Bill James presents. . .

STATS
Major League Handbook
2001

STATS, Inc. • Bill James

Published by STATS Publishing
A division of Sports Team Analysis & Tracking Systems, Inc.

D1568559

Cover by Ryan Balock, Marc Elman and Chuck Miller

Cover photo by Larry Goren

First Edition: November, 2000

Printed in the United States of America

ISBN 1-884064-86-8

Acknowledgments

Publishing the 12th edition of the *STATS Major League Handbook* is a collective effort. The STATS team is successfully anchored by CEO John Dewan and President Alan Leib, and lending invaluable assistance to the guys at the top is Jennifer Manicki. Sue Dewan and Bob Meyerhoff oversee our Research & Development/Special Projects efforts. Sue works on special projects and Bob directs a group composed of Athan Arvanitis, Jim Osborne, Craig Rolling, Joe Sclafani and Andy Tumpowsky. Arthur Ashley provides programming and project support for the development group. Tom Schmitt leads the Technical Operations Department, which includes: Roger Liss, Angie Melecio, Dean Peterson, Brian Spisak and Yingmin Wang.

Marc Elman oversees the Publications Department that produced this book and all of our other sports titles. Getting the numbers programmed appropriately fell into the hands of Jim Henzler, with help from Tim Coletta. Chuck Miller painstakingly manipulated the many columns and graphs that are key to the book's design. Tony Nistler and Thom Henninger oversaw editorial responsibilities, with help from Taylor Bechtold, Marc Carl and Norm DeNosaquo. Getting the word out about the *STATS Major League Handbook* and other STATS publications requires the hard work of Ryan Balock, Mike Janosi, Antoinette Kelly and Mike Sarkis. Ryan designed this book's cover.

We couldn't get the book out without our Operations Department. Managing the collection of these numbers is Allan Spear. His troup includes Jeremy Alpert, Scott Berg, Michelle Blanco, Les Briesemeister, Jon Caplin, Jeff Chernow, Mike Hammer, Derek Kenar, Tony Largo, Jon Passman, Jeff Schinski, Matt Senter, Bill Stephens, Joe Stillwell and Chris Witt. Special thanks to Jeff, who oversees the accuracy of our MLB data.

The efforts of our Commercial, Fantasy, Interactive and Sales departments help pay most of our bills at STATS. Vince Smith heads our Commercial staff, made up of Ethan D. Cooperson, Stefan Kretschmann and Nick Stamm. Steve Byrd oversees the Fantasy Department, which consists of Bill Burke, Sean Bush, Jim Corelis, Consilia DiBartolo, Mike Dreckmann, Dan Ford, Brian Hogan, Walter Lis, Marc Moeller, Jim Pollard, Eric Robin, Jeff Smith, Jake Stein, John Strougal, Michael Trakan, Zach Williams and Rick Wilton. Robert Schur directs an Interactive group that includes Li Chen, Karen Christensen, Walt Cohen, Jake Costello, Chuck Durvis, Jay Fleck, Gregg Kosieniak, Scott Kraatz, Joe Lindholm, Patrick Markey, Will McCleskey, Oscar Palacios, Pat Quinn, John Sasman, Mindy Singer, David Thiel and Brian Tolleson. Jim Capuano heads Sales with the help of Greg Kirkorsky.

Keeping us in the game is the Financial/Administrative/Human Resources/Legal Department. Howard Lanin facilitates the financial and administrative concerns of the company with assistance from Kim Bartlett, Mary Ellen Gomez and Susan Zamecheck. Betty Moy contributes in finance and keeps our headquarters running smoothly. Tracy Lickton is in charge of human resources and is assisted by Megan Bennett while Carol Savier aids with legal matters.

Our Research Department for Fox Sports in Los Angeles is headed by Don Zminda, and his team of sports researchers includes: Mike Berger, Matt Brown, Eric Corwin, Khalid El-Bayoumy, Eddie Garcia, Tracey Graham, Ryan Gunn, Don Hartack, Matt Jenkins, Fred King, Sam Lubeck, Barry Rubinowitz, Meghan Sheehan, Stephanie Sluke, Paul Sobaje, Aneel Trivedi and Randy Williams.

—Chuck Miller

I dedicate this book to my wife Pam and children, Josh and Kaley.
It is your love and support of me that fuels my passion
for life and love. You remind me of those things that are truly
important and meaningful and those that are not.
You always hold a special place in my heart.

—Bobby Schur

Table of Contents

Introduction

Another baseball season has come and gone. The American League now has completed 100 seasons; the National League is 125 years old. Time doesn't stand still, and neither does the game. Even a game as steeped in tradition as baseball.

That's why we bring you the 12th edition of the *STATS Major League Handbook*. We have our own annual ritual to summarize the most recent major league season, and our review of the 2000 campaign can be found in these pages. It's more than just stat lines for every player who made a major league appearance in 2000. It's lefty/righty splits, fielding numbers, tons of leader boards, statistical analysis of the major league parks, and player projections for the 2001 season.

Year after year, the book's the same but the numbers change. Just like the players and parks that make up the storied franchises in baseball. Just as we had to say goodbye to Jackie Robinson and Ebbets Field in the 1950s, we'll soon have to part ways with Tony Gwynn, Cal Ripken and Fenway Park. For now, however, the *Handbook* provides the year-by-year stats and every 2000 number on record for Gwynn and Ripken, as well as plenty of statistical information on the old ballfield on Yawkey Way.

The happier news is, the ever-changing landscape of the game includes a plethora of new stars who will have us marveling at their feats on the field. Carlos Delgado, Todd Helton and Andruw Jones had breakout seasons in 2000, and all three will be mainstays of the new decade. In fact, each is likely to be found on the cover of this annual before his playing days are over. Plus, there are plenty of other up-and-comers who emerged or took the next step during the 2000 campaign: Rick Ankiel, Lance Berkman, Luis Castillo, Darin Erstad, Brad Fullmer, Rafael Furcal, Tim Hudson and Terrence Long.

The promise of these young players makes it more difficult to endure the winter months of the offseason. But just as seasons pass, so does the cold spell without baseball. Soon we'll be compiling the numbers that will spawn future editions.

For now, this 12th edition can fill plenty of hours during these months without the game. With all the statistics it provides, the *Handbook* can help bring the 2000 season back to life. Enjoy.

—Thom Henninger

What's Official and What's Not

The statistics in this book technically are unofficial. The official Major League Baseball averages are not released until December, but we can't wait that long. If you compare these stats with the official ones, you'll find no major differences. That said, we do not agree with the unofficial stats released by Major League Baseball in the following instances:

- Benny Agbayani vs. Jay Powell, NYM@Hou 8/8/00, 9th inning
  Agbayani doubled, although he is not credited as such by MLB

- Scott Rolen vs. Heathcliff Slocumb, Phi@SD 8/1/00, 7th inning
  Rolen drew a non-intentional walk, though MLB credits this as intentional

In both cases, we have confidence in the accuracy of our numbers and confirmed this with multiple STATS reporters and the individual teams involved. As always, we take extraordinary efforts to ensure the accuracy of our data.

Career Register

The Career Register includes the records of all players who saw major league action in 2000, plus the following eight players who did not play in 2000, but who we feel are likely to play in 2001: Wilson Alvarez, Tom Gordon, Mike Jackson, Graeme Lloyd, Dave Nilsson, Juan Pena, Odalis Perez and John Smoltz.

The abbreviations used in the register are defined below:

For all players, **Age** is seasonal age as of June 30, 2001; **Ht** = Height; **Wt** = Weight; **Lg** = Major League (**AL** = American League; **NL** = National League) or minor league classification. Class-A (A+, A, A-) and Rookie (R+, R) have separate classifications to distinguish the level of competition. **IND** = independent minor league.

For Batters, **R** = bats or throws right; **L** = bats or throws left; **B** = bats both right and left; **Pos** = number of games played at each position in 2000; **DH** = designated hitter; **PH** = pinch hitter; **PR** = pinch runner; **G** = games; **AB** = at-bats; **H** = hits; **2B** = doubles; **3B** = triples; **HR** = home runs; **Hm** = home runs at home; **Rd** = home runs on the road; **TB** = total bases; **R** = runs; **RBI** = runs batted in; **TBB** = total bases on balls; **IBB** = intentional bases on balls; **SO** = strikeouts; **HBP** = times hit by pitches; **SH** = sacrifice hits; **SF** = sacrifice flies; **SB** = stolen bases; **CS** = times caught stealing; **SB%** = stolen base percentage; **GDP** = times grounded into double plays; **Avg** = batting average; **OBP** = on-base percentage; **SLG** = slugging percentage.

For pitchers, **Pos** = number of games pitched as a starter and as a reliever; **SP** = starting pitcher; **RP** = relief pitcher; **G** = games pitched; **GS** = games started; **CG** = complete games; **GF** = games finished; **IP** = innings pitched; **BFP** = batters facing pitcher; **H** = hits allowed; **R** = runs allowed; **ER** = earned runs allowed; **HR** = home runs allowed; **SH** = sacrifice hits allowed; **SF** = sacrifice flies allowed; **HB** = hit batsmen; **TBB** = total bases on balls; **IBB** = intentional bases on balls; **SO** = strikeouts; **WP** = wild pitches; **Bk** = balks; **W** = wins; **L** = losses; **Pct.** = winning percentage; **ShO** = shutouts; **Sv** = saves; **Op** = save opportunities; **Hld** = holds; **ERA** = earned run average.

An asterisk (*) by a player's minor league stats indicates that these are his 2000 minor league numbers only; previous minor league experience is not included. Figures in **boldface** indicate the player led the league in that category.

For players who played for more than one major league team in a season, stats for each team are shown just above the bottom-line career totals.

Jeff Abbott

Bats: R **Throws:** L **Pos:** CF-33; LF-20; PH/PR-20; RF-16; DH-7   **Ht:** 6'2" **Wt:** 200 **Born:** 8/17/72 **Age:** 28

							BATTING											BASERUNNING				PERCENTAGES		
Year Team	Lg	G	AB	H	2B	3B	HR	(Hm | Rd)	TB	R	RBI	TBB	IBB	SO	HBP	SH	SF	SB	CS	SB%	GDP	Avg	OBP	SLG
1997 Chicago	AL	19	38	10	1	0	1	(0 | 1)	14	8	2	0	0	6	0	0	0	0	0	—	3	.263	.263	.368
1998 Chicago	AL	89	244	68	14	1	12	(5 | 7)	120	33	41	9	1	28	0	2	5	3	3	.50	2	.279	.298	.492
1999 Chicago	AL	17	57	9	0	0	2	(0 | 2)	15	5	6	5	0	12	0	1	1	1	1	.50	4	.158	.222	.263
2000 Chicago	AL	80	215	59	15	1	3	(1 | 2)	85	31	29	21	1	38	2	2	2	2	1	.67	2	.274	.343	.395
4 ML YEARS		205	554	146	30	2	18	(6 | 12)	234	77	78	35	2	84	2	5	7	6	5	.55	11	.264	.306	.422

Kurt Abbott

Bats: R **Throws:** R **Pos:** SS-39; PH/PR-26; 2B-23; 3B-2; CF-2   **Ht:** 6'0" **Wt:** 200 **Born:** 6/2/69 **Age:** 32

							BATTING											BASERUNNING				PERCENTAGES		
Year Team	Lg	G	AB	H	2B	3B	HR	(Hm | Rd)	TB	R	RBI	TBB	IBB	SO	HBP	SH	SF	SB	CS	SB%	GDP	Avg	OBP	SLG
2000 Norfolk *	AAA	2	4	1	0	0	0	—	—	1	1	0	0	0	0	0	0	0	0	0	—	1	.250	.250	.250
1993 Oakland	AL	20	61	15	1	0	3	(0 | 3)	25	11	9	3	0	20	0	3	0	2	0	1.00	0	.246	.281	.410
1994 Florida	NL	101	345	86	17	3	9	(4 | 5)	136	41	33	16	1	98	5	3	2	3	0	1.00	5	.249	.291	.394
1995 Florida	NL	120	420	107	18	7	17	(12 | 5)	190	60	60	36	4	110	5	2	5	4	3	.57	6	.255	.318	.452
1996 Florida	NL	109	320	81	18	7	8	(6 | 2)	137	37	33	22	1	99	3	4	0	3	3	.50	7	.253	.307	.428
1997 Florida	NL	94	252	69	18	2	6	(1 | 5)	109	35	30	14	3	68	1	6	0	3	1	.75	5	.274	.315	.433
1998 Oak-Col		77	194	51	13	1	5	(3 | 2)	81	26	24	12	0	53	2	1	3	2	1	.67	5	.263	.308	.418
1999 Colorado	NL	96	286	78	17	2	8	(6 | 2)	123	41	41	16	0	69	0	2	1	3	2	.60	4	.273	.310	.430
2000 New York	NL	79	157	34	7	1	6	(3 | 3)	61	22	12	14	2	51	1	1	1	1	1	.50	2	.217	.283	.389
1998 Oakland	AL	35	123	33	7	1	2	(1 | 1)	48	17	9	10	0	34	1	1	1	2	1	.67	3	.268	.326	.390
Colorado	NL	42	71	18	6	0	3	(2 | 1)	33	9	15	2	0	19	1	0	2	0	0	—	2	.254	.276	.465
8 ML YEARS		696	2035	521	109	23	62	(35 | 27)	862	273	242	133	11	568	17	21	12	21	11	.66	37	.256	.305	.424

Paul Abbott

Pitches: Right **Bats:** Right **Pos:** SP-27; RP-8   **Ht:** 6'3" **Wt:** 195 **Born:** 9/15/67 **Age:** 33

		HOW MUCH HE PITCHED						WHAT HE GAVE UP									THE RESULTS					
Year Team	Lg	G	GS	CG	GF	IP	BFP	H	R	ER	HR	SH	SF	HB	TBB	IBB	SO	WP	Bk	W	L	Pct.	ShO	Sv-Op	Hld	ERA
1990 Minnesota	AL	7	7	0	0	34.2	162	37	24	23	0	1	1	1	28	0	25	1	0	0	5	.000	0	0-0	0	5.97
1991 Minnesota	AL	15	3	0	1	47.1	210	38	27	25	5	7	3	0	36	1	43	5	0	3	1	.750	0	0-0	0	4.75
1992 Minnesota	AL	6	0	0	-5	11	50	12	4	4	1	0	1	1	5	0	13	1	0	0	0	—	0	0-0	0	3.27
1993 Cleveland	AL	5	5	0	0	18.1	84	19	15	13	5	0	0	0	11	1	7	1	0	0	1	.000	0	0-0	0	6.38
1998 Seattle	AL	4	4	0	0	24.2	105	24	11	11	2	0	1	0	10	0	22	3	0	3	1	.750	0	0-0	0	4.01
1999 Seattle	AL	25	7	0	8	72.2	298	50	31	25	9	3	4	0	32	3	68	2	0	6	2	.750	0	0-2	0	3.10
2000 Seattle	AL	35	27	0	2	179	766	164	89	84	23	1	4	5	80	4	100	3	0	9	7	.563	0	0-0	4	4.22
7 ML YEARS		97	53	0	16	387.2	1675	344	201	185	45	12	14	7	202	9	278	16	0	21	17	.553	0	0-2	7	4.29

Bobby Abreu

Bats: Left **Throws:** Right **Pos:** RF-152; PH/PR-3   **Ht:** 6'0" **Wt:** 197 **Born:** 3/11/74 **Age:** 27

							BATTING											BASERUNNING				PERCENTAGES		
Year Team	Lg	G	AB	H	2B	3B	HR	(Hm | Rd)	TB	R	RBI	TBB	IBB	SO	HBP	SH	SF	SB	CS	SB%	GDP	Avg	OBP	SLG
1996 Houston	NL	15	22	5	1	0	0	(0 | 0)	6	1	1	2	0	3	0	0	0	0	0	—	1	.227	.292	.273
1997 Houston	NL	59	188	47	10	2	3	(3 | 0)	70	22	26	21	0	48	1	0	0	7	2	.78	0	.250	.329	.372
1998 Philadelphia	NL	151	497	155	29	6	17	(10 | 7)	247	68	74	84	14	133	0	4	4	19	10	.66	6	.312	.409	.497
1999 Philadelphia	NL	152	546	183	35	11	20	(13 | 7)	300	118	93	109	8	113	3	0	4	27	9	.75	13	.335	.446	.549
2000 Philadelphia	NL	154	576	182	42	10	25	(14 | 11)	319	103	79	100	9	116	1	0	3	28	8	.78	12	.316	.416	.554
5 ML YEARS		531	1829	572	117	29	65	(40 | 25)	942	312	273	316	31	413	5	4	11	81	29	.74	32	.313	.413	.515

Juan Acevedo

Pitches: Right **Bats:** Right **Pos:** RP-62   **Ht:** 6'2" **Wt:** 228 **Born:** 5/5/70 **Age:** 31

		HOW MUCH HE PITCHED						WHAT HE GAVE UP									THE RESULTS					
Year Team	Lg	G	GS	CG	GF	IP	BFP	H	R	ER	HR	SH	SF	HB	TBB	IBB	SO	WP	Bk	W	L	Pct.	ShO	Sv-Op	Hld	ERA
2000 Indianapols *	AAA	2	2	0	0	4	15	3	0	0	0	0	0	0	4	0	4	1	0	0	0	—	0	0- —	1	0.00
1995 Colorado	NL	17	11	0	0	65.2	291	82	53	47	15	4	2	6	20	2	40	2	1	4	6	.400	0	0-0	1	6.44
1997 New York	NL	25	2	0	4	47.2	215	52	24	19	6	2	5	4	22	2	33	0	1	3	1	.750	0	0-4	3	3.59
1998 St. Louis	NL	50	9	0	29	98.1	394	83	30	28	7	8	1	4	29	2	56	3	0	8	3	.727	0	15-16	3	2.56
1999 St. Louis	NL	50	12	0	21	102.1	457	115	71	67	17	4	6	4	48	3	52	5	0	6	8	.429	0	4-6	4	5.89
2000 Milwaukee	NL	62	0	0	18	82.2	347	77	38	35	11	1	1	1	31	9	51	3	2	3	7	.300	0	0-2	7	3.81
5 ML YEARS		204	34	0	72	396.2	1704	409	216	196	56	19	15	19	150	18	232	13	4	24	25	.490	0	19-28	18	4.45

Terry Adams

Pitches: Right **Bats:** Right **Pos:** RP-66   **Ht:** 6'3" **Wt:** 215 **Born:** 3/6/73 **Age:** 28

		HOW MUCH HE PITCHED						WHAT HE GAVE UP									THE RESULTS					
Year Team	Lg	G	GS	CG	GF	IP	BFP	H	R	ER	HR	SH	SF	HB	TBB	IBB	SO	WP	Bk	W	L	Pct.	ShO	Sv-Op	Hld	ERA
1995 Chicago	NL	18	0	0	7	18	86	22	15	13	0	0	0	0	10	1	15	1	0	1	1	.500	0	1-1	0	6.50
1996 Chicago	NL	69	0	0	22	101	423	84	36	33	6	7	3	1	49	6	78	5	1	3	6	.333	0	4-8	11	2.94
1997 Chicago	NL	74	0	0	39	74	341	91	43	38	3	1	2	1	40	6	64	6	0	2	9	.182	0	18-22	11	4.62
1998 Chicago	NL	63	0	0	15	72.2	330	72	39	35	7	3	3	1	41	3	73	4	3	7	7	.500	0	1-7	13	4.33
1999 Chicago	NL	52	0	0	38	65	277	60	33	29	9	1	3	0	28	2	57	6	0	6	3	.667	0	13-18	3	4.02
2000 Los Angeles	NL	66	0	0	18	84.1	369	80	42	33	6	3	0	0	39	0	56	5	0	6	9	.400	0	2-7	15	3.52
6 ML YEARS		342	0	0	139	415	1826	409	208	181	31	15	11	3	207	18	343	27	4	25	35	.417	0	39-63	53	3.93

3

Benny Agbayani

Bats: R **Throws:** R **Pos:** LF-102; PH/PR-20; RF-12; CF-3; DH-1   **Ht:** 6'0" **Wt:** 225 **Born:** 12/28/71 **Age:** 29

Year Team	Lg	G	AB	H	2B	3B	HR	(Hm	Rd)	TB	R	RBI	TBB	IBB	SO	HBP	SH	SF	SB	CS	SB%	GDP	Avg	OBP	SLG
1998 New York	NL	11	15	2	0	0	0	(0	0)	2	1	0	1	0	5	0	0	0	0	2	.00	1	.133	.188	.133
1999 New York	NL	101	276	79	18	3	14	(10	4)	145	42	42	32	4	60	3	0	3	6	4	.60	8	.286	.363	.525
2000 New York	NL	119	350	101	20	1	15	(9	6)	168	59	60	54	2	68	7	0	3	5	5	.50	6	.289	.391	.480
3 ML YEARS		231	641	182	38	4	29	(19	10)	315	102	102	87	6	133	10	0	6	11	11	.50	15	.284	.375	.491

Rick Aguilera

Pitches: Right **Bats:** Right **Pos:** RP-54   **Ht:** 6'5" **Wt:** 210 **Born:** 12/31/61 **Age:** 39

Year Team	Lg	G	GS	CG	GF	IP	BFP	H	R	ER	HR	SH	SF	HB	TBB	IBB	SO	WP	Bk	W	L	Pct.	ShO	Sv-Op	Hld	ERA
1985 New York	NL	21	19	2	1	122.1	507	118	49	44	8	7	4	2	37	2	74	5	2	10	7	.588	0	0-0	0	3.24
1986 New York	NL	28	20	2	2	141.2	605	145	70	61	15	6	5	7	36	1	104	5	3	10	7	.588	0	0-1	0	3.88
1987 New York	NL	18	17	1	0	115	494	124	53	46	12	7	2	3	33	2	77	9	0	11	3	.786	0	0-0	1	3.60
1988 New York	NL	11	3	0	2	24.2	111	29	20	19	2	2	0	1	10	2	16	1	1	0	4	.000	0	0-0	0	6.93
1989 NYM-Min		47	11	3	19	145	594	130	51	45	8	7	1	3	38	4	137	4	3	9	11	.450	0	7-11	1	2.79
1990 Minnesota	AL	56	0	0	54	65.1	268	55	27	20	5	0	0	4	19	6	61	3	0	5	3	.625	0	32-39	0	2.76
1991 Minnesota	AL	63	0	0	60	69	275	44	20	18	3	1	1	2	30	6	61	3	0	4	5	.444	0	42-51	0	2.35
1992 Minnesota	AL	64	0	0	61	66.2	273	60	28	21	7	1	2	1	17	4	52	5	0	2	6	.250	0	41-48	0	2.84
1993 Minnesota	AL	65	0	0	61	72.1	287	60	25	25	9	2	1	1	14	3	59	1	0	4	3	.571	0	34-40	0	3.11
1994 Minnesota	AL	44	0	0	40	44.2	201	57	23	18	7	4	1	0	10	3	46	2	0	1	4	.200	0	23-29	0	3.63
1995 Min-Bos	AL	52	0	0	51	55.1	223	46	16	16	6	1	1	1	13	1	52	0	0	3	3	.500	0	32-36	0	2.60
1996 Minnesota	AL	19	19	2	0	111.1	484	124	69	67	20	1	3	3	27	1	83	6	0	8	6	.571	0	0-0	0	5.42
1997 Minnesota	AL	61	0	0	57	66.1	285	65	29	29	9	5	3	2	22	3	68	3	0	5	4	.556	0	26-33	0	3.82
1998 Minnesota	AL	68	0	0	64	74.1	307	75	35	35	8	3	2	1	15	1	57	1	0	4	9	.308	0	38-49	0	4.24
1999 Min-ChC		61	0	0	41	67.2	267	54	25	22	8	4	2	2	12	1	45	1	0	9	4	.692	0	14-21	4	2.93
2000 Chicago	NL	54	0	0	44	47.2	210	47	28	26	11	1	0	4	18	2	38	1	0	1	2	.333	0	29-37	0	4.91
1989 New York	NL	36	0	0	19	69.1	284	59	19	18	3	5	1	2	21	3	80	3	3	6	6	.500	0	7-11	1	2.34
Minnesota	AL	11	11	3	0	75.2	310	71	32	27	5	2	0	1	17	1	57	1	0	3	5	.375	0	0-0	0	3.21
1995 Minnesota	AL	22	0	0	21	25	99	20	7	7	2	0	2	1	6	1	29	0	0	1	1	.500	0	12-15	0	2.52
Boston	AL	30	0	0	30	30.1	124	26	9	9	4	1	2	0	7	0	23	0	0	2	2	.500	0	20-21	0	2.67
1999 Minnesota	AL	17	0	0	16	21.1	76	10	3	3	2	2	0	0	2	0	13	1	1	3	1	.750	0	6-8	0	1.27
Chicago	NL	44	0	0	25	46.1	191	44	22	19	6	4	2	2	10	1	32	3	0	6	3	.667	0	8-13	4	3.69
16 ML YEARS		732	89	10	557	1291.1	5391	1233	568	512	138	52	33	36	351	42	1030	53	10	86	81	.515	0	318-395	7	3.57

Israel Alcantara

Bats: R **Throws:** R **Pos:** DH-8; PH/PR-8; RF-7; 1B-5; LF-1   **Ht:** 6'2" **Wt:** 165 **Born:** 5/6/73 **Age:** 28

Year Team	Lg	G	AB	H	2B	3B	HR	(Hm	Rd)	TB	R	RBI	TBB	IBB	SO	HBP	SH	SF	SB	CS	SB%	GDP	Avg	OBP	SLG
1992 Expos	R	59	224	62	14	2	3	—	—	89	29	37	17	4	35	1	0	2	6	5	.55	4	.277	.328	.397
1993 Burlington	A	126	470	115	26	3	18	—	—	201	65	73	20	2	125	7	1	5	6	7	.46	5	.245	.283	.428
1994 Wst Plm Bch	A+	125	471	134	26	4	15	—	—	213	65	69	26	0	130	3	1	3	9	3	.75	6	.285	.324	.452
1995 Harrisburg	AA	71	237	50	12	2	10	—	—	96	25	29	21	1	81	2	1	1	1	1	.50	5	.211	.280	.405
Wst Plm Bch	A+	39	134	37	7	2	3	—	—	57	16	22	9	0	35	2	2	1	3	0	1.00	0	.276	.329	.425
1996 Harrisburg	AA	62	218	46	5	0	8	—	—	75	26	19	14	0	62	1	0	1	1	1	.50	5	.211	.261	.344
Expos	R	7	30	9	2	0	2	—	—	17	4	10	3	2	6	0	0	0	0	1	.00	1	.300	.364	.567
Wst Plm Bch	A+	15	61	19	2	0	4	—	—	33	11	14	3	0	13	1	0	1	0	0	—	1	.311	.348	.541
1997 Harrisburg	AA	89	301	85	9	2	27	—	—	179	48	68	29	1	84	3	0	3	4	5	.44	5	.282	.348	.595
1998 St. Pete	A+	38	141	47	5	0	10	—	—	82	21	26	21	2	29	2	0	0	1	0	1.00	6	.333	.427	.582
Reading	AA	53	203	63	12	2	15	—	—	124	36	44	17	2	37	2	0	1	1	0	1.00	9	.310	.368	.611
Orlando	AA	15	55	13	4	0	3	—	—	26	8	18	7	0	15	0	0	3	0	1	.00	0	.236	.308	.473
1999 Trenton	AA	77	293	86	26	0	20	—	—	172	48	60	27	0	78	4	0	0	4	2	.67	5	.294	.361	.587
Pawtucket	AA	24	81	22	3	0	9	—	—	52	13	23	9	0	29	3	0	0	0	0	—	0	.272	.366	.642
2000 Pawtucket	AAA	78	299	92	17	1	29	—	—	198	60	76	25	1	84	4	0	4	2	1	.67	3	.308	.364	.662
2000 Boston	AL	21	45	13	1	0	4	(1	3)	26	9	7	3	0	7	0	0	0	0	0	—	0	.289	.333	.578

Scott Aldred

Pitches: Left **Bats:** Left **Pos:** RP-23   **Ht:** 6'4" **Wt:** 220 **Born:** 6/12/68 **Age:** 33

Year Team	Lg	G	GS	CG	GF	IP	BFP	H	R	ER	HR	SH	SF	HB	TBB	IBB	SO	WP	Bk	W	L	Pct.	ShO	Sv-Op	Hld	ERA
1990 Detroit	AL	4	3	0	0	14.1	63	13	6	6	0	2	1	1	10	1	7	0	0	1	2	.333	0	0-0	0	3.77
1991 Detroit	AL	11	11	1	0	57.1	253	58	37	33	9	3	2	0	30	2	35	3	1	2	4	.333	0	0-0	0	5.18
1992 Detroit	AL	16	13	0	0	65	304	80	51	49	12	4	3	3	33	4	34	1	0	3	8	.273	0	0-0	0	6.78
1993 Col-Mon	NL	8	0	0	2	12	65	19	14	12	2	2	0	1	10	1	9	2	0	1	0	1.000	0	0-1	0	9.00
1996 Det-Min	AL	36	25	0	0	165.1	748	194	125	114	29	7	7	6	68	4	111	10	1	6	9	.400	0	0-0	1	6.21
1997 Minnesota	AL	17	15	0	0	77.1	350	102	66	66	20	2	1	3	28	2	33	7	0	2	10	.167	0	0-0	0	7.68
1998 Tampa Bay	AL	48	0	0	8	31.1	135	33	13	13	1	3	0	2	12	3	21	2	0	0	0	—	0	0-0	8	3.73
1999 TB-Phi		66	0	0	14	56.2	254	59	30	28	2	3	6	2	29	3	41	4	0	4	3	.571	0	1-4	6	4.45
2000 Philadelphia	NL	23	0	0	5	20.1	95	23	14	13	3	1	0	0	10	0	21	1	0	1	3	.250	0	0-1	2	5.75
1993 Colorado	NL	5	0	0	1	6.2	40	10	10	8	1	2	0	1	9	1	5	1	0	0	0	—	0	0-0	0	10.80
Montreal	NL	3	0	0	1	5.1	25	9	4	4	1	0	0	0	1	0	4	1	0	1	0	1.000	0	0-1	0	6.75
1996 Detroit	AL	11	8	0	0	43.1	217	60	52	49	9	3	2	3	26	3	36	6	1	0	4	.000	0	0-0	0	9.35
Minnesota	AL	25	17	0	0	122	531	134	73	69	20	4	5	3	42	1	75	4	0	6	5	.545	0	0-0	1	5.09
1999 Tampa Bay	AL	37	0	0	9	24.1	114	26	15	14	1	2	1	2	14	0	22	1	0	3	2	.600	0	0-0	3	5.18
Philadelphia	NL	29	0	0	5	32.1	140	33	15	14	1	1	5	0	15	3	19	3	0	1	1	.500	0	1-4	3	3.90
9 ML YEARS		229	67	1	29	499.2	2267	581	356	334	78	27	22	19	230	20	312	30	2	20	39	.339	0	1-6	17	6.02

Manny Alexander

Bats: R **Throws:** R **Pos:** 3B-63; SS-20; PH/PR-20; 2B-7; DH-3   **Ht:** 5'10" **Wt:** 180 **Born:** 3/20/71 **Age:** 30

Year Team	Lg	G	AB	H	2B	3B	HR	(Hm	Rd)	TB	R	RBI	TBB	IBB	SO	HBP	SH	SF	SB	CS	SB%	GDP	Avg	OBP	SLG
1992 Baltimore	AL	4	5	1	0	0	0	(0	0)	1	1	0	0	0	3	0	0	0	0	0	—	0	.200	.200	.200
1993 Baltimore	AL	3	0	0	0	0	0	(0	0)	0	1	0	0	0	0	0	0	0	0	0	—	0	—	—	—
1995 Baltimore	AL	94	242	57	9	1	3	(2	1)	77	35	23	20	0	30	2	4	0	11	4	.73	2	.236	.299	.318
1996 Baltimore	AL	54	68	7	0	0	0	(0	0)	7	6	4	3	0	27	0	2	0	3	3	.50	2	.103	.141	.103
1997 NYM-ChC	NL	87	248	66	12	4	3	(0	3)	95	37	22	17	3	54	3	3	1	13	1	.93	6	.266	.320	.383
1998 Chicago	NL	108	264	60	10	1	5	(1	4)	87	34	25	18	1	66	1	5	1	4	1	.80	6	.227	.278	.330
1999 Chicago	NL	90	177	48	11	2	0	(0	0)	63	17	15	10	0	38	0	1	1	4	0	1.00	1	.271	.309	.356
2000 Boston	AL	101	194	41	4	3	4	(1	3)	63	30	19	13	0	41	0	2	0	2	0	1.00	0	.211	.261	.325
1997 New York	NL	54	149	37	9	3	2	(0	2)	58	26	15	9	1	38	1	1	3	11	0	1.00	3	.248	.294	.389
Chicago	NL	33	99	29	3	1	1	(0	1)	37	11	7	8	2	16	2	2	0	2	1	.67	3	.293	.358	.374
8 ML YEARS		541	1198	280	46	11	15	(4	11)	393	161	108	81	4	259	6	17	3	37	9	.80	17	.234	.285	.328

Antonio Alfonseca

Pitches: Right **Bats:** Right **Pos:** RP-68   **Ht:** 6'5" **Wt:** 235 **Born:** 4/16/72 **Age:** 29

Year Team	Lg	G	GS	CG	GF	IP	BFP	H	R	ER	HR	SH	SF	HB	TBB	IBB	SO	WP	Bk	W	L	Pct.	ShO	Sv-Op	Hld	ERA
1997 Florida	NL	17	0	0	2	25.2	123	36	16	14	3	1	0	1	10	3	19	1	0	1	3	.250	0	0-2	0	4.91
1998 Florida	NL	58	0	0	27	70.2	316	75	36	32	10	7	6	3	33	9	46	1	0	4	5	.400	0	8-14	9	4.08
1999 Florida	NL	73	0	0	49	77.2	325	79	28	28	4	3	1	4	29	6	46	1	0	4	5	.444	0	21-25	5	3.24
2000 Florida	NL	68	0	0	62	70	311	82	35	33	7	3	1	1	24	3	47	0	2	5	6	.455	0	45-49	0	4.24
4 ML YEARS		216	0	0	140	244	1075	272	115	107	24	14	8	9	96	21	158	3	2	14	20	.412	0	74-90	14	3.95

Edgardo Alfonzo

Bats: Right **Throws:** Right **Pos:** 2B-146; DH-2; PH/PR-2   **Ht:** 5'11" **Wt:** 187 **Born:** 11/8/73 **Age:** 27

Year Team	Lg	G	AB	H	2B	3B	HR	(Hm	Rd)	TB	R	RBI	TBB	IBB	SO	HBP	SH	SF	SB	CS	SB%	GDP	Avg	OBP	SLG
1995 New York	NL	101	335	93	13	5	4	(0	4)	128	26	41	12	1	37	1	4	4	1	1	.50	7	.278	.301	.382
1996 New York	NL	123	368	96	15	2	4	(2	2)	127	36	40	25	2	56	0	9	5	2	0	1.00	8	.261	.304	.345
1997 New York	NL	151	518	163	27	2	10	(4	6)	224	84	72	63	0	56	5	8	5	11	6	.65	4	.315	.391	.432
1998 New York	NL	144	557	155	28	2	17	(8	9)	238	94	78	65	1	77	3	2	3	8	3	.73	11	.278	.355	.427
1999 New York	NL	158	628	191	41	1	27	(11	16)	315	123	108	85	2	85	3	1	9	9	2	.82	14	.304	.385	.502
2000 New York	NL	150	544	176	40	2	25	(13	12)	295	109	94	95	1	70	5	0	6	3	2	.60	12	.324	.425	.542
6 ML YEARS		827	2950	874	164	14	87	(38	49)	1327	472	433	345	7	381	17	24	32	34	14	.71	56	.296	.370	.450

Luis Alicea

Bats: B **Throws:** R **Pos:** 2B-130; 3B-8; DH-5; PH/PR-5; SS-2   **Ht:** 5'9" **Wt:** 176 **Born:** 7/29/65 **Age:** 35

Year Team	Lg	G	AB	H	2B	3B	HR	(Hm	Rd)	TB	R	RBI	TBB	IBB	SO	HBP	SH	SF	SB	CS	SB%	GDP	Avg	OBP	SLG
1988 St. Louis	NL	93	297	63	10	4	1	(1	0)	84	20	24	25	4	32	2	4	2	1	1	.50	12	.212	.276	.283
1991 St. Louis	NL	56	68	13	3	0	0	(0	0)	16	5	0	8	0	19	0	0	0	0	1	.00	0	.191	.276	.235
1992 St. Louis	NL	85	265	65	9	11	2	(2	0)	102	26	32	27	1	40	4	2	4	2	5	.29	5	.245	.320	.385
1993 St. Louis	NL	115	362	101	19	3	3	(2	1)	135	50	46	47	2	54	1	1	7	11	1	.92	9	.279	.362	.373
1994 St. Louis	NL	88	205	57	12	5	5	(3	2)	94	32	29	30	4	38	3	1	3	4	5	.44	1	.278	.373	.459
1995 Boston	AL	132	419	113	20	3	6	(0	6)	157	64	44	63	0	61	7	13	9	13	10	.57	10	.270	.367	.375
1996 Boston	NL	129	380	98	26	3	5	(4	1)	145	54	42	52	10	78	5	4	6	11	3	.79	4	.258	.350	.382
1997 Anaheim	AL	128	388	98	16	7	5	(2	3)	143	59	37	69	3	65	8	4	2	22	8	.73	4	.253	.375	.369
1998 Texas	AL	101	259	71	15	3	6	(1	5)	110	51	33	37	0	40	5	4	3	4	3	.57	1	.274	.372	.425
1999 Texas	AL	68	164	33	10	0	3	(0	3)	52	33	17	28	0	32	0	3	1	2	1	.67	4	.201	.316	.317
2000 Texas	AL	139	540	159	25	8	6	(4	2)	218	85	63	59	1	75	5	7	7	1	3	.25	13	.294	.365	.404
11 ML YEARS		1134	3347	871	165	47	42	(19	23)	1256	479	367	445	25	534	43	43	44	71	41	.63	63	.260	.350	.375

Chad Allen

Bats: Right **Throws:** Right **Pos:** RF-13; LF-2   **Ht:** 6'1" **Wt:** 195 **Born:** 2/6/75 **Age:** 26

Year Team	Lg	G	AB	H	2B	3B	HR	(Hm	Rd)	TB	R	RBI	TBB	IBB	SO	HBP	SH	SF	SB	CS	SB%	GDP	Avg	OBP	SLG
1996 Fort Wayne	A	7	21	9	0	0	0	—	—	9	2	2	3	1	2	0	0	1	1	1	.50	0	.429	.480	.429
1997 Fort Myers	A+	105	401	124	18	4	3	—	—	159	66	45	40	2	51	2	2	2	27	15	.64	9	.309	.373	.397
New Britain	AA	30	115	29	9	1	4	—	—	52	20	18	9	0	21	0	1	1	2	0	1.00	1	.252	.304	.452
1998 New Britain	AA	137	504	132	31	7	8	—	—	201	70	82	51	0	78	6	1	5	21	9	.70	19	.262	.334	.399
2000 Salt Lake	AAA	96	389	121	21	5	9	—	—	179	71	67	31	1	72	1	2	2	10	2	.83	13	.311	.363	.460
1999 Minnesota	AL	137	481	133	21	3	10	(4	6)	190	69	46	37	1	89	2	1	2	14	7	.67	10	.277	.330	.395
2000 Minnesota	AL	15	50	15	3	0	0	(0	0)	18	2	7	3	0	14	1	0	1	0	2	.00	1	.300	.345	.360
2 ML YEARS		152	531	148	24	3	10	(4	6)	208	71	53	40	1	103	3	1	3	14	9	.61	11	.279	.331	.392

Dusty Allen

Bats: R **Throws:** R **Pos:** 1B-18; PH/PR-8; LF-3; DH-1; 3B-1; RF-1   **Ht:** 6'4" **Wt:** 215 **Born:** 8/9/72 **Age:** 28

Year Team	Lg	G	AB	H	2B	3B	HR	(Hm	Rd)	TB	R	RBI	TBB	IBB	SO	HBP	SH	SF	SB	CS	SB%	GDP	Avg	OBP	SLG
1995 Idaho Falls	R+	29	104	34	7	0	4	—	—	53	21	24	21	0	19	0	0	2	1	2	.33	2	.327	.433	.510
Clinton	A	36	139	37	12	1	5	—	—	66	25	31	12	1	29	1	0	0	1	0	1.00	3	.266	.329	.475
1996 Clinton	A	77	243	65	10	3	10	—	—	111	46	46	67	1	59	4	0	3	4	7	.36	3	.267	.429	.457
Rancho Cuc	A+	55	208	62	15	1	10	—	—	109	41	45	38	1	66	5	2	0	3	2	.60	3	.298	.406	.524
1997 Mobile	AA	131	475	120	28	4	17	—	—	207	85	75	81	0	116	0	0	3	1	4	.20	12	.253	.360	.436
1998 Mobile	AA	42	154	39	10	4	6	—	—	75	30	42	32	1	26	1	0	1	1	0	1.00	0	.253	.381	.487
Las Vegas	AAA	87	292	78	21	1	16	—	—	149	42	45	31	0	80	4	0	4	2	0	.00	2	.267	.341	.510

Year Team	Lg	G	AB	H	2B	3B	HR	Hm	Rd	TB	R	RBI	TBB	IBB	SO	HBP	SH	SF	SB	CS	SB%	GDP	Avg	OBP	SLG
1999 Las Vegas	AAA	128	454	124	30	3	18	—	—	214	68	89	79	0	143	1	0	2	3	5	.38	5	.273	.381	.471
2000 Las Vegas	AAA	67	222	69	14	4	14	—	—	133	52	55	58	0	50	0	0	3	3	0	1.00	6	.311	.449	.599
Toledo	AAA	25	90	20	5	0	2	—	—	31	9	12	5	0	27	1	0	0	2	2	.00	2	.222	.271	.344
2000 SD-Det		27	28	7	2	0	2	(1	1)	15	5	2	4	0	12	0	0	0	0	0	—	0	.250	.344	.536
2000 San Diego	NL	9	12	0	0	0	0	(0	0)	0	0	0	2	0	5	0	0	0	0	0	—	1	.000	.143	.000
Detroit	AL	18	16	7	2	0	2	(1	1)	15	5	2	2	0	7	0	0	0	0	0	—	0	.438	.500	.938

Armando Almanza

Pitches: Left **Bats:** Left **Pos:** RP-67 **Ht:** 6'3" **Wt:** 205 **Born:** 10/26/72 **Age:** 28

Year Team	Lg	G	GS	CG	GF	IP	BFP	H	R	ER	HR	SH	SF	HB	TBB	IBB	SO	WP	Bk	W	L	Pct.	ShO	Sv-Op	Hld	ERA
1993 Cardinals	R	20	4	0	6	42	179	38	19	15	2	0	1	3	14	0	56	14	1	4	1	.800	0	0--	—	3.21
Johnson Cty	R+	3	0	0	0	4.1	21	6	2	2	1	0	0	0	3	0	4	0	0	1	1	.500	0	0--	—	4.15
1995 Savannah	A	20	20	0	0	108	476	108	62	47	13	5	4	3	40	1	72	6	1	3	9	.250	0	0--	—	3.92
1996 Peoria	A	52	1	0	18	56	271	50	27	19	2	3	2	2	32	5	67	8	2	8	6	.571	0	0--	—	2.76
1997 Pr William	A+	58	0	0	47	64.2	259	38	18	12	3	1	4	1	32	1	83	8	1	2	3	.400	0	36--	—	1.67
1998 Arkansas	AA	28	0	0	16	32.2	140	27	13	12	2	0	0	2	18	0	46	4	0	4	1	.800	0	8--	—	3.31
Memphis	AAA	31	0	0	9	35.2	163	35	18	12	1	1	1	0	19	1	45	6	2	3	1	.750	0	1--	—	3.03
1999 Calgary	AAA	15	0	0	4	17.1	99	29	27	21	3	0	1	0	18	0	20	2	0	2	2	.500	0	1--	—	10.90
Portland	AA	10	0	0	6	11.1	41	5	5	5	1	1	0	0	4	0	20	0	1	0	0	.000	0	3--	—	3.97
1999 Florida	NL	14	0	0	2	15.2	64	8	4	3	1	1	1	1	9	1	20	0	1	0	1	.000	0	0-0	3	1.72
2000 Florida	NL	67	0	0	8	46.1	216	38	27	25	3	2	2	1	43	6	46	1	0	4	2	.667	0	0-4	13	4.86
2 ML YEARS		81	0	0	10	62	280	46	31	28	4	3	3	1	52	7	66	1	1	4	3	.571	0	0-4	16	4.06

Carlos Almanzar

Pitches: Right **Bats:** Right **Pos:** RP-62 **Ht:** 6'2" **Wt:** 200 **Born:** 11/6/73 **Age:** 27

Year Team	Lg	G	GS	CG	GF	IP	BFP	H	R	ER	HR	SH	SF	HB	TBB	IBB	SO	WP	Bk	W	L	Pct.	ShO	Sv-Op	Hld	ERA
2000 Las Vegas *	AAA	4	0	0	0	6	28	9	4	3	1	0	0	0	0	0	7	0	0	0	0	—	0	0--	0	4.50
1997 Toronto	AL	4	0	0	2	3.1	12	1	1	1	1	0	0	0	1	0	4	0	0	0	1	.000	0	0-0	0	2.70
1998 Toronto	AL	25	0	0	8	28.2	129	34	18	17	4	1	0	1	8	2	20	0	1	2	2	.500	0	0-3	1	5.34
1999 San Diego	NL	28	0	0	11	37.1	173	48	32	31	6	2	1	3	15	2	30	2	0	0	0	—	0	0-0	5	7.47
2000 San Diego	NL	62	0	0	11	69.2	308	73	35	34	12	2	3	4	25	2	56	2	0	4	5	.444	0	0-3	8	4.39
4 ML YEARS		119	0	0	32	139	622	156	86	83	23	5	4	8	49	6	110	4	0	6	8	.429	0	0-6	9	5.37

Roberto Alomar

Bats: Both **Throws:** Right **Pos:** 2B-155; PH/PR-1 **Ht:** 6'0" **Wt:** 185 **Born:** 2/5/68 **Age:** 33

Year Team	Lg	G	AB	H	2B	3B	HR	Hm	Rd	TB	R	RBI	TBB	IBB	SO	HBP	SH	SF	SB	CS	SB%	GDP	Avg	OBP	SLG
1988 San Diego	NL	143	545	145	24	6	9	(4	5)	208	84	41	47	5	83	3	16	0	24	6	.80	15	.266	.328	.382
1989 San Diego	NL	158	623	184	27	1	7	(3	4)	234	82	56	53	4	76	1	17	8	42	17	.71	10	.295	.347	.376
1990 San Diego	NL	147	586	168	27	5	6	(4	2)	223	80	60	48	1	72	2	5	5	24	7	.77	16	.287	.340	.381
1991 Toronto	AL	161	637	188	41	11	9	(5	4)	278	88	69	57	3	86	4	16	5	53	11	.83	5	.295	.354	.436
1992 Toronto	AL	152	571	177	27	8	8	(5	3)	244	105	76	87	5	52	5	6	2	49	9	.84	8	.310	.405	.427
1993 Toronto	AL	153	589	192	35	6	17	(8	9)	290	109	93	80	5	67	5	4	5	55	15	.79	13	.326	.408	.492
1994 Toronto	AL	107	392	120	25	4	8	(4	4)	177	78	38	51	2	41	2	7	3	19	8	.70	14	.306	.386	.452
1995 Toronto	AL	130	517	155	24	7	13	(7	6)	232	71	66	47	3	45	0	7	6	30	3	.91	16	.300	.354	.449
1996 Baltimore	AL	153	588	193	43	4	22	(14	8)	310	132	94	90	10	65	1	8	12	17	6	.74	14	.328	.411	.527
1997 Baltimore	AL	112	412	137	23	2	14	(10	4)	206	64	60	40	2	43	3	7	7	9	3	.75	5	.333	.390	.500
1998 Baltimore	AL	147	588	166	36	1	14	(7	7)	246	86	56	59	3	70	2	3	5	18	5	.78	11	.282	.347	.418
1999 Cleveland	AL	159	563	182	40	3	24	(12	12)	300	138	120	99	3	96	7	12	13	37	6	.86	13	.323	.422	.533
2000 Cleveland	AL	155	610	189	40	2	19	(8	11)	290	111	89	64	4	82	6	11	6	39	4	.91	19	.310	.378	.475
13 ML YEARS		1877	7221	2196	412	60	170	(93	77)	3238	1228	918	822	50	878	41	118	78	416	100	.81	164	.304	.375	.448

Sandy Alomar Jr.

Bats: Right **Throws:** Right **Pos:** C-95; PH/PR-3; DH-1 **Ht:** 6'5" **Wt:** 220 **Born:** 6/18/66 **Age:** 35

Year Team	Lg	G	AB	H	2B	3B	HR	Hm	Rd	TB	R	RBI	TBB	IBB	SO	HBP	SH	SF	SB	CS	SB%	GDP	Avg	OBP	SLG
1988 San Diego	NL	1	1	0	0	0	0	(0	0)	0	0	0	0	0	1	0	0	0	0	0	—	0	.000	.000	.000
1989 San Diego	NL	7	19	4	1	0	1	(1	0)	8	1	6	3	1	3	0	0	0	0	0	—	0	.211	.318	.421
1990 Cleveland	AL	132	445	129	26	2	9	(5	4)	186	60	66	25	2	46	2	5	6	4	1	.80	10	.290	.326	.418
1991 Cleveland	AL	51	184	40	9	0	0	(0	0)	49	10	7	8	1	24	4	2	1	0	4	.00	4	.217	.264	.266
1992 Cleveland	AL	89	299	75	16	0	2	(1	1)	97	22	26	13	3	32	5	3	0	3	3	.50	7	.251	.293	.324
1993 Cleveland	AL	64	215	58	7	1	6	(3	3)	85	24	32	11	0	28	6	1	4	3	1	.75	5	.270	.318	.395
1994 Cleveland	AL	80	292	84	15	1	14	(4	10)	143	44	43	25	2	31	2	0	1	8	4	.67	7	.288	.347	.490
1995 Cleveland	AL	66	203	61	6	0	10	(4	6)	97	32	35	7	0	26	3	4	1	3	1	.75	8	.300	.332	.478
1996 Cleveland	AL	127	418	110	23	0	11	(3	8)	166	53	50	19	0	42	3	2	2	1	0	1.00	20	.263	.299	.397
1997 Cleveland	AL	125	451	146	37	0	21	(9	12)	246	63	83	19	2	48	3	6	1	0	2	.00	16	.324	.354	.545
1998 Cleveland	AL	117	409	96	26	2	6	(3	3)	144	45	44	18	0	45	3	5	3	0	3	.00	15	.235	.270	.352
1999 Cleveland	AL	37	137	42	13	0	6	(4	2)	73	19	25	4	0	20	3	0	2	0	1	.00	1	.307	.322	.533
2000 Cleveland	AL	97	356	103	16	2	7	(5	2)	144	44	42	16	1	41	4	4	4	1	2	.50	9	.289	.324	.404
13 ML YEARS		993	3429	948	195	8	93	(42	51)	1438	417	459	168	12	390	35	33	25	24	22	.52	101	.276	.315	.419

Moises Alou

Bats: R **Throws:** R **Pos:** RF-64; LF-59; PH/PR-5; DH-1 **Ht:** 6'3" **Wt:** 195 **Born:** 7/3/66 **Age:** 34

Year Team	Lg	G	AB	H	2B	3B	HR	Hm	Rd	TB	R	RBI	TBB	IBB	SO	HBP	SH	SF	SB	CS	SB%	GDP	Avg	OBP	SLG
1990 Pit-Mon	NL	16	20	4	0	1	0	(0	0)	6	4	0	0	0	3	0	1	0	0	0	—	1	.200	.200	.300

Year Team	Lg	G	AB	H	2B	3B	HR	Hm	Rd	TB	R	RBI	TBB	IBB	SO	HBP	SH	SF	SB	CS	SB%	GDP	Avg	OBP	SLG
1992 Montreal	NL	115	341	96	28	2	9	(6	3)	155	53	56	25	0	46	1	5	5	16	2	.89	5	.282	.328	.455
1993 Montreal	NL	136	482	138	29	6	18	(10	8)	233	70	85	38	9	53	3	3	7	17	6	.74	9	.286	.340	.483
1994 Montreal	NL	107	422	143	31	5	22	(9	13)	250	81	78	42	10	63	2	0	5	7	6	.54	7	.339	.397	.592
1995 Montreal	NL	93	344	94	22	0	14	(4	10)	158	48	58	29	6	56	9	0	4	4	3	.57	9	.273	.342	.459
1996 Montreal	NL	143	540	152	28	2	21	(14	7)	247	87	96	49	7	83	2	0	7	9	4	.69	15	.281	.339	.457
1997 Florida	NL	150	538	157	29	5	23	(12	11)	265	88	115	70	9	85	4	0	7	9	5	.64	13	.292	.373	.493
1998 Houston	NL	159	584	182	34	5	38	(19	19)	340	104	124	84	11	87	5	0	6	11	3	.79	14	.312	.399	.582
2000 Houston	NL	126	454	161	28	2	30	(17	13)	283	82	114	52	4	45	2	0	9	3	3	.50	21	.355	.416	.623
1990 Pittsburgh	NL	2	5	1	0	0	0	(0	0)	1	0	0	0	0	0	0	0	0	0	0	—	0	.200	.200	.200
Montreal	NL	14	15	3	0	1	0	(0	0)	5	4	0	0	0	3	0	1	0	0	0	—	0	.200	.200	.333
9 ML YEARS		1045	3725	1127	229	28	175	(91	84)	1937	617	726	389	56	521	30	9	50	76	32	.70	94	.303	.369	.520

Clemente Alvarez

Bats: Right **Throws:** Right **Pos:** C-2; PH/PR-1 **Ht:** 5'11" **Wt:** 180 **Born:** 5/18/68 **Age:** 33

Year Team	Lg	G	AB	H	2B	3B	HR	Hm	Rd	TB	R	RBI	TBB	IBB	SO	HBP	SH	SF	SB	CS	SB%	GDP	Avg	OBP	SLG
1987 White Sox	R	25	55	10	1	0	1	—	—	14	8	4	7	0	8	0	0	0	1	1	.50	1	.182	.274	.255
1988 South Bend	A	15	41	3	0	0	0	—	—	3	0	1	3	0	19	0	0	0	0	0	—	0	.073	.136	.073
Utica	A-	53	132	31	5	1	0	—	—	38	15	14	11	0	36	2	4	1	5	2	.71	2	.235	.301	.288
1989 South Bend	A	86	230	51	15	0	0	—	—	66	22	22	16	0	59	0	9	1	4	1	.80	6	.222	.271	.287
1990 Sarasota	A+	37	119	19	4	1	1	—	—	28	9	9	8	0	24	0	2	0	0	0	—	5	.160	.213	.235
South Bend	A	48	127	30	5	0	2	—	—	41	14	12	20	0	38	1	5	2	2	1	.67	1	.236	.340	.323
1991 Sarasota	A+	71	194	40	10	2	1	—	—	57	14	22	20	0	41	4	7	1	3	2	.60	6	.206	.292	.294
1992 Birmingham	AA	57	169	24	8	0	1	—	—	35	7	10	10	0	52	2	3	0	1	1	.50	5	.142	.199	.207
1993 White Sox	R	2	5	0	0	0	0	—	—	0	0	0	1	0	2	0	0	0	0	1	.00	0	.000	.167	.000
Nashville	AAA	11	29	6	0	0	0	—	—	6	1	2	1	0	4	0	2	0	0	0	—	0	.207	.233	.207
Birmingham	AA	35	111	25	4	0	1	—	—	32	8	8	11	0	28	1	1	1	0	4	.00	3	.225	.298	.288
1994 Nashville	AAA	87	223	48	8	1	3	—	—	67	18	14	17	0	48	2	12	2	0	0	—	2	.215	.275	.300
1995 Ottawa	AAA	50	143	33	7	0	4	—	—	52	15	20	10	1	34	2	3	0	0	0	—	2	.231	.290	.364
1997 Winston-Sal	A+	2	4	1	0	0	0	—	—	1	0	1	0	0	2	1	0	0	0	0	—	0	.250	.400	.250
Birmingham	AA	79	242	49	10	1	3	—	—	70	29	23	27	0	49	5	3	1	0	0	—	17	.202	.295	.289
1999 Scrantn-WB	AAA	9	28	7	4	0	0	—	—	11	4	6	3	0	9	0	0	0	0	0	—	1	.250	.323	.393
Reading	AA	48	142	25	5	1	2	—	—	38	12	12	11	0	38	0	5	1	1	1	.50	3	.176	.234	.268
2000 Clearwater	A+	12	41	11	0	0	0	—	—	11	1	1	2	1	7	1	0	0	0	0	—	0	.268	.318	.268
Scrantn-WB	AAA	5	11	0	0	0	0	—	—	0	0	0	0	0	2	1	0	0	0	0	—	1	.000	.083	.000
Reading	AA	9	18	4	1	0	0	—	—	5	2	5	3	0	3	0	2	2	0	0	—	0	.222	.304	.278
2000 Philadelphia	NL	2	5	1	0	0	0	(0	0)	1	1	0	1	0	1	0	0	0	0	0	—	0	.200	.200	.200

Gabe Alvarez

Bats: R **Throws:** R **Pos:** PH/PR-8; 3B-3; LF-2; DH-1 **Ht:** 6'1" **Wt:** 205 **Born:** 3/6/74 **Age:** 27

Year Team	Lg	G	AB	H	2B	3B	HR	Hm	Rd	TB	R	RBI	TBB	IBB	SO	HBP	SH	SF	SB	CS	SB%	GDP	Avg	OBP	SLG
2000 Toledo *	AAA	69	241	50	11	2	8	—	—	89	37	35	47	0	53	1	0	3	0	1	.00	4	.207	.336	.369
Las Vegas *	AAA	43	141	43	11	0	9	—	—	81	33	26	33	0	44	4	1	2	2	0	1.00	3	.305	.444	.574
1998 Detroit	AL	58	199	46	11	0	5	(3	2)	72	16	29	18	1	65	2	0	2	1	3	.25	2	.231	.299	.362
1999 Detroit	AL	22	53	11	3	0	2	(2	0)	20	5	4	3	0	9	0	0	0	0	0	—	0	.208	.250	.377
2000 Det-SD	AL	12	14	2	1	0	0	(0	0)	3	1	0	3	0	2	0	0	0	0	1	.00	0	.143	.294	.214
2000 Detroit	AL	1	1	0	0	0	0	(0	0)	0	0	0	2	0	1	0	0	0	0	0	.00	0	.000	.667	.000
San Diego	NL	11	13	2	1	0	0	(0	0)	3	1	0	1	0	1	0	0	0	0	0	—	0	.154	.214	.231
3 ML YEARS		92	266	59	15	0	7	(5	2)	95	22	33	24	1	76	2	0	2	1	4	.20	2	.222	.289	.357

Juan Alvarez

Pitches: Left **Bats:** Left **Pos:** RP-11 **Ht:** 6'0" **Wt:** 175 **Born:** 8/9/73 **Age:** 27

Year Team	Lg	G	GS	CG	GF	IP	BFP	H	R	ER	HR	SH	SF	HB	TBB	IBB	SO	WP	Bk	W	L	Pct.	ShO	Sv-Op	Hld	ERA
1995 Boise	A-	9	0	0	2	11.2	47	12	1	1	0	0	0	1	2	0	11	0	0	0	0	—	0	0--	—	0.77
1996 Cedar Rapds	A	40	0	0	14	53	238	50	25	20	0	3	1	7	30	1	53	4	0	1	2	.333	0	3--	—	3.40
1997 Lk Elsinore	A+	27	0	0	10	51.1	196	33	9	8	2	2	1	4	13	2	46	2	2	4	2	.667	0	3--	—	1.40
Midland	AA	24	0	0	6	37	199	63	42	34	5	0	1	3	22	1	27	0	3	4	1	.800	0	0--	—	8.27
1998 Midland	AA	40	0	0	31	46	197	40	26	22	5	2	1	2	21	3	41	2	1	3	4	.429	0	12--	—	4.30
Vancouver	AAA	18	0	0	5	14.1	65	14	9	8	2	0	4		8	0	12	0	1	1	1	.500	0	0--	—	5.02
1999 Erie	AA	23	0	0	12	30.2	121	20	14	7	4	1	2	2	6	0	22	1	1	1	2	.333	0	4--	—	2.05
Edmonton	AAA	27	0	0	13	28.1	123	30	13	11	2	1	1	1	8	0	25	0	1	0	3	.000	0	0--	—	3.49
2000 Edmonton	AAA	44	0	0	15	38.1	158	30	12	12	3	3	0	1	19	1	27	2	0	3	1	.750	0	0--	—	2.82
1999 Anaheim	AL	8	0	0	1	3	14	1	1	1	0	1	0	0	4	0	1	1	0	0	1	.000	0	0-0	0	3.00
2000 Anaheim	AL	11	0	0	3	6	38	14	9	9	3	0	1	0	7	1	2	1	0	0	0	—	0	0-0	1	13.50
2 ML YEARS		19	0	0	4	9	52	15	10	10	3	1	1	0	11	1	6	2	0	0	0	.000	0	0-0	1	10.00

Wilson Alvarez

Pitches: Left **Bats:** Left **Pos:** SP **Ht:** 6'1" **Wt:** 245 **Born:** 3/24/70 **Age:** 31

Year Team	Lg	G	GS	CG	GF	IP	BFP	H	R	ER	HR	SH	SF	HB	TBB	IBB	SO	WP	Bk	W	L	Pct.	ShO	Sv-Op	Hld	ERA
1989 Texas	AL	1	1	0	0	0	5	3	3	3	1	0	0	0	0	0	0	0	0	0	1	.000	0	0-0	0	—
1991 Chicago	AL	10	9	2	0	56.1	237	47	26	22	9	3	1	0	29	0	32	2	0	3	2	.600	1	0-0	0	3.51
1992 Chicago	AL	34	9	0	4	100.1	455	103	64	58	12	3	4	4	65	2	66	2	0	5	3	.625	0	1-1	3	5.20
1993 Chicago	AL	31	31	1	0	207.2	877	168	78	68	14	**13**	6	7	122	8	155	2	1	15	8	.652	1	0-0	0	2.95
1994 Chicago	AL	24	24	2	0	161.2	682	147	72	62	16	6	3	0	62	1	108	3	0	12	8	.600	1	0-0	0	3.45
1995 Chicago	AL	29	29	3	0	175	769	171	96	84	21	6	5	2	93	4	118	1	2	8	11	.421	0	0-0	0	4.32
1996 Chicago	AL	35	35	0	0	217.1	946	216	106	102	21	5	2	4	97	3	181	2	0	15	10	.600	0	0-0	0	4.22
1997 CWS-SF	AL	33	33	2	0	212	896	180	97	82	18	10	6	4	91	4	179	5	1	13	11	.542	0	0-0	0	3.48

		HOW MUCH HE PITCHED						WHAT HE GAVE UP												THE RESULTS						
Year Team	Lg	G	GS	CG	GF	IP	BFP	H	R	ER	HR	SH	SF	HB	TBB	IBB	SO	WP	Bk	W	L	Pct.	ShO	Sv-Op	Hld	ERA
1998 Tampa Bay	AL	25	25	0	0	142.2	624	130	78	75	18	1	2	9	68	0	107	4	0	6	14	.300	0	0-0	0	4.73
1999 Tampa Bay	AL	28	28	0	0	160	703	159	92	75	22	3	6		79	1	128	3	0	9	9	.500	0	0-0	0	4.22
1997 Chicago	AL	22	22	2	0	145.2	613	126	61	49	9	6	5	3	55	1	110	4	0	9	8	.529	1	0-0	0	3.03
San Francisco	NL	11	11	0	0	66.1	283	54	36	33	9	4	1	1	36	3	69	1	0	4	3	.571	0	0-0	0	4.48
10 ML YEARS		250	224	11	4	1433	6194	1324	712	631	153	50	32	36	708	23	1074	24	4	86	77	.528	4	1-1	3	3.96

Rich Amaral

Bats: R Throws: R Pos: CF-12; PH/PR-11; DH-5; RF-4; LF-3; 1B-1   **Ht:** 6'0" **Wt:** 175 **Born:** 4/1/62 **Age:** 39

					BATTING														BASERUNNING				PERCENTAGES		
Year Team	Lg	G	AB	H	2B	3B	HR	(Hm	Rd)	TB	R	RBI	TBB	IBB	SO	HBP	SH	SF	SB	CS	SB%	GDP	Avg	OBP	SLG
2000 Richmond *	AAA	7	22	3	1	0	0	—	—	4	3	0	4	0	6	0	0	0	0	0	—	1	.136	.269	.182
1991 Seattle	AL	14	16	1	0	0	0	(0	0)	1	2	0	1	0	5	1	0	0	0	0	—		.063	.167	.063
1992 Seattle	AL	35	100	24	3	0	1	(0	1)	30	9	7	5	0	16	0	4	0	4	2	.67	4	.240	.276	.300
1993 Seattle	AL	110	373	108	24	1	1	(0	1)	137	53	44	33	0	54	3	7	5	19	11	.63	5	.290	.348	.367
1994 Seattle	AL	77	228	60	10	2	4	(2	2)	86	37	18	24	1	28	1	7	2	5	1	.83	3	.263	.333	.377
1995 Seattle	AL	90	238	67	14	2	2	(1	1)	91	45	19	21	0	33	1	1	0	21	2	.91	3	.282	.342	.382
1996 Seattle	AL	118	312	91	11	3	1	(1	0)	111	69	29	47	0	55	5	4	1	25	6	.81	6	.292	.392	.356
1997 Seattle	AL	89	190	54	5	0	1	(0	1)	62	34	21	10	0	34	3	5	2	12	8	.60	7	.284	.327	.326
1998 Seattle	AL	73	134	37	6	0	1	(1	0)	46	25	4	13	0	24	1	0	1	11	1	.92	1	.276	.342	.343
1999 Baltimore	AL	91	137	38	8	1	0	(0	0)	48	21	11	15	0	20	1	1	2	9	6	.60	1	.277	.348	.350
2000 Baltimore	AL	30	60	13	1	1	0	(0	0)	16	10	6	7	0	8	0	0	0	6	2	.75	6	.217	.299	.267
10 ML YEARS		727	1788	493	82	10	11	(5	6)	628	305	159	176	1	277	16	29	13	112	39	.74	37	.276	.344	.351

Brady Anderson

Bats: L Throws: L Pos: CF-88; RF-24; LF-16; DH-11; PH/PR-8   **Ht:** 6'1" **Wt:** 202 **Born:** 1/18/64 **Age:** 37

					BATTING														BASERUNNING				PERCENTAGES		
Year Team	Lg	G	AB	H	2B	3B	HR	(Hm	Rd)	TB	R	RBI	TBB	IBB	SO	HBP	SH	SF	SB	CS	SB%	GDP	Avg	OBP	SLG
1988 Bos-Bal	AL	94	325	69	13	4	1	(1	0)	93	31	21	23	0	75	4	11	1	10	6	.63	3	.212	.272	.286
1989 Baltimore	AL	94	266	55	12	2	4	(2	2)	83	44	16	43	0	45	3	5	0	16	4	.80	4	.207	.324	.312
1990 Baltimore	AL	89	234	54	5	2	3	(1	2)	72	24	24	31	2	46	5	4	5	15	2	.88	4	.231	.327	.308
1991 Baltimore	AL	113	256	59	12	3	2	(1	1)	83	40	27	38	0	44	5	11	3	12	5	.71	1	.230	.338	.324
1992 Baltimore	AL	159	623	169	28	10	21	(15	6)	280	100	80	98	14	98	9	10	9	53	16	.77	2	.271	.373	.449
1993 Baltimore	AL	142	560	147	36	8	13	(2	11)	238	87	66	82	4	99	10	6	6	24	12	.67	4	.263	.363	.425
1994 Baltimore	AL	111	453	119	25	5	12	(7	5)	190	78	48	57	3	75	10	3	2	31	1	.97	7	.263	.356	.419
1995 Baltimore	AL	143	554	145	33	10	16	(10	6)	246	108	64	87	4	111	10	4	2	26	7	.79	3	.262	.371	.444
1996 Baltimore	AL	149	579	172	37	5	50	(19	31)	369	117	110	76	6	106	22	6	4	21	8	.72	11	.297	.396	.637
1997 Baltimore	AL	151	590	170	39	7	18	(8	10)	277	97	73	84	6	105	19	2	1	18	12	.60	1	.288	.393	.469
1998 Baltimore	AL	133	479	113	28	3	18	(7	11)	201	84	51	75	1	78	15	4	1	21	7	.75	7	.236	.356	.420
1999 Baltimore	AL	150	564	159	28	5	24	(10	14)	269	109	81	96	7	105	24	1	7	36	7	.84	6	.282	.404	.477
2000 Baltimore	AL	141	506	130	26	0	19	(9	10)	213	89	50	92	5	103	8	5	7	16	9	.64	4	.257	.375	.421
1988 Boston	AL	41	148	34	5	3	0	(0	0)	45	14	12	15	0	35	4	4	1	4	2	.67	2	.230	.315	.304
Baltimore	AL	53	177	35	8	1	1	(1	0)	48	17	9	8	0	40	0	7	0	6	4	.60	1	.198	.232	.271
13 ML YEARS		1669	5989	1561	322	64	201	(92	109)	2614	1008	711	882	53	1090	144	72	48	299	96	.76	57	.261	.366	.436

Brian Anderson

Pitches: Left Bats: Both Pos: SP-32; RP-1   **Ht:** 6'1" **Wt:** 183 **Born:** 4/26/72 **Age:** 29

				HOW MUCH HE PITCHED				WHAT HE GAVE UP												THE RESULTS						
Year Team	Lg	G	GS	CG	GF	IP	BFP	H	R	ER	HR	SH	SF	HB	TBB	IBB	SO	WP	Bk	W	L	Pct.	ShO	Sv-Op	Hld	ERA
1993 California	AL	4	1	0	3	11.1	45	11	5	5	1	0	0	0	2	0	4	0	0	0	0	—	0	0-0	0	3.97
1994 California	AL	18	18	0	0	101.2	441	120	63	59	13	3	6	5	27	0	47	5	5	7	5	.583	0	0-0	0	5.22
1995 California	AL	18	17	1	0	99.2	433	110	66	65	24	5	5	3	30	2	45	1	3	6	8	.429	0	0-0	0	5.87
1996 Cleveland	AL	10	9	0	0	51.1	215	58	29	28	9	2	3	0	14	1	21	2	0	3	1	.750	0	0-0	1	4.91
1997 Cleveland	AL	8	8	0	0	48	199	55	28	25	7	0	1	0	11	0	22	1	0	4	2	.667	0	0-0	0	4.69
1998 Arizona	NL	32	32	2	0	208	845	221	109	100	39	8	3	4	24	2	95	3	6	12	13	.480	1	0-0	0	4.33
1999 Arizona	NL	31	19	2	4	130	549	144	69	66	18	4	0	1	28	3	75	0	2	8	2	.800	1	1-2	1	4.57
2000 Arizona	NL	33	32	2	0	213.1	876	226	101	96	38	6	6	3	39	7	104	1	4	11	7	.611	0	0-0	0	4.05
8 ML YEARS		154	136	7	7	863.1	3603	945	470	444	149	28	28	16	175	15	413	13	20	51	38	.573	2	1-2	2	4.63

Garret Anderson

Bats: L Throws: L Pos: CF-137; RF-15; DH-10; 1B-1; PH/PR-1   **Ht:** 6'3" **Wt:** 220 **Born:** 6/30/72 **Age:** 29

					BATTING														BASERUNNING				PERCENTAGES		
Year Team	Lg	G	AB	H	2B	3B	HR	(Hm	Rd)	TB	R	RBI	TBB	IBB	SO	HBP	SH	SF	SB	CS	SB%	GDP	Avg	OBP	SLG
1994 California	AL	5	13	5	0	0	0	(0	0)	5	0	1	0	0	2	0	0	0	0	0	—	0	.385	.385	.385
1995 California	AL	106	374	120	19	1	16	(7	9)	189	50	69	19	4	65	1	2	4	6	2	.75	8	.321	.352	.505
1996 California	AL	150	607	173	33	2	12	(5	7)	246	79	72	27	5	84	0	5	3	7	9	.44	22	.285	.314	.405
1997 Anaheim	AL	154	624	189	36	3	8	(5	3)	255	76	92	30	6	70	2	4	5	10	4	.71	20	.303	.334	.409
1998 Anaheim	AL	156	622	183	41	7	15	(4	11)	283	62	79	29	8	80	1	3	3	8	3	.73	13	.294	.325	.455
1999 Anaheim	AL	157	620	188	36	2	21	(10	11)	291	88	80	34	8	81	0	0	6	4	3	.43	15	.303	.336	.469
2000 Anaheim	AL	159	647	185	40	2	35	(20	15)	336	92	117	24	8	87	0	0	1	7	6	.54	21	.286	.307	.519
7 ML YEARS		887	3507	1043	205	18	107	(53	54)	1605	447	510	163	36	469	4	12	30	41	28	.59	99	.297	.327	.458

Jimmy Anderson

Pitches: Left Bats: Left Pos: SP-26; RP-1   **Ht:** 6'1" **Wt:** 207 **Born:** 1/22/76 **Age:** 25

				HOW MUCH HE PITCHED				WHAT HE GAVE UP												THE RESULTS						
Year Team	Lg	G	GS	CG	GF	IP	BFP	H	R	ER	HR	SH	SF	HB	TBB	IBB	SO	WP	Bk	W	L	Pct.	ShO	Sv-Op	Hld	ERA
1994 Pirates	R	10	10	0	0	56.1	230	35	21	10	1	2	1	2	27	0	66	5	1	5	1	.833	0	0-—	—	1.60
1995 Augusta	A	14	14	0	0	76.2	305	51	15	13	1	1	0	4	31	0	75	9	1	4	2	.667	0	0-—	—	1.53
Lynchburg	A+	10	9	0	1	52.1	231	56	29	24	1	4	1	5	21	1	32	7	3	1	5	.167	0	0-—	—	4.13

HOW MUCH HE PITCHED								WHAT HE GAVE UP												THE RESULTS						
Year Team	Lg	G	GS	CG	GF	IP	BFP	H	R	ER	HR	SH	SF	HB	TBB	IBB	SO	WP	Bk	W	L	Pct.	ShO	Sv-Op	Hld	ERA
1996 Lynchburg	A+	11	11	1	0	65.1	267	51	25	14	2	2	0	2	21	0	56	1	0	5	3	.625	1	0--	—	1.93
Carolina	AA	17	16	0	0	97	411	92	40	36	3	1	0	3	44	3	79	13	5	8	3	.727	0	0--	—	3.34
1997 Carolina	AA	4	4	0	0	24.2	98	16	6	4	1	0	0	2	9	0	23	1	0	2	1	.667	0	0--	—	1.46
Calgary	AAA	21	21	0	0	103	486	124	78	65	9	6	5	5	64	3	71	9	4	7	6	.538	0	0--	—	5.68
1998 Nashville	AAA	35	17	0	8	123.2	570	144	87	69	8	11	5	4	72	6	63	13	1	9	10	.474	0	0--	—	5.02
1999 Nashville	AAA	21	21	1	0	133.2	579	153	67	57	5	6	0	3	41	0	93	8	0	11	2	.846	0	0--	—	3.84
2000 Nashville	AAA	2	2	0	0	13	55	18	6	6	0	0	0	1	4	0	7	1	0	0	0	—	0	0--	—	4.15
Altoona	AA	1	1	1	0	9	34	7	1	0	0	0	0	0	1	0	6	0	0	1	0	1.000	0	0--	—	0.00
1999 Pittsburgh	NL	13	4	0	2	29.1	127	25	15	13	2	2	1	1	16	2	13	4	0	2	1	.667	0	0-0	0	3.99
2000 Pittsburgh	NL	27	26	1	0	144	648	169	94	84	13	5	3	7	58	2	73	6	0	5	11	.313	0	0-0	0	5.25
2 ML YEARS		40	30	1	2	173.1	775	194	109	97	15	7	4	8	74	4	86	10	0	7	12	.368	0	0-0	0	5.04

Marlon Anderson

Bats: Left **Throws:** Right **Pos:** 2B-41   **Ht:** 5'11" **Wt:** 198 **Born:** 1/6/74 **Age:** 27

BATTING																		BASERUNNING				PERCENTAGES		
Year Team	Lg	G	AB	H	2B	3B	HR	(Hm	Rd)	TB	R	RBI	TBB	IBB	SO	HBP	SH	SF	SB	CS	SB%	GDP	Avg	OBP	SLG
2000 Scrantn-WB *	AAA	103	397	121	18	8	8	—	—	179	57	53	39	12	43	5	2	5	24	10	.71	2	.305	.370	.451
1998 Philadelphia	NL	17	43	14	3	0	1	(1	0)	20	4	4	1	0	6	0	1	0	2	0	1.00	1	.326	.333	.465
1999 Philadelphia	NL	129	452	114	26	4	5	(4	1)	163	48	54	24	1	61	2	4	2	13	2	.87	6	.252	.292	.361
2000 Philadelphia	NL	41	162	37	8	1	1	(1	0)	50	10	15	12	0	22	0	0	0	2	2	.50	5	.228	.282	.309
3 ML YEARS		187	657	165	37	5	7	(6	1)	233	62	73	37	1	89	2	4	3	17	4	.81	11	.251	.292	.355

Matt Anderson

Pitches: Right **Bats:** Right **Pos:** RP-69   **Ht:** 6'4" **Wt:** 200 **Born:** 8/17/76 **Age:** 24

HOW MUCH HE PITCHED								WHAT HE GAVE UP												THE RESULTS						
Year Team	Lg	G	GS	CG	GF	IP	BFP	H	R	ER	HR	SH	SF	HB	TBB	IBB	SO	WP	Bk	W	L	Pct.	ShO	Sv-Op	Hld	ERA
1998 Detroit	AL	42	0	0	10	44	194	38	16	16	3	6	3	2	44	2	44	1	0	5	1	.833	0	0-4	6	3.27
1999 Detroit	AL	37	0	0	9	38	180	33	27	24	8	0	2	1	35	1	32	3	0	2	1	.667	0	0-2	3	5.68
2000 Detroit	AL	69	0	0	27	74.1	324	61	44	39	8	2	6	3	45	4	71	4	0	3	2	.600	0	1-1	9	4.72
3 ML YEARS		148	0	0	46	156.1	698	132	87	79	19	8	11	6	111	9	147	9	0	10	4	.714	0	1-7	18	4.55

Clayton Andrews

Pitches: Left **Bats:** Right **Pos:** RP-6; SP-2   **Ht:** 6'0" **Wt:** 180 **Born:** 5/15/78 **Age:** 23

HOW MUCH HE PITCHED								WHAT HE GAVE UP												THE RESULTS						
Year Team	Lg	G	GS	CG	GF	IP	BFP	H	R	ER	HR	SH	SF	HB	TBB	IBB	SO	WP	Bk	W	L	Pct.	ShO	Sv-Op	Hld	ERA
1996 Medcine Hat	R+	8	4	0	1	25.2	120	37	23	21	4	0	3	1	10	0	14	1	0	2	4	.333	0	0--	—	7.36
1997 Hagerstown	A	28	15	0	7	114.2	512	120	70	58	8	4	4	5	47	1	112	4	2	7	7	.500	0	0--	—	4.55
1998 Hagerstown	A	27	26	2	0	162	635	112	59	41	7	4	5	6	46	0	193	7	2	10	7	.588	1	0--	—	2.28
1999 Knoxville	AA	25	25	0	0	132.2	593	143	85	58	13	8	3	4	69	0	93	4	2	10	8	.556	0	0--	—	3.93
Syracuse	AAA	3	3	0	0	15	65	10	14	13	5	0	1	0	13	0	9	1	0	0	1	.000	0	0--	—	7.80
2000 Syracuse	AAA	19	18	0	0	102.2	449	114	56	55	8	2	3	2	42	0	59	1	2	8	7	.533	0	0--	—	4.82
2000 Toronto	AL	8	2	0	1	20.2	102	34	23	23	6	1	1	0	9	0	12	0	1	1	2	.333	0	0-0	0	10.02

Shane Andrews

Bats: Right **Throws:** Right **Pos:** 3B-58; PH/PR-15; 1B-6   **Ht:** 6'1" **Wt:** 220 **Born:** 8/28/71 **Age:** 29

BATTING																		BASERUNNING				PERCENTAGES		
Year Team	Lg	G	AB	H	2B	3B	HR	(Hm	Rd)	TB	R	RBI	TBB	IBB	SO	HBP	SH	SF	SB	CS	SB%	GDP	Avg	OBP	SLG
2000 Iowa *	AAA	15	38	7	3	0	2	—	—	16	5	7	7	1	10	0	0	1	0	0	—	2	.184	.304	.421
1995 Montreal	NL	84	220	47	10	1	8	(2	6)	83	27	31	17	2	68	1	1	2	1	1	.50	4	.214	.271	.377
1996 Montreal	NL	127	375	85	15	2	19	(8	11)	161	43	64	35	8	119	2	0	2	3	1	.75	2	.227	.295	.429
1997 Montreal	NL	18	64	13	3	0	4	(2	2)	28	10	9	3	0	20	0	0	2	0	0	—	0	.203	.232	.438
1998 Montreal	NL	150	492	117	30	1	25	(12	13)	224	48	69	58	3	137	0	2	7	1	6	.14	10	.238	.314	.455
1999 Mon-ChC	NL	117	348	68	12	0	16	(9	7)	128	41	51	50	3	109	1	0	5	1	1	.50	10	.195	.295	.368
2000 Chicago	NL	66	192	44	5	0	14	(7	7)	91	25	39	27	1	59	2	0	1	1	1	.50	5	.229	.329	.474
1999 Montreal	NL	98	281	51	8	0	11	(5	6)	92	28	37	43	2	88	0	0	4	1	0	1.00	10	.181	.287	.327
Chicago	NL	19	67	17	4	0	5	(4	1)	36	13	14	7	1	21	1	0	1	0	1	.00	0	.254	.329	.537
6 ML YEARS		562	1691	374	75	4	86	(40	46)	715	194	263	190	17	512	6	3	19	7	10	.41	35	.221	.299	.423

Rick Ankiel

Pitches: Left **Bats:** Left **Pos:** SP-30; RP-1   **Ht:** 6'1" **Wt:** 210 **Born:** 7/19/79 **Age:** 21

HOW MUCH HE PITCHED								WHAT HE GAVE UP												THE RESULTS						
Year Team	Lg	G	GS	CG	GF	IP	BFP	H	R	ER	HR	SH	SF	HB	TBB	IBB	SO	WP	Bk	W	L	Pct.	ShO	Sv-Op	Hld	ERA
1998 Peoria	A	7	7	0	0	35	128	15	8	8	0	1	1	2	12	0	41	1	0	3	0	1.000	0	0--	—	2.06
Pr William	A+	21	21	1	0	126	503	91	46	39	8	5	3	12	38	0	181	10	1	9	6	.600	0	0--	—	2.79
1999 Arkansas	AA	8	8	1	0	49.1	191	25	6	5	2	1	0	2	16	0	75	0	0	6	0	1.000	1	0--	—	0.91
Memphis	AAA	16	16	0	0	88.1	385	73	37	31	7	1	3	7	46	1	119	6	1	7	3	.700	0	0--	—	3.16
1999 St. Louis	NL	9	5	0	1	33	137	26	12	12	2	1	0	1	14	0	39	2	0	0	1	.000	0	1-1	0	3.27
2000 St. Louis	NL	31	30	0	0	175	735	137	80	68	21	8	6	6	90	2	194	12	2	11	7	.611	0	0-0	0	3.50
2 ML YEARS		40	35	0	1	208	872	163	92	80	23	9	6	7	104	2	233	14	2	11	8	.579	0	1-1	1	3.46

Kevin Appier

Pitches: Right **Bats:** Right **Pos:** SP-31   **Ht:** 6'2" **Wt:** 200 **Born:** 12/6/67 **Age:** 33

HOW MUCH HE PITCHED								WHAT HE GAVE UP												THE RESULTS						
Year Team	Lg	G	GS	CG	GF	IP	BFP	H	R	ER	HR	SH	SF	HB	TBB	IBB	SO	WP	Bk	W	L	Pct.	ShO	Sv-Op	Hld	ERA
1989 Kansas City	AL	6	5	0	0	21.2	106	34	22	22	3	0	3	0	12	1	10	0	0	1	4	.200	0	0-0	0	9.14
1990 Kansas City	AL	32	24	3	1	185.2	784	179	67	57	13	5	9	6	54	2	127	6	1	12	8	.600	3	0-0	0	2.76

Year Team	Lg	G	GS	CG	GF	IP	BFP	H	R	ER	HR	SH	SF	HB	TBB	IBB	SO	WP	Bk	W	L	Pct.	ShO	Sv-Op	Hld	ERA
1991 Kansas City	AL	34	31	6	1	207.2	881	205	97	79	13	8	6	2	61	3	158	7	1	13	10	.565	3	0-0	1	3.42
1992 Kansas City	AL	30	30	3	0	208.1	852	167	59	57	10	8	3	2	68	5	150	4	0	15	8	.652	2	0-0	0	2.46
1993 Kansas City	AL	34	34	5	0	238.2	953	183	74	68	8	3	5	1	81	3	186	5	0	18	8	.692	1	0-0	0	2.56
1994 Kansas City	AL	23	23	1	0	155	653	137	68	66	11	9	7	4	63	7	145	11	1	7	6	.538	0	0-0	0	3.83
1995 Kansas City	AL	31	31	4	0	201.1	832	163	90	87	14	3	3	8	80	1	185	5	0	15	10	.600	1	0-0	0	3.89
1996 Kansas City	AL	32	32	5	0	211.1	874	192	87	85	17	7	4	5	75	2	207	10	1	14	11	.560	1	0-0	0	3.62
1997 Kansas City	AL	34	34	4	0	235.2	972	215	96	89	24	4	4	4	74	2	196	14	1	9	13	.409	1	0-0	0	3.40
1998 Kansas City	AL	3	3	0	0	15	69	21	13	13	5	1	0	1	5	1	9	1	0	1	2	.333	0	0-0	0	7.80
1999 KC-Oak	AL	34	34	1	0	209	926	230	131	120	27	7	5	7	84	4	131	10	1	16	14	.533	0	0-0	0	5.17
2000 Oakland	AL	31	31	1	0	195.1	884	200	109	98	23	5	6	9	102	10	129	6	0	15	11	.577	1	0-0	0	4.52
1999 Kansas City	AL	22	22	1	0	140.1	613	153	81	76	18	5	3	6	51	3	78	5	0	9	9	.500	0	0-0	0	4.87
Oakland	AL	12	12	0	0	68.2	313	77	50	44	9	2	2	1	33	1	53	5	0	7	5	.583	0	0-0	0	5.77
12 ML YEARS		324	312	33	2	2084.2	8786	1926	913	841	166	59	56	49	759	41	1633	79	6	136	105	.564	11	0-0	1	3.63

Danny Ardoin

Bats: Right **Throws:** Right **Pos:** C-15; PH/PR-1 **Ht:** 6'0" **Wt:** 218 **Born:** 7/8/74 **Age:** 26

Year Team	Lg	G	AB	H	2B	3B	HR	(Hm	Rd)	TB	R	RBI	TBB	IBB	SO	HBP	SH	SF	SB	CS	SB%	GDP	Avg	OBP	SLG
1995 Sou Oregon	A-	58	175	41	9	1	2	—	—	58	28	23	31	0	50	9	5	4	2	1	.67	2	.234	.370	.331
1996 Modesto	A+	91	317	83	13	3	6	—	—	120	55	34	47	0	81	9	3	2	5	7	.42	9	.262	.371	.379
1997 Huntsville	AA	57	208	48	10	1	4	—	—	72	26	23	17	0	38	3	0	2	2	3	.40	7	.231	.296	.346
Visalia	A+	43	145	34	7	1	3	—	—	52	16	19	21	0	39	4	1	0	0	1	.00	3	.234	.347	.359
1998 Huntsville	AA	109	363	90	21	0	16	—	—	159	67	62	62	0	87	7	6	1	8	4	.67	10	.248	.367	.438
1999 Vancouver	AAA	109	336	85	13	2	8	—	—	126	53	46	50	0	78	9	9	1	3	3	.50	12	.253	.364	.375
2000 Modesto	A+	4	10	3	1	0	0	—	—	4	1	2	0	0	4	1	0	0	0	0	—	0	.300	.364	.400
Sacramento	AAA	67	234	65	16	1	6	—	—	101	42	34	34	3	72	8	3	2	6	0	1.00	5	.278	.385	.432
Salt Lake	AAA	3	9	2	0	0	0	—	—	2	1	0	3	0	4	0	0	0	0	0	—	0	.222	.417	.222
2000 Minnesota	AL	15	32	4	1	0	1	(0	1)	8	4	5	8	0	10	0	0	0	0	0	—	0	.125	.300	.250

Alex Arias

Bats: R **Throws:** R **Pos:** SS-39; PH/PR-21; 3B-10; 2B-1 **Ht:** 6'3" **Wt:** 202 **Born:** 11/20/67 **Age:** 33

Year Team	Lg	G	AB	H	2B	3B	HR	(Hm	Rd)	TB	R	RBI	TBB	IBB	SO	HBP	SH	SF	SB	CS	SB%	GDP	Avg	OBP	SLG
1992 Chicago	NL	32	99	29	6	0	0	(0	0)	35	14	7	11	0	13	2	1	0	0	0	—	4	.293	.375	.354
1993 Florida	NL	96	249	67	5	1	2	(1	1)	80	27	20	27	0	18	3	1	3	1	1	.50	5	.269	.344	.321
1994 Florida	NL	59	113	27	5	0	0	(0	0)	32	4	15	9	0	19	1	1	0	1	0	.00	5	.239	.298	.283
1995 Florida	NL	94	216	58	9	2	3	(2	1)	80	22	26	22	1	20	2	3	3	1	0	1.00	8	.269	.337	.370
1996 Florida	NL	100	224	62	11	2	3	(1	2)	86	27	26	17	1	28	3	1	1	2	0	1.00	7	.277	.335	.384
1997 Florida	NL	74	93	23	2	0	1	(0	1)	28	13	11	12	0	12	3	4	0	2	1	.00	6	.247	.352	.301
1998 Philadelphia	NL	56	133	39	8	0	1	(0	1)	50	17	16	13	3	18	1	1	1	2	0	1.00	6	.293	.358	.376
1999 Philadelphia	NL	118	347	105	20	1	4	(4	0)	139	43	48	36	6	31	4	1	2	2	2	.50	12	.303	.373	.401
2000 Philadelphia	NL	70	155	29	9	0	2	(1	1)	44	17	15	16	2	28	3	3	3	1	0	1.00	1	.187	.271	.284
9 ML YEARS		699	1629	439	75	6	16	(10	6)	574	184	184	163	13	187	22	16	14	9	5	.64	44	.269	.341	.352

Tony Armas Jr.

Pitches: Right **Bats:** Right **Pos:** SP-17 **Ht:** 6'4" **Wt:** 205 **Born:** 4/29/78 **Age:** 23

Year Team	Lg	G	GS	CG	GF	IP	BFP	H	R	ER	HR	SH	SF	HB	TBB	IBB	SO	WP	Bk	W	L	Pct.	ShO	Sv-Op	Hld	ERA
1995 Yankees	R	5	4	0	0	14	61	12	9	1	1	1	0	1	6	0	13	3	1	0	1	.000	0	0--	—	0.64
1996 Oneonta	A-	3	3	0	0	15.2	73	14	12	10	1	0	1	0	11	0	14	4	0	1	1	.500	0	0--	—	5.74
Yankees	R	8	7	0	1	45.2	191	41	18	16	1	0	2	2	13	0	45	4	2	4	1	.800	0	1--	—	3.15
1997 Greensboro	A	9	9	2	0	51.2	207	36	13	6	3	0	0	1	13	0	64	1	1	5	2	.714	1	0--	—	1.05
Tampa	A+	9	9	0	0	46	191	43	23	17	1	3	4	1	16	3	26	2	0	3	1	.750	0	0--	—	3.33
Sarasota	A+	3	3	0	0	17.2	83	18	13	13	2	2	1	2	12	0	9	3	0	2	1	.667	0	0--	—	6.62
1998 Jupiter	A+	27	27	1	0	153.1	656	140	63	49	11	11	1	10	59	0	136	3	0	12	8	.600	1	0--	—	2.88
1999 Harrisburg	AA	24	24	2	0	149.2	611	123	62	48	10	8	1	3	55	0	106	5	1	9	7	.563	1	0--	—	2.89
2000 Jupiter	A+	1	1	0	0	4.2	18	4	0	0	0	0	0	0	4	0	8	0	0	0	0	—	0	0--	—	0.00
Ottawa	AAA	4	4	0	0	19	83	22	11	8	3	0	0	2	4	0	12	0	0	1	2	.333	0	0--	—	3.79
1999 Montreal	NL	1	1	0	0	6	28	8	4	1	1	0	0	0	2	1	2	2	0	0	1	.000	0	0-0	0	1.50
2000 Montreal	NL	17	17	0	0	95	403	74	49	46	10	7	3	3	50	2	59	3	0	7	9	.438	0	0-0	0	4.36
2 ML YEARS		18	18	0	0	101	431	82	53	47	10	7	4	3	52	3	61	3	0	7	10	.412	0	0-0	0	4.19

Jamie Arnold

Pitches: Right **Bats:** Right **Pos:** RP-10; SP-4 **Ht:** 6'2" **Wt:** 188 **Born:** 3/24/74 **Age:** 27

Year Team	Lg	G	GS	CG	GF	IP	BFP	H	R	ER	HR	SH	SF	HB	TBB	IBB	SO	WP	Bk	W	L	Pct.	ShO	Sv-Op	Hld	ERA
1992 Braves	R	7	5	0	2	20	85	16	12	9	0	0	2	4	6	0	22	0	0	0	1	.000	0	0--	—	4.05
1993 Macon	A	27	27	1	0	164.1	692	142	67	57	5	3	4	16	56	0	124	13	2	8	9	.471	0	0--	—	3.12
1994 Durham	A+	25	25	0	0	145	656	144	96	75	26	3	1	14	79	4	91	8	4	7	7	.500	0	0--	—	4.66
1995 Durham	A+	15	14	1	0	80	347	86	42	35	5	4	1	9	21	0	44	4	0	4	8	.333	0	0--	—	3.94
Greenville	AA	10	10	0	0	56.2	266	76	42	40	8	0	2	7	25	1	19	6	0	1	5	.167	0	0--	—	6.35
1996 Greenville	AA	23	23	2	0	128	573	149	79	70	17	0	5	10	44	1	64	6	1	7	7	.500	0	0--	—	4.92
1997 Braves	R	5	5	0	0	19	74	13	6	6	1	0	0	0	6	0	21	0	0	1	0	1.000	0	0--	—	2.84
Durham	A+	5	5	0	0	24.1	115	25	21	16	2	2	0	1	13	0	21	2	0	2	2	.500	0	0--	—	5.92
Greenville	AA	1	1	0	0	4.2	27	10	6	6	3	0	0	1	2	0	3	1	0	1	0	1.000	0	0--	—	11.57
1998 Greenville	AA	32	6	0	7	83.1	387	93	51	41	12	2	1	3	46	2	48	12	0	1	4	.200	0	1--	—	4.43
Richmond	AAA	9	2	0	2	20.2	102	30	22	22	1	1	3	1	17	1	10	3	0	1	0	1.000	0	1--	—	9.58
1999 Albuquerque	AAA	7	2	0	0	19.1	91	28	14	12	1	0	1	2	7	0	13	3	0	0	0	—	0	0--	—	5.59
2000 Albuquerque	AAA	20	13	0	1	92.1	415	94	62	52	5	3	1	6	54	0	47	3	0	4	7	.364	0	0--	—	5.07
Iowa	AAA	3	3	0	0	17.2	83	22	10	9	2	0	0	2	10	0	10	1	0	2	0	.667	0	0--	—	4.58

	HOW MUCH HE PITCHED						WHAT HE GAVE UP											THE RESULTS						
Year Team	Lg	G	GS	CG	GF	IP	BFP	H	R	ER	HR	SH	SF	HB	TBB	IBB	SO	WP	Bk	W	L	Pct.	ShO	Sv-Op	Hld	ERA
1999 Los Angeles	NL	36	3	0	18	69	313	81	50	42	6	3	6	6	34	2	26	3	0	2	4	.333	0	1-3	2	5.48
2000 LA-ChC	NL	14	4	0	5	39.1	181	38	31	27	1	2	4	4	24	0	16	2	0	0	3	.000	0	1-1	0	6.18
2000 Los Angeles	NL	2	0	0	2	6.2	30	4	3	3	0	0	1	1	5	0	3	1	0	0	0	—	0	0-0	0	4.05
Chicago	NL	12	4	0	3	32.2	151	34	28	24	1	2	3	3	19	0	13	1	0	0	3	.000	0	1-1	0	6.61
2 ML YEARS		50	7	0	23	108.1	494	119	81	69	7	5	4	10	58	2	42	5	0	2	7	.222	0	2-4	2	5.73

Rolando Arrojo

Pitches: Right Bats: Right Pos: SP-32 Ht: 6'4" Wt: 220 Born: 7/18/68 Age: 32

	HOW MUCH HE PITCHED						WHAT HE GAVE UP											THE RESULTS						
Year Team	Lg	G	GS	CG	GF	IP	BFP	H	R	ER	HR	SH	SF	HB	TBB	IBB	SO	WP	Bk	W	L	Pct.	ShO	Sv-Op	Hld	ERA
1998 Tampa Bay	AL	32	32	2	0	202	853	195	84	80	21	5	3	19	65	2	152	3	1	14	12	.538	2	0-0	0	3.56
1999 Tampa Bay	AL	24	24	2	0	140.2	630	162	84	81	23	5	3	14	60	2	107	2	0	7	12	.368	0	0-0	0	5.18
2000 Col-Bos		32	32	0	0	172.2	771	187	118	108	24	4	7	16	68	6	124	4	2	10	11	.476	0	0-0	0	5.63
2000 Colorado	NL	19	19	0	0	101.1	470	120	77	68	14	3	7	12	46	6	80	1	2	5	9	.357	0	0-0	0	6.04
Boston	AL	13	13	0	0	71.1	301	67	41	40	10	1	0	4	22	0	44	3	0	5	2	.714	0	0-0	0	5.05
3 ML YEARS		88	88	4	0	515.1	2254	544	286	269	68	14	13	49	193	10	383	9	3	31	35	.470	2	0-0	0	4.70

Bronson Arroyo

Pitches: Right Bats: Right Pos: SP-12; RP-8 Ht: 6'5" Wt: 180 Born: 2/24/77 Age: 24

	HOW MUCH HE PITCHED						WHAT HE GAVE UP											THE RESULTS						
Year Team	Lg	G	GS	CG	GF	IP	BFP	H	R	ER	HR	SH	SF	HB	TBB	IBB	SO	WP	Bk	W	L	Pct.	ShO	Sv-Op	Hld	ERA
1995 Pirates	R	13	9	0	3	61.1	275	72	39	29	4	2	0	4	9	0	48	5	0	5	4	.556	0	1--	—	4.26
1996 Augusta	A	26	26	0	0	135.2	562	123	64	53	11	9	1	7	36	0	107	10	0	8	6	.571	0	0--	—	3.52
1997 Lynchburg	A+	24	24	3	0	160.1	658	154	69	59	17	7	0	3	33	0	121	9	0	12	4	.750	1	0--	—	3.31
1998 Carolina	AA	23	22	1	0	127	573	158	91	77	18	4	6	3	51	0	90	7	0	9	8	.529	0	0--	—	5.46
1999 Altoona	AA	25	25	2	0	153	668	167	73	62	15	5	2	7	58	1	100	6	0	15	4	.789	1	0--	—	3.65
Nashville	AAA	3	3	0	0	13	71	22	15	15	1	0	0	1	10	0	11	0	0	0	2	.000	0	0--	—	10.38
2000 Nashville	AAA	13	13	1	0	88.2	363	82	43	36	7	6	2	3	25	3	52	5	1	8	2	.800	1	0--	—	3.65
Lynchburg	A+	1	1	0	0	7	32	8	3	3	0	0	0	0	2	0	3	0	0	0	0	—	0	0--	—	3.86
2000 Pittsburgh	NL	20	12	0	1	71.2	338	88	61	51	10	5	2	4	36	6	50	3	1	2	6	.250	0	0-0	0	6.40

Andy Ashby

Pitches: Right Bats: Right Pos: SP-31 Ht: 6'5" Wt: 202 Born: 7/11/67 Age: 33

	HOW MUCH HE PITCHED						WHAT HE GAVE UP											THE RESULTS						
Year Team	Lg	G	GS	CG	GF	IP	BFP	H	R	ER	HR	SH	SF	HB	TBB	IBB	SO	WP	Bk	W	L	Pct.	ShO	Sv-Op	Hld	ERA
1991 Philadelphia	NL	8	8	0	0	42	186	41	28	28	5	1	3	3	19	0	26	6	0	1	5	.167	0	0-0	0	6.00
1992 Philadelphia	NL	10	8	0	0	37	171	42	31	31	6	2	2	1	21	0	24	2	0	1	3	.250	0	0-0	0	7.54
1993 Col-SD	NL	32	21	0	3	123	577	168	100	93	19	6	7	4	56	5	77	6	3	3	10	.231	0	1-1	0	6.80
1994 San Diego	NL	24	24	4	0	164.1	682	145	75	62	16	11	3	3	43	12	121	5	0	6	11	.353	0	0-0	0	3.40
1995 San Diego	NL	31	31	2	0	192.2	800	180	79	63	17	10	4	11	62	3	150	7	0	12	10	.545	2	0-0	0	2.94
1996 San Diego	NL	24	24	1	0	150.2	612	147	60	54	17	6	2	3	34	1	85	3	0	9	5	.643	0	0-0	0	3.23
1997 San Diego	NL	30	30	2	0	200.2	862	207	108	92	17	13	6	5	49	2	144	3	0	9	11	.450	0	0-0	0	4.13
1998 San Diego	NL	33	33	5	0	226.2	939	223	90	84	23	8	5	7	58	8	151	7	0	17	9	.654	1	0-0	0	3.34
1999 San Diego	NL	31	31	4	0	206	862	204	95	87	26	10	1	6	61	9	132	6	0	14	10	.583	3	0-0	0	3.80
2000 Phi-Atl	NL	31	31	3	0	199.1	867	216	124	109	29	18	10	6	61	9	106	6	1	12	13	.480	1	0-0	0	4.92
1993 Colorado	NL	20	9	0	3	54	277	89	54	51	5	3	3	3	32	4	33	2	3	0	4	.000	0	1-1	0	8.50
San Diego	NL	12	12	0	0	69	300	79	46	42	14	3	4	1	24	1	44	4	0	3	6	.333	0	0-0	0	5.48
2000 Philadelphia	NL	16	16	1	0	101.1	455	113	75	64	17	11	9	5	38	5	51	4	0	4	7	.364	0	0-0	0	5.68
Atlanta	NL	15	15	2	0	98	412	103	49	45	12	7	1	1	23	4	55	2	1	8	6	.571	1	0-0	0	4.13
10 ML YEARS		254	241	21	3	1542.1	6547	1573	790	703	175	85	43	50	457	44	1016	51	4	84	87	.491	7	1-1	0	4.10

Pedro Astacio

Pitches: Right Bats: Right Pos: SP-32 Ht: 6'2" Wt: 210 Born: 11/28/69 Age: 31

	HOW MUCH HE PITCHED						WHAT HE GAVE UP											THE RESULTS						
Year Team	Lg	G	GS	CG	GF	IP	BFP	H	R	ER	HR	SH	SF	HB	TBB	IBB	SO	WP	Bk	W	L	Pct.	ShO	Sv-Op	Hld	ERA
1992 Los Angeles	NL	11	11	4	0	82	341	80	23	18	1	3	2	2	20	4	43	1	0	5	5	.500	4	0-0	0	1.98
1993 Los Angeles	NL	31	31	3	0	186.1	777	165	80	74	14	7	8	5	68	5	122	8	9	14	9	.609	2	0-0	0	3.57
1994 Los Angeles	NL	23	23	3	0	149	625	142	77	71	18	6	5	4	47	4	108	4	0	6	8	.429	1	0-0	0	4.29
1995 Los Angeles	NL	48	11	1	7	104	436	103	53	49	12	5	3	4	29	5	80	5	0	7	8	.467	1	0-1	2	4.24
1996 Los Angeles	NL	35	32	0	0	211.2	885	207	86	81	18	11	5	9	67	9	130	6	2	9	8	.529	0	0-0	0	3.44
1997 LA-Col	NL	33	31	2	2	202.1	862	200	98	93	24	9	7	9	61	0	166	6	3	12	10	.545	1	0-0	0	4.14
1998 Colorado	NL	35	34	0	0	209.1	938	245	160	145	39	12	3	17	74	0	170	2	0	13	14	.481	0	0-0	0	6.23
1999 Colorado	NL	34	34	7	0	232	1008	258	140	130	38	6	10	11	75	6	210	5	0	17	11	.607	0	0-0	0	5.04
2000 Colorado	NL	32	32	3	0	196.1	875	217	119	115	32	7	4	15	77	5	193	8	0	12	9	.571	0	0-0	0	5.27
1997 Los Angeles	NL	26	24	2	2	153.2	654	151	75	70	15	9	5	4	47	0	115	4	3	7	9	.438	1	0-0	0	4.10
Colorado	NL	7	7	0	0	48.2	208	49	23	23	9	0	2	5	14	0	51	2	0	5	1	.833	0	0-0	0	4.25
9 ML YEARS		282	239	23	9	1573	6747	1617	836	776	196	66	47	76	518	38	1222	45	14	95	82	.537	9	0-1	2	4.44

Rich Aurilia

Bats: Right Throws: Right Pos: SS-140; PH/PR-1 Ht: 6'1" Wt: 185 Born: 9/2/71 Age: 29

	BATTING																	BASERUNNING				PERCENTAGES		
Year Team	Lg	G	AB	H	2B	3B	HR	(Hm	Rd)	TB	R	RBI	TBB	IBB	SO	HBP	SH	SF	SB	CS	SB%	GDP	Avg	OBP	SLG
1995 San Francisco	NL	9	19	9	3	0	2	(0	2)	18	4	4	1	0	2	0	1	1	1	0	1.00	1	.474	.476	.947
1996 San Francisco	NL	105	318	76	7	1	4	(1	2)	94	27	26	25	2	52	1	1	6	4	1	.80	1	.239	.295	.296
1997 San Francisco	NL	46	102	28	8	0	5	(1	4)	51	16	19	8	0	15	0	1	2	1	1	.50	3	.275	.321	.500
1998 San Francisco	NL	122	413	110	27	2	9	(5	4)	168	54	49	31	3	62	2	5	2	3	3	.50	3	.266	.319	.407
1999 San Francisco	NL	152	558	157	23	1	22	(9	13)	248	68	80	43	3	71	5	3	5	2	3	.40	16	.281	.336	.444
2000 San Francisco	NL	141	509	138	24	2	20	(12	8)	226	67	79	54	2	90	0	4	4	1	2	.33	15	.271	.339	.444
6 ML YEARS		575	1919	518	92	6	61	(28	33)	805	236	257	162	10	292	8	20	16	12	10	.55	39	.270	.327	.419

11

Brad Ausmus

Bats: R **Throws:** R **Pos:** C-150; PH/PR-3; 1B-1; 2B-1; 3B-1 **Ht:** 5'11" **Wt:** 195 **Born:** 4/14/69 **Age:** 32

Year Team	Lg	G	AB	H	2B	3B	HR	(Hm	Rd)	TB	R	RBI	TBB	IBB	SO	HBP	SH	SF	SB	CS	SB%	GDP	Avg	OBP	SLG
1993 San Diego	NL	49	160	41	8	1	5	(4	1)	66	18	12	6	0	28	0	0	0	2	0	1.00	2	.256	.283	.413
1994 San Diego	NL	101	327	82	12	1	7	(6	1)	117	45	24	30	12	63	1	6	2	5	1	.83	8	.251	.314	.358
1995 San Diego	NL	103	328	96	16	4	5	(2	3)	135	44	34	31	3	56	2	4	4	16	5	.76	6	.293	.353	.412
1996 SD-Det		125	375	83	16	0	5	(2	3)	114	46	35	39	1	72	5	6	2	4	8	.33	8	.221	.302	.304
1997 Houston	NL	130	425	113	25	1	4	(1	3)	152	45	44	38	4	78	3	6	6	14	6	.70	8	.266	.326	.358
1998 Houston	NL	128	412	111	10	4	6	(2	4)	147	62	45	53	11	60	3	3	1	10	3	.77	18	.269	.356	.357
1999 Detroit	AL	127	458	126	25	6	9	(5	4)	190	62	54	51	0	71	14	3	1	12	9	.57	11	.275	.365	.415
2000 Detroit	AL	150	523	139	25	3	7	(3	4)	191	75	51	69	0	79	6	4	2	11	5	.69	19	.266	.357	.365
1996 San Diego	NL	50	149	27	4	0	1	(0	1)	34	16	13	13	0	27	3	1	0	1	4	.20	4	.181	.261	.228
Detroit	AL	75	226	56	12	0	4	(2	2)	80	30	22	26	1	45	2	5	2	3	4	.43	4	.248	.328	.354
8 ML YEARS		913	3008	791	137	20	48	(25	23)	1112	397	299	317	31	507	34	32	18	74	37	.67	80	.263	.338	.370

Bruce Aven

Bats: R **Throws:** R **Pos:** PH/PR-36; LF-26; RF-20; CF-8 **Ht:** 5'9" **Wt:** 180 **Born:** 3/4/72 **Age:** 29

Year Team	Lg	G	AB	H	2B	3B	HR	(Hm	Rd)	TB	R	RBI	TBB	IBB	SO	HBP	SH	SF	SB	CS	SB%	GDP	Avg	OBP	SLG
2000 Nashville *	AAA	3	10	3	1	0	0	—	—	4	1	3	1	1	3	0	0	0	0	0	—	0	.300	.364	.400
Albuquerque *	AAA	9	32	9	1	0	0	—	—	10	7	3	6	0	6	0	0	0	0	0	—	1	.281	.395	.313
1997 Cleveland	AL	13	19	4	1	0	0	(0	0)	5	4	2	1	0	5	0	0	0	0	1	.00	0	.211	.250	.263
1999 Florida	NL	137	381	110	19	2	12	(3	9)	169	57	70	44	1	82	9	0	6	3	0	1.00	6	.289	.370	.444
2000 Pit-LA	NL	81	168	42	11	0	7	(4	3)	74	20	29	8	0	39	0	0	0	2	3	.40	4	.250	.284	.440
2000 Pittsburgh	NL	72	148	37	11	0	5	(4	1)	63	18	25	5	0	31	0	0	0	2	3	.40	4	.250	.275	.426
Los Angeles	NL	9	20	5	0	0	2	(0	2)	11	2	4	3	0	8	0	0	0	0	0	—	0	.250	.348	.550
3 ML YEARS		231	568	156	31	2	19	(7	12)	248	81	101	53	1	126	9	0	6	5	4	.56	10	.275	.343	.437

Manny Aybar

Pitches: Right **Bats:** Right **Pos:** RP-54 **Ht:** 6'1" **Wt:** 177 **Born:** 10/5/74 **Age:** 26

Year Team	Lg	G	GS	CG	GF	IP	BFP	H	R	ER	HR	SH	SF	HB	TBB	IBB	SO	WP	Bk	W	L	Pct.	ShO	Sv-Op	Hld	ERA
2000 Louisville *	AAA	3	2	0	0	6.2	39	10	10	10	0	0	0	0	10	0	1	1	1	0	2	.000	0	0--	—	13.50
1997 St. Louis	NL	12	12	0	0	68	295	66	33	32	8	7	4	4	29	0	41	1	1	2	4	.333	0	0-0	—	4.24
1998 St. Louis	NL	20	14	0	1	81.1	369	90	58	54	6	4	1	2	42	1	57	2	0	6	6	.500	0	0-0	0	5.98
1999 St. Louis	NL	65	1	0	22	97	430	104	67	59	13	4	3	4	36	3	74	1	2	4	5	.444	0	3-5	12	5.47
2000 Col-Cin-Fla	NL	54	0	0	20	79.1	349	74	42	38	11	5	4	2	35	3	45	7	1	2	2	.500	0	0-1	1	4.31
2000 Colorado	NL	1	0	0	0	1.2	10	5	3	3	1	0	0	0	0	0	0	0	0	1	0	1.000	0	0-0	0	16.20
Cincinnati	NL	32	0	0	10	50.1	226	51	31	27	7	4	3	2	22	2	31	7	1	1	1	.500	0	0-0	1	4.83
Florida	NL	21	0	0	10	27.1	113	18	8	8	3	1	1	0	13	1	14	0	0	0	1	.000	0	0-1	0	2.63
4 ML YEARS		151	27	0	43	325.2	1443	334	200	183	38	20	12	12	142	7	217	11	4	14	17	.452	0	3-6	13	5.06

Jeff Bagwell

Bats: Right **Throws:** Right **Pos:** 1B-158; DH-1 **Ht:** 6'0" **Wt:** 195 **Born:** 5/27/68 **Age:** 33

Year Team	Lg	G	AB	H	2B	3B	HR	(Hm	Rd)	TB	R	RBI	TBB	IBB	SO	HBP	SH	SF	SB	CS	SB%	GDP	Avg	OBP	SLG
1991 Houston	NL	156	554	163	26	4	15	(6	9)	242	79	82	75	5	116	13	1	7	7	4	.64	12	.294	.387	.437
1992 Houston	NL	162	586	160	34	6	18	(8	10)	260	87	96	84	13	97	12	2	13	10	6	.63	17	.273	.368	.444
1993 Houston	NL	142	535	171	37	4	20	(9	11)	276	76	88	62	6	73	3	0	9	13	4	.76	20	.320	.388	.516
1994 Houston	NL	110	400	147	32	2	39	(23	16)	300	104	116	65	14	65	4	0	10	15	4	.79	12	.368	.451	.750
1995 Houston	NL	114	448	130	29	0	21	(10	11)	222	88	87	79	12	102	6	0	5	12	5	.71	9	.290	.399	.496
1996 Houston	NL	162	568	179	48	2	31	(16	15)	324	111	120	135	20	114	10	0	6	21	7	.75	15	.315	.451	.570
1997 Houston	NL	162	566	162	40	2	43	(22	21)	335	109	135	127	27	122	16	0	8	31	10	.76	10	.286	.425	.592
1998 Houston	NL	147	540	164	33	1	34	(20	14)	301	124	111	109	8	90	7	0	5	19	7	.73	14	.304	.424	.557
1999 Houston	NL	162	562	171	35	0	42	(12	30)	332	143	126	149	16	127	11	0	7	30	11	.73	18	.304	.454	.591
2000 Houston	NL	159	590	183	37	1	47	(28	19)	363	152	132	107	11	116	15	0	7	9	6	.60	19	.310	.424	.615
10 ML YEARS		1476	5349	1630	351	22	310	(154	156)	2955	1073	1093	992	132	1022	97	3	78	167	64	.72	146	.305	.417	.552

Harold Baines

Bats: Left **Throws:** Left **Pos:** DH-78; PH/PR-20 **Ht:** 6'2" **Wt:** 195 **Born:** 3/15/59 **Age:** 42

Year Team	Lg	G	AB	H	2B	3B	HR	(Hm	Rd)	TB	R	RBI	TBB	IBB	SO	HBP	SH	SF	SB	CS	SB%	GDP	Avg	OBP	SLG
1980 Chicago	AL	141	491	125	23	6	13	(3	10)	199	55	49	19	7	65	1	2	5	2	4	.33	15	.255	.281	.405
1981 Chicago	AL	82	280	80	11	7	10	(3	7)	135	42	41	12	4	41	2	0	2	6	2	.75	6	.286	.318	.482
1982 Chicago	AL	161	608	165	29	8	25	(11	14)	285	89	105	49	10	95	0	2	9	10	3	.77	12	.271	.321	.469
1983 Chicago	AL	156	596	167	33	2	20	(12	8)	264	76	99	49	13	85	1	3	6	7	5	.58	15	.280	.333	.443
1984 Chicago	AL	147	569	173	28	10	29	(16	13)	308	72	94	54	9	75	0	1	5	1	2	.33	12	.304	.361	.541
1985 Chicago	AL	160	640	198	29	3	22	(13	9)	299	86	113	42	8	89	1	0	10	1	1	.50	23	.309	.348	.467
1986 Chicago	AL	145	570	169	29	2	21	(8	13)	265	72	88	38	9	89	2	0	8	2	1	.67	14	.296	.338	.465
1987 Chicago	AL	132	505	148	26	4	20	(12	8)	242	59	93	46	2	82	1	0	7	0	0	—	14	.293	.352	.479
1988 Chicago	AL	158	599	166	39	1	13	(5	8)	246	55	81	67	14	109	1	0	7	0	0	—	21	.277	.347	.411
1989 CWS-Tex	AL	146	505	156	29	1	16	(5	11)	235	73	72	73	13	79	1	0	3	0	0	—	15	.309	.395	.465
1990 Tex-Oak	AL	135	415	118	15	1	16	(9	7)	183	52	65	67	10	80	0	0	7	0	0	—	15	.284	.378	.441
1991 Oakland	AL	141	488	144	25	1	20	(11	9)	231	76	90	72	22	67	1	1	5	0	1	.00	12	.295	.383	.473
1992 Oakland	AL	140	478	121	18	0	16	(10	6)	187	58	76	59	6	61	0	0	4	0	0	—	10	.253	.331	.391
1993 Baltimore	AL	118	416	130	22	0	20	(12	8)	212	64	78	57	9	52	0	1	6	1	0	—	14	.313	.390	.510
1994 Baltimore	AL	94	326	96	12	1	16	(11	5)	158	44	54	30	6	49	1	0	0	0	0	—	9	.294	.356	.485
1995 Baltimore	AL	127	385	115	19	1	24	(7	17)	208	60	63	70	13	45	0	0	4	0	2	.00	15	.299	.403	.540
1996 Chicago	AL	143	495	154	29	0	22	(9	13)	249	80	95	73	7	62	1	0	3	3	1	.75	20	.311	.399	.503
1997 CWS-Bal	AL	137	452	136	23	0	16	(6	10)	207	55	67	55	11	62	0	0	3	0	1	.00	12	.301	.375	.458

12

Year Team	Lg	G	AB	H	2B	3B	HR	(Hm	Rd)	TB	R	RBI	TBB	IBB	SO	HBP	SH	SF	SB	CS	SB%	GDP	Avg	OBP	SLG
																							BATTING		
1998 Baltimore	AL	104	293	88	17	0	9	(5	4)	132	40	57	32	4	40	1	0	2	0	0	—	17	.300	.369	.451
1999 Bal-Cle	AL	135	430	134	18	1	25	(13	12)	229	62	103	54	3	48	0	0	2	1	2	.33	16	.312	.387	.533
2000 Bal-CWS	AL	96	283	72	13	0	11	(4	7)	118	26	39	36	7	50	0	0	1	0	0	—	6	.254	.338	.417
1989 Chicago	AL	96	333	107	20	1	13	(4	9)	168	55	56	60	13	52	1	0	3	0	1	.00	11	.321	.423	.505
Texas	AL	50	172	49	9	0	3	(1	2)	67	18	16	13	0	27	0	0	1	0	2	.00	4	.285	.333	.390
1990 Texas	AL	103	321	93	10	1	13	(6	7)	144	41	44	47	9	63	0	0	3	0	1	.00	13	.290	.377	.449
Oakland	AL	32	94	25	5	0	3	(3	0)	39	11	21	20	1	17	0	0	4	0	2	.00	4	.266	.381	.415
1997 Chicago	AL	93	318	97	18	0	12	(5	7)	151	40	52	41	10	47	0	0	2	0	1	.00	9	.305	.382	.475
Baltimore	AL	44	134	39	5	0	4	(1	3)	56	15	15	14	1	15	0	0	1	0	0	—	3	.291	.356	.418
1999 Baltimore	AL	107	345	111	16	1	24	(12	12)	201	57	81	43	3	38	0	0	2	1	2	.33	14	.322	.395	.583
Cleveland	AL	28	85	23	2	0	1	(1	0)	28	5	22	11	0	10	0	0	0	0	0	—	2	.271	.354	.329
2000 Baltimore	AL	72	222	59	8	0	10	(4	6)	97	24	30	29	6	39	0	0	1	0	0	—	6	.266	.349	.437
Chicago	AL	24	61	13	5	0	1	(0	1)	21	2	9	7	1	11	0	0	0	0	0	—	0	.213	.294	.344
21 ML YEARS		2798	9824	2855	487	49	384	(185	199)	4592	1296	1622	1054	187	1425	14	9	97	34	34	.50	296	.291	.357	.467

Paul Bako

Bats: Left **Throws:** Right **Pos:** C-80; PH/PR-2; 1B-1   **Ht:** 6'2" **Wt:** 205 **Born:** 6/20/72 **Age:** 29

Year Team	Lg	G	AB	H	2B	3B	HR	(Hm	Rd)	TB	R	RBI	TBB	IBB	SO	HBP	SH	SF	SB	CS	SB%	GDP	Avg	OBP	SLG
1998 Detroit	AL	96	305	83	12	1	3	(2	1)	106	23	30	23	4	82	0	1	4	1	1	.50	3	.272	.319	.348
1999 Houston	NL	73	215	55	14	1	2	(2	0)	77	16	17	26	3	57	0	3	3	1	1	.50	4	.256	.332	.358
2000 Hou-Fla-Atl	NL	81	221	50	10	1	2	(2	0)	68	18	20	27	10	64	1	1	1	0	0	—	6	.226	.312	.308
2000 Houston	NL	1	2	0	0	0	0	(0	0)	0	0	0	0	0	1	0	0	0	0	0	—	0	.000	.000	.000
Florida	NL	56	161	39	6	1	0	(0	0)	47	10	14	22	7	48	1	1	1	0	0	—	4	.242	.335	.292
Atlanta	NL	24	58	11	4	0	2	(2	0)	21	8	6	5	3	15	0	0	0	0	0	—	2	.190	.254	.362
3 ML YEARS		250	741	188	36	3	7	(6	1)	251	57	67	76	17	203	1	5	8	2	2	.50	13	.254	.321	.339

James Baldwin

Pitches: Right **Bats:** Right **Pos:** SP-28; RP-1   **Ht:** 6'3" **Wt:** 210 **Born:** 7/15/71 **Age:** 29

Year Team	Lg	G	GS	CG	GF	IP	BFP	H	R	ER	HR	SH	SF	HB	TBB	IBB	SO	WP	Bk	W	L	Pct.	ShO	Sv-Op	Hld	ERA
1995 Chicago	AL	6	4	0	0	14.2	81	32	22	21	6	0	0	0	9	1	10	1	0	0	1	.000	0	0-0	0	12.89
1996 Chicago	AL	28	28	0	0	169	719	168	88	83	24	2	2	4	57	3	127	12	1	11	6	.647	0	0-0	0	4.42
1997 Chicago	AL	32	32	1	0	200	879	205	128	117	19	3	6	5	83	3	140	14	3	12	15	.444	0	0-0	0	5.27
1998 Chicago	AL	37	24	1	3	159	712	176	103	94	18	3	5	10	60	2	108	5	1	13	6	.684	0	0-1	0	5.32
1999 Chicago	AL	35	33	1	1	199.1	886	219	119	113	34	4	7	1	81	1	123	11	1	12	13	.480	0	0-0	0	5.10
2000 Chicago	AL	29	28	2	0	178	758	185	96	92	34	6	5	8	59	3	116	4	1	14	7	.667	1	0-0	0	4.65
6 ML YEARS		167	149	5	4	920	4035	985	556	520	135	18	25	34	349	13	624	47	7	62	48	.564	1	0-1	0	5.09

John Bale

Pitches: Left **Bats:** Left **Pos:** RP-2   **Ht:** 6'4" **Wt:** 205 **Born:** 5/22/74 **Age:** 27

Year Team	Lg	G	GS	CG	GF	IP	BFP	H	R	ER	HR	SH	SF	HB	TBB	IBB	SO	WP	Bk	W	L	Pct.	ShO	Sv-Op	Hld	ERA
1996 St.Cathrnes	A-	8	8	0	0	33.1	148	39	21	18	2	0	1	0	11	0	35	4	2	3	2	.600	0	0--	—	4.86
1997 Hagerstown	A	25	25	0	0	140.1	633	130	83	67	11	4	3	1	63	1	155	11	0	7	7	.500	0	0--	—	4.30
1998 Dunedin	A+	24	9	0	5	66	290	68	39	34	5	3	5	4	23	1	78	6	1	5	4	.444	0	4--	—	4.64
Knoxville	AA	3	0	0	2	1.1	5	1	1	1	0	0	0	0	0	0	0	0	0	0	0	—	0	0--	—	6.75
1999 Knoxville	AA	33	4	0	9	62.1	265	64	32	26	7	1	0	0	16	1	91	4	0	2	2	.500	0	1--	—	3.75
Syracuse	AAA	6	4	0	0	22.2	92	16	14	10	1	2	3	0	10	0	10	1	0	0	3	.000	0	0--	—	3.97
2000 Syracuse	AAA	21	12	0	2	79	338	68	35	28	4	1	3	2	41	0	70	4	0	3	4	.429	0	0--	—	3.19
1999 Toronto	AL	1	0	0	0	2	10	2	3	3	1	0	0	0	2	0	4	0	0	0	0	—	0	0-0	0	13.50
2000 Toronto	AL	2	0	0	0	3.2	22	5	7	6	1	0	1	2	3	0	6	0	0	0	0	—	0	0-0	0	14.73
2 ML YEARS		3	0	0	0	5.2	32	7	10	9	2	0	1	2	5	0	10	0	0	0	0	—	0	0-0	0	14.29

Rod Barajas

Bats: Right **Throws:** Right **Pos:** C-5   **Ht:** 6'2" **Wt:** 220 **Born:** 9/5/75 **Age:** 25

Year Team	Lg	G	AB	H	2B	3B	HR	(Hm	Rd)	TB	R	RBI	TBB	IBB	SO	HBP	SH	SF	SB	CS	SB%	GDP	Avg	OBP	SLG
1996 Visalia	A+	27	74	12	3	0	0	—	—	15	6	8	7	0	21	1	0	0	0	0	—	3	.162	.244	.203
Lethbridge	R+	51	175	59	9	3	10	—	—	104	47	50	12	0	24	2	0	4	2	1	.67	6	.337	.378	.594
1997 High Desert	A+	57	199	53	11	0	7	—	—	85	24	30	8	0	41	1	0	1	0	2	.00	7	.266	.297	.427
1998 High Desert	A+	113	442	134	26	0	23	—	—	229	67	81	25	2	81	7	0	7	1	1	.50	13	.303	.345	.518
1999 El Paso	AA	127	510	162	41	2	14	—	—	249	77	95	24	6	73	8	0	6	2	0	1.00	8	.318	.354	.488
2000 Tucson	AAA	110	416	94	25	0	13	—	—	158	43	75	14	0	65	5	0	11	4	3	.57	13	.226	.253	.380
1999 Arizona	NL	5	16	4	1	0	1	(1	0)	8	3	3	1	0	1	0	0	0	0	0	—	0	.250	.294	.500
2000 Arizona	NL	5	13	3	0	0	1	(1	0)	6	1	3	0	0	4	0	0	0	0	0	—	0	.231	.231	.462
2 ML YEARS		10	29	7	1	0	2	(2	0)	14	4	6	1	0	5	0	0	0	0	0	—	0	.241	.267	.483

Lorenzo Barcelo

Pitches: Right **Bats:** Right **Pos:** RP-21; SP-1   **Ht:** 6'4" **Wt:** 220 **Born:** 8/10/77 **Age:** 23

Year Team	Lg	G	GS	CG	GF	IP	BFP	H	R	ER	HR	SH	SF	HB	TBB	IBB	SO	WP	Bk	W	L	Pct.	ShO	Sv-Op	Hld	ERA
1995 Bellingham	A-	12	11	0	0	47	198	43	23	18	3	0	1	2	19	0	34	1	1	3	2	.600	0	0--	—	3.45
1996 Burlington	A	26	26	1	0	152.2	633	138	70	60	19	5	5	5	46	0	139	5	5	12	10	.545	0	0--	—	3.54
1997 San Jose	A+	16	16	1	0	89	378	91	45	39	13	1	3	1	30	2	89	1	2	5	4	.556	1	0--	—	3.94
Shreveport	AA	5	5	0	0	31.1	132	30	19	14	4	1	0	0	8	0	20	0	2	3	0	1.000	0	0--	—	4.02
Birmingham	AA	6	6	0	0	33.1	147	36	20	18	2	0	1	4	9	0	29	1	0	2	1	.667	0	0--	—	4.86
1998 White Sox	R	3	3	0	0	6	24	6	1	1	0	1	0	0	0	0	6	0	0	0	1	.000	0	0--	—	1.50

Year Team	Lg	HOW MUCH HE PITCHED						WHAT HE GAVE UP												THE RESULTS						
		G	GS	CG	GF	IP	BFP	H	R	ER	HR	SH	SF	HB	TBB	IBB	SO	WP	Bk	W	L	Pct.	ShO	Sv-Op	Hld	ERA
1999 White Sox	R	9	9	0	0	42.2	171	36	14	8	0	1	0	1	6	0	57	3	2	2	1	.667	0	0--		1.69
Burlington	A	1	1	0	0	5	18	3	2	2	1	1	0	0	0	0	6	0		1	0	1.000	0	0--		3.60
Birmingham	AA	4	4	0	0	20	79	14	8	8	0	1	2	1	6	0	14	0	0	0	1	.000	0	0--		3.60
2000 Charlotte	AAA	17	17	0	0	99.1	433	114	53	47	20	1	4	4	17	1	62	3	2	5	6	.455	0	0--		4.26
2000 Chicago	AL	22	1	0	5	39	157	34	17	16	5	0	1	0	9	1	26	1	0	4	2	.667	0	0-1	0	3.69

Glen Barker

Bats: B Throws: R Pos: CF-63; PH/PR-32; RF-4; LF-2 Ht: 5'10" Wt: 180 Born: 5/10/71 Age: 30

Year Team	Lg	BATTING																	BASERUNNING				PERCENTAGES		
		G	AB	H	2B	3B	HR	(Hm	Rd)	TB	R	RBI	TBB	IBB	SO	HBP	SH	SF	SB	CS	SB%	GDP	Avg	OBP	SLG
1993 Niagara Fal	A-	72	253	55	11	4	5	—	—	89	49	23	24	0	71	4	2	3	37	12	.76	1	.217	.292	.352
1994 Fayettevlle	A	74	267	61	13	5	1	—	—	87	38	30	33	0	79	9	2	1	41	13	.76	5	.228	.332	.326
Lakeland	A+	28	104	19	5	1	2	—	—	32	10	6	4	0	34	2	0	0	5	3	.63	2	.183	.227	.308
1995 Jacksnville	AA	133	507	121	26	4	10	—	—	185	74	49	33	0	143	9	12	1	39	16	.71	1	.239	.296	.365
1996 Fayettevlle	A	37	132	38	1	0	1	—	—	42	23	9	16	1	34	3	3	0	20	6	.77	2	.288	.377	.318
Toledo	AAA	24	80	20	2	1	0	—	—	24	13	2	9	0	25	0	2	0	6	6	.50	1	.250	.326	.300
Jacksnville	AA	43	120	19	2	1	0	—	—	23	9	8	8	0	36	0	1	0	6	4	.60	2	.158	.211	.192
1997 Toledo	AAA	21	47	9	1	0	1	—	—	13	9	3	5	0	15	1	2	0	6	2	.75	0	.191	.283	.277
Lakeland	A+	13	57	18	4	0	1	—	—	25	9	11	4	0	17	0	3	0	7	1	.88	0	.316	.361	.439
Jacksnville	AA	69	257	72	8	4	6	—	—	106	47	29	29	0	72	5	8	3	17	8	.68	4	.280	.361	.412
1998 Jacksnville	AA	110	453	127	29	6	6	—	—	186	95	54	57	1	120	4	7	5	31	7	.82	1	.280	.362	.411
2000 New Orleans	AAA	26	107	29	5	0	2	—	—	40	15	10	10	1	12	0	0	5	11	3	.79	3	.271	.333	.374
1999 Houston	NL	81	73	21	2	0	1	(0	1)	26	23	11	11	0	19	1	4	1	17	6	.74	0	.288	.384	.356
2000 Houston	NL	84	67	15	2	1	2	(2	0)	25	18	6	7	0	23	1	2	0	9	6	.60	0	.224	.307	.373
2 ML YEARS		165	140	36	4	1	3	(2	1)	51	41	17	18	0	42	2	6	1	26	12	.68	0	.257	.348	.364

Kevin Barker

Bats: Left Throws: Left Pos: 1B-32; PH/PR-9 Ht: 6'3" Wt: 205 Born: 7/26/75 Age: 25

Year Team	Lg	BATTING																	BASERUNNING				PERCENTAGES		
		G	AB	H	2B	3B	HR	(Hm	Rd)	TB	R	RBI	TBB	IBB	SO	HBP	SH	SF	SB	CS	SB%	GDP	Avg	OBP	SLG
1996 Ogden	R+	71	281	89	19	4	9	—	—	143	61	56	46	4	54	3	0	5	0	2	.00	4	.317	.412	.509
1997 Stockton	A+	70	267	81	20	5	13	—	—	150	47	45	25	4	60	0	0	1	4	3	.57	6	.303	.362	.562
El Paso	AA	65	238	66	15	6	10	—	—	123	37	63	28	0	40	2	0	5	3	3	.50	5	.277	.352	.517
1998 El Paso	AA	20	85	26	6	0	5	—	—	47	14	14	3	0	21	2	0	2	2	1	.67	2	.306	.337	.553
Louisville	AAA	124	463	128	26	4	23	—	—	231	59	96	36	1	97	3	0	4	2	5	.29	11	.276	.330	.499
1999 Louisville	AAA	121	442	123	27	4	23	—	—	229	89	87	59	5	94	4	0	7	2	2	.50	13	.278	.363	.518
2000 Indianapolis	AAA	85	286	56	10	1	11	—	—	101	41	44	52	3	76	1	0	6	0	1	.00	6	.196	.316	.353
1999 Milwaukee	NL	38	117	33	3	0	3	(1	2)	45	13	23	9	1	19	0	0	1	1	0	1.00	0	.282	.331	.385
2000 Milwaukee	NL	40	100	22	5	0	2	(0	2)	33	14	9	20	0	21	1	0	1	1	0	1.00	1	.220	.352	.330
2 ML YEARS		78	217	55	8	0	5	(1	4)	78	27	32	29	1	40	1	0	2	2	0	1.00	1	.253	.341	.359

John Barnes

Bats: Right Throws: Right Pos: RF-8; LF-2; CF-2 Ht: 6'2" Wt: 205 Born: 4/24/76 Age: 25

Year Team	Lg	BATTING																	BASERUNNING				PERCENTAGES		
		G	AB	H	2B	3B	HR	(Hm	Rd)	TB	R	RBI	TBB	IBB	SO	HBP	SH	SF	SB	CS	SB%	GDP	Avg	OBP	SLG
1996 Red Sox	R	30	101	28	4	0	1	—	—	35	9	17	5	0	17	6	0	5	4	0	1.00	3	.277	.333	.347
1997 Michigan	A	130	490	149	19	5	6	—	—	196	80	73	65	3	42	5	0	6	19	5	.79	7	.304	.387	.400
1998 Trenton	AA	100	380	104	18	0	14	—	—	164	53	36	40	3	47	3	2	4	3	8	.27	11	.274	.344	.432
New Britain	AA	20	71	19	4	1	0	—	—	25	9	8	9	0	9	1	0	1	1	1	.50	2	.268	.354	.352
1999 New Britain	AA	129	452	119	21	1	13	—	—	181	62	58	49	3	40	5	1	4	10	2	.83	15	.263	.339	.400
2000 Salt Lake	AAA	120	441	161	37	6	13	—	—	249	107	87	57	0	48	7	1	7	7	6	.54	10	.365	.439	.565
2000 Minnesota	AL	11	37	13	4	0	0	(0	0)	17	5	2	2	0	6	2	0	0	0	1	.00	3	.351	.415	.459

Michael Barrett

Bats: Right Throws: Right Pos: 3B-55; C-28; PH/PR-7 Ht: 6'2" Wt: 200 Born: 10/22/76 Age: 24

Year Team	Lg	BATTING																	BASERUNNING				PERCENTAGES		
		G	AB	H	2B	3B	HR	(Hm	Rd)	TB	R	RBI	TBB	IBB	SO	HBP	SH	SF	SB	CS	SB%	GDP	Avg	OBP	SLG
2000 Ottawa *	AAA	31	120	43	7	0	2	—	—	56	21	19	13	1	10	2	0	0	1	0	1.00	5	.358	.430	.467
1998 Montreal	NL	8	23	7	2	0	1	(0	1)	12	3	2	3	0	6	1	0	0	0	0	—	0	.304	.407	.522
1999 Montreal	NL	126	433	127	32	3	8	(5	3)	189	53	52	32	4	39	3	0	1	0	2	.00	18	.293	.345	.436
2000 Montreal	NL	89	271	58	15	1	1	(0	1)	78	28	22	23	5	35	1	1	1	0	1	.00	7	.214	.277	.288
3 ML YEARS		223	727	192	49	4	10	(5	5)	279	84	76	58	9	80	5	1	2	0	3	.00	25	.264	.322	.384

Kimera Bartee

Bats: Right Throws: Right Pos: PH/PR-9; LF-2; CF-1 Ht: 6'0" Wt: 200 Born: 7/21/72 Age: 28

Year Team	Lg	BATTING																	BASERUNNING				PERCENTAGES		
		G	AB	H	2B	3B	HR	(Hm	Rd)	TB	R	RBI	TBB	IBB	SO	HBP	SH	SF	SB	CS	SB%	GDP	Avg	OBP	SLG
2000 Louisville *	AAA	119	453	135	19	4	8	—	—	186	69	48	48	0	64	2	8	3	28	11	.72	7	.298	.366	.411
1996 Detroit	AL	110	217	55	6	1	1	(0	1)	66	32	14	17	0	77	0	13	0	20	10	.67	1	.253	.308	.304
1997 Detroit	AL	12	5	1	0	0	0	(0	0)	1	4	0	2	0	2	1	0	0	3	1	.75	0	.200	.500	.200
1998 Detroit	AL	57	98	19	5	1	3	(3	0)	35	20	15	6	0	35	0	0	1	9	5	.64	1	.194	.238	.357
1999 Detroit	AL	41	77	15	1	3	0	(0	0)	22	11	3	9	0	20	0	3	0	3	3	.50	2	.195	.279	.286
2000 Cincinnati	NL	11	4	0	0	0	0	(0	0)	0	2	0	0	0	2	0	0	0	1	0	1.00	0	.000	.200	.000
5 ML YEARS		231	401	90	12	5	4	(3	1)	124	69	32	34	0	136	2	16	1	36	19	.65	4	.224	.288	.309

Miguel Batista

Pitches: Right **Bats:** Right **Pos:** SP-9; RP-9   **Ht:** 6'0" **Wt:** 190 **Born:** 2/19/71 **Age:** 30

Year Team	Lg	G	GS	CG	GF	IP	BFP	H	R	ER	HR	SH	SF	HB	TBB	IBB	SO	WP	Bk	W	L	Pct.	ShO	Sv-Op	Hld	ERA
2000 Omaha *	AAA	18	1	0	12	28.1	127	35	20	19	6	1	1	2	7	0	27	2	0	2	2	.500	0	3- -	—	6.04
1992 Pittsburgh	NL	1	0	0	1	2	13	4	2	2	1	0	0	0	3	0	1	0	0	0	0	—	0	0-0	0	9.00
1996 Florida	NL	9	0	0	4	11.1	49	9	8	7	0	3	0	0	7	2	6	1	0	0	0	—	0	0-0	0	5.56
1997 Chicago	NL	11	6	0	2	36.1	168	36	24	23	4	4	4	1	24	2	27	2	0	0	5	.000	0	0-0	0	5.70
1998 Montreal	NL	56	13	0	12	135	598	141	66	57	12	7	5	6	65	7	92	6	1	3	5	.375	0	0-0	3	3.80
1999 Montreal	NL	39	17	2	3	134.2	606	146	88	73	10	8	11	7	58	2	95	6	0	8	7	.533	1	1-1	0	4.88
2000 Mon-KC		18	9	0	2	65.1	310	85	68	62	19	1	2	2	37	2	37	4	0	2	7	.222	0	0-2	0	8.54
2000 Montreal	NL	4	0	0	0	8.1	49	19	14	13	2	1	1	2	3	0	7	0	0	0	1	.000	0	0-2	0	14.04
Kansas City	AL	14	9	0	2	57	261	66	54	49	17	0	1	0	34	2	30	4	0	2	6	.250	0	0-0	0	7.74
6 ML YEARS		134	45	2	24	384.2	1744	421	256	224	46	23	22	16	194	15	258	19	1	13	24	.351	1	1-3	3	5.24

Tony Batista

Bats: Right **Throws:** Right **Pos:** 3B-154   **Ht:** 6'0" **Wt:** 185 **Born:** 12/9/73 **Age:** 27

Year Team	Lg	G	AB	H	2B	3B	HR	(Hm	Rd)	TB	R	RBI	TBB	IBB	SO	HBP	SH	SF	SB	CS	SB%	GDP	Avg	OBP	SLG
1996 Oakland	AL	74	238	71	10	2	6	(1	5)	103	38	25	19	0	49	1	0	2	7	3	.70	2	.298	.350	.433
1997 Oakland	AL	68	188	38	10	1	4	(0	4)	62	22	18	14	0	31	2	3	0	2	2	.50	8	.202	.265	.330
1998 Arizona	NL	106	293	80	16	1	18	(9	9)	152	46	41	18	0	52	3	0	4	1	1	.50	7	.273	.318	.519
1999 Ari-Tor		142	519	144	30	1	31	(10	21)	269	77	100	38	4	96	6	3	7	4	0	1.00	12	.277	.330	.518
2000 Toronto	AL	154	620	163	32	2	41	(25	16)	322	96	114	35	1	121	6	0	3	4	4	.56	15	.263	.307	.519
1999 Arizona	NL	44	144	37	5	0	5	(1	4)	57	16	21	16	3	17	2	0	2	2	0	1.00	1	.257	.335	.396
Toronto		98	375	107	25	1	26	(9	17)	212	61	79	22	1	79	4	3	5	2	0	1.00	11	.285	.328	.565
5 ML YEARS		544	1858	496	98	7	100	(45	55)	908	279	298	124	5	349	18	6	16	19	10	.66	44	.267	.316	.489

Justin Baughman

Bats: R **Throws:** R **Pos:** PH/PR-6; 2B-5; SS-5; DH-4   **Ht:** 5'11" **Wt:** 180 **Born:** 8/1/74 **Age:** 26

Year Team	Lg	G	AB	H	2B	3B	HR	(Hm	Rd)	TB	R	RBI	TBB	IBB	SO	HBP	SH	SF	SB	CS	SB%	GDP	Avg	OBP	SLG
1995 Boise	A-	58	215	50	4	3	1	—	—	63	26	20	18	0	38	2	4	1	19	4	.83	2	.233	.297	.293
1996 Cedar Rapds	A	127	464	115	17	8	5	—	—	163	78	48	45	2	78	6	15	1	50	17	.75	13	.248	.322	.351
1997 Lk Elsinore	A+	134	478	131	14	3	2	—	—	157	71	48	40	3	79	13	11	5	68	15	.82	5	.274	.343	.328
1998 Vancouver	AAA	54	222	66	10	4	0	—	—	84	35	15	13	0	28	4	5	2	26	8	.76	7	.297	.344	.378
2000 Erie	AA	31	126	36	2	2	1	—	—	45	15	6	8	0	20	1	1	0	11	2	.85	1	.286	.333	.357
Edmonton	AAA	80	303	71	7	2	1	—	—	85	44	35	30	1	41	7	4	6	28	5	.85	6	.234	.312	.281
1998 Anaheim	AL	63	196	50	9	1	1	(0	1)	64	24	20	6	0	36	1	5	3	10	4	.71	4	.255	.277	.327
2000 Anaheim	AL	16	22	5	2	0	0	(0	0)	7	4	0	1	0	2	0	0	0	3	0	1.00	0	.227	.261	.318
2 ML YEARS		79	218	55	11	1	1	(0	1)	71	28	20	7	0	38	1	5	3	13	4	.76	4	.252	.275	.326

Danny Bautista

Bats: R **Throws:** R **Pos:** RF-84; LF-27; CF-26; PH/PR-22   **Ht:** 5'11" **Wt:** 170 **Born:** 5/24/72 **Age:** 29

Year Team	Lg	G	AB	H	2B	3B	HR	(Hm	Rd)	TB	R	RBI	TBB	IBB	SO	HBP	SH	SF	SB	CS	SB%	GDP	Avg	OBP	SLG
1993 Detroit	AL	17	61	19	3	0	1	(0	1)	25	6	9	1	0	10	0	0	1	3	1	.75	1	.311	.317	.410
1994 Detroit	AL	31	99	23	4	1	4	(1	3)	41	12	15	3	0	18	0	0	0	1	2	.33	3	.232	.255	.414
1995 Detroit	AL	89	271	55	9	0	7	(3	4)	85	28	27	12	0	68	0	6	0	4	1	.80	6	.203	.237	.314
1996 Det-Atl		42	84	19	2	0	2	(1	1)	27	13	9	11	0	20	1	0	0	1	2	.33	4	.226	.323	.321
1997 Atlanta	NL	64	103	25	3	2	3	(1	2)	41	14	9	5	1	24	1	2	1	2	0	1.00	3	.243	.282	.398
1998 Atlanta	NL	82	144	36	11	0	3	(2	1)	56	17	17	7	0	21	0	3	2	1	0	1.00	4	.250	.281	.389
1999 Florida	NL	70	205	59	10	1	5	(2	3)	86	32	24	4	0	30	1	0	1	3	0	1.00	5	.288	.303	.420
2000 Fla-Ari	NL	131	351	100	20	7	11	(5	6)	167	54	59	25	4	50	3	4	5	6	2	.75	11	.285	.333	.476
1996 Detroit	AL	25	64	16	2	0	2	(1	1)	24	12	8	9	0	15	0	0	0	1	2	.33	1	.250	.342	.375
Atlanta	NL	17	20	3	0	0	0	(0	0)	3	1	1	2	0	5	1	0	0	0	0	—	3	.150	.261	.150
2000 Florida	NL	44	89	17	4	0	4	(1	3)	33	9	12	5	0	20	0	0	1	1	0	1.00	1	.191	.234	.371
Arizona	NL	87	262	83	16	7	7	(4	3)	134	45	47	20	4	30	3	4	5	5	2	.71	10	.317	.366	.511
8 ML YEARS		526	1318	336	62	11	36	(15	21)	528	176	169	68	5	241	6	15	10	21	8	.72	37	.255	.292	.401

Rod Beck

Pitches: Right **Bats:** Right **Pos:** RP-34   **Ht:** 6'1" **Wt:** 235 **Born:** 8/3/68 **Age:** 32

Year Team	Lg	G	GS	CG	GF	IP	BFP	H	R	ER	HR	SH	SF	HB	TBB	IBB	SO	WP	Bk	W	L	Pct.	ShO	Sv-Op	Hld	ERA
2000 Pawtucket *	AAA	3	0	0	0	6	22	4	0	0	0	0	0	0	0	0	7	0	0	1	0	1.000	0	0- -	—	0.00
1991 San Francisco	NL	31	0	0	10	52.1	214	53	22	22	4	4	2	1	13	2	38	0	0	1	1	.500	0	1-1	1	3.78
1992 San Francisco	NL	65	0	0	42	92	352	62	20	18	4	6	2	2	15	2	87	5	2	3	3	.500	0	17-23	4	1.76
1993 San Francisco	NL	76	0	0	71	79.1	309	57	20	19	11	6	3	3	13	4	86	4	0	3	1	.750	0	48-52	0	2.16
1994 San Francisco	NL	48	0	0	47	48.2	207	49	17	15	10	3	0	1	13	2	39	0	0	2	4	.333	0	28-28	0	2.77
1995 San Francisco	NL	60	0	0	52	58.2	255	60	31	29	7	4	3	2	21	3	42	2	0	5	6	.455	0	33-43	0	4.45
1996 San Francisco	NL	63	0	0	58	62	248	56	23	23	9	0	2	1	10	2	48	1	0	0	9	.000	0	35-42	0	3.34
1997 San Francisco	NL	73	0	0	66	70	281	67	31	27	7	1	0	2	8	2	53	1	0	7	4	.636	0	37-45	0	3.47
1998 Chicago	NL	81	0	0	70	80.1	349	86	33	27	11	2	5	2	20	4	81	2	0	3	4	.429	0	51-58	1	3.02
1999 ChC-Bos		43	0	0	27	44	196	50	29	29	5	2	2	1	18	3	25	1	0	2	5	.286	0	10-15	3	5.93
2000 Boston	AL	34	0	0	8	40.2	169	34	15	14	2	2	0	2	12	1	35	1	0	3	0	1.000	0	0-3	7	3.10
1999 Chicago	NL	31	0	0	19	30	141	41	26	26	2	0	2	1	13	3	13	1	0	2	4	.333	0	7-11	0	7.80
Boston	AL	12	0	0	8	14	55	9	3	3	0	0	0	0	5	0	12	0	0	0	1	.000	0	3-4	2	1.93
10 ML YEARS		574	0	0	451	628	2580	574	241	223	70	30	22	16	143	25	534	17	2	29	37	.439	0	260-310	17	3.20

Rich Becker

Bats: L **Throws:** L **Pos:** RF-48; CF-38; PH/PR-35; LF-22; DH-6   **Ht:** 5'10" **Wt:** 193 **Born:** 2/1/72 **Age:** 29

Year Team	Lg	G	AB	H	2B	3B	HR	(Hm	Rd)	TB	R	RBI	TBB	IBB	SO	HBP	SH	SF	SB	CS	SB%	GDP	Avg	OBP	SLG
1993 Minnesota	AL	3	7	2	2	0	0	(0	0)	4	3	0	5	0	4	0	0	0	1	1	.50	0	.286	.583	.571
1994 Minnesota	AL	28	98	26	3	0	1	(1	0)	32	12	8	13	0	25	0	1	0	6	1	.86	2	.265	.351	.327
1995 Minnesota	AL	106	392	93	15	1	2	(1	1)	116	45	33	34	0	95	4	6	2	8	9	.47	9	.237	.303	.296
1996 Minnesota	AL	148	525	153	31	4	12	(8	4)	228	92	71	68	1	118	2	5	4	19	5	.79	14	.291	.372	.434
1997 Minnesota	AL	132	443	117	22	3	10	(4	6)	175	61	45	62	1	130	1	2	2	17	5	.77	4	.264	.354	.395
1998 NYM-Bal	AL	128	213	42	5	2	6	(4	2)	69	37	21	43	2	76	2	2	0	5	1	.83	7	.197	.337	.324
1999 Mil-Oak	AL	129	264	68	8	2	6	(5	1)	98	36	26	58	0	81	2	3	0	8	2	.80	7	.258	.395	.371
2000 Oak-Det	AL	115	285	69	14	0	8	(4	4)	107	59	39	67	0	87	1	0	4	2	2	.50	1	.242	.384	.375
1998 New York	NL	49	100	19	4	2	3	(3	0)	36	15	10	21	2	42	0	0	0	3	1	.75	1	.190	.331	.360
Baltimore	AL	79	113	23	1	0	3	(1	2)	33	22	11	22	0	34	2	2	0	2	0	1.00	6	.204	.343	.292
1999 Milwaukee	NL	89	139	35	5	2	5	(4	1)	59	15	16	33	0	38	0	2	0	5	0	1.00	4	.252	.395	.424
Oakland	AL	40	125	33	3	0	1	(1	0)	39	21	10	25	0	43	2	1	0	3	2	.60	3	.264	.395	.312
2000 Oakland	AL	23	47	11	2	0	1	(1	0)	16	11	5	11	0	17	1	0	0	1	0	1.00	1	.234	.390	.340
Detroit	AL	92	238	58	12	0	7	(3	4)	91	48	34	56	0	70	0	0	4	1	2	.33	0	.244	.383	.382
8 ML YEARS		789	2227	570	100	12	45	(27	18)	829	345	243	350	4	616	12	19	12	66	26	.72	44	.256	.358	.372

Kevin Beirne

Pitches: Right **Bats:** Left **Pos:** RP-28; SP-1   **Ht:** 6'4" **Wt:** 210 **Born:** 1/1/74 **Age:** 27

Year Team	Lg	G	GS	CG	GF	IP	BFP	H	R	ER	HR	SH	SF	HB	TBB	IBB	SO	WP	Bk	W	L	Pct.	ShO	Sv-Op	Hld	ERA
1995 White Sox	R	2	0	0	2	3.2	15	2	2	1	0	0	0	0	1	0	3	0	0	0	0	--	0	2--	--	2.45
Bristol	R+	9	0	0	7	9	35	4	0	0	0	0	0	0	4	0	12	0	0	1	0	1.000	0	2--	--	0.00
Hickory	A	3	0	0	1	4	16	7	2	2	0	0	0	0	0	0	4	0	0	0	0	--	0	0--	--	4.50
1996 South Bend	A	26	25	1	0	145.1	627	153	85	67	5	5	5	9	60	0	110	12	3	4	11	.267	0	0--	--	4.15
1997 Winston-Sal	A+	13	13	1	0	82.2	338	66	38	28	7	1	2	7	28	1	75	5	0	4	4	.500	0	0--	--	3.05
Birmingham	AA	13	12	0	1	75	336	76	51	41	4	2	3	4	41	0	49	2	1	6	4	.600	0	0--	--	4.92
1998 Birmingham	AA	26	26	2	0	167.1	702	142	77	64	12	6	6	6	87	2	153	4	2	13	9	.591	1	0--	--	3.44
Calgary	AAA	2	2	0	0	8	38	12	5	4	1	1	1	1	4	0	6	0	0	0	0	--	0	0--	--	4.50
1999 Charlotte	AAA	20	20	0	0	113	495	134	75	68	14	1	4	2	36	0	63	12	0	5	5	.500	0	0--	--	5.42
2000 Charlotte	AAA	7	7	0	0	33.1	143	39	13	13	8	1	1	2	7	0	28	5	0	1	2	.333	0	0--	--	3.51
2000 Chicago	AL	29	1	0	8	49.2	220	50	41	37	9	1	5	4	20	1	41	1	0	1	3	.250	0	0-1	0	6.70

Tim Belcher

Pitches: Right **Bats:** Right **Pos:** SP-9   **Ht:** 6'3" **Wt:** 235 **Born:** 10/19/61 **Age:** 39

Year Team	Lg	G	GS	CG	GF	IP	BFP	H	R	ER	HR	SH	SF	HB	TBB	IBB	SO	WP	Bk	W	L	Pct.	ShO	Sv-Op	Hld	ERA
2000 Edmonton *	AAA	3	3	0	0	14	60	12	7	6	2	0	0	1	7	0	6	0	0	1	1	.500	0	0--	--	3.86
Lk Elsinore *	A+	3	3	0	0	14	50	6	5	5	1	1	1	2	2	0	16	0	0	1	0	1.000	0	0--	--	3.21
Erie *	AA	1	1	0	0	7	26	4	0	0	0	0	0	0	2	0	6	0	0	1	0	1.000	0	0--	--	0.00
1987 Los Angeles	NL	6	5	0	1	34	135	30	11	9	2	2	1	0	7	0	23	0	1	4	2	.667	0	0-0	0	2.38
1988 Los Angeles	NL	36	27	4	5	179.2	719	143	65	58	8	6	1	2	51	7	152	4	0	12	6	.667	1	4-5	0	2.91
1989 Los Angeles	NL	39	30	10	0	230	937	182	81	72	20	6	6	7	80	5	200	7	2	15	12	.556	8	1-1	1	2.82
1990 Los Angeles	NL	24	24	5	0	153	627	136	76	68	17	5	6	2	48	0	102	6	1	9	9	.500	2	0-0	0	4.00
1991 Los Angeles	NL	33	33	2	0	209.1	880	189	76	61	16	3	3	2	75	3	156	7	0	10	9	.526	1	0-0	0	2.62
1992 Cincinnati	NL	35	34	2	1	227.2	949	201	104	99	17	12	11	3	80	2	149	3	1	15	14	.517	1	0-0	0	3.91
1993 Cin-CWS		34	33	5	0	208.2	880	198	108	103	19	8	4	6	74	4	135	4	0	12	11	.522	3	0-0	0	4.44
1994 Detroit	AL	25	25	3	0	162	750	192	124	106	21	3	3	4	78	10	76	6	1	7	15	.318	0	0-0	0	5.89
1995 Seattle	AL	28	28	1	0	179.1	802	188	101	90	19	4	5	6	88	5	96	6	0	10	12	.455	0	0-0	0	4.52
1996 Kansas City	AL	35	35	4	0	238.2	1021	262	117	104	28	6	10	6	68	4	113	7	0	15	11	.577	1	0-0	0	3.92
1997 Kansas City	AL	32	32	3	0	213.1	927	242	128	119	31	7	6	5	70	2	113	7	1	13	12	.520	1	0-0	0	5.02
1998 Kansas City	AL	34	34	2	0	234	1003	247	127	111	37	5	5	7	73	0	130	6	1	14	14	.500	0	0-0	0	4.27
1999 Anaheim	AL	24	24	0	0	132.1	600	168	104	99	27	6	9	5	46	0	52	7	1	6	8	.429	0	0-0	0	6.73
2000 Anaheim	AL	9	9	0	0	40.2	186	45	31	31	8	1	1	2	22	1	22	1	1	4	5	.444	0	0-0	0	6.86
1993 Cincinnati	NL	22	22	4	0	137	590	134	72	68	16	6	3	7	47	4	101	6	0	9	6	.600	2	0-0	0	4.47
Chicago	AL	12	11	1	0	71.2	296	64	36	35	8	2	1	1	27	0	34	0	0	3	5	.375	1	0-0	0	4.40
14 ML YEARS		394	373	42	13	2442.2	10422	2423	1253	1130	264	82	73	58	860	43	1519	73	10	146	140	.510	18	5-6	1	4.16

Stan Belinda

Pitches: Right **Bats:** Right **Pos:** RP-56   **Ht:** 6'3" **Wt:** 215 **Born:** 8/6/66 **Age:** 34

Year Team	Lg	G	GS	CG	GF	IP	BFP	H	R	ER	HR	SH	SF	HB	TBB	IBB	SO	WP	Bk	W	L	Pct.	ShO	Sv-Op	Hld	ERA
1989 Pittsburgh	NL	8	0	0	2	10.1	46	13	8	7	0	0	0	0	2	0	10	1	0	0	0	.000	0	0-0	2	6.10
1990 Pittsburgh	NL	55	0	0	17	58.1	245	48	23	23	4	2	2	1	29	3	55	1	0	3	4	.429	0	8-13	3	3.55
1991 Pittsburgh	NL	60	0	0	37	78.1	318	50	30	30	10	4	3	4	35	4	71	2	0	7	5	.583	0	16-20	6	3.45
1992 Pittsburgh	NL	59	0	0	22	71.1	299	58	26	25	8	4	6	4	29	5	57	2	0	6	4	.600	0	18-24	0	3.15
1993 Pit-KC		63	0	0	44	69.2	287	65	31	30	6	3	2	2	17	4	55	2	0	4	2	.667	0	19-23	8	3.88
1994 Kansas City	AL	37	0	0	10	49	220	47	34	28	6	0	3	5	24	3	37	1	0	2	2	.500	0	0-2	5	5.14
1995 Boston	AL	63	0	0	30	69.2	285	51	25	24	5	0	4	4	28	3	57	2	0	8	1	.889	0	10-14	17	3.10
1996 Boston	AL	31	0	0	10	28.2	139	31	22	21	3	1	0	4	20	1	18	2	0	2	1	.667	0	2-4	7	6.59
1997 Cincinnati	NL	84	0	0	18	99.1	420	84	42	41	11	6	6	9	33	6	114	5	0	1	5	.167	0	1-5	28	3.71
1998 Cincinnati	NL	40	0	0	24	61.1	254	46	23	22	7	7	1	2	28	6	57	3	0	4	8	.333	0	1-2	4	3.23
1999 Cincinnati	NL	29	0	0	12	42.2	185	42	26	25	11	2	1	2	17	0	40	3	0	3	3	.750	0	2-2	5	5.27
2000 Col-Atl	NL	56	0	0	17	46.2	220	55	44	40	14	4	4	3	22	5	51	2	0	1	3	.250	0	1-7	5	7.71
1993 Pittsburgh	NL	40	0	0	37	42.1	171	35	18	17	4	1	2	1	11	4	30	0	0	3	1	.750	0	19-22	6	3.61
Kansas City		23	0	0	7	27.1	116	30	13	13	2	2	0	1	6	0	25	2	0	1	1	.500	0	0-1	2	4.28
2000 Colorado	NL	46	0	0	10	35.2	168	39	32	28	10	4	2	4	17	4	40	1	0	1	3	.250	0	1-7	5	7.07
Atlanta	NL	10	0	0	7	11	54	16	12	12	4	0	2	1	5	1	11	0	0	0	0	--	0	0-0	0	9.82
12 ML YEARS		585	0	0	263	685.1	2918	590	336	316	85	33	31	34	285	43	622	25	0	41	37	.526	0	79-116	93	4.15

Todd Belitz

Pitches: Left **Bats:** Left **Pos:** RP-5 **Ht:** 6'3" **Wt:** 200 **Born:** 10/23/75 **Age:** 25

Year Team	Lg	G	GS	CG	GF	IP	BFP	H	R	ER	HR	SH	SF	HB	TBB	IBB	SO	WP	Bk	W	L	Pct.	ShO	Sv-Op	Hld	ERA
1997 Hudson Val	A-	15	15	0	0	74	315	65	41	29	4	1	2	5	18	0	78	0	0	4	5	.444	0	0--	—	3.53
1998 Chston-SC	A	21	21	0	0	130	530	99	44	35	4	8	6	1	8	48	0	123	11	1	6	4	.600	0	0--	—	2.42
St. Pete	A+	7	7	0	0	44.2	188	39	28	25	3	2	3	2	14	0	40	2	0	2	2	.500	0	0--	—	5.04
1999 Orlando	AA	28	28	0	0	160.2	712	169	114	103	23	3	6	11	65	1	118	2	4	9	9	.500	0	0--	—	5.77
2000 Durham	AAA	43	0	0	6	47	199	33	24	20	1	1	3	2	28	1	46	1	0	1	1	.500	0	2--	—	3.83
Sacramento	AAA	12	0	0	1	12.1	52	12	6	6	2	0	0	2	5	0	10	2	0	0	1	.000	0	1--	—	4.38
2000 Oakland	AL	5	0	0	3	3.1	19	4	2	1	0	0	0	0	4	0	3	1	0	0	0	—	0	0-0	0	2.70

David Bell

Bats: R **Throws:** R **Pos:** 3B-93; 2B-48; PH/PR-5; 1B-2; DH-1; SS-1 **Ht:** 5'10" **Wt:** 190 **Born:** 9/14/72 **Age:** 28

Year Team	Lg	G	AB	H	2B	3B	HR	(Hm	Rd)	TB	R	RBI	TBB	IBB	SO	HBP	SH	SF	SB	CS	SB%	GDP	Avg	OBP	SLG
1995 Cle-StL		41	146	36	7	2	2	(1	1)	53	13	19	4	0	25	2	0	1	1	2	.33	0	.247	.275	.363
1996 St. Louis	NL	62	145	31	6	0	1	(1	0)	40	12	9	10	2	22	1	0	1	1	1	.50	3	.214	.268	.276
1997 St. Louis	NL	66	142	30	7	2	1	(1	0)	44	9	12	10	2	28	0	2	1	1	0	1.00	2	.211	.261	.310
1998 StL-Cle-Sea		132	429	117	30	2	10	(2	8)	181	48	49	27	4	65	2	1	5	0	4	.00	11	.273	.315	.422
1999 Seattle	AL	157	597	160	31	2	21	(11	10)	258	92	78	58	0	90	2	3	7	7	4	.64	7	.268	.331	.432
2000 Seattle	AL	133	454	112	24	2	11	(4	7)	173	57	47	42	0	66	6	6	4	2	3	.40	11	.247	.316	.381
1995 Cleveland	AL	2	2	0	0	0	0	(0	0)	0	0	0	0	0	0	0	0	0	0	0	—	0	.000	.000	.000
St. Louis	NL	39	144	36	7	2	2	(1	1)	53	13	19	4	0	25	2	0	1	1	2	.33	0	.250	.278	.368
1998 St. Louis	NL	4	9	2	1	0	0	(0	0)	3	0	0	0	0	3	0	0	0	0	0	—	0	.222	.222	.333
Cleveland	AL	107	340	89	21	2	10	(2	8)	144	37	41	22	4	54	2	1	5	0	4	.00	8	.262	.306	.424
Seattle	AL	21	80	26	8	0	0	(0	0)	34	11	8	5	0	8	0	0	0	0	0	—	3	.325	.365	.425
6 ML YEARS		591	1913	486	105	10	46	(20	26)	749	231	214	151	8	296	13	12	19	12	14	.46	34	.254	.310	.392

Derek Bell

Bats: R **Throws:** R **Pos:** RF-142; CF-5; P-1; PH/PR-1 **Ht:** 6'2" **Wt:** 215 **Born:** 12/11/68 **Age:** 32

Year Team	Lg	G	AB	H	2B	3B	HR	(Hm	Rd)	TB	R	RBI	TBB	IBB	SO	HBP	SH	SF	SB	CS	SB%	GDP	Avg	OBP	SLG
1991 Toronto	AL	18	28	4	0	0	0	(0	0)	4	5	1	6	0	5	1	0	0	3	2	.60	0	.143	.314	.143
1992 Toronto	AL	61	161	39	6	3	2	(2	0)	57	23	15	15	1	34	5	2	1	7	2	.78	6	.242	.324	.354
1993 San Diego	NL	150	542	142	19	1	21	(12	9)	226	73	72	23	5	122	12	0	8	26	5	.84	7	.262	.303	.417
1994 San Diego	NL	108	434	135	20	0	14	(8	6)	197	54	54	29	5	88	1	0	2	24	8	.75	14	.311	.354	.454
1995 Houston	NL	112	452	151	21	2	8	(3	5)	200	63	86	33	2	71	8	0	6	27	9	.75	18	.334	.385	.442
1996 Houston	NL	158	627	165	40	3	17	(8	9)	262	84	113	40	8	123	8	0	9	29	3	.91	18	.263	.311	.418
1997 Houston	NL	129	493	136	29	3	15	(8	7)	216	67	71	40	3	94	12	0	2	15	7	.68	16	.276	.344	.438
1998 Houston	NL	156	630	198	41	2	22	(12	10)	309	111	108	51	0	126	4	0	10	13	3	.81	14	.314	.364	.490
1999 Houston	NL	128	509	120	22	0	12	(5	7)	178	61	66	50	1	129	4	0	5	18	6	.75	20	.236	.306	.350
2000 New York	NL	144	546	145	31	1	18	(8	10)	232	87	69	65	0	125	6	2	3	8	4	.67	14	.266	.348	.425
10 ML YEARS		1164	4422	1235	229	15	129	(65	64)	1881	628	655	352	25	917	61	4	46	170	49	.78	119	.279	.338	.425

Jay Bell

Bats: Right **Throws:** Right **Pos:** 2B-145; PH/PR-4; DH-1 **Ht:** 6'0" **Wt:** 184 **Born:** 12/11/65 **Age:** 35

Year Team	Lg	G	AB	H	2B	3B	HR	(Hm	Rd)	TB	R	RBI	TBB	IBB	SO	HBP	SH	SF	SB	CS	SB%	GDP	Avg	OBP	SLG
1986 Cleveland	AL	5	14	5	2	0	1	(0	1)	10	3	4	2	0	3	0	0	0	0	0	—	0	.357	.438	.714
1987 Cleveland	AL	38	125	27	9	1	2	(1	1)	44	14	13	8	0	31	1	3	0	2	0	1.00	0	.216	.269	.352
1988 Cleveland	AL	73	211	46	5	1	2	(2	0)	59	23	21	21	0	53	1	1	2	4	2	.67	3	.218	.289	.280
1989 Pittsburgh	NL	78	271	70	13	3	2	(1	1)	95	33	27	19	0	47	1	10	2	5	3	.63	9	.258	.307	.351
1990 Pittsburgh	NL	159	583	148	28	7	7	(1	6)	211	93	52	65	0	109	3	39	6	10	6	.63	14	.254	.329	.362
1991 Pittsburgh	NL	157	608	164	32	8	16	(7	9)	260	96	67	52	1	99	4	30	3	10	6	.63	15	.270	.330	.428
1992 Pittsburgh	NL	159	632	167	36	6	9	(5	4)	242	87	55	55	0	103	4	19	2	7	5	.58	12	.264	.326	.383
1993 Pittsburgh	NL	154	604	187	32	9	9	(3	6)	264	102	51	77	6	122	6	11	3	16	10	.62	16	.310	.392	.437
1994 Pittsburgh	NL	110	424	117	35	4	9	(3	6)	187	68	45	49	1	82	3	8	3	2	0	1.00	9	.276	.353	.441
1995 Pittsburgh	NL	138	530	139	28	4	13	(8	5)	214	79	55	55	1	110	4	3	1	2	5	.29	13	.262	.336	.404
1996 Pittsburgh	NL	151	527	132	29	3	13	(6	7)	206	65	71	54	5	108	5	6	6	4	6	.60	10	.250	.323	.391
1997 Kansas City	AL	153	573	167	28	3	21	(10	11)	264	89	92	71	2	101	4	3	9	10	6	.63	18	.291	.368	.461
1998 Arizona	NL	155	549	138	29	5	20	(10	10)	237	79	67	81	3	129	7	5	3	3	5	.38	14	.251	.353	.432
1999 Arizona	NL	151	589	170	32	6	38	(21	17)	328	132	112	82	2	132	4	4	9	7	4	.64	9	.289	.374	.557
2000 Arizona	NL	149	565	151	30	6	18	(9	9)	247	87	68	70	0	88	3	6	5	7	3	.70	7	.267	.348	.437
15 ML YEARS		1830	6805	1828	368	66	180	(89	91)	2868	1050	800	761	21	1317	50	150	52	91	59	.61	150	.269	.344	.421

Mike Bell

Bats: Right **Throws:** Right **Pos:** 3B-13; PH/PR-10 **Ht:** 6'2" **Wt:** 210 **Born:** 12/7/74 **Age:** 26

Year Team	Lg	G	AB	H	2B	3B	HR	(Hm	Rd)	TB	R	RBI	TBB	IBB	SO	HBP	SH	SF	SB	CS	SB%	GDP	Avg	OBP	SLG
1993 Rangers	R	60	230	73	13	6	3	—	—	107	48	34	27	0	23	4	1	2	9	2	.82	2	.317	.395	.465
1994 Chston-SC	A	120	475	125	22	6	6	—	—	177	58	58	47	1	76	3	1	6	16	12	.57	14	.263	.330	.373
1995 Charlotte	A+	129	470	122	20	1	5	—	—	159	49	52	48	0	72	0	3	2	8	8	.53	11	.260	.327	.338
1996 Tulsa	AA	128	484	129	31	3	16	—	—	214	62	59	42	1	75	3	4	0	3	1	.75	13	.267	.329	.442
1997 Okla City	AAA	93	328	77	18	2	5	—	—	114	35	38	29	0	78	4	0	3	4	2	.67	10	.235	.302	.348
Tulsa	AA	33	123	35	11	0	8	—	—	70	17	23	15	0	28	4	2	2	0	1	.00	2	.285	.375	.569
1998 Norfolk	AAA	17	44	8	1	0	2	—	—	15	6	8	8	1	7	0	0	0	0	0	—	0	.182	.302	.341
St. Lucie	A+	18	63	22	5	2	1	—	—	34	11	14	8	2	10	2	2	5	2	1	.67	1	.349	.410	.540
Binghamton	AA	78	275	73	14	1	14	—	—	131	47	56	35	1	50	2	0	6	3	5	.38	5	.265	.346	.476
1999 Norfolk	AAA	39	135	37	11	1	1	—	—	53	11	25	9	1	23	2	0	7	4	2	.67	5	.274	.324	.393
2000 Louisville	AAA	115	429	115	29	2	22	—	—	214	70	78	45	6	76	0	0	7	0	0	—	10	.268	.342	.499
2000 Cincinnati	NL	19	27	6	0	0	2	(1	1)	12	5	4	4	0	7	0	0	0	0	0	—	0	.222	.323	.444

Rob Bell

Pitches: Right **Bats:** Right **Pos:** SP-26   **Ht:** 6'5" **Wt:** 225 **Born:** 1/17/77 **Age:** 24

Year Team	Lg	HOW MUCH HE PITCHED						WHAT HE GAVE UP											THE RESULTS						
		G	GS	CG	GF	IP	BFP	H	R	ER	HR	SH	SF	HB	TBB	IBB	SO	WP	Bk	W	L	Pct.	ShO	Sv-Op	Hld	ERA
1995 Braves	R	10	8	0	0	34	154	38	29	26	2	0	2	4	14	0	33	1	0	1	6	.143	0	0--	—	6.88
1996 Eugene	A-	16	16	0	0	81	356	89	49	46	5	5	3	3	29	1	74	2	0	5	6	.455	0	0--	—	5.11
1997 Macon	A	27	27	1	0	146.2	614	144	72	60	15	5	5	3	41	1	140	7	0	14	7	.667	0	0--	—	3.68
1998 Danville	A+	28	28	2	0	178.1	736	169	79	65	8	6	6	7	46	0	197	8	0	7	9	.438	0	0--	—	3.28
1999 Reds	R	2	2	0	0	8	36	3	1	1	0	1	0	0	0	0	11	1	0	0	0	—	0	0--	—	1.13
Chattanooga	AA	12	12	2	0	72	293	75	30	25	7	2	2	0	17	0	68	1	0	3	6	.333	1	0--	—	3.13
2000 Louisville	AAA	6	6	0	0	41	170	35	18	17	6	0	1	0	13	0	47	1	0	4	0	1.000	0	0--	—	3.73
2000 Cincinnati	NL	26	26	1	0	140.1	618	130	84	78	32	8	2	1	73	6	112	11	0	7	8	.467	0	0-0	0	5.00

Albert Belle

Bats: Right **Throws:** Right **Pos:** RF-110; DH-31   **Ht:** 6'2" **Wt:** 225 **Born:** 8/25/66 **Age:** 34

Year Team	Lg	BATTING															BASERUNNING				PERCENTAGES		
		G	AB	H	2B	3B	HR	(Hm | Rd)	TB	R	RBI	TBB	IBB	SO	HBP	SH	SF	SB	CS	SB%	GDP	Avg	OBP	SLG
1989 Cleveland	AL	62	218	49	8	4	7	(3 | 4)	86	22	37	12	0	55	2	0	2	2	2	.50	4	.225	.269	.394
1990 Cleveland	AL	9	23	4	0	0	1	(1 | 0)	7	1	3	1	0	6	0	1	0	0	0	—	1	.174	.208	.304
1991 Cleveland	AL	123	461	130	31	2	28	(8 | 20)	249	60	95	25	2	99	5	0	5	3	1	.75	24	.282	.323	.540
1992 Cleveland	AL	153	585	152	23	1	34	(15 | 19)	279	81	112	52	5	128	4	1	8	8	2	.80	18	.260	.320	.477
1993 Cleveland	AL	159	594	172	36	3	38	(20 | 18)	328	93	**129**	76	13	96	8	1	**14**	23	12	.66	18	.290	.370	.552
1994 Cleveland	AL	106	412	147	35	2	36	(21 | 15)	**294**	90	101	58	9	71	5	1	4	9	6	.60	5	.357	.438	.714
1995 Cleveland	AL	143	546	173	**52**	1	**50**	(25 | 25)	**377**	121	126	73	5	80	6	0	4	5	2	.71	24	.317	.401	**.690**
1996 Cleveland	AL	158	602	187	38	3	48	(22 | 26)	375	124	148	99	15	87	7	0	7	11	0	1.00	20	.311	.410	.623
1997 Chicago	AL	161	634	174	45	1	30	(14 | 16)	311	90	116	53	6	105	6	0	8	4	4	.50	**26**	.274	.332	.491
1998 Chicago	AL	**163**	609	200	48	2	49	(29 | 20)	**399**	113	152	81	10	84	1	0	**15**	6	4	.60	17	.328	.399	**.655**
1999 Baltimore	AL	161	610	181	36	1	37	(19 | 18)	330	108	117	101	15	82	7	0	4	17	3	.85	19	.297	.400	.541
2000 Baltimore	AL	141	559	157	37	1	23	(14 | 9)	265	71	103	52	11	68	4	0	7	0	5	.00	17	.281	.342	.474
12 ML YEARS		1539	5853	1726	389	21	381	(191 | 190)	3300	974	1239	683	91	961	55	4	78	88	41	.68	193	.295	.369	.564

Mark Bellhorn

Bats: B **Throws:** R **Pos:** PH/PR-7; 2B-2; 3B-2; SS-1   **Ht:** 6'1" **Wt:** 214 **Born:** 8/23/74 **Age:** 26

Year Team	Lg	BATTING															BASERUNNING				PERCENTAGES		
		G	AB	H	2B	3B	HR	(Hm | Rd)	TB	R	RBI	TBB	IBB	SO	HBP	SH	SF	SB	CS	SB%	GDP	Avg	OBP	SLG
2000 Sacramento *	AAA	117	436	116	17	11	24	—	—	227	111	73	94	3	121	5	6	4	20	5	.80	5	.266	.399	.521
1997 Oakland	AL	68	224	51	9	1	6	(3 | 3)	80	33	19	32	0	70	0	5	0	7	1	.88	1	.228	.324	.357
1998 Oakland	AL	11	12	1	1	0	0	(0 | 0)	2	1	1	3	0	4	1	0	0	2	0	1.00	0	.083	.313	.167
2000 Oakland	AL	9	13	2	0	0	0	(0 | 0)	2	2	0	2	0	6	0	0	0	0	0	—	0	.154	.267	.154
3 ML YEARS		88	249	54	10	1	6	(3 | 3)	84	36	20	37	0	80	1	5	0	9	1	.90	1	.217	.321	.337

Ron Belliard

Bats: Right **Throws:** Right **Pos:** 2B-151; PH/PR-2   **Ht:** 5'8" **Wt:** 180 **Born:** 4/7/75 **Age:** 26

Year Team	Lg	BATTING															BASERUNNING				PERCENTAGES		
		G	AB	H	2B	3B	HR	(Hm | Rd)	TB	R	RBI	TBB	IBB	SO	HBP	SH	SF	SB	CS	SB%	GDP	Avg	OBP	SLG
1998 Milwaukee	NL	8	5	1	0	0	0	(0 | 0)	1	1	0	0	0	0	0	0	0	0	0	—	0	.200	.200	.200
1999 Milwaukee	NL	124	457	135	29	4	8	(5 | 3)	196	60	58	64	0	59	0	6	4	4	5	.44	16	.295	.379	.429
2000 Milwaukee	NL	152	571	150	30	9	8	(4 | 4)	222	83	54	82	4	84	3	4	7	7	5	.58	12	.263	.354	.389
3 ML YEARS		284	1033	286	59	13	16	(9 | 7)	419	144	112	146	4	143	3	10	11	11	10	.52	28	.277	.365	.406

Clay Bellinger

Bats: R **Throws:** R **Pos:** CF-26; 2B-21; 3B-18; PH/PR-18; LF-17; 1B-10; SS-6; RF-5   **Ht:** 6'3" **Wt:** 215 **Born:** 11/18/68 **Age:** 32

Year Team	Lg	BATTING															BASERUNNING				PERCENTAGES		
		G	AB	H	2B	3B	HR	(Hm | Rd)	TB	R	RBI	TBB	IBB	SO	HBP	SH	SF	SB	CS	SB%	GDP	Avg	OBP	SLG
1989 Everett	A-	51	185	37	8	1	4	—	—	59	29	16	19	0	47	1	1	0	3	2	.60	4	.200	.278	.319
1990 Clinton	A	109	382	83	17	4	10	—	—	138	52	48	28	0	102	7	5	3	13	6	.68	5	.217	.281	.361
1991 San Jose	A+	105	368	95	29	2	8	—	—	152	65	62	53	3	88	11	7	6	13	4	.76	3	.258	.363	.413
1992 Shreveport	AA	126	433	90	18	3	13	—	—	153	45	50	36	1	82	3	4	4	7	8	.47	15	.208	.271	.353
1993 Phoenix	AAA	122	407	104	20	3	6	—	—	148	50	49	38	4	81	4	7	5	7	7	.50	8	.256	.322	.364
1994 Phoenix	AAA	106	337	90	15	1	7	—	—	128	48	50	18	0	56	7	2	3	6	1	.86	8	.267	.315	.380
1995 Phoenix	AAA	97	277	76	16	1	2	—	—	100	34	32	27	1	52	2	2	3	3	2	.60	5	.274	.340	.361
1996 Rochester	AAA	125	459	138	34	4	15	—	—	225	68	78	33	0	90	6	1	11	8	4	.67	6	.301	.348	.490
1997 Columbus	AAA	111	416	114	31	3	12	—	—	187	55	59	34	2	74	7	2	1	10	4	.71	10	.274	.338	.450
1998 Columbus	AAA	115	397	89	20	2	9	—	—	140	35	40	35	2	79	5	1	4	6	3	.67	10	.224	.293	.353
1999 Columbus	AAA	40	141	33	10	1	2	—	—	51	19	14	13	0	32	2	0	4	6	0	1.00	1	.234	.300	.362
2000 Columbus	AAA	8	28	9	2	0	0	—	—	11	3	2	2	0	5	0	0	0	1	0	1.00	1	.321	.367	.393
1999 New York	AL	32	45	9	2	0	1	(1 | 0)	14	12	2	1	0	10	0	0	0	1	0	1.00	1	.200	.217	.311
2000 New York	AL	98	184	38	8	2	6	(2 | 4)	68	33	21	17	1	48	5	1	2	5	0	1.00	1	.207	.288	.370
2 ML YEARS		130	229	47	10	2	7	(3 | 4)	82	45	23	18	1	58	5	1	2	6	0	1.00	2	.205	.276	.358

Carlos Beltran

Bats: B **Throws:** R **Pos:** CF-83; DH-7; RF-3; PH/PR-3; LF-2   **Ht:** 6'1" **Wt:** 190 **Born:** 4/24/77 **Age:** 24

Year Team	Lg	BATTING															BASERUNNING				PERCENTAGES		
		G	AB	H	2B	3B	HR	(Hm | Rd)	TB	R	RBI	TBB	IBB	SO	HBP	SH	SF	SB	CS	SB%	GDP	Avg	OBP	SLG
2000 Royals *	R	1	4	2	1	0	1	—	—	6	3	1	1	0	0	0	0	0	0	0	—	0	.500	.600	1.500
Wilmington *	A+	3	13	4	0	1	2	—	—	12	2	6	0	0	5	0	0	0	0	0	—	0	.308	.308	.923
Omaha *	AAA	5	18	6	1	0	2	—	—	13	4	2	3	0	3	1	0	0	1	0	1.00	0	.333	.455	.722
1998 Kansas City	AL	14	58	16	5	3	0	(0 | 0)	27	12	7	3	0	12	1	0	0	3	0	1.00	2	.276	.317	.466
1999 Kansas City	AL	156	663	194	27	7	22	(12 | 10)	301	112	108	46	2	123	4	0	10	27	8	.77	17	.293	.337	.454
2000 Kansas City	AL	98	372	92	15	4	7	(4 | 3)	136	49	44	35	2	69	0	2	4	13	0	1.00	12	.247	.309	.366
3 ML YEARS		268	1093	302	47	14	29	(16 | 13)	464	173	159	84	4	204	5	2	15	43	8	.84	31	.276	.327	.425

Rigo Beltran

Pitches: Left **Bats:** Left **Pos:** SP-1   **Ht:** 5'11" **Wt:** 200 **Born:** 11/13/69 **Age:** 31

Year Team	Lg	G	GS	CG	GF	IP	BFP	H	R	ER	HR	SH	SF	HB	TBB	IBB	SO	WP	Bk	W	L	Pct.	ShO	Sv-Op	Hld	ERA
2000 Colo Sprngs *	AAA	25	21	1	1	125	563	132	85	82	15	5	3	7	63	0	95	8	2	6	10	.375	1	0- -	—	5.90
1997 St. Louis	NL	35	4	0	16	54.1	224	47	25	21	3	6	3	0	17	0	50	1	0	1	2	.333	0	1-1	2	3.48
1998 New York	NL	7	0	0	0	8	33	6	3	3	1	0	1	0	4	0	5	0	0	0	0	—	0	0-0	0	3.38
1999 NYM-Col	NL	33	0	0	12	42	195	50	24	21	7	3	0	1	19	3	50	7	0	1	1	.500	0	0-0	1	4.50
2000 Colorado	NL	1	1	0	0	1.1	13	6	6	6	2	0	0	0	3	0	1	0	0	0	0	—	0	0-0	0	40.50
1999 New York	NL	21	0	0	10	31	134	30	15	12	5	2	0	0	12	2	35	6	0	1	1	.500	0	0-0	1	3.48
Colorado	NL	12	0	0	2	11	61	20	9	9	2	1	0	1	7	1	15	1	0	0	0	—	0	0-0	1	7.36
4 ML YEARS		76	5	0	28	105.2	465	109	58	51	13	9	4	1	43	3	106	8	0	2	3	.400	0	1-1	3	4.34

Adrian Beltre

Bats: Right **Throws:** Right **Pos:** 3B-138; SS-1; PH/PR-1   **Ht:** 5'11" **Wt:** 170 **Born:** 4/7/79 **Age:** 22

Year Team	Lg	G	AB	H	2B	3B	HR	(Hm	Rd)	TB	R	RBI	TBB	IBB	SO	HBP	SH	SF	SB	CS	SB%	GDP	Avg	OBP	SLG
1998 Los Angeles	NL	77	195	42	9	0	7	(5	2)	72	18	22	14	0	37	3	2	0	3	1	.75	4	.215	.278	.369
1999 Los Angeles	NL	152	538	148	27	5	15	(6	9)	230	84	67	61	12	105	6	4	5	18	7	.72	4	.275	.352	.428
2000 Los Angeles	NL	138	510	148	30	2	20	(7	13)	242	71	85	56	2	80	2	3	4	12	5	.71	13	.290	.360	.475
3 ML YEARS		367	1243	338	66	7	42	(18	24)	544	173	174	131	14	222	11	9	9	33	13	.72	21	.272	.344	.438

Marvin Benard

Bats: L **Throws:** L **Pos:** CF-128; RF-38; LF-21; PH/PR-16   **Ht:** 5'9" **Wt:** 185 **Born:** 1/20/70 **Age:** 31

Year Team	Lg	G	AB	H	2B	3B	HR	(Hm	Rd)	TB	R	RBI	TBB	IBB	SO	HBP	SH	SF	SB	CS	SB%	GDP	Avg	OBP	SLG
1995 San Francisco	NL	13	34	13	0	1	0	(0	1)	18	5	4	1	0	7	0	0	0	1	0	1.00	1	.382	.400	.529
1996 San Francisco	NL	135	488	121	17	4	5	(2	3)	161	89	27	59	2	84	4	6	1	25	11	.69	8	.248	.333	.330
1997 San Francisco	NL	84	114	26	4	0	1	(0	1)	33	13	13	13	0	29	2	0	1	3	1	.75	2	.228	.315	.289
1998 San Francisco	NL	121	286	92	21	4	1	(2	1)	124	41	36	34	1	39	2	4	1	11	4	.73	3	.322	.396	.434
1999 San Francisco	NL	149	562	163	36	5	16	(9	7)	257	100	64	55	2	97	6	1	1	27	14	.66	5	.290	.359	.457
2000 San Francisco	NL	149	560	147	27	6	12	(6	6)	222	102	55	63	0	97	6	2	2	22	7	.76	4	.263	.342	.396
6 ML YEARS		651	2044	562	107	16	38	(19	19)	815	350	199	225	5	353	20	13	6	89	37	.71	23	.275	.352	.399

Alan Benes

Pitches: Right **Bats:** Right **Pos:** RP-30   **Ht:** 6'5" **Wt:** 235 **Born:** 1/21/72 **Age:** 29

Year Team	Lg	G	GS	CG	GF	IP	BFP	H	R	ER	HR	SH	SF	HB	TBB	IBB	SO	WP	Bk	W	L	Pct.	ShO	Sv-Op	Hld	ERA
2000 Memphis *	AAA	9	8	0	0	39.1	179	45	31	26	7	2	2	1	21	0	26	3	0	1	2	.333	0	0- -	—	5.95
1995 St. Louis	NL	3	3	0	0	16	76	24	15	15	2	1	0	1	4	0	20	3	0	1	2	.333	0	0-0	0	8.44
1996 St. Louis	NL	34	32	3	1	191	840	192	120	104	27	15	9	7	87	3	131	5	1	13	10	.565	1	0-0	0	4.90
1997 St. Louis	NL	23	23	2	0	161.2	666	128	60	52	15	5	4	4	68	3	160	9	2	9	9	.500	0	0-0	0	2.89
1999 St. Louis	NL	2	0	0	2	2	7	2	0	0	0	0	0	0	0	0	2	0	0	0	0	—	0	0-0	0	0.00
2000 St. Louis	NL	30	0	0	16	46	214	54	33	29	7	2	1	2	23	2	26	5	0	2	2	.500	0	0-1	2	5.67
5 ML YEARS		92	58	5	19	416.2	1803	400	228	200	49	23	14	14	182	8	339	22	3	25	23	.521	1	0-1	2	4.32

Andy Benes

Pitches: Right **Bats:** Right **Pos:** SP-27; RP-3   **Ht:** 6'6" **Wt:** 245 **Born:** 8/20/67 **Age:** 33

Year Team	Lg	G	GS	CG	GF	IP	BFP	H	R	ER	HR	SH	SF	HB	TBB	IBB	SO	WP	Bk	W	L	Pct.	ShO	Sv-Op	Hld	ERA
1989 San Diego	NL	10	10	0	0	66.2	280	51	28	26	7	6	2	1	31	0	66	0	3	6	3	.667	0	0-0	0	3.51
1990 San Diego	NL	32	31	2	1	192.1	811	177	87	77	18	5	6	1	69	5	140	2	5	10	11	.476	2	0-0	0	3.60
1991 San Diego	NL	33	33	4	0	223	908	194	76	75	23	5	4	4	59	7	167	3	4	15	11	.577	1	0-0	0	3.03
1992 San Diego	NL	34	34	2	0	231.1	961	230	90	86	14	19	6	5	61	6	169	1	1	13	14	.481	2	0-0	0	3.35
1993 San Diego	NL	34	34	4	0	230.2	968	200	111	97	23	10	6	4	86	7	179	14	2	15	15	.500	2	0-0	0	3.78
1994 San Diego	NL	25	25	2	0	172.1	717	155	82	74	20	11	1	1	51	2	189	4	0	6	14	.300	2	0-0	0	3.86
1995 SD-Sea		31	31	1	0	181.2	809	193	107	96	18	4	8	6	78	5	171	5	0	11	9	.550	1	0-0	0	4.76
1996 St. Louis	NL	36	34	3	1	230.1	963	215	107	98	28	2	6	6	77	7	160	6	0	18	10	.643	1	1-1	0	3.83
1997 St. Louis	NL	26	26	0	0	177	727	149	64	61	9	6	7	5	61	4	175	7	0	10	7	.588	0	0-0	0	3.10
1998 Arizona	NL	34	34	1	0	231.1	979	221	111	102	25	11	8	6	74	3	164	9	1	14	13	.519	0	0-0	0	3.97
1999 Arizona	NL	33	32	0	0	198.1	886	216	117	106	34	6	3	4	82	3	141	10	0	13	12	.520	0	0-0	0	4.81
2000 St. Louis	NL	30	27	1	1	166	719	174	95	90	30	9	8	0	68	0	137	1	0	12	9	.571	0	0-0	1	4.88
1995 San Diego	NL	19	19	1	0	118.2	518	121	65	55	10	3	4	4	45	3	126	3	0	4	7	.364	1	0-0	0	4.17
Seattle	AL	12	12	0	0	63	291	72	42	41	8	1	4	2	33	2	45	2	0	7	2	.778	0	0-0	0	5.86
12 ML YEARS		358	351	20	3	2301	9728	2175	1075	988	249	94	65	44	797	49	1858	62	16	143	128	.528	9	1-1	1	3.86

Armando Benitez

Pitches: Right **Bats:** Right **Pos:** RP-76   **Ht:** 6'4" **Wt:** 229 **Born:** 11/3/72 **Age:** 28

Year Team	Lg	G	GS	CG	GF	IP	BFP	H	R	ER	HR	SH	SF	HB	TBB	IBB	SO	WP	Bk	W	L	Pct.	ShO	Sv-Op	Hld	ERA
1994 Baltimore	AL	3	0	0	1	10	42	8	1	1	0	0	0	1	4	0	14	0	0	0	0	—	0	0-0	0	0.90
1995 Baltimore	AL	44	0	0	18	47.2	221	37	33	30	8	2	3	5	37	2	56	3	1	1	5	.167	0	2-5	6	5.66
1996 Baltimore	AL	18	0	0	8	14.1	56	7	6	6	2	0	1	0	6	0	20	1	0	1	0	1.000	0	4-5	1	3.77
1997 Baltimore	AL	71	0	0	26	73.1	307	49	22	20	7	2	4	1	43	5	106	1	0	4	5	.444	0	9-10	20	2.45
1998 Baltimore	AL	71	0	0	54	68.1	289	48	29	29	10	3	2	4	39	2	87	0	0	5	6	.455	0	22-26	3	3.82
1999 New York	NL	77	0	0	42	78	312	40	17	16	4	0	0	0	41	4	128	2	0	4	3	.571	0	22-28	17	1.85
2000 New York	NL	76	0	0	68	76	304	39	24	22	10	2	1	0	38	2	106	0	0	4	4	.500	0	41-46	0	2.61
7 ML YEARS		360	0	0	217	367.2	1531	228	132	124	41	9	11	11	208	15	517	7	1	19	23	.452	0	100-120	47	3.04

19

Mike Benjamin

Bats: R **Throws:** R **Pos:** 3B-34; SS-30; 2B-27; PH/PR-16; 1B-1   **Ht:** 6'0" **Wt:** 172 **Born:** 11/22/65 **Age:** 35

Year Team	Lg	G	AB	H	2B	3B	HR	(Hm	Rd)	TB	R	RBI	TBB	IBB	SO	HBP	SH	SF	SB	CS	SB%	GDP	Avg	OBP	SLG
1989 San Francisco	NL	14	6	1	0	0	0	(0	0)	1	6	0	0	0	1	0	0	0	0	0	—	0	.167	.167	.167
1990 San Francisco	NL	22	56	12	3	1	2	(2	0)	23	7	3	3	1	10	0	0	0	1	0	1.00	2	.214	.254	.411
1991 San Francisco	NL	54	106	13	3	0	2	(0	2)	22	12	8	7	2	26	2	3	2	3	0	1.00	1	.123	.188	.208
1992 San Francisco	NL	40	75	13	2	1	1	(0	1)	20	4	3	4	1	15	0	3	0	1	0	1.00	0	.173	.215	.267
1993 San Francisco	NL	63	146	29	7	0	4	(3	1)	48	22	16	9	2	23	4	6	0	0	0	—	3	.199	.264	.329
1994 San Francisco	NL	38	62	16	5	1	1	(1	0)	26	9	9	5	1	16	3	5	0	5	0	1.00	1	.258	.343	.419
1995 San Francisco	NL	68	186	41	6	0	3	(1	2)	56	19	12	8	3	51	1	7	0	11	1	.92	3	.220	.256	.301
1996 Philadelphia	NL	35	103	23	5	1	4	(0	4)	42	13	13	12	5	21	2	1	0	3	1	.75	2	.223	.316	.408
1997 Boston	AL	49	116	27	9	1	0	(0	0)	38	12	7	4	0	27	1	1	1	2	3	.40	2	.233	.262	.328
1998 Boston	AL	124	349	95	23	0	4	(2	2)	130	46	39	15	1	73	6	13	2	3	0	1.00	11	.272	.312	.372
1999 Pittsburgh	NL	110	368	91	26	7	1	(1	0)	134	42	37	20	3	90	2	11	3	10	1	.91	3	.247	.288	.364
2000 Pittsburgh	NL	93	233	63	18	2	2	(0	2)	91	28	19	12	0	45	3	6	1	5	4	.56	4	.270	.313	.391
12 ML YEARS		710	1806	424	107	14	24	(10	14)	631	220	166	99	19	398	24	56	9	44	10	.81	33	.235	.282	.349

Gary Bennett

Bats: Right **Throws:** Right **Pos:** C-31; PH/PR-1   **Ht:** 6'0" **Wt:** 208 **Born:** 4/17/72 **Age:** 29

Year Team	Lg	G	AB	H	2B	3B	HR	(Hm	Rd)	TB	R	RBI	TBB	IBB	SO	HBP	SH	SF	SB	CS	SB%	GDP	Avg	OBP	SLG
2000 Scrantn-WB *	AAA	92	317	97	24	0	12	—	—	157	47	52	40	1	44	7	3	2	1	0	1.00	9	.306	.393	.495
1995 Philadelphia	NL	1	1	0	0	0	0	(0	0)	0	0	0	0	0	1	0	0	0	0	0	—	0	.000	.000	.000
1996 Philadelphia	NL	6	16	4	0	0	0	(0	0)	4	0	1	2	1	6	0	0	0	0	0	—	1	.250	.333	.250
1998 Philadelphia	NL	9	31	9	0	0	0	(0	0)	9	4	3	5	0	5	0	0	1	0	0	—	1	.290	.378	.290
1999 Philadelphia	NL	36	88	24	4	0	1	(0	1)	31	7	21	4	0	11	0	0	2	0	0	—	7	.273	.298	.352
2000 Philadelphia	NL	31	74	18	5	0	2	(0	2)	29	8	5	13	0	15	2	0	0	0	0	—	0	.243	.371	.392
5 ML YEARS		83	210	55	9	0	3	(0	3)	73	19	30	24	1	38	2	0	3	0	0	—	8	.262	.339	.348

Kris Benson

Pitches: Right **Bats:** Right **Pos:** SP-32   **Ht:** 6'4" **Wt:** 200 **Born:** 11/7/74 **Age:** 26

Year Team	Lg	G	GS	CG	GF	IP	BFP	H	R	ER	HR	SH	SF	HB	TBB	IBB	SO	WP	Bk	W	L	Pct.	ShO	Sv-Op	Hld	ERA
1997 Lynchburg	A+	10	10	0	0	59.1	241	49	20	17	1	3	1	2	13	0	72	3	1	5	2	.714	0	0-	—	2.58
Carolina	AA	14	14	0	0	68.2	316	81	49	38	11	0	2	2	32	1	66	2	0	3	5	.375	0	0-	—	4.98
1998 Nashville	AAA	28	28	1	0	156	689	162	102	93	26	6	5	5	50	5	129	9	0	8	10	.444	1	0-	—	5.37
1999 Pittsburgh	NL	31	31	2	0	196.2	840	184	105	89	16	6	7	6	83	5	139	2	1	11	14	.440	0	0-0	0	4.07
2000 Pittsburgh	NL	32	32	2	0	217.2	936	206	104	93	24	7	6	10	86	5	184	5	0	10	12	.455	1	0-0	0	3.85
2 ML YEARS		63	63	4	0	414.1	1776	390	209	182	40	13	13	16	169	10	323	7	1	21	26	.447	1	0-0	0	3.95

Jason Bere

Pitches: Right **Bats:** Right **Pos:** SP-31   **Ht:** 6'3" **Wt:** 215 **Born:** 5/26/71 **Age:** 30

Year Team	Lg	G	GS	CG	GF	IP	BFP	H	R	ER	HR	SH	SF	HB	TBB	IBB	SO	WP	Bk	W	L	Pct.	ShO	Sv-Op	Hld	ERA
1993 Chicago	AL	24	24	1	0	142.2	610	109	60	55	12	4	2	5	81	0	129	8	0	12	5	.706	0	0-0	0	3.47
1994 Chicago	AL	24	24	0	0	141.2	608	119	65	60	17	4	4	1	80	0	127	2	0	12	2	.857	0	0-0	0	3.81
1995 Chicago	AL	27	27	1	0	137.2	668	151	120	110	21	4	7	6	106	6	110	8	0	8	15	.348	0	0-0	0	7.19
1996 Chicago	AL	5	5	0	0	16.2	93	26	19	19	3	1	1	1	18	1	19	2	0	1	0	1.000	0	0-0	0	10.26
1997 Chicago	AL	6	6	0	0	28.2	123	20	15	15	4	1	1	3	17	0	21	1	0	4	2	.667	0	0-0	0	4.71
1998 CWS-Cin		27	22	0	2	127.1	588	137	91	80	17	7	7	3	78	0	84	8	0	6	9	.400	0	0-0	0	5.65
1999 Cin-Mil	NL	17	14	0	0	66.2	322	79	52	45	9	6	2	2	50	3	47	6	0	5	0	1.000	0	0-0	0	6.08
2000 Mil-Cle	NL	31	31	0	0	169.1	767	180	107	103	25	12	6	5	89	7	142	5	1	12	10	.545	0	0-0	0	5.47
1998 Chicago	AL	18	15	0	0	83.2	404	98	71	60	14	4	5	2	58	0	53	7	0	3	7	.300	0	0-0	0	6.45
Cincinnati	NL	9	7	0	2	43.2	184	39	20	20	3	3	2	1	20	0	31	1	0	3	2	.600	0	0-0	0	4.12
1999 Cincinnati	NL	12	10	0	0	43.1	220	56	37	33	6	5	1	2	40	3	28	2	0	3	0	1.000	0	0-0	0	6.85
Milwaukee	NL	5	4	0	0	23.1	102	23	15	12	3	1	1	0	10	0	19	4	0	2	0	1.000	0	0-0	0	4.63
2000 Milwaukee	NL	20	20	0	0	115	522	115	66	63	19	12	3	1	63	7	98	3	1	6	7	.462	0	0-0	0	4.93
Cleveland	AL	11	11	0	0	54.1	252	65	41	40	6	0	3	4	26	0	44	2	0	6	3	.667	0	0-0	0	6.63
8 ML YEARS		161	153	2	2	830.2	3779	821	529	487	108	36	30	25	519	17	679	40	1	59	44	.573	0	0-0	0	5.28

Dave Berg

Bats: R **Throws:** R **Pos:** SS-49; PH/PR-17; 3B-13; 2B-11   **Ht:** 5'11" **Wt:** 185 **Born:** 9/3/70 **Age:** 30

Year Team	Lg	G	AB	H	2B	3B	HR	(Hm	Rd)	TB	R	RBI	TBB	IBB	SO	HBP	SH	SF	SB	CS	SB%	GDP	Avg	OBP	SLG
2000 Brevard Cty *	A+	3	11	3	0	0	0	—	—	3	2	2	1	0	3	1	0	0	0	1	.00	1	.273	.385	.273
1998 Florida	NL	81	182	57	11	0	2	(1	1)	74	18	21	26	1	46	0	4	3	3	0	1.00	1	.313	.393	.407
1999 Florida	NL	109	304	87	18	1	3	(1	2)	116	42	25	27	0	59	2	3	0	2	2	.50	7	.286	.348	.382
2000 Florida	NL	82	210	53	14	1	1	(1	0)	72	23	21	25	0	46	5	1	4	3	0	1.00	5	.252	.340	.343
3 ML YEARS		272	696	197	43	2	6	(3	3)	262	83	67	78	1	151	7	8	7	8	2	.80	13	.283	.358	.376

Peter Bergeron

Bats: Left **Throws:** Right **Pos:** CF-117; LF-32; PH/PR-5   **Ht:** 6'0" **Wt:** 185 **Born:** 11/9/77 **Age:** 23

Year Team	Lg	G	AB	H	2B	3B	HR	(Hm	Rd)	TB	R	RBI	TBB	IBB	SO	HBP	SH	SF	SB	CS	SB%	GDP	Avg	OBP	SLG
1996 Yakima	A-	61	232	59	5	3	5	—	—	85	36	21	28	0	59	0	3	0	13	9	.59	2	.254	.335	.366
1997 Savannah	A	131	492	138	18	5	5	—	—	181	89	36	67	3	110	2	5	3	32	21	.60	5	.280	.367	.368
San Berndno	A+	2	8	2	0	0	0	—	—	2	1	1	0	0	2	0	0	0	2	0	1.00	0	.250	.250	.250
1998 San Antonio	AA	109	416	132	17	8	8	—	—	189	81	54	61	1	69	2	9	1	33	9	.79	2	.317	.406	.454
Harrisburg	AA	34	134	33	8	4	0	—	—	49	22	9	17	0	26	0	2	0	8	3	.73	0	.246	.331	.366

Year Team	Lg	G	AB	H	2B	3B	HR	(Hm	Rd)	TB	R	RBI	TBB	IBB	SO	HBP	SH	SF	SB	CS	SB%	GDP	Avg	OBP	SLG
1999 Harrisburg	AA	42	162	53	14	2	4	—	—	83	29	18	24	4	29	0	0	3	9	7	.56	0	.327	.407	.512
Ottawa	AAA	58	194	61	12	3	3	—	—	88	36	20	23	0	40	1	1	2	14	8	.64	1	.314	.386	.454
1999 Montreal	NL	16	45	11	2	0	0	(0	0)	13	12	1	9	0	5	0	1	0	0	0	—	0	.244	.370	.289
2000 Montreal	NL	148	518	127	25	7	5	(3	2)	181	80	31	58	0	100	0	14	2	11	13	.46	4	.245	.320	.349
2 ML YEARS		164	563	138	27	7	5	(3	2)	194	92	32	67	0	105	0	15	2	11	13	.46	4	.245	.324	.345

Sean Bergman

Pitches: Right **Bats:** Right **Pos:** SP-14; RP-1 **Ht:** 6'4" **Wt:** 225 **Born:** 4/11/70 **Age:** 31

Year Team	Lg	G	GS	CG	GF	IP	BFP	H	R	ER	HR	SH	SF	HB	TBB	IBB	SO	WP	Bk	W	L	Pct.	ShO	Sv-Op	Hld	ERA
2000 Calgary *	AAA	13	13	0	0	81.2	363	107	55	52	8	1	3	1	23	1	48	6	0	4	3	.571	0	0--	0	5.73
1993 Detroit	AL	9	6	1	1	39.2	189	47	29	25	6	3	2	1	23	3	19	3	1	1	4	.200	0	0-0	0	5.67
1994 Detroit	AL	3	3	0	0	17.2	82	22	11	11	2	0	1	1	7	0	12	1	0	2	1	.667	0	0-0	0	5.60
1995 Detroit	AL	28	28	1	0	135.1	630	169	95	77	19	5	3	4	67	8	86	13	0	7	10	.412	1	0-0	0	5.12
1996 San Diego	NL	41	14	0	11	113.1	482	119	63	55	14	8	4	2	33	3	85	7	2	6	8	.429	0	0-0	1	4.37
1997 San Diego	NL	44	9	0	13	99	451	126	72	67	11	7	4	3	38	4	74	6	0	2	4	.333	0	0-2	1	6.09
1998 Houston	NL	31	27	1	1	172	733	183	81	71	20	3	1	5	42	3	100	8	1	12	9	.571	0	0-0	0	3.72
1999 Hou-Atl	AL	25	16	2	2	105.1	455	135	62	61	9	4	4	3	29	1	44	3	0	5	6	.455	1	0-1	1	5.21
2000 Minnesota	AL	15	14	0	0	68	337	111	76	73	18	2	3	2	33	1	35	2	0	4	5	.444	0	0-0	0	9.66
1999 Houston	NL	19	16	2	1	99	428	130	60	59	9	3	4	3	26	1	38	3	0	4	6	.400	1	0-0	0	5.36
Atlanta	NL	6	0	0	1	6.1	27	5	2	2	0	1	0	0	3	0	6	0	0	1	0	1.000	0	0-1	1	2.84
8 ML YEARS		196	117	5	28	750.1	3359	912	489	440	99	32	22	21	272	23	455	43	4	39	47	.453	2	0-3	3	5.28

Lance Berkman

Bats: B **Throws:** L **Pos:** RF-63; LF-40; PH/PR-22; 1B-2 **Ht:** 6'1" **Wt:** 205 **Born:** 2/10/76 **Age:** 25

Year Team	Lg	G	AB	H	2B	3B	HR	(Hm	Rd)	TB	R	RBI	TBB	IBB	SO	HBP	SH	SF	SB	CS	SB%	GDP	Avg	OBP	SLG
1997 Kissimmee	A+	53	184	54	10	0	12	—	—	100	31	35	37	4	38	2	0	1	2	1	.67	2	.293	.417	.543
1998 Jackson	AA	122	425	130	34	0	24	—	—	236	82	89	85	10	82	4	0	3	6	4	.60	12	.306	.424	.555
New Orleans	AAA	17	59	16	4	0	6	—	—	38	14	13	12	1	16	2	0	0	0	0	—	1	.271	.411	.644
1999 New Orleans	AAA	64	226	73	20	0	8	—	—	117	42	49	39	1	47	0	0	2	7	1	.88	10	.323	.419	.518
2000 New Orleans	AAA	31	112	37	4	2	6	—	—	63	18	27	31	2	20	1	0	0	4	4	.50	7	.330	.479	.563
1999 Houston	NL	34	93	22	2	0	4	(2	2)	36	10	15	12	0	21	0	0	1	5	1	.83	2	.237	.321	.387
2000 Houston	NL	114	353	105	28	1	21	(10	11)	198	76	67	56	1	73	1	0	7	6	2	.75	6	.297	.388	.561
2 ML YEARS		148	446	127	30	1	25	(12	13)	234	86	82	68	1	94	1	0	8	11	3	.79	8	.285	.375	.525

Adam Bernero

Pitches: Right **Bats:** Right **Pos:** RP-8; SP-4 **Ht:** 6'4" **Wt:** 205 **Born:** 11/28/76 **Age:** 24

Year Team	Lg	G	GS	CG	GF	IP	BFP	H	R	ER	HR	SH	SF	HB	TBB	IBB	SO	WP	Bk	W	L	Pct.	ShO	Sv-Op	Hld	ERA
1999 W Michigan	A	15	15	2	0	95.2	386	75	36	27	8	0	2	4	23	0	80	3	3	8	4	.667	1	0--	—	2.54
2000 Jacksonville	AA	10	10	0	0	61.1	260	54	26	19	6	2	3	3	24	0	46	5	0	2	5	.286	0	0--	—	2.79
Toledo	AAA	7	7	1	0	47.1	182	34	16	13	5	0	0	3	10	0	37	1	0	3	1	.750	1	0--	—	2.47
2000 Detroit	AL	12	4	0	4	34.1	141	33	18	16	3	2	3	1	13	1	20	1	0	0	1	.000	0	0-0	1	4.19

Geronimo Berroa

Bats: R **Throws:** R **Pos:** PH/PR-18; LF-4; 1B-2; RF-2 **Ht:** 6'0" **Wt:** 210 **Born:** 3/18/65 **Age:** 36

Year Team	Lg	G	AB	H	2B	3B	HR	(Hm	Rd)	TB	R	RBI	TBB	IBB	SO	HBP	SH	SF	SB	CS	SB%	GDP	Avg	OBP	SLG
1989 Atlanta	NL	81	136	36	4	0	2	(1	1)	46	7	9	7	1	32	0	0	0	0	1	.00	2	.265	.301	.338
1990 Atlanta	NL	7	4	0	0	0	0	(0	0)	0	0	0	1	1	0	0	0	0	0	0	—	0	.000	.200	.000
1992 Cincinnati	NL	13	15	4	1	0	0	(0	0)	5	2	0	2	0	1	1	0	0	0	1	.00	1	.267	.389	.333
1993 Florida	NL	14	34	4	1	0	0	(0	0)	5	3	0	2	0	7	0	0	0	0	0	—	0	.118	.167	.147
1994 Oakland	AL	96	340	104	18	2	13	(4	9)	165	55	65	41	0	62	3	0	7	7	2	.78	5	.306	.379	.485
1995 Oakland	AL	141	546	152	22	3	22	(10	12)	246	87	88	63	2	98	1	0	6	7	4	.64	12	.278	.351	.451
1996 Oakland	AL	153	586	170	32	1	36	(21	15)	312	101	106	47	0	122	4	0	6	4	3	.00	16	.290	.344	.532
1997 Oak-Bal	AL	156	561	159	25	0	26	(11	15)	262	88	90	76	4	120	4	0	7	4	4	.50	18	.283	.369	.467
1998 Cle-Det	AL	72	191	43	7	2	1	(0	0)	57	23	13	24	1	44	2	0	1	1		.50	5	.225	.318	.298
1999 Toronto	AL	22	62	12	3	0	1	(0	1)	18	11	6	9	0	15	2	0	0	0		—	5	.194	.315	.290
2000 Los Angeles	NL	24	31	8	0	1	0	(0	0)	10	2	5	4	1	8	0	0	0	0	0	—	0	.258	.343	.323
1997 Oakland	AL	73	261	81	12	0	16	(6	10)	141	40	42	36	2	58	1	0	1	3	2	.60	12	.310	.395	.540
Baltimore	AL	83	300	78	13	0	10	(5	5)	121	48	48	40	2	62	3	0	6	1	2	.33	6	.260	.347	.403
1998 Cleveland	AL	20	65	13	3	1	0	(1	0)	18	6	3	7	0	17	0	0	1	1	0	1.00	2	.200	.278	.277
Detroit	AL	52	126	30	4	1	1	(1	0)	39	17	10	17	1	27	2	0	0	0		.00	3	.238	.338	.310
11 ML YEARS		779	2506	692	113	9	101	(48	53)	1126	379	382	276	10	510	17	0	26	19	16	.54	68	.276	.349	.449

Sean Berry

Bats: Right **Throws:** Right **Pos:** PH/PR-24; 3B-10 **Ht:** 5'11" **Wt:** 200 **Born:** 3/22/66 **Age:** 35

Year Team	Lg	G	AB	H	2B	3B	HR	(Hm	Rd)	TB	R	RBI	TBB	IBB	SO	HBP	SH	SF	SB	CS	SB%	GDP	Avg	OBP	SLG
2000 Sarasota *	A+	1	4	1	0	0	0	—	—	1	0	0	0	0	2	0	0	0	0	0	—	1	.250	.250	.250
Pawtucket *	AAA	16	57	21	3	0	2	—	—	30	12	4	6	1	17	2	0	0	0	0	—	1	.368	.446	.526
Buffalo *	AAA	13	48	13	0	0	0	—	—	13	2	8	4	0	3	1	0	1	0	1	1.00	0	.271	.333	.271
1990 Kansas City	AL	8	23	5	1	1	0	(0	0)	8	2	4	2	0	5	0	0	0	0	0	—	0	.217	.280	.348
1991 Kansas City	AL	31	60	8	3	0	0	(0	0)	11	5	1	5	0	23	1	0	0	0	0	—	1	.133	.212	.183
1992 Montreal	NL	24	57	19	1	0	1	(0	1)	23	5	4	1	0	11	0	0	0	2	1	.67	1	.333	.345	.404
1993 Montreal	NL	122	299	78	15	2	14	(5	9)	139	50	49	41	6	70	2	3	6	12	2	.86	4	.261	.348	.465
1994 Montreal	NL	103	320	89	19	2	11	(4	7)	145	43	41	32	7	50	3	2	2	14	0	1.00	7	.278	.347	.453

21

(continued)

Year Team	Lg	G	AB	H	2B	3B	HR	(Hm	Rd)	TB	R	RBI	TBB	IBB	SO	HBP	SH	SF	SB	CS	SB%	GDP	Avg	OBP	SLG
1995 Montreal	NL	103	314	100	22	1	14	(5	9)	166	38	55	25	1	53	2	2	5	3	8	.27	5	.318	.367	.529
1996 Houston	NL	132	431	121	38	1	17	(4	13)	212	55	95	23	1	58	9	2	4	12	6	.67	11	.281	.328	.492
1997 Houston	NL	96	301	77	24	1	8	(4	4)	127	37	43	25	1	53	5	1	6	1	5	.17	8	.256	.318	.422
1998 Houston	NL	102	299	94	17	1	13	(7	6)	152	48	52	31	3	50	7	1	4	3	1	.75	8	.314	.387	.508
1999 Milwaukee	NL	106	259	59	11	1	2	(0	2)	78	26	23	17	0	50	3	0	2	0	0	—	4	.228	.281	.301
2000 Mil-Bos		33	50	7	2	0	1	(1	0)	12	1	2	4	0	15	0	0	0	0	1	.00	1	.140	.204	.240
2000 Milwaukee	NL	32	46	7	2	0	1	(1	0)	12	1	2	4	0	13	0	0	0	0	1	.00	1	.152	.220	.261
Boston	AL	1	4	0	0	0	0	(0	0)	0	0	0	0	0	2	0	0	0	0	0	—	0	.000	.000	.000
11 ML YEARS		860	2413	657	153	10	81	(30	51)	1073	310	369	206	19	438	32	11	29	47	24	.66	50	.272	.334	.445

Dante Bichette

Bats: Right **Throws:** Right **Pos:** RF-121; DH-30; PH/PR-8   **Ht:** 6'2" **Wt:** 235 **Born:** 11/18/63 **Age:** 37

Year Team	Lg	G	AB	H	2B	3B	HR	(Hm	Rd)	TB	R	RBI	TBB	IBB	SO	HBP	SH	SF	SB	CS	SB%	GDP	Avg	OBP	SLG
1988 California	AL	21	46	12	2	0	0	(0	0)	14	1	8	0	0	7	0	0	4	0	0	—	0	.261	.240	.304
1989 California	AL	48	138	29	7	0	3	(2	1)	45	13	15	6	0	24	0	0	2	3	0	1.00	3	.210	.240	.326
1990 California	AL	109	349	89	15	1	15	(8	7)	151	40	53	16	1	79	3	1	2	5	2	.71	9	.255	.292	.433
1991 Milwaukee	AL	134	445	106	18	3	15	(6	9)	175	53	59	22	4	107	1	1	6	14	8	.64	9	.238	.272	.393
1992 Milwaukee	AL	112	387	111	27	2	5	(3	2)	157	37	41	16	3	74	3	2	3	18	7	.72	13	.287	.318	.406
1993 Colorado	NL	141	538	167	43	5	21	(11	10)	283	93	89	28	2	99	7	0	8	14	8	.64	9	.310	.348	.526
1994 Colorado	NL	116	484	147	33	2	27	(15	12)	265	74	95	19	3	70	4	0	2	21	8	.72	17	.304	.334	.548
1995 Colorado	NL	139	579	197	38	2	40	(31	9)	359	102	128	22	5	96	4	0	7	13	9	.59	16	.340	.364	.620
1996 Colorado	NL	159	633	198	39	3	31	(22	9)	336	114	141	45	4	105	6	0	10	31	12	.72	18	.313	.359	.531
1997 Colorado	NL	151	561	173	31	2	26	(20	6)	286	81	118	30	1	90	3	0	7	6	5	.55	13	.308	.343	.510
1998 Colorado	NL	161	662	219	48	2	22	(17	5)	337	97	122	28	2	76	1	0	4	14	4	.78	22	.331	.357	.509
1999 Colorado	NL	151	593	177	38	2	34	(20	14)	321	104	133	54	3	84	2	0	10	6	6	.50	15	.298	.354	.541
2000 Cin-Bos		155	575	169	32	2	23	(15	8)	274	80	90	49	3	91	4	1	7	5	2	.71	21	.294	.350	.477
2000 Cincinnati	NL	125	461	136	27	2	16	(11	5)	215	67	76	41	3	69	4	1	7	5	2	.71	18	.295	.353	.466
Boston	AL	30	114	33	5	0	7	(4	3)	59	13	14	8	0	22	0	0	0	0	0	—	3	.289	.336	.518
13 ML YEARS		1597	5990	1794	371	26	262	(170	92)	3003	889	1092	335	31	1002	38	5	72	150	71	.68	163	.299	.337	.501

Rocky Biddle

Pitches: Right **Bats:** Right **Pos:** SP-4   **Ht:** 6'3" **Wt:** 230 **Born:** 5/21/76 **Age:** 25

Year Team	Lg	G	GS	CG	GF	IP	BFP	H	R	ER	HR	SH	SF	HB	TBB	IBB	SO	WP	Bk	W	L	Pct.	ShO	Sv-Op	Hld	ERA
1997 Hickory	A	13	0	0	4	21.1	96	22	18	11	2	0	1	2	10	0	25	5	0	0	1	.000	0	1- -	—	4.64
1998 White Sox	R	5	2	0	0	16	72	15	9	7	2	0	0	2	8	0	18	5	0	1	0	1.000	0	0- -	—	3.94
Winston-Sal	A+	16	16	0	0	82.2	382	92	55	42	7	0	4	5	45	0	72	5	1	4	5	.444	0	0- -	—	4.57
2000 Birmingham	AA	23	23	2	0	146.1	619	138	63	50	10	2	3	8	54	0	118	4	0	11	6	.647	0	0- -	—	3.08
2000 Chicago	AL	4	4	0	0	22.2	105	31	25	21	5	0	2	0	8	0	7	2	0	1	2	.333	0	0-0	0	8.34

Craig Biggio

Bats: Right **Throws:** Right **Pos:** 2B-100; PH/PR-1   **Ht:** 5'11" **Wt:** 180 **Born:** 12/14/65 **Age:** 35

Year Team	Lg	G	AB	H	2B	3B	HR	(Hm	Rd)	TB	R	RBI	TBB	IBB	SO	HBP	SH	SF	SB	CS	SB%	GDP	Avg	OBP	SLG
1988 Houston	NL	50	123	26	6	1	3	(1	2)	43	14	5	7	2	29	0	1	0	6	1	.86	1	.211	.254	.350
1989 Houston	NL	134	443	114	21	2	13	(6	7)	178	64	60	49	8	64	6	6	5	21	3	.88	7	.257	.336	.402
1990 Houston	NL	150	555	153	24	2	4	(2	2)	193	53	42	53	1	79	3	9	1	25	11	.69	11	.276	.342	.348
1991 Houston	NL	149	546	161	23	4	4	(0	4)	204	79	46	53	3	71	2	5	3	19	6	.76	2	.295	.358	.374
1992 Houston	NL	162	613	170	32	3	6	(3	3)	226	96	39	94	9	95	7	5	2	38	15	.72	5	.277	.378	.369
1993 Houston	NL	155	610	175	41	5	21	(8	13)	289	98	64	77	7	93	10	4	5	15	17	.47	10	.287	.373	.474
1994 Houston	NL	114	437	139	44	5	6	(4	2)	211	88	56	62	1	58	8	2	2	39	4	.91	5	.318	.411	.483
1995 Houston	NL	141	553	167	30	2	22	(6	16)	267	123	77	80	1	85	22	11	7	33	8	.80	6	.302	.406	.483
1996 Houston	NL	162	605	174	24	4	15	(7	8)	251	113	75	75	0	72	27	4	8	25	7	.78	10	.288	.386	.415
1997 Houston	NL	162	619	191	37	8	22	(7	15)	310	146	81	84	6	107	34	0	7	47	10	.82	0	.309	.415	.501
1998 Houston	NL	160	646	210	51	2	20	(10	10)	325	123	88	64	6	113	23	1	4	50	8	.86	10	.325	.403	.503
1999 Houston	NL	160	669	188	56	0	16	(10	6)	292	123	73	88	9	107	11	5	6	28	14	.67	5	.294	.386	.457
2000 Houston	NL	101	377	101	13	5	8	(2	6)	148	67	35	61	3	73	16	7	5	12	2	.86	10	.268	.388	.393
13 ML YEARS		1800	6766	1969	402	43	160	(66	94)	2937	1187	741	847	56	1046	169	64	55	358	106	.77	82	.291	.381	.434

Willie Blair

Pitches: Right **Bats:** Right **Pos:** RP-30; SP-17   **Ht:** 6'1" **Wt:** 185 **Born:** 12/18/65 **Age:** 35

Year Team	Lg	G	GS	CG	GF	IP	BFP	H	R	ER	HR	SH	SF	HB	TBB	IBB	SO	WP	Bk	W	L	Pct.	ShO	Sv-Op	Hld	ERA
1990 Toronto	AL	27	6	0	8	68.2	297	66	33	31	4	0	4	1	28	4	43	3	0	3	5	.375	0	0-0	1	4.06
1991 Cleveland	AL	11	5	0	1	36	168	58	27	27	7	1	2	1	10	0	13	1	0	2	3	.400	0	0-1	0	6.75
1992 Houston	NL	29	8	0	1	78.2	331	74	47	35	5	4	3	2	25	2	48	2	0	5	7	.417	0	0-0	1	4.00
1993 Colorado	NL	46	18	1	5	146	664	184	90	77	20	10	8	3	42	4	84	6	1	6	10	.375	0	0-0	3	4.75
1994 Colorado	NL	47	1	0	13	77.2	365	98	57	50	9	3	1	4	39	1	68	4	0	0	5	.000	0	3-6	3	5.79
1995 San Diego	AL	40	12	0	11	114	485	112	60	55	11	8	2	2	45	3	83	4	0	7	5	.583	0	0-0	0	4.34
1996 San Diego	NL	60	0	0	17	88	377	80	52	45	13	4	3	3	29	5	67	2	0	2	6	.250	0	1-5	3	4.60
1997 Detroit	AL	29	27	2	0	175	739	186	85	81	18	3	6	3	46	2	90	6	1	16	8	.667	0	0-0	0	4.17
1998 Ari-NYM	NL	34	25	0	2	175.1	750	188	101	97	31	4	4	4	61	2	92	6	0	5	16	.238	0	0-0	0	4.98
1999 Detroit	AL	39	16	0	8	134	604	169	107	102	29	3	4	4	44	0	82	5	0	3	11	.214	0	0-0	0	6.85
2000 Detroit	AL	47	17	0	8	156.2	671	185	89	85	20	1	7	2	35	0	74	2	0	10	6	.625	0	0-2	2	4.88
1998 Arizona	NL	23	23	0	0	146.2	634	165	91	87	27	1	3	3	51	2	71	5	0	4	15	.211	0	0-0	0	5.34
New York	NL	11	2	0	2	28.2	116	23	10	10	4	3	1	1	10	0	21	1	0	1	1	.500	0	0-0	0	3.14
11 ML YEARS		409	135	3	74	1250	5451	1400	748	685	167	51	44	33	404	25	744	41	2	59	82	.418	0	4-14	15	4.93

Casey Blake

Bats: R **Throws:** R **Pos:** 3B-5; PH/PR-2; DH-1; 1B-1   **Ht:** 6'2" **Wt:** 200 **Born:** 8/23/73 **Age:** 27

Year Team	Lg	G	AB	H	2B	3B	HR	(Hm	Rd)	TB	R	RBI	TBB	IBB	SO	HBP	SH	SF	SB	CS	SB%	GDP	Avg	OBP	SLG
1996 Hagerstown	A	48	172	43	13	1	2	—	—	64	29	18	11	1	40	7	0	2	5	3	.63	3	.250	.318	.372
1997 Dunedin	A+	129	449	107	21	0	7	—	—	149	56	39	48	2	91	6	2	2	19	9	.68	5	.238	.319	.332
1998 Dunedin	A+	88	340	119	28	3	11	—	—	186	62	65	30	1	81	9	3	7	9	6	.60	5	.350	.409	.547
Knoxville	AA	45	172	64	15	4	7	—	—	108	41	38	22	0	25	2	0	3	10	0	1.00	6	.372	.442	.628
1999 Syracuse	AAA	110	387	95	16	2	22	—	—	181	69	75	61	2	82	7	1	2	9	5	.64	10	.245	.357	.468
St.Cathrnes	A-	1	3	2	0	0	0	—	—	2	0	1	0	0	0	0	0	0	0	0	—	0	.667	.750	.667
2000 Syracuse	AAA	30	106	23	6	1	2	—	—	37	10	7	8	0	23	3	0	0	3	3	.00	2	.217	.291	.349
Salt Lake	AAA	80	293	93	22	2	12	—	—	155	59	52	39	0	59	6	2	2	7	2	.78	4	.317	.406	.529
1999 Toronto	AL	14	39	10	2	0	1	(0	1)	15	6	1	2	0	7	0	0	0	0	0	—	1	.256	.293	.385
2000 Minnesota	AL	7	16	3	2	0	0	(0	0)	5	1	1	3	0	7	1	0	1	0	0	—	1	.188	.333	.313
2 ML YEARS		21	55	13	4	0	1	(0	1)	20	7	2	5	0	14	1	0	1	0	0	—	2	.236	.306	.364

Henry Blanco

Bats: Right **Throws:** Right **Pos:** C-88; PH/PR-6   **Ht:** 5'11" **Wt:** 170 **Born:** 8/29/71 **Age:** 29

Year Team	Lg	G	AB	H	2B	3B	HR	(Hm	Rd)	TB	R	RBI	TBB	IBB	SO	HBP	SH	SF	SB	CS	SB%	GDP	Avg	OBP	SLG
2000 Indianapolis *	AAA	1	3	1	1	0	0	—	—	2	1	0	1	0	0	0	0	0	0	0	—	0	.333	.500	.667
1997 Los Angeles	NL	3	5	2	0	0	1	(0	1)	5	1	1	0	0	1	0	0	0	0	0	—	0	.400	.400	1.000
1999 Colorado	NL	88	263	61	12	3	6	(3	3)	97	30	28	34	1	38	1	3	2	1	1	.50	4	.232	.320	.369
2000 Milwaukee	NL	93	284	67	24	0	7	(3	4)	112	29	31	36	6	60	0	0	4	0	3	.00	9	.236	.318	.394
3 ML YEARS		184	552	130	36	3	14	(6	8)	214	60	60	70	7	99	1	3	6	1	4	.20	13	.236	.320	.388

Matt Blank

Pitches: Left **Bats:** Left **Pos:** RP-13   **Ht:** 6'2" **Wt:** 195 **Born:** 4/5/76 **Age:** 25

Year Team	Lg	G	GS	CG	GF	IP	BFP	H	R	ER	HR	SH	SF	HB	TBB	IBB	SO	WP	Bk	W	L	Pct.	ShO	Sv-Op	Hld	ERA
1997 Vermont	A-	16	15	2	0	95.2	375	74	26	18	2	1	3	2	14	0	84	0	0	6	4	.600	0	0--	—	1.69
1998 Cape Fear	A	21	21	2	0	134.2	539	121	45	39	6	4	2	9	24	0	114	1	1	9	2	.818	2	0--	—	2.61
Jupiter	A+	8	6	0	1	42.1	170	33	14	11	2	0	1	4	10	0	26	0	1	5	1	.833	0	0--	—	2.34
1999 Jupiter	A+	14	14	0	0	90	348	64	26	24	5	3	3	2	19	1	66	1	2	5	3	.643	1	0--	—	2.40
Harrisburg	AA	15	14	0	0	85	363	94	41	37	14	5	2	0	26	0	42	3	0	6	3	.667	0	0--	—	3.92
2000 Montreal	NL	13	0	0	3	14	63	12	8	8	1	2	1	1	5	1	4	0	0	0	1	.000	0	0-1	0	5.14

Geoff Blum

Bats: B **Throws:** R **Pos:** 3B-55; SS-44; PH/PR-26; 2B-13; 1B-11   **Ht:** 6'3" **Wt:** 195 **Born:** 4/26/73 **Age:** 28

Year Team	Lg	G	AB	H	2B	3B	HR	(Hm	Rd)	TB	R	RBI	TBB	IBB	SO	HBP	SH	SF	SB	CS	SB%	GDP	Avg	OBP	SLG
1994 Vermont	A-	63	241	83	15	1	3	—	—	109	48	38	33	0	21	3	1	1	5	5	.50	4	.344	.428	.452
1995 Wst Plm Bch	A+	125	457	120	20	1	1	—	—	147	54	42	34	1	61	3	1	7	6	5	.55	12	.263	.313	.322
1996 Harrisburg	AA	120	396	95	22	2	1	—	—	124	47	41	59	2	51	3	11	3	6	7	.46	11	.240	.341	.313
1997 Ottawa	AAA	118	407	101	21	2	3	—	—	135	59	35	52	1	73	3	12	6	14	6	.70	6	.248	.333	.332
1998 Ottawa	AAA	8	23	4	0	0	0	—	—	4	1	1	3	0	6	0	1	0	0	0	—	0	.174	.269	.174
Expos	R	5	18	3	1	1	0	—	—	6	0	1	1	0	4	0	0	0	0	0	—	0	.167	.211	.333
Jupiter	A+	17	58	16	6	0	0	—	—	22	13	5	13	1	14	1	2	1	1	0	1.00	0	.276	.411	.379
Harrisburg	AA	39	139	43	12	3	6	—	—	79	25	21	17	0	24	4	2	0	2	1	.67	3	.309	.400	.568
1999 Ottawa	AAA	77	268	71	14	1	10	—	—	117	43	37	37	1	39	2	3	7	6	1	.86	5	.265	.350	.437
1999 Montreal	NL	45	133	32	7	2	8	(0	8)	67	21	18	17	3	25	0	3	0	1	0	1.00	3	.241	.327	.504
2000 Montreal	NL	124	343	97	20	2	11	(5	6)	154	40	45	26	2	60	3	3	4	1	4	.20	7	.283	.335	.449
2 ML YEARS		169	476	129	27	4	19	(5	14)	221	61	63	43	5	85	3	6	4	2	4	.33	7	.271	.333	.464

Hiram Bocachica

Bats: Right **Throws:** Right **Pos:** PH/PR-7; 2B-2   **Ht:** 5'11" **Wt:** 165 **Born:** 3/4/76 **Age:** 25

Year Team	Lg	G	AB	H	2B	3B	HR	(Hm	Rd)	TB	R	RBI	TBB	IBB	SO	HBP	SH	SF	SB	CS	SB%	GDP	Avg	OBP	SLG
1994 Expos	R	43	168	47	9	3	5	—	—	71	31	16	15	0	42	2	2	0	11	4	.73	1	.280	.346	.423
1995 Albany	A	96	380	108	20	10	2	—	—	154	65	30	52	3	78	8	3	1	47	17	.73	4	.284	.381	.405
1996 Expos	R	9	32	8	3	0	0	—	—	11	11	2	5	1	3	1	0	0	2	1	.67	0	.250	.368	.344
Wst Plm Bch	A+	71	267	90	17	5	2	—	—	123	50	26	34	0	47	6	3	3	21	3	.88	6	.337	.419	.461
1997 Harrisburg	AA	119	443	123	19	3	11	—	—	181	82	35	41	1	98	13	1	3	29	12	.71	3	.278	.354	.409
1998 Harrisburg	AA	80	296	78	18	4	4	—	—	116	39	27	21	2	61	11	2	1	20	8	.71	1	.264	.334	.392
Ottawa	AAA	12	41	8	3	1	0	—	—	13	5	5	6	0	14	1	0	0	2	0	1.00	1	.195	.313	.317
Albuquerque	AAA	26	101	24	7	1	4	—	—	45	16	16	13	1	24	6	1	0	5	3	.63	1	.238	.358	.446
1999 San Antonio	AA	123	477	139	22	10	11	—	—	214	84	60	60	0	71	13	4	5	30	15	.67	5	.291	.382	.449
2000 Albuquerque	AAA	124	482	155	38	4	23	—	—	270	99	84	40	0	100	15	9	2	10	14	.42	7	.322	.390	.560
2000 Los Angeles	NL	8	10	3	0	0	0	(0	0)	3	2	0	0	0	2	0	0	0	0	0	—	0	.300	.300	.300

Doug Bochtler

Pitches: Right **Bats:** Right **Pos:** RP-6   **Ht:** 6'3" **Wt:** 200 **Born:** 7/5/70 **Age:** 30

Year Team	Lg	G	GS	CG	GF	IP	BFP	H	R	ER	HR	SH	SF	HB	TBB	IBB	SO	WP	Bk	W	L	Pct.	ShO	Sv-Op	Hld	ERA
2000 Omaha *	AAA	27	0	0	13	40.1	179	37	19	18	4	1	2	0	28	6	28	3	0	2	1	.667	0	2--	—	4.02
1995 San Diego	NL	34	0	0	11	45.1	181	38	18	18	5	2	0		19	0	45	1	0	4	4	.500	0	1-4	8	3.57
1996 San Diego	NL	63	0	0	17	65.2	278	45	25	22	6	5	2		39	8	68	8	2	2	4	.333	0	3-7	20	3.02
1997 San Diego	NL	54	0	0	13	60.1	281	51	35	32	3	4	3		50	4	46	5	0	3	6	.333	0	2-3	9	4.77
1998 Detroit	AL	51	0	0	11	67.1	312	73	48	46	17	2	3		42	6	45	6	0	0	2	.000	0	0-2	2	6.15

Year Team	Lg	HOW MUCH HE PITCHED G	GS	CG	GF	IP	BFP	WHAT HE GAVE UP H	R	ER	HR	SH	SF	HB	TBB	IBB	SO	WP	Bk	THE RESULTS W	L	Pct.	ShO	Sv-Op	Hld	ERA
1999 Los Angeles	NL	12	0	0	4	13	58	11	8	8	3	1	1	1	6	1	7	1	0	0	0	—	0	0-0	—	5.54
2000 Kansas City	AL	6	0	0	2	8.1	46	13	6	6	1	1	0	0	10	4	4	1	0	0	2	.000	0	0-0	0	6.48
6 ML YEARS		220	0	0	58	260	1156	231	140	132	36	15	10	6	166	23	215	22	2	9	18	.333	0	6-16	39	4.57

Brian Boehringer

Pitches: Right **Bats:** Both **Pos:** RP-4; SP-3   **Ht:** 6'2" **Wt:** 190 **Born:** 1/8/70 **Age:** 31

Year Team	Lg	HOW MUCH HE PITCHED G	GS	CG	GF	IP	BFP	WHAT HE GAVE UP H	R	ER	HR	SH	SF	HB	TBB	IBB	SO	WP	Bk	THE RESULTS W	L	Pct.	ShO	Sv-Op	Hld	ERA
2000 Rancho Cuc *	A+	4	2	0	0	5	24	8	3	3	0	0	0	2	1	0	5	0	0	0	2	.000	0	0--	—	5.40
1995 New York	AL	7	3	0	0	17.2	99	24	27	27	5	0	1	1	22	1	10	3	0	0	3	.000	0	0-1	0	13.75
1996 New York	AL	15	3	0	1	46.1	205	46	28	28	6	3	3	1	21	2	37	1	0	2	4	.333	0	0-1	4	5.44
1997 New York	AL	34	0	0	11	48	210	39	16	14	4	3	2	0	32	6	53	2	0	3	2	.600	0	0-3	5	2.63
1998 San Diego	NL	56	1	0	18	76.1	347	75	38	37	10	5	4	4	45	4	67	1	0	5	2	.714	0	0-1	7	4.36
1999 San Diego	NL	33	11	0	3	94.1	409	97	38	34	10	6	4	1	35	4	64	2	0	6	5	.545	0	0-2	3	3.24
2000 San Diego	NL	7	3	0	1	15.2	74	18	15	10	4	0	1	0	10	0	9	0	0	0	3	.000	0	0-1	0	5.74
6 ML YEARS		152	21	0	39	298.1	1344	299	162	150	39	17	12	7	165	17	240	9	0	16	19	.457	0	0-9	19	4.53

Tim Bogar

Bats: R **Throws:** R **Pos:** SS-95; PH/PR-14; P-2; 2B-2; 3B-1   **Ht:** 6'2" **Wt:** 198 **Born:** 10/28/66 **Age:** 34

Year Team	Lg	BATTING G	AB	H	2B	3B	HR	(Hm	Rd)	TB	R	RBI	TBB	IBB	SO	HBP	SH	SF	BASERUNNING SB	CS	SB%	GDP	PERCENTAGES Avg	OBP	SLG
1993 New York	NL	78	205	50	13	0	3	(1	2)	72	19	25	14	2	29	3	1	1	0	1	.00	2	.244	.300	.351
1994 New York	NL	50	52	8	0	0	2	(0	2)	14	5	5	4	1	11	0	2	1	1	0	1.00	1	.154	.211	.269
1995 New York	NL	78	145	42	7	0	1	(0	1)	52	17	21	9	0	25	0	2	1	1	0	1.00	2	.290	.329	.359
1996 New York	NL	91	89	19	4	0	0	(0	0)	23	17	6	8	0	20	2	3	2	1	3	.25	0	.213	.287	.258
1997 Houston	NL	97	241	60	14	4	4	(3	1)	94	30	30	24	1	42	3	3	4	4	1	.80	4	.249	.320	.390
1998 Houston	NL	79	156	24	4	1	1	(0	1)	33	12	8	9	2	36	2	1	1	2	1	.67	5	.154	.208	.212
1999 Houston	NL	106	309	74	16	2	4	(2	2)	106	44	31	38	5	52	4	0	3	3	5	.38	10	.239	.328	.343
2000 Houston	NL	110	304	63	9	2	7	(3	4)	97	32	33	35	7	56	3	5	4	1	1	.50	15	.207	.292	.319
8 ML YEARS		689	1501	340	67	9	22	(9	13)	491	176	159	141	18	271	17	17	17	13	12	.52	39	.227	.297	.327

Brian Bohanon

Pitches: Left **Bats:** Left **Pos:** SP-26; RP-8   **Ht:** 6'2" **Wt:** 240 **Born:** 8/1/68 **Age:** 32

Year Team	Lg	HOW MUCH HE PITCHED G	GS	CG	GF	IP	BFP	WHAT HE GAVE UP H	R	ER	HR	SH	SF	HB	TBB	IBB	SO	WP	Bk	THE RESULTS W	L	Pct.	ShO	Sv-Op	Hld	ERA
1990 Texas	AL	11	6	0	1	34	158	40	30	25	4	0	3	2	18	0	15	1	0	0	3	.000	0	0-0	0	6.62
1991 Texas	AL	11	11	1	0	61.1	273	66	35	33	4	2	5	2	23	0	34	3	1	4	3	.571	0	0-0	0	4.84
1992 Texas	AL	18	7	0	3	45.2	220	57	38	32	7	0	2	1	25	0	29	2	0	1	1	.500	0	0-0	0	6.31
1993 Texas	AL	36	8	0	4	92.2	418	107	54	49	8	2	5	4	46	3	45	10	0	4	4	.500	0	0-1	1	4.76
1994 Texas	AL	11	5	0	1	37.1	169	51	31	30	7	1	0	1	8	1	26	5	0	2	2	.500	0	0-0	0	7.23
1995 Detroit	AL	52	10	0	7	105.2	474	121	68	65	10	0	5	4	41	5	63	3	0	1	1	.500	0	1-1	10	5.54
1996 Toronto	AL	20	0	0	6	22	112	27	19	19	4	0	2	2	19	4	17	2	0	0	1	.000	0	1-1	2	7.77
1997 New York	NL	19	14	0	0	94.1	412	95	49	40	9	6	0	4	34	2	66	3	1	6	4	.600	0	0-0	0	3.82
1998 NYM-LA	NL	39	18	2	4	151.2	626	121	56	45	13	7	2	11	57	2	111	3	0	7	11	.389	0	0-1	1	2.67
1999 Colorado	NL	33	33	3	0	197.1	903	236	146	136	30	18	3	14	92	1	120	6	0	12	12	.500	1	0-0	0	6.20
2000 Colorado	NL	34	26	2	0	177.1	772	181	101	92	24	4	3	6	79	4	98	2	0	12	10	.545	1	0-0	0	4.68
1998 New York	NL	25	4	0	4	54.1	230	47	21	19	4	2	0	6	21	2	39	1	0	2	4	.333	0	0-1	1	3.15
Los Angeles	NL	14	14	2	0	97.1	396	74	35	26	9	5	2	5	36	0	72	2	0	5	7	.417	0	0-0	0	2.40
11 ML YEARS		284	138	8	26	1019	4537	1102	627	566	122	40	30	51	442	22	624	40	2	49	52	.485	2	2-4	16	5.00

Barry Bonds

Bats: Left **Throws:** Left **Pos:** LF-141; PH/PR-4   **Ht:** 6'2" **Wt:** 210 **Born:** 7/24/64 **Age:** 36

Year Team	Lg	BATTING G	AB	H	2B	3B	HR	(Hm	Rd)	TB	R	RBI	TBB	IBB	SO	HBP	SH	SF	BASERUNNING SB	CS	SB%	GDP	PERCENTAGES Avg	OBP	SLG
1986 Pittsburgh	NL	113	413	92	26	3	16	(9	7)	172	72	48	65	2	102	2	2	2	36	7	.84	4	.223	.330	.416
1987 Pittsburgh	NL	150	551	144	34	9	25	(12	13)	271	99	59	54	3	88	3	0	3	32	10	.76	4	.261	.329	.492
1988 Pittsburgh	NL	144	538	152	30	5	24	(14	10)	264	97	58	72	14	82	2	0	2	17	11	.61	3	.283	.368	.491
1989 Pittsburgh	NL	159	580	144	34	6	19	(7	12)	247	96	58	93	22	93	1	1	4	32	10	.76	9	.248	.351	.426
1990 Pittsburgh	NL	151	519	156	32	3	33	(14	19)	293	104	114	93	15	83	3	0	6	52	13	.80	8	.301	.406	.565
1991 Pittsburgh	NL	153	510	149	28	5	25	(12	13)	262	95	116	107	25	73	4	0	13	43	13	.77	8	.292	.410	.514
1992 Pittsburgh	NL	140	473	147	36	5	34	(15	19)	295	109	103	127	32	69	5	0	7	39	8	.83	9	.311	.456	.624
1993 San Francisco	NL	159	539	181	38	4	46	(21	25)	365	129	123	126	43	79	2	0	7	29	12	.71	11	.336	.458	.677
1994 San Francisco	NL	112	391	122	18	1	37	(15	22)	253	89	81	74	18	43	6	0	3	29	9	.76	3	.312	.426	.647
1995 San Francisco	NL	144	506	149	30	7	33	(16	17)	292	109	104	120	22	83	5	0	4	31	10	.76	12	.294	.431	.577
1996 San Francisco	NL	158	517	159	27	3	42	(23	19)	318	122	129	151	30	76	1	0	6	40	7	.85	11	.308	.461	.615
1997 San Francisco	NL	159	532	155	26	5	40	(24	16)	311	123	101	145	34	87	8	0	5	37	8	.82	13	.291	.446	.585
1998 San Francisco	NL	156	552	167	44	7	37	(21	16)	336	120	122	130	29	92	8	1	6	28	12	.70	15	.303	.438	.609
1999 San Francisco	NL	102	355	93	20	2	34	(16	18)	219	91	83	73	9	62	3	0	3	15	2	.88	6	.262	.389	.617
2000 San Francisco	NL	143	480	147	28	4	49	(25	24)	330	129	106	117	22	77	3	0	7	11	3	.79	6	.306	.440	.688
15 ML YEARS		2143	7456	2157	451	69	494	(244	250)	4228	1584	1405	1547	320	1189	56	4	78	471	135	.78	122	.289	.412	.567

Ricky Bones

Pitches: Right **Bats:** Right **Pos:** RP-56   **Ht:** 6'0" **Wt:** 202 **Born:** 4/7/69 **Age:** 32

Year Team	Lg	HOW MUCH HE PITCHED G	GS	CG	GF	IP	BFP	WHAT HE GAVE UP H	R	ER	HR	SH	SF	HB	TBB	IBB	SO	WP	Bk	THE RESULTS W	L	Pct.	ShO	Sv-Op	Hld	ERA
1991 San Diego	NL	11	11	0	0	54	234	57	33	29	3	0	4	0	18	0	31	4	0	4	6	.400	0	0-0	0	4.83
1992 Milwaukee	AL	31	28	0	0	163.1	705	169	90	83	27	2	5	9	48	0	65	3	2	9	10	.474	0	0-0	0	4.57
1993 Milwaukee	AL	32	31	3	1	203.2	883	222	122	110	28	5	7	8	63	3	63	6	1	11	11	.500	0	0-0	0	4.86

		HOW MUCH HE PITCHED						WHAT HE GAVE UP												THE RESULTS						
Year Team	Lg	G	GS	CG	GF	IP	BFP	H	R	ER	HR	SH	SF	HB	TBB	IBB	SO	WP	Bk	W	L	Pct.	ShO	Sv-Op	Hld	ERA
1994 Milwaukee	AL	24	24	4	0	170.2	708	166	76	65	17	4	5	3	45	1	57	8	0	10	9	.526	1	0-0	0	3.43
1995 Milwaukee	AL	32	31	3	0	200.1	877	218	108	103	26	3	11	4	83	2	77	5	2	10	12	.455	0	0-0	0	4.63
1996 Mil-NYY	AL	36	24	0	2	152	699	184	115	105	30	5	5	10	68	2	63	2	0	7	14	.333	0	0-0	3	6.22
1997 Cin-KC		30	13	1	4	96	450	133	81	72	12	3	8	7	36	4	44	1	0	4	8	.333	0	0-1	2	6.75
1998 Kansas City	AL	32	0	0	12	53.1	231	49	18	18	4	5	0	1	24	5	38	2	0	2	2	.500	0	1-2	3	3.04
1999 Baltimore	AL	30	0	0	7	43.2	207	59	29	29	7	2	1	2	19	0	26	3	0	0	3	.000	0	0-3	5	5.98
2000 Florida	NL	56	0	0	13	77.1	352	94	43	39	6	6	6	3	27	8	59	2	1	2	3	.400	0	0-3	6	4.54
1996 Milwaukee	AL	32	23	0	2	145	658	170	104	94	28	4	4	9	62	2	59	2	0	7	14	.333	0	0-0	3	5.83
New York	AL	4	1	0	0	7	41	14	11	11	2	1	1	1	6	0	4	0	0	0	0	—	0	0-0	0	14.14
1997 Cincinnati	NL	9	2	0	2	17.2	98	31	22	20	2	1	2	2	11	2	8	0	0	0	1	.000	0	0-0	0	10.19
Kansas City	AL	21	11	1	2	78.1	352	102	59	52	10	2	6	5	25	2	36	1	0	4	7	.364	0	0-1	2	5.97
10 ML YEARS		314	164	11	39	1214.1	5346	1351	715	653	160	35	52	47	431	25	523	36	6	59	78	.431	1	1-9	17	4.84

Bobby Bonilla

Bats: B Throws: R Pos: LF-63; PH/PR-48; DH-1; 3B-1; RF-1   Ht: 6'3" Wt: 240 Born: 2/23/63 Age: 38

		BATTING																BASERUNNING				PERCENTAGES		
Year Team	Lg	G	AB	H	2B	3B	HR	(Hm	Rd)	TB	R	RBI	TBB	IBB	SO	HBP	SH	SF	SB	CS	SB%	GDP	Avg	OBP	SLG
1986 CWS-Pit		138	426	109	16	4	3	(2	1)	142	55	43	62	3	88	2	5	1	8	5	.62	9	.256	.352	.333
1987 Pittsburgh	NL	141	466	140	33	3	15	(7	8)	224	58	77	39	4	64	2	0	8	3	5	.38	8	.300	.351	.481
1988 Pittsburgh	NL	159	584	160	32	7	24	(9	15)	278	87	100	85	19	82	4	0	8	3	5	.38	4	.274	.366	.476
1989 Pittsburgh	NL	163	616	173	37	10	24	(13	11)	302	96	86	76	20	93	1	0	5	8	8	.50	10	.281	.358	.490
1990 Pittsburgh	NL	160	625	175	39	7	32	(13	19)	324	112	120	45	9	103	1	0	15	4	3	.57	11	.280	.322	.518
1991 Pittsburgh	NL	157	577	174	44	6	18	(9	9)	284	102	100	90	8	67	2	0	11	2	4	.33	14	.302	.391	.492
1992 New York	NL	128	438	109	23	0	19	(5	14)	189	62	70	66	10	73	1	0	1	4	3	.57	11	.249	.348	.432
1993 New York	NL	139	502	133	21	3	34	(18	16)	262	81	87	72	11	96	0	0	8	3	3	.50	12	.265	.352	.522
1994 New York	NL	108	403	117	24	1	20	(8	12)	203	60	67	55	9	101	0	0	2	1	3	.25	10	.290	.374	.504
1995 NYM-Bal		141	554	182	37	8	28	(14	14)	319	96	99	54	10	79	2	0	4	0	5	.00	22	.329	.388	.576
1996 Baltimore	AL	159	595	171	27	5	28	(9	19)	292	107	116	75	7	85	5	0	17	1	3	.25	13	.287	.363	.491
1997 Florida	NL	153	562	167	39	3	17	(8	9)	263	77	96	73	8	94	5	0	5	6	6	.50	18	.297	.378	.468
1998 Fla-LA		100	333	83	11	1	11	(8	3)	129	39	45	41	4	59	0	0	6	1	2	.33	16	.249	.326	.387
1999 New York	NL	60	119	19	5	0	4	(2	2)	36	12	18	19	1	16	1	0	2	0	1	.00	4	.160	.277	.303
2000 Atlanta	NL	114	239	61	13	3	5	(4	1)	95	23	28	37	2	51	1	0	1	0	0	—	3	.255	.356	.397
1986 Chicago	AL	75	234	63	10	2	2	(2	0)	83	27	26	33	2	49	1	2	1	4	1	.80	4	.269	.361	.355
Pittsburgh	NL	63	192	46	6	2	1	(0	1)	59	28	17	29	1	39	1	3	0	4	4	.50	5	.240	.342	.307
1995 New York	NL	80	317	103	25	4	18	(7	11)	190	49	53	31	10	48	1	0	2	0	3	.00	11	.325	.385	.599
Baltimore	AL	61	237	79	12	4	10	(7	3)	129	47	46	23	0	31	1	0	2	0	2	.00	11	.333	.392	.544
1998 Florida	NL	28	97	27	5	0	4	(3	1)	44	11	15	12	1	22	0	0	1	0	0	.00	6	.278	.355	.454
Los Angeles	NL	72	236	56	6	1	7	(5	2)	85	28	30	29	3	37	0	0	5	1	1	.50	10	.237	.315	.360
15 ML YEARS		2020	7039	1973	401	61	282	(129	153)	3342	1067	1152	889	125	1151	27	5	97	44	56	.44	165	.280	.359	.475

Aaron Boone

Bats: Right Throws: Right Pos: 3B-84; SS-2; PH/PR-1   Ht: 6'2" Wt: 200 Born: 3/9/73 Age: 28

		BATTING																BASERUNNING				PERCENTAGES		
Year Team	Lg	G	AB	H	2B	3B	HR	(Hm	Rd)	TB	R	RBI	TBB	IBB	SO	HBP	SH	SF	SB	CS	SB%	GDP	Avg	OBP	SLG
1997 Cincinnati	NL	16	49	12	1	0	0	(0	0)	13	5	5	2	0	5	0	1	0	1	0	1.00	1	.245	.275	.265
1998 Cincinnati	NL	58	181	51	13	2	2	(2	0)	74	24	28	15	1	36	5	3	2	6	1	.86	3	.282	.350	.409
1999 Cincinnati	NL	139	472	132	26	5	14	(7	7)	210	56	72	30	2	79	8	5	5	17	6	.74	6	.280	.330	.445
2000 Cincinnati	NL	84	291	83	18	0	12	(5	7)	137	44	43	24	1	52	10	2	4	6	1	.86	5	.285	.356	.471
4 ML YEARS		297	993	278	58	7	28	(14	14)	434	129	148	71	4	172	23	11	11	30	8	.79	15	.280	.339	.437

Bret Boone

Bats: Right Throws: Right Pos: 2B-126; PH/PR-1   Ht: 5'10" Wt: 180 Born: 4/6/69 Age: 32

		BATTING																BASERUNNING				PERCENTAGES		
Year Team	Lg	G	AB	H	2B	3B	HR	(Hm	Rd)	TB	R	RBI	TBB	IBB	SO	HBP	SH	SF	SB	CS	SB%	GDP	Avg	OBP	SLG
1992 Seattle	AL	33	129	25	4	0	4	(2	2)	41	15	15	4	0	34	1	1	0	1	1	.50	4	.194	.224	.318
1993 Seattle	AL	76	271	68	12	2	12	(7	5)	120	31	38	17	1	52	4	6	4	3	2	.40	6	.251	.301	.443
1994 Cincinnati	NL	108	381	122	25	2	12	(5	7)	187	59	68	24	1	74	8	5	6	3	4	.43	10	.320	.368	.491
1995 Cincinnati	NL	138	513	137	34	2	15	(9	6)	220	63	68	41	0	84	6	5	5	5	1	.83	14	.267	.326	.429
1996 Cincinnati	NL	142	520	121	21	3	12	(7	5)	184	56	69	31	0	100	3	5	9	3	2	.60	8	.233	.275	.354
1997 Cincinnati	NL	139	442	99	25	1	7	(4	3)	147	40	46	45	4	101	4	4	5	5	5	.50	11	.223	.298	.332
1998 Cincinnati	NL	157	583	155	38	1	24	(13	11)	267	76	95	48	3	104	4	9	4	6	4	.60	23	.266	.324	.458
1999 Atlanta	NL	152	608	153	38	1	20	(9	11)	253	102	63	47	0	112	5	9	2	14	9	.61	11	.252	.310	.416
2000 San Diego	NL	127	463	116	18	2	19	(8	11)	195	61	74	50	7	97	5	0	7	4	4	.67	11	.251	.326	.421
9 ML YEARS		1072	3911	996	215	14	125	(61	64)	1614	503	536	307	16	758	40	44	42	47	33	.59	99	.255	.312	.413

Pedro Borbon

Pitches: Left Bats: Left Pos: RP-59   Ht: 6'1" Wt: 205 Born: 11/15/67 Age: 33

		HOW MUCH HE PITCHED						WHAT HE GAVE UP												THE RESULTS						
Year Team	Lg	G	GS	CG	GF	IP	BFP	H	R	ER	HR	SH	SF	HB	TBB	IBB	SO	WP	Bk	W	L	Pct.	ShO	Sv-Op	Hld	ERA
1992 Atlanta	NL	2	0	0	2	1.1	7	2	1	1	0	0	0	0	1	1	1	0	0	0	1	.000	0	0-0	0	6.75
1993 Atlanta	NL	3	0	0	1	1.2	11	3	4	4	0	1	0	0	3	0	2	0	0	0	0	—	0	0-0	0	21.60
1995 Atlanta	NL	41	0	0	19	32	143	29	12	11	2	3	1	1	17	4	33	0	1	2	2	.500	0	2-4	6	3.09
1996 Atlanta	NL	43	0	0	19	36	140	26	12	11	1	4	0	1	7	0	31	0	0	3	0	1.000	0	1-1	4	2.75
1999 Los Angeles	NL	70	0	0	11	50.2	220	39	23	23	5	0	3	1	29	1	33	1	0	4	3	.571	0	1-2	15	4.09
2000 Toronto	AL	59	0	0	6	41.2	213	45	37	30	5	2	7	5	38	5	29	0	0	1	1	.500	0	1-1	12	6.48
6 ML YEARS		218	0	0	57	163.1	734	144	89	80	13	10	11	8	95	11	129	1	1	10	7	.588	0	5-8	37	4.41

Mike Bordick

Bats: Right **Throws:** Right **Pos:** SS-156   **Ht:** 5'11" **Wt:** 175 **Born:** 7/21/65 **Age:** 35

Year Team	Lg	G	AB	H	2B	3B	HR	(Hm Rd)	TB	R	RBI	TBB	IBB	SO	HBP	SH	SF	SB	CS	SB%	GDP	Avg	OBP	SLG
1990 Oakland	AL	25	14	1	0	0	0	(0 0)	1	0	0	1	0	4	0	0	0	0	0	—	0	.071	.133	.071
1991 Oakland	AL	90	235	56	5	1	0	(0 0)	63	21	21	14	0	37	3	12	1	3	4	.43	3	.238	.289	.268
1992 Oakland	AL	154	504	151	19	4	3	(3 0)	187	62	48	40	2	59	9	14	5	12	6	.67	10	.300	.358	.371
1993 Oakland	AL	159	546	136	21	2	3	(2 1)	170	60	48	60	2	58	11	10	6	10	10	.50	9	.249	.332	.311
1994 Oakland	AL	114	391	99	18	4	2	(1 1)	131	38	37	38	1	44	3	3	5	7	2	.78	9	.253	.320	.335
1995 Oakland	AL	126	428	113	13	0	8	(2 6)	150	46	44	35	2	48	5	7	3	11	3	.79	8	.264	.325	.350
1996 Oakland	AL	155	525	126	18	4	5	(2 3)	167	46	54	52	0	59	1	4	5	5	6	.45	8	.240	.307	.318
1997 Baltimore	AL	153	509	120	19	1	7	(5 2)	162	55	46	33	1	66	2	12	4	0	2	.00	23	.236	.283	.318
1998 Baltimore	AL	151	465	121	29	1	13	(10 3)	191	59	51	39	0	65	10	15	4	6	7	.46	13	.260	.328	.411
1999 Baltimore	AL	160	631	175	35	7	10	(3 7)	254	93	77	54	1	102	5	8	10	14	4	.78	25	.277	.334	.403
2000 Bal-NYM		156	583	166	30	1	20	(9 11)	258	88	80	49	0	99	3	4	5	9	6	.60	16	.285	.341	.443
2000 Baltimore	AL	100	391	116	22	1	16	(6 10)	188	70	59	34	0	71	1	2	5	6	5	.55	12	.297	.350	.481
New York	NL	56	192	50	8	0	4	(3 1)	70	18	21	15	0	28	2	2	0	3	1	.75	4	.260	.321	.365
11 ML YEARS		1443	4831	1264	207	25	71	(37 34)	1734	568	506	415	9	641	52	89	48	77	50	.61	124	.262	.324	.359

Dave Borkowski

Pitches: Right **Bats:** Right **Pos:** SP-1; RP-1   **Ht:** 6'1" **Wt:** 200 **Born:** 2/7/77 **Age:** 24

Year Team	Lg	G	GS	CG	GF	IP	BFP	H	R	ER	HR	SH	SF	HB	TBB	IBB	SO	WP	Bk	W	L	Pct.	ShO	Sv-Op	Hld	ERA
1995 Tigers	R	10	10	1	0	51.2	212	45	24	17	2	1	0	5	8	0	36	1	2	3	2	.600	0	0--	—	2.96
Lakeland	A+	1	1	0	0	5	17	2	0	0	0	0	0	0	1	0	3	0	0	1	0	1.000	0	0--	—	0.00
1996 Fayettevlle	A	27	27	5	0	178.1	739	158	85	66	7	4	5	15	54	0	117	12	3	10	10	.500	0	0--	—	3.33
1997 W Michigan	A	25	25	4	0	164	670	143	79	63	15	3	3	7	31	0	104	7	0	15	3	.833	2	0--	—	3.46
1998 Jacksnville	AA	28	28	3	0	178.2	775	204	99	92	25	2	7	10	54	0	97	10	2	16	7	.696	1	0--	—	4.63
1999 Toledo	AAA	19	19	3	0	126	530	119	59	49	16	0	3	10	43	0	94	10	0	6	8	.429	0	0--	—	3.50
2000 Toledo	AAA	8	8	0	0	47	202	44	27	23	9	0	1	3	14	0	29	2	0	3	1	.750	0	0--	—	4.40
Tigers	R	3	3	0	0	8	32	7	3	2	0	0	0	0	0	0	6	0	0	0	0	—	0	0--	—	2.25
Lakeland	A+	2	2	0	0	7.1	35	11	7	7	1	0	0	0	4	0	5	0	0	0	1	.000	0	0--	—	8.59
1999 Detroit	AL	17	12	0	2	76.2	351	86	58	52	10	1	2	4	40	0	50	3	0	2	6	.250	0	0-0	0	6.10
2000 Detroit	AL	2	1	0	0	5.1	34	11	13	13	2	0	1	0	7	1	1	0	0	0	1	.000	0	0-0	0	21.94
2 ML YEARS		19	13	0	2	82	385	97	71	65	12	1	3	4	47	1	51	3	0	2	7	.222	0	0-0	0	7.13

Ricky Bottalico

Pitches: Right **Bats:** Left **Pos:** RP-62   **Ht:** 6'1" **Wt:** 215 **Born:** 8/26/69 **Age:** 31

Year Team	Lg	G	GS	CG	GF	IP	BFP	H	R	ER	HR	SH	SF	HB	TBB	IBB	SO	WP	Bk	W	L	Pct.	ShO	Sv-Op	Hld	ERA
1994 Philadelphia	NL	3	0	0	3	3	13	3	0	0	0	0	0	0	1	0	3	0	0	0	0	—	0	0-0	0	0.00
1995 Philadelphia	NL	62	0	0	20	87.2	350	50	25	24	7	3	1	4	42	3	87	1	0	5	3	.625	0	1-5	20	2.46
1996 Philadelphia	NL	61	0	0	56	67.2	269	47	24	24	6	4	2	2	23	2	74	3	0	4	5	.444	0	34-38	0	3.19
1997 Philadelphia	NL	69	0	0	61	74	324	68	31	30	7	1	2	2	42	4	89	3	0	2	5	.286	0	34-41	0	3.65
1998 Philadelphia	NL	39	0	0	28	43.1	206	54	31	31	7	1	2	1	25	5	27	2	0	1	5	.167	0	6-7	3	6.44
1999 St. Louis	NL	68	0	0	40	73.1	347	83	45	40	8	3	0	3	49	1	66	6	0	3	7	.300	0	20-28	8	4.91
2000 Kansas City	AL	62	0	0	50	72.2	319	65	40	39	12	3	1	2	41	3	56	5	1	9	6	.600	0	16-23	1	4.83
7 ML YEARS		364	0	0	258	421.2	1828	370	196	188	47	15	8	14	223	18	402	20	1	24	31	.436	0	111-142	32	4.01

Kent Bottenfield

Pitches: Right **Bats:** Right **Pos:** SP-29   **Ht:** 6'3" **Wt:** 240 **Born:** 11/14/68 **Age:** 32

Year Team	Lg	G	GS	CG	GF	IP	BFP	H	R	ER	HR	SH	SF	HB	TBB	IBB	SO	WP	Bk	W	L	Pct.	ShO	Sv-Op	Hld	ERA
1992 Montreal	NL	10	4	0	2	32.1	135	26	9	8	7	1	2	1	11	1	14	0	0	1	2	.333	0	1-1	1	2.23
1993 Mon-Col	NL	37	25	1	2	159.2	710	179	102	90	24	21	4	6	71	3	63	4	1	5	10	.333	0	0-0	0	5.07
1994 Col-SF	NL	16	1	0	3	26.1	121	33	18	18	2	1	0	2	10	0	15	2	0	3	1	.750	0	1-1	0	6.15
1996 Chicago	NL	48	0	0	10	61.2	258	59	25	18	3	5	0	3	19	4	33	2	0	3	5	.375	0	1-3	4	2.63
1997 Chicago	NL	64	0	0	20	84	361	82	39	36	13	4	4	2	35	7	74	2	0	2	3	.400	0	2-4	8	3.86
1998 St. Louis	NL	44	17	0	11	133.2	578	128	72	66	13	11	3	4	57	3	98	3	2	4	6	.400	0	4-5	5	4.44
1999 St. Louis	NL	31	31	0	0	190.1	843	197	91	84	21	11	9	5	89	5	124	1	0	18	7	.720	0	0-0	0	3.97
2000 Ana-Phi		29	29	1	0	171.2	765	185	106	103	30	2	7	3	77	4	106	1	0	8	10	.444	1	0-0	0	5.40
1993 Montreal	NL	23	11	0	2	83	373	93	49	38	11	11	1	5	33	2	33	4	1	2	5	.286	0	0-0	0	4.12
Colorado	NL	14	14	1	0	76.2	337	86	53	52	13	10	3	1	38	1	30	0	0	3	5	.375	0	0-0	0	6.10
1994 Colorado	NL	15	1	0	3	24.2	112	28	16	16	1	1	0	2	10	0	15	2	0	3	1	.750	0	1-1	0	5.84
San Francisco	NL	1	0	0	0	1.2	9	5	2	2	1	0	0	0	0	0	0	0	0	0	0	—	0	0-0	0	10.80
2000 Anaheim	AL	21	21	0	0	127.2	571	144	82	81	25	2	5	3	56	4	75	1	0	7	8	.467	0	0-0	0	5.71
Philadelphia	NL	8	8	1	0	44	194	41	24	22	5	0	2	0	21	0	31	0	0	1	2	.333	0	0-0	0	4.50
8 ML YEARS		279	107	2	48	859.2	3771	889	462	423	107	56	29	26	369	27	527	15	3	44	44	.500	1	9-14	19	4.43

Jason Boyd

Pitches: Right **Bats:** Right **Pos:** RP-30   **Ht:** 6'3" **Wt:** 173 **Born:** 2/23/73 **Age:** 28

Year Team	Lg	G	GS	CG	GF	IP	BFP	H	R	ER	HR	SH	SF	HB	TBB	IBB	SO	WP	Bk	W	L	Pct.	ShO	Sv-Op	Hld	ERA
1994 Martinsvlle	R+	14	13	1	0	69	306	65	46	32	6	0	1	4	32	0	45	7	6	3	7	.300	0	0--	—	4.17
1995 Piedmont	A	26	24	1	1	151	638	151	77	60	8	5	3	4	44	0	129	18	2	6	8	.429	0	0--	—	3.58
1996 Clearwater	A+	26	26	2	0	161.2	674	160	75	70	12	3	6	3	49	1	120	7	1	11	8	.579	0	0--	—	3.90
1997 Reading	AA	48	7	0	9	115.2	509	113	65	62	16	2	3	3	64	7	98	1	2	10	6	.625	0	0--	—	4.82
1998 Tucson	AAA	15	0	0	3	21.2	109	28	22	15	4	0	0	1	14	1	13	0	1	2	2	.500	0	0--	—	6.23
1999 Tucson	AAA	44	0	0	17	75.2	325	76	42	38	6	2	4	3	27	2	60	6	2	6	5	.545	0	5--	—	4.52
Nashville	AAA	5	0	0	2	4.2	14	2	0	0	0	0	0	0	0	0	3	0	0	0	0	—	0	0--	—	0.00
2000 Clearwater	A+	6	3	0	1	11.1	50	11	4	3	0	0	0	2	4	0	12	0	1	1	0	1.000	0	0--	—	2.38
Scrantn-WB	AAA	11	2	0	1	15.2	66	8	3	3	0	1	0	0	14	0	10	1	0	1	0	1.000	0	0--	—	1.72

Year Team	Lg	G	GS	CG	GF	IP	BFP	H	R	ER	HR	SH	SF	HB	TBB	IBB	SO	WP	Bk	W	L	Pct.	ShO	Sv-Op	Hld	ERA
1999 Pittsburgh	NL	4	0	0	0	5.1	24	5	2	2	0	0	1	1	2	0	4	1	0	0	0	—	0	0-0	0	3.38
2000 Philadelphia	NL	30	0	0	11	34.1	161	39	28	25	2	3	0	1	24	4	32	1	0	0	1	.000	0	0-1	2	6.55
2 ML YEARS		34	0	0	11	39.2	185	44	30	27	2	3	1	2	26	4	36	2	0	0	1	.000	0	0-1	2	6.13

Chad Bradford

Pitches: Right **Bats:** Right **Pos:** RP-12   **Ht:** 6'5" **Wt:** 205 **Born:** 9/14/74 **Age:** 26

Year Team	Lg	G	GS	CG	GF	IP	BFP	H	R	ER	HR	SH	SF	HB	TBB	IBB	SO	WP	Bk	W	L	Pct.	ShO	Sv-Op	Hld	ERA
2000 Charlotte *	AAA	55	0	0	25	53.2	212	38	18	9	2	5	2	3	12	1	42	1	0	2	4	.333	0	10--	-	1.51
1998 Chicago	AL	29	0	0	8	30.2	125	27	16	11	0	0	0	0	7	0	11	1	1	2	1	.667	0	1-3	9	3.23
1999 Chicago	AL	3	0	0	0	3.2	24	9	8	8	1	0	0	0	5	0	0	1	0	0	0	—	0	0-0	0	19.64
2000 Chicago	AL	12	0	0	5	13.2	52	13	4	3	0	0	0	0	1	1	9	0	0	1	0	1.000	0	0-0	2	1.98
3 ML YEARS		44	0	0	13	48	201	49	28	22	1	0	0	0	13	1	20	2	1	3	1	.750	0	1-3	11	4.13

Milton Bradley

Bats: Both **Throws:** Right **Pos:** CF-40; PH/PR-1   **Ht:** 6'0" **Wt:** 180 **Born:** 4/15/78 **Age:** 23

Year Team	Lg	G	AB	H	2B	3B	HR	(Hm	Rd)	TB	R	RBI	TBB	IBB	SO	HBP	SH	SF	SB	CS	SB%	GDP	Avg	OBP	SLG
1996 Expos	R	31	109	27	7	1	1	—	—	39	18	12	13	0	14	1	1	2	7	4	.64	2	.248	.328	.358
1997 Vermont	A-	50	200	60	7	5	3	—	—	86	29	30	17	1	34	0	1	2	7	7	.50	6	.300	.352	.430
Expos	R	9	25	5	2	0	1	—	—	10	6	2	4	0	4	1	0	0	2	2	.50	0	.200	.333	.400
1998 Cape Fear	A	75	281	85	21	4	6	—	—	132	54	50	23	1	57	4	3	3	13	8	.62	7	.302	.360	.470
Jupiter	A+	67	261	75	14	1	5	—	—	106	55	34	30	2	42	5	1	2	17	9	.65	3	.287	.369	.406
1999 Harrisburg	AA	87	346	114	22	5	12	—	—	182	62	50	33	0	61	3	1	2	14	10	.58	5	.329	.391	.526
2000 Ottawa	AAA	88	342	104	20	1	6	—	—	144	58	29	45	3	56	1	1	2	10	15	.40	5	.304	.385	.421
2000 Montreal	NL	42	154	34	8	1	2	(1	1)	50	20	15	14	0	32	1	1	1	2	1	.67	3	.221	.288	.325

Darren Bragg

Bats: Left **Throws:** Right **Pos:** LF-34; PH/PR-31; RF-9   **Ht:** 5'9" **Wt:** 180 **Born:** 9/7/69 **Age:** 31

Year Team	Lg	G	AB	H	2B	3B	HR	(Hm	Rd)	TB	R	RBI	TBB	IBB	SO	HBP	SH	SF	SB	CS	SB%	GDP	Avg	OBP	SLG
1994 Seattle	AL	8	19	3	1	0	0	(0	0)	4	4	2	2	1	5	0	0	0	0	0	—	0	.158	.238	.211
1995 Seattle	AL	52	145	34	5	1	3	(1	2)	50	20	12	18	1	37	4	1	2	9	0	1.00	6	.234	.331	.345
1996 Sea-Bos	AL	127	417	109	26	2	10	(7	3)	169	74	47	69	6	74	4	2	7	14	9	.61	5	.261	.366	.405
1997 Boston	AL	153	513	132	35	2	9	(6	3)	198	65	57	61	5	102	3	5	4	10	6	.63	16	.257	.337	.386
1998 Boston	AL	129	409	114	29	3	8	(3	5)	173	51	57	42	0	99	6	4	4	5	3	.63	16	.279	.351	.423
1999 St. Louis	NL	93	273	71	12	1	6	(4	2)	103	38	26	44	1	67	3	5	0	3	0	1.00	5	.260	.369	.377
2000 Colorado	NL	71	149	33	7	1	3	(3	0)	51	16	21	17	1	41	0	0	3	4	1	.80	5	.221	.296	.342
1996 Seattle	AL	69	195	53	12	1	7	(4	3)	88	36	25	33	4	35	2	1	4	8	5	.62	2	.272	.376	.451
Boston	AL	58	222	56	14	1	3	(3	0)	81	38	22	36	2	39	2	1	3	6	4	.60	3	.252	.357	.365
7 ML YEARS		633	1925	496	115	10	39	(21	18)	748	268	222	253	15	425	20	17	20	45	19	.70	47	.258	.347	.389

Jeff Branson

Bats: L **Throws:** R **Pos:** SS-7; PH/PR-5; 2B-3; 3B-3   **Ht:** 6'0" **Wt:** 180 **Born:** 1/26/67 **Age:** 34

Year Team	Lg	G	AB	H	2B	3B	HR	(Hm	Rd)	TB	R	RBI	TBB	IBB	SO	HBP	SH	SF	SB	CS	SB%	GDP	Avg	OBP	SLG
2000 Albuquerque *	AAA	108	332	96	23	2	5			138	45	41	27	3	71	0	2	4	6	4	.60	3	.289	.339	.416
1992 Cincinnati	NL	72	115	34	7	1	0	(0	0)	43	12	15	5	2	16	0	2	1	0	1	.00	4	.296	.322	.374
1993 Cincinnati	NL	125	381	92	15	1	3	(2	1)	118	40	22	19	2	73	0	8	4	4	1	.80	4	.241	.275	.310
1994 Cincinnati	NL	58	109	31	4	1	6	(1	5)	55	18	16	5	2	16	0	2	0	0	0	—	4	.284	.316	.505
1995 Cincinnati	NL	122	331	86	18	2	12	(9	3)	144	43	45	44	14	69	2	1	6	2	1	.67	9	.260	.345	.435
1996 Cincinnati	NL	129	311	76	16	4	9	(5	4)	127	34	37	31	4	67	1	7	3	2	0	1.00	9	.244	.312	.408
1997 Cin-Cle		94	170	34	7	1	3	(3	0)	52	14	12	14	1	40	1	1	2	1	2	.33	4	.200	.262	.306
1998 Cleveland	AL	63	100	20	4	1	1	(1	0)	29	6	9	3	0	21	0	1	1	0	0	—	1	.200	.221	.290
2000 Los Angeles	NL	18	17	4	1	0	0	(0	0)	5	3	0	1	0	6	0	0	0	0	0	—	1	.235	.278	.294
1997 Cincinnati	NL	65	98	15	3	1	1	(1	0)	23	9	7	7	1	23	0	1	0	1	2	.33	4	.153	.210	.235
Cleveland	AL	29	72	19	4	0	2	(2	0)	29	5	7	7	0	17	1	0	2	0	0	—	0	.264	.329	.403
8 ML YEARS		681	1534	377	72	11	34	(21	13)	573	170	156	122	25	308	4	22	17	9	5	.64	36	.246	.300	.374

Jeff Brantley

Pitches: Right **Bats:** Right **Pos:** RP-55   **Ht:** 5'10" **Wt:** 197 **Born:** 9/5/63 **Age:** 37

Year Team	Lg	G	GS	CG	GF	IP	BFP	H	R	ER	HR	SH	SF	HB	TBB	IBB	SO	WP	Bk	W	L	Pct.	ShO	Sv-Op	Hld	ERA
2000 Clearwater *	A+	9	1	0	0	6	24	5	2	2	0	0	0	0	3	0	5	1	0	2	0	1.000	0	0--	—	3.00
Scrantn-WB *	AAA	5	1	0	1	5	19	3	2	2	1	0	0	0	1	0	4	0	0	0	0	—	0	0--	—	3.60
1988 San Francisco	NL	9	1	0	2	20.2	88	22	13	13	2	1	0	1	6	1	11	0	1	0	1	.000	0	0--	0	5.66
1989 San Francisco	NL	59	1	0	15	97.1	422	101	50	44	10	7	3	2	37	8	69	3	2	7	1	.875	0	0-1	11	4.07
1990 San Francisco	NL	55	0	0	32	86.2	361	77	18	15	3	2	2	3	33	6	61	0	3	5	3	.625	0	19-24	8	1.56
1991 San Francisco	NL	67	0	0	39	95.1	411	78	27	26	8	4	4	5	52	10	81	6	0	5	2	.714	0	15-19	12	2.45
1992 San Francisco	NL	56	4	0	32	91.2	381	67	32	30	8	7	3	4	45	5	86	3	1	7	7	.500	0	7-9	2	2.95
1993 San Francisco	NL	53	12	0	9	113.2	496	112	60	54	19	5	5	7	46	2	76	3	4	5	6	.455	0	0-3	10	4.28
1994 Cincinnati	NL	50	0	0	35	65.1	262	46	20	18	6	5	1	0	28	5	63	1	0	6	6	.500	0	15-21	7	2.48
1995 Cincinnati	NL	56	0	0	49	70.1	283	53	22	22	11	2	3	1	20	3	62	2	1	3	2	.600	0	28-32	0	2.82
1996 Cincinnati	NL	66	0	0	61	71	288	54	21	19	7	4	5	0	28	6	76	2	0	1	2	.333	0	44-49	0	2.41
1997 Cincinnati	NL	13	0	0	9	11.2	53	9	5	5	2	0	0	2	7	1	16	2	0	1	1	.500	0	1-3	0	3.86
1998 St. Louis	NL	48	0	0	33	50.2	209	40	26	25	12	5	3	1	18	3	48	1	0	0	5	.000	0	14-22	3	4.44
1999 Philadelphia	NL	10	0	0	9	8.2	40	5	6	5	0	1	1	0	8	0	11	0	0	1	2	.333	0	5-6	0	5.19
2000 Philadelphia	NL	55	0	0	47	55.1	256	64	36	36	12	1	2	3	29	0	57	2	0	2	7	.222	0	23-28	1	5.86
13 ML YEARS		597	18	0	372	838.1	3550	728	336	312	100	43	32	27	357	50	717	25	13	43	45	.489	0	172-218	49	3.35

Russ Branyan

Bats: L **Throws:** R **Pos:** DH-23; LF-18; RF-15; PH/PR-12; 3B-1   **Ht:** 6'3" **Wt:** 195 **Born:** 12/19/75 **Age:** 25

Year Team	Lg	G	AB	H	2B	3B	HR	(Hm	Rd)	TB	R	RBI	TBB	IBB	SO	HBP	SH	SF	SB	CS	SB%	GDP	Avg	OBP	SLG
1994 Burlington	R+	55	171	36	10	0	5	—	—	61	21	13	25	2	64	4	0	1	4	2	.67	3	.211	.323	.357
1995 Columbus	A	76	277	71	8	6	19	—	—	148	46	55	27	2	120	3	0	3	1	1	.50	6	.256	.326	.534
1996 Columbus	A	130	482	129	20	4	40	—	—	277	102	106	62	5	166	5	0	3	7	4	.64	1	.268	.355	.575
1997 Kinston	A+	83	297	86	26	2	27	—	—	197	59	75	52	4	94	5	0	5	3	1	.75	9	.290	.398	.663
Akron	AA	41	137	32	4	0	12	—	—	72	26	30	28	1	56	2	0	1	0	0	—	1	.234	.369	.526
1998 Akron	AA	43	163	48	11	3	16	—	—	113	35	46	35	4	58	0	0	1	1	1	.50	2	.294	.417	.693
1999 Buffalo	AAA	109	395	82	11	1	30	—	—	185	51	67	52	2	187	4	0	2	8	3	.73	5	.208	.305	.468
2000 Buffalo	AAA	64	229	56	9	2	21	—	—	132	46	60	28	0	93	2	0	2	1	1	.50	2	.245	.330	.576
1998 Cleveland	AL	1	4	0	0	0	0	(0	0)	0	0	0	0	0	2	0	0	0	0	0	—	0	.000	.000	.000
1999 Cleveland	AL	11	38	8	2	0	1	(0	1)	13	4	6	3	0	19	1	0	0	0	0	—	0	.211	.286	.342
2000 Cleveland	AL	67	193	46	7	2	16	(13	3)	105	32	38	22	1	76	4	0	1	0	0	—	2	.238	.327	.544
3 ML YEARS		79	235	54	9	2	17	(13	4)	118	36	44	25	1	97	5	0	1	0	0	—	2	.230	.316	.502

Lesli Brea

Pitches: Right **Bats:** Right **Pos:** RP-5; SP-1   **Ht:** 5'11" **Wt:** 170 **Born:** 10/12/78 **Age:** 22

Year Team	Lg	G	GS	CG	GF	IP	BFP	H	R	ER	HR	SH	SF	HB	TBB	IBB	SO	WP	Bk	W	L	Pct.	ShO	Sv-Op	Hld	ERA
1996 Mariners	R	7	0	0	3	10.2	47	7	10	6	1	0	1	0	6	0	12	1	1	1	0	1.000	0	0- -	—	5.06
1997 Lancaster	A+	1	0	0	0	2	13	5	5	3	1	0	0	0	1	0	1	1	0	0	0	—	0	0- -	—	13.50
Everett	A-	23	0	0	14	32.2	162	34	29	29	3	2	1	3	29	4	49	8	0	2	4	.333	0	3- -	—	7.99
1998 Wisconsin	A	49	0	0	34	58.2	260	47	26	18	1	3	1	2	40	2	86	5	0	3	4	.429	0	12- -	—	2.76
1999 St. Lucie	A	32	18	0	9	120.2	516	95	64	50	4	2	2	4	68	1	136	7	3	1	7	.125	0	3- -	—	3.73
2000 Norfolk	AAA	1	1	0	0	5	23	4	2	0	0	0	1	0	4	0	4	0	0	0	0	—	0	0- -	—	0.00
Binghamton	AA	19	18	0	0	93.1	422	85	53	44	10	3	5	7	61	0	86	8	2	5	8	.385	0	0- -	—	4.24
Bowie	AA	2	2	0	0	12.2	55	12	6	6	1	0	1	0	9	0	3	0	0	1	1	.500	0	0- -	—	4.26
Rochester	AAA	4	4	0	0	19.1	95	27	18	13	3	0	1	1	8	0	13	2	0	1	2	.333	0	0- -	—	6.05
2000 Baltimore	AL	6	1	0	3	9	49	12	11	11	0	1	0	1	10	0	5	1	0	0	1	.000	0	0-0	0	11.00

Jamie Brewington

Pitches: Right **Bats:** Right **Pos:** RP-26   **Ht:** 6'4" **Wt:** 190 **Born:** 9/28/71 **Age:** 29

Year Team	Lg	G	GS	CG	GF	IP	BFP	H	R	ER	HR	SH	SF	HB	TBB	IBB	SO	WP	Bk	W	L	Pct.	ShO	Sv-Op	Hld	ERA
1992 Everett	A-	15	11	1	1	68.2	317	65	40	33	2	0	3	5	47	2	63	9	1	5	2	.714	0	0- -	—	4.33
1993 Clinton	A	26	25	1	0	133.2	580	126	78	71	20	1	3	5	61	1	111	19	2	13	5	.722	0	0- -	—	4.78
1994 Clinton	A	10	10	0	0	53	226	46	29	29	5	1	3	2	24	0	62	7	1	2	4	.333	0	0- -	—	4.92
San Jose	A+	13	13	0	0	76	310	61	38	27	3	2	2	2	25	0	65	7	1	7	3	.700	0	0- -	—	3.20
1995 Shreveport	AA	16	16	1	0	88.1	376	72	39	30	8	2	7	0	55	0	74	4	0	8	3	.727	1	0- -	—	3.06
1996 Phoenix	AAA	35	17	0	7	110.1	526	130	93	86	14	5	8	6	72	1	75	15	0	6	9	.400	0	1- -	—	7.02
1997 Omaha	AAA	7	4	0	0	21.2	98	21	21	20	10	0	1	1	13	0	20	1	1	2	2	.500	0	0- -	—	8.31
Wichita	AA	10	10	0	0	51	245	68	43	38	12	0	1	4	28	0	31	2	0	2	5	.286	0	0- -	—	6.71
Tucson	AAA	6	5	0	0	20.1	112	33	26	23	2	0	1	2	17	0	13	0	0	1	3	.250	0	0- -	—	10.18
1999 Kinston	A+	36	5	0	15	81.1	353	74	42	35	6	4	2	2	37	0	81	8	1	1	10	.091	0	4- -	—	3.87
2000 Buffalo	AAA	17	0	0	6	23.2	99	19	8	8	3	0	1	0	12	0	25	1	0	1	0	1.000	0	0- -	—	3.04
1995 San Francisco	NL	13	13	0	0	75.1	334	68	38	38	8	4	4	4	45	6	45	3	0	6	4	.600	0	0-0	0	4.54
2000 Cleveland	AL	26	0	0	10	45.1	205	56	28	27	3	2	2	2	19	0	34	1	0	3	0	1.000	0	0-0	0	5.36
2 ML YEARS		39	13	0	10	120.2	539	124	66	65	11	6	6	6	64	6	79	4	0	9	4	.692	0	0-0	0	4.85

Doug Brocail

Pitches: Right **Bats:** Left **Pos:** RP-49   **Ht:** 6'5" **Wt:** 235 **Born:** 5/16/67 **Age:** 34

Year Team	Lg	G	GS	CG	GF	IP	BFP	H	R	ER	HR	SH	SF	HB	TBB	IBB	SO	WP	Bk	W	L	Pct.	ShO	Sv-Op	Hld	ERA
1992 San Diego	NL	3	3	0	0	14	64	17	10	10	2	2	0	0	5	0	15	0	0	0	0	—	0	0-0	0	6.43
1993 San Diego	NL	24	24	0	0	128.1	571	143	75	65	16	10	8	4	42	4	70	4	1	4	13	.235	0	0-0	0	4.56
1994 San Diego	NL	12	0	0	4	17	78	21	13	11	1	1	1	2	5	3	11	1	0	0	0	—	0	0-1	0	5.82
1995 Houston	NL	36	7	0	12	77.1	339	87	40	36	10	1	4	4	22	2	39	1	1	6	4	.600	0	1-1	0	4.19
1996 Houston	NL	23	4	0	4	53	231	58	31	27	7	3	2	2	23	1	34	0	0	1	5	.167	0	0-0	1	4.58
1997 Detroit	AL	61	4	0	20	78	332	74	31	28	10	1	3	4	36	4	60	6	0	3	4	.429	0	2-9	16	3.23
1998 Detroit	AL	60	0	0	24	62.2	247	47	23	19	2	2	3	1	18	3	55	6	0	5	2	.714	0	0-1	11	2.73
1999 Detroit	AL	70	0	0	22	82	326	60	23	23	7	4	2	4	25	1	78	4	1	4	4	.500	0	2-4	23	2.52
2000 Detroit	AL	49	0	0	10	50.2	221	57	25	23	5	3	3	1	14	2	41	1	1	5	4	.556	0	0-5	19	4.09
9 ML YEARS		338	42	0	96	563	2409	564	271	242	60	27	23	21	190	20	403	23	5	28	36	.438	0	5-21	70	3.87

Chris Brock

Pitches: Right **Bats:** Right **Pos:** RP-58; SP-5   **Ht:** 6'0" **Wt:** 185 **Born:** 2/5/70 **Age:** 31

Year Team	Lg	G	GS	CG	GF	IP	BFP	H	R	ER	HR	SH	SF	HB	TBB	IBB	SO	WP	Bk	W	L	Pct.	ShO	Sv-Op	Hld	ERA
1997 Atlanta	NL	7	6	0	1	30.2	144	34	23	19	2	3	4	0	19	2	16	2	1	0	0	—	0	0-0	0	5.58
1998 San Francisco	NL	13	0	0	4	27.2	120	31	13	12	3	2	0	0	7	1	19	0	0	0	0	—	0	0-0	0	3.90
1999 San Francisco	NL	19	19	0	0	106.2	479	124	69	65	18	5	3	4	41	2	76	8	2	6	8	.429	0	0-0	0	5.48
2000 Philadelphia	NL	63	5	0	17	93.1	403	85	48	45	21	1	2	3	41	0	69	4	1	7	8	.467	0	1-3	16	4.34
4 ML YEARS		102	30	0	22	258.1	1146	274	153	141	44	11	9	7	108	5	180	14	4	13	16	.448	0	1-3	16	4.91

Tarrik Brock

Bats: Left **Throws:** Left **Pos:** LF-9; PH/PR-4; CF-2 **Ht:** 6'2" **Wt:** 185 **Born:** 12/25/73 **Age:** 27

Year Team	Lg	G	AB	H	2B	3B	HR	(Hm	Rd)	TB	R	RBI	TBB	IBB	SO	HBP	SH	SF	SB	CS	SB%	GDP	Avg	OBP	SLG
1991 Bristol	R+	55	177	47	7	3	1	—	—	63	26	13	22	0	42	3	1	1	14	6	.70	3	.266	.355	.356
1992 Fayetteville	A	100	271	59	5	4	0	—	—	72	35	17	31	1	69	4	5	1	15	10	.60	2	.218	.306	.266
1993 Fayetteville	A	116	427	92	8	4	3	—	—	117	60	47	54	2	108	5	5	4	25	16	.61	5	.215	.308	.274
1994 Lakeland	A+	86	331	77	17	14	2	—	—	128	43	32	38	2	89	2	2	2	15	6	.71	5	.233	.314	.387
Trenton	AA	34	115	16	1	4	2	—	—	31	12	11	13	0	43	2	1	0	3	3	.50	2	.139	.238	.270
1995 Toledo	AAA	9	31	6	1	0	0	—	—	7	4	0	2	0	17	0	0	0	2	2	.50	0	.194	.242	.226
Jacksnville	AA	9	26	3	0	0	0	—	—	3	4	2	3	0	14	1	1	0	2	0	1.00	0	.115	.233	.115
Lakeland	A+	28	91	19	3	0	0	—	—	22	12	5	12	0	32	0	1	0	5	3	.63	2	.209	.301	.242
Visalia	A+	45	138	31	5	2	1	—	—	43	21	15	17	0	52	4	2	0	11	1	.92	2	.225	.327	.312
1996 Lakeland	A+	53	212	59	11	4	5	—	—	93	42	27	17	0	61	5	0	3	9	2	.82	4	.278	.342	.439
Jacksnville	AA	37	102	13	2	0	0	—	—	15	14	6	10	0	36	1	0	0	3	3	.50	0	.127	.212	.147
Fayetteville	A	32	119	35	5	2	1	—	—	47	21	11	14	1	31	4	0	1	4	5	.44	3	.294	.384	.395
1997 Lancaster	A+	132	402	108	21	12	7	—	—	174	88	47	78	1	106	6	6	0	40	8	.83	7	.269	.395	.433
1998 Orlando	AA	111	372	103	28	7	15	—	—	190	76	65	59	4	110	6	1	5	17	9	.65	2	.277	.380	.511
Tacoma	AAA	24	94	23	2	3	1	—	—	34	14	14	9	0	28	0	1	1	5	0	1.00	0	.245	.308	.362
1999 Carolina	AA	66	218	54	10	1	7	—	—	87	40	23	39	0	67	1	1	1	7	4	.64	2	.248	.363	.399
West Tenn	AA	54	189	41	10	4	1	—	—	62	29	9	33	1	60	0	1	1	9	4	.69	0	.217	.332	.328
2000 Iowa	AAA	104	388	102	19	5	12	—	—	167	60	47	43	2	109	1	2	1	15	7	.68	5	.263	.337	.430
2000 Chicago	NL	13	12	2	0	0	0	(0	0)	2	1	0	4	0	4	0	0	0	1	1	.50	0	.167	.375	.167

Rico Brogna

Bats: Left **Throws:** Left **Pos:** 1B-71; PH/PR-17; DH-2 **Ht:** 6'2" **Wt:** 203 **Born:** 4/18/70 **Age:** 31

Year Team	Lg	G	AB	H	2B	3B	HR	(Hm	Rd)	TB	R	RBI	TBB	IBB	SO	HBP	SH	SF	SB	CS	SB%	GDP	Avg	OBP	SLG
2000 Clearwater *	A+	7	32	7	1	0	0	—	—	8	2	2	1	1	4	0	0	0	0	0	—	0	.219	.242	.250
1992 Detroit	AL	9	26	5	1	0	1	(1	0)	9	3	3	3	0	5	0	0	0	0	0	—	0	.192	.276	.346
1994 New York	NL	39	131	46	11	2	7	(2	5)	82	16	20	6	0	29	0	1	0	1	0	1.00	2	.351	.380	.626
1995 New York	NL	134	495	143	27	2	22	(13	9)	240	72	76	39	7	111	2	2	2	0	0	—	10	.289	.342	.485
1996 New York	NL	55	188	48	10	1	7	(5	2)	81	18	30	19	1	50	0	0	4	0	0	—	4	.255	.318	.431
1997 Philadelphia	NL	148	543	137	36	1	20	(9	11)	235	68	81	33	4	116	0	0	4	12	3	.80	12	.252	.293	.433
1998 Philadelphia	NL	153	565	150	36	3	20	(11	9)	252	77	104	49	8	125	0	0	10	7	7	.50	12	.265	.319	.446
1999 Philadelphia	NL	157	619	172	29	4	24	(14	10)	281	90	102	54	7	132	2	0	4	8	5	.62	19	.278	.336	.454
2000 Phi-Bos		81	185	43	17	0	2	(2	0)	66	20	21	10	1	41	2	1	1	1	0	1.00	5	.232	.278	.357
2000 Philadelphia	NL	38	129	32	14	0	1	(1	0)	49	12	13	7	1	28	2	0	1	1	0	1.00	4	.248	.295	.380
Boston	AL	43	56	11	3	0	1	(1	0)	17	8	8	3	0	13	0	1	0	0	0	—	1	.196	.237	.304
8 ML YEARS		776	2752	744	167	13	103	(57	46)	1246	364	437	213	28	609	6	4	25	29	15	.66	64	.270	.321	.453

Scott Brosius

Bats: R **Throws:** R **Pos:** 3B-134; 1B-2; DH-1; LF-1; RF-1; PH/PR-1 **Ht:** 6'1" **Wt:** 202 **Born:** 8/15/66 **Age:** 34

Year Team	Lg	G	AB	H	2B	3B	HR	(Hm	Rd)	TB	R	RBI	TBB	IBB	SO	HBP	SH	SF	SB	CS	SB%	GDP	Avg	OBP	SLG
2000 Tampa *	A+	2	4	1	0	0	0	—	—	1	0	0	1	0	0	0	0	0	0	0	—	0	.250	.400	.250
1991 Oakland	AL	36	68	16	5	0	2	(1	1)	27	9	4	3	0	11	0	1	0	3	1	.75	2	.235	.268	.397
1992 Oakland	AL	38	87	19	2	0	4	(1	3)	33	13	13	3	1	13	2	0	1	3	0	1.00	0	.218	.258	.379
1993 Oakland	AL	70	213	53	10	1	6	(3	3)	83	26	25	14	0	37	1	3	2	6	0	1.00	6	.249	.296	.390
1994 Oakland	AL	96	324	77	14	1	14	(9	5)	135	31	49	24	0	57	2	4	6	2	6	.25	7	.238	.289	.417
1995 Oakland	AL	123	389	102	19	2	17	(12	5)	176	69	46	41	0	67	8	1	4	4	2	.67	5	.262	.342	.452
1996 Oakland	AL	114	428	130	25	0	22	(15	7)	221	73	71	59	4	85	7	1	5	7	2	.78	11	.304	.393	.516
1997 Oakland	AL	129	479	97	20	1	11	(7	4)	152	59	41	34	1	102	4	5	4	9	4	.69	9	.203	.259	.317
1998 New York	AL	152	530	159	34	0	19	(8	11)	250	86	98	52	1	97	10	8	3	11	8	.58	4	.300	.371	.472
1999 New York	AL	133	473	117	26	1	17	(4	13)	196	64	71	39	2	74	6	2	9	9	3	.75	13	.247	.307	.414
2000 New York	AL	135	470	108	20	0	16	(7	9)	176	57	64	45	1	73	2	0	2	0	3	.00	17	.230	.299	.374
10 ML YEARS		1026	3461	878	175	6	128	(67	61)	1449	487	482	314	10	616	42	25	36	54	29	.65	74	.254	.320	.419

Jim Brower

Pitches: Right **Bats:** Right **Pos:** SP-11; RP-6 **Ht:** 6'2" **Wt:** 205 **Born:** 12/29/72 **Age:** 28

Year Team	Lg	G	GS	CG	GF	IP	BFP	H	R	ER	HR	SH	SF	HB	TBB	IBB	SO	WP	Bk	W	L	Pct.	ShO	Sv-Op	Hld	ERA
1994 Hudson Val	A-	4	4	1	0	19.2	83	14	10	7	0	0	2	1	6	0	15	0	1	2	1	.667	0	0--	—	3.20
Chston-SC	A	12	12	3	0	78.2	312	52	18	15	2	1	1	5	26	1	84	6	0	7	3	.700	2	0--	—	1.72
1995 Charlotte	A+	27	27	2	0	173.2	740	170	93	75	16	3	3	8	62	1	110	11	0	7	10	.412	1	0--	—	3.89
1996 Charlotte	A+	23	21	2	2	145	607	148	67	61	11	5	4	4	40	0	86	7	2	9	8	.529	1	0--	—	3.79
Tulsa	AA	5	5	1	0	33.1	140	35	16	14	4	0	1	1	10	0	16	1	0	3	2	.600	1	0--	—	3.78
1997 Tulsa	AA	23	23	1	0	140	602	156	99	81	13	4	7	3	42	1	103	15	1	5	12	.294	0	0--	—	5.21
Okla City	AAA	4	3	0	0	18.2	92	30	17	15	3	0	2	1	8	0	7	3	0	2	1	.667	0	0--	—	7.23
1998 Akron	AA	23	23	2	0	155.2	630	142	60	52	9	4	3	7	38	0	91	5	0	13	5	.722	2	0--	—	3.01
1999 Buffalo	AAA	27	27	0	0	160	689	164	101	84	23	6	8	8	59	6	76	9	2	11	11	.500	0	0--	—	4.73
2000 Buffalo	AAA	16	15	1	1	101.1	425	99	41	35	7	4	3	4	24	1	68	2	0	9	4	.692	0	0--	—	3.11
1999 Cleveland	AL	9	2	0	1	25.2	113	27	13	13	8	1	1	1	10	1	18	0	0	3	1	.750	0	0-0	0	4.56
2000 Cleveland	AL	17	11	0	0	62	293	80	45	43	11	1	0	2	31	1	32	3	0	2	3	.400	0	0-0	0	6.24
2 ML YEARS		26	13	0	1	87.2	406	107	58	56	19	2	1	3	41	2	50	3	0	5	4	.556	0	0-0	0	5.75

Adrian Brown

Bats: B **Throws:** R **Pos:** CF-71; PH/PR-23; RF-15; LF-7 **Ht:** 6'0" **Wt:** 185 **Born:** 2/7/74 **Age:** 27

Year Team	Lg	G	AB	H	2B	3B	HR	(Hm	Rd)	TB	R	RBI	TBB	IBB	SO	HBP	SH	SF	SB	CS	SB%	GDP	Avg	OBP	SLG
2000 Altoona *	AA	2	5	0	0	0	0	—	—	0	1	0	3	0	1	0	0	0	0	0	—	0	.000	.375	.000
Nashville *	AAA	8	26	6	1	0	0	—	—	7	3	2	2	0	4	1	0	0	3	0	1.00	0	.231	.310	.269

(continued)

Year Team	Lg	G	AB	H	2B	3B	HR	(Hm	Rd)	TB	R	RBI	TBB	IBB	SO	HBP	SH	SF	SB	CS	SB%	GDP	Avg	OBP	SLG
1997 Pittsburgh	NL	48	147	28	6	0	1	(0	1)	37	17	10	13	0	18	4	2	1	8	4	.67	3	.190	.273	.252
1998 Pittsburgh	NL	41	152	43	4	1	0	(0	0)	49	20	5	9	0	18	4	4	0	4	0	1.00	3	.283	.323	.322
1999 Pittsburgh	NL	116	226	61	5	2	4	(2	2)	82	34	17	33	2	39	1	6	1	5	3	.63	5	.270	.364	.363
2000 Pittsburgh	NL	104	308	97	18	3	4	(2	2)	133	64	28	29	1	34	0	2	1	13	1	.93	1	.315	.373	.432
4 ML YEARS		309	833	229	33	6	9	(4	5)	301	135	60	84	3	109	5	14	3	30	8	.79	12	.275	.344	.361

Brant Brown

Bats: L **Throws:** L **Pos:** PH/PR-49; LF-26; 1B-12; CF-9; RF-8   **Ht:** 6'3" **Wt:** 220 **Born:** 6/22/71 **Age:** 30

Year Team	Lg	G	AB	H	2B	3B	HR	(Hm	Rd)	TB	R	RBI	TBB	IBB	SO	HBP	SH	SF	SB	CS	SB%	GDP	Avg	OBP	SLG
1996 Chicago	NL	29	69	21	1	0	5	(3	2)	37	11	9	2	1	17	1	0	1	3	3	.50	1	.304	.329	.536
1997 Chicago	NL	46	137	32	7	1	5	(3	2)	56	15	15	7	0	28	3	1	0	2	1	.67	2	.234	.286	.409
1998 Chicago	NL	124	347	101	17	7	14	(10	4)	174	56	48	30	2	95	1	1	1	4	5	.44	1	.291	.348	.501
1999 Pittsburgh	NL	130	341	79	20	3	16	(4	12)	153	49	58	22	3	114	4	0	4	3	4	.43	4	.232	.283	.449
2000 Fla-ChC	NL	95	162	28	7	0	5	(2	3)	50	11	16	13	0	62	1	1	1	3	1	.75	3	.173	.237	.309
2000 Florida	NL	41	73	14	6	0	2	(0	0)	26	4	6	3	0	33	0	0	0	1	0	1.00	1	.192	.224	.356
Chicago	NL	54	89	14	1	0	3	(0	3)	24	7	10	10	0	29	1	1	1	2	1	.67	2	.157	.248	.270
5 ML YEARS		424	1056	261	52	11	45	(22	23)	470	142	146	74	6	316	10	3	7	15	14	.52	11	.247	.301	.445

Dee Brown

Bats: Left **Throws:** Right **Pos:** PH/PR-11; LF-5   **Ht:** 6'0" **Wt:** 215 **Born:** 3/27/78 **Age:** 23

Year Team	Lg	G	AB	H	2B	3B	HR	(Hm	Rd)	TB	R	RBI	TBB	IBB	SO	HBP	SH	SF	SB	CS	SB%	GDP	Avg	OBP	SLG
1996 Royals	R	7	20	1	1	0	0	(—	—)	2	1	1	0	0	6	1	0	0	0	2	.00	0	.050	.095	.100
1997 Spokane	A-	73	298	97	20	6	13	(—	—)	168	67	73	38	5	65	2	0	1	17	4	.81	5	.326	.404	.564
1998 Wilmington	A+	128	442	114	30	2	10	(—	—)	178	64	58	53	5	115	7	1	0	26	10	.72	12	.258	.347	.403
1999 Wilmington	A+	61	221	68	10	2	13	(—	—)	121	49	46	44	6	56	4	0	0	20	8	.71	10	.308	.431	.548
Wichita	AA	65	235	83	14	3	12	(—	—)	139	58	56	35	1	41	3	1	2	10	8	.56	2	.353	.440	.591
2000 Omaha	AAA	125	479	129	25	6	23	(—	—)	235	76	70	37	5	112	3	0	3	20	3	.87	14	.269	.324	.491
1998 Kansas City	AL	5	3	0	0	0	0	(0	0)	0	2	0	0	0	1	0	0	0	0	0	—	0	.000	.000	.000
1999 Kansas City	AL	12	25	2	0	0	0	(0	0)	2	1	0	2	0	7	0	0	0	0	0	—	0	.080	.148	.080
2000 Kansas City	AL	15	25	4	1	0	0	(0	0)	5	4	4	3	0	9	0	0	0	0	0	—	0	.160	.250	.200
3 ML YEARS		32	53	6	1	0	0	(0	0)	7	7	4	5	0	17	0	0	0	0	0	—	0	.113	.190	.132

Emil Brown

Bats: R **Throws:** R **Pos:** RF-18; PH/PR-16; LF-14; CF-12   **Ht:** 6'2" **Wt:** 193 **Born:** 12/29/74 **Age:** 26

Year Team	Lg	G	AB	H	2B	3B	HR	(Hm	Rd)	TB	R	RBI	TBB	IBB	SO	HBP	SH	SF	SB	CS	SB%	GDP	Avg	OBP	SLG
2000 Nashville *	AAA	70	237	74	20	1	5	(—	—)	111	44	25	40	1	44	6	0	1	26	4	.87	8	.312	.423	.468
1997 Pittsburgh	NL	66	95	17	2	1	2	(1	1)	27	16	6	10	1	32	7	0	0	5	1	.83	1	.179	.304	.284
1998 Pittsburgh	NL	13	39	10	1	0	0	(0	0)	11	2	3	1	0	11	1	0	0	0	0	—	0	.256	.293	.282
1999 Pittsburgh	NL	6	14	2	1	0	0	(0	0)	3	0	0	0	0	3	0	0	0	0	0	—	0	.143	.143	.214
2000 Pittsburgh	NL	50	119	26	5	0	3	(2	1)	40	13	16	11	0	34	3	1	1	3	1	.75	3	.218	.299	.336
4 ML YEARS		135	267	55	9	1	5	(3	2)	81	31	25	22	1	80	11	1	1	8	2	.80	4	.206	.292	.303

Kevin Brown

Pitches: Right **Bats:** Right **Pos:** SP-33   **Ht:** 6'4" **Wt:** 200 **Born:** 3/14/65 **Age:** 36

Year Team	Lg	G	GS	CG	GF	IP	BFP	H	R	ER	HR	SH	SF	HB	TBB	IBB	SO	WP	Bk	W	L	Pct.	ShO	Sv-Op	Hld	ERA
1986 Texas	AL	1	1	0	0	5	19	6	2	2	0	0	0	0	0	0	4	0	0	1	0	1.000	0	0-0	0	3.60
1988 Texas	AL	4	4	1	0	23.1	110	33	15	11	2	1	0	0	8	0	12	1	0	1	1	.500	0	0-0	0	4.24
1989 Texas	AL	28	28	7	0	191	798	167	81	71	10	3	6	4	70	2	104	7	2	12	9	.571	0	0-0	0	3.35
1990 Texas	AL	26	26	6	0	180	757	175	84	72	13	2	7	3	60	3	88	9	2	12	10	.545	2	0-0	0	3.60
1991 Texas	AL	33	33	0	0	210.2	934	233	116	103	17	6	4	13	90	5	96	12	3	9	12	.429	0	0-0	0	4.40
1992 Texas	AL	35	35	11	0	265.2	1108	262	117	98	11	7	8	10	76	2	173	8	2	21	11	.656	1	0-0	0	3.32
1993 Texas	AL	34	34	12	0	233	1001	228	105	93	14	5	3	15	74	5	142	4	1	15	12	.556	3	0-0	0	3.59
1994 Texas	AL	26	25	3	1	170	760	218	109	91	18	2	7	6	50	3	123	7	0	7	9	.438	0	0-0	0	4.82
1995 Baltimore	AL	26	26	3	0	172.1	706	155	73	69	10	5	2	9	48	1	117	3	0	10	9	.526	1	0-0	0	3.60
1996 Florida	NL	32	32	5	0	233	900	187	60	49	8	4	4	16	33	2	159	6	1	17	11	.607	3	0-0	0	1.89
1997 Florida	NL	33	33	6	0	237.1	976	214	77	71	10	5	1	14	66	7	205	7	1	16	8	.667	2	0-0	0	2.69
1998 San Diego	NL	36	35	7	0	257	1032	225	77	68	8	13	3	10	49	4	257	10	0	18	7	.720	1	0-0	1	2.38
1999 Los Angeles	NL	35	35	5	0	252.1	1018	210	99	84	19	7	1	7	59	1	221	4	1	18	9	.667	1	0-0	0	3.00
2000 Los Angeles	NL	33	33	5	0	230	921	181	76	66	21	13	4	9	47	1	216	4	0	13	6	.684	1	0-0	0	2.58
14 ML YEARS		382	380	71	1	2660.2	11046	2494	1091	948	161	73	50	117	730	36	1917	86	13	170	114	.599	17	0-0	1	3.21

Kevin L. Brown

Bats: Right **Throws:** Right **Pos:** C-5   **Ht:** 6'2" **Wt:** 215 **Born:** 4/21/73 **Age:** 28

Year Team	Lg	G	AB	H	2B	3B	HR	(Hm	Rd)	TB	R	RBI	TBB	IBB	SO	HBP	SH	SF	SB	CS	SB%	GDP	Avg	OBP	SLG
2000 Syracuse *	AAA	51	179	60	15	1	7	(Hm	Rd)	98	26	29	8	1	46	0	0	1	0	0	—	5	.335	.362	.547
Indianapols *	AAA	23	82	20	5	0	1	(—	—)	28	5	6	6	0	24	1	0	0	0	0	—	0	.244	.303	.341
1996 Texas	AL	3	4	0	0	0	0	(0	0)	0	1	1	2	0	2	1	0	1	0	0	—	0	.000	.375	.000
1997 Texas	AL	4	5	2	0	0	1	(0	0)	5	1	1	0	0	0	0	0	0	0	0	—	0	.400	.400	1.000
1998 Toronto	AL	52	110	29	7	1	2	(1	1)	44	17	15	9	0	31	2	3	4	0	0	—	1	.264	.320	.400
1999 Toronto	AL	2	9	4	2	0	0	(0	0)	6	1	1	0	0	4	0	0	0	0	0	—	0	.444	.444	.667
2000 Milwaukee	NL	5	17	4	3	0	0	(0	0)	7	3	1	1	0	5	0	0	0	0	0	—	1	.235	.278	.412
5 ML YEARS		66	145	39	12	1	3	(1	2)	62	23	19	12	0	41	3	3	5	0	0	—	1	.269	.327	.428

Roosevelt Brown

Bats: L Throws: R Pos: LF-24; PH/PR-17; RF-5; CF-1   Ht: 5'11" Wt: 195 Born: 8/3/75 Age: 25

Year Team	Lg	G	AB	H	2B	3B	HR	(Hm	Rd)	TB	R	RBI	TBB	IBB	SO	HBP	SH	SF	SB	CS	SB%	GDP	Avg	OBP	SLG
1993 Braves	R	26	80	9	1	2	0	—	—	14	4	5	2	0	9	1	1	0	2	0	1.00	2	.113	.145	.175
1994 Idaho Falls	R+	48	160	53	8	1	3	—	—	72	28	22	17	0	15	1	0	1	8	6	.57	2	.331	.397	.450
1995 Eugene	A-	57	165	51	12	4	7	—	—	92	28	32	13	2	30	3	0	2	6	3	.67	1	.309	.366	.558
1996 Macon	A	113	413	115	27	0	19	—	—	199	61	64	33	4	60	3	0	3	21	11	.66	9	.278	.334	.482
Kane County	A	11	40	6	2	0	0	—	—	8	1	3	1	0	10	1	0	0	0	1	.00	0	.150	.190	.200
1997 Kane County	A	61	211	50	7	1	4	—	—	71	29	30	22	2	52	1	0	0	5	4	.56	5	.237	.312	.336
Brevard Cty	A+	33	114	28	7	1	1	—	—	40	8	12	7	0	31	0	1	1	0	3	.00	4	.246	.287	.351
1998 Daytona	A+	68	244	84	15	5	9	—	—	136	49	43	23	3	46	2	0	2	3	2	.60	6	.344	.402	.557
West Tenn	AA	42	160	42	11	0	6	—	—	71	20	24	13	1	30	2	0	1	3	1	.75	6	.263	.324	.444
Iowa	AAA	1	3	1	1	0	0	—	—	2	0	2	0	0	0	0	0	0	0	0	—	0	.333	.333	.667
1999 West Tenn	AA	34	125	37	12	0	3	—	—	58	12	12	14	1	29	2	0	0	6	1	.86	1	.296	.376	.464
Iowa	AAA	74	268	96	25	2	22	—	—	191	50	79	19	1	54	3	0	4	3	3	.50	8	.358	.401	.713
2000 Iowa	AAA	100	363	112	32	0	12	—	—	180	67	55	37	3	60	7	0	2	10	3	.77	5	.309	.381	.496
1999 Chicago	NL	33	64	14	6	1	1	(0	1)	25	6	10	2	0	14	0	3	1	1	0	1.00	2	.219	.239	.391
2000 Chicago	NL	45	91	32	8	0	3	(1	2)	49	11	14	4	0	22	1	0	2	0	1	.00	0	.352	.378	.538
2 ML YEARS		78	155	46	14	1	4	(1	3)	74	17	24	6	0	36	1	3	3	1	1	.50	2	.297	.321	.477

Mark Brownson

Pitches: Right Bats: Left Pos: RP-2   Ht: 6'2" Wt: 185 Born: 6/17/75 Age: 26

Year Team	Lg	G	GS	CG	GF	IP	BFP	H	R	ER	HR	SH	SF	HB	TBB	IBB	SO	WP	Bk	W	L	Pct.	ShO	Sv-Op	Hld	ERA
1994 Rockies	R	19	4	0	6	54.1	224	48	18	10	2	2	2	3	6	0	72	2	2	4	1	.800	0	3- -	—	1.66
1995 Asheville	A	23	12	0	6	98.2	422	106	52	44	12	2	2	4	29	0	94	4	2	6	7	.462	0	1- -	—	4.01
New Haven	AA	1	1	0	0	6	24	4	2	1	1	0	0	0	1	0	4	0	0	0	0	—	0	0- -	—	1.50
Salem	A+	9	1	0	5	15.2	71	16	8	7	0	0	0	1	10	4	9	4	0	2	1	.667	0	1- -	—	4.02
1996 New Haven	AA	37	19	1	10	144	619	141	73	56	10	6	3	6	43	5	155	7	2	8	13	.381	0	3- -	—	3.50
1997 New Haven	AA	29	29	2	0	184.2	779	172	101	86	24	8	5	14	55	1	170	5	2	10	9	.526	0	0- -	—	4.19
1998 Colo Sprngs	AAA	21	21	3	0	124.2	542	131	85	74	22	5	8	14	37	0	82	3	3	6	8	.429	0	0- -	—	5.34
1999 Colo Sprngs	AAA	17	16	2	0	103	446	120	75	71	24	2	6	7	24	0	81	6	2	6	6	.500	0	0- -	—	6.20
2000 Scrantn-WB	AAA	31	20	4	1	132.2	556	134	70	67	15	4	6	6	36	1	104	2	3	10	8	.556	0	0- -	—	4.55
1998 Colorado	NL	2	2	1	0	13.1	57	16	7	7	2	0	0	1	2	0	8	0	0	1	0	1.000	1	0-0	0	4.73
1999 Colorado	NL	7	7	0	0	29.2	139	42	26	26	8	4	0	1	8	0	21	2	0	2	2	.000	0	0-0	0	7.89
2000 Philadelphia	NL	2	0	0	0	5	25	7	4	4	1	1	0	0	3	0	3	0	0	1	0	1.000	0	0-1	1	7.20
3 ML YEARS		11	9	1	0	48	221	65	37	37	11	5	0	2	13	0	32	2	0	2	2	.500	1	0-1	1	6.94

Justin Brunette

Pitches: Left Bats: Left Pos: RP-4   Ht: 6'1" Wt: 200 Born: 10/7/75 Age: 25

Year Team	Lg	G	GS	CG	GF	IP	BFP	H	R	ER	HR	SH	SF	HB	TBB	IBB	SO	WP	Bk	W	L	Pct.	ShO	Sv-Op	Hld	ERA
1997 New Jersey	A-	6	0	0	2	5.2	29	13	6	5	0	0	0	0	0	0	6	1	1	1	0	1.000	0	0- -	—	7.94
1999 Peoria	A	38	0	0	12	44.2	181	34	9	9	2	2	1	1	16	1	44	2	1	3	1	.750	0	2- -	—	1.81
Arkansas	AA	18	0	0	3	18.1	82	21	12	4	3	0	0	0	7	0	23	1	0	1	2	.333	0	0- -	—	1.96
2000 Arkansas	AA	3	0	0	1	3	13	5	4	1	1	0	0	0	0	0	1	0	0	0	0	—	0	0- -	—	3.00
Memphis	AAA	30	0	0	7	33.2	159	42	27	23	4	3	2	1	14	2	27	1	0	1	2	.333	0	0- -	—	6.15
2000 St. Louis	NL	4	0	0	2	4.2	27	8	3	3	0	0	0	0	5	0	2	1	1	0	0	—	0	0-0	0	5.79

Jim Bruske

Pitches: Right Bats: Right Pos: RP-15   Ht: 6'1" Wt: 185 Born: 10/7/64 Age: 36

Year Team	Lg	G	GS	CG	GF	IP	BFP	H	R	ER	HR	SH	SF	HB	TBB	IBB	SO	WP	Bk	W	L	Pct.	ShO	Sv-Op	Hld	ERA
2000 Indianapolis *	AAA	19	2	0	4	32	159	47	36	33	9	3	2	3	14	2	22	2	0	2	4	.333	0	1- -	—	9.28
1995 Los Angeles	NL	9	0	0	3	10	45	12	7	5	0	0	0	1	4	0	5	1	0	0	0	—	0	1-1	0	4.50
1996 Los Angeles	NL	11	0	0	5	12.2	58	17	8	8	2	0	0	1	3	1	12	1	0	0	0	—	0	0-0	0	5.68
1997 San Diego	NL	28	0	0	6	44.2	193	37	22	18	4	2	3	1	25	1	32	4	0	4	1	.800	0	0-1	5	3.63
1998 LA-SD-NYY		42	1	0	11	60	265	66	25	23	5	0	0	3	24	3	38	3	0	4	0	1.000	0	1-2	4	3.45
2000 Milwaukee	NL	15	0	0	1	16.2	85	22	15	12	5	0	1	2	12	1	8	0	0	1	0	1.000	0	0-0	2	6.48
1998 Los Angeles	NL	35	0	0	10	44	195	47	18	17	2	0	0	3	19	1	31	3	0	3	0	1.000	0	1-2	4	3.48
San Diego	NL	4	0	0	1	7	34	10	4	3	1	0	0	0	4	2	4	0	0	0	0	—	0	0-0	1	3.86
New York	AL	3	1	0	0	9	36	9	3	3	2	0	0	0	1	0	3	0	0	1	0	1.000	0	0-0	1	3.00
5 ML YEARS		105	1	0	26	144	646	154	77	66	16	2	4	8	68	6	95	8	0	9	1	.900	0	2-4	11	4.13

Brian Buchanan

Bats: R Throws: R Pos: RF-24; PH/PR-7; DH-2; LF-2   Ht: 6'4" Wt: 230 Born: 7/21/73 Age: 27

Year Team	Lg	G	AB	H	2B	3B	HR	(Hm	Rd)	TB	R	RBI	TBB	IBB	SO	HBP	SH	SF	SB	CS	SB%	GDP	Avg	OBP	SLG
1994 Oneonta	A-	50	177	40	9	2	4	—	—	65	28	26	24	2	53	6	0	2	5	3	.63	2	.226	.335	.367
1995 Greensboro	A	23	96	29	3	0	3	—	—	41	19	12	9	1	17	1	0	0	7	1	.88	1	.302	.368	.427
1996 Tampa	A+	131	526	137	22	4	10	—	—	197	65	58	37	6	108	10	1	1	23	8	.74	14	.260	.321	.375
1997 Columbus	AAA	18	61	17	1	0	4	—	—	30	8	7	4	0	11	3	1	1	2	1	.67	3	.279	.348	.492
Norwich	AA	116	470	145	25	2	10	—	—	204	75	69	32	0	85	11	0	6	11	9	.55	11	.309	.362	.434
1998 Salt Lake	AAA	133	500	139	29	3	17	—	—	225	74	82	36	1	90	9	1	1	14	2	.88	7	.278	.335	.450
1999 Salt Lake	AAA	107	391	116	24	1	10	—	—	172	67	60	28	0	85	9	0	3	11	2	.85	14	.297	.355	.440
2000 Salt Lake	AAA	95	364	108	20	1	27	—	—	211	82	103	41	2	75	3	0	11	5	1	.83	16	.297	.363	.580
2000 Minnesota	AL	30	82	19	3	0	1	(1	0)	25	10	8	8	0	22	1	0	0	0	2	.00	3	.232	.301	.305

Mike Buddie

Pitches: Right **Bats:** Right **Pos:** RP-5 **Ht:** 6'3" **Wt:** 215 **Born:** 12/12/70 **Age:** 30

Year Team	Lg	G	GS	CG	GF	IP	BFP	H	R	ER	HR	SH	SF	HB	TBB	IBB	SO	WP	Bk	W	L	Pct.	ShO	Sv-Op	Hld	ERA
2000 Columbus *	AAA	6	6	0	0	30	145	34	30	25	8	1	2	0	20	1	16	2	0	1	3	.250	0	0--	—	7.50
Indianapols *	AAA	30	0	0	7	58.1	245	40	20	17	4	2	2	5	29	1	39	4	0	7	2	.778	0	2--	—	2.62
1998 New York	AL	24	2	0	8	41.2	180	46	29	26	5	1	1	3	13	1	20	2	1	4	1	.800	0	0-0	—	5.62
1999 New York	AL	2	0	0	0	2	9	3	1	1	0	0	0	0	0	0	1	0	0	0	0	—	0	0-0	—	4.50
2000 Milwaukee	NL	5	0	0	2	6	27	8	3	3	0	1	0	0	1	1	5	0	0	0	0	—	0	0-0	0	4.50
3 ML YEARS		31	2	0	10	49.2	216	57	33	30	6	2	1	3	14	2	26	2	1	4	1	.800	0	0-0	—	5.44

Mark Buehrle

Pitches: Left **Bats:** Left **Pos:** RP-25; SP-3 **Ht:** 6'2" **Wt:** 200 **Born:** 3/23/79 **Age:** 22

Year Team	Lg	G	GS	CG	GF	IP	BFP	H	R	ER	HR	SH	SF	HB	TBB	IBB	SO	WP	Bk	W	L	Pct.	ShO	Sv-Op	Hld	ERA
1999 Burlington	A	20	14	1	4	98.2	412	105	49	45	8	2	2	5	16	1	91	3	6	7	4	.636	1	3--	—	4.10
2000 Birmingham	AA	16	16	1	0	118.2	458	95	37	30	8	1	1	10	17	0	68	1	0	8	4	.667	1	0--	—	2.28
2000 Chicago	AL	28	3	0	6	51.1	225	55	27	24	5	1	0	3	19	1	37	0	0	4	1	.800	0	0-2	3	4.21

Damon Buford

Bats: R **Throws:** R **Pos:** CF-140; PH/PR-10; RF-7; LF-2 **Ht:** 5'10" **Wt:** 180 **Born:** 6/12/70 **Age:** 31

Year Team	Lg	G	AB	H	2B	3B	HR	(Hm	Rd)	TB	R	RBI	TBB	IBB	SO	HBP	SH	SF	SB	CS	SB%	GDP	Avg	OBP	SLG
1993 Baltimore	AL	53	79	18	5	0	2	(0	2)	29	18	9	9	0	19	1	1	0	2	2	.50	1	.228	.315	.367
1994 Baltimore	AL	4	2	1	0	0	0	(0	0)	1	2	0	0	0	1	0	0	0	0	0	—	0	.500	.500	.500
1995 Bal-NYM		68	168	34	5	0	4	(2	2)	51	30	14	25	0	35	5	3	3	10	8	.56	3	.202	.318	.304
1996 Texas	AL	90	145	41	9	0	6	(3	3)	68	30	20	15	0	34	0	1	1	8	5	.62	3	.283	.348	.469
1997 Texas	AL	122	366	82	18	0	8	(4	4)	124	49	39	30	0	83	3	3	2	18	7	.72	8	.224	.287	.339
1998 Boston	AL	86	216	61	14	4	10	(4	6)	113	37	42	22	1	43	1	0	2	5	5	.50	5	.282	.349	.523
1999 Boston	AL	91	297	72	15	2	6	(3	3)	109	39	38	21	0	74	2	1	3	9	2	.82	5	.242	.294	.367
2000 Chicago	NL	150	494	124	18	3	15	(9	6)	193	64	48	47	3	118	8	4	2	4	6	.40	9	.251	.324	.390
1995 Baltimore	AL	24	32	2	0	0	0	(0	0)	2	6	2	6	0	7	0	3	1	3	1	.75	0	.063	.205	.063
New York	NL	44	136	32	5	0	4	(2	2)	49	24	12	19	0	28	5	0	2	7	7	.50	3	.235	.346	.360
8 ML YEARS		664	1768	433	84	9	51	(25	26)	688	269	210	169	4	407	20	13	13	56	35	.62	34	.245	.316	.389

Jay Buhner

Bats: Right **Throws:** Right **Pos:** RF-104; PH/PR-10; DH-1 **Ht:** 6'3" **Wt:** 210 **Born:** 8/13/64 **Age:** 36

Year Team	Lg	G	AB	H	2B	3B	HR	(Hm	Rd)	TB	R	RBI	TBB	IBB	SO	HBP	SH	SF	SB	CS	SB%	GDP	Avg	OBP	SLG
1987 New York	AL	7	22	5	2	0	0	(0	0)	7	0	1	1	0	6	0	0	0	0	0	—	1	.227	.261	.318
1988 NYY-Sea		85	261	56	13	1	13	(8	5)	110	36	38	28	1	93	6	1	3	1	1	.50	5	.215	.302	.421
1989 Seattle	AL	58	204	56	15	1	9	(7	2)	100	27	33	19	0	55	2	0	1	1	4	.20	0	.275	.341	.490
1990 Seattle	AL	51	163	45	12	0	7	(2	5)	78	16	33	17	1	50	4	0	1	2	2	.50	6	.276	.357	.479
1991 Seattle	AL	137	406	99	14	4	27	(14	13)	202	64	77	53	5	117	6	2	4	0	1	.00	10	.244	.337	.498
1992 Seattle	AL	152	543	132	16	3	25	(9	16)	229	69	79	71	2	146	6	1	8	0	6	.00	12	.243	.333	.422
1993 Seattle	AL	158	563	153	28	3	27	(13	14)	268	91	98	100	11	144	2	2	8	2	5	.29	12	.272	.379	.476
1994 Seattle	AL	101	358	100	23	4	21	(8	13)	194	74	68	66	3	63	5	2	5	0	1	.00	7	.279	.394	.542
1995 Seattle	AL	126	470	123	23	0	40	(21	19)	266	86	121	60	7	120	1	2	6	0	0	.00	15	.262	.343	.566
1996 Seattle	AL	150	564	153	29	0	44	(21	23)	314	107	138	84	5	159	9	0	10	0	1	.00	11	.271	.369	.557
1997 Seattle	AL	157	540	131	18	2	40	(13	27)	273	104	109	119	3	175	5	0	1	0	0	—	23	.243	.383	.506
1998 Seattle	AL	72	244	59	7	1	15	(8	7)	113	33	45	38	0	71	1	1	2	0	0	—	2	.242	.344	.463
1999 Seattle	AL	87	266	59	11	0	14	(5	9)	112	37	38	69	0	100	5	0	3	0	0	—	6	.222	.388	.421
2000 Seattle	AL	112	364	92	20	0	26	(15	11)	190	50	82	59	3	98	4	1	2	0	2	.00	10	.253	.361	.522
1988 New York	AL	25	69	13	0	0	3	(1	2)	22	8	13	3	0	25	3	0	1	0	0	—	1	.188	.250	.319
Seattle	AL	60	192	43	13	1	10	(7	3)	88	28	25	25	1	68	3	1	2	1	1	.50	4	.224	.320	.458
14 ML YEARS		1453	4968	1263	231	19	308	(144	164)	2456	794	960	784	41	1397	56	12	54	6	24	.20	120	.254	.359	.494

Kirk Bullinger

Pitches: Right **Bats:** Right **Pos:** RP-3 **Ht:** 6'2" **Wt:** 170 **Born:** 10/28/69 **Age:** 31

Year Team	Lg	G	GS	CG	GF	IP	BFP	H	R	ER	HR	SH	SF	HB	TBB	IBB	SO	WP	Bk	W	L	Pct.	ShO	Sv-Op	Hld	ERA
1992 Hamilton	A-	35	0	0	7	48.2	191	24	7	6	0	1	2		15	4	61	3	1	2	2	.500	0	2--	—	1.11
1993 Springfield	A	50	0	0	46	51.1	208	26	19	13	5	3	2	2	21	1	72	6	0	1	3	.250	0	33--	—	2.28
1994 St. Pete	A+	39	0	0	18	53.2	220	37	16	7	0	4	0	1	20	5	50	4	3	2	0	1.000	0	6--	—	1.17
1995 Harrisburg	AA	56	0	0	39	67	282	61	22	18	4	4	1	0	25	5	42	2	2	5	3	.625	0	7--	—	2.42
1996 Ottawa	AAA	10	0	0	4	15.1	62	10	6	6	3	0	0	0	9	1	9	1	0	2	1	.667	0	0--	—	3.52
Harrisburg	AA	47	0	0	40	45.2	193	46	16	10	5	3	1	1	18	3	29	3	0	3	4	.429	0	22--	—	1.97
1997 Wst Plm Bch	A+	2	0	0	0	3.2	15	3	0	0	0	0	0	0	0	0	7	1	0	1	0	1.000	0	0--	—	0.00
Harrisburg	AA	21	0	0	12	27	106	22	9	8	4	1	0	1	6	0	21	0	0	3	0	1.000	0	6--	—	2.67
Ottawa	AAA	22	0	0	14	31.2	119	17	7	6	0	2	1	0	10	0	15	1	0	3	4	.429	0	5--	—	1.71
1998 Expos	R	2	2	0	0	4	14	2	0	0	0	0	0	0	0	0	7	0	0	0	0	—	0	0--	—	0.00
Jupiter	A+	8	0	0	1	10	42	9	7	6	1	0	0	0	2	0	12	2	0	0	0	—	0	0--	—	5.40
Ottawa	AAA	13	0	0	4	17	72	16	2	2	0	1	0	0	6	1	7	0	0	0	0	—	0	3--	—	1.06
1999 Trenton	AA	17	0	0	17	17	60	6	4	1	0	3	1	1	5	1	16	1	1	1	1	.500	0	10--	—	0.53
Pawtucket	AAA	35	0	0	30	37.2	160	37	14	10	3	4	1	2	13	4	27	0	0	0	1	.000	0	15--	—	2.39
2000 Reading	AA	2	1	0	0	3	12	3	0	0	0	0	0	0	1	0	1	0	0	0	0	—	0	0--	—	0.00
Phillies	R	1	1	0	0	1	3	0	0	0	0	0	0	0	1	0	0	0	0	0	0	—	0	0--	—	0.00
Scrantn-WB	AAA	26	0	0	21	25	99	19	4	2	0	3	0	1	10	2	16	0	0	0	1	.000	0	12--	—	0.72
1998 Montreal	NL	8	0	0	1	7	35	14	8	7	1	0	0	0	3	1	2	0	0	1	0	1.000	0	0-1	—	9.00
1999 Boston	AL	4	0	0	0	2	9	3	1	1	0	0	0	0	2	0	0	0	0	0	0	—	0	0-0	—	4.50
2000 Philadelphia	NL	3	0	0	1	3.1	14	3	2	2	0	0	0	0	1	0	4	0	0	0	0	—	0	0-0	—	5.40
3 ML YEARS		15	0	0	2	12.1	58	20	11	10	1	0	0	0	6	1	6	0	0	1	0	1.000	0	0-1	3	7.30

Dave Burba

Pitches: Right **Bats:** Right **Pos:** SP-32   **Ht:** 6'4" **Wt:** 240 **Born:** 7/7/66 **Age:** 34

		HOW MUCH HE PITCHED					WHAT HE GAVE UP												THE RESULTS					
Year Team	Lg	G	GS	CG	GF	IP	BFP	H	R	ER	HR	SH	SF	HB	TBB	IBB	SO	WP	Bk	W	L	Pct.	ShO	Sv-Op	Hld	ERA
1990 Seattle	AL	6	0	0	2	8	35	8	6	4	2	0	1	0	2	0	4	0	0	0	0	—	0	0-0	0	4.50
1991 Seattle	AL	22	2	0	11	36.2	153	34	16	15	6	0	0	0	14	3	16	1	0	2	2	.500	0	1-1	0	3.68
1992 San Francisco	NL	23	11	0	4	70.2	318	80	43	39	4	2	4	2	31	2	47	1	1	2	7	.222	0	0-0	0	4.97
1993 San Francisco	NL	54	5	0	9	95.1	408	95	49	45	14	6	3	3	37	5	88	4	0	10	3	.769	0	0-0	10	4.25
1994 San Francisco	NL	57	0	0	13	74	322	59	39	36	5	3	1	6	45	3	84	3	0	3	6	.333	0	0-3	11	4.38
1995 SF-Cin	NL	52	9	1	7	106.2	451	90	50	47	9	4	1	0	51	3	96	5	0	10	4	.714	1	0-1	5	3.97
1996 Cincinnati	NL	34	33	0	0	195	849	179	96	83	18	5	12	2	97	9	148	9	1	11	13	.458	0	0-0	0	3.83
1997 Cincinnati	NL	30	27	2	1	160	706	157	88	84	22	6	3	9	73	10	131	6	0	11	10	.524	0	0-0	0	4.73
1998 Cleveland	AL	32	31	0	0	203.2	870	210	100	93	30	3	10	7	69	4	132	6	0	15	10	.600	0	0-0	0	4.11
1999 Cleveland	AL	34	34	1	0	220	940	211	113	104	30	2	3	8	96	3	174	13	0	15	9	.625	0	0-0	0	4.25
2000 Cleveland	AL	32	32	0	0	191.1	848	199	99	95	19	5	5	2	91	2	180	7	0	16	6	.727	0	0-0	0	4.47
1995 San Francisco	NL	37	0	0	7	43.1	191	38	26	24	5	3	1	0	25	2	46	2	0	4	2	.667	0	0-1	5	4.98
Cincinnati	NL	15	9	1	0	63.1	260	52	24	23	4	1	0	0	26	1	50	3	0	6	2	.750	1	0-0	0	3.27
11 ML YEARS		376	184	4	47	1361.1	5900	1322	699	645	157	38	42	40	606	44	1100	55	2	95	70	.576	1	1-5	26	4.26

John Burkett

Pitches: Right **Bats:** Right **Pos:** SP-22; RP-9   **Ht:** 6'3" **Wt:** 215 **Born:** 11/28/64 **Age:** 36

		HOW MUCH HE PITCHED					WHAT HE GAVE UP												THE RESULTS					
Year Team	Lg	G	GS	CG	GF	IP	BFP	H	R	ER	HR	SH	SF	HB	TBB	IBB	SO	WP	Bk	W	L	Pct.	ShO	Sv-Op	Hld	ERA
1987 San Francisco	NL	3	0	0	1	6	28	7	4	3	2	1	0	1	3	0	5	0	0	0	0	0-0	0	0-0	0	4.50
1990 San Francisco	NL	33	32	2	1	204	857	201	92	86	18	6	5	4	61	7	118	3	3	14	7	.667	0	1-1	0	3.79
1991 San Francisco	NL	36	34	3	0	206.2	890	223	103	96	19	8	8	10	60	2	131	5	0	12	11	.522	1	0-0	1	4.18
1992 San Francisco	NL	32	32	3	0	189.2	799	194	96	81	13	11	4	4	45	6	107	0	0	13	9	.591	1	0-0	0	3.84
1993 San Francisco	NL	34	34	2	0	231.2	942	224	100	94	18	8	4	11	40	4	145	1	2	22	7	.759	1	0-0	0	3.65
1994 San Francisco	NL	25	25	0	0	159.1	676	176	72	64	14	12	5	7	36	7	85	2	0	6	8	.429	0	0-0	0	3.62
1995 Florida	NL	30	30	4	0	188.1	810	208	95	90	22	10	0	6	57	5	126	2	1	14	14	.500	1	0-0	0	4.30
1996 Fla-Tex		34	34	2	0	222.2	934	229	117	105	19	12	6	5	58	4	155	0	0	11	12	.478	1	0-0	0	4.24
1997 Texas	AL	30	30	2	0	189.1	828	240	106	96	20	4	7	6	30	1	139	1	0	9	12	.429	0	0-0	0	4.56
1998 Texas	AL	32	32	0	0	195	854	230	131	123	19	7	5	8	46	1	131	3	0	9	13	.409	0	0-0	0	5.68
1999 Texas	AL	30	25	0	1	147.1	656	184	95	92	18	5	3	3	46	1	96	4	0	9	8	.529	0	0-0	0	5.62
2000 Atlanta	NL	31	22	0	4	134.1	603	162	79	73	13	8	5	6	51	2	110	2	0	10	6	.625	0	0-1	0	4.89
1996 Florida	NL	24	24	1	0	154	645	154	84	74	15	11	4	3	42	2	108	0	0	6	10	.375	0	0-0	0	4.32
Texas	AL	10	10	1	0	68.2	289	75	33	31	4	1	2	2	16	2	47	0	0	5	2	.714	1	0-0	0	4.06
12 ML YEARS		350	330	18	7	2074.1	8877	2278	1090	1003	195	92	52	67	533	40	1348	23	6	129	107	.547	4	1-2	1	4.35

Morgan Burkhart

Bats: B **Throws:** L **Pos:** DH-19; 1B-5; PH/PR-3; LF-1   **Ht:** 5'11" **Wt:** 225 **Born:** 1/29/72 **Age:** 29

		BATTING																	BASERUNNING				PERCENTAGES		
Year Team	Lg	G	AB	H	2B	3B	HR	(Hm	Rd)	TB	R	RBI	TBB	IBB	SO	HBP	SH	SF	SB	CS	SB%	GDP	Avg	OBP	SLG
1995 Richmond	IND	70	282	93	28	1	9	—	—	150	58	70	41	4	24	7	0	7	16	7	.70	5	.330	.418	.532
1996 Richmond	IND	74	266	95	27	1	17	—	—	175	60	64	49	4	24	14	0	6	22	4	.85	3	.357	.472	.658
1997 Richmond	IND	80	285	92	22	0	24	—	—	186	76	74	73	8	47	8	0	5	8	4	.67	6	.323	.466	.653
1998 Richmond	IND	80	280	113	18	1	36	—	—	241	97	98	85	9	38	13	0	1	13	1	.93	6	.404	.557	.861
1999 Sarasota	A+	68	245	89	18	0	23	—	—	176	56	67	37	6	33	6	0	7	5	2	.71	4	.363	.447	.718
Trenton	AA	66	239	55	14	1	12	—	—	107	40	41	31	1	43	10	0	3	3	0	1.00	6	.230	.339	.448
2000 Pawtucket	AAA	105	353	90	17	1	23	—	—	178	59	77	69	4	89	12	0	2	0	0	—	6	.255	.392	.504
2000 Boston	AL	25	73	21	3	0	4	(1	3)	36	16	18	17	1	25	4	0	1	0	0	—	1	.288	.442	.493

Ellis Burks

Bats: Right **Throws:** Right **Pos:** RF-108; PH/PR-12; DH-2   **Ht:** 6'2" **Wt:** 205 **Born:** 9/11/64 **Age:** 36

		BATTING																	BASERUNNING				PERCENTAGES		
Year Team	Lg	G	AB	H	2B	3B	HR	(Hm	Rd)	TB	R	RBI	TBB	IBB	SO	HBP	SH	SF	SB	CS	SB%	GDP	Avg	OBP	SLG
1987 Boston	AL	133	558	152	30	2	20	(11	9)	246	94	59	41	0	98	2	4	1	27	6	.82	1	.272	.324	.441
1988 Boston	AL	144	540	159	37	5	18	(8	10)	260	93	92	62	1	89	3	4	6	25	9	.74	8	.294	.367	.481
1989 Boston	AL	97	399	121	19	6	12	(6	6)	188	73	61	36	2	52	5	2	4	21	5	.81	8	.303	.365	.471
1990 Boston	AL	152	588	174	33	8	21	(10	11)	286	89	89	48	4	82	1	2	2	9	11	.45	18	.296	.349	.486
1991 Boston	AL	130	474	119	33	3	14	(8	6)	200	56	56	39	2	81	6	2	3	6	11	.35	7	.251	.314	.422
1992 Boston	AL	66	235	60	8	3	8	(4	4)	98	35	30	25	2	48	1	0	2	5	2	.71	5	.255	.327	.417
1993 Chicago	AL	146	499	137	24	4	17	(7	10)	220	75	74	60	2	97	4	3	8	6	9	.40	11	.275	.352	.441
1994 Colorado	NL	42	149	48	8	3	13	(7	6)	101	33	24	16	3	39	0	0	0	3	1	.75	3	.322	.388	.678
1995 Colorado	NL	103	278	74	10	6	14	(8	6)	138	41	49	39	0	72	2	1	1	7	3	.70	7	.266	.359	.496
1996 Colorado	NL	156	613	211	45	8	40	(23	17)	392	142	128	61	2	114	6	3	2	32	6	.84	19	.344	.408	.639
1997 Colorado	NL	119	424	123	19	2	32	(17	15)	242	91	82	47	0	75	3	1	2	7	2	.78	17	.290	.363	.571
1998 Col-SF	NL	142	504	147	28	6	21	(10	11)	250	76	76	58	4	111	5	6	9	18	8	.58	12	.292	.365	.496
1999 San Francisco	NL	120	390	110	19	0	31	(16	15)	222	73	96	69	2	86	6	0	4	7	5	.58	11	.282	.394	.569
2000 San Francisco	NL	122	393	135	21	5	24	(16	8)	238	74	96	56	5	49	1	0	8	5	1	.83	10	.344	.419	.606
1998 Colorado	NL	100	357	102	22	5	16	(8	8)	182	54	54	39	0	80	2	2	5	3	7	.30	10	.286	.355	.510
San Francisco	NL	42	147	45	6	1	5	(2	3)	68	22	22	19	1	31	3	4	4	8	1	.89	2	.306	.387	.463
14 ML YEARS		1672	6044	1770	334	61	285	(150	135)	3081	1045	1012	657	26	1093	45	28	52	171	79	.68	137	.293	.364	.510

A.J. Burnett

Pitches: Right **Bats:** Right **Pos:** SP-13   **Ht:** 6'5" **Wt:** 205 **Born:** 1/3/77 **Age:** 24

		HOW MUCH HE PITCHED					WHAT HE GAVE UP												THE RESULTS					
Year Team	Lg	G	GS	CG	GF	IP	BFP	H	R	ER	HR	SH	SF	HB	TBB	IBB	SO	WP	Bk	W	L	Pct.	ShO	Sv-Op	Hld	ERA
1995 Mets	R	9	8	1	1	33.2	144	27	16	16	2	0	2	2	23	0	26	7	4	2	3	.400	0	0--	—	4.28
1996 Kingsport	R+	12	12	0	0	58	245	31	26	25	0	1	2	7	54	0	68	16	3	4	0	1.000	0	0--	—	3.88
1997 Mets	R	3	2	0	0	11.1	54	8	8	4	0	0	0	0	8	0	15	3	0	1	0	1.000	0	0--	—	3.18
Pittsfield	A-	9	9	0	0	44	192	28	26	23	3	0	2	6	35	0	48	9	0	3	1	.750	0	0--	—	4.70

33

		HOW MUCH HE PITCHED			WHAT HE GAVE UP			THE RESULTS	
Year Team	Lg	G GS CG GF	IP	BFP	H R ER HR SH SF HB	TBB IBB	SO WP Bk	W L Pct. ShO Sv-Op Hld	ERA
1998 Kane County	A	20 20 0 0	119	469	74 27 26 3 2 0 8	45 0	186 6 2	10 4 .714 0 0-- —	1.97
1999 Portland	AA	26 23 0 1	120.2	552	132 91 74 15 3 4 5	71 0	121 16 2	6 12 .333 0 0-- —	5.52
2000 Brevard Cty	A+	2 2 0 0	7.1	31	4 3 3 0 0 0 0	6 0	6 0 2	0 0 — 0 0-- —	3.68
Calgary	AAA	1 1 0 0	5	18	0 0 0 0 0 0 0	3 0	6 2 0	0 0 — 0 0-- —	0.00
1999 Florida	NL	7 7 0 0	41.1	182	37 23 16 3 1 3 0	25 2	33 0 0	4 2 .667 0 0-0 0	3.48
2000 Florida	NL	13 13 0 0	82.2	364	80 46 44 8 6 3 2	44 3	57 2 0	3 7 .300 0 0-0 0	4.79
2 ML YEARS		20 20 0 0	124	546	117 69 60 11 7 6 2	69 5	90 2 0	7 9 .438 0 0-0 0	4.35

Jeromy Burnitz

Bats: Left **Throws:** Right **Pos:** RF-158; PH/PR-2; DH-1   **Ht:** 6'0" **Wt:** 205 **Born:** 4/15/69 **Age:** 32

		BATTING														BASERUNNING				PERCENTAGES		
Year Team	Lg	G	AB	H	2B	3B	HR	(Hm	Rd)	TB	R	RBI	TBB	IBB	SO	HBP	SH	SF	SB CS SB% GDP	Avg	OBP	SLG
1993 New York	NL	86	263	64	10	6	13	(6	7)	125	49	38	38	4	66	1	1	2	3 6 .33 2	.243	.339	.475
1994 New York	NL	45	143	34	4	0	3	(2	1)	47	26	15	23	0	45	1	1	0	1 1 .50 2	.238	.347	.329
1995 Cleveland	AL	9	7	4	1	0	0	(0	0)	5	4	0	0	0	0	0	0	0	0 0 — 0	.571	.571	.714
1996 Cle-Mil	AL	94	200	53	14	0	9	(5	4)	94	38	40	33	2	47	4	0	2	4 1 .80 4	.265	.377	.470
1997 Milwaukee	AL	153	494	139	37	8	27	(18	9)	273	85	85	75	8	111	5	3	0	20 13 .61 8	.281	.382	.553
1998 Milwaukee	NL	161	609	160	28	1	38	(17	21)	304	92	125	70	7	158	4	1	7	7 4 .64 9	.263	.339	.499
1999 Milwaukee	NL	130	467	126	33	2	33	(12	21)	262	87	103	91	7	124	16	0	6	7 3 .70 11	.270	.402	.561
2000 Milwaukee	NL	161	564	131	29	2	31	(12	19)	257	91	98	99	10	121	14	0	9	6 4 .60 12	.232	.356	.456
1996 Cleveland	AL	71	128	36	10	0	7	(4	3)	67	30	26	25	1	31	2	0	0	2 1 .67 3	.281	.406	.523
Milwaukee		23	72	17	4	0	2	(1	1)	27	8	14	8	1	16	2	0	2	2 0 1.00 1	.236	.321	.375
8 ML YEARS		839	2747	711	156	19	154	(72	82)	1367	472	504	429	38	672	45	7	26	48 32 .60 58	.259	.365	.498

Pat Burrell

Bats: R **Throws:** R **Pos:** 1B-58; LF-48; DH-4; PH/PR-1   **Ht:** 6'4" **Wt:** 225 **Born:** 10/10/76 **Age:** 24

		BATTING														BASERUNNING				PERCENTAGES		
Year Team	Lg	G	AB	H	2B	3B	HR	(Hm	Rd)	TB	R	RBI	TBB	IBB	SO	HBP	SH	SF	SB CS SB% GDP	Avg	OBP	SLG
1998 Clearwater	A+	37	132	40	7	1	7	—	—	70	29	30	27	2	22	0	0	2	2 0 1.00 3	.303	.416	.530
1999 Reading	AA	117	417	139	28	6	28	—	—	263	84	90	79	3	103	0	0	2	3 1 .75 13	.333	.438	.631
Scrantn-WB	AAA	10	33	5	0	0	1	—	—	8	4	4	4	0	8	1	0	0	0 1 .00 0	.152	.263	.242
2000 Scrantn-WB	AAA	40	143	42	15	1	4	—	—	71	31	25	32	0	36	0	0	1	1 1 .50 1	.294	.420	.497
2000 Philadelphia	NL	111	408	106	27	1	18	(7	11)	189	57	79	63	2	139	1	0	2	0 0 — 5	.260	.359	.463

Homer Bush

Bats: Right **Throws:** Right **Pos:** 2B-75; PH/PR-3   **Ht:** 5'10" **Wt:** 180 **Born:** 11/12/72 **Age:** 28

		BATTING														BASERUNNING				PERCENTAGES		
Year Team	Lg	G	AB	H	2B	3B	HR	(Hm	Rd)	TB	R	RBI	TBB	IBB	SO	HBP	SH	SF	SB CS SB% GDP	Avg	OBP	SLG
1997 New York	AL	10	11	4	0	0	0	(0	0)	4	2	3	0	0	0	0	0	0	0 0 — 0	.364	.364	.364
1998 New York	AL	45	71	27	3	0	1	(1	0)	33	17	5	5	0	19	0	2	0	6 3 .67 1	.380	.421	.465
1999 Toronto	AL	128	485	155	26	4	5	(2	3)	204	69	55	21	0	82	6	8	3	32 8 .80 9	.320	.353	.421
2000 Toronto	AL	76	297	64	8	0	1	(1	0)	75	38	18	18	0	60	5	4	1	9 4 .69 10	.215	.271	.253
4 ML YEARS		259	864	250	37	4	7	(4	3)	316	126	81	44	0	161	11	14	4	47 15 .76 20	.289	.330	.366

Paul Byrd

Pitches: Right **Bats:** Right **Pos:** SP-15; RP-2   **Ht:** 6'1" **Wt:** 184 **Born:** 12/3/70 **Age:** 30

		HOW MUCH HE PITCHED			WHAT HE GAVE UP			THE RESULTS	
Year Team	Lg	G GS CG GF	IP	BFP	H R ER HR SH SF HB	TBB IBB	SO WP Bk	W L Pct. ShO Sv-Op Hld	ERA
2000 Scrantn-WB *	AAA	3 3 2 0	26	101	20 6 5 2 1 0 1	6 0	10 0 1	2 0 1.000 0 0-- —	1.73
1995 New York	NL	17 0 0 6	22	91	18 6 5 1 0 2 1	7 1	26 1 0	2 0 1.000 0 0-0 3	2.05
1996 New York	NL	38 0 0 14	46.2	204	48 22 22 7 1 1 0	21 4	31 3 0	1 2 .333 0 0-2 3	4.24
1997 Atlanta	NL	31 4 0 9	53	236	47 34 31 6 2 2 4	28 4	37 3 1	4 4 .500 0 0-0 1	5.26
1998 Atl-Phi	NL	9 8 2 0	57	233	45 19 17 6 2 1 0	18 1	39 2 0	5 2 .714 1 0-0 0	2.68
1999 Philadelphia	NL	32 32 1 0	199.2	872	205 119 102 34 5 6 **17**	70 2	106 11 3	15 11 .577 0 0-0 0	4.60
2000 Philadelphia	NL	17 15 0 0	83	371	89 67 60 17 3 1 3	35 2	53 1 0	2 9 .182 0 0-0 0	6.51
1998 Atlanta	NL	1 0 0 0	2	11	4 3 3 0 0 0 0	1 0	1 0 0	0 0 — 0 0-0 0	13.50
Philadelphia		8 8 2 0	55	222	41 16 14 6 2 1 0	17 1	38 2 0	5 2 .714 1 0-0 0	2.29
6 ML YEARS		144 59 3 29	461.1	2007	452 267 237 71 13 13 25	179 14	292 21 6	29 28 .509 1 0-2 7	4.62

Tim Byrdak

Pitches: Left **Bats:** Left **Pos:** RP-12   **Ht:** 5'11" **Wt:** 180 **Born:** 10/31/73 **Age:** 27

		HOW MUCH HE PITCHED			WHAT HE GAVE UP			THE RESULTS	
Year Team	Lg	G GS CG GF	IP	BFP	H R ER HR SH SF HB	TBB IBB	SO WP Bk	W L Pct. ShO Sv-Op Hld	ERA
2000 Wichita *	AA	4 0 0 1	6.2	29	9 4 4 1 0 0 0	3 0	1 0 0	0 0 — 0 0-- —	5.40
Omaha *	AAA	34 1 0 17	52.2	244	59 27 26 5 4 1 4	29 3	47 3 2	6 2 .750 0 4-- —	4.44
1998 Kansas City	AL	3 0 0 0	1.2	9	5 1 1 1 0 0 0	0 0	1 0 0	0 0 — 0 0-0 0	5.40
1999 Kansas City	AL	33 0 0 5	24.2	128	32 24 21 5 3 0 1	20 2	17 3 1	0 3 .000 0 1-4 10	7.66
2000 Kansas City	AL	12 0 0 1	6.1	34	11 8 8 3 0 0 0	4 0	8 1 0	0 1 .000 0 0-2 3	11.37
3 ML YEARS		48 0 0 6	32.2	171	48 33 30 9 3 0 1	24 2	26 4 1	0 4 .000 0 1-6 13	8.27

Eric Byrnes

Bats: R **Throws:** R **Pos:** PH/PR-8; RF-3; DH-2; LF-1   **Ht:** 6'2" **Wt:** 205 **Born:** 2/16/76 **Age:** 25

		BATTING														BASERUNNING				PERCENTAGES		
Year Team	Lg	G	AB	H	2B	3B	HR	(Hm	Rd)	TB	R	RBI	TBB	IBB	SO	HBP	SH	SF	SB CS SB% GDP	Avg	OBP	SLG
1998 Sou Oregon	A-	42	169	53	10	2	7	—	—	88	36	31	16	1	16	2	0	1	6 1 .86 3	.314	.378	.521
Visalia	A+	29	108	46	9	2	4	—	—	71	26	21	18	0	15	1	0	2	11 1 .92 2	.426	.504	.657

Year Team	Lg	G	AB	H	2B	3B	HR	(Hm	Rd)	TB	R	RBI	TBB	IBB	SO	HBP	SH	SF	SB	CS	SB%	GDP	Avg	OBP	SLG
								BATTING												BASERUNNING			PERCENTAGES		
1999 Midland	AA	43	164	39	14	0	1	—	—	56	25	22	17	0	32	3	2	3	6	3	.67	5	.238	.316	.341
Modesto	A+	96	365	123	28	1	6	—	—	171	86	66	58	2	37	9	0	7	28	8	.78	14	.337	.433	.468
2000 Midland	AA	67	259	78	25	2	5	—	—	122	49	37	43	0	38	1	2	6	21	11	.66	5	.301	.395	.471
Sacramento	AAA	67	243	81	23	1	9	—	—	133	55	47	31	0	30	2	1	2	12	5	.71	3	.333	.410	.547
2000 Oakland	AL	10	10	3	0	0	0	(0	0)	3	5	0	0	0	1	1	0	0	2	1	.67	0	.300	.364	.300

Alex Cabrera

Bats: R **Throws:** R **Pos:** 1B-15; RF-11; PH/PR-8; LF-1   **Ht:** 6'2" **Wt:** 217 **Born:** 12/24/71 **Age:** 29

Year Team	Lg	G	AB	H	2B	3B	HR	(Hm	Rd)	TB	R	RBI	TBB	IBB	SO	HBP	SH	SF	SB	CS	SB%	GDP	Avg	OBP	SLG
								BATTING												BASERUNNING			PERCENTAGES		
1992 Rockies/Cub	R	41	135	28	4	0	1	—	—	35	18	19	9	0	48	6	0	2	1	1	.50	1	.207	.283	.259
1993 Geneva	A-	53	167	41	5	0	5	—	—	61	29	27	9	0	49	5	0	1	4	5	.44	1	.246	.302	.365
1994 Peoria	A	121	432	120	25	1	24	—	—	219	57	73	19	4	92	16	0	4	2	8	.20	4	.278	.329	.507
1995 Daytona	A+	54	214	63	14	0	2	—	—	83	26	35	9	0	36	4	0	2	2	4	.33	8	.294	.332	.388
1996 Bakersfield	A+	89	345	97	18	1	15	—	—	162	45	53	14	0	80	11	0	4	0	1	.00	13	.281	.326	.470
2000 El Paso	AA	53	212	81	19	2	35	—	—	209	56	82	25	6	52	2	0	0	3	2	.60	1	.382	.452	.986
Diamndbcks	R	2	5	1	0	0	0	—	—	1	0	0	0	0	1	0	0	0	0	0	—	0	.200	.200	.200
Tucson	AAA	21	78	22	5	1	4	—	—	41	18	12	5	0	19	2	0	0	0	0	—	1	.282	.341	.526
2000 Arizona	NL	31	80	21	2	1	5	(2	3)	40	10	14	4	0	21	1	0	2	0	0	—	3	.263	.299	.500

Jolbert Cabrera

Bats: R **Throws:** R **Pos:** RF-29; CF-26; PH/PR-25; LF-24; 2B-19; SS-8; DH-2   **Ht:** 6'0" **Wt:** 177 **Born:** 12/8/72 **Age:** 28

Year Team	Lg	G	AB	H	2B	3B	HR	(Hm	Rd)	TB	R	RBI	TBB	IBB	SO	HBP	SH	SF	SB	CS	SB%	GDP	Avg	OBP	SLG
								BATTING												BASERUNNING			PERCENTAGES		
1991 Sumter	A	101	324	66	4	0	1	—	—	73	33	20	19	0	62	4	4	2	10	11	.48	5	.204	.255	.225
1992 Albany	A	118	377	86	9	2	0	—	—	99	44	23	34	0	77	1	6	0	22	11	.67	8	.228	.294	.263
1993 Burlington	A	128	507	129	24	2	0	—	—	157	62	38	39	0	93	7	11	4	31	11	.74	13	.254	.314	.310
1994 Wst Plm Bch	A+	83	266	54	4	0	0	—	—	58	32	13	14	0	48	8	4	0	7	10	.41	4	.203	.264	.218
San Berndno	A+	30	109	27	5	1	0	—	—	34	14	11	14	0	24	0	4	2	2	2	.50	1	.248	.328	.312
Harrisburg	AA	3	2	0	0	0	0	—	—	0	0	0	0	0	1	0	0	0	0	0	—	0	.000	.000	.000
1995 Wst Plm Bch	A+	103	357	102	23	2	1	—	—	132	62	25	38	0	61	8	6	4	19	12	.61	3	.286	.364	.370
Harrisburg	AA	9	35	10	2	0	0	—	—	12	4	1	1	0	3	0	2	0	3	1	.75	1	.286	.306	.343
1996 Harrisburg	AA	107	354	85	18	2	3	—	—	116	40	29	23	3	63	1	5	4	10	5	.67	9	.240	.285	.328
1997 Harrisburg	AA	48	171	43	9	0	2	—	—	58	28	11	28	0	28	1	3	0	5	4	.56	4	.251	.360	.339
Ottawa	AAA	68	191	54	10	4	0	—	—	72	28	12	11	0	31	0	4	1	15	5	.75	5	.283	.320	.377
1998 Buffalo	AAA	129	494	157	24	1	10	—	—	213	94	45	68	0	71	13	8	2	25	15	.63	10	.318	.412	.431
1999 Buffalo	AAA	71	279	74	13	4	0	—	—	95	44	27	26	0	43	2	7	5	20	4	.83	8	.265	.327	.341
2000 Buffalo	AAA	20	74	25	6	1	3	—	—	42	18	11	5	0	8	1	1	1	2	1	.67	3	.338	.383	.568
1998 Cleveland	AL	1	2	0	0	0	0	(0	0)	0	0	0	0	0	1	0	0	0	0	0	—	0	.000	.000	.000
1999 Cleveland	AL	30	37	7	1	0	0	(0	0)	8	6	0	1	0	8	1	0	0	3	0	1.00	0	.189	.231	.216
2000 Cleveland	AL	100	175	44	3	1	2	(2	0)	55	27	15	8	0	15	2	1	1	6	4	.60	1	.251	.290	.314
3 ML YEARS		131	214	51	4	1	2	(2	0)	63	33	15	9	0	24	3	1	1	9	4	.69	1	.238	.278	.294

Jose Cabrera

Pitches: Right **Bats:** Right **Pos:** RP-52   **Ht:** 6'0" **Wt:** 180 **Born:** 3/24/72 **Age:** 29

Year Team	Lg	G	GS	CG	GF	IP	BFP	H	R	ER	HR	SH	SF	HB	TBB	IBB	SO	WP	Bk	W	L	Pct.	ShO	Sv-Op	Hld	ERA
			HOW MUCH HE PITCHED						WHAT HE GAVE UP													THE RESULTS			
2000 New Orleans *	AAA	12	0	0	8	15.1	67	15	6	5	0	1	1	0	5	2	12	0	0	0	0	.000	0	4- —	—	2.93
1997 Houston	NL	12	0	0	6	15.1	57	6	2	2	1	0	3	0	6	0	18	0	0	0	0	—	0	0-1	2	1.17
1998 Houston	NL	3	0	0	1	4.1	19	7	4	4	0	0	0	0	1	1	1	0	0	0	0	—	0	0-0	1	8.31
1999 Houston	NL	26	0	0	11	29.1	119	21	7	7	3	0	3	0	9	2	28	4	0	4	0	1.000	0	0-1	6	2.15
2000 Houston	NL	52	0	0	22	59.1	266	74	40	39	10	3	3	3	17	2	41	1	1	2	3	.400	0	2-3	5	5.92
4 ML YEARS		93	0	0	40	108.1	461	108	53	52	14	3	9	3	33	5	88	5	1	6	3	.667	0	2-5	13	4.32

Orlando Cabrera

Bats: Right **Throws:** Right **Pos:** SS-124; PH/PR-3; 2B-1   **Ht:** 5'10" **Wt:** 175 **Born:** 11/2/74 **Age:** 26

Year Team	Lg	G	AB	H	2B	3B	HR	(Hm	Rd)	TB	R	RBI	TBB	IBB	SO	HBP	SH	SF	SB	CS	SB%	GDP	Avg	OBP	SLG
								BATTING												BASERUNNING			PERCENTAGES		
2000 Ottawa *	AAA	2	6	4	0	0	0	—	—	4	1	0	1	0	0	1	0	0	1	0	1.00	1	.667	.750	.667
1997 Montreal	NL	16	18	4	0	0	0	(0	0)	4	4	2	1	0	3	0	1	0	1	2	.33	1	.222	.263	.222
1998 Montreal	NL	79	261	73	16	5	3	(2	1)	108	44	22	18	1	27	0	5	1	6	2	.75	6	.280	.325	.414
1999 Montreal	NL	104	382	97	23	5	8	(6	2)	154	48	39	18	4	38	3	4	0	2	2	.50	9	.254	.293	.403
2000 Montreal	NL	125	422	100	25	1	13	(7	6)	166	47	55	25	3	28	1	3	3	4	4	.50	12	.237	.279	.393
4 ML YEARS		324	1083	274	64	11	24	(15	9)	432	143	118	62	8	96	4	13	4	13	10	.57	28	.253	.295	.399

Cam Cairncross

Pitches: Left **Bats:** Left **Pos:** RP-15   **Ht:** 6'0" **Wt:** 195 **Born:** 5/11/72 **Age:** 29

Year Team	Lg	G	GS	CG	GF	IP	BFP	H	R	ER	HR	SH	SF	HB	TBB	IBB	SO	WP	Bk	W	L	Pct.	ShO	Sv-Op	Hld	ERA
			HOW MUCH HE PITCHED						WHAT HE GAVE UP													THE RESULTS			
1991 Chston-SC	A	24	24	2	0	131.1	545	111	72	52	10	4	3	7	74	0	102	6	9	8	5	.615	1	0- —	—	3.56
1992 Waterloo	A	24	24	1	0	137	578	127	68	55	14	3	3	14	61	2	138	8	9	8	8	.500	1	0- —	—	3.61
1993 Rancho Cuc	A+	29	26	0	0	154.2	706	182	112	88	10	5	6	13	81	1	122	8	9	10	11	.476	0	0- —	—	5.12
1994 Las Vegas	AAA	4	0	0	0	6.1	32	8	3	3	0	0	0	0	6	2	4	0	0	1	0	1.000	0	0- —	—	4.26
Rancho Cuc	A+	29	0	0	6	34.2	139	26	19	17	3	0	1	2	14	0	40	1	2	3	1	.750	0	3- —	—	4.41
Wichita	AA	31	0	0	13	37	162	37	19	15	5	0	0	2	15	1	33	6	1	3	2	.400	0	3- —	—	3.65
1997 Rancho Cuc	A+	40	0	0	17	64	291	81	46	40	5	4	1	5	15	0	70	4	1	1	3	.250	0	1- —	—	5.63
1999 Kinston	A+	6	0	0	4	9.2	35	5	1	0	0	0	0	1	4	0	11	1	0	2	0	1.000	0	2- —	—	0.00
Buffalo	AAA	19	0	0	5	19	86	22	13	11	2	4	2	0	6	0	13	1	0	0	3	.000	0	0- —	—	5.21

Year Team	Lg	G	GS	CG	GF	IP	BFP	H	R	ER	HR	SH	SF	HB	TBB	IBB	SO	WP	Bk	W	L	Pct.	ShO	Sv-Op	Hld	ERA

		HOW MUCH HE PITCHED						**WHAT HE GAVE UP**												**THE RESULTS**						
Year Team	Lg	G	GS	CG	GF	IP	BFP	H	R	ER	HR	SH	SF	HB	TBB	IBB	SO	WP	Bk	W	L	Pct.	ShO	Sv-Op	Hld	ERA
2000 Akron	AA	28	0	0	15	29.2	114	22	5	5	2	1	1	3	6	2	23	1	0	1	0	1.000	0	4--	—	1.52
Buffalo	AAA	15	0	0	6	8	36	11	2	2	1	0	0	0	4	1	11	0	0	1	-	.000	0	1--	—	2.25
2000 Cleveland	AL	15	0	0	2	9.1	40	11	4	4	1	0	1	0	3	1	8	0	0	1	0	1.000	0	0-0	3	3.86

Miguel Cairo

Bats: Right **Throws:** Right **Pos:** 2B-108; PH/PR-15; DH-2   **Ht:** 6'1" **Wt:** 200 **Born:** 5/4/74 **Age:** 27

		BATTING																**BASERUNNING**				**PERCENTAGES**		
Year Team	Lg	G	AB	H	2B	3B	HR	(Hm | Rd)	TB	R	RBI	TBB	IBB	SO	HBP	SH	SF	SB	CS	SB%	GDP	Avg	OBP	SLG
1996 Toronto	AL	9	27	6	2	0	0	(0 | 0)	8	5	1	2	0	9	1	0	0	0	0	—	1	.222	.300	.296
1997 Chicago	NL	16	29	7	1	0	0	(0 | 0)	8	7	1	2	0	3	1	0	0	0	0	—	0	.241	.313	.276
1998 Tampa Bay	AL	150	515	138	26	5	5	(3 | 2)	189	49	46	24	0	44	6	11	2	19	8	.70	9	.268	.307	.367
1999 Tampa Bay	AL	120	465	137	15	5	3	(1 | 2)	171	61	36	24	0	46	7	7	5	22	7	.76	13	.295	.335	.368
2000 Tampa Bay	AL	119	375	98	18	2	1	(0 | 1)	123	49	34	29	0	34	2	6	5	28	7	.80	7	.261	.314	.328
5 ML YEARS		414	1411	386	62	12	9	(4 | 5)	499	171	118	81	0	136	17	24	12	69	22	.76	30	.274	.318	.354

Mike Cameron

Bats: R **Throws:** R **Pos:** CF-155; PH/PR-6; LF-1; RF-1   **Ht:** 6'2" **Wt:** 190 **Born:** 1/8/73 **Age:** 28

		BATTING																**BASERUNNING**				**PERCENTAGES**		
Year Team	Lg	G	AB	H	2B	3B	HR	(Hm | Rd)	TB	R	RBI	TBB	IBB	SO	HBP	SH	SF	SB	CS	SB%	GDP	Avg	OBP	SLG
1995 Chicago	AL	28	38	7	2	0	1	(0 | 1)	12	4	2	3	0	15	0	3	0	0	0	—	0	.184	.244	.316
1996 Chicago	AL	11	11	1	0	0	0	(0 | 0)	1	1	0	1	0	3	0	0	0	0	1	.00	0	.091	.167	.091
1997 Chicago	AL	116	379	98	18	3	14	(10 | 4)	164	63	55	55	1	105	5	2	5	23	2	.92	6	.259	.356	.433
1998 Chicago	AL	141	396	83	16	5	8	(5 | 3)	133	53	43	37	0	101	6	1	3	27	11	.71	6	.210	.285	.336
1999 Cincinnati	NL	146	542	139	34	9	21	(12 | 9)	254	93	66	80	2	145	6	5	3	38	12	.76	4	.256	.357	.469
2000 Seattle	AL	155	543	145	28	4	19	(5 | 14)	238	96	78	78	0	133	9	7	6	24	7	.77	10	.267	.365	.438
6 ML YEARS		597	1909	473	98	21	63	(32 | 31)	802	310	244	254	4	502	26	18	17	112	33	.77	28	.248	.341	.420

Ken Caminiti

Bats: Both **Throws:** Right **Pos:** 3B-58; PH/PR-3   **Ht:** 6'0" **Wt:** 200 **Born:** 4/21/63 **Age:** 38

		BATTING																**BASERUNNING**				**PERCENTAGES**		
Year Team	Lg	G	AB	H	2B	3B	HR	(Hm | Rd)	TB	R	RBI	TBB	IBB	SO	HBP	SH	SF	SB	CS	SB%	GDP	Avg	OBP	SLG
1987 Houston	NL	63	203	50	7	1	3	(2 | 1)	68	10	23	12	1	44	0	2	1	0	0	—	6	.246	.287	.335
1988 Houston	NL	30	83	15	2	0	1	(0 | 1)	20	5	7	5	0	18	0	0	1	0	0	—	3	.181	.225	.241
1989 Houston	NL	161	585	149	31	3	10	(3 | 7)	216	71	72	51	9	93	3	3	4	4	1	.80	8	.255	.316	.369
1990 Houston	NL	153	541	131	20	2	4	(2 | 2)	167	52	51	48	7	97	0	3	4	9	4	.69	15	.242	.302	.309
1991 Houston	NL	152	574	145	30	3	13	(9 | 4)	220	65	80	46	7	85	5	3	4	4	5	.44	18	.253	.312	.383
1992 Houston	NL	135	506	149	31	2	13	(7 | 6)	223	68	62	44	13	68	1	2	4	10	4	.71	14	.294	.350	.441
1993 Houston	NL	143	543	142	31	0	13	(8 | 5)	212	75	75	49	10	88	0	1	3	8	5	.62	15	.262	.321	.390
1994 Houston	NL	111	406	115	28	2	18	(6 | 12)	201	63	75	43	13	71	2	0	3	4	3	.57	6	.283	.352	.495
1995 San Diego	NL	143	526	159	33	0	26	(16 | 10)	270	74	94	69	8	94	1	0	6	12	5	.71	11	.302	.380	.513
1996 San Diego	NL	146	546	178	37	2	40	(20 | 20)	339	109	130	78	16	99	4	0	10	11	5	.69	15	.326	.408	.621
1997 San Diego	NL	137	486	141	28	0	26	(11 | 15)	247	92	90	80	9	118	3	0	7	11	2	.85	12	.290	.389	.508
1998 San Diego	NL	131	452	114	29	0	29	(14 | 15)	230	87	82	71	4	108	4	0	7	6	2	.75	6	.252	.353	.509
1999 Houston	NL	78	273	78	11	1	13	(4 | 9)	130	45	56	46	3	58	3	0	7	6	2	.75	7	.286	.386	.476
2000 Houston	NL	59	208	63	13	0	15	(6 | 9)	121	42	45	42	8	37	1	0	2	3	0	1.00	7	.303	.419	.582
14 ML YEARS		1642	5932	1629	331	16	224	(112 | 112)	2664	858	942	684	108	1078	27	14	64	88	38	.70	145	.275	.349	.449

Eric Cammack

Pitches: Right **Bats:** Right **Pos:** RP-8   **Ht:** 6'1" **Wt:** 180 **Born:** 8/14/75 **Age:** 25

		HOW MUCH HE PITCHED						**WHAT HE GAVE UP**												**THE RESULTS**						
Year Team	Lg	G	GS	CG	GF	IP	BFP	H	R	ER	HR	SH	SF	HB	TBB	IBB	SO	WP	Bk	W	L	Pct.	ShO	Sv-Op	Hld	ERA
1997 Pittsfield	A-	23	0	0	17	31.1	117	9	4	3	1	3	1	1	14	1	32	1	1	0	1	.000	0	8--	—	0.86
1998 Capital Cty	A	25	0	0	22	32	127	17	13	10	2	0	0	2	13	0	49	1	0	4	0	1.000	0	8--	—	2.81
St. Lucie	A+	29	0	0	24	35.2	142	22	12	8	2	0	1	0	14	2	53	0	0	3	2	.600	0	11--	—	2.02
1999 Binghamton	AA	45	0	0	38	56.2	231	28	17	15	2	5	2	1	38	1	83	0	2	4	2	.667	0	15--	—	2.38
Norfolk	AAA	9	0	0	5	8.2	35	7	3	3	0	0	0	1	1	0	17	1	0	0	0	—	0	4--	—	3.12
2000 Norfolk	AAA	47	0	0	27	63.2	259	38	14	12	2	3	0	2	31	3	67	2	1	6	2	.750	0	9--	—	1.70
2000 New York	NL	8	0	0	0	10	48	7	7	7	1	0	1	1	10	1	9	0	0	0	0	—	0	0-0	0	6.30

Jay Canizaro

Bats: Right **Throws:** Right **Pos:** 2B-90; PH/PR-14; DH-2   **Ht:** 5'9" **Wt:** 178 **Born:** 7/4/73 **Age:** 27

		BATTING																**BASERUNNING**				**PERCENTAGES**		
Year Team	Lg	G	AB	H	2B	3B	HR	(Hm | Rd)	TB	R	RBI	TBB	IBB	SO	HBP	SH	SF	SB	CS	SB%	GDP	Avg	OBP	SLG
2000 Salt Lake *	AAA	27	101	36	9	2	6	—	—	67	21	32	17	2	17	1	0	4	4	1	.80	2	.356	.439	.663
1996 San Francisco	NL	43	120	24	4	1	2	(1	1)	36	11	8	9	0	38	1	1	0	2	.00	5	.200	.260	.300
1999 San Francisco	NL	12	18	8	2	0	1	(0	1)	13	5	9	1	0	2	0	0	0	1	1.00	0	.444	.474	.722
2000 Minnesota	AL	102	346	93	21	1	7	(2 | 5)	137	43	40	24	0	57	1	0	0	4	2	.67	8	.269	.318	.396
3 ML YEARS		157	484	125	27	2	10	(3 | 7)	186	59	57	34	0	97	2	1	0	5	4	.56	13	.258	.309	.384

Jose Canseco

Bats: R **Throws:** R **Pos:** DH-86; PH/PR-8; LF-4; RF-1   **Ht:** 6'4" **Wt:** 240 **Born:** 7/2/64 **Age:** 36

		BATTING																**BASERUNNING**				**PERCENTAGES**		
Year Team	Lg	G	AB	H	2B	3B	HR	(Hm | Rd)	TB	R	RBI	TBB	IBB	SO	HBP	SH	SF	SB	CS	SB%	GDP	Avg	OBP	SLG
1985 Oakland	AL	29	96	29	3	0	5	(4 | 1)	47	16	13	4	0	31	0	0	0	1	1	.50	1	.302	.330	.490
1986 Oakland	AL	157	600	144	29	1	33	(14 | 19)	274	85	117	65	1	175	8	0	9	15	7	.68	12	.240	.318	.457
1987 Oakland	AL	159	630	162	35	3	31	(16 | 15)	296	81	113	50	2	157	2	0	9	15	3	.83	16	.257	.310	.470

Year Team	Lg	G	AB	H	2B	3B	HR	(Hm	Rd)	TB	R	RBI	TBB	IBB	SO	HBP	SH	SF	SB	CS	SB%	GDP	Avg	OBP	SLG
1988 Oakland	AL	158	610	187	34	0	42	(16	26)	347	120	124	78	10	128	10	1	6	40	16	.71	15	.307	.391	**.569**
1989 Oakland	AL	65	227	61	9	1	17	(8	9)	123	40	57	23	4	69	2	0	6	6	3	.67	4	.269	.333	.542
1990 Oakland	AL	131	481	132	14	2	37	(18	19)	261	83	101	72	8	158	5	0	5	19	10	.66	9	.274	.371	.543
1991 Oakland	AL	154	572	152	32	1	44	(16	28)	318	115	122	78	8	152	9	0	6	26	6	.81	16	.266	.359	.556
1992 Oak-Tex	AL	119	439	107	15	0	26	(15	11)	200	74	87	63	2	128	6	0	4	6	7	.46	16	.244	.344	.456
1993 Texas	AL	60	231	59	14	1	10	(6	4)	105	30	46	16	2	62	3	0	3	6	6	.50	6	.255	.308	.455
1994 Texas	AL	111	429	121	19	2	31	(17	14)	237	88	90	69	8	114	5	0	2	15	8	.65	20	.282	.386	.552
1995 Boston	AL	102	396	121	25	1	24	(10	14)	220	64	81	42	4	93	7	0	5	4	0	1.00	9	.306	.378	.556
1996 Boston	AL	96	360	104	22	1	28	(17	11)	212	68	82	63	3	82	6	0	3	3	1	.75	7	.289	.400	.589
1997 Oakland	AL	108	388	91	19	0	23	(10	13)	179	56	74	51	1	122	3	0	4	8	2	.80	15	.235	.325	.461
1998 Toronto	AL	151	583	138	26	0	46	(25	21)	302	98	107	65	5	159	6	0	4	29	17	.63	7	.237	.318	.518
1999 Tampa Bay	AL	113	430	120	18	1	34	(12	22)	242	75	95	58	3	135	7	0	7	3	0	1.00	14	.279	.369	.563
2000 TB-NYY	AL	98	329	83	18	0	15	(6	9)	146	47	49	64	2	102	4	0	4	2	0	1.00	7	.252	.377	.444
1992 Oakland	AL	97	366	90	11	0	22	(12	10)	167	66	72	48	1	104	3	0	4	5	7	.42	15	.246	.335	.456
Texas	AL	22	73	17	4	0	4	(3	1)	33	8	15	15	1	24	3	0	0	1	0	1.00	1	.233	.385	.452
2000 Tampa Bay	AL	61	218	56	15	0	9	(4	5)	98	31	30	41	1	65	4	0	1	2	0	1.00	5	.257	.383	.450
New York	AL	37	111	27	3	0	6	(2	4)	48	16	19	23	1	37	0	0	3	0	0	—	2	.243	.365	.432
16 ML YEARS		1811	6801	1811	332	14	446	(210	236)	3509	1140	1358	861	63	1867	83	1	77	198	87	.69	174	.266	.352	.516

Javier Cardona

Bats: Right **Throws:** Right **Pos:** C-26; PH/PR-2   **Ht:** 6'1" **Wt:** 185 **Born:** 9/15/75 **Age:** 25

Year Team	Lg	G	AB	H	2B	3B	HR	(Hm	Rd)	TB	R	RBI	TBB	IBB	SO	HBP	SH	SF	SB	CS	SB%	GDP	Avg	OBP	SLG
1994 Jamestown	A-	19	46	12	2	0	0	—	—	14	6	5	7	0	9	0	0	0	0	0	—	2	.261	.358	.304
1995 Fayettevlle	A	51	165	34	8	0	3	—	—	51	18	19	13	0	30	1	0	0	1	0	1.00	5	.206	.268	.309
1996 Fayettevlle	A	97	348	98	21	0	4	—	—	131	42	28	28	1	53	2	3	3	1	5	.17	9	.282	.336	.376
1997 Lakeland	A+	85	284	82	15	0	7	—	—	118	28	38	25	1	51	1	2	2	1	3	.25	8	.289	.346	.415
1998 Jacksnville	AA	46	163	54	16	1	4	—	—	84	31	40	15	1	29	1	0	2	0	0	—	6	.331	.387	.515
Toledo	AAA	47	162	31	4	0	5	—	—	50	12	16	9	1	32	1	4	0	0	0	—	3	.191	.238	.309
1999 Jacksnville	AA	108	418	129	31	0	26	—	—	238	84	92	46	0	69	8	0	5	4	2	.67	16	.309	.384	.569
2000 Toledo	AAA	56	218	60	10	0	11	—	—	103	29	43	15	0	33	2	0	2	0	1	.00	7	.275	.325	.472
2000 Detroit	AL	26	40	7	1	0	1	(1	0)	11	1	2	0	0	9	1	0	1	0	0	—	1	.175	.190	.275

Buddy Carlyle

Pitches: Right **Bats:** Left **Pos:** RP-4   **Ht:** 6'3" **Wt:** 175 **Born:** 12/21/77 **Age:** 23

Year Team	Lg	G	GS	CG	GF	IP	BFP	H	R	ER	HR	SH	SF	HB	TBB	IBB	SO	WP	Bk	W	L	Pct.	ShO	Sv-Op	Hld	ERA
1996 Princeton	R+	10	9	1	1	46.1	204	47	33	24	4	2	1	6	16	0	42	8	0	2	4	.333	1	0--	—	4.66
1997 Chstn-WV	A	23	23	4	0	143	579	130	51	44	9	4	4	3	27	0	111	5	1	14	5	.737	1	0--	—	2.77
1998 Chattanooga	AA	1	1	0	0	5	20	6	3	3	0	0	0	0	3	0	3	0	0	1	0	1.000	0	0--	—	5.40
Mobile	AA	27	27	2	0	183.2	763	179	77	69	13	8	3	7	46	0	97	4	1	14	6	.700	1	0--	—	3.38
1999 Las Vegas	AAA	25	25	0	0	160	690	180	99	87	25	5	8	6	42	1	138	6	0	11	8	.579	0	0--	—	4.89
2000 Las Vegas	AAA	27	27	1	0	151	656	165	93	72	25	5	4	4	44	0	127	3	0	8	6	.571	0	0--	—	4.29
1999 San Diego	NL	7	7	0	0	37.2	162	36	28	25	7	1	2	2	17	0	29	1	0	1	3	.250	0	0-0	0	5.97
2000 San Diego	NL	4	0	0	2	3	18	6	7	7	0	0	0	0	3	0	2	0	0	0	0	—	0	0-0	0	21.00
2 ML YEARS		11	7	0	2	40.2	180	42	35	32	7	1	2	2	20	0	31	1	0	1	3	.250	0	0-0	0	7.08

Bubba Carpenter

Bats: L **Throws:** L **Pos:** PH/PR-7; LF-5; DH-2; RF-1   **Ht:** 6'1" **Wt:** 185 **Born:** 7/23/68 **Age:** 32

Year Team	Lg	G	AB	H	2B	3B	HR	(Hm	Rd)	TB	R	RBI	TBB	IBB	SO	HBP	SH	SF	SB	CS	SB%	GDP	Avg	OBP	SLG
1991 Pr William	A+	69	236	66	10	3	6	—	—	100	33	34	40	3	50	2	1	3	4	1	.80	7	.280	.384	.424
1992 Albany-Col	AA	60	221	51	11	5	4	—	—	84	24	31	25	0	41	2	0	1	2	3	.40	8	.231	.313	.380
Pr William	A+	68	240	76	15	2	5	—	—	110	41	41	35	2	44	1	1	6	4	4	.50	4	.317	.397	.458
1993 Albany-Col	AA	14	53	17	4	0	2	—	—	27	8	14	7	0	4	0	0	1	2	2	.50	2	.321	.393	.509
Columbus	AAA	70	199	53	9	0	5	—	—	77	29	17	29	3	35	3	0	1	2	2	.50	4	.266	.366	.387
1994 Albany-Col	AA	116	429	109	14	1	13	—	—	164	47	51	58	5	65	3	3	3	9	5	.64	3	.288	.385	.434
Columbus	AAA	7	15	4	0	0	0	—	—	4	0	2	0	0	7	0	0	0	0	0	—	1	.267	.267	.267
1995 Columbus	AAA	116	410	92	12	3	11	—	—	143	57	49	40	2	70	1	2	3	13	6	.68	2	.246	.318	.382
1996 Columbus	AAA	132	466	114	23	3	7	—	—	164	55	48	48	1	80	0	2	1	10	7	.59	7	.245	.315	.352
1997 Columbus	AAA	85	271	76	12	4	6	—	—	114	47	39	48	0	46	0	3	1	4	8	.33	3	.280	.388	.421
1998 Yankees	R	5	17	4	0	2	1	—	—	11	3	7	2	0	2	0	0	0	0	0	—	0	.235	.316	.647
Columbus	AAA	63	198	45	14	2	7	—	—	84	28	24	36	2	48	1	2	0	3	2	.60	9	.227	.349	.424
1999 Columbus	AAA	101	325	92	20	2	22	—	—	182	78	81	75	7	68	4	1	4	7	3	.70	4	.283	.419	.560
2000 Colo Sprngs	AAA	53	157	35	7	2	4	—	—	58	23	19	33	3	37	0	1	1	3	2	.60	2	.223	.356	.369
2000 Colorado	NL	15	27	6	0	0	3	(1	2)	15	4	5	4	0	13	0	0	0	0	0	—	0	.222	.323	.556

Chris Carpenter

Pitches: Right **Bats:** Right **Pos:** SP-27; RP-7   **Ht:** 6'6" **Wt:** 225 **Born:** 4/27/75 **Age:** 26

Year Team	Lg	G	GS	CG	GF	IP	BFP	H	R	ER	HR	SH	SF	HB	TBB	IBB	SO	WP	Bk	W	L	Pct.	ShO	Sv-Op	Hld	ERA
1997 Toronto	AL	14	13	1	1	81.1	374	108	55	46	7	1	2	2	37	0	55	7	1	3	7	.300	1	0-0	0	5.09
1998 Toronto	AL	33	24	1	4	175	742	177	97	85	18	4	5	5	61	1	136	5	0	12	7	.632	1	0-0	0	4.37
1999 Toronto	AL	24	24	4	0	150	663	177	81	73	16	4	6	3	48	1	106	9	1	9	8	.529	1	0-0	0	4.38
2000 Toronto	AL	34	27	2	1	175.1	795	204	130	122	30	3	1	5	83	1	113	3	0	10	12	.455	0	0-0	0	6.26
4 ML YEARS		105	88	8	6	581.2	2574	666	363	326	71	12	14	15	229	3	410	24	2	34	34	.500	3	0-0	0	5.04

Giovanni Carrara

Pitches: Right **Bats:** Right **Pos:** RP-8   **Ht:** 6'2" **Wt:** 210 **Born:** 3/4/68 **Age:** 33

		HOW MUCH HE PITCHED					WHAT HE GAVE UP										THE RESULTS					
Year Team	Lg	G	GS	CG	GF	IP	BFP	H	R	ER	HR	SH	SF	HB	TBB	IBB	SO	WP	Bk	W	L	Pct.	ShO	Sv-Op	Hld	ERA
2000 Colo Sprngs *	AAA	18	15	0	1	96.2	403	89	39	35	8	3	1	5	30	1	89	4	0	7	2	.778	0	0- -	—	3.26
1995 Toronto	AL	12	7	1	2	48.2	229	64	46	39	10	1	2	1	25	1	27	1	0	2	4	.333	0	0-0	0	7.21
1996 Tor-Cin		19	5	0	4	38	188	54	36	34	11	1	0	2	25	3	23	1	0	1	1	.500	0	0-1	0	8.05
1997 Cincinnati	NL	2	2	0	0	10.1	49	14	9	9	4	1	0	0	6	1	5	0	0	0	1	.000	0	0-0	0	7.84
2000 Colorado	NL	8	0	0	2	13.1	72	21	19	19	5	0	1	1	11	2	15	0	0	0	1	.000	0	0-1	0	12.83
1996 Toronto	AL	11	0	0	3	15	76	23	19	19	5	0	0	0	12	2	10	1	0	0	1	.000	0	0-1	0	11.40
Cincinnati	NL	8	5	0	1	23	112	31	17	15	6	1	0	2	13	1	13	0	0	1	0	1.000	0	0-0	0	5.87
4 ML YEARS		41	14	1	8	110.1	538	153	110	101	30	3	3	4	67	7	70	2	0	3	7	.300	0	0-2	0	8.24

Hector Carrasco

Pitches: Right **Bats:** Right **Pos:** RP-68; SP-1   **Ht:** 6'2" **Wt:** 220 **Born:** 10/22/69 **Age:** 31

		HOW MUCH HE PITCHED					WHAT HE GAVE UP										THE RESULTS					
Year Team	Lg	G	GS	CG	GF	IP	BFP	H	R	ER	HR	SH	SF	HB	TBB	IBB	SO	WP	Bk	W	L	Pct.	ShO	Sv-Op	Hld	ERA
1994 Cincinnati	NL	45	0	0	29	56.1	237	42	17	14	3	5	0	2	30	1	41	3	1	5	6	.455	0	6-8	3	2.24
1995 Cincinnati	NL	64	0	0	28	87.1	391	86	45	40	1	2	6	2	46	5	64	15	0	2	7	.222	0	5-9	11	4.12
1996 Cincinnati	NL	56	0	0	10	74.1	325	58	37	31	6	4	4	1	45	5	59	8	1	4	3	.571	0	0-2	15	3.75
1997 Cin-KC		66	0	0	22	86	388	80	46	42	7	4	3	8	41	5	76	11	2	2	8	.200	0	0-2	4	4.40
1998 Minnesota	AL	63	0	0	10	61.2	287	75	30	30	4	0	1	1	31	1	46	8	0	4	2	.667	0	1-2	10	4.38
1999 Minnesota	AL	39	0	0	10	49	204	48	29	27	3	0	1	1	18	0	35	4	0	2	3	.400	0	1-2	7	4.96
2000 Min-Bos	AL	69	1	0	20	78.2	364	90	46	41	8	8	4	4	38	1	64	14	1	5	4	.556	0	1-6	8	4.69
1997 Cincinnati	NL	38	0	0	11	51.1	237	51	25	21	3	3	1	4	25	2	46	3	2	1	2	.333	0	0-0	5	3.68
Kansas City		28	0	0	11	34.2	151	29	21	21	4	1	2	4	16	3	30	8	0	1	6	.143	0	0-2	3	5.45
2000 Minnesota	AL	61	0	0	18	72	324	75	38	34	6	6	4	3	33	0	57	14	0	4	3	.571	0	1-5	7	4.25
Boston	AL	8	1	0	2	6.2	40	15	8	7	2	2	0	1	5	1	7	0	1	1	1	.500	0	0-1	1	9.45
7 ML YEARS		402	1	0	139	493.1	2196	479	250	225	32	23	26	19	249	18	385	63	5	24	33	.421	0	14-31	62	4.10

Raul Casanova

Bats: Both **Throws:** Right **Pos:** C-72; PH/PR-18; DH-3   **Ht:** 6'0" **Wt:** 195 **Born:** 8/23/72 **Age:** 28

		BATTING																	BASERUNNING				PERCENTAGES		
Year Team	Lg	G	AB	H	2B	3B	HR	(Hm	Rd)	TB	R	RBI	TBB	IBB	SO	HBP	SH	SF	SB	CS	SB%	GDP	Avg	OBP	SLG
2000 Indianapols *	AAA	20	73	21	2	0	5			38	10	12	7	0	10	1	0	1	0	1	.00	3	.288	.354	.521
1996 Detroit	AL	25	85	16	1	0	4	(1	3)	29	6	9	6	0	18	0	0	0	0	0	—	6	.188	.242	.341
1997 Detroit	AL	101	304	74	10	1	5	(5	0)	101	27	24	26	1	48	3	0	1	1	1	.50	10	.243	.308	.332
1998 Detroit	AL	16	42	6	2	0	1	(1	0)	11	4	3	5	0	10	1	0	0	0	0	—	0	.143	.250	.262
2000 Milwaukee	NL	86	231	57	13	3	6	(4	2)	94	20	36	26	1	48	4	2	2	1	2	.33	5	.247	.331	.407
4 ML YEARS		228	662	153	26	4	16	(11	5)	235	57	72	63	2	124	8	2	3	2	3	.40	21	.231	.304	.355

Sean Casey

Bats: Left **Throws:** Right **Pos:** 1B-129; PH/PR-4   **Ht:** 6'4" **Wt:** 225 **Born:** 7/2/74 **Age:** 26

		BATTING																	BASERUNNING				PERCENTAGES		
Year Team	Lg	G	AB	H	2B	3B	HR	(Hm	Rd)	TB	R	RBI	TBB	IBB	SO	HBP	SH	SF	SB	CS	SB%	GDP	Avg	OBP	SLG
1997 Cleveland	AL	6	10	2	0	0	0	(0	0)	2	1	1	1	0	2	1	0	0	0	0	—	0	.200	.333	.200
1998 Cincinnati	NL	96	302	82	21	1	7	(3	4)	126	44	52	43	3	45	3	0	3	1	1	.50	11	.272	.365	.417
1999 Cincinnati	NL	151	594	197	42	3	25	(11	14)	320	103	99	61	13	88	9	0	5	0	2	.00	15	.332	.399	.539
2000 Cincinnati	NL	133	480	151	33	2	20	(9	11)	248	69	85	52	4	80	7	0	6	1	0	1.00	16	.315	.385	.517
4 ML YEARS		386	1386	432	96	6	52	(23	29)	696	217	237	157	20	215	20	0	14	2	3	.40	42	.312	.386	.502

Carlos Casimiro

Bats: Right **Throws:** Right **Pos:** DH-2; PH/PR-1   **Ht:** 5'11" **Wt:** 175 **Born:** 11/8/76 **Age:** 24

		BATTING																	BASERUNNING				PERCENTAGES		
Year Team	Lg	G	AB	H	2B	3B	HR	(Hm	Rd)	TB	R	RBI	TBB	IBB	SO	HBP	SH	SF	SB	CS	SB%	GDP	Avg	OBP	SLG
1995 Orioles	R	32	107	27	4	2	2	—	—	41	14	11	10	0	22	1	1	2	1	3	.25	3	.252	.317	.383
1996 Bluefield	R+	62	239	66	16	0	10	—	—	112	51	33	20	1	52	2	1	2	22	9	.71	3	.276	.335	.469
1997 Delmarva	A	122	457	111	21	8	9	—	—	175	54	51	26	1	108	5	4	2	20	13	.61	11	.243	.290	.383
1998 Frederick	A+	131	478	113	23	9	15	—	—	199	44	61	25	2	98	1	4	6	10	7	.59	16	.236	.273	.416
1999 Bowie	AA	139	526	116	23	1	18	—	—	195	73	64	39	0	101	3	5	5	7	12	.37	10	.221	.276	.371
2000 Bowie	AA	87	290	76	12	2	6	—	—	110	44	32	23	0	66	1	3	1	2	4	.33	5	.262	.317	.379
Rochester	AAA	24	81	18	4	0	4	—	—	34	9	10	4	0	16	0	0	0	0	0	—	1	.222	.259	.420
2000 Baltimore	AL	2	8	1	0	0	0	(0	0)	2	0	3	0	0	2	0	0	0	0	0	—	0	.125	.125	.250

Vinny Castilla

Bats: Right **Throws:** Right **Pos:** 3B-83; PH/PR-2   **Ht:** 6'1" **Wt:** 205 **Born:** 7/4/67 **Age:** 33

		BATTING																	BASERUNNING				PERCENTAGES		
Year Team	Lg	G	AB	H	2B	3B	HR	(Hm	Rd)	TB	R	RBI	TBB	IBB	SO	HBP	SH	SF	SB	CS	SB%	GDP	Avg	OBP	SLG
2000 Durham *	AAA	2	8	3	1	0	1			7	1	3	0	0	1	0	0	0	0	0	—	0	.375	.375	.875
1991 Atlanta	NL	12	5	1	0	0	0	(0	0)	1	1	0	0	0	1	0	0	0	0	0	—	0	.200	.200	.200
1992 Atlanta	NL	9	16	4	1	0	0	(0	0)	5	1	1	1	0	2	1	0	0	0	0	—	0	.250	.333	.313
1993 Colorado	NL	105	337	86	9	7	9	(5	4)	136	36	30	13	4	45	0	5	2	2	5	.29	10	.255	.283	.404
1994 Colorado	NL	52	130	43	11	1	3	(2	1)	65	16	18	7	1	23	0	1	3	2	1	.67	3	.331	.357	.500
1995 Colorado	NL	139	527	163	34	2	32	(23	9)	297	82	90	30	2	87	4	4	6	2	8	.20	15	.309	.347	.564
1996 Colorado	NL	160	629	191	34	0	40	(27	13)	345	97	113	35	7	88	5	0	4	7	2	.78	20	.304	.343	.548
1997 Colorado	NL	159	612	186	25	2	40	(21	19)	335	94	113	44	9	94	1	0	5	2	4	.33	17	.304	.356	.547
1998 Colorado	NL	**162**	645	206	28	4	46	(26	20)	380	108	144	40	4	89	6	0	6	5	4	.33	24	.319	.362	.589
1999 Colorado	NL	158	615	169	24	1	33	(20	13)	294	83	102	53	7	75	1	0	5	3	2	.40	15	.275	.331	.478
2000 Tampa Bay	AL	85	331	73	9	1	6	(2	4)	102	22	42	14	3	41	0	0	6	1	2	.33	9	.221	.254	.308
10 ML YEARS		1041	3847	1122	175	18	209	(125	84)	1960	540	653	237	41	562	30	6	39	23	34	.40	113	.292	.334	.509

38

Alberto Castillo

Bats: Right **Throws:** Right **Pos:** C-66; PH/PR-1   **Ht:** 6'0" **Wt:** 185 **Born:** 2/10/70 **Age:** 31

Year Team	Lg	G	AB	H	2B	3B	HR	(Hm	Rd)	TB	R	RBI	TBB	IBB	SO	HBP	SH	SF	SB	CS	SB%	GDP	Avg	OBP	SLG
1995 New York	NL	13	29	3	0	0	0	(0	0)	3	2	0	3	0	9	1	0	0	1	0	1.00	0	.103	.212	.103
1996 New York	NL	6	11	4	0	0	0	(0	0)	4	1	0	0	0	4	0	0	0	0	0	—	0	.364	.364	.364
1997 New York	NL	35	59	12	1	0	0	(0	0)	13	3	7	9	0	16	0	2	1	0	1	.00	0	.203	.304	.220
1998 New York	NL	38	83	17	4	0	2	(0	2)	27	13	7	9	0	17	1	6	0	0	2	.00	1	.205	.290	.325
1999 St. Louis	NL	93	255	67	8	0	4	(2	2)	87	21	31	24	1	48	2	5	4	0	0	—	6	.263	.326	.341
2000 Toronto	AL	66	185	39	7	0	1	(1	0)	49	14	16	21	0	36	0	2	3	0	0	—	3	.211	.287	.265
6 ML YEARS		251	622	142	20	0	7	(3	4)	183	54	61	66	1	130	4	15	8	1	3	.25	13	.228	.303	.294

Frank Castillo

Pitches: Right **Bats:** Right **Pos:** SP-24; RP-1   **Ht:** 6'1" **Wt:** 200 **Born:** 4/1/69 **Age:** 32

Year Team	Lg	G	GS	CG	GF	IP	BFP	H	R	ER	HR	SH	SF	HB	TBB	IBB	SO	WP	Bk	W	L	Pct.	ShO	Sv-Op	Hld	ERA
1991 Chicago	NL	18	18	4	0	111.2	467	107	56	54	5	6	3	0	33	2	73	5	1	6	7	.462	0	0-0	0	4.35
1992 Chicago	NL	33	33	0	0	205.1	856	179	91	79	19	11	5	6	63	6	135	11	0	10	11	.476	0	0-0	0	3.46
1993 Chicago	NL	29	25	2	0	141.1	614	162	83	76	20	10	3	9	39	4	84	5	3	5	8	.385	0	0-0	0	4.84
1994 Chicago	NL	4	4	1	0	23	96	25	13	11	3	1	0	0	5	0	19	0	0	2	1	.667	0	0-0	0	4.30
1995 Chicago	NL	29	29	2	0	188	795	179	75	67	22	11	3	6	52	4	135	3	1	11	10	.524	2	0-0	0	3.21
1996 Chicago	NL	33	33	1	0	182.1	789	209	112	107	28	4	5	8	46	4	139	2	1	7	16	.304	1	0-0	0	5.28
1997 ChC-Col	NL	34	33	0	0	184.1	830	220	121	111	25	17	2	8	69	4	126	3	0	12	12	.500	0	0-0	0	5.42
1998 Detroit	AL	27	19	0	4	116	531	150	91	88	17	2	6	5	44	0	81	0	0	3	9	.250	0	1-1	0	6.83
2000 Toronto	AL	25	24	0	1	138	576	112	58	55	18	5	2	5	56	0	104	0	0	10	5	.667	0	0-0	0	3.59
1997 Chicago	NL	20	19	0	0	98	446	113	64	59	9	11	0	4	44	1	67	1	0	6	9	.400	0	0-0	0	5.42
Colorado	NL	14	14	0	0	86.1	384	107	57	52	16	6	2	4	25	3	59	2	0	6	3	.667	0	0-0	0	5.42
9 ML YEARS		232	218	10	5	1290	5554	1343	700	648	157	67	29	47	407	24	896	29	6	66	79	.455	3	1-1	0	4.52

Luis Castillo

Bats: Both **Throws:** Right **Pos:** 2B-136; PH/PR-1   **Ht:** 5'11" **Wt:** 175 **Born:** 9/12/75 **Age:** 25

Year Team	Lg	G	AB	H	2B	3B	HR	(Hm	Rd)	TB	R	RBI	TBB	IBB	SO	HBP	SH	SF	SB	CS	SB%	GDP	Avg	OBP	SLG
2000 Calgary *	AAA	4	13	4	1	1	0	—	—	7	4	0	4	0	2	0	0	0	1	0	1.00	0	.308	.471	.538
1996 Florida	NL	41	164	43	2	1	1	(0	1)	50	26	8	14	0	46	0	2	0	17	4	.81	0	.262	.320	.305
1997 Florida	NL	75	263	63	8	0	0	(0	0)	71	27	8	27	0	53	0	1	0	16	10	.62	6	.240	.310	.270
1998 Florida	NL	44	153	31	3	2	1	(0	1)	41	21	10	22	0	33	1	1	0	3	0	1.00	1	.203	.307	.268
1999 Florida	NL	128	487	147	23	4	0	(0	0)	178	76	28	67	0	85	0	6	5	50	17	.75	3	.302	.384	.366
2000 Florida	NL	136	539	180	17	3	2	(1	1)	209	101	17	78	0	86	0	9	0	62	22	.74	11	.334	.418	.388
5 ML YEARS		424	1606	464	53	10	4	(1	3)	549	251	71	208	0	303	1	19	3	148	53	.74	21	.289	.370	.342

Juan Castro

Bats: R **Throws:** R **Pos:** SS-57; 2B-21; 3B-7; PH/PR-1   **Ht:** 5'10" **Wt:** 187 **Born:** 6/20/72 **Age:** 29

Year Team	Lg	G	AB	H	2B	3B	HR	(Hm	Rd)	TB	R	RBI	TBB	IBB	SO	HBP	SH	SF	SB	CS	SB%	GDP	Avg	OBP	SLG
2000 Louisville *	AAA	19	60	19	5	1	2	—	—	32	9	10	12	3	12	0	1	1	0	1	.00	3	.317	.425	.533
1995 Los Angeles	NL	11	4	1	0	0	0	(0	0)	1	0	1	1	0	1	0	0	0	0	0	—	0	.250	.400	.250
1996 Los Angeles	NL	70	132	26	5	3	0	(0	0)	37	16	5	10	0	27	0	4	0	1	0	1.00	3	.197	.254	.280
1997 Los Angeles	NL	40	75	11	3	1	0	(0	0)	16	3	4	7	1	20	0	2	0	0	0	—	2	.147	.220	.213
1998 Los Angeles	NL	89	220	43	7	0	2	(0	2)	56	25	14	15	0	37	0	9	2	0	0	—	5	.195	.245	.255
1999 Los Angeles	NL	2	1	0	0	0	0	(0	0)	0	0	0	0	0	1	0	0	0	0	0	—	0	.000	.000	.000
2000 Cincinnati	NL	82	224	54	12	2	4	(1	3)	82	20	23	14	1	33	0	4	2	0	2	.00	9	.241	.283	.366
6 ML YEARS		294	656	135	27	6	6	(1	5)	192	64	46	47	2	119	0	19	4	1	2	.33	19	.206	.257	.293

Ramon Castro

Bats: Right **Throws:** Right **Pos:** C-50   **Ht:** 6'3" **Wt:** 225 **Born:** 3/1/76 **Age:** 25

Year Team	Lg	G	AB	H	2B	3B	HR	(Hm	Rd)	TB	R	RBI	TBB	IBB	SO	HBP	SH	SF	SB	CS	SB%	GDP	Avg	OBP	SLG
1994 Astros	R	37	123	34	7	0	3	—	—	50	17	14	17	1	14	2	0	0	5	5	.50	4	.276	.373	.407
1995 Kissimmee	A+	36	120	25	5	0	0	—	—	30	6	8	6	0	21	1	0	1	0	0	—	1	.208	.250	.250
Auburn	A-	63	224	67	17	0	9	—	—	111	40	49	24	0	27	0	0	6	0	1	.00	6	.299	.358	.496
1996 Quad City	A	96	314	78	15	0	7	—	—	114	38	43	31	1	61	2	0	3	2	0	1.00	12	.248	.317	.363
1997 Kissimmee	A+	115	410	115	22	1	8	—	—	163	53	65	53	3	73	2	0	11	0	1	1.00	17	.280	.357	.398
1998 Jackson	AA	48	168	43	6	0	8	—	—	73	27	25	13	2	31	4	0	0	1	0	1.00	3	.256	.324	.435
Portland	AA	31	88	22	3	0	3	—	—	34	9	11	8	0	21	0	0	2	0	0	—	3	.250	.306	.386
1999 Calgary	AAA	97	349	90	22	0	15	—	—	157	43	61	24	3	64	2	0	3	0	0	—	11	.258	.307	.450
2000 Calgary	AAA	67	218	73	22	0	14	—	—	137	44	45	16	0	38	0	0	0	0	0	—	5	.335	.380	.628
1999 Florida	NL	24	67	12	4	0	2	(0	2)	22	4	4	10	3	14	0	0	1	0	0	—	1	.179	.282	.328
2000 Florida	NL	50	138	33	4	0	2	(0	2)	43	10	14	16	7	36	1	0	2	0	0	—	1	.239	.318	.312
2 ML YEARS		74	205	45	8	0	4	(0	4)	65	14	18	26	10	50	1	0	3	0	0	—	2	.220	.306	.317

Frank Catalanotto

Bats: L **Throws:** R **Pos:** 2B-49; PH/PR-32; DH-19; 1B-17; RF-1   **Ht:** 6'0" **Wt:** 195 **Born:** 4/27/74 **Age:** 27

Year Team	Lg	G	AB	H	2B	3B	HR	(Hm	Rd)	TB	R	RBI	TBB	IBB	SO	HBP	SH	SF	SB	CS	SB%	GDP	Avg	OBP	SLG
2000 Oklahoma *	AAA	3	11	3	0	0	0	—	—	3	2	1	0	0	4	1	0	0	0	0	—	0	.273	.333	.273
1997 Detroit	AL	13	26	8	2	0	0	(0	0)	10	2	3	3	0	7	0	0	0	0	0	—	0	.308	.379	.385
1998 Detroit	AL	89	213	60	13	2	6	(3	3)	95	23	25	12	1	39	4	0	5	3	2	.60	4	.282	.325	.446
1999 Detroit	AL	100	286	79	19	0	11	(6	5)	131	41	35	15	1	49	9	0	5	3	4	.43	5	.276	.327	.458
2000 Texas	AL	103	282	82	13	2	10	(6	4)	129	55	42	33	0	36	6	3	2	6	2	.75	5	.291	.375	.457
4 ML YEARS		305	807	229	47	4	27	(15	12)	365	121	105	63	2	131	19	3	12	12	8	.60	14	.284	.345	.452

Roger Cedeno

Bats: B **Throws:** R **Pos:** CF-29; LF-23; RF-17; PH/PR-9   **Ht:** 6'1"   **Wt:** 205   **Born:** 8/16/74   **Age:** 26

Year Team	Lg	G	AB	H	2B	3B	HR	(Hm	Rd)	TB	R	RBI	TBB	IBB	SO	HBP	SH	SF	SB	CS	SB%	GDP	Avg	OBP	SLG
2000 New Orleans *	AAA	6	20	7	0	1	0	—	—	9	2	3	2	0	5	0	0	1	1	1	.50	0	.350	.391	.450
1995 Los Angeles	NL	40	42	10	2	0	0	(0	0)	12	4	3	3	0	10	0	0	1	1	0	1.00	1	.238	.283	.286
1996 Los Angeles	NL	86	211	52	11	1	2	(0	2)	71	26	18	24	0	47	1	2	0	5	1	.83	0	.246	.326	.336
1997 Los Angeles	NL	80	194	53	10	2	3	(3	0)	76	31	17	25	2	44	3	3	2	9	1	.90	1	.273	.362	.392
1998 Los Angeles	NL	105	240	58	11	1	2	(2	0)	77	33	17	27	2	57	0	3	1	8	2	.80	1	.242	.317	.321
1999 New York	NL	155	453	142	23	4	4	(4	0)	185	90	36	60	3	100	3	7	2	66	17	.80	5	.313	.396	.408
2000 Houston	NL	74	259	73	2	5	6	(3	3)	103	54	26	43	0	47	0	2	1	25	11	.69	6	.282	.383	.398
6 ML YEARS		540	1399	388	59	13	17	(12	5)	524	238	117	182	7	305	7	17	7	114	32	.78	14	.277	.362	.375

Frank Charles

Bats: Right **Throws:** Right **Pos:** PH/PR-3; C-1   **Ht:** 6'4"   **Wt:** 210   **Born:** 2/23/69   **Age:** 32

Year Team	Lg	G	AB	H	2B	3B	HR	(Hm	Rd)	TB	R	RBI	TBB	IBB	SO	HBP	SH	SF	SB	CS	SB%	GDP	Avg	OBP	SLG
1991 Everett	A-	62	239	76	17	1	9	—	—	122	31	49	21	0	55	1	0	1	1	2	.33	5	.318	.374	.510
1992 Clinton	A	2	5	0	0	0	0	—	—	0	1	0	0	0	3	0	0	0	0	0	—	0	.000	.000	.000
San Jose	A+	87	286	83	16	1	0	—	—	101	27	34	11	2	61	4	1	0	4	4	.50	12	.290	.326	.353
1993 St. Paul	IND	58	216	59	13	0	2	—	—	78	27	37	11	0	33	3	5	1	5	3	.63	9	.273	.316	.361
1994 Charlotte	A+	79	254	67	17	1	2	—	—	92	23	33	16	1	52	3	5	2	2	3	.40	2	.264	.313	.362
1995 Tulsa	AA	126	479	121	24	3	13	—	—	190	51	72	22	0	92	4	1	4	1	0	1.00	19	.253	.289	.397
1996 Okla City	AAA	35	113	21	7	2	1	—	—	35	10	8	4	0	29	1	0	2	0	3	.00	3	.186	.217	.310
Tulsa	AA	41	147	39	6	0	5	—	—	60	18	15	10	0	28	0	0	0	2	0	1.00	1	.265	.312	.408
1997 Tulsa	AA	95	335	77	18	2	9	—	—	126	38	44	24	1	81	3	1	1	2	2	.50	9	.230	.287	.376
1998 Fresno	AAA	4	10	5	0	0	1	—	—	8	2	1	1	0	2	0	0	0	0	0	—	0	.500	.545	.800
Shreveport	AA	108	411	118	39	1	12	—	—	195	49	66	18	0	93	0	0	5	0	2	.00	10	.287	.323	.474
1999 Las Vegas	AAA	80	272	67	19	2	2	—	—	96	25	28	10	2	61	3	0	2	2	0	1.00	16	.246	.279	.353
2000 New Orleans	AAA	84	284	74	10	3	5	—	—	105	29	37	21	0	62	3	2	3	1	3	.25	9	.261	.315	.370
2000 Houston	NL	4	7	3	1	0	0	(0	0)	4	1	2	0	0	2	0	0	0	0	0	—	0	.429	.429	.571

Norm Charlton

Pitches: Left **Bats:** Both **Pos:** RP-2   **Ht:** 6'3"   **Wt:** 205   **Born:** 1/6/63   **Age:** 38

Year Team	Lg	G	GS	CG	GF	IP	BFP	H	R	ER	HR	SH	SF	HB	TBB	IBB	SO	WP	Bk	W	L	Pct.	ShO	Sv-Op	Hld	ERA
2000 Louisville *	AAA	4	0	0	2	2.2	10	0	0	0	0	0	0	0	2	0	5	1	0	0	0	—	0	1--	0	0.00
1988 Cincinnati	NL	10	10	0	0	61.1	259	60	27	27	6	1	2	2	20	2	39	3	2	4	5	.444	0	0-0	0	3.96
1989 Cincinnati	NL	69	0	0	27	95.1	393	67	38	31	5	9	2	2	40	7	98	2	4	8	3	.727	0	0-1	8	2.93
1990 Cincinnati	NL	56	16	1	13	154.1	650	131	53	47	10	7	2	4	70	4	117	9	1	12	9	.571	1	2-3	8	2.74
1991 Cincinnati	NL	39	11	0	10	108.1	438	92	37	35	6	7	1	6	34	4	77	11	0	3	5	.375	0	1-4	3	2.91
1992 Cincinnati	NL	64	0	0	46	81.1	341	79	39	27	7	7	3	3	26	4	90	8	0	4	2	.667	0	26-34	7	2.99
1993 Seattle	AL	34	0	0	29	34.2	141	22	12	9	4	0	1	0	17	0	48	6	0	1	3	.250	0	18-21	1	2.34
1995 Phi-Sea		55	0	0	27	69.2	284	46	31	26	4	1	0	4	31	3	70	6	1	4	6	.400	0	14-16	12	3.36
1996 Seattle	AL	70	0	0	50	75.2	323	68	37	34	7	4	2	4	38	1	73	9	0	4	7	.364	0	20-27	8	4.04
1997 Seattle	AL	71	0	0	38	69.1	343	89	59	56	7	7	2	4	47	2	55	7	1	3	8	.273	0	14-25	9	7.27
1998 Bal-Atl		49	0	0	19	48	231	53	29	29	5	2	4	1	33	0	47	7	0	2	1	.667	0	1-2	5	5.44
1999 Tampa Bay	AL	42	0	0	9	50.2	233	49	29	25	4	5	1	0	36	0	45	4	0	2	3	.400	0	0-1	15	4.44
2000 Cincinnati	NL	2	0	0	2	3	20	6	9	9	1	0	0	0	6	0	1	1	0	0	0	—	0	0-0	0	27.00
1995 Philadelphia	NL	25	0	0	5	22	102	23	19	18	2	1	1	3	15	3	12	1	0	2	5	.286	0	0-1	9	7.36
Seattle		30	0	0	22	47.2	182	23	12	8	2	3	1	1	16	0	58	5	1	2	1	.667	0	14-15	3	1.51
1998 Baltimore	AL	36	0	0	11	35	178	46	27	27	5	1	1	0	25	0	41	5	0	2	1	.667	0	0-1	3	6.94
Atlanta	NL	13	0	0	8	13	53	7	2	2	0	1	1	1	8	0	6	2	0	0	0	—	0	1-1	2	1.38
12 ML YEARS		561	37	1	270	851.2	3656	762	400	355	66	49	20	28	398	27	760	73	9	47	52	.475	1	96-134	77	3.75

Eric Chavez

Bats: L **Throws:** R **Pos:** 3B-146; PH/PR-13; SS-2; DH-1   **Ht:** 6'0"   **Wt:** 204   **Born:** 12/7/77   **Age:** 23

Year Team	Lg	G	AB	H	2B	3B	HR	(Hm	Rd)	TB	R	RBI	TBB	IBB	SO	HBP	SH	SF	SB	CS	SB%	GDP	Avg	OBP	SLG
1998 Oakland	AL	16	45	14	4	1	0	(0	0)	20	6	6	3	1	5	0	0	0	1	1	.50	1	.311	.354	.444
1999 Oakland	AL	115	356	88	21	2	13	(8	5)	152	47	50	46	4	56	0	0	0	1	1	.50	7	.247	.333	.427
2000 Oakland	AL	153	501	139	23	4	26	(15	11)	248	89	86	62	8	94	1	0	5	2	2	.50	9	.277	.355	.495
3 ML YEARS		284	902	241	48	7	39	(23	16)	420	142	142	111	13	155	1	0	5	4	4	.50	17	.267	.346	.466

Raul Chavez

Bats: Right **Throws:** Right **Pos:** C-14   **Ht:** 5'11"   **Wt:** 210   **Born:** 3/18/73   **Age:** 28

Year Team	Lg	G	AB	H	2B	3B	HR	(Hm	Rd)	TB	R	RBI	TBB	IBB	SO	HBP	SH	SF	SB	CS	SB%	GDP	Avg	OBP	SLG
1990 Astros	R	48	155	50	8	1	0	—	—	60	23	23	7	0	12	2	2	1	5	2	.71	5	.323	.358	.387
1991 Burlington	A	114	420	108	17	0	3	—	—	134	54	41	25	1	64	10	3	4	1	4	.20	13	.257	.312	.319
1992 Asheville	A	95	348	99	22	1	2	—	—	129	37	40	16	1	39	4	1	4	1	0	1.00	11	.284	.320	.371
1993 Osceola	A+	58	197	45	5	1	0	—	—	52	13	16	8	0	19	1	1	1	1	1	.50	12	.228	.261	.264
1994 Jackson	AA	89	251	55	7	0	1	—	—	65	17	22	17	3	41	2	2	1	0	1	.00	5	.219	.273	.259
1995 Jackson	AA	58	188	54	8	0	4	—	—	74	16	25	8	1	17	2	1	1	0	0	—	7	.287	.323	.394
Tucson	AAA	32	103	27	5	0	0	—	—	32	14	10	8	0	13	2	1	1	0	0	—	7	.262	.325	.311
1996 Ottawa	AAA	60	198	49	10	0	2	—	—	65	15	24	11	0	31	1	4	0	0	0	—	7	.247	.290	.328
1997 Ottawa	AAA	92	310	76	17	0	4	—	—	105	31	46	18	1	42	4	3	3	1	3	.25	9	.245	.293	.339
1998 Ottawa	AAA	11	31	7	0	0	0	—	—	7	2	4	3	0	6	0	0	0	0	0	—	1	.226	.333	.226
Tacoma	AAA	76	233	52	6	0	4	—	—	70	27	34	22	1	41	4	1	0	1	2	.33	7	.223	.294	.300
1999 Tacoma	AAA	102	354	95	20	1	3	—	—	126	39	40	28	0	63	6	0	5	3	1	.75	11	.268	.331	.356
2000 New Orleans	AAA	99	303	74	13	0	2	—	—	93	31	36	34	5	44	4	4	4	3	3	.50	12	.244	.325	.307

40

Year Team	Lg	G	AB	H	2B	3B	HR	(Hm	Rd)	TB	R	RBI	TBB	IBB	SO	HBP	SH	SF	SB	CS	SB%	GDP	Avg	OBP	SLG
1996 Montreal	NL	4	5	1	0	0	0	(0	0)	1	1	0	1	0	1	0	0	1	1	0	1.00	0	.200	.333	.200
1997 Montreal	NL	13	26	7	0	0	0	(0	0)	7	0	2	0	0	5	0	0	1	1	0	1.00	0	.269	.259	.269
1998 Seattle	AL	1	1	0	0	0	0	(0	0)	0	0	0	0	0	0	0	0	0	0	0	—	0	.000	.000	.000
2000 Houston	NL	14	43	11	2	0	1	(0	1)	16	3	5	3	2	6	0	0	1	0	0	—	5	.256	.298	.372
4 ML YEARS		32	75	19	2	0	1	(0	1)	24	4	7	4	2	12	0	0	2	2	0	1.00	6	.253	.284	.320

Bruce Chen

Pitches: Left Bats: Both Pos: RP-22; SP-15   Ht: 6'2" Wt: 210 Born: 6/19/77 Age: 24

Year Team	Lg	G	GS	CG	GF	IP	BFP	H	R	ER	HR	SH	SF	HB	TBB	IBB	SO	WP	Bk	W	L	Pct.	ShO	Sv-Op	Hld	ERA
2000 Richmond *	AAA	1	1	0	0	6	22	5	0	0	0	0	0	0	1	0	6	1	0	1	0	1.000	0	0--	—	0.00
1998 Atlanta	NL	4	4	0	0	20.1	91	23	9	9	3	1	0	1	9	1	17	0	0	2	0	1.000	0	0-0	0	3.98
1999 Atlanta	NL	16	7	0	3	51	214	38	32	31	11	1	1	2	27	3	45	0	0	2	2	.500	0	0-0	0	5.47
2000 Atl-Phi	NL	37	15	0	4	134	559	116	54	49	18	8	3	2	46	4	112	4	1	7	4	.636	0	0-0	0	3.29
2000 Atlanta	NL	22	0	0	4	39.2	176	35	15	11	4	3	2	1	19	2	32	0	0	4	0	1.000	0	0-0	0	2.50
Philadelphia	NL	15	15	0	0	94.1	383	81	39	38	14	5	1	1	27	2	80	4	0	3	4	.429	0	0-0	0	3.63
3 ML YEARS		57	26	0	7	205.1	864	177	95	89	32	10	4	5	82	8	174	4	1	11	6	.647	0	0-0	0	3.90

Randy Choate

Pitches: Left Bats: Left Pos: RP-22   Ht: 6'3" Wt: 180 Born: 9/5/75 Age: 25

Year Team	Lg	G	GS	CG	GF	IP	BFP	H	R	ER	HR	SH	SF	HB	TBB	IBB	SO	WP	Bk	W	L	Pct.	ShO	Sv-Op	Hld	ERA
1997 Oneonta	A-	10	10	0	0	62.1	242	49	12	12	1	0	0	2	12	1	61	0	2	5	1	.833	0	0--	—	1.73
1998 Tampa	A+	13	13	0	0	70	316	83	57	41	6	4	1	3	22	2	55	2	0	1	8	.111	0	0--	—	5.27
Greensboro	A	8	8	1	0	39	165	46	21	13	1	1	0	0	7	0	32	3	0	1	5	.167	0	0--	—	3.00
1999 Tampa	A+	47	0	0	17	50	224	51	25	25	4	4	0	2	24	5	62	4	0	2	2	.500	0	1--	—	4.50
2000 Columbus	AAA	33	0	0	6	35.1	151	34	8	8	2	0	0	3	14	3	37	0	0	2	0	1.000	0	1--	—	2.04
2000 New York	AL	22	0	0	6	17	75	14	10	9	3	0	1	1	8	0	12	1	0	0	0	.000	0	0-0	2	4.76

Bobby Chouinard

Pitches: Right Bats: Right Pos: RP-31   Ht: 6'1" Wt: 190 Born: 5/1/72 Age: 29

Year Team	Lg	G	GS	CG	GF	IP	BFP	H	R	ER	HR	SH	SF	HB	TBB	IBB	SO	WP	Bk	W	L	Pct.	ShO	Sv-Op	Hld	ERA
2000 Colo Spngs *	AAA	9	0	0	3	17.1	73	18	10	7	3	0	0	0	3	0	12	1	0	0	0	—	0	1--	—	3.63
1996 Oakland	AL	13	11	0	0	59	278	75	41	40	10	3	3	3	32	3	32	0	0	4	2	.667	0	0-0	0	6.10
1998 Mil-Ari	NL	27	2	0	9	41.1	181	46	24	19	5	4	2	0	11	2	27	5	0	0	2	.000	0	0-1	6	4.14
1999 Arizona	NL	32	0	0	9	40.1	161	31	16	12	3	4	4	0	12	2	23	1	0	5	2	.714	0	1-2	7	2.68
2000 Colorado	NL	31	0	0	6	32.2	140	35	17	14	4	1	1	1	9	2	23	0	0	2	2	.500	0	0-2	3	3.86
1998 Milwaukee	NL	1	0	0	0	3	12	5	1	1	0	0	1	0	0	0	1	0	0	0	0	—	0	0-0	0	3.00
Arizona	NL	26	2	0	9	38.1	169	41	23	18	5	4	1	0	11	2	26	5	0	0	2	.000	0	0-1	6	4.23
4 ML YEARS		103	13	0	24	173.1	760	187	98	85	22	12	10	4	64	9	105	6	0	11	8	.579	0	1-5	16	4.41

McKay Christensen

Bats: Left Throws: Left Pos: CF-29; PH/PR-8   Ht: 5'11" Wt: 180 Born: 8/14/75 Age: 25

Year Team	Lg	G	AB	H	2B	3B	HR	(Hm	Rd)	TB	R	RBI	TBB	IBB	SO	HBP	SH	SF	SB	CS	SB%	GDP	Avg	OBP	SLG
1996 White Sox	R	35	133	35	7	5	1	—		55	17	16	10	0	23	3	0	1	10	3	.77	1	.263	.327	.414
Hickory	A	6	11	0	0	0	0	—		0	0	0	1	0	4	0	0	0	0	0	—	0	.000	.083	.000
1997 Hickory	A	127	503	141	12	12	5	—		192	95	47	52	0	61	11	4	6	28	20	.58	2	.280	.357	.382
1998 Winston-Sal	A+	95	361	103	17	6	4	—		144	69	32	53	1	54	11	4	2	20	10	.67	3	.285	.391	.399
1999 Birmingham	AA	75	293	85	8	6	3	—		114	53	28	31	0	46	8	4	1	18	6	.75	6	.290	.372	.389
Charlotte	AAA	1	4	1	0	0	0	—		1	0	0	0	0	0	0	0	0	1	0	1.00	0	.250	.250	.250
2000 Charlotte	AAA	90	337	89	13	2	6	—		124	49	29	32	1	51	1	7	5	28	6	.82	2	.264	.325	.368
1999 Chicago	AL	28	53	12	1	0	1	(1	0)	16	10	6	4	0	7	0	1	2	2	1	.67	1	.226	.271	.302
2000 Chicago	AL	32	19	2	0	0	0	(0	0)	2	4	1	2	0	6	1	0	0	1	1	.50	0	.105	.227	.105
2 ML YEARS		60	72	14	1	0	1	(1	0)	18	14	7	6	0	13	1	1	2	3	2	.60	1	.194	.259	.250

Ryan Christenson

Bats: R Throws: R Pos: LF-76; PH/PR-43; CF-27; RF-14   Ht: 6'0" Wt: 191 Born: 3/28/74 Age: 27

Year Team	Lg	G	AB	H	2B	3B	HR	(Hm	Rd)	TB	R	RBI	TBB	IBB	SO	HBP	SH	SF	SB	CS	SB%	GDP	Avg	OBP	SLG
1998 Oakland	AL	117	370	95	22	2	5	(2	3)	136	64	40	36	0	106	1	10	4	5	6	.45	1	.257	.321	.368
1999 Oakland	AL	106	268	56	12	1	4	(2	2)	82	41	24	38	0	58	1	4	0	7	5	.58	6	.209	.305	.306
2000 Oakland	AL	121	129	32	2	2	4	(3	1)	50	31	18	19	0	33	1	4	0	1	2	.33	1	.248	.349	.388
3 ML YEARS		344	767	183	36	5	13	(7	6)	268	128	82	93	0	197	3	22	8	13	13	.50	8	.239	.320	.349

Jason Christiansen

Pitches: Left Bats: Right Pos: RP-65   Ht: 6'5" Wt: 241 Born: 9/21/69 Age: 31

Year Team	Lg	G	GS	CG	GF	IP	BFP	H	R	ER	HR	SH	SF	HB	TBB	IBB	SO	WP	Bk	W	L	Pct.	ShO	Sv-Op	Hld	ERA
1995 Pittsburgh	NL	63	0	0	13	56.1	255	49	28	26	5	6	3	3	34	9	53	4	1	1	3	.250	0	0-4	12	4.15
1996 Pittsburgh	NL	33	0	0	9	44.1	205	56	34	33	7	2	3	1	19	2	38	4	1	3	3	.500	0	0-2	2	6.70
1997 Pittsburgh	NL	39	0	0	9	33.2	154	37	11	11	2	0	0	2	17	3	37	4	0	3	0	1.000	0	0-2	8	2.94
1998 Pittsburgh	NL	60	0	0	19	64.2	269	51	22	18	2	5	1	0	27	7	71	3	0	3	3	.500	0	6-10	15	2.51
1999 Pittsburgh	NL	39	0	0	17	37.2	158	26	17	17	2	2	1	2	22	4	35	0	0	2	3	.400	0	3-5	7	4.06
2000 Pit-StL	NL	65	0	0	19	48	210	41	29	27	3	4	1	2	27	5	53	3	0	3	8	.273	0	1-4	22	5.06
2000 Pittsburgh	NL	44	0	0	17	38	164	28	22	21	2	3	1	0	25	4	41	3	0	2	8	.200	0	1-3	13	4.97
St. Louis	NL	21	0	0	2	10	46	13	7	6	1	1	0	2	2	1	12	0	0	1	0	1.000	0	0-1	9	5.40
6 ML YEARS		299	0	0	86	284.2	1251	260	141	132	21	19	9	10	146	30	287	18	2	15	20	.429	0	10-27	66	4.17

Jeff Cirillo

Bats: Right **Throws:** Right **Pos:** 3B-155; PH/PR-3 **Ht:** 6'1" **Wt:** 195 **Born:** 9/23/69 **Age:** 31

Year Team	Lg	G	AB	H	2B	3B	HR	(Hm	Rd)	TB	R	RBI	TBB	IBB	SO	HBP	SH	SF	SB	CS	SB%	GDP	Avg	OBP	SLG
1994 Milwaukee	AL	39	126	30	9	0	3	(1	2)	48	17	12	11	0	16	2	0	0	0	1	.00	4	.238	.309	.381
1995 Milwaukee	AL	125	328	91	19	4	9	(6	3)	145	57	39	47	0	42	4	1	4	7	2	.78	8	.277	.371	.442
1996 Milwaukee	AL	158	566	184	46	5	15	(6	9)	285	101	83	58	0	69	7	6	6	4	9	.31	14	.325	.391	.504
1997 Milwaukee	AL	154	580	167	46	2	10	(6	4)	247	74	82	60	0	74	14	4	3	4	3	.57	13	.288	.367	.426
1998 Milwaukee	NL	156	604	194	31	1	14	(6	8)	269	97	68	79	3	88	4	5	2	10	4	.71	26	.321	.402	.445
1999 Milwaukee	NL	157	607	198	35	1	15	(6	9)	280	98	88	75	4	83	5	3	7	7	4	.64	15	.326	.401	.461
2000 Colorado	NL	157	598	195	53	2	11	(9	2)	285	111	115	67	4	72	6	1	12	3	4	.43	19	.326	.392	.477
7 ML YEARS		946	3409	1059	239	15	77	(40	37)	1559	555	487	397	11	444	42	20	34	35	27	.56	99	.311	.386	.457

Chris Clapinski

Bats: B **Throws:** R **Pos:** PH/PR-18; 2B-14; 3B-3; LF-3; SS-1 **Ht:** 6'0" **Wt:** 175 **Born:** 8/20/71 **Age:** 29

Year Team	Lg	G	AB	H	2B	3B	HR	(Hm	Rd)	TB	R	RBI	TBB	IBB	SO	HBP	SH	SF	SB	CS	SB%	GDP	Avg	OBP	SLG
1992 Marlins	R	59	212	51	8	1	1	—	—	64	36	15	49	2	42	4	3	2	5	6	.45	4	.241	.390	.302
1993 Kane County	A	82	214	45	12	1	0	—	—	59	22	27	31	0	55	1	8	4	3	8	.27	3	.210	.308	.276
1994 Brevard Cty	A+	65	157	45	12	3	1	—	—	66	33	13	23	2	28	3	7	1	3	2	.60	2	.287	.386	.420
1995 Portland	AA	87	208	49	9	3	4	—	—	76	32	30	28	2	44	2	5	5	5	2	.71	4	.236	.325	.365
1996 Portland	AA	23	73	19	7	0	3	—	—	35	15	11	13	1	13	2	1	1	3	1	.75	2	.260	.382	.479
Charlotte	AAA	105	362	103	20	1	10	—	—	155	74	39	47	0	54	3	8	5	13	6	.68	7	.285	.367	.428
1997 Charlotte	AAA	110	340	89	24	2	12	—	—	153	62	52	48	4	64	9	6	2	14	2	.88	9	.262	.366	.450
1998 Brevard Cty	A+	5	14	1	0	0	0	—	—	3	1	4	7	2	2	0	0	1	0	0	—	1	.071	.364	.214
Charlotte	AAA	100	312	84	18	1	9	—	—	131	53	35	39	0	53	5	7	1	11	3	.79	7	.269	.359	.420
1999 Calgary	AAA	81	267	86	21	6	8	—	—	143	51	35	30	0	53	2	3	1	5	1	.83	6	.322	.393	.536
2000 Calgary	AAA	62	214	60	10	3	6	—	—	94	41	24	33	0	36	2	1	2	3	3	.50	4	.280	.378	.439
Brevard Cty	A+	4	17	6	0	0	1	—	—	9	4	1	0	0	2	0	0	0	0	0	—	0	.353	.353	.529
1999 Florida	NL	36	56	13	1	2	0	(0	0)	18	6	2	9	0	12	1	0	0	1	0	1.00	1	.232	.348	.321
2000 Florida	NL	34	49	15	4	1	1	(0	1)	24	12	7	5	0	7	0	1	0	0	0	—	0	.306	.370	.490
2 ML YEARS		70	105	28	5	3	1	(0	1)	42	18	9	14	0	19	1	1	0	1	0	1.00	1	.267	.358	.400

Brady Clark

Bats: Right **Throws:** Right **Pos:** PH/PR-8; RF-3; LF-2 **Ht:** 6'2" **Wt:** 195 **Born:** 4/18/73 **Age:** 28

Year Team	Lg	G	AB	H	2B	3B	HR	(Hm	Rd)	TB	R	RBI	TBB	IBB	SO	HBP	SH	SF	SB	CS	SB%	GDP	Avg	OBP	SLG
1997 Burlington	A	126	459	149	29	7	11	—	—	225	108	63	76	3	71	4	1	3	31	18	.63	10	.325	.423	.490
1998 Chattanooga	AA	64	222	60	13	1	2	—	—	81	41	16	31	0	34	4	1	0	12	4	.75	11	.270	.370	.365
1999 Chattanooga	AA	138	506	165	37	4	17	—	—	261	103	75	89	6	58	2	5	5	25	17	.60	6	.326	.425	.516
2000 Louisville	AAA	132	487	148	41	6	16	—	—	249	90	79	72	0	51	9	0	9	12	8	.60	14	.304	.397	.511
2000 Cincinnati	NL	11	11	3	1	0	0	(0	0)	4	1	2	0	0	2	0	0	0	0	0	—	0	.273	.273	.364

Mark Clark

Pitches: Right **Bats:** Right **Pos:** SP-8; RP-4 **Ht:** 6'5" **Wt:** 235 **Born:** 5/12/68 **Age:** 33

Year Team	Lg	G	GS	CG	GF	IP	BFP	H	R	ER	HR	SH	SF	HB	TBB	IBB	SO	WP	Bk	W	L	Pct.	ShO	Sv-Op	Hld	ERA
1991 St. Louis	NL	7	2	0	1	22.1	93	17	10	10	3	0	3	0	11	0	13	2	0	1	1	.500	0	0-0	1	4.03
1992 St. Louis	NL	20	20	1	0	113.1	488	117	59	56	12	7	4	0	36	2	44	4	0	3	10	.231	1	0-0	0	4.45
1993 Cleveland	AL	26	15	1	1	109.1	454	119	55	52	18	1	1	1	25	1	57	1	0	7	5	.583	0	0-0	2	4.28
1994 Cleveland	AL	20	20	4	0	127.1	540	133	61	54	14	2	7	4	40	0	60	9	1	11	3	.786	1	0-0	0	3.82
1995 Cleveland	AL	22	21	2	0	124.2	552	143	77	73	13	6	4	4	42	0	68	8	0	9	7	.563	0	0-0	0	5.27
1996 New York	NL	32	32	2	0	212.1	883	217	99	81	20	8	4	3	48	8	142	6	2	14	11	.560	0	0-0	0	3.43
1997 NYM-ChC	NL	32	31	3	0	205	866	213	96	87	24	9	4	4	59	3	123	4	1	14	8	.636	0	0-0	0	3.82
1998 Chicago	NL	33	33	2	0	213.2	918	236	116	115	23	12	6	4	48	4	161	5	2	9	14	.391	1	0-0	0	4.84
1999 Texas	AL	15	15	0	0	74.1	353	103	71	71	17	1	4	1	34	1	44	7	0	3	7	.300	0	0-0	0	8.60
2000 Texas	AL	12	8	0	1	44	220	66	42	39	10	1	2	3	24	2	16	1	0	3	5	.375	0	0-0	0	7.98
1997 New York	NL	23	22	1	0	142	608	158	74	67	18	9	2	3	47	2	72	4	0	8	7	.533	0	0-0	0	4.25
Chicago	NL	9	9	2	0	63	258	55	22	20	6	0	2	1	12	1	51	0	1	6	1	.857	0	0-0	0	2.86
10 ML YEARS		219	197	15	3	1246.1	5367	1364	687	638	154	44	41	24	367	21	728	47	6	74	71	.510	3	0-0	3	4.61

Tony Clark

Bats: Both **Throws:** Right **Pos:** 1B-58; DH-1; PH/PR-1 **Ht:** 6'7" **Wt:** 245 **Born:** 6/15/72 **Age:** 29

Year Team	Lg	G	AB	H	2B	3B	HR	(Hm	Rd)	TB	R	RBI	TBB	IBB	SO	HBP	SH	SF	SB	CS	SB%	GDP	Avg	OBP	SLG
2000 Toledo *	AAA	6	22	2	1	0	1	—	—	6	1	2	1	0	1	0	0	0	0	0	—	0	.091	.130	.273
1995 Detroit	AL	27	101	24	5	1	3	(0	3)	40	10	11	8	0	30	0	0	0	0	0	—	2	.238	.294	.396
1996 Detroit	AL	100	376	94	14	0	27	(17	10)	189	56	72	29	1	127	0	0	6	0	1	.00	7	.250	.299	.503
1997 Detroit	AL	159	580	160	28	3	32	(18	14)	290	105	117	93	13	144	3	0	5	1	3	.25	11	.276	.376	.500
1998 Detroit	AL	157	602	175	37	0	34	(18	16)	314	84	103	63	5	128	3	0	5	3	3	.50	16	.291	.358	.522
1999 Detroit	AL	143	540	150	29	0	31	(12	19)	272	74	99	64	7	133	6	0	3	2	1	.67	14	.280	.361	.507
2000 Detroit	AL	60	208	57	14	0	13	(6	7)	110	32	37	24	2	51	0	0	0	0	0	—	10	.274	.349	.529
6 ML YEARS		646	2403	660	127	4	140	(71	69)	1215	361	439	281	28	613	12	0	19	6	8	.43	60	.275	.351	.506

Will Clark

Bats: Left **Throws:** Left **Pos:** 1B-122; DH-6; PH/PR-3 **Ht:** 6'1" **Wt:** 200 **Born:** 3/13/64 **Age:** 37

Year Team	Lg	G	AB	H	2B	3B	HR	(Hm	Rd)	TB	R	RBI	TBB	IBB	SO	HBP	SH	SF	SB	CS	SB%	GDP	Avg	OBP	SLG
1986 San Francisco	NL	111	408	117	27	2	11	(7	4)	181	66	41	34	10	76	3	9	4	4	7	.36	3	.287	.343	.444

Batting (continued)

Year Team	Lg	G	AB	H	2B	3B	HR	(Hm	Rd)	TB	R	RBI	TBB	IBB	SO	HBP	SH	SF	SB	CS	SB%	GDP	Avg	OBP	SLG
1987 San Francisco	NL	150	529	163	29	5	35	(22	13)	307	89	91	49	11	98	5	3	2	5	17	.23	2	.308	.371	.580
1988 San Francisco	NL	162	575	162	31	6	29	(14	15)	292	102	**109**	**100**	**27**	129	4	0	10	9	1	.90	9	.282	.386	.508
1989 San Francisco	NL	159	588	196	38	9	23	(9	14)	321	**104**	111	74	14	103	5	0	8	8	3	.73	6	.333	.407	.546
1990 San Francisco	NL	154	600	177	25	5	19	(8	11)	269	91	95	62	9	97	3	0	13	8	2	.80	7	.295	.357	.448
1991 San Francisco	NL	148	565	170	32	7	29	(17	12)	**303**	84	116	51	12	91	2	0	4	4	2	.67	5	.301	.359	**.536**
1992 San Francisco	NL	144	513	154	40	1	16	(11	5)	244	69	73	73	23	82	4	0	11	12	7	.63	5	.300	.384	.476
1993 San Francisco	NL	132	491	139	27	2	14	(5	9)	212	82	73	63	6	68	6	1	6	2	2	.50	10	.283	.367	.432
1994 Texas	AL	110	389	128	24	2	13	(9	4)	195	73	80	71	11	59	3	0	6	5	1	.83	5	.329	.431	.501
1995 Texas	AL	123	454	137	27	3	16	(10	6)	218	85	92	68	6	50	4	0	11	0	1	.00	7	.302	.389	.480
1996 Texas	AL	117	436	124	25	1	13	(9	4)	190	69	72	64	5	67	5	0	7	2	1	.67	10	.284	.377	.436
1997 Texas	AL	110	393	128	29	1	12	(6	6)	195	56	51	49	11	62	3	0	5	0	0	—	4	.326	.400	.496
1998 Texas	AL	149	554	169	41	1	23	(11	12)	281	98	102	72	5	97	3	0	7	1	0	1.00	15	.305	.384	.507
1999 Baltimore	AL	77	251	76	15	0	10	(6	5)	121	40	29	38	2	42	2	0	3	2	2	.50	5	.303	.395	.482
2000 Bal-StL		130	427	136	30	2	21	(12	9)	233	78	70	69	3	69	7	0	4	5	2	.71	7	.319	.418	.546
2000 Baltimore	AL	79	256	77	15	1	9	(6	3)	121	49	28	47	3	45	4	0	3	4	2	.67	4	.301	.413	.473
St. Louis	NL	51	171	59	15	1	12	(6	6)	112	29	42	22	0	24	3	0	1	1	0	1.00	3	.345	.426	.655
15 ML YEARS		1976	7173	2176	440	47	284	(155	129)	3562	1186	1205	937	155	1190	59	13	101	67	48	.58	100	.303	.384	.497

Royce Clayton

Bats: Right **Throws:** Right **Pos:** SS-148   **Ht:** 6'0" **Wt:** 183 **Born:** 1/2/70 **Age:** 31

Year Team	Lg	G	AB	H	2B	3B	HR	(Hm	Rd)	TB	R	RBI	TBB	IBB	SO	HBP	SH	SF	SB	CS	SB%	GDP	Avg	OBP	SLG
1991 San Francisco	NL	9	26	3	1	0	0	(0	0)	4	0	2	1	0	6	0	0	0	0	0	—	1	.115	.148	.154
1992 San Francisco	NL	98	321	72	7	4	4	(3	1)	99	31	24	26	3	63	0	3	2	8	4	.67	11	.224	.281	.308
1993 San Francisco	NL	153	549	155	21	5	6	(5	1)	204	54	70	38	2	91	5	8	7	11	10	.52	16	.282	.331	.372
1994 San Francisco	NL	108	385	91	14	6	3	(1	2)	126	38	30	30	2	74	3	3	2	23	3	.88	7	.236	.295	.327
1995 San Francisco	NL	138	509	124	29	3	5	(2	3)	174	56	58	38	1	109	3	4	3	24	9	.73	7	.244	.298	.342
1996 St. Louis	NL	129	491	136	20	4	6	(6	0)	182	64	35	33	4	89	1	2	4	33	15	.69	13	.277	.321	.371
1997 St. Louis	NL	154	576	153	39	5	9	(5	4)	229	75	61	33	4	109	3	2	5	30	10	.75	19	.266	.306	.398
1998 StL-Tex		142	541	136	31	2	9	(2	7)	198	89	53	53	1	83	3	6	5	24	11	.69	16	.251	.319	.366
1999 Texas	AL	133	465	134	21	5	14	(6	8)	207	69	52	39	1	100	4	9	3	8	6	.57	6	.288	.346	.445
2000 Texas	AL	148	513	124	21	5	14	(9	5)	197	70	54	42	1	92	3	12	3	11	7	.61	21	.242	.301	.384
1998 St. Louis	NL	90	355	83	19	1	4	(1	3)	116	59	29	40	1	51	2	3	2	19	6	.76	10	.234	.313	.327
Texas		52	186	53	12	1	5	(1	4)	82	30	24	13	0	32	1	3	3	5	5	.50	6	.285	.330	.441
10 ML YEARS		1212	4376	1128	204	39	70	(39	31)	1620	546	439	333	19	816	25	49	34	172	75	.70	117	.258	.312	.370

Roger Clemens

Pitches: Right **Bats:** Right **Pos:** SP-32   **Ht:** 6'4" **Wt:** 238 **Born:** 8/4/62 **Age:** 38

Year Team	Lg	G	GS	CG	GF	IP	BFP	H	R	ER	HR	SH	SF	HB	TBB	IBB	SO	WP	Bk	W	L	Pct.	ShO	Sv-Op	Hld	ERA
1984 Boston	AL	21	20	5	0	133.1	575	146	67	64	13	2	3	2	29	3	126	4	0	9	4	.692	1	0-0	0	4.32
1985 Boston	AL	15	15	3	0	98.1	407	83	38	36	5	1	2	3	37	0	74	1	3	7	5	.583	1	0-0	0	3.29
1986 Boston	AL	33	33	10	0	254	997	179	77	70	21	4	6	4	67	0	238	11	3	**24**	4	**.857**	1	0-0	0	**2.48**
1987 Boston	AL	36	36	**18**	0	281.2	1157	248	100	93	19	6	4	9	83	4	256	4	3	**20**	9	.690	**7**	0-0	0	2.97
1988 Boston	AL	35	35	**14**	0	264	1063	217	86	77	17	6	3	6	62	4	**291**	4	0	18	12	.600	**8**	0-0	0	2.93
1989 Boston	AL	35	35	8	0	253.1	1044	215	101	88	20	9	5	8	93	5	230	7	0	17	11	.607	3	0-0	0	3.13
1990 Boston	AL	31	31	7	0	228.1	920	193	59	49	7	7	5	7	54	3	209	8	0	21	6	.778	**4**	0-0	0	**1.93**
1991 Boston	AL	35	**35**	13	0	271.1	1077	219	79	79	15	6	8	5	65	12	241	6	0	18	10	.643	**4**	0-0	0	**2.62**
1992 Boston	AL	32	32	11	0	246.2	989	203	80	66	11	5	5	9	62	5	208	3	0	18	11	.621	**5**	0-0	0	**2.41**
1993 Boston	AL	29	29	2	0	191.2	808	175	99	95	17	5	7	11	67	4	160	3	1	11	14	.440	1	0-0	0	4.46
1994 Boston	AL	24	24	3	0	170.2	692	124	62	54	15	2	5	4	71	1	168	4	0	9	7	.563	1	0-0	0	2.85
1995 Boston	AL	23	23	0	0	140	623	141	70	65	15	2	3	**14**	60	0	132	9	0	10	5	.667	0	0-0	0	4.18
1996 Boston	AL	34	34	6	0	242.2	1032	216	106	98	19	4	7	4	106	2	**257**	8	1	10	13	.435	2	0-0	0	3.63
1997 Toronto	AL	34	34	**9**	0	264	1044	204	65	60	9	5	2	12	68	1	**292**	4	0	**21**	7	.750	**3**	0-0	0	**2.05**
1998 Toronto	AL	33	33	5	0	234.2	961	169	78	69	11	8	2	7	88	0	**271**	6	0	**20**	6	.769	3	0-0	0	**2.65**
1999 New York	AL	30	30	1	0	187.2	822	185	101	96	20	**10**	5	9	90	0	163	8	1	14	10	.583	1	0-0	0	4.60
2000 New York	AL	32	32	1	0	204.1	878	184	96	84	26	9	2	10	84	0	188	2	1	13	8	.619	0	0-0	0	3.70
17 ML YEARS		512	511	116	0	3666.2	15089	3101	1385	1252	260	83	74	124	1186	44	3504	92	19	260	142	.647	45	0-0	0	3.07

Matt Clement

Pitches: Right **Bats:** Right **Pos:** SP-34   **Ht:** 6'3" **Wt:** 195 **Born:** 8/12/74 **Age:** 26

Year Team	Lg	G	GS	CG	GF	IP	BFP	H	R	ER	HR	SH	SF	HB	TBB	IBB	SO	WP	Bk	W	L	Pct.	ShO	Sv-Op	Hld	ERA
1998 San Diego	NL	4	2	0	0	13.2	62	15	8	7	0	2	0	0	7	1	13	2	0	2		1.000	0	0-0	0	4.61
1999 San Diego	NL	31	31	0	0	180.2	803	190	106	90	18	7	6	9	86	2	135	11	0	10	12	.455	0	0-0	0	4.48
2000 San Diego	NL	34	34	0	0	205	940	194	131	117	22	12	5	16	**125**	4	170	**23**	0	13	17	.433	0	0-0	0	5.14
3 ML YEARS		69	67	0	0	399.1	1805	399	245	214	40	21	11	25	218	7	318	36	0	25	29	.463	0	0-0	0	4.82

Edgard Clemente

Bats: R **Throws:** R **Pos:** PH/PR-16; LF-15; RF-12; DH-11; CF-5   **Ht:** 5'11" **Wt:** 188 **Born:** 12/15/75 **Age:** 25

Year Team	Lg	G	AB	H	2B	3B	HR	(Hm	Rd)	TB	R	RBI	TBB	IBB	SO	HBP	SH	SF	SB	CS	SB%	GDP	Avg	OBP	SLG
2000 Edmonton *	AAA	22	87	21	4	1	2	—		33	14	10	9	0	23	2	0	0	0	2	.00	2	.241	.327	.379
1998 Colorado	NL	11	17	6	0	1	0	(0	0)	8	2	2	2	0	8	0	0	0	0	0	—	0	.353	.421	.471
1999 Colorado	NL	57	162	41	10	2	8	(7	1)	79	24	25	7	0	46	0	1	1	0	0	—	1	.253	.282	.488
2000 Anaheim	AL	46	78	17	2	0	0	(0	0)	19	4	5	0	0	27	1	1	0	0	1	.00	0	.218	.228	.244
3 ML YEARS		114	257	64	12	3	8	(7	1)	106	30	32	9	0	81	1	2	1	0	1	.00	4	.249	.276	.412

Brad Clontz

Pitches: Right **Bats:** Right **Pos:** RP-5 **Ht:** 6'1" **Wt:** 203 **Born:** 4/25/71 **Age:** 30

Year Team	Lg	G	GS	CG	GF	IP	BFP	H	R	ER	HR	SH	SF	HB	TBB	IBB	SO	WP	Bk	W	L	Pct.	ShO	Sv-Op	Hld	ERA
2000 Nashville *	AAA	4	0	0	2	4.2	17	1	0	0	0	0	0	0	5	0	5	0	0	0	0	--	0	1--	--	0.00
Altoona *	AA	4	0	0	0	4.2	19	4	2	1	0	1	1	1	1	0	4	0	0	0	0	--	0	0--	--	1.93
1995 Atlanta	NL	59	0	0	14	69	295	71	29	28	5	3	2	4	22	4	55	0	0	8	1	.889	0	4-6	6	3.65
1996 Atlanta	NL	81	0	0	11	80.2	350	78	53	51	11	5	4	2	33	8	49	0	1	6	3	.667	0	1-6	17	5.69
1997 Atlanta	NL	51	0	0	16	48	203	52	24	20	3	0	2	1	18	3	42	1	0	5	1	.833	0	1-2	0	3.75
1998 LA-NYM	NL	20	0	0	6	23.2	101	19	16	16	4	0	0	2	12	4	16	0	0	2	0	1.000	0	0-1	5	6.08
1999 Pittsburgh	NL	56	0	0	16	49.1	223	49	21	15	6	2	1	3	24	5	40	2	0	1	3	.250	0	2-3	9	2.74
2000 Pittsburgh	NL	5	0	0	0	7	37	4	4	4	1	0	0	0	11	2	1	0	0	0	0	--	0	0-0	0	5.14
1998 Los Angeles	NL	18	0	0	6	20.2	87	15	13	13	3	0	0	2	10	4	14	0	0	2	0	1.000	0	0-1	5	5.66
New York	NL	2	0	0	0	3	14	4	3	3	1	0	0	0	2	0	2	0	0	0	0	--	0	0-0	0	9.00
6 ML YEARS		272	0	0	63	277.2	1209	276	147	134	30	10	9	12	120	26	210	4	1	22	8	.733	0	8-18	35	4.34

Pasqual Coco

Pitches: Right **Bats:** Right **Pos:** SP-1 **Ht:** 6'1" **Wt:** 160 **Born:** 9/24/77 **Age:** 23

Year Team	Lg	G	GS	CG	GF	IP	BFP	H	R	ER	HR	SH	SF	HB	TBB	IBB	SO	WP	Bk	W	L	Pct.	ShO	Sv-Op	Hld	ERA
1997 St.Cathrnes	A-	10	8	0	1	46	199	48	32	25	5	0	4	2	16	1	44	6	1	1	4	.200	0	0--	--	4.89
1998 St.Cathrnes	A-	15	15	1	0	81.2	353	62	52	29	4	2	1	9	32	0	84	10	3	3	7	.300	0	0--	--	3.20
1999 Hagerstown	A	14	14	0	0	97.2	384	67	29	24	4	1	1	8	25	1	83	2	0	11	1	.917	0	0--	--	2.21
Dunedin	A+	13	13	2	0	75	338	81	50	47	7	3	3	6	36	0	59	7	2	4	6	.400	0	0--	--	5.64
2000 Tennessee	AA	27	26	2	0	167.2	723	154	83	70	16	1	4	17	68	0	142	6	3	12	7	.632	0	0--	--	3.76
2000 Toronto	AL	1	1	0	0	4	23	5	4	4	1	0	0	1	5	0	2	1	0	0	0	--	0	0-0	0	9.00

Ivanon Coffie

Bats: L **Throws:** R **Pos:** 3B-15; PH/PR-6; SS-4; DH-1 **Ht:** 6'1" **Wt:** 170 **Born:** 5/16/77 **Age:** 24

Year Team	Lg	G	AB	H	2B	3B	HR	(Hm	Rd)	TB	R	RBI	TBB	IBB	SO	HBP	SH	SF	SB	CS	SB%	GDP	Avg	OBP	SLG
1996 Orioles	R	56	193	42	8	4	0	--	--	58	29	20	23	1	26	2	0	0	6	2	.75	4	.218	.307	.301
1997 Delmarva	A	90	305	84	14	5	3	--	--	117	41	48	23	1	45	4	1	6	19	10	.66	5	.275	.328	.384
1998 Frederick	A+	130	473	121	19	2	16	--	--	192	62	75	48	2	109	3	3	9	17	12	.59	11	.256	.323	.406
1999 Bowie	AA	57	195	36	9	3	3	--	--	60	21	23	20	0	46	1	1	3	2	2	.50	3	.185	.260	.308
Frederick	A+	73	276	78	18	4	11	--	--	137	35	53	28	3	62	4	0	3	7	4	.64	5	.283	.354	.496
2000 Bowie	AA	87	341	91	21	3	9	--	--	145	49	44	36	3	53	4	0	3	1	4	.20	6	.267	.341	.425
Rochester	AAA	21	78	17	2	1	0	--	--	21	4	10	6	2	21	1	1	1	0	0	--	1	.218	.244	.269
2000 Baltimore	AL	23	60	13	4	1	0	(0	0)	19	6	5	5	0	11	1	0	0	0	1	1.00	3	.217	.284	.317

Dave Coggin

Pitches: Right **Bats:** Right **Pos:** SP-5 **Ht:** 6'4" **Wt:** 195 **Born:** 10/30/76 **Age:** 24

Year Team	Lg	G	GS	CG	GF	IP	BFP	H	R	ER	HR	SH	SF	HB	TBB	IBB	SO	WP	Bk	W	L	Pct.	ShO	Sv-Op	Hld	ERA
1995 Martinsvlle	R+	11	11	0	0	48	209	45	25	16	1	1	1	5	31	0	37	8	1	5	3	.625	0	0--	--	3.00
1996 Piedmont	A	28	28	3	0	169.1	699	156	87	81	12	3	3	7	46	1	129	12	1	9	12	.429	3	0--	--	4.31
1997 Clearwater	A+	27	27	3	0	155	697	160	96	81	12	5	7	9	86	0	110	24	1	11	8	.579	2	0--	--	4.70
1998 Reading	AA	20	20	0	0	108.2	477	106	58	50	8	2	2	8	62	1	65	14	0	4	8	.333	0	0--	--	4.14
1999 Reading	AA	9	9	0	0	42	203	55	37	35	8	0	3	3	20	0	21	6	0	2	5	.286	0	0--	--	7.50
2000 Clearwater	A+	6	5	0	0	33.2	131	25	11	10	1	1	1	0	13	0	26	0	0	2	2	.500	0	0--	--	2.67
Reading	AA	7	7	0	0	42	181	49	24	23	5	2	2	1	13	0	30	2	0	2	3	.400	0	0--	--	4.93
Scrantn-WB	AAA	9	9	0	0	45.2	204	35	27	22	2	3	1	5	33	0	27	4	0	3	2	.600	0	0--	--	4.34
2000 Philadelphia	NL	5	5	0	0	27	126	35	20	16	2	2	0	1	12	0	17	1	0	2	0	1.000	0	0-0	0	5.33

Greg Colbrunn

Bats: R **Throws:** R **Pos:** 1B-99; PH/PR-28; DH-2; 3B-1 **Ht:** 6'0" **Wt:** 205 **Born:** 7/26/69 **Age:** 31

Year Team	Lg	G	AB	H	2B	3B	HR	(Hm	Rd)	TB	R	RBI	TBB	IBB	SO	HBP	SH	SF	SB	CS	SB%	GDP	Avg	OBP	SLG
1992 Montreal	NL	52	168	45	8	0	2	(1	1)	59	12	18	6	1	34	2	0	4	3	2	.60	1	.268	.294	.351
1993 Montreal	NL	70	153	39	9	0	4	(2	2)	60	15	23	6	1	33	1	1	3	4	2	.67	1	.255	.282	.392
1994 Florida	NL	47	155	47	10	0	6	(3	3)	75	17	31	9	0	27	2	0	2	1	1	.50	3	.303	.345	.484
1995 Florida	NL	138	528	146	22	1	23	(12	11)	239	70	89	22	4	69	6	0	4	11	3	.79	15	.277	.311	.453
1996 Florida	NL	141	511	146	26	2	16	(7	9)	224	60	69	25	1	76	14	0	5	4	5	.44	22	.286	.333	.438
1997 Min-Atl		98	271	76	17	0	7	(3	4)	114	27	35	10	1	49	2	1	2	2	2	.33	8	.280	.309	.421
1998 Col-Atl	NL	90	166	51	11	2	3	(1	2)	75	18	23	10	0	34	4	0	0	4	3	.57	8	.307	.361	.452
1999 Arizona	NL	67	135	44	5	3	5	(2	3)	70	20	24	12	0	23	4	0	2	1	1	.50	3	.326	.392	.519
2000 Arizona	NL	116	329	103	22	1	15	(6	9)	172	48	57	43	2	45	10	0	3	1	0	.00	13	.313	.405	.523
1997 Minnesota	AL	70	217	61	14	0	5	(2	3)	90	24	26	8	1	38	1	0	2	1	2	.33	7	.281	.307	.415
Atlanta	NL	28	54	15	3	0	2	(1	1)	24	3	9	2	0	11	1	1	0	0	0	--	1	.278	.316	.444
1998 Colorado	NL	62	122	38	8	2	2	(1	1)	56	12	13	8	0	23	4	0	0	3	3	.50	1	.311	.359	.459
Atlanta	NL	28	44	13	3	0	1	(0	1)	19	6	10	2	0	11	0	0	0	1	0	1.00	7	.295	.367	.432
9 ML YEARS		819	2416	697	130	9	81	(37	44)	1088	287	369	143	10	390	45	2	25	29	20	.59	67	.288	.337	.450

Lou Collier

Bats: R **Throws:** R **Pos:** CF-7; LF-5; PH/PR-4; 3B-1 **Ht:** 5'10" **Wt:** 182 **Born:** 8/21/73 **Age:** 27

Year Team	Lg	G	AB	H	2B	3B	HR	(Hm	Rd)	TB	R	RBI	TBB	IBB	SO	HBP	SH	SF	SB	CS	SB%	GDP	Avg	OBP	SLG
2000 Indianapols *	AAA	17	56	14	4	1	0	--	--	20	7	12	11	0	9	1	1	2	2	2	.50	1	.250	.371	.357
Huntsville *	AA	50	172	46	4	2	2	--	--	60	29	29	30	1	44	0	0	3	7	3	.70	5	.267	.374	.349

Year Team	Lg	G	AB	H	2B	3B	HR	(Hm	Rd)	TB	R	RBI	TBB	IBB	SO	HBP	SH	SF	SB	CS	SB%	GDP	Avg	OBP	SLG
									BATTING										BASERUNNING				PERCENTAGES		
1997 Pittsburgh	NL	18	37	5	0	0	0	(0	0)	5	3	3	1	0	11	0	0	0	1	0	1.00	1	.135	.158	.135
1998 Pittsburgh	NL	110	334	82	13	6	2	(1	1)	113	30	34	31	6	70	6	3	5	2	2	.50	8	.246	.316	.338
1999 Milwaukee	NL	74	135	35	9	0	2	(2	0)	50	18	21	14	0	32	0	1	2	3	2	.60	2	.259	.325	.370
2000 Milwaukee	NL	14	32	7	1	0	1	(0	1)	11	9	2	6	0	4	0	0	1	0	0	—	1	.219	.333	.344
4 ML YEARS		216	538	129	23	6	5	(3	2)	179	60	60	52	6	117	6	4	8	6	4	.60	12	.240	.310	.333

Bartolo Colon

Pitches: Right **Bats:** Right **Pos:** SP-30 **Ht:** 6'0" **Wt:** 230 **Born:** 5/24/75 **Age:** 26

Year Team	Lg	G	GS	CG	GF	IP	BFP	H	R	ER	HR	SH	SF	HB	TBB	IBB	SO	WP	Bk	W	L	Pct.	ShO	Sv-Op	Hld	ERA
		HOW MUCH HE PITCHED						WHAT HE GAVE UP												THE RESULTS						
2000 Buffalo *	AAA	1	1	0	0	5	21	6	1	1	0	0	0	0	0	0	4	0	0	1	0	1.000	0	0- -	—	1.80
1997 Cleveland	AL	19	17	1	0	94	427	107	66	59	12	4	1	3	45	1	66	5	0	4	7	.364	0	0-0	0	5.65
1998 Cleveland	AL	31	31	6	0	204	883	205	91	84	15	10	2	3	79	5	158	4	0	14	9	.609	2	0-0	0	3.71
1999 Cleveland	AL	32	32	1	0	205	858	185	97	90	24	5	4	7	76	5	161	4	0	18	5	.783	1	0-0	0	3.95
2000 Cleveland	AL	30	30	2	0	188	807	163	86	81	21	2	3	4	98	4	212	4	0	15	8	.652	1	0-0	0	3.88
4 ML YEARS		112	110	10	0	691	2975	660	340	314	72	21	10	17	298	15	597	17	0	51	29	.638	4	0-0	0	4.09

David Cone

Pitches: Right **Bats:** Left **Pos:** SP-29; RP-1 **Ht:** 6'1" **Wt:** 200 **Born:** 1/2/63 **Age:** 38

Year Team	Lg	G	GS	CG	GF	IP	BFP	H	R	ER	HR	SH	SF	HB	TBB	IBB	SO	WP	Bk	W	L	Pct.	ShO	Sv-Op	Hld	ERA
		HOW MUCH HE PITCHED						WHAT HE GAVE UP												THE RESULTS						
1986 Kansas City	AL	11	0	0	5	22.2	108	29	14	14	2	0	0	1	13	1	21	3	0	0	0	—	0	0- -	—	5.56
1987 New York	NL	21	13	1	3	99.1	420	87	46	41	11	4	3	5	44	1	68	2	4	5	6	.455	0	1-1	2	3.71
1988 New York	NL	35	28	8	0	231.1	936	178	67	57	10	11	5	4	80	7	213	10	10	20	3	.870	4	0-0	1	2.22
1989 New York	NL	34	33	7	0	219.2	910	183	92	86	20	6	4	4	74	6	190	14	4	14	8	.636	2	0-0	0	3.52
1990 New York	NL	31	30	6	1	211.2	860	177	84	76	21	4	6	1	65	1	233	10	4	14	10	.583	2	0-0	0	3.23
1991 New York	NL	34	34	5	0	232.2	966	204	95	85	13	13	7	5	73	2	241	17	1	14	14	.500	2	0-0	0	3.29
1992 NYM-Tor		35	34	7	0	249.2	1055	201	91	78	15	6	9	12	111	7	261	12	1	17	10	.630	5	0-0	0	2.81
1993 Kansas City	AL	34	34	6	0	254	1060	205	102	94	20	7	9	10	114	2	191	14	2	11	14	.440	1	0-0	0	3.33
1994 Kansas City	AL	23	23	4	0	171.2	690	130	60	56	15	1	5	7	54	0	132	5	1	16	5	.762	3	0-0	0	2.94
1995 Tor-NYY		30	30	6	0	229.1	954	195	95	91	24	2	3	6	88	2	191	11	1	18	8	.692	2	0-0	0	3.57
1996 New York	AL	11	11	1	0	72	295	50	25	23	3	1	5	2	34	0	71	4	1	7	2	.778	0	0-0	0	2.88
1997 New York	AL	29	29	1	0	195	805	155	67	61	17	3	2	4	86	2	222	14	2	12	6	.667	0	0-0	0	2.82
1998 New York	AL	31	31	3	0	207.2	866	186	89	82	20	4	4	15	59	1	209	6	0	20	7	.741	0	0-0	0	3.55
1999 New York	AL	31	31	1	0	193.1	827	164	84	74	21	5	6	11	90	2	177	7	1	12	9	.571	1	0-0	0	3.44
2000 New York	AL	30	29	0	0	155	733	192	124	119	25	6	8	9	82	3	120	11	0	4	14	.222	0	0-0	0	6.91
1992 New York	NL	27	27	7	0	196.2	831	162	75	63	12	6	6	9	82	5	214	9	1	13	7	.650	5	0-0	0	2.88
Toronto	AL	8	7	0	0	53	224	39	16	15	3	0	3	3	29	2	47	3	0	4	3	.571	0	0-0	0	2.55
1995 Toronto	AL	17	17	5	0	130.1	537	113	53	49	12	2	2	5	41	2	102	6	1	9	6	.600	2	0-0	0	3.38
New York	AL	13	13	1	0	99	417	82	42	42	12	0	1	1	47	0	89	5	0	9	2	.818	0	0-0	0	3.82
15 ML YEARS		420	390	56	9	2745	11485	2336	1135	1037	237	73	76	96	1067	37	2540	140	32	184	116	.613	22	1- -	—	3.40

Jeff Conine

Bats: R **Throws:** R **Pos:** 3B-44; 1B-39; DH-20; RF-12; PH/PR-10; LF-7 **Ht:** 6'1" **Wt:** 220 **Born:** 6/27/66 **Age:** 35

Year Team	Lg	G	AB	H	2B	3B	HR	(Hm	Rd)	TB	R	RBI	TBB	IBB	SO	HBP	SH	SF	SB	CS	SB%	GDP	Avg	OBP	SLG
									BATTING										BASERUNNING				PERCENTAGES		
1990 Kansas City	AL	9	20	5	2	0	0	(0	0)	7	3	2	2	0	5	0	0	0	0	0	—	1	.250	.318	.350
1992 Kansas City	AL	28	91	23	5	2	0	(0	0)	32	10	9	8	1	23	0	0	0	0	0	—	1	.253	.313	.352
1993 Florida	NL	162	595	174	24	3	12	(5	7)	240	75	79	52	2	135	5	0	6	2	2	.50	14	.292	.351	.403
1994 Florida	NL	115	451	144	27	6	18	(8	10)	237	60	82	40	4	92	1	0	4	1	2	.33	8	.319	.373	.525
1995 Florida	NL	133	483	146	26	2	25	(13	12)	251	72	105	66	5	94	1	0	12	2	0	1.00	13	.302	.379	.520
1996 Florida	NL	157	597	175	32	2	26	(15	11)	289	84	95	62	1	121	4	0	7	1	4	.20	17	.293	.360	.484
1997 Florida	NL	151	405	98	13	1	17	(7	10)	164	46	61	57	3	89	2	0	2	2	0	1.00	5	.242	.337	.405
1998 Kansas City	AL	93	309	79	26	0	8	(4	4)	129	30	43	26	1	68	2	0	6	3	0	1.00	8	.256	.312	.417
1999 Baltimore	AL	139	444	129	31	1	13	(7	6)	201	54	75	30	0	40	3	1	7	0	3	.00	12	.291	.335	.453
2000 Baltimore	AL	119	409	116	20	2	13	(6	7)	179	53	46	36	1	53	2	0	4	4	3	.57	12	.284	.341	.438
10 ML YEARS		1106	3804	1089	206	19	132	(65	67)	1729	487	597	379	18	720	20	1	48	15	14	.52	99	.286	.350	.455

Jason Conti

Bats: L **Throws:** R **Pos:** RF-33; PH/PR-18; CF-4; LF-2 **Ht:** 5'11" **Wt:** 180 **Born:** 1/27/75 **Age:** 26

Year Team	Lg	G	AB	H	2B	3B	HR	(Hm	Rd)	TB	R	RBI	TBB	IBB	SO	HBP	SH	SF	SB	CS	SB%	GDP	Avg	OBP	SLG
									BATTING										BASERUNNING				PERCENTAGES		
1996 Lethbridge	R+	63	226	83	15	1	4	—	—	112	63	49	30	0	29	6	0	3	30	7	.81	9	.367	.449	.496
1997 South Bend	A	117	458	142	22	10	3	—	—	193	78	43	45	2	99	11	4	3	30	18	.63	10	.310	.383	.421
High Desert	A+	14	59	21	5	1	2	—	—	34	15	8	10	0	12	1	0	0	1	2	.33	0	.356	.457	.576
1998 Tulsa	AA	130	530	167	31	12	15	—	—	267	125	67	63	4	96	9	1	2	19	13	.59	5	.315	.396	.504
1999 Tucson	AAA	133	520	151	23	8	9	—	—	217	100	50	55	1	99	8	3	6	22	8	.73	8	.290	.360	.417
2000 Tucson	AAA	93	383	117	20	5	11	—	—	180	75	57	23	1	57	5	2	5	11	3	.79	8	.305	.349	.470
2000 Arizona	NL	47	91	21	4	3	1	(1	0)	34	11	15	7	2	30	1	0	0	3	0	1.00	2	.231	.293	.374

Dennis Cook

Pitches: Left **Bats:** Left **Pos:** RP-68 **Ht:** 6'3" **Wt:** 190 **Born:** 10/4/62 **Age:** 38

Year Team	Lg	G	GS	CG	GF	IP	BFP	H	R	ER	HR	SH	SF	HB	TBB	IBB	SO	WP	Bk	W	L	Pct.	ShO	Sv-Op	Hld	ERA
		HOW MUCH HE PITCHED						WHAT HE GAVE UP												THE RESULTS						
1988 San Francisco	NL	4	4	1	0	22	86	9	8	7	1	0	2	0	11	1	13	1	0	2	1	.667	1	0-0	0	2.86
1989 SF-Phi	NL	23	18	2	1	121	499	110	59	50	18	5	2	2	38	6	67	4	2	7	8	.467	1	0-0	1	3.72
1990 Phi-LA	NL	47	16	2	4	156	663	155	74	68	20	7	7	2	56	9	64	6	3	9	4	.692	1	1-2	4	3.92
1991 Los Angeles	NL	20	1	0	5	17.2	69	12	3	1	0	1	2	0	7	1	8	0	0	1	0	1.000	0	0-1	1	0.51

45

Year Team	Lg	G	GS	CG	GF	IP	BFP	H	R	ER	HR	SH	SF	HB	TBB	IBB	SO	WP	Bk	W	L	Pct.	ShO	Sv-Op	Hld	ERA
		HOW MUCH HE PITCHED						**WHAT HE GAVE UP**												**THE RESULTS**						
1992 Cleveland	AL	32	25	1	1	158	669	156	79	67	29	3	3	3	50	2	96	4	5	5	7	.417	0	0-0	0	3.82
1993 Cleveland	AL	25	6	0	2	54	233	62	36	34	9	3	2	2	16	1	34	0	1	5	5	.500	0	0-2	1	5.67
1994 Chicago	AL	38	0	0	8	33	143	29	17	13	4	3	0	0	14	3	26	0	1	3	1	.750	0	0-1	3	3.55
1995 Cle-Tex	AL	46	1	0	10	57.2	255	63	32	29	9	4	5	2	26	3	53	1	0	0	0	.000	0	2-2	6	4.53
1996 Texas	AL	60	0	0	9	70.1	298	53	34	32	2	3	5	7	35	7	64	0	0	5	2	.714	0	0-2	11	4.09
1997 Florida	NL	59	0	0	12	62.1	272	64	28	27	4	1	1	2	28	4	63	0	0	1	2	.333	0	0-2	13	3.90
1998 New York	NL	73	0	0	18	68	286	60	21	18	5	3	3	3	27	4	79	1	1	8	4	.667	0	1-5	21	2.38
1999 New York	NL	71	0	0	12	63	262	50	27	27	11	1	2	1	27	1	68	0	0	10	5	.667	0	3-6	19	3.86
2000 New York	NL	68	0	0	15	59	269	63	35	35	8	0	0	5	31	4	53	3	2	6	3	.667	0	2-8	10	5.34
1989 San Francisco	NL	2	2	1	0	15	58	13	3	3	1	0	0	0	5	0	9	1	0	1	0	1.000	0	0-0	0	1.80
Philadelphia	NL	21	16	1	1	106	441	97	56	47	17	5	2	2	33	6	58	3	2	6	8	.429	1	0-0	1	3.99
1990 Philadelphia	NL	42	13	2	4	141.2	594	132	61	56	13	5	5	2	54	9	58	6	3	8	3	.727	1	1-2	3	3.56
Los Angeles	NL	5	3	0	0	14.1	69	23	13	12	7	2	2	0	2	0	6	0	0	1	1	.500	0	0-1	0	7.53
1995 Cleveland	AL	11	0	0	1	12.2	62	16	9	9	3	1	0	1	10	2	13	0	0	0	0	—	0	0-0	1	6.39
Texas	AL	35	1	0	9	45	193	47	23	20	6	3	5	1	16	1	40	1	0	0	2	.000	0	2-2	5	4.00
13 ML YEARS		566	71	6	97	942	4004	886	453	408	120	34	35	28	366	46	688	20	15	62	44	.585	3	9-31	91	3.90

Ron Coomer

Bats: R **Throws:** R **Pos:** 1B-124; DH-9; 3B-5; PH/PR-4   **Ht:** 5'11" **Wt:** 206 **Born:** 11/18/66 **Age:** 34

Year Team	Lg	G	AB	H	2B	3B	HR	(Hm	Rd)	TB	R	RBI	TBB	IBB	SO	HBP	SH	SF	SB	CS	SB%	GDP	Avg	OBP	SLG
		BATTING																	**BASERUNNING**				**PERCENTAGES**		
1995 Minnesota	AL	37	101	26	3	1	5	(2	3)	46	15	19	9	0	11	1	0	0	0	1	.00	9	.257	.324	.455
1996 Minnesota	AL	95	233	69	12	1	12	(5	7)	119	34	41	17	1	24	0	0	3	3	0	1.00	10	.296	.340	.511
1997 Minnesota	AL	140	523	156	30	2	13	(4	9)	229	63	85	22	5	91	0	0	5	4	3	.57	11	.298	.324	.438
1998 Minnesota	AL	137	529	146	22	1	15	(6	9)	215	64	72	18	1	72	0	0	8	2	2	.50	**22**	.276	.295	.406
1999 Minnesota	AL	127	467	123	25	1	16	(6	10)	198	53	65	30	1	69	1	0	3	2	1	.67	16	.263	.307	.424
2000 Minnesota	AL	140	544	147	29	1	16	(3	13)	226	64	82	36	2	50	4	0	5	2	0	1.00	25	.270	.317	.415
6 ML YEARS		676	2397	667	121	7	77	(26	51)	1033	283	364	132	10	317	6	0	24	13	7	.65	93	.278	.315	.431

Brian Cooper

Pitches: Right **Bats:** Right **Pos:** SP-15   **Ht:** 6'1" **Wt:** 185 **Born:** 8/19/74 **Age:** 26

Year Team	Lg	G	GS	CG	GF	IP	BFP	H	R	ER	HR	SH	SF	HB	TBB	IBB	SO	WP	Bk	W	L	Pct.	ShO	Sv-Op	Hld	ERA
		HOW MUCH HE PITCHED						**WHAT HE GAVE UP**												**THE RESULTS**						
1995 Boise	A-	13	11	0	1	62	264	60	31	27	5	4	1	6	22	1	66	4	1	3	2	.600	0	1--	—	3.92
1996 Lk Elsinore	A+	26	23	1	0	162.1	702	177	100	76	17	5	8	10	39	0	155	4	1	7	9	.438	1	0--	—	4.21
1997 Lk Elsinore	A+	17	17	1	0	117	497	111	56	46	7	5	2	10	27	0	104	6	0	7	3	.700	0	0--	—	3.54
1998 Midland	AA	32	24	5	4	161.2	750	215	138	128	35	5	6	9	59	1	141	7	0	8	10	.444	1	0--	—	7.13
1999 Erie	AA	22	22	6	0	158	640	146	61	58	17	3	1	13	29	0	143	5	1	10	5	.667	0	0--	—	3.30
Edmonton	AAA	5	5	0	0	31	130	30	17	13	0	1	0	0	10	0	32	1	0	2	1	.667	0	0--	—	3.77
2000 Lk Elsinore	A+	1	1	0	0	7	27	4	1	0	0	0	0	1	2	0	3	2	0	0	0	—	0	0--	—	0.00
Edmonton	AAA	11	11	1	0	61	288	87	51	49	12	1	3	3	18	0	37	3	0	3	7	.300	—	0--	—	7.23
1999 Anaheim	AL	5	5	0	0	27.2	124	23	15	15	3	4	0	4	15	0	15	0	0	1	1	.500	0	0-0	—	4.88
2000 Anaheim	AL	15	15	0	0	87	396	105	66	57	18	4	4	2	35	1	36	1	0	4	8	.333	1	0-0	—	5.90
2 ML YEARS		20	20	1	0	114.2	520	128	81	72	21	4	5	6	53	1	51	1	0	5	9	.357	1	0-0	—	5.65

Trace Coquillette

Bats: R **Throws:** R **Pos:** 3B-19; 2B-8; PH/PR-6; LF-2; RF-1   **Ht:** 5'11" **Wt:** 185 **Born:** 6/4/74 **Age:** 27

Year Team	Lg	G	AB	H	2B	3B	HR	(Hm	Rd)	TB	R	RBI	TBB	IBB	SO	HBP	SH	SF	SB	CS	SB%	GDP	Avg	OBP	SLG
		BATTING																	**BASERUNNING**				**PERCENTAGES**		
1993 Wst Plm Bch	A+	6	18	5	3	0	0	—	—	8	2	3	2	0	5	0	1	0	0	0	—	0	.278	.350	.444
Expos	R	44	159	40	4	3	2	—	—	56	27	11	37	0	28	7	1	3	16	3	.84	6	.252	.408	.352
1994 Burlington	A	5	17	3	1	0	0	—	—	4	2	0	1	0	4	0	0	0	1	0	1.00	0	.176	.222	.235
Vermont	A-	70	252	77	11	5	9	—	—	125	54	52	23	0	40	8	1	6	7	2	.78	5	.306	.374	.496
1995 Albany	A	128	458	123	27	4	3	—	—	167	67	57	64	2	91	9	4	6	17	16	.52	8	.269	.365	.365
1996 Expos	R	7	25	4	1	0	0	—	—	5	4	0	4	0	6	0	0	0	1	0	1.00	0	.160	.276	.200
Wst Plm Bch	A+	72	266	67	17	4	1	—	—	95	39	27	27	1	72	8	0	3	9	7	.56	5	.252	.336	.357
1997 Wst Plm Bch	A+	53	188	60	18	2	8	—	—	106	34	33	27	0	27	6	1	1	8	7	.53	1	.319	.419	.564
Harrisburg	AA	81	293	76	17	3	10	—	—	129	46	51	25	0	40	14	1	1	4	4	.69	5	.259	.345	.440
1998 Harrisburg	AA	49	187	62	10	0	9	—	—	99	40	23	15	0	41	6	0	1	10	3	.77	2	.332	.397	.529
Ottawa	AAA	74	252	64	14	0	7	—	—	99	30	40	17	1	38	7	2	3	3	3	.50	9	.254	.315	.393
1999 Ottawa	AAA	98	334	109	32	3	14	—	—	189	56	55	44	1	68	24	0	6	10	4	.71	5	.326	.434	.566
2000 Ottawa	AAA	75	267	64	19	1	1	—	—	88	30	27	24	1	58	11	2	4	2	0	.00	2	.240	.324	.330
1999 Montreal	NL	17	49	13	3	0	0	(0	0)	16	2	4	4	0	7	1	1	0	1	0	1.00	3	.265	.333	.327
2000 Montreal	NL	34	59	12	4	0	1	(0	1)	19	6	8	7	0	19	0	0	1	0	0	—	2	.203	.284	.322
2 ML YEARS		51	108	25	7	0	1	(0	1)	35	8	12	11	0	26	1	1	1	1	0	1.00	5	.231	.306	.324

Alex Cora

Bats: Left **Throws:** Right **Pos:** SS-101; 2B-8; PH/PR-2   **Ht:** 6'0" **Wt:** 180 **Born:** 10/18/75 **Age:** 25

Year Team	Lg	G	AB	H	2B	3B	HR	(Hm	Rd)	TB	R	RBI	TBB	IBB	SO	HBP	SH	SF	SB	CS	SB%	GDP	Avg	OBP	SLG
		BATTING																	**BASERUNNING**				**PERCENTAGES**		
2000 Albuquerque *	AAA	30	110	41	8	3	0	—	—	55	18	20	7	0	10	2	2	1	5	3	.63	1	.373	.417	.500
1998 Los Angeles	NL	29	33	4	0	1	0	(0	0)	6	1	0	2	0	8	1	2	0	0	0	—	0	.121	.194	.182
1999 Los Angeles	NL	11	30	5	1	0	0	(0	0)	6	2	3	0	0	6	1	0	0	0	0	—	1	.167	.194	.200
2000 Los Angeles	NL	109	353	84	18	6	4	(2	2)	126	39	32	26	4	53	7	6	2	4	1	.80	6	.238	.302	.357
3 ML YEARS		149	416	93	19	7	4	(2	2)	138	42	35	28	4	65	9	8	2	4	1	.80	7	.224	.286	.332

Francisco Cordero

Pitches: Right **Bats:** Right **Pos:** RP-56   **Ht:** 6'2" **Wt:** 200 **Born:** 8/11/77 **Age:** 23

		HOW MUCH HE PITCHED					WHAT HE GAVE UP											THE RESULTS						
Year Team	Lg	G	GS	CG	GF	IP	BFP	H	R	ER	HR	SH	SF	HB	TBB	IBB	SO	WP	Bk	W	L	Pct.	ShO	Sv-Op	Hld	ERA
1995 Fayetteville	A	4	4	0	0	20	92	26	16	14	1	2	2	0	12	0	19	4	0	0	3	.000	0	0--	—	6.30
Jamestown	A-	15	14	0	0	88	392	96	62	51	3	3	3	8	37	0	54	11	0	4	7	.364	0	0--	—	5.22
1996 Fayetteville	A	2	1	0	0	7	27	2	2	2	0	0	0	0	6	0	7	0	0	0	0	—	0	0--	—	2.57
Jamestown	A-	2	2	0	0	11	39	5	1	1	0	0	0	0	2	0	10	0	0	0	0	—	0	0--	—	0.82
1997 W Michigan	A	50	0	0	47	54.1	208	36	13	6	2	4	4	2	15	2	67	5	0	6	1	.857	0	35--	—	0.99
1998 Jacksnville	AA	17	0	0	15	16.2	79	19	12	9	1	1	1	1	9	0	18	0	0	1	1	.500	0	8--	—	4.86
Lakeland	A+	1	0	0	0	1	1	1	0	0	0	0	0	0	0	0	0	0	0	0	0	—	0	0--	—	0.00
1999 Jacksnville	AA	47	0	0	43	52.1	218	35	9	8	3	2	0	3	22	0	58	3	0	4	1	.800	0	27--	—	1.38
2000 Oklahoma	AAA	3	0	0	3	4.1	23	7	3	2	0	0	0	0	3	0	5	1	0	0	0	—	0	1--	—	4.15
1999 Detroit	AL	20	0	0	4	19	91	19	7	7	2	2	4	0	18	2	19	1	0	2	2	.500	0	0-0	6	3.32
2000 Texas	AL	56	0	0	13	77.1	365	87	51	46	11	2	6	4	48	3	49	7	0	1	2	.333	0	0-3	4	5.35
2 ML YEARS		76	0	0	17	96.1	456	106	58	53	13	4	10	4	66	5	68	8	0	3	4	.429	0	0-3	10	4.95

Wil Cordero

Bats: Right **Throws:** Right **Pos:** LF-123; PH/PR-4; DH-1   **Ht:** 6'2" **Wt:** 200 **Born:** 10/3/71 **Age:** 29

		BATTING																BASERUNNING				PERCENTAGES		
Year Team	Lg	G	AB	H	2B	3B	HR	(Hm	Rd)	TB	R	RBI	TBB	IBB	SO	HBP	SH	SF	SB	CS	SB%	GDP	Avg	OBP	SLG
1992 Montreal	NL	45	126	38	4	1	2	(1	1)	50	17	8	9	0	31	1	1	0	0	0	—	3	.302	.353	.397
1993 Montreal	NL	138	475	118	32	2	10	(8	2)	184	56	58	34	8	60	7	4	1	12	3	.80	12	.248	.308	.387
1994 Montreal	NL	110	415	122	30	3	15	(5	10)	203	65	63	41	3	62	6	2	3	16	3	.84	8	.294	.363	.489
1995 Montreal	NL	131	514	147	35	2	10	(2	8)	216	64	49	36	4	88	9	1	4	9	5	.64	11	.286	.341	.420
1996 Boston	AL	59	198	57	14	0	3	(2	1)	80	29	37	11	4	31	2	1	1	2	1	.67	8	.288	.330	.404
1997 Boston	AL	140	570	160	26	3	18	(11	7)	246	82	72	31	7	122	4	0	4	1	3	.25	11	.281	.320	.432
1998 Chicago	AL	96	341	91	18	2	13	(5	8)	152	58	49	22	0	66	3	1	4	2	1	.67	7	.267	.314	.446
1999 Cleveland	AL	54	194	58	15	0	8	(3	5)	97	35	32	15	0	37	6	0	2	2	0	1.00	7	.299	.364	.500
2000 Pit-Cle		127	496	137	35	5	16	(8	8)	230	64	68	32	1	76	7	0	1	1	2	.33	18	.276	.328	.464
2000 Pittsburgh	NL	89	348	98	24	3	16	(8	8)	176	46	51	25	1	58	4	0	1	1	2	.33	11	.282	.336	.506
Cleveland	AL	38	148	39	11	2	0	(0	0)	54	18	17	7	0	18	3	0	0	0	0	—	7	.264	.310	.365
9 ML YEARS		900	3329	928	209	18	95	(45	50)	1458	470	436	231	27	573	45	10	20	45	18	.71	85	.279	.332	.438

Francisco Cordova

Pitches: Right **Bats:** Right **Pos:** SP-17; RP-1   **Ht:** 6'1" **Wt:** 197 **Born:** 4/26/72 **Age:** 29

		HOW MUCH HE PITCHED						WHAT HE GAVE UP												THE RESULTS					
Year Team	Lg	G	GS	CG	GF	IP	BFP	H	R	ER	HR	SH	SF	HB	TBB	IBB	SO	WP	Bk	W	L	Pct.	ShO	Sv-Op	Hld	ERA
1996 Pittsburgh	NL	59	6	0	41	99	414	103	49	45	11	1	0	2	20	6	95	2	1	4	7	.364	0	12-18	3	4.09
1997 Pittsburgh	NL	29	29	2	0	178.2	744	175	80	72	14	3	7	9	49	4	121	4	0	11	8	.579	2	0-0	0	3.63
1998 Pittsburgh	NL	33	33	3	0	220.1	921	204	91	81	22	9	6	3	69	5	157	1	1	13	14	.481	2	0-0	0	3.31
1999 Pittsburgh	NL	27	27	2	0	160.2	682	166	83	79	16	7	4	4	59	6	98	5	0	8	10	.444	0	0-0	0	4.43
2000 Pittsburgh	NL	18	17	0	0	95	421	107	63	55	12	3	3	2	38	4	66	3	1	6	8	.429	0	0-0	0	5.21
5 ML YEARS		166	112	7	41	753.2	3182	755	366	332	75	23	20	20	235	25	537	15	3	42	47	.472	4	12-18	3	3.96

Marty Cordova

Bats: R **Throws:** R **Pos:** LF-23; RF-18; DH-15; PH/PR-8   **Ht:** 6'0" **Wt:** 206 **Born:** 7/10/69 **Age:** 31

		BATTING																BASERUNNING				PERCENTAGES		
Year Team	Lg	G	AB	H	2B	3B	HR	(Hm	Rd)	TB	R	RBI	TBB	IBB	SO	HBP	SH	SF	SB	CS	SB%	GDP	Avg	OBP	SLG
1995 Minnesota	AL	137	512	142	27	4	24	(16	8)	249	81	84	52	1	111	10	0	5	20	7	.74	10	.277	.352	.486
1996 Minnesota	AL	145	569	176	46	1	16	(10	6)	272	97	111	53	4	96	8	0	9	11	5	.69	18	.309	.371	.478
1997 Minnesota	AL	103	378	93	18	4	15	(4	11)	164	44	51	30	2	92	3	0	2	5	3	.63	13	.246	.305	.434
1998 Minnesota	AL	119	438	111	20	2	10	(6	4)	165	52	69	50	3	103	5	0	6	3	6	.33	14	.253	.333	.377
1999 Minnesota	AL	124	425	121	28	3	14	(9	5)	197	62	70	48	2	96	9	0	6	13	4	.76	22	.285	.365	.464
2000 Toronto	AL	62	200	49	7	0	4	(3	1)	68	23	18	18	0	35	3	0	0	3	2	.60	6	.245	.317	.340
6 ML YEARS		690	2522	692	146	14	83	(48	35)	1115	359	403	251	12	533	38	0	28	55	27	.67	83	.274	.346	.442

Rheal Cormier

Pitches: Left **Bats:** Left **Pos:** RP-64   **Ht:** 5'10" **Wt:** 187 **Born:** 4/23/67 **Age:** 34

		HOW MUCH HE PITCHED						WHAT HE GAVE UP												THE RESULTS					
Year Team	Lg	G	GS	CG	GF	IP	BFP	H	R	ER	HR	SH	SF	HB	TBB	IBB	SO	WP	Bk	W	L	Pct.	ShO	Sv-Op	Hld	ERA
1991 St. Louis	NL	11	10	2	1	67.2	281	74	35	31	5	1	3	2	8	1	38	2	1	4	5	.444	0	0-0	0	4.12
1992 St. Louis	NL	31	30	3	1	186	772	194	83	76	15	11	3	5	33	2	117	4	2	10	10	.500	0	0-0	0	3.68
1993 St. Louis	NL	38	21	1	4	145.1	619	163	80	70	18	10	4	4	27	3	75	6	0	7	6	.538	0	0-0	0	4.33
1994 St. Louis	NL	7	7	0	0	39.2	169	40	24	24	6	1	2	3	7	0	26	2	0	3	2	.600	0	0-0	0	5.45
1995 Boston	AL	48	12	0	3	115	488	131	60	52	12	6	2	3	31	2	69	4	0	7	5	.583	0	0-2	9	4.07
1996 Montreal	NL	33	27	1	1	159.2	674	165	80	74	16	4	8	9	41	3	100	8	0	7	10	.412	1	0-0	0	4.17
1997 Montreal	NL	1	1	0	0	1.1	9	4	5	5	1	0	0	0	1	0	0	0	0	0	1	.000	0	0-0	0	33.75
1999 Boston	AL	60	0	0	7	63.1	275	61	34	26	4	1	3	5	18	2	39	1	0	2	0	1.000	0	0-3	15	3.69
2000 Boston	AL	64	0	0	12	68.1	293	74	40	35	7	5	2	0	17	2	43	1	0	3	3	.500	0	0-2	9	4.61
9 ML YEARS		293	108	7	29	846.1	3580	906	441	393	84	39	27	31	183	15	507	28	3	43	42	.506	1	0-7	33	4.18

Reid Cornelius

Pitches: Right **Bats:** Right **Pos:** SP-21; RP-1   **Ht:** 6'0" **Wt:** 200 **Born:** 6/2/70 **Age:** 31

		HOW MUCH HE PITCHED						WHAT HE GAVE UP												THE RESULTS					
Year Team	Lg	G	GS	CG	GF	IP	BFP	H	R	ER	HR	SH	SF	HB	TBB	IBB	SO	WP	Bk	W	L	Pct.	ShO	Sv-Op	Hld	ERA
2000 Calgary *	AAA	8	8	0	0	43.1	190	45	23	22	5	2	1	1	18	0	22	1	0	2	2	.500	0	0--	—	4.57
1995 Mon-NYM	NL	18	10	0	1	66.2	301	75	44	41	11	4	3	3	30	5	39	2	1	3	7	.300	0	0-0	0	5.54
1999 Florida	NL	5	2	0	0	19.1	76	16	7	7	0	1	0	0	5	1	12	1	0	1	0	1.000	0	0-0	0	3.26

		HOW MUCH HE PITCHED						WHAT HE GAVE UP												THE RESULTS						
Year Team	Lg	G	GS	CG	GF	IP	BFP	H	R	ER	HR	SH	SF	HB	TBB	IBB	SO	WP	Bk	W	L	Pct.	ShO	Sv-Op	Hld	ERA
2000 Florida	NL	22	21	0	0	125	547	135	74	67	19	9	6	4	50	4	50	8	5	4	10	.286	0	0-0	0	4.82
1995 Montreal	NL	8	0	0	1	9	43	11	8	8	3	0	0	2	5	0	4	1	0							8.00
New York	NL	10	10	0	0	57.2	258	64	36	33	8	4	3	1	25	5	35	1	1	3	7	.300	0	0-0	0	5.15
3 ML YEARS		45	33	0	1	211	924	226	125	115	30	14	9	7	85	10	101	11	6	8	17	.320	0	0-0	0	4.91

Craig Counsell

Bats: L **Throws:** R **Pos:** PH/PR-27; 2B-25; 3B-23; SS-6 **Ht:** 6'0" **Wt:** 175 **Born:** 8/21/70 **Age:** 30

		BATTING																	BASERUNNING				PERCENTAGES		
Year Team	Lg	G	AB	H	2B	3B	HR	(Hm	Rd)	TB	R	RBI	TBB	IBB	SO	HBP	SH	SF	SB	CS	SB%	GDP	Avg	OBP	SLG
2000 Tucson *	AAA	50	198	69	14	3	3	—	—	98	45	27	22	3	20	1	1	2	4	1	.80	1	.348	.413	.495
1995 Colorado	NL	3	1	0	0	0	0	(0	0)	0	0	0	1	0	0	0	0	0	0	0		0	.000	.500	.000
1997 Col-Fla	NL	52	164	49	9	2	1	(1	0)	65	20	16	18	2	17	3	3	1	1	1	.50	5	.299	.376	.396
1998 Florida	NL	107	335	84	19	5	4	(2	2)	125	43	40	51	7	47	4	8	1	3	0	1.00	5	.251	.355	.373
1999 Fla-LA	NL	87	174	38	7	0	0	(0	0)	45	24	11	14	0	24	0	5	2	1	0	1.00	5	.218	.274	.259
2000 Arizona	NL	67	152	48	8	1	2	(0	2)	64	23	11	20	0	18	2	1	1	3	3	.50	4	.316	.400	.421
1997 Colorado	NL	1	0	0	0	0	0	(0	0)	0	0	0	0	0	0	0	0	0	0	0		0			
Florida	NL	51	164	49	9	2	1	(1	0)	65	20	16	18	2	17	3	3	1	1	1	.50	5	.299	.376	.396
1999 Florida	NL	37	66	10	1	0	0	(0	0)	11	4	2	5	0	10	0	2	0	0	0		1	.152	.211	.167
Los Angeles	NL	50	108	28	6	0	0	(0	0)	34	20	9	9	0	14	0	3	2	1	0	1.00		.259	.311	.315
5 ML YEARS		316	826	219	43	8	7	(3	4)	299	110	78	104	9	106	9	17	5	8	4	.67	16	.265	.352	.362

Steve Cox

Bats: L **Throws:** L **Pos:** RF-30; LF-26; PH/PR-25; 1B-24; DH-17 **Ht:** 6'4" **Wt:** 222 **Born:** 10/31/74 **Age:** 26

		BATTING																	BASERUNNING				PERCENTAGES		
Year Team	Lg	G	AB	H	2B	3B	HR	(Hm	Rd)	TB	R	RBI	TBB	IBB	SO	HBP	SH	SF	SB	CS	SB%	GDP	Avg	OBP	SLG
1992 Athletics	R	52	184	43	4	1	1	—	—	52	30	35	27	1	51	3	0	2	2	1	.67	2	.234	.338	.283
1993 Sou Oregon	A-	15	57	18	4	1	2	—	—	30	10	16	5	0	15	0	0	2	0	0			.316	.359	.526
1994 W Michigan	A	99	311	75	19	2	6	—	—	116	37	32	41	3	95	4	1	3	2	6	.25	5	.241	.334	.373
1995 Modesto	A+	132	483	144	29	3	30	—	—	269	95	110	84	6	88	14	0	10	5	4	.56	12	.298	.409	.557
1996 Huntsville	AA	104	381	107	21	1	12	—	—	166	59	61	51	6	65	6	2	3	2	2	.50	17	.281	.372	.436
1997 Edmonton	AAA	131	467	128	34	1	15	—	—	209	84	93	88	4	90	2	2	9	1	3	.25	16	.274	.385	.448
1998 Durham	AAA	119	430	109	23	2	13	—	—	175	64	67	56	6	100	2	2	5	3	4	.43	9	.253	.339	.407
1999 Durham	AAA	134	534	182	49	4	25	—	—	314	107	127	67	11	74	5	0	6	3	3	.50	12	.341	.415	.588
1999 Tampa Bay	AL	6	19	4	1	0	0	(0	0)	5	0	0	0	0	2	0	0	0	0	0			.211	.211	.263
2000 Tampa Bay	AL	116	318	90	19	1	11	(7	4)	144	44	35	46	2	47	4	0	1	1	2	.33	9	.283	.379	.453
2 ML YEARS		122	337	94	20	1	11	(7	4)	149	44	35	46	2	49	4	0	1	1	2	.33	11	.279	.371	.442

Tim Crabtree

Pitches: Right **Bats:** Right **Pos:** RP-68 **Ht:** 6'4" **Wt:** 220 **Born:** 10/13/69 **Age:** 31

		HOW MUCH HE PITCHED						WHAT HE GAVE UP												THE RESULTS						
Year Team	Lg	G	GS	CG	GF	IP	BFP	H	R	ER	HR	SH	SF	HB	TBB	IBB	SO	WP	Bk	W	L	Pct.	ShO	Sv-Op	Hld	ERA
1995 Toronto	AL	31	0	0	19	32	141	30	16	11	1	0	1	2	13	0	21	2	0	0	2	.000	0	0-2	1	3.09
1996 Toronto	AL	53	0	0	16	67.1	284	59	26	19	4	2	2	3	22	4	57	3	0	5	3	.625	0	1-5	17	2.54
1997 Toronto	AL	37	0	0	16	40.2	199	65	32	32	7	4	2	2	17	3	26	4	0	3	3	.500	0	2-5	8	7.08
1998 Texas	AL	64	0	0	14	85.1	371	86	40	34	3	1	6	3	35	2	60	6	0	6	1	.857	0	0-1	10	3.59
1999 Texas	AL	68	0	0	21	65	275	71	26	25	4	1	1	1	18	1	54	5	0	5	1	.833	0	0-3	14	3.46
2000 Texas	AL	68	0	0	28	80.1	352	86	52	46	7	4	1	2	31	6	54	4	0	2	7	.222	0	2-9	11	5.15
6 ML YEARS		321	0	0	119	370.2	1622	397	192	167	26	9	16	13	136	16	272	24	0	21	17	.553	0	5-25	61	4.05

Paxton Crawford

Pitches: Right **Bats:** Right **Pos:** SP-4; RP-3 **Ht:** 6'3" **Wt:** 193 **Born:** 8/4/77 **Age:** 23

		HOW MUCH HE PITCHED						WHAT HE GAVE UP												THE RESULTS						
Year Team	Lg	G	GS	CG	GF	IP	BFP	H	R	ER	HR	SH	SF	HB	TBB	IBB	SO	WP	Bk	W	L	Pct.	ShO	Sv-Op	Hld	ERA
1995 Red Sox	R	12	7	1	4	46	184	38	17	14	2	0	1	4	12	0	44	6	0	2	4	.333	0	2--	—	2.74
1996 Michigan	A	22	22	1	0	128.1	548	120	62	51	5	2	5	8	42	1	105	8	1	6	11	.353	0	0--	—	3.58
1997 Sarasota	A+	12	11	2	0	65.1	289	69	42	33	6	4	2	1	27	2	56	3	0	4	8	.333	1	0--	—	4.55
1998 Trenton	AA	22	20	1	0	108	457	104	53	50	8	3	1	6	39	1	82	7	0	6	5	.545	0	0--	—	4.17
1999 Trenton	AA	28	28	1	0	163.1	696	151	81	74	12	7	4	10	59	1	111	10	1	7	8	.467	1	0--	—	4.08
2000 Trenton	AA	9	9	0	0	52.1	211	50	20	18	3	1	0	0	6	0	54	2	0	2	3	.400	0	0--	—	3.10
Pawtucket	AAA	12	11	1	1	61.1	252	47	32	31	6	6	2	6	22	1	47	0	0	7	4	.636	1	0--	—	4.55
2000 Boston	AL	7	4	0	2	29	123	25	15	11	2	0	1	2	13	2	17	0	0	2	1	.667	0	0-0	0	3.41

Joe Crede

Bats: Right **Throws:** Right **Pos:** 3B-6; DH-1; PH/PR-1 **Ht:** 6'3" **Wt:** 195 **Born:** 4/26/78 **Age:** 23

		BATTING																	BASERUNNING				PERCENTAGES		
Year Team	Lg	G	AB	H	2B	3B	HR	(Hm	Rd)	TB	R	RBI	TBB	IBB	SO	HBP	SH	SF	SB	CS	SB%	GDP	Avg	OBP	SLG
1996 White Sox	R	56	221	66	17	1	4	—	—	97	30	32	9	0	41	2	1	4	1	1	.50	8	.299	.326	.439
1997 Hickory	A	113	402	109	26	0	5	—	—	149	65	62	24	0	83	5	0	2	3	1	.75	6	.271	.319	.371
1998 Winston-Sal	A+	137	492	155	32	3	20	—	—	253	92	88	53	3	98	12	0	11	9	7	.56	10	.315	.387	.514
1999 Birmingham	AA	74	291	73	14	1	4	—	—	101	37	42	22	1	47	1	0	3	2	6	.25	15	.251	.303	.347
2000 Birmingham	AA	138	533	163	35	0	21	—	—	261	84	94	56	10	111	15	1	5	3	4	.43	18	.306	.384	.490
2000 Chicago	AL	7	14	5	1	0	0	(0	0)	6	2	3	0	0	3	0	0	0	0	0			.357	.333	.429

Doug Creek

Pitches: Left Bats: Left Pos: RP-45 Ht: 6'0" Wt: 200 Born: 3/1/69 Age: 32

Year Team	Lg	G	GS	CG	GF	IP	BFP	H	R	ER	HR	SH	SF	HB	TBB	IBB	SO	WP	Bk	W	L	Pct.	ShO	Sv-Op	Hld	ERA
2000 Durham *	AAA	10	1	0	2	18.1	80	10	5	4	1	0	0	0	14	0	22	4	0	0	0	—	0	0--	0	1.96
1995 St. Louis	NL	6	0	0	1	6.2	24	2	0	0	0	0	0	0	3	0	10	0	0	0	0	—	0	0-0	0	0.00
1996 San Francisco	NL	63	0	0	15	48.1	220	45	41	35	11	1	0	2	32	2	38	2	0	0	2	.000	0	0-1	7	6.52
1997 San Francisco	NL	3	3	0	0	13.1	64	12	12	10	1	0	0	0	14	0	14	0	0	1	2	.333	0	0-0	0	6.75
1999 Chicago	NL	3	0	0	2	6	32	6	7	7	1	0	1	0	8	1	6	1	0	0	0	—	0	0-0	0	10.50
2000 Tampa Bay	AL	45	0	0	8	60.2	265	49	33	31	10	2	3	2	39	3	73	3	0	1	3	.250	0	1-3	2	4.60
5 ML YEARS		120	3	0	26	135	605	114	93	83	23	3	4	4	96	6	141	6	0	2	7	.222	0	1-4	9	5.53

Felipe Crespo

Bats: B Throws: R Pos: PH/PR-56; LF-18; 1B-11; RF-9; 2B-7; DH-1 Ht: 5'11" Wt: 200 Born: 3/5/73 Age: 28

Year Team	Lg	G	AB	H	2B	3B	HR	Hm	Rd	TB	R	RBI	TBB	IBB	SO	HBP	SH	SF	SB	CS	SB%	GDP	Avg	OBP	SLG
1996 Toronto	AL	22	49	9	4	0	0	(0	0)	13	6	4	12	0	13	3	0	1	1	0	1.00	0	.184	.375	.265
1997 Toronto	AL	12	28	8	0	1	1	(0	1)	13	3	5	2	0	4	0	1	0	0	0	—	1	.286	.333	.464
1998 Toronto	AL	66	130	34	8	1	1	(0	1)	47	11	15	15	1	27	2	4	2	4	3	.57	1	.262	.342	.362
2000 San Francisco	NL	89	131	38	6	1	4	(1	3)	58	17	29	10	2	23	4	2	3	3	2	.60	5	.290	.351	.443
4 ML YEARS		189	338	89	18	3	6	(1	5)	131	37	53	39	3	67	9	7	5	8	5	.62	5	.263	.350	.388

Jack Cressend

Pitches: Right Bats: Right Pos: RP-11 Ht: 6'1" Wt: 185 Born: 5/13/75 Age: 26

Year Team	Lg	G	GS	CG	GF	IP	BFP	H	R	ER	HR	SH	SF	HB	TBB	IBB	SO	WP	Bk	W	L	Pct.	ShO	Sv-Op	Hld	ERA
1996 Lowell	A-	9	8	0	1	45.2	189	37	15	12	0	2	4	4	17	1	57	6	1	3	2	.600	0	0--	—	2.36
1997 Sarasota	A+	28	25	2	1	165.2	718	163	98	70	15	8	6	2	56	1	149	14	4	8	11	.421	1	0--	—	3.80
1998 Trenton	AA	29	29	3	0	149.1	646	168	86	72	13	10	2	5	55	0	130	6	0	10	11	.476	1	0--	—	4.34
1999 Trenton	AA	3	3	0	0	15	71	19	12	12	3	0	1	0	7	0	11	2	0	1	0	1.000	0	0--	—	7.20
New Britain	AA	25	24	2	0	145	629	152	79	70	10	3	5	5	50	0	125	4	2	7	10	.412	2	0--	—	4.34
2000 Salt Lake	AAA	54	1	0	20	86.1	380	87	40	33	3	4	3	1	39	4	87	6	0	4	4	.500	0	8--	—	3.44
2000 Minnesota	AL	11	0	0	4	13.2	61	20	8	8	0	0	0	0	6	0	6	0	0	0	0	—	0	0-0	0	5.27

D.T. Cromer

Bats: Left Throws: Left Pos: PH/PR-24; 1B-13 Ht: 6'2" Wt: 220 Born: 3/19/71 Age: 30

Year Team	Lg	G	AB	H	2B	3B	HR	Hm	Rd	TB	R	RBI	TBB	IBB	SO	HBP	SH	SF	SB	CS	SB%	GDP	Avg	OBP	SLG
1992 Sou Oregon	A-	50	168	35	7	0	4	—	—	54	17	26	13	1	34	1	1	2	4	3	.57	2	.208	.266	.321
1993 Madison	A	98	321	84	20	4	4	—	—	124	37	41	22	0	72	1	7	2	8	6	.57	1	.262	.309	.386
1994 W Michigan	A	102	349	89	20	5	10	—	—	149	50	58	33	1	76	4	3	2	11	10	.52	5	.255	.325	.427
1995 Modesto	A+	108	378	98	18	5	14	—	—	168	59	52	36	1	66	4	6	6	5	7	.42	10	.259	.325	.444
1996 Modesto	A+	124	505	166	40	10	30	—	—	316	100	130	32	4	67	6	3	4	20	7	.74	5	.329	.373	.626
1997 Huntsville	AA	134	545	176	40	6	15	—	—	273	100	121	60	4	102	3	0	6	12	7	.63	8	.323	.389	.501
1998 Edmonton	AAA	125	504	148	30	3	16	—	—	232	75	85	32	3	93	4	0	4	12	6	.67	9	.294	.338	.460
1999 Indianapols	AAA	136	535	166	37	4	30	—	—	301	83	107	44	3	98	3	0	7	4	2	.67	12	.310	.362	.563
2000 Louisville	AAA	106	415	112	26	3	14	—	—	186	58	67	33	1	84	1	0	7	6	4	.60	11	.270	.320	.448
2000 Cincinnati	NL	35	47	16	4	0	2	(0	2)	26	7	8	1	1	14	1	1	1	0	0	—	0	.340	.360	.553

Tripp Cromer

Bats: R Throws: R Pos: PH/PR-5; 3B-2; 2B-1; SS-1 Ht: 6'2" Wt: 165 Born: 11/21/67 Age: 33

Year Team	Lg	G	AB	H	2B	3B	HR	Hm	Rd	TB	R	RBI	TBB	IBB	SO	HBP	SH	SF	SB	CS	SB%	GDP	Avg	OBP	SLG
2000 New Orleans *	AAA	66	224	48	7	3	4	—	—	73	21	24	17	1	47	0	1	2	1	0	1.00	4	.214	.267	.326
1993 St. Louis	NL	10	23	2	0	0	0	(0	0)	2	1	0	1	0	6	0	0	0	0	0	—	0	.087	.125	.087
1994 St. Louis	NL	1	1	0	0	0	0	(0	0)	0	1	0	0	0	0	0	0	0	0	0	—	0	—	—	—
1995 St. Louis	NL	105	345	78	19	0	5	(2	3)	112	36	18	14	2	66	4	1	5	0	0	—	14	.226	.261	.325
1997 Los Angeles	NL	28	86	25	3	0	4	(2	2)	40	8	20	6	3	16	0	2	1	0	1	.00	2	.291	.333	.465
1998 Los Angeles	NL	6	6	1	0	0	1	(0	1)	4	1	1	0	0	2	0	0	0	0	0	—	0	.167	.167	.667
1999 Los Angeles	NL	33	52	10	0	0	2	(1	1)	16	5	8	5	0	10	0	0	0	0	0	—	4	.192	.263	.308
2000 Houston	NL	9	8	1	0	0	0	(0	0)	1	2	0	1	0	1	0	0	0	0	0	—	0	.125	.222	.125
7 ML YEARS		193	520	117	22	0	12	(5	7)	175	54	47	27	5	101	4	4	6	0	1	.00	20	.225	.266	.337

Rick Croushore

Pitches: Right Bats: Right Pos: RP-11 Ht: 6'4" Wt: 210 Born: 8/7/70 Age: 30

Year Team	Lg	G	GS	CG	GF	IP	BFP	H	R	ER	HR	SH	SF	HB	TBB	IBB	SO	WP	Bk	W	L	Pct.	ShO	Sv-Op	Hld	ERA
2000 Colo Sprngs *	AAA	33	2	0	12	36.2	178	40	31	30	4	2	4	2	32	1	30	6	0	2	4	.333	0	0--	—	7.36
Pawtucket *	AAA	11	0	0	5	21	87	16	8	8	1	0	1	0	10	0	23	2	0	1	1	.000	0	0--	—	3.43
1998 St. Louis	NL	41	0	0	15	54.1	243	44	31	30	6	2	1	4	29	2	47	6	0	0	3	.000	0	8-11	6	4.97
1999 St. Louis	NL	59	0	0	12	71.2	329	68	42	33	9	7	1	3	43	4	88	9	0	3	7	.300	0	3-10	14	4.14
2000 Col-Bos		11	0	0	4	16	80	19	14	14	1	0	1	2	11	2	14	2	0	2	1	.667	0	0-0	0	7.88
2000 Colorado	NL	6	0	0	1	11.1	56	15	11	11	1	0	1	1	6	1	11	1	0	2	0	1.000	0	0-0	0	8.74
Boston	AL	5	0	0	3	4.2	24	4	3	3	0	1	0	1	5	1	3	1	0	0	1	.000	0	0-0	0	5.79
3 ML YEARS		111	0	0	31	142	652	131	87	77	16	10	4	9	83	8	149	17	0	5	11	.313	0	11-21	20	4.88

49

Deivi Cruz

Bats: Right **Throws:** Right **Pos:** SS-156; PH/PR-1   **Ht:** 6'0" **Wt:** 184 **Born:** 11/6/75 **Age:** 25

Year Team	Lg	G	AB	H	2B	3B	HR	(Hm	Rd)	TB	R	RBI	TBB	IBB	SO	HBP	SH	SF	SB	CS	SB%	GDP	Avg	OBP	SLG
1997 Detroit	AL	147	436	105	26	0	2	(0	2)	137	35	40	14	0	55	0	14	3	3	6	.33	9	.241	.263	.314
1998 Detroit	AL	135	454	118	22	3	5	(5	0)	161	52	45	13	0	55	3	5	2	3	4	.43	11	.260	.284	.355
1999 Detroit	AL	155	518	147	35	4	13	(9	4)	221	64	58	12	0	57	4	14	5	1	4	.20	10	.284	.302	.427
2000 Detroit	AL	156	583	176	46	5	10	(1	9)	262	68	82	13	2	43	4	8	7	1	4	.20	25	.302	.318	.449
4 ML YEARS		593	1991	546	129	8	30	(15	15)	781	219	225	52	2	210	11	41	17	8	18	.31	55	.274	.294	.392

Ivan Cruz

Bats: Left **Throws:** Left **Pos:** PH/PR-7; 1B-1   **Ht:** 6'2" **Wt:** 219 **Born:** 5/3/68 **Age:** 33

Year Team	Lg	G	AB	H	2B	3B	HR	(Hm	Rd)	TB	R	RBI	TBB	IBB	SO	HBP	SH	SF	SB	CS	SB%	GDP	Avg	OBP	SLG
1989 Niagara Fal	A-	64	226	62	11	2	7	—	—	98	43	40	27	4	29	3	0	1	2	0	1.00	2	.274	.358	.434
1990 Lakeland	A+	118	414	118	23	2	11	—	—	178	61	73	49	3	71	5	2	4	8	1	.89	8	.285	.364	.430
1991 Toledo	AAA	8	29	4	0	0	1	—	—	7	2	4	2	0	12	1	0	0	0	0	—	0	.138	.219	.241
London	AA	121	443	110	21	0	9	—	—	158	45	47	36	5	74	4	1	2	3	3	.50	12	.248	.309	.357
1992 London	AA	134	524	143	25	1	14	—	—	212	71	104	37	1	102	4	0	6	1	1	.50	16	.273	.322	.405
1993 Toledo	AAA	115	402	91	18	4	13	—	—	156	44	50	30	2	85	3	0	2	1	1	.50	5	.226	.284	.388
1994 Toledo	AAA	97	303	75	11	2	15	—	—	135	36	43	28	0	83	2	0	3	1	0	1.00	7	.248	.313	.446
1995 Toledo	AAA	11	36	7	2	0	0	—	—	9	5	3	6	0	9	0	0	1	0	0	—	1	.194	.302	.250
Jacksnville	AA	108	397	112	17	1	31	—	—	224	65	93	60	15	94	0	0	3	0	0	—	7	.282	.374	.564
1996 Columbus	AAA	130	446	115	26	0	28	—	—	225	84	96	48	3	99	8	2	9	2	4	.33	9	.258	.335	.504
1997 Columbus	AAA	116	417	125	35	1	24	—	—	234	69	95	65	10	78	11	0	4	4	5	.44	8	.300	.404	.561
1998 Yankees	R	5	10	6	3	0	1	—	—	12	2	5	3	0	3	0	0	0	0	0	—	0	.600	.692	1.200
Columbus	AAA	56	204	54	10	0	13	—	—	103	34	36	29	3	44	2	0	1	0	0	—	0	.265	.360	.505
1999 Altoona	AA	3	13	2	1	0	0	—	—	3	1	3	1	0	8	0	0	0	0	0	—	0	.154	.214	.231
Nashville	AAA	75	273	89	20	1	25	—	—	186	57	81	21	4	56	1	0	9	0	2	.00	7	.326	.365	.681
2000 Nashville	AAA	36	121	38	11	0	7	—	—	70	15	28	15	0	26	1	0	1	0	0	—	3	.314	.391	.579
1997 New York	AL	11	20	5	1	0	0	(0	0)	6	0	3	2	0	4	0	0	0	0	0	—	0	.250	.318	.300
1999 Pittsburgh	NL	5	10	4	0	0	1	(1	0)	7	3	2	0	0	2	0	0	0	0	0	—	0	.400	.400	.700
2000 Pittsburgh	NL	8	11	1	0	0	0	(0	0)	1	0	0	0	0	8	0	0	0	0	0	—	1	.091	.091	.091
3 ML YEARS		24	41	10	1	0	1	(1	0)	14	3	5	2	0	14	0	0	0	0	0	—	1	.244	.279	.341

Jacob Cruz

Bats: L **Throws:** L **Pos:** CF-8; DH-2; LF-1; PH/PR-1   **Ht:** 6'0" **Wt:** 215 **Born:** 1/28/73 **Age:** 28

Year Team	Lg	G	AB	H	2B	3B	HR	(Hm	Rd)	TB	R	RBI	TBB	IBB	SO	HBP	SH	SF	SB	CS	SB%	GDP	Avg	OBP	SLG
1996 San Francisco	NL	33	77	18	3	0	3	(3	0)	30	10	10	12	0	24	2	1	0	0	1	.00	2	.234	.352	.390
1997 San Francisco	NL	16	25	4	1	0	0	(0	0)	5	3	3	3	0	4	0	0	1	0	0	—	3	.160	.241	.200
1998 SF-Cle		4	4	0	0	0	0	(0	0)	0	0	0	0	0	3	0	0	0	0	0	—	0	.000	.000	.000
1999 Cleveland	AL	32	88	29	5	1	3	(3	0)	45	14	17	5	0	13	1	1	1	0	2	.00	4	.330	.368	.511
2000 Cleveland	AL	11	29	7	3	0	0	(0	0)	10	3	5	5	0	4	1	0	1	1	0	1.00	0	.241	.361	.345
1998 San Francisco	NL	3	3	0	0	0	0	(0	0)	0	0	0	0	0	2	0	0	0	0	0	—	0	.000	.000	.000
Cleveland	AL	1	1	0	0	0	0	(0	0)	0	0	0	0	0	1	0	0	0	0	0	—	0	.000	.000	.000
5 ML YEARS		96	223	58	12	1	6	(6	0)	90	30	35	25	0	48	4	2	3	1	3	.25	9	.260	.341	.404

Jose Cruz

Bats: Both **Throws:** Right **Pos:** CF-162   **Ht:** 6'0" **Wt:** 200 **Born:** 4/19/74 **Age:** 27

Year Team	Lg	G	AB	H	2B	3B	HR	(Hm	Rd)	TB	R	RBI	TBB	IBB	SO	HBP	SH	SF	SB	CS	SB%	GDP	Avg	OBP	SLG
1997 Sea-Tor	AL	104	395	98	19	1	26	(11	15)	197	59	68	41	2	117	0	1	5	7	2	.78	5	.248	.315	.499
1998 Toronto	AL	105	352	89	14	3	11	(4	7)	142	55	42	57	3	99	0	0	4	11	4	.73	0	.253	.354	.403
1999 Toronto	AL	106	349	84	19	3	14	(8	6)	151	63	45	64	5	91	0	1	0	14	4	.78	6	.241	.358	.433
2000 Toronto	AL	162	603	146	32	5	31	(15	16)	281	91	76	71	3	129	2	2	3	15	5	.75	11	.242	.323	.466
1997 Seattle	AL	49	183	49	12	1	12	(7	5)	99	28	34	13	0	45	0	1	1	1	0	1.00	3	.268	.315	.541
Toronto	AL	55	212	49	7	0	14	(4	10)	98	31	34	28	2	72	0	0	4	6	2	.75	2	.231	.316	.462
4 ML YEARS		477	1699	417	84	12	82	(38	44)	771	268	231	233	13	436	2	4	12	47	15	.76	22	.245	.335	.454

Nelson Cruz

Pitches: Right **Bats:** Right **Pos:** RP-27   **Ht:** 6'1" **Wt:** 185 **Born:** 9/13/72 **Age:** 28

Year Team	Lg	G	GS	CG	GF	IP	BFP	H	R	ER	HR	SH	SF	HB	TBB	IBB	SO	WP	Bk	W	L	Pct.	ShO	Sv-Op	Hld	ERA
2000 Toledo *	AAA	11	10	0	1	52.1	229	54	37	28	9	2	3	1	17	0	39	1	0	2	4	.333	0	0--	—	4.82
1997 Chicago	AL	19	0	0	5	26.1	119	29	19	19	6	1	0	0	9	1	23	3	0	0	2	.000	0	0-0	6	6.49
1999 Detroit	AL	29	6	0	10	66.2	295	74	44	42	11	4	3	3	23	1	46	2	0	2	5	.286	0	0-0	4	5.67
2000 Detroit	AL	27	0	0	12	41	172	39	14	14	4	0	2	3	13	3	34	2	0	5	2	.714	0	0-1	2	3.07
3 ML YEARS		75	6	0	27	134	583	142	77	75	21	3	6	6	45	5	103	7	0	7	9	.438	0	0-1	12	5.04

Darwin Cubillan

Pitches: Right **Bats:** Right **Pos:** RP-20   **Ht:** 6'2" **Wt:** 170 **Born:** 11/15/74 **Age:** 26

Year Team	Lg	G	GS	CG	GF	IP	BFP	H	R	ER	HR	SH	SF	HB	TBB	IBB	SO	WP	Bk	W	L	Pct.	ShO	Sv-Op	Hld	ERA
1994 Yankees	R	13	8	1	1	57.1	222	45	16	15	1	4	1	0	16	0	48	2	1	4	2	.667	1	0--	—	2.35
Greensboro	A	1	0	0	0	2	15	6	5	4	1	0	0	0	2	0	1	0	0	0	0	—	0	0--	—	18.00
1995 Greensboro	A	22	14	1	3	97	409	86	50	39	5	3	1	4	38	1	78	5	0	5	5	.500	1	0--	—	3.62
1997 Yankees	R	1	1	0	0	1.2	7	1	0	0	0	0	0	0	1	0	2	0	0	0	0	—	0	0--	—	0.00
1998 Tampa	A+	45	1	0	13	65	310	79	45	34	3	1	7	1	36	9	70	8	1	9	2	.818	0	1--	—	4.71

Year Team	Lg	G	GS	CG	GF	IP	BFP	H	R	ER	HR	SH	SF	HB	TBB	IBB	SO	WP	Bk	W	L	Pct.	ShO	Sv-Op	Hld	ERA
1999 Tampa	A+	55	0	0	28	75.1	311	57	27	21	6	4	1	3	32	6	76	2	0	7	4	.636	0	3--	—	2.51
2000 Syracuse	AAA	24	0	0	14	32.2	123	14	2	2	0	1	0	1	13	1	41	1	0	3	1	.750	0	6--	—	0.55
Oklahoma	AAA	8	0	0	6	16.2	61	9	2	2	0	0	0	0	4	0	12	0	0	0	0	—	0	2--	—	1.08
2000 Tor-Tex	AL	20	0	0	6	33.1	172	52	36	35	9	0	3	1	25	0	27	1	0	1	0	1.000	0	0-0	0	9.45
2000 Toronto	AL	7	0	0	1	15.2	75	20	14	14	5	0	0	1	11	0	14	0	0	1	0	1.000	0	0-0	0	8.04
Texas	AL	13	0	0	5	17.2	97	32	22	21	4	0	3	0	14	0	13	1	0	0	0	—	0	0-0	0	10.70

Midre Cummings

Bats: L **Throws:** R **Pos:** PH/PR-54; RF-36; DH-16; LF-7; CF-1   **Ht:** 6'0" **Wt:** 195 **Born:** 10/14/71 **Age:** 29

Year Team	Lg	G	AB	H	2B	3B	HR	(Hm	Rd)	TB	R	RBI	TBB	IBB	SO	HBP	SH	SF	SB	CS	SB%	GDP	Avg	OBP	SLG
1993 Pittsburgh	NL	13	36	4	1	0	0	(0	0)	5	5	3	4	0	9	0	0	1	0	0		1	.111	.195	.139
1994 Pittsburgh	NL	24	86	21	4	0	1	(1	0)	28	11	12	4	0	18	1	0	1	0	0		0	.244	.283	.326
1995 Pittsburgh	NL	59	152	37	7	1	2	(1	1)	52	13	15	13	3	30	1	0	0	1	0	1.00	0	.243	.303	.342
1996 Pittsburgh	NL	24	85	19	3	1	3	(2	1)	33	11	7	0	0	16	0	1	0	0	0		0	.224	.221	.388
1997 Pit-Phi	NL	115	314	83	22	6	4	(3	1)	129	35	31	31	0	56	1	2	2	2	3	.40	3	.264	.330	.411
1998 Boston	AL	67	120	34	8	0	5	(4	1)	57	20	15	17	0	19	2	1	0	3	3	.50	3	.283	.381	.475
1999 Minnesota	AL	16	38	10	0	0	1	(0	1)	13	1	9	3	0	7	0	0	1	2	0	1.00	0	.263	.310	.342
2000 Min-Bos	AL	98	206	57	10	0	4	(2	2)	79	29	24	17	1	28	3	1	0	0	0		5	.277	.341	.383
1997 Pittsburgh	NL	52	106	20	6	2	3	(2	1)	39	11	8	8	0	26	1	1	0	0	0		1	.189	.252	.368
Philadelphia		63	208	63	16	4	1	(1	0)	90	24	23	23	0	30	0	1	2	2	3	.40	2	.303	.369	.433
2000 Minnesota	AL	77	181	50	10	0	4	(2	2)	72	28	22	11	1	25	3	1	0	0	0		4	.276	.328	.398
Boston	AL	21	25	7	0	0	0	(0	0)	7	1	2	6	0	3	0	0	0	0	0		1	.280	.419	.280
8 ML YEARS		416	1037	265	55	8	20	(14	6)	396	125	116	89	4	183	7	5	6	8	6	.57	12	.256	.317	.382

Will Cunnane

Pitches: Right **Bats:** Right **Pos:** RP-24; SP-3   **Ht:** 6'2" **Wt:** 200 **Born:** 4/24/74 **Age:** 27

Year Team	Lg	G	GS	CG	GF	IP	BFP	H	R	ER	HR	SH	SF	HB	TBB	IBB	SO	WP	Bk	W	L	Pct.	ShO	Sv-Op	Hld	ERA
2000 Las Vegas *	AAA	17	17	1	0	97.1	407	96	46	43	7	1	3	3	26	0	97	1	0	7	4	.636	1	0--	—	3.98
1997 San Diego	NL	54	8	0	16	91.1	430	114	69	59	11	1	1	5	49	3	79	3	0	6	3	.667	0	0-2	4	5.81
1998 San Diego	NL	3	0	0	1	3	14	4	2	2	1	0	0	0	1	1	1	0	0	0	0	—	0	0-0	0	6.00
1999 San Diego	NL	24	0	0	2	31	130	34	19	18	8	2	0	0	12	3	22	3	0	2	1	.667	0	0-0	5	5.23
2000 San Diego	NL	27	3	0	4	38.1	169	35	21	18	2	1	1	1	21	0	34	1	0	1	1	.500	0	0-0	1	4.23
4 ML YEARS		108	11	0	23	163.2	743	187	111	97	22	4	2	6	83	7	136	7	0	9	5	.643	0	0-2	10	5.33

Chad Curtis

Bats: R **Throws:** R **Pos:** LF-51; RF-30; PH/PR-28; DH-16   **Ht:** 5'10" **Wt:** 185 **Born:** 11/6/68 **Age:** 32

Year Team	Lg	G	AB	H	2B	3B	HR	(Hm	Rd)	TB	R	RBI	TBB	IBB	SO	HBP	SH	SF	SB	CS	SB%	GDP	Avg	OBP	SLG
1992 California	AL	139	441	114	16	2	10	(5	5)	164	59	46	51	2	71	6	5	4	43	18	.70	10	.259	.341	.372
1993 California	AL	152	583	166	25	3	6	(3	3)	215	94	59	70	2	89	4	7	7	48	24	.67	16	.285	.361	.369
1994 California	AL	114	453	116	23	4	11	(8	3)	180	67	50	37	0	69	5	7	4	25	11	.69	10	.256	.317	.397
1995 Detroit	AL	144	586	157	29	3	21	(11	10)	255	96	67	70	3	93	7	0	7	27	15	.64	12	.268	.349	.435
1996 Det-LA	AL	147	504	127	25	1	12	(3	9)	190	85	46	70	0	88	1	6	6	18	11	.62	15	.252	.341	.377
1997 Cle-NYY	AL	115	349	99	22	1	15	(4	11)	168	69	55	43	1	59	5	2	9	12	6	.67	7	.284	.362	.481
1998 New York	AL	151	456	111	21	1	10	(6	4)	164	79	56	75	3	80	7	1	6	21	5	.81	11	.243	.355	.360
1999 New York	AL	96	195	51	6	0	5	(0	5)	72	37	24	43	0	35	3	1	3	8	4	.67	6	.262	.398	.369
2000 Texas	AL	108	335	91	25	1	8	(3	5)	142	48	48	37	0	71	1	5	3	3	3	.50	12	.272	.343	.424
1996 Detroit	AL	104	400	105	20	1	10	(2	8)	157	65	37	53	0	73	1	6	6	16	10	.62	14	.263	.346	.393
Los Angeles	NL	43	104	22	5	0	2	(1	1)	33	20	9	17	0	15	0	0	0	2	1	.67	1	.212	.322	.317
1997 Cleveland	AL	22	29	6	1	0	3	(1	2)	16	8	5	7	0	10	0	0	0	0	0	—	1	.207	.361	.552
New York	AL	93	320	93	21	1	12	(3	9)	152	51	50	36	1	49	5	2	9	12	6	.67	6	.291	.362	.475
9 ML YEARS		1166	3902	1032	192	16	98	(45	53)	1550	624	451	496	11	655	39	34	49	205	97	.68	99	.264	.349	.397

Omar Daal

Pitches: Left **Bats:** Left **Pos:** SP-28; RP-4   **Ht:** 6'3" **Wt:** 195 **Born:** 3/1/72 **Age:** 29

Year Team	Lg	G	GS	CG	GF	IP	BFP	H	R	ER	HR	SH	SF	HB	TBB	IBB	SO	WP	Bk	W	L	Pct.	ShO	Sv-Op	Hld	ERA
1993 Los Angeles	NL	47	0	0	12	35.1	155	36	20	20	5	2	2	0	21	3	19	1	2	2	3	.400	0	0-1	7	5.09
1994 Los Angeles	NL	24	0	0	13	13.2	55	12	5	5	1	1	0	0	5	0	9	1	1	0	0	—	0	0-0	3	3.29
1995 Los Angeles	NL	28	0	0	0	20	100	29	16	16	1	1	1	1	15	4	11	0	1	4	0	1.000	0	0-1	4	7.20
1996 Montreal	NL	64	6	0	9	87.1	366	74	40	39	10	2	2	1	37	3	82	1	1	4	5	.444	0	0-4	9	4.02
1997 Mon-Tor		42	3	0	6	57.1	270	82	48	45	7	7	1	2	21	3	44	2	0	2	3	.400	0	1-3	3	7.06
1998 Arizona	NL	33	23	3	4	162.2	664	146	60	52	12	9	6	3	51	3	132	0	1	8	12	.400	1	0-0	1	2.88
1999 Arizona	NL	32	32	3	0	214.2	895	188	92	87	21	4	7	7	79	3	148	3	2	16	9	.640	1	0-0	0	3.65
2000 Ari-Phi	NL	32	28	0	1	167	775	208	128	114	26	9	4	9	72	11	96	0	2	4	19	.174	0	0-0	0	6.14
1997 Montreal	NL	33	0	0	6	30.1	150	48	35	33	4	5	1	2	15	3	16	1	0	1	2	.333	0	1-3	3	9.79
Toronto	AL	9	3	0	0	27	120	34	13	12	3	2	0	0	6	0	28	1	0	1	1	.500	0	0-0	0	4.00
2000 Arizona	NL	20	16	0	1	96	460	127	88	77	17	3	5	7	42	11	45	0	1	2	10	.167	0	0-0	0	7.22
Philadelphia	NL	12	12	0	0	71	315	81	40	37	9	3	1	2	30	0	51	0	1	2	9	.182	0	0-0	0	4.69
8 ML YEARS		302	92	5	37	758	3280	775	409	378	83	32	25	23	301	30	541	8	10	40	51	.440	2	1-9	27	4.49

Jeff D'Amico

Pitches: Right **Bats:** Right **Pos:** SP-23   **Ht:** 6'7" **Wt:** 250 **Born:** 12/27/75 **Age:** 25

Year Team	Lg	G	GS	CG	GF	IP	BFP	H	R	ER	HR	SH	SF	HB	TBB	IBB	SO	WP	Bk	W	L	Pct.	ShO	Sv-Op	Hld	ERA
2000 Indianapols *	AAA	6	6	0	0	31.1	125	25	11	11	6	0	0	0	11	0	20	0	0	1	1	.500	0	0--	—	3.16

Year Team	Lg	G	GS	CG	GF	IP	BFP	H	R	ER	HR	SH	SF	HB	TBB	IBB	SO	WP	Bk	W	L	Pct.	ShO	Sv-Op	Hld	ERA
1996 Milwaukee	AL	17	17	1	0	86	367	88	53	52	21	3	0		31	0	53	1	1	6	6	.500	0	0-0	0	5.44
1997 Milwaukee	AL	23	23	1	0	135.2	585	139	81	71	25	4	4	8	43	2	94	3	1	9	9	.563	1	0-0	0	4.71
1999 Milwaukee	NL	1	0	0	1	1	4	1	0	0	0	0	0	0	0	0	0	0	0	0	0	—	0	0-0	0	0.00
2000 Milwaukee	NL	23	23	1	0	162.1	667	143	55	48	14	10	3	6	46	5	101	5	0	12	7	.632	1	0-0	0	2.66
4 ML YEARS		64	63	2	1	385	1623	371	189	171	60	17	10	14	120	7	249	9	2	27	20	.574	2	0-0	0	4.00

Jeff M. D'Amico

Pitches: Right **Bats:** Right **Pos:** RP-6; SP-1   **Ht:** 6'3" **Wt:** 200 **Born:** 11/9/74 **Age:** 26

Year Team	Lg	G	GS	CG	GF	IP	BFP	H	R	ER	HR	SH	SF	HB	TBB	IBB	SO	WP	Bk	W	L	Pct.	ShO	Sv-Op	Hld	ERA
1996 Athletics	R	8	0	0	2	19	72	14	3	3	0	0	0	3	1	0	15	0	1	3	0	1.000	0	0--	—	1.42
Modesto	A+	1	0	0	0	1	7	3	3	2	0	0	0	1	0	0	0	0	0	0	0	—	0	0--	—	18.00
1997 Modesto	A+	20	13	0	5	97	442	115	57	41	5	1	4	7	34	1	89	9	1	7	3	.700	0	1--	—	3.80
Edmonton	AAA	10	7	0	1	30.2	141	42	29	28	7	1	2	2	6	0	19	3	0	1	2	.333	0	1--	—	8.22
1998 Athletics	R	4	1	0	0	9.1	34	6	4	4	2	0	0	1	1	0	8	0	0	0	0	—	0	0--	—	3.86
Huntsville	AA	24	8	0	4	61	295	77	57	52	12	1	6	3	34	0	46	6	5	5	5	.500	0	0--	—	7.67
1999 Midland	AA	32	0	0	18	45.1	207	53	31	25	4	3	3	16	2	38	3	0	1	2	.333	0	3--	—	4.96
Vancouver	AAA	14	0	0	11	17	75	16	6	6	5	1	1	0	10	1	10	2	0	2	2	.500	0	3--	—	2.65
Omaha	AAA	12	0	0	10	18.2	88	29	13	9	1	0	0	1	3	0	12	3	1	1	3	.250	0	2--	—	4.34
2000 Omaha	AAA	16	16	1	0	91.2	386	87	39	39	16	1	0	7	26	1	66	6	2	3	3	.500	0	0--	—	3.83
2000 Kansas City	AL	7	1	0	1	13.2	71	19	14	14	2	1	0	0	15	1	9	1	2	1	0	1.000	0	0-0	1	9.22

Johnny Damon

Bats: L **Throws:** L **Pos:** CF-69; LF-67; DH-25; PH/PR-1   **Ht:** 6'2" **Wt:** 190 **Born:** 11/5/73 **Age:** 27

Year Team	Lg	G	AB	H	2B	3B	HR	(Hm	Rd)	TB	R	RBI	TBB	IBB	SO	HBP	SH	SF	SB	CS	SB%	GDP	Avg	OBP	SLG
1995 Kansas City	AL	47	188	53	11	5	3	(1	2)	83	32	23	12	0	22	1	2	3	7	0	1.00	2	.282	.324	.441
1996 Kansas City	AL	145	517	140	22	5	6	(3	3)	190	61	50	31	3	64	3	10	5	25	5	.83	4	.271	.313	.368
1997 Kansas City	AL	146	472	130	12	8	8	(3	5)	182	70	48	42	2	70	3	6	1	16	10	.62	3	.275	.338	.386
1998 Kansas City	AL	161	642	178	30	10	18	(11	7)	282	104	66	58	4	84	4	3	4	26	12	.68	4	.277	.339	.439
1999 Kansas City	AL	145	583	179	39	9	14	(5	9)	278	101	77	67	5	50	3	3	4	36	6	.86	13	.307	.379	.477
2000 Kansas City	AL	159	655	214	42	10	16	(10	6)	324	136	88	65	4	60	1	8	12	46	9	.84	7	.327	.382	.495
6 ML YEARS		803	3057	894	156	47	65	(33	32)	1339	504	352	275	18	350	15	32	28	156	42	.79	33	.292	.351	.438

Vic Darensbourg

Pitches: Left **Bats:** Left **Pos:** RP-56   **Ht:** 5'10" **Wt:** 165 **Born:** 11/13/70 **Age:** 30

Year Team	Lg	G	GS	CG	GF	IP	BFP	H	R	ER	HR	SH	SF	HB	TBB	IBB	SO	WP	Bk	W	L	Pct.	ShO	Sv-Op	Hld	ERA
1998 Florida	NL	59	0	0	10	71	287	52	29	29	5	3	3	0	30	6	74	4	0	0	7	.000	0	1-2	13	3.68
1999 Florida	NL	56	0	0	5	34.2	180	50	36	34	3	5	2	5	21	1	16	1	3	0	1	.000	0	0-1	10	8.83
2000 Florida	NL	56	0	0	17	62	274	61	32	28	7	3	6	2	28	1	59	1	0	5	3	.625	0	0-1	3	4.06
3 ML YEARS		171	0	0	32	167.2	741	163	97	91	15	11	11	7	79	8	149	6	3	5	11	.313	0	1-4	26	4.88

Mike Darr

Bats: L **Throws:** R **Pos:** RF-47; CF-19; LF-8; PH/PR-4   **Ht:** 6'3" **Wt:** 205 **Born:** 3/21/76 **Age:** 25

Year Team	Lg	G	AB	H	2B	3B	HR	(Hm	Rd)	TB	R	RBI	TBB	IBB	SO	HBP	SH	SF	SB	CS	SB%	GDP	Avg	OBP	SLG
1994 Bristol	R+	44	149	41	6	0	1	—	—	50	23	18	23	1	22	1	0	0	4	4	.50	3	.275	.376	.336
1995 Fayettevlle	A	112	395	114	21	2	5	—	—	154	58	66	58	2	88	4	0	6	5	2	.71	5	.289	.380	.390
1996 Lakeland	A+	85	311	77	14	7	0	—	—	105	26	38	28	0	64	0	0	3	7	3	.70	7	.248	.307	.338
1997 Rancho Cuc	A+	134	521	179	32	11	15	—	—	278	104	94	57	1	90	4	0	5	23	7	.77	19	.344	.409	.534
1998 Mobile	AA	132	523	162	41	4	6	—	—	229	105	90	62	2	79	5	1	5	28	8	.78	18	.310	.385	.438
1999 Las Vegas	AAA	100	383	114	34	0	10	—	—	178	57	62	50	0	103	4	0	1	10	3	.77	11	.298	.384	.465
2000 Las Vegas	AAA	91	366	126	23	5	9	—	—	186	79	65	44	0	55	0	0	9	13	6	.68	7	.344	.409	.508
1999 San Diego	NL	25	48	13	1	0	2	(1	1)	20	6	3	5	0	18	0	0	2	1		.67	1	.271	.340	.417
2000 San Diego	NL	58	205	55	14	4	1	(1	0)	80	21	30	23	1	45	0	0	0	9	1	.90	9	.268	.342	.390
2 ML YEARS		83	253	68	15	4	3	(2	1)	100	27	33	28	1	63	0	0	0	11	2	.85	10	.269	.342	.395

Brian Daubach

Bats: L **Throws:** R **Pos:** 1B-83; DH-41; PH/PR-14; LF-7; 3B-1; RF-1   **Ht:** 6'1" **Wt:** 201 **Born:** 2/11/72 **Age:** 29

Year Team	Lg	G	AB	H	2B	3B	HR	(Hm	Rd)	TB	R	RBI	TBB	IBB	SO	HBP	SH	SF	SB	CS	SB%	GDP	Avg	OBP	SLG
1998 Florida	NL	10	15	3	1	0	0	(0	0)	4	0	3	1	0	5	1	0	0	0	0		0	.200	.294	.267
1999 Boston	AL	110	381	112	33	3	21	(11	10)	214	61	73	36	0	92	3	0	0	0	1	.00	0	.294	.360	.562
2000 Boston	AL	142	495	123	32	2	21	(10	11)	222	55	76	44	2	130	6	0	4	1	1	.50	6	.248	.315	.448
3 ML YEARS		262	891	238	66	5	42	(21	21)	440	116	152	81	2	227	10	0	4	1	2	.33	11	.267	.334	.494

Tom Davey

Pitches: Right **Bats:** Right **Pos:** RP-11   **Ht:** 6'7" **Wt:** 230 **Born:** 9/11/73 **Age:** 27

Year Team	Lg	G	GS	CG	GF	IP	BFP	H	R	ER	HR	SH	SF	HB	TBB	IBB	SO	WP	Bk	W	L	Pct.	ShO	Sv-Op	Hld	ERA
1994 Medcine Hat	R+	14	14	0	0	65	318	76	53	37	3	2	2	3	59	0	35	11	0	2	8	.200	0	0--	—	5.12
1995 St.Cathrnes	A-	7	7	0	0	38	160	27	19	14	2	2	3	1	21	0	29	3	1	4	3	.571	0	0--	—	3.32
Hagerstown	A	8	8	0	0	37.1	167	29	23	14	2	1	2	2	31	0	25	9	0	4	1	.800	0	0--	—	3.38
1996 Hagerstown	A	26	26	2	0	155.2	675	132	76	67	7	5	5	15	91	0	98	15	1	10	9	.526	1	0--	—	3.87
1997 Dunedin	A+	7	6	0	0	39.2	172	44	21	19	4	0	0	2	15	0	36	5	1	1	3	.250	0	0--	—	4.31
Knoxville	AA	20	16	0	1	92.2	429	108	65	60	5	1	4	8	50	0	72	14	0	6	7	.462	0	0--	—	5.83

Year Team	Lg	G	GS	CG	GF	IP	BFP	H	R	ER	HR	SH	SF	HB	TBB	IBB	SO	WP	Bk	W	L	Pct.	ShO	Sv-Op	Hld	ERA
1998 Knoxville	AA	48	9	0	32	76.2	348	70	35	33	2	3	2	3	52	3	78	9	1	5	3	.625	0	16--	—	3.87
1999 Syracuse	AAA	6	6	0	0	33.2	144	30	15	13	1	2	1	3	19	0	20	3	0	1	2	.333	0	0--	—	3.48
2000 Tacoma	AAA	28	12	0	6	93.2	418	104	59	48	10	0	1	3	37	0	77	4	0	1	2	.333	0	0--	—	4.61
Las Vegas	AAA	13	0	0	2	15.2	80	27	13	0	0	0	1	0	7	0	17	0	0	1	2	.333	0	0--	—	4.02
1999 Tor-Sea	AL	45	0	0	15	65	298	62	41	34	5	1	2	7	40	1	59	6	0	2	1	.667	0	1-1	4	4.71
2000 San Diego	NL	11	0	0	2	12.2	50	12	1	1	0	0	0	0	2	0	6	1	0	2	1	.667	0	0-1	2	0.71
1999 Toronto	AL	29	0	0	10	44	198	40	28	23	5	1	2	3	26	0	42	6	0	1	1	.500	0	1-1	3	4.70
Seattle	AL	16	0	0	5	21	100	22	13	11	0	0	0	4	14	1	17	0	0	1	0	1.000	0	0-0	1	4.71
2 ML YEARS		56	0	0	17	77.2	348	74	42	35	5	1	2	7	42	1	65	7	0	4	2	.667	0	1-2	6	4.06

Ben Davis

Bats: Both Throws: Right Pos: C-38; PH/PR-5; DH-1 Ht: 6'4" Wt: 215 Born: 3/10/77 Age: 24

Year Team	Lg	G	AB	H	2B	3B	HR	(Hm	Rd)	TB	R	RBI	TBB	IBB	SO	HBP	SH	SF	SB	CS	SB%	GDP	Avg	OBP	SLG
2000 Las Vegas *	AAA	59	221	58	16	1	7	—	—	97	38	40	38	3	43	1	1	0	5	2	.71	5	.262	.373	.439
1998 San Diego	NL	1	1	0	0	0	0	(0	0)	0	0	0	0	0	0	0	0	0	0	0	—	0	.000	.000	.000
1999 San Diego	NL	76	266	65	14	1	5	(1	4)	96	29	30	25	3	70	0	0	2	2	1	.67	9	.244	.307	.361
2000 San Diego	NL	43	130	29	6	0	3	(1	2)	44	12	14	14	1	35	0	3	1	1	1	.50	2	.223	.297	.338
3 ML YEARS		120	397	94	20	1	8	(2	6)	140	41	44	39	4	105	0	3	3	3	2	.60	11	.237	.303	.353

Doug Davis

Pitches: Left Bats: Right Pos: RP-17; SP-13 Ht: 6'3" Wt: 190 Born: 9/21/75 Age: 25

Year Team	Lg	G	GS	CG	GF	IP	BFP	H	R	ER	HR	SH	SF	HB	TBB	IBB	SO	WP	Bk	W	L	Pct.	ShO	Sv-Op	Hld	ERA
1996 Rangers	R	8	7	0	0	42.2	174	28	13	9	0	1	2	0	26	1	49	2	2	3	1	.750	0	0--	—	1.90
1997 Rangers	R	4	4	0	0	21	88	14	5	4	0	0	1	2	15	0	27	1	1	3	1	.750	0	0--	—	1.71
Charlotte	A+	9	8	1	0	49.1	205	29	19	17	2	4	2	0	33	1	52	8	3	5	3	.625	0	0--	—	3.10
1998 Charlotte	A+	27	27	1	0	155.1	665	129	69	56	8	1	3	13	74	0	173	8	0	11	7	.611	1	0--	—	3.24
1999 Tulsa	AA	12	12	1	0	74.1	305	65	26	20	9	1	0	2	25	0	79	2	1	4	4	.500	0	0--	—	2.42
Oklahoma	AAA	13	11	0	0	78	330	77	27	26	4	3	1	2	31	0	74	2	0	7	0	1.000	0	0--	—	3.00
2000 Oklahoma	AAA	12	12	2	0	69.2	290	62	32	22	8	2	2	2	34	1	53	4	0	8	3	.727	0	0--	—	2.84
1999 Texas	AL	2	0	0	0	2.2	20	12	10	10	3	0	0	0	0	0	3	0	0	0	0	—	0	0-0	0	33.75
2000 Texas	AL	30	13	1	4	98.2	450	109	61	59	14	6	4	3	58	3	66	5	1	7	6	.538	0	0-3	2	5.38
2 ML YEARS		32	13	1	4	101.1	470	121	71	69	17	6	4	3	58	3	69	5	1	7	6	.538	0	0-3	2	6.13

Eric Davis

Bats: Right Throws: Right Pos: RF-69; PH/PR-24; DH-4 Ht: 6'3" Wt: 185 Born: 5/29/62 Age: 39

Year Team	Lg	G	AB	H	2B	3B	HR	(Hm	Rd)	TB	R	RBI	TBB	IBB	SO	HBP	SH	SF	SB	CS	SB%	GDP	Avg	OBP	SLG
1984 Cincinnati	NL	57	174	39	10	1	10	(3	7)	81	33	30	24	0	48	1	0	1	10	2	.83	1	.224	.320	.466
1985 Cincinnati	NL	56	122	30	3	3	8	(1	7)	63	26	18	7	0	39	0	2	0	16	3	.84	1	.246	.287	.516
1986 Cincinnati	NL	132	415	115	15	3	27	(12	15)	217	97	71	68	5	100	1	0	3	80	11	.88	6	.277	.378	.523
1987 Cincinnati	NL	129	474	139	23	4	37	(17	20)	281	120	100	84	8	134	1	0	3	50	6	.89	6	.293	.399	.593
1988 Cincinnati	NL	135	472	129	18	3	26	(14	12)	231	81	93	65	10	124	3	0	3	35	3	.92	11	.273	.363	.489
1989 Cincinnati	NL	131	462	130	14	2	34	(15	19)	250	74	101	68	12	116	1	0	11	21	7	.75	16	.281	.367	.541
1990 Cincinnati	NL	127	453	118	26	2	24	(13	11)	220	84	86	60	6	100	2	0	3	21	3	.88	7	.260	.347	.486
1991 Cincinnati	NL	89	285	67	10	0	11	(5	6)	110	39	33	48	5	92	5	0	2	14	2	.88	4	.235	.353	.386
1992 Los Angeles	NL	76	267	61	8	1	5	(1	4)	86	21	32	36	2	71	3	0	2	19	1	.95	9	.228	.325	.322
1993 LA-Det		131	451	107	18	1	20	(10	10)	187	71	68	55	7	106	1	0	4	35	7	.83	12	.237	.319	.415
1994 Detroit	AL	37	120	22	4	0	3	(3	0)	35	19	13	18	0	45	0	0	0	5	0	1.00	2	.183	.290	.292
1996 Cincinnati	NL	129	415	119	20	0	26	(8	18)	217	81	83	70	3	121	6	1	4	23	9	.72	8	.287	.394	.523
1997 Baltimore	AL	42	158	48	11	0	8	(7	1)	83	29	25	14	0	47	1	0	3	6	0	1.00	2	.304	.358	.525
1998 Baltimore	AL	131	452	148	29	1	28	(16	12)	263	81	89	44	0	108	5	0	7	7	6	.54	13	.327	.388	.582
1999 St. Louis	NL	58	191	49	9	2	5	(2	3)	77	27	30	30	1	49	1	0	1	5	4	.56	1	.257	.359	.403
2000 St. Louis	NL	92	254	77	14	0	6	(2	4)	109	38	40	36	0	60	1	0	2	1	1	.50	7	.303	.389	.429
1993 Los Angeles	NL	108	376	88	17	0	14	(7	7)	147	57	53	41	6	88	1	0	4	33	5	.87	8	.234	.308	.391
Detroit	AL	23	75	19	1	1	6	(3	3)	40	14	15	14	1	18	0	0	0	2	2	.50	4	.253	.371	.533
16 ML YEARS		1552	5165	1398	232	23	278	(129	149)	2510	921	912	727	59	1360	32	3	49	348	65	.84	108	.271	.361	.486

Kane Davis

Pitches: Right Bats: Right Pos: RP-6; SP-2 Ht: 6'3" Wt: 194 Born: 6/25/75 Age: 26

Year Team	Lg	G	GS	CG	GF	IP	BFP	H	R	ER	HR	SH	SF	HB	TBB	IBB	SO	WP	Bk	W	L	Pct.	ShO	Sv-Op	Hld	ERA
1993 Pirates	R	11	4	0	5	28	140	34	30	22	0	3	2	0	19	1	24	2	0	0	4	.000	0	0--	—	7.07
1994 Welland	A-	15	15	2	0	98.1	400	90	36	29	4	2	2	3	32	1	74	7	1	5	5	.500	0	0--	—	2.65
1995 Augusta	A	26	25	1	0	139.1	602	136	73	58	4	3	4	9	43	0	78	10	1	12	6	.667	0	0--	—	3.75
1996 Lynchburg	A+	26	26	3	0	157.1	684	160	84	75	12	12	3	10	56	0	116	11	2	11	9	.550	1	0--	—	4.29
1997 Carolina	AA	6	6	0	0	28.2	128	22	17	12	2	2	1	3	16	1	23	2	0	0	3	.000	0	0--	—	3.77
1998 Augusta	A	2	2	0	0	9	36	8	6	6	0	1	1	0	3	0	6	0	2	0	0	—	0	0--	—	6.00
Carolina	AA	18	16	0	0	74	362	102	84	76	12	4	0	7	38	2	39	10	1	1	11	.083	0	0--	—	9.24
1999 Altoona	AA	16	16	0	0	95.1	421	97	51	40	5	2	4	3	41	1	53	4	0	4	6	.400	0	0--	—	3.78
Nashville	AAA	12	9	0	1	49.1	224	65	38	37	8	2	1	3	17	1	31	2	0	3	2	.600	0	0--	—	6.75
2000 Akron	AA	5	5	0	0	20	78	17	7	6	2	0	0	0	5	0	13	3	0	0	1	.000	0	0--	—	2.70
Buffalo	AAA	6	4	0	1	30	131	30	16	14	2	2	0	1	12	0	19	2	0	2	0	1.000	0	0--	—	4.20
Indianapols	AAA	4	4	0	0	20.1	83	19	8	8	2	0	0	0	7	0	12	0	0	1	1	.500	0	0--	—	3.54
2000 Cle-Mil		8	2	0	1	15	85	27	24	21	4	0	0	2	13	0	4	0	1	0	3	.000	0	0-0	0	12.60
2000 Cleveland	AL	5	2	0	0	11	61	20	21	18	3	0	0	1	8	0	2	0	1	0	3	.000	0	0-0	0	14.73
Milwaukee	NL	3	0	0	1	4	24	7	3	3	1	0	0	1	5	0	2	0	0	0	0	—	0	0-0	0	6.75

Russ Davis

Bats: R **Throws:** R **Pos:** 3B-43; PH/PR-33; 1B-6; DH-3   **Ht:** 6'0" **Wt:** 195 **Born:** 9/13/69 **Age:** 31

Year Team	Lg	G	AB	H	2B	3B	HR	(Hm	Rd)	TB	R	RBI	TBB	IBB	SO	HBP	SH	SF	SB	CS	SB%	GDP	Avg	OBP	SLG
1994 New York	AL	4	14	2	0	0	0	(0	0)	2	0	1	0	0	4	0	0	0	0	0	—	1	.143	.143	.143
1995 New York	AL	40	98	27	5	2	2	(2	0)	42	14	12	10	0	26	1	0	0	0	0	—	0	.276	.349	.429
1996 Seattle	AL	51	167	39	9	0	5	(3	2)	63	24	18	17	1	50	2	4	0	2	0	1.00	1	.234	.312	.377
1997 Seattle	AL	119	420	114	29	1	20	(11	9)	205	57	63	27	2	100	2	3	2	6	2	.75	11	.271	.317	.488
1998 Seattle	AL	141	502	130	30	1	20	(7	13)	222	68	82	34	1	134	3	2	9	4	3	.57	10	.259	.305	.442
1999 Seattle	AL	124	432	106	17	1	21	(12	9)	188	55	59	32	1	111	5	7	2	3	3	.50	13	.245	.304	.435
2000 San Francisco	NL	80	180	47	5	0	9	(5	4)	79	27	24	9	0	29	2	0	1	0	3	.00	1	.261	.302	.439
7 ML YEARS		559	1813	465	95	5	77	(40	37)	801	245	259	129	5	454	15	16	14	15	11	.58	37	.256	.309	.442

Gookie Dawkins

Bats: Right **Throws:** Right **Pos:** SS-14   **Ht:** 6'1" **Wt:** 180 **Born:** 5/12/79 **Age:** 22

Year Team	Lg	G	AB	H	2B	3B	HR	(Hm	Rd)	TB	R	RBI	TBB	IBB	SO	HBP	SH	SF	SB	CS	SB%	GDP	Avg	OBP	SLG
1997 Billings	R+	70	253	61	5	0	4	—	—	78	47	37	30	0	38	0	3	6	16	6	.73	6	.241	.315	.308
1998 Burlington	A	102	367	97	7	6	1	—	—	119	52	30	37	0	60	1	2	2	37	10	.79	10	.264	.332	.324
1999 Rockford	A	76	305	83	10	6	8	—	—	129	56	32	35	2	38	0	1	1	38	13	.75	5	.272	.346	.423
Chattanooga	AA	32	129	47	7	0	2	—	—	60	24	13	14	0	17	0	2	0	15	5	.75	5	.364	.427	.465
2000 Chattanooga	AA	95	368	85	20	6	6	—	—	135	54	31	40	0	71	3	2	2	22	10	.69	3	.231	.310	.367
1999 Cincinnati	NL	7	7	1	0	0	0	(0	0)	1	1	0	0	0	4	1	0	0	0	0	—	0	.143	.250	.143
2000 Cincinnati	NL	14	41	9	2	0	0	(0	0)	11	5	3	2	1	7	0	1	0	0	0	—	3	.220	.256	.268
2 ML YEARS		21	48	10	2	0	0	(0	0)	12	6	3	2	1	11	1	1	0	0	0	—	3	.208	.255	.250

Kory DeHaan

Bats: L **Throws:** R **Pos:** RF-49; PH/PR-48; LF-10; CF-4; DH-1   **Ht:** 6'2" **Wt:** 187 **Born:** 7/16/76 **Age:** 24

Year Team	Lg	G	AB	H	2B	3B	HR	(Hm	Rd)	TB	R	RBI	TBB	IBB	SO	HBP	SH	SF	SB	CS	SB%	GDP	Avg	OBP	SLG
1997 Erie	A-	58	205	49	8	6	1	—	—	72	43	18	38	2	43	2	6	4	14	9	.61	4	.239	.357	.351
1998 Augusta	A	132	475	149	39	8	8	—	—	228	85	75	69	3	114	8	8	7	33	13	.72	4	.314	.404	.480
1999 Lynchburg	A+	78	295	96	19	5	7	—	—	146	55	42	36	3	63	4	4	1	32	10	.76	4	.325	.405	.495
Altoona	AA	47	190	51	13	2	3	—	—	77	26	24	11	0	46	2	5	3	14	6	.70	3	.268	.311	.405
2000 Rancho Cuc	A+	4	14	3	1	0	1	—	—	7	2	1	1	0	4	0	0	0	0	0	—	0	.214	.267	.500
Las Vegas	AAA	10	41	12	4	0	0	—	—	16	7	3	2	0	11	1	1	1	3	0	1.00	1	.293	.333	.390
2000 San Diego	NL	90	103	21	7	0	2	(1	1)	34	19	13	5	0	39	0	1	1	4	2	.67	1	.204	.239	.330

Mike DeJean

Pitches: Right **Bats:** Right **Pos:** RP-54   **Ht:** 6'2" **Wt:** 212 **Born:** 9/28/70 **Age:** 30

		HOW MUCH HE PITCHED						WHAT HE GAVE UP											THE RESULTS					
Year Team	Lg	G	GS	CG	GF	IP	BFP	H	R	ER	HR	SH	SF	HB	TBB	IBB	SO	WP	Bk	W	L	Pct.	ShO	Sv-Op	Hld	ERA
2000 Colo Sprngs *	AAA	12	0	0	9	14.1	59	15	4	4	0	0	0	0	4	0	12	1	0	1	1	.500	0	5--	—	2.51
1997 Colorado	NL	55	0	0	15	67.2	295	74	34	30	4	3	1	0	24	2	38	2	0	5	0	1.000	0	2-4	13	3.99
1998 Colorado	NL	59	1	0	9	74.1	307	78	29	25	4	4	4	1	24	1	27	3	0	3	1	.750	0	2-3	11	3.03
1999 Colorado	NL	56	0	0	17	61	288	83	61	57	13	3	3	2	32	8	31	3	0	2	4	.333	0	0-4	9	8.41
2000 Colorado	NL	54	0	0	15	53.1	235	54	31	29	9	3	1	0	30	6	34	5	0	4	4	.500	0	0-4	7	4.89
4 ML YEARS		224	1	0	56	256.1	1125	289	155	141	30	13	9	6	110	17	130	13	0	14	9	.609	0	4-15	40	4.95

Tomas de la Rosa

Bats: Right **Throws:** Right **Pos:** SS-29; PH/PR-6; DH-1   **Ht:** 5'10" **Wt:** 155 **Born:** 1/28/78 **Age:** 23

Year Team	Lg	G	AB	H	2B	3B	HR	(Hm	Rd)	TB	R	RBI	TBB	IBB	SO	HBP	SH	SF	SB	CS	SB%	GDP	Avg	OBP	SLG
1996 Expos	R	53	184	46	7	1	0	—	—	55	34	21	22	0	25	2	4	1	8	5	.62	2	.250	.335	.299
Vermont	A-	3	8	2	0	0	0	—	—	2	1	1	0	0	3	0	0	0	0	0	—	1	.250	.250	.250
1997 Wst Plm Bch	A+	4	9	2	0	0	0	—	—	2	1	0	2	0	3	0	0	0	2	0	1.00	0	.222	.364	.222
Vermont	A-	69	271	72	14	6	2	—	—	104	46	40	32	0	47	2	3	4	19	6	.76	1	.266	.343	.384
1998 Jupiter	A+	117	390	98	22	1	3	—	—	131	56	43	37	0	61	6	10	3	27	7	.79	5	.251	.323	.336
1999 Harrisburg	AA	135	467	122	22	3	6	—	—	168	70	43	42	2	64	1	7	5	28	15	.65	10	.261	.320	.360
2000 Ottawa	AAA	103	340	69	10	1	1	—	—	84	27	36	31	0	43	2	12	5	10	3	.77	9	.203	.270	.247
2000 Montreal	NL	32	66	19	3	1	2	(1	1)	30	7	9	7	0	11	1	3	0	2	1	.67	2	.288	.365	.455

Carlos Delgado

Bats: Left **Throws:** Right **Pos:** 1B-162   **Ht:** 6'3" **Wt:** 225 **Born:** 6/25/72 **Age:** 29

Year Team	Lg	G	AB	H	2B	3B	HR	(Hm	Rd)	TB	R	RBI	TBB	IBB	SO	HBP	SH	SF	SB	CS	SB%	GDP	Avg	OBP	SLG
1993 Toronto	AL	2	1	0	0	0	0	(0	0)	0	0	0	1	0	0	0	0	0	0	0	—	0	.000	.500	.000
1994 Toronto	AL	43	130	28	2	0	9	(5	4)	57	17	24	25	4	46	3	0	1	1	1	.50	5	.215	.352	.438
1995 Toronto	AL	37	91	15	3	0	3	(2	1)	27	7	11	6	0	26	0	0	2	0	0	—	1	.165	.212	.297
1996 Toronto	AL	138	488	132	28	2	25	(12	13)	239	68	92	58	2	139	9	0	8	0	0	—	13	.270	.353	.490
1997 Toronto	AL	153	519	136	42	3	30	(17	13)	274	79	91	64	9	133	8	0	4	0	3	.00	6	.262	.350	.528
1998 Toronto	AL	142	530	155	43	1	38	(20	18)	314	94	115	73	13	139	11	0	6	3	0	1.00	8	.292	.385	.592
1999 Toronto	AL	152	573	156	39	0	44	(17	27)	327	113	134	86	7	141	15	0	7	1	1	.50	11	.272	.377	.571
2000 Toronto	AL	162	569	196	57	1	41	(30	11)	378	115	137	123	18	104	15	0	0	0	1	.00	12	.344	.470	.664
8 ML YEARS		829	2901	818	214	7	190	(103	87)	1616	493	604	436	53	728	61	0	32	5	6	.45	56	.282	.383	.557

Wilson Delgado

Bats: B **Throws:** R **Pos:** 2B-33; SS-23; PH/PR-12; 3B-8   Ht: 5'11" Wt: 165 Born: 7/15/75 **Age:** 25

							BATTING												BASERUNNING				PERCENTAGES		
Year Team	Lg	G	AB	H	2B	3B	HR	(Hm	Rd)	TB	R	RBI	TBB	IBB	SO	HBP	SH	SF	SB	CS	SB%	GDP	Avg	OBP	SLG
1994 Mariners	R	39	149	56	5	4	0	—	—	69	30	10	15	0	24	1	0	0	13	5	.72	2	.376	.436	.463
Appleton	A	9	31	6	0	0	0	—	—	6	2	0	0	0	8	0	0	0	0	0	—	2	.194	.194	.194
1995 Port City	AA	13	41	8	4	0	0	—	—	12	3	1	6	0	8	0	0	0	0	0	—	1	.195	.298	.293
Wisconsin	A	19	70	17	3	0	0	—	—	20	13	7	3	0	15	0	2	0	3	0	1.00	5	.243	.274	.286
Burlington	A	93	365	113	20	3	5	—	—	154	52	37	32	1	57	2	2	1	9	9	.50	7	.310	.368	.422
San Jose	A+	1	2	0	0	0	0	—	—	0	1	0	0	0	0	0	0	0	0	0	—	0	.000	.000	.000
1996 San Jose	A+	121	462	124	19	6	2	—	—	161	59	54	48	0	89	2	4	4	8	2	.80	8	.268	.337	.348
Phoenix	AAA	12	43	6	0	1	0	—	—	8	1	1	3	1	7	0	0	0	0	1	.00	1	.140	.196	.186
1997 Phoenix	AAA	119	416	120	22	4	9	—	—	177	47	59	24	4	70	1	6	4	9	3	.75	9	.288	.326	.425
1998 Fresno	AAA	127	512	142	22	2	12	—	—	204	87	63	52	2	92	3	4	4	9	5	.64	6	.277	.345	.398
1999 Fresno	AAA	57	213	64	10	3	1	—	—	83	28	33	18	1	35	0	3	0	4	2	.67	8	.300	.355	.390
1996 San Francisco	NL	6	22	8	0	0	0	(0	0)	8	3	2	1	0	5	2	0	0	1	0	1.00	0	.364	.440	.364
1997 San Francisco	NL	8	7	1	1	0	0	(0	0)	2	1	0	0	0	2	0	1	0	0	0	—	0	.143	.143	.286
1998 San Francisco	NL	10	12	2	1	0	0	(0	0)	3	1	1	1	0	3	0	0	0	0	0	—	0	.167	.231	.250
1999 San Francisco	NL	35	71	18	2	1	0	(0	0)	22	7	3	5	0	9	1	1	0	1	0	1.00	2	.254	.312	.310
2000 NYY-KC	AL	64	128	33	2	0	1	(0	1)	38	21	11	11	0	26	0	0	2	2	1	.67	2	.258	.312	.297
2000 New York	AL	31	45	11	1	0	1	(0	1)	15	6	4	5	0	9	0	0	1	1	0	1.00	1	.244	.314	.333
Kansas City	AL	33	83	22	1	0	0	(0	0)	23	15	7	6	0	17	0	0	1	1	1	.50	1	.265	.311	.277
5 ML YEARS		123	240	62	6	1	1	(0	1)	73	33	17	18	0	45	3	2	2	4	1	.80	4	.258	.316	.304

David Dellucci

Bats: Left **Throws:** Left **Pos:** PH/PR-23; RF-11; LF-1   Ht: 5'10" Wt: 194 **Born:** 10/31/73 **Age:** 27

							BATTING												BASERUNNING				PERCENTAGES		
Year Team	Lg	G	AB	H	2B	3B	HR	(Hm	Rd)	TB	R	RBI	TBB	IBB	SO	HBP	SH	SF	SB	CS	SB%	GDP	Avg	OBP	SLG
2000 South Bend *	A	2	5	1	1	0	0	—	—	2	3	1	2	0	0	0	0	1	0	0	.00	0	.200	.375	.400
Tucson *	AAA	33	122	28	6	3	3	—	—	49	16	17	13	0	15	0	1	1	4	0	1.00	0	.230	.301	.402
1997 Baltimore	AL	17	27	6	1	0	1	(0	1)	10	3	3	4	1	7	1	0	0	0	0	—	2	.222	.344	.370
1998 Arizona	NL	124	416	108	19	12	5	(1	4)	166	43	51	33	2	103	3	0	1	3	5	.38	6	.260	.318	.399
1999 Arizona	NL	63	109	43	7	1	1	(0	1)	55	27	15	11	0	24	3	0	0	2	0	1.00	3	.394	.463	.505
2000 Arizona	NL	34	50	15	3	0	0	(0	0)	18	2	2	4	0	9	0	0	0	0	2	.00	1	.300	.352	.360
4 ML YEARS		238	602	172	30	13	7	(1	6)	249	75	71	52	3	143	7	0	1	5	7	.42	12	.286	.349	.414

Valerio de los Santos

Pitches: Left **Bats:** Left **Pos:** RP-64; SP-2   Ht: 6'2" Wt: 180 **Born:** 10/6/75 **Age:** 25

		HOW MUCH HE PITCHED						WHAT HE GAVE UP										THE RESULTS					
Year Team	Lg	G	GS	CG	GF	IP	BFP	H	R	ER	HR	SH	SF	HB	TBB	IBB	SO	WP	Bk	W	L	Pct.	ShO	Sv-Op	Hld	ERA
1998 Milwaukee	NL	13	0	0	3	21.2	75	11	7	7	4	0	0	2	0	18	1	0	0	0		0	0-0	0	2.91
1999 Milwaukee	NL	7	0	0	3	8.1	43	12	6	6	1	0	0	5	1	5	1	0	0	1	.000	0	0-0	0	6.48
2000 Milwaukee	NL	66	2	0	15	73.2	320	72	43	42	15	2	1	1	33	7	70	3	1	2	3	.400	0	0-1	9	5.13
3 ML YEARS		86	2	0	21	103.2	438	95	56	55	20	2	1	2	42	7	93	5	1	2	4	.333	0	0-1	9	4.77

Miguel del Toro

Pitches: Right **Bats:** Right **Pos:** RP-8; SP-1   Ht: 6'1" Wt: 160 **Born:** 6/22/72 **Age:** 29

		HOW MUCH HE PITCHED						WHAT HE GAVE UP										THE RESULTS					
Year Team	Lg	G	GS	CG	GF	IP	BFP	H	R	ER	HR	SH	SF	HB	TBB	IBB	SO	WP	Bk	W	L	Pct.	ShO	Sv-Op	Hld	ERA
1992 Pirates	R	11	10	1	1	60.1	266	64	30	23	0	0	3	4	21	0	42	5	5	2	5	.286	0	1--	—	3.43
1999 Fresno	AAA	40	0	0	12	71.1	323	76	41	35	11	5	2	6	29	0	71	5	1	4	2	.667	0	0--	—	4.42
2000 Fresno	AAA	21	20	0	0	112.1	502	117	82	75	17	6	3	7	42	0	98	4	1	6	6	.500	0	0--	—	6.01
1999 San Francisco	NL	14	0	0	2	23.2	102	24	11	11	5	0	0	0	11	0	20	0	0	0	0	—	0	0-0	0	4.18
2000 San Francisco	NL	9	1	0	4	17.1	77	17	10	10	3	1	0	2	6	2	16	2	0	2	0	1.000	0	0-0	0	5.19
2 ML YEARS		23	1	0	6	41	179	41	21	21	8	1	0	2	17	2	36	2	0	2	0	1.000	0	0-0	0	4.61

Ryan Dempster

Pitches: Right **Bats:** Right **Pos:** SP-33   Ht: 6'1" Wt: 201 **Born:** 5/3/77 **Age:** 24

		HOW MUCH HE PITCHED						WHAT HE GAVE UP										THE RESULTS					
Year Team	Lg	G	GS	CG	GF	IP	BFP	H	R	ER	HR	SH	SF	HB	TBB	IBB	SO	WP	Bk	W	L	Pct.	ShO	Sv-Op	Hld	ERA
1998 Florida	NL	14	11	0	1	54.2	272	72	47	43	6	5	6	9	38	1	35	5	0	1	5	.167	0	0-1	0	7.08
1999 Florida	NL	25	25	0	0	147	666	146	77	77	21	3	6	6	93	2	126	8	0	7	8	.467	0	0-0	0	4.71
2000 Florida	NL	33	33	2	0	226.1	974	210	102	92	30	4	5	5	97	7	209	4	0	14	10	.583	1	0-0	0	3.66
3 ML YEARS		72	69	2	1	428	1912	428	226	212	57	12	17	20	228	10	370	17	0	22	23	.489	1	0-1	0	4.46

Sean DePaula

Pitches: Right **Bats:** Right **Pos:** RP-13   Ht: 6'4" Wt: 215 **Born:** 11/7/73 **Age:** 27

		HOW MUCH HE PITCHED						WHAT HE GAVE UP										THE RESULTS					
Year Team	Lg	G	GS	CG	GF	IP	BFP	H	R	ER	HR	SH	SF	HB	TBB	IBB	SO	WP	Bk	W	L	Pct.	ShO	Sv-Op	Hld	ERA
1996 Burlington	R+	23	0	0	11	35.1	151	31	16	15	3	2	2	2	13	0	42	4	3	4	2	.667	0	1--	—	3.82
Watertown	A-	1	0	0	0	2	6	0	0	0	0	0	0	0	0	0	5	0	0	0	0	—	0	0--	—	0.00
1997 Watertown	A-	9	0	0	2	19	86	21	6	6	1	1	1	1	8	0	17	0	0	1	1	.500	0	0--	—	2.84
Columbus	A	29	1	0	7	71	336	71	56	41	4	3	7	4	43	3	75	9	0	4	5	.444	0	0--	—	5.20
1998 Kinston	A+	28	1	0	14	49.2	226	50	20	13	0	4	1	3	18	3	59	6	0	3	2	.600	0	1--	—	2.36
Akron	AA	8	1	0	1	17	81	16	10	9	0	1	0	1	15	0	17	3	0	1	1	.500	0	0--	—	4.76
1999 Kinston	A+	23	0	0	14	51.1	208	36	17	13	6	0	0	3	17	0	75	4	0	4	2	.667	0	7--	—	2.28
Akron	AA	14	0	0	6	28	122	20	11	11	2	2	0	2	17	0	31	2	0	1	0	1.000	0	3--	—	3.54
Buffalo	AAA	5	0	0	5	5	19	0	0	0	0	0	0	0	3	0	7	1	0	0	0	—	0	2--	—	0.00
2000 Akron	AA	4	0	0	1	5	18	1	1	1	0	0	0	1	2	0	4	0	0	0	0	—	0	0--	—	1.80
Buffalo	AAA	9	0	0	4	13	62	16	9	8	1	0	1	0	7	0	11	2	0	0	1	.000	0	1--	—	5.54

HOW MUCH HE PITCHED					WHAT HE GAVE UP											THE RESULTS						
Year Team	Lg	G	GS	CG	GF	IP	BFP	H	R	ER	HR	SH	SF	HB	TBB	IBB	SO	WP	Bk	W	L	Pct.	ShO	Sv-Op	Hld	ERA
1999 Cleveland	AL	11	0	0	4	11.2	45	8	6	6	0	2	0	1	3	0	18	0	0	0	0	—	0	0-0	3	4.63
2000 Cleveland	AL	13	0	0	3	16.2	83	20	11	11	3	0	1	0	14	2	16	0	0	0	0	—	0	0-2	2	5.94
2 ML YEARS		24	0	0	7	28.1	128	28	17	17	3	2	1	0	17	2	34	0	0	0	0	—	0	0-2	5	5.40

Mark DeRosa

Bats: Right **Throws:** Right **Pos:** PH/PR-14; SS-10   **Ht:** 6'1" **Wt:** 195 **Born:** 2/2/75 **Age:** 26

BATTING																		BASERUNNING				PERCENTAGES		
Year Team	Lg	G	AB	H	2B	3B	HR	(Hm | Rd)	TB	R	RBI	TBB	IBB	SO	HBP	SH	SF	SB	CS	SB%	GDP	Avg	OBP	SLG
1996 Eugene	A-	70	255	66	13	1	2	—	—	87	43	28	38	1	48	5	0	2	3	4	.43	10	.259	.363	.341
1997 Durham	A+	92	346	93	11	3	8	—	—	134	51	37	25	2	73	10	2	4	6	8	.43	12	.269	.332	.387
1998 Greenville	AA	125	461	123	26	2	8	—	—	177	67	49	60	2	57	5	5	2	7	13	.35	18	.267	.356	.384
1999 Richmond	AAA	105	364	99	16	2	1	—	—	122	41	40	21	1	49	5	3	4	7	6	.54	5	.272	.317	.335
2000 Richmond	AAA	101	370	108	22	3	3	—	—	145	62	35	38	0	36	3	6	4	13	4	.76	13	.292	.359	.392
1998 Atlanta	NL	5	3	1	0	0	0	(0 | 0)	1	2	0	0	0	1	0	0	0	0	0	—	0	.333	.333	.333
1999 Atlanta	NL	7	8	0	0	0	0	(0 | 0)	0	0	0	0	0	0	0	0	0	0	0	—	0	.000	.000	.000
2000 Atlanta	NL	22	13	4	1	0	0	(0 | 0)	5	9	3	2	0	1	0	0	0	0	0	—	0	.308	.400	.385
3 ML YEARS		34	24	5	1	0	0	(0 | 0)	6	11	3	2	0	4	0	0	0	0	0	—	0	.208	.269	.250

Delino DeShields

Bats: L **Throws:** R **Pos:** 2B-96; LF-39; DH-10; PH/PR-9; CF-2   **Ht:** 6'1" **Wt:** 175 **Born:** 1/15/69 **Age:** 32

BATTING																		BASERUNNING				PERCENTAGES		
Year Team	Lg	G	AB	H	2B	3B	HR	(Hm | Rd)	TB	R	RBI	TBB	IBB	SO	HBP	SH	SF	SB	CS	SB%	GDP	Avg	OBP	SLG
1990 Montreal	NL	129	499	144	28	6	4	(3 | 1)	196	69	45	66	3	96	4	1	2	42	22	.66	10	.289	.375	.393
1991 Montreal	NL	151	563	134	15	4	10	(3 | 7)	187	83	51	95	2	151	2	8	5	56	23	.71	6	.238	.347	.332
1992 Montreal	NL	135	530	155	19	8	7	(1 | 6)	211	82	56	54	4	108	3	9	3	46	15	.75	10	.292	.359	.398
1993 Montreal	NL	123	481	142	17	7	2	(2 | 0)	179	75	29	72	3	64	3	4	2	43	10	.81	6	.295	.389	.372
1994 Los Angeles	NL	89	320	80	11	3	2	(1 | 1)	103	51	33	54	0	53	0	1	1	27	7	.79	9	.250	.357	.322
1995 Los Angeles	NL	127	425	109	18	3	8	(2 | 6)	157	66	37	63	4	83	1	3	1	39	14	.74	6	.256	.353	.369
1996 Los Angeles	NL	154	581	139	12	8	5	(3 | 2)	173	75	41	53	7	124	1	2	5	48	11	.81	12	.224	.288	.298
1997 St. Louis	NL	150	572	169	26	14	11	(6 | 5)	256	92	58	55	1	72	3	7	6	55	14	.80	5	.295	.357	.448
1998 St. Louis	NL	117	420	122	21	8	7	(3 | 4)	180	74	44	56	2	61	0	4	4	26	10	.72	6	.290	.371	.429
1999 Baltimore	AL	96	330	87	11	2	6	(4 | 2)	120	46	34	37	0	52	1	5	1	11	8	.58	5	.264	.339	.364
2000 Baltimore	AL	151	561	166	43	5	10	(4 | 6)	249	84	86	69	2	82	1	3	9	37	10	.79	16	.296	.369	.444
11 ML YEARS		1422	5282	1438	221	68	72	(32 | 40)	2011	797	514	674	28	946	19	47	39	430	144	.75	91	.272	.354	.381

Elmer Dessens

Pitches: Right **Bats:** Right **Pos:** RP-24; SP-16   **Ht:** 6'0" **Wt:** 187 **Born:** 1/13/72 **Age:** 29

HOW MUCH HE PITCHED							WHAT HE GAVE UP										THE RESULTS						
Year Team	Lg	G	GS	CG	GF	IP	BFP	H	R	ER	HR	SH	SF	HB	TBB	IBB	SO	WP	Bk	W	L	Pct.	ShO	Sv-Op	Hld	ERA
2000 Louisville *	AAA	4	4	0	0	22.2	98	24	10	8	1	1	1	0	7	0	14	1	0	2	0	1.000	0	0--	—	3.18
1996 Pittsburgh	NL	15	3	0	1	25	112	40	23	23	2	3	1	0	4	0	13	0	0	0	2	.000	0	0-0	3	8.28
1997 Pittsburgh	NL	3	0	0	1	3.1	13	2	0	0	0	0	0	1	0	0	2	0	0	0	0	—	0	0-0	0	0.00
1998 Pittsburgh	NL	43	5	0	8	74.2	332	90	50	47	10	4	3	0	25	0	43	1	0	2	6	.250	0	0-1	6	5.67
2000 Cincinnati	NL	40	16	1	6	147.1	640	170	73	70	10	12	7	3	43	7	85	4	0	11	5	.688	0	1-1	1	4.28
4 ML YEARS		101	24	1	16	250.1	1097	302	146	140	22	19	11	4	72	9	143	5	0	13	13	.500	0	1-2	10	5.03

Matt DeWitt

Pitches: Right **Bats:** Right **Pos:** RP-8   **Ht:** 6'4" **Wt:** 220 **Born:** 9/4/77 **Age:** 23

HOW MUCH HE PITCHED							WHAT HE GAVE UP										THE RESULTS						
Year Team	Lg	G	GS	CG	GF	IP	BFP	H	R	ER	HR	SH	SF	HB	TBB	IBB	SO	WP	Bk	W	L	Pct.	ShO	Sv-Op	Hld	ERA
1995 Johnson Cty	R+	13	12	0	0	62.2	305	84	56	49	10	0	3	1	32	0	45	5	6	2	6	.250	0	0--	—	7.04
1996 Johnson Cty	R+	14	14	0	0	79.2	353	96	53	48	17	1	0	3	26	0	58	7	0	5	5	.500	0	0--	—	5.42
1997 Peoria	A	27	27	1	0	158.1	672	152	84	72	16	7	8	9	57	2	121	6	1	9	9	.500	0	0--	—	4.09
1998 Pr William	A+	24	24	1	0	148.1	588	132	65	60	13	3	3	7	18	0	118	5	0	6	9	.400	0	0--	—	3.64
1999 Arkansas	AA	26	26	0	0	148.1	644	153	87	73	21	4	3	1	59	0	107	3	1	9	8	.529	0	0--	—	4.43
2000 Syracuse	AAA	31	7	0	23	64.2	296	78	42	35	6	2	5	2	25	0	41	0	0	4	5	.444	0	15--	—	4.87
2000 Toronto	AL	8	0	0	4	13.2	68	20	13	13	4	0	0	2	9	0	6	1	0	1	0	1.000	0	0-0	0	8.56

Einar Diaz

Bats: Right **Throws:** Right **Pos:** C-74; PH/PR-2; 3B-1   **Ht:** 5'10" **Wt:** 185 **Born:** 12/28/72 **Age:** 28

BATTING																		BASERUNNING				PERCENTAGES		
Year Team	Lg	G	AB	H	2B	3B	HR	(Hm | Rd)	TB	R	RBI	TBB	IBB	SO	HBP	SH	SF	SB	CS	SB%	GDP	Avg	OBP	SLG
1996 Cleveland	AL	4	1	0	0	0	0	(0 | 0)	0	0	0	0	0	0	0	0	0	0	0	—	0	.000	.000	.000
1997 Cleveland	AL	5	7	1	0	0	0	(0 | 0)	2	1	1	0	0	2	0	0	0	0	0	—	0	.143	.143	.286
1998 Cleveland	AL	17	48	11	1	0	2	(1 | 1)	18	8	9	3	0	2	2	0	3	0	0	—	2	.229	.286	.375
1999 Cleveland	AL	119	392	110	21	1	3	(2 | 1)	142	43	32	23	0	41	5	6	1	11	4	.73	10	.281	.328	.362
2000 Cleveland	AL	75	250	68	14	2	4	(2 | 2)	98	29	25	11	0	29	8	6	0	4	2	.67	7	.272	.323	.392
5 ML YEARS		220	698	190	37	3	9	(5 | 4)	260	81	67	37	0	74	15	12	4	15	6	.71	19	.272	.321	.372

Jason Dickson

Pitches: Right **Bats:** Left **Pos:** SP-6   **Ht:** 6'0" **Wt:** 195 **Born:** 3/30/73 **Age:** 28

HOW MUCH HE PITCHED							WHAT HE GAVE UP										THE RESULTS						
Year Team	Lg	G	GS	CG	GF	IP	BFP	H	R	ER	HR	SH	SF	HB	TBB	IBB	SO	WP	Bk	W	L	Pct.	ShO	Sv-Op	Hld	ERA
2000 Edmonton *	AAA	2	2	0	0	8	38	13	9	9	1	0	0	0	4	0	4	1	0	0	2	.000	0	0--	—	10.13
1996 California	AL	7	7	0	0	43.1	192	52	22	22	6	2	1	1	18	1	20	1	1	1	2	.200	0	0-0	0	4.57
1997 Anaheim	AL	33	32	2	1	203.2	888	236	111	97	32	4	5	7	56	3	115	4	1	13	9	.591	1	0-0	0	4.29

Year Team	Lg	HOW MUCH HE PITCHED					WHAT HE GAVE UP										THE RESULTS						
		G	GS	CG	GF	IP	BFP	H	R	ER	HR	SH	SF	HB	TBB	IBB	SO	WP	Bk	W	L	Pct.	ShO Sv-Op Hld ERA
1998 Anaheim	AL	27	18	0	5	122	545	147	89	82	17	4	9	6	41	1	61	6	0	10	10	.500	0 0-0 0 6.05
2000 Anaheim	AL	6	6	0	0	28	125	39	20	19	5	1	0	1	7	0	18	0	0	2	2	.500	0 0-0 0 6.11
4 ML YEARS		73	63	2	6	397	1750	474	242	220	60	11	15	15	122	5	214	11	2	26	25	.510	1 0-0 0 4.99

Mike DiFelice

Bats: Right **Throws:** Right **Pos:** C-59; PH/PR-2   **Ht:** 6'2" **Wt:** 205 **Born:** 5/28/69 **Age:** 32

Year Team	Lg	G	AB	H	2B	3B	HR	(Hm	Rd)	TB	R	RBI	TBB	IBB	SO	HBP	SH	SF	SB	CS	SB%	GDP	Avg	OBP	SLG
1996 St. Louis	NL	4	7	2	1	0	0	(0	0)	3	0	2	0	0	1	0	0	0	0	0	—	0	.286	.286	.429
1997 St. Louis	NL	93	260	62	10	1	4	(1	3)	86	16	30	19	0	61	3	6	1	1	1	.50	11	.238	.297	.331
1998 Tampa Bay	AL	84	248	57	12	3	3	(1	2)	84	17	23	15	0	56	1	3	2	0	0	—	12	.230	.274	.339
1999 Tampa Bay	AL	51	179	55	11	0	6	(5	1)	84	21	27	8	0	23	3	0	1	0	0	—	0	.307	.346	.469
2000 Tampa Bay	AL	60	204	49	13	1	6	(4	2)	82	23	19	12	0	40	0	5	2	0	0	—	8	.240	.280	.402
5 ML YEARS		292	898	225	47	5	19	(11	8)	339	77	101	54	0	181	7	14	6	1	1	.50	32	.251	.296	.378

Craig Dingman

Pitches: Right **Bats:** Right **Pos:** RP-10   **Ht:** 6'4" **Wt:** 215 **Born:** 3/12/74 **Age:** 27

Year Team	Lg	G	GS	CG	GF	IP	BFP	H	R	ER	HR	SH	SF	HB	TBB	IBB	SO	WP	Bk	W	L	Pct.	ShO	Sv-Op	Hld	ERA
1994 Yankees	R	17	1	0	11	32	135	27	17	12	0	7	2	3	10	0	51	4	0	0	5	.000	0	1- -	—	3.38
1996 Oneonta	A-	20	0	0	15	35.1	137	17	11	8	0	1	1	1	9	0	52	0	1	0	2	.000	0	9- -	—	2.04
1997 Tampa	A+	19	0	0	11	22.1	92	15	14	13	2	1	0	0	14	2	26	3	0	0	4	.000	0	6- -	—	5.24
Greensboro	A	30	0	0	27	33	131	19	7	7	0	2	1	1	12	0	41	3	0	2	0	1.000	0	19- -	—	1.91
1998 Tampa	A+	50	0	0	28	70.2	293	48	29	25	8	3	2	1	39	9	95	2	0	5	4	.556	0	7- -	—	3.18
1999 Norwich	AA	55	0	0	21	74.1	288	56	16	13	2	2	0	2	12	2	90	2	0	8	6	.571	0	15- -	—	1.57
2000 Columbus	AAA	47	2	0	10	73.2	304	60	31	25	5	3	8	0	20	2	65	1	1	6	1	.857	0	1- -	—	3.05
2000 New York	AL	10	0	0	4	11	51	18	8	8	1	0	0	0	3	0	8	0	0	0	0	—	0	0-0	0	6.55

Jerry Dipoto

Pitches: Right **Bats:** Right **Pos:** RP-17   **Ht:** 6'2" **Wt:** 205 **Born:** 5/24/68 **Age:** 33

Year Team	Lg	G	GS	CG	GF	IP	BFP	H	R	ER	HR	SH	SF	HB	TBB	IBB	SO	WP	Bk	W	L	Pct.	ShO	Sv-Op	Hld	ERA
2000 Colo Sprngs *	AAA	9	0	0	2	9	35	6	2	2	1	0	0	0	3	1	12	0	0	1	0	1.000	0	1- -	—	2.00
1993 Cleveland	AL	46	0	0	26	56.1	247	57	21	15	3	0	3	2	30	7	41	0	0	4	4	.500	0	11-17	6	2.40
1994 Cleveland	AL	7	0	0	1	15.2	79	26	14	14	1	0	4	1	10	0	9	0	0	0	0	—	0	0-0	1	8.04
1995 New York	NL	58	0	0	26	78.2	330	77	41	33	2	6	3	4	29	8	49	3	1	4	6	.400	0	2-6	8	3.78
1996 New York	NL	57	0	0	21	77.1	364	91	44	36	5	7	4	3	45	8	52	3	3	7	2	.778	0	0-5	3	4.19
1997 Colorado	NL	74	0	0	33	95.2	422	108	56	50	6	3	7	4	33	5	74	4	1	5	3	.625	0	16-21	10	4.70
1998 Colorado	NL	68	0	0	51	71.1	295	61	31	28	8	2	2	3	25	3	49	7	0	3	4	.429	0	19-23	7	3.53
1999 Colorado	NL	63	0	0	18	86.2	379	91	44	41	10	1	5	3	44	4	69	6	0	4	5	.444	0	1-1	15	4.26
2000 Colorado	NL	17	0	0	7	13.2	59	16	6	6	1	1	2	0	5	2	9	0	0	0	0	—	0	0-1	3	3.95
8 ML YEARS		390	0	0	183	495.1	2175	527	257	223	33	23	29	19	221	37	352	23	5	27	24	.529	0	49-74	53	4.05

Gary DiSarcina

Bats: Right **Throws:** Right **Pos:** SS-12   **Ht:** 6'2" **Wt:** 195 **Born:** 11/19/67 **Age:** 33

Year Team	Lg	G	AB	H	2B	3B	HR	(Hm	Rd)	TB	R	RBI	TBB	IBB	SO	HBP	SH	SF	SB	CS	SB%	GDP	Avg	OBP	SLG
1989 California	AL	2	0	0	0	0	0	(0	0)	0	0	0	0	0	0	0	0	0	0	0	—	0			
1990 California	AL	18	57	8	1	1	0	(0	0)	11	8	0	3	0	10	0	1	0	1	0	1.00	3	.140	.183	.193
1991 California	AL	18	57	12	2	0	0	(0	0)	14	5	3	3	0	4	2	2	0	0	0	—	0	.211	.274	.246
1992 California	AL	157	518	128	19	0	3	(2	1)	156	48	42	20	0	50	7	5	3	9	7	.56	15	.247	.283	.301
1993 California	AL	126	416	99	20	1	3	(2	1)	130	44	45	15	0	38	6	5	3	5	7	.42	13	.238	.273	.313
1994 California	AL	112	389	101	14	2	3	(2	1)	128	53	33	18	0	28	2	10	2	3	7	.30	10	.260	.294	.329
1995 California	AL	99	362	111	28	6	5	(1	4)	166	61	41	20	0	25	2	7	3	7	4	.64	10	.307	.344	.459
1996 California	AL	150	536	137	26	4	5	(2	3)	186	62	48	21	0	36	2	16	1	2	1	.67	16	.256	.286	.347
1997 Anaheim	AL	154	549	135	28	2	4	(2	2)	179	52	47	17	0	29	4	8	5	7	8	.47	18	.246	.271	.326
1998 Anaheim	AL	157	551	158	39	3	3	(0	3)	212	73	56	21	0	51	8	12	3	11	7	.61	11	.287	.321	.385
1999 Anaheim	AL	81	271	62	7	1	1	(1	0)	74	32	29	15	0	32	2	9	1	2	2	.50	8	.229	.273	.273
2000 Anaheim	AL	12	38	15	2	0	1	(1	0)	20	6	11	1	0	3	1	2	0	0	1	.00	1	.395	.425	.526
12 ML YEARS		1086	3744	966	186	20	28	(13	15)	1276	444	355	154	0	306	36	77	21	47	44	.52	105	.258	.292	.341

Chris Donnels

Bats: L **Throws:** R **Pos:** PH/PR-17; LF-6; 1B-4; 3B-2; 2B-1   **Ht:** 6'0" **Wt:** 185 **Born:** 4/21/66 **Age:** 35

Year Team	Lg	G	AB	H	2B	3B	HR	(Hm	Rd)	TB	R	RBI	TBB	IBB	SO	HBP	SH	SF	SB	CS	SB%	GDP	Avg	OBP	SLG
2000 Albuquerque *	AAA	105	332	109	27	1	27	—	—	219	79	84	66	2	52	2	0	2	6	1	.86	9	.328	.440	.660
1991 New York	NL	37	89	20	2	0	0	(0	0)	22	7	5	14	1	19	0	1	0	1	1	.50	1	.225	.330	.247
1992 New York	NL	45	121	21	4	0	0	(0	0)	25	8	6	17	2	25	0	1	0	1	0	1.00	1	.174	.275	.207
1993 Houston	NL	88	179	46	14	2	2	(0	2)	70	18	24	19	0	33	0	0	1	2	0	1.00	6	.257	.327	.391
1994 Houston	NL	54	86	23	5	0	3	(2	1)	37	12	5	13	0	18	0	0	0	0	0	—	3	.267	.364	.430
1995 Hou-Bos		59	121	32	2	2	2	(0	2)	44	17	13	12	2	24	0	1	0	0	0	—	2	.264	.328	.364
2000 Los Angeles	NL	27	34	10	3	0	4	(3	1)	25	8	9	6	1	7	0	0	1	0	0	—	3	.294	.390	.735
1995 Houston	NL	19	30	9	0	0	0	(0	0)	9	4	2	3	2	6	0	0	0	0	0	—	1	.300	.364	.300
Boston	AL	40	91	23	2	2	2	(0	2)	35	13	11	9	0	18	0	1	0	0	0	—	1	.253	.317	.385
6 ML YEARS		310	630	152	30	4	11	(5	6)	223	70	62	81	4	126	0	2	3	5	1	.83	13	.241	.326	.354

Octavio Dotel

Pitches: Right **Bats:** Right **Pos:** RP-34; SP-16   **Ht:** 6'0" **Wt:** 175 **Born:** 11/25/75 **Age:** 25

Year Team	Lg	G	GS	CG	GF	IP	BFP	H	R	ER	HR	SH	SF	HB	TBB	IBB	SO	WP	Bk	W	L	Pct.	ShO	Sv-Op	Hld	ERA
1995 Mets	R	13	12	2	1	74.1	293	48	23	18	0	1	0	5	17	1	86	9	0	7	4	.636	0	0--	--	2.18
St. Lucie	A+	3	0	0	2	8	38	10	5	5	1	1	2	0	4	0	9	2	0	1	0	1.000	0	0--	--	5.63
1996 Capital Cty	A	22	19	0	3	115.1	480	89	49	46	7	1	4	7	49	0	142	12	4	11	3	.786	0	0--	--	3.59
1997 Mets	R	3	2	0	1	9.1	39	9	1	1	0	0	0	1	2	0	7	0	2	0	0	--	0	1--	--	0.96
St. Lucie	A+	9	8	1	1	50	212	44	18	14	2	0	1	1	23	0	39	5	1	5	2	.714	1	0--	--	2.52
Binghamton	AA	12	12	0	0	55.2	266	66	50	37	5	1	0	0	38	1	40	2	1	3	4	.429	1	0--	--	5.98
1998 Binghamton	AA	10	10	2	0	68.2	261	41	19	15	4	1	1	0	24	1	82	0	1	4	2	.667	1	0--	--	1.97
Norfolk	AAA	17	16	1	0	99	424	82	47	38	9	6	2	2	43	1	118	9	1	8	6	.571	0	0--	--	3.45
1999 Norfolk	AAA	13	13	1	0	70.1	293	52	33	30	9	1	1	2	34	1	90	3	1	5	2	.714	0	0--	--	3.84
1999 New York	NL	19	14	0	1	85.1	368	69	52	51	12	3	5	6	49	1	85	3	2	8	3	.727	0	0-0	0	5.38
2000 Houston	NL	50	16	0	25	125	563	127	80	75	26	7	8	7	61	3	142	6	0	3	7	.300	0	16-23	0	5.40
2 ML YEARS		69	30	0	26	210.1	931	196	132	126	38	10	13	13	110	4	227	9	2	11	10	.524	0	16-23	0	5.39

Scott Downs

Pitches: Left **Bats:** Left **Pos:** SP-19   **Ht:** 6'2" **Wt:** 190 **Born:** 3/17/76 **Age:** 25

Year Team	Lg	G	GS	CG	GF	IP	BFP	H	R	ER	HR	SH	SF	HB	TBB	IBB	SO	WP	Bk	W	L	Pct.	ShO	Sv-Op	Hld	ERA
1997 Williamsprt	A-	5	5	0	0	23	93	15	11	7	0	1	0	1	7	0	28	0	2	0	2	.000	0	0--	--	2.74
Rockford	A	5	5	0	0	36	128	17	5	5	1	1	0	1	8	0	43	2	2	3	0	1.000	0	0--	--	1.25
1998 Daytona	A+	27	27	2	0	161.2	713	179	83	70	12	7	7	4	55	0	117	12	4	8	9	.471	0	0--	--	3.90
1999 New Britain	AA	6	3	0	1	19.2	99	33	21	19	5	0	0	1	10	1	22	0	0	0	0	--	0	0--	--	8.69
Fort Myers	A+	2	2	0	0	9.2	45	7	3	0	0	0	0	1	6	0	9	2	0	0	1	.000	0	0--	--	0.00
Daytona	A+	7	7	1	0	48	185	41	12	10	2	0	0	1	11	0	41	3	1	5	0	1.000	0	0--	--	1.88
West Tenn	AA	13	13	1	0	80	319	56	13	12	2	1	0	1	28	0	101	1	0	8	1	.889	0	0--	--	1.35
2000 ChC-Mon	NL	19	19	0	0	97	442	122	62	57	13	2	4	5	40	1	63	1	0	4	3	.571	0	0-0	0	5.29
2000 Chicago	NL	18	18	0	0	94	426	117	59	54	13	2	4	5	37	1	63	1	0	4	3	.571	0	0-0	0	5.17
Montreal	NL	1	1	0	0	3	16	5	3	3	0	0	0	0	3	0	0	0	0	0	0	--	0	0-0	0	9.00

Kelly Dransfeldt

Bats: Right **Throws:** Right **Pos:** SS-14; PH/PR-4; 2B-2   **Ht:** 6'2" **Wt:** 195 **Born:** 4/16/75 **Age:** 26

Year Team	Lg	G	AB	H	2B	3B	HR	(Hm	Rd)	TB	R	RBI	TBB	IBB	SO	HBP	SH	SF	SB	CS	SB%	GDP	Avg	OBP	SLG
1996 Hudson Val	A-	75	284	67	17	1	7	—	—	107	42	29	27	1	76	4	1	3	13	4	.76	2	.236	.308	.377
1997 Charlotte	A+	135	466	106	20	7	6	—	—	158	64	58	42	0	115	3	4	3	25	16	.61	8	.227	.294	.339
1998 Charlotte	A+	67	245	79	17	0	18	—	—	150	46	76	29	1	67	2	0	6	7	2	.78	4	.322	.390	.612
Tulsa	AA	58	226	57	15	4	9	—	—	107	43	36	18	0	79	2	0	3	8	1	.89	4	.252	.309	.473
1999 Oklahoma	AAA	102	359	85	21	2	10	—	—	140	55	44	24	0	108	3	3	3	6	3	.67	12	.237	.288	.390
2000 Oklahoma	AAA	117	441	109	22	3	8	—	—	161	60	42	38	0	123	4	1	3	10	5	.67	7	.247	.311	.365
1999 Texas	AL	16	53	10	1	0	1	(1	0)	14	3	5	3	0	12	0	1	0	0	0	—	2	.189	.232	.264
2000 Texas	AL	16	26	3	2	0	0	(0	0)	5	2	2	1	0	14	0	1	0	0	0	—	0	.115	.148	.192
2 ML YEARS		32	79	13	3	0	1	(1	0)	19	5	7	4	0	26	0	1	0	0	0	—	2	.165	.205	.241

Darren Dreifort

Pitches: Right **Bats:** Right **Pos:** SP-32   **Ht:** 6'2" **Wt:** 211 **Born:** 5/3/72 **Age:** 29

Year Team	Lg	G	GS	CG	GF	IP	BFP	H	R	ER	HR	SH	SF	HB	TBB	IBB	SO	WP	Bk	W	L	Pct.	ShO	Sv-Op	Hld	ERA
1994 Los Angeles	NL	27	0	0	15	29	148	45	21	20	4	0	3	0	15	3	22	1	0	0	5	.000	0	6-9	3	6.21
1996 Los Angeles	NL	19	0	0	5	23.2	106	23	13	13	2	3	1	0	12	4	24	2	1	1	4	.200	0	0-2	1	4.94
1997 Los Angeles	NL	48	0	0	15	63	265	45	21	20	5	3	2	0	34	2	63	3	1	5	2	.714	0	4-7	9	2.86
1998 Los Angeles	NL	32	26	1	0	180	752	171	84	80	12	11	6	10	57	2	168	9	0	8	12	.400	1	0-0	0	4.00
1999 Los Angeles	NL	30	29	1	0	178.2	773	177	105	95	20	8	2	7	76	2	140	9	4	13	13	.500	1	0-0	0	4.79
2000 Los Angeles	NL	32	32	1	0	192.2	842	175	105	89	31	9	0	12	87	1	164	17	3	12	9	.571	1	0-0	0	4.16
6 ML YEARS		188	87	3	35	667	2886	636	349	317	68	39	11	34	281	14	581	41	9	39	45	.464	3	10-18	13	4.28

J.D. Drew

Bats: L **Throws:** R **Pos:** RF-98; CF-26; LF-24; PH/PR-15   **Ht:** 6'1" **Wt:** 195 **Born:** 11/20/75 **Age:** 25

Year Team	Lg	G	AB	H	2B	3B	HR	(Hm	Rd)	TB	R	RBI	TBB	IBB	SO	HBP	SH	SF	SB	CS	SB%	GDP	Avg	OBP	SLG
1998 St. Louis	NL	14	36	15	3	1	5	(4	1)	35	9	13	4	0	10	0	0	1	0	0	—	4	.417	.463	.972
1999 St. Louis	NL	104	368	89	16	6	13	(5	8)	156	72	39	50	0	77	6	3	3	19	3	.86	6	.242	.340	.424
2000 St. Louis	NL	135	407	120	17	2	18	(11	7)	195	73	57	67	4	99	6	5	1	17	9	.65	3	.295	.401	.479
3 ML YEARS		253	811	224	36	9	36	(20	16)	386	154	109	121	4	186	12	8	5	36	12	.75	11	.276	.376	.476

Tim Drew

Pitches: Right **Bats:** Right **Pos:** SP-3   **Ht:** 6'1" **Wt:** 195 **Born:** 8/31/78 **Age:** 22

Year Team	Lg	G	GS	CG	GF	IP	BFP	H	R	ER	HR	SH	SF	HB	TBB	IBB	SO	WP	Bk	W	L	Pct.	ShO	Sv-Op	Hld	ERA
1997 Burlington	R+	4	4	0	0	11.2	63	16	15	8	0	0	0	6	4	0	14	4	1	0	1	.000	0	0--	--	6.17
Watertown	A-	1	1	0	0	4.2	20	4	1	1	0	0	0	0	3	0	9	0	0	0	0	—	0	0--	--	1.93
1998 Columbus	A	13	13	0	0	71.1	311	68	43	30	5	0	4	6	26	0	64	5	2	4	3	.571	0	0--	--	3.79
Kinston	A+	15	15	0	0	90	392	105	58	52	9	3	5	5	30	1	67	5	2	3	8	.273	0	0--	--	5.20
1999 Kinston	A+	28	28	2	0	169	713	154	79	70	12	5	3	10	60	0	125	7	0	13	5	.722	0	0--	--	3.73
2000 Akron	AA	9	9	0	0	52	210	41	19	14	1	3	2	1	15	0	22	3	1	3	2	.600	0	0--	--	2.42
Buffalo	AAA	16	16	2	0	95	432	122	69	62	12	3	6	1	31	0	53	5	1	7	8	.467	0	0--	--	5.87
2000 Cleveland	AL	3	3	0	0	9	51	17	12	10	1	0	2	1	4	0	5	0	0	1	0	1.000	0	0-0	0	10.00

Rob Ducey

Bats: L **Throws:** R **Pos:** PH/PR-84; LF-30; DH-5; RF-5; CF-2 **Ht:** 6'2" **Wt:** 183 **Born:** 5/24/65 **Age:** 36

Year Team	Lg	G	AB	H	2B	3B	HR	(Hm	Rd)	TB	R	RBI	TBB	IBB	SO	HBP	SH	SF	SB	CS	SB%	GDP	Avg	OBP	SLG
1987 Toronto	AL	34	48	9	1	0	1	(1	0)	13	12	6	8	0	10	0	0	1	2	0	1.00	0	.188	.298	.271
1988 Toronto	AL	27	54	17	4	1	0	(0	0)	23	15	6	5	0	7	0	2	2	1	0	1.00	1	.315	.361	.426
1989 Toronto	AL	41	76	16	4	0	0	(0	0)	20	5	7	9	1	25	0	1	0	2	1	.67	2	.211	.294	.263
1990 Toronto	AL	19	53	16	5	0	0	(0	0)	21	7	7	7	0	15	1	0	1	1	1	.50	2	.302	.387	.396
1991 Toronto	AL	39	68	16	2	2	1	(0	1)	25	8	4	6	0	26	0	1	0	2	0	1.00	1	.235	.297	.368
1992 Tor-Cal	AL	54	80	15	4	0	0	(0	0)	19	7	2	5	0	22	0	0	1	2	4	.33	1	.188	.233	.238
1993 Texas	AL	27	85	24	6	3	2	(2	0)	42	15	9	10	2	17	0	2	2	2	3	.40	1	.282	.351	.494
1994 Texas	AL	11	29	5	1	0	0	(0	0)	6	1	1	2	0	1	0	0	0	0	0	—	1	.172	.226	.207
1997 Seattle	AL	76	143	41	15	2	5	(0	5)	75	25	10	6	0	31	0	0	2	3	3	.50	3	.287	.311	.524
1998 Seattle	AL	97	217	52	18	2	5	(2	3)	89	30	23	23	2	61	9	0	1	4	3	.57	4	.240	.336	.410
1999 Philadelphia	NL	104	188	49	10	2	8	(3	5)	87	29	33	38	1	57	0	0	1	2	1	.67	1	.261	.383	.463
2000 Phi-Tor		117	165	32	5	1	6	(4	2)	57	26	26	31	1	49	0	0	0	1	0	1.00	0	.194	.318	.345
1992 Toronto	AL	23	21	1	1	0	0	(0	0)	2	3	0	0	0	10	0	0	0	0	1	.00	0	.048	.048	.095
California	AL	31	59	14	3	0	0	(0	0)	17	4	2	5	0	12	0	0	1	2	3	.40	1	.237	.292	.288
2000 Philadelphia	NL	112	152	30	4	1	6	(4	2)	54	24	25	29	1	47	0	0	0	1	0	1.00	0	.197	.322	.355
Toronto	AL	5	13	2	1	0	0	(0	0)	3	2	1	2	0	2	0	0	0	0	0	—	0	.154	.267	.231
12 ML YEARS		646	1206	292	75	13	28	(12	16)	477	180	134	150	7	321	10	6	13	22	16	.58	16	.242	.328	.396

Shawon Dunston

Bats: R **Throws:** R **Pos:** LF-41; PH/PR-37; RF-13; CF-9; SS-8; 1B-6; 3B-5; DH-1 **Ht:** 6'1" **Wt:** 180 **Born:** 3/21/63 **Age:** 38

Year Team	Lg	G	AB	H	2B	3B	HR	(Hm	Rd)	TB	R	RBI	TBB	IBB	SO	HBP	SH	SF	SB	CS	SB%	GDP	Avg	OBP	SLG
1985 Chicago	NL	74	250	65	12	4	4	(3	1)	97	40	18	19	3	42	0	1	2	11	3	.79	3	.260	.310	.388
1986 Chicago	NL	150	581	145	37	3	17	(10	7)	239	66	68	21	5	114	3	4	2	13	11	.54	5	.250	.278	.411
1987 Chicago	NL	95	346	85	18	3	5	(3	2)	124	40	22	10	1	68	1	0	2	12	3	.80	6	.246	.267	.358
1988 Chicago	NL	155	575	143	23	6	9	(5	4)	205	69	56	16	8	108	2	4	2	30	9	.77	6	.249	.271	.357
1989 Chicago	NL	138	471	131	20	6	9	(3	6)	190	52	60	30	15	86	1	6	4	19	11	.63	7	.278	.320	.403
1990 Chicago	NL	146	545	143	22	8	17	(7	10)	232	73	66	15	1	87	3	4	6	25	5	.83	9	.262	.283	.426
1991 Chicago	NL	142	492	128	22	7	12	(7	5)	200	59	50	23	5	64	4	4	11	21	6	.78	9	.260	.292	.407
1992 Chicago	NL	18	73	23	3	1	0	(0	0)	28	8	2	3	0	13	0	0	0	2	3	.40	0	.315	.342	.384
1993 Chicago	NL	7	10	4	2	0	0	(0	0)	6	3	2	0	0	1	0	0	0	0	0	—	0	.400	.400	.600
1994 Chicago	NL	88	331	92	19	0	11	(2	9)	144	38	35	16	3	48	2	5	2	3	8	.27	4	.278	.313	.435
1995 Chicago	NL	127	477	141	30	6	14	(8	6)	225	58	69	10	3	75	6	7	3	10	5	.67	8	.296	.317	.472
1996 San Francisco	NL	82	287	86	12	2	5	(3	2)	117	27	25	13	0	40	1	5	1	8	0	1.00	8	.300	.331	.408
1997 ChC-Pit	NL	132	490	147	22	5	14	(10	4)	221	71	57	8	0	75	3	5	5	32	8	.80	9	.300	.312	.451
1998 Cle-SF		98	207	46	13	3	6	(2	4)	83	36	20	6	0	28	4	1	3	9	4	.69	3	.222	.255	.401
1999 StL-NYM	NL	104	243	78	11	3	5	(4	1)	110	35	41	2	0	39	5	3	2	10	4	.71	8	.321	.337	.453
2000 St. Louis	NL	98	216	54	11	2	12	(6	6)	105	28	43	6	0	47	3	4	2	3	1	.75	11	.250	.278	.486
1997 Chicago	NL	114	419	119	18	4	9	(7	2)	172	57	41	8	0	64	3	3	4	29	7	.81	7	.284	.300	.411
Pittsburgh	NL	18	71	28	4	1	5	(3	2)	49	14	16	0	0	11	0	2	1	3	1	.75	2	.394	.389	.690
1998 Cleveland	AL	62	156	37	11	3	3	(1	2)	63	26	12	6	0	18	1	0	3	9	2	.82	2	.237	.265	.404
San Francisco	NL	36	51	9	2	0	3	(1	2)	20	10	8	0	0	10	3	1	0	0	2	.00	1	.176	.222	.392
1999 St. Louis	NL	62	150	46	5	2	5	(4	1)	70	23	25	2	0	23	3	2	1	6	3	.67	4	.307	.327	.467
New York	NL	42	93	32	6	1	0	(0	0)	40	12	16	0	0	16	2	1	1	4	1	.80	4	.344	.354	.430
16 ML YEARS		1654	5594	1511	277	59	140	(73	67)	2326	703	634	198	44	935	38	53	47	208	81	.72	96	.270	.297	.416

Todd Dunwoody

Bats: L **Throws:** L **Pos:** CF-19; PH/PR-15; LF-14; DH-11; RF-9 **Ht:** 6'1" **Wt:** 205 **Born:** 4/11/75 **Age:** 26

Year Team	Lg	G	AB	H	2B	3B	HR	(Hm	Rd)	TB	R	RBI	TBB	IBB	SO	HBP	SH	SF	SB	CS	SB%	GDP	Avg	OBP	SLG
2000 Omaha *	AAA	9	31	10	1	0	1	—	—	14	5	5	4	0	8	1	1	1	1	2	.33	1	.323	.405	.452
1997 Florida	NL	19	50	13	2	2	2	(0	2)	25	7	7	7	0	21	1	0	0	2	0	1.00	1	.260	.362	.500
1998 Florida	NL	116	434	109	27	7	5	(2	3)	165	53	28	21	0	113	4	3	0	5	1	.83	6	.251	.292	.380
1999 Florida	NL	64	186	41	6	3	2	(1	1)	59	20	20	12	0	41	1	0	1	3	4	.43	1	.220	.270	.317
2000 Kansas City	AL	61	178	37	9	0	1	(1	0)	49	12	23	8	0	42	1	2	6	3	0	1.00	4	.208	.238	.275
4 ML YEARS		260	848	200	44	12	10	(4	6)	298	92	78	48	0	217	7	5	7	13	5	.72	12	.236	.280	.351

Erubiel Durazo

Bats: Left **Throws:** Left **Pos:** 1B-60; PH/PR-11 **Ht:** 6'3" **Wt:** 225 **Born:** 1/23/74 **Age:** 27

Year Team	Lg	G	AB	H	2B	3B	HR	(Hm	Rd)	TB	R	RBI	TBB	IBB	SO	HBP	SH	SF	SB	CS	SB%	GDP	Avg	OBP	SLG
1999 El Paso	AA	64	226	91	18	3	14	—	—	157	53	55	44	6	37	2	0	3	2	1	.67	5	.403	.498	.695
Tucson	AAA	30	118	48	7	0	10	—	—	85	27	28	14	0	18	1	0	1	1	0	1.00	1	.407	.470	.720
2000 Diamndbcks	R	2	5	3	0	0	1	—	—	6	2	2	1	0	0	0	0	0	0	0	—	0	.600	.667	1.200
Tucson	AAA	13	43	18	6	0	3	—	—	33	9	10	6	0	7	0	0	0	0	0	—	0	.419	.490	.767
1999 Arizona	NL	52	155	51	4	2	11	(9	2)	92	31	30	26	1	43	1	0	3	1	1	.50	1	.329	.422	.594
2000 Arizona	NL	67	196	52	11	0	8	(3	5)	87	35	33	34	2	43	1	0	2	1	0	1.00	3	.265	.373	.444
2 ML YEARS		119	351	103	15	2	19	(7	12)	179	66	63	60	3	86	2	0	5	2	1	.67	4	.293	.395	.510

Chad Durbin

Pitches: Right **Bats:** Right **Pos:** SP-16 **Ht:** 6'2" **Wt:** 200 **Born:** 12/3/77 **Age:** 23

Year Team	Lg	G	GS	CG	GF	IP	BFP	H	R	ER	HR	SH	SF	HB	TBB	IBB	SO	WP	Bk	W	L	Pct.	ShO	Sv-Op	Hld	ERA
1996 Royals	R	11	8	1	0	44.1	187	34	22	21	3	0	1	1	25	0	43	6	3	2	2	.600	1	0- --	—	4.26
1997 Lansing	A	26	26	0	0	144.2	642	157	85	77	15	6	6	11	53	0	116	12	1	5	8	.385	1	0- --	—	4.79
1998 Wilmington	A+	26	26	0	0	147.2	624	126	57	48	10	5	7	8	59	3	162	13	1	10	7	.588	0	0- --	—	2.93
1999 Wichita	AA	28	27	1	0	157	664	154	88	81	20	1	10	6	49	1	122	12	1	8	10	.444	1	0- --	—	4.64

59

Year Team	Lg	HOW MUCH HE PITCHED						WHAT HE GAVE UP											THE RESULTS						
		G	GS	CG	GF	IP	BFP	H	R	ER	HR	SH	SF	HB	TBB	IBB	SO	WP	Bk	W	L	Pct.	ShO	Sv-Op	Hld	ERA
2000 Omaha	AAA	12	12	0	0	72.2	303	75	37	36	10	0	1	1	22	0	53	0	0	4	4	.500	0	0--	—	4.46
1999 Kansas City	AL	1	0	0	0	2.1	9	1	0	0	0	0	0	1	0	3	1	0	0	—	0	0-0	—	0.00
2000 Kansas City	AL	16	16	0	0	72.1	349	91	71	66	14	1	3	0	43	1	37	7	0	2	5	.286	0	0-0	0	8.21
2 ML YEARS		17	16	0	0	74.2	358	92	71	66	14	1	3	0	44	1	40	8	0	2	5	.286	0	0-0	0	7.96

Ray Durham

Bats: Both **Throws:** Right **Pos:** 2B-151; PH/PR-2   **Ht:** 5'8" **Wt:** 170 **Born:** 11/30/71 **Age:** 29

Year Team	Lg	BATTING																BASERUNNING				PERCENTAGES		
		G	AB	H	2B	3B	HR	(Hm | Rd)	TB	R	RBI	TBB	IBB	SO	HBP	SH	SF	SB	CS	SB%	GDP	Avg	OBP	SLG
1995 Chicago	AL	125	471	121	27	6	7	(1 | 6)	181	68	51	31	2	83	6	5	4	18	5	.78	8	.257	.309	.384
1996 Chicago	AL	156	557	153	33	5	10	(3 | 7)	226	79	65	58	4	95	10	7	7	30	4	.88	6	.275	.350	.406
1997 Chicago	AL	155	634	172	27	5	11	(3 | 8)	242	106	53	61	0	96	6	2	4	33	16	.67	14	.271	.337	.382
1998 Chicago	AL	158	635	181	35	8	19	(10 | 9)	289	126	67	73	3	105	6	6	3	36	9	.80	5	.285	.363	.455
1999 Chicago	AL	153	612	181	30	8	13	(7 | 6)	266	109	60	73	1	105	4	3	2	34	11	.76	9	.296	.373	.435
2000 Chicago	AL	151	614	172	35	9	17	(5 | 12)	276	121	75	75	0	105	7	5	8	25	13	.66	13	.280	.361	.450
6 ML YEARS		898	3523	980	187	41	77	(29 | 48)	1480	609	371	371	10	589	39	28	32	176	58	.75	55	.278	.351	.420

Trent Durrington

Bats: Right **Throws:** Right **Pos:** PH/PR-3; 2B-1   **Ht:** 5'10" **Wt:** 188 **Born:** 8/27/75 **Age:** 25

Year Team	Lg	BATTING																BASERUNNING				PERCENTAGES		
		G	AB	H	2B	3B	HR	(Hm | Rd)	TB	R	RBI	TBB	IBB	SO	HBP	SH	SF	SB	CS	SB%	GDP	Avg	OBP	SLG
1994 Angels	R	16	52	14	3	0	1	—	—	20	13	2	11	0	16	1	0	0	5	1	.83	1	.269	.406	.385
1995 Boise	A-	50	140	24	4	1	3	—	—	39	23	19	17	0	35	2	2	2	2	0	1.00	4	.171	.267	.279
1996 Boise	A-	40	154	43	7	2	0	—	—	54	38	14	31	1	32	13	0	0	24	5	.83	4	.279	.439	.351
Cedar Rapids	A	25	76	19	1	0	0	—	—	20	12	4	33	0	20	2	2	1	15	2	.88	2	.250	.482	.263
1997 Lk Elsinore	A+	123	409	101	21	3	3	—	—	137	60	36	51	1	99	11	17	3	52	18	.74	5	.247	.344	.335
1998 Midland	AA	112	351	79	10	1	1	—	—	94	62	30	50	0	74	17	7	4	24	12	.67	5	.225	.346	.268
1999 Erie	AA	107	396	114	26	1	3	—	—	151	84	34	52	1	66	9	12	5	59	16	.79	4	.288	.379	.381
2000 Edmonton	AAA	28	105	23	4	1	3	—	—	38	19	14	16	0	25	1	3	1	8	6	.57	3	.219	.325	.362
1999 Anaheim	AL	43	122	22	2	0	0	(0 | 0)	24	14	2	9	0	28	0	5	0	4	3	.57	1	.180	.237	.197
2000 Anaheim	AL	4	3	0	0	0	0	(0 | 0)	0	0	0	0	0	0	0	0	0	0	0	—	0	.000	.000	.000
2 ML YEARS		47	125	22	2	0	0	(0 | 0)	24	14	2	9	0	28	0	5	0	4	3	.57	2	.176	.231	.192

Mike Duvall

Pitches: Left **Bats:** Right **Pos:** RP-2   **Ht:** 6'0" **Wt:** 200 **Born:** 10/11/74 **Age:** 26

Year Team	Lg	HOW MUCH HE PITCHED						WHAT HE GAVE UP											THE RESULTS						
		G	GS	CG	GF	IP	BFP	H	R	ER	HR	SH	SF	HB	TBB	IBB	SO	WP	Bk	W	L	Pct.	ShO	Sv-Op	Hld	ERA
1995 Marlins	R	16	1	0	10	28.1	118	15	8	7	1	0	0	2	12	1	34	4	2	5	0	1.000	0	1--	—	2.22
1996 Kane County	A	41	0	0	28	48	210	43	20	11	0	2	0	0	21	2	46	3	0	4	1	.800	0	8--	—	2.06
1997 Brevard Cty	A+	11	0	0	11	12.1	45	7	1	1	0	0	0	0	3	1	9	0	0	1	0	1.000	0	6--	—	0.73
Portland	AA	45	0	0	25	68.1	291	63	20	14	4	9	1	2	20	2	49	2	0	4	6	.400	0	18--	—	1.84
1998 St. Pete	A+	2	0	0	2	3.1	16	4	1	1	0	0	0	0	2	0	3	2	0	0	0	—	0	0--	—	2.70
Durham	AAA	32	9	1	5	72.2	314	74	31	26	3	0	1	2	32	3	55	5	0	5	3	.625	0	0--	—	3.22
1999 Durham	AAA	19	1	0	4	30	131	32	20	18	4	0	0	2	12	1	27	0	0	2	2	.500	0	2--	—	5.40
2000 Durham	AAA	30	8	0	1	80.1	363	85	47	41	8	1	3	3	44	0	49	7	0	6	2	.750	0	0--	—	4.59
1998 Tampa Bay	AL	3	0	0	0	4	17	4	3	3	0	0	0	0	2	0	1	0	0	0	0	—	0	0-0	0	6.75
1999 Tampa Bay	AL	40	0	0	7	40	188	46	21	18	5	1	1	2	27	1	18	4	1	1	1	.500	0	0-1	0	4.05
2000 Tampa Bay	AL	2	0	0	0	2.1	12	5	2	2	0	0	0	0	1	0	0	0	0	0	0	—	0	0-0	1	7.71
3 ML YEARS		45	0	0	7	46.1	217	55	26	23	5	1	1	2	30	1	19	4	1	1	1	.500	0	0-1	1	4.47

Jermaine Dye

Bats: Right **Throws:** Right **Pos:** RF-146; DH-10; PH/PR-1   **Ht:** 6'5" **Wt:** 220 **Born:** 1/28/74 **Age:** 27

Year Team	Lg	BATTING																BASERUNNING				PERCENTAGES		
		G	AB	H	2B	3B	HR	(Hm | Rd)	TB	R	RBI	TBB	IBB	SO	HBP	SH	SF	SB	CS	SB%	GDP	Avg	OBP	SLG
1996 Atlanta	NL	98	292	82	16	0	12	(4 | 8)	134	32	37	8	0	67	3	0	3	1	4	.20	11	.281	.304	.459
1997 Kansas City	AL	75	263	62	14	0	7	(3 | 4)	97	26	22	17	0	51	1	1	1	2	1	.67	6	.236	.284	.369
1998 Kansas City	AL	60	214	50	5	1	5	(3 | 2)	72	24	23	11	2	46	1	0	4	2	2	.50	8	.234	.270	.336
1999 Kansas City	AL	158	608	179	44	8	27	(15 | 12)	320	96	119	58	4	119	1	0	6	2	3	.40	17	.294	.354	.526
2000 Kansas City	AL	157	601	193	41	2	33	(15 | 18)	337	107	118	69	6	99	3	0	6	0	1	.00	12	.321	.390	.561
5 ML YEARS		548	1978	566	120	11	84	(40 | 44)	960	285	319	163	12	382	9	1	20	7	11	.39	54	.286	.340	.485

Damion Easley

Bats: Right **Throws:** Right **Pos:** 2B-125   **Ht:** 5'11" **Wt:** 185 **Born:** 11/11/69 **Age:** 31

Year Team	Lg	BATTING																BASERUNNING				PERCENTAGES		
		G	AB	H	2B	3B	HR	(Hm | Rd)	TB	R	RBI	TBB	IBB	SO	HBP	SH	SF	SB	CS	SB%	GDP	Avg	OBP	SLG
2000 Toledo *	AAA	4	13	3	1	0	1	—	—	7	3	4	4	0	2	2	0	0	0	0	—	0	.231	.474	.538
1992 California	AL	47	151	39	5	0	1	(1 | 0)	47	14	12	8	0	26	3	2	1	9	5	.64	2	.258	.307	.311
1993 California	AL	73	230	72	13	2	2	(0 | 2)	95	33	22	28	2	35	3	1	2	6	6	.50	5	.313	.392	.413
1994 California	AL	88	316	68	16	1	6	(4 | 2)	104	41	30	29	0	48	4	4	2	4	5	.44	8	.215	.288	.329
1995 California	AL	114	357	77	14	2	4	(1 | 3)	107	35	35	32	1	47	6	6	4	5	2	.71	11	.216	.288	.300
1996 Cal-Det	AL	49	112	30	2	0	4	(1 | 3)	44	14	17	10	0	25	1	5	1	3	1	.75	0	.268	.331	.393
1997 Detroit	AL	151	527	139	37	3	22	(12 | 10)	248	97	72	68	3	102	16	4	5	28	13	.68	18	.264	.362	.471
1998 Detroit	AL	153	594	161	38	2	27	(19 | 8)	284	84	100	39	2	112	16	0	2	15	5	.75	8	.271	.332	.478
1999 Detroit	AL	151	549	146	30	1	20	(12 | 8)	238	83	65	51	2	124	19	2	6	11	3	.79	15	.266	.346	.434
2000 Detroit	AL	126	464	120	27	2	14	(5 | 9)	193	76	58	55	1	79	11	4	1	13	4	.76	11	.259	.350	.416
1996 California	AL	28	45	7	1	0	2	(1 | 1)	14	4	7	6	0	12	0	3	0	0	0	—	0	.156	.255	.311
Detroit	AL	21	67	23	1	0	2	(0 | 2)	30	10	10	4	0	13	1	2	1	3	1	.75	0	.343	.384	.448
9 ML YEARS		952	3300	852	182	13	100	(55 | 45)	1360	477	411	320	11	598	79	28	24	94	44	.68	78	.258	.336	.412

Adam Eaton

Pitches: Right **Bats:** Right **Pos:** SP-22 **Ht:** 6'2" **Wt:** 190 **Born:** 11/23/77 **Age:** 23

Year Team	Lg	G	GS	CG	GF	IP	BFP	H	R	ER	HR	SH	SF	HB	TBB	IBB	SO	WP	Bk	W	L	Pct.	ShO	Sv-Op	Hld	ERA
1997 Piedmont	A	14	14	0	0	71.1	318	81	38	33	2	0	2	4	30	0	57	4	2	5	6	.455	0	0- —	—	4.16
1998 Clearwater	A+	24	23	1	0	131.2	578	152	68	65	9	3	5	5	47	1	89	9	1	9	8	.529	0	0- —	—	4.44
1999 Clearwater	A+	13	13	0	0	69	308	81	39	30	2	2	2	4	24	0	50	1	2	5	5	.500	0	0- —	—	3.91
Reading	AA	12	12	2	0	77	317	60	30	25	9	1	2	5	28	1	67	1	2	5	4	.556	1	0- —	—	2.92
Scrantn-WB	AAA	3	3	0	0	21	83	17	10	7	1	0	0	1	6	0	10	0	0	1	1	.500	0	0- —	—	3.00
2000 Mobile	AA	10	10	1	0	57	238	47	20	17	3	1	3	1	18	0	58	4	1	4	1	.800	1	0- —	—	2.68
2000 San Diego	NL	22	22	0	0	135	583	134	63	62	14	1	3	2	61	3	90	3	0	7	4	.636	0	0-0	0	4.13

Angel Echevarria

Bats: R **Throws:** R **Pos:** PH/PR-32; 1B-11; LF-3; RF-3 **Ht:** 6'3" **Wt:** 226 **Born:** 5/25/71 **Age:** 30

Year Team	Lg	G	AB	H	2B	3B	HR	(Hm	Rd)	TB	R	RBI	TBB	IBB	SO	HBP	SH	SF	SB	CS	SB%	GDP	Avg	OBP	SLG
2000 Colo Sprngs *	AAA	74	284	95	23	2	7	—	—	143	46	50	26	4	44	5	0	4	1	1	.50	5	.335	.395	.504
1996 Colorado	NL	26	21	6	0	0	0	(0	0)	6	2	6	2	0	5	1	0	2	0	0	—	0	.286	.346	.286
1997 Colorado	NL	15	20	5	2	0	0	(0	0)	7	4	0	2	0	5	0	0	0	0	0	—	0	.250	.318	.350
1998 Colorado	NL	19	29	11	3	0	1	(1	0)	17	7	9	2	0	3	2	0	0	0	0	—	4	.379	.455	.586
1999 Colorado	NL	102	191	56	7	0	11	(5	6)	96	28	35	17	0	34	3	0	0	1	3	.25	11	.293	.360	.503
2000 Col-Mil	NL	41	51	10	2	0	1	(1	0)	15	3	6	7	0	11	0	0	0	0	0	—	1	.196	.293	.294
2000 Colorado	NL	10	9	1	0	0	0	(0	0)	1	0	2	0	0	2	0	0	0	0	0	—	0	.111	.111	.111
Milwaukee	NL	31	42	9	2	0	1	(1	0)	14	3	4	7	0	9	0	0	0	0	0	—	1	.214	.327	.333
5 ML YEARS		203	312	88	14	0	13	(7	6)	141	44	56	30	0	58	6	0	2	1	3	.25	16	.282	.354	.452

Jim Edmonds

Bats: Left **Throws:** Left **Pos:** CF-146; 1B-6; PH/PR-4 **Ht:** 6'1" **Wt:** 212 **Born:** 6/27/70 **Age:** 31

Year Team	Lg	G	AB	H	2B	3B	HR	(Hm	Rd)	TB	R	RBI	TBB	IBB	SO	HBP	SH	SF	SB	CS	SB%	GDP	Avg	OBP	SLG
1993 California	AL	18	61	15	4	1	0	(0	0)	21	5	4	2	1	16	0	0	0	0	2	.00	1	.246	.270	.344
1994 California	AL	94	289	79	13	1	5	(3	2)	109	35	37	30	3	72	1	1	1	4	2	.67	3	.273	.343	.377
1995 California	AL	141	558	162	30	4	33	(16	17)	299	120	107	51	4	130	5	1	5	1	4	.20	10	.290	.352	.536
1996 California	AL	114	431	131	28	3	27	(17	10)	246	73	66	46	2	101	4	0	2	4	0	1.00	8	.304	.375	.571
1997 Anaheim	AL	133	502	146	21	4	26	(14	12)	251	82	80	60	5	80	4	0	5	5	7	.42	8	.291	.368	.500
1998 Anaheim	AL	154	599	184	42	1	25	(9	16)	303	115	91	57	7	114	1	1	1	7	5	.58	16	.307	.368	.506
1999 Anaheim	AL	55	204	51	17	2	5	(3	2)	87	34	23	28	0	45	0	0	1	5	4	.56	3	.250	.339	.426
2000 St. Louis	NL	152	525	155	25	0	42	(22	20)	306	129	108	103	3	167	6	1	8	10	3	.77	5	.295	.411	.583
8 ML YEARS		861	3169	923	186	12	163	(84	79)	1622	593	516	377	25	725	21	4	23	36	27	.57	54	.291	.368	.512

Dave Eiland

Pitches: Right **Bats:** Right **Pos:** SP-10; RP-7 **Ht:** 6'3" **Wt:** 208 **Born:** 7/5/66 **Age:** 34

Year Team	Lg	G	GS	CG	GF	IP	BFP	H	R	ER	HR	SH	SF	HB	TBB	IBB	SO	WP	Bk	W	L	Pct.	ShO	Sv-Op	Hld	ERA
2000 Orlando *	AA	2	2	0	0	11.1	42	7	3	2	2	0	0	1	1	0	8	0	0	1	0	1.000	0	0- —	—	1.59
Durham *	AAA	4	4	0	0	23.1	99	31	13	12	2	0	0	3	3	0	10	0	0	2	1	.667	0	0- —	—	4.63
1988 New York	AL	3	3	0	0	12.2	57	15	9	9	6	0	0	2	4	0	7	0	0	0	0	—	0	0-0	0	6.39
1989 New York	AL	6	6	0	0	34.1	152	44	25	22	5	1	2	2	13	3	11	0	0	1	3	.250	0	0-0	0	5.77
1990 New York	AL	5	5	0	0	30.1	127	31	14	12	2	0	0	0	5	0	16	0	0	2	1	.667	0	0-0	0	3.56
1991 New York	AL	18	13	0	4	72.2	317	87	51	43	10	0	3	3	23	1	18	0	0	2	5	.286	0	0-0	0	5.33
1992 San Diego	NL	7	7	0	0	27	120	33	21	17	1	0	0	0	5	0	10	0	1	0	2	.000	0	0-0	0	5.67
1993 San Diego	NL	10	9	0	0	48.1	217	58	33	28	5	2	2	1	17	1	14	1	0	0	3	.000	0	0-0	0	5.21
1995 New York	AL	4	1	0	1	10	51	16	10	7	1	0	1	1	3	1	6	1	0	1	1	.500	0	0-0	0	6.30
1998 Tampa Bay	AL	1	1	0	0	2.2	17	6	6	6	0	0	0	0	3	0	1	0	0	0	1	.000	0	0-0	0	20.25
1999 Tampa Bay	AL	21	15	0	0	80.1	369	98	59	50	8	2	4	3	27	1	53	2	1	4	8	.333	0	0-1	0	5.60
2000 Tampa Bay	AL	17	10	0	1	54.2	260	77	46	44	8	0	2	4	18	0	17	1	0	2	3	.400	0	0-0	0	7.24
10 ML YEARS		92	70	0	6	373	1687	465	274	238	46	5	14	16	118	7	153	5	2	12	27	.308	0	0-1	0	5.74

Darrell Einertson

Pitches: Right **Bats:** Right **Pos:** RP-11 **Ht:** 6'2" **Wt:** 196 **Born:** 9/4/72 **Age:** 28

Year Team	Lg	G	GS	CG	GF	IP	BFP	H	R	ER	HR	SH	SF	HB	TBB	IBB	SO	WP	Bk	W	L	Pct.	ShO	Sv-Op	Hld	ERA
1995 Oneonta	A-	25	0	0	8	38.1	167	32	20	8	1	1	0	3	15	1	35	0	1	4	0	.000	0	0- —	—	1.88
1996 Greensboro	A	48	0	0	26	70	306	69	29	21	1	4	2	2	19	3	48	4	1	3	9	.250	0	8- —	—	2.70
1997 Tampa	A+	45	0	0	24	71	287	63	24	17	2	5	0	1	19	8	55	1	0	5	4	.556	0	6- —	—	2.15
1998 Norwich	AA	17	0	0	5	35.1	142	23	7	4	1	3	0	1	10	3	33	2	0	3	1	.750	0	0- —	—	1.02
1999 Yankees	R	1	0	0	1	2	11	3	3	0	0	0	0	0	1	0	4	0	0	0	1	.000	0	0- —	—	0.00
Tampa	A+	2	1	0	0	4.2	19	1	1	1	0	0	0	1	1	0	3	0	0	0	0	—	0	0- —	—	1.93
Norwich	AA	21	0	0	6	29	141	39	23	16	2	4	0	1	10	5	16	4	0	2	2	.500	0	0- —	—	4.97
2000 Columbus	AAA	26	0	0	10	33.1	154	31	19	12	4	1	2	1	18	3	20	5	1	5	3	.625	0	1- —	—	3.24
2000 New York	AL	11	0	0	4	12.2	58	16	9	5	1	0	1	0	4	0	3	0	0	0	0	—	0	0-0	1	3.55

Scott Elarton

Pitches: Right **Bats:** Right **Pos:** SP-30 **Ht:** 6'7" **Wt:** 240 **Born:** 2/23/76 **Age:** 25

Year Team	Lg	G	GS	CG	GF	IP	BFP	H	R	ER	HR	SH	SF	HB	TBB	IBB	SO	WP	Bk	W	L	Pct.	ShO	Sv-Op	Hld	ERA
2000 New Orleans *	AAA	2	2	0	0	12	42	3	1	1	0	0	0	1	4	0	12	0	0	1	0	1.000	0	0- —	—	0.75
Round Rock *	AA	2	2	0	0	6.1	26	7	2	2	1	1	0	0	0	0	7	0	0	1	0	1.000	0	0- —	—	2.84
1998 Houston	NL	28	2	0	7	57	227	40	21	21	5	1	1	4	20	0	56	1	0	2	1	.667	0	2-3	2	3.32

Year Team	Lg	G	GS	CG	GF	IP	BFP	H	R	ER	HR	SH	SF	HB	TBB	IBB	SO	WP	Bk	W	L	Pct.	ShO	Sv-Op	Hld	ERA
1999 Houston	NL	42	15	0	8	124	524	111	55	48	8	7	4	4	43	0	121	3	0	9	5	.643	0	1-4	5	3.48
2000 Houston	NL	30	30	2	0	192.2	855	198	117	103	29	5	7	6	84	1	131	8	0	17	7	.708	0	0-0	0	4.81
3 ML YEARS		100	47	2	15	373.2	1606	349	193	172	42	13	12	11	147	0	308	12	0	28	13	.683	0	3-7	7	4.14

Cal Eldred

Pitches: Right **Bats:** Right **Pos:** SP-20   **Ht:** 6'4" **Wt:** 237 **Born:** 11/24/67 **Age:** 33

Year Team	Lg	G	GS	CG	GF	IP	BFP	H	R	ER	HR	SH	SF	HB	TBB	IBB	SO	WP	Bk	W	L	Pct.	ShO	Sv-Op	Hld	ERA
2000 Charlotte *	AAA	2	2	0	0	5	20	4	4	4	2	0	0	1	0	0	1	0	0	0	1	.000	0	0--	—	7.20
1991 Milwaukee	AL	3	3	0	0	16	73	20	9	8	2	0	0	0	6	0	10	0	0	2	0	1.000	0	0-0	0	4.50
1992 Milwaukee	AL	14	14	2	0	100.1	394	76	21	20	4	1	0	2	23	0	62	3	0	11	2	.846	1	0-0	0	1.79
1993 Milwaukee	AL	36	36	8	0	258	1087	232	120	115	32	5	12	10	91	5	180	2	0	16	16	.500	1	0-0	0	4.01
1994 Milwaukee	AL	25	25	6	0	179	769	158	96	93	23	5	7	4	84	0	98	2	0	11	11	.500	0	0-0	0	4.68
1995 Milwaukee	AL	4	4	0	0	23.2	104	24	10	9	4	1	0	1	10	0	18	1	1	1	1	.500	0	0-0	0	3.42
1996 Milwaukee	AL	15	15	0	0	84.2	363	82	43	42	8	0	4	4	38	0	50	1	0	4	4	.500	0	0-0	0	4.46
1997 Milwaukee	AL	34	34	1	0	202	885	207	118	112	31	4	6	9	89	0	122	5	0	13	15	.464	1	0-0	0	4.99
1998 Milwaukee	NL	23	23	0	0	133	602	157	82	71	14	5	3	4	61	3	86	6	0	4	8	.333	0	0-0	0	4.80
1999 Milwaukee	NL	20	15	0	2	82	392	101	75	71	19	2	3	1	46	0	60	8	1	2	8	.200	0	0-0	0	7.79
2000 Chicago	AL	20	20	2	0	112	492	103	61	57	13	3	2	5	59	0	97	4	0	10	2	.833	1	0-0	0	4.58
10 ML YEARS		194	189	19	2	1190.2	5161	1160	635	598	149	26	37	40	507	8	783	32	2	74	67	.525	4	0-0	0	4.52

Kevin Elster

Bats: R **Throws:** R **Pos:** SS-55; PH/PR-19; 3B-8; 1B-1   **Ht:** 6'2" **Wt:** 205 **Born:** 8/3/64 **Age:** 36

Year Team	Lg	G	AB	H	2B	3B	HR	(Hm	Rd)	TB	R	RBI	TBB	IBB	SO	HBP	SH	SF	SB	CS	SB%	GDP	Avg	OBP	SLG
1986 New York	NL	19	30	5	1	0	0	(0	0)	6	3	0	3	1	8	0	0	0	0	0	—	0	.167	.242	.200
1987 New York	NL	5	10	4	2	0	0	(0	0)	6	1	1	0	0	1	0	0	0	0	0	—	1	.400	.400	.600
1988 New York	NL	149	406	87	11	1	9	(6	3)	127	41	37	35	12	47	3	6	0	2	0	1.00	5	.214	.282	.313
1989 New York	NL	151	458	106	25	2	10	(5	5)	165	52	55	34	11	77	2	6	8	4	3	.57	13	.231	.283	.360
1990 New York	NL	92	314	65	20	1	9	(2	7)	114	36	45	30	2	54	1	1	6	2	0	1.00	4	.207	.274	.363
1991 New York	NL	115	348	84	16	2	6	(3	3)	122	33	36	40	6	53	1	1	4	2	3	.40	4	.241	.318	.351
1992 New York	NL	6	18	4	0	0	0	(0	0)	4	0	0	2	0	0	0	0	0	0	0	—	1	.222	.222	.222
1994 New York	AL	7	20	0	0	0	0	(0	0)	0	0	0	1	0	6	0	1	0	0	0	—	1	.000	.048	.000
1995 NYY-Phi		36	70	13	5	1	1	(0	0)	23	11	9	8	1	19	1	2	2	0	0	—	1	.186	.272	.329
1996 Texas	AL	157	515	130	32	2	24	(9	15)	238	79	99	52	1	138	2	16	11	4	1	.80	8	.252	.317	.462
1997 Pittsburgh	NL	39	138	31	6	2	7	(3	4)	62	14	25	21	0	39	1	2	2	0	2	.00	1	.225	.327	.449
1998 Texas	AL	84	297	69	10	1	8	(3	5)	105	33	37	33	0	66	2	2	2	0	2	.00	7	.232	.311	.354
2000 Los Angeles	NL	80	220	50	8	0	14	(7	7)	100	29	32	38	5	52	0	1	0	0	0	—	0	.227	.341	.455
1995 New York	AL	10	17	2	1	0	0	(0	0)	3	1	0	1	0	5	0	0	0	0	0	—	1	.118	.167	.176
Philadelphia	NL	26	53	11	4	1	1	(0	0)	20	10	9	7	1	14	1	2	2	0	0	—	1	.208	.302	.377
13 ML YEARS		940	2844	648	136	12	88	(39	49)	1072	332	376	295	39	562	13	38	35	14	11	.56	45	.228	.300	.377

Alan Embree

Pitches: Left **Bats:** Left **Pos:** RP-63   **Ht:** 6'2" **Wt:** 190 **Born:** 1/23/70 **Age:** 31

Year Team	Lg	G	GS	CG	GF	IP	BFP	H	R	ER	HR	SH	SF	HB	TBB	IBB	SO	WP	Bk	W	L	Pct.	ShO	Sv-Op	Hld	ERA
1992 Cleveland	AL	4	4	0	0	18	81	19	14	14	3	0	2	1	8	0	12	1	1	0	2	.000	0	0-0	0	7.00
1995 Cleveland	AL	23	0	0	8	24.2	111	23	16	14	2	2	2	0	16	0	23	1	0	3	2	.600	0	1-1	6	5.11
1996 Cleveland	AL	24	0	0	2	31	141	30	26	22	10	1	3	0	21	3	33	3	0	1	1	.500	0	0-0	1	6.39
1997 Atlanta	NL	66	0	0	15	46	190	36	13	13	1	4	1	2	20	2	45	3	1	3	1	.750	0	0-0	16	2.54
1998 Atl-Ari	NL	55	0	0	16	53.2	237	56	32	25	7	4	1	1	23	0	43	3	0	4	2	.667	0	1-3	12	4.19
1999 San Francisco	NL	68	0	0	13	58.2	244	42	22	22	6	3	2	3	26	2	53	3	0	3	2	.600	0	0-3	22	3.38
2000 San Francisco	NL	63	0	0	21	60	263	62	34	33	4	4	5	3	25	2	49	1	0	3	5	.375	0	2-5	9	4.95
1998 Atlanta	NL	20	0	0	5	18.2	87	23	14	9	2	1	1	0	10	0	19	0	0	1	0	1.000	0	0-1	6	4.34
Arizona	NL	35	0	0	11	35	150	33	18	16	5	3	0	1	13	0	24	3	0	3	2	.600	0	1-2	6	4.11
7 ML YEARS		303	4	0	75	292	1267	268	157	143	33	18	16	10	139	9	258	15	2	17	15	.531	0	4-12	66	4.41

Juan Encarnacion

Bats: Right **Throws:** Right **Pos:** CF-141   **Ht:** 6'3" **Wt:** 187 **Born:** 3/8/76 **Age:** 25

Year Team	Lg	G	AB	H	2B	3B	HR	(Hm	Rd)	TB	R	RBI	TBB	IBB	SO	HBP	SH	SF	SB	CS	SB%	GDP	Avg	OBP	SLG
1997 Detroit	AL	11	33	7	1	1	1	(1	0)	13	3	5	3	0	12	2	0	0	3	1	.75	1	.212	.316	.394
1998 Detroit	AL	40	164	54	9	4	7	(4	3)	92	30	21	7	0	31	1	0	3	7	4	.64	2	.329	.354	.561
1999 Detroit	AL	132	509	130	30	6	19	(6	13)	229	62	74	14	1	113	9	4	2	33	12	.73	12	.255	.287	.450
2000 Detroit	AL	141	547	158	25	6	14	(4	10)	237	75	72	29	1	90	7	3	4	16	4	.80	15	.289	.330	.433
4 ML YEARS		324	1253	349	65	17	41	(15	26)	571	170	172	53	2	246	19	7	9	59	21	.74	30	.279	.316	.456

Trevor Enders

Pitches: Left **Bats:** Right **Pos:** RP-9   **Ht:** 6'0" **Wt:** 214 **Born:** 12/22/74 **Age:** 26

Year Team	Lg	G	GS	CG	GF	IP	BFP	H	R	ER	HR	SH	SF	HB	TBB	IBB	SO	WP	Bk	W	L	Pct.	ShO	Sv-Op	Hld	ERA
1996 Butte	R+	19	0	0	6	27.2	132	34	22	15	1	2	2	2	13	1	24	2	0	0	1	.000	0	1--	—	4.88
1997 Chston-SC	A	44	0	0	24	67	271	55	18	14	2	2	1	2	17	3	73	2	1	4	3	.571	0	2--	—	1.88
1998 St. Pete	A+	51	0	0	16	68.2	267	48	20	17	4	2	2	3	15	3	61	5	0	10	1	.909	0	1--	—	2.23
1999 Orlando	AA	60	0	0	11	95.1	394	86	37	35	4	3	5	2	33	1	63	6	0	8	2	.800	0	1--	—	3.30
2000 Orlando	AA	29	5	0	8	67	264	63	26	24	7	0	1	1	11	0	41	5	3	6	3	.667	0	0--	—	3.22
Durham	AAA	15	0	0	5	26.2	104	22	8	8	3	1	0	1	6	0	16	2	0	1	0	.000	0	0--	—	2.70
2000 Tampa Bay	AL	9	0	0	4	9.1	46	14	13	11	2	2	0	0	5	0	5	0	0	0	0	.000	0	0-1	0	10.61

Morgan Ensberg

Bats: Right **Throws:** Right **Pos:** PH/PR-3; 3B-1 **Ht:** 6'2" **Wt:** 210 **Born:** 8/26/75 **Age:** 25

Year Team	Lg	G	AB	H	2B	3B	HR	(Hm	Rd)	TB	R	RBI	TBB	IBB	SO	HBP	SH	SF	SB	CS	SB%	GDP	Avg	OBP	SLG
1998 Auburn	A-	59	196	45	10	1	5	—	—	72	39	31	46	1	51	6	0	2	15	3	.83	5	.230	.388	.367
1999 Kissimmee	A+	123	427	102	25	2	15	—	—	176	72	69	68	0	90	9	1	3	17	6	.74	9	.239	.353	.412
2000 Round Rock	AA	137	483	145	34	0	28	—	—	263	95	90	92	3	107	8	3	6	9	12	.43	15	.300	.416	.545
2000 Houston	NL	4	7	2	0	0	0	(0	0)	2	0	0	0	0	1	0	0	0	0	0	—	0	.286	.286	.286

Todd Erdos

Pitches: Right **Bats:** Right **Pos:** RP-36 **Ht:** 6'1" **Wt:** 204 **Born:** 11/21/73 **Age:** 27

Year Team	Lg	G	GS	CG	GF	IP	BFP	H	R	ER	HR	SH	SF	HB	TBB	IBB	SO	WP	Bk	W	L	Pct.	ShO	Sv-Op	Hld	ERA
1997 San Diego	NL	11	0	0	2	13.2	64	17	9	8	1	0	0	2	4	0	13	3	0	2	0	1.000	0	0-0	0	5.27
1998 New York	AL	2	0	0	1	2	11	5	2	2	1	0	0	1	1	1	0	0	0	0	0	—	0	0-0	0	9.00
1999 New York	AL	4	0	0	1	7	31	5	4	3	2	0	1	0	4	0	4	1	0	0	0	—	0	0-0	0	3.86
2000 NYY-SD		36	0	0	14	54.2	260	63	38	36	7	1	4	7	28	1	34	2	0	0	0	—	0	2-3	1	5.93
2000 New York	AL	14	0	0	6	25	114	31	14	14	2	0	0	1	11	0	18	1	0	0	0	—	0	1-1	0	5.04
San Diego	NL	22	0	0	8	29.2	146	32	24	22	5	1	4	6	17	1	16	1	0	0	0	—	0	1-2	1	6.67
4 ML YEARS		53	0	0	18	77.1	366	90	53	49	10	1	5	9	37	2	51	6	0	2	0	1.000	0	2-3	1	5.70

Scott Erickson

Pitches: Right **Bats:** Right **Pos:** SP-16 **Ht:** 6'4" **Wt:** 230 **Born:** 2/2/68 **Age:** 33

Year Team	Lg	G	GS	CG	GF	IP	BFP	H	R	ER	HR	SH	SF	HB	TBB	IBB	SO	WP	Bk	W	L	Pct.	ShO	Sv-Op	Hld	ERA
2000 Frederick *	A+	1	1	0	0	6.2		3	2	2	0	0	0	0	1	0	5	0	0	0	0	—	0	0--	—	2.70
Bowie *	AA	1	1	0	0	7	25	4	0	0	0	0	0	0	0	0	5	1	0	0	0	—	0	0--	—	0.00
1990 Minnesota	AL	19	17	1	1	113	485	108	49	36	9	5	2	5	51	4	53	3	0	8	4	.667	0	0-0	0	2.87
1991 Minnesota	AL	32	32	5	0	204	851	189	80	72	13	5	7	6	71	3	108	4	0	20	8	.714	3	0-0	0	3.18
1992 Minnesota	AL	32	32	5	0	212	888	197	86	80	18	9	7	8	83	3	101	6	1	13	12	.520	3	0-0	0	3.40
1993 Minnesota	AL	34	34	1	0	218.2	976	266	138	126	17	10	13	10	71	1	116	5	0	8	19	.296	0	0-0	0	5.19
1994 Minnesota	AL	23	23	2	0	144	654	173	95	87	15	3	4	9	59	0	104	10	0	8	11	.421	1	0-0	0	5.44
1995 Min-Bal	AL	32	31	7	1	196.1	836	213	108	105	18	3	3	5	67	0	106	3	2	13	10	.565	2	0-0	0	4.81
1996 Baltimore	AL	34	34	6	0	222.1	968	262	137	124	21	5	5	11	66	4	100	1	0	13	12	.520	0	0-0	0	5.02
1997 Baltimore	AL	34	33	3	0	221.2	922	218	100	91	16	3	4	5	61	5	131	11	0	16	7	.696	2	0-0	0	3.69
1998 Baltimore	AL	36	36	11	0	251.1	1102	284	125	112	23	7	2	13	69	4	186	4	0	16	13	.552	2	0-0	0	4.01
1999 Baltimore	AL	34	34	6	0	230.1	995	244	127	123	27	7	6	11	99	4	106	10	0	15	12	.556	3	0-0	0	4.81
2000 Baltimore	AL	16	16	1	0	92.2	446	127	81	81	14	3	5	5	48	0	41	3	0	5	8	.385	0	0-0	0	7.87
1995 Minnesota	AL	15	15	0	0	87.2	390	102	61	58	11	2	1	4	32	0	45	1	0	4	6	.400	0	0-0	0	5.95
Baltimore	AL	17	16	7	1	108.2	446	111	47	47	7	1	2	1	35	0	61	2	2	9	4	.692	2	0-0	0	3.89
11 ML YEARS		326	322	48	2	2106.1	9123	2281	1126	1037	191	60	58	88	745	28	1152	60	3	135	116	.538	16	0-0	0	4.43

Darin Erstad

Bats: L **Throws:** L **Pos:** LF-112; CF-30; DH-20; 1B-3; PH/PR-1 **Ht:** 6'2" **Wt:** 212 **Born:** 6/4/74 **Age:** 27

Year Team	Lg	G	AB	H	2B	3B	HR	(Hm	Rd)	TB	R	RBI	TBB	IBB	SO	HBP	SH	SF	SB	CS	SB%	GDP	Avg	OBP	SLG
1996 California	AL	57	208	59	5	1	4	(1	3)	78	34	20	17	1	29	0	1	3	3	3	.50	3	.284	.333	.375
1997 Anaheim	AL	139	539	161	34	4	16	(8	8)	251	99	77	51	4	86	4	5	6	23	8	.74	5	.299	.360	.466
1998 Anaheim	AL	133	537	159	39	4	19	(9	10)	261	84	82	43	7	77	6	1	3	20	6	.77	2	.296	.353	.486
1999 Anaheim	AL	142	585	148	22	5	13	(7	6)	219	84	53	47	3	101	1	2	3	13	7	.65	16	.253	.308	.374
2000 Anaheim	AL	157	676	240	39	6	25	(11	14)	366	121	100	64	9	82	1	2	4	28	8	.78	6	.355	.409	.541
5 ML YEARS		628	2545	767	139	19	77	(36	41)	1175	422	332	222	24	375	12	11	19	87	32	.73	34	.301	.358	.462

Kelvim Escobar

Pitches: Right **Bats:** Right **Pos:** SP-24; RP-19 **Ht:** 6'1" **Wt:** 210 **Born:** 4/11/76 **Age:** 25

Year Team	Lg	G	GS	CG	GF	IP	BFP	H	R	ER	HR	SH	SF	HB	TBB	IBB	SO	WP	Bk	W	L	Pct.	ShO	Sv-Op	Hld	ERA
1997 Toronto	AL	27	0	0	23	31	139	28	12	10	1	2	0	0	19	2	36	0	0	3	2	.600	0	14-17	1	2.90
1998 Toronto	AL	22	10	0	2	79.2	342	72	37	33	5	0	3	0	35	0	72	0	0	7	3	.700	0	0-1	5	3.73
1999 Toronto	AL	33	30	1	2	174	795	203	130	110	19	2	8	10	81	2	129	6	1	14	11	.560	0	0-0	0	5.69
2000 Toronto	AL	43	24	3	8	180	794	186	118	107	26	5	4	3	85	3	142	4	0	10	15	.400	1	2-3	3	5.35
4 ML YEARS		125	64	4	35	464.2	2070	489	285	260	51	9	15	13	220	7	379	10	1	34	31	.523	1	16-21	9	5.04

Bobby Estalella

Bats: Right **Throws:** Right **Pos:** C-106; PH/PR-2 **Ht:** 6'1" **Wt:** 205 **Born:** 8/23/74 **Age:** 26

Year Team	Lg	G	AB	H	2B	3B	HR	(Hm	Rd)	TB	R	RBI	TBB	IBB	SO	HBP	SH	SF	SB	CS	SB%	GDP	Avg	OBP	SLG
1996 Philadelphia	NL	7	17	6	0	0	2	(0	2)	12	5	4	1	0	6	0	0	0	1	0	1.00	0	.353	.389	.706
1997 Philadelphia	NL	13	29	10	1	0	4	(1	3)	23	9	9	7	0	7	0	0	0	0	0	—	2	.345	.472	.793
1998 Philadelphia	NL	47	165	31	6	1	8	(3	5)	63	16	20	13	0	49	1	0	3	0	0	—	4	.188	.247	.382
1999 Philadelphia	NL	9	18	3	0	0	0	(0	0)	3	2	1	4	0	7	0	0	0	0	1	.00	0	.167	.318	.167
2000 San Francisco	NL	106	299	70	22	3	14	(6	8)	140	45	53	57	9	92	2	0	3	3	0	1.00	4	.234	.357	.468
5 ML YEARS		182	528	120	29	4	28	(10	18)	241	77	87	82	9	161	3	0	6	4	1	.80	10	.227	.331	.456

Shawn Estes

Pitches: Left **Bats:** Right **Pos:** SP-30 **Ht:** 6'2" **Wt:** 195 **Born:** 2/18/73 **Age:** 28

Year Team	Lg	G	GS	CG	GF	IP	BFP	H	R	ER	HR	SH	SF	HB	TBB	IBB	SO	WP	Bk	W	L	Pct.	ShO	Sv-Op	Hld	ERA
2000 Fresno *	AAA	1	1	0	0	3	19	5	9	3	2	0	0	0	2	0	2	0	0	0	1	.000	0	0- -	—	9.00
San Jose *	A+	1	1	0	0	7	23	2	0	0	0	0	0	1	1	0	11	1	0	1	0	1.000	0	0- -	—	0.00
1995 San Francisco	NL	3	3	0	0	17.1	76	16	14	13	2	0	0	1	5	0	14	4	0	0	3	.000	0	0-0	—	6.75
1996 San Francisco	NL	11	11	0	0	70	305	63	30	28	3	5	0	2	39	3	60	4	0	3	5	.375	0	0-0	—	3.60
1997 San Francisco	NL	32	32	3	0	201	849	162	80	71	12	13	2	8	100	2	181	10	2	19	5	.792	2	0-0	—	3.18
1998 San Francisco	NL	25	25	1	0	149.1	661	150	89	84	14	15	4	5	80	6	136	6	1	7	12	.368	1	0-0	—	5.06
1999 San Francisco	NL	32	32	1	0	203	914	209	121	111	21	14	3	5	112	2	159	15	1	11	11	.500	1	0-0	—	4.92
2000 San Francisco	NL	30	30	4	0	190.1	829	194	99	90	11	7	6	3	108	1	136	11	0	15	6	.714	2	0-0	—	4.26
6 ML YEARS		133	133	9	0	831	3634	794	433	397	63	54	15	24	444	14	686	50	4	55	42	.567	6	0-0	—	4.30

Horacio Estrada

Pitches: Left **Bats:** Left **Pos:** SP-4; RP-3 **Ht:** 6'0" **Wt:** 160 **Born:** 10/19/75 **Age:** 25

Year Team	Lg	G	GS	CG	GF	IP	BFP	H	R	ER	HR	SH	SF	HB	TBB	IBB	SO	WP	Bk	W	L	Pct.	ShO	Sv-Op	Hld	ERA
1992 Brewers	R	12	4	0	3	31	158	40	37	34	2	3	1	7	19	1	16	3	0	0	4	.000	0	0- -	—	9.87
1995 Brewers	R	8	1	0	3	17	73	13	9	7	1	1	1	0	8	0	21	4	2	1	0	1.000	0	2- -	—	3.71
Helena	R+	13	0	0	1	30	144	27	21	18	3	5	0	3	24	0	30	2	0	1	2	.333	0	0- -	—	5.40
1996 Beloit	A	17	0	0	9	29.1	113	21	8	4	2	2	0	0	11	1	34	5	1	2	1	.667	0	1- -	—	1.23
Stockton	A+	29	0	0	11	51	214	43	29	26	7	1	1	2	21	2	62	3	0	1	3	.250	0	4- -	—	4.59
1997 El Paso	AA	29	23	1	2	153.2	694	174	93	81	11	4	4	4	70	0	127	8	3	8	10	.444	0	1- -	—	4.74
1998 El Paso	AA	8	8	0	0	49.2	206	50	27	25	3	6	2	2	21	0	37	4	1	5	0	1.000	0	0- -	—	4.53
Louisville	AAA	2	2	0	0	12	50	10	4	4	1	0	0	0	5	0	4	0	0	0	0	—	0	0- -	—	3.00
1999 Louisville	AAA	25	24	1	0	131.2	575	128	87	83	21	3	8	9	65	1	112	8	1	6	6	.500	0	0- -	—	5.67
2000 Indianapolis	AAA	25	25	3	0	159.1	663	149	63	59	14	7	2	7	45	0	103	9	0	14	4	.778	2	0- -	—	3.33
1999 Milwaukee	NL	4	0	0	2	7.1	36	10	6	6	4	0	0	0	4	0	5	0	0	0	0	—	0	0-0	—	7.36
2000 Milwaukee	NL	7	4	0	2	24.1	123	30	18	17	5	0	1	2	20	4	13	3	0	3	0	1.000	0	0-0	—	6.29
2 ML YEARS		11	4	0	4	31.2	159	40	24	23	9	0	1	2	24	4	18	3	0	3	0	1.000	0	0-0	—	6.54

Leo Estrella

Pitches: Right **Bats:** Right **Pos:** RP-2 **Ht:** 6'1" **Wt:** 172 **Born:** 2/20/75 **Age:** 26

Year Team	Lg	G	GS	CG	GF	IP	BFP	H	R	ER	HR	SH	SF	HB	TBB	IBB	SO	WP	Bk	W	L	Pct.	ShO	Sv-Op	Hld	ERA
1996 Kingsport	R+	15	7	1	3	58	248	54	32	25	3	4	1	1	24	0	52	6	2	6	3	.667	0	0- -	—	3.88
1997 Pittsfield	A-	15	15	0	0	92	395	91	48	31	0	2	1	3	27	0	55	3	2	7	6	.538	0	0- -	—	3.03
1998 Capital Cty	A	20	20	3	0	119	502	120	66	52	10	7	3	8	23	0	97	1	1	10	8	.556	0	0- -	—	3.93
Hagerstown	A	5	5	0	0	30	130	34	19	15	0	2	3	3	13	1	27	2	1	1	3	.250	0	0- -	—	4.50
1999 Dunedin	A+	27	24	2	0	168	696	166	74	60	11	6	5	17	47	0	116	6	1	14	7	.667	2	0- -	—	3.21
2000 Tennessee	AA	13	13	3	0	76	324	68	36	31	6	4	3	10	30	1	63	2	0	5	5	.500	2	0- -	—	3.67
Syracuse	AAA	15	15	3	0	89.2	364	68	42	40	8	1	4	2	40	0	48	2	1	5	4	.556	1	0- -	—	4.01
2000 Toronto	AL	2	0	0	1	4.2	21	9	3	3	1	0	1	0	0	0	3	0	0	0	0	—	0	0-0	0	5.79

Seth Etherton

Pitches: Right **Bats:** Right **Pos:** SP-11 **Ht:** 6'1" **Wt:** 200 **Born:** 10/17/76 **Age:** 24

Year Team	Lg	G	GS	CG	GF	IP	BFP	H	R	ER	HR	SH	SF	HB	TBB	IBB	SO	WP	Bk	W	L	Pct.	ShO	Sv-Op	Hld	ERA
1998 Midland	AA	9	7	1	0	48.1	211	57	36	33	9	3	2	1	12	0	35	1	1	1	5	.167	0	0- -	—	6.14
1999 Erie	AA	24	24	4	0	167.2	694	153	72	61	14	7	5	3	43	0	153	4	4	10	10	.500	1	0- -	—	3.27
Edmonton	AAA	4	4	0	0	21.1	94	25	13	13	7	1	1	0	6	0	19	1	0	2	0	1.000	0	0- -	—	5.48
2000 Edmonton	AAA	9	9	0	0	58.1	248	60	30	26	6	0	1	1	19	0	50	3	0	3	2	.600	0	0- -	—	4.01
2000 Anaheim	AL	11	11	0	0	60.1	270	68	38	37	16	1	1	1	22	0	32	2	0	5	1	.833	0	0-0	0	5.52

Tony Eusebio

Bats: Right **Throws:** Right **Pos:** C-68; PH/PR-7 **Ht:** 6'2" **Wt:** 210 **Born:** 4/27/67 **Age:** 34

Year Team	Lg	G	AB	H	2B	3B	HR	(Hm	Rd)	TB	R	RBI	TBB	IBB	SO	HBP	SH	SF	SB	CS	SB%	GDP	Avg	OBP	SLG
1991 Houston	NL	10	19	2	1	0	0	(0	0)	3	4	0	6	0	8	0	0	0	0	0	—	1	.105	.320	.158
1994 Houston	NL	55	159	47	9	1	5	(1	4)	73	18	30	8	0	33	0	2	5	0	1	.00	4	.296	.320	.459
1995 Houston	NL	113	368	110	21	1	6	(5	1)	151	46	58	31	1	59	3	1	5	0	2	.00	12	.299	.354	.410
1996 Houston	NL	58	152	41	7	2	1	(1	0)	55	15	19	18	2	20	0	0	2	0	1	.00	5	.270	.343	.362
1997 Houston	NL	60	164	45	2	0	1	(0	1)	50	12	18	19	1	27	4	0	0	0	1	.00	4	.274	.364	.305
1998 Houston	NL	66	182	46	6	1	1	(1	0)	57	13	36	18	2	31	1	0	2	0	1	1.00	8	.253	.320	.313
1999 Houston	NL	103	323	88	15	0	4	(2	2)	115	31	33	40	4	67	0	0	9	0	0	—	9	.272	.353	.356
2000 Houston	NL	74	218	61	18	0	7	(2	5)	100	24	33	25	2	45	4	0	2	0	0	—	8	.280	.361	.459
8 ML YEARS		539	1585	440	79	5	25	(12	13)	604	163	227	165	12	290	12	3	16	1	5	.17	51	.278	.347	.381

Tom Evans

Bats: R **Throws:** R **Pos:** 3B-21; PH/PR-3; DH-1; 1B-1 **Ht:** 6'1" **Wt:** 180 **Born:** 7/9/74 **Age:** 26

Year Team	Lg	G	AB	H	2B	3B	HR	(Hm	Rd)	TB	R	RBI	TBB	IBB	SO	HBP	SH	SF	SB	CS	SB%	GDP	Avg	OBP	SLG
1992 Medcine Hat	R+	52	166	36	3	0	1	—	—	42	17	21	33	0	29	1	1	1	4	3	.57	4	.217	.348	.253
1993 Hagerstown	A	119	389	100	25	1	7	—	—	148	47	54	53	2	61	3	0	4	9	2	.82	7	.257	.347	.380
1994 Hagerstown	A	95	322	88	16	2	13	—	—	147	52	48	51	1	80	1	1	1	2	1	.67	3	.273	.373	.457
1995 Dunedin	A+	130	444	124	29	3	9	—	—	186	63	66	51	0	80	8	3	7	7	2	.78	10	.279	.359	.419
1996 Knoxville	AA	120	394	111	27	1	17	—	—	191	87	65	115	0	113	9	0	5	2	0	1.00	7	.282	.452	.485
1997 Dunedin	A+	15	42	11	2	0	2	—	—	19	8	4	11	0	10	4	0	1	0	0	—	0	.262	.448	.452
Syracuse	AAA	107	376	99	17	1	15	—	—	163	60	65	53	1	104	9	1	3	1	2	.33	4	.263	.365	.434

Year Team	Lg	G	AB	H	2B	3B	HR	(Hm	Rd)	TB	R	RBI	TBB	IBB	SO	HBP	SH	SF	SB	CS	SB%	GDP	Avg	OBP	SLG
1998 Syracuse	AAA	109	400	120	32	1	15	—	—	199	57	55	50	1	74	8	0	1	11	7	.61	13	.300	.388	.498
1999 Oklahoma	AAA	128	439	123	35	3	12	—	—	200	84	68	66	1	100	9	1	1	5	4	.56	10	.280	.384	.456
1997 Toronto	AL	12	38	11	2	0	1	(1	0)	16	7	2	2	0	10	1	0	0	0	1	1.00	0	.289	.341	.421
1998 Toronto	AL	7	10	0	0	0	0	(0	0)	0	0	0	1	0	2	0	0	0	0	0	—	0	.000	.091	.000
2000 Texas	AL	23	54	15	4	0	0	(0	0)	19	10	5	10	0	13	1	1	1	0	3	.00	1	.278	.394	.352
3 ML YEARS		42	102	26	6	0	1	(1	0)	35	17	7	13	0	25	2	1	1	0	4	.00	2	.255	.347	.343

Carl Everett

Bats: Both **Throws:** Right **Pos:** CF-126; PH/PR-10; DH-5   **Ht:** 6'0" **Wt:** 215 **Born:** 6/3/71 **Age:** 30

Year Team	Lg	G	AB	H	2B	3B	HR	(Hm	Rd)	TB	R	RBI	TBB	IBB	SO	HBP	SH	SF	SB	CS	SB%	GDP	Avg	OBP	SLG
1993 Florida	NL	11	19	2	0	0	0	(0	0)	2	0	0	1	0	9	0	0	0	1	0	1.00	0	.105	.150	.105
1994 Florida	NL	16	51	11	1	0	2	(2	0)	18	7	6	3	0	15	0	0	0	4	0	1.00	0	.216	.259	.353
1995 New York	NL	79	289	75	13	1	12	(9	3)	126	48	54	39	2	67	2	1	0	2	5	.29	11	.260	.352	.436
1996 New York	NL	101	192	46	8	1	1	(1	0)	59	29	16	21	2	53	4	1	1	6	0	1.00	4	.240	.326	.307
1997 New York	NL	142	443	110	28	3	14	(11	3)	186	58	57	32	3	102	7	3	2	17	9	.65	3	.248	.308	.420
1998 Houston	NL	133	467	138	34	4	15	(5	10)	225	72	76	44	2	102	3	3	2	14	12	.54	11	.296	.359	.482
1999 Houston	NL	123	464	151	33	3	25	(11	14)	265	86	108	50	5	94	11	2	8	27	7	.79	5	.325	.398	.571
2000 Boston	AL	137	496	149	32	4	34	(17	17)	291	82	108	52	5	113	8	0	5	11	4	.73	4	.300	.373	.587
8 ML YEARS		742	2421	682	149	16	103	(56	47)	1172	382	425	242	19	555	35	10	18	82	37	.69	38	.282	.353	.484

Scott Eyre

Pitches: Left **Bats:** Left **Pos:** RP-12; SP-1   **Ht:** 6'1" **Wt:** 200 **Born:** 5/30/72 **Age:** 29

Year Team	Lg	G	GS	CG	GF	IP	BFP	H	R	ER	HR	SH	SF	HB	TBB	IBB	SO	WP	Bk	W	L	Pct.	ShO	Sv-Op	Hld	ERA
2000 Charlotte *	AAA	47	0	0	26	48	191	33	18	16	1	6	0	0	20	3	46	2	0	3	2	.600	0	12--	—	3.00
1997 Chicago	AL	11	11	0	0	60.2	267	62	36	34	11	1	2	1	31	1	36	2	0	4	4	.500	0	0-0	0	5.04
1998 Chicago	AL	33	17	0	10	107	491	114	78	64	24	2	3	2	64	0	73	7	0	3	8	.273	0	0-0	0	5.38
1999 Chicago	AL	21	0	0	8	25	129	38	22	21	6	0	1	1	15	2	17	1	0	1	1	.500	0	0-0	1	7.56
2000 Chicago	AL	13	1	0	3	19	93	29	15	14	3	0	2	1	12	0	16	0	0	1	1	.500	0	0-0	0	6.63
4 ML YEARS		78	29	0	21	211.2	980	243	151	133	44	3	8	5	122	3	142	10	0	9	14	.391	0	0-0	1	5.66

Jorge Fabregas

Bats: Left **Throws:** Right **Pos:** C-39; PH/PR-4; DH-1   **Ht:** 6'3" **Wt:** 215 **Born:** 3/13/70 **Age:** 31

Year Team	Lg	G	AB	H	2B	3B	HR	(Hm	Rd)	TB	R	RBI	TBB	IBB	SO	HBP	SH	SF	SB	CS	SB%	GDP	Avg	OBP	SLG
2000 Omaha *	AAA	37	129	32	5	1	1	—	—	42	8	18	12	1	9	0	0	1	1	1	.50	5	.248	.310	.326
1994 California	AL	43	127	36	3	0	0	(0	0)	39	12	16	7	1	18	0	1	0	2	1	.67	5	.283	.321	.307
1995 California	AL	73	227	56	10	0	1	(1	0)	69	24	22	17	0	28	0	3	1	0	2	.00	9	.247	.298	.304
1996 California	AL	90	254	73	6	0	2	(1	1)	85	18	26	17	3	27	0	3	5	0	1	.00	7	.287	.326	.335
1997 Ana-CWS	AL	121	360	93	11	1	7	(1	6)	127	33	51	14	0	46	1	6	4	1	1	.50	16	.258	.285	.353
1998 Ari-NYM	NL	70	183	36	4	0	2	(0	2)	46	11	20	14	1	32	1	1	2	0	0	—	4	.197	.255	.251
1999 Fla-Atl	NL	88	231	46	10	2	3	(1	2)	69	20	21	26	4	27	2	4	5	0	0	—	7	.199	.280	.299
2000 Kansas City	AL	43	142	40	4	0	3	(2	1)	53	13	17	8	1	11	0	2	0	1	0	1.00	1	.282	.320	.373
1997 Anaheim	AL	21	38	3	1	0	0	(0	0)	4	2	3	3	0	3	0	2	0	0	0	—	2	.079	.146	.105
Chicago	AL	100	322	90	10	1	7	(1	6)	123	31	48	11	0	43	1	4	4	1	1	.50	14	.280	.302	.382
1998 Arizona	AL	50	151	30	4	0	1	(0	1)	37	8	15	13	1	26	1	0	2	0	0	—	3	.199	.263	.245
New York	NL	20	32	6	0	0	1	(0	1)	9	3	5	1	0	6	0	1	0	0	0	—	1	.188	.212	.281
1999 Florida	NL	82	223	46	10	2	3	(1	2)	69	20	21	26	6	27	2	4	5	0	0	—	7	.206	.289	.309
Atlanta	NL	6	8	0	0	0	0	(0	0)	0	0	0	0	0	0	0	0	0	0	0	—	0	.000	.000	.000
7 ML YEARS		528	1524	380	48	3	18	(6	12)	488	131	173	103	12	189	4	20	17	4	5	.44	51	.249	.296	.320

Kyle Farnsworth

Pitches: Right **Bats:** Right **Pos:** RP-41; SP-5   **Ht:** 6'4" **Wt:** 215 **Born:** 4/14/76 **Age:** 25

Year Team	Lg	G	GS	CG	GF	IP	BFP	H	R	ER	HR	SH	SF	HB	TBB	IBB	SO	WP	Bk	W	L	Pct.	ShO	Sv-Op	Hld	ERA
1995 Cubs	R	16	0	0	6	31	120	22	8	3	0	4	2	0	11	0	18	1	1	3	2	.600	0	1--	—	0.87
1996 Rockford	A	20	20	1	0	112	495	122	62	46	7	2	4	9	35	0	82	8	1	9	6	.600	0	0--	—	3.70
1997 Daytona	A+	27	27	2	0	156.1	684	178	91	71	13	6	2	6	47	1	105	5	1	10	10	.500	0	0--	—	4.09
1998 West Tenn	AA	13	13	0	0	81.1	330	70	32	25	6	2	3	1	21	0	73	2	2	8	2	.800	0	0--	—	2.77
Iowa	AAA	18	18	0	0	102.2	469	129	88	79	18	5	7	2	36	0	79	4	1	5	9	.357	0	0--	—	6.93
1999 Iowa	AAA	6	6	0	0	39.1	157	38	16	14	5	3	0	0	9	0	29	1	0	2	2	.500	0	0--	—	3.20
2000 Iowa	AAA	22	0	0	22	25.1	115	24	10	9	1	0	1	0	18	2	22	4	1	0	2	.000	0	9--	—	3.20
1999 Chicago	NL	27	21	1	1	130	579	140	80	73	28	6	2	3	52	1	70	7	1	5	9	.357	1	0-0	0	5.05
2000 Chicago	NL	46	5	0	8	77	371	90	58	55	14	4	4	4	50	8	74	3	0	2	9	.182	0	1-6	6	6.43
2 ML YEARS		73	26	1	9	207	950	230	138	128	42	10	6	7	102	9	144	10	1	7	18	.280	1	1-6	6	5.57

Sal Fasano

Bats: Right **Throws:** Right **Pos:** C-52; PH/PR-1   **Ht:** 6'2" **Wt:** 230 **Born:** 8/10/71 **Age:** 29

Year Team	Lg	G	AB	H	2B	3B	HR	(Hm	Rd)	TB	R	RBI	TBB	IBB	SO	HBP	SH	SF	SB	CS	SB%	GDP	Avg	OBP	SLG
1996 Kansas City	AL	51	143	29	2	0	6	(1	5)	49	20	19	14	0	25	2	1	0	1	1	.50	3	.203	.283	.343
1997 Kansas City	AL	13	38	8	2	0	1	(0	1)	13	4	1	1	0	12	0	0	0	0	0	—	1	.211	.231	.342
1998 Kansas City	AL	74	216	49	10	0	8	(4	4)	83	21	31	10	1	56	16	3	2	1	0	1.00	4	.227	.307	.384
1999 Kansas City	AL	23	60	14	2	0	5	(2	3)	31	11	16	7	0	17	7	0	1	0	1	.00	1	.233	.373	.517
2000 Oakland	AL	52	126	27	6	0	7	(4	3)	54	21	19	14	0	47	3	0	1	0	0	—	3	.214	.306	.429
5 ML YEARS		213	583	127	22	0	27	(11	16)	230	77	86	46	1	157	28	4	4	2	2	.50	12	.218	.304	.395

Jeff Fassero

Pitches: Left Bats: Left Pos: SP-23; RP-15   Ht: 6'1" Wt: 195 Born: 1/5/63 Age: 38

Year Team	Lg	G	GS	CG	GF	IP	BFP	H	R	ER	HR	SH	SF	HB	TBB	IBB	SO	WP	Bk	W	L	Pct.	ShO	Sv-Op	Hld	ERA
1991 Montreal	NL	51	0	0	30	55.1	223	39	17	15	1	6	0	1	17	1	42	4	0	2	5	.286	0	8-11	7	2.44
1992 Montreal	NL	70	0	0	22	85.2	368	81	35	27	1	5	2	2	34	6	63	7	1	8	7	.533	0	1-7	12	2.84
1993 Montreal	NL	56	15	1	10	149.2	616	119	50	38	7	7	4	0	54	0	140	5	0	12	5	.706	0	1-3	6	2.29
1994 Montreal	NL	21	21	1	0	138.2	569	119	54	46	13	7	2	1	40	4	119	6	0	8	6	.571	0	0-0	0	2.99
1995 Montreal	NL	30	30	1	0	189	833	207	102	91	15	19	7	2	74	3	164	7	1	13	14	.481	0	0-0	0	4.33
1996 Montreal	NL	34	34	5	0	231.2	967	217	95	85	20	16	5	3	55	3	222	5	2	15	11	.577	1	0-0	0	3.30
1997 Seattle	AL	35	35	2	0	234.1	1010	226	108	94	21	7	10	3	84	6	189	13	2	16	9	.640	1	0-0	0	3.61
1998 Seattle	AL	32	32	7	0	224.2	954	223	115	99	33	8	8	10	66	2	176	12	0	13	12	.520	0	0-0	0	3.97
1999 Sea-Tex	AL	37	27	0	2	156.1	751	208	135	125	35	2	7	4	83	3	114	9	0	5	14	.263	0	0-0	2	7.20
2000 Boston	AL	38	23	0	4	130	577	153	72	69	16	7	2	1	50	2	97	2	0	4	8	.500	0	0-0	5	4.78
1999 Seattle	AL	30	24	0	1	139	669	188	123	114	34	1	6	4	73	3	101	7	0	4	14	.222	0	0-0	0	7.38
Texas	AL	7	3	0	1	17.1	82	20	12	11	1	1	1	0	10	0	13	2	0	1	0	1.000	0	0-0	0	5.71
10 ML YEARS		404	217	17	68	1595.1	6868	1592	783	689	162	84	47	27	557	30	1326	70	6	100	91	.524	2	10-21	32	3.89

Carlos Febles

Bats: Right Throws: Right Pos: 2B-99; PH/PR-3   Ht: 5'11" Wt: 185 Born: 5/24/76 Age: 25

Year Team	Lg	G	AB	H	2B	3B	HR	(Hm	Rd)	TB	R	RBI	TBB	IBB	SO	HBP	SH	SF	SB	CS	SB%	GDP	Avg	OBP	SLG
2000 Royals *	R	1	3	1	1	0	0	—	—	2	0	0	1	0	0	0	0	0	1	0	1.00	0	.333	.500	.667
Wichita *	AA	4	15	2	0	0	0	—	—	2	2	1	2	0	4	1	0	1	2	0	1.00	0	.133	.263	.133
Omaha *	AAA	11	42	9	4	0	1	—	—	16	6	5	7	0	10	1	0	0	3	3	.50	2	.214	.340	.381
1998 Kansas City	AL	11	25	10	1	2	0	(0	0)	15	5	2	4	0	7	0	0	0	2	1	.67	0	.400	.483	.600
1999 Kansas City	AL	123	453	116	22	9	10	(5	5)	186	71	53	47	0	91	9	12	3	20	4	.83	16	.256	.336	.411
2000 Kansas City	AL	100	339	87	12	1	2	(2	0)	107	59	29	36	1	48	10	13	1	17	6	.74	10	.257	.345	.316
3 ML YEARS		234	817	213	35	12	12	(7	5)	308	135	84	87	1	146	19	25	4	39	11	.78	26	.261	.344	.377

Pedro Feliz

Bats: Right Throws: Right Pos: 3B-4; PH/PR-4   Ht: 6'1" Wt: 180 Born: 4/27/77 Age: 24

Year Team	Lg	G	AB	H	2B	3B	HR	(Hm	Rd)	TB	R	RBI	TBB	IBB	SO	HBP	SH	SF	SB	CS	SB%	GDP	Avg	OBP	SLG
1994 Giants	R	38	119	23	0	0	0	—	—	23	7	3	2	0	20	2	3	0	2	3	.40	3	.193	.220	.193
1995 Bellingham	A-	43	113	31	2	1	0	—	—	35	14	16	7	0	33	0	2	2	1	1	.50	2	.274	.311	.310
1996 Burlington	A	93	321	85	12	2	5	—	—	116	36	36	18	0	65	1	0	3	5	2	.71	11	.265	.303	.361
1997 Bakersfield	A+	135	515	140	25	4	14	—	—	215	59	56	23	0	90	7	3	3	5	7	.42	15	.272	.310	.417
1998 Shreveport	AA	100	364	96	23	2	12	—	—	159	39	50	9	0	62	2	0	4	0	1	.00	15	.264	.282	.437
Fresno	AAA	3	7	3	1	0	1	—	—	7	1	3	1	0	0	0	0	0	0	0	—	0	.429	.500	1.000
1999 Shreveport	AA	131	491	124	24	6	13	—	—	199	52	77	19	0	90	3	1	5	4	2	.67	18	.253	.282	.405
2000 Fresno	AAA	128	503	150	34	2	33	—	—	287	85	105	30	4	94	2	2	5	1	1	.50	18	.298	.337	.571
2000 San Francisco	NL	8	7	2	0	0	0	(0	0)	2	1	0	0	0	0	0	0	0	0	0	—	0	.286	.286	.286

Alex Fernandez

Pitches: Right Bats: Right Pos: SP-8   Ht: 6'1" Wt: 225 Born: 8/13/69 Age: 31

Year Team	Lg	G	GS	CG	GF	IP	BFP	H	R	ER	HR	SH	SF	HB	TBB	IBB	SO	WP	Bk	W	L	Pct.	ShO	Sv-Op	Hld	ERA
1990 Chicago	AL	13	13	3	0	87.2	378	89	46	37	6	5	3	0	34	0	61	1	0	5	5	.500	0	0-0	0	3.80
1991 Chicago	AL	34	32	3	0	191.2	827	186	100	96	16	7	11	2	88	2	145	4	1	9	13	.409	0	0-0	1	4.51
1992 Chicago	AL	29	29	4	0	187.2	804	199	100	89	21	6	4	8	50	3	95	3	0	8	11	.421	2	0-0	0	4.27
1993 Chicago	AL	34	34	3	0	247.1	1004	221	95	86	27	9	3	6	67	5	169	8	0	18	9	.667	1	0-0	0	3.13
1994 Chicago	AL	24	24	4	0	170.1	712	163	83	73	25	4	6	1	50	4	122	3	1	11	7	.611	3	0-0	0	3.86
1995 Chicago	AL	30	30	5	0	203.2	858	200	98	86	19	4	6	0	65	7	159	3	0	12	8	.600	2	0-0	0	3.80
1996 Chicago	AL	35	35	6	0	258	1071	248	110	99	34	5	7	7	72	4	200	5	0	16	10	.615	1	0-0	0	3.45
1997 Florida	NL	32	32	5	0	220.2	904	193	93	88	25	14	5	4	69	2	183	9	0	17	12	.586	1	0-0	0	3.59
1999 Florida	NL	24	24	1	0	141	590	135	60	53	10	3	6	4	41	1	91	2	0	7	8	.467	0	0-0	0	3.38
2000 Florida	NL	8	8	0	0	52.1	222	59	25	24	7	3	1	0	16	1	25	2	0	4	4	.500	0	0-0	0	4.13
10 ML YEARS		263	261	33	1	1760.1	7370	1693	804	731	190	60	49	35	552	29	1252	38	2	107	87	.552	10	0-0	1	3.74

Osvaldo Fernandez

Pitches: Right Bats: Right Pos: SP-14; RP-1   Ht: 6'2" Wt: 193 Born: 11/4/68 Age: 32

Year Team	Lg	G	GS	CG	GF	IP	BFP	H	R	ER	HR	SH	SF	HB	TBB	IBB	SO	WP	Bk	W	L	Pct.	ShO	Sv-Op	Hld	ERA
2000 Chattanooga *	AA	1	1	0	0	5.2	30	11	9	8	2	2	0	0	3	1	1	0	0	0	0	—	0	0--	—	12.71
Louisville *	AAA	10	10	0	0	56.2	243	57	27	26	3	3	0	0	19	0	44	2	0	6	1	.857	0	0--	—	4.13
1996 San Francisco	NL	30	28	2	1	171.2	760	193	95	88	20	12	5	10	57	4	106	6	2	7	13	.350	0	0-0	0	4.61
1997 San Francisco	NL	11	11	0	0	56.1	256	74	39	31	9	4	1	0	15	2	31	2	1	3	4	.429	0	0-0	0	4.95
2000 Cincinnati	NL	15	14	1	0	79.2	327	69	33	32	6	1	3	2	31	2	36	1	1	4	3	.571	0	0-0	0	3.62
3 ML YEARS		56	53	3	1	307.2	1343	336	167	151	35	17	9	12	103	8	173	9	4	14	20	.412	0	0-0	0	4.42

Mike Fetters

Pitches: Right Bats: Right Pos: RP-51   Ht: 6'4" Wt: 226 Born: 12/19/64 Age: 36

Year Team	Lg	G	GS	CG	GF	IP	BFP	H	R	ER	HR	SH	SF	HB	TBB	IBB	SO	WP	Bk	W	L	Pct.	ShO	Sv-Op	Hld	ERA
1989 California	AL	1	0	0	0	3.1	16	5	4	3	1	0	0	0	1	0	4	2	0	0	0	—	0	0-0	0	8.10
1990 California	AL	26	2	0	10	67.2	291	77	33	31	9	1	0	2	20	0	35	3	0	1	1	.500	0	1-1	1	4.12
1991 California	AL	19	4	0	8	44.2	206	53	29	24	4	1	0	3	28	2	24	4	0	2	5	.286	0	0-1	0	4.84
1992 Milwaukee	AL	50	0	0	11	62.2	243	38	15	13	3	5	2	7	24	1	43	1	0	5	1	.833	0	2-5	8	1.87

Year Team	Lg	G	GS	CG	GF	IP	BFP	H	R	ER	HR	SH	SF	HB	TBB	IBB	SO	WP	Bk	W	L	Pct.	ShO	Sv-Op	Hld	ERA
		HOW MUCH HE PITCHED						**WHAT HE GAVE UP**												**THE RESULTS**						
1993 Milwaukee	AL	45	0	0	14	59.1	246	59	29	22	4	5	5	2	22	4	23	0	0	3	3	.500	0	0-0	8	3.34
1994 Milwaukee	AL	42	0	0	31	46	202	41	16	13	0	2	3	1	27	5	31	3	1	1	4	.200	0	17-20	3	2.54
1995 Milwaukee	AL	40	0	0	34	34.2	163	40	16	13	3	2	1	0	20	4	33	5	0	3	0	.000	0	22-27	2	3.38
1996 Milwaukee	AL	61	0	0	55	61.1	268	65	26	23	4	0	4	1	26	4	53	5	0	3	3	.500	0	32-38	1	3.38
1997 Milwaukee	AL	51	0	0	20	70.1	268	62	30	27	4	6	4	1	33	3	62	2	1	1	5	.167	0	6-11	11	3.45
1998 Oak-Ana	AL	60	0	0	28	58.2	264	62	34	28	5	4	2	1	25	2	43	6	0	2	8	.200	0	5-9	11	4.30
1999 Baltimore	AL	27	0	0	10	31	151	35	23	20	5	1	0	2	22	2	22	1	1	1	0	1.000	0	0-3	2	5.81
2000 Los Angeles	NL	51	0	0	20	50	201	35	18	18	7	3	0	2	25	2	40	3	0	6	2	.750	0	5-7	11	3.24
1998 Oakland	AL	48	0	0	22	47.1	214	48	26	21	3	4	2	1	21	2	34	3	0	1	6	.143	0	5-8	10	3.99
Anaheim	AL	12	0	0	6	11.1	50	14	8	7	2	0	0	0	4	0	9	3	0	1	2	.333	0	0-1	1	5.56
12 ML YEARS		473	6	0	241	589.2	2549	572	275	235	49	30	21	22	273	30	413	38	4	25	35	.417	0	90-122	58	3.59

Robert Fick

Bats: L **Throws:** R **Pos:** 1B-34; C-16; PH/PR-14; DH-12 **Ht:** 6'1" **Wt:** 189 **Born:** 3/15/74 **Age:** 27

Year Team	Lg	G	AB	H	2B	3B	HR	(Hm	Rd)	TB	R	RBI	TBB	IBB	SO	HBP	SH	SF	SB	CS	SB%	GDP	Avg	OBP	SLG
		BATTING																	**BASERUNNING**				**PERCENTAGES**		
1996 Jamestown	A-	43	133	33	6	0	1	—	—	42	18	14	12	1	25	0	0	2	3	1	.75	4	.248	.306	.316
1997 W Michigan	A	122	463	158	50	3	16	—	—	262	100	90	75	11	74	1	0	7	13	4	.76	10	.341	.429	.566
1998 Jacksnville	AA	130	515	164	47	6	18	—	—	277	101	114	71	6	83	6	0	9	8	4	.67	8	.318	.401	.538
1999 Tigers	R	3	9	3	1	0	0	—	—	4	2	2	2	0	0	0	0	0	1	0	1.00	0	.333	.455	.444
W Michigan	A	3	11	3	0	0	0	—	—	3	2	0	2	0	0	0	0	0	1	0	1.00	0	.273	.385	.273
Toledo	AAA	14	48	15	0	1	2	—	—	23	11	8	8	0	5	1	0	1	1	0	1.00	0	.313	.414	.479
2000 Toledo	AAA	17	68	10	5	0	1	—	—	18	5	7	6	1	13	2	0	1	1	0	1.00	1	.147	.234	.265
1998 Detroit	AL	7	22	8	1	0	3	(0	3)	18	6	7	2	0	7	0	0	0	1	0	1.00	1	.364	.417	.818
1999 Detroit	AL	15	41	9	0	0	3	(1	2)	18	6	10	7	0	6	0	0	1	1	0	1.00	1	.220	.327	.439
2000 Detroit	AL	66	163	41	7	2	3	(0	3)	61	18	22	22	2	39	1	0	2	2	1	.67	6	.252	.340	.374
3 ML YEARS		88	226	58	8	2	9	(1	8)	97	30	39	31	2	52	1	0	3	4	1	.80	6	.257	.345	.429

Nelson Figueroa

Pitches: Right **Bats:** Both **Pos:** SP-3 **Ht:** 6'1" **Wt:** 155 **Born:** 5/18/74 **Age:** 27

Year Team	Lg	G	GS	CG	GF	IP	BFP	H	R	ER	HR	SH	SF	HB	TBB	IBB	SO	WP	Bk	W	L	Pct.	ShO	Sv-Op	Hld	ERA
		HOW MUCH HE PITCHED						**WHAT HE GAVE UP**												**THE RESULTS**						
1995 Kingsport	R+	12	12	2	0	76.1	304	57	31	26	3	3	2	5	22	1	79	5	0	7	3	.700	2	0--	—	3.07
1996 Capital Cty	A	26	25	8	1	185.1	723	119	55	42	10	3	2	2	58	1	200	9	2	14	7	.667	4	0--	—	2.04
1997 Binghamton	AA	33	22	0	3	143	617	137	76	69	14	7	2	6	68	1	116	7	0	5	11	.313	0	0--	—	4.34
1998 Binghamton	AA	21	21	3	0	123.2	531	133	73	64	19	2	1	0	44	2	116	1	1	13	3	.800	2	0--	—	4.66
Tucson	AAA	7	7	0	0	41.1	180	46	22	17	8	0	2	2	16	1	29	1	0	2	2	.500	0	0--	—	3.70
1999 Diamndbcks	R	1	1	0	0	3	11	3	1	0	0	0	0	0	0	0	2	0	0	0	1	.000	0	0--	—	0.00
Tucson	AAA	24	21	1	0	128	541	128	59	56	16	3	1	5	41	0	106	6	0	11	6	.647	1	0--	—	3.94
2000 Tucson	AAA	17	16	1	0	112	455	101	41	35	9	2	2	0	28	2	78	8	0	9	4	.692	0	0--	—	2.81
Scrantn-WB	AAA	8	8	1	0	50	209	50	28	21	9	2	1	2	11	0	35	2	0	4	3	.571	0	0--	—	3.78
2000 Arizona	NL	3	3	0	0	15.2	68	17	13	13	4	1	2	0	5	0	7	2	0	0	1	.000	0	0-0	0	7.47

Chuck Finley

Pitches: Left **Bats:** Left **Pos:** SP-34 **Ht:** 6'6" **Wt:** 225 **Born:** 11/26/62 **Age:** 38

Year Team	Lg	G	GS	CG	GF	IP	BFP	H	R	ER	HR	SH	SF	HB	TBB	IBB	SO	WP	Bk	W	L	Pct.	ShO	Sv-Op	Hld	ERA
		HOW MUCH HE PITCHED						**WHAT HE GAVE UP**												**THE RESULTS**						
1986 California	AL	25	0	0	7	46.1	198	40	17	17	2	4	0	1	23	1	37	2	0	3	1	.750	0	0-0	1	3.30
1987 California	AL	35	3	0	17	90.2	405	102	54	47	7	2	2	3	43	3	63	4	0	2	7	.222	0	0-2	0	4.67
1988 California	AL	31	31	2	0	194.1	831	191	95	90	15	7	10	6	82	7	111	5	8	9	15	.375	2	0-0	0	4.17
1989 California	AL	29	29	9	0	199.2	827	171	64	57	13	7	3	2	82	0	156	4	2	16	9	.640	1	0-0	0	2.57
1990 California	AL	32	32	7	0	236	962	210	77	63	17	**12**	3	3	81	3	177	9	0	18	9	.667	2	0-0	0	2.40
1991 California	AL	34	34	4	0	227.1	955	205	102	96	23	4	3	8	101	2	171	6	3	18	9	.667	2	0-0	0	3.80
1992 California	AL	31	31	4	0	204.1	885	212	99	90	14	10	10	3	98	2	124	6	0	7	12	.368	1	0-0	0	3.96
1993 California	AL	35	35	**13**	0	251.1	1065	243	108	88	22	11	7	6	82	1	187	8	1	16	14	.533	2	0-0	0	3.15
1994 California	AL	25	**25**	7	0	**183.1**	**774**	178	95	88	21	**9**	6	3	71	0	148	10	0	10	10	.500	2	0-0	0	4.32
1995 California	AL	32	32	2	0	203	880	192	106	95	20	4	5	7	93	1	195	13	1	15	12	.556	1	0-0	0	4.21
1996 California	AL	35	35	4	0	238	1037	241	124	110	27	7	9	11	94	5	215	**17**	2	15	16	.484	1	0-0	0	4.16
1997 Anaheim	AL	25	25	3	0	164	690	152	79	77	20	3	4	5	65	0	155	10	2	13	6	.684	1	0-0	0	4.23
1998 Anaheim	AL	34	34	1	0	223.1	976	210	97	84	20	3	5	6	109	1	212	8	0	11	9	.550	1	0-0	0	3.39
1999 Anaheim	AL	33	33	1	0	213.1	913	197	117	105	23	7	3	8	94	2	200	**15**	0	12	11	.522	0	0-0	0	4.43
2000 Cleveland	AL	34	34	3	0	218	936	211	108	101	23	5	4	2	101	3	189	9	0	16	11	.593	0	0-0	0	4.17
15 ML YEARS		470	413	60	24	2893	12334	2755	1342	1208	277	95	74	73	1219	30	2340	126	22	181	151	.545	14	0-2	1	3.76

Steve Finley

Bats: Left **Throws:** Left **Pos:** CF-148; DH-2; PH/PR-2 **Ht:** 6'2" **Wt:** 180 **Born:** 3/12/65 **Age:** 36

Year Team	Lg	G	AB	H	2B	3B	HR	(Hm	Rd)	TB	R	RBI	TBB	IBB	SO	HBP	SH	SF	SB	CS	SB%	GDP	Avg	OBP	SLG
		BATTING																	**BASERUNNING**				**PERCENTAGES**		
1989 Baltimore	AL	81	217	54	5	2	2	(0	2)	69	35	25	15	1	30	1	6	2	17	3	.85	3	.249	.298	.318
1990 Baltimore	AL	142	464	119	16	4	3	(1	2)	152	46	37	32	3	53	2	10	5	22	9	.71	8	.256	.304	.328
1991 Houston	NL	159	596	170	28	10	8	(0	8)	242	84	54	42	5	65	2	10	6	34	18	.65	8	.285	.331	.406
1992 Houston	NL	**162**	607	177	29	13	5	(5	0)	247	84	55	58	6	63	3	16	2	44	9	.83	10	.292	.355	.407
1993 Houston	NL	142	545	145	15	**13**	8	(1	7)	210	69	44	28	1	65	3	6	3	19	6	.76	8	.266	.304	.385
1994 Houston	NL	94	373	103	16	5	11	(4	7)	162	64	33	28	0	52	2	13	1	13	7	.65	3	.276	.329	.434
1995 San Diego	NL	139	562	167	23	8	10	(4	6)	236	104	44	59	5	62	3	4	2	36	12	.75	8	.297	.366	.420
1996 San Diego	NL	161	655	195	45	9	30	(15	15)	348	126	95	56	5	87	4	1	5	22	8	.73	20	.298	.354	.531
1997 San Diego	NL	143	560	146	26	5	28	(5	23)	266	101	92	43	2	92	3	2	7	15	3	.83	10	.261	.313	.475
1998 San Diego	NL	159	619	156	40	6	14	(8	6)	248	92	67	45	0	103	3	3	4	12	3	.80	9	.249	.301	.401
1999 Arizona	NL	156	590	156	32	10	34	(17	17)	310	100	103	63	7	94	3	2	5	8	4	.67	4	.264	.336	.525
2000 Arizona	NL	152	539	151	27	5	35	(17	18)	293	100	96	65	7	87	6	2	9	12	6	.67	9	.280	.361	.544
12 ML YEARS		1690	6327	1737	302	90	188	(77	111)	2783	1005	745	534	42	853	37	75	51	254	88	.74	100	.275	.332	.440

Tony Fiore

Pitches: Right **Bats:** Right **Pos:** RP-11   **Ht:** 6'4" **Wt:** 210 **Born:** 10/12/71 **Age:** 29

		HOW MUCH HE PITCHED						WHAT HE GAVE UP											THE RESULTS					
Year Team	Lg	G	GS	CG	GF	IP	BFP	H	R	ER	HR	SH	SF	HB	TBB	IBB	SO	WP	Bk	W	L	Pct.	ShO	Sv-Op	Hld	ERA
1992 Martinsville	R+	17	2	0	9	32.1	161	32	20	15	0	2	1	3	31	1	30	11	0	2	3	.400	0	0- –	—	4.18
1993 Batavia	A-	16	16	1	0	97.1	411	82	51	33	1	3	4	4	40	0	55	15	0	2	8	.200	0	0- –	—	3.05
1994 Spartanburg	A	28	28	9	0	166.2	719	162	94	76	10	2	5	4	77	1	113	19	1	12	13	.480	1	0- –	—	4.10
1995 Clearwater	A+	24	10	0	3	70.1	323	70	41	29	4	3	5	2	44	2	45	9	3	6	2	.750	0	0- –	—	3.71
1996 Clearwater	A+	22	22	3	0	128	533	102	61	45	4	1	1	5	56	1	80	13	1	8	4	.667	1	0- –	—	3.16
Reading	AA	5	5	0	0	31	146	32	21	15	2	0	1	1	18	0	19	6	0	1	2	.333	0	0- –	—	4.35
1997 Reading	AA	17	16	0	0	104.2	433	89	47	35	6	8	4	5	40	0	64	10	1	8	3	.727	0	0- –	—	3.01
Scrantn-WB	AAA	9	9	1	0	60.2	268	60	34	26	3	0	1	0	26	1	56	6	1	3	5	.375	0	0- –	—	3.86
1998 Scrantn-WB	AAA	41	7	0	12	94.2	418	92	53	47	4	3	3	1	52	1	71	6	0	4	7	.364	0	1- –	—	4.47
1999 Scrantn-WB	AAA	13	0	0	2	20.1	102	28	19	15	0	0	1	0	15	1	13	4	0	0	0	—	0	0- –	—	6.64
Salt Lake	AAA	40	0	0	35	46.2	205	45	21	18	1	2	2	2	26	3	38	3	1	2	1	.667	0	19- –	—	3.47
2000 Durham	AAA	53	1	0	26	75	317	62	22	19	3	6	0	3	38	6	39	3	1	8	5	.615	0	8- –	—	2.28
2000 Tampa Bay	AL	11	0	0	3	15	74	21	16	14	3	0	0	2	9	2	8	1	0	1	1	.500	0	0-1	0	8.40

John Flaherty

Bats: Right **Throws:** Right **Pos:** C-108; PH/PR-2   **Ht:** 6'1" **Wt:** 200 **Born:** 10/21/67 **Age:** 33

		BATTING																BASERUNNING				PERCENTAGES		
Year Team	Lg	G	AB	H	2B	3B	HR	(Hm	Rd)	TB	R	RBI	TBB	IBB	SO	HBP	SH	SF	SB	CS	SB%	GDP	Avg	OBP	SLG
1992 Boston	AL	35	66	13	2	0	0	(0	0)	15	3	2	3	0	7	0	1	1	0	0	—	0	.197	.229	.227
1993 Boston	AL	13	25	3	2	0	0	(0	0)	5	3	2	2	0	6	1	1	0	0	0	—	0	.120	.214	.200
1994 Detroit	AL	34	40	6	1	0	0	(0	0)	7	2	4	1	0	11	0	2	1	0	1	.00	1	.150	.167	.175
1995 Detroit	AL	112	354	86	22	1	11	(6	5)	143	39	40	18	0	47	3	8	2	0	0	—	8	.243	.284	.404
1996 Det-SD	NL	119	416	118	24	0	13	(6	5)	181	40	64	17	2	61	3	4	4	3	3	.50	13	.284	.314	.435
1997 San Diego	NL	129	439	120	21	1	9	(4	5)	170	38	46	33	7	62	0	2	2	4	4	.50	11	.273	.323	.387
1998 Tampa Bay	AL	91	304	63	11	0	3	(1	2)	83	21	24	22	0	46	1	4	3	0	5	.00	9	.207	.261	.273
1999 Tampa Bay	AL	117	446	124	19	0	14	(3	11)	185	53	71	19	0	64	6	1	10	0	2	.00	14	.278	.310	.415
2000 Tampa Bay	AL	109	394	103	15	0	10	(7	3)	148	36	39	20	2	57	0	2	2	0	0	—	11	.261	.296	.376
1996 Detroit	AL	47	152	38	12	0	4	(2	2)	62	18	23	8	1	25	1	3	1	1	0	1.00	5	.250	.290	.408
San Diego	NL	72	264	80	12	0	9	(6	3)	119	22	41	9	1	36	2	1	3	2	3	.40	8	.303	.327	.451
9 ML YEARS		759	2484	636	117	2	60	(29	31)	937	235	292	135	11	361	14	25	25	7	15	.32	67	.256	.295	.377

Darrin Fletcher

Bats: Left **Throws:** Right **Pos:** C-117; PH/PR-15; DH-2   **Ht:** 6'2" **Wt:** 205 **Born:** 10/3/66 **Age:** 34

		BATTING																BASERUNNING				PERCENTAGES		
Year Team	Lg	G	AB	H	2B	3B	HR	(Hm	Rd)	TB	R	RBI	TBB	IBB	SO	HBP	SH	SF	SB	CS	SB%	GDP	Avg	OBP	SLG
1989 Los Angeles	NL	5	8	4	0	0	1	(1	0)	7	1	2	1	0	0	0	0	0	0	0	—	0	.500	.556	.875
1990 LA-Phi	NL	11	23	3	1	0	0	(0	0)	4	3	1	1	0	6	0	0	0	0	0	—	0	.130	.167	.174
1991 Philadelphia	NL	46	136	31	8	0	1	(1	0)	42	5	12	5	0	15	0	1	0	0	1	.00	0	.228	.255	.309
1992 Montreal	NL	83	222	54	10	2	2	(0	2)	74	13	26	14	3	28	2	2	4	0	2	.00	8	.243	.289	.333
1993 Montreal	NL	133	396	101	20	1	9	(5	4)	150	33	60	34	2	40	6	5	4	0	0	—	7	.255	.320	.379
1994 Montreal	NL	94	285	74	18	1	10	(4	6)	124	28	57	25	4	23	3	0	4	0	0	—	7	.260	.314	.435
1995 Montreal	NL	110	350	100	21	1	11	(3	8)	156	42	45	32	1	23	4	1	2	0	0	—	12	.286	.351	.446
1996 Montreal	NL	127	394	105	22	0	12	(7	5)	163	41	57	27	4	42	6	1	3	0	1	.00	13	.266	.321	.414
1997 Montreal	NL	96	310	86	20	1	17	(10	7)	159	39	55	17	3	35	5	0	2	1	1	.50	6	.277	.323	.513
1998 Toronto	AL	124	407	115	23	1	9	(3	6)	167	37	52	25	7	39	6	1	7	0	0	—	19	.283	.328	.410
1999 Toronto	AL	115	412	120	26	0	18	(10	8)	200	48	80	26	0	47	6	0	4	0	0	—	16	.291	.339	.485
2000 Toronto	AL	122	416	133	19	1	20	(10	10)	214	43	58	20	3	43	5	0	4	1	1	.50	8	.320	.355	.514
1990 Los Angeles	NL	2	1	0	0	0	0	(0	0)	0	0	0	0	0	1	0	0	0	0	0	—	0	.000	.000	.000
Philadelphia	NL	9	22	3	1	0	0	(0	0)	4	3	1	1	0	5	0	0	0	0	0	—	0	.136	.174	.182
12 ML YEARS		1066	3359	926	188	8	110	(54	56)	1460	333	505	227	27	343	43	11	42	2	5	.29	100	.276	.326	.435

Bryce Florie

Pitches: Right **Bats:** Right **Pos:** RP-29   **Ht:** 5'11" **Wt:** 192 **Born:** 5/21/70 **Age:** 31

		HOW MUCH HE PITCHED						WHAT HE GAVE UP											THE RESULTS					
Year Team	Lg	G	GS	CG	GF	IP	BFP	H	R	ER	HR	SH	SF	HB	TBB	IBB	SO	WP	Bk	W	L	Pct.	ShO	Sv-Op	Hld	ERA
2000 Sarasota *	A+	3	1	0	0	3	13	3	1	0	0	0	0	0	1	0	2	0	0	0	0	—	0	0- –	—	0.00
Trenton *	AA	3	1	0	0	5	20	2	0	0	0	0	0	0	2	0	11	0	0	0	0	—	0	0- –	—	0.00
1994 San Diego	NL	9	0	0	4	9.1	37	8	1	1	0	0	1	0	3	0	8	1	0	0	0	—	0	0-0	0	0.96
1995 San Diego	NL	47	0	0	10	68.2	290	49	30	23	4	8	5	1	38	3	68	7	2	2	2	.500	0	1-4	9	3.01
1996 SD-Mil		54	0	0	16	68.1	312	65	40	36	4	1	3	6	40	5	63	6	1	2	3	.400	0	0-3	6	4.74
1997 Milwaukee	AL	32	8	0	6	75	332	74	43	36	4	1	4	3	42	2	53	4	1	4	4	.500	0	0-1	0	4.32
1998 Detroit	AL	42	16	0	6	133	580	141	80	71	16	3	2	4	59	6	97	9	0	8	9	.471	0	0-0	0	4.80
1999 Det-Bos	AL	41	5	0	10	81.1	368	94	50	44	8	3	2	2	35	5	65	8	0	4	1	.800	0	0-0	3	4.65
2000 Boston	AL	29	0	0	14	49.1	223	57	30	25	5	6	3	1	19	6	34	0	0	0	4	.000	0	1-2	1	4.56
1996 San Diego	NL	39	0	0	11	49.1	222	45	24	22	1	0	1	6	27	3	51	3	1	2	2	.500	0	0-1	5	4.01
Milwaukee	AL	15	0	0	5	19	90	20	16	14	3	1	2	0	13	2	12	3	0	0	1	.000	0	0-2	1	6.63
1999 Detroit	AL	27	3	0	6	51.1	234	61	31	26	6	3	1	1	20	2	40	4	0	2	1	.667	0	0-0	2	4.56
Boston	AL	14	2	0	4	30	134	33	19	16	2	0	1	1	15	3	25	4	0	2	0	1.000	0	0-0	1	4.80
7 ML YEARS		254	29	0	66	485	2142	488	274	234	45	19	16	20	236	27	388	35	4	20	23	.465	0	2-10	25	4.34

Cliff Floyd

Bats: Left **Throws:** Right **Pos:** LF-108; PH/PR-13; DH-1   **Ht:** 6'4" **Wt:** 235 **Born:** 12/5/72 **Age:** 28

		BATTING																BASERUNNING				PERCENTAGES		
Year Team	Lg	G	AB	H	2B	3B	HR	(Hm	Rd)	TB	R	RBI	TBB	IBB	SO	HBP	SH	SF	SB	CS	SB%	GDP	Avg	OBP	SLG
1993 Montreal	NL	10	31	7	0	0	1	(0	1)	10	3	2	0	0	9	0	0	0	0	0	—	0	.226	.226	.323
1994 Montreal	NL	100	334	94	19	4	4	(2	2)	133	43	41	24	0	63	3	2	3	10	3	.77	3	.281	.332	.398
1995 Montreal	NL	29	69	9	1	0	1	(1	0)	13	6	8	7	0	22	1	0	0	3	0	1.00	1	.130	.221	.188

Year Team	Lg	G	AB	H	2B	3B	HR	(Hm	Rd)	TB	R	RBI	TBB	IBB	SO	HBP	SH	SF	SB	CS	SB%	GDP	Avg	OBP	SLG
1996 Montreal	NL	117	227	55	15	4	6	(3	3)	96	29	26	30	1	52	5	1	3	7	1	.88	3	.242	.340	.423
1997 Florida	NL	61	137	32	9	1	6	(2	4)	61	23	19	24	0	33	2	1	1	6	2	.75	3	.234	.354	.445
1998 Florida	NL	153	588	166	45	3	22	(10	12)	283	85	90	47	7	112	3	0	3	27	14	.66	10	.282	.337	.481
1999 Florida	NL	69	251	76	19	1	11	(4	7)	130	37	49	30	5	47	2	0	2	5	6	.45	8	.303	.379	.518
2000 Florida	NL	121	420	126	30	0	22	(13	9)	222	75	91	50	5	82	8	0	9	24	3	.89	4	.300	.378	.529
8 ML YEARS		660	2057	565	138	13	73	(35	38)	948	301	326	212	18	420	24	4	21	82	29	.74	32	.275	.346	.461

Ben Ford

Pitches: Right Bats: Right Pos: SP-2; RP-2   Ht: 6'7" Wt: 200 Born: 8/15/75 Age: 25

Year Team	Lg	G	GS	CG	GF	IP	BFP	H	R	ER	HR	SH	SF	HB	TBB	IBB	SO	WP	Bk	W	L	Pct.	ShO	Sv-Op	Hld	ERA
1994 Yankees	R	18	0	0	11	34	143	27	13	9	0	0	0	6	8	0	31	3	0	2	2	.500	0	3- -	—	2.38
1995 Greensboro	A	7	0	0	2	7	31	4	4	4	1	1	0	0	5	1	8	2	0	0	0	—	0	0- -	—	5.14
Oneonta	A-	29	0	0	10	52	224	39	23	5	1	0	2	5	16	0	50	8	0	5	0	1.000	0	0- -	—	0.87
1996 Greensboro	A	43	0	0	16	82.1	359	75	48	39	3	4	1	11	33	6	84	9	0	2	6	.250	0	2- -	—	4.26
1997 Tampa	A+	32	0	0	30	37.1	155	27	8	8	1	2	0	6	14	1	37	4	0	4	0	1.000	0	18- -	—	1.93
Norwich	A+	28	0	0	14	42.2	183	35	28	20	1	1	2	3	19	1	38	4	0	4	3	.571	0	1- -	—	4.22
1998 Tucson	AAA	48	0	0	36	68.1	313	68	41	33	6	3	3	2	33	5	63	7	1	2	5	.286	0	13- -	—	4.35
1999 Columbus	AAA	53	0	0	23	70.1	318	69	42	37	4	2	1	9	39	1	40	11	0	6	3	.667	0	3- -	—	4.73
2000 Columbus	AAA	20	2	0	5	44	194	37	15	15	3	0	1	4	24	0	41	8	0	3	0	1.000	0	0- -	—	3.07
Iowa	AAA	8	8	0	0	36.2	178	36	30	27	4	2	4	3	31	0	30	2	0	1	3	.250	0	0- -	—	6.63
1998 Arizona	NL	8	0	0	2	10	49	13	12	11	2	0	2	3	3	0	5	1	0	0	0	—	0	0-0	0	9.90
2000 New York	AL	4	2	0	0	11	52	14	11	11	1	0	0	3	7	0	5	0	0	0	1	.000	0	0-0	0	9.00
2 ML YEARS		12	2	0	2	21	101	27	23	22	3	0	0	5	10	0	10	1	0	0	1	.000	0	0-0	0	9.43

Brook Fordyce

Bats: Right Throws: Right Pos: C-92; PH/PR-6   Ht: 6'0" Wt: 190 Born: 5/7/70 Age: 31

Year Team	Lg	G	AB	H	2B	3B	HR	(Hm	Rd)	TB	R	RBI	TBB	IBB	SO	HBP	SH	SF	SB	CS	SB%	GDP	Avg	OBP	SLG
2000 Charlotte *	AAA	17	67	16	5	0	2	(Hm	Rd)	27	9	12	8	0	13	0	0	1	0	1	.00	2	.239	.316	.403
1995 New York	NL	4	2	1	1	0	0	(0	0)	4	2	1	1	0	0	0	0	0	0	0	—	0	.500	.667	1.000
1996 Cincinnati	NL	4	7	2	1	0	0	(0	0)	3	0	1	3	0	1	0	0	0	0	0	—	0	.286	.500	.429
1997 Cincinnati	NL	47	96	20	5	0	1	(1	0)	28	7	8	8	1	15	0	0	1	2	0	1.00	0	.208	.267	.292
1998 Cincinnati	NL	57	146	37	9	0	3	(3	0)	55	8	14	11	3	28	0	1	0	0	1	.00	0	.253	.306	.377
1999 Chicago	AL	105	333	99	25	1	9	(5	4)	153	36	49	21	0	48	3	3	2	2	0	1.00	5	.297	.343	.459
2000 CWS-Bal	AL	93	302	91	18	1	14	(8	6)	153	41	49	17	0	50	4	2	5	0	0	—	4	.301	.341	.507
2000 Chicago	AL	40	125	34	7	1	5	(3	2)	58	18	21	6	0	23	2	2	1	0	0	—	0	.272	.313	.464
Baltimore	AL	53	177	57	11	0	9	(5	4)	95	23	28	11	0	27	2	0	4	0	0	—	3	.322	.361	.537
6 ML YEARS		310	886	250	59	2	27	(17	10)	394	93	121	61	4	142	7	6	8	4	1	.80	11	.282	.331	.445

Scott Forster

Pitches: Left Bats: Right Pos: RP-42   Ht: 6'1" Wt: 194 Born: 10/27/71 Age: 29

Year Team	Lg	G	GS	CG	GF	IP	BFP	H	R	ER	HR	SH	SF	HB	TBB	IBB	SO	WP	Bk	W	L	Pct.	ShO	Sv-Op	Hld	ERA
1994 Vermont	A-	12	9	0	0	52.2	236	38	32	19	0	0	1	4	34	0	39	6	2	1	6	.143	0	0- -	—	3.25
1995 Wst Plm Bch	A+	26	26	1	0	146.2	643	129	78	66	6	5	4	7	80	1	92	16	0	6	11	.353	0	0- -	—	4.05
1996 Harrisburg	AA	28	28	0	0	176.1	755	164	94	74	15	3	4	7	67	2	97	5	0	10	7	.588	0	0- -	—	3.78
1997 Harrisburg	AA	17	15	0	2	79.1	365	77	45	20	7	7	6	6	48	0	71	4	0	3	6	.333	0	0- -	—	2.27
1998 Jupiter	A+	6	0	0	1	8	38	9	10	8	0	0	1	1	5	0	7	2	0	0	0	—	0	0- -	—	9.00
Harrisburg	AA	25	1	0	5	77.2	360	90	50	42	8	2	1	6	47	1	54	5	0	7	3	.700	0	0- -	—	4.87
1999 Harrisburg	AA	2	0	0	1	5	16	3	0	0	0	0	0	1	0	0	1	0	0	0	0	—	0	0- -	—	0.00
Ottawa	AAA	53	0	0	27	52.1	249	49	32	30	3	2	1	2	47	2	32	8	0	0	4	.000	0	2- -	—	5.16
2000 Ottawa	AAA	23	0	0	9	31	135	24	11	8	0	1	1	0	22	1	22	5	0	1	0	1.000	0	2- -	—	2.32
2000 Montreal	NL	42	0	0	10	32	154	28	31	28	5	2	3	2	25	1	23	2	0	0	1	.000	0	0-0	4	7.88

Keith Foulke

Pitches: Right Bats: Right Pos: RP-72   Ht: 6'0" Wt: 200 Born: 10/19/72 Age: 28

Year Team	Lg	G	GS	CG	GF	IP	BFP	H	R	ER	HR	SH	SF	HB	TBB	IBB	SO	WP	Bk	W	L	Pct.	ShO	Sv-Op	Hld	ERA
1997 SF-CWS		27	8	0	5	73.1	326	89	52	52	13	3	1	4	23	2	54	1	0	3	6	.444	0	3-6	5	6.38
1998 Chicago	AL	54	0	0	18	65.1	267	51	31	30	9	2	4	4	20	1	57	3	1	3	2	.600	0	1-2	13	4.13
1999 Chicago	AL	67	0	0	31	105.1	411	73	28	26	11	3	0	3	21	4	123	1	0	3	3	.500	0	9-13	22	2.22
2000 Chicago	AL	72	0	0	58	88	350	66	31	29	9	5	2	2	22	2	91	1	0	3	1	.750	0	34-39	3	2.97
1997 San Francisco	NL	11	8	0	0	44.2	209	60	41	41	9	2	0	4	18	1	33	1	0	1	5	.167	0	0-1	0	8.26
Chicago	AL	16	0	0	5	28.2	117	28	11	11	4	1	1	0	5	1	21	0	0	3	0	1.000	0	3-5	5	3.45
4 ML YEARS		220	8	0	112	332	1354	277	142	137	42	13	6	13	86	11	325	6	1	13	11	.542	0	47-60	43	3.71

Andy Fox

Bats: L Throws: R Pos: SS-33; 3B-32; PH/PR-23; LF-10; RF-9; 2B-2; 1B-1; CF-1   Ht: 6'4" Wt: 202 Born: 1/12/71 Age: 30

Year Team	Lg	G	AB	H	2B	3B	HR	(Hm	Rd)	TB	R	RBI	TBB	IBB	SO	HBP	SH	SF	SB	CS	SB%	GDP	Avg	OBP	SLG
2000 El Paso *	AA	4	15	6	2	0	0	(—	—)	8	3	4	2	0	2	0	0	0	1	1	.50	1	.400	.471	.533
Tucson *	AAA	3	13	3	0	1	0	(—	—)	5	1	3	0	0	1	0	0	0	0	0	.00	1	.231	.231	.385
1996 New York	AL	113	189	37	4	0	3	(1	2)	50	26	13	20	0	28	1	9	0	11	3	.79	1	.196	.276	.265
1997 New York	AL	22	31	7	1	0	0	(0	0)	8	13	1	7	0	9	0	0	0	2	1	.67	1	.226	.368	.258
1998 Arizona	NL	139	502	139	21	6	9	(5	4)	199	67	44	43	0	97	18	0	1	14	7	.67	2	.277	.355	.396
1999 Arizona	NL	99	274	70	12	2	6	(4	2)	104	34	33	33	10	61	9	1	3	4	1	.80	4	.255	.351	.380
2000 Ari-Fla	NL	100	250	58	8	2	4	(2	2)	82	29	20	22	4	53	3	0	0	10	4	.71	3	.232	.302	.328
2000 Arizona	NL	31	86	18	4	0	1	(1	0)	25	10	10	4	1	16	0	0	0	2	1	.67	1	.209	.244	.291
Florida	NL	69	164	40	4	2	3	(1	2)	57	19	10	18	3	37	3	0	0	8	3	.73	1	.244	.330	.348
5 ML YEARS		473	1246	311	46	10	22	(12	10)	443	169	111	125	14	248	31	12	4	41	16	.72	11	.250	.332	.356

John Franco

Pitches: Left **Bats:** Left **Pos:** RP-62   **Ht:** 5'10" **Wt:** 185 **Born:** 9/17/60 **Age:** 40

		HOW MUCH HE PITCHED						WHAT HE GAVE UP											THE RESULTS					
Year Team	Lg	G	GS	CG	GF	IP	BFP	H	R	ER	HR	SH	SF	HB	TBB	IBB	SO	WP	Bk	W	L	Pct.	ShO	Sv-Op	Hld	ERA
1984 Cincinnati	NL	54	0	0	30	79.1	335	74	28	23	3	4	4	2	36	4	55	2	0	6	2	.750	0	4-8	2	2.61
1985 Cincinnati	NL	67	0	0	33	99	407	83	27	24	5	11	1	1	40	8	61	4	0	12	3	.800	0	12-14	11	2.18
1986 Cincinnati	NL	74	0	0	52	101	429	90	40	33	7	8	3	2	44	12	84	4	2	6	6	.500	0	29-38	2	2.94
1987 Cincinnati	NL	68	0	0	60	82	344	76	26	23	6	5	2	0	27	6	61	1	0	8	5	.615	0	32-41	0	2.52
1988 Cincinnati	NL	70	0	0	61	86	336	60	18	15	3	5	1	0	27	3	46	1	2	6	6	.500	0	39-42	1	1.57
1989 Cincinnati	NL	60	0	0	50	80.2	345	77	35	28	3	7	3	0	36	8	60	3	2	4	8	.333	0	32-39	1	3.12
1990 New York	NL	55	0	0	48	67.2	287	66	22	19	4	3	1	0	21	2	56	7	3	5	3	.625	0	33-39	0	2.53
1991 New York	NL	52	0	0	48	55.1	247	61	27	18	2	3	0	1	18	4	45	6	0	5	9	.357	0	30-35	0	2.93
1992 New York	NL	31	0	0	30	33	128	24	6	6	1	2	0	0	11	2	20	0	0	6	2	.750	0	15-17	1	1.64
1993 New York	NL	35	0	0	30	36.1	172	46	24	21	6	4	1	1	19	3	29	5	0	4	3	.571	0	10-17	0	5.20
1994 New York	NL	47	0	0	43	50	216	47	20	15	2	2	1	1	19	0	42	1	0	1	4	.200	0	30-36	0	2.70
1995 New York	NL	48	0	0	41	51.2	213	48	17	14	4	4	1	0	17	2	41	0	0	5	3	.625	0	29-36	0	2.44
1996 New York	NL	51	0	0	44	54	235	54	15	11	2	6	0	0	21	0	48	2	0	4	3	.571	0	28-36	0	1.83
1997 New York	NL	59	0	0	53	60	244	49	18	17	3	5	1	1	20	2	53	6	0	5	3	.625	0	36-42	0	2.55
1998 New York	NL	61	0	0	54	64.2	289	66	28	26	4	4	5	4	29	7	59	2	0	0	8	.000	0	38-46	0	3.62
1999 New York	NL	46	0	0	34	40.2	182	40	14	13	1	3	1	2	19	1	41	0	0	0	2	.000	0	19-21	1	2.88
2000 New York	NL	62	0	0	14	55.2	239	46	24	21	6	3	0	2	26	6	56	2	0	5	4	.556	0	4-4	20	3.40
17 ML YEARS		940	0	0	725	1097	4648	1007	389	327	62	77	27	17	430	70	857	46	8	82	74	.526	0	420-511	39	2.68

Matt Franco

Bats: L **Throws:** R **Pos:** PH/PR-62; 1B-28; 3B-22; LF-3; DH-2; 2B-1   **Ht:** 6'1" **Wt:** 210 **Born:** 8/19/69 **Age:** 31

		BATTING										BASERUNNING				PERCENTAGES		
Year Team	Lg	G	AB	H	2B	3B	HR	(Hm	Rd)	TB	R	RBI	TBB	IBB	SO	HBP	SH	SF	SB	CS	SB%	GDP	Avg	OBP	SLG
2000 Norfolk *	AAA	14	51	7	1	0	0			8	3	1	3	0	10	0	0	0	0	0	—	0	.137	.185	.157
1995 Chicago	NL	16	17	5	1	0	0	(0	0)	6	3	1	0	0	4	0	0	0	0	0	—	0	.294	.294	.353
1996 New York	NL	14	31	6	1	0	1	(0	1)	10	3	2	1	0	5	1	0	1	0	0	—	1	.194	.235	.323
1997 New York	NL	112	163	45	5	0	5	(3	2)	65	21	21	13	4	23	0	0	0	1	0	1.00	4	.276	.330	.399
1998 New York	NL	103	161	44	7	1	1	(1	0)	58	20	13	23	6	26	1	1	1	0	1	.00	8	.273	.366	.360
1999 New York	NL	122	132	31	5	0	4	(0	4)	48	18	21	28	3	21	0	0	1	0	0	—	9	.235	.366	.364
2000 New York	NL	101	134	32	4	0	2	(1	1)	42	9	14	21	3	22	0	1	0	0	0	—	3	.239	.340	.313
6 ML YEARS		468	638	163	23	2	13	(5	8)	229	74	72	86	16	101	2	2	4	1	1	.50	25	.255	.344	.359

Wayne Franklin

Pitches: Left **Bats:** Left **Pos:** RP-25   **Ht:** 6'2" **Wt:** 195 **Born:** 3/9/74 **Age:** 27

		HOW MUCH HE PITCHED						WHAT HE GAVE UP											THE RESULTS					
Year Team	Lg	G	GS	CG	GF	IP	BFP	H	R	ER	HR	SH	SF	HB	TBB	IBB	SO	WP	Bk	W	L	Pct.	ShO	Sv-Op	Hld	ERA
1996 Yakima	A-	20	0	0	5	25	115	32	10	7	2	0	0	0	12	3	22	3	1	1	0	1.000	0	1-—	—	2.52
1997 Savannah	A	28	7	1	10	82	362	79	41	29	10	1	1	4	35	0	58	2	1	5	3	.625	0	2-—	—	3.18
San Berndno	A+	1	0	0	0	2	7	2	0	0	0	0	0	0	0	0	1	0	0	0	0	—	0	0-—	—	0.00
1998 Vero Beach	A+	48	0	0	26	86.2	369	81	43	34	7	3	5	2	26	0	78	3	2	9	3	.750	0	10-—	—	3.53
1999 Kissimmee	A+	12	0	0	7	17.2	69	11	4	3	0	1	0	1	6	0	22	0	0	1	0	1.000	0	1-—	—	1.53
Jackson	AA	46	0	0	40	50.1	200	31	11	9	3	3	4	3	16	3	40	1	0	3	1	.750	0	20-—	—	1.61
2000 New Orleans	AAA	48	0	0	15	44.2	208	51	29	18	4	3	1	2	19	3	37	1	0	3	3	.500	0	4-—	—	3.63
2000 Houston	NL	25	0	0	4	21.1	103	24	14	13	2	0	2	4	12	1	21	0	1	0	0	—	0	0-0	8	5.48

John Frascatore

Pitches: Right **Bats:** Right **Pos:** RP-60   **Ht:** 6'1" **Wt:** 223 **Born:** 2/4/70 **Age:** 31

		HOW MUCH HE PITCHED						WHAT HE GAVE UP											THE RESULTS					
Year Team	Lg	G	GS	CG	GF	IP	BFP	H	R	ER	HR	SH	SF	HB	TBB	IBB	SO	WP	Bk	W	L	Pct.	ShO	Sv-Op	Hld	ERA
1994 St. Louis	NL	1	1	0	0	3.1	18	7	6	6	2	0	0	0	2	0	2	1	0	0	1	.000	0	0-0	0	16.20
1995 St. Louis	NL	14	4	0	3	32.2	151	39	19	16	3	1	1	2	16	1	21	0	0	1	1	.500	0	0-0	0	4.41
1997 St. Louis	NL	59	0	0	17	80	348	74	25	22	5	5	5	6	33	5	58	4	0	5	2	.714	0	0-4	3	2.48
1998 St. Louis	NL	69	0	0	15	95.2	415	95	48	44	11	4	1	4	36	3	49	2	0	3	4	.429	0	0-2	13	4.14
1999 Ari-Tor		59	0	0	24	70	297	73	32	29	11	6	3	2	21	8	37	5	0	8	5	.615	0	1-3	10	3.73
2000 Toronto	AL	60	0	0	15	73	335	87	51	44	14	2	4	7	33	2	30	3	0	2	4	.333	0	0-5	13	5.42
1999 Arizona	NL	26	0	0	10	33	136	31	16	15	6	1	1	1	12	4	15	0	0	1	4	.200	0	0-1	4	4.09
Toronto	AL	33	0	0	14	37	161	42	16	14	5	5	2	1	9	4	22	5	0	7	1	.875	0	1-2	6	3.41
6 ML YEARS		262	5	0	74	354.2	1564	375	181	161	46	18	14	20	141	19	197	15	0	19	17	.528	0	1-14	39	4.09

Hanley Frias

Bats: B **Throws:** R **Pos:** PH/PR-45; SS-21; 2B-15; 3B-7   **Ht:** 6'0" **Wt:** 173 **Born:** 12/5/73 **Age:** 27

		BATTING										BASERUNNING				PERCENTAGES		
Year Team	Lg	G	AB	H	2B	3B	HR	(Hm | Rd)	TB	R	RBI	TBB	IBB	SO	HBP	SH	SF	SB	CS	SB%	GDP	Avg	OBP	SLG
1997 Texas	AL	14	26	5	1	0	0	(0 | 0)	6	4	1	1	0	4	0	0	0	0	0	—	1	.192	.222	.231
1998 Arizona	NL	15	23	3	1	0	0	(1 | 0)	8	4	2	0	0	5	0	0	0	0	0	—	0	.130	.130	.348
1999 Arizona	NL	69	150	41	3	2	1	(1 | 0)	51	27	16	29	2	18	0	1	0	4	3	.57	2	.273	.391	.340
2000 Arizona	NL	75	112	23	5	0	2	(2 | 0)	34	18	6	17	0	18	0	0	0	2	2	.50	3	.205	.310	.304
4 ML YEARS		173	311	72	9	3	4	(4 | 0)	99	53	25	47	2	45	0	1	0	6	5	.55	7	.232	.332	.318

Jeff Frye

Bats: R **Throws:** R **Pos:** 2B-80; PH/PR-23; RF-13; 3B-4; DH-3; CF-2; LF-1   **Ht:** 5'9" **Wt:** 170 **Born:** 8/31/66 **Age:** 34

		BATTING										BASERUNNING				PERCENTAGES		
Year Team	Lg	G	AB	H	2B	3B	HR	(Hm | Rd)	TB	R	RBI	TBB	IBB	SO	HBP	SH	SF	SB	CS	SB%	GDP	Avg	OBP	SLG
1992 Texas	AL	67	199	51	9	1	1	(0 | 1)	65	24	12	16	0	27	3	11	1	1	3	.25	2	.256	.320	.327
1994 Texas	AL	57	205	67	20	3	0	(0 | 0)	93	37	18	29	0	23	1	5	3	6	1	.86	1	.327	.408	.454

Year Team	Lg	G	AB	H	2B	3B	HR	(Hm	Rd)	TB	R	RBI	TBB	IBB	SO	HBP	SH	SF	SB	CS	SB%	GDP	Avg	OBP	SLG
1995 Texas	AL	90	313	87	15	2	4	(2	2)	118	38	29	24	0	45	5	8	4	3	3	.50	7	.278	.335	.377
1996 Boston	AL	105	419	120	27	2	4	(3	1)	163	74	41	54	0	57	5	5	3	18	4	.82	6	.286	.372	.389
1997 Boston	AL	127	404	126	36	2	3	(2	1)	175	56	51	27	1	44	2	2	7	19	8	.70	12	.312	.352	.433
1999 Boston	AL	41	114	32	3	0	1	(1	0)	38	14	12	14	1	11	1	1	1	2	2	.50	2	.281	.362	.333
2000 Bos-Col		106	326	100	19	0	1	(0	1)	122	49	16	36	0	54	2	5	2	5	3	.63	8	.307	.377	.374
2000 Boston	AL	69	239	69	13	0	1	(0	1)	85	35	13	28	0	38	1	4	1	3		.25	5	.289	.364	.356
Colorado	NL	37	87	31	6	0	0	(0	0)	37	14	3	8	0	16	1	1	1	4	0	1.00	3	.356	.412	.425
7 ML YEARS		593	1980	583	129	10	14	(8	6)	774	292	179	200	2	261	19	37	21	54	24	.69	38	.294	.361	.391

Travis Fryman

Bats: Right **Throws:** Right **Pos:** 3B-154; DH-1; 1B-1 **Ht:** 6'1" **Wt:** 205 **Born:** 3/25/69 **Age:** 32

Year Team	Lg	G	AB	H	2B	3B	HR	(Hm	Rd)	TB	R	RBI	TBB	IBB	SO	HBP	SH	SF	SB	CS	SB%	GDP	Avg	OBP	SLG
1990 Detroit	AL	66	232	69	11	1	9	(5	4)	109	32	27	17	0	51	1	1	0	3	3	.50	3	.297	.348	.470
1991 Detroit	AL	149	557	144	36	3	21	(8	13)	249	65	91	40	0	149	1	3	6	12	5	.71	13	.259	.309	.447
1992 Detroit	AL	161	659	175	31	4	20	(9	11)	274	87	96	45	1	144	6	5	6	8	4	.67	13	.266	.316	.416
1993 Detroit	AL	151	607	182	37	5	22	(13	9)	295	98	97	77	1	128	4	1	6	9	4	.69	8	.300	.379	.486
1994 Detroit	AL	114	464	122	34	5	18	(10	8)	220	66	85	45	1	128	5	1	13	2	2	.50	6	.263	.326	.474
1995 Detroit	AL	144	567	156	21	5	15	(9	6)	232	79	81	63	4	100	3	0	7	4	2	.67	18	.275	.347	.409
1996 Detroit	AL	157	616	165	32	3	22	(10	12)	269	90	100	57	2	118	4	1	10	4	3	.57	18	.268	.329	.437
1997 Detroit	AL	154	595	163	27	3	22	(13	9)	262	90	102	46	5	113	5	0	11	16	3	.84	15	.274	.326	.440
1998 Cleveland	AL	146	557	160	33	2	28	(16	12)	281	74	96	44	0	125	3	0	4	10	8	.56	12	.287	.340	.504
1999 Cleveland	AL	85	322	82	16	2	10	(6	4)	132	45	48	25	1	57	1	0	2	2	1	.67	13	.255	.309	.410
2000 Cleveland	AL	155	574	184	38	4	22	(9	13)	296	93	106	73	2	111	1	0	10	1	1	.50	15	.321	.392	.516
11 ML YEARS		1482	5750	1602	316	37	209	(108	101)	2619	819	929	532	17	1224	36	15	75	71	36	.66	134	.279	.339	.455

Brad Fullmer

Bats: Left **Throws:** Right **Pos:** DH-129; PH/PR-17; 1B-1 **Ht:** 6'0" **Wt:** 215 **Born:** 1/17/75 **Age:** 26

Year Team	Lg	G	AB	H	2B	3B	HR	(Hm	Rd)	TB	R	RBI	TBB	IBB	SO	HBP	SH	SF	SB	CS	SB%	GDP	Avg	OBP	SLG
1997 Montreal	NL	19	40	12	2	0	3	(1	2)	23	4	8	2	1	7	1	0	0	0	0	—	0	.300	.349	.575
1998 Montreal	NL	140	505	138	44	2	13	(3	10)	225	58	73	39	4	70	2	0	1	6	6	.50	12	.273	.327	.446
1999 Montreal	NL	100	347	96	34	2	9	(4	5)	161	38	47	22	6	35	2	0	3	2	3	.40	14	.277	.321	.464
2000 Toronto	AL	133	482	142	29	1	32	(16	16)	269	76	104	30	3	68	6	0	6	3	1	.75	14	.295	.340	.558
4 ML YEARS		392	1374	388	109	5	57	(24	33)	678	176	232	93	14	180	11	0	10	11	10	.52	40	.282	.331	.493

Aaron Fultz

Pitches: Left **Bats:** Left **Pos:** RP-58 **Ht:** 6'0" **Wt:** 196 **Born:** 9/4/73 **Age:** 27

Year Team	Lg	G	GS	CG	GF	IP	BFP	H	R	ER	HR	SH	SF	HB	TBB	IBB	SO	WP	Bk	W	L	Pct.	ShO	Sv-Op	Hld	ERA
1992 Giants	R	14	14	0	0	67.2	282	51	24	16	0	4	1	4	33	0	72	7	0	3	2	.600	0	0--	—	2.13
1993 Clinton	A	26	25	2	0	148	641	132	63	56	8	12	2	11	64	2	144	10	2	14	8	.636	1	0--	—	3.41
Fort Wayne	A	1	1	0	0	4	21	10	4	4	0	0	0	0	0	0	3	0	0	0	0	—	0	0--	—	9.00
1994 Fort Myers	A+	28	28	3	0	168.1	745	193	95	81	9	6	4	7	60	5	132	9	2	9	10	.474	0	0--	—	4.33
1995 Hardware Cy	AA	3	3	0	0	15	64	11	12	11	1	0	2	0	9	0	12	0	0	0	2	.000	0	0--	—	6.60
Fort Myers	A+	21	21	2	0	122	516	115	52	44	10	4	3	8	41	1	127	7	1	3	6	.333	2	0--	—	3.25
1996 San Jose	A+	36	12	0	11	104.2	460	101	52	46	7	9	3	8	54	2	103	13	0	9	5	.643	0	1--	—	3.96
1997 Shreveport	AA	49	0	0	20	70	293	65	30	22	4	4	5	2	19	0	60	4	1	6	3	.667	0	1--	—	2.83
1998 Shreveport	AA	54	0	0	34	62	273	58	40	26	4	8	3	3	29	10	61	5	1	5	7	.417	0	15--	—	3.77
Fresno	AAA	10	0	0	3	16	68	12	10	9	2	0	0	0	2	1	13	1	0	0	0	—	0	0--	—	5.06
1999 Fresno	AAA	37	20	1	7	137.1	601	141	87	76	32	3	9	7	51	1	151	11	1	9	8	.529	0	0--	—	4.98
2000 San Francisco	NL	58	0	0	18	69.1	299	67	38	36	8	7	6	3	28	0	62	0	2	5	2	.714	0	1-3	7	4.67

Rafael Furcal

Bats: Both **Throws:** Right **Pos:** SS-110; 2B-31; PH/PR-8 **Ht:** 5'10" **Wt:** 165 **Born:** 8/24/80 **Age:** 20

Year Team	Lg	G	AB	H	2B	3B	HR	(Hm	Rd)	TB	R	RBI	TBB	IBB	SO	HBP	SH	SF	SB	CS	SB%	GDP	Avg	OBP	SLG
1997 Braves	R	50	190	49	5	4	1	—	—	65	31	9	20	0	21	2	0	0	15	2	.88	1	.258	.335	.342
1998 Danville	R+	66	268	88	15	4	0	—	—	111	56	23	36	0	29	3	1	1	60	15	.80	2	.328	.412	.414
1999 Macon	A	83	335	113	15	1	1	—	—	133	73	29	41	1	36	5	1	0	73	22	.77	4	.337	.417	.397
Myrtle Bch	A+	43	184	54	9	3	0	—	—	69	32	12	14	0	42	0	6	0	23	8	.74	3	.293	.343	.375
2000 Greenville	AA	3	10	2	0	0	1	—	—	5	1	3	1	0	0	0	0	0	0	0	—	0	.200	.273	.500
2000 Atlanta	NL	131	455	134	20	4	4	(1	3)	174	87	37	73	0	80	3	9	2	40	14	.74	2	.295	.394	.382

Chris Fussell

Pitches: Right **Bats:** Right **Pos:** RP-11; SP-9 **Ht:** 6'2" **Wt:** 200 **Born:** 5/19/76 **Age:** 25

Year Team	Lg	G	GS	CG	GF	IP	BFP	H	R	ER	HR	SH	SF	HB	TBB	IBB	SO	WP	Bk	W	L	Pct.	ShO	Sv-Op	Hld	ERA
2000 Royals *	R	2	2	0	0	3.2	23	6	5	1	0	0	0	2	2	0	6	0	0	0	1	.000	0	0--	—	2.45
Omaha *	AAA	6	6	0	0	21.2	99	22	13	12	5	1	0	3	12	0	12	0	0	1	1	.500	0	0--	—	4.98
1998 Baltimore	AL	3	2	0	0	9.2	47	11	9	9	1	1	1	0	9	1	8	0	0	0	1	.000	0	0-0	—	8.38
1999 Kansas City	AL	17	8	0	3	56	265	72	51	46	9	1	4	5	36	3	37	6	0	5	5	.000	0	2-2	1	7.39
2000 Kansas City	AL	20	9	0	2	70	320	76	52	49	18	3	5	2	44	2	46	3	0	5	3	.625	0	0-0	—	6.30
3 ML YEARS		40	19	0	5	135.2	632	159	112	104	28	5	10	7	89	6	91	9	0	5	9	.357	0	2-2	1	6.90

Mike Fyhrie

Pitches: Right **Bats:** Right **Pos:** RP-32　　　　　　**Ht:** 6'2" **Wt:** 203 **Born:** 12/9/69 **Age:** 31

Year Team		HOW MUCH HE PITCHED						WHAT HE GAVE UP												THE RESULTS						
		G	GS	CG	GF	IP	BFP	H	R	ER	HR	SH	SF	HB	TBB	IBB	SO	WP	Bk	W	L	Pct.	ShO	Sv-Op	Hld	ERA
2000 Edmonton *	AAA	9	0	0	3	15.2	63	6	4	4	1	0	0	0	12	0	9	1	0	2	1	.667	0	1- --		2.30
1996 New York	NL	2	0	0	0	2.1	14	4	4	4	0	0	0	0	3	0	0	0	0	0	1	.000	0	0-0	0	15.43
1999 Anaheim	AL	16	7	0	5	51.2	235	61	32	29	8	0	1	0	21	1	26	0	0	0	4	.000	0	0-0	1	5.05
2000 Anaheim	AL	32	0	0	7	52.2	220	54	14	14	4	1	3	0	15	4	43	0	0	0	0	—	0	0-0	2	2.39
3 ML YEARS		50	7	0	12	106.2	469	119	50	47	12	1	4	0	39	5	69	0	0	0	5	.000	0	0-0	3	3.97

Gary Gaetti

Bats: Right **Throws:** Right **Pos:** DH-5; PH/PR-3　　　　**Ht:** 6'0" **Wt:** 205 **Born:** 8/19/58 **Age:** 42

Year Team	Lg	BATTING																BASERUNNING				PERCENTAGES		
		G	AB	H	2B	3B	HR	(Hm	Rd)	TB	R	RBI	TBB	IBB	SO	HBP	SH	SF	SB	CS	SB%	GDP	Avg	OBP	SLG
1981 Minnesota	AL	9	26	5	0	0	2	(1	1)	11	4	3	0	0	6	0	0	0	0	0	—	1	.192	.192	.423
1982 Minnesota	AL	145	508	117	25	4	25	(15	10)	225	59	84	37	2	107	3	4	13	0	4	.00	16	.230	.280	.443
1983 Minnesota	AL	157	584	143	30	3	21	(7	14)	242	81	78	54	2	121	4	0	8	7	1	.88	18	.245	.309	.414
1984 Minnesota	AL	162	588	154	29	4	5	(2	3)	206	55	65	44	1	81	4	3	5	11	5	.69	9	.262	.315	.350
1985 Minnesota	AL	160	560	138	31	0	20	(10	10)	229	71	63	37	3	89	7	3	1	13	5	.72	15	.246	.301	.409
1986 Minnesota	AL	157	596	171	34	1	34	(16	18)	309	91	108	52	4	108	6	1	6	14	15	.48	18	.287	.347	.518
1987 Minnesota	AL	154	584	150	36	2	31	(18	13)	283	95	109	37	7	92	3	1	3	10	7	.59	25	.257	.303	.485
1988 Minnesota	AL	133	468	141	29	2	28	(9	19)	258	66	88	36	5	85	5	1	6	7	4	.64	10	.301	.353	.551
1989 Minnesota	AL	130	498	125	11	4	19	(10	9)	201	63	75	25	5	87	3	1	9	6	2	.75	12	.251	.286	.404
1990 Minnesota	AL	154	577	132	27	5	16	(7	9)	217	61	85	36	1	101	3	1	8	6	1	.86	22	.229	.274	.376
1991 California	AL	152	586	144	22	1	18	(12	6)	222	58	66	33	3	104	8	2	5	5	5	.50	13	.246	.293	.379
1992 California	AL	130	456	103	13	2	12	(8	4)	156	41	48	21	4	79	6	0	3	3	1	.75	13	.226	.267	.342
1993 Cal-KC	AL	102	331	81	20	1	14	(6	8)	145	40	50	21	0	87	8	2	7	1	3	.25	5	.245	.300	.438
1994 Kansas City	AL	90	327	94	15	3	12	(5	7)	151	53	57	19	3	63	2	1	3	0	2	.00	9	.287	.328	.462
1995 Kansas City	AL	137	514	134	27	0	35	(16	19)	266	76	96	47	6	91	8	3	6	3	3	.50	7	.261	.329	.518
1996 St. Louis	NL	141	522	143	27	4	23	(13	10)	247	71	80	35	6	97	8	4	5	2	2	.50	10	.274	.326	.473
1997 St. Louis	NL	148	502	126	24	1	17	(7	10)	203	63	69	36	3	88	6	4	3	7	3	.70	20	.251	.305	.404
1998 StL-ChC	NL	128	434	122	34	1	19	(9	10)	215	60	70	43	2	62	10	1	4	1	1	.50	12	.281	.356	.495
1999 Chicago	NL	113	280	57	9	1	9	(6	3)	95	22	46	21	0	51	2	0	5	1	0	1.00	9	.204	.260	.339
2000 Boston	AL	5	10	0	0	0	0	(0	0)	0	0	1	0	0	3	0	0	1	0	0	—	0	.000	.000	.000
1993 California	AL	20	50	9	2	0	0	(0	0)	11	3	4	5	0	12	0	0	1	1	0	1.00	3	.180	.250	.220
Kansas City		82	281	72	18	1	14	(6	8)	134	37	46	16	0	75	8	2	6	0	3	.00	2	.256	.309	.477
1998 St. Louis	NL	91	306	81	23	1	11	(1	10)	139	39	43	31	1	39	5	0	3	1	1	.50	10	.265	.339	.454
Chicago	NL	37	128	41	11	0	8	(4	4)	76	21	27	12	1	23	5	1	1	0	0	—	2	.320	.397	.594
20 ML YEARS		2507	8951	2280	443	39	360	(173	187)	3881	1130	1341	634	57	1602	96	32	104	96	65	.60	236	.255	.308	.434

Eric Gagne

Pitches: Right **Bats:** Right **Pos:** SP-19; RP-1　　　　**Ht:** 6'2" **Wt:** 195 **Born:** 1/7/76 **Age:** 25

Year Team		HOW MUCH HE PITCHED						WHAT HE GAVE UP													THE RESULTS					
		G	GS	CG	GF	IP	BFP	H	R	ER	HR	SF	SH	HB	TBB	IBB	SO	WP	Bk	W	L	Pct.	ShO	Sv-Op	Hld	ERA
1996 Savannah	A	23	21	1	0	115.1	474	94	48	42	11	3	2	1	43	1	131	7	5	7	6	.538	1	0- --	—	3.28
1998 Vero Beach	A+	25	25	3	0	139.2	584	118	69	58	16	2	4	4	48	0	144	5	3	9	7	.563	1	0- --	—	3.74
1999 San Antonio	AA	26	26	0	0	167.2	683	122	55	49	17	2	2	8	64	0	185	6	0	12	4	.750	0	0- --	—	2.63
2000 Albuquerque	AAA	9	9	0	0	55.2	233	56	30	24	8	1	2	0	15	0	59	1	0	5	1	.833	0	0- --	—	3.88
1999 Los Angeles	NL	5	5	0	0	30	119	18	8	7	3	1	0	0	15	0	30	1	0	1	1	.500	0	0-0	0	2.10
2000 Los Angeles	NL	20	19	0	0	101.1	464	106	62	58	20	5	3	3	60	1	79	4	0	4	6	.400	0	0-0	0	5.15
2 ML YEARS		25	24	0	0	131.1	583	124	70	65	23	6	3	3	75	1	109	5	0	5	7	.417	0	0-0	0	4.45

Andres Galarraga

Bats: Right **Throws:** Right **Pos:** 1B-132; PH/PR-15; DH-1　　　**Ht:** 6'3" **Wt:** 235 **Born:** 6/18/61 **Age:** 40

Year Team	Lg	BATTING																BASERUNNING				PERCENTAGES		
		G	AB	H	2B	3B	HR	(Hm	Rd)	TB	R	RBI	TBB	IBB	SO	HBP	SH	SF	SB	CS	SB%	GDP	Avg	OBP	SLG
1985 Montreal	NL	24	75	14	1	0	2	(0	2)	21	9	4	3	0	18	1	0	0	1	2	.33	0	.187	.228	.280
1986 Montreal	NL	105	321	87	13	0	10	(4	6)	130	39	42	30	5	79	3	1	1	6	5	.55	8	.271	.338	.405
1987 Montreal	NL	147	551	168	40	3	13	(7	6)	253	72	90	41	13	127	10	0	4	7	10	.41	11	.305	.361	.459
1988 Montreal	NL	157	609	184	42	8	29	(14	15)	329	99	92	39	9	153	10	0	3	13	4	.76	12	.302	.352	.540
1989 Montreal	NL	152	572	147	30	1	23	(13	10)	248	76	85	48	10	158	13	0	3	12	5	.71	12	.257	.327	.434
1990 Montreal	NL	155	579	148	29	0	20	(6	14)	237	65	87	40	8	169	4	0	5	10	1	.91	14	.256	.306	.409
1991 Montreal	NL	107	375	82	13	2	9	(3	6)	126	34	33	23	5	86	2	0	5	5	6	.45	6	.219	.268	.336
1992 St. Louis	NL	95	325	79	14	2	10	(4	6)	127	38	39	11	0	69	8	0	3	5	4	.56	8	.243	.282	.391
1993 Colorado	NL	120	470	174	35	4	22	(13	9)	283	71	98	24	12	73	6	0	4	2	4	.33	9	.370	.403	.602
1994 Colorado	NL	103	417	133	21	0	31	(16	15)	247	77	85	19	8	93	6	0	3	8	3	.73	10	.319	.356	.592
1995 Colorado	NL	143	554	155	29	3	31	(18	13)	283	89	106	32	6	146	13	0	4	12	2	.86	14	.280	.331	.511
1996 Colorado	NL	159	626	190	39	3	47	(32	15)	376	119	150	40	3	157	17	0	8	18	8	.69	16	.304	.357	.601
1997 Colorado	NL	154	600	191	31	3	41	(21	20)	351	120	140	54	2	141	17	0	3	15	8	.65	16	.318	.389	.585
1998 Atlanta	NL	153	555	169	27	1	44	(16	28)	330	103	121	63	11	146	25	0	5	7	6	.54	8	.305	.397	.595
2000 Atlanta	NL	141	494	149	25	1	28	(14	14)	260	67	100	36	5	126	17	0	1	3	5	.38	15	.302	.369	.526
15 ML YEARS		1915	7123	2070	389	31	360	(181	179)	3601	1078	1272	503	97	1741	154	1	52	124	73	.63	149	.291	.348	.506

Ron Gant

Bats: R **Throws:** R **Pos:** LF-105; PH/PR-18; DH-12　　　**Ht:** 6'0" **Wt:** 196 **Born:** 3/2/65 **Age:** 36

Year Team	Lg	BATTING																BASERUNNING				PERCENTAGES		
		G	AB	H	2B	3B	HR	(Hm	Rd)	TB	R	RBI	TBB	IBB	SO	HBP	SH	SF	SB	CS	SB%	GDP	Avg	OBP	SLG
1987 Atlanta	NL	21	83	22	4	0	2	(1	1)	32	9	9	1	0	11	0	1	1	4	2	.67	3	.265	.271	.386
1988 Atlanta	NL	146	563	146	28	8	19	(7	12)	247	85	60	46	4	118	3	2	4	19	10	.66	7	.259	.317	.439
1989 Atlanta	NL	75	260	46	8	3	9	(5	4)	87	26	25	20	0	63	1	2	2	9	6	.60	0	.177	.237	.335
1990 Atlanta	NL	152	575	174	34	3	32	(18	14)	310	107	84	50	0	86	0	0	5	33	16	.67	8	.303	.357	.539

Year Team	Lg	G	AB	H	2B	3B	HR	(Hm	Rd)	TB	R	RBI	TBB	IBB	SO	HBP	SH	SF	SB	CS	SB%	GDP	Avg	OBP	SLG
1991 Atlanta	NL	154	561	141	35	3	32	(18	14)	278	101	105	71	8	104	5	0	5	34	15	.69	6	.251	.338	.496
1992 Atlanta	NL	153	544	141	22	6	17	(10	7)	226	74	80	45	5	101	7	0	6	32	10	.76	10	.259	.321	.415
1993 Atlanta	NL	157	606	166	27	4	36	(17	19)	309	113	117	67	2	117	2	0	7	26	9	.74	14	.274	.345	.510
1995 Cincinnati	NL	119	410	113	19	4	29	(12	17)	227	79	88	74	5	108	3	1	5	23	8	.74	11	.276	.386	.554
1996 St. Louis	NL	122	419	103	14	2	30	(17	13)	211	74	82	73	5	98	3	1	4	13	4	.76	9	.246	.359	.504
1997 St. Louis	NL	139	502	115	21	4	17	(11	6)	195	68	62	58	3	162	1	0	1	14	6	.70	2	.229	.310	.388
1998 St. Louis	NL	121	383	92	17	1	26	(14	12)	189	60	67	51	2	92	2	0	2	8	0	1.00	6	.240	.331	.493
1999 Philadelphia	NL	138	516	134	27	5	17	(6	11)	222	107	77	85	0	112	1	0	3	13	3	.81	6	.260	.364	.430
2000 Phi-Ana	NL	123	425	106	19	3	26	(14	12)	209	69	54	56	1	91	1	1	4	6	6	.50	7	.249	.335	.492
2000 Philadelphia	NL	89	343	87	16	2	20	(9	11)	167	54	38	36	1	73	1	1	3	5	4	.56	7	.254	.324	.487
Anaheim	AL	34	82	19	3	1	6	(5	1)	42	15	16	20	0	18	0	0	1	1	2	.33	0	.232	.379	.512
13 ML YEARS		1620	5847	1499	275	46	292	(150	142)	2742	972	910	697	35	1263	30	9	48	234	95	.71	89	.256	.336	.469

Rich Garces

Pitches: Right Bats: Right Pos: RP-64   Ht: 6'0" Wt: 215 Born: 5/18/71 Age: 30

Year Team	Lg	G	GS	CG	GF	IP	BFP	H	R	ER	HR	SH	SF	HB	TBB	IBB	SO	WP	Bk	W	L	Pct.	ShO	Sv-Op	Hld	ERA
1990 Minnesota	AL	5	0	0	3	5.2	24	4	2	1	0	0	0	0	4	0	1	0	0	0	0	—	0	2-2	0	1.59
1993 Minnesota	AL	3	0	0	1	4	18	4	2	0	0	0	0	0	2	0	3	0	0	0	0	—	0	0-0	0	0.00
1995 ChC-Fla	NL	18	0	0	7	24.1	108	25	15	12	1	1	0	0	11	2	22	0	0	0	2	.000	0	0-1	1	4.44
1996 Boston	AL	37	0	0	9	44	205	42	26	24	5	0	5	0	33	5	55	0	0	3	2	.600	0	0-2	4	4.91
1997 Boston	AL	12	0	0	4	13.2	66	14	9	7	2	0	1	0	9	0	12	0	0	0	1	.000	0	0-2	1	4.61
1998 Boston	AL	30	0	0	11	46	201	36	19	17	6	2	1	2	27	3	34	1	1	1	1	.500	0	1-3	6	3.33
1999 Boston	AL	30	0	0	4	40.2	164	25	9	7	1	0	0	0	18	1	33	0	0	5	1	.833	0	2-3	2	1.55
2000 Boston	AL	64	0	0	9	74.2	309	64	28	27	7	1	4	1	23	5	69	3	0	8	1	.889	0	1-5	17	3.25
1995 Chicago	NL	7	0	0	4	11	46	11	6	4	0	0	0	0	3	0	6	0	0	0	0	—	0	0-0	0	3.27
Florida	NL	11	0	0	3	13.1	62	14	9	8	1	1	0	0	8	2	16	0	0	0	2	.000	0	0-1	1	5.40
8 ML YEARS		199	0	0	48	253	1095	214	110	95	22	4	11	4	127	16	229	4	1	17	8	.680	0	6-18	31	3.38

Freddy Garcia

Pitches: Right Bats: Right Pos: SP-20; RP-1   Ht: 6'4" Wt: 235 Born: 10/6/76 Age: 24

Year Team	Lg	G	GS	CG	GF	IP	BFP	H	R	ER	HR	SH	SF	HB	TBB	IBB	SO	WP	Bk	W	L	Pct.	ShO	Sv-Op	Hld	ERA
1995 Astros	R	11	11	0	0	58.1	256	60	32	29	2	3	3	6	14	0	58	5	0	6	3	.667	0	0--	—	4.47
1996 Quad City	A	13	13	0	0	60.2	265	57	27	21	3	1	1	4	27	0	50	5	5	5	4	.556	0	0--	—	3.12
1997 Kissimmee	A+	27	27	5	0	179	741	165	63	51	6	4	3	4	49	3	131	3	2	10	8	.556	2	0--	—	2.56
1998 Jackson	AA	19	19	2	0	119.1	505	94	48	43	8	4	0	6	58	0	115	8	0	6	7	.462	0	0--	—	3.24
New Orleans	AAA	2	2	0	0	14.1	56	14	5	5	2	0	0	0	1	0	13	2	0	1	0	1.000	0	0--	—	3.14
Tacoma	AAA	5	5	0	0	32.2	137	30	14	14	6	0	0	2	13	0	30	0	1	3	1	.750	0	0--	—	3.86
2000 Everett	A-	2	2	0	0	10	44	11	5	5	1	0	0	0	2	0	15	2	1	0	0	—	0	0--	—	4.50
Tacoma	AAA	1	1	0	0	7	26	5	2	2	0	0	0	0	0	0	11	0	1	1	0	1.000	0	0--	—	2.57
1999 Seattle	AL	33	33	2	0	201.1	888	205	96	91	18	3	6	10	90	4	170	12	3	17	8	.680	1	0-0	0	4.07
2000 Seattle	AL	21	20	0	0	124.1	538	112	62	54	16	6	1	2	64	4	79	4	2	9	5	.643	0	0-0	0	3.91
2 ML YEARS		54	53	2	0	325.2	1426	317	158	145	34	9	7	12	154	8	249	16	5	26	13	.667	1	0-0	0	4.01

Jesse Garcia

Bats: Right Throws: Right Pos: 2B-6; SS-5; PH/PR-4   Ht: 5'10" Wt: 171 Born: 9/24/73 Age: 27

Year Team	Lg	G	AB	H	2B	3B	HR	(Hm	Rd)	TB	R	RBI	TBB	IBB	SO	HBP	SH	SF	SB	CS	SB%	GDP	Avg	OBP	SLG
1993 Orioles	R	48	156	37	4	0	0	—	—	41	20	16	21	1	32	1	8	3	14	6	.70	1	.237	.326	.263
1995 Frederick	A+	124	365	82	11	3	3	—	—	108	52	27	49	0	75	9	7	2	5	10	.33	5	.225	.329	.296
1996 High Desert	A+	137	459	122	21	5	10	—	—	183	94	66	57	0	81	8	20	4	25	7	.78	7	.266	.354	.399
1997 Bowie	AA	141	437	103	18	1	5	—	—	138	52	42	38	0	71	6	24	1	7	7	.50	9	.236	.304	.316
1998 Bowie	AA	86	258	73	13	1	2	—	—	94	46	20	34	1	37	1	6	0	12	3	.80	3	.283	.369	.364
Rochester	AAA	44	160	47	6	4	0	—	—	61	20	18	7	0	22	3	2	3	7	5	.58	3	.294	.329	.381
1999 Rochester	AAA	62	220	56	10	2	2	—	—	76	25	23	11	0	21	0	11	1	9	6	.60	5	.255	.289	.345
2000 Rochester	AAA	106	372	90	12	2	1	—	—	109	44	23	27	0	60	4	16	1	9	4	.69	8	.242	.300	.293
1999 Baltimore	AL	17	29	6	0	0	2	(1	1)	12	6	2	2	0	3	0	3	0	0	0	—	1	.207	.258	.414
2000 Baltimore	AL	14	17	1	0	0	0	(0	0)	1	2	0	2	0	2	0	0	0	0	0	—	0	.059	.158	.059
2 ML YEARS		31	46	7	0	0	2	(1	1)	13	8	2	4	0	5	0	3	0	0	0	—	1	.152	.220	.283

Karim Garcia

Bats: L Throws: L Pos: RF-7; DH-5; PH/PR-5; LF-2   Ht: 6'0" Wt: 172 Born: 10/29/75 Age: 25

Year Team	Lg	G	AB	H	2B	3B	HR	(Hm	Rd)	TB	R	RBI	TBB	IBB	SO	HBP	SH	SF	SB	CS	SB%	GDP	Avg	OBP	SLG
2000 Toledo *	AAA	40	155	46	6	2	15	—	—	101	31	38	11	1	32	3	0	3	2	1	.67	4	.297	.349	.652
Rochester *	AAA	76	270	75	17	1	13	—	—	133	38	54	34	1	70	2	0	4	3	3	.50	7	.278	.358	.493
1995 Los Angeles	NL	13	20	4	0	0	0	(0	0)	4	1	0	0	0	4	0	0	0	0	0	—	0	.200	.200	.200
1996 Los Angeles	NL	1	1	0	0	0	0	(0	0)	0	0	0	0	0	1	0	0	0	0	0	—	0	.000	.000	.000
1997 Los Angeles	NL	15	39	5	0	0	1	(0	1)	8	5	4	6	1	14	0	0	0	0	0	—	0	.128	.239	.205
1998 Arizona	NL	113	333	74	10	8	9	(4	5)	127	39	43	18	1	78	0	0	3	5	4	.56	6	.222	.260	.381
1999 Detroit	AL	96	288	69	10	3	14	(4	10)	127	38	32	20	1	67	0	0	1	2	4	.33	2	.240	.288	.441
2000 Det-Bal	AL	16	33	3	0	0	0	(0	0)	3	1	0	0	0	10	0	0	0	0	0	—	1	.091	.091	.091
2000 Detroit	AL	8	17	3	0	0	0	(0	0)	3	1	0	0	0	4	0	0	0	0	0	—	1	.176	.176	.176
Baltimore	AL	8	16	0	0	0	0	(0	0)	0	0	0	0	0	6	0	0	0	0	0	—	0	.000	.000	.000
6 ML YEARS		254	714	155	20	11	24	(8	16)	269	84	83	44	3	174	0	0	5	7	8	.47	9	.217	.261	.377

Mike Garcia

Pitches: Right **Bats:** Right **Pos:** RP-13

Ht: 6'2" **Wt:** 220 **Born:** 5/11/68 **Age:** 33

Year Team	Lg	G	GS	CG	GF	IP	BFP	H	R	ER	HR	SH	SF	HB	TBB	IBB	SO	WP	Bk	W	L	Pct.	ShO	Sv-Op	Hld	ERA
1989 Bristol	R+	8	0	0	0	15.2	68	17	9	8	0	1	0	1	4	1	13	1	1	0	3	.000	0	0--	—	4.60
Niagara Fal	A-	7	6	1	0	40.1	151	27	12	7	3	1	0	3	7	0	39	0	0	5	1	.833	0	0--	—	1.56
1990 Fayetteville	A	28	28	6	0	180.1	726	152	69	51	7	6	2	6	41	0	113	3	0	12	8	.600	2	0--	—	2.55
1991 Lakeland	A+	25	24	0	0	144	596	130	63	50	5	4	2	6	41	2	109	3	2	6	8	.429	1	0--	—	3.13
1992 London	AA	27	20	1	3	136.2	581	149	69	59	10	4	5	4	35	1	92	2	0	8	8	.500	1	0--	—	3.89
1993 London	AA	6	0	0	2	11.1	55	12	8	7	0	1	0	0	6	0	12	1	0	1	0	1.000	0	0--	—	5.56
Rochester	IND	16	16	1	0	94.2	396	89	36	31	8	1	4	1	27	0	100	5	0	9	2	.818	0	0--	—	2.95
1999 Nashville	AA	23	0	0	10	27.1	114	24	12	12	3	3	1	1	10	2	35	0	0	2	2	.000	0	2--	—	3.95
2000 Nashville	AAA	24	0	0	3	33	137	31	17	13	3	1	2	0	8	0	31	0	0	2	2	.500	0	0--	—	3.55
1999 Pittsburgh	NL	7	0	0	2	7	25	2	1	1	1	0	0	0	3	0	9	0	0	1	0	1.000	0	0-0	1	1.29
2000 Pittsburgh	NL	13	0	0	0	11.1	59	21	15	14	1	0	3	0	7	1	9	1	0	0	2	.000	0	0-1	2	11.12
2 ML YEARS		20	0	0	4	18.1	84	23	16	15	2	0	3	0	10	1	18	1	0	1	2	.333	0	0-1	3	7.36

Nomar Garciaparra

Bats: Right **Throws:** Right **Pos:** SS-136; PH/PR-3; DH-1

Ht: 6'0" **Wt:** 180 **Born:** 7/23/73 **Age:** 27

Year Team	Lg	G	AB	H	2B	3B	HR	(Hm	Rd)	TB	R	RBI	TBB	IBB	SO	HBP	SH	SF	SB	CS	SB%	GDP	Avg	OBP	SLG
1996 Boston	AL	24	87	21	2	3	4	(3	1)	41	11	16	4	0	14	0	1	1	5	0	1.00	5	.241	.272	.471
1997 Boston	AL	153	684	209	44	11	30	(11	19)	365	122	98	35	2	92	6	2	7	22	9	.71	9	.306	.342	.534
1998 Boston	AL	143	604	195	37	8	35	(17	18)	353	111	122	33	1	62	8	0	7	12	6	.67	20	.323	.362	.584
1999 Boston	AL	135	532	190	42	4	27	(14	13)	321	103	104	51	7	39	8	0	4	14	3	.82	11	.357	.418	.603
2000 Boston	AL	140	529	197	51	3	21	(7	14)	317	104	96	61	20	50	2	0	7	5	2	.71	8	.372	.434	.599
5 ML YEARS		595	2436	812	176	29	117	(52	65)	1397	451	436	184	30	257	24	3	26	58	20	.74	48	.333	.382	.573

Mark Gardner

Pitches: Right **Bats:** Right **Pos:** SP-20; RP-10

Ht: 6'1" **Wt:** 220 **Born:** 3/1/62 **Age:** 39

Year Team	Lg	G	GS	CG	GF	IP	BFP	H	R	ER	HR	SH	SF	HB	TBB	IBB	SO	WP	Bk	W	L	Pct.	ShO	Sv-Op	Hld	ERA
1989 Montreal	NL	7	4	0	1	26.1	117	26	16	15	2	0	0	2	11	1	21	0	0	0	3	.000	0	0-0	0	5.13
1990 Montreal	NL	27	26	3	1	152.2	642	129	62	58	13	4	7	9	61	5	135	2	4	7	9	.438	3	0-0	0	3.42
1991 Montreal	NL	27	27	0	0	168.1	692	139	78	72	17	7	2	4	75	1	107	2	1	9	11	.450	0	0-0	0	3.85
1992 Montreal	NL	33	30	0	1	179.2	778	179	91	87	15	12	7	9	60	2	132	2	0	12	10	.545	0	0-0	0	4.36
1993 Kansas City	AL	17	16	0	0	91.2	387	92	65	63	17	1	7	4	36	0	54	2	0	4	6	.400	0	0-0	0	6.19
1994 Florida	NL	20	14	0	3	92.1	391	97	53	50	14	4	5	1	30	2	57	3	1	4	4	.500	0	0-0	0	4.87
1995 Florida	NL	39	11	1	7	102.1	456	109	60	51	14	7	0	5	43	5	87	3	1	5	5	.500	1	1-1	4	4.49
1996 San Francisco	NL	30	28	4	0	179.1	782	200	105	88	29	6	5	8	57	3	145	2	4	12	7	.632	1	0-0	0	4.42
1997 San Francisco	NL	30	30	2	0	180.1	764	188	92	86	20	10	6	1	57	6	136	3	3	12	9	.571	1	0-0	0	4.29
1998 San Francisco	NL	33	33	4	0	212	886	203	106	102	29	6	7	6	65	5	151	5	1	13	6	.684	2	0-0	0	4.33
1999 San Francisco	NL	29	21	1	2	139	613	142	103	100	27	6	10	8	57	2	86	3	1	5	11	.313	0	0-1	1	6.47
2000 San Francisco	NL	30	20	0	3	149	634	155	72	67	16	6	6	8	42	2	92	2	1	11	7	.611	0	0-0	0	4.05
12 ML YEARS		322	260	15	18	1673	7142	1659	903	839	220	69	62	62	594	34	1203	29	13	94	88	.516	8	1-2	6	4.51

Daniel Garibay

Pitches: Left **Bats:** Left **Pos:** RP-22; SP-8

Ht: 5'11" **Wt:** 160 **Born:** 2/14/73 **Age:** 28

Year Team	Lg	G	GS	CG	GF	IP	BFP	H	R	ER	HR	SH	SF	HB	TBB	IBB	SO	WP	Bk	W	L	Pct.	ShO	Sv-Op	Hld	ERA
1994 San Antonio	AA	3	1	0	0	0.2	17	10	10	9	2	0	0	0	4	0	0	1	0	0	1	.000	0	0--	—	121.50
2000 Iowa	AAA	1	1	0	0	4.1	20	3	1	1	0	0	0	0	5	1	2	0	0	0	0	—	0	0--	—	2.08
2000 Chicago	NL	30	8	0	6	74.2	345	88	54	50	9	5	6	1	39	1	46	4	0	2	8	.200	0	0-2	1	6.03

Jon Garland

Pitches: Right **Bats:** Right **Pos:** SP-13; RP-2

Ht: 6'6" **Wt:** 205 **Born:** 9/27/79 **Age:** 21

Year Team	Lg	G	GS	CG	GF	IP	BFP	H	R	ER	HR	SH	SF	HB	TBB	IBB	SO	WP	Bk	W	L	Pct.	ShO	Sv-Op	Hld	ERA
1997 Cubs	R	10	7	0	0	40	161	37	14	12	3	0	0	1	10	0	39	3	3	3	2	.600	0	0--	—	2.70
1998 Rockford	A	19	19	1	0	107.1	467	124	69	60	11	1	1	8	45	0	70	5	1	4	7	.364	0	0--	—	5.03
Hickory	A	5	5	0	0	26.2	126	36	20	16	2	1	2	2	13	0	19	2	0	1	4	.200	0	0--	—	5.40
1999 Winston-Sal	A+	19	19	2	0	119	502	109	57	44	7	4	5	8	39	2	84	7	0	5	7	.417	1	0--	—	3.33
Birmingham	AA	7	7	0	0	39	175	39	22	19	4	2	1	3	18	0	27	4	0	3	1	.750	0	0--	—	4.38
2000 Charlotte	AAA	16	16	2	0	103.2	433	99	28	26	3	4	0	1	32	2	63	2	0	9	2	.818	1	0--	—	2.26
Birmingham	AA	1	1	0	0	6	22	4	0	0	0	1	0	0	1	0	10	0	0	0	0	—	0	0--	—	0.00
2000 Chicago	AL	15	13	0	1	69.2	324	82	55	50	10	0	2	1	40	0	42	4	0	4	8	.333	0	0-0	1	6.46

Jason Giambi

Bats: Left **Throws:** Right **Pos:** 1B-124; DH-24; PH/PR-4

Ht: 6'3" **Wt:** 235 **Born:** 1/8/71 **Age:** 30

Year Team	Lg	G	AB	H	2B	3B	HR	(Hm	Rd)	TB	R	RBI	TBB	IBB	SO	HBP	SH	SF	SB	CS	SB%	GDP	Avg	OBP	SLG
1995 Oakland	AL	54	176	45	7	0	6	(3	3)	70	27	25	28	0	31	3	1	2	2	1	.67	4	.256	.364	.398
1996 Oakland	AL	140	536	156	40	1	20	(6	14)	258	84	79	51	3	95	5	1	5	0	1	.00	15	.291	.355	.481
1997 Oakland	AL	142	519	152	41	2	20	(14	6)	257	66	81	55	3	89	6	0	8	0	1	.00	11	.293	.362	.495
1998 Oakland	AL	153	562	166	28	0	27	(12	15)	275	92	110	81	7	102	5	0	9	2	2	.50	16	.295	.384	.489
1999 Oakland	AL	158	575	181	36	1	33	(17	16)	318	115	123	105	6	106	7	0	8	1	1	.50	11	.315	.422	.553
2000 Oakland	AL	152	510	170	29	1	43	(23	20)	330	108	137	137	6	96	9	0	8	2	0	1.00	9	.333	.476	.647
6 ML YEARS		799	2878	870	181	5	149	(75	74)	1508	492	555	457	25	519	35	2	40	7	6	.54	66	.302	.399	.524

Jeremy Giambi

Bats: L Throws: L Pos: RF-49; PH/PR-33; DH-21; 1B-15; LF-6   Ht: 6'0" Wt: 200 Born: 9/30/74 Age: 26

Year Team	Lg	G	AB	H	2B	3B	HR	(Hm	Rd)	TB	R	RBI	TBB	IBB	SO	HBP	SH	SF	SB	CS	SB%	GDP	Avg	OBP	SLG
2000 Sacramento *	AAA	8	31	11	2	0	2	—	—	19	8	8	8	0	7	0	0	0	1	1	.50	1	.355	.487	.613
1998 Kansas City	AL	18	58	13	4	0	2	(0	2)	23	6	8	11	0	9	0	0	1	0	1	.00	3	.224	.343	.397
1999 Kansas City	AL	90	288	82	13	1	3	(2	1)	106	34	34	40	5	67	3	1	4	0	0	—	7	.285	.373	.368
2000 Oakland	AL	104	260	66	10	2	10	(3	7)	110	42	50	32	2	61	3	3	4	0	0	—	7	.254	.338	.423
3 ML YEARS		212	606	161	27	3	15	(5	10)	239	82	92	83	7	137	6	4	9	0	1	.00	17	.266	.355	.394

Benji Gil

Bats: R Throws: R Pos: SS-94; PH/PR-10; 2B-7; DH-6; 1B-3   Ht: 6'2" Wt: 190 Born: 10/6/72 Age: 28

Year Team	Lg	G	AB	H	2B	3B	HR	(Hm	Rd)	TB	R	RBI	TBB	IBB	SO	HBP	SH	SF	SB	CS	SB%	GDP	Avg	OBP	SLG
1993 Texas	AL	22	57	7	0	0	0	(0	0)	7	3	2	5	0	22	0	4	0	1	2	.33	0	.123	.194	.123
1995 Texas	AL	130	415	91	20	3	9	(5	4)	144	36	46	26	0	147	1	10	2	2	4	.33	5	.219	.266	.347
1996 Texas	AL	5	5	2	0	0	0	(0	0)	2	0	1	1	0	1	0	1	0	0	1	.00	0	.400	.500	.400
1997 Texas	AL	110	317	71	13	2	5	(3	2)	103	35	31	17	0	96	1	6	4	1	2	.33	3	.224	.263	.325
2000 Anaheim	AL	110	301	72	14	1	6	(4	2)	106	28	23	30	0	59	5	5	2	10	6	.63	7	.239	.317	.352
5 ML YEARS		377	1095	243	47	6	20	(12	8)	362	102	103	79	0	325	7	26	8	14	15	.48	15	.222	.277	.331

Shawn Gilbert

Bats: R Throws: R Pos: LF-8; PH/PR-5; CF-4; RF-2   Ht: 5'9" Wt: 185 Born: 3/12/68 Age: 33

Year Team	Lg	G	AB	H	2B	3B	HR	(Hm	Rd)	TB	R	RBI	TBB	IBB	SO	HBP	SH	SF	SB	CS	SB%	GDP	Avg	OBP	SLG
2000 Albuquerque *	AAA	86	297	99	19	4	14	—	—	168	67	49	60	1	69	5	0	1	11	10	.52	3	.333	.452	.566
1997 New York	NL	29	22	3	0	0	1	(1	0)	6	3	1	1	0	8	0	0	0	1	0	1.00	0	.136	.174	.273
1998 NYM-StL	NL	7	5	1	0	0	0	(0	0)	1	1	0	0	0	2	0	0	0	1	0	1.00	0	.200	.200	.200
2000 Los Angeles	NL	15	20	3	1	0	1	(0	1)	7	5	3	2	0	7	0	1	0	0	0	—	0	.150	.227	.350
1998 New York	NL	3	3	0	0	0	0	(0	0)	0	1	0	0	0	1	0	0	0	0	0	—	0	.000	.000	.000
St. Louis	NL	4	2	1	0	0	0	(0	0)	1	0	0	0	0	1	0	0	0	1	0	1.00	0	.500	.500	.500
3 ML YEARS		51	47	7	1	0	2	(1	1)	14	9	4	3	0	17	0	1	0	2	0	1.00	0	.149	.200	.298

Brian Giles

Bats: L Throws: L Pos: CF-72; LF-46; RF-39; PH/PR-1   Ht: 5'10" Wt: 200 Born: 1/20/71 Age: 30

Year Team	Lg	G	AB	H	2B	3B	HR	(Hm	Rd)	TB	R	RBI	TBB	IBB	SO	HBP	SH	SF	SB	CS	SB%	GDP	Avg	OBP	SLG
1995 Cleveland	AL	6	9	5	0	0	1	(0	1)	8	6	3	0	0	1	0	0	0	0	0	—	0	.556	.556	.889
1996 Cleveland	AL	51	121	43	14	1	5	(2	3)	74	26	27	19	4	13	0	0	3	3	0	1.00	6	.355	.434	.612
1997 Cleveland	AL	130	377	101	15	3	17	(7	10)	173	62	61	63	2	50	1	3	7	13	3	.81	10	.268	.368	.459
1998 Cleveland	AL	112	350	94	19	0	16	(10	6)	161	56	66	73	8	75	3	1	3	10	5	.67	7	.269	.396	.460
1999 Pittsburgh	NL	141	521	164	33	4	39	(24	15)	320	109	115	95	7	80	3	0	8	6	2	.75	14	.315	.418	.614
2000 Pittsburgh	NL	156	559	176	37	7	35	(16	19)	332	111	123	114	13	69	7	0	8	6	0	1.00	15	.315	.432	.594
6 ML YEARS		596	1937	583	118	14	113	(59	54)	1068	370	395	364	34	288	14	4	29	38	10	.79	52	.301	.410	.551

Bernard Gilkey

Bats: R Throws: R Pos: PH/PR-34; RF-32; LF-9; DH-8   Ht: 6'0" Wt: 198 Born: 9/24/66 Age: 34

Year Team	Lg	G	AB	H	2B	3B	HR	(Hm	Rd)	TB	R	RBI	TBB	IBB	SO	HBP	SH	SF	SB	CS	SB%	GDP	Avg	OBP	SLG
1990 St. Louis	NL	18	64	19	5	2	1	(0	1)	31	11	3	8	0	5	0	0	0	6	1	.86	1	.297	.375	.484
1991 St. Louis	NL	81	268	58	7	2	5	(2	3)	84	28	20	39	0	33	1	1	2	14	8	.64	14	.216	.316	.313
1992 St. Louis	NL	131	384	116	19	4	7	(3	4)	164	56	43	39	1	52	1	3	4	18	12	.60	13	.302	.364	.427
1993 St. Louis	NL	137	557	170	40	5	16	(7	9)	268	99	70	56	2	66	4	0	5	15	10	.60	16	.305	.370	.481
1994 St. Louis	NL	105	380	96	22	1	6	(0	6)	138	52	45	39	2	65	10	0	2	15	8	.65	6	.253	.336	.363
1995 St. Louis	NL	121	480	143	33	4	17	(5	12)	235	73	69	42	3	70	5	1	3	12	6	.67	17	.298	.358	.490
1996 New York	NL	153	571	181	44	3	30	(14	16)	321	108	117	73	7	125	4	0	8	17	9	.65	18	.317	.393	.562
1997 New York	NL	145	518	129	31	1	18	(7	11)	216	85	78	70	1	111	6	0	12	7	11	.39	9	.249	.338	.417
1998 NYM-Ari	NL	111	365	85	15	0	5	(2	3)	115	41	33	43	1	80	5	3	3	9	3	.75	11	.233	.320	.315
1999 Arizona	NL	94	204	60	16	1	8	(4	4)	102	28	39	29	2	42	2	1	5	2	2	.50	7	.294	.379	.500
2000 Ari-Bos		74	164	29	6	1	3	(1	2)	46	17	15	17	2	28	3	0	0	0	0	—	8	.177	.265	.280
1998 New York	NL	82	264	60	15	0	4	(1	3)	87	33	28	32	1	66	4	2	3	5	1	.83	6	.227	.317	.330
Arizona	NL	29	101	25	0	0	1	(1	0)	28	8	5	11	0	14	1	1	0	4	2	.67	5	.248	.327	.277
2000 Arizona	NL	38	73	8	1	0	2	(1	1)	15	6	6	7	2	16	0	0	0	0	0	—	3	.110	.185	.205
Boston	AL	36	91	21	5	1	1	(0	1)	31	11	9	10	0	12	3	0	0	0	0	—	5	.231	.327	.341
11 ML YEARS		1170	3955	1086	238	24	116	(45	71)	1720	598	532	455	21	677	41	9	45	115	70	.62	112	.275	.352	.435

Keith Ginter

Bats: Right Throws: Right Pos: PH/PR-3; 2B-2   Ht: 5'10" Wt: 190 Born: 5/5/76 Age: 25

Year Team	Lg	G	AB	H	2B	3B	HR	(Hm	Rd)	TB	R	RBI	TBB	IBB	SO	HBP	SH	SF	SB	CS	SB%	GDP	Avg	OBP	SLG
1998 Auburn	A-	71	241	76	22	1	8	—	—	124	55	41	60	0	68	7	0	2	10	7	.59	1	.315	.461	.515
1999 Jackson	AA	9	34	13	1	0	1	—	—	17	9	6	4	0	6	2	0	1	0	0	—	0	.382	.463	.500
Kissimmee	A+	103	376	99	15	4	13	—	—	161	66	46	61	1	90	12	2	2	9	10	.47	7	.263	.381	.428
2000 Round Rock	AA	125	462	154	30	3	26	—	—	268	108	92	82	3	127	24	0	1	24	11	.69	4	.333	.457	.580
2000 Houston	NL	5	8	2	0	0	1	(1	0)	5	3	3	1	0	3	0	0	1	0	0	—	0	.250	.300	.625

Matt Ginter

Pitches: Right Bats: Right Pos: RP-7   Ht: 6'1" Wt: 215 Born: 12/24/77 Age: 23

Year Team	Lg	G	GS	CG	GF	IP	BFP	H	R	ER	HR	SH	SF	HB	TBB	IBB	SO	WP	Bk	W	L	Pct.	ShO	Sv-Op	Hld	ERA
1999 White Sox	R	3	0	0	1	8.1	33	5	4	3	0	0	0	0	3	0	10	0	0	1	0	1.000	0	1- -	-	3.24
Burlington	A	9	9	0	0	40	173	38	20	18	3	1	0	3	19	0	29	1	0	4	2	.667	0	0- -	-	4.05
2000 Birmingham	AA	27	26	0	0	179.2	741	153	72	45	4	5	5	13	60	2	126	12	0	11	8	.579	2	0- -	-	2.25
2000 Chicago	AL	7	0	0	3	9.1	52	18	14	14	5	0	1	0	7	0	6	1	0	1	0	1.000	0	0-1	0	13.50

Charles Gipson

Bats: R Throws: R Pos: RF-29; LF-14; PH/PR-14; CF-8; 3B-5; SS-5; DH-1   Ht: 6'2" Wt: 180 Born: 12/16/72 Age: 28

Year Team	Lg	G	AB	H	2B	3B	HR	(Hm	Rd)	TB	R	RBI	TBB	IBB	SO	HBP	SH	SF	SB	CS	SB%	GDP	Avg	OBP	SLG
2000 Tacoma *	AAA	67	214	53	6	6	1	—	—	74	27	22	31	1	38	3	4	3	16	7	.70	7	.248	.347	.346
1998 Seattle	AL	44	51	12	1	0	0	(0	0)	13	11	2	5	1	9	1	0	0	2	1	.67	1	.235	.316	.255
1999 Seattle	AL	55	80	18	5	2	0	(0	0)	27	16	9	6	0	13	1	2	0	3	4	.43	2	.225	.287	.338
2000 Seattle	AL	59	29	9	1	1	0	(0	0)	12	7	3	4	0	9	0	0	0	2	3	.40	0	.310	.394	.414
3 ML YEARS		158	160	39	7	3	0	(0	0)	52	34	14	15	1	31	2	2	0	7	8	.47	3	.244	.316	.325

Joe Girardi

Bats: Right Throws: Right Pos: C-103; PH/PR-4   Ht: 5'11" Wt: 200 Born: 10/14/64 Age: 36

Year Team	Lg	G	AB	H	2B	3B	HR	(Hm	Rd)	TB	R	RBI	TBB	IBB	SO	HBP	SH	SF	SB	CS	SB%	GDP	Avg	OBP	SLG
1989 Chicago	NL	59	157	39	10	0	1	(0	1)	52	15	14	11	5	26	2	1	1	2	1	.67	4	.248	.304	.331
1990 Chicago	NL	133	419	113	24	2	1	(1	0)	144	36	38	17	11	50	3	4	4	8	3	.73	13	.270	.300	.344
1991 Chicago	NL	21	47	9	2	0	0	(0	0)	11	3	6	1	6	6	0	1	0	0	0	—	0	.191	.283	.234
1992 Chicago	NL	91	270	73	3	1	1	(1	0)	81	19	12	19	3	38	1	0	1	0	2	.00	7	.270	.320	.300
1993 Colorado	NL	86	310	90	14	5	3	(2	1)	123	35	31	24	0	41	3	12	1	6	6	.50	6	.290	.346	.397
1994 Colorado	NL	93	330	91	9	4	4	(1	3)	120	47	34	21	1	48	2	6	2	3	3	.50	13	.276	.321	.364
1995 Colorado	NL	125	462	121	17	2	8	(6	2)	166	63	55	29	0	76	2	2	1	3	3	.50	15	.262	.308	.359
1996 New York	AL	124	422	124	22	3	2	(1	1)	158	55	45	30	1	55	5	11	3	13	4	.76	11	.294	.346	.374
1997 New York	AL	112	398	105	23	1	1	(1	0)	133	38	50	26	1	53	2	3	2	2	3	.40	15	.264	.311	.334
1998 New York	AL	78	254	70	11	4	3	(2	1)	98	31	31	14	1	38	2	2	1	2	4	.33	10	.276	.317	.386
1999 New York	AL	65	209	50	16	1	2	(1	1)	74	23	27	10	0	26	0	8	2	3	1	.75	16	.239	.271	.354
2000 Chicago	NL	106	363	101	15	1	6	(4	2)	136	47	40	32	3	61	3	6	3	1	0	1.00	12	.278	.339	.375
12 ML YEARS		1093	3641	986	166	24	32	(19	13)	1296	412	383	239	27	518	25	74	21	43	30	.59	123	.271	.318	.356

Doug Glanville

Bats: Right Throws: Right Pos: CF-150; PH/PR-6   Ht: 6'2" Wt: 172 Born: 8/25/70 Age: 30

Year Team	Lg	G	AB	H	2B	3B	HR	(Hm	Rd)	TB	R	RBI	TBB	IBB	SO	HBP	SH	SF	SB	CS	SB%	GDP	Avg	OBP	SLG
1996 Chicago	NL	49	83	20	5	1	1	(1	0)	30	10	10	3	0	11	0	2	1	2	0	1.00	4	.241	.264	.361
1997 Chicago	NL	146	474	142	22	5	4	(2	2)	186	79	35	24	0	46	1	9	2	19	11	.63	9	.300	.333	.392
1998 Philadelphia	NL	158	678	189	28	7	8	(3	5)	255	106	49	42	1	89	6	5	4	23	6	.79	7	.279	.325	.376
1999 Philadelphia	NL	150	628	204	38	6	11	(5	6)	287	101	73	48	1	82	6	5	5	34	2	.94	9	.325	.376	.457
2000 Philadelphia	NL	154	637	175	27	6	8	(3	5)	238	89	52	31	1	76	2	12	7	31	8	.79	11	.275	.307	.374
5 ML YEARS		657	2500	730	120	25	32	(14	18)	996	385	219	148	3	304	15	33	19	109	27	.80	36	.292	.333	.398

Keith Glauber

Pitches: Right Bats: Right Pos: RP-4   Ht: 6'2" Wt: 190 Born: 1/18/72 Age: 29

Year Team	Lg	G	GS	CG	GF	IP	BFP	H	R	ER	HR	SH	SF	HB	TBB	IBB	SO	WP	Bk	W	L	Pct.	ShO	Sv-Op	Hld	ERA
1994 New Jersey	A-	17	10	0	3	68.2	289	67	36	32	3	4	2	2	26	1	51	6	0	4	6	.400	0	0- -	-	4.19
1995 Savannah	A	40	0	0	3	62.2	277	50	29	26	2	2	3	5	36	3	62	9	1	2	1	.667	0	0- -	-	3.73
1996 Peoria	A	54	0	0	36	64	276	54	31	22	2	2	5	1	26	2	80	2	1	3	3	.500	0	14- -	-	3.09
1997 Arkansas	AA	50	0	0	22	59	245	48	22	18	3	2	4	2	25	2	53	5	0	5	7	.417	0	3- -	-	2.75
Louisville	AAA	15	0	0	12	15.2	71	18	14	9	1	2	1	0	4	0	14	0	0	1	3	.250	0	5- -	-	5.17
1998 Burlington	A	7	1	0	1	14	73	13	9	6	1	0	0	2	6	0	13	2	0	1	0	1.000	0	0- -	-	3.86
Chattanooga	AA	2	2	0	0	9	35	3	4	4	1	0	0	0	6	0	5	0	0	1	0	1.000	0	0- -	-	4.00
Indianapols	AAA	4	4	0	0	16	78	20	17	16	1	3	2	6	14	0	15	3	0	1	3	.250	0	0- -	-	9.00
1999 Chattanooga	AA	7	7	0	0	50	193	42	12	11	0	1	1	2	8	0	26	3	1	5	0	1.000	0	0- -	-	1.98
Indianapols	AAA	12	12	1	0	68	305	84	49	44	8	2	6	6	20	0	51	1	0	3	3	.500	1	0- -	-	5.82
2000 Chattanooga	AA	32	0	0	9	41	176	42	19	16	2	5	2	4	12	3	27	2	1	0	4	.000	0	2- -	-	3.51
Louisville	AAA	18	0	0	10	29.2	116	26	5	5	1	1	1	0	6	1	15	1	0	1	2	.333	0	4- -	-	1.52
1998 Cincinnati	NL	3	0	0	2	7.2	31	6	2	2	0	0	0	0	1	0	4	2	0	0	0	—	0	0-0	-	2.35
2000 Cincinnati	NL	4	0	0	0	7.1	30	5	3	3	0	0	0	0	2	0	4	0	0	0	0	—	0	0-0	-	3.68
2 ML YEARS		7	0	0	2	15	61	11	5	5	0	0	2	1	3	0	8	2	0	0	0	—	0	0-0	-	3.00

Troy Glaus

Bats: R Throws: R Pos: 3B-156; SS-6; DH-4; PH/PR-1   Ht: 6'5" Wt: 229 Born: 8/3/76 Age: 24

Year Team	Lg	G	AB	H	2B	3B	HR	(Hm	Rd)	TB	R	RBI	TBB	IBB	SO	HBP	SH	SF	SB	CS	SB%	GDP	Avg	OBP	SLG
1998 Anaheim	AL	48	165	36	9	0	1	(0	1)	48	19	23	15	0	51	0	0	2	1	0	1.00	4	.218	.280	.291
1999 Anaheim	AL	154	551	132	29	0	29	(12	17)	248	85	79	71	1	143	6	0	3	5	1	.83	9	.240	.331	.450
2000 Anaheim	AL	159	563	160	37	1	47	(24	23)	340	120	102	112	6	163	2	0	1	14	11	.56	14	.284	.404	.604
3 ML YEARS		361	1279	328	75	1	77	(36	41)	636	224	204	198	7	357	8	0	6	20	12	.63	26	.256	.358	.497

Tom Glavine

Pitches: Left **Bats:** Left **Pos:** SP-35   **Ht:** 6'0" **Wt:** 185 **Born:** 3/25/66 **Age:** 35

		HOW MUCH HE PITCHED						WHAT HE GAVE UP											THE RESULTS						
Year Team	Lg	G	GS	CG	GF	IP	BFP	H	R	ER	HR	SH	SF	HB	TBB	IBB	SO	WP	Bk	W	L	Pct.	ShO	Sv-Op	Hld	ERA
1987 Atlanta	NL	9	9	0	0	50.1	238	55	34	31	5	2	3	3	33	4	20	1	1	2	4	.333	0	0-0	0	5.54
1988 Atlanta	NL	34	34	1	0	195.1	844	201	111	99	12	17	11	8	63	7	84	2	2	7	17	.292	0	0-0	0	4.56
1989 Atlanta	NL	29	29	6	0	186	766	172	88	76	20	11	4	2	40	3	90	2	0	14	8	.636	4	0-0	0	3.68
1990 Atlanta	NL	33	33	1	0	214.1	929	232	111	102	18	21	2	1	78	10	129	8	1	10	12	.455	0	0-0	0	4.28
1991 Atlanta	NL	34	34	9	0	246.2	989	201	83	70	17	7	6	2	69	6	192	10	2	20	11	.645	1	0-0	0	2.55
1992 Atlanta	NL	33	33	7	0	225	919	197	81	69	6	2	6	2	70	7	129	5	0	20	8	.714	5	0-0	0	2.76
1993 Atlanta	NL	36	36	4	0	239.1	1014	236	91	85	16	10	2	2	90	7	120	4	0	22	6	.786	2	0-0	0	3.20
1994 Atlanta	NL	25	25	2	0	165.1	731	173	76	73	10	9	6	1	70	10	140	8	1	13	9	.591	0	0-0	0	3.97
1995 Atlanta	NL	29	29	3	0	198.2	822	182	76	68	9	7	5	5	66	0	127	3	0	16	7	.696	1	0-0	0	3.08
1996 Atlanta	NL	36	36	1	0	235.1	994	222	91	78	14	15	2	0	85	7	181	4	0	15	10	.600	0	0-0	0	2.98
1997 Atlanta	NL	33	33	5	0	240	970	197	86	79	20	11	6	4	79	9	152	3	0	14	7	.667	2	0-0	0	2.96
1998 Atlanta	NL	33	33	4	0	229.1	934	202	67	63	13	6	2	2	74	2	157	3	0	20	6	.769	3	0-0	0	2.47
1999 Atlanta	NL	35	35	2	0	234	1023	259	115	107	18	22	10	4	83	14	138	2	0	14	11	.560	0	0-0	0	4.12
2000 Atlanta	NL	35	35	4	0	241	992	222	101	91	24	9	5	4	65	6	152	0	0	21	9	.700	2	0-0	0	3.40
14 ML YEARS		434	434	49	0	2900.2	12165	2751	1211	1091	202	149	70	40	965	92	1811	55	7	208	125	.625	20	0-0	0	3.39

Ross Gload

Bats: L **Throws:** L **Pos:** PH/PR-9; LF-7; 1B-2; RF-1   **Ht:** 6'2" **Wt:** 210 **Born:** 4/5/76 **Age:** 25

		BATTING																BASERUNNING				PERCENTAGES		
Year Team	Lg	G	AB	H	2B	3B	HR	(Hm | Rd)	TB	R	RBI	TBB	IBB	SO	HBP	SH	SF	SB	CS	SB%	GDP	Avg	OBP	SLG
1997 Utica	A-	68	245	64	15	2	3	—	—	92	28	43	28	0	57	2	0	5	1	1	.50	5	.261	.336	.376
1998 Kane County	A	132	501	157	41	3	12	—	—	240	77	92	58	7	84	3	2	3	7	6	.54	13	.313	.386	.479
1999 Brevard Cty	A+	133	490	146	26	3	10	—	—	208	80	74	53	3	76	5	2	5	1	1	.75	8	.298	.369	.424
2000 Portland	AA	100	401	114	28	4	16	—	—	198	60	65	29	3	53	2	3	4	4	1	.80	4	.284	.333	.494
Iowa	AAA	28	104	42	10	2	14	—	—	98	24	39	9	1	13	1	0	1	1	1	.50	2	.404	.452	.942
2000 Chicago	NL	18	31	6	0	1	1	(0 | 1)	11	4	3	1	0	10	0	0	1	0	0	—	1	.194	.257	.355

Ryan Glynn

Pitches: Right **Bats:** Right **Pos:** SP-16   **Ht:** 6'3" **Wt:** 195 **Born:** 11/1/74 **Age:** 26

		HOW MUCH HE PITCHED						WHAT HE GAVE UP											THE RESULTS						
Year Team	Lg	G	GS	CG	GF	IP	BFP	H	R	ER	HR	SH	SF	HB	TBB	IBB	SO	WP	Bk	W	L	Pct.	ShO	Sv-Op	Hld	ERA
1995 Hudson Val	A-	9	8	0	0	44	192	56	27	23	0	0	1	3	16	1	21	10	3	3	3	.500	1	0--	—	4.70
1996 Chston-SC	A	19	19	2	0	121	526	118	70	61	10	6	6	8	59	2	72	12	0	8	7	.533	1	0--	—	4.54
1997 Charlotte	A+	23	22	5	1	134	579	148	81	74	13	2	7	4	44	0	96	9	1	8	7	.533	1	1--	—	4.97
Tulsa	AA	3	3	0	0	21.1	94	21	9	8	1	1	2	2	10	0	18	2	0	1	1	.500	0	0--	—	3.38
1998 Tulsa	AA	26	24	4	0	157	660	140	66	60	12	4	3	5	64	0	111	9	1	9	6	.600	1	0--	—	3.44
1999 Oklahoma	AAA	16	16	2	0	90.1	385	81	46	34	7	1	4	4	36	1	55	3	0	6	2	.750	1	0--	—	3.39
2000 Oklahoma	AAA	15	14	2	0	83.2	347	72	36	33	5	0	3	3	33	1	66	7	1	4	2	.667	2	0--	—	3.55
1999 Texas	AL	13	10	0	2	54.2	262	71	46	44	10	0	1	1	35	0	39	3	1	2	4	.333	0	0-0	0	7.24
2000 Texas	AL	16	16	0	0	88.2	412	107	65	55	15	3	0	3	41	2	33	3	0	5	7	.417	0	0-0	0	5.58
2 ML YEARS		29	26	0	2	143.1	674	178	111	99	25	3	1	4	76	2	72	6	1	7	11	.389	0	0-0	0	6.22

Wayne Gomes

Pitches: Right **Bats:** Right **Pos:** RP-65   **Ht:** 6'2" **Wt:** 227 **Born:** 1/15/73 **Age:** 28

		HOW MUCH HE PITCHED						WHAT HE GAVE UP											THE RESULTS						
Year Team	Lg	G	GS	CG	GF	IP	BFP	H	R	ER	HR	SH	SF	HB	TBB	IBB	SO	WP	Bk	W	L	Pct.	ShO	Sv-Op	Hld	ERA
2000 Scrantn-WB	AAA	3	0	0	1	4	16	3	1	1	0	0	0	0	1	0	1	0	0	0	0	—	0	0--	—	2.25
1997 Philadelphia	NL	37	0	0	13	42.2	191	45	26	25	4	2	0	1	24	0	24	2	0	5	1	.833	0	0-1	3	5.27
1998 Philadelphia	NL	71	0	0	16	93.1	408	94	48	44	9	5	1	3	35	4	86	6	0	9	6	.600	0	1-8	13	4.24
1999 Philadelphia	NL	73	0	0	58	74	341	70	38	35	5	5	3	2	56	2	58	3	1	5	5	.500	0	19-24	9	4.26
2000 Philadelphia	NL	65	0	0	26	73.2	324	72	41	36	6	7	4	3	35	3	49	10	0	4	6	.400	0	7-11	4	4.40
4 ML YEARS		246	0	0	113	283.2	1264	281	153	140	24	19	8	9	150	9	217	21	1	23	18	.561	0	27-44	29	4.44

Chris Gomez

Bats: Right **Throws:** Right **Pos:** SS-17; PH/PR-14; 2B-3   **Ht:** 6'1" **Wt:** 195 **Born:** 6/16/71 **Age:** 30

		BATTING																BASERUNNING				PERCENTAGES		
Year Team	Lg	G	AB	H	2B	3B	HR	(Hm | Rd)	TB	R	RBI	TBB	IBB	SO	HBP	SH	SF	SB	CS	SB%	GDP	Avg	OBP	SLG
1993 Detroit	AL	46	128	32	7	1	0	(0 | 0)	41	11	11	9	0	17	1	3	0	2	2	.50	2	.250	.304	.320
1994 Detroit	AL	84	296	76	19	0	8	(5 | 3)	119	32	53	33	0	64	3	3	1	5	3	.63	8	.257	.336	.402
1995 Detroit	AL	123	431	96	20	2	11	(5 | 6)	153	49	50	41	0	96	3	3	4	4	1	.80	13	.223	.292	.355
1996 Det-SD		137	456	117	21	1	4	(2 | 2)	152	53	45	57	1	84	7	6	2	3	3	.50	16	.257	.347	.333
1997 San Diego	NL	150	522	132	19	2	5	(2 | 3)	170	62	54	53	1	114	5	3	3	5	8	.38	16	.253	.326	.326
1998 San Diego	NL	145	449	120	32	3	4	(3 | 1)	170	55	39	51	7	87	5	7	3	1	3	.25	11	.267	.346	.379
1999 San Diego	NL	76	234	59	8	1	1	(1 | 0)	72	20	15	27	3	49	1	2	1	1	2	.33	6	.252	.331	.308
2000 San Diego	NL	33	54	12	0	0	0	(0 | 0)	12	4	3	7	0	5	0	1	1	0	0	—	0	.222	.306	.222
1996 Detroit	AL	48	128	31	5	0	1	(1 | 0)	39	21	16	18	0	20	1	3	0	1	1	.50	5	.242	.340	.305
San Diego	NL	89	328	86	16	1	3	(1 | 2)	113	32	29	39	1	64	6	3	2	2	2	.50	11	.262	.349	.345
8 ML YEARS		794	2570	644	126	10	33	(18 | 15)	889	286	270	278	12	516	25	28	15	21	22	.49	73	.251	.328	.346

Alex Gonzalez

Bats: Right **Throws:** Right **Pos:** SS-104; PH/PR-6   **Ht:** 6'0" **Wt:** 170 **Born:** 2/15/77 **Age:** 24

		BATTING																BASERUNNING				PERCENTAGES		
Year Team	Lg	G	AB	H	2B	3B	HR	(Hm | Rd)	TB	R	RBI	TBB	IBB	SO	HBP	SH	SF	SB	CS	SB%	GDP	Avg	OBP	SLG
2000 Brevard Cty *	A+	4	17	2	0	0	0	—	—	2	1	2	1	0	3	0	0	0	1	0	1.00	0	.118	.167	.118
1998 Florida	NL	25	86	13	2	0	3	(1 | 2)	24	11	7	9	0	30	1	2	0	0	0	—	2	.151	.240	.279

Year Team	Lg	G	AB	H	2B	3B	HR	Hm	Rd	TB	R	RBI	TBB	IBB	SO	HBP	SH	SF	SB	CS	SB%	GDP	Avg	OBP	SLG
1999 Florida	NL	136	560	155	28	8	14	7	7	241	81	59	15	0	113	12	1	3	3	5	.38	13	.277	.308	.430
2000 Florida	NL	109	385	77	17	4	7	5	2	123	35	42	13	0	77	2	5	2	7	1	.88	7	.200	.229	.319
3 ML YEARS		270	1031	245	47	12	24	13	11	388	127	108	37	0	220	15	8	5	10	6	.63	22	.238	.273	.376

Alex S. Gonzalez

Bats: Right **Throws:** Right **Pos:** SS-141   **Ht:** 6'0" **Wt:** 200 **Born:** 4/8/73 **Age:** 28

Year Team	Lg	G	AB	H	2B	3B	HR	Hm	Rd	TB	R	RBI	TBB	IBB	SO	HBP	SH	SF	SB	CS	SB%	GDP	Avg	OBP	SLG
2000 Syracuse *	AAA	1	5	0	0	0	0	—	—	0	0	0	0	0	0	0	0	0	0	0	—	0	.000	.000	.000
1994 Toronto	AL	15	53	8	3	1	0	0	0	13	7	1	4	0	17	1	1	0	3	0	1.00	2	.151	.224	.245
1995 Toronto	AL	111	367	89	19	4	10	8	2	146	51	42	44	1	114	1	9	4	4	4	.50	7	.243	.322	.398
1996 Toronto	AL	147	527	124	30	5	14	3	11	206	64	64	45	0	127	5	7	3	16	6	.73	12	.235	.300	.391
1997 Toronto	AL	126	426	102	23	2	12	4	8	165	46	35	34	1	94	5	11	2	15	6	.71	9	.239	.302	.387
1998 Toronto	AL	158	568	136	28	1	13	7	6	205	70	51	28	1	121	6	13	3	21	6	.78	13	.239	.281	.361
1999 Toronto	AL	38	154	45	13	0	2	1	1	64	22	12	16	0	23	3	0	0	4	2	.67	4	.292	.370	.416
2000 Toronto	AL	141	527	133	31	2	15	5	10	213	68	69	43	0	113	4	16	1	4	4	.50	14	.252	.313	.404
7 ML YEARS		736	2622	637	147	15	66	28	38	1012	328	274	214	3	609	25	57	13	67	28	.71	61	.243	.305	.386

Juan Gonzalez

Bats: Right **Throws:** Right **Pos:** RF-66; DH-48; PH/PR-1   **Ht:** 6'3" **Wt:** 220 **Born:** 10/16/69 **Age:** 31

Year Team	Lg	G	AB	H	2B	3B	HR	Hm	Rd	TB	R	RBI	TBB	IBB	SO	HBP	SH	SF	SB	CS	SB%	GDP	Avg	OBP	SLG
1989 Texas	AL	24	60	9	3	0	1	1	0	15	6	7	6	0	17	0	2	0	0	0	—	4	.150	.227	.250
1990 Texas	AL	25	90	26	7	1	4	3	1	47	11	12	2	0	18	2	0	1	0	1	.00	2	.289	.316	.522
1991 Texas	AL	142	545	144	34	1	27	7	20	261	78	102	42	7	118	5	0	3	4	4	.50	10	.264	.321	.479
1992 Texas	AL	155	584	152	24	2	43	19	24	309	77	109	35	1	143	5	0	8	0	1	.00	16	.260	.304	.529
1993 Texas	AL	140	536	166	33	1	46	24	22	339	105	118	37	7	99	13	0	1	4	1	.80	12	.310	.368	.632
1994 Texas	AL	107	422	116	18	4	19	6	13	199	57	85	30	10	66	7	0	4	6	4	.60	18	.275	.330	.472
1995 Texas	AL	90	352	104	20	2	27	15	12	209	57	82	17	3	66	0	0	5	0	0	—	15	.295	.324	.594
1996 Texas	AL	134	541	170	33	2	47	23	24	348	89	144	45	12	82	3	0	3	2	0	1.00	13	.314	.368	.643
1997 Texas	AL	133	533	158	24	3	42	18	24	314	87	131	33	7	107	3	0	10	0	0	—	12	.296	.335	.589
1998 Texas	AL	154	606	193	50	2	45	21	24	382	110	157	46	9	126	6	0	11	2	1	.67	20	.318	.366	.630
1999 Texas	AL	144	562	183	36	1	39	14	25	338	114	128	51	7	105	4	0	2	3	3	.50	10	.326	.378	.601
2000 Detroit	AL	115	461	133	30	2	22	8	14	233	69	67	32	3	84	2	0	1	1	2	.33	13	.289	.337	.505
12 ML YEARS		1363	5292	1554	312	21	362	159	203	2994	860	1142	376	66	1031	50	2	59	22	17	.56	142	.294	.343	.566

Luis Gonzalez

Bats: Left **Throws:** Right **Pos:** LF-162   **Ht:** 6'2" **Wt:** 190 **Born:** 9/2/67 **Age:** 33

Year Team	Lg	G	AB	H	2B	3B	HR	Hm	Rd	TB	R	RBI	TBB	IBB	SO	HBP	SH	SF	SB	CS	SB%	GDP	Avg	OBP	SLG
1990 Houston	NL	12	21	4	2	0	0	0	0	6	1	0	2	1	5	0	0	0	0	0	—	0	.190	.261	.286
1991 Houston	NL	137	473	120	28	9	13	4	9	205	51	69	40	4	101	8	1	4	10	7	.59	9	.254	.320	.433
1992 Houston	NL	122	387	94	19	3	10	4	6	149	40	55	24	3	52	2	1	2	7	7	.50	6	.243	.289	.385
1993 Houston	NL	154	540	162	34	3	15	8	7	247	82	72	47	7	83	10	3	10	20	9	.69	9	.300	.361	.457
1994 Houston	NL	112	392	107	29	4	8	3	5	168	57	67	49	6	57	3	0	6	15	13	.54	10	.273	.353	.429
1995 Hou-ChC	NL	133	471	130	29	8	13	6	7	214	69	69	57	8	63	6	1	6	9	6	.60	13	.276	.357	.454
1996 Chicago	NL	146	483	131	30	4	15	6	9	214	70	79	61	8	49	4	1	6	9	6	.60	13	.271	.354	.443
1997 Houston	NL	152	550	142	31	2	10	4	6	207	78	68	71	7	67	5	0	5	10	7	.59	12	.258	.345	.376
1998 Detroit	AL	154	547	146	35	5	23	15	8	260	84	71	57	7	57	8	0	8	12	7	.63	13	.267	.340	.475
1999 Arizona	NL	153	614	206	45	4	26	10	16	337	112	111	66	6	63	7	1	5	9	5	.64	13	.336	.403	.549
2000 Arizona	NL	162	618	192	47	2	31	14	17	336	106	114	78	6	85	12	2	12	2	4	.33	12	.311	.392	.544
1995 Houston	NL	56	209	54	10	4	6	1	5	90	35	35	18	3	30	3	1	3	1	3	.25	8	.258	.322	.431
Chicago	NL	77	262	76	19	4	7	5	2	124	34	34	39	5	33	3	0	3	5	5	.50	8	.290	.384	.473
11 ML YEARS		1437	5096	1434	329	44	164	74	90	2343	750	775	552	63	687	65	10	64	100	73	.58	109	.281	.355	.460

Raul Gonzalez

Bats: Right **Throws:** Right **Pos:** LF-2; PH/PR-2   **Ht:** 5'9" **Wt:** 190 **Born:** 12/27/73 **Age:** 27

Year Team	Lg	G	AB	H	2B	3B	HR	Hm	Rd	TB	R	RBI	TBB	IBB	SO	HBP	SH	SF	SB	CS	SB%	GDP	Avg	OBP	SLG
1991 Royals	R	47	160	47	5	3	0	—	—	58	24	17	19	0	21	0	1	2	3	4	.43	4	.294	.365	.363
1992 Appleton	A	119	449	115	32	1	9	—	—	176	82	51	57	1	58	2	4	6	13	5	.72	4	.256	.339	.392
1993 Wilmington	A+	127	461	124	30	3	11	—	—	193	59	55	54	1	58	4	1	4	13	5	.72	6	.269	.348	.419
1994 Wilmington	A+	115	414	108	19	8	9	—	—	170	60	51	45	2	50	2	2	4	0	4	.00	8	.261	.333	.411
1995 Wichita	AA	22	79	23	3	2	2	—	—	36	14	11	8	0	13	0	0	0	4	0	1.00	4	.291	.356	.456
Wilmington	A+	86	308	90	19	3	11	—	—	148	36	49	14	3	34	2	3	7	6	4	.60	3	.292	.320	.481
1996 Wichita	AA	23	84	24	5	1	1	—	—	34	17	9	5	0	12	1	0	0	1	2	.33	3	.286	.333	.405
1997 Wichita	AA	129	452	129	30	4	13	—	—	206	66	74	56	3	50	2	3	8	12	8	.60	12	.285	.335	.456
1998 Wichita	AA	118	455	148	31	1	17	—	—	232	84	86	58	3	53	2	1	4	12	8	.60	15	.325	.401	.510
1999 Trenton	AA	127	505	169	33	4	18	—	—	264	80	103	51	3	71	3	1	7	12	3	.80	14	.335	.394	.523
2000 Iowa	AAA	69	241	64	13	1	4	—	—	91	35	33	21	1	20	2	0	1	5	5	.50	6	.266	.328	.378
2000 Chicago	NL	3	2	0	0	0	0	0	0	0	0	0	0	0	0	0	0	0	0	0	—	0	.000	.000	.000

Wiki Gonzalez

Bats: Right **Throws:** Right **Pos:** C-87; PH/PR-9   **Ht:** 5'11" **Wt:** 203 **Born:** 5/17/74 **Age:** 27

Year Team	Lg	G	AB	H	2B	3B	HR	Hm	Rd	TB	R	RBI	TBB	IBB	SO	HBP	SH	SF	SB	CS	SB%	GDP	Avg	OBP	SLG
1994 Pirates	R	41	143	48	8	2	4	—	—	72	25	26	13	1	13	3	1	1	2	4	.33	3	.336	.400	.503
1995 Augusta	A	84	278	67	17	0	3	—	—	93	41	36	26	0	32	2	2	5	5	4	.56	7	.241	.305	.335

Year Team	Lg	G	AB	H	2B	3B	HR	(Hm	Rd)	TB	R	RBI	TBB	IBB	SO	HBP	SH	SF	SB	CS	SB%	GDP	Avg	OBP	SLG
1996 Augusta	A	118	419	106	21	3	4	—	—	145	52	62	58	1	41	7	2	5	4	6	.40	14	.253	.350	.346
1997 Rancho Cuc	A+	33	110	33	9	1	5	—	—	59	18	26	7	1	25	0	1	1	1	1	.50	1	.300	.339	.536
Mobile	AA	47	143	39	7	1	4	—	—	60	15	25	10	0	12	2	0	1	1	1	.50	5	.273	.327	.420
1998 Mobile	AA	22	67	26	9	0	4	—	—	47	20	26	14	0	4	2	0	2	0	0	—	1	.388	.494	.701
Rancho Cuc	A+	75	292	84	24	2	10	—	—	142	51	59	26	1	54	2	0	0	0	0	—	6	.288	.346	.486
1999 Mobile	AA	61	225	76	16	2	10	—	—	126	38	49	29	2	28	7	0	3	0	0	—	3	.338	.424	.560
Las Vegas	AAA	24	92	25	6	0	6	—	—	49	13	12	5	0	10	3	0	0	0	0	—	3	.272	.330	.533
1999 San Diego	NL	30	83	21	2	1	3	(1	2)	34	7	12	1	0	8	1	0	0	0	0	—	5	.253	.271	.410
2000 San Diego	NL	95	284	66	15	1	5	(1	4)	98	25	30	30	4	31	3	1	1	1	2	.33	5	.232	.311	.345
2 ML YEARS		125	367	87	17	2	8	(2	6)	132	32	42	31	4	39	4	1	1	1	2	.33	10	.237	.303	.360

Dwight Gooden

Pitches: Right Bats: Right Pos: SP-14; RP-13   Ht: 6'3" Wt: 210 Born: 11/16/64 Age: 36

Year Team	Lg	G	GS	CG	GF	IP	BFP	H	R	ER	HR	SH	SF	HB	TBB	IBB	SO	WP	Bk	W	L	Pct.	ShO	Sv-Op	Hld	ERA
2000 Yankees *	R	2	2	0	0	8	29	3	0	0	0	0	0	0	1	0	12	0	0	0	0	0- -	0	0-0	0	0.00
1984 New York	NL	31	31	7	0	218	879	161	72	63	7	3	2	2	73	2	276	3	7	17	9	.654	3	0-0	0	2.60
1985 New York	NL	35	35	16	0	276.2	1065	198	51	47	13	6	2	2	69	4	268	6	2	24	4	.857	8	0-0	0	1.53
1986 New York	NL	33	33	12	0	250	1020	197	92	79	17	10	8	4	80	3	200	4	4	17	6	.739	2	0-0	0	2.84
1987 New York	NL	25	25	7	0	179.2	730	162	68	64	11	5	5	2	53	2	148	1	1	15	7	.682	3	0-0	0	3.21
1988 New York	NL	34	34	10	0	248.1	1024	242	98	88	8	10	6	6	57	4	175	5	5	18	9	.667	3	0-0	0	3.19
1989 New York	NL	19	17	0	1	118.1	497	93	42	38	9	4	3	2	47	2	101	7	5	9	4	.692	0	1-1	1	2.89
1990 New York	NL	34	34	2	0	232.2	983	229	106	99	10	10	7	7	70	3	223	6	3	19	7	.731	1	0-0	0	3.83
1991 New York	NL	27	27	3	0	190	789	185	80	76	12	5	4	3	56	2	150	5	2	13	7	.650	1	0-0	0	3.60
1992 New York	NL	31	31	3	0	206	863	197	84	84	11	10	7	3	70	7	145	3	1	10	13	.435	0	0-0	0	3.67
1993 New York	NL	29	29	7	0	208.2	866	188	89	80	16	11	7	9	61	1	149	5	2	12	15	.444	2	0-0	0	3.45
1994 New York	NL	7	7	0	0	41.1	182	46	32	29	9	3	0	1	15	1	40	2	0	3	4	.429	0	0-0	0	6.31
1996 New York	AL	29	29	1	0	170.2	756	169	101	95	19	1	5	9	88	4	126	9	1	11	7	.611	1	0-0	0	5.01
1997 New York	AL	20	19	0	0	106.1	472	116	61	58	14	0	2	7	53	1	66	8	0	9	5	.643	0	0-0	0	4.91
1998 Cleveland	AL	23	23	0	0	134	580	135	59	56	13	1	4	9	51	0	83	3	0	8	6	.571	0	0-0	0	3.76
1999 Cleveland	AL	26	22	0	0	115	532	127	90	80	18	1	4	9	67	3	88	4	0	3	4	.429	0	0-0	0	6.26
2000 Hou-TB-NYY	AL	27	14	0	3	105	467	119	64	55	23	4	2	3	44	3	55	5	0	6	5	.545	0	2-2	2	4.71
2000 Houston	NL	1	1	0	0	4	20	6	4	4	1	0	0	0	3	0	1	2	0	0	0	—	0	0-0	0	9.00
Tampa Bay	AL	8	8	0	0	36.2	173	47	32	27	14	1	0	3	20	0	23	2	0	2	3	.400	0	0-0	0	6.63
New York	AL	18	5	0	3	64.1	274	66	28	24	8	3	2	0	21	3	31	1	0	4	2	.667	0	2-2	2	3.36
16 ML YEARS		430	410	68	4	2800.2	11705	2564	1198	1091	210	84	68	78	954	42	2293	76	33	194	112	.634	24	3-3	3	3.51

Tom Goodwin

Bats: L Throws: R Pos: CF-136; PH/PR-13; LF-10   Ht: 6'1" Wt: 175 Born: 7/27/68 Age: 32

Year Team	Lg	G	AB	H	2B	3B	HR	(Hm	Rd)	TB	R	RBI	TBB	IBB	SO	HBP	SH	SF	SB	CS	SB%	GDP	Avg	OBP	SLG
1991 Los Angeles	NL	16	7	1	0	0	0	(0	0)	1	3	0	0	0	0	0	0	0	1	1	.50	0	.143	.143	.143
1992 Los Angeles	NL	57	73	17	1	1	0	(0	0)	20	15	3	6	0	10	0	0	0	7	3	.70	0	.233	.291	.274
1993 Los Angeles	NL	30	17	5	1	0	0	(0	0)	6	6	1	1	0	4	0	0	0	1	2	.33	1	.294	.333	.353
1994 Kansas City	AL	2	2	0	0	0	0	(0	0)	0	0	0	0	0	1	0	0	0	0	0	—	0	.000	.000	.000
1995 Kansas City	AL	133	480	138	16	3	4	(2	2)	172	72	28	38	0	72	5	14	0	50	18	.74	7	.288	.346	.358
1996 Kansas City	AL	143	524	148	14	4	1	(0	1)	173	80	35	39	0	79	2	21	1	66	22	.75	3	.282	.334	.330
1997 KC-Tex	AL	150	574	149	26	6	2	(0	2)	193	90	39	44	1	88	3	11	3	50	16	.76	7	.260	.314	.336
1998 Texas	AL	154	520	151	13	3	2	(2	0)	176	102	33	73	0	90	2	10	3	38	20	.66	2	.290	.378	.338
1999 Texas	AL	109	405	105	12	6	3	(1	2)	138	63	33	40	0	61	0	7	3	39	11	.78	7	.259	.324	.341
2000 Col-LA	NL	147	528	139	11	9	6	(4	2)	186	94	58	68	2	117	1	5	4	55	10	.85	7	.263	.346	.352
1997 Kansas City	AL	97	367	100	13	4	2	(0	2)	127	51	22	19	0	51	2	11	1	34	10	.77	5	.272	.311	.346
Texas	AL	53	207	49	13	2	0	(0	0)	66	39	17	25	1	37	1	0	2	16	6	.73	2	.237	.319	.319
2000 Colorado	NL	91	317	86	8	8	5	(4	1)	125	65	47	50	2	76	1	5	4	39	7	.85	3	.271	.368	.394
Los Angeles	NL	56	211	53	3	1	1	(0	1)	61	29	11	18	0	41	0	0	0	16	3	.84	4	.251	.310	.289
10 ML YEARS		941	3130	853	94	32	18	(9	9)	1065	525	230	309	3	522	13	68	14	307	103	.75	34	.273	.339	.340

Tom Gordon

Pitches: Right Bats: Right Pos: RP   Ht: 5'9" Wt: 190 Born: 11/18/67 Age: 33

Year Team	Lg	G	GS	CG	GF	IP	BFP	H	R	ER	HR	SH	SF	HB	TBB	IBB	SO	WP	Bk	W	L	Pct.	ShO	Sv-Op	Hld	ERA
1988 Kansas City	AL	5	2	0	0	15.2	67	16	9	9	1	0	0	0	7	0	18	0	0	0	2	.000	0	0-0	2	5.17
1989 Kansas City	AL	49	16	1	16	163	677	122	67	66	10	4	4	1	86	4	153	12	0	17	9	.654	0	1-7	3	3.64
1990 Kansas City	AL	32	32	6	0	195.1	858	192	99	81	17	8	2	3	99	1	175	11	0	12	11	.522	1	0-0	0	3.73
1991 Kansas City	AL	45	14	1	11	158	684	129	76	68	16	5	3	4	87	6	167	5	0	9	14	.391	0	1-4	4	3.87
1992 Kansas City	AL	40	11	0	13	117.2	516	116	67	60	7	6	3	4	55	4	98	5	2	6	10	.375	0	0-2	0	4.59
1993 Kansas City	AL	48	14	2	18	155.2	651	125	65	62	11	6	6	1	77	5	143	17	0	12	6	.667	0	1-6	2	3.58
1994 Kansas City	AL	24	24	0	0	155.1	675	136	79	75	15	3	8	3	87	3	126	12	1	11	7	.611	0	0-0	0	4.35
1995 Kansas City	AL	31	31	2	0	189	843	204	110	93	12	7	11	4	89	4	119	9	0	12	12	.500	0	0-0	0	4.43
1996 Boston	AL	34	34	4	0	215.2	998	249	143	134	28	2	11	4	105	5	171	6	1	12	9	.571	1	0-0	0	5.59
1997 Boston	AL	42	25	2	16	182.2	774	155	85	76	10	3	4	3	78	1	159	5	0	6	10	.375	1	11-13	0	3.74
1998 Boston	AL	73	0	0	69	79.1	317	55	24	24	2	2	2	0	25	1	78	9	0	7	4	.636	0	46-47	0	2.72
1999 Boston	AL	21	0	0	15	17.2	82	17	11	11	2	0	0	1	12	2	24	0	0	0	2	.000	0	11-13	1	5.60
12 ML YEARS		444	203	18	158	1645	7142	1516	835	759	133	42	57	28	807	36	1431	91	4	104	96	.520	4	71-92	12	4.15

Mark Grace

Bats: Left Throws: Left Pos: 1B-140; PH/PR-4   Ht: 6'2" Wt: 200 Born: 6/28/64 Age: 37

Year Team	Lg	G	AB	H	2B	3B	HR	(Hm	Rd)	TB	R	RBI	TBB	IBB	SO	HBP	SH	SF	SB	CS	SB%	GDP	Avg	OBP	SLG
1988 Chicago	NL	134	486	144	23	4	7	(0	7)	196	65	57	60	5	43	0	0	4	3	3	.50	12	.296	.371	.403

(continued)

Year Team	Lg	G	AB	H	2B	3B	HR	Hm	Rd	TB	R	RBI	TBB	IBB	SO	HBP	SH	SF	SB	CS	SB%	GDP	Avg	OBP	SLG
1989 Chicago	NL	142	510	160	28	3	13	(8	5)	233	74	79	80	13	42	0	3	3	14	7	.67	13	.314	.405	.457
1990 Chicago	NL	157	589	182	32	1	9	(4	5)	243	72	82	59	5	54	1	1	5	15	6	.71	10	.309	.372	.413
1991 Chicago	NL	160	619	169	28	5	8	(5	3)	231	87	58	70	7	53	3	4	7	3	4	.43	6	.273	.346	.373
1992 Chicago	NL	158	603	185	37	5	9	(5	4)	259	72	79	72	8	36	4	2	8	6	1	.86	14	.307	.380	.430
1993 Chicago	NL	155	594	193	39	4	14	(5	9)	282	86	98	71	14	32	1	1	9	8	4	.67	**25**	.325	.393	.475
1994 Chicago	NL	106	403	120	23	3	6	(5	1)	167	55	44	48	5	41	0	0	3	0	1	.00	10	.298	.370	.414
1995 Chicago	NL	143	552	180	51	3	16	(4	12)	285	97	92	65	9	46	2	1	7	6	2	.75	10	.326	.395	.516
1996 Chicago	NL	142	547	181	39	1	9	(4	5)	249	88	75	62	8	41	1	0	6	2	3	.40	18	.331	.396	.455
1997 Chicago	NL	151	555	177	32	5	13	(6	7)	258	87	78	88	3	45	2	1	8	4	4	.33	18	.319	.409	.465
1998 Chicago	NL	158	595	184	39	3	17	(7	10)	280	92	89	93	8	56	3	0	7	4	7	.36	17	.309	.401	.471
1999 Chicago	NL	161	593	183	44	5	16	(8	8)	285	107	91	83	4	44	2	0	10	3	4	.43	14	.309	.390	.481
2000 Chicago	NL	143	510	143	41	1	11	(3	8)	219	75	82	95	11	28	6	2	8	1	2	.33	7	.280	.394	.429
13 ML YEARS		1910	7156	2201	456	43	148	(64	84)	3187	1057	1004	946	100	561	29	15	88	67	48	.58	174	.308	.386	.445

Tony Graffanino

Bats: R **Throws:** R **Pos:** 2B-25; SS-22; PH/PR-20; 3B-15; DH-3   **Ht:** 6'1" **Wt:** 195 **Born:** 6/6/72 **Age:** 29

Year Team	Lg	G	AB	H	2B	3B	HR	Hm	Rd	TB	R	RBI	TBB	IBB	SO	HBP	SH	SF	SB	CS	SB%	GDP	Avg	OBP	SLG
2000 Durham *	AAA	10	35	10	3	0	2			19	9	6	7	0	8	0	0	0	2	0	1.00	0	.286	.405	.543
1996 Atlanta	NL	22	46	8	1	1	0	(0	0)	11	7	2	4	0	13	1	0	1	0	0	—	0	.174	.250	.239
1997 Atlanta	NL	104	186	48	9	1	8	(5	3)	83	33	20	26	1	46	1	3	5	6	4	.60	3	.258	.344	.446
1998 Atlanta	NL	105	289	61	14	1	5	(3	2)	92	32	22	24	0	68	2	1	1	1	4	.20	7	.211	.275	.318
1999 Tampa Bay	AL	39	130	41	9	4	2	(0	2)	64	20	19	9	0	22	1	1	2	3	2	.60	1	.315	.364	.492
2000 TB-CWS	AL	70	168	46	6	1	2	(1	1)	60	33	17	22	0	27	2	1	1	7	4	.64	2	.274	.363	.357
2000 Tampa Bay	AL	13	20	6	1	0	0	(0	0)	7	8	1	1	0	2	1	0	0	0	0	—	1	.300	.364	.350
Chicago	AL	57	148	40	5	1	2	(1	1)	53	25	16	21	0	25	1	1	1	7	4	.64	1	.270	.363	.358
5 ML YEARS		340	819	204	39	8	17	(9	8)	310	125	80	85	1	176	7	7	8	17	14	.55	13	.249	.322	.379

Danny Graves

Pitches: Right **Bats:** Right **Pos:** RP-66   **Ht:** 5'11" **Wt:** 185 **Born:** 8/7/73 **Age:** 27

Year Team	Lg	G	GS	CG	GF	IP	BFP	H	R	ER	HR	SH	SF	HB	TBB	IBB	SO	WP	Bk	W	L	Pct.	ShO	Sv-Op	Hld	ERA
1996 Cleveland	AL	15	0	0	5	29.2	129	29	18	15	2	0	1	0	10	0	22	1	0	2	0	1.000	0	0-1	0	4.55
1997 Cle-Cin		15	0	0	3	26	134	41	22	16	2	3	2	0	20	1	11	1	0	0	0	—	0	0-0	1	5.54
1998 Cincinnati	NL	62	0	0	35	81.1	340	76	31	30	6	2	5	2	28	4	44	4	0	2	1	.667	0	8-8	6	3.32
1999 Cincinnati	NL	75	0	0	56	111	454	90	42	38	10	5	2	2	49	4	69	3	0	8	7	.533	0	27-36	0	3.08
2000 Cincinnati	NL	66	0	0	57	91.1	388	81	31	26	8	6	4	2	42	7	53	3	1	10	5	.667	0	30-35	0	2.56
1997 Cleveland	AL	5	0	0	2	11.1	56	15	8	6	2	0	1	0	9	0	4	0	0	0	0	—	0	0-0	1	4.76
Cincinnati	NL	10	0	0	1	14.2	78	26	14	10	0	3	1	0	11	1	7	1	0	0	0	—	0	0-0	0	6.14
5 ML YEARS		233	0	0	156	339.1	1445	317	144	125	28	16	14	7	149	16	199	12	1	22	13	.629	0	65-80	7	3.32

Craig Grebeck

Bats: Right **Throws:** Right **Pos:** 2B-56; SS-8; PH/PR-4   **Ht:** 5'7" **Wt:** 155 **Born:** 12/29/64 **Age:** 36

Year Team	Lg	G	AB	H	2B	3B	HR	Hm	Rd	TB	R	RBI	TBB	IBB	SO	HBP	SH	SF	SB	CS	SB%	GDP	Avg	OBP	SLG
1990 Chicago	AL	59	119	20	3	1	1	(1	0)	28	7	9	8	0	24	2	3	3	0	0	—	2	.168	.227	.235
1991 Chicago	AL	107	224	63	16	3	6	(3	3)	103	37	31	38	0	40	1	4	1	1	3	.25	3	.281	.386	.460
1992 Chicago	AL	88	287	77	21	2	3	(2	1)	111	24	35	30	0	34	3	10	3	0	3	.00	5	.268	.341	.387
1993 Chicago	AL	72	190	43	5	0	1	(0	1)	51	25	12	26	0	26	0	7	0	1	2	.33	9	.226	.319	.268
1994 Chicago	AL	35	97	30	5	0	0	(0	0)	35	17	5	12	0	5	1	3	0	0	0	—	4	.309	.391	.361
1995 Chicago	AL	53	154	40	12	0	1	(0	1)	55	19	18	21	0	23	1	4	0	0	0	—	9	.260	.360	.357
1996 Florida	NL	50	95	20	1	0	1	(0	1)	24	8	9	4	1	14	1	1	2	0	0	—	2	.211	.245	.253
1997 Anaheim	AL	63	126	34	9	0	1	(0	1)	46	12	6	18	1	11	0	5	1	0	1	.00	6	.270	.359	.365
1998 Toronto	AL	102	301	77	17	2	2	(2	0)	104	33	27	29	0	42	4	8	2	2	2	.50	8	.256	.327	.346
1999 Toronto	AL	34	113	41	7	0	0	(0	0)	48	18	10	15	0	13	2	3	1	0	0	—	2	.363	.443	.425
2000 Toronto	AL	66	241	71	19	0	3	(2	1)	99	38	23	25	0	33	2	1	1	0	0	—	7	.295	.364	.411
11 ML YEARS		729	1947	516	115	8	19	(11	8)	704	238	185	226	2	265	19	49	14	4	11	.27	49	.265	.345	.362

Jason Green

Pitches: Right **Bats:** Right **Pos:** RP-14   **Ht:** 6'4" **Wt:** 190 **Born:** 6/5/75 **Age:** 26

Year Team	Lg	G	GS	CG	GF	IP	BFP	H	R	ER	HR	SH	SF	HB	TBB	IBB	SO	WP	Bk	W	L	Pct.	ShO	Sv-Op	Hld	ERA
1994 Astros	R	18	0	0	7	23	96	16	11	7	0	1	1	1	16	0	12	6	4	2	1	.667	0	1--	—	2.74
1995 Auburn	A-	14	14	0	2	82.2	365	82	48	35	1	4	0	10	29	0	48	5	0	8	2	.800	1	0--	—	3.81
1997 Kissimmee	A+	8	0	0	4	8.2	50	11	12	5	0	0	0	0	10	1	3	2	0	0	3	.000	0	0--	—	5.19
Quad City	A	23	22	1	1	125.2	548	126	79	64	9	5	2	8	53	2	96	12	2	7	12	.368	0	0--	—	4.58
1998 Kissimmee	A+	51	3	0	44	67.1	304	64	34	28	4	2	2	4	32	3	67	5	1	2	5	.286	0	14--	—	3.34
1999 Jackson	AA	33	0	0	18	42.1	187	41	20	16	2	0	0	0	20	2	50	0	1	3	3	.500	0	10--	—	3.40
2000 Round Rock	AA	31	0	0	29	41	169	38	10	9	0	0	0	0	11	3	54	1	0	8	2	.800	0	15--	—	1.98
New Orleans	AAA	10	0	0	7	13	55	10	3	3	0	1	0	2	4	2	12	0	0	2	1	.667	0	1--	—	2.08
2000 Houston	NL	14	0	0	1	17.2	87	15	16	13	3	2	0	1	20	1	19	0	0	1	1	.500	0	0-0	0	6.62

Scarborough Green

Bats: B **Throws:** R **Pos:** CF-41; RF-23; PH/PR-22; DH-6; LF-3   **Ht:** 5'10" **Wt:** 170 **Born:** 6/9/74 **Age:** 27

Year Team	Lg	G	AB	H	2B	3B	HR	Hm	Rd	TB	R	RBI	TBB	IBB	SO	HBP	SH	SF	SB	CS	SB%	GDP	Avg	OBP	SLG
1993 Cardinals	R	33	95	21	3	1	0	—	—	26	16	11	7	0	17	3	1	0	3	2	.60	1	.221	.295	.274
1994 Johnson Cty	R+	54	199	48	5	0	0	—	—	53	32	11	25	1	61	0	4	2	22	7	.76	0	.241	.323	.266

Year Team	Lg	G	AB	H	2B	3B	HR	(Hm	Rd)	TB	R	RBI	TBB	IBB	SO	HBP	SH	SF	SB	CS	SB%	GDP	Avg	OBP	SLG
1995 Savannah	A	132	429	98	7	6	1	—	—	120	48	25	55	0	101	3	9	1	26	9	.74	1	.228	.320	.280
1996 St. Pete	A+	36	140	41	4	1	1	—	—	50	26	11	21	1	22	2	2	0	13	9	.59	1	.293	.393	.357
Arkansas	AA	92	300	60	6	3	3	—	—	81	45	24	38	1	58	3	3	1	21	8	.72	3	.200	.295	.270
1997 Arkansas	AA	76	251	77	14	4	2	—	—	105	45	29	36	4	48	2	3	1	11	5	.69	2	.307	.397	.418
Louisville	AAA	52	209	53	11	2	3	—	—	77	26	13	22	0	55	0	1	0	10	7	.59	3	.254	.325	.368
1998 Memphis	AAA	26	81	16	5	0	0	—	—	21	11	2	8	1	22	0	1	0	1	4	.20	2	.198	.270	.259
Arkansas	AA	18	75	27	2	1	2	—	—	37	16	9	6	0	12	0	0	0	9	2	.82	0	.360	.407	.493
1999 Oklahoma	AAA	104	359	89	16	6	3	—	—	126	68	29	34	1	86	3	4	3	26	11	.70	3	.248	.316	.351
2000 Oklahoma	AAA	27	99	31	6	0	1	—	—	40	20	10	22	0	24	1	3	0	14	2	.88	0	.313	.443	.404
1997 St. Louis	NL	20	31	3	0	0	0	(0	0)	3	5	1	2	0	5	0	0	0	0	0	—	0	.097	.152	.097
1999 Texas	AL	18	13	4	0	0	0	(0	0)	4	4	0	1	0	2	0	0	0	0	1	.00	0	.308	.357	.308
2000 Texas	AL	79	124	29	1	1	0	(0	0)	32	21	9	10	0	26	0	5	0	10	6	.63	3	.234	.291	.258
3 ML YEARS		117	168	36	1	1	0	(0	0)	39	30	10	13	0	33	0	5	0	10	7	.59	3	.214	.271	.232

Shawn Green

Bats: Left **Throws:** Left **Pos:** RF-161; CF-1; PH/PR-1 **Ht:** 6'4" **Wt:** 200 **Born:** 11/10/72 **Age:** 28

Year Team	Lg	G	AB	H	2B	3B	HR	(Hm	Rd)	TB	R	RBI	TBB	IBB	SO	HBP	SH	SF	SB	CS	SB%	GDP	Avg	OBP	SLG
1993 Toronto	AL	3	6	0	0	0	0	(0	0)	0	0	0	0	0	1	0	0	0	0	0	—	0	.000	.000	.000
1994 Toronto	AL	14	33	3	1	0	0	(0	0)	4	1	1	1	0	8	0	0	0	1	0	1.00	1	.091	.118	.121
1995 Toronto	AL	121	379	109	31	4	15	(5	10)	193	52	54	20	3	68	3	0	3	1	2	.33	4	.288	.326	.509
1996 Toronto	AL	132	422	118	32	3	11	(7	4)	189	52	45	33	3	75	8	0	2	5	1	.83	9	.280	.342	.448
1997 Toronto	AL	135	429	123	22	4	16	(10	6)	201	57	53	36	4	99	1	1	4	14	3	.82	4	.287	.340	.469
1998 Toronto	AL	158	630	175	33	4	35	(21	14)	321	106	100	50	2	142	5	1	3	35	12	.74	6	.278	.334	.510
1999 Toronto	AL	153	614	190	45	0	42	(20	22)	361	134	123	66	4	117	11	0	5	20	7	.74	13	.309	.384	.588
2000 Los Angeles	NL	162	610	164	44	4	24	(15	9)	288	98	99	90	9	121	8	0	6	24	5	.83	18	.269	.367	.472
8 ML YEARS		878	3123	882	208	19	143	(78	65)	1557	500	475	296	25	631	36	2	23	100	30	.77	55	.282	.349	.499

Charlie Greene

Bats: Right **Throws:** Right **Pos:** C-3 **Ht:** 6'2" **Wt:** 190 **Born:** 1/23/71 **Age:** 30

Year Team	Lg	G	AB	H	2B	3B	HR	(Hm	Rd)	TB	R	RBI	TBB	IBB	SO	HBP	SH	SF	SB	CS	SB%	GDP	Avg	OBP	SLG
1991 Padres	R	49	183	52	15	1	5	—	—	84	27	39	16	0	23	3	2	6	6	1	.86	7	.284	.341	.459
1992 Chston-SC	A	98	298	55	9	1	1	—	—	69	22	24	11	0	60	5	3	2	1	2	.33	7	.185	.225	.232
1993 Waterloo	A	84	213	38	8	0	2	—	—	52	19	20	13	0	33	3	6	3	0	0	—	5	.178	.233	.244
1994 Binghamton	AA	30	106	18	4	0	0	—	—	22	13	2	6	1	18	1	0	1	0	0	—	3	.170	.219	.208
St. Lucie	A+	69	224	57	4	0	0	—	—	61	23	21	9	0	31	4	4	1	0	1	.00	3	.254	.294	.272
1995 Binghamton	AA	100	346	82	13	0	2	—	—	101	26	34	15	4	47	5	3	4	2	1	.67	10	.237	.276	.292
Norfolk	AAA	27	88	17	3	0	0	—	—	20	6	4	3	0	28	0	1	0	0	1	.00	1	.193	.220	.227
1996 Binghamton	AA	100	336	82	17	0	2	—	—	105	35	27	17	0	52	0	2	4	2	0	1.00	8	.244	.277	.313
1997 Norfolk	AAA	76	238	49	7	0	8	—	—	80	27	28	9	0	54	2	0	2	1	0	1.00	4	.206	.239	.336
1998 Rochester	AAA	77	250	53	10	0	4	—	—	75	23	28	9	0	54	3	5	0	1	1	.50	2	.212	.248	.300
1999 Louisville	AAA	56	161	34	8	0	4	—	—	54	16	15	7	1	26	0	0	0	0	0	—	2	.211	.244	.335
2000 Syracuse	AAA	77	267	60	12	0	5	—	—	87	23	26	17	0	46	3	3	0	1	3	.25	5	.225	.279	.326
1996 New York	NL	2	1	0	0	0	0	(0	0)	0	0	0	0	0	1	0	0	0	0	0	—	0	.000	.000	.000
1997 Baltimore	AL	5	2	0	0	0	0	(0	0)	0	0	1	0	0	1	0	0	0	0	0	—	0	.000	.000	.000
1998 Baltimore	AL	13	21	4	1	0	0	(0	0)	5	1	0	0	0	8	0	1	0	0	0	—	1	.190	.190	.238
1999 Milwaukee	NL	32	42	8	1	0	0	(0	0)	9	4	1	5	0	11	0	1	1	0	0	—	1	.190	.271	.214
2000 Toronto	AL	3	9	1	0	0	0	(0	0)	1	0	0	0	0	5	0	0	0	0	0	—	0	.111	.111	.111
5 ML YEARS		55	75	13	2	0	0	(0	0)	15	5	2	5	0	25	0	2	1	0	0	—	1	.173	.222	.200

Todd Greene

Bats: R **Throws:** R **Pos:** DH-23; PH/PR-10; C-2; LF-1 **Ht:** 5'10" **Wt:** 208 **Born:** 5/8/71 **Age:** 30

Year Team	Lg	G	AB	H	2B	3B	HR	(Hm	Rd)	TB	R	RBI	TBB	IBB	SO	HBP	SH	SF	SB	CS	SB%	GDP	Avg	OBP	SLG
2000 Syracuse *	AAA	24	91	27	3	0	7	—	—	51	14	14	6	0	16	0	0	1	1	0	1.00	3	.297	.337	.560
Dunedin *	A+	6	20	4	1	0	1	—	—	8	2	4	2	1	4	1	0	0	0	0	—	0	.200	.304	.400
1996 California	AL	29	79	15	1	0	2	(1	1)	22	9	9	4	0	11	1	0	0	2	0	1.00	4	.190	.238	.278
1997 Anaheim	AL	34	124	36	6	0	9	(5	4)	69	24	24	7	1	25	0	0	0	2	0	1.00	1	.290	.328	.556
1998 Anaheim	AL	29	71	18	4	0	1	(0	1)	25	3	7	2	0	20	0	0	0	0	0	—	0	.254	.274	.352
1999 Anaheim	AL	97	321	78	20	0	14	(7	7)	140	36	42	12	0	63	3	0	2	1	4	.20	8	.243	.275	.436
2000 Toronto	AL	34	85	20	2	0	5	(2	3)	37	11	10	5	0	18	0	0	0	0	0	—	4	.235	.278	.435
5 ML YEARS		223	680	167	33	0	31	(15	16)	293	83	92	30	1	137	4	0	2	5	4	.56	17	.246	.281	.431

Willie Greene

Bats: Left **Throws:** Right **Pos:** 3B-90; PH/PR-17 **Ht:** 5'11" **Wt:** 190 **Born:** 9/23/71 **Age:** 29

Year Team	Lg	G	AB	H	2B	3B	HR	(Hm	Rd)	TB	R	RBI	TBB	IBB	SO	HBP	SH	SF	SB	CS	SB%	GDP	Avg	OBP	SLG
2000 Iowa *	AAA	6	17	5	2	1	0	—	—	10	4	4	3	0	5	0	0	1	1	0	1.00	1	.294	.381	.588
1992 Cincinnati	NL	29	93	25	5	2	2	(2	0)	40	10	13	10	0	23	0	0	1	0	2	.00	1	.269	.337	.430
1993 Cincinnati	NL	15	50	8	1	1	2	(2	0)	17	7	5	2	0	19	0	0	1	0	0	—	1	.160	.189	.340
1994 Cincinnati	NL	16	37	8	2	0	0	(0	0)	10	5	3	6	1	14	0	0	1	0	0	—	1	.216	.318	.270
1995 Cincinnati	NL	8	19	2	0	0	0	(0	0)	2	1	0	3	0	7	0	0	0	0	0	—	1	.105	.227	.105
1996 Cincinnati	NL	115	287	70	5	5	19	(11	8)	142	48	63	36	6	88	0	1	1	0	0	—	5	.244	.327	.495
1997 Cincinnati	NL	151	495	125	22	1	26	(13	13)	227	62	91	78	5	111	1	1	3	6	0	1.00	10	.253	.354	.459
1998 Cin-Bal		135	396	102	19	1	15	(9	6)	168	65	54	69	2	90	3	0	2	7	3	.70	9	.258	.370	.424
1999 Toronto	AL	81	226	46	7	0	12	(8	4)	89	22	41	20	0	56	0	0	2	0	0	—	4	.204	.266	.394
2000 Chicago	NL	105	299	60	15	2	10	(2	8)	109	34	37	36	2	69	2	2	2	4	0	1.00	5	.201	.289	.365
1998 Cincinnati	NL	111	356	96	18	1	14	(8	6)	158	57	49	56	2	80	3	0	2	6	3	.67	7	.270	.372	.444
Baltimore	AL	24	40	6	1	0	1	(1	0)	10	8	5	13	0	10	0	0	0	1	0	1.00	2	.150	.358	.250
9 ML YEARS		655	1902	446	76	12	86	(52	34)	804	254	307	260	16	477	6	2	13	17	6	.74	37	.234	.326	.423

Rusty Greer

Bats: Left **Throws:** Left **Pos:** LF-97; PH/PR-7; DH-2   **Ht:** 6'0" **Wt:** 195 **Born:** 1/21/69 **Age:** 32

Year Team	Lg	G	AB	H	2B	3B	HR	(Hm	Rd)	TB	R	RBI	TBB	IBB	SO	HBP	SH	SF	SB	CS	SB%	GDP	Avg	OBP	SLG
2000 Tulsa *	AA	2	7	1	0	0	0	—	—	1	0	1	1	0	3	0	0	0	0	0	—	0	.143	.250	.143
1994 Texas	AL	80	277	87	16	1	10	(3	7)	135	36	46	46	2	46	2	2	4	0	0	—	3	.314	.410	.487
1995 Texas	AL	131	417	113	21	2	13	(7	6)	177	58	61	55	1	66	1	2	3	3	1	.75	9	.271	.355	.424
1996 Texas	AL	139	542	180	41	6	18	(9	9)	287	96	100	62	4	86	3	0	10	9	0	1.00	9	.332	.397	.530
1997 Texas	AL	157	601	193	42	3	26	(18	8)	319	112	87	83	4	87	3	1	2	9	5	.64	11	.321	.405	.531
1998 Texas	AL	155	598	183	31	5	16	(8	8)	272	107	108	80	1	93	4	0	9	2	4	.33	18	.306	.386	.455
1999 Texas	AL	147	556	167	41	3	20	(10	10)	274	107	101	96	2	67	5	0	5	2	2	.50	17	.300	.405	.493
2000 Texas	AL	105	394	117	34	3	8	(3	5)	181	65	65	51	1	61	3	0	5	4	1	.80	14	.297	.377	.459
7 ML YEARS		914	3385	1040	226	23	111	(58	53)	1645	581	568	473	15	506	21	5	38	29	13	.69	81	.307	.392	.486

Ben Grieve

Bats: Left **Throws:** Right **Pos:** LF-144; DH-12; PH/PR-3   **Ht:** 6'4" **Wt:** 230 **Born:** 5/4/76 **Age:** 25

Year Team	Lg	G	AB	H	2B	3B	HR	(Hm	Rd)	TB	R	RBI	TBB	IBB	SO	HBP	SH	SF	SB	CS	SB%	GDP	Avg	OBP	SLG
1997 Oakland	AL	24	93	29	6	0	3	(3	0)	44	12	24	13	1	25	1	1	0	0	0	—	1	.312	.402	.473
1998 Oakland	AL	155	583	168	41	2	18	(5	13)	267	94	89	85	3	123	9	0	1	2	2	.50	18	.288	.386	.458
1999 Oakland	AL	148	486	129	21	0	28	(13	15)	234	80	86	63	2	108	8	0	1	4	0	1.00	17	.265	.358	.481
2000 Oakland	AL	158	594	166	40	1	27	(13	14)	289	92	104	73	2	130	3	0	5	3	0	1.00	32	.279	.359	.487
4 ML YEARS		485	1756	492	108	3	76	(34	42)	834	278	303	234	8	386	21	1	7	9	2	.82	68	.280	.370	.475

Ken Griffey Jr.

Bats: Left **Throws:** Left **Pos:** CF-141; PH/PR-4   **Ht:** 6'3" **Wt:** 205 **Born:** 11/21/69 **Age:** 31

Year Team	Lg	G	AB	H	2B	3B	HR	(Hm	Rd)	TB	R	RBI	TBB	IBB	SO	HBP	SH	SF	SB	CS	SB%	GDP	Avg	OBP	SLG
1989 Seattle	AL	127	455	120	23	0	16	(10	6)	191	61	61	44	8	83	2	1	4	16	7	.70	4	.264	.329	.420
1990 Seattle	AL	155	597	179	28	7	22	(8	14)	287	91	80	63	12	81	2	0	4	16	11	.59	12	.300	.366	.481
1991 Seattle	AL	154	548	179	42	1	22	(16	6)	289	76	100	71	21	82	1	4	9	18	6	.75	10	.327	.399	.527
1992 Seattle	AL	142	565	174	39	4	27	(16	11)	302	83	103	44	15	67	5	0	3	10	5	.67	15	.308	.361	.535
1993 Seattle	AL	156	582	180	38	3	45	(21	24)	359	113	109	96	25	91	6	0	7	17	9	.65	14	.309	.408	.617
1994 Seattle	AL	111	433	140	24	4	40	(18	22)	292	94	90	56	19	73	2	0	2	11	3	.79	9	.323	.402	.674
1995 Seattle	AL	72	260	67	7	0	17	(13	4)	125	52	42	52	6	53	0	0	2	4	2	.67	4	.258	.379	.481
1996 Seattle	AL	140	545	165	26	2	49	(26	23)	342	125	140	78	13	104	1	1	7	16	1	.94	7	.303	.392	.628
1997 Seattle	AL	157	608	185	34	3	56	(27	29)	393	125	147	76	23	121	8	0	12	15	4	.79	12	.304	.382	.646
1998 Seattle	AL	161	633	180	33	3	56	(30	26)	387	120	146	76	11	121	7	0	4	20	5	.80	14	.284	.365	.611
1999 Seattle	AL	160	606	173	26	3	48	(27	21)	349	123	134	91	17	108	7	0	2	24	7	.77	8	.285	.384	.576
2000 Cincinnati	NL	145	520	141	22	3	40	(22	18)	289	100	118	94	17	117	9	0	8	6	4	.60	7	.271	.387	.556
12 ML YEARS		1680	6352	1883	342	33	438	(234	204)	3605	1163	1270	841	187	1101	56	6	64	173	64	.73	116	.296	.380	.568

Jason Grilli

Pitches: Right **Bats:** Right **Pos:** SP-1   **Ht:** 6'4" **Wt:** 185 **Born:** 11/11/76 **Age:** 24

Year Team	Lg	G	GS	CG	GF	IP	BFP	H	R	ER	HR	SH	SF	HB	TBB	IBB	SO	WP	Bk	W	L	Pct.	ShO	Sv-Op	Hld	ERA
1998 Shreveport	AA	21	21	3	0	123.1	511	113	60	52	11	6	3	4	37	0	100	6	3	7	10	.412	0	0--	—	3.79
Fresno	AAA	8	8	0	0	42	193	49	30	24	7	0	1	5	18	0	37	1	1	2	3	.400	0	0--	—	5.14
1999 Fresno	AAA	19	19	1	0	100.2	461	124	69	62	22	2	3	6	39	0	76	3	0	7	5	.583	0	0--	—	5.54
Calgary	AAA	8	8	0	0	41	205	56	48	35	7	2	1	2	23	0	27	5	1	1	5	.167	0	0--	—	7.68
2000 Calgary	AAA	8	8	0	0	41.1	204	58	37	33	4	3	3	2	23	0	21	6	0	1	4	.200	0	0--	—	7.19
2000 Florida	NL	1	1	0	0	6.2	35	11	4	4	0	2	0	2	3	0	3	0	0	0	1	.000	0	0-0	0	5.40

Jason Grimsley

Pitches: Right **Bats:** Right **Pos:** RP-59; SP-4   **Ht:** 6'3" **Wt:** 205 **Born:** 8/7/67 **Age:** 33

Year Team	Lg	G	GS	CG	GF	IP	BFP	H	R	ER	HR	SH	SF	HB	TBB	IBB	SO	WP	Bk	W	L	Pct.	ShO	Sv-Op	Hld	ERA
1989 Philadelphia	NL	4	4	0	0	18.1	91	19	13	12	2	1	0	0	19	1	7	2	0	1	3	.250	0	0-0	0	5.89
1990 Philadelphia	NL	11	11	0	0	57.1	255	47	21	21	1	2	1	2	43	0	41	6	1	3	2	.600	0	0-0	0	3.30
1991 Philadelphia	NL	12	12	0	0	61	272	54	34	33	4	3	2	3	41	3	42	14	0	1	7	.125	0	0-0	0	4.87
1993 Cleveland	AL	10	6	0	1	42.1	194	52	26	25	3	1	0	1	20	1	27	2	0	3	4	.429	0	0-0	1	5.31
1994 Cleveland	AL	14	13	1	0	82.2	368	91	47	42	7	4	2	6	34	1	59	6	1	5	2	.714	0	0-0	0	4.57
1995 Cleveland	AL	15	2	0	2	34	165	37	24	23	4	1	2	2	32	1	25	7	0	0	0	—	0	1-1	0	6.09
1996 California	AL	35	20	2	4	130.1	620	150	110	99	14	4	5	13	74	5	82	11	0	5	7	.417	0	0-0	0	6.84
1999 New York	AL	55	0	0	25	75	336	66	39	30	7	3	3	4	40	5	49	8	0	7	2	.778	0	1-4	8	3.60
2000 New York	AL	63	4	0	18	96.1	428	100	58	54	10	2	6	5	42	1	53	16	0	3	2	.600	0	1-4	4	5.04
9 ML YEARS		219	72	3	50	597.1	2729	616	372	339	52	21	21	36	345	18	385	72	2	28	29	.491	0	3-9	13	5.11

Marquis Grissom

Bats: Right **Throws:** Right **Pos:** CF-142; PH/PR-4   **Ht:** 5'11" **Wt:** 188 **Born:** 4/17/67 **Age:** 34

Year Team	Lg	G	AB	H	2B	3B	HR	(Hm	Rd)	TB	R	RBI	TBB	IBB	SO	HBP	SH	SF	SB	CS	SB%	GDP	Avg	OBP	SLG
1989 Montreal	NL	26	74	19	2	0	1	(0	1)	24	16	2	12	0	21	0	1	0	1	0	1.00	1	.257	.360	.324
1990 Montreal	NL	98	288	74	14	2	3	(2	1)	101	42	29	27	2	40	0	4	1	22	2	.92	3	.257	.320	.351
1991 Montreal	NL	148	558	149	23	9	6	(3	3)	208	73	39	34	0	89	1	4	0	76	17	.82	8	.267	.310	.373
1992 Montreal	NL	159	653	180	39	6	14	(8	6)	273	99	66	42	6	81	5	3	4	78	13	.86	12	.276	.322	.418
1993 Montreal	NL	157	630	188	27	2	19	(9	10)	276	104	95	52	6	76	3	0	8	53	10	.84	9	.298	.351	.438
1994 Montreal	NL	110	475	137	25	4	11	(4	7)	203	96	45	41	4	66	1	0	4	36	6	.86	10	.288	.344	.427
1995 Atlanta	NL	139	551	142	23	3	12	(5	7)	207	80	42	47	4	61	3	1	4	29	9	.76	8	.258	.317	.376

BATTING

Year Team	Lg	G	AB	H	2B	3B	HR	(Hm	Rd)	TB	R	RBI	TBB	IBB	SO	HBP	SH	SF	SB	CS	SB%	GDP	Avg	OBP	SLG
1996 Atlanta	NL	158	671	207	32	10	23	(11	12)	328	106	74	41	6	73	3	4	4	28	11	.72	12	.308	.349	.489
1997 Cleveland	AL	144	558	146	27	6	12	(5	7)	221	74	66	43	1	89	6	6	9	22	13	.63	12	.262	.317	.396
1998 Milwaukee	NL	142	542	147	28	1	10	(2	8)	207	57	60	24	2	78	2	2	2	13	8	.62	12	.271	.304	.382
1999 Milwaukee	NL	154	603	161	27	1	20	(9	11)	250	92	83	49	4	109	0	4	5	24	6	.80	12	.267	.320	.415
2000 Milwaukee	NL	146	595	145	18	2	14	(4	10)	209	67	62	39	2	99	0	2	4	20	10	.67	9	.244	.288	.351
12 ML YEARS		1581	6198	1695	285	46	145	(62	83)	2507	906	663	451	37	882	24	31	45	402	105	.79	108	.273	.323	.404

Buddy Groom

Pitches: Left **Bats:** Left **Pos:** RP-70 **Ht:** 6'2" **Wt:** 207 **Born:** 7/10/65 **Age:** 35

HOW MUCH HE PITCHED / WHAT HE GAVE UP / THE RESULTS

Year Team	Lg	G	GS	CG	GF	IP	BFP	H	R	ER	HR	SH	SF	HB	TBB	IBB	SO	WP	Bk	W	L	Pct.	ShO	Sv-Op	Hld	ERA
1992 Detroit	AL	12	7	0	3	38.2	177	48	28	25	4	3	2	0	22	4	15	0	1	0	5	.000	0	1-2	0	5.82
1993 Detroit	AL	19	3	0	8	36.2	170	48	25	25	4	2	4	2	13	5	15	2	1	0	2	.000	0	0-0	1	6.14
1994 Detroit	AL	40	0	0	10	32	139	31	14	14	4	0	3	2	13	2	27	0	0	0	1	.000	0	1-1	11	3.94
1995 Det-Fla	AL	37	4	0	11	55.2	274	81	47	46	8	2	2	2	32	4	35	3	0	2	5	.286	0	1-3	0	7.44
1996 Oakland	AL	72	1	0	16	77.1	341	85	37	33	8	2	0	3	34	3	57	5	0	5	0	1.000	0	2-4	10	3.84
1997 Oakland	AL	78	0	0	7	64.2	285	75	38	37	9	0	4	0	24	1	45	3	0	2	2	.500	0	3-5	12	5.15
1998 Oakland	AL	75	0	0	13	57.1	251	62	30	27	4	1	3	1	20	1	36	1	0	3	1	.750	0	0-6	16	4.24
1999 Oakland	AL	76	0	0	6	46	196	48	29	26	1	2	0	1	18	5	32	2	1	3	2	.600	0	0-3	27	5.09
2000 Baltimore	AL	70	0	0	14	59.1	260	63	37	32	5	5	5	0	21	2	44	1	0	6	3	.667	0	4-11	27	4.85
1995 Detroit	AL	23	4	0	8	40.2	203	55	35	34	6	2	2	2	26	4	23	3	0	1	3	.250	0	1-3	0	7.52
Florida	NL	14	0	0	5	15	71	26	12	12	2	0	0	0	6	0	12	0	0	1	2	.333	0	0-0	0	7.20
9 ML YEARS		479	15	0	88	467.2	2093	541	285	265	47	17	23	11	197	27	306	17	3	21	21	.500	0	12-35	104	5.10

Kip Gross

Pitches: Right **Bats:** Right **Pos:** SP-1; RP-1 **Ht:** 6'2" **Wt:** 195 **Born:** 8/24/64 **Age:** 36

HOW MUCH HE PITCHED / WHAT HE GAVE UP / THE RESULTS

Year Team	Lg	G	GS	CG	GF	IP	BFP	H	R	ER	HR	SH	SF	HB	TBB	IBB	SO	WP	Bk	W	L	Pct.	ShO	Sv-Op	Hld	ERA
2000 New Orleans *	AAA	25	25	2	0	157.2	664	156	80	69	20	10	6	4	44	1	94	3	0	8	7	.533	0	0--	—	3.94
1990 Cincinnati	NL	5	0	0	2	6.1	25	6	3	3	0	1	0	2	2	0	3	0	0	0	0	—	0	0-0	0	4.26
1991 Cincinnati	NL	29	9	1	6	85.2	381	93	43	33	8	6	2	0	40	2	40	5	1	6	4	.600	0	0-0	1	3.47
1992 Los Angeles	NL	16	1	0	7	23.2	109	32	14	11	1	0	0	0	10	1	14	1	1	1	1	.500	0	0-0	2	4.18
1993 Los Angeles	NL	10	0	0	0	15	59	13	1	1	0	0	0	0	4	0	12	0	0	0	0	—	0	0-0	3	0.60
1999 Boston	AL	11	1	0	7	12.2	64	15	11	11	3	1	3	0	8	2	9	1	0	0	2	.000	0	0-1	0	7.82
2000 Houston	NL	2	1	0	0	4.1	23	9	8	5	2	0	0	0	3	0	3	0	0	1	0	1.000	0	0-0	1	10.38
6 ML YEARS		73	12	1	22	147.2	661	168	80	64	14	7	4	3	66	5	81	7	2	7	8	.467	0	0-1	7	3.90

Mark Grudzielanek

Bats: Right **Throws:** Right **Pos:** 2B-148; PH/PR-2; SS-1 **Ht:** 6'1" **Wt:** 185 **Born:** 6/30/70 **Age:** 31

BATTING

Year Team	Lg	G	AB	H	2B	3B	HR	(Hm	Rd)	TB	R	RBI	TBB	IBB	SO	HBP	SH	SF	SB	CS	SB%	GDP	Avg	OBP	SLG
1995 Montreal	NL	78	269	66	12	2	1	(1	0)	85	27	20	14	4	47	7	3	0	8	3	.73	7	.245	.300	.316
1996 Montreal	NL	153	657	201	34	4	6	(5	1)	261	99	49	26	3	83	9	1	3	33	7	.83	10	.306	.340	.397
1997 Montreal	NL	156	649	177	54	3	4	(1	3)	249	76	51	23	0	76	10	3	3	25	9	.74	13	.273	.307	.384
1998 Mon-LA	NL	156	589	160	21	1	10	(5	5)	213	62	62	26	2	73	11	8	7	18	5	.78	18	.272	.311	.362
1999 Los Angeles	NL	123	488	159	23	5	7	(4	3)	213	72	46	31	0	65	10	2	3	6	6	.50	13	.326	.376	.436
2000 Los Angeles	NL	148	617	172	35	6	7	(4	3)	240	101	49	45	0	81	9	2	3	12	3	.80	16	.279	.335	.389
1998 Montreal	NL	105	396	109	15	1	8	(3	5)	150	51	41	21	1	50	9	5	4	11	5	.69	11	.275	.323	.379
Los Angeles	NL	51	193	51	6	0	2	(2	0)	63	11	21	5	1	23	2	3	3	7	0	1.00	7	.264	.286	.326
6 ML YEARS		814	3269	935	179	21	35	(20	15)	1261	437	277	165	10	425	56	19	19	102	33	.76	77	.286	.329	.386

Eddie Guardado

Pitches: Left **Bats:** Right **Pos:** RP-70 **Ht:** 6'0" **Wt:** 194 **Born:** 10/2/70 **Age:** 30

HOW MUCH HE PITCHED / WHAT HE GAVE UP / THE RESULTS

Year Team	Lg	G	GS	CG	GF	IP	BFP	H	R	ER	HR	SH	SF	HB	TBB	IBB	SO	WP	Bk	W	L	Pct.	ShO	Sv-Op	Hld	ERA
1993 Minnesota	AL	19	16	0	2	94.2	426	123	68	65	13	1	3	1	36	2	46	0	0	3	8	.273	0	0-0	0	6.18
1994 Minnesota	AL	4	4	0	0	17	81	26	16	16	3	1	2	0	4	0	8	0	0	0	2	.000	0	0-0	0	8.47
1995 Minnesota	AL	51	5	0	10	91.1	410	99	54	52	13	6	5	0	45	2	71	5	1	4	9	.308	0	2-5	5	5.12
1996 Minnesota	AL	83	0	0	17	73.2	313	61	45	43	12	6	4	3	33	4	74	3	0	6	5	.545	0	4-7	18	5.25
1997 Minnesota	AL	69	0	0	20	46	201	45	23	20	7	2	1	2	17	2	54	2	0	0	1	.000	0	1-1	13	3.91
1998 Minnesota	AL	79	0	0	12	65.2	286	66	34	33	10	3	6	0	28	6	53	2	0	3	1	.750	0	0-4	16	4.52
1999 Minnesota	AL	63	0	0	13	48	197	37	24	24	6	2	1	2	25	4	50	0	0	2	5	.286	0	2-4	15	4.50
2000 Minnesota	AL	70	0	0	36	61.2	262	55	27	27	14	3	2	1	25	3	52	1	0	7	4	.636	0	9-11	25	3.94
8 ML YEARS		438	25	0	110	498	2176	512	291	280	78	24	24	9	213	23	408	13	2	25	38	.397	0	18-32	75	5.06

Vladimir Guerrero

Bats: Right **Throws:** Right **Pos:** RF-151; DH-2; PH/PR-1 **Ht:** 6'3" **Wt:** 205 **Born:** 2/9/76 **Age:** 25

BATTING

Year Team	Lg	G	AB	H	2B	3B	HR	(Hm	Rd)	TB	R	RBI	TBB	IBB	SO	HBP	SH	SF	SB	CS	SB%	GDP	Avg	OBP	SLG
1996 Montreal	NL	9	27	5	0	0	1	(0	1)	8	2	1	0	0	3	0	0	0	0	0	—	1	.185	.185	.296
1997 Montreal	NL	90	325	98	22	2	11	(5	6)	157	44	40	19	2	39	7	0	5	3	4	.43	11	.302	.350	.483
1998 Montreal	NL	159	623	202	37	7	38	(19	19)	367	108	109	42	13	95	7	0	5	11	9	.55	15	.324	.371	.589
1999 Montreal	NL	160	610	193	37	5	42	(23	19)	366	102	131	55	14	62	7	0	2	14	7	.67	18	.316	.378	.600
2000 Montreal	NL	154	571	197	28	11	44	(25	19)	379	101	123	58	23	74	8	0	4	9	10	.47	15	.345	.410	.664
5 ML YEARS		572	2156	695	124	25	136	(72	64)	1277	357	404	174	52	273	29	0	14	37	30	.55	60	.322	.378	.592

Wilton Guerrero

Bats: B Throws: R Pos: PH/PR-55; LF-42; RF-24; CF-13; DH-6; 2B-1   Ht: 6'0" Wt: 175 Born: 10/24/74 Age: 26

Year Team	Lg	G	AB	H	2B	3B	HR	(Hm	Rd)	TB	R	RBI	TBB	IBB	SO	HBP	SH	SF	SB	CS	SB%	GDP	Avg	OBP	SLG
1996 Los Angeles	NL	5	2	0	0	0	0	(0	0)	0	1	0	0	0	2	0	0	0	0	0	—	0	.000	.000	.000
1997 Los Angeles	NL	111	357	104	10	9	4	(2	2)	144	39	32	8	1	52	0	13	2	6	5	.55	7	.291	.305	.403
1998 LA-Mon	NL	116	402	114	14	9	2	(0	2)	152	50	27	14	0	63	1	6	3	8	2	.80	4	.284	.307	.378
1999 Montreal	NL	132	315	92	15	7	2	(0	2)	127	42	31	13	0	38	2	10	0	7	6	.54	4	.292	.324	.403
2000 Montreal	NL	127	288	77	7	2	2	(2	0)	94	30	23	19	0	41	0	6	1	8	1	.89	6	.267	.312	.326
1998 Los Angeles	NL	64	180	51	4	3	0	(0	0)	61	21	7	4	0	33	1	3	2	5	2	.71	3	.283	.299	.339
Montreal	NL	52	222	63	10	6	2	(0	2)	91	29	20	10	0	30	0	3	1	3	0	1.00	1	.284	.313	.410
5 ML YEARS		491	1364	387	46	27	10	(4	6)	517	162	113	54	1	196	3	35	6	29	14	.67	21	.284	.311	.379

Carlos Guillen

Bats: Both Throws: Right Pos: 3B-68; SS-23; PH/PR-5   Ht: 6'1" Wt: 180 Born: 9/30/75 Age: 25

Year Team	Lg	G	AB	H	2B	3B	HR	(Hm	Rd)	TB	R	RBI	TBB	IBB	SO	HBP	SH	SF	SB	CS	SB%	GDP	Avg	OBP	SLG
1995 Astros	R	30	105	31	4	2	2	—	—	45	17	15	9	1	17	1	1	2	17	1	.94	0	.295	.350	.429
1996 Quad City	A	29	112	37	7	1	3	—	—	55	23	17	16	2	25	0	0	3	13	6	.68	1	.330	.405	.491
1997 Jackson	AA	115	390	99	16	1	10	—	—	147	47	39	38	1	78	2	4	2	6	5	.55	9	.254	.322	.377
New Orleans	AAA	3	13	4	1	0	0	—	—	5	3	0	0	0	4	0	0	0	0	0	—	0	.308	.308	.385
1998 New Orleans	AAA	100	374	109	18	4	12	—	—	171	67	51	31	1	61	5	6	4	3	4	.43	5	.291	.350	.457
Tacoma	AAA	24	92	21	1	1	1	—	—	27	8	4	9	0	17	0	1	1	1	2	.33	1	.228	.297	.293
2000 Tacoma	AAA	24	87	26	4	1	2	—	—	38	19	11	12	0	17	1	1	1	4	1	.80	3	.299	.386	.437
1998 Seattle	AL	10	39	13	1	1	0	(0	0)	16	9	5	3	0	9	0	0	0	2	0	1.00	0	.333	.381	.410
1999 Seattle	AL	5	19	3	0	0	1	(1	0)	6	2	3	1	0	6	0	1	0	0	0	—	1	.158	.200	.316
2000 Seattle	AL	90	288	74	15	2	7	(3	4)	114	45	42	28	0	53	2	7	3	1	3	.25	6	.257	.324	.396
3 ML YEARS		105	346	90	16	3	8	(4	4)	136	56	50	32	0	68	2	8	3	3	3	.50	7	.260	.324	.393

Jose Guillen

Bats: Right Throws: Right Pos: RF-98; PH/PR-15; CF-1   Ht: 5'11" Wt: 195 Born: 5/17/76 Age: 25

Year Team	Lg	G	AB	H	2B	3B	HR	(Hm	Rd)	TB	R	RBI	TBB	IBB	SO	HBP	SH	SF	SB	CS	SB%	GDP	Avg	OBP	SLG
2000 Durham *	AAA	19	78	33	8	2	9	—	—	72	20	31	8	3	11	1	0	1	0	1	.00	2	.423	.477	.923
1997 Pittsburgh	NL	143	498	133	20	5	14	(5	9)	205	58	70	17	0	88	8	0	3	1	2	.33	16	.267	.300	.412
1998 Pittsburgh	NL	153	573	153	38	2	14	(10	4)	237	60	84	21	0	100	6	1	4	3	5	.38	7	.267	.298	.414
1999 Pit-TB		87	288	73	16	0	3	(1	2)	98	42	31	20	2	57	7	1	2	1	0	1.00	16	.253	.315	.340
2000 Tampa Bay	AL	105	316	80	16	5	10	(5	5)	136	40	41	24	1	65	13	2	0	3	1	.75	6	.253	.320	.430
1999 Pittsburgh	NL	40	120	32	6	0	1	(0	1)	41	18	18	10	1	21	0	1	1	1	0	1.00	7	.267	.321	.342
Tampa Bay	AL	47	168	41	10	0	2	(1	1)	57	24	13	10	1	36	7	0	1	0	0	—	9	.244	.312	.339
4 ML YEARS		488	1675	439	90	12	41	(21	20)	676	200	226	76	3	310	34	4	9	8	8	.50	45	.262	.306	.404

Ozzie Guillen

Bats: L Throws: R Pos: SS-42; PH/PR-13; 3B-11; 1B-5; 2B-2   Ht: 5'11" Wt: 165 Born: 1/20/64 Age: 37

Year Team	Lg	G	AB	H	2B	3B	HR	(Hm	Rd)	TB	R	RBI	TBB	IBB	SO	HBP	SH	SF	SB	CS	SB%	GDP	Avg	OBP	SLG
1985 Chicago	AL	150	491	134	21	9	1	(1	0)	176	71	33	12	1	36	1	8	1	7	4	.64	5	.273	.291	.358
1986 Chicago	AL	159	547	137	19	4	2	(1	1)	170	58	47	12	1	52	1	12	5	8	4	.67	14	.250	.265	.311
1987 Chicago	AL	149	560	156	22	7	2	(2	0)	198	64	51	22	2	52	1	13	8	25	8	.76	10	.279	.303	.354
1988 Chicago	AL	156	566	148	16	7	0	(0	0)	178	58	39	25	3	40	2	10	3	25	13	.66	14	.261	.294	.314
1989 Chicago	AL	155	597	151	20	8	1	(0	1)	190	63	54	15	3	48	0	11	3	36	17	.68	8	.253	.270	.318
1990 Chicago	AL	160	516	144	21	4	1	(0	1)	176	61	58	26	8	37	1	15	5	13	17	.43	6	.279	.312	.341
1991 Chicago	AL	154	524	143	20	3	3	(1	2)	178	52	49	11	1	38	0	13	7	21	15	.58	7	.273	.284	.340
1992 Chicago	AL	12	40	8	4	0	0	(0	0)	12	5	7	1	0	5	0	1	1	1	0	1.00	1	.200	.214	.300
1993 Chicago	AL	134	457	128	23	4	4	(3	1)	171	44	50	10	0	41	0	13	6	5	4	.56	6	.280	.292	.374
1994 Chicago	AL	100	365	105	9	5	1	(0	1)	127	46	39	14	2	35	0	7	4	5	4	.56	5	.288	.311	.348
1995 Chicago	AL	122	415	103	20	3	1	(0	1)	132	50	41	13	1	25	0	4	1	6	7	.46	11	.248	.270	.318
1996 Chicago	AL	150	499	131	24	8	4	(1	3)	183	62	45	10	0	27	0	12	7	6	5	.55	10	.263	.273	.367
1997 Chicago	AL	142	490	120	21	6	4	(1	3)	165	59	52	22	1	24	0	11	4	5	3	.63	7	.245	.275	.337
1998 Bal-Atl		95	280	74	15	1	1	(1	0)	94	37	22	25	0	27	1	5	2	1	5	.17	3	.264	.325	.336
1999 Atlanta	NL	92	232	56	16	0	1	(0	1)	75	21	20	15	2	17	0	5	3	4	2	.67	6	.241	.284	.323
2000 Tampa Bay	AL	63	107	26	4	0	2	(1	1)	36	22	12	6	0	7	0	1	0	1	0	1.00	1	.243	.283	.336
1998 Baltimore	AL	12	16	1	0	0	0	(0	0)	1	2	0	1	0	2	0	1	0	0	1	.00	1	.063	.118	.063
Atlanta	NL	83	264	73	15	1	1	(1	0)	93	35	22	24	0	25	1	4	2	1	4	.20	2	.277	.337	.352
16 ML YEARS		1993	6686	1764	275	69	28	(13	15)	2261	773	619	239	25	511	7	141	60	169	108	.61	114	.264	.287	.338

Eric Gunderson

Pitches: Left Bats: Right Pos: RP-6   Ht: 6'0" Wt: 190 Born: 3/29/66 Age: 35

Year Team	Lg	G	GS	CG	GF	IP	BFP	H	R	ER	HR	SH	SF	HB	TBB	IBB	SO	WP	Bk	W	L	Pct.	ShO	Sv-Op	Hld	ERA
2000 Syracuse *	AAA	33	0	0	10	27	117	26	12	8	2	2	1	1	11	0	17	4	1	0	3	.000	0	2-–	—	2.67
Fresno *	AAA	13	0	0	7	23.1	109	34	18	13	2	1	0	1	7	1	14	0	0	2	1	.667	0	2-–	—	5.01
1990 San Francisco	NL	7	4	0	1	19.2	94	24	14	12	2	1	0	0	11	1	14	0	0	1	2	.333	0	0-0	0	5.49
1991 San Francisco	NL	2	0	0	1	3.1	18	6	4	2	0	0	0	0	1	0	2	0	0	0	0	—	0	1-1	0	5.40
1992 Seattle	AL	9	0	0	4	9.1	45	12	12	9	1	0	2	1	5	3	2	0	0	2	1	.667	0	0-0	0	8.68
1994 New York	NL	14	0	0	3	9	45	5	0	0	0	0	0	0	4	0	4	0	0	0	0	—	0	0-0	2	0.00
1995 NYM-Bos		49	0	0	8	36.2	161	38	17	17	2	2	2	3	17	4	28	1	0	3	2	.600	0	0-3	6	4.17
1996 Boston	AL	28	0	0	8	17.1	82	21	17	16	5	0	2	2	8	2	7	2	0	0	1	.000	0	0-0	3	8.31
1997 Texas	AL	60	0	0	11	49.2	209	45	19	18	5	2	3	2	15	3	31	2	1	2	1	.667	0	1-4	12	3.26
1998 Texas	AL	68	1	0	13	67.2	303	88	43	39	13	1	3	1	19	4	41	4	0	0	3	.000	0	0-2	5	5.19
1999 Texas	AL	11	0	0	3	10	51	20	8	8	1	0	1	0	2	0	6	3	0	0	0	—	0	0-0	1	7.20

Year Team	Lg	G	GS	CG	GF	IP	BFP	H	R	ER	HR	SH	SF	HB	TBB	IBB	SO	WP	Bk	W	L	Pct.	ShO	Sv-Op	Hld	ERA
2000 Toronto	AL	6	0	0	1	6.1	37	15	6	5	0	0	1	1	2	1	2	0	0	0	1	.000	0	0-0	0	7.11
1995 New York	NL	30	0	0	7	24.1	103	25	10	10	2	0	1	1	8	3	19	1	0	1	1	.500	0	0-3	3	3.70
Boston	AL	19	0	0	1	12.1	58	13	7	7	0	2	1	2	9	1	9	0	0	2	1	.667	0	0-0	6	5.11
10 ML YEARS		254	5	0	47	229	1031	274	140	126	29	6	14	10	84	18	137	13	3	8	11	.421	0	2-10	33	4.95

Mark Guthrie

Pitches: Left **Bats:** Right **Pos:** RP-76 **Ht:** 6'4" **Wt:** 215 **Born:** 9/22/65 **Age:** 35

		HOW MUCH HE PITCHED						WHAT HE GAVE UP												THE RESULTS						
Year Team	Lg	G	GS	CG	GF	IP	BFP	H	R	ER	HR	SH	SF	HB	TBB	IBB	SO	WP	Bk	W	L	Pct.	ShO	Sv-Op	Hld	ERA
1989 Minnesota	AL	13	8	0	2	57.1	254	66	32	29	7	1	5	1	21	1	38	1	0	2	4	.333	0	0-0	0	4.55
1990 Minnesota	AL	24	21	3	0	144.2	603	154	65	61	8	6	0	1	39	3	101	9	0	7	9	.438	1	0-0	0	3.79
1991 Minnesota	AL	41	12	0	13	98	432	116	52	47	11	4	3	1	41	2	72	7	0	7	5	.583	0	2-2	5	4.32
1992 Minnesota	AL	54	0	0	15	75	303	59	27	24	7	4	2	0	23	7	76	2	0	2	3	.400	0	5-7	19	2.88
1993 Minnesota	AL	22	0	0	2	21	94	20	11	11	2	1	2	0	16	2	15	1	3	2	1	.667	0	0-1	8	4.71
1994 Minnesota	AL	50	2	0	13	51.1	234	65	43	35	8	2	6	2	18	2	38	7	0	4	2	.667	0	1-3	12	6.14
1995 Min-LA		60	0	0	14	62	272	66	33	29	6	4	0	2	25	5	67	5	1	5	5	.500	0	0-2	15	4.21
1996 Los Angeles	NL	66	0	0	16	73	302	65	21	18	3	4	4	1	22	2	56	1	0	2	3	.400	0	1-3	12	2.22
1997 Los Angeles	NL	62	0	0	18	69.1	305	71	44	41	12	10	3	0	30	6	42	2	1	1	4	.200	0	1-4	13	5.32
1998 Los Angeles	NL	53	0	0	11	54	241	56	26	21	3	5	0	2	24	1	45	2	0	2	1	.667	0	0-1	8	3.50
1999 Bos-ChC		57	0	0	15	58.2	254	57	38	35	10	2	3	2	24	5	45	3	0	1	3	.250	0	2-2	14	5.37
2000 ChC-TB-Tor		76	0	0	15	71.1	315	70	41	37	8	4	4	2	37	9	63	13	0	6	3	.333	0	0-4	10	4.67
1995 Minnesota	AL	36	0	0	7	42.1	181	47	22	21	5	2	0	1	16	3	48	3	1	5	3	.625	0	0-2	10	4.46
Los Angeles	NL	24	0	0	7	19.2	91	19	11	8	1	2	0	1	9	2	19	2	0	0	2	.000	0	0-0	5	3.66
1999 Boston	AL	46	0	0	15	46.1	207	50	32	30	9	0	3	2	20	3	36	2	0	1	1	.500	0	2-2	12	5.83
Chicago	NL	11	0	0	0	12.1	47	7	6	5	1	2	0	0	4	2	9	1	0	0	2	.000	0	0-0	2	3.65
2000 Chicago	NL	19	0	0	3	18.2	82	17	11	10	1	2	3	1	10	4	17	4	0	2	3	.400	0	0-0	3	4.82
Tampa Bay	AL	34	0	0	7	32	145	33	18	16	4	1	0	0	18	5	26	7	0	1	1	.500	0	0-3	4	4.50
Toronto	AL	23	0	0	5	20.2	88	20	12	11	3	1	1	1	9	0	20	2	0	0	2	.000	0	0-1	3	4.79
12 ML YEARS		578	43	3	134	835.2	3609	865	433	388	85	47	32	14	320	45	658	53	5	38	46	.452	1	12-29	116	4.18

Ricky Gutierrez

Bats: Right **Throws:** Right **Pos:** SS-121; PH/PR-5 **Ht:** 6'1" **Wt:** 195 **Born:** 5/23/70 **Age:** 31

		BATTING																	BASERUNNING				PERCENTAGES		
Year Team	Lg	G	AB	H	2B	3B	HR	(Hm	Rd)	TB	R	RBI	TBB	IBB	SO	HBP	SH	SF	SB	CS	SB%	GDP	Avg	OBP	SLG
2000 Daytona *	A+	4	10	4	1	0	0	—	—	5	0	1	2	0	2	0	0	0	1	0	1.00	1	.400	.500	.500
1993 San Diego	NL	133	438	110	10	5	5	(5	0)	145	76	26	50	2	97	5	1	1	4	3	.57	7	.251	.334	.331
1994 San Diego	NL	90	275	66	11	5	1	(1	0)	84	27	28	32	1	54	2	2	3	6	2	.25	8	.240	.321	.305
1995 Houston	NL	52	156	43	6	0	0	(0	0)	49	22	12	10	3	33	1	1	1	5	0	1.00	4	.276	.321	.314
1996 Houston	NL	89	218	62	8	1	1	(1	0)	75	28	15	23	3	42	3	4	1	6	1	.86	4	.284	.359	.344
1997 Houston	NL	102	303	79	14	4	3	(0	3)	110	33	34	21	2	50	3	0	0	5	2	.71	17	.261	.315	.363
1998 Houston	NL	141	491	128	24	3	2	(1	1)	164	55	46	54	5	84	6	3	7	13	7	.65	20	.261	.337	.334
1999 Houston	NL	85	268	70	7	5	1	(1	0)	90	33	25	37	4	45	2	3	1	5	5	.29	9	.261	.354	.336
2000 Chicago	NL	125	449	124	19	2	11	(7	4)	180	73	56	66	0	58	7	16	4	8	2	.80	10	.276	.375	.401
8 ML YEARS		817	2598	682	99	22	24	(16	8)	897	347	242	293	20	463	29	30	18	45	26	.63	79	.263	.342	.345

Cristian Guzman

Bats: Both **Throws:** Right **Pos:** SS-151; PH/PR-8; DH-1 **Ht:** 6'0" **Wt:** 195 **Born:** 3/21/78 **Age:** 23

		BATTING																	BASERUNNING				PERCENTAGES		
Year Team	Lg	G	AB	H	2B	3B	HR	(Hm	Rd)	TB	R	RBI	TBB	IBB	SO	HBP	SH	SF	SB	CS	SB%	GDP	Avg	OBP	SLG
1996 Yankees	R	42	170	50	8	2	1	—	—	65	37	21	10	0	31	3	2	2	7	6	.54	2	.294	.341	.382
1997 Tampa	A+	4	14	4	0	0	0	—	—	4	4	1	1	0	1	0	0	0	0	1	.00	0	.286	.333	.286
Greensboro	A	124	495	135	21	4	4	—	—	176	68	52	17	0	105	10	4	2	23	12	.66	3	.273	.309	.356
1998 New Britain	AA	140	566	157	29	5	1	—	—	199	68	40	21	1	111	1	17	1	23	14	.62	13	.277	.304	.352
1999 Minnesota	AL	131	420	95	12	3	1	(1	0)	116	47	26	22	0	90	3	7	4	9	7	.56	5	.226	.267	.276
2000 Minnesota	AL	156	631	156	25	20	8	(3	5)	245	89	54	46	1	101	2	7	4	28	10	.74	5	.247	.299	.388
2 ML YEARS		287	1051	251	37	23	9	(4	5)	361	136	80	68	1	191	5	14	8	37	17	.69	10	.239	.286	.343

Domingo Guzman

Pitches: Right **Bats:** Right **Pos:** RP-1 **Ht:** 6'0" **Wt:** 210 **Born:** 4/5/75 **Age:** 26

		HOW MUCH HE PITCHED						WHAT HE GAVE UP												THE RESULTS						
Year Team	Lg	G	GS	CG	GF	IP	BFP	H	R	ER	HR	SH	SF	HB	TBB	IBB	SO	WP	Bk	W	L	Pct.	ShO	Sv-Op	Hld	ERA
1994 Padres	R	13	13	0	0	70	309	65	39	32	1	1	2	11	25	0	55	5	2	8	4	.667	0	0--	—	4.11
1995 Idaho Falls	R+	27	0	0	23	25.2	127	25	22	19	2	3	1	1	25	1	33	6	3	2	1	.667	0	11--	—	6.66
1996 Clinton	A	6	5	0	1	20.2	112	32	33	29	2	0	1	1	19	0	18	5	0	0	5	.000	0	0--	—	12.63
Idaho Falls	R+	15	10	1	1	65.1	278	52	41	30	7	2	1	7	29	0	75	13	0	4	2	.667	1	0--	—	4.13
1997 Clinton	A	12	12	5	0	79	320	66	36	28	7	2	2	3	25	0	91	5	2	4	5	.444	2	0--	—	3.19
Rancho Cuc	A+	6	6	0	0	38	168	42	23	23	6	2	1	2	16	0	39	2	0	3	2	.600	0	0--	—	5.45
1998 Rancho Cuc	A+	4	4	0	0	21.2	91	22	11	9	1	0	0	1	6	0	16	3	0	1	1	.500	0	0--	—	3.74
Mobile	AA	12	8	0	2	48	217	51	34	24	7	3	0	3	26	0	39	8	0	5	2	.714	0	1--	—	4.50
1999 Mobile	AA	41	0	0	21	51	240	60	33	31	2	3	3	5	25	1	38	3	0	1	2	.333	0	6--	—	5.47
2000 Mobile	AA	14	1	0	4	17.1	76	13	8	4	2	1	2	0	11	0	14	4	0	0	0	--	0	0--	—	2.08
Las Vegas	AAA	43	3	0	10	63.1	282	56	47	42	10	3	6	8	35	3	54	6	2	3	5	.375	0	1--	—	5.97
1999 San Diego	NL	7	0	0	2	5	33	13	12	12	1	2	0	0	3	2	4	0	0	0	1	.000	0	0-0	0	21.60
2000 San Diego	NL	1	0	0	0	1	6	1	1	1	0	0	0	2	1	0	0	0	0	0	0	—	0	0-0	0	9.00
2 ML YEARS		8	0	0	2	6	39	14	13	13	1	2	0	2	4	2	4	0	0	0	1	.000	0	0-0	0	19.50

Geraldo Guzman

Pitches: Right Bats: Right Pos: SP-10; RP-3 Ht: 6'1" Wt: 160 Born: 11/28/72 Age: 28

Year Team	Lg	G	GS	CG	GF	IP	BFP	H	R	ER	HR	SH	SF	HB	TBB	IBB	SO	WP	Bk	W	L	Pct.	ShO	Sv-Op	Hld	ERA
2000 Tucson	AAA	6	6	1	0	38	148	23	7	6	3	0	0	3	10	1	44	0	0	4	1	.800	1	0- -	—	1.42
El Paso	AA	17	7	0	5	50.1	220	47	23	21	2	3	0	3	22	2	53	3	0	3	3	.500	0	3- -	—	3.75
2000 Arizona	NL	13	10	0	0	60.1	259	66	36	36	8	3	1	2	22	0	52	3	0	5	4	.556	0	0-1	0	5.37

Juan Guzman

Pitches: Right Bats: Right Pos: SP-1 Ht: 5'11" Wt: 195 Born: 10/28/66 Age: 34

Year Team	Lg	G	GS	CG	GF	IP	BFP	H	R	ER	HR	SH	SF	HB	TBB	IBB	SO	WP	Bk	W	L	Pct.	ShO	Sv-Op	Hld	ERA
2000 St. Pete *	A+	1	1	0	0	5	21	4	0	0	0	0	0	0	2	0	6	0	0	1	0	1.000	0	0- -	—	0.00
Orlando *	AA	1	1	0	0	5.1	26	6	6	5	1	1	0	1	3	0	5	0	0	0	1	.000	0	0- -	—	8.44
Durham *	AAA	2	2	0	0	9.2	42	13	6	6	3	0	0	0	1	0	7	0	0	0	2	.000	0	0- -	—	5.59
1991 Toronto	AL	23	23	1	0	138.2	574	98	53	46	6	2	5	4	66	0	123	10	0	10	3	.769	0	0-0	0	2.99
1992 Toronto	AL	28	28	1	0	180.2	733	135	56	53	6	2	5	3	72	0	165	14	2	16	5	.762	0	0-0	0	2.64
1993 Toronto	AL	33	33	2	0	221	963	211	107	98	17	5	9	3	110	2	194	26	1	14	3	.824	1	0-0	0	3.99
1994 Toronto	AL	25	25	2	0	147.1	671	165	102	93	20	1	6	3	76	1	124	13	1	12	11	.522	0	0-0	0	5.68
1995 Toronto	AL	24	24	3	0	135.1	619	151	101	95	13	3	2	3	73	6	94	6	0	4	14	.222	0	0-0	0	6.32
1996 Toronto	AL	27	27	4	0	187.2	756	158	68	61	20	2	2	7	53	3	165	7	0	11	8	.579	1	0-0	0	2.93
1997 Toronto	AL	13	13	0	0	60	261	48	42	33	14	1	2	2	31	0	52	4	0	3	6	.333	0	0-0	0	4.95
1998 Tor-Bal	AL	33	33	2	0	211	918	193	117	102	23	2	5	8	98	2	168	11	0	10	16	.385	0	0-0	0	4.35
1999 Bal-Cin	AL	33	33	2	0	200	864	194	96	83	28	7	4	4	86	6	155	12	2	11	12	.478	1	0-0	0	3.74
2000 Tampa Bay	AL	1	1	0	0	1.2	14	7	8	8	2	1	0	0	2	0	3	0	0	0	1	.000	0	0-0	0	43.20
1998 Toronto	AL	22	22	2	0	145	632	133	83	71	19	2	3	6	65	1	113	6	0	6	12	.333	0	0-0	0	4.41
Baltimore	AL	11	11	0	0	66	286	60	34	31	4	0	2	2	33	1	55	5	0	4	4	.500	0	0-0	0	4.23
1999 Baltimore	AL	21	21	1	0	122.2	544	124	63	57	18	4	3	3	65	3	95	7	2	5	9	.357	1	0-0	0	4.18
Cincinnati	NL	12	12	1	0	77.1	320	70	33	26	10	3	1	1	21	3	60	5	0	6	3	.667	0	0-0	0	3.03
10 ML YEARS		240	240	17	0	1483.1	6373	1360	750	672	149	29	38	35	667	22	1243	105	6	91	79	.535	3	0-0	0	4.08

Tony Gwynn

Bats: Left Throws: Left Pos: RF-26; DH-6; PH/PR-4 Ht: 5'11" Wt: 225 Born: 5/9/60 Age: 41

Year Team	Lg	G	AB	H	2B	3B	HR	(Hm	Rd)	TB	R	RBI	TBB	IBB	SO	HBP	SH	SF	SB	CS	SB%	GDP	Avg	OBP	SLG
1982 San Diego	NL	54	190	55	12	2	1	(0	1)	74	33	17	14	0	16	0	4	1	8	3	.73	5	.289	.337	.389
1983 San Diego	NL	86	304	94	12	2	1	(0	1)	113	34	37	23	5	21	0	4	3	7	4	.64	9	.309	.355	.372
1984 San Diego	NL	158	606	213	21	10	5	(3	2)	269	88	71	59	13	23	2	6	2	33	18	.65	15	.351	.410	.444
1985 San Diego	NL	154	622	197	29	5	6	(3	3)	254	90	46	45	4	33	2	1	6	14	11	.56	17	.317	.364	.408
1986 San Diego	NL	160	642	211	33	7	14	(8	6)	300	107	59	52	11	35	3	2	2	37	9	.80	20	.329	.381	.467
1987 San Diego	NL	157	589	218	36	13	7	(5	2)	301	119	54	82	26	35	3	2	4	56	12	.82	13	.370	.447	.511
1988 San Diego	NL	133	521	163	22	5	7	(3	4)	216	64	70	51	13	40	0	4	4	26	11	.70	11	.313	.373	.415
1989 San Diego	NL	158	604	203	27	7	4	(3	1)	256	82	62	56	16	30	1	1	7	40	16	.71	12	.336	.389	.424
1990 San Diego	NL	141	573	177	29	10	4	(2	2)	238	79	72	44	20	23	1	7	4	17	8	.68	13	.309	.357	.415
1991 San Diego	NL	134	530	168	27	11	4	(1	3)	229	69	62	34	8	19	0	0	5	8	8	.50	11	.317	.355	.432
1992 San Diego	NL	128	520	165	27	3	6	(4	2)	216	77	41	46	12	16	0	0	3	3	6	.33	13	.317	.371	.415
1993 San Diego	NL	122	489	175	41	3	7	(4	3)	243	70	59	36	11	19	1	1	7	14	1	.93	18	.358	.398	.497
1994 San Diego	NL	110	419	165	35	1	12	(4	8)	238	79	64	48	16	19	2	1	5	5	0	1.00	20	.394	.454	.568
1995 San Diego	NL	135	535	197	33	1	9	(5	4)	259	82	90	35	10	15	1	0	6	17	5	.77	20	.368	.404	.484
1996 San Diego	NL	116	451	159	27	2	3	(2	1)	199	67	50	39	12	17	1	1	6	11	4	.73	17	.353	.400	.441
1997 San Diego	NL	149	592	220	49	2	17	(8	9)	324	97	119	43	12	28	3	1	12	12	5	.71	12	.372	.409	.547
1998 San Diego	NL	127	461	148	35	0	16	(5	11)	231	65	69	35	6	18	1	0	8	3	1	.75	14	.321	.364	.501
1999 San Diego	NL	111	411	139	27	0	10	(5	5)	196	59	62	29	5	14	2	0	7	7	2	.78	15	.338	.381	.477
2000 San Diego	NL	36	127	41	12	0	1	(1	0)	56	17	17	9	2	4	1	0	3	0	1	.00	4	.323	.364	.441
19 ML YEARS		2369	9186	3108	534	84	134	(66	68)	4212	1378	1121	780	202	425	24	45	85	318	125	.72	259	.338	.388	.459

Luther Hackman

Pitches: Right Bats: Right Pos: RP-1 Ht: 6'4" Wt: 195 Born: 10/10/74 Age: 26

Year Team	Lg	G	GS	CG	GF	IP	BFP	H	R	ER	HR	SH	SF	HB	TBB	IBB	SO	WP	Bk	W	L	Pct.	ShO	Sv-Op	Hld	ERA
1994 Rockies	R	12	12	0	0	55.2	234	50	21	13	0	1	0	5	16	0	63	5	1	1	3	.250	0	0- -	—	2.10
1995 Asheville	A	28	28	2	0	165	710	162	95	85	11	3	3	14	65	0	108	9	7	11	11	.500	0	0- -	—	4.64
1996 Salem	A+	21	21	1	0	110.1	484	93	60	52	2	4	7	5	69	1	83	6	2	5	7	.417	0	0- -	—	4.24
1997 New Haven	AA	10	10	0	0	50.2	241	58	49	44	11	5	4	2	34	1	34	4	3	0	6	.000	0	0- -	—	7.82
Salem	A+	15	15	2	0	80.2	384	99	60	52	14	4	5	9	37	0	59	8	0	1	4	.200	0	0- -	—	5.80
1998 New Haven	AA	28	23	1	2	139	640	169	102	84	18	7	7	10	54	1	90	10	2	3	12	.200	0	0- -	—	5.44
1999 Carolina	AA	11	10	0	0	62.1	271	53	33	28	4	2	1	4	28	0	50	4	0	4	3	.571	0	0- -	—	4.04
Colo Sprngs	AAA	15	15	1	0	101	445	106	49	42	7	4	3	6	44	2	88	2	2	7	6	.538	1	0- -	—	3.74
2000 Memphis	AAA	21	21	0	0	119.2	522	134	71	63	11	5	3	5	36	1	66	1	0	8	9	.471	0	0- -	—	4.74
1999 Colorado	NL	5	3	0	0	16	86	26	19	19	5	2	0	0	12	0	10	0	0	1	2	.333	0	0-0	0	10.69
2000 St. Louis	NL	1	0	0	0	2.2	17	4	3	3	0	2	0	1	4	1	0	0	0	0	0	—	0	0-0	0	10.13
2 ML YEARS		6	3	0	0	18.2	101	30	22	22	5	4	0	1	16	1	10	0	0	1	2	.333	0	0-0	0	10.61

Jerry Hairston Jr.

Bats: Right Throws: Right Pos: 2B-49 Ht: 5'10" Wt: 175 Born: 5/29/76 Age: 25

Year Team	Lg	G	AB	H	2B	3B	HR	(Hm	Rd)	TB	R	RBI	TBB	IBB	SO	HBP	SH	SF	SB	CS	SB%	GDP	Avg	OBP	SLG
2000 Orioles *	R	4	10	3	2	0	0	—	—	5	3	3	3	0	2	2	0	1	4	0	1.00	0	.300	.500	.500
Frederick *	A+	2	8	3	2	0	0	—	—	5	1	1	0	0	0	0	0	0	0	0	—	0	.375	.444	.625
Rochester *	AAA	58	201	59	15	1	4	—	—	88	43	21	29	0	32	5	2	2	6	4	.60	2	.294	.392	.438
1998 Baltimore	AL	6	7	0	0	0	0	(0	0)	0	2	0	0	0	1	0	0	0	0	0	—	0	.000	.000	.000

86

Year Team	Lg	G	AB	H	2B	3B	HR	(Hm	Rd)	TB	R	RBI	TBB	IBB	SO	HBP	SH	SF	SB	CS	SB%	GDP	Avg	OBP	SLG
								BATTING											**BASERUNNING**				**PERCENTAGES**		
1999 Baltimore	AL	50	175	47	12	1	4	(1	3)	73	26	17	11	0	24	3	4	0	9	4	.69	2	.269	.323	.417
2000 Baltimore	AL	49	180	46	5	0	5	(2	3)	66	27	19	21	0	22	6	5	0	8	5	.62	8	.256	.353	.367
3 ML YEARS		105	362	93	17	1	9	(3	6)	139	55	36	32	0	47	9	9	0	17	9	.65	10	.257	.333	.384

John Halama

Pitches: Left **Bats:** Left **Pos:** SP-30   **Ht:** 6'5" **Wt:** 210 **Born:** 2/22/72 **Age:** 29

Year Team	Lg	G	GS	CG	GF	IP	BFP	H	R	ER	HR	SH	SF	HB	TBB	IBB	SO	WP	Bk	W	L	Pct.	ShO	Sv-Op	Hld	ERA
				HOW MUCH HE PITCHED							**WHAT HE GAVE UP**											**THE RESULTS**				
1998 Houston	NL	6	6	0	0	32.1	147	37	21	21	0	3	4	2	13	0	21	2	1	1	1	.500	0	0-0	0	5.85
1999 Seattle	AL	38	24	1	7	179	763	193	88	84	20	5	9	7	56	3	105	4	1	11	10	.524	1	0-0	1	4.22
2000 Seattle	AL	30	30	1	0	166.2	736	206	108	94	19	4	6	2	56	0	87	4	0	14	9	.609	1	0-0	0	5.08
3 ML YEARS		74	60	2	7	378	1646	436	217	199	39	12	19	11	125	3	213	10	2	26	20	.565	2	0-0	1	4.74

Toby Hall

Bats: Right **Throws:** Right **Pos:** C-4   **Ht:** 6'3" **Wt:** 205 **Born:** 10/21/75 **Age:** 25

Year Team	Lg	G	AB	H	2B	3B	HR	(Hm	Rd)	TB	R	RBI	TBB	IBB	SO	HBP	SH	SF	SB	CS	SB%	GDP	Avg	OBP	SLG
								BATTING											**BASERUNNING**				**PERCENTAGES**		
1997 Hudson Val	A-	55	200	50	3	0	1	—	—	56	25	27	13	1	33	1	1	3	0	0	—	3	.250	.295	.280
1998 Chston-SC	A	105	377	121	25	1	6	—	—	166	59	50	39	2	32	5	0	6	3	7	.30	15	.321	.386	.440
1999 St. Pete	A+	56	212	63	13	1	4	—	—	90	24	36	17	0	9	2	1	3	1	2	.00	7	.297	.350	.425
Orlando	AA	46	173	44	7	0	9	—	—	78	20	34	4	1	10	1	1	4	1	1	.50	7	.254	.269	.451
2000 Orlando	AA	68	271	93	14	0	9	—	—	134	37	50	17	2	24	1	0	5	3	2	.60	6	.343	.378	.494
Durham	AAA	47	184	56	15	0	7	—	—	92	21	35	3	0	19	2	0	5	0	0	—	9	.304	.314	.500
2000 Tampa Bay	AL	4	12	2	0	0	1	(0	1)	5	1	1	1	0	0	0	0	0	0	0	—	0	.167	.231	.417

Roy Halladay

Pitches: Right **Bats:** Right **Pos:** SP-13; RP-6   **Ht:** 6'6" **Wt:** 225 **Born:** 5/14/77 **Age:** 24

Year Team	Lg	G	GS	CG	GF	IP	BFP	H	R	ER	HR	SH	SF	HB	TBB	IBB	SO	WP	Bk	W	L	Pct.	ShO	Sv-Op	Hld	ERA
				HOW MUCH HE PITCHED							**WHAT HE GAVE UP**											**THE RESULTS**				
2000 Syracuse *	AAA	11	11	3	0	73.2	317	85	46	45	10	1	0	2	21	0	38	4	0	2	3	.400	0	0- --		5.50
1998 Toronto	AL	2	2	1	0	14	53	9	4	3	2	0	0	0	2	0	13	0	0	1	0	1.000	0	0-0	0	1.93
1999 Toronto	AL	36	18	1	2	149.1	668	156	76	65	19	3	4	4	79	1	82	6	0	8	7	.533	1	1-1	2	3.92
2000 Toronto	AL	19	13	0	4	67.2	349	107	87	80	14	2	3	2	42	0	44	6	1	4	7	.364	0	0-0	0	10.64
3 ML YEARS		57	33	2	6	231	1070	272	167	148	35	5	7	6	123	1	139	12	1	13	14	.481	1	1-1	2	5.77

Shane Halter

Bats: R **Throws:** R **Pos:** 3B-55; 1B-29; SS-17; 2B-10; PH/PR-10; CF-5; RF-3; C-2; LF-2; P-1 **Ht:** 6'0" **Wt:** 180 **Born:** 11/8/69 **Age:** 31

Year Team	Lg	G	AB	H	2B	3B	HR	(Hm	Rd)	TB	R	RBI	TBB	IBB	SO	HBP	SH	SF	SB	CS	SB%	GDP	Avg	OBP	SLG
								BATTING											**BASERUNNING**				**PERCENTAGES**		
1997 Kansas City	AL	74	123	34	5	1	2	(1	1)	47	16	10	10	0	28	2	4	0	4	3	.57	1	.276	.341	.382
1998 Kansas City	AL	86	204	45	12	0	2	(0	2)	63	17	13	12	0	38	1	7	2	2	5	.29	3	.221	.265	.309
1999 New York	NL	7	0	0	0	0	0	(0	0)	0	0	0	0	0	0	0	0	0	0	0	—	0	—	—	—
2000 Detroit	AL	105	238	62	12	2	3	(0	3)	87	26	27	14	0	49	1	10	2	5	2	.71	5	.261	.302	.366
4 ML YEARS		272	565	141	29	3	7	(1	6)	197	59	50	36	0	115	4	21	4	11	10	.52	9	.250	.297	.349

Darryl Hamilton

Bats: L **Throws:** R **Pos:** LF-17; PH/PR-16; CF-11; RF-8   **Ht:** 6'1" **Wt:** 192 **Born:** 12/3/64 **Age:** 36

Year Team	Lg	G	AB	H	2B	3B	HR	(Hm	Rd)	TB	R	RBI	TBB	IBB	SO	HBP	SH	SF	SB	CS	SB%	GDP	Avg	OBP	SLG
								BATTING											**BASERUNNING**				**PERCENTAGES**		
2000 St. Lucie *	A+	1	3	1	0	0	0	—	—	1	0	0	1	0	0	0	0	0	0	0	—	0	.333	.500	.333
Norfolk *	AAA	10	40	9	0	0	1	—	—	12	3	4	6	0	5	0	0	1	0	2	.00	0	.225	.319	.300
1988 Milwaukee	AL	44	103	19	4	0	1	(1	0)	26	14	11	12	0	9	1	0	1	7	3	.70	2	.184	.274	.252
1990 Milwaukee	AL	89	156	46	5	0	1	(1	0)	54	27	18	9	0	12	0	3	0	10	3	.77	2	.295	.333	.346
1991 Milwaukee	AL	122	405	126	15	6	1	(0	1)	156	64	57	33	2	38	0	7	3	16	6	.73	10	.311	.361	.385
1992 Milwaukee	AL	128	470	140	19	7	5	(1	4)	188	67	62	45	0	42	1	4	1	41	14	.75	10	.298	.356	.400
1993 Milwaukee	AL	135	520	161	21	1	9	(5	4)	211	74	48	45	5	62	3	4	1	21	13	.62	9	.310	.367	.406
1994 Milwaukee	AL	36	141	37	10	1	1	(0	1)	52	23	13	15	1	17	0	2	1	3	0	1.00	3	.262	.331	.369
1995 Milwaukee	AL	112	398	108	20	6	5	(3	2)	155	54	44	47	3	35	3	8	3	11	1	.92	9	.271	.350	.389
1996 Texas	AL	148	627	184	29	4	6	(2	4)	239	94	51	54	4	66	2	7	6	15	5	.75	15	.293	.348	.381
1997 San Francisco	NL	125	460	124	23	3	5	(1	4)	168	78	43	61	1	61	0	6	2	15	10	.60	6	.270	.354	.365
1998 SF-Col	NL	148	561	173	28	3	6	(3	3)	225	95	51	82	1	73	3	12	3	13	9	.59	6	.308	.398	.401
1999 Col-NYM	NL	146	505	159	19	4	9	(5	4)	213	82	45	57	0	39	2	3	1	6	8	.43	9	.315	.386	.422
2000 New York	NL	43	105	29	4	1	1	(0	1)	38	20	6	14	0	20	0	1	0	2	0	1.00	6	.276	.358	.362
1998 San Francisco	NL	97	367	108	19	2	1	(1	0)	134	65	26	59	0	53	2	6	2	9	8	.53	6	.294	.393	.365
Colorado	NL	51	194	65	9	1	5	(2	3)	91	30	25	23	1	20	1	6	1	4	1	.80	0	.335	.406	.469
1999 Colorado	NL	91	337	102	11	3	4	(2	2)	131	63	24	38	0	21	1	2	1	4	5	.44	7	.303	.374	.389
New York	NL	55	168	57	8	1	5	(3	2)	82	19	21	19	0	18	1	1	0	2	3	.40	2	.339	.410	.488
12 ML YEARS		1276	4451	1306	197	36	50	(22	28)	1725	692	449	474	17	474	15	56	29	160	72	.69	80	.293	.361	.388

Joey Hamilton

Pitches: Right **Bats:** Right **Pos:** SP-6   **Ht:** 6'4" **Wt:** 230 **Born:** 9/9/70 **Age:** 30

Year Team	Lg	G	GS	CG	GF	IP	BFP	H	R	ER	HR	SH	SF	HB	TBB	IBB	SO	WP	Bk	W	L	Pct.	ShO	Sv-Op	Hld	ERA
				HOW MUCH HE PITCHED							**WHAT HE GAVE UP**											**THE RESULTS**				
2000 Syracuse *	AAA	6	6	1	0	39.1	167	41	18	16	1	1	4	4	12	0	17	0	0	3	2	.600	0	0- --		3.66
1994 San Diego	NL	16	16	1	0	108.2	447	98	40	36	7	4	2	6	29	3	61	6	0	9	6	.600	1	0-0	0	2.98
1995 San Diego	NL	31	30	2	1	204.1	850	189	89	70	17	12	4	11	56	5	123	2	0	6	9	.400	2	0-0	0	3.08

		HOW MUCH HE PITCHED					WHAT HE GAVE UP											THE RESULTS					
Year Team	Lg	G	GS	CG	GF	IP	BFP	H	R	ER	HR	SH	SF	HB	TBB	IBB	SO	WP	Bk	W	L	Pct.	ShO	Sv-Op	Hld	ERA
1996 San Diego	NL	34	33	3	0	211.2	908	206	100	98	19	6	5	9	83	3	184	14	1	15	9	.625	1	0-0	1	4.17
1997 San Diego	NL	31	29	1	1	192.2	831	199	100	91	22	8	8	12	69	2	124	7	0	12	7	.632	0	0-0	0	4.25
1998 San Diego	NL	34	34	0	0	217.1	958	220	113	103	15	13	6	8	106	10	147	4	0	13	13	.500	0	0-0	0	4.27
1999 Toronto	AL	22	18	0	1	98	440	118	73	71	13	0	2	3	39	0	56	4	1	7	8	.467	0	0-0	1	6.52
2000 Toronto	AL	6	6	0	0	33	135	28	13	13	3	0	1	2	12	0	15	0	0	2	1	.667	0	0-0	0	3.55
7 ML YEARS		174	166	7	3	1065.2	4569	1058	528	482	96	43	28	51	394	23	710	37	2	64	53	.547	4	0-0	2	4.07

Jeffrey Hammonds

Bats: R **Throws:** R **Pos:** RF-85; LF-33; CF-9; PH/PR-6   **Ht:** 6'0" **Wt:** 200 **Born:** 3/5/71 **Age:** 30

		BATTING														BASERUNNING				PERCENTAGES		
Year Team	Lg	G	AB	H	2B	3B	HR	(Hm | Rd)	TB	R	RBI	TBB	IBB	SO	HBP	SH	SF	SB	CS	SB%	GDP	Avg	OBP	SLG
1993 Baltimore	AL	33	105	32	8	0	3	(2 | 1)	49	10	19	2	1	16	0	1	2	4	0	1.00	3	.305	.312	.467
1994 Baltimore	AL	68	250	74	18	2	8	(6 | 2)	120	45	31	17	1	39	2	0	5	5	0	1.00	5	.296	.339	.480
1995 Baltimore	AL	57	178	43	9	1	4	(2 | 2)	66	18	23	9	0	30	1	1	2	4	2	.67	3	.242	.279	.371
1996 Baltimore	AL	71	248	56	10	1	9	(3 | 6)	95	38	27	23	1	53	4	6	1	3	3	.50	7	.226	.301	.383
1997 Baltimore	AL	118	397	105	19	3	21	(9 | 12)	193	71	55	32	1	73	3	0	2	15	1	.94	6	.264	.323	.486
1998 Bal-Cin		89	257	72	16	2	6	(1 | 5)	110	50	39	39	1	56	3	3	4	8	3	.73	2	.280	.376	.428
1999 Cincinnati	NL	123	262	73	13	0	17	(5 | 12)	137	43	41	27	0	64	1	2	1	3	6	.33	4	.279	.347	.523
2000 Colorado	NL	122	454	152	24	2	20	(14 | 6)	240	94	106	44	4	83	5	2	6	14	7	.67	11	.335	.395	.529
1998 Cincinnati	AL	63	171	46	12	1	6	(1 | 5)	78	36	28	26	1	38	3	0	3	7	2	.78	2	.269	.369	.456
Cincinnati	NL	26	86	26	4	1	0	(0 | 0)	32	14	11	13	0	18	0	3	1	1	0	.50	0	.302	.390	.372
8 ML YEARS		681	2151	607	117	11	88	(42 | 46)	1010	369	341	193	9	414	19	15	23	56	22	.72	39	.282	.343	.470

Mike Hampton

Pitches: Left **Bats:** Right **Pos:** SP-33   **Ht:** 5'10" **Wt:** 180 **Born:** 9/9/72 **Age:** 28

		HOW MUCH HE PITCHED						WHAT HE GAVE UP											THE RESULTS					
Year Team	Lg	G	GS	CG	GF	IP	BFP	H	R	ER	HR	SH	SF	HB	TBB	IBB	SO	WP	Bk	W	L	Pct.	ShO	Sv-Op	Hld	ERA
1993 Seattle	AL	13	3	0	2	17	95	28	20	18	3	1	1	0	17	3	8	1	1	1	3	.250	0	1-1	2	9.53
1994 Houston	NL	44	0	0	7	41.1	181	46	19	17	4	0	0	2	16	1	24	5	1	2	1	.667	0	0-1	10	3.70
1995 Houston	NL	24	24	0	0	150.2	641	141	73	56	13	11	5	4	49	3	115	3	1	9	8	.529	0	0-0	0	3.35
1996 Houston	NL	27	27	2	0	160.1	691	175	79	64	12	10	3	3	49	1	101	7	2	10	10	.500	1	0-0	0	3.59
1997 Houston	NL	34	34	7	0	223	941	217	105	95	16	11	7	2	77	2	139	6	1	15	10	.600	2	0-0	0	3.83
1998 Houston	NL	32	32	1	0	211.2	917	227	92	79	18	7	7	5	81	1	137	4	2	11	7	.611	1	0-0	0	3.36
1999 Houston	NL	34	34	3	0	239	979	206	86	77	12	10	9	5	101	2	177	9	0	22	4	.846	2	0-0	0	2.90
2000 New York	NL	33	33	3	0	217.2	929	194	89	76	10	11	5	8	99	5	151	10	0	15	10	.600	1	0-0	0	3.14
8 ML YEARS		241	187	16	9	1260.2	5374	1234	563	482	88	61	37	29	489	18	852	45	8	85	53	.616	7	1-2	12	3.44

Chris Haney

Pitches: Left **Bats:** Left **Pos:** RP-1   **Ht:** 6'3" **Wt:** 210 **Born:** 11/16/68 **Age:** 32

		HOW MUCH HE PITCHED						WHAT HE GAVE UP											THE RESULTS					
Year Team	Lg	G	GS	CG	GF	IP	BFP	H	R	ER	HR	SH	SF	HB	TBB	IBB	SO	WP	Bk	W	L	Pct.	ShO	Sv-Op	Hld	ERA
2000 Buffalo *	AAA	15	13	1	1	92.1	382	87	27	25	8	1	0	8	17	0	70	0	0	8	3	.727	1	0- -	1	2.44
1991 Montreal	NL	16	16	0	0	84.2	387	94	49	38	6	6	1	1	43	1	51	9	0	3	7	.300	0	0-0	0	4.04
1992 Mon-KC		16	13	2	2	80	339	75	43	41	11	0	6	4	26	2	54	5	1	4	6	.400	2	0-0	0	4.61
1993 Kansas City	AL	23	23	1	0	124	556	141	87	83	13	3	4	3	53	2	65	6	1	9	9	.500	1	0-0	0	6.02
1994 Kansas City	AL	6	6	0	0	28.1	127	36	25	23	2	3	4	1	11	1	18	2	0	2	2	.500	0	0-0	0	7.31
1995 Kansas City	AL	16	13	1	0	81.1	338	78	35	33	7	1	4	2	33	0	31	2	0	3	4	.429	0	0-0	2	3.65
1996 Kansas City	AL	35	35	4	0	228	988	267	136	119	29	5	8	6	51	0	115	8	0	10	14	.417	1	0-0	0	4.70
1997 Kansas City	AL	8	3	0	1	24.2	110	29	16	12	1	2	1	2	5	2	16	1	0	1	2	.333	0	0-0	0	4.38
1998 KC-ChC		38	12	0	2	102.1	469	128	82	80	20	2	11	5	37	0	55	4	1	6	6	.500	0	0-1	0	7.04
1999 Cleveland	AL	13	4	0	1	40.1	178	43	22	21	3	0	0	3	16	0	22	0	0	2	2	.500	0	0-0	0	4.69
2000 Cleveland	AL	1	0	0	1	1	5	1	1	1	0	0	1	0	1	0	0	0	0	0	0	—	0	0-0	0	9.00
1992 Montreal	NL	9	6	1	2	38	165	40	25	23	6	0	3	4	10	0	27	5	1	2	3	.400	1	0-0	0	5.45
Kansas City	NL	7	7	1	0	42	174	35	18	18	5	0	3	0	16	2	27	0	0	2	3	.400	1	0-0	0	3.86
1998 Kansas City	AL	33	12	0	2	97.1	450	125	78	76	18	2	11	5	36	0	51	4	1	6	6	.500	0	0-1	0	7.03
Chicago	NL	5	0	0	0	5	19	3	4	4	2	0	0	0	1	0	4	0	0	0	0	—	0	0-0	0	7.20
10 ML YEARS		172	125	8	7	794.2	3497	892	496	451	92	22	40	27	276	6	427	37	3	38	52	.422	4	0-1	3	5.11

Dave Hansen

Bats: L **Throws:** R **Pos:** PH/PR-70; 1B-16; 3B-16; DH-5; LF-3   **Ht:** 6'0" **Wt:** 195 **Born:** 11/24/68 **Age:** 32

		BATTING														BASERUNNING				PERCENTAGES		
Year Team	Lg	G	AB	H	2B	3B	HR	(Hm | Rd)	TB	R	RBI	TBB	IBB	SO	HBP	SH	SF	SB	CS	SB%	GDP	Avg	OBP	SLG
1990 Los Angeles	NL	5	7	1	0	0	0	(0 | 0)	1	0	1	0	0	3	0	0	0	0	0	—	0	.143	.143	.143
1991 Los Angeles	NL	53	56	15	4	0	1	(0 | 1)	22	3	5	2	0	12	0	0	0	1	0	1.00	2	.268	.293	.393
1992 Los Angeles	NL	132	341	73	11	4	6	(1 | 5)	102	30	22	34	3	49	1	0	2	0	2	.00	9	.214	.286	.299
1993 Los Angeles	NL	84	105	38	3	0	4	(2 | 2)	53	13	30	21	3	13	0	0	1	0	1	.00	1	.362	.465	.505
1994 Los Angeles	NL	40	44	15	3	0	0	(0 | 0)	18	3	5	5	0	6	0	0	0	0	0	—	0	.341	.408	.409
1995 Los Angeles	NL	100	181	52	10	0	1	(0 | 1)	65	19	14	28	4	28	1	0	1	0	0	—	4	.287	.384	.359
1996 Los Angeles	NL	80	104	23	1	0	0	(0 | 0)	24	7	6	11	1	22	0	0	1	0	0	—	4	.221	.293	.231
1997 Chicago	NL	90	151	47	8	2	3	(1 | 2)	68	19	21	31	1	32	1	2	1	1	2	.33	0	.311	.429	.450
1999 Los Angeles	NL	100	107	27	8	1	2	(2 | 0)	43	14	17	26	0	20	2	0	1	0	0	—	3	.252	.404	.402
2000 Los Angeles	NL	102	121	35	6	2	8	(4 | 4)	69	18	26	26	0	32	0	0	0	1	0	.00	1	.289	.415	.570
10 ML YEARS		786	1217	326	54	5	25	(10 | 15)	465	126	147	184	12	216	5	2	7	2	6	.25	24	.268	.364	.382

Pete Harnisch

Pitches: Right **Bats:** Right **Pos:** SP-22   **Ht:** 6'0" **Wt:** 228 **Born:** 9/23/66 **Age:** 34

Year Team	Lg	G	GS	CG	GF	IP	BFP	H	R	ER	HR	SH	SF	HB	TBB	IBB	SO	WP	Bk	W	L	Pct.	ShO	Sv-Op	Hld	ERA
2000 Louisville *	AAA	1	1	0	0	5.2	24	6	6	2	1	0	1	0	0	0	6	0	0	0	0	—	0	0--	0	3.18
1988 Baltimore	AL	2	2	0	0	13	61	13	8	8	1	2	0	0	9	1	10	1	0	0	2	.000	0	0-0	0	5.54
1989 Baltimore	AL	18	17	2	1	103.1	468	97	55	53	10	4	5	5	64	1	70	5	1	5	9	.357	0	0-0	0	4.62
1990 Baltimore	AL	31	31	3	0	188.2	821	189	96	91	17	6	5	1	86	5	122	2	2	11	11	.500	0	0-0	0	4.34
1991 Houston	NL	33	33	4	0	216.2	900	169	71	65	14	9	7	5	83	3	172	5	2	12	9	.571	2	0-0	0	2.70
1992 Houston	NL	34	34	0	0	206.2	859	182	92	85	18	5	5	5	64	3	164	4	1	9	10	.474	0	0-0	0	3.70
1993 Houston	NL	33	33	5	0	217.2	896	171	84	72	20	9	4	6	79	5	185	3	1	16	9	.640	4	0-0	0	2.98
1994 Houston	NL	17	17	1	0	95	419	100	59	57	13	3	2	3	39	1	62	2	0	8	5	.615	0	0-0	0	5.40
1995 New York	NL	18	18	0	0	110	462	111	55	45	13	4	3	3	24	4	82	0	1	2	8	.200	0	0-0	0	3.68
1996 New York	NL	31	31	2	0	194.2	839	195	103	91	30	13	9	7	61	5	114	7	3	8	12	.400	1	0-0	0	4.21
1997 NYM-Mil		10	8	0	0	39.2	186	48	33	31	6	0	2	1	23	1	22	2	0	1	2	.333	0	0-0	0	7.03
1998 Cincinnati	NL	32	32	2	0	209	854	176	79	73	24	8	5	6	64	4	157	4	1	14	7	.667	1	0-0	0	3.14
1999 Cincinnati	NL	33	33	2	0	198.1	833	190	86	81	25	10	6	5	57	2	120	3	0	16	10	.615	2	0-0	0	3.68
2000 Cincinnati	NL	22	22	3	0	131	562	133	76	69	23	1	4	1	46	1	71	10	0	8	6	.571	1	0-0	0	4.74
1997 New York	NL	6	5	0	0	25.2	121	35	24	23	5	0	2	1	11	1	12	1	0	0	1	.000	0	0-0	0	8.06
Milwaukee	AL	4	3	0	0	14	65	13	9	8	1	0	0	0	12	0	10	1	0	1	1	.500	0	0-0	0	5.14
13 ML YEARS		314	311	24	1	1923.2	8160	1774	897	821	214	74	60	48	699	38	1351	48	12	110	100	.524	11	0-0	0	3.84

Travis Harper

Pitches: Right **Bats:** Left **Pos:** SP-5; RP-1   **Ht:** 6'4" **Wt:** 190 **Born:** 5/21/76 **Age:** 25

Year Team	Lg	G	GS	CG	GF	IP	BFP	H	R	ER	HR	SH	SF	HB	TBB	IBB	SO	WP	Bk	W	L	Pct.	ShO	Sv-Op	Hld	ERA
1998 Hudson Val	A-	13	10	0	1	56.1	228	38	14	12	2	1	1	8	20	0	81	4	0	6	2	.750	0	0--	—	1.92
1999 St. Pete	A+	14	14	0	0	81.1	347	82	36	31	4	1	4	10	23	0	79	8	0	5	4	.556	0	0--	—	3.43
Orlando	AA	14	14	1	0	72	319	73	45	43	10	0	5	10	26	0	68	7	0	6	3	.667	1	0--	—	5.38
2000 Orlando	AA	9	9	0	0	51.1	215	49	19	15	1	2	3	7	11	0	33	2	1	3	1	.750	0	0--	—	2.63
Durham	AAA	17	17	0	0	104	435	98	53	49	15	1	0	9	26	1	48	5	0	7	4	.636	0	0--	—	4.24
2000 Tampa Bay	AL	6	5	1	0	32	141	30	17	17	5	1	1	1	15	0	14	1	0	1	2	.333	1	0-0	0	4.78

Lenny Harris

Bats: L **Throws:** R **Pos:** PH/PR-61; 3B-36; 1B-10; RF-8; LF-6; 2B-3; DH-1   **Ht:** 5'10" **Wt:** 220 **Born:** 10/28/64 **Age:** 36

Year Team	Lg	G	AB	H	2B	3B	HR	(Hm	Rd)	TB	R	RBI	TBB	IBB	SO	HBP	SH	SF	SB	CS	SB%	GDP	Avg	OBP	SLG
1988 Cincinnati	NL	16	43	16	1	0	0	(0	0)	17	7	8	5	0	4	0	1	2	4	1	.80	0	.372	.420	.395
1989 Cin-LA	NL	115	335	79	10	1	3	(1	2)	100	36	26	20	0	33	2	1	0	14	9	.61	14	.236	.283	.299
1990 Los Angeles	NL	137	431	131	16	4	2	(0	2)	161	61	29	29	2	31	1	3	1	15	10	.60	8	.304	.348	.374
1991 Los Angeles	NL	145	429	123	16	1	3	(1	2)	150	59	38	37	5	32	5	12	2	12	3	.80	16	.287	.349	.350
1992 Los Angeles	NL	135	347	94	11	0	0	(0	0)	105	28	30	24	3	24	1	6	2	19	7	.73	10	.271	.318	.303
1993 Los Angeles	NL	107	160	38	6	1	2	(0	2)	52	20	11	15	4	15	0	1	0	3	1	.75	4	.238	.303	.325
1994 Cincinnati	NL	66	100	31	3	1	0	(0	0)	36	13	14	5	0	13	0	0	1	7	2	.78	5	.310	.340	.360
1995 Cincinnati	NL	101	197	41	8	3	2	(0	2)	61	32	16	14	0	20	0	3	1	10	1	.91	6	.208	.259	.310
1996 Cincinnati	NL	125	302	86	17	2	5	(2	3)	122	33	32	21	1	31	1	6	3	14	6	.70	8	.285	.330	.404
1997 Cincinnati	NL	120	238	65	13	1	3	(2	1)	89	32	28	18	1	18	2	3	2	4	3	.57	10	.273	.327	.374
1998 Cin-NYM	NL	132	290	75	15	0	6	(2	4)	108	30	27	17	3	21	2	4	4	6	5	.55	13	.259	.300	.372
1999 Col-Ari	NL	110	187	58	13	0	1	(1	0)	74	17	20	6	0	7	0	0	1	2	1	.67	7	.310	.330	.396
2000 Ari-NYM	NL	112	223	58	7	4	4	(2	2)	85	31	26	20	2	22	0	0	2	13	1	.93	7	.260	.317	.381
1989 Cincinnati	NL	61	188	42	4	0	2	(0	2)	52	17	11	9	0	20	1	1	0	10	6	.63	5	.223	.263	.277
Los Angeles	NL	54	147	37	6	1	1	(1	0)	48	19	15	11	0	13	1	0	0	4	3	.57	9	.252	.308	.327
1998 Cincinnati	NL	57	122	36	8	0	0	(0	0)	44	12	10	8	2	9	1	0	2	1	3	.25	8	.295	.338	.361
New York	NL	75	168	39	7	0	6	(2	4)	64	18	17	9	1	12	1	4	2	5	2	.71	5	.232	.272	.381
1999 Colorado	NL	91	158	47	12	0	0	(0	0)	59	15	13	6	0	6	0	0	0	1	1	.50	7	.297	.323	.373
Arizona	NL	19	29	11	1	0	1	(1	0)	15	2	7	0	0	1	0	0	1	1	0	1.00	0	.379	.367	.517
2000 Arizona	NL	36	85	16	1	1	1	(1	0)	22	9	13	3	1	5	0	0	3	5	0	1.00	3	.188	.209	.259
New York	NL	76	138	42	6	3	3	(1	2)	63	22	13	17	1	17	0	0	2	8	1	.89	4	.304	.381	.457
13 ML YEARS		1421	3282	895	136	18	31	(11	20)	1160	399	305	231	21	271	14	42	22	123	50	.71	98	.273	.321	.353

Shigetoshi Hasegawa

Pitches: Right **Bats:** Right **Pos:** RP-66   **Ht:** 5'11" **Wt:** 178 **Born:** 8/1/68 **Age:** 32

Year Team	Lg	G	GS	CG	GF	IP	BFP	H	R	ER	HR	SH	SF	HB	TBB	IBB	SO	WP	Bk	W	L	Pct.	ShO	Sv-Op	Hld	ERA
1997 Anaheim	AL	50	7	0	17	116.2	497	118	60	51	14	5	5	3	46	6	83	2	1	3	7	.300	0	0-1	3	3.93
1998 Anaheim	AL	61	0	0	20	97.1	401	86	37	34	14	4	6	2	32	2	73	5	2	8	3	.727	0	5-7	10	3.14
1999 Anaheim	AL	64	1	0	26	77	333	80	45	42	14	3	4	2	34	2	44	4	0	4	6	.400	0	2-5	6	4.91
2000 Anaheim	AL	66	0	0	26	95.2	415	100	43	38	11	2	3	2	38	6	59	2	1	10	6	.625	0	9-18	19	3.57
4 ML YEARS		241	8	0	89	386.2	1646	384	185	165	53	14	18	9	150	16	259	13	4	25	22	.532	0	16-31	38	3.84

Bill Haselman

Bats: Right **Throws:** Right **Pos:** C-62   **Ht:** 6'3" **Wt:** 223 **Born:** 5/25/66 **Age:** 35

Year Team	Lg	G	AB	H	2B	3B	HR	(Hm	Rd)	TB	R	RBI	TBB	IBB	SO	HBP	SH	SF	SB	CS	SB%	GDP	Avg	OBP	SLG
1990 Texas	AL	7	13	2	0	0	0	(0	0)	2	0	3	1	0	5	0	0	0	0	0	—	0	.154	.214	.154
1992 Seattle	AL	8	19	5	0	0	0	(0	0)	5	1	0	0	0	7	0	0	0	0	0	—	1	.263	.263	.263
1993 Seattle	AL	58	137	35	8	0	5	(3	2)	58	21	16	12	0	19	1	2	2	2	1	.67	5	.255	.316	.423
1994 Seattle	AL	38	83	16	7	1	1	(1	0)	28	11	8	3	0	11	1	1	0	1	0	1.00	4	.193	.230	.337
1995 Boston	AL	64	152	37	6	1	5	(3	2)	60	22	23	17	0	30	2	0	3	0	2	.00	4	.243	.322	.395
1996 Boston	AL	77	237	65	13	1	8	(5	3)	104	33	34	19	3	52	1	0	0	4	2	.67	13	.274	.331	.439
1997 Boston	AL	67	212	50	15	0	6	(3	3)	83	22	26	15	2	44	2	1	0	0	2	.00	8	.236	.290	.392

Year Team	Lg	G	AB	H	2B	3B	HR	(Hm	Rd)	TB	R	RBI	TBB	IBB	SO	HBP	SH	SF	SB	CS	SB%	GDP	Avg	OBP	SLG
1998 Texas	AL	40	105	33	6	0	6	(4	2)	57	11	17	3	0	17	0	0	0	0	0	.	2	.314	.327	.543
1999 Detroit	AL	48	143	39	8	0	4	(2	2)	59	13	14	10	1	26	0	0	0	2	0	1.00	4	.273	.320	.413
2000 Texas	AL	62	193	53	18	0	6	(3	3)	89	23	26	15	0	36	1	0	1	0	1	.00	1	.275	.329	.461
10 ML YEARS		469	1294	335	81	3	41	(24	17)	545	157	167	95	6	247	8	4	10	9	5	.53	40	.259	.311	.421

Scott Hatteberg

Bats: L **Throws:** R **Pos:** C-48; PH/PR-28; DH-20; 3B-1   **Ht:** 6'1" **Wt:** 205 **Born:** 12/14/69 **Age:** 31

Year Team	Lg	G	AB	H	2B	3B	HR	(Hm	Rd)	TB	R	RBI	TBB	IBB	SO	HBP	SH	SF	SB	CS	SB%	GDP	Avg	OBP	SLG
1995 Boston	AL	2	2	1	0	0	0	(0	0)	1	1	0	0	0	0	0	0	0	0	0	—		.500	.500	.500
1996 Boston	AL	10	11	2	1	0	0	(0	0)	3	3	0	3	0	2	0	0	0	0	0	—	2	.182	.357	.273
1997 Boston	AL	114	350	97	23	1	10	(5	5)	152	46	44	40	2	70	2	2	1	0	1	.00	11	.277	.354	.434
1998 Boston	AL	112	359	99	23	1	12	(4	8)	160	46	43	43	3	58	5	0	3	0	0	—	11	.276	.359	.446
1999 Boston	AL	30	80	22	5	0	1	(1	0)	30	12	11	18	0	14	1	0	1	0	0	—	2	.275	.410	.375
2000 Texas	AL	92	230	61	15	0	8	(2	6)	100	21	36	38	3	39	0	1	2	0	1	.00	8	.265	.367	.435
6 ML YEARS		360	1032	282	67	2	31	(12	19)	446	129	134	142	8	183	8	3	7	0	2	.00	35	.273	.363	.432

LaTroy Hawkins

Pitches: Right **Bats:** Right **Pos:** RP-66   **Ht:** 6'5" **Wt:** 204 **Born:** 12/21/72 **Age:** 28

Year Team	Lg	G	GS	CG	GF	IP	BFP	H	R	ER	HR	SH	SF	HB	TBB	IBB	SO	WP	Bk	W	L	Pct.	ShO	Sv-Op	Hld	ERA
1995 Minnesota	AL	6	6	1	0	27	131	39	26	26	3	0	3	1	12	0	9	1	1	2	3	.400	0	0-0	0	8.67
1996 Minnesota	AL	7	6	1	0	26.1	124	42	24	24	8	1	1	0	9	0	24	1	1	1	1	.500	0	0-0	0	8.20
1997 Minnesota	AL	20	20	0	0	103.1	478	134	71	67	19	2	2	4	47	0	58	6	3	6	12	.333	0	0-0	0	5.84
1998 Minnesota	AL	33	33	0	0	190.1	840	227	126	111	27	4	10	5	61	1	105	10	2	7	14	.333	0	0-0	0	5.25
1999 Minnesota	AL	33	33	1	0	174.1	803	238	136	129	29	1	5	1	60	2	103	9	0	10	14	.417	0	0-0	0	6.66
2000 Minnesota	AL	66	0	0	38	87.2	370	85	34	33	7	4	1	1	32	1	59	6	0	2	5	.286	0	14-14	7	3.39
6 ML YEARS		165	98	2	39	609	2746	765	420	390	93	12	22	12	221	4	358	33	7	28	49	.364	0	14-14	7	5.76

Charlie Hayes

Bats: R **Throws:** R **Pos:** 3B-59; 1B-57; PH/PR-21; DH-1   **Ht:** 6'0" **Wt:** 215 **Born:** 5/29/65 **Age:** 36

Year Team	Lg	G	AB	H	2B	3B	HR	(Hm	Rd)	TB	R	RBI	TBB	IBB	SO	HBP	SH	SF	SB	CS	SB%	GDP	Avg	OBP	SLG
1988 San Francisco	NL	7	11	1	0	0	0	(0	0)	1	0	0	0	0	3	0	0	0	0	0	—	0	.091	.091	.091
1989 SF-Phi	NL	87	304	78	15	1	8	(3	5)	119	26	43	11	1	50	0	1	6	3	1	.75	6	.257	.280	.391
1990 Philadelphia	NL	152	561	145	20	0	10	(3	7)	195	56	57	28	3	91	2	0	6	4	4	.50	12	.258	.293	.348
1991 Philadelphia	NL	142	460	106	23	1	12	(6	6)	167	34	53	16	3	75	1	2	1	3	3	.50	13	.230	.257	.363
1992 New York	AL	142	509	131	19	2	18	(7	11)	208	52	66	28	0	100	3	3	6	3	5	.38	12	.257	.297	.409
1993 Colorado	NL	157	573	175	45	2	25	(17	8)	299	89	98	43	6	82	5	1	8	11	6	.65	25	.305	.355	.522
1994 Colorado	NL	113	423	122	24	4	10	(4	6)	183	46	50	36	4	71	3	0	11	3	6	.33	11	.288	.348	.433
1995 Philadelphia	NL	141	529	146	30	3	11	(6	5)	215	58	85	50	2	88	4	0	6	5	1	.83	22	.276	.340	.406
1996 Pit-NYY	NL	148	526	133	24	2	12	(5	7)	199	58	75	37	4	90	0	3	4	6	0	1.00	13	.253	.300	.375
1997 New York	AL	100	353	91	16	0	11	(5	6)	140	39	53	40	2	66	1	0	4	3	2	.60	13	.258	.332	.397
1998 San Francisco	NL	111	329	94	8	0	12	(5	7)	138	39	62	34	0	61	0	1	2	3	1	.67	4	.286	.351	.419
1999 San Francisco	NL	95	264	54	9	1	6	(2	4)	83	33	33	33	0	41	1	0	3	3	1	.75	8	.205	.292	.314
2000 Milwaukee	NL	121	370	93	17	0	9	(2	7)	137	46	46	57	4	84	1	0	6	1	1	.50	11	.251	.348	.370
1989 San Francisco	NL	3	5	1	0	0	0	(0	0)	1	0	0	0	0	1	0	0	0	0	0	—	0	.200	.200	.200
Philadelphia	NL	84	299	77	15	1	8	(3	5)	118	26	43	11	1	49	0	2	3	3	1	.75	6	.258	.281	.395
1996 Pittsburgh	NL	128	459	114	21	2	10	(5	5)	169	51	62	36	4	78	0	3	3	6	0	1.00	16	.248	.301	.368
New York	AL	20	67	19	3	0	2	(0	2)	28	7	13	1	0	12	0	0	1	0	0	—	1	.284	.294	.418
13 ML YEARS		1516	5212	1369	249	16	144	(67	77)	2082	576	736	413	29	902	21	12	49	47	31	.60	154	.263	.317	.399

Jimmy Haynes

Pitches: Right **Bats:** Right **Pos:** SP-33   **Ht:** 6'4" **Wt:** 203 **Born:** 9/5/72 **Age:** 28

Year Team	Lg	G	GS	CG	GF	IP	BFP	H	R	ER	HR	SH	SF	HB	TBB	IBB	SO	WP	Bk	W	L	Pct.	ShO	Sv-Op	Hld	ERA
1995 Baltimore	AL	4	3	0	0	24	94	11	6	6	2	1	0	0	12	1	22	0	0	2	1	.667	0	0-0	0	2.25
1996 Baltimore	AL	26	11	0	8	89	435	122	84	82	14	4	5	2	58	1	65	5	0	3	6	.333	0	1-1	0	8.29
1997 Oakland	AL	13	13	0	0	73.1	329	74	38	36	7	1	4	2	40	1	65	4	1	3	6	.333	0	0-0	0	4.42
1998 Oakland	AL	33	33	1	0	194.1	875	229	124	110	25	5	9	5	88	4	134	11	0	11	9	.550	1	0-0	0	5.09
1999 Oakland	AL	30	25	0	2	142	652	158	112	100	21	4	5	2	80	3	93	7	2	7	12	.368	0	0-0	0	6.34
2000 Milwaukee	NL	33	33	0	0	199.1	897	228	128	118	21	10	6	7	100	7	88	7	0	12	13	.480	0	0-0	0	5.33
6 ML YEARS		139	118	1	10	722	3282	822	492	452	90	25	29	18	378	17	467	34	3	38	47	.447	1	1-1	0	5.63

Rick Helling

Pitches: Right **Bats:** Right **Pos:** SP-35   **Ht:** 6'3" **Wt:** 220 **Born:** 12/15/70 **Age:** 30

Year Team	Lg	G	GS	CG	GF	IP	BFP	H	R	ER	HR	SH	SF	HB	TBB	IBB	SO	WP	Bk	W	L	Pct.	ShO	Sv-Op	Hld	ERA
1994 Texas	AL	9	9	1	0	52	228	62	34	34	14	0	0	4	18	0	25	4	1	3	2	.600	1	0-0	0	5.88
1995 Texas	AL	3	3	0	0	12.1	62	17	11	9	2	0	2		5	0	5	0	0	0	2	.000	0	0-0	0	6.57
1996 Tex-Fla		11	6	0	2	48	198	37	23	23	9	1	0	6	16	0	42	1	0	3	3	.500	0	0-0	0	4.31
1997 Fla-Tex		41	16	0	9	131	550	108	67	65	17	3	9	6	69	2	99	3	0	5	9	.357	0	0-1	6	4.47
1998 Texas	AL	33	33	4	0	216.1	922	209	109	106	27	6	10	7	78	6	164	10	0	20	7	.741	2	0-0	0	4.41
1999 Texas	AL	35	35	3	0	219.1	943	228	127	118	41	5	10	6	85	5	131	8	0	13	11	.542	0	0-0	0	4.84
2000 Texas	AL	35	35	0	0	217	963	212	122	108	29	4	9	9	92	2	146	9	0	16	13	.552	0	0-0	0	4.48
1996 Texas	AL	6	2	0	2	20.1	92	23	17	17	7	0	1	0	9	0	16	1	0	1	2	.333	0	0-0	0	7.52
Florida	NL	5	4	0	0	27.2	106	14	6	6	2	1	0	6	7	0	26	0	0	2	1	.667	0	0-0	0	1.95
1997 Florida	NL	31	8	0	8	76	324	61	38	37	12	2	7	4	48	2	53	0	0	2	5	.250	0	0-1	6	4.38
Texas	AL	10	8	0	1	55	226	47	29	28	5	1	2	2	21	0	46	3	0	3	5	.500	0	0-0	0	4.58
7 ML YEARS		167	137	8	11	896	3866	873	493	463	139	19	41	24	373	15	612	28	3	60	47	.561	3	0-1	7	4.65

Wes Helms

Bats: Right **Throws:** Right **Pos:** 3B-5; PH/PR-4 **Ht:** 6'4" **Wt:** 230 **Born:** 5/12/76 **Age:** 25

Year Team	Lg	G	AB	H	2B	3B	HR	(Hm	Rd)	TB	R	RBI	TBB	IBB	SO	HBP	SH	SF	SB	CS	SB%	GDP	Avg	OBP	SLG
1994 Braves	R	56	184	49	15	1	4	—	—	78	22	29	22	0	36	4	0	1	6	1	.86	3	.266	.355	.424
1995 Macon	A	136	539	149	32	1	11	—	—	216	89	85	50	0	107	10	0	3	2	2	.50	8	.276	.347	.401
1996 Durham	A+	67	258	83	19	2	13	—	—	145	40	54	12	0	51	7	0	1	1	1	.50	7	.322	.367	.562
Greenville	AA	64	231	59	13	2	4	—	—	88	24	22	13	2	48	4	1	0	1	0	.67	6	.255	.306	.381
1997 Richmond	AAA	32	110	21	4	0	3	—	—	34	11	15	10	1	34	5	0	1	1	1	.50	4	.191	.286	.309
Greenville	AA	86	314	93	14	1	11	—	—	142	50	44	33	2	50	6	0	3	3	4	.43	14	.296	.371	.452
1998 Richmond	AAA	125	451	124	27	1	13	—	—	192	56	75	35	2	103	13	0	4	6	2	.75	11	.275	.342	.426
1999 Braves	R	9	33	15	2	0	0	—	—	17	1	10	5	0	4	1	0	0	1	0	1.00	1	.455	.538	.515
Greenville	AA	30	113	34	6	0	8	—	—	64	15	26	7	1	34	1	0	0	1	0	1.00	3	.301	.347	.566
2000 Richmond	AAA	136	539	155	27	7	20	—	—	256	74	70	27	2	92	6	2	6	0	6	.00	10	.288	.325	.475
1998 Atlanta	NL	7	13	4	1	0	1	(0	1)	8	2	2	0	0	4	0	0	0	0	0	—	0	.308	.308	.615
2000 Atlanta	NL	6	5	1	0	0	0	(0	0)	1	0	0	0	0	2	0	0	0	0	0	—	0	.200	.200	.200
2 ML YEARS		13	18	5	1	0	1	(0	1)	9	2	2	0	0	6	0	0	0	0	0	—	0	.278	.278	.500

Todd Helton

Bats: Left **Throws:** Left **Pos:** 1B-160; PH/PR-2 **Ht:** 6'2" **Wt:** 206 **Born:** 8/20/73 **Age:** 27

Year Team	Lg	G	AB	H	2B	3B	HR	(Hm	Rd)	TB	R	RBI	TBB	IBB	SO	HBP	SH	SF	SB	CS	SB%	GDP	Avg	OBP	SLG
1997 Colorado	NL	35	93	26	2	1	5	(3	2)	45	13	11	8	0	11	0	0	0	0	1	.00	1	.280	.337	.484
1998 Colorado	NL	152	530	167	37	1	25	(13	12)	281	78	97	53	5	54	6	1	5	3	3	.50	15	.315	.380	.530
1999 Colorado	NL	159	578	185	39	5	35	(23	12)	339	114	113	68	6	77	6	0	4	6	5	.54	14	.320	.395	.587
2000 Colorado	NL	160	580	216	59	2	42	(27	15)	405	138	147	103	22	61	4	0	10	5	3	.63	12	.372	.463	.698
4 ML YEARS		506	1781	594	137	9	107	(66	41)	1070	343	368	232	33	203	16	1	19	15	13	.54	42	.334	.411	.601

Rickey Henderson

Bats: Right **Throws:** Left **Pos:** LF-117; PH/PR-6; DH-2 **Ht:** 5'10" **Wt:** 190 **Born:** 12/25/58 **Age:** 42

Year Team	Lg	G	AB	H	2B	3B	HR	(Hm	Rd)	TB	R	RBI	TBB	IBB	SO	HBP	SH	SF	SB	CS	SB%	GDP	Avg	OBP	SLG
1979 Oakland	AL	89	351	96	13	3	1	(1	0)	118	49	26	34	0	39	2	8	3	33	11	.75	4	.274	.338	.336
1980 Oakland	AL	158	591	179	22	4	9	(3	6)	236	111	53	117	7	54	5	6	3	100	26	.79	6	.303	.420	.399
1981 Oakland	AL	108	423	135	18	7	6	(5	1)	185	89	35	64	4	68	2	0	4	56	22	.72	7	.319	.408	.437
1982 Oakland	AL	149	536	143	24	4	10	(5	5)	205	119	51	116	1	94	2	0	2	130	42	.76	5	.267	.398	.382
1983 Oakland	AL	145	513	150	25	7	9	(4	5)	216	105	48	103	8	80	4	1	1	108	19	.85	11	.292	.414	.421
1984 Oakland	AL	142	502	147	27	4	16	(7	9)	230	113	58	86	1	81	5	1	3	66	18	.79	7	.293	.399	.458
1985 New York	AL	143	547	172	28	5	24	(8	16)	282	146	72	99	1	65	3	0	5	80	10	.89	8	.314	.419	.516
1986 New York	AL	153	608	160	31	5	28	(13	15)	285	130	74	89	2	81	2	0	2	87	18	.83	12	.263	.358	.469
1987 New York	AL	95	358	104	17	3	17	(10	7)	178	78	37	80	1	52	2	0	0	41	8	.84	10	.291	.423	.497
1988 New York	AL	140	554	169	30	2	6	(4	2)	221	118	50	82	1	54	3	2	6	93	13	.88	5	.305	.394	.399
1989 NYY-Oak	AL	150	541	148	26	3	12	(7	5)	216	113	57	126	5	68	3	0	4	77	14	.85	8	.274	.411	.399
1990 Oakland	AL	136	489	159	33	3	28	(8	20)	282	119	61	97	2	60	4	2	2	65	10	.87	13	.325	.439	.577
1991 Oakland	AL	134	470	126	17	1	18	(8	10)	199	105	57	98	7	73	7	0	3	58	18	.76	7	.268	.400	.423
1992 Oakland	AL	117	396	112	18	3	15	(10	5)	181	77	46	95	5	56	6	0	3	48	11	.81	5	.283	.426	.457
1993 Oak-Tor	AL	134	481	139	22	2	21	(10	11)	228	114	59	120	7	65	4	1	4	53	8	.87	9	.289	.432	.474
1994 Oakland	AL	87	296	77	13	0	6	(4	2)	108	66	20	72	1	45	5	1	2	22	7	.76	0	.260	.411	.365
1995 Oakland	AL	112	407	122	31	1	9	(8	1)	182	67	54	72	2	66	4	1	3	32	10	.76	8	.300	.407	.447
1996 San Diego	NL	148	465	112	17	2	9	(6	3)	160	110	29	125	2	90	10	0	4	37	15	.71	5	.241	.410	.344
1997 SD-Ana		120	403	100	14	0	8	(6	2)	138	84	34	97	2	85	6	1	2	45	8	.85	10	.248	.400	.342
1998 Oakland	AL	152	542	128	16	1	14	(6	8)	188	101	57	118	0	114	5	2	3	66	13	.84	8	.236	.376	.347
1999 New York	NL	121	438	138	30	0	12	(1	11)	204	89	42	82	1	82	2	1	3	37	14	.73	4	.315	.423	.466
2000 NYM-Sea		123	420	98	14	2	4	(2	2)	128	75	32	88	1	75	4	3	4	36	11	.77	11	.233	.368	.305
1989 New York	AL	65	235	58	13	1	3	(1	2)	82	41	22	56	0	29	1	0	1	25	8	.76	0	.247	.392	.349
Oakland	AL	85	306	90	13	2	9	(6	3)	134	72	35	70	5	39	2	0	3	52	6	.90	8	.294	.425	.438
1993 Oakland	AL	90	318	104	19	1	17	(8	9)	176	77	47	85	6	46	2	0	2	31	6	.84	8	.327	.469	.553
Toronto	AL	44	163	35	3	1	4	(2	2)	52	37	12	35	1	19	2	1	2	22	2	.92	1	.215	.356	.319
1997 San Diego	NL	88	288	79	11	0	6	(5	1)	108	63	27	71	2	62	4	0	2	29	4	.88	7	.274	.422	.375
Anaheim	AL	32	115	21	3	0	2	(1	1)	30	21	7	26	0	23	2	1	0	16	4	.80	3	.183	.343	.261
2000 New York	NL	31	96	21	1	0	0	(0	0)	22	17	2	25	1	20	2	0	1	5	2	.71	2	.219	.387	.229
Seattle	AL	92	324	77	13	2	4	(2	2)	106	58	30	63	0	55	2	3	3	31	9	.78	9	.238	.362	.327
22 ML YEARS		2856	10331	2914	486	62	282	(130	152)	4370	2178	1052	2060	61	1547	90	30	64	1370	326	.81	161	.282	.404	.423

Doug Henry

Pitches: Right **Bats:** Right **Pos:** RP-72 **Ht:** 6'4" **Wt:** 205 **Born:** 12/10/63 **Age:** 37

Year Team	Lg	G	GS	CG	GF	IP	BFP	H	R	ER	HR	SH	SF	HB	TBB	IBB	SO	WP	Bk	W	L	Pct.	ShO	Sv-Op	Hld	ERA
1991 Milwaukee	AL	32	0	0	25	36	137	16	4	4	1	1	2	0	14	1	28	0	0	2	1	.667	0	15-16	3	1.00
1992 Milwaukee	AL	68	0	0	56	65	277	64	34	29	6	1	2	0	24	4	52	4	0	1	4	.200	0	29-33	1	4.02
1993 Milwaukee	AL	54	0	0	41	55	260	67	37	34	7	5	4	3	25	8	38	4	0	4	4	.500	0	17-24	0	5.56
1994 Milwaukee	AL	25	0	0	7	31.1	143	32	17	16	7	1	0	1	23	1	20	3	0	2	3	.400	0	0-0	4	4.60
1995 New York	NL	51	0	0	20	67	273	48	23	22	7	3	2	1	25	6	62	6	1	3	6	.333	0	4-7	6	2.96
1996 New York	NL	58	0	0	33	75	343	82	48	39	7	3	3	1	36	6	58	6	1	2	8	.200	0	9-14	8	4.68
1997 San Francisco	NL	75	0	0	25	70.2	317	70	45	37	5	4	3	1	41	6	69	3	0	4	5	.444	0	3-6	21	4.71
1998 Houston	NL	59	0	0	25	71	296	55	25	24	9	0	3	0	35	5	59	7	0	8	2	.800	0	2-5	11	3.04
1999 Houston	NL	35	0	0	17	40.2	188	45	24	21	8	1	0	3	24	0	36	0	0	2	3	.400	0	2-4	2	4.65
2000 Hou-SF	NL	72	0	0	21	78.1	335	57	36	33	12	5	2	4	49	3	62	3	1	4	4	.500	0	1-4	12	3.79
2000 Houston	NL	45	0	0	13	53	225	39	26	26	10	2	1	3	28	2	46	2	0	1	3	.250	0	1-2	6	4.42
San Francisco	NL	27	0	0	8	25.1	110	18	10	7	2	3	1	1	21	1	16	1	1	3	1	.750	0	0-2	6	2.49
10 ML YEARS		529	0	0	270	590	2569	536	293	259	69	27	21	14	296	40	484	36	2	32	40	.444	0	82-113	68	3.95

Pat Hentgen

Pitches: Right **Bats:** Right **Pos:** SP-33 **Ht:** 6'2" **Wt:** 195 **Born:** 11/13/68 **Age:** 32

Year Team	Lg	G	GS	CG	GF	IP	BFP	H	R	ER	HR	SH	SF	HB	TBB	IBB	SO	WP	Bk	W	L	Pct.	ShO	Sv-Op	Hld	ERA
1991 Toronto	AL	3	1	0	1	7.1	30	5	2	2	1	1	0	2	3	0	3	1	0	0	0	—	0	0-0	0	2.45
1992 Toronto	AL	28	2	0	10	50.1	229	49	30	30	7	2	2	0	32	5	39	2	1	5	2	.714	0	0-1	1	5.36
1993 Toronto	AL	34	32	3	0	216.1	926	215	103	93	27	6	5	7	74	0	122	11	1	19	9	.679	0	0-0	0	3.87
1994 Toronto	AL	24	24	6	0	174.2	728	158	74	66	21	6	3	3	59	1	147	5	1	13	8	.619	3	0-0	0	3.40
1995 Toronto	AL	30	30	2	0	200.2	913	236	129	114	24	2	1	5	90	6	135	7	2	10	14	.417	0	0-0	0	5.11
1996 Toronto	AL	35	35	10	0	265.2	1100	238	105	.95	20	5	8	5	94	3	177	8	0	20	10	.667	3	0-0	0	3.22
1997 Toronto	AL	35	35	9	0	264	1085	253	116	108	31	9	3	7	71	2	160	6	2	15	10	.600	3	0-0	0	3.68
1998 Toronto	AL	29	29	0	0	177.2	795	208	109	102	28	5	7	5	69	1	94	7	1	12	11	.522	0	0-0	0	5.17
1999 Toronto	AL	34	34	1	0	199	869	225	115	106	32	3	11	3	65	1	118	8	1	11	12	.478	0	0-0	0	4.79
2000 St. Louis	NL	33	33	1	0	194.1	846	202	107	102	24	13	8	3	89	4	118	4	0	15	12	.556	1	0-0	0	4.72
10 ML YEARS		285	255	32	11	1750	7521	1789	890	818	215	52	48	40	646	23	1113	59	9	120	88	.577	10	0-1	1	4.21

Felix Heredia

Pitches: Left **Bats:** Left **Pos:** RP-74 **Ht:** 6'0" **Wt:** 180 **Born:** 6/18/76 **Age:** 25

Year Team	Lg	G	GS	CG	GF	IP	BFP	H	R	ER	HR	SH	SF	HB	TBB	IBB	SO	WP	Bk	W	L	Pct.	ShO	Sv-Op	Hld	ERA
1996 Florida	NL	21	0	0	5	16.2	78	21	8	8	1	0	1	0	10	1	10	2	0	1	1	.500	0	0-0	2	4.32
1997 Florida	NL	56	0	0	10	56.2	259	53	30	27	3	2	2	5	30	1	54	2	0	5	3	.625	0	0-1	7	4.29
1998 Fla-ChC	NL	71	2	0	18	58.2	268	57	39	33	2	1	4	1	38	3	54	6	1	3	3	.500	0	2-5	17	5.06
1999 Chicago	NL	69	0	0	15	52	237	56	35	28	7	1	4	1	25	2	50	2	0	3	1	.750	0	1-7	12	4.85
2000 Chicago	NL	74	0	0	24	58.2	250	46	31	31	6	4	0	2	33	4	52	5	0	7	3	.700	0	2-5	12	4.76
1998 Florida	NL	41	2	0	12	41	194	38	30	25	1	1	2	1	32	2	38	5	1	0	3	.000	0	2-3	9	5.49
Chicago	NL	30	0	0	6	17.2	74	19	9	8	1	0	0	6	6	1	16	1	0	3	0	1.000	0	0-2	8	4.08
5 ML YEARS		291	2	0	72	242.2	1092	233	143	127	19	8	11	9	136	11	220	17	1	19	11	.633	0	5-18	50	4.71

Gil Heredia

Pitches: Right **Bats:** Right **Pos:** SP-32 **Ht:** 6'1" **Wt:** 221 **Born:** 10/26/65 **Age:** 35

Year Team	Lg	G	GS	CG	GF	IP	BFP	H	R	ER	HR	SH	SF	HB	TBB	IBB	SO	WP	Bk	W	L	Pct.	ShO	Sv-Op	Hld	ERA
1991 San Francisco	NL	7	4	0	1	33	126	27	14	14	4	2	1	0	7	2	13	1	0	2	2	.000	0	0-0	0	3.82
1992 SF-Mon	NL	20	5	0	4	44.2	187	44	23	21	4	2	1	1	20	1	22	1	0	2	3	.400	0	0-0	1	4.23
1993 Montreal	NL	20	9	1	2	57.1	246	66	28	25	4	4	1	2	14	2	40	0	0	4	2	.667	0	2-3	1	3.92
1994 Montreal	NL	39	3	0	8	75.1	325	85	34	29	7	3	4	3	13	3	62	4	1	6	3	.667	0	0-0	5	3.46
1995 Montreal	NL	40	18	0	5	119	509	137	60	57	7	9	4	5	21	1	74	1	0	5	6	.455	0	1-3	1	4.31
1996 Texas	AL	44	0	0	21	73.1	320	91	50	48	12	1	2	1	14	2	43	2	0	2	5	.286	0	1-4	7	5.89
1998 Oakland	AL	8	6	0	2	42.2	175	43	14	13	4	1	0	3	3	0	27	0	0	3	3	.500	0	0-0	0	2.74
1999 Oakland	AL	33	33	1	0	200.1	852	228	119	107	22	3	0	8	34	4	117	2	1	13	8	.619	0	0-0	0	4.81
2000 Oakland	AL	32	32	2	0	198.2	860	214	106	91	24	4	6	4	66	5	101	3	0	15	11	.577	0	0-0	0	4.12
1992 San Francisco	NL	13	4	0	3	30	132	32	20	18	3	0	0	1	16	1	15	1	0	2	3	.400	0	0-0	1	5.40
Montreal	NL	7	1	0	1	14.2	55	12	3	3	1	2	1	0	4	0	7	0	0	0	0	—	0	0-0	0	1.84
9 ML YEARS		243	110	4	43	844.1	3600	935	448	405	88	29	19	26	192	20	499	14	2	50	43	.538	0	4-10	15	4.32

Matt Herges

Pitches: Right **Bats:** Left **Pos:** RP-55; SP-4 **Ht:** 6'0" **Wt:** 200 **Born:** 4/1/70 **Age:** 31

Year Team	Lg	G	GS	CG	GF	IP	BFP	H	R	ER	HR	SH	SF	HB	TBB	IBB	SO	WP	Bk	W	L	Pct.	ShO	Sv-Op	Hld	ERA
1992 Yakima	A-	27	0	0	23	44.2	194	33	21	16	2	1	0	3	24	1	57	2	3	2	3	.400	0	9- —	—	3.22
1993 Bakersfield	A+	51	0	0	17	90.1	403	70	49	37	6	6	4	10	56	6	84	4	3	6	2	.250	0	2- —	—	3.69
1994 Vero Beach	A+	48	3	1	12	111	476	115	45	41	8	8	2	4	33	3	61	3	3	8	9	.471	0	3- —	—	3.32
1995 San Antonio	AA	19	0	0	13	27.2	130	34	16	15	2	3	0	0	16	1	18	3	0	0	3	.000	0	8- —	—	4.88
San Berndno	A+	22	2	0	4	51.2	231	58	29	21	3	4	2	2	15	0	35	0	0	5	2	.714	0	1- —	—	3.66
1996 San Antonio	AA	30	6	0	10	83	355	83	38	25	3	2	5	2	28	0	45	5	1	3	2	.600	0	3- —	—	2.71
Albuquerque	AAA	10	4	2	1	34.2	140	33	11	10	2	0	4	0	14	0	15	1	0	4	1	.800	1	0- —	—	2.60
1997 Albuquerque	AAA	31	12	0	5	85	417	120	92	84	13	5	4	9	46	1	61	5	0	0	8	.000	0	0- —	—	8.89
San Antonio	AA	4	3	0	0	15.1	74	22	15	15	2	0	0	2	10	0	12	3	0	0	1	.000	0	0- —	—	8.80
1998 San Antonio	AA	3	0	0	0	6	21	3	0	0	0	0	0	0	2	0	3	0	0	0	0	—	0	0- —	—	0.00
Albuquerque	AAA	34	8	0	9	88.1	406	115	64	56	9	6	4	5	37	1	75	4	0	3	5	.375	0	0- —	—	5.71
1999 Albuquerque	AAA	21	21	2	0	131.1	563	135	82	69	17	5	7	7	47	0	88	4	0	8	3	.727	0	0- —	—	4.73
1999 Los Angeles	NL	17	0	0	9	24.1	104	24	13	11	5	1	0	2	8	0	18	0	0	0	2	.000	0	0-2	1	4.07
2000 Los Angeles	NL	59	4	0	17	110.2	461	100	43	39	7	4	4	6	40	5	75	4	0	11	3	.786	0	1-3	4	3.17
2 ML YEARS		76	4	0	26	135	565	124	56	50	12	5	4	8	48	5	93	4	0	11	5	.688	0	1-5	5	3.33

Chad Hermansen

Bats: Right **Throws:** Right **Pos:** CF-27; RF-4; PH/PR-2 **Ht:** 6'2" **Wt:** 185 **Born:** 9/10/77 **Age:** 23

Year Team	Lg	G	AB	H	2B	3B	HR	(Hm	Rd)	TB	R	RBI	TBB	IBB	SO	HBP	SH	SF	SB	CS	SB%	GDP	Avg	OBP	SLG
1995 Pirates	R	24	92	28	10	1	3	—	—	49	14	17	9	1	19	0	0	1	0	0	—	2	.304	.363	.533
Erie	A-	44	165	45	8	3	6	—	—	77	30	25	18	0	39	4	0	2	4	2	.67	6	.273	.354	.467
1996 Augusta	A	62	226	57	11	3	14	—	—	116	41	41	38	5	65	8	0	1	11	3	.79	1	.252	.377	.513
Lynchburg	A+	66	251	69	11	3	10	—	—	116	40	46	29	1	56	3	0	4	5	1	.83	8	.275	.352	.462
1997 Carolina	AA	129	487	134	31	4	20	—	—	233	87	70	69	5	136	10	0	5	18	6	.75	3	.275	.373	.478
1998 Nashville	AAA	126	458	118	26	5	28	—	—	238	81	78	50	0	152	4	0	3	21	4	.84	3	.258	.334	.520
1999 Nashville	AAA	125	496	134	27	3	32	—	—	263	89	97	35	1	119	4	0	4	19	10	.66	9	.270	.321	.530
2000 Nashville	AAA	78	294	66	12	1	11	—	—	113	47	38	25	0	89	6	0	2	16	4	.80	2	.224	.304	.384
1999 Pittsburgh	NL	19	60	14	3	0	1	(0	1)	20	5	1	7	1	19	1	0	0	2	2	.50	0	.233	.323	.333
2000 Pittsburgh	NL	33	108	20	4	1	2	(2	0)	32	12	8	6	0	37	0	2	1	0	0	—	3	.185	.226	.296
2 ML YEARS		52	168	34	7	1	3	(2	1)	52	17	9	13	1	56	1	3	1	2	2	.50	3	.202	.262	.310

Dustin Hermanson

Pitches: Right **Bats:** Right **Pos:** SP-30; RP-8   **Ht:** 6'2" **Wt:** 200 **Born:** 12/21/72 **Age:** 28

Year Team	Lg	HOW MUCH HE PITCHED						WHAT HE GAVE UP										THE RESULTS						
		G	GS	CG	GF	IP	BFP	H	R	ER	HR	SH	SF	HB	TBB	IBB	SO	WP	Bk	W	L	Pct.	ShO	Sv-Op	Hld	ERA
1995 San Diego	NL	26	0	0	6	31.2	151	35	26	24	8	3	0	1	22	1	19	3	0	3	1	.750	0	0-0	1	6.82
1996 San Diego	NL	8	0	0	4	13.2	62	18	15	13	3	2	3	0	4	0	11	0	1	1	0	1.000	0	0-0	0	8.56
1997 Montreal	NL	32	28	1	0	158.1	656	134	68	65	15	10	6	1	66	2	136	4	1	8	8	.500	1	0-0	0	3.69
1998 Montreal	NL	32	30	1	0	187	768	163	80	65	21	9	3	3	56	3	154	4	3	14	11	.560	0	0-0	1	3.13
1999 Montreal	NL	34	34	0	0	216.1	928	225	110	101	20	16	7	7	69	4	145	4	1	9	14	.391	0	0-0	0	4.20
2000 Montreal	NL	38	30	2	7	198	876	226	128	105	26	10	9	4	75	5	94	5	0	12	14	.462	1	4-7	1	4.77
6 ML YEARS		170	122	4	17	805	3441	801	427	373	93	50	28	16	292	15	559	20	6	47	48	.495	2	4-7	3	4.17

Alex Hernandez

Bats: L **Throws:** L **Pos:** 1B-12; PH/PR-5; LF-3; RF-2   **Ht:** 6'4" **Wt:** 190 **Born:** 5/28/77 **Age:** 24

Year Team	Lg	BATTING																	BASERUNNING				PERCENTAGES		
		G	AB	H	2B	3B	HR	(Hm	Rd)	TB	R	RBI	TBB	IBB	SO	HBP	SH	SF	SB	CS	SB%	GDP	Avg	OBP	SLG
1995 Pirates	R	49	186	50	5	3	1	—	—	64	24	17	17	1	33	1	1	2	4	4	.50	3	.269	.330	.344
1996 Erie	A-	61	225	65	13	4	4	—	—	98	38	30	20	1	47	0	1	2	7	8	.47	1	.289	.344	.436
1997 Lynchburg	A+	131	520	151	37	4	5	—	—	211	75	68	27	2	140	2	2	7	13	8	.62	6	.290	.324	.406
1998 Carolina	AA	115	452	117	22	7	8	—	—	177	62	48	41	2	81	0	5	6	11	4	.73	12	.259	.317	.392
1999 Altoona	AA	126	475	122	26	3	15	—	—	199	76	63	54	1	110	2	3	3	11	8	.58	3	.257	.333	.419
2000 Altoona	AA	50	199	67	16	1	4	—	—	97	28	34	13	2	42	0	1	1	1	2	.33	4	.337	.376	.487
Nashville	AAA	76	276	76	17	2	8	—	—	121	29	37	11	1	60	1	0	0	6	3	.67	6	.275	.306	.438
2000 Pittsburgh	NL	20	60	12	3	0	1	(1	0)	18	4	5	0	0	13	0	0	0	1	1	.50	0	.200	.200	.300

Carlos Hernandez

Bats: Right **Throws:** Right **Pos:** C-70; PH/PR-4; 1B-1   **Ht:** 5'10" **Wt:** 215 **Born:** 5/24/67 **Age:** 34

Year Team	Lg	BATTING																	BASERUNNING				PERCENTAGES		
		G	AB	H	2B	3B	HR	(Hm	Rd)	TB	R	RBI	TBB	IBB	SO	HBP	SH	SF	SB	CS	SB%	GDP	Avg	OBP	SLG
1990 Los Angeles	NL	10	20	4	1	0	0	(0	0)	5	2	1	0	0	2	0	0	0	0	0	—	0	.200	.200	.250
1991 Los Angeles	NL	15	14	3	1	0	0	(0	0)	4	1	1	0	0	5	1	0	1	1	0	1.00	0	.214	.250	.286
1992 Los Angeles	NL	69	173	45	4	0	3	(1	2)	58	11	17	11	1	21	4	0	2	0	1	.00	8	.260	.316	.335
1993 Los Angeles	NL	50	99	25	5	0	2	(1	1)	36	6	7	2	0	11	0	1	0	0	0	—	0	.253	.267	.364
1994 Los Angeles	NL	32	64	14	2	0	2	(0	2)	22	6	6	1	0	14	0	0	0	0	0	—	0	.219	.231	.344
1995 Los Angeles	NL	45	94	14	1	0	2	(1	1)	21	3	8	7	0	25	1	1	0	0	0	—	5	.149	.216	.223
1996 Los Angeles	NL	13	14	4	0	0	0	(0	0)	4	1	0	2	0	2	0	0	0	0	0	—	0	.286	.375	.286
1997 San Diego	NL	50	134	42	7	1	3	(2	1)	60	15	14	3	0	27	0	1	0	0	2	.00	5	.313	.328	.448
1998 San Diego	NL	129	390	102	15	0	9	(7	2)	144	34	52	16	2	54	9	0	2	2	2	.50	19	.262	.305	.369
2000 SD-StL	NL	75	242	62	15	0	3	(2	1)	86	23	35	21	1	35	4	0	3	2	3	.40	4	.256	.322	.355
2000 San Diego	NL	58	191	48	11	0	2	(1	1)	65	16	25	16	1	26	3	0	2	1	3	.25	4	.251	.316	.340
St. Louis	NL	17	51	14	4	0	1	(1	0)	21	7	10	5	0	9	1	0	1	1	0	1.00	0	.275	.345	.412
10 ML YEARS		488	1244	315	51	1	24	(14	10)	440	102	141	63	4	196	19	3	8	5	8	.38	43	.253	.298	.354

Carlos E. Hernandez

Bats: Right **Throws:** Right **Pos:** 3B-2; PH/PR-2   **Ht:** 5'9" **Wt:** 175 **Born:** 12/12/75 **Age:** 25

Year Team	Lg	BATTING																	BASERUNNING				PERCENTAGES		
		G	AB	H	2B	3B	HR	(Hm	Rd)	TB	R	RBI	TBB	IBB	SO	HBP	SH	SF	SB	CS	SB%	GDP	Avg	OBP	SLG
1994 Astros	R	51	192	62	10	1	0	—	—	74	45	23	19	0	22	4	2	1	25	7	.78	1	.323	.394	.385
1995 Quad City	A	126	470	122	19	6	4	—	—	165	74	40	39	1	68	11	9	1	58	21	.73	4	.260	.330	.351
1996 Quad City	A	112	456	123	15	7	5	—	—	167	67	49	27	0	71	4	9	5	41	14	.75	6	.270	.313	.366
1997 Jackson	AA	92	363	106	12	1	4	—	—	132	62	33	33	2	59	4	6	3	17	8	.68	7	.292	.355	.364
1998 New Orleans	AAA	134	494	147	23	2	1	—	—	177	64	54	21	3	81	12	7	1	29	11	.73	10	.298	.341	.358
1999 New Orleans	AAA	94	355	104	14	0	0	—	—	118	56	43	27	1	65	10	3	3	22	13	.63	5	.293	.357	.332
2000 Tacoma	AAA	62	210	50	10	1	0	—	—	62	21	15	15	0	38	3	4	0	9	0	1.00	8	.238	.298	.295
1999 Houston	NL	16	14	2	0	0	0	(0	0)	2	4	1	0	0	0	0	1	0	3	1	.75	0	.143	.143	.143
2000 Seattle	AL	2	1	0	0	0	0	(0	0)	0	0	0	0	0	1	0	0	0	0	1	.00	0	.000	.000	.000
2 ML YEARS		18	15	2	0	0	0	(0	0)	2	4	1	0	0	1	0	1	0	3	2	.60	0	.133	.133	.133

Jose Hernandez

Bats: R **Throws:** R **Pos:** 3B-95; SS-37; PH/PR-4; LF-2   **Ht:** 6'1" **Wt:** 180 **Born:** 7/14/69 **Age:** 31

Year Team	Lg	BATTING																	BASERUNNING				PERCENTAGES		
		G	AB	H	2B	3B	HR	(Hm	Rd)	TB	R	RBI	TBB	IBB	SO	HBP	SH	SF	SB	CS	SB%	GDP	Avg	OBP	SLG
2000 Indianapols *	AAA	2	9	3	0	0	2	—	—	9	2	3	1	0	3	0	0	0	0	0	—	0	.333	.400	1.000
1991 Texas	AL	45	98	18	2	1	0	(0	0)	22	8	4	3	0	31	0	6	0	0	1	.00	2	.184	.208	.224
1992 Cleveland	AL	3	4	0	0	0	0	(0	0)	0	0	0	0	0	2	0	0	0	0	0	—	0	.000	.000	.000
1994 Chicago	NL	56	132	32	2	3	1	(0	1)	43	19	9	8	0	29	1	5	0	2	2	.50	4	.242	.291	.326
1995 Chicago	NL	93	245	60	11	4	13	(6	7)	118	37	40	13	3	69	0	8	2	1	0	1.00	8	.245	.281	.482
1996 Chicago	NL	131	331	81	14	1	10	(4	6)	126	52	41	24	4	97	1	5	2	4	0	1.00	10	.242	.293	.381
1997 Chicago	NL	121	183	50	8	5	7	(4	3)	89	33	26	14	2	42	0	1	1	2	5	.29	5	.273	.323	.486
1998 Chicago	NL	149	488	124	23	7	23	(11	12)	230	76	75	40	3	140	1	2	2	4	6	.40	12	.254	.311	.471
1999 ChC-Atl	NL	147	508	135	20	2	19	(6	13)	216	79	62	52	6	145	5	2	1	11	3	.79	10	.266	.339	.425
2000 Milwaukee	NL	124	446	109	22	1	11	(8	3)	166	51	59	41	3	125	6	0	3	3	7	.30	12	.244	.315	.372
1999 Chicago	NL	99	342	93	12	2	15	(5	10)	154	57	43	40	3	101	5	1	0	7	2	.78	5	.272	.357	.450
Atlanta	NL	48	166	42	8	0	4	(1	3)	62	22	19	12	3	44	0	1	1	4	1	.80	5	.253	.302	.373
9 ML YEARS		869	2435	608	102	24	84	(39	45)	1010	354	316	195	21	680	14	29	11	27	24	.53	63	.250	.308	.415

Livan Hernandez

Pitches: Right **Bats:** Right **Pos:** SP-33   **Ht:** 6'2" **Wt:** 222 **Born:** 2/20/75 **Age:** 26

		HOW MUCH HE PITCHED					WHAT HE GAVE UP										THE RESULTS					
Year Team	Lg	G	GS	CG	GF	IP	BFP	H	R	ER	HR	SH	SF	HB	TBB	IBB	SO	WP	Bk	W	L	Pct.	ShO	Sv-Op	Hld	ERA
1996 Florida	NL	1	0	0	0	3	13	3	0	0	0	0	0	0	2	0	2	0	0	0	0	—	0	0-0	0	0.00
1997 Florida	NL	17	17	0	0	96.1	405	81	39	34	5	4	7	3	38	1	72	0	0	9	3	.750	0	0-0	0	3.18
1998 Florida	NL	33	33	9	0	234.1	1040	265	133	123	37	8	5	6	104	8	162	4	3	10	12	.455	0	0-0	0	4.72
1999 Fla-SF	NL	30	30	2	0	199.2	886	227	110	103	23	7	6	2	76	5	144	2	2	8	12	.400	0	0-0	0	4.64
2000 San Francisco	NL	33	33	5	0	240	1030	254	114	100	22	12	9	4	73	3	165	3	0	17	11	.607	2	0-0	0	3.75
1999 Florida	NL	20	20	2	0	136	612	161	78	72	17	3	4	2	55	3	97	2	1	5	9	.357	0	0-0	0	4.76
San Francisco	NL	10	10	0	0	63.2	274	66	32	31	6	4	2	0	21	2	47	0	1	3	3	.500	0	0-0	0	4.38
5 ML YEARS		114	113	16	0	773.1	3374	830	396	360	87	31	27	15	293	17	545	9	5	44	38	.537	2	0-0	0	4.19

Orlando Hernandez

Pitches: Right **Bats:** Right **Pos:** SP-29   **Ht:** 6'2" **Wt:** 220 **Born:** 10/11/69 **Age:** 31

		HOW MUCH HE PITCHED					WHAT HE GAVE UP										THE RESULTS					
Year Team	Lg	G	GS	CG	GF	IP	BFP	H	R	ER	HR	SH	SF	HB	TBB	IBB	SO	WP	Bk	W	L	Pct.	ShO	Sv-Op	Hld	ERA
2000 Tampa *	A+	1	0	0	0	4	14	1	0	0	0	0	0	0	1	0	5	0	0	0	0	—	0	0- —		0.00
1998 New York	AL	21	21	3	0	141	574	113	53	49	11	3	5	6	52	1	131	5	2	12	4	.750	1	0-0	0	3.13
1999 New York	AL	33	33	2	0	214.1	910	187	108	98	24	3	11	8	87	2	157	4	0	17	9	.654	1	0-0	0	4.12
2000 New York	AL	29	29	3	0	195.2	820	186	104	98	34	4	5	6	51	2	141	1	0	12	13	.480	0	0-0	0	4.51
3 ML YEARS		83	83	8	0	551	2304	486	265	245	69	10	21	20	190	5	429	10	2	41	26	.612	2	0-0	0	4.00

Ramon Hernandez

Bats: Right **Throws:** Right **Pos:** C-142; PH/PR-16   **Ht:** 6'0" **Wt:** 227 **Born:** 5/20/76 **Age:** 25

		BATTING																			BASERUNNING			PERCENTAGES		
Year Team	Lg	G	AB	H	2B	3B	HR	(Hm	Rd)	TB	R	RBI	TBB	IBB	SO	HBP	SH	SF			SB	CS	SB%	GDP	Avg	OBP	SLG
1995 Athletics	R	48	143	52	9	6	4	—	—	85	37	37	39	1	16	8	0	4			6	2	.75	3	.364	.510	.594
1996 W Michigan	A	123	447	114	26	2	12	—	—	180	62	68	69	1	62	4	1	7			2	3	.40	22	.255	.355	.403
1997 Visalia	A+	86	332	120	21	2	15	—	—	190	57	85	35	1	47	9	0	8			2	4	.33	5	.361	.427	.572
Huntsville	AA	44	161	31	3	0	4	—	—	46	27	24	18	0	23	3	0	3			0	0	—	6	.193	.281	.286
1998 Huntsville	AA	127	479	142	24	1	15	—	—	213	83	98	57	2	61	19	2	6			4	5	.44	15	.296	.389	.445
1999 Vancouver	AAA	77	291	76	11	3	13	—	—	132	38	55	23	1	37	7	2	4			1	2	.33	13	.261	.326	.454
1999 Oakland	AL	40	136	38	7	0	3	(1	2)	54	13	21	18	0	11	1	1	2			1	0	1.00	5	.279	.363	.397
2000 Oakland	AL	143	419	101	19	0	14	(7	7)	162	52	62	38	1	64	7	10	5			1	0	1.00	14	.241	.311	.387
2 ML YEARS		183	555	139	26	0	17	(8	9)	216	65	83	56	1	75	8	11	7			2	0	1.00	19	.250	.324	.389

Roberto Hernandez

Pitches: Right **Bats:** Right **Pos:** RP-68   **Ht:** 6'4" **Wt:** 250 **Born:** 11/11/64 **Age:** 36

		HOW MUCH HE PITCHED					WHAT HE GAVE UP										THE RESULTS					
Year Team	Lg	G	GS	CG	GF	IP	BFP	H	R	ER	HR	SH	SF	HB	TBB	IBB	SO	WP	Bk	W	L	Pct.	ShO	Sv-Op	Hld	ERA
1991 Chicago	AL	9	3	0	1	15	69	18	15	13	1	0	0	0	6	1	6	1	0	1	0	1.000	0	0-0	0	7.80
1992 Chicago	AL	43	0	0	27	71	277	45	15	13	4	0	3	4	20	1	68	2	0	7	3	.700	0	12-16	6	1.65
1993 Chicago	AL	70	0	0	67	78.2	314	66	21	20	6	2	2	0	20	1	71	2	0	3	4	.429	0	38-44	5	2.29
1994 Chicago	AL	45	0	0	43	47.2	206	44	29	26	5	0	1	1	19	1	50	1	0	4	4	.500	0	14-20	0	4.91
1995 Chicago	AL	60	0	0	57	59.2	272	63	30	26	9	4	0	3	28	4	84	1	0	3	7	.300	0	32-42	0	3.92
1996 Chicago	AL	72	0	0	61	84.2	355	65	21	18	2	2	2	0	38	5	85	6	0	6	5	.545	0	38-46	0	1.91
1997 CWS-SF		74	0	0	50	80.2	340	67	24	22	7	2	1	1	38	5	82	3	0	10	3	.769	0	31-39	9	2.45
1998 Tampa Bay	AL	67	0	0	58	71.1	310	55	33	32	5	4	0	5	41	4	55	1	0	2	6	.250	0	26-35	0	4.04
1999 Tampa Bay	AL	72	0	0	66	73.1	321	68	27	25	1	2	3	4	33	1	69	3	0	2	3	.400	0	43-47	0	3.07
2000 Tampa Bay	AL	68	0	0	58	73.1	315	76	33	26	9	7	3	3	23	1	61	2	1	4	7	.364	0	32-40	1	3.19
1997 Chicago	AL	46	0	0	43	48	203	38	15	13	5	1	1	1	24	4	47	2	0	5	1	.833	0	27-31	0	2.44
San Francisco	NL	28	0	0	7	32.2	137	29	9	9	2	1	0	0	14	1	35	1	0	5	2	.714	0	4-8	9	2.48
10 ML YEARS		580	3	0	488	655.1	2779	567	248	221	49	23	15	21	267	23	631	22	1	42	42	.500	0	266-329	16	3.04

Orel Hershiser

Pitches: Right **Bats:** Right **Pos:** SP-6; RP-4   **Ht:** 6'3" **Wt:** 195 **Born:** 9/16/58 **Age:** 42

		HOW MUCH HE PITCHED					WHAT HE GAVE UP										THE RESULTS					
Year Team	Lg	G	GS	CG	GF	IP	BFP	H	R	ER	HR	SH	SF	HB	TBB	IBB	SO	WP	Bk	W	L	Pct.	ShO	Sv-Op	Hld	ERA
2000 San Berndno *	A+	3	3	0	0	17.2	73	18	7	6	1	0	1	1	5	1	8	1	0	1	0	1.000	0	0- —	—	3.06
1983 Los Angeles	NL	8	0	0	4	8	37	7	6	3	1	1	0	0	6	0	5	1	0	0	0	—	0	1-1	0	3.38
1984 Los Angeles	NL	45	20	8	10	189.2	771	160	65	56	9	2	3	4	50	6	150	8	1	11	8	.579	4	2-3	0	2.66
1985 Los Angeles	NL	36	34	9	1	239.2	953	179	72	54	8	5	4	6	68	5	157	5	0	19	3	.864	5	0-0	0	2.03
1986 Los Angeles	NL	35	35	8	0	231.1	988	213	112	99	13	14	6	6	86	11	153	12	3	14	14	.500	1	0-0	0	3.85
1987 Los Angeles	NL	37	35	10	2	264.2	1093	247	105	90	17	8	2	9	74	5	190	11	2	16	16	.500	1	1-1	0	3.06
1988 Los Angeles	NL	35	34	15	1	267	1068	208	73	67	18	9	6	4	73	10	178	6	5	23	8	.742	8	1-1	0	2.26
1989 Los Angeles	NL	35	33	8	0	256.2	1047	226	75	66	9	19	6	3	77	14	178	8	4	15	15	.500	4	0-0	0	2.31
1990 Los Angeles	NL	4	4	0	0	25.1	106	26	12	12	1	1	0	1	4	0	16	0	1	1	1	.500	0	0-0	0	4.26
1991 Los Angeles	NL	21	21	0	0	112	473	112	43	43	3	2	1	5	32	6	73	2	4	7	2	.778	0	0-0	0	3.46
1992 Los Angeles	NL	33	33	1	0	210.2	910	209	101	86	15	15	6	8	69	13	130	10	0	10	15	.400	1	0-0	0	3.67
1993 Los Angeles	NL	33	33	5	0	215.2	913	201	106	86	17	12	4	7	72	13	141	7	0	12	14	.462	1	0-0	0	3.59
1994 Los Angeles	NL	21	21	0	0	135.1	575	146	67	57	19	4	3	2	42	6	72	6	0	6	6	.500	0	0-0	0	3.79
1995 Cleveland	AL	26	26	1	0	167.1	683	151	76	72	21	3	4	5	51	1	111	3	0	16	6	.727	1	0-0	0	3.87
1996 Cleveland	AL	33	33	1	0	206	908	238	115	97	21	9	4	12	58	4	125	11	1	15	9	.625	0	0-0	0	4.24
1997 Cleveland	AL	32	32	1	0	195.1	826	199	105	97	26	8	6	11	69	2	107	11	0	14	6	.700	0	0-0	0	4.47
1998 San Francisco	NL	34	34	0	0	202	887	200	105	99	22	12	5	13	85	7	126	12	0	11	10	.524	0	0-0	0	4.41
1999 New York	NL	32	32	0	0	179	776	175	92	91	14	6	8	11	77	2	89	6	0	13	12	.520	0	0-0	0	4.58
2000 Los Angeles	NL	10	6	0	0	24.2	136	42	36	36	5	0	3	11	14	1	13	2	0	1	5	.167	0	0-1	1	13.14
18 ML YEARS		510	466	68	19	3130.1	13150	2939	1366	1211	235	124	73	117	1007	108	2014	121	23	204	150	.576	25	5-7	1	3.48

94

Richard Hidalgo

Bats: R **Throws:** R **Pos:** CF-125; RF-37; LF-36; PH/PR-2   **Ht:** 6'3" **Wt:** 190 **Born:** 7/2/75 **Age:** 25

Year Team	Lg	G	AB	H	2B	3B	HR	(Hm	Rd)	TB	R	RBI	TBB	IBB	SO	HBP	SH	SF	SB	CS	SB%	GDP	Avg	OBP	SLG
1997 Houston	NL	19	62	19	5	0	2	(0	2)	30	8	6	4	0	18	1	0	0	1	0	1.00	0	.306	.358	.484
1998 Houston	NL	74	211	64	15	0	7	(3	4)	100	31	35	17	0	37	2	0	4	3	3	.50	5	.303	.355	.474
1999 Houston	NL	108	383	87	25	2	15	(5	10)	161	49	56	56	2	73	4	0	5	8	5	.62	5	.227	.328	.420
2000 Houston	NL	153	558	175	42	3	44	(16	28)	355	118	122	56	3	110	21	0	9	13	6	.68	13	.314	.391	.636
4 ML YEARS		354	1214	345	87	5	68	(24	44)	646	206	219	133	5	238	28	0	18	25	14	.64	23	.284	.363	.532

Bobby Higginson

Bats: Left **Throws:** Right **Pos:** LF-145; DH-10   **Ht:** 5'11" **Wt:** 195 **Born:** 8/18/70 **Age:** 30

Year Team	Lg	G	AB	H	2B	3B	HR	(Hm	Rd)	TB	R	RBI	TBB	IBB	SO	HBP	SH	SF	SB	CS	SB%	GDP	Avg	OBP	SLG
1995 Detroit	AL	131	410	92	17	5	14	(10	4)	161	61	43	62	3	107	5	2	7	6	4	.60	5	.224	.329	.393
1996 Detroit	AL	130	440	141	35	0	26	(15	11)	254	75	81	65	7	66	1	3	6	6	3	.67	7	.320	.404	.577
1997 Detroit	AL	146	546	163	30	5	27	(16	11)	284	94	101	70	2	85	3	0	4	12	7	.63	10	.299	.379	.520
1998 Detroit	AL	157	612	174	37	4	25	(10	15)	294	92	85	63	2	101	6	0	4	3	3	.50	16	.284	.355	.480
1999 Detroit	AL	107	377	90	18	0	12	(8	4)	144	51	46	64	2	66	2	0	2	4	6	.40	2	.239	.351	.382
2000 Detroit	AL	154	597	179	44	4	30	(12	18)	321	104	102	74	6	99	2	2	3	15	3	.83	5	.300	.377	.538
6 ML YEARS		825	2982	839	181	18	134	(71	63)	1458	477	458	398	22	524	19	7	26	46	26	.64	45	.281	.367	.489

Erik Hiljus

Pitches: Right **Bats:** Right **Pos:** RP-3   **Ht:** 6'5" **Wt:** 230 **Born:** 12/25/72 **Age:** 28

Year Team	Lg	G	GS	CG	GF	IP	BFP	H	R	ER	HR	SH	SF	HB	TBB	IBB	SO	WP	Bk	W	L	Pct.	ShO	Sv-Op	Hld	ERA
1991 Mets	R	9	9	1	0	38	183	31	27	18	1	0	1	1	37	0	38	5	1	2	3	.400	1	0--	—	4.26
1992 Kingsport	R+	12	11	0	1	70.2	317	66	49	40	5	2	2	2	40	0	63	7	2	3	6	.333	0	0--	—	5.09
1993 Capital Cty	A	27	27	1	0	145.2	640	114	76	70	8	2	7	4	111	1	157	17	4	7	10	.412	0	0--	—	4.32
1994 St. Lucie	A+	26	26	3	0	160.2	709	159	85	71	8	6	10	5	90	3	140	10	8	11	10	.524	1	0--	—	3.98
1995 St. Lucie	A+	17	17	0	0	111.1	453	85	46	37	4	6	5	3	50	2	98	10	6	8	4	.667	0	0--	—	2.99
Binghamton	AA	10	10	0	0	55.1	252	60	38	36	8	2	1	1	32	1	40	4	2	2	4	.333	0	0--	—	5.86
1996 Arkansas	AA	10	10	0	0	45.2	221	62	37	31	6	3	2	0	30	1	21	4	0	3	5	.375	0	0--	—	6.11
1998 Jacksnville	AA	42	0	0	17	65.2	280	49	31	27	7	2	3	0	35	0	85	4	0	2	3	.400	0	2--	—	3.70
1999 Lakeland	A+	3	0	0	1	4	15	4	1	1	0	2	0	0	0	0	9	0	1	0	0	—	0	0--	—	2.25
Jacksnville	AA	10	0	0	3	17.1	65	5	4	2	1	3	1	1	5	0	28	1	1	1	0	1.000	0	0--	—	1.04
Toledo	AAA	33	0	0	9	59.1	239	49	31	29	5	5	2	2	16	0	73	5	0	2	3	.400	0	5--	—	4.40
2000 Toledo	AAA	46	0	0	15	70.2	297	67	33	27	3	2	5	0	20	1	81	3	0	5	3	.625	0	2--	—	3.44
1999 Detroit	AL	6	0	0	0	8.2	35	7	5	5	2	0	1	0	5	0	1	0	0	0	0	—	0	0-0	1	5.19
2000 Detroit	AL	3	0	0	2	3.2	16	5	3	3	1	0	0	0	1	0	2	0	0	0	0	—	0	0-0	0	7.36
2 ML YEARS		9	0	0	2	12.1	51	12	8	8	3	0	1	0	6	0	3	0	0	0	0	—	0	0-0	1	5.84

Glenallen Hill

Bats: Right **Throws:** Right **Pos:** LF-41; PH/PR-34; DH-33   **Ht:** 6'3" **Wt:** 230 **Born:** 3/22/65 **Age:** 36

Year Team	Lg	G	AB	H	2B	3B	HR	(Hm	Rd)	TB	R	RBI	TBB	IBB	SO	HBP	SH	SF	SB	CS	SB%	GDP	Avg	OBP	SLG
1989 Toronto	AL	19	52	15	0	0	1	(1	0)	18	4	7	3	0	12	0	0	0	2	1	.67	0	.288	.327	.346
1990 Toronto	AL	84	260	60	11	3	12	(7	5)	113	47	32	18	0	62	0	0	0	8	3	.73	5	.231	.281	.435
1991 Tor-Cle	AL	72	221	57	8	2	8	(3	5)	93	29	25	23	0	54	0	1	3	6	4	.60	7	.258	.324	.421
1992 Cleveland	AL	102	369	89	16	1	18	(7	11)	161	38	49	20	0	73	4	0	1	9	6	.60	11	.241	.287	.436
1993 Cle-ChC		97	261	69	14	2	15	(5	10)	132	33	47	17	1	71	1	1	4	8	3	.73	4	.264	.307	.506
1994 Chicago	NL	89	269	80	12	1	10	(3	7)	124	48	38	29	0	57	0	0	1	19	6	.76	5	.297	.365	.461
1995 San Francisco	NL	132	497	131	29	4	24	(13	11)	240	71	86	39	4	98	1	0	2	25	5	.83	11	.264	.317	.483
1996 San Francisco	NL	98	379	106	26	0	19	(9	10)	189	56	67	33	3	95	6	0	3	6	3	.67	6	.280	.344	.499
1997 San Francisco	NL	128	398	104	28	4	11	(3	8)	173	47	64	19	0	87	4	0	7	7	4	.64	8	.261	.297	.435
1998 Sea-ChC		122	390	121	25	2	20	(11	9)	210	63	56	28	2	79	3	0	1	1	1	.50	16	.310	.360	.538
2000 ChC-NYY	NL	99	253	76	9	1	20	(11	9)	147	43	55	22	1	61	0	0	3	5	1	.83	7	.300	.353	.581
2000 ChC-NYY		104	300	88	9	1	27	(11	16)	180	45	58	19	2	76	1	0	1	0	1	.00	6	.293	.336	.600
1991 Toronto	AL	35	99	25	5	2	3	(2	1)	43	14	11	7	0	24	0	0	2	2	2	.50	2	.253	.296	.434
Cleveland	AL	37	122	32	3	0	5	(1	4)	50	15	14	16	0	30	0	1	1	4	2	.67	5	.262	.345	.410
1993 Cleveland	AL	66	174	39	7	2	5	(5	0)	65	19	25	11	1	50	1	1	4	7	3	.70	0	.224	.268	.374
Chicago	NL	31	87	30	7	0	10	(5	5)	67	14	22	6	0	21	0	0	0	1	0	1.00	1	.345	.387	.770
1998 Seattle	NL	74	259	75	20	2	12	(5	7)	135	37	33	14	1	45	3	0	1	1	1	.50	13	.290	.332	.521
Chicago	NL	48	131	46	5	0	8	(6	2)	75	26	23	14	1	34	0	0	0	0	0		3	.351	.414	.573
2000 Chicago	NL	64	168	44	4	1	11	(6	5)	83	23	29	10	2	43	0	0	0	0	1	.00	5	.262	.303	.494
New York	NL	40	132	44	5	0	16	(11	5)	97	22	29	9	0	33	1	0	1	0	0	—	1	.333	.378	.735
12 ML YEARS		1146	3649	996	187	21	185	(90	95)	1780	524	584	270	13	825	20	2	26	96	38	.72	86	.273	.324	.488

Ken Hill

Pitches: Right **Bats:** Right **Pos:** SP-17; RP-1   **Ht:** 6'2" **Wt:** 215 **Born:** 12/14/65 **Age:** 35

Year Team	Lg	G	GS	CG	GF	IP	BFP	H	R	ER	HR	SH	SF	HB	TBB	IBB	SO	WP	Bk	W	L	Pct.	ShO	Sv-Op	Hld	ERA
2000 Lk Elsinore *	A+	1	1	0	0	4	18	5	2	0	0	0	0	0	1	0	3	0	0	0	0	—	0	0--	—	0.00
Edmonton *	AAA	2	2	0	0	9.2	47	14	8	7	4	1	0	0	8	0	5	0	0	0	0	—	0	0--	—	6.52
Charlotte *	AAA	1	1	0	0	4	18	6	2	2	0	0	0	0	0	0	7	0	0	0	0	—	0	0--	—	4.50
1988 St. Louis	NL	4	1	0	0	14	62	16	9	8	0	0	0	0	6	0	6	1	0	0	0	.000	0	0-0	0	5.14
1989 St. Louis	NL	33	33	2	0	196.2	862	186	92	83	9	14	5	5	99	6	112	11	2	7	15	.318	1	0-0	0	3.80
1990 St. Louis	NL	17	14	1	1	78.2	343	79	49	48	7	5	5	1	33	1	58	5	0	5	6	.455	0	0-1	0	5.49
1991 St. Louis	NL	30	30	1	0	181.1	743	147	76	72	15	7	7	6	67	4	121	7	1	11	10	.524	1	0-0	0	3.57
1992 Montreal	NL	33	33	3	0	218	908	187	76	65	13	15	3	3	75	4	150	11	4	16	9	.640	3	0-0	0	2.68
1993 Montreal	NL	28	28	2	0	183.2	780	163	84	66	7	4	6	6	74	7	90	6	0	9	7	.563	0	0-0	0	3.23

Year Team	Lg	G	GS	CG	GF	IP	BFP	H	R	ER	HR	SH	SF	HB	TBB	IBB	SO	WP	Bk	W	L	Pct.	ShO	Sv-Op	Hld	ERA
1994 Montreal	NL	23	23	2	0	154.2	647	145	61	57	12	6	6	6	44	7	85	3	0	16	5	.762	1	0-0	0	3.32
1995 StL-Cle		30	29	1	0	185	817	202	107	95	21	12	3	1	77	4	98	6	0	10	8	.556	0	0-0	0	4.62
1996 Texas	AL	35	35	7	0	250.2	1061	250	110	101	19	4	7	6	95	3	170	5	4	16	10	.615	3	0-0	0	3.63
1997 Tex-Ana	AL	31	31	1	0	190	833	194	103	96	19	3	7	3	95	3	106	7	0	9	12	.429	0	0-0	0	4.55
1998 Anaheim	AL	19	19	0	0	103	458	123	60	57	6	7	5	4	47	0	57	3	0	9	6	.600	0	0-0	0	4.98
1999 Anaheim	AL	26	22	0	0	128.1	569	129	72	68	14	3	8	4	76	1	76	5	0	4	11	.267	0	0-0	1	4.77
2000 Ana-CWS	AL	18	17	0	0	81.2	399	107	67	65	16	3	8	2	59	1	50	6	0	5	8	.385	0	0-0	0	7.16
1995 St. Louis	NL	18	18	0	0	110.1	493	125	71	62	16	9	2	0	45	4	50	3	0	6	7	.462	0	0-0	0	5.06
Cleveland	AL	12	11	1	0	74.2	324	77	36	33	5	3	1	1	32	0	48	3	0	4	1	.800	0	0-0	0	3.98
1997 Texas	AL	19	19	0	0	111	499	129	69	64	11	2	6	2	56	3	68	5	0	5	8	.385	0	0-0	0	5.19
Anaheim	AL	12	12	1	0	79	334	65	34	32	8	1	1	1	39	0	38	2	0	4	4	.500	0	0-0	0	3.65
2000 Anaheim	AL	16	16	0	0	78.2	380	102	59	57	16	2	7	2	53	1	50	6	0	5	7	.417	0	0-0	0	6.52
Chicago	AL	2	1	0	0	3	19	5	8	8	0	1	1	0	6	0	0	0	0	0	1	.000	0	0-0	0	24.00
13 ML YEARS		327	315	19	3	1965.2	8482	1928	966	881	158	88	71	46	847	41	1179	76	13	117	108	.520	8	0-0	0	4.03

A.J. Hinch

Bats: Right **Throws:** Right **Pos:** C-5; PH/PR-2; DH-1   **Ht:** 6'1" **Wt:** 207 **Born:** 5/15/74 **Age:** 27

Year Team	Lg	G	AB	H	2B	3B	HR	(Hm	Rd)	TB	R	RBI	TBB	IBB	SO	HBP	SH	SF	SB	CS	SB%	GDP	Avg	OBP	SLG
2000 Sacramento *	AAA	109	417	111	23	2	6	(—	—)	156	65	47	45	2	67	7	2	5	5	5	.50	8	.266	.344	.374
1998 Oakland	AL	120	337	78	10	0	9	(4	5)	115	34	35	30	0	89	4	13	7	3	0	1.00	6	.231	.296	.341
1999 Oakland	AL	76	205	44	4	1	7	(3	4)	71	26	24	11	0	41	2	9	1	6	2	.75	4	.215	.260	.346
2000 Oakland	AL	6	8	2	0	0	0	(0	0)	2	1	0	1	0	1	0	0	0	0	0	--	0	.250	.333	.250
3 ML YEARS		202	550	124	14	1	16	(7	9)	188	61	59	42	0	131	6	22	8	9	2	.82	10	.225	.284	.342

Brett Hinchliffe

Pitches: Right **Bats:** Right **Pos:** RP-2   **Ht:** 6'5" **Wt:** 190 **Born:** 7/21/74 **Age:** 26

Year Team	Lg	G	GS	CG	GF	IP	BFP	H	R	ER	HR	SH	SF	HB	TBB	IBB	SO	WP	Bk	W	L	Pct.	ShO	Sv-Op	Hld	ERA
1992 Mariners	R	24	0	0	20	35	161	42	17	9	0	3	0	3	9	0	26	1	1	5	4	.556	0	3- -		2.31
1993 Mariners	R	10	9	0	0	44.1	190	55	32	25	4	1	3	3	5	0	29	4	1	0	4	.000	0	0- -		5.08
1994 Appleton	A	27	27	3	0	173.2	721	140	79	62	16	7	4	10	50	4	160	5	2	11	7	.611	0	0- -		3.21
1995 Riverside	A+	15	15	0	0	77.2	373	110	69	57	10	5	3	8	35	3	68	4	0	3	8	.273	0	0- -		6.61
1996 Lancaster	A+	27	26	0	0	163.1	731	179	105	77	19	6	5	9	64	1	146	10	1	11	10	.524	0	0- -		4.24
1997 Memphis	AA	24	24	5	0	145.2	627	159	81	72	20	3	4	9	45	2	107	2	1	10	10	.500	1	0- -		4.45
1998 Lancaster	A+	3	3	0	0	17	62	8	5	3	2	0	0	0	5	0	26	1	0	1	1	.500	0	0- -		1.59
Tacoma	AAA	25	25	2	0	159.2	681	132	80	71	22	1	5	4	88	2	100	4	2	10	8	.556	1	0- -		4.00
1999 Tacoma	AAA	21	21	3	0	131	563	141	78	75	17	4	5	5	44	1	107	9	0	9	7	.563	0	0- -		5.15
2000 Edmonton	AAA	27	3	0	10	64	272	63	29	27	6	1	2	2	24	0	30	8	1	2	3	.400	0	2- -		3.80
Iowa	AAA	7	4	1	0	32	133	32	10	10	4	1	0	1	8	1	22	0	0	2	0	1.000	0	0- -		2.81
1999 Seattle	AL	11	4	0	2	30.2	153	41	31	30	10	1	0	4	21	0	14	2	0	0	4	.000	0	0-0	0	8.80
2000 Anaheim	AL	2	0	0	0	1.2	7	1	1	1	0	0	0	0	1	0	0	0	0	0	0	--	0	0-0	0	5.40
2 ML YEARS		13	4	0	2	32.1	160	42	32	31	10	1	0	4	22	0	14	2	0	0	4	.000	0	0-0	1	8.63

Sterling Hitchcock

Pitches: Left **Bats:** Left **Pos:** SP-11   **Ht:** 6'0" **Wt:** 205 **Born:** 4/29/71 **Age:** 30

Year Team	Lg	G	GS	CG	GF	IP	BFP	H	R	ER	HR	SH	SF	HB	TBB	IBB	SO	WP	Bk	W	L	Pct.	ShO	Sv-Op	Hld	ERA
1992 New York	AL	3	3	0	0	13	68	23	12	12	2	0	0	1	6	0	6	0	0	0	2	.000	0	0-0	0	8.31
1993 New York	AL	6	6	0	0	31	135	32	18	16	4	0	2	1	14	1	26	3	2	1	2	.333	0	0-0	0	4.65
1994 New York	AL	23	5	1	4	49.1	218	48	24	23	3	1	7	0	29	1	37	5	0	4	1	.800	0	2-2	3	4.20
1995 New York	AL	27	27	4	0	168.1	719	155	91	88	22	5	9	5	68	1	121	5	2	11	10	.524	1	0-0	0	4.70
1996 Seattle	AL	35	35	0	0	196.2	885	245	131	117	27	3	8	7	73	4	132	4	1	13	9	.591	0	0-0	0	5.35
1997 San Diego	NL	32	28	1	1	161	693	172	102	93	24	7	4	4	55	2	106	6	2	10	11	.476	0	0-0	0	5.20
1998 San Diego	NL	39	27	2	3	176.1	743	169	83	77	29	9	3	9	48	2	158	11	1	9	7	.563	1	1-2	3	3.93
1999 San Diego	NL	33	33	1	0	205.2	892	202	99	94	29	6	5	9	76	6	194	15	1	12	14	.462	0	0-0	0	4.11
2000 San Diego	NL	11	11	0	0	65.2	292	69	38	36	12	2	1	5	26	1	61	4	0	1	6	.143	0	0-0	0	4.93
9 ML YEARS		209	175	9	8	1067	4645	1115	598	556	152	36	40	37	395	18	841	53	10	61	62	.496	2	3-4	6	4.69

Denny Hocking

Bats: B **Throws:** R **Pos:** 2B-47; PH/PR-38; CF-21; RF-19; 3B-16; LF-16; SS-15; 1B-12; DH-2 **Ht:** 5'10" **Wt:** 183 **Born:** 4/2/70 **Age:** 31

Year Team	Lg	G	AB	H	2B	3B	HR	(Hm	Rd)	TB	R	RBI	TBB	IBB	SO	HBP	SH	SF	SB	CS	SB%	GDP	Avg	OBP	SLG
1993 Minnesota	AL	15	36	5	1	0	0	(0	0)	6	7	0	6	0	8	0	0	0	1	0	1.00	1	.139	.262	.167
1994 Minnesota	AL	11	31	10	3	0	0	(0	0)	13	3	2	0	0	4	0	0	0	2	0	1.00	1	.323	.323	.419
1995 Minnesota	AL	9	25	5	0	2	0	(0	0)	9	4	3	2	1	2	0	1	0	1	0	1.00	1	.200	.259	.360
1996 Minnesota	AL	49	127	25	6	0	1	(0	1)	34	16	10	8	0	24	0	1	1	3	3	.50	3	.197	.243	.268
1997 Minnesota	AL	115	253	65	12	4	2	(0	2)	91	28	25	18	0	51	1	5	1	3	5	.38	6	.257	.308	.360
1998 Minnesota	AL	110	198	40	6	1	3	(1	2)	57	32	15	16	1	44	0	3	2	2	1	.67	2	.202	.259	.288
1999 Minnesota	AL	136	386	103	18	2	7	(2	5)	146	47	41	22	1	54	3	4	6	11	7	.61	10	.267	.307	.378
2000 Minnesota	AL	134	373	111	24	4	4	(1	3)	155	52	47	48	1	77	0	7	5	7	5	.58	7	.298	.373	.416
8 ML YEARS		579	1429	364	70	13	17	(4	13)	511	189	143	120	4	264	4	21	15	30	21	.59	26	.255	.311	.358

Kevin Hodges

Pitches: Right **Bats:** Right **Pos:** RP-13   **Ht:** 6'4" **Wt:** 200 **Born:** 6/24/73 **Age:** 28

Year Team	Lg	G	GS	CG	GF	IP	BFP	H	R	ER	HR	SH	SF	HB	TBB	IBB	SO	WP	Bk	W	L	Pct.	ShO	Sv-Op	Hld	ERA
1991 Royals	R	9	3	0	0	23	104	22	14	11	0	1	1	4	11	0	13	2	0	1	2	.333	0	0- -	--	4.30

Year Team	Lg	HOW MUCH HE PITCHED						WHAT HE GAVE UP												THE RESULTS						
		G	GS	CG	GF	IP	BFP	H	R	ER	HR	SH	SF	HB	TBB	IBB	SO	WP	Bk	W	L	Pct.	ShO	Sv-Op	Hld	ERA
1992 Royals	R	11	9	0	0	49.2	232	60	30	26	1	2	2	4	25	0	24	1	1	5	3	.625	0	0- -	—	4.71
1993 Royals	R	12	10	0	0	71	299	52	25	16	0	5	0	7	25	0	40	3	0	7	2	.778	0	0- -	—	2.03
Wilmington	A+	3	0	0	1	4.2	18	2	0	0	0	1	0	1	3	0	1	0	0	1	0	1.000	0	0- -	—	0.00
1994 Rockford	A	24	17	2	6	114.1	466	96	53	43	5	3	0	9	35	1	83	7	3	9	6	.600	1	3- -	—	3.38
1995 Wilmington	A+	12	10	0	1	53.2	232	53	31	27	1	1	1	3	25	1	27	4	0	2	3	.400	0	0- -	—	4.53
1996 Lansing	A	9	9	0	0	48.1	208	47	32	25	3	2	1	6	19	0	23	3	1	1	2	.333	0	0- -	—	4.66
Wilmington	A+	8	8	0	0	38.2	172	45	30	23	2	0	3	1	18	0	15	5	1	2	4	.333	0	0- -	—	5.35
1997 Wilmington	AA	28	20	0	4	124.2	563	150	78	62	11	3	6	5	44	7	63	5	2	8	11	.421	0	1- -	—	4.48
1998 Jackson	AA	29	15	0	4	107.1	462	108	55	43	8	5	2	7	38	3	70	6	2	4	5	.444	0	0- -	—	3.61
1999 Jackson	AA	8	8	0	0	49	211	48	22	16	0	2	2	3	16	0	21	0	1	1	4	.200	0	0- -	—	2.94
New Orleans	AAA	5	5	0	0	27.1	126	34	23	22	6	0	2	1	11	1	16	0	0	1	3	.250	0	0- -	—	7.24
Tacoma	AAA	14	12	0	1	83	358	88	31	30	3	3	1	9	27	1	42	3	0	3	3	.500	0	1- -	—	3.25
2000 Tacoma	AAA	30	11	2	6	98	393	87	32	30	3	3	3	8	21	1	73	1	0	4	3	.571	1	3- -	—	2.76
2000 Seattle	AL	13	0	0	7	17.1	73	18	10	10	4	0	1	2	12	0	7	1	0	0	0	—	0	0-0	0	5.19

Trevor Hoffman

Pitches: Right **Bats:** Right **Pos:** RP-70 **Ht:** 6'0" **Wt:** 215 **Born:** 10/13/67 **Age:** 33

Year Team	Lg	HOW MUCH HE PITCHED						WHAT HE GAVE UP												THE RESULTS						
		G	GS	CG	GF	IP	BFP	H	R	ER	HR	SH	SF	HB	TBB	IBB	SO	WP	Bk	W	L	Pct.	ShO	Sv-Op	Hld	ERA
1993 Fla-SD	NL	67	0	0	26	90	391	80	43	39	10	4	5	1	39	13	79	5	0	4	6	.400	0	5-8	15	3.90
1994 San Diego	NL	47	0	0	41	56	225	39	16	16	4	1	2	0	20	6	68	3	0	4	4	.500	0	20-23	1	2.57
1995 San Diego	NL	55	0	0	51	53.1	218	48	25	23	10	0	0	0	14	3	52	1	0	7	4	.636	0	31-38	0	3.88
1996 San Diego	NL	70	0	0	62	88	348	50	23	22	6	2	2	2	31	5	111	2	0	9	5	.643	0	42-49	0	2.25
1997 San Diego	NL	70	0	0	59	81.1	322	59	25	24	9	2	1	0	24	4	111	7	0	6	4	.600	0	37-44	0	2.66
1998 San Diego	NL	66	0	0	61	73	274	41	12	12	2	3	0	1	21	2	86	8	0	4	2	.667	0	53-54	0	1.48
1999 San Diego	NL	64	0	0	54	67.1	263	48	23	16	5	1	3	0	15	2	73	4	0	2	3	.400	0	40-43	0	2.14
2000 San Diego	NL	70	0	0	59	72.1	291	61	29	24	7	3	5	0	11	4	85	4	0	4	7	.364	0	43-50	0	2.99
1993 Florida	NL	28	0	0	13	35.2	152	24	13	13	5	2	1	0	19	7	26	3	0	2	2	.500	0	2-3	8	3.28
San Diego	NL	39	0	0	13	54.1	239	56	30	26	5	2	4	1	20	6	53	2	0	2	4	.333	0	3-5	7	4.31
8 ML YEARS		509	0	0	413	581.1	2332	426	196	176	53	16	18	4	175	39	665	34	0	40	35	.533	0	271-309	16	2.72

Ray Holbert

Bats: Right **Throws:** Right **Pos:** 2B-1; 3B-1; SS-1 **Ht:** 6'0" **Wt:** 185 **Born:** 9/25/70 **Age:** 30

Year Team	Lg	BATTING																		BASERUNNING				PERCENTAGES		
		G	AB	H	2B	3B	HR	(Hm	Rd)	TB	R	RBI	TBB	IBB	SO	HBP	SH	SF		SB	CS	SB%	GDP	Avg	OBP	SLG
2000 Omaha *	AAA	94	338	86	12	1	2	—	—	106	41	40	35	0	49	0	1	2		14	9	.61	10	.254	.323	.314
1994 San Diego	NL	5	5	1	0	0	0	(0	0)	1	1	0	0	0	4	0	0	0		0	0	—	0	.200	.200	.200
1995 San Diego	NL	63	73	13	2	1	2	(1	1)	23	11	5	8	1	20	2	3	0		4	0	1.00	3	.178	.277	.315
1998 Atl-Mon	NL	10	20	2	0	0	0	(0	0)	2	2	1	2	0	5	0	0	1		0	0	—	0	.100	.174	.100
1999 Kansas City	AL	34	100	28	3	0	0	(0	0)	31	14	5	8	0	20	0	6	1		7	4	.64	4	.280	.330	.310
2000 Kansas City	AL	3	4	1	0	0	0	(0	0)	1	0	0	0	0	2	0	0	0		0	0	—	0	.250	.250	.250
1998 Atlanta	NL	8	15	2	0	0	0	(0	0)	2	2	1	2	0	4	0	0	1		0	0	—	0	.133	.222	.133
Montreal	NL	2	5	0	0	0	0	(0	0)	0	0	0	0	0	1	0	0	0		0	0	—	0	.000	.000	.000
5 ML YEARS		115	202	45	5	1	2	(1	1)	58	28	11	18	1	51	2	9	2		11	4	.73	7	.223	.290	.287

Todd Hollandsworth

Bats: L **Throws:** L **Pos:** CF-72; LF-40; PH/PR-30; RF-19 **Ht:** 6'2" **Wt:** 215 **Born:** 4/20/73 **Age:** 28

Year Team	Lg	BATTING																		BASERUNNING				PERCENTAGES		
		G	AB	H	2B	3B	HR	(Hm	Rd)	TB	R	RBI	TBB	IBB	SO	HBP	SH	SF		SB	CS	SB%	GDP	Avg	OBP	SLG
1995 Los Angeles	NL	41	103	24	2	0	5	(3	2)	41	16	13	10	2	29	1	0	1		2	1	.67	1	.233	.304	.398
1996 Los Angeles	NL	149	478	139	26	4	12	(2	10)	209	64	59	41	1	93	2	3	2		21	6	.78	5	.291	.348	.437
1997 Los Angeles	NL	106	296	73	20	2	4	(1	3)	109	39	31	17	2	60	0	2	2		5	5	.50	8	.247	.286	.368
1998 Los Angeles	NL	55	175	47	6	4	3	(1	2)	70	23	20	9	0	42	1	2	0		4	3	.57	2	.269	.308	.400
1999 Los Angeles	NL	92	261	74	12	2	9	(5	4)	117	39	32	24	1	61	1	0	1		5	2	.71	2	.284	.345	.448
2000 LA-Col	NL	137	428	115	20	0	19	(13	6)	192	81	47	41	3	99	1	0	1		18	7	.72	8	.269	.333	.449
2000 Los Angeles	NL	81	261	61	12	0	8	(6	2)	97	42	24	30	2	61	1	0	1		11	4	.73	4	.234	.314	.372
Colorado	NL	56	167	54	8	0	11	(7	4)	95	39	23	11	1	38	0	0	0		7	3	.70	4	.323	.365	.569
6 ML YEARS		580	1741	472	86	12	52	(25	27)	738	262	202	142	9	384	6	7	7		55	24	.70	23	.271	.327	.424

Darren Holmes

Pitches: Right **Bats:** Right **Pos:** RP-18 **Ht:** 6'0" **Wt:** 202 **Born:** 4/25/66 **Age:** 35

Year Team	Lg	HOW MUCH HE PITCHED						WHAT HE GAVE UP												THE RESULTS						
		G	GS	CG	GF	IP	BFP	H	R	ER	HR	SH	SF	HB	TBB	IBB	SO	WP	Bk	W	L	Pct.	ShO	Sv-Op	Hld	ERA
2000 Memphis *	AAA	9	0	0	3	14.2	54	10	4	4	0	2	0	0	3	0	8	1	0	0	0	—	0	—	—	2.45
Tucson *	AAA	3	0	0	3	4.1	20	4	1	1	0	0	0	0	4	1	2	0	0	1	1	.500	0	1- -	—	2.08
1990 Los Angeles	NL	14	0	0	1	17.1	77	15	10	10	1	1	2	0	11	3	19	1	0	0	1	.000	0	0-0	0	5.19
1991 Milwaukee	AL	40	0	0	9	76.1	344	90	43	40	6	8	3	1	27	1	59	6	0	1	4	.200	0	3-6	3	4.72
1992 Milwaukee	AL	41	0	0	25	42.1	173	35	12	12	1	4	0	2	11	4	31	0	0	4	4	.500	0	6-8	2	2.55
1993 Colorado	NL	62	0	0	51	66.2	274	56	31	30	6	0	0	2	20	1	60	2	1	3	3	.500	0	25-29	2	4.05
1994 Colorado	NL	29	0	0	14	28.1	142	35	25	20	5	4	1	1	24	4	33	2	0	0	3	.000	0	3-8	3	6.35
1995 Colorado	NL	68	0	0	33	66.2	286	59	26	24	5	3	3	1	28	3	61	7	1	6	1	.857	0	14-18	13	3.24
1996 Colorado	NL	62	0	0	21	77	333	78	41	34	8	2	1	1	28	2	73	2	0	5	4	.556	0	1-8	7	3.97
1997 Colorado	NL	42	6	0	10	89.1	406	113	58	53	12	6	4	0	36	3	70	4	0	9	2	.818	0	3-4	5	5.34
1998 New York	AL	34	0	0	13	51.1	215	53	19	19	4	0	3	2	14	3	31	1	0	0	3	.000	0	2-3	2	3.33
1999 Arizona	NL	44	0	0	9	48.2	219	50	21	20	3	2	0	1	25	8	35	0	2	4	3	.571	0	0-2	4	3.70
2000 Ari-StL-Bal		18	0	0	4	19.1	103	37	28	28	6	0	3	2	9	0	16	0	0	0	1	.000	0	1-2	1	13.03
2000 Arizona	NL	8	0	0	3	6.1	32	12	6	6	1	0	1	1	5	0	5	0	0	0	0	—	0	1-1	1	8.53
St. Louis	NL	5	0	0	1	8.1	39	12	9	9	2	0	2	1	3	0	6	0	0	0	1	.000	0	0-1	0	9.72
Baltimore	AL	5	0	0	0	4.2	32	13	13	13	3	0	0	0	5	0	5	0	0	0	0	—	0	0-0	0	25.07
11 ML YEARS		454	6	0	190	583.1	2572	621	314	290	55	32	20	13	233	32	488	25	4	32	29	.525	0	58-88	42	4.47

Chris Holt

Pitches: Right **Bats:** Right **Pos:** SP-32; RP-2   **Ht:** 6'4" **Wt:** 205 **Born:** 9/18/71 **Age:** 29

		HOW MUCH HE PITCHED						WHAT HE GAVE UP											THE RESULTS					
Year Team	Lg	G	GS	CG	GF	IP	BFP	H	R	ER	HR	SH	SF	HB	TBB	IBB	SO	WP	Bk	W	L	Pct.	ShO	Sv-Op	Hld	ERA
1996 Houston	NL	4	0	0	3	4.2	22	5	3	3	0	0	0	0	3	1	0	1	0	0	1	.000	0	0-0	0	5.79
1997 Houston	NL	33	32	0	0	209.2	883	211	98	82	17	7	5	8	61	4	95	1	0	8	12	.400	0	0-0	0	3.52
1999 Houston	NL	32	26	0	2	164	720	193	92	85	12	9	8	8	57	1	115	5	0	5	13	.278	0	1-2	0	4.66
2000 Houston	NL	34	32	3	1	207	916	247	131	123	22	7	12	8	75	2	136	10	1	8	16	.333	1	0-0	0	5.35
4 ML YEARS		103	90	3	6	585.1	2541	656	324	293	51	23	25	24	196	8	346	17	1	21	42	.333	1	1-2	0	4.51

Mike Holtz

Pitches: Left **Bats:** Left **Pos:** RP-61   **Ht:** 5'9" **Wt:** 188 **Born:** 10/10/72 **Age:** 28

		HOW MUCH HE PITCHED						WHAT HE GAVE UP											THE RESULTS					
Year Team	Lg	G	GS	CG	GF	IP	BFP	H	R	ER	HR	SH	SF	HB	TBB	IBB	SO	WP	Bk	W	L	Pct.	ShO	Sv-Op	Hld	ERA
2000 Edmonton *	AAA	6	0	0	1	5	22	5	6	6	1	0	0	1	1	0	1	0	0	0	1	.000	0	0--	—	10.80
1996 California	AL	30	0	0	8	29.1	127	21	11	8	1	1	1	3	19	2	31	1	0	3	3	.500	0	0-0	5	2.45
1997 Anaheim	AL	66	0	0	11	43.1	187	38	21	16	7	1	2	2	15	4	40	1	0	3	4	.429	0	2-8	14	3.32
1998 Anaheim	AL	53	0	0	9	30.1	137	38	16	16	0	1	2	1	15	1	29	4	0	2	2	.500	0	1-2	13	4.75
1999 Anaheim	AL	28	0	0	9	22.1	106	26	20	20	3	1	0	2	15	1	17	3	0	2	3	.400	0	0-0	1	8.06
2000 Anaheim	AL	61	0	0	6	41	176	37	26	23	4	4	3	2	18	2	40	1	0	3	3	.500	0	0-0	10	5.05
5 ML YEARS		238	0	0	43	166.1	733	160	94	83	15	8	8	10	82	10	157	10	0	13	15	.464	0	3-10	43	4.49

Mark Holzemer

Pitches: Left **Bats:** Left **Pos:** RP-25   **Ht:** 6'0" **Wt:** 185 **Born:** 8/20/69 **Age:** 31

		HOW MUCH HE PITCHED						WHAT HE GAVE UP											THE RESULTS					
Year Team	Lg	G	GS	CG	GF	IP	BFP	H	R	ER	HR	SH	SF	HB	TBB	IBB	SO	WP	Bk	W	L	Pct.	ShO	Sv-Op	Hld	ERA
2000 Reading *	AA	3	1	0	0	2.2	10	0	0	0	0	0	0	0	2	0	1	0	0	0	0	—	0	0--	—	0.00
Scrantn-WB *	AAA	24	3	0	6	44.2	184	40	19	18	1	3	1	0	16	2	35	1	0	3	2	.600	0	2--	—	3.63
1993 California	AL	5	4	0	1	23.1	117	34	24	23	2	1	0	3	13	0	10	1	0	0	3	.000	0	0-0	0	8.87
1995 California	AL	12	0	0	5	8.1	45	11	6	5	1	1	0	1	7	1	5	0	0	1	0	.000	0	0-0	0	5.40
1996 California	AL	25	0	0	3	24.2	119	35	28	24	7	0	1	3	8	1	20	0	0	1	0	1.000	0	0-0	1	8.76
1997 Seattle	AL	14	0	0	2	9	44	9	6	6	0	0	0	0	8	0	7	0	0	0	1	.000	0	1-1	1	6.00
1998 Oakland	AL	13	0	0	4	9.2	44	13	6	6	1	0	1	1	3	0	3	1	0	1	0	1.000	0	0-0	1	5.59
2000 Philadelphia	NL	25	0	0	9	25.2	121	36	23	22	4	5	0	1	8	1	19	2	0	0	1	.000	0	0-1	1	7.71
6 ML YEARS		94	4	0	24	100.2	490	138	93	86	15	7	2	9	47	3	64	4	0	2	5	.286	0	1-2	5	7.69

Craig House

Pitches: Right **Bats:** Right **Pos:** RP-16   **Ht:** 6'2" **Wt:** 210 **Born:** 7/8/77 **Age:** 23

		HOW MUCH HE PITCHED						WHAT HE GAVE UP											THE RESULTS					
Year Team	Lg	G	GS	CG	GF	IP	BFP	H	R	ER	HR	SH	SF	HB	TBB	IBB	SO	WP	Bk	W	L	Pct.	ShO	Sv-Op	Hld	ERA
1999 Portland	A-	26	0	0	19	34.2	154	28	14	8	0	1	0	5	14	0	58	4	2	2	1	.667	0	11--	—	2.08
2000 Salem	A+	13	0	0	12	16	69	7	4	4	0	0	1	2	10	0	24	7	0	2	0	1.000	0	8--	—	2.25
Carolina	AA	18	0	0	14	21.1	96	14	11	9	0	1	1	0	15	0	28	6	0	0	0	—	0	9--	—	3.80
Colo Spngs	AAA	8	0	0	8	8.1	32	6	4	3	0	0	1	1	2	0	8	1	0	0	0	—	0	4--	—	3.24
2000 Colorado	NL	16	0	0	3	13.2	69	13	11	11	3	0	1	2	17	0	8	0	0	1	1	.500	0	0-0	2	7.24

Tyler Houston

Bats: L **Throws:** R **Pos:** 1B-35; 3B-28; C-23; PH/PR-23   **Ht:** 6'1" **Wt:** 210 **Born:** 1/17/71 **Age:** 30

		BATTING																BASERUNNING				PERCENTAGES		
Year Team	Lg	G	AB	H	2B	3B	HR	(Hm	Rd)	TB	R	RBI	TBB	IBB	SO	HBP	SH	SF	SB	CS	SB%	GDP	Avg	OBP	SLG
1996 Atl-ChC	NL	79	142	45	9	1	3	(1	2)	65	21	27	9	1	27	0	0	0	3	2	.60	5	.317	.358	.458
1997 Chicago	NL	72	196	51	10	0	2	(0	2)	67	15	28	9	1	35	0	0	2	1	0	1.00	4	.260	.290	.342
1998 Chicago	NL	95	255	65	7	1	9	(4	5)	101	26	33	13	1	53	0	0	1	2	2	.50	6	.255	.290	.396
1999 ChC-Cle	NL	113	276	62	10	1	10	(0	8)	104	28	30	31	4	78	0	1	1	1	1	.50	7	.225	.302	.377
2000 Milwaukee	NL	101	284	71	15	0	18	(6	12)	140	30	43	17	3	72	0	4	0	2	1	.67	13	.250	.292	.493
1996 Atlanta	NL	33	27	6	2	1	1	(1	0)	13	3	8	1	0	9	0	0	0	0	0	—	0	.222	.250	.481
Chicago	NL	46	115	39	7	0	2	(0	2)	52	18	19	8	1	18	0	0	0	3	2	.60	4	.339	.382	.452
1999 Chicago	NL	100	249	58	9	1	9	(0	7)	96	26	27	28	4	67	0	1	1	1	1	.50	7	.233	.309	.386
Cleveland	AL	13	27	4	1	0	1	(0	1)	8	2	3	3	0	11	0	0	0	0	0	—	0	.148	.233	.296
5 ML YEARS		460	1153	294	51	3	42	(13	29)	477	120	161	79	10	265	0	6	4	9	6	.60	35	.255	.302	.414

Thomas Howard

Bats: B **Throws:** R **Pos:** PH/PR-60; RF-22; LF-6; DH-3; 1B-1   **Ht:** 6'2" **Wt:** 205 **Born:** 12/11/64 **Age:** 36

		BATTING																BASERUNNING				PERCENTAGES		
Year Team	Lg	G	AB	H	2B	3B	HR	(Hm	Rd)	TB	R	RBI	TBB	IBB	SO	HBP	SH	SF	SB	CS	SB%	GDP	Avg	OBP	SLG
2000 Memphis *	AAA	17	34	9	2	0	0	—	—	11	7	5	7	1	6	2	0	1	0	0	.00	2	.265	.419	.324
1990 San Diego	NL	20	44	12	2	0	0	(0	0)	14	4	0	0	0	11	0	1	0	0	1	.00	1	.273	.273	.318
1991 San Diego	NL	106	281	70	12	3	4	(4	0)	100	30	22	24	4	57	1	2	1	10	7	.59	4	.249	.309	.356
1992 SD-Cle		122	361	100	15	2	2	(1	1)	125	37	32	17	1	60	0	11	2	15	8	.65	4	.277	.308	.346
1993 Cle-Cin		112	319	81	15	3	7	(5	2)	123	48	36	24	0	63	0	0	5	10	7	.59	9	.254	.302	.386
1994 Cincinnati	NL	83	178	47	11	0	5	(4	1)	73	24	24	10	1	30	0	3	1	4	2	.67	3	.264	.302	.410
1995 Cincinnati	NL	113	281	85	15	2	3	(1	2)	113	42	26	20	0	37	1	1	1	17	8	.68	3	.302	.350	.402
1996 Cincinnati	NL	121	360	98	19	10	6	(1	5)	155	50	42	17	3	51	3	2	4	6	5	.55	5	.272	.307	.431
1997 Houston	NL	107	255	63	16	1	3	(0	3)	90	24	22	26	1	48	3	1	1	1	2	.33	3	.247	.323	.353
1998 Los Angeles	NL	47	76	14	4	0	2	(1	1)	24	9	4	3	0	15	0	0	0	0	1	.00	3	.184	.215	.316
1999 St. Louis	NL	98	195	57	10	0	6	(3	3)	85	16	28	17	0	26	0	0	1	1	0	1.00	3	.292	.353	.436
2000 St. Louis	NL	86	133	28	4	1	6	(1	5)	52	13	28	7	0	34	1	0	0	0	1	.00	3	.211	.255	.391
1992 San Diego	NL	5	3	1	0	0	0	(0	0)	1	1	0	0	0	0	0	0	1	0	0	—	0	.333	.333	.333
Cleveland	AL	117	358	99	15	2	2	(1	1)	124	36	32	17	1	60	0	10	2	15	8	.65	4	.277	.308	.346

					BATTING														BASERUNNING				PERCENTAGES		
Year Team	Lg	G	AB	H	2B	3B	HR	(Hm	Rd)	TB	R	RBI	TBB	IBB	SO	HBP	SH	SF	SB	CS	SB%	GDP	Avg	OBP	SLG
1993 Cleveland	AL	74	178	42	7	0	3	(3	0)	58	26	23	12	0	42	0	0	4	5	1	.83	5	.236	.278	.326
Cincinnati	NL	38	141	39	8	3	4	(2	2)	65	22	13	12	0	21	0	0	1	5	6	.45	4	.277	.331	.461
11 ML YEARS		1015	2483	655	123	22	44	(21	23)	954	297	264	165	10	432	11	21	16	66	41	.62	39	.264	.311	.384

Bob Howry

Pitches: Right **Bats:** Left **Pos:** RP-65　　　　**Ht:** 6'5" **Wt:** 215 **Born:** 8/4/73 **Age:** 27

		HOW MUCH HE PITCHED						WHAT HE GAVE UP											THE RESULTS						
Year Team	Lg	G	GS	CG	GF	IP	BFP	H	R	ER	HR	SH	SF	HB	TBB	IBB	SO	WP	Bk	W	L	Pct.	ShO	Sv-Op	Hld	ERA
1998 Chicago	AL	44	0	0	15	54.1	217	37	20	19	7	2	3	2	19	2	51	2	0	0	3	.000	0	9-11	19	3.15
1999 Chicago	AL	69	0	0	54	67.2	298	58	34	27	8	3	1	3	38	3	80	3	1	5	3	.625	0	28-34	1	3.59
2000 Chicago	AL	65	0	0	29	71	289	54	26	25	6	2	4	4	29	2	60	2	0	2	4	.333	0	7-12	14	3.17
3 ML YEARS		178	0	0	98	193	804	149	80	71	21	7	8	9	86	7	191	7	1	7	10	.412	0	44-57	34	3.31

Mike Hubbard

Bats: Right **Throws:** Right **Pos:** C-1; PH/PR-1　　　　**Ht:** 6'1" **Wt:** 205 **Born:** 2/16/71 **Age:** 30

					BATTING														BASERUNNING				PERCENTAGES		
Year Team	Lg	G	AB	H	2B	3B	HR	(Hm	Rd)	TB	R	RBI	TBB	IBB	SO	HBP	SH	SF	SB	CS	SB%	GDP	Avg	OBP	SLG
2000 Louisville *	AAA	8	8	3	1	0	0	—	—	4	1	0	1	0	4	0	0	0	0	0	—	0	.375	.444	.500
Richmond *	AAA	70	224	66	8	1	6	—	—	94	33	31	22	0	24	2	0	2	4	3	.57	6	.295	.360	.420
1995 Chicago	NL	15	23	4	0	0	0	(0	0)	4	2	1	2	0	2	0	0	0	0	0	—	1	.174	.240	.174
1996 Chicago	NL	21	38	4	0	0	1	(1	0)	7	1	4	0	0	15	0	0	0	0	0	—	1	.105	.103	.184
1997 Chicago	NL	29	64	13	0	0	1	(0	1)	16	4	2	2	1	21	0	0	0	0	0	—	1	.203	.227	.250
1998 Montreal	NL	32	55	8	1	0	1	(1	0)	12	3	3	0	0	17	1	0	0	0	0	—	0	.145	.161	.218
2000 Atlanta	NL	2	1	0	0	0	0	(0	0)	0	0	0	0	0	1	0	0	0	0	0	—	0	.000	.000	.000
5 ML YEARS		99	181	29	1	0	3	(2	1)	39	10	10	4	1	56	1	0	0	0	0	—	4	.160	.182	.215

Trenidad Hubbard

Bats: R **Throws:** R **Pos:** LF-47; PH/PR-40; RF-24; DH-6　　　　**Ht:** 5'9" **Wt:** 203 **Born:** 5/11/66 **Age:** 35

					BATTING														BASERUNNING				PERCENTAGES		
Year Team	Lg	G	AB	H	2B	3B	HR	(Hm	Rd)	TB	R	RBI	TBB	IBB	SO	HBP	SH	SF	SB	CS	SB%	GDP	Avg	OBP	SLG
1994 Colorado	NL	18	25	7	1	1	1	(1	0)	13	3	3	3	0	4	0	0	0	0	0	—	1	.280	.357	.520
1995 Colorado	NL	24	58	18	4	0	3	(2	1)	31	13	9	8	0	6	0	1	0	2	1	.67	2	.310	.394	.534
1996 Col-SF	NL	55	89	19	5	2	2	(2	0)	34	15	14	11	0	27	1	0	0	2	0	1.00	0	.213	.307	.382
1997 Cleveland	AL	7	12	3	1	0	0	(0	0)	4	3	0	1	0	3	0	0	0	2	0	1.00	0	.250	.308	.333
1998 Los Angeles	NL	94	208	62	9	1	7	(2	5)	94	29	18	18	0	46	3	3	3	9	5	.64	5	.298	.358	.452
1999 Los Angeles	NL	82	105	33	5	0	1	(0	1)	41	23	13	13	1	24	0	1	1	4	3	.57	2	.314	.387	.390
2000 Atl-Bal		92	108	20	2	2	1	(0	1)	29	18	6	11	0	23	1	3	0	4	2	.67	3	.185	.267	.269
1996 Colorado	NL	45	60	13	5	1	1	(1	0)	23	12	12	9	0	22	1	0	0	2	0	1.00	1	.217	.329	.383
San Francisco		10	29	6	0	1	1	(1	0)	11	3	2	2	0	5	0	0	0	0	0	—	2	.207	.258	.379
2000 Atlanta	NL	61	81	15	2	1	1	(0	1)	22	15	6	11	0	20	1	3	0	2	1	.67	1	.185	.290	.272
Baltimore	AL	31	27	5	0	1	0	(0	0)	7	3	0	0	0	3	0	0	0	2	1	.67	2	.185	.185	.259
7 ML YEARS		372	605	162	27	6	15	(7	8)	246	104	63	65	1	133	5	8	4	23	11	.68	16	.268	.342	.407

Tim Hudson

Pitches: Right **Bats:** Right **Pos:** SP-32　　　　**Ht:** 6'0" **Wt:** 160 **Born:** 7/14/75 **Age:** 25

		HOW MUCH HE PITCHED						WHAT HE GAVE UP											THE RESULTS						
Year Team	Lg	G	GS	CG	GF	IP	BFP	H	R	ER	HR	SH	SF	HB	TBB	IBB	SO	WP	Bk	W	L	Pct.	ShO	Sv-Op	Hld	ERA
1997 Sou Oregon	A-	8	4	0	1	28.2	111	12	8	8	0	0	1	1	15	2	37	3	2	3	1	.750	0	0- -	—	2.51
1998 Modesto	A+	8	5	0	2	37.2	150	19	10	7	0	2	0	2	18	0	48	2	1	4	0	1.000	0	0- -	—	1.67
Huntsville	AA	22	22	2	0	134.2	603	136	84	68	13	7	8	13	71	2	104	13	1	10	9	.526	0	0- -	—	4.54
1999 Midland	AA	3	3	0	0	18	63	9	1	1	0	1	0	0	3	0	18	0	0	3	0	1.000	0	0- -	—	0.50
Vancouver	AAA	8	8	0	0	49	202	38	16	12	2	1	0	1	21	0	61	2	0	4	0	1.000	0	0- -	—	2.20
1999 Oakland	AL	21	21	1	0	136.1	580	121	56	49	8	1	2	4	62	2	132	6	0	11	2	.846	0	0-0	0	3.23
2000 Oakland	AL	32	32	2	0	202.1	847	169	100	93	24	5	7	7	82	5	169	7	0	20	6	.769	2	0-0	0	4.14
2 ML YEARS		53	53	3	0	338.2	1427	290	156	142	32	6	9	11	144	7	301	13	0	31	8	.795	2	0-0	0	3.77

Aubrey Huff

Bats: Left **Throws:** Right **Pos:** 3B-37; PH/PR-3　　　　**Ht:** 6'4" **Wt:** 221 **Born:** 12/20/76 **Age:** 24

					BATTING														BASERUNNING				PERCENTAGES		
Year Team	Lg	G	AB	H	2B	3B	HR	(Hm	Rd)	TB	R	RBI	TBB	IBB	SO	HBP	SH	SF	SB	CS	SB%	GDP	Avg	OBP	SLG
1998 Chston-SC	A	69	265	85	19	1	13	—	—	145	38	54	24	0	40	0	0	5	3	1	.75	5	.321	.371	.547
1999 Orlando	AA	133	491	148	40	3	22	—	—	260	85	78	64	4	77	4	0	2	3	4	.40	14	.301	.385	.530
2000 Durham	AAA	108	408	129	36	3	20	—	—	231	73	76	51	4	72	2	2	1	2	3	.40	15	.316	.394	.566
2000 Tampa Bay	AL	39	122	35	7	0	4	(3	1)	54	12	14	5	1	18	1	0	1	0	0	—	6	.287	.318	.443

Todd Hundley

Bats: Both **Throws:** Right **Pos:** C-84; PH/PR-6; DH-1　　　　**Ht:** 5'11" **Wt:** 199 **Born:** 5/27/69 **Age:** 32

					BATTING														BASERUNNING				PERCENTAGES		
Year Team	Lg	G	AB	H	2B	3B	HR	(Hm	Rd)	TB	R	RBI	TBB	IBB	SO	HBP	SH	SF	SB	CS	SB%	GDP	Avg	OBP	SLG
2000 Albuquerque *	AAA	3	9	5	0	0	1	—	—	8	2	5	1	0	0	0	0	0	0	0	—	1	.556	.600	.889
1990 New York	NL	36	67	14	6	0	0	(0	0)	20	8	2	6	0	18	0	1	0	0	0	—	1	.209	.274	.299
1991 New York	NL	21	60	8	0	1	1	(1	0)	13	5	7	6	0	14	1	1	1	0	0	—	3	.133	.221	.217
1992 New York	NL	123	358	75	17	0	7	(2	5)	113	32	32	19	4	76	4	7	2	3	0	1.00	8	.209	.256	.316
1993 New York	NL	130	417	95	17	2	11	(5	6)	149	40	53	23	7	62	2	2	4	1	1	.50	10	.228	.269	.357
1994 New York	NL	91	291	69	10	1	16	(8	8)	129	45	42	25	4	73	3	3	1	2	1	.67	8	.237	.303	.443
1995 New York	NL	90	275	77	11	0	15	(6	9)	133	39	51	42	5	64	5	1	3	1	0	1.00	4	.280	.382	.484

Year Team	Lg	G	AB	H	2B	3B	HR	(Hm	Rd)	TB	R	RBI	TBB	IBB	SO	HBP	SH	SF	SB	CS	SB%	GDP	Avg	OBP	SLG
1996 New York	NL	153	540	140	32	1	41	(20	21)	297	85	112	79	15	146	3	0	2	1	3	.25	9	.259	.356	.550
1997 New York	NL	132	417	114	21	2	30	(14	16)	229	78	86	83	16	116	3	0	5	2	3	.40	10	.273	.394	.549
1998 New York	NL	53	124	20	4	0	3	(1	2)	33	8	12	16	0	55	1	0	1	1	1	.50	0	.161	.261	.266
1999 Los Angeles	NL	114	376	78	14	0	24	(10	14)	164	49	55	44	3	113	4	1	3	3	0	1.00	5	.207	.295	.436
2000 Los Angeles	NL	90	299	85	16	0	24	(10	14)	173	49	70	45	6	69	2	1	6	0	1	.00	5	.284	.375	.579
11 ML YEARS		1033	3224	775	148	7	172	(77	95)	1453	438	522	388	60	806	28	17	28	14	10	.58	58	.240	.325	.451

Brian Hunter

Bats: R **Throws:** L **Pos:** PH/PR-51; 1B-40; LF-6; RF-3; DH-1 **Ht:** 6'0" **Wt:** 195 **Born:** 3/4/68 **Age:** 33

Year Team	Lg	G	AB	H	2B	3B	HR	(Hm	Rd)	TB	R	RBI	TBB	IBB	SO	HBP	SH	SF	SB	CS	SB%	GDP	Avg	OBP	SLG
2000 Richmond *	AAA	2	8	1	0	0	1	—	—	4	2	1	1	0	1	0	0	0	1	0	1.00	1	.125	.222	.500
1991 Atlanta	NL	97	271	68	16	1	12	(7	5)	122	32	50	17	0	48	1	0	2	0	2	.00	6	.251	.296	.450
1992 Atlanta	NL	102	238	57	13	2	14	(9	5)	116	34	41	21	3	50	0	1	8	1	2	.33	2	.239	.292	.487
1993 Atlanta	NL	37	80	11	3	1	0	(0	0)	16	4	8	2	1	15	0	0	0	0	0	—	1	.138	.153	.200
1994 Pit-Cin	NL	85	256	60	16	1	15	(4	11)	123	34	57	17	2	56	0	0	3	0	0	—	3	.234	.277	.480
1995 Cincinnati	NL	40	79	17	6	0	1	(0	1)	26	9	9	11	1	21	1	0	5	2	1	.67	0	.215	.312	.329
1996 Seattle	AL	75	198	53	10	0	7	(2	5)	84	21	28	15	2	43	4	1	3	0	1	.00	6	.268	.327	.424
1998 St. Louis	NL	62	112	23	9	1	4	(2	2)	46	11	13	7	0	23	1	3	0	1	1	.50	6	.205	.258	.411
1999 Atlanta	NL	114	181	45	12	1	6	(2	4)	77	28	30	31	1	40	4	5	2	0	1	.00	6	.249	.367	.425
2000 Atl-Phi		87	140	30	5	0	8	(4	4)	59	14	23	20	1	39	0	0	0	1	0	1.00	2	.214	.313	.421
1994 Pittsburgh	NL	76	233	53	15	1	11	(4	7)	103	28	47	15	2	55	0	0	4	0	0	—	3	.227	.270	.442
Cincinnati	NL	9	23	7	1	0	4	(0	4)	20	6	10	2	0	1	0	0	1	0	0	—	0	.304	.346	.870
2000 Atlanta	NL	2	2	1	0	0	1	(1	0)	4	1	1	0	0	0	0	0	0	0	0	—	0	.500	.500	2.000
Philadelphia	NL	85	138	29	5	0	7	(3	4)	55	13	22	20	1	39	0	0	0	1	0	1.00	2	.210	.310	.399
9 ML YEARS		699	1555	364	90	7	67	(30	37)	669	187	259	141	11	335	11	10	25	4	9	.31	32	.234	.298	.430

Brian L. Hunter

Bats: R **Throws:** R **Pos:** CF-50; LF-36; PH/PR-30; RF-13 **Ht:** 6'3" **Wt:** 180 **Born:** 3/5/71 **Age:** 30

Year Team	Lg	G	AB	H	2B	3B	HR	(Hm	Rd)	TB	R	RBI	TBB	IBB	SO	HBP	SH	SF	SB	CS	SB%	GDP	Avg	OBP	SLG
1994 Houston	NL	6	24	6	1	0	0	(0	0)	7	2	0	1	0	6	0	1	0	2	1	.67	0	.250	.280	.292
1995 Houston	NL	78	321	97	14	5	2	(0	2)	127	52	28	21	0	52	2	2	3	24	7	.77	2	.302	.346	.396
1996 Houston	NL	132	526	145	27	2	5	(1	4)	191	74	35	17	0	92	2	1	7	35	9	.80	6	.276	.297	.363
1997 Detroit	AL	162	658	177	29	7	4	(2	2)	232	112	45	66	1	121	1	8	5	74	18	.80	13	.269	.334	.353
1998 Detroit	AL	142	595	151	29	3	4	(1	3)	198	67	36	36	0	94	2	2	1	42	12	.78	8	.254	.298	.333
1999 Det-Sea	AL	139	539	125	13	6	4	(0	4)	162	79	34	37	0	91	2	3	4	44	8	.85	8	.232	.280	.301
2000 Col-Cin	NL	104	240	64	5	1	1	(1	0)	74	47	14	27	0	40	1	5	1	20	3	.87	2	.267	.342	.308
1999 Detroit	AL	18	55	13	2	1	0	(0	0)	17	8	0	5	0	11	1	1	0	0	3	.00	1	.236	.311	.309
Seattle		121	484	112	11	5	4	(0	4)	145	71	34	32	0	80	1	3	7	44	5	.90	8	.231	.277	.300
2000 Colorado	NL	72	200	55	4	1	1	(1	0)	64	36	13	21	0	31	1	4	0	15	3	.83	2	.275	.347	.320
Cincinnati		32	40	9	1	0	0	(0	0)	10	11	1	6	0	9	0	1	1	5	0	1.00	0	.225	.319	.250
7 ML YEARS		763	2903	765	118	24	20	(5	15)	991	433	192	205	1	496	10	23	24	241	58	.81	39	.264	.312	.341

Torii Hunter

Bats: Right **Throws:** Right **Pos:** CF-98; PH/PR-3; LF-1 **Ht:** 6'2" **Wt:** 205 **Born:** 7/18/75 **Age:** 25

Year Team	Lg	G	AB	H	2B	3B	HR	(Hm	Rd)	TB	R	RBI	TBB	IBB	SO	HBP	SH	SF	SB	CS	SB%	GDP	Avg	OBP	SLG
2000 Salt Lake *	AAA	55	209	77	17	2	18	—	—	152	58	61	11	0	28	3	1	3	11	3	.79	4	.368	.403	.727
1997 Minnesota	AL	1	0	0	0	0	0	(0	0)	0	0	0	0	0	0	0	0	0	0	0	—	0	—	—	—
1998 Minnesota	AL	6	17	4	1	0	0	(0	0)	5	0	2	2	0	6	0	0	0	0	1	.00	1	.235	.316	.294
1999 Minnesota	AL	135	384	98	17	2	9	(2	7)	146	52	35	26	1	72	6	1	5	10	6	.63	9	.255	.309	.380
2000 Minnesota	AL	99	336	94	14	5	5	(4	1)	137	44	44	18	2	68	2	0	2	4	3	.57	13	.280	.318	.408
4 ML YEARS		241	737	196	32	9	14	(6	8)	288	96	81	46	3	146	8	1	7	14	10	.58	23	.266	.313	.391

Butch Huskey

Bats: R **Throws:** R **Pos:** DH-39; RF-23; PH/PR-23; 1B-17; LF-15 **Ht:** 6'3" **Wt:** 244 **Born:** 11/10/71 **Age:** 29

Year Team	Lg	G	AB	H	2B	3B	HR	(Hm	Rd)	TB	R	RBI	TBB	IBB	SO	HBP	SH	SF	SB	CS	SB%	GDP	Avg	OBP	SLG
2000 Salt Lake *	AAA	2	9	3	0	0	2	—	—	9	2	5	1	0	2	0	0	0	0	0	—	0	.333	.400	1.000
1993 New York	NL	13	41	6	1	0	0	(0	0)	7	2	3	1	1	13	0	0	2	0	0	—	0	.146	.159	.171
1995 New York	NL	28	90	17	1	0	3	(2	1)	27	8	11	10	0	16	0	1	1	1	0	1.00	3	.189	.267	.300
1996 New York	NL	118	414	115	16	2	15	(9	6)	180	43	60	27	3	77	0	0	4	1	0	1.00	3	.278	.319	.435
1997 New York	NL	142	471	135	26	2	24	(7	17)	237	61	81	25	5	84	1	0	8	8	5	.62	21	.287	.319	.503
1998 New York	NL	113	369	93	18	0	13	(4	9)	150	43	59	26	3	66	1	2	4	7	6	.54	13	.252	.300	.407
1999 Sea-Bos	AL	119	386	109	15	0	22	(9	13)	190	62	77	34	1	65	0	0	3	3	1	.75	9	.282	.338	.492
2000 Min-Col		109	307	80	21	0	9	(6	3)	128	40	45	41	2	63	2	0	6	1	3	.25	10	.261	.346	.417
1999 Seattle	AL	74	262	76	9	0	15	(7	8)	130	44	49	27	0	45	0	0	3	3	0	1.00	6	.290	.353	.496
Boston		45	124	33	6	0	7	(2	5)	60	18	28	7	1	20	0	0	0	0	1	.00	3	.266	.305	.484
2000 Minnesota	AL	64	215	48	13	0	5	(4	1)	76	22	27	25	1	49	2	0	3	0	2	.00	5	.223	.306	.353
Colorado	NL	45	92	32	8	0	4	(2	2)	52	18	18	16	1	14	0	0	3	1	1	.50	5	.348	.432	.565
7 ML YEARS		642	2078	555	98	4	86	(37	49)	919	259	336	164	15	384	4	3	28	21	17	.55	66	.267	.318	.442

Jeff Huson

Bats: L **Throws:** R **Pos:** PH/PR-28; 3B-18; 2B-17; SS-17; 1B-1 **Ht:** 6'3" **Wt:** 180 **Born:** 8/15/64 **Age:** 36

Year Team	Lg	G	AB	H	2B	3B	HR	(Hm	Rd)	TB	R	RBI	TBB	IBB	SO	HBP	SH	SF	SB	CS	SB%	GDP	Avg	OBP	SLG
1988 Montreal	NL	20	42	13	2	0	0	(0	0)	15	7	3	4	2	3	0	0	0	2	1	.67	2	.310	.370	.357

Year Team	Lg	G	AB	H	2B	3B	HR	(Hm	Rd)	TB	R	RBI	TBB	IBB	SO	HBP	SH	SF	SB	CS	SB%	GDP	Avg	OBP	SLG
1989 Montreal	NL	32	74	12	5	0	0	(0	0)	17	1	2	6	3	6	0	3	0	3	0	1.00	6	.162	.225	.230
1990 Texas	AL	145	396	95	12	2	0	(0	0)	111	57	28	46	0	54	2	7	3	12	4	.75	8	.240	.320	.280
1991 Texas	AL	119	268	57	8	3	2	(1	1)	77	36	26	39	0	32	0	9	1	8	3	.73	6	.213	.312	.287
1992 Texas	AL	123	318	83	14	3	4	(0	4)	115	49	24	41	2	43	1	8	6	18	6	.75	7	.261	.342	.362
1993 Texas	AL	23	45	6	1	1	0	(0	0)	9	3	2	0	0	10	0	1	0	0	0	—	0	.133	.133	.200
1995 Baltimore	AL	66	161	40	4	2	1	(0	1)	51	24	19	15	1	20	1	2	1	5	4	.56	4	.248	.315	.317
1996 Baltimore	AL	17	28	9	1	0	0	(0	0)	10	5	2	1	0	3	0	0	1	0	0	—	0	.321	.333	.357
1997 Milwaukee	AL	84	143	29	3	0	0	(0	0)	32	12	11	5	0	15	2	2	1	3	0	1.00	7	.203	.238	.224
1998 Seattle	AL	31	49	8	1	0	1	(0	0)	12	8	4	5	0	6	0	0	0	1	1	.50	0	.163	.241	.245
1999 Anaheim	AL	97	225	59	7	1	0	(0	0)	68	21	18	16	0	27	0	1	3	10	1	.91	9	.262	.307	.302
2000 Chicago	NL	70	130	28	7	1	0	(0	0)	37	19	11	13	1	9	0	1	0	2	1	.67	6	.215	.287	.285
12 ML YEARS		827	1879	439	65	13	8	(1	7)	554	242	150	191	9	228	6	34	16	64	21	.75	55	.234	.304	.295

Adam Hyzdu

Bats: Right **Throws:** Right **Pos:** PH/PR-8; RF-4; LF-1   **Ht:** 6'2" **Wt:** 220 **Born:** 12/6/71 **Age:** 29

Year Team	Lg	G	AB	H	2B	3B	HR	(Hm	Rd)	TB	R	RBI	TBB	IBB	SO	HBP	SH	SF	SB	CS	SB%	GDP	Avg	OBP	SLG
1990 Everett	A-	69	253	62	16	1	6	—	—	98	31	34	28	1	78	2	0	5	2	4	.33	4	.245	.319	.387
1991 Clinton	A	124	410	96	14	5	5	—	—	135	47	50	64	1	131	3	7	2	4	5	.44	10	.234	.340	.329
1992 San Jose	A+	128	457	127	25	5	9	—	—	189	60	60	55	4	134	1	1	8	10	5	.67	6	.278	.351	.414
1993 San Jose	A+	44	165	48	11	3	13	—	—	104	35	38	29	0	53	0	1	2	1	1	.50	3	.291	.393	.630
Shreveport	AA	86	302	61	17	0	6	—	—	96	30	25	20	2	82	1	1	1	0	5	.00	5	.202	.253	.318
1994 Winston-Sal	A+	55	210	58	11	1	15	—	—	116	30	39	18	0	33	2	0	2	1	5	.17	3	.276	.336	.552
Chattanooga	AA	38	133	35	10	0	3	—	—	54	17	9	8	0	21	1	1	0	0	2	.00	1	.263	.310	.406
Indianapols	AAA	12	25	3	2	0	0	—	—	5	3	3	1	0	5	0	0	2	0	0	—	0	.120	.143	.200
1995 Chattanooga	AA	102	312	82	14	1	13	—	—	137	55	48	45	2	56	4	2	1	3	2	.60	4	.263	.362	.439
1996 Trenton	AA	109	374	126	24	3	25	—	—	231	71	80	56	6	75	2	0	2	1	8	.11	7	.337	.424	.618
1997 Pawtucket	AAA	119	413	114	21	1	23	—	—	206	77	84	72	0	113	4	1	2	10	6	.63	6	.276	.387	.499
1998 Tucson	AAA	34	100	34	7	1	4	—	—	55	21	14	15	0	23	0	1	2	0	1	.00	2	.340	.419	.550
1999 Pawtucket	AAA	12	35	8	0	0	1	—	--	11	4	6	4	0	13	0	0	0	0	0	—	1	.229	.308	.314
Altoona	AA	91	345	109	26	2	24	—	—	211	64	78	40	1	62	3	0	0	8	4	.67	3	.316	.392	.612
Nashville	AAA	14	44	11	1	0	5	—	—	27	6	13	4	0	11	0	0	0	0	0	—	0	.250	.313	.614
2000 Altoona	AA	142	514	149	39	2	31	—	—	285	96	106	94	7	102	8	0	3	3	7	.30	6	.290	.405	.554
2000 Pittsburgh	NL	12	18	7	2	0	1	(0	1)	12	2	4	0	0	4	0	0	0	0	0	—	0	.389	.389	.667

Raul Ibanez

Bats: L **Throws:** R **Pos:** RF-44; LF-35; PH/PR-27; DH-4; 1B-3   **Ht:** 6'2" **Wt:** 200 **Born:** 6/2/72 **Age:** 29

Year Team	Lg	G	AB	H	2B	3B	HR	(Hm	Rd)	TB	R	RBI	TBB	IBB	SO	HBP	SH	SF	SB	CS	SB%	GDP	Avg	OBP	SLG
2000 Tacoma *	AAA	10	40	10	4	0	0	—	—	14	3	6	1	0	3	0	0	0	0	0	—	0	.250	.268	.350
1996 Seattle	AL	4	5	0	0	0	0	(0	0)	0	0	0	0	0	1	1	0	0	0	0	—	0	.000	.167	.000
1997 Seattle	AL	11	26	4	0	1	1	(1	0)	9	3	4	0	0	6	0	0	0	0	0	—	0	.154	.154	.346
1998 Seattle	AL	37	98	25	7	1	2	(1	1)	40	12	12	5	0	22	0	0	0	0	0	—	4	.255	.291	.408
1999 Seattle	AL	87	209	54	7	0	9	(3	6)	88	23	27	17	1	32	0	0	1	5	1	.83	4	.258	.313	.421
2000 Seattle	AL	92	140	32	8	0	2	(2	0)	46	21	15	14	1	25	1	0	1	2	0	1.00	1	.229	.301	.329
5 ML YEARS		231	478	115	22	2	14	(7	7)	183	59	58	36	2	86	2	0	2	7	1	.88	9	.241	.295	.383

Hideki Irabu

Pitches: Right **Bats:** Right **Pos:** SP-11   **Ht:** 6'4" **Wt:** 240 **Born:** 5/5/69 **Age:** 32

		HOW MUCH HE PITCHED					WHAT HE GAVE UP										THE RESULTS						
Year Team	Lg	G	GS	CG	GF	IP	BFP	H	R	ER	HR	SH	SF	HB	TBB	IBB	SO	WP	Bk	W	L	Pct.	ShO	Sv-Op	Hld	ERA
2000 Jupiter *	A+	2	2	0	0	8.2	34	7	1	1	0	0	0	1	0	9	0	0	1	0	1.000	0	0--	—	1.04
Ottawa *	AAA	1	1	0	0	5.2	23	5	2	2	1	0	0	0	2	0	6	0	0	1	0	.000	0	0--	—	3.18
1997 New York	AL	13	9	0	0	53.1	246	69	47	42	15	1	2	1	20	0	56	4	3	5	4	.556	0	0-0	1	7.09
1998 New York	AL	29	28	2	0	173	732	148	79	78	27	6	6	9	76	1	126	6	1	13	9	.591	1	0-0	0	4.06
1999 New York	AL	32	27	2	2	169.1	733	180	98	91	26	2	4	6	46	0	133	7	0	11	7	.611	1	0-0	0	4.84
2000 Montreal	NL	11	11	0	0	54.2	247	77	45	44	9	3	2	1	14	0	42	5	2	2	5	.286	0	0-0	0	7.24
4 ML YEARS		85	75	4	2	450.1	1958	474	269	255	77	12	14	17	156	1	357	22	6	31	25	.554	2	0-0	1	5.10

Jason Isringhausen

Pitches: Right **Bats:** Right **Pos:** RP-66   **Ht:** 6'3" **Wt:** 210 **Born:** 9/7/72 **Age:** 28

		HOW MUCH HE PITCHED					WHAT HE GAVE UP										THE RESULTS						
Year Team	Lg	G	GS	CG	GF	IP	BFP	H	R	ER	HR	SH	SF	HB	TBB	IBB	SO	WP	Bk	W	L	Pct.	ShO	Sv-Op	Hld	ERA
1995 New York	NL	14	14	1	0	93	385	88	29	29	6	3	3	2	31	2	55	4	1	9	2	.818	0	0-0	0	2.81
1996 New York	NL	27	27	2	0	171.2	766	190	103	91	13	7	9	8	73	5	114	14	0	6	14	.300	1	0-0	0	4.77
1997 New York	NL	6	6	0	0	29.2	145	42	27	25	3	1	2	1	22	0	25	3	0	2	2	.500	0	0-0	0	7.58
1999 NYM-Oak		33	5	0	20	64.2	286	64	35	34	9	0	1	3	34	4	51	4	0	1	4	.200	0	9-9	0	4.73
2000 Oakland	AL	66	0	0	57	69	304	67	34	29	6	2	1	0	32	5	57	5	1	6	4	.600	0	33-40	0	3.78
1999 New York	NL	13	5	0	2	39.1	179	43	29	28	7	0	1	2	22	2	31	2	0	1	3	.250	0	1-1	0	6.41
Oakland	AL	20	0	0	18	25.1	107	21	6	6	2	0	0	1	12	2	20	2	0	0	1	.000	0	8-8	0	2.13
5 ML YEARS		146	52	3	77	428	1886	449	228	208	37	13	16	17	192	16	302	30	2	24	26	.480	1	42-49	0	4.37

Damian Jackson

Bats: R **Throws:** R **Pos:** SS-88; 2B-36; LF-17; PH/PR-9   **Ht:** 5'11" **Wt:** 185 **Born:** 8/16/73 **Age:** 27

Year Team	Lg	G	AB	H	2B	3B	HR	(Hm	Rd)	TB	R	RBI	TBB	IBB	SO	HBP	SH	SF	SB	CS	SB%	GDP	Avg	OBP	SLG
1996 Cleveland	AL	5	10	3	2	0	0	(0	0)	5	2	1	1	0	4	0	0	0	0	0	—	0	.300	.364	.500
1997 Cle-Cin		20	36	7	2	1	1	(0	1)	14	8	2	4	1	8	1	1	0	2	1	.67	0	.194	.293	.389

101

Year Team	Lg	BATTING																	BASERUNNING				PERCENTAGES		
		G	AB	H	2B	3B	HR	(Hm	Rd)	TB	R	RBI	TBB	IBB	SO	HBP	SH	SF	SB	CS	SB%	GDP	Avg	OBP	SLG
1998 Cincinnati	NL	13	38	12	5	0	0	(0	0)	17	4	7	6	0	0	0	1	1	2	0	1.00	1	.316	.400	.447
1999 San Diego	NL	133	388	87	20	2	9	(6	3)	138	56	39	53	3	105	3	0	3	34	10	.77	2	.224	.320	.356
2000 San Diego	NL	138	470	120	27	6	6	(5	1)	177	68	37	62	2	108	3	4	2	28	6	.82	7	.255	.345	.377
1997 Cleveland	AL	8	9	1	0	0	0	(0	0)	1	2	0	0	0	1	1	0	0	1	0	1.00	0	.111	.200	.111
Cincinnati	NL	12	27	6	2	1	1	(0	1)	13	6	2	4	1	7	0	1	0	1	1	.50	0	.222	.323	.481
5 ML YEARS		309	942	229	56	9	16	(11	5)	351	138	86	126	6	229	7	5	6	66	17	.80	10	.243	.335	.373

Mike Jackson

Pitches: Right **Bats:** Right **Pos:** RP **Ht:** 6'2" **Wt:** 225 **Born:** 12/22/64 **Age:** 36

Year Team	Lg	HOW MUCH HE PITCHED						WHAT HE GAVE UP											THE RESULTS						
		G	GS	CG	GF	IP	BFP	H	R	ER	HR	SH	SF	HB	TBB	IBB	SO	WP	Bk	W	L	Pct.	ShO	Sv-Op	Hld	ERA
1986 Philadelphia	NL	9	0	0	4	13.1	54	12	5	5	2	0	0	2	4	1	3	0	0	0	0	—	0	0-1	0	3.38
1987 Philadelphia	NL	55	7	0	8	109.1	468	88	55	51	16	3	4	3	56	6	93	6	8	3	10	.231	0	1-2	6	4.20
1988 Seattle	AL	62	0	0	29	99.1	412	74	37	29	10	3	10	2	43	10	76	6	6	6	5	.545	0	4-11	10	2.63
1989 Seattle	AL	65	0	0	27	99.1	431	81	43	35	8	6	2	6	54	6	94	1	2	4	6	.400	0	7-10	9	3.17
1990 Seattle	AL	63	0	0	28	77.1	338	64	42	39	8	8	5	2	44	12	69	9	2	5	7	.417	0	3-12	13	4.54
1991 Seattle	AL	72	0	0	35	88.2	363	64	35	32	5	4	5	6	34	11	74	3	0	7	7	.500	0	14-22	9	3.25
1992 San Francisco	NL	67	0	0	24	82	346	76	35	34	7	5	2	4	33	10	80	1	0	6	6	.500	0	2-3	9	3.73
1993 San Francisco	NL	81	0	0	17	77.1	317	58	28	26	7	4	2	3	24	6	70	2	2	6	6	.500	0	1-6	34	3.03
1994 San Francisco	NL	36	0	0	12	42.1	158	23	8	7	4	4	1	2	11	0	51	0	0	3	2	.600	0	4-6	9	1.49
1995 Cincinnati	NL	40	0	0	10	49	200	38	13	13	5	1	1	1	19	1	41	1	1	6	1	.857	0	2-4	5	2.39
1996 Seattle	AL	73	0	0	23	72	302	61	32	29	11	0	1	6	24	3	70	2	0	1	1	.500	0	6-8	15	3.63
1997 Cleveland	AL	71	0	0	38	75	313	59	33	27	3	3	3	4	29	5	74	2	0	2	5	.286	0	15-17	14	3.24
1998 Cleveland	AL	69	0	0	57	64	239	43	11	11	4	1	0	4	13	0	55	1	3	1	1	.500	0	40-45	1	1.55
1999 Memphis	AL	72	0	0	65	68.2	291	60	32	31	11	2	2	2	26	1	55	0	1	3	4	.429	0	39-43	0	4.06
14 ML YEARS		835	7	0	377	1017.2	4232	801	409	369	101	44	33	47	414	72	905	34	25	53	61	.465	0	138-190	138	3.26

Tom Jacquez

Pitches: Left **Bats:** Left **Pos:** RP-9 **Ht:** 6'2" **Wt:** 195 **Born:** 12/29/75 **Age:** 25

Year Team	Lg	HOW MUCH HE PITCHED						WHAT HE GAVE UP											THE RESULTS						
		G	GS	CG	GF	IP	BFP	H	R	ER	HR	SH	SF	HB	TBB	IBB	SO	WP	Bk	W	L	Pct.	ShO	Sv-Op	Hld	ERA
1997 Batavia	A-	4	4	0	0	22.1	93	20	6	6	0	0	2	3	2	0	20	0	0	2	1	.667	0	0- -	—	2.42
Piedmont	A	8	8	0	0	41.2	183	45	29	23	2	2	3	3	13	0	26	1	0	2	4	.333	0	0- -	—	4.97
1998 Clearwater	A+	29	28	2	0	169.2	740	215	102	81	12	6	9	6	31	3	108	5	4	9	11	.450	1	0- -	—	4.30
1999 Reading	AA	38	14	0	8	122.2	555	149	84	72	20	3	2	11	32	1	68	1	0	6	5	.545	0	1- -	—	5.28
Scrantn-WB	AAA	3	0	0	1	3.2	15	4	1	1	0	0	0	0	0	0	4	0	0	0	1	.000	0	0- -	—	2.45
2000 Reading	AA	13	0	0	8	27.1	115	26	11	9	2	2	0	0	9	0	21	1	0	0	3	.000	0	3- -	—	2.96
Scrantn-WB	AAA	35	1	0	8	54.2	229	53	15	12	3	2	4	3	20	1	34	1	0	5	1	.833	0	1- -	—	1.98
2000 Philadelphia	NL	9	0	0	2	7.1	34	10	9	9	2	0	1	0	3	1	6	0	0	0	0		0	1-1	2	11.05

John Jaha

Bats: Right **Throws:** Right **Pos:** DH-30; PH/PR-3 **Ht:** 6'1" **Wt:** 224 **Born:** 5/27/66 **Age:** 35

Year Team	Lg	BATTING																	BASERUNNING				PERCENTAGES		
		G	AB	H	2B	3B	HR	(Hm	Rd)	TB	R	RBI	TBB	IBB	SO	HBP	SH	SF	SB	CS	SB%	GDP	Avg	OBP	SLG
2000 Sacramento *	AAA	3	9	4	1	0	0	—	—	5	0	2	4	2	2	0	0	0	0	0	—	0	.444	.615	.556
Modesto *	A+	1	2	0	0	0	0	—	—	0	0	2	0	1	0	0	0	0	0	0	—	0	.000	.500	.000
1992 Milwaukee	AL	47	133	30	3	1	2	(1	1)	41	17	10	12	1	30	2	1	4	10	0	1.00	1	.226	.291	.308
1993 Milwaukee	AL	153	515	136	21	0	19	(5	14)	214	78	70	51	4	109	8	4	4	13	9	.59	6	.264	.337	.416
1994 Milwaukee	AL	84	291	70	14	0	12	(5	7)	120	45	39	32	3	75	10	1	4	3	3	.50	8	.241	.332	.412
1995 Milwaukee	AL	88	316	99	20	2	20	(8	12)	183	59	65	36	0	66	4	0	1	2	1	.67	8	.313	.389	.579
1996 Milwaukee	AL	148	543	163	28	1	34	(17	17)	295	108	118	85	1	118	5	0	3	3	1	.75	16	.300	.398	.543
1997 Milwaukee	AL	46	162	40	7	0	11	(1	10)	80	25	26	25	1	40	3	0	2	1	0	1.00	5	.247	.354	.494
1998 Milwaukee	NL	73	216	45	6	1	7	(2	5)	74	29	38	49	3	66	6	0	2	1	3	.25	5	.208	.366	.343
1999 Oakland	AL	142	457	126	23	0	35	(18	17)	254	93	111	101	2	129	9	0	3	4	0	1.00	14	.276	.414	.556
2000 Oakland	AL	33	97	17	1	0	1	(0	1)	21	14	5	33	0	38	3	0	0	1	0	1.00	4	.175	.398	.216
9 ML YEARS		814	2730	726	123	5	141	(57	84)	1282	468	482	424	15	671	50	6	23	36	17	.68	68	.266	.372	.470

Mike James

Pitches: Right **Bats:** Right **Pos:** RP-51 **Ht:** 6'3" **Wt:** 205 **Born:** 8/15/67 **Age:** 33

Year Team	Lg	HOW MUCH HE PITCHED						WHAT HE GAVE UP											THE RESULTS						
		G	GS	CG	GF	IP	BFP	H	R	ER	HR	SH	SF	HB	TBB	IBB	SO	WP	Bk	W	L	Pct.	ShO	Sv-Op	Hld	ERA
2000 Memphis *	AAA	8	0	0	1	9.2	39	6	3	1	1	0	0	1	4	0	8	1	0	2	1	.667	0	1- -	—	0.93
1995 California	AL	46	0	0	11	55.2	237	49	27	24	6	2	0	3	26	2	36	1	0	3	0	1.000	0	1-2	3	3.88
1996 California	AL	69	0	0	23	81	353	62	27	24	7	6	5	10	42	7	65	5	0	5	5	.500	0	1-6	18	2.67
1997 Anaheim	AL	58	0	0	22	62.2	284	69	32	30	3	6	1	5	28	4	57	1	0	5	5	.500	0	7-13	12	4.31
1998 Anaheim	AL	11	0	0	3	14	55	10	3	3	0	0	0	0	7	0	12	1	0	0	0		0	0-0	2	1.93
2000 St. Louis	NL	51	0	0	10	51.1	213	40	22	18	7	2	1	3	24	2	41	2	0	2	2	.500	0	2-5	12	3.16
5 ML YEARS		235	0	0	69	264.2	1142	230	111	99	23	16	7	21	127	15	211	9	0	15	12	.556	0	11-26	47	3.37

Kevin Jarvis

Pitches: Right **Bats:** Left **Pos:** SP-19; RP-5 **Ht:** 6'2" **Wt:** 200 **Born:** 8/1/69 **Age:** 31

Year Team	Lg	HOW MUCH HE PITCHED						WHAT HE GAVE UP											THE RESULTS						
		G	GS	CG	GF	IP	BFP	H	R	ER	HR	SH	SF	HB	TBB	IBB	SO	WP	Bk	W	L	Pct.	ShO	Sv-Op	Hld	ERA
2000 Colo Spmgs *	AAA	7	7	0	0	39	145	18	6	3	1	1	1	0	13	0	18	3	0	3	2	.600	0	0- -	—	0.69
1994 Cincinnati	NL	6	3	0	0	17.2	79	22	14	14	4	1	0	0	5	0	10	1	0	1	1	.500	0	0-0	0	7.13
1995 Cincinnati	NL	19	11	1	2	79	354	91	56	50	13	2	5	3	32	2	33	0	2	3	4	.429	1	0-0	0	5.70
1996 Cincinnati	NL	24	20	2	2	120.1	552	152	93	80	17	6	2	2	43	5	63	2	0	8	9	.471	1	0-0	0	5.98
1997 Cin-Min-Det		32	5	0	13	68	329	99	62	58	17	4	1	1	29	0	48	4	0	0	4	.000	0	1-1	0	7.68

102

	HOW MUCH HE PITCHED						WHAT HE GAVE UP										THE RESULTS					
Year Team	Lg	G	GS	CG	GF	IP	BFP	H	R	ER	HR	SH	SF	HB	TBB	IBB	SO	WP	Bk	W	L	Pct.	ShO	Sv-Op	Hld	ERA
1999 Oakland	AL	4	1	0	0	14	75	28	19	18	6	0	1	1	6	0	11	0	0	0	1	.000	0	0-0	0	11.57
2000 Colorado	NL	24	19	0	0	115	505	138	83	76	26	6	2	4	33	3	60	2	0	3	4	.429	0	0-0	0	5.95
1997 Cincinnati	NL	9	0	0	3	13.1	70	21	16	15	4	1	0	1	7	0	12	2	0	0	1	.000	0	1-1	0	10.13
Minnesota	AL	6	2	0	1	13	70	23	18	18	4	0	0	0	8	0	9	2	0	0	0	—	0	0-0	0	12.46
Detroit	AL	17	3	0	9	41.2	189	55	28	25	9	1	1	0	14	0	27	0	0	0	3	.000	0	0-0	0	5.40
6 ML YEARS		109	59	3	17	414	1894	530	327	296	83	17	11	11	148	10	225	12	0	15	23	.395	2	1-1	0	6.43

Stan Javier

Bats: B **Throws:** R **Pos:** LF-46; RF-38; PH/PR-23; CF-14; DH-4; 1B-3 **Ht:** 6'0" **Wt:** 200 **Born:** 1/9/64 **Age:** 37

	BATTING																BASERUNNING				PERCENTAGES		
Year Team	Lg	G	AB	H	2B	3B	HR	(Hm | Rd)	TB	R	RBI	TBB	IBB	SO	HBP	SH	SF	SB	CS	SB%	GDP	Avg	OBP	SLG
1984 New York	AL	7	7	1	0	0	0	(0 | 0)	1	1	0	0	0	1	0	0	0	0	0	—	0	.143	.143	.143
1986 Oakland	AL	59	114	23	8	0	0	(0 | 0)	31	13	8	16	0	27	1	0	0	8	0	1.00	1	.202	.305	.272
1987 Oakland	AL	81	151	28	3	1	2	(1 | 1)	39	22	9	19	3	33	0	6	0	3	2	.60	2	.185	.276	.258
1988 Oakland	AL	125	397	102	13	3	2	(0 | 2)	127	49	35	32	1	63	2	6	3	20	1	.95	13	.257	.313	.320
1989 Oakland	AL	112	310	77	12	3	1	(0 | 1)	98	42	28	31	1	45	1	4	2	12	2	.86	6	.248	.317	.316
1990 Oak-LA		123	309	92	9	6	3	(1 | 2)	122	60	27	40	2	50	0	6	2	15	7	.68	6	.298	.376	.395
1991 Los Angeles	NL	121	176	36	5	3	1	(0 | 1)	50	21	11	16	0	36	0	3	2	7	1	.88	4	.205	.268	.284
1992 LA-Phi		130	334	83	17	1	1	(1 | 0)	105	42	29	37	2	54	3	3	2	18	3	.86	4	.249	.327	.314
1993 California	AL	92	237	69	10	4	3	(0 | 3)	96	33	28	27	1	33	1	1	3	12	2	.86	7	.291	.362	.405
1994 Oakland	AL	109	419	114	23	0	10	(1 | 9)	167	75	44	49	1	76	2	7	3	24	7	.77	7	.272	.349	.399
1995 Oakland	AL	130	442	123	20	2	8	(3 | 5)	171	81	56	49	3	63	4	5	4	36	5	.88	8	.278	.353	.387
1996 San Francisco	NL	71	274	74	25	0	2	(1 | 1)	105	44	22	25	0	51	2	5	0	14	2	.88	4	.270	.336	.383
1997 San Francisco	NL	142	440	126	16	4	8	(6 | 2)	174	69	50	56	1	70	5	2	7	25	3	.89	5	.286	.368	.395
1998 San Francisco	NL	135	417	121	13	5	4	(1 | 3)	156	63	49	65	4	63	1	4	3	21	5	.81	13	.290	.385	.374
1999 SF-Hou		132	397	113	19	2	3	(2 | 1)	145	61	34	38	4	63	1	8	2	16	7	.70	6	.285	.347	.365
2000 Seattle	AL	105	342	94	18	5	5	(5 | 0)	137	61	40	42	2	64	0	4	4	4	3	.57	7	.275	.351	.401
1990 Oakland	AL	19	33	8	0	2	0	(0 | 0)	12	4	3	3	0	6	0	0	0	0	0	—	0	.242	.306	.364
Los Angeles	NL	104	276	84	9	4	3	(1 | 2)	110	56	24	37	2	44	0	6	2	15	7	.68	6	.304	.384	.399
1992 Los Angeles	NL	56	58	11	3	0	1	(0 | 0)	17	6	5	6	2	11	1	1	0	1	2	.33	0	.190	.277	.293
Philadelphia	NL	74	276	72	14	1	0	(0 | 0)	88	36	24	31	0	43	2	2	2	17	1	.94	4	.261	.338	.319
1999 San Francisco	NL	112	333	92	15	1	3	(2 | 1)	118	49	30	29	4	55	1	7	1	13	6	.68	4	.276	.335	.354
Houston	NL	20	64	21	4	1	0	(0 | 0)	27	12	4	9	0	8	0	1	1	3	1	.75	2	.328	.405	.422
16 ML YEARS		1674	4766	1276	211	39	53	(23 | 30)	1724	737	470	542	25	792	23	64	37	235	50	.82	94	.268	.343	.362

Gregg Jefferies

Bats: B **Throws:** R **Pos:** 1B-20; 2B-14; 3B-6; PH/PR-4; DH-2; LF-1 **Ht:** 5'10" **Wt:** 185 **Born:** 8/1/67 **Age:** 33

	BATTING																BASERUNNING				PERCENTAGES		
Year Team	Lg	G	AB	H	2B	3B	HR	(Hm | Rd)	TB	R	RBI	TBB	IBB	SO	HBP	SH	SF	SB	CS	SB%	GDP	Avg	OBP	SLG
1987 New York	NL	6	6	3	1	0	0	(0 | 0)	4	0	2	0	0	0	0	0	0	0	0	—	0	.500	.500	.667
1988 New York	NL	29	109	35	8	2	6	(3 | 3)	65	19	17	8	0	10	0	0	1	5	1	.83	1	.321	.364	.596
1989 New York	NL	141	508	131	28	2	12	(7 | 5)	199	72	56	39	8	46	5	2	5	21	6	.78	16	.258	.314	.392
1990 New York	NL	153	604	171	40	3	15	(9 | 6)	262	96	68	46	2	40	5	0	4	11	2	.85	12	.283	.337	.434
1991 New York	NL	136	486	132	19	2	9	(5 | 4)	182	59	62	47	2	38	2	1	3	26	5	.84	12	.272	.336	.374
1992 Kansas City	AL	152	604	172	36	3	10	(3 | 7)	244	66	75	43	4	29	1	0	9	19	9	.68	24	.285	.329	.404
1993 St. Louis	NL	142	544	186	24	3	16	(10 | 6)	264	89	83	62	7	32	2	0	4	46	9	.84	15	.342	.408	.485
1994 St. Louis	NL	103	397	129	27	1	12	(5 | 7)	194	52	55	45	12	26	1	0	4	12	5	.71	9	.325	.391	.489
1995 Philadelphia	NL	114	480	147	31	2	11	(4 | 7)	215	69	56	35	0	26	0	0	6	9	5	.64	15	.306	.349	.448
1996 Philadelphia	NL	104	404	118	17	3	7	(4 | 3)	162	59	51	36	6	21	1	0	5	20	6	.77	9	.292	.348	.401
1997 Philadelphia	NL	130	476	122	25	3	11	(2 | 9)	186	68	48	53	7	27	2	0	0	12	6	.67	8	.256	.333	.391
1998 Phi-Ana		144	555	167	28	3	9	(3 | 6)	228	72	58	29	4	32	1	1	6	12	3	.80	19	.301	.333	.411
1999 Detroit	AL	70	205	41	8	0	6	(5 | 1)	67	22	18	13	1	11	4	0	3	3	4	.43	9	.200	.258	.327
2000 Detroit	AL	41	142	39	8	0	2	(0 | 2)	53	18	14	16	1	10	0	0	2	0	2	.00	7	.275	.344	.373
1998 Philadelphia	NL	125	483	142	22	3	8	(3 | 5)	194	65	48	29	4	27	1	1	6	11	3	.79	17	.294	.331	.402
Anaheim	AL	19	72	25	6	0	1	(0 | 1)	34	7	10	0	0	5	0	0	0	1	0	1.00	2	.347	.347	.472
14 ML YEARS		1465	5520	1593	300	27	126	(62 | 64)	2325	761	663	472	59	348	24	4	52	196	63	.76	156	.289	.344	.421

Geoff Jenkins

Bats: Left **Throws:** Right **Pos:** LF-131; PH/PR-5 **Ht:** 6'1" **Wt:** 204 **Born:** 7/21/74 **Age:** 26

	BATTING																BASERUNNING				PERCENTAGES		
Year Team	Lg	G	AB	H	2B	3B	HR	(Hm | Rd)	TB	R	RBI	TBB	IBB	SO	HBP	SH	SF	SB	CS	SB%	GDP	Avg	OBP	SLG
1998 Milwaukee	NL	84	262	60	12	1	9	(4 | 5)	101	33	28	20	4	61	2	4	0	1	3	.25	7	.229	.288	.385
1999 Milwaukee	NL	135	447	140	43	3	21	(10 | 11)	252	70	82	35	7	87	7	3	1	5	1	.83	10	.313	.371	.564
2000 Milwaukee	NL	135	512	155	36	4	34	(15 | 19)	301	100	94	33	6	135	15	0	4	11	1	.92	9	.303	.360	.588
3 ML YEARS		354	1221	355	91	8	64	(29 | 35)	654	203	204	88	17	283	24	3	6	17	5	.77	26	.291	.349	.536

Marcus Jensen

Bats: Both **Throws:** Right **Pos:** C-49; PH/PR-8; DH-1 **Ht:** 6'4" **Wt:** 204 **Born:** 12/14/72 **Age:** 28

	BATTING																BASERUNNING				PERCENTAGES		
Year Team	Lg	G	AB	H	2B	3B	HR	(Hm | Rd)	TB	R	RBI	TBB	IBB	SO	HBP	SH	SF	SB	CS	SB%	GDP	Avg	OBP	SLG
2000 Salt Lake *	AAA	15	55	16	4	0	1	—	—	23	10	12	11	0	10	2	1	1	0	2	.00	3	.291	.420	.418
1996 San Francisco	NL	9	19	4	1	0	0	(0 | 0)	5	4	4	8	0	7	0	0	0	0	0	—	1	.211	.444	.263
1997 SF-Det		38	85	13	2	0	1	(1 | 0)	18	6	4	8	1	28	0	0	0	0	0	—	2	.153	.226	.212
1998 Milwaukee	NL	2	2	0	0	0	0	(0 | 0)	0	0	0	0	0	2	0	0	0	0	0	—	0	.000	.000	.000
1999 St. Louis	NL	16	34	8	5	0	1	(0 | 1)	16	5	1	6	1	12	0	2	0	0	0	—	1	.235	.350	.471
2000 Minnesota	AL	52	139	29	7	1	3	(2 | 1)	47	16	14	24	0	36	0	1	0	0	0	.00	2	.209	.325	.338
1997 San Francisco	NL	30	74	11	2	0	1	(1 | 0)	16	5	3	7	1	23	0	0	0	0	0	—	0	.149	.222	.216
Detroit	AL	8	11	2	0	0	0	(0 | 0)	2	1	1	1	0	5	0	0	0	0	0	—	2	.182	.250	.182
5 ML YEARS		117	279	54	15	1	5	(3 | 2)	86	31	23	46	2	85	0	3	0	0	0	.00	7	.194	.308	.308

Derek Jeter

Bats: Right Throws: Right Pos: SS-148 Ht: 6'3" Wt: 195 Born: 6/26/74 Age: 27

Year Team	Lg	G	AB	H	2B	3B	HR	(Hm	Rd)	TB	R	RBI	TBB	IBB	SO	HBP	SH	SF	SB	CS	SB%	GDP	Avg	OBP	SLG
2000 Tampa *	A+	1	3	2	1	0	0	(—	—)	3	2	0	0	0	0	0	0	0	0	0	—	0	.667	.667	1.000
1995 New York	AL	15	48	12	4	1	0	(0	0)	18	5	7	3	0	11	0	0	0	0	0	—	0	.250	.294	.375
1996 New York	AL	157	582	183	25	6	10	(3	7)	250	104	78	48	1	102	9	6	9	14	7	.67	13	.314	.370	.430
1997 New York	AL	159	654	190	31	7	10	(5	5)	265	116	70	74	0	125	10	8	2	23	12	.66	14	.291	.370	.405
1998 New York	AL	149	626	203	25	8	19	(9	10)	301	127	84	57	1	119	5	3	6	30	6	.83	13	.324	.384	.481
1999 New York	AL	158	627	219	37	9	24	(15	9)	346	134	102	91	5	116	12	3	6	19	8	.70	12	.349	.438	.552
2000 New York	AL	148	593	201	31	4	15	(8	7)	285	119	73	68	4	99	12	3	3	22	4	.85	14	.339	.416	.481
6 ML YEARS		786	3130	1008	153	35	78	(40	38)	1465	605	414	341	11	572	48	23	23	108	37	.74	66	.322	.394	.468

Jose Jimenez

Pitches: Right Bats: Right Pos: RP-72 Ht: 6'3" Wt: 190 Born: 7/7/73 Age: 27

Year Team	Lg	G	GS	CG	GF	IP	BFP	H	R	ER	HR	SH	SF	HB	TBB	IBB	SO	WP	Bk	W	L	Pct.	ShO	Sv-Op	Hld	ERA
1998 St. Louis	NL	4	3	0	0	21.1	94	22	8	7	0	1	1	0	8	0	12	0	0	3	0	1.000	0	0-0	0	2.95
1999 St. Louis	NL	29	28	2	0	163	727	173	114	106	16	10	6	11	71	2	113	10	1	5	14	.263	2	0-1	0	5.85
2000 Colorado	NL	72	0	0	55	70.2	301	63	27	25	4	4	2	3	28	6	44	5	0	5	2	.714	0	24-30	2	3.18
3 ML YEARS		105	31	2	55	255	1122	258	149	138	20	15	9	14	107	8	169	15	1	13	16	.448	2	24-31	2	4.87

Brian Johnson

Bats: Right Throws: Right Pos: C-37 Ht: 6'2" Wt: 210 Born: 1/8/68 Age: 33

Year Team	Lg	G	AB	H	2B	3B	HR	(Hm	Rd)	TB	R	RBI	TBB	IBB	SO	HBP	SH	SF	SB	CS	SB%	GDP	Avg	OBP	SLG
2000 Memphis *	AAA	15	48	12	6	0	2	(—	—)	24	6	7	4	0	10	2	0	0	0	0	—	2	.250	.333	.500
Columbus *	AAA	18	68	13	5	0	1	(—	—)	21	12	6	8	0	9	0	1	1	0	0	—	1	.191	.273	.309
1994 San Diego	NL	36	93	23	4	1	3	(3	0)	38	7	16	5	0	21	0	2	1	0	0	—	4	.247	.283	.409
1995 San Diego	NL	68	207	52	9	0	3	(1	2)	70	20	29	11	2	39	1	1	4	0	0	—	4	.251	.287	.338
1996 San Diego	NL	82	243	66	13	1	8	(3	5)	105	18	35	4	2	36	4	2	4	0	0	—	8	.272	.290	.432
1997 Det-SF		101	318	83	13	3	13	(8	5)	141	32	45	19	8	45	2	5	4	1	1	.50	11	.261	.303	.443
1998 San Francisco	NL	99	308	73	8	1	13	(7	6)	122	34	34	28	4	67	5	4	1	0	2	.00	11	.237	.310	.396
1999 Cincinnati	NL	45	117	27	7	0	5	(3	2)	49	12	18	9	0	31	0	1	0	0	0	—	2	.231	.286	.419
2000 Kansas City	AL	37	125	26	6	0	4	(3	1)	44	9	18	4	0	28	0	1	2	0	0	—	4	.208	.229	.352
1997 Detroit	AL	45	139	33	6	1	2	(2	0)	47	13	18	5	1	19	0	2	1	0	1	0 1.00	8	.237	.262	.338
San Francisco	NL	56	179	50	7	2	11	(6	5)	94	19	27	14	7	26	2	3	3	1	1	1.00	8	.279	.333	.525
7 ML YEARS		468	1411	350	60	6	49	(28	21)	569	132	195	80	16	267	12	16	16	1	3	.25	42	.248	.291	.403

Charles Johnson

Bats: Right Throws: Right Pos: C-126; PH/PR-3; DH-1 Ht: 6'2" Wt: 220 Born: 7/20/71 Age: 29

Year Team	Lg	G	AB	H	2B	3B	HR	(Hm	Rd)	TB	R	RBI	TBB	IBB	SO	HBP	SH	SF	SB	CS	SB%	GDP	Avg	OBP	SLG
1994 Florida	NL	4	11	5	1	0	1	(1	0)	9	5	4	1	0	4	0	0	1	0	0	—	1	.455	.462	.818
1995 Florida	NL	97	315	79	15	1	11	(3	8)	129	40	39	46	2	71	4	4	2	0	2	.00	11	.251	.351	.410
1996 Florida	NL	120	386	84	13	1	13	(9	4)	138	34	37	40	6	91	2	2	4	1	0	1.00	13	.218	.292	.358
1997 Florida	NL	124	416	104	26	1	19	(7	12)	189	43	63	60	6	109	3	3	2	0	2	.00	13	.250	.347	.454
1998 Fla-LA	NL	133	459	100	18	0	19	(14	5)	175	44	58	45	1	129	1	0	1	0	2	.00	13	.218	.289	.381
1999 Baltimore	AL	135	426	107	19	1	16	(8	8)	176	58	54	55	2	107	4	4	3	0	0	—	13	.251	.340	.413
2000 Bal-CWS	AL	128	421	128	24	0	31	(19	12)	245	76	91	52	0	106	1	1	3	2	0	1.00	8	.304	.379	.582
1998 Florida	NL	31	113	25	5	0	7	(5	2)	51	13	23	16	0	30	0	0	1	0	0	—	8	.221	.315	.451
Los Angeles	NL	102	346	75	13	0	12	(9	3)	124	31	35	29	1	99	1	0	0	0	1	.00	9	.217	.279	.358
2000 Baltimore	AL	84	286	84	16	0	21	(12	9)	163	52	55	32	0	69	0	1	1	2	0	1.00	8	.294	.364	.570
Chicago	AL	44	135	44	8	0	10	(7	3)	82	24	36	20	0	37	1	0	2	0	0	—	0	.326	.411	.607
7 ML YEARS		741	2434	607	116	4	110	(61	49)	1061	300	346	299	17	617	15	14	16	3	6	.33	78	.249	.333	.436

Jason Johnson

Pitches: Right Bats: Right Pos: SP-13; RP-12 Ht: 6'6" Wt: 235 Born: 10/27/73 Age: 27

Year Team	Lg	G	GS	CG	GF	IP	BFP	H	R	ER	HR	SH	SF	HB	TBB	IBB	SO	WP	Bk	W	L	Pct.	ShO	Sv-Op	Hld	ERA
2000 Rochester *	AAA	8	8	1	0	55	216	32	12	9	2	2	2	3	21	0	56	2	0	3	1	.750	0	0- --	--	1.47
1997 Pittsburgh	NL	3	0	0	0	6	27	10	4	4	2	0	1	0	3	0	3	0	0	0	0	—	0	0-0	0	6.00
1998 Tampa Bay	AL	13	13	0	0	60	274	74	38	38	9	1	1	3	27	0	36	2	0	2	5	.286	0	0-0	0	5.70
1999 Baltimore	AL	22	21	0	0	115.1	515	120	74	70	16	2	4	3	55	0	71	5	1	8	7	.533	0	0-0	0	5.46
2000 Baltimore	AL	25	13	0	3	107.2	501	119	95	84	21	3	5	4	61	2	79	3	0	1	10	.091	0	0-0	2	7.02
4 ML YEARS		63	47	0	3	289	1317	323	211	196	48	6	11	10	144	2	189	10	1	11	22	.333	0	0-0	2	6.10

Jonathan Johnson

Pitches: Right Bats: Right Pos: RP-15 Ht: 6'0" Wt: 180 Born: 7/16/74 Age: 26

Year Team	Lg	G	GS	CG	GF	IP	BFP	H	R	ER	HR	SH	SF	HB	TBB	IBB	SO	WP	Bk	W	L	Pct.	ShO	Sv-Op	Hld	ERA
1995 Charlotte	A+	8	7	1	1	43.1	178	34	14	13	2	2	0	1	16	0	25	3	3	1	5	.167	0	0- --	--	2.70
1996 Okla City	AAA	1	1	0	0	9	29	2	0	0	0	0	0	0	1	0	6	0	0	1	0	1.000	1	0- --	--	0.00
Tulsa	AA	26	25	6	1	174.1	728	176	86	69	15	3	5	6	41	1	97	2	3	13	10	.565	0	0- --	--	3.56
1997 Okla City	AAA	13	12	1	1	58	276	83	54	47	9	3	1	3	29	3	33	2	1	1	8	.111	0	1- --	--	7.29
Tulsa	AA	10	10	4	0	71.2	297	70	35	28	3	1	3	2	15	0	47	0	0	5	4	.556	0	0- --	--	3.52
1998 Charlotte	A+	3	3	0	0	11.2	51	10	6	6	2	0	1	2	4	0	11	0	0	0	2	.000	0	0- --	--	4.63
Oklahoma	AAA	19	18	0	0	112	474	109	66	61	15	0	4	11	32	0	94	6	2	6	6	.500	0	0- --	--	4.90
1999 Rangers	R	1	1	0	0	5	18	3	1	1	0	0	0	0	5	0	5	0	0	0	0	—	0	0- --	--	1.80
Tulsa	AA	1	1	0	0	5.2	28	12	6	6	3	1	1	0	4	0	5	1	0	0	0	—	0	0- --	--	9.53
Oklahoma	AAA	21	8	0	5	67.2	308	91	53	47	9	2	3	2	23	0	38	6	0	8	4	.667	0	2- --	--	6.25

		HOW MUCH HE PITCHED						WHAT HE GAVE UP											THE RESULTS						
Year Team	Lg	G	GS	CG	GF	IP	BFP	H	R	ER	HR	SH	SF	HB	TBB	IBB	SO	WP	Bk	W	L	Pct.	ShO	Sv-Op	Hld	ERA
2000 Oklahoma	AAA	36	2	0	18	56.2	243	55	38	32	8	1	2	0	26	2	63	3	1	4	7	.364	0	5- -	—	5.08
1998 Texas	AL	1	1	0	0	4.1	22	5	4	4	0	0	1	0	5	0	3	0	0	0	0	—	0	0-0	0	8.31
1999 Texas	AL	1	0	0	0	3	21	9	5	5	0	0	1	1	2	0	3	0	0	0	0	—	0	0-0	0	15.00
2000 Texas	AL	15	0	0	3	29	144	34	23	20	3	0	2	6	19	2	23	2	0	1	1	.500	0	0-0	0	6.21
3 ML YEARS		17	1	0	3	36.1	187	48	32	29	3	0	4	7	26	2	29	2	0	1	1	.500	0	0-0	0	7.18

Keith Johnson

Bats: R **Throws:** R **Pos:** 1B-3; PH/PR-3; 2B-2; SS-1   **Ht:** 5'11" **Wt:** 200 **Born:** 4/17/71 **Age:** 30

		BATTING															BASERUNNING				PERCENTAGES		
Year Team	Lg	G	AB	H	2B	3B	HR	(Hm | Rd)	TB	R	RBI	TBB	IBB	SO	HBP	SH	SF	SB	CS	SB%	GDP	Avg	OBP	SLG
1992 Yakima	A-	57	197	40	6	0	1	—	—	49	27	17	16	0	37	10	1	1	5	1	.83	4	.203	.295	.249
1993 Vero Beach	A+	111	404	96	22	0	4	—	—	130	37	48	18	0	71	4	6	5	13	13	.50	8	.238	.274	.322
1994 Bakersfield	A+	64	210	42	12	1	2	—	—	62	19	19	16	0	49	5	3	2	13	7	.65	3	.200	.270	.295
1995 San Berndno	A+	111	417	101	26	1	17	—	—	180	64	68	17	0	83	4	11	2	20	12	.63	4	.242	.277	.432
1996 San Antonio	AA	127	521	143	28	6	10	—	—	213	74	57	17	1	82	4	9	3	15	8	.65	15	.274	.301	.409
Albuquerque	AAA	4	16	4	1	0	0	—	—	5	2	2	1	0	1	0	0	0	0	0	—	0	.250	.294	.313
1997 San Antonio	AA	96	298	80	9	3	9	—	—	122	43	52	17	0	48	4	8	3	7	6	.54	4	.268	.314	.409
1998 Albuquerque	AAA	82	254	59	5	1	6	—	—	84	32	26	10	0	51	4	6	1	6	3	.67	4	.232	.271	.331
San Antonio	AA	40	154	46	10	1	3	—	—	67	20	16	10	2	26	3	6	1	10	5	.67	3	.299	.351	.435
1999 El Paso	AA	17	70	21	10	1	3	—	—	42	17	15	4	0	17	0	1	1	0	1	.00	1	.300	.333	.600
Tucson	AAA	107	356	102	19	0	12	—	—	157	61	46	30	2	71	8	4	4	2	4	.33	11	.287	.352	.441
2000 Edmonton	AAA	109	423	130	31	2	13	—	—	204	63	64	19	0	71	7	6	5	7	8	.47	14	.307	.344	.482
2000 Anaheim	AL	6	4	2	0	0	0	(0)	0)	2	2	0	2	0	0	0	1	0	0	0	—	0	.500	.667	.500

Lance Johnson

Bats: L **Throws:** L **Pos:** PH/PR-14; DH-3; LF-2; RF-2   **Ht:** 5'11" **Wt:** 165 **Born:** 7/6/63 **Age:** 37

		BATTING															BASERUNNING				PERCENTAGES		
Year Team	Lg	G	AB	H	2B	3B	HR	(Hm | Rd)	TB	R	RBI	TBB	IBB	SO	HBP	SH	SF	SB	CS	SB%	GDP	Avg	OBP	SLG
1987 St. Louis	NL	33	59	13	2	1	0	(0 | 0)	17	4	7	4	1	6	0	0	0	6	1	.86	2	.220	.270	.288
1988 Chicago	AL	33	124	23	4	1	0	(0 | 0)	29	11	6	6	0	11	0	2	0	6	2	.75	1	.185	.223	.234
1989 Chicago	AL	50	180	54	8	2	0	(0 | 0)	66	28	16	17	0	24	0	2	0	16	3	.84	1	.300	.360	.367
1990 Chicago	AL	151	541	154	18	9	1	(0 | 1)	193	76	51	33	2	45	1	8	4	36	22	.62	12	.285	.325	.357
1991 Chicago	AL	160	588	161	14	13	0	(0 | 0)	201	72	49	26	2	58	1	6	3	26	11	.70	14	.274	.304	.342
1992 Chicago	AL	157	567	158	15	12	3	(2 | 1)	206	67	47	34	4	33	1	4	5	41	14	.75	20	.279	.318	.363
1993 Chicago	AL	147	540	168	18	14	0	(0 | 0)	214	75	47	36	1	33	0	3	0	35	7	.83	10	.311	.354	.396
1994 Chicago	AL	106	412	114	11	14	3	(1 | 2)	162	56	54	26	5	23	2	0	3	26	6	.81	8	.277	.321	.393
1995 Chicago	AL	142	607	186	18	12	10	(2 | 8)	258	98	57	32	2	31	1	2	3	40	6	.87	7	.306	.341	.425
1996 New York	NL	160	682	227	31	21	9	(1 | 8)	327	117	69	33	8	40	1	3	5	50	12	.81	8	.333	.362	.479
1997 NYM-ChC	NL	111	410	126	16	8	5	(4 | 1)	173	60	39	42	3	31	0	0	2	20	12	.63	8	.307	.370	.422
1998 Chicago	NL	85	304	85	8	4	2	(1 | 1)	107	51	21	26	1	22	0	1	1	10	6	.63	5	.280	.335	.352
1999 Chicago	NL	95	335	87	11	6	1	(1 | 0)	113	46	21	37	0	20	0	4	1	13	3	.81	6	.260	.332	.337
2000 New York	AL	18	30	9	1	0	0	(0 | 0)	10	6	2	0	0	7	0	0	0	2	0	1.00	1	.300	.300	.333
1997 New York	NL	72	265	82	10	6	1	(1 | 0)	107	43	24	33	2	21	0	0	1	15	10	.60	6	.309	.385	.404
Chicago	NL	39	145	44	6	2	4	(3 | 1)	66	17	15	9	1	10	0	0	1	5	2	.71	2	.303	.342	.455
14 ML YEARS		1448	5379	1565	175	117	34	(12 | 22)	2076	767	486	352	29	384	7	35	27	327	105	.76	103	.291	.334	.386

Mark Johnson

Pitches: Right **Bats:** Right **Pos:** RP-6; SP-3   **Ht:** 6'3" **Wt:** 226 **Born:** 5/2/75 **Age:** 26

		HOW MUCH HE PITCHED						WHAT HE GAVE UP											THE RESULTS						
Year Team	Lg	G	GS	CG	GF	IP	BFP	H	R	ER	HR	SH	SF	HB	TBB	IBB	SO	WP	Bk	W	L	Pct.	ShO	Sv-Op	Hld	ERA
1997 Kissimmee	A+	26	26	3	0	155.1	652	150	67	53	8	7	5	6	39	1	127	4	6	8	9	.471	1	0- -	—	3.07
1998 Portland	AA	26	26	2	0	142.1	615	147	89	73	12	8	2	4	60	4	120	7	0	5	14	.263	0	0- -	—	4.62
1999 Yankees	R	3	2	0	0	11	53	15	11	10	1	1	1	0	5	1	10	0	0	0	3	.000	0	0- -	—	8.18
Tampa	A+	1	1	0	0	6	22	4	1	1	1	0	0	0	1	0	6	0	0	1	0	1.000	0	0- -	—	1.50
Norwich	AA	16	15	0	0	88	393	88	51	36	7	1	5	4	39	0	52	6	0	9	3	.750	0	0- -	—	3.68
2000 Toledo	AAA	17	17	1	0	100	454	142	81	73	15	3	3	6	26	2	48	1	0	2	11	.154	0	0- -	—	6.57
2000 Detroit	AL	9	3	0	3	24	116	25	23	20	3	1	4	1	16	1	11	2	0	0	1	.000	0	0-0	0	7.50

Mark L. Johnson

Bats: Left **Throws:** Right **Pos:** C-74; DH-1; PH/PR-1   **Ht:** 6'0" **Wt:** 185 **Born:** 9/12/75 **Age:** 25

		BATTING															BASERUNNING				PERCENTAGES		
Year Team	Lg	G	AB	H	2B	3B	HR	(Hm | Rd)	TB	R	RBI	TBB	IBB	SO	HBP	SH	SF	SB	CS	SB%	GDP	Avg	OBP	SLG
1998 Chicago	AL	7	23	2	0	2	0	(0 | 0)	6	2	1	1	0	8	0	0	0	0	0	—	0	.087	.125	.261
1999 Chicago	AL	73	207	47	11	0	4	(2 | 2)	70	27	16	36	0	58	2	1	2	3	1	.75	2	.227	.344	.338
2000 Chicago	AL	75	213	48	11	0	3	(2 | 1)	68	29	23	27	0	40	1	10	0	3	2	.60	3	.225	.315	.319
3 ML YEARS		155	443	97	22	2	7	(4 | 3)	144	58	40	64	0	106	3	11	2	6	3	.67	5	.219	.320	.325

Mark P. Johnson

Bats: L **Throws:** L **Pos:** PH/PR-16; 1B-4; DH-1; LF-1   **Ht:** 6'4" **Wt:** 230 **Born:** 10/17/67 **Age:** 33

		BATTING															BASERUNNING				PERCENTAGES		
Year Team	Lg	G	AB	H	2B	3B	HR	(Hm | Rd)	TB	R	RBI	TBB	IBB	SO	HBP	SH	SF	SB	CS	SB%	GDP	Avg	OBP	SLG
2000 Norfolk *	AAA	94	315	85	21	1	17	—	—	159	49	60	67	4	54	5	0	1	14	2	.88	4	.270	.405	.505
1995 Pittsburgh	NL	79	221	46	6	1	13	(7 | 6)	93	32	28	37	2	66	2	0	1	5	2	.71	2	.208	.326	.421
1996 Pittsburgh	NL	127	343	94	24	0	13	(10 | 3)	157	55	47	44	3	64	5	0	4	6	4	.60	5	.274	.361	.458
1997 Pittsburgh	NL	78	219	47	10	0	4	(2 | 2)	69	30	29	43	1	78	2	0	3	1	1	.50	1	.215	.345	.315
1998 Anaheim	AL	10	14	1	0	0	0	(0 | 0)	1	1	0	0	0	6	0	0	0	0	0	—	1	.071	.071	.071
2000 New York	NL	21	22	4	0	0	1	(1 | 0)	7	2	6	5	0	9	0	0	0	0	0	—	0	.182	.333	.318
5 ML YEARS		315	819	192	40	1	31	(20 | 11)	327	120	110	129	6	223	9	0	8	12	7	.63	10	.234	.342	.399

Mike Johnson

Pitches: Right **Bats:** Left **Pos:** RP-28; SP-13   **Ht:** 6'2" **Wt:** 170 **Born:** 10/3/75 **Age:** 25

Year Team	Lg	G	GS	CG	GF	IP	BFP	H	R	ER	HR	SH	SF	HB	TBB	IBB	SO	WP	Bk	W	L	Pct.	ShO	Sv-Op	Hld	ERA
2000 Ottawa *	AAA	5	5	0	0	30	119	14	8	7	3	1	0	3	14	0	27	1	0	2	0	1.000	0	0- -	—	2.10
1997 Bal-Mon		25	16	0	5	89.2	403	106	70	68	20	2	4	1	37	4	57	5	0	2	6	.250	0	2-2	0	6.83
1998 Montreal	NL	2	2	0	0	7.1	40	16	12	12	4	0	1	2	2	0	4	0	0	2	0	.000	0	0-0	0	14.73
1999 Montreal	NL	3	1	0	0	8.1	44	12	8	8	2	0	0	0	7	1	6	2	0	0	0	—	0	0-0	0	8.64
2000 Montreal	NL	41	13	0	5	101.1	466	107	73	72	18	4	2	9	53	1	70	8	0	5	6	.455	0	0-0	0	6.39
1997 Baltimore	AL	14	5	0	5	39.2	183	52	36	35	12	0	2	1	16	2	29	1	0	0	1	.000	0	2-2	0	7.94
Montreal	NL	11	11	0	0	50	220	54	34	33	8	2	2	0	21	2	28	4	0	2	5	.286	0	0-0	0	5.94
4 ML YEARS		71	32	0	10	206.2	953	241	163	160	44	6	6	11	99	6	137	15	0	7	14	.333	0	2-2	0	6.97

Randy Johnson

Pitches: Left **Bats:** Right **Pos:** SP-35   **Ht:** 6'10" **Wt:** 230 **Born:** 9/10/63 **Age:** 37

Year Team	Lg	G	GS	CG	GF	IP	BFP	H	R	ER	HR	SH	SF	HB	TBB	IBB	SO	WP	Bk	W	L	Pct.	ShO	Sv-Op	Hld	ERA
1988 Montreal	NL	4	4	1	0	26	109	23	8	7	3	0	0	0	7	0	25	3	0	3	0	1.000	0	0-0	0	2.42
1989 Mon-Sea		29	28	2	1	160.2	715	147	100	86	13	10	13	3	96	2	130	7	3	7	13	.350	0	0-0	0	4.82
1990 Seattle	AL	33	33	5	0	219.2	944	174	103	89	26	7	6	5	120	2	194	4	2	14	11	.560	2	0-0	0	3.65
1991 Seattle	AL	33	33	2	0	201.1	855	151	96	89	15	9	8	12	152	0	228	12	2	13	10	.565	1	0-0	0	3.98
1992 Seattle	AL	31	31	6	0	210.1	922	154	104	88	13	3	8	18	144	1	241	13	1	12	14	.462	2	0-0	0	3.77
1993 Seattle	AL	35	34	10	1	255.1	1043	185	97	92	22	8	7	16	99	1	308	8	2	19	8	.704	3	1-1	0	3.24
1994 Seattle	AL	23	23	9	0	172	694	132	65	61	14	3	1	6	72	2	204	5	0	13	6	.684	4	0-0	0	3.19
1995 Seattle	AL	30	30	6	0	214.1	866	159	65	59	12	2	1	6	65	1	294	5	2	18	2	.900	3	0-0	0	2.48
1996 Seattle	AL	14	8	0	2	61.1	256	48	27	25	8	1	2	1	25	0	85	3	1	5	0	1.000	0	1-2	0	3.67
1997 Seattle	AL	30	29	5	0	213	850	147	60	54	20	4	1	10	77	2	291	4	0	20	4	.833	2	0-0	0	2.28
1998 Sea-Hou		34	34	10	0	244.1	1014	203	102	89	23	5	2	14	86	1	329	7	2	19	11	.633	4	0-0	0	3.28
1999 Arizona	NL	35	35	12	0	271.2	1079	207	86	75	30	4	3	9	70	3	364	4	2	17	9	.654	2	0-0	0	2.48
2000 Arizona	NL	35	35	8	0	248.2	1001	202	89	73	23	14	5	6	76	1	347	5	2	19	7	.731	3	0-0	0	2.64
1989 Montreal	NL	7	6	0	1	29.2	143	29	25	22	2	3	4	0	26	1	26	2	2	0	4	.000	0	0-0	0	6.67
Seattle	AL	22	22	2	0	131	572	118	75	64	11	7	9	3	70	1	104	5	5	7	9	.438	0	0-0	0	4.40
1998 Seattle	AL	23	23	6	0	160	685	146	90	77	19	5	1	11	60	0	213	7	2	9	10	.474	2	0-0	0	4.33
Houston	NL	11	11	4	0	84.1	329	57	12	12	4	0	1	3	26	1	116	0	0	10	1	.909	2	0-0	0	1.28
13 ML YEARS		366	357	76	4	2498.2	10382	1932	1002	887	222	70	55	107	1089	16	3040	80	23	179	95	.653	28	2-3	0	3.19

Russ Johnson

Bats: R **Throws:** R **Pos:** 3B-53; PH/PR-32; 2B-21; SS-16   **Ht:** 5'10" **Wt:** 180 **Born:** 2/22/73 **Age:** 28

Year Team	Lg	G	AB	H	2B	3B	HR	(Hm	Rd)	TB	R	RBI	TBB	IBB	SO	HBP	SH	SF	SB	CS	SB%	GDP	Avg	OBP	SLG
1997 Houston	NL	21	60	18	1	0	2	(2	0)	25	7	9	6	0	14	0	1	0	1	1	.50	2	.300	.364	.417
1998 Houston	NL	8	13	3	1	0	0	(0	0)	4	2	0	1	0	5	1	0	0	1	0	1.00	1	.231	.333	.308
1999 Houston	NL	83	156	44	10	0	5	(2	3)	69	24	23	20	0	31	0	4	3	2	3	.40	3	.282	.358	.442
2000 Hou-TB		100	230	55	8	0	2	(2	0)	69	32	20	27	0	40	1	4	1	5	2	.71	7	.239	.320	.300
2000 Houston	NL	26	45	8	0	0	0	(0	0)	8	4	3	2	0	10	0	1	0	1	1	.50	3	.178	.213	.178
Tampa Bay	AL	74	185	47	8	0	2	(2	0)	61	28	17	25	0	30	1	3	1	4	1	.80	4	.254	.344	.330
4 ML YEARS		212	459	120	20	0	9	(6	3)	167	65	52	54	0	90	2	9	4	9	6	.60	13	.261	.339	.364

John Johnstone

Pitches: Right **Bats:** Right **Pos:** RP-47   **Ht:** 6'3" **Wt:** 210 **Born:** 11/25/68 **Age:** 32

Year Team	Lg	G	GS	CG	GF	IP	BFP	H	R	ER	HR	SH	SF	HB	TBB	IBB	SO	WP	Bk	W	L	Pct.	ShO	Sv-Op	Hld	ERA
2000 San Jose *	A+	2	2	0	0	2	10	4	2	2	0	0	0	0	0	0	3	0	0	0	0	—	0	0- -	—	9.00
Giants *	R	1	1	0	0	1	3	0	0	0	0	0	0	0	0	0	1	0	0	0	0	—	0	0.00	—	0.00
Fresno *	AAA	1	1	0	0	2	7	0	0	0	0	0	0	0	1	0	1	0	0	0	0	—	0	0- -	—	0.00
1993 Florida	NL	7	0	0	3	10.2	54	16	8	7	1	0	0	0	7	0	5	1	0	0	2	.000	0	0-0	0	5.91
1994 Florida	NL	17	0	0	7	21.1	105	23	20	14	4	1	0	1	16	5	23	0	0	1	2	.333	0	0-0	3	5.91
1995 Florida	NL	4	0	0	0	4.2	23	7	2	2	1	0	0	0	2	1	3	0	0	0	0	—	0	0-0	0	3.86
1996 Houston	NL	9	0	0	6	13	60	17	8	8	2	0	2	0	5	0	5	0	0	1	0	1.000	0	0-0	0	5.54
1997 SF-Oak		18	0	0	3	25	112	22	9	9	1	2	4	4	14	0	19	0	0	0	0	—	0	0-0	1	3.24
1998 San Francisco	NL	70	0	0	13	88	370	72	32	30	10	4	5	1	38	8	86	4	0	6	5	.545	0	0-0	9	3.07
1999 San Francisco	NL	62	0	0	11	65.2	262	48	24	19	8	4	0	1	20	5	56	2	1	4	6	.400	0	0-1	15	2.60
2000 San Francisco	NL	47	0	0	9	50	222	64	35	35	11	4	4	2	13	2	37	0	0	3	4	.429	0	0-3	6	6.30
1997 San Francisco	NL	13	0	0	2	18.2	80	15	7	7	1	2	3	4	7	0	15	0	0	0	0	—	0	0-0	1	3.38
Oakland	AL	5	0	0	1	6.1	32	7	2	2	0	0	1	0	7	0	4	0	0	0	0	—	0	0-0	0	2.84
8 ML YEARS		234	0	0	52	278.1	1208	269	138	124	38	15	15	9	115	21	234	7	1	15	19	.441	0	3-11	53	4.01

Andruw Jones

Bats: Right **Throws:** Right **Pos:** CF-161   **Ht:** 6'1" **Wt:** 210 **Born:** 4/23/77 **Age:** 24

Year Team	Lg	G	AB	H	2B	3B	HR	(Hm	Rd)	TB	R	RBI	TBB	IBB	SO	HBP	SH	SF	SB	CS	SB%	GDP	Avg	OBP	SLG
1996 Atlanta	NL	31	106	23	7	1	5	(3	2)	47	11	13	7	0	29	0	0	0	3	0	1.00	1	.217	.265	.443
1997 Atlanta	NL	153	399	92	18	1	18	(5	13)	166	60	70	56	2	107	4	5	3	20	11	.65	11	.231	.329	.416
1998 Atlanta	NL	159	582	158	33	8	31	(16	15)	300	89	90	40	8	129	4	1	4	27	4	.87	10	.271	.321	.515
1999 Atlanta	NL	162	592	163	35	5	26	(10	16)	286	97	84	76	11	103	9	0	2	24	12	.67	12	.275	.365	.483
2000 Atlanta	NL	161	656	199	36	6	36	(15	21)	355	122	104	59	0	100	9	0	5	21	6	.78	12	.303	.366	.541
5 ML YEARS		666	2335	635	129	21	116	(49	67)	1154	379	361	238	21	468	26	6	14	95	33	.74	46	.272	.344	.494

Bobby J. Jones

Pitches: Right **Bats:** Right **Pos:** SP-27 **Ht:** 6'4" **Wt:** 225 **Born:** 2/10/70 **Age:** 31

Year Team	Lg	G	GS	CG	GF	IP	BFP	H	R	ER	HR	SH	SF	HB	TBB	IBB	SO	WP	Bk	W	L	Pct.	ShO	Sv-Op	Hld	ERA
2000 Norfolk *	AAA	4	4	0	0	23.2	107	31	14	14	5	0	1	0	4	0	19	0	0	2	0	1.000	0	0- -	—	5.32
1993 New York	NL	9	9	0	0	61.2	265	61	35	25	6	5	3	2	22	3	35	1	0	2	4	.333	0	0-0	0	3.65
1994 New York	NL	24	24	1	0	160	685	157	75	56	10	11	4	4	56	9	80	1	3	12	7	.632	1	0-0	0	3.15
1995 New York	NL	30	30	3	0	195.2	839	209	107	91	20	11	6	7	53	6	127	2	1	10	10	.500	1	0-0	0	4.19
1996 New York	NL	31	31	3	0	195.2	826	219	102	96	26	12	5	3	46	6	116	2	0	12	8	.600	1	0-0	0	4.42
1997 New York	NL	30	30	2	0	193.1	806	177	88	78	24	6	4	2	63	3	125	3	1	15	9	.625	1	0-0	0	3.63
1998 New York	NL	30	30	0	0	195.1	804	192	94	88	23	4	7	8	53	2	115	2	2	9	9	.500	0	0-0	0	4.05
1999 New York	NL	12	9	0	0	59.1	253	69	37	37	3	3	3	2	11	0	31	0	0	3	3	.500	0	0-0	0	5.61
2000 New York	NL	27	27	1	0	154.2	676	171	90	87	25	7	6	5	49	3	85	2	1	11	6	.647	0	0-0	0	5.06
8 ML YEARS		193	190	10	0	1215.2	5154	1255	628	558	137	59	38	33	353	32	714	13	8	74	56	.569	4	0-0	0	4.13

Bobby M. Jones

Pitches: Left **Bats:** Right **Pos:** RP-10; SP-1 **Ht:** 6'0" **Wt:** 178 **Born:** 4/11/72 **Age:** 29

Year Team	Lg	G	GS	CG	GF	IP	BFP	H	R	ER	HR	SH	SF	HB	TBB	IBB	SO	WP	Bk	W	L	Pct.	ShO	Sv-Op	Hld	ERA
2000 Norfolk *	AAA	22	21	4	0	133.1	572	122	66	64	13	0	3	5	58	4	100	6	1	10	8	.556	1	0- -	—	4.32
1997 Colorado	NL	4	4	0	0	19.1	96	30	18	18	2	2	3	0	12	0	5	0	0	1	1	.500	0	0-0	0	8.38
1998 Colorado	NL	35	20	1	1	141.1	630	153	87	82	12	9	6	6	66	0	109	4	1	7	8	.467	0	0-0	1	5.22
1999 Colorado	NL	30	20	0	1	112.1	546	132	91	79	24	7	4	6	77	0	74	4	0	6	10	.375	0	0-0	0	6.33
2000 New York	NL	11	1	0	4	21.2	99	18	11	10	2	0	1	3	14	1	20	0	0	0	1	.000	0	0-0	0	4.15
4 ML YEARS		80	45	1	6	294.2	1371	333	207	189	40	18	14	15	169	1	208	8	1	14	20	.412	0	0-0	1	5.77

Chipper Jones

Bats: Both **Throws:** Right **Pos:** 3B-152; SS-6; PH/PR-1 **Ht:** 6'4" **Wt:** 210 **Born:** 4/24/72 **Age:** 29

Year Team	Lg	G	AB	H	2B	3B	HR	(Hm	Rd)	TB	R	RBI	TBB	IBB	SO	HBP	SH	SF	SB	CS	SB%	GDP	Avg	OBP	SLG
1993 Atlanta	NL	8	3	2	1	0	0	(0	0)	3	2	0	1	0	1	0	0	0	0	0	-	0	.667	.750	1.000
1995 Atlanta	NL	140	524	139	22	3	23	(15	8)	236	87	86	73	1	99	0	1	4	8	4	.67	10	.265	.353	.450
1996 Atlanta	NL	157	598	185	32	5	30	(18	12)	317	114	110	87	0	88	0	1	7	14	1	.93	14	.309	.393	.530
1997 Atlanta	NL	157	597	176	41	3	21	(7	14)	286	100	111	76	8	88	0	0	6	20	5	.80	19	.295	.371	.479
1998 Atlanta	NL	160	601	188	29	5	34	(17	17)	329	123	107	96	1	93	1	1	8	16	6	.73	17	.313	.404	.547
1999 Atlanta	NL	157	567	181	41	1	45	(25	20)	359	116	110	126	18	94	2	0	6	25	3	.89	20	.319	.441	.633
2000 Atlanta	NL	156	579	180	38	1	36	(18	18)	328	118	111	95	10	64	2	0	10	14	7	.67	14	.311	.404	.566
7 ML YEARS		935	3469	1051	204	18	189	(100	89)	1858	660	635	554	38	527	5	3	41	97	26	.79	94	.303	.396	.536

Chris Jones

Bats: Right **Throws:** Right **Pos:** PH/PR-10; RF-2 **Ht:** 6'1" **Wt:** 219 **Born:** 12/16/65 **Age:** 35

Year Team	Lg	G	AB	H	2B	3B	HR	(Hm	Rd)	TB	R	RBI	TBB	IBB	SO	HBP	SH	SF	SB	CS	SB%	GDP	Avg	OBP	SLG
2000 Las Vegas *	AAA	13	26	7	2	0	1	(—	—)	12	6	6	2	0	9	0	0	2	1	0	1.00	0	.269	.300	.462
Indianapolis *	AAA	64	233	71	17	6	3	(—	—)	109	32	25	12	1	58	1	0	2	5	4	.56	3	.305	.339	.468
1991 Cincinnati	NL	52	89	26	1	2	2	(0	2)	37	14	6	2	0	31	0	0	1	2	1	.67	2	.292	.304	.416
1992 Houston	NL	54	63	12	2	1	1	(1	0)	19	7	4	7	0	21	0	3	0	3	0	1.00	1	.190	.271	.302
1993 Colorado	NL	86	209	57	11	4	6	(2	4)	94	29	31	10	1	48	0	5	1	9	4	.69	6	.273	.305	.450
1994 Colorado	NL	21	40	12	2	1	0	(0	0)	16	6	2	2	1	14	0	0	0	0	1	.00	1	.300	.333	.400
1995 New York	NL	79	182	51	6	2	8	(4	4)	85	33	31	9	1	45	1	2	3	2	1	.67	2	.280	.327	.467
1996 New York	NL	89	149	36	7	0	4	(2	2)	55	22	18	12	1	42	0	2	0	1	0	1.00	3	.242	.307	.369
1997 San Diego	NL	92	152	37	9	0	7	(4	3)	67	24	25	16	0	45	2	1	1	7	2	.78	4	.243	.322	.441
1998 Ari-SF	NL	63	121	23	3	1	2	(2	0)	34	17	13	11	0	37	0	0	2	2	1	.67	2	.190	.254	.281
2000 Milwaukee	NL	12	16	3	2	0	0	(0	0)	5	3	1	1	0	4	0	0	0	0	0	—	0	.188	.235	.313
1998 Arizona	NL	20	31	6	1	0	0	(0	0)	7	3	3	3	0	9	0	0	0	0	0	—	0	.194	.265	.226
San Francisco	NL	43	90	17	2	1	2	(2	0)	27	14	10	8	0	28	0	0	2	2	1	.67	0	.189	.250	.300
9 ML YEARS		548	1021	257	43	11	30	(15	15)	412	155	131	74	4	287	5	11	8	26	10	.72	21	.252	.303	.404

Doug Jones

Pitches: Right **Bats:** Right **Pos:** RP-54 **Ht:** 6'2" **Wt:** 224 **Born:** 6/24/57 **Age:** 44

Year Team	Lg	G	GS	CG	GF	IP	BFP	H	R	ER	HR	SH	SF	HB	TBB	IBB	SO	WP	Bk	W	L	Pct.	ShO	Sv-Op	Hld	ERA
1982 Milwaukee	AL	4	0	0	2	2.2	14	5	3	3	1	0	0	0	1	0	1	0	0	0	0	—	0	0-0	0	10.13
1986 Cleveland	AL	11	0	0	5	18	79	18	5	5	0	1	1	1	6	1	12	0	0	1	0	1.000	0	1-3	0	2.50
1987 Cleveland	AL	49	0	0	29	91.1	400	101	45	32	4	5	5	6	24	5	87	0	0	6	5	.545	0	8-12	1	3.15
1988 Cleveland	AL	51	0	0	46	83.1	338	69	26	21	1	3	0	2	16	3	72	2	3	3	4	.429	0	37-43	0	2.27
1989 Cleveland	AL	59	0	0	53	80.2	331	76	25	21	4	8	6	1	13	4	65	1	1	7	10	.412	0	32-41	0	2.34
1990 Cleveland	AL	66	0	0	64	84.1	331	66	26	24	5	2	2	2	22	4	55	2	0	5	5	.500	0	43-51	0	2.56
1991 Cleveland	AL	36	4	0	29	63.1	293	87	42	39	7	2	2	0	17	5	48	1	0	4	8	.333	0	7-12	0	5.54
1992 Houston	NL	80	0	0	70	111.2	440	96	29	23	5	9	0	5	17	5	93	2	1	11	8	.579	0	36-42	0	1.85
1993 Houston	NL	71	0	0	60	85.1	381	102	46	43	7	9	4	5	21	6	66	3	0	4	10	.286	0	26-34	1	4.54
1994 Philadelphia	NL	47	0	0	42	54	226	55	14	13	2	4	0	0	6	0	38	1	0	2	4	.333	0	27-29	0	2.17
1995 Baltimore	AL	52	0	0	47	46.2	213	55	30	26	6	1	0	2	16	2	42	0	0	0	4	.000	0	22-25	0	5.01
1996 ChC-Mil		52	0	0	21	64	282	72	33	30	7	1	2	3	20	6	60	1	0	7	2	.778	0	3-11	2	4.22
1997 Milwaukee	AL	75	0	0	73	80.1	338	62	20	18	4	1	5	3	9	1	82	2	0	6	6	.500	0	36-38	0	2.02
1998 Mil-Cle		69	0	0	42	85.1	372	99	44	43	17	5	6	4	17	4	71	0	1	4	6	.400	0	13-22	5	4.54
1999 Oakland	AL	70	0	0	35	104	430	106	43	41	10	3	3	3	24	3	63	2	0	5	5	.500	0	10-16	11	3.55
2000 Oakland	AL	54	0	0	22	73.1	319	86	34	32	6	2	2	2	18	4	54	1	0	4	2	.667	0	2-2	7	3.93
1996 Chicago	NL	28	0	0	13	32.1	143	41	20	18	4	1	0	1	7	4	26	0	0	2	2	.500	0	2-7	0	5.01
Milwaukee		24	0	0	8	31.2	139	31	13	12	3	0	2	2	13	2	34	1	0	5	0	1.000	0	1-4	2	3.41
1998 Milwaukee	NL	46	0	0	34	54	239	65	32	31	15	3	4	4	11	1	43	0	0	3	4	.429	0	12-20	1	5.17
Cleveland	AL	23	0	0	8	31.1	133	34	12	12	2	2	2	0	6	3	28	0	1	1	2	.333	0	1-2	4	3.45
16 ML YEARS		846	4	0	640	1128.1	4754	1155	465	414	86	56	38	39	247	53	909	18	6	69	79	.466	0	303-381	27	3.30

Jacque Jones

Bats: L Throws: L Pos: LF-90; CF-63; PH/PR-15; RF-1   Ht: 5'10" Wt: 176 Born: 4/25/75 Age: 26

Year Team	Lg	G	AB	H	2B	3B	HR	(Hm	Rd)	TB	R	RBI	TBB	IBB	SO	HBP	SH	SF	SB	CS	SB%	GDP	Avg	OBP	SLG
1996 Fort Myers	A+	1	3	2	1	0	0	—	—	3	0	1	0	0	0	0	0	0	0	1	.00	0	.667	.667	1.000
1997 Fort Myers	A+	131	539	160	33	6	15	—	—	250	84	82	33	3	110	3	0	2	24	12	.67	9	.297	.340	.464
1998 New Britain	AA	134	518	155	39	3	21	—	—	263	78	85	37	8	134	4	4	3	18	11	.62	4	.299	.349	.508
1999 Salt Lake	AAA	52	198	59	13	2	4	—	—	88	32	26	9	1	36	0	1	2	9	2	.82	5	.298	.325	.444
1999 Minnesota	AL	95	322	93	24	2	9	(5	4)	148	54	44	17	1	63	4	1	3	3	4	.43	7	.289	.329	.460
2000 Minnesota	AL	154	523	149	26	5	19	(11	8)	242	66	76	26	4	111	0	1	0	7	5	.58	17	.285	.319	.463
2 ML YEARS		249	845	242	50	7	28	(16	12)	390	120	120	43	5	174	4	2	3	10	9	.53	24	.286	.323	.462

Marcus Jones

Pitches: Right Bats: Right Pos: SP-1   Ht: 6'5" Wt: 235 Born: 3/29/75 Age: 26

Year Team	Lg	G	GS	CG	GF	IP	BFP	H	R	ER	HR	SH	SF	HB	TBB	IBB	SO	WP	Bk	W	L	Pct.	ShO	Sv-Op	Hld	ERA
1997 Sou Oregon	A-	14	10	0	0	56	246	58	37	28	4	0	3	2	22	0	49	4	0	3	3	.500	0	0- —	—	4.50
1998 Visalia	A+	29	20	0	8	131	587	155	79	68	8	2	4	7	45	3	112	2	3	7	9	.438	0	4- —	—	4.67
Edmonton	AAA	2	2	0	0	10.2	50	14	7	3	1	0	0	0	5	0	4	1	0	2	0	1.000	0	0- —	—	2.53
1999 Visalia	A+	18	15	0	0	91	401	103	56	45	7	3	3	4	32	1	82	3	1	6	4	.600	0	0- —	—	4.45
Vancouver	AAA	3	3	0	0	15	73	23	11	4	1	0	0	0	5	0	5	1	0	2	1	.667	0	0- —	—	2.40
Modesto	A+	7	5	0	0	32	137	29	18	10	5	2	0	3	14	0	36	1	0	4	2	.667	0	0- —	—	2.81
2000 Visalia	A+	3	2	0	1	11	49	15	8	8	1	1	1	0	3	0	11	0	0	0	1	.000	0	0- —	—	6.55
Sacramento	AAA	17	17	0	0	101.1	434	108	57	49	7	3	5	2	36	0	51	3	1	6	4	.600	0	0- —	—	4.35
Midland	AA	5	5	0	0	23	92	24	8	7	0	2	1	0	12	0	12	0	1	2	0	1.000	0	0- —	—	2.74
2000 Oakland	AL	1	1	0	0	2.1	15	5	4	4	1	0	0	0	3	0	1	0	0	0	0	—	0	0-0	0	15.43

Terry Jones

Bats: B Throws: R Pos: LF-55; PH/PR-40; CF-26; RF-7   Ht: 5'10" Wt: 165 Born: 2/15/71 Age: 30

Year Team	Lg	G	AB	H	2B	3B	HR	(Hm	Rd)	TB	R	RBI	TBB	IBB	SO	HBP	SH	SF	SB	CS	SB%	GDP	Avg	OBP	SLG
1996 Colorado	NL	12	10	3	0	0	0	(0	0)	3	6	1	0	0	3	0	0	1	0	0	—	0	.300	.273	.300
1998 Montreal	NL	60	212	46	7	2	1	(1	0)	60	30	15	21	1	46	0	15	0	16	4	.80	2	.217	.288	.283
1999 Montreal	NL	17	63	17	1	1	0	(0	0)	20	14	3	3	0	14	0	0	0	1	2	.33	0	.270	.303	.317
2000 Montreal	NL	108	168	42	8	2	0	(0	0)	54	30	13	10	1	32	0	3	0	7	2	.78	3	.250	.292	.321
4 ML YEARS		197	453	108	16	5	1	(1	0)	137	70	32	34	2	95	0	18	1	24	8	.75	5	.238	.291	.302

Todd Jones

Pitches: Right Bats: Left Pos: RP-67   Ht: 6'3" Wt: 230 Born: 4/24/68 Age: 33

Year Team	Lg	G	GS	CG	GF	IP	BFP	H	R	ER	HR	SH	SF	HB	TBB	IBB	SO	WP	Bk	W	L	Pct.	ShO	Sv-Op	Hld	ERA
1993 Houston	NL	27	0	0	8	37.1	150	28	14	13	4	2	1	1	15	2	25	1	1	1	2	.333	0	2-3	6	3.13
1994 Houston	NL	48	0	0	20	72.2	288	52	23	22	3	3	1	1	26	4	63	1	0	5	2	.714	0	5-9	8	2.72
1995 Houston	NL	68	0	0	40	99.2	442	89	38	34	8	4	5	6	52	17	96	5	0	6	5	.545	0	15-20	8	3.07
1996 Houston	NL	51	0	0	37	57.1	263	61	30	28	5	2	1	5	32	6	44	3	0	6	3	.667	0	17-23	1	4.40
1997 Detroit	AL	68	0	0	51	70	301	60	29	24	3	1	4	1	35	2	70	7	0	5	4	.556	0	31-36	5	3.09
1998 Detroit	AL	65	0	0	53	63.1	279	58	38	35	7	2	6	2	36	4	57	5	0	1	4	.200	0	28-32	0	4.97
1999 Detroit	AL	65	0	0	62	66.1	287	64	30	28	7	3	1	1	35	1	64	2	0	4	4	.500	0	30-35	0	3.80
2000 Detroit	AL	67	0	0	60	64	271	67	28	25	6	1	1	1	25	1	67	2	0	2	4	.333	0	42-46	0	3.52
8 ML YEARS		459	0	0	331	530.2	2281	479	230	209	43	19	19	18	256	37	486	26	1	30	28	.517	0	170-204	28	3.54

Brian Jordan

Bats: Right Throws: Right Pos: RF-130; PH/PR-5   Ht: 6'1" Wt: 205 Born: 3/29/67 Age: 34

Year Team	Lg	G	AB	H	2B	3B	HR	(Hm	Rd)	TB	R	RBI	TBB	IBB	SO	HBP	SH	SF	SB	CS	SB%	GDP	Avg	OBP	SLG
1992 St. Louis	NL	55	193	40	9	4	5	(3	2)	72	17	22	10	1	48	1	0	0	7	2	.78	6	.207	.250	.373
1993 St. Louis	NL	67	223	69	10	6	10	(4	6)	121	33	44	12	0	35	4	0	3	6	6	.50	6	.309	.351	.543
1994 St. Louis	NL	53	178	46	8	2	5	(4	1)	73	14	15	16	0	40	1	0	2	4	3	.57	6	.258	.320	.410
1995 St. Louis	NL	131	490	145	20	4	22	(14	8)	239	83	81	22	4	79	11	0	2	24	9	.73	5	.296	.339	.488
1996 St. Louis	NL	140	513	159	36	1	17	(3	14)	248	82	104	29	4	84	7	2	9	22	5	.81	6	.310	.349	.483
1997 St. Louis	NL	47	145	34	5	0	0	(0	0)	39	17	10	10	1	21	6	0	0	6	1	.86	4	.234	.311	.269
1998 St. Louis	NL	150	564	178	34	7	25	(9	16)	301	100	91	40	1	66	9	0	4	17	5	.77	18	.316	.368	.534
1999 Atlanta	NL	153	576	163	28	4	23	(11	12)	268	100	115	51	2	81	9	0	9	13	8	.62	9	.283	.346	.465
2000 Atlanta	NL	133	489	129	26	0	17	(7	10)	206	71	77	38	1	80	5	0	5	10	2	.83	12	.264	.320	.421
9 ML YEARS		929	3371	963	176	28	124	(55	69)	1567	517	559	228	14	534	53	2	34	109	41	.73	72	.286	.337	.465

Kevin Jordan

Bats: R Throws: R Pos: 2B-47; 3B-39; PH/PR-24; 1B-9   Ht: 6'1" Wt: 201 Born: 10/9/69 Age: 31

Year Team	Lg	G	AB	H	2B	3B	HR	(Hm	Rd)	TB	R	RBI	TBB	IBB	SO	HBP	SH	SF	SB	CS	SB%	GDP	Avg	OBP	SLG
1995 Philadelphia	NL	24	54	10	1	0	2	(1	1)	17	6	6	2	1	9	1	0	0	0	0	—	0	.185	.228	.315
1996 Philadelphia	NL	43	131	37	10	0	3	(2	1)	56	15	12	5	0	20	1	3	2	2	1	.67	3	.282	.309	.427
1997 Philadelphia	NL	84	177	47	8	0	6	(4	2)	73	19	30	3	0	26	0	0	3	0	1	.00	5	.266	.273	.412
1998 Philadelphia	NL	112	250	69	13	0	2	(1	1)	88	23	27	8	1	30	2	0	1	0	0	—	12	.276	.300	.352
1999 Philadelphia	NL	120	347	99	17	3	4	(2	2)	134	36	51	24	1	34	6	0	3	0	1	.00	5	.285	.339	.386
2000 Philadelphia	NL	109	337	74	16	2	5	(2	3)	109	30	36	17	0	41	1	0	0	0	1	.00	11	.220	.257	.323
6 ML YEARS		492	1296	336	65	5	22	(12	10)	477	129	162	59	3	160	11	3	12	2	3	.40	36	.259	.295	.368

Felix Jose

Bats: B **Throws:** R **Pos:** PH/PR-10; RF-8; LF-6; DH-2   **Ht:** 6'1" **Wt:** 220 **Born:** 5/8/65 **Age:** 36

Year Team	Lg	G	AB	H	2B	3B	HR	(Hm	Rd)	TB	R	RBI	TBB	IBB	SO	HBP	SH	SF	SB	CS	SB%	GDP	Avg	OBP	SLG
2000 Columbus *	AAA	59	210	65	17	2	11	—	—	119	31	38	23	1	60	1	0	1	4	3	.57	7	.310	.379	.567
1988 Oakland	AL	8	6	2	1	0	0	(0	0)	3	2	1	0	0	1	0	0	0	1	0	1.00	0	.333	.333	.500
1989 Oakland	AL	20	57	11	2	0	0	(0	0)	13	3	5	4	0	13	0	0	0	0	1	.00	2	.193	.246	.228
1990 Oak-StL		126	426	113	16	1	11	(5	6)	164	54	52	24	0	81	5	2	1	12	6	.67	9	.265	.311	.385
1991 St. Louis	NL	154	568	173	40	6	8	(3	5)	249	69	77	50	8	113	0	0	5	20	12	.63	12	.305	.360	.438
1992 St. Louis	NL	131	509	150	22	3	14	(12	2)	220	62	75	40	8	100	1	0	1	28	12	.70	9	.295	.347	.432
1993 Kansas City	AL	149	499	126	24	3	6	(2	4)	174	64	43	36	5	95	1	1	2	31	13	.70	5	.253	.303	.349
1994 Kansas City	AL	99	366	111	28	1	11	(1	10)	174	56	55	35	6	75	0	0	2	10	12	.45	9	.303	.362	.475
1995 Kansas City	AL	9	30	4	1	0	0	(0	0)	5	2	1	2	0	9	0	0	0	0	0	—	1	.133	.188	.167
2000 New York	AL	20	29	7	0	0	1	(0	1)	10	4	5	2	0	9	0	0	1	0	1	.00	1	.241	.281	.345
1990 Oakland	AL	101	341	90	12	0	8	(3	5)	126	42	39	16	0	65	5	2	1	8	2	.80	8	.264	.306	.370
St. Louis	NL	25	85	23	4	1	3	(2	1)	38	12	13	8	0	16	0	0	0	4	4	.50	1	.271	.333	.447
9 ML YEARS		716	2490	697	134	14	51	(23	28)	1012	316	314	193	27	496	9	3	12	102	57	.64	48	.280	.332	.406

Wally Joyner

Bats: Left **Throws:** Left **Pos:** PH/PR-66; 1B-55; DH-7   **Ht:** 6'2" **Wt:** 200 **Born:** 6/16/62 **Age:** 39

Year Team	Lg	G	AB	H	2B	3B	HR	(Hm	Rd)	TB	R	RBI	TBB	IBB	SO	HBP	SH	SF	SB	CS	SB%	GDP	Avg	OBP	SLG
1986 California	AL	154	593	172	27	3	22	(11	11)	271	82	100	57	8	58	2	10	12	5	2	.71	11	.290	.348	.457
1987 California	AL	149	564	161	33	1	34	(19	15)	298	100	117	72	12	64	5	2	10	8	2	.80	14	.285	.366	.528
1988 California	AL	158	597	176	31	2	13	(6	7)	250	81	85	55	14	51	5	0	6	8	2	.80	16	.295	.356	.419
1989 California	AL	159	593	167	30	2	16	(8	8)	249	78	79	46	7	58	6	1	8	3	2	.60	15	.282	.335	.420
1990 California	AL	83	310	83	15	0	8	(5	3)	122	35	41	41	4	34	1	1	5	2	1	.67	10	.268	.350	.394
1991 California	AL	143	551	166	34	3	21	(10	11)	269	79	96	52	4	66	1	2	5	2	0	1.00	11	.301	.360	.488
1992 Kansas City	AL	149	572	154	36	2	9	(1	8)	221	66	66	55	4	50	4	0	2	11	5	.69	19	.269	.336	.386
1993 Kansas City	AL	141	497	145	36	3	15	(4	11)	232	83	65	66	13	67	3	2	5	5	9	.36	6	.292	.375	.467
1994 Kansas City	AL	97	363	113	20	3	8	(2	6)	163	52	57	47	3	43	0	2	5	3	2	.60	12	.311	.386	.449
1995 Kansas City	AL	131	465	144	28	0	12	(6	6)	208	69	83	69	10	65	2	5	9	3	2	.60	13	.310	.394	.447
1996 San Diego	NL	121	433	120	29	1	8	(5	3)	175	59	65	69	8	71	3	1	4	5	3	.63	6	.277	.377	.404
1997 San Diego	NL	135	455	149	29	2	13	(6	7)	221	59	83	51	5	51	2	0	10	3	5	.38	14	.327	.390	.453
1998 San Diego	NL	131	439	131	30	1	12	(4	8)	199	58	80	51	8	44	1	0	3	1	2	.33	11	.298	.370	.453
1999 San Diego	NL	110	323	80	14	2	5	(2	3)	113	34	43	50	6	54	2	0	3	0	1	.00	8	.248	.363	.350
2000 Atlanta	NL	119	224	63	12	0	5	(2	3)	90	24	32	31	3	31	1	0	4	0	0	—	2	.281	.365	.402
15 ML YEARS		1980	6979	2024	404	25	201	(91	110)	3081	959	1092	820	109	807	38	26	91	59	38	.61	165	.290	.364	.441

Mike Judd

Pitches: Right **Bats:** Right **Pos:** SP-1   **Ht:** 6'1" **Wt:** 217 **Born:** 6/30/75 **Age:** 26

Year Team	Lg	G	GS	CG	GF	IP	BFP	H	R	ER	HR	SH	SF	HB	TBB	IBB	SO	WP	Bk	W	L	Pct.	ShO	Sv-Op	Hld	ERA
2000 Albuquerque *	AAA	24	23	1	1	141.2	628	153	86	71	12	7	4	12	62	0	92	9	1	7	6	.538	0	0- -		4.51
1997 Los Angeles	NL	1	0	0	0	2.2	11	4	0	0	0	0	0	0	0	0	4	0	0	0	0	—	0	0-0	0	0.00
1998 Los Angeles	NL	7	0	0	3	11.1	63	19	19	19	4	2	0	1	9	1	14	0	0	0	1	.000	0	0-0	0	15.09
1999 Los Angeles	NL	7	4	0	0	28	120	30	17	17	4	0	1	0	12	0	22	3	0	3	1	.750	0	0-0	0	5.46
2000 Los Angeles	NL	1	1	0	0	4	20	4	7	7	2	0	0	1	3	0	5	0	0	0	1	.000	0	0-0	0	15.75
4 ML YEARS		16	5	0	3	46	214	57	43	43	10	2	0	3	24	1	45	3	0	3	2	.600	0	0-0	0	8.41

David Justice

Bats: L **Throws:** L **Pos:** LF-68; RF-48; DH-38; PH/PR-4; CF-3   **Ht:** 6'3" **Wt:** 200 **Born:** 4/14/66 **Age:** 35

Year Team	Lg	G	AB	H	2B	3B	HR	(Hm	Rd)	TB	R	RBI	TBB	IBB	SO	HBP	SH	SF	SB	CS	SB%	GDP	Avg	OBP	SLG
1989 Atlanta	NL	16	51	12	3	0	1	(1	0)	18	7	3	3	1	9	1	1	0	2	1	.67	1	.235	.291	.353
1990 Atlanta	NL	127	439	124	23	2	28	(19	9)	235	76	78	64	4	92	0	0	1	11	6	.65	2	.282	.373	.535
1991 Atlanta	NL	109	396	109	25	1	21	(11	10)	199	67	87	65	9	81	3	0	5	8	8	.50	4	.275	.377	.503
1992 Atlanta	NL	144	484	124	19	5	21	(10	11)	216	78	72	79	8	85	2	0	6	2	4	.33	1	.256	.359	.446
1993 Atlanta	NL	157	585	158	15	4	40	(18	22)	301	90	120	78	12	90	3	0	5	3	5	.38	4	.270	.357	.515
1994 Atlanta	NL	104	352	110	16	2	19	(9	10)	187	61	59	69	5	45	2	0	1	2	4	.33	8	.313	.427	.531
1995 Atlanta	NL	120	411	104	17	2	24	(15	9)	197	73	78	73	5	68	2	0	5	4	2	.67	5	.253	.365	.479
1996 Atlanta	NL	40	140	45	9	0	6	(5	1)	72	23	25	21	1	22	1	0	2	1	1	.50	5	.321	.409	.514
1997 Cleveland	AL	139	495	163	31	1	33	(17	16)	295	84	101	80	11	79	0	0	7	3	5	.38	12	.329	.418	.596
1998 Cleveland	AL	146	540	151	39	2	21	(7	14)	257	94	88	76	7	98	0	0	9	9	3	.75	4	.280	.363	.476
1999 Cleveland	AL	133	429	123	18	0	21	(11	10)	204	75	88	94	11	90	2	0	5	1	3	.25	14	.287	.413	.476
2000 Cle-NYY	AL	146	524	150	31	1	41	(24	17)	306	89	118	77	3	91	1	0	3	2	1	.67	13	.286	.377	.584
2000 Cleveland	AL	68	249	66	14	1	21	(10	11)	145	46	58	38	2	49	0	0	1	1	1	.50	7	.265	.361	.582
New York	AL	78	275	84	17	0	20	(14	6)	161	43	60	39	1	42	1	0	2	1	0	1.00	6	.305	.391	.585
12 ML YEARS		1381	4846	1373	246	20	276	(147	129)	2487	817	917	779	77	850	17	1	48	48	43	.53	83	.283	.381	.513

Scott Kamieniecki

Pitches: Right **Bats:** Right **Pos:** RP-52   **Ht:** 6'0" **Wt:** 200 **Born:** 4/19/64 **Age:** 37

Year Team	Lg	G	GS	CG	GF	IP	BFP	H	R	ER	HR	SH	SF	HB	TBB	IBB	SO	WP	Bk	W	L	Pct.	ShO	Sv-Op	Hld	ERA
1991 New York	AL	9	9	0	0	55.1	239	54	24	24	8	2	1	3	22	1	34	1	0	4	4	.500	0	0-0	0	3.90
1992 New York	AL	28	28	4	0	188	804	193	100	91	13	3	5	5	74	9	88	9	1	6	14	.300	0	0-0	0	4.36
1993 New York	AL	30	20	2	4	154.1	659	163	73	70	17	3	5	3	59	7	72	2	0	10	7	.588	0	0-0	0	4.08
1994 New York	AL	22	16	1	2	117.1	505	115	53	49	13	4	3	3	59	5	71	4	0	8	6	.571	0	0-0	1	3.76
1995 New York	AL	17	16	1	0	89.2	391	83	43	40	8	1	0	3	49	1	43	4	0	7	6	.538	0	0-0	0	4.01
1996 New York	AL	7	5	0	0	22.2	120	36	30	28	6	0	0	4	19	1	15	1	0	1	2	.333	0	0-1	0	11.12
1997 Baltimore	AL	30	30	0	0	179.1	764	179	83	80	20	1	6	4	67	2	109	5	0	10	6	.625	0	0-0	0	4.01

109

		HOW MUCH HE PITCHED						WHAT HE GAVE UP													THE RESULTS						
Year Team	Lg	G	GS	CG	GF	IP	BFP	H	R	ER	HR	SH	SF	HB	TBB	IBB	SO	WP	Bk	W	L	Pct.	ShO	Sv-Op	Hld	ERA
1998 Baltimore	AL	12	11	0	1	54.2	249	67	41	41	7	3	2	4	26	0	25	2	0	2	6	.250	0	0-0	0	6.75
1999 Baltimore	AL	43	3	0	18	56.1	248	52	32	31	4	4	3	4	29	2	39	4	0	2	4	.333	0	2-2	11	4.95
2000 Cle-Atl		52	0	0	11	58	271	64	40	36	9	1	0	1	42	6	46	3	0	3	4	.429	0	2-2	10	5.59
2000 Cleveland	AL	26	0	0	7	33.1	157	42	22	21	6	1	0	1	20	5	29	3	0	1	3	.250	0	0-0	5	5.67
Atlanta	NL	26	0	0	4	24.2	114	22	18	15	3	0	0	0	22	1	17	0	0	2		.667	0	2-2	5	5.47
10 ML YEARS		250	138	8	37	975.2	4254	1006	519	490	105	22	25	32	446	34	542	35	1	53	59	.473	0	5-6	22	4.52

Gabe Kapler

Bats: Right **Throws:** Right **Pos:** CF-84; RF-40; PH/PR-1 **Ht:** 6'2" **Wt:** 208 **Born:** 8/31/75 **Age:** 25

		BATTING																	BASERUNNING				PERCENTAGES		
Year Team	Lg	G	AB	H	2B	3B	HR	(Hm	Rd)	TB	R	RBI	TBB	IBB	SO	HBP	SH	SF	SB	CS	SB%	GDP	Avg	OBP	SLG
2000 Oklahoma *	AAA	3	9	3	0	0	0	—	—	3	3	0	3	0	2	0	0	0	0	0	—	0	.333	.500	.333
Tulsa *	AA	3	12	7	0	0	1	—	—	10	3	4	1	0	2	0	0	0	0	0	—	0	.583	.615	.833
1998 Detroit	AL	7	25	5	0	1	0	(0	0)	7	3	0	1	0	4	0	0	0	2	0	1.00	0	.200	.231	.280
1999 Detroit	AL	130	416	102	22	4	18	(12	6)	186	60	49	42	0	74	2	4	4	11	5	.69	7	.245	.315	.447
2000 Texas	AL	116	444	134	32	1	14	(11	3)	210	59	66	42	2	57	0	2	3	8	4	.67	12	.302	.360	.473
3 ML YEARS		253	885	241	54	6	32	(23	9)	403	122	115	85	2	135	2	6	7	21	9	.70	19	.272	.335	.455

Matt Karchner

Pitches: Right **Bats:** Right **Pos:** RP-13 **Ht:** 6'4" **Wt:** 220 **Born:** 6/28/67 **Age:** 34

		HOW MUCH HE PITCHED						WHAT HE GAVE UP													THE RESULTS						
Year Team	Lg	G	GS	CG	GF	IP	BFP	H	R	ER	HR	SH	SF	HB	TBB	IBB	SO	WP	Bk	W	L	Pct.	ShO	Sv-Op	Hld	ERA
2000 Iowa *	AAA	20	1	0	5	42.2	189	46	23	19	2	3	3	2	12	1	35	2	0	2	1	.667	0	2--	—	4.01
1995 Chicago	AL	31	0	0	10	32	137	33	8	6	2	4	1	1	12	2	24	1	0	4	2	.667	0	0-0	13	1.69
1996 Chicago	AL	50	0	0	13	59.1	278	61	42	38	10	2	4	1	41	8	46	4	0	7	4	.636	0	1-9	15	5.76
1997 Chicago	AL	52	0	0	25	52.2	235	50	18	17	4	3	1	0	26	4	30	6	0	3	1	.750	0	15-16	12	2.91
1998 CWS-ChC		61	0	0	26	64.2	299	63	39	37	8	5	4	7	33	8	52	1	0	5	5	.500	0	11-18	10	5.15
1999 Chicago	NL	16	0	0	2	18	80	16	5	5	3	1	0	2	9	0	9	1	0	1	0	1.000	0	0-1	2	2.50
2000 Chicago	NL	13	0	0	5	14.2	75	19	11	10	3	2	1	0	11	0	5	1	2	0	1	.500	0	0-0	0	6.14
1998 Chicago	AL	32	0	0	23	36.2	167	33	21	21	2	3	4	5	19	6	30	0	0	2	4	.333	0	11-15	1	5.15
Chicago	NL	29	0	0	3	28	132	30	18	16	6	2	0	2	14	2	22	1	0	3	1	.750	0	0-3	9	5.14
6 ML YEARS		223	0	0	81	241.1	1093	242	123	113	30	13	14	12	132	22	166	15	0	21	13	.618	0	27-44	50	4.21

Scott Karl

Pitches: Left **Bats:** Left **Pos:** SP-13; RP-10 **Ht:** 6'2" **Wt:** 209 **Born:** 8/9/71 **Age:** 29

		HOW MUCH HE PITCHED						WHAT HE GAVE UP													THE RESULTS						
Year Team	Lg	G	GS	CG	GF	IP	BFP	H	R	ER	HR	SH	SF	HB	TBB	IBB	SO	WP	Bk	W	L	Pct.	ShO	Sv-Op	Hld	ERA
2000 Colo Sprngs *	AAA	3	2	0	1	20.2	88	21	17	13	2	1	0	0	4	1	16	0	0	0	3	.000	0	0--	—	5.66
Lk Elsinore *	A+	1	0	0	0	7	27	5	0	0	0	0	0	0	1	0	5	0	0	0	1	1.000	0	0--	—	0.00
1995 Milwaukee	AL	25	18	1	3	124	548	141	65	57	10	3	3	3	50	6	59	0	0	6	7	.462	0	0-0	1	4.14
1996 Milwaukee	AL	32	32	3	0	207.1	905	220	124	112	29	2	7	11	72	0	121	5	1	13	9	.591	1	0-0	0	4.86
1997 Milwaukee	AL	32	32	1	0	193.1	839	212	103	96	23	5	2	4	67	1	119	6	0	10	13	.435	0	0-0	0	4.40
1998 Milwaukee	NL	33	33	0	0	192.1	843	219	104	94	21	14	3	4	66	4	102	6	0	10	11	.476	0	0-0	0	4.40
1999 Milwaukee	NL	33	33	0	0	197.2	885	246	121	105	21	12	7	8	69	4	74	4	0	11	11	.500	0	0-0	0	4.78
2000 Col-Ana		23	13	0	1	87.1	424	126	77	72	16	4	3	3	45	3	38	5	0	4	5	.444	0	0-0	0	7.42
2000 Colorado	NL	17	9	0	1	65.2	319	95	56	56	14	3	3	3	33	3	29	3	0	4	3	.400	0	0-0	0	7.68
Anaheim	AL	6	4	0	0	21.2	105	31	21	16	2	1	0	0	12	0	9	2	0	2	2	.500	0	0-0	0	6.65
6 ML YEARS		178	161	5	4	1002	4444	1164	594	536	120	40	25	33	369	18	513	26	3	54	56	.491	1	0-0	1	4.81

Eric Karros

Bats: Right **Throws:** Right **Pos:** 1B-153; DH-1; PH/PR-1 **Ht:** 6'4" **Wt:** 226 **Born:** 11/4/67 **Age:** 33

		BATTING																	BASERUNNING				PERCENTAGES		
Year Team	Lg	G	AB	H	2B	3B	HR	(Hm	Rd)	TB	R	RBI	TBB	IBB	SO	HBP	SH	SF	SB	CS	SB%	GDP	Avg	OBP	SLG
1991 Los Angeles	NL	14	14	1	1	0	0	(0	0)	2	0	1	1	0	6	0	0	0	0	0	—	0	.071	.133	.143
1992 Los Angeles	NL	149	545	140	30	1	20	(6	14)	232	63	88	37	3	103	2	0	5	2	4	.33	15	.257	.304	.426
1993 Los Angeles	NL	158	619	153	27	2	23	(13	10)	253	74	80	34	1	82	2	0	3	0	1	.00	17	.247	.287	.409
1994 Los Angeles	NL	111	406	108	21	1	14	(5	9)	173	51	46	29	1	53	2	0	11	2	0	1.00	14	.266	.310	.426
1995 Los Angeles	NL	143	551	164	29	3	32	(16	16)	295	83	105	61	4	115	4	0	14	4	4	.50	14	.298	.369	.535
1996 Los Angeles	NL	154	608	158	29	1	34	(16	18)	291	84	111	53	2	121	1	0	8	8	0	1.00	27	.260	.316	.479
1997 Los Angeles	NL	162	628	167	28	0	31	(13	18)	288	86	104	61	2	116	2	0	9	15	7	.68	10	.266	.329	.459
1998 Los Angeles	NL	139	507	150	20	1	23	(9	14)	241	59	87	47	1	93	3	0	7	7	2	.78	7	.296	.355	.475
1999 Los Angeles	NL	153	578	176	40	0	34	(17	17)	318	74	112	53	0	119	2	0	6	8	5	.62	18	.304	.362	.550
2000 Los Angeles	NL	155	584	146	29	0	31	(15	16)	268	84	106	63	2	122	4	0	12	4	3	.57	18	.250	.321	.459
10 ML YEARS		1338	5040	1363	254	9	242	(114	128)	2361	658	840	439	16	930	22	0	65	50	26	.66	139	.270	.328	.468

Steve Karsay

Pitches: Right **Bats:** Right **Pos:** RP-72 **Ht:** 6'3" **Wt:** 215 **Born:** 3/24/72 **Age:** 29

		HOW MUCH HE PITCHED						WHAT HE GAVE UP													THE RESULTS						
Year Team	Lg	G	GS	CG	GF	IP	BFP	H	R	ER	HR	SH	SF	HB	TBB	IBB	SO	WP	Bk	W	L	Pct.	ShO	Sv-Op	Hld	ERA
1993 Oakland	AL	8	8	0	0	49	210	49	23	22	4	0	2	2	16	1	33	1	0	3	3	.500	0	0-0	0	4.04
1994 Oakland	AL	4	4	1	0	28	115	26	8	8	1	2	1	2	8	0	15	0	0	1	1	.500	0	0-0	0	2.57
1997 Oakland	AL	24	24	0	0	132.2	609	166	92	85	20	2	5	9	47	3	92	7	0	3	12	.200	0	0-0	0	5.77
1998 Cleveland	AL	11	1	0	4	24.1	111	31	16	16	3	1	2	2	6	1	13	2	0	0	2	.000	0	0-0	0	5.92
1999 Cleveland	AL	50	3	0	13	78.2	324	71	29	26	6	2	3	2	30	3	68	5	0	10	2	.833	0	1-3	9	2.97
2000 Cleveland	AL	72	0	0	46	76.2	329	79	33	32	5	2	2	3	25	4	66	0	0	5	9	.357	0	20-29	11	3.76
6 ML YEARS		169	40	1	63	389.1	1698	422	201	189	39	9	15	19	132	12	287	15	0	22	29	.431	0	21-32	22	4.37

Randy Keisler

Pitches: Left **Bats:** Left **Pos:** RP-3; SP-1   **Ht:** 6'3" **Wt:** 190 **Born:** 2/24/76 **Age:** 25

		HOW MUCH HE PITCHED						WHAT HE GAVE UP												THE RESULTS						
Year Team	Lg	G	GS	CG	GF	IP	BFP	H	R	ER	HR	SH	SF	HB	TBB	IBB	SO	WP	Bk	W	L	Pct.	ShO	Sv-Op	Hld	ERA
1998 Oneonta	A-	6	2	0	1	9.2	51	14	10	8	0	0	3	0	7	1	11	0	0	1	1	.500	0	1- —	—	7.45
1999 Greensboro	A	4	4	0	0	22.2	91	12	6	6	1	0	0	0	10	0	42	0	0	1	1	.500	0	0- —	—	2.38
Tampa	A+	15	15	1	0	90	375	67	43	33	2	3	1	3	40	0	77	4	1	10	3	.769	0	0- —	—	3.30
Norwich	AA	8	8	0	0	43.1	189	45	24	22	2	1	3	3	17	0	33	2	0	3	4	.429	0	0- —	—	4.57
2000 Norwich	AA	11	11	1	0	72.2	313	63	29	21	4	0	1	1	34	1	70	4	1	6	2	.750	0	0- —	—	2.60
Columbus	AAA	17	17	1	0	113.1	479	104	44	38	9	3	4	4	42	1	86	5	3	8	3	.727	1	0- —	—	3.02
2000 New York	AL	4	1	0	0	10.2	52	16	14	14	1	0	0	0	8	0	6	0	0	1	0	1.000	0	0-0	0	11.81

Kenny Kelly

Bats: Right **Throws:** Right **Pos:** PH/PR-2; DH-1   **Ht:** 6'3" **Wt:** 180 **Born:** 1/26/79 **Age:** 22

		BATTING																	BASERUNNING				PERCENTAGES		
Year Team	Lg	G	AB	H	2B	3B	HR	(Hm	Rd)	TB	R	RBI	TBB	IBB	SO	HBP	SH	SF	SB	CS	SB%	GDP	Avg	OBP	SLG
1997 Devil Rays	R	27	99	21	2	1	2	—	—	31	21	7	11	0	24	2	0	0	6	3	.67	1	.212	.304	.313
1998 Chston-SC	A	54	218	61	7	5	3	—	—	87	46	17	19	0	52	4	0	1	19	4	.83	1	.280	.347	.399
1999 St. Pete	A+	51	206	57	10	4	3	—	—	84	39	21	18	0	46	4	0	0	14	5	.74	1	.277	.346	.408
2000 Orlando	AA	124	489	123	17	8	3	—	—	165	73	29	59	1	119	6	4	2	31	21	.60	9	.252	.338	.337
2000 Tampa Bay	AL	2	1	0	0	0	0	(0	0)	0	0	0	0	0	0	0	0	0	0	0	—	0	.000	.000	.000

Roberto Kelly

Bats: Right **Throws:** Right **Pos:** LF-7; CF-3   **Ht:** 6'2" **Wt:** 198 **Born:** 10/1/64 **Age:** 36

		BATTING																	BASERUNNING				PERCENTAGES		
Year Team	Lg	G	AB	H	2B	3B	HR	(Hm	Rd)	TB	R	RBI	TBB	IBB	SO	HBP	SH	SF	SB	CS	SB%	GDP	Avg	OBP	SLG
1987 New York	AL	23	52	14	3	0	1	(0	1)	20	12	7	5	0	15	0	1	1	9	3	.75	0	.269	.328	.385
1988 New York	AL	38	77	19	4	1	1	(1	0)	28	9	7	3	0	15	0	3	1	5	2	.71	0	.247	.272	.364
1989 New York	AL	137	441	133	18	3	9	(2	7)	184	65	48	41	3	89	6	8	0	35	12	.74	9	.302	.369	.417
1990 New York	AL	162	641	183	32	4	15	(5	10)	268	85	61	33	0	148	4	4	4	42	17	.71	7	.285	.323	.418
1991 New York	AL	126	486	130	22	2	20	(11	9)	216	68	69	45	2	77	5	2	5	32	9	.78	14	.267	.333	.444
1992 New York	AL	152	580	158	31	2	10	(6	4)	223	81	66	41	4	96	4	1	6	28	5	.85	19	.272	.322	.384
1993 Cincinnati	NL	78	320	102	17	3	9	(4	5)	152	44	35	17	0	43	2	0	3	21	5	.81	10	.319	.354	.475
1994 Cin-Atl	NL	110	434	127	23	3	9	(2	5)	183	73	45	35	1	71	3	0	3	19	11	.63	8	.293	.347	.422
1995 Mon-LA	NL	136	504	140	23	2	7	(2	5)	188	58	57	22	6	79	6	0	7	19	10	.66	14	.278	.312	.373
1996 Minnesota	AL	98	322	104	17	4	6	(3	3)	147	41	47	23	0	53	7	0	5	10	2	.83	17	.323	.375	.457
1997 Min-Sea	AL	105	368	107	26	2	12	(8	4)	173	58	59	22	0	67	3	2	3	9	5	.64	6	.291	.333	.470
1998 Texas	AL	75	257	83	7	3	16	(6	10)	144	46	44	8	0	46	3	1	1	0	2	.00	4	.323	.349	.560
1999 Texas	AL	87	290	87	17	1	8	(4	4)	130	41	37	21	0	57	5	0	2	6	1	.86	5	.300	.355	.448
2000 New York	AL	10	25	3	1	0	1	(1	0)	7	4	1	1	0	6	1	0	0	0	0	—	0	.120	.185	.280
1994 Cincinnati	NL	47	179	54	8	0	3	(1	2)	71	29	21	11	1	35	3	0	1	9	8	.53	3	.302	.351	.397
Atlanta	NL	63	255	73	15	3	6	(3	3)	112	44	24	24	0	36	0	0	2	10	3	.77	5	.286	.345	.439
1995 Montreal	NL	24	95	26	4	0	1	(0	1)	33	11	9	7	1	14	2	0	0	4	3	.57	4	.274	.337	.347
Los Angeles	NL	112	409	114	19	2	6	(2	4)	155	47	48	15	5	65	4	0	7	15	7	.68	10	.279	.306	.379
1997 Minnesota	AL	75	247	71	19	2	5	(5	0)	109	39	37	17	0	50	2	1	2	7	4	.64	4	.287	.336	.441
Seattle	AL	30	121	36	7	0	7	(3	4)	64	19	22	5	0	17	1	1	1	2	1	.67	2	.298	.328	.529
14 ML YEARS		1337	4797	1390	241	30	124	(57	67)	2063	687	585	317	16	862	49	22	41	235	84	.74	113	.290	.337	.430

Jason Kendall

Bats: Right **Throws:** Right **Pos:** C-147; PH/PR-5   **Ht:** 6'0" **Wt:** 195 **Born:** 6/26/74 **Age:** 27

		BATTING																	BASERUNNING				PERCENTAGES		
Year Team	Lg	G	AB	H	2B	3B	HR	(Hm	Rd)	TB	R	RBI	TBB	IBB	SO	HBP	SH	SF	SB	CS	SB%	GDP	Avg	OBP	SLG
1996 Pittsburgh	NL	130	414	124	23	5	3	(2	1)	166	54	42	35	11	30	15	3	4	5	2	.71	7	.300	.372	.401
1997 Pittsburgh	NL	144	486	143	36	4	8	(5	3)	211	71	49	49	2	53	31	1	5	18	6	.75	11	.294	.391	.434
1998 Pittsburgh	NL	149	535	175	36	3	12	(6	6)	253	95	75	51	3	55	31	2	8	26	5	.84	6	.327	.411	.473
1999 Pittsburgh	NL	78	280	93	20	3	8	(5	3)	143	61	41	38	3	32	12	0	4	22	3	.88	8	.332	.428	.511
2000 Pittsburgh	NL	152	579	185	33	6	14	(7	7)	272	112	58	79	3	79	15	1	4	22	12	.65	13	.320	.412	.470
5 ML YEARS		653	2294	720	148	21	45	(25	20)	1045	393	265	252	22	245	104	7	25	93	28	.77	45	.314	.402	.456

Adam Kennedy

Bats: Left **Throws:** Right **Pos:** 2B-155; PH/PR-8   **Ht:** 6'1" **Wt:** 180 **Born:** 1/10/76 **Age:** 25

		BATTING																	BASERUNNING				PERCENTAGES		
Year Team	Lg	G	AB	H	2B	3B	HR	(Hm	Rd)	TB	R	RBI	TBB	IBB	SO	HBP	SH	SF	SB	CS	SB%	GDP	Avg	OBP	SLG
1997 New Jersey	A-	29	114	39	6	3	0	—	—	51	20	19	13	0	10	2	1	2	9	1	.90	3	.342	.412	.447
Pr William	A+	35	154	48	9	3	1	—	—	66	24	27	6	1	17	2	1	0	4	3	.57	3	.312	.346	.429
1998 Pr William	A+	17	69	18	6	0	0	—	—	24	9	7	5	0	12	0	0	1	5	2	.71	1	.261	.307	.348
Arkansas	AA	52	205	57	11	2	6	—	—	90	35	24	8	0	21	2	3	3	6	2	.75	4	.278	.307	.439
Memphis	AAA	74	305	93	22	7	4	—	—	141	36	41	12	0	42	1	5	2	15	4	.79	3	.305	.331	.462
1999 Memphis	AAA	91	367	120	22	4	10	—	—	180	69	63	29	0	36	4	0	5	20	6	.77	7	.327	.378	.490
1999 St. Louis	NL	33	102	26	10	1	1	(1	0)	41	12	16	3	0	8	2	1	2	0	1	.00	1	.255	.284	.402
2000 Anaheim	AL	156	598	159	33	11	9	(7	2)	241	82	72	28	5	73	3	8	4	22	8	.73	10	.266	.300	.403
2 ML YEARS		189	700	185	43	12	10	(8	2)	282	94	88	31	5	81	5	9	6	22	9	.71	11	.264	.298	.403

Jeff Kent

Bats: Right **Throws:** Right **Pos:** 2B-150; 1B-16; PH/PR-2   **Ht:** 6'1" **Wt:** 205 **Born:** 3/7/68 **Age:** 33

		BATTING																	BASERUNNING				PERCENTAGES		
Year Team	Lg	G	AB	H	2B	3B	HR	(Hm	Rd)	TB	R	RBI	TBB	IBB	SO	HBP	SH	SF	SB	CS	SB%	GDP	Avg	OBP	SLG
1992 Tor-NYM		102	305	73	21	2	11	(4	7)	131	52	50	27	0	76	7	0	4	2	3	.40	5	.239	.312	.430
1993 New York	NL	140	496	134	24	0	21	(9	12)	221	65	80	30	2	88	8	6	4	4	4	.50	11	.270	.320	.446

Year Team	Lg	G	AB	H	2B	3B	HR	(Hm	Rd)	TB	R	RBI	TBB	IBB	SO	HBP	SH	SF	SB	CS	SB%	GDP	Avg	OBP	SLG
1994 New York	NL	107	415	121	24	5	14	(10	4)	197	53	68	23	3	84	10	1	3	1	4	.20	7	.292	.341	.475
1995 New York	NL	125	472	131	22	3	20	(11	9)	219	65	65	29	3	89	8	1	4	3	3	.50	9	.278	.327	.464
1996 NYM-Cle		128	437	124	27	1	12	(4	8)	189	61	55	31	1	78	2	1	6	6	4	.60	8	.284	.330	.432
1997 San Francisco	NL	155	580	145	38	2	29	(13	16)	274	90	121	48	6	133	13	0	10	11	3	.79	14	.250	.316	.472
1998 San Francisco	NL	137	526	156	37	3	31	(17	14)	292	94	128	48	4	110	9	1	10	9	4	.69	16	.297	.359	.555
1999 San Francisco	NL	138	511	148	40	2	23	(11	12)	261	86	101	61	3	112	5	0	8	13	6	.68	12	.290	.366	.511
2000 San Francisco	NL	159	587	196	41	7	33	(14	19)	350	114	125	90	6	107	9	0	9	12	9	.57	17	.334	.424	.596
1992 Toronto	AL	65	192	46	13	1	8	(2	6)	85	36	35	20	0	47	6	0	4	2	1	.67	3	.240	.324	.443
New York	NL	37	113	27	8	1	3	(2	1)	46	16	15	7	0	29	1	0	0	0	2	.00	2	.239	.289	.407
1996 New York	NL	89	335	97	20	1	9	(2	7)	146	45	39	21	1	56	1	1	3	4	3	.57	7	.290	.331	.436
Cleveland	NL	39	102	27	7	0	3	(2	1)	43	16	16	10	0	22	1	0	1	2	1	.67	1	.265	.328	.422
9 ML YEARS		1191	4329	1228	274	25	194	(93	101)	2134	680	793	387	28	877	71	10	58	61	40	.60	99	.284	.348	.493

Masao Kida

Pitches: Right Bats: Right Pos: RP-2 Ht: 6'3" Wt: 210 Born: 9/12/68 Age: 32

		HOW MUCH HE PITCHED						WHAT HE GAVE UP												THE RESULTS						
Year Team	Lg	G	GS	CG	GF	IP	BFP	H	R	ER	HR	SH	SF	HB	TBB	IBB	SO	WP	Bk	W	L	Pct.	ShO	Sv-Op	Hld	ERA
1999 Toledo	AAA	3	0	0	1	5.2	23	6	2	2	2	0	0	0	1	0	4	0	0	0	0		0	0--	--	3.18
2000 Toledo	AAA	21	0	0	20	25	96	21	6	6	3	1	1	0	4	1	26	1	0	2	1	.667	0	7--	--	2.16
1999 Detroit	AL	49	0	0	21	64.2	292	73	48	45	6	1	4	4	30	3	50	7	0	1	0	1.000	0	1-1	4	6.26
2000 Detroit	AL	2	0	0	0	2.2	13	5	3	3	1	0	0	0	0	0	0	0	0	0	0		0	0-0	0	10.13
2 ML YEARS		51	0	0	21	67.1	305	78	51	48	7	1	4	4	30	3	50	7	0	1	0	1.000	0	1-1	4	6.42

Brooks Kieschnick

Bats: Left Throws: Right Pos: PH/PR-13; 1B-1 Ht: 6'4" Wt: 230 Born: 6/6/72 Age: 29

Year Team	Lg	G	AB	H	2B	3B	HR	(Hm	Rd)	TB	R	RBI	TBB	IBB	SO	HBP	SH	SF	SB	CS	SB%	GDP	Avg	OBP	SLG
2000 Louisville *	AAA	113	440	122	25	0	25	—	—	222	68	90	38	6	107	1	0	2	2	1	.67	10	.277	.335	.527
1996 Chicago	NL	25	29	10	2	0	1	(0	1)	15	6	6	3	0	8	0	0	0	0	0	—	0	.345	.406	.517
1997 Chicago	NL	39	90	18	2	0	4	(3	1)	32	9	12	12	0	21	0	0	0	1	0	1.00	2	.200	.294	.356
2000 Cincinnati	NL	14	12	0	0	0	0	(0	0)	0	0	0	1	0	5	0	0	0	0	0	—	0	.000	.077	.000
3 ML YEARS		78	131	28	4	0	5	(3	2)	47	15	18	16	0	34	0	0	0	1	0	1.00	2	.214	.299	.359

Darryl Kile

Pitches: Right Bats: Right Pos: SP-34 Ht: 6'5" Wt: 212 Born: 12/2/68 Age: 32

		HOW MUCH HE PITCHED						WHAT HE GAVE UP												THE RESULTS						
Year Team	Lg	G	GS	CG	GF	IP	BFP	H	R	ER	HR	SH	SF	HB	TBB	IBB	SO	WP	Bk	W	L	Pct.	ShO	Sv-Op	Hld	ERA
1991 Houston	NL	37	22	0	5	153.2	689	144	81	63	16	9	5	6	84	4	100	5	4	7	11	.389	0	0-1	0	3.69
1992 Houston	NL	22	22	2	0	125.1	554	124	61	55	8	5	4	6	63	4	90	3	4	5	10	.333	0	0-0	0	3.95
1993 Houston	NL	32	26	4	0	171.2	733	152	73	67	12	5	7	15	69	1	141	9	3	15	8	.652	2	0-0	0	3.51
1994 Houston	NL	24	24	0	0	147.2	664	153	84	75	13	14	2	9	82	6	105	10	0	9	6	.600	0	0-0	0	4.57
1995 Houston	NL	25	21	0	1	127	570	114	81	70	5	7	3	12	73	2	113	11	1	4	12	.250	0	0-0	0	4.96
1996 Houston	NL	35	33	4	1	219	975	233	113	102	16	10	9	16	97	8	219	13	3	12	11	.522	0	0-0	0	4.19
1997 Houston	NL	34	34	6	0	255.2	1056	208	87	73	19	17	10	10	94	2	205	7	1	19	7	.731	4	0-0	0	2.57
1998 Colorado	NL	36	35	4	0	230.1	1020	257	141	133	28	15	8	7	96	4	158	12	0	13	17	.433	1	0-0	0	5.20
1999 Colorado	NL	32	32	1	0	190.2	888	225	150	140	33	9	6	6	109	5	116	13	1	8	13	.381	0	0-0	0	6.61
2000 St. Louis	NL	34	34	5	0	232.1	960	215	109	101	33	11	8	13	58	1	192	8	1	20	9	.690	1	0-0	0	3.91
10 ML YEARS		311	283	26	8	1853.1	8109	1825	980	879	183	102	64	98	825	37	1439	91	18	112	104	.519	8	0-1	0	4.27

Byung-Hyun Kim

Pitches: Right Bats: Right Pos: RP-60; SP-1 Ht: 5'11" Wt: 176 Born: 1/19/79 Age: 22

		HOW MUCH HE PITCHED						WHAT HE GAVE UP												THE RESULTS						
Year Team	Lg	G	GS	CG	GF	IP	BFP	H	R	ER	HR	SH	SF	HB	TBB	IBB	SO	WP	Bk	W	L	Pct.	ShO	Sv-Op	Hld	ERA
1999 El Paso	AA	10	0	0	3	21.1	81	6	5	5	0	3	1	3	9	0	32	0	2	2	0	1.000	0	0--	—	2.11
Diamndbcks	R	1	1	0	0	2	7	1	0	0	0	0	0	1	1	0	2	0	0	0	0	—	0	0--	—	0.00
Tucson	AAA	11	3	0	3	30	123	21	9	8	2	0	0	1	15	1	40	1	3	4	0	1.000	0	1--	—	2.40
2000 Tucson	AAA	2	2	0	0	8.1	29	1	0	0	0	0	0	1	4	0	13	1	0	0	0	—	0	0--	—	0.00
1999 Arizona	NL	25	0	0	10	27.1	121	20	15	14	2	1	0	5	20	2	31	4	1	1	2	.333	0	1-4	4	4.61
2000 Arizona	NL	61	1	0	30	70.2	320	52	39	35	9	2	3	9	46	5	111	3	2	6	6	.500	0	14-20	5	4.46
2 ML YEARS		86	1	0	40	98	441	72	54	49	11	3	3	14	66	7	142	7	3	7	8	.467	0	15-24	8	4.50

Ray King

Pitches: Left Bats: Left Pos: RP-36 Ht: 6'1" Wt: 230 Born: 1/15/74 Age: 27

		HOW MUCH HE PITCHED						WHAT HE GAVE UP												THE RESULTS						
Year Team	Lg	G	GS	CG	GF	IP	BFP	H	R	ER	HR	SH	SF	HB	TBB	IBB	SO	WP	Bk	W	L	Pct.	ShO	Sv-Op	Hld	ERA
1995 Billings	R+	28	0	0	15	43	169	31	11	8	1	2	0	0	15	3	43	1	1	3	0	1.000	0	5--	—	1.67
1996 Macon	A	18	10	1	2	70.2	286	63	34	22	4	0	0	0	20	0	63	2	1	3	5	.375	0	0--	—	2.80
Durham	A+	14	14	2	0	82.2	364	104	54	41	3	4	4	3	15	2	52	2	1	3	6	.333	0	0--	—	4.46
1997 Greenville	AA	12	9	0	0	65.2	305	85	53	50	9	0	0	1	24	2	42	4	0	5	5	.500	0	0--	—	6.85
Durham	A+	24	6	0	6	71.2	335	89	54	43	6	7	1	4	26	4	60	4	0	6	9	.400	0	3--	—	5.40
1998 West Tenn	AA	25	0	0	8	29.2	121	23	8	8	1	1	1	1	10	0	26	2	0	1	3	.250	0	3--	—	2.43
Iowa	AAA	37	0	0	7	32.1	143	36	20	18	4	1	0	0	15	1	26	4	0	1	3	.250	0	2--	—	5.01
1999 Iowa	AAA	29	0	0	19	43	183	31	11	9	1	2	0	2	22	3	41	2	0	4	0	1.000	0	2--	—	1.88
2000 Iowa	AAA	1	0	0	1	1.1	9	1	0	0	0	0	0	0	0	0	1	0	0	1	0	1.000	0	0--	—	0.00
Indianapolis	AAA	29	0	0	6	25.2	112	26	15	10	1	3	1	1	12	0	20	3	0		3	.000	0	1--	—	3.51
1999 Chicago	NL	10	0	0	0	10.2	50	11	8	7	2	1	0	3	10	0	5	1	0	0	0	—	0	0-0	0	5.91
2000 Milwaukee	NL	36	0	0	8	28.2	111	18	7	4	1	0	1	0	14	1	19	1	0	3	2	.600	0	0-1	5	1.26
2 ML YEARS		46	0	0	8	39.1	161	29	15	11	3	1	1	3	20	1	24	2	0	3	2	.600	0	0-1	7	2.52

Gene Kingsale

Bats: Both **Throws:** Right **Pos:** CF-24; PH/PR-3; DH-1 **Ht:** 6'3" **Wt:** 194 **Born:** 8/20/76 **Age:** 24

Year Team	Lg	G	AB	H	2B	3B	HR	(Hm	Rd)	TB	R	RBI	TBB	IBB	SO	HBP	SH	SF	SB	CS	SB%	GDP	Avg	OBP	SLG
1994 Orioles	R	50	168	52	2	3	0	—	—	60	26	9	18	0	24	2	1	1	15	8	.65	1	.310	.381	.357
1995 Bluefield	R+	47	171	54	11	2	0	—	—	69	45	16	27	0	31	5	4	2	20	8	.71	0	.316	.420	.404
1996 Frederick	A+	49	166	45	6	4	0	—	—	59	26	9	19	1	32	6	3	2	23	4	.85	1	.271	.363	.355
1997 Orioles	R	6	17	5	0	0	0	—	—	5	2	0	2	0	2	1	0	0	1	0	1.00	0	.294	.400	.294
Bowie	AA	13	46	19	6	0	0	—	—	25	8	4	5	0	4	1	1	0	5	1	.83	2	.413	.481	.543
1998 Rochester	AAA	18	55	12	1	1	0	—	—	15	3	2	4	0	8	1	1	0	3	3	.50	3	.218	.283	.273
Bowie	AA	111	427	112	11	5	1	—	—	136	69	34	48	2	79	12	10	4	29	12	.71	6	.262	.350	.319
1999 Bowie	AA	67	268	63	11	4	3	—	—	91	43	23	33	0	46	1	6	2	13	10	.57	4	.235	.319	.340
Rochester	AAA	48	191	59	9	0	2	—	—	74	31	20	13	0	23	3	3	1	10	9	.53	2	.309	.361	.387
2000 Orioles	R	5	16	5	0	0	0	—	—	5	7	4	4	0	0	0	0	1	2	0	1.00	0	.313	.429	.313
Frederick	A+	6	25	11	3	0	1	—	—	17	8	3	1	0	6	0	0	0	2	1	.67	0	.440	.462	.680
Bowie	AA	3	11	4	2	0	1	—	—	9	5	5	3	0	0	0	0	0	1	0	1.00	0	.364	.500	.818
Rochester	AAA	2	10	4	1	0	0	—	—	5	2	1	0	0	0	0	0	0	1	1	.50	1	.400	.400	.500
1996 Baltimore	AL	3	0	0	0	0	0	(0	0)	0	0	0	0	0	0	0	0	0	0	0	—	0	—	—	—
1998 Baltimore	AL	11	2	0	0	0	0	(0	0)	0	1	0	0	0	1	0	0	0	0	0	—	0	.000	.000	.000
1999 Baltimore	AL	28	85	21	2	0	0	(0	0)	23	9	7	5	0	13	2	2	1	1	3	.25	3	.247	.301	.271
2000 Baltimore	AL	26	88	21	2	1	0	(0	0)	25	13	9	2	0	14	0	0	1	2	2	.33	4	.239	.253	.284
4 ML YEARS		68	175	42	4	1	0	(0	0)	48	23	16	7	0	28	2	2	2	2	5	.29	7	.240	.274	.274

Mike Kinkade

Bats: R **Throws:** R **Pos:** DH-2; PH/PR-2; 1B-1; RF-1 **Ht:** 6'1" **Wt:** 210 **Born:** 5/6/73 **Age:** 28

Year Team	Lg	G	AB	H	2B	3B	HR	(Hm	Rd)	TB	R	RBI	TBB	IBB	SO	HBP	SH	SF	SB	CS	SB%	GDP	Avg	OBP	SLG
1995 Helena	R+	69	266	94	19	1	4	—	—	127	76	39	43	2	38	10	0	6	26	9	.74	6	.353	.452	.477
1996 Beloit	A	135	499	151	33	4	15	—	—	237	105	100	47	7	69	32	3	6	23	12	.66	10	.303	.394	.475
1997 El Paso	AA	125	468	180	35	12	12	—	—	275	112	109	52	0	66	13	1	6	17	4	.81	13	.385	.455	.588
1998 Louisville	AAA	80	291	90	24	6	7	—	—	147	57	46	36	1	52	6	1	2	10	2	.83	7	.309	.394	.505
Norfolk	AAA	30	125	35	5	0	1	—	—	43	12	18	3	0	24	5	1	2	6	1	.86	5	.280	.319	.344
1999 Norfolk	AAA	84	312	96	20	2	7	—	—	141	53	49	21	2	31	5	0	2	7	1	.88	9	.308	.359	.452
2000 Binghamton	AA	90	317	116	24	3	10	—	—	176	66	67	35	4	39	9	0	3	18	7	.72	6	.366	.440	.555
Bowie	AA	8	27	7	1	0	3	—	—	17	4	5	3	1	7	2	0	0	0	0	—	2	.259	.375	.630
Rochester	AAA	15	55	20	5	0	1	—	—	28	10	10	11	0	11	1	0	1	0	1	.00	0	.364	.471	.509
1998 New York	NL	3	2	0	0	0	0	(0	0)	0	2	0	0	0	0	0	0	0	0	0	—	0	.000	.000	.000
1999 New York	NL	28	46	9	2	1	2	(1	1)	19	3	6	3	0	9	2	0	0	1	0	1.00	1	.196	.275	.413
2000 NYM-Bal		5	9	3	1	0	0	(0	0)	4	0	1	0	0	1	1	0	0	0	0	—	0	.333	.400	.444
2000 New York	NL	2	2	0	0	0	0	(0	0)	0	0	0	0	0	1	0	0	0	0	0	—	0	.000	.000	.000
Baltimore	AL	3	7	3	1	0	0	(0	0)	4	0	1	0	0	0	1	0	0	0	0	—	0	.429	.500	.571
3 ML YEARS		36	57	12	3	1	2	(1	1)	23	5	7	3	0	10	3	0	0	1	0	1.00	1	.211	.286	.404

Matt Kinney

Pitches: Right **Bats:** Right **Pos:** SP-8 **Ht:** 6'5" **Wt:** 220 **Born:** 12/16/76 **Age:** 24

Year Team	Lg	G	GS	CG	GF	IP	BFP	H	R	ER	HR	SH	SF	HB	TBB	IBB	SO	WP	Bk	W	L	Pct.	ShO	Sv-Op	Hld	ERA
1995 Red Sox	R	8	2	0	4	27.2	119	29	13	9	0	1	2	2	10	0	11	5	0	1	3	.250	0	2- —	—	2.93
1996 Lowell	A-	15	15	0	0	87.1	387	68	51	26	0	3	3	9	44	2	72	13	1	3	9	.250	0	0- —	—	2.68
1997 Michigan	A	22	22	2	0	117.1	514	93	59	46	4	5	2	0	78	2	123	6	0	8	5	.615	1	0- —	—	3.53
1998 Sarasota	A+	22	20	2	1	121.1	536	109	70	54	5	5	2	2	75	3	96	19	2	9	6	.600	1	1- —	—	4.01
Fort Myers	A+	7	7	0	0	37.1	162	31	18	13	0	2	1	0	18	0	39	6	0	3	2	.600	0	0- —	—	3.13
1999 Twins	R	3	3	0	0	5.2	24	6	4	3	0	0	0	0	3	0	8	0	0	1	0	1.000	0	0- —	—	4.76
New Britain	AA	14	13	0	0	60.2	284	69	54	48	8	2	3	4	36	0	50	6	1	4	7	.364	0	0- —	—	7.12
2000 New Britain	AA	15	15	0	0	86.1	358	74	31	26	7	2	2	1	35	0	93	4	0	6	1	.857	0	0- —	—	2.71
Salt Lake	AAA	9	9	0	0	55	228	42	26	26	5	1	1	1	26	0	59	2	1	5	2	.714	0	0- —	—	4.25
2000 Minnesota	AL	8	8	0	0	42.1	186	41	26	24	7	0	4	0	25	1	24	4	0	2	2	.500	0	0-0	0	5.10

Danny Klassen

Bats: Right **Throws:** Right **Pos:** 3B-25; SS-3; PH/PR-3 **Ht:** 6'0" **Wt:** 175 **Born:** 9/22/75 **Age:** 25

Year Team	Lg	G	AB	H	2B	3B	HR	(Hm	Rd)	TB	R	RBI	TBB	IBB	SO	HBP	SH	SF	SB	CS	SB%	GDP	Avg	OBP	SLG
1993 Brewers	R	38	117	26	5	0	2	—	—	37	26	20	24	3	28	8	1	4	14	3	.82	2	.222	.379	.316
Helena	R+	18	45	9	1	0	0	—	—	10	8	3	7	0	11	2	1	0	2	1	.67	2	.200	.333	.222
1994 Beloit	A	133	458	119	20	3	6	—	—	163	61	54	58	0	123	12	17	3	28	14	.67	3	.260	.356	.356
1995 Beloit	A	59	218	60	15	2	2	—	—	85	27	25	16	0	43	4	0	3	12	4	.75	4	.275	.332	.390
1996 Stockton	A+	118	432	116	22	4	2	—	—	152	58	46	34	0	77	10	5	2	14	8	.64	12	.269	.335	.352
1997 El Paso	AA	135	519	172	30	6	14	—	—	256	112	81	48	1	104	10	4	4	16	9	.64	13	.331	.396	.493
1998 Tucson	AAA	73	281	82	25	2	10	—	—	141	47	47	19	1	54	6	0	5	6	2	.75	11	.292	.344	.502
1999 Diamndbcks	R	6	17	4	1	0	0	—	—	5	2	1	1	0	4	0	0	0	0	0	—	1	.235	.278	.294
Tucson	AAA	64	245	66	16	3	6	—	—	106	38	33	20	1	51	1	0	2	5	3	.63	5	.269	.325	.433
2000 Tucson	AAA	28	97	31	7	2	2	—	—	48	25	14	19	1	23	1	2	0	1	2	.33	2	.320	.436	.495
1998 Arizona	NL	29	108	21	2	1	3	(3	0)	34	12	8	9	0	33	1	0	1	1	1	.50	5	.194	.263	.315
1999 Arizona	NL	1	1	1	0	0	0	(0	0)	1	0	0	0	0	0	0	0	0	0	0	—	0	1.000	1.000	1.000
2000 Arizona	NL	29	76	18	3	0	2	(2	0)	27	13	8	8	0	24	1	2	0	1	1	.50	0	.237	.318	.355
3 ML YEARS		59	185	40	5	1	5	(5	0)	62	25	16	17	0	57	2	2	0	2	2	.50	5	.216	.289	.335

Ryan Klesko

Bats: L Throws: L Pos: 1B-136; PH/PR-15; LF-2; RF-2 **Ht: 6'3" Wt: 220 Born: 6/12/71 Age: 30**

						BATTING												BASERUNNING				PERCENTAGES		
Year Team	Lg	G	AB	H	2B	3B	HR	(Hm | Rd)	TB	R	RBI	TBB	IBB	SO	HBP	SH	SF	SB	CS	SB%	GDP	Avg	OBP	SLG
1992 Atlanta	NL	13	14	0	0	0	0	(0 | 0)	0	0	1	0	0	5	1	0	0	0	0	—	0	.000	.067	.000
1993 Atlanta	NL	22	17	6	1	0	2	(2 | 0)	13	3	5	3	1	4	0	0	0	0	0	—	0	.353	.450	.765
1994 Atlanta	NL	92	245	68	13	3	17	(7 | 10)	138	42	47	26	3	48	1	0	4	1	0	1.00	8	.278	.344	.563
1995 Atlanta	NL	107	329	102	25	2	23	(15 | 8)	200	48	70	47	10	72	2	0	3	5	4	.56	8	.310	.396	.608
1996 Atlanta	NL	153	528	149	21	4	34	(20 | 14)	280	90	93	68	10	129	2	0	4	6	3	.67	10	.282	.364	.530
1997 Atlanta	NL	143	467	122	23	6	24	(10 | 14)	229	67	84	48	5	130	4	1	2	4	4	.50	12	.261	.334	.490
1998 Atlanta	NL	129	427	117	29	1	18	(8 | 10)	202	69	70	56	5	66	3	0	4	5	3	.63	9	.274	.359	.473
1999 Atlanta	NL	133	404	120	28	2	21	(12 | 9)	215	55	80	53	8	69	2	0	7	5	2	.71	6	.297	.376	.532
2000 San Diego	NL	145	494	140	33	2	26	(9 | 17)	255	88	92	91	9	81	1	0	4	23	7	.77	10	.283	.393	.516
9 ML YEARS		937	2925	824	173	20	165	(83 | 82)	1532	462	542	392	51	604	16	1	28	49	23	.68	63	.282	.367	.524

Steve Kline

Pitches: Left Bats: Both Pos: RP-83 **Ht: 6'1" Wt: 215 Born: 8/22/72 Age: 28**

		HOW MUCH HE PITCHED						WHAT HE GAVE UP										THE RESULTS						
Year Team	Lg	G	GS	CG	GF	IP	BFP	H	R	ER	HR	SH	SF	HB	TBB	IBB	SO	WP	Bk	W	L	Pct.	ShO	Sv-Op	Hld	ERA
1997 Cle-Mon		46	1	0	7	52.2	248	73	37	35	10	4	2	2	23	4	37	4	1	4	4	.500	0	0-3	5	5.98
1998 Montreal	NL	78	0	0	18	71.2	319	62	25	22	4	1	3	2	41	7	76	5	0	3	6	.333	0	1-2	18	2.76
1999 Montreal	NL	82	0	0	18	69.2	297	56	32	29	8	3	1	3	33	6	69	2	0	7	4	.636	0	0-2	16	3.75
2000 Montreal	NL	83	0	0	42	82.1	349	88	36	32	8	2	1	3	27	2	64	4	0	1	5	.167	0	14-18	12	3.50
1997 Cleveland	AL	20	1	0	0	26.1	130	42	19	17	6	1	0	1	13	1	17	3	1	3	1	.750	0	0-2	4	5.81
Montreal	NL	26	0	0	7	26.1	118	31	18	18	4	3	2	1	10	3	20	1	0	1	3	.250	0	0-1	1	6.15
4 ML YEARS		289	1	0	85	276.1	1213	279	130	118	30	10	6	11	124	19	246	15	1	15	19	.441	0	15-25	51	3.84

Chuck Knoblauch

Bats: Right Throws: Right Pos: 2B-82; DH-20; PH/PR-1 **Ht: 5'9" Wt: 175 Born: 7/7/68 Age: 32**

						BATTING												BASERUNNING				PERCENTAGES		
Year Team	Lg	G	AB	H	2B	3B	HR	(Hm	Rd)	TB	R	RBI	TBB	IBB	SO	HBP	SH	SF	SB	CS	SB%	GDP	Avg	OBP	SLG
2000 Tampa *	A+	1	1	0	0	0	0	—	—	0	0	0	0	0	1	0	0	0	0	0	—	0	.000	.500	.000
1991 Minnesota	AL	151	565	159	24	6	1	(1	0)	198	78	50	59	0	40	4	1	5	25	5	.83	8	.281	.351	.350
1992 Minnesota	AL	155	600	178	19	6	2	(0	2)	215	104	56	88	1	60	5	2	12	34	13	.72	8	.297	.384	.358
1993 Minnesota	AL	153	602	167	27	4	2	(2	0)	208	82	41	65	1	44	9	4	5	29	11	.73	11	.277	.354	.346
1994 Minnesota	AL	109	445	139	45	3	5	(1	4)	205	85	51	41	2	56	10	0	3	35	6	.85	13	.312	.381	.461
1995 Minnesota	AL	136	538	179	34	8	11	(4	7)	262	107	63	78	3	95	10	0	3	46	18	.72	15	.333	.424	.487
1996 Minnesota	AL	153	578	197	35	14	13	(7	6)	299	140	72	98	6	74	19	0	6	45	14	.76	9	.341	.448	.517
1997 Minnesota	AL	156	611	178	26	10	9	(2	7)	251	117	58	84	6	84	17	1	4	62	10	.86	11	.291	.390	.411
1998 New York	AL	150	603	160	25	4	17	(5	12)	244	117	64	76	1	70	18	2	7	31	12	.72	13	.265	.361	.405
1999 New York	AL	150	603	176	36	4	18	(11	7)	274	120	68	83	0	57	21	3	5	28	9	.76	7	.292	.393	.454
2000 New York	AL	102	400	113	22	2	5	(5	0)	154	75	26	46	0	45	8	1	2	15	7	.68	6	.283	.366	.385
10 ML YEARS		1415	5545	1646	293	61	83	(38	45)	2310	1025	549	718	20	625	121	13	52	350	105	.77	101	.297	.386	.417

Randy Knorr

Bats: Right Throws: Right Pos: C-15 **Ht: 6'2" Wt: 230 Born: 11/12/68 Age: 32**

						BATTING												BASERUNNING				PERCENTAGES		
Year Team	Lg	G	AB	H	2B	3B	HR	(Hm	Rd)	TB	R	RBI	TBB	IBB	SO	HBP	SH	SF	SB	CS	SB%	GDP	Avg	OBP	SLG
2000 Nashville *	AAA	13	40	6	1	0	1	—	—	10	3	4	6	0	11	0	0	0	0	1	.00	0	.150	.261	.250
Oklahoma *	AAA	70	252	64	16	1	6	—	—	100	36	41	22	0	50	0	0	1	0	0	—	12	.254	.313	.397
1991 Toronto	AL	3	1	0	0	0	0	(0	0)	0	0	0	1	0	1	0	0	0	0	0	—	0	.000	.500	.000
1992 Toronto	AL	8	19	5	0	0	1	(0	1)	8	1	2	1	1	5	0	0	0	0	0	—	0	.263	.300	.421
1993 Toronto	AL	39	101	25	3	2	4	(2	2)	44	11	20	9	0	29	0	2	0	0	0	—	2	.248	.309	.436
1994 Toronto	AL	40	124	30	2	0	7	(4	3)	53	20	19	10	0	35	1	0	1	0	0	—	7	.242	.301	.427
1995 Toronto	AL	45	132	28	8	0	3	(2	1)	45	18	16	11	0	28	0	1	0	0	0	—	5	.212	.273	.341
1996 Houston	NL	37	87	17	5	0	1	(1	0)	25	7	7	5	2	18	0	1	0	0	0	—	0	.195	.245	.287
1997 Houston	NL	4	8	3	0	0	1	(1	0)	6	1	1	0	0	2	0	0	0	0	1	.00	0	.375	.375	.750
1998 Florida	NL	15	49	10	4	1	2	(0	2)	22	4	11	1	0	10	0	1	0	0	0	—	1	.204	.216	.449
1999 Houston	NL	13	30	5	1	0	0	(0	0)	6	2	0	1	0	8	0	0	0	0	0	—	0	.167	.194	.200
2000 Texas	AL	15	34	10	2	0	2	(2	0)	18	5	2	0	0	3	0	0	0	0	0	—	1	.294	.294	.529
10 ML YEARS		219	585	133	25	3	21	(12	9)	227	69	78	39	3	139	2	6	3	0	1	.00	16	.227	.277	.388

Billy Koch

Pitches: Right Bats: Right Pos: RP-68 **Ht: 6'3" Wt: 205 Born: 12/14/74 Age: 26**

		HOW MUCH HE PITCHED						WHAT HE GAVE UP										THE RESULTS						
Year Team	Lg	G	GS	CG	GF	IP	BFP	H	R	ER	HR	SH	SF	HB	TBB	IBB	SO	WP	Bk	W	L	Pct.	ShO	Sv-Op	Hld	ERA
1997 Dunedin	A+	3	3	0	0	21.2	88	27	10	5	1	1	1	0	3	0	20	1	1	0	1	.000	0	0--	—	2.08
1998 Dunedin	A+	25	25	0	0	124.2	528	120	65	52	8	2	2	7	41	0	108	4	3	14	7	.667	0	0--	—	3.75
Syracuse	AAA	2	2	0	0	5.2	31	9	9	9	1	0	1	0	5	0	9	0	1	0	1	.000	0	0--	—	14.29
1999 Syracuse	AAA	5	5	0	0	25.2	111	27	11	11	3	0	0	0	10	0	22	0	2	3	0	1.000	0	0--	—	3.86
1999 Toronto	AL	56	0	0	48	63.2	272	55	26	24	5	4	1	3	30	5	57	0	0	0	5	.000	0	31-35	—	3.39
2000 Toronto	AL	68	0	0	62	78.2	326	78	28	23	6	4	0	2	18	4	60	1	0	9	3	.750	0	33-38	—	2.63
2 ML YEARS		124	0	0	110	142.1	598	133	54	47	11	8	1	5	48	9	117	1	0	9	8	.529	0	64-73	—	2.97

Ryan Kohlmeier

Pitches: Right Bats: Right Pos: RP-25 **Ht: 6'2" Wt: 197 Born: 6/25/77 Age: 24**

		HOW MUCH HE PITCHED						WHAT HE GAVE UP										THE RESULTS						
Year Team	Lg	G	GS	CG	GF	IP	BFP	H	R	ER	HR	SH	SF	HB	TBB	IBB	SO	WP	Bk	W	L	Pct.	ShO	Sv-Op	Hld	ERA
1997 Bowie	AA	2	0	0	1	2.2	9	0	0	0	0	0	0	0	2	0	5	0	1	0	0	—	0	1--	—	0.00
Delmarva	A	50	0	0	41	74.2	276	48	22	22	8	2	1	2	17	1	99	2	1	2	2	.500	0	24--	—	2.65

Year Team	Lg	G	GS	CG	GF	IP	BFP	H	R	ER	HR	SH	SF	HB	TBB	IBB	SO	WP	Bk	W	L	Pct.	ShO	Sv-Op	Hld	ERA
1998 Bowie	AA	42	0	0	28	50	219	52	37	34	13	1	1	3	16	1	56	2	1	4	4	.500	0	7- --	—	6.12
Frederick	A+	9	0	0	9	9.2	44	10	9	8	1	0	2	1	3	0	15	0	1	1	2	.333	0	5- --	—	7.45
1999 Bowie	AA	55	0	0	49	62.2	256	44	23	22	10	4	2	1	29	1	78	2	1	3	7	.300	0	23- --	—	3.16
2000 Rochester	AAA	37	0	0	28	46.2	192	33	14	13	4	2	3	2	16	2	49	2	0	1	4	.200	0	10- --	—	2.51
2000 Baltimore	AL	25	0	0	22	26.1	120	30	9	7	1	1	1	0	15	2	17	0	0	0	1	.000	0	13-14	0	2.39

Brandon Kolb

Pitches: Right **Bats:** Right **Pos:** RP-11 **Ht:** 6'1" **Wt:** 190 **Born:** 11/20/73 **Age:** 27

Year Team	Lg	G	GS	CG	GF	IP	BFP	H	R	ER	HR	SH	SF	HB	TBB	IBB	SO	WP	Bk	W	L	Pct.	ShO	Sv-Op	Hld	ERA
1995 Idaho Falls	R+	9	8	0	0	38.1	181	42	33	30	1	2	2	2	29	0	21	5	0	2	3	.400	1	0- --	—	7.04
Padres	R	4	4	1	0	23	100	13	10	3	0	0	0	3	13	0	21	4	0	1	1	.500	1	0- --	—	1.17
1996 Clinton	A	27	27	3	0	181.1	776	170	84	69	7	6	7	8	76	1	138	19	0	16	9	.640	0	0- --	—	3.42
1997 Rancho Cuc	A+	10	10	0	0	63	261	60	29	21	0	1	1	2	22	0	49	5	0	3	2	.600	0	0- --	—	3.00
1998 Rancho Cuc	A+	4	4	0	0	20.2	92	14	8	7	3	0	0	1	18	0	16	0	1	0	2	.000	0	0- --	—	3.05
Mobile	AA	21	6	0	4	62	274	46	33	31	4	3	3	1	40	0	58	6	0	4	3	.571	0	1- --	—	4.50
1999 Mobile	AA	7	0	0	6	11.1	52	8	4	1	0	1	0	1	4	0	14	1	0	0	2	.000	0	2- --	—	0.79
Las Vegas	AAA	42	0	0	16	61.2	281	72	36	27	3	1	3	3	29	1	63	7	0	2	1	.667	0	4- --	—	3.94
2000 Las Vegas	AAA	47	0	0	35	56.1	250	53	35	28	2	0	1	5	21	0	59	2	0	3	3	.500	0	16- --	—	4.47
2000 San Diego	NL	11	0	0	5	14	66	16	8	7	0	0	1	0	11	1	12	3	0	0	1	.000	0	0-1	0	4.50

Danny Kolb

Pitches: Right **Bats:** Right **Pos:** RP-1 **Ht:** 6'4" **Wt:** 215 **Born:** 3/29/75 **Age:** 26

Year Team	Lg	G	GS	CG	GF	IP	BFP	H	R	ER	HR	SH	SF	HB	TBB	IBB	SO	WP	Bk	W	L	Pct.	ShO	Sv-Op	Hld	ERA
1995 Rangers	R	12	11	0	0	53	219	38	22	13	0	0	2	3	28	0	46	8	2	1	7	.125	0	0- --	—	2.21
1996 Chston-SC	A	20	20	4	0	126	514	80	50	36	5	6	0	6	60	2	127	22	4	8	6	.571	2	0- --	—	2.57
Charlotte	A+	6	6	0	0	38	162	38	18	18	1	1	0	1	14	0	28	2	0	2	2	.500	0	0- --	—	4.26
Tulsa	AA	2	2	0	0	11.2	45	5	1	1	0	0	0	1	8	0	7	0	0	1	0	1.000	0	0- --	—	0.77
1997 Tulsa	AA	2	2	0	0	11.1	50	7	7	6	1	0	0	0	11	0	6	4	0	0	2	.000	0	0- --	—	4.76
Charlotte	A+	24	23	3	0	133	600	146	91	72	10	8	5	8	62	1	83	12	0	4	10	.286	0	0- --	—	4.87
1998 Tulsa	AA	28	28	2	0	162.1	730	187	104	87	11	3	5	8	76	1	83	8	1	12	11	.522	0	0- --	—	4.82
Oklahoma	AAA	1	0	0	1	1	5	1	0	0	0	0	0	0	1	0	0	0	0	0	0	—	0	0- --	—	0.00
1999 Tulsa	AA	7	7	1	0	38.2	170	38	16	12	0	3	1	2	18	0	32	2	0	1	2	.333	1	0- --	—	2.79
Oklahoma	AAA	11	8	0	2	60	261	74	35	34	4	2	0	1	27	0	21	2	0	5	3	.625	0	0- --	—	5.10
2000 Oklahoma	AAA	13	0	0	13	18.1	74	11	6	2	0	1	2	0	8	1	18	1	0	4	1	.800	0	4- --	—	0.98
1999 Texas	AL	16	0	0	6	31	139	33	18	16	2	0	1	1	15	0	15	2	0	2	1	.667	0	0-0	0	4.65
2000 Texas	AL	1	0	0	0	0.2	9	5	5	5	0	0	1	0	2	0	0	0	0	0	0	—	0	0-0	0	67.50
2 ML YEARS		17	0	0	6	31.2	148	38	23	21	2	0	1	1	17	0	15	2	0	2	1	.667	0	0-0	0	5.97

Paul Konerko

Bats: R **Throws:** R **Pos:** 1B-122; PH/PR-10; DH-7; 3B-7 **Ht:** 6'3" **Wt:** 211 **Born:** 3/5/76 **Age:** 25

Year Team	Lg	G	AB	H	2B	3B	HR	(Hm	Rd)	TB	R	RBI	TBB	IBB	SO	HBP	SH	SF	SB	CS	SB%	GDP	Avg	OBP	SLG
1997 Los Angeles	NL	6	7	1	0	0	0	(0	0)	1	0	0	1	0	2	0	0	0	0	0	—	1	.143	.250	.143
1998 LA-Cin	NL	75	217	47	4	0	7	(2	5)	72	21	29	16	0	40	3	0	3	0	1	.00	10	.217	.276	.332
1999 Chicago	AL	142	513	151	31	4	24	(16	8)	262	71	81	45	0	68	2	1	3	1	0	1.00	19	.294	.352	.511
2000 Chicago	AL	143	524	156	31	1	21	(10	11)	252	84	97	47	0	72	10	0	5	1	0	1.00	22	.298	.363	.481
1998 Los Angeles	NL	49	144	31	1	0	4	(2	2)	44	14	16	10	0	30	2	0	2	0	1	.00	5	.215	.272	.306
Cincinnati	NL	26	73	16	3	0	3	(0	3)	28	7	13	6	0	10	1	0	1	0	0	—	5	.219	.284	.384
4 ML YEARS		366	1261	355	66	5	52	(28	24)	587	176	207	109	0	182	15	1	11	2	1	.67	52	.282	.343	.466

Corey Koskie

Bats: Left **Throws:** Right **Pos:** 3B-139; PH/PR-11; DH-1 **Ht:** 6'3" **Wt:** 217 **Born:** 6/28/73 **Age:** 28

Year Team	Lg	G	AB	H	2B	3B	HR	(Hm	Rd)	TB	R	RBI	TBB	IBB	SO	HBP	SH	SF	SB	CS	SB%	GDP	Avg	OBP	SLG
1998 Minnesota	AL	11	29	4	0	0	1	(1	0)	7	2	2	2	0	10	0	0	0	0	0	—	0	.138	.194	.241
1999 Minnesota	AL	117	342	106	21	0	11	(4	7)	160	42	58	40	4	72	5	2	3	4	4	.50	4	.310	.387	.468
2000 Minnesota	AL	146	474	142	32	4	9	(1	8)	209	79	65	77	7	104	4	1	3	5	4	.56	11	.300	.400	.441
3 ML YEARS		274	845	252	53	4	21	(6	15)	376	123	125	119	11	186	9	3	6	9	8	.53	17	.298	.388	.445

Mark Kotsay

Bats: L **Throws:** L **Pos:** RF-139; PH/PR-15; CF-9; 1B-2 **Ht:** 6'0" **Wt:** 190 **Born:** 12/2/75 **Age:** 25

Year Team	Lg	G	AB	H	2B	3B	HR	(Hm	Rd)	TB	R	RBI	TBB	IBB	SO	HBP	SH	SF	SB	CS	SB%	GDP	Avg	OBP	SLG
1997 Florida	NL	14	52	10	1	1	0	(0	0)	13	5	4	4	0	7	0	1	0	3	0	1.00	1	.192	.250	.250
1998 Florida	NL	154	578	161	25	7	11	(5	6)	233	72	68	34	2	61	1	7	3	10	5	.67	17	.279	.318	.403
1999 Florida	NL	148	495	134	23	9	8	(5	3)	199	57	50	29	5	50	0	2	9	7	6	.54	11	.271	.306	.402
2000 Florida	NL	152	530	158	31	5	12	(5	7)	235	87	57	42	2	46	0	2	4	19	9	.68	17	.298	.347	.443
4 ML YEARS		468	1655	463	80	22	31	(15	16)	680	221	179	109	9	164	1	12	16	39	20	.66	46	.280	.322	.411

Chad Kreuter

Bats: Both **Throws:** Right **Pos:** C-78; PH/PR-3 **Ht:** 6'2" **Wt:** 200 **Born:** 8/26/64 **Age:** 36

Year Team	Lg	G	AB	H	2B	3B	HR	(Hm	Rd)	TB	R	RBI	TBB	IBB	SO	HBP	SH	SF	SB	CS	SB%	GDP	Avg	OBP	SLG
1988 Texas	AL	16	51	14	2	1	1	(0	1)	21	3	5	7	0	13	0	0	0	0	0	—	1	.275	.362	.412
1989 Texas	AL	87	158	24	3	0	5	(2	3)	42	16	9	27	0	40	0	6	1	0	1	.00	4	.152	.274	.266

Year Team	Lg	G	AB	H	2B	3B	HR	(Hm	Rd)	TB	R	RBI	TBB	IBB	SO	HBP	SH	SF	SB	CS	SB%	GDP	Avg	OBP	SLG
1990 Texas	AL	22	22	1	1	0	0	(0	0)	2	2	2	8	0	9	0	1	1	0	0	—	0	.045	.290	.091
1991 Texas	AL	3	4	0	0	0	0	(0	0)	0	0	0	0	0	1	0	0	0	0	0	—	0	.000	.000	.000
1992 Detroit	AL	67	190	48	9	0	2	(2	0)	63	22	16	20	1	38	0	3	2	0	1	.00	8	.253	.321	.332
1993 Detroit	AL	119	374	107	23	3	15	(9	6)	181	59	51	49	4	92	3	2	3	2	1	.67	5	.286	.371	.484
1994 Detroit	AL	65	170	38	8	0	1	(1	0)	49	17	19	28	0	36	0	2	4	0	1	.00	3	.224	.327	.288
1995 Seattle	AL	26	75	17	5	0	1	(0	1)	25	12	8	5	0	22	2	1	0	0	0	—	0	.227	.293	.333
1996 Chicago	AL	46	114	25	8	0	3	(2	1)	42	14	18	13	0	29	2	2	1	0	0	—	2	.219	.308	.368
1997 CWS-Ana	AL	89	255	59	9	2	5	(3	2)	87	25	21	29	0	66	0	1	0	0	3	.00	7	.231	.310	.341
1998 CWS-Ana	AL	96	252	63	10	1	2	(2	0)	81	27	33	33	1	49	3	5	1	1	0	1.00	6	.250	.343	.321
1999 Kansas City	AL	107	324	73	15	0	5	(2	3)	103	31	35	34	1	65	6	2	2	0	0	—	16	.225	.309	.318
2000 Los Angeles	NL	80	212	56	13	0	6	(4	2)	87	32	28	54	0	48	2	2	1	1	0	1.00	6	.264	.416	.410
1997 Chicago	AL	19	37	8	2	1	1	(1	0)	15	6	3	8	0	9	0	0	0	0	1	.00	0	.216	.356	.405
Anaheim	AL	70	218	51	7	1	4	(2	2)	72	19	18	21	0	57	0	1	0	0	2	.00	7	.234	.301	.330
1998 Chicago	AL	93	245	62	9	1	2	(2	0)	79	26	33	32	1	45	3	5	1	1	0	1.00	8	.253	.345	.322
Anaheim	AL	3	7	1	1	0	0	(0	0)	2	1	0	1	0	4	0	0	0	0	0	—	0	.143	.250	.286
13 ML YEARS		823	2201	525	106	7	46	(27	19)	783	260	245	307	7	508	18	27	16	4	7	.36	60	.239	.334	.356

David Lamb

Bats: B Throws: R Pos: 3B-3; 2B-2; SS-2; PH/PR-2   **Ht: 6'2" Wt: 165 Born: 6/6/75 Age: 26**

Year Team	Lg	G	AB	H	2B	3B	HR	(Hm	Rd)	TB	R	RBI	TBB	IBB	SO	HBP	SH	SF	SB	CS	SB%	GDP	Avg	OBP	SLG
1993 Orioles	R	16	56	10	1	0	0	—	—	11	4	6	10	0	8	0	0	0	2	0	1.00	1	.179	.303	.196
1994 Albany	A	92	436	74	9	2	0	—	—	87	37	29	32	0	40	2	6	0	4	1	.80	4	.240	.316	.282
1995 Bowie	AA	1	4	1	0	0	0	—	—	1	0	1	0	0	1	0	0	0	0	0	—	0	.250	.250	.250
Frederick	A+	124	436	97	14	2	2	—	—	121	39	34	38	5	81	10	8	5	6	7	.46	10	.222	.297	.278
1996 High Desert	A+	116	460	118	24	3	3	—	—	157	63	55	50	1	68	10	5	2	5	6	.45	19	.257	.341	.341
1997 Frederick	A+	70	249	65	21	1	2	—	—	94	30	39	25	2	32	6	3	3	3	1	.75	10	.261	.339	.378
Bowie	AA	73	269	89	20	2	4	—	—	125	46	38	34	0	35	4	4	4	0	0	—	3	.331	.408	.465
1998 Bowie	AA	66	241	73	10	1	2	—	—	91	29	25	27	1	33	1	4	1	1	3	.25	6	.303	.374	.378
Rochester	AAA	48	178	53	7	1	1	—	—	65	24	16	17	1	25	3	1	2	1	5	.17	4	.298	.365	.365
1999 Durham	AAA	7	30	7	3	0	0	—	—	10	7	7	2	0	4	0	2	1	0	1	.00	0	.233	.273	.333
2000 Norfolk	AAA	109	356	80	23	1	2	—	—	111	45	35	40	3	49	8	9	6	8	3	.73	9	.225	.312	.312
1999 Tampa Bay	AL	55	124	28	5	1	1	(0	1)	38	18	13	10	0	18	0	0	0	1	0	1.00	4	.226	.284	.306
2000 New York	NL	7	5	1	0	0	0	(0	0)	1	1	0	1	0	1	0	0	0	0	0	—	0	.200	.333	.200
2 ML YEARS		62	129	29	5	1	1	(0	1)	39	19	13	11	0	19	0	0	0	1	0	1.00	4	.225	.286	.302

Mike Lamb

Bats: Left Throws: Right Pos: 3B-135; PH/PR-3; DH-2   **Ht: 6'1" Wt: 195 Born: 8/9/75 Age: 25**

Year Team	Lg	G	AB	H	2B	3B	HR	(Hm	Rd)	TB	R	RBI	TBB	IBB	SO	HBP	SH	SF	SB	CS	SB%	GDP	Avg	OBP	SLG
1997 Pulaski	R+	60	233	78	19	3	9	—	—	130	59	47	31	2	18	4	2	6	7	2	.78	5	.335	.412	.558
1998 Charlotte	A+	135	566	142	35	3	9	—	—	230	83	93	45	5	63	4	2	7	18	7	.72	10	.302	.356	.429
1999 Tulsa	AA	137	544	176	51	5	21	—	—	300	98	100	53	5	65	7	1	8	4	3	.57	11	.324	.386	.551
Oklahoma	AAA	2	2	1	0	0	0	—	—	1	0	0	1	1	0	1	0	0	0	1	.00	0	.500	.750	.500
2000 Oklahoma	AAA	14	55	14	5	1	2	—	—	27	8	5	5	0	6	0	0	0	2	1	.67	5	.255	.317	.491
2000 Texas	AL	138	493	137	25	2	6	(4	2)	184	65	47	34	6	60	4	5	2	0	2	.00	10	.278	.328	.373

Tom Lampkin

Bats: Left Throws: Right Pos: C-28; PH/PR-7; DH-3   **Ht: 5'11" Wt: 195 Born: 3/4/64 Age: 37**

Year Team	Lg	G	AB	H	2B	3B	HR	(Hm	Rd)	TB	R	RBI	TBB	IBB	SO	HBP	SH	SF	SB	CS	SB%	GDP	Avg	OBP	SLG
2000 Tacoma *	AAA	3	4	2	1	0	0	—	—	3	1	0	3	0	2	0	0	0	0	0	—	0	.250	.455	.375
1988 Cleveland	AL	4	4	0	0	0	0	(0	0)	0	0	0	1	0	0	0	0	0	0	0	—	1	.000	.200	.000
1990 San Diego	NL	26	63	14	0	1	1	(1	0)	19	4	4	4	1	9	0	0	0	0	1	.00	2	.222	.269	.302
1991 San Diego	NL	38	58	11	3	1	0	(0	0)	16	4	3	3	0	9	0	0	0	0	0	—	2	.190	.230	.276
1992 San Diego	NL	9	17	4	0	0	0	(0	0)	4	3	0	6	0	1	1	0	0	2	0	1.00	0	.235	.458	.235
1993 Milwaukee	AL	73	162	32	8	0	4	(1	3)	52	22	25	20	3	26	0	2	4	7	3	.70	2	.198	.280	.321
1995 San Francisco	NL	65	76	21	2	0	1	(1	0)	26	8	9	9	1	8	1	0	0	2	0	1.00	1	.276	.360	.342
1996 San Francisco	NL	66	177	41	8	0	6	(5	1)	67	26	29	20	2	22	5	0	2	1	5	.17	2	.232	.324	.379
1997 St. Louis	NL	108	229	56	8	1	7	(2	5)	87	28	22	28	5	30	4	4	2	2	1	.67	8	.245	.335	.380
1998 St. Louis	NL	93	216	50	12	1	6	(4	2)	82	25	28	24	5	32	7	1	0	3	2	.60	5	.231	.328	.380
1999 Seattle	AL	76	206	60	11	2	9	(5	4)	102	29	34	13	1	32	5	1	2	1	3	.25	2	.291	.345	.495
2000 Seattle	AL	36	103	26	6	1	7	(3	4)	55	15	23	9	1	17	3	0	2	0	0	—	7	.252	.325	.534
11 ML YEARS		594	1311	315	58	7	41	(22	19)	510	164	177	137	19	186	26	8	12	18	15	.55	30	.240	.322	.389

Ray Lankford

Bats: L Throws: L Pos: LF-116; PH/PR-14; CF-2; DH-1   **Ht: 5'11" Wt: 200 Born: 6/5/67 Age: 34**

Year Team	Lg	G	AB	H	2B	3B	HR	(Hm	Rd)	TB	R	RBI	TBB	IBB	SO	HBP	SH	SF	SB	CS	SB%	GDP	Avg	OBP	SLG
1990 St. Louis	NL	39	126	36	10	1	3	(2	1)	57	12	12	13	0	27	0	0	0	8	2	.80	1	.286	.353	.452
1991 St. Louis	NL	151	566	142	23	15	9	(4	5)	222	83	69	41	1	114	1	4	3	44	20	.69	4	.251	.301	.392
1992 St. Louis	NL	153	598	175	40	6	20	(13	7)	287	87	86	72	6	147	5	2	5	42	24	.64	5	.293	.371	.480
1993 St. Louis	NL	127	407	97	17	3	7	(6	1)	141	64	45	81	7	111	3	1	3	14	14	.50	5	.238	.366	.346
1994 St. Louis	NL	109	416	111	25	5	19	(8	11)	203	89	57	58	3	113	4	0	4	11	10	.52	0	.267	.359	.488
1995 St. Louis	NL	132	483	134	35	2	25	(16	9)	248	81	82	63	6	110	2	0	5	24	8	.75	10	.277	.360	.513
1996 St. Louis	NL	149	545	150	36	8	21	(8	13)	266	100	86	79	10	133	3	1	7	35	7	.83	12	.275	.366	.486
1997 St. Louis	NL	133	465	137	36	3	31	(10	21)	272	94	98	95	10	125	0	0	5	21	11	.66	9	.295	.411	.585
1998 St. Louis	NL	154	533	156	37	1	31	(20	11)	288	94	105	86	5	151	3	0	4	26	5	.84	4	.293	.391	.540
1999 St. Louis	NL	122	422	129	32	1	15	(7	8)	208	77	63	49	3	110	3	0	6	14	4	.78	6	.306	.380	.493
2000 St. Louis	NL	128	392	99	16	3	26	(18	8)	199	73	65	70	1	148	4	0	6	5	6	.45	6	.253	.367	.508
11 ML YEARS		1397	4953	1366	307	48	207	(113	94)	2390	854	768	707	52	1289	28	8	44	244	111	.69	62	.276	.367	.483

Mike Lansing

Bats: Right **Throws:** Right **Pos:** 2B-137; PH/PR-4; 3B-1   **Ht:** 6'0" **Wt:** 195 **Born:** 4/3/68 **Age:** 33

Year Team	Lg	G	AB	H	2B	3B	HR	(Hm	Rd)	TB	R	RBI	TBB	IBB	SO	HBP	SH	SF	SB	CS	SB%	GDP	Avg	OBP	SLG
1993 Montreal	NL	141	491	141	29	1	3	(1	2)	181	64	45	46	2	56	5	10	3	23	5	.82	16	.287	.352	.369
1994 Montreal	NL	106	394	105	21	2	5	(3	2)	145	44	35	30	3	37	7	2	2	12	8	.60	10	.266	.328	.368
1995 Montreal	NL	127	467	119	30	2	10	(4	6)	183	47	62	28	2	65	3	1	3	27	4	.87	14	.255	.299	.392
1996 Montreal	NL	159	641	183	40	2	11	(3	8)	260	99	53	44	1	85	10	9	1	23	8	.74	19	.285	.341	.406
1997 Montreal	NL	144	572	161	45	2	20	(11	9)	270	86	70	45	2	92	5	6	3	11	5	.69	9	.281	.338	.472
1998 Colorado	NL	153	584	161	39	2	12	(7	5)	240	73	66	39	4	88	5	7	3	10	3	.77	18	.276	.325	.411
1999 Colorado	NL	35	145	45	9	0	4	(2	2)	66	24	15	7	0	22	1	1	1	2	0	1.00	3	.310	.344	.455
2000 Col-Bos		139	504	121	18	6	11	(9	2)	184	72	60	38	2	75	0	3	3	8	2	.80	20	.240	.292	.365
2000 Colorado	NL	90	365	94	14	6	11	(9	2)	153	62	47	31	1	49	0	3	1	8	2	.80	13	.258	.315	.419
Boston	AL	49	139	27	4	0	0	(0	0)	31	10	13	7	1	26	0	0	2			—	7	.194	.230	.223
8 ML YEARS		1004	3798	1036	231	17	76	(40	36)	1529	509	406	277	16	520	36	39	19	116	35	.77	109	.273	.327	.403

Yovanny Lara

Pitches: Right **Bats:** Right **Pos:** RP-6   **Ht:** 6'4" **Wt:** 180 **Born:** 9/20/75 **Age:** 25

Year Team	Lg	G	GS	CG	GF	IP	BFP	H	R	ER	HR	SH	SF	HB	TBB	IBB	SO	WP	Bk	W	L	Pct.	ShO	Sv-Op	Hld	ERA
1995 Expos	R	11	4	0	1	30	139	35	21	17	4	0	3	2	19	0	16	0	1	1	2	.333	0	0--	—	5.10
1996 Vermont	A-	15	15	2	0	92.1	392	95	54	48	5	3	3	4	27	0	63	7	1	6	3	.667	0	0--	—	4.68
1997 Cape Fear	A	28	27	1	0	170	742	199	107	86	13	9	9	9	45	0	100	13	1	9	12	.429	0	0--	—	4.55
1998 Cape Fear	A	22	9	0	3	54.2	281	61	51	43	5	2	4	7	48	0	31	15	0	2	5	.286	0	0--	—	7.08
1999 Harrisburg	AA	9	0	0	6	13.2	71	19	12	12	2	1	0	0	8	0	10	0	0	0	0	—	0	0--	—	7.90
Jupiter	A+	33	0	0	15	65.1	264	59	24	20	1	7	2	0	18	2	42	2	1	3	1	.750	0	0--	—	2.76
2000 Harrisburg	AA	33	0	0	19	41.1	182	40	15	13	2	3	2	0	22	1	34	3	0	3	2	.600	0	5--	—	2.83
2000 Montreal	NL	6	0	0	2	5.2	29	5	4	4	0	0	1	0	8	0	3	0	0	0	0	—	0	0-0	0	6.35

Andy Larkin

Pitches: Right **Bats:** Right **Pos:** RP-21   **Ht:** 6'4" **Wt:** 210 **Born:** 6/27/74 **Age:** 27

Year Team	Lg	G	GS	CG	GF	IP	BFP	H	R	ER	HR	SH	SF	HB	TBB	IBB	SO	WP	Bk	W	L	Pct.	ShO	Sv-Op	Hld	ERA
2000 Louisville *	AAA	27	0	0	10	41.2	173	30	13	12	4	0	2	2	17	1	40	5	0	1	0	1.000	0	4--	—	2.59
1996 Florida	NL	1	1	0	0	5	22	3	1	1	0	0	0	1	4	0	2	0	0	0	0	—	0	0-0	0	1.80
1998 Florida	NL	17	14	0	0	74.2	373	101	87	80	12	5	2	4	55	3	43	3	0	3	8	.273	0	0-0	0	9.64
2000 Cin-KC		21	0	0	11	26	127	35	24	23	6	2	1	0	16	2	24	2	0	0	3	.000	0	1-3	1	7.96
2000 Cincinnati	NL	3	0	0	2	6.2	30	6	4	4	1	0	0	0	5	0	7	0	0	0	0	—	0	0-0	0	5.40
Kansas City	AL	18	0	0	9	19.1	97	29	20	19	5	2	1	0	11	2	17	2	0	0	3	.000	0	1-3	1	8.84
3 ML YEARS		39	15	0	11	105.2	522	139	112	104	18	7	3	5	75	5	69	5	0	3	11	.214	0	1-3	1	8.86

Barry Larkin

Bats: Right **Throws:** Right **Pos:** SS-102; DH-1; PH/PR-1   **Ht:** 6'0" **Wt:** 185 **Born:** 4/28/64 **Age:** 37

Year Team	Lg	G	AB	H	2B	3B	HR	(Hm	Rd)	TB	R	RBI	TBB	IBB	SO	HBP	SH	SF	SB	CS	SB%	GDP	Avg	OBP	SLG
1986 Cincinnati	NL	41	159	45	4	3	3	(3	0)	64	27	19	9	1	21	0	0	1	8	0	1.00	6	.283	.320	.403
1987 Cincinnati	NL	125	439	107	16	2	12	(6	6)	163	64	43	36	3	52	5	3	5	21	6	.78	8	.244	.306	.371
1988 Cincinnati	NL	151	588	174	32	5	12	(9	3)	252	91	56	41	3	24	8	10	5	40	7	.85	7	.296	.347	.429
1989 Cincinnati	NL	97	325	111	14	4	4	(1	3)	145	47	36	20	5	23	2	2	8	10	5	.67	7	.342	.375	.446
1990 Cincinnati	NL	158	614	185	25	6	7	(4	3)	243	85	67	49	3	49	7	7	4	30	5	.86	14	.301	.358	.396
1991 Cincinnati	NL	123	464	140	27	4	20	(16	4)	235	88	69	55	1	64	3	3	2	24	6	.80	7	.302	.378	.506
1992 Cincinnati	NL	140	533	162	32	6	12	(8	4)	242	76	78	63	8	58	4	2	7	15	4	.79	13	.304	.377	.454
1993 Cincinnati	NL	100	384	121	20	3	8	(4	4)	171	57	51	51	6	33	1	1	3	14	1	.93	13	.315	.394	.445
1994 Cincinnati	NL	110	427	119	23	5	9	(3	6)	179	78	52	64	3	58	0	5	5	26	2	.93	6	.279	.369	.419
1995 Cincinnati	NL	131	496	158	29	6	15	(8	7)	244	98	66	61	2	49	3	3	4	51	5	.91	6	.319	.394	.492
1996 Cincinnati	NL	152	517	154	32	4	33	(14	19)	293	117	89	96	3	52	7	0	7	36	10	.78	20	.298	.410	.567
1997 Cincinnati	NL	73	224	71	17	3	4	(0	4)	106	34	20	47	6	24	3	1	0	14	3	.82	3	.317	.440	.473
1998 Cincinnati	NL	145	538	166	34	10	17	(8	9)	271	93	72	79	5	69	2	4	3	26	3	.90	12	.309	.397	.504
1999 Cincinnati	NL	161	583	171	30	4	12	(7	5)	245	108	75	93	5	57	2	5	4	30	8	.79	12	.293	.390	.420
2000 Cincinnati	NL	102	396	124	26	5	11	(6	5)	193	71	41	48	0	31	1	2	0	14	6	.70	10	.313	.389	.487
15 ML YEARS		1809	6687	2008	361	70	179	(97	82)	3046	1134	834	812	54	664	48	50	57	359	71	.83	140	.300	.377	.456

Greg LaRocca

Bats: R **Throws:** R **Pos:** 3B-8; SS-4; PH/PR-4; 2B-2   **Ht:** 5'11" **Wt:** 185 **Born:** 11/10/72 **Age:** 28

Year Team	Lg	G	AB	H	2B	3B	HR	(Hm	Rd)	TB	R	RBI	TBB	IBB	SO	HBP	SH	SF	SB	CS	SB%	GDP	Avg	OBP	SLG
1994 Spokane	A-	42	158	46	9	2	0	—	—	59	20	14	14	0	18	2	2	0	7	2	.78	4	.291	.356	.373
Rancho Cuc	A+	28	85	14	5	1	1	—	—	24	7	8	7	0	11	2	1	1	3	1	.75	2	.165	.242	.282
1995 Rancho Cuc	A+	125	466	150	36	5	8	—	—	220	77	74	44	0	77	12	0	2	15	4	.79	13	.322	.393	.472
Memphis	AA	2	7	1	0	0	0	—	—	1	0	0	0	0	1	0	0	0	0	1	.00	1	.143	.143	.143
1996 Memphis	AA	128	445	122	22	5	6	—	—	172	66	42	51	4	58	10	5	5	5	9	.36	9	.274	.358	.387
1997 Mobile	AA	76	300	80	16	2	3	—	—	109	44	31	26	0	46	8	0	5	8	3	.73	4	.267	.336	.363
1998 Las Vegas	AAA	95	304	94	22	5	8	—	—	150	55	39	19	0	48	12	2	2	7	4	.64	3	.309	.371	.493
1999 Las Vegas	AAA	14	51	14	2	0	0	—	—	16	3	2	2	0	10	4	0	1	2	2	.50	3	.275	.345	.314
2000 Las Vegas	AAA	137	482	142	42	7	9	—	—	225	90	80	54	1	62	12	1	2	13	4	.76	9	.295	.378	.467
2000 San Diego	NL	13	27	6	2	0	0	(0	0)	8	1	2	1	0	4	0	2	0	0	0	—	1	.222	.250	.296

Jason LaRue

Bats: Right **Throws:** Right **Pos:** C-31   **Ht:** 5'11" **Wt:** 200 **Born:** 3/19/74 **Age:** 27

Year Team	Lg	G	AB	H	2B	3B	HR	(Hm	Rd)	TB	R	RBI	TBB	IBB	SO	HBP	SH	SF	SB	CS	SB%	GDP	Avg	OBP	SLG
1995 Billings	R+	58	183	50	8	1	5	—	—	75	35	31	16	2	28	12	2	2	3	5	.38	2	.273	.366	.410
1996 Chstn-WV	A	37	123	26	8	0	2	—	—	40	17	14	11	0	28	2	1	0	3	0	1.00	2	.211	.287	.325
1997 Chstn-WV	A	132	473	149	50	3	8	—	—	229	78	81	47	0	90	5	1	8	14	4	.78	8	.315	.377	.484
1998 Indianapols	AAA	15	51	12	4	0	0	—	—	16	5	5	4	1	8	0	0	1	0	1	.00	2	.235	.286	.314
Chattanooga	AA	105	386	141	39	8	14	—	—	238	71	82	40	0	60	10	1	9	4	3	.57	13	.365	.429	.617
1999 Indianapols	AAA	70	263	66	12	2	12	—	—	118	42	37	15	1	52	4	0	2	0	3	.00	13	.251	.299	.449
2000 Louisville	AAA	82	307	78	22	1	14	—	—	144	54	48	22	0	52	8	0	0	3	2	.60	4	.254	.320	.469
1999 Cincinnati	NL	36	90	19	7	0	3	(1	2)	35	12	10	11	1	32	4	0	0	4	1	.80	1	.211	.311	.389
2000 Cincinnati	NL	31	98	23	3	0	5	(1	4)	41	12	12	5	2	19	4	0	0	0	0	—	1	.235	.299	.418
2 ML YEARS		67	188	42	10	0	8	(2	6)	76	24	22	16	3	51	6	0	0	4	1	.80	5	.223	.305	.404

Matt Lawton

Bats: L **Throws:** R **Pos:** RF-83; LF-67; DH-9; PH/PR-7; CF-3   **Ht:** 5'10" **Wt:** 186 **Born:** 11/3/71 **Age:** 29

Year Team	Lg	G	AB	H	2B	3B	HR	(Hm	Rd)	TB	R	RBI	TBB	IBB	SO	HBP	SH	SF	SB	CS	SB%	GDP	Avg	OBP	SLG
1995 Minnesota	AL	21	60	19	4	1	1	(1	0)	28	11	12	7	0	11	3	0	0	1	1	.50	1	.317	.414	.467
1996 Minnesota	AL	79	252	65	7	1	6	(1	5)	92	34	42	28	1	28	4	0	2	4	4	.50	6	.258	.339	.365
1997 Minnesota	AL	142	460	114	29	3	14	(8	6)	191	74	60	76	3	81	10	1	1	7	4	.64	7	.248	.366	.415
1998 Minnesota	AL	152	557	155	36	6	21	(11	10)	266	91	77	86	6	64	15	0	4	16	8	.67	10	.278	.387	.478
1999 Minnesota	AL	118	406	105	18	0	7	(2	5)	144	58	54	57	7	42	6	0	7	26	4	.87	11	.259	.353	.355
2000 Minnesota	AL	156	561	171	44	2	13	(8	5)	258	84	88	91	8	63	7	0	5	23	7	.77	10	.305	.405	.460
6 ML YEARS		668	2296	629	138	13	62	(31	31)	979	352	333	345	25	289	45	1	19	77	28	.73	45	.274	.377	.426

Brett Laxton

Pitches: Right **Bats:** Left **Pos:** RP-5; SP-1   **Ht:** 6'1" **Wt:** 210 **Born:** 10/5/73 **Age:** 27

Year Team	Lg	G	GS	CG	GF	IP	BFP	H	R	ER	HR	SH	SF	HB	TBB	IBB	SO	WP	Bk	W	L	Pct.	ShO	Sv-Op	Hld	ERA
1996 Sou Oregon	A-	13	8	0	1	32.2	162	39	34	28	4	1	1	3	26	1	38	5	3	0	5	.000	0	0-—	0	7.71
1997 Visalia	A+	29	22	0	2	138.2	606	141	62	46	7	4	0	11	50	0	121	14	0	11	5	.688	0	0-—	0	2.99
1998 Huntsville	AA	21	21	0	0	129.2	570	109	64	49	4	3	6	10	79	0	82	8	0	11	4	.733	0	0-—	0	3.40
Edmonton	AAA	8	8	0	0	46.1	204	45	35	34	6	1	3	5	24	2	21	7	0	2	4	.333	0	0-—	0	6.60
1999 Vancouver	AAA	25	25	3	0	161.1	662	158	68	62	8	5	4	6	49	0	112	10	0	13	8	.619	1	0-—	0	3.46
2000 Omaha	AAA	21	21	0	0	108.1	492	118	69	64	4	3	5	7	61	0	88	7	0	5	9	.357	0	0-—	0	5.32
1999 Oakland	AL	3	2	0	0	9.2	50	12	12	8	1	0	3	2	7	1	9	3	0	0	1	.000	0	0-0	0	7.45
2000 Kansas City	AL	6	1	0	0	16.2	79	23	15	15	0	1	0	2	10	1	14	1	0	0	1	.000	0	0-0	0	8.10
2 ML YEARS		9	3	0	1	26.1	129	35	27	23	1	1	3	4	17	2	23	4	0	0	2	.000	0	0-0	0	7.86

Matt LeCroy

Bats: R **Throws:** R **Pos:** C-49; DH-3; 1B-3; PH/PR-2   **Ht:** 6'2" **Wt:** 225 **Born:** 12/13/75 **Age:** 25

Year Team	Lg	G	AB	H	2B	3B	HR	(Hm	Rd)	TB	R	RBI	TBB	IBB	SO	HBP	SH	SF	SB	CS	SB%	GDP	Avg	OBP	SLG
1998 Fort Wayne	A	64	225	62	17	1	9	—	—	108	33	40	34	1	45	8	0	2	0	0	—	9	.276	.387	.480
Fort Myers	A+	51	200	61	9	1	12	—	—	108	32	51	21	1	35	4	0	6	2	1	.67	9	.305	.372	.540
Salt Lake	AAA	3	13	4	1	0	2	—	—	11	2	4	0	0	7	0	0	0	0	0	—	0	.308	.308	.846
1999 Fort Myers	A+	89	333	93	20	1	20	—	—	175	54	69	42	3	51	3	0	1	0	1	.00	10	.279	.364	.526
Salt Lake	AAA	29	119	36	4	1	10	—	—	72	23	30	5	0	22	1	0	2	0	1	.00	8	.303	.331	.605
2000 New Britain	AA	54	195	55	12	1	10	—	—	99	33	38	29	3	34	6	0	0	0	0	—	8	.282	.391	.508
Salt Lake	AAA	16	65	20	5	0	5	—	—	40	15	15	4	0	11	0	0	0	0	0	—	4	.308	.348	.615
2000 Minnesota	AL	56	167	29	10	0	5	(2	3)	54	18	17	17	2	38	2	1	3	0	0	—	6	.174	.254	.323

Ricky Ledee

Bats: L **Throws:** L **Pos:** LF-78; RF-49; DH-10; PH/PR-9; CF-7   **Ht:** 6'1" **Wt:** 200 **Born:** 11/22/73 **Age:** 27

Year Team	Lg	G	AB	H	2B	3B	HR	(Hm	Rd)	TB	R	RBI	TBB	IBB	SO	HBP	SH	SF	SB	CS	SB%	GDP	Avg	OBP	SLG
1998 New York	AL	42	79	19	5	2	1	(0	1)	31	13	12	7	0	29	0	0	1	3	1	.75	1	.241	.299	.392
1999 New York	AL	88	250	69	13	5	9	(4	5)	119	45	40	28	5	73	0	0	2	4	3	.57	2	.276	.346	.476
2000 NYY-Cle-Tex		137	467	110	19	5	13	(6	7)	178	59	77	59	4	98	2	0	3	13	6	.68	17	.236	.322	.381
2000 New York	AL	62	191	46	11	1	7	(2	5)	80	23	31	26	2	39	1	0	2	7	3	.70	7	.241	.332	.419
Cleveland	AL	17	63	14	2	1	2	(2	0)	24	13	8	8	0	9	0	0	0	0	0	—	3	.222	.310	.381
Texas	AL	58	213	50	6	3	4	(2	2)	74	23	38	25	2	50	1	0	1	6	3	.67	7	.235	.317	.347
3 ML YEARS		267	796	198	37	12	23	(10	13)	328	117	129	94	9	200	2	0	6	20	10	.67	20	.249	.327	.412

Aaron Ledesma

Bats: Right **Throws:** Right **Pos:** PH/PR-25; 3B-5; 1B-3   **Ht:** 6'2" **Wt:** 200 **Born:** 6/3/71 **Age:** 30

Year Team	Lg	G	AB	H	2B	3B	HR	(Hm	Rd)	TB	R	RBI	TBB	IBB	SO	HBP	SH	SF	SB	CS	SB%	GDP	Avg	OBP	SLG
2000 Colo Spngs *	AAA	59	224	77	9	1	0	—	—	88	31	37	17	1	30	1	2	3	10	1	.91	6	.344	.388	.393
1995 New York	NL	21	33	8	0	0	0	(0	0)	8	4	3	6	1	7	0	0	0	0	0	—	2	.242	.359	.242
1997 Baltimore	AL	43	88	31	5	1	2	(1	1)	44	24	11	13	0	9	1	1	1	1	0	1.00	1	.352	.437	.500
1998 Tampa Bay	AL	95	299	97	16	3	0	(0	0)	119	30	29	9	1	51	1	4	2	9	7	.56	8	.324	.344	.398
1999 Tampa Bay	AL	93	294	78	15	0	0	(0	0)	93	32	30	14	1	35	3	1	0	1	1	.50	14	.265	.305	.265
2000 Colorado	NL	32	40	9	2	0	0	(0	0)	11	4	3	2	0	9	1	0	0	0	0	—	1	.225	.279	.275
5 ML YEARS		284	754	223	38	4	2	(1	1)	275	94	76	44	3	111	6	6	3	11	8	.58	26	.296	.338	.365

Carlos Lee

Bats: Right **Throws:** Right **Pos:** LF-149; PH/PR-3; DH-2

Ht: 6'2" **Wt:** 220 **Born:** 6/20/76 **Age:** 25

Year Team	Lg	G	AB	H	2B	3B	HR	(Hm	Rd)	TB	R	RBI	TBB	IBB	SO	HBP	SH	SF	SB	CS	SB%	GDP	Avg	OBP	SLG
1994 White Sox	R	29	56	7	1	0	0	—	—	8	6	1	4	0	8	0	0	0	0	1	.00	1	.125	.183	.143
1995 Hickory	A	63	218	54	9	1	4	—	—	77	18	30	8	2	34	1	0	0	1	5	.17	7	.248	.278	.353
Bristol	R+	67	269	93	17	1	7	—	—	133	43	45	8	3	34	2	0	3	17	7	.71	6	.346	.365	.494
1996 Hickory	A	119	480	150	23	6	8	—	—	209	65	70	23	5	50	0	0	11	18	13	.58	15	.313	.337	.435
1997 Winston-Sal	A+	139	546	173	50	4	17	—	—	282	81	82	36	2	65	2	2	7	11	5	.69	12	.317	.357	.516
1998 Birmingham	AA	138	549	166	33	2	21	—	—	266	77	106	39	2	55	0	0	2	11	5	.69	32	.302	.350	.485
1999 Charlotte	AAA	25	94	33	5	0	4	—	—	50	16	20	8	1	14	1	0	3	2	1	.67	3	.351	.396	.532
1999 Chicago	AL	127	492	144	32	2	16	(10	6)	228	66	84	13	0	72	4	1	7	4	2	.67	11	.293	.312	.463
2000 Chicago	AL	152	572	172	29	2	24	(12	12)	277	107	92	38	1	94	3	1	5	13	4	.76	17	.301	.345	.484
2 ML YEARS		279	1064	316	61	4	40	(22	18)	505	173	176	51	1	166	7	2	12	17	6	.74	28	.297	.330	.475

David Lee

Pitches: Right **Bats:** Right **Pos:** RP-7

Ht: 6'1" **Wt:** 202 **Born:** 3/12/73 **Age:** 28

Year Team	Lg	G	GS	CG	GF	IP	BFP	H	R	ER	HR	SH	SF	HB	TBB	IBB	SO	WP	Bk	W	L	Pct.	ShO	Sv-Op	Hld	ERA
1996 Portland	A-	17	0	0	16	23	96	13	3	2	0	1	0	3	16	3	24	1	0	5	1	.833	0	7- —	—	0.78
Salem	A+	8	0	0	5	12	56	14	6	3	1	0	0	2	6	0	10	2	0	0	2	.000	0	1- —	—	2.25
1997 Asheville	A	51	0	0	49	53	239	61	30	24	5	3	1	1	23	0	59	4	0	4	8	.333	0	22- —	—	4.08
1998 Salem	A+	54	0	0	52	57.1	244	57	26	24	2	4	4	3	15	1	54	3	1	3	5	.375	0	25- —	—	3.77
1999 Carolina	AA	16	0	0	15	17.1	63	8	3	2	1	0	0	1	3	0	16	0	0	1	0		0	10- —	—	1.04
Colo Sprngs	AAA	6	0	0	6	5.2	20	0	0	0	0	0	0	0	1	0	7	2	0	0	0		0	3- —	—	0.00
2000 Colo Sprngs	AAA	47	0	0	39	48.1	223	50	38	32	9	2	2	2	28	1	44	1	1	2	3	.400	0	12- —	—	5.96
1999 Colorado	NL	36	0	0	11	49	212	43	21	20	4	3	2	4	29	1	38	3	1	3	2	.600	0	0-0	2	3.67
2000 Colorado	NL	7	0	0	3	5.2	35	10	9	7	3	0	0	1	6	0	6	0	0	0	0		0	1-1	1	11.12
2 ML YEARS		43	0	0	14	54.2	247	53	30	27	7	3	2	5	35	1	44	3	1	3	2	.600	0	1-1	3	4.45

Derrek Lee

Bats: Right **Throws:** Right **Pos:** 1B-147; PH/PR-15

Ht: 6'5" **Wt:** 225 **Born:** 9/6/75 **Age:** 25

Year Team	Lg	G	AB	H	2B	3B	HR	(Hm	Rd)	TB	R	RBI	TBB	IBB	SO	HBP	SH	SF	SB	CS	SB%	GDP	Avg	OBP	SLG
1997 San Diego	NL	22	54	14	3	0	1	(0	1)	20	9	4	9	0	24	0	0	0	0	0	—	1	.259	.365	.370
1998 Florida	NL	141	454	106	29	1	17	(4	13)	188	62	74	47	1	120	10	0	2	5	2	.71	12	.233	.318	.414
1999 Florida	NL	70	218	45	9	1	5	(0	5)	71	21	20	17	1	70	0	0	1	2	1	.67	3	.206	.263	.326
2000 Florida	NL	158	477	134	18	2	28	(9	19)	242	70	70	63	6	123	4	0	2	0	3	.00	14	.281	.368	.507
4 ML YEARS		391	1203	299	59	5	51	(13	38)	521	162	168	136	8	337	14	0	5	7	6	.54	30	.249	.331	.433

Sang-Hoon Lee

Pitches: Left **Bats:** Left **Pos:** RP-9

Ht: 6'1" **Wt:** 190 **Born:** 3/11/71 **Age:** 30

Year Team	Lg	G	GS	CG	GF	IP	BFP	H	R	ER	HR	SH	SF	HB	TBB	IBB	SO	WP	Bk	W	L	Pct.	ShO	Sv-Op	Hld	ERA
2000 Pawtucket	AAA	45	1	0	18	71	287	51	23	16	5	3	0	1	24	2	73	1	4	5	2	.714	0	2- —	—	2.03
2000 Boston	AL	9	0	0	1	11.2	49	11	4	4	2	0	1	1	5	0	6	0	0	0	0		0	0-0	0	3.09

Travis Lee

Bats: L **Throws:** L **Pos:** 1B-70; RF-54; LF-10; PH/PR-8; CF-2

Ht: 6'3" **Wt:** 214 **Born:** 5/26/75 **Age:** 26

Year Team	Lg	G	AB	H	2B	3B	HR	(Hm	Rd)	TB	R	RBI	TBB	IBB	SO	HBP	SH	SF	SB	CS	SB%	GDP	Avg	OBP	SLG
2000 El Paso *	AA	3	10	2	0	0	0	—	—	2	0	0	2	0	1	0	0	0	0	0	—	1	.200	.333	.200
Tucson *	AAA	7	30	11	4	0	0	—	—	15	4	3	1	0	6	0	0	0	1	0	1.00	0	.367	.387	.500
1998 Arizona	NL	146	562	151	20	2	22	(12	10)	241	71	72	67	5	123	0	0	1	8	1	.89	13	.269	.346	.429
1999 Arizona	NL	120	375	89	16	2	9	(7	2)	136	57	50	58	4	50	0	0	3	17	3	.85	10	.237	.337	.363
2000 Ari-Phi	NL	128	404	95	24	1	9	(2	7)	148	53	54	65	1	79	2	0	2	8	1	.89	12	.235	.342	.366
2000 Arizona	NL	72	224	52	13	0	8	(1	7)	89	34	40	25	1	46	0	0	1	5	1	.83	6	.232	.308	.397
Philadelphia	NL	56	180	43	11	1	1	(1	0)	59	19	14	40	0	33	2	0	1	3	0	1.00	6	.239	.381	.328
3 ML YEARS		394	1341	335	60	5	40	(21	19)	525	181	176	190	10	252	2	0	6	33	5	.87	35	.250	.342	.391

Al Leiter

Pitches: Left **Bats:** Left **Pos:** SP-31

Ht: 6'3" **Wt:** 220 **Born:** 10/23/65 **Age:** 35

Year Team	Lg	G	GS	CG	GF	IP	BFP	H	R	ER	HR	SH	SF	HB	TBB	IBB	SO	WP	Bk	W	L	Pct.	ShO	Sv-Op	Hld	ERA
1987 New York	AL	4	4	0	0	22.2	104	24	16	16	2	1	0	0	15	0	28	4	0	2	2	.500	0	0-0		6.35
1988 New York	AL	14	14	0	0	57.1	251	49	27	25	7	1	0	5	33	0	60	1	4	4	4	.500	0	0-0		3.92
1989 NYY-Tor	AL	5	5	0	0	33.1	154	32	23	21	2	1	1	2	23	0	26	2	1	1	2	.333	0	0-0		5.67
1990 Toronto	AL	4	0	0	2	6.1	22	1	0	0	0	0	0	0	2	0	5	0	0	0	0		0	0-0		0.00
1991 Toronto	AL	3	0	0	1	1.2	13	3	5	5	0	1	0	0	5	0	1	0	0	0	0	—	0	0-0		27.00
1992 Toronto	AL	1	0	0	0	1	7	1	1	1	0	0	0	0	2	0	0	0	0	0	0		0	0-0		9.00
1993 Toronto	AL	34	12	1	4	105	454	93	52	48	8	3	3	4	56	2	66	2	2	9	6	.600	1	2-3	3	4.11
1994 Toronto	AL	20	20	1	0	111.2	516	125	68	63	6	3	8	2	65	3	100	7	5	6	7	.462	0	0-0		5.08
1995 Toronto	AL	28	28	2	0	183	805	162	80	74	15	6	4	6	108	1	153	14	0	11	11	.500	1	0-0		3.64
1996 Florida	NL	33	33	2	0	215.1	896	153	74	70	14	7	3	11	119	3	200	5	0	16	12	.571	1	0-0		2.93
1997 Florida	NL	27	27	0	0	151.1	668	133	78	73	13	10	3	12	91	4	132	2	0	11	9	.550	0	0-0		4.34
1998 New York	NL	28	28	4	0	193	789	151	55	53	8	6	2	11	71	2	174	4	1	17	6	.739	2	0-0		2.47
1999 New York	NL	32	32	1	0	213	923	209	107	100	19	13	10	9	93	8	162	4	1	13	12	.520	1	0-0		4.23
2000 New York	NL	31	31	2	0	208	874	176	84	74	19	10	6	11	76	1	200	4	1	16	8	.667	1	0-0		3.20
1989 New York	AL	4	4	0	0	26.2	123	23	20	18	1	1	1	2	21	0	22	1	1	1	2	.333	0	0-0		6.08
Toronto	AL	1	1	0	0	6.2	31	9	3	3	1	0	0	0	2	0	4	1	0	0	0		0	0-0		4.05
14 ML YEARS		264	234	13	7	1502.2	6476	1312	670	623	113	62	40	73	759	24	1307	49	15	106	79	.573	7	2-3	3	3.73

119

Brian Lesher

Bats: Right **Throws:** Left **Pos:** PH/PR-5; 1B-4; DH-1   **Ht:** 6'5" **Wt:** 222 **Born:** 3/5/71 **Age:** 30

Year Team	Lg	G	AB	H	2B	3B	HR	(Hm	Rd)	TB	R	RBI	TBB	IBB	SO	HBP	SH	SF	SB	CS	SB%	GDP	Avg	OBP	SLG
2000 Tacoma *	AAA	132	489	141	33	3	25	—	—	255	77	92	70	5	104	2	2	4	4	4	.50	10	.288	.377	.521
1996 Oakland	AL	26	82	19	3	0	5	(2	3)	37	11	16	5	0	17	1	1	1	0	0	—	2	.232	.281	.451
1997 Oakland	AL	46	131	30	4	1	4	(2	2)	48	17	16	9	0	30	0	0	2	4	1	.80	4	.229	.275	.366
1998 Oakland	AL	7	7	1	1	0	0	(0	0)	2	0	1	0	0	3	0	0	0	0	0	—	0	.143	.143	.286
2000 Seattle	AL	5	5	4	1	1	0	(0	0)	7	1	3	1	0	0	0	0	0	1	0	1.00	0	.800	.833	1.400
4 ML YEARS		84	225	54	9	2	9	(4	5)	94	29	36	15	0	50	1	1	3	5	1	.83	6	.240	.287	.418

Curtis Leskanic

Pitches: Right **Bats:** Right **Pos:** RP-73   **Ht:** 6'0" **Wt:** 186 **Born:** 4/2/68 **Age:** 33

Year Team	Lg	G	GS	CG	GF	IP	BFP	H	R	ER	HR	SH	SF	HB	TBB	IBB	SO	WP	Bk	W	L	Pct.	ShO	Sv-Op	Hld	ERA
1993 Colorado	NL	18	8	0	1	57	260	59	40	34	7	5	4	2	27	1	30	8	2	1	5	.167	0	0-0	0	5.37
1994 Colorado	NL	8	3	0	2	22.1	98	27	14	14	2	2	0	0	10	0	17	2	0	1	1	.500	0	0-0	0	5.64
1995 Colorado	NL	76	0	0	27	98	406	83	38	37	7	3	2	0	33	1	107	6	1	6	3	.667	0	10-16	19	3.40
1996 Colorado	NL	70	0	0	32	73.2	334	82	51	51	12	3	3	2	38	1	76	6	2	7	5	.583	0	6-10	9	6.23
1997 Colorado	NL	55	0	0	23	58.1	248	59	36	36	8	2	4	0	24	0	53	4	0	4	0	1.000	0	2-4	6	5.55
1998 Colorado	NL	66	0	0	20	75.2	332	75	37	37	9	0	0	1	40	2	55	3	1	6	4	.600	0	2-5	12	4.40
1999 Colorado	NL	63	0	0	5	85	382	87	54	48	7	5	3	5	49	4	77	5	0	6	2	.750	0	0-3	8	5.08
2000 Milwaukee	NL	73	0	0	39	77.1	333	58	23	22	7	1	4	3	51	5	75	5	0	9	3	.750	0	12-13	11	2.56
8 ML YEARS		429	11	0	149	547.1	2393	530	293	279	59	21	20	13	272	14	490	39	6	40	23	.635	0	32-51	65	4.59

Al Levine

Pitches: Right **Bats:** Left **Pos:** RP-46; SP-5   **Ht:** 6'3" **Wt:** 198 **Born:** 5/22/68 **Age:** 33

Year Team	Lg	G	GS	CG	GF	IP	BFP	H	R	ER	HR	SH	SF	HB	TBB	IBB	SO	WP	Bk	W	L	Pct.	ShO	Sv-Op	Hld	ERA
2000 Erie *	AA	1	1	0	0	2	9	3	2	0	0	0	0	0	0	0	0	0	0	0	0	—	0	0-0		0.00
1996 Chicago	AL	16	0	0	5	18.1	85	22	14	11	1	0	1	1	7	1	12	0	0	0	1	.000	0	0-1	0	5.40
1997 Chicago	AL	25	0	0	6	27.1	133	35	22	21	4	1	2	2	16	1	22	2	0	2	2	.500	0	0-1	3	6.91
1998 Texas	AL	30	0	0	11	58	251	68	30	29	6	1	3	0	16	1	19	5	0	0	1	.000	0	0-0	1	4.50
1999 Anaheim	AL	50	1	0	12	85	349	76	40	32	13	2	7	3	39	2	37	3	0	1	1	.500	0	0-1	3	3.39
2000 Anaheim	AL	51	5	0	12	95.1	426	98	44	41	10	3	3	2	49	5	42	1	0	3	4	.429	0	2-2	5	3.87
5 ML YEARS		172	6	0	46	284	1244	299	150	134	34	7	16	8	117	10	132	11	0	6	9	.400	0	2-5	11	4.25

Allen Levrault

Pitches: Right **Bats:** Right **Pos:** RP-4; SP-1   **Ht:** 6'3" **Wt:** 230 **Born:** 8/15/77 **Age:** 23

Year Team	Lg	G	GS	CG	GF	IP	BFP	H	R	ER	HR	SH	SF	HB	TBB	IBB	SO	WP	Bk	W	L	Pct.	ShO	Sv-Op	Hld	ERA
1996 Helena	R+	18	11	0	2	71	302	70	43	42	9	0	8	8	22	0	68	4	3	4	3	.571	0	1- —	—	5.32
1997 Beloit	A	24	24	1	0	131.1	561	141	89	77	18	1	2	6	40	1	112	3	12	3	10	.231	0	0- —	—	5.28
1998 Stockton	A+	16	15	4	0	97.1	388	76	33	31	8	4	3	2	27	0	86	2	1	9	3	.750	1	0- —	—	2.87
El Paso	AA	11	11	0	0	62.2	281	77	51	41	7	2	2	1	17	0	46	1	1	5	1	.167	0	0- —	—	5.89
1999 Huntsville	AA	16	16	2	0	99.2	404	77	44	38	11	3	2	5	33	0	82	3	3	9	2	.818	1	0- —	—	3.43
Louisville	AAA	9	5	0	1	34.1	169	48	37	33	9	1	2	3	16	0	33	1	0	1	3	.250	0	0- —	—	8.65
2000 Indianapolis	AAA	21	18	1	1	108.1	460	98	55	51	9	7	5	6	46	3	78	5	2	6	8	.429	0	0- —	—	4.24
2000 Milwaukee	NL	5	1	0	2	12	51	10	7	6	0	1	0	0	7	0	9	0	0	0	1	.000	0	0-0	0	4.50

Darren Lewis

Bats: R **Throws:** R **Pos:** CF-41; RF-37; LF-18; PH/PR-15; DH-5   **Ht:** 6'0" **Wt:** 190 **Born:** 8/28/67 **Age:** 33

Year Team	Lg	G	AB	H	2B	3B	HR	(Hm	Rd)	TB	R	RBI	TBB	IBB	SO	HBP	SH	SF	SB	CS	SB%	GDP	Avg	OBP	SLG
2000 Red Sox *	R	2	6	1	0	0	0	—	—	1	0	1	1	0	0	0	0	0	1	0	1.00	0	.167	.286	.167
1990 Oakland	AL	25	35	8	0	0	0	(0	0)	8	4	1	7	0	4	1	3	0	2	0	1.00	2	.229	.372	.229
1991 San Francisco	NL	72	222	55	5	3	1	(0	1)	69	41	15	36	0	30	2	7	0	13	7	.65	1	.248	.358	.311
1992 San Francisco	NL	100	320	74	8	1	1	(1	0)	87	38	18	29	0	46	1	10	2	28	8	.78	3	.231	.295	.272
1993 San Francisco	NL	136	522	132	17	7	2	(2	0)	169	84	48	30	0	40	7	12	1	46	15	.75	4	.253	.302	.324
1994 San Francisco	NL	114	451	116	15	9	4	(4	0)	161	70	29	53	0	50	4	4	1	30	13	.70	6	.257	.340	.357
1995 SF-Cin	NL	132	472	118	13	3	1	(1	0)	140	66	24	34	0	57	8	12	1	32	18	.64	9	.250	.311	.297
1996 Chicago	AL	141	337	77	12	2	4	(0	4)	105	55	53	45	1	40	3	15	5	21	5	.81	9	.228	.321	.312
1997 CWS-LA	NL	107	154	41	4	1	1	(0	1)	50	22	15	17	0	31	0	7	1	14	6	.70	3	.266	.339	.325
1998 Boston	AL	155	585	157	25	3	8	(5	3)	212	95	63	70	0	94	8	2	5	29	12	.71	12	.268	.352	.362
1999 Boston	AL	135	470	113	14	6	2	(1	1)	145	63	40	45	0	52	5	14	4	16	10	.62	5	.240	.311	.309
2000 Boston	AL	97	270	65	12	0	2	(0	2)	83	44	17	22	0	34	3	8	0	10	5	.67	2	.241	.305	.307
1995 San Francisco	NL	74	309	78	10	3	1	(1	0)	97	47	16	17	0	37	6	7	1	21	7	.75	6	.252	.303	.314
Cincinnati	NL	58	163	40	3	0	0	(0	0)	43	19	8	17	0	20	2	5	0	11	11	.50	3	.245	.324	.264
1997 Chicago	AL	81	77	18	1	0	0	(0	0)	19	15	5	11	0	14	0	5	0	11	4	.73	2	.234	.330	.247
Los Angeles	NL	26	77	23	3	1	1	(0	1)	31	7	10	6	0	17	0	2	1	3	2	.60	1	.299	.349	.403
11 ML YEARS		1214	3838	956	125	35	26	(14	12)	1229	582	323	388	1	478	42	94	19	241	99	.71	56	.249	.323	.320

Mark Lewis

Bats: R **Throws:** R **Pos:** 3B-34; PH/PR-22; 2B-21; SS-14; DH-4   **Ht:** 6'1" **Wt:** 195 **Born:** 11/30/69 **Age:** 31

Year Team	Lg	G	AB	H	2B	3B	HR	(Hm	Rd)	TB	R	RBI	TBB	IBB	SO	HBP	SH	SF	SB	CS	SB%	GDP	Avg	OBP	SLG
1991 Cleveland	AL	84	314	83	15	1	0	(0	0)	100	29	30	15	0	45	0	2	5	2	2	.50	12	.264	.293	.318
1992 Cleveland	AL	122	413	109	21	0	5	(2	3)	145	44	30	25	1	69	3	1	4	4	5	.44	12	.264	.308	.351
1993 Cleveland	AL	14	52	13	2	0	1	(1	0)	18	6	5	0	0	7	0	1	0	3	0	1.00	1	.250	.250	.346

Year Team	Lg	G	AB	H	2B	3B	HR	(Hm	Rd)	TB	R	RBI	TBB	IBB	SO	HBP	SH	SF	SB	CS	SB%	GDP	Avg	OBP	SLG
1994 Cleveland	AL	20	73	15	5	0	1	(1	0)	23	6	8	2	0	13	0	1	0	1	0	1.00	2	.205	.227	.315
1995 Cincinnati	NL	81	171	58	13	1	3	(1	2)	82	25	30	21	2	33	0	0	2	0	3	.00	1	.339	.407	.480
1996 Detroit	AL	145	545	147	30	3	11	(8	3)	216	69	55	42	0	109	5	4	3	6	1	.86	12	.270	.326	.396
1997 San Francisco	NL	118	341	91	14	6	10	(4	6)	147	50	42	23	2	62	4	1	3	3	2	.60	8	.267	.318	.431
1998 Philadelphia	NL	142	518	129	21	2	9	(4	5)	181	52	54	48	2	111	3	3	8	3	3	.50	17	.249	.312	.349
1999 Cincinnati	NL	88	173	44	16	0	6	(2	4)	78	18	28	7	1	24	0	2	2	0	0	—	8	.254	.280	.451
2000 Cin-Bal		82	182	46	18	0	2	(1	1)	70	20	24	13	0	34	1	1	1	7	2	.78	6	.253	.305	.385
2000 Cincinnati	NL	11	19	2	1	0	0	(0	0)	3	1	3	1	0	3	0	0	0	0	0	—	1	.105	.150	.158
Baltimore	AL	71	163	44	17	0	2	(1	1)	67	19	21	12	0	31	1	1	1	7	2	.78	5	.270	.322	.411
10 ML YEARS		896	2782	735	155	13	48	(24	24)	1060	319	306	196	8	507	16	16	28	29	18	.62	79	.264	.313	.381

Jim Leyritz

Bats: R **Throws:** R **Pos:** PH/PR-37; DH-15; 1B-9; C-5; LF-5; RF-1   **Ht:** 5'11" **Wt:** 220 **Born:** 12/27/63 **Age:** 37

Year Team	Lg	G	AB	H	2B	3B	HR	(Hm	Rd)	TB	R	RBI	TBB	IBB	SO	HBP	SH	SF	SB	CS	SB%	GDP	Avg	OBP	SLG
1990 New York	AL	92	303	78	13	1	5	(1	4)	108	28	25	27	1	51	7	1	1	2	3	.40	11	.257	.331	.356
1991 New York	AL	32	77	14	3	0	0	(0	0)	17	8	4	13	0	15	0	1	0	0	1	.00	0	.182	.300	.221
1992 New York	AL	63	144	37	6	0	7	(3	4)	64	17	26	14	1	22	6	0	3	0	1	.00	2	.257	.341	.444
1993 New York	AL	95	259	80	14	0	14	(6	8)	136	43	53	37	3	59	8	0	1	0	0	—	12	.309	.410	.525
1994 New York	AL	75	249	66	12	0	17	(4	13)	129	47	58	35	1	61	6	0	3	0	0	—	9	.265	.365	.518
1995 New York	AL	77	264	71	12	0	7	(3	4)	104	37	37	37	2	73	8	0	1	1	1	.50	4	.269	.374	.394
1996 New York	AL	88	265	70	10	0	7	(3	4)	101	23	40	30	3	68	9	2	3	2	0	1.00	11	.264	.355	.381
1997 Ana-Tex	AL	121	379	105	11	0	11	(3	8)	149	58	64	60	2	78	6	4	6	2	1	.67	13	.277	.379	.393
1998 Bos-SD		114	272	75	16	0	12	(7	5)	127	34	42	42	1	74	9	0	5	0	0	—	6	.276	.384	.467
1999 SD-NYY		81	200	47	9	1	8	(4	4)	82	25	26	28	2	54	4	0	1	0	0	—	7	.235	.339	.410
2000 NYY-LA		65	115	24	1	0	2	(2	0)	31	5	12	14	0	26	2	0	0	0	0	—	4	.209	.305	.270
1997 Anaheim	AL	84	294	81	7	0	11	(3	8)	121	47	50	37	2	56	3	3	5	1	1	.50	11	.276	.357	.412
Texas	AL	37	85	24	4	0	0	(0	0)	28	11	14	23	0	22	3	1	1	1	0	1.00	2	.282	.446	.329
1998 Boston	AL	52	129	37	6	0	8	(6	2)	67	17	24	21	1	34	2	0	4	0	0	—	2	.287	.385	.519
San Diego	NL	62	143	38	10	0	4	(1	3)	60	17	18	21	0	40	7	0	1	0	0	—	4	.266	.384	.420
1999 San Diego	NL	50	134	32	5	0	8	(4	4)	61	17	21	15	1	37	4	0	1	0	0	—	4	.239	.331	.455
New York	AL	31	66	15	4	1	0	(0	0)	21	8	5	13	1	17	0	0	0	0	0	—	3	.227	.354	.318
2000 New York	AL	24	55	12	0	0	2	(1	0)	15	2	4	7	0	14	1	0	0	0	0	—	2	.218	.317	.273
Los Angeles	NL	41	60	12	1	0	1	(1	0)	16	3	8	7	0	12	1	0	0	0	0	—	2	.200	.294	.267
11 ML YEARS		903	2527	667	107	2	90	(36	54)	1048	325	387	337	16	581	65	8	24	7	7	.50	79	.264	.362	.415

Cory Lidle

Pitches: Right **Bats:** Right **Pos:** RP-20; SP-11   **Ht:** 5'11" **Wt:** 180 **Born:** 3/22/72 **Age:** 29

Year Team	Lg	G	GS	CG	GF	IP	BFP	H	R	ER	HR	SH	SF	HB	TBB	IBB	SO	WP	Bk	W	L	Pct.	ShO	Sv-Op	Hld	ERA
2000 Durham *	AAA	9	9	0	0	50	205	52	15	14	3	1	0	1	8	0	44	1	0	6	2	.750	0	0- -	-	2.52
1997 New York	NL	54	2	0	20	81.2	345	86	38	32	7	4	4	3	20	4	54	2	0	7	2	.778	0	2-3	9	3.53
1999 Tampa Bay	AL	5	1	0	1	5	24	8	4	4	0	0	0	0	2	0	4	0	0	1	0	1.000	0	0-0	0	7.20
2000 Tampa Bay	AL	31	11	0	5	96.2	424	114	61	54	13	3	1	3	29	3	62	6	0	4	6	.400	0	0-0	2	5.03
3 ML YEARS		90	14	0	26	183.1	793	208	103	90	20	7	5	6	51	7	120	8	0	12	8	.600	0	2-3	11	4.42

Jon Lieber

Pitches: Right **Bats:** Left **Pos:** SP-35   **Ht:** 6'3" **Wt:** 225 **Born:** 4/2/70 **Age:** 31

Year Team	Lg	G	GS	CG	GF	IP	BFP	H	R	ER	HR	SH	SF	HB	TBB	IBB	SO	WP	Bk	W	L	Pct.	ShO	Sv-Op	Hld	ERA
1994 Pittsburgh	NL	17	17	1	0	108.2	460	116	62	45	12	3	3	1	25	3	71	2	3	6	7	.462	0	0-0	0	3.73
1995 Pittsburgh	NL	21	12	0	3	72.2	327	103	56	51	7	5	6	4	14	0	45	3	0	4	7	.364	0	0-1	3	6.32
1996 Pittsburgh	NL	51	15	0	6	142	600	156	70	63	19	7	2	3	28	2	94	0	0	9	5	.643	0	1-4	9	3.99
1997 Pittsburgh	NL	33	32	1	0	188.1	799	193	102	94	23	6	7	1	51	8	160	3	1	11	14	.440	0	0-0	0	4.49
1998 Pittsburgh	NL	29	28	2	1	171	731	182	93	78	23	7	4	3	40	4	138	0	3	8	14	.364	0	1-1	0	4.11
1999 Chicago	NL	31	31	3	0	203.1	875	226	107	92	28	7	11	1	46	6	186	2	2	10	11	.476	1	0-0	0	4.07
2000 Chicago	NL	35	35	6	0	251	1047	248	130	123	36	9	7	10	54	3	192	2	2	12	11	.522	1	0-0	0	4.41
7 ML YEARS		217	170	13	10	1137	4839	1224	620	546	148	44	40	23	258	26	886	12	11	60	69	.465	2	2-6	12	4.32

Mike Lieberthal

Bats: Right **Throws:** Right **Pos:** C-106; PH/PR-5   **Ht:** 6'0" **Wt:** 190 **Born:** 1/18/72 **Age:** 29

Year Team	Lg	G	AB	H	2B	3B	HR	(Hm	Rd)	TB	R	RBI	TBB	IBB	SO	HBP	SH	SF	SB	CS	SB%	GDP	Avg	OBP	SLG
1994 Philadelphia	NL	24	79	21	3	1	1	(1	0)	29	6	5	3	0	5	1	1	0	0	0	—	4	.266	.301	.367
1995 Philadelphia	NL	16	47	12	2	0	0	(0	0)	14	1	4	5	0	5	0	2	0	0	0	—	1	.255	.327	.298
1996 Philadelphia	NL	50	166	42	8	0	7	(4	3)	71	21	23	10	0	30	2	0	4	0	0	—	4	.253	.297	.428
1997 Philadelphia	NL	134	455	112	27	1	20	(11	9)	201	59	77	44	1	76	4	0	7	3	4	.43	10	.246	.314	.442
1998 Philadelphia	NL	86	313	80	15	3	8	(5	3)	125	39	45	17	1	44	7	0	5	2	1	.67	4	.256	.304	.399
1999 Philadelphia	NL	145	510	153	33	1	31	(10	21)	281	84	96	44	7	86	11	1	8	0	0	—	15	.300	.363	.551
2000 Philadelphia	NL	108	389	108	30	0	15	(8	7)	183	55	71	40	3	53	6	0	3	2	0	1.00	12	.278	.352	.470
7 ML YEARS		563	1959	528	118	6	82	(39	43)	904	265	321	163	12	299	31	4	27	7	5	.58	50	.270	.331	.461

Jeff Liefer

Bats: Left **Throws:** Right **Pos:** RF-5; 1B-1; PH/PR-1   **Ht:** 6'3" **Wt:** 195 **Born:** 8/17/74 **Age:** 26

Year Team	Lg	G	AB	H	2B	3B	HR	(Hm	Rd)	TB	R	RBI	TBB	IBB	SO	HBP	SH	SF	SB	CS	SB%	GDP	Avg	OBP	SLG
1996 South Bend	A	74	277	90	14	0	15	—	—	149	60	58	30	3	62	5	0	4	6	5	.55	3	.325	.396	.538
Pr William	A+	37	147	33	6	0	1	—	—	42	17	13	11	2	27	0	0	1	0	0	—	6	.224	.277	.286

		BATTING																	BASERUNNING				PERCENTAGES		
Year Team	Lg	G	AB	H	2B	3B	HR	(Hm	Rd)	TB	R	RBI	TBB	IBB	SO	HBP	SH	SF	SB	CS	SB%	GDP	Avg	OBP	SLG
1997 Birmingham	AA	119	474	113	24	9	15	—	—	200	67	71	38	3	115	7	1	4	2	0	1.00	10	.238	.302	.422
1998 Birmingham	AA	127	471	137	33	6	21	—	—	245	84	89	60	6	125	9	0	1	1	2	.33	9	.291	.381	.520
Calgary	AAA	8	31	8	3	0	1	—	—	14	3	10	2	0	12	0	0	0	0	0	—	1	.258	.303	.452
1999 Charlotte	AAA	46	171	58	17	1	9	—	—	104	36	34	21	3	26	1	1	1	2	1	.67	3	.339	.412	.608
2000 Charlotte	AAA	120	445	125	29	1	32	—	—	252	75	91	53	4	107	2	0	5	2	3	.40	17	.281	.356	.566
1999 Chicago	AL	45	113	28	7	1	0	(0	0)	37	8	14	8	0	28	0	0	1	2	0	1.00	3	.248	.295	.327
2000 Chicago	AL	5	11	2	0	0	0	(0	0)	2	0	0	0	0	4	0	0	0	0	0	—	0	.182	.182	.182
2 ML YEARS		50	124	30	7	1	0	(0	0)	39	8	14	8	0	32	0	0	1	2	0	1.00	3	.242	.286	.315

Kerry Ligtenberg

Pitches: Right **Bats:** Right **Pos:** RP-59   **Ht:** 6'2" **Wt:** 215 **Born:** 5/11/71 **Age:** 30

		HOW MUCH HE PITCHED						WHAT HE GAVE UP												THE RESULTS						
Year Team	Lg	G	GS	CG	GF	IP	BFP	H	R	ER	HR	SH	SF	HB	TBB	IBB	SO	WP	Bk	W	L	Pct.	ShO	Sv-Op	Hld	ERA
2000 Richmond *	AAA	5	0	0	4	5.2	20	0	0	0	0	0	0	0	4	0	7	1	0	0	0	—	0	1--	—	0.00
1997 Atlanta	NL	15	0	0	9	15	61	12	5	5	4	0	0	0	4	2	19	0	0	1	0	1.000	0	1-1	—	3.00
1998 Atlanta	NL	75	0	0	56	73	290	51	24	22	6	1	1	0	24	1	79	3	0	3	2	.600	0	30-34	11	2.71
2000 Atlanta	NL	59	0	0	19	52.1	217	43	21	21	7	2	1	0	24	5	51	0	0	2	3	.400	0	12-14	12	3.61
3 ML YEARS		149	0	0	84	140.1	568	106	50	48	17	3	2	0	52	8	149	3	0	6	5	.545	0	43-49	23	3.08

Ted Lilly

Pitches: Left **Bats:** Left **Pos:** RP-7   **Ht:** 6'0" **Wt:** 185 **Born:** 1/4/76 **Age:** 25

		HOW MUCH HE PITCHED						WHAT HE GAVE UP												THE RESULTS						
Year Team	Lg	G	GS	CG	GF	IP	BFP	H	R	ER	HR	SH	SF	HB	TBB	IBB	SO	WP	Bk	W	L	Pct.	ShO	Sv-Op	Hld	ERA
1996 Yakima	A-	13	8	0	1	53.2	200	25	9	5	0	0	0	1	14	1	75	0	2	4	0	1.000	0	0--	—	0.84
1997 San Berndno	A+	23	21	2	0	134.2	540	116	52	42	9	5	3	4	32	0	158	7	5	7	8	.467	1	0--	—	2.81
1998 San Antonio	AA	17	17	0	0	111.2	471	114	50	41	8	1	2	1	37	0	96	4	3	8	4	.667	0	0--	—	3.30
Albuquerque	AAA	5	5	0	0	31	135	39	20	17	3	0	0	0	9	0	25	1	2	1	3	.250	0	0--	—	4.94
Ottawa	AAA	7	7	0	0	39	182	45	28	21	8	1	1	0	19	0	49	0	0	2	2	.500	0	0--	—	4.85
1999 Ottawa	AAA	16	16	0	0	89	364	81	40	38	12	1	2	2	23	0	78	1	2	8	5	.615	0	0--	—	3.84
2000 Tampa	A+	1	1	0	0	6.2	28	5	3	1	0	1	0	1	1	0	6	1	0	0	0	—	0	0--	—	1.35
Columbus	AAA	22	22	3	0	137.1	610	157	77	64	14	6	5	4	48	0	127	5	4	8	11	.421	1	0--	—	4.19
1999 Montreal	NL	9	3	0	1	23.2	110	30	20	20	7	0	1	3	9	0	28	1	0	1	0	.000	0	0-0	0	7.61
2000 New York	AL	7	0	0	1	8	39	8	6	5	1	0	0	3	5	0	11	1	1	0	0	—	0	0-0	0	5.63
2 ML YEARS		16	3	0	2	31.2	149	38	26	25	8	0	1	3	14	0	39	2	1	0	0	.000	0	0-0	0	7.11

Jose Lima

Pitches: Right **Bats:** Right **Pos:** SP-33   **Ht:** 6'2" **Wt:** 205 **Born:** 9/30/72 **Age:** 28

		HOW MUCH HE PITCHED						WHAT HE GAVE UP												THE RESULTS						
Year Team	Lg	G	GS	CG	GF	IP	BFP	H	R	ER	HR	SH	SF	HB	TBB	IBB	SO	WP	Bk	W	L	Pct.	ShO	Sv-Op	Hld	ERA
1994 Detroit	AL	3	3	0	1	6.2	34	11	10	10	2	0	0	0	3	1	7	1	0	0	1	.000	0	0-0	—	13.50
1995 Detroit	AL	15	15	0	0	73.2	320	85	52	50	10	2	1	4	18	4	37	5	0	3	9	.250	0	0-0	—	6.11
1996 Detroit	AL	39	4	0	15	72.2	329	87	48	46	13	5	3	5	22	4	59	3	0	5	6	.455	0	3-7	5	5.70
1997 Houston	NL	52	1	0	15	75	321	79	45	44	9	6	3	5	16	2	63	2	0	1	6	.143	0	2-2	5	5.28
1998 Houston	NL	33	33	3	0	233.1	950	229	100	96	34	11	5	7	32	1	169	0	0	16	8	.667	1	0-0	—	3.70
1999 Houston	NL	35	35	3	0	246.1	1024	256	108	98	30	5	7	2	44	2	187	8	0	21	10	.677	0	0-0	—	3.58
2000 Houston	NL	33	33	0	0	196.1	895	251	152	145	48	12	12	2	68	3	124	3	0	7	16	.304	0	0-0	—	6.65
7 ML YEARS		210	122	6	31	904	3873	998	515	489	146	41	31	25	203	17	646	26	0	53	56	.486	1	5-9	9	4.87

Mike Lincoln

Pitches: Right **Bats:** Right **Pos:** SP-4; RP-4   **Ht:** 6'2" **Wt:** 210 **Born:** 4/10/75 **Age:** 26

		HOW MUCH HE PITCHED						WHAT HE GAVE UP												THE RESULTS						
Year Team	Lg	G	GS	CG	GF	IP	BFP	H	R	ER	HR	SH	SF	HB	TBB	IBB	SO	WP	Bk	W	L	Pct.	ShO	Sv-Op	Hld	ERA
1996 Fort Myers	A+	12	11	0	0	59.2	263	64	31	27	5	2	4	3	25	0	24	4	1	5	2	.714	0	0--	—	4.07
1997 Fort Myers	A+	20	20	1	0	134	553	130	41	34	4	5	3	4	25	0	75	4	2	13	4	.765	1	0--	—	2.28
1998 New Britain	AA	26	26	1	0	173.1	720	180	80	62	13	8	5	5	35	0	109	5	0	15	7	.682	0	0--	—	3.22
1999 Salt Lake	AAA	9	9	0	0	59	274	82	52	51	12	1	5	2	21	0	39	2	0	5	2	.714	0	0--	—	7.78
2000 Salt Lake	AAA	12	12	2	0	74.1	306	72	35	32	4	0	2	2	16	1	37	0	0	4	1	.800	1	0--	—	3.87
Quad City	A	17	0	0	9	23.1	114	25	16	11	2	0	1	1	19	1	27	4	1	0	0	—	0	0--	—	4.24
1999 Minnesota	AL	18	15	0	0	76.1	353	102	59	58	11	2	6	1	26	0	27	4	0	3	10	.231	0	0-0	1	6.84
2000 Minnesota	AL	8	4	0	1	20.2	109	36	25	25	10	0	0	2	13	0	15	1	0	0	3	.000	0	0-0	0	10.89
2 ML YEARS		26	19	0	1	97	462	138	84	83	21	2	6	3	39	0	42	5	0	3	13	.188	0	0-0	1	7.70

Rod Lindsey

Bats: R **Throws:** R **Pos:** PH/PR-8; CF-4; LF-2; RF-2   **Ht:** 5'8" **Wt:** 175 **Born:** 1/28/76 **Age:** 25

		BATTING																	BASERUNNING				PERCENTAGES		
Year Team	Lg	G	AB	H	2B	3B	HR	(Hm	Rd)	TB	R	RBI	TBB	IBB	SO	HBP	SH	SF	SB	CS	SB%	GDP	Avg	OBP	SLG
1994 Padres	R	48	172	46	3	0	0	—	—	49	29	19	11	0	59	9	0	0	15	8	.65	2	.267	.344	.285
1995 Idaho Falls	R+	35	155	41	4	4	0	—	—	53	30	14	13	0	37	4	0	1	21	7	.75	1	.265	.335	.342
1996 Clinton	A	23	87	14	2	0	0	—	—	16	11	4	11	0	30	3	0	1	12	8	.60	2	.161	.275	.184
Idaho Falls	R+	48	185	56	4	6	5	—	—	87	45	17	23	0	53	2	0	0	16	3	.84	1	.303	.386	.470
1997 Clinton	A	130	502	107	15	8	6	—	—	156	80	49	62	0	161	7	3	2	70	23	.75	8	.213	.307	.311
1998 Clinton	A	40	155	42	4	4	4	—	—	66	32	17	17	1	54	3	1	1	36	4	.90	2	.271	.352	.424
W Michigan	A	45	158	43	7	4	3	—	—	67	37	17	22	1	42	10	0	1	24	8	.75	1	.272	.393	.424
1999 Jacksonville	AA	7	27	5	1	0	0	—	—	6	3	2	1	0	6	0	1	0	0	0	—	0	.185	.214	.222
Lakeland	A+	120	485	129	20	8	7	—	—	186	81	51	25	0	129	18	4	5	61	20	.75	6	.266	.323	.384
2000 Jacksonville	AA	114	393	88	11	4	0	—	—	107	57	20	38	0	100	10	10	1	46	14	.77	4	.224	.308	.272
2000 Detroit	AL	11	3	1	1	0	0	(0	0)	2	6	0	0	0	1	1	1	0	2	1	.67	0	.333	.500	.667

Scott Linebrink

Pitches: Right **Bats:** Right **Pos:** RP-11   **Ht:** 6'3" **Wt:** 185 **Born:** 8/4/76 **Age:** 24

Year Team	Lg	G	GS	CG	GF	IP	BFP	H	R	ER	HR	SH	SF	HB	TBB	IBB	SO	WP	Bk	W	L	Pct.	ShO	Sv-Op	Hld	ERA
1997 Salem-Keizr	A-	3	3	0	0	10	42	7	5	5	1	0	0	0	6	0	6	1	0	0	0	—	0	0--	—	4.50
San Jose	A+	6	6	0	0	28.1	120	29	11	10	2	0	0	0	10	0	40	2	0	2	1	.667	0	0--	—	3.18
1998 Shreveport	AA	21	21	0	0	113	494	101	66	63	12	6	5	7	58	1	128	8	0	10	8	.556	0	0--	—	5.02
1999 Shreveport	AA	10	10	0	0	43.1	190	48	31	31	7	0	4	0	14	0	33	1	0	1	8	.111	0	0--	—	6.44
2000 Fresno	AAA	28	7	0	14	62	255	54	42	36	10	0	2	1	12	0	49	3	1	1	4	.200	0	4--	—	5.23
New Orleans	AAA	11	0	0	4	15	66	15	4	3	0	0	1	0	7	0	22	3	0	2	0	1.000	0	1--	—	1.80
2000 SF-Hou	NL	11	0	0	4	12	63	18	8	8	4	0	0	3	8	0	6	0	0	0	0	—	0	0-0	0	6.00
2000 San Francisco	NL	3	0	0	1	2.1	16	7	3	3	1	0	0	0	2	0	0	0	0	0	0	—	0	0-0	0	11.57
Houston	NL	8	0	0	3	9.2	47	11	5	5	3	0	0	3	6	0	6	0	0	0	0	—	0	0-0	0	4.66

Cole Liniak

Bats: Right **Throws:** Right **Pos:** PH/PR-3   **Ht:** 6'1" **Wt:** 190 **Born:** 8/23/76 **Age:** 24

Year Team	Lg	G	AB	H	2B	3B	HR	(Hm	Rd)	TB	R	RBI	TBB	IBB	SO	HBP	SH	SF	SB	CS	SB%	GDP	Avg	OBP	SLG
1995 Red Sox	R	23	79	21	7	0	1	—	—	31	9	8	4	0	8	1	2	0	2	0	1.00	2	.266	.310	.392
1996 Michigan	A	121	437	115	26	2	3	—	—	154	65	46	59	1	59	10	3	8	7	6	.54	12	.263	.358	.352
1997 Sarasota	A+	64	217	73	16	0	6	—	—	107	32	42	22	1	31	3	3	2	1	2	.33	2	.336	.402	.493
Trenton	AA	53	200	56	11	0	2	—	—	73	20	18	17	0	29	1	3	1	0	1	.00	6	.280	.338	.365
1998 Red Sox	R	2	8	0	0	0	0	—	—	0	1	0	0	0	1	1	0	0	0	0	—	0	.000	.111	.000
Pawtucket	AAA	112	429	112	31	1	17	—	—	196	65	59	39	1	71	5	4	3	4	4	.50	11	.261	.328	.457
1999 Pawtucket	AAA	95	348	92	25	0	12	—	—	153	55	42	40	1	57	1	3	1	0	5	.00	7	.264	.341	.440
2000 Iowa	AAA	123	411	97	24	1	19	—	—	180	63	58	39	0	77	3	4	4	5	3	.63	16	.236	.304	.438
1999 Chicago	NL	12	29	7	2	0	0	(0	0)	9	3	2	1	0	4	0	0	0	0	1	.00	2	.241	.267	.310
2000 Chicago	NL	3	3	0	0	0	0	(0	0)	0	0	0	0	0	2	0	0	0	0	0	—	0	.000	.000	.000
2 ML YEARS		15	32	7	2	0	0	(0	0)	9	3	2	1	0	6	0	0	0	0	1	.00	2	.219	.242	.281

Felipe Lira

Pitches: Right **Bats:** Right **Pos:** RP-46; SP-7   **Ht:** 6'1" **Wt:** 205 **Born:** 4/26/72 **Age:** 29

Year Team	Lg	G	GS	CG	GF	IP	BFP	H	R	ER	HR	SH	SF	HB	TBB	IBB	SO	WP	Bk	W	L	Pct.	ShO	Sv-Op	Hld	ERA
2000 Ottawa *	AAA	4	4	0	0	20	88	24	12	11	3	1	0	1	3	1	10	0	0	0	3	.000	0	0--	—	4.95
1995 Detroit	AL	37	22	0	7	146.1	635	151	74	70	17	4	9	8	56	7	89	5	1	9	13	.409	0	1-3	1	4.31
1996 Detroit	AL	32	32	3	0	194.2	850	204	123	113	30	5	11	10	66	2	113	7	0	6	14	.300	2	0-0	1	5.22
1997 Det-Sea	AL	28	18	1	3	110.2	516	132	82	78	18	2	4	6	55	2	73	7	0	5	11	.313	1	0-0	1	6.34
1998 Seattle	AL	7	0	0	3	15.2	75	22	10	8	5	0	1	0	5	0	16	1	0	1	0	1.000	0	0-0	0	4.60
1999 Detroit	AL	2	0	0	0	3.1	20	7	5	4	2	0	0	0	2	0	3	0	0	0	0	—	0	0-0	0	10.80
2000 Montreal	NL	53	7	0	0	101.2	468	129	71	61	11	3	9	4	36	6	51	2	1	5	8	.385	0	0-0	2	5.40
1997 Detroit	AL	20	15	1	1	92	415	101	61	59	15	2	2	2	45	2	64	7	0	5	7	.417	1	0-0	1	5.77
Seattle	AL	8	3	0	2	18.2	101	31	21	19	3	0	2	4	10	0	9	0	0	0	4	.000	0	0-0	1	9.16
6 ML YEARS		159	79	4	21	572.1	2564	645	365	334	83	14	34	28	220	17	345	22	2	26	46	.361	3	1-3	4	5.25

Graeme Lloyd

Pitches: Left **Bats:** Left **Pos:** RP   **Ht:** 6'7" **Wt:** 225 **Born:** 4/9/67 **Age:** 34

Year Team	Lg	G	GS	CG	GF	IP	BFP	H	R	ER	HR	SH	SF	HB	TBB	IBB	SO	WP	Bk	W	L	Pct.	ShO	Sv-Op	Hld	ERA
1993 Milwaukee	AL	55	0	0	12	63.2	269	64	24	20	5	1	2	3	13	3	31	4	0	3	4	.429	0	0-4	6	2.83
1994 Milwaukee	AL	43	0	0	21	47	203	49	28	27	4	1	2	3	15	6	31	2	0	2	3	.400	0	3-6	3	5.17
1995 Milwaukee	AL	33	0	0	14	32	127	28	16	16	4	1	4	0	8	2	13	3	0	0	5	.000	0	4-6	9	4.50
1996 Mil-NYY	AL	65	0	0	15	56.2	252	61	30	27	4	5	3	1	22	4	30	4	0	2	6	.250	0	0-5	17	4.29
1997 New York	AL	46	0	0	17	49	217	55	24	18	6	3	5	1	20	7	26	3	0	1	1	.500	0	1-1	2	3.31
1998 New York	AL	50	0	0	8	37.2	145	26	10	7	3	0	1	2	6	2	20	2	0	3	0	1.000	0	0-2	9	1.67
1999 Toronto	AL	74	0	0	25	72	301	68	36	29	11	1	1	4	23	4	47	1	0	5	3	.625	0	3-9	22	3.63
1996 Milwaukee	AL	52	0	0	15	51	217	49	19	16	3	5	1	1	17	3	24	0	0	2	4	.333	0	0-3	15	2.82
New York	AL	13	0	0	0	5.2	35	12	11	11	1	0	2	0	5	1	6	4	0	0	2	.000	0	0-2	2	17.47
7 ML YEARS		366	0	0	112	358	1514	351	168	144	37	12	18	14	107	28	198	19	0	16	22	.421	0	11-33	68	3.62

Esteban Loaiza

Pitches: Right **Bats:** Right **Pos:** SP-31; RP-3   **Ht:** 6'3" **Wt:** 210 **Born:** 12/31/71 **Age:** 29

Year Team	Lg	G	GS	CG	GF	IP	BFP	H	R	ER	HR	SH	SF	HB	TBB	IBB	SO	WP	Bk	W	L	Pct.	ShO	Sv-Op	Hld	ERA
1995 Pittsburgh	NL	32	31	1	0	172.2	762	205	115	99	21	10	9	5	55	3	85	6	1	8	9	.471	0	0-0	0	5.16
1996 Pittsburgh	NL	10	10	1	0	52.2	236	66	32	29	11	3	1	2	19	2	32	0	0	2	3	.400	1	0-0	0	4.96
1997 Pittsburgh	NL	33	32	1	0	196.1	851	214	99	90	17	10	7	12	56	9	122	2	3	11	11	.500	0	0-0	0	4.13
1998 Pit-Tex	AL	35	28	1	0	171	751	199	107	98	28	7	12	5	52	4	108	4	2	9	11	.450	0	0-1	0	5.16
1999 Texas	AL	30	15	0	4	120.1	517	128	65	61	10	7	4	0	40	2	77	2	0	9	5	.643	0	0-0	0	4.56
2000 Tex-Tor	AL	34	31	1	2	199.1	871	228	112	101	29	4	5	13	57	1	137	1	0	10	13	.435	1	1-1	0	4.56
1998 Pittsburgh	NL	21	14	0	3	91.2	394	96	50	46	13	5	7	3	30	1	53	1	2	6	5	.545	0	0-1	0	4.52
Texas	AL	14	14	1	0	79.1	357	103	57	52	15	2	5	2	22	3	55	3	0	3	6	.333	0	0-0	0	5.90
2000 Texas	AL	20	17	0	2	107.1	480	133	67	64	21	2	4	3	31	1	75	1	0	5	6	.455	0	1-1	0	5.37
Toronto	AL	14	14	1	0	92	391	95	45	37	8	2	1	10	26	0	62	0	0	5	7	.417	1	0-0	0	3.62
6 ML YEARS		174	147	5	9	912.1	3988	1039	530	478	116	41	38	37	279	21	561	15	6	49	52	.485	2	1-2	0	4.72

Keith Lockhart

Bats: Left **Throws:** Right **Pos:** 2B-74; PH/PR-36; 3B-18   **Ht:** 5'10" **Wt:** 170 **Born:** 11/10/64 **Age:** 36

Year Team	Lg	G	AB	H	2B	3B	HR	(Hm	Rd)	TB	R	RBI	TBB	IBB	SO	HBP	SH	SF	SB	CS	SB%	GDP	Avg	OBP	SLG
1994 San Diego	NL	27	43	9	0	0	2	(2	0)	15	4	6	4	0	10	1	1	1	1	0	1.00	2	.209	.286	.349
1995 Kansas City	AL	94	274	88	19	3	6	(3	3)	131	41	33	14	2	21	4	1	7	8	1	.89	2	.321	.355	.478
1996 Kansas City	AL	138	433	118	33	3	7	(4	3)	178	49	55	30	4	40	2	1	5	11	6	.65	7	.273	.319	.411
1997 Atlanta	NL	96	147	41	5	3	6	(3	3)	70	25	32	14	0	17	1	3	4	0	0	—	4	.279	.337	.476
1998 Atlanta	NL	109	366	94	21	0	9	(4	5)	142	50	37	29	0	37	1	2	3	2	2	.50	2	.257	.311	.388
1999 Atlanta	NL	108	161	42	3	1	1	(0	1)	50	20	21	19	0	21	1	0	3	3	1	.75	3	.261	.337	.311
2000 Atlanta	NL	113	275	73	12	3	2	(1	1)	97	32	32	29	7	31	0	5	4	4	1	.80	10	.265	.331	.353
7 ML YEARS		685	1699	465	93	13	33	(17	16)	683	221	216	139	13	177	10	13	27	29	11	.73	29	.274	.327	.402

Paul LoDuca

Bats: R **Throws:** R **Pos:** C-20; PH/PR-11; LF-7; RF-2; 3B-1   **Ht:** 5'10" **Wt:** 185 **Born:** 4/12/72 **Age:** 29

Year Team	Lg	G	AB	H	2B	3B	HR	(Hm	Rd)	TB	R	RBI	TBB	IBB	SO	HBP	SH	SF	SB	CS	SB%	GDP	Avg	OBP	SLG
1993 Vero Beach	A+	39	134	42	6	0	0	—	—	48	17	13	13	0	22	2	0	1	0	0	—	2	.313	.380	.358
1994 Bakersfield	A+	123	455	141	32	1	6	—	—	193	65	68	52	2	49	3	0	4	16	9	.64	5	.310	.381	.424
1995 San Antonio	AA	61	199	49	8	0	1	—	—	60	27	8	26	0	25	2	0	0	5	5	.50	12	.246	.339	.302
1996 Vero Beach	A+	124	439	134	22	0	3	—	—	165	54	66	70	2	38	2	0	4	8	2	.80	14	.305	.400	.376
1997 San Antonio	AA	105	385	126	28	2	7	—	—	179	63	69	46	3	27	3	4	5	16	8	.67	17	.327	.399	.465
1998 Albuquerque	AAA	126	451	144	30	3	8	—	—	204	69	58	59	2	40	5	7	6	19	7	.73	20	.319	.399	.452
1999 Albuquerque	AAA	26	76	28	9	0	1	—	—	40	17	8	10	0	1	6	0	0	1	1	.50	0	.368	.478	.526
2000 Albuquerque	AAA	78	279	98	27	3	4	—	—	143	47	54	33	0	14	2	2	2	8	5	.62	13	.351	.421	.513
1998 Los Angeles	NL	6	14	4	1	0	0	(0	0)	5	2	1	0	0	1	0	0	0	0	0	—	0	.286	.286	.357
1999 Los Angeles	NL	36	95	22	1	0	3	(1	2)	32	11	11	10	4	9	2	1	2	1	2	.33	3	.232	.312	.337
2000 Los Angeles	NL	34	65	16	2	0	2	(0	2)	24	6	8	6	0	8	0	2	2	0	2	.00	2	.246	.301	.369
3 ML YEARS		76	174	42	4	0	5	(1	4)	61	19	20	16	4	18	2	3	4	1	4	.20	5	.241	.306	.351

Kenny Lofton

Bats: Left **Throws:** Left **Pos:** CF-135; DH-1; PH/PR-1   **Ht:** 6'0" **Wt:** 190 **Born:** 5/31/67 **Age:** 34

Year Team	Lg	G	AB	H	2B	3B	HR	(Hm	Rd)	TB	R	RBI	TBB	IBB	SO	HBP	SH	SF	SB	CS	SB%	GDP	Avg	OBP	SLG
1991 Houston	NL	20	74	15	1	0	0	(0	0)	16	9	0	5	0	19	0	0	0	2	1	.67	0	.203	.253	.216
1992 Cleveland	AL	148	576	164	15	8	5	(3	2)	210	96	42	68	3	54	2	4	1	66	12	.85	7	.285	.362	.365
1993 Cleveland	AL	148	569	185	28	8	1	(1	0)	232	116	42	81	6	83	1	2	4	70	14	.83	8	.325	.408	.408
1994 Cleveland	AL	112	459	160	32	9	12	(10	2)	246	105	57	52	5	56	2	4	6	60	12	.83	5	.349	.412	.536
1995 Cleveland	AL	118	481	149	22	13	7	(5	2)	218	93	53	40	6	49	1	4	3	54	15	.78	6	.310	.362	.453
1996 Cleveland	AL	154	662	210	35	4	14	(7	7)	295	132	67	61	3	82	0	7	6	75	17	.82	7	.317	.372	.446
1997 Atlanta	NL	122	493	164	20	6	5	(3	2)	211	90	48	64	5	83	2	2	3	27	20	.57	10	.333	.409	.428
1998 Cleveland	AL	154	600	169	31	6	12	(6	6)	248	101	64	87	1	80	2	3	6	54	10	.84	7	.282	.371	.413
1999 Cleveland	AL	120	465	140	28	6	7	(1	6)	201	110	39	79	2	84	6	5	5	25	6	.81	6	.301	.405	.432
2000 Cleveland	AL	137	543	151	23	5	15	(10	5)	229	107	73	79	3	72	4	6	8	30	7	.81	11	.278	.369	.422
10 ML YEARS		1233	4922	1507	235	65	78	(46	32)	2106	959	485	616	34	662	20	37	42	463	114	.80	67	.306	.383	.428

Rich Loiselle

Pitches: Right **Bats:** Right **Pos:** RP-40   **Ht:** 6'5" **Wt:** 253 **Born:** 1/12/72 **Age:** 29

Year Team	Lg	G	GS	CG	GF	IP	BFP	H	R	ER	HR	SH	SF	HB	TBB	IBB	SO	WP	Bk	W	L	Pct.	ShO	Sv-Op	Hld	ERA
2000 Altoona *	AA	13	0	0	6	13.2	65	7	9	8	1	1	0	0	6	1	18	1	0	0	1	.000	0	2--	—	5.27
Nashville *	AAA	4	0	0	1	4.2	20	2	0	0	0	1	0	1	2	0	3	0	0	0	0	—	0	0--	—	0.00
1996 Pittsburgh	NL	5	3	0	0	20.2	90	22	8	7	3	0	0	0	8	1	9	3	0	1	0	1.000	0	0-0	—	3.05
1997 Pittsburgh	NL	72	0	0	58	72.2	312	76	29	25	7	2	1	2	24	3	66	4	0	1	5	.167	0	29-34	5	3.10
1998 Pittsburgh	NL	54	0	0	43	55	258	56	26	21	2	5	1	2	36	9	48	0	0	2	7	.222	0	19-27	1	3.44
1999 Pittsburgh	NL	13	0	0	6	15.1	69	16	9	9	2	1	0	2	9	2	14	1	0	3	2	.600	0	0-1	3	5.28
2000 Pittsburgh	NL	40	0	0	13	42.1	203	43	27	24	5	3	3	3	30	5	32	1	0	2	3	.400	0	0-6	7	5.10
5 ML YEARS		184	3	0	120	206	932	213	99	86	19	11	6	8	107	20	169	9	0	9	17	.346	0	48-68	17	3.76

George Lombard

Bats: Left **Throws:** Right **Pos:** PH/PR-17; RF-11; LF-5   **Ht:** 6'0" **Wt:** 212 **Born:** 9/14/75 **Age:** 25

Year Team	Lg	G	AB	H	2B	3B	HR	(Hm	Rd)	TB	R	RBI	TBB	IBB	SO	HBP	SH	SF	SB	CS	SB%	GDP	Avg	OBP	SLG
1994 Braves	R	40	129	18	2	0	0	—	—	20	10	5	18	0	47	3	0	0	10	4	.71	1	.140	.260	.155
1995 Macon	A	49	180	37	6	1	3	—	—	54	32	16	27	3	44	5	1	0	16	4	.80	4	.206	.325	.300
Eugene	A-	68	262	66	5	3	5	—	—	92	38	19	23	0	91	5	2	1	35	13	.73	0	.252	.323	.351
1996 Macon	A	116	444	109	16	8	15	—	—	186	76	51	36	0	122	7	8	2	24	17	.59	4	.245	.311	.419
1997 Durham	A+	131	462	122	25	7	14	—	—	203	65	72	66	9	145	9	2	2	35	7	.83	6	.264	.365	.439
1998 Greenville	AA	122	422	130	25	4	22	—	—	229	84	65	71	10	140	5	5	4	35	5	.88	2	.308	.410	.543
1999 Richmond	AAA	74	233	48	11	3	7	—	—	86	25	29	35	2	98	3	0	0	21	6	.78	2	.206	.317	.369
2000 Richmond	AAA	112	424	117	25	7	10	—	—	186	72	48	55	3	130	6	5	3	32	9	.78	3	.276	.365	.439
1998 Atlanta	NL	6	6	2	0	0	1	(0	1)	5	2	1	0	0	1	0	0	0	1	0	1.00	0	.333	.333	.833
1999 Atlanta	NL	6	6	2	0	0	0	(0	0)	2	1	0	1	0	2	0	0	0	2	0	1.00	0	.333	.429	.333
2000 Atlanta	NL	27	39	4	0	0	0	(0	0)	4	8	2	1	0	14	1	0	0	4	0	1.00	2	.103	.146	.103
3 ML YEARS		39	51	8	0	0	1	(0	1)	11	11	3	2	0	17	1	0	0	7	0	1.00	2	.157	.204	.216

Terrence Long

Bats: Left **Throws:** Left **Pos:** CF-137; PH/PR-5   **Ht:** 6'1" **Wt:** 190 **Born:** 2/29/76 **Age:** 25

							BATTING											BASERUNNING				PERCENTAGES		
Year Team	Lg	G	AB	H	2B	3B	HR	(Hm | Rd)	TB	R	RBI	TBB	IBB	SO	HBP	SH	SF	SB	CS	SB%	GDP	Avg	OBP	SLG
1994 Kingsport	R+	60	215	50	9	2	12	—	—	99	39	39	32	0	52	4	0	2	9	3	.75	2	.233	.340	.460
1995 Capital Cty	A	55	178	35	1	2	2	—	—	46	27	13	28	4	43	1	1	0	8	5	.62	3	.197	.309	.258
Pittsfield	A-	51	187	48	9	4	4	—	—	77	24	31	18	2	36	1	1	1	11	4	.73	2	.257	.324	.412
1996 Capital Cty	A	123	473	136	26	9	12	—	—	216	66	78	36	3	120	5	1	4	32	7	.82	9	.288	.342	.457
1997 St. Lucie	A+	126	470	118	29	7	8	—	—	185	52	61	40	4	102	2	0	4	24	8	.75	6	.251	.310	.394
1998 Binghamton	AA	130	455	135	20	10	16	—	—	223	69	58	62	6	105	2	0	4	23	11	.68	8	.297	.380	.490
1999 Norfolk	AAA	78	304	99	20	4	7	—	—	148	41	47	23	4	41	1	0	1	14	6	.70	6	.326	.374	.487
Vancouver	AAA	40	154	38	6	2	2	—	—	54	16	21	10	2	29	1	0	0	7	4	.64	1	.247	.297	.351
2000 Sacramento	AAA	15	60	24	6	0	3	—	—	39	11	15	4	0	4	0	1	1	0	3	.00	2	.400	.431	.650
1999 New York	NL	3	3	0	(0 | 0)	0	0	0	0	0	0	0	0	2	0	0	0	0	0	—	1	.000	.000	.000
2000 Oakland	AL	138	584	168	34	4	18	(9 | 9)	264	104	80	43	1	77	1	0	3	5	0	1.00	18	.288	.336	.452
2 ML YEARS		141	587	168	34	4	18	(9 | 9)	264	104	80	43	1	79	1	0	3	5	0	1.00	19	.286	.334	.450

Braden Looper

Pitches: Right **Bats:** Right **Pos:** RP-73   **Ht:** 6'5" **Wt:** 225 **Born:** 10/28/74 **Age:** 26

		HOW MUCH HE PITCHED						WHAT HE GAVE UP										THE RESULTS					
Year Team	Lg	G	GS	CG	GF	IP	BFP	H	R	ER	HR	SH	SF	HB	TBB	IBB	SO	WP	Bk	W	L	Pct.	ShO	Sv-Op	Hld	ERA
1998 St. Louis	NL	4	0	0	3	3.1	16	5	4	2	1	0	1	0	1	0	4	1	0	0	1	.000	0	0-2	0	5.40
1999 Florida	NL	72	0	0	22	83	370	96	43	35	7	5	5	1	31	6	50	2	2	3	3	.500	0	0-4	8	3.80
2000 Florida	NL	73	0	0	23	67.1	311	71	41	33	3	3	2	5	36	6	29	5	0	5	1	.833	0	2-5	18	4.41
3 ML YEARS		149	0	0	48	153.2	697	172	88	70	11	8	8	6	68	12	83	8	2	8	5	.615	0	2-11	26	4.10

Albie Lopez

Pitches: Right **Bats:** Right **Pos:** SP-24; RP-21   **Ht:** 6'2" **Wt:** 240 **Born:** 8/18/71 **Age:** 29

		HOW MUCH HE PITCHED						WHAT HE GAVE UP										THE RESULTS					
Year Team	Lg	G	GS	CG	GF	IP	BFP	H	R	ER	HR	SH	SF	HB	TBB	IBB	SO	WP	Bk	W	L	Pct.	ShO	Sv-Op	Hld	ERA
2000 Princeton *	R+	1	0	0	0	0.2	0	0	0	0	0	0	0	0	1	0	0	0	0	0	0	—	0	0-	0	0.00
1993 Cleveland	AL	9	9	0	0	49.2	222	49	34	33	7	1	1	1	32	1	25	0	0	3	1	.750	0	0-0	0	5.98
1994 Cleveland	AL	4	4	1	0	17	76	20	11	8	3	0	0	1	6	0	18	3	0	1	2	.333	1	0-0	0	4.24
1995 Cleveland	AL	6	2	0	0	23	92	17	8	8	4	0	1	1	7	1	22	2	0	0	0	—	0	0-0	0	3.13
1996 Cleveland	AL	13	10	0	0	62	282	80	47	44	14	0	1	2	22	1	45	2	0	5	4	.556	0	0-0	0	6.39
1997 Cleveland	AL	37	6	0	10	76.2	364	101	61	59	11	3	2	4	40	9	63	5	0	3	7	.300	0	0-1	4	6.93
1998 Tampa Bay	AL	54	0	0	12	79.2	335	73	31	23	7	4	3	3	32	4	62	5	0	7	4	.636	0	1-5	4	2.60
1999 Tampa Bay	AL	51	0	0	14	64	281	66	40	33	8	1	4	1	24	2	37	3	0	3	2	.600	0	1-3	12	4.64
2000 Tampa Bay	AL	45	24	4	10	185.1	798	199	95	85	24	6	3	1	70	3	96	4	1	11	13	.458	1	2-4	1	4.13
8 ML YEARS		219	55	5	46	557.1	2450	605	327	293	78	15	15	14	233	21	368	24	1	33	33	.500	2	4-13	21	4.73

Javy Lopez

Bats: Right **Throws:** Right **Pos:** C-132; PH/PR-7   **Ht:** 6'3" **Wt:** 200 **Born:** 11/5/70 **Age:** 30

							BATTING											BASERUNNING				PERCENTAGES		
Year Team	Lg	G	AB	H	2B	3B	HR	(Hm	Rd)	TB	R	RBI	TBB	IBB	SO	HBP	SH	SF	SB	CS	SB%	GDP	Avg	OBP	SLG
1992 Atlanta	NL	9	16	6	2	0	1	(0	0)	8	3	2	0	0	1	0	0	0	0	0	—	0	.375	.375	.500
1993 Atlanta	NL	8	16	6	1	1	1	(0	1)	12	1	2	0	0	2	1	0	0	0	0	—	0	.375	.412	.750
1994 Atlanta	NL	80	277	68	9	0	13	(4	9)	116	27	35	17	0	61	5	2	2	0	2	.00	13	.245	.299	.419
1995 Atlanta	NL	100	333	105	11	4	14	(8	6)	166	37	51	14	0	57	2	0	3	1	1	.00	13	.315	.344	.498
1996 Atlanta	NL	138	489	138	19	1	23	(10	13)	228	56	69	28	5	84	3	1	5	1	6	.14	17	.282	.322	.466
1997 Atlanta	NL	123	414	122	28	1	23	(11	12)	221	52	68	40	10	82	5	1	4	1	1	.50	9	.295	.361	.534
1998 Atlanta	NL	133	489	139	21	1	34	(18	16)	264	73	106	30	1	85	6	1	8	5	3	.63	22	.284	.328	.540
1999 Atlanta	NL	65	246	78	18	1	11	(1	10)	131	34	45	20	2	41	3	0	0	0	3	.00	6	.317	.375	.533
2000 Atlanta	NL	134	481	138	21	1	24	(12	12)	233	60	89	35	3	80	4	0	5	0	0	—	20	.287	.337	.484
9 ML YEARS		790	2761	800	130	10	143	(64	79)	1379	343	467	184	21	493	29	5	27	7	16	.30	99	.290	.338	.499

Luis Lopez

Bats: B **Throws:** R **Pos:** SS-45; 2B-22; PH/PR-22; 3B-6   **Ht:** 5'11" **Wt:** 166 **Born:** 9/4/70 **Age:** 30

							BATTING											BASERUNNING				PERCENTAGES		
Year Team	Lg	G	AB	H	2B	3B	HR	(Hm	Rd)	TB	R	RBI	TBB	IBB	SO	HBP	SH	SF	SB	CS	SB%	GDP	Avg	OBP	SLG
1993 San Diego	NL	17	43	5	1	0	0	(0	0)	6	1	1	0	0	8	0	0	1	0	0	—	0	.116	.114	.140
1994 San Diego	NL	77	235	65	16	1	2	(2	0)	89	29	20	15	2	39	3	2	2	3	2	.60	7	.277	.325	.379
1996 San Diego	NL	63	139	25	3	0	2	(1	1)	34	10	11	9	1	35	1	1	1	0	0	—	7	.180	.233	.245
1997 New York	NL	78	178	48	12	1	1	(1	0)	65	19	19	12	2	42	4	2	0	2	4	.33	7	.270	.330	.365
1998 New York	NL	117	266	67	13	2	2	(1	1)	90	37	22	20	3	60	4	3	2	2	2	.50	10	.252	.312	.338
1999 New York	NL	68	104	22	4	0	2	(1	1)	32	11	13	12	0	33	3	1	1	1	1	.50	1	.212	.308	.308
2000 Milwaukee	NL	78	201	53	14	0	6	(3	3)	85	24	27	9	1	35	5	8	2	1	2	.33	2	.264	.309	.423
7 ML YEARS		498	1166	285	63	4	15	(9	6)	401	131	113	77	9	252	20	17	9	9	11	.45	29	.244	.300	.344

Mendy Lopez

Bats: Right **Throws:** Right **Pos:** PH/PR-4   **Ht:** 6'2" **Wt:** 190 **Born:** 10/15/74 **Age:** 26

							BATTING											BASERUNNING				PERCENTAGES		
Year Team	Lg	G	AB	H	2B	3B	HR	(Hm	Rd)	TB	R	RBI	TBB	IBB	SO	HBP	SH	SF	SB	CS	SB%	GDP	Avg	OBP	SLG
2000 Calgary *	AAA	56	225	73	20	1	7	—	—	116	34	29	13	0	38	0	2	0	1	1	.50	2	.324	.361	.516
1998 Kansas City	AL	74	206	50	10	2	1	(1	0)	67	18	15	12	0	40	1	5	1	5	2	.71	6	.243	.286	.325
1999 Kansas City	AL	7	20	8	0	1	0	(0	0)	10	2	3	0	0	5	1	0	0	0	0	—	0	.400	.429	.500
2000 Florida	NL	4	3	0	0	0	0	(0	0)	0	0	0	1	0	1	0	0	0	0	0	—	0	.000	.250	.000
3 ML YEARS		85	229	58	10	3	1	(1	0)	77	20	18	13	0	46	2	5	1	5	2	.71	6	.253	.298	.336

Rodrigo Lopez

Pitches: Right **Bats:** Right **Pos:** SP-6   **Ht:** 6'1" **Wt:** 180 **Born:** 12/14/75 **Age:** 25

Year Team	Lg	G	GS	CG	GF	IP	BFP	H	R	ER	HR	SH	SF	HB	TBB	IBB	SO	WP	Bk	W	L	Pct.	ShO	Sv-Op	Hld	ERA
1995 Padres	R	11	7	0	3	34.2	162	41	29	21	0	1	0	2	14	0	33	3	1	1	1	.500	0	1--	—	5.45
1996 Idaho Falls	R+	15	14	0	1	71	314	76	52	45	3	4	3	4	34	0	72	8	4	4	4	.500	0	1--	—	5.70
1997 Clinton	A	37	14	2	19	121.2	508	103	49	43	6	7	4	3	42	1	123	3	4	6	8	.429	0	9--	—	3.18
1998 Mobile	AA	4	4	2	0	25.2	101	21	11	4	1	0	1	0	4	0	20	0	0	3	0	1.000	1	0--	—	1.40
1999 Mobile	AA	28	28	2	0	169.1	728	187	91	83	14	6	4	7	58	3	138	5	1	10	8	.556	1	0--	—	4.41
2000 Las Vegas	AAA	20	20	1	0	109.1	483	123	66	57	9	3	7	2	45	1	100	0	0	8	7	.533	0	0--	—	4.69
2000 San Diego	NL	6	6	0	0	24.2	120	40	24	24	5	0	1	0	13	0	17	0	0	0	3	.000	0	0-0	0	8.76

Mark Loretta

Bats: Right **Throws:** Right **Pos:** SS-90; PH/PR-3; 2B-1   **Ht:** 6'0" **Wt:** 180 **Born:** 8/14/71 **Age:** 29

				BATTING														BASERUNNING				PERCENTAGES		
Year Team	Lg	G	AB	H	2B	3B	HR	(Hm	Rd)	TB	R	RBI	TBB	IBB	SO	HBP	SH	SF	SB	CS	SB%	GDP	Avg	OBP	SLG
2000 Indianapols *	AAA	10	25	6	1	0	0			7	6	5	2	0	4	1	0	1	0	0	—	1	.240	.310	.280
1995 Milwaukee	AL	19	50	13	3	0	1	(0	1)	19	13	3	4	0	7	1	1	0	1	1	.50	1	.260	.327	.380
1996 Milwaukee	AL	73	154	43	3	0	1	(0	1)	49	20	13	14	0	15	0	2	0	2	1	.67	7	.279	.339	.318
1997 Milwaukee	AL	132	418	120	17	5	5	(2	3)	162	56	47	47	2	60	2	5	10	5	5	.50	15	.287	.354	.388
1998 Milwaukee	NL	140	434	137	29	0	6	(3	3)	184	55	54	42	1	47	7	4	4	9	6	.60	14	.316	.382	.424
1999 Milwaukee	NL	153	587	170	34	5	5	(2	3)	229	93	67	52	1	59	10	9	6	4	1	.80	14	.290	.354	.390
2000 Milwaukee	NL	91	352	99	21	1	7	(3	4)	143	49	40	37	2	38	1	8	1	0	3	.00	9	.281	.350	.406
6 ML YEARS		608	1995	582	107	11	25	(10	15)	786	286	224	196	6	226	21	29	21	21	17	.55	60	.292	.358	.394

Andrew Lorraine

Pitches: Left **Bats:** Left **Pos:** RP-13; SP-5   **Ht:** 6'3" **Wt:** 200 **Born:** 8/11/72 **Age:** 28

Year Team	Lg	G	GS	CG	GF	IP	BFP	H	R	ER	HR	SH	SF	HB	TBB	IBB	SO	WP	Bk	W	L	Pct.	ShO	Sv-Op	Hld	ERA
2000 Buffalo *	AAA	14	13	0	0	90.2	378	97	37	35	8	0	2	2	24	0	51	1	1	8	3	.727	0	0--	—	3.47
1994 California	AL	4	3	0	0	18.2	96	30	23	22	7	2	1	0	11	0	10	0	0	0	2	.000	0	0-0	0	10.61
1995 Chicago	AL	5	0	0	2	8	30	3	3	3	0	0	1	0	2	0	5	0	0	0	0	—	0	0-0	1	3.38
1997 Oakland	AL	12	6	0	1	29.2	146	45	22	21	2	0	3	1	15	0	18	0	0	3	1	.750	0	0-0	0	6.37
1998 Seattle	AL	4	0	0	1	3.2	16	3	1	1	0	0	0	0	4	0	1	0	0	0	0	—	0	0-0	1	2.45
1999 Chicago	NL	11	11	2	0	61.2	272	71	42	38	9	6	2	0	22	3	40	3	0	2	5	.286	1	0-0	0	5.55
2000 ChC-Cle	AL	18	5	0	3	41.1	189	44	29	27	6	2	2	0	23	1	30	0	1	1	2	.333	0	0-1	3	5.88
2000 Chicago	NL	8	5	0	0	32	148	36	25	23	5	2	2	0	18	1	25	0	1	1	2	.333	0	0-1	0	6.47
Cleveland	AL	10	0	0	3	9.1	41	8	4	4	1	0	0	0	5	0	5	0	0	0	0	—	0	0-0	3	3.86
6 ML YEARS		54	25	2	7	163	749	196	120	112	24	10	8	2	77	4	103	6	1	6	10	.375	1	0-1	3	6.18

Derek Lowe

Pitches: Right **Bats:** Right **Pos:** RP-74   **Ht:** 6'6" **Wt:** 200 **Born:** 6/1/73 **Age:** 28

Year Team	Lg	G	GS	CG	GF	IP	BFP	H	R	ER	HR	SH	SF	HB	TBB	IBB	SO	WP	Bk	W	L	Pct.	ShO	Sv-Op	Hld	ERA
1997 Sea-Bos	AL	20	9	0	1	69	298	74	49	47	11	4	2	4	23	3	52	2	0	2	6	.250	0	0-2	1	6.13
1998 Boston	AL	63	10	0	8	123	527	126	65	55	4	5	4	4	42	5	77	8	0	3	9	.250	0	4-9	12	4.02
1999 Boston	AL	74	0	0	32	109.1	436	84	35	32	7	1	4	2	25	1	80	1	0	6	3	.667	0	15-20	22	2.63
2000 Boston	AL	74	0	0	64	91.1	379	90	27	26	6	4	1	2	22	5	79	2	1	4	4	.500	0	42-47	0	2.56
1997 Seattle	AL	12	9	0	1	53	234	59	43	41	11	2	1	2	20	2	39	2	0	2	4	.333	0	0-0	0	6.96
Boston	AL	8	0	0	0	16	64	15	6	6	0	2	1	2	3	1	13	0	0	0	2	.000	0	0-2	1	3.38
4 ML YEARS		231	19	0	105	392.2	1640	374	176	160	29	13	10	14	112	14	288	13	1	15	22	.405	0	61-78	35	3.67

Sean Lowe

Pitches: Right **Bats:** Right **Pos:** RP-45; SP-5   **Ht:** 6'2" **Wt:** 205 **Born:** 3/29/71 **Age:** 30

Year Team	Lg	G	GS	CG	GF	IP	BFP	H	R	ER	HR	SH	SF	HB	TBB	IBB	SO	WP	Bk	W	L	Pct.	ShO	Sv-Op	Hld	ERA
2000 Charlotte *	AAA	2	1	0	0	3	14	5	1	1	1	0	0	0	1	0	1	0	0	0	0	—	0	0--	—	3.00
1997 St. Louis	NL	6	4	0	1	17.1	89	27	21	18	2	1	2	1	10	0	8	0	0	0	2	.000	0	0-0	0	9.35
1998 St. Louis	NL	4	1	0	2	5.1	31	11	9	9	1	1	0	0	5	0	2	0	0	3	0	.000	0	0-0	0	15.19
1999 Chicago	AL	64	0	0	13	95.2	406	90	39	39	10	3	9	4	46	1	62	4	0	4	1	.800	0	0-3	6	3.67
2000 Chicago	AL	50	5	0	8	70.2	325	78	47	43	10	4	1	6	39	3	53	3	0	4	1	.800	0	0-0	6	5.48
4 ML YEARS		124	10	0	24	189	851	206	116	109	23	9	12	11	100	4	125	7	0	8	7	.533	0	0-3	12	5.19

Mike Lowell

Bats: Right **Throws:** Right **Pos:** 3B-136; PH/PR-4   **Ht:** 6'4" **Wt:** 205 **Born:** 2/24/74 **Age:** 27

				BATTING														BASERUNNING				PERCENTAGES		
Year Team	Lg	G	AB	H	2B	3B	HR	(Hm	Rd)	TB	R	RBI	TBB	IBB	SO	HBP	SH	SF	SB	CS	SB%	GDP	Avg	OBP	SLG
1998 New York	AL	8	15	4	0	0	0	(0	0)	4	1	0	0	0	1	0	0	0	0	0	—	0	.267	.267	.267
1999 Florida	NL	97	308	78	15	0	12	(7	5)	129	32	47	26	1	69	5	0	5	0	0	—	8	.253	.317	.419
2000 Florida	NL	140	508	137	38	0	22	(11	11)	241	73	91	54	4	75	9	0	11	4	0	1.00	4	.270	.344	.474
3 ML YEARS		245	831	219	53	0	34	(18	16)	374	106	138	80	5	145	14	0	16	4	0	1.00	12	.264	.333	.450

Terrell Lowery

Bats: R **Throws:** R **Pos:** LF-13; PH/PR-10; RF-8; DH-1   **Ht:** 6'3" **Wt:** 195 **Born:** 10/25/70 **Age:** 30

				BATTING														BASERUNNING				PERCENTAGES		
Year Team	Lg	G	AB	H	2B	3B	HR	(Hm	Rd)	TB	R	RBI	TBB	IBB	SO	HBP	SH	SF	SB	CS	SB%	GDP	Avg	OBP	SLG
2000 Fresno *	AAA	84	301	60	9	1	16	—	—	119	48	44	36	0	88	3	1	2	6	1	.86	12	.199	.289	.395

(continued)

Year Team	Lg	G	AB	H	2B	3B	HR	(Hm	Rd)	TB	R	RBI	TBB	IBB	SO	HBP	SH	SF	SB	CS	SB%	GDP	Avg	OBP	SLG
1997 Chicago	NL	9	14	4	0	0	0	(0	0)	4	2	0	3	0	3	0	0	0	1	0	1.00		.286	.412	.286
1998 Chicago	NL	24	15	3	1	0	0	(0	0)	4	2	1	3	0	7	0	0	0	0	0		0	.200	.333	.267
1999 Tampa Bay	AL	66	185	48	15	1	2	(0	2)	71	25	17	19	0	53	1	0	1	0	2	.00	1	.259	.330	.384
2000 San Francisco	NL	24	34	15	4	0	1	(0	1)	22	13	5	7	0	8	1	0	0	1	0	1.00	1	.441	.548	.647
4 ML YEARS		123	248	70	20	1	3	(0	3)	101	42	23	32	0	71	2	0	1	2	2	.50	2	.282	.367	.407

Larry Luebbers

Pitches: Right **Bats:** Right **Pos:** RP-13; SP-1 **Ht:** 6'6" **Wt:** 210 **Born:** 10/11/69 **Age:** 31

Year Team	Lg	G	GS	CG	GF	IP	BFP	H	R	ER	HR	SH	SF	HB	TBB	IBB	SO	WP	Bk	W	L	Pct.	ShO	Sv-Op	Hld	ERA
2000 Louisville *	AAA	18	17	2	1	114.2	472	97	50	45	9	4	0	6	40	1	69	2	0	7	6	.538	1	0--	0	3.53
1993 Cincinnati	NL	14	14	0	0	77.1	332	74	49	39	7	4	5	1	38	3	38	4	0	2	5	.286	0	0-0	0	4.54
1999 St. Louis	NL	8	8	1	0	45.2	192	46	27	26	8	4	0	3	16	0	16	1	1	3	3	.500	0	0-0	0	5.12
2000 Cincinnati	NL	14	1	0	4	20.1	94	27	15	14	1	1	0	0	12	2	9	1	0	0	2	.000	0	1-1	4	6.20
3 ML YEARS		36	23	1	4	143.1	625	147	91	79	16	9	5	4	66	5	63	6	1	5	10	.333	0	1-1	4	4.96

Julio Lugo

Bats: R **Throws:** R **Pos:** SS-60; 2B-45; PH/PR-15; LF-3; RF-2; CF-1 **Ht:** 5'10" **Wt:** 165 **Born:** 11/16/75 **Age:** 25

Year Team	Lg	G	AB	H	2B	3B	HR	(Hm	Rd)	TB	R	RBI	TBB	IBB	SO	HBP	SH	SF	SB	CS	SB%	GDP	Avg	OBP	SLG
1995 Auburn	A-	59	230	67	6	3	1	—	—	82	36	16	26	0	31	2	2	0	17	7	.71	7	.291	.368	.357
1996 Quad City	A	101	393	116	18	2	10	—	—	168	60	50	32	0	75	3	4	4	24	11	.69	7	.295	.350	.427
1997 Kissimmee	A+	125	505	135	22	14	7	—	—	206	89	61	46	1	99	2	8	4	35	8	.81	8	.267	.329	.408
1998 Kissimmee	A+	128	509	154	20	14	7	—	—	223	81	62	49	3	72	4	6	2	51	18	.74	13	.303	.367	.438
1999 Jackson	AA	116	445	142	24	5	10	—	—	206	77	42	44	0	53	3	1	4	25	11	.69	6	.319	.381	.463
2000 New Orleans	AAA	24	101	33	4	1	3	—	—	48	22	12	11	0	20	0	2	0	12	7	.63	2	.327	.393	.475
2000 Houston	NL	116	420	119	22	5	10	(6	4)	181	78	40	37	0	93	4	3	1	22	9	.71	9	.283	.346	.431

Fernando Lunar

Bats: Right **Throws:** Right **Pos:** C-31; PH/PR-1 **Ht:** 6'1" **Wt:** 190 **Born:** 5/25/77 **Age:** 24

Year Team	Lg	G	AB	H	2B	3B	HR	(Hm	Rd)	TB	R	RBI	TBB	IBB	SO	HBP	SH	SF	SB	CS	SB%	GDP	Avg	OBP	SLG
1994 Braves	R	33	100	24	5	0	2	—	—	35	9	12	1	0	13	3	1	1	0	0	—	1	.240	.267	.350
1995 Macon	A	39	134	24	2	0	0	—	—	26	13	9	10	0	38	3	3	0	1	0	1.00	3	.179	.252	.194
Eugene	A-	38	131	32	6	0	2	—	—	44	13	16	9	0	28	0	2	0	1	0	.00	2	.244	.293	.336
1996 Macon	A	104	343	63	9	0	7	—	—	93	33	33	20	0	65	12	3	2	3	2	.60	11	.184	.252	.271
1997 Macon	A	105	380	99	26	2	7	—	—	150	41	37	18	1	42	5	2	1	0	1	.00	11	.261	.302	.395
1998 Danville	A+	91	286	63	9	0	3	—	—	81	19	28	6	0	52	12	2	1	1	1	.50	4	.220	.266	.283
1999 Greenville	AA	105	343	77	15	1	3	—	—	103	33	35	12	5	64	12	0	0	0	1	.00	7	.224	.275	.300
2000 Greenville	AA	31	102	17	3	0	0	—	—	20	6	4	8	0	15	0	0	0	0	0	—	2	.167	.227	.196
Bowie	AA	22	80	23	7	1	0	—	—	32	12	8	6	0	8	3	0	0	0	0	—	4	.288	.360	.400
2000 Atl-Bal		31	70	12	1	0	0	(0	0)	13	5	6	3	1	19	4	0	0	0	2	.00	2	.171	.247	.186
2000 Atlanta	NL	22	54	10	1	0	0	(0	0)	11	5	5	3	1	15	3	0	0	0	2	.00	2	.185	.267	.204
Baltimore	AL	9	16	2	0	0	0	(0	0)	2	0	1	0	0	4	1	0	0	0	0	—	0	.125	.176	.125

Keith Luuloa

Bats: Right **Throws:** Right **Pos:** SS-4; 2B-3; PH/PR-1 **Ht:** 6'1" **Wt:** 175 **Born:** 12/24/74 **Age:** 26

Year Team	Lg	G	AB	H	2B	3B	HR	(Hm	Rd)	TB	R	RBI	TBB	IBB	SO	HBP	SH	SF	SB	CS	SB%	GDP	Avg	OBP	SLG
1994 Angels	R	28	97	29	4	1	1	—	—	38	14	10	8	0	14	4	1	3	3	4	.43	0	.299	.366	.392
1995 Lk Elsinore	A+	102	380	100	22	7	5	—	—	151	50	53	24	0	47	6	7	1	1	5	.17	9	.263	.316	.397
1996 Midland	AA	134	531	138	24	2	7	—	—	187	80	44	47	0	54	6	8	3	4	6	.40	14	.260	.325	.352
1997 Midland	AA	120	421	115	29	5	9	—	—	181	67	59	36	0	59	5	10	6	7	4	.64	18	.273	.333	.430
1998 Midland	AA	130	479	160	43	10	17	—	—	274	85	102	75	5	54	7	2	16	6	5	.55	15	.334	.419	.572
Vancouver	AAA	8	30	10	1	0	0	—	—	11	4	3	4	0	3	0	0	1	1	1	.50	1	.333	.400	.367
1999 Edmonton	AAA	115	396	113	23	1	4	—	—	150	54	46	44	0	53	5	4	2	7	7	.50	14	.285	.362	.379
2000 Edmonton	AAA	76	270	66	17	2	8	—	—	111	39	46	30	1	30	2	1	4	2	4	.33	11	.244	.320	.411
Iowa	AAA	4	16	6	1	0	1	—	—	10	4	4	2	0	1	0	0	0	0	1	1.00	0	.375	.444	.625
2000 Anaheim	AL	6	18	6	0	0	0	(0	0)	6	3	0	1	0	1	0	0	0	0	0	—	0	.333	.368	.333

John Mabry

Bats: L **Throws:** R **Pos:** RF-42; PH/PR-30; 3B-22; LF-9; DH-5; 1B-5; P-1 **Ht:** 6'4" **Wt:** 210 **Born:** 10/17/70 **Age:** 30

Year Team	Lg	G	AB	H	2B	3B	HR	(Hm	Rd)	TB	R	RBI	TBB	IBB	SO	HBP	SH	SF	SB	CS	SB%	GDP	Avg	OBP	SLG
2000 Tacoma *	AAA	4	14	3	1	0	0	—	—	4	1	1	0	0	4	0	0	0	0	0	—	0	.214	.214	.286
1994 St. Louis	NL	6	23	7	3	0	0	(0	0)	10	2	3	2	0	4	0	0	0	0	0	—	0	.304	.360	.435
1995 St. Louis	NL	129	388	119	21	1	5	(2	3)	157	35	41	24	5	45	2	0	4	0	3	.00	6	.307	.347	.405
1996 St. Louis	NL	151	543	161	30	2	13	(3	10)	234	63	74	37	11	84	3	3	5	3	2	.60	21	.297	.342	.431
1997 St. Louis	NL	116	388	110	19	0	5	(5	0)	144	40	36	39	9	77	3	2	1	0	1	.00	11	.284	.352	.371
1998 St. Louis	NL	142	377	94	22	0	9	(5	4)	143	41	46	30	6	76	1	3	2	0	2	.00	6	.249	.305	.379
1999 Seattle	AL	87	262	64	14	0	9	(5	4)	105	34	33	20	1	60	0	2	1	2	1	.67	6	.244	.297	.401
2000 Sea-SD		96	226	53	13	0	8	(3	5)	90	35	32	15	0	69	2	0	1	0	1	.00	4	.235	.287	.398
2000 Seattle	AL	48	103	25	5	0	1	(0	1)	33	18	7	10	0	31	2	0	0	0	1	.00	1	.243	.322	.320
San Diego	NL	48	123	28	8	0	7	(3	4)	57	17	25	5	0	38	0	0	1	0	0	—	3	.228	.256	.463
7 ML YEARS		727	2207	608	122	3	49	(22	27)	883	250	265	167	32	415	11	10	15	5	10	.33	54	.275	.328	.400

Robert Machado

Bats: Right **Throws:** Right **Pos:** C-8   **Ht:** 6'1" **Wt:** 205 **Born:** 6/3/73 **Age:** 28

Year Team	Lg	G	AB	H	2B	3B	HR	(Hm	Rd)	TB	R	RBI	TBB	IBB	SO	HBP	SH	SF	SB	CS	SB%	GDP	Avg	OBP	SLG
2000 Tacoma *	AAA	92	330	99	20	0	9	(Hm	Rd)	146	41	58	28	1	43	3	5	3	1	5	.17	10	.300	.357	.442
1996 Chicago	AL	4	6	4	1	0	0	(0	0)	5	1	2	0	0	0	0	0	0	0	0	—	1	.667	.667	.833
1997 Chicago	AL	10	15	3	0	1	0	(0	0)	5	1	2	1	0	6	0	1	0	0	0	—	0	.200	.250	.333
1998 Chicago	AL	34	111	23	6	0	3	(2	1)	38	14	15	7	0	22	0	3	0	0	0	—	3	.207	.254	.342
1999 Montreal	NL	17	22	4	1	0	0	(0	0)	5	3	0	2	0	6	0	0	0	0	0	—	0	.182	.250	.227
2000 Seattle	AL	8	14	3	0	0	1	(1	0)	6	2	1	1	0	4	0	0	0	0	0	—	0	.214	.267	.429
5 ML YEARS		73	168	37	8	1	4	(3	1)	59	21	20	11	0	38	0	4	0	0	0	—	4	.220	.268	.351

Jose Macias

Bats: B **Throws:** R **Pos:** 2B-39; 3B-26; PH/PR-17; RF-2; DH-1; SS-1; CF-1   **Ht:** 5'10" **Wt:** 173 **Born:** 1/25/74 **Age:** 27

Year Team	Lg	G	AB	H	2B	3B	HR	(Hm	Rd)	TB	R	RBI	TBB	IBB	SO	HBP	SH	SF	SB	CS	SB%	GDP	Avg	OBP	SLG
1994 Expos	R	31	104	28	8	2	1	—	—	43	23	6	14	0	15	0	0	0	4	1	.80	3	.269	.356	.413
1995 Vermont	A-	53	176	42	4	2	0	—	—	50	24	9	19	0	19	2	2	0	11	7	.61	3	.239	.320	.284
1996 Delmarva	A	116	369	91	13	4	1	—	—	115	64	33	56	1	48	6	7	2	38	15	.72	2	.247	.353	.312
1997 Lakeland	A+	122	424	113	18	2	2	—	—	141	54	21	52	1	33	2	8	2	10	14	.42	10	.267	.348	.333
1998 Jacksnville	AA	128	511	156	28	10	12	—	—	240	82	71	52	2	46	4	3	3	6	9	.40	4	.305	.372	.470
1999 Toledo	AAA	112	438	107	18	8	2	—	—	147	44	36	36	0	60	4	5	2	10	5	.67	8	.244	.306	.336
2000 Toledo	AAA	33	130	30	5	0	0	—	—	35	19	8	17	0	17	1	4	1	2	3	.40	3	.231	.322	.269
1999 Detroit	AL	5	4	1	0	0	1	(1	0)	4	2	2	0	0	1	0	0	0	0	0	—	0	.250	.250	1.000
2000 Detroit	AL	73	173	44	3	5	2	(2	0)	63	25	24	18	0	24	1	4	0	2	0	1.00	3	.254	.328	.364
2 ML YEARS		78	177	45	3	5	3	(3	0)	67	27	26	18	0	25	1	4	0	2	0	1.00	3	.254	.327	.379

Greg Maddux

Pitches: Right **Bats:** Right **Pos:** SP-35   **Ht:** 6'0" **Wt:** 185 **Born:** 4/14/66 **Age:** 35

Year Team	Lg	G	GS	CG	GF	IP	BFP	H	R	ER	HR	SH	SF	HB	TBB	IBB	SO	WP	Bk	W	L	Pct.	ShO	Sv-Op	Hld	ERA
1986 Chicago	NL	6	5	1	1	31	144	44	20	19	3	1	0	1	11	2	20	2	0	2	4	.333	0	0-0	0	5.52
1987 Chicago	NL	30	27	1	2	155.2	701	181	111	97	17	7	1	4	74	13	101	4	7	6	14	.300	1	0-0	0	5.61
1988 Chicago	NL	34	34	9	0	249	1047	230	97	88	13	11	2	9	81	16	140	3	6	18	8	.692	3	0-0	0	3.18
1989 Chicago	NL	35	35	7	0	238.1	1002	222	90	78	13	18	6	6	82	13	135	5	3	19	12	.613	1	0-0	0	2.95
1990 Chicago	NL	35	35	8	0	237	1011	242	116	91	11	18	5	4	71	10	144	3	3	15	15	.500	2	0-0	0	3.46
1991 Chicago	NL	37	37	7	0	263	1070	232	113	98	18	16	3	6	66	9	198	6	3	15	11	.577	2	0-0	0	3.35
1992 Chicago	NL	35	35	9	0	268	1061	201	68	65	7	15	3	14	70	7	199	5	0	20	11	.645	4	0-0	0	2.18
1993 Atlanta	NL	36	36	8	0	267	1064	228	85	70	14	15	7	6	52	7	197	5	1	20	10	.667	1	0-0	0	2.36
1994 Atlanta	NL	25	25	10	0	202	774	150	44	35	4	6	5	6	31	3	156	3	1	16	6	.727	3	0-0	0	1.56
1995 Atlanta	NL	28	28	10	0	209.2	785	147	39	38	8	9	1	4	23	3	181	1	0	19	2	.905	3	0-0	0	1.63
1996 Atlanta	NL	35	35	5	0	245	978	225	85	74	11	8	5	3	28	11	172	4	0	15	11	.577	1	0-0	0	2.72
1997 Atlanta	NL	33	33	5	0	232.2	893	200	58	57	9	11	7	6	20	6	177	0	0	19	4	.826	2	0-0	0	2.20
1998 Atlanta	NL	34	34	9	0	251	987	201	75	62	13	15	5	7	45	10	204	4	0	18	9	.667	5	0-0	0	2.22
1999 Atlanta	NL	33	33	4	0	219.1	940	258	103	87	16	15	5	4	37	8	136	1	0	19	9	.679	0	0-0	0	3.57
2000 Atlanta	NL	35	35	6	0	249.1	1012	225	91	83	19	8	5	10	42	12	190	1	2	19	9	.679	3	0-0	0	3.00
15 ML YEARS		471	467	99	3	3318	13469	2986	1195	1042	176	173	60	90	733	130	2350	47	26	240	135	.640	31	0-0	0	2.83

Mike Maddux

Pitches: Right **Bats:** Left **Pos:** RP-21   **Ht:** 6'2" **Wt:** 185 **Born:** 8/27/61 **Age:** 39

Year Team	Lg	G	GS	CG	GF	IP	BFP	H	R	ER	HR	SH	SF	HB	TBB	IBB	SO	WP	Bk	W	L	Pct.	ShO	Sv-Op	Hld	ERA
1986 Philadelphia	NL	16	16	0	0	78	351	88	56	47	6	3	3	3	34	4	44	4	2	3	7	.300	0	0-0	0	5.42
1987 Philadelphia	NL	7	2	0	0	17	59	17	5	5	0	0	0	0	5	0	15	1	0	2	0	1.000	0	0-0	0	2.65
1988 Philadelphia	NL	25	11	0	4	88.2	380	91	41	37	6	7	0	5	34	4	59	4	2	3	7	.571	0	0-0	0	3.76
1989 Philadelphia	NL	16	4	2	1	43.2	191	52	29	25	3	3	1	2	14	3	26	3	1	1	3	.250	1	1-1	2	5.15
1990 Los Angeles	NL	11	2	0	3	20.2	88	24	15	15	3	0	1	1	4	0	11	2	0	1	0	1.000	0	0-0	1	6.53
1991 San Diego	NL	64	1	0	27	98.2	388	78	30	27	4	5	2	1	27	3	57	5	0	7	2	.778	0	5-7	9	2.46
1992 San Diego	NL	50	1	0	14	79.2	330	71	25	21	2	2	3	0	24	4	60	4	1	2	2	.500	0	5-9	8	2.37
1993 New York	NL	58	0	0	31	75	320	67	34	30	3	7	6	4	27	7	57	4	1	3	8	.273	0	5-11	3	3.60
1994 New York	NL	27	0	0	12	44	186	45	25	25	7	0	2	0	13	4	32	2	0	2	1	.667	0	2-4	1	5.11
1995 Pit-Bos		44	4	0	7	89.2	409	100	49	45	5	1	1	2	18	4	69	6	0	5	1	.833	0	1-1	6	4.10
1996 Boston	AL	23	7	0	2	64.1	295	76	37	32	12	3	2	5	27	2	32	1	0	3	2	.600	0	0-0	1	4.48
1997 Seattle	AL	6	0	0	1	10.2	59	20	12	12	1	0	0	1	8	2	7	1	0	1	0	1.000	0	0-0	0	10.13
1998 Montreal	NL	51	0	0	20	55.2	228	50	24	23	3	3	3	1	15	1	33	3	1	3	4	.429	0	1-2	7	3.72
1999 Mon-LA	NL	53	0	0	21	59.2	260	63	26	25	6	2	2	5	22	2	45	1	0	1	1	.500	0	0-0	10	3.77
2000 Houston	NL	21	0	0	6	27.1	128	31	20	19	6	3	1	2	12	0	17	0	0	2	2	.500	0	0-0	2	6.26
1995 Pittsburgh	NL	8	0	0	0	9	42	14	9	9	0	0	0	0	3	1	4	1	0	1	0	1.000	0	0-0	2	9.00
Boston	AL	36	4	0	6	89.2	367	86	40	36	5	1	1	2	15	3	65	5	0	4	1	.800	0	1-1	4	3.61
1999 Montreal	NL	4	0	0	2	5	26	9	5	5	1	0	0	1	3	0	4	0	0	0	0	—	0	0-0	0	9.00
Los Angeles	NL	49	0	0	19	54.2	234	54	21	20	5	2	2	4	19	2	41	1	0	1	1	.500	0	0-0	10	3.29
15 ML YEARS		472	48	2	149	861.2	3685	873	428	388	67	39	30	32	284	40	564	41	8	39	37	.513	1	20-35	51	4.05

Calvin Maduro

Pitches: Right **Bats:** Right **Pos:** RP-13; SP-2   **Ht:** 6'0" **Wt:** 180 **Born:** 9/5/74 **Age:** 26

Year Team	Lg	G	GS	CG	GF	IP	BFP	H	R	ER	HR	SH	SF	HB	TBB	IBB	SO	WP	Bk	W	L	Pct.	ShO	Sv-Op	Hld	ERA
2000 Rochester *	AAA	4	1	0	0	4	16	1	1	1	0	0	0	0	4	0	6	0	0	1	0	1.000	0	0- --	—	0.00
Frederick *	A+	1	1	0	0	2	7	1	0	0	0	0	0	0	0	0	6	0	0	0	0	—	0	0- --	—	0.00
1996 Philadelphia	NL	4	2	0	0	15.1	62	13	6	6	1	1	0	2	3	0	11	1	0	0	1	.000	0	0-0	0	3.52
1997 Philadelphia	NL	15	13	0	0	71	331	83	59	57	12	1	4	3	41	5	31	6	2	3	7	.300	0	0-0	0	7.23
2000 Baltimore	AL	15	2	0	6	23.1	113	29	25	25	8	1	2	2	16	1	18	1	0	0	0	—	0	0-0	1	9.64
3 ML YEARS		34	17	0	6	109.2	506	125	90	88	21	3	6	7	60	6	60	8	2	3	8	.273	0	0-0	1	7.22

128

Dave Magadan

Bats: L Throws: R Pos: PH/PR-67; 3B-29; 1B-8; DH-2; SS-2   Ht: 6'4" Wt: 215 Born: 9/30/62 Age: 38

				BATTING														BASERUNNING				PERCENTAGES		
Year Team	Lg	G	AB	H	2B	3B	HR	(Hm	Rd)	TB	R	RBI	TBB	IBB	SO	HBP	SH	SF	SB	CS	SB%	GDP	Avg	OBP	SLG
1986 New York	NL	10	18	8	0	0	0	(0	0)	8	3	3	3	0	1	0	0	0	0	0	—	1	.444	.524	.444
1987 New York	NL	85	192	61	13	1	3	(2	1)	85	21	24	22	2	22	0	1	1	0	0	—	5	.318	.386	.443
1988 New York	NL	112	314	87	15	0	1	(1	0)	105	39	35	60	4	39	2	1	3	0	1	.00	9	.277	.393	.334
1989 New York	NL	127	374	107	22	3	4	(3	1)	147	47	41	49	6	37	1	1	4	1	0	1.00	2	.286	.367	.393
1990 New York	NL	144	451	148	28	6	6	(2	4)	206	74	72	74	4	55	2	4	10	2	1	.67	11	.328	.417	.457
1991 New York	NL	124	418	108	23	0	4	(2	2)	143	58	51	83	3	50	2	7	7	1	1	.50	5	.258	.378	.342
1992 New York	NL	99	321	91	9	1	3	(2	1)	111	33	28	56	3	44	0	2	0	1	0	1.00	6	.283	.390	.346
1993 Fla-Sea		137	455	124	23	0	5	(3	2)	162	49	50	80	7	63	1	2	6	2	1	.67	12	.273	.378	.356
1994 Florida	NL	74	211	58	7	0	1	(1	0)	68	30	17	39	0	25	1	0	3	0	0	—	8	.275	.386	.322
1995 Houston	NL	127	348	109	24	0	2	(0	2)	139	44	51	71	9	56	0	1	2	2	1	.67	9	.313	.428	.399
1996 Chicago	NL	78	169	43	10	0	3	(2	1)	62	23	17	29	3	23	0	1	2	0	2	.00	7	.254	.360	.367
1997 Oakland	AL	128	271	82	10	1	4	(2	2)	106	38	30	50	1	40	2	4	1	1	0	1.00	7	.303	.414	.391
1998 Oakland	AL	35	109	35	8	0	1	(0	1)	46	12	13	13	1	12	0	0	1	0	1	.00	5	.321	.390	.422
1999 San Diego	NL	116	248	68	12	1	2	(1	1)	88	20	30	45	2	36	0	0	7	1	3	.25	10	.274	.377	.355
2000 San Diego	NL	95	132	36	7	0	2	(1	1)	49	13	21	32	1	23	0	0	0	0	0	—	4	.273	.410	.371
1993 Florida	NL	66	227	65	12	0	4	(3	1)	89	22	29	44	4	30	1	0	3	0	1	.00	3	.286	.400	.392
Seattle	AL	71	228	59	11	0	1	(0	1)	73	27	21	36	3	33	0	2	3	2	0	1.00	9	.259	.356	.320
15 ML YEARS		1491	4031	1165	211	13	41	(22	19)	1525	504	483	706	46	526	11	24	49	11	11	.50	97	.289	.392	.378

Wendell Magee

Bats: R Throws: R Pos: RF-56; PH/PR-30; LF-18; DH-6; CF-5   Ht: 6'0" Wt: 220 Born: 8/3/72 Age: 28

				BATTING														BASERUNNING				PERCENTAGES		
Year Team	Lg	G	AB	H	2B	3B	HR	(Hm	Rd)	TB	R	RBI	TBB	IBB	SO	HBP	SH	SF	SB	CS	SB%	GDP	Avg	OBP	SLG
2000 Toledo *	AAA	2	7	4	1	0	0	—	—	5	1	1	1	0	1	0	0	0	0	1	.00	0	.571	.625	.714
1996 Philadelphia	NL	38	142	29	7	0	2	(2	0)	42	9	14	9	0	33	0	0	0	0	0	—	2	.204	.252	.296
1997 Philadelphia	NL	38	115	23	4	0	1	(0	1)	30	7	9	9	1	20	0	0	2	1	4	.20	8	.200	.254	.261
1998 Philadelphia	NL	20	75	22	6	1	1	(0	1)	33	9	11	7	0	11	0	0	0	0	0	—	4	.293	.354	.440
1999 Philadelphia	NL	12	14	5	1	0	2	(1	1)	12	4	5	1	0	4	0	0	0	0	0	—	0	.357	.400	.857
2000 Detroit	AL	91	186	51	4	2	7	(2	5)	80	31	31	10	0	28	0	0	1	1	0	1.00	7	.274	.310	.430
5 ML YEARS		199	532	130	22	3	13	(5	8)	197	60	70	36	1	96	0	0	3	2	4	.33	22	.244	.291	.370

Mike Magnante

Pitches: Left Bats: Left Pos: RP-55   Ht: 6'1" Wt: 185 Born: 6/17/65 Age: 36

		HOW MUCH HE PITCHED						WHAT HE GAVE UP												THE RESULTS					
Year Team	Lg	G	GS	CG	GF	IP	BFP	H	R	ER	HR	SH	SF	HB	TBB	IBB	SO	WP	Bk	W	L	Pct.	ShO	Sv-Op	Hld	ERA
2000 Sacramento *	AAA	5	2	0	0	6.2	27	6	3	3	2	0	0	1	1	0	4	0	0	0	0	—	0	0--	—	4.05
1991 Kansas City	AL	38	0	0	10	55	236	55	19	15	3	2	1	0	23	3	42	1	0	1	0	.000	0	0-0	2	2.45
1992 Kansas City	AL	44	12	0	11	89.1	403	115	53	49	5	5	7	2	35	5	31	2	0	4	9	.308	0	0-3	4	4.94
1993 Kansas City	AL	7	6	0	0	35.1	145	37	16	16	3	1	1	1	11	1	16	1	0	1	2	.333	0	0-0	0	4.08
1994 Kansas City	AL	36	1	0	10	47	211	55	27	24	5	2	3	0	16	1	21	3	0	2	3	.400	0	0-0	6	4.60
1995 Kansas City	AL	28	0	0	7	44.2	190	45	23	21	6	2	2	2	16	1	28	2	0	1	1	.500	0	0-1	5	4.23
1996 Kansas City	AL	38	0	0	9	54	238	58	38	34	5	0	4	4	24	1	32	3	0	2	2	.500	0	0-1	5	5.67
1997 Houston	NL	40	0	0	14	47.2	191	39	16	12	2	3	2	0	11	2	43	2	2	3	1	.750	0	1-5	3	2.27
1998 Houston	NL	48	0	0	20	51.2	237	56	28	28	2	3	1	4	26	4	39	3	0	4	7	.364	0	2-4	8	4.88
1999 Anaheim	AL	53	0	0	13	69.1	299	68	30	26	2	0	7	3	29	4	44	3	1	5	2	.714	0	0-3	4	3.38
2000 Oakland	AL	55	0	0	6	39.2	189	50	22	19	3	6	0	2	19	7	17	1	0	1	1	.500	0	0-3	14	4.31
10 ML YEARS		387	19	0	100	533.2	2339	578	272	244	36	24	28	18	210	29	313	21	3	23	29	.442	0	3-20	46	4.11

Ron Mahay

Pitches: Left Bats: Left Pos: RP-21; SP-2   Ht: 6'2" Wt: 190 Born: 6/28/71 Age: 30

		HOW MUCH HE PITCHED						WHAT HE GAVE UP												THE RESULTS					
Year Team	Lg	G	GS	CG	GF	IP	BFP	H	R	ER	HR	SH	SF	HB	TBB	IBB	SO	WP	Bk	W	L	Pct.	ShO	Sv-Op	Hld	ERA
2000 Calgary *	AAA	8	0	0	3	13	50	7	7	7	1	2	1	0	7	1	15	1	0	0	1	.000	0	0--	—	4.85
1997 Boston	AL	28	0	0	7	25	105	19	7	7	3	1	0	0	11	0	22	3	0	3	0	1.000	0	0-1	5	2.52
1998 Boston	AL	29	0	0	6	26	120	26	16	10	2	0	4	2	15	1	14	3	0	1	1	.500	0	1-2	7	3.46
1999 Oakland	AL	6	1	0	2	19.1	68	8	4	4	2	0	0	0	3	0	15	0	0	2	0	1.000	0	1-1	0	1.86
2000 Oak-Fla		23	2	0	7	41.1	199	57	35	33	10	1	2	0	25	1	32	4	0	1	1	.500	0	0-0	2	7.19
2000 Oakland	AL	5	2	0	1	16	82	26	18	16	4	1	1	0	9	0	5	2	0	1	0	1.000	0	0-0	0	9.00
Florida	NL	18	0	0	6	25.1	117	31	17	17	6	0	1	0	16	1	27	2	0	0	1	1.000	0	0-0	2	6.04
4 ML YEARS		86	3	0	22	111.2	492	110	62	54	17	2	6	2	54	2	83	10	0	7	2	.778	0	2-4	14	4.35

Pat Mahomes

Pitches: Right Bats: Right Pos: RP-48; SP-5   Ht: 6'4" Wt: 212 Born: 8/9/70 Age: 30

		HOW MUCH HE PITCHED						WHAT HE GAVE UP												THE RESULTS					
Year Team	Lg	G	GS	CG	GF	IP	BFP	H	R	ER	HR	SH	SF	HB	TBB	IBB	SO	WP	Bk	W	L	Pct.	ShO	Sv-Op	Hld	ERA
1992 Minnesota	AL	14	13	0	1	69.2	302	73	41	39	5	0	3	0	37	0	44	2	1	3	4	.429	0	0-0	0	5.04
1993 Minnesota	AL	12	5	0	4	37.1	173	47	34	32	8	1	3	1	16	0	23	3	0	1	5	.167	0	0-0	0	7.71
1994 Minnesota	AL	21	21	0	0	120	517	121	68	63	22	1	4	1	62	1	53	3	0	9	5	.643	0	0-0	0	4.73
1995 Minnesota	AL	47	7	0	16	94.2	423	100	74	67	22	3	2	2	47	1	67	6	0	4	10	.286	0	3-7	9	6.37
1996 Min-Bos	AL	31	0	0	9	57.1	271	72	46	44	13	2	2	0	33	0	36	2	0	3	4	.429	0	2-2	4	6.91
1997 Boston	AL	10	0	0	2	10	54	15	10	9	2	0	1	2	10	1	5	1	0	1	0	1.000	0	0-0	1	8.10
1999 New York	NL	39	0	0	12	63.2	265	44	26	26	7	1	2	2	37	5	51	2	0	8	0	1.000	0	0-1	3	3.68
2000 New York	NL	53	5	0	12	94	439	96	63	57	15	3	3	2	66	4	76	5	0	5	3	.625	0	0-1	3	5.46
1996 Minnesota	AL	20	5	0	5	45	220	63	38	36	10	0	2	0	27	0	30	2	0	1	4	.200	0	0-0	3	7.20
Boston	AL	11	0	0	4	12.1	51	9	8	8	3	2	0	0	6	0	6	0	0	2	0	1.000	0	2-2	1	5.84
8 ML YEARS		227	56	0	57	546.2	2444	568	362	337	94	11	20	10	308	12	355	24	1	34	31	.523	0	5-11	18	5.55

Mike Mahoney

Bats: Right **Throws:** Right **Pos:** C-4; PH/PR-1   **Ht:** 6'1" **Wt:** 200 **Born:** 12/5/72 **Age:** 28

Year Team	Lg	G	AB	H	2B	3B	HR	(Hm	Rd)	TB	R	RBI	TBB	IBB	SO	HBP	SH	SF	SB	CS	SB%	GDP	Avg	OBP	SLG
1995 Eugene	A-	43	112	27	6	0	1	—	—	36	14	15	15	1	17	3	1	1	6	2	.75	5	.241	.344	.321
1996 Durham	A+	101	363	94	24	2	9	—	—	149	52	46	23	0	64	7	4	4	4	3	.57	8	.259	.312	.410
1997 Greenville	AA	87	298	68	17	0	8	—	—	109	46	46	28	1	75	3	5	2	1	0	1.00	10	.228	.299	.366
1998 Greenville	AA	20	74	16	5	0	1	—	—	24	3	6	1	0	20	2	0	2	1	1	.50	1	.216	.241	.324
Richmond	AAA	71	208	44	10	0	5	—	—	69	26	28	24	3	49	5	6	5	1	1	.50	10	.212	.332	.332
1999 Richmond	AAA	55	145	33	7	0	2	—	—	46	10	20	6	1	25	1	2	3	0	1	.00	2	.228	.258	.317
2000 West Tenn	AA	24	76	23	7	0	0	—	—	30	12	7	7	0	16	2	0	1	0	0	.00	0	.303	.372	.395
Iowa	AAA	63	181	55	14	0	6	—	—	87	29	28	16	0	28	6	1	3	2	1	.67	2	.304	.374	.481
2000 Chicago	NL	4	7	2	1	0	0	(0	0)	3	1	1	1	0	1	0	0	0	0	0	—	0	.286	.444	.429

Oswaldo Mairena

Pitches: Left **Bats:** Left **Pos:** RP-2   **Ht:** 5'11" **Wt:** 165 **Born:** 7/30/75 **Age:** 25

Year Team	Lg	G	GS	CG	GF	IP	BFP	H	R	ER	HR	SH	SF	HB	TBB	IBB	SO	WP	Bk	W	L	Pct.	ShO	Sv-Op	Hld	ERA
1997 Tampa	A+	3	0	0	0	4.1	19	6	2	2	1	0	0	0	0	0	6	0	0	0	0	—	0	0--	—	4.15
Greensboro	A	49	0	0	20	60.1	241	43	24	17	2	3	1	1	16	3	75	0	3	6	1	.857	0	8--	—	2.54
1998 Tampa	A+	52	0	0	11	54	238	53	24	19	5	2	2	3	23	3	50	0	2	1	5	.167	0	2--	—	3.17
1999 Norwich	AA	49	0	0	16	57.1	252	48	24	17	3	4	4	1	27	4	47	4	0	4	3	.571	0	2--	—	2.67
2000 Columbus	AAA	5	1	0	2	9	43	12	3	3	2	1	0	0	5	1	4	0	0	1	1	.500	0	1--	—	3.00
Norwich	AA	35	0	0	5	32.1	137	29	16	10	0	1	2	1	11	3	30	0	0	0	4	.000	0	0--	—	2.78
West Tenn	AA	2	0	0	1	2	10	3	1	0	0	1	0	1	1	1	0	0	0	0	1	.000	0	1--	—	0.00
Iowa	AAA	11	0	0	3	14.2	62	13	9	8	1	1	0	0	2	0	4	3	0	0	1	1.000	0	0--	—	4.91
2000 Chicago	NL	2	0	1	1	2	14	7	4	4	1	0	0	0	2	0	0	0	0	0	0	—	0	0-0	0	18.00

Jim Mann

Pitches: Right **Bats:** Right **Pos:** RP-2   **Ht:** 6'3" **Wt:** 225 **Born:** 11/17/74 **Age:** 26

Year Team	Lg	G	GS	CG	GF	IP	BFP	H	R	ER	HR	SH	SF	HB	TBB	IBB	SO	WP	Bk	W	L	Pct.	ShO	Sv-Op	Hld	ERA
1994 Blue Jays	R	11	9	0	0	53	236	54	28	22	1	3	1	3	26	1	41	0	1	3	2	.600	0	0--	—	3.74
1995 Medcine Hat	R+	14	14	1	0	77.2	347	78	47	37	5	3	2	7	37	0	66	6	0	5	4	.556	1	0--	—	4.29
1996 St.Cathrnes	A-	26	0	0	23	27.1	117	22	12	11	3	2	2	3	10	1	37	0	1	2	1	.667	0	17--	—	3.62
1997 Hagerstown	A	19	0	0	16	26.2	122	35	18	15	4	0	1	1	11	0	30	2	0	0	0	.000	0	4--	—	5.06
Dunedin	A+	12	0	0	4	18	88	27	12	12	2	0	1	1	6	1	13	1	0	1	0	1.000	0	0--	—	6.00
1998 Dunedin	A+	51	0	0	47	50.1	206	31	19	17	4	0	2	4	24	1	59	2	0	2	2	.000	0	25--	—	3.04
1999 Knoxville	AA	6	0	0	4	9.2	39	6	2	1	1	3	1	2	1	0	12	0	0	1	2	.333	0	0--	—	0.93
Syracuse	AAA	47	0	0	20	66	287	53	35	34	11	1	1	2	39	1	72	6	0	6	5	.545	0	5--	—	4.64
2000 Norfolk	AAA	49	0	0	19	81.2	326	61	27	27	8	3	2	2	33	3	74	3	1	3	4	.429	0	3--	—	2.98
2000 New York	NL	2	0	0	2	2.2	15	6	3	3	1	0	0	0	1	0	0	0	0	0	0	—	0	0-0	0	10.13

Matt Mantei

Pitches: Right **Bats:** Right **Pos:** RP-47   **Ht:** 6'1" **Wt:** 190 **Born:** 7/7/73 **Age:** 27

Year Team	Lg	G	GS	CG	GF	IP	BFP	H	R	ER	HR	SH	SF	HB	TBB	IBB	SO	WP	Bk	W	L	Pct.	ShO	Sv-Op	Hld	ERA
2000 Tucson *	AAA	4	2	0	0	3.2	14	1	1	1	0	0	1	0	3	0	2	0	0	0	0	—	0	0--	—	2.45
1995 Florida	NL	12	0	0	3	13.1	64	12	8	7	1	1	1	0	13	0	15	1	0	0	1	.000	0	0-0	0	4.73
1996 Florida	NL	14	0	0	1	18.1	89	13	13	13	2	1	0	1	21	1	25	2	0	1	0	1.000	0	0-1	0	6.38
1998 Florida	NL	42	0	0	23	54.2	224	38	19	18	1	3	4	7	23	3	63	0	0	3	4	.429	0	9-12	2	2.96
1999 Fla-Ari	NL	65	0	0	60	65.1	284	44	21	20	5	1	1	5	44	1	99	2	0	1	3	.250	0	32-37	0	2.76
2000 Arizona	NL	47	0	0	38	45.1	200	31	24	24	6	1	0	2	35	1	53	1	1	1	1	.500	0	17-20	1	4.57
1999 Florida	NL	35	0	0	32	36.1	157	24	11	11	4	0	1	2	25	1	50	0	0	1	2	.333	0	10-12	0	2.72
Arizona	NL	30	0	0	28	29	127	20	10	9	1	1	0	3	19	0	49	2	0	1	0	1.000	0	22-25	0	2.79
5 ML YEARS		180	0	0	125	197	861	138	85	81	13	8	6	15	136	6	255	10	0	6	9	.400	0	58-70	2	3.70

Jeff Manto

Bats: Right **Throws:** Right **Pos:** PH/PR-6; 1B-1; 3B-1   **Ht:** 6'3" **Wt:** 210 **Born:** 8/23/64 **Age:** 36

Year Team	Lg	G	AB	H	2B	3B	HR	(Hm	Rd)	TB	R	RBI	TBB	IBB	SO	HBP	SH	SF	SB	CS	SB%	GDP	Avg	OBP	SLG
2000 Buffalo *	AAA	94	324	65	14	1	13	—	—	120	39	46	51	0	96	0	0	1	0	0	—	6	.201	.309	.370
1990 Cleveland	AL	30	76	17	5	1	2	(1	1)	30	12	14	21	1	18	0	0	0	0	1	.00	0	.224	.392	.395
1991 Cleveland	AL	47	128	27	7	0	2	(0	2)	40	15	13	14	0	22	4	1	1	2	0	1.00	3	.211	.306	.313
1993 Philadelphia	NL	8	18	1	0	0	0	(0	0)	1	0	0	0	0	3	1	0	0	0	0	—	0	.056	.105	.056
1995 Baltimore	AL	89	254	65	9	0	17	(12	5)	125	31	38	24	0	69	2	0	0	0	3	.00	6	.256	.325	.492
1996 Bos-Sea	AL	43	102	20	6	1	3	(3	0)	37	15	10	17	0	24	1	0	0	0	1	.00	2	.196	.317	.363
1997 Cleveland	AL	16	30	8	3	0	2	(2	0)	17	3	7	1	0	10	0	0	0	0	0	—	2	.267	.290	.567
1998 Cle-Det	AL	31	67	16	3	0	3	(1	2)	28	14	9	5	0	21	1	0	0	1	1	.50	5	.239	.301	.418
1999 Cle-NYY	AL	18	33	6	0	0	1	(1	0)	9	5	2	13	0	15	0	0	0	0	0	—	0	.182	.413	.273
2000 Colorado	NL	7	5	4	2	0	1	(0	1)	9	4	2	2	0	0	0	0	0	0	0	—	0	.800	.857	1.800
1996 Boston	AL	22	48	10	3	1	2	(2	0)	21	8	6	8	0	12	1	0	0	0	0	—	1	.208	.333	.438
Seattle	AL	21	54	10	3	0	1	(1	0)	16	7	4	9	0	12	0	0	0	0	0	.00	1	.185	.302	.296
1998 Cleveland	AL	15	37	8	1	0	2	(1	1)	15	8	6	2	0	11	1	0	0	0	0	.00	4	.216	.256	.405
Detroit	AL	16	30	8	2	0	1	(0	1)	13	6	3	3	0	11	0	0	0	1	0	1.00	1	.267	.353	.433
1999 Cleveland	AL	12	25	5	0	0	1	(1	0)	8	5	2	11	0	11	0	0	0	0	0	—	2	.200	.444	.320
New York	AL	6	8	1	0	0	0	(0	0)	1	0	0	2	0	4	0	0	0	0	0	—	0	.125	.300	.125
9 ML YEARS		289	713	164	35	2	31	(20	11)	296	97	97	97	1	182	9	2	1	3	6	.33	18	.230	.329	.415

Josias Manzanillo

Pitches: Right **Bats:** Right **Pos:** RP-43   **Ht:** 6'0" **Wt:** 205 **Born:** 10/16/67 **Age:** 33

Year Team	Lg	G	GS	CG	GF	IP	BFP	H	R	ER	HR	SH	SF	HB	TBB	IBB	SO	WP	Bk	W	L	Pct.	ShO	Sv-Op	Hld	ERA
2000 Nashville *	AAA	15	0	0	6	23.1	93	19	8	7	0	0	1	2	6	1	23	1	0	0	2	.000	0	3- —	—	2.70
1991 Boston	AL	1	0	0	1	1	8	2	2	2	0	0	0	0	3	0	1	0	0	0	0	—	0	0-0	0	18.00
1993 Mil-NYM		16	1	0	6	29	140	30	27	22	2	3	3	2	19	3	21	1	0	1	1	.500	0	1-2	0	6.83
1994 New York	NL	37	0	0	14	47.1	186	34	15	14	4	0	0	3	13	2	48	2	0	3	2	.600	0	2-5	11	2.66
1995 NYM-NYY		23	0	0	8	33.1	154	37	19	18	4	2	1	2	15	4	25	6	0	1	2	.333	0	0-0	1	4.86
1997 Seattle	AL	16	0	0	4	18.1	88	19	13	11	3	0	2	0	17	1	18	2	0	0	1	.000	0	0-1	1	5.40
1999 New York	NL	12	0	0	1	18.2	80	19	12	12	5	1	1	2	4	1	25	0	0	0	0	—	0	0-0	1	5.79
2000 Pittsburgh	NL	43	0	0	11	58.2	246	50	23	22	6	4	2	0	32	4	39	1	0	2	2	.500	0	0-2	5	3.38
1993 Milwaukee	AL	10	1	0	4	17	86	22	20	18	1	2	2	2	10	3	10	1	0	1	1	.500	0	1-2	0	9.53
New York	NL	6	0	0	2	12	54	8	7	4	1	1	1	0	9	0	11	0	0	0	0	—	0	0-0	0	3.00
1995 New York	NL	12	0	0	4	16	73	18	15	14	3	0	1	0	6	2	14	5	0	1	2	.333	0	0-0	1	7.88
New York		11	0	0	4	17.1	81	19	4	4	1	2	0	2	9	2	11	1	0	0	0	—	0	0-0	0	2.08
7 ML YEARS		148	1	0	45	206.1	902	191	111	101	24	10	9	9	103	15	177	12	0	7	8	.467	0	3-10	18	4.41

Jason Marquis

Pitches: Right **Bats:** Left **Pos:** RP-15   **Ht:** 6'1" **Wt:** 185 **Born:** 8/21/78 **Age:** 22

Year Team	Lg	G	GS	CG	GF	IP	BFP	H	R	ER	HR	SH	SF	HB	TBB	IBB	SO	WP	Bk	W	L	Pct.	ShO	Sv-Op	Hld	ERA
1996 Danville	R+	7	4	0	0	23.1	113	30	18	12	0	0	0	1	7	0	24	2	0	1	1	.500	0	0- —	—	4.63
1997 Macon	A	28	28	0	0	141.2	627	156	78	69	10	2	7	2	55	1	121	8	2	14	10	.583	0	0- —	—	4.38
1998 Danville	A+	22	22	1	0	114.2	500	120	65	62	3	4	3	6	41	0	135	7	0	2	12	.143	0	0- —	—	4.87
1999 Myrtle Bch	A+	6	6	0	0	32	134	22	2	1	0	0	1	1	17	0	41	2	0	3	0	1.000	0	0- —	—	0.28
Greenville	AA	12	12	1	0	55	248	52	33	28	7	0	1	2	29	0	35	1	0	3	4	.429	0	0- —	—	4.58
2000 Greenville	AA	11	11	0	0	68	287	68	35	27	10	1	2	1	23	0	49	2	1	4	2	.667	0	0- —	—	3.57
Richmond	AAA	6	6	0	0	20	97	26	21	20	2	1	2	2	13	0	18	7	0	0	3	.000	0	0- —	—	9.00
2000 Atlanta	NL	15	0	0	7	23.1	103	23	16	13	4	1	1	1	12	1	17	1	0	1	0	1.000	0	0-1	1	5.01

Eli Marrero

Bats: Right **Throws:** Right **Pos:** C-38; PH/PR-20; 1B-7   **Ht:** 6'1" **Wt:** 180 **Born:** 11/17/73 **Age:** 27

Year Team	Lg	G	AB	H	2B	3B	HR	(Hm	Rd)	TB	R	RBI	TBB	IBB	SO	HBP	SH	SF	SB	CS	SB%	GDP	Avg	OBP	SLG
2000 Memphis *	AAA	6	15	1	0	0	0			1	1	0	0	0	2	0	0	0	0	0	—	1	.067	.067	.067
1997 St. Louis	NL	17	45	11	2	0	2	(0	2)	19	4	7	2	1	13	0	0	1	4	0	1.00	1	.244	.271	.422
1998 St. Louis	NL	83	254	62	18	1	4	(2	2)	94	28	20	28	5	42	0	1	1	6	2	.75	5	.244	.318	.370
1999 St. Louis	NL	114	317	61	13	1	6	(3	3)	94	32	34	18	4	56	1	4	3	11	2	.85	14	.192	.236	.297
2000 St. Louis	NL	53	102	23	3	1	5	(2	3)	43	21	17	9	0	16	3	0	2	5	0	1.00	3	.225	.302	.422
4 ML YEARS		267	718	157	36	3	17	(7	10)	250	85	78	57	10	127	4	5	7	26	4	.87	23	.219	.277	.348

Al Martin

Bats: L **Throws:** L **Pos:** LF-109; PH/PR-14; RF-9; CF-7; DH-2   **Ht:** 6'2" **Wt:** 214 **Born:** 11/24/67 **Age:** 33

Year Team	Lg	G	AB	H	2B	3B	HR	(Hm	Rd)	TB	R	RBI	TBB	IBB	SO	HBP	SH	SF	SB	CS	SB%	GDP	Avg	OBP	SLG
1992 Pittsburgh	NL	12	12	2	0	1	0	(0	0)	4	1	2	0	0	5	0	0	1	0	0	—	0	.167	.154	.333
1993 Pittsburgh	NL	143	480	135	26	8	18	(15	3)	231	85	64	42	5	122	1	2	3	16	9	.64	5	.281	.338	.481
1994 Pittsburgh	NL	82	276	79	12	4	9	(6	3)	126	48	33	34	3	56	2	0	1	15	6	.71	3	.286	.367	.457
1995 Pittsburgh	NL	124	439	124	25	3	13	(8	5)	194	70	41	44	6	92	2	1	0	20	11	.65	5	.282	.351	.442
1996 Pittsburgh	NL	155	630	189	40	1	18	(8	10)	285	101	72	54	2	116	2	1	7	38	12	.76	9	.300	.354	.452
1997 Pittsburgh	NL	113	423	123	24	7	13	(8	5)	200	64	59	45	7	83	3	1	5	23	7	.77	7	.291	.359	.473
1998 Pittsburgh	NL	125	440	105	15	2	12	(5	7)	160	57	47	32	2	91	5	0	2	20	3	.87	13	.239	.296	.364
1999 Pittsburgh	NL	143	541	150	36	8	24	(12	12)	274	97	63	49	5	119	1	0	2	20	3	.87	8	.277	.337	.506
2000 SD-Sea		135	480	137	15	10	15	(10	5)	217	81	36	36	5	85	4	0	3	10	9	.53	3	.285	.338	.452
2000 San Diego	NL	93	346	106	13	6	11	(8	3)	164	62	27	28	5	54	2	0	2	6	8	.43	2	.306	.360	.474
Seattle	AL	42	134	31	2	4	4	(2	2)	53	19	9	8	0	31	2	0	1	4	1	.80	1	.231	.283	.396
9 ML YEARS		1032	3721	1044	193	44	122	(72	50)	1691	604	417	336	35	769	20	5	24	162	60	.73	53	.281	.341	.454

Tom Martin

Pitches: Left **Bats:** Left **Pos:** RP-31   **Ht:** 6'1" **Wt:** 200 **Born:** 5/21/70 **Age:** 31

Year Team	Lg	G	GS	CG	GF	IP	BFP	H	R	ER	HR	SH	SF	HB	TBB	IBB	SO	WP	Bk	W	L	Pct.	ShO	Sv-Op	Hld	ERA
2000 Buffalo *	AAA	9	3	0	1	10	42	12	4	4	1	0	1	0	1	0	4	1	0	0	1	.000	0	0- —	—	3.60
1997 Houston	NL	55	0	0	18	56	236	52	13	13	2	6	1	1	23	2	36	3	0	5	3	.625	0	2-3	7	2.09
1998 Cleveland	AL	14	0	0	1	14.2	85	29	21	21	3	1	1	0	12	0	9	2	0	1	1	.500	0	0-0	3	12.89
1999 Cleveland	AL	6	0	0	0	9.1	44	13	9	9	2	0	1	0	3	1	8	0	0	0	1	.000	0	0-0	0	8.68
2000 Cleveland	AL	31	0	0	7	33.1	143	32	16	15	3	0	1	1	15	2	21	1	0	1	0	1.000	0	0-0	0	4.05
4 ML YEARS		106	0	0	26	113.1	508	126	59	58	10	7	4	2	53	5	74	6	0	7	5	.583	0	2-3	10	4.61

Dave Martinez

Bats: L **Throws:** L **Pos:** RF-110; 1B-13; PH/PR-10; LF-9; CF-1   **Ht:** 5'10" **Wt:** 190 **Born:** 9/26/64 **Age:** 36

Year Team	Lg	G	AB	H	2B	3B	HR	(Hm	Rd)	TB	R	RBI	TBB	IBB	SO	HBP	SH	SF	SB	CS	SB%	GDP	Avg	OBP	SLG
1986 Chicago	NL	53	108	15	1	1	1	(1	0)	21	13	7	6	0	22	1	0	0	4	2	.67	1	.139	.190	.194
1987 Chicago	NL	142	459	134	18	8	8	(5	3)	192	70	36	57	4	96	2	1	1	16	8	.67	4	.292	.372	.418
1988 ChC-Mon	NL	138	447	114	13	6	6	(2	4)	157	51	46	38	8	94	2	2	5	23	9	.72	3	.255	.313	.351
1989 Montreal	NL	126	361	99	16	7	3	(1	2)	138	41	27	27	2	57	0	7	1	23	4	.85	1	.274	.324	.382
1990 Montreal	NL	118	391	109	13	5	11	(5	6)	165	60	39	24	2	48	1	3	2	13	11	.54	8	.279	.321	.422

Year Team	Lg	G	AB	H	2B	3B	HR	(Hm	Rd)	TB	R	RBI	TBB	IBB	SO	HBP	SH	SF	SB	CS	SB%	GDP	Avg	OBP	SLG
1991 Montreal	NL	124	396	117	18	5	7	(3	4)	166	47	42	20	3	54	3	5	3	16	7	.70	3	.295	.332	.419
1992 Cincinnati	NL	135	393	100	20	5	3	(3	0)	139	47	31	42	4	54	0	6	4	12	8	.60	6	.254	.323	.354
1993 San Francisco	NL	91	241	58	12	1	5	(1	4)	87	28	27	27	3	39	0	0	0	6	3	.67	5	.241	.317	.361
1994 San Francisco	NL	97	235	58	9	3	4	(1	3)	85	23	27	21	1	22	2	2	0	3	4	.43	6	.247	.314	.362
1995 Chicago	AL	119	303	93	16	4	5	(2	3)	132	49	37	32	2	41	1	9	4	8	2	.80	6	.307	.371	.436
1996 Chicago	AL	146	440	140	20	8	10	(3	7)	206	85	53	52	1	52	3	2	1	15	7	.68	4	.318	.393	.468
1997 Chicago	AL	145	504	144	16	6	12	(5	7)	208	78	55	55	7	69	3	5	6	12	6	.67	4	.286	.356	.413
1998 Tampa Bay	AL	90	309	79	11	0	3	(2	1)	99	31	20	35	4	52	2	0	1	8	7	.53	5	.256	.334	.320
1999 Tampa Bay	AL	143	514	146	25	5	6	(2	4)	199	79	66	60	3	76	5	10	5	13	6	.68	6	.284	.361	.387
2000 4 ML Teams		132	457	125	19	5	5	(3	2)	169	60	47	50	3	73	2	1	3	8	7	.53	12	.274	.346	.370
1988 Chicago	NL	75	256	65	10	1	4	(2	2)	89	27	34	21	5	46	2	0	4	7	3	.70	2	.254	.311	.348
Montreal	NL	63	191	49	3	5	2	(0	2)	68	24	12	17	3	48	0	2	1	16	6	.73	1	.257	.316	.356
2000 Tampa Bay	AL	29	104	27	4	2	1	(0	0)	38	12	12	10	1	17	0	1	2	1	4	.20	1	.260	.319	.365
Chicago	NL	18	54	10	1	1	0	(0	0)	13	5	1	2	0	8	0	0	1	0	1	1.00	1	.185	.214	.241
Texas	AL	38	119	32	4	1	2	(1	1)	44	14	12	14	2	20	1	0	0	2	1	.67	8	.269	.351	.370
Toronto	AL	47	180	56	10	1	2	(1	1)	74	29	22	24	0	28	1	0	1	4	2	.67	1	.311	.393	.411
15 ML YEARS		1799	5558	1531	227	69	89	(39	50)	2163	762	560	546	47	849	27	53	37	180	91	.66	74	.275	.341	.389

Edgar Martinez

Bats: Right **Throws:** Right **Pos:** DH-146; PH/PR-5; 1B-2   **Ht:** 5'11" **Wt:** 200 **Born:** 1/2/63 **Age:** 38

Year Team	Lg	G	AB	H	2B	3B	HR	(Hm	Rd)	TB	R	RBI	TBB	IBB	SO	HBP	SH	SF	SB	CS	SB%	GDP	Avg	OBP	SLG
1987 Seattle	AL	13	43	16	5	2	0	(0	0)	25	6	5	2	0	5	1	0	0	0	0	—	0	.372	.413	.581
1988 Seattle	AL	14	32	9	4	0	0	(0	0)	13	0	5	4	0	7	0	1	1	0	0	—	0	.281	.351	.406
1989 Seattle	AL	65	171	41	5	0	2	(0	2)	52	20	20	17	1	26	3	2	3	2	1	.67	3	.240	.314	.304
1990 Seattle	AL	144	487	147	27	2	11	(3	8)	211	71	49	74	3	62	5	1	3	1	4	.20	13	.302	.397	.433
1991 Seattle	AL	150	544	167	35	1	14	(8	6)	246	98	52	84	9	72	8	2	4	0	3	.00	19	.307	.405	.452
1992 Seattle	AL	135	528	181	46	3	18	(11	7)	287	100	73	54	2	61	4	1	5	14	4	.78	15	.343	.404	.544
1993 Seattle	AL	42	135	32	7	0	4	(1	3)	51	20	13	28	1	19	0	1	1	0	0	—	1	.237	.366	.378
1994 Seattle	AL	89	326	93	23	1	13	(4	9)	157	47	51	53	3	42	3	2	3	6	2	.75	2	.285	.387	.482
1995 Seattle	AL	145	511	182	52	0	29	(16	13)	321	121	113	116	19	87	8	0	3	4	3	.57	11	.356	.479	.628
1996 Seattle	AL	139	499	163	52	2	26	(14	12)	297	121	103	123	12	84	8	0	4	3	3	.50	15	.327	.464	.595
1997 Seattle	AL	155	542	179	35	1	28	(12	16)	300	104	108	119	11	86	11	0	6	2	4	.33	21	.330	.456	.554
1998 Seattle	AL	154	556	179	46	1	29	(17	12)	314	86	102	106	4	96	3	0	7	1	1	.50	13	.322	.429	.565
1999 Seattle	AL	142	502	169	35	1	24	(12	12)	278	86	86	97	6	99	6	0	3	7	2	.78	12	.337	.447	.554
2000 Seattle	AL	153	556	180	31	0	37	(19	18)	322	100	145	96	8	95	4	0	8	3	0	1.00	13	.324	.423	.579
14 ML YEARS		1540	5432	1738	403	14	235	(117	118)	2874	980	925	973	79	841	65	10	52	43	27	.61	141	.320	.426	.529

Felix Martinez

Bats: Both **Throws:** Right **Pos:** SS-106; PH/PR-1   **Ht:** 6'0" **Wt:** 180 **Born:** 5/18/74 **Age:** 27

Year Team	Lg	G	AB	H	2B	3B	HR	(Hm	Rd)	TB	R	RBI	TBB	IBB	SO	HBP	SH	SF	SB	CS	SB%	GDP	Avg	OBP	SLG
1993 Royals	R	57	165	42	5	1	0	—	—	49	23	12	17	0	26	3	1	0	22	5	.81	2	.255	.335	.297
1994 Wilmington	A+	117	400	107	16	4	2	—	—	137	65	43	30	0	91	3	12	2	19	8	.70	10	.268	.322	.343
1995 Wichita	AA	127	426	112	15	3	3	—	—	142	53	30	31	0	71	6	4	1	44	20	.69	5	.263	.321	.333
1996 Omaha	AAA	118	395	93	13	3	5	—	—	127	54	35	44	0	79	5	10	0	18	10	.64	11	.235	.320	.322
1997 Omaha	AAA	112	410	104	19	4	2	—	—	137	55	36	29	0	86	7	5	1	21	11	.66	11	.254	.313	.334
1998 Omaha	AAA	51	164	41	8	3	2	—	—	61	27	16	15	0	40	1	5	1	6	2	.75	1	.250	.315	.372
1999 Omaha	AAA	8	23	7	5	0	0	—	—	12	2	2	2	0	6	0	1	0	1	0	1.00	0	.304	.360	.522
Wichita	AA	87	327	88	22	2	4	—	—	126	57	37	37	0	43	3	8	3	19	12	.61	8	.269	.346	.385
2000 Durham	AAA	42	149	36	7	2	3	—	—	56	17	17	7	0	28	1	5	0	3	3	.50	4	.242	.288	.376
1997 Kansas City	AL	16	31	7	1	1	0	(0	0)	10	3	3	6	0	9	0	1	0	0	0	—	1	.226	.351	.323
1998 Kansas City	AL	34	85	11	1	1	0	(0	0)	14	7	5	5	0	21	1	4	0	3	1	.75	1	.129	.187	.165
1999 Kansas City	AL	6	7	1	0	0	0	(0	0)	1	1	0	0	0	0	0	0	0	0	0	—	0	.143	.143	.143
2000 Tampa Bay	AL	106	299	64	11	4	2	(0	2)	89	42	17	32	0	68	8	12	2	9	3	.75	4	.214	.305	.298
4 ML YEARS		162	422	83	13	6	2	(0	2)	114	53	25	43	0	97	9	17	2	12	4	.75	7	.197	.284	.270

Pedro Martinez

Pitches: Right **Bats:** Right **Pos:** SP-29   **Ht:** 5'11" **Wt:** 170 **Born:** 10/25/71 **Age:** 29

Year Team	Lg	G	GS	CG	GF	IP	BFP	H	R	ER	HR	SH	SF	HB	TBB	IBB	SO	WP	Bk	W	L	Pct.	ShO	Sv-Op	Hld	ERA
1992 Los Angeles	NL	2	1	0	1	8	31	6	2	2	0	0	0	0	1	0	8	0	0	0	0	—	0	0-0	0	2.25
1993 Los Angeles	NL	65	2	0	20	107	444	76	34	31	5	0	5	4	57	4	119	3	1	10	5	.667	0	2-3	14	2.61
1994 Montreal	NL	24	23	1	1	144.2	584	115	58	55	11	2	3	11	45	3	142	6	0	11	5	.688	1	1-1	0	3.42
1995 Montreal	NL	30	30	2	1	194.2	784	158	79	76	21	7	3	11	66	1	174	5	2	14	10	.583	2	0-0	0	3.51
1996 Montreal	NL	33	33	4	0	216.2	901	189	100	89	19	9	6	3	70	3	222	6	0	13	10	.565	1	0-0	0	3.70
1997 Montreal	NL	31	31	13	0	241.1	947	158	65	51	16	9	1	9	67	5	305	3	1	17	8	.680	4	0-0	0	1.90
1998 Boston	AL	33	33	3	0	233.2	951	188	82	75	26	4	7	8	67	3	251	6	0	19	7	.731	0	0-0	0	2.89
1999 Boston	AL	31	29	5	0	213.1	835	160	56	49	9	3	6	9	37	1	313	6	0	23	4	.852	1	0-0	0	2.07
2000 Boston	AL	29	29	7	0	217	817	128	44	42	17	2	1	14	32	0	284	1	0	18	6	.750	4	0-0	0	1.74
9 ML YEARS		278	211	35	23	1576.1	6294	1178	520	470	124	36	32	69	442	20	1818	39	4	125	56	.691	15	3-4	14	2.68

Ramon Martinez

Pitches: Right **Bats:** Both **Pos:** SP-27   **Ht:** 6'4" **Wt:** 184 **Born:** 3/22/68 **Age:** 33

Year Team	Lg	G	GS	CG	GF	IP	BFP	H	R	ER	HR	SH	SF	HB	TBB	IBB	SO	WP	Bk	W	L	Pct.	ShO	Sv-Op	Hld	ERA
2000 Pawtucket *	AAA	2	2	0	0	11.2	46	8	4	3	1	0	1	0	4	0	10	0	0	1	0	1.000	0	0--	0	2.31
1988 Los Angeles	NL	9	6	0	0	35.2	151	27	17	15	1	0	4	0	22	1	23	1	0	1	3	.250	0	0-0	1	3.79
1989 Los Angeles	NL	15	15	2	0	98.2	410	79	39	35	11	4	0	5	41	1	89	1	0	6	4	.600	2	0-0	0	3.19
1990 Los Angeles	NL	33	33	12	0	234.1	950	191	89	76	22	7	5	4	67	5	223	3	3	20	6	.769	3	0-0	0	2.92

(continued)

Year Team	Lg	G	GS	CG	GF	IP	BFP	H	R	ER	HR	SH	SF	HB	TBB	IBB	SO	WP	Bk	W	L	Pct.	ShO	Sv-Op	Hld	ERA
1991 Los Angeles	NL	33	33	6	0	220.1	916	190	89	80	18	8	4	7	69	4	150	6	0	17	13	.567	4	0-0	0	3.27
1992 Los Angeles	NL	25	25	1	0	150.2	662	141	82	67	11	12	1	5	69	4	101	9	0	8	11	.421	1	0-0	0	4.00
1993 Los Angeles	NL	32	32	4	0	211.2	918	202	88	81	15	12	5	4	104	9	127	2	2	10	12	.455	3	0-0	0	3.44
1994 Los Angeles	NL	24	24	4	0	170	718	160	83	75	18	6	8	6	56	2	119	2	0	12	7	.632	3	0-0	0	3.97
1995 Los Angeles	NL	30	30	4	0	206.1	859	176	95	84	19	7	5	5	81	5	138	3	0	17	7	.708	2	0-0	0	3.66
1996 Los Angeles	NL	28	27	2	1	168.2	732	153	76	64	12	7	6	8	86	5	133	2	1	15	6	.714	2	0-0	0	3.42
1997 Los Angeles	NL	22	22	1	0	133.2	590	122	64	54	14	5	4	6	68	1	120	1	1	10	5	.667	0	0-0	0	3.64
1998 Los Angeles	NL	15	15	1	0	101.2	418	76	41	32	8	2	3	3	41	1	91	2	0	7	3	.700	0	0-0	0	2.83
1999 Boston	AL	4	4	0	0	20.2	84	14	8	7	2	0	1	2	8	0	15	0	0	2	1	.667	0	0-0	0	3.05
2000 Boston	AL	27	27	0	0	127.2	590	143	94	87	16	2	7	9	67	3	89	0	0	10	8	.556	0	0-0	1	6.13
13 ML YEARS		297	293	37	1	1880	7998	1675	865	757	166	76	49	64	779	41	1418	32	7	135	86	.611	20	0-0	1	3.62

Ramon E. Martinez

Bats: R **Throws:** R **Pos:** SS-44; 2B-32; PH/PR-20; 1B-2; 3B-2   **Ht:** 6'1" **Wt:** 187 **Born:** 10/10/72 **Age:** 28

Year Team	Lg	G	AB	H	2B	3B	HR	(Hm	Rd)	TB	R	RBI	TBB	IBB	SO	HBP	SH	SF	SB	CS	SB%	GDP	Avg	OBP	SLG
1998 San Francisco	NL	19	19	6	1	0	0	(0	0)	7	4	0	4	0	2	0	1	0	0	0	—	0	.316	.435	.368
1999 San Francisco	NL	61	144	38	6	0	5	(3	2)	59	21	19	14	0	17	0	6	1	1	2	.33	2	.264	.327	.410
2000 San Francisco	NL	88	189	57	13	2	6	(4	2)	92	30	25	15	1	22	1	4	1	3	2	.60	6	.302	.354	.487
3 ML YEARS		168	352	101	20	2	11	(7	4)	158	55	44	33	1	41	1	11	2	4	4	.50	8	.287	.348	.449

Sandy Martinez

Bats: Left **Throws:** Right **Pos:** C-9; PH/PR-1   **Ht:** 6'2" **Wt:** 215 **Born:** 10/3/72 **Age:** 28

Year Team	Lg	G	AB	H	2B	3B	HR	(Hm	Rd)	TB	R	RBI	TBB	IBB	SO	HBP	SH	SF	SB	CS	SB%	GDP	Avg	OBP	SLG
2000 Calgary *	AAA	86	277	83	20	0	15	—	—	148	45	48	16	1	57	2	0	4	2	1	.67	5	.300	.338	.534
1995 Toronto	AL	62	191	46	12	0	2	(1	1)	64	12	25	7	0	45	1	0	1	0	0	—	1	.241	.270	.335
1996 Toronto	AL	76	229	52	9	3	3	(2	1)	76	17	18	16	0	58	4	1	0	0	0	—	4	.227	.288	.332
1997 Toronto	AL	3	2	0	0	0	0	(0	0)	0	1	0	1	0	1	0	0	0	0	0	—	0	.000	.333	.000
1998 Chicago	NL	45	87	23	9	1	0	(0	0)	34	7	7	13	0	21	1	0	1	0	1.00	3	.264	.363	.391
1999 Chicago	NL	17	30	5	0	0	1	(0	1)	8	1	1	0	0	11	0	0	0	0	0	—	0	.167	.167	.267
2000 Florida	NL	10	18	4	2	0	0	(0	0)	6	1	0	0	0	8	0	0	0	0	0	—	0	.222	.222	.333
6 ML YEARS		213	557	130	32	4	6	(3	3)	188	39	51	37	0	144	6	1	3	1	0	1.00	8	.233	.287	.338

Tino Martinez

Bats: Left **Throws:** Right **Pos:** 1B-154; PH/PR-6   **Ht:** 6'2" **Wt:** 210 **Born:** 12/7/67 **Age:** 33

Year Team	Lg	G	AB	H	2B	3B	HR	(Hm	Rd)	TB	R	RBI	TBB	IBB	SO	HBP	SH	SF	SB	CS	SB%	GDP	Avg	OBP	SLG
1990 Seattle	AL	24	68	15	4	0	0	(0	0)	19	4	5	9	0	9	0	0	1	0	0	—	0	.221	.308	.279
1991 Seattle	AL	36	112	23	2	0	4	(3	1)	37	11	9	11	0	24	0	0	2	0	0	—	2	.205	.272	.330
1992 Seattle	AL	136	460	118	19	2	16	(10	6)	189	53	66	42	9	77	2	1	8	2	1	.67	24	.257	.316	.411
1993 Seattle	AL	109	408	108	25	1	17	(9	8)	186	48	60	45	9	56	5	3	3	1	3	.00	7	.265	.343	.456
1994 Seattle	AL	97	329	86	21	0	20	(8	12)	167	42	61	29	2	52	1	4	3	1	2	.33	9	.261	.320	.508
1995 Seattle	AL	141	519	152	35	3	31	(14	17)	286	92	111	62	15	91	4	2	6	0	0	—	10	.293	.369	.551
1996 New York	AL	155	595	174	28	0	25	(9	16)	277	82	117	68	4	85	2	1	5	2	1	.67	18	.292	.364	.466
1997 New York	AL	158	594	176	31	2	44	(18	26)	343	96	141	75	14	75	3	0	13	3	1	.75	15	.296	.371	.577
1998 New York	AL	142	531	149	33	1	28	(12	16)	268	92	123	61	3	83	6	0	10	2	1	.67	18	.281	.355	.505
1999 New York	AL	159	589	155	27	2	28	(7	21)	270	95	105	69	7	86	3	0	4	3	4	.43	14	.263	.341	.458
2000 New York	AL	155	569	147	37	4	16	(12	4)	240	69	91	52	9	74	8	0	3	4	1	.80	16	.258	.328	.422
11 ML YEARS		1312	4774	1303	262	15	229	(102	127)	2282	684	889	523	72	712	34	11	58	17	14	.55	133	.273	.345	.478

Willie Martinez

Pitches: Right **Bats:** Right **Pos:** RP-1   **Ht:** 6'2" **Wt:** 180 **Born:** 1/4/78 **Age:** 23

Year Team	Lg	G	GS	CG	GF	IP	BFP	H	R	ER	HR	SH	SF	HB	TBB	IBB	SO	WP	Bk	W	L	Pct.	ShO	Sv-Op	Hld	ERA
1995 Burlington	R+	11	11	0	0	40	208	64	50	42	1	2	2	4	25	0	36	6	3	0	7	.000	0	0--	—	9.45
1996 Watertown	A-	14	14	1	0	90	358	79	25	24	5	2	0	0	21	2	92	6	0	6	5	.545	1	0--	—	2.40
1997 Kinston	A+	23	23	1	0	137	568	125	61	47	13	4	3	4	42	2	120	4	0	8	2	.800	0	0--	—	3.09
1998 Akron	AA	26	26	2	0	154	661	169	92	75	15	6	2	6	44	0	117	10	1	9	7	.563	1	0--	—	4.38
1999 Akron	AA	24	24	0	0	147.1	639	163	83	67	20	5	2	3	45	0	91	8	0	9	8	.529	0	0--	—	4.09
Buffalo	AAA	4	4	0	0	22.1	101	28	17	17	3	1	0	2	7	1	12	0	0	2	2	.500	0	0--	—	6.85
2000 Buffalo	AAA	28	22	0	3	135.1	598	132	72	67	16	6	3	5	67	1	95	11	1	8	5	.615	0	1--	—	4.46
2000 Cleveland	AL	1	1	0	0	3	11	1	1	1	0	0	1	0	1	0	1	0	0	0	0	—	0	0-0	0	3.00

Onan Masaoka

Pitches: Left **Bats:** Right **Pos:** RP-29   **Ht:** 6'0" **Wt:** 188 **Born:** 10/27/77 **Age:** 23

Year Team	Lg	G	GS	CG	GF	IP	BFP	H	R	ER	HR	SH	SF	HB	TBB	IBB	SO	WP	Bk	W	L	Pct.	ShO	Sv-Op	Hld	ERA
1995 Yakima	A-	15	7	0	5	49.1	225	28	25	20	2	1	0	4	47	0	75	12	4	2	4	.333	0	3--	—	3.65
1996 Savannah	A	13	13	0	0	65	283	55	35	31	7	1	0	6	35	0	80	3	2	2	5	.286	0	4--	—	4.29
1997 Vero Beach	A+	28	24	2	3	148.2	612	113	72	64	16	6	4	10	55	1	132	10	1	6	8	.429	1	1--	—	3.87
1998 San Antonio	AA	27	20	1	2	110	500	114	79	65	11	2	5	6	63	0	94	3	1	6	6	.500	1	1--	—	5.32
2000 Albuquerque	AAA	18	5	0	4	37.1	172	31	17	16	1	1	1	0	36	1	22	2	0	3	1	.750	0	0--	—	3.86
1999 Los Angeles	NL	54	0	0	12	66.2	300	55	33	32	8	1	2	2	47	3	61	3	0	2	4	.333	0	1-2	5	4.32
2000 Los Angeles	NL	29	0	0	3	27	116	23	12	12	2	0	1	0	15	1	27	2	0	1	1	.500	0	0-0	0	4.00
2 ML YEARS		83	0	0	15	93.2	416	78	45	44	10	1	3	3	62	4	88	5	0	3	5	.375	0	1-2	5	4.23

Ruben Mateo

Bats: Right **Throws:** Right **Pos:** CF-52   **Ht:** 6'0" **Wt:** 185 **Born:** 2/10/78 **Age:** 23

Year Team	Lg	G	AB	H	2B	3B	HR	(Hm	Rd)	TB	R	RBI	TBB	IBB	SO	HBP	SH	SF	SB	CS	SB%	GDP	Avg	OBP	SLG
1996 Chston-SC	A	134	496	129	30	8	8	—	—	199	65	58	26	1	78	12	2	7	30	9	.77	8	.260	.309	.401
1997 Charlotte	A+	99	385	121	23	8	12	—	—	196	63	67	22	0	55	6	1	2	20	5	.80	16	.314	.359	.509
1998 Charlotte	A+	1	4	0	0	0	0	—	—	0	0	1	0	0	1	0	0	0	0	0		0	.000	.000	.000
Tulsa	AA	107	433	134	32	3	18	—	—	226	79	75	30	1	56	15	3	4	18	8	.69	7	.309	.371	.522
1999 Oklahoma	AAA	63	253	85	12	0	18	—	—	151	53	62	14	6	36	8	0	3	6	3	.67	5	.336	.385	.597
1999 Texas	AL	32	122	29	9	1	5	(2	3)	55	16	18	4	0	28	1	0	0	3	0	1.00	2	.238	.268	.451
2000 Texas	AL	52	206	60	11	0	7	(3	4)	92	32	19	10	1	34	5	1	0	6	0	1.00	5	.291	.339	.447
2 ML YEARS		84	328	89	20	1	12	(5	7)	147	48	37	14	1	62	6	1	0	9	0	1.00	7	.271	.313	.448

Mike Matheny

Bats: Right **Throws:** Right **Pos:** C-124; 1B-8; PH/PR-2   **Ht:** 6'3" **Wt:** 205 **Born:** 9/22/70 **Age:** 30

Year Team	Lg	G	AB	H	2B	3B	HR	(Hm	Rd)	TB	R	RBI	TBB	IBB	SO	HBP	SH	SF	SB	CS	SB%	GDP	Avg	OBP	SLG
1994 Milwaukee	AL	28	53	12	3	0	1	(1	0)	18	3	2	3	0	13	2	1	0	0	1	.00	1	.226	.293	.340
1995 Milwaukee	AL	80	166	41	9	1	0	(0	0)	52	13	21	12	0	28	2	1	0	2	1	.67	3	.247	.306	.313
1996 Milwaukee	AL	106	313	64	15	2	8	(5	3)	107	31	46	14	0	80	3	7	4	3	2	.60	9	.204	.243	.342
1997 Milwaukee	AL	123	320	78	16	1	4	(2	2)	108	29	32	17	0	68	7	9	3	0	1	.00	9	.244	.294	.338
1998 Milwaukee	NL	108	320	76	13	0	6	(4	2)	107	24	27	11	0	63	7	3	0	1	0	1.00	6	.238	.278	.334
1999 Toronto	AL	57	163	35	6	0	3	(1	2)	50	16	17	12	0	37	1	2	1	0	0		5	.215	.271	.307
2000 St. Louis	NL	128	417	109	22	1	6	(2	4)	151	43	47	32	8	96	4	7	4	0	0		11	.261	.317	.362
7 ML YEARS		630	1752	415	84	5	28	(15	13)	593	159	192	101	8	385	26	30	12	6	5	.55	42	.237	.287	.338

T.J. Mathews

Pitches: Right **Bats:** Right **Pos:** RP-50   **Ht:** 6'1" **Wt:** 214 **Born:** 1/19/70 **Age:** 31

Year Team	Lg	G	GS	CG	GF	IP	BFP	H	R	ER	HR	SH	SF	HB	TBB	IBB	SO	WP	Bk	W	L	Pct.	ShO	Sv-Op	Hld	ERA
2000 Sacramento *	AAA	3	1	0	1	3.2	15	2	1	0	0	0	0	1	1	0	5	2	0	0	0		0	0--	—	0.00
1995 St. Louis	NL	23	0	0	12	29.2	120	21	7	5	1	4	0	0	11	1	28	2	0	1	1	.500	0	2-2	7	1.52
1996 St. Louis	NL	67	0	0	23	83.2	345	62	32	28	8	5	0	2	32	4	80	1	0	2	6	.250	0	6-11	9	3.01
1997 StL-Oak		64	0	0	26	74.2	329	75	32	25	9	8	1	2	30	4	70	1	0	10	6	.625	0	3-9	12	3.01
1998 Oakland	AL	66	0	0	15	72.2	319	71	44	37	6	2	9	4	29	3	53	1	0	7	4	.636	0	1-4	19	4.58
1999 Oakland	AL	50	0	0	15	59	242	46	28	25	9	5	1	2	20	4	42	2	0	9	5	.643	0	3-5	17	3.81
2000 Oakland	AL	50	0	0	19	59.2	273	73	40	40	10	1	4	2	25	5	42	2	0	2	3	.400	0	0-1	9	6.03
1997 St. Louis	NL	40	0	0	12	46	197	41	14	11	4	6	0	1	18	3	46	1	0	4	4	.500	0	0-3	8	2.15
Oakland	AL	24	0	0	14	28.2	132	34	18	14	5	2	1	1	12	1	24	0	0	6	2	.750	0	3-6	4	4.40
6 ML YEARS		320	0	0	110	379.1	1628	348	183	160	43	25	15	12	147	21	315	9	0	31	25	.554	0	15-32	73	3.80

Luis Matos

Bats: R **Throws:** R **Pos:** CF-44; RF-25; PH/PR-5; DH-3; LF-1   **Ht:** 6'0" **Wt:** 179 **Born:** 10/30/78 **Age:** 22

Year Team	Lg	G	AB	H	2B	3B	HR	(Hm	Rd)	TB	R	RBI	TBB	IBB	SO	HBP	SH	SF	SB	CS	SB%	GDP	Avg	OBP	SLG
1996 Orioles	R	43	130	38	2	0	0	—	—	40	21	13	15	0	18	2	4	0	12	7	.63	3	.292	.374	.308
1997 Delmarva	A	36	119	25	1	2	0	—	—	30	10	13	9	0	21	2	2	1	8	5	.62	2	.210	.275	.252
Bluefield	R+	61	240	66	7	3	2	—	—	85	37	35	20	0	36	4	1	1	26	4	.87	5	.275	.340	.354
1998 Delmarva	A	133	503	137	26	6	7	—	—	196	73	62	38	0	90	7	6	7	42	14	.75	9	.272	.328	.390
Bowie	AA	5	19	5	0	0	1	—	—	8	2	3	1	0	1	0	0	0	1	1	.50	0	.263	.300	.421
1999 Frederick	A+	68	273	81	15	1	7	—	—	119	40	41	20	1	35	2	2	5	27	6	.82	6	.297	.343	.436
Bowie	AA	66	283	67	11	1	9	—	—	107	41	36	15	0	39	1	5	6	14	4	.78	6	.237	.272	.378
2000 Rochester	AAA	11	35	6	1	0	0	—	—	7	2	0	3	0	8	1	1	0	2	0	1.00	0	.171	.256	.200
Bowie	AA	50	181	49	7	5	2	—	—	72	26	33	17	0	23	5	1	3	14	8	.64	3	.271	.345	.398
2000 Baltimore	AL	72	182	41	6	3	1	(1	0)	56	21	17	12	0	30	3	2	2	13	4	.76	7	.225	.281	.308

Mike Matthews

Pitches: Left **Bats:** Left **Pos:** RP-14   **Ht:** 6'2" **Wt:** 175 **Born:** 10/24/73 **Age:** 27

Year Team	Lg	G	GS	CG	GF	IP	BFP	H	R	ER	HR	SH	SF	HB	TBB	IBB	SO	WP	Bk	W	L	Pct.	ShO	Sv-Op	Hld	ERA
1992 Burlington	R+	10	10	0	0	62.1	245	33	13	7	1	2	1	3	27	0	55	3	1	7	0	1.000	0	0--	—	1.01
Watertown	A-	2	2	0	0	11	47	10	4	4	0	1	0	0	8	0	5	1	0	1	0	1.000	0	0--	—	3.27
1994 Columbus	A	23	23	0	0	119.2	502	120	53	41	8	3	3	7	44	1	99	7	3	6	8	.429	0	0--	—	3.08
1995 Canton-Akrn	AA	15	15	1	0	74.1	345	82	62	49	6	2	8	2	43	1	37	8	1	5	8	.385	0	0--	—	5.93
1996 Canton-Akrn	AA	27	27	3	0	162.1	713	178	96	84	13	6	7	5	74	3	112	6	1	9	11	.450	0	0--	—	4.66
1997 Buffalo	AAA	5	5	0	0	21	106	32	19	18	7	0	2	0	10	0	17	1	0	0	2	.000	0	0--	—	7.71
Akron	AA	19	19	3	0	113	492	116	62	48	13	3	0	7	57	0	69	5	4	6	8	.429	1	0--	—	3.82
1998 Buffalo	AAA	24	23	0	1	130.1	577	137	79	67	19	4	1	5	68	1	86	5	2	9	6	.600	0	0--	—	4.63
1999 Buffalo	AAA	25	0	0	8	21.1	99	23	18	18	3	1	2	2	18	0	16	0	1	1	2	.333	0	0--	—	7.59
Akron	AA	6	6	0	0	25.2	127	36	30	25	7	0	3	2	15	0	10	0	2	0	5	.000	0	0--	—	8.77
Trenton	AA	3	3	0	0	11.2	52	11	7	6	1	1	1	0	9	0	10	0	0	0	2	.000	0	0--	—	4.63
Arkansas	AA	2	2	1	0	12	39	3	0	0	0	0	0	0	1	0	10	0	0	2	0	1.000	1	0--	—	0.00
2000 Memphis	AAA	9	9	0	0	52	216	33	19	18	4	2	0	1	32	1	50	3	0	3	1	.750	0	0--	—	3.12
2000 St. Louis	NL	14	0	0	4	9.1	54	15	12	12	2	0	0	0	10	2	8	0	0	0	0		—	0	0-0	2	11.57

Gary Matthews Jr.

Bats: B **Throws:** R **Pos:** LF-46; PH/PR-30; CF-21; RF-1   **Ht:** 6'3" **Wt:** 200 **Born:** 8/25/74 **Age:** 26

							BATTING												BASERUNNING				PERCENTAGES		
Year Team	Lg	G	AB	H	2B	3B	HR	(Hm Rd)	TB	R	RBI	TBB	IBB	SO	HBP	SH	SF	SB	CS	SB%	GDP	Avg	OBP	SLG
1994 Spokane	A-	52	191	40	6	1	0	— —	48	23	18	19	1	58	2	0	1	3	5	.38	4	.209	.286	.251
1995 Clinton	A	128	421	100	18	4	2	— —	132	57	40	68	1	109	6	3	3	28	8	.78	8	.238	.349	.314
1996 Rancho Cuc	A+	123	435	118	21	11	7	— —	182	65	54	60	1	102	6	4	2	7	8	.47	11	.271	.366	.418
1997 Rancho Cuc	A+	69	268	81	15	4	8	— —	128	66	40	49	2	57	3	0	0	10	4	.71	4	.302	.416	.478
Mobile	AA	28	90	22	4	1	2	— —	34	14	12	15	1	29	1	0	2	3	1	.75	1	.244	.352	.378
1998 Mobile	AA	72	254	78	15	4	7	— —	122	62	51	55	2	50	1	0	3	11	1	.92	6	.307	.428	.480
1999 Las Vegas	AAA	121	422	108	22	3	9	— —	163	57	52	58	0	104	7	0	4	17	6	.74	13	.256	.352	.386
2000 Iowa	AAA	60	211	51	11	3	5	— —	83	27	22	18	3	41	0	0	1	6	1	.86	4	.242	.300	.393
1999 San Diego	NL	23	36	8	0	0	0	(0 0)	8	4	7	9	0	9	0	0	0	2	0	1.00	1	.222	.378	.222
2000 Chicago	NL	80	158	30	1	2	4	(2 2)	47	24	14	15	1	28	1	1	0	3	0	1.00	2	.190	.264	.297
2 ML YEARS		103	194	38	1	2	4	(2 2)	55	28	21	24	1	37	1	1	0	5	0	1.00	3	.196	.288	.284

Dave Maurer

Pitches: Left **Bats:** Right **Pos:** RP-14   **Ht:** 6'2" **Wt:** 205 **Born:** 2/23/75 **Age:** 26

		HOW MUCH HE PITCHED						WHAT HE GAVE UP												THE RESULTS						
Year Team	Lg	G	GS	CG	GF	IP	BFP	H	R	ER	HR	SH	SF	HB	TBB	IBB	SO	WP	Bk	W	L	Pct.	ShO	Sv-Op	Hld	ERA
1997 Clinton	A	25	0	0	10	34.1	142	24	15	11	1	2	1	0	15	0	43	3	1	0	4	.000	0	3- -	—	2.88
1998 Rancho Cuc	A+	48	0	0	14	83.1	348	56	27	25	1	5	1	1	46	1	93	8	2	5	2	.714	0	5- -	—	2.70
1999 Mobile	AA	54	0	0	33	72	301	59	30	29	7	1	4	3	26	5	59	6	0	4	4	.500	0	3- -	—	3.63
2000 Mobile	AA	24	0	0	8	26.2	98	15	8	8	2	3	0	1	3	1	28	1	0	1	2	.333	0	0- -	—	2.70
Las Vegas	AAA	35	0	0	10	44.1	193	47	19	16	5	0	0	0	15	1	44	1	0	4	1	.800	0	0- -	—	3.25
2000 San Diego	NL	14	0	0	1	14.2	64	15	8	6	2	0	0	2	5	1	13	1	0	1	0	1.000	0	0-1	2	3.68

Jason Maxwell

Bats: R **Throws:** R **Pos:** 2B-30; 3B-19; PH/PR-18; DH-7; SS-5; CF-1; RF-1   **Ht:** 6'1" **Wt:** 180 **Born:** 3/26/72 **Age:** 29

							BATTING												BASERUNNING				PERCENTAGES		
Year Team	Lg	G	AB	H	2B	3B	HR	(Hm Rd)	TB	R	RBI	TBB	IBB	SO	HBP	SH	SF	SB	CS	SB%	GDP	Avg	OBP	SLG
1993 Huntington	R+	61	179	52	7	2	7	— —	84	50	38	35	0	39	4	2	1	6	5	.55	0	.291	.416	.469
1994 Daytona	A+	116	368	85	18	2	10	— —	137	71	32	55	0	96	8	6	2	7	7	.50	6	.231	.342	.372
1995 Daytona	A+	117	388	102	13	3	10	— —	151	66	58	63	1	68	6	1	8	12	7	.63	6	.263	.368	.389
1996 Orlando	AA	126	433	115	20	1	9	— —	164	64	45	56	3	77	6	4	3	19	4	.83	5	.266	.355	.379
1997 Orlando	AA	122	409	114	22	6	14	— —	190	87	58	82	1	72	4	5	9	12	9	.57	6	.279	.397	.465
1998 Iowa	AAA	124	483	144	40	3	15	— —	235	86	60	52	1	93	8	1	4	8	1	.89	6	.298	.373	.487
1999 Toledo	AAA	119	419	99	17	2	15	— —	165	60	62	53	0	87	2	4	4	6	3	.67	4	.236	.322	.394
1998 Chicago	NL	7	3	1	0	0	1	(1 0)	4	2	2	0	0	2	0	1	0	0	0	-	0	.333	.333	1.333
2000 Minnesota	AL	64	111	27	6	0	1	(1 0)	36	14	11	9	0	32	1	0	3	2	1	.67	2	.243	.298	.324
2 ML YEARS		71	114	28	6	0	2	(2 0)	40	16	13	9	0	34	1	1	3	2	1	.67	2	.246	.299	.351

Brent Mayne

Bats: Left **Throws:** Right **Pos:** C-106; PH/PR-22; P-1   **Ht:** 6'1" **Wt:** 192 **Born:** 4/19/68 **Age:** 33

							BATTING												BASERUNNING				PERCENTAGES		
Year Team	Lg	G	AB	H	2B	3B	HR	(Hm Rd)	TB	R	RBI	TBB	IBB	SO	HBP	SH	SF	SB	CS	SB%	GDP	Avg	OBP	SLG
1990 Kansas City	AL	5	13	3	0	0	0	(0 0)	3	2	1	3	0	3	0	0	0	0	1	.00	0	.231	.375	.231
1991 Kansas City	AL	85	231	58	8	0	3	(2 1)	75	22	31	23	4	42	0	2	3	2	4	.33	6	.251	.315	.325
1992 Kansas City	AL	82	213	48	10	0	0	(0 0)	58	16	18	11	0	26	0	2	3	0	4	.00	5	.225	.260	.272
1993 Kansas City	AL	71	205	52	9	1	2	(0 2)	69	22	22	18	7	31	1	3	0	3	2	.60	6	.254	.317	.337
1994 Kansas City	AL	46	144	37	5	1	2	(1 1)	50	19	20	14	1	27	0	0	0	1	0	1.00	3	.257	.323	.347
1995 Kansas City	AL	110	307	77	18	1	1	(1 0)	100	23	27	25	1	41	3	11	1	0	1	.00	16	.251	.313	.326
1996 New York	NL	70	99	26	6	0	1	(0 1)	35	9	6	12	1	22	0	2	0	0	1	.00	4	.263	.342	.354
1997 Oakland	AL	85	256	74	12	0	6	(4 2)	104	29	22	18	1	33	4	2	2	1	0	1.00	6	.289	.343	.406
1998 San Francisco	NL	94	275	75	15	0	3	(0 3)	99	26	32	37	3	47	1	2	2	2	1	.67	8	.273	.359	.360
1999 San Francisco	NL	117	322	97	32	0	2	(1 1)	135	39	39	43	5	65	5	1	3	2	2	.50	16	.301	.389	.419
2000 Colorado	NL	117	335	101	21	0	6	(3 3)	140	36	64	47	13	48	1	4	8	1	3	.25	12	.301	.381	.418
11 ML YEARS		882	2400	648	136	3	26	(12 14)	868	243	282	251	36	385	15	29	22	12	19	.39	82	.270	.340	.362

Joe Mays

Pitches: Right **Bats:** Both **Pos:** SP-28; RP-3   **Ht:** 6'1" **Wt:** 185 **Born:** 12/10/75 **Age:** 25

		HOW MUCH HE PITCHED						WHAT HE GAVE UP												THE RESULTS						
Year Team	Lg	G	GS	CG	GF	IP	BFP	H	R	ER	HR	SH	SF	HB	TBB	IBB	SO	WP	Bk	W	L	Pct.	ShO	Sv-Op	Hld	ERA
1995 Mariners	R	10	10	0	0	44.1	189	41	24	16	0	2	1	0	18	0	44	7	1	2	3	.400	0	0- -	—	3.25
1996 Everett	A-	13	10	0	0	64.1	271	55	33	22	3	3	2	2	22	0	56	9	1	4	4	.500	0	0- -	—	3.08
1997 Wisconsin	A	13	13	1	0	81.2	322	62	20	19	3	1	2	6	23	1	79	1	0	9	3	.750	0	0- -	—	2.09
Lancaster	A+	15	15	1	0	96.1	420	108	55	52	9	2	6	5	34	0	82	2	0	7	4	.636	0	0- -	—	4.86
1998 Fort Myers	A+	16	15	0	0	94.2	409	101	45	32	7	5	2	5	23	0	83	4	0	7	2	.778	0	0- -	—	3.04
New Britain	AA	11	10	0	0	57.2	258	63	40	32	4	2	3	1	21	0	45	2	1	5	3	.625	0	0- -	—	4.99
2000 Salt Lake	AAA	3	3	0	0	15.2	64	16	4	3	0	1	0	1	2	0	18	2	0	2	0	1.000	0	0- -	—	1.72
1999 Minnesota	AL	49	20	2	8	171	746	179	92	83	24	7	6	2	67	2	115	6	0	6	11	.353	1	0-0	2	4.37
2000 Minnesota	AL	31	28	2	1	160.1	723	193	105	99	20	3	5	2	67	1	102	11	0	7	15	.318	1	0-0	—	5.56
2 ML YEARS		80	48	4	9	331.1	1469	372	197	182	44	10	11	4	134	3	217	17	0	13	26	.333	2	0-0	2	4.94

Dave McCarty

Bats: R **Throws:** L **Pos:** 1B-63; PH/PR-29; DH-7; LF-7; RF-4   **Ht:** 6'5" **Wt:** 215 **Born:** 11/23/69 **Age:** 31

							BATTING												BASERUNNING				PERCENTAGES		
Year Team	Lg	G	AB	H	2B	3B	HR	(Hm Rd)	TB	R	RBI	TBB	IBB	SO	HBP	SH	SF	SB	CS	SB%	GDP	Avg	OBP	SLG
1993 Minnesota	AL	98	350	75	15	2	2	(2 0)	100	36	21	19	0	80	1	1	0	2	6	.25	13	.214	.257	.286

Year Team	Lg	G	AB	H	2B	3B	HR	(Hm	Rd)	TB	R	RBI	TBB	IBB	SO	HBP	SH	SF	SB	CS	SB%	GDP	Avg	OBP	SLG
1994 Minnesota	AL	44	131	34	8	2	1	(1	0)	49	21	12	7	1	32	5	0	0	2	1	.67	3	.260	.322	.374
1995 Min-SF		37	75	17	4	1	0	(0	0)	23	11	6	6	0	22	1	0	1	1	1	.50	1	.227	.289	.307
1996 San Francisco	NL	91	175	38	3	0	6	(5	1)	59	16	24	18	0	43	2	0	2	2	1	.67	5	.217	.294	.337
1998 Seattle	AL	8	18	5	0	0	1	(1	0)	8	1	2	5	0	4	0	0	0	1	0	1.00	0	.278	.435	.444
2000 Kansas City	AL	103	270	75	14	2	12	(6	6)	129	34	53	22	1	68	0	0	3	0	0	—	6	.278	.329	.478
1995 Minnesota	AL	25	55	12	3	1	0	(0	0)	17	10	4	4	0	18	1	0	1	0	1	.00	1	.218	.279	.309
San Francisco	NL	12	20	5	1	0	0	(0	0)	6	1	2	2	0	4	0	0	0	1	0	1.00	1	.250	.318	.300
6 ML YEARS		381	1019	244	44	7	22	(15	7)	368	119	118	77	2	249	9	1	6	8	9	.47	28	.239	.297	.361

Quinton McCracken

Bats: Both **Throws:** Right **Pos:** LF-9; PH/PR-7; CF-3   **Ht:** 5'7" **Wt:** 173 **Born:** 8/16/70 **Age:** 30

Year Team	Lg	G	AB	H	2B	3B	HR	(Hm	Rd)	TB	R	RBI	TBB	IBB	SO	HBP	SH	SF	SB	CS	SB%	GDP	Avg	OBP	SLG
2000 Durham *	AAA	85	334	87	18	2	2			115	54	28	34	0	57	2	3	1	13	7	.65	10	.260	.332	.344
1995 Colorado	NL	3	1	0	0	0	0	(0	0)	0	0	0	0	0	1	0	0	0	0	0	—	0	.000	.000	.000
1996 Colorado	NL	124	283	82	13	6	3	(2	1)	116	50	40	32	4	62	1	12	1	17	6	.74	5	.290	.363	.410
1997 Colorado	NL	147	325	95	11	1	3	(1	2)	117	69	36	42	0	62	1	6	1	28	11	.72	6	.292	.374	.360
1998 Tampa Bay	AL	155	614	190	38	7	6	(5	2)	252	77	59	41	1	107	3	9	8	19	10	.66	12	.292	.335	.410
1999 Tampa Bay	AL	40	148	37	6	1	1	(1	0)	48	20	18	14	0	23	1	1	1	6	5	.55	7	.250	.317	.324
2000 Tampa Bay	AL	15	31	4	0	0	0	(0	0)	4	1	2	4	0	4	0	0	0	0	1	.00	3	.129	.270	.129
6 ML YEARS		484	1402	397	68	15	14	(9	5)	537	221	155	135	5	259	6	28	11	70	33	.68	33	.283	.346	.383

Allen McDill

Pitches: Left **Bats:** Left **Pos:** RP-13   **Ht:** 6'0" **Wt:** 170 **Born:** 8/23/71 **Age:** 29

Year Team	Lg	G	GS	CG	GF	IP	BFP	H	R	ER	HR	SH	SF	HB	TBB	IBB	SO	WP	Bk	W	L	Pct.	ShO	Sv-Op	Hld	ERA
1992 Kingsport	R+	1	0	0	0	0.1	3	0	0	0	0	0	0	0	2	0	1	0	0	0	0	—	0	0--	—	0.00
Mets	R	10	9	0	0	53.1	216	36	23	16	3	0	0	4	15	0	60	3	0	3	4	.429	0	0--	—	2.70
1993 Kingsport	R+	9	9	0	0	53.1	224	52	19	13	1	1	2	0	14	0	42	2	2	5	2	.714	0	0--	—	2.19
Pittsfield	A-	5	5	0	0	28.1	132	31	22	17	0	2	2	1	15	0	24	3	0	2	3	.400	0	0--	—	5.40
1994 Capital Cty	A	19	19	1	0	111.2	461	101	52	44	11	5	2	4	38	2	102	9	0	9	6	.600	0	0--	—	3.55
1995 St. Lucie	A+	7	7	1	0	49.1	190	36	11	9	2	1	0	1	13	0	28	3	0	4	2	.667	1	0--	—	1.64
Binghamton	AA	12	12	1	0	73	324	69	42	37	5	1	4	3	38	2	44	3	1	3	5	.375	0	0--	—	4.56
Wichita	AA	12	1	0	5	21.1	85	16	7	5	2	0	0	1	5	0	20	1	0	1	0	1.000	0	1--	—	2.11
1996 Omaha	AAA	2	0	0	0	0.1	5	3	2	2	0	0	0	0	1	0	1	2	0	0	0	1.000	0	0--	—	54.00
Wichita	AA	54	0	0	30	65	288	79	43	40	10	2	4	4	21	3	62	7	0	1	5	.167	0	11--	—	5.54
1997 Omaha	AAA	23	6	0	5	64	295	80	42	42	10	2	1	5	26	2	51	2	0	5	2	.714	0	2--	—	5.88
Wichita	AA	16	0	0	7	17.1	72	18	7	6	0	1	0	0	7	1	14	1	0	1	0	1.000	0	3--	—	3.12
1998 Omaha	AAA	61	0	0	22	60.1	246	54	22	16	4	3	0	0	24	3	62	1	0	6	4	.600	0	4--	—	2.39
1999 Oklahoma	AAA	42	0	0	35	48.1	207	45	22	20	6	1	1	2	17	0	46	4	0	1	3	.250	0	0--	—	3.72
2000 Toledo	AAA	16	0	0	5	18.2	82	21	4	2	0	0	0	0	7	0	15	1	0	1	0	1.000	0	0--	—	0.96
Memphis	AAA	23	0	0	5	24.2	114	24	13	12	1	1	0	0	17	0	28	1	0	2	0	.000	0	0--	—	4.38
1997 Kansas City	AL	3	0	0	1	4	24	3	6	6	1	1	0	1	8	0	2	0	0	0	0	—	0	0-0	—	13.50
1998 Kansas City	AL	7	0	0	1	6	29	9	7	7	3	0	0	0	2	0	3	0	0	0	0	—	0	0-0	1	10.50
2000 Detroit	AL	13	0	0	1	10	43	13	9	8	2	0	0	1	1	0	7	1	0	0	0	—	0	0-0	1	7.20
3 ML YEARS		23	0	0	3	20	96	25	22	21	6	1	0	2	11	0	12	1	0	0	0	—	0	0-0	2	9.45

Jason McDonald

Bats: B **Throws:** R **Pos:** RF-26; LF-11; PH/PR-8; CF-3; DH-1   **Ht:** 5'7" **Wt:** 182 **Born:** 3/20/72 **Age:** 29

Year Team	Lg	G	AB	H	2B	3B	HR	(Hm	Rd)	TB	R	RBI	TBB	IBB	SO	HBP	SH	SF	SB	CS	SB%	GDP	Avg	OBP	SLG
2000 Rangers *	R	3	10	2	0	0	0	—	—	2	0	0	1	0	2	0	1	0	0	0	—	0	.200	.273	.200
Charlotte *	A+	5	15	5	2	0	0	—	—	7	4	1	4	0	5	0	0	0	1	0	1.00	0	.333	.474	.467
Oklahoma *	AAA	32	105	25	6	1	2	—	—	39	13	12	14	0	29	2	2	1	2	4	.33	1	.238	.336	.371
1997 Oakland	AL	78	236	62	11	4	4	(1	3)	93	47	14	36	0	49	1	2	1	13	8	.62	0	.263	.361	.394
1998 Oakland	AL	70	175	44	9	0	1	(1	0)	56	25	16	27	0	33	3	6	1	10	4	.71	2	.251	.359	.320
1999 Oakland	AL	100	187	39	2	1	3	(0	3)	52	26	8	25	0	48	3	4	1	6	3	.67	2	.209	.310	.278
2000 Texas	AL	38	94	22	5	0	3	(3	0)	36	15	13	17	0	25	1	2	0	4	4	.50	2	.234	.357	.383
4 ML YEARS		286	692	167	27	5	11	(5	6)	237	113	51	105	0	155	8	14	3	33	19	.63	6	.241	.347	.342

John McDonald

Bats: Right **Throws:** Right **Pos:** SS-7; 2B-2; PH/PR-2   **Ht:** 5'11" **Wt:** 175 **Born:** 9/24/74 **Age:** 26

Year Team	Lg	G	AB	H	2B	3B	HR	(Hm	Rd)	TB	R	RBI	TBB	IBB	SO	HBP	SH	SF	SB	CS	SB%	GDP	Avg	OBP	SLG
1995 Sonoma Cty	IND	39	129	27	7	0	1	—	—	37	18	11	6	0	37	0	5	0	3	1	.75	4	.209	.244	.287
1996 Watertown	A-	75	278	75	11	0	2	—	—	92	48	26	32	0	49	5	11	1	11	1	.92	3	.270	.354	.331
1997 Kinston	A+	130	541	140	27	3	5	—	—	188	77	53	51	0	75	2	7	2	6	5	.55	12	.259	.324	.348
1998 Akron	AA	132	514	118	18	2	2	—	—	146	68	43	43	0	61	6	11	6	17	6	.74	7	.230	.293	.284
1999 Akron	AA	55	226	67	12	0	1	—	—	82	31	26	19	0	26	2	2	4	7	3	.70	5	.296	.351	.363
Buffalo	AAA	66	237	75	12	1	0	—	—	89	30	25	11	0	23	2	5	2	6	3	.67	5	.316	.349	.376
2000 Mahoning Vy	A-	5	17	2	1	0	0	—	—	3	0	1	0	0	3	0	0	0	0	1	.00	0	.118	.211	.176
Buffalo	AAA	75	286	77	17	2	1	—	—	101	37	36	21	0	29	1	7	6	4	3	.57	7	.269	.315	.353
Kinston	A+	1	3	1	0	0	0	—	—	1	0	0	0	0	0	0	0	0	0	0	—	0	.333	.333	.333
1999 Cleveland	AL	18	21	7	0	0	0	(0	0)	7	2	0	0	0	3	0	0	0	0	1	.00	2	.333	.333	.333
2000 Cleveland	AL	9	9	4	0	0	0	(0	0)	4	0	0	0	0	1	0	0	0	0	0	—	0	.444	.444	.444
2 ML YEARS		27	30	11	0	0	0	(0	0)	11	2	0	0	0	4	0	0	0	0	1	.00	2	.367	.367	.367

Keith McDonald

Bats: Right **Throws:** Right **Pos:** C-4; PH/PR-4 **Ht:** 6'2" **Wt:** 215 **Born:** 2/8/73 **Age:** 28

Year Team	Lg	G	AB	H	2B	3B	HR	(Hm	Rd)	TB	R	RBI	TBB	IBB	SO	HBP	SH	SF	SB	CS	SB%	GDP	Avg	OBP	SLG
1994 Johnson Cty	R+	59	199	49	12	0	6	—	—	79	32	31	27	3	36	5	2	3	3	1	.75	9	.246	.346	.397
1995 Peoria	A	65	179	48	6	0	1	—	—	57	22	20	22	0	38	6	4	0	0	1	.00	2	.268	.367	.318
1996 St. Pete	A+	114	410	111	25	0	2	—	—	142	30	52	34	1	65	5	1	5	1	3	.25	18	.271	.330	.346
1997 Arkansas	AA	79	233	56	16	0	5	—	—	87	32	30	31	0	56	3	1	0	0	1	.00	4	.240	.337	.373
1998 Memphis	AAA	58	170	54	8	0	7	—	—	83	21	22	10	2	30	2	2	0	1	1	.50	2	.318	.363	.488
1999 Arkansas	AA	49	163	50	10	0	2	—	—	66	21	14	15	0	35	3	0	2	1	0	1.00	1	.307	.372	.405
Memphis	AAA	39	113	34	7	0	5	—	—	56	20	27	20	0	25	0	1	2	1	0	1.00	1	.301	.400	.496
2000 Memphis	AAA	83	266	70	15	0	5	—	—	100	34	30	28	1	59	3	5	6	0	2	.00	8	.263	.333	.376
2000 St. Louis	NL	6	7	3	0	0	3	(2	1)	12	3	5	2	0	1	0	0	0	0	0	—	0	.429	.556	1.714

Chuck McElroy

Pitches: Left **Bats:** Left **Pos:** RP-41; SP-2 **Ht:** 6'0" **Wt:** 205 **Born:** 10/1/67 **Age:** 33

Year Team	Lg	G	GS	CG	GF	IP	BFP	H	R	ER	HR	SH	SF	HB	TBB	IBB	SO	WP	Bk	W	L	Pct.	ShO	Sv-Op	Hld	ERA
1989 Philadelphia	NL	11	0	0	4	10.1	46	12	2	2	1	0	0	0	4	1	8	0	0	0	0	—	0	0-0	0	1.74
1990 Philadelphia	NL	16	0	0	8	14	76	24	13	12	0	0	1	0	10	2	16	0	0	0	1	.000	0	0-0	0	7.71
1991 Chicago	NL	71	0	0	12	101.1	419	73	33	22	7	9	6	0	57	7	92	1	0	2		.750	0	3-6	10	1.95
1992 Chicago	NL	72	0	0	30	83.2	369	73	40	33	5	5	5	0	51	10	83	3	0	4	7	.364	0	6-11	3	3.55
1993 Chicago	NL	49	0	0	11	47.1	214	51	30	24	4	5	1	1	25	5	31	3	0	2	2	.500	0	0-0	4	4.56
1994 Cincinnati	NL	52	0	0	13	57.2	230	52	15	15	3	2	0	0	15	2	38	4	0	1	2	.333	0	5-11	10	2.34
1995 Cincinnati	NL	44	0	0	11	40.1	178	46	29	27	5	1	3	1	15	3	27	1	0	3	4	.429	0	0-3	3	6.02
1996 Cin-Cal		52	0	0	12	49	210	45	22	21	4	1	1	2	23	3	45	1	0	7	1	.875	0	0-2	7	3.86
1997 Ana-CWS	AL	61	0	0	16	75	320	73	36	32	5	3	3	2	22	1	62	1	0	1	3	.250	0	1-6	15	3.84
1998 Colorado	NL	78	0	0	27	68.1	281	68	23	22	3	0	3	0	24	0	61	0	0	6	4	.600	0	2-6	19	2.90
1999 Col-NYM	NL	56	0	0	19	54	251	60	34	33	9	1	3	1	36	4	44	5	0	3	1	.750	0	0-3	5	5.50
2000 Baltimore	AL	43	2	0	10	63.1	282	60	36	33	6	0	3	2	34	2	50	6	0	3	0	1.000	0	0-1	2	4.69
1996 Cincinnati	NL	12	0	0	1	12.1	59	13	10	9	2	0	0	0	10	1	13	0	0	2	0	1.000	0	0-0	1	6.57
California	AL	40	0	0	11	36.2	151	32	12	12	2	1	1	2	13	2	32	1	0	5	1	.833	0	0-2	6	2.95
1997 Anaheim	AL	13	0	0	3	15.2	66	17	7	6	2	0	0	0	3	0	18	0	0	0	0	—	0	0-2	4	3.45
Chicago	AL	48	0	0	13	59.1	254	56	29	26	3	3	3	2	19	1	44	1	0	1	3	.250	0	1-4	11	3.94
1999 Colorado	NL	41	0	0	12	40.2	192	48	29	28	9	0	2	0	28	3	37	4	0	3	1	.750	0	0-3	5	6.20
New York	NL	15	0	0	7	13.1	59	12	5	5	0	1	1	1	8	1	7	1	0	0	0	—	0	0-0	0	3.38
12 ML YEARS		605	2	0	173	664.1	2876	637	313	276	52	27	29	9	316	40	557	25	0	36	27	.571	0	17-49	78	3.74

Joe McEwing

Bats: R **Throws:** R **Pos:** LF-43; PH/PR-21; 3B-19; 2B-16; CF-11; RF-6; SS-4 **Ht:** 5'11" **Wt:** 170 **Born:** 10/19/72 **Age:** 28

Year Team	Lg	G	AB	H	2B	3B	HR	(Hm	Rd)	TB	R	RBI	TBB	IBB	SO	HBP	SH	SF	SB	CS	SB%	GDP	Avg	OBP	SLG
2000 Norfolk *	AAA	43	171	44	10	2	5	—	—	73	28	18	16	1	34	0	2	1	7	3	.70	3	.257	.319	.427
1998 St. Louis	NL	10	20	4	1	0	0	(0	0)	5	5	1	1	0	3	1	1	0	0	1	.00	1	.200	.273	.250
1999 St. Louis	NL	152	451	141	28	4	9	(5	4)	204	65	44	41	8	87	6	9	5	7	4	.64	3	.275	.333	.398
2000 New York	NL	87	153	34	14	1	2	(1	1)	56	20	19	5	0	29	1	8	2	3	1	.75	2	.222	.248	.366
3 ML YEARS		249	686	179	43	5	11	(6	5)	265	90	64	47	8	119	8	18	7	10	6	.63	5	.261	.313	.386

Kevin McGlinchy

Pitches: Right **Bats:** Right **Pos:** RP-10 **Ht:** 6'5" **Wt:** 220 **Born:** 6/28/77 **Age:** 24

Year Team	Lg	G	GS	CG	GF	IP	BFP	H	R	ER	HR	SH	SF	HB	TBB	IBB	SO	WP	Bk	W	L	Pct.	ShO	Sv-Op	Hld	ERA
1996 Danville	R+	13	13	0	0	72	283	52	21	9	2	1	2	2	11	0	77	4	4	3	2	.600	0	0--	—	1.13
Eugene	A-	2	2	0	0	6.2	31	7	5	4	2	1	0	0	1	0	5	0	0	0	0	—	0	0--	—	5.40
1997 Durham	A+	26	26	0	0	139.2	595	145	78	76	14	2	4	9	39	2	113	4	2	3	7	.300	0	0--	—	4.90
1998 Danville	A+	22	22	1	0	142.1	566	122	55	46	7	6	3	6	29	0	129	1	0	9	8	.529	0	0--	—	2.91
Greenville	AA	6	6	0	0	33	144	35	19	19	5	1	1	1	15	1	20	0	0	1	1	.500	0	0--	—	5.18
2000 Greenville	AA	4	0	0	0	4	15	2	1	0	0	0	1	0	0	0	7	1	0	0	0	—	0	0--	—	0.00
Braves	R	4	2	0	0	5	29	12	8	5	0	0	1	0	1	0	6	0	0	0	0	—	0	0--	—	9.00
Richmond	AAA	9	0	3	1	10	42	9	4	4	0	2	2	2	3	2	7	0	0	1	0	1.000	0	1--	—	3.60
1999 Atlanta	NL	64	0	0	21	70.1	298	66	25	22	6	4	4	1	30	7	67	1	0	7	3	.700	0	0-2	7	2.82
2000 Atlanta	NL	10	0	0	6	8.1	42	11	4	2	1	1	0	0	6	1	9	1	0	0	0	—	0	0-0	0	2.16
2 ML YEARS		74	0	0	27	78.2	340	77	29	24	7	5	4	1	36	8	76	2	0	7	3	.700	0	0-2	7	2.75

Fred McGriff

Bats: Left **Throws:** Left **Pos:** 1B-144; DH-10; PH/PR-4 **Ht:** 6'3" **Wt:** 215 **Born:** 10/31/63 **Age:** 37

Year Team	Lg	G	AB	H	2B	3B	HR	(Hm	Rd)	TB	R	RBI	TBB	IBB	SO	HBP	SH	SF	SB	CS	SB%	GDP	Avg	OBP	SLG
1986 Toronto	AL	3	5	1	0	0	0	(0	0)	1	1	0	0	0	2	0	0	0	0	0	—	0	.200	.200	.200
1987 Toronto	AL	107	295	73	16	0	20	(7	13)	149	58	43	60	4	104	1	0	0	3	2	.60	3	.247	.376	.505
1988 Toronto	AL	154	536	151	35	4	34	(18	16)	296	100	82	79	3	149	4	0	4	6	1	.86	15	.282	.376	.552
1989 Toronto	AL	161	551	148	27	3	36	(18	18)	289	98	92	119	12	132	4	1	5	7	4	.64	14	.269	.399	.525
1990 Toronto	AL	153	557	167	21	1	35	(14	21)	295	91	88	94	12	108	2	1	4	5	3	.63	7	.300	.400	.530
1991 San Diego	NL	153	528	147	19	1	31	(18	13)	261	84	106	105	26	135	2	0	7	4	1	.80	14	.278	.396	.494
1992 San Diego	NL	152	531	152	30	4	35	(21	14)	295	79	104	96	23	108	1	0	4	8	6	.57	14	.286	.394	.556
1993 SD-Atl	NL	151	557	162	29	2	37	(15	22)	306	111	101	76	6	106	2	0	5	5	3	.63	14	.291	.375	.549
1994 Atlanta	NL	113	424	135	25	1	34	(13	21)	264	81	94	50	8	76	1	0	3	7	3	.70	8	.318	.389	.623
1995 Atlanta	NL	144	528	148	27	1	27	(15	12)	258	85	93	65	6	99	5	0	6	3	6	.33	19	.280	.361	.489
1996 Atlanta	NL	159	617	182	37	1	28	(17	11)	305	81	107	68	12	116	2	0	4	7	3	.70	20	.295	.365	.494
1997 Atlanta	NL	152	564	156	25	1	22	(8	14)	249	77	97	68	4	112	4	0	5	5	0	1.00	22	.277	.356	.441
1998 Tampa Bay	AL	151	564	160	33	0	19	(14	5)	250	73	81	79	9	118	2	0	4	7	2	.78	14	.284	.371	.443

Year Team	Lg	G	AB	H	2B	3B	HR	(Hm	Rd)	TB	R	RBI	TBB	IBB	SO	HBP	SH	SF	SB	CS	SB%	GDP	Avg	OBP	SLG
								BATTING											BASERUNNING				PERCENTAGES		
1999 Tampa Bay	AL	144	529	164	30	1	32	(18	14)	292	75	104	86	11	107	1	0	4	1	0	1.00	12	.310	.405	.552
2000 Tampa Bay	AL	158	566	157	18	0	27	(10	17)	256	82	106	91	10	120	0	0	7	2	0	1.00	16	.277	.373	.452
1993 San Diego	NL	83	302	83	11	1	18	(7	11)	150	52	46	42	4	55	1	0	4	4	3	.57	9	.275	.361	.497
Atlanta	NL	68	255	79	18	1	19	(8	11)	156	59	55	34	2	51	1	0	1	1	0		9	.310	.392	.612
15 ML YEARS		2055	7352	2103	372	20	417	(206	211)	3766	1176	1298	1136	146	1592	31	2	62	70	34	.67	192	.286	.381	.512

Ryan McGuire

Bats: Left **Throws:** Left **Pos:** RF-1

Ht: 6'0" **Wt:** 215 **Born:** 11/23/71 **Age:** 29

Year Team	Lg	G	AB	H	2B	3B	HR	(Hm	Rd)	TB	R	RBI	TBB	IBB	SO	HBP	SH	SF	SB	CS	SB%	GDP	Avg	OBP	SLG
								BATTING											BASERUNNING				PERCENTAGES		
2000 Norfolk *	AAA	122	392	117	23	1	10	—	—	172	63	62	87	5	84	1	1	6	6	3	.67	3	.298	.422	.439
1997 Montreal	NL	84	199	51	15	2	3	(2	1)	79	22	17	19	1	34	0	3	1	1	4	.20	3	.256	.320	.397
1998 Montreal	NL	130	210	39	9	0	1	(1	0)	51	17	10	32	0	55	0	1	5	0	0	—	9	.186	.292	.243
1999 Montreal	NL	88	140	31	7	2	2	(1	1)	48	17	18	27	0	33	0	3	0	1	1	.50	9	.221	.347	.343
2000 New York	NL	1	2	0	0	0	0	(0	0)	0	0	0	1	0	0	0	0	0	0	0	—	1	.000	.333	.000
4 ML YEARS		303	551	121	31	4	6	(4	2)	178	56	45	79	1	122	0	7	2	2	5	.29	22	.220	.316	.323

Mark McGwire

Bats: Right **Throws:** Right **Pos:** 1B-70; PH/PR-13

Ht: 6'5" **Wt:** 250 **Born:** 10/1/63 **Age:** 37

Year Team	Lg	G	AB	H	2B	3B	HR	(Hm	Rd)	TB	R	RBI	TBB	IBB	SO	HBP	SH	SF	SB	CS	SB%	GDP	Avg	OBP	SLG
								BATTING											BASERUNNING				PERCENTAGES		
1986 Oakland	AL	18	53	10	1	0	3	(1	2)	20	10	9	4	0	18	1	0	0	0	1	.00	0	.189	.259	.377
1987 Oakland	AL	151	557	161	28	4	49	(21	28)	344	97	118	71	8	131	5	0	8	1	1	.50	6	.289	.370	**.618**
1988 Oakland	AL	155	550	143	22	1	32	(12	20)	263	87	99	76	4	117	4	1	4	0	0	—	15	.260	.352	.478
1989 Oakland	AL	143	490	113	17	0	33	(12	21)	229	74	95	83	5	94	3	0	11	1	1	.50	23	.231	.339	.467
1990 Oakland	AL	156	523	123	16	0	39	(14	25)	256	87	108	110	9	116	7	1	9	2	1	.67	13	.235	.370	.489
1991 Oakland	AL	154	483	97	22	0	22	(15	7)	185	62	75	93	3	116	3	1	5	2	1	.67	13	.201	.330	.383
1992 Oakland	AL	139	467	125	22	0	42	(24	18)	273	87	104	90	12	105	5	0	9	0	1	.00	10	.268	.385	**.585**
1993 Oakland	AL	27	84	28	6	0	9	(5	4)	61	16	24	21	5	19	1	0	1	0	1	.00	0	.333	.467	.726
1994 Oakland	AL	47	135	34	3	0	9	(3	6)	64	26	25	37	3	40	0	0	0	0	0	—	3	.252	.413	.474
1995 Oakland	AL	104	317	87	13	0	39	(15	24)	217	75	90	88	5	77	11	0	6	1	1	.50	9	.274	.441	.685
1996 Oakland	AL	130	423	132	21	0	52	(24	28)	309	104	113	116	16	112	8	0	1	0	0	—	14	.312	**.467**	**.730**
1997 Oak-StL		156	540	148	27	0	58	(30	28)	349	86	123	101	16	159	9	0	7	3	0	1.00	9	.274	.393	.646
1998 St. Louis	NL	155	509	152	21	0	70	(38	32)	383	130	147	162	28	155	6	0	4	1	0	1.00	8	.299	**.470**	**.752**
1999 St. Louis	NL	153	521	145	21	1	65	(37	28)	363	118	147	133	21	141	2	0	5	0	0	—	12	.278	.424	.697
2000 St. Louis	NL	89	236	72	8	0	32	(18	14)	176	60	73	76	12	78	7	0	2	1	0	1.00	5	.305	.483	.746
1997 Oakland	AL	105	366	104	24	0	34	(17	17)	230	48	81	58	8	98	4	0	5	1	0	1.00	9	.284	.383	.628
St. Louis	NL	51	174	44	3	0	24	(13	11)	119	38	42	43	8	61	5	0	2	2	0	1.00	0	.253	.411	.684
15 ML YEARS		1777	5888	1570	248	6	554	(272	282)	3492	1119	1350	1261	147	1478	72	3	72	12	8	.60	140	.267	.398	.593

Tony McKnight

Pitches: Right **Bats:** Left **Pos:** SP-6

Ht: 6'5" **Wt:** 205 **Born:** 6/29/77 **Age:** 24

Year Team	Lg	G	GS	CG	GF	IP	BFP	H	R	ER	HR	SH	SF	HB	TBB	IBB	SO	WP	Bk	W	L	Pct.	ShO	Sv-Op	Hld	ERA
				HOW MUCH HE PITCHED							WHAT HE GAVE UP											THE RESULTS				
1995 Astros	R	3	3	0	0	11.2	48	14	5	5	0	0	2	0	2	0	1	0	1	1	1	.500	0	0--	—	3.86
1996 Astros	R	8	5	0	0	21.2	108	28	21	15	1	0	2	3	7	0	15	3	0	2	1	.667	0	0--	—	6.23
1997 Quad City	A	20	20	0	0	115.1	504	116	71	60	7	6	3	5	55	5	92	6	3	4	9	.308	0	0--	—	4.68
1998 Kissimmee	A+	28	28	0	0	154.1	701	191	101	80	12	4	3	9	50	2	104	12	2	11	13	.458	0	0--	—	4.67
1999 Jackson	AA	24	24	0	0	160.1	653	134	60	49	15	1	0	4	44	0	118	6	1	9	9	.500	0	0--	—	2.75
2000 Round Rock	AA	6	6	0	0	32	141	39	19	17	4	0	1	1	10	1	24	1	0	4	2	.000	0	0--	—	4.78
New Orleans	AAA	19	19	0	0	118.1	511	129	66	60	10	7	3	5	36	3	63	2	2	4	8	.333	0	0--	—	4.56
2000 Houston	NL	6	6	1	0	35	156	35	19	15	4	1	1	2	9	0	23	2	0	4	1	.800	0	0-0	0	3.86

Mark McLemore

Bats: B **Throws:** R **Pos:** 2B-129; LF-14; PH/PR-4; CF-1

Ht: 5'11" **Wt:** 207 **Born:** 10/4/64 **Age:** 36

Year Team	Lg	G	AB	H	2B	3B	HR	(Hm	Rd)	TB	R	RBI	TBB	IBB	SO	HBP	SH	SF	SB	CS	SB%	GDP	Avg	OBP	SLG
								BATTING											BASERUNNING				PERCENTAGES		
1986 California	AL	5	4	0	0	0	0	(0	0)	0	0	0	1	0	2	0	1	0	1	0	1.00	0	.000	.200	.000
1987 California	AL	138	433	102	13	3	3	(3	0)	130	61	41	48	0	72	0	15	3	25	8	.76	7	.236	.310	.300
1988 California	AL	77	233	56	11	2	2	(1	1)	77	38	16	25	0	28	0	5	2	13	7	.65	6	.240	.312	.330
1989 California	AL	32	103	25	3	1	0	(0	0)	30	12	14	7	0	19	1	3	1	6	1	.86	2	.243	.295	.291
1990 Cal-Cle	AL	28	60	9	2	0	0	(0	0)	11	6	2	4	0	15	0	1	0	1	0	1.00	1	.150	.203	.183
1991 Houston	NL	21	61	9	1	0	0	(0	0)	10	6	2	6	0	13	0	0	1	1	0	1.00	1	.148	.221	.164
1992 Baltimore	AL	101	228	55	7	2	0	(0	0)	67	40	27	21	1	26	0	6	1	11	5	.69	6	.246	.308	.294
1993 Baltimore	AL	148	581	165	27	5	4	(2	2)	214	81	72	64	4	92	1	11	6	21	15	.58	21	.284	.353	.368
1994 Baltimore	AL	104	343	88	11	1	3	(2	1)	110	44	29	51	3	50	1	4	1	20	5	.80	7	.257	.354	.321
1995 Texas	AL	129	467	122	20	5	5	(3	2)	167	73	41	66	5	71	3	10	3	21	11	.66	10	.261	.346	.358
1996 Texas	AL	147	517	150	23	4	5	(3	2)	196	84	46	87	5	69	0	2	5	27	10	.73	16	.290	.389	.379
1997 Texas	AL	89	349	91	17	2	1	(0	1)	115	47	25	40	1	54	2	6	2	7	5	.58	5	.261	.338	.330
1998 Texas	AL	126	461	114	15	1	1	(4	1)	146	79	53	89	1	64	2	12	3	12	4	.75	15	.247	.369	.317
1999 Texas	AL	144	566	155	20	7	6	(2	4)	207	105	45	83	2	79	0	9	6	16	8	.67	8	.274	.363	.366
2000 Seattle	AL	138	481	118	23	3	1	(2	1)	152	72	46	81	2	78	1	11	4	30	**14**	.68	12	.245	.353	.316
1990 California	AL	20	48	7	2	0	0	(0	0)	9	4	2	4	0	9	0	1	0	1	0	1.00	1	.146	.212	.188
Cleveland	AL	8	12	2	0	0	0	(0	0)	2	2	0	0	0	6	0	0	0	0	0	—	0	.167	.167	.167
15 ML YEARS		1427	4887	1260	193	34	37	(22	15)	1632	748	459	666	25	732	11	96	38	210	95	.69	117	.258	.346	.334

Greg McMichael

Pitches: Right **Bats:** Right **Pos:** RP-15   **Ht:** 6'3" **Wt:** 222 **Born:** 12/1/66 **Age:** 34

Year Team	Lg	G	GS	CG	GF	IP	BFP	H	R	ER	HR	SH	SF	HB	TBB	IBB	SO	WP	Bk	W	L	Pct.	ShO	Sv-Op	Hld	ERA
1993 Atlanta	NL	74	0	0	40	91.2	365	68	22	21	3	4	2	0	29	4	89	6	1	2	3	.400	0	19-21	12	2.06
1994 Atlanta	NL	51	0	0	41	58.2	259	66	29	25	1	3	1	0	19	6	47	3	1	4	6	.400	0	21-31	1	3.84
1995 Atlanta	NL	67	0	0	16	80.2	337	64	27	25	8	5	0	0	32	9	74	3	0	7	2	.778	0	2-4	20	2.79
1996 Atlanta	NL	73	0	0	14	86.2	366	84	37	31	4	3	3	1	27	7	78	4	1	5	3	.625	0	2-8	18	3.22
1997 New York	NL	73	0	0	23	87.2	355	73	34	29	8	9	4	2	27	6	81	5	0	7	10	.412	0	7-18	19	2.98
1998 NYM-LA	NL	64	0	0	19	68	317	81	39	31	9	6	3	4	35	10	55	6	1	5	4	.556	0	2-7	10	4.10
1999 NYM-Oak	NL	36	0	0	8	33.2	153	35	19	19	6	2	2	2	20	5	21	4	0	1	1	.500	0	0-1	7	5.08
2000 Atlanta	NL	15	0	0	3	16.1	61	12	8	8	3	0	1	0	4	1	14	1	0	0	0	—	0	0-0	1	4.41
1998 New York	NL	52	0	0	18	53.2	251	64	31	24	8	3	2	3	29	7	44	5	1	5	3	.625	0	1-4	8	4.02
Los Angeles	NL	12	0	0	1	14.1	66	17	8	7	1	3	1	1	6	3	11	1	0	0	1	.000	0	1-3	2	4.40
1999 New York	NL	19	0	0	4	18.2	84	20	10	10	3	1	1	0	8	3	18	4	0	1	1	.500	0	0-1	4	4.82
Oakland	AL	17	0	0	4	15	69	15	9	9	3	1	1	2	12	2	3	0	0	0	0	—	0	0-0	3	5.40
8 ML YEARS		453	0	0	164	523.1	2213	483	215	189	42	32	16	9	193	48	459	32	4	31	29	.517	0	53-90	89	3.25

Billy McMillon

Bats: L **Throws:** L **Pos:** DH-24; RF-13; PH/PR-10; LF-3   **Ht:** 5'11" **Wt:** 179 **Born:** 11/17/71 **Age:** 29

Year Team	Lg	G	AB	H	2B	3B	HR	(Hm	Rd)	TB	R	RBI	TBB	IBB	SO	HBP	SH	SF	SB	CS	SB%	GDP	Avg	OBP	SLG
2000 Toledo *	AAA	105	380	131	30	1	13	(—	—)	202	61	50	71	7	65	2	0	4	3	1	.75	18	.345	.446	.532
1996 Florida	NL	28	51	11	0	0	0	(0	0)	11	4	4	5	1	14	0	0	0	0	0	—	1	.216	.286	.216
1997 Fla-Phi	NL	37	90	23	5	1	2	(0	0)	36	10	14	6	0	24	0	0	3	2	1	.67	1	.256	.293	.400
2000 Detroit	NL	46	123	37	7	1	4	(3	1)	58	20	24	19	0	19	1	2	4	1	0	1.00	2	.301	.388	.472
1997 Florida	NL	13	18	2	1	0	0	(0	0)	3	0	1	0	0	7	0	0	0	0	0	—	0	.111	.111	.167
Philadelphia	NL	24	72	21	4	1	2	(2	0)	33	10	13	6	0	17	0	0	3	2	1	.67	1	.292	.333	.458
3 ML YEARS		111	264	71	12	2	6	(5	1)	105	34	42	30	1	57	1	2	7	3	1	.75	4	.269	.338	.398

Rusty Meacham

Pitches: Right **Bats:** Right **Pos:** RP-5   **Ht:** 6'3" **Wt:** 180 **Born:** 1/27/68 **Age:** 33

Year Team	Lg	G	GS	CG	GF	IP	BFP	H	R	ER	HR	SH	SF	HB	TBB	IBB	SO	WP	Bk	W	L	Pct.	ShO	Sv-Op	Hld	ERA
2000 New Orleans *	AAA	33	4	0	8	57.1	227	43	16	14	5	4	1	3	14	1	56	2	0	4	3	.571	0	0--	1	2.20
1991 Detroit	AL	10	4	0	1	27.2	126	35	17	16	4	1	3	0	11	0	14	0	1	2	1	.667	0	0-0	1	5.20
1992 Kansas City	AL	64	0	0	20	101.2	412	88	39	31	5	3	9	1	21	5	64	4	0	10	4	.714	0	2-6	15	2.74
1993 Kansas City	AL	15	0	0	11	21	104	31	15	13	2	0	1	3	5	1	13	0	0	2	2	.500	0	0-0	1	5.57
1994 Kansas City	AL	36	0	0	15	50.2	213	51	23	21	7	1	4	2	12	1	36	4	0	3	3	.500	0	4-5	7	3.73
1995 Kansas City	AL	49	0	0	26	59.2	262	72	36	33	6	1	4	1	19	5	30	0	4	4	3	.571	0	2-3	7	4.98
1996 Seattle	AL	15	5	0	3	42.1	192	57	28	27	9	0	1	4	13	1	25	1	0	1	1	.500	0	1-1	0	5.74
2000 Houston	NL	5	0	0	2	4.2	23	8	6	6	3	0	0	0	2	0	3	0	0	0	0	—	0	0-0	0	11.57
7 ML YEARS		194	9	0	78	307.2	1332	342	164	147	36	6	22	11	83	13	185	9	4	22	14	.611	0	9-15	31	4.30

Brian Meadows

Pitches: Right **Bats:** Right **Pos:** SP-32; RP-1   **Ht:** 6'4" **Wt:** 220 **Born:** 11/21/75 **Age:** 25

Year Team	Lg	G	GS	CG	GF	IP	BFP	H	R	ER	HR	SH	SF	HB	TBB	IBB	SO	WP	Bk	W	L	Pct.	ShO	Sv-Op	Hld	ERA
1998 Florida	NL	31	31	1	0	174.1	772	222	106	101	20	14	4	3	46	3	88	5	1	11	13	.458	0	0-0	0	5.21
1999 Florida	NL	31	31	0	0	178.1	795	214	117	111	31	16	8	5	57	5	72	4	1	11	15	.423	0	0-0	0	5.60
2000 SD-KC		33	32	0	0	196.1	869	234	119	112	32	7	5	8	64	6	79	3	0	13	10	.565	0	0-0	0	5.13
2000 San Diego	NL	22	22	0	0	124.2	565	150	80	74	24	7	2	8	50	6	53	3	0	7	8	.467	0	0-0	0	5.34
Kansas City	AL	11	10	2	0	71.2	304	84	39	38	8	0	3	0	14	0	26	0	0	6	2	.750	0	0-0	0	4.77
3 ML YEARS		95	94	3	0	549	2436	670	342	324	83	37	17	16	167	14	239	12	2	35	38	.479	0	0-0	0	5.31

Pat Meares

Bats: Right **Throws:** Right **Pos:** SS-126; PH/PR-6   **Ht:** 6'0" **Wt:** 187 **Born:** 9/6/68 **Age:** 32

Year Team	Lg	G	AB	H	2B	3B	HR	(Hm	Rd)	TB	R	RBI	TBB	IBB	SO	HBP	SH	SF	SB	CS	SB%	GDP	Avg	OBP	SLG
1993 Minnesota	AL	111	346	87	14	3	0	(0	0)	107	33	33	7	0	52	1	4	3	4	5	.44	11	.251	.266	.309
1994 Minnesota	AL	80	229	61	12	1	2	(2	0)	81	29	24	14	0	50	2	6	3	5	1	.83	5	.266	.310	.354
1995 Minnesota	AL	116	390	105	19	4	12	(3	9)	168	57	49	15	0	68	11	4	5	10	4	.71	17	.269	.311	.431
1996 Minnesota	AL	152	517	138	26	7	8	(3	5)	202	66	67	17	1	90	9	4	7	9	4	.69	19	.267	.298	.391
1997 Minnesota	AL	134	439	121	23	3	10	(5	5)	180	63	60	18	0	86	16	3	7	7	7	.50	9	.276	.323	.410
1998 Minnesota	AL	149	543	141	26	3	9	(2	7)	200	56	70	24	1	86	6	3	5	7	4	.64	12	.260	.296	.368
1999 Pittsburgh	NL	21	91	28	4	0	0	(0	0)	32	15	7	9	0	20	2	2	0	0	0	—	1	.308	.382	.352
2000 Pittsburgh	NL	132	462	111	22	2	13	(7	6)	176	55	47	36	6	91	8	5	3	1	0	1.00	13	.240	.305	.381
8 ML YEARS		895	3017	792	146	23	54	(20	34)	1146	374	357	140	8	543	55	31	33	43	25	.63	85	.263	.304	.380

Gil Meche

Pitches: Right **Bats:** Right **Pos:** SP-15   **Ht:** 6'3" **Wt:** 200 **Born:** 9/8/78 **Age:** 22

Year Team	Lg	G	GS	CG	GF	IP	BFP	H	R	ER	HR	SH	SF	HB	TBB	IBB	SO	WP	Bk	W	L	Pct.	ShO	Sv-Op	Hld	ERA
1996 Mariners	R	2	2	0	0	3	13	4	2	2	0	0	0	0	1	0	4	0	0	0	1	.000	0	0--	—	6.00
1997 Everett	A-	12	12	1	0	74.2	316	75	40	33	7	3	2	3	24	0	62	7	0	3	4	.429	0	0--	—	3.98
Wisconsin	A	2	2	0	0	12	51	12	5	4	1	0	0	1	4	0	14	2	1	0	2	.000	0	0--	—	3.00
1998 Wisconsin	A	26	26	0	0	149	643	136	77	57	9	2	2	5	63	0	168	12	2	8	7	.533	0	0--	—	3.44
1999 New Haven	A	10	10	0	0	59	250	51	24	20	3	2	1	0	26	0	56	4	0	3	4	.429	0	0--	—	3.05
Tacoma	AAA	6	6	0	0	31	135	31	12	11	0	0	0	0	13	0	24	2	0	2	2	.500	0	0--	—	3.19

Year Team	Lg	HOW MUCH HE PITCHED						WHAT HE GAVE UP												THE RESULTS						
		G	GS	CG	GF	IP	BFP	H	R	ER	HR	SH	SF	HB	TBB	IBB	SO	WP	Bk	W	L	Pct.	ShO	Sv-Op	Hld	ERA
2000 Tacoma	AAA	3	3	0	0	14	61	10	7	6	1	0	1	0	10	0	15	0	0	1	1	.500	0	0--	0	3.86
Wisconsin	A	1	1	0	0	5	17	1	0	0	0	0	0	0	2	0	6	0	0	0	0	.---	0	0--	0	0.00
Everett	A-	1	1	0	0	1	5	1	0	0	0	0	0	0	0	0	0	0	0	0	1	.000	0	0--	0	9.00
1999 Seattle	AL	16	15	0	0	85.2	375	73	48	45	9	5	3	2	57	1	47	1	0	8	4	.667	0	0-0	0	4.73
2000 Seattle	AL	15	15	1	0	85.2	363	75	37	36	7	5	4	1	40	0	60	2	0	4	4	.500	1	0-0	0	3.78
2 ML YEARS		31	30	1	0	171.1	738	148	85	81	16	10	7	3	97	1	107	3	0	12	8	.600	1	0-0	0	4.25

Jim Mecir

Pitches: Right **Bats:** Both **Pos:** RP-63   **Ht:** 6'1" **Wt:** 210 **Born:** 5/16/70 **Age:** 31

Year Team	Lg	HOW MUCH HE PITCHED						WHAT HE GAVE UP												THE RESULTS						
		G	GS	CG	GF	IP	BFP	H	R	ER	HR	SH	SF	HB	TBB	IBB	SO	WP	Bk	W	L	Pct.	ShO	Sv-Op	Hld	ERA
1995 Seattle	AL	2	0	0	1	4.2	21	5	1	0	0	0	0	0	2	0	3	0	0	0	0	.---	0	0-0	0	0.00
1996 New York	AL	26	0	0	10	40.1	185	42	24	23	6	5	4	0	23	4	38	6	0	1	1	.500	0	0-0	0	5.13
1997 New York	AL	25	0	0	11	33.2	142	36	23	22	5	0	1	2	10	1	25	1	0	0	4	.000	0	0-1	0	5.88
1998 Tampa Bay	AL	68	0	0	23	84	343	68	30	29	6	3	2	3	33	5	77	2	0	7	2	.778	0	0-3	14	3.11
1999 Tampa Bay	AL	17	0	0	3	20.2	91	15	7	6	0	0	2	1	14	0	15	0	0	1	1	.500	0	0-2	6	2.61
2000 TB-Oak	AL	63	0	0	17	85	352	70	31	28	4	1	2	2	36	2	70	2	0	10	3	.769	0	5-13	21	2.96
2000 Tampa Bay	AL	38	0	0	10	49.2	199	35	17	17	2	1	1	1	22	0	33	0	0	7	2	.778	0	1-4	11	3.08
Oakland	AL	25	0	0	7	35.1	153	35	14	11	2	0	1	1	14	2	37	2	0	3	1	.750	0	4-9	10	2.80
6 ML YEARS		201	0	0	65	268.1	1134	236	116	108	21	9	11	8	118	12	228	11	0	18	11	.621	0	5-19	42	3.62

Adam Melhuse

Bats: B **Throws:** R **Pos:** PH/PR-22; 1B-3; C-1; RF-1   **Ht:** 6'2" **Wt:** 185 **Born:** 3/27/72 **Age:** 29

Year Team	Lg	BATTING																	BASERUNNING				PERCENTAGES		
		G	AB	H	2B	3B	HR	(Hm	Rd)	TB	R	RBI	TBB	IBB	SO	HBP	SH	SF	SB	CS	SB%	GDP	Avg	OBP	SLG
1993 St.Cathrnes	A-	73	266	68	14	2	5	—	—	101	40	32	45	4	61	0	2	3	4	1	1.00	4	.256	.360	.380
1994 Hagerstown	A	118	422	109	16	3	11	—	—	164	61	58	53	3	77	1	1	6	6	8	.43	13	.258	.338	.389
1995 Dunedin	A+	123	428	92	20	0	4	—	—	124	43	41	61	1	87	1	1	4	6	1	.86	7	.215	.312	.289
1996 Dunedin	A+	97	315	78	23	2	13	—	—	144	50	51	69	2	68	3	0	4	3	1	.75	5	.248	.384	.457
Knoxville	AA	32	94	20	3	0	1	—	—	26	13	6	14	1	29	0	1	1	0	1	1.00	3	.213	.312	.277
1997 Knoxville	AA	31	87	20	3	0	3	—	—	32	14	10	19	1	19	0	1	1	0	0	—	1	.230	.364	.368
Syracuse	AAA	38	118	28	5	1	2	—	—	41	7	9	12	0	18	1	0	1	1	1	.50	2	.237	.311	.347
1998 Syracuse	AAA	12	38	11	3	0	1	—	—	17	4	7	7	0	6	0	1	1	0	0	—	0	.289	.391	.447
Knoxville	AA	76	240	72	22	0	15	—	—	139	56	43	70	1	39	0	0	6	0	1	.50	6	.300	.458	.579
1999 Syracuse	AAA	21	71	20	5	0	2	—	—	31	15	16	10	0	20	0	0	0	1	1	.50	1	.282	.370	.437
Knoxville	AA	107	374	110	25	0	19	—	—	192	79	69	108	7	76	4	0	3	5	6	.45	10	.294	.454	.513
2000 San Antonio	AA	16	58	23	7	0	2	—	—	36	17	9	11	1	9	2	1	1	3	0	1.00	2	.397	.500	.621
Albuquerque	AAA	36	108	37	9	0	1	—	—	49	21	19	22	0	21	0	2	0	4	2	.67	2	.343	.454	.454
Colo Sprngs	AAA	42	140	39	5	1	3	—	—	55	23	18	21	0	35	0	0	0	2	3	.40	4	.279	.373	.393
2000 LA-Col	NL	24	24	4	0	1	0	(0	0)	6	3	4	3	0	6	0	0	0	0	0	—	0	.167	.259	.250
2000 Los Angeles	NL	1	1	0	0	0	0	(0	0)	0	0	0	0	0	0	0	0	0	0	0	—	0	.000	.000	.000
Colorado	NL	23	23	4	0	1	0	(0	0)	6	3	4	3	0	6	0	0	0	0	0	—	0	.174	.269	.261

Juan Melo

Bats: Both **Throws:** Right **Pos:** 2B-6; PH/PR-6   **Ht:** 6'1" **Wt:** 180 **Born:** 11/5/76 **Age:** 24

Year Team	Lg	BATTING																	BASERUNNING				PERCENTAGES		
		G	AB	H	2B	3B	HR	(Hm	Rd)	TB	R	RBI	TBB	IBB	SO	HBP	SH	SF	SB	CS	SB%	GDP	Avg	OBP	SLG
1994 Spokane	A-	3	11	4	1	0	0	—	—	8	4	2	1	0	3	0	0	0	0	0	—	1	.364	.417	.727
Las Vegas	AAA	1	0	0	0	0	0	—	—	0	0	0	0	0	0	0	0	0	0	0	—	0	.---	.---	.---
Padres	R	37	145	41	3	3	0	—	—	50	20	15	10	0	36	6	0	1	3	2	.60	5	.283	.352	.345
1995 Clinton	A	134	479	135	32	1	5	—	—	184	65	46	33	0	88	5	5	2	12	10	.55	11	.282	.333	.384
1996 Rancho Cuc	A+	128	503	153	27	6	8	—	—	216	75	75	22	0	102	10	0	1	6	8	.43	10	.304	.345	.429
1997 Las Vegas	AAA	12	48	13	4	0	1	—	—	20	6	6	1	0	10	1	0	1	0	0	—	0	.271	.294	.417
Mobile	AA	113	456	131	22	2	7	—	—	178	52	67	29	4	90	0	0	2	7	9	.44	16	.287	.329	.390
1998 Las Vegas	AAA	130	467	127	26	1	6	—	—	173	61	47	24	2	91	4	2	3	9	8	.53	15	.272	.311	.370
1999 Las Vegas	AAA	45	169	34	3	2	2	—	—	47	17	13	7	0	34	2	0	0	1	1	.50	5	.201	.242	.278
Syracuse	AAA	41	141	33	9	1	3	—	—	53	21	13	10	0	31	1	0	1	8	4	.67	2	.234	.288	.376
Indianapols	AAA	3	9	3	0	0	1	—	—	6	2	3	0	0	5	0	0	0	1	0	1.00	0	.333	.333	.667
2000 Fresno	AAA	123	417	123	26	6	12	—	—	197	58	50	35	3	89	3	4	1	13	13	.50	8	.295	.353	.472
2000 San Francisco	NL	11	13	1	0	0	0	(0	0)	1	0	1	0	0	5	0	0	0	0	0	—	0	.077	.077	.077

Mitch Meluskey

Bats: Both **Throws:** Right **Pos:** C-103; PH/PR-23; 3B-1   **Ht:** 6'0" **Wt:** 185 **Born:** 9/18/73 **Age:** 27

Year Team	Lg	BATTING																	BASERUNNING				PERCENTAGES		
		G	AB	H	2B	3B	HR	(Hm	Rd)	TB	R	RBI	TBB	IBB	SO	HBP	SH	SF	SB	CS	SB%	GDP	Avg	OBP	SLG
1992 Burlington	R+	43	126	29	7	0	3	—	—	45	23	16	29	0	36	0	0	2	3	0	1.00		.230	.369	.357
1993 Columbus	A	101	342	84	18	3	3	—	—	117	36	47	35	4	69	4	4	7	1	1	.50	5	.246	.317	.342
1994 Kinston	A+	100	319	77	16	1	3	—	—	104	36	41	49	0	62	2	2	4	3	4	.43	6	.241	.342	.326
1995 Kinston	A+	8	29	7	5	0	0	—	—	12	5	2	2	0	9	0	0	0	0	0	—	1	.241	.290	.414
Kissimmee	A+	78	261	56	18	1	3	—	—	85	23	31	27	2	33	1	2	4	3	0	1.00	12	.215	.287	.326
1996 Kissimmee	A+	74	231	77	19	0	1	—	—	99	29	31	29	5	26	1	1	5	1	1	.50	9	.333	.402	.429
Jackson	AA	38	134	42	11	0	0	—	—	53	18	21	18	1	21	1	1	1	0	0	—	6	.313	.396	.396
1997 Jackson	AA	73	241	82	18	0	14	—	—	142	49	46	31	4	39	3	0	3	1	3	.25	7	.340	.417	.589
New Orleans	AAA	51	172	43	7	0	3	—	—	59	22	21	25	1	38	1	0	1	0	0	—	6	.250	.347	.343
1998 New Orleans	AAA	121	397	140	41	0	17	—	—	232	76	71	85	10	59	0	3	5	2	0	1.00	15	.353	.465	.584
1998 Houston	NL	8	8	2	1	0	0	(0	0)	3	1	0	1	0	4	0	0	0	0	0	—	15	.250	.333	.375
1999 Houston	NL	10	33	7	1	0	1	(0	1)	11	4	3	5	1	9	0	0	0	0	0	—	1	.212	.316	.333
2000 Houston	NL	117	337	101	21	0	14	(11	3)	164	47	69	55	10	74	4	1	3	1	0	1.00	7	.300	.401	.487
3 ML YEARS		135	378	110	23	0	15	(11	4)	178	52	72	61	11	84	4	1	3	1	0	1.00	9	.291	.392	.471

Carlos Mendoza

Bats: Left **Throws:** Left **Pos:** PH/PR-10; LF-3   **Ht:** 5'11" **Wt:** 165 **Born:** 11/14/74 **Age:** 26

Year Team	Lg	G	AB	H	2B	3B	HR	(Hm	Rd)	TB	R	RBI	TBB	IBB	SO	HBP	SH	SF	SB	CS	SB%	GDP	Avg	OBP	SLG
1995 Kingsport	R+	51	192	63	9	0	1	—	—	75	56	24	27	0	24	3	4	2	28	6	.82	3	.328	.415	.391
1996 Capital Cty	A	85	300	101	10	2	0	—	—	115	61	37	57	1	46	8	11	2	31	13	.70	2	.337	.452	.383
1997 Binghamton	AA	59	228	87	12	2	1	—	—	106	36	13	14	1	25	4	7	0	14	12	.54	4	.382	.427	.465
Norfolk	AAA	10	35	5	0	1	0	—	—	7	3	0	3	0	4	1	1	0	1	0	1.00	1	.143	.231	.200
1998 Durham	AAA	51	201	54	8	0	0	—	—	62	32	11	16	0	29	1	5	1	9	9	.50	5	.269	.324	.308
St. Pete	A+	8	32	10	2	0	0	—	—	12	6	8	4	0	3	1	2	1	4	2	.67	0	.313	.395	.375
Devil Rays	R	6	18	8	1	0	0	—	—	9	6	4	5	0	3	1	0	1	3	1	.75	1	.444	.560	.500
Orlando	AA	35	139	47	3	3	1	—	—	59	27	19	19	0	18	4	4	0	16	2	.89	6	.338	.432	.424
1999 Durham	AAA	75	266	78	8	3	1	—	—	95	57	25	32	0	38	7	9	0	9	8	.53	5	.293	.384	.357
2000 Colo Sprngs	AAA	107	359	127	16	14	0	—	—	171	79	42	60	2	50	3	8	1	26	13	.67	5	.354	.449	.476
1997 New York	NL	15	12	3	0	0	0	(0	0)	3	6	1	4	0	2	2	0	0	0	0	—	0	.250	.500	.250
2000 Colorado	NL	13	10	1	0	0	0	(0	0)	1	0	0	1	0	4	0	0	0	0	1	.00	0	.100	.182	.100
2 ML YEARS		28	22	4	0	0	0	(0	0)	4	6	1	5	0	6	2	0	0	0	1	.00	0	.182	.379	.182

Ramiro Mendoza

Pitches: Right **Bats:** Right **Pos:** SP-9; RP-5   **Ht:** 6'2" **Wt:** 195 **Born:** 6/15/72 **Age:** 29

Year Team	Lg	G	GS	CG	GF	IP	BFP	H	R	ER	HR	SH	SF	HB	TBB	IBB	SO	WP	Bk	W	L	Pct.	ShO	Sv-Op	Hld	ERA
2000 Tampa *	A+	2	2	0	0	5	22	9	4	4	0	0	0	0	7	0	0	0	0	0	2	.000	0	0--	—	7.20
1996 New York	AL	12	11	0	0	53	249	80	43	40	5	1	1	4	10	1	34	2	1	4	5	.444	0	0-0	0	6.79
1997 New York	AL	39	15	0	9	133.2	578	157	67	63	15	3	5	5	28	2	82	2	1	8	6	.571	0	2-4	4	4.24
1998 New York	AL	41	14	1	6	130.1	548	131	50	47	9	6	7	9	30	6	56	3	0	10	2	.833	1	1-4	5	3.25
1999 New York	AL	53	6	0	15	123.2	536	141	68	59	13	6	4	3	27	3	80	2	0	9	9	.500	0	3-6	4	4.29
2000 New York	AL	14	9	1	0	65.2	281	66	32	31	9	1	2	4	20	1	30	0	0	7	4	.636	1	0-1	0	4.25
5 ML YEARS		159	55	2	30	506.1	2192	575	260	240	51	17	19	25	115	13	282	9	2	38	26	.594	2	6-15	13	4.27

Frank Menechino

Bats: R **Throws:** R **Pos:** 2B-51; PH/PR-16; SS-5; DH-4; 3B-4; P-1   **Ht:** 5'9" **Wt:** 175 **Born:** 1/7/71 **Age:** 30

Year Team	Lg	G	AB	H	2B	3B	HR	(Hm	Rd)	TB	R	RBI	TBB	IBB	SO	HBP	SH	SF	SB	CS	SB%	GDP	Avg	OBP	SLG
1993 White Sox	R	17	45	11	4	1	1	—	—	20	10	9	12	0	4	4	0	0	3	1	.75	1	.244	.443	.444
Hickory	A	50	178	50	6	3	4	—	—	74	35	19	33	0	28	4	1	1	15	2	.85	4	.281	.403	.416
1994 South Bend	A	106	379	113	21	5	5	—	—	159	77	48	78	1	70	9	3	2	15	8	.65	8	.298	.427	.420
1995 Pr William	A+	137	476	124	31	3	6	—	—	179	65	58	96	2	75	11	3	8	6	2	.75	17	.261	.391	.376
1996 Birmingham	AA	125	415	121	25	3	12	—	—	188	77	62	64	0	84	8	3	6	7	9	.44	5	.292	.391	.453
1997 Nashville	AAA	37	113	26	4	0	4	—	—	42	20	11	26	1	31	6	0	1	3	2	.60	2	.230	.397	.372
Birmingham	AA	90	318	95	28	4	12	—	—	167	78	60	79	0	77	11	1	6	7	3	.70	7	.299	.447	.525
1998 Edmonton	AAA	106	378	105	11	7	10	—	—	160	72	40	70	1	75	10	2	1	9	10	.47	11	.278	.403	.423
1999 Vancouver	AAA	130	501	155	31	9	15	—	—	249	103	88	73	7	97	9	1	5	4	5	.44	12	.309	.403	.497
2000 Sacramento	AAA	9	38	12	2	0	2	—	—	20	8	2	5	0	4	0	0	0	1	0	1.00	0	.316	.395	.526
1999 Oakland	AL	9	9	2	0	0	0	(0	0)	2	0	0	0	0	4	0	0	0	0	0	—	0	.222	.222	.222
2000 Oakland	AL	66	145	37	9	1	6	(3	3)	66	31	26	20	0	45	1	1	2	1	4	.20	1	.255	.345	.455
2 ML YEARS		75	154	39	9	1	6	(3	3)	68	31	26	20	0	49	1	1	2	1	4	.20	1	.253	.339	.442

Hector Mercado

Pitches: Left **Bats:** Left **Pos:** RP-12   **Ht:** 6'3" **Wt:** 235 **Born:** 4/29/74 **Age:** 27

Year Team	Lg	G	GS	CG	GF	IP	BFP	H	R	ER	HR	SH	SF	HB	TBB	IBB	SO	WP	Bk	W	L	Pct.	ShO	Sv-Op	Hld	ERA
1992 Astros	R	13	3	0	4	30	140	22	17	14	0	1	0	3	25	0	36	7	6	1	2	.333	0	0--	—	4.20
1993 Osceola	A+	2	2	0	0	8.2	39	9	7	5	0	4	0	0	6	1	5	0	0	1	1	.500	0	0--	—	5.19
Astros	R	11	11	1	0	67	278	49	26	18	1	0	3	1	29	0	59	10	2	5	4	.556	1	0--	—	2.42
1994 Osceola	A+	25	25	1	0	136.2	601	123	75	60	5	11	4	1	79	4	88	9	3	6	13	.316	1	0--	—	3.95
1995 Kissimmee	A+	19	17	2	0	104	433	96	50	40	2	2	3	3	37	0	75	4	1	6	8	.429	0	0--	—	3.46
Jackson	AA	8	7	0	0	30	157	36	33	26	5	2	1	2	32	1	20	4	0	1	4	.200	0	0--	—	7.80
1996 Kissimmee	A+	56	0	0	18	80	353	78	43	37	4	3	1	4	48	1	68	6	0	3	5	.375	0	3--	—	4.16
1997 Charlotte	AAA	1	1	0	0	5	25	5	5	5	2	0	0	0	5	0	1	1	0	0	1	.000	0	0--	—	9.00
Portland	AA	31	17	1	6	129.2	565	129	66	57	10	6	1	3	54	5	125	16	2	11	3	.786	1	0--	—	3.96
1999 Norfolk	AAA	2	2	0	0	6	22	3	1	1	1	0	0	1	1	0	2	0	0	0	0	—	0	0--	—	1.50
2000 Louisville	AAA	47	5	0	10	77	339	69	26	26	2	0	6	2	48	2	67	6	0	1	5	.167	0	2--	—	3.04
2000 Cincinnati	NL	12	0	0	4	14	60	12	7	7	2	1	1	0	8	0	13	2	0	0	0	—	0	0-0	1	4.50

Jose Mercedes

Pitches: Right **Bats:** Right **Pos:** SP-20; RP-16   **Ht:** 6'1" **Wt:** 180 **Born:** 3/5/71 **Age:** 30

Year Team	Lg	G	GS	CG	GF	IP	BFP	H	R	ER	HR	SH	SF	HB	TBB	IBB	SO	WP	Bk	W	L	Pct.	ShO	Sv-Op	Hld	ERA
1994 Milwaukee	AL	19	0	0	5	31	120	22	9	8	4	0	0	2	16	1	11	0	1	2	0	1.000	0	0-1	3	2.32
1995 Milwaukee	AL	5	0	0	0	7.1	42	12	9	8	1	0	2	0	8	0	6	1	0	0	1	.000	0	0-2	1	9.82
1996 Milwaukee	AL	11	0	0	4	16.2	74	20	18	17	6	0	1	0	5	0	6	2	0	0	2	.000	0	0-1	2	9.18
1997 Milwaukee	AL	29	23	2	1	159	653	146	76	67	24	3	4	5	53	2	80	1	1	7	10	.412	1	0-0	1	3.79
1998 Milwaukee	NL	7	5	0	0	32	146	42	25	24	5	1	2	1	9	1	11	0	0	2	2	.500	0	0-0	0	6.75
2000 Baltimore	AL	36	20	1	7	145.2	636	150	71	65	15	7	7	3	64	1	70	3	0	14	7	.667	0	0-0	0	4.02
6 ML YEARS		107	48	3	17	391.2	1671	392	208	189	55	11	16	11	155	5	184	7	2	25	22	.532	1	0-4	7	4.34

Kent Mercker

Pitches: Left **Bats:** Left **Pos:** RP-14; SP-7 **Ht:** 6'2" **Wt:** 200 **Born:** 2/1/68 **Age:** 33

		HOW MUCH HE PITCHED						WHAT HE GAVE UP										THE RESULTS					
Year Team	Lg	G	GS	CG	GF	IP	BFP	H	R	ER	HR	SH	SF	HB	TBB	IBB	SO	WP	Bk	W	L	Pct.	ShO	Sv-Op	Hld	ERA
2000 Lk Elsinore *	A+	1	1	0	0	4	12	0	0	0	0	0	0	0	0	0	3	0	0	0	0	—	0	0--	0	0.00
1989 Atlanta	NL	2	1	0	1	4.1	26	8	6	6	0	0	0	0	6	0	4	0	0	0	0	—	0	0-0	0	12.46
1990 Atlanta	NL	36	0	0	28	48.1	211	43	22	17	6	1	2	2	24	3	39	2	0	4	7	.364	0	7-10	0	3.17
1991 Atlanta	NL	50	4	0	28	73.1	306	56	23	21	5	2	2	1	35	3	62	4	1	5	3	.625	0	6-8	3	2.58
1992 Atlanta	NL	53	0	0	18	68.1	289	51	27	26	4	4	1	3	35	1	49	6	0	3	2	.600	0	6-9	6	3.42
1993 Atlanta	NL	43	6	0	9	66	283	52	24	21	2	0	0	2	36	3	59	5	1	3	1	.750	0	0-3	4	2.86
1994 Atlanta	NL	20	17	2	0	112.1	461	90	46	43	16	4	3	0	45	3	111	4	1	9	4	.692	1	0-0	0	3.45
1995 Atlanta	NL	29	26	0	1	143	622	140	73	66	16	8	7	3	61	2	102	6	2	7	8	.467	0	0-0	0	4.15
1996 Bal-Cle	AL	24	12	0	2	69.2	329	83	60	54	13	6	3	6	38	2	29	3	1	4	6	.400	0	0-0	2	6.98
1997 Cincinnati	NL	28	25	0	0	144.2	616	135	65	63	16	8	4	2	62	6	75	2	1	8	11	.421	0	0-0	0	3.92
1998 St. Louis	NL	30	29	0	0	161.2	716	199	99	91	11	10	9	3	53	4	72	6	4	11	11	.500	0	0-0	0	5.07
1999 StL-Bos	NL	30	23	0	2	129.1	589	148	85	69	16	8	4	3	64	3	81	3	1	8	5	.615	0	0-0	0	4.80
2000 Anaheim	AL	21	7	0	2	48.1	225	57	35	35	12	3	1	2	29	3	30	2	0	1	3	.250	0	0-0	1	6.52
1996 Baltimore	AL	14	12	0	0	58	283	73	56	50	12	3	4	3	35	1	22	3	1	3	6	.333	0	0-0	0	7.76
Cleveland	AL	10	0	0	2	11.2	46	10	4	4	1	0	2	0	3	1	7	0	0	1	0	1.000	0	0-0	2	3.09
1999 St. Louis	NL	25	18	0	2	103.2	476	125	73	59	16	8	3	2	51	3	64	3	1	6	5	.545	0	0-0	0	5.12
Boston	AL	5	5	0	0	25.2	113	23	12	10	0	0	1	1	13	0	17	0	0	2	0	1.000	0	0-0	0	3.51
12 ML YEARS		366	150	2	92	1069.1	4673	1062	565	512	117	51	39	24	488	33	713	43	12	63	61	.508	1	19-30	16	4.31

Lou Merloni

Bats: Right **Throws:** Right **Pos:** 3B-40 **Ht:** 5'10" **Wt:** 200 **Born:** 4/6/71 **Age:** 30

		BATTING																	BASERUNNING				PERCENTAGES		
Year Team	Lg	G	AB	H	2B	3B	HR	(Hm	Rd)	TB	R	RBI	TBB	IBB	SO	HBP	SH	SF	SB	CS	SB%	GDP	Avg	OBP	SLG
2000 Pawtucket *	AAA	11	39	16	2	0	1	—	—	21	6	5	3	0	3	0	0	0	0	1	.00	2	.410	.452	.538
1998 Boston	AL	39	96	27	6	0	1	(1	0)	36	10	15	7	1	20	2	1	0	1	0	1.00	1	.281	.343	.375
1999 Boston	AL	43	126	32	7	0	1	(0	1)	42	18	13	8	0	16	2	3	1	0	0	—	6	.254	.307	.333
2000 Boston	AL	40	128	41	11	2	0	(0	0)	56	10	18	4	1	22	1	4	2	0	1	1.00	8	.320	.341	.438
3 ML YEARS		122	350	100	24	2	2	(1	1)	134	38	46	19	2	58	5	8	3	0	1	1.00	15	.286	.329	.383

Jose Mesa

Pitches: Right **Bats:** Right **Pos:** RP-66 **Ht:** 6'3" **Wt:** 225 **Born:** 5/22/66 **Age:** 35

		HOW MUCH HE PITCHED						WHAT HE GAVE UP										THE RESULTS					
Year Team	Lg	G	GS	CG	GF	IP	BFP	H	R	ER	HR	SH	SF	HB	TBB	IBB	SO	WP	Bk	W	L	Pct.	ShO	Sv-Op	Hld	ERA
1987 Baltimore	AL	6	5	0	0	31.1	143	38	23	21	7	0	0	0	15	0	17	4	0	1	3	.250	0	0-0	1	6.03
1990 Baltimore	AL	7	7	0	0	46.2	202	37	20	20	2	2	2	1	27	2	24	1	1	3	2	.600	0	0-0	0	3.86
1991 Baltimore	AL	23	23	2	0	123.2	566	151	86	82	11	5	4	3	62	2	64	3	0	6	11	.353	1	0-0	0	5.97
1992 Bal-Cle	AL	28	27	1	1	160.2	700	169	86	82	14	2	5	4	70	1	62	2	0	7	12	.368	1	0-0	0	4.59
1993 Cleveland	AL	34	33	3	0	208.2	897	232	122	114	21	9	9	7	62	2	118	8	2	10	12	.455	0	0-0	0	4.92
1994 Cleveland	AL	51	0	0	22	73	315	71	33	31	3	3	4	3	26	7	63	3	0	7	5	.583	0	2-6	8	3.82
1995 Cleveland	AL	62	0	0	57	64	250	49	9	8	3	4	2	0	17	2	58	5	0	3	0	1.000	0	46-48	0	1.13
1996 Cleveland	AL	69	0	0	60	72.1	304	69	32	30	6	2	3	2	28	4	64	4	0	2	7	.222	0	39-44	0	3.73
1997 Cleveland	AL	66	0	0	38	82.1	356	83	28	22	7	2	2	2	28	3	69	1	0	4	4	.500	0	16-21	13	2.40
1998 Cle-SF		76	0	0	36	84.2	383	91	50	43	8	2	4	4	38	5	63	10	0	8	7	.533	0	1-4	13	4.57
1999 Seattle	AL	68	0	0	60	68.2	325	84	42	38	11	2	4	6	40	4	42	7	0	3	6	.333	0	33-38	1	4.98
2000 Seattle	AL	66	0	0	29	80.2	372	89	48	48	11	2	6	5	41	0	84	3	0	4	6	.400	0	1-3	5	5.36
1992 Baltimore	AL	13	12	0	1	67.2	300	77	41	39	9	0	3	2	27	1	22	2	0	3	8	.273	0	0-0	0	5.19
Cleveland	AL	15	15	1	0	93	400	92	45	43	5	2	2	2	43	0	40	0	0	4	4	.500	1	0-0	0	4.16
1998 Cleveland	AL	44	0	0	18	54	244	61	36	31	7	2	2	4	20	3	35	2	0	3	4	.429	0	1-3	7	5.17
San Francisco	NL	32	0	0	18	30.2	139	30	14	12	1	0	2	0	18	2	28	8	0	5	3	.625	0	0-1	6	3.52
12 ML YEARS		556	95	6	303	1096.2	4813	1163	579	539	104	39	42	37	454	32	728	51	3	58	75	.436	2	138-164	43	4.42

Mike Metcalfe

Bats: B **Throws:** R **Pos:** LF-3; 2B-1; CF-1; PH/PR-1 **Ht:** 5'10" **Wt:** 175 **Born:** 1/2/73 **Age:** 28

		BATTING																	BASERUNNING				PERCENTAGES		
Year Team	Lg	G	AB	H	2B	3B	HR	(Hm	Rd)	TB	R	RBI	TBB	IBB	SO	HBP	SH	SF	SB	CS	SB%	GDP	Avg	OBP	SLG
1994 Bakersfield	A+	69	275	78	10	0	0	—	—	88	44	18	28	0	34	1	4	2	41	13	.76	6	.284	.350	.320
1995 San Antonio	AA	10	41	10	1	0	0	—	—	11	10	2	7	0	2	0	1	1	1	2	.33	0	.244	.347	.268
Vero Beach	A+	120	435	131	13	3	3	—	—	159	86	35	60	2	37	3	6	5	60	27	.69	8	.301	.386	.366
1996 Vero Beach	A+	2	5	0	0	0	0	—	—	0	0	0	0	0	0	0	0	0	0	0	—	0	.000	.000	.000
1997 San Berndno	A+	132	519	147	28	7	3	—	—	198	83	47	55	0	79	4	6	1	67	32	.68	5	.283	.356	.382
1998 San Antonio	AA	57	213	60	5	5	3	—	—	84	35	19	30	1	24	1	3	2	19	15	.56	3	.282	.370	.394
1999 San Antonio	AA	123	461	135	25	3	3	—	—	175	78	57	65	1	47	3	9	4	57	21	.73	9	.293	.381	.380
2000 San Antonio	AA	52	196	48	5	3	2	—	—	65	42	25	30	1	18	1	4	1	34	9	.79	0	.245	.346	.332
Albuquerque	AAA	35	149	45	6	3	0	—	—	57	22	21	10	0	16	2	2	2	9	11	.45	2	.302	.350	.383
1998 Los Angeles	NL	4	1	0	0	0	0	(0	0)	0	0	0	0	0	1	0	0	0	0	0	—	0	.000	.000	.000
2000 Los Angeles	NL	4	12	1	0	0	0	(0	0)	1	0	0	1	0	2	0	0	0	2	0	1.00	0	.083	.154	.083
2 ML YEARS		8	13	1	0	0	0	(0	0)	1	0	0	1	0	3	0	0	0	2	0	1.00	0	.077	.143	.077

Chad Meyers

Bats: Right **Throws:** Right **Pos:** PH/PR-24; 2B-8; 3B-8 **Ht:** 6'0" **Wt:** 190 **Born:** 8/8/75 **Age:** 25

		BATTING																	BASERUNNING				PERCENTAGES		
Year Team	Lg	G	AB	H	2B	3B	HR	(Hm	Rd)	TB	R	RBI	TBB	IBB	SO	HBP	SH	SF	SB	CS	SB%	GDP	Avg	OBP	SLG
1996 Williamsprt	A-	67	230	56	9	2	2	—	—	75	46	26	33	0	39	5	2	1	27	6	.82	2	.243	.349	.326
1997 Rockford	A	125	439	132	28	4	4	—	—	180	89	58	74	5	72	10	6	7	54	16	.77	4	.301	.408	.410
1998 Daytona	A+	48	186	60	8	3	3	—	—	83	39	25	33	1	29	5	1	1	23	7	.77	4	.323	.436	.446
West Tenn	AA	77	293	79	14	0	0	—	—	93	36	26	58	0	43	4	1	0	37	9	.80	5	.270	.397	.317
1999 West Tenn	AA	64	238	69	19	2	3	—	—	101	45	29	26	0	40	10	0	0	22	8	.73	6	.290	.383	.424
Iowa	AAA	44	175	62	13	2	0	—	—	79	39	16	29	0	20	3	3	0	17	7	.71	1	.354	.454	.451

Year Team	Lg	G	AB	H	2B	3B	HR	(Hm	Rd)	TB	R	RBI	TBB	IBB	SO	HBP	SH	SF	SB	CS	SB%	GDP	Avg	OBP	SLG
								BATTING											BASERUNNING				PERCENTAGES		
2000 Iowa	AAA	80	301	81	10	0	0	(—	—)	97	54	26	43	0	41	5	4	2	34	15	.69	5	.269	.368	.322
1999 Chicago	NL	43	142	33	9	0	0	(0	0)	42	17	4	9	1	27	3	0	1	4	2	.67	5	.232	.292	.296
2000 Chicago	NL	36	52	9	2	0	0	(0	0)	11	8	5	3	0	11	1	0	1	1	0	1.00	0	.173	.228	.212
2 ML YEARS		79	194	42	11	0	0	(0	0)	53	25	9	12	1	38	4	2	1	5	2	.71	5	.216	.275	.273

Dan Miceli

Pitches: Right **Bats:** Right **Pos:** RP-45   **Ht:** 6'0" **Wt:** 216 **Born:** 9/9/70 **Age:** 30

Year Team	Lg	G	GS	CG	GF	IP	BFP	H	R	ER	HR	SH	SF	HB	TBB	IBB	SO	WP	Bk	W	L	Pct.	ShO	Sv-Op	Hld	ERA
			HOW MUCH HE PITCHED								WHAT HE GAVE UP											THE RESULTS				
2000 Marlins *	R	2	2	0	0	3	10	0	0	0	0	0	0	1	0	3	0	0	0	0	—	0	0--	—	0.00
Brevard Cty *	A+	5	4	0	0	6	21	3	2	2	1	0	0	0	0	0	7	0	0	1	0	1.000	0	0--	—	3.00
1993 Pittsburgh	NL	9	0	0	1	5.1	25	6	3	3	0	0	0	0	3	0	4	0	1	0	0	—	0	0-0	0	5.06
1994 Pittsburgh	NL	28	0	0	9	27.1	121	28	19	18	5	1	2	2	11	2	27	2	0	2	1	.667	0	2-3	4	5.93
1995 Pittsburgh	NL	58	0	0	51	58	264	61	30	30	7	2	4	4	28	5	56	4	0	4	4	.500	0	21-27	2	4.66
1996 Pittsburgh	NL	44	9	0	17	85.2	398	99	65	55	15	3	7	3	45	5	66	9	0	2	10	.167	0	1-1	4	5.78
1997 Detroit	AL	71	0	0	24	82.2	357	77	49	46	13	5	3	1	38	4	79	3	0	3	2	.600	0	3-8	11	5.01
1998 San Diego	NL	67	0	0	18	72.2	302	64	28	26	6	3	2	1	27	4	70	5	1	10	5	.667	0	2-8	20	3.22
1999 San Diego	NL	66	0	0	28	68.2	296	67	39	34	7	4	2	1	36	5	59	2	0	4	5	.444	0	2-4	9	4.46
2000 Florida	NL	45	0	0	9	48.2	207	45	23	23	4	1	1	1	18	2	40	3	0	6	4	.600	0	0-3	11	4.25
8 ML YEARS		388	9	0	157	449	1970	447	256	235	57	19	21	14	206	27	401	28	2	31	31	.500	0	31-54	61	4.71

Doug Mientkiewicz

Bats: Left **Throws:** Right **Pos:** 1B-3   **Ht:** 6'2" **Wt:** 200 **Born:** 6/19/74 **Age:** 27

Year Team	Lg	G	AB	H	2B	3B	HR	(Hm	Rd)	TB	R	RBI	TBB	IBB	SO	HBP	SH	SF	SB	CS	SB%	GDP	Avg	OBP	SLG
								BATTING											BASERUNNING				PERCENTAGES		
2000 Salt Lake *	AAA	130	485	162	32	3	18	—	—	254	96	96	61	2	68	3	3	8	9	5	.64	17	.334	.406	.524
1998 Minnesota	AL	8	25	5	1	0	0	(0	0)	6	1	2	4	0	3	0	0	0	1	1	.50	0	.200	.310	.240
1999 Minnesota	AL	118	327	75	21	3	2	(0	2)	108	34	32	43	3	51	4	3	2	1	1	.50	13	.229	.324	.330
2000 Minnesota	AL	3	14	6	0	0	0	(0	0)	6	0	4	0	0	0	0	0	1	0	0	—	1	.429	.400	.429
3 ML YEARS		129	366	86	22	3	2	(0	2)	120	35	38	47	3	54	4	3	3	2	2	.50	14	.235	.326	.328

Matt Mieske

Bats: Right **Throws:** Right **Pos:** PH/PR-60; LF-14; RF-5   **Ht:** 6'0" **Wt:** 194 **Born:** 2/13/68 **Age:** 33

Year Team	Lg	G	AB	H	2B	3B	HR	(Hm	Rd)	TB	R	RBI	TBB	IBB	SO	HBP	SH	SF	SB	CS	SB%	GDP	Avg	OBP	SLG
								BATTING											BASERUNNING				PERCENTAGES		
2000 Tucson *	AAA	6	25	6	2	0	1	—	—	11	2	3	0	0	7	0	0	1	0	0	—	1	.240	.231	.440
1993 Milwaukee	AL	23	58	14	0	0	3	(1	2)	23	9	7	4	0	14	0	1	0	0	2	.00	1	.241	.290	.397
1994 Milwaukee	AL	84	259	67	13	1	10	(7	3)	112	39	38	21	0	62	3	2	1	3	5	.38	6	.259	.320	.432
1995 Milwaukee	AL	117	267	67	13	1	12	(3	9)	118	42	48	27	0	45	4	0	5	2	4	.33	8	.251	.323	.442
1996 Milwaukee	AL	127	374	104	24	3	14	(9	5)	176	46	64	26	2	76	2	1	6	1	5	.17	9	.278	.324	.471
1997 Milwaukee	AL	84	253	63	15	3	5	(1	4)	99	39	21	19	2	50	0	0	1	1	0	1.00	12	.249	.300	.391
1998 Chicago	NL	77	97	29	7	0	1	(1	0)	39	16	12	11	1	17	1	1	1	0	0	—	4	.299	.373	.402
1999 Sea-Hou		78	150	46	5	0	9	(4	5)	78	24	29	8	2	31	0	1	2	0	0	—	0	.307	.338	.520
2000 Hou-Ari	NL	73	89	16	1	2	2	(2	0)	27	10	7	8	0	18	1	0	0	0	0	—	2	.180	.253	.303
1999 Seattle	AL	24	41	15	0	0	4	(3	1)	27	11	7	2	1	9	0	0	0	0	0	—	0	.366	.395	.659
Houston	NL	54	109	31	5	0	5	(1	4)	51	13	22	6	1	22	0	1	2	0	0	—	0	.284	.316	.468
2000 Houston	NL	62	81	14	1	2	1	(1	0)	22	7	5	7	0	17	1	0	0	0	0	—	2	.173	.247	.272
Arizona	NL	11	8	2	0	0	1	(1	0)	5	3	2	1	0	1	0	0	0	0	0	—	0	.250	.300	.625
8 ML YEARS		663	1547	406	78	10	56	(28	28)	672	225	226	124	7	313	11	6	17	7	16	.30	43	.262	.318	.434

Kevin Millar

Bats: R **Throws:** R **Pos:** PH/PR-56; 1B-34; LF-17; 3B-13; DH-6; RF-1   **Ht:** 6'0" **Wt:** 210 **Born:** 9/24/71 **Age:** 29

Year Team	Lg	G	AB	H	2B	3B	HR	(Hm	Rd)	TB	R	RBI	TBB	IBB	SO	HBP	SH	SF	SB	CS	SB%	GDP	Avg	OBP	SLG
								BATTING											BASERUNNING				PERCENTAGES		
1998 Florida	NL	2	2	1	0	0	0	(0	0)	1	1	0	1	0	0	0	0	0	0	0	—	0	.500	.667	.500
1999 Florida	NL	105	351	100	17	4	9	(3	6)	152	48	67	40	2	64	7	1	8	1	0	1.00	7	.285	.362	.433
2000 Florida	NL	123	259	67	14	3	14	(6	8)	129	36	42	36	0	47	8	0	2	0	0	—	5	.259	.364	.498
3 ML YEARS		230	612	168	31	7	23	(9	14)	282	85	109	77	2	111	15	1	10	1	0	1.00	12	.275	.364	.461

Damian Miller

Bats: Right **Throws:** Right **Pos:** C-97; PH/PR-3; 1B-2   **Ht:** 6'2" **Wt:** 212 **Born:** 10/13/69 **Age:** 31

Year Team	Lg	G	AB	H	2B	3B	HR	(Hm	Rd)	TB	R	RBI	TBB	IBB	SO	HBP	SH	SF	SB	CS	SB%	GDP	Avg	OBP	SLG
								BATTING											BASERUNNING				PERCENTAGES		
1997 Minnesota	AL	25	66	18	1	0	2	(1	1)	25	5	13	2	0	12	0	0	3	0	0	—	2	.273	.282	.379
1998 Arizona	NL	57	168	48	14	2	3	(2	1)	75	17	14	11	2	43	2	2	0	1	0	1.00	6	.286	.337	.446
1999 Arizona	NL	86	296	80	19	0	11	(3	8)	132	35	47	19	3	78	2	0	3	0	0	—	6	.270	.316	.446
2000 Arizona	NL	100	324	89	24	0	10	(6	4)	143	43	44	36	4	74	1	1	2	2	2	.50	6	.275	.347	.441
4 ML YEARS		268	854	235	58	2	26	(12	14)	375	100	118	68	9	207	5	3	8	3	2	.60	16	.275	.329	.439

Travis Miller

Pitches: Left **Bats:** Right **Pos:** RP-67   **Ht:** 6'3" **Wt:** 215 **Born:** 11/2/72 **Age:** 28

Year Team	Lg	G	GS	CG	GF	IP	BFP	H	R	ER	HR	SH	SF	HB	TBB	IBB	SO	WP	Bk	W	L	Pct.	ShO	Sv-Op	Hld	ERA
			HOW MUCH HE PITCHED								WHAT HE GAVE UP											THE RESULTS				
1996 Minnesota	AL	7	7	0	0	26.1	126	45	29	27	7	1	0	0	9	0	15	0	0	1	2	.333	0	0-0	0	9.23
1997 Minnesota	AL	13	7	0	1	48.1	227	64	49	41	8	1	2	1	23	2	26	5	0	1	5	.167	0	0-0	0	7.63
1998 Minnesota	AL	14	0	0	2	23.1	104	25	10	10	0	0	1	0	11	1	23	2	0	0	2	.000	0	0-0	0	3.86

143

		HOW MUCH HE PITCHED						WHAT HE GAVE UP												THE RESULTS						
Year Team	Lg	G	GS	CG	GF	IP	BFP	H	R	ER	HR	SH	SF	HB	TBB	IBB	SO	WP	Bk	W	L	Pct.	ShO	Sv-Op	Hld	ERA
1999 Minnesota	AL	52	0	0	12	49.2	214	55	19	15	3	2	2	0	16	3	40	6	0	2	2	.500	0	0-2	8	2.72
2000 Minnesota	AL	67	0	0	12	67	316	83	35	29	4	1	3	1	32	1	62	2	0	2	3	.400	0	1-4	10	3.90
5 ML YEARS		153	14	0	27	214.2	987	272	142	122	22	5	8	2	91	8	166	15	0	6	14	.300	0	1-6	18	5.11

Trever Miller

Pitches: Left Bats: Right Pos: RP-16   Ht: 6'4" Wt: 195 Born: 5/29/73 Age: 28

		HOW MUCH HE PITCHED						WHAT HE GAVE UP												THE RESULTS						
Year Team	Lg	G	GS	CG	GF	IP	BFP	H	R	ER	HR	SH	SF	HB	TBB	IBB	SO	WP	Bk	W	L	Pct.	ShO	Sv-Op	Hld	ERA
2000 Albuquerque *	AAA	12	9	1	0	58	248	60	29	22	5	2	1	1	20	0	39	2	0	4	2	.667	1	0- -	—	3.41
1996 Detroit	AL	5	4	0	0	16.2	88	28	17	17	3	2	2	2	9	0	8	0	0	0	4	.000	0	0-0	—	9.18
1998 Houston	NL	37	1	0	15	53.1	235	57	21	18	4	0	0	1	20	1	30	1	0	2	0	1.000	0	1-2	1	3.04
1999 Houston	NL	47	0	0	11	49.2	232	58	29	28	6	2	2	5	29	1	37	4	0	3	2	.600	0	1-1	4	5.07
2000 Phi-LA	NL	16	0	0	2	16.1	90	27	22	19	3	1	1	2	12	1	11	1	0	0	0	—	0	0-0	0	10.47
2000 Philadelphia	NL	14	0	0	2	14	72	19	16	13	3	1	1	1	9	1	10	1	0	0	0	—	0	0-0	0	8.36
Los Angeles	NL	2	0	0	0	2.1	18	8	6	6	0	0	0	1	3	0	1	0	0	0	0	—	0	0-0	0	23.14
4 ML YEARS		105	5	0	28	136	645	170	89	82	16	5	5	10	70	3	86	6	0	5	6	.455	0	2-3	5	5.43

Wade Miller

Pitches: Right Bats: Right Pos: SP-16   Ht: 6'2" Wt: 185 Born: 9/13/76 Age: 24

		HOW MUCH HE PITCHED						WHAT HE GAVE UP												THE RESULTS						
Year Team	Lg	G	GS	CG	GF	IP	BFP	H	R	ER	HR	SH	SF	HB	TBB	IBB	SO	WP	Bk	W	L	Pct.	ShO	Sv-Op	Hld	ERA
1996 Astros	R	11	10	0	0	57	233	49	26	24	1	2	5	4	12	0	53	5	0	3	4	.429	0	0-	—	3.79
Auburn	A-	2	2	0	0	9	41	8	9	5	0	0	0	0	4	0	11	0	1	1	1	.500	0	0-	—	5.00
1997 Quad City	A	10	8	2	1	59	235	45	27	22	7	0	1	0	10	0	50	4	0	5	3	.625	0	0-	—	3.36
Kissimmee	A+	14	14	4	0	100	395	79	28	20	3	3	5	4	14	1	76	4	1	10	2	.833	1	0-	—	1.80
1998 Jackson	AA	10	10	0	0	62	262	49	23	16	7	1	0	4	27	2	48	3	1	5	0	1.000	0	0-	—	2.32
1999 New Orleans	AAA	26	26	2	0	162.1	704	156	85	79	16	6	2	4	64	0	135	10	1	11	9	.550	0	0-	—	4.38
2000 New Orleans	AAA	16	15	0	0	105.1	437	95	46	43	6	7	1	3	38	1	81	0	1	4	5	.444	0	0-	—	3.67
1999 Houston	NL	5	1	0	2	10.1	52	17	11	11	4	0	0	0	5	0	8	0	0	0	1	.000	0	0-0	—	9.58
2000 Houston	NL	16	16	2	0	105	453	104	66	60	14	3	1	3	42	1	89	1	0	6	6	.500	0	0-0	—	5.14
2 ML YEARS		21	17	2	2	115.1	505	121	77	71	18	3	1	3	47	1	97	1	0	6	7	.462	0	0-0	—	5.54

Alan Mills

Pitches: Right Bats: Both Pos: RP-41   Ht: 6'1" Wt: 195 Born: 10/18/66 Age: 34

		HOW MUCH HE PITCHED						WHAT HE GAVE UP												THE RESULTS						
Year Team	Lg	G	GS	CG	GF	IP	BFP	H	R	ER	HR	SH	SF	HB	TBB	IBB	SO	WP	Bk	W	L	Pct.	ShO	Sv-Op	Hld	ERA
2000 Frederick *	A+	1	1	0	0	2	8	2	1	1	0	0	0	0	0	0	1	0	0	0	0	—	0	0-	—	4.50
1990 New York	AL	36	0	0	18	41.2	200	48	21	19	4	4	1	1	33	6	24	3	0	1	5	.167	0	0-2	3	4.10
1991 New York	AL	6	2	0	3	16.1	72	16	9	8	1	0	1	0	8	0	11	2	0	1	1	.500	0	0-0	—	4.41
1992 Baltimore	AL	35	3	0	12	103.1	428	78	33	30	5	6	5	1	54	10	60	2	0	10	4	.714	0	2-3	2	2.61
1993 Baltimore	AL	45	0	0	18	100.1	421	80	39	36	14	4	6	4	51	5	68	3	0	5	4	.556	0	4-7	4	3.23
1994 Baltimore	AL	47	0	0	16	45.1	199	43	26	26	7	1	1	2	24	2	44	2	0	3	3	.500	0	2-4	14	5.16
1995 Baltimore	AL	21	0	0	1	23	118	30	20	19	4	0	1	2	18	4	16	1	0	3	0	1.000	0	0-1	1	7.43
1996 Baltimore	AL	49	0	0	23	54.2	233	40	26	26	10	3	2	1	35	2	50	6	0	3	2	.600	0	3-8	9	4.28
1997 Baltimore	AL	39	0	0	11	38.2	192	41	23	21	5	4	1	1	33	1	32	2	0	2	3	.400	0	0-0	7	4.89
1998 Baltimore	AL	72	0	0	13	77	327	55	32	32	8	2	3	1	50	8	57	4	0	3	4	.429	0	2-5	19	3.74
1999 Los Angeles	NL	68	0	0	18	72.1	322	70	33	30	10	3	4	4	43	4	49	3	0	3	4	.429	0	0-5	18	3.73
2000 LA-Bal		41	0	0	12	49.1	234	56	29	29	9	0	0	2	35	1	36	4	0	4	1	.800	0	2-2	8	5.29
2000 Los Angeles	NL	18	0	0	9	25.2	119	31	12	12	3	0	0	1	16	0	18	1	0	2	1	.667	0	1-1	2	4.21
Baltimore	AL	23	0	0	3	23.2	115	25	17	17	6	0	0	1	19	1	18	3	0	2	0	1.000	0	1-1	6	6.46
11 ML YEARS		459	5	0	145	622	2746	557	291	276	77	27	25	19	384	43	447	32	0	38	31	.551	0	15-37	85	3.99

Kevin Millwood

Pitches: Right Bats: Right Pos: SP-35; RP-1   Ht: 6'4" Wt: 220 Born: 12/24/74 Age: 26

		HOW MUCH HE PITCHED						WHAT HE GAVE UP												THE RESULTS						
Year Team	Lg	G	GS	CG	GF	IP	BFP	H	R	ER	HR	SH	SF	HB	TBB	IBB	SO	WP	Bk	W	L	Pct.	ShO	Sv-Op	Hld	ERA
1997 Atlanta	NL	12	8	0	2	51.1	227	55	26	23	1	3	5	2	21	1	42	1	0	5	3	.625	0	0-0	1	4.03
1998 Atlanta	NL	31	29	3	1	174.1	748	175	86	79	18	8	3	3	56	3	163	6	1	17	8	.680	1	0-0	1	4.08
1999 Atlanta	NL	33	33	2	0	228	906	168	80	68	24	9	3	4	59	2	205	5	0	18	7	.720	0	0-0	0	2.68
2000 Atlanta	NL	36	35	0	0	212.2	903	213	115	110	26	8	5	3	62	2	168	4	0	10	13	.435	0	0-0	0	4.66
4 ML YEARS		112	105	5	3	666.1	2784	611	307	280	69	28	16	12	198	8	578	16	1	50	31	.617	1	0-0	1	3.78

Eric Milton

Pitches: Left Bats: Left Pos: SP-33   Ht: 6'3" Wt: 220 Born: 8/4/75 Age: 25

		HOW MUCH HE PITCHED						WHAT HE GAVE UP												THE RESULTS						
Year Team	Lg	G	GS	CG	GF	IP	BFP	H	R	ER	HR	SH	SF	HB	TBB	IBB	SO	WP	Bk	W	L	Pct.	ShO	Sv-Op	Hld	ERA
1998 Minnesota	AL	32	32	1	0	172.1	772	195	113	108	25	2	6	2	70	0	107	1	0	8	14	.364	0	0-0	0	5.64
1999 Minnesota	AL	34	34	5	0	206.1	858	190	111	103	28	3	6	3	63	2	163	2	0	7	11	.389	2	0-0	0	4.49
2000 Minnesota	AL	33	33	0	0	200	849	205	123	108	35	4	6	7	44	0	160	5	0	13	10	.565	0	0-0	0	4.86
3 ML YEARS		99	99	6	0	578.2	2479	590	347	319	88	9	18	12	177	2	430	8	0	28	35	.444	2	0-0	0	4.96

Damon Minor

Bats: Left Throws: Left Pos: PH/PR-7; 1B-4   Ht: 6'7" Wt: 230 Born: 1/5/74 Age: 27

		BATTING																	BASERUNNING				PERCENTAGES		
Year Team	Lg	G	AB	H	2B	3B	HR	(Hm	Rd)	TB	R	RBI	TBB	IBB	SO	HBP	SH	SF	SB	CS	SB%	GDP	Avg	OBP	SLG
1996 Bellingham	A-	75	269	65	11	1	12	—	—	114	44	55	47	4	86	5	1	1	0	2	.00	5	.242	.363	.424

Year Team	Lg	G	AB	H	2B	3B	HR	(Hm	Rd)	TB	R	RBI	TBB	IBB	SO	HBP	SH	SF	SB	CS	SB%	GDP	Avg	OBP	SLG
1997 Bakersfield	A+	140	532	154	34	1	31	—	—	283	98	99	87	8	143	5	0	5	2	1	.67	6	.289	.391	.532
1998 Shreveport	AA	81	289	69	11	1	14	—	—	124	39	52	30	1	51	6	0	2	1	0	1.00	3	.239	.321	.429
San Jose	A+	48	176	50	10	1	7	—	—	83	26	36	28	0	40	2	0	1	0	1	1.00	1	.284	.386	.472
1999 Shreveport	AA	136	473	129	33	4	20	—	—	230	76	82	80	6	115	8	0	3	1	0	1.00	10	.273	.385	.486
2000 Fresno	AAA	133	482	140	27	1	30	—	—	259	84	106	87	4	97	1	0	9	0	0	—	11	.290	.394	.537
2000 San Francisco	NL	10	9	4	0	0	3	(2	1)	13	3	6	2	0	1	0	0	0	0	0	—	0	.444	.545	1.444

Ryan Minor

Bats: Right **Throws:** Right **Pos:** 3B-26; 1B-5; PH/PR-3 **Ht:** 6'7" **Wt:** 245 **Born:** 1/5/74 **Age:** 27

Year Team	Lg	G	AB	H	2B	3B	HR	(Hm	Rd)	TB	R	RBI	TBB	IBB	SO	HBP	SH	SF	SB	CS	SB%	GDP	Avg	OBP	SLG
2000 Orioles *	R	3	13	2	1	0	1	—	—	6	2	4	1	0	6	0	0	0	0	0	—	0	.154	.214	.462
Frederick *	A+	2	9	3	0	0	0	—	—	3	3	0	0	0	4	0	0	0	0	0	—	0	.333	.333	.333
Rochester *	AAA	68	241	71	9	1	14	—	—	124	33	48	32	2	57	5	0	7	1	4	.20	4	.295	.379	.515
1998 Baltimore	AL	9	14	6	1	0	0	(0	0)	7	3	1	0	0	3	0	0	0	0	0	—	0	.429	.429	.500
1999 Baltimore	AL	46	124	24	7	0	3	(3	0)	40	13	10	8	0	43	0	0	1	1	0	1.00	1	.194	.241	.323
2000 Baltimore	AL	32	84	11	1	0	0	(0	0)	12	4	3	3	0	20	1	0	0	0	0	—	0	.131	.170	.143
3 ML YEARS		87	222	41	9	0	3	(3	0)	59	20	14	11	0	66	1	0	1	1	0	1.00	1	.185	.226	.266

Doug Mirabelli

Bats: Right **Throws:** Right **Pos:** C-80; PH/PR-2 **Ht:** 6'1" **Wt:** 218 **Born:** 10/18/70 **Age:** 30

Year Team	Lg	G	AB	H	2B	3B	HR	(Hm	Rd)	TB	R	RBI	TBB	IBB	SO	HBP	SH	SF	SB	CS	SB%	GDP	Avg	OBP	SLG
1992 San Jose	A+	53	177	41	11	1	0	—	—	54	30	21	24	0	18	4	2	2	1	3	.25	7	.232	.333	.305
1993 San Jose	A+	113	371	100	19	2	1	—	—	126	58	48	72	1	55	4	2	4	4	0	.00	7	.270	.390	.340
1994 Shreveport	AA	85	255	56	8	0	4	—	—	76	23	24	36	5	48	0	2	0	3	1	.75	6	.220	.316	.298
1995 Phoenix	AAA	23	66	11	0	1	0	—	—	13	3	7	12	1	10	1	0	2	1	0	1.00	5	.167	.296	.197
Shreveport	AA	40	126	38	13	0	0	—	—	51	14	16	20	1	14	0	2	0	1	0	1.00	3	.302	.397	.405
1996 Phoenix	AAA	14	47	14	7	0	0	—	—	21	10	7	4	0	7	1	0	0	0	0	—	1	.298	.365	.447
Shreveport	AA	115	380	112	23	0	21	—	—	198	60	70	76	0	49	6	1	1	0	1	.00	9	.295	.419	.521
1997 Phoenix	AAA	100	332	88	23	2	8	—	—	139	49	48	58	2	69	7	3	1	1	2	.33	9	.265	.384	.419
1998 Fresno	AAA	85	265	69	12	2	13	—	—	124	45	53	52	6	55	3	3	1	2	0	1.00	9	.260	.386	.468
1999 Fresno	AAA	86	320	100	24	1	14	—	—	168	63	51	48	2	56	1	0	5	8	2	.80	6	.313	.398	.525
1996 San Francisco	NL	9	18	4	1	0	0	(0	0)	5	2	1	3	0	4	0	0	0	0	0	—	0	.222	.333	.278
1997 San Francisco	NL	6	7	1	0	0	0	(0	0)	1	0	0	1	0	3	0	0	0	0	0	—	0	.143	.250	.143
1998 San Francisco	NL	10	17	4	2	0	1	(1	0)	9	2	4	2	0	6	0	0	0	0	0	—	0	.235	.316	.529
1999 San Francisco	NL	33	87	22	6	0	1	(1	0)	31	10	10	9	1	25	1	0	1	0	0	—	6	.253	.327	.356
2000 San Francisco	NL	82	230	53	10	2	6	(2	4)	85	23	28	36	2	57	2	3	2	1	0	1.00	6	.230	.337	.370
5 ML YEARS		140	359	84	19	2	8	(4	4)	131	37	43	51	3	95	3	3	3	1	0	1.00	7	.234	.332	.365

Dave Mlicki

Pitches: Right **Bats:** Right **Pos:** SP-21; RP-3 **Ht:** 6'4" **Wt:** 205 **Born:** 6/8/68 **Age:** 33

Year Team	Lg	G	GS	CG	GF	IP	BFP	H	R	ER	HR	SH	SF	HB	TBB	IBB	SO	WP	Bk	W	L	Pct.	ShO	Sv-Op	Hld	ERA
2000 W Michigan *	A	1	1	0	0	6	21	1	0	0	0	0	0	0	1	0	6	0	0	1	0	1.000	0	0- -	—	0.00
Toledo *	AAA	1	1	0	0	5.2	27	11	5	5	0	0	1	0	0	0	3	0	0	0	1	.000	0	0- -	—	7.94
1992 Cleveland	AL	4	4	0	0	21.2	101	23	14	12	3	2	0	1	16	0	16	1	0	0	2	.000	0	0-0	0	4.98
1993 Cleveland	AL	3	3	0	0	13.1	58	11	6	5	2	0	0	2	6	0	7	2	0	0	0	—	0	0-0	0	3.38
1995 New York	NL	29	25	0	1	160.2	696	160	82	76	23	8	5	4	54	2	123	5	1	9	7	.563	0	0-0	0	4.26
1996 New York	NL	51	2	0	16	90	393	95	46	33	9	8	3	6	33	8	83	7	0	6	7	.462	0	1-3	8	3.30
1997 New York	NL	32	32	1	0	193.2	838	194	89	86	21	3	6	5	76	7	157	5	1	8	12	.400	1	0-0	0	4.00
1998 NYM-LA	NL	30	30	3	0	181.1	789	188	102	92	23	8	7	7	63	5	117	10	0	8	7	.533	1	0-0	0	4.57
1999 LA-Det	AL	33	31	2	0	199	883	219	112	102	25	3	8	12	72	1	120	1	0	14	13	.519	0	0-0	1	4.61
2000 Detroit	AL	24	21	0	1	119.1	547	143	79	74	17	3	6	3	44	1	57	4	0	6	11	.353	0	0-0	0	5.58
1998 New York	NL	10	10	1	0	57	264	68	38	36	8	2	3	5	25	4	39	4	0	1	4	.200	0	0-0	0	5.68
Los Angeles	NL	20	20	2	0	124.1	525	120	64	56	15	6	4	2	38	1	78	6	0	7	3	.700	1	0-0	0	4.05
1999 Los Angeles	NL	2	0	0	0	7.1	33	10	4	4	1	0	0	0	2	0	1	1	0	0	0	1.000	0	0-0	1	4.91
Detroit	AL	31	31	2	0	191.2	850	209	108	98	24	3	8	12	70	1	119	0	0	14	12	.538	0	0-0	0	4.60
8 ML YEARS		206	148	6	18	979	4305	1033	530	480	123	35	35	40	364	24	680	35	2	51	59	.464	2	1-3	9	4.41

Brian Moehler

Pitches: Right **Bats:** Right **Pos:** SP-29 **Ht:** 6'3" **Wt:** 235 **Born:** 12/31/71 **Age:** 29

Year Team	Lg	G	GS	CG	GF	IP	BFP	H	R	ER	HR	SH	SF	HB	TBB	IBB	SO	WP	Bk	W	L	Pct.	ShO	Sv-Op	Hld	ERA
2000 W Michigan *	A	1	1	0	0	6.1	24	5	3	3	1	0	0	0	1	0	4	0	0	0	1	.000	0	0- -	—	4.26
1996 Detroit	AL	2	2	0	0	10.1	51	11	10	5	1	1	0	0	8	1	2	1	0	0	1	.000	0	0-0	0	4.35
1997 Detroit	AL	31	31	2	0	175.1	770	198	97	91	22	1	8	5	61	1	97	3	0	11	12	.478	1	0-0	0	4.67
1998 Detroit	AL	33	33	4	0	221.1	912	220	103	96	30	3	3	2	56	1	123	4	0	14	13	.519	3	0-0	0	3.90
1999 Detroit	AL	32	32	2	0	196.1	859	229	116	110	22	8	5	7	59	5	106	4	0	10	16	.385	2	0-0	0	5.04
2000 Detroit	AL	29	29	2	0	178	776	222	99	89	20	3	4	2	40	0	103	2	1	12	9	.571	0	0-0	0	4.50
5 ML YEARS		127	127	10	0	781.1	3368	880	425	391	95	16	20	16	224	8	431	14	1	47	51	.480	6	0-0	0	4.50

Chad Moeller

Bats: Right **Throws:** Right **Pos:** C-48; PH/PR-1 **Ht:** 6'3" **Wt:** 210 **Born:** 2/18/75 **Age:** 26

Year Team	Lg	G	AB	H	2B	3B	HR	(Hm	Rd)	TB	R	RBI	TBB	IBB	SO	HBP	SH	SF	SB	CS	SB%	GDP	Avg	OBP	SLG
1996 Elizabethtn	R+	17	59	21	4	0	4	—	—	37	17	13	18	0	9	2	0	0	1	2	.33	3	.356	.519	.627
1997 Fort Wayne	A	108	384	111	18	3	9	—	—	162	58	39	48	0	76	13	2	1	11	8	.58	8	.289	.386	.422

Year Team	Lg	G	AB	H	2B	3B	HR	(Hm	Rd)	TB	R	RBI	TBB	IBB	SO	HBP	SH	SF	SB	CS	SB%	GDP	Avg	OBP	SLG
1998 Fort Myers	A+	66	254	83	24	1	6	—	—	127	37	39	31	4	37	3	0	2	2	3	.40	8	.327	.406	.500
New Britain	AA	58	187	44	10	0	6	—	—	72	21	23	24	0	41	3	1	0	2	1	.67	4	.235	.332	.385
1999 New Britain	AA	89	250	62	11	3	4	—	—	91	29	24	21	1	44	6	1	4	0	0	—	7	.248	.317	.364
2000 Salt Lake	AAA	47	167	48	13	1	5	—	—	78	30	20	9	1	45	0	1	1	0	1	.00	6	.287	.322	.467
2000 Minnesota	AL	48	128	27	3	1	1	(1	0)	35	13	9	9	0	33	0	1	1	1	0	1.00	4	.211	.261	.273

Mike Mohler

Pitches: Left **Bats:** Right **Pos:** RP-24 **Ht:** 6'2" **Wt:** 208 **Born:** 7/26/68 **Age:** 32

Year Team	Lg	G	GS	CG	GF	IP	BFP	H	R	ER	HR	SH	SF	HB	TBB	IBB	SO	WP	Bk	W	L	Pct.	ShO	Sv-Op	Hld	ERA
2000 Buffalo *	AAA	3	0	0	2	6	23	3	0	0	0	0	0	0	3	0	3	0	0	0	0	—	0	0- —	—	0.00
Sacramento *	AAA	18	0	0	6	18	91	22	13	13	6	1	0	0	16	1	14	1	0	2	0	1.000	0	1- —	—	6.50
1993 Oakland	AL	42	9	0	4	64.1	290	57	45	40	10	5	2	2	44	4	42	0	1	1	6	.143	0	0-1	1	5.60
1994 Oakland	AL	1	0	0	0	2.1	14	2	3	2	1	0	0	0	2	0	4	0	0	0	1	.000	0	0-0	—	7.71
1995 Oakland	AL	28	0	0	6	23.2	100	16	8	8	0	1	0	0	18	1	15	1	0	1	1	.500	0	1-2	4	3.04
1996 Oakland	AL	72	0	0	30	81	352	79	36	33	9	6	4	1	41	6	64	9	0	6	3	.667	0	7-13	13	3.67
1997 Oakland	AL	62	10	0	16	101.2	462	116	65	58	11	9	7	7	54	8	66	4	0	1	10	.091	0	1-4	11	5.13
1998 Oakland	AL	57	0	0	16	61	277	70	38	35	6	3	2	4	26	3	42	3	1	3	3	.500	0	0-1	8	5.16
1999 St. Louis	NL	48	0	0	16	49.1	211	47	26	24	3	1	1	1	23	2	31	1	0	1	1	.500	0	1-2	6	4.38
2000 StL-Cle		24	0	0	7	20	102	27	21	20	2	0	0	2	15	1	10	2	0	1	2	.333	0	0-3	4	9.00
2000 St. Louis	NL	22	0	0	7	19	98	26	20	19	1	0	0	2	15	1	8	2	0	1	1	.500	0	0-2	4	9.00
Cleveland	AL	2	0	0	0	1	4	1	1	1	1	0	0	0	0	0	2	0	0	0	1	.000	0	0-1	0	9.00
8 ML YEARS		334	20	0	95	403.1	1808	414	242	220	42	25	16	17	223	25	274	20	2	14	27	.341	0	10-26	47	4.91

Ben Molina

Bats: Right **Throws:** Right **Pos:** C-127; DH-2; PH/PR-2 **Ht:** 5'11" **Wt:** 207 **Born:** 7/20/74 **Age:** 26

Year Team	Lg	G	AB	H	2B	3B	HR	(Hm	Rd)	TB	R	RBI	TBB	IBB	SO	HBP	SH	SF	SB	CS	SB%	GDP	Avg	OBP	SLG
1993 Angels	R	27	80	21	6	2	0	—	—	31	9	10	10	0	4	1	0	1	0	2	.00	1	.263	.348	.388
1994 Cedar Rapds	A	48	171	48	8	0	3	—	—	65	14	16	8	0	12	3	1	0	1	2	.33	3	.281	.324	.380
1995 Vancouver	AAA	1	2	0	0	0	0	—	—	0	0	0	0	0	1	0	0	0	0	0	—	0	.000	.000	.000
Cedar Rapds	A	39	133	39	9	0	4	—	—	60	15	17	5	0	11	1	1	1	1	1	.50	4	.293	.367	.451
Lk Elsinore	A+	27	96	37	7	2	2	—	—	54	21	12	8	1	7	4	1	3	0	0	—	2	.385	.450	.563
1996 Midland	AA	108	365	100	21	2	8	—	—	149	45	54	25	1	25	6	4	5	0	0	.00	16	.274	.327	.408
1997 Lk Elsinore	A+	36	149	42	10	2	4	—	—	68	18	33	7	2	9	0	0	3	0	1	.00	5	.282	.308	.456
Midland	AA	29	106	35	8	0	6	—	—	61	18	30	10	0	7	0	0	2	0	0	—	5	.330	.381	.575
1998 Midland	AA	41	154	55	8	0	9	—	—	90	28	39	14	2	7	3	0	1	0	1	.00	7	.357	.419	.584
Vancouver	AAA	49	184	54	9	1	1	—	—	68	13	22	5	0	14	0	1	1	1	1	.50	6	.293	.311	.370
1999 Edmonton	AAA	65	241	69	16	0	7	—	—	106	28	41	15	1	17	6	1	4	1	2	.33	7	.286	.338	.440
1998 Anaheim	AL	2	1	0	0	0	0	(0	0)	0	0	0	0	0	0	0	0	0	0	0	—	0	.000	.000	.000
1999 Anaheim	AL	31	101	26	5	0	1	(0	1)	34	8	10	6	0	6	2	0	0	0	1	.00	5	.257	.312	.337
2000 Anaheim	AL	130	473	133	20	2	14	(11	3)	199	59	71	23	0	33	6	4	7	1	0	1.00	17	.281	.318	.421
3 ML YEARS		163	575	159	25	2	15	(11	4)	233	67	81	29	0	39	8	4	7	1	1	.50	22	.277	.317	.405

Gabe Molina

Pitches: Right **Bats:** Right **Pos:** RP-11 **Ht:** 6'1" **Wt:** 220 **Born:** 5/3/75 **Age:** 26

Year Team	Lg	G	GS	CG	GF	IP	BFP	H	R	ER	HR	SH	SF	HB	TBB	IBB	SO	WP	Bk	W	L	Pct.	ShO	Sv-Op	Hld	ERA
1996 Bluefield	R+	23	0	0	19	30	131	29	12	12	1	1	0	2	13	1	33	5	3	4	0	1.000	0	7- —	—	3.60
1997 Delmarva	A	46	0	0	31	91	364	59	24	22	3	6	1	3	32	5	119	7	2	8	6	.571	0	7- —	—	2.18
1998 Bowie	AA	47	0	0	38	61.2	256	48	24	23	5	3	1	3	27	0	75	5	1	3	2	.600	0	24- —	—	3.36
1999 Rochester	AAA	45	0	0	36	57.1	241	45	22	20	3	2	1	2	23	1	58	6	1	2	2	.500	0	18- —	—	3.14
2000 Rochester	AAA	18	4	0	9	27.1	120	30	16	15	3	2	0	0	10	0	26	2	1	1	2	.333	0	5- —	—	4.94
Richmond	AAA	9	0	0	8	10	41	7	5	4	2	0	2	0	3	0	9	0	1	1	0	1.000	0	3- —	—	3.60
1999 Baltimore	AL	20	0	0	7	23	102	22	19	17	4	0	0	0	16	1	14	4	0	1	2	.333	0	0-1	2	6.65
2000 Bal-Atl		11	0	0	4	15	85	28	18	15	3	0	3	1	10	0	9	0	0	0	0	—	0	0-0	1	9.00
2000 Baltimore	AL	9	0	0	3	13	74	25	14	13	2	0	2	0	9	0	8	0	0	0	0	—	0	0-0	1	9.00
Atlanta	NL	2	0	0	1	2	11	3	4	2	1	0	1	1	1	0	1	0	0	0	0	—	0	0-0	0	9.00
2 ML YEARS		31	0	0	11	38	187	50	37	32	7	0	3	1	26	1	23	4	0	1	2	.333	0	0-1	3	7.58

Raul Mondesi

Bats: Right **Throws:** Right **Pos:** RF-96; PH/PR-1 **Ht:** 5'11" **Wt:** 215 **Born:** 3/12/71 **Age:** 30

Year Team	Lg	G	AB	H	2B	3B	HR	(Hm	Rd)	TB	R	RBI	TBB	IBB	SO	HBP	SH	SF	SB	CS	SB%	GDP	Avg	OBP	SLG
1993 Los Angeles	NL	42	86	25	3	1	4	(2	2)	42	13	10	4	0	16	0	1	0	4	1	.80	1	.291	.322	.488
1994 Los Angeles	NL	112	434	133	27	8	16	(10	6)	224	63	56	16	5	78	2	0	2	11	8	.58	9	.306	.333	.516
1995 Los Angeles	NL	139	536	153	23	6	26	(13	13)	266	91	88	33	4	96	4	0	7	27	4	.87	7	.285	.328	.496
1996 Los Angeles	NL	157	634	188	40	7	24	(11	13)	314	98	88	32	9	122	5	0	2	14	7	.67	6	.297	.334	.495
1997 Los Angeles	NL	159	616	191	42	5	30	(16	14)	333	95	87	44	7	105	6	1	3	32	15	.68	11	.310	.360	.541
1998 Los Angeles	NL	148	580	162	26	4	30	(13	17)	288	85	90	30	4	112	3	0	4	16	10	.62	8	.279	.316	.497
1999 Los Angeles	NL	159	601	152	29	5	33	(18	15)	290	98	99	71	6	134	3	0	5	36	9	.80	3	.253	.332	.483
2000 Toronto	AL	96	388	105	22	2	24	(10	14)	203	78	67	32	0	73	3	0	3	22	6	.79	8	.271	.329	.523
8 ML YEARS		1012	3875	1109	212	39	187	(93	94)	1960	621	585	262	35	736	26	2	26	162	60	.73	53	.286	.333	.506

Steve Montgomery

Pitches: Right **Bats:** Right **Pos:** RP-7   **Ht:** 6'4" **Wt:** 200 **Born:** 12/25/70 **Age:** 30

Year Team	Lg	G	GS	CG	GF	IP	BFP	H	R	ER	HR	SH	SF	HB	TBB	IBB	SO	WP	Bk	W	L	Pct.	ShO	Sv-Op	Hld	ERA
2000 Las Vegas *	AAA	1	1	0	0	0.2	4	2	2	2	0	0	0	0	0	0	1	0	0	0	1	.000	0	0- -	—	27.00
Rancho Cuc *	A+	6	0	0	0	6	29	8	7	5	0	1	1	0	2	0	8	1	0	0	1	.000	0	0- -	—	7.50
1996 Oakland	AL	8	0	0	0	13.2	71	18	14	14	5	0	0	0	13	2	8	3	0	1	0	1.000	0	0-0	0	9.22
1997 Oakland	AL	4	0	0	0	6.1	35	10	7	7	2	0	1	0	8	2	1	0	0	0	1	.000	0	0-0	1	9.95
1999 Philadelphia	NL	53	0	0	21	64.2	268	54	25	24	10	1	0	0	31	3	55	4	0	1	5	.167	0	3-3	11	3.34
2000 San Diego	NL	7	0	0	0	5.2	27	6	6	5	3	1	0	0	4	0	3	0	0	0	2	.000	0	0- -	—	7.94
4 ML YEARS		72	0	0	22	90.1	401	88	52	50	20	2	1	0	56	7	67	7	0	2	8	.200	0	3-3	13	4.98

Trey Moore

Pitches: Left **Bats:** Left **Pos:** SP-8   **Ht:** 6'0" **Wt:** 190 **Born:** 10/2/72 **Age:** 28

Year Team	Lg	G	GS	CG	GF	IP	BFP	H	R	ER	HR	SH	SF	HB	TBB	IBB	SO	WP	Bk	W	L	Pct.	ShO	Sv-Op	Hld	ERA
1994 Bellingham	A-	11	10	1	0	61.2	247	48	18	18	4	0	2	2	24	0	73	4	0	5	2	.714	0	0- -	—	2.63
1995 Riverside	A+	24	24	0	0	148.1	605	122	65	51	6	2	5	2	58	1	134	6	1	14	6	.700	0	0- -	—	3.09
1996 Port City	AA	11	11	0	0	53.2	265	73	54	46	6	2	5	0	33	0	42	4	1	1	6	.143	0	0- -	—	7.71
Lancaster	A+	15	15	2	0	94.1	413	106	57	43	10	2	0	7	31	0	77	7	0	7	5	.583	0	0- -	—	4.10
1997 Harrisburg	AA	27	27	2	0	162.2	701	152	91	75	15	6	3	10	66	1	137	4	0	11	6	.647	2	0- -	—	4.15
1998 Ottawa	AAA	3	3	0	0	13	59	18	8	8	1	0	1	0	4	0	8	1	0	1	1	.500	0	0- -	—	5.54
2000 Ottawa	AAA	12	12	1	0	58.1	250	56	36	27	4	4	2	1	18	0	43	0	0	3	2	.600	0	0- -	—	4.17
1998 Montreal	NL	13	11	0	1	61	277	78	37	34	5	1	3	1	17	3	35	2	0	2	5	.286	0	0-0	0	5.02
2000 Montreal	NL	8	8	0	0	35.1	178	55	31	26	7	2	0	4	21	1	24	1	1	1	5	.167	0	0-0	0	6.62
2 ML YEARS		21	19	0	1	96.1	455	133	68	60	12	3	3	5	38	4	59	3	1	3	10	.231	0	0-0	0	5.61

Melvin Mora

Bats: R **Throws:** R **Pos:** SS-96; CF-16; LF-12; PH/PR-8; 2B-5; 3B-4; RF-3   **Ht:** 5'10" **Wt:** 180 **Born:** 2/2/72 **Age:** 29

Year Team	Lg	G	AB	H	2B	3B	HR	(Hm	Rd)	TB	R	RBI	TBB	IBB	SO	HBP	SH	SF	SB	CS	SB%	GDP	Avg	OBP	SLG
1992 Astros	R	49	144	32	3	0	0	—	—	35	28	8	18	0	16	5	0	1	16	3	.84	2	.222	.327	.243
1993 Asheville	A	108	365	104	22	2	2	—	—	136	66	31	36	0	46	9	5	8	20	13	.61	7	.285	.356	.373
1994 Osceola	A+	118	425	120	29	4	8	—	—	181	57	46	37	1	60	10	3	3	24	16	.60	8	.282	.352	.426
1995 Jackson	AA	123	467	139	32	0	3	—	—	180	63	45	32	1	57	9	7	7	22	11	.67	11	.298	.350	.385
Tucson	AAA	2	5	3	0	1	0	—	—	5	3	1	2	1	0	0	0	0	3	0	1.00	0	.600	.714	1.000
1996 Tucson	AAA	62	228	64	11	2	3	—	—	88	35	26	17	1	27	1	3	4	3	5	.38	7	.281	.328	.386
Jackson	AA	70	255	73	6	1	5	—	—	96	36	23	14	1	23	6	1	2	4	7	.36	4	.286	.336	.376
1997 New Orleans	AAA	119	370	95	15	3	2	—	—	122	55	38	47	0	52	11	9	2	7	7	.50	7	.257	.356	.330
1998 St. Lucie	A+	17	55	15	0	0	0	—	—	15	5	8	5	0	9	0	1	0	1	1	.50	0	.273	.328	.273
Norfolk	AAA	11	28	5	1	0	0	—	—	6	5	2	5	0	7	0	2	0	0	0	—	0	.179	.303	.214
1999 Norfolk	AAA	82	304	92	17	2	8	—	—	137	55	36	41	0	54	7	4	4	18	8	.69	8	.303	.393	.451
2000 Norfolk	AAA	8	27	9	2	0	0	—	—	11	7	7	7	0	3	0	1	0	2	0	1.00	0	.333	.471	.407
1999 New York	NL	66	31	5	0	0	0	(0	0)	5	6	1	4	0	7	1	3	0	2	1	.67	0	.161	.278	.161
2000 NYM-Bal		132	414	114	22	5	8	(5	3)	170	60	47	35	3	80	6	4	5	12	11	.52	5	.275	.337	.411
2000 New York	NL	79	215	56	13	2	6	(4	2)	91	35	30	18	3	48	2	2	5	7	3	.70	3	.260	.317	.423
Baltimore	AL	53	199	58	9	3	2	(1	1)	79	25	17	17	0	32	4	2	0	5	8	.38	2	.291	.359	.397
2 ML YEARS		198	445	119	22	5	8	(5	3)	175	66	48	39	3	87	7	7	5	14	12	.54	5	.267	.333	.393

David Moraga

Pitches: Left **Bats:** Left **Pos:** RP-4   **Ht:** 6'0" **Wt:** 185 **Born:** 7/8/75 **Age:** 25

Year Team	Lg	G	GS	CG	GF	IP	BFP	H	R	ER	HR	SH	SF	HB	TBB	IBB	SO	WP	Bk	W	L	Pct.	ShO	Sv-Op	Hld	ERA
1994 Expos	R	14	0	0	7	23.2	100	23	11	4	0	3	1	0	8	1	13	4	2	3	5	.375	0	2- -	—	1.52
1995 Wst Plm Bch	A+	3	3	0	0	16	75	20	7	7	0	0	0	0	10	0	10	0	0	1	1	.500	0	0- -	—	3.94
Albany	A	25	24	1	0	147.2	620	136	63	44	6	4	6	1	46	0	109	10	0	8	8	.500	0	0- -	—	2.68
1996 Wst Plm Bch	A+	29	20	1	1	125.2	560	138	74	64	6	4	7	4	50	0	96	12	0	7	10	.412	0	0- -	—	4.58
1997 Wst Plm Bch	A+	13	7	0	3	47.2	207	50	27	26	3	1	2	1	18	0	37	6	0	1	4	.200	0	0- -	—	4.91
1998 Jupiter	A+	25	0	0	11	45	180	37	16	14	2	5	2	1	9	0	38	3	0	5	2	.714	0	0- -	—	2.80
Harrisburg	AA	19	4	0	5	40	182	42	27	22	3	2	1	3	22	2	23	5	0	1	4	.200	0	1- -	—	4.95
1999 Ottawa	AAA	4	3	0	0	16	76	24	14	11	4	1	2	0	5	0	10	1	0	1	2	.333	0	0- -	—	6.19
Jupiter	A+	23	23	2	0	137.2	575	124	63	56	8	4	0	4	44	0	91	6	0	8	6	.571	2	0- -	—	3.66
Harrisburg	AA	1	0	0	0	3	11	1	0	0	0	0	0	1	0	0	0	0	0	1	0	1.000	0	0- -	—	0.00
2000 Harrisburg	AA	12	12	1	0	71.1	299	67	28	27	2	2	1	1	24	1	39	0	2	7	3	.700	0	0- -	—	3.41
Carolina	AA	8	8	3	0	59.1	243	52	18	7	3	3	1	3	11	0	53	2	0	3	3	.500	0	0- -	—	1.06
Colo Sprngs	AAA	6	6	2	0	31.1	147	50	27	27	6	1	0	1	7	0	6	0	0	4	1	.800	0	0- -	—	7.76
2000 Mon-Col	NL	4	0	0	2	2.2	22	10	12	12	1	1	2	1	2	0	2	1	0	0	0	—	0	0-0	0	40.50
2000 Montreal	NL	3	0	0	1	1.2	14	6	7	7	0	1	2	0	2	0	2	1	0	0	0	—	0	0-0	0	37.80
Colorado	NL	1	0	0	1	1	8	4	5	5	1	0	0	1	0	0	0	0	0	0	0	—	0	0-0	0	45.00

Willie Morales

Bats: Right **Throws:** Right **Pos:** C-3   **Ht:** 5'11" **Wt:** 185 **Born:** 9/7/72 **Age:** 28

Year Team	Lg	G	AB	H	2B	3B	HR	(Hm	Rd)	TB	R	RBI	TBB	IBB	SO	HBP	SH	SF	SB	CS	SB%	GDP	Avg	OBP	SLG
1993 Sou Oregon	A-	60	208	56	16	0	1	—	—	75	34	27	19	2	36	4	1	4	0	3	.00	2	.269	.336	.361
1994 W Michigan	A	111	380	101	26	0	13	—	—	166	47	51	36	4	64	3	3	2	3	5	.38	12	.266	.333	.437
1995 Modesto	A+	109	419	116	32	0	4	—	—	160	49	60	28	1	75	7	2	4	1	4	.20	13	.277	.330	.382
1996 Huntsville	AA	108	377	110	24	0	18	—	—	188	54	73	38	2	67	7	4	6	0	2	.00	11	.292	.362	.499
1997 Huntsville	AA	36	136	37	11	0	3	—	—	57	19	24	17	0	24	0	0	2	1	0	1.00	4	.272	.346	.419
Edmonton	AAA	56	179	52	12	0	5	—	—	79	23	35	11	0	27	0	3	3	0	2	.00	4	.291	.326	.441
1998 Edmonton	AAA	73	242	47	13	0	5	—	—	75	25	30	17	0	47	1	1	1	0	1	.00	8	.194	.249	.310

147

Year Team	Lg	G	AB	H	2B	3B	HR	(Hm	Rd)	TB	R	RBI	TBB	IBB	SO	HBP	SH	SF	SB	CS	SB%	GDP	Avg	OBP	SLG
BATTING																			**BASERUNNING**				**PERCENTAGES**		
1999 Vancouver	AAA	5	14	2	1	0	0	—	—	3	2	2	1	0	4	0	1	1	0	0	—		.143	.188	.214
Midland	AA	102	343	96	27	0	16	—	—	171	43	71	24	0	54	6	2	4	2	0	1.00	8	.280	.334	.499
2000 Rochester	AAA	73	249	62	12	1	6	—	—	94	21	23	12	0	58	0	2	1	0	3	.00	3	.249	.282	.378
2000 Baltimore	AL	3	11	3	1	0	0	(0	0)	4	1	0	0	0	3	0	0	0	0	0	—		.273	.273	.364

Mickey Morandini

Bats: Left **Throws:** Right **Pos:** 2B-120; PH/PR-8   **Ht:** 5'11" **Wt:** 180 **Born:** 4/22/66 **Age:** 35

Year Team	Lg	G	AB	H	2B	3B	HR	(Hm	Rd)	TB	R	RBI	TBB	IBB	SO	HBP	SH	SF	SB	CS	SB%	GDP	Avg	OBP	SLG
BATTING																			**BASERUNNING**				**PERCENTAGES**		
1990 Philadelphia	NL	25	79	19	4	0	1	(1	0)	26	9	3	6	0	19	0	2	0	3	0	1.00	1	.241	.294	.329
1991 Philadelphia	NL	98	325	81	11	4	1	(1	0)	103	38	20	29	0	45	2	6	2	13	2	.87	7	.249	.313	.317
1992 Philadelphia	NL	127	422	112	8	8	3	(2	1)	145	47	30	25	2	64	0	6	2	8	3	.73	4	.265	.305	.344
1993 Philadelphia	NL	120	425	105	19	9	3	(2	1)	151	57	33	34	2	73	5	4	2	13	2	.87	7	.247	.309	.355
1994 Philadelphia	NL	87	274	80	16	5	2	(1	1)	112	40	26	34	5	33	4	4	0	10	5	.67	1	.292	.378	.409
1995 Philadelphia	NL	127	494	140	34	7	6	(3	3)	206	65	49	42	3	80	9	4	1	9	6	.60	11	.283	.350	.417
1996 Philadelphia	NL	140	539	135	24	6	3	(2	1)	180	64	32	49	0	87	9	5	4	26	5	.84	15	.250	.321	.334
1997 Philadelphia	NL	150	553	163	40	2	1	(1	0)	210	83	39	62	0	91	8	12	5	16	13	.55	8	.295	.371	.380
1998 Chicago	NL	154	582	172	20	4	8	(4	4)	224	93	53	72	4	84	9	4	2	13	1	.93	14	.296	.380	.385
1999 Chicago	NL	144	456	110	18	5	4	(3	1)	150	60	37	48	2	61	6	7	4	6	6	.50	10	.241	.319	.329
2000 Phi-Tor		126	409	105	15	4	0	(0	0)	128	41	29	36	1	77	4	7	1	6	2	.75	13	.257	.322	.313
2000 Philadelphia	NL	91	302	76	13	3	0	(0	0)	95	31	22	29	1	54	4	5	1	5	2	.71	11	.252	.324	.315
Toronto	AL	35	107	29	2	1	0	(0	0)	33	10	7	7	0	23	0	2	0	1	0	1.00	2	.271	.316	.308
11 ML YEARS		1298	4558	1222	209	54	32	(20	12)	1635	597	351	437	19	714	56	61	23	123	45	.73	94	.268	.338	.359

Mike Mordecai

Bats: R **Throws:** R **Pos:** 3B-58; SS-10; 2B-9; PH/PR-9; 1B-3   **Ht:** 5'10" **Wt:** 185 **Born:** 12/13/67 **Age:** 33

Year Team	Lg	G	AB	H	2B	3B	HR	(Hm	Rd)	TB	R	RBI	TBB	IBB	SO	HBP	SH	SF	SB	CS	SB%	GDP	Avg	OBP	SLG
BATTING																			**BASERUNNING**				**PERCENTAGES**		
1994 Atlanta	NL	4	4	1	0	0	1	(1	0)	4	1	3	1	0	0	0	0	0	0	0	—	0	.250	.400	1.000
1995 Atlanta	NL	69	75	21	6	0	3	(1	2)	36	10	11	9	0	16	0	2	1	0	0	—	0	.280	.353	.480
1996 Atlanta	NL	66	108	26	5	0	2	(0	2)	37	12	8	9	1	24	0	4	1	1	0	1.00	1	.241	.297	.343
1997 Atlanta	NL	61	81	14	2	1	0	(0	0)	18	8	3	6	0	16	0	1	1	0	1	.00	4	.173	.227	.222
1998 Montreal	NL	73	119	24	4	2	3	(1	2)	41	12	10	9	0	20	0	2	0	1	0	1.00	2	.202	.258	.345
1999 Montreal	NL	109	226	53	10	2	5	(4	1)	82	29	25	20	0	31	1	1	2	2	5	.29	1	.235	.297	.363
2000 Montreal	NL	86	169	48	16	0	4	(2	2)	76	20	16	12	0	34	1	1	0	2	2	.50	1	.284	.335	.450
7 ML YEARS		468	782	187	43	5	18	(9	9)	294	92	76	66	1	141	2	11	5	6	8	.43	9	.239	.298	.376

Mike Morgan

Pitches: Right **Bats:** Right **Pos:** RP-56; SP-4   **Ht:** 6'2" **Wt:** 220 **Born:** 10/8/59 **Age:** 41

Year Team	Lg	G	GS	CG	GF	IP	BFP	H	R	ER	HR	SH	SF	HB	TBB	IBB	SO	WP	Bk	W	L	Pct.	ShO	Sv-Op	Hld	ERA
HOW MUCH HE PITCHED								**WHAT HE GAVE UP**												**THE RESULTS**						
1978 Oakland	AL	3	3	1	0	12.1	60	19	12	10	1	1	0	0	8	0	0	0	0	0	3	.000	0	0-0	0	7.30
1979 Oakland	AL	13	13	2	0	77.1	368	102	57	51	7	4	4	3	50	0	17	7	0	2	10	.167	0	0-0	0	5.94
1982 New York	AL	30	23	2	2	150.1	661	167	77	73	15	2	4	2	67	5	71	6	0	7	11	.389	0	0-0	0	4.37
1983 Toronto	AL	16	4	0	2	45.1	198	48	26	26	6	0	1	0	21	0	22	3	0	0	3	.000	0	0-0	0	5.16
1985 Seattle	AL	2	2	0	0	6	33	11	8	8	2	0	0	0	5	0	2	1	0	1	1	.500	0	0-0	0	12.00
1986 Seattle	AL	37	33	9	2	216.1	951	243	122	109	24	4	3	4	86	3	116	8	1	11	17	.393	1	1-1	0	4.53
1987 Seattle	AL	34	31	8	2	207	898	245	117	107	25	8	5	5	53	3	85	11	0	12	17	.414	2	0-0	0	4.65
1988 Baltimore	AL	22	10	2	6	71.1	299	70	45	43	8	1	0	1	23	1	29	5	0	1	6	.143	0	0-1	0	5.43
1989 Los Angeles	NL	40	19	0	7	152.2	604	130	51	43	6	8	6	2	33	8	72	6	0	8	11	.421	0	0-1	1	2.53
1990 Los Angeles	NL	33	33	6	0	211	891	216	100	88	19	11	4	5	60	5	106	4	1	11	15	.423	4	0-0	0	3.75
1991 Los Angeles	NL	34	33	5	1	236.1	949	197	85	73	12	10	4	6	61	10	140	6	0	14	10	.583	1	1-1	0	2.78
1992 Chicago	NL	34	34	6	0	240	966	203	80	68	14	10	5	3	79	10	123	11	0	16	8	.667	1	0-0	0	2.55
1993 Chicago	NL	32	32	1	0	207.2	883	206	100	93	15	11	5	7	74	4	111	8	2	10	15	.400	1	0-0	0	4.03
1994 Chicago	NL	15	15	1	0	80.2	380	111	65	60	12	7	6	4	35	2	57	5	0	2	10	.167	0	0-0	0	6.69
1995 ChC-StL	NL	21	21	1	0	131.1	548	133	56	52	12	12	5	6	34	2	61	6	0	7	7	.500	0	0-0	0	3.56
1996 StL-Cin	NL	23	23	0	0	130.1	567	146	72	67	16	6	7	1	47	0	74	2	0	6	11	.353	0	0-0	0	4.63
1997 Cincinnati	NL	31	30	1	0	162	688	165	91	86	13	9	2	8	49	6	103	7	0	9	12	.429	0	0-0	0	4.78
1998 Min-ChC		23	22	0	0	120.2	524	138	62	56	21	3	3	8	39	2	60	1	0	4	3	.571	0	0-0	0	4.18
1999 Texas	AL	34	25	1	1	140	632	184	108	97	25	3	5	7	48	2	61	3	1	13	10	.565	0	0-1	0	6.24
2000 Arizona	NL	60	4	0	15	101.2	448	123	55	55	10	7	4	1	40	5	56	0	0	5	5	.500	0	5-6	5	4.87
1995 Chicago	NL	4	4	0	0	24.2	100	19	8	6	2	2	0	1	9	1	15	0	0	2	1	.667	0	0-0	0	2.19
St. Louis	NL	17	17	1	0	106.2	448	114	48	46	10	10	5	5	25	1	46	6	0	5	6	.455	0	0-0	0	3.88
1996 St. Louis	NL	18	18	0	0	103	452	118	63	60	14	5	6	0	40	0	55	2	0	4	8	.333	0	0-0	0	5.24
Cincinnati	NL	5	5	0	0	27.1	115	28	9	7	2	1	1	1	7	0	19	0	0	2	3	.400	0	0-0	0	2.30
1998 Minnesota	AL	18	17	0	0	98	412	108	41	38	13	0	3	7	24	1	50	1	0	4	2	.667	0	0-0	0	3.49
Chicago	NL	5	5	0	0	22.2	112	30	21	18	8	3	0	1	15	1	10	0	0	0	1	.000	0	0-0	0	7.15
20 ML YEARS		537	410	46	38	2700.1	11548	2857	1389	1265	261	120	73	70	912	72	1366	100	5	139	185	.429	10	8-11	7	4.22

Hal Morris

Bats: L **Throws:** L **Pos:** 1B-54; PH/PR-49; DH-1; LF-1; RF-1   **Ht:** 6'2" **Wt:** 195 **Born:** 4/9/65 **Age:** 36

Year Team	Lg	G	AB	H	2B	3B	HR	(Hm	Rd)	TB	R	RBI	TBB	IBB	SO	HBP	SH	SF	SB	CS	SB%	GDP	Avg	OBP	SLG
BATTING																			**BASERUNNING**				**PERCENTAGES**		
1988 New York	AL	15	20	2	0	0	0	(0	0)	2	1	0	0	0	9	0	0	0	0	0	—	0	.100	.100	.100
1989 New York	AL	15	18	5	0	0	0	(0	0)	5	2	4	1	0	4	0	0	0	0	0	—	2	.278	.316	.278
1990 Cincinnati	NL	107	309	105	22	3	7	(3	4)	154	50	36	21	4	32	1	3	2	9	3	.75	12	.340	.381	.498
1991 Cincinnati	NL	136	478	152	33	1	14	(9	5)	229	72	59	46	7	61	1	5	7	10	4	.71	4	.318	.374	.479
1992 Cincinnati	NL	115	395	107	21	3	6	(1	5)	152	41	53	45	8	53	2	2	2	6	6	.50	12	.271	.347	.385
1993 Cincinnati	NL	101	379	120	18	0	7	(2	5)	159	48	49	34	4	51	2	0	2	2	2	.50	5	.317	.371	.420
1994 Cincinnati	NL	112	436	146	30	4	10	(5	5)	214	60	78	34	8	62	5	2	6	6	2	.75	16	.335	.385	.491

		BATTING																		BASERUNNING				PERCENTAGES		
Year Team	Lg	G	AB	H	2B	3B	HR	(Hm	Rd)	TB	R	RBI	TBB	IBB	SO	HBP	SH	SF		SB	CS	SB%	GDP	Avg	OBP	SLG
1995 Cincinnati	NL	101	359	100	25	2	11	(6	5)	162	53	51	29	7	58	1	1	1		1	1	.50	10	.279	.333	.451
1996 Cincinnati	NL	142	528	165	32	4	16	(7	9)	253	82	80	50	5	76	5	5	6		7	5	.58	12	.313	.374	.479
1997 Cincinnati	NL	96	333	92	20	1	1	(1	0)	117	42	33	23	2	43	3	4	1		3	1	.75	10	.276	.328	.351
1998 Kansas City	AL	127	472	146	27	2	1	(0	1)	180	50	40	32	6	52	1	4	7		1	0	1.00	15	.309	.350	.381
1999 Cincinnati	NL	80	102	29	9	0	0	(0	0)	38	10	16	10	0	21	0	0	0		0	0	—	1	.284	.348	.373
2000 Cin-Det		99	169	47	9	1	3	(1	2)	67	24	14	31	4	26	1	2	1		0	0	—	6	.278	.391	.396
2000 Cincinnati	NL	59	63	14	2	1	2	(1	1)	24	9	6	12	3	10	1	1	1		0	0	—	3	.222	.351	.381
Detroit	AL	40	106	33	7	0	1	(0	1)	43	15	8	19	1	16	0	1	0		0	0	—	3	.311	.416	.406
13 ML YEARS		1246	3998	1216	246	21	76	(37	39)	1732	535	513	356	55	548	22	28	39		45	24	.65	105	.304	.361	.433

Jim Morris

Pitches: Left **Bats:** Left **Pos:** RP-16   **Ht:** 6'3" **Wt:** 215 **Born:** 1/19/64 **Age:** 37

		HOW MUCH HE PITCHED						WHAT HE GAVE UP											THE RESULTS					
Year Team	Lg	G	GS	CG	GF	IP	BFP	H	R	ER	HR	SH	SF	HB	TBB	IBB	SO	WP	Bk	W	L	Pct.	ShO	Sv-Op	Hld	ERA
1983 Paintsville	R+	13	13	0	0	67	—	58	50	38	11	—	—	0	42	0	75	13	1	3	6	.333	0	0- -	—	5.10
1984 Beloit	A	24	22	1	0	112.1	510	107	80	63	8	7	3	1	79	1	109	13	1	8	9	.471	0	0- -	—	5.05
1985 Beloit	A	1	0	0	1	3	9	0	0	0	0	0	0	0	0	0	4	0	0	0	0	—	0	1- -	—	0.00
Stockton	A+	19	13	0	2	73	—	85	63	49	3	—	—	2	57	2	43	7	0	5	6	.455	0	0- -	—	6.04
1987 Stockton	A+	4	0	0	0	12	60	6	5	1	1	0	0	0	12	0	9	0	0	1	0	1.000	0	0- -	—	0.75
1989 Sarasota	A+	2	0	0	1	2.2	14	3	3	3	0	0	1	0	2	0	4	1	0	0	0	—	0	0- -	—	10.13
1999 Orlando	AA	3	0	0	2	5	22	6	1	1	0	0	0	0	1	0	6	1	1	0	0	—	0	1- -	—	1.80
Durham	AAA	18	0	0	5	23	103	21	14	14	3	0	0	1	19	0	16	2	0	3	1	.750	0	0- -	—	5.48
2000 Durham	AAA	1	0	0	0	1	6	1	1	1	1	0	0	0	2	0	1	0	0	0	0	—	0	0- -	—	9.00
1999 Tampa Bay	AL	5	0	0	3	4.2	21	3	3	3	1	0	0	1	2	0	3	0	0	0	0	—	0	0-0	0	5.79
2000 Tampa Bay	AL	16	0	0	3	10.1	48	10	9	5	1	1	0	0	7	1	10	1	0	0	0	—	0	0-0	0	4.35
2 ML YEARS		21	0	0	6	15	69	13	12	8	2	1	0	1	9	1	13	1	0	0	0	—	0	0-0	0	4.80

Matt Morris

Pitches: Right **Bats:** Right **Pos:** RP-31   **Ht:** 6'5" **Wt:** 210 **Born:** 8/9/74 **Age:** 26

		HOW MUCH HE PITCHED						WHAT HE GAVE UP											THE RESULTS					
Year Team	Lg	G	GS	CG	GF	IP	BFP	H	R	ER	HR	SH	SF	HB	TBB	IBB	SO	WP	Bk	W	L	Pct.	ShO	Sv-Op	Hld	ERA
2000 Arkansas *	AA	2	2	0	0	7	31	8	5	5	0	0	0	0	4	0	7	0	0	0	0	—	0	0- -	—	6.43
Memphis *	AAA	3	3	0	0	14.2	67	20	13	13	2	1	2	1	6	1	8	0	0	1	2	.333	0	0- -	—	7.98
1997 St. Louis	NL	33	33	3	0	217	900	208	88	77	12	11	7	7	69	2	149	5	3	12	9	.571	0	0-0	0	3.19
1998 St. Louis	NL	17	17	2	0	113.2	468	101	37	32	8	6	1	3	42	6	79	3	0	7	5	.583	1	0-0	0	2.53
2000 St. Louis	NL	31	0	0	12	53	226	53	22	21	3	3	1	2	17	1	34	0	0	3	3	.500	0	4-7	7	3.57
3 ML YEARS		81	50	5	12	383.2	1594	362	147	130	23	20	9	12	128	9	262	8	3	22	17	.564	1	4-7	7	3.05

Warren Morris

Bats: Left **Throws:** Right **Pos:** 2B-134; PH/PR-12   **Ht:** 5'11" **Wt:** 179 **Born:** 1/11/74 **Age:** 27

		BATTING																		BASERUNNING				PERCENTAGES		
Year Team	Lg	G	AB	H	2B	3B	HR	(Hm	Rd)	TB	R	RBI	TBB	IBB	SO	HBP	SH	SF		SB	CS	SB%	GDP	Avg	OBP	SLG
1997 Charlotte	A+	128	494	151	27	9	12	—	—	232	78	75	62	3	100	7	3	1		16	5	.76	6	.306	.390	.470
Okla City	AAA	8	32	7	1	0	1	—	—	11	3	3	3	0	5	0	0	0		0	0	—	0	.219	.286	.344
1998 Tulsa	AA	95	390	129	22	5	14	—	—	203	59	73	43	2	63	4	1	2		12	7	.63	11	.331	.401	.521
Carolina	AA	44	151	50	8	3	5	—	—	79	28	30	24	1	34	1	0	3		5	2	.71	2	.331	.419	.523
1999 Pittsburgh	NL	147	511	147	20	3	15	(9	6)	218	65	73	59	3	88	2	4	5		3	7	.30	12	.288	.360	.427
2000 Pittsburgh	NL	144	528	137	31	2	3	(3	0)	181	68	43	65	3	78	2	8	3		7	10	.41	7	.259	.341	.343
2 ML YEARS		291	1039	284	51	5	18	(12	6)	399	133	116	124	6	166	4	12	8		10	17	.37	19	.273	.351	.384

Danny Mota

Pitches: Right **Bats:** Right **Pos:** RP-4   **Ht:** 6'0" **Wt:** 180 **Born:** 10/9/75 **Age:** 25

		HOW MUCH HE PITCHED						WHAT HE GAVE UP											THE RESULTS					
Year Team	Lg	G	GS	CG	GF	IP	BFP	H	R	ER	HR	SH	SF	HB	TBB	IBB	SO	WP	Bk	W	L	Pct.	ShO	Sv-Op	Hld	ERA
1995 Yankees	R	14	0	0	9	32.2	133	27	9	8	2	4	0	2	4	0	35	6	3	2	3	.400	0	0- -	—	2.20
1996 Oneonta	A-	10	0	0	8	10	42	10	5	5	0	0	0	0	2	0	11	0	1	0	1	.000	0	7- -	—	4.50
1997 Greensboro	A	20	0	0	9	29.2	111	17	6	6	1	0	0	0	11	1	30	0	0	2	0	1.000	0	1- -	—	1.82
Oneonta	A-	27	0	0	25	28.1	119	21	8	7	0	1	0	0	16	0	40	0	0	1	0	1.000	0	17- -	—	2.22
1998 Fort Wayne	A	25	0	0	20	32	135	24	14	8	2	3	0	2	8	1	39	0	1	4	3	.571	0	7- -	—	2.25
Fort Myers	A+	19	4	0	9	47.1	206	45	21	15	3	1	3	0	22	0	49	6	1	3	5	.375	0	2- -	—	2.85
1999 Fort Myers	A+	11	0	0	3	18.2	79	19	5	5	0	1	1	0	5	0	22	0	0	1	1	.500	0	1- -	—	2.41
New Britain	AA	6	0	0	5	12.2	52	11	5	5	2	1	0	0	5	1	12	0	0	1	0	1.000	0	0- -	—	3.55
2000 Fort Myers	A+	29	1	0	13	48.1	209	38	20	11	0	1	3	1	23	5	52	5	0	2	2	.500	0	4- -	—	2.05
New Britain	AA	24	0	0	16	28.1	110	19	13	9	0	0	1	1	8	1	40	0	0	3	1	.750	0	3- -	—	2.86
Salt Lake	AAA	4	0	0	0	5.2	23	5	1	1	0	0	1	0	1	0	5	0	0	0	0	—	0	0- -	—	1.59
2000 Minnesota	AL	4	0	0	3	5.1	28	10	5	5	1	0	0	0	3	1	3	1	0	0	0	—	0	0-0	0	8.44

Guillermo Mota

Pitches: Right **Bats:** Right **Pos:** RP-29   **Ht:** 6'4" **Wt:** 205 **Born:** 7/25/73 **Age:** 27

		HOW MUCH HE PITCHED						WHAT HE GAVE UP											THE RESULTS					
Year Team	Lg	G	GS	CG	GF	IP	BFP	H	R	ER	HR	SH	SF	HB	TBB	IBB	SO	WP	Bk	W	L	Pct.	ShO	Sv-Op	Hld	ERA
1997 Cape Fear	A	25	23	0	0	126	528	135	65	61	8	2	3	4	33	0	112	1	2	5	10	.333	0	0- -	—	4.36
1998 Jupiter	A+	20	0	0	13	41	149	18	6	3	0	2	1	2	6	0	27	0	0	3	2	.600	0	2- -	—	0.66
Harrisburg	AA	12	0	0	8	17	60	10	2	2	0	0	0	0	2	0	19	2	0	2	0	1.000	0	4- -	—	1.06
1999 Ottawa	AAA	14	0	0	10	19	76	16	6	4	0	4	1	0	5	0	17	0	0	2	0	1.000	0	5- -	—	1.89
2000 Ottawa	AAA	35	0	0	21	63	257	49	16	16	4	1	0	2	31	3	35	1	0	4	5	.444	0	7- -	—	2.29
1999 Montreal	NL	51	0	0	18	55.1	243	54	24	18	5	3	3	2	25	3	27	1	1	2	4	.333	0	0-1	3	2.93
2000 Montreal	NL	29	0	0	7	30	126	27	21	20	3	1	1	2	12	0	24	1	1	1	1	.500	0	0-0	5	6.00
2 ML YEARS		80	0	0	25	85.1	369	81	45	38	8	4	4	4	37	3	51	2	2	3	5	.375	0	0-1	8	4.01

Chad Mottola

Bats: Right **Throws:** Right **Pos:** RF-3 — **Ht:** 6'3" **Wt:** 215 **Born:** 10/15/71 **Age:** 29

Year Team	Lg	G	AB	H	2B	3B	HR	(Hm	Rd)	TB	R	RBI	TBB	IBB	SO	HBP	SH	SF	SB	CS	SB%	GDP	Avg	OBP	SLG
1992 Billings	R+	57	213	61	8	3	12	—	—	111	53	37	25	0	43	0	0	0	12	3	.80	4	.286	.361	.521
1993 Winston-Sal	A+	137	493	138	25	3	21	—	—	232	76	91	62	2	109	2	0	3	13	7	.65	9	.280	.361	.471
1994 Chattanooga	AA	118	402	97	19	1	7	—	—	139	44	41	30	1	68	1	2	2	9	12	.43	12	.241	.294	.346
1995 Chattanooga	AA	51	181	53	13	1	10	—	—	98	32	39	13	0	32	1	0	1	1	2	.33	2	.293	.342	.541
Indianapols	AAA	69	239	62	11	1	8	—	—	99	40	37	20	0	50	0	1	1	8	1	.89	6	.259	.315	.414
1996 Indianapols	AAA	103	362	95	24	3	9	—	—	152	45	47	21	3	93	4	0	4	9	6	.60	10	.262	.307	.420
1997 Chattanooga	AA	46	174	63	9	3	5	—	—	93	35	32	16	1	23	1	1	5	7	1	.88	3	.362	.408	.534
Indianapols	AAA	83	284	82	10	6	7	—	—	125	33	45	16	2	43	4	0	2	12	4	.75	6	.289	.333	.440
1998 Indianapols	AAA	5	12	5	0	0	1	—	—	8	2	2	4	0	0	0	0	0	0	2	.00	0	.417	.563	.667
Tulsa	AA	8	26	13	1	0	1	—	—	17	9	7	10	1	1	0	0	0	3	0	1.00	0	.500	.639	.654
Oklahoma	AAA	74	257	68	13	1	2	—	—	89	29	22	18	1	49	1	0	2	8	3	.73	7	.265	.313	.346
1999 Charlotte	AAA	140	511	164	32	4	20	—	—	264	95	94	60	1	83	3	0	7	18	6	.75	7	.321	.391	.517
2000 Syracuse	AAA	134	505	156	25	3	33	—	—	286	85	102	37	2	99	5	0	11	30	15	.67	11	.309	.359	.566
1996 Cincinnati	NL	35	79	17	3	0	3	(1	2)	29	10	6	6	1	16	0	0	0	2	2	.50	0	.215	.271	.367
2000 Toronto	AL	3	9	2	0	0	0	(0	0)	2	1	2	0	0	4	1	0	0	0	0	—	0	.222	.300	.222
2 ML YEARS		38	88	19	3	0	3	(1	2)	31	11	8	6	1	20	1	0	0	2	2	.50	0	.216	.274	.352

James Mouton

Bats: R **Throws:** R **Pos:** PH/PR-46; CF-23; LF-19; RF-7 — **Ht:** 5'9" **Wt:** 175 **Born:** 12/29/68 **Age:** 32

Year Team	Lg	G	AB	H	2B	3B	HR	(Hm	Rd)	TB	R	RBI	TBB	IBB	SO	HBP	SH	SF	SB	CS	SB%	GDP	Avg	OBP	SLG
1994 Houston	NL	99	310	76	11	0	2	(1	1)	93	43	16	27	0	69	5	2	1	24	5	.83	6	.245	.315	.300
1995 Houston	NL	104	298	78	18	2	4	(2	2)	112	42	27	25	1	59	4	3	1	25	8	.76	5	.262	.326	.376
1996 Houston	NL	122	300	79	15	1	3	(2	1)	105	40	34	38	2	55	0	2	3	21	9	.70	9	.263	.343	.350
1997 Houston	NL	86	180	38	9	1	3	(1	2)	58	24	23	18	0	30	2	2	2	9	7	.56	3	.211	.287	.322
1998 San Diego	NL	55	63	12	2	1	0	(0	0)	16	8	7	7	1	11	0	0	1	4	3	.57	3	.190	.268	.254
1999 Montreal	NL	95	122	32	5	1	2	(1	1)	45	18	13	18	1	31	2	3	1	6	2	.75	2	.262	.364	.369
2000 Milwaukee	NL	87	159	37	7	1	2	(1	1)	52	28	17	30	0	43	3	4	1	13	4	.76	5	.233	.363	.327
7 ML YEARS		648	1432	352	67	7	16	(8	8)	481	203	137	163	5	298	16	16	10	102	38	.73	33	.246	.328	.336

Lyle Mouton

Bats: R **Throws:** R **Pos:** LF-22; PH/PR-20; RF-4; CF-1 — **Ht:** 6'4" **Wt:** 230 **Born:** 5/13/69 **Age:** 32

Year Team	Lg	G	AB	H	2B	3B	HR	(Hm	Rd)	TB	R	RBI	TBB	IBB	SO	HBP	SH	SF	SB	CS	SB%	GDP	Avg	OBP	SLG
2000 Indianapols *	AAA	52	197	60	23	0	12	—	—	119	33	51	23	2	41	4	0	6	4	1	.80	7	.305	.378	.604
1995 Chicago	AL	58	179	54	16	0	5	(4	1)	85	23	27	19	0	46	2	0	1	1	0	1.00	7	.302	.373	.475
1996 Chicago	AL	87	214	63	8	1	7	(4	3)	94	25	39	22	4	50	2	0	3	3	0	1.00	3	.294	.361	.439
1997 Chicago	AL	88	242	65	9	0	5	(4	1)	89	26	23	14	1	66	1	0	3	4	4	.50	8	.269	.308	.368
1998 Baltimore	AL	18	39	12	2	0	2	(0	2)	20	5	7	4	0	8	0	0	0	0	0	—	0	.308	.372	.513
1999 Milwaukee	NL	14	17	3	1	0	1	(1	0)	7	2	3	2	0	3	0	0	0	0	0	—	0	.176	.263	.412
2000 Milwaukee	NL	42	97	27	7	1	2	(2	0)	42	14	16	10	0	29	1	0	1	1	0	1.00	2	.278	.349	.433
6 ML YEARS		307	788	224	43	2	22	(15	7)	337	95	115	71	5	202	6	0	8	9	4	.69	20	.284	.345	.428

Jamie Moyer

Pitches: Left **Bats:** Left **Pos:** SP-26 — **Ht:** 6'0" **Wt:** 175 **Born:** 11/18/62 **Age:** 38

Year Team	Lg	G	GS	CG	GF	IP	BFP	H	R	ER	HR	SH	SF	HB	TBB	IBB	SO	WP	Bk	W	L	Pct.	ShO	Sv-Op	Hld	ERA
1986 Chicago	NL	16	16	1	0	87.1	395	107	52	49	10	3	3	3	42	1	45	3	3	7	4	.636	1	0-0	0	5.05
1987 Chicago	NL	35	33	1	1	201	899	210	127	114	28	14	7	5	97	9	147	11	2	12	15	.444	0	0-0	0	5.10
1988 Chicago	NL	34	30	3	1	202	855	212	84	78	20	14	4	4	55	7	121	4	0	9	15	.375	1	0-2	0	3.48
1989 Texas	AL	15	15	1	0	76	337	84	51	41	10	1	4	2	33	0	44	1	0	4	9	.308	0	0-0	0	4.86
1990 Texas	AL	33	10	1	6	102.1	447	115	59	53	6	1	7	4	39	4	58	1	0	2	6	.250	0	0-0	1	4.66
1991 St. Louis	NL	8	7	0	1	31.1	142	38	21	20	5	4	2	1	16	0	20	2	1	0	5	.000	0	0-0	0	5.74
1993 Baltimore	AL	25	25	3	0	152	630	154	63	58	11	3	1	6	38	2	90	1	1	12	9	.571	1	0-0	0	3.43
1994 Baltimore	AL	23	23	0	0	149	631	158	81	79	23	2	2	2	38	3	87	1	0	5	7	.417	0	0-0	0	4.77
1995 Baltimore	AL	27	18	0	3	115.2	483	117	70	67	18	5	3	3	30	0	65	0	0	8	6	.571	0	0-0	0	5.21
1996 Bos-Sea	AL	34	21	0	1	160.2	703	177	86	71	23	7	6	2	46	5	79	3	1	13	3	.813	0	0-0	1	3.98
1997 Seattle	AL	30	30	2	0	188.2	787	187	82	81	21	6	1	7	43	2	113	3	0	17	5	.773	0	0-0	0	3.86
1998 Seattle	AL	34	34	4	0	234.1	974	234	99	92	23	3	10	4	42	2	158	3	1	15	9	.625	0	0-0	0	3.53
1999 Seattle	AL	32	32	4	0	228	945	235	108	98	23	2	9	4	48	1	137	3	0	14	8	.636	0	0-0	0	3.87
2000 Seattle	AL	26	26	0	0	154	678	173	103	94	22	3	3	3	53	2	98	4	1	13	10	.565	0	0-0	0	5.49
1996 Boston	AL	23	10	0	1	90	405	111	50	45	14	4	3	1	27	2	50	2	1	7	1	.875	0	0-0	0	4.50
Seattle	AL	11	11	0	0	70.2	298	66	36	26	9	3	3	1	19	3	29	1	0	6	2	.750	0	0-0	0	3.31
14 ML YEARS		372	320	20	13	2082.1	8906	2201	1086	995	243	76	48	61	620	38	1262	40	10	131	111	.541	6	0-2	2	4.30

Bill Mueller

Bats: Both **Throws:** Right **Pos:** 3B-145; PH/PR-16; 2B-2 — **Ht:** 5'10" **Wt:** 180 **Born:** 3/17/71 **Age:** 30

Year Team	Lg	G	AB	H	2B	3B	HR	(Hm	Rd)	TB	R	RBI	TBB	IBB	SO	HBP	SH	SF	SB	CS	SB%	GDP	Avg	OBP	SLG
1996 San Francisco	NL	55	200	66	15	1	0	(0	0)	83	31	19	24	0	26	1	1	2	0	0	—	1	.330	.401	.415
1997 San Francisco	NL	128	390	114	26	3	7	(5	2)	167	51	44	48	1	71	3	6	6	4	3	.57	10	.292	.369	.428
1998 San Francisco	NL	145	534	157	27	0	9	(1	8)	211	93	59	79	1	83	1	3	5	3	3	.50	12	.294	.383	.395
1999 San Francisco	NL	116	414	120	24	0	2	(1	1)	150	61	36	65	1	52	3	8	2	4	2	.67	11	.290	.388	.363
2000 San Francisco	NL	153	560	150	29	4	10	(3	7)	217	97	55	52	0	62	6	7	6	4	2	.67	16	.268	.333	.388
5 ML YEARS		597	2098	607	121	8	28	(10	18)	828	333	213	268	3	294	14	25	21	15	10	.60	50	.289	.370	.395

Mark Mulder

Pitches: Left **Bats:** Left **Pos:** SP-27
Ht: 6'6" **Wt:** 200 **Born:** 8/5/77 **Age:** 23

Year Team	Lg	G	GS	CG	GF	IP	BFP	H	R	ER	HR	SH	SF	HB	TBB	IBB	SO	WP	Bk	W	L	Pct.	ShO	Sv-Op	Hld	ERA
1999 Vancouver	AAA	22	22	1	0	128.2	549	152	69	58	13	4	5	3	31	0	81	6	0	6	7	.462	0	0--	—	4.06
2000 Sacramento	AAA	2	2	0	0	8.1	44	15	11	5	1	0	0	0	4	0	6	1	0	1	1	.500	0	0--	—	5.40
2000 Oakland	AL	27	27	0	0	154	705	191	106	93	22	3	8	4	69	3	88	6	0	9	10	.474	0	0-0	0	5.44

Terry Mulholland

Pitches: Left **Bats:** Right **Pos:** RP-34; SP-20
Ht: 6'3" **Wt:** 220 **Born:** 3/9/63 **Age:** 38

Year Team	Lg	G	GS	CG	GF	IP	BFP	H	R	ER	HR	SH	SF	HB	TBB	IBB	SO	WP	Bk	W	L	Pct.	ShO	Sv-Op	Hld	ERA
1986 San Francisco	NL	15	10	0	1	54.2	245	51	33	30	3	5	1	1	35	2	27	6	0	1	7	.125	0	0--	—	4.94
1988 San Francisco	NL	9	6	2	1	46	191	50	20	19	3	5	0	1	7	0	18	1	0	2	1	.667	1	0-0	1	3.72
1989 SF-Phi	NL	25	18	2	4	115.1	513	137	66	63	8	7	1	4	36	3	66	3	0	4	7	.364	1	0-0	1	4.92
1990 Philadelphia	NL	33	26	6	2	180.2	746	172	78	67	15	7	12	4	42	7	75	7	2	9	10	.474	1	0-1	0	3.34
1991 Philadelphia	NL	34	34	8	0	232	956	231	100	93	15	11	6	3	49	2	142	3	0	16	13	.552	3	0-0	0	3.61
1992 Philadelphia	NL	32	32	12	0	229	937	227	101	97	14	10	7	3	46	3	125	3	0	13	11	.542	2	0-0	0	3.81
1993 Philadelphia	NL	29	28	7	0	191	786	177	80	69	20	5	4	3	40	2	116	5	0	12	9	.571	2	0-0	0	3.25
1994 New York	AL	24	19	2	4	120.2	542	150	94	87	24	3	4	3	37	1	72	5	0	6	7	.462	0	0-0	0	6.49
1995 San Francisco	NL	29	24	2	2	149	666	190	112	96	25	11	6	4	38	1	65	4	0	5	13	.278	0	0-0	0	5.80
1996 Phi-Sea		33	33	3	0	202.2	871	232	112	105	22	11	8	5	49	4	86	6	0	13	11	.542	0	0-0	0	4.66
1997 ChC-SF	NL	40	27	1	5	186.2	794	190	100	88	24	17	4	11	51	3	99	3	0	6	13	.316	0	0-0	0	4.24
1998 Chicago	NL	70	6	0	14	112	476	100	49	36	7	5	3	4	39	7	72	4	0	6	5	.545	0	3-5	19	2.89
1999 ChC-Atl	NL	42	24	0	7	170.1	736	201	95	83	21	9	4	1	45	6	83	3	0	10	8	.556	0	1-1	4	4.39
2000 Atlanta	NL	54	20	1	14	156.2	702	198	96	89	24	10	5	4	41	7	78	3	0	9	9	.500	0	1-3	3	5.11
1989 San Francisco	NL	5	1	0	2	11	51	15	5	5	0	0	0	0	4	0	6	0	0	0	0	—	0	0-0	1	4.09
Philadelphia	NL	20	17	2	2	104.1	462	122	61	58	8	7	1	4	32	3	60	3	0	4	7	.364	1	0-0	0	5.00
1996 Philadelphia	NL	21	21	3	0	133.1	571	157	74	69	17	6	5	3	21	1	52	5	0	8	7	.533	0	0-0	0	4.66
Seattle	AL	12	12	0	0	69.1	300	75	38	36	5	5	3	2	28	3	34	1	0	5	4	.556	0	0-0	0	4.67
1997 Chicago	NL	25	25	1	0	157	668	162	79	71	20	13	3	9	45	2	74	2	0	6	12	.333	0	0-0	0	4.07
San Francisco	NL	15	2	0	5	29.2	126	28	21	17	4	4	1	2	6	1	25	1	0	0	1	.000	0	0-0	1	5.16
1999 Chicago	NL	26	16	0	4	110	485	137	71	63	16	6	3	1	32	4	44	2	0	6	6	.500	0	0-0	0	5.15
Atlanta	NL	16	8	0	3	60.1	251	64	24	20	5	3	1	0	13	2	39	1	0	4	2	.667	0	1-1	3	2.98
14 ML YEARS		469	307	46	54	2146.2	9161	2306	1136	1022	225	116	65	49	555	48	1124	56	2	112	124	.475	10	5--	—	4.28

Scott Mullen

Pitches: Left **Bats:** Right **Pos:** RP-11
Ht: 6'2" **Wt:** 190 **Born:** 1/17/75 **Age:** 26

Year Team	Lg	G	GS	CG	GF	IP	BFP	H	R	ER	HR	SH	SF	HB	TBB	IBB	SO	WP	Bk	W	L	Pct.	ShO	Sv-Op	Hld	ERA
1996 Spokane	A-	15	15	0	0	80.1	352	78	45	35	6	1	2	8	29	0	78	1	0	5	6	.455	0	0--	—	3.92
1997 Lansing	A	16	16	0	0	92.1	391	90	46	38	14	0	3	4	31	0	78	2	1	5	2	.714	0	0--	—	3.70
Wilmington	A+	11	11	0	0	59.1	260	64	35	30	5	1	2	1	26	4	43	5	2	4	4	.500	0	0--	—	4.55
1998 Wilmington	A+	14	14	1	0	85.2	344	68	28	21	4	3	1	7	25	0	56	3	1	8	4	.667	1	0--	—	2.21
Wichita	AA	12	12	0	0	70	289	66	34	32	7	0	3	1	26	0	42	7	0	8	2	.800	0	0--	—	4.11
1999 Wichita	AA	9	9	0	0	49.1	216	47	28	22	2	1	4	1	18	1	30	3	0	4	3	.571	0	0--	—	4.01
Omaha	AAA	20	20	0	0	119.1	543	150	91	83	24	4	6	2	53	2	87	7	1	6	7	.462	0	0--	—	6.26
2000 Wichita	AA	33	1	0	16	73.1	299	65	27	26	5	3	1	1	26	1	61	3	0	3	2	.600	0	7--	—	3.19
Omaha	AAA	16	0	0	5	20.2	85	15	10	7	1	0	2	1	8	0	21	0	0	2	1	.667	0	0--	—	3.05
2000 Kansas City	AL	11	0	0	5	10.1	44	10	5	5	2	0	0	0	3	0	7	0	0	0	0	—	0	0-0	2	4.35

Mike Munoz

Pitches: Left **Bats:** Left **Pos:** RP-7
Ht: 6'2" **Wt:** 198 **Born:** 7/12/65 **Age:** 35

Year Team	Lg	G	GS	CG	GF	IP	BFP	H	R	ER	HR	SH	SF	HB	TBB	IBB	SO	WP	Bk	W	L	Pct.	ShO	Sv-Op	Hld	ERA
1989 Los Angeles	NL	3	0	0	1	2.2	14	5	5	5	1	0	0	0	2	0	3	0	0	0	0	—	0	0-0	0	16.88
1990 Los Angeles	NL	8	0	0	3	5.2	24	6	2	2	0	1	0	0	3	0	2	0	0	0	1	.000	0	0-1	2	3.18
1991 Detroit	AL	6	0	0	4	9.1	46	14	10	10	0	0	1	0	5	0	3	1	0	0	0	—	0	0-0	0	9.64
1992 Detroit	AL	65	0	0	15	48	210	44	16	16	3	4	2	0	25	6	23	2	0	1	2	.333	0	2-3	15	3.00
1993 Det-Col		29	0	0	10	21	101	25	14	11	2	3	2	0	15	4	17	2	0	2	2	.500	0	0-2	4	4.71
1994 Colorado	NL	57	0	0	8	45.2	200	37	22	19	3	2	1	0	31	5	32	2	0	4	2	.667	0	1-2	12	3.74
1995 Colorado	NL	64	0	0	19	43.2	208	54	38	36	9	2	2	1	27	0	37	5	0	2	4	.333	0	2-4	12	7.42
1996 Colorado	NL	54	0	0	7	44.2	203	55	33	33	4	3	1	1	16	2	45	0	0	2	2	.500	0	0-3	13	6.65
1997 Colorado	NL	64	0	0	16	45.2	192	52	25	23	4	2	0	2	13	0	26	3	0	3	3	.500	0	2-2	19	4.53
1998 Colorado	NL	40	0	0	13	41.1	189	53	32	26	2	1	1	1	16	2	24	1	0	2	2	.500	0	3-4	11	5.66
1999 Texas	AL	56	0	0	11	52.2	221	52	24	23	5	1	3	1	18	2	27	2	0	2	1	.667	0	1-3	10	3.93
2000 Texas	AL	7	0	0	2	4	25	11	6	6	1	1	0	0	3	1	1	0	0	0	1	.000	0	0-1	0	13.50
1993 Detroit	AL	8	0	0	3	3	19	4	2	1	0	0	0	0	6	1	0	0	0	0	1	.000	0	0-0	1	6.00
Colorado	NL	21	0	0	7	18	82	21	12	9	1	3	2	0	9	3	16	2	0	2	1	.667	0	0-2	1	4.50
12 ML YEARS		453	0	0	109	364.1	1633	408	227	210	34	18	15	4	174	22	240	18	0	18	20	.474	0	11-25	86	5.19

Peter Munro

Pitches: Right **Bats:** Right **Pos:** RP-6; SP-3
Ht: 6'2" **Wt:** 210 **Born:** 6/14/75 **Age:** 26

Year Team	Lg	G	GS	CG	GF	IP	BFP	H	R	ER	HR	SH	SF	HB	TBB	IBB	SO	WP	Bk	W	L	Pct.	ShO	Sv-Op	Hld	ERA
1995 Utica	A-	14	14	0	0	90	389	79	38	26	3	3	3	7	33	1	74	4	0	5	4	.556	0	0--	—	2.60
1996 Sarasota	A+	27	25	2	1	155	667	153	76	62	4	3	2	7	62	1	115	7	1	11	6	.647	2	1--	—	3.60
1997 Trenton	AA	22	22	1	0	116.1	506	113	76	64	12	10	6	8	47	0	109	6	3	7	10	.412	0	0--	—	4.95
1998 Pawtucket	AAA	18	17	0	0	106.2	450	111	49	48	10	2	5	4	35	2	75	8	0	5	4	.556	0	0--	—	4.05
Syracuse	AAA	8	8	0	0	44.2	213	58	42	37	7	2	0	2	23	2	42	4	0	2	5	.286	0	0--	—	7.46
1999 Syracuse	AAA	18	11	0	3	69.2	312	70	29	24	6	0	3	4	33	1	68	3	0	6	1	.857	0	0--	—	3.10

Year Team	Lg	G	GS	CG	GF	IP	BFP	H	R	ER	HR	SH	SF	HB	TBB	IBB	SO	WP	Bk	W	L	Pct.	ShO	Sv-Op	Hld	ERA
2000 Dunedin	A+	3	3	0	0	11.1	47	11	7	7	0	0	0	4	0		12	1	0	0	1	.000	0	0--	—	5.56
Syracuse	AAA	10	10	2	0	61.2	251	52	20	17	1	2	1	2	25	0	45	2	0	4	3	.571	0	0--	—	2.48
Oklahoma	AAA	5	5	1	0	31	136	27	17	16	3	0	1	3	14	0	15	1	0	1	2	.333	1	0--	—	4.65
1999 Toronto	AL	31	2	0	9	55.1	250	70	38	37	6	1	4	2	23	0	38	3	0	0	2	.000	0	0-1	4	6.02
2000 Toronto	AL	9	3	0	2	25.2	127	38	22	17	1	1	0	3	16	0	16	1	0	1	1	.500	0	0-0	0	5.96
2 ML YEARS		40	5	0	11	81	377	108	60	54	7	2	4	5	39	0	54	4	0	1	3	.250	0	0-1	4	6.00

Eric Munson

Bats: Left **Throws:** Right **Pos:** 1B-3   **Ht:** 6'3" **Wt:** 220 **Born:** 10/3/77 **Age:** 23

Year Team	Lg	G	AB	H	2B	3B	HR	(Hm	Rd)	TB	R	RBI	TBB	IBB	SO	HBP	SH	SF	SB	CS	SB%	GDP	Avg	OBP	SLG
1999 Lakeland	A+	2	6	2	0	0	0	—	—	2	0	1	1	0	1	0	0	0	0	0	—	0	.333	.429	.333
W Michigan	A	67	252	67	16	1	14	—	—	127	42	44	37	3	47	9	0	1	3	1	.75	4	.266	.378	.504
2000 Jacksonville	AA	98	365	92	21	4	15	—	—	166	52	68	39	5	96	18	0	6	5	2	.71	8	.252	.348	.455
2000 Detroit	AL	3	5	0	0	0	0	(0	0)	0	0	0	1	0	1	0	0	0	0	0	—	0	.000	.000	.000

Calvin Murray

Bats: Right **Throws:** Right **Pos:** CF-104; PH/PR-24; LF-2   **Ht:** 5'11" **Wt:** 190 **Born:** 7/30/71 **Age:** 29

Year Team	Lg	G	AB	H	2B	3B	HR	(Hm	Rd)	TB	R	RBI	TBB	IBB	SO	HBP	SH	SF	SB	CS	SB%	GDP	Avg	OBP	SLG
1993 Shreveport	AA	37	138	26	6	0	0	—	—	32	15	6	14	0	29	2	3	1	12	6	.67	0	.188	.271	.232
San Jose	A+	85	345	97	24	1	9	—	—	150	61	42	40	0	63	4	2	0	42	10	.81	4	.281	.362	.435
Phoenix	AAA	5	19	6	1	1	0	—	—	9	4	0	2	0	5	0	0	0	1	1	.50	0	.316	.381	.474
1994 Shreveport	AA	129	480	111	19	5	2	—	—	146	67	35	47	0	81	5	8	4	33	13	.72	4	.231	.304	.304
1995 Phoenix	AAA	13	50	9	1	0	4	—	—	22	8	10	4	0	6	0	1	1	2	2	.50	2	.180	.236	.440
Shreveport	AA	110	441	104	17	3	2	—	—	133	77	29	59	2	70	3	5	1	26	10	.72	5	.236	.329	.302
1996 Shreveport	AA	50	169	44	7	0	7	—	—	72	32	24	25	0	33	1	3	4	6	5	.55	5	.260	.352	.426
Phoenix	AAA	83	311	76	16	3	3	—	—	113	50	28	43	0	60	3	5	1	12	6	.67	1	.244	.341	.363
1997 Shreveport	AA	122	419	114	25	3	10	—	—	175	83	56	66	0	73	4	1	2	52	6	.90	7	.272	.375	.418
1998 Shreveport	AA	88	337	104	22	5	8	—	—	160	63	39	58	1	45	5	1	0	34	15	.69	8	.309	.418	.475
Fresno	AAA	33	90	21	3	1	3	—	—	35	16	5	12	0	18	0	1	0	3	1	.75	2	.233	.324	.389
1999 Fresno	AAA	130	548	183	31	7	23	—	—	297	122	73	49	3	88	3	4	6	42	14	.75	6	.334	.389	.542
1999 San Francisco	NL	15	19	5	2	0	0	(0	0)	7	1	5	2	0	4	0	0	0	1	0	1.00	0	.263	.333	.368
2000 San Francisco	NL	108	194	47	12	1	2	(1	1)	67	35	22	29	0	33	3	2	1	9	3	.75	0	.242	.348	.345
2 ML YEARS		123	213	52	14	1	2	(1	1)	74	36	27	31	0	37	3	2	1	10	3	.77	0	.244	.347	.347

Dan Murray

Pitches: Right **Bats:** Right **Pos:** RP-10   **Ht:** 6'1" **Wt:** 195 **Born:** 11/21/73 **Age:** 27

Year Team	Lg	G	GS	CG	GF	IP	BFP	H	R	ER	HR	SH	SF	HB	TBB	IBB	SO	WP	Bk	W	L	Pct.	ShO	Sv-Op	Hld	ERA
1995 Pittsfield	A-	22	0	0	19	32	145	24	17	7	2	0	1	1	16	3	34	3	0	0	6	.000	0	6--	—	1.97
1996 St. Lucie	A+	33	13	0	5	101.2	465	114	60	48	2	3	3	8	53	3	56	11	0	7	5	.583	0	0--	—	4.25
1997 St. Lucie	A+	30	24	4	3	156.1	682	150	75	60	4	5	3	10	55	3	91	13	0	12	10	.545	2	0--	—	3.45
1998 Binghamton	AA	27	27	1	0	164.1	681	153	64	58	13	3	2	8	54	2	159	5	0	11	6	.647	1	0--	—	3.18
1999 Norfolk	AAA	29	27	3	1	145	650	163	91	80	22	7	5	7	70	5	96	11	3	12	10	.545	1	0--	—	4.97
2000 Omaha	AAA	27	22	1	3	140.2	618	148	99	87	22	2	9	7	60	3	102	9	1	10	9	.526	1	1--	—	5.57
1999 NYM-KC		5	0	0	1	10.1	51	13	11	9	4	0	1	1	6	0	9	1	0	0	0	—	0	0-0	0	7.84
2000 Kansas City	AL	10	0	0	3	19.1	86	20	10	10	7	2	1	1	10	0	16	2	0	0	0	—	0	0-0	0	4.66
1999 New York	NL	1	0	0	1	2	12	4	3	3	0	0	1	0	2	0	1	1	0	0	0	—	0	0-0	0	13.50
Kansas City	AL	9	0	0	2	8.1	39	9	8	6	4	0	0	1	4	0	8	0	0	0	0	—	0	0-0	0	6.48
2 ML YEARS		15	0	0	4	29.2	137	33	21	19	11	2	2	2	16	0	25	3	0	0	0	—	0	0-0	0	5.76

Mike Mussina

Pitches: Right **Bats:** Both **Pos:** SP-34   **Ht:** 6'2" **Wt:** 185 **Born:** 12/8/68 **Age:** 32

Year Team	Lg	G	GS	CG	GF	IP	BFP	H	R	ER	HR	SH	SF	HB	TBB	IBB	SO	WP	Bk	W	L	Pct.	ShO	Sv-Op	Hld	ERA
1991 Baltimore	AL	12	12	2	0	87.2	349	77	31	28	7	3	2	1	21	0	52	3	1	4	5	.444	0	0-0	0	2.87
1992 Baltimore	AL	32	32	8	0	241	957	212	70	68	16	13	6	2	48	2	130	6	0	18	5	.783	4	0-0	0	2.54
1993 Baltimore	AL	25	25	3	0	167.2	693	163	84	83	20	6	4	3	44	2	117	5	0	14	6	.700	2	0-0	0	4.46
1994 Baltimore	AL	24	24	3	0	176.1	712	163	63	60	19	3	9	1	42	1	99	0	0	16	5	.762	0	0-0	0	3.06
1995 Baltimore	AL	32	32	7	0	221.2	882	187	86	81	24	2	1	1	50	4	158	2	0	19	9	.679	4	0-0	0	3.29
1996 Baltimore	AL	36	36	4	0	243.1	1039	264	137	130	31	4	4	3	69	0	204	3	0	19	11	.633	1	0-0	0	4.81
1997 Baltimore	AL	33	33	4	0	224.2	905	197	87	80	27	3	2	3	54	3	218	5	0	15	8	.652	4	0-0	0	3.20
1998 Baltimore	AL	29	29	4	0	206.1	835	189	85	80	22	6	3	4	41	0	175	10	0	13	10	.565	2	0-0	0	3.49
1999 Baltimore	AL	31	31	4	0	203.1	842	207	88	79	16	9	7	1	52	0	172	2	0	18	7	.720	0	0-0	0	3.50
2000 Baltimore	AL	34	34	6	0	237.2	987	236	105	100	28	8	6	3	46	0	210	3	0	11	15	.423	1	0-0	0	3.79
10 ML YEARS		288	288	45	0	2009.2	8201	1895	836	789	210	57	45	22	467	15	1535	39	1	147	81	.645	15	0-0	0	3.53

Greg Myers

Bats: Left **Throws:** Right **Pos:** C-28; DH-9; PH/PR-9   **Ht:** 6'2" **Wt:** 225 **Born:** 4/14/66 **Age:** 35

Year Team	Lg	G	AB	H	2B	3B	HR	(Hm	Rd)	TB	R	RBI	TBB	IBB	SO	HBP	SH	SF	SB	CS	SB%	GDP	Avg	OBP	SLG
1987 Toronto	AL	7	9	1	0	0	0	(0	0)	1	1	0	0	0	3	0	0	0	0	0	—	2	.111	.111	.111
1989 Toronto	AL	17	44	5	2	0	0	(0	0)	7	0	1	2	0	9	0	0	0	0	1	.00	2	.114	.152	.159
1990 Toronto	AL	87	250	59	7	1	5	(3	2)	83	33	22	22	0	33	0	1	4	0	1	.00	12	.236	.293	.332
1991 Toronto	AL	107	309	81	22	0	8	(5	3)	127	25	36	21	4	45	0	4	3	0	0	—	13	.262	.306	.411
1992 Tor-Cal	AL	30	78	18	7	0	1	(0	1)	28	4	13	5	0	11	0	1	2	0	0	—	2	.231	.271	.359
1993 California	AL	108	290	74	10	0	7	(4	3)	105	27	40	17	2	47	2	3	3	3	3	.50	8	.255	.298	.362

Year Team	Lg	G	AB	H	2B	3B	HR	(Hm	Rd)	TB	R	RBI	TBB	IBB	SO	HBP	SH	SF	SB	CS	SB%	GDP	Avg	OBP	SLG
1994 California	AL	45	126	31	6	0	2	(1	1)	43	10	8	10	3	27	0	5	1	0	2	.00	3	.246	.299	.341
1995 California	AL	85	273	71	12	2	9	(6	3)	114	35	38	17	3	49	1	1	2	0	1	.00	4	.260	.304	.418
1996 Minnesota	AL	97	329	94	22	3	6	(3	3)	140	37	47	19	3	52	0	0	5	0	0	—	6	.286	.320	.426
1997 Min-Atl	AL	71	174	45	11	1	5	(3	2)	73	24	29	17	2	32	0	0	2	0	0	—	11	.259	.321	.420
1998 San Diego	NL	69	171	42	10	0	4	(1	3)	64	19	20	17	1	36	0	0	1	0	0	—	4	.246	.312	.374
1999 SD-Atl	NL	84	200	53	6	0	5	(3	2)	74	19	24	26	4	30	0	1	1	0	0	—	6	.265	.348	.370
2000 Baltimore	AL	43	125	28	6	0	3	(1	2)	43	9	12	8	0	29	0	1	0	0	0	—	7	.224	.271	.344
1992 Toronto	AL	22	61	14	6	0	1	(0	1)	23	4	13	5	0	5	0	0	2	0	0	—	2	.230	.279	.377
California	AL	8	17	4	1	0	0	(0	0)	5	0	0	0	0	6	0	1	0	0	0	—	0	.235	.235	.294
1997 Minnesota	AL	62	165	44	11	1	5	(3	2)	72	24	28	16	2	29	0	0	2	0	0	—	4	.267	.328	.436
Atlanta	NL	9	9	1	0	0	0	(0	0)	1	0	1	1	0	3	0	1	0	0	0	—	0	.111	.200	.111
1999 San Diego	NL	50	128	37	4	0	3	(2	1)	50	9	15	13	2	14	0	0	0	0	0	—	0	.289	.355	.391
Atlanta	NL	34	72	16	2	0	2	(1	1)	24	10	9	13	2	16	0	0	0	0	0	—	1	.222	.337	.333
13 ML YEARS		850	2378	602	121	7	55	(30	25)	902	243	290	181	22	403	3	12	24	3	9	.25	80	.253	.304	.379

Mike Myers

Pitches: Left **Bats:** Left **Pos:** RP-78   **Ht:** 6'4" **Wt:** 214 **Born:** 6/26/69 **Age:** 32

Year Team	Lg	G	GS	CG	GF	IP	BFP	H	R	ER	HR	SH	SF	HB	TBB	IBB	SO	WP	Bk	W	L	Pct.	ShO	Sv-Op	Hld	ERA
1995 Fla-Det		13	0	0	5	8.1	42	11	7	7	1	0	1	2	7	0	4	0	0	1	0	1.000	0	0-1	1	7.56
1996 Detroit	AL	83	0	0	25	64.2	298	70	41	36	6	2	1	4	34	8	69	2	0	1	5	.167	0	6-8	17	5.01
1997 Detroit	AL	88	0	0	23	53.2	246	58	36	34	12	4	3	2	25	2	50	0	0	0	4	.000	0	2-5	18	5.70
1998 Milwaukee	NL	70	0	0	14	50	211	44	19	15	5	4	2	6	22	1	40	2	1	2	2	.500	0	1-3	23	2.70
1999 Milwaukee	NL	71	0	0	14	41.1	179	46	24	24	7	5	0	3	13	1	35	1	0	2	1	.667	0	0-3	14	5.23
2000 Colorado	NL	78	0	0	22	45.1	177	24	10	10	2	1	0	2	24	3	41	1	0	0	1	.000	0	1-2	15	1.99
1995 Florida	NL	2	0	0	2	2	9	1	0	0	0	0	0	0	3	0	3	0	0	0	0	—	0	0-0	0	0.00
Detroit	AL	11	0	0	3	6.1	33	10	7	7	1	0	1	2	4	0	4	0	0	1	0	1.000	0	0-1	1	9.95
6 ML YEARS		403	0	0	103	263.1	1153	253	137	126	33	16	7	19	125	15	239	6	1	6	13	.316	0	10-22	88	4.31

Rodney Myers

Pitches: Right **Bats:** Right **Pos:** RP-3   **Ht:** 6'1" **Wt:** 215 **Born:** 6/26/69 **Age:** 32

Year Team	Lg	G	GS	CG	GF	IP	BFP	H	R	ER	HR	SH	SF	HB	TBB	IBB	SO	WP	Bk	W	L	Pct.	ShO	Sv-Op	Hld	ERA
2000 Rancho Cuc *	A+	3	2	0	0	4	14	2	0	0	0	1	0	0	4	0	0	0	0	0	0	—	0	0--	0	0.00
1996 Chicago	NL	45	0	0	8	67.1	298	61	38	35	6	1	5	3	38	3	50	4	1	2	1	.667	0	0-0	1	4.68
1997 Chicago	NL	5	1	0	2	9	44	12	6	6	1	0	0	1	7	1	6	0	0	0	0	—	0	0-0	0	6.00
1998 Chicago	NL	12	0	0	3	18	82	26	14	14	3	0	0	0	6	0	15	1	0	0	0	—	0	0-1	0	7.00
1999 Chicago	NL	46	0	0	5	63.2	278	71	34	31	10	4	2	1	25	2	41	2	0	3	1	.750	0	0-1	8	4.38
2000 San Diego	NL	3	0	0	1	2	8	2	1	1	0	0	0	0	0	0	3	1	0	0	0	—	0	0-0	0	4.50
5 ML YEARS		111	1	0	19	160	710	172	93	87	20	5	7	5	76	6	115	8	1	5	2	.714	0	0-2	9	4.89

Aaron Myette

Pitches: Right **Bats:** Right **Pos:** RP-2   **Ht:** 6'4" **Wt:** 195 **Born:** 9/26/77 **Age:** 23

Year Team	Lg	G	GS	CG	GF	IP	BFP	H	R	ER	HR	SH	SF	HB	TBB	IBB	SO	WP	Bk	W	L	Pct.	ShO	Sv-Op	Hld	ERA
1997 Bristol	R+	9	8	1	0	47.1	215	39	28	19	9	0	0	7	20	0	50	2	1	4	3	.571	0	0--	—	3.61
Hickory	A	5	5	0	0	31.2	121	19	6	4	1	1	0	2	11	0	27	2	2	3	1	.750	0	0--	—	1.14
1998 Hickory	A	17	17	0	0	102	421	84	43	28	4	2	3	8	30	0	103	5	2	9	4	.692	0	0--	—	2.47
Winston-Sal	A+	6	6	1	0	44.2	178	32	14	10	4	1	0	1	14	0	54	0	0	4	2	.667	1	0--	—	2.01
1999 Birmingham	AA	28	28	0	0	164.2	711	138	76	67	19	2	3	15	77	0	135	6	1	12	7	.632	0	0--	—	3.66
2000 Birmingham	AA	3	3	0	0	15.1	68	11	7	6	1	0	0	2	8	0	21	1	0	2	0	1.000	0	0--	—	3.52
Charlotte	AAA	19	18	0	0	111.2	488	103	58	54	18	0	4	7	56	0	85	2	1	5	5	.500	0	0--	—	4.35
1999 Chicago	AL	4	3	0	0	15.2	80	17	11	11	2	0	0	2	14	1	11	2	0	0	2	.000	0	0-0	0	6.32
2000 Chicago	AL	2	0	0	1	2.2	12	0	0	0	0	0	0	0	4	0	1	0	0	0	0	—	0	0-0	0	0.00
2 ML YEARS		6	3	0	1	18.1	92	17	11	11	2	0	0	2	18	1	12	2	0	0	2	.000	0	0-0	0	5.40

Xavier Nady

Bats: Right **Throws:** Right **Pos:** PH/PR-1   **Ht:** 6'0" **Wt:** 180 **Born:** 11/14/78 **Age:** 22

Year Team	Lg	G	AB	H	2B	3B	HR	(Hm	Rd)	TB	R	RBI	TBB	IBB	SO	HBP	SH	SF	SB	CS	SB%	GDP	Avg	OBP	SLG
2000 San Diego	NL	1	1	1	0	0	0	(0	0)	1	1	0	0	0	0	0	0	0	0	0	—	0	1.000	1.000	1.000

Charles Nagy

Pitches: Right **Bats:** Left **Pos:** SP-11   **Ht:** 6'3" **Wt:** 200 **Born:** 5/5/67 **Age:** 34

Year Team	Lg	G	GS	CG	GF	IP	BFP	H	R	ER	HR	SH	SF	HB	TBB	IBB	SO	WP	Bk	W	L	Pct.	ShO	Sv-Op	Hld	ERA
2000 Akron *	AA	2	2	0	0	9	33	4	1	1	0	0	0	0	2	0	10	1	0	1	0	1.000	0	0--	—	1.00
Buffalo *	AAA	3	3	0	0	14.2	63	12	7	7	2	0	1	2	4	0	5	0	0	1	1	.500	0	0--	—	4.30
1990 Cleveland	AL	9	8	0	1	45.2	208	58	31	30	7	1	1	1	21	1	26	1	1	2	4	.333	0	0-0	0	5.91
1991 Cleveland	AL	33	33	6	0	211.1	914	228	103	97	15	5	9	6	66	7	109	6	2	10	15	.400	1	0-0	0	4.13
1992 Cleveland	AL	33	33	10	0	252	1018	245	91	83	11	6	9	6	57	1	169	7	0	17	10	.630	3	0-0	0	2.96
1993 Cleveland	AL	9	9	1	0	48.2	223	66	38	34	6	2	1	2	13	1	30	2	0	2	6	.250	0	0-0	0	6.29
1994 Cleveland	AL	23	23	3	0	169.1	717	175	76	65	15	2	2	5	48	1	108	5	1	10	8	.556	0	0-0	0	3.45
1995 Cleveland	AL	29	29	2	0	178	771	194	95	90	20	2	5	6	61	0	139	2	0	16	6	.727	1	0-0	0	4.55
1996 Cleveland	AL	32	32	5	0	222	952	217	91	84	21	2	4	3	61	2	167	7	0	17	5	.773	0	0-0	0	3.41
1997 Cleveland	AL	34	34	1	0	227	991	253	115	108	27	5	6	7	77	4	149	6	0	15	11	.577	1	0-0	0	4.28
1998 Cleveland	AL	33	33	2	0	210.1	930	234	139	122	34	8	6	9	66	12	120	3	0	15	10	.600	0	0-0	0	5.22
1999 Cleveland	AL	33	32	1	0	202	887	238	120	111	26	5	4	6	59	4	126	3	0	17	11	.607	0	0-0	0	4.95
2000 Cleveland	AL	11	11	0	0	57	267	71	53	52	15	5	2	2	21	2	41	1	0	2	7	.222	0	0-0	0	8.21
11 ML YEARS		279	277	31	1	1823.1	7847	1995	950	876	197	43	49	49	550	35	1184	42	4	123	93	.569	6	0-0	0	4.32

Joe Nathan

Pitches: Right **Bats:** Right **Pos:** SP-15; RP-5   **Ht:** 6'4" **Wt:** 195 **Born:** 11/22/74 **Age:** 26

		HOW MUCH HE PITCHED						WHAT HE GAVE UP												THE RESULTS						
Year Team	Lg	G	GS	CG	GF	IP	BFP	H	R	ER	HR	SH	SF	HB	TBB	IBB	SO	WP	Bk	W	L	Pct.	ShO	Sv-Op	Hld	ERA
1997 Salem-Keizr	A-	18	5	0	4	62	254	53	22	17	7	4	2	4	26	0	44	0	0	2	1	.667	0	2--	—	2.47
1998 Shreveport	AA	4	4	0	0	15.1	74	20	15	15	4	0	0	2	9	0	10	0	0	1	3	.250	0	0--	—	8.80
San Jose	A+	22	22	0	0	122	506	100	51	45	13	1	1	10	48	0	118	1	0	8	6	.571	0	0--	—	3.32
1999 Shreveport	AA	2	2	0	0	8.2	38	5	4	3	0	1	1	1	7	0	7	2	1	0	1	.000	0	0--	—	3.12
Fresno	AAA	13	13	1	0	74.2	324	68	44	37	11	3	1	5	36	0	82	6	1	6	4	.600	0	0--	—	4.46
2000 San Jose	A+	1	1	0	0	5	19	4	2	2	1	0	1	0	1	0	2	1	0	0	1	.000	0	0--	—	3.60
Bakersfield	A+	1	1	0	0	5.1	25	2	3	3	0	0	0	1	7	0	6	1	0	1	0	1.000	0	0--	—	5.06
Fresno	AAA	3	3	0	0	14.1	64	15	8	7	4	1	0	0	9	1	8	0	0	0	2	.000	0	0--	—	4.40
1999 San Francisco	NL	19	14	0	2	90.1	395	84	45	42	17	2	0	1	46	0	54	2	0	7	4	.636	0	1-1	0	4.18
2000 San Francisco	NL	20	15	0	0	93.1	426	89	63	54	12	5	5	4	63	4	61	5	0	5	2	.714	0	0-1	0	5.21
2 ML YEARS		39	29	0	2	183.2	821	173	108	96	29	7	5	5	109	4	115	7	0	12	6	.667	0	1-2	0	4.70

Joey Nation

Pitches: Left **Bats:** Left **Pos:** SP-2   **Ht:** 6'2" **Wt:** 205 **Born:** 9/28/78 **Age:** 22

		HOW MUCH HE PITCHED						WHAT HE GAVE UP												THE RESULTS						
Year Team	Lg	G	GS	CG	GF	IP	BFP	H	R	ER	HR	SH	SF	HB	TBB	IBB	SO	WP	Bk	W	L	Pct.	ShO	Sv-Op	Hld	ERA
1997 Danville	R+	8	8	0	0	26.1	107	24	11	8	1	0	0	1	5	0	41	1	0	1	2	.333	0	0--	—	2.73
1998 Macon	A	29	28	1	0	143	640	179	102	80	15	6	6	1	39	0	141	10	2	6	12	.333	0	0--	—	5.03
1999 Macon	A	6	6	0	0	27.1	118	27	10	9	1	0	1	1	9	0	31	2	1	1	1	.500	0	0--	—	2.96
Myrtle Bch	A+	19	17	0	0	96.1	401	88	51	47	7	2	4	2	37	0	87	4	0	5	4	.556	0	0--	—	4.39
Daytona	A+	2	2	0	0	13	47	8	2	2	0	0	0	0	2	0	11	0	0	2	0	1.000	0	0--	—	1.38
2000 West Tenn	AA	27	27	1	0	166	695	137	72	61	17	6	6	6	65	2	165	9	0	11	10	.524	0	0--	—	3.31
2000 Chicago	NL	2	2	0	0	11.2	55	12	9	9	2	1	1	2	8	0	8	0	0	0	2	.000	0	0--	0	6.94

Jaime Navarro

Pitches: Right **Bats:** Right **Pos:** SP-7; RP-5   **Ht:** 6'4" **Wt:** 250 **Born:** 3/27/68 **Age:** 33

		HOW MUCH HE PITCHED						WHAT HE GAVE UP												THE RESULTS						
Year Team	Lg	G	GS	CG	GF	IP	BFP	H	R	ER	HR	SH	SF	HB	TBB	IBB	SO	WP	Bk	W	L	Pct.	ShO	Sv-Op	Hld	ERA
2000 Colo Sprngs *	AAA	5	5	0	0	35.2	160	48	26	21	8	4	0	0	6	0	20	2	0	3	2	.600	0	0--	—	5.30
Buffalo *	AAA	4	4	0	0	26.1	121	36	16	13	1	0	0	0	10	2	13	0	0	1	2	.333	0	0--	—	4.44
1989 Milwaukee	AL	19	17	1	1	109.2	470	119	47	38	6	5	2	1	32	3	56	3	0	7	8	.467	0	0-0	0	3.12
1990 Milwaukee	AL	32	22	3	2	149.1	654	176	83	74	11	4	5	4	41	3	75	6	5	8	7	.533	0	1-2	3	4.46
1991 Milwaukee	AL	34	34	10	0	234	1002	237	117	102	18	7	8	6	73	3	114	10	0	15	12	.556	2	0-0	0	3.92
1992 Milwaukee	AL	34	34	5	0	246	1004	224	98	91	14	9	13	6	64	3	100	6	0	17	11	.607	0	0-0	0	3.33
1993 Milwaukee	AL	35	34	5	0	214.1	955	254	135	127	21	6	17	11	73	4	114	11	0	11	12	.478	1	0-0	0	5.33
1994 Milwaukee	AL	29	10	0	7	89.2	411	115	71	66	10	2	4	4	35	4	65	3	0	4	9	.308	0	0-0	0	6.62
1995 Chicago	NL	29	29	1	0	200.1	837	194	79	73	19	2	3	3	56	7	128	1	0	14	6	.700	1	0-0	0	3.28
1996 Chicago	NL	35	35	4	0	236.2	1007	244	116	103	25	10	7	10	72	5	158	10	0	15	12	.556	1	0-0	0	3.92
1997 Chicago	AL	33	33	2	0	209.2	957	267	155	135	22	2	14	3	73	6	142	14	1	9	14	.391	0	0-0	0	5.79
1998 Chicago	AL	37	27	1	4	172.2	802	223	135	122	30	3	7	7	77	1	71	18	0	8	16	.333	0	1-1	0	6.36
1999 Chicago	AL	32	27	0	1	159.2	748	206	126	108	29	3	4	11	71	1	74	9	0	8	13	.381	0	0-0	0	6.09
2000 Mil-Cle	AL	12	7	0	1	33.1	174	54	44	39	9	2	4	1	23	3	16	1	0	0	6	.000	0	0-2	2	10.53
2000 Milwaukee	NL	5	5	0	0	18.2	105	34	31	26	6	2	2	0	18	3	7	1	0	0	5	.000	0	0-0	0	12.54
Cleveland	AL	7	2	0	1	14.2	69	20	13	13	3	0	2	1	5	0	9	0	0	0	1	.000	0	0-2	2	7.98
12 ML YEARS		361	309	32	16	2055.1	9021	2313	1206	1078	214	55	88	67	690	44	1113	92	6	116	126	.479	8	2-3	5	4.72

Denny Neagle

Pitches: Left **Bats:** Left **Pos:** SP-33; RP-1   **Ht:** 6'3" **Wt:** 225 **Born:** 9/13/68 **Age:** 32

		HOW MUCH HE PITCHED						WHAT HE GAVE UP												THE RESULTS						
Year Team	Lg	G	GS	CG	GF	IP	BFP	H	R	ER	HR	SH	SF	HB	TBB	IBB	SO	WP	Bk	W	L	Pct.	ShO	Sv-Op	Hld	ERA
1991 Minnesota	AL	7	3	0	2	20	92	28	9	9	3	0	0	0	7	2	14	1	0	0	1	.000	0	0-0	0	4.05
1992 Pittsburgh	NL	55	6	0	8	86.1	380	81	46	43	9	4	3	2	43	8	77	3	2	4	6	.400	0	2-4	5	4.48
1993 Pittsburgh	NL	50	7	0	13	81.1	360	82	49	48	10	4	1	3	37	3	73	0	0	3	5	.375	0	1-1	0	5.31
1994 Pittsburgh	NL	24	24	2	0	137	587	135	80	78	18	7	6	3	49	3	122	2	0	9	10	.474	0	0-0	0	5.12
1995 Pittsburgh	NL	31	31	5	0	209.2	876	221	91	80	20	13	6	4	45	3	150	6	0	13	8	.619	1	0-0	0	3.43
1996 Pit-Atl	NL	33	33	2	0	221.1	910	226	93	86	26	10	4	3	48	2	149	3	1	16	9	.640	0	0-0	0	3.50
1997 Atlanta	NL	34	34	4	0	233.1	947	204	87	77	18	12	6	6	49	5	172	3	0	20	5	.800	4	0-0	0	2.97
1998 Atlanta	NL	32	31	5	0	210.1	861	196	91	83	25	7	3	6	60	3	165	6	1	16	11	.593	2	0-0	0	3.55
1999 Cincinnati	NL	20	19	0	0	111.2	467	95	54	53	23	3	5	4	43	3	76	4	0	9	5	.643	0	0-0	0	4.27
2000 Cin-NYY	NL	34	33	1	0	209	906	210	109	105	31	8	6	5	81	4	146	1	1	15	9	.625	0	0-0	0	4.52
1996 Pittsburgh	NL	27	27	1	0	182.2	745	186	67	62	21	9	3	3	34	2	131	2	1	14	6	.700	0	0-0	0	3.05
Atlanta	NL	6	6	1	0	38.2	165	40	26	24	5	1	1	0	14	0	18	1	0	2	3	.400	0	0-0	0	5.59
2000 Cincinnati	NL	18	18	0	0	117.2	506	111	48	46	15	2	1	3	50	3	88	0	0	8	2	.800	0	0-0	0	3.52
New York	AL	16	15	1	0	91.1	400	99	61	59	16	6	5	2	31	1	58	1	0	7	7	.500	0	0-0	0	5.81
10 ML YEARS		320	221	19	23	1520	6386	1478	709	662	183	65	40	35	459	36	1144	40	5	105	69	.603	7	3-5	11	3.92

Jeff Nelson

Pitches: Right **Bats:** Right **Pos:** RP-73   **Ht:** 6'8" **Wt:** 235 **Born:** 11/17/66 **Age:** 34

		HOW MUCH HE PITCHED						WHAT HE GAVE UP												THE RESULTS						
Year Team	Lg	G	GS	CG	GF	IP	BFP	H	R	ER	HR	SH	SF	HB	TBB	IBB	SO	WP	Bk	W	L	Pct.	ShO	Sv-Op	Hld	ERA
1992 Seattle	AL	66	0	0	27	81	352	71	34	31	7	9	3	6	44	12	46	2	0	1	7	.125	0	6-14	6	3.44
1993 Seattle	AL	71	0	0	13	60	269	57	30	29	5	2	4	8	34	10	61	2	0	5	3	.625	0	1-11	17	4.35
1994 Seattle	AL	28	0	0	7	42.1	185	35	18	13	3	1	1	8	20	4	44	0	0	0	0	—	0	0-0	2	2.76
1995 Seattle	AL	62	0	0	24	78.2	318	58	21	19	4	5	3	6	27	5	96	1	0	7	3	.700	0	2-4	14	2.17
1996 New York	AL	73	0	0	27	74.1	328	75	38	36	6	3	1	6	36	1	91	4	0	4	4	.500	0	2-4	10	4.36
1997 New York	AL	77	0	0	22	78.2	327	53	32	25	7	4	3	2	37	12	81	4	0	3	7	.300	0	2-8	22	2.86
1998 New York	AL	45	0	0	13	40.1	192	44	18	17	1	1	3	3	22	4	35	2	0	5	3	.625	0	3-6	10	3.79

154

Year Team	Lg	G	GS	CG	GF	IP	BFP	H	R	ER	HR	SH	SF	HB	TBB	IBB	SO	WP	Bk	W	L	Pct	ShO	Sv-Op	Hld	ERA
1999 New York	AL	39	0	0	8	30.1	139	27	14	14	2	2	2	3	22	2	35	2	1	2	1	.667	0	1-2	10	4.15
2000 New York	AL	73	0	0	13	69.2	296	44	24	19	2	6	2	2	45	1	71	4	0	8	4	.667	0	0-4	15	2.45
9 ML YEARS		534	0	0	154	555.1	2406	464	229	203	37	36	21	47	287	51	560	23	1	35	32	.522	0	17-53	106	3.29

Robb Nen

Pitches: Right Bats: Right Pos: RP-68 Ht: 6'5" Wt: 215 Born: 11/28/69 Age: 31

Year Team	Lg	G	GS	CG	GF	IP	BFP	H	R	ER	HR	SH	SF	HB	TBB	IBB	SO	WP	Bk	W	L	Pct	ShO	Sv-Op	Hld	ERA
1993 Tex-Fla	AL	24	4	0	5	56	272	63	45	42	6	1	2	0	46	0	39	6	1	2	1	.667	0	0-0	0	6.75
1994 Florida	NL	44	0	0	28	58	228	46	20	19	6	3	1	0	17	2	60	3	2	5	5	.500	0	15-15	1	2.95
1995 Florida	NL	62	0	0	54	65.2	279	62	26	24	6	0	1	1	23	3	68	2	0	0	7	.000	0	23-29	4	3.29
1996 Florida	NL	75	0	0	66	83	326	67	21	18	2	5	1	1	21	6	92	4	0	5	1	.833	0	35-42	0	1.95
1997 Florida	NL	73	0	0	65	74	332	72	35	32	7	1	3	0	40	7	81	5	0	9	3	.750	0	35-42	0	3.89
1998 San Francisco	NL	78	0	0	67	88.2	357	59	21	15	4	2	2	1	25	5	110	3	0	7	7	.500	0	40-45	0	1.52
1999 San Francisco	NL	72	0	0	64	72.1	320	79	36	32	8	5	1	0	27	3	77	5	0	3	8	.273	0	37-46	0	3.98
2000 San Francisco	NL	68	0	0	63	66	256	37	15	11	4	4	3	2	19	1	92	5	0	4	3	.571	0	41-46	0	1.50
1993 Texas	AL	9	3	0	3	22.2	113	28	17	16	1	0	1	0	26	0	12	2	1	1	1	.500	0	0-0	0	6.35
Florida	NL	15	1	0	2	33.1	159	35	28	26	5	1	1	0	20	0	27	4	0	1	0	1.000	0	0-0	0	7.02
8 ML YEARS		496	4	0	412	563.2	2370	485	219	193	43	21	14	5	218	27	619	33	3	35	35	.500	0	226-265	1	3.08

Phil Nevin

Bats: Right Throws: Right Pos: 3B-142; PH/PR-1 Ht: 6'2" Wt: 231 Born: 1/19/71 Age: 30

Year Team	Lg	G	AB	H	2B	3B	HR	Hm	Rd	TB	R	RBI	TBB	IBB	SO	HBP	SH	SF	SB	CS	SB%	GDP	Avg	OBP	SLG
1995 Hou-Det		47	156	28	4	1	2	(2	0)	40	13	13	18	1	40	4	1	0	1	0	1.00	5	.179	.281	.256
1996 Detroit	AL	38	120	35	5	0	8	(3	5)	64	15	19	8	0	39	1	0	1	1	0	1.00	1	.292	.338	.533
1997 Detroit	AL	93	251	59	16	1	9	(4	5)	104	32	35	25	1	68	1	0	1	0	1	.00	5	.235	.306	.414
1998 Anaheim	AL	75	237	54	8	1	8	(3	5)	88	27	27	17	0	67	5	0	2	0	0	—	6	.228	.291	.371
1999 San Diego	NL	128	383	103	27	0	24	(12	12)	202	52	85	51	1	82	1	1	5	1	0	1.00	5	.269	.352	.527
2000 San Diego	NL	143	538	163	34	1	31	(13	18)	292	87	107	59	9	121	4	0	4	2	0	1.00	17	.303	.374	.543
1995 Houston	NL	18	60	7	1	0	0	(0	0)	8	4	1	7	1	13	1	1	0	1	0	1.00	2	.117	.221	.133
Detroit	AL	29	96	21	3	1	2	(2	0)	32	9	12	11	0	27	3	0	0	0	0	—	3	.219	.318	.333
6 ML YEARS		524	1685	442	94	4	82	(37	45)	790	226	286	178	12	417	16	2	13	5	1	.83	41	.262	.336	.469

David Newhan

Bats: L Throws: R Pos: PH/PR-13; 2B-8; RF-5; 3B-2 Ht: 5'10" Wt: 180 Born: 9/7/73 Age: 27

Year Team	Lg	G	AB	H	2B	3B	HR	Hm	Rd	TB	R	RBI	TBB	IBB	SO	HBP	SH	SF	SB	CS	SB%	GDP	Avg	OBP	SLG
1995 Sou Oregon	A-	42	145	39	8	1	6	—	—	67	25	21	29	1	30	1	1	3	10	5	.67	2	.269	.388	.462
W Michigan	A	25	96	21	5	0	3	—	—	35	9	8	13	1	26	1	1	1	3	2	.60	2	.219	.315	.365
1996 Modesto	A+	117	455	137	27	3	25	—	—	245	96	75	62	1	106	2	6	2	17	8	.68	8	.301	.386	.538
1997 Visalia	A+	67	241	67	15	2	7	—	—	107	52	48	44	2	58	3	2	5	9	3	.75	5	.278	.389	.444
Huntsville	AA	57	212	67	13	2	5	—	—	99	40	35	28	2	59	2	1	2	5	5	.50	4	.316	.398	.467
1998 Mobile	AA	121	491	128	26	3	12	—	—	196	89	45	68	1	110	2	2	1	27	8	.77	8	.261	.352	.399
1999 Las Vegas	AAA	98	374	107	25	1	14	—	—	176	49	49	30	0	84	2	4	1	22	4	.85	5	.286	.342	.471
2000 Las Vegas	AAA	66	244	62	5	2	5	—	—	86	41	35	37	1	61	0	2	1	9	3	.75	4	.254	.351	.352
Scrantn-WB	AAA	25	83	21	3	0	3	—	—	33	10	8	11	0	15	0	1	0	3	1	.75	0	.253	.337	.398
1999 San Diego	NL	32	43	6	1	0	2	(1	1)	13	7	6	1	0	11	0	0	1	2	1	.67	0	.140	.159	.302
2000 SD-Phi	NL	24	37	6	1	0	1	(1	0)	10	8	2	8	1	13	0	0	0	0	0	—	2	.162	.311	.270
2000 San Diego	NL	14	20	3	1	0	1	(1	0)	7	5	2	6	1	7	0	0	0	0	0	—	0	.150	.346	.350
Philadelphia	NL	10	17	3	0	0	0	(0	0)	3	3	0	2	0	6	0	0	0	0	0	—	2	.176	.263	.176
2 ML YEARS		56	80	12	2	0	3	(2	1)	23	15	8	9	1	24	0	0	1	2	1	.67	2	.150	.236	.288

Alan Newman

Pitches: Left Bats: Left Pos: RP-1 Ht: 6'6" Wt: 240 Born: 10/2/69 Age: 31

Year Team	Lg	G	GS	CG	GF	IP	BFP	H	R	ER	HR	SH	SF	HB	TBB	IBB	SO	WP	Bk	W	L	Pct	ShO	Sv-Op	Hld	ERA
1988 Elizabethtn	R+	13	12	2	0	55.1	279	57	62	50	3	2	2	2	56	0	51	17	3	2	8	.200	0	0-	—	8.13
1989 Kenosha	A	18	18	1	0	88.2	398	65	41	28	2	5	0	4	74	0	82	3	9	3	9	.250	0	0-	—	2.84
1990 Kenosha	A	22	22	5	0	154	614	94	41	28	2	4	0	6	78	2	158	10	2	10	4	.714	1	0-	—	1.64
Visalia	A+	5	5	0	0	36.1	155	29	15	9	0	3	2	1	22	0	42	1	0	3	1	.750	0	0-	—	2.23
1991 Visalia	A+	15	15	0	0	92.1	411	86	49	36	2	4	0	6	49	2	79	11	0	6	5	.545	0	0-	—	3.51
Orlando	AA	11	11	2	0	67	275	53	28	20	0	2	1	1	30	1	53	8	0	5	4	.556	0	0-	—	2.69
1992 Orlando	AA	18	18	2	0	102	454	94	54	47	3	4	3	4	67	0	86	9	3	4	8	.333	1	0-	—	4.15
1993 Nashville	AA	14	11	1	1	65.2	304	75	52	44	4	4	2	1	40	0	35	5	0	1	6	.143	0	0-	—	6.03
Indianapols	AAA	8	3	0	3	20	111	24	23	19	3	0	2	1	27	0	15	5	1	1	3	.250	0	0-	—	8.55
1995 Alexandria	IND	23	21	5	1	137	612	141	87	79	9	13	0	2	74	2	129	12	0	10	8	.556	2	0-	—	5.19
1996 Alexandria	IND	35	11	0	10	118.1	522	136	70	60	8	7	4	4	43	1	82	6	0	6	6	.500	0	2-	—	4.56
1997 Birmingham	AA	44	0	0	33	72.1	314	55	34	20	0	4	2	0	40	4	64	9	0	7	3	.700	0	10-	—	2.49
1998 Las Vegas	AAA	63	0	0	23	76.1	332	58	29	28	2	5	3	3	50	3	76	0	0	3	3	.500	0	7-	—	3.30
1999 Durham	AAA	50	0	0	7	80.1	316	59	24	20	2	2	2	3	20	0	76	3	1	10	0	1.000	0	0-	—	2.24
2000 Buffalo	AAA	32	6	0	7	71.2	303	71	34	27	9	4	1	1	22	0	63	0	0	7	4	.636	0	0-	—	3.39
1999 Tampa Bay	AL	18	0	0	5	15.2	76	22	12	12	2	0	0	1	9	0	20	2	1	2	2	.500	0	0-1	0	6.89
2000 Cleveland	AL	1	0	0	1	1.1	10	6	3	3	1	0	0	0	1	0	0	0	0	0	0	—	0	0-0	0	20.25
2 ML YEARS		19	0	0	6	17	86	28	15	15	3	0	0	1	10	0	20	2	1	2	2	.500	0	0-1	0	7.94

Kevin Nicholson

Bats: Both **Throws:** Right **Pos:** SS-30; PH/PR-5; 2B-4   **Ht:** 5'10" **Wt:** 190 **Born:** 3/29/76 **Age:** 25

								BATTING										BASERUNNING				PERCENTAGES		
Year Team	Lg	G	AB	H	2B	3B	HR	(Hm | Rd)	TB	R	RBI	TBB	IBB	SO	HBP	SH	SF	SB	CS	SB%	GDP	Avg	OBP	SLG
1997 Padres	R	7	34	9	1	0	2	—	—	16	7	8	2	0	5	0	0	0	0	2	.00	2	.265	.306	.471
Rancho Cuc	A+	17	65	21	5	0	1	—	—	29	7	9	4	0	15	2	2	0	2	1	.67	1	.323	.380	.446
1998 Mobile	AA	132	488	105	27	3	5	—	—	153	64	52	47	7	114	3	5	6	9	5	.64	10	.215	.285	.314
1999 Mobile	AA	127	489	141	38	3	13	—	—	224	84	81	46	1	92	5	1	6	16	5	.76	15	.288	.352	.458
2000 Las Vegas	AAA	91	326	91	26	3	6	—	—	141	48	44	35	0	62	1	1	5	4	4	.50	5	.279	.350	.433
2000 San Diego	NL	37	97	21	6	1	1	(0 | 1)	32	7	8	4	0	31	1	3	0	1	0	1.00	2	.216	.255	.330

Chris Nichting

Pitches: Right **Bats:** Right **Pos:** RP-7   **Ht:** 6'1" **Wt:** 205 **Born:** 5/13/66 **Age:** 35

		HOW MUCH HE PITCHED						WHAT HE GAVE UP											THE RESULTS						
Year Team	Lg	G	GS	CG	GF	IP	BFP	H	R	ER	HR	SH	SF	HB	TBB	IBB	SO	WP	Bk	W	L	Pct.	ShO	Sv-Op	Hld	ERA
1988 Vero Beach	A+	21	19	5	2	138	545	90	40	32	7	0	2	2	51	0	151	7	0	11	4	.733	1	1--	—	2.09
1989 San Antonio	AA	26	26	2	0	154	698	160	96	86	13	9	6	6	101	6	136	14	4	4	14	.222	1	0--	—	5.03
1992 Albuquerque	AAA	10	9	0	0	42	205	64	42	37	2	2	0	0	23	1	25	5	1	1	3	.250	0	0--	—	7.93
San Antonio	AA	13	13	0	0	78.2	309	58	25	22	3	4	0	1	37	0	81	4	0	4	5	.444	0	0--	—	2.52
1993 Vero Beach	A+	4	4	0	0	17.1	75	18	9	8	2	0	0	0	6	0	18	1	0	1	0	1.000	0	0--	—	4.15
1994 Albuquerque	AAA	10	7	0	1	41.1	209	61	39	34	5	0	0	3	28	1	25	6	0	2	2	.500	0	1--	—	7.40
San Antonio	AA	21	8	0	8	65.2	277	47	21	12	1	4	1	2	34	1	74	7	1	3	4	.429	0	1--	—	1.64
1995 Okla City	AAA	23	7	3	8	67.2	275	58	19	16	4	4	2	2	19	0	72	2	0	5	5	.500	2	1--	—	2.13
1996 Okla City	AAA	4	1	0	1	9	37	9	1	1	0	0	0	0	3	0	7	0	0	1	0	1.000	0	0--	—	1.00
1997 Edmonton	AAA	33	24	3	3	131	602	170	120	113	21	0	7	3	46	2	90	8	1	7	13	.350	0	1--	—	7.76
1998 Buffalo	AAA	43	5	0	17	96.1	428	104	54	47	9	6	4	3	37	4	97	11	1	8	6	.571	0	1--	—	4.39
1999 Columbus	AAA	25	21	2	0	127.2	552	135	80	75	22	2	4	3	47	0	110	6	0	8	5	.615	0	0--	—	5.29
2000 Buffalo	AAA	47	3	0	36	66	275	65	31	31	6	2	1	3	16	1	60	0	0	2	3	.400	0	26--	—	4.23
1995 Texas	AL	13	0	0	3	24.1	122	36	19	19	1	1	2	1	13	1	6	3	0	0	0	—	0	0-0	1	7.03
2000 Cleveland	AL	7	0	0	1	9	46	13	7	7	0	0	1	2	5	1	7	1	0	0	0	—	0	0-1	0	7.00
2 ML YEARS		20	0	0	4	33.1	168	49	26	26	1	1	3	3	18	2	13	4	0	0	0	—	0	0-1	1	7.02

Doug Nickle

Pitches: Right **Bats:** Right **Pos:** RP-4   **Ht:** 6'4" **Wt:** 210 **Born:** 10/2/74 **Age:** 26

		HOW MUCH HE PITCHED						WHAT HE GAVE UP											THE RESULTS						
Year Team	Lg	G	GS	CG	GF	IP	BFP	H	R	ER	HR	SH	SF	HB	TBB	IBB	SO	WP	Bk	W	L	Pct.	ShO	Sv-Op	Hld	ERA
1997 Boise	A-	17	2	0	7	19.2	96	27	17	14	3	0	2	1	8	1	22	0	0	0	1	.000	0	0--	—	6.41
1998 Cedar Rapds	A	20	7	1	3	69	285	66	30	29	2	2	3	4	20	0	59	11	0	4	2	.667	1	0--	—	3.78
Lk Elsinore	A+	11	10	1	0	66.1	285	68	40	33	3	0	1	3	25	0	69	13	1	3	4	.429	0	0--	—	4.48
1999 Clearwater	A+	60	0	0	50	70.2	299	60	25	18	1	1	4	4	23	3	70	6	0	2	4	.333	0	28--	—	2.29
2000 Reading	AA	49	0	0	36	77.1	311	55	25	21	4	4	1	3	22	2	58	4	0	8	3	.727	0	16--	—	2.44
2000 Philadelphia	NL	4	0	0	3	2.2	15	5	4	4	0	0	1	0	2	0	0	0	0	0	0	—	0	0-0	0	13.50

Jose Nieves

Bats: R **Throws:** R **Pos:** 3B-39; PH/PR-25; SS-24; 2B-7   **Ht:** 6'1" **Wt:** 180 **Born:** 6/16/75 **Age:** 26

								BATTING										BASERUNNING				PERCENTAGES		
Year Team	Lg	G	AB	H	2B	3B	HR	(Hm	Rd)	TB	R	RBI	TBB	IBB	SO	HBP	SH	SF	SB	CS	SB%	GDP	Avg	OBP	SLG
2000 Daytona *	A+	2	6	1	0	0	0	—	—	1	2	0	1	0	0	0	0	0	0	0	—	0	.167	.286	.167
West Tenn *	AA	2	7	4	0	0	2	—	—	10	2	2	0	0	0	0	0	0	0	0	—	0	.571	.571	1.429
Iowa *	AAA	7	32	9	4	1	1	—	—	18	7	7	2	0	5	0	0	0	1	0	1.00	0	.281	.324	.563
1998 Chicago	NL	2	1	0	0	0	0	(0	0)	0	0	0	0	0	0	0	0	0	0	0	—	0	.000	.000	.000
1999 Chicago	NL	54	181	45	9	1	2	(2	0)	62	16	18	8	0	25	4	3	3	0	2	.00	5	.249	.291	.343
2000 Chicago	NL	82	198	42	6	3	5	(1	4)	69	17	24	11	1	43	0	2	2	1	1	.50	8	.212	.251	.348
3 ML YEARS		138	380	87	15	4	7	(3	4)	131	33	42	19	1	68	4	6	5	1	3	.25	13	.229	.270	.345

Dave Nilsson

Bats: Left **Throws:** Right **Pos:** C/PH/PR/DH   **Ht:** 6'3" **Wt:** 229 **Born:** 12/14/69 **Age:** 31

								BATTING										BASERUNNING				PERCENTAGES		
Year Team	Lg	G	AB	H	2B	3B	HR	(Hm	Rd)	TB	R	RBI	TBB	IBB	SO	HBP	SH	SF	SB	CS	SB%	GDP	Avg	OBP	SLG
1992 Milwaukee	AL	51	164	38	8	0	4	(1	3)	58	15	25	17	1	18	0	2	0	2	2	.50	1	.232	.304	.354
1993 Milwaukee	AL	100	296	76	10	2	7	(5	2)	111	35	40	37	5	36	0	4	3	3	6	.33	10	.257	.336	.375
1994 Milwaukee	AL	109	397	109	28	3	12	(4	8)	179	51	69	34	9	61	0	1	7	1	0	1.00	7	.275	.326	.451
1995 Milwaukee	AL	81	263	73	12	1	12	(7	5)	123	41	53	24	4	41	2	0	5	2	0	1.00	9	.278	.337	.468
1996 Milwaukee	AL	123	453	150	33	2	17	(3	14)	238	81	84	57	6	68	3	0	3	2	3	.40	4	.331	.407	.525
1997 Milwaukee	AL	156	554	154	33	4	20	(5	15)	247	71	81	65	8	88	2	1	7	2	3	.40	7	.278	.352	.446
1998 Milwaukee	NL	102	309	83	14	1	12	(6	6)	135	39	56	33	1	48	1	2	2	5	2	.50	12	.269	.339	.437
1999 Milwaukee	NL	115	343	106	19	1	21	(9	12)	190	56	62	53	6	64	2	2	4	3	2	.33	7	.309	.400	.554
8 ML YEARS		837	2779	789	157	10	105	(40	65)	1281	389	470	320	40	424	10	12	32	15	18	.45	57	.284	.356	.461

C.J. Nitkowski

Pitches: Left **Bats:** Left **Pos:** RP-56; SP-11   **Ht:** 6'3" **Wt:** 205 **Born:** 3/9/73 **Age:** 28

		HOW MUCH HE PITCHED						WHAT HE GAVE UP											THE RESULTS						
Year Team	Lg	G	GS	CG	GF	IP	BFP	H	R	ER	HR	SH	SF	HB	TBB	IBB	SO	WP	Bk	W	L	Pct.	ShO	Sv-Op	Hld	ERA
1995 Cin-Det		20	18	0	0	71.2	338	94	57	53	11	2	4	5	35	3	31	2	2	2	7	.222	0	0-1	0	6.66
1996 Detroit	AL	11	8	0	0	45.2	234	62	44	41	7	0	2	7	38	1	36	2	0	2	3	.400	0	0-0	0	8.08
1998 Houston	NL	43	0	0	11	59.2	266	49	27	25	4	4	2	6	23	2	44	3	1	3	3	.500	0	3-5	8	3.77
1999 Detroit	AL	68	7	0	7	81.2	349	63	44	39	11	4	4	3	45	3	66	4	3	4	5	.444	0	0-0	11	4.30
2000 Detroit	AL	67	11	0	7	109.2	497	124	79	64	13	8	4	8	49	3	81	3	1	4	9	.308	0	0-2	15	5.25
1995 Cincinnati	NL	9	7	0	0	32.1	154	41	25	22	4	2	1	2	15	1	18	1	2	1	3	.250	0	0-1	0	6.12
Detroit	AL	11	11	0	0	39.1	184	53	32	31	7	0	3	3	20	2	13	1	0	1	4	.200	0	0-0	0	7.09
5 ML YEARS		209	44	0	25	368.1	1668	392	251	222	46	10	20	25	190	12	258	14	7	15	27	.357	0	3-8	34	5.42

Trot Nixon

Bats: L **Throws:** L **Pos:** RF-115; PH/PR-13; CF-6; DH-1   **Ht:** 6'2" **Wt:** 200 **Born:** 4/11/74 **Age:** 27

Year Team	Lg	G	AB	H	2B	3B	HR	(Hm	Rd)	TB	R	RBI	TBB	IBB	SO	HBP	SH	SF	SB	CS	SB%	GDP	Avg	OBP	SLG
2000 Red Sox *	R	3	10	4	0	0	1	—	—	7	3	5	2	1	0	1	0	0	0	0	—	0	.400	.538	.700
1996 Boston	AL	2	4	2	1	0	0	(0	0)	3	2	0	0	0	1	0	0	0	1	0	1.00	0	.500	.500	.750
1998 Boston	AL	13	27	7	1	0	0	(0	0)	8	3	0	1	0	3	0	0	0	0	0	—	0	.259	.286	.296
1999 Boston	AL	124	381	103	22	5	15	(3	12)	180	67	52	53	1	75	3	2	8	3	1	.75	7	.270	.357	.472
2000 Boston	AL	123	427	118	27	8	12	(4	8)	197	66	60	63	2	85	2	5	5	8	1	.89	11	.276	.368	.461
4 ML YEARS		262	839	230	51	13	27	(7	20)	388	138	112	117	3	164	5	7	13	12	2	.86	18	.274	.361	.462

Hideo Nomo

Pitches: Right **Bats:** Right **Pos:** SP-31; RP-1   **Ht:** 6'2" **Wt:** 200 **Born:** 8/31/68 **Age:** 32

Year Team	Lg	G	GS	CG	GF	IP	BFP	H	R	ER	HR	SH	SF	HB	TBB	IBB	SO	WP	Bk	W	L	Pct.	ShO	Sv-Op	Hld	ERA
1995 Los Angeles	NL	28	28	4	0	191.1	780	124	63	54	14	11	4	5	78	2	236	19	5	13	6	.684	3	0-0	0	2.54
1996 Los Angeles	NL	33	33	3	0	228.1	932	180	93	81	23	12	6	2	85	6	234	11	3	16	11	.593	2	0-0	0	3.19
1997 Los Angeles	NL	33	33	1	0	207.1	904	193	104	98	23	7	1	9	92	2	233	10	4	14	12	.538	0	0-0	0	4.25
1998 LA-NYM	NL	29	28	0	0	157.1	687	130	88	86	19	8	5	4	94	2	167	13	4	6	12	.333	0	0-0	0	4.92
1999 Milwaukee	NL	28	28	0	0	176.1	767	173	96	89	27	5	5	3	78	2	161	10	1	12	8	.600	0	0-0	0	4.54
2000 Detroit	AL	32	31	1	0	190	828	191	102	100	31	6	3	3	89	1	181	16	0	8	12	.400	0	0-0	0	4.74
1998 Los Angeles	NL	12	12	2	0	67.2	295	57	39	38	8	2	2	3	38	0	73	4	1	2	7	.222	0	0-0	0	5.05
New York	NL	17	16	1	0	89.2	392	73	49	48	11	6	3	1	56	2	94	9	3	4	5	.444	0	0-0	0	4.82
6 ML YEARS		183	181	12	0	1150.2	4898	991	546	508	137	49	24	26	516	15	1212	79	17	69	61	.531	5	0-0	0	3.97

Greg Norton

Bats: B **Throws:** R **Pos:** 3B-47; 1B-17; PH/PR-14; DH-3   **Ht:** 6'1" **Wt:** 205 **Born:** 7/6/72 **Age:** 28

Year Team	Lg	G	AB	H	2B	3B	HR	(Hm	Rd)	TB	R	RBI	TBB	IBB	SO	HBP	SH	SF	SB	CS	SB%	GDP	Avg	OBP	SLG
2000 Charlotte *	AAA	29	97	28	4	0	5	—	—	47	18	17	24	3	23	2	0	1	1	0	1.00	0	.289	.435	.485
1996 Chicago	AL	11	23	5	0	0	2	(0	2)	11	4	3	4	0	6	0	0	0	0	1	.00	0	.217	.333	.478
1997 Chicago	AL	18	34	9	2	2	0	(0	0)	15	5	1	2	0	8	0	1	0	0	0	—	0	.265	.306	.441
1998 Chicago	AL	105	299	71	17	2	9	(6	3)	119	38	36	26	1	77	2	1	2	3	3	.50	11	.237	.301	.398
1999 Chicago	AL	132	436	111	26	0	16	(5	11)	185	62	50	69	3	93	2	1	2	4	4	.50	11	.255	.358	.424
2000 Chicago	AL	71	201	49	6	1	6	(4	2)	75	25	28	26	0	47	2	0	2	1	0	1.00	2	.244	.333	.373
5 ML YEARS		337	993	245	51	5	33	(15	18)	405	134	118	127	4	231	6	3	6	8	8	.50	24	.247	.334	.408

Phil Norton

Pitches: Left **Bats:** Right **Pos:** SP-2   **Ht:** 6'1" **Wt:** 190 **Born:** 2/1/76 **Age:** 25

Year Team	Lg	G	GS	CG	GF	IP	BFP	H	R	ER	HR	SH	SF	HB	TBB	IBB	SO	WP	Bk	W	L	Pct.	ShO	Sv-Op	Hld	ERA
1996 Cubs	R	1	0	0	1	3	10	1	0	0	0	0	0	0	0	0	6	0	1	0	0	—	0	0-—	—	0.00
Williamsprt	A-	15	13	2	1	85	364	68	33	24	1	3	2	3	33	2	77	7	3	7	4	.636	1	0-—	—	2.54
1997 Rockford	A	18	18	3	0	109	460	92	51	39	4	3	3	1	44	1	114	12	1	9	3	.750	0	0-—	—	3.22
Daytona	A+	7	6	3	0	42.1	171	40	11	11	5	1	0	0	12	0	44	0	0	3	2	.600	0	0-—	—	2.34
Orlando	AA	2	1	0	1	7	28	8	2	2	0	0	0	0	2	1	7	0	0	1	0	1.000	0	0-—	—	2.57
1998 Daytona	A+	10	10	0	0	66	275	57	30	24	4	1	1	2	26	1	54	4	1	4	3	.571	0	0-—	—	3.27
West Tenn	AA	19	19	1	0	120.1	515	118	60	47	14	4	3	5	50	1	119	6	1	6	6	.500	1	0-—	—	3.52
1999 West Tenn	AA	14	13	0	0	86.2	365	72	32	23	5	3	4	3	42	4	81	9	0	7	4	.636	0	0-—	—	2.39
Iowa	AAA	14	14	0	0	79.2	361	98	63	59	20	0	2	5	33	0	61	3	1	5	6	.455	0	0-—	—	6.67
2000 Iowa	AAA	28	26	2	0	159.2	733	166	100	88	16	9	6	2	104	4	126	8	2	8	13	.381	1	0-—	—	4.96
2000 Chicago	NL	2	2	0	0	8.2	47	14	10	9	5	0	0	0	7	0	6	0	0	0	1	.000	0	0-0	0	9.35

Abraham Nunez

Bats: Both **Throws:** Right **Pos:** SS-21; PH/PR-15; 2B-6   **Ht:** 5'11" **Wt:** 185 **Born:** 3/16/76 **Age:** 25

Year Team	Lg	G	AB	H	2B	3B	HR	(Hm	Rd)	TB	R	RBI	TBB	IBB	SO	HBP	SH	SF	SB	CS	SB%	GDP	Avg	OBP	SLG
2000 Nashville *	AAA	90	351	97	11	3	1	—	—	119	49	29	36	0	46	1	4	2	20	5	.80	7	.276	.344	.339
1997 Pittsburgh	NL	19	40	9	2	2	0	(0	0)	15	3	6	3	0	10	1	0	1	0	0	1.00	1	.225	.289	.375
1998 Pittsburgh	NL	24	52	10	2	0	1	(0	1)	15	6	2	12	0	14	0	3	0	4	2	.67	1	.192	.344	.288
1999 Pittsburgh	NL	90	259	57	8	0	0	(0	0)	65	25	17	28	0	54	1	13	0	9	1	.90	2	.220	.299	.251
2000 Pittsburgh	NL	40	91	20	1	0	1	(0	1)	24	10	8	8	1	14	0	0	0	0	0	—	3	.220	.283	.264
4 ML YEARS		173	442	96	13	2	2	(0	2)	119	44	33	51	1	92	2	16	1	14	3	.82	7	.217	.300	.269

Vladimir Nunez

Pitches: Right **Bats:** Right **Pos:** SP-12; RP-5   **Ht:** 6'4" **Wt:** 224 **Born:** 3/15/75 **Age:** 26

Year Team	Lg	G	GS	CG	GF	IP	BFP	H	R	ER	HR	SH	SF	HB	TBB	IBB	SO	WP	Bk	W	L	Pct.	ShO	Sv-Op	Hld	ERA
2000 Calgary *	AAA	15	15	1	0	89.2	385	92	43	41	9	3	4	2	38	1	95	6	0	6	7	.462	0	0-0	0	4.12
1998 Arizona	NL	4	0	0	2	5.1	25	7	6	6	0	0	1	0	2	0	2	0	1	0	0	—	0	0-0	0	10.13
1999 Ari-Fla	NL	44	12	0	12	108.2	463	95	63	49	11	7	6	4	54	6	86	8	1	7	10	.412	0	1-3	4	4.06
2000 Florida	NL	17	12	0	3	68.1	322	88	63	60	12	5	5	2	34	2	45	5	0	0	6	.000	0	0-0	1	7.90
1999 Arizona	NL	27	0	0	11	34	146	29	15	11	2	2	3	1	20	5	28	3	0	3	2	.600	0	1-2	3	2.91
Florida	NL	17	12	0	1	74.2	317	66	48	38	9	5	3	3	34	1	58	5	1	4	8	.333	0	0-1	1	4.58
3 ML YEARS		65	24	0	17	182.1	810	190	132	115	23	12	12	6	90	8	133	13	2	7	16	.304	0	1-3	5	5.68

Jon Nunnally

Bats: L **Throws:** R **Pos:** PH/PR-29; LF-26; CF-10; RF-4   **Ht:** 5'10" **Wt:** 190 **Born:** 11/9/71 **Age:** 29

Year Team	Lg	G	AB	H	2B	3B	HR	(Hm	Rd)	TB	R	RBI	TBB	IBB	SO	HBP	SH	SF	SB	CS	SB%	GDP	Avg	OBP	SLG
1995 Kansas City	AL	119	303	74	15	6	14	(6	8)	143	51	42	51	5	86	2	4	0	6	4	.60	4	.244	.357	.472
1996 Kansas City	AL	35	90	19	5	1	5	(2	3)	41	16	17	13	2	25	0	0	1	0	0	—	0	.211	.308	.456
1997 KC-Cin		78	230	71	12	4	14	(7	7)	133	46	39	31	0	58	2	1	1	7	3	.70	2	.309	.394	.578
1998 Cincinnati	NL	74	174	36	9	0	7	(2	5)	66	29	20	34	3	38	1	1	3	3	4	.43	4	.207	.335	.379
1999 Boston	AL	10	14	4	1	0	0	(0	0)	5	4	1	0	0	6	0	0	0	0	0	—	0	.286	.286	.357
2000 New York	NL	48	74	14	5	1	2	(0	2)	27	16	6	17	0	26	0	0	1	3	1	.75	1	.189	.337	.365
1997 Kansas City	AL	13	29	7	0	1	1	(1	0)	12	8	4	5	0	7	0	0	0	0	0	—	0	.241	.353	.414
Cincinnati	NL	65	201	64	12	3	13	(6	7)	121	38	35	26	0	51	2	1	1	7	3	.70	2	.318	.400	.602
6 ML YEARS		364	885	218	47	12	42	(17	25)	415	162	125	146	10	239	5	6	6	19	12	.61	11	.246	.354	.469

Talmadge Nunnari

Bats: Left **Throws:** Left **Pos:** 1B-14; PH/PR-5   **Ht:** 6'1" **Wt:** 200 **Born:** 4/9/75 **Age:** 26

Year Team	Lg	G	AB	H	2B	3B	HR	(Hm	Rd)	TB	R	RBI	TBB	IBB	SO	HBP	SH	SF	SB	CS	SB%	GDP	Avg	OBP	SLG
1997 Vermont	A-	62	236	75	11	3	4	—	—	104	30	42	31	4	37	3	0	4	6	3	.67	4	.318	.398	.441
Cape Fear	A	9	35	13	1	1	1	—	—	19	8	6	1	0	5	0	0	0	2	0	1.00	0	.371	.389	.543
1998 Cape Fear	A	79	289	88	18	0	2	—	—	112	51	51	42	2	44	1	0	0	4	4	.50	5	.304	.395	.388
Jupiter	A+	56	201	59	14	0	2	—	—	79	18	34	30	1	39	0	0	6	1	2	.33	2	.294	.376	.393
1999 Jupiter	A+	71	261	93	17	1	5	—	—	127	41	44	27	1	36	3	1	0	10	0	1.00	5	.356	.423	.487
Harrisburg	AA	63	239	79	17	1	6	—	—	116	45	29	39	3	46	1	2	2	7	2	.78	3	.331	.423	.485
2000 Harrisburg	AA	92	317	85	16	2	5	—	—	120	46	54	48	1	66	2	0	5	10	6	.63	6	.268	.363	.379
Ottawa	AAA	44	135	38	12	1	0	—	—	52	17	12	23	1	31	2	0	1	0	1	.00	1	.281	.391	.385
2000 Montreal	NL	18	5	1	0	0	0	(0	0)	1	2	1	6	1	2	0	0	0	0	0	—	0	.200	.583	.200

Charlie O'Brien

Bats: Right **Throws:** Right **Pos:** C-9   **Ht:** 6'2" **Wt:** 205 **Born:** 5/1/61 **Age:** 40

Year Team	Lg	G	AB	H	2B	3B	HR	(Hm	Rd)	TB	R	RBI	TBB	IBB	SO	HBP	SH	SF	SB	CS	SB%	GDP	Avg	OBP	SLG
2000 Harrisburg *	AA	5	18	4	2	0	1	—	—	9	3	5	2	0	5	0	0	0	0	0	—	0	.222	.300	.500
1985 Oakland	AL	16	11	3	1	0	0	(0	0)	4	3	1	3	0	3	0	0	0	0	0	—	0	.273	.429	.364
1987 Milwaukee	AL	10	35	7	3	1	0	(0	0)	12	2	0	4	0	4	0	1	0	0	1	.00	0	.200	.282	.343
1988 Milwaukee	AL	40	118	26	6	0	2	(2	0)	38	12	9	5	0	16	0	4	0	0	1	.00	3	.220	.252	.322
1989 Milwaukee	AL	62	188	44	10	0	6	(4	2)	72	22	35	21	1	11	9	8	0	0	0	—	11	.234	.339	.383
1990 Mil-NYM		74	213	38	10	2	0	(0	0)	52	17	20	21	3	34	3	10	2	0	0	—	4	.178	.259	.244
1991 New York	NL	69	168	31	6	0	2	(1	1)	43	16	14	17	1	25	4	0	2	0	0	—	5	.185	.272	.256
1992 New York	NL	68	156	33	12	0	2	(1	1)	51	15	13	16	1	18	1	4	0	0	1	.00	6	.212	.289	.327
1993 New York	NL	67	188	48	11	0	4	(3	1)	71	15	23	14	1	14	2	3	1	1	1	.50	4	.255	.312	.378
1994 Atlanta	NL	51	152	37	11	0	8	(6	2)	72	24	28	15	2	24	3	1	1	0	0	—	5	.243	.322	.474
1995 Atlanta	NL	67	198	45	7	0	9	(4	5)	79	18	23	29	2	40	6	0	0	0	1	.00	8	.227	.343	.399
1996 Toronto	AL	109	324	77	17	0	13	(8	5)	133	33	44	29	1	68	17	3	2	0	1	.00	8	.238	.331	.410
1997 Toronto	AL	69	225	49	15	1	4	(2	2)	78	22	27	22	1	45	11	3	6	0	2	.00	6	.218	.311	.347
1998 CWS-Ana	AL	62	175	45	9	0	4	(0	4)	66	13	18	10	0	33	2	3	3	0	0	—	6	.257	.300	.377
1999 Anaheim	AL	27	62	6	0	0	1	(0	1)	9	3	4	1	0	12	2	1	1	0	0	—	1	.097	.136	.145
2000 Montreal	NL	9	19	4	1	0	1	(0	1)	8	1	2	2	1	7	0	0	0	0	0	—	0	.211	.286	.421
1990 Milwaukee	AL	46	145	27	7	2	0	(0	0)	38	11	11	11	1	26	2	8	0	0	0	—	4	.186	.253	.262
New York	NL	28	68	11	3	0	0	(0	0)	14	6	9	10	2	8	1	2	2	0	0	—	0	.162	.272	.206
1998 Chicago	AL	57	164	43	9	0	4	(0	4)	64	12	18	9	0	31	2	3	3	0	0	—	5	.262	.303	.390
Anaheim	AL	5	11	2	0	0	0	(0	0)	2	1	0	1	0	2	0	0	0	0	0	—	1	.182	.250	.182
15 ML YEARS		800	2232	493	119	4	56	(29	27)	788	216	261	209	14	354	60	41	18	1	10	.09	62	.221	.303	.353

Alex Ochoa

Bats: R **Throws:** R **Pos:** LF-74; PH/PR-41; RF-37; CF-3   **Ht:** 6'0" **Wt:** 195 **Born:** 3/29/72 **Age:** 29

Year Team	Lg	G	AB	H	2B	3B	HR	(Hm	Rd)	TB	R	RBI	TBB	IBB	SO	HBP	SH	SF	SB	CS	SB%	GDP	Avg	OBP	SLG
2000 Chattanooga *	AA	4	16	3	2	0	1	—	—	8	3	2	2	0	1	0	0	0	1	0	1.00	2	.188	.316	.500
1995 New York	NL	11	37	11	1	0	0	(0	0)	12	7	0	2	0	10	0	0	0	1	0	1.00	1	.297	.333	.324
1996 New York	NL	82	282	83	19	3	4	(1	3)	120	37	33	17	0	30	2	0	3	4	3	.57	2	.294	.336	.426
1997 New York	NL	113	238	58	14	1	3	(1	2)	83	31	22	18	0	32	2	2	2	3	4	.43	7	.244	.300	.349
1998 Minnesota	AL	94	249	64	14	2	2	(1	1)	88	35	25	10	0	35	1	0	0	6	3	.67	7	.257	.288	.353
1999 Milwaukee	NL	119	277	83	16	3	8	(8	0)	129	47	40	45	2	43	5	0	2	6	4	.60	4	.300	.404	.466
2000 Cincinnati	NL	118	244	77	21	3	13	(9	4)	143	50	58	24	3	27	3	0	4	8	4	.67	7	.316	.378	.586
6 ML YEARS		537	1327	376	85	12	30	(20	10)	575	207	178	116	5	177	13	2	11	28	18	.61	28	.283	.344	.433

Brian O'Connor

Pitches: Left **Bats:** Left **Pos:** RP-5; SP-1   **Ht:** 6'2" **Wt:** 170 **Born:** 1/4/77 **Age:** 24

Year Team	Lg	G	GS	CG	GF	IP	BFP	H	R	ER	HR	SH	SF	HB	TBB	IBB	SO	WP	Bk	W	L	Pct.	ShO	Sv-Op	Hld	ERA
1995 Pirates	R	14	5	0	5	43	183	33	22	9	1	0	1	0	13	0	43	4	2	2	2	.500	0	1--	—	1.88
1996 Augusta	A	19	0	0	5	35.1	147	33	13	12	2	1	1	1	8	0	37	6	0	0	1	.000	0	1--	—	3.06
Erie	A-	15	15	0	0	67.2	329	75	60	44	4	3	2	3	47	0	60	10	1	4	10	.286	0	0--	—	5.85
1997 Augusta	A	25	14	0	3	85.2	385	90	54	42	6	4	1	2	39	1	91	11	0	7	2	.222	0	0--	—	4.41
Lynchburg	A+	11	0	0	6	13	55	11	5	5	0	0	0	1	6	1	14	3	0	2	1	.667	0	2--	—	3.46
1998 Lynchburg	A+	14	14	1	0	86.2	371	86	34	25	3	3	1	1	22	1	84	7	0	6	2	.750	0	0--	—	2.60
Carolina	AA	14	13	0	0	64.1	318	86	65	59	11	3	4	3	53	1	41	12	0	2	4	.333	0	0--	—	8.25
1999 Altoona	AA	28	27	1	0	153.1	698	152	98	77	10	11	3	6	92	2	106	21	0	7	11	.389	0	0--	—	4.52
2000 Altoona	AA	22	22	4	0	129.1	562	120	69	54	4	4	2	7	61	0	76	12	0	12	4	.750	0	0--	—	3.76
Nashville	AAA	5	5	0	0	26.1	121	30	23	20	2	1	1	1	14	0	19	5	0	2	2	.500	0	0--	—	6.84
2000 Pittsburgh	NL	6	1	0	2	12.1	62	12	11	7	2	0	1	0	11	0	7	4	0	0	0	—	0	0-0	0	5.11

Jose Offerman

Bats: B **Throws:** R **Pos:** 2B-80; 1B-39; DH-9; PH/PR-1   **Ht:** 6'0" **Wt:** 190 **Born:** 11/8/68 **Age:** 32

Year Team	Lg	G	AB	H	2B	3B	HR	(Hm	Rd)	TB	R	RBI	TBB	IBB	SO	HBP	SH	SF	SB	CS	SB%	GDP	Avg	OBP	SLG
1990 Los Angeles	NL	29	58	9	0	0	1	(1	0)	12	7	7	4	1	14	0	1	0	1	0	1.00	0	.155	.210	.207
1991 Los Angeles	NL	52	113	22	2	0	0	(0	0)	24	10	3	25	2	32	1	1	0	3	2	.60	5	.195	.345	.212
1992 Los Angeles	NL	149	534	139	20	8	1	(1	0)	178	67	30	57	4	98	0	5	2	23	16	.59	5	.260	.331	.333
1993 Los Angeles	NL	158	590	159	21	6	1	(1	0)	195	77	62	71	7	75	2	25	8	30	13	.70	12	.269	.346	.331
1994 Los Angeles	NL	72	243	51	8	4	1	(0	1)	70	27	25	38	4	38	0	6	2	2	1	.67	6	.210	.314	.288
1995 Los Angeles	NL	119	429	123	14	6	4	(2	2)	161	69	33	69	0	67	3	10	0	2	7	.22	5	.287	.389	.375
1996 Kansas City	AL	151	561	170	33	8	5	(1	4)	234	85	47	74	3	98	1	7	2	24	10	.71	9	.303	.384	.417
1997 Kansas City	AL	106	424	126	23	6	2	(2	0)	167	59	39	41	3	64	0	6	0	9	10	.47	5	.297	.359	.394
1998 Kansas City	AL	158	607	191	28	13	7	(4	3)	266	102	66	89	1	96	5	2	6	45	12	.79	7	.315	.403	.438
1999 Boston	AL	149	586	172	37	11	8	(5	3)	255	107	69	96	5	79	2	2	7	18	12	.60	11	.294	.391	.435
2000 Boston	AL	116	451	115	14	3	9	(3	6)	162	73	41	70	0	70	1	2	3	0	8	.00	9	.255	.354	.359
11 ML YEARS		1259	4596	1277	200	65	39	(20	19)	1724	683	422	634	30	731	15	67	30	157	91	.63	74	.278	.365	.375

Tomokazu Ohka

Pitches: Right **Bats:** Right **Pos:** SP-12; RP-1   **Ht:** 6'1" **Wt:** 179 **Born:** 3/18/76 **Age:** 25

Year Team	Lg	G	GS	CG	GF	IP	BFP	H	R	ER	HR	SH	SF	HB	TBB	IBB	SO	WP	Bk	W	L	Pct.	ShO	Sv-Op	Hld	ERA
1999 Trenton	AA	12	12	0	0	72	298	63	26	24	9	0	0	3	25	0	53	3	0	8	0	1.000	0	0--	—	3.00
Pawtucket	AAA	12	12	1	0	68.1	274	60	17	12	5	1	1	0	11	0	63	1	0	7	0	1.000	1	0--	—	1.58
2000 Pawtucket	AAA	19	19	3	0	130.2	513	111	52	43	15	2	7	3	23	1	78	2	0	9	6	.600	2	0--	—	2.96
1999 Boston	AL	8	2	0	3	13	65	21	12	9	2	0	1	0	6	0	8	0	0	1	2	.333	0	0-0	0	6.23
2000 Boston	AL	13	12	0	1	69.1	297	70	25	24	7	1	2	2	26	0	40	3	0	3	6	.333	0	0-0	0	3.12
2 ML YEARS		21	14	0	4	82.1	362	91	37	33	9	1	3	2	32	0	48	3	0	4	8	.333	0	0-0	0	3.61

Will Ohman

Pitches: Left **Bats:** Left **Pos:** RP-6   **Ht:** 6'2" **Wt:** 195 **Born:** 8/13/77 **Age:** 23

Year Team	Lg	G	GS	CG	GF	IP	BFP	H	R	ER	HR	SH	SF	HB	TBB	IBB	SO	WP	Bk	W	L	Pct.	ShO	Sv-Op	Hld	ERA
1998 Williamsprt	A-	10	7	0	0	39	167	39	32	28	6	0	3	1	13	0	35	0	0	4	4	.500	0	0--	—	6.46
Rockford	A	4	4	0	0	24.1	104	25	13	12	3	2	0	2	7	0	21	1	0	1	1	.500	0	0--	—	4.44
1999 Daytona	A+	31	15	2	12	106.2	457	102	59	41	11	2	4	8	41	1	97	6	1	4	7	.364	2	5--	—	3.46
2000 West Tenn	AA	59	0	0	23	71.1	312	53	20	15	3	3	5	3	36	5	85	8	0	4	6	.400	0	3--	—	1.89
2000 Chicago	NL	6	0	0	2	3.1	17	4	3	3	0	0	0	0	4	1	2	1	0	1	0	1.000	0	0-0	1	8.10

Augie Ojeda

Bats: Both **Throws:** Right **Pos:** SS-25; 2B-4; PH/PR-1   **Ht:** 5'9" **Wt:** 170 **Born:** 12/20/74 **Age:** 26

Year Team	Lg	G	AB	H	2B	3B	HR	(Hm	Rd)	TB	R	RBI	TBB	IBB	SO	HBP	SH	SF	SB	CS	SB%	GDP	Avg	OBP	SLG
1997 Frederick	A+	34	128	44	11	1	1	—	—	60	25	20	18	1	18	1	4	0	2	5	.29	1	.344	.429	.469
Bowie	AA	58	204	60	9	1	2	—	—	77	33	23	31	1	17	3	4	3	7	0	1.00	6	.294	.390	.377
Rochester	AAA	15	47	11	3	1	0	—	—	16	5	6	8	0	4	0	3	0	1	2	.33	2	.234	.345	.340
1998 Orioles	R	4	15	6	2	0	0	—	—	8	6	2	3	0	1	2	0	0	3	0	1.00	0	.400	.550	.533
Bowie	AA	73	254	65	10	2	1	—	—	82	36	19	36	0	30	3	5	1	0	3	.00	5	.256	.354	.323
1999 Rochester	AAA	1	0	0	0	0	0	—	—	0	1	0	0	0	0	0	0	0	0	0	—	0	.000	.000	.000
Bowie	AA	134	460	123	18	4	10	—	—	179	73	60	57	0	47	11	25	4	6	2	.75	7	.267	.359	.389
2000 Iowa	AAA	113	396	111	23	2	8	—	—	162	56	43	33	1	27	7	3	4	16	6	.73	10	.280	.343	.409
2000 Chicago	NL	28	77	17	3	1	2	(1	1)	28	10	8	10	1	9	0	1	0	0	1	.00	1	.221	.307	.364

Troy O'Leary

Bats: Left **Throws:** Left **Pos:** LF-137; PH/PR-1   **Ht:** 6'0" **Wt:** 200 **Born:** 8/4/69 **Age:** 31

Year Team	Lg	G	AB	H	2B	3B	HR	(Hm	Rd)	TB	R	RBI	TBB	IBB	SO	HBP	SH	SF	SB	CS	SB%	GDP	Avg	OBP	SLG
2000 Red Sox *	R	3	8	6	1	0	0	—	—	7	3	1	3	0	1	0	0	0	0	0	—	0	.750	.818	.875
1993 Milwaukee	AL	19	41	12	3	0	0	(0	0)	15	3	3	5	0	9	0	3	0	0	0	—	1	.293	.370	.366
1994 Milwaukee	AL	27	66	18	1	1	2	(0	2)	27	9	7	5	0	12	1	0	1	1	1	.50	0	.273	.329	.409
1995 Boston	AL	112	399	123	31	6	10	(5	5)	196	60	49	29	4	64	1	3	2	5	3	.63	8	.308	.355	.491
1996 Boston	AL	149	497	129	28	5	15	(10	5)	212	68	81	47	3	80	4	1	3	3	2	.60	13	.260	.327	.427
1997 Boston	AL	146	499	154	32	4	15	(5	10)	239	65	80	39	7	70	2	1	4	0	5	.00	13	.309	.358	.479
1998 Boston	AL	156	611	165	36	8	23	(12	11)	286	95	83	36	2	108	5	0	5	2	2	.50	17	.270	.314	.468
1999 Boston	AL	157	596	167	36	4	28	(13	15)	295	84	103	56	5	91	4	0	5	1	2	.33	21	.280	.343	.495
2000 Boston	AL	138	513	134	30	4	13	(7	6)	211	68	70	44	2	76	2	0	4	0	2	.00	12	.261	.320	.411
8 ML YEARS		904	3222	902	197	32	106	(52	54)	1481	452	476	261	23	510	19	8	24	12	17	.41	85	.280	.335	.460

John Olerud

Bats: Left **Throws:** Left **Pos:** 1B-158; PH/PR-2   **Ht:** 6'5" **Wt:** 220 **Born:** 8/5/68 **Age:** 32

Year Team	Lg	G	AB	H	2B	3B	HR	(Hm	Rd)	TB	R	RBI	TBB	IBB	SO	HBP	SH	SF	SB	CS	SB%	GDP	Avg	OBP	SLG
1989 Toronto	AL	6	8	3	0	0	0	(0	0)	3	2	0	0	0	1	0	0	0	0	0	—	0	.375	.375	.375
1990 Toronto	AL	111	358	95	15	1	14	(11	3)	154	43	48	57	6	75	1	1	4	0	2	.00	5	.265	.364	.430
1991 Toronto	AL	139	454	116	30	1	17	(7	10)	199	64	68	68	9	84	6	3	10	0	2	.00	12	.256	.353	.438
1992 Toronto	AL	138	458	130	28	0	16	(4	12)	206	68	66	70	11	61	1	1	7	1	0	1.00	6	.284	.375	.450
1993 Toronto	AL	158	551	200	54	2	24	(9	15)	330	109	107	114	33	65	7	0	7	0	2	.00	12	.363	.473	.599
1994 Toronto	AL	108	384	114	29	2	12	(6	6)	183	47	67	61	12	53	3	0	5	1	2	.33	11	.297	.393	.477
1995 Toronto	AL	135	492	143	32	0	8	(1	7)	199	72	54	84	10	54	4	0	1	0	0	—	17	.291	.398	.404
1996 Toronto	AL	125	398	109	25	0	18	(9	9)	188	59	61	60	6	37	10	0	1	1	0	1.00	10	.274	.382	.472

Year Team	Lg	G	AB	H	2B	3B	HR	(Hm	Rd)	TB	R	RBI	TBB	IBB	SO	HBP	SH	SF	SB	CS	SB%	GDP	Avg	OBP	SLG
						BATTING													BASERUNNING				PERCENTAGES		
1997 New York	NL	154	524	154	34	1	22	(13	9)	256	90	102	85	5	67	13	0	8	0	0	—	19	.294	.400	.489
1998 New York	NL	160	557	197	36	4	22	(13	9)	307	91	93	96	11	73	4	1	7	2	2	.50	15	.354	.447	.551
1999 New York	NL	162	581	173	39	0	19	(11	8)	269	107	96	125	5	66	11	0	6	3	0	1.00	22	.298	.427	.463
2000 Seattle	AL	159	565	161	45	0	14	(8	6)	248	84	103	102	11	96	4	2	10	0	2	.00	17	.285	.392	.439
12 ML YEARS		1555	5330	1595	367	11	186	(92	94)	2542	836	865	922	119	732	64	8	66	8	12	.40	155	.299	.404	.477

Omar Olivares

Pitches: Right **Bats:** Right **Pos:** SP-16; RP-5   **Ht:** 6'1" **Wt:** 205 **Born:** 7/6/67 **Age:** 33

Year Team	Lg	G	GS	CG	GF	IP	BFP	H	R	ER	HR	SH	SF	HB	TBB	IBB	SO	WP	Bk	W	L	Pct.	ShO	Sv-Op	Hld	ERA
			HOW	MUCH	HE PITCHED						WHAT HE GAVE UP											THE RESULTS				
2000 Modesto *	A+	2	2	0	0	6	21	3	1	1	0	0	0	0	1	0	3	0	0	0	0	—	0	0--		1.50
Sacramento *	AAA	1	1	0	0	6	21	3	1	0	0	0	0	0	2	0	3	0	0	0	0	—	0	0--		0.00
1990 St. Louis	NL	9	6	0	0	49.1	201	45	17	16	2	1	0	2	17	0	20	1	1	0	0	.500	0	0-0	1	2.92
1991 St. Louis	NL	28	24	0	2	167.1	688	148	72	69	13	11	2	5	61	1	91	3	1	11	7	.611	0	1-1	0	3.71
1992 St. Louis	NL	32	30	1	1	197	818	189	84	84	20	8	7	4	63	5	124	2	0	9	9	.500	0	0-0	0	3.84
1993 St. Louis	NL	58	9	0	11	118.2	537	134	60	55	10	4	4	9	54	7	63	4	3	5	3	.625	0	1-5	2	4.17
1994 St. Louis	NL	14	12	1	2	73.2	333	84	53	47	10	3	3	4	37	0	26	5	0	3	4	.429	0	1-1	0	5.74
1995 Col-Phi	NL	16	6	0	4	41.2	195	55	34	32	5	2	2	3	23	0	22	4	0	1	4	.200	0	0-0	0	6.91
1996 Detroit	AL	25	25	4	0	160	708	169	90	87	16	3	6	9	75	4	81	4	1	7	11	.389	0	0-0	0	4.89
1997 Det-Sea	AL	32	31	3	0	177.1	794	191	109	98	18	2	7	13	81	4	103	5	0	6	10	.375	2	0-0	0	4.97
1998 Anaheim	AL	37	26	1	6	183	805	189	92	82	19	6	4	5	91	1	112	5	0	9	9	.500	0	0-0	0	4.03
1999 Ana-Oak	AL	32	32	4	0	205.2	885	217	105	95	19	3	7	9	81	0	85	6	0	15	11	.577	0	0-0	0	4.16
2000 Oakland	AL	21	16	1	1	108	508	134	86	81	10	0	7	7	60	0	57	4	0	4	8	.333	0	0-0	0	6.75
1995 Colorado	NL	11	6	0	1	31.2	151	44	28	26	4	1	1	2	21	0	15	4	0	1	3	.250	0	0-0	0	7.39
Philadelphia	NL	5	0	0	3	10	44	11	6	6	1	1	1	1	2	0	7	0	0	0	1	.000	0	0-0	0	5.40
1997 Detroit	AL	19	19	3	0	115	502	110	68	60	8	2	4	9	53	1	74	5	0	5	6	.455	2	0-0	0	4.70
Seattle	AL	13	12	0	0	62.1	292	81	41	38	10	0	3	4	28	3	29	0	0	1	4	.200	0	0-0	0	5.49
1999 Anaheim	AL	20	20	3	0	131	558	135	62	59	11	3	5	6	49	0	49	4	0	8	9	.471	0	0-0	0	4.05
Oakland	AL	12	12	1	0	74.2	327	82	43	36	8	0	2	3	32	0	36	2	0	7	2	.778	0	0-0	0	4.34
11 ML YEARS		304	217	15	27	1481.2	6472	1555	802	746	142	43	49	70	643	22	784	43	6	71	77	.480	2	3-7	3	4.53

Darren Oliver

Pitches: Left **Bats:** Right **Pos:** SP-21   **Ht:** 6'2" **Wt:** 210 **Born:** 10/6/70 **Age:** 30

Year Team	Lg	G	GS	CG	GF	IP	BFP	H	R	ER	HR	SH	SF	HB	TBB	IBB	SO	WP	Bk	W	L	Pct.	ShO	Sv-Op	Hld	ERA
			HOW	MUCH	HE PITCHED						WHAT HE GAVE UP											THE RESULTS				
2000 Tulsa *	AA	1	1	0	0	4.2	27	10	7	6	0	0	1	0	2	0	5	1	0	0	1	.000	0	0--	—	11.57
Oklahoma *	AAA	7	7	1	0	32	128	22	11	7	2	0	1	1	14	0	28	0	0	2	1	.667	1	0--	—	1.97
1993 Texas	AL	2	0	0	0	3.1	14	2	1	1	1	0	0	1	1	1	4	0	0	0	0	—	0	0-0	0	2.70
1994 Texas	AL	43	0	0	10	50	226	40	24	19	4	6	0	6	35	4	50	2	2	4	0	1.000	0	2-3	9	3.42
1995 Texas	AL	17	7	0	2	49	222	47	25	23	3	5	1	1	32	1	39	4	0	4	2	.667	0	0-0	0	4.22
1996 Texas	AL	30	30	1	0	173.2	777	190	97	90	20	2	7	10	76	3	112	5	1	14	6	.700	1	0-0	0	4.66
1997 Texas	AL	32	32	3	0	201.1	887	213	111	94	29	2	5	11	82	3	104	7	0	13	12	.520	1	0-0	0	4.20
1998 Tex-StL	AL	29	29	2	0	160.1	749	204	115	102	18	8	8	10	66	2	87	7	4	10	11	.476	0	0-0	0	5.73
1999 St. Louis	NL	30	30	2	0	196.1	842	197	96	93	16	11	4	11	74	4	119	6	2	9	9	.500	1	0-0	0	4.26
2000 St. Louis	NL	21	21	0	0	108	501	151	95	89	16	5	4	4	42	3	49	4	1	2	9	.182	0	0-0	0	7.42
1998 Texas	AL	19	19	2	0	103.1	493	140	84	75	11	3	6	10	43	1	58	6	1	6	7	.462	0	0-0	0	6.53
St. Louis	NL	10	10	0	0	57	256	64	31	27	7	5	2	0	23	1	29	1	3	4	4	.500	0	0-0	0	4.26
8 ML YEARS		204	149	8	12	942	4218	1044	564	511	107	39	29	53	408	21	564	35	10	56	49	.533	3	2-3	9	4.88

Joe Oliver

Bats: R **Throws:** R **Pos:** C-66; PH/PR-3; DH-1; 1B-1   **Ht:** 6'3" **Wt:** 220 **Born:** 7/24/65 **Age:** 35

Year Team	Lg	G	AB	H	2B	3B	HR	(Hm	Rd)	TB	R	RBI	TBB	IBB	SO	HBP	SH	SF	SB	CS	SB%	GDP	Avg	OBP	SLG
						BATTING													BASERUNNING				PERCENTAGES		
2000 Tacoma *	AAA	18	61	12	2	0	0	—		14	2	8	5	0	12	1	0	1	0	0	—	3	.197	.265	.230
1989 Cincinnati	NL	49	151	41	8	0	3	(1	2)	58	13	23	6	1	28	1	1	2	0	0	—	5	.272	.300	.384
1990 Cincinnati	NL	121	364	84	23	0	8	(3	5)	131	34	52	37	15	75	2	5	1	1	1	.50	6	.231	.304	.360
1991 Cincinnati	NL	94	269	58	11	0	11	(7	4)	102	21	41	18	5	53	0	4	0	0	0	—	14	.216	.265	.379
1992 Cincinnati	NL	143	485	131	25	1	10	(7	3)	188	42	57	35	19	75	1	6	7	2	3	.40	12	.270	.316	.388
1993 Cincinnati	NL	139	482	115	28	0	14	(7	7)	185	40	75	27	2	91	1	2	9	0	0	—	13	.239	.276	.384
1994 Cincinnati	NL	6	19	4	0	0	1	(1	0)	7	1	5	2	1	3	0	0	0	0	0	—	1	.211	.286	.368
1995 Milwaukee	AL	97	337	92	20	0	12	(4	8)	148	43	51	27	1	66	3	2	0	2	4	.33	11	.273	.332	.439
1996 Cincinnati	NL	106	289	70	12	1	11	(6	5)	117	31	46	28	6	54	2	3	3	2	0	1.00	8	.242	.311	.405
1997 Cincinnati	NL	111	349	90	13	0	14	(7	7)	145	28	43	25	1	58	5	2	5	1	3	.25	7	.258	.313	.415
1998 Det-Sea	AL	79	240	54	11	0	6	(3	3)	83	20	32	17	0	48	0	2	4	1	1	.50	8	.225	.272	.346
1999 Pittsburgh	NL	45	134	27	8	0	1	(1	0)	38	10	13	10	0	33	0	0	2	2	0	1.00	4	.201	.253	.284
2000 Seattle	AL	69	200	53	13	1	10	(6	4)	98	33	35	14	1	38	0	5	0	2	1	.67	6	.265	.313	.490
1998 Detroit	AL	50	155	35	8	0	4	(2	2)	55	8	22	7	0	33	0	0	4	1	0	.00	5	.226	.253	.355
Seattle	AL	29	85	19	3	0	2	(1	1)	28	12	10	10	0	15	0	2	0	0	1	1.00	3	.224	.305	.329
12 ML YEARS		1059	3319	819	172	3	101	(53	48)	1300	316	473	246	52	622	15	32	33	13	13	.50	93	.247	.299	.392

Gregg Olson

Pitches: Right **Bats:** Right **Pos:** RP-13   **Ht:** 6'4" **Wt:** 208 **Born:** 10/11/66 **Age:** 34

Year Team	Lg	G	GS	CG	GF	IP	BFP	H	R	ER	HR	SH	SF	HB	TBB	IBB	SO	WP	Bk	W	L	Pct.	ShO	Sv-Op	Hld	ERA
			HOW	MUCH	HE PITCHED						WHAT HE GAVE UP											THE RESULTS				
2000 San Berndno *	A+	6	4	0	0	6.2	31	8	4	3	0	0	0	0	4	0	8	2	0	0	0	—	0	0--	0	4.05
Albuquerque *	AAA	4	0	0	0	4	16	3	2	2	0	0	0	0	2	0	2	1	0	0	0	—	0	0--	0	4.50
1988 Baltimore	AL	10	0	0	4	11	51	10	4	4	1	0	0	0	10	1	9	0	1	1	1	.500	0	0-1	0	3.27
1989 Baltimore	AL	64	0	0	52	85	356	57	17	16	1	4	1	1	46	10	90	9	3	5	2	.714	0	27-33	0	1.69
1990 Baltimore	AL	64	0	0	58	74.1	305	57	20	20	3	1	2	3	31	3	74	5	0	6	5	.545	0	37-42	0	2.42
1991 Baltimore	AL	72	0	0	62	73.2	319	74	28	26	1	5	1	1	29	5	72	8	1	4	6	.400	0	31-39	1	3.18

Year Team	Lg	HOW MUCH HE PITCHED						WHAT HE GAVE UP												THE RESULTS						
		G	GS	CG	GF	IP	BFP	H	R	ER	HR	SH	SF	HB	TBB	IBB	SO	WP	Bk	W	L	Pct.	ShO	Sv-Op	Hld	ERA
1992 Baltimore	AL	60	0	0	56	61.1	244	46	14	14	3	0	2	0	24	0	58	4	0	1	5	.167	0	36-44	0	2.05
1993 Baltimore	AL	50	0	0	45	45	188	37	9	8	1	2	2	0	18	3	44	5	0	0	2	.000	0	29-35	0	1.60
1994 Atlanta	NL	16	0	0	6	14.2	77	19	15	15	1	2	1	1	13	3	10	0	2	0	0	.000	0	1-1	1	9.20
1995 Cle-KC	AL	23	0	0	12	33	141	28	15	15	4	1	2	0	19	2	21	1	0	3	3	.500	0	3-5	2	4.09
1996 Det-Hou		52	0	0	30	52.1	243	55	30	29	7	1	1	1	35	6	37	6	0	4	0	1.000	0	8-10	1	4.99
1997 Min-KC	AL	45	0	0	18	50	226	58	35	31	3	2	1	1	28	4	34	1	0	4	3	.571	0	1-4	5	5.58
1998 Arizona	NL	64	0	0	49	68.2	281	56	25	23	4	3	1	1	25	1	55	2	0	3	4	.429	0	30-34	0	3.01
1999 Arizona	NL	61	0	0	36	60.2	257	54	28	25	9	1	2	2	25	2	45	1	0	9	4	.692	0	14-23	9	3.71
2000 Los Angeles	NL	13	0	0	9	17.2	81	21	11	10	4	1	1	1	7	0	15	0	0	0	1	.000	0	0-1	0	5.09
1995 Cleveland	AL	3	0	0	2	2.2	14	5	4	4	1	0	0	0	2	0	0	0	0	0	0	—	0	0-0	0	13.50
Kansas City	AL	20	0	0	10	30.1	127	23	11	11	3	1	2	0	17	2	21	1	0	3	3	.500	0	3-5	2	3.26
1996 Detroit	AL	43	0	0	28	43	196	43	25	24	6	1	0	1	28	4	29	5	0	3	0	1.000	0	8-10	1	5.02
Houston	NL	9	0	0	2	9.1	47	12	5	5	1	0	1	0	7	2	8	1	0	1	0	1.000	0	0-0	0	4.82
1997 Minnesota	AL	11	0	0	5	8.1	55	19	17	17	0	0	0	0	11	1	6	0	0	0	0	—	0	0-0	1	18.36
Kansas City	AL	34	0	0	13	41.2	171	39	18	14	3	2	1	1	17	3	28	1	0	4	3	.571	0	1-4	4	3.02
13 ML YEARS		594	0	0	437	647.1	2769	572	251	236	42	23	17	12	310	40	564	42	7	40	38	.513	0	217-272	21	3.28

Paul O'Neill

Bats: Left **Throws:** Left **Pos:** RF-140; DH-2; PH/PR-1   **Ht:** 6'4" **Wt:** 215 **Born:** 2/25/63 **Age:** 38

Year Team	Lg	BATTING																	BASERUNNING				PERCENTAGES		
		G	AB	H	2B	3B	HR	(Hm	Rd)	TB	R	RBI	TBB	IBB	SO	HBP	SH	SF	SB	CS	SB%	GDP	Avg	OBP	SLG
1985 Cincinnati	NL	5	12	4	1	0	0	(0	0)	5	1	1	0	0	2	0	0	0	0	0	—	0	.333	.333	.417
1986 Cincinnati	NL	3	2	0	0	0	0	(0	0)	0	0	0	1	0	1	0	0	0	0	0	—	0	.000	.333	.000
1987 Cincinnati	NL	84	160	41	14	1	7	(4	3)	78	24	28	18	1	29	0	0	0	2	1	.67	3	.256	.331	.488
1988 Cincinnati	NL	145	485	122	25	3	16	(12	4)	201	58	73	38	5	65	2	3	5	8	6	.57	7	.252	.306	.414
1989 Cincinnati	NL	117	428	118	24	2	15	(11	4)	191	49	74	46	8	64	2	0	4	20	5	.80	7	.276	.346	.446
1990 Cincinnati	NL	145	503	136	28	0	16	(10	6)	212	59	78	53	13	103	2	1	5	13	11	.54	12	.270	.339	.421
1991 Cincinnati	NL	152	532	136	36	0	28	(20	8)	256	71	91	73	14	107	1	0	1	12	7	.63	8	.256	.346	.481
1992 Cincinnati	NL	148	496	122	19	1	14	(6	8)	185	59	66	77	15	85	2	3	6	6	3	.67	10	.246	.346	.373
1993 New York	AL	141	498	155	34	1	20	(8	12)	251	71	75	44	5	69	2	0	3	2	4	.33	13	.311	.367	.504
1994 New York	AL	103	368	132	25	1	21	(10	11)	222	68	83	72	13	56	0	0	3	5	4	.56	16	.359	.460	.603
1995 New York	AL	127	460	138	30	4	22	(12	10)	242	82	96	71	8	76	1	0	11	1	2	.33	25	.300	.387	.526
1996 New York	AL	150	546	165	35	1	19	(7	12)	259	89	91	102	8	76	4	0	8	0	1	.00	21	.302	.411	.474
1997 New York	AL	149	553	179	42	0	21	(10	11)	284	89	117	75	8	92	0	0	9	10	7	.59	16	.324	.399	.514
1998 New York	AL	152	602	191	40	2	24	(10	14)	307	95	116	57	2	103	2	0	11	15	1	.94	22	.317	.372	.510
1999 New York	AL	153	597	170	39	4	19	(10	9)	274	70	110	66	1	89	2	0	10	11	9	.55	24	.285	.353	.459
2000 New York	AL	142	566	160	26	0	18	(10	8)	240	79	100	51	2	90	0	0	11	14	9	.61	17	.283	.336	.424
16 ML YEARS		1916	6808	1969	418	20	260	(139	121)	3207	964	1199	844	103	1107	20	7	87	119	70	.63	201	.289	.365	.471

Steve Ontiveros

Pitches: Right **Bats:** Right **Pos:** RP-2; SP-1   **Ht:** 6'0" **Wt:** 190 **Born:** 3/5/61 **Age:** 40

Year Team	Lg	HOW MUCH HE PITCHED						WHAT HE GAVE UP												THE RESULTS						
		G	GS	CG	GF	IP	BFP	H	R	ER	HR	SH	SF	HB	TBB	IBB	SO	WP	Bk	W	L	Pct.	ShO	Sv-Op	Hld	ERA
2000 Valley *	IND	9	9	2	0	62.2	262	56	31	25	5	1	0	4	16	0	55	0	0	4	4	.500	1	0--	—	3.59
Colo Spngs *	AAA	8	8	0	0	43.1	177	36	15	14	6	1	0	3	10	1	33	2	0	4	1	.800	0	0--	—	2.91
1985 Oakland	AL	39	0	0	18	74.2	284	45	17	16	4	2	2	2	19	2	36	1	0	1	3	.250	0	8--	—	1.93
1986 Oakland	AL	46	4	0	27	72.2	305	72	40	38	10	1	6	1	25	3	54	4	0	2	2	.500	0	10--	—	4.71
1987 Oakland	AL	35	22	2	6	150.2	645	141	78	67	19	6	2	4	50	3	97	4	1	10	8	.556	1	1-4	1	4.00
1988 Oakland	AL	10	10	0	0	54.2	241	57	32	28	4	5	0	0	21	1	30	5	3	4	.429	0	0-0	0	4.61
1989 Philadelphia	NL	6	5	0	0	30.2	134	34	15	13	2	1	0	0	15	1	12	2	0	2	1	.667	0	0-0	0	3.82
1990 Philadelphia	NL	5	0	0	1	10	43	9	3	3	1	0	0	0	3	0	6	0	0	0	0	—	0	0-0	1	2.70
1993 Seattle	AL	14	0	0	8	18	72	18	3	2	0	1	0	0	6	2	13	1	0	0	2	.000	0	0-0	0	1.00
1994 Oakland	AL	27	13	2	5	115.1	463	93	39	34	7	2	1	6	26	1	56	5	0	6	4	.600	0	0-0	1	2.65
1995 Oakland	AL	22	22	2	0	129.2	558	144	75	63	12	2	6	4	38	0	77	5	0	9	6	.600	1	0-0	0	4.37
2000 Boston	AL	3	1	0	0	5.1	28	9	6	6	1	0	0	0	4	0	1	2	0	1	1	.500	0	0-0	0	10.13
10 ML YEARS		207	73	6	65	661.2	2773	622	308	270	60	20	17	17	207	13	382	29	6	34	31	.523	2	19--	—	3.67

Luis Ordaz

Bats: Right **Throws:** Right **Pos:** SS-38; 2B-22; PH/PR-20   **Ht:** 5'11" **Wt:** 170 **Born:** 8/12/75 **Age:** 25

Year Team	Lg	BATTING																	BASERUNNING				PERCENTAGES		
		G	AB	H	2B	3B	HR	(Hm	Rd)	TB	R	RBI	TBB	IBB	SO	HBP	SH	SF	SB	CS	SB%	GDP	Avg	OBP	SLG
1997 St. Louis	NL	12	22	6	1	0	0	(0	0)	7	3	1	1	0	2	0	0	0	0	0	1.00	0	.273	.304	.318
1998 St. Louis	NL	57	153	31	5	0	0	(0	0)	36	9	8	12	1	18	0	4	0	2	0	1.00	3	.203	.261	.235
1999 St. Louis	NL	10	9	1	0	0	0	(0	0)	1	3	2	1	0	2	0	1	0	1	0	1.00	0	.111	.200	.111
2000 Kansas City	AL	65	104	23	2	0	0	(0	0)	25	17	11	5	0	10	1	4	3	4	2	.67	6	.221	.257	.240
4 ML YEARS		144	288	61	8	0	0	(0	0)	69	32	22	19	1	32	1	9	3	10	2	.83	9	.212	.260	.240

Magglio Ordonez

Bats: Right **Throws:** Right **Pos:** RF-152; PH/PR-1   **Ht:** 6'0" **Wt:** 200 **Born:** 1/28/74 **Age:** 27

Year Team	Lg	BATTING																	BASERUNNING				PERCENTAGES		
		G	AB	H	2B	3B	HR	(Hm	Rd)	TB	R	RBI	TBB	IBB	SO	HBP	SH	SF	SB	CS	SB%	GDP	Avg	OBP	SLG
1997 Chicago	AL	21	69	22	6	0	4	(2	2)	40	12	11	2	0	8	0	1	0	1	2	.33	1	.319	.338	.580
1998 Chicago	AL	145	535	151	25	2	14	(8	6)	222	70	65	28	1	53	9	2	4	9	7	.56	19	.282	.326	.415
1999 Chicago	AL	157	624	188	34	3	30	(16	14)	318	100	117	47	4	64	1	0	5	13	6	.68	24	.301	.349	.510
2000 Chicago	AL	153	588	185	34	3	32	(21	11)	321	102	126	60	3	64	2	0	15	18	4	.82	28	.315	.371	.546
4 ML YEARS		476	1816	546	99	8	80	(47	33)	901	284	319	137	8	189	12	3	24	41	19	.68	72	.301	.349	.496

Rey Ordonez

Bats: Right **Throws:** Right **Pos:** SS-44; PH/PR-1   **Ht:** 5'9" **Wt:** 159 **Born:** 11/11/72 **Age:** 28

								BATTING											BASERUNNING				PERCENTAGES		
Year Team	Lg	G	AB	H	2B	3B	HR	(Hm	Rd)	TB	R	RBI	TBB	IBB	SO	HBP	SH	SF	SB	CS	SB%	GDP	Avg	OBP	SLG
1996 New York	NL	151	502	129	12	4	1	(0	1)	152	51	30	22	12	53	1	4	1	1	3	.25	12	.257	.289	.303
1997 New York	NL	120	356	77	5	3	1	(1	0)	91	35	33	18	3	36	1	14	2	11	5	.69	10	.216	.255	.256
1998 New York	NL	153	505	124	20	2	1	(0	1)	151	46	42	23	7	60	1	15	4	3	6	.33	11	.246	.278	.299
1999 New York	NL	154	520	134	24	2	1	(1	0)	165	49	60	49	12	59	1	11	7	8	4	.67	16	.258	.319	.317
2000 New York	NL	45	133	25	5	0	0	(0	0)	30	10	9	17	2	16	0	4	1	0	0	—	4	.188	.278	.266
5 ML YEARS		623	2016	489	66	11	4	(2	2)	589	191	174	129	36	224	4	48	15	23	18	.56	53	.243	.287	.292

Jesse Orosco

Pitches: Left **Bats:** Right **Pos:** RP-6   **Ht:** 6'2" **Wt:** 205 **Born:** 4/21/57 **Age:** 44

		HOW MUCH HE PITCHED						WHAT HE GAVE UP												THE RESULTS						
Year Team	Lg	G	GS	CG	GF	IP	BFP	H	R	ER	HR	SH	SF	HB	TBB	IBB	SO	WP	Bk	W	L	Pct.	ShO	Sv-Op	Hld	ERA
2000 Peoria *	A	2	2	0	0	1.2	6	0	0	0	0	0	0	0	1	0	1	0	0	0	0	—	0	0--	—	0.00
Memphis *	AAA	2	1	0	0	1	4	1	1	1	0	0	0	0	0	0	0	0	1	0	0	1	.000	0	0--	—	9.00
1979 New York	NL	18	2	0	6	35	154	33	20	19	4	3	0	2	22	0	22	0	0	1	2	.333	0	0-0	0	4.89
1981 New York	NL	8	0	0	4	17.1	69	13	4	3	2	2	0	0	6	2	18	0	1	0	1	1.000	0	1-1	0	1.56
1982 New York	NL	54	2	0	22	109.1	451	92	37	33	7	5	4	2	40	2	89	3	2	4	10	.286	0	4-5	5	2.72
1983 New York	NL	62	0	0	42	110	432	76	27	18	3	4	3	1	38	7	84	1	2	13	7	.650	0	17-22	1	1.47
1984 New York	NL	60	0	0	52	87	355	58	29	25	7	3	3	2	34	6	85	1	1	10	6	.625	0	31-38	0	2.59
1985 New York	NL	54	0	0	39	79	331	66	26	24	6	1	1	0	34	7	68	4	0	8	6	.571	0	17-25	1	2.73
1986 New York	NL	58	0	0	40	81	338	64	23	21	6	2	3	3	35	3	62	2	0	8	6	.571	0	21-29	1	2.33
1987 New York	NL	58	0	0	41	77	335	78	41	38	5	5	4	2	31	9	78	2	0	3	9	.250	0	16-22	4	4.44
1988 Los Angeles	NL	55	0	0	21	53	229	41	18	16	4	3	3	2	30	3	43	1	0	3	2	.600	0	9-15	14	2.72
1989 Cleveland	AL	69	0	0	29	78	312	54	20	18	7	8	3	2	26	4	79	0	0	3	4	.429	0	3-7	12	2.08
1990 Cleveland	AL	55	0	0	28	64.2	289	58	35	28	9	5	3	0	38	7	55	1	0	5	4	.556	0	2-3	2	3.90
1991 Cleveland	AL	47	0	0	20	45.2	202	52	20	19	4	1	3	1	15	8	36	1	1	2	0	1.000	0	0-0	3	3.74
1992 Milwaukee	AL	59	0	0	14	39	158	33	15	14	5	0	2	1	13	1	40	2	0	3	1	.750	0	1-2	11	3.23
1993 Milwaukee	AL	57	0	0	27	56.2	233	47	25	20	2	1	2	3	17	3	67	3	1	3	5	.375	0	8-13	11	3.18
1994 Milwaukee	AL	40	0	0	5	39	174	32	26	22	4	0	2	2	26	2	36	0	0	3	1	.750	0	0-4	8	5.08
1995 Baltimore	AL	65	0	0	23	49.2	200	28	19	18	4	2	4	1	27	7	58	2	1	2	4	.333	0	3-6	15	3.26
1996 Baltimore	AL	66	0	0	10	55.2	236	42	22	21	5	2	1	2	28	4	52	2	0	3	1	.750	0	0-3	19	3.40
1997 Baltimore	AL	71	0	0	12	50.1	205	29	13	13	6	1	2	0	30	0	46	1	0	6	3	.667	0	0-4	21	2.32
1998 Baltimore	AL	69	0	0	26	56.2	243	46	20	20	6	2	2	1	28	1	50	3	1	4	1	.800	0	7-9	9	3.18
1999 Baltimore	AL	65	0	0	12	32	144	28	21	19	5	2	3	2	20	3	35	2	0	0	2	.000	0	1-4	12	5.34
2000 St. Louis	NL	6	0	0	0	2.1	16	3	3	1	1	0	0	2	3	2	4	0	0	0	0	—	0	0-0	3	3.86
21 ML YEARS		1096	4	0	473	1218.1	5106	973	464	410	102	54	48	31	541	81	1107	31	11	84	75	.528	0	141-212	152	3.03

David Ortiz

Bats: Left **Throws:** Left **Pos:** DH-88; 1B-27; PH/PR-21   **Ht:** 6'4" **Wt:** 230 **Born:** 11/18/75 **Age:** 25

								BATTING											BASERUNNING				PERCENTAGES		
Year Team	Lg	G	AB	H	2B	3B	HR	(Hm	Rd)	TB	R	RBI	TBB	IBB	SO	HBP	SH	SF	SB	CS	SB%	GDP	Avg	OBP	SLG
1997 Minnesota	AL	15	49	16	3	0	1	(0	1)	22	10	6	2	0	19	0	0	0	0	0	—	1	.327	.353	.449
1998 Minnesota	AL	86	278	77	20	0	9	(2	7)	124	47	46	39	3	72	5	0	4	1	0	1.00	8	.277	.371	.446
1999 Minnesota	AL	10	20	0	0	0	0	(0	0)	0	1	0	5	0	12	0	0	0	0	0	—	0	.000	.200	.000
2000 Minnesota	AL	130	415	117	36	1	10	(7	3)	185	59	63	57	2	81	0	0	6	1	0	1.00	13	.282	.364	.446
4 ML YEARS		241	762	210	59	1	20	(9	11)	331	117	115	103	5	184	5	0	10	2	0	1.00	24	.276	.361	.434

Hector Ortiz

Bats: Right **Throws:** Right **Pos:** C-26   **Ht:** 6'0" **Wt:** 205 **Born:** 10/14/69 **Age:** 31

								BATTING											BASERUNNING				PERCENTAGES		
Year Team	Lg	G	AB	H	2B	3B	HR	(Hm	Rd)	TB	R	RBI	TBB	IBB	SO	HBP	SH	SF	SB	CS	SB%	GDP	Avg	OBP	SLG
1988 Salem	A-	32	77	11	1	0	0	—	—	12	5	4	5	0	16	1	1	0	0	2	.00	5	.143	.205	.156
1989 Vero Beach	A+	42	85	12	0	1	0	—	—	14	5	4	6	0	15	2	4	0	0	0	—	1	.141	.215	.165
Salem	A-	44	140	32	3	1	0	—	—	37	13	12	4	0	24	1	2	0	2	1	.67	6	.229	.255	.264
1990 Yakima	A-	52	173	47	3	1	0	—	—	52	16	12	5	0	15	1	1	0	1	1	.50	6	.272	.296	.301
1991 Vero Beach	A+	42	123	28	2	0	0	—	—	30	3	8	5	0	8	3	0	0	0	0	—	2	.228	.275	.244
1992 Bakersfield	A+	63	206	58	8	1	1	—	—	71	19	31	21	0	16	5	3	2	2	3	.40	8	.282	.359	.345
San Antonio	AA	26	59	12	1	0	0	—	—	13	1	5	11	0	13	1	1	0	0	0	—	3	.203	.338	.220
1993 San Antonio	AA	49	131	28	5	0	1	—	—	36	6	6	9	2	17	0	3	0	0	2	.00	3	.214	.264	.275
Albuquerque	AAA	18	44	8	1	1	0	—	—	11	0	3	0	0	6	1	2	0	0	0	—	1	.182	.200	.250
1994 Albuquerque	AAA	34	93	28	1	1	0	—	—	31	7	10	0	0	12	0	0	1	0	0	—	3	.301	.320	.333
San Antonio	AA	24	75	9	0	0	0	—	—	9	4	4	2	0	7	1	0	0	0	0	—	0	.120	.150	.120
1995 Orlando	AA	96	299	70	12	0	0	—	—	82	13	18	20	0	39	1	4	1	0	5	.00	10	.234	.281	.274
1996 Orlando	AA	78	216	47	8	0	0	—	—	55	16	15	26	0	23	0	1	3	1	2	.33	12	.218	.298	.255
Iowa	AAA	27	79	19	2	0	0	—	—	21	6	3	3	1	16	0	0	1	0	0	—	5	.241	.265	.266
1997 Omaha	AAA	21	63	12	3	0	0	—	—	15	7	3	13	0	15	0	1	0	0	0	—	0	.190	.329	.238
Wichita	AA	59	180	45	3	0	1	—	—	51	20	25	21	0	15	2	4	2	1	2	.33	10	.250	.332	.283
1998 Wichita	AA	4	13	2	0	0	0	—	—	2	1	0	2	0	1	0	0	0	0	0	—	0	.154	.267	.154
Omaha	AAA	63	191	43	7	0	0	—	—	50	17	12	9	0	26	1	2	0	0	0	—	10	.225	.264	.262
1999 San Antonio	AA	40	121	29	4	0	0	—	—	33	10	13	10	0	17	1	0	2	0	1	.00	2	.240	.291	.273
Albuquerque	AAA	55	164	50	9	0	6	—	—	77	21	20	7	1	27	1	0	3	2	3	.40	9	.305	.331	.470
2000 Omaha	AAA	68	227	73	12	0	6	—	—	103	30	24	22	2	18	1	3	1	4	3	.57	8	.322	.382	.454
1998 Kansas City	AL	4	4	0	0	0	0	(0	0)	0	1	0	0	0	0	0	0	0	0	0	—	0	.000	.000	.000
2000 Kansas City	AL	26	88	34	6	0	0	(0	0)	40	15	5	1	1	8	1	2	0	0	0	—	0	.386	.443	.455
2 ML YEARS		30	92	34	6	0	0	(0	0)	40	16	5	1	1	8	1	2	0	0	0	—	0	.370	.426	.435

Jose Ortiz

Bats: Right **Throws:** Right **Pos:** PH/PR-5; DH-4; 2B-3   **Ht:** 5'9" **Wt:** 177 **Born:** 6/13/77 **Age:** 24

							BATTING												BASERUNNING				PERCENTAGES		
Year Team	Lg	G	AB	H	2B	3B	HR	(Hm	Rd)	TB	R	RBI	TBB	IBB	SO	HBP	SH	SF	SB	CS	SB%	GDP	Avg	OBP	SLG
1996 Athletics	R	52	200	66	12	8	4	—	—	106	43	25	20	2	34	1	1	1	16	5	.76	1	.330	.392	.530
Modesto	A+	1	4	1	0	0	0	—	—	1	0	0	0	0	1	0	0	0	0	0	—	0	.250	.250	.250
1997 Modesto	A+	128	497	122	25	7	16	—	—	209	92	58	60	2	107	6	3	4	22	14	.61	7	.245	.332	.421
1998 Huntsville	AA	94	354	98	24	2	6	—	—	144	70	55	48	0	63	5	6	2	22	8	.73	6	.277	.369	.407
1999 Vancouver	AAA	107	377	107	29	2	9	—	—	167	66	45	29	1	50	9	3	4	13	4	.76	8	.284	.346	.443
2000 Sacramento	AAA	131	518	182	34	5	24	—	—	298	107	108	47	0	64	4	0	2	22	9	.71	21	.351	.408	.575
2000 Oakland	AL	7	11	2	0	0	0	(0	0)	2	4	1	2	0	3	0	0	0	0	0	—	0	.182	.308	.182

Ramon Ortiz

Pitches: Right **Bats:** Right **Pos:** SP-18   **Ht:** 6'0" **Wt:** 175 **Born:** 3/23/76 **Age:** 25

		HOW MUCH HE PITCHED						WHAT HE GAVE UP											THE RESULTS					
Year Team	Lg	G	GS	CG	GF	IP	BFP	H	R	ER	HR	SH	SF	HB	TBB	IBB	SO	WP	Bk	W	L	Pct.	ShO	Sv-Op	Hld	ERA
1996 Angels	R	16	8	2	5	68	285	55	28	16	5	0	1	2	27	0	78	5	2	5	4	.556	2	1- -	—	2.12
Boise	A-	3	3	0	0	19.2	89	21	10	8	3	2	0	1	6	0	18	0	1	1	1	.500	0	0- -	—	3.66
1997 Cedar Rapds	A	27	27	8	0	181	740	156	78	72	22	2	1	7	53	0	225	14	5	11	10	.524	4	0- -	—	3.58
1998 Midland	AA	7	7	0	0	47	202	50	31	29	10	1	2	1	16	0	53	3	1	2	1	.667	0	0- -	—	5.55
1999 Erie	AA	15	15	2	0	102	419	88	38	32	12	3	2	2	40	0	86	1	0	9	4	.692	2	0- -	—	2.82
Edmonton	AAA	9	9	0	0	53.1	224	46	26	24	7	0	0	2	19	0	64	6	2	5	3	.625	0	0- -	—	4.05
2000 Lk Elsinore	A+	1	1	0	0	6	26	8	2	2	0	0	0	0	2	0	7	0	0	1	0	1.000	0	0- -	—	3.00
Edmonton	AAA	15	15	1	0	89	381	74	49	45	7	1	4	4	37	0	76	7	1	6	6	.500	0	0- -	—	4.55
1999 Anaheim	AL	9	9	0	0	48.1	218	50	35	35	7	0	2	2	25	0	44	2	2	2	3	.400	0	0-0	0	6.52
2000 Anaheim	AL	18	18	2	0	111.1	472	96	69	63	18	4	4	2	55	0	73	7	4	8	6	.571	0	0-0	0	5.09
2 ML YEARS		27	27	2	0	159.2	690	146	104	98	25	4	6	4	80	0	117	9	6	10	9	.526	0	0-0	0	5.52

Russ Ortiz

Pitches: Right **Bats:** Right **Pos:** SP-32; RP-1   **Ht:** 6'1" **Wt:** 210 **Born:** 6/5/74 **Age:** 27

		HOW MUCH HE PITCHED						WHAT HE GAVE UP											THE RESULTS					
Year Team	Lg	G	GS	CG	GF	IP	BFP	H	R	ER	HR	SH	SF	HB	TBB	IBB	SO	WP	Bk	W	L	Pct.	ShO	Sv-Op	Hld	ERA
1998 San Francisco	NL	22	13	0	3	88.1	394	90	51	49	11	5	4	4	46	1	75	3	0	4	4	.500	0	0-0	1	4.99
1999 San Francisco	NL	33	33	3	0	207.2	922	189	109	88	24	11	6	6	125	5	164	13	0	18	9	.667	0	0-0	0	3.81
2000 San Francisco	NL	33	32	0	0	195.2	871	192	117	109	28	10	6	7	112	1	167	8	0	14	12	.538	0	0-0	0	5.01
3 ML YEARS		88	78	3	3	491.2	2187	471	277	246	63	26	16	17	283	7	406	24	0	36	25	.590	0	0-0	1	4.50

Keith Osik

Bats: R **Throws:** R **Pos:** C-26; 3B-12; PH/PR-10; 1B-5; DH-1; P-1   **Ht:** 6'0" **Wt:** 192 **Born:** 10/22/68 **Age:** 32

							BATTING												BASERUNNING				PERCENTAGES		
Year Team	Lg	G	AB	H	2B	3B	HR	(Hm	Rd)	TB	R	RBI	TBB	IBB	SO	HBP	SH	SF	SB	CS	SB%	GDP	Avg	OBP	SLG
1996 Pittsburgh	NL	48	140	41	14	1	1	(0	1)	60	18	14	14	1	22	1	1	0	1	0	1.00	3	.293	.361	.429
1997 Pittsburgh	NL	49	105	27	9	1	0	(0	0)	38	10	7	9	1	21	1	2	0	0	1	.00	1	.257	.322	.362
1998 Pittsburgh	NL	39	98	21	4	0	0	(0	0)	25	8	7	13	2	16	2	2	1	1	2	.33	4	.214	.316	.255
1999 Pittsburgh	NL	66	167	31	3	1	2	(1	1)	42	12	13	11	0	30	1	1	1	0	0	—	8	.186	.239	.251
2000 Pittsburgh	NL	46	123	36	6	1	4	(1	3)	56	11	22	14	0	11	5	1	0	3	0	1.00	2	.293	.387	.455
5 ML YEARS		248	633	156	36	4	7	(2	5)	221	59	63	61	4	100	10	7	2	5	3	.63	18	.246	.322	.349

Antonio Osuna

Pitches: Right **Bats:** Right **Pos:** RP-46   **Ht:** 5'11" **Wt:** 206 **Born:** 4/12/73 **Age:** 28

		HOW MUCH HE PITCHED						WHAT HE GAVE UP											THE RESULTS					
Year Team	Lg	G	GS	CG	GF	IP	BFP	H	R	ER	HR	SH	SF	HB	TBB	IBB	SO	WP	Bk	W	L	Pct.	ShO	Sv-Op	Hld	ERA
2000 San Berndno *	A+	3	3	0	0	7.1	28	4	4	4	2	0	0	1	3	0	11	0	0	0	2	.000	0	0- -	—	4.91
Albuquerque *	AAA	3	1	0	0	5.2	27	2	0	0	0	0	0	1	5	0	7	0	0	0	0	0- -	—		0.00
1995 Los Angeles	NL	39	0	0	8	44.2	186	39	22	22	5	2	1	1	20	2	46	1	0	2	4	.333	0	0-2	11	4.43
1996 Los Angeles	NL	73	0	0	21	84	342	65	33	28	6	7	5	2	32	12	85	3	2	9	6	.600	0	4-9	16	3.00
1997 Los Angeles	NL	48	0	0	18	61.2	245	46	15	15	6	4	1	1	19	2	68	2	0	3	4	.429	0	0-0	10	2.19
1998 Los Angeles	NL	54	0	0	25	64.2	272	50	26	22	8	2	2	2	32	0	72	1	0	7	1	.875	0	6-11	12	3.06
1999 Los Angeles	NL	5	0	0	1	4.2	22	4	5	4	0	0	0	1	3	0	5	1	0	0	0	—	0	0-0	2	7.71
2000 Los Angeles	NL	46	0	0	16	67.1	293	57	30	28	7	4	3	2	35	2	70	1	2	3	6	.333	0	0-3	4	3.74
6 ML YEARS		265	0	0	89	327	1360	261	131	119	32	19	12	9	141	18	346	9	4	24	21	.533	0	10-25	55	3.28

Eric Owens

Bats: R **Throws:** R **Pos:** RF-68; LF-65; CF-34; PH/PR-3; 2B-1   **Ht:** 6'0" **Wt:** 198 **Born:** 2/3/71 **Age:** 30

							BATTING												BASERUNNING				PERCENTAGES		
Year Team	Lg	G	AB	H	2B	3B	HR	(Hm	Rd)	TB	R	RBI	TBB	IBB	SO	HBP	SH	SF	SB	CS	SB%	GDP	Avg	OBP	SLG
1995 Cincinnati	NL	2	2	2	0	0	0	(0	0)	2	0	1	0	0	0	0	1	0	0	0	—	0	1.000	1.000	1.000
1996 Cincinnati	NL	88	205	41	6	0	0	(0	0)	47	26	9	23	1	38	1	1	2	16	2	.89	2	.200	.281	.229
1997 Cincinnati	NL	27	57	15	0	0	0	(0	0)	15	8	3	4	0	11	0	0	0	3	2	.60	2	.263	.311	.263
1998 Milwaukee	NL	34	40	5	2	0	1	(0	1)	10	5	4	2	0	6	0	1	0	0	0	—	3	.125	.167	.250
1999 San Diego	NL	149	440	117	22	3	9	(2	7)	172	55	61	38	2	50	3	2	3	33	7	.83	12	.266	.327	.391
2000 San Diego	NL	145	583	171	19	7	6	(4	2)	222	87	51	45	4	63	4	0	4	29	14	.67	16	.293	.346	.381
6 ML YEARS		445	1327	351	49	10	16	(6	10)	468	181	129	112	7	168	8	5	8	81	25	.76	35	.265	.324	.353

Pablo Ozuna

Bats: Right **Throws:** Right **Pos:** 2B-7; PH/PR-7 **Ht:** 6'0" **Wt:** 160 **Born:** 8/25/78 **Age:** 22

Year Team	Lg	G	AB	H	2B	3B	HR	(Hm	Rd)	TB	R	RBI	TBB	IBB	SO	HBP	SH	SF	SB	CS	SB%	GDP	Avg	OBP	SLG
1997 Johnson Cty	R+	56	232	75	13	1	5	—	—	105	40	24	10	0	24	1	6	2	23	5	.82	2	.323	.351	.453
1998 Peoria	A	133	538	192	27	10	9	—	—	266	122	62	29	3	56	11	12	2	62	26	.70	6	.357	.400	.494
1999 Portland	AA	117	502	141	25	7	7	—	—	201	62	46	13	0	50	13	7	3	31	15	.67	8	.281	.315	.400
2000 Portland	AA	118	464	143	25	6	7	—	—	201	74	59	40	0	55	7	5	5	35	24	.59	9	.308	.368	.433
2000 Florida	NL	14	24	8	1	0	0	(0	0)	9	2	0	0	0	2	0	2	0	1	0	1.00	0	.333	.333	.375

Vicente Padilla

Pitches: Right **Bats:** Right **Pos:** RP-55 **Ht:** 6'2" **Wt:** 200 **Born:** 9/27/77 **Age:** 23

Year Team	Lg	G	GS	CG	GF	IP	BFP	H	R	ER	HR	SH	SF	HB	TBB	IBB	SO	WP	Bk	W	L	Pct.	ShO	Sv-Op	Hld	ERA
1999 High Desert	A+	9	9	0	0	50.2	220	50	27	21	3	1	2	1	17	0	55	2	2	4	1	.800	0	0--	—	3.73
Tucson	AAA	18	14	0	0	93.2	405	107	47	39	6	5	2	7	24	7	58	0	1	7	4	.636	0	0--	—	3.75
2000 Tucson	AAA	12	3	0	4	18.1	82	22	9	9	2	2	0	0	8	0	22	2	0	1	0	1.000	0	1--	—	4.42
1999 Arizona	NL	5	0	0	2	2.2	19	7	5	5	1	1	0	0	3	0	0	0	0	0	1	.000	0	0-1	1	16.88
2000 Ari-Phi	NL	55	0	0	16	65.1	291	72	33	27	3	5	3	1	28	7	51	1	0	4	7	.364	0	2-7	15	3.72
2000 Arizona	NL	27	0	0	12	35	143	32	10	9	0	0	1	0	10	2	30	0	0	2	1	.667	0	0-1	7	2.31
Philadelphia	NL	28	0	0	4	30.1	148	40	23	18	3	5	2	1	18	5	21	1	0	2	6	.250	0	2-6	8	5.34
2 ML YEARS		60	0	0	18	68	310	79	38	32	4	6	3	1	31	7	51	1	0	4	8	.333	0	2-8	16	4.24

Lance Painter

Pitches: Left **Bats:** Left **Pos:** RP-40; SP-2 **Ht:** 6'1" **Wt:** 200 **Born:** 7/21/67 **Age:** 33

Year Team	Lg	G	GS	CG	GF	IP	BFP	H	R	ER	HR	SH	SF	HB	TBB	IBB	SO	WP	Bk	W	L	Pct.	ShO	Sv-Op	Hld	ERA
2000 Dunedin *	A+	1	1	0	0	1	3	0	0	0	0	0	0	0	0	0	0	0	0	0	0	—	0	0--	—	0.00
1993 Colorado	NL	10	6	1	2	39	166	52	26	26	5	1	0	0	9	0	16	2	0	2	2	.500	0	0-0	0	6.00
1994 Colorado	NL	15	14	0	1	73.2	336	91	51	50	9	3	5	1	26	2	41	3	1	4	6	.400	0	0-0	0	6.11
1995 Colorado	NL	33	1	0	7	45.1	198	55	23	22	9	0	0	2	10	0	36	4	1	3	0	1.000	0	1-1	4	4.37
1996 Colorado	NL	34	1	0	4	50.2	234	56	37	33	12	3	3	0	25	3	48	4	1	2	4	.667	0	0-1	4	5.86
1997 St. Louis	NL	14	0	0	4	17	69	13	9	9	1	0	0	3	8	2	11	0	0	1	1	.500	0	0-0	3	4.76
1998 St. Louis	NL	65	0	0	9	47.1	207	42	24	21	5	4	2	4	28	3	39	2	0	4	0	1.000	0	1-2	21	3.99
1999 St. Louis	NL	56	4	0	10	63.1	272	63	37	34	6	4	3	2	25	1	56	4	0	4	5	.444	0	1-3	10	4.83
2000 Toronto	AL	42	2	0	11	66.2	285	69	37	35	9	5	1	2	22	1	53	1	0	2	0	1.000	0	0-1	5	4.73
8 ML YEARS		269	28	1	48	440	1767	441	244	230	56	20	14	14	153	12	300	20	2	24	16	.600	0	3-8	47	5.14

Vicente Palacios

Pitches: Right **Bats:** Right **Pos:** RP-7 **Ht:** 6'2" **Wt:** 180 **Born:** 7/19/63 **Age:** 37

Year Team	Lg	G	GS	CG	GF	IP	BFP	H	R	ER	HR	SH	SF	HB	TBB	IBB	SO	WP	Bk	W	L	Pct.	ShO	Sv-Op	Hld	ERA
2000 Las Vegas *	AAA	36	0	0	23	47.1	199	41	20	18	5	1	3	2	17	2	40	0	0	4	1	.800	0	7--	—	3.42
Iowa *	AAA	6	5	1	0	30	133	39	20	19	3	1	1	2	6	1	23	0	1	2	2	.500	0	0--	—	5.70
1987 Pittsburgh	NL	6	4	0	0	29.1	120	27	14	14	1	2	0	1	9	1	13	0	2	2	1	.667	0	0-0	0	4.30
1988 Pittsburgh	NL	7	3	0	0	24.1	113	28	18	18	3	2	1	0	15	1	15	2	3	1	2	.333	0	0-0	1	6.66
1990 Pittsburgh	NL	7	0	0	4	15	50	4	0	0	0	0	0	0	2	0	8	2	0	0	0	—	0	3-3	0	0.00
1991 Pittsburgh	NL	36	7	1	8	81.2	347	69	34	34	12	4	1	4	38	2	64	6	2	6	3	.667	1	3-5	5	3.75
1992 Pittsburgh	NL	20	8	0	4	53	232	56	25	25	1	4	1	0	27	1	33	7	0	3	2	.600	0	0-0	4	4.25
1994 St. Louis	NL	31	17	1	5	117.2	484	104	60	58	16	7	7	3	43	2	95	4	0	3	8	.273	1	1-1	4	4.44
1995 St. Louis	NL	20	5	0	3	40.1	184	48	29	26	7	2	1	2	19	1	34	1	0	2	3	.400	0	0-0	1	5.80
2000 San Diego	NL	7	0	0	2	10.2	46	12	10	8	4	1	0	0	5	1	8	0	0	0	1	.000	0	0-0	1	6.75
8 ML YEARS		134	44	2	26	372	1576	348	190	183	44	22	12	7	158	9	270	22	7	17	20	.459	2	7-9	11	4.43

Orlando Palmeiro

Bats: L **Throws:** L **Pos:** LF-40; PH/PR-37; RF-31; DH-19; CF-2 **Ht:** 5'11" **Wt:** 175 **Born:** 1/19/69 **Age:** 32

Year Team	Lg	G	AB	H	2B	3B	HR	(Hm	Rd)	TB	R	RBI	TBB	IBB	SO	HBP	SH	SF	SB	CS	SB%	GDP	Avg	OBP	SLG
1995 California	AL	15	20	7	0	0	0	(0	0)	7	3	1	1	0	1	0	0	0	0	0	—	0	.350	.381	.350
1996 California	AL	50	87	25	6	1	0	(0	0)	33	6	6	8	1	13	2	1	0	1	0	.00	1	.287	.361	.379
1997 Anaheim	AL	74	134	29	2	2	0	(0	0)	35	19	8	17	1	11	1	3	1	2	2	.50	4	.216	.307	.261
1998 Anaheim	AL	75	165	53	7	2	0	(0	0)	64	28	21	20	1	11	0	7	0	5	4	.56	4	.321	.395	.388
1999 Anaheim	AL	109	317	88	12	1	1	(0	1)	105	46	23	39	1	30	6	6	3	5	5	.50	4	.278	.364	.331
2000 Anaheim	AL	108	243	73	20	2	0	(0	0)	97	38	25	38	0	20	2	10	3	4	1	.80	4	.300	.395	.399
6 ML YEARS		431	966	275	47	8	1	(0	1)	341	140	84	123	4	86	11	27	7	16	13	.55	15	.285	.369	.353

Rafael Palmeiro

Bats: Left **Throws:** Left **Pos:** 1B-108; DH-46; PH/PR-5 **Ht:** 6'0" **Wt:** 190 **Born:** 9/24/64 **Age:** 36

Year Team	Lg	G	AB	H	2B	3B	HR	(Hm	Rd)	TB	R	RBI	TBB	IBB	SO	HBP	SH	SF	SB	CS	SB%	GDP	Avg	OBP	SLG
1986 Chicago	NL	22	73	18	4	0	3	(1	2)	31	9	12	4	0	6	1	0	0	1	1	.50	4	.247	.295	.425
1987 Chicago	NL	84	221	61	15	1	14	(5	9)	120	32	30	20	1	26	1	0	2	2	2	.50	4	.276	.336	.543
1988 Chicago	NL	152	580	178	41	5	8	(8	0)	253	75	53	38	6	34	3	2	6	12	2	.86	11	.307	.349	.436
1989 Texas	AL	156	559	154	23	4	8	(4	4)	209	76	64	63	3	48	6	2	2	4	3	.57	18	.275	.354	.374
1990 Texas	AL	154	598	191	35	6	14	(9	5)	280	72	89	40	6	59	3	2	8	3	3	.50	24	.319	.361	.468
1991 Texas	AL	159	631	203	49	3	26	(12	14)	336	115	88	68	10	72	6	2	7	4	3	.57	17	.322	.389	.532
1992 Texas	AL	159	608	163	27	4	22	(8	14)	264	84	85	72	8	83	10	5	6	2	3	.40	10	.268	.352	.434
1993 Texas	AL	160	597	176	40	2	37	(22	15)	331	124	105	73	22	85	5	2	9	22	3	.88	8	.295	.371	.554
1994 Baltimore	AL	111	436	139	32	0	23	(11	12)	240	82	76	54	1	63	2	0	6	7	3	.70	11	.319	.392	.550

164

Year Team	Lg	G	AB	H	2B	3B	HR	(Hm	Rd)	TB	R	RBI	TBB	IBB	SO	HBP	SH	SF	SB	CS	SB%	GDP	Avg	OBP	SLG
1995 Baltimore	AL	143	554	172	30	2	39	(21	18)	323	89	104	62	5	65	3	0	5	3	1	.75	12	.310	.380	.583
1996 Baltimore	AL	162	626	181	40	2	39	(21	18)	342	110	142	95	12	96	3	0	8	8	0	1.00	9	.289	.381	.546
1997 Baltimore	AL	158	614	156	24	2	38	(20	18)	298	95	110	67	7	109	5	0	6	5	2	.71	14	.254	.329	.485
1998 Baltimore	AL	162	619	183	36	1	43	(25	18)	350	98	121	79	8	91	7	0	4	11	7	.61	14	.296	.379	.565
1999 Texas	AL	158	565	183	30	1	47	(28	19)	356	96	148	97	14	69	3	0	9	2	4	.33	13	.324	.420	.630
2000 Texas	AL	158	565	163	29	3	39	(26	13)	315	102	120	103	17	77	3	0	7	2	1	.67	14	.288	.397	.558
15 ML YEARS		2098	7846	2321	455	36	400	(221	179)	4048	1259	1347	935	120	983	61	15	85	88	38	.70	183	.296	.372	.516

Dean Palmer

Bats: R **Throws:** R **Pos:** 3B-115; 1B-20; DH-14; PH/PR-3   **Ht:** 6'1" **Wt:** 210 **Born:** 12/27/68 **Age:** 32

Year Team	Lg	G	AB	H	2B	3B	HR	(Hm	Rd)	TB	R	RBI	TBB	IBB	SO	HBP	SH	SF	SB	CS	SB%	GDP	Avg	OBP	SLG
1989 Texas	AL	16	19	2	2	0	0	(0	0)	4	0	1	0	0	12	0	0	1	0	0	—	0	.105	.100	.211
1991 Texas	AL	81	268	50	9	2	15	(6	9)	108	38	37	32	0	98	3	1	0	0	2	.00	4	.187	.281	.403
1992 Texas	AL	152	541	124	25	0	26	(11	15)	227	74	72	62	2	154	4	2	4	10	4	.71	9	.229	.311	.420
1993 Texas	AL	148	519	127	31	2	33	(12	21)	261	88	96	53	4	154	8	0	5	11	10	.52	5	.245	.321	.503
1994 Texas	AL	93	342	84	14	2	19	(11	8)	159	50	59	26	0	89	2	0	1	3	4	.43	7	.246	.302	.465
1995 Texas	AL	36	119	40	6	0	9	(5	4)	73	30	24	21	1	21	4	0	1	1	1	.50	2	.336	.448	.613
1996 Texas	AL	154	582	163	26	2	38	(19	19)	307	98	107	59	4	145	5	0	6	2	0	1.00	15	.280	.348	.527
1997 Tex-KC	AL	143	542	139	31	1	23	(10	13)	241	70	86	41	2	134	3	1	5	2	2	.50	7	.256	.310	.445
1998 Kansas City	AL	152	572	159	27	2	34	(21	13)	292	84	119	48	3	134	6	0	13	8	2	.80	18	.278	.333	.510
1999 Detroit	AL	150	560	147	25	2	38	(24	14)	290	92	100	57	3	153	10	0	4	3	3	.50	12	.263	.339	.518
2000 Detroit	AL	145	524	134	22	2	29	(15	14)	247	73	102	66	2	146	4	0	10	4	2	.67	9	.256	.338	.471
1997 Texas	AL	94	355	87	21	0	14	(6	8)	150	47	55	26	2	84	1	1	3	1	0	1.00	4	.245	.296	.423
Kansas City	AL	49	187	52	10	1	9	(4	5)	91	23	31	15	0	50	2	0	2	1	2	.33	3	.278	.335	.487
11 ML YEARS		1270	4588	1169	218	15	264	(134	130)	2209	697	803	465	21	1240	49	4	50	44	30	.59	88	.255	.327	.481

Jose Paniagua

Pitches: Right **Bats:** Right **Pos:** RP-69   **Ht:** 6'2" **Wt:** 190 **Born:** 8/20/73 **Age:** 27

Year Team	Lg	G	GS	CG	GF	IP	BFP	H	R	ER	HR	SH	SF	HB	TBB	IBB	SO	WP	Bk	W	L	Pct.	ShO	Sv-Op	Hld	ERA
1996 Montreal	NL	13	11	0	0	51	223	55	24	20	7	1	1	3	23	0	27	2	2	2	4	.333	0	0-0	0	3.53
1997 Montreal	NL	9	3	0	0	18	100	29	24	24	2	1	1	4	16	1	8	1	0	1	2	.333	0	0-0	0	12.00
1998 Seattle	AL	18	0	0	2	22	83	15	5	5	3	0	0	3	5	0	16	2	0	2	0	1.000	0	1-2	6	2.05
1999 Seattle	AL	59	0	0	16	77.2	350	75	37	35	5	4	3	7	52	4	74	6	0	6	11	.353	0	3-12	16	4.06
2000 Seattle	AL	69	0	0	26	80.1	344	68	31	31	6	3	5	7	38	3	71	4	1	3	0	1.000	0	5-8	14	3.47
5 ML YEARS		168	14	0	44	249	1100	242	121	115	23	9	10	24	134	8	196	15	3	14	17	.452	0	9-22	36	4.16

Craig Paquette

Bats: R **Throws:** R **Pos:** 3B-86; 1B-28; LF-18; RF-16; PH/PR-15; 2B-13   **Ht:** 6'0" **Wt:** 190 **Born:** 3/28/69 **Age:** 32

Year Team	Lg	G	AB	H	2B	3B	HR	(Hm	Rd)	TB	R	RBI	TBB	IBB	SO	HBP	SH	SF	SB	CS	SB%	GDP	Avg	OBP	SLG
1993 Oakland	AL	105	393	86	20	4	12	(8	4)	150	35	46	14	2	108	0	1	1	4	2	.67	4	.219	.245	.382
1994 Oakland	AL	14	49	7	2	0	0	(0	0)	9	0	0	0	0	14	0	1	0	1	0	1.00	0	.143	.143	.184
1995 Oakland	AL	105	283	64	13	1	13	(8	5)	118	42	49	12	0	88	1	3	5	5	2	.71	5	.226	.256	.417
1996 Kansas City	AL	118	429	111	15	1	22	(12	10)	194	61	67	23	2	101	2	3	5	5	3	.63	11	.259	.296	.452
1997 Kansas City	AL	77	252	58	15	1	8	(7	1)	99	26	33	10	0	57	2	1	2	2	2	.50	13	.230	.263	.393
1998 New York	NL	7	19	5	2	0	0	(0	0)	7	3	0	0	0	6	0	0	0	1	0	1.00	1	.263	.263	.368
1999 St. Louis	NL	48	157	45	6	0	10	(7	3)	81	21	37	6	0	38	0	1	2	1	0	1.00	6	.287	.309	.516
2000 St. Louis	NL	134	384	94	24	2	15	(13	2)	167	47	61	27	1	83	2	1	6	4	3	.57	5	.245	.294	.435
8 ML YEARS		608	1966	470	97	9	80	(55	25)	825	235	293	92	5	495	7	11	21	23	12	.66	50	.239	.273	.420

Chan Ho Park

Pitches: Right **Bats:** Right **Pos:** SP-34   **Ht:** 6'2" **Wt:** 204 **Born:** 6/30/73 **Age:** 28

Year Team	Lg	G	GS	CG	GF	IP	BFP	H	R	ER	HR	SH	SF	HB	TBB	IBB	SO	WP	Bk	W	L	Pct.	ShO	Sv-Op	Hld	ERA
1994 Los Angeles	NL	2	0	0	1	4	23	5	5	5	1	0	0	1	5	0	6	0	0	0	0	—	0	0-0	0	11.25
1995 Los Angeles	NL	2	1	0	0	4	16	2	2	2	1	0	0	0	2	0	7	0	1	0	0	—	0	0-0	0	4.50
1996 Los Angeles	NL	48	10	0	7	108.2	477	82	48	44	7	8	1	4	71	3	119	4	3	5	5	.500	0	0-0	4	3.64
1997 Los Angeles	NL	32	29	2	1	192	792	149	80	72	24	9	5	8	70	1	166	4	1	14	8	.636	0	0-0	0	3.38
1998 Los Angeles	NL	34	34	2	0	220.2	946	199	101	91	16	11	10	11	97	1	191	6	2	15	9	.625	0	0-0	0	3.71
1999 Los Angeles	NL	33	33	0	0	194.1	883	208	120	113	31	10	5	14	100	4	174	11	1	13	11	.542	0	0-0	0	5.23
2000 Los Angeles	NL	34	34	3	0	226	963	173	92	82	21	12	5	12	124	4	217	13	0	18	10	.643	1	0-0	0	3.27
7 ML YEARS		185	141	7	9	949.2	4100	818	448	409	101	50	26	50	469	13	880	38	8	65	43	.602	1	0-0	4	3.88

Jim Parque

Pitches: Left **Bats:** Left **Pos:** SP-32; RP-1   **Ht:** 5'11" **Wt:** 165 **Born:** 2/8/76 **Age:** 25

Year Team	Lg	G	GS	CG	GF	IP	BFP	H	R	ER	HR	SH	SF	HB	TBB	IBB	SO	WP	Bk	W	L	Pct.	ShO	Sv-Op	Hld	ERA
1998 Chicago	AL	21	21	0	0	113	507	135	72	64	14	1	0	6	49	0	77	0	3	7	5	.583	0	0-0	0	5.10
1999 Chicago	AL	31	30	1	0	173.2	804	210	111	99	23	5	8	10	79	2	111	3	2	9	15	.375	0	0-0	0	5.13
2000 Chicago	AL	33	32	0	0	187	828	208	105	89	21	5	5	11	71	1	111	2	5	13	6	.684	0	0-0	0	4.28
3 ML YEARS		85	83	1	0	473.2	2139	553	288	252	58	11	13	27	199	3	299	5	10	29	26	.527	0	0-0	0	4.79

Jose Parra

Pitches: Right **Bats:** Right **Pos:** RP-4; SP-2   **Ht:** 5'11" **Wt:** 175 **Born:** 11/28/72 **Age:** 28

Year Team	Lg	G	GS	CG	GF	IP	BFP	H	R	ER	HR	SH	SF	HB	TBB	IBB	SO	WP	Bk	W	L	Pct.	ShO	Sv-Op	Hld	ERA
2000 Nashville *	AAA	23	21	0	1	101.2	466	106	66	59	7	5	2	7	65		68	14	0	6	5	.545	0	1--		5.22
1995 LA-Min		20	12	0	0	72	339	93	67	57	13	0	4	3	28	1	36	3	1	1	5	.167	0	0-0	0	7.13
1996 Minnesota	AL	27	5	0	7	70	320	88	48	47	15	1	3	3	27	0	50	4	1	5	5	.500	0	0-1	0	6.04
2000 Pittsburgh	NL	6	2	0	1	11.2	57	17	9	9	3	1	0	1	7	0	9	0	0	0	1	.000	0	0-0	0	6.94
1995 Los Angeles	NL	8	0	0	0	10.1	47	10	8	5	2	0	1	1	6	1	7	0	1	0	0	—	0	0-0	0	4.35
Minnesota	AL	12	12	0	0	61.2	292	83	59	52	11	0	3	2	22	0	29	3	0	1	5	.167	0	0-0	0	7.59
3 ML YEARS		53	19	0	8	153.2	716	198	124	113	31	2	7	7	62	1	95	7	2	6	11	.353	0	0-1	0	6.62

Steve Parris

Pitches: Right **Bats:** Right **Pos:** SP-33   **Ht:** 6'0" **Wt:** 195 **Born:** 12/17/67 **Age:** 33

Year Team	Lg	G	GS	CG	GF	IP	BFP	H	R	ER	HR	SH	SF	HB	TBB	IBB	SO	WP	Bk	W	L	Pct.	ShO	Sv-Op	Hld	ERA
1995 Pittsburgh	NL	15	15	1	0	82	360	89	49	49	6	3	2	7	33	1	61	4	0	6	6	.500	1	0-0	0	5.38
1996 Pittsburgh	NL	8	4	0	3	26.1	123	35	22	21	4	1	1	1	11	0	27	2	0	0	3	.000	0	0-0	0	7.18
1998 Cincinnati	NL	18	16	1	0	99	421	89	44	41	9	7	1	4	32	3	77	1	1	6	5	.545	1	0-0	0	3.73
1999 Cincinnati	NL	22	21	2	0	128.2	545	124	59	50	16	7	3	6	52	4	86	3	0	11	4	.733	1	0-0	0	3.50
2000 Cincinnati	NL	33	33	0	0	192.2	861	227	109	103	30	10	3	4	71	5	117	9	1	12	17	.414	0	0-0	0	4.81
5 ML YEARS		96	89	4	3	528.2	2310	564	283	264	71	28	10	22	199	13	368	19	2	35	35	.500	3	0-0	0	4.49

John Parrish

Pitches: Left **Bats:** Left **Pos:** SP-8   **Ht:** 5'11" **Wt:** 181 **Born:** 11/26/77 **Age:** 23

Year Team	Lg	G	GS	CG	GF	IP	BFP	H	R	ER	HR	SH	SF	HB	TBB	IBB	SO	WP	Bk	W	L	Pct.	ShO	Sv-Op	Hld	ERA
1996 Orioles	R	11	0	0	6	19.1	83	13	5	4	0	0	0	0	11	0	33	2	0	2	0	1.000	0	2--	—	1.86
Bluefield	R+	8	0	0	5	13.1	60	11	6	4	0	1	2	0	9	1	18	2	0	1	0	.667	0	1--	—	2.70
1997 Bowie	AA	1	1	0	0	5	20	3	1	1	0	0	0	0	2	0	3	0	0	1	0	1.000	0	0--	—	1.80
Frederick	A+	5	5	0	0	22.1	103	23	18	15	3	1	0	2	16	0	17	3	0	1	3	.250	0	0--	—	6.04
Delmarva	A	23	10	0	5	72.2	315	69	39	31	7	2	3	2	32	3	76	9	0	4	4	.500	0	1--	—	3.84
1998 Frederick	A+	16	16	1	0	82.2	352	77	39	30	5	3	4	5	27	1	81	9	0	4	4	.500	0	0--	—	3.27
1999 Delmarva	A	4	0	0	1	10	47	9	8	8	1	0	0	1	6	1	10	3	0	1	0	1.000	0	0--	—	7.20
Frederick	A+	6	6	0	0	36.2	151	34	17	17	4	1	2	0	12	0	44	5	0	2	2	.500	0	0--	—	4.17
Bowie	AA	12	10	0	2	55.2	248	49	28	25	4	7	5	3	43	1	42	3	1	2	0	1.000	0	0--	—	4.04
2000 Bowie	AA	3	3	0	0	16	64	12	3	3	0	0	1	0	7	0	16	0	0	2	0	1.000	0	0--	—	1.69
Rochester	AAA	18	18	0	0	104	426	85	54	49	10	3	4	2	56	1	87	6	2	6	7	.462	0	0--	—	4.24
2000 Baltimore	AL	8	8	0	0	36.1	180	40	32	29	6	1	4	1	35	0	28	1	0	2	4	.333	0	0-0	0	7.18

Corey Patterson

Bats: Left **Throws:** Right **Pos:** CF-11; PH/PR-1   **Ht:** 5'10" **Wt:** 180 **Born:** 8/13/79 **Age:** 21

Year Team	Lg	G	AB	H	2B	3B	HR	(Hm	Rd)	TB	R	RBI	TBB	IBB	SO	HBP	SH	SF	SB	CS	SB%	GDP	Avg	OBP	SLG
1999 Lansing	A	112	475	152	35	17	20	—	—	281	94	79	25	1	85	5	0	4	33	9	.79	5	.320	.358	.592
2000 West Tenn	AA	118	444	116	26	5	22	—	—	218	73	82	45	5	115	10	0	7	27	14	.66	7	.261	.338	.491
2000 Chicago	NL	11	42	7	1	0	2	(1	1)	14	9	2	3	0	14	1	1	0	1	1	.50	0	.167	.239	.333

Danny Patterson

Pitches: Right **Bats:** Right **Pos:** RP-58   **Ht:** 6'0" **Wt:** 225 **Born:** 2/17/71 **Age:** 30

Year Team	Lg	G	GS	CG	GF	IP	BFP	H	R	ER	HR	SH	SF	HB	TBB	IBB	SO	WP	Bk	W	L	Pct.	ShO	Sv-Op	Hld	ERA
1996 Texas	AL	7	0	0	5	8.2	38	10	4	0	0	0	0	0	3	1	5	0	0	0	0	—	0	0-0	0	0.00
1997 Texas	AL	54	0	0	17	71	296	70	29	27	3	4	3	0	23	4	69	7	1	10	6	.625	0	1-8	9	3.42
1998 Texas	AL	56	0	0	21	60.2	257	64	31	30	11	1	1	2	19	2	33	3	0	2	5	.286	0	2-2	19	4.45
1999 Texas	AL	53	0	0	18	60.1	275	77	38	38	5	0	2	1	19	3	43	2	0	2	0	1.000	0	0-1	4	5.67
2000 Detroit	AL	58	0	0	12	56.2	244	69	26	25	4	3	2	2	14	2	29	1	0	5	1	.833	0	0-2	12	3.97
5 ML YEARS		228	0	0	73	257.1	1110	290	128	120	23	8	8	5	78	12	179	13	1	19	12	.613	0	3-13	44	4.20

Josh Paul

Bats: Right **Throws:** Right **Pos:** C-34; PH/PR-6; LF-1   **Ht:** 6'1" **Wt:** 185 **Born:** 5/19/75 **Age:** 26

Year Team	Lg	G	AB	H	2B	3B	HR	(Hm	Rd)	TB	R	RBI	TBB	IBB	SO	HBP	SH	SF	SB	CS	SB%	GDP	Avg	OBP	SLG
1996 White Sox	R	1	0	0	0	0	0	—	—	0	0	0	1	0	0	0	0	0	0	0	—	0	1.000		
Hickory	A	59	226	74	16	0	8	—	—	114	41	37	21	3	53	1	3	1	13	4	.76	2	.327	.386	.504
1997 White Sox	R	5	14	6	0	1	0	—	—	8	3	0	1	0	3	0	1	0	1	0	1.00	1	.429	.467	.571
Birmingham	AA	34	115	34	5	0	1	—	—	42	18	16	12	0	25	1	3	0	6	2	.75	4	.296	.367	.365
1998 Winston-Sal	A+	123	444	132	20	7	11	—	—	180	66	63	38	2	91	5	7	2	20	8	.71	11	.255	.319	.405
1999 Birmingham	AA	93	319	89	19	3	4	—	—	126	47	42	29	1	68	5	3	4	6	6	.50	6	.279	.345	.395
2000 Charlotte	AAA	51	168	40	5	1	4	—	—	59	28	19	13	0	38	2	6	1	6	2	.75	3	.238	.299	.351
1999 Chicago	AL	6	18	4	1	0	0	(0	0)	5	2	1	0	0	4	0	0	0	0	0	—	0	.222	.222	.278
2000 Chicago	AL	36	71	20	3	2	1	(1	0)	30	15	8	5	0	17	1	2	0	1	0	1.00	3	.282	.338	.423
2 ML YEARS		42	89	24	4	2	1	(1	0)	35	17	9	5	0	21	1	2	0	1	0	1.00	3	.270	.316	.393

166

Carl Pavano

Pitches: Right **Bats:** Right **Pos:** SP-15
Ht: 6'5" **Wt:** 230 **Born:** 1/8/76 **Age:** 25

Year Team	Lg	G	GS	CG	GF	IP	BFP	H	R	ER	HR	SH	SF	HB	TBB	IBB	SO	WP	Bk	W	L	Pct.	ShO	Sv-Op	Hld	ERA
1998 Montreal	NL	24	23	0	0	134.2	580	130	70	63	18	5	6	8	43	1	83	1	0	6	9	.400	0	0-0	0	4.21
1999 Montreal	NL	19	18	1	0	104	457	117	66	65	8	5	2	4	35	1	70	1	3	6	8	.429	1	0-0	0	5.63
2000 Montreal	NL	15	15	0	0	97	408	89	40	33	8	4	3	8	34	1	64	1	1	8	4	.667	0	0-0	0	3.06
3 ML YEARS		58	56	1	0	335.2	1445	336	176	161	34	14	11	20	112	3	217	3	4	20	21	.488	1	0-0	0	4.32

Jay Payton

Bats: Right **Throws:** Right **Pos:** CF-143; PH/PR-11; LF-4
Ht: 5'10" **Wt:** 185 **Born:** 11/22/72 **Age:** 28

Year Team	Lg	G	AB	H	2B	3B	HR	Hm	Rd	TB	R	RBI	TBB	IBB	SO	HBP	SH	SF	SB	CS	SB%	GDP	Avg	OBP	SLG
1994 Pittsfield	A-	58	219	80	16	2	3	—	—	109	47	37	23	2	18	9	0	4	10	2	.83	1	.365	.439	.498
Binghamton	AA	8	25	7	1	0	0	—	—	8	3	1	2	0	3	1	0	0	1	1	.50	1	.280	.357	.320
1995 Binghamton	AA	85	357	123	20	3	14	—	—	191	59	54	29	2	32	2	0	2	16	7	.70	11	.345	.395	.535
Norfolk	AAA	50	196	47	11	4	4	—	—	78	33	30	11	0	22	2	4	2	11	3	.79	5	.240	.284	.398
1996 Mets	R	3	13	5	1	0	1	—	—	9	3	2	0	0	1	0	0	0	1	0	1.00	0	.385	.385	.692
Binghamton	AA	4	10	2	0	0	0	—	—	2	0	2	2	1	2	0	0	2	0	1	.00	0	.200	.286	.200
St. Lucie	A+	9	26	8	2	0	0	—	—	10	4	1	4	1	5	0	0	0	2	1	.67	1	.308	.400	.385
Norfolk	AAA	55	153	47	6	3	6	—	—	77	30	26	11	1	25	3	0	1	0	0	—	0	.307	.363	.503
1998 St. Lucie	A+	3	7	1	0	0	0	—	—	1	0	0	3	2	1	0	0	0	0	0	—	0	.143	.400	.143
Norfolk	AAA	82	322	84	14	4	8	—	—	130	45	30	26	0	50	1	1	0	12	7	.63	5	.261	.318	.404
1999 St. Lucie	A+	7	26	9	1	1	0	—	—	12	3	3	4	0	5	0	0	0	1	0	1.00	1	.346	.433	.462
Norfolk	AAA	38	144	56	13	2	8	—	—	97	27	35	12	1	13	1	0	1	2	2	.50	2	.389	.437	.674
1998 New York	NL	15	22	7	1	0	0	(0	0)	8	2	0	1	0	4	0	0	0	1	2	.33	0	.318	.348	.364
1999 New York	NL	13	8	2	1	0	0	(0	0)	3	1	1	0	0	2	1	0	0	1	1	.33	0	.250	.333	.375
2000 New York	NL	149	488	142	23	1	17	(9	8)	218	63	62	30	0	60	3	0	8	5	11	.31	9	.291	.331	.447
3 ML YEARS		177	518	151	25	1	17	(9	8)	229	66	63	31	0	66	4	0	8	6	13	.32	9	.292	.332	.442

Elvis Pena

Bats: Both **Throws:** Right **Pos:** PH/PR-7; SS-4; 2B-1
Ht: 5'11" **Wt:** 155 **Born:** 9/15/76 **Age:** 24

Year Team	Lg	G	AB	H	2B	3B	HR	Hm	Rd	TB	R	RBI	TBB	IBB	SO	HBP	SH	SF	SB	CS	SB%	GDP	Avg	OBP	SLG
1994 Rockies	R	49	171	39	5	2	0	—	—	48	31	9	35	0	47	6	1	0	20	12	.63	1	.228	.377	.281
1995 Asheville	A	48	145	33	2	0	0	—	—	35	27	4	28	0	32	4	3	0	23	6	.79	1	.228	.367	.241
Portland	A-	58	215	54	6	3	0	—	—	66	29	18	26	0	45	1	3	0	28	7	.80	2	.251	.335	.307
1996 Salem	A+	102	341	76	9	4	0	—	—	93	48	28	61	2	70	3	13	1	30	16	.65	12	.223	.345	.273
1997 Salem	A+	93	279	62	9	2	1	—	—	78	41	30	37	0	53	2	14	3	16	6	.73	1	.222	.315	.280
1998 Asheville	A	115	428	123	24	4	6	—	—	173	93	48	70	2	85	14	7	2	41	12	.77	5	.287	.403	.404
1999 Colo Spngs	AAA	13	43	7	1	0	0	—	—	8	5	1	3	0	7	1	0	0	4	1	.80	0	.163	.234	.186
Carolina	AA	110	356	107	24	6	2	—	—	149	57	31	48	2	64	6	8	2	21	6	.78	6	.301	.391	.419
2000 Carolina	AA	126	477	143	16	7	3	—	—	182	92	37	69	2	76	10	4	1	48	13	.79	11	.300	.399	.382
2000 Colorado	NL	10	9	3	1	0	0	(0	0)	4	1	1	1	0	1	0	0	0	1	0	1.00	3	.333	.400	.444

Jesus Pena

Pitches: Left **Bats:** Left **Pos:** RP-22
Ht: 6'0" **Wt:** 170 **Born:** 3/8/75 **Age:** 26

Year Team	Lg	G	GS	CG	GF	IP	BFP	H	R	ER	HR	SH	SF	HB	TBB	IBB	SO	WP	Bk	W	L	Pct.	ShO	Sv-Op	Hld	ERA
1995 Erie	A-	3	3	0	0	10.2	56	18	16	15	1	1	0	2	7	0	5	0	1	0	3	.000	0	0--	—	12.66
Pirates	R	7	6	0	0	35	138	20	11	10	0	0	0	0	19	0	36	4	0	0	0	—	0	0--	—	2.57
1996 Erie	A-	21	3	0	5	35.2	164	32	24	19	3	2	0	2	24	1	34	2	0	2	5	.286	0	0--	—	4.79
1997 Hickory	A	43	0	0	32	65	263	55	24	16	3	4	3	0	19	1	57	3	0	3	4	.429	0	8--	—	2.22
1998 Winston-Sal	A+	23	0	0	13	31.2	125	20	11	11	2	2	2	1	12	1	37	0	1	3	4	.429	0	5--	—	3.13
Birmingham	AA	22	0	0	12	23.1	100	20	12	10	3	2	1	0	10	0	28	2	2	0	2	.000	0	2--	—	3.86
1999 Birmingham	AA	40	0	0	18	45.2	183	31	12	12	2	1	1	0	18	1	49	2	1	3	2	.600	0	5--	—	2.36
2000 Charlotte	AAA	21	0	0	9	17.1	69	10	6	6	1	0	0	0	10	0	19	1	1	0	0	—	0	4--	—	3.12
Birmingham	AA	23	0	0	20	21.1	89	19	9	8	2	1	0	2	6	2	25	0	1	1	2	.333	0	0-1	2	3.38
1999 Chicago	AL	26	0	0	1	20.1	106	21	15	12	3	1	0	1	23	5	20	3	0	0	0	—	0	0-1	2	5.31
2000 CWS-Bos	AL	22	0	0	0	26.1	123	28	19	15	7	0	2	1	19	0	20	1	0	2	1	.667	0	1-1	0	5.13
2000 Chicago	AL	20	0	0	7	23.1	109	25	18	14	6	0	2	1	16	0	19	1	0	2	1	.667	0	1-1	0	5.40
Boston	AL	2	0	0	0	3	14	3	1	1	0	0	0	0	3	0	1	0	0	0	0	—	0	0-0	0	3.00
2 ML YEARS		48	0	0	8	46.2	229	49	34	27	10	1	2	2	42	5	40	4	0	2	1	.667	0	1-2	2	5.21

Juan Pena

Pitches: Right **Bats:** Right **Pos:** SP
Ht: 6'5" **Wt:** 215 **Born:** 6/27/77 **Age:** 24

Year Team	Lg	G	GS	CG	GF	IP	BFP	H	R	ER	HR	SH	SF	HB	TBB	IBB	SO	WP	Bk	W	L	Pct.	ShO	Sv-Op	Hld	ERA
1995 Red Sox	R	13	4	2	6	55.1	217	41	17	12	2	1	2	1	6	0	47	2	1	3	2	.600	0	1--	—	1.95
Sarasota	A+	2	2	0	0	7.1	35	8	4	4	0	0	0	2	3	0	5	1	1	1	1	.500	0	0--	—	4.91
1996 Michigan	A	26	26	4	0	187.2	743	149	70	62	16	9	5	10	34	2	156	10	2	12	10	.545	0	0--	—	2.97
1997 Sarasota	A+	13	13	3	0	91.1	359	67	39	30	8	1	2	2	23	1	88	1	0	4	6	.400	0	0--	—	2.96
Trenton	AA	16	14	0	2	97	418	98	56	51	13	6	3	2	31	0	79	5	1	5	6	.455	0	0--	—	4.73
1998 Pawtucket	AAA	24	23	1	0	139.2	606	141	73	68	17	4	2	8	51	3	146	14	2	8	10	.444	1	0--	—	4.38
1999 Red Sox	R	1	1	0	0	2	7	0	0	0	0	0	0	0	0	0	4	0	0	0	0	—	0	0--	—	0.00
Sarasota	A+	2	2	0	0	6.1	28	12	6	5	0	0	0	0	5	0	4	0	0	1	0	1.000	0	0--	—	7.11
Pawtucket	AAA	10	10	0	0	48	206	44	28	22	8	0	0	4	13	0	61	1	3	4	2	.667	0	0--	—	4.13
1999 Boston	AL	2	2	0	0	13	49	9	1	1	0	0	0	0	3	0	15	0	0	2	0	1.000	0	0-0	0	0.69

Brad Penny

Pitches: Right **Bats:** Right **Pos:** SP-22; RP-1   **Ht:** 6'4" **Wt:** 200 **Born:** 5/24/78 **Age:** 23

Year Team	Lg	G	GS	CG	GF	IP	BFP	H	R	ER	HR	SH	SF	HB	TBB	IBB	SO	WP	Bk	W	L	Pct.	ShO	Sv-Op	Hld	ERA
1996 Diamndbcks	R	11	8	0	1	49.2	201	36	18	13	1	0	1	3	14	0	52	3	2	2	2	.500	0	0-–	—	2.36
1997 South Bend	A	25	25	0	0	118.2	489	91	44	36	4	5	0	4	43	2	116	10	2	10	5	.667	0	0-–	—	2.73
1998 High Desert	A+	28	28	1	0	164	661	138	65	54	15	3	2	9	35	0	207	4	0	14	5	.737	0	0-–	—	2.96
1999 El Paso	AA	17	17	0	0	90	391	109	56	48	9	1	2	4	25	0	100	4	2	2	7	.222	0	0-–	—	4.80
Portland	AAA	6	6	0	0	32.1	139	28	15	14	3	0	1	3	14	0	35	3	2	1	0	1.000	0	0-–	—	3.90
2000 Brevard Cty	A+	2	2	0	0	8	33	5	2	1	0	0	0	0	4	0	11	0	1	0	1	.000	0	0-–	—	1.13
Calgary	AAA	3	3	0	0	15	65	8	8	3	1	0	1	3	10	0	16	0	0	2	0	1.000	0	0-–	—	1.80
2000 Florida	NL	23	22	0	0	119.2	529	120	70	64	13	6	2	5	60	4	80	4	1	8	7	.533	0	0-0	0	4.81

Troy Percival

Pitches: Right **Bats:** Right **Pos:** RP-54   **Ht:** 6'3" **Wt:** 236 **Born:** 8/9/69 **Age:** 31

Year Team	Lg	G	GS	CG	GF	IP	BFP	H	R	ER	HR	SH	SF	HB	TBB	IBB	SO	WP	Bk	W	L	Pct.	ShO	Sv-Op	Hld	ERA
2000 Lk Elsinore *	A+	2	2	0	0	2	8	1	1	1	0	0	0	0	1	0	1	0	0	0	0	—	0	0-–	—	4.50
1995 California	AL	62	0	0	16	74	284	37	19	16	6	4	1	1	26	2	94	2	2	3	2	.600	0	3-6	29	1.95
1996 California	AL	62	0	0	52	74	291	38	20	19	8	2	1	2	31	4	100	2	0	0	2	.000	0	36-39	2	2.31
1997 Anaheim	AL	55	0	0	46	52	224	40	20	20	6	1	2	4	22	2	72	5	0	5	5	.500	0	27-31	0	3.46
1998 Anaheim	AL	67	0	0	60	66.2	287	45	31	27	5	3	2	3	37	4	87	3	0	2	7	.222	0	42-48	0	3.65
1999 Anaheim	AL	60	0	0	50	57	230	38	24	24	9	0	1	3	22	0	58	0	0	4	6	.400	0	31-39	0	3.79
2000 Anaheim	AL	54	0	0	45	50	221	42	27	25	7	3	2	2	30	4	49	1	0	5	5	.500	0	32-42	0	4.50
6 ML YEARS		360	0	0	269	373.2	1537	240	141	131	41	13	9	15	168	16	460	16	2	19	27	.413	0	171-205	31	3.16

Carlos Perez

Pitches: Left **Bats:** Left **Pos:** SP-22; RP-8   **Ht:** 6'3" **Wt:** 210 **Born:** 1/14/71 **Age:** 30

Year Team	Lg	G	GS	CG	GF	IP	BFP	H	R	ER	HR	SH	SF	HB	TBB	IBB	SO	WP	Bk	W	L	Pct.	ShO	Sv-Op	Hld	ERA
1995 Montreal	NL	28	23	2	2	141.1	592	142	61	58	18	6	1	5	28	2	106	8	4	10	8	.556	1	0-0	1	3.69
1997 Montreal	NL	33	32	8	0	206.2	857	206	109	89	21	5	7	4	48	1	110	2	1	12	13	.480	5	0-0	0	3.88
1998 Mon-LA	NL	34	34	7	0	241	1009	244	109	96	21	14	3	3	63	4	128	7	1	11	14	.440	0	0-0	0	3.59
1999 Los Angeles	NL	17	16	0	0	89.2	420	116	77	74	23	6	3	6	39	1	40	2	3	2	10	.167	0	0-0	0	7.43
2000 Los Angeles	NL	30	22	0	1	144	641	192	95	89	25	6	2	8	33	1	64	3	1	5	8	.385	0	0-1	0	5.56
1998 Montreal	NL	23	23	3	0	163.1	690	177	79	68	12	11	3	3	33	3	82	5	1	7	10	.412	0	0-0	0	3.75
Los Angeles	NL	11	11	4	0	77.2	319	67	30	28	9	3	0	0	30	1	46	2	0	4	4	.500	2	0-0	0	3.24
5 ML YEARS		142	127	17	3	822.2	3519	900	451	406	108	37	16	26	211	9	448	22	10	40	53	.430	8	0-1	1	4.44

Eddie Perez

Bats: Right **Throws:** Right **Pos:** C-7   **Ht:** 6'1" **Wt:** 185 **Born:** 5/4/68 **Age:** 33

Year Team	Lg	G	AB	H	2B	3B	HR	(Hm	Rd)	TB	R	RBI	TBB	IBB	SO	HBP	SH	SF	SB	CS	SB%	GDP	Avg	OBP	SLG
1995 Atlanta	NL	7	13	4	1	0	1	(0	1)	8	1	4	0	0	2	0	0	0	0	0	—	0	.308	.308	.615
1996 Atlanta	NL	68	156	40	9	1	4	(2	2)	63	19	17	8	0	19	1	0	2	0	0	—	6	.256	.293	.404
1997 Atlanta	NL	73	191	41	5	0	6	(4	2)	64	20	18	10	0	35	2	1	2	0	1	.00	8	.215	.259	.335
1998 Atlanta	NL	61	149	50	12	0	6	(3	3)	80	18	32	15	0	28	2	1	0	1	1	.50	3	.336	.404	.537
1999 Atlanta	NL	104	309	77	17	0	7	(0	7)	115	30	30	17	4	40	6	4	3	0	1	.00	9	.249	.299	.372
2000 Atlanta	NL	7	22	4	1	0	0	(0	0)	5	0	3	0	0	2	0	0	0	0	0	—	0	.182	.182	.227
6 ML YEARS		320	840	216	45	1	24	(9	15)	335	88	104	50	4	126	11	6	7	1	3	.25	26	.257	.305	.399

Eduardo Perez

Bats: R **Throws:** R **Pos:** 1B-24; PH/PR-8; LF-4; 3B-2   **Ht:** 6'4" **Wt:** 215 **Born:** 9/11/69 **Age:** 31

Year Team	Lg	G	AB	H	2B	3B	HR	(Hm	Rd)	TB	R	RBI	TBB	IBB	SO	HBP	SH	SF	SB	CS	SB%	GDP	Avg	OBP	SLG
2000 Memphis *	AAA	77	277	80	12	3	19	—	—	155	57	66	43	1	48	1	0	3	10	3	.77	9	.289	.383	.560
1993 California	AL	52	180	45	6	2	4	(2	2)	67	16	30	9	0	39	2	0	1	4	4	.56	4	.250	.292	.372
1994 California	AL	38	129	27	7	0	5	(3	2)	49	10	16	12	1	29	0	1	1	3	0	1.00	5	.209	.275	.380
1995 California	AL	29	71	12	4	1	1	(0	1)	21	7	7	12	0	9	2	0	0	0	2	.00	3	.169	.302	.296
1996 Cincinnati	NL	18	36	8	0	0	3	(3	0)	17	5	5	1	0	9	2	0	1	0	0	—	2	.222	.317	.472
1997 Cincinnati	NL	106	297	75	18	0	16	(7	9)	141	44	52	29	1	76	2	0	2	5	1	.83	6	.253	.321	.475
1998 Cincinnati	NL	84	172	41	4	0	4	(1	3)	57	20	30	21	2	45	2	1	0	1	0	.00	2	.238	.325	.331
1999 St. Louis	NL	21	32	11	2	0	1	(0	1)	16	6	9	7	0	6	0	0	0	0	0	—	0	.344	.462	.500
2000 St. Louis	NL	35	91	27	4	0	3	(0	3)	40	9	10	5	0	19	3	2	1	1	0	1.00	2	.297	.350	.440
8 ML YEARS		383	1008	246	45	3	37	(16	21)	408	122	159	100	5	232	11	4	8	14	8	.64	24	.244	.317	.405

Neifi Perez

Bats: Both **Throws:** Right **Pos:** SS-162; PH/PR-1   **Ht:** 6'0" **Wt:** 175 **Born:** 2/2/75 **Age:** 26

Year Team	Lg	G	AB	H	2B	3B	HR	(Hm	Rd)	TB	R	RBI	TBB	IBB	SO	HBP	SH	SF	SB	CS	SB%	GDP	Avg	OBP	SLG
1996 Colorado	NL	17	45	7	2	0	0	(0	0)	9	4	3	0	0	8	0	1	0	2	2	.50	2	.156	.156	.200
1997 Colorado	NL	83	313	91	13	10	5	(3	2)	139	46	31	21	4	43	1	4	3	4	3	.57	3	.291	.333	.444
1998 Colorado	NL	162	647	177	25	9	9	(6	3)	247	80	59	38	0	70	1	22	4	5	6	.45	8	.274	.313	.382
1999 Colorado	NL	157	690	193	27	11	12	(8	4)	278	108	70	28	0	54	1	9	4	13	5	.72	4	.280	.307	.403
2000 Colorado	NL	162	651	187	39	11	10	(7	3)	278	92	71	30	6	63	0	7	11	3	6	.33	9	.287	.314	.427
5 ML YEARS		581	2346	655	106	41	36	(24	12)	951	330	234	117	10	238	3	44	23	27	22	.55	26	.279	.311	.405

168

Santiago Perez

Bats: Both Throws: Right Pos: SS-20; PH/PR-9 Ht: 6'2" Wt: 150 Born: 12/30/75 Age: 25

Year Team	Lg	G	AB	H	2B	3B	HR	(Hm	Rd)	TB	R	RBI	TBB	IBB	SO	HBP	SH	SF	SB	CS	SB%	GDP	Avg	OBP	SLG
1995 Fayettevle	A	130	425	101	15	1	4	—	—	130	54	44	30	0	98	1	7	7	10	9	.53	6	.238	.285	.306
1996 Lakeland	A+	122	418	105	18	2	1	—	—	130	33	27	16	1	88	3	7	2	6	5	.55	9	.251	.282	.311
1997 Lakeland	A+	111	445	122	20	12	4	—	—	178	66	46	20	1	98	2	8	5	21	9	.70	6	.274	.305	.400
1998 El Paso	AA	107	454	139	20	13	11	—	—	218	73	64	28	3	70	4	4	5	21	11	.66	7	.306	.348	.480
Louisville	AAA	36	133	36	4	3	3	—	—	55	18	14	6	0	31	0	2	1	6	3	.67	3	.271	.300	.414
1999 Louisville	AAA	108	407	107	23	8	7	—	—	167	57	38	31	1	94	2	2	5	21	4	.84	7	.263	.315	.410
2000 Indianapols	AAA	106	408	112	26	7	5	—	—	167	74	34	44	3	96	1	3	1	31	8	.79	2	.275	.346	.409
2000 Milwaukee	NL	24	52	9	2	0	0	(0	0)	11	8	2	8	2	9	1	1	1	4	0	1.00	1	.173	.290	.212

Timoniel Perez

Bats: L Throws: L Pos: PH/PR-10; LF-8; RF-8; CF-7 Ht: 5'9" Wt: 167 Born: 4/8/77 Age: 24

Year Team	Lg	G	AB	H	2B	3B	HR	(Hm	Rd)	TB	R	RBI	TBB	IBB	SO	HBP	SH	SF	SB	CS	SB%	GDP	Avg	OBP	SLG
2000 St. Lucie	A+	8	31	11	4	0	1	—	—	18	3	8	2	0	1	1	2	1	3	3	.50	0	.355	.400	.581
Norfolk	AAA	72	291	104	17	5	6	—	—	149	45	37	16	1	25	3	4	4	13	7	.65	4	.357	.392	.512
2000 New York	NL	24	49	14	4	1	1	(0	1)	23	11	3	3	0	5	1	0	1	1	1	.50	0	.286	.333	.469

Tomas Perez

Bats: Both Throws: Right Pos: SS-44; PH/PR-1 Ht: 5'11" Wt: 177 Born: 12/29/73 Age: 27

Year Team	Lg	G	AB	H	2B	3B	HR	(Hm	Rd)	TB	R	RBI	TBB	IBB	SO	HBP	SH	SF	SB	CS	SB%	GDP	Avg	OBP	SLG
2000 Scrantn-WB *	AAA	77	279	82	16	2	10	—	—	132	44	56	16	1	48	2	1	2	4	1	.80	5	.294	.334	.473
1995 Toronto	AL	41	98	24	3	1	1	(1	0)	32	12	8	7	0	18	0	0	1	0	1	.00	6	.245	.292	.327
1996 Toronto	AL	91	295	74	13	4	1	(1	0)	98	24	19	25	0	29	1	6	1	1	2	.33	10	.251	.311	.332
1997 Toronto	AL	40	123	24	3	2	0	(0	0)	31	9	9	11	0	28	1	3	0	1	1	.50	2	.195	.267	.252
1998 Toronto	AL	6	9	1	0	0	0	(0	0)	1	1	0	1	0	3	0	1	0	0	0	—	1	.111	.200	.111
2000 Philadelphia	NL	45	140	31	7	1	1	(0	1)	43	17	13	11	2	30	0	1	0	1	1	.50	3	.221	.278	.307
5 ML YEARS		223	665	154	26	8	3	(2	1)	205	63	49	55	2	108	2	11	2	3	5	.38	22	.232	.291	.308

Yorkis Perez

Pitches: Left Bats: Both Pos: RP-33 Ht: 6'0" Wt: 213 Born: 9/30/67 Age: 33

Year Team	Lg	G	GS	CG	GF	IP	BFP	H	R	ER	HR	SH	SF	HB	TBB	IBB	SO	WP	Bk	W	L	Pct.	ShO	Sv-Op	Hld	ERA
1991 Chicago	NL	3	0	0	0	4.1	16	2	1	1	0	0	2	0	2	0	3	2	0	1	0	1.000	0	0-1	0	2.08
1994 Florida	NL	44	0	0	11	40.2	167	33	18	16	4	2	0	1	14	3	41	4	1	3	0	1.000	0	0-2	15	3.54
1995 Florida	NL	69	0	0	11	46.2	205	35	29	27	6	2	1	2	28	4	47	2	0	2	6	.250	0	1-4	16	5.21
1996 Florida	NL	64	0	0	15	47.2	222	51	28	28	2	2	2	1	31	4	47	2	0	3	4	.429	0	0-2	10	5.29
1997 New York	NL	9	0	0	1	8.2	45	15	8	8	2	0	1	0	4	0	7	1	0	0	1	.000	0	0-1	1	8.31
1998 Philadelphia	NL	57	0	0	7	52	221	40	23	22	3	2	3	0	25	0	42	7	0	0	2	.000	0	0-0	13	3.81
1999 Philadelphia	NL	35	0	0	4	32	137	29	15	14	4	2	1	0	15	1	26	5	0	3	1	.750	0	0-1	5	3.94
2000 Houston	NL	33	0	0	9	22.2	111	25	18	13	4	1	2	0	14	2	21	1	0	2	1	.667	0	0-2	3	5.16
8 ML YEARS		314	0	0	58	254.2	1124	230	140	129	25	11	12	4	133	14	234	24	1	14	15	.483	0	1-13	63	4.56

Matt Perisho

Pitches: Left Bats: Left Pos: RP-21; SP-13 Ht: 6'0" Wt: 205 Born: 6/8/75 Age: 26

Year Team	Lg	G	GS	CG	GF	IP	BFP	H	R	ER	HR	SH	SF	HB	TBB	IBB	SO	WP	Bk	W	L	Pct.	ShO	Sv-Op	Hld	ERA
1997 Anaheim	AL	11	8	0	2	45	217	59	34	30	6	2	2	3	28	0	35	5	2	0	2	.000	0	0-0	0	6.00
1998 Texas	AL	2	2	0	0	5	40	15	17	15	2	0	0	2	8	0	2	0	0	0	2	.000	0	0-0	0	27.00
1999 Texas	AL	4	1	0	3	10.1	40	8	3	3	0	0	0	0	2	1	17	1	0	0	0	—	0	0-0	0	2.61
2000 Texas	AL	34	13	0	4	105	515	136	99	86	20	6	5	6	67	3	74	4	0	2	7	.222	0	0-1	0	7.37
4 ML YEARS		51	24	0	9	165.1	812	218	153	134	28	8	7	11	105	4	128	10	2	2	11	.154	0	0-1	0	7.29

Chan Perry

Bats: R Throws: R Pos: PH/PR-7; RF-6; DH-4; 1B-1; LF-1 Ht: 6'2" Wt: 200 Born: 9/13/72 Age: 28

Year Team	Lg	G	AB	H	2B	3B	HR	(Hm	Rd)	TB	R	RBI	TBB	IBB	SO	HBP	SH	SF	SB	CS	SB%	GDP	Avg	OBP	SLG
1994 Burlington	R+	52	185	58	16	1	5	—	—	91	28	32	18	0	28	1	0	4	6	0	1.00	9	.314	.370	.492
1995 Columbus	A	113	411	117	30	4	9	—	—	182	64	50	53	1	49	2	2	4	7	2	.78	6	.285	.366	.443
1996 Kinston	A+	96	358	104	27	1	10	—	—	163	44	62	36	3	33	2	3	3	2	3	.40	9	.291	.356	.455
1997 Akron	AA	119	476	150	34	2	20	—	—	248	74	96	28	0	61	5	1	6	3	3	.50	14	.315	.355	.521
1998 Buffalo	AAA	13	49	11	4	0	0	—	—	15	8	3	6	0	10	2	0	0	1	0	1.00	0	.224	.333	.306
Akron	AA	54	203	57	17	2	5	—	—	93	36	27	23	1	43	0	0	1	3	2	.60	2	.281	.352	.458
1999 Akron	AA	37	154	43	14	0	7	—	—	78	24	30	11	0	27	1	0	1	1	0	1.00	3	.279	.329	.506
Buffalo	AAA	79	273	77	17	0	10	—	—	124	44	59	19	0	34	3	3	7	5	1	.83	9	.282	.328	.454
2000 Buffalo	AAA	92	362	107	18	1	10	—	—	157	48	65	21	0	55	3	0	4	1	2	.33	9	.296	.336	.434
2000 Cleveland	AL	13	14	1	0	0	0	(0	0)	1	1	0	0	0	5	0	0	0	0	0	—	1	.071	.071	.071

Herbert Perry

Bats: R Throws: R Pos: 3B-111; PH/PR-9; 1B-4; DH-3 Ht: 6'2" Wt: 220 Born: 9/15/69 Age: 31

Year Team	Lg	G	AB	H	2B	3B	HR	(Hm	Rd)	TB	R	RBI	TBB	IBB	SO	HBP	SH	SF	SB	CS	SB%	GDP	Avg	OBP	SLG
1994 Cleveland	AL	4	9	1	0	0	0	(0	0)	1	1	1	3	1	1	0	1	0	0	0	—	0	.111	.357	.111

Year Team	Lg	G	AB	H	2B	3B	HR	(Hm	Rd)	TB	R	RBI	TBB	IBB	SO	HBP	SH	SF	SB	CS	SB%	GDP	Avg	OBP	SLG
1995 Cleveland	AL	52	162	51	13	1	3	(3	0)	75	23	23	13	0	28	4	3	2	1	3	.25	5	.315	.376	.463
1996 Cleveland	AL	7	12	1	1	0	0	(0	0)	2	1	0	1	0	2	0	0	0	1	0	1.00		.083	.154	.167
1999 Tampa Bay	AL	66	209	53	10	1	6	(5	1)	83	29	32	16	1	42	10	0	4	0	0	—	13	.254	.331	.397
2000 TB-CWS	AL	116	411	124	30	1	12	(7	5)	192	71	62	24	1	75	9	2	4	4	1	.80	13	.302	.350	.467
2000 Tampa Bay	AL	7	28	6	1	0	0	(0	0)	7	2	1	2	0	7	0	0	0	0	0	—	13	.214	.267	.250
Chicago	AL	109	383	118	29	1	12	(7	5)	185	69	61	22	1	68	9	2	4	4	1	.80	13	.308	.356	.483
5 ML YEARS		245	803	230	54	3	21	(15	6)	353	125	118	57	3	148	24	5	11	6	4	.60	31	.286	.347	.440

Robert Person

Pitches: Right **Bats:** Right **Pos:** SP-28

Ht: 6'0" **Wt:** 194 **Born:** 10/6/69 **Age:** 31

	HOW MUCH HE PITCHED						WHAT HE GAVE UP											THE RESULTS						
Year Team	Lg	G	GS	CG	GF	IP	BFP	H	R	ER	HR	SH	SF	HB	TBB	IBB	SO	WP	Bk	W	L	Pct.	ShO	Sv-Op	Hld	ERA
2000 Clearwater *	A+	1	1	0	0	2.2	12	3	2	2	0	0	0	0	1	0	2	0	0	0	0		0	0--	—	6.75
Reading *	AA	1	0	0	0	4.2	20	3	3	3	1	0	0	0	3	0	7	0	0	1	0	1.000	0	0--		5.79
1995 New York	NL	3	1	0	0	12	44	5	1	1	1	0	0	0	2	0	10	0	0	1	0	1.000	0	0-0	0	0.75
1996 New York	NL	27	13	0	0	89.2	390	86	50	45	16	1	4	2	35	3	76	3	0	4	5	.444	0	0-0	1	4.52
1997 Toronto	AL	23	22	0	0	128.1	566	125	86	80	19	4	6	5	60	2	99	7	0	5	10	.333	0	0-0	0	5.61
1998 Toronto	AL	27	0	0	14	38.1	184	45	31	30	9	2	5	2	22	1	31	0	0	3	1	.750	0	6-8	0	7.04
1999 Tor-Phi		42	22	0	8	148	659	139	84	77	24	7	6	6	85	2	139	5	1	10	7	.588	0	2-2	1	4.68
2000 Philadelphia	NL	28	28	1	0	173.1	743	144	73	70	13	4	9	6	95	1	164	10	1	9	7	.563	1	0-0	0	3.63
1999 Toronto	AL	11	0	0	7	11	60	9	12	12	1	0	2	4	15	1	12	2	0	0	2	.000	0	2-2	1	9.82
Philadelphia	NL	31	22	0	1	137	599	130	72	65	23	7	4	2	70	1	127	3	1	10	5	.667	0	0-0	0	4.27
6 ML YEARS		150	86	1	23	589.2	2586	544	325	303	82	18	30	21	299	9	519	25	2	32	30	.516	1	8-10	2	4.62

Chris Peters

Pitches: Left **Bats:** Left **Pos:** RP-18

Ht: 6'1" **Wt:** 170 **Born:** 1/28/72 **Age:** 29

	HOW MUCH HE PITCHED						WHAT HE GAVE UP											THE RESULTS						
Year Team	Lg	G	GS	CG	GF	IP	BFP	H	R	ER	HR	SH	SF	HB	TBB	IBB	SO	WP	Bk	W	L	Pct.	ShO	Sv-Op	Hld	ERA
2000 Nashville *	AAA	11	11	0	0	52.2	252	71	38	32	6	3	1	6	26	1	32	6	0	2	4	.333	0	0--		5.47
1996 Pittsburgh	NL	16	10	0	0	64	283	72	43	40	9	3	3	1	25	0	28	4	0	2	4	.333	0	0-0	2	5.63
1997 Pittsburgh	NL	31	1	0	5	37.1	167	38	23	19	6	5	1	3	21	4	17	4	0	2	2	.500	0	0-1	2	4.58
1998 Pittsburgh	NL	39	21	1	7	148	630	142	63	57	13	4	5	3	55	4	103	4	1	8	10	.444	0	1-1	2	3.47
1999 Pittsburgh	NL	19	11	0	2	71	343	98	59	52	17	4	4	4	27	0	46	2	1	5	4	.556	0	0-0	1	6.59
2000 Pittsburgh	NL	18	0	0	4	28.1	121	23	9	9	2	2	0	1	14	2	16	3	0	0	1	.000	0	1-1	1	2.86
5 ML YEARS		123	43	1	18	348.2	1544	373	197	177	47	18	13	12	142	10	210	17	2	17	21	.447	0	2-3	8	4.57

Mark Petkovsek

Pitches: Right **Bats:** Right **Pos:** RP-63; SP-1

Ht: 6'0" **Wt:** 198 **Born:** 11/18/65 **Age:** 35

	HOW MUCH HE PITCHED						WHAT HE GAVE UP											THE RESULTS						
Year Team	Lg	G	GS	CG	GF	IP	BFP	H	R	ER	HR	SH	SF	HB	TBB	IBB	SO	WP	Bk	W	L	Pct.	ShO	Sv-Op	Hld	ERA
2000 Lk Elsinore *	A+	2	0	0	0	2.2	13	3	1	1	0	0	0	0	3	0	3	0	0	0	0		0	0--	—	3.38
1991 Texas	AL	4	1	0	1	9.1	53	21	16	15	4	0	1	0	3	0	6	2	0	0	1	.000	0	0-0	0	14.46
1993 Pittsburgh	NL	26	0	0	8	32.1	145	43	25	25	7	4	1	0	9	2	14	0	0	3	0	1.000	0	0-0	0	6.96
1995 St. Louis	NL	26	21	1	1	137.1	569	136	71	61	11	4	4	6	35	3	71	1	1	6	6	.500	1	0-0	0	4.00
1996 St. Louis	NL	48	6	0	7	88.2	377	83	37	35	9	5	1	5	35	2	45	2	1	11	2	.846	0	0-3	10	3.55
1997 St. Louis	NL	55	2	0	19	96	414	109	61	54	14	2	2	6	31	4	51	2	0	4	7	.364	0	2-2	5	5.06
1998 St. Louis	NL	48	10	0	7	105.2	476	131	63	56	9	9	3	8	36	3	55	1	1	7	4	.636	0	0-5	6	4.77
1999 Anaheim	AL	64	0	0	18	83	349	85	37	32	6	5	5	2	21	2	43	3	1	10	4	.714	0	1-4	12	3.47
2000 Anaheim	AL	64	1	0	21	81	341	86	39	38	8	4	1	3	23	6	31	3	0	4	2	.667	0	2-4	16	4.22
8 ML YEARS		335	41	1	82	633.1	2724	694	349	316	68	33	18	30	194	22	316	18	4	45	26	.634	1	5-18	49	4.49

Ben Petrick

Bats: Right **Throws:** Right **Pos:** C-48; PH/PR-8

Ht: 6'0" **Wt:** 205 **Born:** 4/7/77 **Age:** 24

	BATTING																		BASERUNNING				PERCENTAGES		
Year Team	Lg	G	AB	H	2B	3B	HR	(Hm	Rd)	TB	R	RBI	TBB	IBB	SO	HBP	SH	SF	SB	CS	SB%	GDP	Avg	OBP	SLG
1996 Asheville	A	122	446	105	24	2	14	—	—	175	74	52	75	1	98	5	2	3	19	9	.68	5	.235	.350	.392
1997 Salem	A+	121	412	102	23	3	15	—	—	176	68	56	62	2	100	2	4	2	30	11	.73	6	.248	.347	.427
1998 New Haven	AA	106	349	83	21	3	18	—	—	164	52	50	56	1	89	3	0	3	7	7	.50	5	.238	.345	.470
1999 Carolina	AA	20	68	21	5	1	4	—	—	40	18	22	9	0	15	1	0	2	3	1	.75	0	.309	.388	.588
Colo Sprngs	AAA	84	282	88	16	5	19	—	—	171	56	64	44	1	58	3	0	6	9	6	.60	4	.312	.403	.606
2000 Colo Sprngs	AAA	63	248	78	22	3	9	—	—	133	38	47	32	1	40	0	0	2	7	2	.78	2	.315	.390	.536
1999 Colorado	NL	19	62	20	3	0	4	(4	0)	35	13	12	10	0	13	0	0	0	1	0	1.00	1	.323	.417	.565
2000 Colorado	NL	52	146	47	10	1	3	(2	1)	68	32	20	20	2	33	2	1	4	1	2	.33	1	.322	.401	.466
2 ML YEARS		71	208	67	13	1	7	(6	1)	103	45	32	30	2	46	2	1	4	2	2	.50	2	.322	.406	.495

Andy Pettitte

Pitches: Left **Bats:** Left **Pos:** SP-32

Ht: 6'5" **Wt:** 225 **Born:** 6/15/72 **Age:** 29

	HOW MUCH HE PITCHED						WHAT HE GAVE UP											THE RESULTS						
Year Team	Lg	G	GS	CG	GF	IP	BFP	H	R	ER	HR	SH	SF	HB	TBB	IBB	SO	WP	Bk	W	L	Pct.	ShO	Sv-Op	Hld	ERA
1995 New York	AL	31	26	3	1	175	745	183	86	81	15	4	5	1	63	3	114	8	1	12	9	.571	0	0-0	0	4.17
1996 New York	AL	35	34	2	1	221	929	229	105	95	23	7	3	3	72	2	162	6	1	21	8	.724	0	0-0	0	3.87
1997 New York	AL	35	35	4	0	240.1	986	233	86	77	7	6	2	3	65	0	166	7	0	18	7	.720	1	0-0	0	2.88
1998 New York	AL	33	32	5	0	216.1	932	226	110	102	20	6	7	6	87	1	146	5	0	16	11	.593	0	0-0	0	4.24
1999 New York	AL	31	31	0	0	191.2	851	216	105	100	20	6	6	3	89	3	121	3	0	14	11	.560	0	0-0	0	4.70
2000 New York	AL	32	32	3	0	204.2	903	219	111	99	17	7	4	4	80	4	125	2	3	19	9	.679	1	0-0	0	4.35
6 ML YEARS		197	190	17	2	1249	5346	1306	603	554	102	36	27	20	456	13	834	31	6	100	55	.645	2	0-0	0	3.99

Josh Phelps

Bats: Right **Throws:** Right **Pos:** C-1   **Ht:** 6'3" **Wt:** 215 **Born:** 5/12/78 **Age:** 23

					BATTING												BASERUNNING				PERCENTAGES		
Year Team	Lg	G	AB	H	2B	3B	HR	(Hm | Rd)	TB	R	RBI	TBB	IBB	SO	HBP	SH	SF	SB	CS	SB%	GDP	Avg	OBP	SLG
1996 Medcine Hat	R+	59	191	46	3	0	5	—	—	64	28	29	27	0	65	6	2	1	5	3	.63	5	.241	.351	.335
1997 Hagerstown	A	68	233	49	9	1	7	—	—	81	26	24	15	0	72	8	0	2	3	2	.60	6	.210	.279	.348
1998 Hagerstown	A	117	385	102	24	1	8	—	—	152	48	44	40	1	80	8	1	5	2	0	1.00	12	.265	.342	.395
1999 Dunedin	A+	110	406	133	27	4	20	—	—	228	72	84	28	0	104	8	2	4	6	3	.67	13	.328	.379	.562
2000 Tennessee	AA	56	184	42	9	1	9	—	—	80	23	28	15	0	66	7	1	2	0	1	1.00	6	.228	.308	.435
Dunedin	A+	30	113	36	7	0	12	—	—	79	26	34	12	0	34	1	0	1	0	0	—	2	.319	.386	.699
2000 Toronto	AL	1	1	0	0	0	0	(0 | 0)	0	0	0	0	0	1	0	0	0	0	0	—	0	.000	.000	.000

Adam Piatt

Bats: R **Throws:** R **Pos:** RF-22; PH/PR-15; DH-13; 3B-13; LF-8; 1B-3   **Ht:** 6'2" **Wt:** 195 **Born:** 2/8/76 **Age:** 25

					BATTING												BASERUNNING				PERCENTAGES		
Year Team	Lg	G	AB	H	2B	3B	HR	(Hm	Rd)	TB	R	RBI	TBB	IBB	SO	HBP	SH	SF	SB	CS	SB%	GDP	Avg	OBP	SLG
1997 Sou Oregon	A-	57	216	63	9	1	13	—	—	113	63	35	35	1	58	1	0	1	19	4	.83	4	.292	.391	.523
1998 Modesto	A+	133	500	144	40	3	20	—	—	250	91	107	80	1	99	0	1	8	20	6	.77	15	.288	.381	.500
1999 Midland	AA	129	476	164	48	3	39	—	—	335	128	135	93	10	101	7	0	9	7	3	.70	11	.345	.451	.704
Vancouver	AAA	6	18	4	1	0	0	—	—	5	1	3	6	0	2	0	0	0	0	0	—	2	.222	.417	.278
2000 Sacramento	AAA	65	254	72	15	0	8	—	—	111	36	42	26	1	57	4	0	3	3	2	.60	3	.283	.355	.437
2000 Oakland	AL	60	157	47	5	5	5	(3	2)	77	24	23	23	0	44	1	1	0	0	1	.00	1	.299	.392	.490

Mike Piazza

Bats: Right **Throws:** Right **Pos:** C-124; PH/PR-7; DH-5   **Ht:** 6'3" **Wt:** 215 **Born:** 9/4/68 **Age:** 32

					BATTING												BASERUNNING				PERCENTAGES		
Year Team	Lg	G	AB	H	2B	3B	HR	(Hm	Rd)	TB	R	RBI	TBB	IBB	SO	HBP	SH	SF	SB	CS	SB%	GDP	Avg	OBP	SLG
1992 Los Angeles	NL	21	69	16	3	0	1	(1	0)	22	5	7	4	0	12	1	0	0	0	0	—	1	.232	.284	.319
1993 Los Angeles	NL	149	547	174	24	2	35	(21	14)	307	81	112	46	6	86	3	0	6	3	4	.43	10	.318	.370	.561
1994 Los Angeles	NL	107	405	129	18	0	24	(13	11)	219	64	92	33	10	65	1	0	2	1	3	.25	11	.319	.370	.541
1995 Los Angeles	NL	112	434	150	17	0	32	(9	23)	263	82	93	39	10	80	1	0	1	1	0	1.00	10	.346	.400	.606
1996 Los Angeles	NL	148	547	184	16	0	36	(14	22)	308	87	105	81	21	93	1	0	2	0	3	.00	21	.336	.422	.563
1997 Los Angeles	NL	152	556	201	32	1	40	(22	18)	355	104	124	69	11	77	3	0	5	5	1	.83	19	.362	.431	.638
1998 LA-Fla-NYM	NL	151	561	184	38	1	32	(15	17)	320	88	111	58	14	80	2	0	5	1	0	1.00	15	.328	.390	.570
1999 New York	NL	141	534	162	25	0	40	(18	22)	307	100	124	51	11	70	1	0	7	2	2	.50	27	.303	.361	.575
2000 New York	NL	136	482	156	26	0	38	(17	21)	296	90	113	58	10	69	3	0	2	4	2	.67	15	.324	.398	.614
1998 Los Angeles	NL	37	149	42	5	0	9	(5	4)	74	20	30	11	4	27	0	0	1	0	0	—	3	.282	.329	.497
Florida	NL	5	18	5	0	1	0	(0	0)	7	1	5	0	0	0	0	0	0	0	0	—	0	.278	.263	.389
New York	NL	109	394	137	33	0	23	(10	13)	239	67	76	47	10	53	2	0	3	1	0	1.00	12	.348	.417	.607
9 ML YEARS		1117	4135	1356	199	4	278	(130	148)	2397	701	881	439	93	632	16	0	30	17	15	.53	129	.328	.392	.580

Hipolito Pichardo

Pitches: Right **Bats:** Right **Pos:** RP-37; SP-1   **Ht:** 6'1" **Wt:** 195 **Born:** 8/22/69 **Age:** 31

		HOW MUCH HE PITCHED					WHAT HE GAVE UP											THE RESULTS						
Year Team	Lg	G	GS	CG	GF	IP	BFP	H	R	ER	HR	SH	SF	HB	TBB	IBB	SO	WP	Bk	W	L	Pct.	ShO	Sv-Op	Hld	ERA
2000 Sarasota *	A+	7	2	0	2	13	51	9	3	2	1	0	0	2	0	0	12	0	0	1	1	.500	0	0--	—	1.38
Pawtucket *	AAA	3	0	0	3	4.2	16	2	0	0	0	0	0	0	0	0	4	0	0	0	0	—	0	0--	—	0.00
1992 Kansas City	AL	31	24	1	0	143.2	615	148	71	63	9	4	5	3	49	1	59	3	1	9	6	.600	1	0-0	0	3.95
1993 Kansas City	AL	30	25	2	2	165	720	183	85	74	10	3	8	6	53	2	70	5	3	7	8	.467	0	0-0	1	4.04
1994 Kansas City	AL	45	0	0	19	67.2	303	82	42	37	4	4	2	7	24	5	36	3	0	5	3	.625	0	3-5	6	4.92
1995 Kansas City	AL	44	0	0	16	64	287	66	34	31	4	3	1	4	30	7	43	4	1	8	4	.667	0	1-2	7	4.36
1996 Kansas City	AL	57	0	0	28	68	294	74	41	41	5	3	2	2	26	5	43	4	0	3	5	.375	0	3-5	15	5.43
1997 Kansas City	AL	47	0	0	26	49	215	51	24	23	7	2	0	1	24	8	34	2	1	3	5	.375	0	11-13	4	4.22
1998 Kansas City	AL	27	18	0	2	112.1	503	126	73	64	11	3	3	4	43	2	55	2	0	7	8	.467	0	1-1	2	5.13
2000 Boston	AL	38	1	0	5	65	275	63	29	25	1	2	2	3	26	2	37	2	0	6	3	.667	0	1-2	4	3.46
8 ML YEARS		319	68	3	98	734.2	3212	793	399	358	51	24	23	30	275	32	377	25	6	48	42	.533	1	20-28	39	4.39

Juan Pierre

Bats: Left **Throws:** Left **Pos:** CF-50; PH/PR-4   **Ht:** 6'0" **Wt:** 170 **Born:** 8/14/77 **Age:** 23

					BATTING												BASERUNNING				PERCENTAGES		
Year Team	Lg	G	AB	H	2B	3B	HR	(Hm	Rd)	TB	R	RBI	TBB	IBB	SO	HBP	SH	SF	SB	CS	SB%	GDP	Avg	OBP	SLG
1998 Portland	A-	64	264	93	9	2	0	—	—	106	55	30	19	0	11	2	4	1	38	9	.81	3	.352	.399	.402
1999 Asheville	A	140	585	187	28	5	1	—	—	228	93	55	38	2	37	8	11	6	66	19	.78	12	.320	.366	.390
2000 Carolina	AA	107	439	143	16	4	0	—	—	167	63	32	33	0	26	5	8	4	46	12	.79	4	.326	.376	.380
Colo Sprngs	AAA	4	17	8	0	1	0	—	—	10	3	1	0	0	0	0	0	0	1	1	.50	0	.471	.471	.588
2000 Colorado	NL	51	200	62	2	0	0	(0	0)	64	26	20	13	0	15	1	4	1	7	6	.54	2	.310	.353	.320

A.J. Pierzynski

Bats: Left **Throws:** Right **Pos:** C-32; PH/PR-1   **Ht:** 6'3" **Wt:** 220 **Born:** 12/30/76 **Age:** 24

					BATTING												BASERUNNING				PERCENTAGES		
Year Team	Lg	G	AB	H	2B	3B	HR	(Hm	Rd)	TB	R	RBI	TBB	IBB	SO	HBP	SH	SF	SB	CS	SB%	GDP	Avg	OBP	SLG
1994 Twins	R	43	152	44	8	1	1	—	—	57	21	19	12	0	19	0	0	2	0	2	.00	3	.289	.337	.375
1995 Fort Wayne	A	22	84	26	5	1	2	—	—	39	10	14	2	0	10	0	0	1	0	0	—	1	.310	.322	.464
Elizabethtn	R+	56	205	68	13	1	7	—	—	104	29	45	14	1	23	0	0	1	0	2	.00	6	.332	.373	.507
1996 Fort Wayne	A	114	431	118	30	3	7	—	—	175	48	70	22	1	53	2	0	6	0	4	.00	10	.274	.308	.406
1997 Fort Myers	A	118	412	115	21	1	9	—	—	167	49	64	16	1	59	6	1	4	2	1	.67	9	.279	.313	.405
1998 New Britain	AA	59	212	63	11	0	3	—	—	83	30	17	10	4	25	2	2	1	0	2	.00	4	.297	.333	.392
Salt Lake	AAA	59	208	53	7	2	7	—	—	85	29	30	9	2	24	0	2	1	3	1	.75	4	.255	.284	.409
1999 Salt Lake	AAA	67	228	59	10	0	1	—	—	72	29	25	16	0	29	0	2	0	0	0	—	11	.259	.307	.316

BATTING																		BASERUNNING				PERCENTAGES		
Year Team	Lg	G	AB	H	2B	3B	HR	(Hm Rd)	TB	R	RBI	TBB	IBB	SO	HBP	SH	SF	SB	CS	SB%	GDP	Avg	OBP	SLG
2000 New Britain	AA	62	228	68	17	2	4	— —	101	36	34	8	0	22	9	0	4	0	0	—	13	.298	.341	.443
Salt Lake	AAA	41	155	52	14	1	4	— —	80	22	25	5	1	22	1	2	3	1	1	.50	3	.335	.354	.516
1998 Minnesota	AL	7	10	3	0	0	0	(0 0)	3	1	1	1	0	2	1	0	1	0	0	—	0	.300	.385	.300
1999 Minnesota	AL	9	22	6	2	0	0	(0 0)	8	3	3	1	0	4	1	0	0	0	0	—	0	.273	.333	.364
2000 Minnesota	AL	33	88	27	5	1	2	(1 1)	40	12	11	5	0	14	2	0	1	1	0	1.00	1	.307	.354	.455
3 ML YEARS		49	120	36	7	1	2	(1 1)	51	16	15	7	0	20	4	0	2	1	0	1.00	1	.300	.353	.425

Joel Pineiro

Pitches: Right **Bats:** Right **Pos:** RP-7; SP-1   **Ht:** 6'1" **Wt:** 180 **Born:** 9/25/78 **Age:** 22

HOW MUCH HE PITCHED							WHAT HE GAVE UP												THE RESULTS						
Year Team	Lg	G	GS	CG	GF	IP	BFP	H	R	ER	HR	SH	SF	HB	TBB	IBB	SO	WP	Bk	W	L	Pct.	ShO	Sv-Op	Hld	ERA
1997 Mariners	R	1	0	0	0	3	11	1	0	0	0	0	0	1	0	0	4	0	0	1	0	1.000	0	0- -	—	0.00
Everett	A-	18	6	0	9	49	223	54	33	29	2	0	0	3	18	1	59	3	2	4	2	.667	0	2- -	—	5.33
1998 Wisconsin	A	16	16	1	0	96	401	92	40	34	8	3	2	3	28	1	84	3	1	8	4	.667	0	0- -	—	3.19
Lancaster	A+	9	9	1	0	45	217	58	40	39	6	0	6	2	22	0	48	2	3	2	0	1.000	1	0- -	—	7.80
Orlando	AA	1	1	0	0	5	22	7	4	3	0	0	1	0	2	0	2	0	0	1	0	1.000	0	0- -	—	5.40
1999 New Haven	AA	28	25	4	0	166	724	190	105	87	18	6	5	5	52	0	116	11	0	10	15	.400	0	0- -	—	4.72
2000 New Haven	AA	9	9	0	0	52.1	207	42	25	24	6	0	1	1	12	0	43	0	0	2	1	.667	0	0- -	—	4.13
Tacoma	AAA	10	9	2	0	61	256	53	20	19	3	2	1	3	22	1	41	2	0	7	1	.875	2	0- -	—	2.80
2000 Seattle	AL	8	1	0	5	19.1	94	25	13	12	3	0	2	0	13	0	10	0	0	1	0	1.000	0	0-0	0	5.59

Dan Plesac

Pitches: Left **Bats:** Left **Pos:** RP-62   **Ht:** 6'5" **Wt:** 217 **Born:** 2/4/62 **Age:** 39

HOW MUCH HE PITCHED							WHAT HE GAVE UP												THE RESULTS						
Year Team	Lg	G	GS	CG	GF	IP	BFP	H	R	ER	HR	SH	SF	HB	TBB	IBB	SO	WP	Bk	W	L	Pct.	ShO	Sv-Op	Hld	ERA
1986 Milwaukee	AL	51	0	0	33	91	377	81	34	30	5	6	5	0	29	1	75	4	0	10	7	.588	0	14-20	5	2.97
1987 Milwaukee	AL	57	0	0	47	79.1	325	63	30	23	8	1	2	3	23	1	89	6	0	5	6	.455	0	23-36	6	2.61
1988 Milwaukee	AL	50	0	0	48	52.1	211	46	14	14	2	2	0	0	12	2	52	4	6	1	2	.333	0	30-35	0	2.41
1989 Milwaukee	AL	52	0	0	51	61.1	242	47	16	16	6	0	4	0	17	1	52	0	0	3	4	.429	0	33-40	0	2.35
1990 Milwaukee	AL	66	0	0	52	69	299	67	36	34	5	2	2	3	31	6	65	2	0	3	7	.300	0	24-34	2	4.43
1991 Milwaukee	AL	45	10	0	25	92.1	402	92	49	44	12	3	3	7	39	1	61	2	1	2	7	.222	0	8-12	1	4.29
1992 Milwaukee	AL	44	4	0	13	79	330	64	28	26	5	8	4	3	35	5	54	3	1	5	4	.556	0	1-3	1	2.96
1993 Chicago	NL	57	0	0	12	62.2	276	74	37	33	10	4	3	0	21	6	47	5	2	2	1	.667	0	0-2	12	4.74
1994 Chicago	NL	54	0	0	14	54.2	235	61	30	28	9	1	1	1	13	0	53	0	0	2	3	.400	0	1-3	14	4.57
1995 Pittsburgh	NL	58	0	0	16	60.1	259	53	26	24	3	4	3	1	27	7	57	1	0	4	4	.500	0	3-5	11	3.58
1996 Pittsburgh	NL	73	0	0	30	70.1	300	67	35	32	4	2	3	0	24	6	76	4	0	6	5	.545	0	11-17	11	4.09
1997 Toronto	AL	73	0	0	18	50.1	215	47	22	20	8	2	1	0	19	4	61	2	0	2	4	.333	0	1-5	27	3.58
1998 Toronto	AL	78	0	0	16	50	203	41	23	21	4	0	3	1	16	1	55	0	0	4	3	.571	0	4-5	27	3.78
1999 Tor-Ari	NL	64	0	0	11	44.1	198	50	30	29	7	4	1	0	17	2	53	3	0	1	3	.333	0	1-3	15	5.89
2000 Arizona	NL	62	0	0	14	40	182	34	21	14	4	6	1	0	26	2	45	3	0	5	1	.833	0	0-4	9	3.15
1999 Toronto	AL	30	0	0	5	22.2	104	28	21	21	4	3	1	0	9	1	26	2	0	0	3	.000	0	0-2	9	8.34
Arizona	NL	34	0	0	6	21.2	94	22	9	8	3	1	0	0	8	1	27	1	0	2	1	.667	0	1-1	6	3.32
15 ML YEARS		884	14	0	400	957	4054	887	431	388	92	45	40	15	349	45	895	39	10	56	62	.475	0	154-224	135	3.65

Placido Polanco

Bats: R **Throws:** R **Pos:** 2B-51; 3B-35; SS-29; PH/PR-20; 1B-1   **Ht:** 5'10" **Wt:** 168 **Born:** 10/10/75 **Age:** 25

BATTING																		BASERUNNING				PERCENTAGES		
Year Team	Lg	G	AB	H	2B	3B	HR	(Hm Rd)	TB	R	RBI	TBB	IBB	SO	HBP	SH	SF	SB	CS	SB%	GDP	Avg	OBP	SLG
1998 St. Louis	NL	45	114	29	3	2	1	(1 0)	39	10	11	5	0	9	1	2	0	2	0	1.00	1	.254	.292	.342
1999 St. Louis	NL	88	220	61	9	3	1	(0 1)	79	24	19	15	1	24	0	3	2	1	3	.25	7	.277	.321	.359
2000 St. Louis	NL	118	323	102	12	3	5	(2 3)	135	50	39	16	0	26	1	1	3	4	4	.50	8	.316	.347	.418
3 ML YEARS		251	657	192	24	8	7	(3 4)	253	84	69	36	1	59	2	12	5	7	7	.50	16	.292	.329	.385

Cliff Politte

Pitches: Right **Bats:** Right **Pos:** SP-8; RP-4   **Ht:** 5'11" **Wt:** 185 **Born:** 2/27/74 **Age:** 27

HOW MUCH HE PITCHED							WHAT HE GAVE UP												THE RESULTS						
Year Team	Lg	G	GS	CG	GF	IP	BFP	H	R	ER	HR	SH	SF	HB	TBB	IBB	SO	WP	Bk	W	L	Pct.	ShO	Sv-Op	Hld	ERA
1996 Peoria	A	25	25	0	0	149.2	603	108	50	43	8	3	2	7	47	0	151	5	1	14	6	.700	0	0- -	—	2.59
1997 Pr William	A+	19	19	0	0	120.1	475	89	37	30	11	0	3	2	31	0	118	2	2	11	1	.917	0	0- -	—	2.24
Arkansas	AA	6	6	0	0	37.2	152	35	15	9	3	6	1	0	9	1	26	0	0	4	1	.800	0	0- -	—	2.15
1998 Memphis	AAA	10	10	0	0	50.2	244	71	46	43	10	3	2	0	24	0	42	3	0	1	4	.200	0	0- -	—	7.64
Arkansas	AA	10	10	1	0	67	265	56	25	22	6	3	1	1	16	0	61	0	0	5	3	.625	1	0- -	—	2.96
1999 Reading	AA	37	13	1	16	109	460	112	49	45	12	6	1	5	33	3	97	4	0	9	8	.529	0	5- -	—	3.63
2000 Scrantn-WB	AAA	21	20	1	0	112.2	467	94	45	39	8	5	4	2	41	2	106	3	1	8	4	.667	0	0- -	—	3.12
1998 St. Louis	NL	8	8	0	0	37	172	45	32	26	6	3	1	1	18	0	22	2	1	2	3	.400	0	0-0	0	6.32
1999 Philadelphia	NL	13	0	0	0	17.2	85	19	14	14	2	1	0	0	15	0	15	2	0	1	0	1.000	0	0-0	0	7.13
2000 Philadelphia	NL	12	8	0	0	59	251	55	24	24	8	1	1	0	27	1	50	3	0	4	3	.571	0	0-0	0	3.66
3 ML YEARS		33	16	0	0	113.2	508	119	70	64	16	5	2	1	60	1	87	7	1	7	6	.538	0	0-0	1	5.07

Luis Polonia

Bats: L **Throws:** L **Pos:** DH-51; RF-32; PH/PR-30; LF-23   **Ht:** 5'8" **Wt:** 160 **Born:** 12/10/64 **Age:** 36

BATTING																		BASERUNNING				PERCENTAGES		
Year Team	Lg	G	AB	H	2B	3B	HR	(Hm Rd)	TB	R	RBI	TBB	IBB	SO	HBP	SH	SF	SB	CS	SB%	GDP	Avg	OBP	SLG
1987 Oakland	AL	125	435	125	16	10	4	(1 3)	173	78	49	32	1	64	0	1	1	29	7	.81	4	.287	.335	.398
1988 Oakland	AL	84	288	84	11	4	2	(1 1)	109	51	27	21	0	40	0	2	2	24	9	.73	3	.292	.338	.378
1989 Oak-NYY	AL	125	433	130	17	6	3	(1 2)	168	70	46	25	1	44	2	2	4	22	8	.73	13	.300	.338	.388
1990 NYY-Cal	AL	120	403	135	7	9	2	(2 0)	166	52	35	25	1	43	1	3	4	21	14	.60	9	.335	.372	.412
1991 California	AL	150	604	179	28	8	2	(1 1)	229	92	50	52	4	74	1	2	3	48	23	.68	11	.296	.352	.379

Batting

Year Team	Lg	G	AB	H	2B	3B	HR	(Hm	Rd)	TB	R	RBI	TBB	IBB	SO	HBP	SH	SF	SB	CS	SB%	GDP	Avg	OBP	SLG
1992 California	AL	149	577	165	17	4	0	(0	0)	190	83	35	45	6	64	1	8	4	51	21	.71	18	.286	.337	.329
1993 California	AL	152	576	156	17	6	1	(0	1)	188	75	32	48	7	53	2	8	3	55	24	.70	7	.271	.328	.326
1994 New York	AL	95	350	109	21	6	1	(0	1)	145	62	36	37	1	36	4	2	1	20	12	.63	7	.311	.383	.414
1995 NYY-Atl		95	291	76	16	3	2	(2	0)	104	43	17	28	1	38	0	3	4	13	4	.76	3	.261	.322	.357
1996 Bal-Atl		80	206	55	4	1	2	(2	0)	67	28	16	11	0	23	1	1	1	9	7	.56	10	.267	.306	.325
1999 Detroit	AL	87	333	108	21	8	10	(8	2)	175	46	32	16	0	32	2	2	2	17	9	.65	2	.324	.357	.526
2000 Det-NYY	AL	117	344	95	14	5	7	(4	3)	140	48	30	29	1	32	1	3	6	12	7	.63	4	.276	.329	.407
1989 Oakland	AL	59	206	59	6	4	1	(0	1)	76	31	17	9	0	15	0	2	1	13	4	.76	5	.286	.315	.369
New York	AL	66	227	71	11	2	2	(1	1)	92	39	29	16	1	29	2	0	3	9	4	.69	8	.313	.359	.405
1990 New York	AL	11	22	7	0	0	0	(0	0)	7	2	3	0	0	1	0	0	1	1	0	1.00	1	.318	.304	.318
California	AL	109	381	128	7	9	2	(2	0)	159	50	32	25	1	42	1	3	3	20	14	.59	8	.336	.376	.417
1995 New York	AL	67	238	62	9	3	2	(2	0)	83	37	15	25	1	29	0	2	4	10	4	.71	3	.261	.326	.349
Atlanta	NL	28	53	14	7	0	0	(0	0)	21	6	2	3	0	9	0	1	0	3	0	1.00		.264	.304	.396
1996 Baltimore	AL	58	175	42	4	1	2	(2	0)	54	25	14	10	0	20	1	1	0	8	6	.57	10	.240	.285	.309
Atlanta	NL	22	31	13	0	0	0	(0	0)	13	3	2	1	0	3	0	0	1	1	1	.50	0	.419	.424	.419
2000 Detroit	AL	80	267	73	10	5	6	(3	3)	111	37	25	22	1	25	1	3	5	8	5	.62	2	.273	.325	.416
New York	AL	37	77	22	4	0	1	(1	0)	29	11	5	7	0	7	0	0	1	4	2	.67	2	.286	.341	.377
12 ML YEARS		1379	4840	1417	189	70	36	(22	14)	1854	728	405	369	23	543	15	37	35	321	145	.69	91	.293	.342	.383

Sidney Ponson

Pitches: Right **Bats:** Right **Pos:** SP-32   **Ht:** 6'1" **Wt:** 225 **Born:** 11/2/76 **Age:** 24

Year Team	Lg	G	GS	CG	GF	IP	BFP	H	R	ER	HR	SH	SF	HB	TBB	IBB	SO	WP	Bk	W	L	Pct.	ShO	Sv-Op	Hld	ERA
1998 Baltimore	AL	31	20	0	5	135	588	157	82	79	19	3	4	3	42	2	85	4	1	8	9	.471	0	1-2	0	5.27
1999 Baltimore	AL	32	32	6	0	210	897	227	118	110	35	4	7	1	80	2	112	4	0	12	12	.500	0	0-0	0	4.71
2000 Baltimore	AL	32	32	6	0	222	953	223	125	119	30	3	3	1	83	0	152	5	0	9	13	.409	1	0-0	0	4.82
3 ML YEARS		95	84	12	5	567	2438	607	325	308	84	10	14	5	205	4	349	13	1	29	34	.460	1	1-2	0	4.89

Jim Poole

Pitches: Left **Bats:** Left **Pos:** RP-23   **Ht:** 6'1" **Wt:** 203 **Born:** 4/28/66 **Age:** 35

Year Team	Lg	G	GS	CG	GF	IP	BFP	H	R	ER	HR	SH	SF	HB	TBB	IBB	SO	WP	Bk	W	L	Pct.	ShO	Sv-Op	Hld	ERA
2000 Buffalo *	AAA	10	0	0	2	12	60	16	10	8	2	1	2	0	6	0	8	1	0	2	2	.500	0	1- -	—	6.00
1990 Los Angeles	NL	16	0	0	4	10.2	46	7	5	5	1	0	0	0	8	4	6	1	0	0	0	—	0	0-0	2	4.22
1991 Tex-Bal		29	0	0	5	42	166	29	14	11	3	3	3	0	12	2	38	2	0	3	2	.600	0	1-1	4	2.36
1992 Baltimore	AL	6	0	0	1	3.1	14	3	3	0	0	0	0	0	1	0	3	0	0	0	0	—	0	0-1	1	0.00
1993 Baltimore	AL	55	0	0	11	50.1	197	30	18	12	2	3	2	0	21	5	29	0	0	2	1	.667	0	2-3	14	2.15
1994 Baltimore	AL	38	0	0	10	20.1	100	32	15	4	0	3	0	0	11	2	18	1	0	1	0	1.000	0	0-2	10	6.64
1995 Cleveland	AL	42	0	0	9	50.1	206	40	22	21	7	1	2	2	17	0	41	2	1	3	3	.500	0	0-0	6	3.75
1996 Cle-SF		67	0	0	13	50.1	218	44	22	16	5	3	1	1	27	7	38	3	0	6	1	.857	0	0-4	10	2.86
1997 San Francisco	NL	63	0	0	11	49.1	242	73	44	39	6	4	2	4	25	4	26	5	0	3	1	.750	0	0-0	9	7.11
1998 SF-Cle		38	0	0	9	39.1	174	47	24	23	5	4	1	1	12	6	27	2	0	1	3	.250	0	0-3	6	5.26
1999 Phi-Cle		54	0	0	12	36.1	173	50	22	19	3	1		3	18	2	22	4	1	2	1	.667	0	1-2	12	4.71
2000 Det-Mon		23	0	0	2	10.2	58	21	14	13	5	1	2	1	4	1	8	0	0	1	0	1.000	0	0-1	2	10.97
1991 Texas	AL	5	0	0	2	6	31	10	4	3	0	0	1	0	3	0	4	0	0	0	0	—	0	1-1	1	4.50
Baltimore		24	0	0	3	36	135	19	10	8	3	3	2	0	9	2	34	2	0	3	2	.600	0	0-0	4	2.00
1996 Cleveland	AL	32	0	0	8	26.2	121	29	15	9	3	0	1	0	14	4	19	2	0	4	0	1.000	0	0-1	5	3.04
San Francisco	NL	35	0	0	5	23.2	97	15	7	7	2	3	0	1	13	3	19	1	0	2	1	.667	0	0-3	5	2.66
1998 Cleveland	AL	26	0	0	8	32.1	140	38	20	19	5	4	1	0	9	5	16	2	0	1	3	.250	0	0-2	3	5.29
Cleveland		12	0	0	1	7	34	9	4	4	0	0	0	1	3	1	11	0	0	0	0	—	0	0-1	3	5.14
1999 Philadelphia	NL	51	0	0	12	35.1	166	48	20	17	3	1	0	3	15	1	22	4	1	1	1	.500	0	1-2	12	4.33
Cleveland		3	0	0	0	1	7	2	2	2	0	0	1	0	3	1	0	0	0	0	0	—	0	0-0	0	18.00
2000 Detroit	AL	18	0	0	1	8.2	41	13	8	7	4	1	2	1	1	0	5	0	0	1	0	1.000	0	0-1	1	7.27
Montreal	NL	5	0	0	1	2	17	8	6	6	1	0	0	0	3	1	3	0	0	0	0	—	0	0-0	1	27.00
11 ML YEARS		431	0	0	87	363	1594	376	203	174	41	20	17	12	156	33	256	20	2	22	12	.647	0	4-17	75	4.31

Bo Porter

Bats: R **Throws:** R **Pos:** RF-14; PH/PR-7; CF-2; LF-1   **Ht:** 6'2" **Wt:** 195 **Born:** 7/5/72 **Age:** 28

Year Team	Lg	G	AB	H	2B	3B	HR	(Hm	Rd)	TB	R	RBI	TBB	IBB	SO	HBP	SH	SF	SB	CS	SB%	GDP	Avg	OBP	SLG
1994 Peoria	A	66	221	60	11	2	6	—	—	93	40	29	27	0	59	2	6	4	6	5	.55	5	.271	.350	.421
1995 Daytona	A+	113	336	73	12	2	3	—	—	98	54	19	32	0	104	2	4	3	22	10	.69	5	.217	.287	.292
1996 Daytona	A+	20	63	11	4	1	0	—	—	17	9	6	6	0	24	0	0	2	5	1	.83	6	.175	.239	.270
Rockford	A	105	378	91	22	3	7	—	—	140	83	44	72	1	107	1	3	4	30	14	.68	7	.241	.360	.370
1997 Daytona	A+	122	440	135	20	6	17	—	—	218	87	65	61	1	115	3	1	3	23	13	.64	8	.307	.393	.495
Orlando	AA	8	31	8	1	0	1	—	—	12	4	3	0	0	11	1	0	0	0	1	.00	1	.258	.281	.387
1998 West Tenn	AA	125	464	134	26	11	10	—	—	212	91	68	82	4	117	6	3	5	50	17	.75	9	.289	.399	.457
Iowa	AAA	4	11	4	1	0	0	—	—	5	2	3	4	0	4	0	0	0	1	2	.33	0	.364	.533	.455
1999 Iowa	AAA	111	414	121	24	2	27	—	—	230	86	64	65	0	121	8	1	3	15	17	.47	7	.292	.396	.556
2000 Sacramento	AAA	129	481	131	21	3	14	—	—	200	94	64	88	1	117	5	4	6	39	10	.80	9	.272	.386	.416
1999 Chicago	NL	24	26	5	1	0	0	(0	0)	6	2	0	2	0	13	0	1	0	0	0	—	1	.192	.250	.231
2000 Oakland	AL	17	13	2	0	0	1	(0	1)	5	3	2	2	0	5	0	0	0	0	0	—	0	.154	.267	.385
2 ML YEARS		41	39	7	1	0	1	(0	1)	11	5	2	4	0	18	0	1	0	0	0	—	1	.179	.256	.282

Jorge Posada

Bats: B **Throws:** R **Pos:** C-142; 1B-12; DH-4; PH/PR-4   **Ht:** 6'2" **Wt:** 200 **Born:** 8/17/71 **Age:** 29

Year Team	Lg	G	AB	H	2B	3B	HR	(Hm	Rd)	TB	R	RBI	TBB	IBB	SO	HBP	SH	SF	SB	CS	SB%	GDP	Avg	OBP	SLG
1995 New York	AL	1	0	0	0	0	0	(0	0)	0	0	0	0	0	0	0	0	0	0	0	—	0	—	—	—
1996 New York	AL	8	14	1	0	0	0	(0	0)	1	1	0	1	0	6	0	0	0	0	0	—	1	.071	.133	.071

Year Team	Lg	G	AB	H	2B	3B	HR	(Hm	Rd)	TB	R	RBI	TBB	IBB	SO	HBP	SH	SF	SB	CS	SB%	GDP	Avg	OBP	SLG
						BATTING															BASERUNNING			PERCENTAGES		
1997 New York	AL	60	188	47	12	0	6	(2	4)	77	29	25	30	2	33	3	1	2	1	2	.33	2	.250	.359	.410
1998 New York	AL	111	358	96	23	0	17	(6	11)	170	56	63	47	7	92	0	1	4	0	1	.00	14	.268	.350	.475
1999 New York	AL	112	379	93	19	2	12	(4	8)	152	50	57	53	2	91	3	0	2	1	0	1.00	9	.245	.341	.401
2000 New York	AL	151	505	145	35	1	28	(18	10)	266	92	86	107	10	151	8	0	4	2	2	.50	11	.287	.417	.527
6 ML YEARS		443	1444	382	89	3	63	(30	33)	666	228	231	238	21	373	14	1	12	4	5	.44	37	.265	.371	.461

Scott Pose

Bats: L **Throws:** R **Pos:** PH/PR-35; RF-7; DH-4; LF-3; CF-2   **Ht:** 5'11" **Wt:** 190 **Born:** 2/11/67 **Age:** 34

Year Team	Lg	G	AB	H	2B	3B	HR	(Hm	Rd)	TB	R	RBI	TBB	IBB	SO	HBP	SH	SF	SB	CS	SB%	GDP	Avg	OBP	SLG
						BATTING															BASERUNNING			PERCENTAGES		
1993 Florida	NL	15	41	8	2	0	0	(0	0)	10	0	3	2	0	4	0	0	0	0	2	.00	0	.195	.233	.244
1997 New York	AL	54	87	19	2	1	0	(0	0)	23	19	5	9	0	11	0	0	0	3	1	.75	1	.218	.292	.264
1999 Kansas City	AL	86	137	39	3	0	0	(0	0)	42	27	12	21	1	22	0	1	1	6	2	.75	3	.285	.377	.307
2000 Kansas City	AL	47	48	9	0	0	0	(0	0)	9	6	1	6	0	13	0	0	0	0	1	.00	1	.188	.278	.188
4 ML YEARS		202	313	75	7	1	0	(0	0)	84	52	21	38	1	50	0	1	1	9	6	.60	5	.240	.321	.268

Lou Pote

Pitches: Right **Bats:** Right **Pos:** RP-31; SP-1   **Ht:** 6'3" **Wt:** 208 **Born:** 8/21/71 **Age:** 29

Year Team	Lg	G	GS	CG	GF	IP	BFP	H	R	ER	HR	SH	SF	HB	TBB	IBB	SO	WP	Bk	W	L	Pct.	ShO	Sv-Op	Hld	ERA
				HOW MUCH HE PITCHED						WHAT HE GAVE UP											THE RESULTS				
1991 Giants	R	8	8	0	0	42.1	184	38	23	12	0	0	1	0	18	0	41	5	0	2	3	.400	0	0--	—	2.55
Everett	A-	5	4	0	0	28.2	117	24	8	8	2	0	1	0	7	0	26	2	0	2	0	1.000	0	0--	—	2.51
1992 Shreveport	AA	20	3	0	9	37.2	146	32	7	4	1	3	1	1	15	2	26	3	0	4	2	.667	0	0--	—	0.96
San Jose	A+	4	3	0	1	9.2	46	11	5	5	0	1	0	0	7	0	8	3	0	1	0	1.000	0	0--	—	4.66
1993 Shreveport	AA	19	19	0	0	108.1	458	111	53	49	10	1	3	0	45	1	81	3	1	8	7	.533	0	0--	—	4.07
1994 Giants	R	4	4	0	0	19.2	73	9	0	0	0	1	0	0	6	0	30	0	0	1	0	1.000	0	0--	—	0.00
Shreveport	AA	5	5	0	0	28.2	122	31	11	9	2	2	0	2	7	0	15	1	1	2	2	.500	0	0--	—	2.83
1995 Shreveport	AA	28	0	0	11	50.2	226	53	41	30	8	4	1	0	26	1	30	4	0	2	2	.500	0	3--	—	5.33
Harrisburg	AA	9	4	0	2	28.1	123	32	17	17	3	0	2	1	7	0	24	1	0	0	1	.000	0	0--	—	5.40
1996 Harrisburg	AA	25	18	0	3	104.2	467	114	66	59	15	3	2	2	48	2	61	8	0	1	7	.125	0	1--	—	5.07
1997 Arkansas	AA	7	3	0	1	23.1	94	15	10	4	1	1	0	0	8	0	21	2	0	0	0	—	0	0--	—	1.54
1998 Midland	AA	32	19	6	7	154.1	700	194	110	91	18	5	6	6	54	1	117	8	0	8	10	.444	1	0--	—	5.31
1999 Edmonton	AAA	24	23	3	1	150	637	171	80	75	19	2	2	2	41	0	118	6	0	7	9	.438	0	0--	—	4.50
2000 Edmonton	AAA	24	0	0	22	30.2	133	27	14	12	2	1	1	0	14	0	28	3	0	2	1	.667	0	12--	—	3.52
1999 Anaheim	AL	20	0	0	10	29.1	118	23	9	7	1	1	0	0	12	1	20	1	0	1	1	.500	0	3-3	3	2.15
2000 Anaheim	AL	32	1	0	12	50.1	214	52	23	19	4	1	1	0	17	1	44	3	0	1	1	.500	0	1-1	2	3.40
2 ML YEARS		52	1	0	22	79.2	332	75	32	26	5	2	1	0	29	2	64	4	0	2	2	.500	0	4-4	5	2.94

Brian Powell

Pitches: Right **Bats:** Right **Pos:** SP-5; RP-4   **Ht:** 6'2" **Wt:** 205 **Born:** 10/10/73 **Age:** 27

Year Team	Lg	G	GS	CG	GF	IP	BFP	H	R	ER	HR	SH	SF	HB	TBB	IBB	SO	WP	Bk	W	L	Pct.	ShO	Sv-Op	Hld	ERA
				HOW MUCH HE PITCHED						WHAT HE GAVE UP											THE RESULTS				
1995 Jamestown	A-	5	5	0	0	26.1	108	19	12	9	1	0	1	5	8	0	15	3	0	2	1	.667	0	0--	—	3.08
Fayettevlle	A	5	5	0	0	28	111	15	5	5	0	1	1	2	11	0	37	2	0	4	0	1.000	0	0--	—	1.61
1996 Lakeland	A+	29	27	5	2	174.1	746	195	106	95	12	9	2	7	47	0	84	1	2	8	13	.381	0	0--	—	4.90
1997 Lakeland	A+	27	27	8	0	183.1	732	153	70	51	9	4	5	6	35	2	122	5	0	13	9	.591	2	0--	—	2.50
1998 Jacksnville	AA	14	14	2	0	93.2	379	84	37	32	5	0	3	4	24	0	51	3	2	10	2	.833	1	0--	—	3.07
Toledo	AAA	1	1	0	0	7	27	5	0	0	0	0	0	0	0	0	7	0	0	0	0	—	0	0--	—	0.00
1999 New Orleans	AAA	9	9	0	0	48	214	54	39	33	5	3	0	0	21	0	36	5	1	4	4	.500	0	0--	—	6.19
2000 New Orleans	AAA	18	18	1	0	103.2	442	103	63	57	9	1	4	5	41	1	57	3	1	9	4	.692	0	0--	—	4.95
1998 Detroit	AL	18	16	0	1	83.2	383	101	67	59	17	1	1	2	36	2	46	3	0	3	8	.273	0	0-0	—	6.35
2000 Houston	NL	9	5	0	1	31.1	140	34	21	20	8	2	2	1	13	0	14	0	0	2	1	.667	0	0-0	0	5.74
2 ML YEARS		27	21	0	2	115	523	135	88	79	25	3	3	3	49	2	60	3	0	5	9	.357	0	0-0	0	6.18

Jay Powell

Pitches: Right **Bats:** Right **Pos:** RP-29   **Ht:** 6'4" **Wt:** 225 **Born:** 1/9/72 **Age:** 29

Year Team	Lg	G	GS	CG	GF	IP	BFP	H	R	ER	HR	SH	SF	HB	TBB	IBB	SO	WP	Bk	W	L	Pct.	ShO	Sv-Op	Hld	ERA
				HOW MUCH HE PITCHED						WHAT HE GAVE UP											THE RESULTS				
2000 New Orleans *	AAA	2	1	0	0	2	9	2	1	1	0	0	0	0	2	0	2	0	0	0	0	—	0	0--	—	4.50
Round Rock *	AA	1	1	0	0	2	6	0	0	0	0	0	0	0	1	0	1	0	0	0	0	—	0	0--	—	0.00
1995 Florida	NL	9	0	0	1	8.1	38	7	2	1	0	1	0	2	6	1	4	0	0	0	0	—	0	0-0	2	1.08
1996 Florida	NL	67	0	0	16	71.1	321	71	41	36	5	2	1	4	36	1	52	3	0	4	3	.571	0	2-5	10	4.54
1997 Florida	NL	74	0	0	23	79.2	337	71	35	29	3	6	4	4	30	3	65	3	0	7	2	.778	0	2-4	24	3.28
1998 Fla-Hou	NL	62	0	0	35	70.1	302	58	28	26	6	3	1	3	37	9	62	1	0	7	7	.500	0	7-11	9	3.33
1999 Houston	NL	67	0	0	26	75	341	82	38	36	3	5	2	3	40	4	77	5	0	5	4	.556	0	4-7	16	4.32
2000 Houston	NL	29	0	0	10	27	127	29	18	17	1	1	0	0	19	1	16	0	0	1	1	.500	0	0-0	0	5.67
1998 Houston	NL	33	0	0	26	36.1	165	36	19	17	5	3	1	2	22	6	24	1	0	4	4	.500	0	3-6	0	4.21
Houston	NL	29	0	0	9	34	137	22	9	9	1	4	1	1	15	3	38	0	0	3	3	.500	0	4-5	3	2.38
6 ML YEARS		308	0	0	111	331.2	1466	318	162	145	18	18	8	16	168	19	276	12	0	24	17	.585	0	15-27	60	3.93

Jeremy Powell

Pitches: Right **Bats:** Right **Pos:** RP-7; SP-4   **Ht:** 6'5" **Wt:** 230 **Born:** 6/18/76 **Age:** 25

Year Team	Lg	G	GS	CG	GF	IP	BFP	H	R	ER	HR	SH	SF	HB	TBB	IBB	SO	WP	Bk	W	L	Pct.	ShO	Sv-Op	Hld	ERA
				HOW MUCH HE PITCHED						WHAT HE GAVE UP											THE RESULTS				
2000 Ottawa *	AAA	25	24	0	1	126.1	592	160	101	97	16	2	9	9	55	1	99	8	3	5	13	.278	0	0--	—	6.91
1998 Montreal	NL	7	6	0	1	25	112	27	25	22	5	2	2	4	11	0	14	0	0	1	5	.167	0	0-0	0	7.92
1999 Montreal	NL	17	17	0	0	97	438	113	60	51	14	9	3	8	44	2	44	4	1	4	8	.333	0	0-0	0	4.73
2000 Montreal	NL	11	4	0	6	26	121	35	27	23	6	2	1	0	9	0	19	1	0	0	3	.000	0	0-0	0	7.96
3 ML YEARS		35	27	0	7	148	671	175	112	96	25	13	6	12	64	2	77	5	1	5	16	.238	0	0-0	0	5.84

Todd Pratt

Bats: Right **Throws:** Right **Pos:** C-71; PH/PR-16; DH-1 **Ht:** 6'3" **Wt:** 230 **Born:** 2/9/67 **Age:** 34

Year Team	Lg	G	AB	H	2B	3B	HR	(Hm	Rd)	TB	R	RBI	TBB	IBB	SO	HBP	SH	SF	SB	CS	SB%	GDP	Avg	OBP	SLG
1992 Philadelphia	NL	16	46	13	1	0	2	(2	0)	20	6	10	4	0	12	0	0	0	0	0	—	2	.283	.340	.435
1993 Philadelphia	NL	33	87	25	6	0	5	(4	1)	46	8	13	5	0	19	1	1	1	0	0	—	2	.287	.330	.529
1994 Philadelphia	NL	28	102	20	6	1	2	(1	1)	34	10	9	12	0	29	0	0	0	0	1	.00	3	.196	.281	.333
1995 Chicago	NL	25	60	8	2	0	0	(0	0)	10	3	4	6	1	21	0	0	1	0	0	—	1	.133	.209	.167
1997 New York	NL	39	106	30	6	0	2	(1	1)	42	12	19	13	0	32	2	0	0	0	1	.00	0	.283	.372	.396
1998 New York	NL	41	69	19	9	1	2	(1	1)	36	9	18	2	0	20	0	0	0	0	0	—	0	.275	.296	.522
1999 New York	NL	71	140	41	4	0	3	(1	2)	54	18	21	15	0	32	3	0	2	2	0	1.00	0	.293	.369	.386
2000 New York	NL	80	160	44	6	0	8	(2	6)	74	33	25	22	1	31	5	2	1	0	0	—	5	.275	.378	.463
8 ML YEARS		333	770	200	40	2	24	(12	12)	316	99	119	79	2	196	11	3	5	2	2	.50	15	.260	.335	.410

Curtis Pride

Bats: L **Throws:** R **Pos:** LF-7; PH/PR-3; CF-2; DH-1 **Ht:** 6'0" **Wt:** 210 **Born:** 12/17/68 **Age:** 32

Year Team	Lg	G	AB	H	2B	3B	HR	(Hm	Rd)	TB	R	RBI	TBB	IBB	SO	HBP	SH	SF	SB	CS	SB%	GDP	Avg	OBP	SLG
2000 Norfolk *	AAA	15	31	9	2	2	1	—	—	18	9	4	11	0	7	1	0	0	3	2	.60	0	.290	.488	.581
Pawtucket *	AAA	48	154	47	10	2	9	—	—	88	44	31	38	1	31	1	5	2	12	1	.92	3	.305	.441	.571
Albuquerque *	AAA	38	133	39	7	3	6	—	—	70	30	17	20	3	37	0	2	1	7	5	.58	2	.293	.383	.526
1993 Montreal	NL	10	9	4	1	1	1	(0	1)	10	3	5	0	0	3	0	0	0	1	0	1.00	0	.444	.444	1.111
1995 Montreal	NL	48	63	11	1	0	0	(0	0)	12	10	2	5	0	16	0	1	0	3	2	.60	2	.175	.235	.190
1996 Detroit	AL	95	267	80	17	5	10	(5	5)	137	52	31	31	1	63	0	3	0	11	6	.65	2	.300	.372	.513
1997 Det-Bos	AL	81	164	35	4	4	3	(3	0)	56	22	20	24	1	46	1	2	1	6	4	.60	4	.213	.316	.341
1998 Atlanta	NL	70	107	27	6	1	3	(1	2)	44	19	9	9	0	29	3	1	1	4	0	1.00	2	.252	.325	.411
2000 Boston	AL	9	20	5	1	0	0	(0	0)	6	4	0	1	0	7	0	0	0	0	0	—	0	.250	.286	.300
1997 Detroit	AL	79	162	34	4	4	2	(2	0)	52	21	19	24	1	45	1	2	1	6	4	.60	4	.210	.314	.321
Boston	AL	2	2	1	0	0	1	(1	0)	4	1	1	0	0	1	0	0	0	0	0	—	0	.500	.500	2.000
6 ML YEARS		313	630	162	30	11	17	(9	8)	265	110	67	70	2	164	4	7	2	25	12	.68	10	.257	.334	.421

Ariel Prieto

Pitches: Right **Bats:** Right **Pos:** SP-6; RP-2 **Ht:** 6'2" **Wt:** 247 **Born:** 10/22/69 **Age:** 31

Year Team	Lg	G	GS	CG	GF	IP	BFP	H	R	ER	HR	SH	SF	HB	TBB	IBB	SO	WP	Bk	W	L	Pct.	ShO	Sv-Op	Hld	ERA
2000 Sacramento *	AAA	20	18	0	1	113	469	110	51	41	9	1	3	1	31	1	79	4	1	8	4	.667	0	0--	—	3.27
1995 Oakland	AL	14	9	1	1	58	258	57	35	32	4	3	2	5	32	1	37	4	1	2	6	.250	0	0-0	0	4.97
1996 Oakland	AL	21	21	2	0	125.2	547	130	66	58	9	5	5	7	54	2	75	6	2	6	7	.462	0	0-0	0	4.15
1997 Oakland	AL	22	22	0	0	125	588	155	84	70	16	3	4	5	70	3	90	7	1	6	8	.429	0	0-0	0	5.04
1998 Oakland	AL	2	2	0	0	8.1	47	17	11	11	2	0	0	1	5	1	8	0	0	0	1	.000	0	0-0	0	11.88
2000 Oakland	AL	8	6	0	2	31.2	148	42	21	18	3	2	1	1	13	0	19	0	0	1	2	.333	0	0-0	0	5.12
5 ML YEARS		67	60	3	3	348.2	1588	401	217	189	34	13	12	19	174	7	229	17	4	15	24	.385	0	0-0	0	4.88

Tom Prince

Bats: Right **Throws:** Right **Pos:** C-46; PH/PR-2 **Ht:** 5'11" **Wt:** 206 **Born:** 8/13/64 **Age:** 36

Year Team	Lg	G	AB	H	2B	3B	HR	(Hm	Rd)	TB	R	RBI	TBB	IBB	SO	HBP	SH	SF	SB	CS	SB%	GDP	Avg	OBP	SLG
1987 Pittsburgh	NL	4	9	2	1	0	1	(0	1)	6	1	2	0	0	2	0	0	0	0	0	—	0	.222	.222	.667
1988 Pittsburgh	NL	29	74	13	2	0	0	(0	0)	15	3	6	4	0	15	0	2	0	0	0	—	5	.176	.218	.203
1989 Pittsburgh	NL	21	52	7	4	0	0	(0	0)	11	1	5	6	1	12	0	0	1	1	1	.50	1	.135	.220	.212
1990 Pittsburgh	NL	4	10	1	0	0	0	(0	0)	1	1	0	1	0	2	0	0	0	0	1	.00	0	.100	.182	.100
1991 Pittsburgh	NL	26	34	9	3	0	1	(0	1)	15	4	2	7	0	3	1	0	0	1	1	.50	0	.265	.405	.441
1992 Pittsburgh	NL	27	44	4	2	0	0	(0	0)	6	1	5	6	0	9	0	0	2	1	1	.50	2	.091	.192	.136
1993 Pittsburgh	NL	66	179	35	14	0	2	(2	0)	55	14	24	13	2	38	7	2	3	1	1	.50	5	.196	.272	.307
1994 Los Angeles	NL	3	6	2	0	0	0	(0	0)	2	2	1	1	0	3	0	0	0	0	0	—	0	.333	.429	.333
1995 Los Angeles	NL	18	40	8	2	1	1	(0	1)	15	3	4	4	0	10	0	0	0	0	0	—	0	.200	.273	.375
1996 Los Angeles	NL	40	64	19	6	0	1	(0	1)	28	6	11	6	2	15	2	3	2	0	0	—	0	.297	.365	.438
1997 Los Angeles	NL	47	100	22	5	0	3	(2	1)	36	17	14	5	0	15	3	4	1	0	0	—	2	.220	.275	.360
1998 Los Angeles	NL	37	81	15	5	1	0	(0	0)	22	7	5	7	1	24	2	2	0	0	0	—	0	.185	.267	.272
1999 Philadelphia	NL	4	6	1	0	0	0	(0	0)	1	1	0	1	0	1	0	0	0	0	0	—	0	.167	.286	.167
2000 Philadelphia	NL	46	122	29	9	0	2	(0	2)	44	14	16	13	0	31	2	3	0	1	0	1.00	6	.238	.321	.361
14 ML YEARS		372	821	167	53	2	11	(4	7)	257	75	95	74	6	180	17	16	9	4	4	.50	25	.203	.280	.313

Chris Pritchett

Bats: Left **Throws:** Right **Pos:** 1B-3; PH/PR-2 **Ht:** 6'4" **Wt:** 212 **Born:** 1/31/70 **Age:** 31

Year Team	Lg	G	AB	H	2B	3B	HR	(Hm	Rd)	TB	R	RBI	TBB	IBB	SO	HBP	SH	SF	SB	CS	SB%	GDP	Avg	OBP	SLG
2000 Scrantn-WB *	AAA	117	391	93	18	2	6	—	—	133	55	60	56	3	65	5	1	6	5	2	.71	6	.238	.336	.340
1996 California	AL	5	13	2	0	0	0	(0	0)	2	1	1	0	0	3	0	0	0	0	0	—	1	.154	.154	.154
1998 Anaheim	AL	31	80	23	2	1	2	(0	2)	33	12	8	4	0	16	0	0	0	2	0	1.00	3	.288	.321	.413
1999 Anaheim	AL	20	45	7	1	0	1	(1	0)	11	3	2	2	0	9	0	1	1	1	1	.50	0	.156	.188	.244
2000 Philadelphia	NL	5	11	1	0	0	0	(0	0)	1	0	0	1	0	3	0	0	0	0	0	—	1	.091	.167	.091
4 ML YEARS		61	149	33	3	1	3	(1	2)	47	16	11	7	0	31	0	1	1	3	1	.75	4	.221	.255	.315

Luke Prokopec

Pitches: Right **Bats:** Left **Pos:** SP-3; RP-2 **Ht:** 5'11" **Wt:** 166 **Born:** 2/23/78 **Age:** 23

Year Team	Lg	G	GS	CG	GF	IP	BFP	H	R	ER	HR	SH	SF	HB	TBB	IBB	SO	WP	Bk	W	L	Pct.	ShO	Sv-Op	Hld	ERA
1997 Savannah	A	13	6	0	5	42	175	37	21	19	8	1	3	1	12	0	45	1	0	3	1	.750	0	0--	—	4.07

Year Team	Lg	G	GS	CG	GF	IP	BFP	H	R	ER	HR	SH	SF	HB	TBB	IBB	SO	WP	Bk	W	L	Pct.	ShO	Sv-Op	Hld	ERA
1998 San Berndno	A+	20	20	0	0	110.1	460	98	43	33	11	3	2	3	33	1	148	5	1	8	5	.615	0	0- --	—	2.69
San Antonio	AA	5	5	0	0	26	106	16	5	4	0	1	1	1	13	0	25	2	1	3	0	1.000	0	0- --	—	1.38
1999 San Antonio	AA	27	27	0	0	157.2	685	172	113	95	18	7	8	7	46	0	128	3	1	8	12	.400	0	0- --	—	5.42
2000 San Antonio	AA	22	22	1	0	128.2	524	118	40	35	8	4	3	7	23	1	124	0	1	3	7	.700	0	0- --	—	2.45
2000 Los Angeles	NL	5	3	0	1	21	88	19	10	7	2	1	1	2	9	0	12	0	0	1	1	.500	0	0-0	0	3.00

Bill Pulsipher

Pitches: Left **Bats:** Left **Pos:** SP-2   **Ht:** 6'3" **Wt:** 200 **Born:** 10/9/73 **Age:** 27

Year Team	Lg	G	GS	CG	GF	IP	BFP	H	R	ER	HR	SH	SF	HB	TBB	IBB	SO	WP	Bk	W	L	Pct.	ShO	Sv-Op	Hld	ERA
2000 Norfolk *	AAA	7	5	0	0	33	150	41	28	24	5	0	2	0	15	1	25	0	0	2	3	.400	0	0- --	—	6.55
Diamndbcks *	R	3	3	0	0	6	24	8	3	3	0	0	0	1	0	0	4	1	0	0	0	—	0	0- --	—	4.50
Tucson *	AAA	13	13	0	0	70.2	309	73	39	31	7	1	1	1	37	0	51	1	2	3	8	.273	0	0- --	—	3.95
1995 New York	NL	17	17	2	0	126.2	530	122	58	56	11	2	1	4	45	0	81	2	1	5	7	.417	0	0-0	0	3.98
1998 NYM-Mil	NL	26	11	0	2	72.1	320	86	41	41	8	4	1	4	31	4	51	2	2	3	4	.429	0	0-1	0	5.10
1999 Milwaukee	NL	19	16	0	1	87.1	398	100	65	58	19	6	4	2	36	2	42	4	0	5	6	.455	0	0-0	0	5.98
2000 New York	NL	2	2	0	0	6.2	39	12	9	9	1	0	1	0	6	0	7	0	0	0	2	.000	0	0-0	0	12.15
1998 New York	NL	15	1	0	1	14.1	68	23	11	11	2	1	0	0	5	1	13	0	0	0	0	—	0	0-1	2	6.91
Milwaukee	NL	11	10	0	1	58	252	63	30	30	6	3	1	4	26	3	38	2	2	3	4	.429	0	0-0	0	4.66
4 ML YEARS		64	46	2	3	293	1287	320	173	164	39	13	9	8	118	6	181	8	3	13	19	.406	0	0-1	2	5.04

Paul Quantrill

Pitches: Right **Bats:** Left **Pos:** RP-68   **Ht:** 6'1" **Wt:** 190 **Born:** 11/3/68 **Age:** 32

Year Team	Lg	G	GS	CG	GF	IP	BFP	H	R	ER	HR	SH	SF	HB	TBB	IBB	SO	WP	Bk	W	L	Pct.	ShO	Sv-Op	Hld	ERA
1992 Boston	AL	27	0	0	10	49.1	213	55	18	12	1	4	2	1	15	5	24	1	0	2	3	.400	0	1-5	3	2.19
1993 Boston	AL	49	14	0	8	138	594	151	73	60	13	4	2	2	44	14	66	0	1	6	12	.333	1	1-2	3	3.91
1994 Bos-Phi		35	1	0	9	53	236	64	31	29	7	5	3	5	15	4	28	0	2	3	3	.500	0	1-4	3	4.92
1995 Philadelphia	NL	33	29	0	1	179.1	784	212	102	93	20	9	6	6	44	3	103	0	3	11	12	.478	0	0-0	0	4.67
1996 Toronto	AL	38	20	0	7	134.1	609	172	90	81	27	5	7	2	51	3	86	1	1	5	14	.263	0	0-2	1	5.43
1997 Toronto	AL	77	0	0	29	88	373	103	25	19	5	5	3	1	17	3	56	1	0	6	7	.462	0	5-10	16	1.94
1998 Toronto	AL	82	0	0	32	80	345	88	26	23	5	7	4	3	22	6	59	1	0	3	4	.429	0	7-14	27	2.59
1999 Toronto	AL	41	0	0	13	48.2	212	53	19	18	5	1	2	4	17	1	28	0	0	3	2	.600	0	0-4	8	3.33
2000 Toronto	AL	68	0	0	24	83.2	367	100	45	42	7	1	3	2	25	1	47	1	0	2	5	.286	0	1-3	13	4.52
1994 Boston	AL	17	0	0	4	23	101	25	10	9	4	2	2	2	5	1	15	0	0	1	1	.500	0	0-2	2	3.52
Philadelphia	NL	18	1	0	5	30	135	39	21	20	3	3	1	3	10	3	13	0	2	2	2	.500	0	1-2	1	6.00
9 ML YEARS		450	64	1	133	854.1	3733	998	429	377	90	41	32	26	250	40	497	5	7	41	62	.398	1	16-44	74	3.97

Ruben Quevedo

Pitches: Right **Bats:** Right **Pos:** SP-15; RP-6   **Ht:** 6'1" **Wt:** 230 **Born:** 1/5/79 **Age:** 22

Year Team	Lg	G	GS	CG	GF	IP	BFP	H	R	ER	HR	SH	SF	HB	TBB	IBB	SO	WP	Bk	W	L	Pct.	ShO	Sv-Op	Hld	ERA
1996 Braves	R	10	10	0	0	55	221	50	19	14	1	4	1	1	9	0	49	3	2	2	6	.250	0	0- --	—	2.29
1997 Danville	R+	13	11	0	0	68.1	286	46	37	27	6	3	5	4	27	0	78	3	1	1	5	.167	0	0- --	—	3.56
1998 Macon	A	21	21	1	0	112	470	114	50	39	13	3	4	1	31	0	117	5	1	11	3	.786	0	0- --	—	3.13
Danville	A+	6	6	0	0	32.2	143	28	22	13	2	1	2	3	13	1	35	2	0	0	2	.000	0	0- --	—	3.58
1999 Richmond	AAA	21	21	0	0	105.2	440	112	65	63	26	2	2	1	34	0	98	4	0	6	5	.545	0	0- --	—	5.37
Iowa	AAA	7	7	1	0	44.1	185	34	18	17	1	2	3	0	21	0	50	0	0	3	1	.750	1	0- --	—	3.45
2000 Iowa	AAA	13	13	0	0	74.2	322	68	37	35	7	4	3	1	31	0	77	1	1	7	2	.778	0	0- --	—	4.22
2000 Chicago	NL	21	15	1	1	88	418	96	81	73	21	4	3	3	54	4	65	2	0	3	10	.231	0	0-0	0	7.47

Mark Quinn

Bats: R **Throws:** R **Pos:** LF-78; DH-48; PH/PR-7; RF-4; CF-1   **Ht:** 6'1" **Wt:** 195 **Born:** 5/21/74 **Age:** 27

Year Team	Lg	G	AB	H	2B	3B	HR	(Hm	Rd)	TB	R	RBI	TBB	IBB	SO	HBP	SH	SF	SB	CS	SB%	GDP	Avg	OBP	SLG
1995 Spokane	A-	44	162	46	12	2	6	—	—	80	28	37	15	0	28	5	0	5	0	1	.00	5	.284	.357	.494
1996 Lansing	A	113	437	132	23	3	9	—	—	188	63	71	43	2	54	5	0	6	14	8	.64	12	.302	.367	.430
1997 Wilmington	A+	87	299	92	22	3	16	—	—	168	51	71	42	4	47	8	0	6	3	2	.60	10	.308	.400	.562
Wichita	AA	26	96	36	13	0	2	—	—	55	26	19	15	0	19	3	0	1	1	1	.50	2	.375	.474	.573
1998 Wichita	AA	100	372	130	26	6	16	—	—	216	82	84	43	1	54	10	0	7	4	1	.80	5	.349	.424	.581
1999 Omaha	AAA	107	428	154	27	0	25	—	—	256	67	84	28	3	69	10	0	4	7	9	.44	9	.360	.409	.598
2000 Omaha	AAA	13	61	23	5	0	3	—	—	37	8	13	0	0	8	0	0	1	0	1	.00	5	.377	.371	.607
1999 Kansas City	AL	17	60	20	4	1	6	(2	4)	44	11	18	4	0	11	1	0	0	1	0	1.00	1	.333	.385	.733
2000 Kansas City	AL	135	500	147	33	2	20	(12	8)	244	76	78	35	4	91	3	3	3	5	2	.71	11	.294	.342	.488
2 ML YEARS		152	560	167	37	3	26	(14	12)	288	87	96	39	4	102	4	3	3	6	2	.75	12	.298	.347	.514

Scott Radinsky

Pitches: Left **Bats:** Left **Pos:** RP-1   **Ht:** 6'3" **Wt:** 215 **Born:** 3/3/68 **Age:** 33

Year Team	Lg	G	GS	CG	GF	IP	BFP	H	R	ER	HR	SH	SF	HB	TBB	IBB	SO	WP	Bk	W	L	Pct.	ShO	Sv-Op	Hld	ERA
1990 Chicago	AL	62	0	0	18	52.1	237	47	29	28	1	2	2	2	36	1	46	2	1	6	1	.857	0	4-5	10	4.82
1991 Chicago	AL	67	0	0	19	71.1	289	53	18	16	4	4	4	1	23	2	49	0	0	5	5	.500	0	8-15	15	2.02
1992 Chicago	AL	68	0	0	33	59.1	261	54	21	18	3	2	1	2	34	5	48	3	0	3	7	.300	0	15-23	16	2.73
1993 Chicago	AL	73	0	0	24	54.2	250	61	33	26	3	2	0	1	19	3	44	0	1	8	2	.800	0	4-5	12	4.28
1995 Chicago	AL	46	0	0	10	38	171	46	23	23	7	1	4	0	17	4	14	0	0	2	1	.667	0	1-3	5	5.45
1996 Los Angeles	NL	58	0	0	19	52.1	221	52	19	14	2	4	3	0	17	5	48	0	3	5	1	.833	0	1-4	7	2.41
1997 Los Angeles	NL	75	0	0	14	62.1	258	54	22	20	2	4	1	4	21	5	44	0	0	5	1	.833	0	3-5	26	2.89
1998 Los Angeles	NL	62	0	0	30	61.2	264	63	21	18	5	6	2	4	20	1	45	0	3	6	6	.500	0	13-24	8	2.63

176

Year Team	Lg	G	GS	CG	GF	IP	BFP	H	R	ER	HR	SH	SF	HB	TBB	IBB	SO	WP	Bk	W	L	Pct.	ShO	Sv-Op	Hld	ERA
1999 St. Louis	NL	43	0	0	13	27.2	126	27	16	15	2	2	5	1	18	3	17	3	1	2	1	.667	0	3-3	11	4.88
2000 St. Louis	NL	1	0	0	0	0	1	0	0	0	0	0	0	0	1	0	0	0	0	0	0	.---	0	0-0	0	.--
10 ML YEARS		555	0	0	180	479.2	2078	457	202	178	31	26	25	12	206	29	355	8	12	42	25	.627	0	52-87	113	3.34

Brad Radke

Pitches: Right **Bats:** Right **Pos:** SP-34 **Ht:** 6'2" **Wt:** 188 **Born:** 10/27/72 **Age:** 28

Year Team	Lg	G	GS	CG	GF	IP	BFP	H	R	ER	HR	SH	SF	HB	TBB	IBB	SO	WP	Bk	W	L	Pct.	ShO	Sv-Op	Hld	ERA
1995 Minnesota	AL	29	28	2	0	181	772	195	112	107	32	2	9	4	47	0	75	4	0	11	14	.440	1	0-0	0	5.32
1996 Minnesota	AL	35	35	3	0	232	973	231	125	115	40	5	6	4	57	2	148	1	1	11	16	.407	0	0-0	0	4.46
1997 Minnesota	AL	35	35	4	0	239.2	989	238	114	103	28	2	9	3	48	1	174	1	1	20	10	.667	1	0-0	0	3.87
1998 Minnesota	AL	32	32	5	0	213.2	904	238	109	102	23	9	3	9	43	1	146	3	1	12	14	.462	1	0-0	0	4.30
1999 Minnesota	AL	33	33	4	0	218.2	910	239	91	91	28	5	5	1	44	0	121	4	0	12	14	.462	0	0-0	0	3.75
2000 Minnesota	AL	34	34	4	0	226.2	978	261	119	112	27	7	4	5	51	1	141	5	0	12	16	.429	1	0-0	0	4.45
6 ML YEARS		198	197	22	0	1311.2	5526	1402	676	630	178	30	36	26	290	5	805	18	2	78	84	.481	4	0-0	0	4.32

Steve Rain

Pitches: Right **Bats:** Right **Pos:** RP-37 **Ht:** 6'6" **Wt:** 260 **Born:** 6/2/75 **Age:** 26

Year Team	Lg	G	GS	CG	GF	IP	BFP	H	R	ER	HR	SH	SF	HB	TBB	IBB	SO	WP	Bk	W	L	Pct.	ShO	Sv-Op	Hld	ERA
1993 Cubs	R	10	6	0	3	37	162	37	20	16	0	1	1	2	17	0	29	5	1	1	3	.250	0	0--	—	3.89
1994 Huntington	R+	14	10	1	1	68	272	55	26	20	2	2	1	2	19	0	55	4	4	3	3	.500	1	0--	—	2.65
1995 Rockford	A	53	0	0	51	59.1	234	38	12	8	0	3	2	2	23	3	66	8	0	5	2	.714	0	23--	—	1.21
1996 Orlando	AA	35	0	0	29	38.2	163	32	15	11	4	0	0	3	12	1	48	2	1	1	0	1.000	0	10--	—	2.56
Iowa	AAA	26	0	0	26	26	103	17	9	9	3	3	3	0	8	3	23	1	0	2	1	.667	0	10--	—	3.12
1997 Iowa	AAA	40	0	0	17	44.1	217	51	30	29	8	2	1	0	34	4	50	4	1	7	1	.875	0	1--	—	5.89
Orlando	AA	14	0	0	12	14.2	69	16	7	5	2	0	0	1	8	0	11	0	0	1	2	.333	0	4--	—	3.07
1998 Iowa	AAA	29	14	1	4	103.2	487	118	82	77	14	6	2	7	64	0	83	16	0	4	6	.400	0	0--	—	6.68
1999 West Tenn	AA	40	0	0	39	45.1	188	32	9	8	3	0	2	1	16	3	55	5	1	3	1	.750	0	24--	—	1.59
Iowa	AAA	8	0	0	7	9	38	7	2	2	1	0	0	0	4	0	9	0	0	0	1	.000	0	2--	—	2.00
2000 Iowa	AAA	28	0	0	21	31.1	132	31	14	12	4	2	1	0	6	1	34	2	0	0	2	.000	0	6--	—	3.45
1999 Chicago	NL	16	0	0	5	14.2	79	28	17	15	1	3	1	1	7	0	12	1	0	0	1	.000	0	0-0	0	9.20
2000 Chicago	NL	37	0	0	6	49.2	214	46	25	24	10	1	1	1	27	0	54	4	0	3	4	.429	0	0-3	8	4.35
2 ML YEARS		53	0	0	11	64.1	293	74	42	39	11	4	2	2	34	0	66	5	0	3	5	.375	0	0-3	8	5.46

Jason Rakers

Pitches: Right **Bats:** Right **Pos:** RP-11 **Ht:** 6'2" **Wt:** 200 **Born:** 6/29/73 **Age:** 28

Year Team	Lg	G	GS	CG	GF	IP	BFP	H	R	ER	HR	SH	SF	HB	TBB	IBB	SO	WP	Bk	W	L	Pct.	ShO	Sv-Op	Hld	ERA
1995 Watertown	A-	14	14	1	0	75	315	72	27	25	3	0	2	0	24	1	73	6	2	4	3	.571	1	0--	—	3.00
1996 Columbus	A	14	14	1	0	77.1	319	84	37	31	5	1	1	3	17	0	64	8	1	5	4	.556	1	0--	—	3.61
1997 Kinston	A+	17	17	2	0	102.2	405	93	41	35	10	1	0	1	18	0	105	2	1	8	5	.615	2	0--	—	3.07
Buffalo	AAA	1	1	0	0	7	26	5	0	0	0	0	0	0	1	0	3	0	0	1	0	1.000	0	0--	—	0.00
Akron	AA	7	7	1	0	41	168	36	21	20	3	1	2	4	11	0	31	1	0	1	4	.200	1	0--	—	4.39
1998 Akron	AA	5	5	0	0	31.1	130	35	10	9	2	2	1	0	7	0	27	2	0	3	1	.750	0	0--	—	2.59
Buffalo	AAA	21	21	1	0	126	542	134	70	64	13	2	6	8	38	0	89	7	1	8	6	.571	0	0--	—	4.57
1999 Buffalo	AAA	23	20	1	1	131.2	577	151	83	72	17	4	2	6	31	2	85	4	3	7	8	.467	0	0--	—	4.92
2000 Omaha	AAA	32	6	0	9	75	319	83	49	46	14	0	2	1	17	2	68	2	1	3	2	.600	0	2--	—	5.52
1998 Cleveland	AL	1	0	0	1	1	6	0	1	1	0	0	1	0	3	0	0	0	0	0	0	.--	0	0-0	0	9.00
1999 Cleveland	AL	1	0	0	0	2	9	2	1	1	1	0	0	0	1	0	0	0	0	0	0	.--	0	0-0	0	4.50
2000 Kansas City	AL	11	0	0	3	21.2	102	33	22	22	5	0	1	0	7	0	16	3	0	2	0	1.000	0	0-0	1	9.14
3 ML YEARS		13	0	0	4	24.2	117	35	24	24	6	0	2	0	11	0	16	3	0	2	0	1.000	0	0-0	1	8.76

Alex Ramirez

Bats: R **Throws:** R **Pos:** RF-47; PH/PR-21; LF-15; DH-6; 1B-1; CF-1 **Ht:** 5'11" **Wt:** 200 **Born:** 10/3/74 **Age:** 26

Year Team	Lg	G	AB	H	2B	3B	HR	(Hm	Rd)	TB	R	RBI	TBB	IBB	SO	HBP	SH	SF	SB	CS	SB%	GDP	Avg	OBP	SLG
1993 Burlington	R+	64	252	68	14	4	13	—	—	129	44	58	13	1	52	4	0	3	12	8	.60	4	.270	.313	.512
Kinston	A+	3	12	2	0	0	0	—	—	2	0	1	0	0	5	0	0	0	0	1	.00	0	.167	.167	.167
1994 Columbus	A	125	458	115	23	3	18	—	—	198	64	57	26	0	100	4	0	4	7	5	.58	11	.251	.295	.432
1995 Bakersfield	A+	98	406	131	25	2	10	—	—	190	56	52	18	1	76	3	0	1	13	9	.59	6	.323	.355	.468
Canton-Akrn	AA	33	133	33	3	4	1	—	—	47	15	11	5	1	24	0	1	1	3	5	.38	5	.248	.273	.353
1996 Canton-Akrn	AA	131	513	169	28	12	14	—	—	263	79	85	16	1	74	3	1	1	18	10	.64	8	.329	.353	.513
1997 Buffalo	AAA	119	416	119	19	8	11	—	—	187	59	44	24	0	95	4	6	3	10	5	.67	9	.286	.329	.450
1998 Buffalo	AAA	121	521	156	21	8	34	—	—	295	94	103	16	4	101	5	0	4	6	4	.60	11	.299	.324	.566
1999 Buffalo	AAA	75	305	93	20	2	12	—	—	153	50	50	17	2	52	4	0	4	5	5	.50	10	.305	.345	.502
1998 Cleveland	AL	3	8	1	0	0	0	(0	0)	1	1	0	0	0	3	0	0	0	0	0	.--	0	.125	.125	.125
1999 Cleveland	AL	48	97	29	6	1	3	(2	1)	46	11	18	3	0	26	1	1	0	1	1	.50	1	.299	.327	.474
2000 Cle-Pit		84	227	56	11	2	9	(4	5)	98	26	30	12	2	49	0	1	0	2	0	1.00	9	.247	.285	.432
2000 Cleveland	AL	41	112	32	5	1	5	(3	2)	54	13	12	5	0	17	0	0	0	1	0	1.00	3	.286	.316	.482
Pittsburgh	NL	43	115	24	6	1	4	(1	3)	44	13	18	7	2	32	0	1	0	1	0	1.00	6	.209	.254	.383
3 ML YEARS		135	332	86	17	3	12	(6	6)	145	38	48	15	2	78	1	2	0	3	1	.75	10	.259	.293	.437

Aramis Ramirez

Bats: Right **Throws:** Right **Pos:** 3B-72; PH/PR-2 **Ht:** 6'1" **Wt:** 219 **Born:** 6/25/78 **Age:** 23

Year Team	Lg	G	AB	H	2B	3B	HR	(Hm	Rd)	TB	R	RBI	TBB	IBB	SO	HBP	SH	SF	SB	CS	SB%	GDP	Avg	OBP	SLG
2000 Nashville *	AAA	44	167	59	12	2	4	—	—	87	28	26	11	0	26	4	0	0	2	1	.67	5	.353	.407	.521

Year Team	Lg	G	AB	H	2B	3B	HR	(Hm	Rd)	TB	R	RBI	TBB	IBB	SO	HBP	SH	SF	SB	CS	SB%	GDP	Avg	OBP	SLG
1998 Pittsburgh	NL	72	251	59	11	0	6	(3	3)	88	23	24	18	0	72	4	1	1	0	1	.00	3	.235	.296	.351
1999 Pittsburgh	NL	18	56	10	2	1	0	(0	0)	14	2	7	6	0	9	1	0	1	0	0	—	0	.179	.254	.250
2000 Pittsburgh	NL	73	254	65	15	2	6	(4	2)	102	19	35	10	0	36	5	1	4	0	0	—	9	.256	.293	.402
3 ML YEARS		163	561	134	26	4	12	(7	5)	204	44	66	34	0	117	9	3	6	0	1	.00	12	.239	.290	.364

Hector Ramirez

Pitches: Right **Bats:** Right **Pos:** RP-6   **Ht:** 6'3" **Wt:** 218 **Born:** 12/15/71 **Age:** 29

Year Team	Lg	G	GS	CG	GF	IP	BFP	H	R	ER	HR	SH	SF	HB	TBB	IBB	SO	WP	Bk	W	L	Pct.	ShO	Sv-Op	Hld	ERA
1989 Mets	R	15	5	0	8	42	189	35	29	21	0	0	3	3	24	0	14	8	2	0	5	.000	0	0--	—	4.50
1990 Mets	R	11	8	1	1	50.2	226	54	34	23	2	1	1	4	21	1	43	2	2	3	5	.375	0	0--	—	4.09
1991 Kingsport	R+	14	13	1	0	85	364	83	39	24	5	0	5	4	28	2	64	9	0	8	2	.800	0	0--	—	2.54
1992 Columbia	A	17	17	1	0	94.2	404	93	50	38	5	3	3	3	33	1	53	4	3	5	4	.556	0	0--	—	3.61
1993 Mets	R	1	1	0	0	7	26	5	1	0	0	0	0	1	0	0	6	0	0	1	0	1.000	0	0--	—	0.00
Capital Cty	A	14	14	0	0	64	294	86	51	38	2	3	4	2	23	0	42	7	0	4	6	.400	0	0--	—	5.34
1994 St. Lucie	A+	27	27	6	0	194	802	202	86	74	10	10	6	5	50	2	110	6	8	11	12	.478	1	0--	—	3.43
1995 Binghamton	AA	20	20	2	0	123.1	534	127	69	63	12	2	2	3	48	2	63	3	5	4	12	.250	0	0--	—	4.60
1996 Norfolk	AAA	3	1	0	1	10.2	49	13	7	4	1	1	1	0	3	0	8	1	0	1	0	1.000	0	0--	—	3.38
Binghamton	AA	38	0	0	17	56	245	51	34	32	3	5	3	6	23	5	49	4	2	1	5	.167	0	6--	—	5.14
1997 Rochester	AAA	39	9	0	10	102.2	456	114	65	56	11	1	8	7	38	2	50	11	3	8	7	.533	0	3--	—	4.91
1998 Charlotte	AAA	55	0	0	21	86.2	385	106	68	65	15	3	4	0	30	1	50	8	0	3	3	.500	0	3--	—	6.75
1999 Louisville	AAA	58	0	0	26	94.2	398	91	46	40	13	4	2	2	33	0	55	4	0	3	3	.500	0	9--	—	3.80
2000 Indianapolis	AAA	15	0	0	6	23.2	98	24	9	8	5	1	0	1	5	0	18	5	0	3	0	1.000	0	0--	—	3.04
Rochester	AAA	26	0	0	8	41.2	193	55	36	34	8	2	1	0	19	2	28	3	4	2	2	.500	0	1--	—	7.34
New Orleans	AAA	5	0	0	4	5	22	6	1	1	0	0	1	0	1	0	4	0	0	0	0	—	0	0--	—	1.80
1999 Milwaukee	NL	15	0	0	5	21	88	19	8	8	1	0	0	0	11	2	9	0	1	1	2	.333	0	0-3	5	3.43
2000 Milwaukee	NL	6	0	0	1	9	43	11	10	10	1	0	0	0	5	0	4	0	0	0	1	.000	0	0-0	0	10.00
2 ML YEARS		21	0	0	6	30	131	30	18	18	2	0	0	0	16	2	13	0	1	1	3	.250	0	0-3	5	5.40

Manny Ramirez

Bats: Right **Throws:** Right **Pos:** RF-93; DH-25   **Ht:** 6'0" **Wt:** 205 **Born:** 5/30/72 **Age:** 29

Year Team	Lg	G	AB	H	2B	3B	HR	(Hm	Rd)	TB	R	RBI	TBB	IBB	SO	HBP	SH	SF	SB	CS	SB%	GDP	Avg	OBP	SLG
2000 Akron *	AA	1	2	1	0	0	1	(—	—)	4	1	2	2	0	1	0	0	0	0	0	—	0	.500	.750	2.000
Buffalo *	AAA	5	11	5	1	0	3	(—	—)	15	5	7	6	1	1	0	0	0	0	0	—	1	.455	.647	1.364
1993 Cleveland	AL	22	53	9	1	0	2	(0	2)	16	5	5	2	0	8	0	0	0	0	0	—	0	.170	.200	.302
1994 Cleveland	AL	91	290	78	22	0	17	(9	8)	151	51	60	42	4	72	0	0	4	4	2	.67	6	.269	.357	.521
1995 Cleveland	AL	137	484	149	26	1	31	(12	19)	270	85	107	75	6	112	5	2	5	6	6	.50	13	.308	.402	.558
1996 Cleveland	AL	152	550	170	45	3	33	(19	14)	320	94	112	85	8	104	3	0	9	8	5	.62	18	.309	.399	.582
1997 Cleveland	AL	150	561	184	40	0	26	(14	12)	302	99	88	79	5	115	7	0	4	2	3	.40	19	.328	.415	.538
1998 Cleveland	AL	150	571	168	35	2	45	(25	20)	342	108	145	76	6	121	6	0	10	5	3	.63	18	.294	.377	.599
1999 Cleveland	AL	147	522	174	34	3	44	(21	23)	346	131	165	96	9	131	13	0	9	2	4	.33	12	.333	.442	.663
2000 Cleveland	AL	118	439	154	34	2	38	(22	16)	306	92	122	86	9	117	3	0	4	1	1	.50	9	.351	.457	.697
8 ML YEARS		967	3470	1086	237	11	236	(122	114)	2053	665	804	541	47	780	37	0	45	28	24	.54	98	.313	.407	.592

Rob Ramsay

Pitches: Left **Bats:** Left **Pos:** RP-36; SP-1   **Ht:** 6'5" **Wt:** 215 **Born:** 12/3/73 **Age:** 27

Year Team	Lg	G	GS	CG	GF	IP	BFP	H	R	ER	HR	SH	SF	HB	TBB	IBB	SO	WP	Bk	W	L	Pct.	ShO	Sv-Op	Hld	ERA
1996 Red Sox	R	2	0	0	1	3.2	19	5	2	2	0	0	0	1	3	0	5	0	0	0	1	.000	0	0--	—	4.91
Sarasota	A+	12	7	0	0	34	165	42	23	23	1	1	1	1	27	0	32	2	2	2	2	.500	0	0--	—	6.09
1997 Sarasota	A+	23	22	1	0	135.2	603	134	90	72	16	1	3	5	63	0	115	7	0	9	9	.500	0	0--	—	4.78
1998 Trenton	AA	27	27	1	0	162.2	659	137	67	63	10	5	5	3	50	1	166	8	3	12	6	.667	1	0--	—	3.49
1999 Pawtucket	AAA	20	20	0	0	114.1	498	114	81	68	21	4	4	4	36	1	79	5	3	6	6	.500	0	0--	—	5.35
Tacoma	AAA	5	5	0	0	33.1	130	20	6	4	2	0	1	0	14	1	37	1	0	4	1	.800	0	0--	—	1.08
2000 Tacoma	AAA	3	3	0	0	16	68	16	8	8	1	0	0	0	6	0	6	0	0	1	0	1.000	0	0--	—	4.50
Everett	A-	1	1	0	0	2	8	2	0	0	0	0	0	0	0	0	4	0	0	0	0	—	0	0--	—	0.00
1999 Seattle	AL	6	3	0	1	18.1	81	23	13	13	3	0	1	0	9	1	11	1	0	0	2	.000	0	0--	—	6.38
2000 Seattle	AL	37	1	0	6	50.1	230	43	22	19	3	2	3	1	40	3	32	4	0	1	1	.500	0	0-0	5	3.40
2 ML YEARS		43	4	0	7	68.2	311	66	35	32	6	2	3	1	49	4	43	5	0	1	3	.250	0	0-0	5	4.19

Joe Randa

Bats: Right **Throws:** Right **Pos:** 3B-156; DH-1; PH/PR-1   **Ht:** 5'11" **Wt:** 190 **Born:** 12/18/69 **Age:** 31

Year Team	Lg	G	AB	H	2B	3B	HR	(Hm	Rd)	TB	R	RBI	TBB	IBB	SO	HBP	SH	SF	SB	CS	SB%	GDP	Avg	OBP	SLG
1995 Kansas City	AL	34	70	12	2	0	1	(1	0)	17	6	5	6	0	17	0	0	0	0	1	.00	2	.171	.237	.243
1996 Kansas City	AL	110	337	102	24	1	6	(2	4)	146	36	47	26	4	47	1	2	4	13	4	.76	10	.303	.351	.433
1997 Pittsburgh	NL	126	443	134	27	9	7	(5	2)	200	58	60	41	1	64	6	4	5	4	2	.67	10	.303	.366	.451
1998 Detroit	AL	138	460	117	21	2	9	(6	3)	169	56	50	41	1	70	7	3	3	8	7	.53	9	.254	.323	.367
1999 Kansas City	AL	156	628	197	36	8	16	(7	9)	297	92	84	50	4	80	3	1	7	5	4	.56	15	.314	.363	.473
2000 Kansas City	AL	158	612	186	29	4	15	(9	6)	268	88	106	36	3	66	6	1	10	3	6	.67	19	.304	.343	.438
6 ML YEARS		722	2550	748	139	24	54	(27	27)	1097	336	352	200	13	344	23	11	29	36	21	.63	65	.293	.347	.430

Pat Rapp

Pitches: Right **Bats:** Right **Pos:** SP-30; RP-1   **Ht:** 6'3" **Wt:** 215 **Born:** 7/13/67 **Age:** 33

Year Team	Lg	G	GS	CG	GF	IP	BFP	H	R	ER	HR	SH	SF	HB	TBB	IBB	SO	WP	Bk	W	L	Pct.	ShO	Sv-Op	Hld	ERA
1992 San Francisco	NL	3	2	0	1	10	43	8	8	8	0	2	0	1	6	1	3	0	0	0	2	.000	0	0-0	0	7.20

Year Team	Lg	G	GS	CG	GF	IP	BFP	H	R	ER	HR	SH	SF	HB	TBB	IBB	SO	WP	Bk	W	L	Pct.	ShO	Sv-Op	Hld	ERA
1993 Florida	NL	16	16	1	0	94	412	101	49	42	7	8	4	2	39	1	57	6	0	4	6	.400	1	0-0	0	4.02
1994 Florida	NL	24	23	2	1	133.1	584	132	67	57	13	8	4	7	69	3	75	5	1	7	8	.467	1	0-0	0	3.85
1995 Florida	NL	28	28	3	0	167.1	716	158	72	64	10	8	0	7	76	2	102	7	0	14	7	.667	2	0-0	0	3.44
1996 Florida	NL	30	29	0	1	162.1	728	184	95	92	12	15	8	3	91	6	86	13	0	8	16	.333	0	0-0	0	5.10
1997 Fla-SF	NL	27	25	1	0	141.2	638	158	83	76	16	6	6	5	72	4	92	8	0	5	8	.385	1	0-0	0	4.83
1998 Kansas City	AL	32	32	1	0	188.1	855	208	117	111	24	3	6	10	107	7	132	14	0	12	13	.480	1	0-0	0	5.30
1999 Boston	AL	37	26	0	3	146.1	638	147	78	67	13	3	0	7	69	1	90	5	0	6	7	.462	0	0-0	1	4.12
2000 Baltimore	AL	31	30	0	0	174	798	203	125	114	18	1	7	5	83	5	106	8	0	9	12	.429	0	0-0	0	5.90
1997 Florida	NL	19	19	1	0	108.2	484	121	59	54	11	4	3	3	51	3	64	5	0	4	6	.400	1	0-0	0	4.47
San Francisco	NL	8	6	0	0	33	154	37	24	22	5	2	3	2	21	1	28	3	0	1	2	.333	0	0-0	0	6.00
9 ML YEARS		228	211	8	6	1217.1	5412	1299	694	631	113	54	35	47	612	30	743	66	1	65	79	.451	5	0-0	1	4.67

Jon Ratliff

Pitches: Right **Bats:** Right **Pos:** RP-1 **Ht:** 6'4" **Wt:** 195 **Born:** 12/22/71 **Age:** 29

Year Team	Lg	G	GS	CG	GF	IP	BFP	H	R	ER	HR	SH	SF	HB	TBB	IBB	SO	WP	Bk	W	L	Pct.	ShO	Sv-Op	Hld	ERA
1993 Geneva	A-	3	3	0	0	14	65	12	8	5	0	0	0	2	8	0	7	0	0	1	1	.500	0	0- -	—	3.21
Daytona	A+	8	8	0	0	41	194	50	29	18	0	2	3	5	23	0	15	3	1	2	4	.333	0	0- -	—	3.95
1994 Daytona	A+	8	8	1	0	54	227	64	23	21	5	2	1	4	5	0	17	4	0	3	2	.600	0	0- -	—	3.50
Iowa	AAA	5	4	0	0	28.1	131	39	19	17	7	1	1	2	7	0	10	3	0	1	3	.250	0	0- -	—	5.40
Orlando	AA	12	12	1	0	62.1	292	78	44	39	4	4	5	8	26	1	19	5	0	1	9	.100	0	0- -	—	5.63
1995 Orlando	AA	26	25	1	1	140	599	143	67	54	9	2	8	10	42	1	94	13	0	10	5	.667	1	0- -	—	3.47
1996 Iowa	AAA	32	13	0	5	93.2	419	107	63	55	10	3	6	6	31	2	59	3	0	4	8	.333	0	1- -	—	5.28
1997 Iowa	AAA	9	4	0	1	32.1	134	30	20	20	6	1	0	2	7	0	25	2	0	1	3	.250	0	1- -	—	5.57
Orlando	AA	18	15	0	1	101.1	443	112	59	49	10	5	2	1	32	3	68	12	1	6	4	.600	0	0- -	—	4.35
1998 Richmond	AAA	29	29	2	0	151.1	671	167	90	83	18	4	9	4	65	0	143	9	0	12	13	.480	0	0- -	—	4.94
1999 Richmond	AAA	27	27	0	0	157.2	660	154	88	78	24	3	6	3	44	2	129	5	0	5	12	.294	0	0- -	—	4.45
2000 Sacramento	AAA	20	18	0	1	107.1	442	102	48	41	12	2	3	4	31	2	72	7	1	8	4	.667	0	1- -	—	3.44
2000 Oakland	AL	1	0	0	1	1	3	0	0	0	0	0	0	0	0	0	0	0	0	0	0	—	0	0-0	0	0.00

Britt Reames

Pitches: Right **Bats:** Right **Pos:** SP-7; RP-1 **Ht:** 5'11" **Wt:** 175 **Born:** 8/19/73 **Age:** 27

Year Team	Lg	G	GS	CG	GF	IP	BFP	H	R	ER	HR	SH	SF	HB	TBB	IBB	SO	WP	Bk	W	L	Pct.	ShO	Sv-Op	Hld	ERA
1995 New Jersey	A-	5	5	0	0	29.2	121	19	7	5	1	1	0	3	12	0	42	5	0	2	1	.667	0	0- -	—	1.52
Savannah	A	10	10	1	0	54.2	227	41	23	21	7	0	0	5	15	0	63	9	1	3	5	.375	0	0- -	—	3.46
1996 Peoria	A	25	25	2	0	161	620	97	43	34	5	3	2	4	41	0	167	7	0	15	7	.682	1	0- -	—	1.90
1999 Potomac	A+	10	8	0	0	36.2	163	34	21	13	2	2	1	3	21	0	22	4	0	3	2	.600	0	0- -	—	3.19
2000 Arkansas	AA	8	8	0	0	39.2	178	46	28	27	4	0	2	0	18	0	39	1	0	2	3	.400	0	0- -	—	6.13
Memphis	AAA	13	13	2	0	75	289	55	20	19	2	3	4	2	20	0	77	1	0	6	2	.750	1	0- -	—	2.28
2000 St. Louis	NL	8	7	0	0	40.2	170	30	17	13	4	0	1	1	23	1	31	2	1	2	1	.667	0	0-0	0	2.88

Jeff Reboulet

Bats: R **Throws:** R **Pos:** 2B-50; 3B-11; SS-5; PH/PR-4; DH-1 **Ht:** 6'0" **Wt:** 175 **Born:** 4/30/64 **Age:** 37

Year Team	Lg	G	AB	H	2B	3B	HR	(Hm	Rd)	TB	R	RBI	TBB	IBB	SO	HBP	SH	SF	SB	CS	SB%	GDP	Avg	OBP	SLG
1992 Minnesota	AL	73	137	26	7	1	1	(1	0)	38	15	16	23	0	26	1	7	0	3	2	.60	0	.190	.311	.277
1993 Minnesota	AL	109	240	62	8	0	1	(0	1)	73	33	15	35	0	37	2	5	1	5	5	.50	6	.258	.356	.304
1994 Minnesota	AL	74	189	49	11	1	3	(2	1)	71	28	23	18	0	23	1	2	0	0	0	—	6	.259	.327	.376
1995 Minnesota	AL	87	216	63	11	0	4	(1	3)	86	39	23	27	0	34	1	2	0	1	2	.33	3	.292	.373	.398
1996 Minnesota	AL	107	234	52	9	0	0	(0	0)	61	20	23	25	1	34	1	4	2	4	2	.67	10	.222	.298	.261
1997 Baltimore	AL	99	228	54	9	0	4	(2	2)	75	26	27	23	0	44	1	11	2	3	0	1.00	3	.237	.307	.329
1998 Baltimore	AL	79	126	31	6	0	1	(1	0)	40	20	8	19	0	34	2	7	1	0	1	.00	3	.246	.351	.317
1999 Baltimore	AL	99	154	25	4	0	0	(0	0)	29	25	4	33	0	29	2	3	0	1	0	1.00	1	.162	.317	.188
2000 Kansas City	AL	66	182	44	7	0	0	(0	0)	51	29	14	23	0	32	0	6	1	3	1	.75	8	.242	.325	.280
9 ML YEARS		793	1706	406	72	2	14	(7	7)	524	235	153	226	1	293	11	47	7	20	13	.61	40	.238	.330	.307

Mark Redman

Pitches: Left **Bats:** Left **Pos:** SP-24; RP-8 **Ht:** 6'5" **Wt:** 220 **Born:** 1/5/74 **Age:** 27

Year Team	Lg	G	GS	CG	GF	IP	BFP	H	R	ER	HR	SH	SF	HB	TBB	IBB	SO	WP	Bk	W	L	Pct.	ShO	Sv-Op	Hld	ERA
1995 Fort Myers	A+	8	5	0	0	32.2	134	28	13	10	4	1	2	1	13	0	26	2	0	2	1	.667	0	0- -	—	2.76
1996 Fort Myers	A+	13	13	1	0	82.2	335	63	24	17	1	6	3	5	34	0	75	4	1	3	4	.429	0	0- -	—	1.85
Hardware Cy	A	16	16	3	0	106.1	467	101	51	45	5	1	6	8	50	1	96	4	1	7	7	.500	0	0- -	—	3.81
Salt Lake	AAA	1	1	0	0	4	21	7	4	4	1	0	0	1	2	0	4	0	0	0	0	—	0	0- -	—	9.00
1997 Salt Lake	AAA	29	28	0	1	158.1	739	204	123	111	19	3	6	4	80	3	125	12	2	8	15	.348	0	1- -	—	6.31
1998 New Britain	AA	8	8	0	0	47.1	190	40	11	8	3	1	0	3	17	0	51	1	1	4	2	.667	0	0- -	—	1.52
Salt Lake	AAA	19	18	0	1	99.1	446	111	75	61	13	2	5	5	41	1	88	3	3	6	7	.462	0	0- -	—	5.53
1999 Salt Lake	AAA	24	24	1	0	133.2	583	141	87	75	12	5	4	4	51	1	114	3	0	9	9	.500	0	0- -	—	5.05
1999 Minnesota	AL	5	1	0	0	12.2	65	17	13	12	3	0	0	1	7	0	11	0	0	1	0	1.000	0	0-0	0	8.53
2000 Minnesota	AL	32	24	0	3	151.1	651	168	81	80	22	3	2	3	45	0	117	6	0	12	9	.571	0	0-0	0	4.76
2 ML YEARS		37	25	0	3	164	716	185	94	92	25	3	2	4	52	0	128	6	0	13	9	.591	0	0-0	0	5.05

Tike Redman

Bats: Left **Throws:** Left **Pos:** RF-4; PH/PR-3; LF-2 **Ht:** 5'11" **Wt:** 166 **Born:** 3/10/77 **Age:** 24

Year Team	Lg	G	AB	H	2B	3B	HR	(Hm	Rd)	TB	R	RBI	TBB	IBB	SO	HBP	SH	SF	SB	CS	SB%	GDP	Avg	OBP	SLG
1996 Pirates	R	26	104	31	4	1	1	—	—	40	20	16	12	1	12	0	0	1	15	3	.83	0	.298	.368	.385
Erie	A-	43	170	50	4	6	2	—	—	72	31	21	17	0	30	0	2	3	7	3	.70	2	.294	.353	.424

						BATTING													BASERUNNING				PERCENTAGES		
Year Team	Lg	G	AB	H	2B	3B	HR	(Hm	Rd)	TB	R	RBI	TBB	IBB	SO	HBP	SH	SF	SB	CS	SB%	GDP	Avg	OBP	SLG
1997 Lynchburg	A+	125	415	104	18	5	4	—	—	144	55	45	45	0	82	7	8	1	21	8	.72	8	.251	.333	.347
1998 Lynchburg	A+	131	525	135	26	10	6	—	—	199	70	46	32	2	73	1	3	5	36	16	.69	5	.257	.298	.379
1999 Altoona	AA	136	532	143	20	12	3	—	—	196	84	60	52	1	52	3	6	10	29	16	.64	6	.269	.332	.368
2000 Nashville	AAA	121	506	132	24	11	4	—	—	190	62	51	32	0	73	3	2	4	24	18	.57	4	.261	.306	.375
2000 Pittsburgh	NL	9	18	6	1	0	1	(0	1)	10	2	1	1	0	7	0	0	0	1	0	1.00	0	.333	.368	.556

Mike Redmond

Bats: Right **Throws:** Right **Pos:** C-85; PH/PR-2   **Ht:** 6'1" **Wt:** 185 **Born:** 5/5/71 **Age:** 30

						BATTING													BASERUNNING				PERCENTAGES		
Year Team	Lg	G	AB	H	2B	3B	HR	(Hm	Rd)	TB	R	RBI	TBB	IBB	SO	HBP	SH	SF	SB	CS	SB%	GDP	Avg	OBP	SLG
1998 Florida	NL	37	118	39	9	0	2	(1	1)	54	10	12	5	2	16	2	4	0	0	0	—	6	.331	.368	.458
1999 Florida	NL	84	242	73	9	0	1	(0	1)	85	22	27	26	2	34	5	5	0	0	0	—	8	.302	.381	.351
2000 Florida	NL	87	210	53	8	0	1	(0	0)	63	17	15	13	3	19	8	1	0	0	0	—	6	.252	.316	.300
3 ML YEARS		208	570	165	26	1	3	(1	2)	202	49	54	44	7	69	15	10	3	0	0	—	19	.289	.354	.354

Jeff Reed

Bats: Left **Throws:** Right **Pos:** C-71; PH/PR-22   **Ht:** 6'2" **Wt:** 200 **Born:** 11/12/62 **Age:** 38

						BATTING													BASERUNNING				PERCENTAGES		
Year Team	Lg	G	AB	H	2B	3B	HR	(Hm	Rd)	TB	R	RBI	TBB	IBB	SO	HBP	SH	SF	SB	CS	SB%	GDP	Avg	OBP	SLG
1984 Minnesota	AL	18	21	3	0	0	0	(0	0)	6	3	1	2	0	6	0	1	0	0	0	—	0	.143	.217	.286
1985 Minnesota	AL	7	10	2	0	0	0	(0	0)	2	2	0	0	0	3	0	0	0	0	0	—	0	.200	.200	.200
1986 Minnesota	AL	68	165	39	6	1	2	(1	1)	53	13	9	16	0	19	1	3	0	1	0	1.00	2	.236	.308	.321
1987 Montreal	NL	75	207	44	11	0	1	(1	0)	58	15	21	12	1	20	1	4	4	0	1	.00	8	.213	.254	.280
1988 Mon-Cin	NL	92	265	60	9	2	1	(1	0)	76	20	16	28	1	41	0	1	4	1	0	1.00	5	.226	.299	.287
1989 Cincinnati	NL	102	287	64	11	0	3	(1	2)	84	16	23	34	5	46	2	3	4	0	0	—	6	.223	.306	.293
1990 Cincinnati	NL	72	175	44	8	1	3	(2	1)	63	12	16	24	5	26	0	5	1	0	0	—	4	.251	.340	.360
1991 Cincinnati	NL	91	270	72	15	2	3	(1	2)	100	20	31	23	3	38	1	1	5	0	1	.00	6	.267	.321	.370
1992 Cincinnati	NL	15	25	4	0	0	0	(0	0)	4	2	2	1	1	4	0	0	0	0	0	—	1	.160	.192	.160
1993 San Francisco	NL	66	119	31	3	0	6	(5	1)	52	10	12	16	4	22	0	0	1	0	1	.00	2	.261	.346	.437
1994 San Francisco	NL	50	103	18	3	0	1	(0	1)	24	11	7	11	4	21	0	0	0	0	0	—	3	.175	.254	.233
1995 San Francisco	NL	66	113	30	2	0	0	(0	0)	32	12	9	20	3	17	0	1	0	0	0	—	3	.265	.376	.283
1996 Colorado	NL	116	341	97	20	1	8	(7	1)	143	34	37	43	8	65	2	6	3	2	2	.50	8	.284	.365	.419
1997 Colorado	NL	90	256	76	10	0	17	(9	8)	137	43	47	35	1	55	2	5	0	2	1	.67	8	.297	.386	.535
1998 Colorado	NL	113	259	75	17	1	9	(6	3)	121	43	39	37	4	57	1	3	3	0	0	—	6	.290	.377	.467
1999 Col-ChC	NL	103	256	66	16	2	3	(0	3)	95	29	29	45	1	58	3	0	2	1	2	.33	7	.258	.373	.371
2000 Chicago	NL	90	229	49	10	0	4	(0	4)	71	26	25	44	2	68	1	2	1	0	1	.00	5	.214	.342	.310
1988 Montreal	NL	43	123	27	3	2	0	(0	0)	34	10	9	13	1	22	0	1	1	1	0	1.00	3	.220	.292	.276
Cincinnati	NL	49	142	33	6	0	1	(1	0)	42	10	7	15	0	19	0	0	0	0	0	—	2	.232	.306	.296
1999 Colorado	NL	46	106	27	5	0	2	(0	2)	38	11	11	17	1	24	1	0	1	1	0	.00	3	.255	.360	.358
Chicago	NL	57	150	39	11	2	1	(0	1)	57	18	17	28	0	34	2	0	1	1	1	.50	4	.260	.381	.380
17 ML YEARS		1234	3101	774	144	10	61	(34	27)	1121	311	323	391	43	566	14	35	25	7	9	.44	74	.250	.334	.361

Rick Reed

Pitches: Right **Bats:** Right **Pos:** SP-30   **Ht:** 6'1" **Wt:** 195 **Born:** 8/16/65 **Age:** 35

		HOW MUCH HE PITCHED						WHAT HE GAVE UP												THE RESULTS					
Year Team	Lg	G	GS	CG	GF	IP	BFP	H	R	ER	HR	SH	SF	HB	TBB	IBB	SO	WP	Bk	W	L	Pct.	ShO	Sv-Op	Hld	ERA
1988 Pittsburgh	NL	2	2	0	0	12	47	10	4	4	1	2	0	0	2	0	6	0	0	1	0	1.000	0	0-0	0	3.00
1989 Pittsburgh	NL	15	7	0	2	54.2	232	62	35	34	5	2	3	2	11	3	34	0	3	1	4	.200	0	0-0	0	5.60
1990 Pittsburgh	NL	13	8	1	2	53.2	238	62	32	26	6	2	1	1	12	6	27	0	0	2	3	.400	1	1-1	1	4.36
1991 Pittsburgh	NL	1	1	0	0	4.1	21	8	6	5	1	0	0	0	1	0	2	0	0	0	0	—	0	0-0	0	10.38
1992 Kansas City	AL	19	18	1	0	100.1	419	105	47	41	10	2	5	5	20	3	49	0	0	3	7	.300	0	0-0	0	3.68
1993 KC-Tex	AL	3	0	0	0	7.2	36	12	5	5	1	0	2	0	2	0	5	0	0	1	0	1.000	0	0-0	0	5.87
1994 Texas	AL	4	3	0	0	16.2	75	17	13	11	3	0	0	1	7	0	12	0	0	1	1	.500	0	0-0	0	5.94
1995 Cincinnati	NL	4	3	0	1	17	70	18	12	11	5	1	0	0	3	0	10	0	0	0	0	—	0	0-0	0	5.82
1997 New York	NL	33	31	2	0	208.1	824	186	76	67	19	7	3	5	31	4	113	0	0	13	9	.591	2	0-0	0	2.89
1998 New York	NL	31	31	2	0	212.1	845	208	84	82	30	8	5	6	29	2	153	1	0	16	11	.593	1	0-0	0	3.48
1999 New York	NL	26	26	1	0	149.1	637	163	77	76	23	6	1	1	47	2	104	1	0	11	5	.688	1	0-0	0	4.58
2000 New York	NL	30	30	0	0	184	768	192	90	84	28	3	5	5	34	3	121	2	1	11	5	.688	0	0-0	0	4.11
1993 Kansas City	AL	1	0	0	0	3.2	18	6	4	4	0	0	0	1	1	0	3	0	0	0	0	—	0	0-0	0	9.82
Texas	AL	2	0	0	0	4	18	6	1	1	1	0	0	0	1	0	2	0	0	1	0	1.000	0	0-0	0	2.25
12 ML YEARS		181	160	7	5	1020.1	4212	1043	481	446	132	33	25	28	199	23	636	4	4	60	45	.571	4	1-1	1	3.93

Steve Reed

Pitches: Right **Bats:** Right **Pos:** RP-57   **Ht:** 6'2" **Wt:** 212 **Born:** 3/11/66 **Age:** 35

		HOW MUCH HE PITCHED						WHAT HE GAVE UP												THE RESULTS					
Year Team	Lg	G	GS	CG	GF	IP	BFP	H	R	ER	HR	SH	SF	HB	TBB	IBB	SO	WP	Bk	W	L	Pct.	ShO	Sv-Op	Hld	ERA
1992 San Francisco	NL	18	0	0	2	15.2	63	13	5	4	2	0	0	1	3	0	11	0	0	1	0	1.000	0	0-0	0	2.30
1993 Colorado	NL	64	0	0	14	84.1	347	80	47	42	13	2	3	3	30	5	51	1	0	9	5	.643	0	3-6	9	4.48
1994 Colorado	NL	61	0	0	11	64	297	79	33	28	9	0	7	6	26	3	51	1	0	3	2	.600	0	3-10	14	3.94
1995 Colorado	NL	71	0	0	15	84	327	61	24	20	8	3	1	1	21	3	79	0	2	3	2	.714	0	3-6	11	2.14
1996 Colorado	NL	70	0	0	7	75	307	66	38	33	11	2	4	6	19	0	51	1	0	4	3	.571	0	0-6	22	3.96
1997 Colorado	NL	63	0	0	23	62.1	260	49	28	28	10	3	1	5	27	1	43	0	0	4	6	.400	0	6-13	10	4.04
1998 SF-Cle		70	0	0	19	80.1	322	56	29	28	8	2	0	5	27	5	73	0	0	4	5	.571	0	1-6	21	3.14
1999 Cleveland	AL	63	0	0	15	61.2	274	69	33	29	10	4	5	3	20	5	44	2	0	3	2	.600	0	0-3	8	4.23
2000 Cleveland	AL	57	0	0	16	56	243	58	30	27	7	4	1	1	21	4	39	2	1	2	1	1.000	0	0-1	9	4.34
1998 San Francisco	NL	50	0	0	14	54.2	213	30	10	9	4	2	0	4	19	5	50	0	0	2	1	.667	0	1-5	13	1.48
Cleveland	AL	20	0	0	5	25.2	109	26	19	19	4	0	0	1	8	0	23	0	0	2	4	.500	0	0-1	8	6.66
9 ML YEARS		537	0	0	122	583.1	2440	531	267	239	78	20	22	31	194	26	442	7	3	35	23	.603	0	16-51	105	3.69

180

Pokey Reese

Bats: Right **Throws:** Right **Pos:** 2B-133; PH/PR-3 **Ht:** 5'11" **Wt:** 180 **Born:** 6/10/73 **Age:** 28

							BATTING													BASERUNNING				PERCENTAGES		
Year Team	Lg	G	AB	H	2B	3B	HR	(Hm	Rd)	TB	R	RBI	TBB	IBB	SO	HBP	SH	SF		SB	CS	SB%	GDP	Avg	OBP	SLG
1997 Cincinnati	NL	128	397	87	15	4	4	(3	1)	114	48	26	31	2	82	5	4	0		25	7	.78	1	.219	.284	.287
1998 Cincinnati	NL	59	133	34	2	2	1	(0	1)	43	20	16	14	1	28	0	2	2		3	2	.60	3	.256	.322	.323
1999 Cincinnati	NL	149	585	167	37	5	10	(5	5)	244	85	52	35	3	81	6	5	5		38	7	.84	9	.285	.330	.417
2000 Cincinnati	NL	135	518	132	20	6	12	(3	9)	200	76	46	45	5	86	6	3	5		29	3	**.91**	8	.255	.319	.386
4 ML YEARS		471	1633	420	74	13	27	(11	16)	601	229	140	125	11	277	17	14	12		95	19	.83	21	.257	.314	.368

Dan Reichert

Pitches: Right **Bats:** Right **Pos:** RP-26; SP-18 **Ht:** 6'3" **Wt:** 175 **Born:** 7/12/76 **Age:** 24

		HOW MUCH HE PITCHED						WHAT HE GAVE UP												THE RESULTS					
Year Team	Lg	G	GS	CG	GF	IP	BFP	H	R	ER	HR	SH	SF	HB	TBB	IBB	SO	WP	Bk		W	L	Pct.	ShO	Sv-Op	Hld	ERA
1997 Spokane	A-	9	9	0	0	38	178	40	25	12	2	0	2	3	16	0	39	2	2		3	4	.429	0	0--	—	2.84
1998 Wichita	AA	8	8	0	0	36	186	52	40	39	7	1	1	4	29	1	24	2	1		1	4	.200	0	0--	—	9.75
Lansing	A	13	6	0	1	35.2	152	25	16	13	0	1	2	3	20	0	35	4	1		1	1	.500	0	0--	—	3.28
Wilmington	A+	2	2	0	0	14	55	13	5	5	0	0	0	0	4	0	10	5	0		2	0	1.000	0	0--	—	3.21
Omaha	AAA	3	3	0	0	17.1	68	14	10	9	2	0	2	1	2	0	11	1	0		1	1	.500	0	0--	—	4.67
1999 Omaha	AAA	17	17	1	0	111.2	464	92	51	46	9	2	2	6	50	0	123	9	0		9	2	.818	0	0--	—	3.71
1999 Kansas City	AL	8	8	0	0	36.2	183	48	38	37	2	1	1	2	32	1	20	1	0		2	2	.500	0	0-0	0	9.08
2000 Kansas City	AL	44	18	1	11	153.1	690	157	92	80	15	5	7	7	91	1	94	**18**	0		8	10	.444	1	2-6	4	4.70
2 ML YEARS		52	26	1	11	190	873	205	130	117	17	6	8	9	123	2	114	19	0		10	12	.455	1	2-6	4	5.54

Bryan Rekar

Pitches: Right **Bats:** Right **Pos:** SP-27; RP-3 **Ht:** 6'3" **Wt:** 220 **Born:** 6/3/72 **Age:** 29

		HOW MUCH HE PITCHED						WHAT HE GAVE UP												THE RESULTS					
Year Team	Lg	G	GS	CG	GF	IP	BFP	H	R	ER	HR	SH	SF	HB	TBB	IBB	SO	WP	Bk		W	L	Pct.	ShO	Sv-Op	Hld	ERA
2000 Durham *	AAA	4	4	0	0	22	85	16	5	5	1	1	1	3	4	0	18	1	0		3	0	1.000	0	0--	—	2.05
1995 Colorado	NL	15	14	1	0	85	375	95	51	47	11	7	4	3	24	2	60	3	2		4	6	.400	0	0-0	1	4.98
1996 Colorado	NL	14	11	0	0	58.1	289	87	61	58	11	3	3	5	26	1	25	4	0		2	4	.333	0	0-1	0	8.95
1997 Colorado	NL	2	2	0	0	9.1	46	11	7	6	3	1	0	0	6	0	4	0	0		1	0	1.000	0	0-0	0	5.79
1998 Tampa Bay	AL	16	15	1	1	86.2	369	95	56	48	16	1	8	2	21	0	55	1	0		2	8	.200	0	0-0	0	4.98
1999 Tampa Bay	AL	27	12	0	2	94.2	437	121	68	61	14	3	2	5	41	2	55	4	0		6	6	.500	0	0-0	1	5.80
2000 Tampa Bay	AL	30	27	2	2	173.1	743	200	92	85	22	3	**9**	4	39	0	95	5	0		7	10	.412	0	0-0	0	4.41
6 ML YEARS		104	81	4	5	507.1	2259	609	335	305	77	18	26	19	157	5	294	17	2		22	34	.393	0	0-1	2	5.41

Desi Relaford

Bats: Both **Throws:** Right **Pos:** SS-126; PH/PR-5 **Ht:** 5'9" **Wt:** 174 **Born:** 9/16/73 **Age:** 27

							BATTING													BASERUNNING				PERCENTAGES		
Year Team	Lg	G	AB	H	2B	3B	HR	(Hm	Rd)	TB	R	RBI	TBB	IBB	SO	HBP	SH	SF		SB	CS	SB%	GDP	Avg	OBP	SLG
1996 Philadelphia	NL	15	40	7	2	0	0	(0	0)	9	2	1	3	0	9	0	1	0		1	0	1.00	1	.175	.233	.225
1997 Philadelphia	NL	15	38	7	1	2	0	(0	0)	12	3	6	5	0	6	0	1	0		3	0	1.00	0	.184	.279	.316
1998 Philadelphia	NL	142	494	121	25	3	5	(4	1)	167	45	41	33	4	87	3	10	6		9	5	.64	9	.245	.293	.338
1999 Philadelphia	NL	65	211	51	11	2	1	(0	1)	69	31	26	19	2	34	6	6	0		4	3	.57	5	.242	.322	.327
2000 Phi-SD	NL	128	410	88	14	3	5	(0	5)	123	55	46	75	7	71	12	3	2		13	0	1.00	10	.215	.351	.300
2000 Philadelphia	NL	83	253	56	12	3	3	(0	3)	83	29	30	48	7	45	9	2	1		5	0	1.00	7	.221	.363	.328
San Diego	NL	45	157	32	2	0	2	(0	2)	40	26	16	27	0	26	3	1	1		8	0	1.00	3	.204	.330	.255
5 ML YEARS		365	1193	274	53	10	11	(4	7)	380	136	120	135	13	207	21	21	8		30	8	.79	25	.230	.317	.319

Mike Remlinger

Pitches: Left **Bats:** Left **Pos:** RP-71 **Ht:** 6'1" **Wt:** 210 **Born:** 3/23/66 **Age:** 35

		HOW MUCH HE PITCHED						WHAT HE GAVE UP												THE RESULTS					
Year Team	Lg	G	GS	CG	GF	IP	BFP	H	R	ER	HR	SH	SF	HB	TBB	IBB	SO	WP	Bk		W	L	Pct.	ShO	Sv-Op	Hld	ERA
1991 San Francisco	NL	8	6	1	1	35	155	36	17	17	5	1	1	0	20	1	19	2	1		2	1	.667	1	0-0	0	4.37
1994 New York	NL	10	9	0	0	54.2	252	55	30	28	9	2	3	1	35	4	33	3	0		1	5	.167	0	0-0	1	4.61
1995 NYM-Cin	NL	7	0	0	4	6.2	34	9	6	5	1	1	0	0	5	0	7	0	0		0	1	.000	0	0-1	0	6.75
1996 Cincinnati	NL	19	4	0	2	27.1	125	24	17	17	4	3	1	3	19	2	19	2	2		0	1	.000	0	0-0	1	5.60
1997 Cincinnati	NL	69	12	2	10	124	525	100	61	57	11	6	4	7	60	6	145	**12**	2		8	8	.500	0	2-2	14	4.14
1998 Cincinnati	NL	35	28	1	0	164.1	727	164	96	88	23	12	7	5	87	1	144	11	1		8	15	.348	1	0-0	0	4.82
1999 Atlanta	NL	73	0	0	14	83.2	346	66	24	22	9	2	1	1	35	5	81	5	0		10	1	.909	0	1-3	21	2.37
2000 Atlanta	NL	71	0	0	18	72.2	311	55	29	28	6	2	3	3	37	1	72	3	0		5	3	.625	0	12-16	23	3.47
1995 New York	NL	5	0	0	4	5.2	27	7	5	4	1	1	0	0	2	0	6	0	0		0	1	.000	0	0-1	0	6.35
Cincinnati	NL	2	0	0	0	1	7	2	1	1	0	0	0	0	3	0	1	0	0		0	0	—	0	0-0	0	9.00
8 ML YEARS		292	59	4	49	568.1	2475	509	280	262	68	30	19	20	298	20	520	38	6		34	35	.493	2	15-22	60	4.15

Edgar Renteria

Bats: Right **Throws:** Right **Pos:** SS-149; PH/PR-1 **Ht:** 6'1" **Wt:** 180 **Born:** 8/7/75 **Age:** 25

							BATTING													BASERUNNING				PERCENTAGES		
Year Team	Lg	G	AB	H	2B	3B	HR	(Hm	Rd)	TB	R	RBI	TBB	IBB	SO	HBP	SH	SF		SB	CS	SB%	GDP	Avg	OBP	SLG
1996 Florida	NL	106	431	133	18	3	5	(2	3)	172	68	31	33	0	68	2	2	3		16	2	.89	12	.309	.358	.399
1997 Florida	NL	154	617	171	21	3	4	(3	1)	210	90	52	45	1	108	4	**19**	6		32	15	.68	17	.277	.327	.340
1998 Florida	NL	133	517	146	18	3	3	(2	1)	177	79	31	48	1	78	4	9	2		41	**22**	.65	13	.282	.347	.342
1999 St. Louis	NL	154	585	161	36	2	11	(6	5)	234	92	63	53	0	82	2	6	7		37	8	.82	16	.275	.334	.400
2000 St. Louis	NL	150	562	156	32	1	16	(4	12)	238	94	76	63	3	77	1	8	9		21	13	.62	19	.278	.346	.423
5 ML YEARS		697	2712	767	125	11	39	(17	22)	1031	423	253	242	5	413	13	44	27		147	60	.71	77	.283	.341	.380

Al Reyes

Pitches: Right **Bats:** Right **Pos:** RP-19   **Ht:** 6'1" **Wt:** 206 **Born:** 4/10/71 **Age:** 30

Year Team	Lg	G	GS	CG	GF	IP	BFP	H	R	ER	HR	SH	SF	HB	TBB	IBB	SO	WP	Bk	W	L	Pct.	ShO	Sv-Op	Hld	ERA
2000 Rochester *	AAA	9	0	0	8	11.2	57	13	11	10	2	0	0	0	9	1	17	2	0	0	1	.000	0	2--	—	7.71
Albuquerque *	AAA	30	0	0	22	38.2	173	33	20	16	5	3	2	1	21	0	39	4	0	3	2	.600	0	8--	—	3.72
1995 Milwaukee	AL	27	0	0	13	33.1	138	19	9	9	3	1	2	3	18	2	29	4	0	1	1	.500	0	1-1	4	2.43
1996 Milwaukee	AL	5	0	0	2	5.2	27	8	5	5	1	0	0	0	2	0	2	2	0	1	0	1.000	0	0-0	0	7.94
1997 Milwaukee	AL	19	0	0	7	29.2	131	32	19	18	4	2	0	3	9	0	28	1	0	1	2	.333	0	1-1	1	5.46
1998 Milwaukee	NL	50	0	0	13	57	253	55	26	25	9	2	1	2	31	1	58	2	0	5	1	.833	0	0-1	10	3.95
1999 Mil-Bal		53	0	0	12	65.2	287	50	33	33	9	4	3	6	41	3	67	3	0	4	3	.571	0	0-4	6	4.52
2000 Bal-LA		19	0	0	6	19.2	86	15	10	10	2	1	0	0	12	1	18	0	0	1	0	1.000	0	0-1	3	4.58
1999 Milwaukee	NL	26	0	0	6	36	161	27	17	17	5	1	1	3	25	1	39	2	0	2	0	1.000	0	0-1	2	4.25
Baltimore	AL	27	0	0	6	29.2	126	23	16	16	4	3	2	3	16	2	28	1	0	2	3	.400	0	0-3	4	4.85
2000 Baltimore	AL	13	0	0	2	13	62	13	10	10	2	1	0	0	11	1	10	0	0	1	0	1.000	0	0-1	2	6.92
Los Angeles	NL	6	0	0	4	6.2	24	2	0	0	0	0	0	0	1	0	8	0	0	0	0	—	0	0-0	1	0.00
6 ML YEARS		173	0	0	53	211	922	179	102	100	28	10	8	14	113	7	202	8	0	13	7	.650	0	2-8	24	4.27

Carlos Reyes

Pitches: Right **Bats:** Both **Pos:** RP-22   **Ht:** 6'0" **Wt:** 190 **Born:** 4/4/69 **Age:** 32

Year Team	Lg	G	GS	CG	GF	IP	BFP	H	R	ER	HR	SH	SF	HB	TBB	IBB	SO	WP	Bk	W	L	Pct.	ShO	Sv-Op	Hld	ERA
2000 Reading *	AA	2	0	0	0	3	9	1	0	0	0	0	0	0	0	0	3	0	0	0	0	—	0	0--	—	0.00
Las Vegas *	AAA	16	0	0	5	28.1	125	28	13	9	5	2	1	0	9	1	24	1	0	0	2	.000	0	1--	—	2.86
1994 Oakland	AL	27	9	0	8	78	344	71	38	36	10	2	3	2	44	1	57	3	0	0	3	.000	0	1-1	0	4.15
1995 Oakland	AL	40	1	0	19	69	306	71	43	39	10	4	0	5	28	4	48	5	0	4	6	.400	0	0-1	4	5.09
1996 Oakland	AL	46	10	0	14	122.1	550	134	71	65	19	2	8	2	61	8	78	2	1	7	10	.412	0	0-0	1	4.78
1997 Oakland	AL	37	6	0	9	77.1	352	101	52	50	13	3	2	2	25	2	43	2	1	3	4	.429	0	0-1	1	5.82
1998 SD-Bos		46	0	0	18	66	267	58	26	26	6	2	3	3	20	2	47	3	1	3	3	.500	0	1-2	3	3.55
1999 San Diego	NL	65	0	0	23	77.1	331	76	38	32	11	5	3	0	24	4	57	7	1	2	4	.333	0	1-2	6	3.72
2000 Phi-SD	NL	22	0	0	9	28.1	121	25	18	18	7	2	0	1	13	0	17	1	1	1	3	.250	0	1-3	2	5.72
1998 San Diego	NL	22	0	0	8	27.2	109	23	11	11	4	2	1	2	6	0	24	0	1	2	2	.500	0	1-2	1	3.58
Boston	AL	24	0	0	10	38.1	158	35	15	15	2	0	1	1	14	2	23	3	0	1	1	.500	0	0-0	2	3.52
2000 Philadelphia	NL	10	0	0	5	10.1	44	10	6	6	2	2	0	0	5	0	4	1	0	0	2	.000	0	0-0	0	5.23
San Diego	NL	12	0	0	4	18	77	15	12	12	5	0	0	1	8	0	13	0	1	1	1	.500	0	1-3	2	6.00
7 ML YEARS		283	26	0	100	518.1	2271	536	286	266	76	20	18	15	215	21	347	23	5	20	33	.377	0	4-10	17	4.62

Dennys Reyes

Pitches: Left **Bats:** Right **Pos:** RP-62   **Ht:** 6'3" **Wt:** 246 **Born:** 4/19/77 **Age:** 24

Year Team	Lg	G	GS	CG	GF	IP	BFP	H	R	ER	HR	SH	SF	HB	TBB	IBB	SO	WP	Bk	W	L	Pct.	ShO	Sv-Op	Hld	ERA
1997 Los Angeles	NL	14	5	0	0	47	207	51	21	20	4	5	1	1	18	3	36	2	1	2	3	.400	0	0-0	0	3.83
1998 LA-Cin	NL	19	10	0	4	67.1	300	62	36	34	3	7	2	1	47	5	77	6	1	3	5	.375	0	0-0	0	4.54
1999 Cincinnati	NL	65	1	0	12	61.2	277	53	30	26	5	4	3	3	39	1	72	5	1	2	2	.500	0	2-3	14	3.79
2000 Cincinnati	NL	62	0	0	15	43.2	200	43	31	22	5	3	3	1	29	0	36	6	0	2	1	.667	0	0-1	10	4.53
1998 Los Angeles	NL	11	3	0	4	28.2	130	27	17	15	1	3	0	1	20	4	33	1	0	0	4	.000	0	0-0	0	4.71
Cincinnati	NL	8	7	0	0	38.2	170	35	19	19	2	4	1	1	27	1	44	5	0	3	1	.750	0	0-0	0	4.42
4 ML YEARS		160	16	0	31	219.2	984	209	118	102	17	19	9	6	133	9	221	19	3	9	11	.450	0	2-4	24	4.18

Shane Reynolds

Pitches: Right **Bats:** Right **Pos:** SP-22   **Ht:** 6'3" **Wt:** 210 **Born:** 3/26/68 **Age:** 33

Year Team	Lg	G	GS	CG	GF	IP	BFP	H	R	ER	HR	SH	SF	HB	TBB	IBB	SO	WP	Bk	W	L	Pct.	ShO	Sv-Op	Hld	ERA
1992 Houston	NL	8	5	0	0	25.1	122	42	22	20	2	6	1	0	6	1	10	1	1	1	3	.250	0	0-0	0	7.11
1993 Houston	NL	5	1	0	0	11	49	11	4	1	0	0	0	0	6	1	10	0	0	0	0	—	0	0-0	0	0.82
1994 Houston	NL	33	14	1	5	124	517	128	46	42	10	4	0	2	21	3	110	3	2	8	5	.615	1	0-0	5	3.05
1995 Houston	NL	30	30	3	0	189.1	792	196	87	73	15	8	0	2	37	6	175	7	1	10	11	.476	2	0-0	0	3.47
1996 Houston	NL	35	35	4	0	239	981	227	103	97	20	11	7	8	44	3	204	5	1	16	10	.615	1	0-0	0	3.65
1997 Houston	NL	30	30	2	0	181	773	189	92	85	19	9	5	3	47	5	152	5	2	9	10	.474	0	0-0	0	4.23
1998 Houston	NL	35	35	3	0	233.1	980	257	99	91	25	5	7	2	53	2	209	5	0	19	8	.704	3	0-0	0	3.51
1999 Houston	NL	35	35	4	0	231.2	963	250	108	99	23	11	5	1	37	0	197	4	0	16	14	.533	2	0-0	0	3.85
2000 Houston	NL	22	22	0	0	131	588	150	86	76	20	6	8	6	45	2	93	5	0	7	8	.467	0	0-0	0	5.22
9 ML YEARS		233	207	17	5	1365.2	5771	1450	647	584	134	60	33	28	296	23	1160	35	7	86	69	.555	7	0-0	5	3.85

Armando Reynoso

Pitches: Right **Bats:** Right **Pos:** SP-30; RP-1   **Ht:** 6'0" **Wt:** 204 **Born:** 5/1/66 **Age:** 35

Year Team	Lg	G	GS	CG	GF	IP	BFP	H	R	ER	HR	SH	SF	HB	TBB	IBB	SO	WP	Bk	W	L	Pct.	ShO	Sv-Op	Hld	ERA
1991 Atlanta	NL	6	5	0	1	23.1	103	26	18	16	4	3	0	3	10	1	10	2	0	2	1	.667	0	0-0	0	6.17
1992 Atlanta	NL	3	1	0	1	7.2	32	11	4	4	2	1	0	1	2	1	2	0	0	1	0	1.000	0	1-1	0	4.70
1993 Colorado	NL	30	30	4	0	189	830	206	101	84	22	5	8	9	63	7	117	7	6	12	11	.522	0	0-0	0	4.00
1994 Colorado	NL	9	9	1	0	52.1	226	54	30	28	5	2	2	6	22	1	25	2	2	3	4	.429	0	0-0	0	4.82
1995 Colorado	NL	20	18	0	0	93	418	116	61	55	12	8	3	5	36	3	40	2	0	7	7	.500	0	0-0	0	5.32
1996 Colorado	NL	30	30	0	0	168.2	733	195	97	93	27	3	3	9	49	0	88	4	3	8	9	.471	0	0-0	0	4.96
1997 New York	NL	16	16	1	0	91.1	388	95	47	46	7	3	5	6	29	4	47	4	1	6	3	.667	1	0-0	0	4.53
1998 New York	NL	11	11	0	0	68.1	292	64	31	29	4	4	1	5	32	3	40	2	2	7	3	.700	0	0-0	0	3.82
1999 Arizona	NL	31	27	0	1	167	730	178	90	81	20	6	6	6	67	7	79	7	1	10	6	.625	0	0-0	1	4.37
2000 Arizona	NL	31	30	2	0	170.2	730	179	102	100	22	11	5	6	52	5	89	3	0	11	12	.478	0	0-0	0	5.27
10 ML YEARS		187	177	8	3	1031.0	4482	1124	581	536	125	46	32	56	362	32	537	33	15	67	56	.545	1	1-1	1	4.68

Arthur Rhodes

Pitches: Left **Bats:** Left **Pos:** RP-72 **Ht:** 6'2" **Wt:** 205 **Born:** 10/24/69 **Age:** 31

Year Team	Lg	G	GS	CG	GF	IP	BFP	H	R	ER	HR	SH	SF	HB	TBB	IBB	SO	WP	Bk	W	L	Pct.	ShO	Sv-Op	Hld	ERA
1991 Baltimore	AL	8	8	0	0	36	174	47	35	32	4	1	3	0	23	0	23	2	0	0	3	.000	0	0-0	0	8.00
1992 Baltimore	AL	15	15	2	0	94.1	394	87	39	38	6	5	1	1	38	2	77	2	1	7	5	.583	1	0-0	0	3.63
1993 Baltimore	AL	17	17	0	0	85.2	387	91	62	62	16	2	3	1	49	1	49	2	0	5	6	.455	0	0-0	0	6.51
1994 Baltimore	AL	10	10	3	0	52.2	238	51	34	34	8	2	3	2	30	1	47	3	0	3	5	.375	2	0-0	0	5.81
1995 Baltimore	AL	19	9	0	3	75.1	336	68	53	52	13	4	0	0	48	1	77	3	1	2	5	.286	0	0-1	0	6.21
1996 Baltimore	AL	28	2	0	5	53	224	48	28	24	6	1	1	0	23	3	62	0	0	9	1	.900	0	1-1	2	4.08
1997 Baltimore	AL	53	0	0	6	95.1	378	75	32	32	9	0	4	4	26	5	102	2	0	10	3	.769	0	1-2	9	3.02
1998 Baltimore	AL	45	0	0	10	77	321	65	30	30	8	2	5	1	34	2	83	1	1	4	4	.500	0	4-8	10	3.51
1999 Baltimore	AL	43	0	0	11	53	244	43	37	32	9	2	2	0	45	6	59	4	0	3	4	.429	0	3-5	5	5.43
2000 Seattle	AL	72	0	0	9	69.1	281	51	34	33	6	1	2	0	29	3	77	4	0	5	8	.385	0	0-7	24	4.28
10 ML YEARS		310	61	5	44	691.2	2977	626	384	369	85	20	24	9	345	24	656	23	3	48	44	.522	3	9-24	50	4.80

Chris Richard

Bats: L **Throws:** L **Pos:** 1B-55; RF-3; PH/PR-3; DH-1; LF-1 **Ht:** 6'2" **Wt:** 190 **Born:** 6/7/74 **Age:** 27

Year Team	Lg	G	AB	H	2B	3B	HR	(Hm	Rd)	TB	R	RBI	TBB	IBB	SO	HBP	SH	SF	SB	CS	SB%	GDP	Avg	OBP	SLG
1995 New Jersey	A-	75	284	80	14	3	3	—	—	109	36	43	47	3	31	6	0	2	6	6	.50	3	.282	.392	.384
1996 St. Pete	A+	129	460	130	28	6	14	—	—	212	65	82	57	6	50	9	0	5	7	3	.70	11	.283	.369	.461
1997 Arkansas	AA	113	390	105	24	3	11	—	—	168	62	58	60	1	59	5	0	3	6	4	.60	8	.269	.371	.431
1998 Pr William	A+	8	30	8	2	0	0	—	—	10	5	1	1	0	5	0	0	0	1	0	1.00	0	.267	.290	.333
Arkansas	AA	28	89	18	5	1	2	—	—	31	7	17	9	0	10	1	0	1	0	1	.00	1	.202	.280	.348
1999 Arkansas	AA	133	442	130	26	3	29	—	—	249	78	94	43	5	75	8	0	6	7	7	.50	14	.294	.363	.563
Memphis	AAA	4	17	7	2	0	1	—	—	12	3	4	1	0	2	0	0	0	0	0	—	1	.412	.444	.706
2000 Memphis	AAA	95	375	104	24	0	16	—	—	176	64	75	50	4	70	4	0	3	9	3	.75	5	.277	.366	.469
2000 StL-Bal		62	215	57	14	2	14	(4	10)	117	39	37	17	3	40	4	0	5	7	5	.58	5	.265	.326	.544
2000 St. Louis	NL	6	16	2	0	0	1	(0	1)	5	1	1	2	0	2	0	0	0	0	0	—	0	.125	.222	.313
Baltimore	AL	56	199	55	14	2	13	(4	9)	112	38	36	15	3	38	4	0	3	7	5	.58	5	.276	.335	.563

John Riedling

Pitches: Right **Bats:** Right **Pos:** RP-13 **Ht:** 5'11" **Wt:** 190 **Born:** 8/29/75 **Age:** 25

Year Team	Lg	G	GS	CG	GF	IP	BFP	H	R	ER	HR	SH	SF	HB	TBB	IBB	SO	WP	Bk	W	L	Pct.	ShO	Sv-Op	Hld	ERA
1994 Billings	R+	15	5	0	2	44.1	221	62	36	27	0	2	2	3	28	0	27	7	0	4	1	.800	0	0--	—	5.48
1995 Billings	R+	13	7	0	2	38.1	192	51	38	30	4	0	3	1	21	2	28	8	0	2	2	.500	0	1--	—	7.04
1996 Chstn-WV	A	26	26	0	0	140	615	135	85	62	2	10	6	10	66	6	90	6	1	6	10	.375	0	0--	—	3.99
1997 Burlington	A	35	16	0	11	102.2	461	101	70	60	8	3	5	7	47	0	104	10	0	7	6	.538	0	0--	—	5.26
1998 Chattanooga	AA	24	20	0	1	102.2	475	112	70	57	10	1	5	4	60	5	86	5	0	3	10	.231	0	0--	—	5.00
1999 Chattanooga	AA	40	0	0	23	42	186	41	23	16	2	1	2	1	20	3	38	7	0	9	5	.643	0	5--	—	3.43
Indianapols	AAA	24	0	0		35	142	19	9	6	1	2	0	3	18	2	26	2	0	1	0	1.000	0	1--	—	1.54
2000 Louisville	AAA	53	0	0	18	75	315	63	24	21	7	4	1	1	30	3	75	8	0	2	1	.667	0	5--	—	2.52
2000 Cincinnati	NL	13	0	0	5	15.1	63	11	7	4	1	1	0	1	8	0	18	1	0	3	1	.750	0	1-2	2	2.35

Brad Rigby

Pitches: Right **Bats:** Right **Pos:** RP-10 **Ht:** 6'6" **Wt:** 215 **Born:** 5/14/73 **Age:** 28

Year Team	Lg	G	GS	CG	GF	IP	BFP	H	R	ER	HR	SH	SF	HB	TBB	IBB	SO	WP	Bk	W	L	Pct.	ShO	Sv-Op	Hld	ERA
2000 Ottawa *	AAA	24	14	0	2	83.2	396	117	77	62	8	2	5	9	26	0	51	4	2	3	10	.231	0	0--	—	6.67
1997 Oakland	AL	14	14	0	0	77.2	339	92	44	42	14	2	8	2	22	2	34	3	0	1	7	.125	0	0-0	0	4.87
1999 Oak-KC	AL	49	0	0	11	83.2	382	102	51	47	11	2	5	7	31	7	36	6	0	4	6	.400	0	0-2	5	5.06
2000 KC-Mon		10	0	0	5	13.2	78	27	21	18	6	0	0	2	8	0	5	0	0	0	0	—	0	2-2	0	11.85
1999 Oakland	AL	29	0	0	6	62.1	278	69	31	30	5	1	3	5	26	7	26	3	0	3	4	.429	0	0-1	2	4.33
Kansas City	AL	20	0	0	6	21.1	104	33	20	17	6	1	2	2	5	0	10	3	0	1	2	.333	0	0-1	3	7.17
2000 Kansas City	AL	4	0	0	1	8.1	51	19	16	15	6	0	0	1	5	0	3	0	0	0	0	—	0	1-1	0	16.20
Montreal	NL	6	0	0	4	5.1	27	8	5	3	0	0	0	1	3	0	2	0	0	0	0	—	0	1-1	0	5.06
3 ML YEARS		73	14	0	16	175	799	221	116	107	31	4	13	11	61	9	75	9	0	5	13	.278	0	2-4	5	5.50

Paul Rigdon

Pitches: Right **Bats:** Right **Pos:** SP-16; RP-1 **Ht:** 6'5" **Wt:** 210 **Born:** 11/2/75 **Age:** 25

Year Team	Lg	G	GS	CG	GF	IP	BFP	H	R	ER	HR	SH	SF	HB	TBB	IBB	SO	WP	Bk	W	L	Pct.	ShO	Sv-Op	Hld	ERA
1996 Watertown	A-	22	0	0	21	39.2	174	41	24	18	4	1	0	2	10	0	46	1	1	2	2	.500	0	6--	—	4.08
1998 Kinston	A+	24	24	0	0	127.1	532	126	65	57	9	2	6	9	35	1	97	3	0	11	7	.611	0	0--	—	4.03
1999 Akron	AA	8	7	0	0	50	177	20	5	5	2	0	1	2	10	0	25	1	0	7	0	1.000	0	0--	—	0.90
Buffalo	AAA	19	19	0	0	103.1	451	114	60	52	11	3	2	1	28	0	60	4	2	7	4	.636	0	0--	—	4.53
2000 Buffalo	AAA	12	12	1	0	71	291	72	27	26	4	2	1	1	18	0	41	1	0	6	1	.857	0	0--	—	3.30
2000 Cle-Mil		17	16	0	0	87.1	381	89	52	50	18	3	5	1	35	0	63	2	0	5	5	.500	0	0-0	0	5.15
2000 Cleveland	AL	5	4	0	0	17.2	79	21	15	15	4	0	0	0	9	1	15	0	0	1	1	.500	0	0-0	0	7.64
Milwaukee	NL	12	12	0	0	69.2	302	68	37	35	14	3	5	1	26	4	48	2	0	4	4	.500	0	0-0	0	4.52

Jerrod Riggan

Pitches: Right **Bats:** Right **Pos:** RP-1 **Ht:** 6'4" **Wt:** 185 **Born:** 5/16/74 **Age:** 27

Year Team	Lg	G	GS	CG	GF	IP	BFP	H	R	ER	HR	SH	SF	HB	TBB	IBB	SO	WP	Bk	W	L	Pct.	ShO	Sv-Op	Hld	ERA
1996 Boise	A-	15	15	1	0	89.1	395	90	62	46	10	3	6	5	38	5	80	6	0	3	5	.375	0	0--	—	4.63
1997 Lk Elsinore	A+	8	8	0	0	43	202	60	36	29	1	4	2	4	16	0	31	6	2	2	5	.286	0	0--	—	6.07
Cedar Rapds	A	19	19	3	0	116	506	132	70	63	15	3	7	2	36	2	65	12	2	9	8	.529	1	0--	—	4.89

Year Team	Lg	G	GS	CG	GF	IP	BFP	H	R	ER	HR	SH	SF	HB	TBB	IBB	SO	WP	Bk	W	L	Pct.	ShO	Sv-Op	Hld	ERA
1998 Capital Cty	A	14	0	0	7	41.1	177	38	21	17	5	3	1	1	14	1	40	2	0	4	1	.800	0	1--	—	3.70
1999 St. Lucie	A+	44	0	0	26	73	305	69	33	27	4	6	1	5	24	5	66	4	0	5	5	.500	0	12--	—	3.33
2000 Binghamton	AA	52	0	0	41	65	252	43	9	8	2	3	2	2	18	0	79	1	0	2	0	1.000	0	28--	—	1.11
2000 New York	NL	1	0	0	0	2	10	3	2	0	0	0	0	0	0	0	1	0	0	0	0	—	0	0-0	0	0.00

Ricky Rincon

Pitches: Left **Bats:** Left **Pos:** RP-35 **Ht:** 5'9" **Wt:** 190 **Born:** 4/13/70 **Age:** 31

Year Team	Lg	G	GS	CG	GF	IP	BFP	H	R	ER	HR	SH	SF	HB	TBB	IBB	SO	WP	Bk	W	L	Pct.	ShO	Sv-Op	Hld	ERA
2000 Buffalo *	AAA	2	0	0	1	2	9	1	1	0	0	0	0	0	0	0	2	0	0	0	0	—	0	0--	—	0.00
1997 Pittsburgh	NL	62	0	0	23	60	254	51	26	23	5	5	1	2	24	6	71	2	3	4	8	.333	0	4-6	18	3.45
1998 Pittsburgh	NL	60	0	0	27	65	272	50	31	21	6	1	2	0	29	2	64	2	0	0	2	.000	0	14-17	11	2.91
1999 Cleveland	AL	59	0	0	14	44.2	193	41	22	22	6	2	1	1	24	5	30	2	1	2	3	.400	0	0-2	11	4.43
2000 Cleveland	AL	35	0	0	4	20	90	17	7	6	1	0	0	1	13	1	20	1	0	2	0	1.000	0	0-0	10	2.70
4 ML YEARS		216	0	0	68	189.2	809	159	86	72	18	8	4	4	90	14	185	7	4	8	13	.381	0	18-25	50	3.42

Armando Rios

Bats: L **Throws:** L **Pos:** RF-76; PH/PR-33; LF-19; 1B-1 **Ht:** 5'9" **Wt:** 185 **Born:** 9/13/71 **Age:** 29

Year Team	Lg	G	AB	H	2B	3B	HR	(Hm	Rd)	TB	R	RBI	TBB	IBB	SO	HBP	SH	SF	SB	CS	SB%	GDP	Avg	OBP	SLG
1994 Clinton	A	119	407	120	23	4	8	—	—	175	67	60	59	2	69	4	1	7	16	12	.57	7	.295	.384	.430
1995 San Jose	A+	128	488	143	34	3	8	—	—	207	74	75	74	3	75	1	4	7	51	10	.84	8	.293	.382	.424
1996 Shreveport	AA	92	329	93	22	2	12	—	—	155	62	49	44	3	42	1	3	4	9	9	.50	2	.283	.365	.471
1997 Shreveport	AA	127	461	133	30	6	14	—	—	217	86	79	63	1	85	0	4	6	17	7	.71	11	.289	.370	.471
1998 Fresno	AAA	125	445	134	23	1	26	—	—	237	85	103	55	4	73	3	4	5	17	5	.77	9	.301	.378	.533
1999 Fresno	AAA	31	109	30	3	0	4	—	—	45	24	21	11	0	22	4	0	0	3	1	.75	2	.275	.363	.413
1998 San Francisco	NL	12	7	4	0	0	2	(0	2)	10	3	3	3	0	2	0	0	0	0	0	—	0	.571	.700	1.429
1999 San Francisco	NL	72	150	49	9	0	7	(4	3)	79	32	29	24	1	35	1	1	1	7	4	.64	3	.327	.420	.527
2000 San Francisco	NL	115	233	62	15	5	10	(2	8)	117	38	50	31	4	43	0	1	4	3	2	.60	9	.266	.347	.502
3 ML YEARS		199	390	115	24	5	19	(6	13)	206	73	82	58	5	80	1	2	5	10	6	.63	12	.295	.383	.528

Cal Ripken Jr.

Bats: Right **Throws:** Right **Pos:** 3B-73; DH-10 **Ht:** 6'4" **Wt:** 220 **Born:** 8/24/60 **Age:** 40

Year Team	Lg	G	AB	H	2B	3B	HR	(Hm	Rd)	TB	R	RBI	TBB	IBB	SO	HBP	SH	SF	SB	CS	SB%	GDP	Avg	OBP	SLG
1981 Baltimore	AL	23	39	5	0	0	0	(0	0)	5	1	0	1	0	8	0	0	0	0	0	—	4	.128	.150	.128
1982 Baltimore	AL	160	598	158	32	5	28	(11	17)	284	90	93	46	3	95	3	2	6	3	3	.50	16	.264	.317	.475
1983 Baltimore	AL	162	663	211	47	2	27	(12	15)	343	121	102	58	0	97	0	0	5	0	4	.00	24	.318	.371	.517
1984 Baltimore	AL	162	641	195	37	7	27	(16	11)	327	103	86	71	1	89	2	0	2	2	1	.67	16	.304	.374	.510
1985 Baltimore	AL	161	642	181	32	5	26	(15	11)	301	116	110	67	1	68	1	0	8	2	3	.40	32	.282	.347	.469
1986 Baltimore	AL	162	627	177	35	1	25	(10	15)	289	98	81	70	5	60	4	0	6	4	2	.67	19	.282	.355	.461
1987 Baltimore	AL	162	624	157	28	3	27	(17	10)	272	97	98	81	0	77	1	0	11	3	5	.38	19	.252	.333	.436
1988 Baltimore	AL	161	575	152	25	1	23	(11	12)	248	87	81	102	7	69	2	0	10	2	2	.50	10	.264	.372	.431
1989 Baltimore	AL	162	646	166	30	0	21	(13	8)	259	80	93	57	5	72	3	0	6	2	3	.60	22	.257	.317	.401
1990 Baltimore	AL	161	600	150	28	4	21	(8	13)	249	78	84	82	18	66	5	1	7	3	1	.75	12	.250	.341	.415
1991 Baltimore	AL	162	650	210	46	5	34	(16	18)	368	99	114	53	15	46	5	0	9	6	1	.86	19	.323	.374	.566
1992 Baltimore	AL	162	637	160	29	1	14	(5	9)	233	73	72	64	14	50	7	0	7	4	3	.57	13	.251	.323	.366
1993 Baltimore	AL	162	641	165	26	3	24	(14	10)	269	87	90	65	19	58	6	0	6	1	4	.20	17	.257	.329	.420
1994 Baltimore	AL	112	444	140	19	3	13	(5	8)	204	71	75	32	3	41	4	0	4	0	1	1.00	16	.315	.364	.459
1995 Baltimore	AL	144	550	144	33	2	17	(10	7)	232	71	88	52	6	59	2	1	8	0	1	.00	15	.262	.324	.422
1996 Baltimore	AL	163	640	178	40	1	26	(10	16)	298	94	102	59	3	78	4	0	4	1	2	.33	28	.278	.341	.466
1997 Baltimore	AL	162	615	166	30	0	17	(10	7)	247	79	84	56	3	73	5	0	10	1	0	1.00	19	.270	.331	.402
1998 Baltimore	AL	161	601	163	27	1	14	(8	6)	234	65	61	51	0	68	4	1	2	0	2	.00	9	.271	.331	.389
1999 Baltimore	AL	86	332	113	27	0	18	(12	6)	194	51	57	13	3	31	3	3	3	0	1	.00	14	.340	.368	.584
2000 Baltimore	AL	83	309	79	16	0	15	(8	7)	140	43	56	23	0	37	3	0	0	0	0	—	10	.256	.310	.453
20 ML YEARS		2873	11074	3070	587	44	417	(211	206)	4996	1604	1627	1103	106	1242	64	8	118	36	37	.49	335	.277	.343	.451

Todd Ritchie

Pitches: Right **Bats:** Right **Pos:** SP-31 **Ht:** 6'3" **Wt:** 222 **Born:** 11/7/71 **Age:** 29

Year Team	Lg	G	GS	CG	GF	IP	BFP	H	R	ER	HR	SH	SF	HB	TBB	IBB	SO	WP	Bk	W	L	Pct.	ShO	Sv-Op	Hld	ERA
1997 Minnesota	AL	42	0	0	19	74.2	331	87	41	38	11	0	1	2	28	0	44	11	0	2	3	.400	0	0-2	4	4.58
1998 Minnesota	AL	15	0	0	7	24	113	30	17	15	1	0	0	0	9	0	21	0	0	0	0	—	0	0-0	0	5.63
1999 Pittsburgh	NL	28	26	2	0	172.1	715	169	79	67	17	3	2	4	54	3	107	7	0	15	9	.625	0	0-0	1	3.50
2000 Pittsburgh	NL	31	31	1	0	187	804	208	111	100	26	8	5	3	51	1	124	5	1	9	8	.529	1	0-2	4	4.81
4 ML YEARS		116	57	3	26	458	1963	494	248	220	55	11	8	9	142	4	296	26	1	26	20	.565	1	0-2	4	4.32

Luis Rivas

Bats: Right **Throws:** Right **Pos:** 2B-14; SS-2; PH/PR-2 **Ht:** 5'11" **Wt:** 175 **Born:** 8/30/79 **Age:** 21

Year Team	Lg	G	AB	H	2B	3B	HR	(Hm	Rd)	TB	R	RBI	TBB	IBB	SO	HBP	SH	SF	SB	CS	SB%	GDP	Avg	OBP	SLG
1996 Twins	R	53	201	52	12	1	1	—	—	69	29	13	18	0	37	0	1	0	35	10	.78	2	.259	.320	.343
1997 Fort Wayne	A	121	419	100	20	6	1	—	—	135	61	30	33	1	90	5	6	2	28	18	.61	5	.239	.301	.374
1998 Fort Myers	A+	126	463	130	21	5	4	—	—	173	58	51	14	0	75	3	4	6	34	8	.81	11	.281	.302	.374
1999 New Britain	AA	132	527	134	30	7	7	—	—	199	78	49	41	1	92	4	2	3	31	14	.69	16	.254	.309	.378
2000 New Britain	AA	82	328	82	23	6	3	—	—	126	56	40	36	0	41	4	1	3	11	4	.73	3	.250	.329	.384
Salt Lake	AAA	41	157	50	14	1	3	—	—	75	33	25	13	0	21	2	0	1	7	4	.64	2	.318	.376	.478
2000 Minnesota	AL	16	58	18	4	1	0	(0	0)	24	8	6	2	0	4	0	0	2	2	0	1.00	2	.310	.323	.414

Luis Rivera

Pitches: Right **Bats:** Right **Pos:** RP-6   **Ht:** 6'3" **Wt:** 163 **Born:** 6/21/78 **Age:** 23

Year Team	Lg	G	GS	CG	GF	IP	BFP	H	R	ER	HR	SH	SF	HB	TBB	IBB	SO	WP	Bk	W	L	Pct.	ShO	Sv-Op	Hld	ERA
1996 Braves	R	8	6	0	0	24.1	97	18	9	7	0	0	0	1	7	1	26	5	0	1	1	.500	0	0- -	—	2.59
1997 Danville	R+	9	9	0	0	41	169	28	15	11	2	1	1	1	17	0	57	5	0	3	1	.750	0	0- -	—	2.41
Macon	A	4	4	0	0	21	81	13	4	3	1	0	1	1	7	0	27	2	0	2	0	1.000	0	0- -	—	1.29
1998 Macon	A	20	20	0	0	92.2	405	78	53	41	8	3	3	6	41	0	118	8	2	5	5	.500	0	0- -	—	3.98
1999 Myrtle Bch	A+	25	13	0	0	66.2	262	45	25	23	3	2	1	1	23	0	81	7	0	2	2	.500	0	0- -	—	3.11
2000 Braves	R	3	3	0	0	4	16	2	0	0	0	1	0	0	1	0	2	1	0	0	0	—	0	0- -	—	0.00
Richmond	AAA	8	7	0	0	22.1	111	29	20	20	3	1	0	1	18	0	12	1	4	0	2	.000	0	0- -	—	8.06
Rochester	AAA	3	3	0	0	8	42	11	5	3	0	1	1	1	5	0	4	2	0	0	1	.000	0	0- -	—	3.38
2000 Atl-Bal		6	0	0	3	7.1	32	5	1	1	0	2	0	0	6	1	5	0	0	1	0	1.000	0	0-0	2	1.23
2000 Atlanta	NL	5	0	0	3	6.2	28	4	1	1	0	2	0	0	5	1	5	0	0	1	0	1.000	0	0-0	1	1.35
Baltimore	AL	1	0	0	0	0.2	4	1	0	0	0	0	0	0	1	0	0	0	0	0	0	—	0	0-0	1	0.00

Mariano Rivera

Pitches: Right **Bats:** Right **Pos:** RP-66   **Ht:** 6'2" **Wt:** 185 **Born:** 11/29/69 **Age:** 31

Year Team	Lg	G	GS	CG	GF	IP	BFP	H	R	ER	HR	SH	SF	HB	TBB	IBB	SO	WP	Bk	W	L	Pct.	ShO	Sv-Op	Hld	ERA
1995 New York	AL	19	10	0	2	67	301	71	43	41	11	0	2	4	30	0	51	0	1	5	3	.625	0	0-1	0	5.51
1996 New York	AL	61	0	0	14	107.2	425	73	25	25	1	2	1	2	34	3	130	1	0	8	3	.727	0	5-8	27	2.09
1997 New York	AL	66	0	0	56	71.2	301	65	17	15	5	3	4	0	20	6	68	2	0	6	4	.600	0	43-52	0	1.88
1998 New York	AL	54	0	0	49	61.1	246	48	13	13	2	3	2	1	17	1	36	0	0	3	0	1.000	0	36-41	0	1.91
1999 New York	AL	66	0	0	63	69	268	43	15	14	2	0	2	3	18	3	52	2	1	4	3	.571	0	45-49	0	1.83
2000 New York	AL	66	0	0	61	75.2	311	58	26	24	4	5	2	0	25	3	58	2	0	7	4	.636	0	36-41	0	2.85
6 ML YEARS		332	10	0	245	452.1	1852	358	139	132	26	12	14	8	144	16	395	7	2	33	17	.660	0	165-192	27	2.63

Ruben Rivera

Bats: Right **Throws:** Right **Pos:** CF-131; PH/PR-8; LF-1   **Ht:** 6'3" **Wt:** 208 **Born:** 11/14/73 **Age:** 27

Year Team	Lg	G	AB	H	2B	3B	HR	(Hm	Rd)	TB	R	RBI	TBB	IBB	SO	HBP	SH	SF	SB	CS	SB%	GDP	Avg	OBP	SLG
2000 Las Vegas *	AAA	2	10	2	0	0	0	(—	—)	2	1	1	0	0	3	0	0	0	0	0	—	0	.200	.200	.200
1995 New York	AL	5	1	0	0	0	0	(0	0)	0	0	0	0	0	1	0	0	0	0	0	—	0	.000	.000	.000
1996 New York	AL	46	88	25	6	1	2	(0	2)	39	17	16	13	0	26	2	1	2	6	2	.75	1	.284	.381	.443
1997 San Diego	NL	17	20	5	1	0	0	(0	0)	6	2	1	2	0	9	0	0	0	2	1	.67	0	.250	.318	.300
1998 San Diego	NL	95	172	36	7	2	6	(2	4)	65	31	29	28	0	52	2	1	1	5	1	.83	1	.209	.325	.378
1999 San Diego	NL	147	411	80	16	1	23	(10	13)	167	65	48	55	1	143	5	0	4	18	7	.72	9	.195	.295	.406
2000 San Diego	NL	135	423	88	18	6	17	(8	9)	169	62	57	44	1	137	10	0	2	8	4	.67	8	.208	.296	.400
6 ML YEARS		445	1115	234	48	10	48	(20	28)	446	177	151	142	2	368	19	2	9	39	15	.72	19	.210	.307	.400

Dave Roberts

Bats: L **Throws:** L **Pos:** LF-12; PH/PR-8; CF-5; RF-1   **Ht:** 5'10" **Wt:** 180 **Born:** 5/31/72 **Age:** 29

Year Team	Lg	G	AB	H	2B	3B	HR	(Hm	Rd)	TB	R	RBI	TBB	IBB	SO	HBP	SH	SF	SB	CS	SB%	GDP	Avg	OBP	SLG
1994 Jamestown	A-	54	178	52	7	2	0	—	—	63	33	12	29	4	27	1	3	1	12	8	.60	0	.292	.392	.354
1995 Lakeland	A+	92	357	108	10	5	3	—	—	137	67	30	39	2	43	1	2	7	30	8	.79	7	.303	.371	.384
1996 Visalia	A+	126	482	131	24	7	5	—	—	184	112	37	98	0	105	1	3	7	65	21	.76	6	.272	.391	.382
Jacksnville	AA	3	9	2	0	0	0	—	—	2	0	0	1	0	0	0	0	0	0	1	.00	0	.222	.300	.222
1997 Jacksnville	AA	105	415	123	24	2	4	—	—	163	76	41	45	1	62	2	9	2	23	5	.82	5	.296	.366	.393
1998 Jacksnville	AA	69	279	91	14	5	5	—	—	130	71	42	53	1	59	3	3	4	21	9	.70	4	.326	.434	.466
Buffalo	AAA	5	15	2	0	0	0	—	—	2	2	2	0	0	3	0	0	1	2	0	1.00	0	.133	.125	.133
Akron	AA	56	227	82	10	5	7	—	—	123	49	33	35	5	30	1	5	1	28	6	.82	3	.361	.447	.542
1999 Buffalo	AAA	89	350	95	17	10	0	—	—	132	65	38	43	1	52	2	8	4	39	3	.93	1	.271	.351	.377
2000 Buffalo	AAA	120	462	135	16	3	13	—	—	196	93	55	59	2	68	2	7	2	39	11	.78	3	.292	.373	.424
1999 Cleveland	AL	41	143	34	4	0	2	(1	1)	44	26	12	9	0	16	0	3	1	11	3	.79	0	.238	.281	.308
2000 Cleveland	AL	19	10	2	0	0	0	(0	0)	2	1	0	2	0	2	0	1	0	1	1	.50	0	.200	.333	.200
2 ML YEARS		60	153	36	4	0	2	(1	1)	46	27	12	11	0	18	0	4	1	12	4	.75	0	.235	.285	.301

Grant Roberts

Pitches: Right **Bats:** Right **Pos:** RP-3; SP-1   **Ht:** 6'3" **Wt:** 205 **Born:** 9/13/77 **Age:** 23

Year Team	Lg	G	GS	CG	GF	IP	BFP	H	R	ER	HR	SH	SF	HB	TBB	IBB	SO	WP	Bk	W	L	Pct.	ShO	Sv-Op	Hld	ERA
1995 Mets	R	11	3	0	4	29.1	121	19	13	7	1	1	1	3	14	1	24	4	1	2	1	.667	0	0- -	—	2.15
1996 Kingsport	R+	13	13	2	0	68.2	285	43	18	16	3	1	0	7	37	1	92	4	0	9	1	.900	2	0- -	—	2.10
1997 Capital Cty	A	22	22	2	0	129.2	530	98	37	34	1	3	3	8	44	0	122	5	0	11	3	.786	1	0- -	—	2.36
1998 St. Lucie	A+	17	17	0	0	72.1	323	72	37	34	11	1	1	5	37	0	70	2	0	5	4	.556	0	0- -	—	4.23
1999 Binghamton	AA	23	23	5	0	131.1	576	135	81	71	9	6	3	12	49	0	94	8	0	7	6	.538	0	0- -	—	4.87
Norfolk	AAA	5	5	0	0	28	122	32	15	14	1	0	1	0	11	2	30	3	0	2	1	.667	0	0- -	—	4.50
2000 Norfolk	AAA	25	25	5	0	157.1	686	154	67	59	6	5	3	8	63	5	115	12	2	7	8	.467	0	0- -	—	3.38
2000 New York	NL	4	1	0	0	7	38	11	10	9	0	0	2	0	4	1	6	0	0	0	0	—	0	0-0	0	11.57

John Rocker

Pitches: Left **Bats:** Right **Pos:** RP-59   **Ht:** 6'4" **Wt:** 225 **Born:** 10/17/74 **Age:** 26

Year Team	Lg	G	GS	CG	GF	IP	BFP	H	R	ER	HR	SH	SF	HB	TBB	IBB	SO	WP	Bk	W	L	Pct.	ShO	Sv-Op	Hld	ERA
2000 Richmond *	AAA	3	0	0	3	3	13	3	1	1	0	0	1	0	1	0	6	0	0	0	0	—	0	1- -	—	3.00
1998 Atlanta	NL	47	0	0	16	38	156	22	10	9	4	3	0	3	22	4	42	6	0	1	3	.250	0	2-4	15	2.13
1999 Atlanta	NL	74	0	0	61	72.1	301	47	24	20	5	2	0	1	37	4	104	7	0	4	5	.444	0	38-45	6	2.49
2000 Atlanta	NL	59	0	0	41	53	251	42	25	17	5	1	0	2	48	4	77	5	2	1	2	.333	0	24-27	4	2.89
3 ML YEARS		180	0	0	118	163.1	708	111	59	46	14	6	0	6	107	12	223	18	2	6	10	.375	0	64-76	19	2.53

Alex Rodriguez

Bats: Right **Throws:** Right **Pos:** SS-148   **Ht:** 6'3" **Wt:** 210 **Born:** 7/27/75 **Age:** 25

Year Team	Lg	G	AB	H	2B	3B	HR	(Hm	Rd)	TB	R	RBI	TBB	IBB	SO	HBP	SH	SF	SB	CS	SB%	GDP	Avg	OBP	SLG
1994 Seattle	AL	17	54	11	0	0	0	(0	0)	11	4	2	3	0	20	0	1	1	3	0	1.00	0	.204	.241	.204
1995 Seattle	AL	48	142	33	6	2	5	(1	4)	58	15	19	6	0	42	0	1	0	4	2	.67	0	.232	.264	.408
1996 Seattle	AL	146	601	215	**54**	1	36	(18	18)	**379**	141	123	59	1	104	4	6	7	15	4	.79	15	**.358**	.414	.631
1997 Seattle	AL	141	587	176	40	3	23	(16	7)	291	100	84	41	1	99	5	4	1	29	6	.83	14	.300	.350	.496
1998 Seattle	AL	161	**686**	**213**	35	5	42	(18	24)	384	123	124	45	0	121	10	3	4	46	13	.78	12	.310	.360	.560
1999 Seattle	AL	129	502	143	25	0	42	(20	22)	294	110	111	56	2	109	5	1	8	21	7	.75	12	.285	.357	.586
2000 Seattle	AL	148	554	175	34	2	41	(13	**28**)	336	134	132	100	5	121	7	0	11	15	4	.79	10	.316	.420	.606
7 ML YEARS		790	3126	966	194	13	189	(86	103)	1753	627	595	310	9	616	31	16	32	133	36	.79	63	.309	.374	.561

Felix Rodriguez

Pitches: Right **Bats:** Right **Pos:** RP-76   **Ht:** 6'1" **Wt:** 190 **Born:** 12/5/72 **Age:** 28

Year Team	Lg	G	GS	CG	GF	IP	BFP	H	R	ER	HR	SH	SF	HB	TBB	IBB	SO	WP	Bk	W	L	Pct.	ShO	Sv-Op	Hld	ERA
1995 Los Angeles	NL	11	0	0	5	10.2	45	11	3	3	2	0	0	0	5	0	5	0	0	1	1	.500	0	0-1	0	2.53
1997 Cincinnati	NL	26	1	0	13	46	212	48	23	22	2	0	1	6	28	2	34	4	1	0	0	—	0	0-0	0	4.30
1998 Arizona	NL	43	0	0	23	44	207	44	31	30	5	4	3	1	29	1	36	5	2	0	2	.000	0	5-8	0	6.14
1999 San Francisco	NL	47	0	0	26	66.1	292	67	32	28	6	2	3	2	29	2	55	2	0	2	3	.400	0	0-1	3	3.80
2000 San Francisco	NL	76	0	0	19	81.2	346	65	29	24	5	2	3	3	42	2	95	3	1	4	2	.667	0	3-8	**30**	2.64
5 ML YEARS		203	1	0	86	248.2	1102	235	118	107	20	8	10	12	133	7	225	14	4	7	8	.467	0	8-18	33	3.87

Frank Rodriguez

Pitches: Right **Bats:** Right **Pos:** RP-23   **Ht:** 6'0" **Wt:** 210 **Born:** 12/11/72 **Age:** 28

Year Team	Lg	G	GS	CG	GF	IP	BFP	H	R	ER	HR	SH	SF	HB	TBB	IBB	SO	WP	Bk	W	L	Pct.	ShO	Sv-Op	Hld	ERA
2000 Tacoma *	AAA	9	6	0	1	35.1	148	30	20	19	1	0	1	4	11	0	26	0	0	2	1	.667	0	0- -	—	4.84
1995 Bos-Min	AL	25	18	0	1	105.2	478	114	83	72	11	4	4	5	57	1	59	9	0	5	8	.385	0	0-0	1	6.13
1996 Minnesota	AL	38	33	3	4	206.2	899	218	129	116	27	6	8	5	78	1	110	2	0	13	14	.481	0	2-2	0	5.05
1997 Minnesota	AL	43	15	0	5	142.1	613	147	82	73	12	4	2	4	60	9	65	6	0	3	6	.333	0	0-2	4	4.62
1998 Minnesota	AL	20	11	0	4	70	329	88	58	51	6	1	5	3	30	0	62	6	1	4	6	.400	0	0-0	0	6.56
1999 Seattle	AL	28	5	0	10	73.1	334	94	47	46	11	0	1	4	30	2	47	1	0	2	4	.333	0	3-4	3	5.65
2000 Seattle	AL	23	0	0	5	47.1	214	60	33	33	8	0	3	0	22	2	19	3	0	2	1	.667	0	0-0	2	6.27
1995 Boston	AL	9	2	0	1	15.1	75	21	19	18	3	0	0	0	10	1	14	4	0	0	2	.000	0	0-0	1	10.57
Minnesota	AL	16	16	0	0	90.1	403	93	64	54	8	4	4	5	47	0	45	5	0	5	6	.455	0	0-0	0	5.38
6 ML YEARS		177	82	3	29	645.1	2867	721	432	391	75	12	23	21	277	15	362	27	1	29	39	.426	0	5-8	10	5.45

Henry Rodriguez

Bats: Left **Throws:** Left **Pos:** LF-94; PH/PR-13; RF-7   **Ht:** 6'2" **Wt:** 225 **Born:** 11/8/67 **Age:** 33

Year Team	Lg	G	AB	H	2B	3B	HR	(Hm	Rd)	TB	R	RBI	TBB	IBB	SO	HBP	SH	SF	SB	CS	SB%	GDP	Avg	OBP	SLG
1992 Los Angeles	NL	53	146	32	7	0	3	(2	1)	48	11	14	8	0	30	0	1	1	0	0	—	1	.219	.258	.329
1993 Los Angeles	NL	76	176	39	10	0	8	(5	3)	73	20	23	11	2	39	1	0	1	1	0	1.00	1	.222	.266	.415
1994 Los Angeles	NL	104	306	82	14	2	8	(5	3)	124	33	49	17	2	58	2	1	4	0	1	.00	9	.268	.307	.405
1995 LA-Mon	NL	45	138	33	4	1	2	(1	1)	45	13	15	11	2	28	0	0	1	0	1	.00	5	.239	.293	.326
1996 Montreal	NL	145	532	147	42	1	36	(20	16)	299	81	103	37	7	**160**	3	0	4	2	0	1.00	10	.276	.325	.562
1997 Montreal	NL	132	476	116	28	3	26	(14	12)	228	55	83	42	5	149	2	0	3	3	3	.50	6	.244	.306	.479
1998 Chicago	NL	128	415	104	21	1	31	(16	15)	220	56	85	54	7	113	0	0	4	1	3	.25	6	.251	.334	.530
1999 Chicago	NL	130	447	136	29	0	26	(14	12)	243	72	87	56	6	113	0	0	1	2	4	.33	8	.304	.381	.544
2000 ChC-Fla	NL	112	367	94	21	1	20	(7	13)	177	47	61	36	2	99	4	0	3	1	2	.33	5	.256	.327	.482
1995 Los Angeles	NL	21	80	21	4	1	1	(0	1)	30	6	10	5	2	17	0	0	0	0	1	.00	3	.263	.306	.375
Montreal	NL	24	58	12	0	0	1	(1	0)	15	7	5	6	0	11	0	0	1	0	0	—	2	.207	.277	.259
2000 Chicago	NL	76	259	65	15	1	18	(6	12)	136	37	51	22	2	76	3	0	3	1	2	.33	4	.251	.314	.525
Florida	NL	36	108	29	6	0	2	(1	1)	41	10	10	14	0	23	1	0	0	0	0	—	1	.269	.358	.380
9 ML YEARS		925	3003	783	176	9	160	(84	76)	1457	388	520	272	33	789	11	2	22	10	14	.42	53	.261	.322	.485

Ivan Rodriguez

Bats: Right **Throws:** Right **Pos:** C-87; PH/PR-4; DH-1   **Ht:** 5'9" **Wt:** 205 **Born:** 11/30/71 **Age:** 29

Year Team	Lg	G	AB	H	2B	3B	HR	(Hm	Rd)	TB	R	RBI	TBB	IBB	SO	HBP	SH	SF	SB	CS	SB%	GDP	Avg	OBP	SLG
1991 Texas	AL	88	280	74	16	0	3	(3	0)	99	24	27	5	0	42	0	2	1	0	1	.00	10	.264	.276	.354
1992 Texas	AL	123	420	109	16	1	8	(4	4)	151	39	37	24	2	73	1	7	2	0	0	—	15	.260	.300	.360
1993 Texas	AL	137	473	129	28	4	10	(7	3)	195	56	66	29	3	70	4	5	8	8	7	.53	16	.273	.315	.412
1994 Texas	AL	99	363	108	19	1	16	(7	9)	177	56	57	31	5	42	7	0	4	6	3	.67	10	.298	.360	.488
1995 Texas	AL	130	492	149	32	2	12	(5	7)	221	56	67	16	2	48	4	0	5	0	0	—	11	.303	.327	.449
1996 Texas	AL	153	639	192	47	3	19	(10	9)	302	116	86	38	7	55	4	0	4	5	0	1.00	15	.300	.342	.473
1997 Texas	AL	150	597	187	34	4	20	(12	8)	289	98	77	38	7	89	8	1	4	7	3	.70	18	.313	.360	.484
1998 Texas	AL	145	579	186	40	4	21	(12	9)	297	88	91	32	4	88	3	0	3	9	0	1.00	18	.321	.358	.513
1999 Texas	AL	144	600	199	29	1	35	(12	23)	335	116	113	24	2	64	1	0	5	25	12	.68	**31**	.332	.356	.558
2000 Texas	AL	91	363	126	27	4	27	(16	11)	242	66	83	19	5	48	1	0	6	5	5	.50	17	.347	.375	.667
10 ML YEARS		1260	4806	1459	288	24	171	(88	83)	2308	715	704	256	37	619	33	15	42	65	33	.66	161	.304	.340	.480

Jose Rodriguez

Pitches: Left **Bats:** Left **Pos:** RP-6   **Ht:** 6'1" **Wt:** 215 **Born:** 12/18/74 **Age:** 26

Year Team	Lg	G	GS	CG	GF	IP	BFP	H	R	ER	HR	SH	SF	HB	TBB	IBB	SO	WP	Bk	W	L	Pct.	ShO	Sv-Op	Hld	ERA
1997 Johnson Cty	R+	4	0	0	1	6.2	27	4	3	3	1	1	0	1	3	1	8	1	0	0	0	—	0	0- -	—	4.05

Year Team	Lg	G	GS	CG	GF	IP	BFP	H	R	ER	HR	SH	SF	HB	TBB	IBB	SO	WP	Bk	W	L	Pct.	ShO	Sv-Op	Hld	ERA
1998 Peoria	A	40	0	0	12	39.1	191	47	32	20	0	6	1	2	19	1	30	3	0	2	4	.333	0	0- -	—	4.58
1999 Arkansas	AA	30	0	0	9	36	173	38	16	13	6	2	0	0	25	0	30	4	0	1	2	.333	0	0- -	—	3.25
Peoria	A	15	0	0	2	16.1	74	14	7	6	1	3	0	0	8	0	15	0	0	2	3	.400	0	0- -	—	3.31
2000 Arkansas	AA	10	0	0	2	11	47	7	3	3	0	2	0	0	4	2	8	0	0	3	0	1.000	0	0- -	—	2.45
Memphis	AAA	40	0	0	17	47.1	200	48	21	20	4	5	1	0	19	1	37	0	1	4	2	.667	0	3- -	—	3.80
2000 St. Louis	NL	6	0	0	1	4	19	2	2	0	0	0	1	1	3	0	2	0	0	0	0	—	0	0-0	1	0.00

Rich Rodriguez

Pitches: Left **Bats:** Left **Pos:** RP-32 **Ht:** 6'0" **Wt:** 205 **Born:** 3/1/63 **Age:** 38

Year Team	Lg	G	GS	CG	GF	IP	BFP	H	R	ER	HR	SH	SF	HB	TBB	IBB	SO	WP	Bk	W	L	Pct.	ShO	Sv-Op	Hld	ERA
2000 Norfolk *	AAA	14	3	0	7	20.2	84	17	7	7	2	1	0	0	6	3	16	0	0	0	0	.000	0	1- -	—	3.05
1990 San Diego	NL	32	0	0	12	47.2	201	52	17	15	2	2	1	1	16	4	22	1	1	1	1	.500	0	1-1	3	2.83
1991 San Diego	NL	64	1	0	19	80	335	66	31	29	8	7	2	0	44	8	40	4	1	3	1	.750	0	0-2	8	3.26
1992 San Diego	NL	61	1	0	15	91	369	77	28	24	4	2	2	0	29	4	64	1	1	6	3	.667	0	0-1	5	2.37
1993 SD-Fla	NL	70	0	0	21	76	331	73	38	32	10	5	0	2	33	8	43	3	0	2	4	.333	0	3-7	10	3.79
1994 St. Louis	NL	56	0	0	15	60.1	260	62	30	27	6	2	1	1	26	4	43	4	0	3	5	.375	0	0-3	15	4.03
1995 St. Louis	NL	1	0	0	0	1.2	4	0	0	0	0	0	0	0	0	0	0	0	0	0	0	—	0	0-0	0	0.00
1997 San Francisco	NL	71	0	0	15	65.1	271	65	24	23	7	3	0	1	21	4	32	0	0	4	3	.571	0	1-5	14	3.17
1998 San Francisco	NL	68	0	0	11	65.2	278	69	28	27	7	2	2	0	20	5	44	3	0	4	0	1.000	0	2-6	22	3.70
1999 San Francisco	NL	62	0	0	8	56.2	255	60	33	33	8	5	2	1	28	5	44	1	0	3	0	1.000	0	0-2	11	5.24
2000 New York	NL	32	0	0	13	37	185	59	40	32	7	0	5	3	15	0	18	2	1	0	1	.000	0	0-0	6	7.78
1993 San Diego	NL	34	0	0	10	30	133	34	15	11	2	2	0	1	9	3	22	1	0	2	3	.400	0	2-5	8	3.30
Florida	NL	36	0	0	11	46	198	39	23	21	8	3	0	1	24	5	21	2	0	0	1	.000	0	1-2	2	4.11
10 ML YEARS		517	2	0	132	581.1	2489	583	269	242	59	28	15	9	232	42	350	19	4	26	18	.591	0	7-27	88	3.75

Kenny Rogers

Pitches: Left **Bats:** Left **Pos:** SP-34 **Ht:** 6'1" **Wt:** 217 **Born:** 11/10/64 **Age:** 36

Year Team	Lg	G	GS	CG	GF	IP	BFP	H	R	ER	HR	SH	SF	HB	TBB	IBB	SO	WP	Bk	W	L	Pct.	ShO	Sv-Op	Hld	ERA
1989 Texas	AL	73	0	0	24	73.2	314	60	28	24	2	6	3	4	42	9	63	6	0	3	4	.429	0	2-5	16	2.93
1990 Texas	AL	69	3	0	46	97.2	428	93	40	34	6	7	4	1	42	5	74	5	0	10	6	.625	0	15-23	6	3.13
1991 Texas	AL	63	9	0	20	109.2	511	121	80	66	14	9	5	6	61	7	73	3	1	10	10	.500	0	5-6	11	5.42
1992 Texas	AL	81	0	0	38	78.2	337	80	32	27	7	4	1	0	26	8	70	4	1	3	6	.333	0	6-10	16	3.09
1993 Texas	AL	35	33	5	0	208.1	885	210	108	95	18	7	5	4	71	2	140	6	5	16	10	.615	0	0-0	1	4.10
1994 Texas	AL	24	24	6	0	167.1	714	169	93	83	24	3	6	3	52	1	120	3	1	11	8	.579	2	0-0	0	4.46
1995 Texas	AL	31	31	3	0	208	877	192	87	78	26	3	5	2	76	1	140	8	1	17	7	.708	1	0-0	0	3.38
1996 New York	AL	30	30	2	0	179	786	179	97	93	16	6	3	8	83	2	92	5	0	12	8	.600	1	0-0	0	4.68
1997 New York	AL	31	22	1	4	145	651	161	100	91	18	2	4	7	62	1	78	2	2	6	7	.462	0	0-0	1	5.65
1998 Oakland	AL	34	34	7	0	238.2	970	215	96	84	19	4	5	7	62	0	138	5	2	16	8	.667	1	0-0	0	3.17
1999 Oak-NYM	AL	31	31	5	0	195.1	845	206	101	91	16	7	7	13	69	1	126	4	1	10	4	.714	1	0-0	0	4.19
2000 Texas	AL	34	34	2	0	227.1	998	257	126	115	20	3	4	11	78	2	127	1	1	13	13	.500	0	0-0	0	4.55
1999 Oakland	AL	19	19	3	0	119.1	528	135	66	57	8	4	6	9	41	0	68	3	1	5	3	.625	0	0-0	0	4.30
New York	NL	12	12	2	0	76	317	71	35	34	8	3	1	4	28	1	58	1	0	5	1	.833	1	0-0	0	4.03
12 ML YEARS		536	251	31	132	1928.2	8316	1943	988	881	186	61	52	66	729	39	1241	52	15	127	91	.583	6	28-44	51	4.11

Scott Rolen

Bats: Right **Throws:** Right **Pos:** 3B-128; PH/PR-1 **Ht:** 6'4" **Wt:** 226 **Born:** 4/4/75 **Age:** 26

Year Team	Lg	G	AB	H	2B	3B	HR	(Hm	Rd)	TB	R	RBI	TBB	IBB	SO	HBP	SH	SF	SB	CS	SB%	GDP	Avg	OBP	SLG
1996 Philadelphia	NL	37	130	33	7	0	4	(2	2)	52	10	18	13	0	27	1	0	2	0	2	.00	4	.254	.322	.400
1997 Philadelphia	NL	156	561	159	35	3	21	(11	10)	263	93	92	76	4	138	13	0	7	16	6	.73	6	.283	.377	.469
1998 Philadelphia	NL	160	601	174	45	4	31	(19	12)	320	120	110	93	6	141	11	0	6	14	7	.67	10	.290	.391	.532
1999 Philadelphia	NL	112	421	113	28	1	26	(9	17)	221	74	77	67	2	114	3	0	6	12	2	.86	8	.268	.368	.525
2000 Philadelphia	NL	128	483	144	32	6	26	(12	14)	266	88	89	51	9	99	5	0	2	8	1	.89	4	.298	.370	.551
5 ML YEARS		593	2196	623	147	14	108	(53	55)	1122	385	386	300	21	519	33	0	23	50	18	.74	32	.284	.375	.511

Nate Rolison

Bats: Left **Throws:** Right **Pos:** 1B-4; PH/PR-4 **Ht:** 6'6" **Wt:** 240 **Born:** 3/27/77 **Age:** 24

Year Team	Lg	G	AB	H	2B	3B	HR	(Hm	Rd)	TB	R	RBI	TBB	IBB	SO	HBP	SH	SF	SB	CS	SB%	GDP	Avg	OBP	SLG
1995 Marlins	R	37	134	37	10	2	1	—	—	54	22	19	15	1	34	8	0	1	0	0	—	0	.276	.380	.403
1996 Kane County	A	131	474	115	28	1	14	—	—	187	63	75	66	9	170	8	1	0	3	3	.50	9	.243	.345	.395
1997 Brevard Cty	A+	122	473	121	22	0	16	—	—	191	59	65	38	1	143	2	0	1	3	1	.75	16	.256	.313	.404
1998 Portland	AA	131	484	134	35	2	16	—	—	221	80	83	64	6	150	7	0	6	5	0	1.00	16	.277	.365	.457
1999 Portland	AA	124	438	131	20	1	17	—	—	204	71	69	68	3	112	6	0	2	3	1	.00	16	.299	.399	.466
2000 Calgary	AAA	123	443	146	37	3	23	—	—	258	88	88	70	5	117	3	0	2	3	1	.75	7	.330	.423	.582
2000 Florida	NL	8	13	1	0	0	0	(0	0)	1	0	2	1	0	4	0	0	2	0	0	—	0	.077	.125	.077

Jimmy Rollins

Bats: Both **Throws:** Right **Pos:** SS-13; PH/PR-1 **Ht:** 5'8" **Wt:** 160 **Born:** 11/27/78 **Age:** 22

Year Team	Lg	G	AB	H	2B	3B	HR	(Hm	Rd)	TB	R	RBI	TBB	IBB	SO	HBP	SH	SF	SB	CS	SB%	GDP	Avg	OBP	SLG
1996 Martinsville	R+	49	172	41	3	1	1	—	—	49	22	16	28	1	20	2	1	3	11	5	.69	2	.238	.351	.285
1997 Piedmont	A	139	560	151	22	8	6	—	—	207	94	59	52	2	80	0	9	3	46	6	.88	4	.270	.330	.370
1998 Clearwater	A+	119	495	121	18	9	6	—	—	175	72	35	41	1	62	4	4	3	23	9	.72	9	.244	.306	.354
1999 Reading	AA	133	532	145	21	8	11	—	—	215	81	56	51	1	47	1	12	3	24	12	.67	8	.273	.336	.404
Scrantn-WB	AAA	4	13	1	1	0	0	—	—	2	1	0	1	0	1	0	1	0	1	0	1.00	0	.077	.143	.154
2000 Scrantn-WB	AAA	133	470	129	28	11	12	—	—	215	67	69	49	1	55	2	5	7	24	7	.77	4	.274	.341	.457
2000 Philadelphia	NL	14	53	17	1	1	0	(0	0)	20	5	5	2	0	7	0	0	0	3	0	1.00	0	.321	.345	.377

Damian Rolls

Bats: Right **Throws:** Right **Pos:** PH/PR-3; DH-1; 3B-1   **Ht:** 6'2" **Wt:** 205 **Born:** 9/15/77 **Age:** 23

Year Team	Lg	G	AB	H	2B	3B	HR	(Hm	Rd)	TB	R	RBI	TBB	IBB	SO	HBP	SH	SF	SB	CS	SB%	GDP	Avg	OBP	SLG
1996 Yakima	A-	66	257	68	11	1	4	—	—	93	31	27	7	0	46	3	2	1	8	3	.73	5	.265	.291	.362
1997 Savannah	A	130	475	100	17	5	5	—	—	142	57	47	38	0	83	5	3	4	11	3	.79	9	.211	.274	.299
1998 Vero Beach	A+	73	266	65	9	0	0	—	—	74	28	30	23	0	43	2	1	2	13	3	.81	6	.244	.307	.278
San Antonio	AA	50	160	35	6	0	1	—	—	44	19	9	6	0	28	0	1	1	2	0	1.00	9	.219	.246	.275
1999 Vero Beach	A+	127	474	141	26	2	9	—	—	198	68	54	36	2	66	14	4	5	24	13	.65	6	.297	.361	.418
2000 St. Pete	A+	5	16	3	2	0	0	—	—	5	2	0	2	0	3	1	1	0	1	0	1.00	0	.188	.316	.313
Orlando	AA	14	51	13	5	0	0	—	—	18	6	3	7	0	6	1	0	1	1	1	.50	0	.255	.350	.353
2000 Tampa Bay	AL	4	3	1	0	0	0	(0	0)	1	0	0	0	0	1	0	0	0	0	0	—	0	.333	.333	.333

J.C. Romero

Pitches: Left **Bats:** Both **Pos:** SP-11; RP-1   **Ht:** 5'11" **Wt:** 195 **Born:** 6/4/76 **Age:** 25

Year Team	Lg	G	GS	CG	GF	IP	BFP	H	R	ER	HR	SH	SF	HB	TBB	IBB	SO	WP	Bk	W	L	Pct.	ShO	Sv-Op	Hld	ERA
1997 Elizabethtn	R+	18	0	0	12	24	110	27	16	13	4	1	0	4	7	0	29	0	4	3	2	.600	0	3--	—	4.88
Fort Myers	A+	7	1	0	3	12.1	50	11	6	6	1	0	0	1	4	0	9	0	0	1	1	.500	0	0--	—	4.38
1998 New Britain	AA	51	1	0	14	78	324	48	28	19	3	6	2	4	43	3	79	13	0	6	3	.667	0	2--	—	2.19
1999 New Britain	AA	36	1	0	17	53	244	51	25	20	6	3	2	4	34	0	53	2	1	4	4	.500	0	7--	—	3.40
Salt Lake	AAA	15	0	0	7	19.2	89	18	11	7	1	1	1	1	14	0	20	3	0	4	1	.800	0	1--	—	3.20
2000 Fort Myers	A+	2	0	0	0	4.2	20	4	1	1	0	0	0	1	1	0	3	0	0	0	0	—	0	0--	—	1.93
Salt Lake	AAA	17	11	1	4	65.1	278	60	40	25	6	1	2	4	25	0	38	3	0	4	2	.667	0	4--	—	3.44
1999 Minnesota	AL	5	0	0	3	9.2	39	13	4	4	0	0	0	0	6	0	4	0	0	0	0	—	0	0-0	0	3.72
2000 Minnesota	AL	12	11	0	0	57.2	268	72	51	45	8	4	2	1	30	0	50	2	1	2	7	.222	0	0-0	0	7.02
2 ML YEARS		17	11	0	3	67.1	307	85	55	49	8	4	2	1	30	0	54	2	1	2	7	.222	0	0-0	0	6.55

Rafael Roque

Pitches: Left **Bats:** Left **Pos:** RP-4   **Ht:** 6'4" **Wt:** 189 **Born:** 10/27/73 **Age:** 27

Year Team	Lg	G	GS	CG	GF	IP	BFP	H	R	ER	HR	SH	SF	HB	TBB	IBB	SO	WP	Bk	W	L	Pct.	ShO	Sv-Op	Hld	ERA
2000 Indianapols *	AAA	25	20	1	0	132.1	576	127	66	61	18	7	2	6	63	0	111	2	0	9	4	.692	0	0-0	0	4.15
1998 Milwaukee	NL	9	9	0	0	48	206	42	28	26	9	4	0	1	24	0	34	3	1	4	2	.667	0	0-0	0	4.88
1999 Milwaukee	NL	43	9	0	7	84.1	386	96	52	50	16	1	3	4	42	1	66	4	1	1	6	.143	0	1-2	8	5.34
2000 Milwaukee	NL	4	0	0	1	5.1	29	7	6	6	1	0	1	0	7	1	4	0	0	0	0	—	0	0-0	0	10.13
3 ML YEARS		56	18	0	8	137.2	621	145	86	82	26	5	4	5	73	2	104	7	2	5	8	.385	0	1-2	8	5.36

Jose Rosado

Pitches: Left **Bats:** Left **Pos:** SP-5   **Ht:** 6'0" **Wt:** 185 **Born:** 11/9/74 **Age:** 26

Year Team	Lg	G	GS	CG	GF	IP	BFP	H	R	ER	HR	SH	SF	HB	TBB	IBB	SO	WP	Bk	W	L	Pct.	ShO	Sv-Op	Hld	ERA
1996 Kansas City	AL	16	16	2	0	106.2	441	101	39	38	7	1	4	4	26	1	64	5	1	8	6	.571	0	0-0	0	3.21
1997 Kansas City	AL	33	33	2	0	203.1	881	208	117	106	26	6	11	4	73	3	129	4	2	9	12	.429	0	0-0	0	4.69
1998 Kansas City	AL	38	25	2	1	174.2	757	180	106	91	25	1	3	5	57	2	135	6	1	8	11	.421	0	1-1	2	4.69
1999 Kansas City	AL	33	33	5	0	208	882	197	103	89	24	8	4	5	72	1	141	9	0	10	14	.417	2	0-0	0	3.85
2000 Kansas City	AL	5	5	0	0	27.2	122	29	18	18	4	1	1	4	9	0	15	0	1	2	2	.500	0	0-0	0	5.86
5 ML YEARS		125	112	11	1	720.1	3083	715	383	342	86	17	23	22	237	7	484	24	5	37	45	.451	2	1-1	2	4.27

Brian Rose

Pitches: Right **Bats:** Right **Pos:** SP-24; RP-3   **Ht:** 6'3" **Wt:** 215 **Born:** 2/13/76 **Age:** 25

Year Team	Lg	G	GS	CG	GF	IP	BFP	H	R	ER	HR	SH	SF	HB	TBB	IBB	SO	WP	Bk	W	L	Pct.	ShO	Sv-Op	Hld	ERA
2000 Pawtucket *	AAA	5	5	1	0	31	134	28	13	11	2	0	2	1	13	0	20	0	0	4	1	.800	0	0--	—	3.19
1997 Boston	AL	1	1	0	0	3	16	5	4	4	0	0	0	2	0	0	3	0	0	0	0	—	0	0-0	0	12.00
1998 Boston	AL	8	8	0	0	37.2	168	43	32	29	9	0	1	2	14	0	18	0	0	1	4	.200	0	0-0	0	6.93
1999 Boston	AL	22	18	0	1	98	433	112	59	53	19	2	0	2	29	2	51	0	0	7	6	.538	0	0-0	0	4.87
2000 Bos-Col		27	24	0	1	116.2	532	130	78	75	21	4	3	6	51	9	64	4	1	7	10	.412	0	0-0	0	5.79
2000 Boston	AL	15	12	0	1	53	239	58	37	36	11	1	2	3	21	3	24	2	0	3	5	.375	0	0-0	0	6.11
Colorado	NL	12	12	0	0	63.2	293	72	41	39	10	2	2	3	30	6	40	2	1	4	5	.444	0	0-0	0	5.51
4 ML YEARS		58	51	0	2	255.1	1149	290	173	161	49	5	5	10	96	11	136	4	1	15	20	.429	0	0-0	0	5.67

John Roskos

Bats: R **Throws:** R **Pos:** PH/PR-7; LF-4; 1B-2; RF-2   **Ht:** 5'11" **Wt:** 195 **Born:** 11/19/74 **Age:** 26

Year Team	Lg	G	AB	H	2B	3B	HR	(Hm	Rd)	TB	R	RBI	TBB	IBB	SO	HBP	SH	SF	SB	CS	SB%	GDP	Avg	OBP	SLG
1993 Marlins	R	11	40	7	1	0	1	—	—	11	6	3	5	0	11	1	0	0	1	1	.50	0	.175	.283	.275
1994 Elmira	A-	39	136	38	7	0	4	—	—	57	11	23	27	0	37	0	0	2	0	1	.00	1	.279	.394	.419
1995 Kane County	A	114	418	124	36	3	12	—	—	202	74	88	42	1	86	6	0	6	2	0	1.00	5	.297	.364	.483
1996 Portland	AA	121	396	109	26	3	9	—	—	168	53	58	67	4	102	5	0	2	4	4	.43	5	.275	.385	.424
1997 Portland	AA	123	451	139	31	1	24	—	—	244	66	84	50	2	81	0	0	6	4	6	.40	17	.308	.373	.541
1998 Charlotte	AAA	115	416	118	23	1	10	—	—	173	54	62	43	0	84	3	0	3	0	4	.00	15	.284	.353	.416
1999 Calgary	AAA	134	506	162	44	0	24	—	—	278	85	90	52	2	112	3	0	9	2	1	.67	18	.320	.381	.549
2000 Las Vegas	AAA	99	377	120	29	0	18	—	—	203	75	74	53	1	67	2	0	4	2	5	.29	14	.318	.401	.538
1998 Florida	NL	10	10	1	0	0	0	(0	0)	1	1	0	1	0	5	0	0	0	0	0	—	0	.100	.100	.100
1999 Florida	NL	13	12	2	0	0	0	(0	0)	4	0	1	1	0	7	0	0	0	0	0	—	0	.167	.231	.333
2000 San Diego	NL	14	27	1	1	0	0	(0	0)	2	0	1	3	0	7	0	0	0	0	0	—	1	.037	.133	.074
3 ML YEARS		37	49	4	3	0	0	(0	0)	7	1	2	4	0	19	0	0	0	0	0	—	1	.082	.151	.143

Kirk Rueter

Pitches: Left **Bats:** Left **Pos:** SP-31; RP-1 **Ht:** 6'2" **Wt:** 205 **Born:** 12/1/70 **Age:** 30

Year Team	Lg	G	GS	CG	GF	IP	BFP	H	R	ER	HR	SH	SF	HB	TBB	IBB	SO	WP	Bk	W	L	Pct.	ShO	Sv-Op	Hld	ERA
1993 Montreal	NL	14	14	1	0	85.2	341	85	33	26	5	1	0	0	18	1	31	0	0	8	0	1.000	0	0-0	0	2.73
1994 Montreal	NL	20	20	0	0	92.1	397	106	60	53	11	6	6	2	23	1	50	2	0	7	3	.700	0	0-0	0	5.17
1995 Montreal	NL	9	9	1	0	47.1	184	38	17	17	3	4	0	1	9	0	28	0	0	5	3	.625	1	0-0	0	3.23
1996 Mon-SF	NL	20	19	0	0	102	430	109	50	45	12	4	1	2	27	0	46	2	0	6	8	.429	0	0-0	0	3.97
1997 San Francisco	NL	32	32	0	0	190.2	802	194	83	73	17	10	6	1	51	8	115	3	0	13	6	.684	0	0-0	0	3.45
1998 San Francisco	NL	33	33	1	0	187.2	806	193	100	91	27	5	8	7	57	3	102	6	0	16	9	.640	0	0-0	0	4.36
1999 San Francisco	NL	33	33	1	0	184.2	804	219	118	111	28	6	4	2	55	2	94	2	0	15	10	.600	0	0-0	0	5.41
2000 San Francisco	NL	32	31	0	0	184	799	205	92	81	23	19	9	2	62	5	71	1	0	11	9	.550	0	0-0	0	3.96
1996 Montreal	NL	16	16	0	0	78.2	338	91	44	40	12	4	1	2	22	0	30	0	0	5	6	.455	0	0-0	0	4.58
San Francisco	NL	4	3	0	0	23.1	92	18	6	5	0	0	0	0	5	0	16	2	0	1	2	.333	0	0-0	0	1.93
8 ML YEARS		193	191	4	0	1074.1	4563	1149	553	497	126	55	34	17	302	20	537	16	0	81	48	.628	1	0-0	0	4.16

Johnny Ruffin

Pitches: Right **Bats:** Right **Pos:** RP-5 **Ht:** 6'3" **Wt:** 170 **Born:** 7/29/71 **Age:** 29

Year Team	Lg	G	GS	CG	GF	IP	BFP	H	R	ER	HR	SH	SF	HB	TBB	IBB	SO	WP	Bk	W	L	Pct.	ShO	Sv-Op	Hld	ERA
2000 Tucson *	AAA	45	0	0	36	57.1	245	48	21	19	4	1	0	0	25	1	66	2	0	5	3	.625	0	20--	—	2.98
1993 Cincinnati	NL	21	0	0	5	37.2	159	36	16	15	4	1	0	1	11	1	30	2	0	2	1	.667	0	2-3	2	3.58
1994 Cincinnati	NL	51	0	0	13	70	287	57	26	24	7	2	2	0	27	3	44	5	1	7	2	.778	0	1-3	11	3.09
1995 Cincinnati	NL	10	0	0	6	13.1	54	4	3	2	0	0	0	0	11	0	11	3	0	0	0	—	0	0-0	1	1.35
1996 Cincinnati	NL	49	0	0	13	62.1	289	71	42	38	10	4	3	2	37	5	69	8	0	1	3	.250	0	0-1	1	5.49
2000 Arizona	NL	5	0	0	2	9	43	14	9	9	4	0	0	0	3	1	5	0	0	0	0	—	0	0-0	0	9.00
5 ML YEARS		136	0	0	39	192.1	832	182	96	88	25	7	5	3	89	10	159	18	1	10	6	.625	0	3-7	15	4.12

Sean Runyan

Pitches: Left **Bats:** Left **Pos:** RP-3 **Ht:** 6'3" **Wt:** 210 **Born:** 6/21/74 **Age:** 27

Year Team	Lg	G	GS	CG	GF	IP	BFP	H	R	ER	HR	SH	SF	HB	TBB	IBB	SO	WP	Bk	W	L	Pct.	ShO	Sv-Op	Hld	ERA
2000 Jacksonville *	AA	3	0	0	1	1.2	11	4	4	4	0	0	0	0	2	0	1	0	0	0	0	—	0	0--	—	21.60
Toledo *	AAA	44	0	0	11	49.1	238	58	36	32	8	1	4	0	35	1	32	6	0	1	2	.333	0	1--	—	5.84
1998 Detroit	AL	88	0	0	11	50.1	223	47	23	20	7	2	7	2	28	3	39	5	0	1	4	.200	0	1-3	11	3.58
1999 Detroit	AL	12	0	0	2	10.2	45	9	4	4	2	1	2	1	3	1	6	2	0	0	1	.000	0	0-0	1	3.38
2000 Detroit	AL	3	0	0	0	3	12	2	2	2	0	0	1	0	2	0	1	0	0	0	0	—	0	0-0	0	6.00
3 ML YEARS		103	0	0	13	64	280	58	29	26	9	3	10	3	33	4	46	7	0	1	5	.167	0	1-3	12	3.66

Ryan Rupe

Pitches: Right **Bats:** Right **Pos:** SP-18 **Ht:** 6'5" **Wt:** 230 **Born:** 3/31/75 **Age:** 26

Year Team	Lg	G	GS	CG	GF	IP	BFP	H	R	ER	HR	SH	SF	HB	TBB	IBB	SO	WP	Bk	W	L	Pct.	ShO	Sv-Op	Hld	ERA
1998 Hudson Val	A-	3	3	0	0	13.1	50	8	1	1	0	1	0	0	2	0	18	1	0	1	0	1.000	0	0--	—	0.68
Chston-SC	A	10	10	0	0	56.1	215	33	18	15	3	0	1	6	9	0	62	3	0	6	1	.857	0	0--	—	2.40
1999 Orlando	AA	5	5	0	0	26.1	109	18	13	8	1	0	0	2	6	0	22	1	1	2	2	.500	0	0--	—	2.73
2000 Durham	AAA	5	5	0	0	19.1	87	24	16	14	3	0	0	1	7	0	18	2	0	1	0	1.000	0	0--	—	6.52
1999 Tampa Bay	AL	24	24	0	0	142.1	614	136	81	72	17	1	7	12	57	2	97	4	1	8	9	.471	0	0-0	0	4.55
2000 Tampa Bay	AL	18	18	0	0	91	425	121	75	70	19	2	6	9	31	3	61	4	0	5	6	.455	0	0-0	0	6.92
2 ML YEARS		42	42	0	0	233.1	1039	257	156	142	36	3	13	21	88	5	158	8	1	13	15	.464	0	0-0	0	5.48

Glendon Rusch

Pitches: Left **Bats:** Left **Pos:** SP-30; RP-1 **Ht:** 6'1" **Wt:** 200 **Born:** 11/7/74 **Age:** 26

Year Team	Lg	G	GS	CG	GF	IP	BFP	H	R	ER	HR	SH	SF	HB	TBB	IBB	SO	WP	Bk	W	L	Pct.	ShO	Sv-Op	Hld	ERA
1997 Kansas City	AL	30	27	1	0	170.1	758	206	111	104	28	8	7	7	52	0	116	0	1	6	9	.400	0	0-0	0	5.50
1998 Kansas City	AL	29	24	1	2	154.2	686	191	104	101	22	1	2	4	50	0	94	1	0	6	15	.286	1	1-1	0	5.88
1999 KC-NYM		4	0	0	2	5	26	8	7	7	1	0	0	0	3	0	4	0	0	0	1	.000	0	0-0	0	12.60
2000 New York	NL	31	30	2	0	190.2	802	196	91	85	18	10	7	6	44	2	157	2	0	11	11	.500	0	0-0	0	4.01
1999 Kansas City	AL	3	0	0	1	4	23	7	7	7	1	0	0	0	3	0	4	0	0	0	1	.000	0	0-0	0	15.75
New York	NL	1	0	0	1	1	3	1	0	0	0	0	0	0	0	0	0	0	0	0	0	—	0	0-0	0	0.00
4 ML YEARS		94	81	4	4	520.2	2272	601	313	297	69	19	16	18	149	2	371	3	1	23	36	.390	1	1-1	0	5.13

B.J. Ryan

Pitches: Left **Bats:** Left **Pos:** RP-42 **Ht:** 6'6" **Wt:** 230 **Born:** 12/28/75 **Age:** 25

Year Team	Lg	G	GS	CG	GF	IP	BFP	H	R	ER	HR	SH	SF	HB	TBB	IBB	SO	WP	Bk	W	L	Pct.	ShO	Sv-Op	Hld	ERA
1998 Billings	R+	14	0	0	11	18.2	76	15	4	4	0	0	0	0	5	0	25	0	3	2	1	.667	0	4--	—	1.93
Chstn-WV	A	3	0	0	3	4.1	15	1	1	1	0	1	0	0	1	0	5	1	0	0	0	—	0	2--	—	2.08
Chattanooga	AA	16	0	0	6	16.1	67	13	4	4	0	1	1	0	6	0	21	0	0	1	0	1.000	0	4--	—	2.20
1999 Chattanooga	AA	35	0	0	23	41.2	172	33	13	12	1	2	1	0	17	0	46	2	2	2	1	.667	0	6--	—	2.59
Indianapolis	AAA	11	0	0	4	9	37	9	4	4	0	0	0	0	3	1	12	1	0	1	0	1.000	0	0--	—	4.00
Rochester	AAA	11	0	0	3	14.1	55	8	4	4	2	1	0	0	4	1	20	1	0	0	0	—	0	1--	—	2.51
2000 Rochester	AAA	14	4	0	3	24.2	105	23	13	13	4	1	1	1	9	0	28	2	0	1	0	1.000	0	0--	—	4.74
1999 Cin-Bal		14	0	0	3	20.1	82	13	7	7	0	0	1	0	13	1	29	1	0	1	0	1.000	0	0-0	0	3.10
2000 Baltimore	AL	42	0	0	9	42.2	193	36	29	28	7	1	1	0	31	1	41	2	1	2	3	.400	0	0-3	7	5.91
1999 Cincinnati	NL	1	0	0	0	2	9	4	1	1	0	0	0	0	1	0	1	0	0	0	0	—	0	0-0	0	4.50
Baltimore	AL	13	0	0	3	18.1	73	9	6	6	0	0	1	0	12	1	28	1	0	1	0	1.000	0	0-0	0	2.95
2 ML YEARS		56	0	0	12	63	275	49	36	35	7	1	2	0	44	2	70	3	1	3	3	.500	0	0-3	7	5.00

Jason Ryan

Pitches: Right **Bats:** Both **Pos:** RP-15; SP-1   **Ht:** 6'3" **Wt:** 195 **Born:** 1/23/76 **Age:** 25

Year Team	Lg	G	GS	CG	GF	IP	BFP	H	R	ER	HR	SH	SF	HB	TBB	IBB	SO	WP	Bk	W	L	Pct.	ShO	Sv-Op	Hld	ERA
1994 Cubs	R	7	7	0	0	33	143	32	19	15	2	1	1	2	4	0	30	5	0	1	2	.333	0	0--	—	4.09
Huntington	R+	4	4	1	0	26	93	7	1	1	0	1	0	1	8	0	32	0	0	2	0	1.000	1	0--	—	0.35
Orlando	AA	2	2	0	0	11	45	6	3	3	1	0	0	1	6	0	12	0	0	2	0	1.000	0	0--	—	2.45
1995 Daytona	A+	26	26	0	0	134.2	579	128	61	52	10	3	2	9	54	0	98	13	1	11	5	.688	0	0--	—	3.48
1996 Orlando	AA	7	7	0	0	34.2	169	39	30	22	6	1	0	4	24	0	25	2	0	2	5	.286	0	0--	—	5.71
Daytona	A+	17	10	0	3	67	298	72	42	39	8	5	2	4	33	0	49	1	0	1	8	.111	0	1--	—	5.24
1997 Daytona	A+	27	27	5	0	170.1	740	168	105	84	22	3	10	6	55	2	140	12	0	9	8	.529	0	0--	—	4.44
1998 West Tenn	AA	30	25	2	3	147.2	661	172	97	80	20	7	4	10	57	3	121	10	1	3	13	.188	0	0--	—	4.88
1999 West Tenn	AA	8	7	0	0	44.2	185	29	12	7	1	1	4	1	15	1	53	1	0	5	0	1.000	0	0--	—	1.41
New Britain	AA	8	8	0	0	50.2	217	48	29	27	6	1	0	1	24	0	42	3	0	2	4	.333	0	0--	—	4.80
Salt Lake	AAA	9	9	0	0	54.1	240	57	36	31	8	1	3	1	24	1	34	0	0	4	4	.500	0	0--	—	5.13
2000 Salt Lake	AAA	17	17	2	0	96.2	419	94	52	47	16	1	2	6	31	0	66	6	0	9	2	.818	1	0--	—	4.38
1999 Minnesota	AL	8	8	1	0	40.2	182	46	23	22	9	0	1	3	17	0	15	0	0	1	4	.200	0	0-0	0	4.87
2000 Minnesota	AL	16	1	0	6	26	125	37	24	22	8	0	2	1	10	0	19	2	0	0	1	.000	0	0-0	0	7.62
2 ML YEARS		24	9	1	6	66.2	307	83	47	44	17	0	3	4	27	0	34	2	0	1	5	.167	0	0-0	0	5.94

Rob Ryan

Bats: Left **Throws:** Left **Pos:** PH/PR-24; RF-2; DH-1   **Ht:** 5'11" **Wt:** 190 **Born:** 6/24/73 **Age:** 28

Year Team	Lg	G	AB	H	2B	3B	HR	(Hm	Rd)	TB	R	RBI	TBB	IBB	SO	HBP	SH	SF	SB	CS	SB%	GDP	Avg	OBP	SLG
1996 Lethbridge	R+	59	211	64	8	1	4	—	—	86	55	37	43	1	33	2	5	3	23	6	.79	2	.303	.421	.408
1997 South Bend	A	121	421	132	35	5	8	—	—	201	71	73	89	5	58	2	0	5	12	1	.92	7	.314	.431	.477
1998 Tucson	AAA	116	394	125	18	2	17	—	—	198	71	66	63	3	61	10	0	5	9	3	.75	5	.317	.419	.503
1999 Tucson	AAA	117	414	120	30	5	19	—	—	217	72	88	56	2	70	12	0	5	4	3	.57	13	.290	.386	.524
2000 Tucson	AAA	92	332	102	19	1	8	—	—	147	56	55	45	5	35	11	0	2	1	1	.50	9	.307	.405	.443
1999 Arizona	NL	20	29	7	1	0	2	(1	1)	14	4	5	1	0	8	0	0	0	0	0	—	0	.241	.267	.483
2000 Arizona	NL	27	27	8	1	1	0	(0	0)	11	4	2	4	0	7	1	0	0	0	0	—	0	.296	.406	.407
2 ML YEARS		47	56	15	2	1	2	(1	1)	25	8	7	5	0	15	1	0	0	0	0	—	0	.268	.339	.446

Donnie Sadler

Bats: R **Throws:** R **Pos:** SS-19; CF-13; 2B-12; PH/PR-7; 3B-3; LF-3; DH-2; RF-1   **Ht:** 5'6" **Wt:** 175 **Born:** 6/17/75 **Age:** 26

Year Team	Lg	G	AB	H	2B	3B	HR	(Hm	Rd)	TB	R	RBI	TBB	IBB	SO	HBP	SH	SF	SB	CS	SB%	GDP	Avg	OBP	SLG
2000 Pawtucket *	AAA	91	313	63	6	5	5	—	—	94	45	23	45	0	60	4	10	4	10	1	.91	8	.201	.306	.300
1998 Boston	AL	58	124	28	4	4	3	(0	3)	49	21	15	6	0	28	3	5	1	4	0	1.00	1	.226	.276	.395
1999 Boston	AL	49	107	30	5	1	0	(0	0)	37	18	4	5	0	20	0	3	0	2	1	.67	1	.280	.313	.346
2000 Boston	AL	49	99	22	5	0	1	(0	1)	30	14	10	5	0	18	1	5	2	3	1	.75	1	.222	.262	.303
3 ML YEARS		156	330	80	14	5	4	(0	4)	116	53	29	16	0	66	4	13	3	9	2	.82	3	.242	.283	.352

Olmedo Saenz

Bats: R **Throws:** R **Pos:** DH-27; PH/PR-24; 3B-18; 1B-17   **Ht:** 6'0" **Wt:** 185 **Born:** 10/8/70 **Age:** 30

Year Team	Lg	G	AB	H	2B	3B	HR	(Hm	Rd)	TB	R	RBI	TBB	IBB	SO	HBP	SH	SF	SB	CS	SB%	GDP	Avg	OBP	SLG
2000 Sacramento *	AAA	1	4	2	0	0	0	—	—	2	1	1	0	0	0	0	0	0	0	0	—	0	.500	.500	.500
1994 Chicago	AL	5	14	2	0	0	0	(0	0)	2	2	0	0	0	5	0	1	0	0	0	—	1	.143	.143	.286
1999 Oakland	AL	97	255	70	18	0	11	(8	3)	121	41	41	22	1	47	15	0	3	1	1	.50	6	.275	.363	.475
2000 Oakland	AL	76	214	67	12	2	9	(3	6)	110	40	33	25	2	40	7	0	1	0	0	1.00	6	.313	.401	.514
3 ML YEARS		178	483	139	30	2	20	(11	9)	235	83	74	47	3	92	22	1	4	2	1	.67	13	.288	.374	.487

Tim Salmon

Bats: Right **Throws:** Right **Pos:** RF-124; DH-33; PH/PR-2   **Ht:** 6'3" **Wt:** 231 **Born:** 8/24/68 **Age:** 32

Year Team	Lg	G	AB	H	2B	3B	HR	(Hm	Rd)	TB	R	RBI	TBB	IBB	SO	HBP	SH	SF	SB	CS	SB%	GDP	Avg	OBP	SLG
1992 California	AL	23	79	14	1	0	2	(1	1)	21	8	6	11	1	23	1	0	1	1	1	.50	1	.177	.283	.266
1993 California	AL	142	515	146	35	1	31	(23	8)	276	93	95	82	5	135	5	0	8	5	6	.45	6	.283	.382	.536
1994 California	AL	100	373	107	18	2	23	(11	12)	198	67	70	54	2	102	5	0	3	1	3	.25	3	.287	.382	.531
1995 California	AL	143	537	177	34	3	34	(15	19)	319	111	105	91	2	111	6	0	4	5	5	.50	9	.330	.429	.594
1996 California	AL	156	581	166	27	4	30	(18	12)	291	90	98	93	7	125	4	0	3	4	2	.67	8	.286	.386	.501
1997 Anaheim	AL	157	582	172	28	1	33	(17	16)	301	95	129	95	5	142	7	0	11	9	12	.43	7	.296	.394	.517
1998 Anaheim	AL	136	463	139	28	1	26	(13	13)	247	84	88	90	5	100	3	0	10	0	1	.00	4	.300	.410	.533
1999 Anaheim	AL	98	353	94	24	2	17	(7	10)	173	60	69	63	2	82	0	0	6	4	1	.80	7	.266	.372	.490
2000 Anaheim	AL	158	568	165	36	2	34	(17	17)	307	108	97	104	5	139	6	0	2	0	2	.00	14	.290	.404	.540
9 ML YEARS		1113	4051	1180	231	16	230	(123	107)	2133	716	757	683	34	959	37	0	48	29	33	.47	59	.291	.394	.527

Jesus Sanchez

Pitches: Left **Bats:** Left **Pos:** SP-32   **Ht:** 5'10" **Wt:** 155 **Born:** 10/11/74 **Age:** 26

Year Team	Lg	G	GS	CG	GF	IP	BFP	H	R	ER	HR	SH	SF	HB	TBB	IBB	SO	WP	Bk	W	L	Pct.	ShO	Sv-Op	Hld	ERA
1998 Florida	NL	35	29	0	1	173	765	178	98	86	18	12	4	4	91	2	137	8	5	7	9	.438	0	0-1	0	4.47
1999 Florida	NL	59	10	0	8	76.1	362	84	53	51	16	2	7	4	60	11	62	5	2	5	7	.417	0	0-2	11	6.01
2000 Florida	NL	32	32	2	0	182	805	197	118	108	32	9	12	4	76	4	123	4	0	9	12	.429	2	0-0	0	5.34
3 ML YEARS		126	71	2	9	431.1	1932	459	269	245	66	23	23	12	227	17	322	17	7	21	28	.429	2	0-3	11	5.11

Rey Sanchez

Bats: Right **Throws:** Right **Pos:** SS-143; PH/PR-2   **Ht:** 5'9" **Wt:** 175 **Born:** 10/5/67 **Age:** 33

Year Team	Lg	G	AB	H	2B	3B	HR	(Hm	Rd)	TB	R	RBI	TBB	IBB	SO	HBP	SH	SF	SB	CS	SB%	GDP	Avg	OBP	SLG
1991 Chicago	NL	13	23	6	0	0	0	(0	0)	6	1	2	4	0	3	0	0	0	0	0	—	0	.261	.370	.261
1992 Chicago	NL	74	255	64	14	3	1	(1	0)	87	24	19	10	1	17	3	5	2	2	1	.67	7	.251	.285	.341
1993 Chicago	NL	105	344	97	11	2	0	(0	0)	112	35	28	15	7	22	3	9	2	1	1	.50	8	.282	.316	.326
1994 Chicago	NL	96	291	83	13	1	0	(0	0)	98	26	24	20	4	29	7	4	1	2	5	.29	9	.285	.345	.337
1995 Chicago	NL	114	428	119	22	2	3	(0	3)	154	57	27	14	2	48	1	8	2	6	4	.60	9	.278	.301	.360
1996 Chicago	NL	95	289	61	9	0	1	(1	0)	73	28	12	22	6	42	3	8	2	7	1	.88	6	.211	.272	.253
1997 ChC-NYY		135	343	94	21	0	2	(1	1)	121	35	27	16	2	47	1	9	1	4	6	.40	8	.274	.307	.353
1998 San Francisco	NL	109	316	90	14	2	2	(0	2)	114	44	30	16	0	47	4	1	2	0	0	—	11	.285	.325	.361
1999 Kansas City	AL	134	479	141	18	6	2	(1	1)	177	66	56	22	2	48	4	10	3	11	5	.69	14	.294	.329	.370
2000 Kansas City	AL	143	509	139	18	2	1	(1	0)	164	68	38	28	0	55	4	11	3	7	3	.70	17	.273	.314	.322
1997 Chicago	NL	97	205	51	9	0	1	(1	0)	63	14	12	11	2	26	0	4	0	4	2	.67	7	.249	.287	.307
New York	AL	38	138	43	12	0	1	(0	1)	58	21	15	5	0	21	1	5	1	0	4	.00	1	.312	.338	.420
10 ML YEARS		1018	3277	894	140	18	12	(5	7)	1106	384	263	167	24	358	30	65	18	40	26	.61	89	.273	.312	.338

Anthony Sanders

Bats: Right **Throws:** Right **Pos:** RF-1; PH/PR-1   **Ht:** 6'2" **Wt:** 200 **Born:** 3/2/74 **Age:** 27

Year Team	Lg	G	AB	H	2B	3B	HR	(Hm	Rd)	TB	R	RBI	TBB	IBB	SO	HBP	SH	SF	SB	CS	SB%	GDP	Avg	OBP	SLG
1993 Medcine Hat	R+	63	225	59	9	3	4	—	—	86	44	33	20	0	49	2	3	1	6	5	.55	2	.262	.327	.382
1994 St.Cathrnes	A-	74	258	66	17	3	6	—	—	107	36	45	27	0	53	1	4	2	8	7	.53	2	.256	.326	.415
1995 Hagerstown	A	133	512	119	28	1	8	—	—	173	72	48	52	0	103	5	9	5	26	14	.65	8	.232	.307	.338
1996 Dunedin	A+	102	417	108	25	0	17	—	—	184	75	50	34	0	93	6	0	0	16	12	.57	5	.259	.324	.441
Knoxville	AA	38	133	36	8	0	1	—	—	47	16	18	7	0	33	2	1	0	1	3	.25	0	.271	.317	.353
1997 Dunedin	A+	1	5	1	1	0	0	—	—	2	0	1	1	0	1	0	0	0	0	0	—	0	.200	.333	.400
Knoxville	AA	111	429	114	20	4	26	—	—	220	68	69	44	3	121	3	4	4	20	12	.63	9	.266	.335	.513
1998 Syracuse	AAA	60	209	40	9	2	4	—	—	65	23	19	20	1	65	3	3	1	5	2	.71	3	.191	.270	.311
Knoxville	AA	6	25	10	2	0	4	—	—	24	9	9	2	0	6	0	0	0	1	0	1.00	0	.400	.444	.960
1999 Syracuse	AAA	124	496	121	22	5	18	—	—	207	71	59	46	0	111	3	8	5	18	10	.64	6	.244	.309	.417
2000 Tacoma	AAA	114	428	131	21	3	20	—	—	218	72	80	33	2	109	6	2	9	9	8	.53	9	.306	.357	.509
1999 Toronto	AL	3	7	2	1	0	0	(0	0)	3	1	2	0	0	2	0	0	0	0	0	—	1	.286	.286	.429
2000 Seattle	AL	1	1	1	0	0	0	(0	0)	1	1	0	0	0	0	0	0	0	0	0	—	0	1.000	1.000	1.000
2 ML YEARS		4	8	3	1	0	0	(0	0)	4	2	2	0	0	2	0	0	0	0	0	—	1	.375	.375	.500

Reggie Sanders

Bats: R **Throws:** R **Pos:** LF-69; RF-27; PH/PR-12; CF-1   **Ht:** 6'1" **Wt:** 185 **Born:** 12/1/67 **Age:** 33

Year Team	Lg	G	AB	H	2B	3B	HR	(Hm	Rd)	TB	R	RBI	TBB	IBB	SO	HBP	SH	SF	SB	CS	SB%	GDP	Avg	OBP	SLG
1991 Cincinnati	NL	9	40	8	0	0	1	(0	1)	11	6	3	0	0	9	0	0	0	1	1	.50	1	.200	.200	.275
1992 Cincinnati	NL	116	385	104	26	6	12	(6	6)	178	62	36	48	2	98	4	0	1	16	7	.70	6	.270	.356	.462
1993 Cincinnati	NL	138	496	136	16	4	20	(8	12)	220	90	83	51	7	118	5	3	8	27	10	.73	10	.274	.343	.444
1994 Cincinnati	NL	107	400	105	20	8	17	(10	7)	192	66	62	41	1	114	2	1	5	21	9	.70	2	.263	.332	.480
1995 Cincinnati	NL	133	484	148	36	6	28	(9	19)	280	91	99	69	4	122	8	0	6	36	12	.75	9	.306	.397	.579
1996 Cincinnati	NL	81	287	72	17	1	14	(7	7)	133	49	33	44	4	86	2	0	1	24	8	.75	8	.251	.353	.463
1997 Cincinnati	NL	86	312	79	19	2	19	(11	8)	159	52	56	42	3	93	3	1	0	13	7	.65	9	.253	.347	.510
1998 Cincinnati	NL	135	481	129	18	6	14	(7	7)	201	83	59	51	2	137	7	4	2	20	9	.69	10	.268	.346	.418
1999 San Diego	NL	133	478	136	24	7	26	(11	15)	252	92	72	65	1	108	6	0	1	36	13	.73	10	.285	.376	.527
2000 Atlanta	NL	103	340	79	23	1	11	(4	7)	137	43	37	32	2	78	2	3	0	21	4	.84	9	.232	.302	.403
10 ML YEARS		1041	3703	996	199	41	162	(73	89)	1763	634	540	443	26	963	39	12	22	215	80	.73	74	.269	.351	.476

Johan Santana

Pitches: Left **Bats:** Left **Pos:** RP-25; SP-5   **Ht:** 6'0" **Wt:** 195 **Born:** 3/13/79 **Age:** 22

Year Team	Lg	G	GS	CG	GF	IP	BFP	H	R	ER	HR	SH	SF	HB	TBB	IBB	SO	WP	Bk	W	L	Pct.	ShO	Sv-Op	Hld	ERA
1997 Auburn	A-	1	1	0	0	4	19	1	1	1	0	0	1	0	6	0	5	0	0	0	0	—	0	0- -	—	2.25
Astros	R	9	5	1	0	36.1	176	49	36	32	2	3	1	2	18	0	25	5	1	0	4	.000	0	0- -	—	7.93
1998 Quad City	A	2	1	0	0	6.2	36	14	7	7	1	2	0	0	3	0	6	1	0	0	1	.000	0	0- -	—	9.45
Auburn	A-	15	15	1	0	86.2	370	81	52	42	9	3	3	10	21	0	88	7	0	7	5	.583	1	0- -	—	4.36
1999 Michigan	A	27	26	1	0	160.1	688	162	94	83	14	1	6	10	55	0	150	10	1	8	8	.500	0	0- -	—	4.66
2000 Minnesota	AL	30	5	0	9	86	398	102	64	62	11	4	3	2	54	0	64	5	2	2	3	.400	0	0-0	0	6.49

Julio Santana

Pitches: Right **Bats:** Right **Pos:** RP-32; SP-4   **Ht:** 6'0" **Wt:** 225 **Born:** 1/20/74 **Age:** 27

Year Team	Lg	G	GS	CG	GF	IP	BFP	H	R	ER	HR	SH	SF	HB	TBB	IBB	SO	WP	Bk	W	L	Pct.	ShO	Sv-Op	Hld	ERA
2000 Pawtucket *	AAA	12	12	0	0	65	271	61	34	34	7	1	0	2	23	0	55	0	2	5	3	.625	0	0- -	—	4.71
1997 Texas	AL	30	14	0	3	104	496	141	86	78	16	1	5	4	49	2	64	8	1	4	6	.400	0	0-1	1	6.75
1998 Tex-TB	AL	35	19	1	5	145.2	630	151	77	71	18	2	5	5	62	3	61	3	0	5	6	.455	0	0-0	0	4.39
1999 Tampa Bay	AL	22	5	0	7	55.1	261	66	49	45	10	1	1	7	32	0	34	0	0	1	4	.200	0	0-0	0	7.32
2000 Montreal	NL	36	4	0	9	66.2	293	69	45	42	11	1	2	2	33	2	58	2	0	1	5	.167	0	0-2	1	5.67
1998 Texas	AL	3	0	0	0	5.1	27	7	5	5	0	0	0	0	4	1	2	0	0	0	0	—	0	0-0	0	8.44
Tampa Bay	AL	32	19	1	5	140.1	603	144	72	66	18	2	5	5	58	2	60	3	0	5	6	.455	0	0-0	0	4.23
4 ML YEARS		123	42	1	24	371.2	1680	427	257	236	55	5	13	18	176	7	217	13	1	11	21	.344	0	0-3	2	5.71

191

F.P. Santangelo

Bats: B **Throws:** R **Pos:** PH/PR-34; CF-27; LF-26; 2B-7; RF-1   **Ht:** 5'10" **Wt:** 165 **Born:** 10/24/67 **Age:** 33

Year Team	Lg	G	AB	H	2B	3B	HR	(Hm	Rd)	TB	R	RBI	TBB	IBB	SO	HBP	SH	SF	SB	CS	SB%	GDP	Avg	OBP	SLG
2000 San Berndno *	A+	7	19	9	2	1	0	—	—	13	2	1	2	1	2	0	0	0	1	1	.50	0	.474	.524	.684
1995 Montreal	NL	35	98	29	5	1	1	(1	0)	39	11	9	12	0	9	2	1	0	1	1	.50	1	.296	.384	.398
1996 Montreal	NL	152	393	109	20	5	7	(5	2)	160	54	56	49	4	61	11	9	5	5	2	.71	6	.277	.369	.407
1997 Montreal	NL	130	350	87	19	5	5	(5	0)	131	56	31	50	1	73	25	12	3	8	5	.62	1	.249	.379	.374
1998 Montreal	NL	122	383	82	18	0	4	(2	2)	112	53	23	44	1	72	23	11	1	7	3	.70	5	.214	.330	.292
1999 San Francisco	NL	113	254	66	17	3	3	(2	1)	98	49	26	53	0	54	11	5	2	12	4	.75	1	.260	.406	.386
2000 Los Angeles	NL	81	142	28	4	0	1	(0	1)	35	19	9	21	0	33	6	6	2	3	2	.60	5	.197	.322	.246
6 ML YEARS		633	1620	401	83	14	21	(15	6)	575	242	154	229	6	302	78	44	13	36	17	.68	18	.248	.365	.355

Benito Santiago

Bats: Right **Throws:** Right **Pos:** C-84; PH/PR-14   **Ht:** 6'1" **Wt:** 195 **Born:** 3/9/65 **Age:** 36

Year Team	Lg	G	AB	H	2B	3B	HR	(Hm	Rd)	TB	R	RBI	TBB	IBB	SO	HBP	SH	SF	SB	CS	SB%	GDP	Avg	OBP	SLG
1986 San Diego	NL	17	62	18	2	0	3	(2	1)	29	10	6	2	0	12	0	0	1	0	1	.00	0	.290	.308	.468
1987 San Diego	NL	146	546	164	33	2	18	(11	7)	255	64	79	16	2	112	5	1	4	21	12	.64	12	.300	.324	.467
1988 San Diego	NL	139	492	122	22	2	10	(3	7)	178	49	46	24	2	82	1	5	5	15	7	.68	18	.248	.282	.362
1989 San Diego	NL	129	462	109	16	3	16	(8	8)	179	50	62	26	6	89	1	3	2	11	6	.65	9	.236	.277	.387
1990 San Diego	NL	100	344	93	8	5	11	(5	6)	144	42	53	27	2	55	3	1	7	5	5	.50	4	.270	.323	.419
1991 San Diego	NL	152	580	155	22	3	17	(6	11)	234	60	87	23	5	114	4	0	7	8	10	.44	21	.267	.296	.403
1992 San Diego	NL	106	386	97	21	0	10	(8	2)	148	37	42	21	1	52	0	0	4	2	5	.29	14	.251	.287	.383
1993 Florida	NL	139	469	108	19	6	13	(6	7)	178	49	50	37	2	88	5	0	4	10	7	.59	9	.230	.291	.380
1994 Florida	NL	101	337	92	14	2	11	(4	7)	143	35	41	25	1	57	1	2	4	1	2	.33	11	.273	.322	.424
1995 Cincinnati	NL	81	266	76	20	0	11	(7	4)	129	40	44	24	1	48	4	0	2	2	2	.50	7	.286	.351	.485
1996 Philadelphia	NL	136	481	127	21	2	30	(8	22)	242	71	85	49	7	104	1	0	2	2	0	1.00	8	.264	.332	.503
1997 Toronto	AL	97	341	83	10	0	13	(7	6)	132	31	42	17	1	80	2	1	5	1	0	1.00	10	.243	.279	.387
1998 Toronto	AL	15	29	9	5	0	0	(0	0)	14	3	4	1	0	6	0	0	0	0	0	—	1	.310	.333	.483
1999 Chicago	NL	109	350	87	18	3	7	(2	5)	132	28	36	32	6	71	2	0	2	1	1	.50	12	.249	.313	.377
2000 Cincinnati	NL	89	252	66	11	1	8	(7	1)	103	22	45	19	8	45	1	0	5	2	2	.50	7	.262	.310	.409
15 ML YEARS		1556	5397	1406	242	29	178	(84	94)	2240	591	722	343	44	1015	30	13	54	81	60	.57	143	.261	.305	.415

Jose Santiago

Pitches: Right **Bats:** Right **Pos:** RP-45   **Ht:** 6'3" **Wt:** 215 **Born:** 11/5/74 **Age:** 26

Year Team	Lg	G	GS	CG	GF	IP	BFP	H	R	ER	HR	SH	SF	HB	TBB	IBB	SO	WP	Bk	W	L	Pct.	ShO	Sv-Op	Hld	ERA
2000 Omaha *	AAA	11	0	0	7	17	71	19	7	6	2	0	0	0	3	1	14	1	0	0	1	.000	0	4- -	—	3.18
1997 Kansas City	AL	4	0	0	3	4.2	24	7	2	1	0	0	0	1	2	1	1	0	0	0	0	—	0	0-0	—	1.93
1998 Kansas City	AL	2	0	0	2	2	9	4	2	2	0	0	0	0	0	0	2	0	0	0	0	—	0	0-0	—	9.00
1999 Kansas City	AL	34	0	0	15	47.1	203	46	23	18	7	1	3	2	14	2	15	2	1	3	4	.429	0	2-3	4	3.42
2000 Kansas City	AL	45	0	0	20	69	302	70	33	30	7	1	3	3	26	3	44	0	0	8	6	.571	0	2-8	5	3.91
4 ML YEARS		85	0	0	40	123	538	127	60	51	14	2	6	6	42	6	62	2	1	11	10	.524	0	4-11	9	3.73

Kazuhiro Sasaki

Pitches: Right **Bats:** Right **Pos:** RP-63   **Ht:** 6'4" **Wt:** 209 **Born:** 2/22/68 **Age:** 33

Year Team	Lg	G	GS	CG	GF	IP	BFP	H	R	ER	HR	SH	SF	HB	TBB	IBB	SO	WP	Bk	W	L	Pct.	ShO	Sv-Op	Hld	ERA
2000 Seattle	AL	63	0	0	58	62.2	265	42	25	22	10	2	2	2	31	5	78	1	0	2	5	.286	0	37-40	0	3.16

Luis Saturria

Bats: Right **Throws:** Right **Pos:** CF-5; RF-4; PH/PR-4   **Ht:** 6'2" **Wt:** 165 **Born:** 7/21/76 **Age:** 24

Year Team	Lg	G	AB	H	2B	3B	HR	(Hm	Rd)	TB	R	RBI	TBB	IBB	SO	HBP	SH	SF	SB	CS	SB%	GDP	Avg	OBP	SLG
1996 Johnson Cty	R+	57	227	58	7	1	5	—	—	82	43	40	24	0	61	7	1	0	12	1	.92	11	.256	.345	.361
1997 Peoria	A	122	445	122	19	5	11	—	—	184	81	51	44	3	95	3	3	3	23	10	.70	5	.274	.341	.413
1998 Pr William	A+	129	462	136	25	9	12	—	—	215	70	73	28	1	104	8	1	7	26	15	.63	12	.294	.341	.465
1999 Arkansas	AA	139	484	118	30	4	16	—	—	204	66	61	35	1	134	5	2	5	16	8	.67	12	.244	.299	.421
2000 Arkansas	AA	129	478	131	25	10	20	—	—	236	78	76	45	5	124	6	2	6	18	11	.62	7	.274	.340	.494
2000 St. Louis	NL	12	5	0	0	0	0	(0	0)	0	1	0	1	0	3	0	0	0	0	0	—	0	.000	.167	.000

Scott Sauerbeck

Pitches: Left **Bats:** Right **Pos:** RP-75   **Ht:** 6'3" **Wt:** 197 **Born:** 11/9/71 **Age:** 29

Year Team	Lg	G	GS	CG	GF	IP	BFP	H	R	ER	HR	SH	SF	HB	TBB	IBB	SO	WP	Bk	W	L	Pct.	ShO	Sv-Op	Hld	ERA
1994 Pittsfield	A-	21	0	0	9	48.1	200	39	16	11	0	3	1	1	19	2	39	4	0	3	1	.750	0	1- -	—	2.05
1995 St. Lucie	A+	20	1	0	4	26.2	116	26	10	6	0	0	2	0	14	1	25	2	2	0	1	.000	0	0- -	—	2.03
Capital Cty	A	19	0	0	13	33	139	28	14	12	2	2	0	1	14	1	33	3	1	5	4	.556	0	2- -	—	3.27
1996 St. Lucie	A+	17	16	2	0	99.1	406	101	37	25	1	3	0	1	27	0	62	4	1	6	6	.500	2	0- -	—	2.27
Binghamton	AA	8	8	2	0	46.2	191	48	24	18	4	1	2	1	12	0	30	0	0	3	3	.500	2	0- -	—	3.47
1997 Norfolk	AAA	1	1	0	0	5	20	3	2	2	0	0	1	0	4	0	4	1	0	1	0	1.000	0	0- -	—	3.60
Binghamton	AA	27	20	2	1	131.1	575	144	89	72	15	7	1	3	50	0	88	4	2	9	10	.471	0	0- -	—	4.93
1998 Norfolk	AAA	27	27	2	0	160.1	701	178	82	70	8	7	2	3	68	1	119	8	2	7	13	.350	0	0- -	—	3.93
2000 Nashville	AAA	2	0	0	0	2	6	1	0	0	0	0	0	0	0	0	0	0	0	0	0	—	0	0- -	—	0.00
1999 Pittsburgh	NL	65	0	0	16	67.2	287	53	19	15	6	4	0	4	38	5	55	3	0	4	1	.800	0	2-5	10	2.00
2000 Pittsburgh	NL	75	0	0	13	75.2	349	76	36	34	4	3	3	1	61	8	83	9	2	5	4	.556	0	1-4	13	4.04
2 ML YEARS		140	0	0	29	143.1	636	129	55	49	10	7	3	5	99	13	138	12	2	9	5	.643	0	3-9	23	3.08

Rich Sauveur

Pitches: Left **Bats:** Left **Pos:** RP-10   Ht: 6'4" **Wt:** 185 **Born:** 11/23/63 **Age:** 37

Year Team	Lg	G	GS	CG	GF	IP	BFP	H	R	ER	HR	SH	SF	HB	TBB	IBB	SO	WP	Bk	W	L	Pct.	ShO	Sv-Op	Hld	ERA
2000 Sacramento *	AAA	25	11	0	2	82.2	357	88	48	42	7	0	3	4	25	1	59	0	0	5	2	.714	0	1- -	—	4.57
1986 Pittsburgh	NL	3	3	0	0	12	57	17	8	8	3	1	0	2	6	0	6	0	2	0	0	—	0	0-0	0	6.00
1988 Montreal	NL	4	0	0	0	3	14	3	2	2	1	0	0	0	2	0	3	0	0	0	0	—	0	0-0	1	6.00
1991 New York	NL	6	0	0	0	3.1	19	7	4	4	1	2	0	0	2	0	4	0	0	0	0	—	0	0-2	2	10.80
1992 Kansas City	AL	8	0	0	2	14.1	65	15	7	7	1	0	0	2	8	1	7	0	1	0	1	.000	0	0-0	1	4.40
1996 Chicago	AL	3	0	0	0	3	15	3	5	5	1	0	0	1	5	0	1	0	0	0	0	—	0	0-0	0	15.00
2000 Oakland	AL	10	0	0	4	10.1	43	13	5	5	3	0	0	0	1	0	7	0	0	0	0	—	0	0-0	0	4.35
6 ML YEARS		34	3	0	6	46	213	58	31	31	10	3	0	5	24	1	28	0	3	0	1	.000	0	0-2	4	6.07

Bob Scanlan

Pitches: Right **Bats:** Right **Pos:** RP-2   Ht: 6'7" **Wt:** 215 **Born:** 8/9/66 **Age:** 34

Year Team	Lg	G	GS	CG	GF	IP	BFP	H	R	ER	HR	SH	SF	HB	TBB	IBB	SO	WP	Bk	W	L	Pct.	ShO	Sv-Op	Hld	ERA
2000 Indianapols *	AAA	57	0	0	51	60.1	243	42	16	12	4	4	1	2	18	4	23	1	0	2	2	.500	0	35- -	—	1.79
1991 Chicago	NL	40	13	0	16	111	482	114	60	48	5	8	6	3	40	3	44	5	1	7	8	.467	0	1-2	0	3.89
1992 Chicago	NL	69	0	0	41	87.1	360	76	32	28	4	4	2	1	30	6	42	6	4	3	6	.333	0	14-18	7	2.89
1993 Chicago	NL	70	0	0	13	75.1	323	79	41	38	6	2	6	3	28	7	44	0	2	4	5	.444	0	0-3	25	4.54
1994 Milwaukee	AL	30	12	0	9	103	441	117	53	47	11	1	2	4	28	2	65	3	1	2	6	.250	0	2-3	3	4.11
1995 Milwaukee	AL	17	14	0	1	83.1	389	101	66	61	9	0	6	7	44	3	29	3	0	4	7	.364	0	0-0	0	6.59
1996 Det-KC	AL	17	0	0	4	22.1	105	29	19	17	2	1	0	2	12	2	6	1	0	0	1	.000	0	0-1	5	6.85
1998 Houston	NL	27	0	0	9	26.1	118	24	12	9	4	3	3	1	13	0	9	5	0	0	1	.000	0	0-0	3	3.08
2000 Milwaukee	NL	2	0	0	1	1.2	13	6	6	5	0	1	1	1	0	0	1	0	0	0	0	—	0	0-0	0	27.00
1996 Detroit	AL	8	0	0	2	11	57	16	15	13	1	1	0	1	9	1	3	1	0	0	0	—	0	0-0	0	10.64
Kansas City	AL	9	0	0	2	11.1	48	13	4	4	1	0	0	1	3	1	3	0	0	0	1	.000	0	0-1	5	3.18
8 ML YEARS		272	39	0	94	510.1	2231	546	289	253	41	20	26	22	195	23	240	23	8	20	34	.370	0	17-27	45	4.46

Curt Schilling

Pitches: Right **Bats:** Right **Pos:** SP-29   Ht: 6'4" **Wt:** 231 **Born:** 11/14/66 **Age:** 34

Year Team	Lg	G	GS	CG	GF	IP	BFP	H	R	ER	HR	SH	SF	HB	TBB	IBB	SO	WP	Bk	W	L	Pct.	ShO	Sv-Op	Hld	ERA
2000 Clearwater *	A+	4	4	0	0	20.2	76	10	3	3	0	0	0	0	2	0	23	1	0	1	0	1.000	0	0- -	—	1.31
Scrantn-WB *	AAA	1	1	0	0	5	25	9	2	2	0	0	0	0	1	0	7	0	0	0	0	—	0	0- -	—	3.60
1988 Baltimore	AL	4	4	0	0	14.2	76	22	19	16	3	0	3	1	10	1	4	2	0	0	3	.000	0	0-0	0	9.82
1989 Baltimore	AL	5	1	0	0	8.2	38	10	6	6	2	0	0	0	3	0	6	1	0	0	1	.000	0	0-0	0	6.23
1990 Baltimore	AL	35	0	0	16	46	191	38	13	13	1	2	4	0	19	0	32	0	0	1	2	.333	0	3-9	5	2.54
1991 Houston	NL	56	0	0	34	75.2	336	79	35	32	2	5	1	0	39	7	71	4	1	3	5	.375	0	8-11	5	3.81
1992 Philadelphia	NL	42	26	10	10	226.1	895	165	67	59	11	7	8	1	59	4	147	4	0	14	11	.560	4	2-3	0	2.35
1993 Philadelphia	NL	34	34	7	0	235.1	982	234	114	105	23	9	7	4	57	6	186	9	3	16	7	.696	2	0-0	0	4.02
1994 Philadelphia	NL	13	13	1	0	82.1	360	87	42	41	10	6	1	3	28	3	58	3	1	2	8	.200	0	0-0	0	4.48
1995 Philadelphia	NL	17	17	1	0	116	473	96	52	46	12	5	2	3	26	2	114	0	1	7	5	.583	0	0-0	0	3.57
1996 Philadelphia	NL	26	26	8	0	183.1	732	149	69	65	16	6	4	3	50	5	182	5	0	9	10	.474	2	0-0	0	3.19
1997 Philadelphia	NL	35	35	7	0	254.1	1009	208	96	84	25	8	8	5	58	3	319	5	1	17	11	.607	2	0-0	0	2.97
1998 Philadelphia	NL	35	35	15	0	268.2	1089	236	101	97	23	14	7	6	61	3	300	12	0	15	14	.517	2	0-0	0	3.25
1999 Philadelphia	NL	24	24	8	0	180.1	735	159	74	71	25	11	3	5	44	0	152	4	0	15	6	.714	1	0-0	0	3.54
2000 Phi-Ari	NL	29	29	8	0	210.1	862	204	90	89	27	11	4	1	45	4	168	4	0	11	12	.478	2	0-0	0	3.81
2000 Philadelphia	NL	16	16	4	0	112.2	474	110	49	49	17	5	1	1	32	4	96	4	0	6	6	.500	1	0-0	0	3.91
Arizona	NL	13	13	4	0	97.2	388	94	41	40	10	6	3	0	13	0	72	0	0	5	6	.455	1	0-0	0	3.69
13 ML YEARS		355	244	65	60	1902	7778	1687	778	724	180	84	52	32	499	38	1739	53	7	110	95	.537	15	13-23	10	3.43

Jason Schmidt

Pitches: Right **Bats:** Right **Pos:** SP-11   Ht: 6'5" **Wt:** 213 **Born:** 1/29/73 **Age:** 28

Year Team	Lg	G	GS	CG	GF	IP	BFP	H	R	ER	HR	SH	SF	HB	TBB	IBB	SO	WP	Bk	W	L	Pct.	ShO	Sv-Op	Hld	ERA
2000 Pirates *	R	1	1	0	0	4	16	4	2	1	0	0	0	0	1	0	1	1	0	0	0	—	0	0- -	—	2.25
1995 Atlanta	NL	9	2	0	1	25	119	27	17	16	2	2	4	1	18	3	19	1	0	2	2	.500	0	0-1	0	5.76
1996 Atl-Pit	NL	19	17	1	0	96.1	445	108	67	61	10	4	9	2	53	0	74	8	1	5	6	.455	0	0-0	0	5.70
1997 Pittsburgh	NL	32	32	2	0	187.2	825	193	106	96	16	10	3	9	76	2	136	8	0	10	9	.526	0	0-0	0	4.60
1998 Pittsburgh	NL	33	33	0	0	214.1	916	228	106	97	24	10	3	4	71	3	158	15	1	11	14	.440	0	0-0	0	4.07
1999 Pittsburgh	NL	33	33	2	0	212.2	937	219	110	99	24	7	7	3	85	4	148	6	4	13	11	.542	0	0-0	0	4.19
2000 Pittsburgh	NL	11	11	0	0	63.1	295	71	43	38	6	1	2	1	41	2	51	1	0	2	5	.286	0	0-0	0	5.40
1996 Atlanta	NL	13	11	0	0	58.2	274	69	48	44	8	3	6	0	32	0	48	5	1	3	4	.429	0	0-0	0	6.75
Pittsburgh	NL	6	6	1	0	37.2	171	39	19	17	2	1	3	2	21	0	26	3	0	2	2	.500	0	0-0	0	4.06
6 ML YEARS		137	128	5	1	799.1	3537	846	449	407	82	34	28	20	344	14	586	39	6	43	47	.478	0	0-1	0	4.58

Brian Schneider

Bats: Left **Throws:** Right **Pos:** C-43; PH/PR-2   Ht: 6'1" **Wt:** 200 **Born:** 11/26/76 **Age:** 24

Year Team	Lg	G	AB	H	2B	3B	HR	(Hm	Rd)	TB	R	RBI	TBB	IBB	SO	HBP	SH	SF	SB	CS	SB%	GDP	Avg	OBP	SLG
1995 Expos	R	30	97	22	3	0	0	—	—	25	7	4	14	0	23	1	0	0	2	4	.33	1	.227	.330	.258
1996 Expos	R	52	164	44	5	2	0	—	—	53	26	23	24	3	15	3	2	0	2	3	.40	3	.268	.372	.323
Delmarva	A	5	9	3	0	0	0	—	—	3	0	1	1	0	1	1	0	0	0	0	—	1	.333	.455	.333
1997 Cape Fear	A	113	381	96	20	1	4	—	—	130	46	49	53	2	45	4	6	5	3	6	.33	9	.252	.345	.341
1998 Cape Fear	A	38	134	40	7	2	7	—	—	72	33	30	16	1	9	3	4	2	6	3	.67	3	.299	.381	.537
Jupiter	A+	82	302	82	12	1	3	—	—	105	32	30	22	1	38	1	0	2	4	4	.50	9	.272	.321	.348
1999 Harrisburg	AA	121	421	111	19	1	17	—	—	183	48	66	32	2	56	2	3	1	2	2	.50	6	.264	.318	.435
2000 Ottawa	AAA	67	238	59	22	3	4	—	—	99	22	31	16	1	42	0	2	9	1	0	1.00	5	.248	.285	.416
2000 Montreal	NL	45	115	27	6	0	0	(0	0)	33	6	11	7	2	24	0	0	1	0	1	.00	1	.235	.276	.287

Scott Schoeneweis

Pitches: Left **Bats:** Left **Pos:** SP-27   **Ht:** 6'0" **Wt:** 186 **Born:** 10/2/73 **Age:** 27

Year Team	Lg	G	GS	CG	GF	IP	BFP	H	R	ER	HR	SH	SF	HB	TBB	IBB	SO	WP	Bk	W	L	Pct.	ShO	Sv-Op	Hld	ERA
1996 Lk Elsinore	A+	14	12	0	1	93.2	387	86	47	41	6	3	2	2	27	0	83	2	1	8	3	.727	0	0--	—	3.94
1997 Midland	AA	20	20	3	0	113.1	510	145	84	75	7	1	5	1	39	0	94	8	1	7	5	.583	0	0--	—	5.96
1998 Vancouver	AAA	27	27	2	0	180	787	188	102	90	18	6	5	9	59	0	133	9	1	11	8	.579	0	0--	—	4.50
1999 Edmonton	AAA	9	7	0	0	35.1	177	58	35	30	6	0	1	3	12	0	29	4	0	2	4	.333	0	0--	—	7.64
2000 Lk Elsinore	A+	1	1	0	0	4.2	19	3	1	1	0	0	0	1	3	0	3	0	0	0	0	—	0	0--	—	1.93
Edmonton	AAA	1	1	0	0	7	25	2	1	0	0	0	0	0	1	0	6	0	0	0	0	—	0	0--	—	0.00
1999 Anaheim	AL	31	0	0	6	39.1	175	47	27	24	4	0	1	0	14	1	22	1	0	1	1	.500	0	0-0	3	5.49
2000 Anaheim	AL	27	27	1	0	170	742	183	112	103	21	2	5	6	67	2	78	4	3	7	10	.412	1	0-0	0	5.45
2 ML YEARS		58	27	1	6	209.1	917	230	139	127	25	2	6	6	81	3	100	5	3	8	11	.421	1	0-0	3	5.46

Pete Schourek

Pitches: Left **Bats:** Left **Pos:** SP-21   **Ht:** 6'5" **Wt:** 220 **Born:** 5/10/69 **Age:** 32

Year Team	Lg	G	GS	CG	GF	IP	BFP	H	R	ER	HR	SH	SF	HB	TBB	IBB	SO	WP	Bk	W	L	Pct.	ShO	Sv-Op	Hld	ERA
2000 Pawtucket *	AAA	1	1	0	0	3	11	1	0	0	0	0	0	0	1	0	1	0	0	0	0	—	0	0--	—	0.00
Sarasota *	A+	1	1	0	0	4.1	15	2	1	1	0	0	0	0	0	0	5	0	0	0	0	—	0	2--	—	2.08
1991 New York	NL	35	8	1	7	86.1	385	82	49	41	7	5	4	2	43	4	67	1	0	5	4	.556	1	2-3	3	4.27
1992 New York	NL	22	21	0	0	136	578	137	60	55	9	4	4	2	44	6	60	4	2	6	8	.429	0	0-0	0	3.64
1993 New York	NL	41	18	0	6	128.1	586	168	90	85	13	3	8	3	45	7	72	1	2	5	12	.294	0	0-1	2	5.96
1994 Cincinnati	NL	22	10	0	3	81.1	354	90	39	37	11	6	3	3	29	4	69	0	0	7	2	.778	0	0-0	0	4.09
1995 Cincinnati	NL	29	29	2	0	190.1	754	158	72	68	17	4	4	8	45	3	160	11	1	18	7	.720	0	0-0	0	3.22
1996 Cincinnati	NL	12	12	0	0	67.1	304	79	48	45	7	3	4	2	24	1	54	3	0	4	5	.444	0	0-0	0	6.01
1997 Cincinnati	NL	18	17	0	0	84.2	371	78	59	51	18	4	1	4	38	0	59	2	0	5	8	.385	0	0-0	0	5.42
1998 Hou-Bos		25	23	0	0	124	537	127	64	61	17	5	7	5	50	1	95	7	0	8	9	.471	0	0-0	1	4.43
1999 Pittsburgh	NL	30	17	0	2	113	511	128	75	67	20	3	8	5	49	5	94	0	0	4	7	.364	0	0-0	0	5.34
2000 Boston	AL	21	21	0	0	107.1	464	116	67	61	17	4	4	3	38	2	63	5	0	3	10	.231	0	0-0	0	5.11
1998 Houston	NL	15	15	0	0	80	354	82	43	40	10	5	4	4	36	0	59	5	0	7	6	.538	0	0-0	0	4.50
Boston	AL	10	8	0	0	44	183	45	21	21	7	0	3	1	14	1	36	2	0	1	3	.250	0	0-0	1	4.30
10 ML YEARS		255	176	3	18	1118.2	4844	1163	623	571	136	41	43	38	405	33	793	24	5	65	72	.474	1	2-4	6	4.59

Steve Schrenk

Pitches: Right **Bats:** Right **Pos:** RP-20   **Ht:** 6'3" **Wt:** 215 **Born:** 11/20/68 **Age:** 32

Year Team	Lg	G	GS	CG	GF	IP	BFP	H	R	ER	HR	SH	SF	HB	TBB	IBB	SO	WP	Bk	W	L	Pct.	ShO	Sv-Op	Hld	ERA
1987 White Sox	R	8	6	1	0	28.1	115	23	10	3	0	3	0	2	12	0	19	2	1	1	2	.333	1	0--	—	0.95
1988 South Bend	A	21	18	1	0	90	417	95	63	50	4	0	3	13	37	0	58	7	2	3	7	.300	0	0--	—	5.00
1989 South Bend	A	16	16	1	0	79	353	71	44	38	6	2	0	8	44	1	49	9	0	5	2	.714	0	0--	—	4.33
1990 South Bend	A	20	14	2	2	103.2	419	79	44	34	7	3	3	11	25	0	92	7	1	7	6	.538	1	0--	—	2.95
1991 White Sox	R	11	7	0	2	37	144	30	20	12	0	1	0	5	6	0	39	1	0	1	3	.250	0	0--	—	2.92
1992 Sarasota	A+	25	22	4	2	154	621	130	48	35	1	4	6	7	40	2	113	7	6	15	2	.882	2	1--	—	2.05
Birmingham	AA	2	2	0	0	12.1	59	13	5	5	0	0	1	0	11	0	9	1	0	1	1	.500	0	0--	—	3.65
1993 Birmingham	AA	8	8	2	0	61.2	224	31	11	8	2	1	1	1	7	0	51	3	0	5	1	.833	1	0--	—	1.17
Nashville	AAA	21	20	0	0	122.1	526	117	61	53	11	5	2	3	47	3	78	6	3	8	6	.429	0	0--	—	3.90
1994 Nashville	AAA	29	28	2	0	178.2	769	175	82	69	15	10	4	6	69	3	134	14	1	14	6	.700	1	0--	—	3.48
1995 White Sox	R	2	2	0	0	7	27	5	2	0	0	0	0	0	0	0	6	0	0	0	1	.000	0	0--	—	0.00
1996 Nashville	AAA	16	15	1	1	95.2	395	93	54	47	12	3	1	3	29	2	58	3	0	4	10	.286	0	0--	—	4.42
1997 Rochester	AAA	25	24	1	0	125.2	539	127	73	65	21	2	1	6	36	0	99	3	2	4	7	.364	0	0--	—	4.66
1998 Pawtucket	AAA	34	0	0	6	60.2	265	60	27	19	8	4	2	2	23	1	45	6	0	8	3	.727	0	0--	—	2.82
1999 Scrantn-WB	AAA	32	0	0	13	43	185	38	17	14	2	3	2	0	21	6	34	2	0	3	1	.750	0	2--	—	2.93
2000 Scrantn-WB	AAA	26	0	0	15	34.1	126	18	5	5	1	2	1	2	5	2	27	0	0	2	1	.667	0	3--	—	1.31
1999 Philadelphia	NL	32	2	0	8	50.1	209	41	24	24	6	3	1	7	14	4	36	2	0	1	3	.250	0	1-1	1	4.29
2000 Philadelphia	NL	20	0	0	6	23.1	109	25	20	19	3	1	1	5	13	0	19	0	0	2	3	.400	0	0-0	0	7.33
2 ML YEARS		52	2	0	14	73.2	318	66	44	43	9	4	2	8	27	4	55	2	0	3	6	.333	0	1-1	1	5.25

Rudy Seanez

Pitches: Right **Bats:** Right **Pos:** RP-23   **Ht:** 5'11" **Wt:** 205 **Born:** 10/20/68 **Age:** 32

Year Team	Lg	G	GS	CG	GF	IP	BFP	H	R	ER	HR	SH	SF	HB	TBB	IBB	SO	WP	Bk	W	L	Pct.	ShO	Sv-Op	Hld	ERA
2000 Greenville *	AA	2	1	0	0	2	8	2	0	0	0	0	0	0	0	0	3	0	0	0	0	—	0	0--	—	0.00
1989 Cleveland	AL	5	0	0	2	5	20	1	2	2	0	0	0	0	4	1	7	1	1	0	0	—	0	0-0	0	3.60
1990 Cleveland	AL	24	0	0	12	27.1	127	22	17	17	2	0	1	1	25	1	24	5	0	2	1	.667	0	0-0	3	5.60
1991 Cleveland	AL	5	0	0	0	5	33	10	12	9	2	0	0	0	7	0	7	2	0	0	0	—	0	0-1	0	16.20
1993 San Diego	NL	3	0	0	3	3.1	20	8	6	5	1	1	0	0	2	0	1	0	0	0	0	—	0	0-0	0	13.50
1994 Los Angeles	NL	17	0	0	6	23.2	104	24	7	7	2	4	2	1	9	1	18	3	0	1	1	.500	0	0-1	1	2.66
1995 Los Angeles	NL	37	0	0	12	34.2	159	39	27	26	5	3	0	1	18	3	29	0	0	1	3	.250	0	3-4	6	6.75
1998 Atlanta	NL	34	0	0	8	36	148	25	13	11	2	1	2	1	16	0	50	2	0	4	1	.800	0	2-4	8	2.75
1999 Atlanta	NL	56	0	0	13	53.2	225	47	21	20	3	0	2	1	21	1	41	3	0	6	1	.857	0	3-8	18	3.35
2000 Atlanta	NL	23	0	0	8	21	89	15	11	10	3	1	0	1	9	1	20	0	0	2	4	.333	0	2-3	6	4.29
9 ML YEARS		204	0	0	64	209.2	925	191	116	107	20	10	9	6	111	8	197	16	1	16	11	.593	0	10-21	42	4.59

Chris Seelbach

Pitches: Right **Bats:** Right **Pos:** RP-2   **Ht:** 6'4" **Wt:** 180 **Born:** 12/18/72 **Age:** 28

Year Team	Lg	G	GS	CG	GF	IP	BFP	H	R	ER	HR	SH	SF	HB	TBB	IBB	SO	WP	Bk	W	L	Pct.	ShO	Sv-Op	Hld	ERA
1991 Braves	R	4	4	0	0	15	65	13	7	7	3	1	0	0	6	0	19	3	1	0	1	.000	0	0--	—	4.20
1992 Macon	A	27	27	1	0	157.1	662	134	65	58	11	3	5	9	68	0	144	5	1	9	11	.450	0	0--	—	3.32
1993 Durham	A+	25	25	0	0	131.1	590	133	85	72	15	4	4	7	74	1	112	10	0	9	9	.500	0	0--	—	4.93

Year Team	Lg	G	GS	CG	GF	IP	BFP	H	R	ER	HR	SH	SF	HB	TBB	IBB	SO	WP	Bk	W	L	Pct.	ShO	Sv-Op	Hld	ERA
1994 Greenville	AA	15	15	2	0	92.2	363	64	26	24	3	5	3	4	38	2	79	5	0	4	6	.400	0	0--	—	2.33
Richmond	AAA	12	11	0	0	61.1	273	68	37	33	6	2	3	0	36	2	35	3	0	3	5	.375	0	0--	—	4.84
1995 Greenville	AA	9	9	1	0	60.1	249	38	15	11	2	5	3	4	30	0	65	3	1	6	0	1.000	1	0--	—	1.64
Richmond	AAA	14	14	1	0	73.1	314	64	39	38	7	0	3	2	39	0	65	3	0	4	6	.400	0	0--	—	4.66
1996 Charlotte	AAA	25	25	1	0	138.1	650	167	123	113	26	2	5	5	76	3	98	9	1	6	13	.316	0	0--	—	7.35
1997 Charlotte	AAA	16	6	0	1	50.1	241	58	36	35	7	3	3	1	34	2	50	3	0	5	0	1.000	0	0--	—	6.26
1998 Tacoma	AAA	6	0	0	4	11.2	53	13	9	8	5	0	0	0	2	0	10	0	0	1	0	1.000	0	0--	—	6.17
Orlando	AA	23	21	0	0	116	500	103	63	52	5	4	6	4	52	0	106	6	1	8	3	.727	0	0--	—	4.03
1999 Greenville	AA	8	6	1	0	39.1	170	31	18	17	5	1	1	2	19	2	47	2	0	3	2	.600	0	0--	—	3.89
Richmond	AAA	13	8	1	2	57.2	255	51	34	33	4	1	1	2	34	1	48	3	0	6	1	.857	0	0--	—	5.15
2000 Richmond	AAA	29	22	1	2	118.2	520	118	71	63	12	2	4	5	55	1	96	8	1	5	9	.357	1	2--	—	4.78
2000 Atlanta	NL	2	0	0	2	1.2	7	3	2	2	0	0	1	0	0	0	1	0	0	0	1	.000	0	0-0	0	10.80

Kevin Sefcik

Bats: R **Throws:** R **Pos:** PH/PR-62; LF-25; CF-20; RF-9; DH-1   **Ht:** 5'10" **Wt:** 182 **Born:** 2/10/71 **Age:** 30

Year Team	Lg	G	AB	H	2B	3B	HR	(Hm	Rd)	TB	R	RBI	TBB	IBB	SO	HBP	SH	SF	SB	CS	SB%	GDP	Avg	OBP	SLG
1995 Philadelphia	NL	5	4	0	0	0	0	(0	0)	0	1	0	0	0	2	0	0	0	0	0	--	0	.000	.000	.000
1996 Philadelphia	NL	44	116	33	5	3	0	(0	0)	44	10	9	9	3	16	2	1	2	3	0	1.00	4	.284	.341	.379
1997 Philadelphia	NL	61	119	32	3	0	2	(2	0)	41	11	6	4	0	9	1	7	0	1	2	.33	4	.269	.298	.345
1998 Philadelphia	NL	104	169	53	7	2	3	(2	1)	73	27	20	25	0	32	7	3	1	4	2	.67	3	.314	.421	.432
1999 Philadelphia	NL	111	209	58	15	3	1	(0	1)	82	28	11	29	0	24	1	3	0	9	4	.69	4	.278	.368	.392
2000 Philadelphia	NL	99	153	36	6	2	0	(0	0)	46	15	10	13	0	19	2	1	2	4	2	.67	4	.235	.300	.301
6 ML YEARS		424	770	212	36	10	6	(5	1)	286	92	56	80	3	102	13	15	5	21	10	.68	19	.275	.351	.371

David Segui

Bats: B **Throws:** L **Pos:** 1B-73; DH-67; RF-7; PH/PR-5   **Ht:** 6'1" **Wt:** 202 **Born:** 7/19/66 **Age:** 34

Year Team	Lg	G	AB	H	2B	3B	HR	(Hm	Rd)	TB	R	RBI	TBB	IBB	SO	HBP	SH	SF	SB	CS	SB%	GDP	Avg	OBP	SLG
1990 Baltimore	AL	40	123	30	7	0	2	(1	1)	43	14	15	11	2	15	1	1	0	0	0	--	12	.244	.311	.350
1991 Baltimore	AL	86	212	59	7	0	2	(1	1)	72	15	22	12	2	19	0	3	1	1	1	.50	7	.278	.316	.340
1992 Baltimore	AL	115	189	44	9	0	1	(1	0)	56	21	17	20	3	23	0	2	0	1	0	1.00	4	.233	.306	.296
1993 Baltimore	AL	146	450	123	27	0	10	(6	4)	180	54	60	58	4	53	0	3	8	2	1	.67	18	.273	.351	.400
1994 New York	AL	92	336	81	17	1	10	(5	5)	130	46	43	33	6	43	1	1	3	0	0	--	6	.241	.308	.387
1995 NYM-Mon	NL	130	456	141	25	4	12	(6	6)	210	68	68	40	5	47	3	8	3	2	7	.22	10	.309	.367	.461
1996 Montreal	NL	115	416	119	30	1	11	(6	5)	184	69	58	60	4	54	0	0	1	4	4	.50	8	.286	.375	.442
1997 Montreal	NL	125	459	141	22	3	21	(10	11)	232	75	68	57	12	66	1	0	6	1	0	1.00	8	.307	.380	.505
1998 Seattle	AL	143	522	159	36	1	19	(10	9)	254	79	84	49	4	80	0	0	9	3	1	.75	12	.305	.359	.487
1999 Sea-Tor	AL	121	440	131	27	3	14	(5	9)	206	57	52	40	4	60	1	1	4	1	2	.33	10	.298	.355	.468
2000 Tex-Cle	AL	150	574	192	42	1	19	(8	11)	293	93	103	53	2	84	1	0	6	0	1	.00	20	.334	.388	.510
1995 New York	NL	33	73	24	3	1	2	(2	0)	35	9	11	12	1	9	1	4	2	1	3	.25	2	.329	.420	.479
Montreal	NL	97	383	117	22	3	10	(4	6)	175	59	57	28	4	38	2	4	1	1	4	.20	8	.305	.355	.457
1999 Seattle	AL	90	345	101	22	3	9	(4	5)	156	43	39	32	4	43	1	1	3	1	2	.33	9	.293	.352	.452
Toronto	AL	31	95	30	5	0	5	(1	4)	50	14	13	8	0	17	0	0	1	0	0	--	1	.316	.365	.526
2000 Texas	AL	93	351	118	29	1	11	(4	7)	182	52	57	34	1	51	0	0	4	0	1	.00	12	.336	.391	.519
Cleveland	AL	57	223	74	13	0	8	(4	4)	111	41	46	19	1	33	1	0	2	0	0	--	8	.332	.384	.498
11 ML YEARS		1263	4177	1220	249	14	121	(59	62)	1860	591	590	433	48	544	8	19	41	15	17	.47	116	.292	.357	.445

Fernando Seguignol

Bats: B **Throws:** R **Pos:** 1B-30; PH/PR-26; LF-17; RF-14; DH-1   **Ht:** 6'5" **Wt:** 230 **Born:** 1/19/75 **Age:** 26

Year Team	Lg	G	AB	H	2B	3B	HR	(Hm	Rd)	TB	R	RBI	TBB	IBB	SO	HBP	SH	SF	SB	CS	SB%	GDP	Avg	OBP	SLG
2000 Ottawa *	AAA	41	141	39	16	0	8	—	—	79	20	31	13	2	26	5	0	3	1	1	.50	8	.277	.352	.560
1998 Montreal	NL	16	42	11	4	0	2	(2	0)	21	6	3	3	0	15	0	0	1	0	0	—	1	.262	.304	.500
1999 Montreal	NL	35	105	27	9	0	5	(3	2)	51	14	10	5	1	33	7	0	2	0	0	—	1	.257	.328	.486
2000 Montreal	NL	76	162	45	8	0	10	(1	9)	83	22	22	9	0	46	3	0	1	0	1	.00	5	.278	.326	.512
3 ML YEARS		127	309	83	21	0	17	(6	11)	155	42	35	17	1	94	10	0	4	0	1	.00	7	.269	.324	.502

Bill Selby

Bats: L **Throws:** R **Pos:** PH/PR-13; DH-6; 2B-6; RF-6; 3B-4; LF-4   **Ht:** 5'9" **Wt:** 190 **Born:** 6/11/70 **Age:** 31

Year Team	Lg	G	AB	H	2B	3B	HR	(Hm	Rd)	TB	R	RBI	TBB	IBB	SO	HBP	SH	SF	SB	CS	SB%	GDP	Avg	OBP	SLG
1992 Elmira	A-	73	275	72	16	1	10	—	—	120	38	41	31	6	53	2	2	2	4	4	.50	3	.262	.339	.436
1993 Lynchburg	A+	113	394	99	22	1	7	—	—	144	57	38	24	2	66	3	2	7	1	2	.33	6	.251	.294	.365
1994 Lynchburg	A+	97	352	109	20	2	19	—	—	190	58	69	28	0	62	5	2	2	3	1	.75	7	.310	.367	.540
New Britain	AA	35	107	28	5	0	1	—	—	36	15	18	15	0	16	0	0	6	0	1	.00	2	.262	.336	.336
1995 Trenton	AA	117	451	129	29	2	13	—	—	201	64	68	46	3	52	3	2	8	4	6	.40	14	.286	.350	.446
1996 Pawtucket	AAA	71	260	66	14	5	11	—	—	123	39	47	22	0	39	2	0	4	0	3	.00	5	.254	.313	.473
1998 Akron	AA	20	77	30	7	1	3	—	—	48	15	10	3	1	11	1	0	1	0	0	—	0	.390	.415	.623
Buffalo	AAA	97	334	85	23	0	14	—	—	150	45	52	38	7	50	0	0	3	3	0	1.00	6	.254	.328	.449
1999 Buffalo	AAA	122	447	132	32	5	20	—	—	234	75	85	57	3	63	2	0	8	4	3	.57	11	.295	.372	.523
2000 Buffalo	AAA	100	384	106	21	6	21	—	—	202	69	86	48	0	61	3	3	7	1	1	.50	9	.276	.355	.526
1996 Boston	AL	40	95	26	4	0	3	(0	3)	39	12	6	9	1	11	0	1	0	1	1	.50	3	.274	.337	.411
2000 Cleveland	AL	30	46	11	1	0	0	(0	0)	12	8	4	1	0	9	1	0	0	0	0	—	1	.239	.271	.261
2 ML YEARS		70	141	37	5	0	3	(0	3)	51	20	10	10	1	20	1	1	0	1	1	.50	4	.262	.316	.362

Aaron Sele

Pitches: Right **Bats:** Right **Pos:** SP-34   **Ht:** 6'5" **Wt:** 215 **Born:** 6/25/70 **Age:** 31

Year Team	Lg	G	GS	CG	GF	IP	BFP	H	R	ER	HR	SH	SF	HB	TBB	IBB	SO	WP	Bk	W	L	Pct.	ShO	Sv-Op	Hld	ERA
1993 Boston	AL	18	18	0	0	111.2	484	100	42	34	5	2	5	7	48	2	93	5	0	7	2	.778	0	0-0	0	2.74
1994 Boston	AL	22	22	2	0	143.1	615	140	68	61	13	4	5	9	60	2	105	4	0	8	7	.533	0	0-0	0	3.83
1995 Boston	AL	6	6	0	0	32.1	146	32	14	11	3	1	1	3	14	0	21	3	0	3	1	.750	0	0-0	0	3.06
1996 Boston	AL	29	29	1	0	157.1	722	192	110	93	14	6	7	8	67	2	137	2	0	7	11	.389	0	0-0	0	5.32
1997 Boston	AL	33	33	1	0	177.1	810	196	115	106	25	5	7	15	80	4	122	7	0	13	12	.520	0	0-0	0	5.38
1998 Texas	AL	33	33	3	0	212.2	954	239	116	100	14	5	7	13	84	6	167	4	0	19	11	.633	2	0-0	0	4.23
1999 Texas	AL	33	33	2	0	205	920	244	115	109	21	1	3	12	70	3	186	4	0	18	9	.667	2	0-0	0	4.79
2000 Seattle	AL	34	34	2	0	211.2	908	221	110	106	17	5	8	5	74	7	137	5	0	17	10	.630	2	0-0	0	4.51
8 ML YEARS		208	208	11	0	1251.1	5559	1364	690	620	112	29	43	72	497	26	968	34	0	92	63	.594	6	0-0	0	4.46

Dan Serafini

Pitches: Left **Bats:** Both **Pos:** SP-11; RP-3   **Ht:** 6'1" **Wt:** 195 **Born:** 1/25/74 **Age:** 27

Year Team	Lg	G	GS	CG	GF	IP	BFP	H	R	ER	HR	SH	SF	HB	TBB	IBB	SO	WP	Bk	W	L	Pct.	ShO	Sv-Op	Hld	ERA
2000 Las Vegas *	AAA	26	4	0	1	51	255	74	44	39	6	3	4	6	23	1	45	4	0	2	4	.333	0	0- -	—	6.88
Nashville *	AAA	7	7	0	0	47	193	39	17	14	4	2	1	1	18	1	22	0	0	4	3	.571	0	0- -	—	2.68
1996 Minnesota	AL	1	1	0	0	4.1	23	7	5	5	1	0	1	1	2	0	1	0	0	0	1	.000	0	0-0	0	10.38
1997 Minnesota	AL	6	4	1	0	26.1	111	27	11	10	1	1	0	1	11	0	15	1	0	2	1	.667	0	0-0	0	3.42
1998 Minnesota	AL	28	9	0	3	75	345	95	58	54	10	3	6	1	29	1	46	2	0	7	4	.636	0	0-0	2	6.48
1999 Chicago	NL	42	4	0	8	62.1	302	86	51	48	9	8	3	1	32	3	17	3	0	3	2	.600	0	1-1	6	6.93
2000 SD-Pit	NL	14	11	0	1	65.1	300	79	41	40	11	8	2	4	28	1	35	3	0	2	5	.286	0	0-0	0	5.51
2000 San Diego	NL	3	0	0	1	3	20	9	6	6	2	0	0	0	2	0	3	1	0	0	0	—	0	0-0	0	18.00
Pittsburgh	NL	11	11	0	0	62.1	280	70	35	34	9	8	2	4	26	1	32	2	0	2	5	.286	0	0-0	0	4.91
5 ML YEARS		91	29	1	13	233.1	1081	294	166	157	32	20	12	7	102	5	114	9	0	14	13	.519	0	1-1	7	6.06

Scott Servais

Bats: Right **Throws:** Right **Pos:** C-38; PH/PR-3   **Ht:** 6'2" **Wt:** 210 **Born:** 6/4/67 **Age:** 34

Year Team	Lg	G	AB	H	2B	3B	HR	(Hm	Rd)	TB	R	RBI	TBB	IBB	SO	HBP	SH	SF	SB	CS	SB%	GDP	Avg	OBP	SLG
2000 Colo Sprngs *	AAA	20	65	19	2	1	3	—	—	32	7	12	4	0	8	1	1	0	0	1	.00	1	.292	.343	.492
1991 Houston	NL	16	37	6	3	0	0	(0	0)	9	0	6	4	0	8	0	1	0	0	0	—	0	.162	.244	.243
1992 Houston	NL	77	205	49	9	0	0	(0	0)	58	12	15	11	2	25	5	6	0	0	0	—	0	.239	.294	.283
1993 Houston	NL	85	258	63	11	0	11	(5	6)	107	24	32	22	2	45	5	3	3	0	0	—	7	.244	.313	.415
1994 Houston	NL	78	251	49	15	1	9	(3	6)	93	27	41	10	0	44	4	7	3	0	0	—	6	.195	.235	.371
1995 Hou-ChC	NL	80	264	70	22	0	13	(8	5)	131	38	47	32	8	52	3	2	3	2	2	.50	8	.265	.348	.496
1996 Chicago	NL	129	445	118	20	0	11	(6	5)	171	42	63	30	1	75	14	3	7	0	1	.00	18	.265	.327	.384
1997 Chicago	NL	122	385	100	21	0	6	(4	2)	139	36	45	24	7	56	6	7	3	0	1	.00	7	.260	.311	.361
1998 Chicago	NL	113	325	72	15	1	7	(5	2)	110	35	36	26	6	51	3	3	1	1	0	1.00	12	.222	.289	.338
1999 San Francisco	NL	69	198	54	10	0	5	(0	5)	79	21	21	13	2	31	3	3	0	0	0	—	7	.273	.327	.399
2000 Col-SF	NL	40	109	24	4	0	1	(1	0)	31	7	13	9	3	17	1	1	0	0	1	.00	1	.220	.283	.284
1995 Houston	NL	28	89	20	10	0	1	(1	0)	33	7	12	9	2	15	1	1	1	0	1	.00	4	.225	.300	.371
Chicago	NL	52	175	50	12	0	12	(7	5)	98	31	35	23	6	37	2	1	2	2	1	.67	4	.286	.371	.560
2000 Colorado	NL	33	101	22	4	0	1	(1	0)	29	6	13	7	2	16	1	0	0	0	1	.00	1	.218	.273	.287
San Francisco	NL	7	8	2	0	0	0	(0	0)	2	1	0	2	1	1	0	1	0	0	0	—	0	.250	.400	.250
10 ML YEARS		809	2477	605	130	2	63	(32	31)	928	242	319	181	31	404	46	35	21	3	6	.33	73	.244	.305	.375

Scott Service

Pitches: Right **Bats:** Right **Pos:** RP-20   **Ht:** 6'6" **Wt:** 240 **Born:** 2/26/67 **Age:** 34

Year Team	Lg	G	GS	CG	GF	IP	BFP	H	R	ER	HR	SH	SF	HB	TBB	IBB	SO	WP	Bk	W	L	Pct.	ShO	Sv-Op	Hld	ERA
2000 Sacramento *	AAA	33	0	0	31	41.2	166	27	8	6	1	1	0	0	11	4	50	5	1	6	2	.750	0	13- -	—	1.30
1988 Philadelphia	NL	5	0	0	1	5.1	23	7	1	1	0	0	0	1	1	0	6	0	0	0	0	—	0	0-0	0	1.69
1992 Montreal	NL	5	0	0	0	7	41	15	11	11	1	0	0	0	5	0	11	0	0	0	0	—	0	0-0	1	14.14
1993 Col-Cin	NL	29	0	0	7	46	197	44	24	22	6	2	4	2	16	4	43	0	0	2	2	.500	0	2-2	3	4.30
1994 Cincinnati	NL	6	0	0	2	7.1	35	8	9	6	2	2	0	0	3	0	5	0	0	1	2	.333	0	0-0	3	7.36
1995 San Francisco	NL	28	0	0	4	31	129	18	11	11	4	3	2	2	20	4	30	3	0	3	1	.750	0	0-0	7	3.19
1996 Cincinnati	NL	34	1	0	5	48	213	51	21	21	7	4	1	6	18	4	46	5	0	1	0	1.000	0	0-0	8	3.94
1997 Cin-KC	NL	16	0	0	3	22.1	95	28	16	16	2	2	1	0	6	0	22	2	0	0	3	.000	0	0-1	1	6.45
1998 Kansas City	AL	73	0	0	26	82.2	353	70	35	32	8	2	5	9	34	4	95	10	1	6	4	.600	0	4-8	18	3.48
1999 Kansas City	AL	68	0	0	29	75.1	352	87	51	51	13	4	7	3	42	8	68	3	0	5	5	.500	0	8-15	8	6.09
2000 Oakland	AL	20	0	0	6	36.2	172	45	31	26	4	0	0	1	19	1	35	0	0	1	2	.333	0	1-1	1	6.38
1993 Colorado	NL	3	0	0	0	4.2	24	8	5	5	1	0	2	1	1	0	3	0	0	0	0	—	0	0-0	0	9.64
Cincinnati	NL	26	0	0	7	41.1	173	36	19	17	5	2	2	1	15	4	40	0	0	2	2	.500	0	2-2	3	3.70
1997 Cincinnati	NL	4	0	0	1	5.1	26	11	7	7	1	1	0	0	3	0	3	2	0	0	0	—	0	0-0	1	11.81
Kansas City	AL	12	0	0	2	17	69	17	9	9	1	1	1	0	3	0	19	0	0	0	3	.000	0	0-1	0	4.76
10 ML YEARS		284	1	0	85	361.2	1610	373	210	197	47	20	22	24	164	25	361	23	1	19	19	.500	0	15-27	44	4.90

Richie Sexson

Bats: R **Throws:** R **Pos:** 1B-84; LF-58; DH-10; PH/PR-8   **Ht:** 6'7" **Wt:** 225 **Born:** 12/29/74 **Age:** 26

Year Team	Lg	G	AB	H	2B	3B	HR	(Hm	Rd)	TB	R	RBI	TBB	IBB	SO	HBP	SH	SF	SB	CS	SB%	GDP	Avg	OBP	SLG
1997 Cleveland	AL	5	11	3	0	0	0	(0	0)	3	1	0	0	0	2	0	0	0	0	0	—	2	.273	.273	.273
1998 Cleveland	AL	49	174	54	14	1	11	(9	2)	103	28	35	6	0	42	3	0	4	1	1	.50	3	.310	.344	.592
1999 Cleveland	AL	134	479	122	17	7	31	(18	13)	246	72	116	34	4	117	4	0	8	3	3	.50	19	.255	.305	.514
2000 Cle-Mil		148	537	146	30	1	30	(15	15)	268	89	91	59	2	159	7	0	4	2	0	1.00	11	.272	.349	.499
2000 Cleveland	AL	91	324	83	16	1	16	(8	8)	149	45	44	25	0	96	4	0	3	1	0	1.00	8	.256	.315	.460
Milwaukee	NL	57	213	63	14	0	14	(7	7)	119	44	47	34	2	63	3	0	1	1	0	1.00	3	.296	.398	.559
4 ML YEARS		336	1201	325	61	9	72	(42	30)	620	190	242	99	2	320	14	0	12	6	4	.60	35	.271	.330	.516

Chris Sexton

Bats: R **Throws:** R **Pos:** SS-14; 2B-12; PH/PR-7; 3B-3   **Ht:** 5'11"   **Wt:** 180   **Born:** 8/3/71   **Age:** 29

							BATTING											BASERUNNING				PERCENTAGES		
Year Team	Lg	G	AB	H	2B	3B	HR	(Hm | Rd)	TB	R	RBI	TBB	IBB	SO	HBP	SH	SF	SB	CS	SB%	GDP	Avg	OBP	SLG
1993 Billings	R+	72	273	91	14	4	4	—	—	125	63	46	35	1	27	1	0	8	13	4	.76	6	.333	.401	.458
1994 Chstn-WV	A	133	467	140	21	4	5	—	—	184	82	59	91	3	67	2	6	6	18	11	.62	9	.300	.412	.394
1995 Winston-Sal	A+	4	15	6	0	0	1	—	—	9	3	5	4	0	0	0	0	0	0	0	—	0	.400	.526	.600
Salem	A+	123	461	123	16	6	4	—	—	163	81	32	93	2	55	1	12	1	14	11	.56	11	.267	.390	.354
New Haven	AA	1	3	0	0	0	0	—	—	0	0	0	0	0	0	0	0	0	0	0	—	0	.000	.000	.000
1996 New Haven	AA	127	444	96	12	2	0	—	—	112	50	28	71	2	68	1	7	3	8	5	.62	10	.216	.324	.252
1997 New Haven	AA	98	360	107	22	4	1	—	—	140	65	38	62	0	37	2	11	4	8	16	.33	8	.297	.400	.389
Colo Sprngs	AAA	33	112	30	3	1	1	—	—	38	18	8	16	0	21	0	1	0	1	1	.50	4	.268	.359	.339
1998 Colo Sprngs	AAA	132	462	131	22	6	2	—	—	171	88	43	72	2	67	1	6	4	7	3	.70	17	.284	.378	.370
1999 Colo Sprngs	AAA	60	171	58	9	0	0	—	—	67	23	17	28	0	22	0	5	1	5	1	.83	7	.339	.430	.392
2000 Louisville	AAA	99	389	126	19	1	7	—	—	168	79	50	63	0	45	0	1	2	8	4	.67	14	.324	.416	.432
1999 Colorado	NL	35	59	14	0	1	1	(0 | 1)	19	9	7	11	1	10	0	0	0	4	2	.67	2	.237	.357	.322
2000 Cincinnati	NL	35	100	21	4	0	0	(0 | 0)	25	9	10	13	1	12	2	2	1	4	2	.67	5	.210	.310	.250
2 ML YEARS		70	159	35	4	1	1	(0 | 1)	44	18	17	24	2	22	2	2	1	8	4	.67	7	.220	.328	.277

Jeff Shaw

Pitches: Right   **Bats:** Right   **Pos:** RP-60   **Ht:** 6'2"   **Wt:** 200   **Born:** 7/7/66   **Age:** 34

		HOW MUCH HE PITCHED						WHAT HE GAVE UP											THE RESULTS						
Year Team	Lg	G	GS	CG	GF	IP	BFP	H	R	ER	HR	SH	SF	HB	TBB	IBB	SO	WP	Bk	W	L	Pct.	ShO	Sv-Op	Hld	ERA
1990 Cleveland	AL	12	9	0	0	48.2	229	73	38	36	11	1	3	0	20	0	25	3	0	3	4	.429	0	0-0	0	6.66
1991 Cleveland	AL	29	1	0	9	72.1	311	72	34	27	6	1	4	4	27	5	31	6	0	0	5	.000	0	1-4	0	3.36
1992 Cleveland	AL	2	1	0	1	7.2	33	7	7	7	2	2	0	0	4	0	3	0	0	1	0	1.000	0	0-0	0	8.22
1993 Montreal	NL	55	8	0	13	95.2	404	91	47	44	12	5	2	7	32	2	50	2	0	2	7	.222	0	0-1	4	4.14
1994 Montreal	NL	46	0	0	15	67.1	287	67	32	29	8	2	4	2	15	2	47	5	0	5	2	.714	0	1-2	10	3.88
1995 Mon-CWS		59	0	0	18	72	309	70	42	39	6	7	1	4	27	4	51	0	0	1	6	.143	0	3-5	6	4.88
1996 Cincinnati	NL	78	0	0	24	104.2	434	99	34	29	8	5	5	2	29	11	69	0	0	8	6	.571	0	4-11	22	2.49
1997 Cincinnati	NL	78	0	0	62	94.2	367	79	26	25	7	3	3	1	12	3	74	1	0	4	2	.667	0	42-49	5	2.38
1998 Cin-LA	NL	73	0	0	69	85	339	75	22	20	8	5	2	1	19	5	55	0	0	3	8	.273	0	48-57	0	2.12
1999 Los Angeles	NL	64	0	0	56	68	284	64	25	21	6	1	2	1	15	1	43	1	0	2	4	.333	0	34-39	0	2.78
2000 Los Angeles	NL	60	0	0	51	57.1	249	61	29	27	7	2	0	1	16	3	39	0	0	3	4	.429	0	27-34	0	4.24
1995 Montreal	NL	50	0	0	17	62.1	268	58	35	32	4	6	1	3	26	4	45	0	0	1	6	.143	0	3-5	5	4.62
Chicago	AL	9	0	0	1	9.2	41	12	7	7	2	1	0	1	1	0	6	0	0	0	0	—	0	0-0	1	6.52
1998 Cincinnati	NL	39	0	0	35	49.2	192	40	11	10	2	4	2	1	12	4	29	0	0	2	4	.333	0	23-28	0	1.81
Los Angeles	NL	34	0	0	34	35.1	147	35	11	10	6	1	0	0	7	1	26	0	0	1	4	.200	0	25-29	0	2.55
11 ML YEARS		556	19	0	318	773.1	3246	758	336	304	81	34	26	23	216	36	487	18	0	31	49	.388	0	160-202	47	3.54

Andy Sheets

Bats: R **Throws:** R **Pos:** SS-10; DH-2; 1B-1; PH/PR-1   **Ht:** 6'2"   **Wt:** 180   **Born:** 11/19/71   **Age:** 29

							BATTING											BASERUNNING				PERCENTAGES		
Year Team	Lg	G	AB	H	2B	3B	HR	(Hm	Rd)	TB	R	RBI	TBB	IBB	SO	HBP	SH	SF	SB	CS	SB%	GDP	Avg	OBP	SLG
2000 Pawtucket *	AAA	83	281	64	9	3	8	—	—	103	38	36	38	0	48	1	3	1	4	2	.67	7	.228	.325	.367
1996 Seattle	AL	47	110	21	8	0	0	(0	0)	29	18	9	10	0	41	1	2	1	2	0	1.00	6	.191	.262	.264
1997 Seattle	AL	32	89	22	3	0	4	(2	2)	37	18	9	7	0	34	0	5	1	2	0	1.00	1	.247	.299	.416
1998 San Diego	NL	88	194	47	5	3	7	(2	5)	79	31	29	21	3	62	1	2	1	7	2	.78	4	.242	.318	.407
1999 Anaheim	AL	87	244	48	10	0	3	(3	0)	67	22	29	14	0	59	0	6	5	1	2	.33	6	.197	.236	.275
2000 Boston	AL	12	21	2	0	0	0	(0	0)	2	1	1	0	0	3	0	0	0	0	0	—	1	.095	.095	.095
5 ML YEARS		266	658	140	26	3	14	(7	7)	214	90	77	52	3	199	2	15	8	12	4	.75	14	.213	.269	.325

Gary Sheffield

Bats: Right **Throws:** Right **Pos:** LF-139; DH-2   **Ht:** 5'11"   **Wt:** 205   **Born:** 11/18/68   **Age:** 32

							BATTING											BASERUNNING				PERCENTAGES		
Year Team	Lg	G	AB	H	2B	3B	HR	(Hm	Rd)	TB	R	RBI	TBB	IBB	SO	HBP	SH	SF	SB	CS	SB%	GDP	Avg	OBP	SLG
1988 Milwaukee	AL	24	80	19	1	0	4	(1	3)	32	12	12	7	0	7	0	1	1	3	1	.75	5	.238	.295	.400
1989 Milwaukee	AL	95	368	91	18	0	5	(2	3)	124	34	32	27	0	33	4	3	3	10	6	.63	4	.247	.303	.337
1990 Milwaukee	AL	125	487	143	30	1	10	(3	7)	205	67	67	44	1	41	3	4	9	25	10	.71	11	.294	.350	.421
1991 Milwaukee	AL	50	175	34	12	2	2	(2	0)	56	25	22	19	1	15	3	1	5	5	5	.50	3	.194	.277	.320
1992 San Diego	NL	146	557	184	34	3	33	(23	10)	323	87	100	48	5	40	6	0	7	5	6	.45	19	.330	.385	.580
1993 SD-Fla	NL	140	494	145	20	5	20	(10	10)	235	67	73	47	6	64	9	0	7	17	5	.77	11	.294	.361	.476
1994 Florida	NL	87	322	89	16	1	27	(15	12)	188	61	78	51	11	50	6	0	5	12	6	.67	10	.276	.380	.584
1995 Florida	NL	63	213	69	8	0	16	(4	12)	125	46	46	55	8	45	4	0	2	19	4	.83	3	.324	.467	.587
1996 Florida	NL	161	519	163	33	1	42	(19	23)	324	118	120	142	19	66	10	0	6	16	9	.64	16	.314	.465	.624
1997 Florida	NL	135	444	111	22	1	21	(13	8)	198	86	71	121	11	79	15	0	2	11	7	.61	7	.250	.424	.446
1998 Fla-LA	NL	130	437	132	27	2	22	(11	11)	229	73	85	95	12	46	8	0	9	22	7	.76	7	.302	.428	.524
1999 Los Angeles	NL	152	549	165	20	0	34	(15	19)	287	103	101	101	4	64	4	0	9	11	5	.69	10	.301	.407	.523
2000 Los Angeles	NL	141	501	163	24	3	43	(23	20)	322	105	109	101	7	71	4	0	6	4	6	.40	13	.325	.438	.643
1993 San Diego	NL	68	258	76	12	2	10	(6	4)	122	34	36	18	0	30	3	0	3	5	1	.83	5	.295	.344	.473
Florida	NL	72	236	69	8	3	10	(4	6)	113	33	37	29	6	34	6	0	4	12	4	.75	2	.292	.378	.479
1998 Florida	NL	40	136	37	11	1	6	(1	0)	68	21	28	26	1	16	2	0	2	4	2	.67	3	.272	.392	.500
Los Angeles	NL	90	301	95	16	1	16	(5	11)	161	52	57	69	11	30	6	0	7	18	5	.78	4	.316	.444	.535
13 ML YEARS		1449	5146	1508	265	19	279	(141	138)	2648	884	916	858	85	621	76	9	71	160	77	.68	119	.293	.397	.515

Scott Sheldon

B: R **T:** R **Pos:** SS-22; 3B-15; 2B-12; 1B-10; PH/PR-8; C-3; LF-2; DH-1; P-1; CF-1; RF-1   **Ht:** 6'3"   **Wt:** 215   **Born:** 11/20/68   **Age:** 32

							BATTING											BASERUNNING				PERCENTAGES		
Year Team	Lg	G	AB	H	2B	3B	HR	(Hm	Rd)	TB	R	RBI	TBB	IBB	SO	HBP	SH	SF	SB	CS	SB%	GDP	Avg	OBP	SLG
1991 Sou Oregon	A-	65	229	58	10	3	0	—	—	74	34	24	23	0	44	2	3	1	9	5	.64	5	.253	.325	.323
1992 Madison	A	74	279	76	16	0	6	—	—	110	41	24	32	1	78	1	3	4	5	4	.56	2	.272	.345	.394

Batting (continued)

Year Team	Lg	G	AB	H	2B	3B	HR	(Hm	Rd)	TB	R	RBI	TBB	IBB	SO	HBP	SH	SF	SB	CS	SB%	GDP	Avg	OBP	SLG
1993 Madison	A	131	428	91	22	1	8	—	—	139	67	67	49	3	121	8	3	8	8	7	.53	8	.213	.300	.325
1994 Huntsville	AA	91	268	62	10	1	0	—	—	74	31	28	28	1	69	7	7	3	7	1	.88	4	.231	.317	.276
1995 Edmonton	AAA	45	128	33	7	1	4	—	—	54	21	12	15	0	15	2	4	1	4	2	.67	0	.258	.342	.422
Huntsville	AA	66	235	51	10	2	4	—	—	77	25	15	23	0	60	1	3	1	5	0	1.00	7	.217	.288	.328
1996 Edmonton	AAA	98	350	105	27	3	10	—	—	168	61	60	43	3	83	4	3	4	5	3	.63	8	.300	.379	.480
1997 Edmonton	AAA	118	422	133	39	6	19	—	—	241	89	77	59	4	104	6	3	3	5	2	.71	11	.315	.404	.571
1998 Oklahoma	AAA	131	493	126	31	4	29	—	—	252	74	96	62	3	143	3	0	6	2	2	.50	7	.256	.339	.511
1999 Oklahoma	AAA	122	453	141	35	3	28	—	—	266	94	97	56	3	112	3	0	7	12	2	.86	11	.311	.385	.587
1997 Oakland	AL	13	24	6	0	0	1	(1	0)	9	2	2	1	0	6	1	1	0	0	0	—	0	.250	.308	.375
1998 Texas	AL	7	16	2	0	0	0	(0	0)	2	0	1	1	0	6	0	0	0	0	0	—	1	.125	.176	.125
1999 Texas	AL	2	1	0	0	0	0	(0	0)	0	0	0	0	0	0	0	0	0	0	0	—	0	.000	.000	.000
2000 Texas	AL	58	124	35	11	0	4	(1	3)	58	21	19	10	0	37	1	1	2	0	0	—	0	.282	.336	.468
4 ML YEARS		80	165	43	11	0	5	(2	3)	69	23	22	12	0	49	2	2	2	0	0	—	3	.261	.315	.418

Paul Shuey

Pitches: Right **Bats:** Right **Pos:** RP-57
Ht: 6'3" **Wt:** 215 **Born:** 9/16/70 **Age:** 30

HOW MUCH HE PITCHED / WHAT HE GAVE UP / THE RESULTS

Year Team	Lg	G	GS	CG	GF	IP	BFP	H	R	ER	HR	SH	SF	HB	TBB	IBB	SO	WP	Bk	W	L	Pct.	ShO	Sv-Op	Hld	ERA
2000 Akron *	AA	2	1	0	0	2	8	1	1	1	0	0	0	0	1	0	1	0	0	0	0	—	0	0--	—	4.50
1994 Cleveland	AL	14	0	0	11	11.2	62	14	11	11	1	0	0	0	12	1	16	4	0	0	1	.000	0	5-5	1	8.49
1995 Cleveland	AL	7	0	0	3	6.1	28	5	4	3	0	2	0	0	5	0	5	1	0	0	0	.000	0	0-0	0	4.26
1996 Cleveland	AL	42	0	0	18	53.2	225	45	19	17	6	1	3	0	26	3	44	3	1	5	2	.714	0	4-7	7	2.85
1997 Cleveland	AL	40	0	0	16	45	212	52	31	31	5	4	2	1	28	3	46	2	0	2	1	.667	0	2-3	4	6.20
1998 Cleveland	AL	43	0	0	16	51	222	44	19	17	6	2	0	3	25	5	58	3	0	5	4	.556	0	2-5	12	3.00
1999 Cleveland	AL	72	0	0	28	81.2	351	68	37	32	8	4	1	1	40	7	103	8	0	8	5	.615	0	6-12	19	3.53
2000 Cleveland	AL	57	0	0	12	63.2	270	51	25	24	4	1	3	3	30	3	69	0	0	4	2	.667	0	0-5	**28**	3.39
7 ML YEARS		275	0	0	104	313	1370	279	146	135	30	14	9	8	166	22	341	21	1	26	18	.591	0	19-37	71	3.88

Terry Shumpert

Bats: R **Throws:** R **Pos:** PH/PR-53; LF-40; 2B-23; 3B-15; SS-7; 1B-6; DH-1
Ht: 6'0" **Wt:** 200 **Born:** 8/16/66 **Age:** 34

BATTING / BASERUNNING / PERCENTAGES

Year Team	Lg	G	AB	H	2B	3B	HR	(Hm	Rd)	TB	R	RBI	TBB	IBB	SO	HBP	SH	SF	SB	CS	SB%	GDP	Avg	OBP	SLG
1990 Kansas City	AL	32	91	25	6	1	0	(0	0)	33	7	8	2	0	17	1	0	2	3	3	.50	4	.275	.292	.363
1991 Kansas City	AL	144	369	80	16	4	5	(1	4)	119	45	34	30	0	75	5	10	3	17	11	.61	10	.217	.283	.322
1992 Kansas City	AL	36	94	14	5	1	1	(0	1)	24	6	11	3	0	17	0	2	0	2	2	.50	2	.149	.175	.255
1993 Kansas City	AL	8	10	1	0	0	0	(0	0)	1	0	0	2	0	2	0	0	0	1	0	1.00	0	.100	.250	.100
1994 Kansas City	AL	64	183	44	6	2	8	(2	6)	78	28	24	13	0	39	0	5	1	18	3	.86	0	.240	.289	.426
1995 Boston	AL	21	47	11	3	0	0	(0	0)	14	6	4	4	0	13	0	0	1	3	1	.75	0	.234	.294	.298
1996 Chicago	NL	27	31	7	1	0	2	(2	0)	14	5	6	2	0	11	1	0	1	0	1	.00	0	.226	.286	.452
1997 San Diego	NL	13	33	9	3	0	1	(0	1)	15	4	6	3	0	4	0	0	1	0	0	—	0	.273	.324	.455
1998 Colorado	NL	23	26	6	1	0	1	(0	1)	10	3	2	1	0	8	0	0	0	0	0	—	0	.231	.286	.385
1999 Colorado	NL	92	262	91	26	3	10	(8	2)	153	58	37	31	2	41	2	4	5	14	0	1.00	2	.347	.413	.584
2000 Colorado	NL	115	263	68	11	7	9	(7	2)	120	52	40	28	1	40	0	2	3	8	4	.67	3	.259	.340	.456
11 ML YEARS		575	1409	356	78	18	37	(20	17)	581	214	171	120	3	267	15	21	16	66	25	.73	22	.253	.315	.412

Ruben Sierra

Bats: Both **Throws:** Right **Pos:** DH-14; PH/PR-8
Ht: 6'1" **Wt:** 200 **Born:** 10/6/65 **Age:** 35

BATTING / BASERUNNING / PERCENTAGES

Year Team	Lg	G	AB	H	2B	3B	HR	(Hm	Rd)	TB	R	RBI	TBB	IBB	SO	HBP	SH	SF	SB	CS	SB%	GDP	Avg	OBP	SLG
2000 Oklahoma *	AAA	112	439	143	26	3	18	—	—	229	70	82	55	6	63	0	0	4	5	2	.71	24	.326	.398	.522
1986 Texas	AL	113	382	101	13	10	16	(8	8)	182	50	55	22	3	65	1	1	5	7	8	.47	8	.264	.302	.476
1987 Texas	AL	158	643	169	35	4	30	(15	15)	302	97	109	39	4	114	2	0	12	16	11	.59	18	.263	.302	.470
1988 Texas	AL	156	615	156	32	2	23	(15	8)	261	77	91	44	10	91	1	0	4	18	4	.82	15	.254	.301	.424
1989 Texas	AL	162	634	194	35	14	29	(21	8)	344	101	119	43	2	82	2	0	10	8	2	.80	7	.306	.347	**.543**
1990 Texas	AL	159	608	170	37	2	16	(10	6)	259	70	96	49	13	86	1	0	9	9	0	1.00	15	.280	.330	.426
1991 Texas	AL	161	661	203	44	5	25	(12	13)	332	110	116	56	7	91	0	0	4	16	4	.80	15	.307	.357	.502
1992 Tex-Oak	AL	151	601	167	34	7	17	(10	7)	266	83	87	45	12	68	0	0	10	14	4	.78	11	.278	.323	.443
1993 Oakland	AL	158	630	147	23	5	22	(9	13)	246	77	101	52	16	97	0	0	10	25	5	.83	17	.233	.288	.390
1994 Oakland	AL	110	426	114	21	1	23	(11	12)	206	71	92	23	4	64	0	0	11	8	5	.62	15	.268	.298	.484
1995 Oak-NYY	AL	126	479	126	32	0	19	(8	11)	215	73	86	46	4	76	0	0	8	5	4	.56	8	.263	.323	.449
1996 NYY-Det	AL	142	518	128	26	2	12	(4	8)	194	61	72	60	12	83	0	0	6	4	4	.50	12	.247	.320	.375
1997 Cin-Tor		39	138	32	5	3	4	(0	4)	52	10	12	9	2	34	0	0	1	0	0	—	1	.232	.277	.377
2000 Texas	AL	20	60	14	0	0	1	(0	1)	17	5	7	4	0	9	0	0	0	0	1	.00	1	.233	.281	.283
1992 Texas	AL	124	500	139	30	6	14	(8	6)	223	66	70	31	6	59	0	0	8	12	4	.75	9	.278	.315	.446
Oakland	AL	27	101	28	4	1	3	(2	1)	43	17	17	14	6	9	0	0	2	2	0	1.00	2	.277	.359	.426
1995 Oakland	AL	70	264	70	17	0	12	(8	4)	123	40	42	24	2	42	0	0	3	4	4	.50	2	.265	.323	.466
New York	AL	56	215	56	15	0	7	(0	7)	92	33	44	22	2	34	0	0	5	1	0	1.00	6	.260	.322	.428
1996 New York	AL	96	360	93	17	1	11	(4	7)	145	39	52	40	11	58	0	0	7	3	3	.25	10	.258	.327	.403
Detroit	AL	46	158	35	9	1	1	(0	1)	49	22	20	20	1	25	0	0	0	1	1	.75	2	.222	.306	.310
1997 Cincinnati	NL	25	90	22	5	1	2	(2	0)	35	6	7	5	1	21	0	0	0	0	0	—	0	.244	.292	.389
Toronto	AL	14	48	10	0	2	1	(1	0)	17	4	5	3	1	13	0	0	1	0	0	—	1	.208	.250	.354
14 ML YEARS		1682	6469	1737	341	56	240	(126	114)	2910	892	1054	495	89	971	7	1	101	133	51	.72	147	.269	.317	.450

Brian Sikorski

Pitches: Right **Bats:** Right **Pos:** SP-5; RP-5
Ht: 6'1" **Wt:** 190 **Born:** 7/27/74 **Age:** 26

HOW MUCH HE PITCHED / WHAT HE GAVE UP / THE RESULTS

Year Team	Lg	G	GS	CG	GF	IP	BFP	H	R	ER	HR	SH	SF	HB	TBB	IBB	SO	WP	Bk	W	L	Pct.	ShO	Sv-Op	Hld	ERA
1995 Auburn	A-	23	0	0	19	34.1	137	22	8	8	1	0	1	0	14	2	35	1	0	1	2	.333	0	12--	—	2.10
Quad City	A	2	0	0	1	3	11	1	0	0	0	0	0	0	0	0	4	0	0	1	0	1.000	0	0--	—	0.00

Year Team	Lg	G	GS	CG	GF	IP	BFP	H	R	ER	HR	SH	SF	HB	TBB	IBB	SO	WP	Bk	W	L	Pct.	ShO	Sv-Op	Hld	ERA
1996 Quad City	A	26	25	1	0	166.2	704	140	79	58	12	4	7	10	70	2	150	7	9	11	8	.579	0	0--	—	3.13
1997 Kissimmee	A+	11	11	0	0	67.2	279	64	29	23	2	0	1	6	16	0	46	0	3	8	2	.800	0	0--	—	3.06
Jackson	AA	17	17	0	0	93.1	402	91	55	48	8	5	2	4	31	2	74	0	2	5	5	.500	0	0--	—	4.63
1998 Jackson	AA	15	15	0	0	97.1	419	83	50	44	13	3	2	6	44	1	80	3	1	6	4	.600	0	0--	—	4.07
New Orleans	AAA	15	14	1	0	84	371	86	57	54	9	2	4	6	32	1	64	2	1	5	8	.385	0	0--	—	5.79
1999 New Orleans	AAA	28	27	2	0	158.1	699	169	92	87	25	8	1	9	58	1	122	6	2	7	10	.412	1	0--	—	4.95
2000 Oklahoma	AAA	24	23	5	1	140.1	591	131	73	63	9	2	8	3	60	1	99	3	5	10	9	.526	2	1--	—	4.04
2000 Texas	AL	10	5	0	2	37.2	187	46	31	24	9	0	1	1	25	1	32	1	0	1	3	.250	0	0-0	0	5.73

Jose Silva

Pitches: Right **Bats:** Right **Pos:** RP-32; SP-19   **Ht:** 6'5" **Wt:** 235 **Born:** 12/19/73 **Age:** 27

Year Team	Lg	G	GS	CG	GF	IP	BFP	H	R	ER	HR	SH	SF	HB	TBB	IBB	SO	WP	Bk	W	L	Pct.	ShO	Sv-Op	Hld	ERA
1996 Toronto	AL	2	0	0	0	2	11	5	3	3	1	0	0	0	0	0	0	0	0	0	0		0	0-0	0	13.50
1997 Pittsburgh	NL	11	4	0	0	36.1	174	52	26	24	4	4	3	1	16	3	30	0	1	2	1	.667	0	0-0	0	5.94
1998 Pittsburgh	NL	18	18	1	0	100.1	425	104	55	49	7	5	5	1	30	2	64	2	2	6	7	.462	0	0-0	0	4.40
1999 Pittsburgh	NL	34	12	0	9	97.1	433	108	70	62	10	3	3	3	39	0	77	4	3	2	8	.200	0	4-5	2	5.73
2000 Pittsburgh	NL	51	19	1	12	136	631	178	96	84	16	9	5	5	50	7	98	6	1	11	9	.550	0	0-2	1	5.56
5 ML YEARS		116	53	2	21	372	1674	447	250	222	38	21	16	10	135	12	269	12	7	21	25	.457	0	4-7	3	5.37

Bill Simas

Pitches: Right **Bats:** Left **Pos:** RP-60   **Ht:** 6'3" **Wt:** 235 **Born:** 11/28/71 **Age:** 29

Year Team	Lg	G	GS	CG	GF	IP	BFP	H	R	ER	HR	SH	SF	HB	TBB	IBB	SO	WP	Bk	W	L	Pct.	ShO	Sv-Op	Hld	ERA
1995 Chicago	AL	14	0	0	4	14	66	15	5	4	1	0	0	1	10	2	16	1	0	1	1	.500	0	0-0	3	2.57
1996 Chicago	AL	64	0	0	16	72.2	328	75	39	37	5	1	2	3	39	6	65	0	0	2	8	.200	0	2-8	15	4.58
1997 Chicago	AL	40	0	0	11	41.1	193	46	23	19	6	1	1	2	24	3	38	2	0	3	1	.750	0	1-2	3	4.14
1998 Chicago	AL	60	0	0	41	70.2	287	54	29	28	12	2	0	1	22	4	56	1	0	4	3	.571	0	18-24	6	3.57
1999 Chicago	AL	70	0	0	21	72	324	73	36	30	6	4	4	6	32	6	41	4	1	6	3	.667	0	2-5	12	3.75
2000 Chicago	AL	60	0	0	9	67.2	283	69	27	26	9	6	4	1	22	6	49	1	0	2	3	.400	0	0-5	13	3.46
6 ML YEARS		308	0	0	102	338.1	1481	332	159	144	39	14	11	14	149	27	265	9	1	18	19	.486	0	23-44	52	3.83

Chris Singleton

Bats: L **Throws:** L **Pos:** CF-143; LF-19; PH/PR-4; DH-1   **Ht:** 6'2" **Wt:** 195 **Born:** 8/15/72 **Age:** 28

Year Team	Lg	G	AB	H	2B	3B	HR	(Hm	Rd)	TB	R	RBI	TBB	IBB	SO	HBP	SH	SF	SB	CS	SB%	GDP	Avg	OBP	SLG
1993 Everett	A-	58	219	58	14	4	3	—	—	89	39	18	18	0	46	1	5	1	14	3	.82	3	.265	.322	.406
1994 San Jose	A+	113	425	106	17	5	2	—	—	139	51	49	27	0	62	3	5	3	19	6	.76	9	.249	.297	.327
1995 San Jose	A+	94	405	112	13	5	2	—	—	141	55	31	17	1	49	5	5	1	33	13	.72	5	.277	.313	.348
1996 Shreveport	AA	129	500	149	31	9	5	—	—	213	68	72	24	2	58	6	3	8	27	12	.69	12	.298	.333	.426
Phoenix	AAA	9	32	4	0	0	0	—	—	4	3	0	1	0	2	0	1	0	0	0	—	0	.125	.152	.125
1997 Shreveport	AA	126	464	147	26	10	9	—	—	220	85	61	22	4	50	1	2	9	27	11	.71	7	.317	.343	.474
1998 Columbus	AAA	121	413	105	17	10	6	—	—	160	55	45	27	0	78	4	7	4	9	3	.75	7	.254	.304	.387
1999 Chicago	AL	133	496	149	31	6	17	(5	12)	243	72	72	22	1	45	1	4	6	20	5	.80	10	.300	.328	.490
2000 Chicago	AL	147	511	130	22	5	11	(5	6)	195	83	62	35	2	85	1	12	4	22	7	.76	6	.254	.301	.382
2 ML YEARS		280	1007	279	53	11	28	(10	18)	438	155	134	57	3	130	2	16	10	42	12	.78	16	.277	.314	.435

Mike Sirotka

Pitches: Left **Bats:** Left **Pos:** SP-32   **Ht:** 6'1" **Wt:** 200 **Born:** 5/13/71 **Age:** 30

Year Team	Lg	G	GS	CG	GF	IP	BFP	H	R	ER	HR	SH	SF	HB	TBB	IBB	SO	WP	Bk	W	L	Pct.	ShO	Sv-Op	Hld	ERA
1995 Chicago	AL	6	6	0	0	34.1	152	39	16	16	2	1	3	0	17	0	19	2	0	1	2	.333	0	0-0	0	4.19
1996 Chicago	AL	15	4	0	2	26.1	122	34	27	21	3	0	2	0	12	0	11	1	0	1	2	.333	0	0-0	0	7.18
1997 Chicago	AL	7	4	0	1	32	130	36	9	8	4	0	0	1	5	1	24	0	0	3	1	1.000	0	0-0	1	2.25
1998 Chicago	AL	33	33	5	0	211.2	911	255	137	119	30	5	7	2	47	0	128	3	1	14	15	.483	0	0-0	0	5.06
1999 Chicago	AL	32	32	3	0	209	909	236	108	93	24	5	9	3	57	2	125	4	0	11	13	.458	1	0-0	0	4.00
2000 Chicago	AL	32	32	1	0	197	832	203	101	83	23	4	3	1	69	1	128	8	2	15	10	.600	0	0-0	0	3.79
6 ML YEARS		125	111	9	3	710.1	3056	803	398	340	86	15	24	7	207	4	435	18	3	45	42	.517	1	0-0	1	4.31

Steve Sisco

Bats: R **Throws:** R **Pos:** PH/PR-20; 2B-5; LF-5; 3B-2; DH-1; RF-1   **Ht:** 5'10" **Wt:** 190 **Born:** 12/2/69 **Age:** 31

Year Team	Lg	G	AB	H	2B	3B	HR	(Hm	Rd)	TB	R	RBI	TBB	IBB	SO	HBP	SH	SF	SB	CS	SB%	GDP	Avg	OBP	SLG
1992 Eugene	A-	67	261	86	7	1	0	—	—	95	41	30	26	0	32	4	2	2	22	12	.65	7	.330	.396	.364
Appleton	A	1	4	1	0	0	0	—	—	1	1	0	0	0	0	1	0	0	0	0	—	0	.250	.250	.250
1993 Rockford	A	124	460	132	22	4	2	—	—	168	62	57	42	2	65	2	4	5	25	10	.71	14	.287	.346	.365
1994 Wilmington	A+	76	270	74	11	4	3	—	—	102	41	32	37	0	39	2	6	4	5	6	.45	2	.274	.361	.378
1995 Omaha	AAA	7	24	5	1	0	0	—	—	6	4	0	2	0	8	0	1	0	0	0	—	0	.208	.269	.250
Wichita	AA	54	209	63	12	1	3	—	—	86	29	23	15	0	31	1	1	1	3	1	.75	5	.301	.350	.411
1996 Wichita	AA	122	462	137	24	1	13	—	—	202	80	74	40	0	69	3	5	5	4	2	.67	14	.297	.353	.437
1997 Wichita	AA	55	182	52	8	2	3	—	—	73	34	24	24	0	29	0	1	2	3	1	.75	5	.286	.365	.401
Omaha	AAA	54	188	49	8	0	3	—	—	66	23	12	8	0	34	0	3	1	2	1	.67	4	.261	.289	.351
1998 Omaha	AAA	109	371	104	20	0	20	—	—	184	58	58	26	1	58	0	5	3	4	6	.40	11	.280	.325	.496
1999 Richmond	AAA	128	495	154	36	2	18	—	—	248	80	76	38	0	74	1	3	8	13	7	.65	7	.311	.356	.501
2000 Richmond	AAA	75	275	81	16	0	12	—	—	133	46	35	21	2	46	2	3	2	3	2	.60	4	.295	.347	.484
2000 Atlanta	NL	25	27	5	0	0	1	(0	1)	8	4	2	3	0	4	0	0	0	0	0	—	1	.185	.267	.296

Matt Skrmetta

Pitches: Right Bats: Both Pos: RP-14   Ht: 6'3" Wt: 215 Born: 11/6/72 Age: 28

Year Team	Lg	G	GS	CG	GF	IP	BFP	H	R	ER	HR	SH	SF	HB	TBB	IBB	SO	WP	Bk	W	L	Pct.	ShO	Sv-Op	Hld	ERA
1993 Bristol	R+	8	5	0	1	35	158	30	23	19	1	0	3	3	22	1	29	6	3	2	3	.400	0	0- -	—	4.89
1994 Jamestown	A-	17	15	1	1	93.2	389	74	42	33	4	2	3	7	37	0	56	2	3	5	3	.625	0	0- -	—	3.17
1995 Fayetteville	A	44	2	0	15	89.2	371	66	36	27	9	6	1	3	35	2	105	2	0	9	4	.692	0	2- -	—	2.71
1996 Jacksnville	AA	4	0	0	1	6	27	4	3	3	0	0	1	0	5	1	7	1	0	0	0	—	0	0- -	—	4.50
Lakeland	A+	40	0	0	20	52.2	223	44	23	21	5	2	0	2	19	1	52	2	1	5	5	.500	0	5- -	—	3.59
1997 Mobile	AA	21	0	0	7	32.2	154	32	21	19	4	0	1	2	21	3	30	3	0	2	3	.400	0	1- -	—	5.23
Rancho Cuc	A+	17	0	0	8	28.1	122	27	7	5	2	1	0	1	10	0	36	4	0	0	1	.000	0	1- -	—	1.59
1998 Mobile	AA	51	0	0	16	78	323	66	32	29	9	5	2	2	31	1	77	1	3	9	2	.818	0	0- -	—	3.35
1999 Mobile	AA	25	1	0	9	37.1	181	42	28	26	3	1	2	3	24	1	45	5	0	1	3	.250	0	1- -	—	6.27
Las Vegas	AAA	20	0	0	11	28.2	117	20	13	11	4	0	1	1	11	0	25	0	0	2	1	.667	0	1- -	—	3.45
2000 Ottawa	AAA	32	0	0	27	34.2	154	32	23	21	4	1	1	2	19	0	38	2	0	0	3	.000	0	10- -	—	5.45
Nashville	AAA	7	0	0	6	8.1	34	6	6	3	2	0	0	0	2	0	13	1	0	1	0	1.000	0	2- -	—	3.24
2000 Mon-Pit	NL	14	0	0	3	14.2	73	19	22	19	3	1	1	1	9	0	11	3	0	2	2	.500	0	0-0	1	11.66
2000 Montreal	NL	6	0	0	3	5.1	29	6	10	9	1	0	1	0	6	0	4	2	0	0	0	—	0	0-0	1	15.19
Pittsburgh	NL	8	0	0	0	9.1	44	13	12	10	2	1	0	1	3	0	7	1	0	2	2	.500	0	0-0	0	9.64

Heathcliff Slocumb

Pitches: Right Bats: Right Pos: RP-65   Ht: 6'3" Wt: 220 Born: 6/7/66 Age: 35

Year Team	Lg	G	GS	CG	GF	IP	BFP	H	R	ER	HR	SH	SF	HB	TBB	IBB	SO	WP	Bk	W	L	Pct.	ShO	Sv-Op	Hld	ERA
1991 Chicago	NL	52	0	0	21	62.2	274	53	29	24	3	6	6	3	30	6	34	9	0	2	1	.667	0	1-3	6	3.45
1992 Chicago	NL	30	0	0	11	36	174	52	27	26	3	2	2	1	21	3	27	1	0	0	3	.000	0	1-1	1	6.50
1993 ChC-Cle		30	0	0	9	38	164	35	19	17	3	1	3	0	20	2	22	0	0	4	1	.800	0	0-2	3	4.03
1994 Philadelphia	NL	52	0	0	16	72.1	322	75	32	23	0	2	4	2	28	4	58	9	0	5	1	.833	0	0-5	18	2.86
1995 Philadelphia	NL	61	0	0	54	65.1	289	64	26	21	2	4	0	1	35	3	63	3	0	5	6	.455	0	32-38	3	2.89
1996 Boston	AL	75	0	0	60	83.1	368	68	31	28	2	1	3	3	55	5	88	10	0	5	5	.500	0	31-39	2	3.02
1997 Bos-Sea	AL	76	0	0	61	75	353	84	45	43	6	4	2	4	49	5	64	10	0	0	9	.000	0	27-33	3	5.16
1998 Seattle	AL	57	0	0	29	67.2	313	72	40	40	5	4	2	1	44	1	51	11	0	2	5	.286	0	3-4	2	5.32
1999 Bal-StL	AL	50	0	0	19	62	287	64	28	26	5	4	1	3	39	7	60	4	0	3	2	.600	0	2-3	5	3.77
2000 StL-SD	NL	65	0	0	17	68.2	309	69	43	38	9	4	5	3	37	4	46	1	2	2	4	.333	0	1-1	12	4.98
1993 Chicago	NL	10	0	0	4	10.2	42	7	5	4	0	1	0	0	4	0	4	0	0	1	0	1.000	0	0-0	2	3.38
Cleveland	AL	20	0	0	5	27.1	122	28	14	13	3	0	3	0	16	2	18	0	0	3	1	.750	0	0-2	1	4.28
1997 Boston	AL	49	0	0	37	46.2	227	58	32	30	4	2	2	3	34	4	36	6	0	5	5	.500	0	17-22	1	5.79
Seattle	AL	27	0	0	24	28.1	126	26	13	13	2	2	0	1	15	1	28	4	0	0	4	.000	0	10-11	2	4.13
1999 Baltimore	AL	10	0	0	7	8.2	49	15	12	12	1	0	0	2	9	2	12	1	0	0	0	—	0	0-0	0	12.46
St. Louis	NL	40	0	0	12	53.1	238	49	16	14	3	4	1	1	30	5	48	3	0	3	2	.600	0	2-3	5	2.36
2000 St. Louis	NL	43	0	0	11	49.2	218	50	32	30	9	3	2	1	24	1	34	1	1	2	3	.400	0	1-1	9	5.44
San Diego	NL	22	0	0	6	19	91	19	11	8	0	1	3	2	13	3	12	0	1	0	1	.000	0	0-0	3	3.79
10 ML YEARS		548	0	0	297	631	2853	636	320	286	38	32	28	21	358	40	513	57	2	28	37	.431	0	98-129	55	4.08

Joe Slusarski

Pitches: Right Bats: Right Pos: RP-54   Ht: 6'4" Wt: 195 Born: 12/19/66 Age: 34

Year Team	Lg	G	GS	CG	GF	IP	BFP	H	R	ER	HR	SH	SF	HB	TBB	IBB	SO	WP	Bk	W	L	Pct.	ShO	Sv-Op	Hld	ERA
2000 New Orleans *	AAA	13	0	0	6	20	84	14	9	5	2	0	0	1	7	5	21	0	0	2	1	.667	0	0- -	—	2.25
1991 Oakland	AL	20	19	1	0	109.1	486	121	69	64	14	0	3	4	52	1	60	4	0	5	7	.417	0	0-0	0	5.27
1992 Oakland	AL	15	14	0	1	76	338	85	52	46	15	1	5	6	27	0	38	0	1	5	5	.500	0	0-0	0	5.45
1993 Oakland	AL	2	1	0	0	8.2	43	9	5	5	1	2	0	0	11	3	1	0	0	0	0	—	0	0-0	0	5.19
1995 Milwaukee	AL	12	0	0	6	15	73	21	11	9	3	1	1	2	6	1	6	0	0	1	1	.500	0	0-0	0	5.40
1999 Houston	NL	3	0	0	1	3.2	15	1	0	0	0	0	0	0	3	1	3	0	0	0	0	—	0	0-0	0	0.00
2000 Houston	NL	54	0	0	16	77	327	80	36	36	8	2	2	3	22	3	54	6	0	2	7	.222	0	3-4	7	4.21
6 ML YEARS		106	34	1	24	289.2	1282	317	173	160	41	6	11	15	121	9	162	10	1	13	20	.394	0	3-4	7	4.97

Bobby Smith

Bats: Right Throws: Right Pos: 2B-45; 3B-5; PH/PR-2   Ht: 6'3" Wt: 190 Born: 5/10/74 Age: 27

Year Team	Lg	G	AB	H	2B	3B	HR	(Hm	Rd)	TB	R	RBI	TBB	IBB	SO	HBP	SH	SF	SB	CS	SB%	GDP	Avg	OBP	SLG
2000 Durham *	AAA	66	261	76	20	2	17	—	—	151	48	58	23	3	61	3	0	4	15	2	.88	5	.291	.351	.579
1998 Tampa Bay	AL	117	370	102	15	3	11	(4	7)	156	44	55	34	0	110	6	2	4	5	3	.63	9	.276	.343	.422
1999 Tampa Bay	AL	68	199	36	4	1	3	(1	2)	51	18	19	16	0	64	1	2	1	4	4	.50	8	.181	.244	.256
2000 Tampa Bay	AL	49	175	41	8	0	6	(2	4)	67	21	26	14	1	59	1	0	1	2	2	.50	6	.234	.293	.383
3 ML YEARS		234	744	179	27	4	20	(7	13)	274	83	100	64	1	233	8	4	6	11	9	.55	23	.241	.305	.368

Brian Smith

Pitches: Right Bats: Right Pos: RP-3   Ht: 6'0" Wt: 190 Born: 9/17/72 Age: 28

Year Team	Lg	G	GS	CG	GF	IP	BFP	H	R	ER	HR	SH	SF	HB	TBB	IBB	SO	WP	Bk	W	L	Pct.	ShO	Sv-Op	Hld	ERA
1994 Medcine Hat	R+	20	5	0	11	64	268	58	36	24	3	2	4	5	20	0	53	6	3	5	4	.556	0	4- -	—	3.38
1995 Hagerstown	A	47	0	0	36	104	402	77	18	10	1	5	0	5	16	1	101	2	1	9	1	.900	0	21- -	—	0.87
1996 Knoxville	AA	54	0	0	43	75.2	333	76	42	32	7	6	3	4	31	6	58	4	0	3	5	.375	0	16- -	—	3.81
1997 Knoxville	AA	1	0	0	0	1	4	0	0	0	0	0	0	0	1	0	1	0	0	0	0	—	0	0- -	—	0.00
Syracuse	AAA	31	21	0	2	137.1	619	169	89	82	12	2	6	8	51	1	73	4	3	7	11	.389	0	0- -	—	5.37
1998 Dunedin	A+	4	0	0	2	10.2	42	8	4	4	0	0	0	1	3	1	9	0	0	1	0	1.000	0	2- -	—	3.38
Knoxville	AA	42	0	0	15	71	307	72	39	32	7	4	3	3	25	3	50	2	0	4	2	.667	0	7- -	—	4.06
1999 Knoxville	AA	29	0	0	21	35	154	42	25	20	4	0	1	3	6	0	27	2	1	2	3	.333	0	13- -	—	5.14
Syracuse	AAA	29	0	0	23	46.1	210	45	22	18	7	5	1	2	24	4	46	2	0	7	4	.636	0	7- -	—	3.50
2000 Pirates	R	5	2	0	1	6	19	0	0	0	0	0	0	0	1	0	5	0	0	0	0	—	0	0-0	0	0.00
2000 Pittsburgh	NL	3	0	0	1	4.1	20	6	5	5	1	1	0	1	0	0	3	0	0	0	0	—	0	0-0	0	10.38

Chuck Smith

Pitches: Right **Bats:** Right **Pos:** SP-19 **Ht:** 6'1" **Wt:** 185 **Born:** 10/21/69 **Age:** 31

Year Team	Lg	G	GS	CG	GF	IP	BFP	H	R	ER	HR	SH	SF	HB	TBB	IBB	SO	WP	Bk	W	L	Pct.	ShO	Sv-Op	Hld	ERA
1991 Astros	R	15	7	1	2	59.1	272	56	36	23	2	3	0	7	37	0	64	7	5	4	3	.571	0	0- –	—	3.49
1992 Asheville	A	28	20	1	3	132	596	128	93	76	14	5	4	4	78	1	117	4	7	9	9	.500	0	1- –	—	5.18
1993 Quad City	A	22	17	2	3	110.2	488	109	73	57	16	3	2	6	52	0	103	7	4	7	5	.583	0	0- –	—	4.64
1994 Jackson	AA	2	0	0	0	6	30	6	6	3	0	2	0	0	5	0	7	0	1	0	0	—	0	0- –	—	4.50
Osceola	A+	35	2	0	11	84.2	376	73	41	35	2	2	2	2	49	3	60	7	3	4	4	.500	0	0- –	—	3.72
1995 South Bend	A	26	25	4	1	167	688	128	70	50	8	7	2	13	61	0	145	21	11	10	10	.500	2	0- –	—	2.69
1996 Pr William	A+	20	20	2	0	123.1	545	125	65	55	7	3	2	10	49	1	99	13	1	6	6	.500	0	0- –	—	4.01
Birmingham	AA	7	3	0	2	30.2	124	25	11	9	1	0	0	1	15	2	30	0	1	2	1	.667	0	1- –	—	2.64
Nashville	AAA	1	0	0	0	0.2	5	2	2	2	0	0	0	0	1	0	1	0	0	0	0	—	0	0- –	—	27.00
1997 Birmingham	AA	25	0	0	6	62.2	280	63	35	22	4	1	2	5	27	5	57	8	3	2	2	.500	0	0- –	—	3.16
Nashville	AAA	20	1	0	12	31.2	156	39	33	31	8	2	3	2	23	2	29	8	2	0	3	.000	0	0- –	—	8.81
1998 Sioux Falls	IND	8	8	2	0	55	226	44	18	16	1	0	0	3	21	1	70	1	0	5	3	.625	1	0- –	—	2.62
1999 Oklahoma	AAA	32	4	2	13	85	341	73	31	28	7	1	3	1	28	0	76	5	0	5	4	.556	0	4- –	—	2.96
2000 Oklahoma	AAA	11	11	0	0	66.2	300	73	31	28	3	2	2	2	38	1	73	5	0	5	3	.625	0	0- –	—	3.78
2000 Florida	NL	19	19	1	0	122.2	513	111	53	44	6	4	5	3	54	2	118	6	1	6	6	.500	0	0-0	0	3.23

Dan Smith

Pitches: Right **Bats:** Right **Pos:** RP-2 **Ht:** 6'3" **Wt:** 210 **Born:** 9/15/75 **Age:** 25

Year Team	Lg	G	GS	CG	GF	IP	BFP	H	R	ER	HR	SH	SF	HB	TBB	IBB	SO	WP	Bk	W	L	Pct.	ShO	Sv-Op	Hld	ERA
1993 Rangers	R	12	10	1	0	53.1	212	50	19	17	1	1	2	3	8	0	27	3	1	3	2	.600	0	0- –	—	2.87
1994 Chston-SC	A	27	27	4	0	157.1	715	171	111	86	12	5	2	19	55	0	86	5	2	7	10	.412	0	0- –	—	4.92
1995 Rangers	R	4	3	0	0	19	81	19	9	9	0	0	1	2	5	0	12	0	0	0	3	.000	0	0- –	—	4.26
Charlotte	A+	9	9	1	0	58	242	53	23	19	4	1	2	3	16	0	34	1	0	5	1	.833	1	0- –	—	2.95
1996 Charlotte	A+	18	18	1	0	87	403	100	61	49	6	5	5	4	38	0	55	3	0	3	7	.300	0	0- –	—	5.07
1997 Charlotte	A+	26	25	2	0	160.2	705	169	93	79	17	6	4	11	66	1	113	9	0	8	10	.444	0	0- –	—	4.43
1998 Tulsa	AA	26	25	1	0	153.1	675	162	101	99	27	1	7	11	58	1	105	9	1	13	9	.591	0	0- –	—	5.81
Oklahoma	AAA	1	1	0	0	6	25	6	4	4	2	1	0	1	1	0	3	0	0	0	0	—	0	0- –	—	6.00
1999 Ottawa	AAA	11	11	0	0	71	298	61	31	29	7	3	0	7	27	0	59	3	0	5	4	.556	0	0- –	—	3.68
2000 Pawtucket	AAA	24	21	2	1	124.2	546	134	72	67	15	2	3	9	41	1	70	7	0	7	10	.412	1	0- –	—	4.84
1999 Montreal	NL	20	17	0	0	89.2	407	104	64	60	12	7	2	4	39	0	72	3	0	4	9	.308	0	0-1	0	6.02
2000 Boston	AL	2	0	0	0	3.1	15	2	3	3	0	1	3	0	3	0	1	0	0	0	0	—	0	0-0	0	8.10
2 ML YEARS		22	17	0	0	93	422	106	67	63	12	8	5	4	42	0	73	3	0	4	9	.308	0	0-1	0	6.10

Mark Smith

Bats: R **Throws:** R **Pos:** PH/PR-58; LF-29; RF-25; DH-1 **Ht:** 6'3" **Wt:** 225 **Born:** 5/7/70 **Age:** 31

Year Team	Lg	G	AB	H	2B	3B	HR	(Hm	Rd)	TB	R	RBI	TBB	IBB	SO	HBP	SH	SF	SB	CS	SB%	GDP	Avg	OBP	SLG
1994 Baltimore	AL	3	7	1	0	0	0	(0	0)	1	0	2	0	0	2	0	0	0	0	0	—	0	.143	.143	.143
1995 Baltimore	AL	37	104	24	5	0	3	(1	2)	38	11	15	12	2	22	1	2	1	3	0	1.00	4	.231	.314	.365
1996 Baltimore	AL	27	78	19	2	0	4	(3	1)	33	9	10	3	0	20	3	0	0	0	2	.00	0	.244	.298	.423
1997 Pittsburgh	NL	71	193	55	13	1	9	(6	3)	97	29	35	28	1	36	0	0	1	3	1	.75	3	.285	.374	.503
1998 Pittsburgh	NL	59	128	25	6	0	2	(1	1)	37	18	13	10	0	26	3	0	2	7	0	1.00	1	.195	.264	.289
2000 Florida	NL	104	192	47	8	1	5	(2	3)	72	22	27	17	1	54	2	0	2	2	0	1.00	2	.245	.310	.375
6 ML YEARS		301	702	171	34	2	23	(13	10)	278	89	102	70	4	160	9	2	7	15	3	.83	10	.244	.317	.396

John Smoltz

Pitches: Right **Bats:** Right **Pos:** SP **Ht:** 6'3" **Wt:** 220 **Born:** 5/15/67 **Age:** 34

Year Team	Lg	G	GS	CG	GF	IP	BFP	H	R	ER	HR	SH	SF	HB	TBB	IBB	SO	WP	Bk	W	L	Pct.	ShO	Sv-Op	Hld	ERA
1988 Atlanta	NL	12	12	0	0	64	297	74	40	39	10	2	0	2	33	4	37	2	1	2	7	.222	0	0-0	0	5.48
1989 Atlanta	NL	29	29	5	0	208	847	160	79	68	15	10	7	2	72	2	168	8	3	12	11	.522	0	0-0	0	2.94
1990 Atlanta	NL	34	34	6	0	231.1	966	206	109	99	20	9	8	1	90	3	170	14	3	14	11	.560	2	0-0	0	3.85
1991 Atlanta	NL	36	36	5	0	229.2	947	206	101	97	16	9	9	3	77	1	148	20	1	14	13	.519	0	0-0	0	3.80
1992 Atlanta	NL	35	35	9	0	246.2	1021	206	90	78	17	7	8	5	80	5	215	17	1	15	12	.556	3	0-0	0	2.85
1993 Atlanta	NL	35	35	3	0	243.2	1028	208	104	98	23	13	4	6	100	12	208	13	1	15	11	.577	1	0-0	0	3.62
1994 Atlanta	NL	21	21	1	0	134.2	568	120	69	62	15	7	6	4	48	4	113	7	0	6	10	.375	0	0-0	0	4.14
1995 Atlanta	NL	29	29	2	0	192.2	808	166	76	68	15	13	5	4	72	8	193	13	0	12	7	.632	1	0-0	0	3.18
1996 Atlanta	NL	35	35	6	0	253.2	995	199	93	83	19	12	4	2	55	3	276	10	1	24	8	.750	2	0-0	0	2.94
1997 Atlanta	NL	35	35	7	0	256	1043	234	97	86	21	10	3	1	63	9	241	10	1	15	12	.556	2	0-0	0	3.02
1998 Atlanta	NL	26	26	2	0	167.2	681	145	58	54	10	4	2	4	44	2	173	3	1	17	3	.850	1	0-0	0	2.90
1999 Atlanta	NL	29	29	1	0	186.1	746	168	70	66	14	10	5	4	40	2	156	2	0	11	8	.579	1	0-0	0	3.19
12 ML YEARS		356	356	47	0	2414.1	9947	2092	986	898	195	106	61	38	774	55	2098	119	14	157	113	.581	14	0-0	0	3.35

J.T. Snow

Bats: Left **Throws:** Left **Pos:** 1B-153; PH/PR-4 **Ht:** 6'2" **Wt:** 205 **Born:** 2/26/68 **Age:** 33

Year Team	Lg	G	AB	H	2B	3B	HR	(Hm	Rd)	TB	R	RBI	TBB	IBB	SO	HBP	SH	SF	SB	CS	SB%	GDP	Avg	OBP	SLG
1992 New York	AL	7	14	2	1	0	0	(0	0)	3	1	2	5	1	5	0	0	0	0	0	—	0	.143	.368	.214
1993 California	AL	129	419	101	18	2	16	(10	6)	171	60	57	55	4	88	2	7	6	3	0	1.00	10	.241	.328	.408
1994 California	AL	61	223	49	4	0	8	(7	1)	77	22	30	19	1	48	3	2	1	0	0	.00	2	.220	.289	.345
1995 California	AL	143	544	157	22	1	24	(14	10)	253	80	102	52	4	91	3	5	2	2	1	.67	16	.289	.353	.465
1996 California	AL	155	575	148	20	1	17	(8	9)	221	69	67	56	6	96	5	2	3	1	6	.14	19	.257	.327	.384
1997 San Francisco	NL	157	531	149	36	1	28	(14	14)	271	81	104	96	13	124	1	2	7	6	4	.60	8	.281	.387	.510
1998 San Francisco	NL	138	435	108	29	1	15	(9	6)	184	65	79	58	3	84	0	0	7	1	2	.33	12	.248	.332	.423
1999 San Francisco	NL	161	570	156	25	2	24	(7	17)	257	93	98	86	7	121	5	1	6	0	4	.00	16	.274	.370	.451
2000 San Francisco	NL	155	536	152	33	2	19	(10	9)	246	82	96	66	6	129	11	0	14	1	3	.25	20	.284	.365	.459
9 ML YEARS		1106	3847	1022	188	10	151	(79	72)	1683	553	635	493	45	786	30	19	46	14	21	.40	103	.266	.350	.437

John Snyder

Pitches: Right **Bats:** Right **Pos:** SP-23   **Ht:** 6'3" **Wt:** 200 **Born:** 8/16/74 **Age:** 26

		HOW MUCH HE PITCHED						WHAT HE GAVE UP													THE RESULTS				
Year Team	Lg	G	GS	CG	GF	IP	BFP	H	R	ER	HR	SH	SF	HB	TBB	IBB	SO	WP	Bk	W	L	Pct.	ShO	Sv-Op	Hld	ERA
2000 Huntsville *	AA	2	2	0	0	12.1	46	6	3	3	1	1	0	1	5	0	6	0	0	1	1	.500	0	0--	—	2.19
Indianapols *	AAA	1	1	0	0	7	26	6	2	2	1	0	0	0	0	0	5	0	0	1	0	1.000	0	0--	—	2.57
1998 Chicago	AL	15	14	1	0	86.1	367	96	49	46	14	2	4	2	23	1	52	2	0	7	2	.778	0	0-0	0	4.80
1999 Chicago	AL	25	25	1	0	129.1	602	167	103	96	27	3	7	6	49	0	67	11	0	9	12	.429	0	0-0	0	6.68
2000 Milwaukee	NL	23	23	0	0	127	596	147	95	87	8	6	7	9	77	10	69	6	0	3	10	.231	0	0-0	0	6.17
3 ML YEARS		63	62	2	0	342.2	1565	410	247	229	49	11	18	17	149	11	188	19	0	19	24	.442	0	0-0	0	6.01

Luis Sojo

Bats: R **Throws:** R **Pos:** 3B-60; 2B-26; PH/PR-12; 1B-7; SS-2   **Ht:** 5'11" **Wt:** 185 **Born:** 1/3/66 **Age:** 35

		BATTING																	BASERUNNING				PERCENTAGES		
Year Team	Lg	G	AB	H	2B	3B	HR	(Hm	Rd)	TB	R	RBI	TBB	IBB	SO	HBP	SH	SF	SB	CS	SB%	GDP	Avg	OBP	SLG
1990 Toronto	AL	33	80	18	3	0	1	(0	1)	24	14	9	5	0	5	0	0	0	1	1	.50	1	.225	.271	.300
1991 California	AL	113	364	94	14	1	3	(1	2)	119	38	20	14	0	26	5	19	0	4	2	.67	12	.258	.295	.327
1992 California	AL	106	368	100	12	3	7	(2	5)	139	37	43	14	0	24	1	7	1	7	11	.39	14	.272	.299	.378
1993 Toronto	AL	19	47	8	2	0	0	(0	0)	10	5	6	4	0	2	0	2	1	0	0	—	3	.170	.231	.213
1994 Seattle	AL	63	213	59	9	2	6	(4	2)	90	32	22	8	0	25	2	3	1	2	1	.67	3	.277	.308	.423
1995 Seattle	AL	102	339	98	18	2	7	(4	3)	141	50	39	23	0	19	1	6	1	4	2	.67	9	.289	.335	.416
1996 Sea-NYY	AL	95	287	63	10	1	1	(1	0)	78	23	21	11	0	17	1	8	1	2	2	.50	10	.220	.250	.272
1997 New York	AL	77	215	66	6	1	2	(2	0)	80	27	25	16	0	14	1	5	2	3	1	.75	5	.307	.345	.372
1998 New York	AL	54	147	34	3	1	0	(0	0)	39	16	14	4	0	15	0	1	1	1	0	1.00	4	.231	.250	.265
1999 New York	AL	49	127	32	6	0	2	(1	1)	44	20	16	4	0	17	0	2	0	1	0	1.00	4	.252	.275	.346
2000 Pit-NYY	AL	95	301	86	18	1	7	(4	3)	127	33	37	17	3	22	1	3	1	2	0	1.00	11	.286	.325	.422
1996 Seattle	AL	77	247	52	8	1	1	(1	0)	65	20	16	10	0	13	1	6	0	2	2	.50	8	.211	.244	.263
New York	AL	18	40	11	2	0	0	(0	0)	13	3	5	1	0	4	0	2	1	0	0	—	2	.275	.286	.325
2000 Pittsburgh	NL	61	176	50	11	0	5	(2	3)	76	14	20	11	3	16	1	0	1	1	0	1.00	6	.284	.328	.432
New York	AL	34	125	36	7	1	2	(2	0)	51	19	17	6	0	6	0	3	0	1	0	1.00	5	.288	.321	.408
11 ML YEARS		806	2488	658	101	12	36	(19	17)	891	295	252	120	3	186	12	56	9	27	20	.57	76	.264	.300	.358

Alfonso Soriano

Bats: R **Throws:** R **Pos:** 3B-10; SS-9; PH/PR-2; DH-1; 2B-1   **Ht:** 6'1" **Wt:** 180 **Born:** 1/7/78 **Age:** 23

		BATTING																	BASERUNNING				PERCENTAGES		
Year Team	Lg	G	AB	H	2B	3B	HR	(Hm	Rd)	TB	R	RBI	TBB	IBB	SO	HBP	SH	SF	SB	CS	SB%	GDP	Avg	OBP	SLG
1999 Norwich	AA	89	361	110	20	3	15	(—	—)	181	57	68	32	1	67	4	0	5	24	16	.60	9	.305	.363	.501
Yankees	R	5	19	5	2	0	1	(—	—)	10	7	5	1	0	3	1	0	1	0	0	—	1	.263	.318	.526
Columbus	AAA	20	82	15	5	1	2	(—	—)	28	8	11	5	0	18	0	0	2	1	1	.50	1	.183	.225	.341
2000 Columbus	AAA	111	459	133	32	6	12	(—	—)	213	90	66	25	1	85	3	2	6	14	7	.67	8	.290	.327	.464
1999 New York	AL	9	8	1	0	0	1	(1	0)	4	2	1	0	0	3	0	0	0	0	1	.00	0	.125	.125	.500
2000 New York	AL	22	50	9	3	0	2	(0	2)	18	5	3	1	0	15	0	2	0	2	1	1.00	0	.180	.196	.360
2 ML YEARS		31	58	10	3	0	3	(1	2)	22	7	4	1	0	18	0	2	0	2	1	.67	0	.172	.186	.379

Sammy Sosa

Bats: Right **Throws:** Right **Pos:** RF-156; CF-2   **Ht:** 6'0" **Wt:** 220 **Born:** 11/12/68 **Age:** 32

		BATTING																	BASERUNNING				PERCENTAGES		
Year Team	Lg	G	AB	H	2B	3B	HR	(Hm	Rd)	TB	R	RBI	TBB	IBB	SO	HBP	SH	SF	SB	CS	SB%	GDP	Avg	OBP	SLG
1989 Tex-CWS	AL	58	183	47	8	0	4	(1	3)	67	27	13	11	2	47	2	5	2	7	5	.58	6	.257	.303	.366
1990 Chicago	AL	153	532	124	26	10	15	(10	5)	215	72	70	33	4	150	6	2	6	32	16	.67	10	.233	.282	.404
1991 Chicago	AL	116	316	64	10	1	10	(3	7)	106	39	33	14	2	98	2	5	1	13	6	.68	5	.203	.240	.335
1992 Chicago	NL	67	262	68	7	2	8	(4	4)	103	41	25	19	1	63	4	4	2	15	7	.68	4	.260	.317	.393
1993 Chicago	NL	159	598	156	25	5	33	(23	10)	290	92	93	38	6	135	4	0	1	36	11	.77	14	.261	.309	.485
1994 Chicago	NL	105	426	128	17	6	25	(11	14)	232	59	70	25	1	92	2	1	4	22	13	.63	7	.300	.339	.545
1995 Chicago	NL	144	564	151	17	3	36	(19	17)	282	89	119	58	11	134	5	0	2	34	7	.83	8	.268	.340	.500
1996 Chicago	NL	124	498	136	21	2	40	(26	14)	281	84	100	34	6	134	5	0	4	18	5	.78	14	.273	.323	.564
1997 Chicago	NL	162	642	161	31	4	36	(25	11)	308	90	119	45	9	174	2	0	5	22	12	.65	16	.251	.300	.480
1998 Chicago	NL	159	643	198	20	0	66	(35	31)	416	134	158	73	14	171	5	0	5	18	9	.67	20	.308	.377	.647
1999 Chicago	NL	162	625	180	24	2	63	(33	30)	397	114	141	78	6	171	3	0	6	7	8	.47	17	.288	.367	.635
2000 Chicago	NL	156	604	193	38	1	50	(22	28)	383	106	138	91	19	168	2	0	8	7	4	.64	12	.320	.406	.634
1989 Texas	AL	25	84	20	3	0	1	(0	1)	26	8	3	0	0	20	0	4	0	0	2	.00	3	.238	.238	.310
Chicago	AL	33	99	27	5	0	3	(1	2)	41	19	10	11	2	27	2	1	2	7	3	.70	3	.273	.351	.414
12 ML YEARS		1565	5893	1606	244	36	386	(212	174)	3080	947	1079	519	83	1537	38	17	46	231	103	.69	133	.273	.333	.523

Jeff Sparks

Pitches: Right **Bats:** Right **Pos:** RP-15   **Ht:** 6'3" **Wt:** 220 **Born:** 4/4/72 **Age:** 29

		HOW MUCH HE PITCHED						WHAT HE GAVE UP													THE RESULTS				
Year Team	Lg	G	GS	CG	GF	IP	BFP	H	R	ER	HR	SH	SF	HB	TBB	IBB	SO	WP	Bk	W	L	Pct.	ShO	Sv-Op	Hld	ERA
1995 Princeton	R+	16	2	0	7	39	172	32	19	14	2	0	6	6	27	2	49	2	1	2	0	1.000	0	0--	—	3.23
1996 Chattanooga	AA	3	0	0	0	2	10	5	1	1	1	0	0	0	1	0	2	0	0	0	0	—	0	0--	—	4.50
Chstn-WV	A	46	3	0	14	89.1	394	79	51	47	4	4	4	9	46	6	94	10	1	2	7	.222	0	0--	—	4.74
1997 Burlington	A	22	9	0	5	61.1	281	61	49	39	7	2	3	0	39	1	72	6	1	2	5	.286	0	0--	—	5.72
1998 Winnipeg	IND	38	0	0	36	49	221	30	21	17	5	2	1	1	42	1	85	4	0	2	1	.667	0	17--	—	3.12
1999 Nashville	AAA	34	0	0	4	49.1	209	37	25	21	4	1	2	4	23	1	69	7	0	5	3	.625	0	0--	—	3.83
Durham	AAA	18	0	0	5	24	106	16	11	9	2	0	1	1	14	0	31	3	0	3	0	1.000	0	0--	—	3.38
2000 Durham	AAA	9	1	0	2	12.2	75	11	21	20	2	1	0	3	23	0	17	2	0	1	4	.200	0	0--	—	14.21
St. Pete	A+	1	1	0	6	28	121	9	13	10	0	2	1	0	26	0	33	3	0	1	4	.200	0	3--	—	3.21
Orlando	AA	3	3	0	0	10.2	55	9	13	8	2	1	0	0	11	0	8	4	0	0	2	.000	0	0--	—	6.75
1999 Tampa Bay	AL	8	0	0	2	10	49	6	6	6	1	1	0	1	12	1	17	1	0	0	0	—	0	1-1	0	5.40
2000 Tampa Bay	AL	15	0	0	0	20.1	90	13	8	8	2	0	0	2	18	1	24	3	0	0	1	.000	0	0-0	1	3.54
2 ML YEARS		23	0	0	6	30.1	139	19	14	14	3	1	0	3	30	2	41	4	0	0	1	.000	0	1-1	1	4.15

Steve Sparks

Pitches: Right **Bats:** Right **Pos:** RP-3

Ht: 6'4" **Wt:** 210 **Born:** 3/28/75 **Age:** 26

Year Team	Lg	G	GS	CG	GF	IP	BFP	H	R	ER	HR	SH	SF	HB	TBB	IBB	SO	WP	Bk	W	L	Pct.	ShO	Sv-Op	Hld	ERA
1998 Erie	A-	14	10	0	0	63	282	55	38	31	3	0	2	9	30	1	61	5	3	2	7	.222	0	0- -	—	4.43
Augusta	A	2	2	0	0	8.2	43	11	9	6	1	0	1	0	4	0	12	1	0	0	1	.000	0	0- -	—	6.23
1999 Hickory	A	25	12	1	2	88.2	407	97	60	44	3	3	3	5	51	0	72	7	0	4	6	.400	1	0- -	—	4.47
Lynchburg	A+	5	5	1	0	26	124	36	20	18	3	0	2	1	15	0	20	2	0	2	3	.400	0	0- -	—	6.23
2000 Altoona	AA	23	17	3	3	109.1	484	103	66	58	6	3	4	11	54	0	66	8	0	6	7	.462	2	0- -	—	4.77
2000 Pittsburgh	NL	3	0	0	2	4	20	4	3	3	0	0	0	0	5	0	2	2	0	0	0	—	0	0-0	0	6.75

Steve W. Sparks

Pitches: Right **Bats:** Right **Pos:** SP-15; RP-5

Ht: 6'0" **Wt:** 180 **Born:** 7/2/65 **Age:** 35

Year Team	Lg	G	GS	CG	GF	IP	BFP	H	R	ER	HR	SH	SF	HB	TBB	IBB	SO	WP	Bk	W	L	Pct.	ShO	Sv-Op	Hld	ERA
2000 Toledo *	AAA	16	14	1	0	90.2	397	86	53	38	8	4	4	4	41	0	44	0	1	5	7	.417	0	0-0	0	3.77
1995 Milwaukee	AL	33	27	3	2	202	875	210	111	104	17	5	12	5	86	1	96	5	1	9	11	.450	0	0-0	0	4.63
1996 Milwaukee	AL	20	13	1	2	88.2	406	103	66	65	19	3	1	3	52	0	21	6	0	4	7	.364	0	0-0	0	6.60
1998 Anaheim	AL	22	20	0	1	128.2	562	130	66	62	14	2	3	5	58	0	90	6	0	9	4	.692	0	0-0	0	4.34
1999 Anaheim	AL	28	26	0	1	147.2	688	165	101	89	21	2	8	9	82	0	73	8	0	5	11	.313	0	0-0	0	5.42
2000 Detroit	AL	20	15	1	5	104	446	108	55	47	7	1	1	4	29	0	53	6	0	7	5	.583	1	1-1	0	4.07
5 ML YEARS		123	101	5	11	671	2977	716	399	367	78	13	25	26	307	1	333	31	1	34	38	.472	1	1-1	0	4.92

Justin Speier

Pitches: Right **Bats:** Right **Pos:** RP-47

Ht: 6'4" **Wt:** 205 **Born:** 11/6/73 **Age:** 27

Year Team	Lg	G	GS	CG	GF	IP	BFP	H	R	ER	HR	SH	SF	HB	TBB	IBB	SO	WP	Bk	W	L	Pct.	ShO	Sv-Op	Hld	ERA
2000 Buffalo *	AAA	13	0	0	13	13	55	13	6	6	0	1	0	0	3	0	12	0	0	0	0	—	0	9- -	1	4.15
1998 ChC-Fla	NL	19	0	0	10	20.2	99	27	20	20	7	2	1	0	13	1	17	3	0	0	3	.000	0	0-1	1	8.71
1999 Atlanta	NL	19	0	0	8	28.2	127	28	18	18	8	0	1	0	13	1	22	0	0	0	0	—	0	0-0	0	5.65
2000 Cleveland	AL	47	0	0	12	68.1	290	57	27	25	9	2	4	4	28	3	69	7	1	5	2	.714	0	0-1	6	3.29
1998 Chicago	NL	1	0	0	0	1.1	7	2	2	2	0	0	0	0	1	0	2	1	0	0	0	—	0	0-0	0	13.50
Florida	NL	18	0	0	10	19.1	92	25	18	18	7	2	1	0	12	1	15	2	0	0	3	.000	0	0-1	1	8.38
3 ML YEARS		85	0	0	30	117.2	516	112	65	63	24	4	6	4	54	5	108	10	1	5	5	.500	0	0-2	7	4.82

Sean Spencer

Pitches: Left **Bats:** Left **Pos:** RP-8

Ht: 5'11" **Wt:** 185 **Born:** 5/29/75 **Age:** 26

Year Team	Lg	G	GS	CG	GF	IP	BFP	H	R	ER	HR	SH	SF	HB	TBB	IBB	SO	WP	Bk	W	L	Pct.	ShO	Sv-Op	Hld	ERA
1997 Lancaster	A+	39	0	0	32	60.1	227	41	12	11	4	4	1	2	15	0	72	2	0	2	3	.400	0	18- -	—	1.64
1998 Orlando	AA	37	0	0	32	42.2	178	33	18	14	3	3	1	1	18	1	43	5	1	2	1	.667	0	18- -	—	2.95
Tacoma	AAA	9	0	0	3	13	56	10	7	7	0	0	0	1	7	0	16	1	0	2	0	1.000	0	1- -	—	4.85
1999 Tacoma	AAA	44	0	0	28	49.1	205	41	21	19	6	1	0	1	23	2	53	4	0	2	1	.667	0	7- -	—	3.47
2000 Tacoma	AAA	42	0	0	20	45.1	208	35	21	17	3	5	2	1	37	3	46	3	2	3	2	.600	0	0- -	—	3.38
Ottawa	AAA	10	0	0	5	10	52	15	12	11	2	0	1	1	6	0	8	0	0	1	1	.500	0	1- -	—	9.90
1999 Seattle	AL	2	0	0	0	1.2	12	5	4	4	0	0	0	0	3	0	2	0	0	0	0	—	0	0-0	0	21.60
2000 Montreal	NL	8	0	0	1	6.2	28	7	4	4	2	0	1	0	3	0	6	4	0	0	0	—	0	0-0	0	5.40
2 ML YEARS		10	0	0	1	8.1	40	12	8	8	2	0	1	0	6	0	8	4	0	0	0	—	0	0-0	0	8.64

Shane Spencer

Bats: R **Throws:** R **Pos:** DH-33; LF-33; RF-7; PH/PR-1

Ht: 5'11" **Wt:** 225 **Born:** 2/20/72 **Age:** 29

Year Team	Lg	G	AB	H	2B	3B	HR	(Hm	Rd)	TB	R	RBI	TBB	IBB	SO	HBP	SH	SF	SB	CS	SB%	GDP	Avg	OBP	SLG
1998 New York	AL	27	67	25	6	0	10	(8	2)	61	18	27	5	0	12	0	0	1	0	1	.00	0	.373	.411	.910
1999 New York	AL	71	205	48	8	0	8	(2	6)	80	25	20	18	0	51	2	0	1	0	4	.00	1	.234	.301	.390
2000 New York	AL	73	248	70	11	3	9	(4	5)	114	33	40	19	0	45	2	0	7	1	2	.33	4	.282	.330	.460
3 ML YEARS		171	520	143	25	3	27	(14	13)	255	76	87	42	0	108	4	0	9	1	7	.13	5	.275	.329	.490

Stan Spencer

Pitches: Right **Bats:** Right **Pos:** SP-8

Ht: 6'4" **Wt:** 223 **Born:** 8/7/69 **Age:** 31

Year Team	Lg	G	GS	CG	GF	IP	BFP	H	R	ER	HR	SH	SF	HB	TBB	IBB	SO	WP	Bk	W	L	Pct.	ShO	Sv-Op	Hld	ERA
2000 Las Vegas *	AAA	6	6	0	0	36.2	146	29	9	7	2	1	3	1	7	0	40	3	1	4	0	1.000	0	0- -	—	1.72
1998 San Diego	NL	6	5	0	0	30.2	124	29	16	16	5	0	0	1	4	0	31	0	0	1	0	1.000	0	0-0	0	4.70
1999 San Diego	NL	8	8	0	1	38.1	183	56	44	39	11	4	0	1	11	1	36	1	1	0	7	.000	0	0-0	0	9.16
2000 San Diego	NL	8	8	0	0	49.2	208	44	22	18	7	2	1	2	19	1	40	0	1	2	2	.500	0	0-0	0	3.26
3 ML YEARS		23	21	0	1	118.2	515	129	82	73	23	6	1	4	34	2	107	1	2	3	9	.250	0	0-0	0	5.54

Bill Spiers

Bats: L **Throws:** R **Pos:** 3B-51; PH/PR-35; SS-27; 2B-26; LF-6; RF-4

Ht: 6'2" **Wt:** 190 **Born:** 6/5/66 **Age:** 35

Year Team	Lg	G	AB	H	2B	3B	HR	(Hm	Rd)	TB	R	RBI	TBB	IBB	SO	HBP	SH	SF	SB	CS	SB%	GDP	Avg	OBP	SLG
1989 Milwaukee	AL	114	345	88	9	3	4	(1	3)	115	44	33	21	1	63	1	4	2	10	2	.83	2	.255	.298	.333
1990 Milwaukee	AL	112	363	88	15	3	2	(2	0)	115	44	36	16	0	45	1	6	3	11	6	.65	12	.242	.274	.317
1991 Milwaukee	AL	133	414	117	13	6	8	(1	7)	166	71	54	34	0	55	2	10	4	14	8	.64	9	.283	.337	.401
1992 Milwaukee	AL	12	16	5	2	0	0	(0	0)	7	2	2	1	0	4	0	1	0	1	1	.50	0	.313	.353	.438
1993 Milwaukee	AL	113	340	81	8	4	2	(2	0)	103	43	36	29	2	51	4	9	4	9	8	.53	11	.238	.302	.303

203

		BATTING																	BASERUNNING				PERCENTAGES		
Year Team	Lg	G	AB	H	2B	3B	HR	(Hm	Rd)	TB	R	RBI	TBB	IBB	SO	HBP	SH	SF	SB	CS	SB%	GDP	Avg	OBP	SLG
1994 Milwaukee	AL	73	214	54	10	1	0	(0	0)	66	27	17	19	1	42	1	3	0	7	1	.88	5	.252	.316	.308
1995 New York	NL	63	72	15	2	1	0	(0	0)	19	5	11	12	1	15	0	1	2	0	1	.00	0	.208	.314	.264
1996 Houston	NL	122	218	55	10	1	6	(3	3)	85	27	26	20	4	34	2	1	1	7	0	1.00	3	.252	.320	.390
1997 Houston	NL	132	291	93	27	4	4	(0	4)	140	51	48	61	6	42	1	1	1	10	5	.67	4	.320	.438	.481
1998 Houston	NL	123	384	105	27	4	4	(1	3)	152	66	43	45	0	62	5	1	2	11	2	.85	9	.273	.356	.396
1999 Houston	NL	127	393	113	18	5	4	(1	3)	153	56	39	47	2	45	0	3	1	10	5	.67	10	.288	.363	.392
2000 Houston	NL	124	355	107	17	3	3	(2	1)	139	41	43	49	3	38	1	2	2	7	4	.64	8	.301	.386	.392
12 ML YEARS		1248	3405	921	158	35	37	(13	24)	1260	477	388	354	20	496	18	42	22	97	43	.69	73	.270	.340	.370

Scott Spiezio

Bats: B **Throws:** R **Pos:** DH-50; PH/PR-39; 1B-29; 3B-15; LF-9; 2B-2; RF-2   **Ht:** 6'2" **Wt:** 225 **Born:** 9/21/72 **Age:** 28

		BATTING																	BASERUNNING				PERCENTAGES		
Year Team	Lg	G	AB	H	2B	3B	HR	(Hm	Rd)	TB	R	RBI	TBB	IBB	SO	HBP	SH	SF	SB	CS	SB%	GDP	Avg	OBP	SLG
1996 Oakland	AL	9	29	9	2	0	2	(1	1)	17	6	8	4	1	4	0	2	0	0	1	.00	0	.310	.394	.586
1997 Oakland	AL	147	538	131	28	4	14	(6	8)	209	58	65	44	2	75	1	3	4	9	3	.75	13	.243	.300	.388
1998 Oakland	AL	114	406	105	19	1	9	(3	6)	153	54	50	44	3	56	2	7	2	1	3	.25	10	.259	.333	.377
1999 Oakland	AL	89	247	60	24	0	8	(3	5)	108	31	33	29	3	36	2	1	3	0	0	—	5	.243	.324	.437
2000 Anaheim	AL	123	297	72	11	2	17	(10	7)	138	47	49	40	2	56	3	1	4	1	2	.33	5	.242	.334	.465
5 ML YEARS		482	1517	377	84	7	50	(26	24)	625	196	205	161	11	227	8	14	13	11	9	.55	33	.249	.321	.412

Paul Spoljaric

Pitches: Left **Bats:** Right **Pos:** RP-13   **Ht:** 6'3" **Wt:** 210 **Born:** 9/24/70 **Age:** 30

		HOW MUCH HE PITCHED						WHAT HE GAVE UP											THE RESULTS						
Year Team	Lg	G	GS	CG	GF	IP	BFP	H	R	ER	HR	SH	SF	HB	TBB	IBB	SO	WP	Bk	W	L	Pct.	ShO	Sv-Op	Hld	ERA
2000 Omaha *	AAA	43	0	0	25	51	210	44	17	16	5	1	4	0	19	0	56	4	0	1	2	.333	0	7- —	—	2.82
1994 Toronto	AL	2	1	0	0	2.1	21	5	10	10	3	0	0	0	9	1	2	0	0	0	1	.000	0	0-0	—	38.57
1996 Toronto	AL	28	0	0	12	38	163	30	17	13	6	1	1	2	19	1	38	0	0	2	2	.500	0	1-1	5	3.08
1997 Tor-Sea	AL	57	0	0	10	70.2	302	61	30	29	4	2	2	3	36	6	70	6	3	0	3	.000	0	3-5	10	3.69
1998 Seattle	AL	53	6	0	10	83.1	387	85	67	60	14	5	3	1	55	3	89	10	0	4	6	.400	0	0-2	9	6.48
1999 Phi-Tor	AL	42	5	0	8	73.1	346	85	65	51	10	6	4	3	39	2	73	1	0	2	5	.286	0	0-1	2	6.26
2000 Kansas City	AL	13	0	0	4	9.2	40	9	7	7	4	1	0	0	5	0	6	0	0	0	0	—	0	0-0	0	6.52
1997 Toronto	AL	37	0	0	10	48	198	37	17	17	3	1	2	2	21	4	43	5	1	0	3	.000	0	3-3	8	3.19
Seattle		20	0	0	0	22.2	104	24	13	12	1	1	0	1	15	2	27	1	2	0	0	—	0	0-2	2	4.76
1999 Philadelphia	NL	5	3	0	1	11.1	64	23	24	19	1	1	1	1	7	0	10	0	0	0	3	.000	0	0-0	0	15.09
Toronto	AL	37	2	0	7	62	282	62	41	32	9	5	3	2	32	2	63	1	0	2	2	.500	0	0-1	2	4.65
6 ML YEARS		195	12	0	44	277.1	1259	275	196	170	41	15	10	9	163	13	278	17	3	8	17	.320	0	4-9	26	5.52

Jerry Spradlin

Pitches: Right **Bats:** Both **Pos:** RP-57; SP-1   **Ht:** 6'7" **Wt:** 260 **Born:** 6/14/67 **Age:** 34

		HOW MUCH HE PITCHED						WHAT HE GAVE UP											THE RESULTS						
Year Team	Lg	G	GS	CG	GF	IP	BFP	H	R	ER	HR	SH	SF	HB	TBB	IBB	SO	WP	Bk	W	L	Pct.	ShO	Sv-Op	Hld	ERA
1993 Cincinnati	NL	37	0	0	16	49	193	44	20	19	4	3	4	0	9	0	24	3	1	2	1	.667	0	2-3	0	3.49
1994 Cincinnati	NL	6	0	0	2	8	38	12	11	9	2	0	2	0	2	0	4	0	0	0	0	—	0	0-0	0	10.13
1996 Cincinnati	NL	1	0	0	1	0.1	5	0	0	0	0	0	0	0	0	0	1	0	0	0	0	—	0	0-0	0	0.00
1997 Philadelphia	NL	76	0	0	23	81.2	345	86	45	43	9	1	2	1	27	3	67	5	2	4	8	.333	0	1-5	18	4.74
1998 Philadelphia	NL	69	0	0	20	81.2	319	63	34	32	9	4	2	2	20	1	76	6	1	4	4	.500	0	1-4	5	3.53
1999 Cle-SF		63	0	0	15	61	286	65	37	33	5	1	0	10	32	6	54	2	0	3	1	.750	0	0-1	11	4.87
2000 KC-ChC		58	1	0	32	90	390	101	64	60	11	4	3	4	32	3	67	2	0	4	5	.444	0	7-11	4	6.00
1999 Cleveland	AL	4	0	0	1	3	18	6	6	6	1	0	0	0	3	0	2	0	0	0	0	—	0	0-0	0	18.00
San Francisco	NL	59	0	0	14	58	268	59	31	27	4	1	0	10	29	6	52	2	0	3	1	.750	0	0-1	11	4.19
2000 Kansas City	AL	50	0	0	30	75	320	81	49	46	9	3	1	3	27	2	54	1	0	4	5	.500	0	7-11	4	5.52
Chicago	NL	8	1	0	2	15	70	20	15	14	2	1	2	1	5	1	13	1	0	0	0	1.000	0	0-0	0	8.40
7 ML YEARS		310	1	0	109	371.2	1572	371	211	196	40	13	13	17	122	13	292	19	4	17	19	.472	0	11-24	38	4.75

Ed Sprague

Bats: R **Throws:** R **Pos:** 3B-41; PH/PR-40; 1B-28; LF-6; DH-1; 2B-1; RF-1   **Ht:** 6'2" **Wt:** 205 **Born:** 7/25/67 **Age:** 33

		BATTING																	BASERUNNING				PERCENTAGES		
Year Team	Lg	G	AB	H	2B	3B	HR	(Hm	Rd)	TB	R	RBI	TBB	IBB	SO	HBP	SH	SF	SB	CS	SB%	GDP	Avg	OBP	SLG
2000 Rancho Cuc *	A+	2	7	2	0	0	1	—	5	1	2	1	0	0	0	0	0	0	0	—	0	.286	.375	.714
1991 Toronto	AL	61	160	44	7	0	4	(3	1)	63	17	20	19	2	43	3	0	1	0	3	.00	2	.275	.361	.394
1992 Toronto	AL	22	47	11	2	0	1	(1	0)	16	6	7	3	0	7	0	0	0	0	0	—	2	.234	.280	.340
1993 Toronto	AL	150	546	142	31	1	12	(8	4)	211	50	73	32	1	85	10	2	6	1	0	1.00	23	.260	.310	.386
1994 Toronto	AL	109	405	97	19	1	11	(6	5)	151	38	44	23	1	95	11	2	4	1	0	1.00	11	.240	.296	.373
1995 Toronto	AL	144	521	127	27	2	18	(7	11)	212	77	74	58	3	96	15	1	7	0	0	—	19	.244	.333	.407
1996 Toronto	AL	159	591	146	35	2	36	(17	19)	293	88	101	60	3	146	12	0	7	0	0	—	7	.247	.325	.496
1997 Toronto	AL	138	504	115	29	4	14	(5	9)	194	63	48	51	0	102	6	0	1	0	1	.00	10	.228	.306	.385
1998 Tor-Oak		132	469	104	25	0	20	(9	11)	189	57	58	26	2	90	13	0	2	1	2	.33	16	.222	.280	.403
1999 Pittsburgh	NL	137	490	131	27	2	22	(10	12)	228	71	81	50	6	93	17	1	6	3	6	.33	12	.267	.352	.465
2000 SD-Bos		106	268	65	16	0	12	(5	7)	117	30	36	25	2	58	3	0	2	0	0	—	3	.243	.312	.437
1998 Toronto	AL	105	382	91	20	0	17	(6	11)	162	49	51	24	1	73	11	0	2	0	2	.00	15	.238	.301	.424
Oakland	AL	27	87	13	5	0	3	(3	0)	27	8	7	2	1	17	2	0	0	1	0	1.00	1	.149	.187	.310
2000 San Diego	NL	73	157	41	12	0	10	(4	6)	83	19	27	13	2	40	3	0	2	0	0	—	1	.261	.325	.529
Boston	AL	33	111	24	4	0	2	(1	1)	34	11	9	12	0	18	0	0	0	0	0	—	2	.216	.293	.306
10 ML YEARS		1158	4001	982	218	12	150	(76	74)	1674	497	542	347	20	815	90	6	36	6	12	.33	103	.245	.317	.418

Dennis Springer

Pitches: Right Bats: Right Pos: SP-2   Ht: 5'10" Wt: 185 Born: 2/12/65 Age: 36

Year Team	Lg	G	GS	CG	GF	IP	BFP	H	R	ER	HR	SH	SF	HB	TBB	IBB	SO	WP	Bk	W	L	Pct.	ShO	Sv-Op	Hld	ERA
2000 Norfolk *	AAA	25	17	1	1	117	501	120	65	57	15	3	4	6	35	1	35	7	1	5	5	.500	1	0- –	–	4.38
1995 Philadelphia	NL	4	4	0	0	22.1	94	21	15	12	3	2	0	1	9	1	15	1	0	0	3	.000	0	0-0	0	4.84
1996 California	AL	20	15	2	3	94.2	413	91	65	58	24	0	1	6	43	0	64	1	0	5	6	.455	1	0-0	1	5.51
1997 Anaheim	AL	32	28	3	0	194.2	846	199	118	112	32	4	13	10	73	0	75	7	0	9	9	.500	1	0-0	0	5.18
1998 Tampa Bay	AL	29	17	1	8	115.2	517	120	77	70	21	1	2	12	60	1	46	6	0	3	11	.214	0	0-0	0	5.45
1999 Florida	NL	38	29	3	3	196.1	855	231	121	106	23	12	10	7	64	3	83	2	0	6	16	.273	2	1-1	1	4.86
2000 New York	NL	2	2	0	0	11.1	59	20	11	11	2	0	0	1	5	0	5	2	0	0	1	.000	0	0-0	0	8.74
6 ML YEARS		125	95	9	14	635	2784	682	407	369	105	19	26	37	254	5	288	19	0	23	46	.333	4	1-1	2	5.23

Russ Springer

Pitches: Right Bats: Right Pos: RP-52   Ht: 6'4" Wt: 205 Born: 11/7/68 Age: 32

Year Team	Lg	G	GS	CG	GF	IP	BFP	H	R	ER	HR	SH	SF	HB	TBB	IBB	SO	WP	Bk	W	L	Pct.	ShO	Sv-Op	Hld	ERA
1992 New York	AL	14	0	0	5	16	75	18	11	11	0	0	0	1	10	0	12	0	0	0	0	–	0	0-0	2	6.19
1993 California	AL	14	9	1	3	60	278	73	48	48	11	1	1	3	32	1	31	6	0	1	6	.143	0	0-0	1	7.20
1994 California	AL	18	5	0	6	45.2	198	53	28	28	9	1	1	0	14	0	28	2	0	2	2	.500	0	2-3	1	5.52
1995 Cal-Phi		33	6	0	6	78.1	350	82	48	46	16	2	2	7	35	4	70	2	0	1	2	.333	0	1-2	0	5.29
1996 Philadelphia	NL	51	7	0	12	96.2	437	106	60	50	12	5	3	1	38	6	94	5	0	3	10	.231	0	0-3	6	4.66
1997 Houston	NL	54	0	0	13	55.1	241	48	28	26	4	1	2	4	27	2	74	4	0	3	3	.500	0	3-7	9	4.23
1998 Ari-Atl	NL	48	0	0	14	52.2	232	51	26	24	4	2	1	1	30	4	56	5	0	5	4	.556	0	0-4	7	4.10
1999 Atlanta	NL	49	0	0	8	47.1	194	31	20	18	5	0	2	2	22	2	49	0	0	2	1	.667	0	1-1	8	3.42
2000 Arizona	NL	52	0	0	10	62	282	63	36	35	11	2	3	2	34	6	53	4	0	2	4	.333	0	0-2	5	5.08
1995 California	AL	19	6	0	3	51.2	238	60	37	35	11	1	0	5	25	1	38	1	0	1	2	.333	0	1-2	0	6.10
Philadelphia	NL	14	0	0	3	26.2	112	22	11	11	5	1	2	2	10	3	32	1	0	0	0	–	0	0-0	0	3.71
1998 Arizona	NL	26	0	0	13	32.2	140	29	16	15	4	0	0	1	14	1	37	3	0	4	3	.571	0	0-3	1	4.13
Atlanta	NL	22	0	0	1	20	92	22	10	9	0	2	1	0	16	3	19	2	0	1	1	.500	0	0-1	6	4.05
9 ML YEARS		333	27	1	77	514	2287	525	305	286	72	14	15	21	242	25	473	27	0	19	32	.373	0	7-22	36	5.01

Jay Spurgeon

Pitches: Right Bats: Right Pos: SP-4; RP-3   Ht: 6'6" Wt: 211 Born: 7/5/76 Age: 24

Year Team	Lg	G	GS	CG	GF	IP	BFP	H	R	ER	HR	SH	SF	HB	TBB	IBB	SO	WP	Bk	W	L	Pct.	ShO	Sv-Op	Hld	ERA
1998 Delmarva	A	27	20	0	0	136.1	547	112	49	40	8	5	5	6	48	0	103	3	0	11	3	.786	0	0- –	–	2.64
1999 Frederick	A+	26	26	1	0	146	659	176	99	77	14	4	4	4	53	2	87	12	2	6	9	.400	0	0- –	–	4.75
2000 Frederick	A+	16	15	1	0	91.2	379	75	47	42	8	3	7	3	31	0	92	8	0	8	2	.800	0	0- –	–	4.12
Bowie	AA	6	6	2	0	39	152	32	10	7	3	0	1	2	7	0	27	0	0	3	1	.750	1	0- –	–	1.62
Rochester	AAA	2	2	0	0	13.2	54	5	1	1	1	0	0	1	9	0	10	0	0	2	0	1.000	0	0- –	–	0.66
2000 Baltimore	AL	7	4	0	1	24	110	26	16	16	5	1	0	2	15	0	11	3	0	1	1	.500	0	0-0	0	6.00

Matt Stairs

Bats: L Throws: R Pos: RF-102; DH-37; PH/PR-12; 1B-1; CF-1   Ht: 5'9" Wt: 217 Born: 2/27/68 Age: 33

Year Team	Lg	G	AB	H	2B	3B	HR	(Hm	Rd)	TB	R	RBI	TBB	IBB	SO	HBP	SH	SF	SB	CS	SB%	GDP	Avg	OBP	SLG
1992 Montreal	NL	13	30	5	2	0	0	(0	0)	7	2	5	7	0	7	0	0	1	0	0	–	0	.167	.316	.233
1993 Montreal	NL	6	8	3	1	0	0	(0	0)	4	1	2	0	0	1	0	0	0	0	0	–	1	.375	.375	.500
1995 Boston	AL	39	88	23	7	1	1	(0	1)	35	8	17	4	0	14	1	1	1	1	0	1.00	4	.261	.298	.398
1996 Oakland	AL	61	137	38	5	1	10	(5	5)	75	21	23	19	2	23	1	0	1	1	1	.50	2	.277	.367	.547
1997 Oakland	AL	133	352	105	19	0	27	(20	7)	205	62	73	50	1	60	3	1	4	3	2	.60	6	.298	.386	.582
1998 Oakland	AL	149	523	154	33	1	26	(16	10)	267	88	106	59	4	93	6	1	4	8	3	.73	13	.294	.370	.511
1999 Oakland	AL	146	531	137	26	3	38	(15	23)	283	94	102	89	6	124	2	0	1	2	7	.22	8	.258	.366	.533
2000 Oakland	AL	143	476	108	26	0	21	(9	12)	197	74	81	78	4	122	1	1	6	2	2	.71	7	.227	.333	.414
8 ML YEARS		690	2145	573	119	6	123	(65	58)	1073	350	409	306	17	444	14	4	18	19	16	.54	41	.267	.360	.500

Rob Stanifer

Pitches: Right Bats: Right Pos: RP-8   Ht: 6'3" Wt: 205 Born: 3/10/72 Age: 29

Year Team	Lg	G	GS	CG	GF	IP	BFP	H	R	ER	HR	SH	SF	HB	TBB	IBB	SO	WP	Bk	W	L	Pct.	ShO	Sv-Op	Hld	ERA
2000 Pawtucket *	AAA	41	0	0	35	52.1	204	40	13	11	6	4	1	1	20	1	42	4	0	3	4	.429	0	16- –	–	1.89
1997 Florida	NL	36	0	0	10	45	188	43	23	23	9	4	0	3	16	0	28	1	0	1	2	.333	0	1-2	4	4.60
1998 Florida	NL	38	0	0	11	48	222	54	33	30	5	2	3	0	22	2	30	1	0	2	4	.333	0	1-3	3	5.63
2000 Boston	AL	8	0	0	3	13	66	22	19	11	3	0	0	0	4	1	3	0	0	0	0	–	0	0-0	0	7.62
3 ML YEARS		82	0	0	24	106	476	119	75	64	17	6	3	3	42	3	61	2	0	3	6	.333	0	2-5	7	5.43

Mike Stanley

Bats: Right Throws: Right Pos: 1B-58; DH-26; PH/PR-11   Ht: 6'0" Wt: 205 Born: 6/25/63 Age: 38

Year Team	Lg	G	AB	H	2B	3B	HR	(Hm	Rd)	TB	R	RBI	TBB	IBB	SO	HBP	SH	SF	SB	CS	SB%	GDP	Avg	OBP	SLG
1986 Texas	AL	15	30	10	3	0	1	(0	1)	16	4	1	3	0	7	0	0	0	1	0	1.00	0	.333	.394	.533
1987 Texas	AL	78	216	59	8	1	6	(3	3)	87	34	37	31	0	48	1	1	4	3	0	1.00	6	.273	.361	.403
1988 Texas	AL	94	249	57	8	0	3	(1	2)	74	21	27	37	0	62	0	1	5	0	0	–	5	.229	.323	.297
1989 Texas	AL	67	122	30	3	1	1	(1	0)	38	9	11	12	1	29	2	1	0	1	0	1.00	5	.246	.324	.311
1990 Texas	AL	103	189	47	8	1	2	(1	1)	63	21	19	30	2	25	0	6	1	1	0	1.00	4	.249	.350	.333
1991 Texas	AL	95	181	45	13	1	3	(1	2)	69	25	25	34	0	44	2	5	1	0	0	–	6	.249	.372	.381
1992 New York	AL	68	173	43	7	0	8	(5	3)	74	24	27	33	0	45	1	0	0	0	0	–	6	.249	.372	.428
1993 New York	AL	130	423	129	17	1	26	(17	9)	226	70	84	57	4	85	5	0	6	1	1	.50	10	.305	.389	.534

Year Team	Lg	G	AB	H	2B	3B	HR	BATTING (Hm	Rd)	TB	R	RBI	TBB	IBB	SO	HBP	SH	SF	BASERUNNING SB	CS	SB%	GDP	PERCENTAGES Avg	OBP	SLG
1994 New York	AL	82	290	87	20	0	17	(8	9)	158	54	57	39	2	56	2	0	2	0	0	—	10	.300	.384	.545
1995 New York	AL	118	399	107	29	1	18	(13	5)	192	63	83	57	1	106	5	0	9	1	1	.50	14	.268	.360	.481
1996 Boston	AL	121	397	107	20	1	24	(10	14)	201	73	69	69	3	62	5	0	2	2	0	1.00	8	.270	.383	.506
1997 Bos-NYY	AL	125	347	103	25	0	16	(6	10)	176	61	65	54	4	72	6	0	8	0	1	.00	13	.297	.393	.507
1998 Tor-Bos	AL	145	497	127	25	0	29	(12	17)	239	74	79	82	5	129	7	0	7	3	1	.75	12	.256	.364	.481
1999 Boston	AL	136	427	120	22	0	19	(8	11)	199	59	72	70	3	94	11	0	4	0	0	—	8	.281	.393	.466
2000 Bos-Oak	AL	90	282	67	12	0	14	(8	6)	121	33	46	44	0	65	1	1	3	0	0	—	4	.238	.339	.429
1997 Boston	AL	97	260	78	17	0	13	(5	8)	134	45	53	39	0	50	6	0	7	0	1	.00	9	.300	.394	.515
New York	AL	28	87	25	8	0	3	(1	2)	42	16	12	15	4	22	0	0	1	0	0	—	4	.287	.388	.483
1998 Toronto	AL	98	341	82	13	0	22	(11	11)	161	49	47	56	3	86	5	0	3	2	1	.67	6	.240	.353	.472
Boston	AL	47	156	45	12	0	7	(1	6)	78	25	32	26	2	43	2	0	4	1	0	1.00	6	.288	.388	.500
2000 Boston	AL	58	185	41	5	0	10	(5	5)	76	22	28	30	0	44	0	1	2	0	0	—	1	.222	.327	.411
Oakland	AL	32	97	26	7	0	4	(3	1)	45	11	18	14	0	21	1	0	1	0	0	—	3	.268	.363	.464
15 ML YEARS		1467	4222	1138	220	7	187	(94	93)	1933	625	702	652	25	929	48	15	52	13	4	.76	108	.270	.370	.458

Mike Stanton

Pitches: Left **Bats:** Left **Pos:** RP-69 **Ht:** 6'1" **Wt:** 215 **Born:** 6/2/67 **Age:** 34

Year Team	Lg	HOW MUCH HE PITCHED G	GS	CG	GF	IP	BFP	WHAT HE GAVE UP H	R	ER	HR	SH	SF	HB	TBB	IBB	SO	WP	Bk	THE RESULTS W	L	Pct.	ShO	Sv-Op	Hld	ERA
1989 Atlanta	NL	20	0	0	10	24	94	17	4	4	0	4	0	0	8	1	27	1	0	0	1	.000	0	7-8	2	1.50
1990 Atlanta	NL	7	0	0	4	7	42	16	16	14	1	1	0	1	4	2	7	1	0	0	3	.000	0	2-3	0	18.00
1991 Atlanta	NL	74	0	0	20	78	314	62	27	25	6	6	0	1	21	6	54	0	0	5	5	.500	0	7-10	15	2.88
1992 Atlanta	NL	65	0	0	23	63.2	264	59	32	29	6	1	2	2	20	2	44	3	0	5	4	.556	0	8-11	15	4.10
1993 Atlanta	NL	63	0	0	41	52	236	51	35	27	4	5	2	0	29	7	43	1	0	4	6	.400	0	27-33	5	4.67
1994 Atlanta	NL	49	0	0	15	45.2	197	41	18	18	2	2	1	0	26	3	35	1	0	3	1	.750	0	3-4	10	3.55
1995 Atl-Bos		48	0	0	22	40.1	178	48	23	19	6	1	1	1	14	2	23	2	1	2	1	.667	0	1-3	8	4.24
1996 Bos-Tex	AL	81	0	0	28	78.2	327	78	32	32	11	4	2	0	27	5	60	3	2	4	4	.500	0	1-6	22	3.66
1997 New York	AL	64	0	0	15	66.2	283	50	19	19	3	4	2	0	34	2	70	3	2	6	1	.857	0	3-5	26	2.57
1998 New York	AL	67	0	0	26	79	330	71	51	48	13	1	2	4	26	1	69	0	0	4	1	.800	0	6-10	18	5.47
1999 New York	AL	73	1	0	10	62.1	271	71	30	30	5	4	2	1	18	4	59	3	0	2	2	.500	0	0-5	21	4.33
2000 New York	AL	69	0	0	20	68	291	68	32	31	5	2	4	2	24	2	75	1	0	2	3	.400	0	0-4	15	4.10
1995 Atlanta	NL	26	0	0	10	19.1	94	31	14	12	3	2	1	1	6	2	13	1	1	1	1	.500	0	1-2	4	5.59
Boston	AL	22	0	0	12	21	84	17	9	7	3	0	0	0	8	0	10	1	0	1	0	1.000	0	0-1	4	3.00
1996 Boston	AL	59	0	0	19	56.1	239	58	24	24	9	3	2	0	23	4	46	3	2	4	3	.571	0	1-5	15	3.83
Texas	AL	22	0	0	9	22.1	88	20	8	8	2	1	0	0	4	1	14	0	0	0	1	.000	0	0-1	7	3.22
12 ML YEARS		680	1	0	234	665.1	2827	632	319	296	62	34	16	18	251	37	566	19	5	37	32	.536	0	65-102	157	4.00

Gene Stechschulte

Pitches: Right **Bats:** Right **Pos:** RP-20 **Ht:** 6'5" **Wt:** 210 **Born:** 8/12/73 **Age:** 27

Year Team	Lg	HOW MUCH HE PITCHED G	GS	CG	GF	IP	BFP	WHAT HE GAVE UP H	R	ER	HR	SH	SF	HB	TBB	IBB	SO	WP	Bk	THE RESULTS W	L	Pct.	ShO	Sv-Op	Hld	ERA
1996 New Jersey	A-	20	1	0	6	33	159	41	17	12	0	2	1	2	16	2	27	4	0	1	2	.333	0	0--	—	3.27
1997 New Jersey	A-	30	0	0	9	36.1	164	45	16	13	2	0	1	2	16	0	28	3	0	1	1	.500	0	1--	—	3.22
1998 Peoria	A	57	0	0	51	66	279	58	26	19	1	5	2	2	21	2	70	2	0	4	8	.333	0	33--	—	2.59
1999 Memphis	AAA	2	0	0	0	2.1	14	2	2	2	0	1	0	0	5	0	2	0	0	0	0	--	0	0--	—	7.71
Arkansas	AA	39	0	0	33	42.1	191	41	26	16	4	4	1	4	20	1	41	3	0	2	6	.250	0	19--	—	3.40
2000 Memphis	AAA	41	0	0	38	47.2	195	38	13	13	4	5	0	1	18	4	37	1	0	4	1	.800	0	26--	—	2.45
Arkansas	AA	2	0	0	1	2	8	0	0	0	0	0	0	1	0	0	3	0	0	0	0	--	0	0--	—	0.00
2000 St. Louis	NL	20	0	0	7	25.2	116	24	22	18	6	0	2	0	17	1	12	2	0	1	0	1.000	0	0-1	3	6.31

Blake Stein

Pitches: Right **Bats:** Right **Pos:** SP-17 **Ht:** 6'7" **Wt:** 240 **Born:** 8/3/73 **Age:** 27

Year Team	Lg	HOW MUCH HE PITCHED G	GS	CG	GF	IP	BFP	WHAT HE GAVE UP H	R	ER	HR	SH	SF	HB	TBB	IBB	SO	WP	Bk	THE RESULTS W	L	Pct.	ShO	Sv-Op	Hld	ERA
2000 Wilmington *	A+	2	2	0	0	5.1	24	6	4	4	1	0	0	0	2	0	12	1	0	0	0	--	0	0--	—	6.75
Wichita *	AA	2	2	0	0	8.2	37	10	6	6	2	0	0	0	1	0	12	1	0	1	0	1.000	0	0--	—	6.23
Omaha *	AAA	2	2	0	0	12.1	49	9	1	1	1	0	0	0	2	0	14	0	0	1	0	1.000	0	0--	—	0.73
1998 Oakland	AL	24	20	1	0	117.1	538	117	92	83	22	1	2	5	71	3	89	15	0	5	9	.357	1	0-0	0	6.37
1999 Oak-KC	AL	13	12	0	0	73	327	65	38	37	11	2	1	7	47	1	47	3	0	1	2	.333	0	0-0	0	4.56
2000 Kansas City	AL	17	17	1	0	107.2	464	98	57	56	19	3	4	3	57	1	78	7	0	8	5	.615	0	0-0	0	4.68
1999 Oakland	AL	1	1	0	0	2.2	19	6	5	5	1	0	0	0	6	0	4	1	0	0	0	--	0	0-0	0	16.88
Kansas City	AL	12	11	0	0	70.1	308	59	33	32	10	2	1	7	41	1	43	2	0	1	2	.333	0	0-0	0	4.09
3 ML YEARS		54	49	2	0	298	1329	280	187	176	52	6	7	15	175	5	214	25	0	14	16	.467	1	0-0	0	5.32

Garrett Stephenson

Pitches: Right **Bats:** Right **Pos:** SP-31; RP-1 **Ht:** 6'5" **Wt:** 208 **Born:** 1/2/72 **Age:** 29

Year Team	Lg	HOW MUCH HE PITCHED G	GS	CG	GF	IP	BFP	WHAT HE GAVE UP H	R	ER	HR	SH	SF	HB	TBB	IBB	SO	WP	Bk	THE RESULTS W	L	Pct.	ShO	Sv-Op	Hld	ERA
1996 Baltimore	AL	3	0	0	2	6.1	35	13	9	9	1	0	1	0	3	1	3	0	0	0	1	.000	0	0-0	0	12.79
1997 Philadelphia	NL	20	18	2	0	117	474	104	45	41	11	2	5	3	38	0	81	1	0	8	6	.571	0	0-0	0	3.15
1998 Philadelphia	NL	6	6	0	0	23	118	31	24	23	3	1	0	0	19	0	17	0	1	0	2	.000	0	0-0	0	9.00
1999 St. Louis	NL	18	12	0	1	85.1	371	90	43	40	11	5	5	3	29	1	59	0	0	6	3	.667	0	0-0	0	4.22
2000 St. Louis	NL	32	31	3	0	200.1	858	209	105	100	31	6	7	7	63	0	123	2	2	16	9	.640	2	0-0	1	4.49
5 ML YEARS		79	67	5	3	432	1856	447	226	213	57	15	17	16	152	2	283	3	3	30	21	.588	2	0-0	1	4.44

Dave Stevens

Pitches: Right Bats: Right Pos: RP-2   Ht: 6'3" Wt: 215 Born: 3/4/70 Age: 31

		HOW MUCH HE PITCHED						WHAT HE GAVE UP											THE RESULTS					
Year Team	Lg	G	GS	CG	GF	IP	BFP	H	R	ER	HR	SH	SF	HB	TBB	IBB	SO	WP	Bk	W	L	Pct.	ShO	Sv-Op	Hld	ERA
2000 Richmond *	AAA	51	0	0	32	72	318	73	44	40	10	1	6	2	31	3	50	7	1	1	9	.100	0	7- -	—	5.00
1994 Minnesota	AL	24	0	0	6	45	208	55	35	34	6	2	0	1	23	2	24	3	0	5	2	.714	0	0-0	1	6.80
1995 Minnesota	AL	56	0	0	34	65.2	302	74	40	37	14	4	5	1	32	1	47	2	0	5	4	.556	0	10-12	5	5.07
1996 Minnesota	AL	49	0	0	38	58	251	58	31	30	12	3	3	0	25	2	29	1	0	3	3	.500	0	11-16	0	4.66
1997 Min-ChC		16	6	0	0	32.1	174	54	34	33	8	0	1	1	26	0	29	1	3	1	5	.167	0	0-0	0	9.19
1998 Chicago	NL	31	0	0	13	38	169	42	20	20	6	4	1	1	17	5	31	1	1	1	2	.333	0	0-0	0	4.74
1999 Cleveland	AL	5	0	0	0	9	44	10	10	10	1	0	1	0	8	1	6	1	0	0	0	—	0	0-0	0	10.00
2000 Atlanta	NL	2	0	0	2	3	15	5	4	4	2	0	0	0	1	0	4	0	0	0	0	—	0	0-0	0	12.00
1997 Minnesota	AL	6	6	0	0	23	124	41	23	23	8	0	0	0	17	0	16	1	2	1	3	.250	0	0-0	0	9.00
Chicago	NL	10	0	0	0	9.1	50	13	11	10	0	0	1	1	9	0	13	0	1	0	2	.000	0	0-0	0	9.64
7 ML YEARS		183	6	0	93	251	1163	298	174	168	49	13	11	4	132	11	170	9	4	15	16	.484	0	21-28	6	6.02

Lee Stevens

Bats: Left Throws: Left Pos: 1B-123; PH/PR-1   Ht: 6'4" Wt: 235 Born: 7/10/67 Age: 33

		BATTING																BASERUNNING				PERCENTAGES		
Year Team	Lg	G	AB	H	2B	3B	HR	(Hm	Rd)	TB	R	RBI	TBB	IBB	SO	HBP	SH	SF	SB	CS	SB%	GDP	Avg	OBP	SLG
1990 California	AL	67	248	53	10	0	7	(4	3)	84	28	32	22	3	75	0	2	3	1	1	.50	8	.214	.275	.339
1991 California	AL	18	58	17	7	0	0	(0	0)	24	8	9	6	2	12	0	1	1	1	2	.33	0	.293	.354	.414
1992 California	AL	106	312	69	19	0	7	(2	5)	109	25	37	29	6	64	1	1	2	1	4	.20	4	.221	.288	.349
1996 Texas	AL	27	78	18	2	3	3	(2	1)	35	6	12	6	0	22	1	0	1	0	0	—	2	.231	.291	.449
1997 Texas	AL	137	426	128	24	2	21	(12	9)	219	58	74	23	2	83	1	1	3	1	3	.25	18	.300	.336	.514
1998 Texas	AL	120	344	91	17	4	20	(13	7)	176	52	59	31	4	93	0	0	1	0	2	.00	6	.265	.324	.512
1999 Texas	AL	146	517	146	31	1	24	(10	14)	251	76	81	52	10	132	0	0	7	2	3	.40	19	.282	.344	.485
2000 Montreal	NL	123	449	119	27	2	22	(14	8)	216	60	75	48	6	105	2	0	2	0	0	—	10	.265	.337	.481
8 ML YEARS		744	2432	641	137	12	104	(57	47)	1114	313	379	217	33	586	5	5	20	6	15	.29	67	.264	.323	.458

Shannon Stewart

Bats: Right Throws: Right Pos: LF-136; CF-1   Ht: 6'1" Wt: 205 Born: 2/25/74 Age: 27

		BATTING																BASERUNNING				PERCENTAGES		
Year Team	Lg	G	AB	H	2B	3B	HR	(Hm	Rd)	TB	R	RBI	TBB	IBB	SO	HBP	SH	SF	SB	CS	SB%	GDP	Avg	OBP	SLG
2000 Dunedin *	A+	1	3	3	1	0	0	—	—	4	2	1	2	1	0	0	0	0	0	1	.00	0	1.000	1.000	1.333
1995 Toronto	AL	12	38	8	0	0	0	(0	0)	8	2	1	5	0	5	1	0	0	0	2	.00	0	.211	.318	.211
1996 Toronto	AL	7	17	3	1	0	0	(0	0)	4	2	2	1	0	4	0	0	0	1	0	1.00	1	.176	.222	.235
1997 Toronto	AL	44	168	48	13	7	0	(0	0)	75	25	22	19	1	24	4	0	2	10	3	.77	3	.286	.368	.446
1998 Toronto	AL	144	516	144	29	3	12	(6	6)	215	90	55	67	1	77	15	6	1	51	18	.74	5	.279	.377	.417
1999 Toronto	AL	145	608	185	28	2	11	(4	7)	250	102	67	59	0	83	8	3	4	37	14	.73	12	.304	.371	.411
2000 Toronto	AL	136	583	186	43	5	21	(12	9)	302	107	69	37	1	79	6	1	4	20	5	.80	12	.319	.363	.518
6 ML YEARS		488	1930	574	114	17	44	(22	22)	854	328	216	188	3	272	34	10	11	121	40	.75	33	.297	.368	.442

Kelly Stinnett

Bats: Right Throws: Right Pos: C-74; PH/PR-3   Ht: 5'11" Wt: 225 Born: 2/4/70 Age: 31

		BATTING																BASERUNNING				PERCENTAGES		
Year Team	Lg	G	AB	H	2B	3B	HR	(Hm	Rd)	TB	R	RBI	TBB	IBB	SO	HBP	SH	SF	SB	CS	SB%	GDP	Avg	OBP	SLG
1994 New York	NL	47	150	38	6	2	2	(0	2)	54	20	14	11	1	28	5	0	1	2	0	1.00	3	.253	.323	.360
1995 New York	NL	77	196	43	8	1	4	(1	3)	65	23	18	29	3	65	6	0	0	2	0	1.00	3	.219	.338	.332
1996 Milwaukee	AL	14	26	2	0	0	0	(0	0)	2	1	0	2	0	11	1	0	0	0	0	—	0	.077	.172	.077
1997 Milwaukee	AL	30	36	9	4	0	0	(0	0)	13	2	3	3	0	9	0	0	0	0	0	—	0	.250	.308	.361
1998 Arizona	NL	92	274	71	14	1	11	(5	6)	120	35	34	35	3	74	6	1	2	0	1	.00	9	.259	.353	.438
1999 Arizona	NL	88	284	66	13	0	14	(3	11)	121	36	38	24	2	83	5	2	2	2	1	.67	4	.232	.302	.426
2000 Arizona	NL	76	240	52	7	0	8	(2	6)	83	22	33	19	4	56	6	0	0	0	1	.00	5	.217	.291	.346
7 ML YEARS		424	1206	281	52	4	39	(11	28)	458	139	140	123	13	326	29	3	5	6	3	.67	24	.233	.318	.380

Kevin Stocker

Bats: Both Throws: Right Pos: SS-109; PH/PR-7   Ht: 6'1" Wt: 180 Born: 2/13/70 Age: 31

		BATTING																BASERUNNING				PERCENTAGES		
Year Team	Lg	G	AB	H	2B	3B	HR	(Hm	Rd)	TB	R	RBI	TBB	IBB	SO	HBP	SH	SF	SB	CS	SB%	GDP	Avg	OBP	SLG
1993 Philadelphia	NL	70	259	84	12	3	2	(1	1)	108	46	31	30	11	43	8	4	1	5	0	1.00	4	.324	.409	.417
1994 Philadelphia	NL	82	271	74	11	2	2	(2	0)	95	38	28	44	8	41	7	4	4	2	2	.50	3	.273	.383	.351
1995 Philadelphia	NL	125	412	90	14	3	1	(1	0)	113	42	32	43	9	75	9	10	3	6	1	.86	7	.218	.304	.274
1996 Philadelphia	NL	119	394	100	22	6	5	(0	5)	149	46	41	43	9	89	8	3	4	6	4	.60	6	.254	.336	.378
1997 Philadelphia	NL	149	504	134	23	5	4	(2	2)	179	51	40	51	7	91	2	2	1	11	6	.65	14	.266	.335	.355
1998 Tampa Bay	AL	112	336	70	11	3	6	(4	2)	105	37	25	27	1	80	8	8	2	5	3	.63	7	.208	.282	.313
1999 Tampa Bay	AL	79	254	76	11	2	1	(1	0)	94	39	27	24	0	41	4	4	0	9	7	.56	4	.299	.369	.370
2000 TB-Ana	AL	110	343	75	20	4	2	(0	2)	109	41	24	51	0	81	4	10	1	1	5	.17	11	.219	.326	.318
2000 Tampa Bay	AL	40	114	30	7	1	2	(0	2)	45	20	8	19	0	27	2	2	0	1	2	.33	3	.263	.378	.395
Anaheim	AL	70	229	45	13	3	0	(0	0)	64	21	16	32	0	54	2	8	1	0	3	.00	8	.197	.299	.279
8 ML YEARS		846	2773	703	124	28	23	(11	12)	952	340	248	313	45	541	50	45	16	45	28	.62	60	.254	.338	.343

Todd Stottlemyre

Pitches: Right Bats: Left Pos: SP-18   Ht: 6'3" Wt: 215 Born: 5/20/65 Age: 36

		HOW MUCH HE PITCHED						WHAT HE GAVE UP											THE RESULTS					
Year Team	Lg	G	GS	CG	GF	IP	BFP	H	R	ER	HR	SH	SF	HB	TBB	IBB	SO	WP	Bk	W	L	Pct.	ShO	Sv-Op	Hld	ERA
2000 Diamndbcks *	R	2	2	0	0	10	40	10	4	4	0	0	2	1	1	0	10	2	0	1	1	.500	0	0- -	—	3.60
1988 Toronto	AL	28	16	0	2	98	443	109	70	62	15	5	3	4	46	5	67	2	3	4	8	.333	0	0-1	0	5.69
1989 Toronto	AL	27	18	0	4	127.2	545	137	56	55	11	3	7	5	44	4	63	4	1	7	7	.500	0	0-0	0	3.88

Year Team	Lg	G	GS	CG	GF	IP	BFP	H	R	ER	HR	SH	SF	HB	TBB	IBB	SO	WP	Bk	W	L	Pct.	ShO	Sv-Op	Hld	ERA
1990 Toronto	AL	33	33	4	0	203	866	214	101	98	18	3	5	8	69	4	115	6	1	13	17	.433	0	0-0	0	4.34
1991 Toronto	AL	34	34	1	0	219	921	194	97	92	21	0	8	12	75	3	116	4	0	15	8	.652	0	0-0	0	3.78
1992 Toronto	AL	28	27	6	0	174	755	175	99	87	20	2	11	10	63	4	98	7	0	12	11	.522	2	0-0	0	4.50
1993 Toronto	AL	30	28	1	0	176.2	786	204	107	95	11	5	11	3	69	5	98	7	1	11	12	.478	1	0-0	0	4.84
1994 Toronto	AL	26	19	3	5	140.2	605	149	67	66	19	4	5	7	48	2	105	0	0	7	7	.500	1	1-3	0	4.22
1995 Oakland	AL	31	31	2	0	209.2	944	228	117	106	26	4	4	6	80	7	205	11	0	14	7	.667	0	0-0	0	4.55
1996 St. Louis	NL	34	33	5	0	223.1	944	191	100	96	30	12	9	4	93	8	194	8	1	14	11	.560	2	0-0	0	3.87
1997 St. Louis	NL	28	28	0	0	181	761	155	86	78	16	8	5	12	65	3	160	6	0	12	9	.571	0	0-0	0	3.88
1998 StL-Tex		33	33	3	0	221.2	949	214	107	92	25	8	6	4	81	1	204	5	2	14	13	.519	0	0-0	0	3.74
1999 Arizona	NL	17	17	0	0	101.1	446	106	51	46	12	3	1	6	40	1	74	2	0	6	3	.667	0	0-0	0	4.09
2000 Arizona	NL	18	18	0	0	95.1	408	98	55	52	18	3	2	2	36	2	76	2	1	9	6	.600	0	0-0	0	4.91
1998 St. Louis	NL	23	23	3	0	161.1	674	146	74	63	20	7	3	4	51	0	147	4	2	9	9	.500	0	0-0	0	3.51
Texas	AL	10	10	0	0	60.1	275	68	33	29	5	1	3	0	30	1	57	1	0	4	4	.556	0	0-0	0	4.33
13 ML YEARS		367	335	25	11	2171.1	9349	2174	1113	1025	242	60	77	83	809	49	1575	64	10	138	119	.537	6	1-4		4.25

Scott Strickland

Pitches: Right **Bats:** Right **Pos:** RP-49   **Ht:** 5'11" **Wt:** 180 **Born:** 4/26/76 **Age:** 25

Year Team	Lg	G	GS	CG	GF	IP	BFP	H	R	ER	HR	SH	SF	HB	TBB	IBB	SO	WP	Bk	W	L	Pct.	ShO	Sv-Op	Hld	ERA
1997 Vermont	A-	15	9	1	5	61.1	255	56	27	26	5	3	2	6	20	0	69	3	1	5	2	.714	0	0--	—	3.82
Cape Fear	A	3	1	0	2	5.2	26	8	7	4	0	0	0	0	1	0	8	1	0	0	0	.000	0	1--	—	6.35
1998 Cape Fear	A	15	2	0	11	36.1	161	36	19	18	3	3	1	3	12	0	53	1	0	0	3	.000	0	4--	—	4.46
Jupiter	A+	22	11	0	7	69	282	64	28	26	5	4	2	1	20	0	51	0	1	4	3	.571	0	2--	—	3.39
1999 Jupiter	A+	12	1	0	7	25.2	103	21	11	10	1	1	1	2	4	1	33	1	0	1	1	.500	0	2--	—	3.51
Harrisburg	AA	14	1	0	6	29	117	25	8	8	1	1	0	1	10	0	36	0	0	1	1	.500	0	3--	—	2.48
Ottawa	AAA	19	0	0	12	27.2	116	23	5	5	0	0	1	1	11	2	34	1	0	3	0	1.000	0	5--	—	1.63
2000 Ottawa	AAA	3	0	0	2	4	13	1	0	0	0	0	0	0	1	0	1	0	0	0	0		0	0--	—	0.00
1999 Montreal	NL	17	0	0	5	18	78	15	10	9	3	2	0	0	11	0	23	0	0	1	0	.000	0	0-0	2	4.50
2000 Montreal	NL	49	0	0	20	48	200	38	18	16	3	3	3	1	16	2	48	2	0	4	3	.571	0	9-13	6	3.00
2 ML YEARS		66	0	0	25	66	278	53	28	25	6	5	3	1	27	2	71	2	0	4	4	.500	0	9-13	8	3.41

Joe Strong

Pitches: Right **Bats:** Both **Pos:** RP-18   **Ht:** 6'0" **Wt:** 200 **Born:** 9/9/62 **Age:** 38

Year Team	Lg	G	GS	CG	GF	IP	BFP	H	R	ER	HR	SH	SF	HB	TBB	IBB	SO	WP	Bk	W	L	Pct.	ShO	Sv-Op	Hld	ERA
1993 Las Vegas	AAA	21	0	0	5	27	129	37	23	17	4	1	2	2	10	1	18	0	1	1	3	.250	0	0--	—	5.67
Rancho Cuc	A+	7	0	0	6	10	42	10	3	3	0	0	0	0	2	0	13	2	0	1	0	1.000	0	1--	—	2.70
Wichita	AA	4	3	0	1	14.2	68	13	13	11	2	2	1	0	11	0	13	0	1	1	0	1.000	0	0--	—	6.75
1994 San Berndno	A+	12	11	0	0	53.2	246	60	46	40	11	0	4	3	27	0	43	6	2	2	3	.400	0	0--	—	6.71
1995 Surrey	IND	20	19	9	0	131	555	120	55	40	7	1	1	7	48	1	129	3	1	8	9	.471	2	0--	—	2.75
1999 Orlando	AA	11	7	2	3	38	163	40	24	24	6	1	1	0	18	1	34	0	1	1	4	.200	0	0--	—	5.68
Durham	AA	6	1	0	1	14.2	71	20	13	13	4	0	0	0	8	0	12	0	0	0	1	.000	0	1--	—	7.98
2000 Calgary	AAA	29	1	0	21	44.2	198	44	21	20	1	1	2	4	20	1	33	7	0	1	2	.667	0	9--	—	4.03
2000 Florida	NL	18	0	0	5	19.2	95	26	16	16	3	1	0	2	12	1	18	2	0	1	1	.500	0	1-2	2	7.32

Everett Stull

Pitches: Right **Bats:** Right **Pos:** RP-16; SP-4   **Ht:** 6'3" **Wt:** 200 **Born:** 8/24/71 **Age:** 29

Year Team	Lg	G	GS	CG	GF	IP	BFP	H	R	ER	HR	SH	SF	HB	TBB	IBB	SO	WP	Bk	W	L	Pct.	ShO	Sv-Op	Hld	ERA
1992 Jamestown	A-	14	14	0	0	63.1	303	52	49	38	2	2	3	3	61	0	64	18	4	3	5	.375	0	0--	—	5.40
1993 Burlington	A	15	15	1	0	82.1	366	68	44	35	8	2	1	3	59	0	85	11	4	4	9	.308	0	0--	—	3.83
1994 Wst Plm Bch	A+	27	26	3	0	147	627	116	60	54	3	7	3	12	78	0	165	15	6	10	10	.500	1	0--	—	3.31
1995 Harrisburg	AA	24	24	0	0	126.2	569	114	88	78	12	5	5	9	79	2	132	7	1	3	12	.200	0	0--	—	5.54
1996 Harrisburg	AA	14	14	0	0	80	345	64	31	28	8	3	3	3	52	1	81	6	0	6	3	.667	0	0--	—	3.15
Ottawa	AAA	13	13	1	0	69.2	331	87	57	49	7	3	3	3	39	1	69	5	0	2	6	.250	0	0--	—	6.33
1997 Ottawa	AAA	27	27	1	0	159.1	710	166	110	103	25	4	4	13	86	0	130	9	0	8	10	.444	0	0--	—	5.82
1998 Rochester	AAA	21	7	0	6	42.2	222	49	44	42	9	0	3	5	45	0	39	6	0	1	4	.200	0	0--	—	8.86
1999 Richmond	AAA	30	22	0	0	139	603	124	75	69	17	4	7	8	73	0	126	12	2	8	8	.500	0	0--	—	4.47
2000 Indianapols	AAA	16	16	1	0	103.2	439	95	41	34	3	3	5	4	43	0	74	5	2	7	5	.583	1	0--	—	2.95
1997 Montreal	NL	3	0	0	1	3.1	17	7	7	6	1	1	0	0	4	0	2	0	0	0	1	.000	0	0-0	0	16.20
1999 Atlanta	NL	1	0	0	0	0.2	7	2	3	1	0	0	0	0	2	0	0	0	0	0	0	—	0	0-0	0	13.50
2000 Milwaukee	NL	20	4	0	3	43.1	199	41	30	28	7	2	3	4	30	3	33	5	0	2	3	.400	0	0-0	0	5.82
3 ML YEARS		24	4	0	4	47.1	227	50	40	35	8	3	4	4	36	3	35	5	0	2	4	.333	0	0-0	0	6.65

Tanyon Sturtze

Pitches: Right **Bats:** Right **Pos:** RP-23; SP-6   **Ht:** 6'5" **Wt:** 205 **Born:** 10/12/70 **Age:** 30

Year Team	Lg	G	GS	CG	GF	IP	BFP	H	R	ER	HR	SH	SF	HB	TBB	IBB	SO	WP	Bk	W	L	Pct.	ShO	Sv-Op	Hld	ERA
1995 Chicago	NL	2	0	0	0	2	9	2	2	2	1	0	0	0	1	0	0	0	0	0	0	—	0	0-0	0	9.00
1996 Chicago	NL	6	0	0	3	11	51	16	11	11	3	0	0	0	5	0	7	0	0	0	0	—	0	0-0	0	9.00
1997 Texas	AL	9	5	0	1	32.2	155	45	30	30	6	0	4	0	18	0	18	1	1	1	1	.500	0	0-0	0	8.27
1999 Chicago	AL	1	1	0	0	6	22	4	0	0	0	0	0	0	2	0	2	0	0	0	0	—	0	0-0	0	0.00
2000 CWS-TB	AL	29	6	0	9	68.1	300	72	39	36	8	1	2	3	29	1	44	2	0	5	2	.714	0	0-0	0	4.74
2000 Chicago	AL	10	1	0	2	15.2	85	25	23	21	4	0	2	2	15	0	6	1	0	1	2	.333	0	0-0	0	12.06
Tampa Bay	AL	19	5	0	7	52.2	215	47	16	15	4	1	0	1	14	1	38	1	0	4	0	1.000	0	0-0	0	2.56
5 ML YEARS		47	12	0	13	120	537	139	82	79	18	1	6	3	55	1	71	3	1	7	3	.700	0	0-0	0	5.93

Chris Stynes

Bats: R **Throws:** R **Pos:** 3B-77; PH/PR-26; 2B-15; LF-6; RF-2   **Ht:** 5'10" **Wt:** 185 **Born:** 1/19/73 **Age:** 28

								BATTING											BASERUNNING				PERCENTAGES		
Year Team	Lg	G	AB	H	2B	3B	HR	(Hm	Rd)	TB	R	RBI	TBB	IBB	SO	HBP	SH	SF	SB	CS	SB%	GDP	Avg	OBP	SLG
1995 Kansas City	AL	22	35	6	1	0	0	(0	0)	7	7	2	4	0	3	0	0	0	0	0	—	3	.171	.256	.200
1996 Kansas City	AL	36	92	27	6	0	0	(0	0)	33	8	6	2	0	5	0	1	0	5	2	.71	1	.293	.309	.359
1997 Cincinnati	NL	49	198	69	7	1	6	(2	4)	96	31	28	11	1	13	4	2	0	11	2	.85	5	.348	.394	.485
1998 Cincinnati	NL	123	347	88	10	1	6	(3	3)	118	52	27	32	1	36	4	4	1	15	1	.94	5	.254	.323	.340
1999 Cincinnati	NL	73	113	27	1	0	2	(1	1)	34	18	14	12	1	13	0	3	1	5	2	.71	2	.239	.310	.301
2000 Cincinnati	NL	119	380	127	24	1	12	(8	4)	189	71	40	32	2	54	2	3	3	5	2	.71	5	.334	.386	.497
6 ML YEARS		422	1165	344	49	3	26	(14	12)	477	187	117	93	5	124	10	13	5	41	9	.82	21	.295	.351	.409

Scott Sullivan

Pitches: Right **Bats:** Right **Pos:** RP-79   **Ht:** 6'3" **Wt:** 210 **Born:** 3/13/71 **Age:** 30

		HOW MUCH HE PITCHED						WHAT HE GAVE UP												THE RESULTS						
Year Team	Lg	G	GS	CG	GF	IP	BFP	H	R	ER	HR	SH	SF	HB	TBB	IBB	SO	WP	Bk	W	L	Pct.	ShO	Sv-Op	Hld	ERA
1995 Cincinnati	NL	3	0	0	1	3.2	17	4	2	2	0	1	0	0	2	0	2	0	0	0	0	—	0	0-0	0	4.91
1996 Cincinnati	NL	7	0	0	4	8	35	7	2	2	0	1	0	1	5	0	3	1	0	0	0	—	0	0-0	0	2.25
1997 Cincinnati	NL	59	0	0	15	97.1	402	79	36	35	12	3	3	7	30	8	96	7	1	5	3	.625	0	1-2	13	3.24
1998 Cincinnati	NL	67	0	0	13	102	440	98	62	59	14	3	4	9	36	4	86	4	0	5	5	.500	0	1-4	5	5.21
1999 Cincinnati	NL	79	0	0	16	113.2	470	88	41	38	10	4	4	8	47	4	78	6	1	5	4	.556	0	3-5	13	3.01
2000 Cincinnati	NL	79	0	0	22	106.1	439	87	44	41	14	2	5	9	38	8	96	7	0	3	6	.333	0	3-6	22	3.47
6 ML YEARS		294	0	0	71	431	1803	363	187	177	50	14	16	34	158	24	361	25	2	18	18	.500	0	8-17	53	3.70

Jeff Suppan

Pitches: Right **Bats:** Right **Pos:** SP-33; RP-2   **Ht:** 6'2" **Wt:** 210 **Born:** 1/2/75 **Age:** 26

		HOW MUCH HE PITCHED						WHAT HE GAVE UP												THE RESULTS						
Year Team	Lg	G	GS	CG	GF	IP	BFP	H	R	ER	HR	SH	SF	HB	TBB	IBB	SO	WP	Bk	W	L	Pct.	ShO	Sv-Op	Hld	ERA
1995 Boston	AL	8	3	0	1	22.2	100	29	15	15	4	1	1	0	5	1	19	0	1	1	2	.333	0	0-0	0	5.96
1996 Boston	AL	8	4	0	2	22.2	107	29	19	19	3	1	4	1	13	0	13	3	0	1	1	.500	0	0-0	0	7.54
1997 Boston	AL	23	22	0	1	112.1	503	140	75	71	12	0	4	4	36	1	67	5	0	7	3	.700	0	0-0	0	5.69
1998 Ari-KC		17	14	1	2	78.2	345	91	56	50	13	3	2	1	22	1	51	2	0	1	7	.125	0	0-0	0	5.72
1999 Kansas City	AL	32	32	4	0	208.2	887	222	113	105	28	7	5	3	62	4	103	5	1	10	12	.455	1	0-0	0	4.53
2000 Kansas City	AL	35	33	3	0	217	948	240	121	119	36	5	6	7	84	3	128	7	1	10	9	.526	1	0-0	0	4.94
1998 Arizona	NL	13	13	1	0	66	299	82	55	49	12	3	2	1	21	1	39	2	0	1	7	.125	0	0-0	0	6.68
Kansas City	AL	4	1	0	2	12.2	46	9	1	1	0	0	0	0	1	0	12	0	0	0	0	—	0	0-0	0	0.71
6 ML YEARS		123	108	8	6	662	2890	751	399	379	96	17	22	16	222	10	381	22	2	30	34	.469	2	0-0	1	5.15

B.J. Surhoff

Bats: Left **Throws:** Right **Pos:** LF-134; PH/PR-12; DH-1   **Ht:** 6'1" **Wt:** 200 **Born:** 8/4/64 **Age:** 36

								BATTING											BASERUNNING				PERCENTAGES		
Year Team	Lg	G	AB	H	2B	3B	HR	(Hm	Rd)	TB	R	RBI	TBB	IBB	SO	HBP	SH	SF	SB	CS	SB%	GDP	Avg	OBP	SLG
1987 Milwaukee	AL	115	395	118	22	3	7	(5	2)	167	50	68	36	1	30	0	5	9	11	10	.52	13	.299	.350	.423
1988 Milwaukee	AL	139	493	121	21	0	5	(2	3)	157	47	38	31	9	49	3	11	3	21	6	.78	12	.245	.292	.318
1989 Milwaukee	AL	126	436	108	17	4	5	(3	2)	148	42	55	25	1	29	3	3	10	14	12	.54	8	.248	.287	.339
1990 Milwaukee	AL	135	474	131	21	4	6	(4	2)	178	55	59	41	5	37	1	7	7	18	7	.72	8	.276	.331	.376
1991 Milwaukee	AL	143	505	146	19	4	5	(3	2)	188	57	68	26	2	33	0	13	9	5	8	.38	21	.289	.319	.372
1992 Milwaukee	AL	139	480	121	19	1	4	(3	1)	154	63	62	46	8	41	2	5	10	14	8	.64	9	.252	.314	.321
1993 Milwaukee	AL	148	552	151	38	3	7	(4	3)	216	66	79	36	5	47	2	4	5	12	9	.57	9	.274	.318	.391
1994 Milwaukee	AL	40	134	35	11	2	5	(2	3)	65	20	22	16	0	14	0	2	2	0	1	.00	5	.261	.336	.485
1995 Milwaukee	AL	117	415	133	26	3	13	(7	6)	204	72	73	37	4	43	4	2	4	7	3	.70	7	.320	.378	.492
1996 Baltimore	AL	143	537	157	27	6	21	(12	9)	259	74	82	47	8	79	3	2	1	0	1	.00	7	.292	.352	.482
1997 Baltimore	AL	147	528	150	30	4	18	(10	8)	242	80	88	49	14	60	5	3	10	1	1	.50	7	.284	.345	.458
1998 Baltimore	AL	162	573	160	34	1	22	(9	13)	262	79	92	49	9	81	1	1	10	9	7	.56	13	.279	.332	.457
1999 Baltimore	AL	**162**	**673**	207	38	1	28	(9	19)	331	104	107	43	1	78	2	1	8	5	1	.83	15	.308	.347	.492
2000 Bal-Atl		147	539	157	36	2	14	(7	7)	239	69	68	41	3	58	3	2	2	10	2	.83	10	.291	.344	.443
2000 Baltimore	AL	103	411	120	27	0	13	(6	7)	186	56	57	29	3	46	2	1	1	7	2	.78	5	.292	.341	.453
Atlanta	NL	44	128	37	9	2	1	(1	0)	53	13	11	12	0	12	1	1	1	3	0	1.00	5	.289	.352	.414
14 ML YEARS		1863	6734	1895	359	38	160	(80	80)	2810	878	961	523	70	679	29	61	90	127	76	.63	144	.281	.332	.417

Larry Sutton

Bats: L **Throws:** L **Pos:** PH/PR-15; 1B-6; LF-3; RF-1   **Ht:** 6'0" **Wt:** 185 **Born:** 5/14/70 **Age:** 31

								BATTING											BASERUNNING				PERCENTAGES		
Year Team	Lg	G	AB	H	2B	3B	HR	(Hm	Rd)	TB	R	RBI	TBB	IBB	SO	HBP	SH	SF	SB	CS	SB%	GDP	Avg	OBP	SLG
2000 Memphis *	AAA	95	347	89	21	2	12	(—	—)	150	61	70	67	5	56	3	0	5	4	1	.80	12	.256	.377	.432
1997 Kansas City	AL	27	69	20	2	0	2	(1	1)	28	9	8	5	0	12	0	1	0	0	0	—	0	.290	.338	.406
1998 Kansas City	AL	111	310	76	14	2	5	(3	2)	109	29	42	29	3	46	3	4	5	3	3	.50	5	.245	.311	.352
1999 Kansas City	AL	43	102	23	6	0	2	(2	0)	35	14	15	13	0	17	0	1	2	1	0	1.00	4	.225	.308	.343
2000 St. Louis	NL	23	25	8	0	0	1	(0	1)	11	5	6	5	0	7	0	1	2	0	0	—	0	.320	.406	.440
4 ML YEARS		204	506	127	22	2	10	(6	4)	183	57	71	52	3	82	3	7	9	4	3	.57	9	.251	.319	.362

Makoto Suzuki

Pitches: Right **Bats:** Right **Pos:** SP-29; RP-3   **Ht:** 6'3" **Wt:** 205 **Born:** 5/31/75 **Age:** 26

		HOW MUCH HE PITCHED						WHAT HE GAVE UP												THE RESULTS						
Year Team	Lg	G	GS	CG	GF	IP	BFP	H	R	ER	HR	SH	SF	HB	TBB	IBB	SO	WP	Bk	W	L	Pct.	ShO	Sv-Op	Hld	ERA
1996 Seattle	AL	1	0	0	0	1.1	8	2	3	3	0	0	0	0	2	1	1	0	0	0	0	—	0	0-0	0	20.25
1998 Seattle	AL	6	5	0	0	26.1	127	34	23	21	3	0	0	0	15	0	19	0	0	1	2	.333	0	0-0	0	7.18
1999 Sea-KC	AL	38	13	0	6	110	510	124	92	83	16	2	3	7	64	3	68	11	0	2	5	.286	0	0-0	0	6.79

Year Team	Lg	G	GS	CG	GF	IP	BFP	H	R	ER	HR	SH	SF	HB	TBB	IBB	SO	WP	Bk	W	L	Pct.	ShO	Sv-Op	Hld	ERA
2000 Kansas City	AL	32	29	1	0	188.2	839	195	100	91	26	2	3	3	94	6	135	11	0	8	10	.444	1	0-0	0	4.34
1999 Seattle	AL	16	4	0	3	42	207	47	47	44	7	0	3	4	34	2	32	2	0	0	2	.000	0	0-0	0	9.43
Kansas City	AL	22	9	0	3	68	303	77	45	39	9	2	0	3	30	1	36	9	0	2	3	.400	0	0-0	0	5.16
4 ML YEARS		77	47	1	6	326.1	1484	355	218	198	45	4	6	10	175	10	223	22	0	11	17	.393	1	0-0	0	5.46

Pedro Swann

Bats: L **Throws:** R **Pos:** RF-2; PH/PR-2; LF-1; CF-1   **Ht:** 6'0" **Wt:** 200 **Born:** 10/27/70 **Age:** 30

Year Team	Lg	G	AB	H	2B	3B	HR	(Hm	Rd)	TB	R	RBI	TBB	IBB	SO	HBP	SH	SF	SB	CS	SB%	GDP	Avg	OBP	SLG
1991 Idaho Falls	R+	55	174	48	6	1	3	—	—	65	35	28	33	0	45	2	1	2	8	5	.62	4	.276	.393	.374
1992 Pulaski	R+	59	203	61	18	1	5	—	—	96	36	34	32	3	33	7	0	1	13	6	.68	6	.300	.412	.473
1993 Durham	A+	61	182	63	8	2	6	—	—	93	27	27	19	0	38	1	0	0	6	12	.33	2	.346	.411	.511
Greenville	AA	44	157	48	9	2	3	—	—	70	19	21	9	0	23	1	1	0	2	2	.50	5	.306	.347	.446
1994 Greenville	AA	126	428	121	25	2	10	—	—	180	55	49	46	2	85	4	0	2	16	9	.64	14	.283	.356	.421
1995 Richmond	AAA	15	38	8	1	0	0	—	—	9	2	3	1	0	2	1	0	0	0	2	.00	0	.211	.250	.237
Greenville	AA	102	339	110	24	2	11	—	—	171	57	64	45	2	63	3	0	3	14	11	.56	8	.324	.405	.504
1996 Richmond	AAA	35	129	40	5	0	3	—	—	54	15	20	18	2	23	3	1	1	4	4	.50	3	.310	.404	.419
Richmond	AA	93	296	74	11	4	4	—	—	105	42	35	22	2	56	4	2	3	7	7	.50	5	.250	.308	.355
1997 Greenville	AA	124	465	133	29	2	24	—	—	238	78	83	49	5	75	4	0	1	5	5	.50	14	.286	.358	.475
1998 Toledo	AAA	120	419	122	28	2	15	—	—	199	56	66	41	4	74	3	1	4	6	3	.67	11	.291	.355	.475
1999 Toledo	AAA	103	332	86	14	2	10	—	—	134	51	37	36	0	67	6	0	5	3	1	.75	7	.259	.338	.404
2000 Richmond	AAA	125	442	135	22	2	9	—	—	188	70	57	54	6	68	5	2	1	6	5	.55	10	.305	.386	.425
2000 Atlanta	NL	4	2	0	0	0	0	(0	0)	0	0	0	0	0	2	0	0	0	0	0	—	0	.000	.000	.000

Mark Sweeney

Bats: L **Throws:** L **Pos:** PH/PR-65; DH-4; LF-3; 1B-2   **Ht:** 6'1" **Wt:** 215 **Born:** 10/26/69 **Age:** 31

Year Team	Lg	G	AB	H	2B	3B	HR	(Hm	Rd)	TB	R	RBI	TBB	IBB	SO	HBP	SH	SF	SB	CS	SB%	GDP	Avg	OBP	SLG
2000 Indianapls *	AAA	18	55	28	8	0	2	—	—	42	13	14	10	0	8	0	0	0	0	0	—	3	.509	.585	.764
1995 St. Louis	NL	37	77	21	2	0	2	(0	2)	29	5	13	10	0	15	0	1	2	1	1	.50	3	.273	.348	.377
1996 St. Louis	NL	98	170	45	9	0	3	(0	3)	63	32	22	33	2	29	1	5	0	3	0	1.00	4	.265	.387	.371
1997 StL-SD	NL	115	164	46	7	0	2	(2	0)	59	16	23	20	1	32	1	1	2	2	3	.40	3	.280	.358	.360
1998 San Diego	NL	122	192	45	8	3	2	(1	1)	65	17	15	26	0	37	1	0	3	1	2	.33	5	.234	.324	.339
1999 Cincinnati	NL	37	31	11	3	0	2	(1	1)	20	6	7	4	1	9	0	0	0	0	0	—	2	.355	.429	.645
2000 Milwaukee	NL	71	73	16	6	0	1	(0	1)	25	9	6	12	1	18	1	1	0	0	0	—	1	.219	.337	.342
1997 St. Louis	NL	44	61	13	3	0	0	(0	0)	16	5	4	9	1	14	1	1	1	0	1	.00	2	.213	.319	.262
San Diego	NL	71	103	33	4	0	2	(2	0)	43	11	19	11	0	18	0	0	1	2	2	.50	1	.320	.383	.417
6 ML YEARS		480	707	184	35	3	12	(4	8)	261	85	86	105	5	140	4	8	7	7	6	.54	18	.260	.356	.369

Mike Sweeney

Bats: Right **Throws:** Right **Pos:** 1B-114; DH-45   **Ht:** 6'3" **Wt:** 225 **Born:** 7/22/73 **Age:** 27

Year Team	Lg	G	AB	H	2B	3B	HR	(Hm	Rd)	TB	R	RBI	TBB	IBB	SO	HBP	SH	SF	SB	CS	SB%	GDP	Avg	OBP	SLG
1995 Kansas City	AL	4	4	1	0	0	0	(0	0)	1	1	0	0	0	0	0	0	0	0	0	—	0	.250	.250	.250
1996 Kansas City	AL	50	165	46	10	0	4	(1	3)	68	23	24	18	0	21	4	0	3	1	2	.33	7	.279	.358	.412
1997 Kansas City	AL	84	240	58	8	0	7	(5	2)	87	30	31	17	0	33	6	1	2	3	2	.60	8	.242	.306	.363
1998 Kansas City	AL	92	282	73	18	0	8	(6	2)	115	32	35	24	1	38	2	2	1	2	3	.40	7	.259	.320	.408
1999 Kansas City	AL	150	575	185	44	2	22	(10	12)	299	101	102	54	0	48	10	0	4	6	1	.86	21	.322	.387	.520
2000 Kansas City	AL	159	618	206	30	0	29	(17	12)	323	105	144	71	5	67	15	0	13	8	3	.73	15	.333	.407	.523
6 ML YEARS		539	1884	569	110	2	70	(39	31)	893	292	336	184	6	207	37	3	23	20	11	.65	58	.302	.371	.474

Greg Swindell

Pitches: Left **Bats:** Right **Pos:** RP-64   **Ht:** 6'3" **Wt:** 230 **Born:** 1/2/65 **Age:** 36

Year Team	Lg	G	GS	CG	GF	IP	BFP	H	R	ER	HR	SH	SF	HB	TBB	IBB	SO	WP	Bk	W	L	Pct.	ShO	Sv-Op	Hld	ERA
1986 Cleveland	AL	9	9	1	0	61.2	255	57	35	29	9	3	1	1	15	0	46	3	2	5	2	.714	0	0-0	0	4.23
1987 Cleveland	AL	16	15	4	0	102.1	441	112	62	58	18	4	3	1	37	1	97	0	1	3	8	.273	1	0-0	1	5.10
1988 Cleveland	AL	33	33	12	0	242	988	234	97	86	18	9	5	1	45	3	180	5	0	18	14	.563	4	0-0	0	3.20
1989 Cleveland	AL	28	28	5	0	184.1	749	170	71	69	16	4	4	0	51	1	129	3	1	13	6	.684	2	0-0	0	3.37
1990 Cleveland	AL	34	34	3	0	214.2	912	245	110	105	27	8	6	1	47	2	135	3	2	12	9	.571	0	0-0	0	4.40
1991 Cleveland	AL	33	33	7	0	238	971	241	112	92	21	13	8	3	31	1	169	3	1	9	16	.360	0	0-0	0	3.48
1992 Cincinnati	NL	31	30	5	0	213.2	867	210	72	64	14	9	7	2	41	4	138	3	2	12	8	.600	3	0-0	0	2.70
1993 Houston	NL	31	30	1	0	190.1	818	215	98	88	24	13	3	1	40	3	124	2	2	12	13	.480	1	0-0	0	4.16
1994 Houston	NL	24	24	1	0	148.1	623	175	80	72	20	9	7	1	26	2	74	1	1	8	9	.471	0	0-0	0	4.37
1995 Houston	NL	33	26	1	3	153	659	180	86	76	21	4	8	3	39	2	96	3	0	10	9	.526	1	0-2	0	4.47
1996 Hou-Cle		21	6	0	4	51.2	237	66	46	41	13	1	2	1	19	0	36	0	0	1	4	.200	0	0-2	1	7.14
1997 Minnesota	AL	65	1	0	12	79.1	343	102	46	46	12	2	3	2	25	3	75	0	0	7	4	.636	0	1-7	12	5.22
1998 Min-Bos		81	0	0	15	90.1	385	92	40	36	13	4	2	3	31	3	63	3	0	5	6	.455	0	2-5	24	3.59
1999 Arizona	NL	63	0	0	15	64.2	261	54	19	18	8	4	0	1	21	1	51	0	0	4	0	1.000	0	1-2	19	2.51
2000 Arizona	NL	64	0	0	21	76	318	71	29	27	7	6	3	1	20	5	64	0	0	2	6	.250	0	1-1	9	3.20
1996 Houston	NL	8	4	0	3	23	116	35	25	20	5	0	1	1	11	0	15	0	0	0	3	.000	0	0-2	0	7.83
Cleveland	AL	13	2	0	1	28.2	121	31	21	21	8	1	1	0	8	0	21	0	0	1	1	.500	0	0-0	1	6.59
1998 Minnesota	AL	52	0	0	12	66.1	281	67	27	27	10	3	2	3	18	2	45	3	0	3	3	.500	0	2-4	18	3.66
Boston	AL	29	0	0	3	24	104	25	13	9	3	1	0	0	13	1	18	0	0	2	3	.400	0	0-1	6	3.38
15 ML YEARS		566	269	40	70	2146.2	8944	2224	1003	907	241	93	62	21	488	31	1477	29	12	121	114	.515	12	5-19	66	3.80

210

Jeff Tam

Pitches: Right **Bats:** Right **Pos:** RP-72 **Ht:** 6'1" **Wt:** 202 **Born:** 8/19/70 **Age:** 30

Year Team	Lg	G	GS	CG	GF	IP	BFP	H	R	ER	HR	SH	SF	HB	TBB	IBB	SO	WP	Bk	W	L	Pct.	ShO	Sv-Op	Hld	ERA
1998 New York	NL	15	0	0	5	14.1	60	13	10	10	2	0	0	2	4	1	8	0	0	1	1	.500	0	0-1	1	6.28
1999 Cle-NYM		10	0	0	3	11.2	47	8	7	7	3	1	0	0	4	1	8	0	0	0	0	—	0	0-0	0	5.40
2000 Oakland	AL	72	0	0	23	85.2	351	86	30	25	3	2	4	1	23	8	46	3	0	3	3	.500	0	3-6	19	2.63
1999 Cleveland	AL	1	0	0	0	0.1	4	2	3	3	0	1	0	1	1	1	0	0	0	0	0	—	0	0-0	0	81.00
New York	NL	9	0	0	3	11.1	43	6	4	4	3	0	0	0	3	0	8	0	0	0	0	—	0	0-0	0	3.18
3 ML YEARS		97	0	0	31	111.2	458	107	47	42	8	3	4	3	31	10	62	3	0	4	4	.500	0	3-7	20	3.39

Kevin Tapani

Pitches: Right **Bats:** Right **Pos:** SP-30 **Ht:** 6'1" **Wt:** 190 **Born:** 2/18/64 **Age:** 37

Year Team	Lg	G	GS	CG	GF	IP	BFP	H	R	ER	HR	SH	SF	HB	TBB	IBB	SO	WP	Bk	W	L	Pct.	ShO	Sv-Op	Hld	ERA
1989 NYM-Min		8	5	0	1	40	169	39	18	17	3	1	2	0	12	1	23	0	1	2	2	.500	0	0-0	0	3.83
1990 Minnesota	AL	28	28	1	0	159.1	659	164	75	72	12	3	4	2	29	2	101	1	0	12	8	.600	1	0-0	0	4.07
1991 Minnesota	AL	34	34	4	0	244	974	225	84	81	23	9	6	2	40	0	135	3	3	16	9	.640	1	0-0	0	2.99
1992 Minnesota	AL	34	34	4	0	220	911	226	103	97	17	8	11	5	48	2	138	4	0	16	11	.593	1	0-0	0	3.97
1993 Minnesota	AL	36	35	3	0	225.2	964	243	123	111	21	3	5	6	57	1	150	4	0	12	15	.444	1	0-0	0	4.43
1994 Minnesota	AL	24	24	4	0	156	672	181	86	80	13	2	5	4	39	0	91	0	1	11	7	.611	1	0-0	0	4.62
1995 Min-LA		33	31	3	0	190.2	834	227	116	105	29	6	5	5	48	4	131	4	0	10	13	.435	1	0-0	0	4.96
1996 Chicago	AL	34	34	1	0	225.1	971	236	123	115	34	6	6	3	76	5	150	13	0	13	10	.565	1	0-0	0	4.59
1997 Chicago	NL	13	13	1	0	85	352	77	33	32	7	7	2	2	23	2	55	0	2	9	3	.750	1	0-0	0	3.39
1998 Chicago	NL	35	34	2	0	219	945	244	120	118	30	11	9	5	62	4	136	7	0	19	9	.679	2	0-0	0	4.85
1999 Chicago	NL	23	23	1	0	136	591	151	81	73	12	8	7	4	33	2	73	3	0	6	12	.333	0	0-0	0	4.83
2000 Chicago	NL	30	30	2	0	195.2	829	208	113	109	35	4	3	8	47	1	150	1	0	8	12	.400	0	0-0	0	5.01
1989 New York	NL	3	0	0	1	7.1	31	5	3	3	1	0	1	0	4	0	2	0	1	0	0	—	0	0-0	0	3.68
Minnesota	AL	5	5	0	0	32.2	138	34	15	14	2	1	1	0	8	1	21	0	0	2	2	.500	0	0-0	0	3.86
1995 Minnesota	AL	20	20	3	0	133.2	579	155	79	73	21	3	3	4	34	2	88	3	0	6	11	.353	1	0-0	0	4.92
Los Angeles	NL	13	11	0	0	57	255	72	37	32	8	3	2	1	14	2	43	1	0	4	2	.667	0	0-0	0	5.05
12 ML YEARS		332	325	26	1	2096.2	8871	2221	1075	1010	236	68	65	46	514	24	1333	41	6	134	111	.547	9	0-0	0	4.34

Fernando Tatis

Bats: R **Throws:** R **Pos:** 3B-91; DH-2; PH/PR-2; 1B-1 **Ht:** 5'10" **Wt:** 170 **Born:** 1/1/75 **Age:** 26

Year Team	Lg	G	AB	H	2B	3B	HR	(Hm	Rd)	TB	R	RBI	TBB	IBB	SO	HBP	SH	SF	SB	CS	SB%	GDP	Avg	OBP	SLG
2000 Memphis *	AAA	3	9	0	0	0	0	—	—	0	0	0	1	0	3	0	0	0	0	0	—	0	.000	.100	.000
1997 Texas	AL	60	223	57	9	0	8	(6	2)	90	29	29	14	0	42	0	2	2	3	0	1.00	6	.256	.297	.404
1998 Tex-StL		150	532	147	33	4	11	(6	5)	221	69	58	36	3	123	6	4	1	13	5	.72	16	.276	.329	.415
1999 St. Louis	NL	149	537	160	31	2	34	(16	18)	297	104	107	82	4	128	16	0	4	21	9	.70	11	.298	.404	.553
2000 St. Louis	NL	96	324	82	21	1	18	(11	7)	159	59	64	57	1	94	10	1	2	3	4	.40	13	.253	.379	.491
1998 Texas	AL	95	330	89	17	2	3	(1	2)	119	41	32	12	2	66	4	4	0	6	2	.75	10	.270	.303	.361
St. Louis	NL	55	202	58	16	2	8	(5	3)	102	28	26	24	1	57	2	0	1	7	3	.70	6	.287	.367	.505
4 ML YEARS		455	1616	446	94	7	71	(39	32)	767	261	258	189	8	387	32	7	9	39	17	.70	46	.276	.361	.475

Eddie Taubensee

Bats: Left **Throws:** Right **Pos:** C-76; PH/PR-11 **Ht:** 6'3" **Wt:** 230 **Born:** 10/31/68 **Age:** 32

Year Team	Lg	G	AB	H	2B	3B	HR	(Hm	Rd)	TB	R	RBI	TBB	IBB	SO	HBP	SH	SF	SB	CS	SB%	GDP	Avg	OBP	SLG
1991 Cleveland	AL	26	66	16	2	1	0	(0	0)	20	5	8	5	1	16	0	0	2	0	0	—	1	.242	.288	.303
1992 Houston	NL	104	297	66	15	0	5	(2	3)	96	23	28	31	3	78	2	0	1	2	1	.67	4	.222	.299	.323
1993 Houston	NL	94	288	72	11	1	9	(4	5)	112	26	42	21	5	44	0	1	2	1	0	1.00	8	.250	.299	.389
1994 Hou-Cin	NL	66	187	53	8	2	8	(2	6)	89	29	21	15	2	31	0	1	2	2	0	1.00	3	.283	.333	.476
1995 Cincinnati	NL	80	218	62	14	2	9	(4	5)	107	32	44	22	2	52	2	1	1	2	2	.50	2	.284	.354	.491
1996 Cincinnati	NL	108	327	95	20	0	12	(6	6)	151	46	48	26	5	64	0	1	5	3	4	.43	4	.291	.338	.462
1997 Cincinnati	NL	108	254	68	18	0	10	(7	3)	116	26	34	22	2	66	1	1	1	0	1	.00	4	.268	.323	.457
1998 Cincinnati	NL	130	431	120	27	0	11	(8	3)	180	61	72	52	6	93	0	2	6	1	0	1.00	4	.278	.352	.418
1999 Cincinnati	NL	126	424	132	22	2	21	(8	13)	221	58	87	30	1	67	1	1	5	2	0	.00	11	.311	.354	.521
2000 Cincinnati	NL	81	266	71	12	0	6	(0	6)	101	29	24	21	1	44	2	1	1	0	0	—	7	.267	.324	.380
1994 Houston	NL	5	10	1	0	0	0	(0	0)	1	0	0	0	0	3	0	0	0	0	0	—	0	.100	.100	.100
Cincinnati	NL	61	177	52	8	2	8	(2	6)	88	29	21	15	2	28	0	1	2	2	0	1.00	2	.294	.345	.497
10 ML YEARS		923	2758	755	149	8	91	(41	50)	1193	335	408	245	28	555	8	9	30	11	10	.52	47	.274	.331	.433

Julian Tavarez

Pitches: Right **Bats:** Left **Pos:** RP-39; SP-12 **Ht:** 6'2" **Wt:** 190 **Born:** 5/22/73 **Age:** 28

Year Team	Lg	G	GS	CG	GF	IP	BFP	H	R	ER	HR	SH	SF	HB	TBB	IBB	SO	WP	Bk	W	L	Pct.	ShO	Sv-Op	Hld	ERA
1993 Cleveland	AL	8	7	0	0	37	172	53	29	27	7	0	1	2	13	2	19	3	1	2	2	.500	0	0-0	0	6.57
1994 Cleveland	AL	1	1	0	0	1.2	14	6	8	4	1	0	1	0	1	1	0	0	0	0	1	.000	0	0-0	0	21.60
1995 Cleveland	AL	57	0	0	15	85	350	76	36	23	7	0	2	3	21	0	68	3	2	10	2	.833	0	0-4	19	2.44
1996 Cleveland	AL	51	4	0	13	80.2	353	101	49	48	9	5	4	1	22	5	46	1	0	4	7	.364	0	0-0	13	5.36
1997 San Francisco	NL	89	0	0	13	88.1	378	91	43	38	6	3	8	4	34	5	38	4	0	6	4	.600	0	0-3	26	3.87
1998 San Francisco	NL	60	0	0	12	85.1	374	96	41	36	5	5	3	8	36	11	52	1	1	5	3	.625	0	1-6	10	3.80
1999 San Francisco	NL	47	0	0	12	54.2	258	65	38	36	7	3	2	8	25	3	33	4	1	2	0	1.000	0	0-2	5	5.93
2000 Colorado	NL	51	12	1	8	120	530	124	68	59	11	3	4	7	53	9	62	2	1	11	5	.688	0	1-1	6	4.43
8 ML YEARS		364	24	1	73	552.2	2429	612	312	271	53	19	25	33	205	36	318	18	6	40	24	.625	0	2-16	79	4.41

Billy Taylor

Pitches: Right **Bats:** Right **Pos:** RP-17   **Ht:** 6'8" **Wt:** 235 **Born:** 10/16/61 **Age:** 39

			HOW MUCH HE PITCHED						WHAT HE GAVE UP										THE RESULTS					
Year Team	Lg	G	GS	CG	GF	IP	BFP	H	R	ER	HR	SH	SF	HB	TBB	IBB	SO	WP	Bk	W	L	Pct.	ShO	Sv-Op	Hld	ERA
2000 Durham *	AAA	42	0	0	36	45.1	194	47	22	21	7	1	0	0	17	5	47	2	0	4	0	1.000	0	26- –		4.17
1994 Oakland	AL	41	0	0	11	46.1	195	38	24	18	4	1	1	2	18	5	48	0	0	1	3	.250	0	1-3	2	3.50
1996 Oakland	AL	55	0	0	30	60.1	261	52	30	29	5	4	3	4	25	4	67	1	0	6	3	.667	0	17-19	4	4.33
1997 Oakland	AL	72	0	0	45	73	320	70	32	31	3	1	2	5	36	9	66	0	0	3	4	.429	0	23-30	7	3.82
1998 Oakland	AL	70	0	0	58	73	311	71	37	29	7	3	5	3	22	4	58	0	1	4	9	.308	0	33-37	0	3.58
1999 Oak-NYM		61	0	0	43	56.1	257	68	35	31	5	5	2	2	23	8	52	1	1	1	6	.143	0	26-34	1	4.95
2000 Tampa Bay	AL	17	0	0	7	13.2	62	13	13	13	2	0	0	2	9	2	13	0	0	1	3	.250	0	0-2	2	8.56
1999 Oakland	AL	43	0	0	38	43	189	48	23	19	3	4	2	2	14	3	38	1	1	1	5	.167	0	26-33	0	3.98
New York	NL	18	0	0	5	13.1	68	20	12	12	2	1	0	0	9	5	14	0	0	0	1	.000	0	0-1	1	8.10
6 ML YEARS		316	0	0	194	322.2	1406	312	171	151	26	14	13	18	133	32	304	2	2	16	28	.364	0	100-125	16	4.21

Reggie Taylor

Bats: Left **Throws:** Right **Pos:** PH/PR-6; CF-3   **Ht:** 6'1" **Wt:** 178 **Born:** 1/12/77 **Age:** 24

								BATTING											BASERUNNING				PERCENTAGES		
Year Team	Lg	G	AB	H	2B	3B	HR	(Hm	Rd)	TB	R	RBI	TBB	IBB	SO	HBP	SH	SF	SB	CS	SB%	GDP	Avg	OBP	SLG
1995 Martinsvlle	R+	64	239	53	4	6	2	—	—	75	36	32	23	0	58	6	0	4	18	7	.72	5	.222	.301	.314
1996 Piedmont	A	128	499	131	20	6	0	—	—	163	68	31	29	0	136	3	3	2	36	17	.68	10	.263	.305	.327
1997 Clearwater	A+	134	545	133	18	6	12	—	—	199	73	47	30	4	130	4	5	6	40	23	.63	3	.244	.285	.365
1998 Reading	AA	79	337	92	14	6	5	—	—	133	49	22	12	0	73	2	0	2	22	10	.69	2	.273	.300	.395
1999 Reading	AA	127	526	140	17	10	15	—	—	222	75	61	18	1	79	3	3	3	38	20	.66	11	.266	.293	.422
2000 Scrantn-WB	AAA	98	422	116	10	8	15	—	—	187	60	43	21	3	87	2	5	4	23	12	.66	4	.275	.310	.443
2000 Philadelphia	NL	9	11	1	0	0	0	(0	0)	1	1	0	0	0	8	0	0	0	1	0	1.00	0	.091	.091	.091

Miguel Tejada

Bats: Right **Throws:** Right **Pos:** SS-160; PH/PR-1   **Ht:** 5'9" **Wt:** 188 **Born:** 5/25/76 **Age:** 25

								BATTING											BASERUNNING				PERCENTAGES		
Year Team	Lg	G	AB	H	2B	3B	HR	(Hm	Rd)	TB	R	RBI	TBB	IBB	SO	HBP	SH	SF	SB	CS	SB%	GDP	Avg	OBP	SLG
1997 Oakland	AL	26	99	20	3	2	2	(1	1)	33	10	10	2	0	22	3	0	0	2	0	1.00	3	.202	.240	.333
1998 Oakland	AL	105	365	85	20	1	11	(5	6)	140	53	45	28	0	86	7	4	3	5	6	.45	8	.233	.298	.384
1999 Oakland	AL	159	593	149	33	4	21	(12	9)	253	93	84	57	3	94	10	9	5	8	7	.53	11	.251	.325	.427
2000 Oakland	AL	160	607	167	32	1	30	(16	14)	291	105	115	66	6	102	4	2	2	6	0	1.00	15	.275	.349	.479
4 ML YEARS		450	1664	421	88	8	64	(34	30)	717	261	254	153	9	304	24	15	10	21	13	.62	37	.253	.323	.431

Amaury Telemaco

Pitches: Right **Bats:** Right **Pos:** RP-11; SP-2   **Ht:** 6'3" **Wt:** 222 **Born:** 1/19/74 **Age:** 27

					HOW MUCH HE PITCHED					WHAT HE GAVE UP										THE RESULTS					
Year Team	Lg	G	GS	CG	GF	IP	BFP	H	R	ER	HR	SH	SF	HB	TBB	IBB	SO	WP	Bk	W	L	Pct.	ShO	Sv-Op	Hld	ERA
2000 Scrantn-WB *	AAA	21	21	0	0	123.1	514	115	60	53	15	4	4	0	42	0	88	5	0	8	3	.727	0	0- –	—	3.87
1996 Chicago	NL	25	17	0	2	97.1	427	108	67	59	20	5	3	3	31	2	64	3	0	5	7	.417	0	0-0	0	5.46
1997 Chicago	NL	10	5	0	2	38	169	47	26	26	4	2	1	0	11	0	29	1	0	0	3	.000	0	0-0	0	6.16
1998 ChC-Ari	NL	41	18	0	5	148.2	637	150	75	65	18	8	6	4	46	2	78	7	0	7	10	.412	0	0-0	1	3.93
1999 Ari-Phi	NL	49	0	0	10	53	249	52	34	34	10	4	1	2	26	4	43	5	0	4	0	1.000	0	0-1	3	5.77
2000 Philadelphia	NL	13	2	0	2	24.1	107	25	22	18	6	0	2	0	14	0	22	1	0	1	3	.250	0	0-1	0	6.66
1998 Chicago	NL	14	0	0	4	27.2	118	23	12	12	5	0	0	0	13	0	18	3	0	1	1	.500	0	0-0	1	3.90
Arizona	NL	27	18	0	1	121	519	127	63	53	13	8	6	4	33	2	60	4	0	6	9	.400	0	0-0	0	3.94
1999 Arizona	NL	5	0	0	3	6	28	7	5	5	2	1	0	0	6	1	2	0	0	1	0	1.000	0	0-0	0	7.50
Philadelphia	NL	44	0	0	7	47	206	45	29	29	8	3	1	2	20	3	41	5	0	3	0	1.000	0	0-1	3	5.55
5 ML YEARS		138	42	0	21	361.1	1574	382	224	202	58	19	13	9	128	8	236	17	0	17	23	.425	0	0-2	4	5.03

Anthony Telford

Pitches: Right **Bats:** Right **Pos:** RP-64   **Ht:** 6'0" **Wt:** 195 **Born:** 3/6/66 **Age:** 35

					HOW MUCH HE PITCHED					WHAT HE GAVE UP										THE RESULTS					
Year Team	Lg	G	GS	CG	GF	IP	BFP	H	R	ER	HR	SH	SF	HB	TBB	IBB	SO	WP	Bk	W	L	Pct.	ShO	Sv-Op	Hld	ERA
1990 Baltimore	AL	8	8	0	0	36.1	168	43	22	20	4	0	2	1	19	0	20	1	0	3	3	.500	0	0-0	0	4.95
1991 Baltimore	AL	9	1	0	4	26.2	109	27	12	12	3	0	1	0	6	1	24	1	0	0	0		0	0-0	0	4.05
1993 Baltimore	AL	3	0	0	2	7.1	34	11	8	8	3	0	0	1	1	0	6	1	0	0	0		0	0-0	0	9.82
1997 Montreal	NL	65	0	0	17	89	369	77	34	32	11	4	1	5	33	4	61	6	0	4	6	.400	0	1-5	11	3.24
1998 Montreal	NL	77	0	0	24	91	398	85	45	39	9	10	4	4	36	1	59	8	1	3	6	.333	0	1-5	8	3.86
1999 Montreal	NL	79	0	0	21	96	429	112	52	42	3	3	5	3	38	3	69	3	1	5	4	.556	0	2-9	18	3.94
2000 Montreal	NL	64	0	0	18	78.1	330	76	38	33	10	2	4	5	23	1	68	4	1	5	4	.556	0	3-5	11	3.79
7 ML YEARS		305	9	0	86	424.2	1837	431	211	186	43	19	17	19	156	10	307	24	3	20	23	.465	0	7-24	48	3.94

Jay Tessmer

Pitches: Right **Bats:** Right **Pos:** RP-7   **Ht:** 6'3" **Wt:** 188 **Born:** 12/26/71 **Age:** 29

					HOW MUCH HE PITCHED					WHAT HE GAVE UP										THE RESULTS					
Year Team	Lg	G	GS	CG	GF	IP	BFP	H	R	ER	HR	SH	SF	HB	TBB	IBB	SO	WP	Bk	W	L	Pct.	ShO	Sv-Op	Hld	ERA
1995 Oneonta	A-	34	0	0	33	38	156	27	8	4	0	0	0	3	12	2	52	3	2	2	0	1.000	0	20- –		0.95
1996 Tampa	A+	68	0	0	63	97.1	381	68	18	16	2	6	0	6	19	3	104	1	0	12	4	.750	0	35- –		1.48
1997 Norwich	AA	55	0	0	49	62.2	289	78	41	39	7	3	2	2	24	2	51	4	0	3	6	.333	0	17- –		5.31
1998 Norwich	AA	45	0	0	44	49.2	208	50	8	6	0	3	0	0	13	5	57	0	1	3	4	.429	0	29- –		1.09
Columbus	AAA	12	0	0	11	18.1	64	8	2	1	1	0	1	1	4	0	14	0	0	1	1	.500	0	5- –		0.49
1999 Columbus	AAA	51	0	0	48	56.2	232	52	22	21	4	5	0	1	12	1	42	3	0	3	3	.500	0	28- –		3.34
2000 Columbus	AAA	60	0	0	53	66.1	293	73	36	28	7	6	3	1	19	7	40	1	0	4	8	.333	0	34- –		3.80
1998 New York	AL	7	0	0	3	8.2	33	11	3	3	1	0	0	0	2	1	4	0	0	1	0	1.000	0	0-0		3.12
1999 New York	AL	6	0	0	4	6.2	41	16	11	11	1	0	0	1	4	2	3	0	0	0	0		0	0-0	1	14.85
2000 New York	AL	7	0	0	5	6.2	31	9	6	5	3	0	0	0	3	0	7	1	0	0	0		0	0-0	0	6.75
3 ML YEARS		20	0	0	12	22	105	29	20	19	5	0	0	1	9	3	14	1	0	1	0	1.000	0	0-0	1	7.77

Frank Thomas

Bats: Right **Throws:** Right **Pos:** DH-127; 1B-30; PH/PR-2 **Ht:** 6'5" **Wt:** 270 **Born:** 5/27/68 **Age:** 33

Year Team	Lg	G	AB	H	2B	3B	HR	(Hm	Rd)	TB	R	RBI	TBB	IBB	SO	HBP	SH	SF	SB	CS	SB%	GDP	Avg	OBP	SLG
1990 Chicago	AL	60	191	63	11	3	7	(2	5)	101	39	31	44	0	54	2	0	3	0	1	.00	5	.330	.454	.529
1991 Chicago	AL	158	559	178	31	2	32	(24	8)	309	104	109	138	13	112	1	0	8	1	2	.33	20	.318	.453	.553
1992 Chicago	AL	160	573	185	46	2	24	(10	14)	307	108	115	122	6	88	5	0	11	6	3	.67	19	.323	.439	.536
1993 Chicago	AL	153	549	174	36	0	41	(26	15)	333	106	128	112	23	54	2	0	13	4	2	.67	10	.317	.426	.607
1994 Chicago	AL	113	399	141	34	1	38	(22	16)	291	106	101	109	12	61	2	0	7	2	3	.40	15	.353	.487	.729
1995 Chicago	AL	145	493	152	27	0	40	(15	25)	299	102	111	136	29	74	6	0	12	3	2	.60	14	.308	.454	.606
1996 Chicago	AL	141	527	184	26	0	40	(16	24)	330	110	134	109	26	70	5	0	8	1	1	.50	25	.349	.459	.626
1997 Chicago	AL	146	530	184	35	0	35	(16	19)	324	110	125	109	9	69	3	0	7	1	1	.50	15	.347	.456	.611
1998 Chicago	AL	160	585	155	35	2	29	(15	14)	281	109	109	110	2	93	6	0	11	7	0	1.00	14	.265	.381	.480
1999 Chicago	AL	135	486	148	36	0	15	(9	6)	239	74	77	87	13	66	9	0	8	3	3	.50	15	.305	.414	.471
2000 Chicago	AL	159	582	191	44	0	43	(30	13)	364	115	143	112	18	94	5	0	8	1	3	.25	13	.328	.436	.625
11 ML YEARS		1530	5474	1755	361	10	344	(185	159)	3168	1083	1183	1188	151	835	46	0	90	29	21	.58	165	.321	.440	.579

Jim Thome

Bats: Left **Throws:** Right **Pos:** 1B-107; DH-49; PH/PR-4 **Ht:** 6'4" **Wt:** 240 **Born:** 8/27/70 **Age:** 30

Year Team	Lg	G	AB	H	2B	3B	HR	(Hm	Rd)	TB	R	RBI	TBB	IBB	SO	HBP	SH	SF	SB	CS	SB%	GDP	Avg	OBP	SLG
1991 Cleveland	AL	27	98	25	4	2	1	(0	1)	36	7	9	5	1	16	1	0	0	1	1	.50	4	.255	.298	.367
1992 Cleveland	AL	40	117	24	3	1	2	(1	1)	35	8	12	10	2	34	2	0	2	2	0	1.00	3	.205	.275	.299
1993 Cleveland	AL	47	154	41	11	0	7	(5	2)	73	28	22	29	1	36	4	0	5	2	1	.67	3	.266	.385	.474
1994 Cleveland	AL	98	321	86	20	1	20	(10	10)	168	58	52	46	5	84	0	1	1	3	3	.50	11	.268	.359	.523
1995 Cleveland	AL	137	452	142	29	3	25	(13	12)	252	92	73	97	3	113	5	0	3	4	3	.57	8	.314	.438	.558
1996 Cleveland	AL	151	505	157	28	5	38	(18	20)	309	122	116	123	8	141	6	0	2	2	2	.50	13	.311	.450	.612
1997 Cleveland	AL	147	496	142	25	0	40	(17	23)	287	104	102	120	9	146	3	0	8	1	1	.50	9	.286	.423	.579
1998 Cleveland	AL	123	440	129	34	2	30	(18	12)	267	89	85	89	8	141	4	0	4	1	0	1.00	7	.293	.413	.584
1999 Cleveland	AL	146	494	137	27	2	33	(19	14)	267	101	108	127	13	171	4	0	4	0	0	—	6	.277	.426	.540
2000 Cleveland	AL	158	557	150	33	1	37	(21	16)	296	106	106	118	4	171	4	0	5	1	0	1.00	8	.269	.398	.531
10 ML YEARS		1074	3634	1033	214	17	233	(122	111)	1980	715	685	764	54	1053	33	1	34	17	11	.61	72	.284	.410	.545

Andy Thompson

Bats: Right **Throws:** Right **Pos:** LF-2 **Ht:** 6'3" **Wt:** 215 **Born:** 10/8/75 **Age:** 25

Year Team	Lg	G	AB	H	2B	3B	HR	(Hm	Rd)	TB	R	RBI	TBB	IBB	SO	HBP	SH	SF	SB	CS	SB%	GDP	Avg	OBP	SLG
1995 Hagerstown	A	124	461	110	19	2	6	—	—	151	48	57	29	2	108	8	1	3	2	3	.40	15	.239	.293	.328
1996 Dunedin	A+	129	425	120	26	5	11	—	—	189	64	50	60	1	108	1	1	3	16	4	.80	5	.282	.370	.445
1997 Knoxville	AA	124	448	128	25	3	15	—	—	204	75	71	63	3	76	6	1	4	0	5	.00	18	.286	.378	.455
1998 Knoxville	AA	125	481	137	33	2	14	—	—	216	74	88	54	2	69	3	0	5	8	3	.73	10	.285	.357	.449
1999 Knoxville	AA	67	254	62	16	3	15	—	—	129	56	53	34	2	55	8	0	5	7	3	.70	2	.244	.346	.508
Syracuse	AAA	62	229	67	17	2	16	—	—	136	42	42	21	0	45	2	0	0	5	0	1.00	4	.293	.357	.594
2000 Syracuse	AAA	121	426	105	27	2	22	—	—	202	59	65	50	1	95	9	0	6	9	2	.82	4	.246	.334	.474
2000 Toronto	AL	2	6	1	0	0	0	(0	0)	1	2	1	3	0	2	0	0	0	0	0	—	0	.167	.444	.167

Mark Thompson

Pitches: Right **Bats:** Right **Pos:** RP-20 **Ht:** 6'2" **Wt:** 212 **Born:** 4/7/71 **Age:** 30

Year Team	Lg	G	GS	CG	GF	IP	BFP	H	R	ER	HR	SH	SF	HB	TBB	IBB	SO	WP	Bk	W	L	Pct.	ShO	Sv-Op	Hld	ERA
2000 Arkansas *	AA	1	1	0	0	3.2	16	6	2	2	0	0	0	0	0	0	3	0	0	0	0	—	0	0--	—	4.91
Memphis *	AAA	6	5	0	0	31	126	31	9	7	1	2	0	2	5	0	15	0	0	2	0	1.000	0	0--	—	2.03
1994 Colorado	NL	2	2	0	0	9	49	16	9	9	2	0	0	1	8	0	5	0	0	1	1	.500	0	0-0	0	9.00
1995 Colorado	NL	21	5	0	3	51	240	73	42	37	7	4	4	1	22	2	30	2	0	2	3	.400	0	0-0	2	6.53
1996 Colorado	NL	34	28	3	2	169.2	763	189	109	100	25	10	3	13	74	1	99	1	1	9	11	.450	1	0-1	0	5.30
1997 Colorado	NL	6	6	0	0	29.2	146	40	27	26	8	3	2	4	13	0	9	0	1	3	3	.500	0	0-0	0	7.89
1998 Colorado	NL	6	6	0	0	23.1	116	36	22	20	8	2	2	5	12	0	14	1	0	1	2	.333	0	0-0	0	7.71
1999 St. Louis	NL	5	5	0	0	29.1	130	26	12	9	1	3	0	2	17	1	22	1	0	1	3	.250	0	0-0	0	2.76
2000 St. Louis	NL	20	0	0	4	25	116	24	21	14	4	1	1	3	15	0	19	3	0	1	1	.500	0	0-1	1	5.04
7 ML YEARS		94	52	3	9	337	1560	404	242	215	55	23	12	29	161	4	198	8	2	18	24	.429	1	0-2	3	5.74

Ryan Thompson

Bats: R **Throws:** R **Pos:** LF-20; PH/PR-11; CF-9; RF-6 **Ht:** 6'3" **Wt:** 215 **Born:** 11/4/67 **Age:** 33

Year Team	Lg	G	AB	H	2B	3B	HR	(Hm	Rd)	TB	R	RBI	TBB	IBB	SO	HBP	SH	SF	SB	CS	SB%	GDP	Avg	OBP	SLG
2000 Columbus *	AAA	86	326	93	23	3	23	—	—	191	45	75	27	0	72	1	0	2	10	3	.77	8	.285	.342	.586
1992 New York	NL	30	108	24	7	1	3	(3	0)	42	15	10	8	0	24	0	0	1	2	2	.50	2	.222	.274	.389
1993 New York	NL	80	288	72	19	2	11	(5	6)	128	34	26	19	4	81	3	5	1	2	7	.22	5	.250	.302	.444
1994 New York	NL	98	334	75	14	1	18	(5	13)	145	39	59	28	7	94	10	3	4	1	1	.50	8	.225	.301	.434
1995 New York	NL	75	267	67	13	0	7	(3	4)	101	39	31	19	1	77	4	0	4	3	1	.75	12	.251	.306	.378
1996 Cleveland	AL	8	22	7	0	1	0	(1	0)	10	2	5	1	0	6	0	0	0	0	0	—	1	.318	.348	.455
1999 Houston	NL	12	20	4	1	0	1	(0	1)	8	2	5	2	0	7	0	0	0	0	0	—	0	.200	.273	.400
2000	AL	33	50	13	3	0	3	(2	1)	25	12	14	5	0	12	1	0	0	0	0	1.00	0	.260	.339	.500
7 ML YEARS		336	1089	262	57	4	44	(19	25)	459	143	150	82	12	301	18	8	10	8	12	.40	28	.241	.302	.421

Mike Thurman

Pitches: Right **Bats:** Right **Pos:** SP-17   **Ht:** 6'5" **Wt:** 210 **Born:** 7/22/73 **Age:** 27

Year Team	Lg	G	GS	CG	GF	IP	BFP	H	R	ER	HR	SH	SF	HB	TBB	IBB	SO	WP	Bk	W	L	Pct.	ShO	Sv-Op	Hld	ERA
2000 Jupiter *	A+	3	3	0	0	13	50	14	3	3	1	0	0	0	0	0	6	0	0	1	1	.500	0	0--	—	2.08
Harrisburg *	AA	1	0	0	0	4.1	19	4	2	2	0	0	1	0	3	0	1	0	0	0	0	—	0	0--	—	4.15
Ottawa *	AAA	4	4	0	0	16.1	76	23	14	14	1	2	1	0	9	0	8	0	0	0	3	.000	0	0--	—	7.71
1997 Montreal	NL	5	2	0	1	11.2	48	8	9	7	3	0	0	1	4	0	8	0	0	1	0	1.000	0	0-0	0	5.40
1998 Montreal	NL	14	13	0	1	67	287	60	38	35	7	2	4	3	26	2	32	3	0	4	5	.444	0	0-0	0	4.70
1999 Montreal	NL	29	27	0	1	146.2	627	140	84	66	17	8	3	7	52	4	85	4	1	7	11	.389	0	0-0	0	4.05
2000 Montreal	NL	17	17	0	0	88.1	415	112	69	63	9	5	3	3	46	4	52	2	0	4	9	.308	0	0-0	0	6.42
4 ML YEARS		65	59	0	3	313.2	1377	320	200	171	36	15	13	14	128	10	177	9	1	16	25	.390	0	0-0	0	4.91

Mike Timlin

Pitches: Right **Bats:** Right **Pos:** RP-62   **Ht:** 6'4" **Wt:** 210 **Born:** 3/10/66 **Age:** 35

Year Team	Lg	G	GS	CG	GF	IP	BFP	H	R	ER	HR	SH	SF	HB	TBB	IBB	SO	WP	Bk	W	L	Pct.	ShO	Sv-Op	Hld	ERA
1991 Toronto	AL	63	3	0	17	108.1	463	94	43	38	6	2	4	1	50	11	85	5	0	11	6	.647	0	3-8	9	3.16
1992 Toronto	AL	26	0	0	14	43.2	190	45	23	20	0	2	1	1	20	5	35	0	0	0	2	.000	0	1-1	1	4.12
1993 Toronto	AL	54	0	0	27	55.2	254	63	32	29	7	1	3	1	27	3	49	1	0	4	2	.667	0	1-4	9	4.69
1994 Toronto	AL	34	0	0	16	40	179	41	25	23	5	0	0	2	20	0	38	3	0	0	1	.000	0	2-4	5	5.18
1995 Toronto	AL	31	0	0	19	42	179	38	13	10	1	3	0	2	17	5	36	3	1	4	3	.571	0	5-9	4	2.14
1996 Toronto	AL	59	0	0	56	56.2	230	47	25	23	4	2	3	2	18	4	52	3	0	1	6	.143	0	31-38	2	3.65
1997 Tor-Sea	AL	64	0	0	31	72.2	297	69	30	26	8	6	1	1	20	5	45	1	1	6	4	.600	0	10-18	9	3.22
1998 Seattle	AL	70	0	0	40	79.1	321	78	26	26	5	4	2	3	16	2	60	0	0	3	3	.500	0	19-24	6	2.95
1999 Baltimore	AL	62	0	0	52	63	261	51	30	25	9	1	1	5	23	3	50	1	0	3	9	.250	0	27-36	5	3.57
2000 Bal-StL	AL	62	0	0	40	64.2	295	67	33	30	8	7	2	4	35	6	52	0	0	5	4	.556	0	12-18	6	4.18
1997 Toronto	AL	38	0	0	26	47	190	41	17	15	6	4	1	1	15	4	36	1	1	3	2	.600	0	9-13	2	2.87
Seattle	AL	26	0	0	5	25.2	107	28	13	11	2	2	0	0	5	1	9	0	0	3	2	.600	0	1-5	7	3.86
2000 Baltimore	AL	37	0	0	31	35	157	37	22	19	6	5	1	2	15	3	26	0	0	2	3	.400	0	11-15	1	4.89
St. Louis	NL	25	0	0	9	29.2	138	30	11	11	2	2	1	2	20	3	26	0	0	3	1	.750	0	1-3	5	3.34
10 ML YEARS		525	3	0	312	626	2669	593	280	250	53	32	15	22	246	44	502	17	2	37	40	.481	0	111-160	51	3.59

Ozzie Timmons

Bats: R **Throws:** R **Pos:** RF-7; LF-2; PH/PR-2; DH-1   **Ht:** 6'2" **Wt:** 225 **Born:** 9/18/70 **Age:** 30

Year Team	Lg	G	AB	H	2B	3B	HR	(Hm	Rd)	TB	R	RBI	TBB	IBB	SO	HBP	SH	SF	SB	CS	SB%	GDP	Avg	OBP	SLG
2000 Durham *	AAA	137	506	152	32	1	29			273	100	104	73	5	105	7	0	5	5	4	.56	6	.300	.393	.540
1995 Chicago	NL	77	177	46	10	1	8	(5	3)	81	30	28	13	2	32	0	0	1	3	0	1.00	8	.263	.314	.474
1996 Chicago	NL	65	140	28	4	0	7	(6	1)	53	18	16	15	0	30	1	1	0	1	0	1.00	1	.200	.282	.379
1997 Cincinnati	NL	6	9	3	1	0	0	(0	0)	4	1	0	0	0	1	0	0	0	0	0	—	0	.333	.333	.444
1999 Seattle	AL	26	44	5	2	0	1	(0	1)	10	4	3	4	0	12	0	0	0	0	1	.00	0	.114	.188	.227
2000 Tampa Bay	AL	12	41	14	3	0	4	(3	1)	29	9	13	1	0	7	0	0	0	0	0	—	2	.341	.357	.707
5 ML YEARS		186	405	95	20	1	20	(14	6)	177	62	60	33	2	82	1	1	1	4	1	.80	11	.235	.293	.437

Jorge Toca

Bats: Right **Throws:** Right **Pos:** 1B-5; PH/PR-4; LF-1   **Ht:** 6'3" **Wt:** 220 **Born:** 1/7/75 **Age:** 26

Year Team	Lg	G	AB	H	2B	3B	HR	(Hm	Rd)	TB	R	RBI	TBB	IBB	SO	HBP	SH	SF	SB	CS	SB%	GDP	Avg	OBP	SLG
1999 Binghamton	AA	75	279	86	15	1	20	—	—	163	60	67	32	3	43	5	0	4	5	5	.50	9	.308	.384	.584
Norfolk	AAA	49	176	59	12	1	5	—	—	88	25	29	6	0	23	1	0	2	0	3	.00	9	.335	.357	.500
2000 Binghamton	AA	3	11	1	1	0	0	—	—	2	1	0	0	0	0	0	0	0	0	0	—	0	.091	.091	.182
Norfolk	AAA	120	453	123	25	3	11	—	—	187	58	70	17	3	72	4	0	3	9	8	.53	18	.272	.302	.413
1999 New York	NL	4	3	1	0	0	0	(0	0)	1	0	0	0	0	2	0	0	0	0	0	—	0	.333	.333	.333
2000 New York	NL	8	7	3	1	0	0	(0	0)	4	1	4	0	0	1	0	0	0	0	0	—	0	.429	.429	.571
2 ML YEARS		12	10	4	1	0	0	(0	0)	5	1	4	0	0	3	0	0	0	0	0	—	0	.400	.400	.500

Kevin Tolar

Pitches: Left **Bats:** Right **Pos:** RP-5   **Ht:** 6'3" **Wt:** 225 **Born:** 1/28/71 **Age:** 30

Year Team	Lg	G	GS	CG	GF	IP	BFP	H	R	ER	HR	SH	SF	HB	TBB	IBB	SO	WP	Bk	W	L	Pct.	ShO	Sv-Op	Hld	ERA
1989 White Sox	R	13	12	1	0	60	256	29	16	11	0	1	4	1	54	0	58	10	0	6	2	.750	0	0--	—	1.65
1990 Utica	A-	15	15	1	0	90.1	407	80	44	33	2	1	3	4	61	1	69	9	1	4	6	.400	0	0--	—	3.29
1991 South Bend	A	30	19	0	6	114.2	507	87	54	35	3	5	5	8	85	0	87	6	0	8	5	.615	0	1--	—	2.75
1992 Salinas	A+	14	8	3	3	53.1	255	55	43	36	4	1	7	5	46	0	24	6	0	1	8	.111	0	0--	—	6.08
South Bend	A	18	10	0	6	81.1	359	84	34	26	5	7	4	2	41	0	81	5	1	6	5	.545	0	0--	—	2.88
1993 Sarasota	A+	23	11	0	8	77.1	358	75	55	46	1	5	7	6	51	1	60	8	0	2	6	.250	0	1--	—	5.35
1995 Lynchburg	A+	18	0	0	4	19.1	77	13	7	6	1	0	1	1	6	0	19	3	0	2	0	1.000	0	0--	—	2.79
Carolina	AA	12	0	0	3	12.1	59	16	5	5	0	0	2	0	7	0	9	2	0	1	0	1.000	0	0--	—	3.65
1996 Canton-Akrn	AA	50	0	0	15	44.2	201	42	19	13	1	4	2	3	26	2	39	5	0	1	3	.250	0	1--	—	2.62
1997 Binghamton	AA	22	0	0	9	31.2	155	38	20	18	3	4	1	2	22	1	26	6	0	1	1	.500	0	1--	—	5.12
St. Lucie	A+	9	0	0	3	13.1	54	9	3	3	0	0	0	0	6	0	8	1	0	0	0	—	0	1--	—	2.03
1998 Nashville	AAA	1	0	0	0	3	14	2	2	2	0	0	0	0	4	0	1	1	0	0	0	—	0	0--	—	6.00
Carolina	AA	42	0	0	15	48.2	211	35	12	12	1	4	1	2	33	0	48	1	0	1	2	.333	0	1--	—	2.22
Indianapols	AAA	19	0	0	0	14.2	82	21	18	17	3	1	0	0	17	1	19	3	0	0	1	.000	0	1--	—	10.43
1999 Chattanooga	AA	47	1	0	16	54.1	262	61	32	30	2	2	4	4	45	4	60	4	0	4	4	.500	0	1--	—	4.97
Indianapols	AAA	8	0	0	3	13	53	8	4	3	1	0	1	0	7	1	18	1	0	1	0	1.000	0	0--	—	2.08
2000 Jacksnville	AAA	9	0	0	2	17.1	66	7	3	1	0	0	0	0	8	0	19	1	0	2	0	1.000	0	0--	—	0.52
Toledo	AAA	33	0	0	12	46.1	203	37	23	17	4	0	0	0	26	1	42	4	0	4	2	.667	0	2--	—	3.30
2000 Detroit	AL	5	0	0	1	3	12	1	1	1	0	0	0	0	1	0	3	0	0	0	0	—	0	0-0	0	3.00

Brian Tollberg

Pitches: Right **Bats:** Right **Pos:** SP-19 **Ht:** 6'3" **Wt:** 195 **Born:** 9/16/72 **Age:** 28

Year Team	Lg	G	GS	CG	GF	IP	BFP	H	R	ER	HR	SH	SF	HB	TBB	IBB	SO	WP	Bk	W	L	Pct.	ShO	Sv-Op	Hld	ERA
1994 Chillicothe	IND	13	13	4	0	94.2	402	90	34	30	5	2	2	8	27	2	69	8	0	7	4	.636	0	0- -	—	2.85
1995 Beloit	A	22	22	1	0	132	529	119	59	50	10	2	5	6	27	0	110	5	4	13	4	.765	1	0- -	—	3.41
1996 El Paso	AA	26	26	0	0	154.1	663	183	90	84	15	2	3	10	23	0	109	4	1	7	5	.583	0	0- -	—	4.90
1997 Mobile	AA	31	13	1	5	123.1	512	123	60	51	15	2	1	4	24	2	108	4	0	6	3	.667	0	0- -	—	3.72
1998 Mobile	AA	6	6	1	0	41	152	31	11	11	3	1	0	1	4	0	45	0	1	3	2	.600	0	0- -	—	2.41
Las Vegas	AAA	33	15	1	7	110	492	138	85	78	21	2	2	12	27	2	109	0	1	6	6	.500	0	3- -	—	6.38
1999 Las Vegas	AAA	5	5	0	0	29.2	123	34	17	16	3	1	0	2	6	0	23	1	0	1	2	.333	0	0- -	—	4.85
Padres	R	2	2	0	0	4	16	4	2	2	0	0	0	0	0	0	0	0	0	0	0	—	0	0- -	—	4.50
2000 Las Vegas	AAA	13	13	0	0	76.1	311	72	28	24	5	1	2	2	11	0	60	0	0	6	0	1.000	0	0- -	—	2.83
2000 San Diego	NL	19	19	1	0	118	506	126	58	47	13	6	0	5	35	4	76	2	1	4	5	.444	0	0-0	0	3.58

Brett Tomko

Pitches: Right **Bats:** Right **Pos:** RP-24; SP-8 **Ht:** 6'4" **Wt:** 215 **Born:** 4/7/73 **Age:** 28

Year Team	Lg	G	GS	CG	GF	IP	BFP	H	R	ER	HR	SH	SF	HB	TBB	IBB	SO	WP	Bk	W	L	Pct.	ShO	Sv-Op	Hld	ERA
2000 Tacoma *	AAA	2	2	0	0	12.2	53	13	4	4	1	0	0	0	5	1	8	0	0	1	0	1.000	0	0- -	—	2.84
1997 Cincinnati	NL	22	19	0	1	126	519	106	50	48	14	5	9	4	47	4	95	5	0	11	7	.611	0	0-0	0	3.43
1998 Cincinnati	NL	34	34	1	0	210.2	887	198	111	104	22	12	2	7	64	3	162	9	1	13	12	.520	0	0-0	0	4.44
1999 Cincinnati	NL	33	26	1	1	172	744	175	103	94	31	9	5	4	60	10	132	8	0	5	7	.417	0	0-0	1	4.92
2000 Seattle	AL	32	8	0	10	92.1	401	92	53	48	12	5	5	3	40	4	59	1	1	7	5	.583	0	1-2	3	4.68
4 ML YEARS		121	87	2	12	601	2551	571	317	294	79	31	21	18	211	21	448	23	2	36	31	.537	0	1-2	4	4.40

Steve Trachsel

Pitches: Right **Bats:** Right **Pos:** SP-34 **Ht:** 6'4" **Wt:** 205 **Born:** 10/31/70 **Age:** 30

Year Team	Lg	G	GS	CG	GF	IP	BFP	H	R	ER	HR	SH	SF	HB	TBB	IBB	SO	WP	Bk	W	L	Pct.	ShO	Sv-Op	Hld	ERA
1993 Chicago	NL	3	3	0	0	19.2	78	16	10	10	4	1	0	0	3	0	14	1	0	0	2	.000	0	0-0	0	4.58
1994 Chicago	NL	22	22	1	0	146	612	133	57	52	19	3	3	3	54	4	108	6	0	9	7	.563	0	0-0	0	3.21
1995 Chicago	NL	30	29	2	0	160.2	722	174	104	92	25	12	5	0	76	8	117	2	1	7	13	.350	0	0-0	0	5.15
1996 Chicago	NL	31	31	3	0	205	845	181	82	69	30	3	3	8	62	3	132	5	2	13	9	.591	2	0-0	0	3.03
1997 Chicago	NL	34	34	0	0	201.1	878	225	110	101	32	8	11	5	69	6	160	4	1	8	12	.400	0	0-0	0	4.51
1998 Chicago	NL	33	33	1	0	208	894	204	107	103	27	9	7	8	84	5	149	3	2	15	8	.652	0	0-0	0	4.46
1999 Chicago	NL	34	34	4	0	205.2	894	226	133	127	32	6	14	3	64	4	149	8	3	8	18	.308	0	0-0	0	5.56
2000 TB-Tor	AL	34	34	3	0	200.2	882	232	116	107	26	6	6	6	74	2	110	4	0	8	15	.348	1	0-0	0	4.80
2000 Tampa Bay	AL	23	23	3	0	137.2	606	160	76	70	16	2	5	6	49	1	78	3	0	6	10	.375	1	0-0	0	4.58
Toronto	AL	11	11	0	0	63	276	72	40	37	10	4	1	0	25	1	32	1	0	2	5	.286	0	0-0	0	5.29
8 ML YEARS		221	220	14	0	1347	5805	1391	719	661	195	48	50	33	486	32	939	33	9	68	84	.447	3	0-0	0	4.42

Andy Tracy

Bats: Left **Throws:** Right **Pos:** 3B-34; PH/PR-32; 1B-28 **Ht:** 6'3" **Wt:** 220 **Born:** 12/11/73 **Age:** 27

Year Team	Lg	G	AB	H	2B	3B	HR	(Hm	Rd)	TB	R	RBI	TBB	IBB	SO	HBP	SH	SF	SB	CS	SB%	GDP	Avg	OBP	SLG
1996 Vermont	A-	57	175	47	11	1	4	—	—	72	26	24	32	2	37	2	1	2	1	1	.50	8	.269	.384	.411
1997 Cape Fear	A	59	210	63	9	2	8	—	—	100	31	43	21	4	47	3	0	2	6	1	.86	4	.300	.369	.476
1998 Jupiter	A+	71	251	67	16	1	11	—	—	118	37	34	39	3	69	3	0	5	4	6	.40	3	.267	.366	.470
Harrisburg	AA	62	211	48	12	3	10	—	—	96	33	33	24	3	62	4	0	3	1	2	.33	5	.227	.314	.455
1999 Harrisburg	AA	134	493	135	26	2	37	—	—	276	96	128	70	4	139	6	1	3	6	1	.86	10	.274	.369	.560
2000 Ottawa	AAA	55	195	60	18	0	10	—	—	108	28	36	34	3	63	0	0	3	2	2	.50	2	.308	.410	.554
2000 Montreal	NL	83	192	50	8	1	11	(6	5)	93	29	32	22	1	61	2	0	2	1	0	1.00	3	.260	.339	.484

Bubba Trammell

Bats: R **Throws:** R **Pos:** RF-40; PH/PR-40; LF-37; DH-9 **Ht:** 6'2" **Wt:** 220 **Born:** 11/6/71 **Age:** 29

Year Team	Lg	G	AB	H	2B	3B	HR	(Hm	Rd)	TB	R	RBI	TBB	IBB	SO	HBP	SH	SF	SB	CS	SB%	GDP	Avg	OBP	SLG
1997 Detroit	AL	44	123	28	5	0	4	(2	2)	45	14	13	15	0	35	0	0	0	3	1	.75	2	.228	.307	.366
1998 Tampa Bay	AL	59	199	57	18	1	12	(6	6)	113	28	35	16	0	45	0	0	1	0	2	.00	4	.286	.338	.568
1999 Tampa Bay	AL	82	283	82	19	0	14	(6	8)	143	49	39	43	1	37	1	0	1	0	2	.00	7	.290	.384	.505
2000 TB-NYM		102	245	65	13	2	10	(6	4)	112	28	45	29	0	49	2	0	2	4	0	1.00	8	.265	.345	.457
2000 Tampa Bay	AL	66	189	52	11	2	7	(5	2)	88	19	33	21	0	30	2	0	1	3	0	1.00	5	.275	.352	.466
New York	NL	36	56	13	2	0	3	(1	2)	24	9	12	8	0	19	0	0	1	1	0	1.00	3	.232	.323	.429
4 ML YEARS		287	850	232	55	3	40	(20	20)	413	119	132	103	1	166	3	0	6	7	5	.58	21	.273	.351	.486

Mike Trombley

Pitches: Right **Bats:** Right **Pos:** RP-75 **Ht:** 6'2" **Wt:** 204 **Born:** 4/14/67 **Age:** 34

Year Team	Lg	G	GS	CG	GF	IP	BFP	H	R	ER	HR	SH	SF	HB	TBB	IBB	SO	WP	Bk	W	L	Pct.	ShO	Sv-Op	Hld	ERA
1992 Minnesota	AL	10	7	0	0	46.1	194	43	20	17	5	2	0	1	17	0	38	0	0	3	2	.600	0	0-0	0	3.30
1993 Minnesota	AL	44	10	0	8	114.1	506	131	72	62	15	3	7	3	41	4	85	5	0	6	6	.500	0	2-5	8	4.88
1994 Minnesota	AL	24	0	0	8	48.1	219	56	36	34	10	1	2	3	18	2	32	3	0	2	0	1.000	0	0-1	1	6.33
1995 Minnesota	AL	20	18	0	0	97.2	442	107	68	61	18	3	2	3	42	1	68	4	0	4	8	.333	0	0-0	0	5.62
1996 Minnesota	AL	43	0	0	19	68.2	292	61	24	23	2	0	3	5	25	8	57	4	0	5	1	.833	0	6-9	4	3.01
1997 Minnesota	AL	67	0	0	21	82.1	349	77	43	40	7	2	3	2	31	4	74	5	0	3	4	.400	0	1-1	11	4.37
1998 Minnesota	AL	77	1	0	17	96.2	413	90	41	39	16	2	1	5	41	3	89	6	1	4	5	.545	0	1-4	23	3.63
1999 Minnesota	AL	75	0	0	56	87.1	377	93	42	42	15	2	3	2	28	2	82	6	0	2	8	.200	0	24-30	5	4.33
2000 Baltimore	AL	75	0	0	32	72	322	67	34	33	15	7	2	4	38	8	72	8	0	4	5	.444	0	4-11	18	4.13
9 ML YEARS		435	36	0	161	713.2	3114	725	380	351	103	22	23	28	281	32	597	41	1	34	38	.472	0	38-61	68	4.43

Chris Truby

Bats: Right **Throws:** Right **Pos:** 3B-74; PH/PR-5   **Ht:** 6'2" **Wt:** 190 **Born:** 12/9/73 **Age:** 27

					BATTING													BASERUNNING				PERCENTAGES		
Year Team	Lg	G	AB	H	2B	3B	HR	(Hm | Rd)	TB	R	RBI	TBB	IBB	SO	HBP	SH	SF	SB	CS	SB%	GDP	Avg	OBP	SLG
1993 Astros	R	57	215	49	10	2	1	—	—	66	30	24	22	0	30	1	2	1	16	1	.94	5	.228	.301	.307
Osceola	A+	3	13	0	0	0	0	—	—	0	0	0	0	0	2	0	0	0	0	0	—	0	.000	.000	.000
1994 Quad City	A	36	111	24	4	1	2	—	—	36	12	19	3	0	29	2	0	2	1	1	.50	3	.216	.246	.324
Auburn	A-	73	282	91	17	6	7	—	—	141	56	61	23	0	48	3	1	8	20	4	.83	8	.323	.370	.500
1995 Quad City	A	118	400	93	23	4	9	—	—	151	68	64	41	0	66	3	3	3	27	8	.77	11	.233	.306	.378
1996 Quad City	A	109	362	91	15	3	8	—	—	136	45	37	28	1	74	2	6	5	6	10	.38	8	.251	.305	.376
1997 Quad City	A	68	268	75	14	1	7	—	—	112	34	46	22	0	32	1	1	2	13	4	.76	8	.280	.334	.418
Kissimmee	A+	57	199	49	11	0	2	—	—	66	23	29	8	0	40	2	4	3	8	3	.73	4	.246	.278	.332
1998 Kissimmee	A+	52	212	66	16	1	14	—	—	126	36	48	19	3	30	3	0	2	6	1	.86	2	.311	.373	.594
Jackson	AA	80	308	89	20	5	16	—	—	167	46	63	20	0	50	4	0	5	8	3	.73	5	.289	.335	.542
New Orleans	AAA	5	17	7	1	1	1	—	—	13	6	1	1	0	3	0	0	0	1	0	1.00	0	.412	.444	.765
1999 Jackson	AA	124	465	131	21	3	28	—	—	242	78	87	36	1	88	3	0	12	20	8	.71	11	.282	.329	.520
2000 New Orleans	AAA	64	268	76	11	3	2	—	—	99	31	30	17	2	32	0	0	7	6	2	.75	7	.284	.318	.369
2000 Houston	NL	78	258	67	15	4	11	(9 | 2)	123	28	59	10	1	56	1	1	5	2	1	.67	4	.260	.295	.477

Michael Tucker

Bats: L **Throws:** R **Pos:** RF-67; LF-41; PH/PR-37; CF-28; 2B-1   **Ht:** 6'2" **Wt:** 185 **Born:** 6/25/71 **Age:** 30

					BATTING													BASERUNNING				PERCENTAGES		
Year Team	Lg	G	AB	H	2B	3B	HR	(Hm	Rd)	TB	R	RBI	TBB	IBB	SO	HBP	SH	SF	SB	CS	SB%	GDP	Avg	OBP	SLG
1995 Kansas City	AL	62	177	46	10	0	4	(1	3)	68	23	17	18	2	51	1	2	0	2	3	.40	3	.260	.332	.384
1996 Kansas City	AL	108	339	88	18	4	12	(2	10)	150	55	53	40	1	69	7	3	4	10	4	.71	7	.260	.346	.442
1997 Atlanta	NL	138	499	141	25	7	14	(5	9)	222	80	56	44	0	116	6	4	1	12	7	.63	7	.283	.347	.445
1998 Atlanta	NL	130	414	101	27	3	13	(10	3)	173	54	46	49	10	112	3	1	2	8	3	.73	4	.244	.327	.418
1999 Cincinnati	NL	133	296	75	8	5	11	(5	6)	126	55	44	37	3	81	3	0	4	11	4	.73	5	.253	.338	.426
2000 Cincinnati	NL	148	270	72	13	4	15	(7	8)	138	55	36	44	1	64	7	0	2	13	6	.68	6	.267	.381	.511
6 ML YEARS		719	1995	523	101	23	69	(30	39)	877	322	252	232	17	493	27	10	13	56	27	.67	32	.262	.345	.440

T.J. Tucker

Pitches: Right **Bats:** Right **Pos:** SP-2   **Ht:** 6'3" **Wt:** 245 **Born:** 8/20/78 **Age:** 22

		HOW MUCH HE PITCHED						WHAT HE GAVE UP												THE RESULTS					
Year Team	Lg	G	GS	CG	GF	IP	BFP	H	R	ER	HR	SH	SF	HB	TBB	IBB	SO	WP	Bk	W	L	Pct.	ShO	Sv-Op	Hld	ERA
1997 Expos	R	3	2	0	0	4.2	19	5	1	1	0	0	0	0	1	0	11	0	0	1	0	1.000	0	0- -	—	1.93
1998 Expos	R	7	7	0	0	36	134	23	5	3	1	0	0	0	5	0	40	0	0	1	0	1.000	0	0- -	—	0.75
Vermont	A-	6	6	0	0	33	135	24	9	8	0	1	0	2	15	0	34	3	0	3	1	.750	0	0- -	—	2.18
Jupiter	A+	2	1	0	1	9	32	5	1	1	0	1	0	0	1	0	10	1	0	1	1	.500	0	0- -	—	1.00
1999 Jupiter	A+	7	7	0	0	44	171	24	7	6	2	0	1	0	16	0	35	1	0	5	1	.833	0	0- -	—	1.23
Harrisburg	AA	19	19	1	0	116.1	489	110	55	53	12	4	1	4	38	0	85	5	1	8	5	.615	1	0- -	—	4.10
2000 Harrisburg	AA	8	8	0	0	45	182	33	19	18	7	2	1	3	17	0	24	1	0	2	1	.667	0	0- -	—	3.60
2000 Montreal	NL	2	2	0	0	7	35	11	9	9	5	0	0	0	3	0	2	1	0	0	1	.000	0	0-0	0	11.57

Derrick Turnbow

Pitches: Right **Bats:** Right **Pos:** RP-23; SP-1   **Ht:** 6'3" **Wt:** 180 **Born:** 1/25/78 **Age:** 23

		HOW MUCH HE PITCHED						WHAT HE GAVE UP												THE RESULTS					
Year Team	Lg	G	GS	CG	GF	IP	BFP	H	R	ER	HR	SH	SF	HB	TBB	IBB	SO	WP	Bk	W	L	Pct.	ShO	Sv-Op	Hld	ERA
1997 Martinsvlle	R+	7	7	0	0	24.1	121	34	29	20	5	0	6	3	16	1	7	5	0	1	3	.250	0	0- -	—	7.40
1998 Martinsvlle	R+	13	13	1	0	70	300	66	44	39	7	3	5	1	26	1	45	5	0	2	6	.250	0	0- -	—	5.01
1999 Piedmont	A	26	26	4	0	161	651	130	67	60	10	1	2	7	53	0	149	8	0	12	8	.600	1	0- -	—	3.35
2000 Anaheim	AL	24	1	0	16	38	181	36	21	20	7	0	1	2	36	0	25	3	1	0	0	—	0	0-0	1	4.74

Chris Turner

Bats: Right **Throws:** Right **Pos:** C-36; PH/PR-3; 1B-1   **Ht:** 6'3" **Wt:** 200 **Born:** 3/23/69 **Age:** 32

					BATTING													BASERUNNING				PERCENTAGES		
Year Team	Lg	G	AB	H	2B	3B	HR	(Hm	Rd)	TB	R	RBI	TBB	IBB	SO	HBP	SH	SF	SB	CS	SB%	GDP	Avg	OBP	SLG
2000 Columbus *	AAA	14	44	12	3	0	2	—	—	21	6	3	3	0	11	0	0	0	0	0	—	2	.273	.319	.477
1993 California	AL	25	75	21	5	0	1	(0	1)	29	9	13	9	0	16	1	0	1	1	1	.50	1	.280	.360	.387
1994 California	AL	58	149	36	7	1	1	(1	0)	48	23	12	10	0	29	1	1	2	3	0	1.00	2	.242	.290	.322
1995 California	AL	5	10	1	0	0	0	(0	0)	1	0	1	0	0	3	0	0	0	0	0	—	0	.100	.100	.100
1996 California	AL	4	3	1	0	0	0	(0	0)	1	1	1	1	0	0	0	0	1	0	0	—	0	.333	.400	.333
1997 Anaheim	AL	13	23	6	1	1	1	(0	1)	12	4	2	5	0	8	0	0	0	0	1	.00	0	.261	.393	.522
1998 Kansas City	AL	9	4	0	0	0	0	(0	0)	0	0	0	0	0	4	1	0	0	0	0	—	1	.000	.100	.000
1999 Cleveland	AL	12	21	4	0	0	0	(0	0)	4	3	0	1	0	8	0	0	0	1	0	1.00	0	.190	.227	.190
2000 New York	AL	37	89	21	3	0	1	(0	1)	27	9	7	10	0	21	1	2	0	0	1	.00	2	.236	.320	.303
8 ML YEARS		158	379	90	16	2	4	(1	3)	122	49	36	36	0	89	4	4	4	5	2	.71	6	.237	.307	.322

Jason Tyner

Bats: L **Throws:** L **Pos:** LF-39; PH/PR-11; CF-6; DH-1   **Ht:** 6'1" **Wt:** 170 **Born:** 4/23/77 **Age:** 24

					BATTING													BASERUNNING				PERCENTAGES		
Year Team	Lg	G	AB	H	2B	3B	HR	(Hm	Rd)	TB	R	RBI	TBB	IBB	SO	HBP	SH	SF	SB	CS	SB%	GDP	Avg	OBP	SLG
1998 St. Lucie	A+	50	201	61	2	3	0	—	—	69	30	16	17	0	20	1	3	0	15	11	.58	3	.303	.361	.343
1999 Binghamton	AA	129	518	162	19	5	0	—	—	191	91	33	62	0	46	1	8	1	49	15	.77	8	.313	.387	.369
Norfolk	AAA	3	8	0	0	0	0	—	—	0	0	0	0	0	0	0	0	0	0	0	—	0	.000	.000	.000
2000 Norfolk	AAA	84	327	105	5	2	0	—	—	114	54	28	30	1	32	2	8	2	33	14	.70	3	.321	.380	.349
2000 NYM-TB		50	124	28	4	0	0	(0	0)	32	9	13	5	0	16	2	8	3	7	2	.78	2	.226	.261	.258
2000 New York	NL	13	41	8	2	0	0	(0	0)	10	3	5	1	0	4	1	3	2	1	1	.50	1	.195	.222	.244
Tampa Bay	AL	37	83	20	2	0	0	(0	0)	22	6	8	4	0	12	1	5	1	6	1	.86	1	.241	.281	.265

Tim Unroe

Bats: Right **Throws:** Right **Pos:** 1B-2; PH/PR-2; LF-1   **Ht:** 6'3" **Wt:** 220 **Born:** 10/7/70 **Age:** 30

							BATTING											BASERUNNING				PERCENTAGES		
Year Team	Lg	G	AB	H	2B	3B	HR	(Hm | Rd)	TB	R	RBI	TBB	IBB	SO	HBP	SH	SF	SB	CS	SB%	GDP	Avg	OBP	SLG
2000 Richmond *	AAA	121	418	116	28	2	24	—	—	220	59	87	27	0	114	7	1	2	2	4	.33	10	.278	.330	.526
1995 Milwaukee	AL	2	4	1	0	0	0	(0 | 0)	1	0	0	0	0	0	0	0	0	0	0	—	0	.250	.250	.250
1996 Milwaukee	AL	14	16	3	0	0	0	(0 | 0)	3	5	0	4	0	5	0	0	0	0	1	.00	0	.188	.350	.188
1997 Milwaukee	AL	32	16	4	1	0	2	(1 | 1)	11	3	5	2	0	9	0	0	0	2	0	1.00	0	.250	.333	.688
1999 Anaheim	AL	27	54	13	2	0	1	(1 | 0)	18	5	6	4	0	16	1	0	0	0	0	—	0	.241	.305	.333
2000 Atlanta	NL	4	5	0	0	0	0	(0 | 0)	0	0	0	1	0	2	0	1	0	0	0	—	0	.000	.167	.000
5 ML YEARS		79	95	21	3	0	3	(2 | 1)	33	13	11	11	0	32	1	1	0	2	1	.67	0	.221	.308	.347

Ugueth Urbina

Pitches: Right **Bats:** Right **Pos:** RP-13   **Ht:** 6'2" **Wt:** 205 **Born:** 2/15/74 **Age:** 27

		HOW MUCH HE PITCHED						WHAT HE GAVE UP											THE RESULTS					
Year Team	Lg	G	GS	CG	GF	IP	BFP	H	R	ER	HR	SH	SF	HB	TBB	IBB	SO	WP	Bk	W	L	Pct.	ShO	Sv-Op	Hld	ERA
1995 Montreal	NL	7	4	0	0	23.1	109	26	17	16	6	2	0	0	14	1	15	2	0	2	2	.500	0	0-0	0	6.17
1996 Montreal	NL	33	17	0	2	114	484	102	54	47	18	1	3	1	44	4	108	3	1	10	5	.667	0	0-1	6	3.71
1997 Montreal	NL	63	0	0	50	64.1	276	52	29	27	9	3	0	1	29	2	84	2	0	5	8	.385	0	27-32	1	3.78
1998 Montreal	NL	64	0	0	59	69.1	272	37	11	10	2	2	1	0	33	2	94	3	2	6	3	.667	0	34-38	0	1.30
1999 Montreal	NL	71	0	0	62	75.2	323	59	35	31	6	1	2	0	36	6	100	6	0	6	6	.500	0	41-50	0	3.69
2000 Montreal	NL	13	0	0	11	13.1	54	11	6	6	1	0	0	0	5	0	22	1	0	0	1	.000	0	8-10	0	4.05
6 ML YEARS		251	21	0	184	360	1518	287	152	137	42	9	6	2	161	15	423	17	3	29	25	.537	0	110-131	7	3.43

Ismael Valdes

Pitches: Right **Bats:** Right **Pos:** SP-20; RP-1   **Ht:** 6'4" **Wt:** 225 **Born:** 8/21/73 **Age:** 27

		HOW MUCH HE PITCHED						WHAT HE GAVE UP											THE RESULTS					
Year Team	Lg	G	GS	CG	GF	IP	BFP	H	R	ER	HR	SH	SF	HB	TBB	IBB	SO	WP	Bk	W	L	Pct.	ShO	Sv-Op	Hld	ERA
2000 Daytona *	A+	1	1	0	0	5	20	3	2	1	0	0	0	0	3	0	5	0	0	1	0	1.000	0	0--	0	1.80
1994 Los Angeles	NL	21	1	0	7	28.1	115	21	10	10	2	3	0	0	10	2	28	1	0	3	1	.750	0	0-0	4	3.18
1995 Los Angeles	NL	33	27	6	1	197.2	804	168	76	67	17	10	5	1	51	5	150	1	3	13	11	.542	2	1-1	2	3.05
1996 Los Angeles	NL	33	33	0	0	225	945	219	94	83	20	7	7	3	54	10	173	1	5	15	7	.682	0	0-0	0	3.32
1997 Los Angeles	NL	30	30	0	0	196.2	795	171	68	58	16	11	3	3	47	1	140	3	2	10	11	.476	0	0-0	0	2.65
1998 Los Angeles	NL	27	27	2	0	174	745	171	82	77	17	5	3	2	66	4	122	4	2	11	10	.524	2	0-0	0	3.98
1999 Los Angeles	NL	32	32	2	0	203.1	871	213	97	90	32	9	8	6	58	2	143	6	0	9	14	.391	1	0-0	0	3.98
2000 ChC-LA	NL	21	20	0	1	107	469	124	69	67	22	0	4	3	40	2	74	0	0	2	7	.222	0	0-0	0	5.64
2000 Chicago	NL	12	12	0	0	67	291	71	40	40	17	0	2	2	27	2	45	0	0	2	4	.333	0	0-0	0	5.37
Los Angeles	NL	9	8	0	1	40	178	53	29	27	5	0	2	1	13	0	29	0	0	0	3	.000	0	0-0	0	6.08
7 ML YEARS		197	170	10	9	1132	4744	1087	496	452	126	45	30	18	326	26	830	16	14	63	61	.508	5	1-1	6	3.59

Marc Valdes

Pitches: Right **Bats:** Right **Pos:** RP-53   **Ht:** 6'0" **Wt:** 185 **Born:** 12/20/71 **Age:** 29

		HOW MUCH HE PITCHED						WHAT HE GAVE UP											THE RESULTS					
Year Team	Lg	G	GS	CG	GF	IP	BFP	H	R	ER	HR	SH	SF	HB	TBB	IBB	SO	WP	Bk	W	L	Pct.	ShO	Sv-Op	Hld	ERA
2000 Durham *	AAA	9	9	0	0	47.2	204	52	25	22	7	1	0	4	17	1	25	0	1	5	2	.714	0	0--	—	4.15
1995 Florida	NL	3	3	0	0	7	49	17	13	11	1	1	1	1	9	0	2	1	0	0	0	—	0	0-0	0	14.14
1996 Florida	NL	11	8	0	0	48.2	228	63	32	26	5	1	3	1	23	0	13	3	2	1	3	.250	0	0-1	0	4.81
1997 Montreal	NL	48	7	0	9	95	407	84	36	33	2	5	5	8	39	5	54	2	0	4	4	.500	0	2-2	1	3.13
1998 Montreal	NL	20	4	0	3	36.1	169	41	34	30	6	1	2	1	21	2	28	4	0	1	3	.250	0	0-0	1	7.43
2000 Houston	NL	53	0	0	20	56.2	264	69	41	32	3	3	2	5	25	1	35	1	0	5	5	.500	0	2-6	8	5.08
5 ML YEARS		135	22	0	32	243.2	1117	274	156	132	17	11	13	16	117	8	132	11	2	11	15	.423	0	4-9	10	4.88

Pedro Valdes

Bats: L **Throws:** L **Pos:** PH/PR-15; RF-13; DH-3; LF-1   **Ht:** 6'1" **Wt:** 180 **Born:** 6/29/73 **Age:** 28

							BATTING											BASERUNNING				PERCENTAGES		
Year Team	Lg	G	AB	H	2B	3B	HR	(Hm	Rd)	TB	R	RBI	TBB	IBB	SO	HBP	SH	SF	SB	CS	SB%	GDP	Avg	OBP	SLG
1991 Huntington	R+	50	157	45	11	1	0	—	—	58	18	16	17	3	31	2	1	5	5	1	.83	5	.287	.354	.369
1992 Peoria	A	33	112	26	7	0	0	—	—	33	8	20	7	3	32	0	0	4	0	0	—	1	.232	.268	.295
Geneva	A-	66	254	69	10	0	5	—	—	94	27	24	3	1	33	3	2	2	4	5	.44	2	.272	.286	.370
1993 Peoria	A	65	234	74	11	1	7	—	—	108	33	36	10	4	40	0	5	4	2	2	.50	3	.316	.339	.462
Daytona	A+	60	230	66	16	1	8	—	—	108	27	49	9	1	30	2	0	5	3	4	.43	8	.287	.313	.470
1994 Orlando	AA	116	365	103	14	4	1	—	—	128	39	37	20	3	45	2	2	1	2	6	.25	10	.282	.322	.351
1995 Orlando	AA	114	426	128	28	3	7	—	—	183	57	68	37	3	77	5	0	6	3	6	.33	7	.300	.359	.430
1996 Iowa	AAA	103	397	117	23	0	15	—	—	185	61	60	31	1	57	1	1	5	2	0	1.00	12	.295	.343	.466
1997 Iowa	AAA	125	464	132	30	1	14	—	—	206	65	60	48	5	67	2	1	6	9	2	.82	13	.284	.350	.444
1998 Iowa	AAA	65	229	72	12	0	17	—	—	135	49	40	27	3	38	0	0	2	2	1	.67	6	.314	.384	.590
1999 Tulsa	AA	11	34	12	4	0	1	—	—	19	3	4	8	0	6	0	0	0	0	0	—	0	.353	.476	.559
Oklahoma	AAA	110	394	129	27	1	21	—	—	221	72	72	52	6	60	6	0	4	1	2	.33	6	.327	.410	.561
2000 Oklahoma	AAA	92	352	117	30	2	16	—	—	199	64	78	45	4	41	3	0	5	2	0	1.00	7	.332	.407	.565
1996 Chicago	NL	9	8	1	1	0	0	(0	0)	2	2	1	1	0	5	0	0	0	0	0	—	0	.125	.222	.250
1998 Chicago	NL	14	23	5	1	1	0	(0	0)	8	1	2	1	0	3	0	0	0	0	1	.00	1	.217	.250	.348
2000 Texas	AL	30	54	15	5	0	1	(1	0)	23	4	5	6	0	7	0	0	0	0	0	—	0	.278	.350	.426
3 ML YEARS		53	85	21	7	1	1	(1	0)	33	7	8	8	0	15	0	0	0	0	1	.00	1	.247	.312	.388

Mario Valdez

Bats: Left **Throws:** Right **Pos:** 1B-4; PH/PR-1   **Ht:** 6'2" **Wt:** 190 **Born:** 11/19/74 **Age:** 26

							BATTING											BASERUNNING				PERCENTAGES		
Year Team	Lg	G	AB	H	2B	3B	HR	(Hm	Rd)	TB	R	RBI	TBB	IBB	SO	HBP	SH	SF	SB	CS	SB%	GDP	Avg	OBP	SLG
1994 White Sox	R	53	157	37	11	2	2	—	—	58	20	25	30	0	28	2	0	1	0	6	.00	3	.236	.363	.369

Year Team	Lg	G	AB	H	2B	3B	HR	(Hm	Rd)	TB	R	RBI	TBB	IBB	SO	HBP	SH	SF	SB	CS	SB%	GDP	Avg	OBP	SLG
1995 Hickory	A	130	441	120	30	5	11	—	—	193	65	56	67	2	107	5	0	3	9	7	.56	5	.272	.372	.438
1996 South Bend	A	61	202	76	19	0	10	—	—	125	46	43	36	2	42	6	0	2	2	4	.33	3	.376	.480	.619
Birmingham	AA	51	168	46	10	2	3	—	—	69	22	28	32	2	34	5	0	3	0	0	—	3	.274	.399	.411
1997 Nashville	AAA	81	282	79	20	1	15	—	—	146	44	61	43	3	77	9	1	4	1	1	.50	8	.280	.388	.518
1998 Calgary	AAA	123	448	148	32	0	20	—	—	240	86	81	60	3	102	12	0	4	1	2	.33	14	.330	.420	.536
1999 Charlotte	AAA	121	402	110	17	2	26	—	—	209	78	76	76	4	91	12	0	1	1	0	1.00	8	.274	.403	.520
2000 Salt Lake	AAA	88	317	116	24	1	18	—	—	196	76	85	57	3	46	3	1	6	1	1	.50	10	.366	.460	.618
Visalia	A+	1	2	1	0	0	0	—	—	1	0	0	1	0	1	0	0	0	0	0	—	0	.500	.667	.500
Sacramento	AAA	17	61	14	3	0	2	—	—	23	11	11	9	1	13	2	0	1	0	0	—	3	.230	.342	.377
1997 Chicago	AL	54	115	28	7	0	1	(0	1)	38	11	13	17	0	39	3	0	2	1	0	1.00	3	.243	.350	.330
2000 Oakland	AL	5	12	0	0	0	0	(0	0)	0	0	0	0	0	3	0	0	0	0	0	—	0	.000	.000	.000
2 ML YEARS		59	127	28	7	0	1	(0	1)	38	11	13	17	0	42	3	0	2	1	0	1.00	3	.220	.322	.299

John Valentin

Bats: Right **Throws:** Right **Pos:** 3B-10   **Ht:** 6'0" **Wt:** 185 **Born:** 2/18/67 **Age:** 34

Year Team	Lg	G	AB	H	2B	3B	HR	(Hm	Rd)	TB	R	RBI	TBB	IBB	SO	HBP	SH	SF	SB	CS	SB%	GDP	Avg	OBP	SLG
1992 Boston	AL	58	185	51	13	0	5	(1	4)	79	21	25	20	0	17	2	4	1	1	0	1.00	5	.276	.351	.427
1993 Boston	AL	144	468	130	40	3	11	(7	4)	209	50	66	49	2	77	2	16	4	3	4	.43	9	.278	.346	.447
1994 Boston	AL	84	301	95	26	2	9	(6	3)	152	53	49	42	1	38	3	5	4	3	1	.75	3	.316	.400	.505
1995 Boston	AL	135	520	155	37	2	27	(11	16)	277	108	102	81	2	67	10	4	6	20	5	.80	7	.298	.399	.533
1996 Boston	AL	131	527	156	29	3	13	(9	4)	230	84	59	63	0	59	7	2	7	9	10	.47	15	.296	.374	.436
1997 Boston	AL	143	575	176	47	5	18	(11	7)	287	95	77	58	5	66	5	1	5	7	4	.64	21	.306	.372	.499
1998 Boston	AL	153	588	145	44	1	23	(11	12)	260	113	73	77	3	82	9	2	5	4	5	.44	9	.247	.340	.442
1999 Boston	AL	113	450	114	27	1	12	(5	7)	179	58	70	40	2	68	4	1	8	0	1	.00	11	.253	.315	.398
2000 Boston	AL	10	35	9	1	0	2	(0	2)	16	6	2	2	0	5	0	0	1	0	1	.00	1	.257	.297	.457
9 ML YEARS		971	3649	1031	264	17	120	(61	59)	1689	588	523	432	15	479	42	36	40	47	31	.60	81	.283	.362	.463

Jose Valentin

Bats: Both **Throws:** Right **Pos:** SS-141; PH/PR-5; RF-1   **Ht:** 5'10" **Wt:** 173 **Born:** 10/12/69 **Age:** 31

Year Team	Lg	G	AB	H	2B	3B	HR	(Hm	Rd)	TB	R	RBI	TBB	IBB	SO	HBP	SH	SF	SB	CS	SB%	GDP	Avg	OBP	SLG
1992 Milwaukee	AL	4	3	0	0	0	0	(0	0)	0	1	1	0	0	0	0	0	1	0	0	—	0	.000	.000	.000
1993 Milwaukee	AL	19	53	13	1	2	1	(1	0)	21	10	7	7	1	16	1	2	0	1	0	1.00	1	.245	.344	.396
1994 Milwaukee	AL	97	285	68	19	0	11	(8	3)	120	47	46	38	1	75	2	4	2	12	3	.80	1	.239	.330	.421
1995 Milwaukee	AL	112	338	74	23	3	11	(3	8)	136	62	49	37	0	83	0	7	4	16	8	.67	0	.219	.293	.402
1996 Milwaukee	AL	154	552	143	33	7	24	(10	14)	262	90	95	66	9	145	0	6	4	17	4	.81	4	.259	.336	.475
1997 Milwaukee	AL	136	494	125	23	1	17	(4	13)	201	58	58	39	4	109	4	4	5	19	8	.70	5	.253	.310	.407
1998 Milwaukee	NL	151	428	96	24	0	16	(7	9)	168	65	49	63	8	105	1	2	3	10	7	.59	2	.224	.323	.393
1999 Milwaukee	NL	89	256	58	9	5	10	(3	7)	107	45	38	48	7	52	2	2	5	3	2	.60	3	.227	.347	.418
2000 Chicago	AL	144	568	155	37	6	25	(16	9)	279	107	92	59	1	106	4	13	4	19	2	.90	11	.273	.343	.491
9 ML YEARS		906	2977	732	169	24	115	(52	63)	1294	485	435	357	31	691	14	40	28	97	34	.74	27	.246	.327	.435

Yohanny Valera

Bats: Right **Throws:** Right **Pos:** C-7   **Ht:** 6'1" **Wt:** 196 **Born:** 8/17/76 **Age:** 24

Year Team	Lg	G	AB	H	2B	3B	HR	(Hm	Rd)	TB	R	RBI	TBB	IBB	SO	HBP	SH	SF	SB	CS	SB%	GDP	Avg	OBP	SLG
1995 Kingsport	R+	56	204	60	13	0	3	—	—	82	30	36	11	0	33	5	2	1	2	1	.67	6	.294	.344	.402
1996 Capital Cty	A	108	372	79	18	0	6	—	—	115	38	38	17	3	78	13	1	7	2	4	.33	9	.212	.267	.309
1997 Capital Cty	A	94	293	56	14	0	8	—	—	94	32	33	21	0	101	5	2	1	2	0	1.00	4	.191	.256	.321
1998 St. Lucie	A+	91	298	61	21	1	14	—	—	126	37	42	21	0	92	7	1	1	1	1	.50	7	.205	.272	.423
1999 Norfolk	AAA	23	65	10	2	0	1	—	—	15	3	6	4	0	16	1	1	0	0	0	—	0	.154	.214	.231
Binghamton	AA	57	204	59	14	3	9	—	—	106	33	39	17	1	57	2	0	2	2	1	.67	0	.289	.347	.520
2000 Ottawa	AAA	21	68	10	1	0	2	—	—	17	6	10	4	0	19	2	0	0	0	0	—	1	.147	.216	.250
Harrisburg	AA	92	281	66	8	3	3	—	—	89	28	34	24	1	56	9	5	2	1	3	.25	4	.235	.313	.317
2000 Montreal	NL	7	10	0	0	0	0	(0	0)	0	1	1	1	0	5	1	1	0	0	0	—	0	.000	.167	.000

John Vander Wal

Bats: L **Throws:** L **Pos:** RF-65; 1B-33; PH/PR-30; LF-13; DH-3   **Ht:** 6'2" **Wt:** 197 **Born:** 4/29/66 **Age:** 35

Year Team	Lg	G	AB	H	2B	3B	HR	(Hm	Rd)	TB	R	RBI	TBB	IBB	SO	HBP	SH	SF	SB	CS	SB%	GDP	Avg	OBP	SLG
1991 Montreal	NL	21	61	13	4	1	1	(0	1)	22	4	8	1	0	18	0	0	1	0	0	—	2	.213	.222	.361
1992 Montreal	NL	105	213	51	8	2	4	(2	2)	75	21	20	24	2	36	0	0	0	3	0	1.00	3	.239	.316	.352
1993 Montreal	NL	106	215	50	7	4	5	(1	4)	80	34	30	27	2	30	1	0	1	6	3	.67	4	.233	.320	.372
1994 Colorado	NL	91	110	27	3	1	5	(1	4)	47	12	15	16	0	31	0	0	1	2	1	.67	4	.245	.339	.427
1995 Colorado	NL	105	101	35	8	1	5	(2	3)	60	15	21	16	5	23	0	0	1	1	1	.50	2	.347	.432	.594
1996 Colorado	NL	104	151	38	6	2	5	(5	0)	63	20	31	19	2	38	1	0	2	2	2	.50	1	.252	.335	.417
1997 Colorado	NL	76	92	16	2	0	1	(0	1)	21	7	11	10	0	33	0	0	0	1	1	.50	2	.174	.255	.228
1998 Col-SD	NL	109	129	36	13	1	5	(3	2)	66	21	20	22	0	34	0	0	1	0	0	—	2	.279	.382	.512
1999 San Diego	NL	132	246	67	18	0	6	(2	4)	103	26	41	37	1	59	2	0	3	2	1	.67	5	.272	.368	.419
2000 Pittsburgh	NL	134	384	115	29	2	24	(13	11)	216	74	94	72	5	92	2	0	3	11	2	.85	7	.299	.410	.563
1998 Colorado	NL	89	104	30	10	1	5	(3	2)	57	18	20	16	0	29	0	0	1	0	0	—	1	.288	.380	.548
San Diego	NL	20	25	6	3	0	0	(0	0)	9	3	0	6	0	5	0	0	0	0	0	—	1	.240	.387	.360
10 ML YEARS		983	1702	448	98	12	61	(29	32)	753	234	291	244	17	394	6	0	13	28	11	.72	31	.263	.355	.442

Todd Van Poppel

Pitches: Right **Bats:** Right **Pos:** RP-49; SP-2   **Ht:** 6'5" **Wt:** 230 **Born:** 12/9/71 **Age:** 29

Year Team	Lg	G	GS	CG	GF	IP	BFP	H	R	ER	HR	SH	SF	HB	TBB	IBB	SO	WP	Bk	W	L	Pct.	ShO	Sv-Op	Hld	ERA
2000 Iowa *	AAA	10	6	0	2	40.2	172	37	18	14	2	1	0	5	10	0	52	6	0	3	4	.429	0	0- -	0	3.10
1991 Oakland	AL	1	1	0	0	4.2	21	7	5	5	1	0	0	0	2	0	6	0	0	0	0	—	0	0-0	0	9.64
1993 Oakland	AL	16	16	0	0	84	380	76	50	47	10	1	2	2	62	0	47	3	0	6	6	.500	0	0-0	0	5.04
1994 Oakland	AL	23	23	0	0	116.2	532	108	80	79	20	4	4	3	89	2	83	3	1	7	10	.412	0	0-0	0	6.09
1995 Oakland	AL	36	14	1	10	138.1	582	125	77	75	16	3	6	4	56	1	122	4	0	4	8	.333	0	0-0	1	4.88
1996 Oak-Det	AL	37	15	1	8	99.1	491	139	107	100	24	4	7	3	62	3	53	7	0	3	9	.250	1	1-2	0	9.06
1998 Tex-Pit		22	11	0	3	66.1	303	79	52	47	9	3	3	1	28	3	42	7	3	2	4	.333	0	0-0	0	6.38
2000 Chicago	NL	51	2	0	13	86.1	378	80	38	36	10	4	3	2	48	2	77	4	0	4	5	.444	0	2-5	7	3.75
1996 Oakland	AL	28	6	0	8	63	301	86	56	54	13	3	5	2	33	3	37	4	0	1	5	.167	0	1-2	0	7.71
Detroit		9	9	1	0	36.1	190	53	51	46	11	1	2	1	29	0	16	3	0	2	4	.333	1	0-0	0	11.39
1998 Texas	AL	4	4	0	0	19.1	95	26	20	19	5	0	1	1	10	0	10	2	0	1	2	.333	0	0-0	0	8.84
Pittsburgh	NL	18	7	0	3	47	208	53	32	28	4	3	2	0	18	3	32	5	3	1	2	.333	0	0-0	0	5.36
7 ML YEARS		186	82	2	34	595.2	2687	614	409	389	90	19	25	15	347	11	430	28	4	26	42	.382	1	3-7	8	5.88

Jason Varitek

Bats: Both **Throws:** Right **Pos:** C-128; PH/PR-18; DH-1   **Ht:** 6'2" **Wt:** 220 **Born:** 4/11/72 **Age:** 29

Year Team	Lg	G	AB	H	2B	3B	HR	(Hm	Rd)	TB	R	RBI	TBB	IBB	SO	HBP	SH	SF	SB	CS	SB%	GDP	Avg	OBP	SLG
1997 Boston	AL	1	1	1	0	0	0	(0	0)	1	0	0	0	0	0	0	0	0	0	0	—	0	1.000	1.000	1.000
1998 Boston	AL	86	221	56	13	0	7	(1	6)	90	31	33	17	1	45	2	4	3	2	2	.50	8	.253	.309	.407
1999 Boston	AL	144	483	130	39	2	20	(12	8)	233	70	76	46	2	85	2	5	8	1	2	.33	13	.269	.330	.482
2000 Boston	AL	139	448	111	31	1	10	(2	8)	174	55	65	60	3	84	6	1	4	1	1	.50	16	.248	.342	.388
4 ML YEARS		370	1153	298	83	3	37	(15	22)	498	156	174	123	6	214	10	10	15	4	5	.44	37	.258	.331	.432

Greg Vaughn

Bats: Right **Throws:** Right **Pos:** LF-72; DH-52; PH/PR-3   **Ht:** 6'0" **Wt:** 202 **Born:** 7/3/65 **Age:** 35

Year Team	Lg	G	AB	H	2B	3B	HR	(Hm	Rd)	TB	R	RBI	TBB	IBB	SO	HBP	SH	SF	SB	CS	SB%	GDP	Avg	OBP	SLG
1989 Milwaukee	AL	38	113	30	3	0	5	(1	4)	48	18	23	13	0	23	0	0	2	4	1	.80	0	.265	.336	.425
1990 Milwaukee	AL	120	382	84	26	2	17	(9	8)	165	51	61	33	1	91	1	7	6	7	4	.64	11	.220	.280	.432
1991 Milwaukee	AL	145	542	132	24	5	27	(16	11)	247	81	98	62	2	125	1	2	7	2	2	.50	5	.244	.319	.456
1992 Milwaukee	AL	141	501	114	18	2	23	(11	12)	205	77	78	60	1	123	5	2	5	15	15	.50	8	.228	.313	.409
1993 Milwaukee	AL	154	569	152	28	2	30	(12	18)	274	97	97	89	14	118	5	0	4	10	7	.59	6	.267	.369	.482
1994 Milwaukee	AL	95	370	94	24	1	19	(9	10)	177	59	55	51	6	93	1	0	1	9	5	.64	6	.254	.345	.478
1995 Milwaukee	AL	108	392	88	19	1	17	(8	9)	160	67	59	55	3	89	0	0	4	10	4	.71	10	.224	.317	.408
1996 Mil-SD		145	516	134	19	1	41	(22	19)	278	98	117	82	6	130	6	0	5	9	3	.75	7	.260	.365	.539
1997 San Diego	NL	120	361	78	10	0	18	(11	7)	142	60	57	56	1	110	2	0	3	7	4	.64	7	.216	.322	.393
1998 San Diego	NL	158	573	156	28	4	50	(23	27)	342	112	119	79	6	121	5	0	4	11	4	.73	7	.272	.363	.597
1999 Cincinnati	NL	153	550	135	20	2	45	(20	25)	294	104	118	85	3	137	3	0	5	15	2	.88	9	.245	.347	.535
2000 Tampa Bay	AL	127	461	117	27	1	28	(13	15)	230	83	74	80	3	128	2	0	2	8	1	.89	10	.254	.365	.499
1996 Milwaukee	AL	102	375	105	16	0	31	(16	15)	214	78	95	58	4	99	4	0	5	5	2	.71	6	.280	.378	.571
San Diego	NL	43	141	29	3	1	10	(6	4)	64	20	22	24	2	31	2	0	0	4	1	.80	1	.206	.329	.454
12 ML YEARS		1504	5330	1314	246	21	320	(155	165)	2562	907	956	745	46	1288	31	11	48	107	52	.67	86	.247	.340	.481

Mo Vaughn

Bats: L **Throws:** R **Pos:** 1B-147; DH-14; CF-1; PH/PR-1   **Ht:** 6'1" **Wt:** 268 **Born:** 12/15/67 **Age:** 33

Year Team	Lg	G	AB	H	2B	3B	HR	(Hm	Rd)	TB	R	RBI	TBB	IBB	SO	HBP	SH	SF	SB	CS	SB%	GDP	Avg	OBP	SLG
1991 Boston	AL	74	219	57	12	0	4	(1	3)	81	21	32	26	2	43	2	0	4	2	1	.67	7	.260	.339	.370
1992 Boston	AL	113	355	83	16	2	13	(8	5)	142	42	57	47	7	67	3	0	3	3	3	.50	6	.234	.326	.400
1993 Boston	AL	152	539	160	34	1	29	(13	16)	283	86	101	79	23	130	8	0	7	4	3	.57	14	.297	.390	.525
1994 Boston	AL	111	394	122	25	1	26	(15	11)	227	65	82	57	20	112	10	0	2	4	4	.50	7	.310	.408	.576
1995 Boston	AL	140	550	165	28	3	39	(15	24)	316	98	126	68	17	150	14	0	4	11	4	.73	17	.300	.388	.575
1996 Boston	AL	161	635	207	29	1	44	(27	17)	370	118	143	95	19	154	14	0	8	2	0	1.00	17	.326	.420	.583
1997 Boston	AL	141	527	166	24	0	35	(20	15)	295	91	96	86	17	154	12	0	3	2	2	.50	10	.315	.420	.560
1998 Boston	AL	154	609	205	31	2	40	(19	21)	360	107	115	61	13	144	8	0	3	0	0	—	13	.337	.402	.591
1999 Anaheim	AL	139	524	147	20	0	33	(16	17)	266	63	108	54	7	127	11	0	3	0	0	—	11	.281	.358	.508
2000 Anaheim	AL	161	614	167	31	0	36	(18	18)	306	93	117	79	11	181	14	0	5	2	0	1.00	14	.272	.365	.498
10 ML YEARS		1346	4966	1479	250	10	299	(152	147)	2646	784	977	652	136	1262	96	0	42	30	17	.64	118	.298	.387	.533

Javier Vazquez

Pitches: Right **Bats:** Right **Pos:** SP-33   **Ht:** 6'2" **Wt:** 195 **Born:** 7/25/76 **Age:** 24

Year Team	Lg	G	GS	CG	GF	IP	BFP	H	R	ER	HR	SH	SF	HB	TBB	IBB	SO	WP	Bk	W	L	Pct.	ShO	Sv-Op	Hld	ERA
1998 Montreal	NL	33	32	0	1	172.1	764	196	121	116	31	9	4	11	68	2	139	2	0	5	15	.250	0	0-0	0	6.06
1999 Montreal	NL	26	26	3	0	154.2	667	154	98	86	20	3	3	4	52	4	113	2	0	9	8	.529	1	0-0	0	5.00
2000 Montreal	NL	33	33	2	0	217.2	945	247	104	98	24	11	3	5	61	10	196	3	0	11	9	.550	1	0-0	0	4.05
3 ML YEARS		92	91	5	1	544.2	2376	597	323	300	75	23	10	20	181	16	448	7	0	25	32	.439	2	0-0	0	4.96

Jorge Velandia

Bats: R **Throws:** R **Pos:** 2B-22; SS-11; PH/PR-8; 3B-3   **Ht:** 5'9" **Wt:** 185 **Born:** 1/12/75 **Age:** 26

Year Team	Lg	G	AB	H	2B	3B	HR	(Hm	Rd)	TB	R	RBI	TBB	IBB	SO	HBP	SH	SF	SB	CS	SB%	GDP	Avg	OBP	SLG
2000 Sacramento *	AAA	83	302	84	20	1	9	—	—	133	56	57	34	0	52	5	2	2	4	3	.57	8	.278	.359	.440
Norfolk *	AAA	4	10	1	0	0	0	—	—	1	0	0	1	0	1	0	0	0	1	0	1.00	0	.100	.182	.100

Year Team	Lg	BATTING																	BASERUNNING				PERCENTAGES		
		G	AB	H	2B	3B	HR	(Hm	Rd)	TB	R	RBI	TBB	IBB	SO	HBP	SH	SF	SB	CS	SB%	GDP	Avg	OBP	SLG
1997 San Diego	NL	14	29	3	2	0	0	(0	0)	5	0	0	1	0	7	0	0	0	0	0	—	0	.103	.133	.172
1998 Oakland	AL	8	4	1	0	0	0	(0	0)	1	0	0	0	0	1	0	0	0	0	0	—	0	.250	.250	.250
1999 Oakland	AL	63	48	9	1	0	0	(0	0)	10	4	2	2	0	13	1	0	0	2	0	1.00	0	.188	.235	.208
2000 Oak-NYM		33	31	3	1	0	0	(0	0)	4	2	2	2	0	8	1	0	0	0	0	—	0	.097	.176	.129
2000 Oakland	AL	18	24	3	1	0	0	(0	0)	4	1	2	0	0	6	1	0	0	0	0	—	0	.125	.160	.167
New York	NL	15	7	0	0	0	0	(0	0)	0	1	0	2	0	2	0	0	0	0	0	—	0	.000	.222	.000
4 ML YEARS		118	112	16	4	0	0	(0	0)	20	6	4	5	0	29	2	0	0	2	0	1.00	0	.143	.193	.179

Randy Velarde

Bats: Right **Throws:** Right **Pos:** 2B-122; PH/PR-1   **Ht:** 6'0" **Wt:** 200 **Born:** 11/24/62 **Age:** 38

Year Team	Lg	BATTING																	BASERUNNING				PERCENTAGES		
		G	AB	H	2B	3B	HR	(Hm	Rd)	TB	R	RBI	TBB	IBB	SO	HBP	SH	SF	SB	CS	SB%	GDP	Avg	OBP	SLG
2000 Midland *	AA	5	16	2	0	0	1	—		5	4	1	4	0	4	0	0	0	0	0	—	0	.125	.300	.313
Sacramento *	AAA	3	11	5	0	0	0	—		5	3	2	4	0	2	1	0	0	2	0	1.00	0	.455	.625	.455
1987 New York	AL	8	22	4	0	0	0	(0	0)	4	1	1	0	0	6	0	0	0	0	0	—	1	.182	.182	.182
1988 New York	AL	48	115	20	6	0	5	(2	3)	41	18	12	8	0	24	2	0	0	1	1	.50	3	.174	.240	.357
1989 New York	AL	33	100	34	4	2	2	(1	1)	48	12	11	7	0	14	1	3	0	0	3	.00	6	.340	.389	.480
1990 New York	AL	95	229	48	6	2	5	(1	4)	73	21	19	20	0	53	1	2	1	0	3	.00	6	.210	.275	.319
1991 New York	AL	80	184	45	11	1	1	(0	1)	61	19	15	18	0	43	3	5	0	3	1	.75	6	.245	.322	.332
1992 New York	AL	121	412	112	24	1	7	(2	5)	159	57	46	38	1	78	2	4	5	7	2	.78	13	.272	.333	.386
1993 New York	AL	85	226	68	13	2	7	(4	3)	106	28	24	18	2	39	4	3	2	2	2	.50	12	.301	.360	.469
1994 New York	AL	77	280	78	16	1	9	(3	6)	123	47	34	22	0	61	4	2	4	4	2	.67	7	.279	.338	.439
1995 New York	AL	111	367	102	19	1	7	(2	5)	144	60	46	55	0	64	4	3	3	5	1	.83	9	.278	.375	.392
1996 California	AL	136	530	151	27	3	14	(8	6)	226	82	54	70	0	118	5	4	2	7	7	.50	7	.285	.372	.426
1997 Anaheim	AL	1	0	0	0	0	0	(0	0)	0	0	0	0	0	0	0	0	0	0	0	—	0	—	—	—
1998 Anaheim	AL	51	188	49	13	1	4	(1	3)	76	29	26	34	0	42	1	0	1	7	2	.78	8	.261	.375	.404
1999 Ana-Oak	AL	156	631	200	25	7	16	(8	8)	287	105	76	70	2	98	6	4	0	24	8	.75	19	.317	.390	.455
2000 Oakland	AL	122	485	135	23	0	12	(11	1)	194	82	41	54	0	95	3	3	1	9	3	.75	15	.278	.354	.400
1999 Anaheim	AL	95	376	115	15	4	9	(4	5)	165	57	48	43	1	56	4	2	0	13	4	.76	8	.306	.383	.439
Oakland	AL	61	255	85	10	3	7	(4	3)	122	48	28	27	1	42	2	2	0	11	4	.73	11	.333	.401	.478
14 ML YEARS		1124	3769	1046	187	21	89	(43	46)	1542	561	405	414	5	735	36	33	17	69	35	.66	106	.278	.353	.409

Mike Venafro

Pitches: Left **Bats:** Left **Pos:** RP-77   **Ht:** 5'10" **Wt:** 180 **Born:** 8/2/73 **Age:** 27

Year Team	Lg	HOW MUCH HE PITCHED						WHAT HE GAVE UP											THE RESULTS						
		G	GS	CG	GF	IP	BFP	H	R	ER	HR	SH	SF	HB	TBB	IBB	SO	WP	Bk	W	L	Pct.	ShO	Sv-Op	Hld	ERA
1995 Hudson Val	A-	32	0	0	12	50.2	200	37	13	12	0	2	1	5	21	2	32	1	3	9	1	.900	0	2- -	—	2.13
1996 Chston-SC	A	50	0	0	42	59	258	57	27	23	0	4	2	3	21	3	62	13	0	1	3	.250	0	19- -	—	3.51
1997 Charlotte	A+	35	0	0	27	44.2	196	51	17	17	2	4	3	1	21	1	35	1	0	4	2	.667	0	10- -	—	3.43
Tulsa	AA	11	0	0	9	15.2	75	13	12	6	1	0	2	2	12	0	13	1	0	1	0	1.000	0	1- -	—	3.45
1998 Tulsa	AA	46	0	0	39	52.1	223	42	21	18	5	3	1	1	26	0	45	3	0	3	4	.429	0	14- -	—	3.10
Oklahoma	AAA	13	0	0	4	17	82	19	12	12	3	0	0	2	10	0	15	1	0	0	0	—	0	0- -	—	6.35
1999 Oklahoma	AAA	6	0	0	3	11.2	46	16	7	7	2	0	0	0	7	0	7	0	0	0	0	—	0	1- -	—	5.40
1999 Texas	AL	65	0	0	11	68.1	283	63	29	25	4	5	2	3	22	0	37	0	0	3	2	.600	0	0-1	19	3.29
2000 Texas	AL	77	0	0	21	56.1	248	64	27	24	2	2	4	4	21	4	32	1	0	3	1	.750	0	1-2	17	3.83
2 ML YEARS		142	0	0	32	124.2	531	127	56	49	6	7	6	7	43	4	69	1	0	6	3	.667	0	1-3	36	3.54

Robin Ventura

Bats: Left **Throws:** Right **Pos:** 3B-137; PH/PR-5; 1B-1   **Ht:** 6'1" **Wt:** 198 **Born:** 7/14/67 **Age:** 33

Year Team	Lg	BATTING																	BASERUNNING				PERCENTAGES		
		G	AB	H	2B	3B	HR	(Hm	Rd)	TB	R	RBI	TBB	IBB	SO	HBP	SH	SF	SB	CS	SB%	GDP	Avg	OBP	SLG
1989 Chicago	AL	16	45	8	3	0	0	(0	0)	11	5	7	8	0	6	1	1	3	0	0	—	1	.178	.298	.244
1990 Chicago	AL	150	493	123	17	1	5	(2	3)	157	48	54	55	2	53	1	13	3	1	4	.20	5	.249	.324	.318
1991 Chicago	AL	157	606	172	25	1	23	(16	7)	268	92	100	80	3	67	4	8	7	2	4	.33	22	.284	.367	.442
1992 Chicago	AL	157	592	167	38	1	16	(7	9)	255	85	93	93	9	71	0	1	6	2	4	.33	14	.282	.375	.431
1993 Chicago	AL	157	554	145	27	1	22	(12	10)	240	85	94	105	16	82	3	1	6	1	6	.14	19	.262	.379	.433
1994 Chicago	AL	109	401	113	15	1	18	(8	10)	184	57	78	61	15	69	2	2	8	3	1	.75	8	.282	.373	.459
1995 Chicago	AL	135	492	145	22	0	26	(8	18)	245	79	93	75	11	98	1	1	9	4	3	.57	8	.295	.384	.498
1996 Chicago	AL	158	586	168	31	2	34	(13	21)	305	96	105	78	10	81	2	0	8	1	3	.25	18	.287	.368	.520
1997 Chicago	AL	54	183	48	10	1	6	(2	4)	78	27	26	34	5	21	0	0	3	0	0	—	3	.262	.373	.426
1998 Chicago	AL	161	590	155	31	4	21	(15	6)	257	84	91	79	15	111	1	1	3	1	1	.50	10	.263	.349	.436
1999 New York	NL	161	588	177	38	0	32	(13	19)	311	88	120	74	10	109	3	1	5	1	1	.50	14	.301	.379	.529
2000 New York	NL	141	469	109	23	1	24	(12	12)	206	61	84	75	12	91	2	1	4	3	5	.38	14	.232	.338	.439
12 ML YEARS		1556	5599	1530	280	13	227	(108	119)	2517	807	945	817	108	859	20	30	66	19	32	.37	135	.273	.364	.450

Quilvio Veras

Bats: Both **Throws:** Right **Pos:** 2B-82; PH/PR-2   **Ht:** 5'10" **Wt:** 183 **Born:** 4/3/71 **Age:** 30

Year Team	Lg	BATTING																	BASERUNNING				PERCENTAGES		
		G	AB	H	2B	3B	HR	(Hm	Rd)	TB	R	RBI	TBB	IBB	SO	HBP	SH	SF	SB	CS	SB%	GDP	Avg	OBP	SLG
1995 Florida	NL	124	440	115	20	7	5	(2	3)	164	86	32	80	0	68	9	7	2	56	21	.73	7	.261	.384	.373
1996 Florida	NL	73	253	64	8	1	4	(1	3)	86	40	14	51	1	42	2	1	1	8	8	.50	3	.253	.381	.340
1997 San Diego	NL	145	539	143	23	1	3	(3	0)	177	74	45	72	0	84	7	9	4	33	12	.73	9	.265	.357	.328
1998 San Diego	NL	138	517	138	24	2	6	(5	1)	184	79	45	84	2	78	6	1	4	24	9	.73	6	.267	.373	.356
1999 San Diego	NL	132	475	133	25	2	6	(4	2)	180	95	41	65	0	88	2	1	2	30	17	.64	7	.280	.368	.379
2000 Atlanta	NL	84	298	92	15	0	5	(2	3)	122	56	37	51	0	50	5	6	4	25	12	.68	8	.309	.413	.409
6 ML YEARS		696	2522	685	115	13	29	(17	12)	913	430	214	403	3	410	31	25	17	176	79	.69	40	.272	.376	.362

Wilton Veras

Bats: Right **Throws:** Right **Pos:** 3B-49; PH/PR-1 **Ht:** 6'2" **Wt:** 198 **Born:** 1/19/78 **Age:** 23

Year Team	Lg	G	AB	H	2B	3B	HR	(Hm	Rd)	TB	R	RBI	TBB	IBB	SO	HBP	SH	SF	SB	CS	SB%	GDP	Avg	OBP	SLG
1995 Red Sox	R	31	91	24	1	0	0	—	—	25	7	5	7	0	9	3	0	0	1	2	.33	2	.264	.337	.275
1996 Lowell	A-	67	250	60	15	0	0	—	—	75	22	19	13	0	29	0	1	2	2	1	.67	9	.240	.275	.300
1997 Michigan	A	131	489	141	21	3	8	—	—	192	51	68	31	0	51	6	1	3	3	2	.60	19	.288	.336	.393
1998 Trenton	AA	126	470	137	27	4	16	—	—	220	70	67	15	1	66	6	6	5	5	4	.56	14	.291	.319	.468
1999 Trenton	AA	116	474	133	23	2	11	—	—	193	65	75	23	1	55	5	1	5	7	6	.54	23	.281	.318	.407
2000 Pawtucket	AAA	60	218	46	9	0	3	—	—	64	18	25	12	1	18	2	1	1	0	1	1.00	6	.211	.258	.294
1999 Boston	AL	36	118	34	5	1	2	(0	2)	47	14	13	5	0	14	2	0	2	0	2	.00	5	.288	.323	.398
2000 Boston	AL	49	164	40	7	1	0	(0	0)	49	21	14	7	0	20	2	3	3	0	0	—	2	.244	.278	.299
2 ML YEARS		85	282	74	12	2	2	(0	2)	96	35	27	12	0	34	4	3	5	0	2	.00	7	.262	.297	.340

Dave Veres

Pitches: Right **Bats:** Right **Pos:** RP-71 **Ht:** 6'2" **Wt:** 220 **Born:** 10/19/66 **Age:** 34

Year Team	Lg	G	GS	CG	GF	IP	BFP	H	R	ER	HR	SH	SF	HB	TBB	IBB	SO	WP	Bk	W	L	Pct.	ShO	Sv-Op	Hld	ERA
1994 Houston	NL	32	0	0	7	41	168	39	13	11	4	0	2	1	7	3	28	2	0	3	3	.500	0	1-1	3	2.41
1995 Houston	NL	72	0	0	15	103.1	418	89	29	26	5	6	8	4	30	6	94	4	0	5	1	.833	0	1-3	19	2.26
1996 Montreal	NL	68	0	0	22	77.2	351	85	39	36	10	3	3	6	32	2	81	3	2	6	3	.667	0	4-6	15	4.17
1997 Montreal	NL	53	0	0	11	62	281	68	28	24	5	6	1	2	27	3	47	7	0	2	3	.400	0	1-4	10	3.48
1998 Colorado	NL	63	0	0	26	76.1	319	67	26	24	6	0	2	2	27	2	74	2	2	3	1	.750	0	8-13	8	2.83
1999 Colorado	NL	73	0	0	63	77	349	88	46	44	14	5	2	2	37	7	71	8	1	4	8	.333	0	31-39	0	5.14
2000 St. Louis	NL	71	0	0	61	75.2	310	65	26	24	6	5	2	6	25	2	67	3	1	3	5	.375	0	29-36	1	2.85
7 ML YEARS		432	0	0	205	513	2196	501	207	189	50	25	20	23	185	25	462	29	6	26	24	.520	0	75-102	56	3.32

Jose Vidro

Bats: Both **Throws:** Right **Pos:** 2B-153 **Ht:** 5'11" **Wt:** 190 **Born:** 8/27/74 **Age:** 26

Year Team	Lg	G	AB	H	2B	3B	HR	(Hm	Rd)	TB	R	RBI	TBB	IBB	SO	HBP	SH	SF	SB	CS	SB%	GDP	Avg	OBP	SLG
1997 Montreal	NL	67	169	42	12	1	2	(0	2)	62	19	17	11	0	20	2	0	3	2	0	1.00	1	.249	.297	.367
1998 Montreal	NL	83	205	45	12	0	0	(0	0)	57	24	18	27	0	33	4	6	3	2	2	.50	5	.220	.318	.278
1999 Montreal	NL	140	494	150	45	2	12	(5	7)	235	67	59	29	2	51	4	2	2	0	4	.00	12	.304	.346	.476
2000 Montreal	NL	153	606	200	51	2	24	(11	13)	327	101	97	49	4	69	2	0	6	5	4	.56	17	.330	.379	.540
4 ML YEARS		443	1474	437	120	5	38	(16	22)	681	211	191	116	6	173	12	8	14	8	10	.44	35	.296	.350	.462

Brandon Villafuerte

Pitches: Right **Bats:** Right **Pos:** RP-3 **Ht:** 5'11" **Wt:** 180 **Born:** 12/17/75 **Age:** 25

Year Team	Lg	G	GS	CG	GF	IP	BFP	H	R	ER	HR	SH	SF	HB	TBB	IBB	SO	WP	Bk	W	L	Pct.	ShO	Sv-Op	Hld	ERA
1995 Kingsport	R+	20	0	0	6	32	144	28	21	20	0	1	1	1	26	0	42	8	0	5	1	.833	0	1--	—	5.63
1996 Pittsfield	A-	18	7	1	4	62.2	267	53	21	21	5	2	3	6	27	0	59	4	0	8	3	.727	0	1--	—	3.02
1997 Capital Cty	A	47	3	0	31	75.2	308	58	23	20	6	2	1	4	33	0	88	12	0	3	1	.750	0	7--	—	2.38
1998 Brevard Cty	A+	3	0	0	0	9.2	34	7	3	1	0	0	0	0	1	0	6	0	0	1	0	1.000	0	0--	—	0.93
Portland	AA	30	0	0	11	54.1	262	68	35	30	3	6	0	4	33	2	52	3	0	1	0	1.000	0	1--	—	4.97
Charlotte	AAA	10	0	0	1	11.1	55	15	8	8	2	1	0	1	8	0	9	1	0	1	0	1.000	0	1--	—	6.35
1999 Portland	AA	22	12	0	4	100.1	422	97	45	39	11	4	2	5	40	3	85	2	1	6	8	.429	0	0--	—	3.50
Jacksnville	AA	15	0	0	10	24	101	17	6	5	0	2	1	1	12	0	20	1	0	2	0	.000	0	5--	—	1.88
2000 Toledo	AAA	46	6	0	21	87.2	417	112	70	65	7	2	3	1	49	1	85	12	1	4	9	.308	0	4--	—	6.67
2000 Detroit	AL	3	0	0	2	4.1	20	4	5	5	0	0	0	0	4	0	1	1	0	0	0	—	0	0-0	0	10.38

Ismael Villegas

Pitches: Right **Bats:** Right **Pos:** RP-1 **Ht:** 6'1" **Wt:** 188 **Born:** 8/12/76 **Age:** 24

Year Team	Lg	G	GS	CG	GF	IP	BFP	H	R	ER	HR	SH	SF	HB	TBB	IBB	SO	WP	Bk	W	L	Pct.	ShO	Sv-Op	Hld	ERA
1995 Cubs	R	11	10	0	0	41.1	168	33	17	11	1	2	6	2	11	0	26	3	2	3	2	.600	0	0--	—	2.40
1996 Rockford	A	10	10	1	0	47.1	223	63	40	27	5	1	2	3	11	0	30	3	1	2	5	.286	0	0--	—	5.13
Williamsprt	A-	2	2	0	0	7	31	7	3	2	0	0	0	0	4	0	5	1	0	0	0	—	0	0--	—	2.57
Danville	R+	1	0	0	0	3	11	2	1	1	0	0	0	0	1	0	4	1	0	0	0	—	0	0--	—	3.00
Macon	A	12	12	2	0	72	313	80	46	40	8	2	4	1	19	1	60	6	0	3	7	.300	1	0--	—	5.00
1997 Durham	A+	30	1	0	5	55	255	60	33	31	5	2	2	4	32	0	44	5	0	2	5	.286	0	1--	—	5.07
1998 Greenville	AA	40	17	1	11	124.1	567	134	78	73	11	3	3	3	71	1	120	11	2	7	6	.538	0	3--	—	5.28
1999 Richmond	AAA	44	2	0	8	92	400	93	51	45	7	6	3	2	39	3	61	8	0	6	7	.462	0	1--	—	4.40
2000 Richmond	AAA	41	0	0	13	63.2	286	66	38	34	7	5	6	2	31	1	51	1	0	5	5	.500	0	3--	—	4.81
Greenville	AA	8	0	0	3	16	75	20	12	8	2	2	1	0	7	1	16	1	0	2	1	.667	0	1--	—	4.50
2000 Atlanta	NL	1	0	0	0	2.2	15	4	4	4	2	0	0	0	2	0	2	0	0	0	0	—	0	0-0	0	13.50

Ron Villone

Pitches: Left **Bats:** Left **Pos:** SP-23; RP-12 **Ht:** 6'3" **Wt:** 237 **Born:** 1/16/70 **Age:** 31

Year Team	Lg	G	GS	CG	GF	IP	BFP	H	R	ER	HR	SH	SF	HB	TBB	IBB	SO	WP	Bk	W	L	Pct.	ShO	Sv-Op	Hld	ERA
1995 Sea-SD		38	0	0	15	45	212	44	31	29	11	3	1	1	34	0	63	3	0	2	3	.400	0	1-5	6	5.80
1996 SD-Mil		44	0	0	19	43	182	31	15	15	6	0	2	5	25	0	38	2	0	1	1	.500	0	2-3	9	3.14
1997 Milwaukee	AL	50	0	0	15	52.2	238	54	23	20	4	2	0	1	36	2	40	3	0	1	0	1.000	0	0-2	8	3.42
1998 Cleveland	AL	25	0	0	6	27	129	30	18	18	3	2	2	2	22	0	15	0	0	0	0	—	0	0-0	1	6.00
1999 Cincinnati	NL	29	22	0	2	142.2	610	114	70	67	8	9	3	5	73	2	97	6	0	9	7	.563	0	2-2	0	4.23
2000 Cincinnati	NL	35	23	2	5	141	643	154	95	85	22	10	8	9	78	3	77	7	0	10	10	.500	0	0-1	1	5.43

		HOW MUCH HE PITCHED			WHAT HE GAVE UP				THE RESULTS				
Year Team	Lg	G GS CG GF	IP	BFP	H R ER HR SH SF HB	TBB IBB	SO	WP Bk	W L	Pct.	ShO	Sv-Op	Hld	ERA
1995 Seattle	AL	19 0 0 7	19.1	101	20 19 17 6 3 0 1	23 0	26	1 0	0 2	.000	0	0-3	3	7.91
San Diego	NL	19 0 0 8	25.2	111	24 12 12 5 0 1 0	11 0	37	2 0	1 1	.667	0	1-2	3	4.21
1996 San Diego	NL	21 0 0 9	18.1	78	17 6 6 2 0 0 1	7 0	19	0 0	1 1	.500	0	0-1	4	2.95
Milwaukee	AL	23 0 0 10	24.2	104	14 9 9 4 0 2 4	18 0	19	2 0	0 0	—	0	2-2	5	3.28
6 ML YEARS		221 45 2 62	451.1	2014	427 252 234 54 26 16 23	268 7	330	21 0	23 21	.523	0	5-12	25	4.67

Fernando Vina

Bats: Left Throws: Right Pos: 2B-122; PH/PR-3   Ht: 5'9" Wt: 174 Born: 4/16/69 Age: 32

		BATTING									BASERUNNING	PERCENTAGES		
Year Team	Lg	G AB H	2B 3B HR	(Hm Rd)	TB	R RBI	TBB IBB	SO	HBP SH SF	SB CS SB% GDP	Avg	OBP	SLG
1993 Seattle	AL	24 45 10	2 0 0	(0 0)	12	5 2	4 0	3	1 0	6 0 1.00 0	.222	.327	.267
1994 New York	NL	79 124 31	6 0 0	(0 0)	37	20 6	12 0	11	12 2 1 0	3 1 .75 4	.250	.372	.298
1995 Milwaukee	AL	113 288 74	7 7 3	(1 2)	104	46 29	22 0	28	9 4 2	6 3 .67 6	.257	.327	.361
1996 Milwaukee	AL	140 554 157	19 10 7	(3 4)	217	94 46	38 3	35	13 6 4	16 7 .70 15	.283	.342	.392
1997 Milwaukee	AL	79 324 89	12 2 4	(1 3)	117	37 28	12 1	23	7 2 3	8 7 .53 4	.275	.312	.361
1998 Milwaukee	NL	159 637 198	39 7 7	(2 5)	272	101 45	54 2	46	25 5 1	22 16 .58 7	.311	.386	.427
1999 Milwaukee	NL	37 154 41	7 0 1	(0 1)	51	17 16	14 0	6	4 3 2	5 2 .71 1	.266	.339	.331
2000 St. Louis	NL	123 487 146	24 6 4	(1 3)	194	81 31	36 0	36	28 2 1	10 8 .56 5	.300	.380	.398
8 ML YEARS		754 2613 746	116 32 26	(8 18)	1004	401 203	192 6	188	101 25 13	76 44 .63 42	.285	.356	.384

Joe Vitiello

Bats: Right Throws: Right Pos: PH/PR-22; 1B-17; RF-1   Ht: 6'3" Wt: 230 Born: 4/11/70 Age: 31

		BATTING									BASERUNNING	PERCENTAGES		
Year Team	Lg	G AB H	2B 3B HR	(Hm Rd)	TB	R RBI	TBB IBB	SO	HBP SH SF	SB CS SB% GDP	Avg	OBP	SLG
2000 Las Vegas *	AAA	77 274 96	31 0 11	— —	160	43 46	27 0	59	2 0 1	2 0 1.00 11	.350	.411	.584
1995 Kansas City	AL	53 130 33	4 0 7	(3 4)	58	13 21	8 0	25	4 0 0	0 0 — 4	.254	.317	.446
1996 Kansas City	AL	85 257 62	15 1 8	(3 5)	103	29 40	38 2	69	3 0 0	2 0 1.00 6	.241	.342	.401
1997 Kansas City	AL	51 130 31	6 0 5	(4 1)	52	11 18	14 1	37	2 0 0	0 0 — 2	.238	.322	.400
1998 Kansas City	AL	3 7 1	0 0 0	(0 0)	1	0 0	1 0	2	0 0 0	0 0 — 0	.143	.250	.143
1999 Kansas City	AL	13 41 6	0 0 1	(0 1)	10	4 4	2 0	9	2 0 0	0 0 — 1	.146	.222	.244
2000 San Diego	NL	39 52 13	3 0 2	(1 1)	22	7 8	10 0	9	0 0 1	0 0 — 1	.250	.365	.423
6 ML YEARS		244 617 146	29 1 23	(11 12)	246	64 91	73 3	151	11 0 4	2 0 1.00 21	.237	.326	.399

Jose Vizcaino

Bats: B Throws: R Pos: 2B-65; PH/PR-24; SS-21; 3B-18; DH-5; 1B-1   Ht: 6'1" Wt: 180 Born: 3/26/68 Age: 33

		BATTING									BASERUNNING	PERCENTAGES		
Year Team	Lg	G AB H	2B 3B HR	(Hm Rd)	TB	R RBI	TBB IBB	SO	HBP SH SF	SB CS SB% GDP	Avg	OBP	SLG
1989 Los Angeles	NL	7 10 2	0 0 0	(0 0)	2	2 0	0 0	1	0 1 0	0 0 — 0	.200	.200	.200
1990 Los Angeles	NL	37 51 14	1 1 0	(0 0)	17	3 2	4 1	8	0 0 0	1 1 .50 1	.275	.327	.333
1991 Chicago	NL	93 145 38	5 0 0	(0 0)	43	7 10	5 0	18	0 2 2	2 1 .67 1	.262	.283	.297
1992 Chicago	NL	86 285 64	10 4 1	(0 1)	85	25 17	14 2	35	0 5 1	3 0 1.00 4	.225	.260	.298
1993 Chicago	NL	151 551 158	19 4 4	(1 3)	197	74 54	46 2	71	3 8 9	12 9 .57 9	.287	.340	.358
1994 New York	NL	103 410 105	13 3 3	(1 2)	133	47 33	33 3	62	2 5 6	1 11 .08 5	.256	.310	.324
1995 New York	NL	135 509 146	21 5 3	(2 1)	186	66 56	35 4	76	1 13 3	8 3 .73 14	.287	.332	.365
1996 NYM-Cle		144 542 161	17 8 1	(1 0)	197	70 45	30 0	82	3 10 3	15 7 .68 8	.297	.341	.363
1997 San Francisco	NL	151 568 151	19 7 5	(1 4)	199	77 50	48 1	87	0 13 1	8 8 .50 13	.266	.323	.350
1998 Los Angeles	NL	67 237 62	9 0 3	(0 3)	80	30 29	17 0	35	1 10 2	7 3 .70 4	.262	.311	.338
1999 Los Angeles	NL	94 266 67	9 0 1	(1 0)	79	27 29	20 0	23	1 9 2	2 1 .67 9	.252	.304	.297
2000 LA-NYY		113 267 67	10 2 0	(0 0)	81	32 14	22 3	43	1 5 2	6 7 .46 6	.251	.308	.303
1996 New York	NL	96 363 110	12 6 1	(1 0)	137	47 32	28 0	58	3 6 2	9 5 .64 6	.303	.356	.377
Cleveland	AL	48 179 51	5 2 0	(0 0)	60	23 13	7 0	24	0 4 1	6 2 .75 2	.285	.310	.335
2000 Los Angeles	NL	40 93 19	2 1 0	(0 0)	23	9 4	10 3	15	1 2 0	1 0 1.00 3	.204	.288	.247
New York	AL	73 174 48	8 1 0	(0 0)	58	23 10	12 0	28	0 3 2	5 7 .42 3	.276	.319	.333
12 ML YEARS		1181 3841 1035	133 34 21	(7 14)	1299	460 339	279 16	541	12 81 31	65 51 .56 74	.269	.319	.338

Luis Vizcaino

Pitches: Right Bats: Right Pos: RP-12   Ht: 5'11" Wt: 169 Born: 6/1/77 Age: 24

		HOW MUCH HE PITCHED			WHAT HE GAVE UP				THE RESULTS				
Year Team	Lg	G GS CG GF	IP	BFP	H R ER HR SH SF HB	TBB IBB	SO	WP Bk	W L	Pct.	ShO	Sv-Op	Hld	ERA
1996 Athletics	R	15 10 0 4	59.2	264	58 36 27 1 1 1 2	24 1	52	6 3	6 3	.667	0	1- —	—	4.07
1997 Modesto	A+	7 0 0 3	14.1	76	24 24 21 4 1 0 0	13 4	15	0 2	0 3	.000	0	0- —	—	13.19
Sou Oregon	A-	22 5 0 7	47.2	237	62 51 42 5 1 5 3	27 0	42	14 0	1 6	.143	0	0- —	—	7.93
1998 Modesto	A+	23 16 0 2	102	421	72 39 31 5 1 4 5	43 1	108	6 4	6 3	.667	0	0- —	—	2.74
Huntsville	AA	7 7 0 0	38.2	182	43 27 20 8 0 3 3	22 0	26	2 0	3 2	.600	0	0- —	—	4.66
1999 Midland	AA	25 19 0 1	104.2	473	120 74 68 18 1 3 3	48 2	88	6 0	8 7	.533	0	0- —	—	5.85
Vancouver	AAA	7 0 0 3	13	56	13 4 2 0 0 0 0	6 0	7	1 0	1 0	1.000	0	1- —	—	1.38
2000 Sacramento	AAA	33 2 0 12	48.1	204	48 27 27 4 5 3 1	21 0	41	1 0	6 2	.750	0	5- —	—	5.03
1999 Oakland	AL	1 0 0 1	3.1	16	3 2 2 1 0 0 0	3 0	2	1 0	0 0	—	0	0-0	0	5.40
2000 Oakland	AL	12 0 0 1	19.1	96	25 17 16 2 0 1 2	11 0	18	1 0	0 1	.000	0	0-0	0	7.45
2 ML YEARS		13 0 0 2	22.2	112	28 19 18 3 0 1 2	14 0	20	2 0	0 1	.000	0	0-0	0	7.15

Omar Vizquel

Bats: Both Throws: Right Pos: SS-156; PH/PR-1   Ht: 5'9" Wt: 185 Born: 4/24/67 Age: 34

		BATTING									BASERUNNING	PERCENTAGES		
Year Team	Lg	G AB H	2B 3B HR	(Hm Rd)	TB	R RBI	TBB IBB	SO	HBP SH SF	SB CS SB% GDP	Avg	OBP	SLG
1989 Seattle	AL	143 387 85	7 3 1	(1 0)	101	45 20	28 0	40	1 13 2	1 4 .20 6	.220	.273	.261
1990 Seattle	AL	81 255 63	3 2 2	(0 2)	76	19 18	18 0	22	0 10 2	4 1 .80 7	.247	.295	.298
1991 Seattle	AL	142 426 98	16 4 1	(1 0)	125	42 41	45 0	37	0 8 3	7 2 .78 8	.230	.302	.293

Year Team	Lg	G	AB	H	2B	3B	HR	(Hm	Rd)	TB	R	RBI	TBB	IBB	SO	HBP	SH	SF	SB	CS	SB%	GDP	Avg	OBP	SLG
1992 Seattle	AL	136	483	142	20	4	0	(0	0)	170	49	21	32	0	38	2	9	1	15	13	.54	14	.294	.340	.352
1993 Seattle	AL	158	560	143	14	2	2	(1	1)	167	68	31	50	2	71	4	13	3	12	14	.46	7	.255	.319	.298
1994 Cleveland	AL	69	286	78	10	1	1	(0	1)	93	39	23	23	0	23	0	11	2	13	4	.76	4	.273	.325	.325
1995 Cleveland	AL	136	542	144	28	0	6	(3	3)	190	87	56	59	0	59	1	10	10	29	11	.73	4	.266	.333	.351
1996 Cleveland	AL	151	542	161	36	1	9	(2	7)	226	98	64	56	0	42	4	12	9	35	9	.80	10	.297	.362	.417
1997 Cleveland	AL	153	565	158	23	6	5	(3	2)	208	89	49	57	1	58	2	16	2	43	12	.78	16	.280	.347	.368
1998 Cleveland	AL	151	576	166	30	6	2	(0	2)	214	86	50	62	1	64	4	12	6	37	12	.76	10	.288	.358	.372
1999 Cleveland	AL	144	574	191	36	4	5	(3	2)	250	112	66	65	0	50	1	17	7	42	9	.82	8	.333	.397	.436
2000 Cleveland	AL	156	613	176	27	3	7	(1	6)	230	101	66	87	0	72	5	7	5	22	10	.69	13	.287	.377	.375
12 ML YEARS		1620	5809	1605	250	36	41	(15	26)	2050	835	515	582	4	576	24	138	52	260	101	.72	107	.276	.342	.353

Ryan Vogelsong

Pitches: Right **Bats:** Right **Pos:** RP-4   **Ht:** 6'3" **Wt:** 195 **Born:** 7/22/77 **Age:** 23

Year Team	Lg	G	GS	CG	GF	IP	BFP	H	R	ER	HR	SH	SF	HB	TBB	IBB	SO	WP	Bk	W	L	Pct.	ShO	Sv-Op	Hld	ERA
1998 San Jose	A+	4	4	0	0	19	83	23	16	16	3	1	2	1	4	0	26	2	4	0	0		0	0--	—	7.58
Salem-Keizr	A-	10	10	0	0	56	221	37	15	11	5	3	2	1	16	0	66	2	2	6	1	.857	0	0--	—	1.77
1999 San Jose	A+	13	13	0	0	69.2	274	37	26	19	3	1	2	3	27	0	86	3	0	4	4	.500	0	0--	—	2.45
Shreveport	AA	6	6	0	0	28.1	137	40	25	23	7	0	1	2	15	0	23	1	1	0	2	.000	0	0--	—	7.31
2000 Shreveport	AA	27	27	1	0	155.1	682	153	82	73	15	5	7	13	69	2	147	5	4	6	10	.375	0	0--	—	4.23
2000 San Francisco	NL	4	0	0	3	6	24	4	0	0	0	0	0	0	2	0	6	0	0	0	0	—	0	0-0	0	0.00

Ed Vosberg

Pitches: Left **Bats:** Left **Pos:** RP-31   **Ht:** 6'1" **Wt:** 210 **Born:** 9/28/61 **Age:** 39

Year Team	Lg	G	GS	CG	GF	IP	BFP	H	R	ER	HR	SH	SF	HB	TBB	IBB	SO	WP	Bk	W	L	Pct.	ShO	Sv-Op	Hld	ERA
2000 Colo Sprngs *	AAA	29	3	0	4	42	204	59	41	32	4	3	2	1	20	0	37	4	1	1	2	.333	0	2--	—	6.86
Scrantn-WB *	AAA	1	0	0	0	2	6	0	0	0	0	0	0	0	0	0	2	0	0	0	0	—	0	0--	—	0.00
1986 San Diego	NL	5	3	0	0	13.2	65	17	11	10	1	0	0	0	9	1	8	0	1	0	1	.000	0	0--	—	6.59
1990 San Francisco	NL	18	0	0	5	24.1	104	21	16	15	3	2	0	0	12	2	12	0	0	1	1	.500	0	0-0	0	5.55
1994 Oakland	NL	16	0	0	2	13.2	56	16	7	6	2	1	0	0	5	0	12	1	1	0	2	.000	0	0-1	2	3.95
1995 Texas	AL	44	0	0	20	36	154	32	15	12	3	2	3	0	16	1	36	3	2	5	5	.500	0	4-8	5	3.00
1996 Texas	AL	52	0	0	21	44	195	51	17	16	4	2	1	0	21	4	32	1	2	1	1	.500	0	8-9	11	3.27
1997 Tex-Fla		59	0	0	22	53	239	59	30	26	3	2	4	5	21	6	37	2	1	2	3	.400	0	1-3	8	4.42
1999 SD-Ari	NL	19	0	0	3	11	60	22	12	10	1	2	2	2	3	0	11	0	1	0	0	.000	0	0-2	4	8.18
2000 Philadelphia	NL	31	0	0	5	24	106	21	11	11	4	1	0	0	18	0	23	1	0	0	0	—	0	0-2	11	4.13
1997 Texas	AL	42	0	0	16	41	180	44	23	21	3	1	3	2	15	6	29	1	1		2	.333	0	0-1	5	4.61
Florida		17	0	0	6	12	59	15	7	5	0	1	1	3	6	0	8	1	1	1	1	.500	0	1-2	3	3.75
1999 San Diego	NL	15	0	0	3	8.1	47	16	11	9	1	2	2	2	3	0	6	1	0	0	0	—	0	0-2	4	9.72
Arizona	NL	4	0	0	2	2.2	13	6	1	1	0	0	0	0	0	0	2	0	0	1		.000	0	0-0	1	3.38
8 ML YEARS		244	3	0	78	219.2	979	239	119	106	21	12	10	7	105	14	168	9	7	10	15	.400	0	13--	—	4.34

Billy Wagner

Pitches: Left **Bats:** Left **Pos:** RP-28   **Ht:** 5'11" **Wt:** 180 **Born:** 7/25/71 **Age:** 29

Year Team	Lg	G	GS	CG	GF	IP	BFP	H	R	ER	HR	SH	SF	HB	TBB	IBB	SO	WP	Bk	W	L	Pct.	ShO	Sv-Op	Hld	ERA
1995 Houston	NL	1	0	0	0	0.1	1	0	0	0	0	0	0	0	0	0	0	0	0	0	0	—	0	0-0	0	0.00
1996 Houston	NL	37	0	0	20	51.2	212	28	16	14	6	7	2	3	30	2	67	1	0	2	2	.500	0	9-13	3	2.44
1997 Houston	NL	62	0	0	49	66.1	277	49	23	21	5	3	1	3	30	1	106	3	0	7	8	.467	0	23-29	1	2.85
1998 Houston	NL	58	0	0	50	60	247	46	19	18	6	4	0	0	25	1	97	2	0	4	3	.571	0	30-35	1	2.70
1999 Houston	NL	66	0	0	55	74.2	286	35	14	13	5	2	1	1	23	1	124	2	0	4	1	.800	0	39-42	4	1.57
2000 Houston	NL	28	0	0	19	27.2	129	28	19	19	6	0	0	1	18	0	28	7	0	2	4	.333	0	6-15	0	6.18
6 ML YEARS		252	0	0	193	280.2	1152	186	91	85	28	16	4	8	126	5	422	15	0	19	18	.514	0	107-134	6	2.73

Dave Wainhouse

Pitches: Right **Bats:** Left **Pos:** RP-9   **Ht:** 6'2" **Wt:** 196 **Born:** 11/7/67 **Age:** 33

Year Team	Lg	G	GS	CG	GF	IP	BFP	H	R	ER	HR	SH	SF	HB	TBB	IBB	SO	WP	Bk	W	L	Pct.	ShO	Sv-Op	Hld	ERA
2000 Memphis *	AAA	20	6	0	2	43	199	55	32	30	8	1	2	3	20	0	20	1	0	4	4	.500	0	0--	—	6.28
1991 Montreal	NL	2	0	0	1	2.2	14	2	2	2	0	1	0	1	4	0	1	2	0	0	1	.000	0	0-0	0	6.75
1993 Seattle	AL	3	0	0	0	2.1	20	7	7	7	1	0	0	1	5	0	2	0	0	0	0	—	0	0-0	0	27.00
1996 Pittsburgh	NL	17	0	0	6	23.2	101	22	16	15	3	1	2	0	10	1	16	2	0	1	0	1.000	0	0-0	1	5.70
1997 Pittsburgh	NL	25	0	0	6	28	137	34	28	25	2	3	1	3	17	0	21	1	0	1	0	1.000	0	0-0	1	8.04
1998 Colorado	NL	10	0	0	3	11	51	15	6	6	1	0	0	2	5	0	3	0	0	1	0	1.000	0	0-1	0	4.91
1999 Colorado	NL	19	0	0	11	28.2	131	37	22	22	6	0	3	0	16	0	18	1	0	0	0	—	0	0-0	1	6.91
2000 St. Louis	NL	9	0	0	4	8.2	44	13	10	9	2	1	0	2	4	1	5	1	0	0	1	.000	0	0-0	1	9.35
7 ML YEARS		85	0	0	31	105	498	130	91	86	15	5	7	8	61	2	66	7	1	2	3	.400	0	0-1	3	7.37

Tim Wakefield

Pitches: Right **Bats:** Right **Pos:** RP-34; SP-17   **Ht:** 6'2" **Wt:** 210 **Born:** 8/2/66 **Age:** 34

Year Team	Lg	G	GS	CG	GF	IP	BFP	H	R	ER	HR	SH	SF	HB	TBB	IBB	SO	WP	Bk	W	L	Pct.	ShO	Sv-Op	Hld	ERA
1992 Pittsburgh	NL	13	13	4	0	92	373	76	26	22	3	6	4	1	35	1	51	3	1	8	1	.889	1	0-0	0	2.15
1993 Pittsburgh	NL	24	20	3	1	128.1	595	145	83	80	14	7	5	9	75	2	59	6	0	6	11	.353	2	0-0	0	5.61
1995 Boston	AL	27	27	6	0	195.1	804	163	76	64	22	3	7	8	68	0	119	11	0	16	8	.667	1	0-0	0	2.95
1996 Boston	AL	32	32	6	0	211.2	963	238	151	121	38	1	9	12	90	0	140	4	1	14	13	.519	0	0-0	0	5.14
1997 Boston	AL	35	29	4	2	201.1	866	193	109	95	24	3	7	16	87	5	151	6	0	12	15	.444	2	0-0	1	4.25
1998 Boston	AL	36	33	2	1	216	939	211	123	110	30	1	8	14	79	1	146	6	1	17	8	.680	0	0-0	0	4.58

		HOW MUCH HE PITCHED					WHAT HE GAVE UP												THE RESULTS						
Year Team	Lg	G	GS	CG	GF	IP	BFP	H	R	ER	HR	SH	SF	HB	TBB	IBB	SO	WP	Bk	W	L	Pct.	ShO	Sv-Op	Hld	ERA
1999 Boston	AL	49	17	0	28	140	635	146	93	79	19	1	8	5	72	2	104	1	0	6	11	.353	0	15-18	0	5.08
2000 Boston	AL	51	17	0	13	159.1	706	170	107	97	31	4	8	5	65	3	102	4	0	6	10	.375	0	0-1		5.48
8 ML YEARS		267	188	25	45	1344	5881	1342	768	668	181	26	56	70	571	14	872	41	3	85	77	.525	6	15-19	4	4.47

Matt Walbeck

Bats: B **Throws:** R **Pos:** C-44; 1B-2; PH/PR-2; DH-1   **Ht:** 5'11" **Wt:** 188 **Born:** 10/2/69 **Age:** 31

		BATTING															BASERUNNING				PERCENTAGES		
Year Team	Lg	G	AB	H	2B	3B	HR	(Hm | Rd)	TB	R	RBI	TBB	IBB	SO	HBP	SH	SF	SB	CS	SB%	GDP	Avg	OBP	SLG
1993 Chicago	NL	11	30	6	2	0	1	(1 | 0)	11	2	6	1	0	6	0	0	0	0	0	—	0	.200	.226	.367
1994 Minnesota	AL	97	338	69	12	0	5	(0 | 5)	96	31	35	17	1	37	2	1	1	1	1	.50	7	.204	.246	.284
1995 Minnesota	AL	115	393	101	18	1	1	(1 | 0)	124	40	44	25	2	71	1	1	2	3	1	.75	11	.257	.302	.316
1996 Minnesota	AL	63	215	48	10	0	2	(1 | 1)	64	25	24	9	0	34	0	1	2	3	1	.75	6	.223	.252	.298
1997 Detroit	AL	47	137	38	3	0	3	(1 | 2)	50	18	10	12	0	19	0	0	2	3	3	.50	4	.277	.331	.365
1998 Anaheim	AL	108	338	87	15	2	6	(3 | 3)	124	41	46	30	0	68	2	5	5	1	1	.50	9	.257	.317	.367
1999 Anaheim	AL	107	288	69	8	1	3	(1 | 2)	88	26	22	26	1	46	3	3	1	2	3	.40	12	.240	.308	.306
2000 Anaheim	AL	47	146	29	5	0	6	(2 | 4)	52	17	12	7	0	22	1	1	0	0	1	.00	2	.199	.240	.356
8 ML YEARS		595	1885	447	73	4	27	(10 | 17)	609	200	199	127	4	303	9	12	13	13	11	.54	51	.237	.287	.323

Kevin Walker

Pitches: Left **Bats:** Left **Pos:** RP-70   **Ht:** 6'4" **Wt:** 190 **Born:** 9/20/76 **Age:** 24

		HOW MUCH HE PITCHED						WHAT HE GAVE UP												THE RESULTS						
Year Team	Lg	G	GS	CG	GF	IP	BFP	H	R	ER	HR	SH	SF	HB	TBB	IBB	SO	WP	Bk	W	L	Pct.	ShO	Sv-Op	Hld	ERA
1995 Padres	R	13	12	0	0	71.2	295	74	34	24	1	1	3	2	12	0	69	1	3	5	5	.500	0	0- -	—	3.01
1996 Idaho Falls	R+	1	1	0	0	6	24	4	3	2	1	0	0	0	2	0	4	1	0	1	0	1.000	0	0- -	—	3.00
Clinton	A	13	13	0	0	76	339	80	46	40	9	1	6	9	33	0	43	1	0	4	6	.400	0	0- -	—	4.74
1997 Clinton	A	19	19	3	0	110.2	495	133	80	60	9	2	5	4	37	0	80	5	2	6	10	.375	1	0- -	—	4.88
1998 Clinton	A	2	2	0	0	14.2	59	11	2	2	0	0	0	1	7	0	10	2	0	2	0	1.000	0	0- -	—	1.23
Rancho Cuc	A+	22	22	0	0	121.1	514	122	62	56	10	2	3	4	48	0	94	3	2	11	7	.611	0	0- -	—	4.15
1999 Rancho Cuc	A+	27	1	0	9	39	169	35	19	15	2	1	2	3	19	3	35	1	0	1	1	.500	0	0- -	—	3.46
2000 Mobile	AA	4	0	0	1	4	14	1	1	1	0	0	0	0	1	0	6	0	0	1	0	1.000	0	0- -	—	2.25
2000 San Diego	NL	70	0	0	14	66.2	287	49	35	31	5	4	2	5	38	6	56	2	1	7	1	.875	0	0-0	19	4.19

Larry Walker

Bats: L **Throws:** R **Pos:** RF-52; LF-31; PH/PR-4; DH-3   **Ht:** 6'3" **Wt:** 237 **Born:** 12/1/66 **Age:** 34

		BATTING															BASERUNNING				PERCENTAGES		
Year Team	Lg	G	AB	H	2B	3B	HR	(Hm	Rd)	TB	R	RBI	TBB	IBB	SO	HBP	SH	SF	SB	CS	SB%	GDP	Avg	OBP	SLG
1989 Montreal	NL	20	47	8	0	0	0	(0	0)	8	4	4	5	0	13	1	3	0	1	1	.50	0	.170	.264	.170
1990 Montreal	NL	133	419	101	18	3	19	(9	10)	182	59	51	49	5	112	5	3	2	21	7	.75	8	.241	.326	.434
1991 Montreal	NL	137	487	141	30	2	16	(5	11)	223	59	64	42	2	102	5	1	4	14	9	.61	7	.290	.349	.458
1992 Montreal	NL	143	528	159	31	4	23	(13	10)	267	85	93	41	10	97	5	0	8	18	6	.75	9	.301	.353	.506
1993 Montreal	NL	138	490	130	24	5	22	(13	9)	230	85	86	80	20	76	6	0	6	29	7	.81	8	.265	.371	.469
1994 Montreal	NL	103	395	127	44	2	19	(7	12)	232	76	86	47	5	74	4	0	6	15	5	.75	9	.322	.394	.587
1995 Colorado	NL	131	494	151	31	5	36	(24	12)	300	96	101	49	13	72	14	0	5	16	3	.84	13	.306	.381	.607
1996 Colorado	NL	83	272	75	18	4	18	(12	6)	155	58	58	20	2	58	9	0	3	18	2	.90	7	.276	.342	.570
1997 Colorado	NL	153	568	208	46	4	49	(20	29)	409	143	130	78	14	90	14	0	4	33	8	.80	15	.366	.452	.720
1998 Colorado	NL	130	454	165	46	3	23	(17	6)	286	113	67	64	2	61	4	0	2	14	4	.78	11	.363	.445	.630
1999 Colorado	NL	127	438	166	26	4	37	(26	11)	311	108	115	57	8	52	12	0	6	11	4	.73	10	.379	.458	.710
2000 Colorado	NL	87	314	97	21	7	9	(7	2)	159	64	51	46	4	40	9	0	3	5	5	.50	12	.309	.409	.506
12 ML YEARS		1385	4906	1528	335	43	271	(153	118)	2762	950	906	578	85	847	89	7	49	195	61	.76	110	.311	.390	.563

Pete Walker

Pitches: Right **Bats:** Right **Pos:** RP-3   **Ht:** 6'2" **Wt:** 195 **Born:** 4/8/69 **Age:** 32

		HOW MUCH HE PITCHED						WHAT HE GAVE UP												THE RESULTS						
Year Team	Lg	G	GS	CG	GF	IP	BFP	H	R	ER	HR	SH	SF	HB	TBB	IBB	SO	WP	Bk	W	L	Pct.	ShO	Sv-Op	Hld	ERA
2000 Colo Sprngs *	AAA	58	0	0	22	73.1	315	64	29	25	3	4	1	3	30	1	61	6	0	7	3	.700	0	5- -	—	3.07
1995 New York	NL	13	0	0	10	17.2	79	24	9	9	3	0	1	0	5	0	5	0	0	1	0	1.000	0	0-0	1	4.58
1996 San Diego	NL	1	0	0	0	0.2	5	0	0	0	0	0	0	0	3	0	1	0	0	0	0	—	0	0-0	0	0.00
2000 Colorado	NL	3	0	0	1	4.2	27	10	9	9	1	0	0	0	4	0	2	0	0	0	0	—	0	0-0	0	17.36
3 ML YEARS		17	0	0	11	23	111	34	18	18	4	0	1	0	12	0	8	0	0	1	0	1.000	0	0-0	1	7.04

Todd Walker

Bats: Left **Throws:** Right **Pos:** 2B-71; PH/PR-14; DH-2   **Ht:** 6'0" **Wt:** 181 **Born:** 5/25/73 **Age:** 28

		BATTING															BASERUNNING				PERCENTAGES		
Year Team	Lg	G	AB	H	2B	3B	HR	(Hm	Rd)	TB	R	RBI	TBB	IBB	SO	HBP	SH	SF	SB	CS	SB%	GDP	Avg	OBP	SLG
2000 Salt Lake *	AAA	63	249	81	14	1	2	—	—	103	51	37	32	0	32	0	3	3	8	3	.73	6	.325	.398	.414
1996 Minnesota	AL	25	82	21	6	0	0	(0	0)	27	8	6	4	0	13	0	0	3	2	0	1.00	4	.256	.281	.329
1997 Minnesota	AL	52	156	37	7	1	3	(1	2)	55	15	16	11	1	30	1	1	2	7	0	1.00	5	.237	.288	.353
1998 Minnesota	AL	143	528	167	41	3	12	(7	5)	250	85	62	47	9	65	2	0	4	19	7	.73	13	.316	.372	.473
1999 Minnesota	AL	143	531	148	37	4	6	(4	2)	211	62	46	52	5	83	1	0	2	18	10	.64	15	.279	.343	.397
2000 Min-Col		80	248	72	11	4	9	(5	4)	118	42	44	27	0	29	1	0	1	7	1	.88	6	.290	.355	.476
2000 Minnesota	AL	23	77	18	1	0	2	(0	2)	25	14	8	7	0	10	0	0	0	3	0	1.00	3	.234	.287	.325
Colorado	NL	57	171	54	10	4	7	(5	2)	93	28	36	20	0	19	1	0	1	4	1	.80	3	.316	.385	.544
5 ML YEARS		443	1545	445	102	12	30	(17	13)	661	212	174	141	15	220	5	2	17	53	18	.75	42	.288	.346	.428

Donne Wall

Pitches: Right **Bats:** Right **Pos:** RP-44
Ht: 6'1" **Wt:** 205 **Born:** 7/11/67 **Age:** 33

Year Team	Lg	G	GS	CG	GF	IP	BFP	H	R	ER	HR	SH	SF	HB	TBB	IBB	SO	WP	Bk	W	L	Pct.	ShO	Sv-Op	Hld	ERA
2000 Las Vegas *	AAA	2	0	0	0	2	10	3	0	0	0	0	0	0	2	0	1	1	0	0	0	0--	—			0.00
1995 Houston	NL	6	5	0	0	24.1	110	33	19	15	5	0	2	0	5	0	16	1	0	3	1	.750	0	0-0	1	5.55
1996 Houston	NL	26	23	2	1	150	643	170	84	76	17	4	5	6	34	3	99	3	2	9	8	.529	1	0-0	0	4.56
1997 Houston	NL	8	8	0	0	41.2	186	53	31	29	8	0	0	2	16	0	25	2	1	2	5	.286	0	0-0	0	6.26
1998 San Diego	NL	46	1	0	14	70.1	287	50	20	19	6	4	2	1	32	2	56	3	1	5	4	.556	0	1-4	16	2.43
1999 San Diego	NL	55	0	0	12	70.1	290	58	31	24	11	1	1	0	23	3	53	6	0	7	4	.636	0	0-6	18	3.07
2000 San Diego	NL	44	0	0	14	53.2	211	36	20	20	4	3	0	0	21	1	29	1	0	5	2	.714	0	1-5	12	3.35
6 ML YEARS		185	37	2	41	410.1	1727	400	205	183	51	12	10	9	131	9	278	16	4	31	24	.564	1	2-15	47	4.01

Jeff Wallace

Pitches: Left **Bats:** Left **Pos:** RP-38
Ht: 6'2" **Wt:** 238 **Born:** 4/12/76 **Age:** 25

Year Team	Lg	G	GS	CG	GF	IP	BFP	H	R	ER	HR	SH	SF	HB	TBB	IBB	SO	WP	Bk	W	L	Pct.	ShO	Sv-Op	Hld	ERA
2000 Nashville *	AAA	13	0	0	6	14	56	11	1	1	1	0	1	1	6	1	12	2	0	0	0		0	1--	—	0.64
1997 Pittsburgh	NL	11	0	0	1	12	50	8	2	1	0	1	1	0	8	1	14	1	0	0	0		0	0-1	3	0.75
1999 Pittsburgh	NL	41	0	0	7	39	176	26	17	16	2	4	1	0	38	1	41	5	0	1	0	1.000	0	0-1	7	3.69
2000 Pittsburgh	NL	38	0	0	6	35.2	185	42	32	28	5	0	2	4	34	1	27	5	0	2	0	1.000	0	0-0	3	7.07
3 ML YEARS		90	0	0	14	86.2	411	76	51	45	7	5	4	4	80	3	82	11	0	3	0	1.000	0	0-2	13	4.67

Bryan Ward

Pitches: Left **Bats:** Left **Pos:** RP-27
Ht: 6'2" **Wt:** 205 **Born:** 1/25/72 **Age:** 29

Year Team	Lg	G	GS	CG	GF	IP	BFP	H	R	ER	HR	SH	SF	HB	TBB	IBB	SO	WP	Bk	W	L	Pct.	ShO	Sv-Op	Hld	ERA
2000 Scrantn-WB *	AAA	22	0	0	14	27.1	113	23	11	7	1	4	0	1	8	0	17	3	0	3	2	.600	0	6--	—	2.30
Edmonton *	AAA	6	0	0	2	6.1	30	12	4	3	0	0	0	1	1	1	3	0	0	0	0		0	1--	—	4.26
1998 Chicago	AL	28	0	0	9	27	116	30	13	10	4	0	1	0	7	0	17	0	0	1	2	.333	0	1-4	3	3.33
1999 Chicago	AL	40	0	0	8	39.1	183	63	36	33	10	0	1	0	11	1	35	2	0	0	1	.000	0	0-0	7	7.55
2000 Phi-Ana		27	0	0	10	27.1	115	22	11	10	3	1	2	0	10	0	14	3	0	0	0		0	0-0	4	3.29
2000 Philadelphia	NL	20	0	0	8	19.1	79	14	5	5	2	1	2	0	8	0	11	1	0	0	0		0	0-0	4	2.33
Anaheim	AL	7	0	0	2	8	36	8	6	5	1	0	0	0	2	0	3	2	0	0	0		0	0-0	0	5.63
3 ML YEARS		95	0	0	27	93.2	414	115	60	53	17	1	4	0	28	1	66	5	0	1	3	.250	0	1-4	10	5.09

Daryle Ward

Bats: L **Throws:** L **Pos:** PH/PR-55; LF-43; 1B-19; DH-4; RF-4
Ht: 6'2" **Wt:** 230 **Born:** 6/27/75 **Age:** 26

Year Team	Lg	G	AB	H	2B	3B	HR	Hm	Rd	TB	R	RBI	TBB	IBB	SO	HBP	SH	SF	SB	CS	SB%	GDP	Avg	OBP	SLG
1998 Houston	NL	4	3	1	0	0	0	0	0	1	1	0	1	0	2	0	0	0	0	0	—	0	.333	.500	.333
1999 Houston	NL	64	150	41	6	0	8	2	6	71	11	30	9	0	31	0	0	2	0	0	—	3	.273	.311	.473
2000 Houston	NL	119	264	68	10	2	20	13	7	142	36	47	15	2	61	0	0	6	0	0	—	6	.258	.295	.538
3 ML YEARS		187	417	110	16	2	28	15	13	214	48	77	25	2	94	0	0	4	0	0	—	9	.264	.303	.513

Turner Ward

Bats: Both **Throws:** Right **Pos:** RF-14; CF-1
Ht: 6'2" **Wt:** 204 **Born:** 4/11/65 **Age:** 36

Year Team	Lg	G	AB	H	2B	3B	HR	Hm	Rd	TB	R	RBI	TBB	IBB	SO	HBP	SH	SF	SB	CS	SB%	GDP	Avg	OBP	SLG
2000 Tucson *	AAA	32	82	31	10	1	4			55	24	16	17	2	7	0	0	0	0	1	.00	3	.378	.485	.671
1990 Cleveland	AL	14	46	16	2	1	1	0	1	23	10	10	3	0	8	0	0	0	0	0	—	2	.348	.388	.500
1991 Cle-Tor	AL	48	113	27	7	0	0	0	0	34	12	7	11	0	18	0	4	0	0	0	—	2	.239	.306	.301
1992 Toronto	AL	18	29	10	3	0	1	0	1	16	7	3	4	0	4	0	0	0	1	0	.00	1	.345	.424	.552
1993 Toronto	AL	72	167	32	4	2	4	2	2	52	20	28	23	2	26	1	3	4	3	3	.50	7	.192	.287	.311
1994 Milwaukee	AL	102	367	85	15	2	9	3	6	131	55	45	52	4	68	3	0	5	6	2	.75	9	.232	.328	.357
1995 Milwaukee	AL	44	129	34	3	1	4	3	1	51	19	16	14	1	21	1	1	1	6	1	.86	2	.264	.338	.395
1996 Milwaukee	AL	43	67	12	2	1	2	2	0	22	7	10	13	0	17	1	1	1	3	0	1.00	3	.179	.309	.328
1997 Pittsburgh	NL	71	167	59	16	1	7	5	2	98	33	33	18	2	17	2	3	1	5	1	.80	4	.353	.420	.587
1998 Pittsburgh	NL	123	282	74	13	3	9	6	3	120	33	46	27	1	40	4	4	7	5	4	.56	4	.262	.328	.426
1999 Pit-Ari	NL	59	114	27	3	0	2	2	0	36	8	15	15	0	15	1	3	2	2	2	.50	2	.237	.326	.316
2000 Arizona	NL	15	52	9	0	0	0	0	0	13	5	4	5	0	7	0	1	1	1	1	.50	3	.173	.241	.250
1991 Cleveland	AL	40	100	23	7	0	0	0	0	30	11	5	10	0	16	0	4	0	0	0	—	1	.230	.300	.300
Toronto	AL	8	13	4	0	0	0	0	0	4	1	2	1	0	2	0	0	0	0	0	—	1	.308	.357	.308
1999 Pittsburgh	NL	49	91	19	2	0	0	0	0	21	2	8	13	0	9	1	3	1	2	2	.50	2	.209	.311	.231
Arizona	NL	10	23	8	1	0	2	2	0	15	6	7	2	0	6	0	0	0	0	0	—	0	.348	.385	.652
11 ML YEARS		609	1533	385	72	11	39	23	16	596	209	217	185	10	241	12	20	22	33	15	.69	35	.251	.332	.389

John Wasdin

Pitches: Right **Bats:** Right **Pos:** RP-35; SP-4
Ht: 6'2" **Wt:** 195 **Born:** 8/5/72 **Age:** 28

Year Team	Lg	G	GS	CG	GF	IP	BFP	H	R	ER	HR	SH	SF	HB	TBB	IBB	SO	WP	Bk	W	L	Pct.	ShO	Sv-Op	Hld	ERA
2000 Pawtucket *	AAA	5	3	0	2	16	57	7	4	4	0	0	0	1	2	0	11	0	0	1	0	1.000	0	1--	—	2.25
1995 Oakland	AL	5	2	0	3	17.1	69	14	9	9	4	0	0	1	3	0	6	0	0	1	1	.500	0	0-0	0	4.67
1996 Oakland	AL	25	21	1	2	131.1	575	145	96	87	24	3	6	4	50	5	75	2	2	8	7	.533	0	0-1	0	5.96
1997 Boston	AL	53	0	0	10	124.2	534	121	68	61	18	4	7	3	38	4	84	4	0	4	6	.400	0	0-2	11	4.40
1998 Boston	AL	47	8	0	13	96	424	111	57	56	14	3	6	2	27	8	59	1	0	6	4	.600	0	0-1	4	5.25
1999 Boston	AL	45	0	0	17	74.1	302	66	38	34	14	2	2	0	18	0	57	2	0	8	3	.727	0	2-5	2	4.12
2000 Bos-Col		39	4	1	12	80.1	352	90	48	48	14	1	7	5	24	3	71	3	0	1	6	.143	0	1-2	5	5.38
2000 Bos-Col	AL	25	1	0	10	44.2	198	48	25	25	8	0	5	2	15	1	36	1	0	1	3	.250	0	1-2	0	5.04
Colorado	NL	14	3	1	2	35.2	154	42	23	23	6	1	2	3	9	2	35	2	0	0	3	.000	0	0-0	5	5.80
6 ML YEARS		214	42	2	57	524	2256	547	316	295	88	13	28	15	160	20	352	12	2	28	27	.509	0	3-11	17	5.07

Jarrod Washburn

Pitches: Left **Bats:** Left **Pos:** SP-14   **Ht:** 6'1" **Wt:** 198 **Born:** 8/13/74 **Age:** 26

Year Team	Lg	G	GS	CG	GF	IP	BFP	H	R	ER	HR	SH	SF	HB	TBB	IBB	SO	WP	Bk	W	L	Pct.	ShO	Sv-Op	Hld	ERA
2000 Lk Elsinore *	A+	1	1	0	0	3	14	3	2	2	0	0	0	0	2	0	7	0	1	0	0	—	0	0--	—	6.00
Edmonton *	AAA	5	5	0	0	30.2	131	35	13	12	2	0	1	0	13	0	20	3	0	3	0	1.000	0	0--	—	3.52
1998 Anaheim	AL	15	11	0	0	74	317	70	40	38	11	2	3	3	27	1	48	0	0	6	3	.667	0	0-0	1	4.62
1999 Anaheim	AL	16	10	0	3	61.2	264	61	36	36	6	1	2	1	26	0	39	2	0	4	5	.444	0	0-0	1	5.25
2000 Anaheim	AL	14	14	0	0	84.1	340	64	38	35	16	1	3	1	37	0	49	1	0	7	2	.778	0	0-0	0	3.74
3 ML YEARS		45	35	0	3	220	921	195	114	109	33	4	8	5	90	1	136	3	0	17	10	.630	0	0-0	2	4.46

B.J. Waszgis

Bats: Right **Throws:** Right **Pos:** C-23; 1B-3   **Ht:** 6'2" **Wt:** 215 **Born:** 8/24/70 **Age:** 30

Year Team	Lg	G	AB	H	2B	3B	HR	(Hm	Rd)	TB	R	RBI	TBB	IBB	SO	HBP	SH	SF	SB	CS	SB%	GDP	Avg	OBP	SLG
1991 Bluefield	R+	12	35	8	1	0	3	—	—	18	8	8	5	0	11	1	0	0	3	0	1.00	1	.229	.341	.514
1992 Kane County	A	111	340	73	18	1	11	—	—	126	39	47	54	2	94	4	3	2	3	2	.60	8	.215	.328	.371
1993 Frederick	A+	31	109	27	4	0	3	—	—	40	12	9	9	0	30	2	0	1	1	1	.50	2	.248	.314	.367
Albany	A	86	300	92	25	3	8	—	—	147	45	52	27	0	55	6	0	5	4	0	1.00	8	.307	.370	.490
1994 Frederick	A+	122	426	120	16	3	21	—	—	205	76	100	65	2	94	5	3	4	6	1	.86	5	.282	.380	.481
1995 Bowie	AA	130	438	111	22	0	10	—	—	163	53	50	70	1	91	9	1	3	2	4	.33	5	.253	.365	.372
1996 Rochester	AAA	96	304	81	16	0	11	—	—	130	37	48	41	0	87	4	1	1	2	3	.40	7	.266	.360	.428
1997 Rochester	AAA	100	315	82	15	1	13	—	—	138	61	48	56	1	78	9	4	4	1	1	.50	5	.260	.383	.438
1998 Pawtucket	AAA	66	208	42	9	0	9	—	—	78	31	41	26	0	52	0	4	3	2	4	.33	7	.202	.287	.375
1999 Columbus	AAA	63	191	53	12	0	6	—	—	83	36	31	27	2	55	6	2	1	4	2	.67	4	.277	.382	.435
2000 Oklahoma	AAA	77	259	68	11	3	13	—	—	124	45	62	55	0	68	4	0	1	2	2	.50	8	.263	.398	.479
2000 Texas	AL	24	45	10	1	0	0	(0	0)	11	6	4	4	0	10	1	0	1	0	0	—	1	.222	.294	.244

Allen Watson

Pitches: Left **Bats:** Left **Pos:** RP-17   **Ht:** 6'1" **Wt:** 224 **Born:** 11/18/70 **Age:** 30

Year Team	Lg	G	GS	CG	GF	IP	BFP	H	R	ER	HR	SH	SF	HB	TBB	IBB	SO	WP	Bk	W	L	Pct.	ShO	Sv-Op	Hld	ERA
2000 Columbus *	AAA	5	1	0	0	6.2	26	3	2	1	1	0	0	0	2	0	4	1	0	0	1	.000	0	0--	—	1.35
Tampa *	A+	1	1	0	0	2	6	0	0	0	0	0	0	0	1	0	1	0	0	0	0	—	0	0--	—	0.00
Yankees *	R	1	1	0	0	1	4	1	0	0	0	0	0	0	0	0	2	0	0	0	0	—	0	0--	—	0.00
1993 St. Louis	NL	16	15	0	1	86	373	90	53	44	11	6	4	3	28	2	49	2	1	6	7	.462	0	0-1	0	4.60
1994 St. Louis	NL	22	22	0	0	115.2	523	130	73	71	15	7	0	8	53	0	74	2	2	6	5	.545	0	0-0	0	5.52
1995 St. Louis	NL	21	19	0	1	114.1	491	126	68	63	17	2	1	5	41	0	49	2	2	7	9	.438	0	0-0	0	4.96
1996 San Francisco	NL	29	29	2	0	185.2	793	189	105	95	28	18	9	5	69	2	128	9	2	8	12	.400	1	0-0	0	4.61
1997 Anaheim	AL	35	34	0	0	199	880	220	121	109	37	5	6	8	73	0	141	8	2	12	12	.500	0	0-0	0	4.93
1998 Anaheim	AL	28	14	1	4	92.1	421	122	67	62	12	0	6	3	34	0	64	6	1	6	7	.462	0	0-0	0	6.04
1999 NYM-Sea-NYY	AL	38	4	0	14	77	329	72	35	30	13	3	5	1	35	3	64	4	0	6	3	.667	0	1-2	2	3.51
2000 New York	AL	17	0	0	9	22	115	30	25	25	6	2	2	2	18	0	20	2	0	0	0	—	0	0-0	0	10.23
1999 New York	NL	14	4	0	6	39.2	173	36	18	18	5	3	4	1	22	3	32	2	0	2	2	.500	0	1-1	1	4.08
Seattle	AL	3	0	0	2	3	19	6	9	4	5	0	1	0	3	0	2	1	0	0	1	.000	0	0-0	0	12.00
New York	AL	21	0	0	6	34.1	137	30	8	8	3	0	0	0	10	0	30	1	0	4	0	1.000	0	0-1	1	2.10
8 ML YEARS		206	137	3	29	892	3925	979	547	499	139	43	33	35	351	7	589	35	10	51	55	.481	0	1-3	0	5.03

Mark Watson

Pitches: Left **Bats:** Right **Pos:** RP-6   **Ht:** 6'4" **Wt:** 215 **Born:** 1/23/74 **Age:** 27

Year Team	Lg	G	GS	CG	GF	IP	BFP	H	R	ER	HR	SH	SF	HB	TBB	IBB	SO	WP	Bk	W	L	Pct.	ShO	Sv-Op	Hld	ERA
1996 Helena	R+	13	13	0	0	60.1	262	59	43	32	2	1	2	1	28	0	68	7	0	5	2	.714	0	0--	—	4.77
1997 Beloit	A	8	7	0	0	32.1	153	40	33	24	3	0	3	1	20	0	33	3	0	0	3	.000	0	0--	—	6.68
Ogden	R+	10	10	1	0	47.2	202	44	26	22	4	1	2	0	19	0	49	2	0	4	3	.571	0	0--	—	4.15
1998 Columbus	A	31	12	1	8	97.2	408	95	53	44	10	3	3	3	32	0	77	6	2	3	4	.429	0	0--	—	4.05
Kinston	A+	1	1	0	0	6.1	26	3	4	0	0	0	1	0	2	0	8	0	0	1	0	1.000	0	0--	—	0.00
1999 Kinston	A+	11	4	0	1	43.1	163	28	7	5	1	0	0	0	10	0	40	1	1	6	0	1.000	0	0--	—	1.04
Akron	AA	19	17	0	1	110	500	143	64	53	9	6	7	6	38	0	57	6	2	9	8	.529	0	0--	—	4.34
2000 Buffalo	AAA	16	0	0	3	20.1	91	18	11	10	4	1	1	2	12	6	16	1	0	1	2	.333	0	1--	—	4.43
Tacoma	AAA	16	0	0	4	25	111	30	16	11	3	0	3	0	6	0	17	0	1	2	1	.667	0	0--	—	3.96
2000 Cleveland	AL	6	0	0	0	6.1	33	12	7	6	0	0	0	0	2	0	4	0	0	0	1	.000	0	0-0	0	8.53

Dave Weathers

Pitches: Right **Bats:** Right **Pos:** RP-69   **Ht:** 6'3" **Wt:** 230 **Born:** 9/25/69 **Age:** 31

Year Team	Lg	G	GS	CG	GF	IP	BFP	H	R	ER	HR	SH	SF	HB	TBB	IBB	SO	WP	Bk	W	L	Pct.	ShO	Sv-Op	Hld	ERA
1991 Toronto	AL	15	0	0	4	14.2	79	15	9	8	1	2	1	2	17	3	13	0	0	1	0	1.000	0	0-0	1	4.91
1992 Toronto	AL	2	0	0	0	3.1	15	5	3	3	1	0	0	0	2	0	3	0	0	0	0	—	0	0-0	0	8.10
1993 Florida	NL	14	6	0	2	45.2	202	57	26	26	3	2	0	1	13	1	34	6	0	2	3	.400	0	0-0	0	5.12
1994 Florida	NL	24	24	0	0	135	621	166	87	79	13	12	4	4	59	9	72	7	1	8	12	.400	0	0-0	0	5.27
1995 Florida	NL	28	15	0	0	90.1	419	104	68	60	8	7	3	4	52	3	60	3	0	4	5	.444	0	0-0	1	5.98
1996 Fla-NYY		42	12	0	9	88.2	409	108	60	54	8	6	2	6	42	5	53	3	0	2	4	.333	0	0-0	3	5.48
1997 NYY-Cle	AL	19	1	0	5	25.2	126	38	24	24	3	2	1	1	15	0	18	1	3	1	3	.250	0	0-1	0	8.42
1998 Cin-Mil	NL	44	9	0	9	110	492	130	69	60	6	6	2	3	41	3	94	2	2	6	5	.545	0	0-0	3	4.91
1999 Milwaukee	NL	63	0	0	14	93	414	102	49	48	14	4	4	2	38	3	74	1	1	7	4	.636	0	2-6	9	4.65
2000 Milwaukee	NL	69	0	0	23	76.1	320	73	29	26	7	4	1	2	32	8	50	0	0	3	5	.375	0	1-7	14	3.07
1996 New York	NL	31	8	0	8	71.1	319	85	41	36	5	1	4	2	28	4	40	2	0	2	2	.500	0	0-0	3	4.54
New York	AL	11	4	0	1	17.1	90	23	19	18	1	0	1	0	7	0	13	1	0	0	2	.000	0	0-0	0	9.35
1997 New York	AL	10	1	0	3	9	47	15	10	10	1	0	0	0	7	0	4	0	1	0	1	.000	0	0-1	0	10.00
Cleveland	AL	9	0	0	2	16.2	79	23	14	14	2	2	1	1	8	0	14	1	1	1	2	.333	0			7.56

Year Team	Lg	G	GS	CG	GF	IP	BFP	H	R	ER	HR	SH	SF	HB	TBB	IBB	SO	WP	Bk	W	L	Pct.	ShO	Sv-Op	Hld	ERA
1998 Cincinnati	NL	16	9	0	0	62.1	294	86	47	43	3	4	1	1	27	2	51	5	1	2	4	.333	0	0-0	0	6.21
Milwaukee	NL	28	0	0	9	47.2	198	44	22	17	3	2	1	2	14	1	43	2	1	4	1	.800	0	0-1	3	3.21
10 ML YEARS		320	67	0	66	682.2	3097	798	424	388	64	44	18	26	311	35	471	30	4	34	41	.453	0	3-15	31	5.12

Eric Weaver

Pitches: Right **Bats:** Right **Pos:** RP-17 **Ht:** 6'5" **Wt:** 230 **Born:** 8/4/73 **Age:** 27

Year Team	Lg	G	GS	CG	GF	IP	BFP	H	R	ER	HR	SH	SF	HB	TBB	IBB	SO	WP	Bk	W	L	Pct.	ShO	Sv-Op	Hld	ERA
2000 Edmonton *	AAA	34	0	0	28	37	164	37	20	17	5	1	1	2	13	0	36	3	0	1	2	.333	0	13--	—	4.14
1998 Los Angeles	NL	7	0	0	4	9.2	35	5	1	1	1	1	0	0	6	0	5	0	0	2	0	1.000	0	0-0	0	0.93
1999 Seattle	AL	8	0	0	2	9.1	52	14	12	11	2	0	0	0	8	1	14	5	0	0	1	.000	0	0-1	0	10.61
2000 Anaheim	AL	17	0	0	4	18.1	92	20	16	14	5	0	1	0	16	1	8	1	0	0	2	.000	0	0-1	2	6.87
3 ML YEARS		32	0	0	10	37.1	179	39	29	26	8	1	1	0	30	2	27	6	0	2	3	.400	0	0-2	2	6.27

Jeff Weaver

Pitches: Right **Bats:** Right **Pos:** SP-30; RP-1 **Ht:** 6'5" **Wt:** 210 **Born:** 8/22/76 **Age:** 24

Year Team	Lg	G	GS	CG	GF	IP	BFP	H	R	ER	HR	SH	SF	HB	TBB	IBB	SO	WP	Bk	W	L	Pct.	ShO	Sv-Op	Hld	ERA
1998 Jamestown	A-	3	3	0	0	12	44	6	4	2	0	0	0	1	1	0	12	0	1	1	0	1.000	0	0--	—	1.50
W Michigan	A	2	2	0	0	13	46	8	3	2	1	1	1	0	0	0	21	1	0	1	0	1.000	0	0--	—	1.38
1999 Jacksnville	AA	1	1	0	0	6	22	5	2	2	0	0	0	0	0	0	6	0	0	0	0	—	0	0--	—	3.00
2000 Toledo	AAA	1	1	0	0	5.1	22	5	2	2	1	0	0	0	1	0	10	0	0	0	1	.000	0	0--	—	3.38
1999 Detroit	AL	30	29	0	1	163.2	717	176	104	101	27	5	5	17	56	2	114	0	0	9	12	.429	0	0-0	0	5.55
2000 Detroit	AL	31	30	2	0	200	849	205	102	96	26	3	9	15	52	2	136	3	2	11	15	.423	0	0-0	0	4.32
2 ML YEARS		61	59	2	1	363.2	1566	381	206	197	53	8	14	32	108	4	250	3	2	20	27	.426	0	0-0	0	4.88

Ben Weber

Pitches: Right **Bats:** Right **Pos:** RP-19 **Ht:** 6'4" **Wt:** 180 **Born:** 11/17/69 **Age:** 31

Year Team	Lg	G	GS	CG	GF	IP	BFP	H	R	ER	HR	SH	SF	HB	TBB	IBB	SO	WP	Bk	W	L	Pct.	ShO	Sv-Op	Hld	ERA
1991 St.Cathrnes	A-	16	14	1	2	97.1	417	105	43	35	3	4	2	4	24	2	60	7	2	6	3	.667	0	0--	—	3.24
1992 Myrtle Bch	A	41	1	0	23	98.2	406	83	27	18	1	2	3	7	29	3	65	7	0	4	7	.364	0	6--	—	1.64
1993 Dunedin	A+	55	0	0	36	83.1	355	87	36	27	4	9	0	7	25	5	45	7	1	8	3	.727	0	12--	—	2.92
1994 Dunedin	A+	18	0	0	14	26.1	110	25	8	8	1	6	0	2	5	3	19	1	0	3	2	.600	0	3--	—	2.73
Knoxville	AA	25	10	0	6	95.2	400	103	49	40	8	3	1	2	16	0	55	4	0	4	3	.571	0	1--	—	3.76
1995 Knoxville	AA	12	1	0	6	25.1	104	26	12	11	3	0	0	0	6	0	16	0	0	4	1	.800	0	0--	—	3.91
Syracuse	AAA	25	15	0	3	91.2	403	111	62	55	10	2	1	3	27	1	38	5	0	4	5	.444	0	1--	—	5.40
1996 Salinas	IND	22	22	2	0	148.1	618	138	68	57	11	11	1	8	42	1	102	15	0	12	6	.667	0	0--	—	3.46
1999 Fresno	AAA	51	0	0	19	86.1	358	78	34	32	6	3	3	5	28	2	67	9	0	2	4	.333	0	8--	—	3.34
2000 Fresno	AAA	38	3	0	26	78	328	72	31	21	7	7	4	3	20	0	66	6	2	4	8	.333	0	7--	—	2.42
Erie	AA	2	0	0	0	1.2	11	3	5	3	1	0	0	0	2	0	2	0	0	0	1	.000	0	0--	—	16.20
2000 SF-Ana		19	0	0	3	22.2	103	28	19	16	0	0	0	1	6	1	14	2	0	1	1	.500	0	0-2	2	6.35
2000 San Francisco	NL	9	0	0	2	8	44	16	13	13	0	0	0	0	4	0	6	1	0	0	1	.000	0	0-2	1	14.63
Anaheim	AL	10	0	0	1	14.2	59	12	6	3	0	0	1	0	2	1	8	1	0	1	0	1.000	0	0-0	1	1.84

Lenny Webster

Bats: Right **Throws:** Right **Pos:** C-32; PH/PR-7 **Ht:** 5'9" **Wt:** 200 **Born:** 2/10/65 **Age:** 36

Year Team	Lg	G	AB	H	2B	3B	HR	Hm	Rd	TB	R	RBI	TBB	IBB	SO	HBP	SH	SF	SB	CS	SB%	GDP	Avg	OBP	SLG
1989 Minnesota	AL	14	20	6	2	0	0	(0	0)	8	3	1	3	0	2	0	0	0	0	0	—	0	.300	.391	.400
1990 Minnesota	AL	2	6	2	1	0	0	(0	0)	3	1	0	1	0	1	0	0	0	0	0	—	2	.333	.429	.500
1991 Minnesota	AL	18	34	10	1	0	3	(1	2)	20	7	8	6	0	10	0	0	0	0	0	—	2	.294	.390	.588
1992 Minnesota	AL	53	118	33	10	1	1	(1	0)	48	10	13	9	0	11	0	2	0	0	2	.00	3	.280	.331	.407
1993 Minnesota	AL	49	106	21	2	0	1	(1	0)	26	14	8	11	1	8	0	0	0	1	0	1.00	4	.198	.274	.245
1994 Montreal	NL	57	143	39	10	0	5	(2	3)	64	13	23	16	1	24	6	1	0	0	0	—	7	.273	.370	.448
1995 Philadelphia	NL	49	150	40	9	0	4	(1	3)	61	18	14	16	0	27	0	1	0	0	0	—	4	.267	.337	.407
1996 Baltimore	AL	78	174	40	10	0	2	(1	1)	56	18	17	25	2	21	2	1	1	0	0	—	10	.230	.332	.322
1997 Baltimore	AL	98	259	66	8	1	7	(3	4)	97	29	37	22	0	46	2	3	1	0	1	.00	10	.255	.317	.375
1998 Baltimore	AL	108	309	88	16	0	10	(6	4)	134	37	46	15	0	38	0	3	1	0	0	—	10	.285	.371	.434
1999 Bal-Bos	AL	22	50	6	1	0	0	(0	0)	7	1	4	10	0	7	2	0	0	0	0	—	0	.120	.290	.140
2000 Montreal	NL	39	81	17	3	0	0	(0	0)	20	6	5	6	1	14	0	0	0	0	0	—	5	.210	.264	.247
1999 Baltimore	AL	16	36	6	1	0	0	(0	0)	7	1	3	8	0	5	1	0	0	0	0	—	0	.167	.333	.194
Boston	AL	6	14	0	0	0	0	(0	0)	0	0	1	2	0	2	1	0	0	0	0	—	0	.000	.176	.000
12 ML YEARS		587	1450	368	73	2	33	(16	17)	544	157	176	140	5	209	12	11	4	1	3	.25	53	.254	.324	.375

John Wehner

Bats: Right **Throws:** Right **Pos:** 3B-16; PH/PR-7; LF-1 **Ht:** 6'3" **Wt:** 205 **Born:** 6/29/67 **Age:** 34

Year Team	Lg	G	AB	H	2B	3B	HR	Hm	Rd	TB	R	RBI	TBB	IBB	SO	HBP	SH	SF	SB	CS	SB%	GDP	Avg	OBP	SLG
2000 Nashville *	AAA	121	427	109	23	0	16	—	—	180	57	63	56	1	65	4	0	2	14	5	.74	11	.255	.346	.422
1991 Pittsburgh	NL	37	106	36	7	0	0	(0	0)	43	15	7	7	0	17	0	0	0	3	0	1.00	0	.340	.381	.406
1992 Pittsburgh	NL	55	123	22	6	0	0	(0	0)	28	11	4	12	2	22	0	2	0	3	0	1.00	4	.179	.252	.228
1993 Pittsburgh	NL	29	35	5	0	0	0	(0	0)	5	3	0	6	1	10	0	2	0	0	0	—	0	.143	.268	.143
1994 Pittsburgh	NL	2	4	1	1	0	0	(0	0)	2	1	3	0	0	0	0	0	0	0	0	—	0	.250	.250	.500
1995 Pittsburgh	NL	52	107	33	0	3	0	(0	0)	39	13	5	10	1	17	0	4	2	3	1	.75	2	.308	.361	.364
1996 Pittsburgh	NL	86	139	36	9	1	2	(1	1)	53	19	13	8	1	22	0	2	0	1	5	.17	3	.259	.299	.381
1997 Florida	NL	44	36	10	2	0	0	(0	0)	12	8	2	2	0	5	1	1	0	1	0	1.00	0	.278	.333	.333
1998 Florida	NL	53	88	20	2	0	0	(0	0)	22	10	5	7	0	12	0	0	0	1	0	1.00	3	.227	.281	.250

		BATTING																		BASERUNNING				PERCENTAGES		
Year Team	Lg	G	AB	H	2B	3B	HR	(Hm	Rd)	TB	R	RBI	TBB	IBB	SO	HBP	SH	SF		SB	CS	SB%	GDP		Avg	OBP	SLG
1999 Pittsburgh	NL	39	65	12	2	0	1	(0	1)	17	6	4	7	0	12	0	3	0		1	0	1.00	1		.185	.264	.262
2000 Pittsburgh	NL	21	50	15	3	0	1	(1	0)	21	10	9	4	0	6	0	1	0		0	0	—	1		.300	.352	.420
10 ML YEARS		418	753	190	32	4	4	(2	2)	242	96	52	63	5	124	1	15	3		13	6	.68	16		.252	.310	.321

Walt Weiss

Bats: Both **Throws:** Right **Pos:** SS-69; PH/PR-14　　　　　**Ht:** 6'0" **Wt:** 188 **Born:** 11/28/63 **Age:** 37

		BATTING																		BASERUNNING				PERCENTAGES		
Year Team	Lg	G	AB	H	2B	3B	HR	(Hm	Rd)	TB	R	RBI	TBB	IBB	SO	HBP	SH	SF		SB	CS	SB%	GDP		Avg	OBP	SLG
1987 Oakland	AL	16	26	12	4	0	0	(0	0)	16	3	1	2	0	2	0	1	0		1	2	.33	1		.462	.500	.615
1988 Oakland	AL	147	452	113	17	3	3	(0	3)	145	44	39	35	1	56	9	8	7		4	4	.50	9		.250	.312	.321
1989 Oakland	AL	84	236	55	11	0	3	(2	1)	75	30	21	21	0	39	1	5	0		6	1	.86	5		.233	.298	.318
1990 Oakland	AL	138	445	118	17	1	2	(1	1)	143	50	35	46	5	53	4	6	4		9	3	.75	7		.265	.337	.321
1991 Oakland	AL	40	133	30	6	1	0	(0	0)	38	15	13	12	0	14	0	1	2		6	0	1.00	3		.226	.286	.286
1992 Oakland	AL	103	316	67	5	2	0	(0	0)	76	36	21	43	1	39	1	11	4		6	3	.67	10		.212	.305	.241
1993 Florida	NL	158	500	133	14	2	1	(0	1)	154	50	39	79	13	73	3	5	4		7	3	.70	5		.266	.367	.308
1994 Colorado	NL	110	423	106	11	4	1	(0	1)	128	58	32	56	0	58	0	4	3		12	7	.63	6		.251	.336	.303
1995 Colorado	NL	137	427	111	17	3	1	(0	1)	137	65	25	98	8	57	5	6	1		15	3	.83	7		.260	.403	.321
1996 Colorado	NL	155	517	146	20	2	8	(5	3)	194	89	48	80	5	78	6	14	6		10	2	.83	9		.282	.381	.375
1997 Colorado	NL	121	393	106	23	5	4	(2	2)	151	52	38	66	3	56	2	7	1		5	2	.71	7		.270	.377	.384
1998 Atlanta	NL	96	347	97	18	2	0	(0	0)	119	64	27	59	0	53	3	12	3		7	1	.88	4		.280	.386	.343
1999 Atlanta	NL	110	279	63	13	4	2	(0	2)	90	38	29	35	1	48	3	6	4		7	3	.70	4		.226	.315	.323
2000 Atlanta	NL	80	192	50	6	2	0	(0	0)	60	29	18	26	1	32	3	3	3		1	1	.50	3		.260	.353	.313
14 ML YEARS		1495	4686	1207	182	31	25	(11	14)	1526	623	386	658	38	658	40	89	42		96	35	.73	75		.258	.351	.326

Bob Wells

Pitches: Right **Bats:** Right **Pos:** RP-76　　　　　**Ht:** 6'0" **Wt:** 200 **Born:** 11/1/66 **Age:** 34

		HOW MUCH HE PITCHED						WHAT HE GAVE UP											THE RESULTS						
Year Team	Lg	G	GS	CG	GF	IP	BFP	H	R	ER	HR	SH	SF	HB	TBB	IBB	SO	WP	Bk	W	L	Pct.	ShO	Sv-Op	Hld	ERA
1994 Phi-Sea		7	0	0	2	9	38	8	2	2	0	0	0	1	4	0	6	0	0	2	0	1.000	0	0-0	0	2.00
1995 Seattle	AL	30	4	0	3	76.2	358	88	51	49	11	1	5	3	39	3	38	1	0	4	3	.571	0	0-1	0	5.75
1996 Seattle	AL	36	16	1	6	130.2	574	141	78	77	25	3	4	6	46	5	94	0	0	12	7	.632	1	0-0	1	5.30
1997 Seattle	AL	46	1	0	19	67.1	304	88	44	43	11	1	2	3	18	1	51	1	0	2	0	1.000	0	2-4	5	5.75
1998 Seattle	AL	30	0	0	4	51.2	228	54	38	35	12	2	1	2	16	1	29	1	0	2	2	.500	0	0-1	1	6.10
1999 Minnesota	AL	76	0	0	18	87.1	364	79	41	37	8	5	3	5	28	4	44	4	0	8	3	.727	0	1-5	17	3.81
2000 Minnesota	AL	76	0	0	25	86.1	351	80	39	35	14	3	5	4	15	2	76	1	0	2	7	.000	0	10-20	11	3.65
1994 Philadelphia	NL	6	0	0	2	5	21	4	1	1	0	0	0	1	3	0	3	0	0	1	0	1.000	0	0-0	0	1.80
Seattle	AL	1	0	0	0	4	17	4	1	1	0	0	0	0	1	0	3	0	0	1	0	1.000	0	0-0	0	2.25
7 ML YEARS		301	21	1	77	509	2217	538	298	278	81	15	20	24	166	16	338	8	0	30	22	.577	1	13-31	35	4.92

David Wells

Pitches: Left **Bats:** Left **Pos:** SP-35　　　　　**Ht:** 6'4" **Wt:** 235 **Born:** 5/20/63 **Age:** 38

		HOW MUCH HE PITCHED						WHAT HE GAVE UP											THE RESULTS						
Year Team	Lg	G	GS	CG	GF	IP	BFP	H	R	ER	HR	SH	SF	HB	TBB	IBB	SO	WP	Bk	W	L	Pct.	ShO	Sv-Op	Hld	ERA
1987 Toronto	AL	18	2	0	6	29.1	132	37	14	13	0	1	0	0	12	0	32	4	0	4	3	.571	0	1-2	3	3.99
1988 Toronto	AL	41	0	0	15	64.1	279	65	36	33	12	2	2	2	31	9	56	6	2	3	5	.375	0	4-6	9	4.62
1989 Toronto	AL	54	0	0	19	86.1	352	66	25	23	5	2	2	0	28	7	78	6	3	7	4	.636	0	2-9	8	2.40
1990 Toronto	AL	43	25	0	8	189	759	165	72	66	14	9	2	2	45	3	115	7	1	11	6	.647	0	3-3	3	3.14
1991 Toronto	AL	40	28	2	3	198.1	811	188	88	82	24	6	6	2	49	1	106	10	3	15	10	.600	0	1-2	3	3.72
1992 Toronto	AL	41	14	0	14	120	529	138	84	72	16	3	4	8	36	6	62	3	1	7	9	.438	0	2-4	3	5.40
1993 Detroit	AL	32	30	0	0	187	776	183	93	87	26	3	3	7	42	6	139	13	0	11	9	.550	0	0-0	1	4.19
1994 Detroit	AL	16	16	5	0	111.1	464	113	54	49	13	3	1	2	24	6	71	5	0	5	7	.417	1	0-0	0	3.96
1995 Det-Cin		29	29	6	0	203	839	194	88	73	23	7	3	2	53	9	133	7	2	16	8	.667	1	0-0	0	3.24
1996 Baltimore	AL	34	34	3	0	224.1	946	247	132	128	32	8	14	7	51	7	130	4	2	11	14	.440	0	0-0	0	5.14
1997 New York	AL	32	32	5	0	218	922	239	109	102	24	7	3	6	45	0	156	8	0	16	10	.615	2	0-0	0	4.21
1998 New York	AL	30	30	8	0	214.1	851	195	86	83	29	2	2	1	29	0	163	2	0	18	4	.818	5	0-0	0	3.49
1999 Toronto	AL	34	34	7	0	231.2	987	246	132	124	32	6	6	6	62	2	169	1	0	17	10	.630	1	0-0	0	4.82
2000 Toronto	AL	35	35	9	0	229.2	972	266	115	105	23	6	7	8	31	0	166	9	1	20	8	.714	1	0-0	0	4.11
1995 Detroit	AL	18	18	3	0	130.1	539	120	54	44	17	3	2	2	37	5	83	6	1	10	3	.769	0	0-0	0	3.04
Cincinnati	NL	11	11	3	0	72.2	300	74	34	29	6	4	1	0	16	4	50	1	1	6	5	.545	1	0-0	0	3.59
14 ML YEARS		479	309	45	65	2306.2	9619	2342	1128	1040	273	66	55	53	538	56	1576	85	15	161	107	.601	10	13-26	30	4.06

Kip Wells

Pitches: Right **Bats:** Right **Pos:** SP-20　　　　　**Ht:** 6'3" **Wt:** 196 **Born:** 4/21/77 **Age:** 24

		HOW MUCH HE PITCHED						WHAT HE GAVE UP											THE RESULTS						
Year Team	Lg	G	GS	CG	GF	IP	BFP	H	R	ER	HR	SH	SF	HB	TBB	IBB	SO	WP	Bk	W	L	Pct.	ShO	Sv-Op	Hld	ERA
1999 Winston-Sal	A+	14	14	0	0	85.2	353	78	39	34	4	2	2	6	34	1	95	7	0	5	6	.455	0	0--	—	3.57
Birmingham	AA	11	11	0	0	70.1	283	49	24	23	5	0	0	4	31	0	44	1	1	8	2	.800	1	0--	—	2.94
2000 Charlotte	AAA	12	12	2	0	62	275	67	38	37	10	1	1	0	27	1	38	6	0	5	3	.625	1	0--	—	5.37
1999 Chicago	AL	7	7	0	0	35.2	153	33	17	16	2	0	2	3	15	0	29	1	2	4	1	.800	0	0-0	0	4.04
2000 Chicago	AL	20	20	0	0	98.2	468	126	76	66	15	1	3	2	58	4	71	7	0	6	9	.400	0	0-0	0	6.02
2 ML YEARS		27	27	0	0	134.1	621	159	93	82	17	1	5	5	73	4	100	8	2	10	10	.500	0	0-0	0	5.49

Vernon Wells

Bats: Right **Throws:** Right **Pos:** CF-3　　　　　**Ht:** 6'1" **Wt:** 210 **Born:** 12/8/78 **Age:** 22

		BATTING																		BASERUNNING				PERCENTAGES		
Year Team	Lg	G	AB	H	2B	3B	HR	(Hm	Rd)	TB	R	RBI	TBB	IBB	SO	HBP	SH	SF		SB	CS	SB%	GDP		Avg	OBP	SLG
1997 St.Cathrnes	A-	66	264	81	20	1	10	—	—	133	52	31	30	1	44	1	0	2		8	6	.57	2		.307	.377	.504
1998 Hagerstown	A	134	509	145	35	2	11	—	—	217	86	65	49	1	84	1	1	2		13	8	.62	8		.285	.348	.426

		BATTING																		BASERUNNING				PERCENTAGES		
Year Team	Lg	G	AB	H	2B	3B	HR	(Hm	Rd)	TB	R	RBI	TBB	IBB	SO	HBP	SH	SF		SB	CS	SB%	GDP		Avg	OBP	SLG
1999 Dunedin	A+	70	265	91	16	2	11	—	—	144	43	43	26	0	34	1	0	1		13	2	.87	6		.343	.403	.543
Knoxville	AA	26	106	36	6	2	3	—	—	55	18	17	12	1	15	0	0	2		6	2	.75	0		.340	.400	.519
Syracuse	AAA	33	129	40	8	1	4	—	—	62	20	21	10	0	22	1	0	3		5	1	.83	3		.310	.357	.481
2000 Syracuse	AAA	127	493	120	31	7	16	—	—	213	76	66	48	1	88	4	1	5		23	4	.85	8		.243	.313	.432
1999 Toronto	AL	24	88	23	5	0	1	(1	0)	31	8	8	4	0	18	0	0	0		1	1	.50	6		.261	.293	.352
2000 Toronto	AL	3	2	0	0	0	0	(0	0)	0	0	0	0	0	0	0	0	0		0	0	—	0		.000	.000	.000
2 ML YEARS		27	90	23	5	0	1	(1	0)	31	8	8	4	0	18	0	0	0		1	1	.50	6		.256	.287	.344

Turk Wendell

Pitches: Right **Bats:** Left **Pos:** RP-77   **Ht:** 6'2" **Wt:** 205 **Born:** 5/19/67 **Age:** 34

		HOW MUCH HE PITCHED						WHAT HE GAVE UP											THE RESULTS					
Year Team	Lg	G	GS	CG	GF	IP	BFP	H	R	ER	HR	SH	SF	HB	TBB	IBB	SO	WP	Bk	W	L	Pct.	ShO	Sv-Op	Hld	ERA
1993 Chicago	NL	7	4	0	1	22.2	98	24	13	11	0	2	0	0	8	1	15	1	1	1	2	.333	0	0-0	0	4.37
1994 Chicago	NL	6	2	0	1	14.1	76	22	20	19	3	2	1	0	10	1	9	1	0	0	1	.000	0	0-0	0	11.93
1995 Chicago	NL	43	0	0	17	60.1	270	71	35	33	11	3	3	2	24	4	50	1	0	3	1	.750	0	0-0	3	4.92
1996 Chicago	NL	70	0	0	49	79.1	339	58	26	25	8	3	1	3	44	4	75	3	2	4	5	.444	0	18-21	6	2.84
1997 ChC-NYM	NL	65	0	0	21	76.1	345	68	42	37	7	4	3	2	53	6	64	4	0	3	5	.375	0	5-7	2	4.36
1998 New York	NL	66	0	0	17	76.2	319	62	25	25	4	2	1	2	33	9	58	1	0	5	1	.833	0	4-8	11	2.93
1999 New York	NL	80	0	0	14	85.2	369	80	31	29	9	2	1	2	37	8	77	2	1	5	4	.556	0	3-6	21	3.05
2000 New York	NL	77	0	0	17	82.2	346	60	36	33	9	6	3	5	41	7	73	0	1	8	6	.571	0	1-5	16	3.59
1997 Chicago	NL	52	0	0	18	60	269	53	32	28	4	3	3	1	39	5	54	4	0	3	5	.375	0	4-5	2	4.20
New York	NL	13	0	0	3	16.1	76	15	10	9	3	1	0	1	14	1	10	0	0	0	0	—	0	1-2	0	4.96
8 ML YEARS		414	6	0	137	498	2162	445	228	212	51	24	13	16	250	40	421	13	5	29	25	.537	0	31-47	59	3.83

Don Wengert

Pitches: Right **Bats:** Right **Pos:** RP-10   **Ht:** 6'3" **Wt:** 205 **Born:** 11/6/69 **Age:** 31

		HOW MUCH HE PITCHED						WHAT HE GAVE UP											THE RESULTS					
Year Team	Lg	G	GS	CG	GF	IP	BFP	H	R	ER	HR	SH	SF	HB	TBB	IBB	SO	WP	Bk	W	L	Pct.	ShO	Sv-Op	Hld	ERA
2000 Richmond *	AAA	29	12	1	1	110.2	462	117	55	52	9	3	4	4	22	0	83	2	0	4	7	.364	0	0--	0	4.23
1995 Oakland	AL	19	0	0	10	29.2	129	30	14	11	3	1	1	1	12	2	16	1	0	1	1	.500	0	0-0	1	3.34
1996 Oakland	AL	36	25	1	2	161.1	725	200	102	100	29	3	5	6	60	5	75	4	0	7	11	.389	1	0-0	2	5.58
1997 Oakland	AL	49	12	1	16	134	612	177	96	90	21	5	7	8	41	4	68	2	0	5	11	.313	0	2-3	0	6.04
1998 SD-ChC	NL	31	6	0	9	63.1	288	76	38	37	10	1	0	3	28	0	46	1	0	1	5	.167	0	1-1	0	5.26
1999 Kansas City	AL	11	1	0	2	24.1	116	41	26	25	6	0	2	0	5	0	10	0	0	0	1	.000	0	0-3	1	9.25
2000 Atlanta	NL	10	0	0	6	10	47	12	9	8	2	0	0	0	5	0	7	0	0	0	0	—	0	0-0	0	7.20
1998 San Diego	NL	10	0	0	3	13.2	64	21	9	9	2	0	0	0	5	0	5	0	0	0	0	—	0	1-1	0	5.93
Chicago	NL	21	6	0	6	49.2	224	55	29	28	8	1	0	3	23	0	41	1	0	1	5	.167	0	0-0	0	5.07
6 ML YEARS		156	44	2	45	422.2	1917	536	285	271	71	10	15	18	151	11	222	8	0	14	30	.318	1	3-7	4	5.77

Jake Westbrook

Pitches: Right **Bats:** Right **Pos:** SP-2; RP-1   **Ht:** 6'3" **Wt:** 185 **Born:** 9/29/77 **Age:** 23

		HOW MUCH HE PITCHED						WHAT HE GAVE UP											THE RESULTS					
Year Team	Lg	G	GS	CG	GF	IP	BFP	H	R	ER	HR	SH	SF	HB	TBB	IBB	SO	WP	Bk	W	L	Pct.	ShO	Sv-Op	Hld	ERA
1996 Rockies	R	11	11	0	0	62.2	271	66	33	20	0	3	1	8	14	0	57	4	0	4	2	.667	0	0--	—	2.87
Portland	A-	4	4	0	0	24.2	99	22	8	7	1	0	0	1	5	0	19	2	0	1	1	.500	0	0--	—	2.55
1997 Asheville	A	28	27	3	0	170	736	176	93	81	16	5	6	15	55	0	92	3	0	14	11	.560	2	0--	—	4.29
1998 Jupiter	A+	27	27	2	0	171	720	169	70	62	11	5	3	11	60	0	79	4	0	11	6	.647	0	0--	—	3.26
1999 Harrisburg	AA	27	27	2	0	174.2	748	180	88	76	14	12	3	13	63	1	90	2	1	11	5	.688	2	0--	—	3.92
2000 Columbus	AAA	16	15	2	0	89	393	94	53	46	3	4	1	4	38	0	61	2	0	5	7	.417	0	0--	—	4.65
2000 New York	AL	3	2	0	1	6.2	38	15	10	10	1	0	2	0	4	1	1	0	0	0	2	.000	0	0--	0	13.50

John Wetteland

Pitches: Right **Bats:** Right **Pos:** RP-62   **Ht:** 6'2" **Wt:** 215 **Born:** 8/21/66 **Age:** 34

		HOW MUCH HE PITCHED						WHAT HE GAVE UP											THE RESULTS					
Year Team	Lg	G	GS	CG	GF	IP	BFP	H	R	ER	HR	SH	SF	HB	TBB	IBB	SO	WP	Bk	W	L	Pct.	ShO	Sv-Op	Hld	ERA
1989 Los Angeles	NL	31	12	0	7	102.2	411	81	46	43	8	4	2	0	34	4	96	16	1	5	8	.385	0	1-1	1	3.77
1990 Los Angeles	NL	22	5	0	7	43	190	44	28	23	6	1	1	4	17	3	36	8	0	2	4	.333	0	0-1	0	4.81
1991 Los Angeles	NL	6	0	0	3	9	36	5	2	0	0	1	0	1	3	0	9	1	0	1	0	1.000	0	0-0	0	0.00
1992 Montreal	NL	67	0	0	58	83.1	347	64	27	27	6	5	1	4	36	3	99	4	0	4	4	.500	0	37-46	0	2.92
1993 Montreal	NL	70	0	0	58	85.1	344	58	17	13	3	5	1	2	28	3	113	7	0	9	3	.750	0	43-49	0	1.37
1994 Montreal	NL	52	0	0	43	63.2	261	46	22	20	5	5	4	3	21	4	68	0	0	4	6	.400	0	25-35	0	2.83
1995 New York	AL	60	0	0	56	61.1	233	40	22	20	6	1	2	0	14	2	66	1	0	1	5	.167	0	31-37	0	2.93
1996 New York	AL	62	0	0	58	63.2	265	54	23	20	9	1	2	0	21	4	69	1	0	2	3	.400	0	**43-47**	0	2.83
1997 Texas	AL	61	0	0	58	65	259	43	18	14	5	1	1	0	21	3	63	1	0	7	2	.778	0	31-37	0	1.94
1998 Texas	AL	63	0	0	59	62	249	47	17	14	6	2	2	0	14	1	72	1	0	3	1	.750	0	42-47	0	2.03
1999 Texas	AL	62	0	0	59	66	281	67	30	27	9	1	5	0	19	1	60	0	0	4	4	.500	0	**43-50**	0	3.68
2000 Texas	AL	62	0	0	57	60	269	67	35	28	10	4	4	2	24	2	53	0	0	6	5	.545	0	34-43	0	4.20
12 ML YEARS		618	17	0	523	765	3145	616	287	249	73	30	26	16	252	30	804	40	1	48	45	.516	0	330-393	1	2.93

Dan Wheeler

Pitches: Right **Bats:** Right **Pos:** RP-9; SP-2   **Ht:** 6'3" **Wt:** 222 **Born:** 12/10/77 **Age:** 23

		HOW MUCH HE PITCHED						WHAT HE GAVE UP											THE RESULTS					
Year Team	Lg	G	GS	CG	GF	IP	BFP	H	R	ER	HR	SH	SF	HB	TBB	IBB	SO	WP	Bk	W	L	Pct.	ShO	Sv-Op	Hld	ERA
1997 Hudson Val	A-	15	15	0	0	84	351	75	36	28	2	1	1	3	17	0	81	4	2	6	7	.462	0	0--	—	3.00
1998 Chston-SC	A	29	29	3	0	181	763	206	96	89	16	7	6	11	29	0	136	4	0	12	14	.462	1	0--	—	4.43
1999 Orlando	AA	9	9	0	0	58	236	56	27	21	7	0	2	4	8	0	53	1	1	3	0	1.000	0	0--	—	3.26
Durham	AAA	14	14	2	0	82.1	369	103	59	45	16	1	3	4	25	0	58	1	0	7	5	.583	1	0--	—	4.92
2000 Durham	AAA	26	26	0	0	150.1	668	183	109	94	35	2	6	7	42	1	91	4	0	5	11	.313	0	0--	—	5.63

		HOW MUCH HE PITCHED				WHAT HE GAVE UP								THE RESULTS					
Year Team	Lg	G GS CG GF	IP	BFP	H R ER	HR SH SF HB	TBB IBB	SO	WP Bk	W L	Pct.	ShO	Sv-Op	Hld	ERA
1999 Tampa Bay	AL	6 6 0 0	30.2	136	35 20 20	7 1 0 0	13 1	32	1 0	0 4	.000	0	0-0	0	5.87
2000 Tampa Bay	AL	11 2 0 6	23	111	29 14 14	2 1 1 2	11 2	17	2 0	1 1	.500	0	0-1	1	5.48
2 ML YEARS		17 8 0 6	53.2	247	64 34 34	9 2 1 2	24 3	49	3 0	1 5	.167	0	0-1	1	5.70

Matt Whisenant

Pitches: Left **Bats:** Right **Pos:** RP-24   **Ht:** 6'3" **Wt:** 215 **Born:** 6/8/71 **Age:** 30

		HOW MUCH HE PITCHED				WHAT HE GAVE UP								THE RESULTS					
Year Team	Lg	G GS CG GF	IP	BFP	H R ER	HR SH SF HB	TBB IBB	SO	WP Bk	W L	Pct.	ShO	Sv-Op	Hld	ERA
2000 Las Vegas *	AAA	33 0 0 8	39	190	49 26 23	3 0 0 3	26 2	24	4 0	0 3	.000	0	0- -	—	5.31
1997 Fla-KC		28 0 0 5	21.2	105	19 13 11	0 1 0 3	18 0	20	3 0	1 0	1.000	0	0-0	5	4.57
1998 Kansas City	AL	70 0 0 23	60.2	267	61 37 33	3 1 5 3	33 2	45	9 0	2 1	.667	0	2-5	16	4.90
1999 KC-SD		67 0 0 25	54.1	244	50 34 34	4 1 0 7	36 2	37	1 0	4 5	.444	0	1-5	11	5.63
2000 San Diego	NL	24 0 0 12	21.1	95	16 12 9	1 1 0 2	17 1	12	5 0	2 2	.500	0	0-3	1	3.80
1997 Florida	NL	4 0 0 2	2.2	19	4 6 5	0 1 0 0	6 0	4	0 0	0 0	—	0	0-0	0	16.88
Kansas City	AL	24 0 0 3	19	86	15 7 6	0 0 0 3	12 0	16	3 0	1 0	1.000	0	0-0	5	2.84
1999 Kansas City	AL	48 0 0 21	39.2	184	40 28 28	4 1 0 7	26 1	27	1 0	4 4	.500	0	1-4	6	6.35
San Diego	NL	19 0 0 4	14.2	60	10 6 6	0 0 0 0	10 1	10	0 0	0 1	.000	0	0-1	5	3.68
4 ML YEARS		189 0 0 65	158	711	146 96 87	8 4 7 13	104 5	114	18 0	9 8	.529	0	3-13	33	4.96

Devon White

Bats: Both **Throws:** Right **Pos:** CF-40; PH/PR-9   **Ht:** 6'2" **Wt:** 190 **Born:** 12/29/62 **Age:** 38

		BATTING															BASERUNNING				PERCENTAGES		
Year Team	Lg	G	AB	H	2B	3B	HR	(Hm Rd)	TB	R	RBI	TBB	IBB	SO	HBP	SH	SF	SB	CS	SB%	GDP	Avg	OBP	SLG
2000 San Berndno *	A+	2	5	2	1	0	0	— —	3	2	1	1	0	1	1	0	0	0	0	0	0	.400	.571	.600
1985 California	AL	21	7	1	0	0	0	(0 0)	1	7	0	1	0	3	1	0	0	3	1	.75	0	.143	.333	.143
1986 California	AL	29	51	12	1	1	1	(0 1)	18	8	3	6	0	8	0	0	0	6	0	1.00	0	.235	.316	.353
1987 California	AL	159	639	168	33	5	24	(11 13)	283	103	87	39	2	135	2	14	2	32	11	.74	8	.263	.306	.443
1988 California	AL	122	455	118	22	2	11	(3 8)	177	76	51	23	1	84	2	5	1	17	8	.68	5	.259	.297	.389
1989 California	AL	156	636	156	18	13	12	(9 3)	236	86	56	31	3	129	2	7	2	44	16	.73	12	.245	.282	.371
1990 California	AL	125	443	96	17	3	11	(5 6)	152	57	44	44	5	116	3	10	0	21	6	.78	6	.217	.290	.343
1991 Toronto	AL	156	642	181	40	10	17	(9 8)	292	110	60	55	1	135	7	5	6	33	10	.77	7	.282	.342	.455
1992 Toronto	AL	153	641	159	26	7	17	(7 10)	250	98	60	47	0	133	5	0	3	37	4	.90	9	.248	.303	.390
1993 Toronto	AL	146	598	163	42	6	15	(10 5)	262	116	52	57	1	127	7	3	3	34	4	.89	3	.273	.341	.438
1994 Toronto	AL	100	403	109	24	6	13	(5 8)	184	67	49	21	3	80	5	4	2	11	3	.79	4	.270	.313	.457
1995 Toronto	AL	101	427	121	23	5	10	(4 6)	184	61	53	29	1	97	5	1	2	11	2	.85	5	.283	.334	.431
1996 Florida	NL	146	552	151	37	6	17	(5 12)	251	77	84	38	6	99	8	4	9	22	6	.79	6	.274	.325	.455
1997 Florida	NL	74	265	65	13	1	6	(4 2)	98	37	34	32	2	65	7	0	4	13	5	.72	3	.245	.338	.370
1998 Arizona	NL	146	563	157	32	1	22	(11 11)	257	84	85	42	4	102	9	7	6	22	8	.73	9	.279	.335	.456
1999 Los Angeles	NL	134	474	127	20	2	14	(8 6)	193	60	68	39	2	88	11	0	2	19	5	.79	10	.268	.337	.407
2000 Los Angeles	NL	47	158	42	5	1	4	(2 2)	61	26	13	9	0	30	1	0	0	3	6	.33	3	.266	.310	.386
16 ML YEARS		1815	6954	1826	353	69	194	(93 101)	2899	1073	799	513	31	1431	75	60	46	328	95	.78	92	.263	.318	.417

Gabe White

Pitches: Left **Bats:** Left **Pos:** RP-68   **Ht:** 6'2" **Wt:** 200 **Born:** 11/20/71 **Age:** 29

		HOW MUCH HE PITCHED				WHAT HE GAVE UP								THE RESULTS					
Year Team	Lg	G GS CG GF	IP	BFP	H R ER	HR SH SF HB	TBB IBB	SO	WP Bk	W L	Pct.	ShO	Sv-Op	Hld	ERA
1994 Montreal	NL	7 5 0 2	23.2	106	24 16 16	4 1 1 1	11 0	17	0 0	1 1	.500	0	1-1	0	6.08
1995 Montreal	NL	19 1 0 8	25.2	115	26 21 20	7 2 1 1	9 0	25	0 0	1 2	.333	0	0-0	0	7.01
1997 Cincinnati	NL	12 6 0 2	41	168	39 20 20	6 3 2 1	8 1	25	0 0	2 2	.500	0	1-1	3	4.39
1998 Cincinnati	NL	69 3 0 29	98.2	404	86 46 44	17 2 2 1	27 6	83	3 0	5 5	.500	0	9-13	6	4.01
1999 Cincinnati	NL	50 0 0 18	61	261	68 31 30	13 2 1 2	14 1	61	0 0	1 2	.333	0	0-1	3	4.43
2000 Cin-Col	NL	68 0 0 17	84	329	64 23 22	6 2 6 3	15 2	84	1 0	11 2	.846	0	5-9	19	2.36
2000 Cincinnati	NL	1 0 0 0	1	6	2 2 2	1 0 0 0	1 0	2	0 0	0 0	—	0	0-0	0	18.00
Colorado	NL	67 0 0 17	83	323	62 21 20	5 2 6 3	14 2	82	1 0	11 2	.846	0	5-9	19	2.17
6 ML YEARS		225 15 0 76	334	1383	307 157 152	53 12 15 9	84 10	295	4 0	21 14	.600	0	16-25	31	4.10

Rick White

Pitches: Right **Bats:** Right **Pos:** RP-66   **Ht:** 6'4" **Wt:** 230 **Born:** 12/23/68 **Age:** 32

		HOW MUCH HE PITCHED				WHAT HE GAVE UP								THE RESULTS					
Year Team	Lg	G GS CG GF	IP	BFP	H R ER	HR SH SF HB	TBB IBB	SO	WP Bk	W L	Pct.	ShO	Sv-Op	Hld	ERA
1994 Pittsburgh	NL	43 5 0 23	75.1	317	79 35 32	9 7 5 6	17 3	38	2 2	4 5	.444	0	6-9	3	3.82
1995 Pittsburgh	NL	15 9 0 2	55	247	66 33 29	3 3 3 2	18 0	29	2 0	2 3	.400	0	0-0	0	4.75
1998 Tampa Bay	AL	38 3 0 12	68.2	289	66 32 29	8 0 3 2	23 2	39	3 0	2 6	.250	0	0-0	0	3.80
1999 Tampa Bay	AL	63 1 0 11	108	480	132 56 49	8 2 5 1	38 5	81	3 0	5 3	.625	0	0-2	4	4.08
2000 TB-NYM		66 0 0 14	99.2	420	83 44 39	9 1 3 7	38 5	67	3 0	5 9	.357	0	3-7	6	3.52
2000 Tampa Bay	AL	44 0 0 8	71.1	293	57 30 27	7 1 2 5	26 3	47	3 0	3 6	.333	0	2-5	2	3.41
New York	NL	22 0 0 6	28.1	127	26 14 12	2 0 1 2	12 2	20	0 0	2 3	.400	0	1-2	2	3.81
5 ML YEARS		225 18 0 62	406.2	1753	426 200 178	37 13 19 18	134 15	254	13 2	18 26	.409	0	9-18	13	3.94

Rondell White

Bats: Right **Throws:** Right **Pos:** LF-92; PH/PR-2   **Ht:** 6'0" **Wt:** 210 **Born:** 2/23/72 **Age:** 29

		BATTING															BASERUNNING				PERCENTAGES		
Year Team	Lg	G	AB	H	2B	3B	HR	(Hm Rd)	TB	R	RBI	TBB	IBB	SO	HBP	SH	SF	SB	CS	SB%	GDP	Avg	OBP	SLG
1993 Montreal	NL	23	73	19	3	1	2	(1 1)	30	9	15	7	0	16	0	2	1	1	2	.33	2	.260	.321	.411
1994 Montreal	NL	40	97	27	10	1	2	(1 1)	45	16	13	9	0	18	3	0	0	1	1	.50	1	.278	.358	.464
1995 Montreal	NL	130	474	140	33	4	13	(6 7)	220	87	57	41	1	87	6	0	4	25	5	.83	11	.295	.356	.464
1996 Montreal	NL	88	334	98	19	4	6	(2 4)	143	35	41	22	0	53	2	0	1	14	6	.70	11	.293	.340	.428
1997 Montreal	NL	151	592	160	29	5	28	(9 19)	283	84	82	31	3	111	10	1	4	16	8	.67	18	.270	.316	.478

BATTING																			BASERUNNING				PERCENTAGES		
Year Team	Lg	G	AB	H	2B	3B	HR	(Hm	Rd)	TB	R	RBI	TBB	IBB	SO	HBP	SH	SF	SB	CS	SB%	GDP	Avg	OBP	SLG
1998 Montreal	NL	97	357	107	21	2	17	(9	8)	183	54	58	30	2	57	7	0	3	16	7	.70	7	.300	.363	.513
1999 Montreal	NL	138	539	168	26	6	22	(10	12)	272	83	64	32	2	85	11	0	6	10	6	.63	17	.312	.359	.505
2000 Mon-ChC	NL	94	357	111	26	0	13	(3	10)	176	59	61	33	0	79	4	0	2	5	3	.63	4	.311	.374	.493
2000 Montreal	NL	75	290	89	24	0	11	(3	8)	146	52	54	28	0	67	2	0	2	5	1	.83	4	.307	.370	.503
Chicago	NL	19	67	22	2	0	2	(0	2)	30	7	7	5	0	12	2	0	0	0	2	.00	0	.328	.392	.448
8 ML YEARS		761	2823	830	167	23	103	(41	62)	1352	427	391	205	8	506	43	3	21	88	38	.70	71	.294	.349	.479

Mark Whiten

Bats: Both **Throws:** Right **Pos:** CF-5; PH/PR-3   **Ht:** 6'3" **Wt:** 235 **Born:** 11/25/66 **Age:** 34

BATTING																			BASERUNNING				PERCENTAGES		
Year Team	Lg	G	AB	H	2B	3B	HR	(Hm	Rd)	TB	R	RBI	TBB	IBB	SO	HBP	SH	SF	SB	CS	SB%	GDP	Avg	OBP	SLG
2000 Buffalo *	AAA	98	355	98	27	1	10	(—	—)	157	59	59	33	1	72	0	0	1	5	2	.71	6	.276	.337	.442
1990 Toronto	AL	33	88	24	1	1	2	(1	1)	33	12	7	7	0	14	0	1	0	2	0	1.00	1	.273	.323	.375
1991 Tor-Cle	AL	116	407	99	18	7	9	(4	5)	158	46	45	30	2	85	3	0	5	4	3	.57	13	.243	.297	.388
1992 Cleveland	AL	148	508	129	19	4	9	(6	3)	183	73	43	72	10	102	2	3	3	16	12	.57	12	.254	.347	.360
1993 St. Louis	NL	152	562	142	13	4	25	(12	13)	238	81	99	58	9	110	2	0	4	15	8	.65	11	.253	.323	.423
1994 St. Louis	NL	92	334	98	18	2	14	(6	8)	162	57	53	37	9	75	1	0	2	10	5	.67	8	.293	.364	.485
1995 Bos-Phi		92	320	77	13	1	12	(5	7)	128	51	47	39	1	86	1	0	1	8	0	1.00	9	.241	.324	.400
1996 Phi-Atl-Sea		136	412	108	20	1	22	(9	13)	196	76	71	70	6	127	3	0	1	17	9	.65	12	.262	.372	.476
1997 New York	AL	69	215	57	11	0	5	(4	1)	83	34	24	30	5	47	2	1	0	4	2	.67	6	.265	.360	.386
1998 Cleveland	AL	88	226	64	14	0	6	(3	3)	96	31	29	29	0	60	3	1	0	2	1	.67	7	.283	.372	.425
1999 Cleveland	AL	8	25	4	1	0	1	(0	1)	8	2	4	3	0	4	0	0	0	0	0	—	1	.160	.250	.320
2000 Cleveland	AL	6	7	2	1	0	0	(0	0)	3	2	1	3	0	2	0	0	0	0	0	—	0	.286	.500	.429
1991 Toronto	AL	46	149	33	4	3	2	(2	0)	49	12	19	11	1	35	1	0	3	0	1	.00	5	.221	.274	.329
Cleveland		70	258	66	14	4	7	(2	5)	109	34	26	19	1	50	2	0	2	4	2	.67	8	.256	.310	.422
1995 Boston		32	108	20	3	0	1	(0	1)	26	13	10	8	0	23	0	0	1	1	0	1.00	5	.185	.239	.241
Philadelphia	NL	60	212	57	10	1	11	(5	6)	102	38	37	31	1	63	1	0	0	7	0	1.00	4	.269	.365	.481
1996 Philadelphia	NL	60	182	43	8	0	7	(4	3)	72	33	21	33	2	62	1	0	0	13	3	.81	9	.236	.356	.396
Atlanta	NL	36	90	23	5	1	3	(1	2)	39	12	17	16	0	25	0	0	1	2	5	.29	2	.256	.364	.433
Seattle	AL	40	140	42	7	0	12	(4	8)	85	31	33	21	4	40	2	0	0	2	1	.67	1	.300	.399	.607
11 ML YEARS		940	3104	804	129	20	105	(50	55)	1288	465	423	378	42	712	17	5	17	78	40	.66	81	.259	.341	.415

Matt Whiteside

Pitches: Right **Bats:** Right **Pos:** RP-28   **Ht:** 6'0" **Wt:** 200 **Born:** 8/8/67 **Age:** 33

HOW MUCH HE PITCHED							WHAT HE GAVE UP												THE RESULTS					
Year Team	Lg	G	GS	CG	GF	IP	BFP	H	R	ER	HR	SH	SF	HB	TBB	IBB	SO	WP	Bk	W	L	Pct.	ShO	Sv-Op	Hld	ERA
2000 Las Vegas *	AAA	23	1	0	5	30.2	144	34	21	18	6	2	2	3	15	2	31	1	1	2	5	.286	0	0- -	—	5.28
1992 Texas	AL	20	0	0	8	28	118	26	8	6	1	0	1	0	11	2	13	2	0	1	1	.500	0	4-4	0	1.93
1993 Texas	AL	60	0	0	10	73	305	78	37	35	7	2	1	1	23	6	39	0	2	2	1	.667	0	1-5	14	4.32
1994 Texas	AL	47	0	0	16	61	272	68	40	34	6	3	2	1	28	3	37	1	0	2	2	.500	0	1-3	7	5.02
1995 Texas	AL	40	0	0	18	53	223	48	24	24	5	2	3	1	19	2	46	4	0	5	4	.556	0	3-4	7	4.08
1996 Texas	AL	14	0	0	7	32.1	148	43	24	24	8	1	2	0	11	1	15	1	0	0	1	.000	0	0-0	1	6.68
1997 Texas	AL	42	1	0	8	72.2	323	85	45	41	4	2	5	3	26	3	44	3	2	4	1	.800	0	0-4	2	5.08
1998 Philadelphia	NL	10	0	0	1	18	85	27	18	17	6	0	0	0	5	0	14	0	1	1	1	.500	0	0-0	0	8.50
1999 San Diego	NL	10	0	0	4	11	55	19	17	17	1	1	1	0	5	0	9	1	0	1	0	1.000	0	0-0	1	13.91
2000 San Diego	NL	28	0	0	9	37	159	32	21	17	6	2	1	1	17	3	27	2	1	2	3	.400	0	0-0	6	4.14
9 ML YEARS		271	1	0	81	386	1688	426	234	215	44	13	16	7	145	20	244	14	6	18	14	.563	0	9-20	37	5.01

Bob Wickman

Pitches: Right **Bats:** Right **Pos:** RP-69   **Ht:** 6'1" **Wt:** 234 **Born:** 2/6/69 **Age:** 32

HOW MUCH HE PITCHED							WHAT HE GAVE UP												THE RESULTS					
Year Team	Lg	G	GS	CG	GF	IP	BFP	H	R	ER	HR	SH	SF	HB	TBB	IBB	SO	WP	Bk	W	L	Pct.	ShO	Sv-Op	Hld	ERA
1992 New York	AL	8	8	0	0	50.1	213	51	25	23	2	1	3	2	20	0	21	3	0	6	1	.857	0	0-0	0	4.11
1993 New York	AL	41	19	1	9	140	629	156	82	72	13	4	1	5	69	7	70	2	0	14	4	.778	1	4-8	2	4.63
1994 New York	AL	53	0	0	19	70	286	54	26	24	3	0	5	1	27	3	56	2	0	5	4	.556	0	6-10	11	3.09
1995 New York	AL	63	1	0	14	80	347	77	38	36	6	4	1	5	33	3	51	2	0	2	4	.333	0	1-10	21	4.05
1996 NYY-Mil		70	0	0	18	95.2	429	106	50	47	10	2	4	1	44	5	75	4	0	7	1	.875	0	0-4	10	4.42
1997 Milwaukee	AL	74	0	0	20	95.2	405	89	32	29	8	6	2	3	41	7	78	8	0	7	6	.538	0	1-5	28	2.73
1998 Milwaukee	NL	72	0	0	51	82.1	357	79	38	34	5	10	3	4	39	2	71	1	0	6	9	.400	0	25-32	9	3.72
1999 Milwaukee	NL	71	0	0	63	74.1	331	75	31	28	6	3	2	2	38	6	60	2	0	3	8	.273	0	37-45	0	3.39
2000 Mil-Cle		69	0	0	60	72.2	309	64	30	25	1	3	1	1	32	5	55	2	0	3	5	.375	0	30-37	0	3.10
1996 New York	AL	58	0	0	14	79	358	94	44	41	7	1	4	5	34	1	61	3	0	4	1	.800	0	0-3	6	4.67
Milwaukee		12	0	0	4	16.2	71	12	6	6	3	1	0	0	10	2	14	1	0	3	0	1.000	0	0-1	4	3.24
2000 Milwaukee	NL	43	0	0	36	46	194	37	18	15	1	0	1	1	20	2	44	2	0	2	2	.500	0	16-20	0	2.93
Cleveland	AL	26	0	0	24	26.2	115	27	12	10	0	3	0	0	12	3	11	0	0	1	3	.250	0	14-17	0	3.38
9 ML YEARS		521	28	1	254	761	3306	751	352	318	54	33	22	28	343	36	537	26	0	53	42	.558	1	104-151	81	3.76

Chris Widger

Bats: R **Throws:** R **Pos:** C-91; PH/PR-3; DH-2; 1B-2; RF-1   **Ht:** 6'2" **Wt:** 215 **Born:** 5/21/71 **Age:** 30

BATTING																			BASERUNNING				PERCENTAGES		
Year Team	Lg	G	AB	H	2B	3B	HR	(Hm	Rd)	TB	R	RBI	TBB	IBB	SO	HBP	SH	SF	SB	CS	SB%	GDP	Avg	OBP	SLG
1995 Seattle	AL	23	45	9	0	0	1	(1	0)	12	2	2	3	0	11	0	0	1	0	0	—	0	.200	.245	.267
1996 Seattle	AL	8	11	2	0	0	0	(0	0)	2	1	0	0	0	5	1	0	0	0	0	—	0	.182	.250	.182
1997 Montreal	NL	91	278	65	20	3	7	(4	3)	112	30	37	22	1	59	1	2	2	2	0	1.00	7	.234	.290	.403
1998 Montreal	NL	125	417	97	18	1	15	(6	9)	162	36	53	29	2	85	0	0	2	6	1	.86	5	.233	.281	.388
1999 Montreal	NL	124	383	101	24	1	14	(11	3)	169	42	56	28	0	86	7	0	1	1	4	.20	5	.264	.325	.441
2000 Mon-Sea		96	292	68	17	2	13	(6	7)	128	32	35	30	3	63	1	0	1	2	3	.33	5	.233	.306	.438
2000 Montreal	NL	86	281	67	17	2	12	(6	6)	124	31	34	29	3	61	1	0	1	1	2	.33	5	.238	.311	.441
Seattle	AL	10	11	1	0	0	1	(0	1)	4	1	1	1	0	2	0	0	0	1	1	.50	0	.091	.167	.364
6 ML YEARS		467	1426	342	79	7	50	(28	22)	585	143	183	112	6	309	10	2	7	10	7	.59	22	.240	.298	.410

Marc Wilkins

Pitches: Right **Bats:** Right **Pos:** RP-52 | **Ht:** 5'11" **Wt:** 212 **Born:** 10/21/70 **Age:** 30

		HOW MUCH HE PITCHED						WHAT HE GAVE UP												THE RESULTS						
Year Team	Lg	G	GS	CG	GF	IP	BFP	H	R	ER	HR	SH	SF	HB	TBB	IBB	SO	WP	Bk	W	L	Pct.	ShO	Sv-Op	Hld	ERA
2000 Nashville *	AAA	17	4	0	7	38	172	34	23	21	4	3	0	4	24	1	33	7	0	2	3	.400	0	3--	—	4.97
1996 Pittsburgh	NL	47	2	0	11	75	331	75	36	32	6	3	4	6	36	6	62	5	0	4	3	.571	0	1-5	4	3.84
1997 Pittsburgh	NL	70	0	0	21	75.2	310	65	33	31	7	4	0	4	33	2	47	5	0	9	5	.643	0	2-4	15	3.69
1998 Pittsburgh	NL	16	0	0	6	15.1	67	13	6	6	1	0	1	2	9	2	17	1	1	0	0	—	0	0-1	4	3.52
1999 Pittsburgh	NL	46	0	0	14	51	227	49	28	24	3	4	2	4	26	1	44	4	1	2	3	.400	0	0-0	8	4.24
2000 Pittsburgh	NL	52	0	0	8	60.1	277	54	34	34	4	3	7	6	43	3	37	3	0	4	2	.667	0	0-0	9	5.07
5 ML YEARS		231	2	0	60	277.1	1212	256	137	127	21	14	14	22	147	14	207	18	2	19	13	.594	0	3-10	40	4.12

Rick Wilkins

Bats: Left **Throws:** Right **Pos:** C-3; PH/PR-1 | **Ht:** 6'2" **Wt:** 215 **Born:** 6/4/67 **Age:** 34

		BATTING																		BASERUNNING				PERCENTAGES		
Year Team	Lg	G	AB	H	2B	3B	HR	(Hm	Rd)	TB	R	RBI	TBB	IBB	SO	HBP	SH	SF		SB	CS	SB%	GDP	Avg	OBP	SLG
2000 Memphis *	AAA	63	187	43	6	1	4	(—	—)	63	23	25	27	1	57	2	1	1		0	1	.00	1	.230	.332	.337
1991 Chicago	NL	86	203	45	9	0	6	(2	4)	72	21	22	19	2	56	6	7	0		3	3	.50	3	.222	.307	.355
1992 Chicago	NL	83	244	66	9	1	8	(3	5)	101	20	22	28	7	53	0	1	1		0	2	.00	6	.270	.344	.414
1993 Chicago	NL	136	446	135	23	1	30	(10	20)	250	78	73	50	13	99	3	0	1		2	1	.67	6	.303	.376	.561
1994 Chicago	NL	100	313	71	25	2	7	(4	3)	121	44	39	40	5	86	2	1	2		4	3	.57	3	.227	.317	.387
1995 ChC-Hou	NL	65	202	41	3	0	7	(3	4)	65	30	19	46	2	61	1	0	2		0	0	—	9	.203	.351	.322
1996 Hou-SF	NL	136	411	100	18	2	14	(6	8)	164	53	59	67	13	121	1	0	10		0	3	.00	5	.243	.344	.399
1997 SF-Sea	NL	71	202	40	6	0	7	(2	5)	67	20	27	18	0	67	0	0	1		0	0	—	1	.198	.259	.332
1998 Sea-NYM		24	56	10	1	1	1	(1	0)	16	8	5	6	0	16	0	0	1		0	0	—	1	.179	.254	.286
1999 Los Angeles	NL	3	4	0	0	0	0	(0	0)	0	0	0	2	0	2	0	0	0		0	0	—	0	.000	.000	.000
2000 St. Louis	NL	4	11	3	0	0	0	(0	0)	3	3	1	2	0	2	0	0	0		0	0	—	0	.273	.385	.273
1995 Chicago	NL	50	162	31	2	0	6	(3	3)	51	24	14	36	1	51	1	0	1		0	0	—	1	.191	.340	.315
Houston	NL	15	40	10	1	0	1	(0	1)	14	6	5	10	1	10	0	0	1		0	0	—	1	.250	.392	.350
1996 Houston	NL	84	254	54	8	2	6	(3	3)	84	34	23	46	10	81	0	0	5		0	1	.00	1	.213	.330	.331
San Francisco	NL	52	157	46	10	0	8	(3	5)	80	19	36	21	3	40	0	0	5		0	2	.00	4	.293	.366	.510
1997 San Francisco	NL	66	190	37	6	0	6	(1	5)	60	18	23	17	0	65	0	0	3		0	0	—	1	.195	.257	.316
Seattle	AL	5	12	3	1	0	1	(1	0)	7	2	4	1	0	2	0	0	1		0	0	—	0	.250	.286	.583
1998 Seattle	AL	19	41	8	1	1	1	(1	0)	14	5	4	4	0	14	0	0	1		0	0	—	1	.195	.261	.341
New York	NL	5	15	2	0	0	0	(0	0)	2	3	1	2	0	2	0	0	0		0	0	—	0	.133	.235	.133
10 ML YEARS		708	2092	511	94	7	80	(31	49)	859	277	267	276	42	563	13	9	21		9	12	.43	33	.244	.333	.411

Bernie Williams

Bats: Both **Throws:** Right **Pos:** CF-137; DH-4; PH/PR-1 | **Ht:** 6'2" **Wt:** 205 **Born:** 9/13/68 **Age:** 32

		BATTING																		BASERUNNING				PERCENTAGES		
Year Team	Lg	G	AB	H	2B	3B	HR	(Hm	Rd)	TB	R	RBI	TBB	IBB	SO	HBP	SH	SF		SB	CS	SB%	GDP	Avg	OBP	SLG
1991 New York	AL	85	320	76	19	4	3	(1	2)	112	43	34	48	0	57	1	2	3		10	5	.67	4	.238	.336	.350
1992 New York	AL	62	261	73	14	2	5	(3	2)	106	39	26	29	1	36	1	2	0		7	6	.54	5	.280	.354	.406
1993 New York	AL	139	567	152	31	4	12	(5	7)	227	67	68	53	4	106	4	1	3		9	9	.50	17	.268	.333	.400
1994 New York	AL	108	408	118	29	1	12	(4	8)	185	80	57	61	2	54	3	1	2		16	9	.64	11	.289	.384	.453
1995 New York	AL	144	563	173	29	9	18	(7	11)	274	93	82	75	1	98	5	2	3		8	6	.57	12	.307	.392	.487
1996 New York	AL	143	551	168	26	7	29	(12	17)	295	108	102	82	8	72	0	1	7		17	4	.81	15	.305	.391	.535
1997 New York	AL	129	509	167	35	6	21	(13	8)	277	107	100	73	7	80	1	0	8		15	8	.65	10	.328	.408	.544
1998 New York	AL	128	499	169	30	5	26	(14	12)	287	101	97	74	9	81	1	0	4		15	9	.63	19	.339	.422	.575
1999 New York	AL	158	591	202	28	6	25	(11	14)	317	116	115	100	17	95	1	0	5		9	10	.47	11	.342	.435	.536
2000 New York	AL	141	537	165	37	6	30	(15	15)	304	108	121	71	11	84	5	0	3		13	5	.72	15	.307	.391	.566
10 ML YEARS		1237	4806	1463	278	50	181	(85	96)	2384	862	802	666	60	763	22	9	38		119	71	.63	119	.304	.389	.496

Brian Williams

Pitches: Right **Bats:** Right **Pos:** RP-29 | **Ht:** 6'3" **Wt:** 230 **Born:** 2/15/69 **Age:** 32

		HOW MUCH HE PITCHED						WHAT HE GAVE UP												THE RESULTS						
Year Team	Lg	G	GS	CG	GF	IP	BFP	H	R	ER	HR	SH	SF	HB	TBB	IBB	SO	WP	Bk	W	L	Pct.	ShO	Sv-Op	Hld	ERA
2000 Buffalo *	AAA	18	0	0	8	21	95	23	7	6	1	4	1	0	11	2	21	2	0	4	3	.571	0	3--	—	2.57
1991 Houston	NL	2	2	0	0	12	49	11	5	5	2	0	0	1	4	0	4	0	0	0	1	.000	0	0-0	0	3.75
1992 Houston	NL	16	16	0	0	96.1	413	92	44	42	10	7	3	0	42	1	54	2	1	7	6	.538	0	0-0	0	3.92
1993 Houston	NL	42	5	0	12	82	357	76	48	44	7	5	4	4	38	4	56	9	2	4	4	.500	0	3-6	2	4.83
1994 Houston	NL	20	13	0	2	78.1	384	112	64	50	9	7	5	4	41	4	49	3	1	6	5	.545	0	2-4	1	5.74
1995 San Diego	NL	44	6	0	7	72	337	79	54	48	3	7	1	6	38	4	75	7	1	3	10	.231	0	0-2	7	6.00
1996 Detroit	AL	40	17	2	17	121	579	145	107	91	21	5	6	8	85	2	72	8	0	3	10	.231	1	2-4	0	6.77
1997 Baltimore	AL	13	0	0	8	24	110	20	8	8	0	0	1	0	18	0	14	1	0	0	0	—	0	0-1	0	3.00
1999 Houston	NL	50	0	0	15	67.1	303	69	35	33	4	5	4	5	35	2	53	7	0	2	1	.667	0	0-0	2	4.41
2000 ChC-Cle		29	0	0	6	42.1	203	51	36	34	4	3	2	4	31	3	20	4	0	1	1	.500	0	1-2	2	7.23
2000 Chicago	NL	22	0	0	5	24.1	122	28	27	26	4	3	1	3	23	2	14	3	0	1	1	.500	0	1-2	2	9.62
Cleveland	AL	7	0	0	1	18	81	23	9	8	2	0	1	1	8	1	6	1	0	0	0	—	0	0-0	0	4.00
9 ML YEARS		256	59	2	67	595.1	2735	655	401	355	62	39	25	32	332	20	397	41	5	26	38	.406	1	6-17	14	5.37

George Williams

Bats: Both **Throws:** Right **Pos:** C-6; PH/PR-6 | **Ht:** 5'10" **Wt:** 214 **Born:** 4/22/69 **Age:** 32

		BATTING																		BASERUNNING				PERCENTAGES		
Year Team	Lg	G	AB	H	2B	3B	HR	(Hm	Rd)	TB	R	RBI	TBB	IBB	SO	HBP	SH	SF		SB	CS	SB%	GDP	Avg	OBP	SLG
2000 Las Vegas *	AAA	63	176	42	8	2	6	(—	—)	78	27	35	36	1	44	3	0	3		0	1	.00	5	.239	.372	.443
1995 Oakland	AL	29	79	23	5	1	3	(1	2)	39	13	14	11	2	21	2	0	2		0	0	—	1	.291	.383	.494
1996 Oakland	AL	56	132	20	5	0	3	(0	3)	34	17	10	28	1	32	3	2	1		0	0	—	3	.152	.311	.258
1997 Oakland	AL	76	201	58	9	1	3	(2	1)	78	30	22	35	0	46	2	2	1		0	0	.00	2	.289	.397	.388
2000 San Diego	NL	11	16	3	0	0	1	(1	0)	6	2	2	0	0	4	1	0	0		0	0	—	0	.188	.235	.375
4 ML YEARS		172	428	104	19	2	10	(4	6)	157	62	48	74	3	103	8	4	4		0	1	.00	6	.243	.362	.367

Gerald Williams

Bats: Right **Throws:** Right **Pos:** CF-138; DH-7; PH/PR-1   **Ht:** 6'2" **Wt:** 187 **Born:** 8/10/66 **Age:** 34

Year Team	Lg	G	AB	H	2B	3B	HR	(Hm	Rd)	TB	R	RBI	TBB	IBB	SO	HBP	SH	SF	SB	CS	SB%	GDP	Avg	OBP	SLG
1992 New York	AL	15	27	8	2	0	3	(2	1)	19	7	6	0	0	3	0	0	0	2	0	1.00	0	.296	.296	.704
1993 New York	AL	42	67	10	2	3	0	(0	0)	18	11	6	1	0	14	2	0	1	2	0	1.00	2	.149	.183	.269
1994 New York	AL	57	86	25	8	0	4	(2	2)	45	19	13	4	0	17	0	0	1	1	3	.25	6	.291	.319	.523
1995 New York	AL	100	182	45	18	2	6	(4	2)	85	33	28	22	1	34	1	0	3	4	2	.67	4	.247	.327	.467
1996 NYY-Mil	AL	125	325	82	19	4	5	(3	2)	124	43	34	19	3	57	5	3	5	10	9	.53	8	.252	.299	.382
1997 Milwaukee	AL	155	566	143	32	2	10	(3	7)	209	73	41	19	1	90	6	5	5	23	9	.72	9	.253	.282	.369
1998 Atlanta	NL	129	266	81	19	2	10	(5	5)	134	46	44	17	1	48	3	2	1	11	5	.69	5	.305	.352	.504
1999 Atlanta	NL	143	422	116	24	1	17	(7	10)	193	76	68	33	1	67	6	4	2	19	11	.63	8	.275	.335	.457
2000 Tampa Bay	AL	146	632	173	30	2	21	(6	15)	270	87	89	34	0	103	3	9	4	12	12	.50	5	.274	.312	.427
1996 New York	AL	99	233	63	15	4	5	(3	2)	101	37	30	15	2	39	4	1	5	7	8	.47	5	.270	.319	.433
Milwaukee	AL	26	92	19	4	0	0	(0	0)	23	6	4	4	1	18	1	2	0	3	1	.75	1	.207	.247	.250
9 ML YEARS		912	2573	683	154	16	76	(32	44)	1097	395	329	149	7	433	26	23	22	84	51	.62	47	.265	.310	.426

Jeff Williams

Pitches: Left **Bats:** Right **Pos:** RP-7   **Ht:** 6'0" **Wt:** 185 **Born:** 6/6/72 **Age:** 29

Year Team	Lg	G	GS	CG	GF	IP	BFP	H	R	ER	HR	SH	SF	HB	TBB	IBB	SO	WP	Bk	W	L	Pct.	ShO	Sv-Op	Hld	ERA
1997 San Antonio	AA	5	5	0	0	28.1	119	30	17	17	2	2	2	0	7	0	14	3	1	2	1	.667	0	0--	—	5.40
San Berndno	A+	18	18	0	0	116	472	101	52	40	8	4	2	2	34	0	72	7	3	10	4	.714	0	0--	—	3.10
1998 San Antonio	AA	7	7	0	0	41.2	182	43	19	12	3	1	3	0	13	1	35	1	1	3	0	1.000	0	0--	—	2.59
Albuquerque	AAA	21	21	0	0	121	556	160	87	67	14	3	3	6	49	0	93	6	4	8	8	.500	0	0--	—	4.98
1999 Albuquerque	AAA	42	14	1	10	125.2	558	151	77	70	14	4	8	9	47	2	86	3	0	9	7	.563	1	4--	—	5.01
2000 Albuquerque	AAA	12	12	0	0	63.1	266	64	33	30	6	2	1	2	28	0	38	7	0	4	3	.571	0	0--	—	4.26
1999 Los Angeles	NL	5	3	0	1	17.2	73	12	10	8	2	1	0	0	9	0	7	0	0	2	0	1.000	0	0-0	—	4.08
2000 Los Angeles	NL	7	0	0	0	5.2	35	12	11	10	1	0	1	0	8	0	3	0	0	0	0	—	0	0-1	1	15.88
2 ML YEARS		12	3	0	1	23.1	108	24	21	18	3	1	1	0	17	0	10	0	0	2	0	1.000	0	0-1	1	6.94

Matt Williams

Bats: Right **Throws:** Right **Pos:** 3B-94; DH-1; PH/PR-1   **Ht:** 6'2" **Wt:** 214 **Born:** 11/28/65 **Age:** 35

Year Team	Lg	G	AB	H	2B	3B	HR	(Hm	Rd)	TB	R	RBI	TBB	IBB	SO	HBP	SH	SF	SB	CS	SB%	GDP	Avg	OBP	SLG
2000 El Paso *	AA	5	13	6	2	0	0	(Hm	—)	8	3	1	2	0	1	0	0	0	0	0	—	0	.462	.533	.615
High Desert *	A+	2	8	3	0	0	1	—	—	6	1	1	0	0	1	0	0	0	0	0	—	0	.375	.375	.750
1987 San Francisco	NL	84	245	46	9	2	8	(5	3)	83	28	21	16	4	68	1	3	1	4	3	.57	5	.188	.240	.339
1988 San Francisco	NL	52	156	32	6	1	8	(7	1)	64	17	19	8	0	41	2	3	1	0	1	.00	7	.205	.251	.410
1989 San Francisco	NL	84	292	59	18	1	18	(10	8)	133	31	50	14	1	72	2	1	2	1	2	.33	5	.202	.242	.455
1990 San Francisco	NL	159	617	171	27	2	33	(20	13)	301	87	122	33	9	138	7	2	5	7	4	.64	13	.277	.319	.488
1991 San Francisco	NL	157	589	158	24	5	34	(17	17)	294	72	98	33	6	128	6	0	7	5	5	.50	11	.268	.310	.499
1992 San Francisco	NL	146	529	120	13	5	20	(9	11)	203	58	66	39	11	109	6	0	2	7	7	.50	15	.227	.286	.384
1993 San Francisco	NL	145	579	170	33	4	38	(19	19)	325	105	110	27	4	80	4	0	9	1	3	.25	12	.294	.325	.561
1994 San Francisco	NL	112	445	119	16	3	43	(20	23)	290	74	96	33	7	87	2	0	3	1	0	1.00	11	.267	.319	.607
1995 San Francisco	NL	76	283	95	17	1	23	(9	14)	183	53	65	30	8	58	2	0	3	2	0	1.00	8	.336	.399	.647
1996 San Francisco	NL	105	404	122	16	1	22	(13	9)	206	69	85	39	9	91	6	0	6	1	2	.33	10	.302	.367	.510
1997 Cleveland	NL	151	596	157	32	3	32	(7	25)	291	86	105	34	4	108	4	0	2	12	4	.75	14	.263	.307	.488
1998 Arizona	NL	135	510	136	26	1	20	(11	9)	224	72	71	43	8	102	3	0	1	5	1	.83	19	.267	.327	.439
1999 Arizona	NL	154	627	190	37	2	35	(17	18)	336	98	142	41	9	93	2	0	8	2	0	1.00	17	.303	.344	.536
2000 Arizona	NL	96	371	102	18	2	12	(5	7)	160	43	47	20	1	51	3	0	3	1	2	.33	11	.275	.315	.431
14 ML YEARS		1656	6243	1677	292	33	346	(169	177)	3073	893	1097	410	81	1226	50	9	53	49	34	.59	158	.269	.316	.492

Matt T. Williams

Pitches: Left **Bats:** Both **Pos:** RP-11   **Ht:** 6'0" **Wt:** 190 **Born:** 4/12/71 **Age:** 30

Year Team	Lg	G	GS	CG	GF	IP	BFP	H	R	ER	HR	SH	SF	HB	TBB	IBB	SO	WP	Bk	W	L	Pct.	ShO	Sv-Op	Hld	ERA
1992 Watertown	A-	6	6	0	0	32.2	130	22	15	8	2	0	4	3	9	0	29	1	2	1	0	1.000	0	0--	—	2.20
1993 Kinston	A+	27	27	2	0	153.1	672	125	65	54	6	7	5	8	100	0	134	12	6	12	12	.500	1	0--	—	3.17
1994 Canton-Akrn	AA	5	4	0	1	23.2	112	30	22	20	3	1	3	1	14	0	9	1	0	0	3	.000	0	1--	—	7.61
Kinston	A+	15	15	1	0	81.1	358	86	63	55	17	0	2	2	33	0	67	4	2	4	6	.400	0	0--	—	6.09
1995 Bakersfield	A+	7	7	0	0	34.1	150	34	9	9	1	3	2	3	14	0	30	1	1	2	0	1.000	0	0--	—	2.36
Kissimmee	A+	19	18	2	0	101	446	115	60	52	7	5	3	2	44	1	71	5	1	4	6	.400	0	0--	—	4.63
1996 Lynchburg	A+	23	0	0	5	41.1	189	40	27	24	9	0	1	2	28	1	45	3	1	0	0	—	0	0--	—	5.23
1997 St. Pete	A+	43	0	0	15	63.2	267	57	26	21	4	2	0	2	24	3	50	3	3	9	5	.643	0	1--	—	2.97
1998 Norwich	AA	31	28	2	0	160.1	719	186	93	82	14	3	7	4	66	2	112	8	2	8	11	.421	0	0--	—	4.60
1999 Norwich	AA	22	0	0	3	30	128	22	9	8	3	0	1	1	18	3	44	3	0	1	1	.500	0	0--	—	2.40
Columbus	AAA	13	1	0	3	21	87	15	9	9	1	0	0	0	11	0	22	0	1	0	2	.000	0	0--	—	3.86
2000 Columbus	AAA	27	0	0	14	36	160	37	24	21	4	0	1	0	16	1	35	3	0	4	2	.667	0	2--	—	5.25
2000 Milwaukee	NL	11	0	0	1	9	46	7	7	7	2	0	0	1	13	0	7	0	0	0	0	—	0	0-0	2	7.00

Mike Williams

Pitches: Right **Bats:** Right **Pos:** RP-72   **Ht:** 6'2" **Wt:** 204 **Born:** 7/29/68 **Age:** 32

Year Team	Lg	G	GS	CG	GF	IP	BFP	H	R	ER	HR	SH	SF	HB	TBB	IBB	SO	WP	Bk	W	L	Pct.	ShO	Sv-Op	Hld	ERA
1992 Philadelphia	NL	5	5	1	0	28.2	121	29	20	17	3	1	1	0	7	0	5	0	0	1	1	.500	0	0-0	0	5.34
1993 Philadelphia	NL	17	4	0	2	51	221	50	32	30	5	1	0	0	22	2	33	2	0	1	3	.250	0	0-0	0	5.29
1994 Philadelphia	NL	12	8	0	2	50.1	222	61	31	28	7	2	3	0	20	3	29	0	0	2	4	.333	0	0-0	0	5.01
1995 Philadelphia	NL	33	8	0	7	87.2	367	78	37	32	10	5	3	3	29	2	57	7	0	3	3	.500	0	0-0	1	3.29
1996 Philadelphia	NL	32	29	0	1	167	732	188	107	101	25	6	5	6	67	6	103	16	1	6	14	.300	0	0-0	0	5.44

233

Year Team	Lg	G	GS	CG	GF	IP	BFP	H	R	ER	HR	SH	SF	HB	TBB	IBB	SO	WP	Bk	W	L	Pct.	ShO	Sv-Op	Hld	ERA
HOW MUCH HE PITCHED								**WHAT HE GAVE UP**												**THE RESULTS**						
1997 Kansas City	AL	10	0	0	4	14	70	20	11	10	1	0	1	1	8	1	10	0	0	0	2	.000	0	1-1	1	6.43
1998 Pittsburgh	NL	37	1	0	9	51	204	39	12	11	1	1	2	0	16	4	59	3	0	4	2	.667	0	0-1	7	1.94
1999 Pittsburgh	NL	58	0	0	50	58.1	269	63	36	33	9	2	1	1	37	7	76	4	0	3	4	.429	0	23-28	1	5.09
2000 Pittsburgh	NL	72	0	0	63	72	307	56	34	28	8	2	4	4	40	3	71	1	0	3	4	.429	0	24-29	1	3.50
9 ML YEARS		276	55	1	138	580	2513	584	320	290	69	20	20	15	246	28	443	33	1	23	37	.383	0	48-59	10	4.50

Woody Williams

Pitches: Right **Bats:** Right **Pos:** SP-23

Ht: 6'0" **Wt:** 195 **Born:** 8/19/66 **Age:** 34

Year Team	Lg	G	GS	CG	GF	IP	BFP	H	R	ER	HR	SH	SF	HB	TBB	IBB	SO	WP	Bk	W	L	Pct.	ShO	Sv-Op	Hld	ERA
HOW MUCH HE PITCHED								**WHAT HE GAVE UP**												**THE RESULTS**						
2000 Rancho Cuc *	A+	1	1	0	0	5	18	3	0	0	0	0	0	0	0	0	10	1	0	0	0	—	0	0- —	—	0.00
Las Vegas *	AAA	1	1	0	0	6	24	7	2	1	1	0	0	0	0	0	5	0	0	0	0	—	0	0- —	—	1.50
1993 Toronto	AL	30	0	0	0	37	172	40	18	18	2	2	1	1	22	3	24	2	1	3	1	.750	0	0-2	4	4.38
1994 Toronto	AL	38	0	0	14	59.1	253	44	24	24	5	1	2	2	33	1	56	4	0	1	3	.250	0	0-0	5	3.64
1995 Toronto	AL	23	0	0	10	53.2	232	44	23	22	6	2	0	2	28	1	41	0	0	1	2	.333	0	0-1	1	3.69
1996 Toronto	AL	12	10	1	0	59	255	64	33	31	8	2	1	1	21	1	43	2	0	4	5	.444	0	0-0	0	4.73
1997 Toronto	AL	31	31	0	0	194.2	833	201	98	94	31	6	8	5	66	3	124	7	0	9	14	.391	0	0-0	0	4.35
1998 Toronto	AL	32	32	1	0	209.2	894	196	112	104	36	5	6	2	81	3	151	2	1	10	9	.526	1	0-0	0	4.46
1999 San Diego	NL	33	33	0	0	208.1	887	213	106	102	33	9	9	2	73	5	137	9	0	12	12	.500	0	0-0	0	4.41
2000 San Diego	NL	23	23	4	0	168	700	152	74	70	23	4	3	3	54	2	111	4	0	10	8	.556	0	0-0	0	3.75
8 ML YEARS		222	132	6	33	989.2	4226	954	488	465	144	31	30	18	378	19	687	30	2	50	54	.481	1	0-3	10	4.23

Scott Williamson

Pitches: Right **Bats:** Right **Pos:** RP-38; SP-10

Ht: 6'0" **Wt:** 185 **Born:** 2/17/76 **Age:** 25

Year Team	Lg	G	GS	CG	GF	IP	BFP	H	R	ER	HR	SH	SF	HB	TBB	IBB	SO	WP	Bk	W	L	Pct.	ShO	Sv-Op	Hld	ERA
HOW MUCH HE PITCHED								**WHAT HE GAVE UP**												**THE RESULTS**						
1997 Billings	R+	13	13	2	0	86	346	66	25	17	5	1	2	4	23	0	101	12	2	8	2	.800	1	0- —	—	1.78
1998 Chattanooga	AA	18	18	0	0	100	420	85	49	42	4	2	6	3	46	4	105	13	2	4	5	.444	0	0- —	—	3.78
Indianapolis	AAA	5	5	0	0	20.2	87	20	9	8	2	0	0	1	9	0	17	0	0	0	0	—	0	0- —	—	3.48
1999 Cincinnati	NL	62	0	0	40	93.1	366	54	29	25	8	5	2	1	43	6	107	13	0	12	7	.632	0	19-26	5	2.41
2000 Cincinnati	NL	48	10	0	13	112	495	92	45	41	7	4	2	3	75	7	136	21	1	5	8	.385	0	6-8	6	3.29
2 ML YEARS		110	10	0	53	205.1	861	146	74	66	15	9	4	4	118	13	243	34	1	17	15	.531	0	25-34	11	2.89

Craig Wilson

Bats: R **Throws:** R **Pos:** 3B-15; SS-10; PH/PR-5; 2B-4

Ht: 6'0" **Wt:** 185 **Born:** 9/3/70 **Age:** 30

Year Team	Lg	G	AB	H	2B	3B	HR	(Hm	Rd)	TB	R	RBI	TBB	IBB	SO	HBP	SH	SF	SB	CS	SB%	GDP	Avg	OBP	SLG
																			BASERUNNING				**PERCENTAGES**		
2000 Charlotte *	AAA	62	230	85	14	2	3	(—	—)	112	43	34	32	0	26	4	0	1	0	1	.00	7	.370	.448	.487
1998 Chicago	AL	13	47	22	5	0	3	(1	2)	36	14	10	3	0	6	0	2	1	1	0	1.00	6	.468	.490	.766
1999 Chicago	AL	98	252	60	8	1	4	(0	4)	82	28	26	23	0	22	0	6	1	1	1	.50	5	.238	.301	.325
2000 Chicago	AL	28	73	19	3	0	0	(0	0)	22	12	4	5	0	11	1	4	0	1	0	1.00	5	.260	.316	.301
3 ML YEARS		139	372	101	16	1	7	(1	6)	140	54	40	31	0	39	1	12	2	3	1	.75	10	.272	.328	.376

Dan Wilson

Bats: R **Throws:** R **Pos:** C-88; PH/PR-4; 1B-1; 3B-1

Ht: 6'3" **Wt:** 202 **Born:** 3/25/69 **Age:** 32

Year Team	Lg	G	AB	H	2B	3B	HR	(Hm	Rd)	TB	R	RBI	TBB	IBB	SO	HBP	SH	SF	SB	CS	SB%	GDP	Avg	OBP	SLG
																			BASERUNNING				**PERCENTAGES**		
2000 Everett *	A-	1	2	1	0	0	0	(—	—)	4	2	1	1	0	0	0	0	0	0	0	—	0	.500	.667	2.000
Tacoma *	AAA	1	4	1	1	0	0	(—	—)	2	0	0	0	0	1	0	0	0	0	0	—	0	.250	.250	.500
1992 Cincinnati	NL	12	25	9	1	0	0	(0	0)	10	2	3	3	0	8	0	0	0	0	0	—	2	.360	.429	.400
1993 Cincinnati	NL	36	76	17	3	0	0	(0	0)	20	6	8	9	4	16	0	2	1	0	0	—	2	.224	.302	.263
1994 Seattle	AL	91	282	61	14	2	3	(1	2)	88	24	27	10	0	57	1	8	2	1	2	.33	11	.216	.244	.312
1995 Seattle	AL	119	399	111	22	3	9	(5	4)	166	40	51	33	1	63	2	5	1	2	1	.67	12	.278	.336	.416
1996 Seattle	AL	138	491	140	24	0	18	(7	11)	218	51	83	32	2	88	3	9	5	1	2	.33	15	.285	.330	.444
1997 Seattle	AL	146	508	137	31	1	15	(9	6)	215	66	74	39	1	72	5	8	3	7	2	.78	12	.270	.326	.423
1998 Seattle	AL	96	325	82	17	1	9	(6	3)	128	39	44	24	0	56	5	8	6	2	1	.67	6	.252	.308	.394
1999 Seattle	AL	123	414	110	23	2	7	(3	4)	158	46	38	29	4	83	2	10	2	5	0	1.00	6	.266	.315	.382
2000 Seattle	AL	90	268	63	12	0	5	(2	3)	90	31	27	22	0	51	0	11	2	1	2	.33	8	.235	.291	.336
9 ML YEARS		851	2788	730	147	9	66	(33	33)	1093	305	355	201	12	494	18	61	22	19	10	.66	78	.262	.313	.392

Enrique Wilson

Bats: B **Throws:** R **Pos:** 3B-28; PH/PR-20; 2B-18; SS-15; DH-8

Ht: 5'11" **Wt:** 180 **Born:** 7/27/75 **Age:** 25

Year Team	Lg	G	AB	H	2B	3B	HR	(Hm	Rd)	TB	R	RBI	TBB	IBB	SO	HBP	SH	SF	SB	CS	SB%	GDP	Avg	OBP	SLG
																			BASERUNNING				**PERCENTAGES**		
2000 Nashville *	AAA	2	7	2	0	0	0	(—	—)	2	0	1	0	0	0	0	0	0	0	0	—	0	.286	.286	.286
1997 Cleveland	AL	5	15	5	0	0	0	(0	0)	5	2	1	0	0	2	0	0	0	0	0	—	0	.333	.333	.333
1998 Cleveland	AL	32	90	29	6	0	2	(1	1)	41	13	12	4	0	8	1	1	1	2	1	.33	4	.322	.354	.456
1999 Cleveland	AL	113	332	87	22	1	2	(1	1)	117	41	24	25	1	41	1	4	6	5	4	.56	12	.262	.310	.352
2000 Cle-Pit		80	239	70	15	1	5	(3	2)	102	27	27	18	2	24	0	4	2	2	2	.50	6	.293	.340	.427
2000 Cleveland	AL	40	117	38	9	0	2	(2	0)	53	16	12	7	0	11	0	2	1	0	1	.00	2	.325	.360	.453
Pittsburgh	NL	40	122	32	6	1	3	(1	2)	49	11	15	11	2	13	0	2	1	2	1	.67	4	.262	.321	.402
4 ML YEARS		230	676	191	43	2	9	(5	4)	265	83	64	47	3	75	2	9	9	9	10	.47	19	.283	.327	.392

Kris Wilson

Pitches: Right **Bats:** Right **Pos:** RP-20   **Ht:** 6'4" **Wt:** 225 **Born:** 8/6/76 **Age:** 24

Year Team	Lg	G	GS	CG	GF	IP	BFP	H	R	ER	HR	SH	SF	HB	TBB	IBB	SO	WP	Bk	W	L	Pct.	ShO	Sv-Op	Hld	ERA
1997 Spokane	A-	15	15	0	0	73.2	345	101	50	37	6	0	3	5	21	1	72	1	2	5	3	.625	0	0- --	—	4.52
1998 Wilmington	A+	10	2	0	4	24	96	19	10	10	0	2	2	3	6	1	20	1	0	0	3	.000	0	1- --	—	3.75
Lansing	A	18	18	1	0	117.1	470	119	50	46	7	3	3	3	15	0	74	2	0	10	5	.667	0	0- --	—	3.53
1999 Wilmington	A+	14	4	0	1	48	169	25	7	6	0	0	0	0	11	0	45	1	0	8	1	.889	0	0- --	—	1.13
Omaha	AAA	1	1	0	0	5.1	23	8	5	5	3	0	0	0	0	0	3	0	0	0	1	.000	0	0- --	—	8.44
Wichita	AA	23	10	0	2	74.1	323	91	51	45	11	2	2	3	14	0	45	1	2	5	7	.417	0	0- --	—	5.45
2000 Wichita	AA	21	15	1	1	102.2	425	99	52	40	12	1	4	6	21	0	69	4	1	7	3	.700	0	0- --	—	3.51
2000 Kansas City	AL	20	0	0	5	34.1	145	38	16	16	3	1	1	0	11	3	17	0	0	0	1	.000	0	0-1	0	4.19

Paul Wilson

Pitches: Right **Bats:** Right **Pos:** SP-7; RP-4   **Ht:** 6'5" **Wt:** 235 **Born:** 3/28/73 **Age:** 28

Year Team	Lg	G	GS	CG	GF	IP	BFP	H	R	ER	HR	SH	SF	HB	TBB	IBB	SO	WP	Bk	W	L	Pct.	ShO	Sv-Op	Hld	ERA
1994 Mets	R	3	3	0	0	12	47	8	4	4	0	1	0	0	4	0	13	0	2	0	2	.000	0	0- --	—	3.00
St. Lucie	A+	8	8	0	0	37.1	160	32	23	21	3	0	1	3	17	1	37	0	5	0	5	.000	0	0- --	—	5.06
1995 Binghamton	AA	16	16	4	0	120.1	464	89	34	29	5	3	4	5	24	2	127	4	3	6	3	.667	1	0- --	—	2.17
Norfolk	AAA	10	10	4	0	66.1	270	59	25	21	3	2	1	3	20	0	67	2	0	5	3	.625	2	0- --	—	2.85
1996 St. Lucie	A+	2	2	0	0	8	36	6	5	3	0	0	1	0	4	0	5	0	0	0	1	.000	0	0- --	—	3.38
Binghamton	AA	1	1	0	0	5	25	6	4	4	0	0	1	0	5	0	5	2	0	0	1	.000	0	0- --	—	7.20
1997 St. Lucie	A+	1	1	0	0	7	26	6	2	2	1	0	0	0	0	0	6	0	0	0	0	—	0	0- --	—	2.57
Mets	R	4	3	0	1	18.2	77	14	7	3	0	1	0	3	4	0	18	0	0	1	0	1.000	0	1- --	—	1.45
1998 St. Lucie	A+	5	5	0	0	18.1	78	23	13	13	2	0	1	0	4	0	16	1	0	0	1	.000	0	0- --	—	6.38
Norfolk	AAA	7	7	0	0	38.2	168	42	19	19	2	3	0	2	9	0	30	1	0	4	1	.800	0	0- --	—	4.42
2000 St. Lucie	A+	5	5	0	0	25.2	100	22	9	4	0	0	1	1	4	0	19	0	0	2	0	1.000	0	0- --	—	1.40
Norfolk	AAA	15	13	0	0	83	350	85	40	39	7	0	4	2	21	1	56	3	1	5	5	.500	0	0- --	—	4.23
1996 New York	NL	26	26	1	0	149	677	157	102	89	15	7	3	10	71	11	109	3	3	5	12	.294	0	0-0	0	5.38
2000 Tampa Bay	AL	11	7	0	0	51	206	38	20	19	1	2	2	4	16	2	40	1	0	1	4	.200	0	0-0	0	3.35
2 ML YEARS		37	33	1	0	200	883	195	122	108	16	9	5	14	87	13	149	4	3	6	16	.273	0	0-0	0	4.86

Preston Wilson

Bats: Right **Throws:** Right **Pos:** CF-158; PH/PR-3   **Ht:** 6'2" **Wt:** 193 **Born:** 7/19/74 **Age:** 26

Year Team	Lg	G	AB	H	2B	3B	HR	(Hm	Rd)	TB	R	RBI	TBB	IBB	SO	HBP	SH	SF	SB	CS	SB%	GDP	Avg	OBP	SLG
1998 NYM-Fla	NL	22	51	8	2	0	1	(1	0)	13	7	3	6	0	21	1	2	0	1	1	.50	0	.157	.259	.255
1999 Florida	NL	149	482	135	21	4	26	(8	18)	242	67	71	46	3	156	9	0	6	11	4	.73	15	.280	.350	.502
2000 Florida	NL	161	605	160	35	3	31	(12	19)	294	94	121	55	1	187	8	0	6	36	14	.72	11	.264	.331	.486
1998 New York	NL	8	20	6	2	0	0	(0	0)	8	3	2	2	0	8	0	0	0	1	1	.50	0	.300	.364	.400
Florida	NL	14	31	2	0	0	1	(1	0)	5	4	1	4	0	13	1	2	0	0	0	—	0	.065	.194	.161
3 ML YEARS		332	1138	303	58	7	58	(21	37)	549	168	195	107	4	364	18	2	12	48	19	.72	26	.266	.336	.482

Vance Wilson

Bats: Right **Throws:** Right **Pos:** C-3; PH/PR-1   **Ht:** 5'11" **Wt:** 190 **Born:** 3/17/73 **Age:** 28

Year Team	Lg	G	AB	H	2B	3B	HR	(Hm	Rd)	TB	R	RBI	TBB	IBB	SO	HBP	SH	SF	SB	CS	SB%	GDP	Avg	OBP	SLG
1994 Pittsfield	A-	44	166	51	12	0	2	—	—	69	22	20	5	2	27	5	0	2	4	1	.80	1	.307	.343	.416
1995 Capital Cty	A	91	324	81	11	0	6	—	—	110	34	32	19	1	45	8	1	2	4	3	.57	6	.250	.306	.340
1996 St. Lucie	A+	93	311	76	14	2	6	—	—	112	29	44	31	2	41	6	0	4	2	4	.33	7	.244	.321	.360
1997 Binghamton	AA	92	322	89	17	0	15	—	—	151	46	40	20	0	46	5	3	1	2	5	.29	6	.276	.328	.469
1998 Mets	R	10	28	10	5	0	2	—	—	21	5	9	0	0	0	1	0	1	0	1	.00	2	.357	.367	.750
St. Lucie	A+	4	16	1	0	0	0	—	—	1	0	0	0	0	5	0	0	0	0	0	—	0	.063	.063	.063
Norfolk	AAA	46	154	40	3	0	4	—	—	55	18	16	9	0	29	1	3	0	0	3	.00	5	.260	.305	.357
1999 Norfolk	AAA	15	53	14	3	0	3	—	—	26	10	5	4	2	8	1	0	0	1	0	1.00	4	.264	.328	.491
2000 Norfolk	AAA	111	400	104	23	1	16	—	—	177	47	62	24	1	65	12	1	3	11	6	.65	12	.260	.319	.443
1999 New York	NL	1	0	0	0	0	0	(0	0)	0	0	0	0	0	0	0	0	0	0	0	—	0	—	—	—
2000 New York	NL	4	4	0	0	0	0	(0	0)	0	0	0	0	0	2	0	0	0	0	0	—	0	.000	.000	.000
2 ML YEARS		5	4	0	0	0	0	(0	0)	0	0	0	0	0	2	0	0	0	0	0	—	0	.000	.000	.000

Scott Winchester

Pitches: Right **Bats:** Right **Pos:** RP-5   **Ht:** 6'2" **Wt:** 210 **Born:** 4/20/73 **Age:** 28

Year Team	Lg	G	GS	CG	GF	IP	BFP	H	R	ER	HR	SH	SF	HB	TBB	IBB	SO	WP	Bk	W	L	Pct.	ShO	Sv-Op	Hld	ERA
2000 Louisville *	AAA	43	0	0	16	57.1	249	67	29	26	4	3	3	0	15	2	33	3	0	1	2	.333	0	3- --	—	4.08
1997 Cincinnati	NL	5	0	0	4	6	30	9	5	4	1	2	0	1	2	0	3	0	0	0	0	—	0	0-0	0	6.00
1998 Cincinnati	NL	16	16	1	0	79	359	101	56	51	12	2	2	4	27	2	40	3	0	3	6	.333	0	0-0	0	5.81
2000 Cincinnati	NL	5	0	0	3	7.1	35	10	4	3	1	0	1	0	2	0	3	0	0	0	0	—	0	0-0	0	3.68
3 ML YEARS		26	16	1	7	92.1	424	120	65	58	14	4	3	5	31	2	46	3	0	3	6	.333	0	0-0	0	5.65

Randy Winn

Bats: B **Throws:** R **Pos:** LF-29; CF-18; PH/PR-8; DH-1   **Ht:** 6'2" **Wt:** 193 **Born:** 6/9/74 **Age:** 27

Year Team	Lg	G	AB	H	2B	3B	HR	(Hm	Rd)	TB	R	RBI	TBB	IBB	SO	HBP	SH	SF	SB	CS	SB%	GDP	Avg	OBP	SLG
2000 Durham *	AAA	79	303	100	24	5	7	—	—	155	67	40	48	1	53	3	3	1	18	5	.78	5	.330	.425	.512
1998 Tampa Bay	AL	109	338	94	9	9	1	(0	1)	124	51	17	29	0	69	1	11	0	26	12	.68	2	.278	.337	.366
1999 Tampa Bay	AL	79	303	81	16	4	2	(2	0)	111	44	24	17	0	63	1	0	2	9	9	.50	3	.267	.307	.366
2000 Tampa Bay	AL	51	159	40	5	0	1	(1	0)	48	28	16	26	0	25	2	2	1	6	7	.46	2	.252	.362	.302
3 ML YEARS		239	800	215	30	13	4	(3	1)	283	123	57	72	0	157	4	14	3	41	28	.59	7	.269	.331	.354

Dewayne Wise

Bats: L **Throws:** L **Pos:** LF-14; PH/PR-13; RF-3; DH-2; CF-1 **Ht:** 6'1" **Wt:** 180 **Born:** 2/24/78 **Age:** 23

Year Team	Lg	G	AB	H	2B	3B	HR	(Hm	Rd)	TB	R	RBI	TBB	IBB	SO	HBP	SH	SF	SB	CS	SB%	GDP	Avg	OBP	SLG
1997 Billings	R+	62	268	84	13	9	7	—	—	136	53	41	9	0	47	2	1	3	18	8	.69	2	.313	.337	.507
1998 Burlington	A	127	496	111	15	9	2	—	—	150	61	44	41	1	111	1	7	9	27	17	.61	4	.224	.280	.302
1999 Rockford	A	131	502	127	20	13	11	—	—	206	70	81	42	2	81	7	5	14	35	13	.73	6	.253	.312	.410
2000 Tennessee	AA	15	56	14	5	2	2	—	—	29	10	8	7	0	13	0	0	0	3	2	.60	2	.250	.333	.518
2000 Toronto	AL	28	22	3	0	0	0	(0	0)	3	3	0	1	0	5	0	0	0	1	0	1.00	0	.136	.208	.136

Matt Wise

Pitches: Right **Bats:** Right **Pos:** SP-6; RP-2 **Ht:** 6'4" **Wt:** 190 **Born:** 11/18/75 **Age:** 25

Year Team	Lg	G	GS	CG	GF	IP	BFP	H	R	ER	HR	SH	SF	HB	TBB	IBB	SO	WP	Bk	W	L	Pct.	ShO	Sv-Op	Hld	ERA
1997 Boise	A-	15	15	0	0	83	342	62	37	30	5	0	1	2	34	0	86	7	3	9	1	.900	0	0--	—	3.25
1998 Midland	AA	27	27	3	0	167.2	735	195	111	101	23	4	5	6	46	0	131	9	0	9	10	.474	1	0--	—	5.42
1999 Erie	AA	16	16	3	0	98	416	102	48	41	10	4	3	4	24	0	72	1	0	8	5	.615	0	0--	—	3.77
2000 Edmonton	AAA	19	19	2	0	124.1	510	122	54	51	10	2	7	2	26	0	82	0	1	9	6	.600	1	0--	—	3.69
2000 Anaheim	AL	8	6	0	0	37.1	163	40	23	23	7	0	2	1	13	1	20	1	0	3	3	.500	0	0--	—	5.54

Jay Witasick

Pitches: Right **Bats:** Right **Pos:** SP-25; RP-8 **Ht:** 6'4" **Wt:** 235 **Born:** 8/28/72 **Age:** 28

Year Team	Lg	G	GS	CG	GF	IP	BFP	H	R	ER	HR	SH	SF	HB	TBB	IBB	SO	WP	Bk	W	L	Pct.	ShO	Sv-Op	Hld	ERA
1996 Oakland	AL	12	0	0	6	13	55	12	9	9	5	0	1	0	5	0	12	2	0	1	1	.500	0	0-1	0	6.23
1997 Oakland	AL	8	0	0	1	11	53	14	7	7	2	1	0	0	6	0	8	0	0	0	0	—	0	0-0	1	5.73
1998 Oakland	AL	7	3	0	1	27	131	36	24	19	9	0	0	0	15	1	29	2	0	1	3	.250	0	0-0	0	6.33
1999 Kansas City	AL	32	28	1	2	158.1	732	191	100	98	23	4	8	8	83	1	102	5	2	9	12	.429	1	0-0	0	5.57
2000 KC-SD		33	25	2	2	150	697	178	107	97	24	8	4	7	73	5	121	5	1	6	10	.375	0	0-0	0	5.82
2000 Kansas City	AL	22	14	2	2	89.1	410	109	65	59	15	3	3	4	38	0	67	3	0	3	8	.273	0	0-0	0	5.94
San Diego	NL	11	11	0	0	60.2	287	69	42	38	9	5	1	3	35	5	54	2	1	3	2	.600	0	0-0	0	5.64
5 ML YEARS		92	56	3	12	359.1	1668	431	255	230	63	13	13	15	182	7	272	14	3	17	26	.395	1	0-1	1	5.76

Bobby Witt

Pitches: Right **Bats:** Right **Pos:** RP-5; SP-2 **Ht:** 6'2" **Wt:** 215 **Born:** 5/11/64 **Age:** 37

Year Team	Lg	G	GS	CG	GF	IP	BFP	H	R	ER	HR	SH	SF	HB	TBB	IBB	SO	WP	Bk	W	L	Pct.	ShO	Sv-Op	Hld	ERA
1986 Texas	AL	31	31	0	0	157.2	741	130	104	96	18	3	9	3	143	2	174	22	3	11	9	.550	0	0-0	0	5.48
1987 Texas	AL	26	25	1	0	143	673	114	82	78	10	5	5	3	140	1	160	7	2	8	10	.444	0	0-0	0	4.91
1988 Texas	AL	22	22	13	0	174.1	736	134	83	76	13	7	6	1	101	2	148	16	8	8	10	.444	2	0-0	0	3.92
1989 Texas	AL	31	31	5	0	194.1	869	182	123	111	14	11	8	2	114	3	166	7	4	12	13	.480	1	0-0	0	5.14
1990 Texas	AL	33	32	7	1	222	954	197	98	83	12	5	6	4	110	3	221	11	2	17	10	.630	1	0-0	0	3.36
1991 Texas	AL	17	16	1	0	88.2	413	84	66	60	4	3	4	1	74	1	82	8	0	3	7	.300	1	0-0	0	6.09
1992 Tex-Oak	AL	31	31	0	0	193	848	183	99	92	16	7	10	2	114	2	125	9	1	10	14	.417	0	0-0	0	4.29
1993 Oakland	AL	35	33	5	0	220	950	226	112	103	16	9	8	3	91	5	131	8	1	14	13	.519	1	0-0	0	4.21
1994 Oakland	AL	24	24	5	0	135.2	618	151	88	76	22	2	7	5	70	4	111	6	1	8	10	.444	3	0-0	0	5.04
1995 Fla-Tex		29	29	2	0	172	748	185	87	79	12	7	5	3	68	2	141	7	0	5	11	.313	0	0-0	0	4.13
1996 Texas	AL	33	32	2	1	199.2	903	235	129	120	28	2	7	2	96	3	157	4	1	16	12	.571	0	0-0	0	5.41
1997 Texas	AL	34	32	3	1	209	919	245	118	112	33	3	7	0	74	4	121	7	0	12	12	.500	0	0-0	0	4.82
1998 Tex-StL		31	18	0	8	116.2	546	150	94	85	21	6	5	2	53	2	58	3	2	7	9	.438	0	0-0	0	6.56
1999 Tampa Bay	AL	32	32	3	0	180.1	815	213	130	117	23	7	8	3	96	1	123	9	1	7	15	.318	2	0-0	0	5.84
2000 Cleveland	AL	7	2	0	2	15.1	77	28	13	13	4	0	0	0	6	1	6	2	0	2	0	1.000	0	0-0	0	7.63
1992 Texas	AL	25	25	0	0	161.1	708	152	87	80	14	5	8	2	95	1	100	6	1	9	13	.409	0	0-0	0	4.46
Oakland	AL	6	6	0	0	31.2	140	31	12	12	2	2	2	0	19	1	25	3	0	1	1	.500	0	0-0	0	3.41
1995 Florida	NL	19	19	1	0	110.2	472	104	52	48	8	5	3	2	47	1	95	2	0	2	7	.222	0	0-0	0	3.90
Texas	AL	10	10	1	0	61.1	276	81	35	31	4	2	2	1	21	1	46	5	0	3	4	.429	0	0-0	0	4.55
1998 Texas	AL	14	13	0	0	69.1	329	95	62	59	14	2	4	0	33	1	30	2	1	5	4	.556	0	0-0	0	7.66
St. Louis	NL	17	5	0	8	47.1	217	55	32	26	7	4	1	2	20	1	28	1	1	2	5	.286	0	0-0	0	4.94
15 ML YEARS		416	390	47	13	2421.2	10810	2457	1426	1301	246	77	95	36	1350	36	1924	126	26	138	156	.469	11	0-0	0	4.84

Mark Wohlers

Pitches: Right **Bats:** Right **Pos:** RP-20 **Ht:** 6'4" **Wt:** 207 **Born:** 1/23/70 **Age:** 31

Year Team	Lg	G	GS	CG	GF	IP	BFP	H	R	ER	HR	SH	SF	HB	TBB	IBB	SO	WP	Bk	W	L	Pct.	ShO	Sv-Op	Hld	ERA
2000 Dayton *	A	3	3	0	0	3	11	1	1	1	0	0	0	0	1	0	7	0	0	0	0	—	0	0--	—	3.00
Louisville *	AAA	17	2	0	6	20.2	103	30	21	14	4	1	2	0	9	0	16	5	0	1	2	.333	0	0--	—	6.10
1991 Atlanta	NL	17	0	0	4	19.2	89	17	7	7	1	2	1	2	13	1	13	0	0	3	1	.750	0	2-4	2	3.20
1992 Atlanta	NL	32	0	0	16	35.1	140	28	11	10	0	5	1	1	14	4	17	1	0	1	2	.333	0	4-6	2	2.55
1993 Atlanta	NL	46	0	0	13	48	199	37	25	24	2	5	1	1	22	3	45	0	0	6	2	.750	0	0-0	12	4.50
1994 Atlanta	NL	51	0	0	15	51	236	51	35	26	1	4	6	0	33	9	58	2	0	7	2	.778	0	1-2	7	4.59
1995 Atlanta	NL	65	0	0	49	64.2	269	51	16	15	2	2	0	1	24	3	90	4	0	7	3	.700	0	25-29	2	2.09
1996 Atlanta	NL	77	0	0	64	77.1	323	71	30	26	8	2	2	2	21	3	100	10	0	2	4	.333	0	39-44	3	3.03
1997 Atlanta	NL	71	0	0	55	69.1	300	57	29	27	4	4	4	0	38	0	92	6	0	5	7	.417	0	33-40	1	3.50
1998 Atlanta	NL	27	0	0	17	20.1	113	18	23	23	2	1	0	1	33	0	22	7	0	0	1	.000	0	8-8	0	10.18
1999 Atlanta	NL	2	0	0	0	0.2	10	1	2	2	0	1	0	0	6	0	0	0	0	0	0	—	0	0-0	0	27.00
2000 Cincinnati	NL	20	0	0	7	28	119	19	14	14	3	2	1	0	17	0	20	2	0	1	2	.333	0	0-0	0	4.50
10 ML YEARS		408	0	0	240	414.1	1798	350	192	174	23	28	16	8	221	25	457	32	0	32	24	.571	0	112-133	26	3.78

Randy Wolf

Pitches: Left **Bats:** Left **Pos:** SP-32

Ht: 6'0" **Wt:** 194 **Born:** 8/22/76 **Age:** 24

		HOW MUCH HE PITCHED						WHAT HE GAVE UP										THE RESULTS						
Year Team	Lg	G	GS	CG	GF	IP	BFP	H	R	ER	HR	SH	SF	HB	TBB	IBB	SO	WP	Bk	W	L	Pct.	ShO	Sv-Op	Hld	ERA
1997 Batavia	A-	7	7	0	0	40	153	29	8	7	1	0	1	2	8	0	53	0	0	4	0	1.000	0	0- —	—	1.58
1998 Reading	AA	4	4	0	0	25	92	15	4	4	0	0	0	1	4	0	33	0	0	2	0	1.000	0	0- —	—	1.44
Scrantn-WB	AAA	24	23	1	0	148	650	167	88	76	16	2	10	4	48	4	118	6	1	9	7	.563	0	0- —	—	4.62
1999 Scrantn-WB	AAA	12	12	0	0	77.1	329	73	36	31	8	1	2	1	29	1	72	4	0	4	5	.444	0	0- —	—	3.61
1999 Philadelphia	NL	22	21	0	0	121.2	552	126	78	75	20	5	1	5	67	0	116	4	0	6	9	.400	0	0-0	0	5.55
2000 Philadelphia	NL	32	32	1	0	206.1	889	210	107	100	25	10	8	8	83	2	160	1	0	11	9	.550	0	0-0	0	4.36
2 ML YEARS		54	53	1	0	328	1441	336	185	175	45	15	9	13	150	2	276	5	0	17	18	.486	0	0-0	0	4.80

Tony Womack

Bats: Left **Throws:** Right **Pos:** SS-143; PH/PR-3; RF-2

Ht: 5'9" **Wt:** 159 **Born:** 9/25/69 **Age:** 31

		BATTING																BASERUNNING				PERCENTAGES		
Year Team	Lg	G	AB	H	2B	3B	HR	(Hm	Rd)	TB	R	RBI	TBB	IBB	SO	HBP	SH	SF	SB	CS	SB%	GDP	Avg	OBP	SLG
1993 Pittsburgh	NL	15	24	2	0	0	0	(0	0)	2	5	0	3	0	3	0	1	0	2	0	1.00	1	.083	.185	.083
1994 Pittsburgh	NL	5	12	4	0	0	0	(0	0)	4	4	1	2	0	3	0	0	0	0	0	—	0	.333	.429	.333
1996 Pittsburgh	NL	17	30	10	3	1	0	(0	0)	15	11	7	6	0	1	1	3	0	2	0	1.00	0	.333	.459	.500
1997 Pittsburgh	NL	155	641	178	26	9	6	(5	1)	240	85	50	43	2	109	3	2	0	60	7	.90	6	.278	.326	.374
1998 Pittsburgh	NL	159	655	185	26	7	3	(2	1)	234	85	45	38	1	94	0	6	5	58	8	.88	4	.282	.319	.357
1999 Arizona	NL	144	614	170	25	10	4	(1	3)	227	111	41	52	0	68	2	9	7	72	13	.85	4	.277	.332	.370
2000 Arizona	NL	146	617	167	21	14	7	(4	3)	237	95	57	30	0	74	5	2	5	45	11	.80	6	.271	.307	.384
7 ML YEARS		641	2593	716	101	41	20	(12	8)	959	396	201	174	3	352	11	23	17	239	39	.86	20	.276	.322	.370

Kerry Wood

Pitches: Right **Bats:** Right **Pos:** SP-23

Ht: 6'5" **Wt:** 230 **Born:** 6/16/77 **Age:** 24

		HOW MUCH HE PITCHED						WHAT HE GAVE UP										THE RESULTS						
Year Team	Lg	G	GS	CG	GF	IP	BFP	H	R	ER	HR	SH	SF	HB	TBB	IBB	SO	WP	Bk	W	L	Pct.	ShO	Sv-Op	Hld	ERA
1995 Cubs	R	1	1	0	0	3	9	0	0	0	0	0	0	1	0	2	0	0	0	0	—	0	0- —		0.00
Williamsprt	A-	2	2	0	0	4.1	23	5	8	5	0	0	0	0	5	0	5	1	0	0	0	—	0	0- —		10.38
1996 Daytona	A+	22	22	0	0	114.1	495	72	51	37	6	5	4	14	70	0	136	10	7	10	2	.833	0	0- —		2.91
1997 Orlando	AA	19	19	0	0	94	416	58	49	47	2	0	6	10	79	2	106	10	4	6	7	.462	0	0- —		4.50
Iowa	AAA	10	10	0	0	57.2	254	35	35	30	2	3	0	6	52	0	80	8	2	4	2	.667	0	0- —		4.68
1998 Iowa	AAA	1	1	0	0	5	17	1	0	0	0	0	0	0	2	0	11	0	0	1	0	1.000	0	0- —		0.00
2000 Daytona	A+	2	2	0	0	12	42	3	2	2	0	0	0	0	5	0	17	0	1	2	0	1.000	0	0- —		1.50
Iowa	AAA	1	1	0	0	7	27	4	2	2	1	0	0	0	4	0	7	1	0	0	0	—	0	0- —		2.57
1998 Chicago	NL	26	26	1	0	166.2	699	117	69	63	14	2	4	11	85	1	233	6	3	13	6	.684	1	0-0	0	3.40
2000 Chicago	NL	23	23	1	0	137	603	112	77	73	17	7	5	9	87	0	132	5	1	8	7	.533	0	0-0	0	4.80
2 ML YEARS		49	49	2	0	303.2	1302	229	146	136	31	9	9	20	172	1	365	11	4	21	13	.618	1	0-0	0	4.03

Steve Woodard

Pitches: Right **Bats:** Left **Pos:** SP-22; RP-18

Ht: 6'4" **Wt:** 217 **Born:** 5/15/75 **Age:** 26

		HOW MUCH HE PITCHED						WHAT HE GAVE UP										THE RESULTS						
Year Team	Lg	G	GS	CG	GF	IP	BFP	H	R	ER	HR	SH	SF	HB	TBB	IBB	SO	WP	Bk	W	L	Pct.	ShO	Sv-Op	Hld	ERA
1997 Milwaukee	AL	7	7	0	0	36.2	153	39	25	21	5	0	0	2	6	0	32	0	0	3	3	.500	0	0-0	0	5.15
1998 Milwaukee	NL	34	26	0	2	165.2	692	170	83	77	19	2	4	9	33	4	135	3	2	10	12	.455	0	0-0	0	4.18
1999 Milwaukee	NL	31	29	2	0	185	801	219	101	93	23	9	4	6	36	7	119	4	1	11	8	.579	0	0-0	0	4.52
2000 Mil-Cle		40	22	1	7	147.2	659	182	105	96	26	8	4	6	44	5	100	8	0	4	10	.286	0	0-0	0	5.85
2000 Milwaukee	NL	27	11	1	6	93.2	432	125	70	62	16	7	3	4	33	4	65	5	0	1	7	.125	0	0-0	0	5.96
Cleveland	AL	13	11	0	1	54	227	57	35	34	10	1	1	2	11	1	35	3	0	3	3	.500	0	0-0	0	5.67
4 ML YEARS		112	84	3	9	535	2305	610	314	287	73	19	12	23	119	16	386	15	3	28	33	.459	0	0-0	0	4.83

Chris Woodward

Bats: R **Throws:** R **Pos:** SS-22; 3B-9; 1B-3; 2B-3; PH/PR-3

Ht: 6'0" **Wt:** 173 **Born:** 6/27/76 **Age:** 25

		BATTING																BASERUNNING				PERCENTAGES		
Year Team	Lg	G	AB	H	2B	3B	HR	(Hm	Rd)	TB	R	RBI	TBB	IBB	SO	HBP	SH	SF	SB	CS	SB%	GDP	Avg	OBP	SLG
1995 Medcine Hat	R+	72	241	56	8	0	3	—	—	73	44	21	33	1	41	6	5	3	9	4	.69	1	.232	.336	.303
1996 Hagerstown	A	123	424	95	24	2	1	—	—	126	41	48	43	1	70	5	7	5	11	3	.79	3	.224	.300	.297
1997 Dunedin	A+	91	314	92	13	4	1	—	—	116	38	38	52	0	52	5	3	4	4	8	.33	3	.293	.397	.369
1998 Knoxville	AA	73	253	62	12	0	3	—	—	83	36	27	26	1	47	3	3	3	3	5	.38	4	.245	.319	.328
Syracuse	AAA	25	85	17	6	0	2	—	—	29	9	6	7	0	20	0	1	0	1	1	.50	4	.200	.261	.341
1999 Syracuse	AAA	75	281	82	20	3	1	—	—	111	46	20	38	1	49	1	1	0	4	1	.80	5	.292	.378	.395
2000 Syracuse	AAA	37	143	46	13	2	5	—	—	78	23	25	11	0	30	0	1	0	2	0	1.00	3	.322	.370	.545
1999 Toronto	AL	14	26	6	1	0	0	(0	0)	7	1	2	2	0	6	0	0	1	0	0	—	1	.231	.276	.269
2000 Toronto	AL	37	104	19	7	0	3	(1	2)	35	16	14	10	3	28	0	1	0	1	0	1.00	1	.183	.254	.337
2 ML YEARS		51	130	25	8	0	3	(1	2)	42	17	16	12	3	34	0	1	1	1	0	1.00	2	.192	.259	.323

Shawn Wooten

Bats: Right **Throws:** Right **Pos:** C-4; 1B-3; PH/PR-1

Ht: 5'10" **Wt:** 205 **Born:** 7/24/72 **Age:** 28

		BATTING																BASERUNNING				PERCENTAGES		
Year Team	Lg	G	AB	H	2B	3B	HR	(Hm	Rd)	TB	R	RBI	TBB	IBB	SO	HBP	SH	SF	SB	CS	SB%	GDP	Avg	OBP	SLG
1993 Bristol	R+	52	177	62	12	2	8	—	—	102	26	39	24	2	20	3	0	2	1	2	.33	1	.350	.432	.576
Fayettevlle	A	5	16	4	0	0	1	—	—	7	2	5	3	0	3	0	0	0	0	0	—	0	.250	.368	.438
1994 Fayettevlle	A	121	439	118	25	1	3	—	—	154	45	61	27	0	84	11	3	4	1	3	.25	11	.269	.324	.351
1995 Jacksnville	AA	20	70	9	1	0	2	—	—	16	4	7	1	0	17	1	0	1	0	0	3	.129	.151	.229
Lakeland	A+	38	135	31	10	1	2	—	—	49	11	11	10	0	28	2	0	1	0	1	.00	2	.230	.291	.363
1996 Moose Jaw	IND	77	292	89	17	0	12	—	—	142	44	57	18	2	46	2	0	1	2	0	1.00	8	.305	.348	.486
1997 Cedar Rapds	A	108	353	102	23	1	15	—	—	172	43	75	49	0	71	6	3	6	0	1	.00	8	.289	.379	.487

		BATTING										BASERUNNING				PERCENTAGES		
Year Team	Lg	G AB H	2B 3B HR	(Hm Rd)	TB	R RBI	TBB IBB SO HBP SH SF					SB CS SB% GDP				Avg OBP SLG		
1998 Midland	AA	8 28 9	4 0 1	— —	16	3 6	3 0 4 0 0 0					0 0 — 0				.321 .387 .571		
Lk Elsinore	A+	105 395 116	31 0 16	— —	195	56 74	38 3 82 3 0 4					0 2 .00 9				.294 .357 .494		
1999 Erie	AA	137 518 151	27 1 19	— —	237	70 88	50 1 102 10 1 8					3 1 .75 12				.292 .360 .458		
2000 Erie	AA	51 191 56	12 2 9	— —	99	32 35	17 0 30 2 0 4					4 1 .80 3				.293 .350 .518		
Edmonton	AAA	66 252 89	21 3 11	— —	149	43 42	18 0 38 3 0 1					0 0 — 4				.353 .401 .591		
2000 Anaheim	AL	7 9 5	1 0 0	(0 0)	6	2 1	0 0 0 0 0 0					0 0 — 0				.556 .556 .667		

Tim Worrell

Pitches: Right **Bats:** Right **Pos:** RP-59   **Ht:** 6'4" **Wt:** 231 **Born:** 7/5/67 **Age:** 33

		HOW MUCH HE PITCHED		WHAT HE GAVE UP			THE RESULTS		
Year Team	Lg	G GS CG GF	IP BFP	H R ER HR SH SF HB	TBB IBB SO WP Bk		W L Pct. ShO Sv-Op Hld		ERA
2000 Iowa *	AAA	6 0 0 0	10.2 44	9 6 6 3 0 0 1	5 1 7 2 0		2 0 1.000 0 0-– —		5.06
1993 San Diego	NL	21 16 0 1	100.2 443	104 63 55 11 8 5 0	43 5 52 3 0		2 7 .222 0 0-0 1		4.92
1994 San Diego	NL	3 3 0 0	14.2 59	9 7 6 1 0 1 0	5 0 14 0 0		0 1 .000 0 0-0 4		3.68
1995 San Diego	NL	9 0 0 4	13.1 63	16 7 7 2 1 0 1	6 0 13 1 0		1 0 1.000 0 0-0 4		4.73
1996 San Diego	NL	50 11 0 8	121 510	109 45 41 9 3 1 6	39 1 99 0 0		9 7 .563 0 1-2 10		3.05
1997 San Diego	NL	60 10 0 14	106.1 483	116 67 61 14 6 6 7	50 2 81 2 1		4 8 .333 0 3-7 16		5.16
1998 Det-Cle-Oak	AL	43 9 0 5	103 440	106 62 60 16 2 3 1	29 3 82 2 0		2 7 .222 0 0-3 6		5.24
1999 Oakland	AL	53 0 0 17	69.1 309	69 38 32 6 1 1 3	34 1 62 1 0		2 2 .500 0 0-5 5		4.15
2000 Bal-ChC	AL	59 0 0 29	69.1 307	72 26 23 10 4 1 1	29 11 57 1 0		5 6 .455 0 3-6 12		2.99
1998 Detroit	AL	15 9 0 0	61.2 265	66 42 41 11 0 1 1	19 2 47 0 0		2 6 .250 0 0-1 0		5.98
Cleveland	AL	3 0 0 1	5.1 24	6 3 3 0 0 2 0	2 0 2 0 0		0 0 — 0 0-0 0		5.06
Oakland	AL	25 0 0 4	36 151	34 17 16 5 2 0 0	8 1 33 2 0		0 1 .000 0 0-2 6		4.00
2000 Baltimore	AL	5 0 0 2	7.1 39	12 6 6 3 0 0 0	5 3 5 0 0		2 1 .500 0 0-0 0		7.36
Chicago	NL	54 0 0 27	62 268	60 20 17 7 4 1 1	24 8 52 1 0		3 4 .429 0 3-6 12		2.47
8 ML YEARS		298 49 0 78	597.2 2614	601 315 285 68 25 18 19	235 23 460 10 1		25 38 .397 0 7-23 50		4.29

Jamey Wright

Pitches: Right **Bats:** Right **Pos:** SP-25; RP-1   **Ht:** 6'5" **Wt:** 221 **Born:** 12/24/74 **Age:** 26

		HOW MUCH HE PITCHED		WHAT HE GAVE UP			THE RESULTS		
Year Team	Lg	G GS CG GF	IP BFP	H R ER HR SH SF HB	TBB IBB SO WP Bk		W L Pct. ShO Sv-Op Hld		ERA
2000 Huntsville *	AA	2 2 0 0	12.1 46	7 0 0 0 0 0 1	5 0 10 1 0		2 0 1.000 0 0-– —		0.00
Indianapols *	AAA	1 1 0 0	5 25	8 5 1 0 0 0 0	3 0 7 0 0		0 0 — 0 0-– —		1.80
1996 Colorado	NL	16 15 0 0	91.1 406	105 60 50 8 4 2 7	41 1 45 1 2		4 4 .500 0 0-0 1		4.93
1997 Colorado	NL	26 26 1 0	149.2 698	198 113 104 19 8 3 11	71 3 59 6 2		8 12 .400 0 0-0 0		6.25
1998 Colorado	NL	34 34 1 0	206.1 919	235 143 130 24 8 6 11	95 3 86 6 3		9 14 .391 0 0-0 0		5.67
1999 Colorado	NL	16 16 0 0	94.1 423	110 52 51 10 3 4 4	54 3 49 3 0		4 3 .571 0 0-0 0		4.87
2000 Milwaukee	NL	26 25 0 1	164.2 718	157 81 75 12 4 6 18	88 5 96 9 2		4 5 .438 0 0-0 0		4.10
5 ML YEARS		118 116 2 1	706.1 3164	805 449 410 73 27 21 51	349 15 335 25 9		32 42 .432 0 0-0 1		5.22

Jaret Wright

Pitches: Right **Bats:** Right **Pos:** SP-9   **Ht:** 6'2" **Wt:** 230 **Born:** 12/29/75 **Age:** 25

		HOW MUCH HE PITCHED		WHAT HE GAVE UP			THE RESULTS		
Year Team	Lg	G GS CG GF	IP BFP	H R ER HR SH SF HB	TBB IBB SO WP Bk		W L Pct. ShO Sv-Op Hld		ERA
2000 Buffalo *	AAA	1 1 0 0	2 6	0 0 0 0 0 0 0	1 0 1 0 0		0 0 — 0 0-– —		0.00
Akron *	AA	2 2 0 0	8 33	4 3 3 0 0 0 0	3 0 5 1 1		0 0 — 0 0-– —		3.38
1997 Cleveland	AL	16 16 0 0	90.1 381	81 45 44 9 3 4 5	35 0 63 1 0		8 3 .727 0 0-0 0		4.38
1998 Cleveland	AL	32 32 1 0	192.2 855	207 109 101 22 4 6 11	87 4 140 6 0		12 10 .545 1 0-0 0		4.72
1999 Cleveland	AL	26 26 0 0	133.2 609	144 99 90 18 3 3 7	77 1 91 4 0		8 10 .444 0 0-0 0		6.06
2000 Cleveland	AL	9 9 1 0	51.2 217	44 27 27 6 0 1 1	28 0 36 2 0		3 4 .429 1 0-0 0		4.70
4 ML YEARS		83 83 2 0	468.1 2069	476 280 262 55 10 14 24	227 5 330 13 0		31 27 .534 2 0-0 0		5.03

Kelly Wunsch

Pitches: Left **Bats:** Left **Pos:** RP-83   **Ht:** 6'5" **Wt:** 192 **Born:** 7/12/72 **Age:** 28

		HOW MUCH HE PITCHED		WHAT HE GAVE UP			THE RESULTS		
Year Team	Lg	G GS CG GF	IP BFP	H R ER HR SH SF HB	TBB IBB SO WP Bk		W L Pct. ShO Sv-Op Hld		ERA
1993 Beloit	A	12 12 0 0	63.1 282	58 39 34 5 4 1 1	39 1 61 5 2		1 5 .167 0 0-– —		4.83
1994 Beloit	A	17 17 0 0	83.1 400	88 69 57 11 4 3 13	47 1 77 6 0		3 10 .231 0 0-– —		6.16
Helena	R+	9 9 1 0	51 238	52 39 29 7 1 2 10	30 0 37 6 1		4 2 .667 0 0-– —		5.12
1995 Beloit	A	14 14 0 0	85.2 364	90 47 40 7 2 3 7	37 0 62 6 0		4 7 .364 1 0-– —		4.20
1997 Stockton	A+	24 22 2 0	143 627	141 65 55 11 10 4 14	62 0 98 9 2		7 9 .438 2 0-– —		3.46
1998 El Paso	AA	17 17 1 0	101.1 469	127 81 67 11 4 3 9	31 0 70 7 0		5 6 .455 0 0-– —		5.95
Louisville	AAA	9 8 0 0	51.2 220	53 23 22 6 0 1 3	15 0 36 2 0		3 1 .750 0 0-– —		3.83
1999 Huntsville	AA	22 3 0 7	50.2 204	40 13 11 1 1 1 4	23 1 35 0 0		4 1 .800 0 1-– —		1.95
Louisville	AAA	16 2 0 3	41.2 189	52 23 22 4 0 2 6	14 0 20 3 0		2 1 .667 0 0-– —		4.75
2000 Chicago	AL	83 0 0 12	61.1 259	50 22 20 4 0 2 2	29 1 51 0 0		6 3 .667 0 1-5 25		2.93

Esteban Yan

Pitches: Right **Bats:** Right **Pos:** RP-23; SP-20   **Ht:** 6'4" **Wt:** 230 **Born:** 6/22/74 **Age:** 27

		HOW MUCH HE PITCHED		WHAT HE GAVE UP			THE RESULTS		
Year Team	Lg	G GS CG GF	IP BFP	H R ER HR SH SF HB	TBB IBB SO WP Bk		W L Pct. ShO Sv-Op Hld		ERA
1996 Baltimore	AL	4 0 0 2	9.1 42	13 7 6 3 0 0 0	3 1 7 0 0		0 0 — 0 0-0 0		5.79
1997 Baltimore	AL	3 2 0 0	9.2 58	20 18 17 3 0 1 2	7 0 4 1 0		0 1 .000 0 0-0 0		15.83
1998 Tampa Bay	AL	64 0 0 18	88.2 381	78 41 38 11 1 3 5	42 1 77 6 0		5 4 .556 0 1-5 3		3.86
1999 Tampa Bay	AL	50 1 0 15	61 286	77 41 40 8 6 3 9	32 4 46 2 0		3 4 .429 0 0-3 7		5.90
2000 Tampa Bay	AL	43 20 0 8	137.2 618	158 98 95 26 4 6 11	40 0 111 7 1		7 8 .467 0 0-2 3		6.21
5 ML YEARS		164 23 0 43	306.1 1385	346 205 196 51 11 13 27	125 7 245 16 1		15 17 .469 0 1-10 18		5.76

Ed Yarnall

Pitches: Left **Bats:** Left **Pos:** SP-1; RP-1

Ht: 6'3" **Wt:** 234 **Born:** 12/4/75 **Age:** 25

Year Team	Lg	G	GS	CG	GF	IP	BFP	H	R	ER	HR	SH	SF	HB	TBB	IBB	SO	WP	Bk	W	L	Pct.	ShO	Sv-Op	Hld	ERA
1997 St. Lucie	A+	18	18	2	0	105.1	435	93	33	29	5	2	1	2	30	0	114	2	4	5	8	.385	0	0- --	—	2.48
Norfolk	AAA	1	1	0	0	5	29	11	8	8	1	0	0	0	7	2	2	0	0	1	0	1.000	0	0- --	—	14.40
Binghamton	AA	5	5	0	0	32.1	127	20	11	11	2	2	1	0	11	0	32	0	0	3	2	.600	0	0- --	—	3.06
1998 Binghamton	AA	7	7	0	0	46.2	177	20	5	2	0	0	1	1	17	0	52	1	1	7	0	1.000	0	0- --	—	0.39
Portland	AA	2	2	0	0	15.1	59	9	5	5	2	1	0	1	4	0	15	1	0	2	0	1.000	0	0- --	—	2.93
Charlotte	AAA	15	13	2	0	69.2	331	79	60	48	11	5	3	3	39	4	47	2	1	4	5	.444	0	0- --	—	6.20
1999 Columbus	AAA	23	23	1	0	145.1	611	136	61	56	5	3	8	3	57	0	146	2	1	13	4	.765	1	0- --	—	3.47
2000 Columbus	AAA	10	10	1	0	49.1	210	43	27	25	4	3	4	4	26	1	34	2	0	2	1	.667	0	0- --	—	4.56
Louisville	AAA	11	11	0	0	67.2	306	72	32	29	7	2	1	2	34	0	59	2	0	3	4	.429	0	0- --	—	3.86
1999 New York	AL	5	2	0	2	17	77	17	8	7	1	0	0	0	10	0	13	0	0	1	0	1.000	0	0-0	0	3.71
2000 New York	AL	2	1	0	1	3	16	5	5	5	1	0	0	1	3	0	1	0	0	0	0	—	0	0-0	0	15.00
2 ML YEARS		7	3	0	3	20	93	22	13	12	2	0	0	1	13	0	14	0	0	1	0	1.000	0	0-0	0	5.40

Masato Yoshii

Pitches: Right **Bats:** Right **Pos:** SP-29

Ht: 6'2" **Wt:** 210 **Born:** 4/20/65 **Age:** 36

Year Team	Lg	G	GS	CG	GF	IP	BFP	H	R	ER	HR	SH	SF	HB	TBB	IBB	SO	WP	Bk	W	L	Pct.	ShO	Sv-Op	Hld	ERA
1998 New York	NL	29	29	1	0	171.2	724	166	79	75	22	9	4	6	53	5	117	5	1	6	8	.429	0	0-0	0	3.93
1999 New York	NL	31	29	1	1	174	723	168	86	85	25	7	6	6	58	3	105	1	0	12	8	.600	0	0-0	0	4.40
2000 Colorado	NL	29	29	0	0	167.1	726	201	112	109	32	8	7	2	53	6	88	2	1	6	15	.286	0	0-0	0	5.86
3 ML YEARS		89	87	2	1	513	2173	535	277	269	79	24	17	14	164	14	310	8	2	24	31	.436	0	0-0	0	4.72

Danny Young

Pitches: Left **Bats:** Right **Pos:** RP-4

Ht: 6'4" **Wt:** 210 **Born:** 11/3/71 **Age:** 29

Year Team	Lg	G	GS	CG	GF	IP	BFP	H	R	ER	HR	SH	SF	HB	TBB	IBB	SO	WP	Bk	W	L	Pct.	ShO	Sv-Op	Hld	ERA
1991 Astros	R	13	7	0	0	32.2	170	32	33	29	1	0	1	2	39	0	41	12	1	1	4	.200	0	0- --	—	7.99
1992 Asheville	A	20	20	0	0	94.2	438	106	65	45	5	2	1	2	70	1	64	11	3	3	10	.231	0	0- --	—	4.28
1993 Asheville	A	32	24	2	0	142.2	679	174	114	97	13	6	7	7	95	1	101	16	3	5	14	.263	1	0- --	—	6.12
1994 Salem	A+	10	0	0	2	18.2	94	32	17	16	2	0	1	0	9	0	12	3	0	2	0	1.000	0	0- --	—	7.71
Augusta	A	21	9	0	3	66.2	290	58	32	25	2	2	3	2	33	0	73	6	1	2	5	.286	0	0- --	—	3.38
1995 Augusta	A	6	2	0	1	14.1	66	9	6	4	0	0	1	0	16	0	11	2	0	1	0	1.000	0	0- --	—	2.51
Lynchburg	A+	24	2	0	7	41.1	196	52	37	34	3	1	2	2	27	1	34	5	0	2	4	.333	0	0- --	—	7.40
1996 Augusta	A	22	1	0	6	33.2	171	36	33	22	1	2	3	3	29	2	36	12	2	0	4	.000	0	2- --	—	5.88
1997 Lynchburg	A+	15	0	0	8	24.1	113	27	17	16	2	1	1	1	14	0	22	0	0	0	0	—	0	0- --	—	5.92
Augusta	A	3	2	0	0	7.1	42	16	15	8	1	0	0	2	5	0	5	0	0	2	0	.000	0	0- --	—	9.82
1998 Daytona	A+	7	0	0	3	8.2	42	9	5	5	0	0	0	0	8	0	6	1	0	1	1	.500	0	0- --	—	5.19
West Tenn	AA	23	1	0	4	27	114	22	13	11	1	2	0	1	15	0	20	2	0	0	2	.000	0	0- --	—	3.67
Iowa	AAA	2	0	0	0	2	7	1	0	0	0	0	0	0	1	0	1	0	0	0	0	—	0	0- --	—	0.00
1999 West Tenn	AA	27	8	0	2	60.1	258	48	25	22	2	1	2	0	38	0	67	5	3	3	5	.375	0	0- --	—	3.28
2000 Iowa	AAA	27	0	0	10	37	169	36	27	23	3	3	1	2	22	1	30	3	0	2	1	.667	0	1- --	—	5.59
2000 Chicago	NL	4	0	0	2	3	20	5	7	7	1	0	0	0	6	0	0	0	0	1	0	1.000	0	0-0	0	21.00

Dmitri Young

Bats: B **Throws:** R **Pos:** LF-111; 1B-36; PH/PR-13; DH-4; RF-1

Ht: 6'2" **Wt:** 235 **Born:** 10/11/73 **Age:** 27

Year Team	Lg	G	AB	H	2B	3B	HR	(Hm	Rd)	TB	R	RBI	TBB	IBB	SO	HBP	SH	SF	SB	CS	SB%	GDP	Avg	OBP	SLG
1996 St. Louis	NL	16	29	7	0	0	0	(0	0)	7	3	2	4	0	5	1	0	0	0	1	.00	1	.241	.353	.241
1997 St. Louis	NL	110	333	86	14	3	5	(2	3)	121	38	34	38	3	63	2	1	3	6	5	.55	8	.258	.335	.363
1998 Cincinnati	NL	144	536	166	48	1	14	(3	11)	258	81	83	47	4	94	2	0	5	2	4	.33	16	.310	.364	.481
1999 Cincinnati	NL	127	373	112	30	2	14	(9	5)	188	63	56	30	1	71	2	0	4	3	1	.75	11	.300	.352	.504
2000 Cincinnati	NL	152	548	166	37	6	18	(6	12)	269	68	88	36	6	80	3	1	5	0	3	.00	16	.303	.346	.491
5 ML YEARS		549	1819	537	129	12	51	(20	31)	843	253	263	155	14	313	10	2	17	11	14	.44	52	.295	.351	.463

Eric Young

Bats: Right **Throws:** Right **Pos:** 2B-150; PH/PR-4

Ht: 5'8" **Wt:** 175 **Born:** 5/18/67 **Age:** 34

Year Team	Lg	G	AB	H	2B	3B	HR	(Hm	Rd)	TB	R	RBI	TBB	IBB	SO	HBP	SH	SF	SB	CS	SB%	GDP	Avg	OBP	SLG
1992 Los Angeles	NL	49	132	34	1	0	1	(0	1)	38	9	11	8	0	9	4	0	1	6	1	.86	3	.258	.300	.288
1993 Colorado	NL	144	490	132	16	8	3	(3	0)	173	82	42	63	3	41	4	4	4	42	19	.69	9	.269	.355	.353
1994 Colorado	NL	90	228	62	13	1	7	(6	1)	98	37	30	38	1	17	2	5	2	18	7	.72	3	.272	.378	.430
1995 Colorado	NL	120	366	116	21	9	6	(5	1)	173	68	36	49	3	29	5	3	1	35	12	.74	4	.317	.404	.473
1996 Colorado	NL	141	568	184	23	4	8	(7	1)	239	113	74	47	1	31	21	2	5	53	19	.74	9	.324	.393	.421
1997 Col-LA	NL	155	622	174	33	8	8	(2	6)	247	106	61	71	1	54	9	10	6	45	14	.76	18	.280	.359	.397
1998 Los Angeles	NL	117	452	129	24	1	8	(7	1)	179	78	43	45	0	32	5	9	2	42	13	.76	4	.285	.355	.396
1999 Los Angeles	NL	119	456	128	24	2	2	(2	0)	162	73	41	63	0	26	5	6	4	51	22	.70	12	.281	.371	.355
2000 Chicago	NL	153	607	180	40	2	6	(5	1)	242	98	47	63	1	39	8	7	5	54	7	.89	12	.297	.367	.399
1997 Colorado	NL	118	468	132	29	6	6	(2	4)	191	78	45	57	0	37	5	8	5	32	12	.73	16	.282	.363	.408
Los Angeles		37	154	42	4	2	2	(0	2)	56	28	16	14	1	17	4	2	1	13	2	.87	2	.273	.347	.364
9 ML YEARS		1088	3921	1139	195	35	49	(37	12)	1551	664	385	447	10	278	59	50	29	346	114	.75	74	.290	.369	.396

Kevin Young

Bats: Right **Throws:** Right **Pos:** 1B-129; PH/PR-5; DH-1   **Ht:** 6'3" **Wt:** 222 **Born:** 6/16/69 **Age:** 32

Year Team	Lg	G	AB	H	2B	3B	HR	(Hm	Rd)	TB	R	RBI	TBB	IBB	SO	HBP	SH	SF	SB	CS	SB%	GDP	Avg	OBP	SLG
1992 Pittsburgh	NL	10	7	4	0	0	0	(0	0)	4	2	4	2	0	1	0	0	0	1	0	1.00	0	.571	.667	.571
1993 Pittsburgh	NL	141	449	106	24	3	6	(6	0)	154	38	47	36	3	82	9	5	9	2	2	.50	10	.236	.300	.343
1994 Pittsburgh	NL	59	122	25	7	2	1	(1	0)	39	15	11	8	2	34	1	2	1	0	2	.00	3	.205	.258	.320
1995 Pittsburgh	NL	56	181	42	9	0	6	(5	1)	69	13	22	8	0	53	2	1	3	1	3	.25	5	.232	.268	.381
1996 Kansas City	AL	55	132	32	6	0	8	(4	4)	62	20	23	11	0	32	0	0	0	3	3	.50	2	.242	.301	.470
1997 Pittsburgh	NL	97	333	100	18	3	18	(11	7)	178	59	74	16	1	89	4	1	8	11	2	.85	6	.300	.332	.535
1998 Pittsburgh	NL	159	592	160	40	2	27	(15	12)	285	88	108	44	1	127	11	0	9	15	7	.68	20	.270	.328	.481
1999 Pittsburgh	NL	156	584	174	41	6	26	(16	10)	305	103	106	75	5	124	12	0	4	22	10	.69	13	.298	.387	.522
2000 Pittsburgh	NL	132	496	128	27	0	20	(11	9)	215	77	88	32	1	96	8	0	5	8	3	.73	15	.258	.311	.433
9 ML YEARS		865	2896	771	172	16	112	(69	43)	1311	415	483	232	13	637	47	9	39	63	32	.66	74	.266	.327	.453

Mike Young

Bats: Right **Throws:** Right **Pos:** 2B-1; PH/PR-1   **Ht:** 6'0" **Wt:** 185 **Born:** 10/19/76 **Age:** 24

Year Team	Lg	G	AB	H	2B	3B	HR	(Hm	Rd)	TB	R	RBI	TBB	IBB	SO	HBP	SH	SF	SB	CS	SB%	GDP	Avg	OBP	SLG
1997 St.Cathrnes	A-	74	276	85	18	3	9	—	—	136	49	48	33	1	59	7	0	3	9	5	.64	6	.308	.392	.493
1998 Hagerstown	A	140	522	147	33	5	16	—	—	238	86	87	55	1	96	7	7	7	16	8	.67	12	.282	.354	.456
1999 Dunedin	A+	129	495	155	36	3	5	—	—	212	86	83	61	2	78	4	1	5	30	6	.83	10	.313	.389	.428
2000 Tennessee	AA	91	345	95	24	5	6	—	—	147	51	47	36	1	72	1	4	6	16	5	.76	5	.275	.340	.426
Tulsa	AA	43	188	60	13	5	1	—	—	86	30	32	17	1	28	0	3	4	9	3	.75	4	.319	.368	.457
2000 Texas	AL	2	2	0	0	0	0	(0	0)	0	0	0	0	0	1	0	0	0	0	0	—	0	.000	.000	.000

Tim Young

Pitches: Left **Bats:** Left **Pos:** RP-8   **Ht:** 5'9" **Wt:** 170 **Born:** 10/15/73 **Age:** 27

Year Team	Lg	G	GS	CG	GF	IP	BFP	H	R	ER	HR	SH	SF	HB	TBB	IBB	SO	WP	Bk	W	L	Pct.	ShO	Sv-Op	Hld	ERA
1996 Vermont	A-	27	0	0	26	29.1	106	14	1	1	1	2	1	2	4	0	46	0	1	1	0	1.000	0	18-—	—	0.31
1997 Cape Fear	A	45	0	0	41	54	214	33	12	9	0	1	2	2	15	0	66	8	0	1	1	.500	0	18-—	—	1.50
Wst Plm Bch	A+	11	0	0	8	15.2	56	8	1	1	0	2	0	1	4	0	13	0	0	0	0	—	0	5-—	—	0.57
Harrisburg	AA	1	0	0	0	2	7	1	0	0	0	0	0	0	0	0	3	0	0	0	0	—	0	0-—	—	0.00
1998 Harrisburg	AA	26	0	0	19	35.2	146	28	17	15	3	5	0	1	10	0	52	1	0	3	3	.500	0	3-—	—	3.79
Ottawa	AAA	20	0	0	10	26.2	119	26	14	6	1	0	0	1	12	2	34	0	0	1	1	.500	0	2-—	—	2.03
1999 Trenton	AA	31	0	0	12	45.1	204	38	26	22	1	6	1	5	26	0	52	4	0	4	4	.500	0	2-—	—	4.37
2000 Pawtucket	AAA	32	0	0	11	41.1	171	35	13	11	5	1	0	3	12	1	43	0	0	1	1	.500	0	6-—	—	2.40
1998 Montreal	NL	10	0	0	0	6	29	6	4	4	0	1	0	0	4	0	7	0	0	0	0	—	0	0-0	3	6.00
2000 Boston	AL	8	0	0	3	7	29	7	5	5	3	0	0	1	2	0	6	0	0	0	0	—	0	0-0	0	6.43
2 ML YEARS		18	0	0	3	13	58	13	9	9	3	1	0	1	6	0	13	0	0	0	0	—	0	0-0	3	6.23

Gregg Zaun

Bats: B **Throws:** R **Pos:** C-76; PH/PR-16; 1B-1; 2B-1   **Ht:** 5'10" **Wt:** 190 **Born:** 4/14/71 **Age:** 30

Year Team	Lg	G	AB	H	2B	3B	HR	(Hm	Rd)	TB	R	RBI	TBB	IBB	SO	HBP	SH	SF	SB	CS	SB%	GDP	Avg	OBP	SLG
2000 Omaha *	AAA	9	25	7	3	0	0	—	—	10	7	3	4	1	3	0	0	0	1	1	.50	1	.280	.379	.400
1995 Baltimore	AL	40	104	27	5	0	3	(1	2)	41	18	14	16	0	14	0	2	0	1	1	.50	2	.260	.358	.394
1996 Bal-Fla	AL	60	139	34	9	1	2	(1	1)	51	20	15	14	3	20	2	1	2	1	0	1.00	5	.245	.318	.367
1997 Florida	NL	58	143	43	10	2	2	(0	2)	63	21	20	26	4	18	2	1	0	1	0	1.00	3	.301	.415	.441
1998 Florida	NL	106	298	56	12	2	5	(3	2)	87	19	29	35	2	52	1	2	2	5	2	.71	7	.188	.274	.292
1999 Texas	AL	43	93	23	2	1	1	(0	1)	30	12	12	10	0	17	1	2	1	1	0	1.00	5	.247	.314	.323
2000 Kansas City	AL	83	234	64	11	0	7	(2	5)	96	36	33	43	3	34	3	0	1	7	3	.70	4	.274	.390	.410
1996 Baltimore	AL	50	108	25	8	1	1	(1	0)	38	16	13	11	2	15	2	0	2	0	0	—	3	.231	.309	.352
Florida	NL	10	31	9	1	0	1	(0	1)	13	4	2	3	1	5	0	1	0	1	0	1.00	1	.290	.353	.419
6 ML YEARS		390	1011	247	49	6	20	(6	14)	368	126	124	144	12	145	8	7	8	16	6	.73	23	.244	.341	.364

Todd Zeile

Bats: Right **Throws:** Right **Pos:** 1B-151; PH/PR-3   **Ht:** 6'1" **Wt:** 200 **Born:** 9/9/65 **Age:** 35

Year Team	Lg	G	AB	H	2B	3B	HR	(Hm	Rd)	TB	R	RBI	TBB	IBB	SO	HBP	SH	SF	SB	CS	SB%	GDP	Avg	OBP	SLG
1989 St. Louis	NL	28	82	21	3	1	1	(0	1)	29	7	8	9	1	14	0	1	1	0	0	—	1	.256	.326	.354
1990 St. Louis	NL	144	495	121	25	3	15	(8	7)	197	62	57	67	3	77	2	0	6	2	4	.33	11	.244	.333	.398
1991 St. Louis	NL	155	565	158	36	3	11	(7	4)	233	76	81	62	3	94	5	0	6	17	11	.61	15	.280	.353	.412
1992 St. Louis	NL	126	439	113	18	4	7	(4	3)	160	51	48	68	4	70	0	0	7	7	10	.41	11	.257	.352	.364
1993 St. Louis	NL	157	571	158	36	1	17	(8	9)	247	82	103	70	5	76	0	0	7	5	5	.50	15	.277	.352	.433
1994 St. Louis	NL	113	415	111	25	1	19	(9	10)	195	62	75	52	3	56	0	0	7	1	3	.25	9	.267	.348	.470
1995 StL-ChC	NL	113	426	105	22	0	14	(8	6)	169	50	52	34	1	76	4	4	5	1	0	1.00	13	.246	.305	.397
1996 Phi-Bal		163	617	162	32	0	25	(10	15)	269	78	99	82	4	104	1	0	1	1	1	.50	18	.263	.348	.436
1997 Los Angeles	NL	160	575	154	17	0	31	(17	14)	264	89	90	85	7	112	6	0	6	8	7	.53	18	.268	.365	.459
1998 LA-Fla-Tex		158	572	155	32	3	19	(7	12)	250	85	94	69	2	90	4	1	7	4	4	.50	18	.271	.352	.437
1999 Texas	AL	156	588	172	41	1	24	(13	11)	287	98	98	56	3	94	4	1	7	1	2	.33	20	.293	.354	.488
2000 New York	NL	153	544	146	36	3	22	(8	14)	254	67	79	74	4	85	2	0	3	3	4	.43	15	.268	.356	.467
1995 St. Louis	NL	34	127	37	6	0	5	(2	3)	58	16	22	18	1	23	1	0	2	1	0	1.00	3	.291	.378	.457
Chicago	NL	79	299	68	16	0	9	(6	3)	111	34	30	16	0	53	3	4	3	0	0	—	11	.227	.271	.371
1996 Philadelphia	NL	134	500	134	24	0	20	(9	11)	218	61	80	67	4	89	1	0	1	1	1	.50	16	.268	.353	.436
Baltimore	AL	29	117	28	8	0	5	(1	4)	51	17	19	15	0	16	0	0	0	0	0	—	2	.239	.326	.436
1998 Los Angeles	NL	40	158	40	6	1	7	(1	6)	69	22	27	10	0	24	1	0	1	1	1	.50	5	.253	.300	.437
Florida	NL	66	234	68	12	1	6	(2	4)	100	37	39	31	2	34	0	0	3	2	3	.40	4	.291	.374	.427
Texas	AL	52	180	47	14	1	6	(4	2)	81	26	28	28	0	32	1	1	3	1	0	1.00	3	.261	.358	.450
12 ML YEARS		1626	5889	1576	323	20	205	(99	106)	2554	789	884	728	40	948	31	7	65	50	50	.50	162	.268	.348	.434

Chad Zerbe

Pitches: Left **Bats:** Left **Pos:** RP-4   **Ht:** 6'0" **Wt:** 190 **Born:** 4/27/72 **Age:** 29

Year Team	Lg	G	GS	CG	GF	IP	BFP	H	R	ER	HR	SH	SF	HB	TBB	IBB	SO	WP	Bk	W	L	Pct.	ShO	Sv-Op	Hld	ERA
1991 Dodgers	R	16	1	0	4	32.2	145	31	19	8	1	0	3	1	15	0	23	6	3	0	2	.000	0	0--	—	2.20
1992 Great Falls	R+	15	15	1	0	92.1	378	75	27	22	2	1	1	5	26	0	70	5	0	8	3	.727	1	0--	—	2.14
1993 Bakersfield	A+	14	12	1	1	67	326	83	60	44	2	1	2	2	47	0	41	2	2	0	10	.000	0	0--	—	5.91
Vero Beach	A+	10	0	0	1	12.1	64	12	10	9	0	0	2	2	13	1	11	3	1	1	0	1.000	0	0--	—	6.57
1994 Vero Beach	A+	18	18	1	0	98.1	412	88	50	37	6	0	4	2	32	0	68	6	0	5	5	.500	0	0--	—	3.39
1995 San Berndno	A+	28	27	1	0	163.1	718	168	103	83	15	10	5	3	64	0	94	4	0	11	7	.611	0	0--	—	4.57
1996 San Antonio	AA	17	11	1	1	86	384	98	52	43	9	5	2	2	37	0	38	4	0	4	6	.400	0	1--	—	4.50
1997 High Desert	A+	9	8	0	0	36.1	192	61	49	30	7	0	3	1	15	0	26	1	0	1	6	.143	0	0--	—	7.43
Sonoma Cty	IND	14	13	2	0	89.2	417	117	70	54	7	5	4	3	36	1	52	1	0	4	5	.444	0	0--	—	5.42
1998 Shreveport	AA	1	0	0	0	0	0	0	0	0	0	0	0	0	0	0	0	0	0	0	0	—	0	0--	—	
San Jose	A+	23	0	0	12	37.2	159	37	16	14	3	0	1	3	12	0	28	1	0	2	0	1.000	0	1--	—	3.35
1999 Bakersfield	A+	21	21	0	0	126	533	124	66	51	4	0	5	2	33	0	81	6	0	7	7	.500	0	0--	—	3.64
Shreveport	AA	7	6	0	1	41.1	164	32	13	9	2	1	2	3	10	0	16	0	1	1	3	.250	0	0--	—	1.96
2000 Shreveport	AA	9	9	0	0	38.2	156	37	11	10	1	1	1	1	9	0	34	0	0	2	1	.667	0	0--	—	2.33
Fresno	AAA	17	11	0	1	81.1	347	94	46	39	5	3	2	5	17	0	41	1	1	7	3	.700	0	0--	—	4.32
2000 San Francisco	NL	4	0	0	2	6	24	6	3	3	1	1	0	0	1	0	5	0	0	0	0	—	0	0-0	0	4.50

Jeff Zimmerman

Pitches: Right **Bats:** Right **Pos:** RP-65   **Ht:** 6'1" **Wt:** 200 **Born:** 8/9/72 **Age:** 28

Year Team	Lg	G	GS	CG	GF	IP	BFP	H	R	ER	HR	SH	SF	HB	TBB	IBB	SO	WP	Bk	W	L	Pct.	ShO	Sv-Op	Hld	ERA
1997 Winnipeg	IND	38	16	3	0	118	479	94	49	37	7	2	2	7	35	0	140	6	1	9	2	.818	0	0--	—	2.82
1998 Charlotte	A+	10	0	0	3	14.1	52	10	2	2	1	1	0	0	1	0	14	0	0	2	1	.667	0	0--	—	1.26
Tulsa	AA	41	0	0	28	63	249	38	16	9	5	2	3	0	20	3	67	3	2	3	1	.750	0	9--	—	1.29
1999 Oklahoma	AAA	2	0	0	2	3.2	10	0	0	0	0	0	0	0	0	0	2	0	0	1	0	1.000	0	1--	—	0.00
1999 Texas	AL	65	0	0	14	87.2	336	50	24	23	9	3	6	2	23	1	67	2	0	9	3	.750	0	3-7	24	2.36
2000 Texas	AL	65	0	0	17	69.2	323	80	45	41	10	2	5	2	34	3	74	3	3	4	5	.444	0	1-3	21	5.30
2 ML YEARS		130	0	0	31	157.1	659	130	69	64	19	5	11	4	57	4	141	5	3	13	8	.619	0	4-10	45	3.66

Barry Zito

Pitches: Left **Bats:** Left **Pos:** SP-14   **Ht:** 6'4" **Wt:** 205 **Born:** 5/13/78 **Age:** 23

Year Team	Lg	G	GS	CG	GF	IP	BFP	H	R	ER	HR	SH	SF	HB	TBB	IBB	SO	WP	Bk	W	L	Pct.	ShO	Sv-Op	Hld	ERA
1999 Visalia	A+	8	8	0	0	40.1	157	21	13	11	3	0	1	0	22	0	62	3	0	3	0	1.000	0	0--	—	2.45
Midland	AA	4	4	0	0	22	99	22	15	12	1	0	0	1	11	0	29	2	0	2	1	.667	0	0--	—	4.91
Vancouver	AAA	1	1	0	0	6	24	5	1	1	0	0	0	0	2	0	6	2	0	1	0	1.000	0	0--	—	1.50
2000 Sacramento	AAA	18	18	0	0	101.2	437	88	44	36	4	5	3	2	45	0	91	5	0	8	5	.615	0	0--	—	3.19
2000 Oakland	AL	14	14	1	0	92.2	376	64	30	28	6	1	0	2	45	2	78	2	0	7	4	.636	0	0-0	—	2.72

Eddie Zosky

Bats: Right **Throws:** Right **Pos:** PH/PR-4   **Ht:** 6'0" **Wt:** 180 **Born:** 2/10/68 **Age:** 33

Year Team	Lg	G	AB	H	2B	3B	HR	(Hm	Rd)	TB	R	RBI	TBB	IBB	SO	HBP	SH	SF	SB	CS	SB%	GDP	Avg	OBP	SLG
1989 Knoxville	AA	56	208	46	5	3	2	—	—	63	21	14	10	0	32	0	2	1	1	1	.50	4	.221	.256	.303
1990 Knoxville	AA	115	450	122	20	7	3	—	—	165	53	45	26	1	73	5	6	3	3	13	.19	7	.271	.316	.367
1991 Syracuse	AAA	119	511	135	18	4	6	—	—	179	69	39	35	1	82	5	7	5	9	4	.69	11	.264	.315	.350
1992 Syracuse	AAA	96	342	79	11	6	4	—	—	114	31	38	19	0	53	1	7	4	3	4	.43	10	.231	.270	.333
1993 Hagerstown	A	5	20	2	0	0	0	—	—	2	2	1	2	0	1	0	0	0	0	0	—	0	.100	.174	.100
Syracuse	AAA	28	93	20	5	0	0	—	—	25	9	8	1	0	20	4	2	3	0	1	.00	1	.215	.248	.269
1994 Syracuse	AAA	85	284	75	15	3	7	—	—	117	41	37	9	0	46	2	6	5	3	1	.75	8	.264	.287	.412
1995 Charlotte	AAA	92	312	77	15	2	3	—	—	105	27	42	7	0	48	1	5	1	2	3	.40	8	.247	.265	.337
1996 Orioles	R	1	3	1	1	0	0	—	—	2	1	0	1	0	0	0	0	0	0	0	—	0	.333	.500	.667
Rochester	AAA	95	340	87	22	4	3	—	—	126	42	34	21	1	40	2	3	6	5	2	.71	5	.256	.298	.371
1997 Phoenix	AAA	86	241	67	10	4	9	—	—	112	38	45	16	2	38	1	1	2	3	3	.50	5	.278	.323	.465
1998 Louisville	AAA	90	257	63	12	1	8	—	—	101	36	35	15	2	47	1	4	1	1	3	.25	3	.245	.288	.393
1999 Louisville	AAA	116	415	122	22	3	12	—	—	186	60	47	23	0	68	3	4	3	5	1	.83	6	.294	.333	.448
2000 Nashville	AAA	53	131	29	5	2	2	—	—	44	14	16	6	0	24	1	2	2	0	1	.00	2	.221	.257	.336
Pirates	R	8	30	10	6	0	0	—	—	16	7	3	3	0	1	0	0	0	1	0	1.00	1	.333	.394	.533
New Orleans	AAA	11	33	9	0	0	0	—	—	9	3	3	4	0	8	1	0	0	0	1	.00	2	.273	.368	.273
1991 Toronto	AL	18	27	4	1	1	0	(0	0)	7	2	2	0	0	8	0	1	0	0	0	—	0	.148	.148	.259
1992 Toronto	AL	8	7	2	0	1	0	(0	0)	4	1	1	0	0	2	0	1	0	0	0	—	0	.286	.250	.571
1995 Florida	NL	6	5	1	0	0	0	(0	0)	1	0	0	0	0	0	0	0	0	0	0	—	0	.200	.200	.200
1999 Milwaukee	NL	8	7	1	0	0	0	(0	0)	1	1	0	1	0	2	0	0	0	0	0	—	0	.143	.250	.143
2000 Houston	NL	4	4	0	0	0	0	(0	0)	0	0	0	0	0	1	0	0	0	0	0	—	0	.000	.000	.000
5 ML YEARS		44	50	8	1	2	0	(0	0)	13	4	3	1	0	13	0	1	1	0	0	—	1	.160	.173	.260

Julio Zuleta

Bats: Right **Throws:** Right **Pos:** 1B-14; PH/PR-14; LF-6   **Ht:** 6'6" **Wt:** 230 **Born:** 3/28/75 **Age:** 26

Year Team	Lg	G	AB	H	2B	3B	HR	(Hm	Rd)	TB	R	RBI	TBB	IBB	SO	HBP	SH	SF	SB	CS	SB%	GDP	Avg	OBP	SLG
1993 Cubs	R	17	53	13	0	1	0	—	—	15	3	6	3	0	12	0	0	0	0	0	—	3	.245	.322	.283
1994 Huntington	R+	6	15	1	0	0	0	—	—	1	0	2	4	0	4	0	0	0	0	0	—	1	.067	.263	.067
Cubs	R	30	100	31	1	0	0	—	—	32	11	8	8	0	18	2	0	1	5	1	.83	0	.310	.373	.320
1995 Williamsprt	A-	30	75	13	3	1	0	—	—	18	9	6	11	1	12	2	0	0	0	1	.00	4	.173	.295	.240
1996 Williamsprt	A-	62	221	57	12	2	1	—	—	76	35	29	19	2	36	8	0	2	7	4	.64	8	.258	.336	.344
1997 Rockford	A	119	430	124	30	5	6	—	—	182	59	77	35	6	88	12	3	8	5	5	.50	7	.288	.353	.423

241

		BATTING																		BASERUNNING				PERCENTAGES		
Year Team	Lg	G	AB	H	2B	3B	HR	(Hm	Rd)	TB	R	RBI	TBB	IBB	SO	HBP	SH	SF	SB	CS	SB%	GDP	Avg	OBP	SLG
1998 Daytona	A+	94	366	126	25	1	16	—	—	201	69	86	35	1	59	15	1	5	6	3	.67	12	.344	.418	.549
West Tenn	AA	40	139	41	9	0	2	—	—	56	18	20	10	0	30	3	0	3	0	1	.00	3	.295	.348	.403
1999 West Tenn	AA	133	482	142	37	4	21	—	—	250	75	97	35	6	122	20	0	8	4	3	.57	11	.295	.361	.519
2000 Iowa	AAA	107	392	122	25	1	26	—	—	227	76	94	31	2	77	9	0	4	5	4	.56	14	.311	.372	.579
2000 Chicago	NL	30	68	20	8	0	3	(1	2)	37	13	12	2	0	19	3	0	0	0	1	.00	2	.294	.342	.544

2000 Team Statistics

All the statistics you need to know about your favorite team are here. Final standings, record breakdowns, team batting, pitching and fielding all can be found in this section. Also included here are teams' records against the other league. American League teams have a split vs. NL teams and National League teams have a split vs. AL teams.

Keep in mind that hitting totals in each league will not necessarily mirror hitting totals allowed by that league's pitchers. For example, home runs hit in the American League may not equal the home runs allowed by American League pitchers. The reason is interleague play.

Some of the abbreviations need an explanation. They are:

LD1st = Last date team was in first place; **1st** = number of days team spent in first place (including days tied for the lead); **Lead** = largest first-place lead, if any, during the season; **LHS** = record in games started by opposing lefthanded pitchers; **RHS** = record in games started by opposing righthanded pitchers; **1-R** = record in games decided by one run; **5+R** = record in games decided by five or more runs.

2000 American League Final Standings

Overall

EAST

Team	W-L	Pct	GB	LD1st	1st	Lead
New York Yankees	87-74	.540	—	10/1	148	9
Boston Red Sox	85-77	.525	2.5	6/22	32	1.5
Toronto Blue Jays	83-79	.512	4.5	7/6	22	3
Baltimore Orioles	74-88	.457	13.5	4/25	14	2
Tampa Bay Devil Rays	69-92	.429	18	4/3	6	0

CENTRAL

Team	W-L	Pct	GB	LD1st	1st	Lead
Chicago White Sox	95-67	.586	—	10/1	172	11.5
Cleveland Indians	90-72	.556	5	5/18	22	1
Detroit Tigers	79-83	.488	16	4/3	6	0
Kansas City Royals	77-85	.475	18	4/8	8	0
Minnesota Twins	69-93	.426	26	4/6	7	0.5

WEST

Team	W-L	Pct	GB	LD1st	1st	Lead
Oakland Athletics	91-70	.565	—	10/1	35	2
Seattle Mariners*	91-71	.562	0.5	9/28	156	7
Anaheim Angels	82-80	.506	9.5	4/13	8	0.5
Texas Rangers	71-91	.438	20.5	5/25	9	1

* represents playoff wild-card berth. Clinch Dates: Chicago 9/24, New York 9/29, Oakland 10/1, Seattle 10/1.

East Division

Team	Home	Road	East	Cent	West	NL	LHS	RHS	Grass	Turf	Day	Night	XInn	1-R	5+R	Apr	May	June	July	Aug	Sep	Pre	Post
New York	44-36	43-38	25-24	26-28	25-16	11-6	22-14	65-50	80-62	7-12	34-25	53-49	4-4	20-18	29-26	15-8	13-13	10-15	18-8	18-12	13-18	45-38	42-36
Boston	42-39	43-38	23-26	32-24	21-18	9-9	20-22	65-55	77-66	8-11	22-24	63-53	5-8	20-23	18-17	12-9	17-10	9-18	16-11	15-13	16-16	43-41	42-36
Toronto	45-36	38-43	28-21	28-25	18-24	9-9	19-24	64-55	31-38	52-41	28-28	55-51	2-6	21-19	27-33	12-14	16-12	16-10	11-16	15-11	13-16	48-41	35-38
Baltimore	44-37	30-51	25-25	24-24	18-28	7-11	23-24	51-64	63-74	11-14	25-30	49-58	4-7	29-25	18-28	14-10	9-17	10-17	13-14	14-15	14-15	38-48	36-40
Tampa Bay	36-44	33-48	22-27	22-27	16-29	9-9	11-25	58-67	25-41	44-51	22-30	47-62	9-5	26-26	18-22	9-15	8-19	15-11	12-14	15-15	10-18	34-51	35-41

Central Division

Team	Home	Road	East	Cent	West	NL	LHS	RHS	Grass	Turf	Day	Night	XInn	1-R	5+R	Apr	May	June	July	Aug	Sep	Pre	Post
Chicago	46-35	49-32	30-24	29-20	24-17	12-6	21-10	74-57	81-62	14-5	26-30	69-37	7-4	28-18	36-23	17-8	13-14	20-7	14-12	15-13	16-13	55-32	40-35
Cleveland	48-33	42-39	31-22	21-30	25-15	13-5	17-21	73-51	79-62	11-10	37-15	53-57	6-5	17-24	34-21	13-8	14-14	13-16	12-12	18-10	20-12	44-42	46-30
Detroit	43-38	36-45	24-31	22-28	23-16	10-8	22-24	57-59	72-71	7-12	21-28	58-55	8-4	20-18	25-29	6-17	12-14	15-12	15-13	18-10	13-17	38-46	41-37
Kansas City	42-39	35-46	24-26	28-20	17-29	8-10	18-24	59-61	68-75	9-10	29-19	48-66	7-8	21-26	18-21	12-13	14-12	11-15	10-17	15-14	15-14	39-46	38-39
Minnesota	36-45	33-48	19-29	24-26	19-27	7-11	11-29	58-64	28-37	41-56	22-27	47-66	7-9	22-26	17-30	11-15	13-14	12-16	12-15	11-14	10-19	38-52	31-41

West Division

Team	Home	Road	East	Cent	West	NL	LHS	RHS	Grass	Turf	Day	Night	XInn	1-R	5+R	Apr	May	June	July	Aug	Sep	Pre	Post
Oakland	47-34	44-36	30-20	28-27	22-16	11-7	21-26	70-44	79-67	12-3	35-25	56-45	8-5	21-19	34-23	12-13	15-13	18-7	13-14	11-16	22-7	48-38	43-32
Seattle	47-34	44-37	35-17	26-28	19-19	11-7	20-11	71-60	79-67	12-4	32-24	59-47	3-4	15-22	35-26	13-10	13-14	19-8	16-12	11-17	19-10	51-35	40-36
Anaheim	46-35	36-45	28-27	25-26	17-21	12-6	21-25	61-55	73-71	9-9	18-24	64-56	9-7	32-23	22-22	13-13	14-13	14-12	16-12	11-15	14-15	47-41	35-39
Texas	42-39	29-52	22-34	25-27	17-19	7-11	19-15	52-76	66-80	5-11	16-23	55-68	5-5	27-25	22-30	9-15	18-10	10-15	13-13	9-21	12-17	42-43	29-48

Team vs. Team Breakdown

	NYY	Bos	Tor	Bal	TB	CWS	Cle	Det	KC	Min	Oak	Sea	Ana	Tex
New York Yankees	—	7	5	7	6	4	5	4	8	5	6	4	5	10
Boston Red Sox	6	—	4	7	6	7	6	7	4	8	5	5	4	7
Toronto Blue Jays	7	8	—	6	7	5	4	9	6	4	3	2	7	6
Baltimore Orioles	5	5	7	—	8	4	5	6	3	6	4	3	5	6
Tampa Bay Devil Rays	6	6	5	5	—	4	2	5	5	6	2	3	6	5
Chicago White Sox	8	5	5	6	6	—	8	9	5	8	7	6	6	5
Cleveland Indians	5	6	8	4	8	5	—	6	5	5	6	7	6	6
Detroit Tigers	8	5	3	4	4	3	7	—	5	7	6	7	5	5
Kansas City Royals	2	6	4	7	5	7	7	7	—	7	4	4	6	3
Minnesota Twins	5	2	5	3	4	5	8	6	5	—	5	3	3	8
Oakland Athletics	3	5	7	8	7	3	6	4	8	7	—	9	8	5
Seattle Mariners	6	5	8	7	9	5	2	2	8	9	4	—	8	7
Anaheim Angels	5	5	5	7	6	4	3	5	6	7	5	5	—	7
Texas Rangers	2	3	4	6	7	5	4	5	7	4	7	5	5	—

(read wins across and losses down)

2000 National League Final Standings

Overall

EAST

Team	W-L	Pct	GB	LD1st	1st	Lead
Atlanta Braves	95-67	.586	—	10/1	173	7
New York Mets*	94-68	.580	1	9/1	10	0.5
Florida Marlins	79-82	.491	15.5	4/18	9	1
Montreal Expos	67-95	.414	28	4/19	8	0.5
Philadelphia Phillies	65-97	.401	30	3/29	1	0

CENTRAL

Team	W-L	Pct	GB	LD1st	1st	Lead
St. Louis Cardinals	95-67	.586	—	10/1	181	11.5
Cincinnati Reds	85-77	.525	10	6/5	9	0.5
Milwaukee Brewers	73-89	.451	22	4/7	3	0
Houston Astros	72-90	.444	23	4/5	2	0
Pittsburgh Pirates	69-93	.426	26	—	—	—
Chicago Cubs	65-97	.401	30	4/2	5	0.5

WEST

Team	W-L	Pct	GB	LD1st	1st	Lead
San Francisco Giants	97-65	.599	—	10/1	71	11.5
Los Angeles Dodgers	86-76	.531	11	4/23	8	0.5
Arizona Diamondbacks	85-77	.525	12	7/30	118	6.5
Colorado Rockies	82-80	.506	15	7/3	7	0
San Diego Padres	76-86	.469	21	4/7	6	0

* represents playoff wild-card berth. Clinch Dates: St. Louis 9/20, San Francisco 9/21, Atlanta 9/27, New York 9/27.

East Division

Team	AT Home	AT Road	VERSUS East	VERSUS Cent	VERSUS West	VERSUS AL	LHS	RHS	Grass	Turf	Day	Night	XInn	1-R	5+R	Apr	May	June	July	Aug	Sep	Pre	Post
Atlanta	51-30	44-37	27-24	25-23	32-13	11-7	21-14	74-53	82-57	13-10	30-20	65-47	3-5	18-18	21-18	18-6	17-10	13-15	17-9	14-15	16-12	52-36	43-31
New York	55-26	39-42	27-23	34-16	24-20	9-9	18-13	76-55	79-56	15-12	33-24	61-44	10-8	29-20	23-19	15-9	13-14	16-8	14-13	20-9	15-14	48-38	46-30
Florida	43-38	36-44	28-22	26-23	17-28	8-9	17-22	62-60	63-70	16-12	25-21	54-61	9-5	32-20	17-24	13-13	11-17	15-11	12-13	13-14	15-14	45-43	34-39
Montreal	37-44	30-51	21-29	23-27	16-28	7-11	19-24	48-71	21-39	46-56	18-39	49-66	4-4	23-24	19-37	14-9	12-14	12-14	9-18	8-20	12-20	42-42	25-53
Philadelphia	34-47	31-50	23-28	21-29	12-31	9-9	14-22	51-75	22-43	43-54	21-20	44-77	4-12	25-35	15-29	7-17	11-16	15-11	13-14	10-18	9-21	39-47	26-50

Central Division

Team	AT Home	AT Road	VERSUS East	VERSUS Cent	VERSUS West	VERSUS AL	LHS	RHS	Grass	Turf	Day	Night	XInn	1-R	5+R	Apr	May	June	July	Aug	Sep	Pre	Post
St. Louis	50-31	45-36	25-16	37-25	26-18	7-8	17-23	78-44	79-58	16-9	38-20	57-47	5-2	28-16	31-16	17-8	13-14	17-10	11-15	17-11	20-9	51-36	44-31
Cincinnati	43-38	42-39	22-19	34-29	22-21	7-8	25-12	60-65	34-34	51-43	35-27	50-50	9-7	25-23	24-12	12-11	16-11	10-17	16-11	13-15	18-11	43-44	42-33
Milwaukee	42-39	31-50	15-26	33-30	19-24	6-9	14-21	59-68	63-77	10-12	21-29	52-60	13-9	26-21	19-27	9-15	13-16	10-16	12-15	14-13	15-14	37-51	36-38
Houston	39-42	33-48	20-22	35-27	11-32	6-9	15-21	57-69	62-79	10-11	22-31	50-59	6-9	15-31	28-26	9-14	10-19	8-19	12-14	16-12	17-12	30-57	42-33
Pittsburgh	37-44	32-49	18-23	27-35	18-26	6-9	15-22	54-71	23-42	46-51	15-33	54-60	8-11	17-30	22-29	9-15	14-13	11-16	11-14	8-21	16-14	38-48	31-45
Chicago	38-43	27-54	18-23	21-41	18-26	8-7	14-21	51-76	12-36	56-29	29-41	36-56	9-13	17-30	11-26	9-16	15-16	12-13	17-9	9-20	7-22	35-51	30-46

West Division

Team	AT Home	AT Road	VERSUS East	VERSUS Cent	VERSUS West	VERSUS AL	LHS	RHS	Grass	Turf	Day	Night	XInn	1-R	5+R	Apr	May	June	July	Aug	Sep	Pre	Post
San Francisco	55-26	42-39	27-17	36-17	26-24	8-7	19-20	78-45	89-60	8-5	37-29	60-36	7-5	18-22	33-19	10-13	15-12	13-13	19-8	19-10	21-9	46-39	51-26
Los Angeles	44-37	42-39	23-21	27-25	30-31	6-9	19-25	67-51	78-71	8-5	23-22	63-54	9-5	25-21	32-19	14-10	14-12	13-15	14-12	15-15	16-12	44-42	42-34
Arizona	47-34	38-43	21-24	29-21	29-23	6-9	23-17	62-60	74-70	11-7	22-24	63-53	5-8	22-27	26-21	16-9	17-10	13-14	12-14	15-12	16-12	51-37	34-40
Colorado	48-33	34-47	24-21	29-24	23-29	6-6	24-13	58-67	70-74	12-6	27-30	55-50	6-5	23-20	34-25	11-14	17-8	15-10	7-22	18-11	14-15	45-40	37-40
San Diego	41-40	35-46	25-18	26-27	20-31	5-10	19-30	57-56	69-74	7-12	23-26	53-60	11-13	25-27	13-23	11-14	13-14	11-15	12-15	18-11	11-17	38-49	38-37

Team vs. Team Breakdown

Team	Atl	NYM	Fla	Mon	Phi	StL	Cin	Mil	Hou	Pit	ChC	SF	LA	Ari	Col	SD
Atlanta Braves	—	7	6	6	8	3	2	6	5	5	4	6	7	6	5	8
New York Mets	6	—	6	9	6	6	4	7	5	7	5	5	7	6	6	3
Florida Marlins	6	6	—	7	9	3	6	3	3	5	6	3	2	5	5	2
Montreal Expos	7	3	6	—	5	2	3	5	5	3	5	3	3	5	2	3
Philadelphia Phillies	5	7	4	7	—	2	4	5	4	3	3	2	4	1	3	2
St. Louis Cardinals	4	3	6	5	7	—	6	7	6	8	10	4	6	4	3	9
Cincinnati Reds	5	5	3	6	3	7	—	5	7	7	8	3	4	5	6	4
Milwaukee Brewers	3	2	4	4	2	5	8	—	6	7	3	4	5	5	5	2
Houston Astros	4	2	5	4	5	6	5	7	—	10	7	1	3	1	4	2
Pittsburgh Pirates	2	2	4	4	6	4	6	5	3	—	9	2	5	2	2	7
Chicago Cubs	5	2	1	6	6	3	4	6	5	3	—	4	3	4	4	3
San Francisco Giants	3	5	6	6	7	5	6	6	8	6	5	—	5	7	7	7
Los Angeles Dodgers	2	4	7	5	5	3	5	3	6	4	6	7	—	6	9	8
Arizona Diamondbacks	3	2	4	4	8	5	2	4	6	7	5	6	7	—	7	9
Colorado Rockies	4	3	5	4	7	6	5	3	4	5	7	5	6	4	—	7
San Diego Padres	1	6	7	6	5	0	5	7	7	2	5	5	5	4	6	—

(read wins across and losses down)

American League Batting

Tm	G	AB	H	2B	3B	HR	(Hm	Rd)	TB	R	RBI	TBB	IBB	SO	HBP	SH	SF	ShO	SB	CS	SB%	GDP	LOB	Avg	OBP	SLG
CWS	162	5646	1615	325	33	216	(125	91)	2654	978	926	591	28	960	53	55	61	3	119	42	.74	140	1127	.286	.356	.470
Cle	162	5683	1639	310	30	221	(122	99)	2672	950	889	685	27	1057	51	41	52	4	113	34	.77	134	1260	.288	.367	.458
Oak	161	5560	1501	281	23	239	(126	113)	2545	947	908	750	32	1159	52	26	44	7	40	15	.73	147	1210	.270	.360	.458
Sea	162	5497	1481	300	26	198	(92	106)	2427	907	869	775	34	1073	48	63	61	5	122	56	.69	129	1247	.269	.361	.442
KC	162	5709	1644	281	27	150	(84	66)	2429	879	831	511	28	840	48	56	70	4	121	35	.78	139	1184	.288	.348	.425
NYY	161	5556	1541	294	25	205	(117	88)	2500	871	833	631	42	1007	57	16	50	7	99	48	.67	134	1189	.277	.354	.450
Ana	162	5628	1574	309	34	236	(130	106)	2659	864	837	608	43	1024	47	47	43	5	93	52	.64	126	1173	.280	.352	.472
Tor	162	5677	1562	328	21	244	(134	110)	2664	861	826	526	32	1026	60	29	34	7	89	34	.72	130	1152	.275	.341	.469
Tex	162	5648	1601	330	35	173	(104	69)	2520	848	806	580	39	922	39	48	48	6	69	47	.59	161	1198	.283	.352	.446
Det	162	5644	1553	307	41	177	(69	108)	2473	823	785	562	22	982	43	42	49	15	83	38	.69	142	1185	.275	.343	.438
Bal	162	5549	1508	310	22	184	(90	94)	2414	794	750	558	34	900	49	27	54	8	126	65	.66	148	1129	.272	.341	.435
Bos	162	5630	1503	316	32	167	(66	101)	2384	792	755	611	40	1019	42	40	48	8	43	30	.59	115	1226	.267	.341	.423
Min	162	5615	1516	325	49	116	(54	62)	2287	748	711	556	31	1021	35	24	51	8	90	45	.67	143	1198	.270	.337	.407
TB	161	5505	1414	253	22	162	(76	86)	2197	733	692	559	25	1022	50	52	40	8	90	46	.66	126	1140	.257	.329	.399
AL	1133	78547	21652	4269	420	2688	(1389	1299)	34625	11995	11418	8503	457	14012	674	566	705	95	1297	587	.69	1914	16618	.276	.349	.443

American League Pitching

Tm	G	CG	Rel	IP	BFP	H	R	ER	HR	SH	SF	HB	TBB	IBB	SO	WP	Bk	W	L	Pct.	ShO	Sv-Op	Hld	OAvg	OOBP	OSLG	ERA
Bos	162	7	425	1452.2	6225	1433	745	683	173	46	49	57	499	40	1121	33	2	85	77	.525	12	46-65	47	.257	.322	.411	4.23
Sea	162	4	383	1441.2	6269	1442	780	720	167	39	55	38	634	37	998	43	6	91	71	.562	10	44-60	63	.262	.339	.416	4.49
Oak	161	7	381	1435.1	6355	1535	813	730	158	35	51	48	615	57	963	46	1	91	70	.565	11	43-62	60	.274	.348	.423	4.58
NYY	161	9	382	1424.1	6256	1458	814	753	177	45	48	52	577	23	1040	49	6	87	74	.540	6	40-57	39	.263	.336	.422	4.76
Cle	162	6	462	1442.1	6380	1511	816	775	173	34	42	42	666	45	1213	50	3	90	72	.556	5	34-57	77	.270	.350	.425	4.84
Det	162	6	429	1443.1	6295	1583	827	755	177	33	63	47	496	22	978	51	5	79	83	.488	6	44-61	62	.280	.340	.443	4.71
CWS	162	5	466	1450.1	6337	1509	839	751	195	39	49	54	614	27	1037	43	8	95	67	.586	7	43-67	65	.270	.346	.434	4.66
TB	161	10	401	1431.1	6283	1553	842	773	198	42	45	66	533	33	955	57	3	69	92	.429	8	38-66	32	.278	.345	.451	4.86
Ana	162	5	441	1448	6401	1534	869	805	228	40	53	36	662	44	846	47	10	82	80	.506	3	46-68	60	.273	.351	.453	5.00
Min	162	6	412	1432.2	6336	1634	880	819	212	41	46	35	516	12	1042	68	4	69	93	.426	4	35-54	44	.287	.347	.466	5.14
Tor	162	15	388	1437.1	6377	1615	908	821	195	44	40	64	560	19	978	37	3	83	79	.512	4	37-52	49	.285	.354	.456	5.14
Bal	162	14	396	1433.1	6433	1547	913	855	202	48	57	36	665	32	1017	51	1	74	88	.457	6	33-57	68	.275	.352	.449	5.37
KC	162	10	329	1439.1	6443	1585	930	876	239	39	45	42	693	35	927	77	5	77	85	.475	6	29-55	22	.282	.362	.474	5.48
Tex	162	3	415	1429	6559	1683	974	876	202	42	62	63	661	40	918	40	6	71	91	.438	4	39-66	55	.294	.369	.475	5.52
AL	1133	107	5710	20141	88949	21622	11950	10992	2696	567	705	680	8391	466	14033	692	63	1143	1122	.505	92	551-847	745	.275	.347	.443	4.91

American League Fielding

Team	G	PO	Ast	OFAst	E	(Throw	Field)	TC	DP	GDP Opp	GDP	GDP%	PB	OSB	OCS	OSB%	CPkof	PPkof	AVG
Cleveland	162	4327	1665	26	72	(38	34)	6064	147	236	125	.530	10	109	42	.72	0	2	.988
Seattle	162	4325	1629	21	99	(36	63)	6053	176	248	154	.621	8	82	38	.68	0	4	.984
Toronto	162	4312	1679	29	100	(42	58)	6091	176	234	143	.611	11	99	38	.72	3	5	.984
Kansas City	162	4318	1751	33	102	(41	61)	6171	185	248	159	.641	7	118	38	.76	3	6	.983
Detroit	162	4330	1754	33	105	(46	59)	6189	172	233	144	.618	7	55	42	.57	1	3	.983
Minnesota	162	4298	1526	41	102	(55	47)	5926	155	192	120	.625	13	64	33	.66	0	2	.983
Boston	162	4358	1647	34	109	(51	58)	6114	120	198	98	.495	26	159	47	.77	0	3	.982
New York	161	4273	1487	18	109	(52	57)	5869	132	211	108	.512	13	91	37	.71	1	5	.981
Tampa Bay	161	4294	1814	38	118	(51	67)	6226	169	234	136	.581	14	114	46	.71	1	2	.981
Baltimore	162	4300	1578	26	116	(45	71)	5994	151	234	126	.538	6	104	31	.77	0	0	.981
Anaheim	162	4344	1746	35	134	(64	70)	6224	182	252	158	.627	6	101	56	.64	1	4	.978
Chicago	162	4351	1686	34	134	(56	77)	6170	190	239	151	.632	13	79	58	.58	0	8	.978
Oakland	161	4306	1726	21	134	(67	67)	6166	164	230	137	.596	8	92	39	.70	2	3	.978
Texas	162	4287	1594	33	135	(70	65)	6016	162	253	133	.526	8	65	37	.64	1	9	.978
American League	1133	60423	23282	422	1568	(714	854)	85273	2281	3242	1892	.584	150	1332	582	.70	13	56	.982

National League Batting

Tm	G	AB	H	2B	3B	HR	(Hm	Rd)	TB	R	RBI	TBB	IBB	SO	HBP	SH	SF	ShO	SB	CS	SB%	GDP	LOB	Avg	OBP	SLG
Col	162	5660	1664	320	53	161	(112	49)	2573	968	905	601	64	907	42	75	75	8	131	61	.68	127	1198	.294	.362	.455
Hou	162	5570	1547	289	36	249	(135	114)	2655	938	900	673	57	1129	83	57	61	3	114	52	.69	154	1171	.278	.361	.477
SF	162	5519	1535	304	44	226	(110	116)	2605	925	889	709	60	1032	51	73	66	5	79	39	.67	131	1213	.278	.362	.472
StL	162	5478	1481	259	25	235	(124	111)	2495	887	841	675	33	1253	84	79	53	5	87	51	.63	116	1214	.270	.356	.455
Cin	163	5635	1545	302	36	200	(98	102)	2519	825	794	559	60	995	64	56	58	0	99	38	.72	137	1189	.274	.343	.447
Atl	162	5489	1490	274	26	179	(84	95)	2353	810	758	595	38	1010	59	87	45	7	148	56	.73	127	1192	.271	.346	.429
NYM	162	5486	1445	282	20	198	(93	105)	2361	807	761	675	42	1037	45	70	51	9	66	46	.59	122	1214	.263	.346	.430
LA	162	5481	1408	265	28	211	(108	103)	2362	798	756	668	42	1083	51	66	46	11	95	42	.69	129	1188	.257	.341	.431
Pit	162	5643	1506	320	31	168	(86	82)	2392	793	749	564	41	1032	66	59	37	7	86	40	.68	133	1202	.267	.339	.424
Ari	162	5527	1466	282	44	179	(84	95)	2373	792	756	535	37	975	59	61	58	7	97	44	.69	114	1128	.265	.333	.429
ChC	162	5577	1426	272	23	183	(84	99)	2293	764	722	632	50	1120	54	89	45	8	93	37	.72	114	1215	.256	.335	.411
SD	162	5560	1413	279	37	157	(72	85)	2237	752	714	602	50	1177	46	39	43	7	131	53	.71	123	1155	.254	.330	.402
Mil	163	5563	1366	297	25	177	(78	99)	2244	740	708	620	47	1245	61	61	49	7	72	44	.62	126	1183	.246	.325	.403
Mon	162	5535	1475	310	35	178	(88	90)	2389	738	705	476	53	1048	29	78	34	9	58	48	.55	111	1100	.266	.326	.432
Fla	161	5509	1441	274	29	160	(71	89)	2253	731	691	540	39	1184	60	42	51	8	168	55	.75	100	1168	.262	.331	.409
Phi	162	5511	1386	304	40	144	(66	78)	2202	708	668	611	40	1117	44	70	37	8	102	30	.77	115	1209	.251	.329	.400
NL	1297	88743	23594	4633	532	3005	(1493	1512)	38306	12976	12317	9735	753	17344	898	1062	809	109	1626	736	.69	1979	18939	.266	.342	.432

National League Pitching

Tm	G	CG	Rel	IP	BFP	H	R	ER	HR	SH	SF	HB	TBB	IBB	SO	WP	Bk	W	L	Pct.	ShO	Sv-Op	Hld	OAvg	OOBP	OSLG	ERA
Atl	162	13	376	1440.1	6165	1428	714	648	165	64	37	37	484	52	1093	23	6	95	67	.586	9	53-67	56	.258	.319	.402	4.05
LA	162	9	371	1445	6249	1379	729	659	176	68	30	75	600	22	1154	60	6	86	76	.531	11	36-59	39	.252	.332	.407	4.10
NYM	162	8	411	1450	6276	1398	738	670	164	56	46	60	574	42	1164	34	7	94	68	.580	10	49-66	51	.252	.327	.403	4.16
SF	162	9	384	1444.1	6270	1452	747	675	151	85	63	41	623	26	1076	43	4	97	65	.599	15	47-70	59	.266	.342	.412	4.21
Ari	162	16	390	1443.2	6158	1441	754	698	190	72	45	42	500	53	1220	30	10	85	77	.525	8	38-56	39	.262	.326	.424	4.35
Cin	163	8	387	1456.1	6362	1446	765	700	190	68	48	43	659	53	1015	96	5	85	77	.525	7	42-54	48	.261	.341	.438	4.33
StL	162	10	386	1433.2	6200	1403	771	696	196	69	52	62	606	28	1100	49	9	95	67	.586	7	37-59	63	.259	.338	.434	4.38
Fla	161	5	429	1429.2	6307	1477	797	729	169	68	59	43	650	56	1051	49	10	79	82	.491	4	48-68	56	.269	.348	.429	4.59
SD	162	5	443	1459.1	6414	1443	815	733	191	59	41	68	649	50	1071	66	7	76	86	.469	5	46-70	58	.258	.340	.416	4.52
Mil	163	2	433	1466.1	6497	1501	826	763	174	67	52	65	728	87	967	60	6	73	89	.451	7	29-44	50	.269	.357	.420	4.63
Phi	162	8	414	1438.2	6314	1458	830	763	201	74	53	42	640	32	1123	54	3	65	97	.401	6	34-54	53	.265	.343	.448	4.77
Pit	162	5	466	1449	6514	1554	888	794	163	70	55	60	711	61	1070	67	6	69	93	.426	7	27-48	55	.277	.361	.432	4.93
Col	162	7	479	1430	6340	1568	897	835	221	53	52	72	588	72	1001	40	5	82	80	.506	2	33-58	65	.281	.354	.471	5.26
Mon	162	4	452	1424.2	6340	1575	902	812	181	66	58	60	579	40	1011	55	7	67	95	.414	7	39-59	43	.282	.353	.449	5.13
ChC	162	10	421	1454.2	6427	1505	904	849	231	62	54	62	658	45	1143	45	4	65	97	.401	5	39-68	52	.288	.348	.452	5.25
Hou	162	8	410	1437.2	6455	1596	944	864	234	60	64	60	598	25	1064	55	3	72	90	.444	2	30-55	45	.281	.353	.476	5.41
NL	1297	127	6652	23103.1	101312	23624	13021	11882	2997	1061	809	892	9847	744	17323	826	98	1285	1306	.496	112	627-955	832	.266	.343	.432	4.63

National League Fielding

Team	G	PO	Ast	OFAst	E	(Throw	Field)	TC	DP	GDP Opp	GDP	GDP%	PB	OSB	OCS	OSB%	CPkof	PPkof	AVG
San Francisco	162	4333	1644	31	93	(36	57)	6070	173	223	137	.614	15	97	48	.67	2	2	.985
Colorado	162	4290	1727	36	94	(38	56)	6111	176	247	141	.571	15	102	34	.75	0	3	.985
Chicago	162	4364	1573	19	100	(34	66)	6037	139	200	105	.525	6	94	54	.64	2	3	.983
Philadelphia	162	4316	1491	33	100	(43	57)	5907	136	204	110	.539	4	77	44	.64	0	5	.983
Arizona	162	4331	1541	29	107	(54	53)	5979	138	183	112	.612	4	102	56	.65	1	10	.982
Cincinnati	163	4369	1639	40	111	(46	65)	6119	156	215	129	.600	12	81	33	.71	0	8	.982
St. Louis	162	4301	1524	24	111	(45	66)	5936	148	188	118	.628	8	69	66	.51	4	2	.981
Milwaukee	163	4399	1745	38	118	(45	73)	6262	187	246	156	.634	12	86	58	.60	3	3	.981
New York	162	4350	1582	28	118	(50	68)	6050	121	203	97	.478	8	133	46	.74	0	8	.980
Florida	161	4289	1710	38	125	(57	68)	6124	144	188	112	.596	12	104	55	.65	1	5	.980
Atlanta	162	4321	1735	28	129	(50	79)	6185	138	215	122	.567	9	99	33	.75	2	3	.979
Pittsburgh	162	4347	1828	34	132	(54	78)	6307	169	268	144	.537	12	101	42	.71	1	8	.979
Montreal	162	4274	1702	47	132	(61	71)	6108	151	220	128	.582	19	123	38	.76	1	5	.978
Los Angeles	162	4335	1717	25	135	(67	68)	6187	151	209	125	.598	15	106	52	.67	0	7	.978
Houston	162	4313	1561	22	133	(59	74)	6007	149	206	121	.587	6	111	32	.78	2	5	.978
San Diego	162	4378	1669	32	141	(65	76)	6188	155	237	124	.523	13	106	50	.68	2	5	.977
National League	1297	69310	26388	504	1879	(804	1075)	97577	2431	3452	1981	.574	170	1591	741	.68	21	82	.981

247

2000 Fielding Statistics

Fielding statistics have come a long way since the days when all we had were games, putouts, assists, errors, fielding percentage and double plays. On the following pages, you'll see that we've added games started and defensive innings, as well as range factor. In the STATS *All-Time Major League Handbook*, range factor is calculated as (putouts plus assists) per game. On the following pages, we've used the formula (putouts plus assists) *per nine innings*, which is a bit more precise. The catchers have an additional section of special stats, where you'll find opponents' stolen base/caught stealing data and team ERA with a particular catcher behind the plate. Although these stats are unofficial, we don't expect that the official ones will be substantially different when they arrive in a few months.

First Basemen - Regulars

Player	Tm	G	GS	Inn	PO	A	E	DP	Pct.	Rng
Segui, David	TOT	73	72	640.0	556	61	0	59	1.000	—
Grace, Mark	ChC	140	136	1216.1	1098	103	4	99	.997	—
Olerud, John	Sea	158	155	1358.2	1271	132	5	154	.996	—
Daubach, Brian	Bos	83	80	672.0	642	51	3	49	.996	—
Palmeiro, Rafael	Tex	108	107	919.0	820	56	4	86	.995	—
Coomer, Ron	Min	124	122	1064.2	1020	67	5	102	.995	—
Snow, J.T.	SF	153	144	1273.1	1197	91	6	135	.995	—
Helton, Todd	Col	160	156	1349.0	1328	148	7	143	.995	—
Karros, Eric	LA	153	153	1331.2	1296	138	7	123	.995	—
Giambi, Jason	Oak	124	124	1064.1	1161	59	6	114	.995	—
Casey, Sean	Cin	129	126	1079.0	1064	60	6	106	.995	—
Thome, Jim	Cle	107	105	923.0	834	91	5	101	.995	—
Martinez, Tino	NYY	154	149	1290.2	1154	88	7	110	.994	—
Bagwell, Jeff	Hou	158	157	1362.0	1264	116	9	128	.994	—
Lee, Derrek	Fla	147	123	1133.0	1101	102	8	104	.993	—
McGriff, Fred	TB	144	144	1255.1	1300	82	10	137	.993	—
Zeile, Todd	NYM	151	148	1270.0	1205	95	10	88	.992	—
Sexson, Richie	TOT	84	80	707.2	668	91	6	61	.992	—
Klesko, Ryan	SD	136	128	1126.0	1029	90	9	104	.992	—
Sweeney, Mike	KC	114	114	977.1	960	88	9	107	.991	—
Delgado, Carlos	Tor	162	162	1429.1	1416	82	13	157	.991	—
Clark, Will	TOT	122	117	1011.0	947	71	9	92	.991	—
Konerko, Paul	CWS	122	121	1068.1	1051	67	10	118	.991	—
Stevens, Lee	Mon	123	121	1036.1	1072	85	11	99	.991	—
Vaughn, Mo	Ana	147	147	1265.1	1257	69	14	156	.990	—
Colbrunn, Greg	Ari	99	82	732.1	649	52	8	60	.989	—
Galarraga, Andres	Atl	132	122	1078.0	1105	61	14	98	.988	—
Young, Kevin	Pit	129	122	1071.1	1109	59	17	121	.986	—
Average	—	130	126	1096.2	1056	84	8	108	.993	—

First Basemen - The Rest

Player	Tm	G	GS	Inn	PO	A	E	DP	Pct.	Rng
Alcantara, Israel	Bos	5	0	7.0	9	0	0	1	1.000	—
Allen, Dusty	SD	1	0	1.0	0	0	0	0	.000	—
Allen, Dusty	Det	17	2	45.0	45	1	0	5	1.000	—
Amaral, Rich	Bal	1	0	6.0	5	4	0	4	1.000	—
Anderson, Garret	Ana	1	0	0.1	0	0	0	0	.000	—
Andrews, Shane	ChC	6	4	34.1	36	7	0	3	1.000	—
Ausmus, Brad	Det	1	0	2.0	2	0	0	1	1.000	—
Bako, Paul	Atl	1	0	1.2	2	0	0	1	1.000	—
Barker, Kevin	Mil	32	29	251.2	250	15	2	24	.993	—
Bell, David	Sea	2	1	7.0	4	0	0	0	1.000	—
Bellinger, Clay	NYY	10	3	36.0	29	1	0	3	1.000	—
Benjamin, Mike	Pit	1	0	3.0	4	0	0	0	1.000	—
Berkman, Lance	Hou	2	0	5.0	2	1	0	0	1.000	—
Berroa, Geronimo	LA	2	2	12.0	11	2	1	3	.929	—
Blake, Casey	Min	1	1	9.0	5	0	0	1	1.000	—
Blum, Geoff	Mon	11	3	31.2	33	2	0	2	1.000	—
Brogna, Rico	Phi	34	32	276.2	248	17	1	22	.996	—
Brogna, Rico	Bos	37	14	161.2	165	9	3	13	.983	—
Brosius, Scott	NYY	2	0	3.0	3	0	0	0	1.000	—
Brown, Brant	Fla	5	4	34.2	30	3	0	2	1.000	—
Brown, Brant	ChC	7	4	36.0	20	3	1	0	.958	—
Burkhart, Morgan	Bos	5	2	26.0	26	1	1	1	.964	—
Burrell, Pat	Phi	58	58	500.0	460	22	6	37	.988	—
Cabrera, Alex	Ari	15	12	102.0	101	6	0	9	1.000	—

First Basemen - The Rest

Player	Tm	G	GS	Inn	PO	A	E	DP	Pct.	Rng
Catalanotto, Frank	Tex	17	12	107.1	100	7	3	12	.973	—
Clark, Tony	Det	58	58	472.1	488	45	4	49	.993	—
Clark, Will	Bal	72	71	607.1	583	44	6	58	.991	—
Clark, Will	StL	50	46	403.2	364	27	3	34	.992	—
Conine, Jeff	Bal	39	36	324.2	304	31	5	27	.985	—
Cox, Steve	TB	24	17	165.0	160	10	2	12	.988	—
Crespo, Felipe	SF	11	2	33.2	30	1	0	1	1.000	—
Cromer, D.T.	Cin	13	5	59.2	50	3	2	8	.964	—
Cruz, Ivan	Pit	1	1	9.0	6	0	0	0	1.000	—
Davis, Russ	SF	6	4	31.0	23	1	2	4	.923	—
Donnels, Chris	LA	4	2	22.0	19	0	1	2	.950	—
Dunston, Shawon	StL	6	1	19.1	21	0	1	3	.955	—
Durazo, Erubiel	Ari	60	56	471.2	422	23	5	36	.989	—
Echevarria, Angel	Col	2	0	4.0	3	0	0	1	1.000	—
Echevarria, Angel	Mil	9	2	34.1	27	3	0	4	1.000	—
Edmonds, Jim	StL	6	6	42.0	40	4	0	6	1.000	—
Elster, Kevin	LA	1	0	1.0	0	0	1	0	.000	—
Erstad, Darin	Ana	3	0	3.2	5	0	0	1	1.000	—
Evans, Tom	Tex	1	0	2.0	1	2	0	0	1.000	—
Fick, Robert	Det	34	20	200.2	222	18	4	19	.984	—
Fox, Andy	Ari	1	1	8.0	7	0	0	3	1.000	—
Franco, Matt	NYM	28	8	109.0	89	8	1	10	.990	—
Fryman, Travis	Cle	1	0	3.0	4	0	0	1	1.000	—
Fullmer, Brad	Tor	1	0	2.0	2	1	0	0	1.000	—
Giambi, Jeremy	Oak	15	3	60.1	55	5	0	5	1.000	—
Gil, Benji	Ana	3	0	5.0	4	0	0	0	1.000	—
Gload, Ross	ChC	2	1	10.0	6	0	0	2	1.000	—
Guillen, Ozzie	TB	5	0	8.0	7	1	0	0	1.000	—
Halter, Shane	Det	29	18	157.1	172	14	1	21	.995	—
Hansen, Dave	LA	16	3	46.0	44	5	1	5	.980	—
Harris, Lenny	NYM	10	5	50.1	36	6	2	3	.955	—
Hayes, Charlie	Mil	57	46	419.2	407	30	4	57	.991	—
Hernandez, Alex	Pit	12	11	105.0	123	3	1	14	.992	—
Hernandez, Carlos	SD	1	0	3.0	2	0	0	1	1.000	—
Hocking, Denny	Min	12	3	40.0	35	5	0	6	1.000	—
Houston, Tyler	Mil	35	29	261.0	257	21	5	30	.982	—
Howard, Thomas	StL	1	0	4.0	4	0	0	0	1.000	—
Hunter, Brian	Phi	40	20	205.1	159	16	1	12	.994	—
Huskey, Butch	Min	9	7	65.0	61	5	2	2	.971	—
Huskey, Butch	Col	8	2	25.0	24	1	0	6	1.000	—
Huson, Jeff	ChC	1	0	1.0	1	0	0	0	1.000	—
Ibanez, Raul	Sea	3	1	11.0	13	0	0	2	1.000	—
Javier, Stan	Sea	3	2	18.0	21	1	0	2	1.000	—
Jefferies, Gregg	Det	20	18	156.0	163	15	1	18	.994	—
Johnson, Keith	Ana	3	0	3.2	0	0	0	0	1.000	—
Johnson, Mark P.	NYM	4	1	10.1	9	0	0	1	1.000	—
Jordan, Kevin	Phi	9	6	56.0	54	5	2	11	.967	—
Joyner, Wally	Atl	55	39	350.2	353	30	3	33	.992	—
Kent, Jeff	SF	16	11	92.1	73	0	2	10	.973	—
Kieschnick, Brooks	Cin	1	0	1.0	1	0	0	0	1.000	—
Kinkade, Mike	Bal	1	1	1.0	1	0	0	0	1.000	—
Kotsay, Mark	Fla	2	0	3.0	1	0	0	0	1.000	—
LeCroy, Matt	Min	3	1	12.0	13	0	0	1	1.000	—
Ledesma, Aaron	Col	3	2	25.0	28	4	0	6	1.000	—
Lee, Travis	Ari	23	11	126.2	112	8	2	16	.984	—
Lee, Travis	Phi	47	43	375.2	338	35	0	42	1.000	—
Lesher, Brian	Sea	4	0	9.0	4	1	0	0	1.000	—
Leyritz, Jim	NYY	1	0	3.0	2	0	0	0	1.000	—

First Basemen - The Rest

Player	Tm	G	GS	Inn	PO	A	E	DP	Pct.	Rng
Leyritz, Jim	LA	8	2	31.1	27	2	0	3	1.000	—
Liefer, Jeff	CWS	1	1	6.0	6	1	1	1	.875	—
Mabry, John	Sea	3	0	7.0	8	1	0	1	1.000	—
Mabry, John	SD	2	1	8.0	8	1	0	0	1.000	—
Magadan, Dave	SD	8	4	43.2	47	10	0	7	1.000	—
Manto, Jeff	Col	1	0	1.0	1	0	0	1	1.000	—
Marrero, Eli	StL	7	0	11.0	16	0	0	1	1.000	—
Martinez, Dave	ChC	9	8	66.1	65	5	1	3	.986	—
Martinez, Dave	Tex	4	1	13.0	11	0	0	0	1.000	—
Martinez, Edgar	Sea	2	2	14.0	12	1	0	3	1.000	—
Martinez, Ramon	SF	2	0	2.0	1	0	0	1	1.000	—
Matheny, Mike	StL	8	0	12.0	12	1	0	0	1.000	—
McCarty, Dave	KC	63	48	459.0	463	59	4	62	.992	—
McGwire, Mark	StL	70	70	587.0	535	23	1	49	.998	—
Melhuse, Adam	Col	1	1	14.0	11	1	0	1	1.000	—
Mientkiewicz, Doug	Min	3	3	26.2	22	0	0	3	1.000	—
Millar, Kevin	Fla	34	31	236.0	233	29	3	18	.989	—
Miller, Damian	Ari	2	0	3.0	2	0	1	0	.667	—
Minor, Damon	SF	4	1	11.0	5	0	0	0	1.000	—
Minor, Ryan	Bal	5	3	29.0	26	3	0	1	1.000	—
Mordecai, Mike	Mon	3	0	7.2	6	1	1	3	.875	—
Morris, Hal	Cin	16	4	65.0	50	12	0	6	1.000	—
Morris, Hal	Det	38	30	269.1	263	23	3	27	.990	—
Munson, Eric	Det	3	1	12.0	16	0	1	2	.941	—
Norton, Greg	CWS	17	10	107.2	94	10	1	12	.990	—
Nunnari, Talmadge	Mon	14	0	28.1	23	2	0	1	1.000	—
Offerman, Jose	Bos	39	31	262.2	253	29	4	19	.986	—
Oliver, Joe	Sea	1	0	4.0	5	0	0	1	1.000	—
Ortiz, David	Min	27	25	215.1	210	12	1	17	.996	—
Osik, Keith	Pit	5	3	30.0	29	0	0	3	1.000	—
Palmer, Dean	Det	20	15	128.2	122	5	2	13	.984	—
Paquette, Craig	StL	28	17	151.1	129	9	1	15	.993	—
Perez, Eduardo	StL	24	19	163.2	156	13	0	18	1.000	—
Perry, Chan	Cle	1	0	1.0	3	0	0	0	1.000	—
Perry, Herbert	TB	1	0	3.0	2	0	0	0	1.000	—
Perry, Herbert	CWS	3	0	10.0	10	0	0	1	1.000	—
Piatt, Adam	Oak	3	0	5.0	5	0	0	0	1.000	—
Polanco, Placido	StL	1	0	3.0	2	1	0	0	1.000	—
Posada, Jorge	NYY	12	8	68.0	63	8	1	6	.986	—
Pritchett, Chris	Phi	3	3	25.0	15	4	0	1	1.000	—
Ramirez, Alex	Pit	1	0	1.0	0	0	0	0	.000	—
Richard, Chris	StL	2	0	3.2	3	0	0	0	1.000	—
Richard, Chris	Bal	53	52	465.1	440	18	5	52	.989	—
Rios, Armando	SF	1	0	1.0	0	0	0	0	.000	—
Rolison, Nate	Fla	4	3	23.0	21	2	0	1	1.000	—
Roskos, John	SD	2	0	5.1	0	1	0	0	1.000	—
Saenz, Olmedo	Oak	17	13	119.2	126	8	1	14	.993	—
Segui, David	Tex	38	38	334.2	295	28	0	38	1.000	—
Segui, David	Cle	35	34	305.1	261	33	0	21	1.000	—
Seguignol, F.	Mon	30	19	157.2	144	11	2	16	.987	—
Sexson, Richie	Cle	27	23	210.0	198	25	1	11	.996	—
Sexson, Richie	Mil	57	57	497.2	470	66	5	50	.991	—
Sheets, Andy	Bos	1	0	1.0	0	1	0	0	1.000	—
Sheldon, Scott	Tex	10	4	48.0	42	2	0	6	1.000	—
Shumpert, Terry	Col	6	1	12.0	8	1	2	2	.818	—
Sojo, Luis	NYY	7	1	21.2	20	4	1	0	.960	—
Spiezio, Scott	Ana	29	15	157.0	141	4	1	12	.993	—
Sprague, Ed	SD	25	20	180.2	181	10	7	14	.965	—

First Basemen - The Rest

Player	Tm	G	GS	Inn	PO	A	E	DP	Pct.	Rng
Sprague, Ed	Bos	3	1	21.0	17	4	0	1	1.000	—
Stairs, Matt	Oak	1	0	1.0	2	0	0	0	1.000	—
Stanley, Mike	Bos	39	34	301.1	264	31	1	26	.997	—
Stanley, Mike	Oak	19	18	157.0	146	13	2	18	.988	—
Sutton, Larry	StL	6	2	25.0	26	2	0	2	1.000	—
Sweeney, Mark	Mil	2	0	2.0	3	0	0	0	1.000	—
Tatis, Fernando	StL	1	1	8.0	7	1	0	2	1.000	—
Thomas, Frank	CWS	30	30	258.1	267	15	1	38	.996	—
Toca, Jorge	NYM	5	0	9.1	9	0	0	0	1.000	—
Tracy, Andy	Mon	28	18	163.0	177	11	0	15	1.000	—
Turner, Chris	NYY	1	0	2.0	1	0	0	0	1.000	—
Unroe, Tim	Atl	2	1	10.0	12	2	0	0	1.000	—
Valdez, Mario	Oak	4	3	28.0	26	2	0	2	1.000	—
Vander Wal, John	Pit	33	25	229.2	251	10	1	21	.996	—
Ventura, Robin	NYM	1	0	1.0	1	0	0	0	1.000	—
Vitiello, Joe	SD	17	9	91.2	77	7	3	11	.966	—
Vizcaino, Jose	LA	1	0	1.0	1	0	0	0	1.000	—
Walbeck, Matt	Ana	2	0	4.0	1	0	0	1	1.000	—
Ward, Daryle	Hou	19	5	70.2	55	3	0	5	1.000	—
Waszgis, B.J.	Tex	3	0	5.0	4	0	0	1	1.000	—
Widger, Chris	Sea	2	1	9.0	9	0	0	2	1.000	—
Wilson, Dan	Sea	1	0	4.0	3	0	0	0	1.000	—
Woodward, Chris	Tor	3	0	6.0	6	1	0	1	1.000	—
Wooten, Shawn	Ana	3	0	9.0	10	1	0	2	1.000	—
Young, Dmitri	Cin	36	28	251.2	229	16	4	18	.984	—
Zaun, Gregg	KC	1	0	3.0	1	0	0	0	1.000	—
Zuleta, Julio	ChC	14	9	90.2	77	8	3	9	.966	—

Second Basemen - Regulars

Player	Tm	G	GS	Inn	PO	A	E	DP	Pct.	Rng
Bush, Homer	Tor	75	73	653.0	165	246	6	68	.986	5.66
Velarde, Randy	Oak	122	119	1032.0	243	399	12	94	.982	5.60
Morris, Warren	Pit	134	131	1166.2	291	414	15	92	.979	5.44
Reese, Pokey	Cin	133	129	1129.0	289	393	14	88	.980	5.44
Cairo, Miguel	TB	108	96	870.0	218	302	9	76	.983	5.38
Belliard, Ron	Mil	151	149	1318.2	336	437	19	130	.976	5.28
Vina, Fernando	StL	122	118	1009.0	261	325	7	85	.988	5.23
Kennedy, Adam	Ana	155	147	1324.1	337	425	19	106	.976	5.18
Boone, Bret	SD	126	126	1097.1	292	334	15	83	.977	5.13
Offerman, Jose	Bos	80	71	618.0	150	202	7	43	.981	5.13
Easley, Damion	Det	125	124	1069.2	198	411	6	98	.990	5.12
Alomar, Roberto	Cle	155	154	1309.1	293	437	15	109	.980	5.02
McLemore, Mark	Sea	129	122	1091.1	262	346	8	87	.987	5.01
Young, Eric	ChC	150	147	1284.2	313	400	15	86	.979	5.00
Kent, Jeff	SF	150	146	1258.0	302	394	10	96	.986	4.98
Durham, Ray	CWS	151	149	1303.1	299	419	15	126	.980	4.96
Castillo, Luis	Fla	136	135	1176.1	282	365	11	83	.983	4.95
Febles, Carlos	KC	99	93	821.2	165	285	10	76	.978	4.93
Alfonzo, Edgardo	NYM	146	145	1240.2	316	362	10	84	.985	4.92
Veras, Quilvio	Atl	82	82	676.2	146	223	6	42	.984	4.91
Grudzielanek, Mark	LA	148	145	1284.2	286	414	17	97	.976	4.90
Biggio, Craig	Hou	100	99	852.2	181	280	6	57	.987	4.87
Vidro, Jose	Mon	153	153	1300.2	260	442	10	102	.986	4.86
Alicea, Luis	Tex	130	122	1048.2	247	318	13	85	.978	4.85
Morandini, Mickey	TOT	120	113	1002.2	237	288	6	73	.989	4.71
Lansing, Mike	TOT	137	124	1098.2	248	327	7	69	.988	4.71

Second Basemen - Regulars

Player	Tm	G	GS	Inn	PO	A	E	DP	Pct.	Rng
DeShields, Delino	Bal	96	93	813.1	171	254	11	46	.975	4.70
Bell, Jay	Ari	145	142	1243.2	290	345	8	86	.988	4.60
Knoblauch, Chuck	NYY	82	82	666.0	149	190	15	42	.958	4.58
Canizaro, Jay	Min	90	85	732.1	120	199	6	41	.982	3.92
Average	—	124	120	1049.2	245	339	11	82	.982	5.01

Second Basemen - The Rest

Player	Tm	G	GS	Inn	PO	A	E	DP	Pct.	Rng
Abbott, Kurt	NYM	23	8	104.0	23	29	1	3	.981	4.50
Alexander, Manny	Bos	7	2	26.0	5	7	0	1	1.000	4.15
Anderson, Marlon	Phi	41	41	362.1	87	100	2	32	.989	4.64
Arias, Alex	Phi	1	1	9.0	2	4	0	0	1.000	6.00
Ausmus, Brad	Det	1	0	0.0	0	0	0	0	.000	.00
Baughman, Justin	Ana	5	4	34.0	8	15	1	4	.958	6.09
Bell, David	Sea	48	40	350.1	85	102	3	33	.984	4.80
Bellhorn, Mark	Oak	2	1	8.0	0	1	0	0	1.000	1.13
Bellinger, Clay	NYY	21	12	119.0	19	49	0	5	1.000	5.14
Benjamin, Mike	Pit	27	20	186.0	57	71	0	18	1.000	6.19
Berg, Dave	Fla	11	9	80.0	17	25	0	3	1.000	4.72
Blum, Geoff	Mon	13	8	82.0	20	26	0	6	1.000	5.05
Bocachica, Hiram	LA	2	1	11.0	3	9	0	2	1.000	9.82
Bogar, Tim	Hou	2	0	6.0	1	2	1	1	.750	4.50
Branson, Jeff	LA	3	2	19.0	3	6	1	2	.900	4.26
Cabrera, Jolbert	Cle	19	4	68.0	13	19	0	7	1.000	4.24
Cabrera, Orlando	Mon	1	0	3.0	0	0	0	0	.000	.00
Castro, Juan	Cin	21	16	159.1	47	46	1	13	.989	5.25
Catalanotto, Frank	Tex	49	35	322.0	69	103	6	21	.966	4.81
Clapinski, Chris	Fla	14	10	101.1	25	31	4	5	.933	4.97
Coquillette, Trace	Mon	8	0	15.1	1	6	0	0	1.000	4.11
Cora, Alex	LA	8	7	59.0	11	13	0	5	1.000	3.66
Counsell, Craig	Ari	25	15	145.1	32	43	2	12	.974	4.64
Crespo, Felipe	SF	7	0	8.0	2	3	0	1	1.000	5.63
Cromer, Tripp	Hou	1	0	0.1	0	0	0	0	.000	.00
Delgado, Wilson	NYY	14	7	73.0	16	22	2	3	.950	4.68
Delgado, Wilson	KC	19	15	130.2	28	70	0	15	1.000	6.75
Donnels, Chris	LA	1	0	2.0	1	0	0	0	1.000	4.50
Dransfeldt, Kelly	Tex	2	0	3.0	0	1	0	0	1.000	3.00
Durrington, Trent	Ana	1	1	9.0	1	2	0	0	1.000	3.00
Fox, Andy	Fla	2	1	16.0	4	6	0	1	1.000	5.63
Franco, Matt	NYM	1	0	1.0	0	0	0	0	.000	.00
Frias, Hanley	Ari	15	5	54.2	11	13	1	3	.960	3.95
Frye, Jeff	Bos	53	43	399.0	95	122	2	20	.991	4.89
Frye, Jeff	Col	27	18	168.1	37	58	1	15	.990	5.08
Furcal, Rafael	Atl	31	26	223.0	45	72	1	18	.992	4.72
Garcia, Jesse	Bal	6	3	32.0	5	18	0	3	1.000	6.47
Gil, Benji	Ana	7	6	44.2	20	19	0	10	1.000	7.86
Ginter, Keith	Hou	2	2	18.0	4	5	0	2	1.000	4.50
Gomez, Chris	SD	3	0	11.0	3	3	0	2	1.000	4.91
Graffanino, Tony	TB	6	4	39.2	12	16	0	4	1.000	6.35
Graffanino, Tony	CWS	19	12	128.2	27	53	3	12	.964	5.60
Grebeck, Craig	Tor	56	55	479.0	100	174	9	34	.968	5.15
Guerrero, Wilton	Mon	1	0	1.0	0	0	0	0	.000	.00
Guillen, Ozzie	TB	2	1	7.2	3	2	0	1	1.000	5.87
Hairston Jr., Jerry	Bal	49	49	433.0	101	156	5	45	.981	5.34
Halter, Shane	Det	10	1	32.2	12	14	0	2	1.000	7.16
Harris, Lenny	NYM	3	2	15.0	2	3	0	0	1.000	3.00

Second Basemen - The Rest

Player	Tm	G	GS	Inn	PO	A	E	DP	Pct.	Rng
Hocking, Denny	Min	47	33	293.2	56	75	3	19	.978	4.01
Holbert, Ray	KC	1	0	3.0	3	1	0	1	1.000	12.00
Huson, Jeff	ChC	17	7	82.1	19	21	2	7	.952	4.37
Jackson, Damian	SD	36	33	307.2	70	104	5	24	.972	5.09
Jefferies, Gregg	Det	14	14	111.0	23	33	0	6	1.000	4.54
Johnson, Keith	Ana	2	1	11.0	2	7	0	0	1.000	7.36
Johnson, Russ	Hou	3	1	19.0	5	2	1	0	.875	3.32
Johnson, Russ	TB	18	15	129.1	27	55	2	9	.976	5.71
Jordan, Kevin	Phi	47	34	314.1	67	97	2	16	.988	4.70
Lamb, David	NYM	2	0	1.2	0	0	0	0	.000	.00
Lansing, Mike	Col	88	86	747.0	175	221	7	57	.983	4.77
Lansing, Mike	Bos	49	38	351.2	73	106	0	12	1.000	4.58
LaRocca, Greg	SD	2	2	18.0	3	6	2	0	.818	4.50
Lewis, Mark	Bal	21	17	152.0	37	51	2	11	.978	5.21
Lockhart, Keith	Atl	74	53	525.2	103	177	6	32	.979	4.79
Lopez, Luis	Mil	22	14	146.2	31	44	1	11	.987	4.60
Loretta, Mark	Mil	1	0	1.0	1	0	0	0	1.000	9.00
Lugo, Julio	Hou	45	40	366.1	92	108	5	26	.976	4.91
Luuloa, Keith	Ana	3	3	22.0	6	9	0	3	1.000	6.14
Macias, Jose	Det	39	22	230.0	39	85	3	19	.976	4.85
Martinez, Ramon	SF	32	15	150.1	43	35	0	11	1.000	4.67
Maxwell, Jason	Min	30	13	144.0	28	61	3	13	.967	5.56
McDonald, John	Cle	2	0	4.0	2	2	0	0	1.000	9.00
McEwing, Joe	NYM	16	6	63.2	16	15	2	4	.939	4.38
McGwire, Mark	StL	2	0	0.0	0	0	0	0	.000	.00
Melo, Juan	SF	6	1	23.0	3	4	0	0	1.000	2.74
Menechino, Frank	Oak	51	32	319.2	83	131	6	30	.973	6.03
Metcalfe, Mike	LA	1	1	7.0	0	1	0	0	1.000	1.29
Meyers, Chad	ChC	8	5	46.2	9	14	0	4	1.000	4.44
Mora, Melvin	NYM	4	1	14.0	3	11	0	1	1.000	9.00
Mora, Melvin	Bal	1	0	3.0	2	1	0	1	1.000	9.00
Morandini, Mickey	Phi	85	82	722.1	179	196	5	45	.987	4.67
Morandini, Mickey	Tor	35	31	280.1	58	92	1	28	.993	4.82
Mordecai, Mike	Mon	9	1	22.2	8	6	0	2	1.000	5.56
Mueller, Bill	SF	2	0	5.0	1	0	0	0	1.000	1.80
Newhan, David	SD	3	0	6.2	3	3	0	0	1.000	8.10
Newhan, David	Phi	5	4	30.2	9	15	0	5	1.000	7.04
Nicholson, Kevin	SD	4	1	16.2	2	8	2	2	.833	5.40
Nieves, Jose	ChC	7	1	24.0	2	11	0	4	1.000	4.88
Nunez, Abraham	Pit	6	3	33.0	12	8	0	4	1.000	5.45
Ojeda, Augie	ChC	4	2	17.0	2	2	0	1	1.000	2.12
Ordaz, Luis	KC	22	15	127.0	27	30	0	10	1.000	4.04
Ortiz, Jose	Oak	3	2	17.0	2	4	1	1	.857	3.18
Owens, Eric	SD	1	0	1.0	0	0	0	0	.000	.00
Ozuna, Pablo	Fla	7	6	56.0	12	17	1	3	.967	4.66
Paquette, Craig	StL	13	8	75.2	19	24	4	7	.915	5.11
Pena, Elvis	Col	1	0	1.0	0	0	0	0	.000	.00
Polanco, Placido	StL	51	32	349.0	80	107	3	18	.984	4.82
Reboulet, Jeff	KC	50	39	356.0	71	143	4	36	.982	5.41
Rivas, Luis	Min	14	13	117.2	30	28	1	8	.983	4.44
Sadler, Donnie	Bos	12	7	58.0	9	18	0	3	1.000	4.19
Santangelo, F.P.	LA	7	6	59.0	18	15	1	2	.971	5.03
Selby, Bill	Cle	6	0	11.0	3	2	0	0	1.000	4.09
Sexton, Chris	Cin	12	11	95.0	17	26	0	6	1.000	4.07
Sheldon, Scott	Tex	12	4	52.1	12	15	2	2	.931	4.64
Shumpert, Terry	Col	23	12	121.1	33	35	0	10	1.000	5.04
Sisco, Steve	Atl	5	1	15.0	3	4	0	2	1.000	4.20
Smith, Bobby	TB	45	45	384.2	84	144	7	26	.970	5.33

Second Basemen - The Rest

Player	Tm	G	GS	Inn	PO	A	E	DP	Pct.	Rng
Sojo, Luis	Pit	1	0	3.0	0	0	0	0	.000	.00
Sojo, Luis	NYY	25	22	177.2	33	59	1	7	.989	4.66
Soriano, Alfonso	NYY	1	0	3.0	0	0	1	0	.000	.00
Spiers, Bill	Hou	26	19	175.1	40	53	2	13	.979	4.77
Spiezio, Scott	Ana	2	0	3.0	0	0	0	0	.000	.00
Sprague, Ed	SD	1	0	1.0	0	1	0	0	1.000	9.00
Stynes, Chris	Cin	15	7	72.0	19	25	1	9	.978	5.50
Tucker, Michael	Cin	1	0	1.0	0	0	0	0	.000	.00
Velandia, Jorge	Oak	14	7	58.2	15	22	0	6	1.000	5.68
Velandia, Jorge	NYM	8	0	10.0	3	1	0	0	1.000	3.60
Vizcaino, Jose	LA	3	0	3.1	0	1	0	0	1.000	2.70
Vizcaino, Jose	NYY	62	38	385.2	83	120	2	28	.990	4.74
Walker, Todd	Min	19	18	145.0	34	36	4	12	.946	4.34
Walker, Todd	Col	52	46	392.1	81	118	5	25	.975	4.56
Wilson, Craig	CWS	4	1	18.1	11	8	1	3	.950	9.33
Wilson, Enrique	Cle	7	4	50.0	10	12	0	2	1.000	3.96
Wilson, Enrique	Pit	11	9	60.1	10	22	1	4	.970	4.77
Woodward, Chris	Tor	3	3	25.0	5	11	1	1	.941	5.76
Young, Mike	Tex	1	0	3.0	0	0	0	0	.000	.00
Zaun, Gregg	KC	1	0	1.0	0	0	0	0	.000	.00

Third Basemen - Regulars

Player	Tm	G	GS	Inn	PO	A	E	DP	Pct.	Rng
Glaus, Troy	Ana	156	155	1373.0	111	349	33	33	.933	3.02
Hernandez, Jose	Mil	95	85	753.0	81	165	13	23	.950	2.94
Castilla, Vinny	TB	83	83	720.0	50	185	8	20	.967	2.94
Beltre, Adrian	LA	138	136	1200.1	116	273	23	30	.944	2.92
Perry, Herbert	TOT	111	105	922.1	87	210	10	18	.967	2.90
Ventura, Robin	NYM	137	131	1110.2	95	261	17	27	.954	2.88
Batista, Tony	Tor	154	154	1367.0	120	318	17	35	.963	2.88
Ripken Jr., Cal	Bal	73	73	608.1	56	134	5	17	.974	2.81
Randa, Joe	KC	156	155	1361.1	132	293	19	30	.957	2.81
Rolen, Scott	Phi	128	127	1080.0	89	245	10	14	.971	2.78
Boone, Aaron	Cin	84	80	702.1	62	154	8	21	.964	2.77
Lamb, Mike	Tex	135	129	1137.0	118	230	33	24	.913	2.75
Lowell, Mike	Fla	136	135	1191.1	102	260	12	19	.968	2.73
Cirillo, Jeff	Col	155	151	1321.0	92	303	15	41	.963	2.69
Williams, Matt	Ari	94	93	804.0	68	172	9	19	.964	2.69
Greene, Willie	ChC	90	77	686.0	46	158	7	18	.967	2.68
Mueller, Bill	SF	145	129	1155.1	99	244	9	24	.974	2.67
Jones, Chipper	Atl	152	152	1311.1	90	297	23	23	.944	2.66
Koskie, Corey	Min	139	133	1164.1	96	241	12	27	.966	2.60
Brosius, Scott	NYY	134	133	1150.1	101	231	11	23	.968	2.60
Chavez, Eric	Oak	146	135	1206.1	91	256	18	17	.951	2.59
Nevin, Phil	SD	142	141	1212.2	96	242	26	22	.929	2.51
Bell, David	Sea	93	81	738.1	50	151	12	14	.944	2.45
Stynes, Chris	Cin	77	72	637.1	53	119	6	14	.966	2.42
Fryman, Travis	Cle	154	153	1346.1	79	276	8	20	.978	2.37
Palmer, Dean	Det	115	114	955.0	66	180	23	14	.914	2.32
Tatis, Fernando	StL	91	90	725.1	35	128	8	15	.953	2.02
Average	—	123	119	1034.2	84	225	15	22	.955	2.69

Third Basemen - The Rest

Player	Tm	G	GS	Inn	PO	A	E	DP	Pct.	Rng
Abbott, Kurt	NYM	2	2	17.0	4	1	0	0	1.000	2.65
Alexander, Manny	Bos	63	38	388.1	39	79	7	5	.944	2.73
Alicea, Luis	Tex	8	5	42.1	5	7	5	1	.706	2.55
Allen, Dusty	Det	1	0	2.0	1	0	0	0	1.000	4.50
Alvarez, Gabe	SD	3	0	7.0	0	1	0	0	1.000	1.29
Andrews, Shane	ChC	58	41	395.2	23	94	12	10	.907	2.66
Arias, Alex	Phi	10	2	37.1	2	6	0	1	1.000	1.93
Ausmus, Brad	Det	1	0	1.0	0	0	0	0	.000	.00
Barrett, Michael	Mon	55	49	421.2	23	83	13	10	.891	2.26
Bell, Mike	Cin	13	4	49.2	2	16	2	2	.900	3.26
Bell, Rob	Cin	0	0	0.0	0	0	0	0	.000	.00
Bellhorn, Mark	Oak	2	0	8.0	0	4	0	0	1.000	4.50
Bellinger, Clay	NYY	18	10	107.0	10	25	3	4	.921	2.94
Benjamin, Mike	Pit	34	19	187.1	13	61	2	5	.974	3.56
Berg, Dave	Fla	13	5	64.1	2	12	1	1	.933	1.96
Berry, Sean	Mil	9	6	55.1	3	4	0	1	1.000	1.14
Berry, Sean	Bos	1	1	9.0	0	0	0	0	.000	.00
Blake, Casey	Min	5	3	31.0	2	5	0	0	1.000	2.03
Blum, Geoff	Mon	55	46	386.1	26	93	6	6	.952	2.77
Bogar, Tim	Hou	1	0	1.0	0	0	0	0	.000	.00
Bonilla, Bobby	Atl	1	1	4.0	0	0	0	0	.000	.00
Branson, Jeff	LA	3	0	6.0	0	2	0	0	1.000	3.00
Branyan, Russ	Cle	1	1	7.2	0	1	1	1	.500	1.17
Caminiti, Ken	Hou	58	56	475.2	37	81	11	8	.915	2.23
Castro, Juan	Cin	7	1	15.1	0	2	0	0	1.000	1.17
Clapinski, Chris	Fla	3	1	9.0	2	2	0	0	1.000	4.00
Coffie, Ivanon	Bal	15	12	116.1	6	27	1	1	.971	2.55
Colbrunn, Greg	Ari	1	0	1.0	0	0	0	0	.000	.00
Collier, Lou	Mil	1	0	3.0	0	0	0	0	.000	.00
Conine, Jeff	Bal	44	38	342.1	21	75	7	10	.932	2.52
Coomer, Ron	Min	5	4	38.0	3	15	0	2	1.000	4.26
Coquillette, Trace	Mon	19	11	97.0	2	21	1	2	.958	2.13
Counsell, Craig	Ari	23	13	130.2	3	37	2	6	.952	2.76
Crede, Joe	CWS	6	2	31.0	5	9	1	1	.933	4.06
Cromer, Tripp	Hou	2	0	3.2	0	1	1	0	.500	2.45
Daubach, Brian	Bos	1	0	1.0	0	1	0	0	1.000	9.00
Davis, Russ	SF	43	33	276.0	14	42	4	3	.933	1.83
Delgado, Wilson	NYY	5	1	13.0	1	1	1	0	.667	1.38
Delgado, Wilson	KC	3	1	12.0	0	2	0	0	1.000	1.50
Diaz, Einar	Cle	1	0	3.0	0	0	0	0	.000	.00
Donnels, Chris	LA	2	1	8.0	1	1	0	0	1.000	2.25
Dunston, Shawon	StL	5	1	13.0	0	3	0	1	1.000	2.08
Elster, Kevin	LA	8	7	64.2	6	16	2	0	.917	3.06
Ensberg, Morgan	Hou	1	1	9.0	1	1	1	0	.667	2.00
Evans, Tom	Tex	21	17	154.1	12	38	5	5	.909	2.92
Feliz, Pedro	SF	4	0	8.0	0	0	0	0	.000	.00
Fox, Andy	Ari	20	17	153.2	11	29	2	3	.952	2.34
Fox, Andy	Fla	12	8	73.0	4	22	1	4	.963	3.21
Franco, Matt	NYM	22	7	86.2	9	18	3	0	.900	2.80
Frias, Hanley	Ari	7	1	16.2	0	3	0	1	1.000	1.62
Frye, Jeff	Bos	3	2	15.0	1	2	0	0	1.000	1.80
Frye, Jeff	Col	1	0	1.0	0	2	0	1	1.000	18.00
Gipson, Charles	Sea	5	2	23.0	1	9	0	1	1.000	3.91
Graffanino, Tony	TB	3	0	5.0	2	1	0	0	1.000	5.40
Graffanino, Tony	CWS	12	4	48.0	10	8	0	2	1.000	3.38
Guillen, Carlos	Sea	68	64	551.1	57	116	17	7	.911	2.82
Guillen, Ozzie	TB	11	9	78.0	4	22	0	2	1.000	3.00
Halter, Shane	Det	55	28	295.2	26	63	6	11	.937	2.71

Third Basemen - The Rest

Player	Tm	G	GS	Inn	PO	A	E	DP	Pct.	Rng
Hansen, Dave	LA	16	9	82.1	4	17	1	2	.955	2.30
Harris, Lenny	Ari	20	18	156.1	11	29	4	1	.909	2.30
Harris, Lenny	NYM	16	12	109.0	15	26	7	2	.854	3.39
Hatteberg, Scott	Bos	1	0	1.0	0	0	0	0	.000	.00
Hayes, Charlie	Mil	59	48	434.0	31	89	3	6	.976	2.49
Helms, Wes	Atl	5	0	11.0	1	4	1	1	.833	4.09
Hernandez, C. E.	Sea	2	0	3.0	1	0	0	0	1.000	3.00
Hocking, Denny	Min	16	8	83.1	3	20	1	2	.958	2.48
Holbert, Ray	KC	1	0	5.0	0	0	0	0	.000	.00
Houston, Tyler	Mil	28	23	202.1	12	50	4	6	.939	2.76
Huff, Aubrey	TB	37	35	278.0	24	53	5	3	.939	2.49
Huson, Jeff	ChC	18	12	90.2	10	16	0	1	1.000	2.58
Jefferies, Gregg	Det	6	4	31.0	2	4	0	1	1.000	1.74
Johnson, Russ	Hou	4	2	14.2	1	4	0	0	1.000	3.07
Johnson, Russ	TB	49	25	270.2	14	74	3	6	.967	2.93
Jordan, Kevin	Phi	39	33	321.1	26	61	3	8	.967	2.44
Klassen, Danny	Ari	25	20	181.1	11	39	2	4	.962	2.48
Konerko, Paul	CWS	7	6	58.2	2	7	1	1	.900	1.38
Lamb, David	NYM	3	0	3.0	0	1	0	0	1.000	3.00
Lansing, Mike	Bos	1	0	1.0	0	0	0	0	.000	.00
LaRocca, Greg	SD	8	2	27.0	3	3	0	0	1.000	2.00
Ledesma, Aaron	Col	5	1	16.1	0	2	0	0	1.000	1.10
Lewis, Mark	Cin	5	3	27.2	2	8	1	0	.909	3.25
Lewis, Mark	Bal	29	19	181.0	8	34	7	2	.857	2.09
Lockhart, Keith	Atl	18	8	103.0	8	27	2	2	.946	3.06
LoDuca, Paul	LA	1	1	6.0	0	1	0	0	1.000	1.50
Lopez, Luis	Mil	6	1	18.2	2	8	0	2	1.000	4.82
Mabry, John	Sea	22	15	122.0	6	19	4	3	.862	1.84
Macias, Jose	Det	26	16	158.2	11	29	1	3	.976	2.27
Magadan, Dave	SD	29	15	152.1	11	29	2	2	.952	2.36
Manto, Jeff	Col	1	0	1.0	0	1	0	0	1.000	9.00
Martinez, Ramon	SF	2	0	5.0	1	1	0	0	1.000	3.60
Maxwell, Jason	Min	19	14	116.0	5	24	2	4	.935	2.25
McEwing, Joe	NYM	19	9	101.2	6	26	3	1	.914	2.83
Meluskey, Mitch	Hou	1	0	2.0	0	0	1	0	.000	.00
Menechino, Frank	Oak	4	2	15.0	3	4	0	1	1.000	4.20
Merloni, Lou	Bos	40	35	299.2	26	64	7	3	.928	2.70
Meyers, Chad	ChC	8	4	30.1	2	5	2	1	.778	2.08
Millar, Kevin	Fla	13	12	92.0	11	23	2	1	.944	3.33
Minor, Ryan	Bal	26	20	185.1	18	32	4	5	.926	2.43
Mora, Melvin	NYM	4	1	14.0	1	0	0	0	1.000	0.64
Mordecai, Mike	Mon	58	33	322.1	21	68	6	9	.937	2.49
Newhan, David	SD	2	0	7.0	0	1	0	0	1.000	1.29
Nieves, Jose	ChC	39	28	252.0	17	58	4	2	.949	2.68
Norton, Greg	CWS	47	45	368.2	32	56	7	5	.926	2.15
Osik, Keith	Pit	12	9	78.2	9	14	1	2	.958	2.63
Paquette, Craig	StL	86	51	505.1	41	88	8	9	.942	2.30
Perez, Eduardo	StL	2	1	3.0	0	0	0	0	.000	.00
Perry, Herbert	TB	7	7	56.2	5	10	1	1	.938	2.38
Perry, Herbert	CWS	104	98	865.2	82	200	9	17	.969	2.93
Piatt, Adam	Oak	13	8	76.0	4	11	0	0	1.000	1.78
Polanco, Placido	StL	35	19	187.0	18	41	0	8	1.000	2.84
Ramirez, Aramis	Pit	72	71	583.0	26	128	14	7	.917	2.38
Reboulet, Jeff	KC	11	6	61.0	4	9	3	2	.813	1.92
Rolls, Damian	TB	1	0	2.0	0	0	0	0	.000	.00
Sadler, Donnie	Bos	3	1	10.0	0	3	0	1	1.000	2.70
Saenz, Olmedo	Oak	18	16	130.0	11	25	3	2	.923	2.49
Selby, Bill	Cle	4	0	10.0	0	1	0	1	1.000	0.90

Third Basemen - The Rest

Player	Tm	G	GS	Inn	PO	A	E	DP	Pct.	Rng
Sexton, Chris	Cin	3	3	24.0	2	4	0	0	1.000	2.25
Sheldon, Scott	Tex	15	11	95.1	11	28	1	6	.975	3.68
Shumpert, Terry	Col	15	10	90.2	8	13	0	0	1.000	2.08
Sisco, Steve	Atl	2	1	11.0	1	1	0	0	1.000	1.64
Smith, Bobby	TB	5	2	21.0	0	7	1	0	.875	3.00
Sojo, Luis	Pit	50	40	373.0	24	97	5	5	.960	2.92
Sojo, Luis	NYY	10	7	63.0	9	10	0	0	1.000	2.71
Soriano, Alfonso	NYY	10	8	65.0	11	11	4	2	.846	3.05
Spiers, Bill	Hou	51	36	340.0	33	85	5	8	.959	3.12
Spiezio, Scott	Ana	15	7	75.0	9	17	2	4	.929	3.12
Sprague, Ed	SD	10	4	53.1	3	9	0	1	1.000	2.03
Sprague, Ed	Bos	31	30	243.0	19	50	2	1	.972	2.56
Tracy, Andy	Mon	34	23	197.1	10	35	6	2	.882	2.05
Truby, Chris	Hou	74	67	591.2	51	125	14	15	.926	2.68
Valentin, John	Bos	10	10	81.0	6	9	0	1	1.000	1.67
Velandia, Jorge	NYM	3	0	8.0	2	2	1	0	.800	4.50
Veras, Wilton	Bos	49	45	403.2	33	94	13	11	.907	2.83
Vizcaino, Jose	LA	12	8	77.2	8	19	2	2	.931	3.13
Vizcaino, Jose	NYY	6	2	26.0	3	5	0	1	1.000	2.77
Wehner, John	Pit	16	10	101.0	14	22	1	0	.973	3.21
Wilson, Craig	CWS	15	7	78.1	6	24	2	2	.938	3.45
Wilson, Dan	Sea	1	0	4.0	0	0	0	0	.000	.00
Wilson, Enrique	Cle	8	2	75.1	2	17	1	0	.950	2.27
Wilson, Enrique	Pit	16	14	126.0	7	30	3	1	.925	2.64
Woodward, Chris	Tor	9	8	70.1	5	18	0	3	1.000	2.94

Shortstops - Regulars

Player	Tm	G	GS	Inn	PO	A	E	DP	Pct.	Rng
Martinez, Felix	TB	106	103	887.2	191	368	14	80	.976	5.67
Perez, Neifi	Col	162	160	1402.2	288	522	18	120	.978	5.20
Jackson, Damian	SD	88	80	704.0	144	258	19	50	.955	5.14
Valentin, Jose	CWS	141	136	1212.1	233	456	36	117	.950	5.11
Sanchez, Rey	KC	143	140	1198.0	224	446	4	106	.994	5.03
Meares, Pat	Pit	126	125	1075.0	191	401	20	99	.967	4.96
Clayton, Royce	Tex	148	144	1237.0	265	411	16	94	.977	4.92
Gil, Benji	Ana	94	84	741.2	140	261	18	59	.957	4.87
Rodriguez, Alex	Sea	148	148	1285.0	243	438	10	123	.986	4.77
Stocker, Kevin	TOT	109	101	881.0	141	321	18	74	.963	4.72
Tejada, Miguel	Oak	160	159	1400.1	233	501	21	115	.972	4.72
Furcal, Rafael	Atl	110	92	839.1	147	290	23	54	.950	4.69
Aurilia, Rich	SF	140	139	1193.0	218	403	21	110	.967	4.68
Cruz, Deivi	Det	156	154	1355.1	222	482	13	116	.982	4.67
Cabrera, Orlando	Mon	124	118	987.2	167	338	10	77	.981	4.60
Garciaparra, N.	Bos	136	135	1185.0	201	402	18	65	.971	4.58
Gonzalez, Alex S.	Tor	141	140	1225.1	213	407	16	100	.975	4.55
Mora, Melvin	TOT	96	92	794.2	134	264	19	48	.954	4.51
Loretta, Mark	Mil	90	88	750.1	121	254	2	54	.995	4.50
Gonzalez, Alex	Fla	104	98	855.2	139	288	19	63	.957	4.49
Bogar, Tim	Hou	95	82	729.1	120	243	11	55	.971	4.48
Cora, Alex	LA	101	94	828.1	152	260	12	70	.972	4.48
Guzman, Cristian	Min	151	148	1307.0	228	413	22	96	.967	4.41
Vizquel, Omar	Cle	156	154	1328.2	231	414	3	99	.995	4.37
Renteria, Edgar	StL	149	144	1258.0	231	379	27	79	.958	4.36
Larkin, Barry	Cin	102	100	844.2	153	249	11	43	.973	4.28
Bordick, Mike	TOT	156	155	1324.1	232	398	16	81	.975	4.28
Relaford, Desi	TOT	126	122	1080.1	189	322	31	79	.943	4.26

254

Shortstops - Regulars

Player	Tm	G	GS	Inn	PO	A	E	DP	Pct.	Rng
Gutierrez, Ricky	ChC	121	118	1018.1	190	290	7	60	.986	4.24
Womack, Tony	Ari	143	142	1244.0	217	365	18	72	.970	4.21
Jeter, Derek	NYY	148	148	1278.2	237	349	24	78	.961	4.12
Average	—	128	124	1079.0	195	361	17	82	.971	4.63

Shortstops - The Rest

Player	Tm	G	GS	Inn	PO	A	E	DP	Pct.	Rng
Abbott, Kurt	NYM	39	25	250.0	47	75	6	10	.953	4.39
Alexander, Manny	Bos	20	9	94.0	16	33	0	7	1.000	4.69
Alicea, Luis	Tex	2	0	6.0	1	3	0	0	1.000	6.00
Arias, Alex	Phi	39	32	300.0	41	88	5	19	.963	3.87
Baughman, Justin	Ana	5	1	17.0	4	2	0	0	1.000	3.18
Bell, David	Sea	1	0	1.0	0	0	0	0	.000	.00
Bellhorn, Mark	Oak	1	0	2.0	0	0	0	0	.000	.00
Bellinger, Clay	NYY	6	5	42.0	9	11	0	1	1.000	4.29
Beltre, Adrian	LA	1	0	1.0	1	0	0	0	1.000	9.00
Benjamin, Mike	Pit	30	15	162.2	30	74	2	13	.981	5.75
Berg, Dave	Fla	49	35	332.2	52	105	7	27	.957	4.25
Blum, Geoff	Mon	44	23	225.2	43	89	3	22	.978	5.26
Boone, Aaron	Cin	2	0	9.1	1	3	0	0	1.000	3.86
Bordick, Mike	Bal	100	100	865.0	161	258	9	57	.979	4.36
Bordick, Mike	NYM	56	55	459.1	71	140	7	24	.968	4.13
Branson, Jeff	LA	7	1	22.2	5	5	0	0	1.000	3.97
Cabrera, Jolbert	Cle	8	2	39.0	7	17	0	2	1.000	5.54
Castro, Juan	Cin	57	38	381.1	55	117	1	27	.994	4.06
Chavez, Eric	Oak	2	0	3.0	1	0	0	0	1.000	3.00
Clapinski, Chris	Fla	1	0	1.0	0	0	0	0	.000	.00
Coffie, Ivanon	Bal	4	2	22.0	7	5	0	1	1.000	4.91
Counsell, Craig	Ari	6	5	44.1	3	15	2	2	.900	3.65
Cromer, Tripp	Hou	1	0	4.1	0	1	0	0	1.000	2.08
Dawkins, Gookie	Cin	14	12	103.0	21	34	2	13	.965	4.81
de la Rosa, Tomas	Mon	29	17	171.1	39	58	2	7	.980	5.10
Delgado, Wilson	NYY	11	3	41.0	6	14	0	2	1.000	4.39
Delgado, Wilson	KC	12	6	58.2	10	25	1	8	.972	5.37
DeRosa, Mark	Atl	10	4	36.1	6	7	0	2	1.000	3.22
DiSarcina, Gary	Ana	12	12	99.0	24	47	5	12	.934	6.45
Dransfeldt, Kelly	Tex	14	6	64.1	13	28	0	8	1.000	5.74
Dunston, Shawon	StL	8	3	24.0	4	6	0	2	1.000	3.75
Elster, Kevin	LA	55	52	456.0	60	133	11	25	.946	3.81
Fox, Andy	Fla	33	28	240.1	37	86	9	12	.932	4.61
Frias, Hanley	Ari	21	13	137.1	18	43	4	12	.938	4.00
Garcia, Jesse	Bal	5	1	18.0	4	4	0	2	1.000	4.00
Gipson, Charles	Sea	5	0	7.2	0	2	0	0	1.000	2.35
Glaus, Troy	Ana	6	0	9.0	1	4	0	1	1.000	5.00
Gomez, Chris	SD	17	13	114.2	24	40	5	10	.928	5.02
Graffanino, Tony	TB	1	0	2.0	0	2	0	0	1.000	9.00
Graffanino, Tony	CWS	21	19	162.1	24	61	3	16	.966	4.71
Grebeck, Craig	Tor	8	5	48.0	10	19	0	4	1.000	5.44
Grudzielanek, Mark	LA	1	1	8.0	2	2	0	1	1.000	4.50
Guillen, Carlos	Sea	23	14	148.0	28	44	4	14	.947	4.38
Guillen, Ozzie	TB	42	17	181.0	26	65	5	12	.948	4.52
Halter, Shane	Det	17	8	85.0	19	33	1	8	.981	5.51
Hernandez, Jose	Mil	37	33	283.2	59	93	5	32	.968	4.82
Hocking, Denny	Min	15	12	98.2	19	38	1	10	.983	5.20
Holbert, Ray	KC	1	0	1.0	1	1	0	1	1.000	18.00
Huson, Jeff	ChC	17	10	111.1	23	33	1	7	.982	4.53

Shortstops - The Rest

Player	Tm	G	GS	Inn	PO	A	E	DP	Pct.	Rng
Johnson, Keith	Ana	1	0	4.0	2	2	0	0	1.000	9.00
Johnson, Russ	Hou	5	4	38.1	5	8	0	2	1.000	3.05
Johnson, Russ	TB	11	3	36.0	4	14	0	1	1.000	4.50
Jones, Chipper	Atl	6	3	36.2	6	8	2	2	.875	3.44
Klassen, Danny	Ari	3	2	18.0	3	3	0	0	1.000	3.00
Lamb, David	NYM	2	1	10.0	2	2	0	0	1.000	3.60
LaRocca, Greg	SD	4	3	26.0	4	3	0	1	1.000	2.42
Lewis, Mark	Bal	14	7	80.1	19	20	1	5	.975	4.37
Lopez, Luis	Mil	45	28	297.1	68	94	7	27	.959	4.90
Lugo, Julio	Hou	60	53	481.1	93	141	12	30	.951	4.38
Luuloa, Keith	Ana	4	2	21.0	2	3	1	1	.833	2.14
Macias, Jose	Det	1	0	3.0	1	2	0	1	1.000	9.00
Magadan, Dave	SD	2	0	3.0	0	2	0	1	1.000	6.00
Martinez, Ramon	SF	44	23	251.1	43	72	1	20	.991	4.12
Maxwell, Jason	Min	5	2	23.0	2	10	1	1	.923	4.70
McDonald, John	Cle	7	0	19.0	2	6	0	1	1.000	3.79
McEwing, Joe	NYM	4	0	14.0	3	3	0	0	1.000	3.86
McGwire, Mark	StL	0	0	0.0	0	0	0	0	.000	.00
Menechino, Frank	Oak	5	2	22.0	4	4	0	0	1.000	3.27
Mora, Melvin	NYM	44	40	346.2	56	104	7	16	.958	4.15
Mora, Melvin	Bal	52	52	448.0	78	160	12	32	.952	4.78
Mordecai, Mike	Mon	10	4	40.0	7	13	1	2	.952	4.50
Nicholson, Kevin	SD	30	24	224.1	37	79	2	11	.983	4.65
Nieves, Jose	ChC	24	14	140.1	27	34	1	10	.984	3.91
Nunez, Abraham	Pit	21	15	149.1	31	57	2	10	.978	5.30
Ojeda, Augie	ChC	25	20	184.2	28	63	1	11	.989	4.44
Ordaz, Luis	KC	38	12	147.0	37	35	1	14	.986	4.41
Ordonez, Rey	NYM	44	41	354.2	58	108	6	20	.965	4.21
Pena, Elvis	Col	4	0	6.0	1	2	0	1	1.000	4.50
Perez, Santiago	Mil	20	14	135.0	21	45	6	11	.917	4.40
Perez, Tomas	Phi	44	39	343.2	76	89	4	20	.976	4.32
Polanco, Placido	StL	29	14	151.2	31	53	0	11	1.000	4.98
Reboulet, Jeff	KC	5	4	34.2	9	15	2	3	.923	6.23
Relaford, Desi	Phi	81	80	693.0	116	202	24	46	.930	4.13
Relaford, Desi	SD	45	42	387.1	73	120	7	33	.965	4.48
Rivas, Luis	Min	2	0	4.0	1	1	0	1	1.000	4.50
Rollins, Jimmy	Phi	13	11	102.0	23	22	1	9	.978	3.97
Sadler, Donnie	Bos	19	14	127.1	19	50	3	7	.958	4.88
Sexton, Chris	Cin	14	13	118.0	25	37	3	6	.954	4.73
Sheets, Andy	Bos	10	3	46.1	7	17	0	4	1.000	4.66
Sheldon, Scott	Tex	22	12	121.2	25	40	2	6	.970	4.81
Shumpert, Terry	Col	7	2	21.1	4	7	0	3	1.000	4.64
Sojo, Luis	NYY	2	1	11.0	2	2	0	0	1.000	3.27
Soriano, Alfonso	NYY	9	4	45.2	7	7	2	1	.875	2.76
Spiers, Bill	Hou	27	23	184.1	40	57	1	18	.990	4.74
Stocker, Kevin	TB	40	38	324.2	43	111	11	25	.933	4.27
Stocker, Kevin	Ana	69	63	556.1	98	210	7	49	.978	4.98
Velandia, Jorge	Oak	4	0	8.0	2	2	0	1	1.000	4.50
Velandia, Jorge	NYM	7	0	15.1	3	2	0	0	1.000	2.93
Vizcaino, Jose	LA	19	14	129.0	15	43	0	6	1.000	4.05
Vizcaino, Jose	NYY	2	0	6.0	2	2	0	2	1.000	6.00
Weiss, Walt	Atl	69	63	528.0	83	197	15	38	.949	4.77
Wilson, Craig	CWS	10	7	75.2	14	29	0	4	1.000	5.11
Wilson, Enrique	Cle	7	6	55.2	8	15	0	5	1.000	3.72
Wilson, Enrique	Pit	8	7	62.0	7	21	2	7	.933	4.06
Woodward, Chris	Tor	22	17	164.0	26	58	4	9	.955	4.61

Left Fielders - Regulars

Player	Tm	G	GS	Inn	PO	A	E	DP	Pct.	Rng
Erstad, Darin	Ana	112	111	968.1	274	9	3	2	.990	2.63
White, Rondell	TOT	92	92	758.1	199	4	1	1	.995	2.41
Higginson, Bobby	Det	145	144	1256.1	308	19	7	3	.979	2.34
Stewart, Shannon	Tor	136	136	1169.0	297	6	2	2	.993	2.33
Gant, Ron	TOT	105	98	858.2	217	5	7	1	.969	2.33
Jones, Jacque	Min	90	81	722.2	176	7	2	1	.989	2.28
Vaughn, Greg	TB	72	72	617.0	145	6	1	1	.993	2.20
Surhoff, B.J.	TOT	134	134	1152.1	276	6	3	1	.989	2.20
Jenkins, Geoff	Mil	131	129	1126.1	263	12	7	3	.975	2.20
Henderson, Rickey	TOT	117	115	905.0	217	0	5	0	.977	2.16
Quinn, Mark	KC	78	76	666.0	150	7	1	1	.994	2.12
Greer, Rusty	Tex	97	96	836.0	194	3	3	0	.985	2.12
Bonds, Barry	SF	141	138	1151.2	255	8	3	4	.989	2.06
Lee, Carlos	CWS	149	146	1272.2	273	10	3	0	.990	2.00
O'Leary, Troy	Bos	137	133	1182.2	243	9	3	0	.988	1.92
Grieve, Ben	Oak	144	144	1160.1	237	6	3	0	.988	1.88
Gonzalez, Luis	Ari	162	162	1430.2	293	4	3	1	.990	1.87
Young, Dmitri	Cin	111	104	848.1	172	4	4	1	.978	1.87
Martin, Al	TOT	109	101	867.0	174	5	9	0	.952	1.86
Lankford, Ray	StL	116	105	909.0	178	3	5	0	.973	1.79
Agbayani, Benny	NYM	102	88	719.2	140	3	3	0	.979	1.79
Floyd, Cliff	Fla	108	107	889.2	168	7	9	0	.951	1.77
Rodriguez, Henry	TOT	94	90	748.1	137	6	2	2	.986	1.72
Sheffield, Gary	LA	139	139	1133.0	203	5	10	0	.954	1.65
Cordero, Wil	TOT	123	121	1062.0	189	5	2	0	.990	1.64
Average	—	118	114	976.1	215	6	4	1	.982	2.04

Left Fielders - The Rest

Player	Tm	G	GS	Inn	PO	A	E	DP	Pct.	Rng
Abbott, Jeff	CWS	20	14	131.2	23	0	0	0	1.000	1.57
Alcantara, Israel	Bos	1	0	2.0	0	0	0	0	.000	.00
Allen, Chad	Min	2	2	18.0	6	0	0	0	1.000	3.00
Allen, Dusty	SD	2	2	14.0	2	0	0	0	1.000	1.29
Allen, Dusty	Det	1	0	2.0	0	0	0	0	.000	.00
Alou, Moises	Hou	59	56	477.2	91	0	5	0	.948	1.71
Alvarez, Gabe	SD	2	0	6.0	0	0	0	0	.000	.00
Amaral, Rich	Bal	3	1	11.1	3	0	0	0	1.000	2.38
Anderson, Brady	Bal	16	16	134.2	26	0	0	0	1.000	1.74
Aven, Bruce	Pit	17	10	89.0	17	0	0	0	1.000	1.72
Aven, Bruce	LA	9	6	60.0	12	0	0	0	1.000	1.80
Barker, Glen	Hou	2	0	4.0	3	0	0	0	1.000	6.75
Barnes, John	Min	2	2	16.0	0	0	0	0	.000	.00
Bartee, Kimera	Cin	2	0	4.0	0	0	0	0	.000	.00
Bautista, Danny	Fla	25	2	67.2	19	0	1	0	.950	2.53
Bautista, Danny	Ari	2	0	2.0	1	0	0	0	1.000	4.50
Becker, Rich	Oak	8	0	12.2	4	0	0	0	1.000	2.84
Becker, Rich	Det	14	5	59.0	16	1	2	0	.895	2.59
Bellinger, Clay	NYY	17	0	36.2	5	1	0	0	1.000	1.47
Beltran, Carlos	KC	2	2	18.2	6	0	0	0	1.000	2.89
Benard, Marvin	SF	21	4	55.1	18	0	0	0	1.000	2.93
Bergeron, Peter	Mon	32	26	226.2	45	1	0	0	1.000	1.83
Berkman, Lance	Hou	40	31	269.1	69	1	0	0	1.000	2.34
Berroa, Geronimo	LA	4	1	19.0	4	0	0	0	1.000	1.89
Bonilla, Bobby	Atl	63	62	416.0	47	1	4	0	.923	1.04
Bragg, Darren	Col	34	29	234.0	46	0	0	0	1.000	1.77
Branyan, Russ	Cle	18	16	120.0	28	0	1	0	.966	2.10

Left Fielders - The Rest

Player	Tm	G	GS	Inn	PO	A	E	DP	Pct.	Rng
Brock, Tarrik	ChC	9	0	19.1	5	0	0	0	1.000	2.33
Brosius, Scott	NYY	1	0	2.0	0	0	0	0	.000	.00
Brown, Adrian	Pit	7	1	18.2	5	1	0	1	1.000	2.89
Brown, Brant	Fla	8	4	32.0	9	0	0	0	1.000	2.53
Brown, Brant	ChC	18	4	57.2	10	0	0	0	1.000	1.56
Brown, Dee	KC	5	3	33.0	12	0	0	0	1.000	3.27
Brown, Emil	Pit	14	10	90.2	21	0	0	0	1.000	2.08
Brown, Roosevelt	ChC	24	19	152.0	35	1	0	0	1.000	2.13
Buchanan, Brian	Min	2	2	9.0	2	0	0	0	1.000	2.00
Buford, Damon	ChC	2	0	3.0	1	0	0	0	1.000	3.00
Burkhart, Morgan	Bos	1	0	1.0	0	0	0	0	.000	.00
Burrell, Pat	Phi	48	48	410.0	74	6	2	0	.976	1.76
Byrnes, Eric	Oak	1	0	2.0	0	0	0	0	.000	.00
Cabrera, Alex	Ari	1	0	1.0	2	0	0	0	1.000	18.00
Cabrera, Jolbert	Cle	24	4	71.0	17	0	0	0	1.000	2.15
Cameron, Mike	Sea	1	1	6.0	1	0	0	0	1.000	1.50
Canseco, Jose	NYY	4	4	27.0	6	0	0	0	1.000	2.00
Carpenter, Bubba	Col	5	4	32.0	3	0	0	0	1.000	0.84
Cedeno, Roger	Hou	23	20	176.0	38	1	1	0	.975	1.99
Christenson, Ryan	Oak	76	5	164.2	28	0	3	0	.903	1.53
Clapinski, Chris	Fla	3	0	4.0	1	0	0	0	1.000	2.25
Clark, Brady	Cin	2	0	5.0	1	0	0	0	1.000	1.80
Clemente, Edgard	Ana	15	9	77.1	18	0	0	0	1.000	2.09
Collier, Lou	Mil	5	2	20.2	3	1	0	0	1.000	1.74
Conine, Jeff	Bal	7	4	47.1	8	1	0	0	1.000	1.71
Conti, Jason	Ari	2	0	4.0	3	0	0	0	1.000	6.75
Coquillette, Trace	Mon	2	0	4.2	1	0	0	0	1.000	1.93
Cordero, Wil	Pit	85	83	743.1	110	3	2	0	.983	1.37
Cordero, Wil	Cle	38	38	318.2	79	2	0	0	1.000	2.29
Cordova, Marty	Tor	23	21	189.0	30	0	1	0	.968	1.43
Cox, Steve	TB	26	24	192.0	61	2	4	0	.940	2.95
Crespo, Felipe	SF	18	11	100.2	12	0	1	0	.923	1.07
Cruz, Jacob	Cle	1	1	9.0	0	0	0	0	.000	.00
Cummings, Midre	Min	7	2	27.0	6	0	0	0	1.000	2.00
Curtis, Chad	Tex	51	49	414.0	95	3	5	0	.951	2.13
Damon, Johnny	KC	67	65	570.0	147	2	3	0	.980	2.35
Darr, Mike	SD	8	7	56.1	11	1	0	0	1.000	1.92
Daubach, Brian	Bos	7	7	58.2	20	0	0	0	1.000	3.07
DeHaan, Kory	SD	10	2	33.0	11	0	0	0	1.000	3.00
Dellucci, David	Ari	1	0	1.0	0	0	0	0	.000	.00
DeShields, Delino	Bal	39	39	329.2	73	3	1	1	.987	2.07
Donnels, Chris	LA	6	3	26.0	8	0	0	0	1.000	2.77
Drew, J.D.	StL	24	13	134.2	25	2	2	1	.931	1.80
Ducey, Rob	Phi	28	18	161.0	37	1	3	0	.927	2.12
Ducey, Rob	Tor	2	1	17.1	4	0	1	0	.800	2.08
Dunston, Shawon	StL	41	27	228.0	54	0	1	0	.982	2.13
Dunwoody, Todd	KC	14	11	104.2	20	0	2	0	.909	1.72
Echevarria, Angel	Col	1	0	1.0	0	0	0	0	.000	.00
Echevarria, Angel	Mil	2	0	7.0	0	0	0	0	.000	.00
Fox, Andy	Ari	1	0	1.0	1	0	0	0	1.000	9.00
Fox, Andy	Fla	9	0	13.0	3	0	0	0	1.000	2.08
Franco, Matt	NYM	3	1	11.0	2	0	0	0	1.000	1.64
Frye, Jeff	Bos	1	1	9.0	2	0	0	0	1.000	2.00
Gant, Ron	Phi	84	84	726.1	175	4	6	0	.968	2.22
Gant, Ron	Ana	21	14	132.1	42	1	1	1	.977	2.92
Garcia, Karim	Bal	2	0	4.0	2	0	0	0	1.000	4.50
Giambi, Jeremy	Oak	6	4	34.2	2	0	1	0	.667	0.52
Gilbert, Shawn	LA	8	1	16.1	3	0	0	0	1.000	1.65

Left Fielders - The Rest

Player	Tm	G	GS	Inn	PO	A	E	DP	Pct.	Rng
Giles, Brian	Pit	46	45	387.2	74	2	1	0	.987	1.76
Gilkey, Bernard	Ari	2	0	4.0	0	0	0	0	.000	.00
Gilkey, Bernard	Bos	7	2	21.2	6	1	0	0	1.000	2.91
Gipson, Charles	Sea	14	1	30.2	5	0	0	0	1.000	1.47
Gload, Ross	ChC	7	6	42.2	9	0	0	0	1.000	1.90
Gonzalez, Raul	ChC	2	0	3.0	0	0	0	0	.000	.00
Goodwin, Tom	LA	10	4	46.0	15	0	0	0	1.000	2.93
Green, Sc.	Tex	3	1	13.0	2	1	0	0	1.000	2.08
Greene, Todd	Tor	1	0	1.0	0	0	0	0	.000	.00
Guerrero, Wilton	Mon	42	36	283.2	69	3	1	1	.986	2.28
Halter, Shane	Det	2	1	8.0	3	1	0	0	1.000	4.50
Hamilton, Darryl	NYM	17	12	94.1	20	2	0	2	1.000	2.10
Hammonds, Jeffrey	Col	33	30	256.2	52	3	1	0	.982	1.93
Hansen, Dave	LA	3	1	11.0	3	0	0	0	1.000	2.45
Harris, Lenny	NYM	6	4	30.0	9	1	1	0	.909	3.00
Henderson, Rickey	NYM	29	28	214.0	36	0	2	0	.947	1.51
Henderson, Rickey	Sea	88	87	691.0	181	0	3	0	.984	2.36
Hernandez, Alex	Pit	3	0	4.0	0	1	0	0	1.000	2.25
Hernandez, Jose	Mil	2	0	7.0	1	0	1	0	.500	1.29
Hidalgo, Richard	Hou	36	7	115.2	36	0	2	1	.947	2.80
Hill, Glenallen	ChC	29	25	205.1	39	3	2	2	.955	1.84
Hill, Glenallen	NYY	12	11	77.0	19	0	0	0	1.000	2.22
Hocking, Denny	Min	16	11	97.0	18	3	0	2	1.000	1.95
Hollandsworth, T.	LA	9	0	16.0	4	0	0	0	1.000	2.25
Hollandsworth, T.	Col	31	23	214.1	41	2	0	0	1.000	1.81
Howard, Thomas	StL	6	4	28.0	1	0	0	0	1.000	0.32
Hubbard, Trenidad	Atl	36	4	143.2	27	1	0	0	1.000	1.75
Hubbard, Trenidad	Bal	11	0	27.0	4	0	1	0	.800	1.33
Hunter, Brian	Phi	6	1	18.2	3	0	0	0	1.000	1.45
Hunter, Brian L.	Col	27	4	77.0	15	1	0	0	1.000	1.87
Hunter, Brian L.	Cin	9	4	40.0	15	3	0	0	1.000	4.05
Hunter, Torii	Min	1	0	2.0	0	0	0	0	.000	.00
Huskey, Butch	Col	15	13	106.1	25	1	0	0	1.000	2.20
Hyzdu, Adam	Pit	1	1	9.0	1	0	0	0	1.000	1.00
Ibanez, Raul	Sea	35	11	148.2	40	1	1	1	.976	2.48
Jackson, Damian	SD	17	11	91.0	20	0	1	0	.952	1.98
Javier, Stan	Sea	46	32	315.0	52	3	0	0	1.000	1.57
Jefferies, Gregg	Det	1	0	1.0	0	0	0	0	.000	.00
Johnson, Lance	NYY	2	0	8.2	1	0	0	0	1.000	1.04
Johnson, Mark P.	NYM	1	1	6.0	1	1	0	0	1.000	3.00
Jones, Terry	Mon	55	14	215.0	46	3	1	0	.980	2.05
Jose, Felix	NYY	6	2	31.0	5	0	1	0	.833	1.45
Justice, David	Cle	25	24	209.2	38	1	0	1	1.000	1.67
Justice, David	NYY	43	41	326.2	81	5	2	0	.977	2.37
Kelly, Roberto	NYY	7	7	57.0	15	0	0	0	1.000	2.37
Klesko, Ryan	SD	2	0	3.0	1	0	0	0	1.000	3.00
Lawton, Matt	Min	67	62	541.0	107	2	1	1	.991	1.81
Ledee, Ricky	NYY	46	41	365.2	88	1	2	0	.978	2.19
Ledee, Ricky	Cle	12	12	101.0	22	0	0	0	1.000	1.96
Ledee, Ricky	Tex	20	13	125.0	28	0	1	0	.966	2.02
Lee, Travis	Phi	10	9	74.2	9	0	0	0	1.000	1.08
Lewis, Darren	Bos	18	13	118.2	22	3	0	0	1.000	1.90
Leyritz, Jim	LA	5	5	39.0	4	0	0	0	1.000	0.92
Lindsey, Rod	Det	2	0	4.0	0	0	0	0	.000	.00
LoDuca, Paul	LA	7	0	12.0	6	0	0	0	1.000	4.50
Lombard, George	Atl	5	2	31.0	4	0	0	0	1.000	1.16
Lowery, Terrell	SF	13	3	49.1	5	0	1	0	.833	0.91
Lugo, Julio	Hou	3	0	3.1	0	0	0	0	.000	.00

Left Fielders - The Rest

Player	Tm	G	GS	Inn	PO	A	E	DP	Pct.	Rng
Mabry, John	Sea	7	3	28.1	4	0	0	0	1.000	1.27
Mabry, John	SD	2	2	14.0	3	0	0	0	1.000	1.93
Magee, Wendell	Det	18	10	93.0	18	1	0	0	1.000	1.84
Martin, Al	SD	89	84	725.2	128	4	7	0	.950	1.64
Martin, Al	Sea	20	17	141.1	46	1	2	0	.959	2.99
Martinez, Dave	ChC	9	3	40.2	10	0	0	0	1.000	2.21
Matos, Luis	Bal	1	0	1.0	0	0	0	0	.000	.00
Matthews Jr., Gary	ChC	46	16	190.2	55	2	2	1	.966	2.69
McCarty, Dave	KC	7	3	30.0	7	1	0	1	1.000	2.40
McCracken, Q.	TB	9	4	46.0	12	0	0	0	1.000	2.35
McDonald, Jason	Tex	11	3	39.0	12	0	0	0	1.000	2.77
McEwing, Joe	NYM	43	6	113.0	24	0	0	0	1.000	1.91
McGwire, Mark	StL	0	0	0.0	0	0	0	0	.000	.00
McLemore, Mark	Sea	14	10	80.2	22	0	0	0	1.000	2.45
McMillon, Billy	Det	3	1	10.0	4	0	0	0	1.000	3.60
Mendoza, Carlos	Col	3	0	6.0	0	0	1	0	.000	.00
Metcalfe, Mike	LA	3	1	10.0	4	0	0	0	1.000	3.60
Mieske, Matt	Hou	14	6	55.1	9	0	1	0	.900	1.46
Millar, Kevin	Fla	17	13	100.0	23	0	0	0	1.000	2.07
Mora, Melvin	NYM	12	1	26.0	5	0	0	0	1.000	1.73
Morris, Hal	Det	1	0	1.0	1	0	0	0	1.000	9.00
Mouton, James	Mil	19	13	125.1	19	2	1	0	.955	1.51
Mouton, Lyle	Mil	22	18	168.2	37	4	1	1	.976	2.19
Murray, Calvin	SF	2	0	3.0	0	0	0	0	.000	.00
Nunnally, Jon	NYM	26	6	79.1	13	2	1	0	.938	1.70
Ochoa, Alex	Cin	74	24	293.0	65	3	1	0	.986	2.09
Owens, Eric	SD	65	45	447.1	113	1	0	0	1.000	2.29
Palmeiro, Orlando	Ana	40	24	235.2	67	3	1	0	.986	2.67
Paquette, Craig	StL	18	8	94.2	19	1	1	1	.952	1.90
Paul, Josh	CWS	1	0	1.0	0	0	0	0	.000	.00
Payton, Jay	NYM	4	0	7.2	2	0	0	0	1.000	2.35
Perez, Eduardo	StL	4	3	24.0	11	0	0	0	1.000	4.13
Perez, Timoniel	NYM	8	3	26.1	9	1	0	0	1.000	3.42
Perry, Chan	Cle	1	0	3.0	1	0	0	0	1.000	3.00
Piatt, Adam	Oak	8	7	55.0	12	0	1	0	.923	1.96
Polonia, Luis	Det	1	1	9.0	4	0	0	0	1.000	4.00
Polonia, Luis	NYY	22	15	136.0	30	0	1	0	.968	1.99
Porter, Bo	Oak	1	1	6.0	1	0	0	0	1.000	1.50
Pose, Scott	KC	3	2	17.0	4	0	0	0	1.000	2.12
Pride, Curtis	Bos	7	4	40.2	12	0	0	0	1.000	2.66
Ramirez, Alex	Cle	15	11	93.0	18	1	0	0	1.000	1.84
Redman, Tike	Pit	2	1	9.0	3	0	0	0	1.000	3.00
Richard, Chris	StL	1	1	9.0	2	0	0	0	1.000	2.00
Rios, Armando	SF	19	6	84.1	13	3	1	0	.941	1.71
Rivera, Ruben	SD	1	0	1.0	0	0	0	0	.000	.00
Roberts, Dave	Cle	12	1	25.0	3	0	0	0	1.000	1.08
Rodriguez, Henry	ChC	70	67	566.2	110	5	2	2	.983	1.83
Rodriguez, Henry	Fla	24	23	181.2	27	1	0	0	1.000	1.39
Roskos, John	SD	4	4	29.0	6	0	0	0	1.000	1.86
Sadler, Donnie	Bos	3	2	18.1	7	0	0	0	1.000	3.44
Sanders, Reggie	Atl	69	62	564.2	104	4	4	0	.964	1.72
Santangelo, F.P.	LA	26	1	56.2	8	0	0	0	1.000	1.27
Sefcik, Kevin	Phi	25	2	48.0	11	0	0	0	1.000	2.06
Seguignol, F.	Mon	17	12	80.0	7	0	2	0	.778	0.79
Selby, Bill	Cle	4	4	29.0	10	0	0	0	1.000	3.10
Sexson, Richie	Cle	58	51	463.0	79	3	0	0	1.000	1.59
Sheldon, Scott	Tex	2	0	1.1	0	0	0	0	.000	.00
Shumpert, Terry	Col	40	29	246.2	56	2	2	0	.967	2.12

Left Fielders - The Rest

Player	Tm	G	GS	Inn	PO	A	E	DP	Pct.	Rng
Singleton, Chris	CWS	19	2	45.0	16	0	0	0	1.000	3.20
Sisco, Steve	Atl	5	0	8.0	3	0	0	0	1.000	3.38
Smith, Mark	Fla	29	12	141.2	31	3	0	0	1.000	2.16
Spencer, Shane	NYY	33	31	263.1	65	3	1	1	.986	2.32
Spiers, Bill	Hou	6	1	14.1	2	1	0	0	1.000	1.88
Spiezio, Scott	Ana	9	4	34.1	12	0	0	0	1.000	3.15
Sprague, Ed	SD	6	5	39.0	10	0	0	0	1.000	2.31
Stynes, Chris	Cin	6	4	40.2	11	1	0	0	1.000	2.66
Surhoff, B.J.	Bal	102	102	878.1	226	5	3	1	.987	2.37
Surhoff, B.J.	Atl	32	32	274.0	50	1	0	0	1.000	1.68
Sutton, Larry	StL	3	0	6.1	2	0	0	0	1.000	2.84
Swann, Pedro	Atl	1	0	2.0	0	0	0	0	.000	.00
Sweeney, Mark	Mil	3	1	11.1	8	0	0	0	1.000	6.35
Thompson, Andy	Tor	2	2	18.0	2	0	0	0	1.000	1.00
Thompson, Ryan	NYY	20	9	93.1	19	0	0	0	1.000	1.83
Timmons, Ozzie	TB	2	1	12.0	3	0	0	0	1.000	2.25
Toca, Jorge	NYM	1	0	2.0	0	0	0	0	.000	.00
Trammell, Bubba	TB	26	20	181.0	34	1	0	0	1.000	1.74
Trammell, Bubba	NYM	11	1	37.0	7	0	0	0	1.000	1.70
Tucker, Michael	Cin	41	27	225.1	47	2	2	0	.961	1.96
Tyner, Jason	NYM	12	10	83.2	21	1	2	1	.917	2.37
Tyner, Jason	TB	27	17	169.2	39	4	0	0	1.000	2.28
Unroe, Tim	Atl	1	0	1.0	0	0	0	0	.000	.00
Valdes, Pedro	Tex	1	0	0.2	1	0	0	0	1.000	13.50
Vander Wal, John	Pit	13	11	96.2	19	1	1	0	.952	1.86
Walker, Larry	Col	31	30	256.0	66	2	0	0	1.000	2.39
Ward, Daryle	Hou	43	41	322.0	65	1	1	1	.985	1.84
Wehner, John	Pit	1	0	1.0	0	0	0	0	.000	.00
White, Rondell	Mon	74	74	614.2	158	4	1	1	.994	2.37
White, Rondell	ChC	18	18	143.2	41	0	0	0	1.000	2.57
Winn, Randy	TB	29	23	213.2	51	4	1	1	.982	2.32
Wise, Dewayne	Tor	14	2	43.0	12	0	0	0	1.000	2.51
Zuleta, Julio	ChC	6	4	30.0	6	0	0	0	1.000	1.80

Center Fielders - Regulars

Player	Tm	G	GS	Inn	PO	A	E	DP	Pct.	Rng
Hunter, Torii	Min	98	94	824.2	270	12	3	3	.989	3.08
Hidalgo, Richard	Hou	125	124	1008.2	333	5	5	0	.985	3.02
Kapler, Gabe	Tex	84	82	701.1	221	4	8	3	.966	2.89
Cameron, Mike	Sea	155	141	1263.2	394	6	6	3	.985	2.85
Singleton, Chris	CWS	143	133	1157.2	357	9	3	0	.992	2.85
Jones, Andruw	Atl	161	161	1430.1	439	9	2	2	.996	2.82
Griffey Jr., Ken	Cin	141	141	1227.1	374	10	5	3	.987	2.82
Beltran, Carlos	KC	83	82	723.1	219	5	6	2	.979	2.79
Goodwin, Tom	TOT	136	122	1092.0	331	5	3	3	.991	2.77
Anderson, Brady	Bal	88	85	751.2	230	1	1	1	.996	2.77
Lofton, Kenny	Cle	135	133	1152.0	348	4	4	1	.989	2.75
Glanville, Doug	Phi	150	145	1275.1	380	9	4	4	.990	2.75
Williams, Bernie	NYY	137	136	1170.0	353	2	0	1	1.000	2.73
Rivera, Ruben	SD	131	112	1036.2	303	10	5	3	.984	2.72
Encarnacion, Juan	Det	141	138	1212.2	363	3	5	2	.987	2.72
Bergeron, Peter	Mon	117	101	909.2	258	15	5	3	.982	2.70
Anderson, Garret	Ana	137	135	1203.0	354	5	3	0	.992	2.69
Edmonds, Jim	StL	146	138	1210.2	351	9	4	2	.989	2.68
Williams, Gerald	TB	138	138	1216.2	349	6	6	0	.983	2.63
Cruz, Jose	Tor	162	162	1423.1	405	9	3	1	.993	2.62

Center Fielders - Regulars

Player	Tm	G	GS	Inn	PO	A	E	DP	Pct.	Rng
Wilson, Preston	Fla	158	152	1362.2	387	9	5	2	.988	2.62
Benard, Marvin	SF	128	121	977.0	273	9	1	1	.996	2.60
Payton, Jay	NYM	143	124	1097.0	308	7	6	2	.981	2.58
Giles, Brian	Pit	72	71	621.1	168	9	4	1	.978	2.56
Long, Terrence	Oak	137	131	1166.1	328	2	10	1	.971	2.55
Grissom, Marquis	Mil	142	141	1258.2	352	4	3	1	.992	2.55
Buford, Damon	ChC	140	124	1128.0	311	4	4	0	.987	2.51
Finley, Steve	Ari	148	145	1283.2	343	10	3	2	.992	2.47
Everett, Carl	Bos	126	122	1063.2	277	11	6	4	.980	2.44
Average	—	131	125	1101.2	323	7	4	2	.987	2.70

Center Fielders - The Rest

Player	Tm	G	GS	Inn	PO	A	E	DP	Pct.	Rng
Abbott, Jeff	CWS	33	26	218.2	52	1	1	0	.981	2.18
Abbott, Kurt	NYM	2	0	3.0	0	0	0	0	.000	.00
Agbayani, Benny	NYM	3	3	18.0	9	0	0	0	1.000	4.50
Amaral, Rich	Bal	12	11	97.0	36	0	0	0	1.000	3.34
Aven, Bruce	Pit	8	5	45.2	11	0	0	0	1.000	2.17
Barker, Glen	Hou	63	10	186.0	61	1	1	0	.984	3.00
Barnes, John	Min	2	2	16.0	6	0	0	0	1.000	3.38
Bartee, Kimera	Cin	1	0	2.0	1	0	0	0	1.000	4.50
Bautista, Danny	Fla	5	1	12.0	5	0	0	0	1.000	3.75
Bautista, Danny	Ari	21	13	125.0	28	2	0	0	1.000	2.16
Becker, Rich	Oak	14	11	92.0	30	2	2	2	.941	3.13
Becker, Rich	Det	24	19	168.2	54	0	0	0	1.000	2.88
Bell, Derek	NYM	5	4	30.0	9	0	0	0	1.000	2.70
Bellinger, Clay	NYY	26	20	187.1	52	0	2	0	.963	2.50
Bradley, Milton	Mon	40	38	325.2	89	6	2	0	.979	2.63
Brock, Tarrik	ChC	2	2	15.0	3	0	1	0	.750	1.80
Brown, Adrian	Pit	71	55	513.2	130	5	3	0	.978	2.37
Brown, Brant	ChC	9	9	76.0	27	0	0	0	1.000	3.20
Brown, Emil	Pit	12	5	51.2	11	0	0	0	1.000	1.92
Brown, Roosevelt	ChC	1	1	5.0	1	0	0	0	1.000	1.80
Cabrera, Jolbert	Cle	26	21	184.1	56	2	1	1	.983	2.83
Cedeno, Roger	Hou	29	26	241.0	68	0	0	0	1.000	2.54
Christensen, M.	CWS	29	3	74.0	20	1	0	0	1.000	2.55
Christenson, Ryan	Oak	27	19	172.0	53	1	2	1	.964	2.83
Clemente, Edgard	Ana	5	2	22.0	10	1	0	0	1.000	4.50
Collier, Lou	Mil	7	5	47.0	13	1	0	0	1.000	2.68
Conti, Jason	Ari	4	2	16.0	3	0	0	0	1.000	1.69
Cruz, Jacob	Cle	8	5	56.0	16	1	0	1	1.000	2.73
Cummings, Midre	Bos	1	0	2.0	1	0	0	0	1.000	4.50
Damon, Johnny	KC	69	67	579.2	187	4	2	1	.990	2.97
Darr, Mike	SD	19	17	127.2	36	1	0	0	1.000	2.61
DeHaan, Kory	SD	4	1	12.0	6	0	0	0	1.000	4.50
DeShields, Delino	Bal	2	1	9.0	2	0	1	0	.667	2.00
Drew, J.D.	StL	26	17	156.1	45	0	2	0	.957	2.59
Ducey, Rob	Phi	2	1	7.0	3	0	0	0	1.000	3.86
Dunston, Shawon	StL	9	5	45.1	14	0	0	0	1.000	2.78
Dunwoody, Todd	KC	19	12	123.1	44	0	0	0	1.000	3.21
Erstad, Darin	Ana	30	25	218.2	76	0	0	0	1.000	3.13
Fox, Andy	Ari	1	0	2.0	0	0	0	0	.000	.00
Frye, Jeff	Bos	2	0	3.0	0	0	0	0	.000	.00
Gilbert, Shawn	LA	4	3	26.2	7	1	1	1	.889	2.70
Gipson, Charles	Sea	8	2	26.0	3	1	0	0	1.000	1.38
Goodwin, Tom	Col	88	76	687.1	208	3	3	1	.986	2.76

Center Fielders - The Rest

Player	Tm	G	GS	Inn	PO	A	E	DP	Pct.	Rng
Goodwin, Tom	LA	48	46	404.2	123	2	0	2	1.000	2.78
Green, Sc.	Tex	41	23	229.0	80	5	0	1	1.000	3.34
Green, Shawn	LA	1	0	1.0	0	0	0	0	.000	.00
Guerrero, Wilton	Mon	13	8	64.0	20	0	1	0	.952	2.81
Guillen, Jose	TB	1	0	2.0	2	0	0	0	1.000	9.00
Halter, Shane	Det	5	3	30.0	11	0	0	0	1.000	3.30
Hamilton, Darryl	NYM	11	7	66.2	12	0	0	0	1.000	1.62
Hammonds, Jeffrey	Col	9	7	51.0	12	0	0	0	1.000	2.12
Hermansen, Chad	Pit	27	26	216.2	35	2	1	0	.974	1.54
Hocking, Denny	Min	21	12	107.0	36	1	0	0	1.000	3.11
Hollandsworth, T.	LA	68	55	521.1	139	6	2	0	.986	2.50
Hollandsworth, T.	Col	4	3	22.2	5	1	0	0	1.000	2.38
Hunter, Brian L.	Col	34	33	264.1	74	2	1	0	.987	2.59
Hunter, Brian L.	Cin	16	5	60.0	15	1	1	0	.941	2.40
Javier, Stan	Sea	14	12	100.0	28	2	0	0	1.000	2.70
Jones, Jacque	Min	63	51	461.0	159	2	0	0	1.000	3.14
Jones, Terry	Mon	26	14	125.1	45	1	2	0	.958	3.30
Justice, David	Cle	2	0	4.0	3	0	0	0	1.000	6.75
Justice, David	NYY	1	0	1.0	0	0	0	0	.000	.00
Kelly, Roberto	NYY	3	1	10.0	3	0	0	0	1.000	2.70
Kingsale, Gene	Bal	24	22	195.2	61	2	3	0	.955	2.90
Kotsay, Mark	Fla	9	8	55.0	20	1	0	0	1.000	3.44
Lankford, Ray	StL	2	1	10.0	1	1	0	0	1.000	1.80
Lawton, Matt	Min	3	3	21.0	7	0	1	0	.875	3.00
Ledee, Ricky	NYY	4	3	28.0	6	0	0	0	1.000	1.93
Ledee, Ricky	Tex	3	2	18.0	4	0	0	0	1.000	2.00
Lee, Travis	Ari	2	1	9.0	3	0	1	0	.750	3.00
Lewis, Darren	Bos	41	31	287.1	69	1	2	1	.972	2.19
Lindsey, Rod	Det	4	0	9.0	2	0	0	0	1.000	2.00
Lugo, Julio	Hou	1	1	2.0	0	0	0	0	.000	.00
Macias, Jose	Det	1	0	1.0	0	0	0	0	.000	.00
Magee, Wendell	Det	5	2	22.0	9	0	0	0	1.000	3.68
Martin, Al	Sea	7	7	51.0	11	1	1	0	.923	2.12
Martinez, Dave	ChC	1	1	10.0	2	0	0	0	1.000	1.80
Mateo, Ruben	Tex	52	52	457.0	140	4	3	0	.980	2.84
Matos, Luis	Bal	44	43	380.0	123	0	2	0	.984	2.91
Matthews Jr., Gary	ChC	21	14	125.0	28	1	0	0	1.000	2.09
Maxwell, Jason	Min	1	0	3.0	2	0	0	0	1.000	6.00
McCracken, Q.	TB	3	3	23.0	7	0	0	0	1.000	2.74
McDonald, Jason	Tex	3	3	23.0	8	0	0	0	1.000	3.13
McEwing, Joe	NYM	11	10	70.0	17	1	0	0	1.000	2.31
McLemore, Mark	Sea	1	0	1.0	2	0	0	0	1.000	18.00
Metcalfe, Mike	LA	1	1	8.0	1	0	0	0	1.000	1.13
Mora, Melvin	NYM	16	7	81.0	22	0	1	0	.957	2.44
Mouton, James	Mil	23	17	158.2	52	1	0	0	1.000	3.01
Mouton, Lyle	Mil	1	0	2.0	0	0	0	0	.000	.00
Murray, Calvin	SF	104	41	467.1	143	2	3	1	.980	2.79
Nixon, Trot	Bos	6	4	36.2	13	0	0	0	1.000	3.19
Nunnally, Jon	NYM	10	5	48.0	18	2	0	2	1.000	3.75
Ochoa, Alex	Cin	3	0	6.0	4	0	0	0	1.000	6.00
Owens, Eric	SD	34	32	283.0	74	2	0	0	1.000	2.42
Palmeiro, Orlando	Ana	2	0	4.0	1	0	0	0	1.000	2.25
Patterson, Corey	ChC	11	9	85.2	26	0	1	0	.963	2.73
Perez, Timoniel	NYM	7	2	33.1	13	0	0	0	1.000	3.51
Pierre, Juan	Col	50	43	404.2	115	2	3	0	.975	2.60
Porter, Bo	Oak	2	0	4.0	2	0	0	0	1.000	4.50
Pose, Scott	KC	2	0	6.0	0	0	0	0	.000	.00
Pride, Curtis	Bos	2	1	10.0	3	0	0	0	1.000	2.70

Center Fielders - The Rest

Player	Tm	G	GS	Inn	PO	A	E	DP	Pct.	Rng
Quinn, Mark	KC	1	1	7.0	2	1	0	0	1.000	3.86
Ramirez, Alex	Cle	1	1	9.0	1	0	0	0	1.000	1.00
Roberts, Dave	Cle	5	1	20.0	7	0	0	0	1.000	3.15
Sadler, Donnie	Bos	13	4	50.0	14	0	0	0	1.000	2.52
Sanders, Reggie	Atl	1	1	9.0	1	0	0	0	1.000	1.00
Santangelo, F.P.	LA	27	22	187.0	48	0	1	0	.980	2.31
Saturria, Luis	StL	5	1	11.1	2	0	0	0	1.000	1.59
Sefcik, Kevin	Phi	20	14	137.1	49	0	0	0	1.000	3.21
Sheldon, Scott	Tex	1	0	0.2	0	0	0	0	.000	.00
Sosa, Sammy	ChC	2	2	10.0	2	0	0	0	1.000	1.80
Stairs, Matt	Oak	1	0	1.0	0	0	0	0	.000	.00
Stewart, Shannon	Tor	1	0	5.0	1	0	0	0	1.000	1.80
Swann, Pedro	Atl	1	0	1.0	0	0	0	0	.000	.00
Taylor, Reggie	Phi	3	2	19.0	4	0	1	0	.800	1.89
Thompson, Ryan	NYY	9	1	28.0	12	0	0	0	1.000	3.86
Tucker, Michael	Cin	28	17	161.0	48	2	2	0	.962	2.80
Tyner, Jason	NYM	2	0	3.0	1	0	0	0	1.000	3.00
Tyner, Jason	TB	4	3	34.2	12	0	0	0	1.000	3.12
Vaughn, Mo	Ana	1	0	0.1	0	0	0	0	.000	.00
Ward, Turner	Ari	1	1	8.0	1	0	0	0	1.000	1.13
Wells, Vernon	Tor	3	0	7.0	2	0	0	0	1.000	2.57
White, Devon	LA	40	35	296.1	68	2	2	0	.972	2.13
Whiten, Mark	Cle	5	1	17.0	3	0	0	0	1.000	1.59
Winn, Randy	TB	18	17	155.0	41	0	0	0	1.000	2.38
Wise, Dewayne	Tor	1	0	2.0	1	0	0	0	1.000	4.50

Right Fielders - Regulars

Player	Tm	G	GS	Inn	PO	A	E	DP	Pct.	Rng
Martinez, Dave	TOT	110	102	896.1	229	15	2	4	.992	2.45
Salmon, Tim	Ana	124	123	1069.2	275	12	6	4	.980	2.41
Jordan, Brian	Atl	130	127	1108.0	287	7	3	0	.990	2.39
Kotsay, Mark	Fla	139	113	1052.1	266	13	3	3	.989	2.39
Abreu, Bobby	Phi	152	150	1330.2	337	13	4	2	.989	2.37
Drew, J.D.	StL	98	78	697.1	178	4	5	1	.973	2.35
Burks, Ellis	SF	108	108	847.1	215	4	4	1	.982	2.33
O'Neill, Paul	NYY	140	139	1153.1	293	5	2	3	.993	2.33
Lawton, Matt	Min	83	76	647.0	163	2	3	0	.982	2.30
Bichette, Dante	Cin	121	119	987.0	236	11	8	3	.969	2.25
Mondesi, Raul	Tor	96	95	831.2	203	5	7	3	.967	2.25
Guerrero, Vladimir	Mon	151	151	1268.0	299	12	10	3	.969	2.21
Burnitz, Jeromy	Mil	158	155	1386.0	318	12	7	2	.979	2.14
Guillen, Jose	TB	98	79	741.2	167	8	4	3	.978	2.12
Sosa, Sammy	ChC	156	154	1373.1	316	3	10	1	.970	2.09
Belle, Albert	Bal	110	110	953.1	211	8	3	2	.986	2.07
Nixon, Trot	Bos	115	104	917.1	202	8	2	4	.991	2.06
Dye, Jermaine	KC	146	145	1260.1	277	11	7	3	.976	2.06
Stairs, Matt	Oak	102	96	844.0	185	5	4	1	.979	2.03
Buhner, Jay	Sea	104	101	803.0	176	4	0	0	1.000	2.02
Ordonez, Magglio	CWS	152	150	1322.2	280	12	5	3	.983	1.99
Hammonds, Jeffrey	Col	85	78	695.1	143	5	1	0	.993	1.92
Bell, Derek	NYM	142	136	1168.0	243	5	3	1	.988	1.91
Green, Shawn	LA	161	161	1425.0	280	9	6	3	.980	1.83
Ramirez, Manny	Cle	93	93	799.1	134	7	2	1	.986	1.59
Average	—	123	118	1023.0	237	8	4	2	.982	2.15

Right Fielders - The Rest

Player	Tm	G	GS	Inn	PO	A	E	DP	Pct.	Rng
Abbott, Jeff	CWS	16	10	102.0	26	1	1	0	.964	2.38
Agbayani, Benny	NYM	12	3	38.2	9	0	1	0	.900	2.09
Alcantara, Israel	Bos	7	3	35.2	8	0	1	0	.889	2.02
Allen, Chad	Min	13	13	108.0	20	2	0	2	1.000	1.83
Allen, Dusty	Det	1	1	2.0	1	0	0	0	1.000	4.50
Alou, Moises	Hou	64	64	535.0	102	5	1	0	.991	1.80
Amaral, Rich	Bal	4	1	16.0	6	1	0	0	1.000	3.94
Anderson, Brady	Bal	24	23	190.0	45	0	0	0	1.000	2.13
Anderson, Garret	Ana	15	12	105.1	26	0	1	0	.963	2.22
Aven, Bruce	Pit	20	11	104.1	21	0	1	0	.955	1.81
Barker, Glen	Hou	4	0	8.0	0	0	0	0	.000	.00
Barnes, John	Min	8	7	67.2	22	2	0	2	1.000	3.19
Bautista, Danny	Fla	17	14	113.2	23	2	0	1	1.000	1.98
Bautista, Danny	Ari	67	50	459.1	113	4	2	0	.983	2.29
Becker, Rich	Oak	1	0	3.0	1	0	0	0	1.000	3.00
Becker, Rich	Det	47	31	308.1	57	2	4	2	.937	1.72
Bellinger, Clay	NYY	5	1	13.0	3	0	0	0	1.000	2.08
Beltran, Carlos	KC	3	3	27.0	6	0	0	0	1.000	2.00
Benard, Marvin	SF	38	5	111.1	32	2	0	0	1.000	2.75
Berkman, Lance	Hou	63	59	505.1	104	5	6	0	.948	1.94
Berroa, Geronimo	LA	2	0	5.0	3	0	0	0	1.000	5.40
Bonilla, Bobby	Atl	1	1	7.0	2	0	0	0	1.000	2.57
Bragg, Darren	Col	9	5	52.0	7	0	0	0	1.000	1.21
Branyan, Russ	Cle	15	15	112.0	31	2	1	0	.971	2.65
Brosius, Scott	NYY	1	0	2.0	0	0	0	0	.000	.00
Brown, Adrian	Pit	15	7	71.1	19	1	1	0	.952	2.52
Brown, Brant	Fla	5	4	31.0	3	0	1	0	.750	0.87
Brown, Brant	ChC	3	0	4.0	1	0	0	0	1.000	2.25
Brown, Emil	Pit	18	11	108.2	22	3	0	1	1.000	2.07
Brown, Roosevelt	ChC	5	1	11.0	2	0	0	0	1.000	1.64
Buchanan, Brian	Min	24	21	184.1	32	1	0	0	1.000	1.61
Buford, Damon	ChC	7	6	58.1	24	0	1	1	.960	3.70
Byrnes, Eric	Oak	3	1	11.0	4	0	0	0	1.000	3.27
Cabrera, Alex	Ari	11	9	64.2	19	1	1	0	.952	2.78
Cabrera, Jolbert	Cle	29	4	82.2	16	1	0	0	1.000	1.85
Cameron, Mike	Sea	1	0	4.0	2	0	0	0	1.000	4.50
Canseco, Jose	NYY	1	1	6.0	1	0	2	0	.600	4.50
Carpenter, Bubba	Col	1	0	3.0	0	0	0	0	.000	.00
Catalanotto, Frank	Tex	1	0	1.0	0	0	0	0	.000	.00
Cedeno, Roger	Hou	17	14	128.0	29	0	2	0	.935	2.04
Christenson, Ryan	Oak	14	3	48.2	14	1	0	0	1.000	2.77
Clark, Brady	Cin	3	0	6.0	5	0	0	0	1.000	7.50
Clemente, Edgard	Ana	12	4	49.0	8	1	0	0	1.000	1.65
Conine, Jeff	Bal	12	12	98.1	30	1	3	1	.912	2.84
Conti, Jason	Ari	33	17	178.1	47	4	1	2	.981	2.57
Coquillette, Trace	Mon	1	0	2.0	1	0	0	0	1.000	4.50
Cordova, Marty	Tor	18	17	158.1	25	1	0	1	1.000	1.48
Cox, Steve	TB	30	30	227.0	46	1	2	0	.959	1.86
Crespo, Felipe	SF	9	4	38.1	13	0	0	0	1.000	3.05
Cummings, Midre	Min	33	22	203.0	52	4	0	2	1.000	2.48
Cummings, Midre	Bos	3	3	26.2	6	0	0	0	1.000	2.03
Curtis, Chad	Tex	30	20	182.0	40	2	0	0	1.000	2.08
Darr, Mike	SD	47	28	288.1	77	5	0	1	1.000	2.56
Daubach, Brian	Bos	1	0	2.0	0	0	0	0	.000	.00
Davis, Eric	StL	69	61	493.0	121	1	4	0	.968	2.23
DeHaan, Kory	SD	49	11	171.0	33	3	0	1	1.000	1.89
Dellucci, David	Ari	11	8	60.2	15	0	0	0	1.000	2.23
Ducey, Rob	Phi	4	2	21.0	3	0	0	0	1.000	1.29
Ducey, Rob	Tor	1	1	8.0	4	0	0	0	1.000	4.50
Dunston, Shawon	StL	13	5	54.0	17	1	0	0	1.000	3.00
Dunwoody, Todd	KC	9	8	72.0	17	0	0	0	1.000	2.13
Echevarria, Angel	Mil	3	2	18.0	2	1	0	0	1.000	1.50
Fox, Andy	Ari	4	1	15.0	2	0	0	0	1.000	1.20
Fox, Andy	Fla	5	3	27.2	3	1	1	0	.800	1.30
Frye, Jeff	Bos	13	8	84.2	18	0	0	0	1.000	1.91
Garcia, Karim	Det	7	5	47.0	8	0	0	0	1.000	1.53
Giambi, Jeremy	Oak	49	43	347.2	79	3	2	0	.976	2.12
Gilbert, Shawn	LA	2	1	6.0	5	0	0	0	1.000	7.50
Giles, Brian	Pit	39	38	342.2	74	3	1	0	.987	2.02
Gilkey, Bernard	Ari	16	15	123.2	29	1	0	0	1.000	2.18
Gilkey, Bernard	Bos	16	12	114.1	30	0	0	0	1.000	2.36
Gipson, Charles	Sea	29	0	47.1	14	0	0	0	1.000	2.66
Gload, Ross	ChC	1	0	1.0	0	0	0	0	.000	.00
Gonzalez, Juan	Det	66	66	544.0	118	2	1	1	.992	1.99
Green, Sc.	Tex	23	6	75.0	20	2	0	0	1.000	2.64
Guerrero, Wilton	Mon	24	8	99.0	27	1	2	0	.933	2.55
Gwynn, Tony	SD	26	26	201.2	31	1	0	0	1.000	1.43
Halter, Shane	Det	3	1	9.0	1	0	0	0	1.000	1.00
Hamilton, Darryl	NYM	8	7	57.0	9	0	0	0	1.000	1.42
Harris, Lenny	Ari	3	0	8.2	0	0	0	0	.000	.00
Harris, Lenny	NYM	5	1	17.1	5	0	1	0	.833	2.60
Hermansen, Chad	Pit	4	4	35.2	9	0	0	0	1.000	2.27
Hernandez, Alex	Pit	2	1	9.2	4	0	0	0	1.000	3.72
Hidalgo, Richard	Hou	37	17	174.2	56	2	0	1	1.000	2.99
Hocking, Denny	Min	19	6	83.0	16	1	0	1	1.000	1.84
Hollandsworth, T.	LA	1	0	1.0	0	0	0	0	.000	.00
Hollandsworth, T.	Col	18	15	136.1	28	3	1	0	.969	2.05
Howard, Thomas	StL	22	12	109.2	22	1	1	1	.958	1.89
Hubbard, Trenidad	Atl	10	7	63.1	13	0	0	0	1.000	1.85
Hubbard, Trenidad	Bal	14	3	44.0	8	1	0	0	1.000	1.84
Hunter, Brian	Phi	3	2	17.0	5	0	0	0	1.000	2.65
Hunter, Brian L.	Col	13	7	69.0	14	0	1	0	.933	1.83
Huskey, Butch	Min	15	15	130.2	37	2	1	0	.975	2.69
Huskey, Butch	Col	8	7	50.2	11	0	0	0	1.000	1.95
Hyzdu, Adam	Pit	4	1	15.0	4	0	0	0	1.000	2.40
Ibanez, Raul	Sea	44	16	181.0	46	0	1	0	.979	2.29
Javier, Stan	Sea	38	28	259.1	62	1	1	0	.984	2.19
Johnson, Lance	NYY	2	0	8.0	1	0	0	0	1.000	1.13
Jones, Chris	Mil	2	2	16.0	6	0	0	0	1.000	3.38
Jones, Jacque	Min	1	1	5.0	0	0	0	0	.000	.00
Jones, Terry	Mon	7	0	10.0	3	0	0	0	1.000	2.70
Jose, Felix	NYY	8	0	24.0	8	0	0	0	1.000	3.00
Justice, David	Cle	23	22	188.1	43	1	2	0	.957	2.10
Justice, David	NYY	25	16	148.1	46	1	0	1	1.000	2.85
Kapler, Gabe	Tex	40	33	298.1	86	1	2	1	.978	2.62
Kinkade, Mike	NYM	1	0	1.2	0	0	0	0	.000	.00
Klesko, Ryan	SD	2	1	11.0	1	0	0	0	1.000	0.82
Ledee, Ricky	NYY	1	0	2.0	0	0	0	0	.000	.00
Ledee, Ricky	Cle	6	5	47.0	17	1	0	0	1.000	3.45
Ledee, Ricky	Tex	42	41	343.0	96	0	2	0	.980	2.52
Lee, Travis	Ari	54	47	397.2	112	3	1	1	.991	2.60
Lewis, Darren	Bos	37	31	264.0	61	1	1	0	.984	2.11
Leyritz, Jim	LA	1	0	1.0	0	0	0	0	.000	.00
Liefer, Jeff	CWS	5	1	16.2	2	0	0	0	1.000	1.08
Lindsey, Rod	Det	2	0	2.0	0	0	0	0	.000	.00
LoDuca, Paul	LA	2	0	4.0	2	0	0	0	1.000	4.50

Right Fielders - The Rest

Player	Tm	G	GS	Inn	PO	A	E	DP	Pct.	Rng
Lombard, George	Atl	11	4	51.0	13	1	0	0	1.000	2.47
Lowery, Terrell	SF	8	1	21.0	6	0	0	0	1.000	2.57
Lugo, Julio	Hou	2	1	14.0	4	0	0	0	1.000	2.57
Mabry, John	Sea	12	7	69.0	19	0	0	0	1.000	2.48
Mabry, John	SD	30	27	209.2	46	1	1	0	.979	2.02
Macias, Jose	Det	2	1	6.0	2	0	0	0	1.000	3.00
Magee, Wendell	Det	56	30	297.2	59	2	0	0	1.000	1.84
Martin, Al	Sea	9	9	70.0	19	1	0	0	1.000	2.57
Martinez, Dave	TB	28	24	227.0	46	5	0	1	1.000	2.02
Martinez, Dave	Tex	35	32	266.0	82	2	0	1	1.000	2.84
Martinez, Dave	Tor	47	46	403.1	101	8	2	2	.982	2.43
Matos, Luis	Bal	25	12	122.2	45	3	0	0	1.000	3.52
Matthews Jr., Gary	ChC	1	0	2.0	1	0	0	0	1.000	4.50
Maxwell, Jason	Min	1	1	4.0	0	0	0	0	.000	.00
McCarty, Dave	KC	4	3	32.0	12	1	1	0	.929	3.66
McDonald, Jason	Tex	26	21	186.1	55	6	1	2	.984	2.95
McEwing, Joe	NYM	6	1	11.2	1	0	0	0	1.000	0.77
McGuire, Ryan	NYM	1	1	6.0	3	0	0	0	1.000	4.50
McMillon, Billy	Det	13	8	75.0	23	0	1	0	.958	2.76
Melhuse, Adam	Col	1	0	2.0	0	0	0	0	.000	.00
Mieske, Matt	Hou	4	3	29.0	5	0	0	0	1.000	1.55
Mieske, Matt	Ari	1	0	1.0	2	0	0	0	1.000	18.00
Millar, Kevin	Fla	1	0	2.0	2	0	0	0	1.000	9.00
Mora, Melvin	NYM	3	0	6.0	2	0	0	0	1.000	3.00
Morris, Hal	Cin	1	0	2.0	0	0	0	0	.000	.00
Mottola, Chad	Tor	3	2	21.0	5	0	0	0	1.000	2.14
Mouton, James	Mil	7	3	37.0	12	0	0	0	1.000	2.92
Mouton, Lyle	Mil	4	1	9.1	4	0	0	0	1.000	3.86
Newhan, David	SD	5	4	42.0	6	0	0	0	1.000	1.29
Nunnally, Jon	NYM	4	2	17.0	4	0	0	0	1.000	2.12
Ochoa, Alex	Cin	37	25	213.0	56	1	2	0	.966	2.41
Owens, Eric	SD	68	61	508.0	128	3	0	2	1.000	2.32
Palmeiro, Orlando	Ana	31	23	220.0	49	3	1	0	.981	2.13
Paquette, Craig	StL	16	3	45.2	8	1	1	1	.900	1.77
Perez, Timoniel	NYM	8	5	46.1	8	1	1	0	.900	1.75
Perry, Chan	Cle	6	1	18.0	4	0	0	0	1.000	2.00
Piatt, Adam	Oak	22	18	144.0	25	1	1	0	.963	1.63
Polonia, Luis	Det	26	19	152.1	40	2	0	0	1.000	2.48
Polonia, Luis	NYY	6	0	17.0	2	0	0	0	1.000	1.06
Porter, Bo	Oak	14	0	37.0	10	0	0	0	1.000	2.43
Pose, Scott	KC	7	0	21.0	2	0	0	0	1.000	0.86
Quinn, Mark	KC	4	3	27.0	6	1	1	0	.875	2.33
Ramirez, Alex	Cle	16	11	106.0	25	0	0	0	.962	2.12
Ramirez, Alex	Pit	31	27	233.1	55	1	3	0	.949	2.16
Redman, Tike	Pit	4	2	22.0	9	1	0	0	1.000	4.09
Richard, Chris	StL	2	2	17.0	5	0	0	0	1.000	2.65
Richard, Chris	Bal	1	1	9.0	3	0	0	0	1.000	3.00
Rios, Armando	SF	76	44	426.1	120	3	5	1	.961	2.60
Roberts, Dave	Cle	1	0	2.0	0	0	0	0	.000	.00
Rodriguez, Henry	ChC	1	1	5.0	0	0	0	0	.000	.00
Rodriguez, Henry	Fla	6	6	41.1	14	0	0	0	1.000	3.05
Roskos, John	SD	2	2	13.2	1	0	1	0	.500	0.66
Ryan, Rob	Ari	2	2	10.1	1	0	0	0	1.000	0.87
Sadler, Donnie	Bos	1	1	8.0	0	0	0	0	.000	.00
Sanders, Anthony	Sea	1	0	1.0	1	0	0	0	1.000	9.00
Sanders, Reggie	Atl	27	23	207.0	50	3	2	1	.964	2.30
Santangelo, F.P.	LA	1	0	3.0	2	0	0	0	1.000	6.00
Saturria, Luis	StL	4	0	9.0	1	0	0	0	1.000	1.00

Right Fielders - The Rest

Player	Tm	G	GS	Inn	PO	A	E	DP	Pct.	Rng
Sefcik, Kevin	Phi	9	8	70.0	14	0	0	0	1.000	1.80
Segui, David	Cle	7	7	55.0	6	0	0	0	1.000	0.98
Seguignol, F.	Mon	14	3	45.2	8	1	1	0	.900	1.77
Selby, Bill	Cle	6	4	32.0	6	0	0	0	1.000	1.69
Sheldon, Scott	Tex	1	0	0.1	0	0	0	0	.000	.00
Sisco, Steve	Atl	1	0	2.0	0	1	0	0	1.000	4.50
Smith, Mark	Fla	25	21	161.2	34	1	0	1	1.000	1.95
Spencer, Shane	NYY	7	4	42.0	18	0	0	0	1.000	3.86
Spiers, Bill	Hou	4	0	9.2	3	0	0	0	1.000	2.79
Spiezio, Scott	Ana	2	0	4.0	2	0	0	0	1.000	4.50
Sprague, Ed	SD	1	1	8.0	0	0	0	0	.000	.00
Stynes, Chris	Cin	2	0	3.2	0	0	0	0	.000	.00
Sutton, Larry	StL	1	1	8.0	3	0	0	0	1.000	3.38
Swann, Pedro	Atl	2	0	2.0	0	0	0	0	.000	.00
Thompson, Ryan	NYY	6	0	8.2	2	0	0	0	1.000	2.08
Timmons, Ozzie	TB	7	7	63.2	5	0	0	0	1.000	0.71
Trammell, Bubba	TB	24	21	172.0	32	1	0	1	1.000	1.73
Trammell, Bubba	NYM	16	7	80.1	18	1	1	0	.950	2.13
Tucker, Michael	Cin	67	19	244.0	58	2	1	0	.984	2.21
Valdes, Pedro	Tex	13	9	77.0	16	0	0	0	1.000	1.87
Valentin, Jose	CWS	1	1	9.0	0	0	0	0	.000	.00
Vander Wal, John	Pit	65	60	506.1	115	1	4	0	.967	2.06
Vitiello, Joe	SD	1	1	6.0	1	0	0	0	1.000	1.50
Walker, Larry	Col	52	50	421.2	95	9	1	4	.990	2.22
Ward, Daryle	Hou	4	4	34.0	5	0	0	0	1.000	1.32
Ward, Turner	Ari	14	13	119.1	34	0	0	0	1.000	2.56
Widger, Chris	Sea	1	1	7.0	0	0	0	0	.000	.00
Wise, Dewayne	Tor	3	1	15.0	7	0	0	0	1.000	4.20
Womack, Tony	Ari	2	0	5.0	1	0	0	0	1.000	1.80
Young, Dmitri	Cin	1	0	0.2	0	0	0	0	.000	.00

Catchers - Regulars

Player	Tm	G	GS	Inn	PO	A	E	DP	PB	Pct.
Piazza, Mike	NYM	124	124	1026.1	862	38	3	10	3	.997
Rodriguez, Ivan	Tex	87	85	736.1	507	34	2	10	2	.996
Matheny, Mike	StL	124	117	1031.2	803	75	5	7	4	.994
Fletcher, Darrin	Tor	117	103	909.2	621	39	4	7	6	.994
Diaz, Einar	Cle	74	69	624.2	579	48	4	4	4	.994
Santiago, Benito	Cin	84	66	608.2	428	36	3	4	4	.994
Lieberthal, Mike	Phi	106	102	896.0	724	40	5	4	2	.993
Girardi, Joe	ChC	103	97	873.0	706	43	5	5	3	.993
Fordyce, Brook	TOT	92	80	731.1	564	33	4	4	5	.993
Lopez, Javy	Atl	132	121	1085.2	817	62	6	6	8	.993
Estalella, Bobby	SF	106	89	791.1	654	49	5	14	10	.993
Posada, Jorge	NYY	142	136	1182.0	892	56	7	7	11	.993
Flaherty, John	TB	108	101	907.2	611	51	5	9	4	.993
Varitek, Jason	Bos	128	119	1076.0	867	46	7	3	14	.992
Johnson, Charles	TOT	126	121	1060.0	722	42	6	7	5	.992
Johnson, Mark L.	CWS	74	69	602.0	466	27	4	4	7	.992
Miller, Damian	Ari	97	91	805.2	681	47	6	4	3	.992
Ausmus, Brad	Det	150	140	1231.1	898	68	8	9	3	.992
Gonzalez, Wiki	SD	87	72	680.2	525	42	5	13	7	.991
Blanco, Henry	Mil	88	83	732.1	506	58	5	13	5	.991
Kendall, Jason	Pit	147	145	1280.2	990	81	10	12	11	.991
Molina, Ben	Ana	127	123	1092.0	683	61	7	9	6	.991
Mayne, Brent	Col	106	93	809.2	582	35	6	2	5	.990
Wilson, Dan	Sea	88	77	677.0	482	30	5	5	6	.990
Stinnett, Kelly	Ari	74	68	610.0	539	40	6	4	1	.990
Alomar Jr., Sandy	Cle	95	93	817.2	661	42	8	6	6	.989
Widger, Chris	TOT	91	80	683.1	514	38	8	4	5	.986
Mirabelli, Doug	SF	80	71	632.0	429	38	7	4	5	.985
Hernandez, Ramon	Oak	142	118	1062.2	764	43	13	7	7	.984
Meluskey, Mitch	Hou	103	88	778.0	623	31	12	6	3	.982
Hundley, Todd	LA	84	82	700.2	554	38	13	3	8	.979
Average	—	106	98	862.1	653	46	6	7	6	.991

Catchers - The Rest

Player	Tm	G	GS	Inn	PO	A	E	DP	PB	Pct.
Alvarez, Clemente	Phi	2	1	8.0	10	0	0	0	0	1.000
Ardoin, Danny	Min	15	10	97.0	80	8	1	0	3	.989
Bako, Paul	Hou	1	0	4.0	2	1	0	0	0	1.000
Bako, Paul	Fla	56	48	424.0	318	21	3	2	3	.991
Bako, Paul	Atl	23	17	156.1	116	9	1	1	0	.992
Barajas, Rod	Ari	5	3	28.0	23	0	0	0	0	1.000
Barrett, Michael	Mon	28	24	211.2	163	12	2	1	5	.989
Bennett, Gary	Phi	31	23	209.1	173	11	1	2	0	.995
Brown, Kevin L.	Mil	5	5	40.0	20	2	1	0	0	.957
Cardona, Javier	Det	26	12	118.0	66	7	2	0	2	.973
Casanova, Raul	Mil	72	55	527.0	358	28	4	6	3	.990
Castillo, Alberto	Tor	66	57	501.2	372	31	3	2	5	.993
Castro, Ramon	Fla	50	43	370.0	274	24	6	4	3	.980
Charles, Frank	Hou	1	1	9.0	7	2	0	1	0	1.000
Chavez, Raul	Hou	14	12	110.0	67	6	1	1	0	.986
Davis, Ben	SD	38	34	303.2	236	17	1	2	3	.996
DiFelice, Mike	TB	59	57	496.2	351	35	8	6	10	.980
Eusebio, Tony	Hou	68	61	536.2	411	17	5	2	3	.988
Fabregas, Jorge	KC	39	36	328.1	219	21	2	2	1	.992
Fasano, Sal	Oak	52	41	353.2	231	22	5	2	1	.981
Fick, Robert	Det	16	10	92.0	50	3	1	1	2	.981

Catchers - The Rest

Player	Tm	G	GS	Inn	PO	A	E	DP	PB	Pct.
Fordyce, Brook	CWS	40	32	299.0	251	13	0	2	2	1.000
Fordyce, Brook	Bal	52	48	432.1	313	20	4	2	3	.988
Greene, Charlie	Tor	3	2	19.0	13	0	0	0	0	1.000
Greene, Todd	Tor	2	0	4.0	2	0	0	0	0	1.000
Hall, Toby	TB	4	3	27.0	19	2	0	0	0	1.000
Halter, Shane	Det	2	0	2.0	1	0	0	0	0	1.000
Haselman, Bill	Tex	62	55	478.1	336	20	4	4	1	.989
Hatteberg, Scott	Bos	48	43	376.2	297	16	6	3	12	.981
Hernandez, Carlos	SD	54	54	448.2	343	33	5	3	3	.987
Hernandez, Carlos	StL	16	15	126.0	96	9	4	0	2	.963
Hinch, A.J.	Oak	5	2	19.0	9	0	1	0	0	.900
Houston, Tyler	Mil	23	20	167.0	130	9	4	1	4	.972
Hubbard, Mike	Atl	1	0	1.0	3	0	0	0	0	1.000
Jensen, Marcus	Min	49	37	345.1	261	13	2	3	4	.993
Johnson, Brian	KC	37	35	304.1	221	12	2	1	4	.991
Johnson, Charles	Bal	83	80	704.0	498	30	3	4	3	.994
Johnson, Charles	CWS	43	41	356.0	224	12	3	3	2	.987
Knorr, Randy	Tex	15	11	94.0	64	2	1	0	1	.985
Kreuter, Chad	LA	78	64	590.1	483	35	3	1	7	.994
Lampkin, Tom	Sea	28	25	213.0	138	13	2	2	1	.987
LaRue, Jason	Cin	31	31	257.0	190	22	2	3	1	.991
LeCroy, Matt	Min	49	48	410.2	317	16	4	8	4	.988
Leyritz, Jim	NYY	2	2	16.0	13	0	0	0	0	1.000
Leyritz, Jim	LA	3	2	19.0	10	1	0	0	0	1.000
LoDuca, Paul	LA	20	14	135.0	114	13	1	0	0	.992
Lunar, Fernando	Atl	22	17	144.2	125	12	1	2	0	.993
Lunar, Fernando	Bal	9	4	41.0	43	2	0	0	0	1.000
Machado, Robert	Sea	8	3	38.0	35	2	0	1	0	1.000
Mahoney, Mike	ChC	4	1	15.0	9	0	0	0	0	1.000
Marrero, Eli	StL	38	26	239.0	196	14	0	2	2	1.000
Martinez, Sandy	Fla	9	5	49.0	43	2	0	0	0	1.000
McDonald, Keith	StL	4	1	12.0	13	1	0	0	0	1.000
Melhuse, Adam	Col	1	0	1.0	0	1	0	0	1	1.000
Moeller, Chad	Min	48	40	343.0	266	13	6	0	0	.979
Morales, Willie	Bal	3	3	26.0	22	2	0	1	0	1.000
Myers, Greg	Bal	28	27	230.0	166	14	0	1	0	1.000
O'Brien, Charlie	Mon	9	5	44.1	25	2	0	0	0	1.000
Oliver, Joe	Sea	66	57	498.2	354	18	2	1	0	.995
Ortiz, Hector	KC	26	26	223.0	130	18	1	1	0	.993
Osik, Keith	Pit	26	17	168.1	118	9	1	1	1	.992
Paul, Josh	CWS	34	20	193.1	130	17	4	5	2	.974
Perez, Eddie	Atl	7	7	52.2	39	2	1	0	1	.976
Petrick, Ben	Col	48	40	370.0	248	19	4	4	8	.985
Phelps, Josh	Tor	1	0	3.0	1	0	0	0	0	1.000
Pierzynski, A.J.	Min	32	27	236.2	160	10	0	3	2	1.000
Pratt, Todd	NYM	71	38	411.2	314	24	1	4	5	.997
Prince, Tom	Phi	46	36	325.1	250	20	1	2	2	.996
Redmond, Mike	Fla	85	65	586.2	446	40	2	9	6	.996
Reed, Jeff	ChC	71	64	566.2	469	19	5	7	3	.990
Schneider, Brian	Mon	43	32	283.0	205	19	6	2	5	.974
Servais, Scott	Col	32	29	249.1	204	17	3	1	1	.987
Servais, Scott	SF	6	2	21.0	18	0	0	0	0	1.000
Sheldon, Scott	Tex	3	0	3.1	3	0	0	0	0	1.000
Taubensee, Eddie	Cin	76	66	590.2	420	26	5	8	6	.989
Turner, Chris	NYY	36	23	226.1	171	5	0	0	2	1.000
Valera, Yohanny	Mon	7	2	28.0	24	2	0	0	1	1.000
Walbeck, Matt	Ana	44	38	343.0	200	16	2	0	0	.991
Waszgis, B.J.	Tex	23	12	117.0	66	2	0	1	4	1.000

Catchers - The Rest

Player	Tm	G	GS	Inn	PO	A	E	DP	PB	Pct.
Webster, Lenny	Mon	32	19	189.1	126	9	0	1	4	1.000
Widger, Chris	Mon	85	80	668.1	503	38	8	4	4	.985
Widger, Chris	Sea	6	0	15.0	11	0	0	0	1	1.000
Wilkins, Rick	StL	3	3	25.0	28	3	0	0	0	1.000
Williams, George	SD	6	2	26.1	16	2	0	0	0	1.000
Wilson, Vance	NYM	3	0	12.0	14	0	0	0	0	1.000
Wooten, Shawn	Ana	4	1	13.0	5	0	0	0	0	1.000
Zaun, Gregg	KC	76	65	583.2	376	31	5	4	2	.988

Catchers - Regulars - Special

Player	Tm	G	GS	Inn	SBA	CS	PCS	CS%	ER	CERA
Mirabelli, Doug	SF	80	71	632.0	67	22	1	.32	265	3.77
Piazza, Mike	NYM	124	124	1026.1	142	32	16	.13	441	3.87
Miller, Damian	Ari	97	91	805.2	83	33	11	.31	351	3.92
Varitek, Jason	Bos	128	119	1076.0	138	34	10	.19	473	3.96
Lopez, Javy	Atl	132	121	1085.2	92	23	5	.21	504	4.18
Santiago, Benito	Cin	84	66	608.2	33	14	2	.39	284	4.20
Hundley, Todd	LA	84	82	700.2	100	24	5	.20	336	4.32
Matheny, Mike	StL	124	117	1031.2	93	49	3	.51	497	4.34
Diaz, Einar	Cle	74	69	624.2	53	19	2	.33	301	4.34
Gonzalez, Wiki	SD	87	72	680.2	70	25	2	.34	330	4.36
Blanco, Henry	Mil	88	83	732.1	67	39	1	.58	360	4.42
Wilson, Dan	Sea	88	77	677.0	51	20	7	.30	338	4.49
Hernandez, Ra.	Oak	142	118	1062.2	95	27	8	.22	534	4.52
Estalella, Bobby	SF	106	89	791.1	78	26	4	.30	400	4.55
Fordyce, Brook	TOT	92	80	731.1	71	16	5	.17	371	4.57
Ausmus, Brad	Det	150	140	1231.1	80	38	6	.43	634	4.63
Posada, Jorge	NYY	142	136	1182.0	104	34	4	.30	612	4.66
Lieberthal, Mike	Phi	106	102	896.0	73	29	5	.35	470	4.72
Flaherty, John	TB	108	101	907.2	108	29	2	.25	486	4.82
Stinnett, Kelly	Ari	74	68	610.0	75	23	4	.27	331	4.88
Molina, Ben	Ana	127	123	1092.0	110	40	6	.33	597	4.92
Johnson, Mark L.	CWS	74	69	602.0	66	28	9	.33	334	4.99
Kendall, Jason	Pit	147	145	1280.2	125	38	4	.28	715	5.02
Alomar Jr., Sandy	Cle	95	93	817.2	98	23	2	.22	474	5.22
Widger, Chris	TOT	91	80	683.1	73	20	1	.26	397	5.23
Fletcher, Darrin	Tor	117	103	909.2	94	21	1	.22	535	5.29
Rodriguez, Ivan	Tex	87	85	736.1	39	19	5	.41	438	5.35
Johnson, Charles	TOT	126	121	1060.0	78	24	4	.27	644	5.47
Meluskey, Mitch	Hou	103	88	778.0	84	20	2	.22	477	5.52
Girardi, Joe	ChC	103	97	873.0	101	38	13	.28	536	5.53
Mayne, Brent	Col	106	93	809.2	73	19	2	.24	499	5.55
Average	—	106	98	862.1	84	27	5	.32	450	4.70

Catchers - The Rest - Special

Player	Tm	G	GS	Inn	SBA	CS	PCS	CS%	ER	CERA
Alvarez, Clemente	Phi	2	1	8.0	2	0	0	0	3	3.38
Ardoin, Danny	Min	15	10	97.0	9	5	1	.50	64	5.94
Bako, Paul	Hou	1	0	4.0	0	0	0	0	1	2.25
Bako, Paul	Fla	56	48	424.0	49	17	7	.24	213	4.52
Bako, Paul	Atl	23	17	156.1	13	4	0	.31	64	3.68
Barajas, Rod	Ari	5	3	28.0	0	0	0	0	16	5.14
Barrett, Michael	Mon	28	24	211.2	19	4	0	.21	131	5.57
Bennett, Gary	Phi	31	23	209.1	19	6	1	.28	119	5.12
Brown, Kevin L.	Mil	5	5	40.0	4	0	0	0	27	6.07
Cardona, Javier	Det	26	12	118.0	10	2	1	.11	56	4.27
Casanova, Raul	Mil	72	55	527.0	50	11	2	.19	255	4.35
Castillo, Alberto	Tor	66	57	501.2	42	17	1	.39	266	4.77
Castro, Ramon	Fla	50	43	370.0	41	15	5	.28	197	4.79
Charles, Frank	Hou	1	1	9.0	1	0	0	0	0	0.00
Chavez, Raul	Hou	14	12	110.0	11	2	0	.18	76	6.22
Davis, Ben	SD	38	34	303.2	27	7	0	.26	169	5.01
DiFelice, Mike	TB	59	57	496.2	52	17	1	.31	282	5.11
Eusebio, Tony	Hou	68	61	536.2	47	10	2	.18	310	5.20
Fabregas, Jorge	KC	39	36	328.1	25	10	0	.40	211	5.78
Fasano, Sal	Oak	52	41	353.2	34	11	3	.26	193	4.91
Fick, Robert	Det	16	10	92.0	7	2	1	.17	62	6.07

Catchers - The Rest - Special

Player	Tm	G	GS	Inn	SBA	CS	PCS	CS%	ER	CERA
Fordyce, Brook	CWS	40	32	299.0	24	10	3	.33	154	4.64
Fordyce, Brook	Bal	52	48	432.1	47	6	2	.09	217	4.52
Greene, Charlie	Tor	3	2	19.0	0	0	0	0	15	7.11
Greene, Todd	Tor	2	0	4.0	1	0	0	0	4	9.00
Hall, Toby	TB	4	3	27.0	0	0	0	0	5	1.67
Halter, Shane	Det	2	0	2.0	0	0	0	0	3	13.50
Haselman, Bill	Tex	62	55	478.1	47	13	2	.24	263	4.95
Hatteberg, Scott	Bos	48	43	376.2	68	13	4	.14	210	5.02
Hernandez, C.	SD	54	54	448.2	56	18	1	.31	222	4.45
Hernandez, C.	StL	16	15	126.0	25	7	0	.28	53	3.79
Hinch, A.J.	Oak	5	2	19.0	2	1	1	0	3	1.42
Houston, Tyler	Mil	23	20	167.0	23	8	1	.32	113	6.09
Hubbard, Mike	Atl	1	0	1.0	0	0	0	0	6	54.00
Jensen, Marcus	Min	49	37	345.1	23	8	2	.29	213	5.55
Johnson, Brian	KC	37	35	304.1	37	8	2	.17	197	5.83
Johnson, Charles	Bal	83	80	704.0	52	14	2	.24	468	5.98
Johnson, Charles	CWS	43	41	356.0	26	10	2	.33	176	4.45
Knorr, Randy	Tex	15	11	94.0	11	4	2	.22	69	6.61
Kreuter, Chad	LA	78	64	590.1	40	19	5	.40	231	3.52
Lampkin, Tom	Sea	28	25	213.0	25	8	2	.26	125	5.28
LaRue, Jason	Cin	31	31	257.0	17	5	1	.25	107	3.75
LeCroy, Matt	Min	49	48	410.2	31	9	2	.24	232	5.08
Leyritz, Jim	NYY	2	2	16.0	2	0	0	0	11	6.19
Leyritz, Jim	LA	3	2	19.0	1	0	0	0	13	6.16
LoDuca, Paul	LA	20	14	135.0	17	9	2	.47	79	5.27
Lunar, Fernando	Atl	22	17	144.2	21	5	0	.24	57	3.55
Lunar, Fernando	Bal	9	4	41.0	2	2	0	1.00	26	5.71
Machado, Robert	Sea	8	3	38.0	1	0	0	0	13	3.08
Mahoney, Mike	ChC	4	1	15.0	1	0	0	0	10	6.00
Marrero, Eli	StL	38	26	239.0	15	9	1	.57	109	4.10
Martinez, Sandy	Fla	9	5	49.0	2	0	0	0	17	3.12
McDonald, Keith	StL	4	1	12.0	1	0	0	0	13	9.75
Melhuse, Adam	Col	1	0	1.0	1	0	0	0	0	0.00
Moeller, Chad	Min	48	40	343.0	18	5	2	.19	196	5.14
Morales, Willie	Bal	3	3	26.0	2	2	0	1.00	8	2.77
Myers, Greg	Bal	28	27	230.0	32	7	2	.17	136	5.32
O'Brien, Charlie	Mon	9	5	44.1	7	0	0	0	34	6.90
Oliver, Joe	Sea	66	57	498.2	43	10	6	.11	237	4.28
Ortiz, Hector	KC	26	26	223.0	24	7	1	.26	135	5.45
Osik, Keith	Pit	26	17	168.1	18	4	0	.22	79	4.22
Paul, Josh	CWS	34	20	193.1	21	10	2	.42	87	4.05
Perez, Eddie	Atl	7	7	52.2	6	1	0	.17	17	2.91
Petrick, Ben	Col	48	40	370.0	33	7	1	.19	206	5.01
Phelps, Josh	Tor	1	0	3.0	0	0	0	0	1	3.00
Pierzynski, A.J.	Min	32	27	236.2	16	6	1	.33	114	4.34
Pratt, Todd	NYM	71	38	411.2	36	14	7	.24	226	4.94
Prince, Tom	Phi	46	36	325.1	27	9	1	.31	171	4.73
Redmond, Mike	Fla	85	65	586.2	67	23	2	.32	302	4.63
Reed, Jeff	ChC	71	64	566.2	46	16	4	.29	303	4.81
Schneider, Brian	Mon	43	32	283.0	38	10	0	.26	133	4.23
Servais, Scott	Col	32	29	249.1	29	8	0	.28	130	4.69
Servais, Scott	SF	6	2	21.0	0	0	0	0	10	4.29
Sheldon, Scott	Tex	3	0	3.1	1	0	0	0	2	5.40
Taubensee, Eddie	Cin	76	66	590.2	64	14	2	.19	309	4.71
Turner, Chris	NYY	36	23	226.1	22	3	1	.10	130	5.17
Valera, Yohanny	Mon	7	2	28.0	3	1	0	.33	26	8.36
Walbeck, Matt	Ana	44	38	343.0	47	16	2	.31	193	5.06
Waszgis, B.J.	Tex	23	12	117.0	4	1	0	.25	104	8.00

Catchers - The Rest - Special

Player	Tm	G	GS	Inn	SBA	CS	PCS	CS%	ER	CERA
Webster, Lenny	Mon	32	19	189.1	21	3	0	.14	98	4.66
Widger, Chris	Mon	85	80	668.1	73	20	1	.26	390	5.25
Widger, Chris	Sea	6	0	15.0	0	0	0	0	7	4.20
Wilkins, Rick	StL	3	3	25.0	1	1	0	1.00	26	9.36
Williams, George	SD	6	2	26.1	3	0	0	0	12	4.10
Wilson, Vance	NYM	3	0	12.0	1	0	0	0	3	2.25
Wooten, Shawn	Ana	4	1	13.0	0	0	0	0	15	10.38
Zaun, Gregg	KC	76	65	583.2	70	13	0	.19	333	5.13

Pitchers Hitting & Fielding
and Hitters Pitching

Free-agent pitcher Mike Hampton might want to consider signing with St. Louis, where manager Tony La Russa has been known to occasionally move his pitcher out of the No. 9 hole on the lineup card. For a second straight year, among pitchers with more than 25 at-bats, Hampton won the batting title in 2000—and that might warrant a higher spot in the Cardinals' order. In 1999, Hampton batted .311 with three doubles, three triples and 10 RBI in 74 at-bats. Last summer he finished with a .274 mark and eight RBI, though he failed to record an extra-base hit and was thrown out in his only stolen-base attempt. Still, his solid bat and robust .296 career on-base percentage would be a nice addition to a potent Cardinals lineup.

Darren Dreifort snatched the home-run crown away from Alex Fernandez. Three dingers by Fernandez claimed the title a year ago, and that number was enough to seal the deal in 2000. The 28-year-old Dreifort already has five homers in his brief career, and among active pitchers, only Dwight Gooden (8) and Andy Benes (7) have more.

The pitcher with the best defensive game in 2000 was Livan Hernandez, who handled 62 chances without committing an error. Hernandez recorded 18 putouts and 44 assists en route to a 1.000 fielding percentage, and Pedro Astacio produced the second-best errorless streak last summer by handling 42 opportunities without a miscue. In the American League, Dave Burba led the way with 37 errorless chances, and two of his teammates, Jason Bere and Steve Woodard—both acquired from Milwaukee during the season—came to Cleveland with error-free streaks that reached 36 by season's end.

With the help of his catchers, Darryl Kile controlled the running game as successfully as anyone, seeing 11 of 13 potential steal attempts thwarted by his batterymate. A trio of lefthanders played a major role themselves in slowing the running game, as Brian Anderson, John Halama and Al Leiter executed 10 successful pickoffs each in 2000. Halama's contribution led to a caught-stealing rate of 64 percent in 14 attempts.

Among non-pitchers who took the mound last summer, Tim Bogar led the way with two appearances. Bogar, Keith Osik and Scott Sheldon recorded strikeouts, but Brent Mayne was the only non-pitcher to pick up a win. On August 22, he pitched a scoreless 12th inning at Coors Field against Atlanta, and his team rallied in the bottom half of the inning to give him the "W."

Pitchers Hitting

	2000 Hitting														Career Hitting													
Pitcher, Team	Avg	OBP	SLG	AB	H	2B	3B	HR	R	RBI	BB	SO	SH	SB-CS	Avg	OBP	SLG	AB	H	2B	3B	HR	R	RBI	BB	SO	SH	SB-CS
Abbott, Paul, Sea	.400	.400	.600	5	2	1	0	0	1	0	0	1	1	0-0	.400	.400	.600	5	2	1	0	0	1	0	0	1	1	0-0
Acevedo, Juan, Mil	.000	.500	.000	1	0	0	0	0	1	0	1	1	0	0-0	.081	.123	.097	62	5	1	0	0	3	0	3	33	5	0-0
Adams, Terry, LA	.000	.000	.000	2	0	0	0	0	0	0	0	1	1	0-0	.000	.071	.000	13	0	0	0	0	0	0	1	8	1	0-0
Aguilera, Rick, ChC	.000	.000	.000	0	0	0	0	0	0	0	0	0	0	0-0	.201	.234	.288	139	28	3	0	3	12	11	6	37	16	0-0
Aldred, Scott, Phi	.000	.000	.000	0	0	0	0	0	0	0	0	0	0	0-0	.000	.000	.000	1	0	0	0	0	0	0	0	1	0	0-0
Alfonseca, Antonio, Fla	.000	.000	.000	0	0	0	0	0	0	0	0	0	0	0-0	.000	.000	.000	9	0	0	0	0	0	0	0	7	0	0-0
Almanza, Armando, Fla	.000	.000	.000	1	0	0	0	0	0	0	0	0	1	0-0	.000	.000	.000	4	0	0	0	0	0	0	0	2	1	0-0
Almanzar, Carlos, SD	.000	.000	.000	3	0	0	0	0	0	0	0	2	0	0-0	.000	.000	.000	4	0	0	0	0	0	0	0	3	0	0-0
Alvarez, Juan, Ana	.000	.000	.000	0	0	0	0	0	0	0	0	0	0	0-0	.000	.000	.000	0	0	0	0	0	0	0	0	0	0	0-0
Anderson, Brian, Ari	.188	.194	.232	69	13	3	0	0	4	4	1	10	9	0-0	.145	.170	.191	173	25	3	1	1	14	6	6	39	16	2-0
Anderson, Jimmy, Pit	.140	.140	.160	50	7	1	0	0	5	1	0	11	4	0-0	.169	.169	.203	59	10	2	0	0	7	2	0	13	4	0-0
Anderson, Matt, Det	.000	.000	.000	0	0	0	0	0	0	0	0	0	0	0-0	.000	.000	.000	0	0	0	0	0	0	0	0	0	0	0-0
Andrews, Clayton, Tor	.000	.000	.000	3	0	0	0	0	0	0	0	2	0	0-0	.000	.000	.000	3	0	0	0	0	0	0	0	2	0	0-0
Ankiel, Rick, StL	.250	.292	.382	68	17	1	1	2	8	9	4	20	1	0-0	.231	.268	.346	78	18	1	1	2	8	9	4	23	2	0-0
Appier, Kevin, Oak	.167	.167	.167	6	1	0	0	0	0	0	0	3	0	0-0	.071	.071	.071	14	1	0	0	0	0	0	0	9	0	0-0
Armas Jr., Tony, Mon	.038	.074	.038	26	1	0	0	0	1	1	1	12	3	0-0	.036	.069	.036	28	1	0	0	0	1	1	1	13	3	0-0
Arnold, Jamie, LA-ChC	.111	.200	.222	9	1	1	0	0	0	0	0	3	0	0-0	.158	.200	.211	19	3	1	0	0	1	1	0	6	1	0-0
Arrojo, R., Col-Bos	.107	.138	.143	28	3	1	0	0	2	3	1	13	3	0-0	.097	.125	.129	31	3	1	0	0	2	3	1	15	3	0-0
Arroyo, Bronson, Pit	.143	.143	.238	21	3	2	0	0	2	0	0	10	2	0-0	.143	.143	.238	21	3	2	0	0	2	0	0	10	2	0-0
Ashby, Andy, Phi-Atl	.148	.175	.148	61	9	0	0	0	2	6	2	22	9	0-0	.138	.161	.166	457	63	13	0	0	20	21	13	187	72	1-0
Astacio, Pedro, Col	.098	.108	.098	82	8	0	0	0	2	6	1	25	1	0-0	.134	.144	.149	509	68	6	1	0	22	23	4	193	56	0-1
Aybar, M., Col-Cin-Fla	.000	.250	.000	6	0	0	0	0	1	0	2	3	1	0-0	.152	.176	.197	66	10	0	0	1	5	5	2	28	3	0-0
Baldwin, James, CWS	.000	.000	.000	4	0	0	0	0	0	0	0	2	1	0-0	.091	.091	.273	11	1	0	1	0	1	1	0	6	2	0-0
Bale, John, Tor	.000	.000	.000	0	0	0	0	0	0	0	0	0	0	0-0	.000	.000	.000	0	0	0	0	0	0	0	0	0	0	0-0
Barcelo, Lorenzo, CWS	.000	.000	.000	0	0	0	0	0	0	0	0	0	0	0-0	.000	.000	.000	0	0	0	0	0	0	0	0	0	0	0-0
Batista, M., Mon-KC	.000	.200	.000	4	0	0	0	0	0	0	1	3	0	0-0	.089	.122	.139	79	7	1	0	1	6	3	3	48	6	0-0
Beck, Rod, Bos	.000	.000	.000	0	0	0	0	0	0	0	0	0	0	0-0	.222	.222	.222	18	4	0	0	0	0	1	0	9	1	0-0
Beirne, Kevin, CWS	.000	.000	.000	0	0	0	0	0	0	0	0	0	0	0-0	.000	.000	.000	0	0	0	0	0	0	0	0	0	0	0-0
Belcher, Tim, Ana	.000	.000	.000	0	0	0	0	0	0	0	0	0	0	0-0	.124	.137	.162	388	48	9	0	2	19	25	2	147	42	0-1
Belinda, Stan, Col-Atl	.000	.000	.000	1	0	0	0	0	0	0	0	1	0	0-0	.160	.222	.200	25	4	1	0	0	1	3	2	13	3	0-0
Belitz, Todd, Oak	.000	.000	.000	0	0	0	0	0	0	0	0	0	0	0-0	.000	.000	.000	0	0	0	0	0	0	0	0	0	0	0-0
Bell, Rob, Cin	.067	.087	.089	45	3	1	0	0	1	0	1	27	3	0-0	.067	.087	.089	45	3	1	0	0	1	0	1	27	3	0-0
Beltran, Rigo, Col	.000	.000	.000	0	0	0	0	0	0	0	0	0	0	0-0	.182	.182	.273	11	2	1	0	0	1	0	0	1	0	0-0
Benes, Alan, StL	.500	.500	.750	4	2	1	0	0	0	0	0	1	0	0-0	.163	.176	.211	123	20	6	0	0	5	8	2	45	9	0-0
Benes, Andy, StL	.080	.148	.140	50	4	0	0	1	1	1	4	19	6	0-0	.139	.184	.196	675	94	17	0	7	44	44	32	283	91	0-0
Benitez, A., NYM	.000	.000	.000	0	0	0	0	0	0	0	0	0	0	0-0	.000	.000	.000	5	0	0	0	0	0	1	0	2	0	0-0
Benson, Kris, Pit	.092	.157	.123	65	6	2	0	0	3	1	4	29	9	0-0	.123	.174	.162	130	16	5	0	0	10	8	7	53	15	0-0
Bere, Jason, Mil-Cle	.205	.205	.256	39	8	0	1	0	3	2	0	17	1	0-0	.200	.241	.227	75	15	0	1	0	6	3	3	31	3	0-0
Bergman, Sean, Min	.500	.500	1.000	2	1	1	0	0	0	0	0	1	0	0-0	.113	.113	.211	133	15	4	0	3	10	11	0	59	12	0-0
Bernero, Adam, Det	.000	.000	.000	0	0	0	0	0	0	0	0	0	0	0-0	.000	.000	.000	0	0	0	0	0	0	0	0	0	0	0-0
Biddle, Rocky, CWS	.000	.000	.000	0	0	0	0	0	0	0	0	0	0	0-0	.000	.000	.000	0	0	0	0	0	0	0	0	0	0	0-0
Blair, Willie, Det	.333	.333	.333	3	1	0	0	0	0	0	0	2	0	0-0	.075	.112	.082	146	11	1	0	0	6	5	6	88	12	0-0
Blank, Matt, Mon	.000	.000	.000	1	0	0	0	0	0	0	0	1	0	0-0	.000	.000	.000	1	0	0	0	0	0	0	0	1	0	0-0
Bochtler, Doug, KC	.000	.000	.000	0	0	0	0	0	0	0	0	0	0	0-0	.000	.000	.000	2	0	0	0	0	0	0	0	0	0	0-0
Boehringer, Brian, SD	.250	.250	.500	4	1	1	0	0	0	2	0	0	1	0-0	.074	.167	.111	27	2	1	0	0	0	2	3	13	3	0-0
Bohanon, Brian, Col	.208	.232	.377	53	11	3	0	2	6	11	2	14	11	0-0	.215	.246	.305	200	43	7	1	3	13	27	9	62	21	0-0
Bones, Ricky, Fla	.000	.250	.000	2	0	0	0	0	1	1	1	0	0	0-0	.056	.182	.056	18	1	0	0	0	3	2	3	5	4	0-0
Borbon, Pedro, Tor	.000	.000	.000	0	0	0	0	0	0	0	0	0	0	0-0	.250	.250	.250	4	1	0	0	0	0	0	0	1	1	0-0
Borkowski, Dave, Det	.000	.000	.000	0	0	0	0	0	0	0	0	0	0	0-0	.000	.000	.000	3	0	0	0	0	0	1	0	2	0	0-0
Bottalico, Ricky, KC	.000	.000	.000	0	0	0	0	0	0	0	0	0	0	0-0	.083	.083	.167	12	1	1	0	0	0	0	0	8	1	0-0
Bottenfield, K., Ana-Phi	.118	.118	.118	17	2	0	0	0	3	0	0	4	3	0-0	.164	.178	.181	177	29	3	0	0	13	10	2	61	25	1-0
Boyd, Jason, Phi	.000	.000	.000	0	0	0	0	0	0	0	0	0	0	0-0	.000	.000	.000	1	0	0	0	0	0	0	0	1	0	0-0
Bradford, Chad, CWS	.000	.000	.000	0	0	0	0	0	0	0	0	0	0	0-0	.000	.000	.000	0	0	0	0	0	0	0	0	0	0	0-0
Brantley, Jeff, Phi	.000	.000	.000	0	0	0	0	0	0	0	0	0	0	0-0	.118	.143	.132	68	8	1	0	0	5	5	2	23	11	0-0
Brea, Lesli, Bal	.000	.000	.000	0	0	0	0	0	0	0	0	0	0	0-0	.000	.000	.000	0	0	0	0	0	0	0	0	0	0	0-0
Brewington, Jamie, Cle	.000	.500	.000	1	0	0	0	0	1	0	1	0	0	0-0	.208	.240	.208	24	5	0	0	0	4	1	1	7	4	0-0
Brocail, Doug, Det	.000	.000	.000	0	0	0	0	0	0	0	0	0	0	0-0	.164	.164	.194	67	11	0	1	0	9	1	0	18	15	2-0
Brock, Chris, Phi	.222	.222	.667	9	2	1	0	1	1	2	0	2	2	0-0	.190	.230	.259	58	11	1	0	1	5	7	3	12	6	0-0
Brower, Jim, Cle	.000	.000	.000	3	0	0	0	0	0	0	0	2	0	0-0	.000	.000	.000	3	0	0	0	0	0	0	0	2	0	0-0
Brown, Kevin, LA	.076	.129	.076	66	5	0	0	0	2	3	2	29	14	0-0	.120	.167	.134	374	45	5	0	0	12	23	19	135	44	0-0
Brownson, Mark, Phi	.000	1.000	.000	0	0	0	0	0	0	0	1	0	0	0-0	.071	.133	.071	14	1	0	0	0	1	0	1	2	2	0-0
Brunette, Justin, StL	1.000	1.000	1.000	1	1	0	0	0	0	0	0	0	0	0-0	1.000	1.000	1.000	1	1	0	0	0	0	0	0	0	0	0-0
Bruske, Jim, Mil	.000	.000	.000	1	0	0	0	0	0	0	0	0	0	0-0	.100	.100	.200	10	1	1	0	0	0	0	0	2	0	0-0
Buddie, Mike, Mil	.000	.000	.000	0	0	0	0	0	0	0	0	0	0	0-0	.000	.000	.000	0	0	0	0	0	0	0	0	0	0	0-0
Buehrle, Mark, CWS	.000	.000	.000	0	0	0	0	0	0	0	0	0	0	0-0	.000	.000	.000	0	0	0	0	0	0	0	0	0	0	0-0
Bullinger, Kirk, Phi	.000	.000	.000	0	0	0	0	0	0	0	0	0	0	0-0	.000	.000	.000	1	0	0	0	0	0	0	0	0	0	0-0
Burba, Dave, Cle	.000	.000	.000	1	0	0	0	0	0	0	0	1	2	0-0	.145	.200	.202	173	25	1	0	3	9	12	10	72	19	0-0
Burkett, John, Atl	.143	.200	.167	42	6	1	0	0	2	3	3	15	6	0-0	.093	.137	.106	471	44	6	0	0	20	17	23	196	53	0-0
Burnett, A.J., Fla	.280	.357	.520	25	7	1	1	1	3	3	3	10	2	0-0	.214	.267	.357	42	9	1	1	1	4	3	3	20	2	0-0
Byrd, Paul, Phi	.150	.227	.150	20	3	0	0	0	2	0	1	6	2	0-0	.146	.214	.146	103	15	0	0	0	9	6	7	26	15	0-0
Byrdak, Tim, KC	.000	.000	.000	0	0	0	0	0	0	0	0	0	0	0-0	.500	.500	1.000	2	1	1	0	0	1	0	0	0	0	0-0
Cabrera, Jose, Hou	.000	.000	.000	1	0	0	0	0	0	0	0	1	0	0-0	.000	.000	.000	3	0	0	0	0	0	0	0	1	0	0-0
Cairncross, Cam, Cle	.000	.000	.000	0	0	0	0	0	0	0	0	0	0	0-0	.000	.000	.000	0	0	0	0	0	0	0	0	0	0	0-0
Cammack, Eric, NYM	1.000	1.000	3.000	1	1	0	1	0	0	1	0	0	0	0-0	1.000	1.000	3.000	1	1	0	1	0	0	1	0	0	0	0-0
Carlyle, Buddy, SD	.000	.000	.000	0	0	0	0	0	0	0	0	0	0	0-0	.222	.364	.222	9	2	0	0	0	1	1	2	3	0	0-0
Carpenter, Chris, Tor	.000	.000	.000	2	0	0	0	0	0	0	0	1	0	0-0	.000	.200	.000	4	0	0	0	0	0	0	1	2	0	0-0
Carrara, Giovanni, Col	.000	.000	.000	1	0	0	0	0	0	0	0	1	0	0-0	.000	.000	.000	10	0	0	0	0	1	0	0	4	2	0-0
Carrasco, H., Min-Bos	.000	.000	.000	0	0	0	0	0	0	0	0	0	0	0-0	.056	.056	.056	18	1	0	0	0	0	0	0	12	0	0-0
Castillo, Frank, Tor	.143	.143	.143	7	1	0	0	0	0	0	0	3	0	0-0	.111	.144	.111	334	37	0	0	0	7	13	13	109	40	0-1
Charlton, Norm, Cin	.000	.000	.000	0	0	0	0	0	0	0	0	0	0	0-0	.092	.151	.115	87	8	2	0	0	6	1	3	50	10	0-0
Chen, Bruce, Atl-Phi	.033	.065	.033	30	1	0	0	0	0	1	1	20	7	0-0	.042	.061	.042	48	2	0	0	0	0	2	1	30	10	0-0
Choate, Randy, NYY	.000	.000	.000	0	0	0	0	0	0	0	0	0	0	0-0	.000	.000	.000	0	0	0	0	0	0	0	0	0	0	0-0
Chouinard, Bobby, Col	.333	.333	.333	3	1	0	0	0	1	0	0	1	0	0-0	.125	.125	.125	8	1	0	0	0	1	0	0	5	1	0-0
Christiansen, J., Pit-StL	.000	.000	.000	0	0	0	0	0	0	0	0	0	0	0-0	.100	.100	.100	10	1	0	0	0	0	1	0	7	1	0-0
Clark, Mark, Tex	.000	.000	.000	0	0	0	0	0	0	0	0	0	0	0-0	.058	.088	.083	242	14	3	0	1	7	9	8	106	29	0-0
Clemens, Roger, NYY	.000	.000	.000	3	0	0	0	0	0	0	0	1	0	0-0	.143	.250	.214	14	2	1	0	0	1	0	2	4	2	0-0
Clement, Matt, SD	.067	.125	.100	60	4	0	1	0	3	2	4	33	5	0-0	.070	.131	.088	114	8	0	1	0	10	3	8	63	13	0-0
Clontz, Brad, Pit	.000	1.000	.000	0	0	0	0	0	1	0	0	0	0	0-0	.000	.231	.000	10	0	0	0	0	2	0	2	6	1	0-0
Coco, Pasqual, Tor	.000	.000	.000	0	0	0	0	0	0	0	0	0	0	0-0	.000	.000	.000	0	0	0	0	0	0	0	0	0	0	0-0

	2000 Hitting														Career Hitting													
Pitcher, Team	Avg	OBP	SLG	AB	H	2B	3B	HR	R	RBI	BB	SO	SH	SB-CS	Avg	OBP	SLG	AB	H	2B	3B	HR	R	RBI	BB	SO	SH	SB-CS
Coggin, Dave, Phi	.000	.000	.000	7	0	0	0	0	0	0	0	4	1	0-0	.000	.000	.000	7	0	0	0	0	0	0	0	4	1	0-0
Colon, Bartolo, Cle	.000	.000	.000	5	0	0	0	0	0	0	0	5	0	0-0	.133	.133	.133	15	2	0	0	0	0	1	0	12	1	0-0
Cone, David, NYY	.333	.333	.333	3	1	0	0	0	0	0	0	1	0	0-0	.155	.192	.177	407	63	9	0	0	28	22	16	89	37	0-1
Cook, Dennis, NYM	.000	.000	.000	0	0	0	0	0	0	0	0	0	1	0-0	.266	.286	.358	109	29	2	1	2	15	9	3	13	9	0-0
Cooper, Brian, Ana	.000	.000	.000	4	0	0	0	0	0	0	0	3	0	0-0	.000	.000	.000	4	0	0	0	0	0	0	0	3	0	0-0
Cordero, F., Tex	.000	.000	.000	0	0	0	0	0	0	0	0	0	0	0-0	.000	.000	.000	0	0	0	0	0	0	0	0	0	0	0-0
Cordova, Francisco, Pit	.114	.162	.114	35	4	0	0	0	0	3	2	15	0	0-0	.121	.158	.134	231	28	1	1	0	8	8	10	92	17	0-0
Cormier, Rheal, Bos	.000	.000	.000	0	0	0	0	0	0	0	0	0	0	0-0	.185	.202	.217	184	34	4	1	0	14	12	3	43	28	0-0
Cornelius, Reid, Fla	.135	.135	.189	37	5	2	0	0	1	1	0	12	4	0-0	.129	.129	.161	62	8	2	0	0	1	1	0	21	5	0-0
Crabtree, Tim, Tex	.000	.000	.000	0	0	0	0	0	0	0	0	0	0	0-0	.000	.000	.000	1	0	0	0	0	0	0	0	0	0	0-0
Crawford, Paxton, Bos	.000	.000	.000	0	0	0	0	0	0	0	0	0	0	0-0	.000	.000	.000	0	0	0	0	0	0	0	0	0	0	0-0
Creek, Doug, TB	.000	.000	.000	0	0	0	0	0	0	0	0	0	0	0-0	.250	.250	.250	4	1	0	0	0	1	0	0	2	3	0-0
Cressend, Jack, Min	.000	.000	.000	0	0	0	0	0	0	0	0	0	0	0-0	.000	.000	.000	0	0	0	0	0	0	0	0	0	0	0-0
Croushore, R., Col-Bos	1.000	1.000	1.000	1	1	0	0	0	0	0	0	0	1	0-0	.500	.600	.500	4	2	0	0	0	1	0	1	1	3	0-0
Cruz, Nelson, Det	.000	.000	.000	1	0	0	0	0	0	0	0	0	0	0-0	.000	.000	.000	1	0	0	0	0	0	0	0	0	0	0-0
Cubillan, D., Tor-Tex	.000	.000	.000	1	0	0	0	0	0	0	0	0	0	0-0	.000	.000	.000	1	0	0	0	0	0	0	0	0	0	0-0
Cunnane, Will, SD	.143	.143	.286	7	1	1	0	0	0	0	0	3	0	0-0	.250	.308	.375	24	6	1	1	0	4	4	2	8	1	0-0
D'Amico, Jeff, Mil	.091	.146	.182	44	4	1	0	1	2	2	3	19	6	0-0	.083	.135	.167	48	4	1	0	1	2	2	3	22	7	0-0
D'Amico, Jeff M., KC	.000	.000	.000	0	0	0	0	0	0	0	0	0	0	0-0	.000	.000	.000	0	0	0	0	0	0	0	0	0	0	0-0
Daal, Omar, Ari-Phi	.267	.327	.400	45	12	3	0	1	3	6	4	8	5	0-0	.193	.245	.239	176	34	5	0	1	14	12	12	40	16	0-0
Darensbourg, Vic, Fla	.250	.250	.250	8	2	0	0	0	0	0	0	2	0	0-0	.125	.222	.125	16	2	0	0	0	0	0	2	5	0	0-0
Davey, Tom, SD	.000	.000	.000	0	0	0	0	0	0	0	0	0	0	0-0	.000	.000	.000	0	0	0	0	0	0	0	0	0	0	0-0
Davis, Doug, Tex	.000	.000	.000	0	0	0	0	0	0	0	0	0	0	0-0	.000	.000	.000	0	0	0	0	0	0	0	0	0	0	0-0
Davis, Kane, Cle-Mil	.000	.000	.000	1	0	0	0	0	0	0	0	1	0	0-0	.000	.000	.000	1	0	0	0	0	0	0	0	1	0	0-0
de los Santos, V., Mil	.000	.000	.000	6	0	0	0	0	0	0	0	4	0	0-0	.000	.000	.000	6	0	0	0	0	0	0	0	4	0	0-0
DeJean, Mike, Col	.000	.000	.000	2	0	0	0	0	0	0	0	0	0	0-0	.083	.083	.167	12	1	1	0	0	0	0	0	6	1	0-0
del Toro, Miguel, SF	.500	.500	.500	2	1	0	0	0	1	2	0	0	0	0-0	.167	.167	.167	6	1	0	0	0	1	2	0	3	1	0-0
Dempster, Ryan, Fla	.078	.090	.104	77	6	2	0	0	3	2	1	29	4	0-0	.079	.092	.101	139	11	3	0	0	8	4	2	59	6	0-0
DePaula, Sean, Cle	.000	.000	.000	0	0	0	0	0	0	0	0	0	0	0-0	.000	.000	.000	0	0	0	0	0	0	0	0	0	0	0-0
Dessens, Elmer, Cin	.100	.234	.100	40	4	0	0	0	6	0	7	16	1	0-0	.113	.230	.113	53	6	0	0	0	7	3	8	20	4	0-0
DeWitt, Matt, Tor	.000	.000	.000	0	0	0	0	0	0	0	0	0	0	0-0	.000	.000	.000	0	0	0	0	0	0	0	0	0	0	0-0
Dickson, Jason, Ana	.000	.000	.000	0	0	0	0	0	0	0	0	0	0	0-0	.000	.143	.000	6	0	0	0	0	1	0	1	3	0	0-0
Dingman, Craig, NYY	.000	.000	.000	0	0	0	0	0	0	0	0	0	0	0-0	.000	.000	.000	0	0	0	0	0	0	0	0	0	0	0-0
Dipoto, Jerry, Col	.000	.000	.000	1	0	0	0	0	0	0	0	1	0	0-0	.045	.125	.045	22	1	0	0	0	0	0	2	12	1	0-0
Dotel, Octavio, Hou	.031	.061	.031	32	1	0	0	0	1	0	1	16	7	0-0	.071	.161	.071	56	4	0	0	0	3	1	5	33	8	0-0
Downs, S., ChC-Mon	.071	.133	.071	28	2	0	0	0	2	1	2	10	4	0-0	.071	.133	.071	28	2	0	0	0	2	1	2	10	4	0-0
Dreifort, Darren, LA	.162	.186	.338	68	11	3	0	3	5	8	1	25	1	0-0	.195	.223	.311	190	37	7	0	5	22	20	6	77	11	1-0
Drew, Tim, Cle	.000	.000	.000	0	0	0	0	0	0	0	0	0	0	0-0	.000	.000	.000	0	0	0	0	0	0	0	0	0	0	0-0
Durbin, Chad, KC	.000	.000	.000	0	0	0	0	0	0	0	0	0	0	0-0	.000	.000	.000	0	0	0	0	0	0	0	0	0	0	0-0
Duvall, Mike, TB	.000	.000	.000	0	0	0	0	0	0	0	0	0	0	0-0	.000	1.000	.000	0	0	0	0	0	0	0	1	0	0	0-0
Eaton, Adam, SD	.289	.400	.342	38	11	2	0	0	6	4	6	10	0	2-0	.289	.400	.342	38	11	2	0	0	6	4	6	10	0	2-0
Eiland, Dave, TB	.000	.000	.000	0	0	0	0	0	0	0	0	0	0	0-0	.091	.091	.227	22	2	0	0	1	2	2	0	8	5	0-0
Einertson, Darrell, NYY	.000	.000	.000	0	0	0	0	0	0	0	0	0	0	0-0	.000	.000	.000	0	0	0	0	0	0	0	0	0	0	0-0
Elarton, Scott, Hou	.159	.197	.190	63	10	2	0	0	6	0	1	20	6	0-0	.156	.182	.177	96	15	2	0	0	7	1	1	34	16	0-0
Eldred, Cal, CWS	.250	.500	.250	4	1	0	0	0	3	0	2	1	0	0-0	.111	.188	.143	63	7	2	0	0	7	4	6	33	10	0-1
Embree, Alan, SF	.000	.000	.000	0	0	0	0	0	0	0	0	0	0	0-0	.000	.500	.000	1	0	0	0	0	0	0	1	1	0	0-0
Enders, Trevor, TB	.000	.000	.000	0	0	0	0	0	0	0	0	0	0	0-0	.000	.000	.000	0	0	0	0	0	0	0	0	0	0	0-0
Erdos, Todd, NYY-SD	.000	.000	.000	2	0	0	0	0	0	0	0	0	0	0-0	.000	.000	.000	3	0	0	0	0	0	0	0	1	0	0-0
Erickson, Scott, Bal	.400	.400	.600	5	2	1	0	0	2	1	0	0	0	0-0	.133	.316	.200	15	2	1	0	0	4	1	4	6	4	0-0
Escobar, Kelvim, Tor	.000	.000	.000	7	0	0	0	0	0	0	0	4	0	0-0	.000	.000	.000	8	0	0	0	0	0	0	0	5	0	0-0
Estes, Shawn, SF	.206	.229	.309	68	14	4	0	1	4	10	2	28	11	0-0	.171	.204	.228	263	45	9	0	2	27	19	8	100	42	0-1
Estrada, Horacio, Mil	.143	.143	.143	7	1	0	0	0	1	0	0	2	1	0-0	.111	.111	.111	9	1	0	0	0	1	0	0	2	1	0-0
Estrella, Leo, Tor	.000	.000	.000	0	0	0	0	0	0	0	0	0	0	0-0	.000	.000	.000	0	0	0	0	0	0	0	0	0	0	0-0
Etherton, Seth, Ana	.000	.333	.000	2	0	0	0	0	1	0	1	0	0	0-0	.000	.333	.000	2	0	0	0	0	1	0	1	0	0	0-0
Eyre, Scott, CWS	.000	.000	.000	0	0	0	0	0	0	0	0	0	0	0-0	.200	.200	.200	5	1	0	0	0	0	0	0	3	0	0-0
Farnsworth, Kyle, ChC	.071	.071	.143	14	1	1	0	0	0	0	0	6	2	0-0	.082	.135	.102	49	4	1	0	0	3	2	2	16	8	0-0
Fassero, Jeff, Bos	.000	.000	.000	2	0	0	0	0	1	0	0	2	1	0-0	.076	.140	.094	224	17	2	1	0	16	5	17	127	40	1-0
Fernandez, Alex, Fla	.118	.250	.176	17	2	1	0	0	1	3	3	10	0	0-0	.175	.228	.310	126	22	8	0	3	7	14	9	35	10	0-0
Fernandez, O., Cin	.091	.167	.091	22	2	0	0	0	0	1	2	10	5	0-0	.073	.110	.073	96	7	0	0	0	0	2	3	48	12	0-0
Fetters, Mike, LA	.000	.000	.000	0	0	0	0	0	0	0	0	0	0	0-0	.000	.000	.000	0	0	0	0	0	0	0	0	0	0	0-0
Figueroa, Nelson, Ari	.333	.333	.333	3	1	0	0	0	1	0	0	1	1	0-0	.333	.333	.333	3	1	0	0	0	1	0	0	1	1	0-0
Finley, Chuck, Cle	.000	.000	.000	7	0	0	0	0	0	0	0	4	0	0-0	.000	.000	.000	21	0	0	0	0	1	0	0	12	1	0-0
Fiore, Tony, TB	.000	.000	.000	0	0	0	0	0	0	0	0	0	0	0-0	.000	.000	.000	0	0	0	0	0	0	0	0	0	0	0-0
Florie, Bryce, Bos	.000	.000	.000	0	0	0	0	0	0	0	0	0	0	0-0	.111	.273	.111	9	1	0	0	0	0	0	2	5	1	0-0
Ford, Ben, NYY	.000	.000	.000	0	0	0	0	0	0	0	0	0	0	0-0	.000	.000	.000	0	0	0	0	0	0	0	0	0	0	0-0
Forster, Scott, Mon	.000	.000	.000	0	0	0	0	0	0	0	0	0	0	0-0	.000	.000	.000	0	0	0	0	0	0	0	0	0	0	0-0
Foulke, Keith, CWS	.000	.000	.000	0	0	0	0	0	0	0	0	0	0	0-0	.133	.133	.133	15	2	0	0	0	0	0	0	5	2	0-0
Franco, John, NYM	.000	.000	.000	1	0	0	0	0	0	0	0	1	0	0-0	.088	.088	.088	34	3	0	0	0	2	1	0	14	3	0-0
Franklin, Wayne, Hou	.000	.000	.000	2	0	0	0	0	0	0	0	1	0	0-0	.000	.000	.000	2	0	0	0	0	0	0	0	1	0	0-0
Frascatore, John, Tor	.000	.000	.000	0	0	0	0	0	0	0	0	0	0	0-0	.059	.111	.059	17	1	0	0	0	0	0	1	12	1	0-0
Fultz, Aaron, SF	.333	.333	.333	6	2	0	0	0	0	0	0	1	1	0-0	.333	.333	.333	6	2	0	0	0	0	0	0	1	1	0-0
Fussell, Chris, KC	.000	.000	.000	2	0	0	0	0	0	0	0	2	0	0-0	.000	.000	.000	2	0	0	0	0	0	0	0	2	0	0-0
Fyhrie, Mike, Ana	.000	.000	.000	0	0	0	0	0	0	0	0	0	0	0-0	.000	.000	.000	0	0	0	0	0	0	0	0	0	0	0-0
Gagne, Eric, LA	.143	.143	.143	28	4	0	0	0	1	0	0	5	6	0-0	.158	.158	.158	38	6	0	0	0	2	1	0	8	6	0-0
Garces, Rich, Bos	.000	.000	.000	0	0	0	0	0	0	0	0	0	0	0-0	.000	.000	.000	1	0	0	0	0	0	0	0	0	0	0-0
Garcia, Freddy, Sea	.667	.667	.667	3	2	0	0	0	0	0	0	0	3	0-0	.429	.429	.429	7	3	0	0	0	0	1	0	1	5	0-0
Garcia, Mike, Pit	.333	.333	.333	3	1	0	0	0	1	0	0	2	0	0-0	.333	.333	.333	3	1	0	0	0	1	0	0	2	0	0-0
Gardner, Mark, SF	.116	.116	.116	43	5	0	0	0	1	0	0	22	7	0-0	.128	.160	.148	485	62	3	2	1	21	21	15	198	57	0-0
Garibay, Daniel, ChC	.133	.133	.133	15	2	0	0	0	1	1	0	6	4	0-0	.133	.133	.133	15	2	0	0	0	1	1	0	6	4	0-0
Garland, Jon, CWS	.000	.000	.000	0	0	0	0	0	0	0	0	0	0	0-0	.000	.000	.000	0	0	0	0	0	0	0	0	0	0	0-0
Ginter, Matt, CWS	.000	.000	.000	0	0	0	0	0	0	0	0	0	0	0-0	.000	.000	.000	0	0	0	0	0	0	0	0	0	0	0-0
Glauber, Keith, Cin	.000	.000	.000	1	0	0	0	0	0	0	0	1	0	0-0	.000	.000	.000	3	0	0	0	0	0	0	0	1	0	0-0
Glavine, Tom, Atl	.147	.227	.162	68	10	1	0	0	5	2	7	20	14	0-0	.196	.249	.222	899	176	17	2	1	67	64	62	231	138	1-0
Glynn, Ryan, Tex	.000	.000	.000	2	0	0	0	0	0	0	0	1	0	0-0	.000	.000	.000	3	0	0	0	0	0	0	0	1	0	0-0
Gomes, Wayne, Phi	.000	.000	.000	0	0	0	0	0	0	0	0	0	0	0-0	.000	.167	.000	5	0	0	0	0	0	0	1	4	0	0-0
Gooden, Hou-TB-NYY	.000	.000	.000	3	0	0	0	0	0	0	0	1	0	0-0	.196	.212	.262	741	145	15	5	8	60	67	14	135	85	1-1
Graves, Danny, Cin	.500	.667	2.000	2	1	0	0	1	1	1	1	0	0	0-0	.083	.154	.333	12	1	0	0	1	1	1	1	6	0	0-0
Green, Jason, Hou	.000	.000	.000	1	0	0	0	0	0	0	0	0	0	0-0	.000	.000	.000	1	0	0	0	0	0	0	0	0	0	0-0
Grilli, Jason, Fla	.500	.500	.500	2	1	0	0	0	0	1	0	0	0	0-0	.500	.500	.500	2	1	0	0	0	0	1	0	0	0	0-0
Grimsley, Jason, NYY	.000	.667	.000	1	0	0	0	0	0	0	2	1	0	0-0	.103	.205	.103	39	4	0	0	0	3	2	5	11	5	0-0
Groom, Buddy, Bal	.000	.000	.000	0	0	0	0	0	0	0	0	0	0	0-0	.000	.000	.000	0	0	0	0	0	0	0	0	0	0	0-0
Gross, Kip, Hou	.000	.000	.000	1	0	0	0	0	0	0	0	0	0	0-0	.160	.160	.160	25	4	0	0	0	2	2	0	6	4	0-0

	2000 Hitting														Career Hitting													
Pitcher, Team	Avg	OBP	SLG	AB	H	2B	3B	HR	R	RBI	BB	SO	SH	SB-CS	Avg	OBP	SLG	AB	H	2B	3B	HR	R	RBI	BB	SO	SH	SB-CS
Guardado, Eddie, Min	.000	.000	.000	0	0	0	0	0	0	0	0	0	0	0-0	.000	.000	.000	0	0	0	0	0	0	0	0	0	0	0-0
Gunderson, Eric, Tor	.000	.000	.000	0	0	0	0	0	0	0	0	0	0	0-0	.000	.143	.000	6	0	0	0	0	1	0	0	4	0	0-0
Guthrie, ChC-TB-Tor	.000	.000	.000	2	0	0	0	0	0	0	0	1	0	0-0	.091	.091	.091	11	1	0	0	0	0	0	0	1	1	0-0
Guzman, Domingo, SD	.000	.000	.000	0	0	0	0	0	0	0	0	0	0	0-0	.000	.000	.000	0	0	0	0	0	0	0	0	0	0	0-0
Guzman, Geraldo, Ari	.000	.000	.000	19	0	0	0	0	0	0	0	13	3	0-0	.000	.000	.000	19	0	0	0	0	0	0	0	13	3	0-0
Guzman, Juan, TB	.000	.000	.000	0	0	0	0	0	0	0	0	0	0	0-0	.118	.143	.118	34	4	0	0	0	1	3	1	14	3	0-0
Hackman, Luther, StL	.000	.000	.000	0	0	0	0	0	0	0	0	0	0	0-0	.200	.200	.200	5	1	0	0	0	1	0	0	3	0	0-0
Halama, John, Sea	.500	.500	.500	2	1	0	0	0	0	0	0	1	1	0-0	.118	.250	.176	17	2	1	0	0	2	0	3	10	2	0-0
Halladay, Roy, Tor	.000	.000	.000	0	0	0	0	0	0	0	0	0	0	0-0	.000	.000	.000	2	0	0	0	0	0	0	0	2	1	0-0
Hamilton, Joey, Tor	.000	.000	.000	0	0	0	0	0	0	0	0	0	0	0-0	.117	.138	.177	300	35	4	1	4	16	20	8	152	32	0-0
Hampton, Mike, NYM	.274	.313	.274	73	20	0	0	0	7	8	5	20	4	0-1	.231	.296	.277	372	86	9	4	0	42	31	32	97	37	2-2
Haney, Chris, Cle	.000	.000	.000	0	0	0	0	0	0	0	0	0	0	0-0	.111	.111	.111	36	4	0	0	0	2	4	0	4	4	0-0
Harnisch, Pete, Cin	.186	.186	.302	43	8	2	0	1	4	8	0	14	6	0-0	.125	.147	.173	502	63	18	0	2	38	29	12	145	61	0-2
Harper, Travis, TB	.000	.000	.000	0	0	0	0	0	0	0	0	0	0	0-0	.000	.000	.000	0	0	0	0	0	0	0	0	0	0	0-0
Hasegawa, S., Ana	.000	.000	.000	1	0	0	0	0	0	0	0	0	0	0-0	.000	.000	.000	1	0	0	0	0	0	0	0	0	0	0-0
Hawkins, LaTroy, Min	.000	.000	.000	1	0	0	0	0	0	0	0	1	0	0-0	.000	.000	.000	5	0	0	0	0	0	0	0	4	0	0-0
Haynes, Jimmy, Mil	.125	.138	.188	64	8	4	0	0	3	4	1	30	5	0-0	.110	.133	.164	73	8	4	0	0	4	4	2	35	6	0-0
Helling, Rick, Tex	.000	.000	.000	5	0	0	0	0	0	0	0	2	0	0-0	.086	.086	.086	35	3	0	0	0	1	0	0	14	2	0-0
Henry, Doug, Hou-SF	.000	.000	.000	1	0	0	0	0	0	0	0	0	0	0-0	.059	.059	.059	17	1	0	0	0	1	0	0	6	2	0-0
Hentgen, Pat, StL	.133	.188	.133	60	8	0	0	0	4	0	4	17	8	0-0	.115	.159	.115	78	9	0	0	0	4	0	4	25	9	0-0
Heredia, Felix, ChC	.000	.000	.000	2	0	0	0	0	0	0	0	1	0	0-0	.273	.273	.273	11	3	0	0	0	0	1	0	3	1	0-0
Heredia, Gil, Oak	.500	.500	.500	2	1	0	0	0	0	0	0	0	1	0-0	.209	.236	.221	86	18	1	0	0	3	3	3	11	12	0-0
Herges, Matt, LA	.077	.077	.077	13	1	0	0	0	0	0	0	8	1	0-0	.071	.071	.071	14	1	0	0	0	0	0	0	9	1	0-0
Hermanson, D., Mon	.145	.175	.182	55	8	2	0	0	1	1	2	21	8	0-0	.100	.169	.146	219	22	4	0	2	10	6	17	113	26	0-0
Hernandez, Livan, SF	.236	.244	.303	89	21	3	0	1	6	9	1	14	9	0-0	.227	.241	.299	264	60	10	0	3	18	25	3	50	20	0-0
Hernandez, O., NYY	.000	.000	.000	9	0	0	0	0	0	0	0	7	1	0-0	.053	.053	.053	19	1	0	0	0	1	0	0	12	2	0-0
Hernandez, R., TB	.000	.000	.000	0	0	0	0	0	0	0	0	0	0	0-0	.500	.500	.500	2	1	0	0	0	0	0	0	1	0	0-0
Hershiser, Orel, LA	.000	.000	.000	7	0	0	0	0	0	0	0	2	0	0-0	.201	.230	.242	810	163	29	2	0	65	50	27	182	101	8-3
Hiljus, Erik, Det	.000	.000	.000	0	0	0	0	0	0	0	0	0	0	0-0	.000	.000	.000	0	0	0	0	0	0	0	0	0	0	0-0
Hill, Ken, Ana-CWS	.333	.333	.333	3	1	0	0	0	0	0	0	0	1	0-0	.150	.209	.186	333	50	7	1	1	22	21	24	94	67	0-0
Hinchliffe, Brett, Ana	.000	.000	.000	0	0	0	0	0	0	0	0	0	0	0-0	.000	.000	.000	0	0	0	0	0	0	0	0	0	0	0-0
Hitchcock, Sterling, SD	.000	.000	.000	22	0	0	0	0	0	1	0	12	1	0-0	.093	.126	.093	183	17	0	0	0	13	4	7	97	21	0-1
Hodges, Kevin, Sea	.000	.000	.000	0	0	0	0	0	0	0	0	0	0	0-0	.000	.000	.000	0	0	0	0	0	0	0	0	0	0	0-0
Hoffman, Trevor, SD	.000	.000	.000	0	0	0	0	0	0	0	0	0	0	0-0	.138	.138	.207	29	4	2	0	0	1	5	0	9	2	0-0
Holmes, D., Ari-StL-Bal	.000	.000	.000	1	0	0	0	0	0	0	0	1	0	0-0	.115	.143	.231	26	3	0	0	1	2	2	1	14	6	0-0
Holt, Chris, Hou	.100	.169	.117	60	6	1	0	0	3	3	4	33	5	0-0	.087	.132	.092	173	15	1	0	0	12	6	8	80	21	0-0
Holtz, Mike, Ana	.000	.000	.000	0	0	0	0	0	0	0	0	0	0	0-0	.000	.000	.000	1	0	0	0	0	0	0	0	1	0	0-0
Holzemer, Mark, Phi	.000	.000	.000	1	0	0	0	0	0	0	0	0	0	0-0	.000	.000	.000	1	0	0	0	0	0	0	0	0	0	0-0
House, Craig, Col	.000	.000	.000	0	0	0	0	0	0	0	0	0	0	0-0	.000	.000	.000	0	0	0	0	0	0	0	0	0	0	0-0
Howry, Bob, CWS	.000	.000	.000	0	0	0	0	0	0	0	0	0	0	0-0	.000	.000	.000	0	0	0	0	0	0	0	0	0	0	0-0
Hudson, Tim, Oak	.000	.000	.000	3	0	0	0	0	0	0	0	1	0	0-0	.143	.250	.143	7	1	0	0	0	0	0	1	3	0	0-0
Irabu, Hideki, Mon	.125	.125	.125	16	2	0	0	0	1	1	0	7	2	0-0	.120	.154	.120	25	3	0	0	0	1	1	1	13	5	0-0
Isringhausen, J., Oak	.000	.000	.000	0	0	0	0	0	0	0	0	0	0	0-0	.196	.238	.299	97	19	4	0	2	10	11	5	33	8	0-0
Jacquez, Tom, Phi	.000	.000	.000	0	0	0	0	0	0	0	0	0	0	0-0	.000	.000	.000	0	0	0	0	0	0	0	0	0	0	0-0
James, Mike, StL	.000	.000	.000	1	0	0	0	0	1	0	0	0	0	0-0	.000	.000	.000	1	0	0	0	0	1	0	0	0	0	0-0
Jarvis, Kevin, Col	.088	.162	.118	34	3	1	0	0	4	0	2	11	3	0-0	.135	.170	.167	96	13	3	0	0	8	2	2	32	14	0-0
Jimenez, Jose, Col	.500	.500	.500	4	2	0	0	0	0	1	0	2	1	0-0	.111	.111	.143	63	7	0	1	0	5	4	0	28	5	0-0
Johnson, Jason, Bal	.000	.000	.000	3	0	0	0	0	0	0	0	2	2	0-0	.000	.000	.000	8	0	0	0	0	0	0	0	6	2	0-0
Johnson, J., Tex	.000	.000	.000	0	0	0	0	0	0	0	0	0	0	0-0	.000	.000	.000	0	0	0	0	0	0	0	0	0	0	0-0
Johnson, Mark, Det	.000	.000	.000	0	0	0	0	0	0	0	0	0	0	0-0	.000	.000	.000	0	0	0	0	0	0	0	0	0	0	0-0
Johnson, Mike, Mon	.182	.217	.182	22	4	0	0	0	1	3	1	8	3	0-0	.167	.186	.167	42	7	0	0	0	3	5	1	15	5	0-0
Johnson, Randy, Ari	.157	.195	.181	83	13	2	0	0	4	8	3	35	5	0-0	.128	.142	.157	235	30	7	0	0	8	16	3	109	17	0-0
Johnstone, John, SF	.000	.000	.000	2	0	0	0	0	0	0	0	2	0	0-0	.000	.000	.000	6	0	0	0	0	0	0	0	3	2	0-0
Jones, Bobby J., NYM	.045	.125	.045	44	2	0	0	0	4	0	3	21	7	0-0	.131	.162	.156	352	46	6	0	1	22	14	12	135	61	0-0
Jones, Bobby M., NYM	.500	.667	.500	2	1	0	0	0	0	0	1	1	1	0-0	.177	.214	.203	79	14	2	0	0	7	8	4	22	11	0-0
Jones, Doug, Oak	.000	.000	.000	0	0	0	0	0	0	0	0	0	0	0-0	.143	.250	.143	7	1	0	0	0	0	0	1	4	0	0-0
Jones, Marcus, Oak	.000	.000	.000	2	0	0	0	0	0	0	0	0	0	0-0	.000	.000	.000	2	0	0	0	0	0	0	0	0	0	0-0
Jones, Todd, Det	.000	.000	.000	0	0	0	0	0	0	0	0	0	0	0-0	.273	.273	.364	11	3	1	0	0	1	0	0	1	0	0-0
Judd, Mike, LA	1.000	1.000	1.000	1	1	0	0	0	1	0	0	0	1	0-0	.125	.222	.125	8	1	0	0	0	1	0	1	2	4	0-0
Kamieniecki, S., Cle-Atl	.000	.000	.000	0	0	0	0	0	0	0	0	0	0	0-0	.000	.000	.000	2	0	0	0	0	0	0	0	2	0	0-0
Karchner, Matt, ChC	.000	1.000	.000	0	0	0	0	0	0	0	1	0	1	0-0	.000	1.000	.000	0	0	0	0	0	0	0	1	0	1	0-0
Karl, Scott, Col-Ana	.286	.375	.286	14	4	0	0	0	3	0	1	5	2	0-1	.142	.194	.216	134	19	2	1	2	11	7	8	42	23	0-1
Karsay, Steve, Cle	.000	.000	.000	1	0	0	0	0	0	0	0	0	0	0-0	.000	.000	.000	1	0	0	0	0	1	0	0	0	0	0-0
Keisler, Randy, NYY	.000	.000	.000	0	0	0	0	0	0	0	0	0	0	0-0	.000	.000	.000	0	0	0	0	0	0	0	0	0	0	0-0
Kida, Masao, Det	.000	.000	.000	0	0	0	0	0	0	0	0	0	0	0-0	.000	.000	.000	0	0	0	0	0	0	0	0	0	0	0-0
Kile, Darryl, StL	.123	.229	.137	73	9	1	0	0	5	3	10	38	8	0-0	.135	.193	.174	564	76	19	0	1	33	36	37	258	73	0-0
Kim, Byung-Hyun, Ari	.000	.250	.000	3	0	0	0	0	0	0	1	2	0	0-0	.000	.200	.000	4	0	0	0	0	0	0	1	2	0	0-0
King, Ray, Mil	.000	.000	.000	0	0	0	0	0	0	0	0	0	0	0-0	.000	.000	.000	1	0	0	0	0	0	0	0	1	0	0-0
Kinney, Matt, Min	.000	.000	.000	0	0	0	0	0	0	0	0	0	0	0-0	.000	.000	.000	1	0	0	0	0	0	0	0	0	0	0-0
Kline, Steve, Mon	.000	.000	.000	2	0	0	0	0	0	0	0	1	0	0-0	.000	.000	.000	8	0	0	0	0	0	0	0	4	2	0-0
Koch, Billy, Tor	.000	.000	.000	1	0	0	0	0	0	0	0	1	0	0-0	.000	.000	.000	2	0	0	0	0	0	0	0	2	0	0-0
Kohlmeier, Ryan, Bal	.000	.000	.000	0	0	0	0	0	0	0	0	0	0	0-0	.000	.000	.000	0	0	0	0	0	0	0	0	0	0	0-0
Kolb, Brandon, SD	.000	.000	.000	1	0	0	0	0	1	0	0	0	0	0-0	.000	.000	.000	1	0	0	0	0	1	0	0	0	0	0-0
Kolb, Danny, Tex	.000	.000	.000	0	0	0	0	0	0	0	0	0	0	0-0	.000	.000	.000	0	0	0	0	0	0	0	0	0	0	0-0
Lara, Yovanny, Mon	.000	.000	.000	0	0	0	0	0	0	0	0	0	0	0-0	.000	.000	.000	0	0	0	0	0	0	0	0	0	0	0-0
Larkin, Andy, Cin-KC	.000	.000	.000	1	0	0	0	0	0	0	0	1	0	0-0	.125	.152	.125	32	4	0	0	0	1	0	1	21	2	0-0
Laxton, Brett, KC	.000	.000	.000	0	0	0	0	0	0	0	0	0	0	0-0	.000	.000	.000	0	0	0	0	0	0	0	0	0	0	0-0
Lee, David, Col	.000	.000	.000	0	0	0	0	0	0	0	0	0	0	0-0	.200	.200	.200	5	1	0	0	0	1	0	0	2	0	0-0
Lee, Sang-Hoon, Bos	.000	.000	.000	0	0	0	0	0	0	0	0	0	0	0-0	.000	.000	.000	0	0	0	0	0	0	0	0	0	0	0-0
Leiter, Al, NYM	.052	.113	.052	58	3	0	0	0	1	0	4	33	9	0-0	.093	.152	.110	290	27	5	0	0	8	11	20	164	34	0-0
Leskanic, Curtis, Mil	.000	.000	.000	2	0	0	0	0	0	0	0	2	0	0-0	.184	.205	.342	38	7	3	0	1	4	7	1	17	5	0-0
Levine, Al, Ana	.000	.000	.000	0	0	0	0	0	0	0	0	0	0	0-0	.000	.000	.000	0	0	0	0	0	0	0	0	0	0	0-0
Levrault, Allen, Mil	.000	.000	.000	3	0	0	0	0	0	0	0	2	0	0-0	.000	.000	.000	3	0	0	0	0	0	0	0	2	0	0-0
Lidle, Cory, TB	.000	.000	.000	2	0	0	0	0	0	0	0	1	0	0-0	.000	.125	.000	7	0	0	0	0	1	0	1	5	0	0-0
Lieber, Jon, ChC	.220	.238	.268	82	18	4	0	0	3	4	2	28	10	0-0	.152	.194	.187	342	52	12	0	0	22	18	18	133	31	0-0
Ligtenberg, Kerry, Atl	.000	.000	.000	0	0	0	0	0	0	0	0	0	0	0-0	.000	.000	.000	0	0	0	0	0	0	0	0	0	0	0-0
Lilly, Ted, NYY	.000	.000	.000	0	0	0	0	0	0	0	0	0	0	0-0	.200	.200	.200	5	1	0	0	0	0	0	0	1	1	0-0
Lima, Jose, Hou	.167	.180	.200	60	10	2	0	0	6	2	1	17	8	0-0	.124	.147	.143	217	27	4	0	0	16	8	6	71	32	0-0
Lincoln, Mike, Min	.000	.000	.000	0	0	0	0	0	0	0	0	0	0	0-0	.000	.000	.000	1	0	0	0	0	0	0	0	0	0	0-0
Linebrink, S., SF-Hou	1.000	1.000	1.000	1	1	0	0	0	0	0	0	0	0	0-0	1.000	1.000	1.000	1	1	0	0	0	0	0	0	0	0	0-0
Lira, Felipe, Mon	.211	.200	.526	19	4	0	0	2	3	3	0	13	1	0-0	.211	.200	.526	19	4	0	0	2	3	3	0	13	1	0-0
Loaiza, E., Tex-Tor	.000	.000	.000	3	0	0	0	0	0	0	0	0	0	0-0	.180	.194	.205	161	29	2	1	0	11	11	3	35	23	0-0

	2000 Hitting														Career Hitting													
Pitcher, Team	Avg	OBP	SLG	AB	H	2B	3B	HR	R	RBI	BB	SO	SH	SB-CS	Avg	OBP	SLG	AB	H	2B	3B	HR	R	RBI	BB	SO	SH	SB-CS
Loiselle, Rich, Pit	.000	.000	.000	0	0	0	0	0	0	0	0	0	0	0-0	.222	.222	.333	9	2	1	0	0	0	2	0	4	2	0-0
Looper, Braden, Fla	.000	.000	.000	2	0	0	0	0	0	0	0	2	0	0-0	.000	.000	.000	2	0	0	0	0	0	0	0	2	0	0-0
Lopez, Albie, TB	.000	.000	.000	6	0	0	0	0	0	0	0	5	1	0-0	.000	.000	.000	8	0	0	0	0	0	0	0	6	1	0-0
Lopez, Rodrigo, SD	.111	.111	.111	9	1	0	0	0	1	0	0	4	0	0-0	.111	.111	.111	9	1	0	0	0	1	0	0	4	0	0-0
Lorraine, A., ChC-Cle	.125	.222	.125	8	1	0	0	0	2	0	1	4	2	0-0	.130	.200	.174	23	3	1	0	0	3	0	2	13	6	0-0
Lowe, Derek, Bos	.000	.000	.000	1	0	0	0	0	0	0	0	1	0	0-0	.000	.111	.000	8	0	0	0	0	0	0	1	6	0	0-0
Lowe, Sean, CWS	.000	.000	.000	0	0	0	0	0	0	0	0	0	0	0-0	.200	.200	.200	5	1	0	0	0	0	0	0	1	0	0-0
Luebbers, Larry, Cin	.000	.000	.000	0	0	0	0	0	0	1	0	0	0	0-0	.200	.233	.225	40	8	1	0	0	2	1	1	10	2	0-0
Maddux, Greg, Atl	.188	.217	.238	80	15	2	1	0	2	5	2	19	7	0-1	.179	.200	.217	1070	191	25	2	4	77	57	26	288	113	4-3
Maddux, Mike, Hou	.000	.000	.000	2	0	0	0	0	0	0	0	2	0	0-0	.065	.122	.076	92	6	1	0	0	4	4	6	34	14	0-0
Maduro, Calvin, Bal	.000	.000	.000	0	0	0	0	0	0	0	0	0	0	0-0	.042	.042	.042	24	1	0	0	0	1	0	0	14	1	0-0
Magnante, Mike, Oak	.000	.000	.000	1	0	0	0	0	0	0	0	0	0	0-0	.333	.333	.333	6	2	0	0	0	0	1	0	2	0	0-0
Mahay, Ron, Oak-Fla	.500	.500	.750	4	2	1	0	0	0	0	0	1	0	0-0	.250	.308	.500	24	6	3	0	1	3	3	1	7	0	0-0
Mahomes, Pat, NYM	.235	.278	.294	17	4	1	0	0	1	1	1	5	2	0-0	.273	.294	.394	33	9	4	0	0	4	4	1	11	2	0-0
Mairena, O., ChC	.000	.000	.000	0	0	0	0	0	0	0	0	0	0	0-0	.000	.000	.000	0	0	0	0	0	0	0	0	0	0	0-0
Mann, Jim, NYM	.000	.000	.000	0	0	0	0	0	0	0	0	0	0	0-0	.000	.000	.000	0	0	0	0	0	0	0	0	0	0	0-0
Mantei, Matt, Ari	.000	.000	.000	0	0	0	0	0	0	0	0	0	0	0-0	.200	.200	.200	5	1	0	0	0	0	0	0	2	0	0-0
Manzanillo, Josias, Pit	.000	.000	.000	3	0	0	0	0	0	0	0	2	1	0-0	.100	.100	.100	10	1	0	0	0	0	0	0	5	2	0-0
Marquis, Jason, Atl	.000	.000	.000	2	0	0	0	0	0	0	0	0	0	0-0	.000	.000	.000	2	0	0	0	0	0	0	0	0	0	0-0
Martin, Tom, Cle	.000	.000	.000	0	0	0	0	0	0	0	0	0	0	0-0	.000	.000	.000	3	0	0	0	0	0	0	0	1	0	0-0
Martinez, Pedro, Bos	.000	.000	.000	0	0	0	0	0	0	0	0	0	0	0-0	.098	.140	.125	255	25	3	2	0	13	11	10	117	37	0-0
Martinez, Ramon, Bos	.200	.200	.200	5	1	0	0	0	1	0	0	1	0	0-0	.154	.165	.183	591	91	12	1	1	33	33	7	198	68	0-2
Martinez, Willie, Cle	.000	.000	.000	0	0	0	0	0	0	0	0	0	0	0-0	.000	.000	.000	0	0	0	0	0	0	0	0	0	0	0-0
Masaoka, Onan, LA	.000	.000	.000	0	0	0	0	0	0	0	0	0	0	0-0	.000	.000	.000	4	0	0	0	0	0	0	0	2	1	0-0
Mathews, T.J., Oak	.000	1.000	.000	0	0	0	0	0	0	0	1	0	0	0-0	.000	.125	.000	7	0	0	0	0	0	0	1	4	0	0-0
Matthews, Mike, StL	.000	.000	.000	0	0	0	0	0	0	0	0	0	0	0-0	.000	.000	.000	0	0	0	0	0	0	0	0	0	0	0-0
Maurer, Dave, SD	.000	.000	.000	0	0	0	0	0	0	0	0	0	0	0-0	.000	.000	.000	0	0	0	0	0	0	0	0	0	0	0-0
Mays, Joe, Min	.400	.400	.600	5	2	1	0	0	1	0	0	2	1	0-0	.250	.400	.375	8	2	1	0	0	1	0	2	3	1	0-0
McDill, Allen, Det	.000	.000	.000	0	0	0	0	0	0	0	0	0	0	0-0	.000	.000	.000	0	0	0	0	0	0	0	0	0	0	0-0
McElroy, Chuck, Bal	.000	.000	.000	0	0	0	0	0	0	0	0	0	0	0-0	.231	.231	.359	39	9	3	1	0	4	4	0	12	2	0-1
McGlinchy, Kevin, Atl	.000	.000	.000	0	0	0	0	0	0	0	0	0	0	0-0	.000	.000	.000	2	0	0	0	0	0	0	0	1	0	0-0
McKnight, Tony, Hou	.000	.000	.000	13	0	0	0	0	1	0	0	6	1	0-0	.000	.000	.000	13	0	0	0	0	1	0	0	6	1	0-0
McMichael, Greg, Atl	.000	.000	.000	0	0	0	0	0	0	0	0	0	0	0-0	.133	.188	.133	15	2	0	0	0	0	0	1	7	0	0-0
Meacham, Rusty, Hou	.000	.000	.000	0	0	0	0	0	0	0	0	0	0	0-0	.000	.000	.000	0	0	0	0	0	0	0	0	0	0	0-0
Meadows, B., SD-KC	.150	.150	.150	40	6	0	0	0	2	2	0	17	4	0-0	.139	.172	.160	144	20	3	0	0	12	6	6	57	13	0-0
Meche, Gil, Sea	.000	.000	.000	0	0	0	0	0	0	0	0	0	0	0-0	.000	.000	.000	0	0	0	0	0	0	0	0	0	0	0-0
Mecir, Jim, TB-Oak	.000	.000	.000	0	0	0	0	0	0	0	0	0	0	0-0	.000	.000	.000	1	0	0	0	0	0	0	0	0	0	0-0
Mendoza, Ramiro, NYY	.000	.000	.000	0	0	0	0	0	0	0	0	0	0	0-0	.000	.000	.000	0	0	0	0	0	0	0	0	0	1	0-0
Mercado, Hector, Cin	.000	.000	.000	1	0	0	0	0	0	0	0	1	0	0-0	.000	.000	.000	1	0	0	0	0	0	0	0	1	0	0-0
Mercedes, Jose, Bal	.000	.000	.000	1	0	0	0	0	0	0	0	0	0	0-0	.071	.133	.071	14	1	0	0	0	0	0	0	8	0	0-0
Mercker, Kent, Ana	.000	.000	.000	0	0	0	0	0	0	0	0	0	0	0-0	.115	.152	.164	244	28	5	2	1	12	18	11	114	22	0-0
Mesa, Jose, Sea	.000	.000	.000	0	0	0	0	0	0	0	0	0	0	0-0	.000	1.000	.000	0	0	0	0	0	1	0	1	0	0	0-0
Miceli, Dan, Fla	.000	.000	.000	0	0	0	0	0	0	0	0	0	0	0-0	.053	.053	.053	19	1	0	0	0	0	0	0	8	0	0-0
Miller, Travis, Min	.000	.000	.000	0	0	0	0	0	0	0	0	0	0	0-0	.000	.000	.000	0	0	0	0	0	0	0	0	0	0	0-0
Miller, Trever, Phi-LA	.000	.000	.000	0	0	0	0	0	0	0	0	0	0	0-0	.167	.167	.333	6	1	1	0	0	1	0	0	1	2	0-0
Miller, Wade, Hou	.100	.100	.125	40	4	1	0	0	1	3	0	16	1	0-0	.098	.098	.122	41	4	1	0	0	1	3	0	17	1	0-0
Mills, Alan, LA-Bal	.000	.250	.000	3	0	0	0	0	0	1	1	2	0	0-0	.000	.167	.000	5	0	0	0	0	0	1	1	3	0	0-0
Millwood, Kevin, Atl	.119	.148	.153	59	7	2	0	0	1	2	2	30	14	0-0	.116	.162	.156	199	23	5	0	1	6	9	11	89	27	0-0
Milton, Eric, Min	.000	.000	.000	2	0	0	0	0	0	0	0	0	0	0-0	.308	.357	.308	13	4	0	0	0	0	1	1	5	0	0-0
Mlicki, Dave, Det	.000	.000	.000	2	0	0	0	0	0	0	0	1	0	0-0	.117	.208	.143	154	18	4	0	0	9	5	18	56	27	0-0
Moehler, Brian, Det	.000	.000	.000	4	0	0	0	0	0	0	0	1	0	0-0	.000	.077	.000	12	0	0	0	0	1	0	1	6	0	0-0
Mohler, Mike, StL-Cle	1.000	1.000	1.000	1	1	0	0	0	0	0	0	0	0	0-0	.250	.250	.250	4	1	0	0	0	0	0	0	1	0	0-0
Molina, Gabe, Bal-Atl	.000	.000	.000	0	0	0	0	0	0	0	0	0	0	0-0	.000	.000	.000	0	0	0	0	0	0	0	0	0	0	0-0
Montgomery, S., SD	.000	.000	.000	0	0	0	0	0	0	0	0	0	0	0-0	1.000	1.000	1.000	1	1	0	0	0	1	0	0	0	0	0-0
Moore, Trey, Mon	.125	.222	.125	8	1	0	0	0	0	0	1	2	2	0-0	.200	.259	.240	25	5	1	0	0	1	0	2	5	3	0-0
Moraga, D., Mon-Col	.000	.000	.000	0	0	0	0	0	0	0	0	0	0	0-0	.000	.000	.000	0	0	0	0	0	0	0	0	0	0	0-0
Morgan, Mike, Ari	.438	.438	.438	16	7	0	0	0	0	1	0	5	1	0-0	.109	.131	.119	497	54	3	1	0	13	15	12	151	59	0-0
Morris, Jim, TB	.000	.000	.000	0	0	0	0	0	0	0	0	0	0	0-0	.000	.000	.000	0	0	0	0	0	0	0	0	0	0	0-0
Morris, Matt, StL	.333	.333	.333	3	1	0	0	0	0	0	0	1	3	0-0	.171	.243	.200	105	18	3	0	0	5	9	10	53	12	0-1
Mota, Danny, Min	.000	.000	.000	0	0	0	0	0	0	0	0	0	0	0-0	.000	.000	.000	0	0	0	0	0	0	0	0	0	0	0-0
Mota, Guillermo, Mon	.000	.000	.000	1	0	0	0	0	0	0	0	0	0	0-0	.500	.500	2.000	2	1	0	0	1	1	3	0	0	0	0-0
Moyer, Jamie, Sea	.000	.000	.000	2	0	0	0	0	0	0	0	1	0	0-0	.144	.216	.156	160	23	2	0	0	10	4	15	53	20	0-0
Mulder, Mark, Oak	.000	.000	.000	4	0	0	0	0	0	0	0	3	0	0-0	.000	.000	.000	4	0	0	0	0	0	0	0	3	0	0-0
Mulholland, Terry, Atl	.250	.250	.333	36	9	3	0	0	3	4	0	16	9	0-0	.114	.134	.149	606	69	13	1	2	26	23	13	274	53	1-1
Mullen, Scott, KC	.000	.000	.000	0	0	0	0	0	0	0	0	0	0	0-0	.000	.000	.000	0	0	0	0	0	0	0	0	0	0	0-0
Munoz, Mike, Tex	.000	.000	.000	0	0	0	0	0	0	0	0	0	0	0-0	.143	.400	.286	7	1	1	0	0	2	1	3	6	1	0-0
Munro, Peter, Tor	.000	.000	.000	1	0	0	0	0	0	0	0	1	0	0-0	.000	.000	.000	1	0	0	0	0	0	0	0	1	0	0-0
Murray, Dan, KC	.000	.000	.000	0	0	0	0	0	0	0	0	0	0	0-0	.000	.000	.000	0	0	0	0	0	0	0	0	0	0	0-0
Mussina, Mike, Bal	.000	.000	.000	6	0	0	0	0	0	0	0	1	0	0-0	.174	.174	.217	23	4	1	0	0	1	4	0	4	0	0-0
Myers, Mike, Col	.000	.000	.000	0	0	0	0	0	0	0	0	0	0	0-0	.000	.000	.000	1	0	0	0	0	0	0	0	1	0	0-0
Myers, Rodney, SD	.000	.000	.000	0	0	0	0	0	0	0	0	0	0	0-0	.231	.231	.308	13	3	1	0	0	2	1	0	7	0	0-0
Myette, Aaron, CWS	.000	.000	.000	0	0	0	0	0	0	0	0	0	0	0-0	.000	.000	.000	0	0	0	0	0	0	0	0	0	0	0-0
Nagy, Charles, Cle	.000	.000	.000	0	0	0	0	0	0	0	0	0	0	0-0	.063	.063	.063	16	1	0	0	0	1	0	0	10	0	0-0
Nathan, Joe, SF	.156	.176	.406	32	5	2	0	2	3	3	1	9	4	0-0	.167	.203	.317	60	10	3	0	2	4	4	3	15	9	0-0
Nation, Joey, ChC	.500	.500	.500	4	2	0	0	0	0	0	0	1	0	0-0	.500	.500	.500	4	2	0	0	0	0	0	0	1	0	0-0
Navarro, Jaime, Mil-Cle	.000	.000	.000	5	0	0	0	0	0	0	0	2	0	0-0	.145	.156	.184	152	22	6	0	0	1	10	1	54	18	0-0
Neagle, D., Cin-NYY	.189	.231	.243	37	7	2	0	0	1	3	2	9	7	0-0	.153	.185	.196	419	64	9	0	3	20	34	17	128	60	0-1
Nelson, Jeff, NYY	.000	.000	.000	1	0	0	0	0	0	0	0	0	0	0-0	.000	.000	.000	2	0	0	0	0	0	0	0	0	1	0-0
Nen, Robb, SF	.000	.000	.000	0	0	0	0	0	0	0	0	0	0	0-0	.000	.000	.000	12	0	0	0	0	0	0	0	3	0	0-0
Newman, Alan, Cle	.000	.000	.000	0	0	0	0	0	0	0	0	0	0	0-0	.000	.000	.000	0	0	0	0	0	0	0	0	0	0	0-0
Nichting, Chris, Cle	.000	.000	.000	0	0	0	0	0	0	0	0	0	0	0-0	.000	.000	.000	0	0	0	0	0	0	0	0	0	0	0-0
Nickle, Doug, Phi	.000	.000	.000	0	0	0	0	0	0	0	0	0	0	0-0	.000	.000	.000	0	0	0	0	0	0	0	0	0	0	0-0
Nitkowski, C.J., Det	.000	.000	.000	0	0	0	0	0	0	0	0	0	0	0-0	.133	.133	.133	15	2	0	0	0	1	1	0	10	1	0-0
Nomo, Hideo, Det	.000	.000	.000	6	0	0	0	0	0	0	0	2	0	0-0	.149	.162	.199	322	48	11	1	1	13	19	5	144	31	0-0
Norton, Phil, ChC	.667	.667	.667	3	2	0	0	0	1	0	0	0	1	0-0	.667	.667	.667	3	2	0	0	0	1	0	0	0	1	0-0
Nunez, Vladimir, Fla	.118	.118	.294	17	2	0	0	1	2	3	0	5	4	0-0	.133	.133	.200	45	6	0	0	1	2	5	0	11	6	0-0
O'Connor, Brian, Pit	.500	.500	.500	2	1	0	0	0	0	0	0	1	0	0-0	.500	.500	.500	2	1	0	0	0	0	0	0	1	0	0-0
Ohka, Tomokazu, Bos	.000	.000	.000	0	0	0	0	0	0	0	0	0	0	0-0	.000	.000	.000	0	0	0	0	0	0	0	0	0	0	0-0
Ohman, Will, ChC	.000	.000	.000	0	0	0	0	0	0	0	0	0	0	0-0	.000	.000	.000	0	0	0	0	0	0	0	0	0	0	0-0
Olivares, Omar, Oak	1.000	1.000	1.000	1	1	0	0	0	0	0	0	0	0	0-0	.242	.261	.344	215	52	8	1	4	22	23	6	61	14	0-0
Oliver, Darren, Tex	.000	.333	.000	2	0	0	0	0	0	0	0	1	0	0-0	.226	.268	.283	106	24	6	0	0	9	9	4	39	8	0-0
Olson, Gregg, LA	.000	.000	.000	0	0	0	0	0	0	0	0	0	0	0-0	.250	.400	1.000	4	1	0	0	1	1	2	1	3	0	0-0

	2000 Hitting														Career Hitting													
Pitcher, Team	Avg	OBP	SLG	AB	H	2B	3B	HR	R	RBI	BB	SO	SH	SB-CS	Avg	OBP	SLG	AB	H	2B	3B	HR	R	RBI	BB	SO	SH	SB-CS
Ontiveros, Steve, Bos	.000	.000	.000	0	0	0	0	0	0	0	0	0	0	0-0	.083	.154	.167	12	1	1	0	0	3	3	1	2	0	0-0
Orosco, Jesse, StL	.000	.000	.000	0	0	0	0	0	0	0	0	0	0	0-0	.169	.250	.169	59	10	0	0	0	2	4	7	25	7	0-0
Ortiz, Ramon, Ana	.000	.000	.000	0	0	0	0	0	0	0	0	0	0	0-0	.000	.000	.000	0	0	0	0	0	0	0	0	0	0	0-0
Ortiz, Russ, SF	.197	.290	.230	61	12	2	0	0	7	5	8	16	6	0-0	.210	.271	.274	157	33	4	0	2	17	15	13	42	18	0-0
Osuna, Antonio, LA	.000	.000	.000	2	0	0	0	0	0	0	0	1	0	0-0	.111	.182	.111	9	1	0	0	0	0	1	1	1	0	0-0
Padilla, Vicente, Ari-Phi	1.000	1.000	1.000	1	1	0	0	0	0	0	0	0	0	0-0	1.000	1.000	1.000	1	1	0	0	0	0	0	0	0	0	0-0
Painter, Lance, Tor	.000	.000	.000	0	0	0	0	0	0	0	0	0	0	0-0	.156	.176	.219	64	10	2	1	0	6	5	2	33	8	0-0
Palacios, Vicente, SD	.000	.000	.000	0	0	0	0	0	0	0	0	0	0	0-0	.045	.067	.045	88	4	0	0	0	2	0	2	43	11	0-0
Paniagua, Jose, Sea	.000	.000	.000	1	0	0	0	0	0	0	0	1	0	0-0	.000	.105	.000	17	0	0	0	0	1	0	2	11	1	0-0
Park, Chan Ho, LA	.214	.236	.357	70	15	4	0	2	6	6	2	16	6	0-0	.176	.207	.250	272	48	12	1	2	17	19	11	103	32	0-0
Parque, Jim, CWS	.000	.000	.000	4	0	0	0	0	0	0	0	3	0	0-0	.200	.200	.200	10	2	0	0	0	0	0	0	4	3	0-0
Parra, Jose, Pit	.000	1.000	.000	0	0	0	0	0	0	0	2	0	0	0-0	.000	1.000	.000	0	0	0	0	0	0	0	2	0	2	0-0
Parris, Steve, Cin	.127	.155	.164	55	7	2	0	0	4	4	2	19	4	0-1	.160	.175	.186	156	25	4	0	0	8	15	3	50	15	0-1
Parrish, John, Bal	.000	.000	.000	0	0	0	0	0	0	0	0	0	0	0-0	.000	.000	.000	0	0	0	0	0	0	0	0	0	0	0-0
Patterson, Danny, Det	.000	.000	.000	0	0	0	0	0	0	0	0	0	0	0-0	.000	.000	.000	1	0	0	0	0	0	0	0	0	0	0-0
Pavano, Carl, Mon	.143	.143	.171	35	5	1	0	0	2	0	0	16	3	0-0	.123	.131	.142	106	13	2	0	0	4	5	1	44	14	0-0
Pena, Jesus, CWS-Bos	.000	.000	.000	0	0	0	0	0	0	0	0	0	0	0-0	.000	.000	.000	0	0	0	0	0	0	0	0	0	0	0-0
Penny, Brad, Fla	.111	.111	.111	45	5	0	0	0	2	2	0	17	1	0-0	.111	.111	.111	45	5	0	0	0	2	2	0	17	1	0-0
Percival, Troy, Ana	.000	.000	.000	0	0	0	0	0	0	0	0	0	0	0-0	.000	.000	.000	1	0	0	0	0	0	0	0	1	0	0-0
Perez, Carlos, LA	.047	.047	.116	43	2	1	1	0	0	3	0	15	7	0-0	.152	.191	.248	250	38	8	2	4	11	15	12	107	33	0-0
Perez, Yorkis, Hou	.000	.000	.000	1	0	0	0	0	0	0	0	1	0	0-0	.000	.000	.000	11	0	0	0	0	0	0	0	8	0	0-0
Perisho, Matt, Tex	.000	.000	.000	4	0	0	0	0	0	0	0	4	0	0-0	.000	.000	.000	5	0	0	0	0	0	0	0	5	0	0-0
Person, Robert, Phi	.132	.175	.189	53	7	3	0	0	1	2	3	29	8	0-0	.123	.163	.156	122	15	4	0	0	6	3	5	65	17	0-0
Peters, Chris, Pit	.167	.167	.167	6	1	0	0	0	1	1	0	1	0	0-0	.233	.258	.244	90	21	1	0	0	10	7	3	30	6	2-0
Petkovsek, Mark, Ana	.000	.000	.000	0	0	0	0	0	0	0	0	0	0	0-0	.163	.232	.174	86	14	1	0	0	10	3	7	18	6	0-0
Pettitte, Andy, NYY	.000	.000	.000	5	0	0	0	0	0	0	0	2	0	0-0	.071	.133	.071	14	1	0	0	0	0	0	1	7	2	0-0
Pichardo, Hipolito, Bos	.000	.000	.000	1	0	0	0	0	0	0	0	1	0	0-0	.000	.000	.000	5	0	0	0	0	0	0	0	3	0	0-0
Pineiro, Joel, Sea	.000	.000	.000	0	0	0	0	0	0	0	0	0	0	0-0	.000	.000	.000	0	0	0	0	0	0	0	0	0	0	0-0
Plesac, Dan, Ari	.000	.000	.000	0	0	0	0	0	0	0	0	0	0	0-0	.067	.067	.067	15	1	0	0	0	0	0	0	10	0	0-0
Politte, Cliff, Phi	.133	.176	.200	15	2	1	0	0	1	2	1	4	2	0-0	.103	.156	.138	29	3	1	0	0	1	2	2	12	3	0-0
Ponson, Sidney, Bal	.000	.000	.000	1	0	0	0	0	0	0	0	1	2	0-0	.250	.250	.250	8	2	0	0	0	1	0	0	3	3	0-0
Poole, Jim, Det-Mon	.000	.000	.000	0	0	0	0	0	0	0	0	0	0	0-0	.125	.125	.250	8	1	1	0	0	1	0	0	2	3	0-0
Pote, Lou, Ana	.000	.000	.000	0	0	0	0	0	0	0	0	0	0	0-0	.000	.000	.000	0	0	0	0	0	0	0	0	0	0	0-0
Powell, Brian, Hou	.222	.300	.333	9	2	1	0	0	2	0	1	4	0	0-0	.200	.273	.300	10	2	1	0	0	2	0	1	5	0	0-0
Powell, Jay, Hou	.000	.000	.000	1	0	0	0	0	0	0	0	1	0	0-0	.182	.182	.182	11	2	0	0	0	0	1	0	7	1	0-0
Powell, Jeremy, Mon	.600	.600	.800	5	3	1	0	0	1	1	0	1	0	0-0	.171	.227	.220	41	7	2	0	0	3	1	3	12	1	0-0
Prieto, Ariel, Oak	.000	.000	.000	2	0	0	0	0	0	0	0	1	0	0-0	.000	.000	.000	2	0	0	0	0	0	0	0	1	0	0-0
Prokopec, Luke, LA	.000	.000	.000	5	0	0	0	0	0	0	0	2	1	0-0	.000	.000	.000	5	0	0	0	0	0	0	0	2	1	0-0
Pulsipher, Bill, NYM	.000	.000	.000	2	0	0	0	0	0	0	0	1	0	0-0	.123	.170	.148	81	10	2	0	0	7	4	5	40	13	0-0
Quantrill, Paul, Tor	.000	1.000	.000	0	0	0	0	0	0	0	1	0	0	0-0	.098	.154	.098	61	6	0	0	0	5	0	4	26	7	0-0
Quevedo, Ruben, ChC	.133	.133	.133	30	4	0	0	0	1	1	0	10	1	0-0	.133	.133	.133	30	4	0	0	0	1	1	0	10	1	0-0
Radinsky, Scott, StL	.000	.000	.000	0	0	0	0	0	0	0	0	0	0	0-0	.000	.000	.000	5	0	0	0	0	0	0	0	4	0	0-0
Radke, Brad, Min	.000	.000	.000	2	0	0	0	0	0	0	0	2	0	0-0	.000	.000	.000	12	0	0	0	0	0	0	0	5	1	0-0
Rain, Steve, ChC	.000	.333	.000	2	0	0	0	0	0	0	1	2	0	0-0	.000	.333	.000	2	0	0	0	0	0	0	1	2	0	0-0
Rakers, Jason, KC	.000	.000	.000	0	0	0	0	0	0	0	0	0	0	0-0	.000	.000	.000	0	0	0	0	0	0	0	0	0	0	0-0
Ramirez, Hector, Mil	1.000	1.000	1.000	1	1	0	0	0	0	0	0	0	0	0-0	.250	.250	.250	4	1	0	0	0	0	0	0	2	0	0-0
Ramsay, Rob, Sea	.000	.000	.000	0	0	0	0	0	0	0	0	0	0	0-0	.000	.000	.000	0	0	0	0	0	0	0	0	0	0	0-0
Rapp, Pat, Bal	.000	.000	.000	3	0	0	0	0	0	0	0	0	0	0-0	.120	.123	.149	242	29	4	0	1	10	13	1	90	21	0-0
Ratliff, Jon, Oak	.000	.000	.000	0	0	0	0	0	0	0	0	0	0	0-0	.000	.000	.000	0	0	0	0	0	0	0	0	0	0	0-0
Reames, Britt, StL	.167	.167	.167	12	2	0	0	0	1	0	0	2	1	0-0	.167	.167	.167	12	2	0	0	0	1	0	0	2	1	0-0
Redman, Mark, Min	.000	.000	.000	4	0	0	0	0	0	0	0	3	1	0-0	.000	.000	.000	4	0	0	0	0	0	0	0	3	1	0-0
Reed, Rick, NYM	.204	.226	.204	49	10	0	0	0	6	2	1	11	14	0-0	.178	.213	.233	253	45	8	0	2	21	20	11	76	42	0-0
Reed, Steve, Cle	.000	.000	.000	0	0	0	0	0	0	0	0	0	0	0-0	.143	.143	.143	21	3	0	0	0	0	0	0	6	2	0-0
Reichert, Dan, KC	.000	.000	.000	1	0	0	0	0	0	0	0	0	0	0-0	.250	.250	.250	4	1	0	0	0	0	0	0	2	1	0-0
Rekar, Bryan, TB	.333	.333	.667	3	1	1	0	0	0	1	0	1	0	0-0	.151	.211	.189	53	8	2	0	0	4	1	4	24	5	0-1
Remlinger, Mike, Atl	.000	.250	.000	3	0	0	0	0	0	0	1	2	0	0-0	.077	.143	.106	104	8	3	0	0	5	8	8	33	19	0-1
Reyes, Al, Bal-LA	.000	.000	.000	0	0	0	0	0	0	0	0	0	0	0-0	.143	.143	.143	7	1	0	0	0	1	0	0	4	0	0-0
Reyes, Carlos, Phi-SD	.000	.000	.000	1	0	0	0	0	0	0	0	0	0	0-0	.000	.000	.000	2	0	0	0	0	0	0	0	1	1	0-0
Reyes, Dennys, Cin	.000	.333	.000	2	0	0	0	0	0	0	1	1	0	0-0	.031	.088	.063	32	1	1	0	0	2	0	2	14	2	1-0
Reynolds, Shane, Hou	.225	.262	.325	40	9	1	0	1	2	2	1	13	4	0-0	.160	.187	.222	419	67	14	0	4	30	33	12	183	68	0-0
Reynoso, Armando, Ari	.104	.140	.104	48	5	0	0	0	0	0	2	24	7	0-0	.150	.189	.193	327	49	5	0	3	17	11	16	146	35	0-0
Rhodes, Arthur, Sea	.000	.000	.000	0	0	0	0	0	0	0	0	0	0	0-0	.333	.333	.333	3	1	0	0	0	0	0	0	2	0	0-0
Riedling, John, Cin	.000	.000	.000	2	0	0	0	0	0	0	0	2	0	0-0	.000	.000	.000	2	0	0	0	0	0	0	0	2	0	0-0
Rigby, Brad, KC-Mon	.000	.000	.000	1	0	0	0	0	0	0	0	0	0	0-0	.000	.000	.000	4	0	0	0	0	0	0	0	2	0	0-0
Rigdon, Paul, Cle-Mil	.188	.278	.375	16	3	0	0	1	3	1	2	6	7	0-0	.188	.278	.375	16	3	0	0	1	3	1	2	6	7	0-0
Riggan, Jerrod, NYM	.000	.000	.000	0	0	0	0	0	0	0	0	0	0	0-0	.000	.000	.000	0	0	0	0	0	0	0	0	0	0	0-0
Rincon, Ricky, Cle	.000	.000	.000	0	0	0	0	0	0	0	0	0	0	0-0	.000	.000	.000	3	0	0	0	0	0	0	0	1	1	0-0
Ritchie, Todd, Pit	.217	.242	.250	60	13	2	0	0	4	2	2	22	2	0-0	.183	.203	.209	115	21	3	0	0	7	3	3	39	10	0-0
Rivera, Luis, Atl-Bal	.000	.000	.000	0	0	0	0	0	0	0	0	0	0	0-0	.000	.000	.000	0	0	0	0	0	0	0	0	0	0	0-0
Rivera, Mariano, NYY	.000	.000	.000	0	0	0	0	0	0	0	0	0	0	0-0	.000	.000	.000	0	0	0	0	0	0	0	0	0	0	0-0
Roberts, Grant, NYM	.000	.000	.000	0	0	0	0	0	0	0	0	0	1	0-0	.000	.000	.000	0	0	0	0	0	0	0	0	0	1	0-0
Rocker, John, Atl	.000	.000	.000	0	0	0	0	0	0	0	0	0	0	0-0	.000	.000	.000	0	0	0	0	0	0	0	0	0	0	0-0
Rodriguez, Felix, SF	.000	.000	.000	4	0	0	0	0	0	0	0	3	0	0-0	.154	.214	.462	13	2	1	0	1	3	3	0	4	2	0-0
Rodriguez, Frank, Sea	.000	.000	.000	1	0	0	0	0	0	0	0	1	0	0-0	.200	.200	.200	5	1	0	0	0	1	1	0	1	0	0-0
Rodriguez, Jose, StL	.000	.000	.000	1	0	0	0	0	0	0	0	1	0	0-0	.000	.000	.000	1	0	0	0	0	0	0	0	1	0	0-0
Rodriguez, Rich, NYM	.000	.000	.000	1	0	0	0	0	0	0	0	1	0	0-0	.107	.194	.107	28	3	0	0	0	3	1	3	9	4	0-0
Rogers, Kenny, Tex	.500	.500	.500	4	2	0	0	0	0	0	0	1	1	0-0	.128	.171	.128	39	5	0	0	0	3	2	2	14	4	0-0
Romero, J.C., Min	.000	.000	.000	0	0	0	0	0	0	0	0	0	0	0-0	.000	.000	.000	0	0	0	0	0	0	0	0	0	0	0-0
Roque, Rafael, Mil	.000	.000	.000	0	0	0	0	0	0	0	0	0	0	0-0	.067	.125	.067	30	2	0	0	0	0	1	2	16	5	0-0
Rosado, Jose, KC	.000	.000	.000	0	0	0	0	0	0	0	0	0	0	0-0	.111	.111	.111	9	1	0	0	0	0	0	0	5	0	0-0
Rose, Brian, Bos-Col	.042	.080	.042	24	1	0	0	0	1	0	1	11	3	0-0	.038	.074	.038	26	1	0	0	0	1	0	1	11	4	0-0
Rueter, Kirk, SF	.200	.213	.250	60	12	3	0	0	5	5	1	11	10	0-0	.151	.182	.168	358	54	6	0	0	26	26	14	72	48	0-1
Ruffin, Johnny, Ari	.000	.000	.000	0	0	0	0	0	0	0	0	0	0	0-0	.176	.176	.176	17	3	0	0	0	1	0	0	5	0	1-0
Runyan, Sean, Det	.000	.000	.000	0	0	0	0	0	0	0	0	0	0	0-0	.000	.000	.000	0	0	0	0	0	0	0	0	0	0	0-0
Rupe, Ryan, TB	.000	.000	.000	1	0	0	0	0	0	0	0	0	0	0-0	.000	.000	.000	5	0	0	0	0	0	0	0	1	0	0-0
Rusch, Glendon, NYM	.060	.113	.060	50	3	0	0	0	2	1	3	19	4	0-0	.054	.102	.054	56	3	0	0	0	2	1	3	21	4	0-0
Ryan, B.J., Bal	.000	.000	.000	0	0	0	0	0	0	0	0	0	0	0-0	.000	.000	.000	0	0	0	0	0	0	0	0	0	0	0-0
Ryan, Jason, Min	.000	.000	.000	0	0	0	0	0	0	0	0	0	0	0-0	.000	.000	.000	0	0	0	0	0	0	0	0	0	0	0-0
Sanchez, Jesus, Fla	.232	.246	.232	56	13	0	0	0	6	4	1	15	3	0-0	.175	.195	.192	120	21	0	1	0	8	5	3	35	9	0-0
Santana, Johan, Min	.000	.000	.000	1	0	0	0	0	0	0	0	0	0	0-0	.000	.000	.000	1	0	0	0	0	0	0	0	0	0	0-0
Santana, Julio, Mon	.000	.000	.000	7	0	0	0	0	0	0	0	4	0	0-0	.143	.143	.143	14	2	0	0	0	0	1	0	7	0	0-0
Santiago, Jose, KC	.000	.000	.000	0	0	0	0	0	0	0	0	0	0	0-0	.000	.000	.000	0	0	0	0	0	0	0	0	0	0	0-0

Pitcher, Team	2000 Hitting														Career Hitting													
	Avg	OBP	SLG	AB	H	2B	3B	HR	R	RBI	BB	SO	SH	SB-CS	Avg	OBP	SLG	AB	H	2B	3B	HR	R	RBI	BB	SO	SH	SB-CS
Sasaki, Kazuhiro, Sea	.000	.000	.000	0	0	0	0	0	0	0	0	0	0	0-0	.000	.000	.000	0	0	0	0	0	0	0	0	0	0	0-0
Sauerbeck, Scott, Pit	.000	.000	.000	1	0	0	0	0	0	0	0	0	0	0-0	.000	.000	.000	2	0	0	0	0	0	0	0	1	1	0-0
Sauveur, Rich, Oak	.000	.000	.000	0	0	0	0	0	0	0	0	0	0	0-0	.333	.333	.333	3	1	0	0	0	0	0	0	1	1	0-0
Scanlan, Bob, Mil	.000	.000	.000	0	0	0	0	0	0	0	0	0	0	0-0	.067	.094	.067	30	2	0	0	0	1	3	1	12	3	0-0
Schilling, Curt, Phi-Ari	.213	.226	.262	61	13	3	0	0	2	4	1	15	9	0-1	.157	.182	.183	541	85	12	1	0	24	25	17	191	76	1-1
Schmidt, Jason, Pit	.000	.050	.000	19	0	0	0	0	1	0	1	9	2	0-0	.082	.130	.099	233	19	4	0	0	7	8	13	110	38	0-0
Schoeneweis, S., Ana	.333	.333	.333	3	1	0	0	0	0	1	0	0	0	0-0	.333	.333	.333	3	1	0	0	0	0	1	0	0	0	0-0
Schourek, Pete, Bos	.500	.500	.500	4	2	0	0	0	0	0	0	1	0	0-0	.164	.192	.201	269	44	4	0	2	15	20	10	81	37	2-0
Schrenk, Steve, Phi	.000	.000	.000	0	0	0	0	0	0	0	0	0	0	0-0	.000	.000	.000	3	0	0	0	0	0	0	0	2	1	0-0
Seanez, Rudy, Atl	.000	.000	.000	0	0	0	0	0	0	0	0	0	0	0-0	.000	.200	.000	4	0	0	0	0	1	0	1	4	0	0-0
Seelbach, Chris, Atl	.000	.000	.000	0	0	0	0	0	0	0	0	0	0	0-0	.000	.000	.000	0	0	0	0	0	0	0	0	0	0	0-0
Sele, Aaron, Sea	.000	.000	.000	3	0	0	0	0	0	0	0	0	1	0-0	.077	.143	.154	13	1	1	0	0	0	0	1	3	2	0-0
Serafini, Dan, SD-Pit	.083	.083	.083	24	2	0	0	0	1	2	0	9	3	0-0	.081	.150	.081	37	3	0	0	0	2	2	3	17	4	0-0
Service, Scott, Oak	.000	.000	.000	0	0	0	0	0	0	0	0	0	0	0-0	.063	.063	.063	16	1	0	0	0	0	1	0	9	0	0-0
Shaw, Jeff, LA	.000	.000	.000	0	0	0	0	0	0	0	0	0	0	0-0	.079	.167	.079	38	3	0	0	0	4	0	4	20	3	0-0
Shuey, Paul, Cle	.000	.000	.000	0	0	0	0	0	0	0	0	0	0	0-0	.000	.000	.000	2	0	0	0	0	0	0	0	1	0	0-0
Sikorski, Brian, Tex	.000	.000	.000	0	0	0	0	0	0	0	0	0	0	0-0	.000	.000	.000	0	0	0	0	0	0	0	0	0	0	0-0
Silva, Jose, Pit	.176	.222	.176	34	6	0	0	0	0	2	1	12	5	0-0	.114	.161	.125	88	10	1	0	0	1	5	3	36	15	0-0
Simas, Bill, CWS	.000	.000	.000	0	0	0	0	0	0	0	0	0	0	0-0	.000	.000	.000	0	0	0	0	0	0	0	0	0	0	0-0
Sirotka, Mike, CWS	.000	.200	.000	4	0	0	0	0	0	0	1	2	0	0-0	.118	.211	.118	17	2	0	0	0	1	0	2	6	0	0-0
Skrmetta, Matt, Mon-Pit	.000	.000	.000	2	0	0	0	0	0	0	0	1	0	0-0	.000	.000	.000	2	0	0	0	0	0	0	0	1	0	0-0
Slocumb, H., StL-SD	.000	.000	.000	1	0	0	0	0	0	0	0	1	0	0-0	.083	.083	.083	12	1	0	0	0	0	2	0	7	1	0-0
Slusarski, Joe, Hou	.111	.111	.111	9	1	0	0	0	1	1	0	5	0	0-0	.111	.111	.111	9	1	0	0	0	1	1	0	5	0	0-0
Smith, Brian, Pit	.000	.000	.000	0	0	0	0	0	0	0	0	0	0	0-0	.000	.000	.000	0	0	0	0	0	0	0	0	0	0	0-0
Smith, Chuck, Fla	.100	.100	.100	40	4	0	0	0	2	2	0	19	1	0-0	.100	.100	.100	40	4	0	0	0	2	2	0	19	1	0-0
Smith, Dan, Bos	.000	.000	.000	0	0	0	0	0	0	0	0	0	0	0-0	.083	.185	.083	24	2	0	0	0	3	1	3	15	3	0-0
Snyder, John, Mil	.079	.146	.105	38	3	1	0	0	1	0	2	7	1	0-0	.079	.146	.105	38	3	1	0	0	1	0	2	7	1	0-0
Sparks, Jeff, TB	.000	.000	.000	0	0	0	0	0	0	0	0	0	0	0-0	.000	.000	.000	0	0	0	0	0	0	0	0	0	0	0-0
Sparks, Steve, Pit	.000	.000	.000	0	0	0	0	0	0	0	0	0	0	0-0	.000	.000	.000	0	0	0	0	0	0	0	0	0	0	0-0
Sparks, Steve W., Det	.000	.000	.000	0	0	0	0	0	0	0	0	0	0	0-0	.250	.400	.500	4	1	1	0	0	1	2	1	1	1	0-0
Speier, Justin, Cle	.500	.500	.500	2	1	0	0	0	0	0	0	1	0	0-0	.400	.400	.400	5	2	0	0	0	0	0	0	3	0	0-0
Spencer, Sean, Mon	.000	.000	.000	0	0	0	0	0	0	0	0	0	0	0-0	.000	.000	.000	0	0	0	0	0	0	0	0	0	0	0-0
Spencer, Stan, SD	.333	.333	.417	12	4	1	0	0	0	1	0	6	2	0-0	.161	.188	.226	31	5	2	0	0	0	1	0	13	6	0-0
Spoljaric, Paul, KC	.000	.000	.000	0	0	0	0	0	0	0	0	0	0	0-0	.000	.000	.000	3	0	0	0	0	0	0	0	0	2	0-0
Spradlin, J., KC-ChC	.000	.000	.000	1	0	0	0	0	0	0	0	1	0	0-0	.167	.167	.333	6	1	1	0	0	0	0	0	3	0	0-0
Springer, Dennis, NYM	.000	.000	.000	4	0	0	0	0	0	0	0	3	0	0-0	.106	.104	.121	66	7	1	0	0	2	2	0	27	3	0-0
Springer, Russ, Ari	.200	.200	.200	5	1	0	0	0	0	0	0	1	0	0-0	.080	.080	.080	25	2	0	0	0	1	0	0	15	3	0-0
Spurgeon, Jay, Bal	.000	.000	.000	0	0	0	0	0	0	0	0	0	0	0-0	.000	.000	.000	0	0	0	0	0	0	0	0	0	0	0-0
Stanifer, Rob, Bos	.000	.000	.000	0	0	0	0	0	0	0	0	0	0	0-0	.250	.333	.375	8	2	1	0	0	1	1	0	3	0	0-0
Stanton, Mike, NYY	1.000	1.000	1.000	1	1	0	0	0	1	0	0	0	0	0-0	.500	.533	.571	14	7	1	0	0	2	2	1	2	1	0-0
Stechschulte, G., StL	.000	.000	.000	0	0	0	0	0	0	0	0	0	0	0-0	.000	.000	.000	0	0	0	0	0	0	0	0	0	0	0-0
Stein, Blake, KC	.000	.000	.000	2	0	0	0	0	0	0	0	2	0	0-0	.000	.000	.000	7	0	0	0	0	0	0	0	6	1	0-0
Stephenson, G., StL	.051	.111	.051	59	3	0	0	0	0	4	4	23	13	0-0	.073	.115	.089	124	9	2	0	0	1	5	5	45	22	0-0
Stevens, Dave, Atl	.000	.000	.000	1	0	0	0	0	0	0	0	0	0	0-0	.167	.167	.167	6	1	0	0	0	0	0	0	2	0	0-0
Stottlemyre, Todd, Ari	.194	.265	.355	31	6	2	0	1	6	4	3	14	3	0-0	.210	.291	.261	238	50	7	1	1	23	11	27	91	25	1-1
Strickland, Scott, Mon	.000	.000	.000	2	0	0	0	0	0	0	0	2	0	0-0	.000	.000	.000	2	0	0	0	0	0	0	0	2	0	0-0
Strong, Joe, Fla	.000	.000	.000	1	0	0	0	0	0	0	0	1	0	0-0	.000	.000	.000	1	0	0	0	0	0	0	0	1	0	0-0
Stull, Everett, Mil	.000	.100	.000	9	0	0	0	0	0	0	1	9	0	0-0	.000	.100	.000	9	0	0	0	0	0	0	1	9	1	0-0
Sturtze, T., CWS-TB	.000	.000	.000	0	0	0	0	0	0	0	0	0	0	0-0	.000	.000	.000	1	0	0	0	0	0	0	0	0	1	0-0
Sullivan, Scott, Cin	.286	.286	.286	7	2	0	0	0	0	0	0	2	0	0-0	.071	.071	.071	42	3	0	0	0	1	1	0	24	3	0-0
Suppan, Jeff, KC	.000	.000	.000	3	0	0	0	0	0	0	0	0	0	0-0	.219	.242	.219	32	7	0	0	0	1	2	0	7	1	1-0
Suzuki, Makoto, KC	.200	.200	.200	5	1	0	0	0	1	0	0	2	1	0-0	.200	.200	.200	5	1	0	0	0	1	0	0	2	1	0-0
Swindell, Greg, Ari	.000	.000	.000	1	0	0	0	0	0	0	0	1	1	0-0	.188	.200	.229	245	46	10	0	0	10	13	4	57	36	0-0
Tam, Jeff, Oak	.000	.000	.000	0	0	0	0	0	0	0	0	0	0	0-0	.000	.000	.000	1	0	0	0	0	0	0	0	0	0	0-0
Tapani, Kevin, ChC	.179	.220	.268	56	10	2	0	1	3	4	3	20	9	0-1	.133	.189	.190	211	28	6	0	2	13	20	15	91	26	1-1
Tavarez, Julian, Col	.086	.086	.086	35	3	0	0	0	1	0	0	14	3	0-0	.100	.100	.100	50	5	0	0	0	1	0	0	21	4	0-0
Taylor, Billy, TB	.000	.000	.000	0	0	0	0	0	0	0	0	0	0	0-0	.000	.000	.000	0	0	0	0	0	0	0	0	0	0	0-0
Telemaco, Amaury, Phi	.000	.200	.000	4	0	0	0	0	0	0	1	1	0	0-0	.104	.146	.143	77	8	1	1	0	3	3	4	38	5	0-0
Telford, Anthony, Mon	.000	.000	.000	2	0	0	0	0	0	0	0	0	1	0-0	.174	.208	.217	23	4	1	0	0	0	3	1	4	4	0-0
Tessmer, Jay, NYY	.000	.000	.000	0	0	0	0	0	0	0	0	0	0	0-0	.000	.000	.000	0	0	0	0	0	0	0	0	0	0	0-0
Thompson, Mark, StL	.000	.000	.000	3	0	0	0	0	0	0	0	1	0	0-0	.154	.162	.221	104	16	4	0	1	7	3	1	47	10	0-0
Thurman, Mike, Mon	.042	.115	.042	24	1	0	0	0	3	0	2	17	6	0-0	.034	.095	.034	89	3	0	0	0	6	0	5	66	13	0-0
Timlin, Mike, Bal-StL	.000	.000	.000	0	0	0	0	0	0	0	0	0	0	0-0	.000	.000	.000	0	0	0	0	0	0	0	0	0	0	0-0
Tolar, Kevin, Det	.000	.000	.000	0	0	0	0	0	0	0	0	0	0	0-0	.000	.000	.000	0	0	0	0	0	0	0	0	0	0	0-0
Tollberg, Brian, SD	.094	.094	.094	32	3	0	0	0	1	1	0	11	6	0-0	.094	.094	.094	32	3	0	0	0	1	1	0	11	6	0-0
Tomko, Brett, Sea	.000	.000	.000	0	0	0	0	0	0	0	0	0	0	0-0	.149	.191	.176	148	22	4	0	0	9	8	8	60	20	0-0
Trachsel, Steve, TB-Tor	.250	.400	.250	4	1	0	0	0	0	0	1	1	0	0-0	.172	.213	.223	355	61	12	0	2	30	23	18	111	47	1-1
Trombley, Mike, Bal	.000	.000	.000	1	0	0	0	0	0	0	0	1	0	0-0	.000	.000	.000	2	0	0	0	0	0	0	0	2	0	0-0
Tucker, T.J., Mon	1.000	1.000	1.000	1	1	0	0	0	1	0	0	0	0	0-0	1.000	1.000	1.000	1	1	0	0	0	1	0	0	0	0	0-0
Turnbow, Derrick, Ana	.000	.000	.000	0	0	0	0	0	0	0	0	0	0	0-0	.000	.000	.000	0	0	0	0	0	0	0	0	0	0	0-0
Urbina, Ugueth, Mon	.000	.000	.000	1	0	0	0	0	0	0	0	1	0	0-0	.096	.130	.096	52	5	0	0	0	3	1	2	31	3	0-0
Valdes, I., ChC-LA	.200	.231	.400	25	5	2	0	1	2	3	1	10	7	0-0	.121	.148	.146	322	39	5	0	1	14	11	10	103	52	3-0
Valdes, Marc, Hou	.000	.000	.000	3	0	0	0	0	0	0	0	2	0	0-0	.093	.152	.093	43	4	0	0	0	1	1	2	15	0	0-0
Van Poppel, Todd, ChC	.000	.000	.000	9	0	0	0	0	0	0	0	4	2	0-0	.130	.167	.174	23	3	1	0	0	3	1	1	8	5	0-0
Vazquez, Javier, Mon	.231	.254	.262	65	15	2	0	0	4	1	2	15	13	0-0	.226	.257	.277	159	36	6	1	0	11	11	7	30	27	0-0
Venafro, Mike, Tex	.000	.000	.000	0	0	0	0	0	0	0	0	0	0	0-0	.000	.000	.000	0	0	0	0	0	0	0	0	0	0	0-0
Veres, Dave, StL	.000	.000	.000	1	0	0	0	0	0	0	0	0	0	0-0	.286	.318	.333	21	6	1	0	0	1	1	1	10	2	0-0
Villafuerte, B., Det	.000	.000	.000	0	0	0	0	0	0	0	0	0	0	0-0	.000	.000	.000	0	0	0	0	0	0	0	0	0	0	0-0
Villegas, Ismael, Atl	.000	.000	.000	1	0	0	0	0	0	0	0	0	0	0-0	.000	.000	.000	1	0	0	0	0	0	0	0	0	0	0-0
Villone, Ron, Cin	.163	.163	.186	43	7	1	0	0	2	4	0	9	2	0-0	.114	.124	.125	88	10	1	0	0	2	4	1	20	7	0-0
Vizcaino, Luis, Oak	.000	.000	.000	0	0	0	0	0	0	0	0	0	0	0-0	.000	.000	.000	0	0	0	0	0	0	0	0	0	0	0-0
Vogelsong, Ryan, SF	.000	.000	.000	0	0	0	0	0	0	0	0	0	0	0-0	.000	.000	.000	0	0	0	0	0	0	0	0	0	0	0-0
Vosberg, Ed, Phi	.000	.000	.000	0	0	0	0	0	0	0	0	0	0	0-0	.000	.000	.000	2	0	0	0	0	0	0	0	1	0	0-0
Wagner, Billy, Hou	.000	.000	.000	2	0	0	0	0	0	0	0	2	0	0-0	.091	.091	.091	11	1	0	0	0	0	0	0	6	0	0-0
Wainhouse, Dave, StL	.000	.000	.000	0	0	0	0	0	0	0	0	0	0	0-0	.000	.000	.000	5	0	0	0	0	0	0	0	1	0	0-0
Wakefield, Tim, Bos	.000	.000	.000	2	0	0	0	0	0	0	0	2	1	0-0	.114	.136	.177	79	9	2	0	1	3	3	2	27	11	0-0
Walker, Kevin, SD	.250	.250	.250	4	1	0	0	0	0	0	0	1	0	0-0	.250	.250	.250	4	1	0	0	0	0	0	0	1	0	0-0
Walker, Pete, Col	.000	.000	.000	0	0	0	0	0	0	0	0	0	0	0-0	.000	.000	.000	0	0	0	0	0	0	0	0	0	0	0-0
Wall, Donne, SD	.000	.000	.000	1	0	0	0	0	0	0	0	1	1	0-0	.176	.211	.191	68	12	1	0	0	5	1	3	22	13	0-0
Wallace, Jeff, Pit	.000	.000	.000	1	0	0	0	0	0	0	0	0	0	0-0	.000	.500	.000	1	0	0	0	0	0	0	1	0	0	0-0
Ward, Bryan, Phi-Ana	.000	.000	.000	0	0	0	0	0	0	0	0	0	0	0-0	.000	1.000	.000	0	0	0	0	0	0	0	1	0	0	0-0
Wasdin, John, Bos-Col	.250	.250	.250	8	2	0	0	0	0	0	0	2	1	0-0	.250	.333	.250	8	2	0	0	0	1	0	1	2	1	0-0

Pitcher, Team	2000 Hitting														Career Hitting													
	Avg	OBP	SLG	AB	H	2B	3B	HR	R	RBI	BB	SO	SH	SB-CS	Avg	OBP	SLG	AB	H	2B	3B	HR	R	RBI	BB	SO	SH	SB-CS
Washburn, Jarrod, Ana	.333	.500	.333	3	1	0	0	0	0	2	1	0	2	0-0	.250	.400	.250	4	1	0	0	0	0	2	1	1	4	0-0
Watson, Allen, NYY	.000	.000	.000	0	0	0	0	0	0	0	0	0	0	0-0	.257	.293	.343	175	45	13	1	0	13	19	9	22	13	0-0
Watson, Mark, Cle	.000	.000	.000	0	0	0	0	0	0	0	0	0	0	0-0	.000	.000	.000	0	0	0	0	0	0	0	0	0	0	0-0
Weathers, Dave, Mil	.000	.000	.000	1	0	0	0	0	0	0	1	0	0	0-0	.108	.153	.154	130	14	0	0	2	7	4	6	81	16	0-0
Weaver, Eric, Ana	.000	.000	.000	0	0	0	0	0	0	0	0	0	0	0-0	.000	.000	.000	1	0	0	0	0	0	0	0	1	0	0-0
Weaver, Jeff, Det	.000	.000	.000	3	0	0	0	0	0	0	2	0	0	0-0	.286	.286	.429	7	2	1	0	0	2	0	0	3	1	0-0
Weber, Ben, SF-Ana	.000	.000	.000	0	0	0	0	0	0	0	0	0	0	0-0	.000	.000	.000	0	0	0	0	0	0	0	0	0	0	0-0
Wells, Bob, Min	.000	.000	.000	0	0	0	0	0	0	0	0	0	0	0-0	.000	1.000	.000	0	0	0	0	0	1	0	1	0	0	0-0
Wells, David, Tor	.167	.167	.167	6	1	0	0	0	0	0	2	0	0	0-0	.136	.136	.136	44	6	0	0	0	2	0	0	8	2	0-0
Wells, Kip, CWS	.000	.000	.000	2	0	0	0	0	0	0	2	0	0	0-0	.000	.000	.000	2	0	0	0	0	0	0	0	2	0	0-0
Wendell, Turk, NYM	.250	.250	.250	4	1	0	0	0	0	0	0	0	0	0-0	.081	.190	.081	37	3	0	0	0	1	0	5	16	1	0-0
Wengert, Don, Atl	.000	.000	.000	0	0	0	0	0	0	0	0	0	0	0-0	.000	.059	.000	16	0	0	0	0	0	0	1	3	1	0-0
Westbrook, Jake, NYY	.000	.000	.000	0	0	0	0	0	0	0	0	0	0	0-0	.000	.000	.000	0	0	0	0	0	0	0	0	0	0	0-0
Wetteland, John, Tex	.000	.000	.000	0	0	0	0	0	0	0	0	0	0	0-0	.167	.167	.286	42	7	2	0	1	4	8	0	19	9	0-0
Wheeler, Dan, TB	.000	.000	.000	0	0	0	0	0	0	0	0	0	0	0-0	.000	.000	.000	0	0	0	0	0	0	0	0	0	0	0-0
Whisenant, Matt, SD	.000	.000	.000	0	0	0	0	0	0	0	0	0	0	0-0	.000	.000	.000	0	0	0	0	0	0	0	0	0	0	0-0
White, Gabe, Cin-Col	.222	.222	.556	9	2	0	0	1	1	2	0	5	1	0-0	.129	.156	.226	31	4	0	0	1	1	3	1	19	9	0-0
White, Rick, TB-NYM	.200	.200	.200	5	1	0	0	0	0	1	0	1	0	0-0	.111	.135	.139	36	4	1	0	0	1	1	0	9	2	0-0
Whiteside, Matt, SD	.000	.000	.000	0	0	0	0	0	0	0	0	0	0	0-0	.000	.000	.000	2	0	0	0	0	0	0	0	2	0	0-0
Wickman, Bob, Mil-Cle	.000	.000	.000	0	0	0	0	0	0	0	0	0	0	0-0	.000	.000	.000	2	0	0	0	0	0	0	0	0	0	0-0
Wilkins, Marc, Pit	.167	.167	.167	6	1	0	0	0	0	0	0	4	0	0-0	.150	.227	.150	20	3	0	0	0	1	2	2	14	1	0-0
Williams, B., ChC-Cle	.500	.500	1.000	2	1	1	0	0	0	1	0	0	0	0-0	.176	.174	.224	85	15	4	0	0	5	9	0	26	15	0-0
Williams, Jeff, LA	.000	.000	.000	0	0	0	0	0	0	0	0	0	0	0-0	.200	.333	.200	5	1	0	0	0	2	0	1	4	1	0-0
Williams, Matt T., Mil	.000	.000	.000	1	0	0	0	0	0	0	1	0	0	0-0	.000	.000	.000	1	0	0	0	0	0	0	0	1	0	0-0
Williams, Mike, Pit	.000	.000	.000	1	0	0	0	0	0	0	0	0	0	0-0	.159	.182	.178	107	17	2	0	0	7	7	3	32	24	1-0
Williams, Woody, SD	.259	.308	.379	58	15	4	0	1	10	9	4	26	1	0-0	.223	.255	.302	139	31	8	0	1	14	15	6	47	5	0-1
Williamson, Scott, Cin	.063	.167	.063	16	1	0	0	0	1	0	2	8	4	0-0	.043	.154	.043	23	1	0	0	0	1	0	3	14	7	0-0
Wilson, Kris, KC	.000	.000	.000	0	0	0	0	0	0	0	0	0	0	0-0	.000	.000	.000	0	0	0	0	0	0	0	0	0	0	0-0
Wilson, Paul, TB	.000	.000	.000	0	0	0	0	0	0	0	0	0	0	0-0	.080	.115	.140	50	4	0	0	1	3	4	1	32	4	0-0
Winchester, Scott, Cin	.000	.000	.000	0	0	0	0	0	0	0	0	0	0	0-0	.130	.167	.130	23	3	0	0	0	0	1	0	9	2	0-0
Wise, Matt, Ana	.000	.000	.000	0	0	0	0	0	0	0	0	0	0	0-0	.000	.000	.000	0	0	0	0	0	0	0	0	0	0	0-0
Witasick, Jay, KC-SD	.115	.148	.115	26	3	0	0	0	0	3	1	12	2	0-0	.097	.125	.097	31	3	0	0	0	0	3	1	16	2	0-0
Witt, Bobby, Cle	.000	.000	.000	0	0	0	0	0	0	0	0	0	0	0-0	.115	.145	.231	52	6	3	0	1	2	5	2	18	5	0-0
Wohlers, Mark, Cin	.000	.000	.000	0	0	0	0	0	0	0	0	0	0	0-0	.083	.083	.083	12	1	0	0	0	1	0	0	11	1	0-0
Wolf, Randy, Phi	.193	.230	.228	57	11	2	0	0	5	4	3	19	10	0-0	.207	.247	.241	87	18	3	0	0	7	4	5	27	17	0-0
Wood, Kerry, ChC	.250	.286	.325	40	10	0	0	1	6	4	2	10	4	0-0	.181	.206	.277	94	17	0	0	3	9	12	3	26	12	0-0
Woodard, S., Mil-Cle	.045	.125	.045	22	1	0	0	0	0	2	1	6	2	0-0	.120	.173	.144	125	15	3	0	0	6	6	7	34	14	0-0
Worrell, Tim, Bal-ChC	.000	.000	.000	2	0	0	0	0	0	0	0	1	0	0-0	.113	.160	.127	71	8	1	0	0	6	4	4	35	9	0-0
Wright, Jamey, Mil	.065	.065	.087	46	3	1	0	0	0	0	0	17	4	0-0	.120	.152	.177	209	25	7	1	1	12	9	8	94	23	0-0
Wright, Jaret, Cle	.000	.000	.000	1	0	0	0	0	0	0	1	1	1	0-0	.250	.250	.250	12	3	0	0	0	2	1	0	5	3	0-0
Wunsch, Kelly, CWS	.000	.000	.000	0	0	0	0	0	0	0	0	0	0	0-0	.000	.000	.000	0	0	0	0	0	0	0	0	0	0	0-0
Yan, Esteban, TB	1.000	1.000	4.000	1	1	0	0	1	1	1	0	0	1	0-0	1.000	1.000	4.000	1	1	0	0	1	1	1	0	0	1	0-0
Yarnall, Ed, NYY	.000	.000	.000	0	0	0	0	0	0	0	0	0	0	0-0	.000	.000	.000	0	0	0	0	0	0	0	0	0	0	0-0
Yoshii, Masato, Col	.180	.212	.260	50	9	1	0	1	4	8	2	13	12	1-0	.137	.165	.170	153	21	2	0	1	8	13	5	56	26	1-1
Young, Danny, ChC	.000	.000	.000	0	0	0	0	0	0	0	0	0	0	0-0	.000	.000	.000	0	0	0	0	0	0	0	0	0	0	0-0
Young, Tim, Bos	.000	.000	.000	0	0	0	0	0	0	0	0	0	0	0-0	.000	.000	.000	0	0	0	0	0	0	0	0	0	0	0-0
Zerbe, Chad, SF	.000	.000	.000	0	0	0	0	0	0	0	0	0	0	0-0	.000	.000	.000	0	0	0	0	0	0	0	0	0	0	0-0
Zimmerman, Jeff, Tex	.000	.000	.000	0	0	0	0	0	0	0	0	0	0	0-0	.000	.000	.000	0	0	0	0	0	0	0	0	0	0	0-0
Zito, Barry, Oak	.000	.000	.000	0	0	0	0	0	0	0	0	0	0	0-0	.000	.000	.000	0	0	0	0	0	0	0	0	0	0	0-0

Pitchers Fielding and Holding Runners

2000 Fielding and Holding Runners

Pitcher, Team	G	Inn	PO	A	E	DP	Pct.	SBA	CS	PCS	PPO	CS%
Abbott, Paul, Sea	35	179.0	12	19	1	3	.969	10	4	0	0	.40
Acevedo, Juan, Mil	62	82.2	8	8	0	0	1.000	12	6	0	0	.50
Adams, Terry, LA	66	84.1	14	21	2	0	.946	3	2	0	0	.67
Aguilera, Rick, ChC	54	47.2	6	7	0	0	1.000	4	0	0	0	.00
Aldred, Scott, Phi	23	20.1	1	2	0	0	1.000	2	0	0	0	.00
Alfonseca, Antonio, Fla	68	70.0	1	14	1	1	.938	2	0	0	0	.00
Almanza, Armando, Fla	67	46.1	1	3	0	0	1.000	7	2	1	0	.43
Almanzar, Carlos, SD	62	69.2	3	11	0	0	1.000	9	1	0	0	.11
Alvarez, Juan, Ana	11	6.0	2	0	0	1	1.000	0	0	0	0	.00
Anderson, Brian, Ari	33	213.1	13	47	1	4	.984	15	0	7	3	.47
Anderson, Jimmy, Pit	27	144.0	5	31	1	2	.973	15	4	0	0	.27
Anderson, Matt, Det	69	74.1	4	6	0	0	1.000	10	3	1	0	.40
Andrews, Clayton, Tor	8	20.2	0	1	0	0	1.000	2	1	0	0	.50
Ankiel, Rick, StL	31	175.0	8	14	7	2	.759	16	6	1	0	.44
Appier, Kevin, Oak	31	195.1	8	14	1	1	.957	16	7	0	0	.44
Armas Jr., Tony, Mon	17	95.0	7	12	0	1	1.000	7	2	0	1	.29
Arnold, Jamie, LA-ChC	14	39.1	1	4	0	0	1.000	4	2	0	0	.50
Arrojo, R., Col-Bos	32	172.2	16	28	4	5	.917	16	5	1	2	.38
Arroyo, Bronson, Pit	20	71.2	3	5	1	0	.889	8	3	0	0	.38
Ashby, Andy, Phi-Atl	31	199.1	14	30	3	0	.936	21	6	0	0	.29
Astacio, Pedro, Col	32	196.1	20	22	0	0	1.000	23	8	0	0	.35
Aybar, M., Col-Cin-Fla	54	79.1	9	14	0	0	1.000	3	0	1	0	.33
Baldwin, James, CWS	29	178.0	14	26	2	2	.952	16	8	0	2	.50
Bale, John, Tor	2	3.2	0	0	0	0	.000	1	0	0	0	.00
Barcelo, Lorenzo, CWS	22	39.0	0	1	0	0	1.000	3	3	0	0	1.00
Batista, M., Mon-KC	18	65.1	4	4	1	0	.889	10	4	0	0	.40
Beck, Rod, Bos	34	40.2	0	3	0	0	1.000	3	1	0	0	.33
Beirne, Kevin, CWS	29	49.2	2	4	1	0	.857	5	0	2	0	.40
Belcher, Tim, Ana	9	40.2	1	5	0	0	1.000	1	1	0	0	1.00
Belinda, Stan, Col-Atl	56	46.2	3	3	1	0	.857	6	0	0	0	.00
Belitz, Todd, Oak	5	3.1	0	0	0	0	.000	0	0	0	0	.00
Bell, Rob, Cin	26	140.1	8	14	2	0	.917	20	1	0	0	.05
Beltran, Rigo, Col	1	1.1	0	0	0	0	.000	0	0	0	0	.00
Benes, Alan, StL	30	46.0	2	4	0	0	1.000	2	0	0	0	.00
Benes, Andy, StL	30	166.0	4	17	0	1	1.000	22	7	0	0	.32
Benitez, Armando, NYM	76	76.0	2	2	0	0	1.000	11	1	1	0	.18
Benson, Kris, Pit	32	217.2	8	28	2	0	.947	17	5	1	1	.35
Bere, Jason, Mil-Cle	31	169.1	17	19	0	2	1.000	9	6	0	0	.67
Bergman, Sean, Min	15	68.0	8	12	1	2	.952	12	0	0	0	.00
Bernero, Adam, Det	12	34.1	2	6	0	2	1.000	2	0	0	0	.00
Biddle, Rocky, CWS	4	22.2	1	3	1	0	.800	3	1	0	1	.33
Blair, Willie, Det	47	156.2	4	13	0	1	1.000	3	1	0	0	.33
Blank, Matt, Mon	13	14.0	1	1	0	0	1.000	0	0	0	0	.00
Bochtler, Doug, KC	6	8.1	0	0	0	0	.000	3	0	0	0	.00
Boehringer, Brian, SD	7	15.2	0	0	0	0	.000	3	3	0	0	1.00
Bohanon, Brian, Col	34	177.0	11	23	1	3	.971	19	2	2	0	.21
Bones, Ricky, Fla	56	77.1	3	11	0	0	1.000	10	0	0	0	.00
Borbon, Pedro, Tor	59	41.2	2	9	0	1	1.000	5	0	0	0	.00
Borkowski, Dave, Det	2	5.1	0	0	0	0	.000	1	0	0	0	.00
Bottalico, Ricky, KC	62	72.2	6	7	1	1	.929	9	5	0	0	.56
Bottenfield, K., Ana-Phi	29	171.2	9	26	1	1	.972	13	6	1	2	.54
Boyd, Jason, Phi	30	34.1	2	5	0	0	1.000	3	1	0	0	.33
Bradford, Chad, CWS	12	13.2	0	2	0	0	1.000	2	1	0	0	.50
Brantley, Jeff, Phi	55	55.1	3	2	0	0	1.000	8	2	0	0	.25
Brea, Lesli, Bal	6	9.0	0	0	0	0	.000	3	0	0	0	.00
Brewington, Jamie, Cle	26	45.1	4	4	0	1	1.000	3	0	0	0	.00
Brocail, Doug, Det	49	50.2	7	7	1	0	.933	1	1	0	0	1.00
Brock, Chris, Phi	63	93.1	4	7	0	0	1.000	6	0	0	1	.00
Brower, Jim, Cle	17	62.0	9	12	1	1	.955	12	4	0	0	.33
Brown, Kevin, LA	33	230.0	35	33	4	1	.944	25	4	1	1	.20
Brownson, Mark, Phi	2	5.0	1	1	0	0	1.000	0	0	0	0	.00
Brunette, Justin, StL	4	4.2	0	1	0	0	1.000	0	0	0	0	.00
Bruske, Jim, Mil	15	16.2	1	1	0	0	1.000	2	0	0	0	.00
Buddie, Mike, Mil	5	6.0	0	0	0	0	.000	2	0	0	0	.00
Buehrle, Mark, CWS	28	51.1	1	9	1	2	.909	4	1	2	2	.75
Bullinger, Kirk, Phi	3	3.1	0	1	0	0	1.000	0	0	0	0	.00
Burba, Dave, Cle	32	191.1	10	27	0	0	1.000	27	4	0	1	.15
Burkett, John, Atl	31	134.1	10	15	1	1	.962	9	1	1	1	.22
Burnett, A.J., Fla	13	82.2	2	8	1	1	.909	12	4	0	1	.33
Byrd, Paul, Phi	17	83.0	6	9	1	1	.938	9	3	0	0	.33
Byrdak, Tim, KC	12	6.1	1	0	0	0	1.000	0	0	0	0	.00
Cabrera, Jose, Hou	52	59.1	4	5	0	0	1.000	5	1	0	1	.20
Cairncross, Cam, Cle	15	9.1	0	1	1	0	.500	2	0	1	0	.50
Cammack, Eric, NYM	8	10.0	1	1	0	0	1.000	3	0	0	0	.00
Carlyle, Buddy, SD	4	3.0	1	0	0	0	1.000	0	0	0	0	.00
Carpenter, Chris, Tor	34	175.1	7	12	1	2	.950	11	7	0	0	.64
Carrara, Giovanni, Col	8	13.1	3	0	0	0	1.000	2	0	0	0	.00
Carrasco, H., Min-Bos	69	78.2	2	12	1	0	.933	7	3	0	0	.43
Castillo, Frank, Tor	25	138.0	8	19	1	4	.964	20	5	1	0	.30
Charlton, Norm, Cin	2	3.0	0	1	0	0	1.000	0	0	0	0	.00
Chen, Bruce, Atl-Phi	37	134.0	1	14	0	1	1.000	11	2	3	0	.45
Choate, Randy, NYY	22	17.0	0	3	1	0	.750	3	0	0	0	.00
Chouinard, Bobby, Col	31	32.2	2	2	0	0	1.000	5	1	0	0	.20
Christiansen, J., Pit-StL	65	48.0	1	9	0	0	1.000	2	1	0	0	.50
Clark, Mark, Tex	12	44.0	1	6	0	3	1.000	1	1	0	0	1.00
Clemens, Roger, NYY	32	204.1	14	32	2	2	.958	22	5	0	2	.23
Clement, Matt, SD	34	205.0	27	25	4	4	.929	17	5	0	0	.29
Clontz, Brad, Pit	5	7.0	0	1	0	0	1.000	4	2	0	0	.50
Coco, Pasqual, Tor	1	4.0	0	0	0	0	.000	1	0	0	0	.00

2000 Fielding and Holding Runners

Pitcher, Team	G	Inn	PO	A	E	DP	Pct.	SBA	CS	PCS	PPO	CS%
Coggin, Dave, Phi	5	27.0	0	4	1	0	.800	4	1	0	0	.25
Colon, Bartolo, Cle	30	188.0	17	18	2	1	.946	7	2	2	0	.57
Cone, David, NYY	30	155.0	9	20	2	0	.935	23	7	0	0	.30
Cook, Dennis, NYM	68	59.0	4	10	0	2	1.000	9	0	1	2	.11
Cooper, Brian, Ana	15	87.0	3	12	2	1	.882	9	1	1	0	.22
Cordero, Francisco, Tex	55	77.1	4	5	1	0	.900	5	2	0	0	.40
Cordova, Francisco, Pit	18	95.0	6	20	3	1	.897	7	2	1	4	.43
Cormier, Rheal, Bos	64	68.1	1	14	0	0	1.000	7	0	1	0	.14
Cornelius, Reid, Fla	22	125.0	8	26	0	3	1.000	10	3	2	0	.50
Crabtree, Tim, Tex	68	80.1	5	11	0	3	1.000	6	3	0	0	.50
Crawford, Paxton, Bos	7	29.0	1	0	0	0	1.000	5	1	0	0	.20
Creek, Doug, TB	45	60.2	2	9	0	1	1.000	8	2	1	0	.38
Cressend, Jack, Min	11	13.2	1	0	0	0	1.000	0	0	0	0	.00
Croushore, R., Col-Bos	11	16.0	0	1	0	0	1.000	2	0	0	0	.00
Cruz, Nelson, Det	26	41.0	1	6	0	1	1.000	2	1	0	1	.50
Cubillan, D., Tor-Tex	20	33.1	2	4	0	1	1.000	2	1	1	0	1.00
Cunnane, Will, SD	27	38.1	4	4	0	0	1.000	5	3	1	0	.80
D'Amico, Jeff, Mil	23	162.1	9	13	0	1	1.000	11	8	0	0	.73
D'Amico, Jeff M., KC	7	13.2	1	1	0	0	1.000	1	1	0	0	1.00
Daal, Omar, Ari-Phi	32	167.0	8	31	4	1	.907	6	3	1	2	.67
Darensbourg, Vic, Fla	56	62.0	6	12	0	1	1.000	10	1	2	0	.30
Davey, Tom, SD	11	12.2	0	4	0	0	1.000	0	0	0	1	.00
Davis, Doug, Tex	30	98.2	3	17	1	0	.952	6	3	0	1	.50
Davis, Kane, Cle-Mil	8	15.0	1	3	0	0	1.000	1	0	0	0	.00
de los Santos, V., Mil	66	73.2	4	8	0	1	1.000	3	0	0	0	.00
DeJean, Mike, Col	54	53.1	2	8	0	1	1.000	5	1	0	0	.20
del Toro, Miguel, SF	9	17.1	0	3	0	0	1.000	1	0	0	0	.00
Dempster, Ryan, Fla	33	226.1	11	29	4	2	.909	22	8	1	0	.41
DePaula, Sean, Cle	13	16.2	4	2	0	0	1.000	7	0	0	0	.00
Dessens, Elmer, Cin	40	147.1	10	26	0	3	1.000	6	3	0	1	.50
DeWitt, Matt, Tor	8	13.2	2	1	0	0	1.000	0	0	0	0	.00
Dickson, Jason, Ana	6	28.0	3	2	0	0	1.000	2	2	0	0	1.00
Dingman, Craig, NYY	10	11.0	0	0	0	0	.000	1	0	0	0	.00
Dipoto, Jerry, Col	17	13.2	0	2	0	0	1.000	5	1	0	1	.20
Dotel, Octavio, Hou	50	125.0	4	14	1	1	.947	20	1	2	2	.15
Downs, Scott, ChC-Mon	19	97.0	3	11	0	1	1.000	6	2	2	0	.67
Dreifort, Darren, LA	32	192.2	19	36	1	2	.982	29	9	1	0	.34
Drew, Tim, Cle	3	9.0	1	3	1	0	.800	3	2	0	0	.67
Durbin, Chad, KC	16	72.1	8	7	1	2	.938	5	0	0	0	.00
Duvall, Mike, TB	2	2.1	0	1	0	0	1.000	0	0	0	0	.00
Eaton, Adam, SD	22	135.0	7	18	1	2	.962	11	4	0	0	.36
Eiland, Dave, TB	17	54.2	6	15	0	0	1.000	14	3	0	0	.21
Einertson, Darrell, NYY	11	12.2	0	2	0	0	1.000	0	0	0	0	.00
Elarton, Scott, Hou	30	192.2	14	21	0	4	1.000	8	2	0	1	.25
Eldred, Cal, CWS	20	112.0	8	13	0	2	1.000	15	4	0	0	.27
Embree, Alan, SF	63	60.0	0	9	0	3	1.000	7	1	0	0	.14
Enders, Trevor, TB	9	9.1	2	2	0	0	1.000	1	0	0	0	.00
Erdos, Todd, NYY-SD	36	54.2	2	5	0	0	1.000	3	0	0	0	.00
Erickson, Scott, Bal	16	92.2	7	5	3	0	.800	11	1	0	0	.09
Escobar, Kelvim, Tor	43	180.0	11	15	1	1	.963	20	3	0	2	.15
Estes, Shawn, SF	30	190.1	11	43	2	7	.964	20	3	3	0	.30
Estrada, Horacio, Mil	7	24.1	1	6	1	0	.875	2	1	0	0	.50
Estrella, Leo, Tor	2	4.2	0	1	0	0	1.000	1	1	0	0	1.00
Etherton, Seth, Ana	11	60.1	1	11	0	1	1.000	8	2	1	0	.38
Eyre, Scott, CWS	13	19.0	0	3	0	0	1.000	3	1	1	0	.67
Farnsworth, Kyle, ChC	46	77.0	4	6	2	1	.833	10	2	1	0	.30
Fassero, Jeff, Bos	38	130.0	11	18	1	3	.967	23	0	5	0	.22
Fernandez, Alex, Fla	8	52.1	6	8	0	1	1.000	6	3	0	0	.50
Fernandez, O., Cin	15	79.2	6	10	2	3	.889	4	0	1	0	.25
Fetters, Mike, LA	51	50.0	7	7	0	2	1.000	5	1	0	1	.20
Figueroa, Nelson, Ari	3	15.2	1	2	0	0	1.000	3	1	1	0	.67
Finley, Chuck, Cle	34	218.0	11	20	4	1	.886	22	9	0	0	.41
Fiore, Tony, TB	11	15.0	1	1	0	0	1.000	4	1	0	0	.25
Florie, Bryce, Bos	29	49.1	7	12	0	1	1.000	0	0	0	0	.00
Ford, Ben, NYY	4	11.0	0	1	0	0	1.000	1	0	0	0	.00
Forster, Scott, Mon	42	32.0	3	5	0	0	1.000	4	1	0	0	.25
Foulke, Keith, CWS	72	88.0	7	3	0	1	1.000	8	3	0	0	.38
Franco, John, NYM	62	55.2	1	8	1	0	.900	8	0	1	0	.13
Franklin, Wayne, Hou	25	21.1	1	1	0	0	1.000	2	0	0	0	.00
Frascatore, John, Tor	60	73.0	7	5	1	2	.923	6	1	0	0	.17
Fultz, Aaron, SF	58	69.1	5	17	0	2	1.000	3	1	0	1	.33
Fussell, Chris, KC	20	70.0	9	4	1	0	.929	6	2	0	0	.33
Fyhrie, Mike, Ana	32	52.2	1	6	0	0	1.000	1	0	0	0	.00
Gagne, Eric, LA	20	101.1	6	8	0	1	1.000	21	2	0	0	.10
Garces, Rich, Bos	64	74.2	5	6	0	0	1.000	13	2	0	0	.15
Garcia, Freddy, Sea	21	124.1	5	19	3	1	.889	14	0	2	0	.14
Garcia, Mike, Pit	13	11.1	0	1	0	0	1.000	4	2	0	0	.50
Gardner, Mark, SF	30	149.0	5	10	1	1	.938	10	6	0	0	.60
Garibay, Daniel, ChC	30	74.2	8	19	0	0	1.000	14	0	6	0	.43
Garland, Jon, CWS	15	69.2	2	10	2	0	.857	9	3	1	1	.44
Ginter, Matt, CWS	7	9.1	0	1	0	0	1.000	0	0	0	0	.00
Glauber, Keith, Cin	4	7.1	1	0	0	1	1.000	0	0	0	0	.00
Glavine, Tom, Atl	35	241.0	11	42	0	5	1.000	26	7	3	0	.38
Glynn, Ryan, Tex	16	88.2	9	12	0	1	1.000	2	2	0	1	1.00
Gomes, Wayne, Phi	65	73.2	2	6	1	0	.889	7	1	0	0	.14
Gooden, Hou-TB-NYY	27	105.0	4	17	1	3	.955	17	5	1	0	.35
Graves, Danny, Cin	66	91.1	5	24	1	4	.967	6	1	0	0	.17
Green, Jason, Hou	14	17.2	0	2	2	0	.500	10	2	0	0	.20
Grilli, Jason, Fla	1	6.2	0	1	0	0	1.000	1	0	0	0	.00

2000 Fielding and Holding Runners

Pitcher, Team	G	Inn	PO	A	E	DP	Pct.	SBA	CS	PCS	PPO	CS%
Grimsley, Jason, NYY	63	96.1	11	11	2	4	.917	4	1	0	0	.25
Groom, Buddy, Bal	70	59.1	2	10	2	1	.857	3	0	1	0	.33
Gross, Kip, Hou	2	4.1	0	0	1	0	.000	0	0	0	0	.00
Guardado, Eddie, Min	70	61.2	0	3	0	0	1.000	4	1	1	0	.50
Gunderson, Eric, Tor	6	6.1	0	2	1	0	.667	0	0	0	0	.00
Guthrie, ChC-TB-Tor	76	71.1	1	9	0	0	1.000	10	4	1	1	.50
Guzman, Domingo, SD	1	1.0	0	0	0	0	.000	0	0	0	0	.00
Guzman, Geraldo, Ari	13	60.1	0	3	0	0	1.000	4	1	0	0	.25
Guzman, Juan, TB	1	1.2	0	0	0	0	.000	1	0	0	0	.00
Hackman, Luther, StL	1	2.2	0	1	0	0	1.000	0	0	0	0	.00
Halama, John, Sea	30	166.2	4	27	3	3	.912	14	2	7	3	.64
Halladay, Roy, Tor	19	67.2	4	7	0	0	1.000	6	3	0	0	.50
Hamilton, Joey, Tor	6	33.0	2	2	0	1	1.000	3	1	0	0	.33
Hampton, Mike, NYM	33	217.2	10	45	2	2	.965	19	6	4	2	.53
Haney, Chris, Cle	1	1.0	0	1	0	0	1.000	0	0	0	0	.00
Harnisch, Pete, Cin	22	131.0	6	17	0	1	1.000	9	4	0	0	.44
Harper, Travis, TB	6	32.0	1	3	0	0	1.000	4	1	0	0	.25
Hasegawa, S., Ana	66	95.2	6	10	0	1	1.000	4	1	0	0	.25
Hawkins, LaTroy, Min	66	87.2	3	16	2	1	.905	7	1	1	0	.29
Haynes, Jimmy, Mil	33	199.1	16	34	2	5	.962	16	9	0	1	.56
Helling, Rick, Tex	35	217.0	8	17	1	1	.962	21	4	1	0	.24
Henry, Doug, Hou-SF	72	78.1	4	9	1	1	.929	10	2	0	0	.20
Hentgen, Pat, StL	33	194.1	14	23	1	1	.974	29	15	1	0	.55
Heredia, Felix, ChC	74	58.2	2	4	0	0	1.000	1	1	0	0	1.00
Heredia, Gil, Oak	32	198.2	9	29	1	0	.974	19	7	0	0	.37
Herges, Matt, LA	59	110.2	4	20	1	2	.960	13	6	0	0	.46
Hermanson, D., Mon	38	198.0	10	27	3	2	.925	15	7	0	4	.47
Hernandez, Livan, SF	33	240.0	18	44	0	4	1.000	12	8	0	0	.67
Hernandez, O., NYY	29	195.2	12	24	0	4	1.000	19	7	0	0	.37
Hernandez, R., TB	68	73.1	4	11	1	1	.938	8	2	0	0	.25
Hershiser, Orel, LA	10	24.2	1	6	0	0	1.000	5	0	0	0	.00
Hiljus, Erik, Det	3	3.2	0	0	0	0	.000	0	0	0	0	.00
Hill, Ken, Ana-CWS	18	81.2	5	14	1	1	.950	26	11	1	0	.46
Hinchliffe, Brett, Ana	2	1.2	0	0	0	0	.000	0	0	0	0	.00
Hitchcock, Sterling, SD	11	65.2	0	9	0	0	1.000	12	2	1	1	.25
Hodges, Kevin, Sea	13	17.1	1	1	0	0	1.000	2	0	0	0	.00
Hoffman, Trevor, SD	70	72.1	2	7	0	0	1.000	5	1	0	0	.20
Holmes, D., Ari-StL-Bal	18	19.1	3	0	0	0	1.000	1	0	0	0	.00
Holt, Chris, Hou	34	207.0	13	27	3	4	.930	19	7	1	1	.42
Holtz, Mike, Ana	61	41.0	3	7	0	0	1.000	5	0	0	0	.00
Holzemer, Mark, Phi	25	25.2	0	4	0	0	1.000	3	0	0	0	.00
House, Craig, Col	16	13.2	0	3	0	0	1.000	0	0	0	0	.00
Howry, Bob, CWS	65	71.0	3	6	0	1	1.000	9	3	0	0	.33
Hudson, Tim, Oak	32	202.1	15	20	4	1	.897	27	2	1	0	.11
Irabu, Hideki, Mon	11	54.2	2	6	0	0	1.000	13	1	0	0	.08
Isringhausen, J., Oak	66	69.0	1	11	1	0	.923	8	0	0	0	.00
Jacquez, Tom, Phi	9	7.1	1	1	0	0	1.000	1	0	0	0	.00
James, Mike, StL	51	51.1	2	5	0	0	1.000	6	1	1	0	.33
Jarvis, Kevin, Col	24	115.0	14	12	0	4	1.000	6	1	1	1	.33
Jimenez, Jose, Col	72	70.2	5	8	2	1	.867	3	1	0	0	.33
Johnson, Jason, Bal	25	107.2	3	4	0	0	1.000	22	5	0	0	.23
Johnson, Jonathan, Tex	15	29.0	1	7	0	0	1.000	4	0	0	1	.00
Johnson, Mark, Det	9	24.0	1	5	0	0	1.000	0	0	0	0	.00
Johnson, Mike, Mon	41	101.1	4	12	1	1	.941	13	3	0	0	.23
Johnson, Randy, Ari	35	248.2	5	22	3	1	.900	42	12	4	2	.38
Johnstone, John, SF	47	50.0	3	6	0	1	1.000	12	3	0	0	.25
Jones, Bobby J., NYM	27	154.2	9	13	1	0	.957	24	3	0	0	.13
Jones, Bobby M., NYM	11	21.2	3	3	0	0	1.000	0	0	0	0	.00
Jones, Doug, Oak	54	73.1	6	10	1	0	.941	4	1	1	0	.50
Jones, Marcus, Oak	1	2.1	0	0	0	0	.000	1	0	0	0	.00
Jones, Todd, Det	67	64.0	3	2	0	0	1.000	3	2	0	0	.67
Judd, Mike, LA	1	4.0	0	0	0	0	.000	0	0	0	0	.00
Kamieniecki, S., Cle-Atl	52	58.0	3	14	1	1	.944	5	0	0	0	.00
Karchner, Matt, ChC	13	14.2	2	3	0	0	1.000	5	1	0	0	.20
Karl, Scott, Col-Ana	23	87.1	4	13	2	2	.895	8	3	0	0	.38
Karsay, Steve, Cle	72	76.2	9	13	1	0	.957	1	0	0	0	.00
Keisler, Randy, NYY	4	10.2	0	0	0	0	.000	2	2	0	0	1.00
Kida, Masao, Det	2	2.2	2	1	0	0	1.000	0	0	0	0	.00
Kile, Darryl, StL	34	232.1	12	30	1	3	.977	13	11	0	0	.85
Kim, Byung-Hyun, Ari	61	70.2	2	7	1	0	.900	18	3	0	0	.17
King, Ray, Mil	36	28.2	2	6	0	0	1.000	1	1	0	0	1.00
Kinney, Matt, Min	8	42.1	3	5	1	0	.889	3	0	0	0	.00
Kline, Steve, Mon	83	82.1	4	10	1	1	.933	1	0	0	0	.00
Koch, Billy, Tor	68	78.2	5	8	0	2	1.000	5	1	0	0	.20
Kohlmeier, Ryan, Bal	25	26.1	2	2	0	0	1.000	2	0	0	0	.00
Kolb, Brandon, SD	11	14.0	0	1	1	0	.500	0	0	0	0	.00
Kolb, Danny, Tex	1	0.2	0	0	0	0	.000	0	0	0	0	.00
Lara, Yovanny, Mon	6	5.2	0	0	0	0	.000	1	0	0	0	.00
Larkin, Andy, Cin-KC	21	26.0	3	1	0	0	1.000	4	0	0	0	.00
Laxton, Brett, KC	6	16.2	0	0	0	0	.000	0	0	0	0	.00
Lee, David, Col	7	5.2	0	0	1	0	.000	1	0	0	0	.00
Lee, Sang-Hoon, Bos	9	11.2	0	2	0	0	1.000	0	0	0	0	.00
Leiter, Al, NYM	31	208.0	5	34	0	2	1.000	35	3	10	0	.37
Leskanic, Curtis, Mil	73	77.1	12	11	0	0	1.000	7	1	1	0	.29
Levine, Al, Ana	51	95.1	4	13	1	0	.944	12	6	0	0	.50
Levrault, Allen, Mil	5	12.0	1	0	0	0	1.000	2	0	0	0	.00
Lidle, Cory, TB	31	96.2	6	19	1	1	.962	9	1	0	0	.11
Lieber, Jon, ChC	35	251.0	30	31	1	1	.984	14	5	0	0	.36
Ligtenberg, Kerry, Atl	59	52.1	0	4	0	1	1.000	6	0	0	0	.00
Lilly, Ted, NYY	7	8.0	1	1	0	0	1.000	0	0	0	0	.00
Lima, Jose, Hou	33	196.1	16	22	1	3	.974	19	5	0	0	.26
Lincoln, Mike, Min	8	20.2	1	2	0	0	1.000	2	1	0	0	.50

2000 Fielding and Holding Runners

Pitcher, Team	G	Inn	PO	A	E	DP	Pct.	SBA	CS	PCS	PPO	CS%
Linebrink, S., SF-Hou	11	12.0	0	1	0	0	1.000	1	0	0	0	.00
Lira, Felipe, Mon	53	101.2	4	17	0	3	1.000	10	2	0	0	.20
Loaiza, E., Tex-Tor	34	199.1	12	29	3	4	.932	12	4	0	0	.33
Loiselle, Rich, Pit	40	42.1	2	5	1	0	.875	7	2	0	0	.29
Looper, Braden, Fla	73	67.1	6	10	1	1	.941	10	4	0	0	.40
Lopez, Albie, TB	45	185.1	12	17	3	2	.906	18	3	0	0	.17
Lopez, Rodrigo, SD	6	24.2	4	3	0	1	1.000	2	1	0	1	.50
Lorraine, A., ChC-Cle	18	41.1	1	2	0	0	1.000	1	0	1	0	1.00
Lowe, Derek, Bos	74	91.1	8	11	0	0	1.000	9	0	0	0	.00
Lowe, Sean, CWS	50	70.2	3	8	1	0	.917	7	0	3	2	.43
Luebbers, Larry, Cin	14	20.1	1	6	0	0	1.000	2	1	0	0	.50
Maddux, Greg, Atl	35	249.1	25	69	2	5	.979	39	7	0	0	.18
Maddux, Mike, Hou	21	27.1	1	6	0	0	1.000	2	0	0	0	.00
Maduro, Calvin, Bal	15	23.1	1	2	0	0	1.000	1	0	0	0	.00
Magnante, Mike, Oak	55	39.2	3	14	1	1	.944	4	1	1	0	.50
Mahay, Ron, Oak-Fla	23	41.1	2	6	0	0	1.000	4	0	1	0	.25
Mahomes, Pat, NYM	53	94.0	9	15	0	2	1.000	23	4	1	1	.22
Mairena, Oswaldo, ChC	2	2.0	0	0	0	0	.000	0	0	0	0	.00
Mann, Jim, NYM	2	2.2	0	0	0	0	.000	1	0	0	0	.00
Mantei, Matt, Ari	47	45.1	4	2	1	1	.857	10	2	0	0	.20
Manzanillo, Josias, Pit	43	58.2	2	5	0	0	1.000	6	2	0	0	.33
Marquis, Jason, Atl	15	23.1	1	4	0	0	1.000	1	0	0	0	.00
Martin, Tom, Cle	31	33.1	5	3	1	0	.889	2	0	1	0	.50
Martinez, Pedro, Bos	29	217.0	14	28	0	2	1.000	13	3	0	2	.23
Martinez, Ramon, Bos	27	127.2	16	7	0	0	1.000	23	7	1	0	.35
Martinez, Willie, Cle	1	3.0	0	2	0	0	1.000	0	0	0	0	.00
Masaoka, Onan, LA	29	27.0	1	2	0	0	1.000	5	1	1	0	.40
Mathews, T.J., Oak	50	59.2	2	11	0	1	1.000	3	0	0	0	.00
Matthews, Mike, StL	14	9.1	0	1	0	0	1.000	1	0	0	0	.00
Maurer, Dave, SD	14	14.2	2	0	0	0	1.000	3	0	0	0	.00
Mays, Joe, Min	31	160.1	9	24	2	2	.943	10	2	1	0	.30
McDill, Allen, Det	13	10.0	0	1	0	0	1.000	2	0	0	0	.00
McElroy, Chuck, Bal	43	63.1	3	6	1	1	.900	5	0	1	0	.20
McGlinchy, Kevin, Atl	10	8.1	0	2	0	0	1.000	2	0	0	0	.00
McKnight, Tony, Hou	6	35.0	1	6	0	1	1.000	6	0	0	0	.00
McMichael, Greg, Atl	15	16.1	1	2	0	0	1.000	4	2	0	0	.50
Meacham, Rusty, Hou	5	4.2	1	0	0	1	1.000	0	0	0	0	.00
Meadows, B., SD-KC	33	196.1	15	25	1	2	.976	15	5	0	1	.33
Meche, Gil, Sea	15	85.2	7	7	0	0	1.000	4	2	0	0	.50
Mecir, Jim, TB-Oak	63	85.0	3	7	0	1	1.000	15	2	0	1	.13
Mendoza, Ramiro, NYY	14	65.2	2	8	0	0	1.000	6	2	0	0	.33
Mercado, Hector, Cin	12	14.0	0	1	0	0	1.000	1	1	0	0	1.00
Mercedes, Jose, Bal	36	145.2	2	16	0	0	1.000	9	5	0	0	.56
Mercker, Kent, Ana	21	48.1	1	5	1	1	.857	2	0	0	0	.00
Mesa, Jose, Sea	66	80.2	7	8	0	0	1.000	6	0	0	0	.00
Miceli, Dan, Fla	45	48.2	6	1	0	0	1.000	5	2	0	0	.40
Miller, Travis, Min	67	67.0	2	6	0	0	1.000	7	1	1	0	.29
Miller, Trever, Phi-LA	16	16.1	3	1	0	1	1.000	2	0	0	0	.00
Miller, Wade, Hou	16	105.0	9	11	0	4	1.000	10	2	0	0	.20
Mills, Alan, LA-Bal	41	49.1	6	4	1	0	.909	5	1	0	1	.20
Millwood, Kevin, Atl	36	212.2	4	19	0	1	1.000	17	5	1	1	.35
Milton, Eric, Min	33	200.0	7	15	1	0	.957	6	2	0	0	.33
Mlicki, Dave, Det	24	119.1	12	14	0	3	1.000	4	0	0	0	.00
Moehler, Brian, Det	29	178.0	13	30	0	5	1.000	7	1	0	1	.14
Mohler, Mike, StL-Cle	24	20.0	1	0	0	0	1.000	1	1	0	0	1.00
Molina, Gabe, Bal-Atl	11	15.0	1	1	0	0	1.000	2	1	0	0	.50
Montgomery, Steve, SD	7	5.2	0	1	0	0	1.000	0	0	0	0	.00
Moore, Trey, Mon	8	35.1	2	2	1	0	.800	7	2	0	0	.29
Moraga, D., Mon-Col	4	2.2	1	0	0	0	1.000	1	0	0	0	.00
Morgan, Mike, Ari	60	101.2	5	13	0	1	1.000	9	3	1	1	.44
Morris, Jim, TB	16	10.1	0	0	0	0	.000	0	0	0	0	.00
Morris, Matt, StL	31	53.0	3	3	0	1	1.000	7	3	0	0	.43
Mota, Danny, Min	4	5.1	0	0	0	0	.000	0	0	0	0	.00
Mota, Guillermo, Mon	29	30.0	1	3	0	1	1.000	0	0	0	0	.00
Moyer, Jamie, Sea	26	154.0	11	27	1	1	.974	17	2	1	0	.18
Mulder, Mark, Oak	27	154.0	7	22	3	1	.906	14	3	3	0	.43
Mulholland, Terry, Atl	54	156.2	6	18	3	1	.889	4	3	0	1	.75
Mullen, Scott, KC	11	10.1	0	1	0	0	1.000	1	0	0	0	.00
Munoz, Mike, Tex	7	4.0	0	0	0	0	.000	1	1	0	0	1.00
Munro, Peter, Tor	9	25.2	2	3	0	2	1.000	4	1	0	0	.25
Murray, Dan, KC	10	19.1	4	4	0	0	1.000	1	1	0	0	1.00
Mussina, Mike, Bal	34	237.2	17	26	1	1	.977	19	3	0	0	.16
Myers, Mike, Col	78	45.1	3	7	0	3	1.000	3	0	0	0	.00
Myers, Rodney, SD	3	2.0	0	0	0	0	.000	0	0	0	0	.00
Myette, Aaron, CWS	2	2.2	0	0	0	0	.000	1	0	0	0	.00
Nagy, Charles, Cle	11	57.0	12	13	0	0	1.000	6	1	0	0	.17
Nathan, Joe, SF	20	93.1	8	11	0	0	1.000	14	5	0	1	.36
Nation, Joey, ChC	2	11.2	0	3	0	0	1.000	3	0	1	0	.33
Navarro, Jaime, Mil-Cle	12	33.1	1	0	0	0	1.000	6	1	0	0	.17
Neagle, D., Cin-NYY	34	209.0	10	23	2	2	.943	16	6	0	0	.38
Nelson, Jeff, NYY	73	69.2	0	10	1	1	.909	13	2	0	0	.15
Nen, Robb, SF	68	66.0	2	6	2	0	.800	9	0	0	0	.00
Newman, Alan, Cle	1	1.1	0	0	0	0	.000	0	0	0	0	.00
Nichting, Chris, Cle	7	9.0	1	1	0	0	1.000	1	0	0	0	.00
Nickle, Doug, Phi	4	2.2	1	1	0	0	1.000	0	0	0	0	.00
Nitkowski, C.J., Det	67	109.2	7	21	1	2	.966	10	0	3	1	.30
Nomo, Hideo, Det	32	190.0	12	16	1	2	.966	30	14	0	0	.47
Norton, Phil, ChC	2	8.2	1	2	0	0	1.000	1	0	0	0	.00
Nunez, Vladimir, Fla	17	68.1	9	11	2	0	.909	15	1	2	1	.20
O'Connor, Brian, Pit	6	12.1	0	0	0	0	.000	1	0	0	0	.00
Ohka, Tomokazu, Bos	13	69.1	8	7	1	1	.938	12	4	1	0	.42
Ohman, Will, ChC	6	3.1	0	2	0	0	1.000	1	0	1	0	1.00

2000 Fielding and Holding Runners

Pitcher, Team	G	Inn	PO	A	E	DP	Pct.	SBA	CS	PCS	PPO	CS%
Olivares, Omar, Oak	21	108.0	6	16	1	2	.957	5	1	0	1	.20
Oliver, Darren, Tex	21	108.0	7	15	0	0	1.000	11	3	2	0	.45
Olson, Gregg, LA	13	17.2	2	2	0	0	1.000	2	2	0	0	1.00
Ontiveros, Steve, Bos	3	5.1	0	0	0	0	.000	2	0	0	0	.00
Orosco, Jesse, StL	6	2.1	0	0	0	0	.000	1	0	0	0	.00
Ortiz, Ramon, Ana	18	111.1	1	12	0	1	1.000	12	5	0	1	.42
Ortiz, Russ, SF	33	195.2	11	33	0	4	1.000	30	8	1	0	.30
Osuna, Antonio, LA	46	67.1	4	7	1	0	.917	5	1	0	1	.20
Padilla, Vicente, Ari-Phi	55	65.1	6	7	1	0	.929	6	2	0	0	.33
Painter, Lance, Tor	42	66.2	4	17	0	2	1.000	3	0	0	0	.00
Palacios, Vicente, SD	7	10.2	0	3	0	1	1.000	2	2	0	0	1.00
Paniagua, Jose, Sea	69	80.1	8	8	0	1	1.000	3	0	0	0	.00
Park, Chan Ho, LA	34	226.0	20	39	3	4	.952	11	7	1	1	.73
Parque, Jim, CWS	33	187.0	2	25	3	0	.900	14	2	5	0	.50
Parra, Jose, Pit	6	11.2	0	3	0	0	1.000	4	2	0	0	.50
Parris, Steve, Cin	33	192.2	15	22	1	4	.974	15	3	0	1	.20
Parrish, John, Bal	8	36.1	1	4	1	1	.833	5	1	2	0	.60
Patterson, Danny, Det	58	56.2	4	8	0	0	1.000	2	1	0	0	.50
Pavano, Carl, Mon	15	97.0	7	13	2	1	.909	18	5	0	0	.28
Pena, Jesus, CWS-Bos	22	26.1	0	6	1	0	.857	1	0	0	0	.00
Penny, Brad, Fla	23	119.2	11	17	2	1	.933	12	4	0	0	.33
Percival, Troy, Ana	54	50.0	2	3	0	0	1.000	5	1	0	0	.20
Perez, Carlos, LA	30	144.0	8	20	1	2	.966	21	2	7	2	.43
Perez, Yorkis, Hou	33	22.2	0	2	1	0	.667	4	0	0	0	.00
Perisho, Matt, Tex	34	105.0	4	9	3	0	.813	7	4	0	2	.57
Person, Robert, Phi	28	173.1	6	11	0	1	1.000	20	8	0	0	.40
Peters, Chris, Pit	18	28.1	1	5	0	0	1.000	2	0	0	0	.00
Petkovsek, Mark, Ana	64	81.0	4	12	0	0	1.000	6	3	0	0	.50
Pettitte, Andy, NYY	32	204.2	17	33	4	3	.926	8	0	3	1	.38
Pichardo, Hipolito, Bos	38	65.0	7	10	1	1	.944	13	4	0	0	.31
Pineiro, Joel, Sea	8	19.1	1	2	0	0	1.000	2	0	0	0	.00
Plesac, Dan, Ari	62	40.0	0	2	0	0	1.000	6	1	0	0	.17
Politte, Cliff, Phi	12	59.0	5	8	0	0	1.000	4	1	0	0	.25
Ponson, Sidney, Bal	32	222.0	13	22	0	0	1.000	22	4	1	0	.23
Poole, Jim, Det-Mon	23	10.2	0	3	1	0	.750	2	1	0	0	.50
Pote, Lou, Ana	32	50.1	2	9	0	1	1.000	9	1	1	0	.22
Powell, Brian, Hou	9	31.1	3	2	0	0	1.000	3	0	0	0	.00
Powell, Jay, Hou	29	27.0	4	2	0	0	1.000	0	0	0	0	.00
Powell, Jeremy, Mon	11	26.0	2	3	0	0	1.000	3	0	0	0	.00
Prieto, Ariel, Oak	8	31.2	4	5	1	0	.900	6	1	0	1	.17
Prokopec, Luke, LA	5	21.0	0	3	0	1	1.000	1	0	0	0	.00
Pulsipher, Bill, NYM	2	6.2	2	2	0	0	1.000	3	0	0	0	.00
Quantrill, Paul, Tor	68	83.2	3	9	0	0	1.000	10	0	0	2	.00
Quevedo, Ruben, ChC	21	88.0	6	9	1	2	.938	5	2	1	0	.60
Radinsky, Scott, StL	1	0.0	0	0	0	0	.000	0	0	0	0	.00
Radke, Brad, Min	34	226.2	29	25	1	5	.982	20	6	0	0	.30
Rain, Steve, ChC	37	49.2	2	2	0	0	1.000	3	2	0	0	.67
Rakers, Jason, KC	11	21.2	1	0	0	0	1.000	1	0	0	0	.00
Ramirez, Hector, Mil	6	9.0	0	1	0	0	1.000	0	0	0	0	.00
Ramsay, Rob, Sea	37	50.1	3	7	0	1	1.000	5	1	2	0	.60
Rapp, Pat, Bal	31	174.0	4	25	1	2	.967	8	1	1	0	.25
Ratliff, Jon, Oak	1	1.0	0	0	0	0	.000	0	0	0	0	.00
Reames, Britt, StL	8	40.2	4	4	0	2	1.000	4	2	0	0	.50
Redman, Mark, Min	32	151.1	4	17	1	1	.955	8	4	2	1	.75
Reed, Rick, NYM	30	184.0	8	16	2	0	.923	13	4	0	0	.31
Reed, Steve, Cle	57	56.0	6	8	1	0	.933	5	4	0	0	.80
Reichert, Dan, KC	44	153.1	14	16	0	1	1.000	15	3	0	0	.20
Rekar, Bryan, TB	30	173.1	11	21	1	2	.970	11	7	0	1	.64
Remlinger, Mike, Atl	71	72.2	2	8	1	1	.909	1	0	0	0	.00
Reyes, Al, Bal-LA	19	19.2	0	4	0	0	1.000	1	0	0	0	.00
Reyes, Carlos, Phi-SD	22	28.1	1	2	0	0	1.000	3	0	0	0	.00
Reyes, Dennys, Cin	62	43.2	4	5	1	0	.900	2	1	0	1	.50
Reynolds, Shane, Hou	22	131.0	9	20	0	0	1.000	13	4	0	0	.31
Reynoso, Armando, Ari	31	170.2	13	34	1	3	.979	8	4	0	2	.50
Rhodes, Arthur, Sea	72	69.1	2	8	0	1	1.000	3	1	1	0	.67
Riedling, John, Cin	13	15.1	0	0	0	0	.000	0	0	0	0	.00
Rigby, Brad, KC-Mon	10	13.2	3	0	0	0	1.000	0	0	0	0	.00
Rigdon, Paul, Cle-Mil	17	87.1	7	9	0	0	1.000	9	4	0	0	.44
Riggan, Jerrod, NYM	1	2.0	0	0	0	0	.000	0	0	0	0	.00
Rincon, Ricky, Cle	35	20.0	2	3	0	0	1.000	0	0	0	0	.00
Ritchie, Todd, Pit	31	187.0	8	35	1	2	.977	11	3	1	1	.36
Rivera, Luis, Atl-Bal	6	7.1	0	1	0	0	1.000	0	0	0	0	.00
Rivera, Mariano, NYY	66	75.2	8	15	0	0	1.000	6	2	0	0	.33
Roberts, Grant, NYM	4	7.0	0	0	0	0	.000	1	0	0	0	.00
Rocker, John, Atl	59	53.0	1	6	0	0	1.000	6	0	0	0	.00
Rodriguez, Felix, SF	76	81.2	0	3	1	0	.750	10	3	0	0	.30
Rodriguez, Frank, Sea	23	47.1	6	7	1	2	.929	2	0	0	0	.00
Rodriguez, Jose, StL	6	4.0	0	0	0	0	.000	0	0	0	0	.00
Rodriguez, Rich, NYM	32	37.0	3	5	0	1	1.000	5	0	0	0	.00
Rogers, Kenny, Tex	34	227.1	18	46	2	6	.970	11	1	5	4	.55
Romero, J.C., Min	12	57.2	6	10	0	0	1.000	6	2	0	0	.33
Roque, Rafael, Mil	4	5.1	0	0	0	0	.000	2	0	0	0	.00
Rosado, Jose, KC	5	27.2	2	4	0	0	1.000	3	0	1	0	.33
Rose, Brian, Bos-Col	27	116.2	10	12	1	0	.957	12	3	0	0	.25
Rueter, Kirk, SF	32	184.0	8	44	0	4	1.000	6	4	1	0	.83
Ruffin, Johnny, Ari	5	9.0	1	3	0	0	1.000	1	1	0	0	1.00
Runyan, Sean, Det	3	3.0	0	2	0	0	1.000	1	0	1	0	1.00
Rupe, Ryan, TB	18	91.0	2	10	0	0	1.000	12	1	1	0	.17
Rusch, Glendon, NYM	31	190.2	5	25	0	1	1.000	16	2	3	0	.31
Ryan, B.J., Bal	42	42.2	0	4	0	0	1.000	4	1	0	0	.25
Ryan, Jason, Min	16	26.0	2	1	2	0	.600	1	1	0	0	1.00
Sanchez, Jesus, Fla	32	182.0	7	28	3	3	.921	15	2	3	3	.33

2000 Fielding and Holding Runners

Pitcher, Team	G	Inn	PO	A	E	DP	Pct.	SBA	CS	PCS	PPO	CS%
Santana, Johan, Min	30	86.0	5	13	1	2	.947	1	0	1	1	1.00
Santana, Julio, Mon	36	66.2	3	10	0	1	1.000	13	4	0	0	.31
Santiago, Jose, KC	45	69.0	5	9	1	0	.933	4	2	0	0	.50
Sasaki, Kazuhiro, Sea	63	62.2	2	3	0	0	1.000	8	0	0	0	.00
Sauerbeck, Scott, Pit	75	75.2	5	10	0	2	1.000	10	2	0	1	.20
Sauveur, Rich, Oak	10	10.1	0	1	0	0	1.000	0	0	0	0	.00
Scanlan, Bob, Mil	2	1.2	0	0	1	0	.000	3	0	0	0	.00
Schilling, Curt, Phi-Ari	29	210.1	11	19	0	0	1.000	8	6	0	0	.75
Schmidt, Jason, Pit	11	63.1	2	7	0	0	1.000	5	1	0	1	.20
Schoeneweis, S., Ana	27	170.0	5	25	1	4	.968	25	4	1	0	.20
Schourek, Pete, Bos	21	107.1	3	18	3	1	.875	20	4	5	0	.45
Schrenk, Steve, Phi	20	23.1	2	1	0	0	1.000	2	1	0	0	.50
Seanez, Rudy, Atl	23	21.0	1	1	0	0	1.000	3	0	0	0	.00
Seelbach, Chris, Atl	2	1.2	0	0	0	0	.000	1	1	0	0	1.00
Sele, Aaron, Sea	34	211.2	19	34	3	2	.946	24	9	1	0	.42
Serafini, Dan, SD-Pit	14	65.1	2	6	0	0	1.000	3	0	1	0	.33
Service, Scott, Oak	20	36.2	2	3	1	0	.833	2	1	1	0	1.00
Shaw, Jeff, LA	60	57.1	4	14	1	2	.947	3	0	0	0	.00
Shuey, Paul, Cle	57	63.2	7	8	0	0	1.000	9	2	0	0	.22
Sikorski, Brian, Tex	10	37.2	4	1	1	0	.833	1	0	0	0	.00
Silva, Jose, Pit	51	136.0	4	16	2	1	.909	10	4	0	0	.40
Simas, Bill, CWS	60	67.2	1	8	0	0	1.000	1	1	0	0	1.00
Sirotka, Mike, CWS	32	197.0	5	18	1	2	.958	12	3	1	0	.33
Skrmetta, Matt, Mon-Pit	14	14.2	1	2	1	0	.750	4	1	0	0	.25
Slocumb, H., StL-SD	65	68.2	5	9	0	0	1.000	5	1	1	0	.40
Slusarski, Joe, Hou	54	77.0	5	6	0	0	1.000	10	3	0	0	.30
Smith, Brian, Pit	3	4.1	0	1	0	0	1.000	1	0	0	0	.00
Smith, Chuck, Fla	19	122.2	11	14	2	1	.926	16	6	2	0	.50
Smith, Dan, Bos	2	3.1	0	0	0	0	.000	0	0	0	0	.00
Snyder, John, Mil	23	127.0	12	18	2	0	.938	15	5	0	0	.33
Sparks, Jeff, TB	15	20.1	1	0	0	0	1.000	3	1	0	0	.33
Sparks, Steve, Pit	3	4.0	1	1	0	1	1.000	1	0	0	0	.00
Sparks, Steve W., Det	20	104.0	11	17	1	2	.966	3	1	0	0	.33
Speier, Justin, Cle	47	68.1	1	6	1	0	.875	13	0	0	1	.00
Spencer, Sean, Mon	8	6.2	0	0	0	0	.000	0	0	0	0	.00
Spencer, Stan, SD	8	49.2	5	4	0	0	1.000	23	5	0	0	.22
Spoljaric, Paul, KC	13	9.2	1	4	0	1	1.000	3	0	1	0	.33
Spradlin, Jerry, KC-ChC	58	90.0	4	9	1	1	.929	16	3	0	1	.19
Springer, Dennis, NYM	2	11.1	1	2	0	0	1.000	0	0	0	0	.00
Springer, Russ, Ari	52	62.0	1	4	1	1	.833	10	1	0	0	.10
Spurgeon, Jay, Bal	7	24.0	0	2	1	0	.667	4	0	0	0	.00
Stanifer, Rob, Bos	8	13.0	0	2	0	0	1.000	0	0	0	0	.00
Stanton, Mike, NYY	69	68.0	3	11	0	0	1.000	5	0	2	2	.40
Stechschulte, G., StL	20	25.2	1	3	0	0	1.000	0	0	0	0	.00
Stein, Blake, KC	17	107.2	8	8	1	0	.941	15	6	0	0	.40
Stephenson, G., StL	32	200.1	9	30	1	0	.975	12	8	0	1	.67
Stevens, Dave, Atl	2	3.0	0	1	0	0	1.000	0	0	0	0	.00
Stottlemyre, Todd, Ari	18	95.1	4	17	1	1	.955	22	7	1	1	.36
Strickland, Scott, Mon	49	48.0	2	7	1	0	.900	6	0	1	0	.17
Strong, Joe, Fla	18	19.2	2	4	0	0	1.000	4	1	0	0	.25
Stull, Everett, Mil	20	43.1	1	7	0	1	1.000	4	0	0	0	.00
Sturtze, T., CWS-TB	29	68.1	6	3	0	0	1.000	7	1	0	0	.14
Sullivan, Scott, Cin	79	106.1	5	10	1	0	.938	3	1	0	0	.33
Suppan, Jeff, KC	35	217.0	14	20	2	0	.944	13	4	0	3	.31
Suzuki, Makoto, KC	32	188.2	20	15	1	2	.972	28	1	0	0	.04
Swindell, Greg, Ari	64	76.0	1	12	0	0	1.000	1	0	1	0	1.00
Tam, Jeff, Oak	72	85.2	3	16	1	3	.950	3	0	2	0	.67
Tapani, Kevin, ChC	30	195.2	11	19	0	1	1.000	25	7	1	0	.32
Tavarez, Julian, Col	51	120.0	14	23	1	1	.974	13	4	0	0	.31
Taylor, Billy, TB	17	13.2	1	0	0	0	1.000	4	2	0	0	.50
Telemaco, Amaury, Phi	13	24.1	2	0	0	0	1.000	5	1	0	0	.20
Telford, Anthony, Mon	64	78.1	5	9	0	1	1.000	3	1	0	0	.33
Tessmer, Jay, NYY	7	6.2	0	0	0	0	.000	0	0	0	0	.00
Thompson, Mark, StL	20	25.0	2	4	0	0	1.000	4	2	1	0	.75
Thurman, Mike, Mon	17	88.1	0	12	3	0	.800	24	3	0	0	.13
Timlin, Mike, Bal-StL	62	64.2	2	15	0	1	1.000	7	1	0	1	.14
Tolar, Kevin, Det	5	3.0	0	0	0	0	.000	0	0	0	0	.00
Tollberg, Brian, SD	19	118.0	9	15	1	1	.960	16	8	0	2	.50
Tomko, Brett, Sea	32	92.1	6	6	0	1	1.000	6	2	1	1	.50
Trachsel, Steve, TB-Tor	34	200.2	20	29	0	4	1.000	17	7	0	1	.41
Trombley, Mike, Bal	75	72.0	3	11	0	1	1.000	7	2	0	0	.29
Tucker, T.J., Mon	2	7.0	0	1	0	0	1.000	1	0	0	0	.00
Turnbow, Derrick, Ana	24	38.0	0	1	0	0	1.000	2	0	0	0	.00
Urbina, Ugueth, Mon	13	13.1	1	0	0	0	1.000	1	0	0	0	.00
Valdes, Ismael, ChC-LA	21	107.0	10	13	1	2	.958	6	3	1	2	.67
Valdes, Marc, Hou	53	56.2	6	9	0	2	1.000	5	0	1	0	.20
Van Poppel, Todd, ChC	51	86.1	9	11	0	1	1.000	22	4	2	0	.27
Vazquez, Javier, Mon	33	217.2	10	32	2	2	.955	18	6	0	0	.33
Venafro, Mike, Tex	77	56.1	3	9	2	1	.857	5	2	0	0	.40
Veres, Dave, StL	71	75.2	3	9	3	0	.800	8	4	0	0	.50
Villafuerte, B., Det	3	4.1	1	0	0	0	1.000	0	0	0	0	.00
Villegas, Ismael, Atl	1	2.2	0	1	0	0	1.000	0	0	0	0	.00
Villone, Ron, Cin	35	141.0	4	23	4	1	.871	13	3	2	2	.38
Vizcaino, Luis, Oak	12	19.1	1	3	0	0	1.000	3	0	0	0	.00
Vogelsong, Ryan, SF	4	6.0	0	0	0	0	.000	0	0	0	0	.00
Vosberg, Ed, Phi	31	24.0	1	8	0	0	1.000	1	0	1	3	1.00
Wagner, Billy, Hou	28	27.2	1	2	0	0	1.000	3	0	0	0	.00
Wainhouse, Dave, StL	9	8.2	0	2	0	0	1.000	1	0	0	0	.00
Wakefield, Tim, Bos	51	159.1	11	11	2	2	.917	33	2	0	0	.06
Walker, Kevin, SD	70	66.2	2	8	0	0	1.000	3	1	0	0	.33
Walker, Pete, Col	3	4.2	0	1	0	0	1.000	1	0	0	0	.00
Wall, Donne, SD	44	53.2	1	5	0	0	1.000	5	3	0	0	.60

2000 Fielding and Holding Runners

Pitcher, Team	G	Inn	PO	A	E	DP	Pct.	SBA	CS	PCS	PPO	CS%
Wallace, Jeff, Pit	38	35.2	2	3	1	0	.833	3	0	0	0	.00
Ward, Bryan, Phi-Ana	27	27.1	1	3	1	0	.800	4	0	0	0	.00
Wasdin, John, Bos-Col	39	80.1	4	5	0	1	1.000	17	0	0	0	.00
Washburn, Jarrod, Ana	14	84.1	1	14	0	1	1.000	10	3	2	1	.50
Watson, Allen, NYY	17	22.0	1	2	0	0	1.000	3	0	0	0	.00
Watson, Mark, Cle	6	6.1	1	0	0	0	1.000	0	0	0	0	.00
Weathers, Dave, Mil	69	76.1	5	7	0	0	1.000	11	4	0	0	.36
Weaver, Eric, Ana	17	18.1	1	4	0	0	1.000	1	0	0	0	.00
Weaver, Jeff, Det	31	200.0	17	28	1	0	.978	15	8	3	0	.73
Weber, Ben, SF-Ana	19	22.2	1	1	0	0	1.000	4	0	0	0	.00
Wells, Bob, Min	76	86.1	2	9	2	2	.846	5	3	1	0	.80
Wells, David, Tor	35	229.2	8	18	3	1	.897	21	6	1	0	.33
Wells, Kip, CWS	20	98.2	6	5	5	0	.688	16	5	0	0	.31
Wendell, Turk, NYM	77	82.2	12	10	2	0	.917	7	0	2	3	.29
Wengert, Don, Atl	10	10.0	0	1	0	0	1.000	0	0	0	0	.00
Westbrook, Jake, NYY	3	6.2	1	0	0	0	1.000	0	0	0	0	.00
Wetteland, John, Tex	62	60.0	2	5	0	0	1.000	10	2	0	0	.20
Wheeler, Dan, TB	11	23.0	1	4	0	1	1.000	0	0	0	0	.00
Whisenant, Matt, SD	24	21.1	1	3	0	0	1.000	2	0	0	0	.00
White, Gabe, Cin-Col	68	84.0	2	6	0	1	1.000	2	0	0	0	.00
White, Rick, TB-NYM	66	99.2	2	10	0	1	1.000	4	2	0	0	.50
Whiteside, Matt, SD	28	37.0	4	7	1	0	.917	1	1	0	0	1.00
Wickman, Bob, Mil-Cle	69	72.2	4	14	0	2	1.000	7	1	0	0	.14
Wilkins, Marc, Pit	52	60.1	2	9	0	2	1.000	5	1	0	0	.20
Williams, B., ChC-Cle	29	42.1	3	4	0	0	1.000	3	2	0	0	.67
Williams, Jeff, LA	7	5.2	0	0	0	0	.000	1	1	0	0	1.00
Williams, Matt T., Mil	11	9.0	0	2	0	0	1.000	2	1	1	0	1.00
Williams, Mike, Pit	72	72.0	4	11	0	2	1.000	15	2	0	0	.13
Williams, Woody, SD	23	168.0	7	12	2	1	.905	11	2	0	0	.18
Williamson, Scott, Cin	48	112.0	4	10	0	0	1.000	9	3	1	3	.44
Wilson, Kris, KC	20	34.1	2	9	1	0	.917	1	1	0	1	1.00
Wilson, Paul, TB	11	51.0	3	4	0	1	1.000	7	1	0	0	.14
Winchester, Scott, Cin	5	7.1	1	1	0	0	1.000	2	0	0	0	.00
Wise, Matt, Ana	8	37.1	2	5	0	0	1.000	4	1	0	0	.25
Witasick, Jay, KC-SD	33	150.0	10	16	1	1	.963	23	2	1	0	.13
Witt, Bobby, Cle	7	15.1	0	3	0	0	1.000	4	1	0	0	.25
Wohlers, Mark, Cin	20	28.0	2	3	1	0	.833	7	1	1	0	.29
Wolf, Randy, Phi	32	206.1	4	28	1	2	.970	10	5	2	0	.70
Wood, Kerry, ChC	23	137.0	8	14	2	1	.917	16	4	0	1	.25
Woodard, S., Mil-Cle	40	147.2	11	25	0	1	1.000	17	6	0	0	.35
Worrell, Tim, Bal-ChC	59	69.1	1	6	0	0	1.000	6	2	0	0	.33
Wright, Jamey, Mil	26	164.2	17	23	2	0	.952	16	6	2	2	.50
Wright, Jaret, Cle	9	51.2	5	3	0	0	1.000	6	2	0	0	.33
Wunsch, Kelly, CWS	83	61.1	3	8	0	0	1.000	4	2	1	0	.75
Yan, Esteban, TB	43	137.2	11	8	2	1	.905	13	3	0	0	.23
Yarnall, Ed, NYY	2	3.0	0	0	0	0	.000	1	0	0	0	.00
Yoshii, Masato, Col	29	167.1	16	20	0	2	1.000	18	5	0	0	.28
Young, Danny, ChC	4	3.0	0	0	0	0	.000	1	0	0	0	.00
Young, Tim, Bos	8	7.0	1	0	0	0	1.000	0	0	0	0	.00
Zerbe, Chad, SF	4	6.0	1	2	0	0	1.000	0	0	0	0	.00
Zimmerman, Jeff, Tex	65	69.2	2	7	1	0	.900	8	0	0	0	.00
Zito, Barry, Oak	14	92.2	4	9	0	0	1.000	7	2	2	0	.57

Hitters Pitching

Player	2000 Pitching											Career Pitching										
	G	W	L	Sv	IP	H	R	ER	BB	SO	ERA	G	W	L	Sv	IP	H	R	ER	BB	SO	ERA
Alexander, Manny	0	0	0	0	0.0	0	0	0	0	0	0.00	1	0	0	0	0.2	1	5	5	4	0	67.50
Bell, Derek	1	0	0	0	1.0	3	5	4	3	0	36.00	1	0	0	0	1.0	3	5	4	3	0	36.00
Benjamin, Mike	0	0	0	0	0.0	0	0	0	0	0	0.00	1	0	0	0	1.0	0	0	0	0	0	0.00
Bogar, Tim	2	0	0	0	2.0	2	1	1	1	1	4.50	2	0	0	0	2.0	2	1	1	1	1	4.50
Canseco, Jose	0	0	0	0	0.0	0	0	0	0	0	0.00	1	0	0	0	1.0	2	3	3	3	0	27.00
Franco, Matt	0	0	0	0	0.0	0	0	0	0	0	0.00	2	0	0	0	1.1	3	2	2	3	2	13.50
Gaetti, Gary	0	0	0	0	0.0	0	0	0	0	0	0.00	3	0	0	0	2.1	5	2	2	1	1	7.71
Halter, Shane	1	0	0	0	0.0	0	0	0	1	0	0.00	2	0	0	0	1.0	1	0	0	1	0	0.00
Harris, Lenny	0	0	0	0	0.0	0	0	0	0	0	0.00	1	0	0	0	1.0	0	0	0	0	1	0.00
Lee, Derrek	0	0	0	0	0.0	0	0	0	0	0	0.00	0	0	0	0	0.0	0	0	0	0	0	0.00
Mabry, John	1	0	0	0	0.2	3	2	2	1	0	27.00	1	0	0	0	0.2	3	2	2	1	0	27.00
Martinez, Dave	0	0	0	0	0.0	0	0	0	0	0	0.00	2	0	0	0	1.1	2	2	2	4	0	13.50
Mayne, Brent	1	1	0	0	1.0	1	0	0	1	0	0.00	1	1	0	0	1.0	1	0	0	1	0	0.00
Menechino, Frank	1	0	0	0	1.0	6	4	4	0	0	36.00	1	0	0	0	1.0	6	4	4	0	0	36.00
O'Neill, Paul	0	0	0	0	0.0	0	0	0	0	0	0.00	1	0	0	0	2.0	3	3	3	4	2	13.50
Osik, Keith	1	0	0	0	1.0	5	5	5	0	1	45.00	2	0	0	0	2.0	7	9	9	2	2	40.50
Sheldon, Scott	1	0	0	0	0.1	0	0	0	0	1	0.00	1	0	0	0	0.1	0	0	0	0	1	0.00
Whiten, Mark	0	0	0	0	0.0	0	0	0	0	0	0.00	1	0	0	0	1.0	1	1	1	2	3	9.00

Park Data

Did the Houston Astros move into a new park that imitated the hitter-friendly nature of Detroit's historic Tiger Stadium? And did the Tigers find that their new digs played more like Houston's old Astrodome? The numbers on the 2000 season are in, and you'll find the early returns in the pages that follow.

For each park, we show how the home team and its opponents performed, both at home and on the road, with the exception being that we do not include data from interleague games. The differences in interleague opponents and ballparks would skew the data.

By comparing the per-game averages at the home park and on the road, we can evaluate the park's impact. We simply divide the home average by the road average and multiply the result by 100, generating a park index. If the home and road per-game averages are equal, the index equals 100, and we can conclude that the park had no impact. An index above 100 means that the park favors that particular statistic.

The indexes for at-bats, runs, hits, errors, and infield errors are determined on a per-game basis; all other stats are calculated on a per-at-bat basis. "E-infield" denotes infield *fielding* errors. "Alt" is the approximate elevation of the ballpark.

For most parks, data is presented both for 2000 and for the last three years overall. If the park's dimensions have changed over that time, however, we do not combine the data from its old and new configurations. At the end, you'll find a rankings section that shows which parks inflate runs, homers and batting average the most.

Anaheim Angels—Edison Int'l Field of Anaheim

Alt: 160 feet **Surface:** Grass

| | 2000 Season | | | | | | | 1998-2000 | | | | | | |
| | Home Games | | | Away Games | | | Index | Home Games | | | Away Games | | | Index |
	Angels	Opp	Total	Angels	Opp	Total		Angels	Opp	Total	Angels	Opp	Total	
G	72	72	144	72	72	144	—	217	217	434	217	217	434	—
Avg	.279	.279	.279	.274	.275	.275	102	.265	.268	.267	.271	.272	.272	98
AB	2418	2542	4960	2566	2445	5011	99	7220	7563	14783	7718	7243	14961	99
R	378	382	760	377	409	786	97	1019	1121	2140	1089	1105	2194	98
H	675	709	1384	704	673	1377	101	1915	2030	3945	2095	1969	4064	97
2B	123	126	249	143	119	262	96	352	403	755	425	392	817	94
3B	10	6	16	20	11	31	52	40	26	66	35	37	72	93
HR	115	99	214	93	102	195	111	233	271	504	248	231	479	106
BB	271	285	556	270	308	578	97	729	865	1594	722	871	1593	101
SO	424	375	799	471	363	834	97	1311	1296	2607	1418	1213	2631	100
E	64	42	106	58	35	93	114	162	140	302	146	141	287	105
E-Infield	57	33	90	49	27	76	118	140	116	256	130	114	244	105
LHB-Avg	.287	.266	.278	.269	.282	.274	101	.280	.263	.272	.274	.273	.273	100
LHB-HR	57	36	93	52	48	100	95	119	112	231	134	97	231	101
RHB-Avg	.269	.288	.280	.282	.270	.275	102	.249	.272	.262	.269	.271	.270	97
RHB-HR	58	63	121	41	54	95	127	114	159	273	114	134	248	112

ANAHEIM

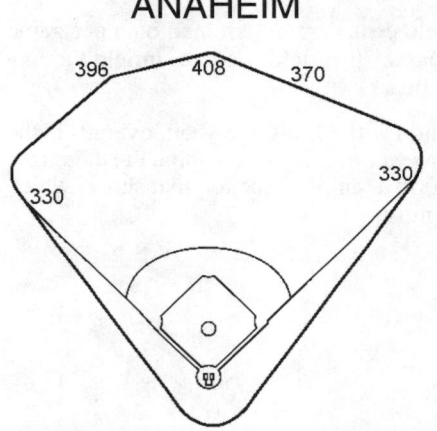

396   408   370
330   330

ARIZONA

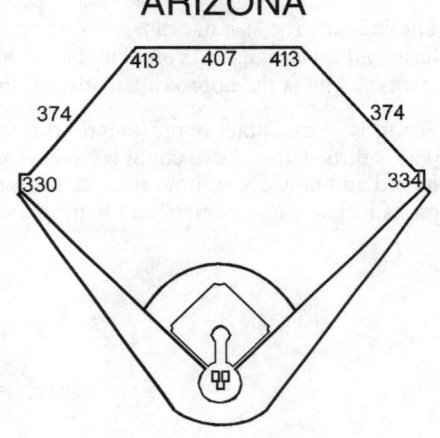

413   407   413
374   374
330   334

Arizona Diamondbacks—BankOne Ballpark

Alt: 1090 feet **Surface:** Grass

| | 2000 Season | | | | | | | 1998-2000 | | | | | | |
| | Home Games | | | Away Games | | | Index | Home Games | | | Away Games | | | Index |
	D'backs	Opp	Total	D'backs	Opp	Total		D'backs	Opp	Total	D'backs	Opp	Total	
G	72	72	144	75	75	150	—	220	220	440	223	223	446	—
Avg	.281	.265	.273	.248	.261	.254	107	.272	.259	.266	.252	.258	.255	104
AB	2425	2490	4915	2576	2494	5070	101	7402	7675	15077	7743	7399	15142	101
R	370	341	711	356	346	702	106	1078	996	2074	1057	1032	2089	101
H	681	659	1340	638	652	1290	108	2014	1990	4004	1950	1912	3862	105
2B	130	118	248	122	118	240	107	358	367	725	369	345	714	102
3B	20	16	36	17	11	28	133	74	57	131	50	32	82	160
HR	75	81	156	90	88	178	90	234	236	470	263	262	525	90
BB	244	218	462	245	234	479	99	728	635	1363	749	754	1503	91
SO	411	525	936	471	585	1056	91	1369	1451	2820	1616	1571	3187	89
E	46	34	80	51	49	100	83	127	141	268	151	152	303	90
E-Infield	42	29	71	43	35	78	95	109	117	226	124	114	238	96
LHB-Avg	.291	.242	.272	.245	.267	.253	108	.276	.253	.267	.257	.265	.260	103
LHB-HR	41	26	67	49	27	76	93	111	71	182	124	77	201	92
RHB-Avg	.269	.275	.273	.250	.259	.255	107	.268	.262	.265	.246	.255	.251	105
RHB-HR	34	55	89	41	61	102	89	123	165	288	139	185	324	88

Atlanta Braves—Turner Field

Alt: 1050 feet **Surface:** Grass

| | 2000 Season | | | | | | | 1998-2000 | | | | | | |
| | Home Games | | | Away Games | | | | Home Games | | | Away Games | | | |
	Braves	Opp	Total	Braves	Opp	Total	Index	Braves	Opp	Total	Braves	Opp	Total	Index
G	72	72	144	72	72	144	—	217	217	434	217	217	434	—
Avg	.278	.255	.266	.264	.257	.261	102	.274	.244	.259	.266	.250	.258	100
AB	2362	2512	4874	2511	2413	4924	99	7105	7446	14551	7634	7236	14870	98
R	353	301	654	356	326	682	96	1084	798	1882	1116	894	2010	94
H	657	641	1298	662	621	1283	101	1946	1819	3765	2027	1807	3834	98
2B	111	109	220	132	116	248	90	385	299	684	400	317	717	97
3B	12	8	20	13	11	24	84	34	30	64	37	27	64	102
HR	75	72	147	83	76	159	93	246	180	426	282	185	467	93
BB	267	206	473	264	210	474	101	773	614	1387	801	669	1470	96
SO	401	494	895	491	478	969	93	1267	1608	2875	1430	1556	2986	98
E	60	87	147	60	66	126	117	153	203	356	146	180	326	109
E-Infield	54	72	126	52	61	113	112	135	164	299	128	154	282	106
LHB-Avg	.296	.280	.288	.244	.267	.254	113	.276	.247	.262	.259	.259	.259	101
LHB-HR	21	26	47	18	22	40	113	82	64	146	76	67	143	102
RHB-Avg	.266	.242	.253	.276	.253	.264	96	.272	.243	.257	.270	.245	.257	100
RHB-HR	54	46	100	65	54	119	87	164	116	280	206	118	324	90

ATLANTA

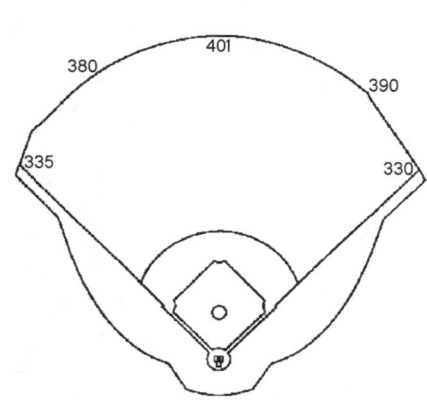

380 401 390 335 330

BALTIMORE

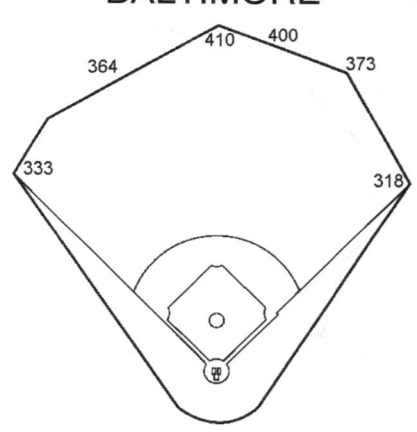

410 400 364 373 333 318

Baltimore Orioles—Oriole Park at Camden Yards

Alt: 20 feet **Surface:** Grass

| | 2000 Season | | | | | | | 1998-2000 | | | | | | |
| | Home Games | | | Away Games | | | | Home Games | | | Away Games | | | |
	Orioles	Opp	Total	Orioles	Opp	Total	Index	Orioles	Opp	Total	Orioles	Opp	Total	Index
G	72	72	144	72	72	144	—	217	217	434	217	217	434	—
Avg	.270	.260	.265	.272	.291	.281	94	.274	.260	.267	.273	.283	.278	96
AB	2348	2515	4863	2583	2492	5075	96	7236	7544	14780	7713	7319	15032	98
R	345	371	716	373	443	816	88	1068	1059	2127	1148	1202	2350	91
H	634	655	1289	702	725	1427	90	1980	1964	3944	2105	2073	4178	94
2B	118	101	219	161	155	316	72	359	319	678	456	419	875	79
3B	8	13	21	14	20	34	64	22	36	58	29	51	80	74
HR	76	96	172	85	86	171	105	260	261	521	274	263	537	99
BB	278	292	570	223	308	531	112	804	805	1609	790	853	1643	100
SO	392	474	866	411	422	833	108	1166	1431	2597	1245	1303	2548	104
E	51	38	89	54	52	106	84	124	120	244	142	139	281	87
E-Infield	43	34	77	44	42	86	90	106	108	214	121	112	233	92
LHB-Avg	.264	.251	.257	.278	.295	.287	90	.271	.248	.259	.277	.290	.284	91
LHB-HR	29	36	65	40	32	72	98	112	98	210	135	111	246	89
RHB-Avg	.275	.268	.271	.267	.287	.277	98	.275	.271	.273	.270	.277	.273	100
RHB-HR	47	60	107	45	54	99	109	148	163	311	139	152	291	107

Boston Red Sox—Fenway Park

Alt: 21 feet **Surface:** Grass

| | 2000 Season | | | | | | | 1998-2000 | | | | | | |
| | Home Games | | | Away Games | | | | Home Games | | | Away Games | | | |
	Red Sox	Opp	Total	Red Sox	Opp	Total	Index	Red Sox	Opp	Total	Red Sox	Opp	Total	Index
G	72	72	144	72	72	144	—	217	217	434	217	217	434	—
Avg	.274	.272	.273	.263	.244	.254	107	.286	.263	.274	.267	.246	.257	107
AB	2445	2573	5018	2579	2394	4973	101	7314	7643	14957	7713	7183	14896	100
R	354	349	703	371	322	693	101	1151	997	2148	1115	951	2066	104
H	671	699	1370	679	584	1263	108	2092	2012	4104	2060	1766	3826	107
2B	152	127	279	135	119	254	109	477	388	865	411	347	758	114
3B	17	16	33	12	10	22	149	53	32	85	46	25	71	119
HR	59	66	125	95	86	181	68	213	205	418	288	237	525	79
BB	268	205	473	274	239	513	91	790	631	1421	788	689	1477	96
SO	439	521	960	459	491	950	100	1305	1551	2856	1349	1416	2765	103
E	59	54	113	41	32	73	155	173	150	323	129	116	245	132
E-Infield	54	40	94	32	24	56	168	152	124	276	115	87	202	137
LHB-Avg	.269	.272	.270	.256	.242	.250	108	.288	.268	.278	.263	.255	.259	107
LHB-HR	36	26	62	57	36	93	69	110	72	182	158	108	266	70
RHB-Avg	.280	.271	.275	.271	.246	.258	107	.285	.259	.271	.271	.238	.255	106
RHB-HR	23	40	63	38	50	88	68	103	133	236	130	129	259	89

BOSTON

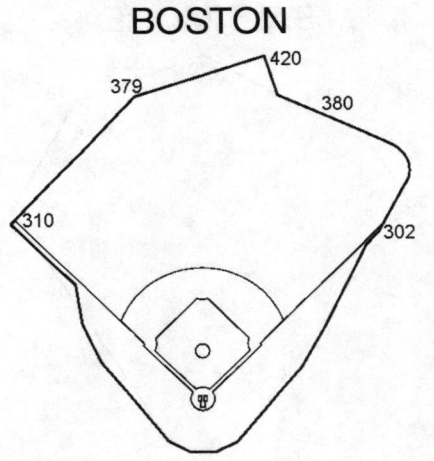

CHICAGO CUBS

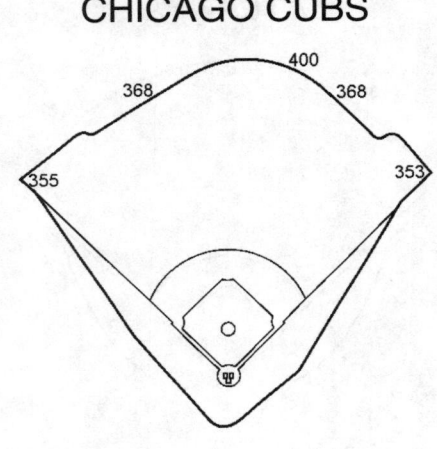

Chicago Cubs—Wrigley Field

Alt: 595 feet **Surface:** Grass

| | 2000 Season | | | | | | | 1998-2000 | | | | | | |
| | Home Games | | | Away Games | | | | Home Games | | | Away Games | | | |
	Cubs	Opp	Total	Cubs	Opp	Total	Index	Cubs	Opp	Total	Cubs	Opp	Total	Index
G	74	74	148	71	71	142	—	223	223	446	219	219	438	—
Avg	.261	.252	.256	.253	.288	.270	95	.268	.266	.267	.251	.278	.265	101
AB	2484	2572	5056	2489	2418	4907	99	7483	7920	15403	7664	7461	15125	100
R	329	364	693	356	466	822	81	1071	1165	2236	1055	1225	2280	96
H	649	647	1296	629	696	1325	94	2004	2108	4112	1925	2076	4001	101
2B	115	109	224	135	143	278	78	355	386	741	354	395	749	97
3B	9	7	16	11	20	31	50	46	34	80	38	61	99	79
HR	75	95	170	87	111	198	83	265	290	555	263	284	547	100
BB	291	299	590	270	302	572	100	845	808	1653	785	796	1581	103
SO	495	532	1027	510	489	999	100	1533	1610	3143	1664	1427	3091	100
E	41	49	90	49	44	93	93	156	145	301	151	146	297	100
E-Infield	29	37	66	40	39	79	80	118	113	231	123	125	248	91
LHB-Avg	.231	.234	.232	.223	.269	.246	94	.270	.269	.269	.251	.276	.263	103
LHB-HR	17	34	51	33	41	74	67	81	104	185	97	104	201	92
RHB-Avg	.278	.263	.271	.270	.299	.284	95	.266	.264	.265	.251	.280	.266	100
RHB-HR	58	61	119	54	70	124	93	184	186	370	166	180	346	104

Chicago White Sox—Comiskey Park

Alt: 595 feet **Surface:** Grass

| | 2000 Season | | | | | | | 1998-2000 | | | | | | |
| | Home Games | | | Away Games | | | | Home Games | | | Away Games | | | |
	White Sox	Opp	Total	White Sox	Opp	Total	Index	White Sox	Opp	Total	White Sox	Opp	Total	Index
G	72	72	144	72	72	144	—	218	218	436	217	217	434	—
Avg	.289	.269	.279	.280	.273	.277	101	.281	.274	.278	.273	.280	.276	100
AB	2416	2503	4919	2579	2444	5023	98	7256	7680	14936	7737	7399	15136	98
R	456	375	831	400	357	757	110	1184	1161	2345	1140	1158	2298	102
H	699	673	1372	722	667	1389	99	2041	2105	4146	2114	2069	4183	99
2B	138	119	257	146	117	263	100	396	382	778	420	377	797	99
3B	18	14	32	11	17	28	117	52	31	83	43	41	84	100
HR	110	88	198	77	78	155	130	276	267	543	236	271	507	109
BB	283	246	529	237	288	525	103	762	756	1518	701	824	1525	101
SO	383	485	868	457	412	869	102	1080	1313	2393	1290	1240	2530	96
E	51	42	93	67	60	127	73	166	148	314	194	182	376	83
E-Infield	50	37	87	59	53	112	78	148	125	273	169	156	325	84
LHB-Avg	.271	.276	.274	.254	.277	.266	103	.266	.281	.274	.266	.290	.278	98
LHB-HR	22	39	61	26	36	62	100	67	123	190	77	119	196	100
RHB-Avg	.298	.264	.282	.294	.270	.283	100	.291	.269	.280	.278	.272	.275	102
RHB-HR	88	49	137	51	42	93	151	209	144	353	159	152	311	113

CHICAGO WHITE SOX

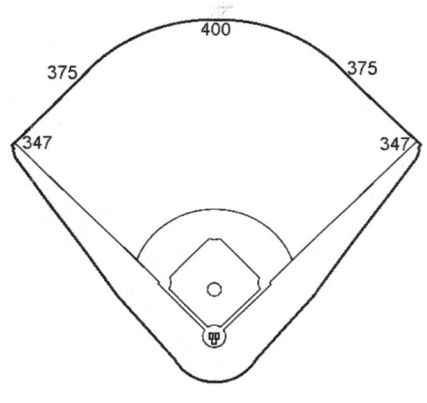

CINCINNATI

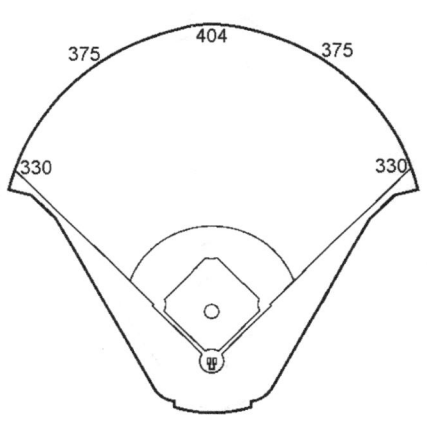

Cincinnati Reds—Cinergy Field

Alt: 550 feet **Surface:** Turf

| | 2000 Season | | | | | | | 1998-2000 | | | | | | |
| | Home Games | | | Away Games | | | | Home Games | | | Away Games | | | |
	Reds	Opp	Total	Reds	Opp	Total	Index	Reds	Opp	Total	Reds	Opp	Total	Index
G	73	73	146	75	75	150	—	222	222	444	223	223	446	—
Avg	.284	.271	.278	.264	.247	.256	109	.269	.251	.259	.268	.251	.260	100
AB	2444	2564	5008	2657	2447	5104	101	7361	7620	14981	7898	7284	15182	99
R	385	370	755	362	318	680	114	1114	1055	2169	1107	968	2075	105
H	695	696	1391	702	604	1306	109	1978	1909	3887	2120	1829	3949	99
2B	144	156	300	135	140	275	111	420	445	865	419	399	818	107
3B	14	18	32	20	15	35	93	40	41	81	54	44	98	84
HR	82	98	180	96	72	168	109	237	273	510	262	220	482	107
BB	268	293	561	239	311	550	104	845	875	1720	736	833	1569	111
SO	402	458	860	503	466	969	90	1386	1488	2874	1575	1422	2997	97
E	46	39	85	55	44	99	88	154	126	280	155	173	328	86
E-Infield	37	31	68	41	36	77	91	124	105	229	117	140	257	90
LHB-Avg	.301	.279	.290	.263	.246	.255	114	.278	.260	.269	.287	.254	.270	99
LHB-HR	35	36	71	51	31	82	93	91	87	178	113	80	193	99
RHB-Avg	.274	.266	.270	.265	.247	.257	105	.264	.244	.254	.258	.249	.254	100
RHB-HR	47	62	109	45	41	86	125	146	186	332	149	140	289	113

Cleveland Indians—Jacobs Field
Alt: 660 feet **Surface:** Grass

| | 2000 Season | | | | | | | 1998-2000 | | | | | | |
| | Home Games | | | Away Games | | | Index | Home Games | | | Away Games | | | Index |
	Indians	Opp	Total	Indians	Opp	Total		Indians	Opp	Total	Indians	Opp	Total	
G	72	72	144	72	72	144	—	217	217	434	217	217	434	—
Avg	.297	.272	.284	.286	.274	.280	101	.293	.279	.286	.274	.265	.270	106
AB	2488	2572	5060	2590	2402	4992	101	7397	7794	15191	7719	7273	14992	101
R	439	366	805	417	372	789	102	1300	1151	2451	1233	1069	2302	106
H	738	700	1438	741	658	1399	103	2170	2174	4344	2117	1930	4047	107
2B	132	146	278	148	123	271	101	404	456	860	456	371	827	103
3B	15	18	33	13	10	23	142	45	42	87	40	42	82	105
HR	106	71	177	84	79	163	107	294	243	537	258	239	497	107
BB	304	291	595	297	302	599	98	917	846	1763	906	815	1721	101
SO	439	545	984	480	538	1018	95	1338	1573	2911	1504	1447	2951	97
E	36	62	98	27	57	84	117	152	172	324	106	158	264	123
E-Infield	30	51	81	22	47	69	117	121	138	259	86	129	215	120
LHB-Avg	.303	.258	.281	.270	.283	.276	102	.298	.276	.287	.271	.267	.269	107
LHB-HR	62	36	98	40	34	74	127	141	126	267	121	109	230	114
RHB-Avg	.290	.284	.287	.301	.267	.284	101	.289	.282	.285	.278	.264	.271	105
RHB-HR	44	35	79	44	45	89	90	153	117	270	137	130	267	100

CLEVELAND

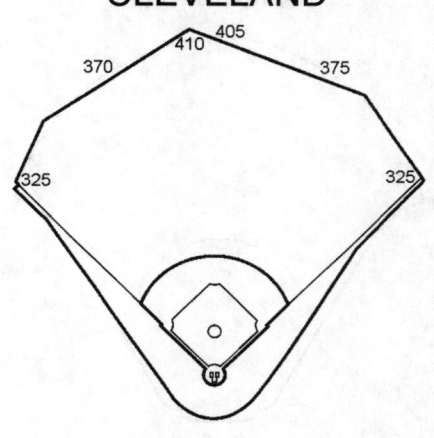

COLORADO

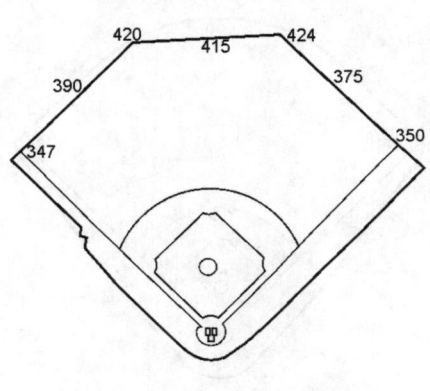

Colorado Rockies—Coors Field
Alt: 5280 feet **Surface:** Grass

| | 2000 Season | | | | | | | 1998-2000 | | | | | | |
| | Home Games | | | Away Games | | | Index | Home Games | | | Away Games | | | Index |
	Rockies	Opp	Total	Rockies	Opp	Total		Rockies	Opp	Total	Rockies	Opp	Total	
G	75	75	150	75	75	150	—	225	225	450	225	225	450	—
Avg	.332	.303	.317	.251	.253	.252	126	.328	.311	.320	.252	.262	.257	124
AB	2654	2721	5375	2573	2424	4997	108	8038	8226	16264	7709	7278	14987	109
R	571	492	1063	316	327	643	165	1588	1538	3126	906	1014	1920	163
H	880	824	1704	647	613	1260	135	2639	2562	5201	1944	1908	3852	135
2B	167	159	326	129	131	260	117	498	471	969	391	392	783	114
3B	31	19	50	17	16	33	141	75	66	141	42	46	88	148
HR	102	122	224	46	77	123	169	339	361	700	188	206	394	164
BB	306	275	581	252	264	516	105	795	880	1675	668	857	1525	101
SO	380	470	850	458	446	904	87	1129	1375	2504	1384	1365	2749	84
E	45	91	136	44	56	100	136	151	210	361	145	160	305	118
E-Infield	37	73	110	39	51	90	122	111	169	280	123	144	267	105
LHB-Avg	.326	.287	.309	.266	.253	.261	119	.336	.309	.323	.270	.272	.271	119
LHB-HR	54	51	105	30	33	63	159	150	140	290	87	85	172	156
RHB-Avg	.338	.313	.324	.236	.253	.245	132	.322	.313	.317	.238	.256	.247	129
RHB-HR	48	71	119	16	44	60	181	189	221	410	101	121	222	169

Detroit Tigers—Comerica Park

Alt: 585 feet   **Surface:** Grass

| | 2000 Season | | | | | | | 1998-1999 (Tiger Stadium) | | | | | | |
| | Home Games | | | Away Games | | | | Home Games | | | Away Games | | | |
	Tigers	Opp	Total	Tigers	Opp	Total	Index	Tigers	Opp	Total	Tigers	Opp	Total	Index
G	72	72	144	72	72	144	—	145	145	290	144	144	288	—
Avg	.280	.281	.280	.275	.281	.278	101	.261	.270	.265	.265	.286	.275	96
AB	2445	2572	5017	2573	2430	5003	100	4857	5087	9944	5085	4849	9934	99
R	350	358	708	396	401	797	89	673	784	1457	633	798	1431	101
H	684	723	1407	708	682	1390	101	1268	1372	2640	1348	1387	2735	96
2B	136	143	279	134	126	260	107	230	251	481	309	256	565	85
3B	20	19	39	16	21	37	105	30	27	57	26	31	57	100
HR	64	58	122	102	98	200	61	185	208	393	142	155	297	132
BB	273	203	476	233	250	483	98	418	536	954	389	515	904	105
SO	388	413	801	476	434	910	88	925	877	1802	938	810	1748	103
E	50	57	107	46	49	95	113	94	120	214	107	83	190	112
E-Infield	39	46	85	38	41	79	108	74	103	177	84	68	152	116
LHB-Avg	.291	.272	.280	.260	.261	.261	107	.260	.271	.266	.275	.295	.286	93
LHB-HR	27	37	64	33	56	89	72	83	94	177	66	88	154	116
RHB-Avg	.273	.289	.281	.282	.300	.290	97	.262	.269	.265	.258	.278	.267	99
RHB-HR	37	21	58	69	42	111	52	102	114	216	76	67	143	150

DETROIT

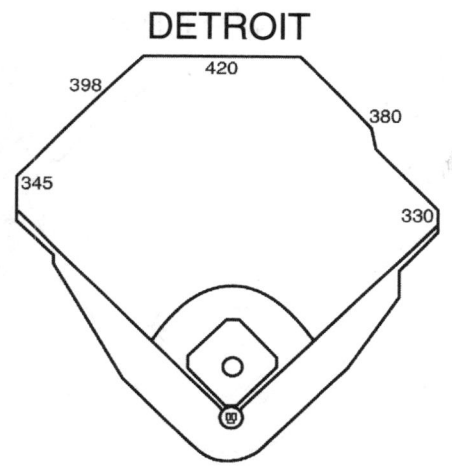

FLORIDA

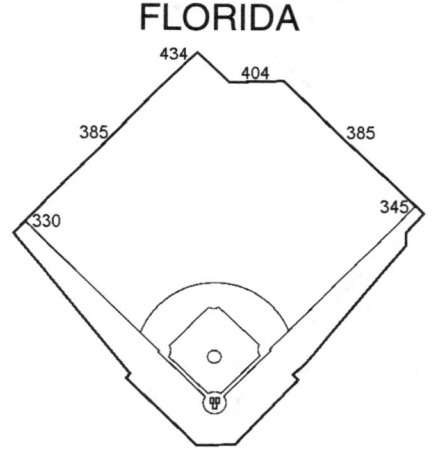

Florida Marlins—Pro Player Stadium

Alt: 10 feet   **Surface:** Grass

| | 2000 Season | | | | | | | 1998-2000 | | | | | | |
| | Home Games | | | Away Games | | | | Home Games | | | Away Games | | | |
	Marlins	Opp	Total	Marlins	Opp	Total	Index	Marlins	Opp	Total	Marlins	Opp	Total	Index
G	72	72	144	72	72	144	—	216	216	432	218	218	436	—
Avg	.262	.253	.257	.256	.280	.268	96	.256	.263	.259	.256	.295	.275	94
AB	2397	2486	4883	2527	2412	4939	99	7302	7562	14864	7567	7309	14876	101
R	314	327	641	329	378	707	91	898	1058	1956	932	1266	2198	90
H	628	629	1257	646	676	1322	95	1867	1989	3856	1934	2156	4090	95
2B	114	122	236	120	130	250	95	352	385	737	364	411	775	95
3B	14	22	36	12	17	29	126	55	64	119	44	50	94	127
HR	62	70	132	81	78	159	84	151	220	371	211	246	457	81
BB	257	284	541	228	302	530	103	744	886	1630	637	952	1589	103
SO	536	511	1047	548	438	986	107	1501	1464	2965	1636	1217	2853	104
E	48	57	105	61	59	120	88	165	173	338	180	141	321	106
E-Infield	44	45	89	50	52	102	87	142	145	287	145	117	262	111
LHB-Avg	.302	.248	.274	.272	.280	.276	99	.264	.268	.266	.264	.303	.283	94
LHB-HR	18	18	36	20	29	49	74	50	77	127	59	102	161	77
RHB-Avg	.240	.256	.248	.247	.280	.263	94	.250	.260	.255	.250	.290	.270	95
RHB-HR	44	52	96	61	49	110	88	101	143	244	152	144	296	84

Houston Astros—Enron Field
Alt: 22 feet   **Surface:** Grass

| | 2000 Season | | | | | | | 1998-1999 (Astrodome) | | | | | | |
| | Home Games | | | Away Games | | | | Home Games | | | Away Games | | | |
	Astros	Opp	Total	Astros	Opp	Total	Index	Astros	Opp	Total	Astros	Opp	Total	Index
G	72	72	144	75	75	150	—	149	149	298	146	146	292	—
Avg	.282	.290	.286	.273	.272	.273	105	.275	.253	.264	.268	.271	.269	98
AB	2422	2617	5039	2644	2548	5192	101	4980	5208	10188	5134	4983	10117	99
R	463	462	925	403	404	807	119	768	571	1339	749	620	1369	96
H	682	760	1442	722	693	1415	106	1369	1319	2688	1377	1348	2725	97
2B	138	154	292	121	134	255	118	307	271	578	260	230	490	117
3B	24	27	51	10	16	26	202	26	28	54	20	29	49	109
HR	123	119	242	104	98	202	123	131	117	248	165	138	303	81
BB	313	273	586	308	280	588	103	645	419	1064	587	453	1040	102
SO	478	492	970	547	463	1010	99	1035	1218	2253	1038	967	2005	112
E	54	41	95	67	56	123	80	96	123	219	100	118	218	98
E-Infield	46	33	79	52	48	100	82	73	110	183	86	100	186	96
LHB-Avg	.283	.320	.307	.293	.287	.290	106	.274	.258	.264	.280	.270	.273	97
LHB-HR	39	58	97	26	46	72	142	29	45	74	41	49	90	77
RHB-Avg	.281	.267	.275	.265	.260	.263	105	.275	.250	.264	.265	.271	.268	99
RHB-HR	84	61	145	78	52	130	113	102	72	174	124	89	213	83

HOUSTON
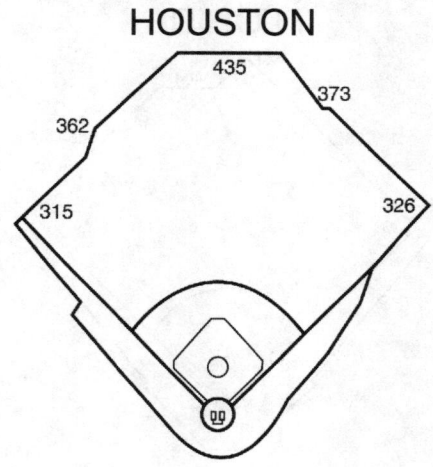

KANSAS CITY
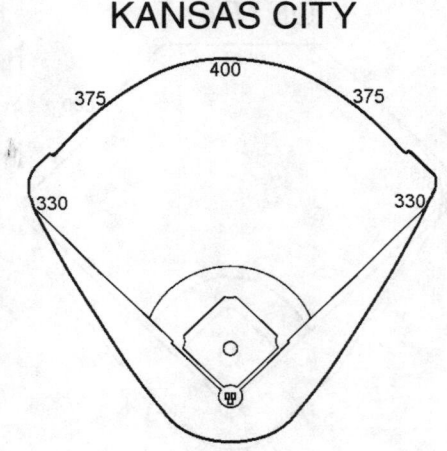

Kansas City Royals—Ewing M. Kauffman Stadium
Alt: 750 feet   **Surface:** Grass

| | 2000 Season | | | | | | | 1998-2000 | | | | | | |
| | Home Games | | | Away Games | | | | Home Games | | | Away Games | | | |
	Royals	Opp	Total	Royals	Opp	Total	Index	Royals	Opp	Total	Royals	Opp	Total	Index
G	72	72	144	72	72	144	—	215	215	430	217	217	434	—
Avg	.304	.292	.298	.273	.272	.273	109	.283	.288	.286	.271	.276	.273	104
AB	2496	2602	5098	2559	2381	4940	103	7352	7735	15087	7659	7254	14913	102
R	408	442	850	373	392	765	111	1109	1262	2371	1065	1189	2254	106
H	758	760	1518	699	648	1347	113	2079	2230	4309	2074	2004	4078	107
2B	124	145	269	123	128	251	104	346	382	728	403	373	776	93
3B	17	14	31	9	11	20	150	68	44	112	36	31	67	165
HR	77	106	183	53	108	161	110	212	288	500	171	284	455	109
BB	212	305	517	229	321	550	91	677	820	1497	668	889	1557	95
SO	330	424	754	403	385	788	93	1133	1213	2346	1293	1213	2506	93
E	46	61	107	43	71	114	94	154	174	328	156	186	342	97
E-Infield	36	51	87	33	63	96	91	128	142	270	130	160	290	94
LHB-Avg	.302	.285	.291	.253	.275	.267	109	.284	.288	.286	.269	.271	.270	106
LHB-HR	15	53	68	9	50	59	108	46	121	167	37	122	159	102
RHB-Avg	.304	.300	.303	.281	.269	.277	109	.282	.288	.285	.272	.280	.275	103
RHB-HR	62	53	115	44	58	102	112	166	167	333	134	162	296	113

Los Angeles Dodgers—Dodger Stadium

Alt: 340 feet **Surface:** Grass

| | 2000 Season | | | | | | | 1998-2000 | | | | | | |
| | Home Games | | | Away Games | | | Index | Home Games | | | Away Games | | | Index |
	Dodgers	Opp	Total	Dodgers	Opp	Total		Dodgers	Opp	Total	Dodgers	Opp	Total	
G	75	75	150	72	72	144	—	223	223	446	220	220	440	—
Avg	.253	.233	.243	.264	.269	.266	91	.258	.240	.249	.257	.265	.261	95
AB	2452	2550	5002	2530	2411	4941	97	7307	7618	14925	7716	7373	15089	98
R	340	315	655	400	342	742	85	973	934	1907	1084	1072	2156	87
H	620	595	1215	667	648	1315	89	1886	1825	3711	1984	1957	3941	93
2B	103	110	213	137	134	271	78	290	335	625	366	389	755	84
3B	9	8	17	16	10	26	65	27	18	45	44	49	93	49
HR	101	79	180	95	85	180	99	257	235	492	255	234	489	102
BB	282	291	573	320	238	558	101	735	807	1542	820	813	1633	95
SO	505	561	1066	469	485	954	110	1391	1589	2980	1486	1516	3002	100
E	70	55	125	56	61	117	103	194	165	359	178	186	364	97
E-Infield	58	42	100	48	53	101	95	165	131	296	152	152	304	96
LHB-Avg	.250	.225	.237	.256	.280	.268	88	.248	.242	.245	.242	.282	.265	92
LHB-HR	41	36	77	34	38	72	102	75	98	173	67	102	169	104
RHB-Avg	.255	.240	.248	.269	.260	.265	94	.263	.238	.251	.264	.252	.259	97
RHB-HR	60	43	103	61	47	108	96	182	137	319	188	132	320	101

LOS ANGELES

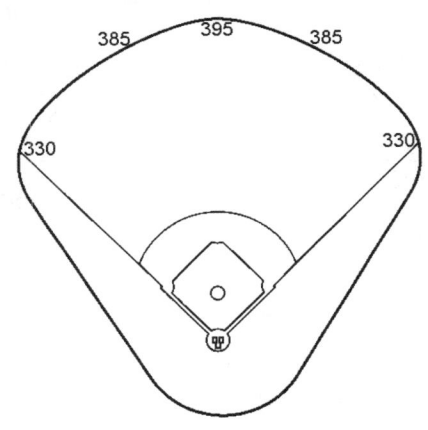

385 395 385
330 330

MILWAUKEE

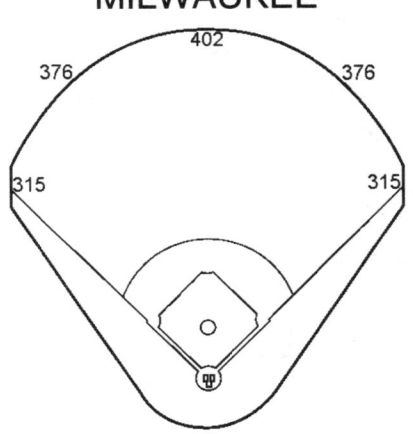

402
376 376
315 315

Milwaukee Brewers—County Stadium

Alt: 635 feet **Surface:** Grass

| | 2000 Season | | | | | | | 1998-2000 | | | | | | |
| | Home Games | | | Away Games | | | Index | Home Games | | | Away Games | | | Index |
	Brewers	Opp	Total	Brewers	Opp	Total		Brewers	Opp	Total	Brewers	Opp	Total	
G	75	75	150	73	73	146	—	222	222	444	221	221	442	—
Avg	.230	.264	.247	.255	.273	.263	94	.252	.277	.265	.261	.273	.267	99
AB	2492	2666	5158	2526	2396	4922	102	7405	7904	15309	7716	7406	15122	101
R	330	359	689	342	383	725	93	980	1172	2152	1054	1122	2176	98
H	572	703	1275	643	653	1296	96	1868	2188	4056	2015	2024	4039	100
2B	119	120	239	139	110	249	92	373	373	746	402	392	794	93
3B	17	10	27	8	20	28	92	33	36	69	33	57	90	76
HR	73	64	137	88	93	181	72	202	247	449	243	277	520	85
BB	295	330	625	276	322	598	100	838	841	1679	810	876	1686	98
SO	534	427	961	578	459	1037	88	1367	1345	2712	1665	1404	3069	87
E	63	71	134	43	49	92	142	161	167	328	155	149	304	107
E-Infield	58	56	114	31	38	69	161	132	129	261	122	118	240	108
LHB-Avg	.234	.266	.252	.271	.272	.272	93	.249	.276	.262	.266	.268	.267	98
LHB-HR	33	28	61	53	31	84	64	109	84	193	144	83	227	83
RHB-Avg	.227	.262	.245	.246	.273	.259	95	.255	.277	.266	.258	.276	.267	100
RHB-HR	40	36	76	35	62	97	78	93	163	256	99	194	293	87

Minnesota Twins—Hubert H. Humphrey Metrodome
Alt: 815 feet **Surface:** Turf

	2000 Season							1998-2000						
	Home Games			Away Games				Home Games			Away Games			
	Twins	Opp	Total	Twins	Opp	Total	Index	Twins	Opp	Total	Twins	Opp	Total	Index
G	72	72	144	72	72	144	—	217	217	434	217	217	434	—
Avg	.280	.293	.286	.264	.283	.273	105	.273	.286	.280	.258	.283	.270	104
AB	2479	2639	5118	2540	2431	4971	103	7420	7924	15344	7578	7331	14909	103
R	374	419	793	312	379	691	115	1026	1194	2220	928	1104	2032	109
H	693	773	1466	671	687	1358	108	2029	2265	4294	1954	2076	4030	107
2B	161	150	311	136	132	268	113	442	471	913	370	387	757	117
3B	30	15	45	14	14	28	156	67	51	118	35	47	82	140
HR	47	97	144	56	94	150	93	133	280	413	166	259	425	94
BB	254	217	471	239	245	484	95	731	682	1413	675	635	1310	105
SO	425	512	937	478	406	884	103	1278	1398	2676	1303	1207	2510	104
E	39	53	92	55	62	117	79	136	163	299	145	178	323	93
E-Infield	35	48	83	48	54	102	81	114	143	257	118	162	280	92
LHB-Avg	.303	.297	.300	.268	.289	.277	108	.285	.286	.285	.260	.288	.272	105
LHB-HR	29	41	70	32	32	64	109	70	141	211	84	90	174	117
RHB-Avg	.250	.291	.274	.259	.278	.270	102	.261	.285	.275	.256	.279	.269	102
RHB-HR	18	56	74	24	62	86	82	63	139	202	82	169	251	79

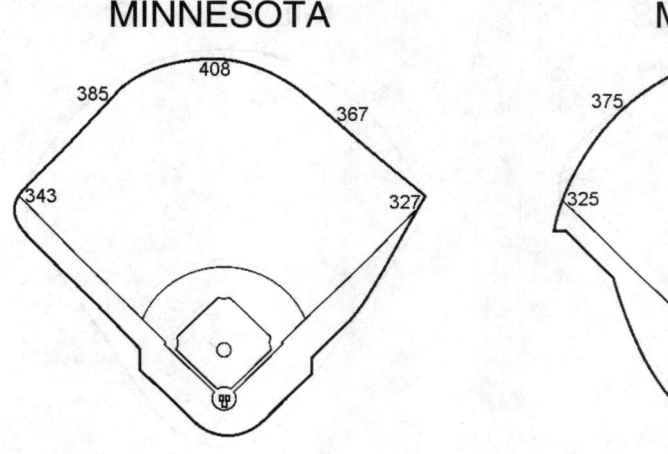

MINNESOTA

408 385 367 343 327

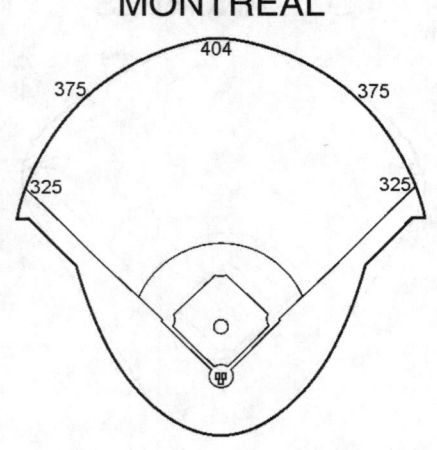

MONTREAL

404 375 375 325 325

Montreal Expos—Olympic Stadium
Alt: 90 feet **Surface:** Turf

	2000 Season							1998-2000						
	Home Games			Away Games				Home Games			Away Games			
	Expos	Opp	Total	Expos	Opp	Total	Index	Expos	Opp	Total	Expos	Opp	Total	Index
G	72	72	144	72	72	144	—	217	217	434	217	217	434	—
Avg	.270	.275	.273	.265	.287	.276	99	.259	.267	.263	.262	.276	.269	98
AB	2412	2534	4946	2525	2426	4951	100	7217	7635	14852	7567	7231	14798	100
R	333	395	728	331	404	735	99	936	1098	2034	956	1167	2123	96
H	652	697	1349	670	696	1366	99	1871	2036	3907	1986	1994	3980	98
2B	143	130	273	130	138	268	102	412	401	813	395	391	786	103
3B	14	19	33	18	18	36	92	48	45	93	56	42	98	95
HR	76	89	165	82	69	151	109	211	206	417	231	226	457	91
BB	200	236	436	225	261	486	90	610	721	1331	608	780	1388	96
SO	430	488	918	493	425	918	100	1291	1427	2718	1422	1339	2761	98
E	58	48	106	64	48	112	95	206	167	373	197	159	356	105
E-Infield	49	40	89	48	38	86	103	158	138	296	151	132	283	105
LHB-Avg	.273	.305	.289	.251	.312	.279	104	.262	.284	.274	.250	.281	.266	103
LHB-HR	31	49	80	30	33	63	132	51	93	144	71	98	169	86
RHB-Avg	.268	.255	.261	.277	.270	.274	95	.258	.254	.256	.270	.272	.271	95
RHB-HR	45	40	85	52	36	88	94	160	113	273	160	128	288	94

New York Mets—Shea Stadium

Alt: 20 feet **Surface:** Grass

	2000 Season							1998-2000						
	Home Games			Away Games				Home Games			Away Games			
	Mets	Opp	Total	Mets	Opp	Total	Index	Mets	Opp	Total	Mets	Opp	Total	Index
G	71	71	142	71	71	142	—	216	216	432	217	217	434	—
Avg	.267	.236	.251	.263	.266	.264	95	.263	.245	.254	.274	.258	.266	95
AB	2329	2465	4794	2474	2387	4861	99	7111	7419	14530	7617	7192	14809	99
R	352	284	636	357	358	715	89	1017	876	1893	1088	982	2070	92
H	622	582	1204	650	634	1284	94	1868	1819	3687	2085	1857	3942	94
2B	126	116	242	125	134	259	95	361	384	745	430	400	830	91
3B	3	9	12	11	19	30	41	15	48	63	29	55	84	76
HR	82	61	143	89	80	169	86	212	188	400	238	231	469	87
BB	294	225	519	309	262	571	92	851	739	1590	908	769	1677	97
SO	449	548	997	474	471	945	107	1318	1631	2949	1428	1465	2893	104
E	59	52	111	49	61	110	101	134	152	286	126	147	273	105
E-Infield	47	43	90	40	53	93	97	106	125	231	103	122	225	103
LHB-Avg	.235	.229	.231	.232	.262	.250	93	.278	.247	.262	.265	.261	.263	100
LHB-HR	15	17	32	17	26	43	80	76	55	131	76	84	160	85
RHB-Avg	.275	.239	.258	.271	.267	.270	96	.254	.244	.249	.279	.257	.268	93
RHB-HR	67	44	111	72	54	126	87	136	133	269	162	147	309	88

NEW YORK METS

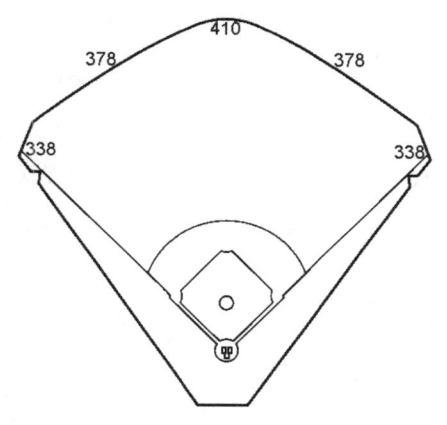

NEW YORK YANKEES

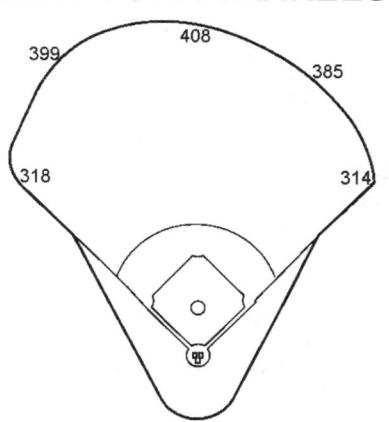

New York Yankees—Yankee Stadium

Alt: 55 feet **Surface:** Grass

	2000 Season							1998-2000						
	Home Games			Away Games				Home Games			Away Games			
	Yankees	Opp	Total	Yankees	Opp	Total	Index	Yankees	Opp	Total	Yankees	Opp	Total	Index
G	72	72	144	72	72	144	—	216	216	432	218	218	436	—
Avg	.280	.261	.270	.272	.271	.272	99	.283	.247	.265	.283	.268	.275	96
AB	2421	2526	4947	2536	2427	4963	100	7249	7497	14746	7778	7319	15097	99
R	400	361	761	373	369	742	103	1184	925	2109	1255	1043	2298	93
H	677	660	1337	691	658	1349	99	2052	1850	3902	2200	1959	4159	95
2B	128	132	260	137	135	272	96	387	366	753	417	372	789	98
3B	11	9	20	12	15	27	74	34	25	59	49	42	91	66
HR	105	78	183	79	76	155	118	264	205	469	275	231	506	95
BB	303	246	549	252	283	535	103	915	691	1606	858	771	1629	101
SO	421	506	927	469	435	904	103	1297	1531	2828	1396	1370	2766	105
E	48	44	92	50	55	105	88	146	137	283	137	165	302	95
E-Infield	41	33	74	44	45	89	83	121	115	236	115	137	252	95
LHB-Avg	.271	.267	.269	.281	.271	.276	97	.273	.256	.265	.287	.271	.279	95
LHB-HR	57	36	93	36	32	68	134	135	107	242	141	109	250	99
RHB-Avg	.288	.256	.271	.265	.271	.268	101	.291	.239	.265	.280	.265	.272	97
RHB-HR	48	42	90	43	44	87	106	129	98	227	134	122	256	91

Oakland Athletics—Network Associates Coliseum   **Alt:** 25 feet   **Surface:** Grass

| | 2000 Season | | | | | | | 1998-2000 | | | | | | |
| | Home Games | | | Away Games | | | | Home Games | | | Away Games | | | |
	Athletics	Opp	Total	Athletics	Opp	Total	Index	Athletics	Opp	Total	Athletics	Opp	Total	Index
G	72	72	144	71	71	142	—	217	217	434	216	216	432	—
Avg	.264	.257	.260	.278	.287	.282	92	.260	.262	.261	.267	.289	.278	94
AB	2381	2521	4902	2565	2434	4999	97	7135	7617	14752	7676	7411	15087	97
R	417	324	741	437	379	816	90	1143	1021	2164	1228	1220	2448	88
H	628	648	1276	713	699	1412	89	1852	1992	3844	2050	2140	4190	91
2B	106	133	239	139	139	278	88	349	408	757	419	438	857	90
3B	11	12	23	11	11	22	107	31	36	67	22	49	71	97
HR	109	56	165	101	76	177	95	265	195	460	286	242	528	89
BB	336	256	592	332	294	626	96	927	727	1654	986	805	1791	94
SO	493	449	942	539	401	940	102	1405	1300	2705	1621	1215	2836	98
E	56	42	98	56	48	104	93	171	159	330	178	160	338	97
E-Infield	41	34	75	44	40	84	88	137	136	273	147	133	280	97
LHB-Avg	.271	.258	.265	.287	.294	.290	91	.272	.268	.270	.280	.284	.282	96
LHB-HR	65	24	89	67	37	104	84	154	87	241	174	102	276	86
RHB-Avg	.254	.257	.256	.268	.282	.276	93	.246	.256	.252	.255	.292	.274	92
RHB-HR	44	32	76	34	39	73	110	111	108	219	112	140	252	92

OAKLAND

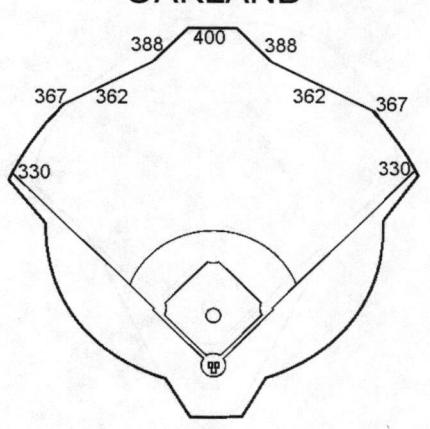

388 400 388
367 362 362 367
330 330

PHILADELPHIA

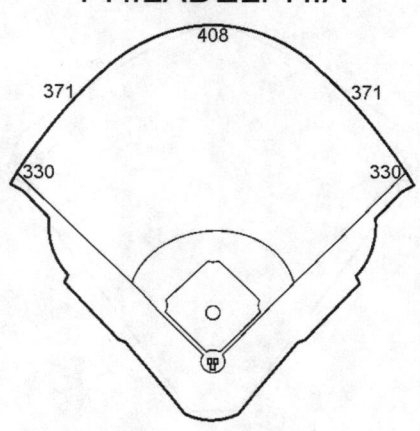

408
371 371
330 330

Philadelphia Phillies—Veterans Stadium   **Alt:** 20 feet   **Surface:** Turf

| | 2000 Season | | | | | | | 1998-2000 | | | | | | |
| | Home Games | | | Away Games | | | | Home Games | | | Away Games | | | |
	Phillies	Opp	Total	Phillies	Opp	Total	Index	Phillies	Opp	Total	Phillies	Opp	Total	Index
G	72	72	144	72	72	144	—	217	217	434	217	217	434	—
Avg	.257	.264	.261	.246	.270	.258	101	.270	.263	.266	.253	.269	.261	102
AB	2392	2511	4903	2472	2348	4820	102	7304	7605	14909	7552	7230	14782	101
R	319	390	709	292	352	644	110	1060	1131	2191	904	1080	1984	110
H	615	664	1279	609	633	1242	103	1973	1998	3971	1910	1942	3852	103
2B	147	190	337	114	115	229	145	415	475	890	349	390	739	119
3B	21	21	42	16	9	25	165	61	48	109	45	33	78	139
HR	58	88	146	63	90	153	94	194	272	466	179	264	443	104
BB	278	305	583	261	258	519	110	822	850	1672	733	752	1485	112
SO	518	565	1083	474	442	916	116	1485	1668	3153	1452	1327	2779	112
E	40	38	78	47	58	105	74	120	139	259	156	163	319	81
E-Infield	32	32	64	35	48	83	77	105	107	212	128	129	257	82
LHB-Avg	.266	.240	.253	.248	.282	.265	96	.289	.264	.276	.253	.279	.267	104
LHB-HR	20	26	46	12	29	41	103	79	100	179	51	89	140	123
RHB-Avg	.252	.278	.266	.246	.263	.254	105	.259	.262	.260	.253	.262	.257	101
RHB-HR	38	62	100	51	61	112	91	115	172	287	128	175	303	96

Pittsburgh Pirates—Three Rivers Stadium

Alt: 730 feet   **Surface:** Turf

| | 2000 Season | | | | | | | 1998-2000 | | | | | | |
| | Home Games | | | Away Games | | | | Home Games | | | Away Games | | | |
	Pirates	Opp	Total	Pirates	Opp	Total	Index	Pirates	Opp	Total	Pirates	Opp	Total	Index
G	72	72	144	75	75	150	—	220	220	440	223	223	446	—
Avg	.261	.269	.265	.272	.287	.279	95	.263	.257	.260	.254	.274	.264	98
AB	2433	2547	4980	2659	2546	5205	100	7300	7614	14914	7753	7512	15265	99
R	355	389	744	371	424	795	97	1043	1036	2079	961	1137	2098	100
H	635	685	1320	722	731	1453	95	1917	1954	3871	1971	2058	4029	97
2B	150	142	292	145	141	286	107	429	421	850	364	413	777	112
3B	17	14	31	11	19	30	108	59	33	92	40	51	91	103
HR	74	77	151	72	73	145	109	208	216	424	185	214	399	109
BB	239	312	551	271	327	598	96	698	819	1517	699	894	1593	97
SO	466	516	982	466	453	919	112	1500	1571	3071	1527	1395	2922	108
E	58	67	125	65	44	109	119	179	183	362	201	153	354	104
E-Infield	50	52	102	52	36	88	121	153	154	307	166	127	293	106
LHB-Avg	.277	.285	.281	.276	.316	.296	95	.274	.261	.267	.257	.302	.279	96
LHB-HR	32	31	63	28	34	62	114	92	86	178	81	95	176	106
RHB-Avg	.252	.260	.256	.269	.269	.269	95	.256	.254	.255	.253	.257	.255	100
RHB-HR	42	46	88	44	39	83	106	116	130	246	104	119	223	112

PITTSBURGH

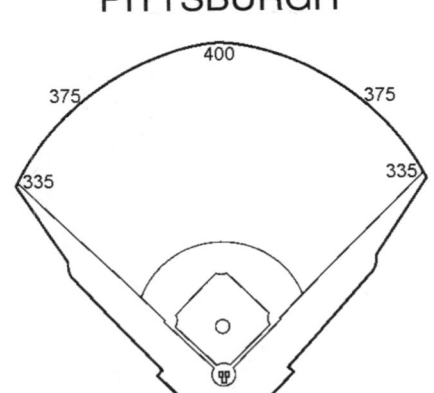

SAN DIEGO

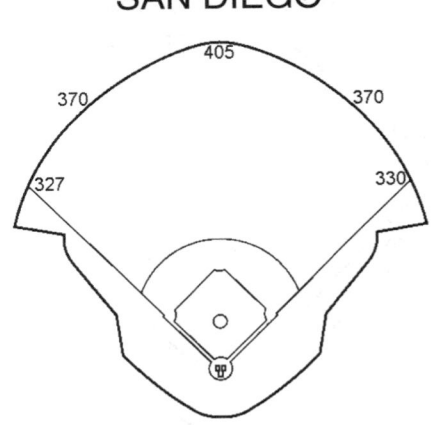

San Diego Padres—Qualcomm Stadium

Alt: 20 feet   **Surface:** Grass

| | 2000 Season | | | | | | | 1998-2000 | | | | | | |
| | Home Games | | | Away Games | | | | Home Games | | | Away Games | | | |
	Padres	Opp	Total	Padres	Opp	Total	Index	Padres	Opp	Total	Padres	Opp	Total	Index
G	75	75	150	72	72	144	—	222	222	444	221	221	442	—
Avg	.252	.243	.247	.263	.277	.270	92	.253	.240	.246	.255	.280	.267	92
AB	2518	2637	5155	2526	2464	4990	99	7326	7649	14975	7656	7482	15138	98
R	328	339	667	369	405	774	83	975	886	1861	1063	1162	2225	83
H	635	640	1275	664	682	1346	91	1853	1835	3688	1949	2095	4044	91
2B	123	104	227	134	130	264	83	341	306	647	409	385	794	82
3B	12	7	19	20	14	34	54	37	25	62	45	47	92	68
HR	65	83	148	79	89	168	85	205	219	424	242	256	498	86
BB	270	264	534	268	321	589	88	848	673	1521	813	829	1642	94
SO	535	528	1063	526	438	964	107	1561	1661	3222	1542	1389	2931	111
E	80	49	129	53	49	102	121	179	158	337	167	153	320	105
E-Infield	72	39	111	47	43	90	118	159	128	287	143	130	273	105
LHB-Avg	.259	.238	.247	.280	.291	.286	86	.264	.243	.253	.272	.292	.282	90
LHB-HR	24	33	57	26	36	62	80	74	74	148	83	98	181	80
RHB-Avg	.249	.247	.248	.255	.266	.260	95	.245	.238	.241	.243	.271	.257	94
RHB-HR	41	50	91	53	53	106	89	131	145	276	159	158	317	90

San Francisco Giants—Pacific Bell Park Alt: 0 feet Surface: Grass

	2000 Season							1998-1999 (3Com Park)						
	Home Games			Away Games				Home Games			Away Games			
	Giants	Opp	Total	Giants	Opp	Total	Index	Giants	Opp	Total	Giants	Opp	Total	Index
G	72	72	144	75	75	150	—	148	148	296	149	149	298	—
Avg	.281	.244	.263	.270	.280	.275	95	.273	.249	.261	.272	.274	.273	96
AB	2356	2416	4772	2634	2526	5160	96	4868	5112	9980	5342	5141	10483	96
R	407	265	672	426	405	831	84	747	630	1377	814	802	1616	86
H	663	590	1253	712	707	1419	92	1328	1275	2603	1455	1407	2862	92
2B	127	107	234	142	129	271	93	254	224	478	286	274	560	90
3B	24	11	35	18	26	44	86	19	21	40	22	29	51	82
HR	99	54	153	100	81	181	91	161	171	332	163	165	328	106
BB	304	251	555	353	307	660	91	626	521	1147	637	582	1219	99
SO	404	475	879	539	507	1046	91	948	1083	2031	952	906	1858	115
E	30	37	67	58	54	112	62	95	105	200	94	100	194	104
E-Infield	28	29	57	42	46	88	67	81	93	174	82	80	162	108
LHB-Avg	.271	.235	.255	.275	.279	.277	92	.286	.255	.272	.279	.272	.276	99
LHB-HR	39	16	55	50	28	78	77	69	64	133	71	48	119	116
RHB-Avg	.290	.249	.267	.267	.280	.274	98	.260	.246	.252	.266	.275	.271	93
RHB-HR	60	38	98	50	53	103	102	92	107	199	92	117	209	101

SAN FRANCISCO

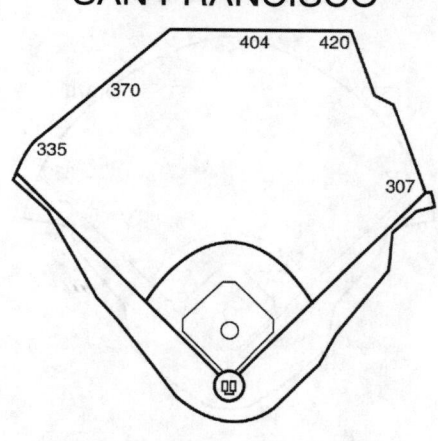

404 420
370
335
307

SEATTLE

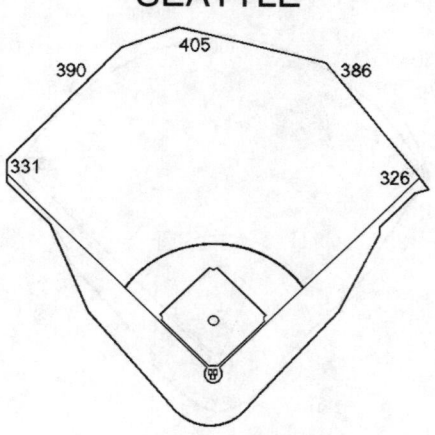

405
390 386
331
326

Seattle Mariners—Safeco Field Alt: -2 feet Surface: Grass

	2000 Season							1999-2000 (post All-Star 1999)						
	Home Games			Away Games				Home Games			Away Games			
	Mariners	Opp	Total	Mariners	Opp	Total	Index	Mariners	Opp	Total	Mariners	Opp	Total	Index
G	72	72	144	72	72	144	—	108	108	216	105	105	210	—
Avg	.249	.249	.249	.292	.279	.286	87	.247	.248	.248	.280	.282	.281	88
AB	2341	2511	4852	2573	2400	4973	98	3496	3735	7231	3717	3519	7236	97
R	375	321	696	453	396	849	82	534	480	1014	599	568	1167	84
H	583	624	1207	751	670	1421	85	864	926	1790	1040	993	2033	86
2B	109	135	244	160	139	299	84	154	192	346	216	206	422	82
3B	10	4	14	13	16	29	49	13	9	22	17	26	43	51
HR	83	66	149	100	90	190	80	124	108	232	146	118	264	88
BB	367	282	649	321	287	608	109	509	413	922	440	426	866	107
SO	499	483	982	463	382	845	119	754	725	1479	726	560	1286	115
E	43	44	87	46	52	98	89	64	64	128	73	75	148	84
E-Infield	34	36	70	40	41	81	86	51	53	104	62	62	124	82
LHB-Avg	.232	.252	.243	.292	.281	.286	85	.238	.240	.239	.279	.285	.282	85
LHB-HR	23	25	48	15	45	60	85	43	38	81	27	60	87	97
RHB-Avg	.259	.246	.252	.292	.278	.286	88	.252	.254	.253	.280	.280	.280	90
RHB-HR	60	41	101	85	45	130	78	81	70	151	119	58	177	84

St. Louis Cardinals—Busch Stadium

Alt: 535 feet **Surface:** Grass

	2000 Season							1998-2000						
	Home Games			Away Games				Home Games			Away Games			
	Cardinals	Opp	Total	Cardinals	Opp	Total	Index	Cardinals	Opp	Total	Cardinals	Opp	Total	Index
G	75	75	150	72	72	144	—	223	223	446	220	220	440	—
Avg	.274	.254	.264	.269	.262	.266	99	.267	.260	.264	.259	.273	.266	99
AB	2463	2544	5007	2509	2375	4884	98	7505	7860	15365	7634	7275	14909	102
R	416	371	787	398	327	725	104	1176	1116	2292	1122	1036	2158	105
H	676	647	1323	676	623	1299	98	2003	2046	4049	1980	1983	3963	101
2B	108	149	257	135	122	257	98	360	422	782	407	391	798	95
3B	13	12	25	10	13	23	106	42	32	74	37	45	82	88
HR	121	99	220	96	83	179	120	322	248	570	279	211	490	113
BB	344	303	647	276	253	529	119	979	873	1852	841	811	1652	109
SO	549	546	1095	589	448	1037	103	1593	1485	3078	1752	1334	3086	97
E	54	56	110	49	54	103	103	199	150	349	158	163	321	107
E-Infield	43	41	84	34	49	83	97	165	116	281	119	132	251	110
LHB-Avg	.295	.262	.278	.291	.264	.278	100	.283	.255	.268	.265	.271	.268	100
LHB-HR	58	37	95	45	34	79	123	110	90	200	89	72	161	124
RHB-Avg	.261	.249	.255	.254	.261	.257	99	.258	.263	.261	.256	.273	.264	99
RHB-HR	63	62	125	51	49	100	118	212	158	370	190	139	329	107

ST. LOUIS

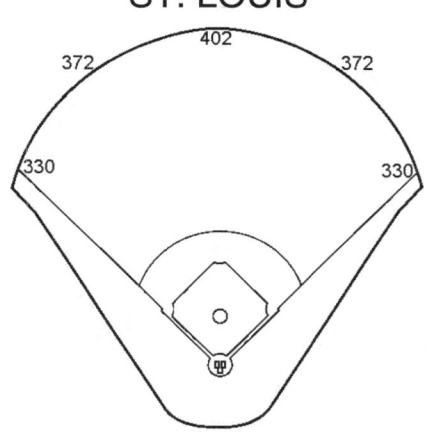

TAMPA BAY

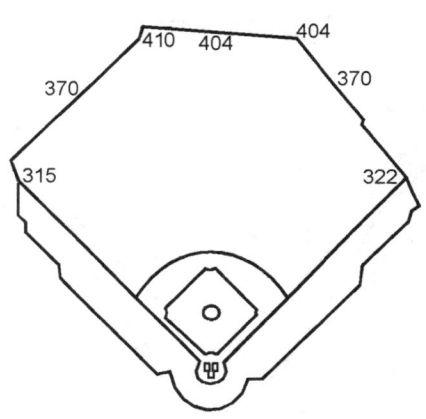

Tampa Bay Devil Rays—Tropicana Field

Alt: 15 feet **Surface:** Turf

	2000 Season							1999						
	Home Games			Away Games				Home Games			Away Games			
	Devil Rays	Opp	Total	Devil Rays	Opp	Total	Index	Devil Rays	Opp	Total	Devil Rays	Opp	Total	Index
G	71	71	142	72	72	144	—	72	72	144	72	72	144	—
Avg	.250	.276	.263	.260	.281	.271	97	.270	.286	.278	.281	.279	.280	99
AB	2372	2575	4947	2511	2400	4911	102	2381	2543	4924	2567	2400	4967	99
R	306	385	691	330	368	698	100	331	403	734	367	380	747	98
H	592	710	1302	654	675	1329	99	642	727	1369	721	670	1391	98
2B	115	138	253	97	134	231	109	110	160	270	137	122	259	105
3B	9	17	26	7	15	22	117	10	17	27	14	11	25	109
HR	68	98	166	77	79	156	106	55	81	136	74	73	147	93
BB	261	226	487	219	245	464	104	244	290	534	239	320	559	96
SO	426	453	879	474	380	854	102	456	494	950	463	438	901	106
E	59	44	103	46	45	91	115	55	43	98	60	50	110	89
E-Infield	52	41	93	38	38	76	124	48	38	86	50	40	90	96
LHB-Avg	.255	.273	.266	.270	.305	.291	91	.290	.296	.293	.276	.276	.276	106
LHB-HR	20	42	62	22	36	58	106	25	38	63	24	37	61	109
RHB-Avg	.247	.278	.261	.256	.257	.256	102	.257	.278	.267	.284	.282	.283	94
RHB-HR	48	56	104	55	43	98	106	30	43	73	50	36	86	83

Texas Rangers—The Ballpark in Arlington

Alt: 551 feet **Surface:** Grass

| | 2000 Season | | | | | | | 1998-2000 | | | | | | |
| | Home Games | | | Away Games | | | | Home Games | | | Away Games | | | |
	Rangers	Opp	Total	Rangers	Opp	Total	Index	Rangers	Opp	Total	Rangers	Opp	Total	Index
G	72	72	144	72	72	144	—	217	217	434	217	217	434	—
Avg	.299	.289	.294	.271	.297	.284	103	.303	.291	.297	.278	.289	.283	105
AB	2489	2631	5120	2531	2461	4992	103	7459	7893	15352	7698	7378	15076	102
R	430	441	871	334	432	766	114	1317	1266	2583	1156	1156	2312	112
H	743	761	1504	687	731	1418	106	2257	2300	4557	2138	2130	4268	107
2B	150	172	322	142	144	286	110	428	488	916	425	442	867	104
3B	14	12	26	14	15	29	87	51	57	108	33	47	80	133
HR	94	100	194	61	84	145	130	283	277	560	264	227	491	112
BB	287	293	580	232	296	528	107	836	719	1555	761	779	1540	99
SO	359	406	765	428	390	818	91	1183	1297	2480	1351	1264	2615	93
E	70	56	126	52	54	106	119	185	148	333	141	159	300	111
E-Infield	54	47	101	45	50	95	106	155	125	280	124	140	264	106
LHB-Avg	.291	.302	.296	.275	.296	.283	104	.295	.292	.294	.276	.283	.280	105
LHB-HR	49	42	91	33	31	64	135	134	127	261	110	105	215	122
RHB-Avg	.307	.281	.292	.268	.298	.285	103	.310	.291	.300	.279	.293	.286	105
RHB-HR	45	58	103	28	53	81	127	149	150	299	154	122	276	104

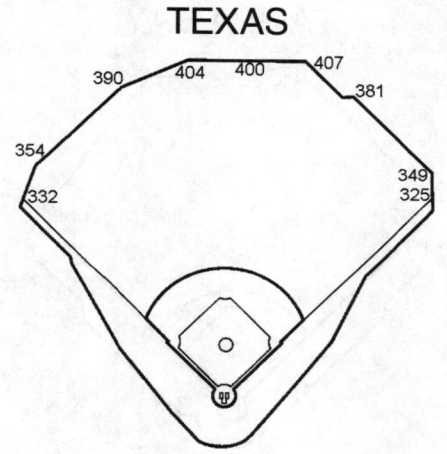

TEXAS

390 404 400 407 381 354 332 349 325

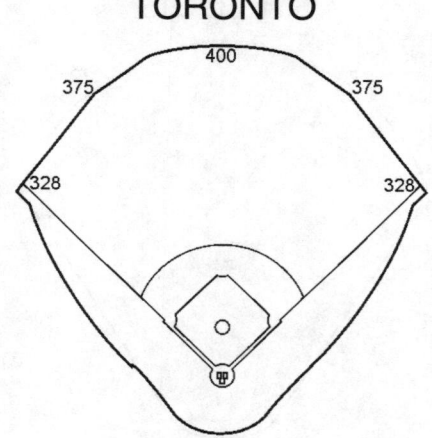

TORONTO

400 375 375 328 328

Toronto Blue Jays—SkyDome

Alt: 300 feet **Surface:** Turf

| | 2000 Season | | | | | | | 1998-2000 | | | | | | |
| | Home Games | | | Away Games | | | | Home Games | | | Away Games | | | |
	Blue Jays	Opp	Total	Blue Jays	Opp	Total	Index	Blue Jays	Opp	Total	Blue Jays	Opp	Total	Index
G	72	72	144	72	72	144	—	217	217	434	218	218	436	—
Avg	.279	.280	.280	.270	.287	.278	101	.274	.268	.271	.273	.278	.275	98
AB	2455	2582	5037	2579	2453	5032	100	7319	7721	15040	7755	7370	15125	100
R	382	409	791	357	395	752	105	1143	1142	2285	1129	1126	2255	102
H	686	723	1409	696	704	1400	101	2005	2067	4072	2120	2046	4166	98
2B	155	159	314	125	137	262	120	464	481	945	409	404	813	117
3B	8	9	17	12	12	24	71	23	28	51	28	51	79	65
HR	117	80	197	96	94	190	104	300	234	534	298	267	565	95
BB	215	241	456	230	246	476	96	748	770	1518	730	797	1527	100
SO	417	460	877	498	396	894	98	1383	1453	2836	1491	1355	2846	100
E	47	47	94	45	47	92	102	154	119	273	141	148	289	95
E-Infield	43	40	83	35	44	79	105	134	101	235	116	129	245	96
LHB-Avg	.310	.277	.293	.282	.290	.286	102	.283	.270	.276	.278	.279	.279	99
LHB-HR	62	35	97	46	48	94	102	163	108	271	155	127	282	94
RHB-Avg	.258	.282	.270	.262	.284	.272	99	.267	.266	.266	.270	.276	.273	98
RHB-HR	55	45	100	50	46	96	105	137	126	263	143	140	283	95

294

1998-2000 Ballpark Index Rankings—Runs per Game

	AMERICAN LEAGUE									NATIONAL LEAGUE								
	Home Games				Away Games						Home Games				Away Games			
	Gm	Team	Opp	Total	Gm	Team	Opp	Total	Index		Gm	Team	Opp	Total	Gm	Team	Opp	Total	Index
Tex	217	1317	1266	2583	217	1156	1156	2312	112	Col	225	1588	1538	3126	225	906	1014	1920	163
Min	217	1026	1194	2220	217	928	1104	2032	109	Hou**	72	463	462	925	75	403	404	807	119
Cle	217	1300	1151	2451	217	1233	1069	2302	106	Phi	217	1060	1131	2191	217	904	1080	1984	110
KC	215	1109	1262	2371	217	1065	1189	2254	106	Cin	222	1114	1055	2169	223	1107	968	2075	105
Bos	217	1151	997	2148	217	1115	951	2066	104	StL	223	1176	1116	2292	220	1122	1036	2158	105
CWS	218	1184	1161	2345	217	1140	1158	2298	102	Ari	220	1078	996	2074	223	1057	1032	2089	101
Tor	217	1143	1142	2285	218	1129	1126	2255	102	Pit	220	1043	1036	2079	223	961	1137	2098	100
TB**	71	306	385	691	72	330	368	698	100	Mil	222	980	1172	2152	221	1054	1122	2176	98
Ana	217	1019	1121	2140	217	1089	1105	2194	98	ChC	223	1071	1165	2236	219	1055	1225	2280	96
NYY	216	1184	925	2109	218	1255	1043	2298	93	Mon	217	936	1098	2034	217	956	1167	2123	96
Bal	217	1068	1059	2127	217	1148	1202	2350	91	Atl	217	1084	798	1882	217	1116	894	2010	94
Det**	72	350	358	708	72	396	401	797	89	NYM	216	1017	876	1893	217	1088	982	2070	92
Oak	217	1143	1021	2164	216	1228	1220	2448	88	Fla	216	898	1058	1956	218	932	1266	2198	90
Sea***	108	534	480	1014	105	599	568	1167	84	LA	223	973	934	1907	220	1084	1072	2156	87
										SF**	72	407	265	672	75	426	405	831	84
										SD	222	975	886	1861	221	1063	1162	2225	83

*—Current dimensions began 1999; **—Current dimensions began 2000; ***—Current dimensions began after 1999 all-star break

1998-2000 Ballpark Index Rankings—Home Runs per At Bat

	AMERICAN LEAGUE									NATIONAL LEAGUE								
	Home Games				Away Games						Home Games				Away Games			
	Gm	Team	Opp	Total	Gm	Team	Opp	Total	Index		Gm	Team	Opp	Total	Gm	Team	Opp	Total	Index
Tex	217	283	277	560	217	264	227	491	112	Col	225	339	361	700	225	188	206	394	164
KC	215	212	288	500	217	171	284	455	109	Hou**	72	123	119	242	75	104	98	202	123
CWS	218	276	267	543	217	236	271	507	109	StL	223	322	248	570	220	279	211	490	113
Cle	217	294	243	537	217	258	239	497	107	Pit	220	208	216	424	223	185	214	399	109
Ana	217	233	271	504	217	248	231	479	106	Cin	222	237	273	510	223	262	220	482	107
TB**	71	68	98	166	72	77	79	156	106	Phi	217	194	272	466	217	179	264	443	104
Bal	217	260	261	521	217	274	263	537	99	LA	223	257	235	492	220	255	234	489	102
Tor	217	300	234	534	218	298	267	565	95	ChC	223	265	290	555	219	263	284	547	100
NYY	216	264	205	469	218	275	231	506	95	Atl	217	246	180	426	217	282	185	467	93
Min	217	133	280	413	217	166	259	425	94	SF**	72	99	54	153	75	100	81	181	91
Oak	217	265	195	460	216	286	242	528	89	Mon	217	211	206	417	217	231	226	457	91
Sea***	108	124	108	232	105	146	118	264	88	Ari	220	234	236	470	223	263	262	525	90
Bos	217	213	205	418	217	288	237	525	79	NYM	216	212	188	400	217	238	231	469	87
Det**	72	64	58	122	72	102	98	200	61	SD	222	205	219	424	221	242	256	498	86
										Mil	222	202	247	449	221	243	277	520	85
										Fla	216	151	220	371	218	211	246	457	81

*—Current dimensions began 1999; **—Current dimensions began 2000; ***—Current dimensions began after 1999 all-star break

1998-2000 Ballpark Index Rankings—Batting Average

	AMERICAN LEAGUE									NATIONAL LEAGUE								
	Home Games				Away Games						Home Games				Away Games			
	Gm	Team	Opp	Avg	Gm	Team	Opp	Avg	Index		Gm	Team	Opp	Avg	Gm	Team	Opp	Avg	Index
Bos	217	.286	.263	.274	217	.267	.246	.257	107	Col	225	.328	.311	.320	225	.252	.262	.257	124
Cle	217	.293	.279	.286	217	.274	.265	.270	106	Hou**	72	.282	.290	.286	75	.273	.272	.273	105
Tex	217	.303	.291	.297	217	.278	.289	.283	105	Ari	220	.272	.259	.266	223	.252	.258	.255	104
KC	215	.283	.288	.286	217	.271	.276	.273	104	Phi	217	.270	.263	.266	217	.253	.269	.261	102
Min	217	.273	.286	.280	217	.258	.283	.270	104	ChC	223	.268	.266	.267	219	.251	.278	.265	101
Det**	72	.280	.281	.280	72	.275	.281	.278	101	Atl	217	.274	.244	.259	217	.266	.250	.258	100
CWS	218	.281	.274	.278	217	.273	.280	.276	100	Cin	222	.269	.251	.259	223	.268	.251	.260	100
Tor	217	.274	.268	.271	218	.273	.278	.275	98	Mil	222	.252	.277	.265	221	.261	.273	.267	99
Ana	217	.265	.268	.267	217	.271	.272	.272	98	StL	223	.267	.260	.264	220	.259	.273	.266	99
TB**	71	.250	.276	.263	72	.260	.281	.271	97	Pit	220	.263	.257	.260	223	.254	.274	.264	98
NYY	216	.283	.247	.265	218	.283	.268	.275	96	Mon	217	.259	.267	.263	217	.262	.276	.269	98
Bal	217	.274	.260	.267	217	.273	.283	.278	96	SF**	72	.281	.244	.263	75	.270	.280	.275	95
Oak	217	.260	.262	.261	216	.267	.289	.278	94	NYM	216	.263	.245	.254	217	.274	.258	.266	95
Sea***	108	.247	.248	.248	105	.280	.282	.281	88	LA	223	.258	.240	.249	220	.257	.265	.261	95
										Fla	216	.256	.263	.259	218	.256	.295	.275	94
										SD	222	.253	.240	.246	221	.255	.280	.267	92

*—Current dimensions began 1999; **—Current dimensions began 2000; ***—Current dimensions began after 1999 all-star break

2000 Lefty/Righty Statistics

These are the numbers that consume managers when they make out lineup cards and when the game is on the line. In the late innings of close contests, managers constantly are making critical platoon decisions regarding pinch-hitters and relief pitchers.

For a second straight season, a pair of American League shortstops had their way against lefthanded pitching.

In 1999, it seemed lefthanded pitchers were better off not pitching to shortstops, as Mike Bordick and Nomar Garciaparra posted the highest batting averages against them in the majors. Not much changed in 2000. While Chipper Jones led the way with a .415 average against southpaws, following closely behind him were Derek Jeter (.395) and Garciaparra (.383).

Against righthanded hurlers, Todd Helton put up numbers that made him a threat to bat .400 last summer. While his push to join the likes of Ted Williams and Rogers Hornsby fell short, Helton finished with a .387 average against righthanders and won the NL batting title with a .372 mark. Garciaparra, who won the AL batting title with an identical .372 average, ranked second against righthanded pitching by batting .369.

Gaining the advantage in a lefty-righty situation obviously is more complicated than simply avoiding pitching to a certain position or team. So check out the 2000 numbers that assisted big league managers every step of the way last season.

Batters vs. Lefthanded and Righthanded Pitchers

Batter	vs	Avg	AB	H	2B	3B	HR	BI	BB	SO	OBP	SLG
Abbott,Jeff	L	.222	63	14	3	0	1	6	6	13	.290	.317
Bats Right	R	.296	152	45	12	1	2	23	15	25	.365	.428
Abbott,Kurt	L	.154	39	6	3	0	2	4	3	11	.214	.385
Bats Right	R	.237	118	28	4	1	4	8	11	40	.305	.390
Abreu,Bobby	L	.243	136	33	4	1	3	10	14	34	.316	.353
Bats Left	R	.339	440	149	38	9	22	69	86	82	.445	.616
Agbayani,B	L	.275	91	25	5	1	3	11	13	15	.362	.451
Bats Right	R	.293	259	76	15	0	12	49	41	53	.401	.490
Alcantara,I	L	.281	32	9	1	0	3	6	3	5	.343	.594
Bats Right	R	.308	13	4	0	0	1	1	0	2	.308	.538
Alexander,M	L	.228	57	13	0	2	1	4	3	10	.267	.351
Bats Right	R	.204	137	28	4	1	3	15	10	31	.259	.314
Alfonzo,E	L	.298	104	31	8	0	5	17	15	16	.390	.519
Bats Right	R	.330	440	145	32	2	20	77	80	54	.433	.548
Alicea,Luis	L	.316	114	36	4	2	0	9	16	8	.394	.386
Bats Both	R	.289	426	123	21	6	6	54	43	67	.357	.408
Allen,Chad	L	.231	13	3	1	0	0	1	1	3	.286	.308
Bats Right	R	.324	37	12	2	0	0	6	2	11	.366	.378
Allen,Dusty	L	.222	18	4	1	0	2	2	3	9	.333	.611
Bats Right	R	.300	10	3	1	0	0	0	1	3	.364	.400
Alomar,R	L	.318	151	48	13	0	3	17	10	24	.364	.464
Bats Both	R	.307	459	141	27	2	16	72	54	58	.382	.479
Alomar Jr.,S	L	.351	74	26	6	1	1	8	4	11	.380	.500
Bats Right	R	.273	282	77	10	1	6	34	12	30	.309	.379
Alou,Moises	L	.370	100	37	7	1	8	27	8	6	.413	.700
Bats Right	R	.350	354	124	21	1	22	87	44	39	.417	.602
Alvarez,C	L	.000	1	0	0	0	0	0	0	0	.000	.000
Bats Right	R	.250	4	1	0	0	0	0	0	1	.250	.250
Alvarez,Gabe	L	.333	6	2	1	0	0	0	2	1	.500	.500
Bats Right	R	.000	8	0	0	0	0	0	1	1	.111	.000
Amaral,Rich	L	.178	45	8	0	1	0	5	3	2	.229	.222
Bats Right	R	.333	15	5	1	0	0	1	4	6	.474	.400
Anderson,B	L	.260	146	38	10	0	3	14	28	33	.384	.390
Bats Left	R	.256	360	92	16	0	16	36	64	70	.372	.433
Anderson,G	L	.333	189	63	15	1	15	42	6	27	.348	.661
Bats Left	R	.266	458	122	25	2	20	75	18	60	.290	.461
Anderson,M	L	.190	21	4	0	0	0	3	2	9	.292	.190
Bats Left	R	.234	141	33	8	1	1	15	9	20	.280	.326
Andrews,S.	L	.295	61	18	3	0	7	21	10	12	.411	.689
Bats Right	R	.198	131	26	2	0	7	18	17	47	.289	.374
Ardoin,Danny	L	.143	7	1	1	0	0	3	0	2	.143	.286
Bats Right	R	.120	25	3	0	0	1	2	8	8	.333	.240
Arias,Alex	L	.240	50	12	2	0	1	5	12	13	.391	.340
Bats Right	R	.162	105	17	7	0	1	10	4	15	.204	.257
Aurilia,Rich	L	.286	119	34	5	1	7	25	16	17	.368	.521
Bats Right	R	.267	390	104	19	1	13	54	38	73	.329	.421
Ausmus,Brad	L	.321	137	44	6	0	3	15	24	12	.422	.431
Bats Right	R	.246	386	95	19	3	4	36	45	67	.333	.342
Aven,Bruce	L	.270	63	17	4	0	2	8	3	11	.303	.429
Bats Right	R	.238	105	25	7	0	5	21	5	28	.273	.448
Bagwell,Jeff	L	.366	112	41	7	1	9	39	30	18	.497	.688
Bats Right	R	.297	478	142	30	0	38	93	77	98	.406	.598
Baines,Harold	L	.192	26	5	0	0	0	3	2	10	.250	.192
Bats Left	R	.261	257	67	13	0	11	36	34	40	.346	.440
Bako,Paul	L	.148	27	4	1	0	1	0	0	11	.179	.296
Bats Left	R	.237	194	46	9	1	1	19	27	53	.329	.309
Barajas,Rod	L	1.000	1	1	0	0	1	2	0	0	1.000	4.000
Bats Right	R	.167	12	2	0	0	0	1	0	4	.167	.167
Barker,Glen	L	.200	20	4	2	0	1	1	2	9	.273	.450
Bats Both	R	.234	47	11	0	1	1	5	5	14	.321	.340
Barker,Kevin	L	.455	11	5	0	0	0	0	0	2	.455	.455
Bats Left	R	.191	89	17	5	0	2	9	20	19	.342	.315
Barnes,John	L	.583	12	7	2	0	0	2	1	1	.615	.750
Bats Right	R	.240	25	6	0	0	0	1	1	5	.321	.320
Barrett,M	L	.160	81	13	4	1	0	5	7	12	.236	.235
Bats Right	R	.237	190	45	11	0	1	17	16	23	.295	.311
Bartee,Kimera	L	.000	2	0	0	0	0	0	0	1	.333	.000
Bats Right	R	.000	2	0	0	0	0	0	0	1	.000	.000
Batista,Tony	L	.235	162	38	9	1	6	23	11	28	.287	.414
Bats Right	R	.273	458	125	23	1	35	91	24	93	.314	.557
Baughman,J	L	.154	13	2	1	0	0	0	1	2	.214	.231
Bats Right	R	.333	9	3	1	0	0	0	0	0	.333	.444
Bautista,D	L	.267	131	35	7	2	4	13	13	20	.333	.443
Bats Right	R	.295	220	65	13	5	7	46	12	30	.333	.495
Becker,Rich	L	.125	32	4	0	0	0	3	6	16	.263	.188
Bats Left	R	.257	253	65	12	0	8	36	61	71	.398	.399
Bell,David	L	.287	108	31	4	1	4	15	8	15	.331	.454
Bats Right	R	.234	346	81	20	1	7	32	34	51	.312	.358
Bell,Derek	L	.156	109	17	4	0	0	5	15	30	.258	.193
Bats Right	R	.293	437	128	27	1	18	64	50	95	.371	.483
Bell,Jay	L	.347	147	51	9	3	6	21	23	23	.430	.571
Bats Right	R	.239	418	100	21	3	12	47	47	65	.318	.390
Bell,Mike	L	.222	9	2	0	0	1	1	2	2	.364	.556
Bats Right	R	.222	18	4	0	0	1	3	2	5	.300	.389
Belle,Albert	L	.343	137	47	12	0	10	33	19	16	.424	.650
Bats Right	R	.261	422	110	25	1	13	70	33	52	.315	.417
Bellhorn,Mark	L	.000	1	0	0	0	0	0	0	1	.000	.000
Bats Both	R	.167	12	2	0	0	0	0	2	5	.286	.167
Belliard,Ron	L	.282	124	35	10	0	1	9	25	14	.400	.387
Bats Right	R	.257	447	115	20	9	7	45	57	70	.341	.389
Bellinger,C	L	.175	57	10	2	0	1	6	1	16	.200	.263
Bats Right	R	.220	127	28	6	2	5	15	16	32	.324	.417
Beltran,C	L	.310	71	22	4	0	4	12	4	16	.338	.535
Bats Both	R	.233	301	70	11	4	3	32	31	53	.302	.326
Beltre,Adrian	L	.277	119	33	4	0	4	21	27	20	.415	.412
Bats Right	R	.294	391	115	26	2	16	64	29	60	.341	.494
Benard,Marvin	L	.216	102	22	3	0	1	5	6	19	.283	.275
Bats Left	R	.273	458	125	24	6	11	50	57	78	.355	.424
Benjamin,Mike	L	.325	80	26	10	0	0	10	4	14	.368	.450
Bats Right	R	.242	153	37	8	2	2	9	8	31	.284	.359

Batters vs. Lefthanded and Righthanded Pitchers

Batter	vs	Avg	AB	H	2B	3B	HR	BI	BB	SO	OBP	SLG	Batter	vs	Avg	AB	H	2B	3B	HR	BI	BB	SO	OBP	SLG
Bennett,Gary	L	.364	22	8	2	0	1	3	3	1	.440	.591	Brown,Adrian	L	.365	52	19	1	0	1	4	4	7	.411	.442
Bats Right	R	.192	52	10	3	0	1	1	10	14	.344	.308	Bats Both	R	.305	256	78	17	3	3	24	25	27	.365	.430
Berg,Dave	L	.270	63	17	3	1	0	4	5	15	.324	.349	Brown,Brant	L	.250	16	4	0	0	0	2	2	6	.368	.250
Bats Right	R	.245	147	36	11	0	1	17	20	31	.347	.340	Bats Left	R	.164	146	24	7	0	5	14	11	56	.222	.315
Bergeron,P	L	.218	87	19	3	0	0	2	10	31	.299	.253	Brown,Dee	L	.000	2	0	0	0	0	0	0	0	.000	.000
Bats Left	R	.251	431	108	22	7	5	29	48	69	.324	.369	Bats Left	R	.174	23	4	1	0	0	4	3	9	.269	.217
Berkman,L.	L	.218	78	17	4	1	2	11	16	20	.347	.372	Brown,Emil	L	.219	32	7	0	0	0	2	3	11	.306	.219
Bats Both	R	.320	275	88	24	0	19	56	40	53	.401	.615	Bats Right	R	.218	87	19	5	0	3	14	8	23	.296	.379
Berroa,G	L	.286	21	6	0	1	0	5	3	5	.375	.381	Brown,K	L	.286	7	2	2	0	0	1	1	2	.375	.571
Bats Right	R	.200	10	2	0	0	0	0	1	3	.273	.200	Bats Right	R	.200	10	2	1	0	0	0	0	3	.200	.300
Berry,Sean	L	.160	25	4	1	0	1	2	0	6	.160	.320	Brown,R	L	.250	4	1	1	0	0	0	0	1	.250	.500
Bats Right	R	.120	25	3	1	0	0	0	4	9	.241	.160	Bats Left	R	.356	87	31	7	0	3	14	4	21	.383	.540
Bichette,D	L	.291	127	37	6	0	8	26	20	20	.382	.528	Buchanan,B	L	.303	33	10	1	0	0	2	5	10	.385	.333
Bats Right	R	.295	448	132	26	2	15	64	29	71	.340	.462	Bats Right	R	.184	49	9	2	0	1	6	3	12	.241	.286
Biggio,Craig	L	.235	68	16	2	1	0	3	21	7	.430	.294	Buford,Damon	L	.326	135	44	8	2	4	20	16	32	.397	.504
Bats Right	R	.275	309	85	11	4	8	32	40	66	.377	.414	Bats Right	R	.222	360	80	10	1	11	28	31	86	.297	.347
Blake,Casey	L	.500	4	2	1	0	0	1	3	2	.625	.750	Buhner,Jay	L	.278	90	25	8	0	6	19	18	22	.405	.567
Bats Right	R	.083	12	1	1	0	0	0	0	5	.154	.167	Bats Right	R	.245	274	67	12	0	20	63	41	76	.346	.507
Blanco,Henry	L	.306	62	19	5	0	2	8	6	12	.362	.484	Burkhart,M	L	.227	22	5	0	0	0	4	4	7	.370	.227
Bats Right	R	.216	222	48	19	0	5	23	30	48	.306	.369	Bats Both	R	.314	51	16	3	0	4	14	13	18	.471	.608
Blum,Geoff	L	.292	72	21	3	0	5	12	2	16	.311	.542	Burks,Ellis	L	.360	100	36	5	1	4	21	16	12	.441	.550
Bats Both	R	.280	271	76	17	2	6	33	24	44	.341	.424	Bats Right	R	.338	293	99	16	4	20	75	40	37	.412	.625
Bocachica,H	L	.143	7	1	0	0	0	0	0	2	.143	.143	Burnitz,J	L	.238	160	38	11	0	7	31	22	30	.347	.438
Bats Right	R	.667	3	2	0	0	0	0	0	0	.667	.667	Bats Left	R	.230	404	93	18	2	24	67	77	91	.359	.463
Bogar,Tim	L	.284	81	23	2	1	2	10	10	14	.359	.407	Burrell,Pat	L	.282	85	24	8	1	5	21	14	28	.380	.576
Bats Right	R	.179	223	40	7	1	5	23	25	42	.268	.287	Bats Right	R	.254	323	82	19	0	13	58	49	111	.353	.433
Bonds,Barry	L	.230	148	34	6	1	12	32	20	33	.320	.527	Bush,Homer	L	.317	41	13	1	0	0	5	4	7	.370	.341
Bats Left	R	.340	332	113	22	3	37	74	97	44	.487	.759	Bats Right	R	.199	256	51	7	0	1	13	14	53	.255	.238
Bonilla,Bobby	L	.372	43	16	7	1	1	8	5	7	.438	.651	Byrnes,Eric	L	.167	6	1	0	0	0	0	0	1	.167	.167
Bats Both	R	.230	196	45	6	2	4	20	32	44	.339	.342	Bats Right	R	.500	4	2	0	0	0	0	0	0	.600	.500
Boone,Aaron	L	.302	53	16	5	0	1	9	10	10	.424	.453	Cabrera,Alex	L	.269	26	7	0	0	5	8	3	7	.355	.846
Bats Right	R	.282	238	67	13	0	11	34	14	42	.338	.475	Bats Right	R	.259	54	14	2	0	0	6	1	14	.268	.333
Boone,Bret	L	.235	132	31	6	0	5	18	16	21	.318	.394	Cabrera,J	L	.210	62	13	1	1	1	6	5	5	.275	.306
Bats Right	R	.257	331	85	12	2	14	56	34	76	.329	.432	Bats Right	R	.274	113	31	2	0	1	9	3	10	.299	.319
Bordick,Mike	L	.307	153	47	14	0	5	21	14	24	.365	.497	Cabrera,O	L	.286	105	30	9	0	2	9	10	5	.342	.429
Bats Right	R	.277	430	119	16	1	15	59	35	75	.332	.423	Bats Right	R	.221	317	70	16	1	11	46	15	23	.257	.382
Bradley,M	L	.261	46	12	1	1	1	9	5	14	.333	.391	Cairo,Miguel	L	.270	74	20	5	0	0	3	3	5	.300	.338
Bats Both	R	.204	108	22	7	0	1	6	9	18	.269	.296	Bats Right	R	.259	301	78	13	2	1	29	26	29	.317	.326
Bragg,Darren	L	.063	16	1	0	0	0	1	1	6	.118	.063	Cameron,Mike	L	.273	110	30	6	1	3	14	13	22	.352	.427
Bats Left	R	.241	133	32	7	1	3	20	16	35	.316	.376	Bats Right	R	.266	433	115	22	3	16	64	65	111	.368	.441
Branson,Jeff	L	.000	5	0	0	0	0	0	0	3	.000	.000	Caminiti,Ken	L	.300	40	12	2	0	1	11	9	5	.429	.425
Bats Left	R	.333	12	4	1	0	0	0	1	3	.385	.417	Bats Both	R	.304	168	51	11	0	14	34	33	32	.417	.619
Branyan,Russ	L	.200	15	3	0	2	0	1	2	4	.278	.467	Canizaro,Jay	L	.269	93	25	7	1	2	15	6	13	.313	.430
Bats Left	R	.242	178	43	7	0	16	37	20	72	.332	.551	Bats Right	R	.269	253	68	14	0	5	25	18	44	.320	.383
Brock,Tarrik	L	1.000	1	1	0	0	0	0	1	0	1.000	1.000	Canseco,Jose	L	.286	77	22	3	0	6	17	15	29	.398	.558
Bats Left	R	.091	11	1	0	0	0	0	3	4	.286	.091	Bats Right	R	.242	252	61	15	0	9	32	49	73	.370	.409
Brogna,Rico	L	.105	38	4	2	0	1	6	1	11	.146	.237	Cardona,J	L	.000	6	0	0	0	0	0	0	3	.000	.000
Bats Left	R	.265	147	39	15	0	1	15	9	30	.312	.388	Bats Right	R	.206	34	7	1	0	1	2	0	6	.222	.324
Brosius,Scott	L	.260	104	27	4	0	6	20	10	16	.325	.471	Carpenter,B	L	.000	1	0	0	0	0	0	0	1	.000	.000
Bats Right	R	.221	366	81	16	0	10	44	35	57	.291	.347	Bats Left	R	.231	26	6	0	0	3	5	4	12	.333	.577

Batters vs. Lefthanded and Righthanded Pitchers

Batter	vs	Avg	AB	H	2B	3B	HR	BI	BB	SO	OBP	SLG
Casanova,Raul	L	.246	57	14	5	1	1	12	7	11	.338	.421
Bats Both	R	.247	174	43	8	2	5	24	19	37	.328	.402
Casey,Sean	L	.250	104	26	6	1	1	18	12	22	.328	.356
Bats Left	R	.332	376	125	27	1	19	67	40	58	.401	.561
Casimiro,C	L	.200	5	1	1	0	0	3	0	1	.200	.400
Bats Right	R	.000	3	0	0	0	0	0	0	1	.000	.000
Castilla,V	L	.203	69	14	2	0	1	7	4	7	.240	.275
Bats Right	R	.225	262	59	7	1	5	35	10	34	.258	.317
Castillo,A	L	.197	71	14	1	0	0	3	12	14	.313	.211
Bats Right	R	.219	114	25	6	0	1	13	9	22	.270	.298
Castillo,Luis	L	.291	148	43	5	2	2	3	18	24	.367	.392
Bats Both	R	.350	391	137	12	1	0	14	60	62	.437	.386
Castro,Juan	L	.244	41	10	4	1	0	2	3	3	.295	.390
Bats Right	R	.240	183	44	8	1	4	21	11	30	.281	.361
Castro,Ramon	L	.200	25	5	1	0	0	2		6	.250	.240
Bats Right	R	.248	113	28	3	0	2	12	14	30	.333	.327
Catalanotto,F	L	.263	19	5	1	0	0	5	6	2	.440	.316
Bats Left	R	.293	263	77	12	2	10	37	27	34	.369	.468
Cedeno,Roger	L	.313	48	15	0	0	3	10	10	8	.431	.500
Bats Both	R	.275	211	58	2	5	3	16	33	39	.371	.374
Charles,Frank	L	.500	2	1	1	0	0	0	0	1	.500	1.000
Bats Right	R	.400	5	2	0	0	0	2	0	1	.400	.400
Chavez,Eric	L	.197	122	24	4	1	3	16	8	32	.244	.320
Bats Left	R	.303	379	115	19	3	23	70	54	62	.388	.551
Chavez,Raul	L	.182	11	2	0	0	0	2	1	0	.231	.182
Bats Right	R	.281	32	9	2	0	1	3	2	6	.324	.438
Christensen,M	L	.500	2	1	0	0	0	1	0	1	.500	.500
Bats Left	R	.059	17	1	0	0	0	0	2	5	.200	.059
Christenson,R	L	.167	54	9	0	0	2	9	8	13	.286	.278
Bats Right	R	.307	75	23	2	2	2	9	11	20	.395	.467
Cirillo,Jeff	L	.379	132	50	14	0	2	32	18	18	.445	.530
Bats Right	R	.311	466	145	39	2	9	83	49	54	.377	.461
Clapinski,C	L	.278	18	5	0	0	0	1	3	2	.381	.278
Bats Both	R	.323	31	10	4	1	1	6	2	5	.364	.613
Clark,Brady	L	.500	2	1	1	0	0	0	0	0	.500	1.000
Bats Right	R	.222	9	2	0	0	0	2	0	2	.222	.222
Clark,Tony	L	.308	39	12	4	0	3	9	2	8	.341	.641
Bats Both	R	.266	169	45	10	0	10	28	22	43	.351	.503
Clark,Will	L	.248	113	28	6	1	2	9	13	20	.344	.372
Bats Left	R	.344	314	108	24	1	19	61	56	49	.444	.608
Clayton,Royce	L	.196	107	21	3	0	4	14	10	26	.263	.336
Bats Right	R	.254	406	103	18	5	10	40	32	66	.312	.397
Clemente,E	L	.227	66	15	2	0	0	4	0	26	.239	.258
Bats Right	R	.167	12	2	0	0	0	1	0	1	.167	.167
Coffie,Ivanon	L	.333	9	3	2	1	0	3	1	1	.400	.778
Bats Left	R	.196	51	10	2	0	0	3	4	10	.263	.235
Colbrunn,Greg	L	.285	137	39	8	1	6	25	21	24	.385	.489
Bats Right	R	.333	192	64	14	0	9	32	22	21	.420	.547
Collier,Lou	L	.182	11	2	0	0	1	2	2	2	.286	.455
Bats Right	R	.238	21	5	1	0	0	0	4	2	.360	.286
Conine,Jeff	L	.333	120	40	7	0	7	16	13	13	.403	.567
Bats Right	R	.263	289	76	13	2	6	30	23	40	.315	.384
Conti,Jason	L	.250	8	2	0	0	0	2	1	1	.400	.250
Bats Left	R	.229	83	19	4	3	1	13	6	29	.281	.386
Coomer,Ron	L	.256	125	32	10	0	5	16	11	6	.321	.456
Bats Right	R	.274	419	115	19	1	11	66	25	44	.316	.403
Coquillette,T	L	.278	18	5	2	0	0	4	3	6	.381	.389
Bats Right	R	.171	41	7	2	0	1	4	4	13	.239	.293
Cora,Alex	L	.226	62	14	1	1	0	5	2	12	.273	.274
Bats Left	R	.241	291	70	17	5	4	27	24	41	.307	.375
Cordero,Wil	L	.323	127	41	12	2	5	24	6	16	.365	.567
Bats Right	R	.260	369	96	23	3	11	44	26	60	.316	.428
Cordova,Marty	L	.212	66	14	2	0	2	8	8	9	.297	.333
Bats Right	R	.261	134	35	5	0	2	10	10	26	.327	.343
Counsell,C	L	.267	15	4	0	1	0	0	0	3	.267	.400
Bats Left	R	.321	137	44	8	0	2	11	20	15	.413	.423
Cox,Steve	L	.245	53	13	3	0	3	7	11	12	.375	.472
Bats Left	R	.291	265	77	16	1	8	28	35	35	.380	.449
Crede,Joe	L	.500	2	1	0	0	0	0	0	1	.500	.500
Bats Right	R	.333	12	4	1	0	0	3	0	2	.308	.417
Crespo,Felipe	L	.174	23	4	1	0	0	2	1	6	.208	.217
Bats Both	R	.315	108	34	5	1	4	27	9	17	.379	.491
Cromer,D.T.	L	.222	9	2	0	0	0	1	1	4	.300	.222
Bats Left	R	.368	38	14	4	0	2	7	0	10	.375	.632
Cromer,Tripp	L	.500	2	1	0	0	0	0	0	0	.500	.500
Bats Right	R	.000	6	0	0	0	0	0	1	1	.143	.000
Cruz,Deivi	L	.345	139	48	12	0	5	27	3	6	.364	.540
Bats Right	R	.288	444	128	34	5	5	55	10	37	.304	.421
Cruz,Ivan	L	.000	0	0	0	0	0	0	0	0	.000	.000
Bats Left	R	.091	11	1	0	0	0	0	0	8	.091	.091
Cruz,Jacob	L	.400	5	2	0	0	0	1	1	0	.571	.400
Bats Left	R	.208	24	5	3	0	0	4	4	4	.310	.333
Cruz,Jose	L	.290	162	47	12	2	5	19	11	21	.339	.481
Bats Both	R	.224	441	99	20	3	26	57	60	108	.317	.460
Cummings,M	L	.360	25	9	2	0	0	3	3	4	.448	.440
Bats Left	R	.265	181	48	8	0	4	21	14	24	.325	.376
Curtis,Chad	L	.328	116	38	11	0	2	17	13	26	.395	.474
Bats Right	R	.242	219	53	14	1	6	31	24	45	.316	.397
Damon,Johnny	L	.357	171	61	14	1	4	33	20	15	.418	.520
Bats Left	R	.316	484	153	28	9	12	55	45	45	.369	.486
Darr,Mike	L	.269	52	14	2	2	0	7	4	8	.321	.385
Bats Left	R	.268	153	41	10	2	1	23	19	37	.349	.392
Daubach,Brian	L	.216	102	22	7	0	3	11	7	30	.274	.373
Bats Left	R	.257	393	101	25	2	18	65	37	100	.326	.468
Davis,Ben	L	.194	36	7	3	0	2	5	6	11	.310	.444
Bats Both	R	.234	94	22	3	0	1	9	8	24	.291	.298
Davis,Eric	L	.390	105	41	7	0	3	18	14	21	.463	.543
Bats Right	R	.242	149	36	7	0	3	22	22	39	.337	.349
Davis,Russ	L	.311	103	32	3	0	7	17	6	12	.355	.544
Bats Right	R	.195	77	15	2	0	2	7	3	17	.232	.299

Batters vs. Lefthanded and Righthanded Pitchers

Batter	vs	Avg	AB	H	2B	3B	HR	BI	BB	SO	OBP	SLG
Dawkins,G	L	.214	14	3	1	0	0	1	0	1	.214	.286
Bats Right	R	.222	27	6	1	0	0	2	2	6	.276	.259
de la Rosa,T	L	.200	30	6	0	1	1	2	3	5	.273	.367
Bats Right	R	.361	36	13	3	0	1	7	4	6	.439	.528
DeHaan,Kory	L	.167	18	3	0	0	0	0	0	8	.167	.167
Bats Left	R	.212	85	18	7	0	2	13	5	31	.253	.365
Delgado,C	L	.319	188	60	21	1	6	36	29	37	.422	.537
Bats Left	R	.357	381	136	36	0	35	101	94	67	.492	.727
Delgado,W	L	.241	29	7	0	0	0	2	2	9	.290	.241
Bats Both	R	.263	99	26	2	0	1	9	9	17	.318	.313
Dellucci,D	L	.000	0	0	0	0	0	0	0	0	.000	.000
Bats Left	R	.300	50	15	3	0	0	2	4	9	.352	.360
DeRosa,Mark	L	.333	6	2	1	0	0	3	2	0	.500	.500
Bats Right	R	.286	7	2	0	0	0	0	0	1	.286	.286
DeShields,D	L	.344	154	53	13	1	2	24	20	24	.415	.481
Bats Left	R	.278	407	113	30	4	8	62	49	58	.351	.430
Diaz,Einar	L	.263	57	15	4	0	0	5	3	8	.323	.333
Bats Right	R	.275	193	53	10	2	4	20	8	21	.324	.409
DiFelice,Mike	L	.225	40	9	3	1	0	1	0	9	.220	.350
Bats Right	R	.244	164	40	10	0	6	18	12	31	.294	.415
DiSarcina,G	L	.250	4	1	0	0	0	0	0	0	.250	.250
Bats Right	R	.412	34	14	2	0	1	11	1	3	.444	.559
Donnels,Chris	L	.000	4	0	0	0	0	0	0	1	.000	.000
Bats Left	R	.333	30	10	3	0	4	9	6	6	.432	.833
Dransfeldt,K	L	.143	7	1	1	0	0	1	0	4	.143	.286
Bats Right	R	.105	19	2	1	0	0	1	1	10	.150	.158
Drew,J.D.	L	.257	74	19	3	0	0	4	8	22	.345	.297
Bats Left	R	.303	333	101	14	2	18	53	59	77	.413	.520
Ducey,Rob	L	.083	12	1	1	0	0	1	2	7	.214	.167
Bats Left	R	.203	153	31	4	1	6	25	29	42	.326	.359
Dunston,S	L	.226	106	24	5	0	6	24	2	23	.245	.443
Bats Right	R	.273	110	30	6	2	6	19	4	24	.308	.527
Dunwoody,T.	L	.176	17	3	1	0	0	3	1	8	.250	.235
Bats Left	R	.211	161	34	8	0	1	20	7	34	.237	.280
Durazo,E	L	.318	22	7	1	0	0	2	4	3	.407	.364
Bats Left	R	.259	174	45	10	0	8	31	30	40	.369	.454
Durham,Ray	L	.248	129	32	6	2	4	16	8	22	.305	.419
Bats Both	R	.289	485	140	29	7	13	59	67	83	.375	.458
Durrington,T	L	.000	3	0	0	0	0	0	0	0	.000	.000
Bats Right	R	.000	0	0	0	0	0	0	0	0	.000	.000
Dye,Jermaine	L	.323	133	43	11	1	7	25	12	11	.379	.579
Bats Right	R	.321	468	150	30	1	26	93	57	88	.393	.556
Easley,Damion	L	.280	125	35	9	0	3	13	14	18	.357	.424
Bats Right	R	.251	339	85	18	2	11	45	41	61	.348	.413
Echevarria,A	L	.136	22	3	1	0	0	2	3	3	.240	.182
Bats Right	R	.241	29	7	1	0	1	4	4	8	.333	.379
Edmonds,Jim	L	.270	152	41	4	0	11	31	28	62	.376	.513
Bats Left	R	.306	373	114	21	0	31	77	75	105	.425	.611
Elster,Kevin	L	.258	89	23	1	0	8	16	20	15	.394	.539
Bats Right	R	.206	131	27	7	0	6	16	18	37	.302	.397
Encarnacion,J	L	.314	140	44	5	2	7	27	7	24	.349	.529
Bats Right	R	.280	407	114	20	4	7	45	22	66	.324	.400
Ensberg,M	L	1.000	1	1	0	0	0	0	0	0	1.000	1.000
Bats Right	R	.167	6	1	0	0	0	0	0	1	.167	.167
Erstad,Darin	L	.338	210	71	11	2	9	34	12	24	.377	.538
Bats Left	R	.363	466	169	28	4	16	66	52	58	.423	.543
Estalella,B	L	.250	72	18	7	1	4	19	17	25	.389	.542
Bats Right	R	.229	227	52	15	2	10	34	40	67	.347	.445
Eusebio,Tony	L	.222	63	14	5	0	2	9	8	17	.310	.397
Bats Right	R	.303	155	47	13	0	5	24	17	28	.382	.484
Evans,Tom	L	.200	20	4	1	0	0	0	2	9	.273	.250
Bats Right	R	.324	34	11	3	0	0	5	8	4	.455	.412
Everett,Carl	L	.348	132	46	10	0	4	23	10	20	.411	.515
Bats Both	R	.283	364	103	22	4	30	85	42	93	.359	.613
Fabregas,J	L	.308	13	4	1	0	0	1	1	2	.357	.385
Bats Left	R	.279	129	36	3	0	3	16	7	9	.316	.372
Fasano,Sal	L	.184	38	7	2	0	3	6	2	13	.225	.474
Bats Right	R	.227	88	20	4	0	4	13	12	34	.337	.409
Febles,Carlos	L	.272	92	25	4	1	0	12	14	11	.370	.337
Bats Right	R	.251	247	62	8	0	2	17	22	37	.335	.308
Feliz,Pedro	L	.000	1	0	0	0	0	0	0	0	.000	.000
Bats Right	R	.333	6	2	0	0	0	0	0	1	.333	.333
Fick,Robert	L	.194	31	6	0	0	0	3	3	10	.257	.194
Bats Left	R	.265	132	35	7	2	3	19	19	29	.359	.417
Finley,Steve	L	.274	157	43	2	3	11	34	13	27	.350	.535
Bats Left	R	.283	382	108	25	2	24	62	52	60	.365	.547
Flaherty,John	L	.270	89	24	6	0	2	9	5	8	.309	.404
Bats Right	R	.259	305	79	9	0	8	30	15	49	.292	.367
Fletcher,D	L	.342	79	27	5	1	1	12	4	15	.391	.468
Bats Left	R	.315	337	106	14	0	19	46	16	30	.346	.525
Floyd,Cliff	L	.333	126	42	9	0	5	26	7	26	.383	.524
Bats Left	R	.286	294	84	21	0	17	65	43	56	.376	.531
Fordyce,Brook	L	.347	72	25	2	0	6	18	5	11	.392	.625
Bats Right	R	.287	230	66	16	1	8	31	12	39	.325	.470
Fox,Andy	L	.250	24	6	2	0	0	1	2	9	.308	.333
Bats Left	R	.230	226	52	6	2	4	19	20	44	.301	.327
Franco,Matt	L	.200	10	2	0	0	0	1	3	2	.385	.200
Bats Left	R	.242	124	30	4	0	2	13	18	20	.336	.323
Frias,Hanley	L	.188	48	9	2	0	1	4	5	5	.264	.292
Bats Both	R	.219	64	14	3	0	1	2	12	13	.342	.313
Frye,Jeff	L	.359	117	42	9	0	1	5	10	23	.411	.462
Bats Right	R	.278	209	58	10	0	0	11	26	31	.359	.325
Fryman,Travis	L	.297	118	35	4	0	4	17	27	25	.422	.432
Bats Right	R	.327	456	149	34	4	18	89	46	86	.384	.537
Fullmer,Brad	L	.226	93	21	4	0	5	19	5	18	.279	.430
Bats Left	R	.311	389	121	25	1	27	85	25	50	.355	.589
Furcal,Rafael	L	.250	96	24	3	0	0	5	15	19	.357	.281
Bats Both	R	.306	359	110	17	4	4	32	58	61	.404	.409
Gaetti,Gary	L	.000	7	0	0	0	0	1	0	2	.000	.000
Bats Right	R	.000	3	0	0	0	0	0	0	1	.000	.000

Batters vs. Lefthanded and Righthanded Pitchers

Batter	vs	Avg	AB	H	2B	3B	HR	BI	BB	SO	OBP	SLG	Batter	vs	Avg	AB	H	2B	3B	HR	BI	BB	SO	OBP	SLG
Galarraga,A	L	.347	118	41	7	0	3	18	8	21	.400	.483	Grace,Mark	L	.305	131	40	7	1	6	23	24	11	.419	.511
Bats Right	R	.287	376	108	18	1	25	82	28	105	.359	.540	Bats Left	R	.272	379	103	34	0	5	59	71	17	.386	.401
Gant,Ron	L	.315	124	39	8	1	7	14	22	23	.412	.565	Graffanino,T	L	.224	58	13	3	0	2	8	13	8	.366	.379
Bats Right	R	.223	301	67	11	2	19	40	34	68	.302	.462	Bats Right	R	.300	110	33	3	1	0	9	9	19	.361	.345
Garcia,Jesse	L	.000	4	0	0	0	0	0	2	0	.333	.000	Grebeck,Craig	L	.272	92	25	4	0	2	10	7	14	.323	.380
Bats Right	R	.077	13	1	0	0	0	0	0	2	.077	.077	Bats Right	R	.309	149	46	15	0	1	13	18	19	.388	.430
Garcia,Karim	L	.000	0	0	0	0	0	0	0	0	.000	.000	Green,S	L	.324	34	11	1	0	0	3	2	7	.361	.353
Bats Left	R	.091	33	3	0	0	0	0	0	10	.091	.091	Bats Both	R	.200	90	18	1	0	6	8	19	.265	.222
Garciaparra,N	L	.383	141	54	12	0	6	29	21	12	.457	.596	Green,Shawn	L	.259	185	48	12	0	4	24	19	40	.333	.389
Bats Right	R	.369	388	143	39	3	15	67	40	38	.425	.601	Bats Left	R	.273	425	116	32	4	20	75	71	81	.381	.508
Giambi,Jason	L	.324	176	57	12	0	7	36	31	26	.427	.511	Greene,C	L	.000	1	0	0	0	0	0	0	1	.000	.000
Bats Left	R	.338	334	113	17	1	36	101	106	70	.499	.719	Bats Right	R	.125	8	1	0	0	0	0	0	4	.125	.125
Giambi,Jeremy	L	.266	64	17	2	0	5	17	6	16	.333	.531	Greene,Todd	L	.260	50	13	2	0	2	6	5	8	.327	.420
Bats Left	R	.250	196	49	8	2	5	33	26	45	.339	.388	Bats Right	R	.200	35	7	0	0	3	4	0	10	.200	.457
Gil,Benji	L	.301	113	34	6	1	2	6	12	16	.378	.425	Greene,Willie	L	.244	45	11	3	0	0	3	4	15	.306	.311
Bats Right	R	.202	188	38	8	0	4	17	18	43	.280	.309	Bats Left	R	.193	254	49	12	2	10	34	32	54	.286	.374
Gilbert,Shawn	L	.143	14	2	0	0	1	1	2	6	.250	.357	Greer,Rusty	L	.245	98	24	7	2	1	12	11	16	.330	.388
Bats Right	R	.167	6	1	1	0	0	2	0	1	.167	.333	Bats Left	R	.314	296	93	27	1	7	53	40	45	.393	.483
Giles,Brian	L	.293	150	44	6	1	5	28	24	23	.393	.447	Grieve,Ben	L	.268	190	51	13	0	8	38	22	50	.338	.463
Bats Left	R	.323	409	132	31	6	30	95	90	46	.446	.648	Bats Left	R	.285	404	115	27	1	19	66	51	80	.368	.498
Gilkey,B	L	.173	104	18	4	1	2	12	10	16	.265	.288	Griffey Jr.,K	L	.263	152	40	5	0	11	32	17	38	.341	.513
Bats Right	R	.183	60	11	2	0	1	3	7	12	.265	.267	Bats Left	R	.274	368	101	17	3	29	86	77	79	.404	.573
Ginter,Keith	L	.000	0	0	0	0	0	1	0	0	.000	.000	Grissom,M	L	.304	125	38	5	1	2	18	9	17	.343	.408
Bats Right	R	.250	8	2	0	0	1	2	1	3	.333	.625	Bats Right	R	.228	470	107	13	1	12	44	30	82	.273	.336
Gipson,C	L	.267	15	4	0	1	0	2	2	5	.353	.400	Grudzielanek	L	.250	168	42	8	2	2	12	16	22	.317	.357
Bats Right	R	.357	14	5	1	0	0	1	2	4	.438	.429	Bats Right	R	.290	449	130	27	4	5	37	29	59	.342	.401
Girardi,Joe	L	.202	114	23	2	0	2	7	16	22	.300	.272	Guerrero,V	L	.376	133	50	7	3	12	32	15	20	.447	.744
Bats Right	R	.313	249	78	13	1	4	33	16	39	.358	.422	Bats Right	R	.336	438	147	21	8	32	91	43	54	.399	.639
Glanville,D	L	.237	139	33	6	0	1	13	10	16	.285	.302	Guerrero,W	L	.292	106	31	2	1	2	13	5	9	.321	.387
Bats Right	R	.285	498	142	21	6	7	39	21	60	.314	.394	Bats Both	R	.253	182	46	5	1	0	10	14	32	.306	.291
Glaus,Troy	L	.369	130	48	12	0	17	32	35	28	.500	.854	Guillen,C	L	.320	50	16	1	0	1	7	1	9	.333	.400
Bats Right	R	.259	433	112	25	1	30	70	77	135	.373	.529	Bats Both	R	.244	238	58	14	2	6	35	27	44	.322	.395
Gload,Ross	L	.000	2	0	0	0	0	0	0	1	.000	.000	Guillen,Jose	L	.195	87	17	2	1	5	14	8	17	.293	.414
Bats Left	R	.207	29	6	0	1	1	3	3	9	.273	.379	Bats Right	R	.275	229	63	14	4	5	27	10	48	.331	.437
Gomez,Chris	L	.227	22	5	0	0	0	1	3	1	.320	.227	Guillen,Ozzie	L	.143	7	1	0	0	0	0	0	1	.143	.143
Bats Right	R	.219	32	7	0	0	0	2	4	4	.297	.219	Bats Left	R	.250	100	25	4	0	2	12	6	6	.292	.350
Gonzalez,Alex	L	.245	98	24	6	0	2	10	3	19	.267	.367	Gutierrez,R	L	.356	90	32	8	0	1	13	10	8	.416	.478
Bats Right	R	.185	287	53	11	4	5	32	10	58	.216	.303	Bats Right	R	.256	359	92	11	2	10	43	56	50	.365	.382
Gonzalez,A	L	.228	114	26	4	1	2	8	13	27	.305	.333	Guzman,C	L	.209	172	36	9	5	4	19	3	24	.225	.390
Bats Right	R	.259	413	107	27	1	13	61	30	86	.315	.424	Bats Both	R	.261	459	120	16	15	4	35	43	77	.325	.388
Gonzalez,Juan	L	.360	114	41	5	1	6	17	9	15	.403	.579	Gwynn,Tony	L	.417	36	15	2	0	1	6	2	2	.462	.556
Bats Right	R	.265	347	92	25	1	16	50	23	69	.315	.481	Bats Left	R	.286	91	26	10	0	0	11	7	2	.327	.396
Gonzalez,Luis	L	.254	177	45	10	0	8	31	20	34	.335	.446	Hairston Jr.,J	L	.244	45	11	1	0	1	6	4	5	.306	.333
Bats Left	R	.333	441	147	37	2	23	83	58	51	.415	.583	Bats Right	R	.259	135	35	4	0	4	13	17	17	.367	.378
Gonzalez,Raul	L	.000	2	0	0	0	0	0	0	2	.000	.000	Hall,Toby	L	.000	1	0	0	0	0	0	0	0	.000	.000
Bats Right	R	.000	0	0	0	0	0	0	0	0	.000	.000	Bats Right	R	.182	11	2	0	0	1	1	1	0	.250	.455
Gonzalez,Wiki	L	.277	83	23	7	0	1	8	9	8	.355	.398	Halter,Shane	L	.286	91	26	6	2	3	14	6	21	.330	.495
Bats Right	R	.214	201	43	8	1	4	22	21	23	.293	.323	Bats Right	R	.245	147	36	6	0	0	13	8	28	.285	.286
Goodwin,Tom	L	.340	106	36	5	1	2	15	9	27	.385	.462	Hamilton,D	L	.000	1	0	0	0	0	0	0	0	.000	.000
Bats Left	R	.244	422	103	6	8	4	43	59	90	.337	.325	Bats Left	R	.279	104	29	4	1	1	6	14	20	.361	.365

302

Batters vs. Lefthanded and Righthanded Pitchers

Batter	vs	Avg	AB	H	2B	3B	HR	BI	BB	SO	OBP	SLG
Hammonds,J	L	.378	98	37	7	0	6	31	12	15	.439	.633
Bats Right	R	.323	356	115	17	2	14	75	32	68	.382	.500
Hansen,Dave	L	.000	8	0	0	0	0	0	0	6	.000	.000
Bats Left	R	.310	113	35	6	2	8	26	26	26	.439	.611
Harris,Lenny	L	.158	19	3	0	0	0	3	0	3	.158	.158
Bats Left	R	.270	204	55	7	4	4	23	20	19	.330	.402
Haselman,Bill	L	.286	35	10	6	0	0	5	4	2	.359	.457
Bats Right	R	.272	158	43	12	0	6	21	11	34	.322	.462
Hatteberg,S	L	.189	37	7	0	0	0	4	6	6	.302	.189
Bats Left	R	.280	193	54	15	0	8	32	32	33	.379	.482
Hayes,Charlie	L	.256	117	30	9	0	4	14	23	20	.373	.436
Bats Right	R	.249	253	63	8	0	5	32	34	64	.336	.340
Helms,Wes	L	.000	0	0	0	0	0	0	0	0	.000	.000
Bats Right	R	.200	5	1	0	0	0	0	0	2	.200	.200
Helton,Todd	L	.329	143	47	15	1	7	31	30	16	.451	.594
Bats Left	R	.387	437	169	44	1	35	116	73	45	.467	.732
Henderson,R	L	.200	90	18	4	0	0	7	26	19	.379	.244
Bats Right	R	.242	330	80	10	2	4	25	62	56	.365	.321
Hermansen,C	L	.188	48	9	3	0	1	3	2	17	.216	.313
Bats Right	R	.183	60	11	1	1	1	5	4	20	.234	.283
Hernandez,A	L	.200	5	1	1	0	0	1	0	1	.200	.400
Bats Left	R	.200	55	11	2	0	1	4	0	12	.200	.291
Hernandez,C	L	.221	68	15	2	0	0	6	6	6	.289	.250
Bats Right	R	.270	174	47	13	0	3	29	15	29	.335	.397
Hernandez,C	L	.000	1	0	0	0	0	0	0	1	.000	.000
Bats Right	R	.000	0	0	0	0	0	0	0	0	.000	.000
Hernandez,J	L	.212	113	24	7	0	2	10	16	35	.310	.327
Bats Right	R	.255	333	85	15	1	9	49	25	90	.316	.387
Hernandez,R	L	.243	107	26	8	0	4	17	17	18	.341	.430
Bats Right	R	.240	312	75	11	0	10	45	21	46	.300	.372
Hidalgo,R	L	.333	117	39	14	1	5	14	12	24	.410	.598
Bats Right	R	.308	441	136	28	2	39	108	44	86	.386	.646
Higginson,B	L	.264	182	48	12	0	4	19	20	34	.338	.396
Bats Left	R	.316	415	131	32	4	26	83	54	65	.394	.600
Hill,G	L	.307	140	43	3	1	13	30	8	35	.342	.621
Bats Right	R	.281	160	45	6	0	14	28	11	41	.331	.581
Hinch,A.J.	L	.000	4	0	0	0	0	0	0	0	.000	.000
Bats Right	R	.500	4	2	0	0	0	0	1	1	.600	.500
Hocking,Denny	L	.279	111	31	3	1	2	20	19	25	.373	.378
Bats Both	R	.305	262	80	21	3	2	27	29	52	.373	.431
Holbert,Ray	L	.000	1	0	0	0	0	0	0	1	.000	.000
Bats Right	R	.333	3	1	0	0	0	0	0	1	.333	.333
Hollandsworth	L	.250	56	14	1	0	0	6	4	19	.295	.268
Bats Left	R	.272	372	101	19	0	19	41	37	80	.339	.476
Houston,Tyler	L	.182	22	4	1	0	2	8	1	7	.217	.500
Bats Left	R	.256	262	67	14	0	16	35	16	65	.299	.492
Howard,T.	L	.000	11	0	0	0	0	1	1	3	.083	.000
Bats Both	R	.230	122	28	4	1	6	27	6	31	.271	.426
Hubbard,Mike	L	.000	0	0	0	0	0	0	0	0	.000	.000
Bats Right	R	.000	1	0	0	0	0	0	0	1	.000	.000

Batter	vs	Avg	AB	H	2B	3B	HR	BI	BB	SO	OBP	SLG
Hubbard,T	L	.244	41	10	2	1	0	3	4	11	.326	.341
Bats Right	R	.149	67	10	0	1	1	3	7	12	.230	.224
Huff,Aubrey	L	.250	12	3	0	0	0	0	1	2	.357	.250
Bats Left	R	.291	110	32	7	0	4	14	4	16	.313	.464
Hundley,Todd	L	.237	76	18	4	0	4	17	9	20	.303	.447
Bats Both	R	.300	223	67	12	0	20	53	36	49	.399	.623
Hunter,Brian	L	.211	71	15	1	0	0	4	8	17	.291	.225
Bats Right	R	.217	69	15	4	0	8	19	12	22	.333	.623
Hunter,B	L	.223	94	21	2	0	0	4	13	18	.318	.245
Bats Right	R	.295	146	43	3	1	1	10	14	22	.358	.349
Hunter,Torii	L	.241	83	20	1	2	2	10	6	17	.289	.373
Bats Right	R	.292	253	74	13	5	3	34	12	51	.328	.419
Huskey,Butch	L	.308	120	37	8	0	3	13	15	22	.382	.450
Bats Right	R	.230	187	43	13	0	6	32	26	41	.323	.396
Huson,Jeff	L	.000	18	0	0	0	0	0	1	2	.053	.000
Bats Left	R	.250	112	28	7	1	0	11	12	7	.323	.330
Hyzdu,Adam	L	.500	4	2	0	0	0	1	0	1	.500	.500
Bats Right	R	.357	14	5	2	0	1	3	0	3	.357	.714
Ibanez,Raul	L	.333	9	3	1	0	0	0	2	3	.500	.444
Bats Left	R	.221	131	29	7	0	2	15	12	22	.285	.321
Jackson,D	L	.223	121	27	6	0	1	6	26	28	.358	.298
Bats Right	R	.266	349	93	21	6	5	31	36	80	.339	.404
Jaha,John	L	.235	34	8	0	0	0	1	11	9	.435	.235
Bats Right	R	.143	63	9	1	0	1	4	22	29	.379	.206
Javier,Stan	L	.291	55	16	2	0	0	7	11	16	.409	.327
Bats Both	R	.272	287	78	16	5	5	33	31	48	.339	.415
Jefferies,G	L	.225	40	9	2	0	0	2	6	0	.326	.275
Bats Both	R	.294	102	30	6	0	2	12	10	10	.351	.412
Jenkins,Geoff	L	.283	120	34	9	1	5	21	6	34	.351	.500
Bats Left	R	.309	392	121	27	3	29	73	27	101	.363	.615
Jensen,Marcus	L	.160	25	4	1	0	0	3	3	5	.250	.200
Bats Both	R	.219	114	25	6	1	3	11	21	31	.341	.368
Jeter,Derek	L	.395	147	58	12	2	4	17	16	22	.461	.585
Bats Right	R	.321	446	143	19	2	11	56	52	77	.401	.446
Johnson,Brian	L	.190	42	8	2	0	2	5	0	8	.190	.381
Bats Right	R	.217	83	18	4	0	2	13	4	20	.247	.337
Johnson,C	L	.252	115	29	6	0	6	21	14	30	.331	.461
Bats Right	R	.324	306	99	18	0	25	70	38	76	.398	.627
Johnson,Keith	L	.333	3	1	0	0	0	0	2	0	.600	.333
Bats Right	R	1.000	1	1	0	0	0	0	0	0	1.000	1.000
Johnson,Lance	L	.333	3	1	0	0	0	0	0	1	.333	.333
Bats Left	R	.296	27	8	1	0	0	2	0	6	.296	.333
Johnson,M	L	.174	23	4	0	0	0	3	4	6	.296	.174
Bats Left	R	.232	190	44	11	0	3	20	23	34	.318	.337
Johnson,M	L	.000	3	0	0	0	0	0	0	2	.000	.000
Bats Left	R	.211	19	4	0	0	1	6	5	7	.375	.368
Johnson,Russ	L	.264	87	23	3	0	1	5	7	12	.316	.333
Bats Right	R	.224	143	32	5	0	1	15	20	28	.323	.280
Jones,Andruw	L	.313	134	42	4	1	4	13	19	23	.403	.448
Bats Right	R	.301	522	157	32	5	32	91	40	77	.357	.565

Batters vs. Lefthanded and Righthanded Pitchers

Batter	vs	Avg	AB	H	2B	3B	HR	BI	BB	SO	OBP	SLG	Batter	vs	Avg	AB	H	2B	3B	HR	BI	BB	SO	OBP	SLG
Jones,Chipper	L	.415	130	54	11	0	12	33	18	17	.480	.777	Kotsay,Mark	L	.308	104	32	4	2	1	13	7	17	.348	.413
Bats Both	R	.281	449	126	27	1	24	78	77	47	.382	.506	Bats Left	R	.296	426	126	27	3	11	44	35	29	.347	.451
Jones,Chris	L	.222	9	2	1	0	0	0	1	3	.300	.333	Kreuter,Chad	L	.288	59	17	5	0	4	8	14	8	.425	.576
Bats Right	R	.143	7	1	1	0	0	1	0	1	.143	.286	Bats Both	R	.255	153	39	8	0	2	20	40	40	.413	.346
Jones,Jacque	L	.230	74	17	2	0	1	8	4	16	.269	.297	Lamb,David	L	.000	2	0	0	0	0	0	0	1	.000	.000
Bats Left	R	.294	449	132	24	5	18	68	22	95	.327	.490	Bats Both	R	.333	3	1	0	0	0	0	1	0	.500	.333
Jones,Terry	L	.243	74	18	4	1	0	6	5	13	.291	.324	Lamb,Mike	L	.286	84	24	4	0	1	10	9	11	.362	.369
Bats Both	R	.255	94	24	4	1	0	7	5	19	.293	.319	Bats Left	R	.276	409	113	21	2	5	37	25	49	.321	.374
Jordan,Brian	L	.402	112	45	12	0	5	27	9	13	.444	.643	Lampkin,Tom	L	.100	10	1	0	0	1	1	1	5	.182	.400
Bats Right	R	.223	377	84	14	0	12	50	29	67	.283	.355	Bats Left	R	.269	93	25	6	1	6	22	8	12	.340	.548
Jordan,Kevin	L	.212	113	24	9	1	1	14	5	17	.244	.336	Lankford,Ray	L	.135	74	10	1	2	2	10	14	37	.286	.284
Bats Right	R	.223	224	50	7	1	4	22	12	24	.264	.317	Bats Left	R	.280	318	89	15	1	24	55	56	111	.386	.560
Jose,Felix	L	.231	13	3	0	0	0	1	1	5	.267	.231	Lansing,Mike	L	.226	115	26	4	1	1	12	9	15	.280	.304
Bats Both	R	.250	16	4	0	0	1	4	1	4	.294	.438	Bats Both	R	.244	389	95	14	5	10	48	29	60	.295	.383
Joyner,Wally	L	.267	15	4	0	0	0	3	2	4	.353	.267	Larkin,Barry	L	.307	75	23	8	1	3	9	13	7	.409	.560
Bats Left	R	.282	209	59	12	0	5	29	29	27	.366	.411	Bats Right	R	.315	321	101	18	4	8	32	35	24	.384	.470
Justice,David	L	.306	134	41	10	0	15	36	13	30	.367	.716	LaRocca,Greg	L	.286	14	4	2	0	0	2	1	2	.333	.429
Bats Left	R	.279	390	109	21	1	26	82	64	61	.380	.538	Bats Right	R	.154	13	2	0	0	0	0	0	2	.154	.154
Kapler,Gabe	L	.286	98	28	4	0	5	13	9	17	.343	.480	LaRue,Jason	L	.300	20	6	1	0	2	7	0	4	.300	.650
Bats Right	R	.306	346	106	28	1	9	53	33	40	.365	.471	Bats Right	R	.218	78	17	2	0	3	5	5	15	.299	.359
Karros,Eric	L	.286	140	40	11	0	5	22	22	21	.383	.471	Lawton,Matt	L	.294	163	48	7	1	2	28	14	15	.355	.387
Bats Right	R	.239	444	106	18	0	26	84	41	101	.301	.455	Bats Left	R	.309	398	123	37	1	11	60	77	48	.424	.490
Kelly,Kenny	L	.000	1	0	0	0	0	0	0	0	.000	.000	LeCroy,Matt	L	.169	59	10	4	0	1	2	9	11	.279	.288
Bats Right	R	.000	0	0	0	0	0	0	0	0	.000	.000	Bats Right	R	.176	108	19	6	0	4	15	8	27	.240	.343
Kelly,Roberto	L	.143	21	3	1	0	1	1	1	5	.217	.333	Ledee,Ricky	L	.241	83	20	3	1	3	15	8	24	.312	.410
Bats Right	R	.000	4	0	0	0	0	0	0	1	.000	.000	Bats Left	R	.234	384	90	16	4	10	62	51	74	.324	.375
Kendall,Jason	L	.331	127	42	11	2	2	14	17	16	.411	.496	Ledesma,A.	L	.200	15	3	1	0	0	0	1	4	.250	.267
Bats Right	R	.316	452	143	22	4	12	44	62	63	.412	.462	Bats Right	R	.240	25	6	1	0	0	3	1	5	.296	.280
Kennedy,Adam	L	.275	142	39	6	2	0	16	7	18	.314	.345	Lee,Carlos	L	.327	98	32	6	0	4	18	7	19	.371	.510
Bats Left	R	.263	456	120	27	9	9	56	21	55	.296	.421	Bats Right	R	.295	474	140	23	2	20	74	31	75	.339	.479
Kent,Jeff	L	.324	145	47	10	2	5	24	35	20	.459	.524	Lee,Derrek	L	.228	101	23	1	1	6	8	15	33	.328	.436
Bats Right	R	.337	442	149	31	5	28	101	55	87	.412	.620	Bats Right	R	.295	376	111	17	2	22	62	48	90	.379	.527
Kieschnick,B	L	.000	0	0	0	0	0	0	0	0	.000	.000	Lee,Travis	L	.205	73	15	4	0	0	8	8	18	.284	.260
Bats Left	R	.000	12	0	0	0	0	0	1	5	.077	.000	Bats Left	R	.242	331	80	20	1	9	46	57	61	.355	.390
Kingsale,Gene	L	.360	25	9	0	0	0	4	1	5	.385	.360	Lesher,Brian	L	.667	3	2	0	1	0	1	1	0	.750	1.333
Bats Both	R	.190	63	12	2	1	0	5	1	9	.200	.254	Bats Right	R	1.000	2	2	1	0	0	2	0	0	1.000	1.500
Kinkade,Mike	L	.000	2	0	0	0	0	0	0	1	.000	.000	Lewis,Darren	L	.277	112	31	6	0	1	8	12	13	.352	.357
Bats Right	R	.429	7	3	1	0	0	1	0	0	.500	.571	Bats Right	R	.215	158	34	6	0	1	9	10	21	.271	.272
Klassen,Danny	L	.243	37	9	1	0	1	3	3	12	.317	.351	Lewis,Mark	L	.277	65	18	6	0	0	7	9	12	.360	.369
Bats Right	R	.231	39	9	2	0	1	5	5	12	.318	.359	Bats Right	R	.239	117	28	12	0	2	17	4	22	.270	.393
Klesko,Ryan	L	.256	121	31	7	1	2	16	16	27	.343	.380	Leyritz,Jim	L	.207	58	12	0	0	1	9	9	13	.333	.259
Bats Left	R	.292	373	109	26	1	24	76	75	54	.408	.560	Bats Right	R	.211	57	12	1	0	1	3	5	13	.274	.281
Knoblauch,C	L	.210	100	21	7	1	2	5	7	10	.266	.360	Lieberthal,M	L	.350	80	28	6	0	4	19	13	7	.447	.575
Bats Right	R	.307	300	92	15	1	3	21	39	35	.398	.393	Bats Right	R	.259	309	80	24	0	11	52	27	46	.326	.443
Knorr,Randy	L	.250	4	1	1	0	0	0	0	0	.250	.500	Liefer,Jeff	L	.000	1	0	0	0	0	0	0	1	.000	.000
Bats Right	R	.300	30	9	1	0	2	2	0	3	.300	.533	Bats Left	R	.200	10	2	0	0	0	0	0	3	.200	.200
Konerko,Paul	L	.302	96	29	7	0	2	20	7	9	.356	.438	Lindsey,Rod	L	.000	1	0	0	0	0	0	0	1	.000	.000
Bats Right	R	.297	428	127	24	1	19	77	40	63	.365	.491	Bats Right	R	.500	2	1	1	0	0	0	0	0	.667	1.000
Koskie,Corey	L	.333	90	30	4	0	0	12	12	26	.419	.378	Liniak,Cole	L	.000	3	0	0	0	0	0	0	2	.000	.000
Bats Left	R	.292	384	112	28	4	9	53	65	78	.395	.456	Bats Right	R	.000	0	0	0	0	0	0	0	0	.000	.000

Batters vs. Lefthanded and Righthanded Pitchers

Batter	vs	Avg	AB	H	2B	3B	HR	BI	BB	SO	OBP	SLG
Lockhart,K	L	.375	32	12	4	0	0	5	3	6	.429	.500
Bats Left	R	.251	243	61	8	3	2	27	26	25	.319	.333
LoDuca,Paul	L	.240	25	6	0	0	0	3	2	2	.286	.240
Bats Right	R	.250	40	10	2	0	2	5	4	6	.311	.450
Lofton,Kenny	L	.260	123	32	8	0	2	20	28	24	.391	.374
Bats Left	R	.283	420	119	15	5	13	53	51	48	.362	.436
Lombard,G	L	.000	5	0	0	0	0	1	0	2	.000	.000
Bats Left	R	.118	34	4	0	0	0	1	1	12	.167	.118
Long,Terrence	L	.263	171	45	13	1	1	11	9	26	.302	.368
Bats Left	R	.298	413	123	21	3	17	69	34	51	.350	.487
Lopez,Javy	L	.277	101	28	3	1	5	22	6	14	.315	.475
Bats Right	R	.289	380	110	18	0	19	67	29	66	.343	.487
Lopez,Luis	L	.255	47	12	3	0	2	5	0	6	.265	.447
Bats Both	R	.266	154	41	11	0	4	22	9	29	.321	.416
Lopez,Mendy	L	.000	0	0	0	0	0	0	0	0	.000	.000
Bats Right	R	.000	3	0	0	0	0	0	1	1	.250	.000
Loretta,Mark	L	.333	78	26	5	0	1	11	10	7	.416	.436
Bats Right	R	.266	274	73	16	1	6	29	27	31	.331	.398
Lowell,Mike	L	.257	105	27	5	0	5	16	8	18	.308	.448
Bats Right	R	.273	403	110	33	0	17	75	46	57	.353	.481
Lowery,T	L	.500	16	8	2	0	1	4	4	3	.600	.813
Bats Right	R	.389	18	7	2	0	0	1	3	5	.500	.500
Lugo,Julio	L	.239	113	27	5	1	1	8	10	25	.301	.327
Bats Right	R	.300	307	92	17	4	9	32	27	68	.363	.469
Lunar,F	L	.421	19	8	1	0	0	4	1	6	.450	.474
Bats Right	R	.078	51	4	0	0	0	2	2	13	.175	.078
Luuloa,Keith	L	.750	4	3	0	0	0	0	0	0	.750	.750
Bats Right	R	.214	14	3	0	0	0	0	1	1	.267	.214
Mabry,John	L	.000	25	0	0	0	0	1	0	10	.000	.000
Bats Left	R	.264	201	53	13	0	8	31	15	59	.320	.448
Machado,R	L	1.000	1	1	0	0	0	0	0	0	1.000	1.000
Bats Right	R	.154	13	2	0	0	1	1	1	4	.214	.385
Macias,Jose	L	.350	40	14	1	2	1	10	1	3	.366	.550
Bats Both	R	.226	133	30	2	3	1	14	17	21	.318	.308
Magadan,Dave	L	.250	20	5	0	0	0	2	8	4	.464	.250
Bats Left	R	.277	112	31	7	0	2	19	24	19	.399	.393
Magee,W.	L	.273	132	36	3	1	2	17	5	19	.297	.356
Bats Right	R	.278	54	15	1	1	5	14	5	9	.339	.611
Mahoney,Mike	L	.000	0	0	0	0	0	0	1	0	1.000	.000
Bats Right	R	.286	7	2	1	0	0	1	0	0	.375	.429
Manto,Jeff	L	.750	4	3	2	0	0	1	1	0	.800	1.250
Bats Right	R	1.000	1	1	0	0	1	3	1	0	1.000	4.000
Marrero,Eli	L	.200	20	4	1	0	2	6	3	1	.346	.550
Bats Right	R	.232	82	19	2	1	3	11	6	15	.289	.390
Martin,Al	L	.156	77	12	1	0	0	3	2	15	.198	.169
Bats Left	R	.310	403	125	14	10	15	33	34	70	.364	.506
Martinez,Dave	L	.292	72	21	5	0	1	9	8	12	.370	.403
Bats Left	R	.270	385	104	14	5	4	38	42	61	.341	.364
Martinez,E	L	.359	92	33	5	0	9	34	18	16	.451	.707
Bats Right	R	.317	464	147	26	0	28	111	78	79	.417	.554

Batter	vs	Avg	AB	H	2B	3B	HR	BI	BB	SO	OBP	SLG
Martinez,F	L	.101	69	7	0	0	0	1	6	23	.205	.101
Bats Both	R	.248	230	57	11	4	2	16	26	45	.335	.357
Martinez,R	L	.297	64	19	3	1	2	6	6	10	.357	.469
Bats Right	R	.304	125	38	10	1	4	19	9	12	.353	.496
Martinez,S	L	.000	2	0	0	0	0	0	0	2	.000	.000
Bats Left	R	.250	16	4	2	0	0	0	0	6	.250	.375
Martinez,Tino	L	.281	171	48	13	1	3	28	11	29	.339	.421
Bats Left	R	.249	398	99	24	3	13	63	41	45	.323	.422
Mateo,Ruben	L	.318	44	14	2	0	3	5	3	6	.375	.568
Bats Right	R	.284	162	46	9	0	4	14	7	28	.329	.414
Matheny,Mike	L	.250	104	26	3	0	2	14	5	23	.288	.337
Bats Right	R	.265	313	83	19	1	4	33	27	73	.327	.371
Matos,Luis	L	.259	58	15	4	2	1	7	3	5	.295	.448
Bats Right	R	.210	124	26	2	1	0	10	9	25	.275	.242
Matthews Jr.,G	L	.250	40	10	1	0	2	4	4	5	.333	.425
Bats Both	R	.169	118	20	0	2	2	10	11	23	.240	.254
Maxwell,Jason	L	.222	72	16	4	0	0	7	7	21	.293	.278
Bats Right	R	.282	39	11	2	0	1	4	2	11	.310	.410
Mayne,Brent	L	.196	46	9	2	0	1	12	5	10	.255	.304
Bats Left	R	.318	289	92	19	0	5	52	42	38	.402	.436
McCarty,Dave	L	.365	104	38	10	1	5	24	6	20	.400	.625
Bats Right	R	.223	166	37	4	1	7	29	16	48	.286	.386
McCracken,Q	L	.250	12	3	0	0	0	0	1	2	.308	.250
Bats Both	R	.053	19	1	0	0	0	2	5	2	.250	.053
McDonald,Ja.	L	.000	8	0	0	0	0	0	1	1	.111	.000
Bats Both	R	.256	86	22	5	0	3	13	16	24	.379	.419
McDonald,Jo.	L	.333	3	1	0	0	0	0	0	1	.333	.333
Bats Right	R	.500	6	3	0	0	0	0	0	0	.500	.500
McDonald,K	L	.500	2	1	0	0	1	2	0	0	.500	2.000
Bats Right	R	.400	5	2	0	0	2	3	2	1	.571	1.600
McEwing,Joe	L	.163	49	8	3	0	1	10	1	6	.173	.286
Bats Right	R	.250	104	26	11	1	1	9	4	23	.284	.404
McGriff,Fred	L	.273	161	44	4	0	10	43	21	32	.355	.484
Bats Left	R	.279	405	113	14	0	17	63	70	88	.380	.440
McGuire,Ryan	L	.000	0	0	0	0	0	0	0	0	.000	.000
Bats Left	R	.000	2	0	0	0	0	0	1	0	.333	.000
McGwire,Mark	L	.321	53	17	3	0	8	13	21	19	.507	.830
Bats Right	R	.301	183	55	5	0	24	60	55	59	.476	.721
McLemore,M.	L	.293	75	22	3	0	1	6	12	14	.393	.373
Bats Both	R	.236	406	96	20	1	2	40	69	64	.345	.305
McMillon,B	L	.267	15	4	1	0	0	4	4	4	.421	.333
Bats Left	R	.306	108	33	6	1	4	20	15	15	.383	.491
Meares,Pat	L	.231	121	28	5	0	3	9	8	22	.306	.347
Bats Right	R	.243	341	83	17	2	10	38	28	69	.304	.393
Melhuse,Adam	L	.091	11	1	0	1	0	3	1	4	.167	.273
Bats Both	R	.231	13	3	0	0	0	1	2	2	.333	.231
Melo,Juan	L	.000	3	0	0	0	0	0	0	2	.000	.000
Bats Both	R	.100	10	1	0	0	0	0	0	3	.100	.100
Meluskey,M	L	.193	57	11	2	0	0	10	13	12	.343	.228
Bats Both	R	.321	280	90	19	0	14	59	42	62	.413	.539

Batters vs. Lefthanded and Righthanded Pitchers

Batter	vs	Avg	AB	H	2B	3B	HR	BI	BB	SO	OBP	SLG	Batter	vs	Avg	AB	H	2B	3B	HR	BI	BB	SO	OBP	SLG
Mendoza,C	L	.000	0	0	0	0	0	0	0	0	.000	.000	Munson,Eric	L	.000	0	0	0	0	0	0	0	0	.000	.000
Bats Left	R	.100	10	1	0	0	0	0	1	4	.182	.100	Bats Left	R	.000	5	0	0	0	0	1	0	1	.000	.000
Menechino,F	L	.224	49	11	3	1	2	13	4	16	.286	.449	Murray,Calvin	L	.270	115	31	8	1	2	18	15	19	.356	.409
Bats Right	R	.271	96	26	6	0	4	13	16	29	.375	.458	Bats Right	R	.203	79	16	4	0	0	4	14	14	.337	.253
Merloni,Lou	L	.294	34	10	4	0	0	5	2	5	.333	.412	Myers,Greg	L	.000	8	0	0	0	0	0	0	2	.000	.000
Bats Right	R	.330	94	31	7	2	0	13	2	17	.343	.447	Bats Left	R	.239	117	28	6	0	3	12	8	27	.288	.368
Metcalfe,Mike	L	.250	4	1	0	0	0	0	0	2	.250	.250	Nady,Xavier	L	1.000	1	1	0	0	0	0	0	0	1.000	1.000
Bats Both	R	.000	8	0	0	0	0	0	1	0	.111	.000	Bats Right	R	.000	0	0	0	0	0	0	0	0	.000	.000
Meyers,Chad	L	.222	18	4	1	0	0	2	1	5	.263	.278	Nevin,Phil	L	.342	146	50	9	1	13	35	26	27	.439	.685
Bats Right	R	.147	34	5	1	0	0	3	2	6	.211	.176	Bats Right	R	.288	392	113	25	0	18	72	33	94	.347	.490
Mientkiewicz,D	L	.500	2	1	0	0	0	3	0	0	.500	.500	Newhan,David	L	.000	5	0	0	0	0	1	3	2	.375	.000
Bats Left	R	.417	12	5	0	0	0	1	0	0	.385	.417	Bats Left	R	.188	32	6	1	0	1	1	5	11	.297	.313
Mieske,Matt	L	.130	46	6	0	0	1	6	4	9	.196	.196	Nicholson,K	L	.189	37	7	3	0	1	2	1	6	.211	.351
Bats Right	R	.233	43	10	1	2	1	1	4	9	.313	.419	Bats Both	R	.233	60	14	3	1	1	6	3	25	.281	.317
Millar,Kevin	L	.254	71	18	1	0	6	14	13	14	.376	.521	Nieves,Jose	L	.213	80	17	3	1	1	12	3	18	.235	.313
Bats Right	R	.261	188	49	13	3	8	28	23	33	.359	.489	Bats Right	R	.212	118	25	3	2	4	12	8	25	.262	.373
Miller,Damian	L	.269	104	28	7	0	3	10	6	18	.306	.423	Nixon,Trot	L	.264	53	14	2	1	1	6	9	15	.371	.396
Bats Right	R	.277	220	61	17	0	7	34	30	56	.365	.450	Bats Left	R	.278	374	104	25	7	11	54	54	70	.368	.471
Minor,Damon	L	.000	0	0	0	0	0	0	1	0	1.000	.000	Norton,Greg	L	.125	16	2	0	0	1	1	2	3	.222	.313
Bats Left	R	.444	9	4	0	0	3	6	1	1	.500	1.444	Bats Both	R	.254	185	47	6	1	5	27	24	44	.343	.378
Minor,Ryan	L	.138	29	4	0	0	0	2	2	5	.219	.138	Nunez,A.	L	.200	10	2	0	0	0	1	3	0	.385	.200
Bats Right	R	.127	55	7	1	0	0	1	1	15	.143	.145	Bats Both	R	.222	81	18	1	0	1	7	5	14	.267	.272
Mirabelli,D	L	.229	48	11	2	0	1	8	14	10	.403	.333	Nunnally,Jon	L	.000	2	0	0	0	0	0	2	0	.500	.000
Bats Right	R	.231	182	42	8	2	5	20	22	47	.317	.379	Bats Left	R	.194	72	14	5	1	2	6	15	26	.330	.375
Moeller,Chad	L	.200	45	9	1	1	0	3	5	10	.275	.267	Nunnari,T	L	.000	2	0	0	0	0	0	0	0	.000	.000
Bats Right	R	.217	83	18	2	0	1	6	4	23	.253	.277	Bats Left	R	.333	3	1	0	0	0	1	6	2	.700	.333
Molina,Ben	L	.293	123	36	6	0	8	28	4	6	.308	.537	O'Brien,C	L	.250	4	1	0	0	1	2	1	1	.400	1.000
Bats Right	R	.277	350	97	14	2	6	43	19	27	.322	.380	Bats Right	R	.200	15	3	1	0	0	0	1	6	.250	.267
Mondesi,Raul	L	.311	74	23	5	0	4	11	7	13	.386	.541	O'Leary,Troy	L	.252	147	37	6	1	3	23	8	21	.291	.367
Bats Right	R	.261	314	82	17	2	20	56	25	60	.315	.519	Bats Left	R	.265	366	97	24	3	10	47	36	55	.331	.429
Mora,Melvin	L	.280	93	26	5	1	3	13	6	18	.317	.452	O'Neill,Paul	L	.346	156	54	9	0	3	28	10	37	.374	.462
Bats Right	R	.274	321	88	17	4	5	34	29	62	.343	.399	Bats Left	R	.259	410	106	17	0	15	72	41	53	.322	.410
Morales,W	L	.333	3	1	0	0	0	0	0	2	.333	.333	Ochoa,Alex	L	.300	90	27	10	0	5	26	16	8	.398	.578
Bats Right	R	.250	8	2	1	0	0	0	0	1	.250	.375	Bats Right	R	.325	154	50	11	3	8	32	8	19	.365	.591
Morandini,M	L	.196	56	11	1	0	0	2	2	18	.237	.214	Offerman,Jose	L	.291	134	39	4	1	4	16	14	21	.358	.425
Bats Left	R	.266	353	94	14	4	0	27	34	59	.335	.329	Bats Both	R	.240	317	76	10	2	5	25	56	49	.353	.331
Mordecai,Mike	L	.309	68	21	7	0	0	5	7	15	.373	.412	Ojeda,Augie	L	.250	24	6	2	0	0	3	2	2	.308	.333
Bats Right	R	.267	101	27	9	0	4	11	5	19	.308	.475	Bats Both	R	.208	53	11	1	1	2	5	8	7	.306	.377
Morris,Hal	L	.231	26	6	1	0	0	1	4	8	.333	.269	Olerud,John	L	.242	124	30	9	0	0	23	19	26	.354	.435
Bats Left	R	.287	143	41	8	1	3	13	27	18	.401	.420	Bats Left	R	.297	441	131	36	0	14	80	83	70	.403	.474
Morris,Warren	L	.230	87	20	4	0	0	8	10	18	.309	.276	Oliver,Joe	L	.179	39	7	3	0	1	5	2	8	.220	.333
Bats Left	R	.265	441	117	27	2	3	35	55	60	.347	.356	Bats Right	R	.286	161	46	10	1	9	30	12	30	.335	.528
Mottola,Chad	L	.167	6	1	0	0	0	0	0	2	.167	.167	Ordaz,Luis	L	.172	29	5	0	0	0	2	0	2	.167	.172
Bats Right	R	.333	3	1	0	0	0	2	0	2	.500	.333	Bats Right	R	.240	75	18	2	0	0	9	5	8	.289	.267
Mouton,James	L	.265	68	18	5	0	1	7	14	17	.390	.382	Ordonez,M	L	.337	98	33	6	1	6	27	11	6	.393	.602
Bats Right	R	.209	91	19	2	1	1	10	16	26	.342	.286	Bats Right	R	.310	490	152	28	2	26	99	49	58	.367	.535
Mouton,Lyle	L	.259	27	7	2	0	0	3	6	10	.394	.333	Ordonez,Rey	L	.192	26	5	2	0	0	4	8	4	.371	.269
Bats Right	R	.286	70	20	5	1	2	13	4	19	.329	.471	Bats Right	R	.187	107	20	3	0	0	5	9	12	.250	.215
Mueller,Bill	L	.306	108	33	5	0	3	11	14	14	.390	.435	Ortiz,David	L	.423	78	33	13	1	1	13	10	11	.483	.654
Bats Both	R	.259	452	117	24	4	7	44	38	48	.319	.376	Bats Left	R	.249	337	84	23	0	9	50	47	70	.337	.398

Batters vs. Lefthanded and Righthanded Pitchers

Batter	vs	Avg	AB	H	2B	3B	HR	BI	BB	SO	OBP	SLG	Batter	vs	Avg	AB	H	2B	3B	HR	BI	BB	SO	OBP	SLG
Ortiz,Hector	L	.326	43	14	2	0	0	4	6	2	.408	.372	Pierre,Juan	L	.500	24	12	0	0	0	5	1	3	.520	.500
Bats Right	R	.444	45	20	4	0	0	1	2	6	.479	.533	Bats Left	R	.284	176	50	2	0	0	15	12	12	.332	.295
Ortiz,Jose	L	.333	3	1	0	0	0	0	1	0	.500	.333	Pierzynski,A	L	.000	4	0	0	0	0	1	0	1	.000	.000
Bats Right	R	.125	8	1	0	0	0	1	1	3	.222	.125	Bats Left	R	.321	84	27	5	1	2	10	5	13	.370	.476
Osik,Keith	L	.371	35	13	3	0	3	9	2	1	.405	.714	Polanco,P	L	.333	87	29	4	1	4	17	3	4	.352	.540
Bats Right	R	.261	88	23	3	1	1	13	12	10	.381	.352	Bats Right	R	.309	236	73	8	2	1	22	13	22	.345	.373
Owens,Eric	L	.307	179	55	9	1	4	12	14	24	.359	.436	Polonia,Luis	L	.212	33	7	1	1	1	6	3	3	.270	.394
Bats Right	R	.287	404	116	10	6	2	39	31	39	.340	.356	Bats Left	R	.283	311	88	13	4	6	24	26	29	.335	.408
Ozuna,Pablo	L	.500	6	3	0	0	0	0	0	0	.500	.500	Porter,Bo	L	.000	6	0	0	0	0	0	0	3	.000	.000
Bats Right	R	.278	18	5	1	0	0	0	0	2	.278	.333	Bats Right	R	.286	7	2	0	0	1	2	2	2	.444	.714
Palmeiro,O	L	.258	31	8	4	0	0	3	2	4	.303	.387	Posada,Jorge	L	.321	159	51	14	1	6	28	22	41	.405	.535
Bats Left	R	.307	212	65	16	2	0	22	36	16	.407	.401	Bats Both	R	.272	346	94	21	0	22	58	85	110	.421	.523
Palmeiro,R	L	.326	144	47	5	0	10	40	24	22	.415	.569	Pose,Scott	L	.250	4	1	0	0	0	0	0	1	.250	.250
Bats Left	R	.276	421	116	24	3	29	80	79	55	.391	.553	Bats Left	R	.182	44	8	0	0	0	1	6	12	.280	.182
Palmer,Dean	L	.228	123	28	5	0	6	20	18	32	.329	.415	Pratt,Todd	L	.256	43	11	2	0	1	5	6	7	.360	.372
Bats Right	R	.264	401	106	17	2	23	82	48	114	.341	.489	Bats Right	R	.282	117	33	4	0	7	20	16	24	.384	.496
Paquette,C	L	.221	113	25	8	0	2	14	11	22	.286	.345	Pride,Curtis	L	.000	3	0	0	0	0	0	0	2	.000	.000
Bats Right	R	.255	271	69	16	2	13	47	16	61	.297	.472	Bats Left	R	.294	17	5	1	0	0	5	1	5	.333	.353
Patterson,C	L	.000	6	0	0	0	0	0	0	2	.000	.000	Prince,Tom	L	.208	24	5	2	0	0	3	4	4	.345	.292
Bats Left	R	.194	36	7	1	0	2	2	3	12	.275	.389	Bats Right	R	.245	98	24	7	0	2	13	9	27	.315	.378
Paul,Josh	L	.333	21	7	2	1	0	3	1	7	.364	.524	Pritchett,C	L	.000	0	0	0	0	0	0	0	0	.000	.000
Bats Right	R	.260	50	13	1	1	1	5	4	10	.327	.380	Bats Right	R	.091	11	1	0	0	0	0	1	3	.167	.091
Payton,Jay	L	.365	104	38	5	0	5	14	11	13	.419	.558	Quinn,Mark	L	.359	103	37	5	0	6	19	9	14	.416	.583
Bats Right	R	.271	384	104	18	1	12	48	19	47	.306	.417	Bats Right	R	.277	397	110	28	2	14	59	26	77	.322	.463
Pena,Elvis	L	.000	1	0	0	0	0	0	0	0	.000	.000	Ramirez,Alex	L	.247	97	24	5	1	1	10	4	17	.277	.351
Bats Both	R	.375	8	3	1	0	0	1	1	1	.444	.500	Bats Right	R	.246	130	32	6	1	8	20	8	32	.290	.492
Perez,Eddie	L	.000	5	0	0	0	0	0	0	0	.000	.000	Ramirez,A	L	.238	63	15	5	0	1	4	2	10	.262	.365
Bats Right	R	.235	17	4	1	0	0	3	0	2	.235	.294	Bats Right	R	.262	191	50	10	2	5	31	8	26	.303	.414
Perez,Eduardo	L	.200	30	6	1	0	1	1	3	6	.314	.333	Ramirez,M.	L	.396	91	36	11	0	7	25	26	20	.525	.747
Bats Right	R	.344	61	21	3	0	2	9	2	13	.369	.492	Bats Right	R	.339	348	118	23	2	31	97	60	97	.437	.684
Perez,Neifi	L	.357	154	55	12	1	7	26	5	18	.366	.584	Randa,Joe	L	.310	126	39	8	2	0	24	9	14	.350	.405
Bats Both	R	.266	497	132	27	10	3	45	25	45	.297	.378	Bats Right	R	.302	486	147	21	2	15	82	27	52	.342	.447
Perez,S	L	.214	14	3	0	0	0	0	3	3	.353	.214	Reboulet,Jeff	L	.297	37	11	3	0	0	4	4	5	.366	.378
Bats Both	R	.158	38	6	2	0	0	2	5	6	.267	.211	Bats Right	R	.228	145	33	4	0	0	10	19	27	.315	.255
Perez,T	L	.125	8	1	0	0	1	1	0	1	.125	.500	Redman,Tike	L	.333	3	1	0	0	0	0	0	1	.333	.333
Bats Left	R	.317	41	13	4	1	0	2	3	4	.370	.463	Bats Left	R	.333	15	5	1	0	1	1	1	6	.375	.600
Perez,Tomas	L	.304	23	7	1	0	0	1	2	6	.360	.348	Redmond,Mike	L	.321	81	26	4	1	0	4	5	7	.368	.395
Bats Both	R	.205	117	24	6	1	1	12	9	24	.262	.299	Bats Right	R	.209	129	27	4	0	0	11	8	12	.286	.240
Perry,Chan	L	.111	9	1	0	0	0	0	0	3	.111	.111	Reed,Jeff	L	.120	25	3	1	0	0	1	4	8	.241	.160
Bats Right	R	.000	5	0	0	0	0	0	0	2	.000	.000	Bats Left	R	.225	204	46	9	0	4	24	40	60	.354	.328
Perry,Herbert	L	.296	81	24	5	0	1	10	6	20	.356	.395	Reese,Pokey	L	.257	109	28	4	2	1	9	13	18	.347	.358
Bats Right	R	.303	330	100	25	1	11	52	18	55	.349	.485	Bats Right	R	.254	409	104	16	4	11	37	32	68	.311	.394
Petrick,Ben	L	.354	48	17	4	1	1	4	1	14	.367	.542	Relaford,Desi	L	.194	93	18	3	1	2	10	25	17	.370	.312
Bats Right	R	.306	98	30	6	0	2	16	19	19	.415	.429	Bats Both	R	.221	317	70	11	2	3	36	50	54	.345	.297
Phelps,Josh	L	.000	0	0	0	0	0	0	0	0	.000	.000	Renteria,E	L	.259	139	36	12	0	5	16	27	18	.381	.453
Bats Right	R	.000	1	0	0	0	0	0	0	1	.000	.000	Bats Both	R	.284	423	120	20	1	11	60	36	59	.334	.414
Piatt,Adam	L	.369	84	31	2	3	5	17	16	23	.470	.643	Richard,Chris	L	.256	39	10	1	0	1	3	2	6	.310	.359
Bats Right	R	.219	73	16	3	2	0	6	7	21	.296	.315	Bats Left	R	.267	176	47	13	2	13	34	15	34	.330	.585
Piazza,Mike	L	.354	79	28	6	0	11	20	10	10	.427	.848	Rios,Armando	L	.167	42	7	1	0	2	10	3	6	.222	.333
Bats Right	R	.318	403	128	20	0	27	93	48	59	.393	.568	Bats Left	R	.288	191	55	14	5	8	40	28	37	.372	.539

Batters vs. Lefthanded and Righthanded Pitchers

Batter	vs	Avg	AB	H	2B	3B	HR	BI	BB	SO	OBP	SLG
Ripken Jr.,C	L	.263	95	25	5	0	2	16	10	7	.330	.379
Bats Right	R	.252	214	54	11	0	13	40	13	30	.300	.486
Rivas,Luis	L	.316	19	6	2	0	0	1	1	1	.350	.421
Bats Right	R	.308	39	12	2	1	0	5	1	3	.310	.410
Rivera,Ruben	L	.188	149	28	4	4	5	16	17	42	.284	.369
Bats Right	R	.219	274	60	14	2	12	41	27	95	.303	.416
Roberts,Dave	L	.000	2	0	0	0	0	0	0	1	.000	.000
Bats Left	R	.250	8	2	0	0	0	0	2	1	.400	.250
Rodriguez,A	L	.366	93	34	5	0	11	29	17	18	.447	.774
Bats Right	R	.306	461	141	29	2	30	103	83	103	.414	.573
Rodriguez,H	L	.245	53	13	3	0	2	4	6	21	.333	.415
Bats Left	R	.258	314	81	18	1	18	57	30	78	.326	.494
Rodriguez,I	L	.342	79	27	1	1	8	18	9	11	.404	.684
Bats Right	R	.349	284	99	26	3	19	65	10	37	.367	.662
Rolen,Scott	L	.283	106	30	3	2	8	20	17	25	.387	.575
Bats Right	R	.302	377	114	29	4	18	69	34	74	.365	.544
Rolison,Nate	L	.000	0	0	0	0	0	1	0	0	.000	.000
Bats Left	R	.077	13	1	0	0	0	1	1	4	.133	.077
Rollins,Jimmy	L	.333	12	4	0	0	0	0	0	0	.333	.333
Bats Both	R	.317	41	13	1	1	0	5	2	7	.349	.390
Rolls,Damian	L	.000	0	0	0	0	0	0	0	0	.000	.000
Bats Right	R	.333	3	1	0	0	0	0	0	1	.333	.333
Roskos,John	L	.000	20	0	0	0	0	0	3	4	.130	.000
Bats Right	R	.143	7	1	1	0	0	1	0	3	.143	.286
Ryan,Rob	L	.000	0	0	0	0	0	0	0	0	.000	.000
Bats Left	R	.296	27	8	1	1	0	2	4	7	.406	.407
Sadler,Donnie	L	.080	25	2	0	0	0	1	2	6	.143	.080
Bats Right	R	.270	74	20	5	0	1	9	3	12	.304	.378
Saenz,Olmedo	L	.319	94	30	5	0	2	10	16	17	.430	.436
Bats Right	R	.308	120	37	7	2	7	23	9	23	.376	.575
Salmon,Tim	L	.226	155	35	6	0	12	22	33	41	.360	.497
Bats Right	R	.315	413	130	30	2	22	75	71	98	.422	.557
Sanchez,Rey	L	.290	131	38	4	0	0	7	7	11	.329	.321
Bats Right	R	.267	378	101	14	2	1	31	21	44	.309	.323
Sanders,A	L	1.000	1	1	0	0	0	0	0	0	1.000	1.000
Bats Right	R	.000	0	0	0	0	0	0	0	0	.000	.000
Sanders,R	L	.264	72	19	5	0	2	13	11	16	.361	.417
Bats Right	R	.224	268	60	18	1	9	24	21	62	.285	.399
Santangelo,F	L	.140	57	8	1	0	0	4	7	15	.275	.158
Bats Both	R	.235	85	20	3	0	1	5	14	18	.353	.306
Santiago,B	L	.268	82	22	5	0	2	10	6	16	.315	.402
Bats Right	R	.259	170	44	6	1	6	35	13	29	.309	.412
Saturria,Luis	L	.000	3	0	0	0	0	0	1	1	.250	.000
Bats Right	R	.000	2	0	0	0	0	0	0	2	.000	.000
Schneider,B	L	.364	22	8	0	0	0	2	1	4	.391	.364
Bats Left	R	.204	93	19	6	0	0	9	6	20	.250	.269
Sefcik,Kevin	L	.246	61	15	1	1	0	4	6	7	.324	.295
Bats Right	R	.228	92	21	5	1	0	6	7	12	.284	.304
Segui,David	L	.310	155	48	10	0	4	23	13	28	.367	.452
Bats Both	R	.344	419	144	32	1	15	80	40	56	.396	.532
Seguignol,F	L	.358	81	29	4	0	6	12	3	18	.381	.630
Bats Both	R	.198	81	16	4	0	4	10	6	28	.275	.395
Selby,Bill	L	.000	4	0	0	0	0	0	0	3	.000	.000
Bats Left	R	.262	42	11	1	0	0	4	1	6	.295	.286
Servais,Scott	L	.255	47	12	3	0	1	7	5	8	.327	.383
Bats Right	R	.194	62	12	1	0	0	6	4	9	.250	.210
Sexson,Richie	L	.220	118	26	6	0	5	19	16	30	.321	.398
Bats Right	R	.286	419	120	24	1	25	72	43	129	.357	.527
Sexton,Chris	L	.105	19	2	1	0	0	2	1	1	.150	.158
Bats Right	R	.235	81	19	3	0	0	8	12	11	.344	.272
Sheets,Andy	L	.000	2	0	0	0	0	0	0	0	.000	.000
Bats Right	R	.105	19	2	0	0	0	1	0	3	.105	.105
Sheffield,G	L	.285	123	35	7	0	7	17	30	16	.425	.512
Bats Right	R	.339	378	128	17	3	36	92	71	55	.442	.685
Sheldon,Scott	L	.372	43	16	5	0	2	12	1	13	.378	.628
Bats Right	R	.235	81	19	6	0	2	7	9	24	.315	.383
Shumpert,T	L	.277	94	26	3	5	3	15	8	10	.340	.511
Bats Right	R	.249	169	42	8	2	6	25	20	30	.340	.426
Sierra,Ruben	L	.400	15	6	0	0	0	2	1	1	.438	.400
Bats Both	R	.178	45	8	0	0	1	5	3	8	.229	.244
Singleton,C	L	.206	68	14	1	1	0	7	6	7	.270	.250
Bats Left	R	.262	443	116	21	4	11	55	29	78	.306	.402
Sisco,Steve	L	.273	11	3	0	0	1	2	3	1	.429	.545
Bats Right	R	.125	16	2	0	0	0	0	0	3	.125	.125
Smith,Bobby	L	.250	48	12	2	0	1	7	6	16	.333	.354
Bats Right	R	.228	127	29	6	0	5	19	8	43	.277	.394
Smith,Mark	L	.173	75	13	1	0	1	5	8	24	.253	.227
Bats Right	R	.291	117	34	7	1	4	22	9	30	.346	.470
Snow,J.T.	L	.256	129	33	6	0	4	27	11	39	.351	.395
Bats Left	R	.292	407	119	27	2	15	69	55	90	.370	.479
Sojo,Luis	L	.238	84	20	5	0	2	11	8	6	.301	.369
Bats Right	R	.304	217	66	13	1	5	26	9	16	.335	.442
Soriano,A	L	.150	20	3	0	0	1	1	1	4	.190	.300
Bats Right	R	.200	30	6	3	0	1	2	0	11	.200	.400
Sosa,Sammy	L	.347	124	43	7	0	8	23	28	36	.461	.597
Bats Right	R	.313	480	150	31	1	42	115	63	132	.390	.644
Spencer,Shane	L	.312	77	24	2	0	3	13	2	13	.317	.455
Bats Right	R	.269	171	46	9	3	6	27	17	32	.335	.462
Spiers,Bill	L	.250	32	8	1	0	0	3	8	7	.400	.281
Bats Left	R	.307	323	99	16	3	3	40	41	31	.384	.402
Spiezio,Scott	L	.250	56	14	3	0	2	6	3	11	.288	.411
Bats Both	R	.241	241	58	8	2	15	43	37	45	.344	.477
Sprague,Ed	L	.292	137	40	12	0	9	25	17	25	.368	.577
Bats Right	R	.191	131	25	4	0	3	11	8	33	.252	.290
Stairs,Matt	L	.202	114	23	4	0	5	23	16	44	.295	.368
Bats Left	R	.235	362	85	22	0	16	58	62	78	.345	.428
Stanley,Mike	L	.301	83	25	4	0	6	21	13	15	.396	.566
Bats Right	R	.211	199	42	8	0	8	25	31	50	.316	.372
Stevens,Lee	L	.281	114	32	9	0	7	28	11	33	.352	.544
Bats Left	R	.260	335	87	18	2	15	47	37	72	.332	.460

Batters vs. Lefthanded and Righthanded Pitchers

Batter	vs	Avg	AB	H	2B	3B	HR	BI	BB	SO	OBP	SLG	Batter	vs	Avg	AB	H	2B	3B	HR	BI	BB	SO	OBP	SLG
Stewart,S	L	.309	139	43	13	0	3	9	6	20	.340	.468	Unroe,Tim	L	.000	1	0	0	0	0	0	1	0	.500	.000
Bats Right	R	.322	444	143	30	5	18	60	31	59	.371	.534	Bats Right	R	.000	4	0	0	0	0	0	0	2	.000	.000
Stinnett,K	L	.250	48	12	0	0	1	4	3	15	.294	.313	Valdes,Pedro	L	.200	5	1	1	0	0	0	0	1	.200	.400
Bats Right	R	.208	192	40	7	0	7	29	16	41	.290	.354	Bats Left	R	.286	49	14	4	0	1	5	6	6	.364	.429
Stocker,Kevin	L	.214	84	18	8	0	0	5	9	14	.290	.310	Valdez,Mario	L	.000	2	0	0	0	0	0	0	0	.000	.000
Bats Both	R	.220	259	57	12	4	2	19	42	67	.337	.320	Bats Left	R	.000	10	0	0	0	0	0	0	3	.000	.000
Stynes,Chris	L	.398	88	35	9	0	3	12	11	14	.471	.602	Valentin,John	L	.400	5	2	1	0	0	0	0	0	.400	.600
Bats Right	R	.315	292	92	15	1	9	28	21	40	.359	.466	Bats Right	R	.233	30	7	0	0	2	2	2	5	.281	.433
Surhoff,B.J.	L	.295	149	44	7	0	6	18	11	17	.350	.463	Valentin,Jose	L	.215	79	17	6	1	1	10	11	15	.319	.354
Bats Left	R	.290	390	113	29	2	8	50	30	41	.341	.436	Bats Both	R	.282	489	138	31	5	24	82	48	91	.348	.513
Sutton,Larry	L	.000	2	0	0	0	0	1	1	1	.333	.000	Valera,Y	L	.000	4	0	0	0	0	1	1	1	.333	.000
Bats Left	R	.348	23	8	0	0	1	5	4	6	.414	.478	Bats Right	R	.000	6	0	0	0	0	0	0	4	.000	.000
Swann,Pedro	L	.000	0	0	0	0	0	0	0	0	.000	.000	Vander Wal,J	L	.200	50	10	0	0	2	7	7	19	.310	.320
Bats Left	R	.000	2	0	0	0	0	0	0	2	.000	.000	Bats Left	R	.314	334	105	29	0	22	87	65	73	.424	.599
Sweeney,Mark	L	.000	1	0	0	0	0	0	1	1	.500	.000	Varitek,Jason	L	.254	130	33	9	0	3	19	13	23	.329	.392
Bats Left	R	.222	72	16	6	0	1	6	11	17	.333	.347	Bats Both	R	.245	318	78	22	1	7	46	47	61	.347	.387
Sweeney,Mike	L	.374	131	49	9	0	6	29	14	12	.443	.580	Vaughn,Greg	L	.264	87	23	6	0	4	11	28	28	.440	.471
Bats Right	R	.322	487	157	21	0	23	115	57	55	.398	.507	Bats Right	R	.251	374	94	21	1	24	63	52	100	.345	.505
Tatis,F	L	.261	88	23	6	0	8	16	17	35	.393	.602	Vaughn,Mo	L	.204	191	39	12	0	6	22	27	65	.323	.361
Bats Right	R	.250	236	59	15	1	10	48	40	59	.374	.449	Bats Left	R	.303	423	128	19	0	30	95	52	116	.385	.560
Taubensee,E	L	.342	38	13	4	0	1	4	3	9	.381	.526	Velandia,J	L	.000	6	0	0	0	0	0	1	2	.143	.000
Bats Left	R	.254	228	58	4	0	5	20	18	35	.315	.355	Bats Right	R	.120	25	3	1	0	0	2	1	6	.185	.160
Taylor,Reggie	L	.000	1	0	0	0	0	0	0	1	.000	.000	Velarde,Randy	L	.262	145	38	10	0	3	9	15	19	.329	.393
Bats Left	R	.100	10	1	0	0	0	0	0	7	.100	.100	Bats Right	R	.285	340	97	13	0	9	32	39	76	.364	.403
Tejada,Miguel	L	.220	168	37	8	0	10	26	23	25	.313	.446	Ventura,Robin	L	.225	102	23	2	1	5	22	14	22	.328	.412
Bats Right	R	.296	439	130	24	1	20	89	43	77	.363	.492	Bats Left	R	.234	367	86	21	0	19	62	61	69	.341	.447
Thomas,Frank	L	.407	91	37	8	0	10	32	30	12	.549	.824	Veras,Quilvio	L	.355	76	27	5	0	3	16	13	7	.451	.539
Bats Right	R	.314	491	154	36	0	33	111	82	82	.412	.589	Bats Both	R	.293	222	65	10	0	2	21	38	43	.401	.365
Thome,Jim	L	.250	152	38	6	0	6	19	22	51	.352	.408	Veras,Wilton	L	.229	35	8	3	0	0	3	1	9	.250	.314
Bats Left	R	.277	405	112	27	1	31	87	96	120	.413	.578	Bats Right	R	.248	129	32	4	1	0	11	6	11	.286	.295
Thompson,A.	L	.333	3	1	0	0	0	1	2	0	.600	.333	Vidro,Jose	L	.373	161	60	14	1	7	25	14	22	.423	.602
Bats Right	R	.000	3	0	0	0	0	0	1	2	.250	.000	Bats Both	R	.315	445	140	37	1	17	72	35	47	.363	.517
Thompson,R.	L	.250	12	3	0	0	0	0	2	4	.357	.250	Vina,Fernando	L	.267	120	32	6	1	0	3	13	12	.380	.333
Bats Right	R	.263	38	10	3	0	3	14	3	8	.333	.579	Bats Left	R	.311	367	114	18	5	4	28	23	24	.380	.420
Timmons,O.	L	.500	8	4	1	0	1	3	1	0	.556	1.000	Vitiello,Joe	L	.268	41	11	3	0	2	7	7	7	.367	.488
Bats Right	R	.303	33	10	2	0	3	10	0	7	.303	.636	Bats Right	R	.182	11	2	0	0	0	1	3	2	.357	.182
Toca,Jorge	L	.000	4	0	0	0	0	1	0	1	.000	.000	Vizcaino,Jose	L	.233	73	17	3	1	0	3	5	12	.288	.301
Bats Right	R	1.000	3	3	1	0	0	3	0	0	1.000	1.333	Bats Both	R	.258	194	50	7	1	0	11	17	31	.316	.304
Tracy,Andy	L	.200	30	6	0	0	1	5	2	10	.273	.300	Vizquel,Omar	L	.218	156	34	7	0	1	16	23	23	.313	.282
Bats Left	R	.272	162	44	8	1	10	27	20	51	.351	.519	Bats Both	R	.311	457	142	20	3	6	50	64	49	.400	.407
Trammell,B	L	.305	82	25	3	1	4	17	11	19	.387	.512	Walbeck,Matt	L	.276	29	8	1	0	2	3	0	3	.276	.517
Bats Right	R	.245	163	40	10	1	6	28	18	30	.324	.429	Bats Both	R	.179	117	21	4	0	4	9	7	19	.232	.316
Truby,Chris	L	.355	76	27	5	4	4	22	5	15	.386	.684	Walker,Larry	L	.341	85	29	2	3	2	17	11	8	.440	.506
Bats Right	R	.220	182	40	10	0	7	37	5	41	.256	.390	Bats Left	R	.297	229	68	19	4	7	34	35	32	.397	.507
Tucker,M	L	.167	24	4	2	0	2	2	6	11	.375	.500	Walker,Todd	L	.357	14	5	1	0	1	5	1	0	.400	.643
Bats Left	R	.276	246	68	11	4	13	34	38	53	.381	.512	Bats Left	R	.286	234	67	10	4	8	39	26	29	.352	.466
Turner,Chris	L	.280	25	7	0	0	0	2	3	6	.379	.280	Ward,Daryle	L	.304	23	7	2	0	2	8	3	2	.385	.652
Bats Right	R	.219	64	14	3	0	1	5	7	15	.296	.313	Bats Left	R	.253	241	61	8	2	18	39	12	59	.286	.527
Tyner,Jason	L	.150	20	3	0	0	0	2	1	3	.227	.150	Ward,Turner	L	.200	5	1	0	0	0	0	1	1	.333	.200
Bats Left	R	.240	104	25	4	0	0	11	4	13	.268	.279	Bats Both	R	.170	47	8	4	0	0	4	4	6	.231	.255

Batters vs. Lefthanded and Righthanded Pitchers

Batter	vs	Avg	AB	H	2B	3B	HR	BI	BB	SO	OBP	SLG
Waszgis,B.J.	L	.111	9	1	0	0	0	1	3	1	.333	.111
Bats Right	R	.250	36	9	1	0	0	3	1	9	.282	.278
Webster,Lenny	L	.207	29	6	1	0	0	2	3	5	.281	.241
Bats Right	R	.212	52	11	2	0	0	3	3	9	.255	.250
Wehner,John	L	.200	10	2	1	0	0	2	0	4	.200	.300
Bats Right	R	.325	40	13	2	0	1	7	4	2	.386	.450
Weiss,Walt	L	.299	67	20	0	1	0	10	5	14	.342	.328
Bats Both	R	.240	125	30	6	1	0	8	21	18	.358	.304
Wells,Vernon	L	.000	0	0	0	0	0	0	0	0	.000	.000
Bats Right	R	.000	2	0	0	0	0	0	0	0	.000	.000
White,Devon	L	.308	65	20	3	1	2	7	4	8	.348	.477
Bats Both	R	.237	93	22	2	0	2	6	5	22	.283	.323
White,Rondell	L	.338	74	25	5	0	3	11	5	18	.388	.527
Bats Right	R	.304	283	86	21	0	10	50	28	61	.370	.484
Whiten,Mark	L	.000	1	0	0	0	0	0	0	0	.000	.000
Bats Both	R	.333	6	2	1	0	0	1	3	2	.556	.500
Widger,Chris	L	.260	77	20	6	2	5	12	9	11	.333	.584
Bats Right	R	.223	215	48	11	0	8	23	21	52	.295	.386
Wilkins,Rick	L	.000	1	0	0	0	0	0	0	1	.000	.000
Bats Left	R	.300	10	3	0	0	0	1	2	1	.417	.300
Williams,B	L	.289	166	48	7	0	9	43	24	22	.381	.494
Bats Both	R	.315	371	117	30	6	21	78	47	62	.396	.598
Williams,G	L	.500	2	1	0	0	0	0	0	0	.500	.500
Bats Both	R	.143	14	2	0	0	1	2	0	4	.200	.357
Williams,G	L	.260	123	32	6	0	5	19	8	15	.303	.431
Bats Right	R	.277	509	141	24	2	16	70	26	88	.314	.426
Williams,Matt	L	.311	106	33	2	0	5	14	9	15	.362	.472
Bats Right	R	.260	265	69	16	2	7	33	11	36	.295	.415
Wilson,Craig	L	.400	25	10	3	0	0	3	2	2	.444	.520
Bats Right	R	.188	48	9	0	0	0	1	3	9	.250	.188
Wilson,Dan	L	.234	64	15	1	0	2	8	8	7	.319	.344
Bats Right	R	.235	204	48	11	0	3	19	14	44	.282	.333
Wilson,E	L	.349	63	22	7	0	2	9	3	4	.373	.556
Bats Both	R	.273	176	48	8	1	3	18	15	20	.328	.381
Wilson,P	L	.250	144	36	8	0	9	31	14	49	.314	.493
Bats Right	R	.269	461	124	27	3	22	90	41	138	.336	.484
Wilson,Vance	L	.000	1	0	0	0	0	0	0	0	.000	.000
Bats Right	R	.000	3	0	0	0	0	0	0	0	.000	.000
Winn,Randy	L	.256	43	11	2	0	1	6	7	3	.360	.372
Bats Both	R	.250	116	29	3	0	0	10	19	22	.362	.276
Wise,Dewayne	L	.333	3	1	0	0	0	0	1	0	.500	.333
Bats Left	R	.105	19	2	0	0	0	0	0	5	.150	.105
Womack,Tony	L	.276	123	34	4	2	1	17	11	18	.331	.366
Bats Left	R	.269	494	133	17	12	6	40	19	56	.301	.389
Woodward,C	L	.235	17	4	2	0	1	7	5	4	.409	.529
Bats Right	R	.172	87	15	5	0	2	7	5	24	.217	.299
Wooten,Shawn	L	.333	6	2	1	0	0	1	0	0	.333	.500
Bats Right	R	1.000	3	3	0	0	0	0	0	0	1.000	1.000
Young,Dmitri	L	.333	141	47	11	2	5	26	7	20	.364	.546
Bats Both	R	.292	407	119	26	4	13	62	29	60	.340	.472

Batter	vs	Avg	AB	H	2B	3B	HR	BI	BB	SO	OBP	SLG
Young,Eric	L	.341	138	47	13	0	2	8	15	12	.404	.478
Bats Right	R	.284	469	133	27	2	4	39	48	27	.357	.375
Young,Kevin	L	.264	129	34	8	0	7	14	10	23	.321	.488
Bats Right	R	.256	367	94	19	0	13	74	22	73	.307	.414
Young,Mike	L	.000	1	0	0	0	0	0	0	0	.000	.000
Bats Right	R	.000	1	0	0	0	0	0	0	1	.000	.000
Zaun,Gregg	L	.324	34	11	0	0	2	3	10	5	.477	.500
Bats Both	R	.265	200	53	11	0	5	30	33	29	.374	.395
Zeile,Todd	L	.248	117	29	7	0	10	21	22	13	.364	.564
Bats Right	R	.274	427	117	29	3	12	58	52	72	.354	.440
Zosky,Eddie	L	.000	3	0	0	0	0	0	0	1	.000	.000
Bats Right	R	.000	1	0	0	0	0	0	0	0	.000	.000
Zuleta,Julio	L	.400	20	8	1	0	2	3	0	3	.429	.750
Bats Right	R	.250	48	12	7	0	1	9	2	16	.308	.458
AL	L	.279	—	—	—	—	—	—	—	—	.350	.440
	R	.275	—	—	—	—	—	—	—	—	.348	.445
NL	L	.267	—	—	—	—	—	—	—	—	.345	.427
	R	.266	—	—	—	—	—	—	—	—	.340	.433
MLB	L	.272	—	—	—	—	—	—	—	—	.348	.433
	R	.270	—	—	—	—	—	—	—	—	.344	.438

Pitchers vs. Lefthanded and Righthanded Batters

Pitcher	vs	Avg	AB	H	2B	3B	HR	BI	BB	SO	OBP	SLG
Abbott,Paul	L	.259	370	96	22	3	9	42	47	59	.343	.408
Throws Right	R	.222	306	68	12	0	14	40	33	41	.304	.399
Acevedo,Juan	L	.287	122	35	7	4	4	15	13	16	.356	.508
Throws Right	R	.220	191	42	8	1	7	30	18	35	.289	.382
Adams,Terry	L	.226	159	36	6	0	1	12	23	31	.324	.283
Throws Right	R	.262	168	44	6	0	5	25	16	25	.326	.387
Aguilera,Rick	L	.257	74	19	1	1	3	11	10	18	.345	.419
Throws Right	R	.248	113	28	4	0	8	22	8	20	.320	.496
Aldred,Scott	L	.303	33	10	1	0	1	7	2	11	.361	.424
Throws Left	R	.271	48	13	2	0	2	7	8	10	.362	.438
Alfonseca,A	L	.277	130	36	7	1	2	16	14	15	.347	.392
Throws Right	R	.303	152	46	6	1	5	19	10	32	.348	.454
Almanza,A	L	.179	67	12	4	1	1	10	21	21	.382	.313
Throws Left	R	.260	100	26	8	0	2	23	22	25	.392	.400
Almanzar,C	L	.212	104	22	3	1	2	19	20	18	.341	.317
Throws Right	R	.300	170	51	7	0	10	33	5	38	.328	.518
Alvarez,Juan	L	.471	17	8	3	0	2	8	4	1	.571	1.000
Throws Left	R	.462	13	6	0	0	1	3	3	1	.529	.692
Anderson,B	L	.266	188	50	11	1	7	19	11	17	.310	.447
Throws Left	R	.278	634	176	30	6	31	77	28	87	.307	.491
Anderson,J	L	.303	119	36	6	1	5	19	11	19	.382	.496
Throws Left	R	.292	456	133	21	5	8	62	47	54	.359	.412
Anderson,Matt	L	.200	110	22	3	1	4	22	26	27	.357	.355
Throws Right	R	.247	158	39	5	1	4	24	19	44	.324	.367
Andrews,C	L	.333	30	10	3	0	1	6	1	2	.355	.533
Throws Left	R	.393	61	24	4	0	5	16	8	10	.457	.705
Ankiel,Rick	L	.253	95	24	5	0	1	5	16	29	.379	.337
Throws Left	R	.213	530	113	21	1	20	65	74	165	.309	.370
Appier,Kevin	L	.296	405	120	24	3	13	57	65	63	.393	.467
Throws Right	R	.224	357	80	22	0	10	36	37	66	.308	.370
Armas Jr.,T	L	.266	143	38	12	0	6	22	32	21	.397	.476
Throws Right	R	.183	197	36	7	1	4	15	18	38	.258	.289
Arnold,Jamie	L	.271	59	16	3	1	1	10	14	10	.416	.407
Throws Right	R	.250	88	22	1	0	0	17	10	6	.333	.261
Arrojo,R	L	.298	332	99	25	3	17	62	35	54	.370	.545
Throws Right	R	.256	344	88	13	5	7	48	33	70	.337	.384
Arroyo,B	L	.300	110	33	7	2	2	20	16	12	.395	.455
Throws Right	R	.304	181	55	13	0	8	33	20	38	.377	.508
Ashby,Andy	L	.313	371	116	20	1	16	54	34	36	.374	.501
Throws Right	R	.249	401	100	26	0	13	57	27	70	.295	.411
Astacio,Pedro	L	.291	358	104	20	2	17	57	40	82	.368	.500
Throws Right	R	.273	414	113	25	2	15	52	37	111	.346	.452
Aybar,Manny	L	.208	106	22	6	2	2	10	18	18	.325	.358
Throws Right	R	.264	197	52	10	3	9	30	17	27	.321	.482
Baldwin,James	L	.279	362	101	19	1	17	42	30	65	.333	.478
Throws Right	R	.264	318	84	10	1	17	41	29	51	.337	.462
Bale,John	L	.375	8	3	0	1	1	7	2	0	.545	1.000
Throws Left	R	.250	8	2	1	0	0	2	1	6	.364	.375
Barcelo,L	L	.197	66	13	1	2	3	10	7	13	.274	.409
Throws Right	R	.259	81	21	5	0	2	9	2	13	.274	.395

Pitcher	vs	Avg	AB	H	2B	3B	HR	BI	BB	SO	OBP	SLG
Batista,M	L	.298	124	37	3	0	8	27	23	15	.405	.516
Throws Right	R	.333	144	48	10	0	11	39	14	22	.398	.632
Beck,Rod	L	.246	69	17	5	0	1	8	4	7	.288	.362
Throws Right	R	.202	84	17	2	0	1	10	8	28	.287	.262
Beirne,Kevin	L	.283	92	26	3	2	5	21	8	19	.349	.522
Throws Right	R	.245	98	24	5	0	4	12	12	22	.327	.418
Belcher,Tim	L	.311	74	23	8	1	2	11	12	11	.409	.527
Throws Right	R	.256	86	22	2	1	6	16	10	11	.340	.512
Belinda,Stan	L	.242	66	16	5	2	4	22	11	19	.357	.561
Throws Right	R	.322	121	39	8	3	10	32	11	32	.379	.686
Belitz,Todd	L	.167	6	1	1	0	0	2	4	1	.500	.333
Throws Left	R	.333	9	3	1	0	0	2	0	2	.333	.444
Bell,Rob	L	.226	234	53	17	1	12	28	33	43	.321	.462
Throws Right	R	.257	300	77	21	1	20	45	40	69	.345	.533
Beltran,Rigo	L	.667	3	2	1	0	1	3	0	0	.667	2.000
Throws Left	R	.571	7	4	1	0	1	2	3	1	.700	1.143
Benes,Alan	L	.273	77	21	3	1	4	11	10	12	.371	.494
Throws Right	R	.303	109	33	7	0	3	18	13	14	.374	.450
Benes,Andy	L	.268	265	71	15	1	15	39	31	66	.341	.502
Throws Right	R	.280	368	103	25	5	15	51	37	71	.343	.497
Benitez,A	L	.133	120	16	4	1	1	10	23	50	.271	.208
Throws Right	R	.161	143	23	3	1	9	27	15	56	.241	.385
Benson,Kris	L	.276	395	109	16	2	16	53	49	75	.359	.448
Throws Right	R	.225	432	97	19	3	8	39	37	109	.293	.338
Bere,Jason	L	.267	281	75	15	2	7	35	40	66	.363	.409
Throws Right	R	.281	374	105	12	1	18	58	49	76	.363	.463
Bergman,Sean	L	.407	135	55	8	1	10	32	23	12	.488	.704
Throws Right	R	.346	162	56	10	1	8	36	10	23	.389	.568
Bernero,Adam	L	.242	62	15	1	0	3	7	9	12	.333	.403
Throws Right	R	.300	60	18	4	1	0	5	4	8	.343	.400
Biddle,Rocky	L	.333	39	13	4	1	0	9	5	6	.391	.487
Throws Right	R	.321	56	18	2	0	5	14	3	1	.356	.625
Blair,Willie	L	.257	288	74	10	3	11	34	20	39	.304	.427
Throws Right	R	.329	337	111	25	3	9	53	15	35	.356	.501
Blank,Matt	L	.286	21	6	0	0	1	5	2	1	.360	.429
Throws Left	R	.188	32	6	2	0	0	0	3	3	.257	.250
Bochtler,Doug	L	.462	13	6	2	0	1	3	5	2	.611	.846
Throws Right	R	.318	22	7	0	0	1	4	5	2	.444	.455
Boehringer,B	L	.280	25	7	0	0	1	2	4	5	.379	.400
Throws Right	R	.289	38	11	1	0	3	8	6	4	.378	.553
Bohanon,Brian	L	.196	163	32	4	2	5	24	14	21	.267	.337
Throws Left	R	.288	517	149	25	3	19	64	65	77	.371	.458
Bones,Ricky	L	.360	111	40	4	0	3	21	11	13	.411	.477
Throws Right	R	.271	199	54	10	1	3	22	16	46	.329	.377
Borbon,Pedro	L	.209	86	18	3	0	2	16	21	20	.363	.314
Throws Left	R	.360	75	27	6	0	3	24	17	9	.480	.560
Borkowski,D	L	.700	10	7	2	1	1	4	5	0	.800	1.400
Throws Right	R	.250	16	4	3	0	1	6	2	1	.316	.625
Bottalico,R	L	.241	133	32	9	2	6	20	20	29	.348	.474
Throws Right	R	.237	139	33	6	0	6	17	21	27	.335	.410

Pitchers vs. Lefthanded and Righthanded Batters

Pitcher	vs	Avg	AB	H	2B	3B	HR	BI	BB	SO	OBP	SLG	Pitcher	vs	Avg	AB	H	2B	3B	HR	BI	BB	SO	OBP	SLG
Bottenfield,K	L	.304	352	107	21	3	13	53	48	51	.386	.491	Carpenter,C	L	.294	327	96	28	2	12	46	46	56	.384	.502
Throws Right	R	.241	324	78	14	0	17	50	29	55	.304	.441	Throws Right	R	.287	376	108	19	2	18	70	37	57	.355	.492
Boyd,Jason	L	.283	46	13	4	0	2	5	9	8	.400	.500	Carrara,G	L	.280	25	7	1	0	4	10	6	7	.438	.800
Throws Right	R	.299	87	26	9	1	0	18	15	24	.408	.425	Throws Right	R	.412	34	14	1	0	1	7	5	8	.475	.529
Bradford,Chad	L	.474	19	9	0	0	0	3	1	2	.500	.474	Carrasco,H	L	.281	114	32	7	1	4	24	17	24	.381	.465
Throws Right	R	.125	32	4	1	0	0	1	0	7	.125	.156	Throws Right	R	.297	195	58	9	0	4	29	21	40	.367	.405
Brantley,Jeff	L	.291	103	30	3	0	2	19	20	23	.403	.379	Castillo,F	L	.225	253	57	15	1	10	27	41	63	.340	.411
Throws Right	R	.286	119	34	6	0	10	17	9	34	.344	.588	Throws Right	R	.216	255	55	10	0	8	23	15	41	.263	.349
Brea,Lesli	L	.500	12	6	2	0	0	7	6	1	.632	.667	Charlton,Norm	L	.167	6	1	0	0	0	1	1	1	.286	.167
Throws Right	R	.240	25	6	0	0	1	6	4	4	.367	.360	Throws Left	R	.625	8	5	2	0	1	8	5	0	.769	1.250
Brewington,J	L	.390	82	32	4	1	3	23	9	15	.441	.573	Chen,Bruce	L	.223	112	25	3	0	3	9	7	29	.276	.330
Throws Right	R	.245	98	24	5	1	0	12	10	19	.327	.316	Throws Left	R	.235	388	91	26	0	15	42	39	83	.304	.418
Brocail,Doug	L	.245	110	27	8	1	5	17	10	25	.309	.473	Choate,Randy	L	.184	38	7	3	0	1	4	3	9	.256	.342
Throws Right	R	.333	90	30	4	3	0	10	4	16	.358	.444	Throws Left	R	.259	27	7	1	1	2	5	5	3	.375	.593
Brock,Chris	L	.222	126	28	5	1	4	11	18	25	.322	.373	Chouinard,B	L	.224	49	11	3	0	1	4	4	9	.283	.347
Throws Right	R	.248	230	57	6	5	17	35	23	44	.320	.539	Throws Right	R	.304	79	24	2	0	3	12	5	14	.349	.443
Brower,Jim	L	.292	120	35	7	0	8	17	18	13	.384	.550	Christiansen,J	L	.246	65	16	4	0	3	12	7	16	.338	.446
Throws Right	R	.324	139	45	6	0	3	23	13	19	.390	.432	Throws Left	R	.225	111	25	6	0	0	13	20	37	.341	.279
Brown,Kevin	L	.226	411	93	22	3	5	33	30	87	.286	.331	Clark,Mark	L	.316	95	30	5	1	6	16	11	8	.394	.579
Throws Right	R	.201	437	88	14	0	16	39	17	129	.236	.343	Throws Right	R	.379	95	36	6	2	4	23	13	8	.455	.611
Brownson,M.	L	.400	5	2	1	0	0	1	0	1	.400	.600	Clemens,R.	L	.206	407	84	14	1	11	30	57	104	.310	.327
Throws Right	R	.313	16	5	2	0	1	3	3	2	.421	.625	Throws Right	R	.267	374	100	16	3	15	60	27	84	.325	.447
Brunette,J	L	.375	8	3	0	0	0	3	1	2	.444	.375	Clement,Matt	L	.267	412	110	21	2	14	78	71	72	.376	.430
Throws Left	R	.357	14	5	0	0	0	1	4	0	.500	.357	Throws Right	R	.227	370	84	15	0	8	29	54	98	.345	.332
Bruske,Jim	L	.265	34	9	1	0	3	11	5	4	.375	.559	Clontz,Brad	L	1.000	3	3	2	0	0	0	5	0	1.000	1.667
Throws Right	R	.361	36	13	3	0	2	8	7	4	.467	.611	Throws Right	R	.174	23	4	1	1	1	3	6	8	.345	.435
Buddie,Mike	L	.250	8	2	0	0	0	1	0	1	.250	.250	Coco,Pasqual	L	1.000	2	2	0	1	0	0	1	0	1.000	2.000
Throws Right	R	.353	17	6	1	1	0	2	1	4	.389	.529	Throws Right	R	.200	15	3	1	0	1	2	4	2	.400	.467
Buehrle,Mark	L	.260	73	19	5	0	2	12	3	18	.308	.411	Coggin,Dave	L	.341	44	15	3	0	2	8	10	7	.463	.545
Throws Left	R	.279	129	36	10	2	3	21	16	19	.363	.457	Throws Right	R	.299	67	20	5	1	0	9	2	10	.329	.403
Bullinger,K	L	.500	6	3	0	0	0	2	0	1	.429	.500	Colon,Bartolo	L	.242	335	81	16	1	12	35	51	95	.344	.403
Throws Right	R	.143	7	1	0	0	0	2	0	3	.143	.143	Throws Right	R	.225	365	82	16	0	9	39	47	117	.316	.342
Burba,Dave	L	.259	351	91	20	2	8	39	48	73	.348	.396	Cone,David	L	.302	318	96	22	2	11	59	50	67	.396	.487
Throws Right	R	.274	394	108	23	3	11	47	43	107	.345	.431	Throws Right	R	.310	310	96	22	0	14	49	32	53	.382	.516
Burkett,John	L	.294	218	64	11	4	4	25	21	48	.363	.436	Cook,Dennis	L	.322	90	29	4	0	3	15	6	17	.390	.467
Throws Right	R	.309	317	98	18	0	9	47	30	62	.366	.451	Throws Left	R	.238	143	34	7	0	5	26	25	36	.355	.392
Burnett,A.J.	L	.302	149	45	10	2	2	13	30	22	.417	.436	Cooper,Brian	L	.303	152	46	14	2	7	26	24	16	.399	.559
Throws Right	R	.219	160	35	7	3	6	22	14	35	.287	.413	Throws Right	R	.298	198	59	7	1	11	33	11	20	.333	.510
Byrd,Paul	L	.333	144	48	13	2	11	32	24	19	.432	.681	Cordero,F	L	.310	113	35	7	1	4	20	35	20	.461	.496
Throws Right	R	.222	185	41	11	3	6	31	11	34	.271	.411	Throws Right	R	.271	192	52	12	2	7	42	13	29	.327	.464
Byrdak,Tim	L	.353	17	6	1	1	2	7	3	6	.450	.882	Cordova,F	L	.349	172	60	13	2	4	18	17	24	.405	.517
Throws Left	R	.385	13	5	1	0	1	7	1	2	.429	.692	Throws Right	R	.232	203	47	15	0	8	32	21	42	.307	.424
Cabrera,Jose	L	.314	105	33	8	2	4	20	10	20	.373	.543	Cormier,Rheal	L	.264	87	23	4	0	1	8	5	14	.304	.345
Throws Right	R	.304	135	41	9	1	6	25	7	21	.345	.519	Throws Left	R	.280	182	51	7	2	6	23	12	29	.321	.440
Cairncross,C	L	.300	20	6	0	0	1	5	1	6	.318	.450	Cornelius,R	L	.283	212	60	2	2	11	30	21	32	.345	.467
Throws Left	R	.313	16	5	2	0	0	2	2	2	.389	.438	Throws Right	R	.282	266	75	18	1	8	33	29	18	.357	.447
Cammack,Eric	L	.273	11	3	1	0	0	2	4	3	.467	.364	Crabtree,Tim	L	.323	127	41	10	0	1	26	18	17	.401	.425
Throws Right	R	.160	25	4	1	0	1	6	6	6	.333	.320	Throws Right	R	.241	187	45	7	0	6	29	13	37	.294	.374
Carlyle,Buddy	L	.444	9	4	2	0	0	1	2	2	.545	.667	Crawford,P	L	.296	54	16	2	0	0	5	5	10	.367	.333
Throws Right	R	.333	6	2	0	0	0	2	1	0	.429	.333	Throws Right	R	.180	50	9	1	0	0	8	8	7	.286	.200

Pitchers vs. Lefthanded and Righthanded Batters

Pitcher	vs	Avg	AB	H	2B	3B	HR	BI	BB	SO	OBP	SLG
Creek,Doug	L	.170	88	15	2	1	1	10	18	31	.303	.250
Throws Left	R	.260	131	34	8	0	9	26	21	42	.370	.527
Cressend,Jack	L	.350	20	7	1	1	0	1	2	2	.409	.500
Throws Right	R	.371	35	13	2	0	0	11	4	4	.436	.429
Croushore,R	L	.263	19	5	1	0	1	5	5	7	.400	.474
Throws Right	R	.311	45	14	3	0	0	12	6	7	.407	.378
Cruz,Nelson	L	.236	72	17	1	0	2	9	10	11	.337	.333
Throws Right	R	.268	82	22	7	0	2	15	3	23	.302	.427
Cubillan,D	L	.351	57	20	6	0	4	20	11	10	.443	.667
Throws Right	R	.372	86	32	7	0	5	17	14	17	.461	.628
Cunnane,Will	L	.243	74	18	4	1	1	11	11	13	.341	.365
Throws Right	R	.239	71	17	2	0	1	6	10	21	.337	.310
D'Amico,Jeff	L	.242	248	60	11	3	5	27	25	32	.308	.371
Throws Right	R	.234	354	83	18	0	9	23	21	69	.289	.362
D'Amico,J	L	.500	26	13	4	0	2	10	7	1	.606	.885
Throws Right	R	.207	29	6	1	0	0	2	8	8	.378	.241
Daal,Omar	L	.298	121	36	6	0	6	28	11	24	.353	.496
Throws Left	R	.307	561	172	36	3	20	90	61	72	.381	.488
Darensbourg,V	L	.190	79	15	2	1	2	6	11	26	.297	.316
Throws Left	R	.295	156	46	11	1	5	24	17	33	.356	.474
Davey,Tom	L	.227	22	5	0	0	0	2	0	3	.227	.227
Throws Right	R	.269	26	7	1	0	0	0	2	3	.321	.308
Davis,Doug	L	.314	86	27	3	0	4	23	12	19	.406	.488
Throws Left	R	.280	293	82	12	1	10	38	46	47	.376	.430
Davis,Kane	L	.355	31	11	4	0	1	4	6	2	.459	.581
Throws Right	R	.410	39	16	0	1	3	14	7	2	.521	.692
de los Santos	L	.273	110	30	6	1	5	19	8	28	.325	.482
Throws Left	R	.243	173	42	6	1	10	31	25	42	.338	.462
DeJean,Mike	L	.293	75	22	3	1	5	10	18	10	.430	.560
Throws Right	R	.254	126	32	7	1	4	15	12	24	.317	.421
del Toro,M	L	.276	29	8	0	0	1	3	1	4	.300	.379
Throws Right	R	.231	39	9	2	2	2	5	5	12	.348	.538
Dempster,R.	L	.245	379	93	12	2	16	40	54	88	.342	.414
Throws Right	R	.242	484	117	25	4	14	53	43	121	.304	.397
DePaula,Sean	L	.464	28	13	1	0	2	8	7	3	.556	.714
Throws Right	R	.175	40	7	1	0	1	9	7	13	.298	.275
Dessens,Elmer	L	.328	259	85	22	2	5	40	23	27	.378	.486
Throws Right	R	.269	316	85	17	1	5	28	20	58	.315	.377
DeWitt,Matt	L	.542	24	13	3	0	2	14	6	0	.633	.917
Throws Right	R	.212	33	7	2	0	2	5	3	6	.316	.455
Dickson,Jason	L	.327	52	17	4	0	2	7	5	7	.397	.519
Throws Right	R	.344	64	22	2	0	3	11	2	11	.364	.516
Dingman,Craig	L	.273	22	6	0	0	0	4	1	4	.304	.273
Throws Right	R	.462	26	12	2	0	1	9	2	4	.500	.654
Dipoto,Jerry	L	.211	19	4	0	0	1	3	1	3	.238	.368
Throws Right	R	.375	32	12	4	0	0	6	4	6	.432	.500
Dotel,Octavio	L	.282	216	61	12	2	12	38	32	70	.376	.523
Throws Right	R	.250	264	66	15	0	14	40	29	72	.329	.466
Downs,Scott	L	.271	70	19	4	0	5	12	8	14	.363	.543
Throws Left	R	.321	321	103	26	5	8	40	32	49	.383	.508
Dreifort,D	L	.264	356	94	18	3	19	57	43	76	.350	.492
Throws Right	R	.214	378	81	19	0	12	35	44	88	.309	.360
Drew,Tim	L	.385	26	10	1	0	0	6	4	4	.452	.423
Throws Right	R	.500	14	7	2	0	1	4	4	1	.600	.857
Durbin,Chad	L	.303	145	44	10	1	8	32	27	22	.408	.552
Throws Right	R	.299	157	47	11	0	6	26	16	15	.362	.484
Duvall,Mike	L	.750	4	3	2	1	0	2	1	0	.800	1.750
Throws Left	R	.286	7	2	0	0	1		0	0	.286	.571
Eaton,Adam	L	.301	269	81	17	4	8	35	39	40	.389	.483
Throws Right	R	.215	247	53	9	0	6	22	22	50	.280	.324
Eiland,Dave	L	.320	122	39	13	2	4	17	17	12	.411	.557
Throws Right	R	.333	114	38	7	0	4	25	1	5	.345	.500
Einertson,D	L	.400	15	6	0	0	1	4	2	2	.471	.600
Throws Right	R	.263	38	10	1	0	0	8	2	1	.293	.289
Elarton,Scott	L	.261	356	93	24	2	16	47	52	71	.357	.475
Throws Right	R	.264	397	105	23	3	13	57	32	60	.321	.436
Eldred,Cal	L	.234	209	49	13	2	7	28	31	60	.337	.416
Throws Right	R	.252	214	54	10	1	5	22	28	37	.346	.379
Embree,Alan	L	.286	91	26	5	0	2	24	11	22	.349	.407
Throws Left	R	.267	135	36	9	0	2	18	14	27	.346	.378
Enders,Trevor	L	.400	20	8	5	0	0	9	3	3	.478	.650
Throws Right	R	.316	19	6	1	0	2	5	2	2	.381	.684
Erdos,Todd	L	.245	110	27	6	0	3	21	12	14	.328	.382
Throws Right	R	.327	110	36	5	0	4	22	16	20	.427	.482
Erickson,S	L	.390	195	76	10	1	8	46	28	21	.463	.574
Throws Right	R	.270	189	51	9	2	6	25	20	20	.346	.434
Escobar,K	L	.282	341	96	24	1	15	55	38	73	.354	.490
Throws Right	R	.253	356	90	21	1	11	50	47	69	.341	.410
Estes,Shawn	L	.216	102	22	5	1	1	13	17	15	.328	.314
Throws Left	R	.285	603	172	28	2	10	62	91	121	.379	.388
Estrada,H	L	.208	24	5	1	0	0	4	4	3	.321	.250
Throws Left	R	.329	76	25	10	2	5	12	16	10	.453	.711
Estrella,Leo	L	.429	7	3	0	0	1	2	0	1	.375	.857
Throws Right	R	.462	13	6	2	0	0	2	0	2	.462	.615
Etherton,Seth	L	.282	124	35	5	1	10	18	14	18	.360	.581
Throws Right	R	.273	121	33	11	0	6	15	8	14	.315	.512
Eyre,Scott	L	.393	28	11	2	1	1	9	7	5	.514	.643
Throws Left	R	.360	50	18	1	1	2	10	5	11	.411	.540
Farnsworth,K	L	.258	124	32	1	0	9	24	21	25	.367	.484
Throws Right	R	.314	185	58	12	1	5	36	29	49	.409	.470
Fassero,Jeff	L	.255	106	27	5	1	2	10	8	24	.307	.377
Throws Left	R	.307	411	126	23	1	14	54	42	73	.371	.470
Fernandez,A	L	.250	84	21	4	2	3	11	5	12	.289	.452
Throws Right	R	.322	118	38	2	1	4	12	11	15	.380	.458
Fernandez,O	L	.213	141	30	8	1	4	14	17	20	.297	.369
Throws Right	R	.262	149	39	9	0	2	16	14	16	.327	.362
Fetters,Mike	L	.189	95	18	1	1	6	11	12	14	.280	.411
Throws Right	R	.224	76	17	2	0	1	7	13	26	.352	.289
Figueroa,N	L	.310	29	9	1	0	1	4	4	3	.382	.448
Throws Right	R	.258	31	8	3	0	3	8	1	4	.273	.645

Pitchers vs. Lefthanded and Righthanded Batters

Pitcher	vs	Avg	AB	H	2B	3B	HR	BI	BB	SO	OBP	SLG	Pitcher	vs	Avg	AB	H	2B	3B	HR	BI	BB	SO	OBP	SLG
Finley,Chuck	L	.240	175	42	6	1	4	18	16	41	.302	.354	Graves,Danny	L	.265	166	44	8	0	4	22	17	24	.333	.386
Throws Left	R	.260	649	169	33	1	19	72	85	148	.346	.402	Throws Right	R	.222	167	37	7	0	4	22	25	29	.327	.335
Fiore,Tony	L	.400	25	10	0	0	1	9	4	2	.500	.520	Green,Jason	L	.333	30	10	0	0	2	7	9	6	.487	.533
Throws Right	R	.289	38	11	0	0	2	4	5	6	.386	.447	Throws Right	R	.147	34	5	1	0	1	6	11	13	.370	.265
Florie,Bryce	L	.346	81	28	9	0	1	12	11	13	.415	.494	Grilli,Jason	L	.429	14	6	1	0	0	1	1	1	.467	.500
Throws Right	R	.259	112	29	4	1	4	22	8	21	.311	.420	Throws Right	R	.333	15	5	1	0	0	3	1	2	.444	.400
Ford,Ben	L	.389	18	7	2	0	1	7	3	0	.476	.667	Grimsley,J	L	.228	162	37	9	0	5	31	14	21	.293	.377
Throws Right	R	.292	24	7	1	2	0	4	4	5	.452	.500	Throws Right	R	.299	211	63	16	0	5	30	28	32	.384	.445
Forster,Scott	L	.289	45	13	2	2	3	12	11	8	.448	.622	Groom,Buddy	L	.193	88	17	1	0	2	10	5	21	.229	.273
Throws Left	R	.195	77	15	5	0	2	14	14	15	.309	.338	Throws Left	R	.326	141	46	7	2	3	30	16	23	.390	.468
Foulke,Keith	L	.221	163	36	9	1	7	23	11	46	.271	.417	Gross,Kip	L	.750	4	3	0	0	1	3	0	0	.750	1.500
Throws Right	R	.192	156	30	2	1	2	10	11	45	.250	.256	Throws Right	R	.353	17	6	1	0	1	3	2	3	.421	.588
Franco,John	L	.209	67	14	0	0	0	2	4	15	.264	.209	Guardado,E	L	.287	87	25	6	0	5	19	8	20	.340	.529
Throws Left	R	.227	141	32	4	0	6	17	22	41	.335	.383	Throws Left	R	.208	144	30	3	0	9	17	17	32	.296	.417
Franklin,W	L	.256	39	10	3	0	0	6	2	11	.340	.333	Gunderson,E	L	.182	11	2	1	0	0	2	1	2	.286	.273
Throws Left	R	.304	46	14	2	0	2	8	10	10	.429	.478	Throws Left	R	.591	22	13	1	1	0	5	1	0	.609	.727
Frascatore,J	L	.324	102	33	6	0	4	20	15	10	.413	.500	Guthrie,Mark	L	.276	98	27	1	0	2	15	12	23	.357	.347
Throws Right	R	.289	187	54	5	1	10	35	18	20	.363	.487	Throws Left	R	.253	170	43	5	1	6	33	25	40	.347	.400
Fultz,Aaron	L	.221	86	19	6	0	3	14	7	27	.281	.395	Guzman,D	L	.333	3	1	0	0	0	0	0	0	.500	.333
Throws Left	R	.284	169	48	10	1	5	30	21	35	.362	.444	Throws Right	R	.000	0	0	0	0	0	0	1	0	1.000	.000
Fussell,Chris	L	.261	138	36	2	1	9	23	23	23	.362	.486	Guzman,G	L	.330	103	34	4	0	5	18	13	12	.407	.515
Throws Right	R	.313	128	40	5	0	9	23	21	23	.409	.563	Throws Right	R	.250	128	32	4	0	3	13	9	40	.304	.352
Fyhrie,Mike	L	.222	81	18	4	0	0	6	6	20	.270	.272	Guzman,Juan	L	.571	7	4	0	0	2	5	1	2	.625	1.429
Throws Right	R	.300	120	36	5	1	4	15	9	23	.346	.458	Throws Right	R	.750	4	3	0	0	0	3	1	1	.800	.750
Gagne,Eric	L	.263	190	50	10	0	11	33	21	33	.336	.489	Hackman,L	L	1.000	1	1	0	0	0	1	1	0	1.000	1.000
Throws Right	R	.276	203	56	13	1	9	26	39	46	.396	.483	Throws Right	R	.333	9	3	0	0	0	2	3	0	.538	.333
Garces,Rich	L	.209	115	24	5	1	2	18	11	26	.273	.322	Halama,John	L	.343	166	57	16	0	4	26	17	30	.403	.512
Throws Right	R	.242	165	40	8	0	5	16	12	43	.294	.382	Throws Left	R	.297	502	149	33	2	15	63	39	57	.346	.460
Garcia,Freddy	L	.272	246	67	12	2	12	37	39	32	.371	.484	Halladay,Roy	L	.364	143	52	10	2	8	36	28	18	.462	.629
Throws Right	R	.205	219	45	11	0	4	14	25	47	.293	.311	Throws Right	R	.350	157	55	11	1	6	34	14	26	.408	.548
Garcia,Mike	L	.636	11	7	3	0	0	1	2	2	.692	.909	Hamilton,Joey	L	.247	73	18	6	0	1	3	5	11	.291	.370
Throws Right	R	.368	38	14	2	0	1	11	5	7	.413	.500	Throws Right	R	.213	47	10	1	1	2	9	7	4	.339	.404
Gardner,Mark	L	.304	240	73	13	2	7	31	22	39	.365	.463	Hampton,Mike	L	.264	148	39	7	2	3	16	9	31	.325	.399
Throws Right	R	.245	335	82	14	4	9	41	20	53	.290	.391	Throws Right	R	.236	658	155	25	1	7	63	90	120	.328	.309
Garibay,D	L	.227	66	15	7	0	0	9	5	15	.284	.333	Haney,Chris	L	.000	0	0	0	0	0	0	0	0	.000	.000
Throws Left	R	.320	228	73	17	1	9	40	34	31	.402	.522	Throws Left	R	.333	3	1	0	0	0	1	1	0	.400	.333
Garland,Jon	L	.304	148	45	13	1	3	27	27	23	.409	.466	Harnisch,Pete	L	.265	226	60	11	3	6	23	26	26	.341	.420
Throws Right	R	.278	133	37	12	0	7	25	13	19	.345	.526	Throws Right	R	.257	284	73	21	1	17	45	20	45	.304	.518
Ginter,Matt	L	.345	29	10	1	0	3	9	6	2	.457	.690	Harper,Travis	L	.234	64	15	2	0	4	6	8	5	.319	.453
Throws Right	R	.533	15	8	2	0	2	7	1	4	.529	1.067	Throws Right	R	.254	59	15	3	1	1	10	7	9	.338	.390
Glauber,Keith	L	.111	9	1	1	0	0	0	1	1	.200	.222	Hasegawa,S	L	.246	171	42	6	0	5	28	20	27	.326	.368
Throws Right	R	.222	18	4	0	1	0	3	1	3	.300	.333	Throws Right	R	.291	199	58	11	1	6	25	18	32	.350	.447
Glavine,Tom	L	.242	190	46	7	2	4	18	14	32	.296	.363	Hawkins,L	L	.242	128	31	5	0	4	16	20	27	.349	.375
Throws Left	R	.245	719	176	29	4	20	66	51	120	.296	.380	Throws Right	R	.265	204	54	10	0	3	19	12	32	.304	.358
Glynn,Ryan	L	.333	174	58	8	1	9	32	29	14	.431	.546	Haynes,Jimmy	L	.319	329	105	12	1	11	48	47	26	.405	.462
Throws Right	R	.257	191	49	12	0	6	27	12	19	.307	.414	Throws Right	R	.276	445	123	22	2	10	61	53	62	.357	.402
Gomes,Wayne	L	.306	108	33	7	1	2	20	12	13	.379	.444	Helling,Rick	L	.238	453	108	31	3	16	56	58	87	.329	.435
Throws Right	R	.234	167	39	8	1	4	23	23	36	.326	.365	Throws Right	R	.267	389	104	31	2	13	54	41	59	.339	.458
Gooden,Dwight	L	.272	184	50	9	0	10	35	29	30	.367	.484	Henry,Doug	L	.222	99	22	5	0	7	16	19	24	.355	.485
Throws Right	R	.300	230	69	15	1	13	26	15	25	.351	.543	Throws Right	R	.199	176	35	7	1	5	23	30	38	.321	.335

Pitchers vs. Lefthanded and Righthanded Batters

Pitcher	vs	Avg	AB	H	2B	3B	HR	BI	BB	SO	OBP	SLG	Pitcher	vs	Avg	AB	H	2B	3B	HR	BI	BB	SO	OBP	SLG
Hentgen,Pat	L	.252	337	85	14	6	7	40	47	58	.342	.392	James,Mike	L	.203	64	13	1	0	3	10	16	13	.358	.359
Throws Right	R	.295	396	117	22	0	17	55	42	60	.363	.480	Throws Right	R	.227	119	27	4	1	4	13	8	28	.292	.378
Heredia,Felix	L	.195	82	16	4	1	2	15	8	24	.283	.341	Jarvis,Kevin	L	.337	205	69	24	1	10	33	15	24	.384	.610
Throws Left	R	.236	127	30	3	0	4	20	25	28	.357	.354	Throws Right	R	.271	255	69	14	1	16	39	18	36	.324	.522
Heredia,Gil	L	.256	395	101	21	2	11	40	48	59	.336	.403	Jimenez,Jose	L	.238	105	25	6	0	2	10	12	18	.319	.352
Throws Right	R	.294	385	113	31	0	13	50	18	42	.327	.475	Throws Right	R	.239	159	38	5	0	2	18	16	26	.315	.308
Herges,Matt	L	.265	170	45	6	1	4	24	22	27	.344	.382	Johnson,Jason	L	.267	195	52	10	2	11	39	26	36	.356	.508
Throws Right	R	.237	232	55	8	1	3	33	18	48	.307	.319	Throws Right	R	.288	233	67	13	0	10	46	35	43	.381	.472
Hermanson,D	L	.321	318	102	29	0	17	60	41	39	.393	.572	Johnson,J	L	.286	42	12	2	0	2	8	10	11	.426	.476
Throws Right	R	.270	460	124	24	3	9	51	34	55	.322	.393	Throws Right	R	.293	75	22	5	1	1	15	9	12	.400	.427
Hernandez,L	L	.271	414	112	24	3	9	46	42	76	.336	.408	Johnson,Mark	L	.302	53	16	2	1	1	11	10	7	.413	.434
Throws Right	R	.274	518	142	23	3	13	54	31	89	.316	.405	Throws Right	R	.220	41	9	3	1	2	9	6	4	.308	.488
Hernandez,O	L	.280	397	111	20	3	20	55	33	51	.339	.496	Johnson,Mike	L	.298	178	53	9	0	11	37	26	22	.396	.534
Throws Right	R	.210	357	75	15	2	14	41	18	90	.250	.381	Throws Right	R	.245	220	54	11	0	7	35	27	48	.341	.391
Hernandez,R	L	.328	131	43	10	0	4	23	15	29	.399	.496	Johnson,R.	L	.229	83	19	2	0	0	4	8	31	.319	.253
Throws Right	R	.223	148	33	5	0	5	15	8	32	.269	.358	Throws Left	R	.224	817	183	43	2	23	74	68	316	.284	.366
Hershiser,O	L	.417	48	20	4	0	1	12	5	5	.464	.563	Johnstone,J	L	.377	77	29	6	1	5	16	6	8	.419	.675
Throws Right	R	.367	60	22	4	0	4	16	9	8	.513	.633	Throws Right	R	.287	122	35	6	2	6	25	7	29	.326	.516
Hiljus,Erik	L	.125	8	1	0	0	1	1	0	1	.125	.500	Jones,B	L	.264	303	80	23	1	15	46	27	52	.324	.495
Throws Right	R	.571	7	4	1	0	0	3	1	1	.625	.714	Throws Right	R	.297	306	91	25	1	10	34	22	33	.348	.484
Hill,Ken	L	.314	137	43	6	0	6	30	29	26	.424	.489	Jones,B	L	.211	19	4	1	0	0	2	1	7	.286	.263
Throws Right	R	.337	190	64	8	1	10	30	30	24	.425	.547	Throws Left	R	.226	62	14	5	1	2	6	13	13	.372	.435
Hinchliffe,B	L	.333	3	1	0	0	0	0	0	0	.333	.420	Jones,Doug	L	.283	138	39	5	1	4	21	13	25	.342	.420
Throws Right	R	.000	3	0	0	0	0	0	1	0	.250	.000	Throws Right	R	.299	157	47	13	1	2	23	5	29	.327	.433
Hitchcock,S	L	.220	50	11	2	0	3	8	3	16	.316	.440	Jones,Marcus	L	.333	6	2	1	0	0	1	3	1	.556	.500
Throws Left	R	.279	208	58	10	2	9	28	23	45	.352	.476	Throws Right	R	.500	6	3	0	0	1	3	0	0	.500	1.000
Hodges,Kevin	L	.400	20	8	0	0	1	3	8	0	.571	.550	Jones,Todd	L	.294	126	37	2	2	3	17	17	34	.375	.413
Throws Right	R	.263	38	10	0	0	3	10	4	7	.356	.500	Throws Right	R	.256	117	30	2	0	3	17	8	33	.310	.350
Hoffman,T	L	.200	130	26	8	1	2	12	7	46	.239	.323	Judd,Mike	L	.000	5	0	0	0	0	0	2	3	.286	.000
Throws Right	R	.246	142	35	4	1	5	18	4	39	.260	.394	Throws Right	R	.364	11	4	1	0	2	7	1	2	.462	1.000
Holmes,Darren	L	.483	29	14	4	0	2	13	4	7	.514	.828	Kamieniecki,S	L	.289	90	26	5	2	4	17	25	19	.448	.522
Throws Right	R	.383	60	23	5	1	4	25	5	9	.441	.700	Throws Right	R	.277	137	38	9	0	5	18	17	27	.357	.453
Holt,Chris	L	.333	378	126	24	4	13	68	39	61	.393	.521	Karchner,Matt	L	.143	14	2	0	1	0	1	5	0	.368	.286
Throws Right	R	.279	434	121	17	5	9	52	36	75	.338	.403	Throws Right	R	.362	47	17	4	1	3	14	6	5	.426	.681
Holtz,Mike	L	.213	89	19	1	0	2	12	9	28	.284	.292	Karl,Scott	L	.294	102	30	9	0	5	25	7	12	.342	.529
Throws Left	R	.300	60	18	2	0	2	8	9	12	.400	.433	Throws Left	R	.360	267	96	16	2	11	53	38	26	.440	.558
Holzemer,Mark	L	.250	36	9	0	1	1	9	4	7	.325	.389	Karsay,Steve	L	.223	139	31	6	3	2	19	16	34	.304	.353
Throws Left	R	.380	71	27	9	1	3	16	4	12	.421	.662	Throws Right	R	.304	158	48	3	1	3	23	9	32	.349	.392
House,Craig	L	.227	22	5	1	0	1	5	11	4	.485	.409	Keisler,Randy	L	.222	9	2	0	0	0	0	3	2	.417	.222
Throws Right	R	.296	27	8	1	0	2	7	6	4	.444	.556	Throws Left	R	.400	35	14	5	0	1	10	5	4	.475	.629
Howry,Bob	L	.174	121	21	1	0	2	7	10	37	.239	.231	Kida,Masao	L	.333	3	1	1	0	0	0	0	0	.333	.667
Throws Right	R	.256	129	33	7	1	4	24	19	23	.359	.419	Throws Right	R	.400	10	4	1	0	1	3	0	0	.400	.800
Hudson,Tim	L	.231	420	97	22	0	17	54	43	88	.301	.405	Kile,Darryl	L	.229	406	93	24	1	15	44	35	91	.293	.404
Throws Right	R	.221	326	72	10	3	7	34	39	81	.313	.334	Throws Right	R	.263	464	122	26	3	18	57	23	101	.309	.448
Irabu,Hideki	L	.356	90	32	8	0	5	19	6	17	.388	.611	Kim,B	L	.239	113	27	3	1	3	17	23	40	.387	.363
Throws Right	R	.328	137	45	5	2	4	19	8	25	.370	.482	Throws Right	R	.170	147	25	4	1	6	19	23	71	.295	.333
Isringhausen,J	L	.242	153	37	4	0	4	19	18	33	.326	.346	King,Ray	L	.204	49	10	2	0	1	2	3	7	.245	.306
Throws Right	R	.265	113	30	4	0	2	15	14	24	.354	.354	Throws Left	R	.157	51	8	1	0	0	4	7	12	.259	.176
Jacquez,Tom	L	.200	10	2	0	0	1	6	1	3	.250	.500	Kinney,Matt	L	.305	95	29	8	1	4	13	15	12	.393	.537
Throws Left	R	.400	20	8	2	0	1	7	2	3	.455	.650	Throws Right	R	.194	62	12	2	0	3	9	10	12	.297	.371

Pitchers vs. Lefthanded and Righthanded Batters

Pitcher	vs	Avg	AB	H	2B	3B	HR	BI	BB	SO	OBP	SLG
Kline,Steve	L	.243	107	26	5	0	1	12	10	34	.314	.318
Throws Left	R	.297	209	62	10	3	7	33	17	30	.354	.474
Koch,Billy	L	.255	145	37	7	1	2	14	7	31	.294	.359
Throws Right	R	.261	157	41	10	0	4	16	11	29	.314	.401
Kohlmeier,R	L	.333	54	18	4	1	1	7	6	6	.400	.500
Throws Right	R	.245	49	12	1	0	0	4	9	11	.356	.265
Kolb,Brandon	L	.200	25	5	1	0	0	5	7	6	.364	.240
Throws Right	R	.379	29	11	2	1	0	5	4	6	.455	.517
Kolb,Danny	L	1.000	3	3	0	0	0	2	1	0	1.000	1.000
Throws Right	R	.667	3	2	1	0	0	3	1	0	.600	1.000
Lara,Yovanny	L	.167	6	1	1	0	0	1	3	2	.444	.333
Throws Right	R	.286	14	4	1	0	0	5	5	1	.450	.357
Larkin,Andy	L	.386	44	17	3	0	3	12	8	10	.481	.659
Throws Right	R	.281	64	18	6	0	3	17	8	14	.356	.516
Laxton,Brett	L	.389	36	14	3	0	0	7	7	8	.500	.472
Throws Right	R	.300	30	9	2	1	0	3	3	6	.382	.433
Lee,David	L	.333	15	5	1	0	2	5	3	4	.444	.800
Throws Right	R	.385	13	5	1	0	1	1	3	2	.529	.692
Lee,Sang-H.	L	.000	5	0	0	0	0	0	2	1	.375	.000
Throws Left	R	.297	37	11	0	0	2	4	3	5	.341	.459
Leiter,Al	L	.119	118	14	5	0	3	12	9	36	.191	.237
Throws Left	R	.248	653	162	31	3	16	67	67	164	.325	.378
Leskanic,C	L	.214	103	22	4	1	2	13	28	35	.378	.330
Throws Right	R	.211	171	36	7	0	5	12	23	40	.310	.339
Levine,Al	L	.263	160	42	13	1	6	22	26	16	.363	.469
Throws Right	R	.268	209	56	8	1	4	22	23	26	.343	.373
Levrault,A	L	.125	16	2	0	0	0	1	5	3	.318	.125
Throws Right	R	.308	26	8	1	0	0	6	2	6	.357	.346
Lidle,Cory	L	.295	190	56	8	2	9	35	14	25	.341	.500
Throws Right	R	.293	198	58	11	0	4	26	15	37	.352	.409
Lieber,Jon	L	.284	436	124	23	4	18	64	33	77	.338	.479
Throws Right	R	.234	530	124	19	2	18	61	21	115	.269	.379
Ligtenberg,K	L	.206	63	13	1	0	2	4	13	14	.342	.317
Throws Right	R	.236	127	30	10	1	5	19	11	37	.295	.449
Lilly,Ted	L	.286	14	4	2	0	0	3	3	5	.412	.429
Throws Left	R	.200	20	4	1	0	1	5	2	6	.273	.400
Lima,Jose	L	.364	360	131	30	6	25	69	41	32	.426	.689
Throws Right	R	.272	441	120	22	2	23	69	27	92	.311	.488
Lincoln,Mike	L	.378	45	17	3	0	3	8	5	7	.451	.644
Throws Right	R	.388	49	19	2	0	7	16	8	8	.483	.857
Linebrink,S	L	.333	24	8	0	0	4	7	5	4	.467	.833
Throws Right	R	.357	28	8	2	0	0	4	3	2	.455	.429
Lira,Felipe	L	.312	154	48	17	1	5	28	20	11	.389	.532
Throws Right	R	.309	262	81	10	2	6	49	16	40	.347	.431
Loaiza,E	L	.287	415	119	32	0	16	50	42	59	.359	.480
Throws Right	R	.289	377	109	14	3	13	42	15	78	.326	.446
Loiselle,Rich	L	.260	50	13	3	0	1	7	9	8	.361	.380
Throws Right	R	.263	114	30	9	0	4	26	21	24	.388	.447
Looper,Braden	L	.359	78	28	6	1	2	17	18	11	.485	.538
Throws Right	R	.230	187	43	7	0	1	30	18	18	.306	.283
Lopez,Albie	L	.306	363	111	18	1	10	45	43	37	.378	.444
Throws Right	R	.248	355	88	18	3	14	47	27	59	.301	.434
Lopez,Rodrigo	L	.444	45	20	3	0	4	12	8	7	.519	.778
Throws Right	R	.328	61	20	3	0	1	7	5	10	.379	.426
Lorraine,A	L	.171	35	6	1	0	0	3	3	8	.231	.200
Throws Left	R	.299	127	38	8	2	6	25	20	22	.392	.535
Lowe,Derek	L	.268	164	44	10	1	3	16	17	28	.339	.396
Throws Right	R	.247	186	46	11	1	3	17	5	51	.271	.366
Lowe,Sean	L	.345	113	39	7	1	4	21	22	14	.449	.531
Throws Right	R	.241	162	39	7	0	6	22	17	39	.335	.395
Luebbers,L	L	.292	24	7	2	0	0	4	8	4	.469	.375
Throws Right	R	.351	57	20	5	2	1	8	4	5	.393	.561
Maddux,Greg	L	.269	401	108	15	0	10	35	25	91	.316	.382
Throws Right	R	.214	546	117	23	0	9	50	17	99	.246	.306
Maddux,Mike	L	.268	41	11	1	1	0	3	4	5	.362	.341
Throws Right	R	.290	69	20	2	0	6	15	8	12	.359	.580
Maduro,Calvin	L	.286	42	12	2	2	1	13	9	8	.426	.500
Throws Right	R	.340	50	17	2	1	7	13	7	10	.414	.840
Magnante,Mike	L	.288	73	21	2	0	2	11	9	5	.381	.397
Throws Left	R	.330	88	29	8	0	1	13	10	12	.398	.455
Mahay,Ron	L	.262	42	11	3	0	1	8	9	11	.377	.405
Throws Left	R	.357	129	46	11	2	9	25	16	21	.428	.682
Mahomes,Pat	L	.256	156	40	13	1	4	23	31	28	.378	.429
Throws Right	R	.268	209	56	16	0	11	53	35	48	.375	.502
Mairena,O	L	.333	3	1	0	0	1	2	1	0	.500	1.333
Throws Left	R	.667	9	6	1	0	0	2	1	0	.700	.778
Mann,Jim	L	.167	6	1	0	0	0	0	1	0	.286	.167
Throws Right	R	.625	8	5	2	0	1	3	0	0	.625	1.250
Mantei,Matt	L	.183	71	13	5	0	2	12	16	28	.348	.338
Throws Right	R	.200	90	18	3	0	2	10	19	25	.339	.300
Manzanillo,J	L	.250	68	17	3	0	1	4	22	13	.429	.338
Throws Right	R	.236	140	33	5	2	5	23	10	26	.285	.407
Marquis,Jason	L	.226	31	7	2	0	1	5	8	5	.385	.387
Throws Right	R	.281	57	16	2	0	3	14	4	12	.333	.474
Martin,Tom	L	.281	57	16	3	0	0	9	5	10	.339	.333
Throws Left	R	.232	69	16	3	0	3	8	10	11	.333	.406
Martinez,P	L	.150	399	60	9	1	5	19	16	136	.190	.216
Throws Right	R	.184	369	68	9	0	12	22	16	148	.238	.306
Martinez,R	L	.275	255	70	17	0	8	40	38	45	.366	.435
Throws Right	R	.292	250	73	18	3	8	38	29	44	.379	.484
Martinez,W	L	.000	5	0	0	0	0	1	0	0	.000	.000
Throws Right	R	.250	4	1	0	0	0	1	1	1	.400	.250
Masaoka,Onan	L	.200	45	9	4	0	0	5	8	15	.333	.289
Throws Left	R	.255	55	14	3	0	2	6	7	12	.339	.418
Mathews,T.J.	L	.306	98	30	5	1	4	14	19	12	.424	.500
Throws Right	R	.301	143	43	8	0	6	26	6	30	.325	.483
Matthews,Mike	L	.227	22	5	2	0	0	6	2	4	.292	.318
Throws Right	R	.476	21	10	2	0	2	11	8	4	.633	.857
Maurer,Dave	L	.296	27	8	1	0	1	3	0	4	.345	.444
Throws Left	R	.233	30	7	0	0	1	2	5	9	.343	.333

Pitchers vs. Lefthanded and Righthanded Batters

Pitcher	vs	Avg	AB	H	2B	3B	HR	BI	BB	SO	OBP	SLG	Pitcher	vs	Avg	AB	H	2B	3B	HR	BI	BB	SO	OBP	SLG
Mays,Joe	L	.300	310	93	17	2	10	44	38	48	.373	.465	Molina,Gabe	L	.450	40	18	2	0	0	8	4	7	.500	.500
Throws Right	R	.298	336	100	14	5	10	43	29	54	.355	.458	Throws Right	R	.323	31	10	0	0	3	10	6	2	.410	.613
McDill,Allen	L	.300	20	6	3	0	2	6	0	4	.300	.750	Montgomery,S	L	.182	11	2	0	0	1	1	3	2	.357	.455
Throws Left	R	.333	21	7	3	0	0	4	1	3	.391	.476	Throws Right	R	.364	11	4	1	0	2	4	1	1	.417	1.000
McElroy,Chuck	L	.204	93	19	7	0	2	12	9	19	.275	.344	Moore,Trey	L	.459	37	17	2	0	1	6	4	5	.545	.595
Throws Left	R	.273	150	41	7	3	4	23	25	31	.378	.440	Throws Left	R	.333	114	38	4	0	6	23	17	19	.424	.526
McGlinchy,K	L	.231	13	3	0	0	0	0	2	5	.333	.231	Moraga,David	L	.400	5	2	1	0	0	4	1	1	.500	.600
Throws Right	R	.364	22	8	1	0	1	6	4	4	.462	.545	Throws Left	R	.727	11	8	3	0	1	9	1	1	.692	1.273
McKnight,Tony	L	.250	60	15	2	0	2	7	5	6	.308	.383	Morgan,Mike	L	.273	139	38	6	1	3	15	13	17	.333	.396
Throws Right	R	.241	83	20	5	0	2	11	4	17	.289	.373	Throws Right	R	.331	257	85	12	1	7	49	27	39	.392	.467
McMichael,G	L	.304	23	7	0	0	3	6	1	2	.320	.696	Morris,Jim	L	.167	18	3	0	0	0	3	5	5	.348	.167
Throws Right	R	.152	33	5	0	0	0	0	3	12	.222	.152	Throws Left	R	.318	22	7	2	0	1	7	2	5	.375	.545
Meacham,R.	L	.667	6	4	0	0	2	4	0	1	.667	1.667	Morris,Matt	L	.255	94	24	8	1	2	10	9	20	.324	.426
Throws Right	R	.267	15	4	0	0	1	3	2	2	.353	.467	Throws Right	R	.266	109	29	7	0	1	10	8	14	.322	.358
Meadows,Brian	L	.309	395	122	25	5	19	57	44	35	.380	.542	Mota,Danny	L	.417	12	5	2	0	0	5	1	2	.462	.583
Throws Right	R	.287	390	112	28	1	13	51	20	44	.329	.464	Throws Right	R	.333	15	5	0	0	1	5	0	1	.333	.533
Meche,Gil	L	.236	178	42	9	1	6	17	14	32	.289	.399	Mota,G	L	.244	41	10	2	0	3	5	3	10	.311	.512
Throws Right	R	.244	135	33	5	0	1	11	26	28	.366	.304	Throws Right	R	.246	69	17	2	1	0	13	9	14	.338	.304
Mecir,Jim	L	.204	152	31	3	0	1	13	21	35	.301	.243	Moyer,Jamie	L	.288	160	46	11	1	5	23	8	16	.331	.463
Throws Right	R	.245	159	39	4	1	3	22	15	35	.315	.340	Throws Left	R	.279	456	127	28	3	17	72	45	82	.342	.465
Mendoza,R	L	.299	127	38	5	1	5	18	11	17	.357	.472	Mulder,Mark	L	.368	155	57	12	0	4	21	22	19	.453	.523
Throws Right	R	.220	127	28	5	1	4	13	9	13	.286	.370	Throws Left	R	.288	466	134	29	2	18	74	47	69	.350	.474
Mercado,H	L	.250	20	5	0	0	2	4	4	9	.375	.550	Mulholland,T	L	.294	119	35	5	0	2	18	8	18	.341	.387
Throws Left	R	.233	30	7	2	0	0	2	4	4	.314	.300	Throws Left	R	.312	523	163	29	0	22	79	33	60	.353	.493
Mercedes,Jose	L	.291	265	77	18	5	8	30	35	33	.368	.487	Mullen,Scott	L	.143	21	3	1	0	1	2	0	5	.143	.333
Throws Right	R	.252	290	73	13	3	7	41	29	37	.323	.390	Throws Left	R	.350	20	7	1	0	1	5	3	2	.435	.550
Mercker,Kent	L	.235	51	12	4	0	2	10	7	11	.350	.431	Munoz,Mike	L	.455	11	5	0	1	0	4	1	0	.500	.636
Throws Left	R	.324	139	45	8	0	10	24	22	19	.414	.597	Throws Left	R	.600	10	6	1	0	1	3	2	1	.667	1.000
Mesa,Jose	L	.262	149	39	8	1	5	25	16	29	.327	.430	Munro,Peter	L	.310	42	13	3	0	0	5	11	2	.453	.381
Throws Right	R	.296	169	50	11	0	6	31	25	55	.396	.467	Throws Right	R	.385	65	25	7	0	1	14	5	14	.452	.538
Miceli,Dan	L	.270	89	24	4	1	2	11	7	14	.327	.404	Murray,Dan	L	.250	32	8	1	0	2	4	5	7	.342	.469
Throws Right	R	.216	97	21	3	0	2	12	11	26	.296	.309	Throws Right	R	.300	40	12	1	0	5	7	5	9	.391	.700
Miller,Travis	L	.248	105	26	4	1	1	10	12	31	.325	.333	Mussina,Mike	L	.223	404	90	13	2	9	42	24	98	.266	.332
Throws Left	R	.328	174	57	12	2	3	27	20	31	.395	.471	Throws Right	R	.281	520	146	34	1	19	59	22	112	.311	.460
Miller,Trever	L	.300	30	9	1	0	1	8	4	7	.405	.433	Myers,Mike	L	.121	91	11	3	1	1	7	7	33	.200	.209
Throws Left	R	.409	44	18	9	1	2	12	8	4	.500	.795	Throws Left	R	.220	59	13	3	1	1	7	17	8	.395	.356
Miller,Wade	L	.309	165	51	11	1	10	30	21	35	.388	.570	Myers,Rodney	L	.250	4	1	0	0	0	0	0	2	.250	.250
Throws Right	R	.222	239	53	10	0	4	24	21	54	.290	.314	Throws Right	R	.250	4	1	0	0	0	0	0	1	.250	.250
Mills,Alan	L	.313	83	26	5	0	3	15	13	14	.412	.482	Myette,Aaron	L	.000	1	0	0	0	0	0	1	0	.500	.000
Throws Right	R	.263	114	30	5	0	6	14	22	22	.387	.465	Throws Right	R	.000	7	0	0	0	0	0	3	1	.300	.000
Millwood,K	L	.289	357	103	18	5	11	50	38	67	.356	.459	Nagy,Charles	L	.303	132	40	7	1	7	18	11	21	.361	.530
Throws Right	R	.235	468	110	28	0	15	56	24	101	.274	.391	Throws Right	R	.295	105	31	5	3	8	29	10	20	.356	.629
Milton,Eric	L	.242	149	36	5	0	7	21	10	32	.286	.416	Nathan,Joe	L	.289	180	52	16	0	4	26	36	29	.402	.444
Throws Left	R	.265	638	169	37	3	28	82	34	128	.307	.464	Throws Right	R	.219	169	37	8	3	8	32	27	32	.337	.444
Mlicki,Dave	L	.281	235	66	16	4	9	36	26	28	.350	.498	Nation,Joey	L	.000	0	0	0	0	0	0	0	0	.000	.000
Throws Right	R	.301	256	77	13	0	8	29	18	29	.349	.445	Throws Left	R	.279	43	12	2	0	2	7	8	8	.407	.465
Moehler,Brian	L	.285	351	100	24	4	13	40	20	57	.326	.487	Navarro,Jaime	L	.333	57	19	5	0	6	19	10	7	.420	.737
Throws Right	R	.324	376	122	21	1	7	46	20	46	.356	.441	Throws Right	R	.402	87	35	10	1	3	23	13	9	.476	.644
Mohler,Mike	L	.351	37	13	5	0	1	12	9	5	.489	.568	Neagle,Denny	L	.295	200	59	10	1	9	16	12	33	.347	.490
Throws Left	R	.292	48	14	2	1	1	7	6	5	.382	.438	Throws Left	R	.249	606	151	33	1	22	84	69	113	.324	.416

Pitchers vs. Lefthanded and Righthanded Batters

Pitcher	vs	Avg	AB	H	2B	3B	HR	BI	BB	SO	OBP	SLG	Pitcher	vs	Avg	AB	H	2B	3B	HR	BI	BB	SO	OBP	SLG
Nelson,Jeff	L	.232	82	19	7	0	1	10	15	24	.351	.354	Parque,Jim	L	.316	187	59	9	1	5	26	14	25	.373	.455
Throws Right	R	.157	159	25	4	0	1	14	30	47	.295	.201	Throws Left	R	.271	549	149	18	4	16	60	57	86	.346	.406
Nen,Robb	L	.193	119	23	4	0	3	11	11	50	.267	.303	Parra,Jose	L	.385	13	5	1	0	0	2	2	1	.467	.462
Throws Right	R	.128	109	14	2	0	1	5	8	42	.190	.174	Throws Right	R	.343	35	12	2	1	3	9	5	8	.439	.714
Newman,Alan	L	.000	1	0	0	0	0	0	0	0	.000	.000	Parris,Steve	L	.311	383	119	33	4	17	46	28	46	.358	.551
Throws Left	R	.750	8	6	0	0	1	4	1	0	.778	1.125	Throws Right	R	.278	389	108	24	3	13	52	43	71	.352	.455
Nichting,C	L	.308	13	4	2	0	0	3	1	2	.375	.462	Parrish,John	L	.182	11	2	1	0	0	3	8	3	.500	.273
Throws Right	R	.360	25	9	3	0	0	6	4	5	.467	.480	Throws Left	R	.297	128	38	7	0	6	28	27	25	.415	.492
Nickle,Doug	L	.667	3	2	0	0	0	1	0	0	.667	.667	Patterson,D	L	.292	96	28	9	0	2	10	4	7	.320	.448
Throws Right	R	.333	9	3	0	0	0	1	2	0	.500	.333	Throws Right	R	.323	127	41	3	0	2	16	10	22	.376	.394
Nitkowski,C	L	.218	147	32	6	0	5	34	15	44	.292	.361	Pavano,Carl	L	.312	173	54	13	2	7	22	17	21	.383	.532
Throws Left	R	.322	286	92	19	2	8	41	34	37	.393	.486	Throws Right	R	.188	186	35	7	1	1	10	17	43	.269	.253
Nomo,Hideo	L	.241	357	86	12	2	16	43	51	112	.340	.420	Pena,Jesus	L	.324	37	12	2	0	2	7	7	4	.413	.541
Throws Right	R	.284	370	105	20	4	15	44	38	69	.349	.481	Throws Left	R	.250	64	16	2	0	5	16	12	16	.377	.516
Norton,Phil	L	.167	6	1	0	0	1	2	2	1	.375	.667	Penny,Brad	L	.249	193	48	13	1	2	16	34	30	.362	.358
Throws Left	R	.382	34	13	1	0	4	7	5	5	.462	.765	Throws Right	R	.274	263	72	12	3	11	46	26	50	.347	.468
Nunez,V	L	.339	112	38	8	0	6	22	20	21	.440	.571	Percival,Troy	L	.237	93	22	7	0	3	13	16	24	.345	.409
Throws Right	R	.305	164	50	11	1	6	36	14	24	.355	.494	Throws Right	R	.220	91	20	2	0	4	15	14	25	.333	.374
O'Connor,B	L	.100	10	1	0	0	0	0	5	5	.438	.100	Perez,Carlos	L	.296	142	42	12	0	6	21	10	20	.346	.507
Throws Left	R	.289	38	11	3	0	2	10	6	2	.378	.526	Throws Left	R	.333	450	150	24	1	19	68	23	44	.374	.518
Ohka,T.	L	.277	159	44	11	0	5	15	12	25	.331	.440	Perez,Yorkis	L	.282	39	11	2	0	1	5	5	10	.356	.410
Throws Right	R	.243	107	26	7	0	2	10	14	15	.331	.364	Throws Left	R	.255	55	14	4	0	3	14	9	11	.354	.491
Ohman,Will	L	.333	9	3	0	0	0	0	1	2	.400	.333	Perisho,Matt	L	.331	142	47	8	0	4	25	21	34	.419	.472
Throws Left	R	.250	4	1	0	0	0	0	3	0	.571	.250	Throws Left	R	.308	289	89	15	1	16	59	46	40	.406	.533
Olivares,Omar	L	.303	195	59	8	1	6	31	32	27	.409	.446	Person,Robert	L	.178	287	51	15	0	6	24	46	80	.297	.293
Throws Right	R	.314	239	75	15	2	4	42	28	30	.384	.444	Throws Right	R	.272	342	93	28	4	7	40	49	84	.361	.439
Oliver,Darren	L	.373	110	41	11	2	1	15	18	10	.469	.536	Peters,Chris	L	.250	40	10	2	0	2	5	5	8	.333	.450
Throws Left	R	.327	336	110	31	2	15	69	24	39	.372	.565	Throws Left	R	.203	64	13	6	0	0	5	9	8	.311	.297
Olson,Gregg	L	.115	26	3	0	0	2	2	3	8	.233	.346	Petkovsek,M	L	.252	127	32	5	0	3	25	12	16	.317	.362
Throws Right	R	.409	44	18	4	0	2	11	4	7	.449	.636	Throws Right	R	.295	183	54	13	1	5	19	11	15	.343	.459
Ontiveros,S	L	.385	13	5	0	1	0	3	1	1	.429	.538	Pettitte,Andy	L	.256	176	45	10	0	1	16	13	27	.309	.330
Throws Right	R	.364	11	4	2	0	1	3	3	0	.500	.818	Throws Left	R	.275	632	174	33	6	16	73	67	98	.346	.422
Orosco,Jesse	L	.500	6	3	0	0	1	2	1	3	.625	1.000	Pichardo,H	L	.287	94	27	6	1	0	14	15	9	.384	.372
Throws Left	R	.000	5	0	0	0	0	0	1	3	.375	.000	Throws Right	R	.243	148	36	4	0	1	18	11	28	.304	.291
Ortiz,Ramon	L	.250	220	55	11	2	11	34	29	26	.340	.468	Pineiro,Joel	L	.357	28	10	0	0	2	8	8	3	.486	.571
Throws Right	R	.219	187	41	6	0	7	25	26	47	.312	.364	Throws Right	R	.294	51	15	4	0	1	7	5	7	.351	.431
Ortiz,Russ	L	.265	358	95	21	3	8	37	62	76	.376	.408	Plesac,Dan	L	.260	77	20	2	0	3	14	9	26	.333	.403
Throws Right	R	.257	378	97	12	1	20	59	50	91	.347	.452	Throws Left	R	.194	72	14	1	0	1	10	17	19	.348	.250
Osuna,Antonio	L	.227	110	25	8	0	1	13	22	30	.351	.327	Politte,Cliff	L	.227	88	20	6	0	1	3	14	21	.333	.330
Throws Right	R	.230	139	32	10	0	6	20	13	40	.303	.432	Throws Right	R	.261	134	35	8	2	7	19	13	29	.324	.507
Padilla,V	L	.337	95	32	9	1	2	19	16	15	.425	.516	Ponson,Sidney	L	.258	422	109	19	1	12	53	53	70	.340	.393
Throws Right	R	.252	159	40	6	1	1	15	12	36	.306	.321	Throws Right	R	.259	441	114	22	2	18	57	30	82	.306	.440
Painter,Lance	L	.291	103	30	9	0	4	28	8	25	.345	.495	Poole,Jim	L	.448	29	13	1	0	4	18	1	4	.438	.897
Throws Left	R	.257	152	39	7	0	5	13	14	28	.323	.401	Throws Left	R	.381	21	8	0	0	1	6	3	4	.480	.524
Palacios,V	L	.389	18	7	1	0	1	4	3	5	.476	.611	Pote,Lou	L	.294	85	25	1	3	2	16	6	18	.341	.447
Throws Right	R	.238	21	5	1	0	3	8	2	3	.292	.714	Throws Right	R	.245	110	27	3	0	2	10	11	26	.311	.327
Paniagua,Jose	L	.206	126	26	7	0	1	16	21	30	.327	.286	Powell,Brian	L	.295	44	13	2	2	2	6	3	7	.354	.568
Throws Right	R	.255	165	42	11	0	5	28	17	41	.335	.412	Throws Right	R	.269	78	21	4	0	6	14	10	7	.344	.551
Park,Chan Ho	L	.228	399	91	14	1	12	41	70	89	.348	.358	Powell,Jay	L	.233	43	10	2	0	1	7	8	8	.353	.349
Throws Right	R	.200	410	82	22	2	9	39	54	128	.303	.329	Throws Right	R	.297	64	19	4	0	0	11	11	8	.400	.359

Pitchers vs. Lefthanded and Righthanded Batters

Pitcher	vs	Avg	AB	H	2B	3B	HR	BI	BB	SO	OBP	SLG
Powell,Jeremy	L	.391	46	18	4	1	2	6	5	5	.451	.652
Throws Right	R	.270	63	17	4	1	4	18	4	14	.309	.556
Prieto,Ariel	L	.260	73	19	2	0	2	10	4	12	.304	.370
Throws Right	R	.397	58	23	3	1	1	9	9	7	.478	.534
Prokopec,Luke	L	.229	48	11	2	0	1	3	5	10	.321	.333
Throws Right	R	.296	27	8	3	0	1	5	4	2	.387	.519
Pulsipher,B	L	.375	8	3	1	0	0	2	1	1	.500	.500
Throws Left	R	.391	23	9	1	0	1	6	5	6	.500	.565
Quantrill,P	L	.299	137	41	9	1	6	30	9	28	.340	.511
Throws Right	R	.296	199	59	10	3	1	27	16	19	.352	.392
Quevedo,R.	L	.248	145	36	3	1	9	24	16	28	.331	.469
Throws Right	R	.287	209	60	16	1	12	51	38	37	.395	.545
Radinsky,S	L	.000	0	0	0	0	0	0	0	0	.000	.000
Throws Left	R	.000	0	0	0	0	0	0	1	0	1.000	.000
Radke,Brad	L	.297	499	148	35	5	16	63	24	68	.331	.483
Throws Right	R	.274	412	113	23	4	11	45	27	73	.321	.430
Rain,Steve	L	.216	74	16	2	0	3	8	10	23	.310	.365
Throws Right	R	.273	110	30	5	0	7	21	17	31	.372	.509
Rakers,Jason	L	.360	50	18	6	0	4	12	2	7	.377	.720
Throws Right	R	.341	44	15	3	0	1	8	5	9	.408	.477
Ramirez,H	L	.222	18	4	1	0	1	4	2	2	.300	.444
Throws Right	R	.350	20	7	1	0	0	4	3	2	.435	.400
Ramsay,Rob	L	.231	78	18	4	0	2	11	15	15	.351	.359
Throws Left	R	.236	106	25	4	0	1	12	25	17	.381	.302
Rapp,Pat	L	.281	335	94	23	7	4	44	47	55	.370	.427
Throws Right	R	.298	366	109	31	1	14	66	36	51	.361	.503
Ratliff,Jon	L	.000	0	0	0	0	0	0	0	0	.000	.000
Throws Right	R	.000	3	0	0	0	0	0	0	0	.000	.000
Reames,Britt	L	.208	77	16	2	1	2	3	14	15	.330	.338
Throws Right	R	.206	68	14	7	0	2	11	9	16	.304	.397
Redman,Mark	L	.282	149	42	10	0	5	20	13	33	.341	.450
Throws Left	R	.281	449	126	27	0	17	63	32	84	.331	.454
Reed,Rick	L	.273	344	94	15	2	13	40	25	64	.324	.442
Throws Right	R	.260	377	98	16	3	15	41	9	57	.281	.438
Reed,Steve	L	.271	59	16	3	0	3	11	11	8	.386	.475
Throws Right	R	.268	157	42	5	0	4	18	10	31	.314	.376
Reichert,Dan	L	.275	295	81	15	3	5	37	48	44	.382	.397
Throws Right	R	.267	285	76	6	0	10	40	43	50	.362	.393
Rekar,Bryan	L	.293	351	103	17	5	11	49	18	43	.328	.464
Throws Right	R	.290	335	97	18	2	11	39	21	52	.331	.454
Remlinger,M	L	.203	79	16	2	0	1	15	11	22	.308	.266
Throws Left	R	.209	187	39	10	0	5	21	26	50	.309	.342
Reyes,Al	L	.111	27	3	0	0	0	0	4	4	.226	.111
Throws Right	R	.273	44	12	5	0	2	13	8	14	.370	.523
Reyes,Carlos	L	.213	47	10	0	0	4	11	8	11	.327	.468
Throws Right	R	.259	58	15	3	0	3	10	5	6	.328	.466
Reyes,Dennys	L	.178	73	13	3	0	2	13	14	23	.303	.301
Throws Left	R	.330	91	30	5	0	3	18	15	13	.426	.484
Reynolds,S	L	.278	234	65	13	3	6	29	25	44	.346	.436
Throws Right	R	.294	289	85	15	2	14	47	20	49	.345	.505

Pitcher	vs	Avg	AB	H	2B	3B	HR	BI	BB	SO	OBP	SLG
Reynoso,A	L	.270	315	85	21	3	11	46	18	44	.313	.460
Throws Right	R	.276	341	94	14	2	11	39	34	45	.345	.425
Rhodes,Arthur	L	.220	109	24	3	0	2	17	13	28	.298	.303
Throws Left	R	.193	140	27	3	2	4	18	16	49	.276	.329
Riedling,John	L	.280	25	7	2	1	1	5	6	5	.419	.560
Throws Right	R	.143	28	4	1	0	0	0	2	13	.226	.179
Rigby,Brad	L	.333	33	11	4	1	2	7	6	3	.436	.697
Throws Right	R	.457	35	16	4	0	4	19	2	2	.513	.914
Rigdon,Paul	L	.259	135	35	7	0	8	18	23	26	.366	.489
Throws Right	R	.267	202	54	10	1	10	31	12	37	.304	.475
Riggan,Jerrod	L	.000	3	0	0	0	0	0	0	1	.000	.000
Throws Right	R	.429	7	3	0	0	0	2	0	0	.429	.429
Rincon,Ricky	L	.216	51	11	5	0	0	0	5	17	.286	.314
Throws Left	R	.240	25	6	1	0	1	3	8	3	.441	.400
Ritchie,Todd	L	.311	334	104	21	6	13	51	39	59	.382	.527
Throws Right	R	.258	403	104	24	1	13	54	12	65	.282	.419
Rivera,Luis	L	.300	10	3	1	0	0	1	4	1	.500	.400
Throws Right	R	.143	14	2	1	0	0	1	2	4	.250	.214
Rivera,M	L	.210	143	30	5	1	1	19	16	26	.289	.280
Throws Right	R	.206	136	28	5	0	3	16	9	32	.252	.309
Roberts,Grant	L	.353	17	6	2	0	0	7	4	5	.435	.471
Throws Right	R	.333	15	5	2	0	0	2	0	1	.333	.467
Rocker,John	L	.243	37	9	0	0	2	6	14	20	.462	.405
Throws Left	R	.202	163	33	3	1	3	12	34	57	.343	.288
Rodriguez,F	L	.158	133	21	4	1	0	11	19	58	.263	.203
Throws Right	R	.270	163	44	7	0	5	26	23	37	.365	.405
Rodriguez,F	L	.256	78	20	3	1	2	13	16	3	.375	.397
Throws Right	R	.360	111	40	7	1	6	20	6	16	.390	.604
Rodriguez,J	L	.000	5	0	0	0	0	1	2	1	.333	.000
Throws Left	R	.222	9	2	1	0	0	0	1	1	.300	.333
Rodriguez,R	L	.289	45	13	3	0	3	12	5	6	.358	.556
Throws Right	R	.393	117	46	11	3	4	26	10	12	.439	.641
Rogers,Kenny	L	.314	220	69	19	4	6	31	18	41	.368	.518
Throws Left	R	.276	682	188	41	2	14	82	60	86	.341	.403
Romero,J.C.	L	.281	57	16	2	0	1	10	4	15	.328	.368
Throws Left	R	.322	174	56	9	0	7	33	26	35	.409	.494
Roque,Rafael	L	.429	7	3	1	1	0	2	2	1	.556	.857
Throws Left	R	.286	14	4	0	1	1	3	5	3	.450	.643
Rosado,Jose	L	.294	17	5	3	0	0	3	2	3	.400	.471
Throws Left	R	.267	90	24	10	0	4	13	7	12	.337	.511
Rose,Brian	L	.319	232	74	8	2	11	42	29	28	.404	.513
Throws Right	R	.238	235	56	15	2	10	32	22	36	.304	.447
Rueter,Kirk	L	.244	135	33	5	2	4	14	12	21	.309	.400
Throws Left	R	.301	572	172	31	5	19	73	50	50	.353	.472
Ruffin,Johnny	L	.278	18	5	1	0	2	4	1	2	.316	.667
Throws Right	R	.409	22	9	1	1	2	7	2	3	.458	.818
Runyan,Sean	L	.333	6	2	0	0	0	3	1	1	.375	.333
Throws Left	R	.000	3	0	0	0	0	0	1	0	.250	.000
Rupe,Ryan	L	.313	201	63	12	3	9	33	17	35	.364	.537
Throws Right	R	.330	176	58	13	1	10	36	14	26	.399	.585

Pitchers vs. Lefthanded and Righthanded Batters

Pitcher	vs	Avg	AB	H	2B	3B	HR	BI	BB	SO	OBP	SLG
Rusch,Glendon	L	.304	158	48	6	1	3	19	14	35	.375	.411
Throws Left	R	.256	577	148	25	5	15	64	30	122	.292	.395
Ryan,B.J.	L	.175	57	10	1	1	1	8	16	22	.351	.281
Throws Left	R	.252	103	26	5	0	6	25	15	19	.347	.476
Ryan,Jason	L	.388	49	19	4	1	5	16	6	8	.446	.816
Throws Right	R	.286	63	18	4	0	3	10	4	11	.333	.492
Sanchez,Jesus	L	.250	112	28	6	0	3	15	15	21	.336	.384
Throws Left	R	.285	592	169	41	5	29	96	61	102	.350	.519
Santana,Johan	L	.263	95	25	8	0	3	14	12	19	.358	.442
Throws Left	R	.317	243	77	13	4	8	38	42	45	.413	.502
Santana,Julio	L	.327	98	32	8	0	5	18	14	22	.414	.561
Throws Right	R	.236	157	37	5	2	6	21	19	36	.318	.408
Santiago,Jose	L	.224	147	33	10	1	2	25	13	22	.286	.347
Throws Right	R	.303	122	37	2	0	5	25	13	22	.379	.443
Sasaki,K	L	.198	116	23	1	0	8	20	17	36	.299	.414
Throws Right	R	.170	112	19	7	1	2	9	14	42	.271	.304
Sauerbeck,S	L	.222	117	26	4	1	2	12	13	41	.303	.325
Throws Left	R	.305	164	50	13	1	2	25	48	42	.458	.433
Sauveur,Rich	L	.353	17	6	0	0	0	3	0	5	.353	.353
Throws Left	R	.280	25	7	1	0	3	8	1	2	.308	.680
Scanlan,Bob	L	.600	5	3	1	0	0	4	0	0	.500	.800
Throws Right	R	.600	5	3	1	0	0	2	0	1	.667	.800
Schilling,C	L	.243	428	104	22	3	10	43	22	91	.279	.379
Throws Right	R	.268	373	100	21	0	17	45	23	77	.311	.461
Schmidt,Jason	L	.250	100	25	6	1	1	10	17	25	.356	.360
Throws Right	R	.307	150	46	9	1	5	25	24	26	.403	.480
Schoeneweis,S	L	.294	153	45	4	0	4	24	18	22	.376	.399
Throws Left	R	.271	509	138	35	2	17	72	49	56	.337	.448
Schourek,Pete	L	.325	80	26	6	0	3	10	7	17	.379	.513
Throws Left	R	.266	338	90	14	2	14	41	31	46	.332	.444
Schrenk,Steve	L	.250	36	9	4	0	1	8	5	6	.341	.444
Throws Right	R	.281	57	16	4	0	2	9	8	13	.373	.456
Seanez,Rudy	L	.294	34	10	1	0	2	5	4	8	.368	.500
Throws Right	R	.114	44	5	0	0	1	4	5	12	.220	.182
Seelbach,C	L	.500	2	1	0	0	0	1	0	0	.333	.500
Throws Right	R	.500	4	2	0	0	0	1	0	1	.500	.500
Sele,Aaron	L	.275	443	122	23	3	10	49	48	81	.347	.409
Throws Right	R	.265	373	99	17	3	7	46	26	56	.314	.383
Serafini,Dan	L	.383	47	18	2	1	1	5	4	10	.463	.532
Throws Left	R	.289	211	61	15	0	10	34	24	25	.361	.502
Service,Scott	L	.299	67	20	2	0	1	8	13	20	.407	.373
Throws Right	R	.305	82	25	11	0	4	20	6	15	.356	.585
Shaw,Jeff	L	.304	112	34	7	2	3	10	9	18	.355	.482
Throws Right	R	.229	118	27	7	0	4	13	7	21	.278	.390
Shuey,Paul	L	.203	118	24	4	0	2	18	19	35	.319	.288
Throws Right	R	.235	115	27	6	0	2	16	11	34	.305	.339
Sikorski,B	L	.247	85	21	6	0	4	17	14	13	.356	.459
Throws Right	R	.333	75	25	5	0	5	15	11	19	.419	.600
Silva,Jose	L	.355	231	82	14	1	10	43	25	45	.421	.554
Throws Right	R	.290	331	96	12	1	6	43	25	53	.341	.387

Pitcher	vs	Avg	AB	H	2B	3B	HR	BI	BB	SO	OBP	SLG
Simas,Bill	L	.287	94	27	6	0	5	16	12	21	.364	.511
Throws Right	R	.269	156	42	9	1	4	21	10	28	.312	.417
Sirotka,Mike	L	.311	177	55	8	0	7	28	20	35	.382	.475
Throws Left	R	.256	578	148	22	2	16	60	49	93	.313	.384
Skrmetta,Matt	L	.300	20	6	2	0	1	6	5	2	.423	.550
Throws Right	R	.317	41	13	1	0	2	11	4	9	.391	.488
Slocumb,H	L	.299	107	32	4	0	6	19	15	10	.381	.505
Throws Right	R	.242	153	37	10	1	3	22	22	36	.341	.379
Slusarski,Joe	L	.319	135	43	10	4	1	22	8	17	.357	.474
Throws Right	R	.227	163	37	3	1	7	29	14	37	.297	.387
Smith,Brian	L	.429	7	3	1	0	0	2	0	1	.429	.571
Throws Right	R	.333	9	3	1	0	1	3	2	2	.417	.778
Smith,Chuck	L	.240	179	43	10	3	2	21	31	45	.355	.363
Throws Right	R	.254	268	68	13	2	4	26	23	73	.312	.362
Smith,Dan	L	.000	3	0	0	0	0	1	1	1	.200	.000
Throws Right	R	.400	5	2	2	0	0	2	2	0	.444	.800
Snyder,John	L	.286	217	62	12	4	5	29	36	31	.392	.447
Throws Right	R	.304	280	85	14	0	3	52	41	38	.397	.386
Sparks,Jeff	L	.091	33	3	0	0	1	4	10	12	.302	.182
Throws Right	R	.270	37	10	2	0	1	3	8	12	.426	.405
Sparks,Steve	L	.600	5	3	0	0	0	4	4	0	.778	.600
Throws Right	R	.100	10	1	1	0	0	1	1	2	.182	.200
Sparks,S	L	.264	216	57	14	3	5	27	15	24	.316	.426
Throws Right	R	.262	195	51	14	0	2	18	14	29	.318	.364
Speier,Justin	L	.171	117	20	5	0	4	14	15	36	.277	.316
Throws Right	R	.274	135	37	8	0	5	17	13	33	.338	.444
Spencer,Sean	L	.286	7	2	0	0	1	4	0	4	.250	.714
Throws Left	R	.294	17	5	2	0	1	4	3	2	.400	.588
Spencer,Stan	L	.212	85	18	3	0	1	7	8	25	.287	.282
Throws Right	R	.263	99	26	4	0	6	13	11	15	.339	.485
Spoljaric,P	L	.150	20	3	0	0	2	5	4	3	.292	.450
Throws Left	R	.429	14	6	3	0	2	4	1	3	.467	1.071
Spradlin,J	L	.269	171	46	11	1	5	32	18	35	.339	.433
Throws Right	R	.313	176	55	11	1	6	30	14	32	.371	.489
Springer,D	L	.414	29	12	5	0	2	9	3	1	.485	.793
Throws Right	R	.333	24	8	3	0	0	1	2	4	.385	.458
Springer,Russ	L	.243	70	17	1	0	3	15	16	16	.391	.386
Throws Right	R	.269	171	46	11	2	8	33	18	43	.337	.497
Spurgeon,Jay	L	.333	54	18	1	0	4	12	11	3	.446	.574
Throws Right	R	.211	38	8	1	0	1	2	4	8	.318	.316
Stanifer,Rob	L	.375	32	12	2	0	1	7	3	0	.429	.531
Throws Right	R	.333	30	10	2	0	2	9	1	3	.355	.667
Stanton,Mike	L	.339	118	40	9	1	3	19	6	41	.362	.508
Throws Left	R	.199	141	28	3	0	2	13	18	34	.296	.262
Stechschulte,G	L	.205	44	9	0	0	3	7	8	5	.327	.409
Throws Right	R	.283	53	15	6	1	3	15	9	7	.375	.604
Stein,Blake	L	.217	184	40	3	0	8	20	31	29	.327	.364
Throws Right	R	.272	213	58	10	0	11	34	26	49	.357	.474
Stephenson,G	L	.310	377	117	39	2	10	40	30	51	.365	.504
Throws Right	R	.231	398	92	14	1	21	58	33	72	.292	.430

Pitchers vs. Lefthanded and Righthanded Batters

Pitcher	vs	Avg	AB	H	2B	3B	HR	BI	BB	SO	OBP	SLG
Stevens,Dave	L	.333	6	2	0	0	1	1	1	1	.429	.833
Throws Right	R	.375	8	3	1	0	1	3	0	3	.375	.875
Stottlemyre,T	L	.273	143	39	5	1	10	21	22	18	.370	.531
Throws Right	R	.266	222	59	10	0	8	31	14	58	.313	.419
Strickland,S	L	.290	62	18	1	3	2	10	6	6	.343	.500
Throws Right	R	.174	115	20	3	1	1	14	10	42	.244	.243
Strong,Joe	L	.217	23	5	1	1	1	5	4	5	.333	.478
Throws Right	R	.368	57	21	3	0	2	16	8	13	.463	.526
Stull,Everett	L	.284	67	19	3	0	3	13	14	10	.393	.463
Throws Right	R	.237	93	22	2	0	4	12	16	23	.372	.387
Sturtze,T	L	.269	134	36	6	0	4	23	13	24	.336	.403
Throws Right	R	.275	131	36	7	1	4	17	16	20	.360	.435
Sullivan,S	L	.214	159	34	9	0	5	15	15	32	.300	.365
Throws Right	R	.235	226	53	9	1	9	28	23	64	.311	.403
Suppan,Jeff	L	.284	457	130	28	5	15	42	47	71	.353	.466
Throws Right	R	.283	389	110	24	2	21	64	37	57	.349	.517
Suzuki,Makoto	L	.273	400	109	17	3	18	51	55	64	.363	.465
Throws Right	R	.255	337	86	20	0	8	39	39	71	.332	.386
Swindell,Greg	L	.159	107	17	2	0	2	8	4	27	.195	.234
Throws Left	R	.298	181	54	11	2	5	23	16	37	.352	.464
Tam,Jeff	L	.360	125	45	8	1	2	18	15	22	.426	.488
Throws Right	R	.209	196	41	6	3	1	14	8	24	.240	.286
Tapani,Kevin	L	.231	312	72	11	1	9	32	18	64	.278	.359
Throws Right	R	.299	455	136	27	0	26	74	29	86	.346	.530
Tavarez,J	L	.261	180	47	13	1	3	28	26	23	.357	.394
Throws Right	R	.272	283	77	19	2	8	31	27	39	.344	.438
Taylor,Billy	L	.304	23	7	2	1	1	6	4	3	.407	.609
Throws Right	R	.214	28	6	0	0	1	6	5	10	.371	.321
Telemaco,A	L	.233	43	10	3	1	3	7	8	9	.346	.558
Throws Right	R	.313	48	15	3	1	3	14	6	13	.382	.604
Telford,A	L	.281	121	34	4	2	7	20	12	26	.338	.521
Throws Right	R	.240	175	42	7	2	3	13	11	42	.302	.354
Tessmer,Jay	L	.167	6	1	0	0	1	2	1	1	.286	.667
Throws Right	R	.333	24	8	1	0	2	7	0	4	.333	.625
Thompson,M.	L	.308	26	8	2	0	2	5	5	4	.438	.615
Throws Right	R	.229	70	16	3	0	2	12	10	15	.337	.357
Thurman,Mike	L	.336	137	46	7	2	3	20	22	9	.417	.482
Throws Right	R	.303	218	66	15	1	6	43	24	43	.377	.463
Timlin,Mike	L	.308	107	33	2	0	3	25	13	17	.380	.411
Throws Right	R	.243	140	34	3	2	5	13	22	35	.359	.400
Tolar,Kevin	L	.000	3	0	0	0	0	1	0	2	.000	.000
Throws Left	R	.125	8	1	0	0	0	0	1	1	.222	.125
Tollberg,B	L	.283	230	65	15	2	6	26	21	46	.343	.443
Throws Right	R	.265	230	61	10	1	7	23	14	30	.321	.409
Tomko,Brett	L	.268	153	41	9	1	6	26	23	24	.360	.458
Throws Right	R	.262	195	51	10	1	6	28	17	35	.326	.415
Trachsel,S	L	.298	386	115	24	0	9	39	36	52	.355	.430
Throws Right	R	.290	404	117	28	6	17	67	38	58	.357	.515
Trombley,Mike	L	.241	108	26	5	0	5	13	17	28	.341	.426
Throws Right	R	.252	163	41	8	0	10	30	21	44	.349	.485

Pitcher	vs	Avg	AB	H	2B	3B	HR	BI	BB	SO	OBP	SLG
Tucker,T.J.	L	.154	13	2	0	0	2	3	3	1	.313	.615
Throws Right	R	.474	19	9	1	0	3	5	0	1	.474	1.000
Turnbow,D	L	.269	67	18	4	0	2	9	15	13	.405	.418
Throws Right	R	.240	75	18	1	1	5	15	21	12	.412	.480
Urbina,Ugueth	L	.269	26	7	1	1	1	4	3	10	.345	.500
Throws Right	R	.174	23	4	0	0	0	3	2	12	.240	.174
Valdes,Ismael	L	.327	202	66	14	0	14	35	26	26	.403	.604
Throws Right	R	.264	220	58	11	1	8	26	14	48	.311	.432
Valdes,Marc	L	.303	89	27	4	2	0	20	15	11	.400	.393
Throws Right	R	.300	140	42	4	1	3	26	10	24	.365	.407
Van Poppel,T	L	.234	145	34	1	2	3	15	25	34	.345	.331
Throws Right	R	.261	176	46	12	1	7	27	23	43	.350	.460
Vazquez,J	L	.279	394	110	25	1	7	38	32	88	.337	.401
Throws Right	R	.291	471	137	25	2	17	57	29	108	.333	.461
Venafro,Mike	L	.252	123	31	6	0	1	21	10	22	.314	.325
Throws Left	R	.351	94	33	9	0	1	14	11	10	.422	.479
Veres,Dave	L	.210	119	25	5	0	1	6	15	33	.301	.277
Throws Right	R	.261	153	40	10	0	5	30	10	34	.325	.425
Villafuerte,B	L	.286	7	2	1	0	0	2	1	1	.375	.429
Throws Right	R	.222	9	2	1	0	0	3	3	0	.417	.333
Villegas,I	L	.250	4	1	1	0	0	0	1	0	.400	.500
Throws Right	R	.375	8	3	0	0	2	6	1	2	.500	1.125
Villone,Ron	L	.256	117	30	7	1	6	18	12	21	.348	.487
Throws Left	R	.295	421	124	29	3	16	68	66	56	.390	.492
Vizcaino,Luis	L	.270	37	10	3	0	1	7	2	8	.300	.432
Throws Right	R	.333	45	15	1	0	1	7	9	10	.464	.422
Vogelsong,R	L	.000	6	0	0	0	0	0	1	3	.143	.000
Throws Right	R	.250	16	4	0	0	0	0	1	3	.294	.250
Vosberg,Ed	L	.286	42	12	0	0	3	5	9	17	.412	.500
Throws Left	R	.200	45	9	4	0	1	5	9	6	.333	.356
Wagner,Billy	L	.321	28	9	1	0	3	13	2	3	.387	.679
Throws Left	R	.232	82	19	6	1	3	10	16	25	.357	.439
Wainhouse,D	L	.500	10	5	0	0	1	1	1	2	.615	.800
Throws Right	R	.296	27	8	3	0	1	8	3	3	.367	.519
Wakefield,Tim	L	.244	283	69	14	1	11	45	29	42	.312	.417
Throws Right	R	.295	342	101	18	2	20	54	36	60	.363	.535
Walker,Kevin	L	.257	105	27	2	0	1	9	9	33	.328	.305
Throws Left	R	.165	133	22	4	0	4	25	29	23	.323	.286
Walker,Pete	L	.615	13	8	2	1	1	8	3	1	.688	1.154
Throws Right	R	.200	10	2	0	0	0	1	1	1	.273	.200
Wall,Donne	L	.209	91	19	2	0	2	13	14	14	.314	.297
Throws Right	R	.177	96	17	5	1	2	7	7	15	.233	.313
Wallace,Jeff	L	.286	49	14	1	0	3	12	15	10	.463	.490
Throws Left	R	.292	96	28	5	0	2	25	19	17	.415	.406
Ward,Bryan	L	.250	40	10	0	1	0	5	8	7	.360	.300
Throws Left	R	.194	62	12	1	0	3	10	2	7	.219	.355
Wasdin,John	L	.275	120	33	6	0	6	18	14	23	.355	.475
Throws Right	R	.292	195	57	14	2	8	41	10	48	.329	.508
Washburn,J	L	.215	65	14	4	1	4	8	9	7	.307	.492
Throws Left	R	.215	233	50	6	0	12	28	28	42	.299	.395

321

Pitcher	vs	Avg	AB	H	2B	3B	HR	BI	BB	SO	OBP	SLG
Watson,Allen	L	.355	31	11	1	0	2	12	6	7	.450	.581
Throws Left	R	.317	60	19	4	0	4	14	12	13	.438	.583
Watson,Mark	L	.385	13	5	0	1	0	2	0	1	.385	.538
Throws Left	R	.412	17	7	2	0	0	3	2	3	.500	.529
Weathers,Dave	L	.223	94	21	3	0	1	10	21	18	.368	.287
Throws Right	R	.278	187	52	9	1	6	24	11	32	.322	.433
Weaver,Eric	L	.313	32	10	2	0	1	5	7	2	.436	.469
Throws Right	R	.233	43	10	0	0	4	10	9	6	.358	.512
Weaver,Jeff	L	.269	402	108	18	4	19	59	29	65	.328	.475
Throws Right	R	.264	367	97	21	1	7	34	23	71	.315	.384
Weber,Ben	L	.316	38	12	2	0	0	4	4	2	.372	.368
Throws Right	R	.276	58	16	3	2	0	10	2	12	.300	.397
Wells,Bob	L	.233	120	28	9	1	1	10	8	32	.285	.350
Throws Right	R	.255	204	52	10	0	13	41	7	44	.284	.495
Wells,David	L	.289	197	57	17	0	5	26	8	28	.325	.452
Throws Left	R	.289	723	209	39	2	18	76	23	138	.313	.423
Wells,Kip	L	.290	221	64	10	2	9	39	32	36	.379	.475
Throws Right	R	.339	183	62	11	1	6	27	26	35	.422	.508
Wendell,Turk	L	.225	102	23	6	0	3	6	20	18	.358	.373
Throws Right	R	.196	189	37	5	3	6	21	21	55	.286	.349
Wengert,Don	L	.400	10	4	1	0	0	5	0	2	.400	.500
Throws Right	R	.250	32	8	0	0	2	4	5	5	.351	.438
Westbrook,J	L	.375	16	6	1	0	0	3	3	1	.450	.438
Throws Right	R	.563	16	9	5	0	1	7	1	0	.556	1.063
Wetteland,J	L	.309	123	38	2	4	7	25	13	24	.377	.561
Throws Right	R	.259	112	29	8	0	3	14	11	29	.323	.411
Wheeler,Dan	L	.412	51	21	10	2	1	11	6	8	.466	.745
Throws Right	R	.178	45	8	0	0	1	4	5	9	.288	.244
Whisenant,M	L	.143	35	5	0	0	0	4	7	6	.279	.143
Throws Left	R	.275	40	11	3	0	1	12	10	6	.412	.425
White,Gabe	L	.200	105	21	1	1	4	20	7	36	.248	.343
Throws Left	R	.217	198	43	13	0	2	19	8	48	.252	.313
White,Rick	L	.268	153	41	4	0	5	17	20	25	.363	.392
Throws Right	R	.193	218	42	15	0	4	26	18	42	.263	.317
Whiteside,M	L	.264	53	14	3	0	1	6	7	10	.344	.377
Throws Right	R	.212	85	18	6	0	5	18	10	17	.302	.459
Wickman,Bob	L	.258	132	34	6	1	0	15	16	32	.338	.318
Throws Right	R	.214	140	30	4	1	1	15	16	23	.297	.279
Wilkins,Marc	L	.250	80	20	6	1	0	12	21	19	.404	.350
Throws Right	R	.246	138	34	8	0	4	24	22	18	.359	.391
Williams,B	L	.224	49	11	2	0	2	7	15	7	.409	.388
Throws Right	R	.351	114	40	10	0	4	33	16	13	.440	.544
Williams,Jeff	L	.400	10	4	0	0	1	3	4	1	.533	.700
Throws Left	R	.500	16	8	2	1	0	3	4	2	.600	.750
Williams,M	L	.250	8	2	2	0	0	3	4	2	.538	.500
Throws Left	R	.208	24	5	0	0	2	8	9	5	.424	.458
Williams,Mike	L	.231	104	24	2	1	6	20	21	28	.364	.442
Throws Right	R	.209	153	32	6	0	2	14	19	43	.301	.288
Williams,W	L	.228	289	66	13	1	4	19	29	54	.300	.322
Throws Right	R	.248	347	86	15	2	19	52	25	57	.301	.467
Williamson,S	L	.251	171	43	9	2	5	25	39	49	.393	.415
Throws Right	R	.204	240	49	11	3	2	21	36	87	.311	.300

Pitcher	vs	Avg	AB	H	2B	3B	HR	BI	BB	SO	OBP	SLG
Wilson,Kris	L	.306	72	22	3	1	2	10	5	10	.351	.458
Throws Right	R	.267	60	16	4	0	1	8	6	7	.328	.383
Wilson,Paul	L	.228	92	21	7	0	0	11	9	18	.301	.304
Throws Right	R	.189	90	17	3	0	1	3	7	22	.267	.256
Winchester,S	L	.333	9	3	1	0	0	0	1	0	.400	.444
Throws Right	R	.304	23	7	1	0	1	4	1	3	.320	.478
Wise,Matt	L	.250	84	21	0	0	4	9	7	11	.315	.393
Throws Right	R	.302	63	19	5	0	3	11	6	9	.352	.524
Witasick,Jay	L	.315	298	94	19	4	15	62	43	57	.402	.557
Throws Right	R	.274	307	84	13	0	9	38	30	64	.347	.404
Witt,Bobby	L	.423	26	11	3	0	2	6	1	0	.444	.769
Throws Right	R	.378	45	17	3	0	2	6	5	6	.440	.578
Wohlers,Mark	L	.205	39	8	1	0	2	2	7	9	.326	.385
Throws Right	R	.183	60	11	2	1	1	8	10	11	.296	.300
Wolf,Randy	L	.227	110	25	8	1	1	12	11	37	.302	.345
Throws Left	R	.276	670	185	47	3	24	89	72	123	.349	.463
Wood,Kerry	L	.223	224	50	12	1	6	27	46	60	.356	.366
Throws Right	R	.229	271	62	11	2	11	42	41	72	.343	.406
Woodard,Steve	L	.287	272	78	13	7	11	55	20	42	.336	.507
Throws Right	R	.320	325	104	19	0	15	50	24	58	.374	.517
Worrell,Tim	L	.225	120	27	6	1	2	8	13	22	.301	.342
Throws Right	R	.296	152	45	11	0	8	22	16	35	.365	.526
Wright,Jamey	L	.267	247	66	7	1	6	31	54	31	.410	.377
Throws Right	R	.256	355	91	6	1	6	39	34	65	.336	.338
Wright,Jaret	L	.295	88	26	3	2	5	13	14	12	.394	.568
Throws Right	R	.182	99	18	7	0	1	10	14	24	.283	.283
Wunsch,Kelly	L	.160	106	17	3	1	1	12	10	35	.235	.236
Throws Left	R	.275	120	33	4	1	3	18	19	16	.379	.400
Yan,Esteban	L	.316	253	80	24	1	8	33	23	43	.372	.514
Throws Right	R	.258	302	78	17	2	18	57	19	68	.319	.507
Yarnall,Ed	L	.500	4	2	0	0	1	1	1	0	.667	1.250
Throws Left	R	.375	8	3	1	0	0	1	2	1	.500	.500
Yoshii,Masato	L	.282	305	86	18	3	14	42	30	37	.343	.498
Throws Right	R	.328	351	115	23	4	18	59	23	51	.369	.570
Young,Danny	L	.200	5	1	0	0	0	0	1	0	.333	.200
Throws Left	R	.444	9	4	2	0	1	4	5	0	.643	1.000
Young,Tim	L	.364	11	4	0	1	3	6	0	4	.417	1.364
Throws Left	R	.200	15	3	1	0	0	0	2	2	.294	.267
Zerbe,Chad	L	.222	9	2	0	0	0	1	0	1	.222	.222
Throws Left	R	.308	13	4	1	0	1	2	1	4	.357	.615
Zimmerman,J	L	.297	111	33	5	1	6	21	23	32	.415	.523
Throws Right	R	.278	169	47	0	0	4	21	11	42	.323	.391
Zito,Barry	L	.194	72	14	4	2	0	2	15	20	.348	.306
Throws Left	R	.195	256	50	8	2	6	26	30	58	.280	.313
AL	L	.275	—	—	—	—	—	—	—	—	.354	.446
	R	.275	—	—	—	—	—	—	—	—	.342	.441
NL	L	.270	—	—	—	—	—	—	—	—	.354	.439
	R	.264	—	—	—	—	—	—	—	—	.335	.427
MLB	L	.273	—	—	—	—	—	—	—	—	.354	.443
	R	.269	—	—	—	—	—	—	—	—	.338	.433

Pitchers vs. Lefthanded and Righthanded Batters

Runs Created/
Component Earned Run Average

Three years ago, STATS produced two books that we feel set the standard for encyclopedic information. Ask any question about baseball, and the chances are good you'll find the answer in either our *All-Time Major League Handbook* or *All-Time Baseball Sourcebook*.

Among the mountain of statistics available in each book, it's likely that two of them—Runs Created per 27 Outs (RC/27) and Component ERA (ERC)—are among the most compelling. For a definition of each stat, please consult the Glossary.

The second edition of our *All-Time Handbook* is complete through the 1999 season. The *All-Time Sourcebook* covers historical data through the 1997 campaign. So, for players who are active, this section provides a comprehensive update of these numbers through the 2000 season.

Runs Created

Player, Team	2000 RC	RC/27	LRC/27	Career RC	RC/27	LRC27
Abbott, Jeff, CWS	27	4.46	5.30	67	4.12	5.13
Abbott, Kurt, NYM	13	2.75	5.00	256	4.33	4.74
Abbott, Paul, Sea	1	6.70	5.30	1	6.70	5.30
Abreu, Bobby, Phi	119	7.67	5.00	384	7.76	4.84
Acevedo, Juan, Mil	0	0.00	5.00	1	0.42	4.75
Adams, Terry, LA	0	0.00	5.00	0	0.00	4.78
Agbayani, Benny, NYM	63	6.44	5.00	108	5.92	4.99
Aguilera, Rick, ChC	0	—	—	10	2.12	4.23
Alcantara, Israel, Bos	9	7.53	5.30	9	7.53	5.30
Aldred, Scott, Phi	0	—	—	0	0.00	5.00
Alexander, Manny, Bos	17	2.94	5.30	113	3.15	4.91
Alfonseca, Antonio, Fla	0	—	—	0	0.00	4.69
Alfonzo, Edgardo, NYM	129	8.94	5.00	520	6.37	4.77
Alicea, Luis, Tex	79	5.15	5.30	460	4.65	4.73
Allen, Chad, Min	6	4.12	5.30	64	4.20	5.19
Allen, Dusty, SD-Det	2	2.44	5.12	2	2.44	5.12
Almanza, Armando, Fla	0	0.00	5.00	0	0.00	5.00
Almanzar, Carlos, SD	0	0.00	5.00	0	0.00	5.00
Alomar, Roberto, Cle	102	5.93	5.30	1245	6.12	4.71
Alomar Jr., Sandy, Cle	47	4.63	5.30	421	4.25	4.90
Alou, Moises, Hou	104	8.58	5.00	706	6.85	4.58
Alvarez, Clemente, Phi	0	0.00	5.00	0	0.00	5.00
Alvarez, Gabe, Det-SD	1	2.07	5.05	29	3.62	5.05
Amaral, Rich, Bal	5	2.43	5.30	219	4.17	5.01
Anderson, Brady, Bal	80	5.34	5.30	1003	5.73	4.87
Anderson, Brian, Ari	0	0.00	5.00	0	0.00	4.85
Anderson, Garret, Ana	91	4.88	5.30	475	4.84	5.15
Anderson, Jimmy, Pit	0	0.00	5.00	2	1.01	5.00
Anderson, Marlon, Phi	8	1.63	5.00	71	3.72	4.98
Andrews, Clayton, Tor	0	0.00	5.30	0	0.00	5.30
Andrews, Shane, ChC	30	5.07	5.00	199	3.88	4.75
Ankiel, Rick, StL	6	3.04	5.00	6	2.56	5.00
Appier, Kevin, Oak	0	0.00	5.30	0	0.00	5.11
Ardoin, Danny, Min	4	3.83	5.30	4	3.83	5.30
Arias, Alex, Phi	15	3.03	5.00	190	4.04	4.68
Armas Jr., Tony, Mon	0	0.00	5.00	0	0.00	5.00
Arnold, Jamie, LA-ChC	0	0.00	5.00	0	0.00	5.00
Arrojo, Rolando, Col-Bos	0	0.00	5.00	0	0.00	5.00
Arroyo, Bronson, Pit	0	0.00	5.00	0	0.00	5.00
Ashby, Andy, Phi-Atl	3	1.30	5.00	10	0.57	4.68
Astacio, Pedro, Col	-1	-0.35	5.00	7	0.38	4.68
Aurilia, Rich, SF	77	5.23	5.00	257	4.66	4.84
Ausmus, Brad, Det	61	3.95	5.30	362	4.09	4.87
Aven, Bruce, Pit-LA	16	3.24	5.00	87	5.42	5.00
Aybar, Manny, Col-Cin-Fla	0	0.00	5.00	2	0.91	4.73
Bagwell, Jeff, Hou	143	8.76	5.00	1202	8.09	4.55
Baines, Harold, Bal-CWS	35	4.30	5.30	1569	5.70	4.66
Bako, Paul, Hou-Fla-Atl	19	2.85	5.00	66	3.05	5.01
Baldwin, James, CWS	0	0.00	5.30	1	2.24	5.12
Barajas, Rod, Ari	1	2.69	5.00	4	4.68	5.00
Barker, Glen, Hou	6	2.69	5.00	20	4.37	5.00
Barker, Kevin, Mil	13	4.37	5.00	34	5.54	5.00
Barnes, John, Min	5	4.78	5.30	5	4.78	5.30
Barrett, Michael, Mon	19	2.29	5.00	82	3.90	4.99
Bartee, Kimera, Cin	0	0.00	5.00	34	2.60	5.24
Batista, Miguel, Mon-KC	0	0.00	5.22	3	1.04	4.80
Batista, Tony, Tor	91	5.09	5.30	281	5.24	5.11
Baughman, Justin, Ana	1	1.58	5.30	19	2.85	5.04
Bautista, Danny, Fla-Ari	57	5.62	5.00	145	3.71	4.96
Beck, Rod, Bos	0	—	—	1	1.80	4.50
Becker, Rich, Oak-Det	50	6.01	5.30	319	4.88	5.12
Belcher, Tim, Ana	0	—	—	3	0.21	4.10
Belinda, Stan, Col-Atl	0	0.00	5.00	2	2.08	4.35
Bell, David, Sea	52	3.81	5.30	215	3.83	5.04
Bell, Derek, NYM	81	5.14	5.00	600	4.75	4.69
Bell, Jay, Ari	90	5.56	5.00	996	4.99	4.51
Bell, Mike, Cin	3	3.84	5.00	3	3.84	5.00
Bell, Rob, Cin	-2	-1.17	5.00	-2	-1.17	5.00
Belle, Albert, Bal	88	5.47	5.30	1145	6.93	4.92
Bellhorn, Mark, Oak	0	0.00	5.30	29	3.86	4.96
Belliard, Ron, Mil	87	5.21	5.00	160	5.34	5.00
Bellinger, Clay, NYY	20	3.57	5.00	22	3.15	5.27
Beltran, Carlos, KC	39	3.51	5.30	161	5.08	5.21
Beltran, Rigo, Col	0	—	—	0	0.00	4.72
Beltre, Adrian, LA	91	6.32	5.00	193	5.43	4.94
Benard, Marvin, SF	76	4.78	5.00	289	4.99	4.84
Benes, Alan, StL	1	13.45	5.00	3	0.72	4.65
Benes, Andy, StL	0	0.00	5.00	20	0.78	4.50

Player, Team	2000 RC	RC/27	LRC/27	Career RC	RC/27	LRC27
Benitez, Armando, NYM	0	—	—	0	0.00	5.00
Benjamin, Mike, Pit	28	4.07	5.00	177	3.20	4.75
Bennett, Gary, Phi	11	5.28	5.00	26	4.22	4.92
Benson, Kris, Pit	0	0.00	5.00	1	0.21	5.00
Bere, Jason, Mil-Cle	1	0.81	5.00	3	1.24	4.91
Berg, Dave, Fla	26	4.19	5.00	99	5.04	4.90
Bergeron, Peter, Mon	54	3.43	5.00	58	3.40	5.00
Bergman, Sean, Min	0	0.00	5.30	1	0.21	4.70
Berkman, Lance, Hou	67	6.85	5.00	77	6.13	5.00
Berroa, Geronimo, LA	5	5.38	5.00	385	5.38	5.05
Berry, Sean, Mil-Bos	1	0.60	5.03	342	4.94	4.64
Bichette, Dante, Cin-Bos	85	5.23	5.06	967	5.79	4.63
Biggio, Craig, Hou	65	5.83	5.00	1201	6.36	4.46
Blair, Willie, Det	0	0.00	5.30	0	0.00	4.52
Blake, Casey, Min	2	3.57	5.30	3	1.78	5.22
Blanco, Henry, Mil	30	3.46	5.00	61	3.66	5.00
Blank, Matt, Mon	0	0.00	5.00	0	0.00	5.00
Blum, Geoff, Mon	48	4.95	5.00	66	4.82	5.00
Bocachica, Hiram, LA	1	3.84	5.00	1	3.84	5.00
Bochtler, Doug, KC	0	—	—	0	0.00	4.63
Boehringer, Brian, SD	0	0.00	5.00	0	0.00	4.91
Bogar, Tim, Hou	32	3.24	5.00	148	3.20	4.76
Bohanon, Brian, Col	4	1.99	5.00	14	2.05	4.86
Bonds, Barry, SF	129	9.94	5.00	1755	8.42	4.40
Bones, Ricky, Fla	0	0.00	5.00	0	0.00	4.31
Bonilla, Bobby, Atl	36	5.32	5.00	1166	5.85	4.44
Boone, Aaron, Cin	48	5.87	5.00	147	5.21	4.91
Boone, Bret, SD	71	5.17	5.00	488	4.20	4.73
Borbon, Pedro, Tor	0	—	—	1	6.74	4.91
Bordick, Mike, Bal-NYM	79	4.73	5.20	540	3.74	4.97
Borkowski, Dave, Det	0	—	—	0	0.00	5.18
Bottalico, Ricky, KC	0	—	—	1	2.08	4.75
Bottenfield, Kent, Ana-Phi	1	1.49	5.02	6	0.93	4.73
Boyd, Jason, Phi	0	—	—	0	0.00	5.00
Bradley, Milton, Mon	19	4.06	5.00	19	4.06	5.00
Bragg, Darren, Col	22	4.81	5.00	269	4.72	5.08
Branson, Jeff, LA	0	0.00	5.00	148	3.23	4.59
Brantley, Jeff, Phi	0	—	—	1	0.37	4.26
Branyan, Russ, Cle	30	5.36	5.30	36	5.24	5.27
Brewington, Jamie, Cle	0	0.00	5.30	1	1.18	4.66
Brocail, Doug, Det	0	—	—	3	1.14	4.52
Brock, Chris, Phi	1	2.99	5.00	4	1.99	4.91
Brock, Tarrik, ChC	1	2.44	5.00	1	2.44	5.00
Brogna, Rico, Phi-Bos	20	3.61	5.10	385	4.91	4.74
Brosius, Scott, NYY	51	3.56	5.30	465	4.54	5.09
Brower, Jim, Cle	0	0.00	5.30	0	0.00	5.30
Brown, Adrian, Pit	53	6.60	5.00	103	4.33	4.85
Brown, Brant, Fla-ChC	13	2.50	5.00	138	4.48	4.81
Brown, Dee, KC	1	1.28	5.30	1	0.57	5.22
Brown, Emil, Pit	12	3.26	5.00	19	2.32	4.80
Brown, Kevin, LA	0	0.00	5.00	6	0.43	4.79
Brown, Kevin L., Mil	2	4.14	5.00	19	4.44	5.03
Brown, Roosevelt, ChC	14	6.07	5.00	21	4.79	5.00
Brownson, Mark, Phi	0	—	—	0	0.00	4.87
Brunette, Justin, StL	1	Inf	—	1	Inf	—
Bruske, Jim, Mil	0	0.00	5.00	0	0.00	4.65
Buchanan, Brian, Min	5	1.91	5.30	5	1.91	5.30
Buford, Damon, ChC	59	4.05	5.00	214	4.02	5.01
Buhner, Jay, Sea	76	7.09	5.30	889	6.11	4.85
Bullinger, Kirk, Phi	0	—	—	0	0.00	4.60
Burba, Dave, Cle	0	0.00	5.30	9	1.42	4.59
Burkett, John, Atl	2	1.28	5.00	-2	-0.11	4.43
Burkhart, Morgan, Bos	15	7.44	5.30	15	7.44	5.30
Burks, Ellis, SF	90	8.74	5.00	1064	6.27	4.61
Burnett, A.J., Fla	7	9.41	5.00	7	5.38	5.00
Burnitz, Jeromy, Mil	91	5.34	5.00	464	5.81	4.86
Burrell, Pat, Phi	72	6.27	5.00	72	6.27	5.00
Bush, Homer, Tor	14	1.49	5.30	100	4.01	5.21
Byrd, Paul, Phi	1	1.42	5.00	6	1.54	4.91
Byrdak, Tim, KC	0	—	—	1	26.71	5.18
Byrnes, Eric, Oak	1	3.35	5.30	1	3.35	5.30
Cabrera, Alex, Ari	9	3.78	5.00	9	3.78	5.00
Cabrera, Jolbert, Cle	17	3.30	5.30	18	2.82	5.27
Cabrera, Jose, Hou	0	0.00	5.00	0	0.00	4.74
Cabrera, Orlando, Mon	48	3.75	5.00	120	3.74	4.90
Cairo, Miguel, TB	53	4.70	5.30	166	4.00	5.14
Cameron, Mike, Sea	90	5.63	5.30	285	5.00	5.08
Caminiti, Ken, Hou	50	8.73	5.00	921	5.46	4.41

324

Player, Team	2000 RC	RC/27	LRC/27	Career RC	RC/27	LRC27
Cammack, Eric, NYM	1	Inf	—	1	Inf	—
Canizaro, Jay, Min	48	4.89	5.30	62	4.41	5.12
Canseco, Jose, TB-NYY	56	5.84	5.30	1227	6.19	4.78
Cardona, Javier, Det	0	0.00	5.30	0	0.00	5.30
Carlyle, Buddy, SD	0	—	—	2	6.73	5.00
Carpenter, Bubba, Col	4	5.12	5.00	4	5.12	5.00
Carpenter, Chris, Tor	0	0.00	5.30	0	0.00	5.19
Carrara, Giovanni, Col	0	0.00	5.00	0	0.00	4.68
Carrasco, Hector, Min-Bos	0	—	—	0	0.00	4.64
Casanova, Raul, Mil	31	4.51	5.00	66	3.30	5.03
Casey, Sean, Cin	94	7.20	5.00	262	6.96	4.91
Casimiro, Carlos, Bal	0	0.00	5.30	0	0.00	5.30
Castilla, Vinny, TB	23	2.24	5.30	598	5.53	4.73
Castillo, Alberto, Tor	13	2.26	5.30	53	2.75	4.97
Castillo, Frank, Tor	0	0.00	5.30	0	0.00	4.43
Castillo, Luis, Fla	81	5.43	5.00	205	4.46	4.86
Castro, Juan, Cin	19	2.73	5.00	44	2.10	4.75
Castro, Ramon, Fla	15	3.74	5.00	18	2.93	5.00
Catalanotto, Frank, Tex	50	6.32	5.30	123	5.36	5.17
Cedeno, Roger, Hou	42	5.48	5.00	207	5.16	4.82
Charles, Frank, Hou	2	13.45	5.00	2	13.45	5.00
Charlton, Norm, Cin	0	—	—	2	0.61	4.07
Chavez, Eric, Oak	82	5.81	5.30	142	5.53	5.23
Chavez, Raul, Hou	2	1.42	5.00	4	1.68	4.85
Chen, Bruce, Atl-Phi	0	0.00	5.00	0	0.00	4.95
Chouinard, Bobby, Col	0	0.00	5.00	0	0.00	4.87
Christensen, McKay, CWS	1	1.49	5.30	3	1.25	5.21
Christenson, Ryan, Oak	20	5.15	5.30	94	3.97	5.12
Christiansen, J., Pit-StL	0	—	—	1	2.70	4.68
Cirillo, Jeff, Col	122	7.47	5.00	593	6.31	5.00
Clapinski, Chris, Fla	9	6.72	5.00	15	5.04	5.00
Clark, Brady, Cin	1	3.36	5.00	1	3.36	5.00
Clark, Mark, Tex	0	—	—	-3	-0.31	4.51
Clark, Tony, Det	33	5.49	5.30	412	6.04	5.12
Clark, Will, Bal-StL	92	8.12	5.18	1385	7.11	4.54
Clayton, Royce, Tex	53	3.29	5.30	465	3.56	4.70
Clemens, Roger, NYY	0	0.00	5.30	1	1.91	5.13
Clement, Matt, SD	-1	-0.44	5.00	-2	-0.45	4.99
Clemente, Edgard, Ana	4	1.70	5.30	26	3.48	5.07
Clontz, Brad, Pit	0	—	—	0	0.00	4.74
Coffie, Ivanon, Bal	7	3.68	5.30	7	3.68	5.30
Coggin, Dave, Phi	0	0.00	5.00	0	0.00	5.00
Colbrunn, Greg, Ari	64	7.08	5.00	345	5.08	4.67
Collier, Lou, Mil	3	2.99	5.00	57	3.52	4.72
Colon, Bartolo, Cle	0	0.00	5.30	0	0.00	5.19
Cone, David, NYY	0	0.00	5.30	9	0.62	4.08
Conine, Jeff, Bal	54	4.61	5.30	570	5.34	4.77
Conti, Jason, Ari	13	4.86	5.00	13	4.86	5.00
Cook, Dennis, NYM	0	0.00	5.00	11	3.24	4.13
Coomer, Ron, Min	71	4.45	5.30	309	4.47	5.13
Cooper, Brian, Ana	0	0.00	5.30	0	0.00	5.30
Coquillette, Trace, Mon	5	2.69	5.00	11	3.29	5.00
Cora, Alex, LA	33	3.12	5.00	34	2.68	4.97
Cordero, Wil, Pit-Cle	71	5.02	5.09	459	4.88	4.82
Cordova, Francisco, Pit	0	0.00	5.00	0	0.00	4.75
Cordova, Marty, Tor	19	3.20	5.30	376	5.13	5.14
Cormier, Rheal, Bos	0	—	—	8	1.21	4.29
Cornelius, Reid, Fla	0	0.00	5.00	1	0.45	4.89
Counsell, Craig, Ari	22	5.24	5.00	113	4.69	4.76
Cox, Steve, TB	49	5.47	5.30	49	5.11	5.29
Crabtree, Tim, Tex	0	—	—	0	0.00	5.01
Crede, Joe, CWS	2	5.36	5.30	2	5.36	5.30
Creek, Doug, TB	0	—	—	0	0.00	4.63
Crespo, Felipe, SF	19	4.96	5.00	51	5.06	5.06
Cromer, D.T., Cin	10	8.15	5.00	10	8.15	5.00
Cromer, Tripp, Hou	0	0.00	5.00	38	2.37	4.67
Croushore, Rick, Col-Bos	1	26.89	5.00	1	5.39	4.84
Cruz, Deivi, Det	76	4.51	5.30	214	3.64	5.12
Cruz, Ivan, Pit	0	0.00	5.00	2	1.68	4.97
Cruz, Jacob, Cle	5	5.82	5.30	27	3.99	4.93
Cruz, Jose, Tor	89	4.99	5.30	262	5.26	5.13
Cruz, Nelson, Det	0	0.00	5.30	0	0.00	5.30
Cubillan, Darwin, Tor-Tex	0	0.00	5.00	0	0.00	5.30
Cummings, M., Min-Bos	19	3.28	5.30	119	4.00	4.81
Cunnane, Will, SD	0	0.00	5.00	4	5.67	4.79
Curtis, Chad, Tex	48	4.82	5.30	540	4.61	4.97
D'Amico, Jeff, Mil	0	0.00	5.00	0	0.00	5.00
Daal, Omar, Ari-Phi	8	5.52	5.00	11	1.82	4.85
Damon, Johnny, KC	134	7.52	5.30	496	5.79	5.16
Darensbourg, Vic, Fla	1	4.48	5.00	1	1.80	4.76

Player, Team	2000 RC	RC/27	LRC/27	Career RC	RC/27	LRC27
Darr, Mike, SD	30	5.04	5.00	36	4.92	5.00
Daubach, Brian, Bos	70	4.90	5.30	149	5.95	5.23
Davis, Ben, SD	13	3.24	5.00	36	3.01	5.00
Davis, Eric, StL	44	6.33	5.00	952	6.45	4.39
Davis, Kane, Cle-Mil	0	0.00	5.30	0	0.00	5.30
Davis, Russ, SF	23	4.48	5.00	236	4.44	5.07
Dawkins, Gookie, Cin	3	2.24	5.00	3	1.92	5.00
de la Rosa, Tomas, Mon	11	5.58	5.00	11	5.58	5.00
de los Santos, Valerio, Mil	0	0.00	5.00	0	0.00	5.00
DeHaan, Kory, SD	9	2.75	5.00	9	2.75	5.00
DeJean, Mike, Col	0	0.00	5.00	1	2.07	4.72
del Toro, Miguel, SF	0	0.00	5.00	0	0.00	5.00
Delgado, Carlos, Tor	161	11.06	5.30	589	7.26	5.16
Delgado, Wilson, NYY-KC	15	4.02	5.30	25	3.59	5.10
Dellucci, David, Ari	6	4.25	5.00	88	5.27	4.71
Dempster, Ryan, Fla	-1	-0.36	5.00	-1	-0.20	4.96
DeRosa, Mark, Atl	3	8.96	5.00	3	4.25	4.96
DeShields, Delino, Bal	102	6.31	5.30	765	4.95	4.55
Dessens, Elmer, Cin	0	0.00	5.00	2	1.06	4.90
Diaz, Einar, Cle	26	3.53	5.30	81	3.95	5.20
Dickson, Jason, Ana	0	—	—	0	0.00	4.98
DiFelice, Mike, TB	18	2.84	5.30	94	3.47	4.98
Dipoto, Jerry, Col	0	0.00	5.00	0	0.00	4.73
DiSarcina, Gary, Ana	9	8.93	5.30	354	3.15	4.94
Donnels, Chris, LA	10	9.60	5.00	71	3.86	4.44
Dotel, Octavio, Hou	0	0.00	5.00	1	0.45	5.00
Downs, Scott, ChC-Mon	0	0.00	5.00	0	0.00	5.00
Dransfeldt, Kelly, Tex	0	0.00	5.30	2	0.77	5.22
Dreifort, Darren, LA	3	1.39	5.00	14	2.27	4.88
Drew, J.D., StL	83	7.32	5.00	155	6.69	4.99
Ducey, Rob, Phi-Tor	24	4.74	5.03	157	4.38	4.80
Dunston, Shawon, StL	29	4.33	5.00	675	4.19	4.36
Dunwoody, Todd, KC	11	1.93	5.30	78	3.10	4.85
Durazo, Erubiel, Ari	33	5.96	5.00	74	7.72	5.00
Durham, Ray, CWS	100	5.57	5.30	524	5.18	5.14
Durrington, Trent, Ana	0	0.00	5.30	4	0.95	5.18
Duvall, Mike, TB	0	—	—	0	—	—
Dye, Jermaine, KC	113	7.09	5.30	283	5.07	5.08
Easley, Damion, Det	65	4.78	5.30	445	4.55	5.05
Eaton, Adam, SD	6	5.76	5.00	6	5.76	5.00
Echevarria, Angel, Col-Mil	6	3.84	5.00	48	5.28	4.92
Edmonds, Jim, StL	122	8.48	5.00	561	6.40	5.08
Eiland, Dave, TB	0	—	—	1	1.08	4.32
Elarton, Scott, Hou	0	0.00	5.00	1	0.27	4.96
Eldred, Cal, CWS	1	8.93	5.30	2	0.79	4.80
Elster, Kevin, LA	33	5.19	5.00	337	3.92	4.50
Embree, Alan, SF	0	—	—	0	0.00	4.60
Encarnacion, Juan, Det	77	4.97	5.30	173	4.77	5.20
Ensberg, Morgan, Hou	0	0.00	5.00	0	0.00	5.00
Erdos, Todd, NYY-SD	0	0.00	5.15	0	0.00	4.97
Erickson, Scott, Bal	1	8.93	5.00	2	3.15	5.11
Erstad, Darin, Ana	140	8.19	5.30	424	6.07	5.14
Escobar, Kelvim, Tor	0	0.00	5.30	0	0.00	5.28
Estalella, Bobby, SF	56	6.38	5.00	79	5.01	4.84
Estes, Shawn, SF	6	2.41	5.00	10	1.02	4.80
Estrada, Horacio, Mil	0	0.00	5.00	0	0.00	5.00
Etherton, Seth, Ana	0	0.00	5.30	0	0.00	5.30
Eusebio, Tony, Hou	32	5.15	5.00	209	4.62	4.75
Evans, Tom, Tex	7	4.17	5.30	11	3.51	5.14
Everett, Carl, Bos	105	7.81	5.30	412	6.02	4.82
Eyre, Scott, CWS	0	—	—	0	0.00	4.99
Fabregas, Jorge, KC	17	4.34	5.30	141	3.07	5.05
Farnsworth, Kyle, ChC	0	0.00	5.00	0	0.00	5.00
Fasano, Sal, Oak	14	3.64	5.30	77	4.32	5.18
Fassero, Jeff, Bos	0	0.00	5.30	0	0.00	4.63
Febles, Carlos, KC	43	4.08	5.30	117	4.67	5.22
Feliz, Pedro, SF	1	5.38	5.00	1	5.38	5.00
Fernandez, Alex, Fla	1	1.58	5.00	6	1.36	4.79
Fernandez, Osvaldo, Cin	0	0.00	5.00	-1	-0.27	4.75
Fick, Robert, Det	25	5.19	5.30	40	6.02	5.25
Figueroa, Nelson, Ari	0	0.00	5.00	0	0.00	5.00
Finley, Chuck, Cle	0	0.00	5.30	0	0.00	5.12
Finley, Steve, Ari	101	6.56	5.00	914	5.03	4.52
Flaherty, John, TB	44	3.85	5.30	253	3.43	4.99
Fletcher, Darrin, Tor	63	5.72	5.30	433	4.50	4.72
Florie, Bryce, Bos	0	—	—	0	0.00	4.84
Floyd, Cliff, Fla	86	7.46	5.00	338	5.77	4.74
Fordyce, Brook, CWS-Bal	47	5.67	5.30	127	5.14	5.05
Foulke, Keith, CWS	0	—	—	0	0.00	4.68
Fox, Andy, Ari-Fla	27	3.67	5.00	159	4.38	4.91

Player, Team	2000 RC	RC/27	LRC/27	Career RC	RC/27	LRC27
Franco, John, NYM	0	0.00	5.00	1	0.80	4.25
Franco, Matt, NYM	15	3.77	5.00	77	4.09	4.78
Franklin, Wayne, Hou	0	0.00	5.00	0	0.00	5.00
Frascatore, John, Tor	0	—		0	0.00	4.61
Frias, Hanley, Ari	8	2.29	5.00	33	3.52	4.96
Frye, Jeff, Bos-Col	45	4.94	5.22	277	4.91	5.07
Fryman, Travis, Cle	112	7.21	5.30	897	5.47	4.91
Fullmer, Brad, Tor	88	6.53	5.00	221	5.68	4.94
Fultz, Aaron, SF	0	0.00	5.00	0	0.00	5.00
Furcal, Rafael, Atl	73	5.64	5.00	73	5.64	5.00
Fussell, Chris, KC	0	0.00	5.30	0	0.00	5.30
Gaetti, Gary, Bos	0	0.00	5.30	1167	4.42	4.59
Gagne, Eric, LA	0	0.00	5.00	0	0.00	5.00
Galarraga, Andres, Atl	84	6.17	5.00	1186	6.02	4.39
Gant, Ron, Phi-Ana	52	4.15	5.06	911	5.37	4.41
Garces, Rich, Bos	0	—		0	0.00	4.63
Garcia, Freddy, Sea	1	6.70	5.30	2	5.94	5.23
Garcia, Jesse, Bal	0	0.00	5.30	1	0.62	5.22
Garcia, Karim, Det-Bal	0	0.00	5.30	68	3.14	4.86
Garcia, Mike, Pit	0	0.00	5.00	0	0.00	5.00
Garciaparra, Nomar, Bos	122	9.36	5.30	493	7.68	5.09
Gardner, Mark, SF	0	0.00	5.00	3	0.16	4.51
Garibay, Daniel, ChC	0	0.00	5.00	0	0.00	5.00
Giambi, Jason, Oak	162	12.15	5.00	620	7.84	5.15
Giambi, Jeremy, Oak	42	5.41	5.30	88	4.95	5.21
Gil, Benji, Ana	23	2.47	5.30	92	2.69	5.07
Gilbert, Shawn, LA	2	2.99	5.00	3	1.97	4.78
Giles, Brian, Pit	132	8.74	5.00	426	7.91	5.01
Gilkey, Bernard, Ari-Bos	10	1.86	5.16	611	5.31	4.54
Ginter, Keith, Hou	3	11.53	5.00	3	11.53	5.00
Gipson, Charles, Sea	3	3.49	5.30	14	2.80	5.15
Girardi, Joe, ChC	46	4.37	5.00	410	3.81	4.70
Glanville, Doug, Phi	71	3.82	5.00	330	4.71	4.81
Glauber, Keith, Cin	0	0.00	5.00	0	0.00	4.73
Glaus, Troy, Ana	117	7.30	5.30	225	6.05	5.21
Glavine, Tom, Atl	1	0.37	5.00	53	1.65	4.44
Gload, Ross, ChC	1	1.00	5.00	1	1.00	5.00
Glynn, Ryan, Tex	0	0.00	5.30	0	0.00	5.24
Gomes, Wayne, Phi	0	—		0	0.00	4.68
Gomez, Chris, SD	1	0.60	5.00	280	3.65	4.85
Gonzalez, Alex, Fla	31	2.58	5.00	103	3.35	4.97
Gonzalez, Alex S., Tor	64	4.00	5.30	281	3.52	5.15
Gonzalez, Juan, Det	64	4.98	5.30	975	6.62	4.92
Gonzalez, Luis, Ari	132	7.78	5.00	820	5.65	4.63
Gonzalez, Raul, ChC	0	0.00	5.00	0	0.00	5.00
Gonzalez, Wiki, SD	25	2.96	5.00	29	2.65	5.00
Gooden, D., Hou-TB-NYY	0	0.00	5.20	40	1.55	4.15
Goodwin, Tom, Col-LA	80	5.18	5.00	397	4.27	5.06
Grace, Mark, ChC	89	6.20	5.00	1229	6.29	4.43
Graffanino, Tony, TB-CWS	24	4.94	5.30	101	4.13	4.82
Graves, Danny, Cin	2	53.79	5.00	2	4.90	4.82
Grebeck, Craig, Tor	36	5.39	5.30	250	4.33	4.80
Green, Jason, Hou	0	0.00	5.00	0	0.00	5.00
Green, Scarborough, Tex	10	2.46	5.30	11	2.01	5.16
Green, Shawn, LA	106	6.00	5.00	513	5.86	5.09
Greene, Charlie, Tor	0	0.00	5.30	1	0.41	5.03
Greene, Todd, Tor	6	2.33	5.00	69	3.45	5.16
Greene, Willie, ChC	37	4.04	5.00	267	4.75	4.72
Greer, Rusty, Tex	72	6.49	5.30	648	7.01	5.14
Grieve, Ben, Oak	101	5.82	5.00	311	6.21	5.15
Griffey Jr., Ken, Cin	108	7.30	5.00	1311	7.47	4.81
Grilli, Jason, Fla	0	0.00	5.00	0	0.00	5.00
Grimsley, Jason, NYY	1	26.78	5.30	2	1.35	4.14
Grissom, Marquis, Mil	61	3.45	5.00	824	4.64	4.56
Gross, Kip, Hou	0	0.00	5.00	1	1.08	4.13
Grudzielanek, Mark, LA	73	4.19	5.00	379	4.12	4.75
Guerrero, Vladimir, Mon	133	8.88	5.00	440	7.57	4.82
Guerrero, Wilton, Mon	26	3.11	5.00	155	3.96	4.78
Guillen, Carlos, Sea	42	4.83	5.30	54	5.22	5.26
Guillen, Jose, TB	41	4.48	5.30	190	3.92	4.82
Guillen, Ozzie, TB	9	2.90	5.30	662	3.33	4.72
Gunderson, Eric, Tor	0	—		0	0.00	4.20
Guthrie, M., ChC-TB-Tor	0	0.00	5.00	0	0.00	4.70
Gutierrez, Ricky, ChC	73	5.50	5.00	291	3.79	4.70
Guzman, Cristian, Min	74	3.96	5.30	101	3.18	5.25
Guzman, Geraldo, Ari	0	0.00	5.00	0	0.00	5.00
Guzman, Juan, TB	0	—		2	1.63	5.03
Gwynn, Tony, SD	17	4.86	5.00	1595	6.55	4.31
Hackman, Luther, StL	0	—		0	0.00	5.00
Hairston Jr., Jerry, Bal	23	4.05	5.30	45	4.05	5.23

Player, Team	2000 RC	RC/27	LRC/27	Career RC	RC/27	LRC27
Halama, John, Sea	0	0.00	5.30	1	1.58	4.82
Hall, Toby, TB	2	5.36	5.30	2	5.36	5.30
Halladay, Roy, Tor	0	—		0	0.00	5.18
Halter, Shane, Det	23	3.16	5.30	45	2.58	5.11
Hamilton, Darryl, NYM	14	4.89	5.00	655	5.22	4.78
Hamilton, Joey, Tor	0	—		3	0.27	4.63
Hammonds, Jeffrey, Col	95	7.79	5.00	339	5.55	5.04
Hampton, Mike, NYM	8	3.59	5.00	35	2.82	4.76
Haney, Chris, Cle	0	—		1	0.73	4.05
Hansen, Dave, LA	26	7.77	5.00	167	4.85	4.44
Harnisch, Pete, Cin	5	3.20	5.00	10	0.53	4.53
Harris, Lenny, Ari-NYM	28	4.23	5.00	374	3.89	4.38
Hasegawa, S., Ana	0	0.00	5.30	0	0.00	5.30
Haselman, Bill, Tex	28	5.24	5.30	154	4.05	5.09
Hatteberg, Scott, Bos	37	5.48	5.30	146	4.92	5.07
Hawkins, LaTroy, Min	0	0.00	5.30	0	0.00	5.12
Hayes, Charlie, Mil	47	4.28	5.00	623	4.11	4.53
Haynes, Jimmy, Mil	0	0.00	5.00	0	0.00	5.01
Helling, Rick, Tex	0	0.00	5.30	0	0.00	4.85
Helms, Wes, Atl	0	0.00	5.00	1	2.07	4.72
Helton, Todd, Col	173	11.96	5.00	410	8.75	4.86
Henderson, R., NYM-Sea	57	4.35	5.23	2035	6.85	4.62
Henry, Doug, Hou-SF	0	0.00	5.00	1	1.42	4.70
Hentgen, Pat, StL	0	0.00	5.00	0	0.00	5.01
Heredia, Felix, ChC	0	0.00	5.00	1	2.99	4.78
Heredia, Gil, Oak	0	0.00	5.30	7	2.36	4.56
Herges, Matt, LA	0	0.00	5.00	0	0.00	5.00
Hermansen, Chad, Pit	6	1.72	5.00	11	2.07	5.00
Hermanson, Dustin, Mon	2	0.98	5.00	2	0.24	4.82
Hernandez, Alex, Pit	0	0.00	5.00	0	0.00	5.00
Hernandez, C., SD-StL	33	4.67	5.00	126	3.43	4.56
Hernandez, Carlos E., Sea	0	0.00	5.30	0	0.00	5.04
Hernandez, Jose, Mil	52	3.90	5.00	297	4.10	4.76
Hernandez, Livan, SF	5	1.66	5.00	15	1.72	4.83
Hernandez, Orlando, NYY	0	0.00	5.30	0	0.00	5.17
Hernandez, Ramon, Oak	57	4.40	5.30	83	4.90	5.27
Hernandez, Roberto, TB	0	—		0	0.00	4.60
Hershiser, Orel, LA	0	0.00	5.00	40	1.42	4.27
Hidalgo, Richard, Hou	117	7.66	5.00	208	6.06	4.92
Higginson, Bobby, Det	126	7.83	5.30	548	6.54	5.13
Hill, Glenallen, ChC-NYY	50	6.10	5.12	536	5.15	4.65
Hill, Ken, Ana-CWS	0	0.00	5.30	11	0.84	4.27
Hinch, A.J., Oak	0	0.00	5.30	53	3.04	5.08
Hitchcock, Sterling, SD	-1	-1.12	5.00	-2	-0.28	4.79
Hocking, Denny, Min	61	5.81	5.30	165	3.85	5.14
Hoffman, Trevor, SD	0	—		3	3.00	4.64
Holbert, Ray, KC	1	8.93	5.30	14	2.10	4.90
Hollandsworth, T., LA-Col	51	4.17	5.00	236	4.78	4.78
Holmes, D., Ari-StL-Bal	0	0.00	5.00	0	0.00	4.65
Holt, Chris, Hou	0	0.00	5.00	-1	-0.15	4.85
Holtz, Mike, Ana	0	—		0	0.00	4.93
Holzemer, Mark, Phi	0	0.00	5.00	0	0.00	5.00
Houston, Tyler, Mil	35	4.07	5.00	143	4.23	4.82
Howard, Thomas, StL	20	4.98	5.00	296	4.11	4.56
Hubbard, Mike, Atl	0	0.00	5.00	1	0.17	4.63
Hubbard, Trenidad, Atl-Bal	9	2.52	5.08	84	4.70	4.78
Hudson, Tim, Oak	0	0.00	5.30	1	4.46	5.24
Huff, Aubrey, TB	18	5.13	5.30	18	5.13	5.30
Hundley, Todd, LA	71	8.41	5.00	476	5.02	4.58
Hunter, Brian, Atl-Phi	19	4.52	5.00	198	4.22	4.58
Hunter, Brian L., Col-Cin	28	4.03	5.00	327	3.85	4.92
Hunter, Torii, Min	43	4.43	5.30	85	3.91	5.23
Huskey, Butch, Min-Col	42	4.58	5.21	268	4.41	4.81
Huson, Jeff, ChC	12	2.93	5.00	170	2.92	4.61
Hyzdu, Adam, Pit	6	14.67	5.00	6	14.67	5.00
Ibanez, Raul, Sea	13	3.17	5.30	51	3.64	5.17
Irabu, Hideki, Mon	0	0.00	5.00	0	0.00	5.04
Isringhausen, Jason, Oak	0	—		9	2.73	4.70
Jackson, Damian, SD	62	4.52	5.00	124	4.44	4.98
Jaha, John, Oak	8	2.55	5.30	486	6.16	5.02
James, Mike, StL	0	0.00	5.00	0	0.00	5.00
Jarvis, Kevin, Col	0	0.00	5.00	1	0.28	4.78
Javier, Stan, Sea	52	5.24	5.30	623	4.49	4.66
Jefferies, Gregg, Det	14	3.29	5.30	767	4.93	4.45
Jenkins, Geoff, Mil	97	7.03	5.00	200	5.94	4.91
Jensen, Marcus, Min	15	3.49	5.30	28	3.19	5.01
Jeter, Derek, NYY	114	7.34	5.30	548	6.48	5.15
Jimenez, Jose, Col	1	8.96	5.00	1	0.43	4.95
Johnson, Brian, KC	10	2.53	5.30	138	3.27	4.75
Johnson, C., Bal-CWS	87	7.64	5.30	329	4.56	4.83

Player, Team	2000 RC	RC/27	LRC/27	Career RC	RC/27	LRC27
Johnson, Jason, Bal	0	0.00	5.30	0	0.00	5.15
Johnson, Keith, Ana	2	17.86	5.30	2	17.86	5.30
Johnson, Lance, NYY	4	4.87	5.30	717	4.73	4.66
Johnson, Mark L., CWS	24	3.57	5.30	46	3.35	5.23
Johnson, Mark P., NYM	3	4.25	5.00	115	4.76	4.66
Johnson, Mike, Mon	0	0.00	5.00	1	0.66	4.85
Johnson, Randy, Ari	3	1.06	5.00	4	0.48	4.87
Johnson, Russ, Hou-TB	22	3.12	5.23	57	4.13	5.06
Johnstone, John, SF	0	0.00	5.00	0	0.00	4.70
Jones, Andruw, Atl	120	6.72	5.00	377	5.64	4.81
Jones, Bobby J., NYM	0	0.00	5.00	4	0.29	4.68
Jones, Bobby M., NYM	1	13.45	5.00	4	1.38	4.75
Jones, Chipper, Atl	120	7.51	5.00	701	7.32	4.75
Jones, Chris, Mil	1	2.07	5.00	134	4.45	4.51
Jones, Doug, Oak	0	—		1	4.52	4.12
Jones, Jacque, Min	71	4.79	5.30	119	4.97	5.25
Jones, Marcus, Oak	0	0.00	5.30	0	0.00	5.30
Jones, Terry, Mon	20	4.01	5.00	44	3.14	4.80
Jones, Todd, Det	0	—		1	3.38	4.63
Jordan, Brian, Atl	70	4.97	5.00	536	5.66	4.69
Jordan, Kevin, Phi	22	2.13	5.00	123	3.27	4.83
Jose, Felix, NYY	2	2.14	5.30	333	4.70	4.41
Joyner, Wally, Atl	40	6.44	5.00	1155	5.90	4.64
Judd, Mike, LA	1	26.89	5.00	1	2.45	4.93
Justice, David, Cle-NYY	107	7.33	5.30	952	7.03	4.64
Kamieniecki, Scott, Cle-Atl	0	—		0	0.00	4.93
Kapler, Gabe, Tex	66	5.34	5.30	123	4.80	5.23
Karchner, Matt, ChC	0	0.00	5.00	0	0.00	5.00
Karl, Scott, Col-Ana	1	2.07	5.00	5	0.96	4.82
Karros, Eric, LA	82	4.68	5.00	724	5.00	4.61
Karsay, Steve, Cle	0	0.00	5.30	0	0.00	5.30
Kelly, Kenny, TB	0	0.00	5.30	0	0.00	5.30
Kelly, Roberto, NYY	1	1.22	5.30	672	4.94	4.62
Kendall, Jason, Pit	110	6.98	5.00	413	6.63	4.77
Kennedy, Adam, Ana	73	4.17	5.30	85	4.14	5.25
Kent, Jeff, SF	136	8.59	5.00	730	5.95	4.68
Kieschnick, Brooks, Cin	0	0.00	5.00	18	4.62	4.66
Kile, Darryl, StL	2	0.75	5.00	12	0.57	4.62
Kim, Byung-Hyun, Ari	0	0.00	5.00	0	0.00	5.00
King, Ray, Mil	0	—		0	0.00	5.00
Kingsale, Gene, Bal	7	2.53	5.30	13	2.33	5.23
Kinkade, Mike, NYM-Bal	3	13.41	5.20	6	3.51	5.01
Klassen, Danny, Ari	9	3.97	5.00	14	2.45	4.76
Klesko, Ryan, SD	105	7.53	5.00	547	6.66	4.74
Kline, Steve, Mon	0	0.00	5.00	0	0.00	4.76
Knoblauch, Chuck, NYY	57	5.04	5.30	969	6.25	4.94
Knorr, Randy, Tex	3	2.98	5.30	58	3.26	4.92
Koch, Billy, Tor	0	0.00	5.30	0	0.00	5.24
Kolb, Brandon, SD	0	0.00	5.00	0	0.00	5.00
Konerko, Paul, CWS	87	5.90	5.30	185	5.10	5.11
Koskie, Corey, Min	83	6.33	5.30	151	6.44	5.24
Kotsay, Mark, Fla	66	4.39	5.00	190	3.98	4.85
Kreuter, Chad, LA	37	6.03	5.00	255	3.84	4.87
Lamb, David, NYM	0	0.00	5.00	10	2.54	5.17
Lamb, Mike, Tex	54	3.86	5.30	54	3.86	5.30
Lampkin, Tom, Sea	16	4.98	5.30	165	4.19	4.72
Lankford, Ray, StL	60	5.19	5.00	870	6.16	4.51
Lansing, Mike, Col-Bos	53	3.46	5.09	495	4.51	4.69
Larkin, Andy, Cin-KC	0	0.00	5.00	0	0.00	4.62
Larkin, Barry, Cin	65	6.03	5.00	1166	6.31	4.42
LaRocca, Greg, SD	1	1.12	5.00	1	1.12	5.00
LaRue, Jason, Cin	14	4.95	5.00	24	4.25	5.00
Lawton, Matt, Min	113	7.35	5.30	401	6.11	5.14
LeCroy, Matt, Min	6	1.09	5.30	6	1.09	5.30
Ledee, R., NYY-Cle-Tex	68	4.76	5.30	122	5.15	5.23
Ledesma, Aaron, Col	3	2.52	5.00	86	4.02	5.05
Lee, Carlos, CWS	88	5.52	5.30	155	5.21	5.24
Lee, David, Col	0	—		0	0.00	5.00
Lee, Derrek, Fla	74	5.50	5.00	158	4.50	4.83
Lee, Travis, Ari-Phi	44	3.65	5.00	168	4.30	4.84
Leiter, Al, NYM	-2	-0.83	5.00	-2	-0.18	4.79
Lesher, Brian, Sea	4	107.14	5.30	26	3.84	5.10
Leskanic, Curtis, Mil	0	0.00	5.00	5	3.65	4.62
Levrault, Allen, Mil	0	0.00	5.00	0	0.00	5.00
Lewis, Darren, Bos	26	3.17	5.30	443	3.79	4.76
Lewis, Mark, Cin-Bal	23	4.22	5.26	327	4.03	4.79
Leyritz, Jim, NYY-LA	12	3.39	5.14	377	5.13	4.88
Lidle, Cory, TB	0	0.00	5.30	0	0.00	4.80
Lieber, Jon, ChC	6	2.18	5.00	12	0.97	4.78
Lieberthal, Mike, Phi	60	5.45	5.00	280	4.97	4.79

Player, Team	2000 RC	RC/27	LRC/27	Career RC	RC/27	LRC27
Liefer, Jeff, CWS	0	0.00	5.30	13	3.54	5.19
Lilly, Ted, NYY	0	—		0	0.00	5.00
Lima, Jose, Hou	0	0.00	5.00	-2	-0.24	4.86
Lincoln, Mike, Min	0	—		0	0.00	5.18
Lindsey, Rod, Det	1	6.70	5.30	1	6.70	5.30
Linebrink, Scott, SF-Hou	1	Inf		1	Inf	—
Liniak, Cole, ChC	0	0.00	5.00	0	0.00	5.00
Lira, Felipe, Mon	0	0.00	5.00	0	0.00	5.00
Loaiza, Esteban, Tex-Tor	0	0.00	5.30	4	0.67	4.63
Lockhart, Keith, Atl	35	4.24	5.00	225	4.61	4.98
LoDuca, Paul, LA	8	3.77	5.00	20	3.64	4.98
Lofton, Kenny, Cle	94	5.94	5.30	865	6.33	4.96
Loiselle, Rich, Pit	0	—		1	2.70	4.70
Lombard, George, Atl	0	0.00	5.00	3	1.79	4.97
Long, Terrence, Oak	97	5.95	5.30	97	5.89	5.29
Looper, Braden, Fla	0	0.00	5.00	0	0.00	5.00
Lopez, Albie, TB	0	0.00	5.30	0	0.00	5.22
Lopez, Javy, Atl	73	5.33	5.00	424	5.43	4.72
Lopez, Luis, Mil	22	3.65	5.00	114	3.25	4.72
Lopez, Mendy, Fla	0	0.00	5.00	25	3.63	5.02
Lopez, Rodrigo, SD	0	0.00	5.00	0	0.00	5.00
Loretta, Mark, Mil	53	5.20	5.00	276	4.82	4.93
Lorraine, Andrew, ChC-Cle	0	0.00	5.00	0	0.00	5.00
Lowe, Derek, Bos	0	0.00	5.30	0	0.00	5.02
Lowe, Sean, CWS	0	—		0	0.00	4.60
Lowell, Mike, Fla	87	6.06	5.00	129	5.42	5.00
Lowery, Terrell, SF	10	13.45	5.00	36	5.26	5.09
Luebbers, Larry, Cin	0	0.00	5.00	2	1.54	4.72
Lugo, Julio, Hou	56	4.66	5.00	56	4.66	5.00
Lunar, Fernando, Atl-Bal	2	0.87	5.07	2	0.87	5.07
Luuloa, Keith, Ana	1	2.23	5.30	1	2.23	5.30
Mabry, John, Sea-SD	25	3.75	5.13	267	4.26	4.75
Machado, Robert, Sea	2	4.87	5.30	15	2.90	5.03
Macias, Jose, Det	24	4.73	5.30	25	4.82	5.29
Maddux, Greg, Atl	2	0.73	5.00	24	0.65	4.41
Maddux, Mike, Hou	0	0.00	5.00	0	0.00	4.10
Maduro, Calvin, Bal	0	—		0	0.00	4.62
Magadan, Dave, SD	21	5.54	5.00	639	5.67	4.41
Magee, Wendell, Det	27	5.06	5.30	58	3.62	4.86
Magnante, Mike, Oak	0	0.00	5.30	1	6.72	4.78
Mahay, Ron, Oak-Fla	0	0.00	5.00	1	1.49	5.06
Mahomes, Pat, NYM	1	1.79	5.00	3	3.10	5.00
Mahoney, Mike, ChC	3	16.14	5.00	3	16.14	5.00
Mantei, Matt, Ari	0	—		0	0.00	4.72
Manto, Jeff, Col	6	161.36	5.00	98	4.58	4.90
Manzanillo, Josias, Pit	0	0.00	5.00	1	2.45	4.78
Marquis, Jason, Atl	0	0.00	5.00	0	0.00	5.00
Marrero, Eli, StL	14	4.48	5.00	61	2.74	4.84
Martin, Al, SD-Sea	60	4.50	5.09	549	5.25	4.72
Martin, Tom, Cle	0	—		0	0.00	4.60
Martinez, D., TB-ChC-Tex-Tor	52	3.93	5.26	732	4.61	4.61
Martinez, Edgar, Sea	134	9.04	5.30	1152	7.89	4.87
Martinez, Felix, TB	25	2.62	5.30	31	2.25	5.21
Martinez, Pedro, Bos	0	—		-1	-0.10	4.64
Martinez, Ramon, Bos	0	0.00	5.30	11	0.52	4.37
Martinez, Ramon E., SF	30	5.56	5.00	52	5.07	4.98
Martinez, Sandy, Fla	0	0.00	5.00	48	2.94	5.12
Martinez, Tino, NYY	79	4.79	5.30	771	5.62	5.00
Masaoka, Onan, LA	0	—		0	0.00	5.00
Mateo, Ruben, Tex	25	4.41	5.30	41	4.44	5.25
Matheny, Mike, StL	43	3.50	5.00	168	3.17	5.02
Mathews, T.J., Oak	0	—		0	0.00	4.66
Matos, Luis, Bal	15	2.58	5.30	15	2.58	5.30
Matthews Jr., Gary, ChC	11	2.26	5.00	17	2.86	5.00
Maxwell, Jason, Min	12	3.57	5.30	13	3.74	5.27
Mayne, Brent, Col	58	5.98	5.00	299	4.23	4.81
Mays, Joe, Min	1	6.70	5.30	1	3.82	5.24
McCarty, Dave, KC	47	6.17	5.30	108	3.55	4.94
McCracken, Quinton, TB	0	0.00	5.30	192	4.65	4.88
McDonald, Jason, Tex	17	5.69	5.30	90	4.26	5.07
McDonald, John, Cle	1	5.36	5.30	2	2.43	5.20
McDonald, Keith, StL	4	26.89	5.00	4	26.89	5.00
McElroy, Chuck, Bal	0	—		5	4.09	4.45
McEwing, Joe, NYM	13	2.65	5.00	78	3.87	4.99
McGlinchy, Kevin, Atl	0	—		0	0.00	5.00
McGriff, Fred, TB	98	6.08	5.30	1365	6.64	4.59
McGuire, Ryan, NYM	0	0.00	5.00	53	3.06	4.71
McGwire, Mark, StL	81	12.74	5.00	1391	8.25	4.68
McKnight, Tony, Hou	0	0.00	5.00	0	0.00	5.00
McLemore, Mark, Sea	62	4.11	5.30	617	4.17	4.96

Player, Team	2000 RC	RC/27	LRC/27	Career RC	RC/27	LRC27
McMichael, Greg, Atl	0	—	—	1	1.93	4.58
McMillon, Billy, Det	26	7.41	5.30	40	5.20	4.93
Meadows, Brian, SD-KC	0	0.00	5.00	1	0.19	4.85
Meares, Pat, Pit	51	3.69	5.00	339	3.80	5.05
Mecir, Jim, TB-Oak	0	—	—	0	0.00	5.01
Melhuse, Adam, LA-Col	1	1.28	5.00	1	1.28	5.00
Melo, Juan, SF	0	0.00	5.00	0	0.00	5.00
Meluskey, Mitch, Hou	76	8.27	5.00	79	7.56	4.99
Mendoza, Carlos, Col	0	0.00	5.00	3	4.25	4.81
Mendoza, Ramiro, NYY	0	—	—	0	0.00	5.01
Menechino, Frank, Oak	24	5.54	5.30	24	5.23	5.29
Mercado, Hector, Cin	0	0.00	5.00	0	0.00	5.00
Mercedes, Jose, Bal	0	0.00	5.30	0	0.00	4.70
Mercker, Kent, Ana	0	—	—	5	0.56	4.61
Merloni, Lou, Bos	19	5.04	5.30	52	5.04	5.18
Mesa, Jose, Sea	0	—	—	0	—	—
Metcalfe, Mike, LA	0	0.00	5.00	0	0.00	4.97
Meyers, Chad, ChC	2	1.22	5.00	12	1.99	5.00
Miceli, Dan, Fla	0	—	—	1	1.42	4.68
Mientkiewicz, Doug, Min	0	0.00	5.30	33	2.92	5.17
Mieske, Matt, Hou-Ari	5	1.77	5.00	198	4.35	5.10
Millar, Kevin, Fla	45	6.08	5.00	109	6.28	5.00
Miller, Damian, Ari	46	5.03	5.00	117	4.86	4.92
Miller, Trever, Phi-LA	0	—	—	1	3.85	4.89
Miller, Wade, Hou	0	0.00	5.00	0	0.00	5.00
Mills, Alan, LA-Bal	0	0.00	5.00	0	0.00	5.00
Millwood, Kevin, Atl	0	0.00	5.00	1	0.13	4.88
Milton, Eric, Min	0	0.00	5.30	3	8.94	5.11
Minor, Damon, SF	6	32.27	5.00	6	32.27	5.00
Minor, Ryan, Bal	1	0.37	5.30	13	1.90	5.22
Mirabelli, Doug, SF	27	3.86	5.00	46	4.30	4.96
Mlicki, Dave, Det	0	0.00	5.30	5	0.82	4.64
Moehler, Brian, Det	0	0.00	5.30	0	0.00	5.10
Moeller, Chad, Min	4	1.00	5.30	4	1.00	5.30
Mohler, Mike, StL-Cle	1	Inf	—	1	8.97	5.00
Molina, Ben, Ana	53	3.86	5.30	63	3.75	5.27
Mondesi, Raul, Tor	63	5.62	5.30	627	5.82	4.75
Montgomery, Steve, SD	0	—	—	1	Inf	—
Moore, Trey, Mon	0	0.00	5.00	2	2.34	4.76
Mora, Melvin, NYM-Bal	56	4.63	5.14	57	4.31	5.13
Morales, Willie, Bal	1	3.35	5.30	1	3.35	5.30
Morandini, Mickey, Phi-Tor	44	3.62	5.08	577	4.38	4.58
Mordecai, Mike, Mon	19	4.09	5.00	80	3.43	4.81
Morgan, Mike, Ari	2	5.38	5.00	-1	-0.05	4.32
Morris, Hal, Cin-Det	21	4.30	5.18	559	5.07	4.52
Morris, Matt, StL	0	0.00	5.00	6	1.62	4.62
Morris, Warren, Pit	59	3.79	5.00	136	4.51	5.00
Mota, Guillermo, Mon	0	0.00	5.00	2	53.79	5.00
Mottola, Chad, Tor	2	7.65	5.30	10	3.81	4.74
Mouton, James, Mil	22	4.35	5.00	156	3.58	4.71
Mouton, Lyle, Mil	19	7.00	5.00	114	5.14	5.09
Moyer, Jamie, Sea	0	0.00	5.30	6	1.01	4.22
Mueller, Bill, SF	63	3.84	5.00	297	5.01	4.80
Mulder, Mark, Oak	0	0.00	5.30	0	0.00	5.30
Mulholland, Terry, Atl	3	2.24	5.00	-1	-0.05	4.38
Munoz, Mike, Tex	0	—	—	1	3.86	4.56
Munro, Peter, Tor	0	0.00	5.30	0	0.00	5.30
Munson, Eric, Det	0	0.00	5.30	0	0.00	5.30
Murray, Calvin, SF	29	5.10	5.00	33	5.31	5.00
Mussina, Mike, Bal	0	0.00	5.30	2	2.82	5.16
Myers, Greg, Bal	9	2.30	5.30	240	3.40	4.83
Myers, Mike, Col	0	—	—	0	0.00	5.00
Myers, Rodney, SD	0	—	—	3	8.10	4.80
Nady, Xavier, SD	1	Inf	—	1	Inf	—
Nagy, Charles, Cle	0	—	—	0	0.00	5.06
Nathan, Joe, SF	1	0.81	5.00	2	0.88	5.00
Nation, Joey, ChC	1	13.45	5.00	1	13.45	5.00
Navarro, Jaime, Mil-Cle	0	0.00	5.00	3	0.54	4.69
Neagle, Denny, Cin-NYY	2	1.45	5.00	17	1.09	4.66
Nelson, Jeff, NYY	0	0.00	5.30	0	0.00	5.11
Nen, Robb, SF	0	—	—	0	0.00	4.58
Nevin, Phil, SD	100	6.79	5.00	271	5.61	5.01
Newhan, David, SD-Phi	3	2.44	5.00	6	2.27	5.00
Nicholson, Kevin, SD	9	2.99	5.00	9	2.99	5.00
Nieves, Jose, ChC	14	2.23	5.00	32	2.69	5.00
Nitkowski, C.J., Det	0	—	—	1	1.93	4.66
Nixon, Trot, Bos	73	5.91	5.30	131	5.40	5.23
Nomo, Hideo, Det	0	0.00	5.30	6	0.53	4.71
Norton, Greg, CWS	26	4.46	5.30	120	4.07	5.15
Norton, Phil, ChC	1	13.45	5.00	1	13.45	5.00

Player, Team	2000 RC	RC/27	LRC/27	Career RC	RC/27	LRC27
Nunez, Abraham, Pit	9	3.27	5.00	40	2.89	4.92
Nunez, Vladimir, Fla	0	0.00	5.00	1	0.60	5.00
Nunnally, Jon, NYM	10	4.27	5.00	146	5.59	4.89
Nunnari, Talmadge, Mon	2	10.76	5.00	2	10.76	5.00
O'Brien, Charlie, Mon	2	3.59	5.00	241	3.47	4.63
O'Connor, Brian, Pit	0	0.00	5.00	0	0.00	5.00
O'Leary, Troy, Bos	67	4.52	5.30	473	5.17	5.14
O'Neill, Paul, NYY	82	4.96	5.30	1141	5.91	4.68
Ochoa, Alex, Cin	53	7.83	5.00	191	5.09	4.85
Offerman, Jose, Bos	52	3.89	5.30	646	4.86	4.80
Ojeda, Augie, ChC	9	3.78	5.00	9	3.78	5.00
Olerud, John, Sea	100	6.16	5.30	1002	6.78	4.82
Olivares, Omar, Oak	1	Inf	—	22	3.32	4.23
Oliver, Darren, Tex	0	0.00	5.30	8	2.37	4.92
Oliver, Joe, Sea	33	5.56	5.00	387	3.91	4.51
Olson, Gregg, LA	0	—	—	1	8.98	4.64
Ontiveros, Steve, Bos	0	—	—	0	0.00	3.94
Ordaz, Luis, KC	4	1.12	5.30	18	1.94	4.88
Ordonez, Magglio, CWS	116	6.90	5.00	300	5.79	5.16
Ordonez, Rey, NYM	6	1.38	5.00	158	2.56	4.75
Orosco, Jesse, StL	0	—	—	4	1.84	4.17
Ortiz, David, Min	60	5.07	5.30	119	5.45	5.17
Ortiz, Hector, KC	21	10.04	5.30	21	9.38	5.28
Ortiz, Jose, Oak	1	2.98	5.30	1	2.98	5.30
Ortiz, Russ, SF	6	2.83	5.00	14	2.60	4.94
Osik, Keith, Pit	23	6.87	5.00	70	3.72	4.81
Osuna, Antonio, LA	0	0.00	5.00	0	0.00	4.74
Owens, Eric, SD	78	4.70	5.00	162	4.16	4.92
Ozuna, Pablo, Fla	3	4.48	5.00	3	4.48	5.00
Padilla, Vicente, Ari-Phi	1	Inf	—	1	Inf	—
Painter, Lance, Tor	0	—	—	5	2.08	4.66
Palacios, Vicente, SD	0	—	—	-2	-0.56	4.32
Palmeiro, Orlando, Ana	39	5.56	5.30	130	4.63	5.16
Palmeiro, Rafael, Tex	120	7.58	5.30	1439	6.63	4.75
Palmer, Dean, Det	88	5.73	5.00	690	5.16	4.96
Paniagua, Jose, Sea	0	0.00	5.30	0	0.00	4.70
Paquette, Craig, StL	51	4.50	5.00	217	3.67	5.03
Park, Chan Ho, LA	4	1.76	5.00	11	1.15	4.79
Parque, Jim, CWS	0	0.00	5.30	1	2.43	5.17
Parra, Jose, Pit	1	Inf	—	1	13.53	4.63
Parris, Steve, Cin	0	0.00	5.00	6	1.09	4.86
Patterson, Corey, ChC	0	0.00	5.00	0	0.00	5.00
Patterson, Danny, Det	0	—	—	0	0.00	5.18
Paul, Josh, CWS	12	5.74	5.30	12	4.59	5.27
Pavano, Carl, Mon	0	0.00	5.00	2	0.50	4.86
Payton, Jay, NYM	63	4.53	5.00	64	4.34	4.99
Pena, Elvis, Col	1	2.99	5.00	1	2.99	5.00
Penny, Brad, Fla	0	0.00	5.00	0	0.00	5.00
Percival, Troy, Ana	0	—	—	0	0.00	5.39
Perez, Carlos, LA	0	0.00	5.00	11	1.21	4.72
Perez, Eddie, Atl	2	2.99	5.00	93	3.76	4.78
Perez, Eduardo, StL	10	3.90	5.00	129	4.31	4.79
Perez, Neifi, Col	80	4.33	5.00	275	4.10	4.83
Perez, Santiago, Mil	4	2.34	5.00	4	2.34	5.00
Perez, Timoniel, NYM	7	5.09	5.00	7	5.09	5.00
Perez, Tomas, Phi	9	2.12	5.00	48	2.34	5.17
Perez, Yorkis, Hou	0	0.00	5.00	0	0.00	4.73
Perisho, Matt, Tex	0	0.00	5.30	0	0.00	5.22
Perry, Chan, Cle	0	0.00	5.30	0	0.00	5.30
Perry, Herbert, TB-CWS	70	6.11	5.30	122	5.23	5.22
Person, Robert, Phi	0	0.00	5.00	1	0.22	4.94
Peters, Chris, Pit	1	5.38	5.00	6	2.13	4.74
Petkovsek, Mark, Ana	0	—	—	5	1.69	4.63
Petrick, Ben, Col	23	5.78	5.00	37	6.64	5.00
Pettitte, Andy, NYY	0	0.00	5.30	0	0.00	5.15
Phelps, Josh, Tor	0	0.00	5.30	0	0.00	5.30
Piatt, Adam, Oak	33	7.82	5.30	33	7.82	5.30
Piazza, Mike, NYM	105	8.18	5.00	847	7.74	4.69
Pichardo, Hipolito, Bos	0	0.00	5.30	0	0.00	5.09
Pierre, Juan, Col	25	4.45	5.00	25	4.45	5.00
Pierzynski, A.J., Min	12	5.10	5.30	18	5.54	5.25
Piesac, Dan, Ari	0	—	—	0	0.00	4.66
Polanco, Placido, StL	48	5.31	5.00	80	4.26	4.93
Politte, Cliff, Phi	0	0.00	5.00	0	0.00	4.81
Polonia, Luis, Det-NYY	44	4.38	5.30	656	4.73	4.71
Ponson, Sidney, Bal	0	0.00	5.30	1	2.97	5.18
Poole, Jim, Det-Mon	0	—	—	1	2.70	4.70
Porter, Bo, Oak	2	4.87	5.30	2	1.58	5.10
Posada, Jorge, NYY	109	7.74	5.30	248	5.95	5.15
Pose, Scott, KC	2	1.31	5.30	28	2.99	5.03

Player, Team	RC	2000 RC/27	LRC/27	RC	Career RC/27	LRC27
Powell, Brian, Hou	1	3.84	5.00	1	3.36	5.01
Powell, Jay, Hou	0	0.00	5.00	1	2.45	4.68
Powell, Jeremy, Mon	2	26.89	5.00	2	1.54	4.93
Pratt, Todd, NYM	24	5.21	5.00	106	4.80	4.70
Pride, Curtis, Bos	1	1.79	5.30	89	4.80	5.03
Prieto, Ariel, Oak	0	0.00	5.30	0	0.00	5.30
Prince, Tom, Phi	11	2.90	5.00	77	2.94	4.46
Pritchett, Chris, Phi	0	0.00	5.00	7	1.53	5.10
Prokopec, Luke, LA	0	0.00	5.00	0	0.00	5.00
Pulsipher, Bill, NYM	0	0.00	5.00	2	0.62	4.75
Quantrill, Paul, Tor	0	—	—	-1	-0.43	4.64
Quevedo, Ruben, ChC	0	0.00	5.00	0	0.00	5.00
Quinn, Mark, KC	81	5.83	5.30	95	6.16	5.28
Radinsky, Scott, StL	0	—	—	0	0.00	4.62
Radke, Brad, Min	0	0.00	5.30	0	0.00	5.09
Rain, Steve, ChC	0	0.00	5.00	0	0.00	5.00
Ramirez, Alex, Cle-Pit	23	3.41	5.14	38	3.93	5.15
Ramirez, Aramis, Pit	26	3.44	5.00	53	3.18	4.82
Ramirez, Hector, Mil	1	Inf	5.00	1	8.97	5.00
Ramirez, Manny, Cle	129	11.56	5.30	781	8.21	5.14
Randa, Joe, KC	97	5.66	5.30	381	5.30	5.10
Rapp, Pat, Bal	0	0.00	5.30	0	0.00	4.63
Reames, Britt, StL	0	0.00	5.00	0	0.00	5.00
Reboulet, Jeff, KC	17	2.96	5.30	187	3.57	5.03
Redman, Mark, Min	0	0.00	5.30	0	0.00	5.30
Redman, Tike, Pit	4	8.96	5.00	4	8.96	5.00
Redmond, Mike, Fla	21	3.40	5.00	73	4.50	4.92
Reed, Jeff, ChC	25	3.56	5.00	362	3.96	4.47
Reed, Rick, NYM	1	0.49	5.00	14	1.49	4.69
Reed, Steve, Cle	0	—	—	1	1.35	4.55
Reese, Pokey, Cin	60	3.98	5.00	184	3.87	4.87
Reichert, Dan, KC	0	0.00	5.30	0	0.00	5.22
Rekar, Bryan, TB	1	13.39	5.30	2	1.02	4.71
Relaford, Desi, Phi-SD	61	4.87	5.00	134	3.68	4.81
Remlinger, Mike, Atl	0	0.00	5.00	-1	-0.23	4.58
Renteria, Edgar, StL	75	4.43	5.00	337	4.22	4.78
Reyes, Al, Bal-LA	0	—	—	0	0.00	4.73
Reyes, Carlos, Phi-SD	0	0.00	5.00	0	0.00	4.87
Reyes, Dennys, Cin	0	0.00	5.00	0	0.00	4.67
Reynolds, Shane, Hou	2	1.49	5.00	12	0.76	4.72
Reynoso, Armando, Ari	0	0.00	5.00	5	0.43	4.70
Rhodes, Arthur, Sea	0	—	—	0	0.00	4.97
Richard, Chris, StL-Bal	32	5.01	5.27	32	5.01	5.27
Riedling, John, Cin	0	0.00	5.00	0	0.00	5.00
Rigby, Brad, KC-Mon	0	0.00	5.00	0	0.00	4.95
Rigdon, Paul, Cle-Mil	1	1.28	5.00	1	1.28	5.00
Rincon, Ricky, Cle	0	—	—	0	0.00	4.60
Rios, Armando, SF	49	7.05	5.00	85	7.62	5.00
Ripken Jr., Cal, Bal	42	4.61	5.30	1660	5.25	4.70
Ritchie, Todd, Pit	0	0.00	5.00	0	0.00	5.00
Rivas, Luis, Min	8	4.66	5.30	8	4.66	5.30
Rivera, Ruben, SD	51	3.93	5.00	134	3.90	4.96
Roberts, Dave, Cle	1	2.68	5.30	16	3.39	5.19
Roberts, Grant, NYM	0	0.00	5.00	0	0.00	5.00
Rodriguez, Alex, Sea	136	9.02	5.30	627	7.29	5.15
Rodriguez, Felix, SF	0	0.00	5.00	1	2.07	4.88
Rodriguez, Frank, Sea	0	0.00	5.30	1	6.69	5.15
Rodriguez, H., ChC-Fla	58	5.51	5.00	470	5.49	4.68
Rodriguez, Ivan, Tex	75	7.58	5.30	713	5.33	4.98
Rodriguez, Jose, StL	0	0.00	5.00	0	0.00	5.00
Rodriguez, Rich, NYM	0	0.00	5.00	3	2.53	4.28
Rogers, Kenny, Tex	0	0.00	5.30	0	0.00	5.04
Rolen, Scott, Phi	89	6.92	5.00	407	6.66	4.77
Rolison, Nate, Fla	0	0.00	5.00	0	0.00	5.00
Rollins, Jimmy, Phi	9	6.72	5.00	9	6.72	5.00
Rolls, Damian, TB	0	0.00	5.30	0	0.00	5.30
Roque, Rafael, Mil	0	—	—	0	0.00	4.81
Rosado, Jose, KC	0	—	—	0	0.00	5.09
Rose, Brian, Bos-Col	0	0.00	5.04	0	0.00	5.05
Roskos, John, SD	0	0.00	5.00	1	0.59	4.92
Rueter, Kirk, SF	1	0.45	5.00	8	0.59	4.74
Ruffin, Johnny, Ari	0	—	—	1	1.69	4.61
Rupe, Ryan, TB	0	0.00	5.30	0	0.00	5.20
Rusch, Glendon, NYM	0	0.00	5.00	0	0.00	5.00
Ryan, Rob, Ari	4	5.66	5.00	8	5.25	5.00
Sadler, Donnie, Bos	9	2.80	5.30	36	3.56	5.15
Saenz, Olmedo, Oak	41	7.13	5.30	78	5.75	5.23
Salmon, Tim, Ana	114	7.25	5.30	832	7.42	5.08
Sanchez, Jesus, Fla	3	1.72	5.00	3	0.74	4.82
Sanchez, Rey, KC	48	3.18	5.30	327	3.41	4.75

Player, Team	RC	2000 RC/27	LRC/27	RC	Career RC/27	LRC27
Sanders, Anthony, Sea	1	Inf	—	2	8.90	5.18
Sanders, Reggie, Atl	41	3.98	5.00	606	5.65	4.61
Santana, Johan, Min	0	0.00	5.30	0	0.00	5.30
Santana, Julio, Mon	0	0.00	5.00	1	2.24	5.00
Santangelo, F.P., LA	13	2.71	5.00	233	4.79	4.72
Santiago, Benito, Cin	31	4.17	5.00	625	3.97	4.40
Saturria, Luis, StL	0	0.00	5.00	0	0.00	5.00
Sauerbeck, Scott, Pit	0	0.00	5.00	0	0.00	5.00
Sauveur, Rich, Oak	0	—	—	0	0.00	4.18
Scanlan, Bob, Mil	0	—	—	1	0.77	4.11
Schilling, Curt, Phi-Ari	1	0.46	5.00	4	0.20	4.60
Schmidt, Jason, Pit	0	0.00	5.00	0	0.00	4.75
Schneider, Brian, Mon	8	2.36	5.00	8	2.36	5.00
Schoeneweis, Scott, Ana	1	13.39	5.30	1	13.39	5.30
Schourek, Pete, Bos	1	13.39	5.30	11	1.10	4.50
Schrenk, Steve, Phi	0	—	—	0	0.00	5.00
Seanez, Rudy, Atl	0	—	—	0	0.00	4.71
Sefcik, Kevin, Phi	14	2.99	5.00	90	4.00	4.80
Segui, David, Tex-Cle	101	6.61	5.30	605	5.17	4.80
Seguignol, Fernando, Mon	19	4.12	5.00	35	3.96	4.95
Selby, Bill, Cle	3	2.23	5.30	12	2.93	5.36
Sele, Aaron, Sea	0	0.00	5.30	1	1.91	5.14
Serafini, Dan, SD-Pit	0	0.00	5.00	0	0.00	5.00
Servais, Scott, Col-SF	8	2.44	5.00	263	3.54	4.59
Service, Scott, Oak	0	—	—	1	1.80	4.52
Sexson, Richie, Cle-Mil	93	6.14	5.19	190	5.49	5.16
Sexton, Chris, Cin	10	3.02	5.00	18	3.51	5.00
Shaw, Jeff, LA	0	—	—	0	0.00	4.58
Sheets, Andy, Bos	0	0.00	5.30	61	2.93	5.02
Sheffield, Gary, LA	132	9.78	5.00	1045	7.20	4.54
Sheldon, Scott, Tex	17	4.84	5.30	22	4.57	5.21
Shuey, Paul, Cle	0	—	—	0	0.00	4.97
Shumpert, Terry, Col	40	5.25	5.00	183	4.34	4.76
Sierra, Ruben, Tex	7	3.99	5.30	962	5.14	4.68
Silva, Jose, Pit	2	1.58	5.00	2	0.57	4.83
Singleton, Chris, CWS	67	4.38	5.30	148	5.06	5.24
Sirotka, Mike, CWS	0	0.00	5.30	0	0.00	5.15
Sisco, Steve, Atl	3	3.51	5.00	3	3.51	5.00
Skrmetta, Matt, Mon-Pit	0	0.00	5.00	0	0.00	5.00
Slocumb, H., StL-SD	0	0.00	5.00	1	2.25	4.35
Slusarski, Joe, Hou	0	0.00	5.00	0	0.00	5.00
Smith, Bobby, TB	19	3.56	5.30	81	3.58	5.13
Smith, Chuck, Fla	0	0.00	5.00	0	0.00	5.00
Smith, Dan, Bos	0	—	—	1	1.04	5.00
Smith, Mark, Fla	24	4.33	5.00	99	4.82	4.88
Snow, J.T., SF	83	5.30	5.00	572	5.11	4.95
Snyder, John, Mil	0	0.00	5.00	0	0.00	5.00
Sojo, Luis, Pit-NYY	38	4.44	5.13	255	3.45	4.88
Soriano, Alfonso, NYY	2	1.25	5.30	2	1.05	5.28
Sosa, Sammy, ChC	138	8.53	5.00	987	5.81	4.60
Sparks, Steve W., Det	0	—	—	2	13.39	5.09
Speier, Justin, Cle	0	0.00	5.30	0	0.00	5.10
Spencer, Shane, NYY	36	5.05	5.30	79	5.31	5.22
Spencer, Stan, SD	1	2.69	5.00	1	0.82	4.86
Spiers, Bill, Hou	62	6.32	5.00	474	4.79	4.66
Spiezio, Scott, Ana	43	4.86	5.30	195	4.33	5.07
Spoljaric, Paul, KC	0	—	—	0	0.00	4.99
Spradlin, Jerry, KC-ChC	0	0.00	5.00	1	5.39	4.72
Sprague, Ed, SD-Bos	33	4.26	5.13	488	4.13	5.02
Springer, Dennis, NYM	0	0.00	5.00	0	0.00	4.96
Springer, Russ, Ari	0	0.00	5.00	0	0.00	4.72
Stairs, Matt, Oak	69	4.81	5.30	385	6.25	5.11
Stanifer, Rob, Bos	0	—	—	2	8.99	4.60
Stanley, Mike, Bos-Oak	38	4.56	5.30	724	5.96	4.91
Stanton, Mike, NYY	1	Inf	5.00	4	13.49	4.45
Stein, Blake, KC	0	0.00	5.30	0	0.00	5.08
Stephenson, Garrett, StL	0	0.00	5.00	0	0.00	4.89
Stevens, Dave, Atl	0	0.00	5.00	0	0.00	4.68
Stevens, Lee, Mon	64	5.03	5.00	340	4.81	4.86
Stewart, Shannon, Tor	94	6.01	5.30	318	5.88	5.14
Stinnett, Kelly, Ari	28	3.88	5.00	147	4.13	4.81
Stocker, Kevin, TB-Ana	31	2.81	5.30	302	3.66	4.81
Stottlemyre, Todd, Ari	4	3.84	5.00	18	2.26	4.74
Strickland, Scott, Mon	0	0.00	5.00	0	0.00	5.00
Strong, Joe, Fla	0	0.00	5.00	0	0.00	5.00
Stull, Everett, Mil	0	0.00	5.00	0	0.00	4.96
Sturtze, Tanyon, CWS-TB	0	—	—	0	0.00	4.68
Stynes, Chris, Cin	65	6.57	5.00	159	4.93	4.85
Sullivan, Scott, Cin	1	5.38	5.00	1	0.64	4.79
Suppan, Jeff, KC	0	0.00	5.30	3	3.10	4.79

Player, Team	2000 RC	RC/27	LRC/27	Career RC	RC/27	LRC27
Surhoff, B.J., Bal-Atl	76	5.12	5.22	940	4.85	4.80
Sutton, Larry, StL	4	5.38	5.00	73	4.81	5.04
Suzuki, Makoto, KC	0	0.00	5.30	0	0.00	5.30
Swann, Pedro, Atl	0	0.00	5.00	0	0.00	5.00
Sweeney, Mark, Mil	10	4.56	5.00	101	4.85	4.68
Sweeney, Mike, KC	140	8.46	5.30	332	6.31	5.17
Swindell, Greg, Ari	0	0.00	5.00	8	0.91	4.37
Tam, Jeff, Oak	0	—	—	0	0.00	4.60
Tapani, Kevin, ChC	2	0.94	5.00	8	1.00	4.78
Tatis, Fernando, StL	57	5.87	5.00	251	5.41	4.95
Taubensee, Eddie, Cin	26	3.43	5.00	391	5.03	4.62
Tavarez, Julian, Col	-1	-0.77	5.00	-1	-0.55	4.92
Taylor, Reggie, Phi	0	0.00	5.00	0	0.00	5.00
Tejada, Miguel, Oak	104	6.07	5.30	241	4.90	5.17
Telemaco, Amaury, Phi	0	0.00	5.00	1	0.35	4.65
Telford, Anthony, Mon	0	0.00	5.00	1	1.17	4.72
Thomas, Frank, CWS	164	10.58	5.30	1348	9.07	4.92
Thome, Jim, Cle	109	6.95	5.30	765	7.55	5.09
Thompson, Andy, Tor	2	10.71	5.30	2	10.71	5.30
Thompson, Mark, StL	0	0.00	5.00	2	0.55	4.70
Thompson, Ryan, NYY	9	6.34	5.30	127	3.88	4.56
Thurman, Mike, Mon	0	0.00	5.00	-1	-0.27	4.89
Timmons, Ozzie, TB	7	6.47	5.30	51	4.25	4.78
Toca, Jorge, NYM	2	13.45	5.00	2	8.97	5.00
Tollberg, Brian, SD	0	0.00	5.00	0	0.00	5.00
Tomko, Brett, Sea	0	—	—	4	0.73	4.72
Trachsel, Steve, TB-Tor	0	0.00	5.30	14	1.08	4.70
Tracy, Andy, Mon	31	5.67	5.00	31	5.67	5.00
Trammell, B., TB-NYM	42	5.93	5.22	136	5.61	5.11
Trombley, Mike, Bal	0	0.00	5.30	0	0.00	5.11
Truby, Chris, Hou	43	5.72	5.00	43	5.72	5.00
Tucker, Michael, Cin	43	5.45	5.00	290	5.02	4.89
Tucker, T.J., Mon	1	Inf	—	1	Inf	—
Turner, Chris, NYY	7	2.57	5.30	43	3.79	5.12
Tyner, Jason, NYM-TB	12	2.90	5.19	12	2.90	5.19
Unroe, Tim, Atl	0	0.00	5.00	12	4.23	5.16
Urbina, Ugueth, Mon	0	0.00	5.00	1	0.54	4.70
Valdes, Ismael, ChC-LA	2	1.99	5.00	3	0.24	4.73
Valdes, Marc, Hou	0	0.00	5.00	1	0.69	4.66
Valdes, Pedro, Tex	9	6.18	5.30	9	3.66	5.02
Valdez, Mario, Oak	0	0.00	5.30	12	3.10	4.97
Valentin, John, Bos	1	0.92	5.30	599	5.73	5.03
Valentin, Jose, CWS	105	6.35	5.30	457	5.18	5.08
Valera, Yohanny, Mon	0	0.00	5.00	0	0.00	5.00
Van Poppel, Todd, ChC	0	0.00	5.00	1	1.08	4.84
Vander Wal, John, Pit	93	8.90	5.00	288	5.94	4.63
Varitek, Jason, Bos	54	4.03	5.30	148	4.30	5.19
Vaughn, Greg, TB	89	6.68	5.30	911	5.82	4.78
Vaughn, Mo, Ana	109	6.26	5.30	989	7.25	5.01
Vazquez, Javier, Mon	3	1.28	5.00	12	2.11	4.87
Velandia, Jorge, Oak-NYM	0	0.00	5.22	3	0.84	5.03
Velarde, Randy, Oak	63	4.54	5.30	542	5.00	4.94
Ventura, Robin, NYM	70	4.90	5.00	923	5.74	4.83
Veras, Quilvio, Atl	53	6.04	5.00	361	4.87	4.74
Veras, Wilton, Bos	15	3.04	5.30	23	2.73	5.25
Veres, Dave, StL	0	0.00	5.00	2	3.18	4.69
Vidro, Jose, Mon	111	6.89	5.00	219	5.34	4.89
Villegas, Ismael, Atl	0	0.00	5.00	0	0.00	5.00
Villone, Ron, Cin	1	0.69	5.00	0	0.00	5.00
Vina, Fernando, StL	77	5.80	5.00	374	5.06	4.96
Vitiello, Joe, SD	8	5.25	5.00	75	4.06	5.18
Vizcaino, Jose, LA-NYY	17	2.07	5.19	423	3.75	4.63
Vizquel, Omar, Cle	88	4.99	5.30	724	4.23	4.89
Vosberg, Ed, Phi	0	—	—	0	0.00	4.18
Wagner, Billy, Hou	0	0.00	5.00	0	0.00	4.72
Wainhouse, Dave, StL	0	—	—	0	0.00	4.70
Wakefield, Tim, Bos	0	0.00	5.30	2	0.67	4.35
Walbeck, Matt, Ana	10	2.21	5.30	177	3.12	5.14
Walker, Kevin, SD	0	0.00	5.00	0	0.00	5.00
Walker, Larry, Col	70	7.94	5.00	998	7.48	4.48
Walker, Todd, Min-Col	39	5.54	5.10	212	4.82	5.10
Wall, Donne, SD	0	0.00	5.00	1	0.39	4.67
Wallace, Jeff, Pit	0	0.00	5.00	0	0.00	5.00
Ward, Bryan, Phi-Ana	0	—	—	0	—	—
Ward, Daryle, Hou	33	4.35	5.00	54	4.54	5.00
Ward, Turner, Ari	2	1.10	5.00	213	4.62	4.86
Wasdin, John, Bos-Col	0	0.00	5.00	0	0.00	5.00
Washburn, Jarrod, Ana	1	6.70	5.30	1	3.83	5.17
Waszgis, B.J., Tex	5	3.62	5.30	5	3.62	5.30
Watson, Allen, NYY	0	—	—	17	3.04	4.65

Player, Team	2000 RC	RC/27	LRC/27	Career RC	RC/27	LRC27
Weathers, Dave, Mil	0	0.00	5.00	1	0.20	4.63
Weaver, Eric, Ana	0	—	—	0	0.00	4.60
Weaver, Jeff, Det	0	0.00	5.30	1	4.46	5.24
Webster, Lenny, Mon	2	0.78	5.00	151	3.53	4.78
Wehner, John, Pit	7	5.09	5.00	58	2.60	4.49
Weiss, Walt, Atl	21	3.74	5.00	560	4.06	4.55
Wells, Bob, Min	0	—	—	0	—	—
Wells, David, Tor	0	0.00	5.30	0	0.00	4.84
Wells, Kip, CWS	0	0.00	5.30	0	0.00	5.30
Wells, Vernon, Tor	0	0.00	5.30	9	3.25	5.18
Wendell, Turk, NYM	0	0.00	5.00	1	0.77	4.70
Wengert, Don, Atl	0	—	—	0	0.00	4.60
Wetteland, John, Tex	0	—	—	3	1.85	4.10
White, Devon, LA	15	3.23	5.00	938	4.66	4.64
White, Gabe, Cin-Col	2	6.72	5.00	3	2.25	4.70
White, Rick, TB-NYM	1	6.72	5.00	1	0.77	4.70
White, Rondell, Mon-ChC	66	6.96	5.00	422	5.35	4.74
Whiten, Mark, Cle	2	10.71	5.30	426	4.71	4.63
Whiteside, Matt, SD	0	—	—	0	0.00	4.60
Wickman, Bob, Mil-Cle	0	—	—	0	0.00	4.80
Widger, Chris, Mon-Sea	32	3.71	5.02	160	3.84	4.81
Wilkins, Marc, Pit	0	0.00	5.00	1	1.50	4.77
Wilkins, Rick, StL	0	0.00	5.00	265	4.32	4.48
Williams, Bernie, NYY	114	7.73	5.30	897	6.73	5.01
Williams, Brian, ChC-Cle	1	26.89	5.00	7	2.18	4.32
Williams, George, SD	1	2.07	5.00	59	4.68	5.12
Williams, Gerald, TB	87	4.77	5.30	329	4.35	5.07
Williams, Jeff, LA	0	—	—	0	0.00	5.00
Williams, Matt, Ari	41	3.87	5.00	931	5.22	4.48
Williams, Matt T., Mil	0	0.00	5.00	0	0.00	5.00
Williams, Mike, Pit	0	0.00	5.00	5	1.18	4.60
Williams, Woody, SD	9	5.15	5.00	13	2.96	5.00
Williamson, Scott, Cin	0	0.00	5.00	0	0.00	5.00
Wilson, Craig, CWS	6	2.55	5.30	52	4.70	5.19
Wilson, Dan, Sea	24	2.82	5.30	343	4.13	5.12
Wilson, Enrique, Cle-Pit	31	4.55	5.14	76	3.83	5.14
Wilson, Paul, TB	0	—	—	1	0.54	4.68
Wilson, Preston, Fla	92	5.20	5.00	166	5.00	4.98
Wilson, Vance, NYM	0	0.00	5.00	0	0.00	5.00
Winchester, Scott, Cin	0	—	—	0	0.00	4.60
Winn, Randy, TB	18	3.68	5.30	84	3.53	5.13
Wise, Dewayne, Tor	0	0.00	5.30	0	0.00	5.30
Witasick, Jay, KC-SD	1	1.03	5.05	1	0.87	5.07
Witt, Bobby, Cle	0	—	—	4	2.08	4.68
Wohlers, Mark, Cin	0	—	—	1	2.25	4.47
Wolf, Randy, Phi	3	1.42	5.00	5	1.55	5.00
Womack, Tony, Ari	82	4.65	5.00	348	4.74	4.79
Wood, Kerry, ChC	6	4.75	5.00	10	3.03	4.75
Woodard, Steve, Mil-Cle	0	0.00	5.00	0	0.00	4.86
Woodward, Chris, Tor	12	3.69	5.30	14	3.44	5.27
Wooten, Shawn, Ana	2	13.39	5.30	2	13.39	5.30
Worrell, Tim, Bal-ChC	0	0.00	5.00	4	1.50	4.59
Wright, Jamey, Mil	-1	-0.57	5.00	4	0.52	4.76
Wright, Jaret, Cle	0	0.00	5.00	2	4.47	5.04
Yan, Esteban, TB	2	53.57	5.30	2	53.57	5.30
Yoshii, Masato, Col	2	0.96	5.00	1	0.16	4.87
Young, Dmitri, Cin	86	5.68	5.00	268	5.28	4.80
Young, Eric, ChC	90	5.28	5.00	600	5.31	4.69
Young, Kevin, Pit	61	4.20	5.00	407	4.81	4.77
Young, Mike, Tex	0	0.00	5.30	0	0.00	5.30
Zaun, Gregg, KC	43	6.43	5.30	138	4.59	4.94
Zeile, Todd, NYM	85	5.44	5.00	849	4.98	4.58
Zosky, Eddie, Hou	0	0.00	5.00	0	0.00	4.59
Zuleta, Julio, ChC	12	6.33	5.00	12	6.33	5.00

Component Earned Run Average

Pitcher, Team	2000 OAvg	2000 OOB	2000 ERC	2000 LERA	Career OAvg	Career OOB	Career ERC	Career LERA
Abbott, Paul, Sea	.243	.325	4.09	4.92	.239	.333	4.09	4.64
Acevedo, Juan, Mil	.246	.315	3.74	4.64	.272	.343	4.66	4.39
Adams, Terry, LA	.245	.325	3.77	4.64	.257	.342	4.15	4.35
Aguilera, Rick, ChC	.251	.330	5.06	4.64	.251	.303	3.44	4.18
Aldred, Scott, Phi	.284	.362	5.65	4.64	.295	.371	5.82	4.56
Alfonseca, Antonio, Fla	.291	.347	4.79	4.64	.287	.355	4.74	4.45
Almanza, Armando, Fla	.228	.388	4.79	4.64	.210	.365	4.05	4.62
Almanzar, Carlos, SD	.266	.333	4.83	4.64	.281	.345	5.18	4.62
Alvarez, Juan, Ana	.467	.553	21.26	4.92	.385	.510	14.28	4.90
Anderson, Brian, Ari	.275	.308	4.15	4.64	.282	.318	4.43	4.57
Anderson, Jimmy, Pit	.294	.364	5.21	4.64	.284	.359	4.93	4.62
Anderson, Matt, Det	.228	.339	4.01	4.92	.235	.361	4.66	4.83
Andrews, Clayton, Tor	.374	.426	10.03	4.92	.374	.426	10.03	4.92
Ankiel, Rick, StL	.219	.320	3.63	4.64	.218	.317	3.51	4.63
Appier, Kevin, Oak	.262	.354	4.89	4.92	.245	.313	3.45	4.50
Armas Jr., Tony, Mon	.218	.321	3.49	4.64	.225	.323	3.55	4.63
Arnold, Jamie, LA-ChC	.259	.369	4.49	4.64	.285	.382	5.32	4.59
Arrojo, Rolando, Col-Bos	.277	.353	5.14	4.75	.274	.351	4.94	4.74
Arroyo, Bronson, Pit	.302	.384	6.18	4.64	.302	.384	6.18	4.64
Ashby, Andy, Phi-Atl	.280	.333	4.52	4.64	.266	.322	3.97	4.27
Astacio, Pedro, Col	.281	.356	5.42	4.64	.268	.331	4.31	4.26
Aybar, Manny, Col-Cin-Fla	.244	.323	4.08	4.64	.266	.343	4.56	4.42
Baldwin, James, CWS	.272	.335	4.91	4.92	.273	.341	4.87	4.79
Bale, John, Tor	.313	.455	11.52	4.92	.292	.438	10.99	4.90
Barcelo, Lorenzo, CWS	.231	.274	2.90	4.92	.231	.274	2.90	4.92
Batista, Miguel, Mon-KC	.317	.401	8.37	4.89	.283	.367	5.30	4.45
Beck, Rod, Bos	.222	.287	2.59	4.92	.242	.288	3.05	4.12
Beirne, Kevin, CWS	.263	.338	4.97	4.92	.263	.338	4.97	4.92
Belcher, Tim, Ana	.281	.373	6.23	4.92	.259	.323	3.98	4.21
Belinda, Stan, Col-Atl	.294	.370	6.93	4.64	.233	.315	3.62	4.20
Belitz, Todd, Oak	.267	.421	7.07	4.92	.267	.421	7.07	4.92
Bell, Derek, NYM	.429	.600	26.61	4.64	.429	.600	26.61	4.64
Bell, Rob, Cin	.243	.334	4.98	4.64	.243	.334	4.98	4.64
Beltran, Rigo, Col	.600	.692	61.44	4.64	.267	.336	4.39	4.35
Benes, Alan, StL	.290	.373	5.96	4.64	.255	.335	4.24	4.26
Benes, Andy, StL	.275	.342	5.05	4.64	.249	.313	3.66	4.09
Benitez, Armando, NYM	.148	.255	2.08	4.64	.176	.294	2.79	4.64
Benson, Kris, Pit	.249	.325	3.97	4.64	.249	.326	3.88	4.60
Bere, Jason, Mil-Cle	.275	.363	5.34	4.73	.259	.365	5.22	4.62
Bergman, Sean, Min	.374	.436	10.16	4.92	.303	.362	5.51	4.44
Bernero, Adam, Det	.270	.338	3.94	4.92	.270	.338	3.94	4.92
Biddle, Rocky, CWS	.326	.371	7.01	4.92	.326	.371	7.01	4.92
Blair, Willie, Det	.296	.332	4.69	4.92	.285	.340	4.78	4.33
Blank, Matt, Mon	.226	.300	2.86	4.64	.226	.300	2.86	4.64
Bochtler, Doug, KC	.371	.511	11.73	4.92	.241	.353	4.62	4.36
Boehringer, Brian, SD	.286	.378	7.15	4.64	.262	.355	4.90	4.56
Bogar, Tim, Hou	.250	.333	7.30	4.64	.250	.333	7.30	4.64
Bohanon, Brian, Col	.266	.346	4.80	4.64	.277	.355	5.01	4.43
Bones, Ricky, Fla	.303	.358	4.85	4.64	.283	.344	4.90	4.52
Borbon, Pedro, Tor	.280	.417	6.91	4.92	.236	.341	3.97	4.49
Borkowski, Dave, Det	.423	.529	17.78	4.92	.294	.385	6.43	4.86
Bottalico, Ricky, KC	.239	.342	4.65	4.92	.236	.335	4.05	4.39
Bottenfield, Kent, Ana-Phi	.274	.347	5.30	4.85	.270	.346	4.65	4.36
Boyd, Jason, Phi	.293	.405	5.71	4.64	.288	.396	5.40	4.63
Bradford, Chad, CWS	.255	.269	2.01	4.92	.261	.308	3.14	4.74
Brantley, Jeff, Phi	.288	.373	6.57	4.64	.236	.317	3.62	3.94
Brea, Lesli, Bal	.324	.469	9.77	4.92	.324	.469	9.77	4.92
Brewington, Jamie, Cle	.311	.379	5.53	4.92	.271	.364	4.84	4.46
Brocail, Doug, Det	.285	.330	4.25	4.92	.263	.325	3.98	4.41
Brock, Chris, Phi	.239	.321	4.71	4.64	.271	.343	5.06	4.51
Brower, Jim, Cle	.309	.387	6.95	4.92	.298	.374	6.67	4.90
Brown, Kevin, LA	.213	.261	2.30	4.64	.248	.305	3.16	4.28
Brownson, Mark, Phi	.333	.417	8.04	4.64	.323	.370	6.76	4.48
Brunette, Justin, StL	.364	.481	10.34	4.64	.364	.481	10.34	4.64
Bruske, Jim, Mil	.314	.424	9.52	4.64	.273	.357	5.01	4.29
Buddie, Mike, Mil	.320	.346	3.91	4.64	.292	.347	4.82	4.66
Buehrle, Mark, CWS	.272	.344	4.56	4.92	.272	.344	4.56	4.92
Bullinger, Kirk, Phi	.308	.286	2.89	4.64	.364	.379	6.61	4.44
Burba, Dave, Cle	.267	.346	4.62	4.92	.256	.336	4.29	4.42
Burkett, John, Atl	.303	.365	5.28	4.64	.280	.328	4.13	4.20
Burnett, A.J., Fla	.259	.352	4.45	4.64	.253	.349	4.30	4.61
Byrd, Paul, Phi	.271	.345	5.42	4.64	.255	.329	4.44	4.44
Byrdak, Tim, KC	.367	.441	13.14	4.92	.336	.435	9.85	4.86
Cabrera, Jose, Hou	.308	.357	5.72	4.64	.262	.314	3.91	4.54
Cairncross, Cam, Cle	.306	.350	4.79	4.92	.306	.350	4.79	4.92
Cammack, Eric, NYM	.194	.375	4.79	4.64	.194	.375	4.79	4.64
Carlyle, Buddy, SD	.400	.500	12.01	4.64	.271	.358	5.45	4.57
Carpenter, Chris, Tor	.290	.369	6.04	4.92	.289	.355	5.20	4.77

Pitcher, Team	2000 OAvg	2000 OOB	2000 ERC	2000 LERA	Career OAvg	Career OOB	Career ERC	Career LERA
Carrara, Giovanni, Col	.356	.458	12.21	4.64	.333	.419	8.95	4.59
Carrasco, Hector, Min-Bos	.291	.372	5.37	4.92	.255	.344	4.11	4.46
Castillo, Frank, Tor	.220	.303	3.42	4.92	.268	.328	4.24	4.14
Charlton, Norm, Cin	.429	.600	21.95	4.64	.241	.329	3.68	4.05
Chen, Bruce, Atl-Phi	.232	.298	3.35	4.64	.232	.309	3.73	4.58
Choate, Randy, NYY	.215	.307	3.99	4.92	.215	.307	3.99	4.92
Chouinard, Bobby, Col	.273	.324	4.16	4.64	.279	.341	4.59	4.64
Christiansen, J., Pit-StL	.233	.340	3.60	4.64	.243	.337	3.77	4.33
Clark, Mark, Tex	.347	.425	9.14	4.92	.279	.330	4.42	4.32
Clemens, Roger, NYY	.236	.317	3.93	4.92	.228	.294	2.89	4.36
Clement, Matt, SD	.248	.361	4.87	4.64	.261	.360	4.86	4.59
Clontz, Brad, Pit	.269	.486	9.01	4.64	.261	.340	4.26	4.28
Coco, Pasqual, Tor	.294	.478	11.69	4.92	.294	.478	11.69	4.92
Coggin, Dave, Phi	.315	.387	5.95	4.64	.315	.387	5.95	4.64
Colon, Bartolo, Cle	.233	.329	3.97	4.92	.251	.330	4.05	4.77
Cone, David, NYY	.306	.389	6.72	4.92	.230	.307	3.25	4.20
Cook, Dennis, NYM	.270	.368	5.49	4.64	.250	.322	3.95	4.14
Cooper, Brian, Ana	.300	.363	6.17	4.92	.284	.363	5.84	4.91
Cordero, Francisco, Tex	.285	.383	6.15	4.92	.285	.389	6.17	4.91
Cordova, Francisco, Pit	.285	.352	5.03	4.64	.262	.320	3.82	4.34
Cormier, Rheal, Bos	.275	.316	3.86	4.92	.275	.316	3.86	4.16
Cornelius, Reid, Fla	.282	.351	5.04	4.64	.280	.350	4.90	4.49
Crabtree, Tim, Tex	.274	.339	4.30	4.92	.274	.338	4.19	4.80
Crawford, Paxton, Bos	.240	.325	2.99	4.92	.240	.325	2.99	4.92
Creek, Doug, TB	.224	.342	4.50	4.92	.229	.355	5.01	4.54
Cressend, Jack, Min	.364	.426	6.65	4.92	.364	.426	6.65	4.92
Croushore, Rick, Col-Bos	.297	.405	6.15	4.72	.240	.347	4.48	4.45
Cruz, Nelson, Det	.253	.320	3.69	4.92	.272	.333	4.68	4.82
Cubillan, Darwin, Tor-Tex	.364	.453	11.03	4.92	.364	.453	11.03	4.92
Cunnane, Will, SD	.241	.339	3.90	4.64	.289	.373	5.74	4.37
D'Amico, Jeff, Mil	.238	.297	3.01	4.64	.254	.314	4.04	4.69
D'Amico, Jeff M., KC	.345	.486	10.15	4.92	.345	.486	10.15	4.92
Daal, Omar, Ari-Phi	.305	.376	6.17	4.64	.267	.338	4.35	4.41
Darensbourg, Vic, Fla	.260	.336	4.33	4.64	.258	.341	4.17	4.45
Davey, Tom, SD	.250	.280	2.33	4.64	.250	.354	4.43	4.82
Davis, Doug, Tex	.288	.383	5.93	4.92	.303	.392	6.63	4.92
Davis, Kane, Cle-Mil	.386	.494	13.77	4.85	.386	.494	13.77	4.85
de los Santos, Valerio, Mil	.254	.333	4.79	4.64	.243	.319	4.28	4.55
DeJean, Mike, Col	.269	.362	5.22	4.64	.293	.364	5.15	4.39
del Toro, Miguel, SF	.250	.329	4.44	4.64	.258	.337	4.95	4.59
Dempster, Ryan, Fla	.243	.322	4.04	4.64	.262	.356	5.02	4.56
DePaula, Sean, Cle	.294	.410	7.49	4.92	.259	.357	4.69	4.90
Dessens, Elmer, Cin	.296	.344	4.31	4.64	.305	.351	4.75	4.47
DeWitt, Matt, Tor	.351	.456	10.93	4.92	.351	.456	10.93	4.92
Dickson, Jason, Ana	.336	.379	6.72	4.92	.299	.351	5.38	4.66
Dingman, Craig, NYY	.375	.412	7.60	4.92	.375	.412	7.60	4.92
Dipoto, Jerry, Col	.314	.362	4.60	4.64	.280	.356	4.46	4.31
Dotel, Octavio, Hou	.265	.351	5.47	4.64	.250	.346	4.99	4.61
Downs, Scott, ChC-Mon	.312	.380	6.19	4.64	.312	.380	6.19	4.64
Dreifort, Darren, LA	.238	.329	4.40	4.64	.252	.334	4.09	4.43
Drew, Tim, Cle	.425	.510	12.94	4.92	.425	.510	12.94	4.92
Durbin, Chad, KC	.301	.385	7.05	4.92	.297	.381	6.81	4.92
Duvall, Mike, TB	.455	.500	11.29	4.92	.301	.403	6.53	4.84
Eaton, Adam, SD	.260	.338	4.34	4.64	.260	.338	4.34	4.64
Eiland, Dave, TB	.326	.381	6.83	4.92	.303	.356	5.46	4.31
Einertson, Darrell, NYY	.302	.345	4.97	4.92	.302	.345	4.97	4.92
Elarton, Scott, Hou	.263	.339	4.82	4.64	.245	.318	3.85	4.55
Eldred, Cal, CWS	.243	.342	4.36	4.92	.255	.332	4.34	4.52
Embree, Alan, SF	.274	.347	4.24	4.64	.247	.334	4.09	4.48
Enders, Trevor, TB	.359	.432	8.73	4.92	.359	.432	8.73	4.92
Erdos, Todd, NYY-SD	.286	.378	6.05	4.77	.287	.373	5.91	4.67
Erickson, Scott, Bal	.331	.407	7.50	4.92	.279	.344	4.49	4.53
Escobar, Kelvim, Tor	.267	.347	4.94	4.92	.270	.350	4.83	4.83
Estes, Shawn, SF	.275	.371	4.75	4.64	.256	.353	4.31	4.39
Estrada, Horacio, Mil	.300	.423	8.17	4.64	.303	.415	8.76	4.62
Estrella, Leo, Tor	.450	.429	9.77	4.92	.450	.429	9.77	4.92
Etherton, Seth, Ana	.278	.338	5.87	4.92	.278	.338	5.87	4.92
Eyre, Scott, CWS	.372	.452	9.49	4.92	.289	.379	6.64	4.67
Farnsworth, Kyle, ChC	.291	.392	6.72	4.64	.279	.361	5.89	4.59
Fassero, Jeff, Bos	.296	.358	5.25	4.92	.259	.321	3.88	4.37
Fernandez, Alex, Fla	.292	.342	4.75	4.64	.254	.312	3.66	4.44
Fernandez, Osvaldo, Cin	.238	.313	3.28	4.64	.280	.340	4.56	4.32
Fetters, Mike, LA	.205	.313	3.34	4.64	.260	.344	4.15	4.46
Figueroa, Nelson, Ari	.283	.328	5.31	4.64	.283	.328	5.31	4.64
Finley, Chuck, Cle	.256	.337	4.26	4.92	.253	.331	3.99	4.43
Fiore, Tony, TB	.333	.432	8.74	4.92	.333	.432	8.74	4.92
Florie, Bryce, Bos	.295	.356	4.71	4.92	.264	.351	4.49	4.59
Ford, Ben, NYY	.333	.462	8.38	4.92	.314	.416	7.62	4.59

	2000				Career			
Pitcher, Team	OAvg	OOB	ERC	LERA	OAvg	OOB	ERC	LERA
Forster, Scott, Mon	.230	.362	5.27	4.64	.230	.362	5.27	4.64
Foulke, Keith, CWS	.207	.261	2.28	4.92	.224	.280	2.91	4.72
Franco, John, NYM	.221	.314	3.36	4.64	.246	.318	3.26	3.90
Franklin, Wayne, Hou	.282	.388	6.01	4.64	.282	.388	6.01	4.64
Frascatore, John, Tor	.301	.381	6.58	4.92	.274	.347	4.75	4.46
Fultz, Aaron, SF	.263	.336	4.19	4.64	.263	.336	4.19	4.64
Fussell, Chris, KC	.286	.385	6.96	4.92	.305	.407	7.37	4.88
Fyhrie, Mike, Ana	.269	.315	3.53	4.92	.280	.338	4.59	4.87
Gagne, Eric, LA	.270	.368	5.97	4.64	.250	.350	5.09	4.62
Garces, Rich, Bos	.229	.286	2.85	4.92	.226	.316	3.44	4.75
Garcia, Freddy, Sea	.241	.335	4.20	4.92	.255	.341	4.36	4.88
Garcia, Mike, Pit	.429	.475	10.47	4.64	.324	.393	6.31	4.61
Gardner, Mark, SF	.270	.322	4.01	4.64	.261	.327	4.22	4.11
Garibay, Daniel, ChC	.299	.376	5.80	4.64	.299	.376	5.80	4.64
Garland, Jon, CWS	.292	.380	6.26	4.92	.292	.380	6.26	4.92
Ginter, Matt, CWS	.409	.481	16.24	4.92	.409	.481	16.24	4.92
Glauber, Keith, Cin	.185	.267	1.82	4.64	.200	.246	1.61	4.43
Glavine, Tom, Atl	.244	.296	3.19	4.64	.251	.313	3.35	4.03
Glynn, Ryan, Tex	.293	.369	6.12	4.92	.302	.385	6.74	4.90
Gomes, Wayne, Phi	.262	.347	4.20	4.64	.261	.353	4.48	4.42
Gooden, D., Hou-TB-NYY	.287	.359	5.95	4.91	.244	.309	3.32	3.95
Graves, Danny, Cin	.243	.330	3.64	4.64	.252	.331	3.79	4.52
Green, Jason, Hou	.234	.424	6.88	4.64	.234	.424	6.88	4.64
Grilli, Jason, Fla	.379	.455	7.84	4.64	.379	.455	7.84	4.64
Grimsley, Jason, NYY	.268	.345	4.63	4.92	.267	.368	5.05	4.58
Groom, Buddy, Bal	.275	.329	4.01	4.92	.293	.361	5.09	4.67
Gross, Kip, Hou	.429	.478	15.39	4.64	.290	.363	5.07	3.82
Guardado, Eddie, Min	.238	.313	4.34	4.92	.269	.341	4.77	4.70
Gunderson, Eric, Tor	.455	.486	11.80	4.92	.299	.359	5.32	4.49
Guthrie, M., ChC-TB-Tor	.261	.350	4.44	4.85	.271	.337	4.22	4.26
Guzman, Domingo, SD	.333	.667	16.22	4.64	.452	.541	15.07	4.57
Guzman, Geraldo, Ari	.286	.352	4.97	4.64	.286	.352	4.97	4.64
Guzman, Juan, TB	.636	.692	47.43	4.92	.243	.325	3.88	4.54
Hackman, Luther, StL	.400	.600	11.43	4.64	.375	.485	11.71	4.57
Halama, John, Sea	.308	.361	5.42	4.92	.295	.350	4.87	4.83
Halladay, Roy, Tor	.357	.435	9.70	4.92	.293	.377	6.17	4.86
Halter, Shane, Det	—	1.000	Inf	—	.333	.500	6.99	4.65
Hamilton, Joey, Tor	.233	.311	3.38	4.92	.261	.332	4.03	4.29
Hampton, Mike, NYM	.241	.328	3.44	4.64	.259	.330	3.80	4.35
Haney, Chris, Cle	.333	.400	5.48	4.92	.285	.344	4.81	4.52
Harnisch, Pete, Cin	.261	.321	4.51	4.64	.244	.312	3.63	4.08
Harper, Travis, TB	.244	.329	4.46	4.92	.244	.329	4.46	4.92
Hasegawa, S., Ana	.270	.339	4.44	4.92	.264	.333	4.34	4.73
Hawkins, LaTroy, Min	.256	.322	3.70	4.92	.309	.365	5.94	4.75
Haynes, Jimmy, Mil	.295	.378	5.54	4.64	.290	.374	5.69	4.72
Helling, Rick, Tex	.252	.334	4.50	4.92	.256	.330	4.48	4.73
Henry, Doug, Hou-SF	.207	.333	4.00	4.64	.242	.333	4.05	4.29
Hentgen, Pat, StL	.276	.353	4.81	4.64	.266	.331	4.34	4.67
Heredia, Felix, ChC	.220	.329	3.59	4.64	.252	.349	4.34	4.39
Heredia, Gil, Oak	.274	.332	4.44	4.92	.280	.323	4.12	4.55
Herges, Matt, LA	.249	.323	3.35	4.64	.250	.323	3.58	4.62
Hermanson, Dustin, Mon	.290	.352	5.10	4.64	.262	.327	4.07	4.41
Hernandez, Livan, SF	.273	.325	4.01	4.64	.276	.340	4.55	4.44
Hernandez, Orlando, NYY	.247	.298	3.82	4.92	.236	.303	3.52	4.83
Hernandez, Roberto, TB	.272	.331	4.24	4.92	.231	.310	3.25	4.61
Hershiser, Orel, LA	.389	.493	12.48	4.64	.249	.312	3.37	4.00
Hiljus, Erik, Det	.333	.375	7.34	4.92	.273	.353	5.65	4.88
Hill, Ken, Ana-CWS	.327	.424	8.36	4.92	.259	.336	4.03	4.22
Hinchliffe, Brett, Ana	.167	.286	2.03	4.92	.316	.428	9.60	4.86
Hitchcock, Sterling, SD	.267	.345	5.22	4.64	.270	.336	4.63	4.56
Hodges, Kevin, Sea	.310	.438	8.02	4.92	.310	.438	8.02	4.92
Hoffman, Trevor, SD	.224	.250	2.18	4.64	.201	.261	2.19	4.28
Holmes, D., Ari-StL-Bal	.416	.466	12.92	4.71	.273	.341	4.37	4.22
Holt, Chris, Hou	.304	.364	5.31	4.64	.289	.348	4.61	4.46
Holtz, Mike, Ana	.248	.331	3.79	4.92	.256	.348	4.30	4.78
Holzemer, Mark, Phi	.336	.388	6.54	4.64	.325	.402	7.24	4.65
House, Craig, Col	.265	.464	9.36	4.64	.265	.464	9.36	4.64
Howry, Bob, CWS	.216	.303	2.96	4.92	.215	.306	3.22	4.82
Hudson, Tim, Oak	.227	.306	3.43	4.92	.231	.313	3.46	4.90
Irabu, Hideki, Mon	.339	.377	6.58	4.64	.269	.332	4.81	4.72
Isringhausen, Jason, Oak	.252	.338	4.09	4.92	.272	.351	4.58	4.39
Jacquez, Tom, Phi	.333	.382	7.50	4.64	.333	.382	7.50	4.64
James, Mike, StL	.219	.318	3.62	4.64	.237	.336	3.80	4.74
Jarvis, Kevin, Col	.300	.351	5.86	4.64	.311	.367	6.39	4.39
Jimenez, Jose, Col	.239	.316	3.18	4.64	.264	.342	4.21	4.55
Johnson, Jason, Bal	.278	.369	6.18	4.92	.282	.364	5.79	4.82
Johnson, Jonathan, Tex	.291	.410	6.84	4.92	.320	.433	7.84	4.88
Johnson, Mark, Det	.266	.365	5.44	4.92	.266	.365	5.44	4.92
Johnson, Mike, Mon	.269	.366	5.81	4.64	.290	.371	6.42	4.50
Johnson, Randy, Ari	.224	.288	2.80	4.64	.213	.303	3.09	4.37

	2000				Career			
Pitcher, Team	OAvg	OOB	ERC	LERA	OAvg	OOB	ERC	LERA
Johnstone, John, SF	.322	.362	6.21	4.64	.255	.329	4.18	4.38
Jones, Bobby J., NYM	.281	.336	4.88	4.64	.269	.322	4.00	4.27
Jones, Bobby M., NYM	.222	.354	4.43	4.64	.289	.382	6.03	4.38
Jones, Doug, Oak	.292	.334	4.32	4.92	.264	.307	3.38	4.26
Jones, Marcus, Oak	.417	.533	19.41	4.92	.417	.533	19.41	4.92
Jones, Todd, Det	.276	.344	4.43	4.92	.243	.333	3.77	4.46
Judd, Mike, LA	.250	.400	9.87	4.64	.308	.396	7.32	4.47
Kamieniecki, Scott, Cle-Atl	.282	.396	6.44	4.80	.270	.351	4.68	4.47
Karchner, Matt, ChC	.311	.411	7.96	4.64	.263	.358	4.86	4.67
Karl, Scott, Col-Ana	.341	.414	8.11	4.71	.293	.356	5.16	4.62
Karsay, Steve, Cle	.266	.327	3.79	4.92	.277	.339	4.47	4.69
Keisler, Randy, NYY	.364	.462	9.10	4.92	.364	.462	9.10	4.92
Kida, Masao, Det	.385	.385	9.86	4.92	.293	.368	5.41	4.86
Kile, Darryl, StL	.247	.301	3.59	4.64	.260	.343	4.35	4.19
Kim, Byung-Hyun, Ari	.200	.336	4.04	4.64	.203	.347	4.13	4.62
King, Ray, Mil	.180	.252	1.64	4.64	.210	.313	3.06	4.62
Kinney, Matt, Min	.261	.355	5.20	4.92	.261	.355	5.20	4.92
Kline, Steve, Mon	.278	.340	4.37	4.64	.263	.344	4.44	4.46
Koch, Billy, Tor	.258	.304	3.25	4.92	.248	.315	3.37	4.89
Kohlmeier, Ryan, Bal	.291	.378	4.98	4.92	.291	.378	4.98	4.92
Kolb, Brandon, SD	.296	.409	5.61	4.64	.296	.409	5.61	4.64
Kolb, Danny, Tex	.833	.778	69.84	4.92	.295	.378	5.61	4.86
Lara, Yovanny, Mon	.250	.448	6.61	4.64	.250	.448	6.61	4.64
Larkin, Andy, Cin-KC	.324	.408	8.00	4.85	.322	.425	8.06	4.38
Laxton, Brett, KC	.348	.449	7.06	4.92	.337	.438	7.18	4.90
Lee, David, Col	.357	.486	16.73	4.64	.262	.381	5.52	4.57
Lee, Sang-Hoon, Bos	.262	.347	4.94	4.92	.262	.347	4.94	4.92
Leiter, Al, NYM	.228	.304	3.23	4.64	.237	.334	3.79	4.42
Leskanic, Curtis, Mil	.212	.337	3.72	4.64	.257	.344	4.41	4.30
Levine, Al, Ana	.266	.352	4.71	4.92	.273	.343	4.64	4.82
Levrault, Allen, Mil	.238	.340	3.21	4.64	.238	.340	3.21	4.64
Lidle, Cory, TB	.294	.347	5.06	4.92	.287	.337	4.51	4.60
Lieber, Jon, ChC	.257	.301	3.70	4.64	.274	.314	4.05	4.37
Ligtenberg, Kerry, Atl	.226	.312	3.46	4.64	.207	.280	2.73	4.38
Lilly, Ted, NYY	.235	.333	4.76	4.92	.290	.369	6.94	4.65
Lima, Jose, Hou	.313	.364	6.59	4.64	.279	.320	4.45	4.51
Lincoln, Mike, Min	.383	.468	14.32	4.92	.335	.391	7.72	4.87
Linebrink, Scott, SF-Hou	.346	.460	11.88	4.64	.346	.460	11.88	4.64
Lira, Felipe, Mon	.310	.363	5.51	4.64	.285	.350	5.20	4.76
Loaiza, Esteban, Tex-Tor	.288	.344	5.07	4.92	.289	.343	4.83	4.48
Loiselle, Rich, Pit	.262	.380	5.48	4.64	.266	.356	4.63	4.33
Looper, Braden, Fla	.268	.364	4.55	4.64	.283	.357	4.68	4.59
Lopez, Albie, TB	.277	.341	4.68	4.92	.279	.350	5.02	4.77
Lopez, Rodrigo, SD	.377	.442	9.78	4.64	.377	.442	9.78	4.64
Lorraine, Andrew, ChC-Cle	.272	.358	5.32	4.70	.301	.372	5.92	4.63
Lowe, Derek, Bos	.257	.304	3.17	4.92	.251	.307	3.29	4.76
Lowe, Sean, CWS	.284	.383	5.95	4.92	.287	.377	5.58	4.80
Luebbers, Larry, Cin	.333	.419	6.46	4.64	.272	.352	4.67	4.29
Mabry, John, Sea	.600	.667	34.64	4.92	.600	.667	34.64	4.92
Maddux, Greg, Atl	.238	.276	2.60	4.64	.241	.286	2.63	4.00
Maddux, Mike, Hou	.282	.360	6.05	4.64	.265	.326	3.80	4.05
Maduro, Calvin, Bal	.315	.420	9.30	4.92	.291	.382	6.45	4.36
Magnante, Mike, Oak	.311	.390	5.49	4.92	.281	.348	4.35	4.47
Mahay, Ron, Oak-Fla	.333	.414	8.55	4.75	.257	.339	4.73	4.70
Mahomes, Pat, NYM	.263	.376	5.87	4.64	.271	.364	5.62	4.60
Mairena, Oswaldo, ChC	.583	.643	32.37	4.64	.583	.643	32.37	4.64
Mann, Jim, NYM	.429	.467	14.72	4.64	.429	.467	14.72	4.64
Mantei, Matt, Ari	.193	.343	3.80	4.64	.198	.339	3.54	4.43
Manzanillo, Josias, Pit	.240	.339	3.85	4.64	.248	.340	4.22	4.43
Marquis, Jason, Atl	.261	.353	5.13	4.64	.261	.353	5.13	4.64
Martin, Tom, Cle	.254	.336	4.05	4.92	.285	.361	4.91	4.52
Martinez, Pedro, Bos	.167	.213	1.39	4.92	.206	.270	2.34	4.44
Martinez, Ramon, Bos	.283	.372	5.71	4.92	.238	.318	3.55	4.02
Martinez, Willie, Cle	.111	.182	0.69	4.92	.111	.182	0.69	4.92
Masaoka, Onan, LA	.230	.336	3.81	4.64	.224	.345	4.25	4.58
Mathews, T.J., Oak	.303	.368	5.98	4.92	.244	.316	3.66	4.53
Matthews, Mike, StL	.349	.481	11.83	4.64	.349	.481	11.83	4.64
Maurer, Dave, SD	.263	.344	4.71	4.64	.263	.344	4.71	4.64
Mayne, Brent, Col	.250	.400	5.48	4.64	.250	.400	5.48	4.64
Mays, Joe, Min	.299	.364	5.59	4.92	.284	.350	5.08	4.89
McDill, Allen, Det	.317	.349	5.88	4.92	.305	.400	8.32	4.77
McElroy, Chuck, Bal	.247	.340	4.31	4.92	.255	.338	3.96	4.19
McGlinchy, Kevin, Atl	.314	.415	7.10	4.64	.262	.340	4.02	4.57
McKnight, Tony, Hou	.245	.297	3.61	4.64	.245	.297	3.61	4.64
McMichael, Greg, Atl	.214	.262	2.68	4.64	.246	.314	3.32	4.22
Meacham, Rusty, Hou	.381	.435	14.02	4.64	.283	.329	4.37	4.43
Meadows, Brian, SD-KC	.298	.355	5.52	4.74	.305	.356	5.44	4.52
Meche, Gil, Sea	.240	.324	3.60	4.92	.238	.341	4.03	4.89
Mecir, Jim, TB-Oak	.225	.308	2.95	4.92	.239	.322	3.50	4.79
Mendoza, Ramiro, NYY	.260	.321	4.21	4.92	.285	.329	4.30	4.75

	2000				Career			
Pitcher, Team	OAvg	OOB	ERC	LERA	OAvg	OOB	ERC	LERA
Menechino, Frank, Oak	.750	.750	61.17	4.92	.750	.750	61.17	4.92
Mercado, Hector, Cin	.240	.339	4.32	4.64	.240	.339	4.32	4.64
Mercedes, Jose, Bal	.270	.345	4.52	4.92	.265	.336	4.52	4.71
Mercker, Kent, Ana	.300	.396	7.35	4.92	.261	.341	4.37	4.23
Mesa, Jose, Sea	.280	.365	5.60	4.92	.274	.346	4.55	4.43
Miceli, Dan, Fla	.242	.311	3.42	4.64	.261	.342	4.51	4.37
Miller, Travis, Min	.297	.368	5.35	4.92	.309	.372	5.72	4.80
Miller, Trever, Phi-LA	.365	.461	10.68	4.64	.306	.391	6.42	4.49
Miller, Wade, Hou	.257	.331	4.37	4.64	.268	.341	4.90	4.63
Mills, Alan, LA-Bal	.284	.397	7.03	4.77	.243	.353	4.56	4.45
Millwood, Kevin, Atl	.258	.311	3.83	4.64	.242	.298	3.28	4.47
Milton, Eric, Min	.260	.303	4.09	4.92	.261	.316	4.22	4.82
Mlicki, Dave, Det	.291	.349	5.39	4.92	.270	.337	4.56	4.42
Moehler, Brian, Det	.305	.342	4.95	4.92	.285	.334	4.59	4.75
Mohler, Mike, StL-Cle	.318	.431	7.98	4.65	.271	.367	4.97	4.64
Molina, Gabe, Bal-Atl	.394	.459	11.76	4.88	.318	.412	7.97	4.87
Montgomery, Steve, SD	.273	.385	9.01	4.64	.257	.361	5.69	4.63
Moore, Trey, Mon	.364	.455	9.97	4.64	.328	.389	6.66	4.38
Moraga, David, Mon-Col	.625	.619	29.94	4.64	.625	.619	29.94	4.64
Morgan, Mike, Ari	.311	.372	5.34	4.64	.275	.336	4.25	4.08
Morris, Jim, TB	.250	.362	4.68	4.92	.224	.338	4.33	4.90
Morris, Matt, StL	.261	.323	3.58	4.64	.254	.319	3.38	4.27
Mota, Danny, Min	.370	.393	8.84	4.92	.370	.393	8.84	4.92
Mota, Guillermo, Mon	.245	.328	3.86	4.64	.253	.334	4.02	4.59
Moyer, Jamie, Sea	.281	.339	4.91	4.92	.272	.326	4.21	4.41
Mulder, Mark, Oak	.308	.376	6.14	4.92	.308	.376	6.14	4.92
Mulholland, Terry, Atl	.308	.351	5.43	4.64	.275	.322	4.02	4.08
Mullen, Scott, KC	.244	.295	4.00	4.92	.244	.295	4.00	4.92
Munoz, Mike, Tex	.524	.583	19.41	4.92	.287	.363	4.99	4.25
Munro, Peter, Tor	.355	.452	8.18	4.92	.330	.405	6.71	4.88
Murray, Dan, KC	.278	.369	7.09	4.92	.287	.378	7.78	4.88
Mussina, Mike, Bal	.255	.291	3.37	4.92	.249	.293	3.21	4.62
Myers, Mike, Col	.160	.284	1.94	4.64	.257	.349	4.56	4.62
Myers, Rodney, SD	.250	.250	1.95	4.64	.279	.359	5.11	4.36
Myette, Aaron, CWS	.000	.333	1.96	4.92	.236	.402	6.25	4.87
Nagy, Charles, Cle	.300	.359	6.54	4.92	.279	.332	4.38	4.54
Nathan, Joe, SF	.255	.371	5.23	4.64	.249	.353	5.02	4.60
Nation, Joey, ChC	.279	.407	6.81	4.64	.279	.407	6.81	4.64
Navarro, Jaime, Mil-Cle	.375	.453	10.82	4.76	.285	.342	4.66	4.29
Neagle, Denny, Cin-NYY	.261	.330	4.45	4.76	.255	.312	3.74	4.26
Nelson, Jeff, NYY	.183	.314	2.61	4.92	.230	.337	3.56	4.61
Nen, Robb, SF	.162	.230	1.44	4.64	.230	.301	3.05	4.30
Newman, Alan, Cle	.667	.700	45.29	4.92	.373	.453	10.19	4.86
Nichting, Chris, Cle	.342	.435	7.21	4.92	.343	.419	7.07	4.77
Nickle, Doug, Phi	.417	.533	12.52	4.64	.417	.533	12.52	4.64
Nitkowski, C.J., Det	.286	.358	5.23	4.92	.275	.366	5.34	4.72
Nomo, Hideo, Det	.263	.344	4.95	4.92	.231	.316	3.69	4.38
Norton, Phil, ChC	.350	.447	14.18	4.64	.350	.447	14.18	4.64
Nunez, Vladimir, Fla	.319	.391	6.88	4.64	.275	.358	4.98	4.58
O'Connor, Brian, Pit	.250	.393	6.50	4.64	.250	.393	6.50	4.64
Ohka, Tomokazu, Bos	.263	.331	4.19	4.92	.281	.346	4.83	4.91
Ohman, Will, ChC	.308	.471	7.25	4.64	.308	.471	7.25	4.64
Olivares, Omar, Oak	.309	.396	6.42	4.92	.274	.353	4.70	4.35
Oliver, Darren, Tex	.339	.397	7.04	4.92	.283	.360	5.15	4.69
Olson, Gregg, LA	.300	.367	6.32	4.64	.238	.326	3.48	4.25
Ontiveros, Steve, Bos	.375	.464	10.99	4.92	.248	.307	3.42	4.41
Orosco, Jesse, StL	.273	.500	13.85	4.64	.220	.306	3.04	4.00
Ortiz, Ramon, Ana	.236	.327	4.24	4.92	.245	.335	4.54	4.90
Ortiz, Russ, SF	.261	.361	5.17	4.64	.255	.357	4.89	4.53
Osik, Keith, Pit	.625	.700	57.07	4.64	.538	.667	38.63	4.60
Osuna, Antonio, LA	.229	.325	3.74	4.64	.221	.306	3.13	4.30
Padilla, Vicente, Ari-Phi	.283	.353	4.22	4.64	.294	.365	4.75	4.63
Painter, Lance, Tor	.271	.332	4.37	4.92	.282	.348	4.94	4.37
Palacios, Vicente, SD	.308	.378	7.37	4.64	.253	.330	4.04	3.93
Paniagua, Jose, Sea	.234	.331	3.64	4.92	.262	.367	4.84	4.68
Park, Chan Ho, LA	.214	.325	3.51	4.64	.233	.330	3.90	4.39
Parque, Jim, CWS	.283	.352	4.99	4.92	.293	.366	5.56	4.83
Parra, Jose, Pit	.354	.446	9.86	4.64	.310	.374	6.76	4.80
Parris, Steve, Cin	.294	.355	5.44	4.64	.275	.344	4.76	4.45
Parrish, John, Bal	.288	.425	7.75	4.92	.288	.425	7.75	4.92
Patterson, Danny, Det	.309	.353	4.68	4.92	.287	.338	4.37	4.75
Pavano, Carl, Mon	.248	.324	3.67	4.64	.261	.327	4.05	4.45
Pena, Jesus, CWS-Bos	.277	.390	7.39	4.92	.269	.408	7.35	4.89
Penny, Brad, Fla	.263	.354	4.70	4.64	.263	.354	4.70	4.64
Percival, Troy, Ana	.228	.339	4.24	4.92	.180	.278	2.50	4.79
Perez, Carlos, LA	.324	.367	6.21	4.64	.279	.327	4.38	4.32
Perez, Yorkis, Hou	.266	.355	5.64	4.64	.239	.330	3.90	4.28
Perisho, Matt, Tex	.316	.411	7.79	4.92	.320	.415	7.83	4.81
Person, Robert, Phi	.229	.332	3.70	4.64	.245	.336	4.45	4.53
Peters, Chris, Pit	.221	.319	3.22	4.64	.274	.345	4.83	4.32

	2000				Career			
Pitcher, Team	OAvg	OOB	ERC	LERA	OAvg	OOB	ERC	LERA
Petkovsek, Mark, Ana	.277	.332	4.07	4.92	.283	.341	4.49	4.37
Pettitte, Andy, NYY	.271	.338	4.32	4.92	.272	.336	4.17	4.78
Pichardo, Hipolito, Bos	.260	.337	3.51	4.92	.277	.345	4.31	4.51
Pineiro, Joel, Sea	.316	.404	7.44	4.92	.316	.404	7.44	4.92
Plesac, Dan, Ari	.228	.341	3.98	4.64	.246	.312	3.49	4.21
Politte, Cliff, Phi	.248	.328	4.20	4.64	.271	.359	5.21	4.49
Ponson, Sidney, Bal	.258	.323	4.26	4.92	.275	.336	4.75	4.83
Poole, Jim, Det-Mon	.420	.456	13.78	4.87	.271	.346	4.48	4.42
Pote, Lou, Ana	.267	.324	3.87	4.92	.250	.315	3.37	4.90
Powell, Brian, Hou	.279	.348	5.88	4.64	.290	.360	6.15	4.65
Powell, Jay, Hou	.271	.381	5.10	4.64	.253	.347	4.01	4.33
Powell, Jeremy, Mon	.321	.370	6.84	4.64	.304	.381	6.22	4.52
Prieto, Ariel, Oak	.321	.384	6.12	4.92	.293	.377	5.57	4.78
Prokopec, Luke, LA	.253	.345	4.15	4.64	.253	.345	4.15	4.64
Pulsipher, Bill, NYM	.387	.500	12.44	4.64	.281	.350	4.97	4.32
Quantrill, Paul, Tor	.298	.347	4.78	4.92	.295	.345	4.71	4.53
Quevedo, Ruben, ChC	.271	.370	6.49	4.64	.271	.370	6.49	4.64
Radinsky, Scott, StL	—	1.000	Inf	—	.253	.329	3.66	4.20
Radke, Brad, Min	.286	.326	4.44	4.92	.273	.313	4.08	4.78
Rain, Steve, ChC	.250	.347	5.17	4.64	.295	.381	6.25	4.62
Rakers, Jason, KC	.351	.392	8.07	4.92	.337	.393	8.03	4.91
Ramirez, Hector, Mil	.289	.372	5.96	4.64	.261	.351	4.31	4.58
Ramsay, Rob, Sea	.234	.368	4.44	4.92	.259	.375	5.02	4.90
Rapp, Pat, Bal	.290	.366	5.42	4.92	.279	.366	5.00	4.43
Ratliff, Jon, Oak	.000	.000	0.00	4.92	.000	.000	0.00	4.92
Reames, Britt, StL	.207	.318	3.39	4.64	.207	.318	3.39	4.64
Redman, Mark, Min	.281	.333	4.73	4.92	.282	.338	4.96	4.92
Reed, Rick, NYM	.266	.302	3.90	4.64	.266	.304	3.70	4.25
Reed, Steve, Cle	.269	.335	4.31	4.92	.244	.312	3.72	4.32
Reichert, Dan, KC	.271	.372	5.22	4.92	.282	.389	5.72	4.91
Rekar, Bryan, TB	.292	.329	4.56	4.92	.299	.351	5.38	4.64
Remlinger, Mike, Atl	.207	.308	3.15	4.64	.242	.338	4.21	4.29
Reyes, Al, Bal-LA	.211	.318	3.43	4.83	.231	.336	4.19	4.57
Reyes, Carlos, Phi-SD	.238	.328	4.85	4.64	.268	.340	4.72	4.71
Reyes, Dennys, Cin	.262	.371	5.24	4.64	.256	.361	4.48	4.40
Reynolds, Shane, Hou	.287	.345	5.17	4.64	.271	.311	3.73	4.29
Reynoso, Armando, Ari	.273	.330	4.29	4.64	.282	.348	4.78	4.29
Rhodes, Arthur, Sea	.205	.286	2.62	4.92	.243	.332	4.12	4.56
Riedling, John, Cin	.208	.323	3.12	4.64	.208	.323	3.12	4.64
Rigby, Brad, KC-Mon	.397	.474	15.19	4.81	.311	.369	6.19	4.72
Rigdon, Paul, Cle-Mil	.264	.331	4.87	4.69	.264	.331	4.87	4.69
Riggan, Jerrod, NYM	.300	.300	3.96	4.64	.300	.300	3.96	4.64
Rincon, Ricky, Cle	.224	.344	3.89	4.92	.226	.316	3.39	4.44
Ritchie, Todd, Pit	.282	.329	4.55	4.64	.276	.330	4.40	4.60
Rivera, Luis, Atl-Bal	.208	.367	2.98	4.66	.208	.367	2.98	4.66
Rivera, Mariano, NYY	.208	.271	2.20	4.92	.214	.277	2.40	4.80
Roberts, Grant, NYM	.344	.395	6.53	4.64	.344	.395	6.53	4.64
Rocker, John, Atl	.210	.368	4.72	4.64	.188	.319	3.18	4.51
Rodriguez, Felix, SF	.220	.320	3.26	4.64	.250	.347	4.29	4.44
Rodriguez, Frank, Sea	.317	.383	6.56	4.92	.285	.357	5.13	4.79
Rodriguez, Jose, StL	.143	.316	2.62	4.64	.143	.316	2.62	4.64
Rodriguez, Rich, NYM	.364	.416	8.86	4.64	.264	.335	4.09	4.03
Rogers, Kenny, Tex	.285	.348	4.72	4.92	.262	.332	4.12	4.57
Romero, J.C., Min	.312	.390	6.48	4.92	.315	.383	6.10	4.91
Roque, Rafael, Mil	.333	.483	10.54	4.64	.272	.362	5.73	4.45
Rosado, Jose, KC	.271	.347	4.98	4.92	.257	.318	3.98	4.75
Rose, Brian, Bos-Col	.278	.354	5.50	4.77	.281	.346	5.48	4.78
Rueter, Kirk, SF	.290	.345	4.68	4.64	.277	.326	4.18	4.33
Ruffin, Johnny, Ari	.350	.395	9.93	4.64	.250	.332	4.22	4.20
Runyan, Sean, Det	.222	.333	2.79	4.92	.251	.339	4.38	4.70
Rupe, Ryan, TB	.321	.381	7.02	4.92	.281	.353	5.33	4.88
Rusch, Glendon, NYM	.267	.311	3.64	4.64	.290	.341	4.89	4.62
Ryan, B.J., Bal	.225	.349	4.87	4.92	.215	.339	4.05	4.89
Ryan, Jason, Min	.330	.384	8.35	4.92	.304	.371	7.04	4.88
Sanchez, Jesus, Fla	.280	.348	5.24	4.64	.279	.366	5.46	4.46
Santana, Johan, Min	.302	.398	6.59	4.92	.302	.398	6.59	4.92
Santana, Julio, Mon	.271	.356	5.31	4.64	.291	.371	5.85	4.65
Santiago, Jose, KC	.260	.329	4.14	4.92	.263	.326	4.19	4.88
Sasaki, Kazuhiro, Sea	.184	.285	2.98	4.92	.184	.285	2.98	4.92
Sauerbeck, Scott, Pit	.270	.399	5.31	4.64	.247	.370	4.49	4.60
Sauveur, Rich, Oak	.310	.326	5.79	4.92	.320	.414	7.82	4.12
Scanlan, Bob, Mil	.600	.583	20.55	4.64	.278	.345	4.38	4.19
Schilling, Curt, Phi-Ari	.255	.294	3.38	4.64	.237	.288	2.95	4.15
Schmidt, Jason, Pit	.284	.384	5.77	4.64	.272	.345	4.61	4.34
Schoeneweis, Scott, Ana	.276	.346	4.84	4.92	.280	.346	4.87	4.91
Schourek, Pete, Bos	.278	.341	4.91	4.92	.269	.334	4.40	4.18
Schrenk, Steve, Phi	.269	.361	5.39	4.64	.238	.322	3.83	[illegible]
Seanez, Rudy, Atl	.192	.284	2.95	4.64	.242	.337	[illegible]	[illegible]
Seelbach, Chris, Atl	.500	.429	7.19	4.64	.500	.429	[illegible]	[illegible]
Sele, Aaron, Sea	.271	.332	4.06	4.92	.277	.350	[illegible]	[illegible]

Pitcher, Team	2000				Career			
	OAvg	OOB	ERC	LERA	OAvg	OOB	ERC	LERA
Serafini, Dan, SD-Pit	.306	.380	6.19	4.64	.313	.380	6.12	4.62
Service, Scott, Oak	.302	.380	6.22	4.92	.270	.353	4.84	4.49
Shaw, Jeff, LA	.265	.316	4.02	4.64	.257	.310	3.58	4.22
Sheldon, Scott, Tex	.000	.000	0.00	4.92	.000	.000	0.00	4.92
Shuey, Paul, Cle	.219	.312	3.11	4.92	.238	.334	3.91	4.81
Sikorski, Brian, Tex	.288	.385	7.48	4.92	.288	.385	7.48	4.92
Silva, Jose, Pit	.317	.375	5.91	4.64	.300	.358	5.14	4.47
Simas, Bill, CWS	.276	.332	4.13	4.92	.257	.337	4.26	4.81
Sirotka, Mike, CWS	.269	.330	4.26	4.92	.286	.334	4.60	4.80
Skrmetta, Matt, Mon-Pit	.311	.403	7.77	4.64	.311	.403	7.77	4.64
Slocumb, H., StL-SD	.265	.357	4.95	4.64	.263	.360	4.48	4.39
Slusarski, Joe, Hou	.268	.323	3.99	4.64	.281	.355	5.21	4.24
Smith, Brian, Pit	.375	.421	7.97	4.64	.375	.421	7.97	4.64
Smith, Chuck, Fla	.248	.330	3.51	4.92	.248	.330	3.51	4.64
Smith, Dan, Bos	.250	.357	2.96	4.92	.292	.367	5.49	4.57
Snyder, John, Mil	.296	.395	5.71	4.64	.299	.371	5.86	4.72
Sparks, Jeff, TB	.186	.367	4.32	4.92	.181	.377	4.54	4.90
Sparks, Steve, Pit	.267	.450	6.80	4.64	.267	.450	6.80	4.64
Sparks, Steve W., Det	.263	.317	3.71	4.92	.275	.354	5.00	4.80
Speier, Justin, Cle	.226	.309	3.56	4.92	.250	.332	4.82	4.71
Spencer, Sean, Mon	.292	.357	6.38	4.64	.364	.450	9.96	4.68
Spencer, Stan, SD	.239	.316	3.83	4.64	.274	.328	4.86	4.51
Spoljaric, Paul, KC	.265	.359	6.81	4.92	.259	.359	5.16	4.73
Spradlin, Jerry, KC-ChC	.291	.355	5.00	4.87	.264	.327	4.02	4.41
Springer, Dennis, NYM	.377	.441	10.14	4.64	.279	.352	5.28	4.63
Springer, Russ, Ari	.261	.354	5.25	4.64	.263	.347	4.84	4.40
Spurgeon, Jay, Bal	.283	.394	6.88	4.92	.283	.394	6.88	4.92
Stanifer, Rob, Bos	.355	.394	8.60	4.92	.282	.349	5.23	4.30
Stanton, Mike, NYY	.263	.325	3.78	4.92	.252	.323	3.70	4.37
Stechschulte, Gene, StL	.247	.353	5.69	4.64	.247	.353	5.69	4.64
Stein, Blake, KC	.247	.343	4.82	4.92	.249	.355	5.24	4.80
Stephenson, Garrett, StL	.270	.327	4.53	4.64	.270	.334	4.49	4.49
Stevens, Dave, Atl	.357	.400	12.68	4.64	.297	.377	6.43	4.69
Stottlemyre, Todd, Ari	.268	.336	4.90	4.64	.261	.330	4.19	4.26
Strickland, Scott, Mon	.215	.279	2.44	4.64	.219	.297	2.95	4.62
Strong, Joe, Fla	.325	.426	7.85	4.64	.325	.426	7.85	4.64
Stull, Everett, Mil	.256	.381	5.72	4.64	.278	.402	6.69	4.61
Sturtze, Tanyon, CWS-TB	.272	.348	4.80	4.64	.294	.368	5.80	4.74
Sullivan, Scott, Cin	.226	.307	3.40	4.64	.230	.310	3.44	4.41
Suppan, Jeff, KC	.284	.351	5.31	4.92	.287	.344	5.03	4.76
Suzuki, Makoto, KC	.265	.349	4.96	4.92	.275	.365	5.51	4.88
Swindell, Greg, Ari	.247	.295	3.05	4.64	.269	.309	3.72	4.11
Tam, Jeff, Oak	.268	.315	3.14	4.92	.257	.310	3.22	4.80
Tapani, Kevin, ChC	.271	.319	4.52	4.64	.272	.316	3.96	4.37
Tavarez, Julian, Col	.268	.349	4.49	4.64	.285	.353	4.72	4.54
Taylor, Billy, TB	.255	.387	5.67	4.64	.254	.333	3.84	4.75
Telemaco, Amaury, Phi	.275	.364	6.24	4.64	.272	.334	4.70	4.30
Telford, Anthony, Mon	.257	.317	3.95	4.64	.265	.333	4.19	4.34
Tessmer, Jay, NYY	.300	.323	7.01	4.92	.309	.371	6.81	4.79
Thompson, Mark, StL	.250	.365	5.52	4.64	.303	.386	6.45	4.27
Thurman, Mike, Mon	.315	.393	6.25	4.64	.265	.339	4.44	4.50
Timlin, Mike, Bal-StL	.271	.368	5.08	4.79	.252	.327	3.69	4.54
Tolar, Kevin, Det	.091	.167	0.63	4.92	.091	.167	0.63	4.92
Tollberg, Brian, SD	.274	.332	4.26	4.64	.274	.332	4.26	4.64
Tomko, Brett, Sea	.264	.341	4.49	4.92	.252	.318	3.89	4.42
Trachsel, Steve, TB-Tor	.294	.356	5.25	4.92	.268	.332	4.50	4.37
Trombley, Mike, Bal	.247	.346	4.96	4.64	.263	.335	4.53	4.65
Tucker, T.J., Mon	.344	.400	12.90	4.64	.344	.400	12.90	4.64
Turnbow, Derrick, Ana	.254	.409	7.05	4.92	.254	.409	7.05	4.92
Urbina, Ugueth, Mon	.224	.296	2.95	4.64	.214	.298	3.19	4.30
Valdes, Ismael, ChC-LA	.294	.356	5.89	4.64	.251	.305	3.52	4.31
Valdes, Marc, Hou	.301	.379	5.43	4.64	.285	.368	5.06	4.31
Van Poppel, Todd, ChC	.249	.348	4.48	4.64	.269	.366	5.49	4.66
Vazquez, Javier, Mon	.286	.335	4.45	4.64	.279	.339	4.73	4.49
Venafro, Mike, Tex	.295	.362	4.49	4.92	.271	.338	3.83	4.89
Veres, Dave, StL	.239	.315	3.25	4.92	.258	.327	3.88	4.32
Villafuerte, Brandon, Det	.250	.400	5.01	4.92	.250	.400	5.01	4.92
Villegas, Ismael, Atl	.333	.467	16.82	4.64	.333	.467	16.82	4.64
Villone, Ron, Cin	.286	.381	5.97	4.64	.254	.361	4.90	4.58
Vizcaino, Luis, Oak	.305	.396	6.83	4.92	.295	.393	6.86	4.91
Vogelsong, Ryan, SF	.182	.250	1.57	4.64	.182	.250	1.57	4.64
Vosberg, Ed, Phi	.241	.371	5.42	4.64	.283	.363	4.92	4.54
Wagner, Billy, Hou	.255	.364	6.15	4.64	.186	.282	2.54	4.35
Wainhouse, Dave, StL	.351	.442	9.40	4.64	.312	.404	6.95	4.33
Wakefield, Tim, Bos	.272	.340	5.23	4.92	.260	.339	4.62	4.62
Walker, Kevin, SD	.206	.325	3.23	4.64	.206	.325	3.23	4.64
Walker, Pete, Col	.435	.519	15.29	4.64	.347	.414	8.27	4.27
Wall, Donne, SD	.193	.274	2.21	4.64	.256	.315	3.86	4.33
Wallace, Jeff, Pit	.290	.432	8.15	4.64	.239	.394	5.40	4.54
Ward, Bryan, Phi-Ana	.216	.281	2.88	4.72	.302	.346	5.58	4.76

Pitcher, Team	2000				Career			
	OAvg	OOB	ERC	LERA	OAvg	OOB	ERC	LERA
Wasdin, John, Bos-Col	.286	.339	5.09	4.80	.268	.322	4.46	4.77
Washburn, Jarrod, Ana	.215	.301	3.66	4.92	.240	.316	3.96	4.81
Watson, Allen, NYY	.330	.442	10.00	4.92	.283	.352	5.21	4.38
Watson, Mark, Cle	.400	.455	9.18	4.92	.400	.455	9.18	4.92
Weathers, Dave, Mil	.260	.339	3.90	4.64	.296	.372	5.32	4.32
Weaver, Eric, Ana	.267	.391	7.69	4.92	.265	.388	6.76	4.73
Weaver, Jeff, Det	.267	.322	4.18	4.92	.272	.335	4.64	4.89
Weber, Ben, SF-Ana	.292	.330	3.91	4.82	.292	.330	3.91	4.82
Wells, Bob, Min	.247	.284	3.35	4.92	.270	.331	4.64	4.81
Wells, David, Tor	.289	.316	4.05	4.92	.263	.307	3.70	4.50
Wells, Kip, CWS	.312	.398	7.01	4.92	.296	.382	6.10	4.90
Wendell, Turk, NYM	.206	.312	3.14	4.64	.239	.333	3.89	4.33
Wengert, Don, Atl	.286	.362	6.31	4.64	.311	.370	6.18	4.71
Westbrook, Jake, NYY	.469	.500	13.53	4.92	.469	.500	13.53	4.92
Wetteland, John, Tex	.285	.351	5.28	4.92	.218	.284	2.75	4.27
Wheeler, Dan, TB	.302	.382	5.87	4.92	.294	.367	5.94	4.88
Whisenant, Matt, SD	.213	.351	3.73	4.64	.250	.372	4.61	4.67
White, Gabe, Cin-Col	.211	.251	1.98	4.64	.243	.292	3.48	4.38
White, Rick, TB-NYM	.224	.305	3.21	4.84	.272	.332	4.13	4.61
Whiteside, Matt, SD	.232	.318	3.94	4.64	.283	.345	4.69	4.56
Wickman, Bob, Mil-Cle	.235	.317	2.92	4.74	.261	.343	4.09	4.55
Wilkins, Marc, Pit	.248	.376	4.76	4.64	.252	.355	4.27	4.37
Williams, Brian, ChC-Cle	.313	.430	7.50	4.76	.284	.378	5.50	4.31
Williams, Jeff, LA	.462	.571	17.89	4.64	.270	.383	5.83	4.58
Williams, Matt T., Mil	.219	.457	8.82	4.64	.219	.457	8.82	4.64
Williams, Mike, Pit	.218	.328	3.72	4.64	.264	.339	4.40	4.26
Williams, Woody, SD	.239	.300	3.55	4.64	.253	.322	4.17	4.63
Williamson, Scott, Cin	.224	.346	3.85	4.64	.201	.315	3.00	4.60
Wilson, Kris, KC	.288	.340	4.25	4.92	.288	.340	4.25	4.92
Wilson, Paul, TB	.209	.284	2.17	4.92	.254	.339	4.06	4.39
Winchester, Scott, Cin	.313	.343	5.64	4.64	.315	.371	6.16	4.26
Wise, Matt, Ana	.272	.331	4.96	4.92	.272	.331	4.96	4.92
Witasick, Jay, KC-SD	.294	.374	6.09	4.81	.298	.379	6.43	4.82
Witt, Bobby, Cle	.394	.442	10.80	4.92	.266	.358	4.86	4.34
Wohlers, Mark, Cin	.192	.308	3.14	4.64	.230	.327	3.37	4.13
Wolf, Randy, Phi	.269	.342	4.54	4.64	.268	.350	4.91	4.61
Wood, Kerry, ChC	.226	.349	4.43	4.64	.210	.326	3.64	4.41
Woodard, Steve, Mil-Cle	.305	.356	5.71	4.74	.286	.329	4.55	4.51
Worrell, Tim, Bal-ChC	.265	.337	4.42	4.67	.259	.330	4.20	4.38
Wright, Jamey, Mil	.261	.368	4.67	4.64	.297	.384	5.71	4.36
Wright, Jaret, Cle	.235	.336	4.13	4.92	.265	.353	4.87	4.72
Wunsch, Kelly, CWS	.221	.313	3.22	4.92	.221	.313	3.22	4.92
Yan, Esteban, TB	.285	.344	5.46	4.92	.286	.362	5.70	4.82
Yarnall, Ed, NYY	.417	.563	16.77	4.92	.278	.387	5.94	4.87
Yoshii, Masato, Col	.306	.357	5.70	4.64	.274	.332	4.52	4.48
Young, Danny, ChC	.357	.550	18.23	4.64	.357	.550	18.23	4.64
Young, Tim, Bos	.269	.345	6.90	4.92	.260	.351	5.59	4.60
Zerbe, Chad, SF	.273	.304	3.69	4.64	.273	.304	3.69	4.64
Zimmerman, Jeff, Tex	.286	.361	5.58	4.92	.223	.292	3.15	4.89
Zito, Barry, Oak	.195	.296	2.63	4.92	.195	.296	2.63	4.92

2000 Leader Boards

Our extensive leader boards always generate some interesting table talk. Here are a few of the choice nuggets from the 2000 season:

After the 1999 campaign, Larry Walker's name appeared three times across the top of the page of National League batting leaders, by virtue of finishing first in batting average, on-base percentage and slugging. For the 2000 season, simply erase Walker's name three times and write in Todd Helton's. The four-year veteran is among the best of a new wave of young hitters coming into their own in baseball, and he did it all last summer. No one in the National League got on base more than Helton (323), and hardly anyone was better with teammates on the sacks. Helton produced NL-best marks with runners in scoring position (.392) and in late-and-close situations (.393). Plus, his .770 slugging percentage in the No. 4 hole ranked first among all cleanup hitters in the game.

A number of bright young stars sparkled like never before in the American League. Darin Erstad delivered 240 hits, the highest AL total since Wade Boggs led the circuit with the same number in 1985. Not only did Erstad finish second to Nomar Garciaparra for the AL batting title, he also ranked first among all AL leadoff hitters in on-base percentage with a .409 mark. Teammate Troy Glaus, in just his second full season in the league, claimed his first home-run title with 47 longballs. Glaus especially pummeled lefthanded pitching, finishing first against them in on-base percentage (.500) and slugging (.874). Last but not least, Carlos Delgado threatened to win the first Triple Crown in more than 30 years with his fine 2000 season. He finished in the top five in each Triple Crown category, but led the American League in doubles (57), total bases (378), times on base (334), and best slugging percentage against righthanded pitching (.727).

Once again, Pedro Martinez was dominant on all pitching fronts. He easily won the ERA title in the American League with a 1.74 mark. In fact, his ERA could have been double that figure, and it would have been good enough to finish ahead of the second-place finisher, Roger Clemens (3.70). Martinez clearly outdistanced his AL competition in strikeouts, quality starts, shutouts, fewest baserunners per nine innings, and in each of the three opponent hitting percentages.

That kind of dominance is hard to miss. But did you know that Jamie Moyer led all of baseball by allowing the lowest on-base percentage to the first batter faced each inning (.225)? Or that Shawn Estes induced the most groundball double plays in the majors (40)?

There's plenty more where these stats came from. Check out the leader boards that follow.

2000 American League Batting Leaders

Batting Average
minimum 502 PA

Player, Team	AB	H	AVG
N Garciaparra, Bos	**529**	**197**	**.372**
D Erstad, Ana	676	240	.355
M Ramirez, Cle	439	154	.351
C Delgado, Tor	569	196	.344
D Jeter, NYY	593	201	.339
D Segui, Tex-Cle	574	192	.334
M Sweeney, KC	618	206	.333
J Giambi, Oak	510	170	.333
F Thomas, CWS	582	191	.328
J Damon, KC	655	214	.327

On-Base Percentage
minimum 502 PA

Player, Team	PA*	OB	OBP
J Giambi, Oak	**664**	**316**	**.476**
C Delgado, Tor	711	334	.470
M Ramirez, Cle	532	243	.457
F Thomas, CWS	707	308	.436
N Garciaparra, Bos	599	260	.434
E Martinez, Sea	665	281	.423
A Rodriguez, Sea	672	282	.420
J Posada, NYY	624	260	.417
D Jeter, NYY	676	281	.416
D Erstad, Ana	745	305	.409

* AB + BB + HBP + SF

Slugging Percentage
minimum 502 PA

Player, Team	AB	TB	SLG
M Ramirez, Cle	**439**	**306**	**.697**
C Delgado, Tor	569	378	.664
J Giambi, Oak	510	330	.647
F Thomas, CWS	582	364	.625
A Rodriguez, Sea	554	336	.606
T Glaus, Ana	563	340	.604
N Garciaparra, Bos	529	317	.599
C Everett, Bos	496	291	.587
D Justice, Cle-NYY	524	306	.584
E Martinez, Sea	556	322	.579

Games

J Cruz, Tor	**162**
C Delgado, Tor	162
M Vaughn, Ana	161
M Tejada, Oak	160
6 tied with	159

Plate Appearances

D Erstad, Ana	**747**
J Damon, KC	741
M Sweeney, KC	717
O Vizquel, Cle	717
M Vaughn, Ana	712

At-Bats

D Erstad, Ana	**676**
J Damon, KC	655
G Anderson, Ana	647
G Williams, TB	632
C Guzman, Min	631

Hits

D Erstad, Ana	**240**
J Damon, KC	214
M Sweeney, KC	206
D Jeter, NYY	201
N Garciaparra, Bos	197

Singles

D Erstad, Ana	**170**
D Jeter, NYY	151
M Sweeney, KC	147
J Damon, KC	146
O Vizquel, Cle	139

Doubles

C Delgado, Tor	**57**
N Garciaparra, Bos	51
D Cruz, Det	46
J Olerud, Sea	45
3 tied with	44

Triples

C Guzman, Min	**20**
A Kennedy, Ana	11
J Damon, KC	10
R Durham, CWS	9
2 tied with	8

Home Runs

T Glaus, Ana	**47**
J Giambi, Oak	43
F Thomas, CWS	43
4 tied with	41

Total Bases

C Delgado, Tor	**378**
D Erstad, Ana	366
F Thomas, CWS	364
T Glaus, Ana	340
J Dye, KC	337

Runs Scored

J Damon, KC	**136**
A Rodriguez, Sea	134
R Durham, CWS	121
D Erstad, Ana	121
T Glaus, Ana	120

Runs Batted In

E Martinez, Sea	**145**
M Sweeney, KC	144
F Thomas, CWS	143
C Delgado, Tor	137
J Giambi, Oak	137

GDP

B Grieve, Oak	**32**
M Ordonez, CWS	28
R Coomer, Min	25
D Cruz, Det	25
P Konerko, CWS	22

Sacrifice Hits

A Gonzalez, Tor	**16**
C Febles, KC	13
J Valentin, CWS	13
3 tied with	12

Sacrifice Flies

M Ordonez, CWS	**15**
M Sweeney, KC	13
J Damon, KC	12
P O'Neill, NYY	11
A Rodriguez, Sea	11

Stolen Bases

J Damon, KC	**46**
R Alomar, Cle	39
D DeShields, Bal	37
R Henderson, Sea	31
2 tied with	30

Caught Stealing

M McLemore, Sea	**14**
R Durham, CWS	13
G Williams, TB	12
T Glaus, Ana	11
3 tied with	10

Walks

J Giambi, Oak	**137**
C Delgado, Tor	123
J Thome, Cle	118
T Glaus, Ana	112
F Thomas, CWS	112

Intentional Walks

N Garciaparra, Bos	**20**
C Delgado, Tor	18
F Thomas, CWS	18
R Palmeiro, Tex	17
4 tied with	11

Hit by Pitch

C Delgado, Tor	**15**
M Sweeney, KC	**15**
M Vaughn, Ana	14
J Guillen, TB	13
D Jeter, NYY	12

Strikeouts

M Vaughn, Ana	**181**
J Thome, Cle	171
T Glaus, Ana	163
J Posada, NYY	151
D Palmer, Det	146

2000 National League Batting Leaders

Batting Average
minimum 502 PA

Player, Team	AB	H	AVG
T Helton, Col	**580**	**216**	**.372**
M Alou, Hou	454	161	.355
V Guerrero, Mon	571	197	.345
J Hammonds, Col	454	152	.335
L Castillo, Fla	539	180	.334
J Kent, SF	587	196	.334
J Vidro, Mon	606	200	.330
J Cirillo, Col	598	195	.326
G Sheffield, LA	501	163	.325
M Piazza, NYM	482	156	.324

On-Base Percentage
minimum 502 PA

Player, Team	PA*	OB	OBP
T Helton, Col	**697**	**323**	**.463**
B Bonds, SF	607	267	.440
G Sheffield, LA	612	268	.438
B Giles, Pit	688	297	.432
E Alfonzo, NYM	650	276	.425
J Kent, SF	695	295	.424
J Bagwell, Hou	719	305	.424
L Castillo, Fla	617	258	.418
B Abreu, Phi	680	283	.416
M Alou, Hou	517	215	.416

* AB + BB + HBP + SF

Slugging Percentage
minimum 502 PA

Player, Team	AB	TB	SLG
T Helton, Col	**580**	**405**	**.698**
B Bonds, SF	480	330	.688
V Guerrero, Mon	571	379	.664
G Sheffield, LA	501	322	.643
R Hidalgo, Hou	558	355	.636
S Sosa, ChC	604	383	.634
M Alou, Hou	454	283	.623
J Bagwell, Hou	590	363	.615
M Piazza, NYM	482	296	.614
J Kent, SF	587	350	.596

Games

L Gonzalez, Ari	**162**
S Green, LA	**162**
N Perez, Col	**162**
3 tied with	161

Plate Appearances

A Jones, Atl	**729**
L Gonzalez, Ari	722
J Bagwell, Hou	719
S Green, LA	714
S Sosa, ChC	705

At-Bats

A Jones, Atl	**656**
N Perez, Col	651
D Glanville, Phi	637
L Gonzalez, Ari	618
2 tied with	617

Hits

T Helton, Col	**216**
J Vidro, Mon	200
A Jones, Atl	199
V Guerrero, Mon	197
J Kent, SF	196

Singles

L Castillo, Fla	**158**
E Owens, SD	139
D Glanville, Phi	134
J Kendall, Pit	132
E Young, ChC	132

Doubles

T Helton, Col	**59**
J Cirillo, Col	53
J Vidro, Mon	51
L Gonzalez, Ari	47
S Green, LA	44

Triples

T Womack, Ari	**14**
V Guerrero, Mon	11
N Perez, Col	11
B Abreu, Phi	10
2 tied with	9

Home Runs

S Sosa, ChC	**50**
B Bonds, SF	49
J Bagwell, Hou	47
V Guerrero, Mon	44
R Hidalgo, Hou	44

Total Bases

T Helton, Col	**405**
S Sosa, ChC	383
V Guerrero, Mon	379
J Bagwell, Hou	363
2 tied with	355

Runs Scored

J Bagwell, Hou	**152**
T Helton, Col	138
B Bonds, SF	129
J Edmonds, StL	129
A Jones, Atl	122

Runs Batted In

T Helton, Col	**147**
S Sosa, ChC	138
J Bagwell, Hou	132
J Kent, SF	125
2 tied with	123

GDP

M Alou, Hou	**21**
J Lopez, Atl	20
J Snow, SF	20
3 tied with	19

Sacrifice Hits

R Gutierrez, ChC	**16**
5 tied with	14

Sacrifice Flies

J Snow, SF	**14**
J Cirillo, Col	12
L Gonzalez, Ari	12
E Karros, LA	12
2 tied with	11

Stolen Bases

L Castillo, Fla	**62**
T Goodwin, Col-LA	55
E Young, ChC	54
T Womack, Ari	45
R Furcal, Atl	40

Caught Stealing

L Castillo, Fla	**22**
R Furcal, Atl	14
E Owens, SD	14
P Wilson, Fla	14
2 tied with	13

Walks

B Bonds, SF	**117**
B Giles, Pit	114
J Bagwell, Hou	107
J Edmonds, StL	103
T Helton, Col	103

Intentional Walks

V Guerrero, Mon	**23**
B Bonds, SF	22
T Helton, Col	22
S Sosa, ChC	19
K Griffey Jr., Cin	17

Hit by Pitch

F Vina, StL	**28**
R Hidalgo, Hou	21
A Galarraga, Atl	17
C Biggio, Hou	16
3 tied with	15

Strikeouts

P Wilson, Fla	**187**
S Sosa, ChC	168
J Edmonds, StL	167
R Lankford, StL	148
P Burrell, Phi	139

2000 American League Pitching Leaders

Earned Run Average
minimum 162 IP

Pitcher, Team	IP	ER	ERA
P Martinez, Bos	**217.0**	**42**	**1.74**
R Clemens, NYY	204.1	84	3.70
M Mussina, Bal	237.2	100	3.79
M Sirotka, CWS	197.0	83	3.79
B Colon, Cle	188.0	81	3.88
D Wells, Tor	229.2	105	4.11
G Heredia, Oak	198.2	91	4.12
A Lopez, TB	185.1	85	4.13
T Hudson, Oak	202.1	93	4.14
C Finley, Cle	218.0	101	4.17

Won-Lost Percentage
minimum 15 decisions

Pitcher, Team	W	L	Pct
T Hudson, Oak	**20**	**6**	**.769**
P Martinez, Bos	18	6	.750
D Burba, Cle	16	6	.727
D Wells, Tor	20	8	.714
J Parque, CWS	13	6	.684
A Pettitte, NYY	19	9	.679
J Mercedes, Bal	14	7	.667
J Baldwin, CWS	14	7	.667
F Castillo, Tor	10	5	.667
B Colon, Cle	15	8	.652

Opposition AVG
minimum 162 IP

Pitcher, Team	AB	H	AVG
P Martinez, Bos	**768**	**128**	**.167**
T Hudson, Oak	746	169	.227
B Colon, Cle	700	163	.233
R Clemens, NYY	781	184	.236
P Abbott, Sea	676	164	.243
O Hernandez, NYY	754	186	.247
R Helling, Tex	842	212	.252
M Mussina, Bal	924	236	.255
C Finley, Cle	824	211	.256
S Ponson, Bal	863	223	.258

Games

K Wunsch, CWS	**83**
M Venafro, Tex	77
B Wells, Min	76
M Trombley, Bal	75
D Lowe, Bos	74

Games Started

R Helling, Tex	**35**
D Wells, Tor	**35**
6 tied with	34

Complete Games

D Wells, Tor	**9**
P Martinez, Bos	7
M Mussina, Bal	6
S Ponson, Bal	6
2 tied with	4

Games Finished

D Lowe, Bos	**64**
B Koch, Tor	62
M Rivera, NYY	61
T Jones, Det	60
3 tied with	58

Wins

T Hudson, Oak	**20**
D Wells, Tor	20
A Pettitte, NYY	19
P Martinez, Bos	18
A Sele, Sea	17

Losses

B Radke, Min	**16**
5 tied with	15

Saves

T Jones, Det	**42**
D Lowe, Bos	**42**
K Sasaki, Sea	37
M Rivera, NYY	36
2 tied with	34

Shutouts

P Martinez, Bos	**4**
T Hudson, Oak	2
A Sele, Sea	2
26 tied with	1

Hits Allowed

D Wells, Tor	**266**
B Radke, Min	261
K Rogers, Tex	257
J Suppan, KC	240
M Mussina, Bal	236

Doubles Allowed

R Helling, Tex	**66**
K Rogers, Tex	60
B Radke, Min	58
D Wells, Tor	56
P Rapp, Bal	54

Triples Allowed

B Radke, Min	**9**
J Mercedes, Bal	8
P Rapp, Bal	8
3 tied with	7

Home Runs Allowed

J Suppan, KC	**36**
E Milton, Min	35
J Baldwin, CWS	34
O Hernandez, NYY	34
2 tied with	31

Batters Faced

K Rogers, Tex	**998**
M Mussina, Bal	987
B Radke, Min	978
D Wells, Tor	972
R Helling, Tex	963

Innings Pitched

M Mussina, Bal	**237.2**
D Wells, Tor	229.2
K Rogers, Tex	227.1
B Radke, Min	226.2
S Ponson, Bal	222.0

Runs Allowed

C Carpenter, Tor	**130**
K Rogers, Tex	126
S Ponson, Bal	125
P Rapp, Bal	125
D Cone, NYY	124

Strikeouts

P Martinez, Bos	**284**
B Colon, Cle	212
M Mussina, Bal	210
C Finley, Cle	189
R Clemens, NYY	188

Walks Allowed

K Appier, Oak	**102**
C Finley, Cle	101
R Helling, Tex	99
B Colon, Cle	98
M Suzuki, KC	94

Hit Batsmen

J Weaver, Det	**15**
P Martinez, Bos	14
E Loaiza, Tex-Tor	13
3 tied with	11

Wild Pitches

D Reichert, KC	**18**
J Grimsley, NYY	16
H Nomo, Det	16
H Carrasco, Min-Bos	14
3 tied with	11

Balks

J Parque, CWS	**5**
R Ortiz, Ana	4
A Pettitte, NYY	3
S Schoeneweis, Ana	3
J Zimmerman, Tex	3

2000 National League Pitching Leaders

Earned Run Average
minimum 162 IP

Pitcher, Team	IP	ER	ERA
K Brown, LA	**230.0**	**66**	**2.58**
R Johnson, Ari	248.2	73	2.64
J D'Amico, Mil	162.1	48	2.66
G Maddux, Atl	249.1	83	3.00
M Hampton, NYM	217.2	76	3.14
A Leiter, NYM	208.0	74	3.20
C Park, LA	226.0	82	3.27
T Glavine, Atl	241.0	91	3.40
R Ankiel, StL	175.0	68	3.50
R Person, Phi	173.1	70	3.63

Won-Lost Percentage
minimum 15 decisions

Pitcher, Team	W	L	Pct
R Johnson, Ari	**19**	**7**	**.731**
S Estes, SF	15	6	.714
S Elarton, Hou	17	7	.708
T Glavine, Atl	21	9	.700
D Kile, StL	20	9	.690
R Reed, NYM	11	5	.688
J Tavarez, Col	11	5	.688
E Dessens, Cin	11	5	.688
K Brown, LA	13	6	.684
G Maddux, Atl	19	9	.679

Opposition AVG
minimum 162 IP

Pitcher, Team	AB	H	AVG
K Brown, LA	**848**	**181**	**.213**
C Park, LA	809	173	.214
R Ankiel, StL	625	137	.219
R Johnson, Ari	900	202	.224
A Leiter, NYM	771	176	.228
R Person, Phi	629	144	.229
G Maddux, Atl	947	225	.238
J D'Amico, Mil	602	143	.238
D Dreifort, LA	734	175	.238
W Williams, SD	636	152	.239

Games

S Kline, Mon	**83**
S Sullivan, Cin	79
M Myers, Col	78
T Wendell, NYM	77
2 tied with	76

Games Started

T Glavine, Atl	**35**
R Johnson, Ari	**35**
J Lieber, ChC	**35**
G Maddux, Atl	**35**
K Millwood, Atl	**35**

Complete Games

R Johnson, Ari	**8**
C Schilling, Phi-Ari	**8**
J Lieber, ChC	6
G Maddux, Atl	6
3 tied with	5

Games Finished

A Benitez, NYM	**68**
R Nen, SF	63
M Williams, Pit	63
A Alfonseca, Fla	62
D Veres, StL	61

Wins

T Glavine, Atl	**21**
D Kile, StL	20
R Johnson, Ari	19
G Maddux, Atl	19
C Park, LA	18

Losses

O Daal, Ari-Phi	**19**
M Clement, SD	17
S Parris, Cin	17
C Holt, Hou	16
J Lima, Hou	16

Saves

A Alfonseca, Fla	**45**
T Hoffman, SD	43
A Benitez, NYM	41
R Nen, SF	41
D Graves, Cin	30

Shutouts

R Johnson, Ari	**3**
G Maddux, Atl	**3**
6 tied with	2

Hits Allowed

L Hernandez, SF	**254**
J Lima, Hou	251
J Lieber, ChC	248
C Holt, Hou	247
J Vazquez, Mon	247

Doubles Allowed

S Parris, Cin	**57**
R Wolf, Phi	55
D Hermanson, Mon	53
G Stephenson, StL	53
J Lima, Hou	52

Triples Allowed

C Holt, Hou	**9**
J Lima, Hou	8
5 tied with	7

Home Runs Allowed

J Lima, Hou	**48**
B Anderson, Ari	38
J Lieber, ChC	36
K Tapani, ChC	35
D Kile, StL	33

Batters Faced

J Lieber, ChC	**1047**
L Hernandez, SF	1030
G Maddux, Atl	1012
R Johnson, Ari	1001
T Glavine, Atl	992

Innings Pitched

J Lieber, ChC	**251.0**
G Maddux, Atl	249.1
R Johnson, Ari	248.2
T Glavine, Atl	241.0
L Hernandez, SF	240.0

Runs Allowed

J Lima, Hou	**152**
M Clement, SD	131
C Holt, Hou	131
J Lieber, ChC	130
3 tied with	128

Strikeouts

R Johnson, Ari	**347**
C Park, LA	217
K Brown, LA	216
R Dempster, Fla	209
A Leiter, NYM	200

Walks Allowed

M Clement, SD	**125**
C Park, LA	124
R Ortiz, SF	112
S Estes, SF	108
J Haynes, Mil	100

Hit Batsmen

J Wright, Mil	**18**
M Clement, SD	16
P Astacio, Col	15
D Kile, StL	13
3 tied with	12

Wild Pitches

M Clement, SD	**23**
S Williamson, Cin	21
D Dreifort, LA	17
C Park, LA	13
R Ankiel, StL	12

Balks

R Cornelius, Fla	**5**
B Anderson, Ari	4
D Dreifort, LA	3
18 tied with	2

2000 American League Special Batting Leaders

Scoring Position AVG
minimum 100 PA

Player, Team	AB	H	AVG
M Sweeney, KC	**205**	**79**	**.385**
C Delgado, Tor	172	66	.384
F Thomas, CWS	159	60	.377
N Garciaparra, Bos	131	49	.374
T Long, Oak	111	41	.369
J Giambi, Oak	118	42	.356
M Ramirez, Cle	147	52	.354
J Randa, KC	176	61	.347
D DeShields, Bal	130	45	.346
D Erstad, Ana	136	47	.346

Leadoff Hitters OBP
minimum 150 PA

Player, Team	PA*	OB	OBP
D Erstad, Ana	**744**	**304**	**.409**
T Nixon, Bos	166	66	.398
R Becker, Oak-Det	179	71	.397
J Damon, KC	732	279	.381
B Anderson, Bal	609	228	.374
D Easley, Det	212	79	.373
C Knoblauch, NYY	455	167	.367
S Stewart, Tor	630	229	.363
L Alicea, Tex	501	182	.363
R Henderson, Sea	392	142	.362

* AB + BB + HBP + SF

Cleanup Hitters SLG
minimum 150 PA

Player, Team	AB	TB	SLG
M Ramirez, Cle	**439**	**306**	**.697**
C Delgado, Tor	569	378	.664
N Garciaparra, Bos	438	267	.610
B Williams, NYY	458	270	.590
J Dye, KC	600	336	.560
B Grieve, Oak	233	129	.554
E Martinez, Sea	387	214	.553
R Palmeiro, Tex	367	201	.548
M Ordonez, CWS	587	321	.547
T Salmon, Ana	517	279	.540

Avg vs LHP
minimum 125 PA

D Jeter, NYY	**.395**
N Garciaparra, Bos	.383
M Sweeney, KC	.374
T Glaus, Ana	.369
J Damon, KC	.357

Avg vs RHP
minimum 377 PA

N Garciaparra, Bos	**.369**
D Erstad, Ana	.363
C Delgado, Tor	.357
D Segui, Tex-Cle	.344
M Ramirez, Cle	.339

AVG at Home
minimum 251 PA

D Erstad, Ana	**.388**
N Garciaparra, Bos	.375
J Damon, KC	.361
C Delgado, Tor	.360
M Ramirez, Cle	.357

AVG on the Road
minimum 251 PA

N Garciaparra, Bos	**.370**
M Sweeney, KC	.359
A Rodriguez, Sea	.356
S Stewart, Tor	.349
M Ramirez, Cle	.345

OBP vs LHP
minimum 125 PA

T Glaus, Ana	**.500**
D Jeter, NYY	.461
N Garciaparra, Bos	.457
M Sweeney, KC	.443
J Giambi, Oak	.427

OBP vs RHP
minimum 377 PA

J Giambi, Oak	**.499**
C Delgado, Tor	.492
M Ramirez, Cle	.437
N Garciaparra, Bos	.425
M Lawton, Min	.424

Late & Close
minimum 50 PA

M Ramirez, Cle	**.444**
M Bordick, Bal	.404
G Zaun, KC	.400
J Randa, KC	.391
M Lawton, Min	.376

Bases Loaded
minimum 10 PA

B Williams, NYY	**.692**
J Damon, KC	.667
J Giambi, Oak	.636
A Belle, Bal	.625
F McGriff, TB	.615

SLG vs LHP
minimum 125 PA

T Glaus, Ana	**.854**
D Justice, Cle-NYY	.716
G Anderson, Ana	.661
A Belle, Bal	.650
N Garciaparra, Bos	.596

SLG vs RHP
minimum 377 PA

C Delgado, Tor	**.727**
J Giambi, Oak	.719
M Ramirez, Cle	.684
C Everett, Bos	.613
N Garciaparra, Bos	.601

AB per HR
minimum 502 PA

M Ramirez, Cle	**11.6**
J Giambi, Oak	11.9
T Glaus, Ana	12.0
D Justice, Cle-NYY	12.8
A Rodriguez, Sea	13.5

Times on Base

C Delgado, Tor	**334**
J Giambi, Oak	316
F Thomas, CWS	308
D Erstad, Ana	305
M Sweeney, KC	292

Pitches Seen

C Delgado, Tor	**2938**
J Thome, Cle	2869
T Glaus, Ana	2843
A Rodriguez, Sea	2842
F Thomas, CWS	2806

Pitches per PA
minimum 502 PA

M Ramirez, Cle	**4.27**
A Rodriguez, Sea	4.23
J Thome, Cle	4.19
T Glaus, Ana	4.19
M Cameron, Sea	4.16

% Pitches Taken
minimum 1500 pitches

R Becker, Oak-Det	**66.6**
M McLemore, Sea	64.6
J Giambi, Oak	64.5
R Henderson, Sea	64.4
E Martinez, Sea	64.0

Ground/Fly Ratio
minimum 502 PA

R Sanchez, KC	**3.35**
D Jeter, NYY	2.10
J Jones, Min	2.07
C Guzman, Min	1.99
B Williams, NYY	1.83

GDP/GDP Opp
minimum 50 PA

R Becker, Oak-Det	**0.02**
C Everett, Bos	0.03
D Hocking, Min	0.03
B Higginson, Det	0.03
B Anderson, Bal	0.04

SB Success %
minimum 20 SB attempts

R Alomar, Cle	**90.7**
J Valentin, CWS	90.5
D Jeter, NYY	84.6
J Damon, KC	83.6
M Ordonez, CWS	81.8

Steals of Third

R Alomar, Cle	**12**
O Vizquel, Cle	7
D DeShields, Bal	6
J Damon, KC	5
R Henderson, Sea	5

% CS by Catchers
minimum 70 SB attempts

B Ausmus, Det	**43.2**
B Molina, Ana	32.7
J Posada, NYY	30.0
C Johnson, Bal-CWS	27.0
J Flaherty, TB	25.5

2000 National League Special Batting Leaders

Scoring Position AVG
minimum 100 PA

Player, Team	AB	H	AVG
T Helton, Col	**153**	**60**	**.392**
J Cirillo, Col	169	66	.391
M Meluskey, Hou	107	40	.374
S Casey, Cin	120	44	.367
T Hundley, LA	77	28	.364
B Mayne, Col	95	34	.358
G Sheffield, LA	126	45	.357
J Hammonds, Col	159	56	.352
R White, Mon-ChC	100	35	.350
J Vander Wal, Pit	109	38	.349

Leadoff Hitters OBP
minimum 150 PA

Player, Team	PA*	OB	OBP
L Castillo, Fla	**616**	**258**	**.419**
C Biggio, Hou	206	85	.413
Q Veras, Atl	324	131	.404
R Furcal, Atl	397	159	.400
C Stynes, Cin	230	92	.400
R Cedeno, Hou	178	69	.388
F Vina, StL	547	209	.382
J Lugo, Hou	221	83	.376
E Young, ChC	679	251	.370
A Brown, Pit	261	96	.368

* AB + BB + HBP + SF

Cleanup Hitters SLG
minimum 150 PA

Player, Team	AB	TB	SLG
T Helton, Col	**243**	**187**	**.770**
M McGwire, StL	199	153	.769
L Berkman, Hou	168	117	.696
S Sosa, ChC	207	142	.686
V Guerrero, Mon	570	379	.665
W Clark, StL	150	98	.653
M Piazza, NYM	446	266	.596
J Kent, SF	566	337	.595
K Caminiti, Hou	205	120	.585
B Giles, Pit	326	189	.580

Avg vs LHP
minimum 125 PA

C Jones, Atl	**.415**
J Cirillo, Col	.379
V Guerrero, Mon	.376
J Vidro, Mon	.373
J Bagwell, Hou	.366

Avg vs RHP
minimum 377 PA

T Helton, Col	**.387**
L Castillo, Fla	.350
M Alou, Hou	.350
B Bonds, SF	.340
B Abreu, Phi	.339

AVG at Home
minimum 251 PA

J Cirillo, Col	**.403**
J Hammonds, Col	.399
T Helton, Col	.391
L Castillo, Fla	.372
J Vidro, Mon	.368

AVG on the Road
minimum 251 PA

M Piazza, NYM	**.377**
M Alou, Hou	.362
T Helton, Col	.353
V Guerrero, Mon	.353
P Nevin, SD	.348

OBP vs LHP
minimum 125 PA

J Bagwell, Hou	**.496**
C Jones, Atl	.480
S Sosa, ChC	.461
J Kent, SF	.459
T Helton, Col	.451

OBP vs RHP
minimum 377 PA

B Bonds, SF	**.487**
T Helton, Col	.467
B Giles, Pit	.446
B Abreu, Phi	.445
G Sheffield, LA	.442

Late & Close
minimum 50 PA

T Helton, Col	**.393**
S Rolen, Phi	.384
L Lopez, Mil	.381
D Lee, Fla	.366
A Galarraga, Atl	.365

Bases Loaded
minimum 10 PA

P Burrell, Phi	**.727**
J Cirillo, Col	.667
M Meluskey, Hou	.625
L Stevens, Mon	.625
C Hernandez, SD-StL	.625

SLG vs LHP
minimum 125 PA

C Jones, Atl	**.777**
V Guerrero, Mon	.744
J Bagwell, Hou	.688
P Nevin, SD	.685
J Vidro, Mon	.602

SLG vs RHP
minimum 377 PA

B Bonds, SF	**.759**
T Helton, Col	.732
G Sheffield, LA	.685
B Giles, Pit	.648
R Hidalgo, Hou	.646

AB per HR
minimum 502 PA

B Bonds, SF	**9.8**
G Sheffield, LA	11.7
S Sosa, ChC	12.1
J Edmonds, StL	12.5
J Bagwell, Hou	12.6

Times on Base

T Helton, Col	**323**
J Bagwell, Hou	305
B Giles, Pit	297
J Kent, SF	295
S Sosa, ChC	286

Pitches Seen

S Sosa, ChC	**2877**
B Abreu, Phi	2833
J Bagwell, Hou	2812
J Burnitz, Mil	2784
S Green, LA	2784

Pitches per PA
minimum 502 PA

L Castillo, Fla	**4.30**
J Edmonds, StL	4.29
T Zeile, NYM	4.22
B Abreu, Phi	4.17
J Bell, Ari	4.16

% Pitches Taken
minimum 1500 pitches

T Zeile, NYM	**65.8**
B Abreu, Phi	63.7
T Goodwin, Col-LA	62.5
M Grace, ChC	62.4
J Vander Wal, Pit	62.3

Ground/Fly Ratio
minimum 502 PA

L Castillo, Fla	**4.74**
E Owens, SD	2.82
R Furcal, Atl	2.24
P Bergeron, Mon	2.23
R Gutierrez, ChC	2.17

GDP/GDP Opp
minimum 50 PA

K Elster, LA	**0.00**
R Furcal, Atl	0.03
J Edmonds, StL	0.03
J Drew, StL	0.03
A Martin, SD	0.03

SB Success %
minimum 20 SB attempts

P Reese, Cin	**90.6**
C Floyd, Fla	88.9
E Young, ChC	88.5
B Hunter, Col-Cin	87.0
T Goodwin, Col-LA	84.6

Steals of Third

R Sanders, Atl	**9**
L Castillo, Fla	7
T Goodwin, Col-LA	7
D Jackson, SD	7
E Young, ChC	7

% CS by Catchers
minimum 70 SB attempts

M Matheny, StL	**51.1**
D Miller, Ari	30.6
C Hernandez, SD-StL	30.0
B Estalella, SF	29.7
J Girardi, ChC	28.4

2000 American League Special Pitching Leaders

Baserunners per 9 IP
minimum 162 IP

Player, Team	IP	BR	BR/9
P Martinez, Bos	**217.0**	**174**	**7.22**
M Mussina, Bal	237.2	285	10.79
O Hernandez, NYY	195.2	243	11.18
T Hudson, Oak	202.1	258	11.48
E Milton, Min	200.0	256	11.52
D Wells, Tor	229.2	305	11.95
J Weaver, Det	200.0	272	12.24
R Clemens, NYY	204.1	278	12.24
S Ponson, Bal	222.0	307	12.45
M Sirotka, CWS	197.0	273	12.47

Strikeouts per 9 IP
minimum 162 IP

Player, Team	IP	SO	SO/9
P Martinez, Bos	**217.0**	**284**	**11.78**
B Colon, Cle	188.0	212	10.15
H Nomo, Det	190.0	181	8.57
D Burba, Cle	191.1	180	8.47
R Clemens, NYY	204.1	188	8.28
M Mussina, Bal	237.2	210	7.95
C Finley, Cle	218.0	189	7.80
T Hudson, Oak	202.1	169	7.52
E Milton, Min	200.0	160	7.20
K Escobar, Tor	180.0	142	7.10

Run Support per 9 IP
minimum 162 IP

Player, Team	IP	R	R/9
A Pettitte, NYY	**204.2**	**173**	**7.61**
T Hudson, Oak	202.1	165	7.34
P Rapp, Bal	174.0	138	7.14
K Appier, Oak	195.1	154	7.10
J Parque, CWS	187.0	141	6.79
A Sele, Sea	211.2	156	6.63
J Halama, Sea	166.2	120	6.48
D Burba, Cle	191.1	137	6.44
J Baldwin, CWS	178.0	127	6.42
B Colon, Cle	188.0	132	6.32

Opposition OBP
minimum 162 IP

P Martinez, Bos	**.213**
M Mussina, Bal	.291
O Hernandez, NYY	.298
E Milton, Min	.303
T Hudson, Oak	.306

Opposition SLG
minimum 162 IP

P Martinez, Bos	**.259**
B Colon, Cle	.371
T Hudson, Oak	.374
R Clemens, NYY	.384
C Finley, Cle	.392

Hits per 9 IP
minimum 162 IP

P Martinez, Bos	**5.31**
T Hudson, Oak	7.52
B Colon, Cle	7.80
R Clemens, NYY	8.10
P Abbott, Sea	8.25

Home Runs per 9 IP
minimum 162 IP

P Martinez, Bos	**0.71**
A Sele, Sea	0.72
A Pettitte, NYY	0.75
K Rogers, Tex	0.79
D Burba, Cle	0.89

AVG vs LHB
minimum 125 BFP

P Martinez, Bos	**.150**
J Speier, Cle	.171
B Howry, CWS	.174
K Sasaki, Sea	.198
M Anderson, Det	.200

AVG vs RHB
minimum 225 BFP

P Martinez, Bos	**.184**
B Zito, Oak	.195
F Garcia, Sea	.205
O Hernandez, NYY	.210
J Washburn, Ana	.215

AVG Allowed ScPos
minimum 125 BFP

P Martinez, Bos	**.133**
F Castillo, Tor	.195
M Suzuki, KC	.197
A Levine, Ana	.200
B Colon, Cle	.205

OBP Lead Off Inning
minimum 150 BFP

J Moyer, Sea	**.225**
T Hudson, Oak	.241
P Martinez, Bos	.242
J Weaver, Det	.263
D Burba, Cle	.289

K/BB Ratio
minimum 162 IP

P Martinez, Bos	**8.88**
D Wells, Tor	5.35
M Mussina, Bal	4.57
E Milton, Min	3.64
B Radke, Min	2.76

Grd/Fly Ratio Off
minimum 162 IP

S Schoeneweis, Ana	**2.44**
T Hudson, Oak	2.02
C Finley, Cle	1.80
B Moehler, Det	1.79
A Lopez, TB	1.76

Pitches per Start
minimum 30 games started

R Helling, Tex	**108.3**
B Colon, Cle	108.0
M Mussina, Bal	107.6
A Pettitte, NYY	107.3
S Ponson, Bal	107.3

Pitches per Batter
minimum 162 IP

D Wells, Tor	**3.37**
S Schoeneweis, Ana	3.47
B Moehler, Det	3.49
G Heredia, Oak	3.50
J Halama, Sea	3.54

Steals Allowed

T Wakefield, Bos	**31**
M Suzuki, KC	27
T Hudson, Oak	24
D Burba, Cle	23
S Schoeneweis, Ana	20

Caught Stealing Off

H Nomo, Det	**14**
K Hill, Ana-CWS	12
J Weaver, Det	11
A Sele, Sea	10
3 tied with	9

SB% Allowed
minimum 162 IP

J Weaver, Det	**26.7**
J Halama, Sea	35.7
C Carpenter, Tor	36.4
B Rekar, TB	36.4
B Colon, Cle	42.9

Pickoffs

J Halama, Sea	**10**
K Rogers, Tex	9
4 tied with	5

PkOf Throw/Runner
minimum 162 IP

M Sirotka, CWS	**0.74**
G Heredia, Oak	0.74
S Trachsel, TB-Tor	0.71
K Rogers, Tex	0.68
R Clemens, NYY	0.66

GDP Induced

S Schoeneweis, Ana	**30**
A Lopez, TB	29
K Rogers, Tex	29
D Reichert, KC	28
M Sirotka, CWS	25

GDP per 9 IP
minimum 162 IP

S Schoeneweis, Ana	**1.6**
A Lopez, TB	1.4
J Halama, Sea	1.2
K Rogers, Tex	1.1
M Sirotka, CWS	1.1

Quality Starts

P Martinez, Bos	**25**
R Helling, Tex	22
R Clemens, NYY	21
M Mussina, Bal	21
M Sirotka, CWS	21

2000 National League Special Pitching Leaders

Baserunners per 9 IP
minimum 162 IP

Player, Team	IP	BR	BR/9
K Brown, LA	230.0	237	9.27
G Maddux, Atl	249.1	277	10.00
R Johnson, Ari	248.2	284	10.28
C Schilling, Phi-Ari	210.1	250	10.70
J D'Amico, Mil	162.1	195	10.81
T Glavine, Atl	241.0	291	10.87
D Kile, StL	232.1	286	11.08
J Lieber, ChC	251.0	312	11.19
W Williams, SD	168.0	209	11.20
R Reed, NYM	184.0	231	11.30

Strikeouts per 9 IP
minimum 162 IP

Player, Team	IP	SO	SO/9
R Johnson, Ari	248.2	347	12.56
R Ankiel, StL	175.0	194	9.98
P Astacio, Col	196.1	193	8.85
A Leiter, NYM	208.0	200	8.65
C Park, LA	226.0	217	8.64
R Person, Phi	173.1	164	8.52
K Brown, LA	230.0	216	8.45
R Dempster, Fla	226.1	209	8.31
J Vazquez, Mon	217.2	196	8.10
R Ortiz, SF	195.2	167	7.68

Run Support per 9 IP
minimum 162 IP

Player, Team	IP	R	R/9
S Estes, SF	190.1	183	8.65
A Benes, StL	166.0	132	7.16
S Elarton, Hou	192.2	152	7.10
G Stephenson, StL	200.1	153	6.87
D Dreifort, LA	192.2	139	6.49
R Ankiel, StL	175.0	124	6.38
P Astacio, Col	196.1	139	6.37
B Bohanon, Col	177.0	125	6.36
P Hentgen, StL	194.1	134	6.21
M Yoshii, Col	167.1	114	6.13

Opposition OBP
minimum 162 IP

K Brown, LA	.261
G Maddux, Atl	.276
R Johnson, Ari	.288
C Schilling, Phi-Ari	.294
T Glavine, Atl	.296

Opposition SLG
minimum 162 IP

M Hampton, NYM	.325
K Brown, LA	.337
G Maddux, Atl	.338
C Park, LA	.344
J Wright, Mil	.354

Hits per 9 IP
minimum 162 IP

C Park, LA	6.89
R Ankiel, StL	7.05
K Brown, LA	7.08
R Johnson, Ari	7.31
R Person, Phi	7.48

Home Runs per 9 IP
minimum 162 IP

M Hampton, NYM	0.41
S Estes, SF	0.52
J Wright, Mil	0.66
R Person, Phi	0.68
G Maddux, Atl	0.69

AVG vs LHB
minimum 125 BFP

A Leiter, NYM	.119
A Benitez, NYM	.133
F Rodriguez, SF	.158
R Person, Phi	.178
R Nen, SF	.193

AVG vs RHB
minimum 225 BFP

C Park, LA	.200
K Brown, LA	.201
S Williamson, Cin	.204
R Ankiel, StL	.213
2 tied with	.214

AVG Allowed ScPos
minimum 125 BFP

C Park, LA	.159
S Williamson, Cin	.163
R Person, Phi	.190
K Brown, LA	.191
D Dreifort, LA	.194

OBP Lead Off Inning
minimum 150 BFP

G Maddux, Atl	.248
J D'Amico, Mil	.261
K Millwood, Atl	.261
W Williams, SD	.264
B Anderson, Ari	.267

K/BB Ratio
minimum 162 IP

K Brown, LA	4.60
R Johnson, Ari	4.57
G Maddux, Atl	4.52
C Schilling, Phi-Ari	3.73
G Rusch, NYM	3.57

Grd/Fly Ratio Off
minimum 162 IP

G Maddux, Atl	2.66
M Hampton, NYM	2.51
J Wright, Mil	2.15
K Brown, LA	2.11
S Estes, SF	2.06

Pitches per Start
minimum 30 games started

L Hernandez, SF	115.9
R Johnson, Ari	115.0
A Leiter, NYM	112.2
R Wolf, Phi	110.3
R Dempster, Fla	109.1

Pitches per Batter
minimum 162 IP

G Maddux, Atl	3.18
A Ashby, Phi-Atl	3.38
B Anderson, Ari	3.42
O Daal, Ari-Phi	3.48
J D'Amico, Mil	3.50

Steals Allowed

G Maddux, Atl	32
R Johnson, Ari	26
A Leiter, NYM	22
3 tied with	21

Caught Stealing Off

P Hentgen, StL	16
R Johnson, Ari	16
A Leiter, NYM	13
D Kile, StL	11
3 tied with	10

SB% Allowed
minimum 162 IP

D Kile, StL	15.4
K Rueter, SF	16.7
C Schilling, Phi-Ari	25.0
C Park, LA	27.3
J D'Amico, Mil	27.3

Pickoffs

B Anderson, Ari	10
A Leiter, NYM	10
C Perez, LA	9
4 tied with	6

PkOf Throw/Runner
minimum 162 IP

A Reynoso, Ari	1.09
A Leiter, NYM	0.91
B Jones, NYM	0.87
K Brown, LA	0.80
K Millwood, Atl	0.70

GDP Induced

S Estes, SF	40
C Holt, Hou	31
J Haynes, Mil	29
M Hampton, NYM	26
2 tied with	25

GDP per 9 IP
minimum 162 IP

S Estes, SF	1.9
J Wright, Mil	1.4
C Holt, Hou	1.3
J Haynes, Mil	1.3
B Bohanon, Col	1.1

Quality Starts

K Brown, LA	26
T Glavine, Atl	26
R Johnson, Ari	25
G Maddux, Atl	25
J Vazquez, Mon	24

2000 American League Relief Pitching Leaders

Saves

Player, Team	Saves
T Jones, Det	42
D Lowe, Bos	42
K Sasaki, Sea	37
M Rivera, NYY	36
K Foulke, CWS	34
J Wetteland, Tex	34
J Isringhausen, Oak	33
B Koch, Tor	33
R Hernandez, TB	32
T Percival, Ana	32

Save Percentage
minimum 20 SvOp

Player, Team	Sv	Op	Pct
K Sasaki, Sea	37	40	92.5
T Jones, Det	42	46	91.3
D Lowe, Bos	42	47	89.4
M Rivera, NYY	36	41	87.8
K Foulke, CWS	34	39	87.2
B Koch, Tor	33	38	86.8
J Isringhausen, Oak	33	40	82.5
R Hernandez, TB	32	40	80.0
J Wetteland, Tex	34	43	79.1
T Percival, Ana	32	42	76.2

Relief ERA
minimum 50 relief IP

Player, Team	IP	ER	ERA
M Fyhrie, Ana	52.2	14	2.39
J Nelson, NYY	69.2	19	2.45
D Lowe, Bos	91.1	26	2.56
J Tam, Oak	85.2	25	2.63
B Koch, Tor	78.2	23	2.63
M Rivera, NYY	75.2	24	2.85
K Wunsch, CWS	61.1	20	2.93
J Mecir, TB-Oak	85.0	28	2.96
K Foulke, CWS	88.0	29	2.97
H Pichardo, Bos	61.0	21	3.10

Relief Wins

S Hasegawa, Ana	10
J Mecir, TB-Oak	10
R Bottalico, KC	9
B Koch, Tor	9
3 tied with	8

Relief Losses

S Karsay, Cle	9
A Rhodes, Sea	8
T Crabtree, Tex	7
R Hernandez, TB	7
B Wells, Min	7

Holds

P Shuey, Cle	28
B Groom, Bal	27
K Wunsch, CWS	25
A Rhodes, Sea	24
2 tied with	21

Blown Saves

T Percival, Ana	10
B Wells, Min	10
S Hasegawa, Ana	9
S Karsay, Cle	9
J Wetteland, Tex	9

Relief Games

K Wunsch, CWS	83
M Venafro, Tex	77
B Wells, Min	76
M Trombley, Bal	75
D Lowe, Bos	74

Games Finished

D Lowe, Bos	64
B Koch, Tor	62
M Rivera, NYY	61
T Jones, Det	60
3 tied with	58

Relief Innings

S Hasegawa, Ana	95.2
D Lowe, Bos	91.1
K Foulke, CWS	88.0
L Hawkins, Min	87.2
B Wells, Min	86.1

% Inherited Scored
minimum 30 inherited runnrs

R Ramsay, Sea	14.7
A Levine, Ana	16.1
S Reed, Cle	16.7
M Holtz, Ana	16.9
L Hawkins, Min	18.2

Opposition AVG
minimum 50 relief IP

J Nelson, NYY	.183
K Sasaki, Sea	.184
A Rhodes, Sea	.205
K Foulke, CWS	.207
M Rivera, NYY	.208

Opposition OBP
minimum 50 relief IP

K Foulke, CWS	.261
M Rivera, NYY	.271
B Wells, Min	.284
K Sasaki, Sea	.285
2 tied with	.286

Opposition SLG
minimum 50 relief IP

J Nelson, NYY	.253
H Pichardo, Bos	.290
J Mecir, TB-Oak	.293
M Rivera, NYY	.294
P Shuey, Cle	.313

1st Batter AVG
minimum 40 first BFP

J Nelson, NYY	.155
M Rivera, NYY	.177
A Levine, Ana	.179
F Cordero, Tex	.189
K Wunsch, CWS	.192

Avg vs. LHB
minimum 50 relief IP

K Wunsch, CWS	.160
D Creek, TB	.170
J Speier, Cle	.171
B Howry, CWS	.174
C Nitkowski, Det	.189

Avg vs. RHB
minimum 50 relief IP

J Nelson, NYY	.157
K Sasaki, Sea	.170
R White, TB	.172
K Foulke, CWS	.192
A Rhodes, Sea	.193

AVG Runners On
minimum 50 relief IP

K Sasaki, Sea	.168
J Nelson, NYY	.181
R White, TB	.182
A Levine, Ana	.201
J Mecir, TB-Oak	.206

AVG Allowed ScPos
minimum 50 relief IP

R White, TB	.138
M Trombley, Bal	.172
J Nelson, NYY	.173
K Sasaki, Sea	.173
A Levine, Ana	.175

Easy Saves

T Jones, Det	27
J Isringhausen, Oak	21
D Lowe, Bos	20
R Hernandez, TB	19
2 tied with	16

Regular Saves

D Lowe, Bos	20
K Foulke, CWS	19
B Koch, Tor	18
J Wetteland, Tex	18
2 tied with	17

Tough Saves

K Foulke, CWS	6
T Jones, Det	4
M Rivera, NYY	3
J Spradlin, KC	3
7 tied with	2

Pitches per Batter
minimum 50 relief IP

D Patterson, Det	3.31
J Frascatore, Tor	3.40
J Grimsley, NYY	3.44
W Blair, Det	3.48
R Cormier, Bos	3.49

2000 National League Relief Pitching Leaders

Saves

Player, Team	Saves
A Alfonseca, Fla	45
T Hoffman, SD	43
A Benitez, NYM	41
R Nen, SF	41
D Graves, Cin	30
R Aguilera, ChC	29
D Veres, StL	29
J Shaw, LA	27
3 tied with	24

Save Percentage
minimum 20 SvOp

Player, Team	Sv	Op	Pct
A Alfonseca, Fla	45	49	91.8
R Nen, SF	41	46	89.1
A Benitez, NYM	41	46	89.1
J Rocker, Atl	24	27	88.9
T Hoffman, SD	43	50	86.0
D Graves, Cin	30	35	85.7
M Mantei, Ari	17	20	85.0
M Williams, Pit	24	29	82.8
J Brantley, Phi	23	28	82.1
D Veres, StL	29	36	80.6

Relief ERA
minimum 50 relief IP

Player, Team	IP	ER	ERA
R Nen, SF	66.0	11	1.50
G White, Cin-Col	84.0	22	2.36
T Worrell, ChC	62.0	17	2.47
C Leskanic, Mil	77.1	22	2.56
D Graves, Cin	91.1	26	2.56
M Herges, LA	87.2	25	2.57
A Benitez, NYM	76.0	22	2.61
F Rodriguez, SF	81.2	24	2.64
D Veres, StL	75.2	24	2.85
J Rocker, Atl	53.0	17	2.89

Relief Wins

M Herges, LA	11
G White, Cin-Col	11
D Graves, Cin	10
C Leskanic, Mil	9
T Wendell, NYM	8

Relief Losses

T Adams, LA	9
J Christiansen, Pit-StL	8
5 tied with	7

Holds

F Rodriguez, SF	30
M Remlinger, Atl	23
J Christiansen, Pit-StL	22
S Sullivan, Cin	22
J Franco, NYM	20

Blown Saves

B Wagner, Hou	9
R Aguilera, ChC	8
4 tied with	7

Relief Games

S Kline, Mon	83
S Sullivan, Cin	79
M Myers, Col	78
T Wendell, NYM	77
2 tied with	76

Games Finished

A Benitez, NYM	68
R Nen, SF	63
M Williams, Pit	63
A Alfonseca, Fla	62
D Veres, StL	61

Relief Innings

S Sullivan, Cin	106.1
D Graves, Cin	91.1
M Herges, LA	87.2
T Adams, LA	84.1
G White, Cin-Col	84.0

% Inherited Scored
minimum 30 inherited runnrs

C Leskanic, Mil	9.7
M Myers, Col	14.1
T Wendell, NYM	15.0
V Darensbourg, Fla	15.9
J Christiansen, Pit-StL	21.6

Opposition AVG
minimum 50 relief IP

A Benitez, NYM	.148
R Nen, SF	.162
D Wall, SD	.193
B Kim, Ari	.193
M Fetters, LA	.205

Opposition OBP
minimum 50 relief IP

R Nen, SF	.230
T Hoffman, SD	.250
G White, Cin-Col	.251
A Benitez, NYM	.255
D Wall, SD	.274

Opposition SLG
minimum 50 relief IP

R Nen, SF	.241
K Walker, SD	.294
A Benitez, NYM	.304
D Wall, SD	.305
J Rocker, Atl	.310

1st Batter AVG
minimum 40 first BFP

K Walker, SD	.119
T Wendell, NYM	.119
D Wall, SD	.128
R Nen, SF	.133
A Benitez, NYM	.143

Avg vs. LHB
minimum 50 relief IP

A Benitez, NYM	.133
F Rodriguez, SF	.158
G Swindell, Ari	.159
M Fetters, LA	.189
V Darensbourg, Fla	.190

Avg vs. RHB
minimum 50 relief IP

R Nen, SF	.128
B Kim, Ari	.159
A Benitez, NYM	.161
K Walker, SD	.165
D Wall, SD	.177

AVG Runners On
minimum 50 relief IP

R Nen, SF	.138
A Benitez, NYM	.171
J Rocker, Atl	.175
C Leskanic, Mil	.182
M Fetters, LA	.187

AVG Allowed ScPos
minimum 50 relief IP

R Nen, SF	.091
C Leskanic, Mil	.115
J Rocker, Atl	.133
K Ligtenberg, Atl	.138
J Manzanillo, Pit	.164

Easy Saves

A Alfonseca, Fla	31
R Nen, SF	31
T Hoffman, SD	25
A Benitez, NYM	20
2 tied with	17

Regular Saves

A Benitez, NYM	18
T Hoffman, SD	16
D Graves, Cin	15
A Alfonseca, Fla	14
J Jimenez, Col	14

Tough Saves

D Veres, StL	8
O Dotel, Hou	5
D Graves, Cin	4
M Remlinger, Atl	4
3 tied with	3

Pitches per Batter
minimum 50 relief IP

F Lira, Mon	3.38
A Alfonseca, Fla	3.42
M DeJean, Col	3.46
V Padilla, Ari-Phi	3.49
J Jimenez, Col	3.52

2000 American League Bill James Leaders

Top Game Scores of the Year

Pitcher	Date	Opp	IP	H	R	ER	BB	K	SC
P Martinez, Bos	5/12	Bal	9.0	2	0	0	0	15	98
P Martinez, Bos	8/29	TB	9.0	1	0	0	0	13	98
M Mussina, Bal	8/1	Min	9.0	1	0	0	2	15	98
B Colon, Cle	9/18	NYY	9.0	1	0	0	1	13	97
T Hudson, Oak	8/28	CWS	9.0	1	0	0	1	8	92
P Martinez, Bos	7/23	CWS	9.0	6	0	0	0	15	90
P Martinez, Bos	6/8	Cle	8.0	1	0	0	1	10	89
S Trachsel, TB-Tor	5/6	Bos	9.0	3	0	0	3	11	89
J Baldwin, CWS	5/9	Bos	9.0	3	0	0	1	8	88
4 tied with									87

Worst Game Scores of the Year

Pitcher	Date	Opp	IP	H	R	ER	BB	K	SC
J Moyer, Sea	8/9	CWS	3.2	13	11	11	2	2	-9
K Hill, Ana-CWS	4/19	Tor	3.1	11	10	10	3	0	-5
B Moehler, Det	7/28	Tex	2.2	11	10	10	2	2	-4
M Mulder, Oak	8/10	NYY	3.1	11	10	10	3	1	-4
R Ortiz, Ana	9/3	CWS	0.2	8	9	9	2	0	-2
C Durbin, KC	5/11	Cle	1.1	9	9	9	1	2	1
J Johnson, Bal	8/15	CWS	5.0	11	12	10	4	4	1
C Carpenter, Tor	6/20	Det	2.0	7	9	9	4	0	2
O Hernandez, NYY	6/18	CWS	0.2	6	9	9	3	1	2
2 tied with									3

Runs Created

F Thomas, CWS	164
J Giambi, Oak	162
C Delgado, Tor	161
D Erstad, Ana	140
M Sweeney, KC	140
A Rodriguez, Sea	136
J Damon, KC	134
E Martinez, Sea	134
M Ramirez, Cle	129
B Higginson, Det	126

Runs Created per 27 Outs
minimum 502 PA

J Giambi, Oak	12.2
M Ramirez, Cle	11.6
C Delgado, Tor	11.1
F Thomas, CWS	10.6
N Garciaparra, Bos	9.4
E Martinez, Sea	9.0
A Rodriguez, Sea	9.0
M Sweeney, KC	8.5
D Erstad, Ana	8.2
B Higginson, Det	7.8

Offensive Win Percentage
minimum 502 PA

J Giambi, Oak	.840
M Ramirez, Cle	.826
C Delgado, Tor	.813
F Thomas, CWS	.800
N Garciaparra, Bos	.758
E Martinez, Sea	.745
A Rodriguez, Sea	.744
M Sweeney, KC	.719
D Erstad, Ana	.705
B Higginson, Det	.686

Secondary Average
minimum 502 PA

J Giambi, Oak	.586
M Ramirez, Cle	.542
C Delgado, Tor	.534
T Glaus, Ana	.524
A Rodriguez, Sea	.491
F Thomas, CWS	.486
J Thome, Cle	.476
R Palmeiro, Tex	.453
J Posada, NYY	.451
D Justice, Cle-NYY	.447

Isolated Power
minimum 502 PA

M Ramirez, Cle	.346
C Delgado, Tor	.320
T Glaus, Ana	.320
J Giambi, Oak	.314
D Justice, Cle-NYY	.298
F Thomas, CWS	.297
A Rodriguez, Sea	.291
C Everett, Bos	.286
R Palmeiro, Tex	.269
B Fullmer, Tor	.263

Power/Speed Number

D Erstad, Ana	26.4
R Alomar, Cle	25.6
J Damon, KC	23.7
M Ordonez, CWS	23.0
R Mondesi, Tor	23.0
A Rodriguez, Sea	22.0
J Valentin, CWS	21.6
T Glaus, Ana	21.6
M Cameron, Sea	21.2
S Stewart, Tor	20.5

Speed Scores
minimum 800 AB over last two years

C Guzman, Min	7.99
J Damon, KC	7.79
K Lofton, Cle	7.66
C Singleton, CWS	7.48
C Beltran, KC	7.16
R Durham, CWS	6.94
B Anderson, Bal	6.84
J Encarnacion, Det	6.80
D Erstad, Ana	6.65
S Stewart, Tor	6.55

Cheap Wins

J Halama, Sea	8
J Parque, CWS	8
K Appier, Oak	6
W Blair, Det	6
A Pettitte, NYY	6
D Burba, Cle	5
P Rapp, Bal	5
A Sele, Sea	5
5 tied with	4

Tough Losses

P Martinez, Bos	6
M Mussina, Bal	6
S Ponson, Bal	6
J Weaver, Det	6
P Rapp, Bal	5
M Sirotka, CWS	5
M Suzuki, KC	5
S Trachsel, TB-Tor	5
3 tied with	4

2000 National League Bill James Leaders

Top Game Scores of the Year

Pitcher	Date	Opp	IP	H	R	ER	BB	K	SC
C Park, LA	9/29	SD	9.0	2	0	0	1	13	95
R Villone, Cin	9/29	StL	9.0	2	1	0	5	16	92
K Brown, LA	9/23	SD	9.0	2	1	1	1	13	91
P Hentgen, StL	9/14	ChC	9.0	3	0	0	0	9	90
R Johnson, Ari	4/9	Pit	9.0	5	0	0	0	13	90
K Brown, LA	6/15	Ari	9.0	4	0	0	0	10	89
R Dempster, Fla	5/7	NYM	9.0	1	0	0	4	8	89
A Leiter, NYM	8/13	SF	8.0	2	0	0	1	12	89
5 tied with									87

Worst Game Scores of the Year

Pitcher	Date	Opp	IP	H	R	ER	BB	K	SC
J Nathan, SF	5/12	Col	2.2	9	12	10	4	3	-5
J Lima, Hou	4/27	ChC	5.0	13	12	12	3	6	-4
W Miller, Hou	8/23	ChC	4.2	12	12	8	2	0	-2
C Holt, Hou	4/16	SD	3.0	12	10	9	0	4	1
D Kile, StL	4/13	Col	1.2	8	11	8	1	1	1
A Reynoso, Ari	6/18	Col	2.0	10	9	9	0	1	1
B Arroyo, Pit	6/23	NYM	2.2	9	10	9	3	3	2
J Lieber, ChC	8/19	Ari	2.2	10	9	9	2	2	2
J Lima, Hou	5/2	ChC	4.2	13	10	9	3	5	2
J Silva, Pit	8/14	Hou	2.2	9	9	9	3	1	2

Runs Created

T Helton, Col	173
J Bagwell, Hou	143
S Sosa, ChC	138
J Kent, SF	136
V Guerrero, Mon	133
B Giles, Pit	132
L Gonzalez, Ari	132
G Sheffield, LA	132
E Alfonzo, NYM	129
B Bonds, SF	129

Runs Created per 27 Outs
minimum 502 PA

T Helton, Col	12.0
B Bonds, SF	9.9
G Sheffield, LA	9.8
E Alfonzo, NYM	8.9
V Guerrero, Mon	8.9
J Bagwell, Hou	8.8
B Giles, Pit	8.7
J Kent, SF	8.6
M Alou, Hou	8.6
S Sosa, ChC	8.5

Offensive Win Percentage
minimum 502 PA

T Helton, Col	.851
B Bonds, SF	.798
G Sheffield, LA	.792
E Alfonzo, NYM	.761
V Guerrero, Mon	.759
J Bagwell, Hou	.754
B Giles, Pit	.753
J Kent, SF	.746
M Alou, Hou	.746
S Sosa, ChC	.744

Secondary Average
minimum 502 PA

B Bonds, SF	.642
G Sheffield, LA	.515
T Helton, Col	.507
J Edmonds, StL	.497
B Giles, Pit	.494
J Bagwell, Hou	.492
S Sosa, ChC	.470
K Griffey Jr., Cin	.469
R Klesko, SD	.449
B Abreu, Phi	.446

Isolated Power
minimum 502 PA

B Bonds, SF	.381
T Helton, Col	.326
R Hidalgo, Hou	.323
V Guerrero, Mon	.319
G Sheffield, LA	.317
S Sosa, ChC	.315
J Bagwell, Hou	.305
M Piazza, NYM	.290
J Edmonds, StL	.288
G Jenkins, Mil	.285

Power/Speed Number

P Wilson, Fla	33.3
A Jones, Atl	26.5
B Abreu, Phi	26.4
R Klesko, SD	24.4
S Green, LA	24.0
C Floyd, Fla	23.0
C Jones, Atl	20.2
R Hidalgo, Hou	20.1
T Hollandsworth, LA-Col	18.5
E Renteria, StL	18.2

Speed Scores
minimum 800 AB over last two years

T Womack, Ari	8.95
D Glanville, Phi	7.56
P Reese, Cin	7.50
M Benard, SF	7.47
N Perez, Col	7.35
L Castillo, Fla	7.17
A Martin, SD	7.13
D Jackson, SD	7.04
E Young, ChC	7.02
B Abreu, Phi	6.93

Cheap Wins

T Glavine, Atl	6
J Haynes, Mil	6
E Dessens, Cin	5
G Stephenson, StL	5
7 tied with	4

Tough Losses

O Daal, Ari-Phi	7
M Clement, SD	5
M Yoshii, Col	5
C Holt, Hou	4
J Lima, Hou	4
G Maddux, Atl	4
G Rusch, NYM	4
C Smith, Fla	4
J Vazquez, Mon	4
W Williams, SD	4

2000 Active Career Batting Leaders

Batting Average
minimum 1000 PA

Player, Team	AB	H	AVG
1 Tony Gwynn	9186	3108	.338
2 Todd Helton	1781	594	.334
3 Nomar Garciaparra	2436	812	.333
4 Mike Piazza	4135	1356	.328
5 Vladimir Guerrero	2156	695	.322
6 Derek Jeter	3130	1008	.322
7 Frank Thomas	5474	1755	.321
8 Edgar Martinez	5432	1738	.320
9 Jason Kendall	2294	720	.314
10 Manny Ramirez	3470	1086	.313
11 Bobby Abreu	1829	572	.313
12 Sean Casey	1386	432	.312
13 Larry Walker	4906	1528	.311
14 Jeff Cirillo	3409	1059	.311
15 Alex Rodriguez	3126	966	.309
16 Mark Grace	7156	2201	.308
17 Rusty Greer	3385	1040	.307
18 Kenny Lofton	4922	1507	.306
19 Jeff Bagwell	5349	1630	.305
20 Bernie Williams	4806	1463	.304
21 Hal Morris	3998	1216	.304
22 Roberto Alomar	7221	2196	.304
23 Ivan Rodriguez	4806	1459	.304
24 Will Clark	7173	2176	.303
25 Chipper Jones	3469	1051	.303

On-Base Percentage
minimum 1000 PA

Player, Team	PA*	OB	OBP
1 Frank Thomas	6798	2989	.440
2 Edgar Martinez	6522	2776	.426
3 Jeff Bagwell	6516	2719	.417
4 Bobby Abreu	2161	893	.413
5 Barry Bonds	9137	3760	.412
6 Todd Helton	2048	842	.411
7 Brian Giles	2344	961	.410
8 Jim Thome	4465	1830	.410
9 Manny Ramirez	4093	1664	.407
10 John Olerud	6382	2581	.404
11 Rickey Henderson	12545	5064	.404
12 Jason Kendall	2675	1076	.402
13 Jason Giambi	3410	1362	.399
14 Mark McGwire	7293	2903	.398
15 Gary Sheffield	6151	2442	.397
16 Chipper Jones	4069	1610	.396
17 Derek Jeter	3542	1397	.394
18 Tim Salmon	4819	1900	.394
19 Dave Magadan	4797	1882	.392
20 Mike Piazza	4620	1811	.392
21 Rusty Greer	3917	1534	.392
22 Larry Walker	5622	2195	.390
23 Bernie Williams	5532	2151	.389
24 Tony Gwynn	10075	3912	.388
25 Mo Vaughn	5756	2227	.387

* AB + BB + HBP + SF

Slugging Percentage
minimum 1000 PA

Player, Team	AB	TB	SLG
1 Todd Helton	1781	1070	.601
2 Mark McGwire	5888	3492	.593
3 Vladimir Guerrero	2156	1277	.592
4 Manny Ramirez	3470	2053	.592
5 Mike Piazza	4135	2397	.580
6 Frank Thomas	5474	3168	.579
7 Nomar Garciaparra	2436	1397	.573
8 Ken Griffey Jr.	6352	3605	.568
9 Barry Bonds	7456	4228	.567
10 Juan Gonzalez	5292	2994	.566
11 Albert Belle	5853	3300	.564
12 Larry Walker	4906	2762	.563
13 Alex Rodriguez	3126	1753	.561
14 Carlos Delgado	2901	1616	.557
15 Jeff Bagwell	5349	2955	.552
16 Brian Giles	1937	1068	.551
17 Jim Thome	3634	1980	.545
18 Geoff Jenkins	1221	654	.536
19 Chipper Jones	3469	1858	.536
20 Mo Vaughn	4966	2646	.533
21 Richard Hidalgo	1214	646	.532
22 Edgar Martinez	5432	2874	.529
23 Tim Salmon	4051	2133	.527
24 Jason Giambi	2878	1508	.524
25 Ryan Klesko	2925	1532	.524

Hits

Tony Gwynn	3108
Cal Ripken Jr.	3070
Rickey Henderson	2914
Harold Baines	2855
Rafael Palmeiro	2321
Gary Gaetti	2280
Mark Grace	2201
Roberto Alomar	2196
Will Clark	2176
Barry Bonds	2157
Fred McGriff	2103
Andres Galarraga	2070
Wally Joyner	2024
Barry Larkin	2008
Bobby Bonilla	1973
Craig Biggio	1969
Paul O'Neill	1969
B.J. Surhoff	1895
Ken Griffey Jr.	1883
Jay Bell	1828

Home Runs

Mark McGwire	554
Barry Bonds	494
Jose Canseco	446
Ken Griffey Jr.	438
Fred McGriff	417
Cal Ripken Jr.	417
Rafael Palmeiro	400
Sammy Sosa	386
Harold Baines	384
Albert Belle	381
Juan Gonzalez	362
Gary Gaetti	360
Andres Galarraga	360
Matt Williams	346
Frank Thomas	344
Greg Vaughn	320
Jeff Bagwell	310
Jay Buhner	308
Mo Vaughn	299
Ron Gant	292

Runs Batted In

Cal Ripken Jr.	1627
Harold Baines	1622
Barry Bonds	1405
Jose Canseco	1358
Mark McGwire	1350
Rafael Palmeiro	1347
Gary Gaetti	1341
Fred McGriff	1298
Andres Galarraga	1272
Ken Griffey Jr.	1270
Albert Belle	1239
Will Clark	1205
Paul O'Neill	1199
Frank Thomas	1183
Bobby Bonilla	1152
Juan Gonzalez	1142
Tony Gwynn	1121
Matt Williams	1097
Jeff Bagwell	1093
2 tied with	1092

Stolen Bases

Rickey Henderson	1370
Barry Bonds	471
Kenny Lofton	463
Delino DeShields	430
Roberto Alomar	416
Marquis Grissom	402
Barry Larkin	359
Craig Biggio	358
Chuck Knoblauch	350
Eric Davis	348
Eric Young	346
Devon White	328
Lance Johnson	327
Luis Polonia	321
Tony Gwynn	318
Tom Goodwin	307
Brady Anderson	299
Omar Vizquel	260
Steve Finley	254
Ray Lankford	244

Seasons Played

Rickey Henderson	**22**
Harold Baines	21
Jesse Orosco	21
Gary Gaetti	20
Mike Morgan	20
Cal Ripken Jr.	20
Tony Gwynn	19
Orel Hershiser	18
3 tied with	17

Games

Cal Ripken Jr.	**2873**
Rickey Henderson	2856
Harold Baines	2798
Gary Gaetti	2507
Tony Gwynn	2369
Barry Bonds	2143
Rafael Palmeiro	2098
Fred McGriff	2055
Bobby Bonilla	2020
Ozzie Guillen	1993

At-Bats

Cal Ripken Jr.	**11074**
Rickey Henderson	10331
Harold Baines	9824
Tony Gwynn	9186
Gary Gaetti	8951
Rafael Palmeiro	7846
Barry Bonds	7456
Fred McGriff	7352
Roberto Alomar	7221
Will Clark	7173

Runs Scored

Rickey Henderson	**2178**
Cal Ripken Jr.	1604
Barry Bonds	1584
Tony Gwynn	1378
Harold Baines	1296
Rafael Palmeiro	1259
Roberto Alomar	1228
Craig Biggio	1187
Will Clark	1186
Fred McGriff	1176

Doubles

Cal Ripken Jr.	**587**
Tony Gwynn	534
Harold Baines	487
Rickey Henderson	486
Mark Grace	456
Rafael Palmeiro	455
Barry Bonds	451
Gary Gaetti	443
Will Clark	440
Paul O'Neill	418

Triples

Lance Johnson	**117**
Steve Finley	90
Tony Gwynn	84
Barry Larkin	70
Luis Polonia	70
Barry Bonds	69
Ozzie Guillen	69
Dave Martinez	69
Devon White	69
Delino DeShields	68

AB per HR
minimum 1000 AB

Mark McGwire	**10.6**
Ken Griffey Jr.	14.5
Juan Gonzalez	14.6
Manny Ramirez	14.7
Mike Piazza	14.9
Barry Bonds	15.1
Jose Canseco	15.2
Sammy Sosa	15.3
Carlos Delgado	15.3
Albert Belle	15.4

AB per RBI
minimum 1000 AB

Manny Ramirez	**4.3**
Mark McGwire	4.4
Frank Thomas	4.6
Juan Gonzalez	4.6
Mike Piazza	4.7
Albert Belle	4.7
Carlos Delgado	4.8
Todd Helton	4.8
Jeff Bagwell	4.9
Brian Giles	4.9

Total Bases

Cal Ripken Jr.	**4996**
Harold Baines	4592
Rickey Henderson	4370
Barry Bonds	4228
Tony Gwynn	4212
Rafael Palmeiro	4048
Gary Gaetti	3881
Fred McGriff	3766
Ken Griffey Jr.	3605
Andres Galarraga	3601

Walks

Rickey Henderson	**2060**
Barry Bonds	1547
Mark McGwire	1261
Frank Thomas	1188
Fred McGriff	1136
Cal Ripken Jr.	1103
Harold Baines	1054
Jeff Bagwell	992
Edgar Martinez	973
Mark Grace	946

Intentional Walks

Barry Bonds	**320**
Tony Gwynn	202
Harold Baines	187
Ken Griffey Jr.	187
Will Clark	155
Frank Thomas	151
Mark McGwire	147
Fred McGriff	146
Mo Vaughn	136
Jeff Bagwell	132

Hit by Pitch

Craig Biggio	**169**
Andres Galarraga	154
Brady Anderson	144
Chuck Knoblauch	121
Jason Kendall	104
Fernando Vina	101
Jeff Bagwell	97
Gary Gaetti	96
Mo Vaughn	96
2 tied with	90

Strikeouts

Jose Canseco	**1867**
Andres Galarraga	1741
Gary Gaetti	1602
Fred McGriff	1592
Rickey Henderson	1547
Sammy Sosa	1537
Mark McGwire	1478
Devon White	1431
Harold Baines	1425
Jay Buhner	1397

K/BB Ratio
minimum 1000 AB

Tony Gwynn	**.545**
Mark Grace	.593
Eric Young	.622
Frank Thomas	.703
Gary Sheffield	.724
Gregg Jefferies	.737
Dave Magadan	.745
Rickey Henderson	.751
Barry Bonds	.769
Brian Giles	.791

Sacrifice Hits

Jay Bell	**150**
Ozzie Guillen	141
Omar Vizquel	138
Roberto Alomar	118
Greg Maddux	113
Mark McLemore	96
Darren Lewis	94
Mike Bordick	89
Walt Weiss	89
Jose Vizcaino	81

Sacrifice Flies

Cal Ripken Jr.	**118**
Gary Gaetti	104
Will Clark	101
Ruben Sierra	101
Harold Baines	97
Bobby Bonilla	97
Wally Joyner	91
B.J. Surhoff	90
Frank Thomas	90
Mark Grace	88

SB Success %
minimum 100 SB attempts

Tony Womack	**86.0**
Eric Davis	84.3
Barry Larkin	83.5
Pokey Reese	83.3
Stan Javier	82.5
Rickey Henderson	80.8
Roberto Alomar	80.6
Brian L. Hunter	80.6
Kenny Lofton	80.2
Doug Glanville	80.1

Caught Stealing

Rickey Henderson	**326**
Luis Polonia	145
Delino DeShields	144
Barry Bonds	135
Tony Gwynn	125
Kenny Lofton	114
Eric Young	114
Ray Lankford	111
Ozzie Guillen	108
Craig Biggio	106

GDP

Cal Ripken Jr.	**335**
Harold Baines	296
Tony Gwynn	259
Gary Gaetti	236
Paul O'Neill	201
Albert Belle	193
Fred McGriff	192
Rafael Palmeiro	183
Jose Canseco	174
Mark Grace	174

AB per GDP
minimum 1000 AB

Greg Maddux	**178.3**
Tony Womack	129.6
Andy Fox	113.3
Jose Valentin	110.3
Cristian Guzman	105.1
Brady Anderson	105.1
Roger Cedeno	99.9
Brant Brown	96.0
Johnny Damon	92.6
Tom Goodwin	92.1

2000 Active Career Pitching Leaders

Wins

Roger Clemens	**260**
Greg Maddux	240
Tom Glavine	208
Orel Hershiser	204
Dwight Gooden	194
David Cone	184
Chuck Finley	181
Randy Johnson	179
Kevin Brown	170
David Wells	161

Losses

Mike Morgan	**185**
Bobby Witt	156
Chuck Finley	151
Orel Hershiser	150
Roger Clemens	142
Tim Belcher	140
Greg Maddux	135
Andy Benes	128
Jaime Navarro	126
Tom Glavine	125

Winning Percentage
minimum 100 decisions

Pedro Martinez	**.691**
Randy Johnson	.653
Roger Clemens	.647
Andy Pettitte	.645
Mike Mussina	.645
Greg Maddux	.640
Dwight Gooden	.634
Kirk Rueter	.628
Tom Glavine	.625
Mike Hampton	.616

ERA
minimum 750 IP

John Franco	**2.68**
Pedro Martinez	2.68
Greg Maddux	2.83
John Wetteland	2.93
Jesse Orosco	3.03
Roger Clemens	3.07
Randy Johnson	3.19
Kevin Brown	3.21
Doug Jones	3.30
Jeff Brantley	3.35

Games

Jesse Orosco	**1096**
John Franco	940
Dan Plesac	884
Doug Jones	846
Rick Aguilera	732
Mike Stanton	680
John Wetteland	618
Chuck McElroy	605
Jeff Brantley	597
Gregg Olson	594

Games Started

Roger Clemens	**511**
Greg Maddux	467
Orel Hershiser	466
Tom Glavine	434
Chuck Finley	413
Dwight Gooden	410
Mike Morgan	410
David Cone	390
Bobby Witt	390
Kevin Brown	380

Innings Pitched

Roger Clemens	**3666.2**
Greg Maddux	3318.0
Orel Hershiser	3130.1
Tom Glavine	2900.2
Chuck Finley	2893.0
Dwight Gooden	2800.2
David Cone	2745.0
Mike Morgan	2700.1
Kevin Brown	2660.2
Randy Johnson	2498.2

Batters Faced

Roger Clemens	**15089**
Greg Maddux	13469
Orel Hershiser	13150
Chuck Finley	12334
Tom Glavine	12165
Dwight Gooden	11705
Mike Morgan	11548
David Cone	11485
Kevin Brown	11046
Bobby Witt	10810

Complete Games

Roger Clemens	**116**
Greg Maddux	99
Randy Johnson	76
Kevin Brown	71
Dwight Gooden	68
Orel Hershiser	68
Curt Schilling	65
Chuck Finley	60
David Cone	56
Tom Glavine	49

Complete Game %
minimum 100 GS

Curt Schilling	**0.27**
Roger Clemens	0.23
Randy Johnson	0.21
Greg Maddux	0.21
Kevin Brown	0.19
Pedro Martinez	0.17
Dwight Gooden	0.17
Mike Mussina	0.16
Terry Mulholland	0.15
Scott Erickson	0.15

Shutouts

Roger Clemens	**45**
Greg Maddux	31
Randy Johnson	28
Orel Hershiser	25
Dwight Gooden	24
David Cone	22
Tom Glavine	20
Ramon Martinez	20
Tim Belcher	18
Kevin Brown	17

Quality Start %*
minimum 100 GS

Pedro Martinez	**70.6**
Greg Maddux	70.1
Kevin Brown	68.3
Randy Johnson	67.5
Roger Clemens	67.5
Curt Schilling	65.6
Tom Glavine	65.0
David Cone	63.6
Mike Mussina	63.5
Andy Benes	62.7

*since 1987

Strikeouts

Roger Clemens	**3504**
Randy Johnson	3040
David Cone	2540
Greg Maddux	2350
Chuck Finley	2340
Dwight Gooden	2293
Orel Hershiser	2014
Bobby Witt	1924
Kevin Brown	1917
Andy Benes	1858

Walks Allowed

Bobby Witt	**1350**
Chuck Finley	1219
Roger Clemens	1186
Randy Johnson	1089
David Cone	1067
Orel Hershiser	1007
Tom Glavine	965
Dwight Gooden	954
Mike Morgan	912
Tim Belcher	860

Strikeouts/9 IP
minimum 750 IP

Randy Johnson	**10.95**
Pedro Martinez	10.38
Hideo Nomo	9.48
John Wetteland	9.46
Roger Clemens	8.60
Dan Plesac	8.42
Chan Ho Park	8.34
David Cone	8.33
Curt Schilling	8.23
Jesse Orosco	8.18

Walks per 9 Innings
minimum 750 IP

Rick Reed	**1.76**
Brian Anderson	1.82
Rheal Cormier	1.95
Shane Reynolds	1.95
Doug Jones	1.97
Greg Maddux	1.99
Brad Radke	1.99
Jose Lima	2.02
Jon Lieber	2.04
Greg Swindell	2.05

K/BB Ratio

minimum 750 IP

Pedro Martinez	**4.11**
Shane Reynolds	3.92
Doug Jones	3.68
Curt Schilling	3.48
Jon Lieber	3.43
Mike Mussina	3.29
Greg Maddux	3.21
Rick Reed	3.20
John Wetteland	3.19
Jose Lima	3.18

Hits per 9 Innings

Pedro Martinez	**6.73**
Randy Johnson	6.96
Jesse Orosco	7.19
John Wetteland	7.25
Roger Clemens	7.61
David Cone	7.66
Hideo Nomo	7.75
Chan Ho Park	7.75
Jeff Brantley	7.82
Al Leiter	7.86

Baserunners/9 IP

minimum 750 IP

Pedro Martinez	**9.64**
Greg Maddux	10.33
John Wetteland	10.40
Curt Schilling	10.50
Mike Mussina	10.68
Roger Clemens	10.83
Rick Reed	11.20
Randy Johnson	11.27
Rick Aguilera	11.29
Kevin Brown	11.30

Home Runs/9 IP

minimum 750 IP

Greg Maddux	**0.48**
John Franco	0.51
Kevin Brown	0.54
Tom Glavine	0.63
Mike Hampton	0.63
Roger Clemens	0.64
Bob Wickman	0.64
Dwight Gooden	0.67
Orel Hershiser	0.68
Al Leiter	0.68

Opposition AVG*

minimum 750 IP

Pedro Martinez	**.206**
Randy Johnson	.213
John Wetteland	.218
Roger Clemens	.228
David Cone	.229
Hideo Nomo	.231
Chan Ho Park	.233
Jeff Brantley	.236
Al Leiter	.237
Curt Schilling	.237

*since 1987

Opposition OBP*

minimum 750 IP

Pedro Martinez	**.270**
John Wetteland	.284
Greg Maddux	.285
Curt Schilling	.288
Mike Mussina	.293
Roger Clemens	.296
Rick Aguilera	.301
Randy Johnson	.303
Rick Reed	.304
Kevin Brown	.304

*since 1987

Opposition SLG*

minimum 750 IP

Pedro Martinez	**.319**
Greg Maddux	.329
John Franco	.333
Randy Johnson	.335
Roger Clemens	.337
Kevin Brown	.343
John Wetteland	.347
David Cone	.354
Al Leiter	.356
Norm Charlton	.357

*since 1987

Home Runs Allowed

Chuck Finley	**277**
David Wells	273
Tim Belcher	264
Mike Morgan	261
Roger Clemens	260
Andy Benes	249
Bobby Witt	246
Jamie Moyer	243
Todd Stottlemyre	242
Greg Swindell	241

Hit Batsmen

Roger Clemens	**124**
Kevin Brown	117
Orel Hershiser	117
Randy Johnson	107
Darryl Kile	98
David Cone	96
Greg Maddux	90
Scott Erickson	88
Todd Stottlemyre	83
Dwight Gooden	78

Wild Pitches

David Cone	**140**
Chuck Finley	126
Bobby Witt	126
Orel Hershiser	121
Juan Guzman	105
Mike Morgan	100
Roger Clemens	92
Jaime Navarro	92
Darryl Kile	91
Kevin Brown	86

GDP Induced*

Greg Maddux	**277**
Scott Erickson	275
Chuck Finley	273
Tom Glavine	267
Kevin Brown	265
Orel Hershiser	253
Mike Morgan	253
Roger Clemens	221
Bobby Witt	207
Terry Mulholland	197

*since 1987

GDP/9 IP*

minimum 750 IP

Bob Wickman	**1.21**
Scott Erickson	1.18
Shawn Estes	1.17
Mike Hampton	1.14
Andy Pettitte	1.12
Omar Olivares	1.12
Pat Rapp	1.07
Scott Karl	1.07
Mike Morgan	1.04
Scott Kamieniecki	1.01

*since 1987

Saves

John Franco	**420**
John Wetteland	330
Rick Aguilera	318
Doug Jones	303
Trevor Hoffman	271
Roberto Hernandez	266
Rod Beck	260
Robb Nen	226
Gregg Olson	217
Jeff Brantley	172

Save %

minimum 50 SvOp

Trevor Hoffman	**87.7**
Billy Koch	87.7
Mariano Rivera	85.9
Robb Nen	85.3
John Rocker	84.2
Mark Wohlers	84.2
Jose Mesa	84.1
Ugueth Urbina	84.0
John Wetteland	84.0
Rod Beck	83.9

Games Finished

John Franco	**725**
Doug Jones	640
Rick Aguilera	557
John Wetteland	523
Roberto Hernandez	488
Jesse Orosco	473
Rod Beck	451
Gregg Olson	437
Trevor Hoffman	413
Robb Nen	412

SB % Allowed*

minimum 750 IP

Terry Mulholland	**36.4**
Kirk Rueter	36.8
Omar Daal	39.2
Kenny Rogers	41.2
Chan Ho Park	46.4
Greg Swindell	51.3
Brian Anderson	53.3
Tim Belcher	53.6
Alex Fernandez	53.8
Pat Rapp	53.9

*since 1987

Player Profiles

There were plenty of guys who had career years in 2000, including seasoned veterans Barry Bonds, Darryl Kile, Jeff Bagwell, Jeff Kent, Pedro Martinez and Jason Giambi. Then there's the game's crop of young players who excelled in 2000 and enhanced their credentials as budding stars. Guys like Alex Rodriguez, Nomar Garciaparra, Andruw Jones, Tim Hudson, Todd Helton, Carlos Delgado Rick Ankiel and Darin Erstad took their game to new heights last summer.

While all of them deserve a closer look at their 2000 numbers, we have space to focus on just three: Delgado, Helton and Kile. Their profiles provide a wealth of information.

A couple of similarities between the two lefthanded hitters jump out at you. Both are dangerous first-ball hitters. Over the last five seasons, Helton has batted .385 and Delgado has hit .387 when they pounce on the first pitch. If they get ahead in the count, they become .400 hitters. Plus, both post whopping slugging percentages when pitchers fall behind against them. What a dilemma these guys present to pitchers. It's critical to throw a strike in the early going, yet they are menacing when they jump on the first pitch.

A key ingredient to Helton's run at hitting .400 was his astounding .461 average when he got ahead in the count during the 2000 season. If he makes another run at .400 later in his career, it's in his favor that he has posted a much better average and slugging percentage during the second half of the season in his big league years. He's a .395 career hitter in August, though he drops off to .307 in September and October.

On the other hand, Delgado's batting average and slugging percentage dip substantially in the second half, and that hurt his Triple Crown bid last summer. Still, he's a .300 hitter in the No. 4 spot—demonstrating the gifts of making frequent contact *and* driving the ball deep in one package. In 2000, Delgado was especially dangerous when he made contact on the first pitch, batting a remarkable .531 with nine doubles, four homers and a 1.000 slugging percentage in 49 at-bats.

These guys wouldn't have struck fear into the righthanded Kile, who defied his past history and actually fared better against lefties than righties in 2000. Lefthanded hitters batted just .229 against him last season, and all hitters managed just a .238 average in the first six innings of Kile's starts. That's 32 points better than his average allowed over his first six innings in his five previous seasons—and that difference had a lot to do with why Kile won 20 games for the first time in his career.

Winning 20 games also had a lot to do with his 5-0 mark and 2.86 ERA in September. In September and October in his five seasons prior to 2000, Kile was 7-9 with a 4.68 ERA. The bottom line is, no matter how you look at Kile's 2000 season, it's apparent he was a strong finisher. He ranked among league leaders with five complete games, and his .190 opponent batting average after his 105th pitch demonstrated his ability to finish business.

The *Major League Handbook's* companion volume, *STATS Player Profiles 2001*, contains breakdowns like these for every 2000 major leaguer.

Carlos Delgado — Blue Jays

Age 29 – Bats Left (flyball hitter)

	Avg	G	AB	R	H	2B	3B	HR	RBI	BB	SO	HBP	GDP	SB	CS	OBP	SLG	IBB	SH	SF	#Pit	#P/PA	GB	FB	G/F
2000 Season	.344	162	569	115	196	57	1	41	137	123	104	15	12	0	1	.470	.664	18	0	4	2938	4.13	206	155	1.33
Last Five Years	.289	747	2679	469	775	209	7	178	569	404	656	58	50	4	5	.390	.572	49	0	29	12887	4.07	759	846	0.90

2000 Season

	Avg	AB	H	2B	3B	HR	RBI	BB	SO	OBP	SLG		Avg	AB	H	2B	3B	HR	RBI	BB	SO	OBP	SLG
vs. Left	.319	188	60	21	1	6	36	29	37	.422	.537	First Pitch	.531	49	26	9	1	4	18	11	0	.636	1.000
vs. Right	.357	381	136	36	0	35	101	94	67	.492	.727	Ahead in Count	.404	151	61	21	0	11	40	64	0	.581	.762
Groundball	.308	133	41	14	1	4	24	30	28	.446	.519	Behind in Count	.280	232	65	14	0	15	51	0	75	.299	.534
Flyball	.352	122	43	8	0	13	33	25	25	.467	.738	Two Strikes	.272	290	79	19	0	19	61	47	104	.386	.534
Home	.360	283	102	28	0	30	75	59	42	.477	.777	Total	.344	569	196	57	1	41	137	123	104	.470	.664
Away	.329	286	94	29	1	11	62	64	62	.463	.552	Batting #4	.344	569	196	57	1	41	137	123	104	.470	.664
Day	.311	206	64	19	0	19	60	38	38	.427	.680	Other	.000	0	0	0	0	0	0	0	0	.000	.000
Night	.364	363	132	38	1	22	77	85	66	.492	.656	March/April	.319	94	30	8	0	8	20	15	22	.430	.660
Grass	.328	244	80	24	1	10	57	53	54	.461	.557	May	.340	103	35	7	0	10	26	19	25	.439	.699
Turf	.357	325	116	33	0	31	80	70	50	.476	.745	June	.411	95	39	6	0	9	26	20	15	.517	.758
Pre-All Star	.363	320	116	27	0	28	80	66	64	.476	.709	July	.386	88	34	19	0	5	21	27	12	.538	.773
Post-All Star	.321	249	80	30	1	13	57	57	40	.462	.606	August	.368	95	35	9	1	7	31	19	9	.487	.705
Scoring Posn	.384	172	66	18	0	13	102	38	34	.495	.715	Sept/Oct	.245	94	23	8	0	2	13	23	21	.390	.394
Close & Late	.257	70	18	2	0	5	14	16	16	.402	.500	vs. AL	.341	511	174	48	1	34	116	101	93	.458	.638
None on/out	.366	153	56	18	1	16	16	28	27	.476	.810	vs. NL	.379	58	22	9	0	7	21	22	11	.561	.897

2000 By Position

Position	Avg	AB	H	2B	3B	HR	RBI	BB	SO	OBP	SLG	G	GS	Innings	PO	A	E	DP	Fld Pct	Rng Fctr	In Zone	Outs	Zone Rtg	MLB Zone
As 1b	.344	569	196	57	1	41	137	123	104	.470	.664	162	162	1429.1	1416	82	13	157	.991	—	271	228	.841	.846

Last Five Years

	Avg	AB	H	2B	3B	HR	RBI	BB	SO	OBP	SLG		Avg	AB	H	2B	3B	HR	RBI	BB	SO	OBP	SLG
vs. Left	.280	721	202	61	4	27	134	91	195	.373	.488	First Pitch	.387	261	101	24	2	21	73	34	0	.477	.736
vs. Right	.293	1958	573	148	3	151	435	313	461	.396	.603	Ahead in Count	.400	597	239	68	0	72	195	204	0	.552	.876
Groundball	.288	664	191	57	3	41	144	119	146	.406	.568	Behind in Count	.221	1254	277	76	3	46	192	0	513	.235	.396
Flyball	.300	446	134	33	0	32	93	77	121	.408	.590	Two Strikes	.206	1436	296	80	5	54	197	165	656	.295	.382
Home	.299	1323	395	118	4	96	285	206	330	.400	.611	Batting #3	.263	407	107	28	1	17	72	49	107	.350	.462
Away	.280	1356	380	91	3	82	284	198	326	.381	.533	Batting #4	.300	1737	521	145	3	125	398	287	414	.408	.603
Day	.294	918	270	73	3	63	218	138	232	.395	.586	Other	.275	535	147	36	3	36	99	68	135	.362	.555
Night	.287	1761	505	136	4	115	351	266	424	.388	.564	March/April	.305	354	108	20	0	25	66	56	88	.406	.573
Grass	.276	1087	300	78	3	58	221	155	265	.376	.513	May	.301	509	153	49	3	26	90	62	136	.383	.562
Turf	.298	1592	475	131	4	120	348	249	421	.400	.612	June	.277	470	130	32	1	30	101	72	129	.381	.566
Pre-All Star	.294	1457	428	112	4	97	317	216	388	.392	.576	July	.279	452	126	41	1	32	100	78	120	.393	.586
Post-All Star	.284	1222	347	97	3	81	252	188	268	.388	.567	August	.311	485	151	41	1	37	129	64	93	.398	.629
Scoring Posn	.302	774	234	55	3	54	410	182		.407	.590	Sept/Oct	.262	409	107	26	1	24	63	72	90	.379	.506
Close & Late	.259	386	100	21	0	24	71	63	109	.374	.500	vs. AL	.289	2368	685	185	5	147	487	354	570	.389	.558
None on/out	.304	671	204	63	1	56	56	87	151	.395	.651	vs. NL	.289	311	90	24	2	31	82	50	86	.399	.678

Batter vs. Pitcher (career)

Hits Best Against	Avg	AB	H	2B	3B	HR	RBI	BB	SO	OBP	SLG	Hits Worst Against	Avg	AB	H	2B	3B	HR	RBI	BB	SO	OBP	SLG
Dustin Hermanson	.667	9	6	1	0	3	7	3	0	.769	1.778	Wilson Alvarez	.000	12	0	0	0	0	0	1	2	.077	.000
Jason Johnson	.556	9	5	0	0	1	3	3	1	.667	.889	Arthur Rhodes	.067	15	1	1	0	0	0	1	5	.125	.133
Freddy Garcia	.500	12	6	3	0	3	6	2	1	.571	1.500	Tom Gordon	.077	26	2	0	0	0	1	4	8	.194	.077
Ramon Ortiz	.455	11	5	2	0	2	4	2	1	.538	1.182	Rocky Coppinger	.091	11	1	0	0	0	0	1	2	.167	.091
Curt Schilling	.385	13	5	2	1	2	5	1	5	.429	1.154	Gil Heredia	.100	10	1	0	0	0	1	1	1	.182	.100

Todd Helton — Rockies

Age 27 – Bats Left

	Avg	G	AB	R	H	2B	3B	HR	RBI	BB	SO	HBP	GDP	SB	CS	OBP	SLG	IBB	SH	SF	#Pit	#P/PA	GB	FB	G/F
2000 Season	.372	160	580	138	216	59	2	42	147	103	61	4	12	5	3	.463	.698	22	0	10	2688	3.86	204	189	1.08
Career (1997-2000)	.334	506	1781	343	594	137	9	107	368	232	203	16	42	15	13	.411	.601	33	1	19	7824	3.82	654	579	1.13

2000 Season

	Avg	AB	H	2B	3B	HR	RBI	BB	SO	OBP	SLG		Avg	AB	H	2B	3B	HR	RBI	BB	SO	OBP	SLG
vs. Left	.329	143	47	15	1	7	31	30	16	.451	.594	First Pitch	.375	96	36	9	0	6	18	18	0	.479	.656
vs. Right	.387	437	169	44	1	35	116	73	45	.467	.732	Ahead in Count	.461	128	59	15	0	17	47	58	0	.620	.977
Groundball	.307	140	43	10	1	8	27	22	12	.406	.564	Behind in Count	.359	234	84	22	2	9	51	0	41	.354	.585
Flyball	.422	161	68	22	0	11	47	28	14	.495	.764	Two Strikes	.336	268	90	23	2	12	63	27	61	.393	.571
Home	.391	302	118	28	1	27	88	58	30	.484	.758	Batting #4	.391	243	95	24	1	22	75	57	31	.497	.770
Away	.353	278	98	31	1	15	59	45	31	.441	.633	Batting #5	.380	245	93	26	1	17	57	34	19	.459	.702
Day	.391	215	84	22	0	18	56	52	20	.470	.744	Other	.304	92	28	9	0	3	15	12	11	.377	.500
Night	.362	365	132	37	2	24	91	68	35	.459	.671	March/April	.337	89	30	7	2	6	25	17	10	.440	.663
Grass	.367	521	191	52	2	37	128	90	55	.457	.687	May	.512	82	42	7	0	11	26	18	9	.588	1.000
Turf	.424	59	25	7	0	5	19	13	6	.520	.797	June	.315	92	29	11	0	4	17	17	11	.422	.565
Pre-All Star	.383	298	114	28	2	21	70	58	32	.479	.701	July	.340	106	36	10	0	4	19	16	6	.427	.547
Post-All Star	.362	282	102	31	0	21	77	45	29	.446	.695	August	.476	105	50	18	0	7	32	17	7	.548	.848
Scoring Posn	.392	153	60	16	0	15	110	52	20	.525	.791	Sept/Oct	.274	106	29	6	0	10	28	18	18	.370	.613
Close & Late	.393	84	33	5	0	9	22	17	6	.495	.774	vs. AL	.319	47	15	4	0	2	7	7	7	.407	.532
None on/out	.314	140	44	14	1	9	9	14	10	.377	.621	vs. NL	.377	533	201	55	2	40	140	96	54	.468	.713

2000 By Position

Position	Avg	AB	H	2B	3B	HR	RBI	BB	SO	OBP	SLG	G	GS	Innings	PO	A	E	DP	Fld Pct	Rng Fctr	In Zone	Outs	Zone Rtg	MLB Zone
As 1b	.374	578	216	59	2	42	147	103	61	.465	.701	160	156	1349.0	1328	148	7	143	.995	—	325	280	.862	.846

Career (1997-2000)

	Avg	AB	H	2B	3B	HR	RBI	BB	SO	OBP	SLG		Avg	AB	H	2B	3B	HR	RBI	BB	SO	OBP	SLG
vs. Left	.287	428	123	27	2	16	80	58	53	.383	.472	First Pitch	.385	275	106	26	2	16	56	27	0	.447	.669
vs. Right	.348	1353	471	110	7	91	288	174	150	.420	.642	Ahead in Count	.402	403	162	35	2	38	113	128	0	.541	.782
Groundball	.317	502	159	37	2	21	90	57	49	.389	.524	Behind in Count	.295	735	217	47	4	29	118	0	154	.298	.488
Flyball	.363	383	139	37	2	27	92	52	50	.436	.681	Two Strikes	.271	811	220	54	3	33	133	77	203	.334	.467
Home	.373	923	344	74	7	66	232	130	84	.449	.683	Batting #5	.362	500	181	42	3	38	114	62	46	.436	.686
Away	.291	858	250	63	2	41	136	102	119	.369	.513	Batting #6	.318	696	221	52	4	35	125	76	73	.389	.555
Day	.338	680	230	51	4	44	140	90	85	.416	.619	Other	.328	585	192	43	2	34	129	94	84	.415	.583
Night	.331	1101	364	86	5	63	228	142	118	.408	.589	March/April	.280	243	68	21	2	9	50	33	35	.367	.494
Grass	.333	1526	508	118	9	87	316	198	169	.409	.593	May	.371	267	99	17	1	24	57	44	27	.459	.712
Turf	.337	255	86	19	0	20	52	34	34	.421	.647	June	.306	265	81	19	2	14	57	34	39	.387	.551
Pre-All Star	.319	869	277	64	5	50	171	120	100	.403	.577	July	.315	292	92	22	0	14	43	30	22	.384	.534
Post-All Star	.348	912	317	73	4	57	197	112	94	.419	.624	August	.395	392	155	42	1	23	95	41	40	.451	.684
Scoring Posn	.354	469	166	38	1	37	270	98	68	.456	.676	Sept/Oct	.307	322	99	16	3	23	66	50	40	.398	.590
Close & Late	.295	258	76	12	2	17	59	48	37	.408	.554	vs. AL	.242	128	31	7	0	6	24	18	14	.340	.438
None on/out	.299	428	128	38	4	25	25	41	45	.362	.582	vs. NL	.341	1653	563	130	9	101	344	214	189	.417	.613

Batter vs. Pitcher (career)

Hits Best Against	Avg	AB	H	2B	3B	HR	RBI	BB	SO	OBP	SLG	Hits Worst Against	Avg	AB	H	2B	3B	HR	RBI	BB	SO	OBP	SLG
Bobby J. Jones	.692	13	9	3	0	3	8	1	0	.714	1.615	Mike Remlinger	.000	9	0	0	0	0	2	1	4	.091	.000
G. Stephenson	.667	9	6	3	0	0	3	2	0	.667	1.000	Dave Mlicki	.071	14	1	0	0	0	0	0	1	.071	.071
Matt Clement	.615	13	8	1	0	1	5	6	1	.737	.923	Omar Daal	.176	17	3	1	0	0	3	1	5	.222	.235
Kent Bottenfield	.545	11	6	1	0	1	6	2	0	.615	.909	Curt Schilling	.200	15	3	1	0	0	0	2	4	.294	.267
Steve Trachsel	.417	12	5	1	0	2	3	5	2	.588	1.000	Pete Harnisch	.238	21	5	2	0	0	0	0	2	.238	.333

Darryl Kile — Cardinals

	ERA	W	L	Sv	G	GS	IP	BB	SO	Avg	H	2B	3B	HR	RBI	OBP	SLG	CG	ShO	Sup	QS	#P/S	SB	CS	GB	FB	G/F
2000 Season	3.91	20	9	0	34	34	232.1	58	192	.247	215		4	33	101	.301	.428	5	1	5.58	20	104	2	11	291	236	1.23
Last Five Years	4.38	72	57	0	171	168	1128.0	454	890	.266	1138	209	32	129	534	.340	.420	20	6	5.26	95	105	71	31	1524	1184	1.29

2000 Season

	ERA	W	L	Sv	G	GS	IP	H	HR	BB	SO		Avg	AB	H	2B	3B	HR	RBI	BB	SO	OBP	SLG
Home	3.67	11	5	0	18	18	125.0	105	20	30	115	vs. Left	.229	406	93	24	1	15	44	35	91	.293	.404
Away	4.19	9	4	0	16	16	107.1	110	13	28	77	vs. Right	.263	464	122	26	3	18	57	23	101	.309	.448
Day	3.05	11	2	0	16	16	112.0	90	12	26	86	Inning 1-6	.238	713	170	41	2	28	82	54	165	.300	.419
Night	4.71	9	7	0	18	18	120.1	125	21	32	106	Inning 7+	.287	157	45	9	2	5	19	4	27	.307	.465
Grass	4.30	15	9	0	28	28	190.1	174	29	49	161	None on	.239	569	136	31	3	19	19	27	139	.280	.404
Turf	2.14	5	0	0	6	6	42.0	41	4	9	31	Runners on	.262	301	79	19	1	14	82	31	53	.339	.472
March/April	5.40	5	1	0	6	6	35.0	34	5	8	34	Scoring Posn	.255	165	42	13	0	8	68	16	34	.332	.479
May	5.13	2	2	0	5	5	33.1	33	8	11	31	Close & Late	.280	75	21	4	1	4	11	3	16	.316	.520
June	3.20	4	1	0	6	6	39.1	33	5	11	35	None on/out	.249	237	59	16	0	6	6	7	58	.276	.392
July	3.09	2	2	0	6	6	43.2	40	7	8	38	vs. 1st Batr (relief)	.000	0	0	0	0	0	0	0	0	.000	.000
August	4.38	2	3	0	5	5	37.0	40	4	8	24	1st Inning Pitched	.252	131	33	9	0	6	19	10	28	.313	.458
Sept/Oct	2.86	5	0	0	6	6	44.0	35	4	12	30	First 75 Pitches	.238	579	138	31	2	23	64	42	132	.298	.418
Starter	3.91	20	9	0	34	34	232.1	215	33	58	192	Pitch 76-90	.288	132	38	5	1	8	19	3	26	.312	.523
Reliever	0.00	0	0	0	0	0	0.0	0	0	0	0	Pitch 91-105	.277	101	28	10	1	2	12	12	21	.362	.455
0-3 Days Rest (Start)	3.68	1	0	0	1	1	7.1	8	2	0	5	Pitch 106+	.190	58	11	4	0	0	6	1	13	.200	.259
4 Days Rest	3.56	11	5	0	20	20	139.0	126	19	36	123	First Pitch	.270	111	30	9	1	3	15	1	0	.282	.450
5+ Days Rest	4.50	8	4	0	13	13	86.0	81	12	22	64	Ahead in Count	.181	425	77	16	2	11	36	0	170	.194	.306
vs. AL	3.74	2	1	0	3	3	21.2	18	2	6	23	Behind in Count	.331	178	59	16	0	12	33	32	0	.438	.624
vs. NL	3.93	18	8	0	31	31	210.2	197	31	52	169	Two Strikes	.168	428	72	13	0	10	30	25	192	.224	.269
Pre-All Star	4.51	11	5	0	19	19	121.2	113	22	33	115	Pre-All Star	.247	458	113	25	3	22	61	33	115	.308	.459
Post-All Star	3.25	9	4	0	15	15	110.2	102	11	25	77	Post-All Star	.248	412	102	25	1	11	40	25	77	.294	.393

Last Five Years

	ERA	W	L	Sv	G	GS	IP	H	HR	BB	SO		Avg	AB	H	2B	3B	HR	RBI	BB	SO	OBP	SLG
Home	4.53	35	26	0	84	83	564.2	574	79	195	472	vs. Left	.280	2133	597	118	16	59	264	244	410	.353	.433
Away	4.23	37	31	0	87	85	563.1	564	50	259	418	vs. Right	.251	2152	541	91	16	70	270	210	480	.327	.406
Day	4.30	34	22	0	74	72	491.1	484	56	195	379	Inning 1-6	.269	3564	957	165	27	110	463	400	747	.346	.423
Night	4.44	38	35	0	97	96	636.2	654	73	259	511	Inning 7+	.251	721	181	44	5	19	71	54	143	.311	.405
Grass	4.84	43	40	0	110	109	721.0	748	94	307	523	None on	.261	2440	636	119	19	73	73	239	514	.332	.415
Turf	3.56	29	17	0	61	59	407.0	390	35	147	367	Runners on	.272	1845	502	90	13	56	461	215	376	.350	.426
March/April	4.57	14	10	0	30	29	187.0	183	21	87	136	Scoring Posn	.253	1039	263	62	7	28	388	154	242	.347	.407
May	3.20	14	7	0	28	28	194.1	172	18	95	152	Close & Late	.254	394	100	22	3	13	43	26	83	.311	.424
June	4.32	8	10	0	29	29	193.2	196	24	80	158	None on/out	.289	1099	318	55	11	34	34	101	209	.355	.452
July	4.64	14	10	0	31	30	197.2	207	26	64	149	vs. 1st Batr (relief)	.333	3	1	0	0	0	0	0	0	.333	.333
August	5.45	10	11	0	28	27	181.2	223	24	63	150	1st Inning Pitched	.283	667	189	41	5	17	99	80	130	.361	.436
Sept/Oct	4.15	12	9	0	25	25	173.2	157	16	65	145	First 75 Pitches	.269	2924	787	137	22	87	362	307	602	.341	.420
Starter	4.39	72	57	0	168	168	1123.0	1135	128	451	887	Pitch 76-90	.262	546	143	24	5	22	75	61	119	.340	.445
Reliever	1.80	0	0	0	3	0	5.0	3	1	3	3	Pitch 91-105	.259	482	125	32	3	13	58	57	100	.343	.419
0-3 Days Rest (Start)	5.38	5	7	0	13	13	82.0	99	16	29	62	Pitch 106+	.249	333	83	16	2	7	39	29	69	.323	.372
4 Days Rest	3.98	50	26	0	98	98	677.2	652	67	275	545	First Pitch	.332	630	209	44	6	19	87	9	0	.352	.511
5+ Days Rest	4.93	17	24	0	57	57	363.1	384	45	147	280	Ahead in Count	.197	1887	371	65	13	37	159	0	768	.203	.304
vs. AL	5.48	2	6	0	11	11	70.2	76	14	26	60	Behind in Count	.331	1054	349	63	7	51	188	258	0	.461	.549
vs. NL	4.31	70	51	0	160	157	1057.1	1062	115	428	830	Two Strikes	.179	1913	342	58	10	35	153	187	890	.257	.274
Pre-All Star	4.18	39	31	0	96	94	627.0	611	75	281	493	Pre-All Star	.258	2367	611	107	20	75	289	281	493	.342	.415
Post-All Star	4.63	33	26	0	75	74	501.0	527	54	173	397	Post-All Star	.275	1918	527	102	12	54	245	173	397	.337	.415

Pitcher vs. Batter (career)

Pitches Best Vs.	Avg	AB	H	2B	3B	HR	RBI	BB	SO	OBP	SLG	Pitches Worst Vs.	Avg	AB	H	2B	3B	HR	RBI	BB	SO	OBP	SLG
Aaron Boone	.000	11	0	0	0	0	0	0	3	.000	.000	Mark Loretta	.684	19	13	2	1	1	4	1	2	.667	1.053
Chris Widger	.000	10	0	0	0	0	0	2	1	.167	.000	Travis Lee	.545	11	6	2	1	1	2	5	1	.688	1.182
Fernando Vina	.067	15	1	0	0	0	0	0	2	.067	.067	John Olerud	.500	18	9	1	0	2	4	3	0	.571	.889
Carlos Hernandez	.077	13	1	0	0	0	0	0	2	.077	.077	Glenallen Hill	.500	16	8	2	1	1	8	6	4	.640	.938
Midre Cummings	.083	12	1	0	0	0	0	0	2	.083	.083	Brian Giles	.455	11	5	1	0	3	6	3	1	.571	1.364

Manager Tendencies

One of the things about baseball which appeals to many of us is the game's endless opportunity for analysis. . . and few things are analyzed more than managerial decisions. Major league skippers may not have batting averages and slugging percentages to point to at the end of the season, but when it comes time to judge their performance and production, there's no reason we can't take a look at their statistics.

Which manager posted the best stolen-base success rate?

Which skippers were constantly tinkering with their lineups?

Which managers wore out a path to the pitching mound?

It's questions like these that get our second-guessing juices going, and it's questions like these that inspired the following pages, which look at managerial tendencies in a number of situations. Once again, the skippers are compared based on offense, defense, lineups, and pitching use. We don't rank the managers; there is plenty of room for argument on whether certain moves are good or bad. We are simply providing fodder for the discussion.

Offensively, managers have control over bunting, stealing and the timing of hit-and-runs. The *Handbook* looks at the quantity, timing and success of these moves.

Defensively, the *Handbook* looks at the success of pitchouts, the frequency of intentional walks, and the pattern of defensive substitutions.

Most managers spend large amounts of their time devising lineups. The *Handbook* shows the number of lineups used, as well as the platoon percentage. The use of pinch-hitters and pinch-runners is also explored.

Finally, how does the manager use pitchers? For starters, the *Handbook* shows slow and quick hooks, along with the number of times a starter was allowed to throw more than 120 and 140 pitches. For relievers, we look at the number of relief appearances, mid-inning changes and how often a pitcher gets a save going more than one inning (a rare occurrence these days).

For the purposes of this section, it is assumed that a coach filling in for his manager will make his decisions based on what the manager would do in a given situation.

The categories include:

Stolen Base Success Percentage: Stolen bases divided by attempts.

Pitchout Runners Moving: The number of times the opposition is running when a manager calls a pitchout.

Double Steals: The number of double steals attempted in 2000.

Out Percentage: The proportion of stolen bases with that number of outs.

Sacrifice Bunt Attempts: A bunt is considered a sac attempt if no runner is on third, there are no outs, or the pitcher attempts a bunt.

Sacrifice Bunt Success%: A bunt that results in a sacrifice or a hit, divided by the number of attempts.

Favorite Inning: The most common inning in which an event occurred.

Hit-and-Run Success: The hit-and-run results in baserunner advancement with no double play.

Intentional Walk Situation: Runners on base, first base open, and anyone but the pitcher up. The teams must be within two runs of each other, or the tying run must be on base, at bat or on deck.

Defensive Substitutions: Straight defensive substitutions, with the team leading by four runs or less.

Number of Lineups: Based on batting order, 1-8 for National Leaguers, 1-9 for American Leaguers.

Percent LHB vs. RHSP and RHB vs. LHSP: A measure of platooning. A batter is considered to always have the platoon advantage if he is a switch-hitter.

Percent PH platoon: Frequency the manager gets his pinch-hitter the platoon advantage. Switch-hitters always have the advantage.

Score Diff: The most common score differential on which an intentional walk is called for.

Slow and Quick Hooks: See the glossary for complete information. This measures how often a pitcher is left in longer than is standard practice, or pulled earlier than normal.

Mid-Inning Change: The number of times a manager changed pitchers in the middle of an inning.

1-Batter Appearances: The number of times a pitcher was brought in to face only one batter. Called the "Tony La Russa special" because of his penchant for trying to orchestrate specific matchups for specific situations.

3 Pitchers (2 runs or less): The club gives up two runs or less in a game, but uses at least three pitchers.

OFFENSE

	G	Att	SB%	Ptchout Rn Mvg	2nd SB-CS	3rd SB-CS	Home SB-CS	Double Steals	Out Percentage 0	1	2	Sacrifice Bunts Suc. Att	%	Fav. Inning	Sqz	Hit & Run Att	Suc. %
AL Managers																	
Fregosi, Jim, Tor	162	123	72.4	3	81-32	8-2	0-0	1	22.0	33.3	44.7	45	75.6	1	1	42	28.6
Garner, Phil, Det	162	121	68.6	4	74-32	9-5	0-1	4	24.8	29.8	45.5	58	79.3	9	2	62	33.9
Hargrove, Mike, Bal	162	191	66.0	9	106-52	19-9	1-4	6	12.0	37.7	50.3	36	80.6	8	1	74	28.4
Howe, Art, Oak	161	55	72.7	0	32-12	6-2	2-1	4	9.1	49.1	41.8	40	77.5	6	1	32	15.6
Kelly, Tom, Min	162	135	66.7	6	85-41	4-4	1-0	3	13.3	44.4	42.2	37	75.7	3	5	72	36.1
Manuel, Charlie, Cle	162	147	76.9	4	85-31	26-3	2-0	6	21.8	29.3	49.0	59	84.7	1	1	54	37.0
Manuel, Jerry, CWS	162	161	73.9	5	108-36	11-5	0-1	5	18.0	42.2	39.8	75	86.7	7	3	77	33.8
Muser, Tony, KC	162	156	77.6	5	112-26	9-6	0-3	4	21.2	34.0	44.9	72	87.5	7	6	80	33.8
Oates, Johnny, Tex	162	116	59.5	4	64-39	3-7	2-1	1	15.5	35.3	49.1	66	83.3	8	1	57	47.4
Piniella, Lou, Sea	162	178	68.5	6	108-46	14-9	0-1	7	19.1	36.5	44.4	73	87.7	5	0	65	30.8
Rothschild, Larry, TB	161	136	66.2	6	76-39	13-4	1-3	3	23.5	30.9	45.6	73	79.5	7	3	66	36.4
Scioscia, Mike, Ana	162	145	64.1	3	80-47	13-4	0-1	2	17.9	26.9	55.2	63	84.1	7	9	100	37.0
Torre, Joe, NYY	161	147	67.3	2	90-44	9-2	0-2	3	21.1	29.3	49.7	22	81.8	3	1	58	46.6
Williams, Jimy, Bos	162	73	58.9	1	38-27	5-3	0-0	0	31.5	30.1	38.4	49	89.8	7	2	64	38.1
NL Managers																	
Alou, Felipe, Mon	162	106	54.7	2	55-42	3-4	0-2	1	21.7	38.7	39.6	103	83.5	3	5	54	37.0
Baker, Dusty, SF	162	118	66.9	1	72-34	7-5	0-0	2	23.7	37.3	39.0	86	90.7	3	1	59	47.5
Baylor, Don, ChC	162	130	71.5	4	79-33	13-4	1-0	5	20.8	42.3	36.9	115	84.3	3	4	79	25.3
Bell, Buddy, Col	162	192	68.2	14	111-50	18-8	2-3	8	20.8	35.9	43.2	100	83.0	4	5	93	36.6
Bochy, Bruce, SD	162	184	71.2	2	119-48	10-3	2-2	5	24.5	37.5	38.0	52	76.9	2	4	74	31.1
Boles, John, Fla	161	223	75.3	5	154-51	12-4	2-0	4	21.1	38.6	40.4	61	78.7	3	4	79	25.3
Cox, Bobby, Atl	162	204	72.5	4	123-51	24-4	1-1	10	17.2	40.2	42.6	109	80.7	2	11	61	34.4
Dierker, Larry, Hou	162	166	68.7	6	98-41	16-9	0-2	4	23.5	36.7	39.8	77	79.2	4	4	87	34.5
Francona, Terry, Phi	162	132	77.3	6	91-25	11-13	0-2	3	16.7	42.4	40.9	89	84.3	3	7	60	36.7
Johnson, Davey, LA	162	137	69.3	2	84-38	11-4	0-0	2	22.6	37.2	40.1	80	81.3	2	5	45	22.2
La Russa, Tony, StL	162	138	63.0	0	81-45	6-4	0-2	2	22.5	39.1	38.4	107	79.4	2	3	98	43.9
Lamont, Gene, Pit	162	126	68.3	4	72-35	14-5	0-0	3	14.3	33.3	52.4	78	76.9	3	7	70	31.4
Lopes, Davey, Mil	163	116	62.1	2	64-40	8-3	0-1	1	17.2	32.8	50.0	78	78.2	3	5	89	30.3
McKeon, Jack, Cin	163	137	72.3	2	83-34	15-4	1-0	5	15.3	36.5	48.2	82	76.8	3	3	64	31.3
Showalter, Buck, Ari	162	141	68.8	5	85-34	12-8	0-2	5	24.1	34.0	41.8	89	75.3	3	5	54	40.7
Valentine, Bobby, NYM	162	112	58.9	3	57-41	9-4	0-1	3	18.8	45.5	35.7	84	85.7	2	6	107	32.7

DEFENSE

	G	Pitchout Total	Runners Moving	CS%	Non-PO CS%	Intentional BB IBB	Pct. of Situations	Favorite Score Diff.	Defensive Subs Total	Favorite Inning	Pos. 1	Pos. 2	Pos. 3
AL Managers													
Fregosi, Jim, Tor	162	11	2	50.0	27.4	14	2.3	0	10	8	c-4	lf-3	ss-2
Garner, Phil, Det	162	26	6	66.7	41.8	13	2.1	-1	25	8	rf-9	3b-7	2b-4
Hargrove, Mike, Bal	162	31	7	57.1	21.1	21	3.2	-2	19	9	rf-12	c-3	lf-3
Howe, Art, Oak	161	38	11	18.2	30.8	45	7.0	-1	39	9	lf-25	c-3	2b-3
Kelly, Tom, Min	162	10	2	0.0	34.7	9	1.5	-2	11	8	2b-4	c-3	1b-1
Manuel, Charlie, Cle	162	30	7	0.0	42.2	38	6.3	-2	26	8	rf-11	lf-9	2b-2
Manuel, Jerry, CWS	162	32	9	44.4	42.2	21	3.8	-2	20	8	cf-11	3b-5	rf-3
Muser, Tony, KC	162	17	4	50.0	23.7	25	3.6	0	14	8	1b-9	rf-2	2b-1
Oates, Johnny, Tex	162	4	0	-	36.3	29	4.4	-1	18	9	rf-6	cf-5	2b-3
Piniella, Lou, Sea	162	22	3	66.7	30.8	32	5.6	1	52	9	rf-23	lf-14	cf-7
Rothschild, Larry, TB	161	19	5	40.0	28.4	26	3.6	-2	28	9	3b-9	lf-7	rf-7
Scioscia, Mike, Ana	162	40	13	69.2	32.6	32	5.4	0	4	7	ss-2	lf-2	ph-0
Torre, Joe, NYY	161	8	3	0.0	29.6	16	2.8	-2	27	9	2b-11	lf-7	rf-3
Williams, Jimy, Bos	162	114	34	35.3	20.3	28	4.0	-2	30	9	1b-10	3b-8	2b-7
NL Managers													
Alou, Felipe, Mon	162	18	7	42.9	22.7	29	4.2	-2	32	8	lf-7	cf-7	c-6
Baker, Dusty, SF	162	37	6	100.0	30.2	16	2.6	0	22	9	cf-8	1b-5	2b-3
Baylor, Don, ChC	162	34	9	33.3	36.7	37	6.1	-2	20	9	lf-13	cf-4	1b-1
Bell, Buddy, Col	162	40	6	33.3	24.6	53	8.7	-2	8	8	1b-2	lf-2	cf-2
Bochy, Bruce, SD	162	27	8	50.0	31.1	40	6.3	0	14	7	rf-6	lf-3	cf-3
Boles, John, Fla	161	33	7	28.6	34.9	40	5.8	-2	26	7	1b-8	rf-2	3b-4
Cox, Bobby, Atl	162	59	17	35.3	23.5	34	5.9	-2	11	6	lf-8	rf-2	3b-1
Dierker, Larry, Hou	162	7	3	66.7	21.4	18	2.8	-1	23	9	cf-15	c-2	ss-2
Francona, Terry, Phi	162	16	3	66.7	35.6	17	2.6	-2	14	9	lf-5	1b-4	ss-3
Johnson, Davey, LA	162	11	2	50.0	32.7	14	2.2	0	11	9	lf-4	3b-3	ss-3
La Russa, Tony, StL	162	34	11	81.8	46.0	21	3.6	-2	25	8	3b-8	ss-1	rf-1
Lamont, Gene, Pit	162	24	3	0.0	30.0	47	6.5	-2	4	8	2b-2	ss-1	rf-1
Lopes, Davey, Mil	163	50	15	53.3	38.8	56	9.3	0	8	7	ss-3	2b-1	3b-1
McKeon, Jack, Cin	163	24	5	40.0	38.8	43	6.0	1	41	9	rf-12	c-4	cf-2
Showalter, Buck, Ari	162	10	3	33.3	35.5	36	6.3	-1	11	7	1b-4	rf-4	cf-2
Valentine, Bobby, NYM	162	49	9	22.2	25.9	34	5.2	-1	32	7	lf-16	cf-5	2b-3

LINEUPS

		Starting Lineup			Substitutions					
	G	Lineups Used	%LHB vs. RHSP	%RHB vs. LHSP	#PH	Percent PH Platoon	PH BA	PH HR	#PR	PR SB-CS
AL Managers										
Fregosi, Jim, Tor	162	74	47.4	79.8	60	65.0	.333	0	20	1-1
Garner, Phil, Det	162	128	40.7	85.2	126	80.2	.299	3	30	3-1
Hargrove, Mike, Bal	162	107	48.5	68.6	77	74.0	.213	1	42	4-4
Howe, Art, Oak	161	119	58.8	57.9	162	58.6	.212	2	81	2-2
Kelly, Tom, Min	162	131	66.1	74.7	182	89.6	.253	1	27	1-2
Manuel, Charlie, Cle	162	102	59.9	78.4	73	83.6	.231	1	40	2-2
Manuel, Jerry, CWS	162	84	43.3	93.9	84	69.0	.192	3	35	3-0
Muser, Tony, KC	162	111	32.0	89.4	134	72.4	.250	1	25	2-0
Oates, Johnny, Tex	162	108	60.6	74.8	123	87.8	.340	4	39	1-5
Piniella, Lou, Sea	162	130	41.1	90.0	109	86.2	.202	0	43	3-4
Rothschild, Larry, TB	161	138	39.1	84.3	113	65.5	.265	3	52	7-0
Scioscia, Mike, Ana	162	75	62.5	59.2	110	85.5	.232	2	41	1-0
Torre, Joe, NYY	161	112	57.4	78.3	86	70.9	.237	4	49	0-1
Williams, Jimy, Bos	162	140	61.0	82.8	158	88.0	.256	3	52	0-1
NL Managers										
Alou, Felipe, Mon	162	120	51.9	85.8	211	90.5	.246	3	24	2-0
Baker, Dusty, SF	162	82	49.1	76.6	233	73.4	.235	7	26	0-0
Baylor, Don, ChC	162	130	42.5	81.3	280	73.6	.188	8	26	1-1
Bell, Buddy, Col	162	106	60.7	75.4	285	68.4	.246	5	21	1-1
Bochy, Bruce, SD	162	134	37.8	85.5	285	74.0	.224	7	44	5-0
Boles, John, Fla	161	104	42.0	87.2	253	49.0	.230	5	48	0-1
Cox, Bobby, Atl	162	103	48.6	94.9	252	78.2	.235	3	72	5-1
Dierker, Larry, Hou	162	122	34.0	98.8	272	68.8	.184	3	40	5-7
Francona, Terry, Phi	162	108	44.0	83.3	278	63.7	.199	2	17	2-0
Johnson, Davey, LA	162	89	47.1	80.3	252	86.9	.233	12	26	0-0
La Russa, Tony, StL	162	137	45.4	77.5	240	66.7	.199	9	35	6-0
Lamont, Gene, Pit	162	117	41.9	82.9	235	56.6	.246	7	13	0-1
Lopes, Davey, Mil	163	126	38.1	81.9	285	69.1	.224	3	37	6-1
McKeon, Jack, Cin	163	117	42.8	80.8	270	67.0	.258	6	31	3-1
Showalter, Buck, Ari	162	99	57.5	69.4	250	83.6	.234	2	32	2-2
Valentine, Bobby, NYM	162	118	22.1	87.5	299	75.3	.245	7	39	1-2

PITCHING

		Starters					Relievers					
	G	Slow Hooks	Quick Hooks	>120 Pitches	>140 Pitches	3 Days Rest	Relief App	Mid-Inning Change	Save >1 IP	1st Batter Platoon Pct	1-Batter App	3 Pitchers (<=2 runs)
AL Managers												
Fregosi, Jim, Tor	162	24	13	16	0	1	388	179	16	71.6	31	23
Garner, Phil, Det	162	18	18	8	0	3	429	228	3	61.1	41	21
Hargrove, Mike, Bal	162	30	7	24	0	1	396	161	2	61.9	39	23
Howe, Art, Oak	161	17	14	9	1	0	381	201	12	60.1	37	24
Kelly, Tom, Min	162	20	8	9	0	5	412	193	10	63.1	33	18
Manuel, Charlie, Cle	162	12	21	20	0	4	462	219	7	61.9	38	19
Manuel, Jerry, CWS	162	18	30	8	0	1	466	208	18	63.7	44	23
Muser, Tony, KC	162	12	12	19	0	1	329	150	8	53.2	16	7
Oates, Johnny, Tex	162	27	9	20	1	1	415	233	6	66.5	43	12
Piniella, Lou, Sea	162	12	25	1	0	1	383	175	11	63.2	18	26
Rothschild, Larry, TB	161	21	21	7	0	1	401	164	7	58.9	18	18
Scioscia, Mike, Ana	162	21	27	6	0	0	441	204	9	66.9	35	18
Torre, Joe, NYY	161	21	13	27	0	4	382	177	16	64.1	32	30
Williams, Jimy, Bos	162	8	39	9	0	1	425	163	16	57.6	20	22
NL Managers												
Alou, Felipe, Mon	162	16	22	5	0	1	452	190	15	61.4	34	20
Baker, Dusty, SF	162	17	8	25	1	0	384	138	3	58.9	27	31
Baylor, Don, ChC	162	24	13	15	0	4	421	151	6	57.7	41	15
Bell, Buddy, Col	162	18	12	10	0	4	480	207	8	64.2	57	20
Bochy, Bruce, SD	162	21	17	14	0	0	443	154	5	58.5	30	25
Boles, John, Fla	161	11	17	8	0	0	429	164	3	60.8	38	24
Cox, Bobby, Atl	162	16	7	6	0	7	376	120	13	52.9	26	27
Dierker, Larry, Hou	162	29	8	19	0	1	410	158	10	58.8	30	12
Francona, Terry, Phi	162	19	11	25	0	0	414	130	5	64.1	27	21
Johnson, Davey, LA	162	15	20	10	0	3	371	80	6	51.5	13	19
La Russa, Tony, StL	162	8	17	11	1	2	386	143	18	58.0	27	25
Lamont, Gene, Pit	162	13	16	13	0	1	466	172	2	63.5	44	22
Lopes, Davey, Mil	163	16	10	10	0	0	433	133	1	64.0	39	24
McKeon, Jack, Cin	163	9	16	10	1	1	387	146	24	65.6	31	20
Showalter, Buck, Ari	162	14	13	18	1	0	390	163	12	66.2	38	21
Valentine, Bobby, NYM	162	14	15	18	0	3	411	134	7	54.3	25	28

2001 Batter Projections

Setting aside braggadocio, self-promotion, false modesty, true modesty, apologies, excuses and hype, there are really only two things to be said about the projections we run here each year for what players will do the next season. Sometimes they're right, and sometimes they're wrong. Starting on the waste products end of the animal, our worst projection last year was for Vinny Castilla. Castilla, playing for the Rockies, had hit 40, 40, 46 and 33 homers over the previous four seasons. We projected that he would hit 38 home runs in year 2000.

We did not know, obviously, that Castilla
a) would be traded to Tampa Bay in December, and
b) would develop nagging back troubles in June.
So
a) We made a bad projection, or
b) Castilla had a bad year, or
c) Both.

Anyway, he didn't do what we said he would:

Vinny Castilla

	Avg	G	AB	R	H	2B	3B	HR	RBI	BB	SO	SB	CS	RC/27
Actual 2000	.221	85	331	22	73	9	1	6	42	14	41	1	2	2.6
Projected 2000	.297	155	607	91	180	28	2	38	114	45	90	4	4	6.8

We score the similarity between the projection and the actual season at 649, by which standard we give ourselves an "F" for that one. Anything under 760 is an F. We had 17 "Fs" last year, not counting players for whom we printed projections, but who didn't play in the majors for one reason or another. Our second-worst projection was for Vernon Wells, a Toronto outfielder.

Vernon Wells

	Avg	G	AB	R	H	2B	3B	HR	RBI	BB	SO	SB	CS	RC/27
Actual 2000	.000	3	2	0	0	0	0	0	0	0	0	0	0	0.0
Projected 2000	.285	124	421	51	120	23	1	8	51	26	77	12	5	4.9

We had projected Wells as a near-regular based on his fine 1999 season in the minor leagues, a decent performance in September in the majors, and the Blue Jays' perceived need for help in the outfield. We were wrong; he was a regular, but for Syracuse, and he didn't play particularly well at Syracuse.

We were wrong, but. . . just myself, I'll live with that. John Dewan and I have argued about this for many years. It is my view that if a player may play, we should project that he will play, because it's our job to tell you what kind of hitter somebody is as best we know, rather than to speculate about things that we don't know. We don't know which rookies will become regulars in the year 2001; we don't have any way of knowing. What we can say is, if this man plays, this is what we expect him to do. John takes a different view: that even though we may not know who will play next year, we should do the best we can to figure it out, and make the projections on that basis.

Our third-worst projection was the same thing, a projection for Quinton (Coo Coo) McCracken, who wound up playing 85 games for the Durham Bulls, and our fourth-worst was the same, a projection for John (Yee-Haw!) Jaha, who missed most of the season with shoulder miseries.

There is nothing we can do about that, either, but for our fifth-worst projection a few words of contrition may be in order. For reasons that can charitably be described as obscure, we had projected that Cole Liniak would bat 404 times in 2000:

Cole Liniak

	Avg	G	AB	R	H	2B	3B	HR	RBI	BB	SO	SB	CS	RC/27
Actual 2000	.000	3	3	0	0	0	0	0	0	0	2	0	0	0.0
Projected 2000	.252	120	404	50	102	29	0	11	44	32	63	2	2	4.3

Let's be honest: that was just stupid. Our thinking, apparently, was that the Cubs needed a third baseman, Liniak was a young third baseman, they were saying nice things about him, maybe we should project him to play. The problem with this logic is that, in the modern world, players change teams—and managers—with great regularity. We just don't know how much the Cubs will need a third baseman or a second baseman or a relief ace by next May.

What we should have known, and should have had the sense to focus on, is that guys like Cole Liniak do not break through as major league regulars. I'm not apologizing because we make mistakes—everybody makes mistakes—but that one, in all candor, is as dumb a projection as we have ever made in these pages.

Most of our other "F" projections are variations on the theme of Wells and Jaha—players who, for one reason or another, didn't play. Karim Garcia, Gary Disarcina, Edgard Clemente, Erubiel Durazo, Chad Hermansen, Chad Meyers. . . Sally, take a note. Let's not project playing time for anybody named "Chad". We got "Fs" for all of those, plus Roberto Kelly, Angel Echevarria, Rico Brogna, Carlos Beltran and Mike Barrett. Mike Barrett. . . that was a bad one:

Michael Barrett

	Avg	G	AB	R	H	2B	3B	HR	RBI	BB	SO	SB	CS	RC/27
Actual 2000	.214	89	271	28	58	15	1	1	22	23	35	0	1	2.6
Projected 2000	.300	146	507	70	152	38	2	14	74	32	47	4	3	5.9

Occasionally we have an "F" projection for a different reason: because a player plays far better than we thought he would. The most conspicuous example of this, in 2000, was Richard Hidalgo:

Richard Hidalgo

	Avg	G	AB	R	H	2B	3B	HR	RBI	BB	SO	SB	CS	RC/27
Actual 2000	.314	153	558	118	175	42	3	44	122	56	110	13	6	9.2
Projected 2000	.253	113	380	49	96	26	2	12	52	35	59	6	6	4.7

Hidalgo hit 10 to 14 homers every year in the minors from 1993 through 1997, and 15 in the majors in 1999, so sue us; how did we know he was going to turn into an animal? John Vander Wal will file a friend-of-the-court brief:

John Vander Wal

	Avg	G	AB	R	H	2B	3B	HR	RBI	BB	SO	SB	CS	RC/27
Actual 2000	.299	134	384	74	115	29	0	24	94	72	92	11	2	8.8
Projected 2000	.246	114	179	22	44	10	1	4	26	25	50	1	1	4.4

When Vander Wal hit 6 home runs in 1999, he was then 33 years old, and the 6 homers was his career high. He had hit exactly 5 home runs in 1993, 1994, 1995, 1996 and 1998, and had hit 4 in 1992. We projected him for 4 in 2000. He hit 24. Who knew?

No one else had a Great Leap Forward sufficient to cause us to have an "F" projection, but many other players played significantly better than we had expected them to. Among these were Gary Sheffield, Jason Giambi, Todd Helton, Ben Molina, Darin Erstad, Jose Vidro and Chris Stynes:

Gary Sheffield

	Avg	G	AB	R	H	2B	3B	HR	RBI	BB	SO	SB	CS	RC/27
Actual 2000	.325	141	501	105	163	24	3	43	109	101	71	4	6	10.9
Projected 2000	.285	142	484	89	138	27	1	27	91	109	65	12	7	7.9

Jason Giambi

	Avg	G	AB	R	H	2B	3B	HR	RBI	BB	SO	SB	CS	RC/27
Actual 2000	.333	152	510	108	170	29	1	43	137	137	96	2	0	12.0
Projected 2000	.298	148	497	85	148	35	1	25	92	76	89	1	1	7.6

Todd Helton

	Avg	G	AB	R	H	2B	3B	HR	RBI	BB	SO	SB	CS	RC/27
Actual 2000	.372	160	580	138	216	59	2	42	147	103	61	5	3	13.6
Projected 2000	.329	158	563	101	185	41	3	30	107	66	72	4	4	8.9

Ben Molina

	Avg	G	AB	R	H	2B	3B	HR	RBI	BB	SO	SB	CS	RC/27
Actual 2000	.281	130	473	59	133	20	2	14	71	23	33	1	0	4.8
Projected 2000	.260	57	181	17	47	9	0	3	23	8	11	0	1	3.6

Darin Erstad

	Avg	G	AB	R	H	2B	3B	HR	RBI	BB	SO	SB	CS	RC/27
Actual 2000	.355	157	676	121	240	39	6	25	100	64	82	28	8	9.3
Projected 2000	.285	140	554	94	158	32	4	16	72	49	85	16	8	5.6

Jose Vidro

	Avg	G	AB	R	H	2B	3B	HR	RBI	BB	SO	SB	CS	RC/27
Actual 2000	.330	153	606	101	200	51	2	24	97	49	69	5	4	8.0
Projected 2000	.274	154	493	62	135	36	2	10	65	39	60	3	2	4.9

Chris Stynes

	Avg	G	AB	R	H	2B	3B	HR	RBI	BB	SO	SB	CS	RC/27
Actual 2000	.334	119	380	71	127	24	1	12	40	32	54	5	2	7.6
Projected 2000	.270	69	122	17	33	5	0	2	13	8	10	3	1	4.2

These guys all had unexpectedly good years. We did not know they would be having good years, since we are not omniscient, and therefore we made what we could call, generically speaking, bad projections. One other bad projection is interesting enough to warrant a note. We had projected that Ben Petrick, Colorado Rockies catcher, would play 133 games, hitting .282 with 24 homers, 82 RBI. The Rockies sent Petrick back to the minor leagues for most of the summer. When he finally got to play, however, Petrick was actually even better than we had said he would be:

Ben Petrick

	Avg	G	AB	R	H	2B	3B	HR	RBI	BB	SO	SB	CS	RC/27
Actual 2000	.322	52	146	32	47	10	1	3	20	20	33	1	2	7.2
Projected 2000	.282	133	479	83	135	30	5	24	82	65	96	10	8	6.9

A few players every year will perform in an unexpected manner. A great many players every year, however, will perform in a manner which is completely consistent with their previous seasons. When this happens, this creates what we like to call a good projection. Last year, we had a nearly perfect projection for Chipper Jones:

Chipper Jones

	Avg	G	AB	R	H	2B	3B	HR	RBI	BB	SO	SB	CS	RC/27
Actual 2000	.311	156	579	118	180	38	1	36	111	95	64	14	7	8.9
Projected 2000	.306	159	592	118	181	36	3	36	112	105	91	17	4	8.8

We score that at 986, an A+ projection. We rarely do that well for a star; high-scoring projections are more common for less talented players. The more things a player does well, the greater the chance that he will do something more or less often than we had expected him to. We also had a 986 projection for Jeff Huson:

Jeff Huson

	Avg	G	AB	R	H	2B	3B	HR	RBI	BB	SO	SB	CS	RC/27
Actual 2000	.215	70	130	19	28	7	1	0	11	13	9	2	1	2.7
Projected 2000	.236	77	140	13	33	6	1	0	12	8	18	3	1	2.8

And a 985 for Lee Stevens:

Lee Stevens

	Avg	G	AB	R	H	2B	3B	HR	RBI	BB	SO	SB	CS	RC/27
Actual 2000	.265	123	449	60	119	27	2	22	75	48	105	0	0	5.7
Projected 2000	.271	137	435	58	118	27	2	21	69	36	106	1	1	5.7

We had five other A+ projections, those being for Dave Martinez, Mike Cameron, Ramon Hernandez, John Flaherty and Randy Velarde. I'll show Cameron's:

Mike Cameron

	Avg	G	AB	R	H	2B	3B	HR	RBI	BB	SO	SB	CS	RC/27
Actual 2000	.267	155	543	96	145	28	4	19	78	78	133	24	7	5.8
Projected 2000	.250	151	552	98	138	28	6	21	71	75	145	33	12	5.4

We had straight A projections for 59 other players. We just missed an A+ for Neifi Perez:

Neifi Perez

	Avg	G	AB	R	H	2B	3B	HR	RBI	BB	SO	SB	CS	RC/27
Actual 2000	.287	162	651	92	187	39	11	10	71	30	63	3	6	4.9
Projected 2000	.295	160	661	95	195	35	10	12	70	36	63	10	8	5.3

We had projected that Dave Magadan would hit .275 with 2 homers, 23 RBI; he hit .273 with 2 and 21. We just missed an A+ on Fernando Vina and Shane Spencer. We had good or fairly good projections for every regular on the Cleveland Indians:

Sandy Alomar Jr.

	Avg	G	AB	R	H	2B	3B	HR	RBI	BB	SO	SB	CS	RC/27
Actual 2000	.289	97	356	44	103	16	2	7	42	16	41	2	2	4.7
Projected 2000	.272	96	313	39	85	17	0	9	43	14	37	1	1	4.4

Jim Thome

	Avg	G	AB	R	H	2B	3B	HR	RBI	BB	SO	SB	CS	RC/27
Actual 2000	.269	158	557	106	150	33	1	37	106	118	171	1	0	7.5
Projected 2000	.276	150	550	114	152	31	2	38	110	136	176	1	1	8.3

Roberto Alomar

	Avg	G	AB	R	H	2B	3B	HR	RBI	BB	SO	SB	CS	RC/27
Actual 2000	.310	155	610	111	189	40	2	19	89	64	82	39	4	7.2
Projected 2000	.297	155	575	106	171	32	4	19	84	74	78	17	6	6.7

Travis Fryman

	Avg	G	AB	R	H	2B	3B	HR	RBI	BB	SO	SB	CS	RC/27
Actual 2000	.321	155	574	93	184	38	4	22	106	73	111	1	1	7.8
Projected 2000	.277	144	542	78	150	31	3	22	94	43	111	7	4	5.6

Omar Vizquel

	Avg	G	AB	R	H	2B	3B	HR	RBI	BB	SO	SB	CS	RC/27
Actual 2000	.287	156	613	101	176	27	3	7	66	87	72	22	10	5.3
Projected 2000	.275	146	559	87	154	22	2	4	50	61	58	31	10	4.5

Wil Cordero

	Avg	G	AB	R	H	2B	3B	HR	RBI	BB	SO	SB	CS	RC/27
Actual 2000	.276	127	496	64	137	35	5	16	68	32	76	1	2	5.3
Projected 2000	.276	92	337	53	93	22	1	12	51	23	67	2	1	5.3

Kenny Lofton

	Avg	G	AB	R	H	2B	3B	HR	RBI	BB	SO	SB	CS	RC/27
Actual 2000	.278	137	543	107	151	23	5	15	73	79	72	30	7	5.9
Projected 2000	.298	134	523	101	156	26	6	8	50	79	85	36	13	6.4

Manny Ramirez

	Avg	G	AB	R	H	2B	3B	HR	RBI	BB	SO	SB	CS	RC/27
Actual 2000	.351	118	439	92	154	34	2	38	122	86	117	1	1	12.8
Projected 2000	.311	152	559	112	174	38	1	41	130	89	123	4	3	9.3

Those score as follows:

C	Sandy Alomar	969	A
1B	Jim Thome	977	A
2B	Roberto Alomar	962	A
3B	Travis Fryman	928	B+
SS	Omar Vizquel	937	B+
LF	Wilfredo Cordero	939	B+
CF	Kenny Lofton	952	A-
RF	Manny Ramirez	896	C+

We had good luck with Cleveland because they're a veteran team with a lot of "known" players. If we reviewed a team with more unknowns, like the Oakland A's, we'd find more poor projections. Timo Perez next year. . . we don't have a clue what he's going to do. We're just guessing, based on the evidence we have, which is limited.

We have never, in the years we have been doing this, projected a regular player's triple crown stats exactly right. We just missed last year; we got Brad Ausmus' home runs right (7), and nailed his batting average (.266)—but missed by two RBI. We said he would have 49; he had 51. We had a good projection for Paul O'Neill:

Paul O'Neill

	Avg	G	AB	R	H	2B	3B	HR	RBI	BB	SO	SB	CS	RC/27
Actual 2000	.283	142	566	79	160	26	0	18	100	51	90	14	9	5.3
Projected 2000	.285	142	544	72	155	30	1	18	92	61	92	6	4	5.8

That scores at 974, which is a straight A. As I said, we had 59 of those, including Brady Anderson, Ben Grieve, Rafael Palmeiro, Hal Morris, Rich Becker, Ray Durham, Ruben Rivera and Alex Rodriguez:

Brady Anderson

	Avg	G	AB	R	H	2B	3B	HR	RBI	BB	SO	SB	CS	RC/27
Actual 2000	.257	141	506	89	130	26	0	19	50	92	103	16	9	5.6
Projected 2000	.255	139	518	85	132	26	4	20	64	80	95	18	8	5.5

Ben Grieve

	Avg	G	AB	R	H	2B	3B	HR	RBI	BB	SO	SB	CS	RC/27
Actual 2000	.279	158	594	92	166	40	1	27	104	73	130	3	0	6.3
Projected 2000	.292	153	555	104	162	34	1	27	107	81	115	3	2	7.1

Rafael Palmeiro

	Avg	G	AB	R	H	2B	3B	HR	RBI	BB	SO	SB	CS	RC/27
Actual 2000	.288	158	565	102	163	29	3	39	120	103	77	2	1	8.1
Projected 2000	.280	157	564	87	158	32	2	37	119	75	89	5	3	7.1

Hal Morris

	Avg	G	AB	R	H	2B	3B	HR	RBI	BB	SO	SB	CS	RC/27
Actual 2000	.278	99	169	24	47	9	1	3	14	31	26	0	0	5.6
Projected 2000	.301	93	133	15	40	8	0	1	15	9	18	1	1	4.9

Rich Becker

	Avg	G	AB	R	H	2B	3B	HR	RBI	BB	SO	SB	CS	RC/27
Actual 2000	.242	115	285	59	69	14	0	8	39	67	87	2	2	5.0
Projected 2000	.246	137	321	51	79	18	2	8	36	60	99	10	3	5.1

Ray Durham

	Avg	G	AB	R	H	2B	3B	HR	RBI	BB	SO	SB	CS	RC/27
Actual 2000	.280	151	614	121	172	35	9	17	75	75	105	25	13	6.0
Projected 2000	.281	157	631	110	177	34	6	15	66	73	102	32	11	5.7

Ruben Rivera

	Avg	G	AB	R	H	2B	3B	HR	RBI	BB	SO	SB	CS	RC/27
Actual 2000	.208	135	423	62	88	18	6	17	57	44	137	8	4	3.7
Projected 2000	.207	136	334	56	69	18	3	16	46	43	116	11	6	4.2

Alex Rodriguez

	Avg	G	AB	R	H	2B	3B	HR	RBI	BB	SO	SB	CS	RC/27
Actual 2000	.316	148	554	134	175	34	2	41	132	100	121	15	4	9.9
Projected 2000	.312	145	596	128	186	36	3	42	118	51	106	27	8	8.4

Ray Durham may be the most consistent player in the majors today. The last three years his strikeout totals have been 105, 105 and 105. Next year we project him for 105. Durham has scored 106 to 126 runs in each of the last four seasons, with 172 to 181 hits each year. The last three years his walk totals have been 73, 73 and 75. His batting averages for the last five years are all within a 25-point range (.271 to .296), and in a six-year career he has never hit fewer than 27 doubles or more than 35. He's sort of the opposite of Timo Perez: it is fairly obvious what kind of numbers we should project for him next season.

We said last year that Doug Glanville would bat 637 times and hit 8 home runs. He did. We had projected 143 hits, 26 homers, 90 RBI for Scott Rolen; he wound up with 144, 26 and 89. We had projected 86 RBI for Eric Chavez, which was 36 more than his previous career high, but which turned out to be the right number. Chavez, Jacque Jones, Mark Quinn and Mike Lowell demonstrate once more the feasability of projecting major league performance based on minor league numbers:

Eric Chavez

	Avg	G	AB	R	H	2B	3B	HR	RBI	BB	SO	SB	CS	RC/27
Actual 2000	.277	153	501	89	139	23	4	26	86	62	94	2	2	6.4
Projected 2000	.287	141	478	76	137	36	2	21	86	47	75	6	5	6.4

Jacque Jones

	Avg	G	AB	R	H	2B	3B	HR	RBI	BB	SO	SB	CS	RC/27
Actual 2000	.285	154	523	66	149	26	5	19	76	26	111	7	5	5.4
Projected 2000	.289	136	471	69	136	35	2	14	66	24	105	11	8	5.4

Mark Quinn

	Avg	G	AB	R	H	2B	3B	HR	RBI	BB	SO	SB	CS	RC/27
Actual 2000	.294	135	500	76	147	33	2	20	78	35	91	5	2	6.1
Projected 2000	.312	144	504	86	157	34	3	25	95	35	76	4	4	7.2

Mike Lowell

	Avg	G	AB	R	H	2B	3B	HR	RBI	BB	SO	SB	CS	RC/27
Actual 2000	.270	140	508	73	137	38	0	22	91	54	75	4	0	5.8
Projected 2000	.277	136	462	63	128	25	0	20	72	39	75	2	1	5.5

We had equally good projections for other young players, including Ron Belliard, Adrian Beltre and Frank Catalanotto, and a B+ projection for Adam Kennedy. Minor league stats had enabled us to peg fairly well the regression of Pokey Reese:

Pokey Reese

	Avg	G	AB	R	H	2B	3B	HR	RBI	BB	SO	SB	CS	RC/27
Actual 2000	.255	135	518	76	132	20	6	12	46	45	86	29	3	4.5
Projected 2000	.250	153	573	75	143	27	2	8	51	44	96	26	8	3.8

Although we were completely off on Warren Morris. Mike Piazza is easy, of course:

Mike Piazza

	Avg	G	AB	R	H	2B	3B	HR	RBI	BB	SO	SB	CS	RC/27
Actual 2000	.324	136	482	90	156	26	0	38	113	58	69	4	2	9.4
Projected 2000	.335	148	550	94	184	28	0	38	119	61	76	2	1	9.3

We had projected Rickey Henderson fairly accurately:

Rickey Henderson

	Avg	G	AB	R	H	2B	3B	HR	RBI	BB	SO	SB	CS	RC/27
Actual 2000	.233	123	420	75	98	14	2	4	32	88	75	36	11	4.3
Projected 2000	.246	122	422	77	104	19	1	9	36	90	89	30	10	5.1

Which was dumb luck, because in any given season Rickey Henderson may play anywhere from 80 games to 150 and bat anywhere between .225 and .325. We had guessed that Jeremy Burnitz would hit 29 doubles, 32 homers, 103 RBI and 89 runs scored; he had 29 doubles, 31 homers, 98 RBI and 91 runs scored.

One odd note was that Alex Gonzalez of Toronto produced almost exactly the numbers we had projected for Alex Gonzalez of Florida:

Alex Gonzalez

	Avg	G	AB	R	H	2B	3B	HR	RBI	BB	SO	SB	CS	RC/27
Actual 2000	.252	141	527	68	133	31	2	15	69	43	113	4	4	4.3
Projected 2000	.253	138	561	79	142	23	7	15	62	25	109	4	6	3.9

While Alex Gonzalez of Florida was fairly close to the numbers we had projected for Alex Gonzalez of Toronto:

Alex Gonzalez

	Avg	G	AB	R	H	2B	3B	HR	RBI	BB	SO	SB	CS	RC/27
Actual 2000	.200	109	385	35	77	17	4	7	42	13	77	7	1	2.4
Projected 2000	.249	99	345	42	86	20	2	9	36	25	70	11	4	4.2

Who says two wrongs don't make a right?

—Bill James

Projections for 2001 Batters

Batter	Age	Avg	G	AB	R	H	2B	3B	HR	RBI	BB	SO	SB	CS	OBP	SLG
Abbott,Jeff, CWS	28	.281	81	217	32	61	14	0	6	28	14	29	3	2	.325	.429
Abbott,Kurt, NYM	32	.257	67	148	21	38	10	2	4	19	10	41	1	1	.304	.432
Abreu,Bobby, Phi	27	.311	156	550	99	171	32	9	22	85	105	121	23	10	.421	.522
Agbayani,Benny, NYM	29	.275	125	371	59	102	20	2	15	55	53	75	10	6	.366	.461
Alexander,Manny, Bos	30	.229	87	175	22	40	7	1	2	16	12	40	3	1	.278	.314
Alfonzo,Edgardo, NYM	27	.301	155	592	113	178	32	3	24	96	88	78	7	4	.391	.486
Alicea,Luis, Tex	35	.257	110	335	51	86	15	3	4	35	43	54	5	3	.341	.355
Alomar,Roberto, Cle	33	.302	150	570	100	172	33	4	18	82	73	83	21	6	.381	.468
Alomar Jr.,Sandy, Cle	35	.267	97	330	39	88	18	1	8	43	15	41	1	1	.299	.400
Alou,Moises, Hou	34	.305	136	492	83	150	30	2	28	108	66	65	6	3	.387	.545
Anderson,Brady, Bal	37	.248	135	488	82	121	25	3	17	54	82	94	17	8	.356	.416
Anderson,Garret, Ana	28	.297	159	637	86	189	39	3	25	102	31	83	6	4	.329	.485
Anderson,Marlon, Phi	27	.270	93	344	45	93	18	4	6	41	21	45	11	4	.312	.398
Andrews,Shane, ChC	29	.220	103	309	36	68	14	1	17	48	42	91	1	1	.313	.437
Arias,Alex, Phi	33	.267	85	165	20	44	7	0	2	20	17	21	1	1	.335	.345
Aurilia,Rich, SF	29	.272	149	530	71	144	26	1	20	76	48	80	3	2	.332	.438
Ausmus,Brad, Det	32	.264	137	470	64	124	20	2	7	49	59	72	11	6	.346	.360
Aven,Bruce, LA	29	.276	96	239	35	66	16	1	8	41	25	54	3	2	.345	.452
Bagwell,Jeff, Hou	33	.305	151	545	124	166	35	2	44	128	120	111	17	8	.430	.618
Baines,Harold, CWS	42	.274	95	270	30	74	15	1	10	47	32	39	0	0	.351	.448
Bako,Paul, Atl	29	.257	64	191	15	49	10	0	2	19	18	47	1	1	.321	.340
Barker,Kevin, Mil	25	.246	76	175	24	43	8	1	6	29	19	37	1	1	.320	.406
Barrett,Michael, Mon	24	.288	105	351	47	101	25	1	7	47	25	34	2	2	.335	.425
Batista,Tony, Tor	27	.270	153	608	99	164	31	2	40	110	41	112	4	3	.316	.525
Bautista,Danny, Ari	29	.268	124	313	45	84	15	2	9	43	17	45	3	2	.306	.415
Becker,Rich, Det	29	.240	130	263	45	63	17	2	7	31	61	84	6	2	.383	.399
Bell,David, Sea	28	.254	102	358	46	91	20	1	10	42	32	53	2	2	.315	.399
Bell,Derek, NYM	32	.269	143	561	83	151	28	1	17	79	56	129	12	6	.335	.414
Bell,Jay, Ari	35	.257	145	541	85	139	29	3	21	76	73	116	5	4	.345	.438
Belle,Albert, Bal	34	.299	149	568	90	170	38	1	32	116	76	78	6	4	.382	.539
Belliard,Ron, Mil	26	.276	153	555	88	153	34	5	9	63	75	78	13	8	.362	.404
Beltran,Carlos, KC	24	.293	144	535	96	157	25	7	18	86	45	89	19	5	.348	.467
Beltre,Adrian, LA	22	.282	148	503	76	142	30	3	19	79	56	81	16	7	.354	.467
Benard,Marvin, SF	31	.281	144	524	89	147	28	3	12	57	58	88	19	10	.352	.414
Benjamin,Mike, Pit	35	.236	70	195	20	46	10	1	1	16	10	45	3	2	.273	.313
Bennett,Gary, Phi	29	.256	54	121	13	31	6	0	3	16	13	17	0	0	.328	.380
Berg,Dave, Fla	30	.275	87	218	28	60	13	1	2	21	25	43	3	2	.350	.372
Bergeron,Peter, Mon	23	.273	91	326	55	89	17	4	4	29	37	58	13	8	.347	.387
Berkman,Lance, Hou	25	.307	143	462	88	142	36	1	27	94	79	89	8	5	.409	.565
Bichette,Dante, Bos	37	.292	145	565	82	165	32	1	22	92	40	81	6	4	.339	.469
Biggio,Craig, Hou	35	.277	151	591	107	164	35	3	14	64	75	109	28	9	.359	.418
Blanco,Henry, Mil	29	.245	109	319	35	78	19	1	8	38	38	54	2	2	.325	.386
Blum,Geoff, Mon	28	.252	114	341	46	86	21	1	10	40	35	59	4	2	.322	.408
Bonds,Barry, SF	36	.280	144	492	112	138	29	3	40	102	112	85	18	6	.414	.596
Bonilla,Bobby, Atl	38	.260	87	204	24	53	16	1	6	32	28	38	1	1	.349	.436
Boone,Aaron, Cin	28	.264	117	398	53	105	26	2	11	55	31	74	10	4	.317	.422
Boone,Bret, SD	32	.254	145	548	74	139	29	2	20	75	49	106	8	6	.315	.423
Bordick,Mike, NYM	35	.249	148	530	68	132	21	2	12	57	44	88	6	4	.307	.364
Bradley,Milton, Mon	23	.290	90	324	50	94	20	2	6	36	31	56	9	9	.352	.420
Branyan,Russ, Cle	25	.248	77	254	44	63	9	1	23	56	33	103	1	1	.334	.563

Projections for 2001 Batters

Batter	Age	Avg	G	AB	R	H	2B	3B	HR	RBI	BB	SO	SB	CS	OBP	SLG
Brogna,Rico, Bos	31	.267	115	225	30	60	14	1	7	37	19	49	3	2	.324	.431
Brosius,Scott, NYY	34	.250	122	420	58	105	20	0	14	61	40	72	5	4	.315	.398
Brown,Adrian, Pit	27	.277	122	343	57	95	15	3	3	28	35	45	14	5	.344	.364
Brown,Brant, ChC	30	.237	80	186	25	44	12	2	8	26	14	60	2	2	.290	.452
Brown,Dee, KC	23	.279	128	319	56	89	16	4	14	51	28	66	9	5	.337	.486
Brown,Emil, Pit	26	.296	67	159	28	47	9	1	4	19	14	29	6	3	.353	.440
Buford,Damon, ChC	31	.247	120	361	50	89	15	1	10	43	33	85	8	5	.310	.377
Buhner,Jay, Sea	36	.235	101	310	45	73	15	1	19	59	58	100	0	0	.356	.474
Burkhart,Morgan, Bos	29	.238	75	185	28	44	10	0	9	31	28	43	0	0	.338	.438
Burks,Ellis, SF	36	.284	127	419	71	119	24	3	23	81	59	83	6	4	.372	.520
Burnitz,Jeromy, Mil	32	.252	149	539	88	136	28	3	32	101	87	135	9	6	.356	.494
Burrell,Pat, Phi	24	.293	144	518	88	152	38	3	25	99	84	142	2	1	.392	.523
Bush,Homer, Tor	28	.291	99	309	44	90	14	1	3	30	17	53	14	6	.328	.372
Cabrera,Jolbert, Cle	28	.276	63	152	25	42	7	1	2	13	15	22	6	3	.341	.375
Cabrera,Orlando, Mon	26	.253	129	454	65	115	26	4	10	52	30	37	10	6	.300	.394
Cairo,Miguel, TB	27	.271	130	450	55	122	22	3	3	38	27	40	22	8	.312	.353
Cameron,Mike, Sea	28	.257	155	545	91	140	30	6	19	73	75	138	30	10	.347	.439
Caminiti,Ken, Hou	38	.255	98	326	56	83	19	1	17	57	54	73	4	2	.361	.475
Canizaro,Jay, Min	27	.251	104	351	55	88	18	1	13	53	39	67	5	3	.326	.419
Canseco,Jose, NYY	36	.248	122	444	67	110	21	1	28	82	61	136	9	5	.339	.489
Cardona,Javier, Det	25	.263	63	167	24	44	10	0	6	28	11	28	0	0	.309	.431
Casanova,Raul, Mil	28	.228	84	246	23	56	11	1	7	29	23	42	1	1	.294	.366
Casey,Sean, Cin	26	.325	145	520	86	169	39	2	22	99	62	72	1	1	.397	.535
Castilla,Vinny, TB	33	.276	100	377	50	104	17	1	17	64	26	50	2	2	.323	.462
Castillo,Alberto, Tor	31	.220	57	123	10	27	4	0	1	13	14	22	0	0	.299	.276
Castillo,Luis, Fla	25	.294	141	528	89	155	17	3	1	27	81	90	46	19	.388	.343
Castro,Juan, Cin	29	.228	74	184	17	42	8	1	2	17	13	29	0	1	.279	.315
Castro,Ramon, Fla	25	.242	120	351	38	85	19	0	11	45	25	68	0	0	.293	.390
Catalanotto,Frank, Tex	27	.281	117	317	47	89	22	2	11	45	27	52	4	4	.337	.467
Cedeno,Roger, Hou	26	.281	116	327	59	92	12	3	5	29	46	68	28	10	.370	.382
Chavez,Eric, Oak	23	.290	150	548	98	159	34	2	29	103	62	89	6	4	.362	.518
Chavez,Raul, Hou	28	.235	50	119	11	28	5	0	1	13	11	19	0	0	.300	.303
Christenson,Ryan, Oak	27	.258	93	151	29	39	8	1	2	17	20	34	3	2	.345	.364
Cirillo,Jeff, Col	31	.321	155	595	101	191	40	2	12	103	74	81	5	4	.396	.455
Clark,Tony, Det	29	.281	151	558	84	157	29	1	33	104	65	128	2	2	.356	.514
Clark,Will, StL	37	.290	119	404	64	117	25	2	16	59	58	71	1	1	.379	.480
Clayton,Royce, Tex	31	.258	143	512	76	132	25	4	12	54	47	94	16	9	.320	.393
Colbrunn,Greg, Ari	31	.291	107	234	30	68	17	1	8	37	25	38	2	1	.359	.474
Conine,Jeff, Bal	35	.290	118	307	35	89	16	1	10	46	24	45	1	1	.341	.446
Conti,Jason, Ari	26	.276	64	170	30	47	8	2	3	19	13	30	4	3	.328	.400
Coomer,Ron, Min	34	.270	119	445	49	120	21	1	13	64	25	57	2	1	.309	.409
Cora,Alex, LA	25	.239	121	377	42	90	17	4	3	38	18	48	7	6	.273	.329
Cordero,Wil, Cle	29	.280	118	429	65	120	29	2	15	62	31	74	2	1	.328	.462
Cordova,Marty, Tor	31	.270	62	185	24	50	11	1	5	27	21	41	3	2	.345	.422
Counsell,Craig, Ari	30	.281	74	167	25	47	10	1	2	18	20	20	2	1	.358	.389
Cox,Steve, TB	26	.272	123	408	59	111	28	1	14	64	46	72	2	2	.346	.449
Crede,Joe, CWS	23	.289	93	287	45	83	17	0	9	48	23	53	2	3	.342	.443
Crespo,Felipe, SF	28	.275	85	189	31	52	14	1	7	28	26	35	4	3	.363	.471
Cruz,Deivi, Det	25	.282	157	571	67	161	36	2	11	69	15	55	3	4	.300	.410
Cruz,Jacob, Cle	28	.281	77	192	29	54	11	1	7	30	19	34	3	2	.346	.458

Projections for 2001 Batters

Batter	Age	Avg	G	AB	R	H	2B	3B	HR	RBI	BB	SO	SB	CS	OBP	SLG
Cruz,Jose, Tor	27	.247	153	591	100	146	30	3	29	84	99	140	16	6	.355	.455
Cummings,Midre, Bos	29	.278	94	230	32	64	15	2	6	32	22	38	2	2	.341	.439
Curtis,Chad, Tex	32	.255	100	212	34	54	10	1	5	28	34	41	6	3	.358	.382
Damon,Johnny, KC	27	.300	156	631	114	189	32	9	16	78	67	64	32	10	.367	.455
Darr,Mike, SD	25	.285	76	260	39	74	17	2	4	36	25	51	8	4	.347	.412
Daubach,Brian, Bos	29	.268	137	462	64	124	33	1	22	82	52	118	2	3	.342	.487
Davis,Ben, SD	24	.254	89	295	35	75	17	0	7	41	28	57	3	2	.319	.383
Davis,Eric, StL	39	.270	90	274	39	74	11	1	9	40	33	69	4	2	.349	.416
Davis,Russ, SF	31	.254	82	185	25	47	10	0	8	28	13	46	1	1	.303	.438
Delgado,Carlos, Tor	29	.303	160	584	110	177	42	1	42	127	103	134	1	1	.408	.594
Delgado,Wilson, KC	25	.258	75	221	27	57	9	1	2	23	18	38	3	2	.314	.335
DeShields,Delino, Bal	32	.279	128	452	69	126	20	5	8	49	57	70	28	11	.360	.398
Diaz,Einar, Cle	28	.277	97	321	39	89	18	1	4	35	17	31	4	3	.314	.377
DiFelice,Mike, TB	32	.257	85	257	23	66	13	1	6	30	15	44	0	0	.298	.385
DiSarcina,Gary, Ana	33	.252	110	341	38	86	17	1	2	33	15	36	4	4	.284	.326
Drew,J.D., StL	25	.289	147	501	97	145	25	4	22	73	78	105	19	9	.385	.487
Dunston,Shawon, StL	38	.259	84	170	23	44	13	2	5	23	4	30	5	2	.276	.447
Dunwoody,Todd, KC	26	.251	59	187	23	47	10	2	4	21	10	46	4	3	.289	.390
Durazo,Erubiel, Ari	27	.322	110	367	72	118	22	2	22	72	55	70	1	1	.410	.572
Durham,Ray, CWS	29	.281	154	620	117	174	33	6	16	66	77	105	29	12	.360	.431
Dye,Jermaine, KC	27	.288	159	600	95	173	34	2	30	105	62	109	3	2	.355	.502
Easley,Damion, Det	31	.256	145	539	80	138	28	2	19	71	50	107	14	6	.319	.421
Edmonds,Jim, StL	31	.285	149	512	102	146	30	2	29	86	74	127	7	5	.375	.521
Elster,Kevin, LA	36	.230	60	165	22	38	6	0	11	24	29	39	0	0	.345	.467
Encarnacion,Juan, Det	25	.282	144	553	79	156	30	5	18	78	27	109	22	8	.316	.452
Erstad,Darin, Ana	27	.313	155	642	109	201	36	4	21	89	58	91	21	8	.370	.480
Estalella,Bobby, SF	26	.233	119	369	57	86	23	1	17	58	64	100	2	1	.346	.439
Eusebio,Tony, Hou	34	.265	96	272	24	72	14	1	5	38	32	56	0	0	.342	.379
Everett,Adam, Hou	24	.232	68	211	34	49	11	0	2	15	31	49	4	2	.331	.313
Everett,Carl, Bos	30	.291	140	505	83	147	29	2	26	93	53	110	17	9	.358	.511
Fabregas,Jorge, KC	31	.240	71	183	15	44	7	0	2	22	16	21	0	0	.302	.311
Fasano,Sal, Oak	29	.230	63	165	26	38	6	0	9	25	17	42	1	0	.302	.430
Febles,Carlos, KC	25	.281	141	533	102	150	27	8	10	59	66	87	32	12	.361	.418
Fick,Robert, Det	27	.277	81	249	39	69	17	2	7	43	29	43	2	2	.353	.446
Finley,Steve, Ari	36	.258	146	546	92	141	25	5	27	83	53	92	9	4	.324	.471
Flaherty,John, TB	33	.249	115	406	36	101	17	0	9	46	22	62	1	2	.287	.357
Fletcher,Darrin, Tor	34	.273	124	418	41	114	22	1	16	61	24	46	0	0	.312	.445
Floyd,Cliff, Fla	28	.288	141	500	79	144	34	2	23	90	52	96	20	9	.355	.502
Fordyce,Brook, Bal	31	.278	125	407	44	113	25	1	13	57	27	60	1	1	.323	.440
Fox,Andy, Fla	30	.250	75	188	25	47	7	1	3	18	18	39	5	3	.316	.346
Frias,Hanley, Ari	27	.250	60	116	16	29	4	1	1	10	14	19	4	2	.331	.328
Frye,Jeff, Col	34	.273	66	187	25	51	11	0	1	16	22	29	5	3	.349	.348
Fryman,Travis, Cle	32	.279	154	577	83	161	33	3	21	97	57	120	7	4	.344	.456
Fullmer,Brad, Tor	26	.284	132	468	68	133	36	1	23	83	34	58	4	3	.333	.513
Furcal,Rafael, Atl	20	.300	149	523	103	157	24	4	5	53	87	82	46	18	.400	.390
Galarraga,Andres, Atl	40	.275	133	469	71	129	25	1	27	91	44	127	5	4	.337	.505
Gant,Ron, Ana	36	.245	126	432	72	106	21	2	20	62	62	100	8	4	.340	.442
Garcia,Karim, Bal	25	.248	73	202	29	50	8	2	10	33	16	48	3	2	.303	.455
Garciaparra,N., Bos	27	.343	147	583	114	200	45	6	29	109	53	52	13	5	.398	.590
Giambi,Jason, Oak	30	.305	156	554	102	169	37	1	34	117	111	103	1	1	.421	.560

Projections for 2001 Batters

Batter	Age	Avg	G	AB	R	H	2B	3B	HR	RBI	BB	SO	SB	CS	OBP	SLG
Giambi,Jeremy, Oak	26	.309	115	346	60	107	18	2	15	61	55	70	2	2	.404	.503
Gil,Benji, Ana	28	.236	48	127	16	30	6	0	3	13	9	29	3	2	.287	.354
Giles,Brian, Pit	30	.297	154	536	101	159	31	3	33	109	106	85	8	4	.413	.550
Girardi,Joe, ChC	36	.262	96	302	34	79	14	1	4	36	20	48	2	2	.307	.354
Glanville,Doug, Phi	30	.289	155	651	100	188	30	5	9	58	41	84	25	8	.331	.392
Glaus,Troy, Ana	24	.271	159	561	107	152	35	1	41	102	85	140	8	5	.367	.556
Gload,Ross, ChC	25	.268	84	246	33	66	15	2	11	40	14	38	1	1	.308	.480
Gomez,Chris, SD	30	.255	83	255	28	65	12	1	2	23	29	50	2	2	.331	.333
Gonzalez,Alex, Fla	24	.243	114	428	56	104	18	5	10	48	19	87	4	4	.275	.379
Gonzalez,Alex S., Tor	28	.252	140	524	65	132	31	3	13	56	38	107	12	6	.302	.397
Gonzalez,Juan, Det	31	.297	141	553	91	164	33	2	34	117	45	108	2	1	.349	.548
Gonzalez,Luis, Ari	33	.302	151	573	92	173	35	4	25	101	66	70	7	5	.374	.508
Gonzalez,Wiki, SD	27	.264	106	322	37	85	18	1	10	48	28	33	1	1	.323	.419
Goodwin,Tom, LA	32	.264	139	489	87	129	14	4	4	38	62	92	40	15	.347	.333
Grace,Mark, ChC	37	.297	144	525	80	156	33	2	13	75	83	41	2	3	.393	.442
Graffanino,Tony, CWS	29	.264	68	201	29	53	11	1	4	22	19	37	5	3	.327	.388
Grebeck,Craig, Tor	36	.261	57	222	26	58	12	1	2	17	23	31	1	1	.331	.351
Green,Shawn, LA	28	.284	160	626	110	178	40	3	33	104	73	127	24	8	.359	.516
Greene,Willie, ChC	29	.239	101	285	38	68	12	1	13	45	40	68	3	1	.332	.425
Greer,Rusty, Tex	32	.301	138	521	92	157	34	2	15	85	78	77	4	3	.392	.461
Grieve,Ben, Oak	25	.287	157	564	104	162	37	1	28	111	79	118	3	1	.375	.505
Griffey Jr.,Ken, Cin	31	.286	154	580	114	166	32	3	48	135	88	115	14	5	.380	.600
Grissom,Marquis, Mil	34	.257	126	491	61	126	22	2	12	59	32	84	13	7	.302	.383
Grudzielanek,Mark, LA	31	.288	144	570	77	164	33	3	7	51	35	74	13	6	.329	.393
Guerrero,Vladimir, Mon	25	.330	158	600	110	198	37	7	44	123	54	74	10	8	.385	.635
Guerrero,Wilton, Mon	26	.284	119	324	39	92	12	6	2	29	16	43	8	4	.318	.377
Guillen,Carlos, Sea	25	.271	87	295	45	80	13	2	7	35	27	51	3	3	.332	.400
Guillen,Jose, TB	25	.275	110	378	51	104	22	2	12	57	21	68	2	1	.313	.439
Gutierrez,Ricky, ChC	31	.268	126	425	57	114	15	2	6	45	57	67	7	5	.355	.355
Guzman,Cristian, Min	23	.251	151	565	72	142	21	13	4	46	31	101	20	9	.290	.356
Gwynn,Tony, SD	41	.321	110	368	47	118	20	2	8	55	27	14	4	2	.367	.451
Hairston Jr.,Jerry, Bal	25	.279	136	452	77	126	25	2	9	54	40	56	15	10	.337	.403
Halter,Shane, Det	31	.246	80	191	23	47	9	1	2	16	16	38	4	4	.304	.335
Hamilton,Darryl, NYM	36	.288	46	132	21	38	6	1	2	12	17	16	2	2	.369	.394
Hammonds,Jeffrey, Col	30	.283	132	488	89	138	27	2	21	82	56	103	13	7	.357	.475
Hansen,Dave, LA	32	.257	79	70	9	18	5	0	3	11	16	16	0	0	.395	.457
Harris,Lenny, NYM	36	.268	82	157	18	42	6	1	2	16	10	12	3	2	.311	.357
Haselman,Bill, Tex	35	.267	73	195	20	52	12	0	6	24	12	32	1	1	.309	.421
Hatteberg,Scott, Bos	31	.275	97	265	33	73	18	0	8	36	39	40	0	0	.368	.434
Hayes,Charlie, Mil	36	.247	88	251	29	62	11	1	7	40	32	50	1	1	.332	.382
Helton,Todd, Col	27	.341	160	574	118	196	47	3	37	125	80	64	4	3	.422	.627
Henderson,Rickey, Sea	42	.246	91	305	52	75	14	1	5	27	62	61	22	7	.373	.348
Hermansen,Chad, Pit	23	.241	72	232	34	56	12	1	10	31	17	71	7	3	.293	.431
Hernandez,Carlos, StL	34	.257	68	218	21	56	14	0	3	32	19	32	2	3	.316	.362
Hernandez,Jose, Mil	31	.250	133	452	64	113	16	3	15	58	42	130	5	5	.314	.398
Hernandez,R., Oak	25	.263	124	438	65	115	19	1	15	77	42	54	2	2	.327	.413
Hidalgo,Richard, Hou	25	.283	149	547	98	155	40	2	34	104	64	99	9	7	.358	.550
Higginson,Bobby, Det	30	.281	144	545	86	153	32	3	24	85	70	92	7	5	.363	.483
Hill,Glenallen, NYY	36	.266	113	319	46	85	18	1	19	55	23	76	2	1	.316	.508
Hinch,A.J., Oak	27	.252	54	135	17	34	5	0	3	15	11	26	1	1	.308	.356

Projections for 2001 Batters

Batter	Age	Avg	G	AB	R	H	2B	3B	HR	RBI	BB	SO	SB	CS	OBP	SLG
Hocking,Denny, Min	31	.258	133	330	43	85	17	2	4	34	30	61	6	5	.319	.358
Hollandsworth,T., Col	28	.271	119	358	61	97	18	2	13	44	32	83	9	6	.331	.441
Houston,Tyler, Mil	30	.252	119	309	33	78	14	1	15	45	24	70	2	1	.306	.450
Huff,Aubrey, TB	24	.295	146	525	79	155	42	2	22	80	50	84	2	2	.357	.509
Hundley,Todd, LA	32	.223	102	301	41	67	14	1	18	53	43	91	1	1	.320	.455
Hunter,Brian L., Cin	30	.259	94	216	32	56	9	1	1	15	16	36	16	5	.310	.324
Hunter,Torii, Min	25	.268	124	399	54	107	23	3	10	51	21	75	8	7	.305	.416
Huskey,Butch, Col	29	.264	81	231	31	61	11	0	10	43	23	42	3	2	.331	.442
Ibanez,Raul, Sea	29	.243	78	181	25	44	12	1	5	26	15	36	2	1	.301	.403
Jackson,Damian, SD	27	.242	129	430	68	104	24	3	6	36	55	105	23	7	.328	.353
Jaha,John, Oak	35	.232	66	194	31	45	8	0	10	35	46	62	1	1	.379	.428
Javier,Stan, Sea	37	.262	114	344	50	90	14	1	4	33	43	59	11	4	.344	.343
Jefferies,Gregg, Det	33	.284	62	197	25	56	12	1	4	21	13	12	3	2	.329	.416
Jenkins,Geoff, Mil	26	.289	142	539	91	156	38	4	30	98	39	118	5	2	.337	.542
Jeter,Derek, NYY	27	.330	154	624	130	206	32	6	19	87	76	111	22	8	.403	.492
Jimenez,D'A., NYY	23	.292	98	202	29	59	11	1	4	27	17	31	7	3	.347	.416
Johnson,Charles, CWS	29	.254	138	453	58	115	22	1	23	70	55	119	1	1	.335	.459
Johnson,Mark L., CWS	25	.251	72	211	34	53	10	1	4	26	41	43	2	1	.373	.365
Johnson,Russ, TB	28	.284	97	257	43	73	15	1	4	29	41	43	4	4	.383	.397
Jones,Andruw, Atl	24	.290	162	613	108	178	33	5	34	103	62	107	26	10	.356	.527
Jones,Chipper, Atl	29	.308	158	582	120	179	36	2	37	112	111	84	17	6	.418	.567
Jones,Jacque, Min	26	.290	152	555	79	161	36	3	19	80	28	118	11	8	.324	.468
Jordan,Brian, Atl	34	.283	139	516	83	146	26	3	20	86	42	75	11	5	.337	.461
Jordan,Kevin, Phi	31	.262	104	271	27	71	14	1	4	34	15	31	0	0	.301	.365
Joyner,Wally, Atl	39	.275	114	240	27	66	13	0	5	36	34	33	1	1	.365	.392
Justice,David, NYY	35	.273	141	505	81	138	25	1	28	94	83	99	3	3	.376	.493
Kapler,Gabe, Tex	25	.291	147	557	91	162	41	4	22	99	56	84	9	6	.356	.497
Karros,Eric, LA	33	.265	152	565	71	150	28	1	30	102	56	116	6	4	.332	.478
Kendall,Jason, Pit	27	.316	152	557	105	176	36	5	14	70	71	63	24	8	.393	.474
Kennedy,Adam, Ana	25	.281	153	580	82	163	36	7	11	76	27	62	18	8	.313	.424
Kent,Jeff, SF	33	.285	143	533	90	152	32	2	26	109	67	111	9	5	.365	.499
Klesko,Ryan, SD	30	.291	146	474	77	138	28	3	25	88	73	78	9	5	.386	.521
Knoblauch,Chuck, NYY	32	.289	133	498	97	144	26	4	11	50	65	54	26	9	.371	.424
Konerko,Paul, CWS	25	.288	148	513	75	148	27	1	24	93	47	70	1	1	.348	.485
Koskie,Corey, Min	28	.284	148	543	76	154	30	3	16	78	66	121	7	6	.361	.438
Kotsay,Mark, Fla	25	.286	154	548	81	157	29	6	12	67	38	52	13	7	.333	.427
Kreuter,Chad, LA	36	.236	83	212	23	50	9	1	4	24	32	45	0	0	.336	.344
Lamb,Mike, Tex	25	.296	110	399	60	118	30	2	10	54	30	45	1	1	.345	.456
Lankford,Ray, StL	34	.255	134	444	73	113	29	3	22	74	69	140	11	6	.355	.482
Lansing,Mike, Bos	33	.264	112	296	39	78	18	1	7	33	21	46	4	2	.312	.402
Larkin,Barry, Cin	37	.288	131	482	78	139	25	3	11	52	69	52	18	6	.377	.421
LaRue,Jason, Cin	27	.265	62	196	29	52	13	1	8	28	14	36	1	1	.314	.464
Lawton,Matt, Min	29	.281	152	555	86	156	33	2	14	77	90	62	18	7	.381	.423
LeCroy,Matt, Min	25	.239	69	222	30	53	12	0	10	33	18	44	0	0	.296	.428
Ledee,Ricky, Tex	27	.255	122	384	61	98	22	3	13	57	48	103	7	4	.338	.430
Lee,Carlos, CWS	25	.306	152	582	95	178	35	2	24	107	32	74	8	4	.342	.497
Lee,Derrek, Fla	25	.262	150	550	82	144	28	1	25	81	58	147	5	4	.332	.453
Lee,Travis, Phi	26	.261	123	414	58	108	21	1	13	57	60	71	8	2	.354	.411
Lewis,Darren, Bos	33	.244	77	225	32	55	7	2	2	20	24	31	8	5	.317	.320
Lewis,Mark, Bal	31	.257	87	237	27	61	13	1	5	29	19	46	2	1	.313	.384

Projections for 2001 Batters

Batter	Age	Avg	G	AB	R	H	2B	3B	HR	RBI	BB	SO	SB	CS	OBP	SLG
Lieberthal,Mike, Phi	29	.272	131	464	66	126	28	1	21	80	41	70	2	1	.331	.472
Liefer,Jeff, CWS	26	.278	96	277	48	77	18	2	14	52	29	65	1	1	.346	.509
Lockhart,Keith, Atl	36	.260	92	215	27	56	11	1	3	27	20	25	2	1	.323	.363
Lofton,Kenny, Cle	34	.291	136	529	103	154	26	5	11	57	82	81	28	11	.386	.422
Long,Terrence, Oak	25	.290	133	500	75	145	27	5	14	69	39	80	11	7	.341	.448
Lopez,Javy, Atl	30	.290	124	449	58	130	21	1	24	82	32	77	2	2	.337	.501
Lopez,Luis, Mil	30	.248	97	202	25	50	14	1	4	21	15	46	2	2	.300	.386
Loretta,Mark, Mil	29	.293	152	518	73	152	29	2	7	61	51	55	5	4	.357	.398
Lowell,Mike, Fla	27	.269	140	517	70	139	32	1	22	83	44	92	2	1	.326	.462
Lugo,Julio, Hou	25	.308	124	428	80	132	23	4	10	46	38	69	22	11	.365	.451
Mabry,John, SD	30	.253	88	225	27	57	14	0	6	28	17	54	0	1	.306	.396
Macias,Jose, Det	27	.250	70	232	28	58	10	3	2	24	19	26	3	3	.307	.345
Magadan,Dave, SD	38	.273	67	110	11	30	8	0	1	14	20	17	0	0	.385	.373
Magee,Wendell, Det	28	.264	81	193	27	51	11	1	7	25	16	41	2	3	.321	.440
Marrero,Eli, StL	27	.225	96	262	33	59	13	1	8	32	22	44	6	3	.285	.374
Martin,Al, Sea	33	.274	128	354	55	97	18	3	12	38	29	74	11	4	.329	.444
Martinez,Dave, Tor	36	.267	108	288	37	77	11	2	3	29	32	47	5	4	.341	.351
Martinez,Edgar, Sea	38	.311	144	527	84	164	37	1	27	101	97	98	2	1	.418	.539
Martinez,Felix, TB	27	.227	85	256	34	58	11	3	2	21	21	50	8	4	.285	.316
Martinez,Ramon E., SF	28	.279	100	265	39	74	17	2	6	34	23	33	2	2	.337	.426
Martinez,Tino, NYY	33	.269	136	502	71	135	27	1	22	96	55	74	2	1	.341	.458
Mateo,Ruben, Tex	23	.300	156	564	97	169	36	2	26	93	28	81	14	6	.333	.509
Matheny,Mike, StL	30	.236	119	360	32	85	16	1	5	36	22	79	0	0	.280	.328
Matos,Luis, Bal	22	.231	54	169	21	39	5	1	2	19	10	24	9	4	.274	.308
Matthews Jr.,G., ChC	26	.236	48	127	18	30	5	1	3	15	15	27	3	1	.317	.362
Maxwell,Jason, Min	29	.248	66	117	17	29	6	0	3	13	11	26	1	1	.313	.376
Mayne,Brent, Col	33	.269	107	275	29	74	15	0	3	33	38	49	1	1	.358	.356
McCarty,Dave, KC	31	.261	109	291	43	76	15	1	11	43	36	73	3	2	.343	.433
McEwing,Joe, NYM	28	.269	90	156	21	42	9	1	3	18	11	24	2	2	.317	.397
McGriff,Fred, TB	37	.277	141	516	69	143	25	1	23	88	79	112	2	1	.373	.463
McGwire,Mark, StL	37	.265	129	404	79	107	17	0	43	94	117	124	1	0	.430	.626
McLemore,Mark, Sea	36	.253	126	459	74	116	16	2	4	40	76	70	13	7	.359	.322
McMillon,Billy, Det	29	.292	131	332	52	97	25	1	10	48	46	64	4	2	.378	.464
Meares,Pat, Pit	32	.256	113	398	50	102	18	2	9	48	25	73	3	3	.300	.379
Meluskey,Mitch, Hou	27	.318	129	412	70	131	33	0	18	73	76	71	1	1	.424	.529
Menechino,Frank, Oak	30	.274	76	237	44	65	13	2	7	34	34	52	3	3	.365	.435
Merloni,Lou, Bos	30	.286	137	454	60	130	27	1	7	58	37	67	2	2	.340	.396
Mientkiewicz,Doug, Min	27	.271	87	188	27	51	13	1	4	25	23	27	3	2	.351	.415
Millar,Kevin, Fla	29	.272	128	357	51	97	23	2	15	65	43	62	1	1	.350	.473
Miller,Damian, Ari	31	.276	109	340	40	94	23	1	10	51	30	74	2	1	.335	.438
Mirabelli,Doug, SF	30	.245	90	261	33	64	16	1	7	34	36	60	1	1	.337	.395
Molina,Ben, Ana	26	.272	121	427	47	116	21	1	11	63	21	27	1	1	.306	.403
Mondesi,Raul, Tor	30	.277	141	545	90	151	31	4	31	88	47	112	22	10	.334	.519
Mora,Melvin, Bal	29	.255	120	419	62	107	18	2	7	43	45	81	11	9	.328	.358
Morandini,Mickey, Tor	35	.261	104	283	37	74	13	2	2	22	30	46	5	3	.332	.343
Mordecai,Mike, Mon	33	.239	99	180	22	43	10	1	4	16	15	30	1	2	.297	.372
Morris,Hal, Det	36	.299	98	167	20	50	10	1	1	17	16	23	0	0	.361	.389
Morris,Warren, Pit	27	.292	149	542	73	158	28	4	11	73	63	84	7	7	.365	.419
Mouton,James, Mil	32	.245	70	106	16	26	7	1	1	13	14	24	5	3	.333	.358
Mueller,Bill, SF	30	.287	146	530	84	152	29	2	8	56	70	69	4	3	.370	.394

Projections for 2001 Batters

Batter	Age	Avg	G	AB	R	H	2B	3B	HR	RBI	BB	SO	SB	CS	OBP	SLG
Murray,Calvin, SF	29	.270	98	174	31	47	9	1	4	20	19	29	10	4	.342	.402
Nevin,Phil, SD	30	.269	144	535	76	144	30	1	28	96	59	126	1	1	.342	.486
Nieves,Jose, ChC	26	.257	81	261	31	67	16	2	7	33	13	42	5	5	.292	.414
Nilsson,Dave, Mil	31	.282	112	358	52	101	22	1	15	60	45	59	2	2	.362	.475
Nixon,Trot, Bos	27	.266	133	443	71	118	22	4	15	56	62	81	8	4	.356	.436
Norton,Greg, CWS	28	.256	73	207	31	53	11	1	8	28	30	48	2	2	.350	.435
O'Leary,Troy, Bos	31	.276	145	551	76	152	32	4	20	83	44	89	1	2	.329	.457
O'Neill,Paul, NYY	38	.280	132	517	67	145	27	1	16	89	50	86	8	5	.344	.429
Ochoa,Alex, Cin	29	.284	129	299	52	85	21	3	10	46	32	40	6	4	.353	.475
Offerman,Jose, Bos	32	.281	142	549	91	154	22	6	8	54	87	83	17	11	.379	.386
Olerud,John, Sea	32	.298	156	551	89	164	37	1	17	94	107	78	1	1	.412	.461
Oliver,Joe, Sea	35	.232	72	194	16	45	10	0	5	25	11	44	1	1	.273	.361
Ordaz,Luis, KC	25	.254	55	138	14	35	7	1	1	15	9	14	3	2	.299	.341
Ordonez,Magglio, CWS	27	.301	156	599	94	180	37	2	30	114	49	61	12	7	.353	.519
Ordonez,Rey, NYM	28	.243	151	511	49	124	18	2	1	49	41	59	7	5	.299	.292
Ortiz,David, Min	25	.288	131	423	64	122	33	1	16	71	58	92	2	2	.374	.485
Ortiz,Hector, KC	31	.251	71	195	19	49	6	0	2	16	11	23	1	1	.291	.313
Osik,Keith, Pit	32	.235	55	115	10	27	7	1	2	13	11	15	1	1	.302	.365
Owens,Eric, SD	30	.275	150	483	64	133	18	3	5	51	42	56	23	10	.333	.369
Palmeiro,Orlando, Ana	32	.282	107	241	36	68	12	2	0	25	31	20	4	3	.364	.349
Palmeiro,Rafael, Tex	36	.285	149	543	88	155	31	2	37	115	86	77	4	3	.383	.554
Palmer,Dean, Det	32	.255	148	545	79	139	25	1	31	100	57	145	4	2	.326	.475
Paquette,Craig, StL	32	.248	76	210	25	52	10	1	9	35	10	45	2	1	.282	.433
Patterson,Corey, ChC	21	.248	114	399	67	99	21	3	19	69	34	113	18	7	.307	.459
Paul,Josh, CWS	26	.267	65	191	31	51	8	1	3	24	14	40	4	3	.317	.366
Payton,Jay, NYM	28	.286	152	556	74	159	24	3	18	70	37	69	10	11	.331	.437
Pena,Angel, LA	26	.254	57	142	17	36	4	0	5	20	9	38	1	1	.298	.387
Perez,Eddie, Atl	33	.266	67	199	20	53	10	0	5	25	14	26	1	1	.315	.392
Perez,Neifi, Col	26	.294	161	664	99	195	35	11	12	73	34	61	7	5	.328	.434
Perez,Timoniel, NYM	24	.311	112	357	52	111	20	4	5	36	17	34	11	9	.342	.431
Perez,Tomas, Phi	27	.239	42	134	14	32	6	1	2	15	7	24	1	1	.277	.343
Perry,Herbert, CWS	31	.292	113	377	60	110	26	1	11	57	23	66	1	1	.333	.454
Petrick,Ben, Col	24	.316	119	389	68	123	27	4	22	69	53	73	7	6	.398	.576
Piatt,Adam, Oak	25	.297	151	543	97	161	38	4	25	102	69	120	4	3	.376	.519
Piazza,Mike, NYM	32	.326	143	525	94	171	26	0	38	117	57	74	2	1	.392	.592
Pierre,Juan, Col	23	.323	123	436	62	141	13	3	0	35	28	26	29	14	.364	.367
Pierzynski,A.J., Min	24	.261	105	341	39	89	18	1	4	35	12	42	1	1	.286	.355
Polanco,Placido, StL	25	.283	122	346	47	98	15	2	3	35	18	26	6	4	.319	.364
Polonia,Luis, NYY	36	.287	74	237	29	68	9	2	5	21	15	28	9	5	.329	.405
Posada,Jorge, NYY	29	.261	150	548	88	143	30	1	25	87	96	147	2	1	.371	.456
Pratt,Todd, NYM	34	.279	74	136	20	38	8	0	5	25	15	26	0	0	.351	.449
Quinn,Mark, KC	27	.329	136	510	88	168	36	3	25	98	36	78	4	3	.374	.559
Ramirez,Alex, Pit	26	.290	93	314	49	91	16	4	14	51	13	63	4	3	.318	.500
Ramirez,Aramis, Pit	23	.278	146	508	61	141	32	2	14	65	48	81	2	1	.340	.431
Ramirez,Manny, Cle	29	.310	149	532	111	165	37	1	41	132	96	128	2	2	.416	.615
Randa,Joe, KC	31	.294	150	564	77	166	30	4	13	79	43	72	5	4	.344	.431
Reboulet,Jeff, KC	37	.220	65	100	14	22	5	0	0	8	16	21	1	0	.328	.270
Redmond,Mike, Fla	30	.277	100	271	24	75	13	0	1	26	19	28	0	0	.324	.336
Reed,Jeff, ChC	38	.226	95	217	25	49	10	0	5	24	36	55	1	1	.336	.341
Reese,Pokey, Cin	28	.259	145	521	75	135	24	3	10	49	42	81	27	7	.314	.374

Projections for 2001 Batters

Batter	Age	Avg	G	AB	R	H	2B	3B	HR	RBI	BB	SO	SB	CS	OBP	SLG
Relaford,Desi, NYM	27	.234	67	175	22	41	9	1	2	17	21	30	5	2	.316	.331
Renteria,Edgar, StL	25	.287	154	585	101	168	29	2	12	64	61	80	34	16	.354	.405
Richard,Chris, Bal	27	.264	146	507	80	134	31	2	26	89	45	84	7	6	.324	.487
Rios,Armando, SF	29	.272	116	235	41	64	13	1	9	43	29	46	5	3	.352	.451
Ripken Jr.,Cal, Bal	40	.269	102	372	45	100	19	1	13	51	26	42	0	0	.317	.430
Rivas,Luis, Min	21	.249	76	233	32	58	14	2	2	23	15	35	8	4	.294	.352
Rivera,Ruben, SD	27	.199	139	376	58	75	17	3	17	50	47	125	10	4	.288	.396
Rodriguez,Alex, Sea	25	.311	150	594	134	185	37	2	45	127	72	115	28	8	.386	.608
Rodriguez,Henry, Fla	33	.256	128	418	54	107	24	1	24	75	51	114	2	2	.337	.490
Rodriguez,Ivan, Tex	29	.308	134	539	92	166	33	2	28	91	28	70	9	4	.342	.532
Rolen,Scott, Phi	26	.291	133	495	97	144	37	3	29	94	73	113	11	4	.382	.554
Rollins,Jimmy, Phi	22	.264	139	470	61	124	25	7	9	54	39	49	17	7	.320	.404
Saenz,Olmedo, Oak	30	.282	103	308	48	87	19	1	13	50	27	42	1	1	.340	.477
Salmon,Tim, Ana	32	.288	148	517	92	149	29	2	29	101	98	122	3	4	.402	.520
Sanchez,Rey, KC	33	.269	131	438	53	118	18	2	2	38	23	52	5	3	.306	.333
Sanders,Reggie, Atl	33	.265	111	377	61	100	20	3	16	53	44	97	17	7	.342	.462
Santiago,Benito, Cin	36	.250	87	244	20	61	13	1	6	31	19	49	1	1	.304	.385
Schneider,Brian, Mon	24	.243	61	185	17	45	11	0	4	23	11	28	0	0	.286	.368
Sefcik,Kevin, Phi	30	.285	78	123	16	35	8	2	1	11	16	16	3	2	.367	.407
Segui,David, Cle	34	.284	141	457	62	130	27	1	14	64	43	69	1	1	.346	.440
Seguignol,F., Mon	26	.274	87	259	40	71	17	0	16	47	22	73	2	2	.331	.525
Sexson,Richie, Mil	26	.273	148	543	87	148	30	2	35	113	54	134	3	2	.338	.529
Sexton,Chris, Cin	29	.287	59	150	23	43	6	1	1	14	21	20	2	2	.374	.360
Sheffield,Gary, LA	32	.292	142	496	93	145	26	1	32	97	101	62	10	6	.412	.542
Sheldon,Scott, Tex	32	.260	39	100	16	26	8	1	4	17	11	29	1	0	.333	.480
Shumpert,Terry, Col	34	.277	93	249	40	69	14	2	8	29	23	39	6	3	.338	.446
Singleton,Chris, CWS	28	.267	148	544	83	145	29	6	13	68	32	81	18	7	.307	.414
Smith,Bobby, TB	27	.251	82	267	35	67	13	1	10	39	23	78	5	3	.310	.419
Smith,Mark, Fla	31	.259	83	162	22	42	13	0	6	27	14	37	2	1	.318	.451
Snow,J.T., SF	33	.258	148	500	71	129	25	1	18	84	70	112	2	2	.349	.420
Sojo,Luis, NYY	35	.252	85	230	25	58	10	1	3	25	10	22	1	1	.283	.343
Soriano,Alfonso, NYY	23	.264	78	182	27	48	10	1	5	25	10	35	6	3	.302	.412
Sosa,Sammy, ChC	32	.272	155	607	103	165	24	3	49	128	80	169	12	8	.357	.563
Spencer,Shane, NYY	29	.267	95	303	45	81	18	1	14	48	29	60	1	2	.331	.472
Spiers,Bill, Hou	35	.273	106	245	32	67	11	2	2	26	30	33	5	3	.353	.359
Spiezio,Scott, Ana	28	.252	121	282	41	71	16	1	11	41	36	44	2	1	.336	.433
Sprague,Ed, SD	33	.244	95	242	31	59	13	1	10	32	20	49	1	1	.302	.430
Stairs,Matt, Oak	33	.259	141	490	79	127	25	1	28	91	74	112	4	3	.356	.486
Stanley,Mike, Oak	38	.250	88	220	30	55	11	0	10	35	35	55	0	0	.353	.436
Stevens,Lee, Mon	33	.261	132	441	59	115	26	1	21	70	45	114	1	1	.329	.467
Stewart,Shannon, Tor	27	.302	145	579	103	175	36	5	16	70	58	79	31	12	.366	.465
Stinnett,Kelly, Ari	31	.241	87	257	32	62	12	1	10	35	26	69	1	0	.311	.412
Stocker,Kevin, Ana	31	.244	73	205	24	50	9	1	2	16	23	45	3	3	.320	.327
Stynes,Chris, Cin	28	.287	118	310	51	89	19	1	8	37	29	38	8	2	.348	.432
Surhoff,B.J., Atl	36	.272	147	556	72	151	27	2	17	78	41	70	5	3	.322	.419
Sweeney,Mike, KC	27	.309	158	589	95	182	37	1	25	116	62	60	6	3	.375	.503
Tatis,Fernando, StL	26	.280	139	483	86	135	30	2	26	80	63	116	12	6	.363	.511
Taubensee,Eddie, Cin	32	.278	121	395	49	110	20	1	13	61	37	73	1	1	.340	.433
Taylor,Reggie, Phi	24	.258	45	159	21	41	5	2	4	15	5	30	8	3	.280	.390
Tejada,Miguel, Oak	25	.263	160	589	102	155	32	3	26	100	59	102	9	6	.330	.460

Projections for 2001 Batters

Batter	Age	Avg	G	AB	R	H	2B	3B	HR	RBI	BB	SO	SB	CS	OBP	SLG
Thomas,Frank, CWS	33	.318	148	537	98	171	34	1	35	122	102	85	2	2	.427	.581
Thome,Jim, Cle	30	.270	156	544	105	147	32	2	36	105	125	178	1	0	.407	.535
Tracy,Andy, Mon	27	.262	82	252	41	66	15	1	14	49	29	73	1	1	.338	.496
Trammell,Bubba, NYM	29	.272	112	353	51	96	23	1	17	59	42	67	3	2	.349	.487
Truby,Chris, Hou	27	.280	111	396	55	111	21	3	17	70	21	66	8	4	.317	.477
Tucker,Michael, Cin	30	.256	148	351	60	90	21	4	14	46	47	93	9	5	.344	.459
Tyner,Jason, TB	24	.286	82	266	37	76	7	1	0	21	21	26	18	7	.338	.320
Valentin,John, Bos	34	.266	119	305	50	81	21	1	10	41	35	46	2	2	.341	.439
Valentin,Jose, CWS	31	.253	141	538	89	136	32	3	22	76	75	114	14	6	.344	.446
Vander Wal,John, Pit	35	.265	126	249	38	66	13	1	10	44	43	64	3	2	.373	.446
Varitek,Jason, Bos	29	.253	146	454	62	115	31	1	15	66	51	84	1	1	.329	.425
Vaughn,Greg, TB	35	.241	141	507	87	122	23	1	34	92	77	130	8	3	.341	.491
Vaughn,Mo, Ana	33	.289	148	567	83	164	27	1	35	107	64	151	1	0	.361	.526
Velarde,Randy, Oak	38	.272	112	430	65	117	17	1	9	42	52	82	9	4	.351	.379
Ventura,Robin, NYM	33	.259	153	532	74	138	27	1	25	92	75	103	2	2	.351	.455
Veras,Quilvio, Atl	30	.273	131	487	82	133	23	2	6	47	77	82	26	13	.372	.366
Veras,Wilton, Bos	23	.258	57	186	21	48	9	1	3	21	6	22	1	1	.281	.366
Vidro,Jose, Mon	26	.296	152	594	88	176	39	2	17	80	51	67	4	3	.352	.455
Vina,Fernando, StL	32	.288	129	504	73	145	23	5	4	37	42	35	13	10	.342	.377
Vizcaino,Jose, NYY	33	.266	87	229	28	61	10	2	1	22	18	31	3	3	.320	.341
Vizquel,Omar, Cle	34	.273	146	567	89	155	22	2	5	50	70	62	28	10	.353	.346
Walbeck,Matt, Ana	31	.236	52	127	14	30	6	0	3	13	11	23	1	1	.297	.354
Walker,Larry, Col	34	.324	120	413	88	134	28	2	23	74	58	54	12	5	.408	.569
Walker,Todd, Col	28	.302	142	529	81	160	35	3	14	73	53	72	15	7	.366	.459
Ward,Daryle, Hou	26	.306	116	402	66	123	22	0	31	86	31	72	1	1	.356	.592
Weiss,Walt, Atl	37	.241	79	187	26	45	7	1	1	15	27	32	2	1	.336	.305
Wells,Vernon, Tor	22	.263	83	240	35	63	15	2	7	32	20	41	8	4	.319	.429
White,Devon, LA	38	.261	76	257	34	67	13	2	7	35	19	49	7	4	.312	.409
White,Rondell, ChC	29	.298	122	460	70	137	27	3	19	67	37	81	11	6	.350	.493
Widger,Chris, Mon	30	.246	95	293	31	72	16	1	11	39	24	63	2	1	.303	.420
Williams,Bernie, NYY	32	.305	143	541	105	165	32	4	25	104	83	88	11	7	.397	.518
Williams,Gerald, TB	34	.264	138	432	65	114	23	2	14	55	28	74	12	8	.309	.424
Williams,Matt, Ari	35	.273	129	494	66	135	22	2	20	80	34	84	4	2	.320	.447
Wilson,Dan, Sea	32	.251	109	343	39	86	18	1	7	40	26	66	3	1	.304	.370
Wilson,Enrique, Pit	25	.284	109	334	48	95	19	1	5	33	25	34	6	5	.334	.392
Wilson,Preston, Fla	26	.265	158	551	85	146	30	3	30	101	50	178	19	9	.326	.494
Winn,Randy, TB	27	.284	86	296	48	84	15	4	3	27	28	51	14	8	.346	.392
Womack,Tony, Ari	31	.278	150	627	92	174	23	7	5	48	41	80	51	12	.322	.360
Woodward,Chris, Tor	25	.250	47	148	21	37	9	0	2	15	14	29	1	1	.315	.351
Young,Dmitri, Cin	27	.299	150	548	78	164	37	3	18	84	45	90	3	3	.352	.476
Young,Eric, ChC	34	.283	131	505	81	143	23	3	5	44	58	34	38	14	.357	.370
Young,Kevin, Pit	32	.268	134	497	78	133	26	2	21	88	46	105	12	6	.330	.455
Zaun,Gregg, KC	30	.245	93	241	28	59	12	1	5	29	35	32	3	2	.341	.365
Zeile,Todd, NYM	35	.262	148	538	69	141	28	1	20	80	62	89	3	3	.338	.429
Zuleta,Julio, ChC	26	.301	108	332	56	100	24	1	18	67	21	74	2	2	.343	.542

These Guys Can Play Too and Might Get A Shot

It's difficult to predict which players will end up getting significant playing time in the major leagues next year. That said, we can say with confidence that if the following players land major league jobs, their final numbers should be consistent with the stats listed below. These players generally fit into one of two categories: they either have a decent chance to play in the majors in 2001, or we think they deserve that chance. What you'll find below are the players' Major League Equivalencies (or MLEs) for their 2000 seasons. An MLE is not a projection for what a player will do in the future; it is an interpretation of what he did in the minors last year. The MLE method adjusts the player's minor league stats and re-expresses them in major league terms. In short, an MLE shows you what a player would have hit if he'd been playing in the majors. It has just as much predictive value as a major leaguer's 2000 stats, but no more. Ages as of June 30, 2001.

Batter	Age	Avg	G	AB	R	H	2B	3B	HR	RBI	BB	SO	SB	CS	OBP	SLG
Abernathy,Brent	23	.273	119	439	53	120	26	1	3	43	32	44	17	14	.323	.358
Barnes,John	25	.315	120	409	71	129	31	4	8	57	38	51	4	6	.374	.469
Burroughs,Sean	20	.255	108	373	36	95	23	2	1	32	37	48	4	8	.322	.335
Byrnes,Eric	25	.282	134	478	80	135	40	1	10	65	49	69	22	10	.349	.433
Cabrera,Alex	29	.322	74	276	58	89	20	1	30	73	19	74	2	2	.366	.728
Clark,Brady	28	.271	132	465	67	126	37	4	12	59	56	53	8	7	.349	.445
Clark,Jermaine	24	.279	133	438	80	122	21	7	2	44	75	75	30	11	.384	.372
Cust,Jack	22	.265	129	430	79	114	28	4	15	59	78	160	7	9	.378	.453
Escobar,Alex	22	.258	122	419	64	108	21	5	12	55	39	122	16	6	.321	.418
Gerut,Jody	23	.307	109	374	51	115	36	3	3	61	69	53	14	11	.415	.444
Giles,Marcus	23	.265	132	442	59	117	25	1	13	50	50	76	17	6	.339	.414
Ginter,Keith	25	.314	125	449	90	141	28	2	22	76	58	136	16	6	.393	.532
Hart,Jason	23	.282	140	531	74	150	36	2	21	91	42	124	2	0	.335	.476
Hernandez,Alex	24	.277	126	459	45	127	30	1	9	57	17	108	4	3	.303	.405
Jennings,Robin	29	.286	123	440	59	126	40	4	10	60	30	63	2	3	.332	.464
Johnson,Nick*	21	.319	132	404	95	129	29	3	11	72	86	93	5	6	.439	.488
McClain,Scott	29	.283	123	442	63	125	24	2	27	72	51	86	5	9	.357	.529
Ortega,Bill	25	.304	86	322	44	98	16	3	10	54	20	44	0	5	.345	.466
Ortiz,Jose	24	.321	131	495	88	159	30	3	19	89	37	65	16	6	.368	.509
Overbay,Lyle	24	.319	62	232	33	74	14	1	6	38	18	41	2	2	.368	.466
Ozuna,Pablo	22	.274	118	442	57	121	21	4	5	45	26	58	24	9	.314	.373
Pena,Carlos	23	.282	138	517	99	146	33	1	25	89	72	114	8	0	.370	.495
Pena,Elvis	24	.329	126	498	99	164	19	9	4	39	63	72	38	15	.405	.428
Rolison,Nate	24	.276	123	410	58	113	29	2	13	58	47	122	1	1	.350	.451
Roskos,John	26	.276	99	355	53	98	22	0	12	53	37	71	1	5	.344	.439
Sears,Todd	25	.314	129	455	71	143	30	0	17	91	78	120	9	3	.415	.492
Stenson,Dernell	23	.245	98	368	47	90	13	0	16	56	35	103	0	0	.310	.410
Valdes,Pedro	28	.319	92	345	56	110	28	1	15	68	39	42	1	0	.388	.536
Valdez,Mario	26	.299	105	354	59	106	22	0	13	65	45	62	0	1	.378	.472
Valent,Eric	24	.240	128	458	67	110	21	4	18	75	50	97	1	3	.315	.421
Vazquez,Ramon	24	.272	124	397	58	108	23	3	8	59	44	83	0	5	.345	.406
Wilkerson,Brad	24	.275	129	429	78	118	44	1	13	66	67	102	8	6	.373	.473
Wilson,Craig	24	.257	124	382	65	98	22	1	26	67	34	128	0	1	.317	.524
Wooten,Shawn	28	.296	117	423	61	125	27	3	16	63	26	71	2	1	.336	.487
Young,Mike	24	.279	134	524	73	146	35	8	5	71	41	106	18	7	.331	.405

* Did not play in 2000, MLE based upon 1999 season.

2001 Pitcher Projections

Making statistical projections for major league pitchers is a very inexact science. The truth is, it's really a crapshoot because of all the variables that come into play. Defensive lineups change. Favorite catchers come and go. And for a pitcher coming off a solid season, the slightest, unconscious change in his mechanics the next spring can affect his velocity, pitch movement or command. Last year's magic can be elusive.

Despite these vagaries of pitching, we take an annual stab at pitching projections. STATS CEO John Dewan and Mike Canter devised a formula that we have used to predict pitching performances for 2000. Pitchers who have 150 games or 500 innings in the big leagues are covered.

Examples of success at this difficult task include Rick Helling and Randy Johnson:

Rick Helling

	W	L	ERA	G	IP	H	BB	SO	BR/9
Actual 2000	16	13	4.48	35	217	212	99	146	12.9
Projected 2000	14	12	4.42	34	218	207	85	148	12.1

Randy Johnson

	W	L	ERA	G	IP	H	BB	SO	BR/9
Actual 2000	19	7	2.64	35	249	202	76	347	10.1
Projected 2000	20	9	2.67	35	263	201	68	353	9.2

As a reminder that projecting pitchers isn't easy, we supply a couple cases where we predicted better results for hurlers. We didn't anticipate that Enron Field would lead to Jose Lima's demise, but we suspect there was more to Lima's struggles than just a new ballpark. We also expected David Cone's decline to be more of a slow-rolling snowball than an avalanche:

Jose Lima

	W	L	ERA	G	IP	H	BB	SO	BR/9
Actual 2000	7	16	6.65	33	196	251	68	124	14.6
Projected 2000	15	13	3.98	34	242	251	43	180	10.9

David Cone

	W	L	ERA	G	IP	H	BB	SO	BR/9
Actual 2000	4	14	6.91	30	155	192	82	120	15.9
Projected 2000	14	9	3.91	31	198	173	92	191	12.0

There are plenty of new ballparks to make the projection process more complicated, intriguing and entertaining. We hope that two of those three words describe your time spent inside the pages that follow.

—Thom Henninger

Projections for 2001 Pitchers

Pitcher	Age	ERA	W	L	Sv	G	GS	IP	H	HR	BB	SO	BR/9
Acevedo,Juan, Mil	31	4.15	4	4	0	58	4	89	88	11	34	50	12.3
Adams,Terry, LA	28	4.04	5	4	0	61	0	78	75	7	38	65	13.0
Aguilera,Rick, ChC	39	3.67	4	3	15	56	0	54	47	9	14	39	10.2
Aldred,Scott, Phi	33	5.34	2	3	0	37	0	32	38	5	15	25	14.9
Alfonseca,Antonio, Fla	29	4.56	2	5	43	70	0	73	81	7	29	46	13.6
Alvarez,Wilson, TB	31	4.61	7	9	0	22	22	125	126	15	70	111	14.1
Anderson,Brian, Ari	29	4.45	10	11	0	32	28	186	200	32	34	97	11.3
Appier,Kevin, Oak	33	4.95	12	11	0	32	32	200	203	23	104	129	13.8
Arrojo,Rolando, Bos	32	4.78	10	10	0	29	29	162	171	21	64	119	13.1
Ashby,Andy, Atl	33	4.14	13	11	0	31	31	202	206	23	62	118	11.9
Astacio,Pedro, Col	31	5.19	12	13	0	33	33	208	228	33	82	196	13.4
Aybar,Manny, Fla	26	4.45	4	5	0	58	0	85	87	10	37	58	13.1
Baldwin,James, CWS	29	4.72	12	10	0	31	30	185	197	26	61	117	12.6
Beck,Rod, Bos	32	3.86	3	2	0	37	0	42	42	4	13	36	11.8
Belcher,Tim, Ana	39	6.72	3	6	0	14	14	71	88	14	39	30	16.1
Belinda,Stan, Atl	34	4.40	3	3	0	47	0	45	41	8	20	45	12.2
Benes,Andy, StL	33	4.47	11	11	0	31	29	177	174	22	72	135	12.5
Benitez,Armando, NYM	28	2.57	3	3	47	76	0	77	46	8	41	111	10.2
Bere,Jason, Cle	30	5.33	8	9	0	26	25	135	143	19	71	108	14.3
Bergman,Sean, Min	31	5.96	3	7	0	18	15	80	100	11	39	37	15.6
Blair,Willie, Det	35	5.07	5	6	0	44	17	149	173	26	45	79	13.2
Boehringer,Brian, SD	31	4.29	1	2	0	16	6	42	41	5	20	31	13.1
Bohanon,Brian, Col	32	4.74	11	10	0	34	28	184	188	23	82	107	13.2
Bones,Ricky, Fla	32	5.18	3	4	0	47	1	66	82	7	27	47	14.9
Borbon,Pedro, Tor	33	4.60	3	3	0	63	0	45	41	5	32	30	14.6
Bottalico,Ricky, KC	31	4.93	4	5	19	64	0	73	75	9	44	57	14.7
Bottenfield,Kent, Phi	32	4.80	10	12	0	30	30	178	182	24	80	113	13.2
Brantley,Jeff, Phi	37	5.63	2	3	18	40	0	40	43	7	23	42	14.9
Brocail,Doug, Det	34	3.10	5	2	0	56	0	61	53	5	18	54	10.5
Brown,Kevin, LA	36	2.51	19	7	0	34	34	237	198	15	49	215	9.4
Burba,Dave, Cle	34	4.79	13	11	0	33	33	201	201	26	96	173	13.3
Burkett,John, Atl	36	5.24	7	9	0	31	23	139	168	15	53	101	14.3
Carpenter,Chris, Tor	26	5.28	9	11	0	27	27	167	186	20	79	112	14.3
Carrasco,Hector, Bos	31	4.30	4	4	0	59	1	69	73	5	32	53	13.7
Castillo,Frank, Tor	32	5.09	8	9	0	25	24	138	152	19	56	104	13.6
Christiansen,Jason, StL	31	3.20	4	2	0	56	0	45	38	2	23	47	12.2
Clark,Mark, Tex	33	5.83	3	4	0	13	10	54	62	7	30	27	15.3
Clemens,Roger, NYY	38	4.21	13	10	0	31	31	199	187	23	82	178	12.2
Colon,Bartolo, Cle	26	4.36	13	10	0	31	31	194	177	20	101	184	12.9
Cone,David, NYY	38	5.09	10	11	0	30	30	168	171	22	89	143	13.9
Cook,Dennis, NYM	38	4.35	4	4	0	69	0	60	56	9	29	60	12.8
Cordova,Francisco, Pit	29	4.23	7	7	0	21	20	117	116	11	47	75	12.5
Cormier,Rheal, Bos	34	3.76	5	3	0	63	0	67	70	6	18	42	11.8
Crabtree,Tim, Tex	31	4.44	5	4	2	60	0	75	85	6	27	55	13.4
Daal,Omar, Phi	29	4.62	10	11	0	32	29	183	190	20	79	117	13.2
Darensbourg,Vic, Fla	30	4.08	3	3	0	56	0	53	51	5	25	47	12.9
DeJean,Mike, Col	30	4.98	3	3	0	55	0	56	63	7	25	27	14.1
Dipoto,Jerry, Col	33	4.26	2	2	0	32	0	38	39	4	16	28	13.0
Dreifort,Darren, LA	29	4.16	11	11	0	31	31	188	174	20	85	154	12.4
Eldred,Cal, CWS	33	5.21	6	7	0	19	19	102	107	14	54	83	14.2

Projections for 2001 Pitchers

Pitcher	Age	ERA	W	L	Sv	G	GS	IP	H	HR	BB	SO	BR/9
Embree,Alan, SF	31	3.60	5	3	4	65	0	60	53	5	26	50	11.9
Erickson,Scott, Bal	33	5.18	7	9	0	22	22	139	152	14	72	63	14.5
Estes,Shawn, SF	28	4.52	12	11	0	31	31	195	187	15	110	146	13.7
Fassero,Jeff, Bos	38	5.57	4	5	0	47	8	97	112	17	37	71	13.8
Fernandez,Alex, Fla	31	3.63	8	7	0	20	20	129	121	13	39	79	11.2
Fetters,Mike, LA	36	4.09	3	3	2	43	0	44	39	5	23	33	12.7
Finley,Chuck, Cle	38	4.29	15	11	0	34	34	216	205	23	100	195	12.7
Florie,Bryce, Bos	31	4.50	3	3	0	33	2	65	65	6	26	45	13.6
Foulke,Keith, CWS	28	3.06	4	3	38	70	0	94	78	12	23	98	9.7
Franco,John, NYM	40	3.53	4	3	2	57	0	51	46	4	24	51	12.4
Frascatore,John, Tor	31	4.38	4	4	0	60	0	72	74	9	27	35	12.6
Garces,Rich, Bos	30	3.14	5	2	0	53	0	63	50	6	27	53	11.0
Gardner,Mark, SF	39	4.44	8	8	0	30	20	146	150	22	41	90	11.8
Glavine,Tom, Atl	35	3.50	17	11	0	35	35	239	231	19	64	146	11.1
Gomes,Wayne, Phi	28	4.26	5	4	0	68	0	74	73	6	39	59	13.6
Gooden,Dwight, NYY	36	5.19	4	4	0	35	6	85	91	13	36	55	13.4
Graves,Danny, Cin	27	3.67	3	4	36	69	0	98	91	8	41	57	12.1
Grimsley,Jason, NYY	33	4.15	5	4	5	60	3	89	86	9	43	53	13.0
Groom,Buddy, Bal	35	3.93	4	3	0	72	0	55	58	3	20	38	12.8
Guardado,Eddie, Min	30	4.42	4	4	6	68	0	57	52	10	25	50	12.2
Guthrie,Mark, Tor	35	4.30	5	4	0	70	0	67	67	8	31	56	13.2
Guzman,Juan, TB	34	4.38	7	7	0	20	20	113	106	16	49	89	12.3
Hamilton,Joey, Tor	30	4.42	4	3	0	11	10	55	57	5	20	30	12.6
Hampton,Mike, NYM	28	3.92	14	12	0	33	33	225	213	14	102	161	12.6
Harnisch,Pete, Cin	34	4.12	10	9	0	26	26	153	145	21	54	89	11.7
Hasegawa,S., Ana	32	4.25	5	4	5	65	0	89	89	12	34	58	12.4
Hawkins,LaTroy, Min	28	4.60	2	5	22	65	0	86	98	10	29	51	13.3
Haynes,Jimmy, Mil	28	5.45	8	14	0	32	30	180	204	22	90	96	14.7
Helling,Rick, Tex	30	4.71	14	12	0	35	35	218	210	32	99	138	12.8
Henry,Doug, SF	37	4.50	4	4	0	60	0	66	56	11	40	54	13.1
Hentgen,Pat, StL	32	5.10	10	13	0	33	33	196	208	27	90	118	13.7
Heredia,Felix, ChC	25	4.02	4	4	2	72	0	56	53	4	32	52	13.7
Heredia,Gil, Oak	35	4.61	13	11	0	32	32	199	219	23	66	109	12.9
Hermanson,D., Mon	28	4.19	12	12	0	32	32	204	201	22	77	118	12.3
Hernandez,Livan, SF	26	4.40	13	12	0	32	32	227	243	26	69	159	12.4
Hernandez,O., NYY	31	3.43	15	8	0	30	30	202	178	25	53	147	10.3
Hernandez,Roberto, TB	36	3.58	3	4	31	69	0	73	67	5	33	62	12.3
Hitchcock,Sterling, SD	30	4.74	6	8	0	18	18	112	113	17	44	106	12.6
Hoffman,Trevor, SD	33	2.03	3	2	47	68	0	71	50	6	16	81	8.4
Holt,Chris, Hou	29	4.62	12	10	0	33	30	193	216	17	70	130	13.3
Holtz,Mike, Ana	28	4.37	3	2	0	50	0	35	35	4	18	32	13.6
Howry,Bob, CWS	27	3.21	6	3	6	66	0	70	54	8	31	69	10.9
James,Mike, StL	33	3.71	4	3	0	51	0	51	48	4	24	42	12.7
Johnson,Randy, Ari	37	2.95	19	10	0	35	35	256	201	26	78	350	9.8
Johnstone,John, SF	32	3.76	4	3	0	52	0	55	50	7	19	49	11.3
Jones,Bobby J., NYM	31	4.23	9	9	0	26	26	149	151	19	47	81	12.0
Jones,Doug, Oak	44	3.86	6	3	0	59	0	84	90	8	20	55	11.8
Jones,Todd, Det	33	4.02	2	4	39	66	0	65	61	6	32	63	12.9
Kamieniecki,Scott, Atl	37	4.89	3	4	0	49	1	57	58	7	36	43	14.8
Karl,Scott, Ana	29	5.81	6	9	0	26	20	124	149	15	64	49	15.5

Projections for 2001 Pitchers

Pitcher	Age	ERA	W	L	Sv	G	GS	IP	H	HR	BB	SO	BR/9
Karsay,Steve, Cle	29	4.09	5	4	5	65	1	77	82	7	26	63	12.6
Kile,Darryl, StL	32	3.92	14	11	0	33	33	218	217	27	55	159	11.2
Kline,Steve, Mon	28	4.27	5	5	9	83	0	78	79	8	35	73	13.2
Leiter,Al, NYM	35	3.34	15	10	0	31	31	210	183	16	77	180	11.1
Leskanic,Curtis, Mil	33	4.39	4	5	17	70	0	80	75	8	47	70	13.7
Levine,Al, Ana	33	4.40	5	4	0	51	4	92	96	11	36	38	12.9
Lieber,Jon, ChC	31	4.10	14	13	0	34	34	235	245	32	51	196	11.3
Lima,Jose, Hou	28	4.99	13	12	0	34	34	213	231	34	74	150	12.9
Lira,Felipe, Mon	29	5.48	2	4	0	36	5	69	86	11	25	40	14.5
Loaiza,Esteban, Tor	29	4.63	10	10	0	33	26	173	194	21	49	116	12.6
Loiselle,Rich, Pit	29	4.91	2	2	0	31	0	33	34	3	22	28	15.3
Lopez,Albie, TB	29	4.76	11	13	0	32	32	204	221	25	77	109	13.1
Lowe,Derek, Bos	28	3.25	4	4	46	74	0	97	92	7	27	71	11.0
Maddux,Greg, Atl	35	2.94	19	9	0	34	34	239	227	16	40	166	10.1
Maddux,Mike, Hou	39	4.74	2	2	0	32	0	38	41	5	15	27	13.3
Magnante,Mike, Oak	36	4.14	4	3	0	54	0	50	54	2	23	31	13.9
Mahomes,Pat, NYM	30	4.71	4	4	0	48	3	84	78	12	55	68	14.3
Mantei,Matt, Ari	27	2.94	2	2	39	53	0	52	36	3	32	68	11.8
Manzanillo,Josias, Pit	33	4.20	2	2	0	33	0	45	42	7	21	38	12.6
Martinez,Pedro, Bos	29	1.75	21	3	0	30	29	216	151	16	32	299	7.6
Martinez,Ramon, Bos	33	4.43	9	8	0	24	24	138	128	14	72	97	13.0
Mathews,T.J., Oak	31	4.27	4	3	0	50	0	59	59	8	23	43	12.5
McElroy,Chuck, Bal	33	4.20	3	3	0	47	1	60	60	5	30	50	13.5
Meadows,Brian, KC	25	5.49	10	13	0	32	32	190	232	29	62	77	13.9
Mecir,Jim, Oak	31	3.23	5	2	6	48	0	64	54	4	28	55	11.5
Mendoza,Ramiro, NYY	29	4.34	5	4	0	27	8	85	93	9	26	49	12.6
Mercker,Kent, Ana	33	4.80	5	4	0	24	12	75	84	9	32	41	13.9
Mesa,Jose, Sea	35	5.14	4	5	0	67	0	77	86	10	39	62	14.6
Miceli,Dan, Fla	30	3.93	3	3	0	52	0	55	51	6	24	49	12.3
Miller,Travis, Min	28	4.87	3	4	0	62	0	61	74	5	26	55	14.8
Mills,Alan, Bal	34	4.74	3	3	0	50	0	57	53	8	37	41	14.2
Millwood,Kevin, Atl	26	3.51	16	10	0	35	34	218	200	23	63	184	10.9
Milton,Eric, Min	25	4.14	12	12	0	33	33	202	206	31	44	161	11.1
Mlicki,Dave, Det	33	4.68	9	9	0	25	25	146	157	18	54	81	13.0
Moehler,Brian, Det	29	4.45	11	11	0	30	30	184	208	22	41	103	12.2
Mohler,Mike, Cle	32	4.80	2	2	0	32	0	30	33	3	15	19	14.4
Morgan,Mike, Ari	41	5.53	4	6	0	51	11	114	145	17	42	55	14.8
Moyer,Jamie, Sea	38	4.53	11	10	0	28	28	179	191	21	61	110	12.7
Mulholland,Terry, Atl	38	4.95	5	6	0	60	11	131	160	18	34	64	13.3
Mussina,Mike, Bal	32	3.38	16	10	0	33	33	226	215	24	44	196	10.3
Myers,Mike, Col	32	4.09	4	3	0	76	0	44	40	6	19	37	12.1
Nagy,Charles, Cle	34	5.31	6	7	0	18	18	105	123	15	39	68	13.9
Neagle,Denny, NYY	32	4.07	12	9	0	29	28	177	163	22	68	122	11.7
Nelson,Jeff, NYY	34	3.32	5	2	0	62	0	57	43	3	36	57	12.5
Nen,Robb, SF	31	2.78	3	2	40	69	0	68	56	5	21	84	10.2
Nitkowski,C.J., Det	28	4.05	6	4	0	67	10	100	94	11	47	76	12.7
Nomo,Hideo, Det	32	4.52	11	11	0	30	30	185	174	25	87	173	12.7
Olivares,Omar, Oak	33	5.23	8	8	0	25	21	141	152	14	78	64	14.7
Oliver,Darren, Tex	30	5.12	8	9	0	24	24	137	158	16	53	76	13.9
Olson,Gregg, LA	34	3.94	2	2	0	29	0	32	31	3	12	25	12.1

Projections for 2001 Pitchers

Pitcher	Age	ERA	W	L	Sv	G	GS	IP	H	HR	BB	SO	BR/9
Osuna,Antonio, LA	28	3.52	4	3	0	45	0	64	51	7	33	69	11.8
Painter,Lance, Tor	33	3.95	4	3	0	47	3	66	63	7	28	55	12.4
Paniagua,Jose, Sea	27	3.99	5	4	6	66	0	79	75	6	42	71	13.3
Park,Chan Ho, LA	28	4.06	13	12	0	34	34	215	184	21	118	200	12.6
Parris,Steve, Cin	33	4.63	10	11	0	29	29	171	179	22	63	108	12.7
Patterson,Danny, Det	30	4.19	4	3	0	56	0	58	65	5	17	34	12.7
Percival,Troy, Ana	31	3.29	2	2	32	56	0	52	38	6	27	58	11.3
Perez,Carlos, LA	30	4.47	8	9	0	26	24	135	150	18	31	60	12.1
Person,Robert, Phi	31	4.60	11	12	0	31	31	184	166	25	101	174	13.1
Petkovsek,Mark, Ana	35	4.17	5	4	2	64	1	82	92	7	24	39	12.7
Pettitte,Andy, NYY	29	4.28	13	10	0	32	32	200	210	15	78	124	13.0
Pichardo,Hipolito, Bos	31	4.15	4	3	0	38	1	65	69	5	25	34	13.0
Plesac,Dan, Ari	39	4.61	3	3	0	63	0	41	41	5	21	48	13.6
Ponson,Sidney, Bal	24	4.91	11	14	0	32	32	218	233	32	82	133	13.0
Powell,Jay, Hou	29	3.98	3	2	0	42	0	43	41	2	24	39	13.6
Quantrill,Paul, Tor	32	4.25	5	4	0	59	0	72	82	5	22	45	13.0
Radke,Brad, Min	28	4.22	13	13	0	34	34	224	243	26	50	132	11.8
Rapp,Pat, Bal	33	5.13	9	11	0	33	29	165	181	18	79	101	14.2
Reed,Rick, NYM	35	4.08	11	10	0	29	29	172	178	26	32	116	11.0
Reed,Steve, Cle	35	3.72	5	3	0	59	0	58	54	7	20	46	11.5
Rekar,Bryan, TB	29	4.90	7	10	0	29	22	147	173	22	33	82	12.6
Remlinger,Mike, Atl	35	4.03	5	4	3	72	0	76	68	9	38	70	12.6
Reyes,Al, LA	30	4.37	2	2	0	30	0	35	31	5	21	35	13.4
Reyes,Carlos, SD	32	4.40	2	3	0	36	0	45	47	7	15	31	12.4
Reyes,Dennys, Cin	24	4.32	4	3	0	63	0	50	47	4	33	53	14.4
Reynolds,Shane, Hou	33	4.58	11	9	0	26	26	165	179	18	57	132	12.9
Reynoso,Armando, Ari	35	4.21	10	10	0	31	29	169	176	19	52	84	12.1
Rhodes,Arthur, Sea	31	3.66	5	3	0	62	0	64	51	7	35	70	12.1
Rivera,Mariano, NYY	31	2.34	3	2	38	66	0	73	56	4	21	52	9.5
Rocker,John, Atl	26	3.20	2	3	44	64	0	59	40	5	39	81	12.1
Rodriguez,Felix, SF	28	3.97	5	4	0	66	0	77	72	6	40	74	13.1
Rodriguez,Frank, Sea	28	4.98	2	3	0	25	2	56	65	6	24	38	14.3
Rodriguez,Rich, NYM	38	5.93	2	3	0	42	0	44	55	7	20	29	15.3
Rogers,Kenny, Tex	36	4.27	14	11	0	33	33	217	232	18	74	130	12.7
Rosado,Jose, KC	26	4.28	8	7	0	20	20	122	122	16	40	81	12.0
Rueter,Kirk, SF	30	4.70	11	11	0	32	32	184	200	23	62	82	12.8
Rusch,Glendon, NYM	26	4.43	11	12	0	30	30	187	206	25	43	154	12.0
Schilling,Curt, Ari	34	3.15	14	8	0	27	27	200	177	22	43	164	9.9
Schmidt,Jason, Pit	28	5.42	7	11	0	24	24	151	158	16	98	109	15.3
Schourek,Pete, Bos	32	4.87	7	7	0	24	20	109	114	18	39	78	12.6
Seanez,Rudy, Atl	32	2.81	3	1	0	34	0	32	25	2	13	32	10.7
Sele,Aaron, Sea	31	4.61	13	12	0	34	34	209	234	20	73	162	13.2
Service,Scott, Oak	34	4.68	3	2	0	36	0	50	53	6	24	51	13.9
Shaw,Jeff, LA	34	3.10	2	3	31	61	0	61	56	6	14	40	10.3
Shuey,Paul, Cle	30	3.73	5	3	0	62	0	70	62	7	34	82	12.3
Simas,Bill, CWS	29	4.04	5	3	0	63	0	69	66	9	25	48	11.9
Sirotka,Mike, CWS	30	4.66	13	11	0	32	32	201	216	25	70	125	12.8
Slocumb,Heathcliff, SD	35	4.77	3	5	0	60	0	66	69	6	40	53	14.9
Smoltz,John, Atl	34	3.68	12	7	0	24	24	154	140	13	38	140	10.4
Sparks,Steve W., Det	35	4.24	8	6	0	23	19	119	126	13	33	59	12.0

Projections for 2001 Pitchers

Pitcher	Age	ERA	W	L	Sv	G	GS	IP	H	HR	BB	SO	BR/9
Spoljaric,Paul, KC	30	4.94	2	2	0	23	2	31	31	4	18	31	14.2
Spradlin,Jerry, ChC	34	4.05	5	4	0	60	1	80	81	9	29	68	12.4
Springer,Dennis, NYM	36	5.42	3	5	0	14	11	73	84	10	32	31	14.3
Springer,Russ, Ari	32	3.95	4	3	0	51	0	57	51	6	30	58	12.8
Stanton,Mike, NYY	34	3.55	5	3	0	70	0	66	62	6	21	64	11.3
Stottlemyre,Todd, Ari	36	4.44	9	9	0	26	26	142	142	19	54	108	12.4
Sullivan,Scott, Cin	30	3.39	7	4	2	79	0	109	91	13	41	88	10.9
Suppan,Jeff, KC	26	5.09	11	14	0	34	33	214	236	31	83	116	13.4
Swindell,Greg, Ari	36	3.75	5	4	0	64	0	72	68	9	23	56	11.4
Tapani,Kevin, ChC	37	4.45	10	11	0	28	28	176	190	25	42	118	11.9
Tavarez,Julian, Col	28	4.38	11	9	0	33	26	181	195	15	79	102	13.6
Telford,Anthony, Mon	35	3.96	5	4	0	69	0	84	87	7	31	62	12.6
Thompson,Justin, Tex	28	4.59	7	7	0	17	17	102	111	15	45	72	13.8
Timlin,Mike, StL	35	3.80	5	3	4	62	0	64	61	7	23	50	11.8
Tomko,Brett, Sea	28	3.90	5	3	0	40	5	90	86	12	31	67	11.7
Trachsel,Steve, Tor	30	4.95	12	13	0	34	34	202	220	29	75	129	13.1
Trombley,Mike, Bal	34	4.44	5	5	2	75	0	77	74	12	32	73	12.4
Urbina,Ugueth, Mon	27	2.83	2	2	33	49	0	54	39	4	25	74	10.7
Valdes,Ismael, LA	27	4.40	8	9	0	25	24	139	139	18	52	97	12.4
Van Poppel,Todd, ChC	29	4.71	4	5	0	51	2	86	90	11	43	67	13.9
Vazquez,Javier, Mon	24	4.61	11	12	0	31	31	197	216	27	55	163	12.4
Veres,Dave, StL	34	4.03	3	4	22	72	0	76	75	8	30	70	12.4
Villone,Ron, Cin	31	4.69	8	9	0	33	23	142	137	14	78	87	13.6
Wagner,Billy, Hou	29	3.40	2	2	20	49	0	53	43	7	22	81	11.0
Wakefield,Tim, Bos	34	4.65	6	6	0	50	17	153	154	25	64	104	12.8
Wall,Donne, SD	33	3.51	4	3	0	48	0	59	49	7	23	42	11.0
Wasdin,John, Col	28	4.38	4	3	0	41	3	78	81	13	22	58	11.9
Watson,Allen, NYY	30	5.40	2	2	0	24	1	40	46	7	18	31	14.4
Weathers,Dave, Mil	31	4.61	4	5	0	67	0	82	92	8	33	64	13.7
Wells,Bob, Min	34	4.24	5	5	6	76	0	87	89	13	23	58	11.6
Wells,David, Tor	38	4.03	15	11	0	35	35	230	256	27	31	167	11.2
Wendell,Turk, NYM	34	3.43	6	4	0	78	0	84	70	8	38	71	11.6
Wetteland,John, Tex	34	3.77	2	3	34	62	0	62	60	7	19	61	11.5
Whisenant,Matt, SD	30	3.94	2	2	0	38	0	32	30	2	20	22	14.1
White,Gabe, Col	29	3.55	6	3	5	62	0	76	69	11	18	71	10.3
White,Rick, NYM	32	3.97	6	5	0	65	0	102	104	9	37	69	12.4
Wickman,Bob, Cle	32	3.70	3	3	29	70	0	73	69	5	35	59	12.8
Wilkins,Marc, Oak	30	3.79	4	2	0	50	0	57	50	4	35	42	13.4
Williams,Brian, Cle	32	4.59	3	2	0	36	0	51	53	4	30	34	14.6
Williams,Mike, Pit	32	3.90	2	4	25	67	0	67	61	7	35	77	12.9
Williams,Woody, SD	34	4.38	9	11	0	26	26	181	177	29	58	120	11.7
Woodard,Steve, Cle	26	4.89	10	9	0	37	24	160	183	22	48	105	13.0
Worrell,Tim, ChC	33	4.43	4	4	2	57	0	69	72	9	26	57	12.8
Wright,Jamey, Mil	26	4.85	9	12	0	28	28	180	187	16	96	101	14.1
Yan,Esteban, TB	27	5.09	3	5	0	55	0	76	85	12	30	62	13.6
Yoshii,Masato, Col	36	4.61	11	10	0	30	29	170	177	26	54	96	12.2

Career Assessments

AARON WATCH

For the first time in at least five seasons, Henry Aaron's career home run record is in less jeopardy now than it was one year ago. Although the year 2000 was a good year for hitters and a good year for home run hitters, it was an off season for the three men who are the most serious threats to Aaron's record—Mark McGwire, Sammy Sosa, and Ken Griffey Jr.

Mark McGwire, interestingly enough, almost matched his 1998 ratio of home runs to at-bats, which was the best of his career—one home run every 7.27 at-bats. Last year he was at 7.37, his second-best ratio. He did so in a season limited by injuries to 236 at-bats, and thus his chance to catch Aaron dropped from 48% to 23%. Griffey did not have a good year, and he dipped slightly, from 44% to 36%. Sammy Sosa led the majors in home runs, with 50, but even so, that number was 20% off his previous two seasons, and so his chance to get 756 home runs did not improve, hanging steady at 35%.

Still, the long-term outlook for Aaron's record is not good; there is still a 79% chance that some active player will break the record. Ten years ago there was no active player who had established himself as a threat to hit 756 home runs. A year ago there were seven players who had established a shot at Aaron's mark; now there are eight. Juan Gonzalez has dropped off the list, at least for now, but Carlos Delgado and Barry Bonds have moved onto the list. Vladimir Guerrero one year ago had a 1% chance to hit 756 home runs. Now he has an 11% chance. Alex Rodriguez in the last year has moved from 11% to 16%. Essentially, what is happening is that the new home run levels, having been explored by Mark McGwire and Sammy Sosa, are now being settled by other hitters. After Babe Ruth became the first man to hit 30 home runs, the first man to hit 40 home runs, the first man to hit 50 home runs and the first man to hit 60 home runs, within a few years there were many other players who hit 30, some others who hit 40, and a few others who hit 50. The same thing with the 100-stolen base level; after it was explored by Maury Wills, it was settled by several other players.

More players strike out 100 times every year now than did so in all of baseball history up to 1961. The 100-strikeout level, having been explored by Harlond Clift and Vince DiMaggio, was settled by Ralph Kiner and Eddie Mathews and Bob Lemon, was developed by Dave Kingman and Bobby Bonds, and has now been thickly populated. We are now almost ten years into the Mark McGwire era, and the 600-home run level is about to be invaded en masse.

A year ago there were seven players who had a shot at Aaron's other record, 2,297 career RBI; now there are nine players on that list. Despite Griffey's off season, it remains likely that some active player will break that record.

Derek Jeter remains the only player who has any visible chance to threaten Pete Rose's hit record, and that remains very much a longshot. Rickey Henderson may get his 3,000th hit this year, and Roberto Alomar has emerged as the best candidate among the next group, the players born after 1963. Three years ago, Roberto Alomar and Chuck Knoblauch were almost even as 3,000-hit candidates, but Alomar has gone from 28% to 64%, while Knoblauch has gone from 23% to 8%. Vladimir, Alex, Nomar and Erstad are exploding as 3,000-hit candidates, while Palmeiro and Sosa and Frank Thomas are trying to grind it out at 180 hits a year. The 3,000 hit standard remains an imposing barrier—but players will continue to rise to the task.

—Bill James

Player	Age	H	HR	RBI	Home Runs					Hits			RBI	
					500	600	700	756	800	3000	4000	4257	2000	2298
Mark McGwire	36	1570	554	1350	8/5/99	97%	51%	23%	10%	—	—	—	1%	—
Barry Bonds	35	2157	494	1405	100%	89%	21%	6%	—	5%	—	—	9%	—
Ken Griffey Jr.	30	1883	438	1270	96%	90%	54%	36%	25%	35%	—	—	55%	25%
Sammy Sosa	31	1606	386	1079	94%	89%	50%	35%	26%	25%	—	—	35%	14%
Jose Canseco	35	1811	446	1358	94%	10%	—	—	—	—	—	—	35%	—
Rafael Palmeiro	35	2321	400	1347	93%	24%	—	—	—	39%	—	—	19%	—
Juan Gonzalez	30	1554	362	1142	87%	29%	6%	—	—	16%	—	—	22%	3%
Albert Belle	33	1726	381	1239	71%	16%	—	—	—	11%	—	—	18%	—
Alex Rodriguez	24	966	189	595	70%	41%	23%	16%	11%	26%	1%	—	29%	15%
Jeff Bagwell	32	1630	310	1093	64%	24%	5%	—	—	14%	—	—	20%	2%
Manny Ramirez	28	1086	236	804	59%	29%	12%	5%	1%	10%	—	—	32%	16%
Vladimir Guerrero	24	695	136	404	55%	32%	18%	11%	7%	27%	4%	—	20%	9%
Frank Thomas	32	1755	344	1183	53%	13%	—	—	—	19%	—	—	21%	2%
Fred McGriff	36	2103	417	1298	49%	—	—	—	—	3%	—	—	—	—
Carlos Delgado	28	818	190	604	44%	21%	7%	1%	—	6%	—	—	16%	5%
Gary Sheffield	31	1508	279	916	41%	13%	—	—	—	8%	—	—	2%	—
Mo Vaughn	32	1479	299	977	39%	9%	—	—	—	5%	—	—	6%	—
Chipper Jones	28	1051	189	635	37%	16%	3%	—	—	15%	—	—	6%	—
Jim Thome	29	1033	233	685	34%	11%	—	—	—	—	—	—	1%	—
Greg Vaughn	34	1314	320	956	33%	3%	—	—	—	—	—	—	—	—
Troy Glaus	23	328	77	204	29%	14%	4%	—	—	—	—	—	—	—
Andruw Jones	23	635	116	361	29%	12%	2%	—	—	22%	1%	—	5%	—
Dean Palmer	31	1169	264	803	27%	4%	—	—	—	—	—	—	—	—
Todd Helton	26	594	107	368	25%	10%	—	—	—	16%	—	—	12%	3%
Richard Hidalgo	24	345	68	219	19%	6%	—	—	—	—	—	—	—	—
Jason Giambi	29	870	149	555	19%	3%	—	—	—	3%	—	—	8%	—
Tony Batista	26	496	100	298	18%	4%	—	—	—	—	—	—	—	—
Shawn Green	27	882	143	475	17%	2%	—	—	—	12%	—	—	3%	—
Mike Piazza	31	1356	278	881	15%	—	—	—	—	—	—	—	—	—
Eric Karros	32	1363	242	840	9%	—	—	—	—	—	—	—	—	—
Raul Mondesi	29	1109	187	585	8%	—	—	—	—	—	—	—	—	—
Scott Rolen	25	623	108	386	8%	—	—	—	—	—	—	—	—	—
Jim Edmonds	30	923	163	516	6%	—	—	—	—	—	—	—	—	—
Brian Giles	29	583	113	395	6%	—	—	—	—	—	—	—	—	—
Ben Grieve	24	492	76	303	5%	—	—	—	—	5%	—	—	1%	—
Matt Williams	34	1677	346	1097	5%	—	—	—	—	—	—	—	—	—
David Justice	34	1373	276	917	5%	—	—	—	—	—	—	—	—	—
Tim Salmon	31	1180	230	757	5%	—	—	—	—	—	—	—	—	—
Magglio Ordonez	26	546	80	319	4%	—	—	—	—	9%	—	—	4%	—
Richie Sexson	25	325	72	242	4%	—	—	—	—	—	—	—	—	—
Nomar Garciaparra	26	812	117	436	3%	—	—	—	—	21%	—	—	3%	—
Jeromy Burnitz	31	711	154	504	2%	—	—	—	—	—	—	—	—	—
Jermaine Dye	26	566	84	319	1%	—	—	—	—	4%	—	—	—	—
Cal Ripken Jr.	39	3070	417	1627	—	—	—	—	—	4/15/00	—	—	—	—
Tony Gwynn	40	3108	134	1121	—	—	—	—	—	8/6/99	—	—	—	—
Rickey Henderson	41	2914	282	1052	—	—	—	—	—	80%	—	—	—	—
Roberto Alomar	32	2196	170	918	—	—	—	—	—	64%	1%	—	—	—
Derek Jeter	26	1008	78	414	—	—	—	—	—	33%	5%	1%	—	—
Johnny Damon	26	894	65	352	—	—	—	—	—	25%	1%	—	—	—
Darin Erstad	26	767	77	332	—	—	—	—	—	20%	—	—	—	—

Player	Age	Current H	Current HR	Current RBI	Home Runs 500	600	700	756	800	Hits 3000	4000	4257	RBI 2000	2298
Neifi Perez	25	655	36	234	—	—	—	—	—	18%	—	—	—	—
John Olerud	31	1595	186	865	—	—	—	—	—	17%	—	—	—	—
Edgardo Alfonzo	26	874	87	433	—	—	—	—	—	17%	—	—	—	—
Garret Anderson	28	1043	107	510	—	—	—	—	—	16%	—	—	—	—
Bernie Williams	31	1463	181	802	—	—	—	—	—	14%	—	—	3%	—
Edgar Renteria	24	767	39	253	—	—	—	—	—	13%	—	—	—	—
Mark Grace	36	2201	148	1004	—	—	—	—	—	11%	—	—	—	—
Jeff Cirillo	30	1059	77	487	—	—	—	—	—	11%	—	—	—	—
Ray Durham	28	980	77	371	—	—	—	—	—	11%	—	—	—	—
Luis Gonzalez	32	1434	164	775	—	—	—	—	—	10%	—	—	—	—
Shannon Stewart	26	574	44	216	—	—	—	—	—	9%	—	—	—	—
Bobby Abreu	26	572	65	273	—	—	—	—	—	9%	—	—	—	—
Mike Sweeney	26	569	70	336	—	—	—	—	—	8%	—	—	4%	—
Omar Vizquel	33	1605	41	515	—	—	—	—	—	8%	—	—	—	—
Chuck Knoblauch	31	1646	83	549	—	—	—	—	—	8%	—	—	—	—
Craig Biggio	34	1969	160	741	—	—	—	—	—	7%	—	—	—	—
Travis Fryman	31	1602	209	929	—	—	—	—	—	7%	—	—	—	—
Deivi Cruz	24	546	30	225	—	—	—	—	—	7%	—	—	—	—
B.J. Surhoff	35	1895	160	961	—	—	—	—	—	5%	—	—	—	—
Doug Glanville	29	730	32	219	—	—	—	—	—	4%	—	—	—	—
Jay Bell	34	1828	180	800	—	—	—	—	—	3%	—	—	—	—
Mark Kotsay	24	463	31	179	—	—	—	—	—	3%	—	—	—	—
Marquis Grissom	33	1695	145	663	—	—	—	—	—	2%	—	—	—	—
Jose Vidro	25	437	38	191	—	—	—	—	—	2%	—	—	—	—
Ivan Rodriguez	28	1459	171	704	—	—	—	—	—	1%	—	—	—	—
Luis Castillo	24	464	4	71	—	—	—	—	—	1%	—	—	—	—
Miguel Tejada	24	421	64	254	—	—	—	—	—	1%	—	—	—	—
Sean Casey	25	432	52	237	—	—	—	—	—	1%	—	—	—	—
Adrian Beltre	21	338	42	174	—	—	—	—	—	1%	—	—	—	—

Note: A date in place of a percentage indicates the date on which the player achieved the specific milestone.

Glossary

% Inherited Scored
A Relief Pitching statistic indicating the percentage of runners on base at the time a relief pitcher enters a game that he allows to score.

% Pitches Taken
The number of pitches a batter does not swing at divided by the total number of pitches he sees.

1st Batter Average
The batting average allowed by a relief pitcher to the first batter he faces in a game.

1st Batter OBP
The On-Base Percentage allowed by a relief pitcher to the first batter he faces in a game.

Active Career Batting Leaders
Minimum of 1,000 At-Bats required for Batting Average, On-Base Percentage, Slugging Percentage, At-Bats Per HR, At-Bats Per GDP, At-Bats Per RBI, and Strikeout-to-Walk Ratio. One hundred (100) Stolen Base Attempts required for Stolen Base Success %. Any player who appeared in 2000 is eligible for inclusion provided he meets the category's minimum requirements.

Active Career Pitching Leaders
Minimum of 750 Innings Pitched required for Earned Run Average, Opponent Batting Average, all of the "Per 9 Innings" categories, and Strikeout-to-Walk Ratio. Two hundred fifty (250) Games Started required for Complete Game Frequency. One hundred (100) decisions required for Win-Loss Percentage. Any player who appeared in 2000 is eligible for inclusion provided he meets the category's minimum requirements.

AVG Allowed ScPos
Batting Average Allowed with Runners in Scoring Position.

AVG Bases Loaded
Batting Average with the Bases Loaded.

Batting Average
Hits divided by At-Bats.

Blown Save
Entering a game in a Save Situation (see Save Situation in Glossary) and allowing the tying or go-ahead run to score.

Career Assessments
Once known as the Favorite Toy, this method is used to estimate a player's chance of achieving a specific goal. In the following example, we'll say 3,000 hits. Four things are considered:

1. Need Hits, the number of hits needed to reach the goal. (Of course, this also could be Need Home Runs, Need Doubles, etc.)

2. Years Remaining. The number of years remaining to meet the goal is estimated by (42 minus Age) divided by two. This formula assigns a 20-year-old player 11.0 remaining seasons, a 25-year-old player 8.5 remaining seasons, a 30-year-old player 6.0 remaining seasons, and a 35-year-old player 3.5 remaining seasons. Any active player is assumed to have at least half a season remaining, regardless of his age. Additionally, if a player is coming off a year with at least 100 hits *and* an offensive winning percentage of at least .500, he's assumed to have at least 1.5 remaining seasons. And if a player is coming off a year with at least 100 hits *or* an offensive winning percentage of at least .500, he's assumed to have at least 1.0 remaining seasons.

3. Established Hit Level. For 2000, the established hit level would be found by adding 1997 Hits, (1998 Hits multiplied by two) and (1999 Hits multiplied by three), then dividing by six. A player can't have an established performance level that is less than 80 percent of his most recent performance. In other words, a player who had 200 hits in 1999 can't have an established hit level less than 160.

4. Projected Remaining Hits. This is found by multiplying Years Remaining by the Established Hit Level.

Once you get the projected remaining hits, the chance of getting to the goal is figured by dividing Projected Remaining Hits by Need Hits, then subtracting .5. Thus if Need Hits and Projected Remaining Hits are the same, the chance of reaching the goal is 50 percent. A player's chance of continuing to progress toward a goal can't be more than .97 raised to the power of Years Remaining. This prevents a player from figuring to have a 148 percent chance of reaching a goal.

Catcher's ERA

The Earned Run Average of a club's pitchers with a particular catcher behind the plate. To figure this for a catcher, multiply the Earned Runs Allowed by pitchers while he was catching times nine and divide that by his number of Innings Caught.

Cheap Win

To determine the starting pitcher's Game Score: (1) Start with 50. (2) Add 1 point for each out recorded by the starting pitcher. (3) Add 2 points for each inning the pitcher completes after the fourth inning. (4) Add 1 point for each strikeout. (5) Subtract 2 points for each hit allowed. (6) Subtract 4 points for each earned run allowed. (7) Subtract 2 points for an unearned run. (8) Subtract 1 point for each walk.

If he wins with a game score under 50, it's a Cheap Win. The 2000 leaders in Cheap Wins are listed in the Leader Board section.

Cleanup Slugging%

The Slugging Percentage of a player when batting fourth in the batting order.

Complete Game Frequency

Complete Games divided by Games Started.

Component ERA (ERC)

A statistic that estimates what a pitcher's ERA should have been, based on his pitching performance. The steps in calculating an ERC are:

1. Subtract the pitcher's Home Runs Allowed from his Hits Allowed.

2. Multiply Step 1 by 1.255.

3. Multiply his Home Runs allowed by four.

4. Add Steps 2 and 3 together.

5. Multiply Step 4 by .89.

6. Add his Walks and Hit Batsmen.

7. Multiply Step 6 by .475.

8. Add Steps 5 and 7 together.

This yields the pitcher's total base esitmate (PTB), which is:

$$((((H-HR) * 1.255) + (HR * 4)) * .89 + ((BB + HB) * .475)$$

For those pitchers for whom there is intentional walk data, use this formula instead:

$$((((H-HR) * 1.255) + (HR * 4)) * .89 + ((BB + HB - IBB) * .56)$$

9. Add Hits and Walks and Hit Batsmen.

10. Multiply Step 9 by PTB.

11. Divide Step 10 by Batters Facing Pitcher. If BFP data is unavailable, approximate it by multiplying Innings Pitched by 2.9, then adding Step 9.

12. Multiply Step 11 by 9.

13. Divide Step 12 by Innings Pitched.

14. Subtract .56 from Step 13.

This is the pitcher's ERC, which is:

$$(((((H + BB + HB) * PTB) / BFP) * 9) / IP) - .56$$

If the result after Step 13 is less than 2.24, adjust the formula as follows:

$$(((((H + BB + HB) * PTB) / BFP) * 9) / IP) * .75$$

Earned Run Average

(Earned Runs * 9) divided by Innings Pitched.

Easy Save

This distinction is made to gauge the difficulty of a save. An Easy Save occurs when the first batter faced doesn't represent the tying run and the reliever pitches one inning or less.

Fielding Percentage

(Putouts plus Assists) divided by (Putouts plus Assists plus Errors).

Games Finished

The last relief pitcher for either team in any given game is credited with a Game Finished.

Game Scores

To determine the starting pitcher's Game Score: (1) Start with 50. (2) Add 1 point for each out recorded by the starting pitcher. (3) Add 2 points for each inning the pitcher completes after the fourth inning. (4) Add 1 point for each strikeout. (5) Subtract 2 points for each hit allowed. (6) Subtract 4 points for each earned run allowed. (7) Subtract 2 points for an unearned run. (8) Subtract 1 point for each walk.

The top Game Scores of 2000 are listed in the Leader Board section.

GDP

Ground into Double Play.

GDP Opportunity

Any situation with a runner on first and less than two out.

Ground/Fly Ratio (Grd/Fly)

For batters, groundballs hit divided by flyballs hit. For pitchers, groundballs allowed divided by flyballs allowed. All batted balls except line drives and bunts are included.

Hold

A hold is credited any time a relief pitcher enters a game in a Save Situation (see definition, except for point 3c.), records at least one out and leaves the game never having relinquished the lead. Note: a pitcher cannot finish the game and receive credit for a hold, nor can he earn a hold and a save in the same game.

Inherited Runners

Any runner on base when a reliever enters a game is considered inherited by that pitcher.

Isolated Power

Slugging Percentage minus Batting Average.

K/BB Ratio

Strikeouts divided by Walks.

Late & Close

A Late & Close situation meets the following requirements: (1) the game is in the seventh inning or later, and (2) the batting team is either leading by one run, tied, or has the potential tying run on base, at bat, or on deck. Note: this situation is very similar to the characteristics of a Save Situation.

Leadoff On Base%

The On-Base Percentage of a player when batting first in the batting order.

LHS

Lefthanded Starting Pitcher.

Major League Equivalency (MLE)

A translation of a Double-A or Triple-A hitter's statistics into a big league equivalent. The formula considers the player's level of competition, league, home ballpark and parent club's ballpark.

Offensive Winning Percentage

A player's offensive winning percentage (OWP) equals the percentage of games a team would win with nine of that player in its lineup, given average pitching and defense. The formula is the square of Runs Created per 27 Outs, divided by the sum of the square of Runs Created per 27 Outs and the square of the league average of runs per game.

On-Base Percentage

(Hits plus Walks plus Hit by Pitcher) divided by (At-Bats plus Walks plus Hit by Pitcher plus Sacrifice Flies).

Opponent Batting Average

Hits Allowed divided by (Batters Faced minus Walks minus Hit Batsmen minus Sacrifice Hits minus Sacrifice Flies minus Catcher's Interference).

PA*

The divisor for On-Base Percentage: At-Bats plus walks plus Hit By Pitcher plus Sacrifice Flies; or Plate Appearances minus Sacrifice Hits and Times Reached Base on Defensive Interference.

Park Index

A method of measuring the extent to which a given ballpark influences a given statistic. Using home runs as an example, here's how the index is calculated:

1. Add Home Runs and Opponent Home Runs in home games.

2. Add At-Bats and Opponent At-Bats in home games. (If At-Bats are unavailable, use home games.)

3. Divide Step 1 by Step 2.

4. Add Home Runs and Opponent Home Runs in road games.

5. Add At-Bats and Opponent At-Bats in road games. (If At-Bats are unavailable, use road games.)

6. Divide Step 4 by Step 5.

7. Divide Step 3 by Step 6.

8. Multiply Step 7 by 100.

An index of 100 means the park is completely neutral. A park index of 118 for home runs indicates that games played in the park feature 18 percent more home runs than the average park.

PCS (Pitchers Caught Stealing)

The number of runners retired when the pitcher, not the catcher, throws to a base to keep the runner close and the runner breaks to the next base before he is tagged out. Note: such plays are often referred to as pickoffs, but appear in official records as Caught Stealing. The most common scoring for a Pitcher Caught Stealing is a 1-3-6 play. The runner is officially charged with a Caught Stealing because he broke for the next base. A pickoff (with a fielding play of 1-3 being the most common) is not an official statistic.

Pitches per PA

For a hitter, the total number of pitches seen divided by total number of At-Bats.

PkOf Throw/Runner

The number of Pickoff Throws made by a pitcher divided by the number of runners on first base.

Plate Appearances

At-Bats plus Total Walks plus Hit By Pitcher plus Sacrifice Hits plus Sacrifice Flies plus Times Reached on Defensive Interference.

Power/Speed Number

A way to look at power and speed in one number. A player must score high in both areas to earn a high Power/Speed Number. The formula: (HR * SB * 2) divided by (HR + SB).

PPO (Pitcher Pickoff)

The number of runners retired when the pitcher throws to a base to keep the runner close and the runner is out trying to return to that base. A Pitcher Pickoff is not an official stat and does not count as a Caught Stealing.

Quality Start

A Quality Start is an outing in which a starting pitcher works at least six innings and allows three earned runs or less.

Quality Start Percentage

Quality Starts divided by Games Started.

Quick Hooks and Slow Hooks

A quick Hook is the removal of a pitcher who has pitched less than six innings and given up three runs or less. A Slow Hook occurs when a pitcher pitches more than nine innings, or allows seven or more runs, or whose combined innings pitched and runs allowed totals 13 or more.

Range Factor

The number of Successful Chances (Putouts plus Assists) times nine divided by the number of Defensive Innings Played. The average for a player at each position in 2000:

Second Base:	4.99	Left Field:	2.02
Third Base:	2.65	Center Field:	2.69
Shortstop:	4.61	Right Field:	2.14

RHS

Righthanded Starting Pitcher.

Run Support Per 9 IP

The number of runs scored by a pitcher's team while he was still in the game times nine divided by his Innings Pitched.

Runs Created

Bill James has devised 24 different Runs Created formulas, depending on the statistics available in a given year. The current method is as follows:

1. Add hits plus walks plus hit by pitcher.

2. Subtract caught stealings and grounded into double plays from Step 1. This is the A Factor.

3. Add unintentional walks plus hit by pitcher.

4. Multiply Step 3 by .24.

5. Multiply stolen bases by .62.

6. Add sacrifice hits plus sacrifice flies.

7. Multiply Step 6 by .5.

8. Add total bases plus Step 4 plus Step 5 plus Step 7.

9. Multiply strikeouts by .03.

10. Subtract Step 9 from Step 8. This is the B Factor.

11. Add at-bats plus walks plus hit by pitcher plus sacrifice hits plus sacrifice flies. This is the C Factor.

To summarize:

$$A = H + BB + HBP - CS - GDP$$

$$B = ((BB - IBB + HBP) * .24) + (SB * .62) + ((SH + SF) * .5) + TB - (SO * .03)$$

$$C = AB + BB + HBP + SH + SF$$

Each player's runs created is determined as if he were operating in a context of eight other players of average skill. The final steps are:

12. Multiply C by 2.4.

13. Add A plus Step 12.

14. Multiply C by 3.

15. Add B plus Step 14.

16. Multiply Step 13 by Step 15.

17. Multiply C by 9.

18. Divide Step 16 by Step 17.

19. Multiply C by .9.

20. Subtract Step 19 from Step 18.

Expressed as an equation, that's:

$$(((((C * 2.4) + A) * ((C * 3) + B)) / (C * 9)) - (C * .9)$$

Where home runs with men on base and batting average with runners in scoring position are available, we make further adjustments. First, figure out the player's home run percentage by dividing his home runs by his at-bats. Then multiply that number by his at-bats with men on base to find his expected home runs in that situation. Subtract the expected total from the real total, and add the result to his runs created. For example, a player with 20 homers in 600 overall at-bats who hit 10 homers in 150 at-bats with men on base would get an extra five runs created because he would have been expected to hit five. If he hit three homers in 150 at-bats with men on base, he would lose two runs created.

The runners-in-scoring-position adjustment works in similar fashion. Multiply a player's batting average by his at-bats with runners in scoring position to determine his expected hits in that situation. Subtract the expected number from the real number, and again add the result to his runs created. A .300 hitter who batted .350 in 200 at-bats with runners in scoring position would get 10 extra runs created (70 hits minus 60 expected hits). If he batted .280 in that situation, he would lose four runs created (56 hits minus 60 expected hits).

The second-to-last step is to round a player's runs created to the nearest integer. Finally, once all of a team's individual players' runs created have been calculated, compare their total to the team's runs scored and reconcile the difference proportionally. For instance, if a team's players created 700 runs and the club scored 728 runs, increase each player's runs created by 4 percent (728 / 700 = 1.04) and round each off to the nearest integer once again. Repeat if necessary until the two are equal.

Runs Created per 27 Outs (RC/27)

This statistic estimates how many runs per game a team made up of nine of the same player would score. The name is actually a misnomer, however, because Bill James has based his revised formula on the number of league outs per team game rather than 27. The calculation is runs created multiplied by league outs per team game, divided by outs made (the sum of a player's at-bats plus sacrifice hits plus sacrifice flies plus caught stealings plus grounded into double plays, less his hits), or:

$$((RC * ((3 * LgIP) / (2 * LgG))) / (AB - H + SH + SF + CS + GDP)$$

Save Percentage

Saves (SV) divided by Save Opportunities (OP).

Save Situation

Credit a pitcher with a save when he meets all three of the following conditions:

1. He is the finishing pitcher in a game won by his club.

2. He is not the winning pitcher.

3. He qualifies under one of the following conditions:

a. He enters the game with a lead of no more than three runs and pitches for at least one inning.

b. He enters the game, regardless of the count, with the potential tying run either on base, or at-bat, or on deck (that is, the potential tying run is either already on base or is one of the first two batsmen he faces).

c. He pitches effectively for at least three innings.

No more than one save may be credited in each game.

SB Success%

Stolen Bases divided by (Stolen Bases plus Caught Stealing).

Secondary Average

A way to look at a player's extra bases gained, independent of Batting Average. The formula:

$$(TB - H + BB + SB - CS) / AB$$

Similarity Score

A method of measuring the degree of similarity of two statistical lines for a player or a team. Two identical stat lines would generate a score of 1,000.

Slugging Percentage

Total Bases divided by At-Bats.

Speed Score

To figure speed scores, start with the player's record over the last two seasons combined. With that record, you figure six elements of the speed score:

1. The stolen base percentage. Figure the score here as $((SB + 3) / (SB + CS + 7) - .4) * 20$.

2. The frequency of stolen base attempts. Figure the score here as $(SB + CS) / (Singles + BB + HBP)$. Take the square root of that, and divide that by .07. If a player attempts to steal one-tenth of the time when he is on first base, you take the square root of .10 (.316) and divide that by .07, yielding a speed score of 4.52.

3. Triples. Figure the player's triples as a percentage of balls in play (3B) / (AB - HR - SO). From this assign an integer from 0 to 10, based on the following chart:

Less than .001	0
.001-.0023	1
.0023-.0039	2
.0039-.0058	3
.0058-.0080	4
.0080-.0105	5
.0105-.013	6
.013-.0158	7
.0158-.0189	8
.0189-.0223	9
.0223 or higher	10

4. The number of runs scored as a percentage of times on base. Figure first the percentage as (R - HR) / (H + HBP + BB - HR). From this subtract .1, and then divide by .04. Thus, if a player has 150 hits, five hit by pitcher and 95 walks, hits 30 home runs and scores 100 runs, you would figure (100 - 30) / (150 + 5 + 95 - 30), or $70/220$, which is .318. Subtract .1, and you have .218. Divide by .04, and his speed score on this point would be 5.45.

5. The frequency of grounding into double play. The formula here is ((.055 - (GDP / (AB - HR - SO)) / .005).

6. Range factor. If the player is a catcher, his speed score on this point is 1; if a first baseman, 2; if a designated hitter, 1.5. If he plays second base, then his speed score element six is 1.25 times his range factor; if third base, 1.51 times his range factor; if shortstop, 1.52 times his range factor; if the outfield, 3 times his range factor. Remember to figure range factors over a two-year period.

If any speed score is over 10.00, then move it down to 10; if it is less than zero, move it up to zero. No element can be outside the 0 to 10 range. When you have the six elements of the speed score, throw out the lowest one. The player's speed score is the average of the other five.

Times on Base
Hits plus Bases on Balls plus times Hit by Pitches.

Total Bases
Hits plus Doubles plus (2 * Triples) plus (3 * Home Runs).

Tough Loss
To determine the starting pitcher's Game Score: (1) Start with 50. (2) Add 1 point for each out recorded by the starting pitcher. (3) Add 2 points for each inning the pitcher completes after the fourth inning. (4) Add 1 point for each strikeout. (5) Subtract 2 points for each hit allowed. (6) Subtract 4 points for each earned run allowed. (7) Subtract 2 points for an unearned run. (8) Subtract 1 point for each walk.

If the starting pitcher scores over 50 and loses, it's a Tough Loss. The 2000 leaders in Tough Losses are listed in the Leader Board section.

Tough Save
This distinction is made to gauge the difficulty of a save. A Tough Save occurs if the reliever enters with the tying run anywhere on base.

Win-Loss Percentage or Winning Percentage
Wins divided by (Wins plus Losses).

About STATS, Inc.

STATS, Inc. is the nation's leading sports information and statistical analysis company, providing detailed sports services for a wide array of commercial clients. In January 2000, STATS was purchased by News Digital Media, the digital division of News Corporation. News Digital Media engages in three primary activities: operating FOXNews.com, FOX-Sports.com, FOXMarketwire.com and FOX.com; developing related interactive services; and directing investment activities and strategy for News Corporation, as they relate to digital media.

As one of the fastest growing companies in sports, STATS provides the most detailed, up-to-the-minute sports information to professional teams, print and broadcast media, software developers and interactive service providers around the country. STATS recently was recognized as "one of Chicago's 100 most influential technology players" by *Crain's Chicago Business* and has been one of 16 finalists for KPMG/Peat Marwick's Illinois High Tech Award for three consecutive years. Some of our major clients include Fox Sports, the Associated Press, America Online, *The Sporting News*, ESPN, Electronic Arts, MSNBC, SONY and Topps. Much of the information we provide is available to the public via STATS On-Line. With a computer and a modem, you can follow action in the four major professional sports, as well as NCAA football and basketball and other professional and college sports.

STATS Publishing, a division of STATS, Inc., produces 12 annual books, including the *Major League Handbook*, *The Scouting Notebook*, the *Pro Football Handbook*, the *Pro Basketball Handbook* and the *Hockey Handbook*. In 1998, we introduced two baseball encyclopedias, the *All-Time Major League Handbook* and the *All-Time Baseball Sourcebook*. Together they combine for more than 5,000 pages of baseball history. Also available is *From Abba Dabba to Zorro: The World of Baseball Nicknames*, a wacky look at monikers and their origins. A new football title was launched in 1999, the *Pro Football Scoreboard*, and we added the *Pro Football Sourcebook* in 2000. All of our publications deliver STATS' expertise to fans, scouts, general managers and media around the country.

In addition, STATS Fantasy Sports is at the forefront of the booming fantasy sports industry. We develop fantasy baseball, football, basketball, hockey, golf and auto racing games for FOXSports.com. We also feature the first historical baseball simulation game created specifically for the Internet—FOX Diamond Legends. No matter what time of year, STATS Fantasy Sports has a fantasy game to keep even the most passionate sports fan satisfied.

Information technology has grown by leaps and bounds in the last decade, and STATS will continue to be at the forefront as both a vendor and supplier of the most up-to-date, in-depth sports information available. For those of you on the information superhighway, you always can catch STATS in our area on America Online or at our Internet site.

For more information on our products, or on joining our reporter network, contact us via:

America Online — Keyword: STATS

Internet — www.stats.com

Toll Free in the USA at 1-800-63-STATS (1-800-637-8287)

Outside the USA at 1-847-470-8798

Or write to:

STATS, Inc.
8130 Lehigh Ave.
Morton Grove, IL 60053

Notes

Notes

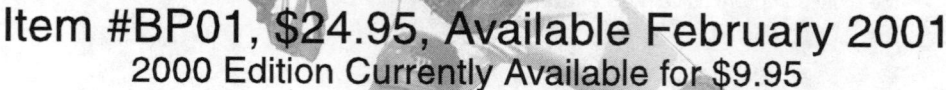

Straight From the Gridiron Into Your Hands

Diamond Legends
BASEBALL SIMULATION GAME

Enter the timeless realm of FOX Diamond Legends baseball simulation game where baseball's eternal mystery of greatness is contested 365 days a year. Surrender to a wondrous journey of baseball realism where the stars of the past century return to compete under your direction on the World Wide Web.

Diamond Legends creates the ultimate second chance for greatness that nature has previously denied. Relive some of the game's most treasured players and place yourself in the middle of baseball's illustrious history with Diamond Legends at FOXSports.com.

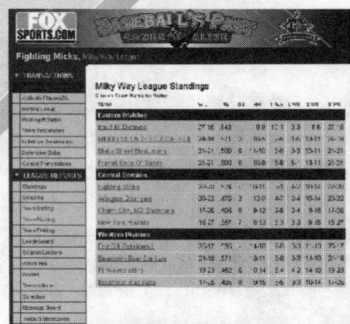

POWERED BY
STATS INC.
FANTASY SPORTS

DIAMOND LEGENDS BASEBALL

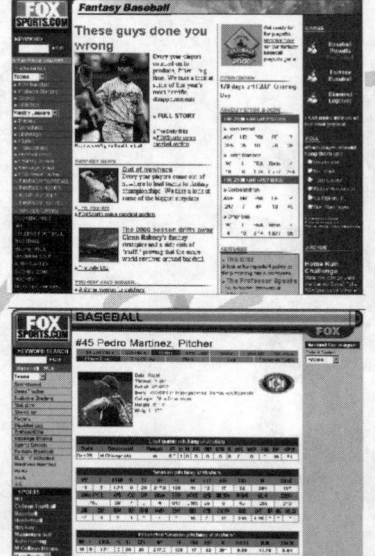
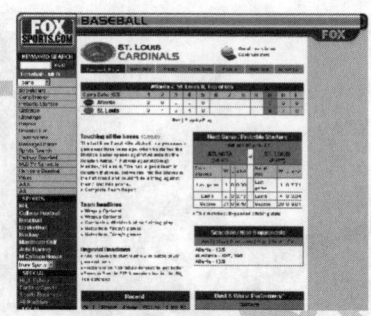

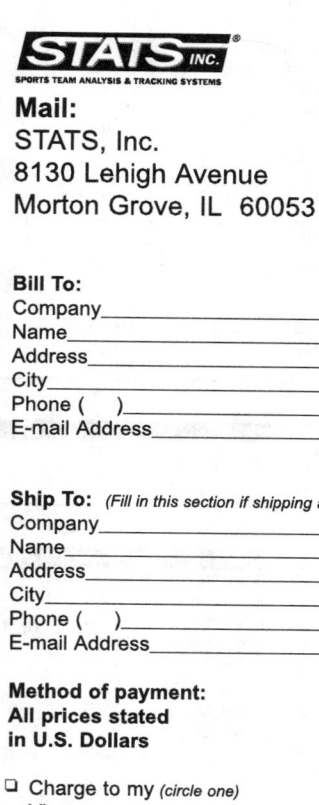

STATS INC. ®
SPORTS TEAM ANALYSIS & TRACKING SYSTEMS

Mail:
STATS, Inc.
8130 Lehigh Avenue
Morton Grove, IL 60053

Phone:
1-800-63-STATS
(847) 677-3322

Fax:
(847) 470-9140

Bill To:
Company_____
Name_____
Address_____
City_____State_____Zip_____
Phone (   )_____Ext.____Fax (   )_____
E-mail Address_____

Ship To: *(Fill in this section if shipping address differs from billing address)*
Company_____
Name_____
Address_____
City_____State_____Zip_____
Phone (   )_____Ext.____Fax (   )_____
E-mail Address_____

Method of payment:
**All prices stated
in U.S. Dollars**

❑ Charge to my *(circle one)*
   Visa
   MasterCard
   American Express
   Discover

❑ Check or Money Order
   (U.S. funds only)

Please include credit card number
and expiration date with charge orders!

Exp. Date ┌──────────┐
           │   / │
           └──────────┘
       Month Year

X_____
Signature *(as shown on credit card)*

Totals for STATS Products:

Books	
Books Under $10 *	
Prior Book Editions *	
order 2 or more books/subtract: $1.00/book *(Does not include prior editions)*	
Illinois residents add 8.5% sales tax	
Sub Total	

Shipping Costs

Canada	Add $4.00/book	
* All books under $10	Add $2.00/book	
	Grand Total	

(No other discounts apply)

(Orders subject to availability)

Free First-Class Shipping for Books Over $10

Books (Free first-class shipping for books over $10)

Qty	Product Name	Item Number	Price	Total
	STATS Major League Handbook 2001	HB01	$ 19.95	
	STATS Major League Handbook 2001 (Comb-bound)	HC01	$ 24.95	
	The Scouting Notebook 2001	SN01	$ 19.95	
	The Scouting Notebook 2001 (Comb-bound)	SC01	$ 24.95	
	STATS Minor League Handbook 2001	MH01	$ 19.95	
	STATS Minor League Handbook 2001 (Comb-bound)	MC01	$ 24.95	
	STATS Player Profiles 2001	PP01	$ 19.95	
	STATS Player Profiles 2001 (Comb-bound)	PC01	$ 24.95	
	STATS Minor League Scouting Notebook 2001	MN01	$ 19.95	
	STATS Batter Vs. Pitcher Match-Ups! 2001	BP01	$ 24.95	
	STATS Ballpark Sourcebook: Diamond Diagrams	BSDD	$ 24.95	
	STATS Baseball Scoreboard 2001	SB01	$ 19.95	
	STATS Pro Football Handbook 2000	FH00	$ 19.95	
	STATS Pro Football Handbook 2000 (Comb-bound)	FC00	$ 24.95	
	STATS Pro Football Scoreboard 2000	SF00	$ 19.95	
	STATS Pro Football Sourcebook 2000	PF00	$ 19.95	
	STATS Hockey Handbook 2000-01	HH01	$ 19.95	
	STATS Pro Basketball Handbook 2000-01	BH01	$ 19.95	
	STATS All-Time Major League Handbook, 2nd Edition	ATHB	$ 79.95	
			Total	

Books Under $10 (Please include $2.00 S&H for each book/magazine)

Qty	Product Name	Item Number	Price	Total
	From Abba Dabba to Zorro: The World of Baseball Nicknames	ABBA	$ 9.95	
	STATS Baseball's Terrific 20	KID1	$ 9.95	
	STATS Player Projections Update 2001	PJUP	$ 9.95	
			Total	

Previous Editions (Please Circle appropriate years and include $2 00 S&H for each book)

Qty	Product Name	Years	Price	Total
	STATS Major League Handbook	'91 '92 '93 '94 '95 '96 '97 '98 '99 '00	$ 9.95	
	The Scouting Notebook/Report	'94 '95 '96 '97 '98 '99 '00	$ 9.95	
	STATS Player Profiles	'93 '94 '95 '96 '97 '98 '99 '00	$ 9.95	
	STATS Minor League Handbook	'92 '93 '94 '95 '96 '97 '98 '99 '00	$ 9.95	
	STATS Minor League Scouting Notebook	'95 '96 '97 '98 '99 '00	$ 9.95	
	STATS Batter Vs. Pitcher Match-Ups!	'94 '95 '96 '97 '98 '99 '00	$ 9.95	
	STATS Diamond Chronicles	'97 '98 '99 '00	$ 9.95	
	STATS Baseball Scoreboard	'92 '93 '94 '95 '96 '97 '98 '99 '00	$ 9.95	
	Pro Football Revealed: The 100-Yard War	'94 '95 '96 '97 '98	$ 9.95	
	STATS Pro Football Handbook	'95 '96 '97 '98 '99	$ 9.95	
	STATS Pro Football Scoreboard	'99	$ 9.95	
	STATS Hockey Handbook	'96-97 '97-98 '98-99 '99-00	$ 9.95	
	STATS Pro Basketball Handbook	'93-94 '94-95 '95-96 '96-97 '97-98 '98-99 '99-00	$ 9.95	
	All-Time Major League Handbook (Slightly dinged)	First Edition	$ 45.00	
	All-Time Major League Sourcebook (Slightly dinged)	First Edition	$ 45.00	
			Total	

TOTAL [   ]